D1710415

# *Sentencing Law and Policy*

ASPEN CASEBOOK SERIES

# Sentencing Law and Policy

## Cases, Statutes, and Guidelines

### Third Edition

**Nora V. Demleitner**

*Dean*
*Roy L. Steinheimer, Jr. Professor of Law*
*Washington and Lee University School of Law*

**Douglas A. Berman**

*Robert J. Watkins/Procter & Gamble Professor of Law*
*The Ohio State University*
*Moritz College of Law*

**Marc L. Miller**

*Dean and Ralph W. Bilby Professor of Law*
*The University of Arizona*
*James E. Rogers College of Law*

**Ronald F. Wright**

*Needham Yancy Gulley Professor of Criminal Law*
*Wake Forest University School of Law*

Wolters Kluwer
Law & Business

Published by Wolters Kluwer Law & Business in New York.

Wolters Kluwer Law & Business serves customers worldwide with CCH, Aspen Publishers, and Kluwer Law International products. (www.wolterskluwerlb.com)

To contact Customer Service, e-mail customer.service@wolterskluwer.com, call 1-800-234-1660, fax 1-800-901-9075, or mail correspondence to:

Wolters Kluwer Law & Business
Attn: Order Department
PO Box 990
Frederick, MD 21705

Printed in the United States of America.

1 2 3 4 5 6 7 8 9 0

ISBN 978-0-7355-0709-8

**Library of Congress Cataloging-in-Publication Data**

Demleitner, Nora V., 1966-
Sentencing law and policy : cases, statutes, and guidelines / Nora V. Demleitner, Dean, Roy L. Steinheimer, Jr. Professor of Law, Washington and Lee University School of Law; Douglas A. Berman, Robert J. Watkins/Procter & Gamble Professor of Law, Ohio State University, Moritz College of Law; Marc L. Miller, Vice Dean, Ralph W. Bilby Professor of Law, University of Arizona, James E. Rogers College of Law; Ronald F. Wright, Needham Yancy Gulley Professor of Criminal Law, Wake Forest University School of Law. — Third edition.
    pages cm. — (Aspen casebook series)
    Includes index.
    ISBN 978-0-7355-0709-8
    1. Sentences (Criminal procedure) — United States. I. Berman, Douglas A., 1968- II. Miller, Marc L. (Marc Louis), 1959- III. Wright, Ronald F., 1959- IV. Title.

KF9685.D459 2013
345.73'07720264 — dc23                                              2013026533

# About Wolters Kluwer Law & Business

Wolters Kluwer Law & Business is a leading global provider of intelligent information and digital solutions for legal and business professionals in key specialty areas, and respected educational resources for professors and law students. Wolters Kluwer Law & Business connects legal and business professionals as well as those in the education market with timely, specialized authoritative content and information-enabled solutions to support success through productivity, accuracy and mobility.

Serving customers worldwide, Wolters Kluwer Law & Business products include those under the Aspen Publishers, CCH, Kluwer Law International, Loislaw, ftwilliam.com and MediRegs family of products.

**CCH** products have been a trusted resource since 1913, and are highly regarded resources for legal, securities, antitrust and trade regulation, government contracting, banking, pension, payroll, employment and labor, and healthcare reimbursement and compliance professionals.

**Aspen Publishers** products provide essential information to attorneys, business professionals and law students. Written by preeminent authorities, the product line offers analytical and practical information in a range of specialty practice areas from securities law and intellectual property to mergers and acquisitions and pension/benefits. Aspen's trusted legal education resources provide professors and students with high-quality, up-to-date and effective resources for successful instruction and study in all areas of the law.

**Kluwer Law International** products provide the global business community with reliable international legal information in English. Legal practitioners, corporate counsel and business executives around the world rely on Kluwer Law journals, looseleafs, books, and electronic products for comprehensive information in many areas of international legal practice.

**Loislaw** is a comprehensive online legal research product providing legal content to law firm practitioners of various specializations. Loislaw provides attorneys with the ability to quickly and efficiently find the necessary legal information they need, when and where they need it, by facilitating access to primary law as well as state-specific law, records, forms and treatises.

**ftwilliam.com** offers employee benefits professionals the highest quality plan documents (retirement, welfare and non-qualified) and government forms (5500/PBGC, 1099 and IRS) software at highly competitive prices.

**MediRegs** products provide integrated health care compliance content and software solutions for professionals in healthcare, higher education and life sciences, including professionals in accounting, law and consulting.

Wolters Kluwer Law & Business, a division of Wolters Kluwer, is headquartered in New York. Wolters Kluwer is a market-leading global information services company focused on professionals.

To my parents, Alfred and
Walburga Demleitner.
*NVD*


To my grandfather and mother,
Seymour Kleinman and Dale Berman.
*DAB*


To Daniel J. Freed.
*MLM*


To my mother, Marian Stallings Wright.
*RFW*

# Summary of Contents

# Contents

# — 2 —

## ‖ Who Sentences? ‖

— 3 —

‖ *Regulating Discretion* ‖     *139*

# — 5 —

## *Sentencing Inputs: The Offender's Record and Background*

*359*

## — 6 —

## *Procedure and Proof at Sentencing* 443

— 7 —

|| *Sentencing Outcomes: The Scale of Imprisonment* ||    549

# — 8 —

## ‖ *Sentencing Outcomes: Nonprison Punishments* ‖ 625

# — 9 —

## ‖ *Race, Class, and Gender* ‖

# — 10 —

## Alternatives to Criminal Sentences

789

## — 11 —

### ‖ *Sentences Reconsidered* ‖        *841*

# ‖ *Preface* ‖

What claim does sentencing have in the modern law school curriculum, which already seems filled to capacity? We believe that the law of sentencing has plenty to offer all law students, even those not inclined toward a career in criminal law. This field provides an insightful case study in the dynamics of law reform; requires synthesis of theoretical and practical issues of doctrine, procedure, and policy; and touches deep and abiding issues about the nature and structure of law in society. Sentencing, in our view, illustrates superbly what advanced courses should offer, with its virtues extending to all law students by building effectively on the themes and goals pursued in an introductory criminal law and procedure class.

Of course, for students interested in a career in criminal law, the law of sentencing will serve as the central legal framework defining their day-to-day practice. Sentencing outcomes are the true bottom line of criminal law practice, and thoughtful defense attorneys and candid prosecutors regularly state that sentencing rules should be a lawyer's very first consideration in a criminal case. Moreover, because sentencing issues are frequently the focal point of criminal justice policy debates, many lawyers working for the government or for public interest groups are regularly engaged with sentencing controversies and concerns. Since criminal cases occupy such a large part of the courts' dockets, all judges (and their law clerks) spend a considerable portion of their working days on issues of sentencing law and policy.

## *A Law Reform Experiment*

Criminal sentences involve some of the most severe actions that governments take against their own citizens and residents. Because every criminal conviction results in some kind of sentence, sentencing occurs all the time and involves a huge number of people. In an average year, federal, state, and local governments make more than 15 million arrests and obtain around 1 million felony convictions and several million additional misdemeanor convictions. Right now, more than 1.5 million people are serving time in U.S. prisons. Another 750,000 are held in jail, and an additional 5 million are on probation or parole. Sentences are essential (though often hidden) elements of every substantive crime and every criminal process. Teachers in the first-year criminal law course point again and again to issues that will be resolved at sentencing; they explain that finer gradations or more subtle principles are possible at sentencing than in the rough-cut efforts to define crimes. Teachers of criminal procedure often note that defendants and their lawyers, as well as prosecutors, care most about the sentence because it represents the bottom line of all their procedural transactions.

Given the elemental role of sentencing in criminal law and procedure and the large social costs and benefits of criminal sentences, one might expect the law in this area to be highly evolved. In fact, for much of our history there has been very little law of sentencing. While some sentencing principles and punishments are ancient, the body of law that regulates sentences has remained undeveloped and unexamined until recently.

Rules prescribing the punishment for wrongdoers are found in the Bible and in the Koran. The earliest recorded legal codes, such as the Babylonian Code of Hammurabi (c. 1780 B.C.E.), spell out sanctions for various harms. Yet by the late twentieth century, 4,000 years of world civilization had resulted in sentencing systems in the United States (and in many other countries) that reflected only the most rudimentary qualities of law — for most offenses, only broad legislative specification of sentencing ranges, an absence of rules to guide judges in sentencing within those ranges, and actual determinations of sentences made not by judges but by executive release authorities.

Social and legal evolution can occur in the blink of an eye, and that has been the case for the law of sentencing. Since the 1970s, sentencing has undergone a political and legal revolution; it has become an area replete with law. Various kinds of "structured" or "guideline" systems now govern felony sentencing in many states and in the federal system; another intricate body of law now applies to capital sentencing, driven by an ongoing constitutional and policy dialogue between courts and legislatures. The emergence of sentencing law is one of the most dramatic and interesting law reform experiments in American legal history.

## Sentencing, Law School, and the Nature of Law

Though young in its details, the law of sentencing wrestles with profound and ancient themes of justice and the nature of law. These themes echo throughout the law: what makes rules and procedures wise, which institutions should design and implement these rules, how much discretion should (or must) be allowed in each case, and what impact the law will have on human lives. This combination of new laws and long-standing problems, of the familiar and the unfamiliar, gives students an opportunity to synthesize many aspects of the lawyer's art.

Some law students end their first year of studies (or their second) and yearn for more opportunities to confront questions of justice, fairness, politics, and efficiency. Even the most cursory reading of daily newspapers will confirm that sentencing is an area in which all these concepts remain openly in play. Indeed, media coverage of current sentencing debates enriches students' appreciation of the importance of this field and enables teachers to place current controversies within the enduring theoretical and doctrinal issues of sentencing law and policy.

Advanced courses should move beyond the mastery of doctrines and the already honed skill of reading appellate decisions. Sentencing integrates substantive criminal law with criminal procedure, and it often does so through institutions other than appellate courts. Sentencing law adds a strong dose of a subject not taught in most law schools — criminal justice policy (or criminology). The emergence of a language and grammar for sentencing has made it possible to explore the substantive, procedural, and policy aspects of criminal justice together in one place in the law school curriculum.

## The Approach of This Book

Two particular areas of sentencing law have received the most attention in law schools. The promulgation of the federal sentencing guidelines has interested many scholars, and courses and seminars on federal sentencing have been developed at a number of schools. The persistence of capital sentencing in the American agenda has also sparked substantial scholarly and classroom interest in the death penalty.

But these dramatic areas of sentencing turn out to be only two slices of a much larger pie. The rapid emergence of sentencing as an area of law has created legal flux and remarkable variety. Drawing from a rich background, the book presents the common themes and trends in this emerging field of law, looking to its practical, political, social, and historical roots. We do not focus on a single system or jurisdiction, but rather try to capture the central issues and elements for all systems in all places.

This book has no separate sections for guideline versus indeterminate sentencing, state versus federal systems, or domestic versus foreign systems. Nor are constitutional issues segregated into a separate unit. This is because lawyers do not think about all of the constitutional doctrine together. Instead, they think about stages of the process, and how various sources of law — constitutional and otherwise — have some bearing on a particular stage. Throughout the book, we draw on the most relevant examples from three distinct sentencing worlds: guideline/determinate, indeterminate, and capital. The examples from structured guideline jurisdictions — the dominant modern sentencing reform — occupy the center of attention. There is simply more "law" in a determinate system than in an indeterminate one, and more explicit discussion of what remains implicit in the older, discretionary systems. Because the federal system is so well funded and closely critiqued, the book devotes thorough attention to that system, but it features several key state systems as well.

We also examine capital punishment materials from time to time. Although detailed coverage of capital sentencing merits a full course and a full book in its own right, we focus here on the revealing comparisons between capital and noncapital sentencing practices.

## Organization and Selection of Materials

An introductory unit surveys the social purposes (Chapter 1) and social institutions at work (Chapter 2) in the sentencing area, and then presents two case studies—involving guideline and capital regimes—showing how the legal system regulates the exercise of sentencing discretion (Chapter 3). After this introduction, the volume follows an intuitive organization that tracks the basic sequence of decisions made in criminal sentencing. The book first reviews the basic "inputs" to the sentencing decision: Chapter 4 weighs the importance of the crime and its effects, and Chapter 5 considers the background of the offender. Chapter 6 reviews the distinctive procedures that shape how judges and others evaluate these sentencing inputs, both before and during the sentencing hearing.

The next three chapters explore the "outputs" of sentencing: prison (Chapter 7), nonprison punishments (Chapter 8), and the patterns of race, gender, and class that emerge in sentencing outcomes (Chapter 9). The book closes by discussing punishment choices that arise in institutional settings other than the criminal trial court. Chapter 10 looks at alternatives to criminal sentences, and Chapter 11 highlights the important judicial and executive review that can occur after sentences are imposed. Our principal materials come from many sources, reflecting the many institutions that shape and apply sentencing law. The U.S. Supreme Court makes occasional forays into the noncapital sentencing realm, but it leaves the great majority of the legal questions for others to address. We blend decisions from the U.S. Supreme Court, state high courts, and the federal appellate courts, along with a sprinkling of cases from foreign jurisdictions and supranational tribunals.

State cases carry substantial weight in this book, since well over 95% of criminal defendants are sentenced in state court and many of the most interesting modern sentencing reforms have occurred in the states. The amazing variety among state systems also allows instructive class discussions about the sentencing choices available.

We do not reprint only appellate judicial opinions as principal materials. We often use statutes or guideline provisions to lay out the common choices made by those who try to change sentencing practices. Reports and data from sentencing commissions and other agencies also help set the scene. To keep track of the options and to prevent our celebration of variety from obscuring core concepts, we strive in the notes to tell readers directly what the most common practices are in various U.S. jurisdictions. The principal materials usually explain (and often embody) this majority position, but we also underscore it in the notes. To the extent possible in an emerging field of law such as sentencing, we estimate in the notes how often a lawyer is likely to encounter a given practice in American jurisdictions.

## Central Themes in This Book

A small number of themes are central to the study of sentencing; these themes are present throughout the study of the law, even in areas completely unrelated to the criminal process. The book returns regularly to five major themes:

1. *Variety and change.* There is no single law of sentencing but rather many laws of sentencing, providing varied answers to a range of similar problems. This variation is apparent both across jurisdictions and within

jurisdictions over time. Why are there different answers to similar questions?

2. *Multiple institutions.* One of the most striking aspects of sentencing is the variety of participants, both in lawmaking and in application. These participants include not only the top officials within the legislative, executive, and judicial branches but also various lowerlevel actors and institutions. Thus, we highlight distinctions between the roles of sentencing judges and appellate judges, spotlight the role of prosecutors, and consider the special role of sentencing commissions, parole boards, and probation officers. We continually ask students to compare decision makers both descriptively and normatively: when does it (and when should it) matter whether judges or legislators make a certain type of decision?

3. *Purposes and politics.* Sentencing and punishment serve many different purposes — some explicit and others implicit, some philosophical and others practical and perhaps base. We repeatedly ask students to consider the connections between specific sentencing rules and the purposes, politics, and practicalities of criminal justice.

4. *Impact and knowledge.* Modern sentencing law sometimes invokes the optimistic belief that knowledge and research can form a sound basis for creating and improving legal systems. Most research considers the visible impact of different sentencing rules on crime and on actual sentencing patterns. Experience, however, tempers the perhaps naïve hope for empirically grounded reform. Still, the materials in this book aim to identify the effects of sentencing practices on the work of judges and attorneys and on defendants of different social groups.

5. *Discretion and equality.* A major theme of sentencing across systems has been the need to individualize sentences to account for relevant variations among convicted offenders. At the same time, one of the major goals of modern sentencing reform has been to regulate the discretion of those who sentence and punish individuals, with the aim of reducing or eliminating unjust disparity. Of particular concern here are sentencing disparities based on race, class, or gender. We believe it is impossible toassess properly any aspect of criminal justice in the United States, including sentencing, without explicit and steady attention to issues of race. One chapter in the book specifically addresses issues of race, class, and gender, but these themes are raised throughout the volume.

Each of these larger lessons attends to the nature of law. The dramatic construction of a new field over a relatively short time — although a field replete with links to ancient puzzles and problems — provides a special kind of clarity into these deeper themes.

## The Second Edition

Sentencing remains an active — and at times a hyperactive — field. This activity reflects the relative youth of sentencing as a discrete area of law and the focus of politicians, system participants, and the public on issues of crime and punishment.

This new edition reflects widely noted and dramatic shifts in constitutional sentencing law along with a host of significant changes in law and policy at the federal and state levels. This edition also reflects our education as teachers and editors as we have taught sentencing courses and heard from teachers around the country about which cases and materials have proved most effective in the classroom and which less so.

The pressures for change in sentencing policy and practice come from many directions. The United States Supreme Court has taken a dramatic turn in constitutionalizing aspects of charging, crime definition, and punishment through the *Apprendi-Blakely* line of cases. These cases have had widely varying impacts in different jurisdictions, but even if most systems find ways to accommodate these decisions, or if in the end the federal constitutional mandates of *Apprendi* and *Blakely* are watered down, these cases have become a pervasive part of sentencing discussions. This constitutional sentencing revolution demands explicit attention — at times in passing, at times as a focal point — throughout this volume and prompted the production of a second edition of this casebook. The world-leading level and rate of imprisonment in the United States have drawn increasing attention in states confronting the "bill due" for so much punishment. A quieter but emerging theme in both national and state discourse is the idea of shifting from the maximum punishment to "smart" punishment. The "smart" punishment (and parallel "smart policing" and nascent "smart prosecution") movements are, among other things, a more policy-centered way of rejuvenating debates over the purposes and value of punishment.

Commentators have raised questions not only about the efficiency of modern punishment regimes, but also about the fairness of modern sentencing systems and the criminal justice systems that generate convictions and sentencing in the first place. The gentle but continuing stream of DNA-related and other innocence cases, often nullifying convictions and long punishments (or the threat of the death penalty), have been one motivation for this renewed attention to fairness. Also burbling at the margins of social and legal policy are voices concerned with race and class bias in United States criminal justice and punishment systems.

Most sentencing commissions have established a role as a steady voice for punishment moderation and sound policy. In particular, the commissions have reminded legislatures and executive branch agencies of the prospects for rational and cost-effective punishment. They seem to have blunted some of the more extreme policies that tend to result from public and political debate uninformed by bureaucratic expertise.

All of these pressures for change combine to produce a dramatic field of study. We have developed this second edition with the continuing sense of intellectual challenge, real-world demands, and drama that led us to produce the first one.

## Our Hopes

We continue to believe that sentencing has blossomed into one of the most provocative and revealing areas of the law. It has become a powerful entry point into the workings of the law itself and into the nature of our social order. We wrote this book in the belief that the study of sentencing will be valuable to all lawyers and law students, not only to those with a commitment to criminal justice practice and policy.

Sentencing law itself is still a legal toddler. For sentencing law to become not only an illustration of the striking change taking place in the law but a model of legal reform and justice as well, the sentencing arena is in desperate need of excellent lawyers, well-informed legislators, and knowledgeable commissioners. We hope that some of those who study sentencing will be ready and willing to join the fray and work to produce better systems and greater justice.

## The Third Edition

While America has changed considerably over the half-decade since the last edition, these years have not slowed the emergence of sentencing law as a distinct and distinctly important field of legal doctrine and policy. In fact, after having described sentencing law as a "legal toddler" in the updated preface of the Second Edition, we might view the last few years of sentencing law's growth and development as a period of awkward adolescence. It is now hard not to notice how large the field of sentencing law has become, and it is also now hard to be sure just what this field will mature into.

The largest changes to be found in the text of this latest edition reflect the U.S. Supreme Court opening two new important frontiers of constitutional sentencing jurisprudence. Through expanded application of the Sixth Amendment addressing defense counsel responsibilities in the plea bargaining process, and through expanded application of the Eighth Amendment limiting imposition of life without parole sentences, the Supreme Court has now further ensured that constitutional considerations are to be an even more integral part of the work and analysis of system-wide and case-specific sentencing decision-makers. But with these rulings emerging from a deeply split Supreme Court, and with dissenting Justices warning and lamenting where new constitutional sentencing jurisprudence might lead, it may take years or even decades to be confident about the evolution and impact of the new constitutional sentencing doctrines now covered this latest edition.

And while the judiciary has engendered new constitutional sentencing jurisprudence, new economic and political realities at local, state and national levels have engendered more dynamic discussions of sentencing reform in other governmental branches. Barack Obama's first campaign for the presidency included a pledge to change the structure of federal crack cocaine sentencing and to promote drug courts and other innovations to reduce reliance on incarceration as the punishment response to drug offending. And, in the wake of the 2010 election in which a number of Republican governors took over states with pressing budgetary problems, a new movement labeled "Right on Crime" began to advocate for GOP elected officials to explore alternatives to incarceration for a range of less serious offenders. Now, it seems, it is no longer politically foolish to resist the "tough on crime" mantra that had been a campaign staple for decade, and it now seems in some jurisdictions some politicians can generate more positive buzz from discussing the need to send few offenders to prison rather than more. Still, as a slow economic recovery reduces budgetary pressures and public perceptions of new crime problems persist, it is difficult to predict whether and how a newly emerging political order around crime and punishment issues will persist.

Last but not least, the world of law schools continues to evolve as well. We continue to believe that a course (or even multiple courses) focused on sentencing law can provide a very effective vehicle (1) to place greater emphasis on experiential learning, (2) to help student emerge from law school with more practice-ready skills and values, and/or (3) to highlight how many individuals and criminal justice institutions still desperately need the input of excellent lawyers and well-informed legal actors. We persist in our hope that some of those who study sentencing will be ready and willing to join the fray and work to produce better systems and greater justice.

*Nora V. Demleitner*
*Douglas A. Berman*
*Marc L. Miller*
*Ronald F. Wright*

July 2013

# Acknowledgments

Modern sentencing law, with structured sentencing at its core, has emerged over the past 30 years, and a community of sentencing scholars, judges, and practitioners has emerged along with it. We have all spent part of our scholarly careers nurturing and critiquing the work that takes place in this field; it is terrifically gratifying for us to see criminal sentencing treated, at long last, as a "field" for study.

Course books reflect not only the immediate work of the editors but also the influence of colleagues and friends. Some of the most important influences on this book came from our close collaborators on other sentencing projects, most notably our fellow editors of the *Federal Sentencing Reporter* over the years: Dan Freed, Frank Bowman, Steve Chanenson, Michael O'Hear, Mark Harris, and Aaron Rappaport.

A special word is in order about Dan Freed: there is a part of Dan in everything we see or do in the area of sentencing. His farsighted and impassioned work for sentencing justice draws others, including us, to this corner of the world. We hope this book reflects Dan's joyful engagement with the ideas and realities of criminal sentencing.

Colleagues in this field around the country have been generous with their observations and encouragement during this project. Steve Chanenson and Michael E. Smith gave us crucial feedback on this book by teaching from the manuscripts and offering us wise suggestions along the way. There are a number of scholars and teachers whose work in sentencing and related areas have influenced this volume. On this score, we thank Albert Alschuler, Rachel Barkow, Sara Sun Beale, Stephanos Bibas, David Boerner, Dennis Curtis, Kara Dansky, George Fisher, George Fletcher, Richard Frase, Jim Jacobs, Eric Janus, Pam Karlan, Joe Kennedy, Nancy King, Susan Klein, Dan Markel, Tracy Meares, Michael O'Hear, Kevin Reitz, Alice Ristroph, Max Schanzenbach, Michael Simons, Kate Stith, Kimberly Thomas, Sandra Guerra Thompson, Michael Tonry, Robert Weisberg, Bert Westbrook, James Q. Whitman, and Deborah Young.

Advice and support also came from our home institutions, and we want to thank Jack Chin, Jennifer Collins, Sharon Davies, Terry Gordon, Kay Levine,

Alan Michaels, Nancy Rogers, Charley Rose, Robert Schapiro, Charlie Shanor, Kami Simmons, and David Yellen. Assistance with this volume also came from Kristie Gallardo, Melissa Haun, Barbara Lopez, and Marissa White. We received timely and thorough research assistance from several students, including Kris Armstrong, Leslie Cory, Jon Cowley, Jeffrey Davis, Amy DeWitt, Rudolph Fusco, Andrew Harris, Christine Robek, Daniel Smith, Jennifer Wiggins, and Robert Zayac. And, of course, the long-suffering students in our courses and seminars tolerated many drafts and many false starts to help us bring the book to its present form.

It is encouraging to meet so many judges around the country who offer important insights about the work of sentencing, which commands so much of their time and energy. We particularly want to thank Justice Samuel Alito Jr., Myron Bright, Guido Calabresi, Paul Cassell, Avern Cohen, Nancy Gertner, John Godbold, Frank Johnson, Gerard Lynch, John Martin, Michael Mihm, Jon O. Newman, Jim Rosenbaum, and Jack Weinstein. Prosecutors and defense attorneys, such as Stephen Bright, Judy Clarke, Roger Haines, Tom Hillier, Margy Love, Jon Sands, and Benson Weintraub, prevented us from losing sight of the realities on the ground as we observe events from our academic vantage points. In addition, probation officers, including Maggie Jensen and Matt Rowland, have provided us with useful glimpses into the difficulties of their work. Finally, our gratitude extends to scholars and researchers outside the United States. Their contributions to sentencing have informed our thinking about reforms and other changes. Among them are Hans-Jörg Albrecht, Andrew Ashworth, Albin Eser, Andrew von Hirsch, Geraldine Mackenzie, Stephan Terblanche, Dirk van Zyl Smit, Andrew Vincent, Susanne Walther, John Zeleznikow, and Emily Zimmerman.

Sentencing law and policy benefit from the vision and tireless work of reformers, based at institutions such as the Vera Institute, the Sentencing Project, the Urban Institute, the U.S. Sentencing Commission, and many state sentencing commissions. We are grateful for insights from Mark Bergstrom, Adam Gelb, Paul Hofer, Kim Hunt, Susan Katzenelson, Cynthia Kempenin, Rick Kearn, Robin Lubitz, Marc Mauer, Linda Drazga Maxfield, John O'Connell, Tom Ross, Julie Stewart, Chris Stone, Barbara Toombs, Jeremy Travis, Nick Turner, Ronald Weich, and Dan Wilhelm.

All writers of texts for students come to appreciate their own teachers even more. We are grateful, more than ever, to Steven Duke, Dan Freed, Owen Fiss, Edward Levi, Norval Morris, and Frank Zimring.

The editors at Aspen Publishers remained supportive throughout. Richard Mixter got the ball rolling and shared with us his wisdom about the nature of learning and the direction of legal education. We deeply value the encouragement and advice we received from Carol McGeehan, whose work with us — including discussions about when it would be appropriate to produce a volume on sentencing law — now stretches back over a decade. The book also profited from the great talents of Curt Berkowitz, Melody Davies, John Devins, Michael Gregory, Katy Guimon, Leslie Keros, and Barbara Roth.

Books do not take shape only in professional surroundings; this book followed us home and lived among our families. We are grateful to our families for playing host to this book in their lives, even though the guest may have overstayed its welcome. Our thanks and our love go to Michael D. Smith, Cordell

Demleitner Smith, Walburga Demleitner, Christine Anne Berman, Charlotte Lindsay Berman, Rebecca Elise Berman, Chris Cutshaw, Owen Miller, Evelyn Miller, Wyatt Miller, Amy Wright, Andrew Wright, and Joanna Wright. Without them, the creation of this book, like everything else we do, would be unthinkable.

---

The authors acknowledge the following authors and copyright holders for permission to use material reprinted in this book.

American Bar Association, Standards for Criminal Justice Sentencing (3d ed. 1994). Copyright © 1994 by the American Bar Association. Reprinted with permission.

Hugo Adam Bedau, The Death Penalty in America (3d ed. 1982). Copyright © 1982 by Oxford University Press, Inc. Used by permission of Oxford University Press, Inc.

Walter Berns, For Capital Punishment: The Morality of Anger, Harper's (April 1979) at 15-20. Copyright © 1979 by Harper's. Reprinted with permission.

Alfred Blumstein, Jacqueline Cohen, Susan E. Martin, and Michael H. Tonry, Research on Sentencing: The Search for Reform (1983). Copyright © 1983 by National Academy Press. Reprinted with permission.

William J. Bowers, The Capital Jury Project: Rationale, Design, and Preview of Early Findings, 70 Ind. L.J. 1043 (1995). Copyright © 1995 by the Indiana Law Journal. Reprinted with permission.

Teresa Carns, Michael Hotchkin, and Elaine Andrews, Therapeutic Justice in Alaska's Courts, 19 Alaska L. Rev. 1 (2002). Copyright © 2002 by the Alaska Law Review. Reprinted with permission.

Leslie A. Cory, Looking at the Federal Sentencing Process One Judge at a Time, One Probation Officer at a Time, 51 Emory L.J. 379 (2002). Copyright © 2002 Emory Law Journal. Reprinted with permission.

Anthony N. Doob & Cheryl Marie Webster, Countering Punitiveness: Understanding Stability in Canada's Imprisonment Rate, 40 Law & Soc'y Rev. 325 (2006). Copyright © 2006. Basil Blackwell, Publishing. Reprinted with permission.

Michel Foucault, Discipline and Punish: The Birth of the Prison (1977). Copyright © 1977 by Pantheon Books. Reprinted with permission.

Marvin E. Frankel, Criminal Sentencing: Law Without Order (1973). Copyright © 1973 by Hill and Wang Publishers. Reprinted with permission.

Richard S. Frase, Sentencing Guidelines in Minnesota, Other States, and the Federal Courts: A Twenty-Year Retrospective, 12 Fed. Sent'g Rep. 69 (1999). Copyright © 1999 by the University of California Press. Reprinted with permission.

Karen Gelb, Myths and Misconceptions: Public Opinion versus Public Judgment about Sentencing, Sentencing Advisory Council (July 2006). Copyright © 2006 Victoria Sentencing Advisory Council. Reprinted with permission.

Catharine M. Goodwin, The Independent Role of the Probation Officer at Sentencing and in Applying Koon v. United States, 60 Fed. Probation 71 (1996). Copyright © 1996. Reprinted with permission.

*Sentencing Law and Policy*

# =1=

## *The Purposes of Punishment and Sentencing*

The simplest question about sentencing is also one of the hardest to answer: what purposes does society achieve, or hope to achieve, when it sentences people convicted of crimes? One long-standing and straightforward view is that society wants to punish individuals who violate social norms and that sentencing systems are the means to impose such punishment. But this initial answer raises many questions of its own. For one thing, what makes a punishment criminal if governments sometimes punish individuals outside of the criminal justice system? And if criminal sentencing is about imposing punishment, is such a purpose tautological? What is to be accomplished through the imposition of punishment?

Such fundamental issues concerning the purposes of punishment confront all organized societies, but they are especially important in the United States, which is now a world leader in punishing its citizens. As of 2010, more than 2.2 million persons are incarcerated in prisons and jails in the United States, and almost 5 million others are subject to criminal justice supervision through probation or parole. Altogether, more than 7 million people in the United States are under the control of the criminal justice system. (For point of reference, this is a group larger than the resident populations of all but the 12 largest states — or roughly equal to the population of Switzerland or Honduras.) These basic numbers, however, mask enormous variation across the United States in how offenders are sentenced and punished.

Although sentencing is an important and dynamic field, decisions about sentencing often take place without any explicit reference to its underlying purposes. It is possible to study the law of sentencing without considering its fundamental purposes, but doing so would only produce expertise in technical rules and procedures without a deep understanding of the reasons (or lack of reasons) for those rules. Consequently, to acquire knowledge and make sound policy about sentencing, and more generally about law and society, we must address the purposes of sentencing up front and maintain an awareness of the theoretical underpinning of different rules and procedures.

The first part of this chapter surveys the various stated or implicit purposes that society tries to achieve through the sentencing process. This analysis reveals that none of the "traditional" justifications for punishment — retribution, deterrence, incapacitation, and rehabilitation — is self-defining, and that each is contested, both conceptually and practically. This discussion also examines other social purposes that have been suggested formally by philosophers and informally by observers of actual punishment and sentencing systems.

The second part of this chapter illuminates three fundamental reasons why it is unrealistic and probably inappropriate to posit a single purpose for sentencing and punishment. First, several different purposes may operate together to justify or limit punishment structures or sentencing systems. Second, the purposes that may justify certain systemwide sentencing rules or procedures may differ from those that justify case-specific sentencing outcomes. Third, purposes are constantly contested in both political and legal realms, and the focal points for debate and policy change over time.

## A.   SOCIAL PURPOSES OF SENTENCING

Organized societies devise many ways to sanction individuals who violate social norms. But formal and substantial punishments are delivered through the criminal justice system, where governments intentionally condemn wrongdoers. All aspects of criminal law — substantive, procedural, and political — must grapple with the core question of purpose and justification: Why should governments condemn and harm their own citizens?

In answering this question, philosophers have traditionally fallen into two camps. *Consequentialist philosophers*, who judge actions based on their consequences, justify state punishment as a means of reducing the overall harms created by criminal behavior. *Deontological philosophers*, who judge actions based on notions of moral duty, justify state punishment as a means of righting the moral wrongs of criminal behavior. Consequentialist philosophers generally endorse forward-looking, utilitarian theories of punishment, believing that punishment can benefit society through *deterrence* of potential offenders from committing future crimes, through *incapacitation* to render the current offender unable to commit future crimes, or through *rehabilitation* of the offender to prevent any further wrongdoing. Deontological philosophers generally endorse backward-looking theories of punishment, described in terms of *retribution* or *just deserts* and based on the notion that punishment is just when it restores the moral balance that criminal behavior upsets.

The materials in this section raise a number of questions: What purposes should a sentencing system seek? Is it possible or helpful to state those purposes explicitly? Do any unstated purposes operate at the same time? Can a system pursue multiple purposes, and if so, can it produce reasonably coherent and consistent outcomes across cases? We also consider whether it is possible to describe and implement a decent system without any guiding purpose or purposes.

It is useful to stop at this point and articulate for yourself an initial reason or set of reasons why a government is justified in condemning and harming its own citizens through criminal punishment. You should attempt to rank the importance of these reasons if you list more than one. Then you can compare the purposes as described in this chapter with your own initial beliefs, testing them along the way for coherence and relevance.

## 1.  Stated Purposes

How can we tell what purposes a system serves? Actors in a variety of settings often make explicit claims about the purposes of a system of criminal punishments. This section surveys some of the most commonly encountered purposes.

### a.  Purposes Statutes

When legislators consider the purposes of criminal sentences and punishment, they often articulate goals that do not fit neatly into the traditional philosophical categories. They also likely do not think about individual offenders, but rather imagine more broadly the values and interests that they hope their entire criminal justice system will pursue. An ever-present challenge in modern sentencing systems is to connect legislative statements of purpose with the traditional purposes discussed by philosophers and with actual offenders who confront judges. Consider first in the abstract the various kinds of purposes and goals identified in the following state statutes, and then try to effectuate those purposes and goals in the context of the case study presented in Problem 1-2. Ask yourself whether legislators provide useful guidance to prosecutors or sentencing judges, and why legislators may highlight purposes different in some important ways from the classic philosophical justifications.

This section begins with an effort by model law reformers (in this case the American Bar Association) to state explicitly which purposes legislatures should consider when designing a sentencing system. Is this statement of purposes complete? If not, what is missing? Is it too sweeping? Is it helpful? We then compare this statement of purposes in model legislation with declarations of purposes enacted in three different legislatures.

*ABA Standards for Criminal Justice,*
*Sentencing 18-2.1*
(3d ed. 1994)

MULTIPLE PURPOSES; CONSEQUENTIAL AND
RETRIBUTIVE APPROACHES

(a) The legislature should consider at least five different societal purposes in designing a sentencing system:
(i) To foster respect for the law and to deter criminal conduct.
(ii) To incapacitate offenders.

(iii) To punish offenders.

(iv) To provide restitution or reparation to victims of crimes.

(v) To rehabilitate offenders.

(b) Determination of the societal purposes for sentencing is a primary element of the legislative function. . . .

## COMMENTARY

Every aspect of a criminal justice system, including sentencing, derives legitimacy from the advancement of social ends.[2] Current criminal codes are generally lacking in useful articulation of the policy objectives sought in the sentencing of offenders. This Standard calls attention to the vital need for a policy foundation upon which the sentencing system can be built. Without reasonably clear identification of goals and purposes, the administration of criminal justice will be inconsistent, incoherent, and ineffectual.

## THE CHOICE OF SOCIETAL PURPOSES

The Standards' drafters recognized that there is no national consensus regarding the operative purposes of criminal sentencing. Indeed, even among philosophers there has been unceasing disagreement over the goals of sanctions. Some current systems have been characterized as predominantly retributive in nature. Other observers have claimed that the prevailing penology of the 1980s and early 1990s has been that of incapacitation. One need not go far back in time to find periods in which theories of rehabilitation and deterrence were of high prominence. Indeed, the resurgence of interest in community-based sanctions signals that, at least for the sentencing of some offenders, rehabilitative theory is alive and flourishing.

Paragraph (a) catalogs five different societal purposes a legislature should consider when designing a sentencing system. No hierarchy of importance is intended in the ordering of the five subsections, nor is it contemplated that every jurisdiction must implement all five purposes. Rather, the Standard is drafted in recognition of the wide diversity of viewpoints that exist concerning ultimate goals, and is meant to express a conclusion that different schemas can be imagined consistent with rational and desirable public policy.

Subparagraph (a)(i) recognizes that criminal sanctions may be used in an attempt to foster respect for the law and deter criminal conduct. This goal might be understood as "general deterrence," which operates through the exemplary and educative force of criminal law.[7] If the public is made to believe that

---

2. This statement is meant to encompass both consequentialist and retributive views of criminal justice policy. Consequentialists seek to promote the prospective social good of reducing future crime. Retributivists find a different social end in the punishment of past criminal acts, even where no forward-looking benefits result.

7. Some theorists have spoken in terms of "general deterrence" and "specific deterrence." The latter term refers to the tendency of painful punishments to deter the offender, who experiences them directly, from future criminal conduct. Under this Standard, such offender-specific effects are classified as "rehabilitation."

criminal behavior will be answered by painful consequences, it is hoped that some individuals will be discouraged from risking such consequences. On a more abstract plane, the imposition of punishment may disseminate a generalized message that criminal transgressions are treated seriously by society. Thus, information about criminal sentences may encourage people to respect the law as a whole and increase the numbers of law-abiding citizens.

Subparagraph (a)(ii) states that a jurisdiction may legitimately consider the goal of incapacitating offenders in designing a sentencing system. There is no question that some degree of disablement occurs whenever groups of offenders are incarcerated or are subjected to the restraint and surveillance of non-prison sanctions. To this extent, all sentencing systems are incapacitative, intentionally or not. A jurisdiction may further choose to pursue incapacitation in deliberate and targeted ways, however, and such choices are matters of fair policy debate.

Subparagraph (a)(iii) acknowledges that the punishment of offenders is a reasonable objective that legislatures may incorporate into a sentencing system. While retributivism had fallen from favor in the middle of this century, at least in the academic community, the theory has enjoyed both a scholarly and political rejuvenation since the 1970s. Today, a number of states have identified punishment or the meting out of "just deserts" as the central objective of their sentencing laws.

Subparagraph (a)(iv) identifies victim restitution and reparation as an eligible goal of sentencing. This consequentialist purpose aims toward the restoration of losses suffered by crime victims, when possible. Obviously, restitution cannot adequately be achieved in all criminal cases. Some injuries defy compensation and most offenders lack the resources to make adequate payments. Where restitution can be made, however, it is hard to posit a reason not to provide for it in the criminal justice system. Accordingly, the Standards elsewhere take the position that victim restitution should be given priority over the assessment and collection of other economic sanctions.

Last, subparagraph (a)(v) states that the legislature should consider the goal of rehabilitation of offenders when designing a sentencing system. As recently as the 1960s and early 1970s, rehabilitation was the prevailing theory of sentencing and corrections, and was the principal justification for the traditional structure of indeterminate sentences and parole. In the intervening years rehabilitation has lost its position of preeminence almost everywhere, but has hardly disappeared from view. Many incarcerative and nonincarcerative programs continue to attempt to reform offenders while at the same time serving other goals, such as punishment, deterrence, and incapacitation. The Standards endorse this as a worthy aim. It should be noted, in this regard, that the Standards take the view that rehabilitation, standing alone, is never an adequate basis for criminal punishment. In effect, reform should be attempted only in connection with sentences that are independently justified on some other ground.

The preceding description of eligible purposes is only a starting point in the development of a meaningful statement of societal goals for a working sentencing system. To be useful, such a statement must identify which purpose or purposes the legislature wishes to pursue. If multiple goals are selected, a system of priorities is needed so that when two purposes conflict, decision makers have a guidepost for choosing between competing objectives. [The] legislature may even wish the hierarchy of relevant goals to change for crimes of lesser and greater severity.

## 18 United States Code §3553

### IMPOSITION OF A SENTENCE

(a) Factors to be considered in imposing a sentence. — The court shall impose a sentence sufficient, but not greater than necessary, to comply with the purposes set forth in paragraph (2) of this subsection. The court, in determining the particular sentence to be imposed, shall consider —

(1) the nature and circumstances of the offense and the history and characteristics of the defendant;

(2) the need for the sentence imposed —

(A) to reflect the seriousness of the offense, to promote respect for the law, and to provide just punishment for the offense;

(B) to afford adequate deterrence to criminal conduct;

(C) to protect the public from further crimes of the defendant; and

(D) to provide the defendant with needed educational or vocational training, medical care, or other correctional treatment in the most effective manner;

(3) the kinds of sentences available;

(4) the kinds of sentence and the sentencing range established [in the federal sentencing guidelines]; . . .

(6) the need to avoid unwarranted sentence disparities among defendants with similar records who have been found guilty of similar conduct; and

(7) the need to provide restitution to any victims of the offense.

## Tennessee Code §40-35-102

### PURPOSE AND INTENT

The foremost purpose of this chapter [on criminal sentencing] is to promote justice [and] in so doing, the following principles are hereby adopted:

(1) Every defendant shall be punished by the imposition of a sentence justly deserved in relation to the seriousness of the offense;

(2) This chapter is to assure fair and consistent treatment of all defendants by eliminating unjustified disparity in sentencing and providing a fair sense of predictability of the criminal law and its sanctions;

(3) Punishment shall be imposed to prevent crime and promote respect for the law by:

(A) Providing an effective general deterrent to those likely to violate the criminal laws of this state;

(B) Restraining defendants with a lengthy history of criminal conduct;

(C) Encouraging effective rehabilitation of those defendants, where reasonably feasible, by promoting the use of alternative sentencing and correctional programs that elicit voluntary cooperation of defendants; and

(D) Encouraging restitution to victims where appropriate;

(4) Sentencing should exclude all considerations respecting race, gender, creed, religion, national origin and social status of the individual;

(5) In recognition that state prison capacities and the funds to build and maintain them are limited, convicted felons committing the most severe offenses, possessing criminal histories evincing a clear disregard for the laws and morals of society, and evincing failure of past efforts at rehabilitation shall be given first priority regarding sentencing involving incarceration; and

(6) . . . A defendant who does not fall within the parameters of subdivision (5), and who is an especially mitigated or standard offender convicted of a Class C, D or E felony, should be considered as a favorable candidate for alternative sentencing options in the absence of evidence to the contrary; however, a defendant's prior convictions shall be considered evidence to the contrary and, therefore, a defendant who is being sentenced for a third or subsequent felony conviction involving separate periods of incarceration or supervision shall not be considered a favorable candidate for alternative sentencing. . . .

## NOTES

1. *Parsimony as a purpose.* The structure and language of the "purposes" statutes reprinted above vary considerably. Which theory or theories of punishment are adopted in the federal system? In Tennessee? Which theory or theories of punishment do these jurisdictions reject? Note that the opening line in the federal statute provides what has been called a "parsimony" requirement by stating that the court "shall impose a sentence sufficient, but not greater than necessary, to comply with the purposes" of punishment. Why do you think Congress included this provision, and does it reflect one of the traditional theories of punishment or a different set of values? Do subdivisions (5) and (6) of Tennessee's statute pursue related interests?

2. *Historical trends in punishment theory.* Adoption of particular theories of sentencing and punishment has varied greatly by jurisdiction and especially by era. Retribution is perhaps the oldest theory of punishment, with clear biblical roots and a beautiful illustration in the Code of Hammurabi, a set of laws created by a ruler of Babylon in the eighteenth century B.C. (excerpts reprinted in Chapter 2). More modern history marks a turn in punishment theory in the late 1700s and early 1800s due to the influential writings of Jeremy Bentham, an English philosopher and social scientist who argued against natural law theories and urged an approach to law and punishment grounded in principles of utility. Writing around this same period, the equally influential German philosopher Immanuel Kant provided a more contemporary argument that retribution is the proper moral justification for punishment.

As a result of a variety of social forces, including the development of prison systems and modern American optimism concerning the ability of humans to improve one another, during the nineteenth and early twentieth centuries rehabilitation took center stage as the dominant (though not the only) theory justifying punishment. See Williams v. New York, 337 U.S. 241 (1949). But rehabilitation as a general justifying theory came under a sustained attack in the 1960s and 1970s, as illustrated by Professor Francis Allen's famous book *The Decline of the Rehabilitative Ideal: Penal Policy and Social Purpose* (1981). These attacks were capped by Robert Martinson's widely discussed short paper What Works? — Questions and Answers About Prison Reform, 25 The Public Interest 25 (1974), which reviewed numerous studies evaluating efforts at penal rehabilitation. Martinson's conclusions, which were generally discouraging, quickly became oversimplified into the assertion that "nothing works."

Commentators and others have tended to overstate the prior dominance of rehabilitation, as well as the modern failings of rehabilitative efforts and the general decline of the role of rehabilitation in sentencing. Indeed, recent Supreme Court opinions have reaffirmed the value of rehabilitation in some sentencing contexts. See Pepper v. United States, 131 S. Ct. 1229 (2011) (sentencing court may consider post-sentence rehabilitation of defendant who appears for resentencing after his original sentence was set aside on appeal, despite an advisory federal sentencing guideline to the contrary); Tapia v. United States, 131 S. Ct. 2382 (2011) (federal statute prevents judge from lengthening prison sentence of defendant solely to make her eligible for rehabilitative drug abuse program in prison). Although different theories of punishment have been expressly favored or disfavored in different eras, a thoughtful observer can probably identify the impact of each classic theory in nearly every punishment or sentencing system throughout history.

3. *Modern views of punishment theory.* As the ABA excerpt highlights, the academic debates and practical realities surrounding punishment theories remain dynamic and contested today. It is probably fair to say that most systems now recognize, either expressly or implicitly, some combination of retribution, deterrence, and incapacitation, along with a sprinkling of other rationales. One of the most interesting developments in modern thinking about punishment is the decline of the once-dominant theory of rehabilitation: note that the ABA states expressly that "rehabilitation, standing alone, is never an adequate basis for criminal punishment [and] reform should be attempted only in connection with sentences that are independently justified on some other ground." Why do you think the ABA declared rehabilitation to be the one traditional theory that cannot alone provide an adequate justification for punishment?

The refinement of retributive theory into various subtypes has proven to be an especially fruitful area for scholarship in recent years. See Mitchell N. Berman, Two Kinds of Retributivism, in Philosophical Foundations of Criminal Law 433 (R.A. Duff & Stuart Green, eds. 2011); R.A Duff, Retrieving Retributivism, in Retributivism: Essays on Theory and Policy 3 (Mark D. White, ed. 2011); Dan Markel, What Might Retributive Justice Be? An Argument for the Confrontational Concept of Retributivism, in Retributivism: Essays on Theory and Policy 49 (Mark D. White, ed. 2011). Some scholars assert that a dominant modern rationale has emerged through the idea of "limiting retributivism," an idea often attributed to Professors H. L. A. Hart and Norval Morris (writing separately). This theory suggests that retribution sets the upper and lower boundaries of just punishment, within which other purposes can hold sway, including utilitarian theories of deterrence, incapacitation, and rehabilitation. See Richard Frase, Limiting Retributivism: The Consensus Model of Criminal Punishment, in Michael Tonry, ed., The Future of Imprisonment (2004). This theory has been endorsed by the American Law Institute during its ongoing effort to revise the Model Penal Code's sentencing provisions, although the exact meaning and the appropriateness of this decision is debated in academic circles. See Paul Robinson, The A.L.I.'s Proposed Distributive Principle of "Limiting Retributivism": Does It Mean in Practice Pure Desert?, 7 Buff. Crim. L. Rev. 3 (2004); Edward Rubin, Just Say No to Retribution, 7 Buff. Crim. L. Rev. 17 (2003).

4. *Single or multiple theories?*  Some philosophers have contended that utilitarian and retributive theories of punishment are incommensurable and that an initial choice must be made between them to develop a truly principled sentencing system. Others, however, perhaps because of the strong intuitive appeal of both approaches, have endeavored to develop hybrid theories of punishment that are compatible with both theoretical perspectives. See Michael Cahill, Punishment Pluralism, Retributivism: Essays on Theory and Policy 25 (Mark D. White, ed. 2011). The theory of limiting retributivism may be popular in large part because it seems to be one of the more satisfying hybrid theories. The ABA sentencing standards suggest that a legislature may legitimately select multiple purposes for its sentencing system, but if multiple goals are selected, "a system of priorities is needed so that when two purposes conflict, decision makers have a guidepost for choosing between competing objectives."

Punishment and sentencing choices frequently reflect a variety of purposes, as Professor Norval Morris astutely observed more than 50 years ago:

> No one theory explains the different punitive measures to be found in our criminal law. . . . *All too often the purposes of punishment are discussed as if they could be treated as a single problem. . . . Surely the truth is that we have a series of related problems rather than a single problem. . . .* Surely, at the present level of our knowledge, we aim at a whole congeries of various purposes in respect not only of various types of crime but various types of criminals. [Because] we do not seek any single purpose or set of purposes through our penal sanctions, we must not suppose we are facing an academic and impractical problem. . . . Prevention, reformation, deterrence, retribution, expiation, vindication of the law, and the Kantian argument that punishment is an end in itself all mingle in the wild dialectic confusion which constitutes most discussions of the purposes of punishment. . . .

Norval Morris, Sentencing Convicted Criminals, 27 Austl. L.J. 186, 188-189 (1953) (emphasis added).

5. *Inherent conundrums in applying punishment theory.*  Though selection of multiple purposes creates the added challenge of establishing priorities, even a jurisdiction's decision to pursue only one theory of punishment does not magically simplify the conundrums inherent in developing a sound sentencing system. For one thing, each theory of punishment has conceptual variations. Rehabilitation can be understood simply in terms of offenders no longer committing crimes or more dynamically in terms of offenders becoming productive contributors to the community. Retributive principles of just deserts can focus on the subjective culpability of an offender or the objective harms created by the offense; retributive theories also conflict over whether the aim of punishment is to inflict *suffering* in response to wrongdoing (perhaps adjusting the punishment to reflect an individual offender's capacity to endure pain), or to experience

*punishment* in proportion to the offense committed. Compare Adam Kolber, The Subjective Experience of Punishment, 109 Colum. L. Rev. 182 (2009) and John Bronsteen, Christopher Buccafusco, and Jonathan Masur, Happiness and Punishment, 76 U. Chi. L. Rev. 1037 (2009) with Dan Markel and Chad Flanders, Bentham on Stilts: The Bare Relevance of Subjectivity to Retributive Justice, 98 Cal. L. Rev. 907 (2010) and David Gray, Punishment as Suffering, 63 Vand. L. Rev. 619 (2010).

In addition, each goal raises challenging (and perhaps unanswerable) empirical and factual questions. Rarely do we have unassailable evidence about what punishments will deter (or rehabilitate) which offenders, and rarely can we establish indisputably what an offender thought (or did) to assess just deserts. One major variant of retributivism, known as "empirical desert," turns on evidence of shared community intuitions about just sentences, because criminal law's moral credibility is essential to its power to control crime. See Paul H. Robinson, Competing Conceptions of Modern Desert: Vengeful, Deontological, and Empirical, 67 Cambridge L.J. 145 (2008) but cf. Christopher Slobogin, Some Hypotheses About Empirical Desert, 42 Ariz. St. L.J. 1189 (2011); Donald Braman, Dan M. Kahan, and David A. Hoffman, Some Realism about Punishment Naturalism, 77 U. Chi. L. Rev. 1531 (2010).

Further, punishment goals must be reconciled with a jurisdiction's various other commitments and limitations; a commitment to the right of due process, for example, may make a particular theory of punishment more difficult to pursue, as can limitations on the resources that a jurisdiction is able to devote to these matters. Should an offender's moral desert overcome illegal police searches or the passage of time that triggers the statutes of limitation? See Douglas N. Husak, Why Punish the Deserving? 26 Nous 447 (1992).

## PROBLEM 1-1.   RICHARD GRAVES

One summer evening, Betsy Baker and her boyfriend ate dinner and had several beers at a local bar. As they drove home, Betsy's boyfriend was arrested for driving while under the influence (DUI). Richard Graves, a stranger, approached Betsy and offered to drive her truck home. Betsy agreed. After Richard returned with Betsy to her trailer, he followed Betsy inside. Betsy allowed Richard to stay, but told him he could sleep either on the bed or on the couch and she would stay on the other because they were not sleeping together.

Betsy awakened when she felt someone penetrating her vagina from behind her. She dove off of the bed and yelled at Richard to leave. Richard told Betsy to "hold on" and calm down, but she kept yelling for him to get out. Before he left, Betsy asked Richard, "Did we make love?" Richard replied, "I didn't mean to hurt you," then ran out the door. Betsy's loud crying brought a neighbor to her door, and she asked the neighbor to call the police. An officer arrived, who recognized Betsy from the earlier DUI stop and arrest. After Betsy calmed down, she told the officer that a man offered to drive her home after the arrest and that she had been raped.

The officer located Richard Graves based on Betsy's description. When the officer asked what had happened that night, Richard said, "What? Nothing happened." When the officer said he knew something happened, Richard told him that Betsy offered to let him sleep in the bed, but that he declined, telling Betsy, "No, that's your bed. I'll sleep on the couch." Richard then said Betsy was with him on the bed and began touching him, but then they fell asleep and that "nothing really happened after that." After Richard became evasive answering follow-up questions, the officer advised him of his rights.

After Richard was booked, a rape examination of Betsy revealed sperm, biologically consistent with Richard. Richard was charged with the offense of sexual intercourse without consent. He was tried before a jury and testified on his own behalf. Richard claimed that, as he drove Betsy home, she flirted with him and gave him a hug and kissed him affectionately. Richard also testified that after he had fallen asleep in her trailer, he awoke to find Betsy fondling his groin area. He testified that after brief foreplay, intercourse took place.

Based on Betsy's testimony and other corroborating evidence, the jury found Richard Graves guilty of sexual intercourse without consent. Montana law provides that a person convicted of sexual intercourse without consent "shall be punished by life imprisonment or by imprisonment in the state prison for a term of not less than 2 years or more than 100 years and may be fined not more than $50,000."

At a hearing before the judge at sentencing, Richard again admitted to having sexual intercourse with Betsy, and he suggested that any mistake as to consent might have resulted from the fact that he had a lot to drink that night. Richard said he was sorry for any harm he caused, and also indicated that he had enrolled in a treatment program to deal with his alcohol problems. Richard also noted that despite a disadvantaged upbringing, which included a brief stint in a juvenile corrections facility following an assault conviction, he had only minor contacts with the criminal justice system as an adult. The Montana Codes provides the following guidance about purposes at sentencing.

## *Montana Code Annotated §46-18-101*

### CORRECTIONAL AND SENTENCING POLICY

(1) It is the purpose of this section to establish the correctional and sentencing policy of the state of Montana. Laws for the punishment of crime are drawn to implement the policy established by this section.

(2) The correctional and sentencing policy of the state of Montana is to:

(a) punish each offender commensurate with the nature and degree of harm caused by the offense and to hold an offender accountable;

(b) protect the public, reduce crime, and increase the public sense of safety by incarcerating violent offenders and serious repeat offenders;

(c) provide restitution, reparation, and restoration to the victim of the offense; and

(d) encourage and provide opportunities for the offender's self-improvement to provide rehabilitation and reintegration of offenders back into the community.

(3) To achieve the policy outlined in subsection (2), the state of Montana adopts the following principles:

(a) Sentencing and punishment must be certain, timely, consistent, and understandable.

(b) Sentences should be commensurate with the punishment imposed on other persons committing the same offenses.

(c) Sentencing practices must be neutral with respect to the offender's race, gender, religion, national origin, or social or economic status.

(d) Sentencing practices must permit judicial discretion to consider aggravating and mitigating circumstances.

(e) Sentencing practices must include punishing violent and serious repeat felony offenders with incarceration.

(f) Sentencing practices must provide alternatives to imprisonment for the punishment of those nonviolent felony offenders who do not have serious criminal records.

(g) Sentencing and correctional practices must emphasize that the offender is responsible for obeying the law and must hold the offender accountable for the offender's actions.

(h) Sentencing practices must emphasize restitution to the victim by the offender. . . .

(i) Sentencing practices should promote and support practices, policies, and programs that focus on restorative justice principles.

If you were the prosecutor in Richard Graves's case, what sentence would you recommend? If you were a defense attorney assigned to represent Richard Graves, what sentence would you recommend? How would the provisions of Mont. Code Ann. §46-18-101 influence your recommendation?

If you were the sentencing judge in Richard Graves's case, what sentence would you impose? How would the provisions of Mont. Code Ann. §46-18-101 influence your decision? In each of these roles, would you seek additional information before making a specific recommendation or decision? Would you emphasize a particular theory or theories of punishment in your recommendation or decision?

Cf. State v. Graves, 901 P.2d 549 (Mont. 1995).

## NOTES

1. *Deterrence.*   Deterrence is not only a plausible concept but one that most people rely on in their everyday activities. Indeed, no one seriously disputes that creating a criminal justice system that punishes wrongdoing has some deterrent impact. But far more debatable — indeed, hotly debated — is the concept of marginal deterrence, which postulates that an additional quantum of punishment can lead to a measurable decrease in a particular crime (or all crimes). Complicating this issue is the likelihood, according to many researchers, that extralegal factors such as moral views, family or community structures, and other social dynamics have more of a deterrent impact than specific legal sanctions.

Defenders of deterrence as a justification for punishment must confront the argument that it is immoral to punish one person to deter others.

Philosopher Immanuel Kant's arguments eloquently set out the terms of this debate:

> [Punishment by government for crime] can never be administered merely as a means for promoting another good either with regard to the criminal himself or to civil society, but must in all cases be imposed only because the individual on whom it is inflicted has committed a crime. For one man ought never to be dealt with merely as a means subservient to the purpose of another, nor be mixed up with the subjects of real right. . . . He must first be found guilty and punishable, before there can be any thought of drawing from his punishment any benefit for himself or his fellow-citizens. The penal law is a categorical imperative; and woe to him who creeps through the serpent-windings of utilitarianism to discover some advantage that may discharge him from the justice of punishment, or even from the due measure of it. . . .

Immanuel Kant, The Science of Right 195 (W. Hastie trans., 1790). This statement is often read solely as a justification for retribution or just deserts. But notice that Kant argues that it is immoral to punish an individual "merely" to promote another good. Kant recognizes that if a person is guilty of crime, then utilitarian reasons might come into play.

A growing body of social science research suggests that we should not expect to decrease crime rates significantly through changes in criminal law rules or through the specific distribution of criminal punishments. See Paul H. Robinson and John M. Darley, Does Criminal Law Deter? A Behavioral Science Investigation, 24 Oxford J. Legal Stud. 173 (2004). Professor Michael Tonry summarizes the state of empirical knowledge about deterrence:

> Current knowledge concerning deterrence is little different than eighteenth-century theorists such as Beccaria ([1764] 1995) supposed it to be: certainty and promptness of punishment are more powerful deterrents than severity. This does not mean that punishments do not deter. No one doubts that having a system of punishment has crime-preventive effects. The important question is whether changes in punishments have marginal deterrent effects, that is, whether a new policy causes crime rates to fall from whatever level they would otherwise have been at. Modern deterrent strategies, through sentencing law changes, take two forms: increases in punishments for particular offenses and mandatory minimum sentence (including "three-strikes") laws.
>
> Imaginable increases in severity of punishments do not yield significant (if any) marginal deterrent effects. Three National Academy of Sciences panels, all appointed by Republican presidents, reached that conclusion, as has every major survey of the evidence. There are a number of good practical reasons why this widely reached conclusion makes sense. First, serious sexual and violent crimes are generally committed under circumstances of extreme emotion, often exacerbated by the influence of alcohol or drugs. Detached reflection on possible penalties or recent changes in penalties seldom if ever occurs in such circumstances. Second, most minor and middling and many serious crimes do not result in arrests or prosecutions; most offenders committing them, naively but realistically, do not expect to be caught. Third, those who are caught and prosecuted almost always are offered plea bargains that break the link between the crime and the prescribed punishment. Fourth, when penalties are especially severe, they are often, albeit inconsistently, circumvented by prosecutors and judges. Fifth, for many crimes including drug trafficking, prostitution, and much gang-related activity, removing individual offenders does not alter the structural circumstances conducing to the crime. Sixth, even when one ignores all those considerations, the idea that increased penalties

have sizable marginal deterrent effects requires heroic and unrealistic assumptions about "threat communication," the process by which would-be offenders learn that penalty increases have been legislated or are being implemented.

Michael Tonry, Purposes and Functions of Sentencing, 34 Crime & Just. 28-29 (2006).

2. *Incapacitation.*    Because of the indisputable efficacy of some punishments to incapacitate offenders, one could reasonably view incapacitation as the most tangible and certain goal for punishment. (In addition, one could, after examining the history of punishment laws and the realities of punishment practices, reasonably conclude that incapacitation has been the goal most regularly and consistently pursued.) But because of the almost limitless reach of a theory of incapacitation and the obvious costs of its blind pursuit — to achieve "perfect" incapacitation, every offender would be executed — deciding how to pursue the theory poses a very serious challenge. See Kevin Bennardo, Incarceration's Incapacitative Shortcomings, available at www.ssrn.com/abstract=2191128 (Dec. 2012).

In the mid-twentieth century, a somewhat refined approach to incapacitation — operating under the label "selective incapacitation" — gained adherents based on the contention that judges and parole officials could accurately determine which offenders were especially dangerous to society and thus should serve longer prison terms than typical offenders. But much research conducted over the past four decades has shown that it is exceedingly difficult to predict future serious criminal behavior. Researchers generally concluded that even with the best information, predictions of future dangerousness would be wrong more often than right, and the challenge of obtaining all needed information for these assessments only increased the risk of "false positives." See Norval Morris and Marc Miller, Predictions of Dangerousness, 6 Crime & Just. 1 (1985).

Anthony Bottoms and Andrew Von Hirsch summarize the empirical research on selective incapacitation and general incapacitation:

> Where does this [research on selective incapacitation] leave us? A limited capacity to forecast risk has long existed: persons with extensive criminal histories, drug habits, and no jobs tend to re-offend at a higher rate than other offenders. However, the limitations in that forecasting capacity must be recognized, especially as regards the difficult issue of estimating residual criminal careers. Research shows that the potential aggregate crime-prevention impact of selective incapacitation on crime rates is well below proponents' initial estimates. [We] also need to recognize the degree to which existing criminal justice practices [such as imposition of longer sentences on those with longer criminal records] in many jurisdictions already incorporate risk-related strategies.
>
> [As for general incapacitation, two] principal research strategies have been deployed in this field. Most analyses are based on what has been described as a "bottom-up" methodology [which] involves projecting, form an analysis of individual criminal careers, an average annual rate of offenses prevented by incarcerating specific groups of offenders. [This research produces] estimates of the amount of crime prevented by a given incapacitative policy [that] often vary widely, even where researchers are using similar data sets. . . . Divergences arise especially in relation to: (i) how to calculate the average offending frequency . . . of various groups of offenders, especially given evidence of considerable heterogeneity in offending rates by age and locality; (ii) issues of co-offending and of "offender replacement" [as when new sellers replace incarcerated drug dealers]; and (iii) the likely length of criminal careers. . . .

The second method of studying general incapacitation is the so-called "top-down" approach. [Studies] of this kind treat the aggregate crime rate as the dependent variable (i.e., the variable to be statistically explained), and they then construct a model which seeks to account for variations in crime rates using data on age, gender, unemployment, and so forth. Among these "independent" (explanatory) variables is the size of the prison population; thus, estimates can be made of the extent to which changes in the prison population affect the crime rate. [Once again], the projected incapacitative effects vary widely in different studies. [In the most recent and sophisticated top-down studies], the estimated percentage reduction in crime rates arising from a 10% increase in incarceration varies between 2.6% and 4.4%.

Anthony Bottoms and Andrew Von Hirsch, The Crime-Preventive Impact of Penal Sanctions, in The Oxford Handbook of Empirical Legal Research 116-119 (Peter Cane and Herbert Kritzer, eds., 2010). Bottoms and Von Hirsch conclude that prison expansion usually does have some incapacitative effect. It is, however, difficult to assess the size of this effect. Moreover, the effect might not be cost-effective: extra prison capacity might cost more than the social cost of the crimes prevented, because after prison expansion begins, "substantially diminishing returns are likely to set in."

3. *Retribution.* Though it has intuitive appeal, the seemingly simple retributivist notion that offenders deserve to be punished proves to be a difficult concept to pin down. Retribution can function as vindication for the victims of crime. See Jean Hampton, Correcting Harms Versus Righting Wrongs: The Goal of Retribution, 39 UCLA L. Rev. 1659 (1992). Retributive theory could also emphasize the rule-of-law values that might flow from punishment. Dan Markel explains the distinction between political justifications for retribution and "moral balance" justifications:

> [Some] versions of retributive theory directed attention at the infliction of suffering in the offender—in some cases, emphasizing that such inflictions of suffering should follow *lex talionis* and thus be equal to the pain and suffering he has caused (or, under some views, threatened). Those accounts, however, have often stumbled on explaining *why* the offender deserves pain and suffering, as well as whether to address wrongful actions that do not actually cause any harm. Hand-waving references to intuition or "fittingness" were often the only support that the pain and suffering version of retribution could muster. Thus, relying on cultural leitmotifs dating back to the Bible, it somehow made cosmic sense that the wicked should suffer and that the good be made happy . . . .
> My sense is that this desire to cause the offender suffering is misguided. [In modern accounts of state retribution], the goal is not to vindicate an agent-neutral duty to cause the offender unvariegated suffering but to implement punishment that is conceived in a relational manner, one that allows and encourages the *polity* to communicate to the offender the wrongness of her action, using particular deprivations to signal that condemnation.

In Markel's account of retributive theory, punishment reaffirms the essential equality of citizens and communicates disapproval to an offender who implicitly claims superiority by violating the law. See Dan Markel, What Might Retributive Justice Be? An Argument for the Confrontational Conception of Retributivism, in Retributivism: Essays on Theory and Policy 49, 60-61 (Mark D. White, ed., 2011).

Though the concept of just deserts has broad appeal in the abstract, the difficulty of deciding exactly what punishment and how much punishment is "deserved" has proven to be the greatest enduring challenge in turning retributive theory into sentencing practice. For one example of a pathway through these challenges, see Andrew Von Hirsch and Andrew Ashworth, Proportionate Sentencing: Exploring the Principles (2005).

4. *Rehabilitation.*   As a theory of punishment, rehabilitation is at once inevitable and oxymoronic. Interest in rehabilitation is inevitable because, unless every offender is to be executed or locked away for life, jurisdictions will want their punishment systems to reduce the likelihood that past offenders will re-offend when returned to the community. Yet a commitment to rehabilitation is oxymoronic because efforts by the state to improve the life and behavior of criminal offenders — through counseling, treatment, education, or training — do not seem like a form of punishment at all. These practical tensions have persistently burdened the concept of rehabilitation as a theory of punishment: jurisdictions have always recognized the importance of rehabilitating criminals, but they have rarely devoted sufficient money and energy to the programs most likely to succeed.

The conclusion drawn from Robert Martinson's famous article that "nothing works" to rehabilitate criminals is now well known to be a gross over-statement. Martinson himself came to recognize this, and within several years he published partial retractions of his position, noting that many rehabilitation programs had some modest impacts on individual behavior. See Robert Martinson, New Findings, New Views: A Note of Caution Regarding Sentencing Reform, 7 Hofstra L. Rev. 243 (1979). But continued research on rehabilitative efforts has tended to support a pessimistic view of the criminal justice system's ability to effectively reform offenders, although a few programs do have a track record of success. See Gerald G. Gaes et al., Adult Correction Treatment, 26 Crime & Just. 361 (1999); see also Rick Sarre, Beyond "What Works?" A 25-Year Jubilee Retrospective of Robert Martinson's Famous Article, 34 Austl. & N.Z. J. Criminology 1 (April 2001).

Michael Tonry summarizes the empirical work on rehabilitation:

> Prevention through rehabilitation looks to be a considerably more viable strategy in the early twenty-first century than it did during the closing decades of the twentieth. The view that "nothing works" was an important backdrop to the shift toward determinate sentencing, the abolition of parole, and adoption of incapacitative and deterrent crime control strategies. If we do not know how to reduce offenders' prospects for later offending, it is hard to justify giving judges and parole boards broad discretion to individualize sentencing.
>
> The prospects for rehabilitation, however, have changed radically. Evidence is accumulating from many sources — individual evaluations, meta-analyses, literature reviews, and practical experience — that well-managed, well-targeted programs can reduce participants' probability of reoffending. A wide range of programs, including drug treatment, anger management, cognitive-skills programs, sex offender treatment, and various educational- and vocational-skills programs, have been shown to reduce reoffending. A report from the English Home Office, which underpinned a massive reorganization of the English criminal justice system mandated by the Criminal Justice Act of 2003, concluded that "a reasonable estimate at this stage is that, if the [treatment] programmes are developed and applied as intended, to the maximum

extent possible, reconviction rates might be reduced by 5-25 percentage points (i.e., from the present level of 56 percent within two years to (perhaps) 40 percent)." The most recent meta-analysis of the effects of cognitive-behavioral programs concluded that, on average, they reduced reoffending by 27 percent. The proliferation of drug courts and prisoner reentry programs in the United States bears witness to the widely shared perception that some things work.

That litany of positive findings does not mean that reducing reoffending rates is easy. The results obtained from a well-funded pilot project, led by motivated people, cannot automatically be obtained by institutionalizing a new program model throughout a jurisdiction. A recent survey of violence prevention programs by the U.S. Surgeon General (2001) concluded that many programs can reduce violent offending but that the challenge is broad-based implementation. This is nonetheless much better news than the state of the evidence twenty-five years ago. We now know what we do; we need to figure out how to do it on a large scale.

An important implication is that rigid sentencing policies obstruct efforts to prevent crime through rehabilitation of offenders. For drug and other treatment programs to work, they must be targeted to the characteristics and needs of particular offenders, and this requires sentences to be individualized. With the fall of the nothing works psychology goes much of the case for rigid sentencing standards.

Michael Tonry, Purposes and Functions of Sentencing, 34 Crime & Just. 32-33 (2006); see also Daniel M. Filler and Austin E. Smith, The New Rehabilitation, 91 Iowa L. Rev. 951 (2006) (focusing on rehabilitative aspects of juvenile justice).

5. *Politicians' purposes.*  Politicians and political party platforms often make statements about crime policy during campaigns, statements that hint at or assume certain justifications for punishment. Should the political parties take an explicit position on the role and justifications for punishment? Should voters expect individual politicians to have a substantial answer to the question "what is the purpose of punishment?" or, more broadly, "what is the purpose of the criminal justice system?" The question may be more important than the answer. Would the answer change (for a party or an individual) if the question were "what is your policy on public safety?"

## b.  Community Purposes

Although debate over the traditional theories of punishment has raged for centuries and continues to be quite lively, a number of philosophers and policymakers who have found the traditional debate unsatisfying or unhelpful have explored other approaches to punishment and sentencing. Notice that the ABA sentencing standards, for example, endorse sentencing systems that "foster respect for the law" and "provide restitution or reparation to victims of crimes." Michael Tonry notes:

> Deterrence, incapacitation, and rehabilitation are not needed to restrain most adults from selling drugs, burglarizing houses, holding up convenience stores, or mugging passersby. Most people's personal norms and values make predatory crime almost unthinkable. European scholars and theorists have long observed that the criminal law's main function is "general prevention": reinforcement of basic social norms that are learned in the home, the church, the school, and the neighborhood. These primary socializing institutions must do

the heavy lifting—what the criminal courts can do is too little and too late for
the criminal justice system to serve as a primary socializing institution—but it is
important that law and the legal system reinforce those norms and not undermine them.

Michael Tonry, Purposes and Functions of Sentencing, 34 Crime & Just. 34
(2006).

Stressing the role and importance of the criminal law in establishing norms
of behavior in society, modern philosophers have often spoken of the "educative" or "expressive" value of punishment and have stressed the ways in which
criminal justice systems can and should shape and reinforce societal norms.
Some retributive theories stress the communicative function of a punishment,
because it reflects existing public values as embodied in the condemnatory
deprivationes aimed at the offender. See R. A. Duff, Punishment, Communication, and Community (2003). This "expressive" theory of punishment, however,
isolates something distinct: the power of the criminal law to shape and reinforce
public values, apart from any effect the punishment might have on the offender.
See Joel Feinberg, The Expressive Function of Punishment, in Doing and
Deserving 98 (1970); Dan M. Kahan, What Do Alternative Sanctions Mean?,
63 U. Chi. L. Rev. 591 (1996).

Highlighting harms suffered by both offenders and their victims in traditional sentencing and punishment schemes, many modern advocates of reform
have urged the application of "restorative justice" principles throughout the
criminal justice system. In its broadest terms, restorative justice is fundamentally
concerned with restoring social relationships; in the context of crime and punishment, restorative justice has been described as a process through which all the
parties with a stake in a particular offense come together to resolve collectively
how to deal with the aftermath of the offense and its implications for the future.
The growing interest in restorative justice ideas can be seen in Montana's 2001
amendment to the statute reprinted in Problem 1-1, which added subsection (i),
stating that "[s]entencing practices should promote and support practices,
policies, and programs that focus on restorative justice principles." See also
David Dolinko, Restorative Justice and the Justification of Punishment, 2003
Utah L. Rev. 319; but see Dan Markel, Wrong Turns on the Road to Alternative
Sanctions: Reflections on the Future of Shaming Punishments and Restorative
Justice, 85 Tex. L. Rev. 1385 (2007).

One of the most tangible expressions of restorative justice concepts is the
use of sentencing circles in some criminal justice systems. Sentencing circles are
based on sentencing practices typical of Native communities in Canada, the
United States, and Australia. Their value is being increasingly emphasized by
those interested in broadening the applicability and usefulness of restorative
justice ideas to all members of society.

A sentencing circle is typically a community-directed process, conducted in
partnership with the criminal justice system, to develop consensus on an appropriate sentencing plan that addresses the concerns of all interested parties.
Sentencing circles are traditional peacemaking rituals and are structured to
involve the victim, victim supporters, the offender, offender supporters, traditional criminal justice personnel, and other community members. Within
the circle, people are asked to speak from the heart in a shared search for

understanding of the event, and together try to identify the steps necessary to assist in healing all affected parties and prevent future crimes.

Modern sentencing circles have been developed most extensively in Saskatchewan, Manitoba, and the Yukon and have been used occasionally in several other communities. Their use spread to the United States in 1996, when a pilot project was initiated in Minnesota. As you review the following discussion of one sentencing circle experience, consider what values and goals find expression in this sort of response to criminal wrongdoing. Also consider whether sentencing circles, and the ideas of restorative justice more generally, have the potential to transform traditional perspectives on theories of punishment.

### A Healing Circle in the Innu Community of Sheshashit
#### Justice as Healing (Native Law Centre of Canada), Summer 1997

[During the fall of 1994 Gavin Sellon, while attending a clinic for alcohol and substance abuse, disclosed to counsellors that he had committed a sexual assault the year before. On his return to Sheshashit, Labrador, Mr. Sellon went to the Royal Canadian Mounted Police detachment and gave a cautioned statement admitting to having intercourse with L. without her consent. The police then began to investigate the incident.

The accused first appeared in provincial court on June 12, 1995, where he elected to be tried in the Newfoundland Supreme Court, Trial Division, waiving the preliminary inquiry. On August 9, 1995, in the supreme court, the accused indicated that he wished to plead guilty and to make an application for a sentencing circle. The Crown opposed the motion and the matter was set over to December 18, 1995, for argument, at which time the application for a sentencing circle was withdrawn. Counsel for the accused indicated that he intended to pursue an informal healing circle outside the courtroom setting and in the community of Sheshashit, and asked Judge O'Regan to give strong consideration to viewing the sentencing of Sellon with a restorative approach rather than a punitive approach. Counsel for the Crown argued that the accused, being a non-native, should be treated using the traditional methods of sentencing. Judge O'Regan indicated to both counsel that if they wished to attend the healing circle they could do so and he would place what he deemed to be appropriate weight on the results of the healing circle.]

On Sunday January 21, 1996 a circle was held in the Alcohol Centre in Sheshashit. This circle was unique because unlike previous circles that have been held, the participants of this circle were aware in advance of the circle that a written report about the circle would be completed to share with the court. The following is a report of that circle.

Much thought and discussion went into the planning and preparation for this circle. Initially Innu Nation workers in health and justice were involved in this planning. Workers all began by referring to this circle as a "sentencing" circle. Workers discussed what needs and whose needs were to be met with this circle and how best to try and meet these varied needs. There was a great deal of concern expressed that the circle needed to be witnessed by members of the justice system so that Innu would not be open to seemingly inevitable criticism that we had something to hide or fear in the circle process. The same concern was raised should we not have witnesses from the Innu public.

Those involved in planning the circle were all able to agree that as the service provider, Innu Nation has a real need to demonstrate, both to Innu and the non-Innu public and justice system, that Innu can develop and deliver services best suited to meet the needs of Innu. . . . We knew that this particular circle, with its direct connection to the court, would have a bearing on any future circles, court related or not. . . .

Therefore a conscious decision was made to be clear and specific about what needs and whose needs we were trying to meet through this process. We could then evaluate the effectiveness of the circle based clearly on what we set out to do. It was decided to tailor the circle to meet L.'s need for an opportunity to be heard within a supportive circle of those most directly affected by and involved with what happened between Gavin and her.

We also made a deliberate decision that it was not suitable or accurate to call this planned circle a "sentencing" circle. Sentencing is a justice system process to be done in court by court participants and the Judge. This circle would be held as a circle of concern and support for L. and Gavin. Included in the circle as part of the process would be recommendations made by the participants which would be shared with the court to be used by the Judge as he saw fit. . . .

We are able to determine the purpose of this circle as twofold:

1.  to provide Gavin an opportunity to acknowledge responsibility for his actions and
2.  to provide L. an opportunity to say what needed to happen for her to feel that the situation was being made more right.

Several weeks prior to the circle Jack Penashue met with L. to ask if she would be willing and able to participate in a circle with Gavin and others to deal with the incident which had resulted in a charge of sexual assault against Gavin. L. said she was willing and able to participate. After this, separate meetings were held with her father and then her mother to determine their support for their daughter's decision to participate as well as their own willingness to participate. They said they supported their daughter in her decision and were themselves willing to participate if asked by L.

Another meeting was then held with L. and Lyla Andrew [the facilitator]. Again she was asked if she felt comfortable about participating and was asked who she wanted to have participate in the circle. She said she wanted to have her sisters and parents be present. The names of other possible participants, Innu and non Innu . . . were given to L. and she indicated that "it was fine" if they wanted to attend. More information was shared with L. about the purpose of the circle and about the way it was thought the circle would happen. L. again indicated her willingness to participate. Her only request was that the circle take place soon. When she was told that her Dad would be working in Davis Inlet and not able to attend anytime soon, L. asked that the circle go ahead anyway and so the January 21 date was set.

Once this date was set Lyla met with Gavin Sellon to invite his participation in the circle. He was told who L. had invited and was asked if there were people he wanted to invite. He requested his mother, stepfather and his spouse. L. had already agreed to their participation and Gavin was told this. He also asked if Jack Penashue could attend and was informed that Jack would be a facilitator of the circle. . . .

Sunday there were 10 participants: L., G. (L.'s mom), R.N. (L.'s sister), Gavin Sellon, Patricia Nuna (Gavin's spouse), Lynne Gregory (Gavin's mom), Apenam Pone (Gavin's stepfather), Germaine Benuen [Labrador Legal Services court liaison in Sheshashit], Jack Penashue (facilitator) and Lyla Andrew (facilitator).

The participants had coffee and tea prior to the circle starting. Then all participants moved into the large meeting room and sat in a circle on the floor. With joined hands a prayer was shared. Jack then explained to the participants the symbolism of burning sweetgrass and smudging. If participants found it meaningful, they were invited to smudge and Jack went around the circle. He spoke Innuaimum first and then in English. When this was completed, Jack asked Lyla to explain the process.

It was explained to participants that what happened in the circle should be guided by the participants' acceptance and use of four principles: honesty, kindness, sharing and respect. Each person in turn would have the chance to speak uninterrupted. If they chose not to speak, they would pass the small "talking stone" on to the next person because no one would be forced to speak. There were four rounds of the circle so there were four opportunities for speaking.

The first round of the circle was for each participant to explain why they were present in the circle. The second round was a chance for each participant to speak directly to L., to share concern, support and encouragement. The third round was for each participant to speak directly to Gavin, to share with him directly feelings about him. The fourth round was the chance for each participant to make recommendations to those in the circle, and especially to Gavin, about what could or should be done at this point in time to help bring about resolution to this situation.

Before the facilitators began the rounds, the possible need for interpretation between Innuaimum and English was discussed. It was agreed that participants would speak the language of their choice and anyone could request interpretation. Jack Penashue agreed to provide the interpretation. . . .

When the fourth and final round was completed . . . participants joined hands and closed the circle with a shared prayer.

It is very difficult to put into words an assessment of the effectiveness and power of this circle. Participants in circles learn the power of the circle through their active participation and learn that equally important to what is said by the participants is the atmosphere or feeling created within the circle by the participants. The comments which follow are those of the facilitators and Germaine Benuen in relation to their impressions about the intangibles of the circle process, about why it was effective and powerful.

As the participants began arriving at the building there was a noticeable tension among some. L. arrived with her mom and was quiet, almost sad, speaking little, standing off to the side while others chatted in twos or threes. All the participants seemed to be nervous. The facilitators had to be very direct to get participants into the room to start the circle. L.'s mother (G.) was the third participant to speak and she said directly that she was scared. The tension noticeably lessened and participants explained why they were present. It seemed to help that all participants had equal opportunity to say something. Even when L. did not speak in the first round, she began to appear less tense and less pressured, perhaps because she was not put on the spot to speak. We felt that in a way the process, and the participants in the process, showed respect to L. by not forcing her to speak. . . . When the circle started L. was seated in between her mom and Gavin's mom. She sat herself in such a way that she could look at her mom and at her cousin, but she had her back to almost everyone else in the circle. By the fourth round she had shifted around so that she could see and be seen by all the participants. She was smiling sometimes and by the end of the circle was laughing when appropriate with the other participants.

Another important aspect of the circle process was the expression of emotion by participants. Facilitators had no way to know what emotions, whether anger, sadness or frustration, might be voiced and/or displayed by the participants. Facilitators knew from previous experiences that the process of the circle was powerful because honesty and emotion are an integral part of the process. How people spoke would in many ways be just as important to the impact of the circle as what people had to say.

There were two occasions when participants broke down weeping. Both L. and Gavin's mom wept. The other circle participants remained seated without speaking and waited for the person to compose themselves and then proceed when they were able. . . . G. commented that if she had been crying and someone had asked that there be a break to give her time to stop crying that it would feel like a rejection of her and her genuine feelings. She felt it was respectful of people to let them show emotion in a setting that was safe. If participants had taken a break, it would have been more because of participants' discomfort than anything else. Participants had been asked to try and be honest and respectful, and accepting the expression of emotion seemed very much a part of that honesty and respect. . . .

An assumption is made that the recommendations of the circle participants in the final round are of most importance to the court. Prior to the circle meeting, participants had been asked in preparation for the circle to think about recommendations they would want to make to be shared with the court. However, it is important to stress that what was said in the earlier three rounds and how that was expressed, had great influence on, indeed shaped the recommendations which eventually were made.

Probably the single most important comments made by any participant affecting the recommendations finally offered, were the comments made by Gavin. In the first round Gavin spoke in a clear voice, in a direct way that he had come to the circle to apologize to everyone that he had hurt for what he had done. He said that he wanted to find out what people wanted from him, what they expected from him and he repeated that he had come to apologize and to say that he was sorry for his behaviour. In the round when everyone was invited to speak to L. Gavin spoke emphasizing that L. was in no way to blame for what had happened, that he took full responsibility for his actions. He explained that when he had gone to the Brentwood Treatment Centre that he had shared a lot of things that had happened in his life and that one of those things was what had happened between him and L. He said the reason he shared that at treatment was because of his shame. He told us that he knew that what he had done was wrong and he thought that if he shared how he felt about what he had done that it might help him to get better. He also thanked people for coming to the circle.

Because of the seating, L. had the opportunity in each round to speak before Gavin. She didn't speak in the first or second rounds but she spoke in the third round to Gavin and said that she was happy that he had opened up about what had happened between them. She said she would not have been strong enough to open up to others about what happened but she was glad he had. She also told participants she was happy to be a part of the circle. After this when Gavin spoke he said he wanted L. to know that what had happened was his fault. He also wanted his family to know that he was not blaming them in any way, that his actions were his own and he was responsible for his behaviour. . . .

Jack began the final round by saying that he felt what needed to be said had been said. He said he saw what had happened in the circle . . . and he felt honoured to have been a part of the process where participants who cared about each other were able to say the things they needed to say. Jack spoke about his hesitation to say anything more but on a very personal note he said that he wanted to say what he felt should now happen, what could now happen. He said he thought that L. and Gavin should start talking to one another if they were not already doing so, that they both needed to accept what had happened because it was his experience that people sometimes "over say things and over think things." He said maybe it wouldn't happen right now but what needed to happen was for L. and Gavin to start having contact again maybe to try and hug each other. . . .

Lyla then began speaking and said she too found the last round the most difficult even though she knew that the earlier rounds had been difficult because what was said and expressed was more painful. The difficulty with making recommendations came with a sense of having to satisfy someone or [some] group outside the circle, someone who hadn't experienced what had happened in the circle.

She then shared the same concern as Jack that where there had been friendships and family ties connecting Gavin and L. and Gavin's spouse and children, and where those connections had been broken or damaged, that through Gavin's actions, with the permission and agreement of others, that he needed to try and mend those connections. . . .

One recommendation was shared with L. This was that she accept and use . . . the caring that her family clearly has for her . . . to grow into being her own person. . . .

Another specific recommendation was made about Gavin. If he were to be placed on probation, and obviously we couldn't know this, but if he was, it was recommended that rather than being supervised directly by the adult probation office, that he be made accountable through a period of probation to people in the community to whom he is connected and who know why he would be on probation and who would have real concern about how he was going to do while on probation. . . .

Through interpretation L.'s mom G. said that she was really happy that Gavin had come to the circle and shared what he had with the participants. It was her opinion that Gavin was a strong young man because he had shared so much and taken responsibility. . . .

Apenam [Gavin's stepfather] recommended to Gavin that he continue to work at what Apenam knew Gavin had learned from going to the Brentwood treatment program. Apenam recommended this because he himself had gone to Brentwood many years before Gavin to change his own behaviour. . . .

Apenam said he wanted to say openly that he loves Gavin. Apenam said he doesn't always know how to show his love and that this is one of the biggest problems in his own life. He said he knows Gavin has a birth father but that he still wants to continue to be a father to Gavin as he has tried to be for many years, and if Gavin needs his help, Apenam offers it to him. . . .

In Innuaimum, L. was asked by Jack if she understood and she made a reply right away. . . . Everyone agreed to close the circle and stood up with hands joined and together repeated the "serenity prayer."

At this point the tape was turned off and participants embraced one another at their own choosing. It is noted that L.'s mom went over to Gavin and embraced him and most significantly that L. and Gavin embraced one another. . . .

[A report of the circle was prepared and attached to the decision of Judge O'Regan of the Newfoundland Supreme Court, Trial Division. In considering sentencing, Judge O'Regan found that "the concern of the Crown" that Gavin was non Inuit was "a non-issue," especially since Gavin "did grow up in the community of Sheshashit and was exposed to the Innu Culture and thus can benefit from the community's involvement in such things as a 'healing circle' which he attended." Judge O'Regan accepted the recommendations of the healing circle and imposed a noncustodial sentence.]

## NOTES

1. *Sentencing circles, restorative justice, and traditional purposes.*   Do sentencing circles serve all, or even any, of the traditional purposes of punishment? Which traditional purposes were served by the healing circle involving Gavin, L., and their families? See Julian V. Roberts & Carol LaPrairie, Sentencing Circles: Some Unanswered Questions, 39 Crim. L.Q. 69 (1997) (exploring the relationship of sentencing circles to traditional purposes of punishment).

What nontraditional purposes were served in the sentencing of Gavin? Proponents of sentencing circles say the goals of the process are to promote healing for all affected parties; to provide an opportunity for the offender to make amends; to empower victims, community members, families, and offenders by giving them a voice and a shared responsibility in finding constructive resolutions; to address the underlying causes of criminal behavior; to build a sense of community and enhance its capacity for resolving conflict; and to promote and share community values. Do you think sentencing circles represent a radically different substantive approach to crime and punishment? Or do they simply represent a more meaningful and effective means to achieve traditional goals?

Proponents of sentencing circles readily concede that the process is not appropriate for all offenders. They stress the importance of several factors in determining whether a case is appropriate for a sentencing circle, including the strength of the offender's connection to the community, the sincerity and nature of the offender's efforts to be healed, the input of victims, and the dedication of the offender's support group. What about the nature of the offense itself? Would a sentencing circle be useful for an offender convicted of murder? For an offender convicted of stock fraud? For an offender convicted of trafficking in cocaine? For an offender convicted of domestic violence? Cf. Rashmi Goel, No Women at the Center: The Use of the Canadian Sentencing Circle in Domestic Violence Cases, 15 Wis. Women's L.J. 293 (2000).

2. *Assessing the efficacy of sentencing circles.*  Very little research has been conducted to date on the effectiveness of sentencing circles, in part because most punishment systems are judged in terms of crime rates whereas sentencing circles are clearly concerned with a range of other interests. There have been a number of positive anecdotal reports about sentencing circles, but they have not been seriously examined empirically. See Roberts & LaPrairie, Sentencing Circles at 82-83 (arguing that before sentencing circles are used broadly, "it is incumbent upon advocates to produce the kind of rigorous scientific evidence that sentencing circles are more effective than the current system").

Should sentencing circles be an option in all criminal justice settings — that is, should jurisdictions explore the possibility of using sentencing circles for all sorts of crimes and all sorts of offenders? Consider the following sentencing and justice experiment.

3. *Other approaches to restorative justice.*  The movement toward restorative justice finds many manifestations besides sentencing circles. Especially for less serious offenses, a number of jurisdictions have developed various novel criminal justice forums and procedures that emphasize repairing harm, healing, and rebuilding relations among victims, offenders, and communities. In addition to sentencing circles, popular restorative justice practices include victim-offender mediation, family group conferencing, citizen panels, and various restitution initiatives. See generally Leena Kurki, Restorative and Community Justice in the United States, 27 Crime & Just. 235 (2000); Frederick W. Gay, Restorative Justice and the Prosecutor, 27 Fordham Urb. L.J. 1651 (2000). A parallel development is the recognition by both traditional and specialty courts of "therapeutic jurisprudence," which treats the law and its institutions and agents as potentially organized around problem solving and individualized justice. David Wexler, Dennis Stolle & Bruce Winick, eds., Practicing Therapeutic Jurisprudence: Law as a Helping Profession (2000); David Wexler, Therapeutic Jurisprudence: It's Not Just for Problem-Solving Courts and Calendars Anymore, in National Center for State Courts, Future Trends in State Courts 2004 87 (2004).

## PROBLEM 1-2.  RED HOOK COMMUNITY COURT

Red Hook, a Brooklyn neighborhood once notorious for drugs and crime, is home to one of New York's oldest and largest public housing developments. It is also home to a multi-jurisdictional community court, the Red Hook Community Justice Center. In the court, one judge hears cases that would otherwise be divided among civil, family, and criminal courts. Typical cases involve common neighborhood problems: drugs, domestic violence, and landlord-tenant disputes. The judge has a variety of sanctions and services available, and the judge, prosecutor, and public defender work together to achieve the best plan for the particular individual. For example, the court can require drug treatment or counseling for mental health or domestic violence. Offenders can also be required to participate in community restitution projects. There are on-site educational workshops as well, including job training and GED classes. These programs are available to all community members, regardless of court involvement.

You work for the District Attorney's office of a community similarly plagued by chronic street crime, drugs, and unemployment. Your boss has heard of Red Hook and other community courts, as well as funding sources in the Department of Justice to underwrite experimental community courts. You are tasked with proposing the jurisdiction for the court, and presenting the idea to city officials, community leaders, and members of the public. How would you explain the benefits of a community court? Would you focus on the success of other courts by highlighting the decline in recidivism rates or would you emphasize the long-term benefits of increased community involvement? What are the similarities between a community court and a traditional court? What would you say to those concerned that the lack of an adversarial process is damaging the rights of the individuals sentenced by community courts?

For a firsthand account of the Red Hook Community Justice Center, see Greg Berman & Aubrey Fox, Justice in Red Hook, 26 Just. Sys. J. 77 (2005).

## 2.  Implicit Purposes

The American Bar Association states in its model sentencing standards that without "reasonably clear identification of goals and purposes, the administration of criminal justice will be inconsistent, incoherent, and ineffectual." In practice, most criminal justice systems operate without reasonably clear identification of goals and purposes. But just because goals and purposes have not been articulated does not mean that they do not operate. And even in systems with explicit purposes, truer and deeper implicit purposes may operate. Consider whether the implicit purposes of punishment described in the following materials offer better tools to explain the actual behavior of legislators, prosecutors, and judges.

## Purposes and Functions of Sentencing, Michael Tonry
### 34 Crime & Just. 10-12, 42-43 (2006)

The fundamental purposes and primary functions of sentencing are clear, and are the same: to punish criminals and prevent crimes. There are, however, other functions that concern officials and policy makers. They range from encouraging most defendants to plead guilty and managing criminal justice budgets to reassuring the public and getting reelected.

People concerned primarily with the word "justice" in "criminal justice" would say that the overriding purpose of sentencing is the imposition of punishments that are just relative to prevailing normative criteria; the overriding functional goal would be to ensure, or at least maximize the likelihood of, imposition of just punishments according to those criteria. People concerned primarily with the word "criminal" would say that the overriding purpose of sentencing is the prevention of crime and accordingly that the overriding functional goal is to minimize the incidence of crime and its consequences. To distinguish the question of what purposes should be pursued from the question of whether laws have been fairly and effectively applied relative to those purposes, I refer to the first as purposes and the second as distributive functions. . . .

All mainstream contemporary theories include crime prevention among the purposes of punishment, though they vary widely in what ways, with what weight, and subject to what constraints prevention may be taken into account. Most people, however, believe that prevention and diminution of crime, fear of crime, and their consequences are important and legitimate functions of sentencing. These are the preventive functions.

Many practitioners would also include efficiency, cost-effectiveness, and resource management among the functional goals of an acceptable sentencing system. Managers need to set and pursue substantive priorities, allocate personnel and resources, meet performance goals, and operate within their budgets. They also need to maintain good working relations with other agencies and officials who can make their work easier or harder, and thereby make achievement of other goals easier or harder. These are management functions.

Some policy makers and analysts urge that it is important that governments reassure the public, maintain confidence in the legal system, denounce wrongful behavior, and reinforce basic social norms. Contemporary analyses of "expressive" policies emphasize government officials' wishes and needs to assure the public that things are being done to address subjects that trouble them [David Garland, The Culture of Control: Crime and Social Order in Contemporary Society (Univ. of Chicago Press 2001)]. Recent work on legitimacy and procedural justice emphasizes that justice needs to be seen to be done [Tom R. Tyler, Procedural Justice, Legitimacy, and the Effective Rule of Law, 30 Crime & Just. 431 (2003)]. Durkheimian analyses portray criminal law as a primary contributor to maintenance and refinement of basic social norms and its dramaturgical features as key sources of social cohesion [Emile Durkheim, Division of Labor in Society (1893/1933)]. These are communicative functions.

The first two of these, distribution and prevention, concern primary goals (what sentencing "is supposed to do"). The third, management, is an ancillary goal (how institutional imperatives can be acknowledged while pursuing primary goals).

The fourth, communication, is the most complex and multifaceted and operates at all three functional levels. Communication of legal threats and acknowledgment in court processes and outcomes of basic social norms are necessary to achieve the primary goals of distribution and prevention.

Communication about court processes and procedures and likely punishments is key to achievement of a variety of management goals. These might, however, be thought of as incidental components of primary and ancillary functions. . . .

The more controversial forms of communication relate to latent functions. Practitioners and policy makers are sometimes moved by personal, ideological, and partisan objectives. People sometimes make decisions or support policies because it is in their personal self-interest, because they want to bear witness to their ideological beliefs, or because they want to pursue partisan political advantage. [To summarize:]

A. Purposes ( . . . these could be called normative functions)
B. Primary functions
   1. Distribution (consistency, evenhandedness, fairness)
   2. Prevention (crime, fear of crime, costs and consequences of both)
   3. Communication (threat communication, denunciation of wrongful behavior, reinforcement of basic social norms)
C. Ancillary functions
   1. Management (efficiency, cost-effectiveness, resource management)
   2. Communication (procedural justice, legitimacy, public confidence)
D. Latent functions
   1. Self-interest
   2. Ideology
   3. Partisanship
   4. Communication. . . .

Purely personal ambitions and self-serving motives are illegitimate considerations in decision making by prosecutors and judges about individual cases. Performance of the distributive, preventive, and communicative functions is undermined when cases are dealt with in a particular way because a practitioner believes she is likelier to gain a nomination, win an election, or obtain a new job. . . . When a prosecutor or judge treats an offender in a particular way to realize a purely personal goal, there is no arguable public benefit that can be said to outweigh or counterbalance the harm done the offender. When an entirely self-motivated legislator votes to support a particular policy for which there is little substantive justification, but claims in good faith to be trying to reassure the public or, more complicatedly, claims a need to vote in a particular way on this subject in order to win others' support for a vote on a more important subject, it is almost impossible to assess what the real motives are. The governing ethical premise, however, should be the same as for a prosecutor or a judge: only disinterested motives are legitimate. . . .

Sometimes penal policies are proposed for reasons having nothing to do with the goals of punishment per se. The prison guards union in California, for example, is often said to promote harsher policies as means to the ends of job creation and maintenance. Many communities have sought placement of prisons within their boundaries and, implicitly, increased use of imprisonment, as a form of economic development. On the face of it these considerations are entirely unrelated to punishment and prevention. . . .

Crime control policy in our time has become entangled in ideological conflict. Recent conflicts over medical use of marijuana and Oregon's assisted-suicide law offer front-page examples. . . .

Ideology is at least as powerful an influence on sentencing policy. Drug policy offers stark examples. The federal 100-to-one law punishes people, mostly black, convicted of crack cocaine offenses as severely as people, many white, convicted of powder cocaine offenses involving amounts that are 100 times larger. The law was enacted in 1986, after the much-publicized death, generally attributed to a crack overdose, of Len Bias, a University of Maryland basketball player forecast to become a National Basketball Association superstar. The law's role in exacerbating racial disparities in federal prisons soon became clear, and the U.S. Sentencing Commission proposed that the differential be eliminated. Both the Clinton White House and the Congress opposed any change, and none was made. In later years Attorney General Janet Reno, Drug Czar Barry McCaffrey, and the U.S. Sentencing Commission proposed that the differential be reduced. The Clinton and Bush II White Houses opposed all changes, and the differential remains. No one presumably wants federal sentencing laws to worsen racial disparities, but neither successive administration nor congressional leaders have been willing to risk being accused of condoning drug use or trafficking.

Mandatory minimum and three-strikes laws, for other examples, often are primarily based on ideology. Research findings discussed in earlier sections make it clear, and for at least a century have made it clear, that such laws seldom achieve their putative goals and always produce undesirable and unwanted consequences. Ideological posturing is no better an explanation for why an offender is punished unjustly than is a judge's hope for reelection.

Pursuit of partisan advantage is the most cynical of the latent functions. Ideological influences grow out of deeply held beliefs; those beliefs may sometimes be blinding. . . . Decisions made for partisan reasons, by contrast, are made in cold calculation. Partisan influences often result in the passage of laws that cannot be justified on the substantive merits and foreseeably produce unjust results. Republican Senator Orrin Hatch, according to a member of his staff, for example, long believed reducing sentences for drug offenders "was the right thing to do, but he couldn't do it for political reasons."

California's three-strikes law, according to Frank Zimring's account, resulted from politicians' competing attempts to use punishment policies to pursue partisan advantage. It was enacted not because thoughtful policy makers really believed that people who stole pizza slices in schoolyards or handfuls of compact discs from Wal-Mart deserved decades-long prison sentences, but because Republican Governor Pete Wilson and California Assembly leader Willie Brown played a game of chicken in which, in the end, neither backed down. Democratic legislators agreed among themselves to pass any proposal Governor Wilson offered, in hopes "that he would back down from an unqualified 'get tough' stand or be politically neutralized if he persisted." . . . Neither Wilson nor Brown was willing to propose refinements to Wilson's extreme initial proposal and thereby expose himself and his party to the other's accusation of softness. As a result California adopted the most far-reaching, rigid, and unjust three-strikes law in the country. . . .

## Discipline and Punish: The Birth of the Prison, Michel Foucault
### Pages 3-8, 16-30, 200-221 (1977)

On 1 March 1757 Damiens the regicide was condemned "to make the *amende honorable* before the main door of the Church of Paris," where he was to be "taken and conveyed in a cart, wearing nothing but a shirt, holding a torch of burning wax weighing two pounds"; then, "in the said cart, to the Place de Grève, where, on a scaffold that will be erected there, the flesh will be torn from his breasts, arms, thighs and calves with red-hot pincers, his right hand, holding the knife with which he committed the said parricide, burnt with sulphur, and, on those places where the flesh will be torn away, poured molten lead, boiling oil, burning resin, wax and sulphur melted together and then his body drawn and quartered by four horses and his limbs and body consumed by fire, reduced to ashes and his ashes thrown to the winds" (*Pièces originales*, 372-4).

"Finally, he was quartered," recounts the *Gazette d'Amsterdam* of 1 April 1757. "This last operation was very long, because the horses used were not accustomed to drawing; consequently, instead of four, six were needed; and when that did not suffice, they were forced, in order to cut off the wretch's thighs, to sever the sinews and hack at the joints. . . . It is said that, though he was always a great swearer, no blashemy escaped his lips; but the excessive pain made him utter horrible cries, and he often repeated: 'My God, have pity on me! Jesus, help me!' The spectators were all edified by the solicitude of the parish priest of St Paul's who despite his great age did not spare himself in offering consolation to the patient." . . .

Eighty years later, Léon Faucher drew up his rules "for the House of young prisoners in Paris":

> Art. 17. The prisoners' day will begin at six in the morning in winter and at five in summer. They will work for nine hours a day throughout the year. Two hours a day will be devoted to instruction. Work and the day will end at nine o'clock in winter and at eight in summer.
>
> Art. 18. *Rising.* At the first drum-roll, the prisoners must rise and dress in silence, as the supervisor opens the cell doors. At the second drum-roll, they must be dressed and make their beds. At the third, they must line up and proceed to the chapel for morning prayer. There is a five-minute interval between each drum-roll.
>
> Art. 19. The prayers are conducted by the chaplain and followed by a moral or religious reading. This exercise must not last more than half an hour.
>
> Art. 20. *Work.* At a quarter to six in the summer, a quarter to seven in winter, the prisoners go down into the courtyard where they must wash their hands and faces, and receive their first ration of bread. Immediately afterwards, they form into work-teams and go off to work, which must begin at six in summer and seven in winter.
>
> Art. 21. *Meal.* At ten o'clock the prisoners leave their work and go to the refectory; they wash their hands in their courtyards and assemble in divisions. After the dinner, there is recreation until twenty minutes to eleven.

> Art. 22. *School.* At twenty minutes to eleven, at the drum-roll, the prisoners
> form into ranks, and proceed in divisions to the school. The class
> lasts two hours and consists alternately of reading, writing, drawing
> and arithmetic.
>
> Art. 23. At twenty minutes to one, the prisoners leave the school, in divi-
> sions, and return to their courtyards for recreation. At five minutes
> to one, at the drum-roll, they form into workteams.
>
> Art. 24. At one o'clock they must be back in the workshops: they work until
> four o'clock.
>
> Art. 25. At four o'clock the prisoners leave their workshops and go into the
> courtyards where they wash their hands and form into divisions for
> the refectory.
>
> Art. 26. Supper and the recreation that follows it last until five o'clock: the
> prisoners then return to the workshops.
>
> Art. 27. At seven o'clock in the summer, at eight in winter, work stops;
> bread is distributed for the last time in the workshops. For a quarter
> of an hour one of the prisoners or supervisors reads a passage from
> some instructive or uplifting work. This is followed by evening
> prayer.
>
> Art. 28. At half-past seven in summer, half-past eight in winter, the prison-
> ers must be back in their cells after the washing of hands and the
> inspection of clothes in the courtyard; at the first drum-roll, they
> must undress, and at the second get into bed. The cell doors are
> closed and the supervisors go the rounds in the corridors, to ensure
> order and silence" (Faucher, 274, 82).

We have, then, [from the two distinct examples] a public execution and a timetable. They do not punish the same crimes or the same type of delinquent. But they each define a certain penal style. Less than a century separates them. [Between 1760 and 1840] in Europe and in the United States, the entire economy of punishment was redistributed. It was a time of great "scandals" for traditional justice, a time of innumerable projects for reform. It saw a new theory of law and crime, a new moral or political justification of the right to punish; old laws were abolished, old customs died out. "Modern" codes were planned or drawn up: Russia, 1769; Prussia, 1780; Pennsylvania and Tuscany, 1786; Austria, 1788; France, 1791, Year IV, 1808 and 1810. It was a new age for penal justice.

Among so many changes, I shall consider one: the disappearance of torture as a public spectacle. Today we are rather inclined to ignore it; perhaps, in its time, it gave rise to too much inflated rhetoric; perhaps it has been attributed too readily and too emphatically to a process of "humanization," thus dispensing with the need for further analysis. And, in any case, how important is such a change, when compared with the great institutional transformations, the formulation of explicit, general codes and unified rules of procedure; with the almost universal adoption of the jury system, the definition of the essentially corrective character of the penalty and the tendency, which has become increasingly marked since the nineteenth century, to adapt punishment to the individual offender? Punishment of a less immediately physical kind, a certain discretion in the art of inflicting pain, a combination of more subtle, more subdued sufferings, deprived of their visible display, should not all this be treated as a special case, an incidental effect of deeper changes? And yet the fact remains that a few decades saw the disappearance of the tortured, dismembered, amputated body, symbolically branded on face or shoulder, exposed alive or dead to public view. The body as the major target of penal repression disappeared.

If the penalty in its most severe forms no longer addresses itself to the body, on what does it lay hold? The answer of the theoreticians — those who, about 1760, opened up a new period that is not yet at an end — is simple, almost obvious. It seems to be contained in the question itself: since it is no longer the body, it must be the soul. The expiation that once rained down upon the body must be replaced by a punishment that acts in depth on the heart, the thoughts, the will, the inclinations. Mably formulated the principle once and for all: "Punishment, if I may so put it, should strike the soul rather than the body." . . .

Bentham's Panopticon is the architectural figure of this composition. We know the principle on which it was based: at the periphery, an annular building; at the centre, a tower; this tower is pierced with wide windows that open onto the inner side of the ring; the peripheric building is divided into cells, each of which extends the whole width of the building; they have two windows, one on the inside, corresponding to the windows of the tower; the other, on the outside, allows the light to cross the cell from one end to the other. All that is needed, then, is to place a supervisor in a central tower and to shut up in each cell a madman, a patient, a condemned man, a worker or a schoolboy. By the effect of backlighting, one can observe from the tower, standing out precisely against the light, the small captive shadows in the cells of the periphery. They are like so many cages, so many small theaters, in which each actor is alone, perfectly individualized and constantly visible. . . .

Each individual, in his place, is securely confined to a cell from which he is seen from the front by the supervisor; but the side walls prevent him from coming into contact with his companions. He is seen, but he does not see; he is the object of information, never a subject in communication. The arrangement of his room, opposite the central tower, imposes on him an axial visibility. And this invisibility is a guarantee of order. If the inmates are convicts, there is no danger of a plot, an attempt at collective escape, the planning of new crimes for the future, bad reciprocal influences; if they are patients, there is no danger of contagion; if they are madmen there is no risk of their committing violence upon one another; if they are schoolchildren, there is no copying, no noise, no chatter, no waste of time; if they are workers, there are no disorders, no theft, no coalitions, none of those distractions that slow down the rate of work, make it less perfect or cause accidents. The crowd, a compact mass, a locus of multiple exchanges, individualities merging together, a collective effect, is abolished and replaced by a collection of separated individualities. . . . (Bentham, 60-64).

Hence the major effect of the Panopticon: to induce in the inmate a state of conscious and permanent visibility that assures the automatic functioning of power. So to arrange things that the surveillance is permanent in its effects, even if it is discontinuous in its action; that the perfection of power should tend to render its actual exercise unnecessary; that this architectural apparatus should be a machine for creating and sustaining a power relation independent of the person who exercises it; in short, that the inmates should be caught up in a power situation of which they are themselves the bearers. . . .

So much for the question of observation. But the Panopticon was also a laboratory; it could be used as a machine to carry out experiments, to alter behaviour, to train or correct individuals. To experiment with medicines and monitor their effects. To try out different punishments on prisoners, according to their crimes and character, and to seek the most effective ones. To teach different techniques simultaneously to the workers, to decide which is the best. To try out pedagogical experiments. . . . The Panopticon is a privileged place for experiment on men, and for analysing with complete certainty the transformations that may be obtained from them. The Panopticon may even provide an apparatus for supervising its own mechanisms. In this central tower, the director may spy on all the employees that he has under his orders: nurses, doctors, foremen, teachers, warders; he will be able to judge them continuously, alter their behaviour, impose upon them the methods he thinks best; and it will even be possible to observe the director himself. . . .

The Panopticon . . . is polyvalent in its applications; it serves to reform prisoners, but also to treat patients, to instruct schoolchildren, to confine the insane, to supervise workers, to put beggars and idlers to work. It is a type of location of bodies in space, of distribution of individuals in relation to one another, of hierarchical organization, of disposition of centres and channels of power, of definition of the instruments and modes of intervention of power, which can be implemented in hospitals, workshops, schools, prisons.

[It] is not that the beautiful totality of the individual is amputate, repressed, altered by our social order, it is rather that the individual is carefully fabricated in it, according to a whole technique of forces and bodies. . . . The panoptic modality of power . . . is not under the immediate dependence or a direct extension of the great juridical-political structures of a society; it is none-theless not absolutely independent. Historically, the process by which the bour-geoisie became in the course of the eighteenth century the politically dominant class was masked by the establishment of an explicit, coded and formally egalitarian juridical framework, made possible by the organization of a parlia-mentary, representative regime. But the development and generalization of disciplinary mechanisms constituted the other, dark side of these processes. The general juridical form that guaranteed a system of rights that were egalitarian in principle was supported by these tiny, everyday, physical mechan-isms, by all those systems of micro-power that are essentially non-egalitarian and asymmetrical that we call the disciplines. And although, in a formal way, the representative regime makes it possible . . . for the will of all to form the fundamental authority of sovereignty, the disciplines provide, at the base, a guarantee of the submission of forces and bodies. The real, corporal disciplines constituted the foundation of the formal, juridical liberties. The contract may have been regarded as the ideal foundation of law and political power; panopti-cism constituted the technique, universally widespread, of coercion. It continued to work in depth on the juridical structures of society, in order to make the effective mechanisms of power function in opposition to the formal framework that it had acquired. The "Enlightenment," which discovered the liberties, also invented the disciplines.

How can we determine any implicit purposes of sentencing in the United States early in the twenty-first century? Perhaps one way is to offer a snapshot of current punishment—what sanctions are used, for how many, and for whom. Imagine this is not a country you know, but a foreign country. If you look only at the picture of punishment described below, what possible theories of implicit purpose can you discern (despite whatever explicit claims might be made)?

- At the end of 2010 the nation's prisons and jails incarcerated 2,266,800 persons. Prisoners in the custody of the 50 states and the federal system accounted for two-thirds of the incarcerated population (1,518,104 inmates). The other third were held in local jails (748,728), not including persons in community-based programs.
- The rate of incarceration in prison and jail was 732 inmates per 100,000 residents in 2010, up from 601 in 1995.
- The five states with the highest incarceration rates in 2010 were all in the South: Louisiana, Mississippi, Alabama, Texas, and Oklahoma. The five states with the lowest incarceration rates at midyear 2010 were all in the Northeast and upper Midwest: Maine, Minnesota, Rhode Island, Massachusetts, and New Hampshire.
- At the end of 2010, black non-Hispanic males had an imprisonment rate (3,059 per 100,000 U.S. black male residents) that was nearly 7 times higher than white non-Hispanic males (456 per 100,000).
- In 2010 a total of 46 persons were executed in 12 states (13 of those executions occurred in Texas). Thirty-six states and the federal government had capital statutes as of 2010.
- At the end of 2010 there were 3,158 prisoners under sentence of death. California held the largest number on death row (699), followed by Florida (392), Texas (315), and Pennsylvania (215). Men made up 98% (3,100) of all prisoners under sentence of death. Whites accounted for 55%, blacks 42%, and other races 3%.

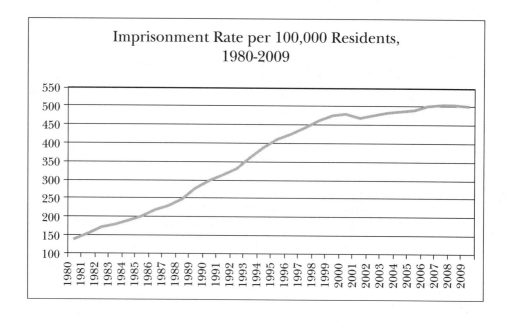

Imprisonment Rate per 100,000 Residents, 1980-2009

## NOTES

1. *Inferring purposes from historical trends in punishment.* What purpose or purposes can be inferred from many societies' reliance on brutal physical punishments throughout history and up to the eighteenth century? What purpose or purposes can be inferred from the United States' increased reliance on incarceration in recent decades?

As Foucault suggests, there have been significant shifts in the overall approach to punishment throughout Western history. While modern sentencing systems usually consider imprisonment as the primary mode of punishment, the very concept of incarceration was largely unknown before the nineteenth century. Physical and financial punishments were the norm in medieval times, and the sanctions imposed by the state could be quite harsh and brutal for even minor offenses. Serious crimes were punished with death or banishment, and nearly all punishments were carried out in public for members of the community to witness. See Arthur W. Campbell, Law of Sentencing, §1 (1978).

Influenced in part by the development and ascendancy of imprisonment as a principal mode of punishment, nearly all Western societies have abandoned the official use of brutal physical punishments, and rarely are punishments carried out in public settings. Though these "modernizing" trends seem to make our systems of punishment more "civilized," the Foucault reading should lead you to consider whether torturing the human soul may in fact be worse than torturing the human body. Another question to consider is whether the "civilization" of our methods of punishment may make them less effective when judged against our theories of punishment. Might certain theories of punishment be better served by forms of physical torture imposed in public than by terms of imprisonment served in private?

2. *Modern variations in types of punishment.* The cumulative statistics presented above do not reveal the significant variations in how individuals are incarcerated and how terms of probation and parole are structured and controlled. The experience of incarceration for offenders can and does vary greatly depending in part on whether the time is served in halfway houses, local jails, minimum-security prisons, general state or federal prisons, or high-security (supermax) prisons. See generally Norval Morris, The Contemporary Prison: 1965-Present, in The Oxford History of the Prison 227 (1995). The experience of probation or parole likewise varies considerably, depending on the conditions placed on probationers or parolees and on other forms of sanctions (both official and unofficial) that can accompany community supervision. See generally Andrew Horwitz, Coercion, Pop-Psychology, and Judicial Moralizing: Some Proposals for Curbing Judicial Abuse of Probation Conditions, 57 Wash. & Lee L. Rev. 75 (2000); Nora V. Demleitner, Preventing Internal Exile: The Need for Restrictions on Collateral Sentencing Consequences, 11 Stan. L. & Pol'y Rev. 153 (1999). Similar issues arise in the context of pretrial release conditions. See Dan Markel and Eric J. Miller, Bowling, as Bail Condition, N.Y. Times, July 13, 2012.

3. *Trends in U.S. punishment practices.* Which of the statistics reflecting modern sentencing and punishment dynamics in the United States surprises

you the most? Which of the statistics disturbs you the most? What other trends (for instance, the use of the death penalty in different regions across time) could tell you something about the implicit purposes of punishment in a society? The Bureau of Justice Statistics, a research arm of the U.S. Department of Justice, collects data on the use of correctional resources.

## B.  PURPOSES IN PRACTICAL CONTEXT

For several millennia philosophers have discussed the ins and outs, the pros and cons, of different theories of punishment. English philosopher H. L. A. Hart advanced the theoretical debate when he observed that these discussions involve three conceptually distinct issues:

(1) The "general justifying aim" — the general goal of the social institution of punishment
(2) The question of liability — who specifically should be punished for certain behavior
(3) The question of amount — exactly how much punishment should be administered

See H. L. A. Hart, Prolegomenon to the Principles of Punishment, in Punishment and Responsibility 1-28 (1968). Hart's insight reinforces the fact that while philosophers have the luxury of discussing theoretical issues in the abstract, societies must confront the complicated practical realities of constructing and operating a workable criminal justice system and then distributing specific punishments to offenders. The materials in this section demonstrate that administering a sentencing and corrections system is even more complex than questions of punishment theory. Rather than working through these issues by starting with general questions and then moving to specific cases, we will begin with a specific case and then telescope out to broader, systemwide questions.

## 1.  Use of Purposes in Sentencing an Individual Offender

Though the purposes of punishment are often debated at a high level of abstraction, individual decision makers (usually judges) necessarily confront them when deciding what sentence to impose in a particular case. Norval Morris, writing in 1953, noted not only the inevitability of considering purposes when sentencing individual offenders but also the importance of blending purposes on a case-by-case basis:

> When a court decides what sentence to impose on a criminal . . . , it must do so with reference to some purpose or purposes, conscious or unconscious, articulate or inarticulate. [A] compass is desirable . . . , even if only for a short distance and over a particular part of the journey. [For] certain types of criminals reformation is one important aim. None will dispute that our hope of

deterring the criminal from repeating his crime by the punishment we inflict and by that same punishment deterring others who are like-minded also plays a considerable part. Few will deny that there is in the community a deep-rooted hatred of the criminal . . . and that in our penal sanctions we must take into account these emotional demands of the community. The extent to which these aims of reformation, deterrence and community satisfaction blend in relation to any particular offender will vary considerably.

Norval Morris, Sentencing Convicted Criminals, 27 Austl. L.J. 186, 192-198 (1953).

Many modern sentencing systems that structure how judges can exercise their sentencing power often prescribe certain sentencing ranges for particular offenders committing particular offenses, but then allow the judge to move outside these ranges in "extraordinary" circumstances or for "substantial and compelling" reasons. Judges in these systems thus have an opportunity to consider the purposes of sentencing in the selection of specific sentences both within and outside of the prescribed ranges.

For example, the Washington State Sentencing Reform Act of 1981 provides that the purposes of sentencing are to: (1) ensure that the punishment for a criminal offense is proportionate to the seriousness of the offense and the offender's criminal history; (2) promote respect for the law by providing punishment that is just; (3) impose punishment that is commensurate with the punishment imposed on others committing similar offenses; (4) protect the public; (5) offer offenders an opportunity to improve themselves; and (6) make frugal use of the state's resources. See Wash. Rev. Code §9.94A.010. The following case comes not from the Northwest but from the Southeast—and to make matters even more interesting, it is from the southeastern Australian territory of Victoria! There are untold riches in the sentencing practices and decisions of several Australian jurisdictions, nicely illustrated by this decision. In the following sentencing decision, consider the role of purposes and the kinds of purposes the court uses to decide whether an exceptional sentence was appropriate.

---

## The Queen v. Robert James Arnautovic
### [2007] VCC 597 (9 June 2005),
### County Court of Victoria,
### Melbourne Criminal Division

---

Her Honour, Judge Gaynor:

1. Robert James Arnautovic, you have pleaded guilty before me to seven counts of burglary, seven counts of theft and one count of armed robbery and have admitted prior convictions. The facts underlying the offending which took place between November 1998 and March 2002 are as follows.

2. Counts 1 and 2 relate to an incident which occurred on the afternoon of 13 November 1998 when you entered the rear yard of a house at 56 Stafford Street, Abbotsford, smashing two windows to gain entry. You stole from that house property to the value of approximately $18,300 consisting of electronic equipment, computer equipment, a mobile phone, a watch, cameras, camera equipment, VCRs, CD players, disk players and CDs. . . .

3. [Counts 3-10 relate to similar criminal incidents during 1999 and 2000.]

7. Count 11 refers to an incident on the morning of 4 December 2001 when you forced a side window of a house at 5 York Street, Albion through which you gained entry and then stole a bag which you filled with items of property. While you were in the house the occupier, one Xavier Haveraux and his three year old daughter Kemely returned home entering through the front door. You rushed at Mr. Haveraux striking him to the head three times with a flat instrument similar to a small jemmy bar causing Mr. Haveraux to fall on the floor. Whilst he was on the floor you searched him taking his watch which was valued at $65 and demanding money from him, you ultimately being given $10. Whilst this was occurring you kept accusing Mr. Haveraux of "ripping you off" to the tune of $50 a couple of weeks earlier and claimed you had followed him home.

8. You then asked Mr. Haveraux to drive you in his car to get more money but Mr. Haveraux talked you out of this and got you to leave. You then left the premises and walked down the street before which you apologised to Mr. Haveraux's three year old daughter who was present during the entire incident. Once you had left Mr. Haveraux grabbed an old cricket bat and followed you to see where you were going and as he followed you down the street you turned back towards him and approached him saying, "Come on."

9. You and Mr. Haveraux then struggled, wrestling to the ground during the course of which Mr. Haveraux managed to hit you over the head with the cricket bat causing you to bleed. Eventually you both stood up and you walked off, Mr. Haveraux going back to his house and calling police. A sample of your bloodstains obtained from the footpath in York Street was subsequently obtained and examined.

10. Counts 12 and 13 relate to an incident which occurred on 8 December 2001 when you entered the back yard of a house at 1 Cowper Street, Footscray, smashing the window with a pitchfork you obtained from a garden shed, thereby gaining entry to the house from which you stole an IBM laptop computer, a Packlite backpack, a Kathmandu backpack, gold jewellery, a camera, a watch and a Sharp remote control valued at approximately $10,190.

11. Counts 14 and 15 relate to an incident 14 March 2002 when you entered the back yard of a house at 36 Princess Street, Kew, smashing and removing slats from a louvre window to gain access to the house from which you stole UK Sterling cash, a video game unit, confectionary, a Samsung mobile telephone, sunglasses, a video game, a Walkman and a backpack to the value of approximately $600.

12. This offending was ultimately linked to you because in each case police obtained blood samples from the scenes of the crimes left by you on entering premises via broken windows or in the case of Count 11 from the pavement of York Street, Albion, following the contretemps with Mr. Haveraux. You were arrested on 4 March 2004. . . .

13. You have admitted extensive prior convictions, they being 39 prior convictions for burglary, 57 prior convictions for theft, and you have in the course of your offending previously received eight gaol terms and in that course breaching three suspended sentences imposed upon you.

14. You are now 30 years of age, the youngest of three children born to your parents who separated when you were still a baby. Your mother was a heroin addict who now resides in a nursing home after suffering a stroke as a result of a

heroin overdose about five years ago. You have had virtually no contact with your
father who remarried, had further children and was himself gaoled for
subsequent criminal behaviour.

15. At the age of one you were placed in foster care and remained in
departmental care for the next 15 years. Your placements were changed every
two to three years. You were rarely visited by your mother who continued with
drug problems and was apparently regularly in and out of gaol.

16. You have one sister who remained in your father's care but you and your
brother went into the foster care system. You had difficulty with learning due to a
hearing problem and needed to attend speech therapy and physiotherapy.
Despite the disruption to your early years, it appears your offending behaviour
did not begin until your adolescence which began promisingly when you were
initially attending St Bernard's College in Essendon where you were an excellent
sportsman being a Victorian champion in running. However your behaviour
deteriorated, you were expelled from that school in Year 9, then attended St
Albans High School, then Kensington Community School.

17. At the age of 15 you were placed to live with your mother for six months,
she then just having come out of gaol. She introduced you to heroin. You quickly
became addicted and this has been the drug that has bedevilled you ever since
although there is also some history of earlier amphetamine use.

18. You have a limited employment history, in 1997 working as a furniture
removalist for about eight months, then briefly as a truck jockey and then with a
garden program. The dominating theme of your life however from the age of 15
until two years ago was your heroin addiction and associated offending in
support of that habit. [That offending saw you] in July 1999 placed on a combined custody and treatment order and in August 2000 you were sentenced to a
total effective sentence of 14 months. . . .

19. You were released in October 2001 and it is clear that both your heroin
addiction and associated offending continued as shown in Counts 11 to 15 on
the presentment in this matter, being the armed robbery, burglaries and theft
committed between 4 December 2001 and 14 March 2002.

20. On your release from prison in October 2001, you admitted yourself to
a rehabilitation centre to detoxify but stayed only eight weeks before moving to
various boarding houses in Footscray. In that time you met Rebecca Gibbons,
also a heroin user with whom you commenced a relationship. On 15 October
2002 your daughter Shakira was born. Her birth saw a remarkable transformation by you in terms of your drug addiction and lifestyle.

21. Before turning to this aspect of your life however, the observations and
psychological testing upon you by forensic psychologist Dr. Carla Lechner as
contained in her report of 27 May 2005 are important. . . .

22. It is Dr. Lechner's view that you demonstrate symptoms [consistent]
with a diagnosis of clinical depression and states that you told her you had been
depressed for as long as you can remember, your mood at present being further
lowered by an intense anxiety over the outcome of this proceeding and your fear
of prison and of course the effect of that upon your daughter, Shakira.

23. Dr. Lechner says you impressed as cognitively and emotionally
immature, which she attributed to a retardation of your emotional development
in the years of your heavy drug use. Formal psychological testing to determine
your level of comprehension, reason and judgment skills rated you in the low

average borderline range of verbal intelligence with approximately 91 per cent of the adult population performing better than you.

24. I now return to the issue of your daughter. Shakira, as I have stated, was born on 15 October 2002. According to the report of Dr. Juliana Antolovic, a paediatrician in child development and rehabilitation at the Royal Children's Hospital, whose report, dated 20 March 2005, was tendered on your behalf, Shakira was born with a significant medical condition, Pierre Robin Syndrome, which is associated with abnormal development of the jaw, tongue and mouth, and children with this condition often have a cleft palate and can have significant problems with breathing and feeding.

25. Indeed, according to Dr. Antolovic, who appears to have been Shakira's paediatrician since her birth, Shakira had a number of complications related to this condition and since her birth has had multiple admissions to hospital, a number of investigations and surgery to repair her very large cleft palate. For the first 18 months of her life she was dependent upon tube feeding for her growth and nutrition. Dr. Antolovic states: "Shakira's care needs have been extremely high. In addition to two weekly visits to the Child Development and Rehabilitation Centre, Shakira and her family have also regularly attended the Royal Children's Hospital for routine follow up with a dietician and in a cleft palate splint. During the time Shakira was fed by a nasogastric tube (the first 18 months of her life) there were multiple visits to the emergency department for replacement of her neo-gastric tube. These visits sometimes occurred up to three times a week, which is not uncommon in the circumstances."

26. At the age of 17 a daughter was born to you and your then partner, a lady named Narelle. That daughter and her mother were taken in by the maternal grandmother with whom they still live and with whom you continue to have contact. However, you did not play a significant parenting role in that daughter's life, you remaining in the grip of your heroin addiction and continuing to offend in support of it and to be gaoled regularly by the court.

27. However, it is clear that the birth of this second gravely physically compromised daughter has wrought the transformation in you and you have entirely devoted yourself to her care since her birth. You have been her primary caregiver since her birth. Concomitant with this dedication to your daughter and her various needs, you have entirely ceased heroin use and criminal offending.

28. In December 2004 the Department of Human Services became involved because of concerns over verbal domestic violence taking place between yourself and Rebecca, who had remained a drug user, you perceiving that she was failing to fulfil her role as Shakira's mother.

29. Shakira was removed from your care for one night then returned to you as her sole carer and you remain in that position to this day. You and the child's mother, Rebecca, remained in a relationship until December 2004. . . .

30. You and Shakira were initially placed by DHS for a six week period in a caravan park by way of emergency housing whilst arrangements were made for more appropriate accommodation which was ultimately provided through Hanover Family Services. . . .

40. Howard Draper, a solicitor who represented you in the Children's Court proceedings relating to Shakira [notes that in] February 2005 the Children's Court made an interim protection order placing the child in your care on

certain conditions and that by the return of that order on 16 May 2005 DHS was recommending that there was no need for any further involvement by that department due to the progress made by you. He states: "According to the latest DHS report, 16 May 2005, my client is currently on methadone and is no longer required to provide drug screens to DHS. It appears that DHS is satisfied that my client is not abusing substances." . . .

42. Mr. Draper concludes, "As a legal practitioner I have been practising in the Children's Court for about 21 years and for the past seven to eight years most of my practice has involved Children's Court matters. I have no hesitation in noting that the efforts of Mr. Arnautovic in addressing the protective concerns and providing a safe and secure environment for his daughter, have been exceptional."

43. . . . During the plea evidence was given by Daheyamima Matthew, a senior Child Protection worker, who is the case manager for Shakira from the Child Protection Unit. Ms. Matthew has been employed with DHS for ten years.

44. She stated that since December you have been the sole carer for Shakira. She said that Rebecca, Shakira's mother, continues to have access to her daughter, which was initially supervised and which is supposed to occur for about two and a half hours a week. This, she said, is either usually cancelled or shortened by Rebecca, who generally wants the child for an hour only. She stated that Rebecca had no capacity to care for Shakira and in the department's view she was not an option as a carer for her daughter. She said Shakira's best interests were the first priority in your life and that, unusually in her experience, you had welcomed DHS's involvement.

45. Ms. Matthew said she had no concerns regarding your heroin use and noted that you were keen to ultimately get off methadone. She said she had never seen you under the influence of any drug. Ms. Matthew said DHS had linked you in with a number of anger management programs which you had undertaken and describes you as honest and open in your dealings with various services. Ms. Matthew said Shakira had a severe deformity and consequent hearing and speech problems requiring regular attendance upon a paediatrician and other services, which was carried out by you. She said there was a strong attachment and bond between yourself and your daughter, and she said that when Shakira was taken to access with her mother you made sure she was well clothed and that appropriate food and nappies went with her. Shakira currently attends crèche two days a week and staff there have requested the attendance of a speech therapist at that crèche to address Shakira's apprehended delay in those areas of her development. . . .

47. Ms. Matthew said it was imperative that Shakira have a constant carer to reach her potentials in life. She said that the only extended family with whom you have contact is your sister who, however, lives in Ballarat, but this was not a close relationship either between your sister and yourself, and Shakira and that sister, and further, given Shakira's medical needs, she must be able to continue with those services in Melbourne. She said there could be some difficulties initially in placing Shakira in foster care given her special needs. . . .

52. I am satisfied that since the birth of Shakira you have ceased to use heroin. You did admit, when giving evidence in the pre-sentence before me, to occasionally smoking marijuana at night after Shakira was in bed. I am satisfied that you have ceased offending and have carried out to the fullest extent to

which you are capable, care which has proved difficult and demanding, of your disabled child.

53. This is, however, not the only aspect to which the court must have regard. A medical report dated 8 October 2003 from Dr. Denis Yeung of the Sunshine Brimbank Clinic, notes that the victim of the armed robbery, Mr. Haveraux, sustained the following injuries as a result upon your assault upon him — bruising on the left side of his skull, sore fingers on the left hand, abrasions on the right little finger, bruises on the back of the right hand and wrist, and whilst X-ray did not show any fracture, a diagnosis of ligamentous strain was made.

54. In his victim impact statement dated 27 May 2005 Mr. Haveraux stated: "For the next week after the attack I found it difficult to enter the empty house. This was the reason for installing the alarm as it would give me prior warning. I do feel that I have been affected psychologically as I now tend to enter empty rooms as if somebody may be waiting around the corner for me."

55. He further states: "I feel that no mercy should be shown because of the fact that the attack took place in front of my three year old daughter and that he wanted to take a hostage to the bank so we could give him all we had. If this attack had involved a weaker person (that is somebody that hadn't played soccer for 20 years) what damage could he have caused? Put him away before he really hurts somebody."

56. Your counsel informed me that regularly throughout the years of your drug addiction you would turn to the use of prescription drugs when your heroin supply failed and at the time of the armed robbery you had taken Rohypnol to this end. . . . These courts are sadly familiar with the elevation in violent offending that can occur when the offender is under the influence of this prescription drug. This appears to have been the case at the time of the armed robbery, the violence involved not being characteristic of your previous offending. . . .

58. Appallingly, this violent offending, however, took place before the undoubtedly terrified gaze of a three year old child. This offending in particular was abhorrent in the extreme. In the absence of mitigatory material, indeed in the absence of any but the most compelling mitigatory material, the court would, in a case such as this involving the intrusion into a home, a violent attack upon the occupier of the house, the terrifying of a little girl in her own home, watching her father being assaulted, would undoubtedly result in a sentence of imprisonment to be served immediately. Such offending cannot and should not be tolerated. I make it clear to you, Mr. Arnautovic, that I condemn your behaviour and I do so in the strongest possible terms. The fact of your difficult personal history, the fact of your heroin addiction, the fact of your Rohypnol use at the time, are of no moment. This was an appalling and dangerous attack and one cannot wonder at the sentiments expressed by Mr. Haveraux in the victim impact statement. . . .

60. The question is whether your undoubted reformation, together with the needs of your highly dependent little daughter, are such that a sentence of imprisonment to be immediately served should be averted. This is the course that I am urged to take by your counsel on the basis of your reformation and the needs of your daughter. This course is resisted by the prosecution, which contends that a sentence of imprisonment to be immediately served should indeed

be visited upon you. It is their contention firstly that the hardship to your daughter, should you be incarcerated, would not be such as to answer the "test" contained in the judgment of Wells, J. in *Worth* (1976) 14 S.A.S.R. 291 where . . . His Honour stated: "the hardship caused directly or indirectly by a proposed sentence of imprisonment to the family of or to others closely associated with the offender [should] be taken into account by the court in mitigation of that sentence . . . where the circumstances are highly exceptional where it would be, in effect, inhuman to refuse to do so."

61. Insofar as your rehabilitation is concerned the prosecution referred to the case of *DPP v. Jovasici*, a decision of the Court of Appeal of the Supreme Court of Victoria delivered on March 22, 2001. There, in essence, it was held that notwithstanding the demonstrated rehabilitation of two professional burglars, including drug rehabilitation, the requirement for general and specific deterrence, denunciation and punishment, were such that gaol sentences to be immediately served, which had been received in the first instance, were in fact manifestly inadequate and were, accordingly, increased by the Court of Appeal. There are, however, in my view, important distinguishing factors between those authorities and this case. Dealing first with the case of *Jovasici*, this involves the participation of perpetrators in a highly organised professional ring of burglars which targeted goods of particular value centring around a particular receiver of stolen goods and the activities of which clearly resulted in the theft and on selling of a vast array of valuable items stolen from a myriad of residences. It involved organised and sophisticated offending. Further, it was not accepted by the sentencing judge in that case that either of the perpetrators, neither of whom gave evidence in their hearings, were remorseful, nor was it accepted that the offending occurred solely to support the drug addiction suffered by both men.

62. During the plea before me you did give evidence on oath, saying there were no apologies you could make to Mr. Haveraux that he could accept. You said you did not blame him for his comments relating to you and described what you had done to him as the "lowest act" you had committed in your life. You said you were still dealing with what you had done in that it continued to play on your conscience. You were concerned that you could have "devastated that little girl" and said that you thought about what you have done all the time. . . .

64. In relation to your daughter reference is also made by the prosecution to the decision of *R v. Holland*, a decision of the Court of Appeal of the Supreme Court of Victoria delivered on 12 August 2002. There the sole ground of appeal by the appellant, who had been incarcerated for cultivating a commercial quantity of narcotic plants, was the effect of her imprisonment on her seven year old daughter who was in the care of her grandparents who did not believe they could continue to care for her. This case was tendered in support of the prosecution's contention that Shakira's plight, should you be incarcerated, would not amount to the exceptional circumstances I have previously referred to as outlined by Wells, J.

65. Importantly, in . . . the case of *Holland*, in disallowing the appeal, the court expressed a doubt that the grandparents would not in fact continue to be able to care for their grandchild in the months remaining of her mother's sentence, and in the words of Batt, J., . . . "In the circumstances of this case the incarceration of both parents of one healthy child of seven is not sufficient to constitute exceptional circumstances."

66. I am satisfied, however, that the hardship which would be faced by Shakira if you were incarcerated would amount to be extreme and exceptional circumstances as demanded by the authority. Shakira is only two and a half years old, a far more vulnerable age than the child in the case of *Holland.* She has disabilities that require particular care and according to the evidence of Ms. Matthew, this will be ongoing for some four years.

67. Further, and unusually, she has no meaningful relationships with any adult other than yourself, thus she is in familial terms, apart from yourself, an isolated, disabled toddler, and your removal from her life would see her placed either in foster care with strangers or, if the department was willing to consider the few persons named by you when pressed in cross-examination as possibly suitable, with adults who are neither related to her or whom it appears she knows particularly well. Mention has been made in more than one report and by myself earlier in this judgment of your social isolation as a result of your change of lifestyle. . . .

69. [It] is my view that Shakira's case is one in which mercy should be exercised. If I be wrong in that it is my view that Shakira's dependence upon you, coupled with your personal transformation and general remorse, are sufficient that I should sentence you in a way which does not require your immediate incarceration. I should add, Mr. Arnautovic, however, that I have made this decision only after anxiously considering all the competing sentencing demands and emphasise that I am fully alive to the appalling and noxious nature of your offending. It is my view, however, that the long term interests of the community and Shakira are best served by your continuing on your path of reformation and your care of your daughter. It is my view that were you to be incarcerated and separated from Shakira the effects upon her would be grievous, long lasting and possibly irretrievable. The effect upon yourself would likely ignite such anxiety in view of your daughter's position that you could well collapse, and even did you not, the additional problems faced by you on your release insofar as the traumatising effects upon Shakira as a result of your separation, could interfere substantially with, if not destroy, your capacity to continue to care for her and her to respond and thus the exceptional work of the past two years be totally undone.

70. I therefore propose to deal with you by way of a non-custodial disposition which will involve not only suspended sentences but the imposition of a community based order for which you have been assessed as suitable. . . .

71. I am including a community based order in the disposition, both because I think the gravity of your offending requires it and because, in my view, you have ongoing personal difficulties and frailties which require attention and you have indicated through your work with DHS that you are capable of taking advantage of assistance offered to you and, indeed, have been reliant upon it to such an extent that it appears your main social interaction in life is with DHS workers. That support is to be withdrawn in June of this year and it is my view that replacement of it with the supports that can be obtained by a Community Based Order is important in terms of your ongoing reform which is, of course, inextricably linked with Shakira's welfare. . . .

73. I therefore sentence you as follows, and can you stand up, please? On counts 1, 3, 5, 7, 9, 12 and 14 you are sentenced to 12 months' imprisonment. On Count 4 you are sentenced to six months' imprisonment. On counts 6, 8, 10, 13

and 15 you are sentenced to nine months' imprisonment. On Count 11 you are sentenced to two years and nine months' imprisonment. I order that 12 days of each of the sentences imposed on counts 1, 3, 5, 7, 9, 12 and 14 be served cumulatively to the sentence imposed on Count 11 and to each other, giving a total effective sentence of three years. This sentence is to be wholly suspended for a period of three years. On Count 2 you are placed on a community based order for two years. . . .

75. The order will last for two years. You must attend at the Sunshine Community Corrections Centre at 10 Foundry Road, Sunshine within two clear working days, all right? . . . You must report to and receive visits from a Community Corrections officer. You must notify an officer at the specified Community Corrections Centre of any change of address or employment within two clear working days of that change. You may not leave Victoria without the consent of the specified Community Corrections officer and you must obey all lawful instructions and directions of the Community Corrections officer.

76. I order that you perform 150 hours of unpaid community work over a 24 month period as directed. I order that you be under the supervision of a Community Corrections officer. [The comment of Ms. Evans was that an onerous level of unpaid community work may place you under a detrimental amount of pressure and may affect your ability to successfully negotiate both your parenting and order commitments.] I order that you undergo assessment and treatment for alcohol or drug addiction or submit to medical, psychological or psychiatric assessment and treatment as directed by the regional manager. I order that you submit to testing for alcohol or drug use as directed by the regional manager and I further order, as a special condition, that you undergo programs to reduce the risk of re-offending and participate in such programs as directed by the Community Corrections officer. . . .

100. . . . Can you stand up Mr. Arnautovic? Because before you leave I have to explain to you the consequences of breaching the suspended sentence. You need to understand that any offending which can result in a sentence of imprisonment, it does not have to, so, for example, if you commit a very small shoplifting offence you might not get a sentence of imprisonment but because that is an offence that you can be sentenced to gaol for, you would have breached the suspended sentence.

101. The legislation makes it very clear that unless there are exceptional circumstances, if a person breaches a suspended sentence the court must make that person serve the whole of the sentence that was suspended. So if you commit an offence — you need to have a look at your marijuana smoking in that respect as well, OK?

102. PRISONER: Yes.

103. HER HONOUR: If you commit an offence you will be looking at three years' imprisonment. I imagine that would ruin your life and it would certainly ruin Shakira's life. Do you understand? All right. I am confident enough in your progress to place you on a disposition which can be very dangerous for persons who have got long offending histories and drug addictions, all right? You just keep going the way you are going and all will be well, but you need to understand that for the next three years you have got to be incredibly careful. All right?

104. PRISONER: Yes.

105. HER HONOUR: Thank you. You can have a seat.

*NOTES*

1. *Applying purposes in individual cases.*   Is the application of punishment purposes in individual sentencing decisions a factual issue or a legal issue? Is it a decision best made by legislatures, trial courts, appellate courts, or some other decision maker? Was the Australian court in *Arnautovic* making judgments that are better left to the legislature? Does the legislature make its own attempt to accommodate the purposes of punishment through the establishment of the standard sentencing terms? Compare State v. Gaines, 859 P.2d 36 (Wash. 1993).

2. *"Consistency" affecting the application of purposes.*   If courts make case-specific judgments as we saw in *Arautovic*, what techniques might be available to ensure reasonable consistency from case to case? Perhaps appellate review of sentencing decisions could exert some unifying force on the choices of sentencing judges. What purpose does consistency serve? Is furthering consistency across cases more important than furthering the purposes of punishment in individual cases?

## PROBLEM 1-3.   BROMLEY HEATH

A federal grand jury indicted John Thompson, a 24-year-old African American man, on narcotics violations stemming from an investigation of crack cocaine trafficking at the Bromley Heath Housing Development in Jamaica Plain, Massachusetts. The charges grew out of a joint federal-state investigation of crack cocaine trafficking at Bromley Heath. Pursuant to a plea agreement, the defendant pled guilty to one count of distributing cocaine base in violation of 21 U.S.C. §841(a)(1).

Thompson has one prior conviction but has never been incarcerated. His criminal record includes possession of a controlled substance at age 17, a charge that was dismissed; assault and battery at age 19, a conviction that resulted in a six-month probation term; drinking alcohol in public at age 20, a charge that was dismissed; and possession with intent to distribute a controlled substance, a charge brought shortly after the events that form the basis of the current charge, to which he pled guilty.

Thompson lived his entire life in Bromley Heath. He describes his childhood as rough; the majority of it was spent without his father, who was incarcerated much of the time. Thompson dropped out of high school in the eleventh grade when he learned that his girlfriend, Breii Murray, was pregnant with their first child. Thompson was determined to provide for her and their daughter, Jabria, despite his youth and lack of education.

Thompson became a member of Union Local 223 and maintained steady employment until his arrest on these charges. At the time of his arrest, he was employed by M. Solberg Enterprises Corp. and earned about $2,000 per month setting planks, drilling cords, and cutting concrete. His employer has provided a letter saying that Thompson was wanted back at his job.

Murray and Thompson have been in a steady relationship for seven years and are engaged to be married. They now have two daughters together. Thompson is a good father who spends a lot of time with his daughters and enjoys a solid relationship with both of them, particularly Jabria, the elder daughter. He supports his fiancée, their children, and his fiancée's family both economically and emotionally. Murray, along with Murray's mother, aunt, and grandmother, are all supportive of Thompson. They describe him as a wonderful person who has substantially assisted in the upkeep of their home by running errands, doing chores, and contributing $100 per week. All of the women stressed that Thompson's incarceration would make a detrimental impact on their lives, and particularly on the lives of his daughters.

What should Thompson's sentence be? What purposes should guide that sentence? See United States v. Thompson, 190 F. Supp. 2d 138 (D. Mass. 2002).

## 2.   Use of Purposes in System Components

Not only do judges and other decision makers face challenges in trying to integrate purposes into case-specific sentencing judgments, but legislators and other rule makers also confront challenges when integrating purposes into structural aspects of a sentencing system. Institutions responsible for creating sentencing rules that apply to a range of cases must consider whether and to what extent particular purposes should be considered for certain types of crimes, certain types of offenders, and certain types of punishment.

As you review the materials in the following sections, consider how your initial beliefs about the purposes of punishment bear on issues such as the appropriate sentencing rules for repeat offenders or the appropriateness of the death penalty.

### a.   The Relevance of Prior Crimes to Current Punishment

The justifications for punishment may help to explain specific sentencing rules. Consider some of the most basic sentencing questions: Should an offender be punished more severely if she has a prior conviction? Multiple convictions? Does it matter if the prior offense is the same as the current offense? How old the prior offense is? How the offender was punished for the prior offense?

First write down your answers to these questions. Then, informed by your own instincts and insights, consider the following report, where the U.S. Sentencing Commission explores options for developing criminal history rules for the federal guideline sentencing system.

> ### Simplification Paper: Criminal History
> **U.S. Sentencing Commission, reprinted in**
> **9 Fed. Sent'g Rep. 216 (1997)**

Criminal history [is incorporated in the federal sentencing guidelines through a series of rules that, in conjunction with rules for defining the seriousness of the current offense, determines the guideline range. This paper discusses Chapter Four, which establishes the rules for sentencing consideration of criminal history].

There are both philosophical and practical reasons for including criminal history as a major component of the federal sentencing guidelines. Criminal history can serve several important functions in setting sentencing recommendations. It can be used to measure increased culpability, predict future criminality, and selectively target dangerous offenders. . . .

There have been various debates as to propriety and purpose of using criminal history to determine a defendant's sentence. Retributionists or those who believe in the "just deserts" philosophy argue that punishment should be proportionate to the defendant's culpability for his/her current offense of conviction. Those who argue that retribution is a key principle in sentencing argue for a significantly reduced role for criminal history. For example, Richard Singer (1978) argues that criminal history is inappropriate to consider at sentencing because the defendant has already been punished for the previous offense. He contends that a defendant has no greater culpability (blameworthiness) because of having committed the prior offense; nor is victimization greater in the current offense as a result of the prior offense.

Andrew Von Hirsch, a noted retributionist, argues that criminal history should play only a minor role at sentencing, impacting sentence only to the extent that the defendant's culpability is enhanced due to his/her prior offenses. Von Hirsch argues that offenders who are being sentenced for their first offense have less culpability due to their not having been punished previously. According to Von Hirsch, the first sentence communicates that the behavior is wrong and will not be tolerated. A sentence for a second violation can reflect the "full" weight of the law because the offender has been alerted previously to the unacceptability of the behavior.[2]

A contrary theory of the role of criminal justice is incapacitation. This approach advocates the expanded use of imprisonment to incapacitate offenders. Incapacitation takes two forms: collective and selective. Both forms assume that while offenders are incarcerated they will not be able to engage in additional criminal behavior. Collective incapacitation seeks to prevent crime by increasing the rate and duration of imprisonment for a broad range of offenders, without specific prediction of future criminality. In contrast, selective incapacitation seeks to prevent crime by using certain criteria to identify for restraint a smaller number of offenders who are predicted to commit more crime and/or serious crime. Selective incapacitation also can reduce punishment for persons who are predicted to be less likely to commit additional crimes or to commit serious crimes.

Society and its elected representatives have reached a level of frustration with crime so that current policies more frequently tend to reflect the selective incapacitation philosophy in sentencing practices in general and criminal history in particular. Advocates of selective incapacitation argue that some offenders have shown themselves to be too dangerous (given the frequency or severity of their criminal conduct) to be permitted to remain in society. These advocates have successfully swayed Congress and state legislators that, for the safety of

---

2. Currently, no guideline system completely disregards the defendant's prior record in the determination of sentence. However, some states do consider aspects of retributionist theory. Minnesota, for example, used this theory in a modified format by adjusting the slope of its imprisonment/non-imprisonment line to focus more on the current offense.

society, presence of an extensive or violent prior record warrants severe sanction for the current offense (e.g., habitual offender provisions in the states and career offender provision in the federal system).[3] Consequently, in many criminal justice systems, criminal history is seen as a crucial component of the determination of an offender's sentence because of its use as a predictor of future criminality.

The Commission determined that criminal history was a major factor in past sentencing practices and should be a major component in the sentencing guidelines. In addition, the Commission believed that with its congressional mandate to consider the breadth of sentencing purposes (rehabilitation, deterrence, incapacitation, and just punishment), it had to consider criminal history as a major component of the guideline sentence. In designing Chapter Four, the Commission considered various philosophical arguments regarding the appropriate use of prior record in determining a defendant's sentence, including arguments regarding "just deserts" and selective incapacitation. The Commission hoped to diminish the conflict between the two ideologies by incorporating elements from both in assessing criminal history.

A defendant with a record of prior criminal behavior is more culpable than a first offender and thus deserving of a greater punishment. General deterrence of criminal conduct dictates that a clear message be sent to society that repeated criminal behavior will aggravate the need for punishment with each recurrence. To protect the public from further crimes of the particular defendant, the likelihood of recidivism and future criminal behavior must be considered. Repeated criminal behavior is an indicator of a limited likelihood of successful rehabilitation.

In the end, Chapter Four was designed to address the frequency, seriousness, and recency of the defendant's prior record. The Commission believed these items were reliable predictors of future criminal conduct.

[The] federal sentencing guidelines are unique in their approach to criminal history. It is the only system that measures the severity of the prior offense by the length of the sentence imposed for the previous conviction. Specifically, the guidelines give three points for each sentence greater than one year and one month, two points for each sentence of 60 days but not more than one year and one month, and one point for any other sentence. Up to three points also can be assigned if the defendant was under a criminal justice sentence at the time the instant offense was committed, and he/she had been released from a sentence of imprisonment within two years of the commencement of the instant offense. This criminal history score is translated into one of six criminal history categories in the Sentencing Table. The higher the category, the higher the guideline sentence for any given offense level. . . .

---

3. States vary in their use of selective incapacitation. For example, in the Pennsylvania guidelines, all prior convictions are included in the computation of the criminal history score, although some offenses are weighed more heavily than others. Because the focus is on the number of prior offenses, little distinction is made between types of offender. In contrast, Oregon uses a typography classification of offenders that focuses not on the number of prior convictions, but, instead, the type of prior offenses committed with violent offenders and repeat non-violent felony offenders targeted for longer sentences. Each prior conviction does not necessarily contribute to the criminal history score.

While there is some variation in approach, almost every sentencing guideline system considers a defendant's prior record in the determination of the sentence. Most states measure both the number and seriousness of prior convictions. Some states weigh prior convictions depending on their severity. Minnesota, for example, assigns prior felony offenses from one-half to two points depending upon the offense's "severity level." [I]n the Pennsylvania Sentencing Guidelines, the most serious category of prior convictions includes murder, voluntary manslaughter, kidnapping, rape, involuntary deviate intercourse, arson, and robbery. Convictions for these offenses receive four points, the maximum amount assessable for a prior conviction. Similarly, in Oregon, criminal history is categorized by prior offense type specifically violent versus nonviolent offenses.

[One] criticism of the federal guidelines' present scheme is its lack of precision in measuring the severity of prior record. For example, because three points are given for each sentence of more than one year and one month, the guidelines make no distinction between a 14-month sentence and a 15-year sentence. Arguably, these two sentences may reflect the seriousness of substantially different prior offenses. Under the current system, there is no differentiation between a fraud and a rape if they both receive sentences of imprisonment of more than one year and one month.

Another area in which the current criminal history score treats seemingly different offenders the same is in Criminal History Category I. . . . Currently, Criminal History Category I treats a wide range of defendants similarly despite the fact that they have dissimilar levels of previous contact with the criminal justice system. For example, defendants who have no prior record (no prior arrests, no pending charges, no dismissed charges, no prior convictions) are in Category I along with defendants who have at least one prior conviction that received a sentence of imprisonment of at least 60 days.[13] Title 28, section 994(j) requires the Commission to "insure that the guidelines reflect the general appropriateness of imposing a sentence other than imprisonment in cases in which the defendant is a first offender who has not been convicted of a crime of violence or an otherwise serious offense. . . ." By not incorporating a "first offender category" in the guidelines, critics argue that the Commission did not adequately address the statutory directive at Title 28, section 994(j) related to first offenders. However, the Commission's compliance with this directive has been challenged in a number of cases and uniformly rejected. . . .

There is general agreement among sentencing theorists that the importance of a previous conviction diminishes over time. In keeping with this theory, the Commission chose to limit the impact of "decaying" prior convictions by requiring that they fall within various time periods. It is not the limitation of old prior convictions that adds complexity. The complexity results because the guidelines have five different applicable time periods for the assessment of criminal history points. These time periods depend upon both the length of

---

13. This category includes the following defendants: (1) a person with no contact with any criminal justice system of any kind, (2) a person who may have had contact with the criminal justice system, such as arrests or dismissed charges, and (3) a person with convictions not countable under the guidelines for a variety of reasons, such as the "age" of the conviction, the locality where the conviction occurred, and the minor nature of the offense.

the sentence imposed and the age of the defendant when the prior offense was committed, and in one instance, whether the prior was imposed as an adult or juvenile sentence.

State guideline systems vary in their use of applicable time periods. States that limit consideration of offenses generally use one applicable time period for all offenses. . . . Some states that do not restrict the time period in which prior offenses can be counted instead have "crime-free" periods from which the defendant benefits. In these states, if the defendant remains "conviction free" for a period of time (usually 10 or 15 years not including periods of imprisonment or release on probation or parole) prior to the instant offense, any convictions prior to that period are not counted. Others leave this item as a departure consideration.

One of the frequently debated issues regarding the prior record measurement is whether to include juvenile adjudications, and if so, to what extent. Currently, the federal guidelines consider offenses that occurred prior to the defendant's eighteenth birthday, except under certain circumstances. Some would argue that juvenile adjudications should not contribute to the criminal history score because juvenile courts typically focus on the juvenile's welfare and treatment, and generally have a more informal process. Moreover, the juvenile courts' standard of proof may be somewhat lower than adult courts. More importantly, juvenile records are less reliable than adult records because of different jurisdictional policies on recording and disclosing juvenile offenses. This inconsistency can result in great disparity in the criminal history score computation.

Nonetheless, most states include juvenile adjudications in the computation of criminal history score because many argue that juvenile record, in particular violent behavior, is a strong predictor of future criminal conduct. In fact, some restrict the use of juvenile offenses to include only convictions for violent offenses. Others restrict the use of juvenile offenses if the defendant is an older offender. For example, in Maryland, juvenile convictions are not included in the sentence determination if the defendant is 26 years of age or older at the time of commission of the instant offense; the argument being that as the offender gets older, the use of a juvenile record as predictor of criminality diminishes. . . .

## NOTES

1. *Recidivism and punishment theory in practice.* The above discussion of criminal history rules in the federal sentencing guidelines begins by highlighting the linkage between considerations of prior criminal history and sentencing theories, as well as the robust debate among theorists about these matters. But note the conclusion of this theoretical discussion:

> In designing Chapter Four, the Commission considered various philosophical arguments regarding the appropriate use of prior record in determining a defendant's sentence, including arguments regarding "just deserts" and selective incapacitation. The Commission hoped to diminish the conflict between the two ideologies by incorporating elements from both in assessing criminal history.

Is it possible to design sentencing rules to "diminish the conflict" between the just-deserts and incapacitation theories? Do the rules for considering criminal history under the federal sentencing guidelines as described in this excerpt succeed in diminishing the conflict? Consider the following assessment of the actual rules developed for the federal sentencing guidelines:

> [The] arguments for viewing the criminal history guidelines as utilitarian in orientation are powerful. Utilitarianism offers a coherent justification for taking prior criminal records into account generally. It helps to explain specific structural features of the Commission's rules. It is consistent with the considerations the Commission actually took into account when developing these guidelines. In its Supplementary Report on the original guidelines, the Commission virtually acknowledged that utilitarianism was the dominant justification for the criminal history rules [by stating the rules were] "included primarily for crime-control considerations."

Aaron J. Rappaport, Rationalizing the Commission: The Philosophical Premises of the U.S. Sentencing Guidelines, 52 Emory L.J. 558, 594-595 (2003). For an exploration of the punishment theory relevant to recidivism more generally, see Youngjae Lee, Recidivism as Omission: A Relational Account, 87 Tex. L. Rev. 571 (2009).

2. *Detailed sentencing rules and punishment theory in practice.*   As the excerpt above highlights, many complications and intricate details arise in the development of structured sentencing rules. This is true not only for criminal history issues but for all areas of sentencing, as we shall see throughout the book. Can the resolution of these complications and details turn on matters of punishment theory? Should they?

## b.  Justifying Particular Forms of Punishment Such as the Death Penalty

Should the application of theories of punishment change when particular forms of punishment are being considered? Historically, there has been a direct connection between the forms of punishment employed and the theories of punishment being pursued. Theories of punishment may also shift for different crimes and different classes of offenders.

For example, one of the most important (and ironic) modern sentencing developments concerns the evolution of imprisonment as a form of punishment and of prisons as an institution for punishment. The penitentiary was developed and structured as a form of punishment with the express goal of "curing" offenders of their criminal tendencies. The belief in the nineteenth century was that imprisonment, by removing an offender from certain corrupting influences in his community while also providing an offender with the time and opportunity to reflect on his misdeeds, would rehabilitate criminals in ways that physical punishment could not. See generally David J. Rothman, Perfecting the Prison: United States, 1789-1865, in The Oxford History of the Prison 111 (1995). For more than a century, many proponents of imprisonment continued to argue that rehabilitation could be furthered through incarceration.

But by the mid-1980s, many observers had come to recognize that most prison environments, in which prisoners were more often warehoused than treated, were more likely to provide criminal training than to rehabilitate effectively. Consequently, in the Sentencing Reform Act of 1984, Congress expressly instructed the U.S. Sentencing Commission that its development of federal sentencing rules should "reflect the inappropriateness of imposing a sentence to a term of imprisonment for the purpose of rehabilitating the defendant or providing the defendant with needed educational or vocational training, medical care, or other correctional treatment." 28 U.S.C. §994(k). But even today, despite the widespread belief that prison is not an effective environment for rehabilitation, many state sentencing systems (and even aspects of the federal system) continue to pursue rehabilitative goals through incarceration. Indeed, at least one scholar has recently asserted that the "only rationale for the design of prison programs that is possible and acceptable in this society is rehabilitation." Edward Rubin, The Inevitability of Rehabilitation, 19 Law & Ineq. 343 (2001).

Perhaps even more than imprisonment, the use of the death penalty has generated considerable debate about the connection between certain forms of punishment and the purposes of punishment. In fact, though most public debates over sentencing issues are rarely cast in theoretical terms, modern public debates over the death penalty frequently explore whether it is an effective deterrent to murder, whether a life sentence without the possibility of parole can incapacitate as well as an execution, whether concepts of retribution justify use of this ultimate punishment for the most heinous of crimes, and whether the death penalty can be administered fairly or efficiently.

Many insights can be drawn from a close examination of the classic theoretical debates surrounding the death penalty. Part of what makes the death penalty so worthy of study is that making a life-and-death decision helps ensure that we do not become complacent in our consideration of the issues. To seize on a well-worn phrase in these debates, "death is different," and that difference informs our thinking about sentencing theory in ways that few other punishments can.

Public debate about capital punishment in recent years has taken place in the shadow of the "innocence movement," an effort by lawyers, journalists, students, and scholars to establish that some defendants—including several on death row—were wrongly convicted of their alleged crimes. Other current concerns about capital punishment include the high cost of death penalty prosecutions and the massive cost of high-profile death cases; participation of medical personnel in executions; the small number of executions compared with the larger numbers on death row; and continuing concern for racial and new concern for geographic inequalities. Taken together, such concerns about the death penalty have convinced legislators in four states over the last decade (Illinois, New Mexico, New Jersey, and New York) to discontinue the use of this punishment.

Pointing in the other direction, recent studies by economists have renewed interest in the deterrent effect of the death penalty. A number of studies since 2001, mostly by economists, have purported to establish that the death penalty has a deterrent impact in modern times. As with prior studies making such claims, the data and conclusions in these papers are hotly disputed, and it still is (and likely will always be) difficult to make conclusive statements about the deterrent effect of capital punishment. Though strong proof of deterrence may always be elusive, would a truly conclusive and indisputable study resolve the debate over the death penalty? Suppose we could be absolutely positive that each execution of a convicted murderer would deter ten murders and thus save ten innocent lives. In light of such data, could there be any conclusive argument against the death penalty? Imagine the empirical evidence running the other way. Suppose we could be absolutely positive that each execution of a convicted murderer would cause ten additional murders (because of the brutalization impact of having society in the business of state killing) and thus cost ten innocent lives. In light of such data, could there be any conclusive argument for the death penalty?

The next set of readings turn on the moral questions sitting before, under, around, and after the deterrence debates. The first is a short statement about the moral justifications for the death penalty. The second reading responds to two prominent legal scholars, Cass Sunstein and Adrian Vermeule, who have taken the position that, in light of the new deterrence data, society (including those with a liberal bent) should as a moral matter support the imposition of the death penalty. See Cass R. Sunstein & Adrian Vermeule, Is Capital Punishment Morally Required? Acts, Omissions, and Life-Life Tradeoffs, 58 Stan. L. Rev. 703 (2005).

## For Capital Punishment: The Morality of Anger,
### Walter Berns
#### Harper's, Apr. 1979, at 15-20

Anger is expressed or manifested on those occasions when someone has acted in a manner that is thought to be unjust, and one of its origins is the opinion that men are responsible, and should be held responsible, for what they do. Thus, as Aristotle teaches us, anger is accompanied not only by the pain caused by the one who is the object of anger, but by the pleasure arising from the expectation of inflicting revenge on someone who is thought to deserve it. We can become angry with an inanimate object (the door we run into and then kick in return) only by foolishly attributing responsibility to it, and we cannot do that for long, which is why we do not think of returning later to revenge ourselves on the door. For the same reason, we cannot be more than momentarily angry with any one creature other than man; only a fool and worse would dream of taking revenge on a dog. And, finally, we tend to pity rather than to be angry with men who — because they are insane, for example — are not responsible for their acts. Anger, then, is a very human passion not only because only a human being can be angry, but also because anger acknowledges the humanity of its objects: it holds them accountable for what they do. And in holding particular men responsible, it pays them the respect that is due them as men. Anger recognizes that only men have the capacity to be moral beings and, in so doing, acknowledges the dignity of human beings. Anger is somehow connected with justice, and it is this that modern penology has not understood; it tends, on the whole, to regard anger as a selfish indulgence. . . .

Criminals are properly the objects of anger, and the perpetrators of terrible crimes — for example, Lee Harvey Oswald and James Earl Ray — are properly the objects of great anger. They have done more than inflict an injury on an isolated individual; they have violated the foundations of trust and friendship, the necessary elements of a moral community, the only community worth living in. A moral community, unlike a hive of bees or a hill of ants, is one whose members are expected freely to obey the laws, and unlike those in a tyranny, are trusted to obey the laws. The criminal has violated that trust, and in so doing has injured not merely his immediate victim but the community as such. He has called into question the very possibility of that community by suggesting that men cannot be trusted to respect freely the property, the person, and the dignity of those with whom they are associated. If, then, men are not angry when someone else is robbed, raped, or murdered, the implication is that no moral community exists, because those men do not care for anyone other than themselves. Anger is an expression of that caring, and society needs men who care for one another, who share their pleasures and their pains, and do so for the sake of the others. It is the passion that can cause us to act for reasons having nothing to do with selfish or mean calculation; indeed, when educated, it can become a generous passion, the passion that protects the community or country by demanding punishment for its enemies. It is the stuff from which heroes are made. . . .

The law must not be understood to be merely a statute that we enact or repeal at our will, and obey or disobey at our convenience — especially not the criminal law. Wherever law is regarded as merely statutory, men will soon enough disobey it, and will learn how to do so without any inconvenience to themselves. The criminal law must possess a dignity far beyond that possessed by mere statutory enactment or utilitarian and self-interested calculations. The most powerful means we have to give it that dignity is to authorize it to impose the ultimate penalty. The criminal law must be made awful, by which I mean inspiring, or commanding "profound respect or reverential fear." It must remind us of the moral order by which alone we can live as *human* beings, and in America, now that the Supreme Court has outlawed banishment, the only punishment that can do this is capital punishment.

The founder of modern criminology, the eighteenth-century Italian Cesare Beccaria, opposed both banishment and capital punishment because he understood that both were inconsistent with the principle of self-interest, and self-interest was the basis of the political order he favored. If a man's first and only duty is to himself, of course he will prefer his money to his country; he will also prefer his money to his brother. In fact, he will prefer his brother's money to his brother, and a people of this description, or a country that understands itself in this Beccarian manner, can put the mark of Cain on no one. For the same reason, such a country can have no legitimate reason to execute its criminals, or, indeed, to punish them in any manner. What would be accomplished by punishment in such a place? Punishment arises out of the demand for justice, and justice is demanded by angry, morally indignant men; its purpose is to satisfy that moral indignation and thereby promote the law-abidingness that, it is assumed, accompanies it. But the principle of self-interest denies the moral basis of that indignation.

Not only will a country based solely on self-interest have no legitimate reason to punish; it may have no need to punish. It may be able to solve what we call the crime problem by substituting a law of contracts for a law of crimes. According to Beccaria's social contract, men agree to yield their natural freedom to the "sovereign" in exchange for his promise to keep the peace. As it becomes more difficult for the sovereign to fulfill his part of the contract, there is a demand that he be made to pay for his nonperformance. From this comes compensation or insurance schemes embodied in statutes whereby the sovereign (or state), being unable to keep the peace by punishing criminals, agrees to compensate its contractual partners for injuries suffered at the hands of criminals, injuries the police are unable to prevent. The insurance policy takes the place of law enforcement and the *posse comitatus*, and John Wayne and Gary Cooper give way to Mutual of Omaha. There is no anger in this kind of law, and none (or no reason for any) in the society. . . .

---

## No, Capital Punishment Is Not Morally Required: Deterrence, Deontology, and the Death Penalty, Carol S. Steiker
### 58 Stan. L. Rev. 751-756, 765-770, 773-774 (2005)

As an opponent of capital punishment, I have participated in many (and witnessed many more) debates about the morality and wisdom of the death penalty. The debate usually begins with one of two dramatic gambits by the proponent of capital punishment, both of which derive their power from the grievous harms suffered by murder victims and their loved ones. The first gambit is to consider in detail the facts of one or more capital murders and to propose that only the punishment of death is an adequate and proportional response to the terrible suffering of the victim intentionally inflicted by the perpetrator—a predominantly retributive argument. The second gambit—a modified version of which Cass Sunstein and Adrian Vermeule use to begin their provocative article[1]—is predominantly consequentialist. This gambit is to suggest that if the death penalty can prevent—through incapacitation of the offender or general deterrence—the loss to murder of even one innocent life, then it is a morally justified or perhaps even morally required penal response. A common response to both of these gambits is to ask why it is we do not rape rapists, torture torturers, or rape and then murder those who rape and murder in order to provide a proportional response to the suffering they have inflicted or to adequately deter future rapists, torturers, and rapist/murderers. This response suggests that our rejection of such extreme punishments points the way to a categorical, deontological limitation on the kinds of punishments we are justified in imposing, on either retributive or consequentialist grounds. The usual counter to this response is to acknowledge that we do not and should not impose such extreme punishments—that there is some moral limit to what we can justify as punishment—but to deny that the use of the death penalty crosses that line.

---

1. Cass R. Sunstein & Adrian Vermeule, Is Capital Punishment Morally Required? Acts, Omissions, and Life-Life Tradeoffs, 58 Stan. L. Rev. 703, 705 (2005) (suggesting that "on certain empirical assumptions, capital punishment may be morally required, not for retributive reasons, but rather to prevent the taking of innocent lives").

The debate — like a stylized form of dance — then tends to move from consideration of capital punishment in the abstract to its application in contemporary society. Here the opponent of the death penalty goes on the offensive, arguing that regardless of whether capital punishment is justified in the abstract, the fact that it is too often imposed arbitrarily, invidiously, or in error in our imperfect legal system renders it a morally unacceptable practice in contemporary society. The usual counter here is some combination of denying that the problems are as big as the opponent claims (citing the opponent's abolitionist bias), denying that problems of arbitrariness and discrimination affect the justice of imposing the death penalty if the defendant is guilty, and acknowledging that the erroneous conviction and execution of innocents is unjust but maintaining that the problem is either small enough to be acceptable (in light of the greater number of innocent lives saved) or fixable.

Sunstein and Vermeule want to dance to a very different tune. They start with some recent statistical studies of the impact of capital punishment on homicide rates — studies that claim to find strong deterrent effects after controlling for potentially confounding variables with multiple regression analysis.[2] Sunstein and Vermeule do not purport to vouch for the validity of this recent spate of studies, acknowledging that "it remains possible that the recent findings will be exposed as statistical artifacts or found to rest on flawed econometric methods." This is a prudent concession, given the powerful reasons that are offered by John Donohue and Justin Wolfers,[4] along with many other experts,[5] to reject this body of work as the basis for any public policy initiative. Rather, Sunstein and Vermeule argue that if such deterrent effects could ever be reliably proven or even if the evidence demonstrated a "significant possibility" that the use of capital punishment saves a substantial number of lives by preventing future murders, then consequentialists and deontologists alike should join in supporting the retention and vigorous use of the death penalty. Indeed, they

---

2. Id. at 706 & n.9 (citing Hashem Dezhbakhsh et al., Does Capital Punishment Have a Deterrent Effect? New Evidence from Postmoratorium Panel Data, 5 Am. L. & Econ. Rev. 344 (2003) (suggesting that each execution on average prevents eighteen murders)).

4. See John J. Donohue & Justin Wolfers, Uses and Abuses of Empirical Evidence in the Death Penalty Debate, 58 Stan. L. Rev. 791, 794 (2005) (reviewing the studies relied upon by Sunstein and Vermeule and finding "that the existing evidence for deterrence is surprisingly fragile").

5. See Richard Berk, New Claims About Executions and General Deterrence: Déjà Vu All Over Again?, 2 J. Empirical Legal Stud. 303, 328 (2005) (noting that "it would be bad statistics and bad social policy" to generalize from one percent of the data to the remaining ninety-nine percent, and concluding that "for the vast majority of states for the vast majority of years there is no evidence for deterrence" and that even for the remaining one percent, "credible evidence for deterrence is lacking"); see also Deterrence and the Death Penalty: A Critical Review of New Evidence: Hearings on the Future of Capital Punishment in the State of New York Before the New York State Assemb. Standing Comm. on Codes, Assemb. Standing Comm. on Judiciary, and Assemb. Standing Comm. on Correction, 2005 Leg., 228th Sess. 1-12 (N.Y. 2005) (statement of Jeffrey Fagan, Professor of Law and Pub. Health, Columbia Univ.), available at www.deathpenaltyinfo.org/FaganTestimony.pdf; Jeffrey Fagan, Death and Deterrence Redux: Science, Law, and Causal Reasoning on Capital Punishment, 4 Ohio St. J. Crim. L. 255 (2006); Ted Goertzel, Capital Punishment and Homicide: Sociological Realities and Econometric Illusions, Skeptical Inquirer, July-Aug. 2004, available at http://www.findarticles.com/p/articles/mi_m2843/is_4_28/ai_n6145278.

contend that under such conditions, capital punishment should be considered not merely morally permissible (as any consequentialist would hold) but actually "morally obligatory." What Sunstein and Vermeule add to prior debates between consequentialists and deontologists regarding the death penalty is their insistence that recognition of the inapplicability of the act/omission distinction to the government as a distinctive kind of moral agent should strengthen the consequentialist argument in favor of capital punishment and undermine deontological objections to capital punishment, under the stipulated conditions of deterrence from which the argument proceeds.

This argument neatly sidesteps some of the central wrangles in the typical death penalty debate described above. First, under the terms of Sunstein and Vermeule's argument, there is no need to "draw the line" excluding some extreme punishments (like torture), because the argument denies the existence of any such categorical line prohibiting extreme punishments as a moral matter; the only question is whether the government can prevent more suffering inflicted by future offenders than it metes out as punishment on current offenders. Second, there is no need to address the vexing issue of how to weigh innocent lives of murder victims against (usually, but not always) guilty lives of convicted capital defendants because the argument holds that the government is equally responsible for the harms that flow from its failure to impose the death penalty and for those that flow from its imposition. Thus, all lives (innocent or guilty) are counted equally, and all that remains to do is count: if more private murders would be prevented than executions imposed, the balance favors executions. Third, the argument insists that the distributional problems of arbitrary or invidious infliction of the death penalty disappear as moral problems, at least when there is reason to believe that private murders are at least equally arbitrary or invidious in their distribution. Sunstein and Vermeule contend that the belief that there is a categorical prohibition of extreme punishments or the belief that arbitrariness, discrimination, or error in the distribution of capital punishment count as distinctive moral failures are examples of the operation of a "moral heuristic" — by which they mean a form of moral shorthand that leads to error. Specifically, they refer to error arising from the failure to fully appreciate the distinctiveness of the government as a moral agent that must treat the death penalty as an example of a "life-life tradeoff."

The problem with Sunstein and Vermeule's argument is not their general premise regarding the government's distinctive moral agency, which, as they acknowledge, is likely to be far more congenial to the political opponents of capital punishment than to its supporters. Rather, Sunstein and Vermeule's argument runs into serious problems when they attempt to transplant their insight about government agency from the arena of civil regulation to the arena of criminal justice. Sunstein and Vermeule's assertion that the state's execution of murderers is equivalent to its failure to adequately deter murders by private actors ignores the ways in which the construction of a governmental choice as a "life-life tradeoff" in the regulatory context does not map congruently onto the criminal justice context, either as a matter of morality or as a matter of justice.

As a matter of morality, Sunstein and Vermeule fail to grapple adequately with the fact that for their argument to succeed in the criminal context, they must jettison not only the act/omission distinction in the context of government action but also—and less convincingly—the distinction between purposeful wrongdoing on the one hand and merely reckless or even knowing wrongdoing on the other. Even more problematic is Sunstein and Vermeule's failure to acknowledge the social and political fact that executions are not mere fungible "killings" but rather are part of a practice of state punishment that can be unjust in ways quite distinct from the general wrongness of killing. Sunstein and Vermeule's reduction of the deontological objections to capital punishment to some version of the moral intuition that "killing is wrong" thus evades and fails even to acknowledge long-standing and widely discussed deontological objections to capital punishment qua punishment.

Moreover, despite their protestations to the contrary, Sunstein and Vermeule's argument in favor of capital punishment presents some conceptual slippery slopes upon which only the deontological arguments that they evade can offer some purchase. Their argument is unable to explain why we might not, under conceivable circumstances, be morally obligated to adopt punishments far more brutal and extreme even than execution, or to inflict similarly brutal and extreme harms on innocent members of an offender's family (as punishment of the offender, not of the innocent), or to extend the use of capital punishment to contexts in which many deaths result from behavior far less culpable than murder, such as highway fatalities due to drunkenness or negligence. From their moral position, the only arguments available to Sunstein and Vermeule against any of these practices are unsatisfactorily contingent on prudential considerations, which will not always provide plausible reasons to avoid such practices.

Sunstein and Vermeule wish to avoid making an exclusively consequentialist argument that appeals only to precommitted consequentialists. Thus, they insist that their argument not only puts consequentialist justifications for capital punishment on a surer footing but also should be persuasive to some deontologists (at least if the number of lives saved by capital punishment reaches a certain level). Here, too, they fail to see that the context of criminal punishment changes arguments about "threshold" deontology—the acknowledgement by some deontologists that at some "threshold" of catastrophic consequences, categorical moral prohibitions should give way to consequentialist concerns.

Perhaps most surprising, it is not only deontologists who will fail to be moved by Sunstein and Vermeule's arguments. If one applies to the question of how deterrence works (when it does) some of the same nuanced consideration of the operation of human cognition upon which Sunstein and Vermeule seek to draw to make their argument in favor of capital punishment, one sees that even committed consequentialists should not be convinced by Sunstein and Vermeule's argument for the retention and use of capital punishment, even under the hypothetical conditions of deterrence that they assume. . . .

A venerable deontological tradition with roots in Kantian retributivism holds that punishment is justified only as a response to wrongdoing by the offender and not by its consequential effects. In its strongest form, retributivism imposes a duty to punish offenders according to their desert. In its weakest and perhaps most widely accepted form—as a side constraint on the useful deterrent, incapacitative, or rehabilitative functions that punishment can serve in a society—retributivism requires, at a bare minimum, that the uses of punishment be limited to situations in which the punishment is deserved by the offender and is proportional to the offender's wrongdoing. Under this theory, if the suffering caused by punishment is not deserved and is not proportional to the wrongdoing of those upon whom it is inflicted, then the infliction of such suffering constitutes a wrong — the imposition of unjust punishment — distinct from and worse than merely the suffering itself.

At first glance, a retributive argument might seem an odd one to make against capital punishment, as it is retributivism that offers some of the strongest arguments in favor of the death penalty. (Reconsider the depiction of a generic death penalty debate with which I began, in which retributive arguments are deployed by the proponent of capital punishment.) Kant's famous injunction — that a desert-island society about to disperse would still have an obligation to kill its last murderer — stands for the strong form of retributivism. This form of retributivism holds that the duty to impose deserved punishment exists regardless of any beneficial consequences that might be thought to flow from it. Kant's use of the death penalty as the quintessential example of deserved punishment for the crime of murder seems, at first blush, natural and unobjectionable.

But there is good reason to think that capital punishment — at least as imposed in our contemporary society — routinely and inevitably runs afoul of retributivism's bedrock proportionality constraint. It is rarely the case that execution as a form of suffering can confidently be viewed as disproportionate to the harms inflicted on the victims of capital murders.[47] Rather, the strongest argument for such disproportionality lies in the reduced culpability of most convicted capital offenders; this is an argument that remains powerful even today, after the Supreme Court has recently declared that mentally retarded and juvenile offenders may no longer be executed for their crimes. Though capital defendants have usually committed (or participated in) heinous murders, they very frequently are extremely intellectually limited, are suffering from some form of mental illness, are in the powerful grip of a drug or alcohol addiction, are survivors of childhood abuse, or are the victims of some sort of societal deprivation (be it poverty, racism, poor education, inadequate health care, or some noxious combination of the above). In such circumstances, it is difficult to say that these defendants deserve all of the blame for their terrible acts; if their families or societies share responsibility — even in some small measure — for the tragic results, then the extreme punishment of death should be considered undeserved. Indeed, this point follows directly from Sunstein and Vermeule's own logic. If the government is responsible for private murders that it fails to prevent by providing adequate deterrence, is it not also responsible for private murders that it fails to prevent by providing adequate poverty relief, support for families, education, health care, and initiatives to promote racial equality? This recognition of the conflict between collective responsibility for crimogenic conditions and the imposition of individual criminal responsibility for crime is best captured by a New Yorker cartoon in which a jury foreperson

47. The lengthy waits on death row in anticipation of execution are the strongest current argument for this sort of disproportionality. See, e.g., Soering v. United Kingdom, 11 Eur. Ct. H.R. 439 (1989) (holding that a person sought for extradition from the United Kingdom to the United States could not be extradited because of the likelihood that he would suffer "death row phenomenon" in the prolonged and uncertain wait for his execution, which would violate the European Convention on Human Rights). . . .

delivers the following verdict: "We find that all of us, as a society, are to blame, but only the defendant is guilty."

For this point to hold, it is not necessary to say that there are no capital defendants in our society who could be deemed sufficiently blameworthy so as to deserve the death penalty, or that all capital defendants not sufficiently blameworthy for capital punishment are blameless for their actions and deserve no punishment at all, or that criminal defendants in general are blameless and undeserving of any criminal punishment. Rather, the more modest point is simply the uncontroversial empirical fact that in our contemporary society, those most likely to commit the worst crimes (capital murders) are, as a group, also most likely to have had their volitional capacities affected or impaired by societal conditions for which we collectively bear some responsibility. Thus, it cannot fairly be said that this group is deserving of our worst punishment, or, more affirmatively, it must be acknowledged that there is a retributive gap between the culpability of such offenders and the punishment inflicted upon them.

Moreover, from the standpoint of retributive justice, the strong evidence of discrimination (on the basis of race) or mere arbitrariness (on the basis of geography, among other things) in the imposition of capital punishment takes on a new and different significance from the disparate impact of the private murders that the government might fail to deter. The fact that the race of the defendant and/or the race of the victim frequently have been found to have salience in predicting whether a defendant will be sentenced to death shows not only that there is some racial skewing in the distribution of capital sentences, but also that there is reason to question the underlying moral and legal judgment that any particular murder is one for which capital punishment is a proportional response. Similarly, the fact that defendants from otherwise similar counties in the same state face radically different prospects of receiving capital punishment calls into question not only the procedures by which those deserving of capital punishment are chosen but also the reliability of the underlying judgment that any particular defendant so chosen deserves the death penalty. Unless one takes the position that capital punishment is a deserved and proportional response to every intentional killing no matter what the circumstances (a position neither required by retributivism nor permitted by American law), one can take no recourse in the argument that discrimination and arbitrariness merely exclude some deserving defendants from execution. Rather, discrimination and arbitrariness undermine our confidence in the very attribution of desert to the defendants chosen for execution.

The strongest case for a retributive gap, of course, lies in the conviction and execution of the innocent — a moral wrong that we have new reason to believe is disturbingly prevalent in our capital punishment system. . . .

There is a second and distinct flaw in the equivalence that Sunstein and Vermeule seek to maintain between racial inequality in the administration of capital punishment and racial inequality in the distribution of private murders. The racial inequalities in the administration of capital punishment — both the failure to give equal weight to the deaths of black victims as compared to white victims in similar cases and the greater willingness to take the lives of black defendants as compared to white defendants in similar cases — give rise to an inference of racial animus on the part of state actors (prosecutors and jurors). That is, these disparities reveal the unwillingness or inability, whether conscious or unconscious, of governmental actors to treat black citizens with equal concern and respect. But the racial inequality in the distribution of private murders does not plausibly reflect such pervasive animus on the part either of the murderers or the government. . . .

A third major wellspring of deontological objection to the justice of capital punishment is the claim that, unlike many ordinary punishments, it violates human dignity. This view has been given its most prominent exposition in Justice Brennan's concurring opinion on the unconstitutionality of the death penalty as "cruel and unusual punishment" under the Eighth Amendment in Furman v. Georgia. This claim has an abstract, slippery quality to it that makes it difficult to assess whether the violence done to human dignity through the imposition of death as punishment is different in any meaningful way from the violence done to human dignity through the crime of murder. . . .

The imposition of extreme punishments such as execution (or rape or torture), even in cases involving the most deserving of murderers (or rapists or torturers), violates human dignity — not because of what it does to the punished, but rather because of what it does to all of us. Death, from either execution or murder, by definition destroys the human capacities of the person killed, but inflicting death (or rape or torture) as punishment can, in addition, damage or destroy the human capacities of those of us in whose name the punishment is publicly inflicted.

This threat to dignity stems from certain sociological facts about the way punishment works as a social practice. Punishment is a public act; it is generally presented by the government as deserved by the recipient, and that imputation of desert is generally accepted by the public; the imposition of punishment tends to elicit gratifying emotions of satisfaction because the public condemnation and suffering of an offender assuage to some degree the anger and hatred provoked by the offense. Nothing in this characterization is meant as a normative justification of punishment practices. I mean to take no position here on whether the "retributive hatred" that wrongdoing inspires is a moral good,[72] or whether the public satisfaction of vengeful urges offers a satisfactory consequentialist defense of punishment. Rather, I mean simply to suggest that when the purposeful infliction of extreme suffering is yoked with emotions of righteousness and satisfaction, it will inevitably suppress our ordinary human capacities for compassion and empathy. To be sure, the desire to punish may itself spring, at least in part, from compassion and empathy for crime victims. And not every kind of punishment necessarily suppresses to any great extent our capacities for compassion and empathy. But the inherent moral satisfaction that attends the practice of punishment when it includes the infliction of death or other very extreme forms of suffering does seem to permit, or even require, the weakening of important psychological constraints against brutality. In this way, brutal punishment poses threats to our human capacities distinct from and more insidious than other forms of brutality that might be authorized or tolerated by the government because punishment has a distinctive connection to powerful human emotions. . . .

---

72. See, e.g., Jeffrie G. Murphy, Hatred: A Qualified Defense, in Forgiveness and Mercy 88, 91-92 (Jeffrie G. Murphy & Jean Hampton eds., 1988) (defending "retributive hatred" as an appropriate moral response to certain types of wrongdoing).

## NOTES

1. *Arguments for and against the death penalty.*  For many observers, the fundamental question about the legitimacy of the death penalty turns on moral arguments. Walter Berns has developed the argument presented above in more detail in his book, For Capital Punishment (1979). More recently, Sunstein and Vermeule made a sustained moral argument in favor of the death penalty under some circumstances. In response critics argue that the taking of life is immoral, even when done by the state. Other critics attack the barbarity of the sanction itself. Yet others question whether any government can be trusted with such an awesome power, even if the morality of retribution itself is recognized. The literature is vast and impassioned, and includes striking historical, geographical, social, and comparative arguments. See, e.g., Encyclopedia of Capital Punishment (1998); Franklin Zimring, The Contradictions of American Capital Punishment (2003).

2. *New deterrence literature.*  The question whether the death penalty deters has a long history. Professor Bernard Harcourt observes:

> Beccaria, the first true rational choice theorist, did not believe that capital punishment fell within the domain of the sovereign's right to punish, but instead within the domain of war, which, he argued, was ruled by necessity and utility. But the death penalty, according to Beccaria, served neither interest. It was not necessary because long-drawn-out punishments, such as penal servitude or slavery for life, were more effective and fear-inducing than the fleeting shock of death. It was also not useful because capital punishment had a brutalizing effect on society. Jeremy Bentham — the very spokesman for the theory of marginal deterrence in the modern era — agreed entirely: "the more attention one gives to the punishment of death the more he will be inclined to adopt the opinion of Beccaria — that it ought to be disused. This subject is so ably discussed in his book that to treat it after him is a work that may well be dispensed with."

See Bernard Harcourt, Randomization and Social Physics: Post-Modern Meditations on Punishment, A Polemic and Manifesto for the 21st Century (working draft, February 2007).

Neither scholars nor politicians in the United States have treated Beccaria and Bentham as having the last word on the subject. In 1975 Professor Isaac Ehrlich influenced the course of this debate when he concluded, based on a sophisticated study on data from 1933 to 1969 in the United States, that "an additional execution per year . . . may have resulted (on the average) in 7 or 8 fewer murders." Isaac Ehrlich, The Deterrent Effect of Capital Punishment: A Question of Life and Death, 65 Am. Econ. Rev. 414 (June 1975). Sharply critical reviews of Ehrlich's studies led most observers in the 1980s and 1990s to treat the deterrent impact of the death penalty as an open question. Ehrlich's work was conducted before the modern reconstruction of the death penalty in America, a story told in brief in Chapter 3 of this volume. A number of new studies, however, have purported to establish that the death penalty has a deterrent impact in modern times.

3. *At what price?*  One fairly isolated argument concerning the death penalty involves the financial cost of operating a functional capital punishment system. Death penalty cases are enormously expensive. See The Costs of the

Death Penalty, testimony of Richard C. Deiter, executive director of the Death Penalty Information Center, before the Massachusetts Legislature, Joint Committee on Criminal Justice (available at http://www.deathpenaltyinfo.org/Mass CostTestimony.pdf) (reporting various calculations and estimates of the cost of capital cases in different jurisdictions). Indeed, many prosecutors with capital charging authority use it rarely or not at all, in part to shepherd resources for the full range of cases, apart from moral, philosophical, or political concerns. See E. Michael McCann, Opposing Capital Punishment: A Prosecutor's Perspective, 79 Marq. L. Rev. 649 (1996) (noting prosecutors' concerns about the costs of the death penalty). Death penalty proponents respond that the costs are high in part because of excessive relitigation of capital claims, and that even at a high cost, a capital sentence may be justified. Other observers find the entire conversation about the cost of the capital system distasteful, holding that moral arguments should be determinative. Some people consider the idea of assessing economic costs in the absence of measures of human cost stilted.

4. *Death as the appropriate penalty for what types of crimes?*   Walter Berns points to the atrocities of the Nazi regime, including genocide and crimes against humanity, as offenses meriting death. Compared with the magnitude of those crimes, what other crimes, if any, deserve the death penalty? See Matthew H. Kramer, The Ethics of Capital Punishment: A Philosophical Investigation of Evil and Its Consequences (2012) (developing a limited "purgative" rationale for capital punishment under narrow circumstances); but see Dan Markel, State, Be Not Proud: A Retributivist Defense of the Commutation of Death Row and the Abolition of the Death Penalty, 40 Harv. C.R.–C.L. L. Rev. 407 (2005). Does it not denigrate the enormity and brutality of genocide and crimes against humanity if death becomes the punishment for any murder? Consider also that the judges of the recently instituted International Criminal Court cannot impose death sentences even though they try cases of genocide, crimes against humanity, war crimes, and the crime of aggression.

### 3.   Politics, Philosophy, and Economics ("PP&E")

Criminal punishments are the product of a series of public acts. It is striking to look at the justifications offered by politicians both for expanding and for restricting or regulating the use of punishment. Often the justifications for particular crimes, sanctions, or policies are unarticulated or poorly articulated. But compared with philosophical claims, public officials in the legislative and executive branch (but typically not judges) more often resort to claims based on concerns of equal treatment (either for its own sake, or to achieve equal severity or leniency for a class of offenses or offenders) or concerns for the public fisc. This part of the chapter introduces these functional and political claims, which sometimes are visible and often are found to underlie policy initiatives.

#### a.   Equality/Disparity Concerns

Ohio Rev. Code §2929.11(C) provides that a court "shall not base the sentence upon the race, ethnic background, gender, or religion of the offender."

Tennessee similarly provides that sentencing "should exclude all considerations respecting race, gender, creed, religion, national origin and social status of the individual," and Montana states that sentencing practices "must be neutral with respect to the offender's race, gender, religion, national origin, or social or economic status." Federal law has a similar provision, 28 U.S.C. §994(d), which instructs the U.S. Sentencing Commission to "assure that the [sentencing] guidelines and policy statements are entirely neutral as to the race, sex, national origin, creed, and socioeconomic status of offenders."

Do you think these requirements of equality are readily integrated with traditional purposes of punishment, or can you envision some tensions between traditional notions of equality and traditional theories of punishment? Consider the following recommendation from the ABA, which focuses on the importance of ensuring that principles of equality are safeguarded in sentencing systems.

## ABA Standards for Criminal Justice, Sentencing 18-2.5
### (3d ed. 1994)

(a) The legislature should create a sentencing structure that enables the agency performing the intermediate function to make reasonably accurate forecasts of the aggregate of sentencing decisions, including forecasts of the types of sanctions and severity of sentences imposed, so that the legislature can make informed changes in sentence patterns through amendment of the criminal code, or the agency can do so through revised guidance to sentencing courts.

(b) The legislature should create a sentencing structure that sufficiently guides the exercise of sentencing courts' discretion to the end that unwarranted and inequitable disparities in sentences are avoided. . . .

### COMMENTARY

Systems of "indeterminate" sentencing, which invest sentencing judges and parole boards with broad discretion in making sentencing decisions, have resulted in unwarranted disparity in individual sentences. . . .[1] Prior editions of these Standards have noted the prevalence of unwarranted sentencing disparities in specific cases, demonstrated in analyses of sentence patterns for similar offenses and in studies of sentence choices by different judges considering identical cases. Some observers have condemned the arbitrary and random nature of indeterminate sentences; others have claimed that such a sentencing structure allows racial and class biases to infect sentencing decisions.

At every level of the drafting process (in the Task Force, the Standards Committee, and the Criminal Justice Section Council), the ABA consistently

---

1. As to the injustices of individualized disparities, the classic work is Marvin E. Frankel, Criminal Sentences: Law Without Order (1973). A valuable study of the unplanned expansion of American prison systems since the 1970s is Franklin E. Zimring & Gordon Hawkins, The Scale of Imprisonment (1991).

decided that the traditional practices of indeterminate sentencing, still followed in most states, should be rejected. It is a telling point that through four years of ABA debate, no defense was raised of the old practices of indeterminacy. . . .

The third edition adds an important new component of the requirement of determinacy: Standard 18-2.5(a) states that the sentencing structure should be sufficiently determinate to allow for reasonably accurate forecasts of aggregate sentencing decisions so that the legislature can make informed changes in sentence patterns through amendment of the criminal code, or the agency can do so through revised guidance to sentencing courts. Thus, the Standard contemplates a system in which policy decisions can be made to have predictable impacts on the system as a whole. Also, with adequate determinacy the legislature and agency can address discrete problems in targeted ways. For example, a jurisdiction that wants to heighten the severity of sentences for violent crimes can do so with some precision. If the resulting changes will overload the prison system, the agency can propose offsetting amendments, such as fractional reductions in sentences for nonviolent crimes. Substantial state experience through the 1980s has shown that the related goals of predictability and manageability can be realized in determinate sentencing structures.

This Standard must be read in conjunction with Standard 18-2.6 regarding the "individualization of sentences." Determinacy, as a systemic and case-specific value, is not an absolute good that must be pursued to the exclusion of other concerns. As argued by Kenneth Culp Davis, predictable and uniform rules must always coexist with a degree of flexibility and discretion. The problem is finding the optimum balance between rule and discretion. In the realm of sentencing, this tension is vividly pronounced. . . .

### NOTES

1. *The goal of reducing sentencing disparity.* As discussed more fully in Chapter 3, one of the most prominent goals of modern sentencing reform has been to reduce unwarranted sentencing disparity. The problems of defining, measuring, and finding solutions to disparity arise throughout sentencing systems. Some of these problems are endemic to discussions of equality and disparity in all contexts. When, for example, are two individuals similar and when are they different? Other problems are especially acute in sentencing: these include the difficulty of describing each offense and offender (for example, is similarity based on the offenders' "actual" behavior or the charges for which offenders are convicted?) and the difficulty of measuring actual sentences (for instance, should fines of fixed dollar amounts be the same if offenders have vastly different resources?).

In practice, among the greatest areas of concern in modern reforms are disparities in treatment by race and, to a lesser extent, gender. Yet one can also find wide sentencing disparities based on socioeconomic class, geography, and other "status" characteristics. Are there certain types of disparity that call for extra attention? In considering this question, examine again the somewhat different groups and commands articulated in the equality provisions of the state statutes reprinted above.

2. *Surface equality and a deep understanding of disparity.* Concepts of disparity and equality in sentencing can be baffling in part because of three additional puzzles that are worth noting as an introduction to this topic. First, what might be seen as apparent equality—such as giving every offender a five-year sentence—can in fact represent great inequality if offenders or their offenses or both are different in pertinent ways. Because equality means not only treating like cases alike, but also treating different cases differently, an example of two cases sentenced in the same way could actually be evidence of *inequality* if these cases were different in ways that should have led to different sentences. Second, even when two convicted offenders who are similar are sentenced in the same way, inequality can exist if a third, similar offender either escapes without being charged or is prosecuted in a different jurisdiction or is charged with a different offense. Finally, the very ability to assess what factors can and should matter in judging equality and disparity depends in large part on initially selecting an underlying theory of punishment. Two offenders committing similar crimes might deserve similar punishments if sentenced according to retributivist theory, but their personal backgrounds might call for quite different punishments if sentencing is based on the goal of rehabilitation. If we cannot or do not adopt defined theories of punishment, it becomes very hard to distinguish *warranted* from *unwarranted* sentencing disparity. See Marc Miller, Sentencing Equality Pathology, 53 Emory L.J. 271 (2005); Kevin Cole, The Empty Idea of Sentencing Disparity, 91 Nw. U. L. Rev. 1336 (1997).

### b. Cents and Sentencing Ability

A central aspect of most legislative sentencing discussions does not concern traditional justifications for punishment at all. Consider the following document developed by criminal justice policy experts in Ohio to explain to the public what factors influence criminal punishments in that state. What non-philosophical justifications do they offer to define, justify, or limit sentences?

## The State of Crime and Criminal Justice in Ohio
### The Office of Criminal Justice Services (Jan. 1995)

*HOW SHOULD CRIME BE PUNISHED?*

The question, itself, testifies to the complexity of the issue in that it wrongly assumes that punishment (e.g., imprisonment, death) is the only legitimate function of justice at the sentencing level. Incapacitation, deterrence, rehabilitation, restitution and, more recently, forfeiture, are other goals which can and do drive the decisions of legislators, judges, parole officials, corrections authorities, and others who administer criminal sanctions—the carrying out of court sentences—in this State.

For these reasons and others (e.g., legal issues, humane and equitable treatment of offenders) prisons and jails are not necessarily the best sanctions for all felony offenders, as is often assumed. "Alternatives to incarceration," rather than suggesting a second or third preferred choice in the sanctioning process, may in fact provide the best means at a government's disposal for dealing with certain kinds of offenders. . . .

Resources can also dictate choice of sanctions, where judges are given such sentencing discretion. Sometimes judges, faced with severely crowded local jails and little in the way of intermediate options, must choose between the polar extremes of prison and probation in felony sentencing. The problem has grown more extreme in recent years in the face of a dramatic increase in drug-related prison sentences which could be diminished, in number and perhaps severity, by sufficient resources devoted to treatment programs.

Ohioans' attitudes and opinions about sanctions reflect uncertainty about appropriate responses to criminal offenders. There appears to be a general presumption that citizens are frustrated by the leniency and inefficiency of the Criminal Justice System, that they are continually seeking harsher felony punishments than those being handed down in Ohio's criminal courts. Research in Ohio and at the national level suggests that key decision makers, such as legislators, rather consistently assume that the public will not support sanctions which propose something in lieu of prison/jail sentences. However, citizen attitude surveys in Ohio and elsewhere have found that these assumptions overestimate public inflexibility, and that given sufficient information regarding the circumstances of the criminal behavior citizens will support a wide range of other sanction options.

Less than one-third of the citizen respondents in a statewide Office of Criminal Justice Services (OCJS) survey readied for release in 1993 stated a preference for building our way out of the prison/jail crowding crisis in Ohio, while more than half opted for community treatment centers (35%), emergency releases (18%), and more use of probation (7%).

When presented a list of six specific options which could be used to replace or ease incarceration for non-violent offenders the same respondents found five of the six options agreeable by margins ranging from 68% to 76%. Only "fines" fell below the level of public acceptability (48%). "Victim compensation" (68%), "community supervision" (69%), "work release" (73%), "education release" (76%), and "early release" (78%) all found solid support. These results were virtually unchanged from those obtained in a 1984 survey which examined the same question.

Five critical issues largely determine Ohio's capacity to administer effective criminal justice sanctions.

*Institutional crowding:* Both the Departments of Youth Services (DYS) and Rehabilitation and Correction (DRC) have experienced unprecedented increases in institutional populations during the past decade. DYS populations have risen by half, while DRC's numbers have doubled. Virtually all of the 24 DRC institutions are operating above capacity—180% statewide. The tremendous growth in numbers appears largely unrelated to broader crime trends, instead being driven by decision choices within the criminal justice system (i.e., legislative, prosecutorial/judicial, parole). Every aspect of Ohio's sanctioning procedures is negatively affected by the institutional crowding crisis.

*Impact of substance abuse:* This nationwide problem has created special stress for the sanctioning function in criminal justice. Tougher laws and sentencing relative to drunk driving and drug abuse, combined with the usage explosion of crack-cocaine in the latter 1980s have proven especially burdensome for already crowded prisons, jails, youth detention facilities, and treatment programs.

*Escalating costs:* Funding for new institutional construction is not the major economic cost concern relative to sanctions; the cost of running those institutions is. The average per-year, per-prisoner operational cost to DRC exceeds $12,000, ballooning that agency's annual budget to the three-quarters of a billion dollar range. Meeting the basic needs of county jail inmates and juvenile offenders adds more hundreds of millions of dollars each year. In the aftermath of the Lucasville uprising it appears that security costs will dramatically increase in at least some state facilities. While technology promises hope for minimizing the costs of some sanctions (e.g., ankle bracelets for electronic monitoring of house arrestees, hair testing for drug usage supervision of parolees, etc.), the fact remains that Ohio's expenditures on criminal sanctions are increasing dramatically at a time when most items in government budgets are holding level or being reduced.

*Effectiveness of treatment:* Sentenced criminal offenders bring a wide range of social disorders relating to sexual problems, gambling, child abuse, substance addiction, learning disabilities, and others. Frequently, criminal sanctions include treatment provisions for these disorders, but it is difficult to determine how effective these treatment programs are, especially in light of very limited treatment resources. Much of the future of criminal sanctions may ride on treatment programs with a proven capacity to interrupt criminal careers.

*Availability of sanctioning options:* Ohio's institutional crowding crisis alone, with its enormous implications for state and local budgets, strongly suggests the development of non-incarceration options for at least some types of offenders. Other issues of justice are also linked to this development, such as sentencing equity, long-term crime costs to society, and the potential tapping of resources outside of the traditional criminal justice arena (e.g., public health).

## NOTES

1. *Functional purposes: politics.* Why does this excerpt discuss at some length the results of a survey of Ohio citizens about their attitudes concerning punishment and sentencing? Why should decision makers, who presumably have more knowledge about and time to consider the consequences of particular punishments, be concerned with the opinions of average citizens? Do any of the traditional purposes of punishment depend on or incorporate the perspectives of a majority of average citizens?

Although one can debate whether the views of the general public should matter in sentencing and punishment decision making, there is little question that they do have a profound influence on sentencing systems in the United States. Every legislature making sentencing rules in the United States is elected by popular vote, and most judges and prosecutors in state systems are also elected officials. A profound and enduring issue in modern sentencing systems, and in many specific sentencing decisions, is the role of politics in the development of sentencing rules. See generally Stephen B. Bright & Patrick J. Keenen, Judges and the Politics of Death: Deciding Between the Bill of Rights and the Next Election in Capital Cases, 75 B.U. L. Rev. 760 (1995).

2. *Functional purposes: costs.*   An obvious theme running through the "five critical issues" influencing Ohio's capacity to administer effective criminal justice sanctions is money (or the lack thereof). In other words, limited resources are another powerful purpose guiding sentencing decision making, especially in states where punishment resources (prisons, jails, probation officers) and prosecutorial and judicial resources are always scarce. Sometimes resource constraints provide the superstructure within which policymakers must allocate sentences. An illustration of this approach is the "capacity constraint" provision in some states, which directs sentencing commissions to design sentencing rules that take into account limitations in available prison space. Some states explain punishment priorities in light of limited resources. For instance, Florida's legislature has decided that punishment is the primary purpose of sentencing. Along with other limitations, the Florida legislature prioritizes the incarceration of serious offenders and recidivists "in order to maximize the finite capacities of state and local correctional facilities." Fla. Stat. §921.002.

3. *State decarceration trends?*   After strong increases during the 1980s and 1990s, and slower increases for much of the 2000s, incarceration rates in state systems declined for several years in a row, starting in 2008. What made such a reversal politically acceptable? Part of the explanation could be falling crime rates, although the rate of violent crime fell throughout the late 1990s and early 2000s without producing decreases in the incarceration rate. The economic downturn that began in 2008 could also account for the change: reduced tax revenues combined with increased needs for other state spending (such as unemployment benefits) left less room in state budgets for increases in prison costs. Does a reduced reliance on prison need to serve an explicit purpose — apart from meeting a budget under difficult conditions — if the decarceration trend is to continue? See Mary Fan, Beyond Budget-Cut Criminal Justice, 90 N.C. L. Rev. 581 (2012).

## PROBLEM 1-4.   SENTENCING WITHOUT PRISON OR DEATH

If prisons and the death penalty were declared unconstitutional or became wildly unpopular politically (perhaps on moral or economic grounds), would the only option be anarchy? How might policymakers respond to a world with crime but without prisons or capital punishment as sentencing options?

## PROBLEM 1-5.   SENTENCING BUDGETS

Given the profound difficulty of specifying, finding political agreement on, and applying purposes of punishment, do functional justifications or other practical resource limits offer the best hope for "forcing" relatively principled sentencing and use of punishment?

Should a legislature decide how many prison beds it wants, and then tell an executive agency to allocate those beds to best achieve one or more stated purposes as opposed to serving whatever mix of purposes the executive agency decides? Are there more profound kinds of budgets that might produce a fairer or more decent society? What if legislatures specified a particular number of prosecutions, convictions, or prison cells for a specific crime — say, 300 person-years for persons convicted of possession of narcotics with intent to sell?

### c.   Public Sentiment

In democratic systems there is a strong belief that fundamental normative choices ought to be made by the people. Few political systems function in such a purely democratic form, and the relationship between legislative and executive representatives and citizens is a relationship reflecting the puzzles of agency and political accountability. The next reading explores the difference between uninformed and informed public preference about punishment. Consider the relevance of these materials for politicians, prosecutors, policy advocates — and for theories of just punishment.

> ### Myths and Misconceptions:
> ### Public Opinion versus Public Judgment
> ### about Sentencing, Karen Gelb
> ### Sentencing Advisory Council (July 2006),
> ### pp. 4, 11-14, 17, 24-25

[The Sentencing Advisory Council (SAC) in Canada was established in Victoria in 2004 as an "independent statutory body." The SAC funnels informed public opinion about the sentencing process to advise the necessary lawmakers, including Victoria's Court of Appeal and Attorney General. The following report examines national and international public opinions on sentencing. The report was the product of a year-long study where the SAC wanted to ascertain current public opinions on sentencing, to analyze the methodologies used to obtain the information and whether certain methodologies influenced the results, and to develop a toolkit of methodologies that can provide the most accurate public opinion to aid review of the sentencing process.]

Most Western governments now routinely conduct public opinion polls about attitudes to important issues in criminal justice. Recent surveys measuring levels of public confidence in the criminal justice system have found that public trust and confidence are at critically low levels around the world. Such findings have led to attempts to promote public confidence and to ensure that the system — in particular the court component — does not lose touch with the community that it serves. In Australia one manifestation of this concern has been a focus for court administrators on ways to improve the relationship between the courts and their various publics.

To some degree, this heightened sensitivity to the views of the public reflects an element of penal populism. Anthony Bottoms recently coined the phrase "populist punitiveness" to describe "the notion of politicians tapping into, and using for their own purposes, what they believe to be the public's generally punitive stance." Policies are populist if they are used for winning votes without regard for their effectiveness in reducing crime or promoting justice—allowing the electoral advantage of a policy to take precedence over its penal effectiveness.

The central tool of penal populism is imprisonment. Penal populism provides a framework within which to understand increasing imprisonment rates around the world as well as the proliferation of punitive sentencing policies. Justification for policies such as three-strikes legislation, mandatory minimum sentences and sex offender notification laws is found in this framework of penal populism, which describes a punitive public fed up with crime and with the perceived leniency of the criminal justice system. . . .

When representative surveys first came into widespread use, the most common way of measuring public opinion on sentencing was to use the general question of whether sentences are "too harsh, about right or too lenient." This question, in some variant or another, has been used in opinion polls across the world for the last forty years. Responses to this question have been remarkably consistent both over time (from the 1970s to current research) and across countries (from North America and Australia to the United Kingdom and Europe): over the past three decades about 70%-80% of respondents in these countries reported that sentences are too lenient, with slightly lower rates in Canada in recent years (60%-70%) and slightly higher rates in the United States (up to 85%). When asked about juvenile offenders, slightly higher proportions of respondents felt that sentences are too lenient: ranging from 71% in a 2003 Office of National Statistics Omnibus Survey in the United Kingdom to 88% of respondents in a 1997 Canadian survey. . . .

In more recent years, however, this conclusion has been called into question. In particular, researchers have hypothesized that the finding of a highly punitive public is merely a methodological artifact—a result of the way in which public opinion has been measured. Since the 1980s researchers have attempted to go beyond the single question poll to include further questions in representative surveys that can clarify and further explain the apparent harshness of public attitudes. In this way the research has attempted to address the methodological limitations of using a single abstract question to measure complex and nuanced public attitudes.

*In the abstract, people tend to think about violent and repeat offenders when reporting that sentencing is too lenient.*

A simple yet highly effective way of explaining public punitiveness has been the inclusion of a second question in representative surveys that asks people about the kind of offender they were thinking about when answering the question about perceived leniency of sentencing. Doob and Roberts [An Analysis of the Public's View of Sentencing: A Report to the Department of Justice, Canada (1983)] developed this approach, which has provided valuable insight into the stereotypical offender: most people (57%) report that they had been thinking about a violent or repeat offender when stating that sentences are too lenient. These same results have been found when asking respondents about juvenile offenders. Violent crimes account for only a very small proportion (no more than about 10% in the United States, the United Kingdom, Canada and Australia) of all crimes recorded by police. Repeat offenders also only account for a small proportion of all offenders. Despite these facts, the public thinks of violent recidivists when claiming that sentences are too lenient.

Doob and Roberts conducted a series of studies examining public opinion on crime and justice. One of these involved a representative nationwide survey in Canada and found that 80% of respondents felt that sentences were not severe enough. [Seventy-four percent] of respondents greatly overestimated the proportion of crimes involving violence; 34% greatly overestimated the proportion of property offenders who would be reconvicted in 5 years; and 45% greatly overestimated the proportion of violent offenders who would be reconvicted in 5 years. . . .

*People have very little accurate knowledge of crime and the criminal justice system.*

Misunderstanding of the facts is not restricted to the prevalence of violent offenders in the criminal justice system. Indeed, research has shown that public misperceptions are rife in relation to every stage of the criminal justice system.

Looking at large-scale surveys of public opinion about crime and punishment in the United States, United Kingdom, Canada, Australia and New Zealand, Roberts et al. [Penal Populism and Public Opinion: Lessons from Five Countries (2003)] conclude that the public has very little accurate knowledge about the criminal justice system. Of particular relevance to attitudes to sentencing are findings that show that people have extensive misperceptions about the nature and extent of crime, about court outcomes and about the use of imprisonment and parole. Consistent results from many of the studies in this field show that people tend to:

- perceive crime to be constantly increasing, particularly crimes of violence;
- over-estimate the proportion of recorded crime that involves violence;
- over-estimate the proportion of juvenile crime that involves violence;
- over-estimate the proportion of crime for which juveniles are responsible;
- over-estimate the number of homicides committed;
- over-estimate the percentage of offenders who re-offend;
- under-estimate the severity of maximum penalties;
- under-estimate the severity of sentencing practices (e.g., the incarceration rate);
- have little accurate knowledge of statutory sentencing;
- have little accurate knowledge of the juvenile justice system;
- know little about sentencing alternatives and focus instead on imprisonment;
- under-estimate the severity of sentencing practices for specific offences;
- under-estimate the severity of prison life;
- over-estimate the percentage of offenders released on parole;
- over-estimate the proportion of prison terms served in the community on parole;

- over-estimate the percentage of parolees who will re-offend while on parole; and
- over-estimate the proportion of young offenders who will be reconvicted of a criminal offence.

It is clear that the public lacks accurate information about crime and criminal justice system practices. Despite this lack of knowledge, people nonetheless have strongly held and confident opinions about crime and justice issues. In fact, representative surveys have shown that it is those who have the lowest levels of knowledge who also hold the most punitive views. For example, Doob and Roberts (1983) found that those who think that sentences are too lenient are more likely to think that crime overall is violent and to underestimate the proportion of offenders convicted of robbery and assault who are sent to prison. . . .

*When people are given more information, their levels of putitiveness drop dramatically.*

There is substantial evidence that the public's lack of knowledge about crime and justice is related to the high levels of punitiveness reported as a response to a general, abstract question about sentencing. Based upon the conclusion that increasing the provision of information will decrease levels of punitiveness, many researchers have moved from traditional survey questions to those which provide much more information to people before asking for a response. The crime vignette approach in a representative survey is a way in which to provide more information about the offence, the offender and the impact on the victim. This approach uses brief case studies to achieve two goals:

- to provide a more accurate picture of public opinion based on an *informed* public; and
- to determine the effect of information provision on respondents' perceptions of sentencing.

By providing the opportunity to ascertain a more informed public opinion, crime vignettes address one of the disadvantages of the traditional survey question — that such questions cannot adequately uncover the nuances of public opinion on the complex issues of crime and justice.

[In a groundbreaking study, two researchers] conducted a series of 13 studies for the Canadian Department of Justice. In a small study of 116 randomly selected respondents, [the researchers] contrasted the response given to brief descriptions of unusual sentences (only offence and sentence information) to those given to more complete descriptions of the same cases (including a case summary). Respondents were initially asked a general question about their perceptions of court sentencing practice. In the abstract, over 90% of the total group reported that in general the courts are too lenient.

Respondents were then randomly assigned to one of two groups, one to receive a brief description of a manslaughter case (similar to a media report) and one to receive a more detailed description with information on incident and offender characteristics.

Most of the respondents provided with a short description of the case felt that the sentence was too lenient (80%), while only 7% felt the sentence was about right. For those given a longer description of the case, 15% felt that the sentence was too lenient and 30% felt that the sentence was about right. It is interesting to note that fully 45% of this group described the sentence as too harsh (citation omitted).

[These] studies show that sentences described in the media are perceived by most people as being too lenient, while those described in detail in court transcripts are mostly seen as appropriate. [The researchers] conclude that, were the public to form opinions from court-based information instead of through the lens of the mass media, there would be fewer instances of calls for harsher sentences. Caution should thus be exercised in responding to calls for harsher penalties as a fully informed public could well be quite content with the current level of severity of penalties. . . .

Rethinking Crime & Punishment (RCP) was set up in 2001 in response to widespread concern about the United Kingdom's growing reliance on imprisonment. A key reason for this has been the perceived pressure of public opinion, as politicians, judges and magistrates have responded to a supposed climate of opinion that demands an increasingly harsh response to crime. The specific aims of RCP have been to increase public knowledge and improve public debate about prison and alternatives. It has been suggested that studies on attitudes to imprisonment might be tapping top-of-the-head reactions, rather than enduring and well-considered beliefs.

In [a] 1996 British Crime Survey, respondents were given a description of a real case and were asked to impose one or more sentences for a 23 year-old male repeat offender convicted of the burglary of an elderly man's house. Half the sample was given a menu of options from which to choose, while the other half was asked to give unprompted responses. This allowed testing of the hypothesis that there would be less support for imprisonment when respondents were made aware of alternative options.

While a majority of respondents in both groups [favored] imprisonment, the figure was significantly higher for those without the menu of options (67%) than for those given information on other sentencing options available (54%). Respondents with the sentencing menu were more likely to favour non-custodial options such as suspended sentences, community service, compensation and probation (citation omitted).

[When exposed to additional, accurate information about current sentencing tools, such as mandatory sentencing, the public also shows a lack of a punitive bent.] The main justification for [mandatory sentencing] has been supposed public demand for more severe sentencing.

People have little knowledge about mandatory sentencing, the offences that attract this response and the actual minimum and maximum penalties that apply. They are also unaware of the extent to which mandatory sentencing laws affect large numbers of offenders convicted of non-violent offences, particularly drug crimes. . . .

In a study that specifically examined public attitudes to "three-strikes" laws, a random sample of Ohio residents [were asked] whether they supported or opposed implementing such a law in their state. In response to a single question with no context provided, 88% expressed support for the proposal.

But when asked to impose sentences for a number of case studies, the percentage endorsing the "three-strikes" sentence dropped to only 17%.

A more recent national survey of 2,000 adults in the United States found even lower levels of support for mandatory sentencing. Respondents were first asked a general question: "In recent years, some states have required that certain crimes, including non-violent crimes, carry a mandatory minimum prison sentence regardless of the circumstances of the crime. Do you support or oppose the idea of mandatory prison sentences for non-violent crime?" In response to this question, 61% were opposed to mandatory prison terms while 35% supported them. . . . Clearly there is less support for mandatory prison terms in the United States than is suggested by the proliferation of such laws. . . .

Evidence of the often contradictory nature of public opinion on sentencing can be found when people are asked how to "fix" the criminal justice system. The responses vary based on the nature of the question (whether the question is the open-ended "what is the most effective way to reduce crime" or the binary "which would you choose to reduce prison over-crowding: build more prisons or increase the use of alternative prisons").

Despite a lack of knowledge about the criminal justice system, public sentencing preferences are actually very similar to those expressed by the judiciary or actually used by the courts. To test the hypothesis that the public is more punitive than judges, [researchers] looked at a 1986 representative survey conducted by Gallup for the Canadian Sentencing Commission. The survey asked respondents what proportion of offenders should be incarcerated for various crimes. These preferences were then compared to the proportion of convictions for this offence that actually resulted in custody in the Canadian courts. No significant difference was found between the two groups—average incarceration rates across ten offences (both violent and property offences) were 66% for the public and 67% for the courts.

A similar approach was adopted [in a] 1989 comparison of lay and judicial responses to case study vignettes in Illinois, in which respondents were asked to impose sentences on the same four moderately severe cases in which prison was a possible, but not inevitable sentencing outcome. A total of 325 respondents participated in the research: [including] state judges who participated as part of seminars on sentencing; . . . jurors who reported for jury duty but who were not needed by the court that day; and . . . university students who participated for course credit.

Respondents were presented with detailed information about each of the four cases, including a presentence report (including information on the nature of the offence and on the offender's background) and a video of the sentencing hearing. Respondents were told the range of possible sentencing options legally available for that case and then completed a questionnaire indicating sentencing preferences. The non-judicial respondents were also told that offenders sentenced to prison would typically serve about half of their prison terms.

[The results] found that there was no evidence in any of the four cases that judicial sentences were more lenient than the sentences of the lay respondents. Judges' sentences in this study were as severe or more severe than those of lay respondents. They conclude that the perception that judges are more lenient than the public is simply a myth. . . .

Evidence of the often contradictory nature of public opinion on sentencing can be found in the literature showing that people favour non-imprisonment mechanisms, even when they have reported that they perceive sentences to
be overly lenient. This result has been found in surveys asking two types of
questions: those that ask respondents about the most effective way to reduce
crime and those that offer respondents a choice between building more prisons
and increasing the use of alternatives to prison as possible options for reducing
prison over-crowding.

### What Do We Know About Public Opinion Internationally?

The Canadian Sentencing Commission commissioned a survey in 1986
that asked respondents about the most effective way of controlling crime.
While 28% of respondents felt that sentences should be made harsher, fully
43% suggested that reducing unemployment would be most effective. A
further 14% favoured increasing the use of alternatives to incarceration and
11% suggested increasing the number of social programs. Respondents were
then asked a follow-up question asking them to choose between spending
money on building more prisons or on developing alternatives to incarceration. While 23% favoured the prison approach, fully 70% chose alternatives to
imprisonment.

A more recent Canadian survey examined people's attitudes to sentencing for adults and juveniles separately. Respondents were asked about the
most effective way to control crime. Half were asked about controlling youth
crime, while the others were asked about controlling adult crime. Fewer than
a third of respondents thought that making sentences harsher was the best
way to control adult crime, and fewer than a quarter of respondents thought
that this was the best way to reduce youth crime. Incapacitation is seen as
being more important for adult offenders than for youth, for whom expressions of community disapproval and rehabilitation are seen as being more
important.

A 2001 survey of 1,056 adults in the United States found that Americans
clearly preferred prevention as the best strategy for dealing with crime. More
respondents felt that prevention in the form of education and youth programs
was the most effective way to control crime (37%), while 20% preferred punishment in the form of longer sentences and more prisons. Enforcement
(more police officers) was considered the best approach by 19% of respondents, while prison rehabilitation and education programs were favoured by
17% of respondents. This same study also found that 65% of adults surveyed
favoured dealing with the root causes of crime while only 32% preferred the
punitive approach in the form of strict sentencing. Respondents reported that
they strongly favoured rehabilitation and re-entry programs over incapacitation
as the best method of ensuring public safety: 66% felt that the best way to
reduce crime was to rehabilitate offenders while only 28% felt that keeping
criminals off the street through long prison sentences would be more effective.
The authors of this report concluded that conventional wisdom about public
punitiveness misjudges the mood of the voters, who now see the "lock-'em-up"
strategy as having failed.

The most recent study to examine public opinion about crime control strategies asked victims of crime about the effectiveness of various methods for reducing re-offending. The survey of 982 victims in the United Kingdom, conducted on behalf of the Smart Justice and Victim Support agencies, found that 61% of respondents believed that prison does not reduce re-offending. Rather, 80% of respondents believed that better supervision of young people by parents is effective in reducing crime in the long run while 83% felt that more constructive activities for young people would be effective in reducing crime.

Representatives of the sponsoring agencies concluded from this research that victims do not want retribution and vengeance but instead want constructive and effective methods to tackle the root causes of offending and thus prevent further offending. . . .

## NOTES

1. *Public opinion and sentencing.*   Politicians, criminal justice scholars in general, and desert theorists in particular often refer to public opinion to justify particular sanctions or policy recommendations. Typically the unstated assumption in such assertions is that the public belief is innate or static. Why should anyone assume that uninformed rather than informed opinion is the proper basis for any policy or decision? Are juries — one model of citizen involvement in the criminal justice process — more fairly described as "informed" or "uninformed" actors?

2. *Political conservatives and criminal punishments.*   In general terms, political discussion in the United States assumes that conservatives favor more severe penalties for crimes and heavier use of prisons, while progressives tend to prefer less severe penalties and heavier use of non-prison punishments. Complex political reality, however, sometimes confounds these categories. For instance, some conservatives draw on traditions of fiscal restraint and mistrust of governmental power to advocate "smart on crime" strategies for limiting the reach of the criminal law and economizing on the use of the most expensive sanctions such as prison. A group known as "Right on Crime" touts positions that "fight crime, prioritize victims, and protect taxpayers" simultaneously. See http://www.rightoncrime.com. What positions might such a conservative coalition take that might differ from progressive positions on criminal punishment?

3. *Crime in America.*   In discussing the purposes of sentencing, it is critical to "frame" the question properly. In this chapter we have emphasized the different jurisprudential roles that the purposes of punishment play at the case, rule, and systemic levels. We have noted the variety of functional and political goals (both legitimate and illegitimate, express and implied, conscious and unintentional) that may be served by criminal sanctions. But perhaps the proper question is not how punishment is justified, but what role punishment (or the criminal justice system as a whole) serves relative to other forms of social control, including education, labor, housing, health and welfare policies, systems for responding to mental health issues and drug and alcohol dependency, and other private or public tools and initiatives.

## PROBLEM 1-6.   CRIME IN AMERICA

Imagine that you are a member of the state legislature who has been elected on a "public safety" platform. You now wish to join committees and to introduce and support legislation and funding consistent with your public commitments. You meet with your staff and several invited "public safety" experts for a nonpublic discussion. You ask the following question: what are the top ten policies that will reduce crime in America, or that will reduce the particular kinds of crime that are most in the news, or that are the most socially costly? You encourage each person at the meeting to think silently for ten minutes and then to write down those ten policies, with a short explanation of the assumptions underlying the recommendations. Now you go around the room and ask: how many of the top ten policies involve changes in sentencing or punishment? Indeed, how many of the policies involve the criminal justice system at all?

Now, in your role as one of the sentencing experts in the room and based on the results of this exercise, does this discussion make you rethink your response to the question of the justifications for sentencing and punishment?

# ═2═
## ‖ *Who Sentences?* ‖

In most criminal justice systems, several institutions share the decision about the proper sentence to impose: Legislatures and judges always have a say in the sentence, and juries, parole boards, and sentencing commissions may participate. But the precise division of labor in setting general sentencing policy and sentences in particular cases varies a great deal from place to place. We begin with a survey of the actors, and then we take a closer look at the distinctive capabilities of each.

‖ ***Research on Sentencing: The Search for Reform,*** ‖
***Alfred Blumstein, Jacqueline Cohen, Susan***
***Martin, and Michael Tonry***
**Vol. 1, pp. 41-47 (1983)**

Any effort . . . to understand sentencing must take into account the existence of the many participants and decisions that together constitute "sentencing" and the conflicting values, perspectives, and interests among them. This very complexity, however, frustrates efforts to change the criminal justice process in America.

*Victims and Witnesses.*   Victims initiate criminal justice action when they decide to complain to the police. They also, subsequently, affect the likelihood of conviction and punishment through their ability and willingness to cooperate with the prosecution. Victim and witness noncooperation is a major cause of charge dismissal in the United States. . . .

*Police.*   Police decide whom to notice, to stop, to arrest, to book, and (in some jurisdictions) to charge. Police officers have the primary authority to decide who will *not* be pursued by the criminal justice system. . . . The exercise of discretion in the police decision to arrest largely dictates the outcome in [misdemeanor cases involving public disorder, family violence, and small-scale drug trafficking]. The police also possess substantial autonomy in handling serious crimes of violence and investigating organized illegal activities and large property loss or damage. Police are relatively free to decide which complaints to follow up, with what diligence and resources, and to select their means of investigation. . . .

   ***Prosecutors.***   Prosecutors establish priorities and determine the vigor with which various kinds of cases will be pursued. In the 1970s, for example, many prosecutors ceased prosecuting marijuana possession cases; in effect, those prosecutors decriminalized marijuana use in their jurisdictions.
   Prosecutors also exercise substantial discretion over individual cases. Prosecutors decide what charges to file or, if the police file charges, what to dismiss. Like the decisions of police officers, prosecutors' decisions to [dismiss or reduce charges] are not subject to independent review. . . .
   Plea bargaining takes diverse forms. In *horizontal charge bargains,* a prosecutor agrees to drop several charges for an offense type if the defendant pleads guilty to the remaining charges (e.g., three burglary charges are dropped when the defendant pleads guilty to a fourth). In *vertical charge bargains,* a prosecutor agrees to drop the highest charge if the defendant pleads guilty to a less serious charge (e.g., a narcotics trafficking charge is dropped if the defendant pleads guilty to a narcotics possession charge, or a charge of armed robbery is dropped if the defendant pleads guilty to a charge of robbery). In sentence bargains, a prosecutor agrees that the defendant will receive a specific sentence in return for a guilty plea. In fact bargains, a prosecutor agrees not to introduce evidence of specific aggravating circumstances. Other plea bargaining variants involve prosecutorial agreements to recommend or not to oppose particular sentences or to dismiss charges in consideration of the defendant's cooperation in other prosecutions or investigations. Whatever form plea bargaining takes, the prosecutor and to a lesser extent the defense counsel often stand supreme. The judge sometimes has little choice but to ratify their decisions. . . .

   ***Judges.***   Judges impose sentences. They decide who goes to prison and who does not; they set the terms of nonincarcerative sentences; and (depending on whether there is a parole board and on the rules governing parole eligibility) they set minimum, maximum, or actual lengths of jail and prison terms. . . .
   Judges' powers [are also] informally but importantly affected by the work of other court personnel. First, in jurisdictions in which sentence bargaining is common, often a judge's choice is whether to ratify the negotiated sentence. Second, where charge bargaining is prevalent, a judge usually accedes to proposed charge dismissals and may impose a sentence only within the constraints set by any statutory sentence provisions. Third, probation officers devote more time to investigation of the offender's circumstances and to consideration of the case than judges possibly can, and so they control the flow of information to judges. Probation officers are attached to most modern felony courts;

presentence reports containing their recommendations are commonly provided to judges, and these recommendations are usually followed.

*Parole Boards.*  Although parole boards have been abolished in some jurisdictions—and in others they have lost their authority to determine release dates—in the majority of states they retain control over parole release. Judges often set maximum sentences (and in some states minimums as well), but the maximum is often very long; parole boards decide who and when to release prior to sentence expiration; the conditions to which a parolee will be subject while on parole; when and why parole can be revoked; and when after revocation, if at all, an offender can be re-released prior to the end of the maximum sentence. . . .

Parole boards traditionally make individualized release decisions, taking account of a wide variety of offender characteristics. In establishing uniform criteria for releasing offenders, they, too, face the basic dilemma in criminal justice: How much emphasis should be placed on the seriousness of the conviction offense in attempting to follow the injunction to "treat like cases alike" and how much on the characteristics of the defendant, including prior record and employment status, in predicting whether the release constitutes a danger to the community?

*Corrections Administrators.*   Corrections administrators affect the duration of imprisonment by the award, withdrawal, or denial of time off for good behavior and by their recommendations and reports to parole boards when a prisoner is being considered for early release. Corrections administrators also influence the quality of a prisoner's confinement through decisions about institutional assignments and participation in various kinds of furlough programs. Whether an inmate spends time in a maximum security prison, in a less restrictive minimum security facility, or in a group home in his or her hometown is almost entirely in the hands of corrections authorities. . . .

*Executive Clemency: Commutations and Pardons.*  Although pardons and similar executive release mechanisms once played a major part in prison releases, these ad hoc powers are no longer extensively used in most states.

*Legislatures.*  Legislative influence in sentencing is first and last: it is first because a legislature constructs and can always alter the basic statutory framework that other officials are charged to carry out; it is last because most punishments prescribed by law are not self-executing but can be realized only through other officials. If those officials behave inconsistently with the law, there is little a legislature can do. Even such seemingly authoritative laws as those calling for mandatory minimum sentences can be effected only through others; if prosecutors and judges choose to circumvent the law, mandatory terms will not be imposed. . . . Sometimes statutes are drafted so broadly that they provide little guidance in individual cases. For example, the maximum prison terms authorized for most offenses—5 or 10 or 25 years—are so much longer than the sentences typically imposed or served that the legislative decision has little significance for the operation of the system.

*The System as a Whole.*   The operations of this complex system of criminal justice, with its network of multiple, overlapping, and interconnecting discretions and conflicting goals, are not easily altered; like the operation of any complex system, they are influenced by powerful forces of tradition, institutional convenience, scarcity of resources, and self-interest. Officials who wish to circumvent or undermine a new law can usually find ways to do so; legislative changes are impositions from outside and are often resisted. . . .

Such reactions are foreseeable. The staffs of prosecutors' offices and the courts have institutional goals and personal interests to serve and limited resources to expend. Sometimes their personal views of justice and injustice may not easily accept legislative solutions to the crime problem. Since new laws are seldom accompanied by appropriation of funds sufficient to permit literal and wholehearted compliance with them, something must give, and that something is often compliance. The complexity of the system also often confounds reform initiatives by merely shifting the locus of decision-making power from one agency to another. . . .

## NOTES

1. *Victim participation in sentencing.*   Victim participation in criminal justice has grown more important since the original publication of the passage reprinted above. Legislation in all 50 states now formalizes victim participation at various stages in the criminal process. For instance, laws in many states require the prosecutor to notify the victim before dismissing any serious charges, and the law often gives the victim the opportunity to speak at the offender's sentencing hearing and sometimes to recommend a sentence. Victims also figure prominently in some parole hearings. Do these contacts between the victim and various government officials amount to a grant of "sentencing" power to the victim?

In 2004 Congress passed the Crime Victims' Rights Act (CVRA), Pub. L. No. 108-405, §§101-104, 118 Stat. 2260, 2261-2265 (2004) (codified at 18 U.S.C. §3771). The CVRA guarantees crime victims eight different rights, and unlike the prior crime victims' rights statute, allows both the government and the victims to enforce them. One of the rights guaranteed by the CVRA is the "right to be reasonably heard at any public proceeding in the district court involving release, plea, sentencing, or any parole proceeding." 18 U.S.C. §3771(a)(4).

Does the timing of the victim's statement matter? Imagine, for instance, the difference between a pre-sentencing impact statement by the victim that aims to influence the sentencing judge's decision, versus a post-sentencing statement by the victim that aims to communicate to the offender the nature of the wrong committed. Would you favor one of these over the other?

2. *Pardon and clemency boards.*   The passage above mentions that executive clemency is "no longer extensively used in most states," and it is true that governors today grant pardons and commute sentences far less often than they once did. Governors do still grant pardons, however, and there are now active and elaborate bureaucracies at work in many states to assist the governor

in deciding when to grant pardons and when to commute sentences. About two-thirds of the states leave the pardon decision entirely to the discretion of the governor. In about ten states, the governor can consider only clemency recommendations issued by a clemency board. We discuss the pardon and clemency power in Chapter 11.

3. *Involvement of unexpected actors.* In various settings and in various ways, additional actors can play a direct or indirect role in the development of sentencing policies and punishment practices. For example, concerns about the post-release activities of sex offenders has led numerous localities to enact regional residency restrictions on persons previously convicted of certain crimes. And in recent debates and litigation over execution methods, doctors and other medical professionals have sometimes been requested—and have sometimes refused—to assess and participate in lethal injection protocols. Can you identify any other types of unexpected actors who may, either systematically or sporadically, have a role in sentencing decision making?

## A. SENTENCING IN THE COURTROOM

The immediate answer to the question of "who sentences" may be the judge who announces a sentence in the courtroom. But the legal framework for sentencing is always more complex. In the United States, the closest approximation to the pure, unadulterated image of the judge as law giver and law applier is found in "indeterminate" sentencing systems, which traditionally vest enormous discretion in the sentencing judge and provide little review of the sentences imposed. But even in indeterminate systems, the seemingly vast power of the judge is circumscribed by modest guidance from legislatures and, more important, by post-sentence executive branch review by parole boards.

The materials that follow illuminate the nature of sentencing by judges and parole boards in indeterminate systems. If one of the purposes of criminal sentences is to reflect the community's response to the violation of social norms, should a group of representative community members, in the familiar form of a jury, decide the sentence? While conceptually intriguing, jury sentencing has played a major role in the United States only in capital cases. The second section below examines one special noncapital setting and the handful of states that grant juries the authority to sentence.

### 1. Judges and Parole Boards in Indeterminate Sentencing

Until recently, sentencing in the United States was characterized more by discretion than by law. In 1950 every state and the federal system used indeterminate sentencing. Under this type of system, the legislature prescribes broad potential sentencing ranges and the trial judge sentences without meaningful legal guidance and typically without offering a detailed explanation for the sentence. An executive branch agency (usually a parole board) ultimately determines the actual sentence each defendant serves. There are virtually no judicial opinions explaining or reviewing a sentence, and legal counsel ordinarily makes oral arguments at sentencing hearings without any written submissions to the court. The unwritten nature of the arguments and the decisions make it difficult for anyone to get a handle on sentencing law and practice. Perhaps that reality demonstrates the most important point about such a system: sentencing occurs without much law. For a more thorough overview, see Kevin R. Reitz, The "Traditional" Indeterminate Sentencing Model, in The Oxford Handbook of Sentencing and Corrections 270 (Joan Petersilia and Kevin R. Reitz, eds., 2012).

The following materials offer a glimpse of indeterminate sentencing systems at work. The U.S. Supreme Court's 1949 decision in Williams v. New York, which came at the high-water mark of indeterminate sentencing, reveals not only the extensive discretion given to trial judges but also some of the principles underlying that discretion.

## Samuel Williams v. New York
### 337 U.S. 241 (1949)

BLACK, J.

A jury in a New York state court found appellant guilty of murder in the first degree. The jury recommended life imprisonment, but the trial judge imposed a sentence of death. In giving his reasons for imposing the death sentence the judge discussed in open court the evidence upon which the jury had convicted stating that this evidence had been considered in the light of additional information obtained through the court's "Probation Department, and through other sources." [A New York statute authorized the court to consider "any information that will aid the court in determining the proper treatment of such defendant." Williams claimed that the sentence, which was based on information supplied by witnesses, violated his due process rights because he had no chance to confront or cross-examine the witnesses or to rebut the evidence.]

The record shows a carefully conducted trial lasting more than two weeks in which appellant was represented by three appointed lawyers who conducted his defense with fidelity and zeal. The evidence proved a wholly indefensible murder committed by a person engaged in a burglary. . . .

About five weeks after the verdict of guilty with recommendation of life imprisonment, and after a statutory pre-sentence investigation report to the judge, the defendant was brought to court to be sentenced. [The] judge gave reasons why he felt that the death sentence should be imposed. . . . He stated that the pre-sentence investigation revealed many material facts concerning appellant's background which though relevant to the question of punishment could not properly have been brought to the attention of the jury in its consideration of the question of guilt. He referred to the experience appellant "had had on 30 other burglaries in and about the same vicinity" where the murder had been committed. The appellant had not been convicted of these burglaries although the judge had information that he had confessed to some and had been identified as the perpetrator of some of the others. The judge also referred to certain activities of appellant as shown by the probation report that indicated appellant possessed "a morbid sexuality" and classified him as a "menace to society." The accuracy of the statements made by the judge as to appellant's background and past practices [was] not challenged by appellant or his counsel, nor was the judge asked to disregard any of them or to afford appellant a chance to refute or discredit any of them by cross-examination or otherwise.

The case presents a serious and difficult question. The question relates to the rules of evidence applicable to the manner in which a judge may obtain information to guide him in the imposition of sentence upon an already convicted defendant. . . . To aid a judge in exercising this discretion intelligently the New York procedural policy encourages him to consider information about the convicted person's past life, health, habits, conduct, and mental and moral propensities. The sentencing judge may consider such information even though obtained outside the courtroom from persons whom a defendant has not been permitted to confront or cross-examine. . . .

Tribunals passing on the guilt of a defendant always have been hedged in by strict evidentiary procedural limitations. But both before and since the American colonies became a nation, courts in this country and in England practiced a policy under which a sentencing judge could exercise a wide discretion in the sources and types of evidence used to assist him in determining the kind and the extent of punishment to be imposed within limits fixed by law. Out-of-court affidavits have been used frequently, and of course in the smaller communities sentencing judges naturally have in mind their knowledge of the personalities and backgrounds of convicted offenders. . . .

In addition to the historical basis for different evidentiary rules governing trial and sentencing procedures there are sound practical reasons for the distinction. In a trial before verdict the issue is whether a defendant is guilty of having engaged in certain criminal conduct of which he has been specifically accused. Rules of evidence have been fashioned for criminal trials which narrowly confine the trial contest to evidence that is strictly relevant to the particular offense charged. These rules rest in part on a necessity to prevent a time-consuming and confusing trial of collateral issues. They were also designed to prevent tribunals concerned solely with the issue of guilt of a particular offense from being influenced to convict for that offense by evidence that the defendant had habitually engaged in other misconduct. A sentencing judge, however, is not confined to the narrow issue of guilt. His task within fixed statutory or constitutional limits is to determine the type and extent of punishment after the issue of guilt has been determined. Highly relevant — if not essential — to his selection of an appropriate sentence is the possession of the fullest information possible concerning the defendant's life and characteristics. And modern concepts individualizing punishment have made it all the more necessary that a sentencing judge not be denied an opportunity to obtain pertinent information by a requirement of rigid adherence to restrictive rules of evidence properly applicable to the trial.

Undoubtedly the New York statutes emphasize a prevalent modern philosophy of penology that the punishment should fit the offender and not merely the crime. The belief no longer prevails that every offense in a like legal category calls for an identical punishment without regard to the past life and habits of a particular offender. This whole country has traveled far from the period in which the death sentence was an automatic and commonplace result of convictions — even for offenses today deemed trivial. . . . Indeterminate sentences, the ultimate termination of which are sometimes decided by nonjudicial agencies, have to a large extent taken the place of the old rigidly fixed punishments. . . . Retribution is no longer the dominant objective of the criminal law. Reformation and rehabilitation of offenders have become important goals of criminal jurisprudence. . . .

Under the practice of individualizing punishments, investigation techniques have been given an important role. Probation workers making reports of their investigations have not been trained to prosecute but to aid offenders. Their reports have been given a high value by conscientious judges who want to sentence persons on the best available information rather than on guesswork and inadequate information. To deprive sentencing judges of this kind of information would undermine modern penological procedural policies that have been cautiously adopted throughout the nation after careful consideration and experimentation. We must recognize that most of the information now relied upon by judges to guide them in the intelligent imposition of sentences would be unavailable if information were restricted to that given in open court by witnesses subject to cross-examination. And the modern probation report draws on information concerning every aspect of a defendant's life. The type and extent of this information make totally impractical if not impossible open court testimony with cross-examination. Such a procedure could endlessly delay criminal administration in a retrial of collateral issues. The considerations we have set out admonish us against treating the due-process clause as a uniform command that courts throughout the nation abandon their age-old practice of seeking information from out-of-court sources to guide their judgment toward a more enlightened and just sentence. . . . So to treat the due-process clause would hinder if not preclude all courts — state and federal — from making progressive efforts to improve the administration of criminal justice. We hold that appellant was not denied due process of law. . . .

### NOTES

1. *Informal procedure at sentencing: majority position.* The New York statute discussed in *Williams*, allowing the sentencing judge to consider evidence inadmissible at trial under the rules of evidence, typifies sentencing practices in most states. See Tex. Crim. Proc. Code Ann. §37.07(3). The informal presentation of evidence supposedly supports an effort to obtain the most information possible about the offender and the offense and to make an individualized (perhaps even clinical) decision. Over time, many different actors participate in the decision about how best to respond to an individual offender. Thus, the indeterminate sentencing system is one of "multiple discretions." More than half the states use this system for large groups of cases, although many of these states use more narrowly circumscribed sentencing rules for some crimes.

As discussed more fully in Chapter 6, recent Supreme Court decisions that are primarily concerned with the Sixth Amendment right to a jury trial have arguably undercut some of the principles of *Williams*, although *Williams* remains good law. See generally Douglas A. Berman, Beyond *Blakely* and *Booker*: Pondering Modern Sentencing Process, 95 J. Crim. L. & Criminology 654 (2005).

2. Williams *revisited.*   Samuel Titto Williams, a black man, was 18 years old at the time he killed 15-year-old Selma Graff, who surprised him during a burglary. Williams had no record of prior convictions, but he had been accused of burglary at age 11. The judgment in juvenile court was suspended. The probation report—a report prepared by probation officers prior to sentencing, also called a presentence investigation report—informed the judge that Williams was suspected of (but not charged with) committing 30 burglaries during the two months before the murder. A 7-year-old girl who was present during one of those burglaries told the probation officer that Williams had sexually molested her. She identified Williams as the perpetrator two weeks after the incident. The probation report also stated that Williams was living with two women, and brought different men into the apartment for the purpose of having sexual relations with the women. It alleged that Williams had once gone to a local school to photograph "private parts of young children." Finally, the sentencing judge relied on injuries inflicted on the murder victim's brother during the burglary. The prosecutor did not bring any charges based on the assault. See Kevin Reitz, Sentencing Facts: Travesties of Real-Offense Sentencing, 45 Stan. L. Rev. 523 (1993). Is the problem in *Williams* the presentation of new offender information at sentencing or the fact that Williams did not know the judge would hear these allegations?

3. *Capital punishment and informal procedure.*   Although the *Williams* Court emphasized that rehabilitative purposes of sentencing required far-reaching information about an offender, the proposed "treatment" for Williams was execution. It brings to mind the statement attributed to the comedian W. C. Fields, who quoted a condemned prisoner on his way to the electric chair, saying, "This will certainly be a lesson to me." *Williams* is still cited with approval in support of informal sentencing procedures generally, but it has been partially overruled in the context of capital sentencing. In Gardner v. Florida, 430 U.S. 349 (1977), the trial judge sentenced a defendant to death after consulting confidential and unrebutted information in the presentence investigation report. A plurality of the Supreme Court found that due process required, at least in capital cases, that the defendant have access to information that will influence the sentencing judge and have an opportunity to test its reliability.

4. *Styles of argument in indeterminate sentencing.*   When judges describe the factors they consider in sentencing under an indeterminate system, they often discuss the traditional purposes of sentencing examined in Chapter 1 and try to operationalize those purposes in light of the specific facts of the offense and the background of the offender. One study of sentences in federal white-collar crime cases concluded that judges considered three common principles during sentencing: (1) the harm the offense produced; (2) the blameworthiness of the defendant, judged from the defendant's criminal intent, from other details of the crime, and from the defendant's earlier life; and (3) the consequences of the punishment, both for deterring future wrongdoing and for the well-being of the defendant's family and community. Despite the presence of these common principles for sentencing, judges selected very different sentences because they did not agree on how to measure each of the principles or the relative weight to place on each. See Stanton Wheeler, Kenneth Mann & Austin Sarat, Sitting in Judgment: The Sentencing of White-Collar Criminals (1988).

Observers in higher-volume courts, such as state misdemeanor courts, describe a very different reality. During plea bargaining the parties settle quickly on a proper sentence, which hinges largely on the charges filed and the parties' interpretation of the facts as reflected in the police reports. These negotiations do not often involve individualized haggling; rather, they are "more akin to modern supermarkets in which prices for various commodities have been clearly established and labeled." Malcolm Feeley, The Process Is the Punishment: Handling Cases in a Lower Criminal Court 187 (1979). What determines whether a given case will receive the "supermarket" form of sentencing or a more individualized assessment?

5. *Probation officers.*   Judges who sentence a defendant after a guilty plea have not heard an extensive presentation of the evidence at trial and thus depend heavily on the presentence investigation that probation officers perform to provide information about the offender and the offense. How might a prosecutor or a defense attorney influence the recommendations of the probation officer? What institutional or individual biases might the probation officer bring to her assessment (and recommendation) of proper sentences? We consider further the work of probation officers and their interaction with attorneys and judges in Chapter 6.

## PROBLEM 2-1.   DETERMINING THE INDETERMINABLE

On February 20 at The Station nightclub in West Warwick, Rhode Island, the metal band Great White took the stage around 11 P.M. and broke into their first song. Daniel Biechele, the tour manager for Great White, then ignited the pyrotechnics he set up to accompany the band's performance. Almost instantly, the combustible soundproofing material that surrounded the stage caught on fire, and the fire quickly spread throughout the wood-paneled club.

Exactly 100 persons died in the resulting blaze: rescue teams pulled 96 bodies from the nightclub after the fire was contained, and 4 more people died in the hospital. Almost 200 other people were treated for their injuries. The victims included teens, married couples, and roadies.

As part of a plea agreement, Biechele ultimately pleaded guilty to 100 counts of involuntary manslaughter for his role in this tragedy. In exchange for a recommended sentence from the prosecution of 10 years in prison and 5 years on probation, Biechele admitted that he set off the pyrotechnics without a permit or license. The plea agreement clarifies that the Rhode Island sentencing judge will have complete discretion to adjust the balance of the prison time against probation as long as the total term does not exceed 15 years.

Representatives from many victims' families have expressed outrage at the plea deal. The sentencing judge has scheduled a set of hearings in which he will permit any and every victim and family member to address the court before the judge determines Biechele's sentence.

If you were the lawyer representing Biechele, what sentence would you request and what sorts of evidence and arguments would you marshal in support of that request?

## PROBLEM 2-2.   DUE NORTH

Oliver North was a marine lieutenant colonel assigned in 1981 to the National Security Council (NSC) staff. By 1984 North was responsible for two principal areas: counterterrorism and Central America. North was prosecuted by an independent counsel and was convicted of aiding and abetting an obstruction of Congress, for his removal and destruction of the permanent historical records of the NSC and for receiving an illegal gratuity. North was a very controversial public figure. The battle between the independent counsel and North's defense lawyers — and between critics and supporters of the Reagan administration policies with respect to Central America — turned on whether North would receive any time in prison. Because of the high-profile nature of the case, the attorneys submitted written sentencing briefs and the judge issued a written sentencing opinion, even though sentencing arguments in the indeterminate sentencing era typically were only addressed through oral statements that went unreported.

The independent counsel wrote in his sentencing memorandum:

> The most striking thing about North's posture on the eve of sentencing is his insistence that he has done nothing wrong. Instead, on the day of the verdict, he declared that his "vindication" was not "complete," and promised to "continue the fight" until it is. . . .
>
> [North] apparently sees nothing wrong with alteration and destruction of official national security records. His participation in the preparation of a false and misleading chronology [to present during a congressional hearing on the Iran-Contra affair] has not led to any acknowledgment of wrongdoing. Certainly, he sees nothing wrong with lying to Congress, when in the view of himself and his superiors lying is necessary. . . .
>
> In fashioning a just sentence in this case, we urge the Court to consider the seriousness of North's abuse of the public trust, the need for deterrence, North's failure to accept personal responsibility for his actions, his lack of remorse and his perjury on the witness stand. Taking all of these factors into account . . . the Government submits that a term of incarceration is appropriate and necessary.
>
> [The] Court, in its sentence, should [demonstrate] that if officials engaging in such conduct are caught and convicted, the punishment will be severe. Further, the private citizens of this country, who continue to follow this case closely, are entitled to the reassurance only this Court can give that these are serious crimes and that powerful government officials are not accorded special treatment. . . .
>
> A sentence in this case that included no period of incarceration would send exactly the wrong message to government officials and to the public. It would be a statement that 15 years after Watergate, government officials can participate in a brazen cover-up, lie to Congress and collect a substantial gratuity and still receive only a slap on the wrist. . . .
>
> Oliver North's sentence will be known to, and closely evaluated by, all who view the perversion of government as a permissible means to the attainment of their goals. The sentence will also be carefully considered by those officials who may now be weighing the advantages of deception, obstruction and personal greed against the risks of punishment. It will also be noted by those serving substantial prison sentences for more personal crimes far less damaging to the nation. Most importantly, the sentence will be closely scrutinized by a citizenry whose confidence in government and the political system has been seriously undermined by the activities of this defendant. . . . Under all these

circumstances, we respectfully submit that a term of incarceration is appropriate and necessary.

North's lawyers responded as follows:

Lt. Col. Oliver L. North is before the court for sentencing upon being found guilty of 3 of the 16 charges brought against him by the IC. . . . The IC's memorandum demonstrates that it will stop at nothing in its effort to crush Oliver North. . . .

We submit that Lt. Col. North has already been punished sufficiently for the three offenses of which he was found guilty. He was fired from his job at the NSC. He has lost his career as a Marine Corps officer. He may lose his Marine Corps pension after 20 years of service. He remains under threat of assassination by a dangerous terrorist organization as a direct result of his service to this country. He has been subjected to unrelenting and often hostile press scrutiny for the past two-and-a-half years. Every detail of his life has been probed, first in nationally televised hearings conducted by the joint Iran/Contra committee and then by the IC. He has heard himself likened to Hitler by a prosecutor who appears to lack any sense of fairness and [has heard] rumors in the press, before Congress, in court, in a nationally televised "docudrama," and now in the IC's memorandum. His children have been tormented. By any standard, the toll that this ordeal has already taken on Lt. Col. North and his family fulfills every legitimate purpose of punishment. If the Court accepts the IC's view that this punishment is not enough — that Oliver North must be punished further for the three offenses of which he was found guilty — then that punishment should take the form of probation conditioned on community service. . . .

In determining the proper sentence for Oliver North, the Court should consider the man as an individual, not — as the IC would have it — merely as a vehicle through which to send a "public message." The Court should weigh carefully Lt. Col. North's service to this country and to society, the devastating impact that imprisonment would have on his family, and the unique confluence of circumstances that gave rise to his conduct. This careful, individualized sentencing is essential to ensure that "the punishment should fit the offender and not merely the crime." Williams v. New York, 337 U.S. 241 (1949).

Oliver North devoted 20 years to the service of this country, from Vietnam to Tehran to Beirut. He has risked his own life and saved the lives of others. We submit that the Court should weigh this service in Lt. Col. North's favor at sentencing. . . .

Oliver North . . . has worked to improve society in other ways as well. Since the Congressional hearings of 1987, he has put his unsought and unwanted notoriety to use in service of his fellow citizens, particularly America's youth. Two examples illustrate Lt. Col. North's compassion and concern — and put the lie to the IC's claim that Lt. Col. North displays "contempt for the public."

First, shortly after his Congressional testimony, Lt. Col. North learned that it was the dream of a terminally ill boy to see him before the boy died. Lt. Col. North agreed to meet the boy to give him courage in his final days. The woman who arranged the meeting describes what happened in her letter to the Court:

[The boy] told me he wanted to meet Lt. Col. North because this was the strongest person that he could ever know. [The boy] said that he needed this man to teach him how to become stronger mentally so that he could deal with his fast-approaching death. . . .

To my amazement and delight, Lt. Col. North brought with him a large Bible with certain scriptures marked throughout the Bible that he said he lives by, that his strength comes from his faith in God. He sat down and read with the child from the Bible and they prayed together that [the boy] would find his answers. Lt. Col. North spent one and a half hours alone with [the boy] helping him to find the strength that the child was very much in need of. . . .

Lt. Col. North placed the following inscription on a photograph for the dying boy: "Courageous Hero, Inspiration, Fighter — Semper Fidelis. 18 September '87, Oliver L. North.'

Second, Lt. Col. North has spoken out throughout America against drug use and in favor of improved drug prevention and rehabilitation. As but one example, he delivered a speech on behalf of the drug-prevention organization Reach Out America. . . .

Criminal punishment serves four legitimate purposes: it incapacitates the offender, to prevent him from harming society; it rehabilitates him; it deters him and others from committing further offenses; and it reflects the seriousness of the offenses. The punishment that Oliver North and his family have suffered to date more than adequately fulfills each of these purposes.

1. *Incapacitation.* There is no need to incapacitate Oliver North. Far from representing a threat to society, Lt. Col. North devoted his professional life to ensuring the safety of Americans at home and abroad. . . .
2. *Rehabilitation.* No one can seriously contend that Oliver North needs rehabilitation, and it would be preposterous to suggest that, if rehabilitation *were* necessary, it would occur in prison. . . .
3. *Deterrence.* The punishment that Oliver North has suffered to date fully satisfied any need for deterrence; no additional sentence is necessary. First, there is no need for a harsh punishment to achieve *specific* deterrence — deterrence of Lt. Col. North from future unlawful acts. In light of his record of service to this country and the excruciating ordeal that he and his family have endured, there is no chance that he will commit offenses in the future. Second, *general* deterrence — deterrence of those other than Lt. Col. North — provides no basis for harsh punishment. The punishment that Lt. Col. North has suffered to date — including the loss of his position at the NSC, the loss of his career in the Marine Corps, and the minute and public scrutiny of his most private affairs by Congress, the IC, and frequently the media — should amply deter others. . . .
4. *The Seriousness of the Offense.* The punishment that Lt. Col. North has suffered to date more than adequately reflects the gravity of the offenses of which he was found guilty. The three offenses — aiding and abetting an obstruction of Congress, destroying, altering, and/or removing official NSC documents, and accepting an unlawful gratuity — are serious. Each is a felony; each has a maximum prison term of between two and five years; and each carries a maximum fine of $250,000. But the seriousness of these offenses is significantly reduced by the unique circumstances of this case. . . .

Can both of these pictures be true? Is purpose-driven picture painting a useful way to help courts decide on a proper sentence? If not, are there any virtues or lessons to be learned from such advocacy?

## NOTE

1. *The sentencing judge speaks.* In United States v. Oliver North, Judge Gerhard Gesell of the United States District Court for the District of Columbia acknowledged North's service, but pointed out that the "case has little to do with your military behavior, commitment or expertise" (Transcript, D.D.C., July 5, 1989). At the same time, Judge Gesell observed that North was "really a low

ranking subordinate working to carry out initiatives of a few cynical superiors."
Judge Gesell sentenced North as follows:

> I fashioned a sentence that punishes you. It is my duty to do that. But it leaves
> the future up to you. . . . On count six where you are found guilty of aiding and
> abetting [an] obstruction of Congress, I'm going to impose a sentence of three
> years and suspend the execution of the sentence, place you on probation for two
> years, fine you $100,000 and I have to impose a special assessment of $50. Under
> count nine, altering, removing and destroying the permanent historical records
> of the National Security Council, I impose a sentence of two years, suspend the
> execution of sentence, place you on probation for two years, fine you $35,000
> and impose a special assessment of $50 and I am required by the statute to
> impose another mandatory penalty. You are hereby disqualified from holding
> any office under the United States. Under count ten, receiving an illegal gra-
> tuity, I'll impose a sentence of one year, suspend the execution of that sentence,
> place you on probation for two years, fine you $15,000 and impose a special
> assessment again of $50. These sentences and the probation are to run concur-
> rently. The fines are to run consecutively. Your probation shall consist . . . of
> community service in a total amount of 1200, 800 the first year, and 400 the
> second year. . . .

North's conviction was later reversed on the ground that witnesses in his
trial had been exposed to North's immunized congressional testimony. United
States v. North, 920 F.2d 940 (D.C. Cir. 1990).

## *Parole Consideration and Eligibility, Georgia Board of Pardons and Paroles*
### http://www.pap.state.ga.us/parole_considera-tion.htm (2003)

. . . Before the Board considers an inmate for parole, it conducts investigations, detailed reports of which become a part of the Board's case file. . . . First, a
parole officer studies arrest and court records and may talk with arresting officers, court officials, victims, and witnesses in order to write a Legal Investigation
report on the details of the inmate's current offense and a summary of any prior
offenses in the same county. Next, a parole officer interviews the inmate and
completes a Personal History Statement questionnaire. The inmate is asked,
among other things, where he has resided and worked; who his family members
are and where they live; where he plans to live and work; and what his own
account is of his crime. Finally, a parole officer conducts a Social Investigation,
which includes interviews with persons mentioned in the Personal History Statement as well as others. The written report presents a revealing picture of the
inmate's life from birth to current imprisonment and may also indicate the
degree of his truthfulness.

Before the inmate is paroled, the Board receives a Parole Review Summary
from the Department of Corrections. This discusses the inmate's behavior, attitude, physical status, mental and emotional condition, participation in activities,
and performance in work and training. The Board may, at its discretion, request
detailed psychological or psychiatric opinions. Other documents in the case file
usually include a Federal Bureau of Investigation or Georgia Crime Information
Center record of arrests and convictions. . . .

For inmates serving non-life sentences, the Board generally establishes a Tentative Parole Month within eight to ten months after the inmate enters state prison. . . . The Parole Board requires all violent offenders as well as residential burglars to serve a minimum of 90 percent of their court-imposed terms of incarceration. The policy affects offenders convicted . . . for twenty crimes not covered under two strikes legislation. That legislation, passed in 1994, already requires offenders convicted of murder, rape, aggravated sodomy, armed robbery, kidnapping, aggravated child molestation, and aggravated sexual battery to serve 100 percent of their prison sentence.

Crimes covered under the Board's 90-percent policy are: attempted rape, voluntary manslaughter, aggravated battery on a police officer, aggravated battery, child molestation, hijacking a motor vehicle, robbery, aggravated assault on a police officer, aggravated assault (with injury or weapon), enticing a child for indecent purposes, cruelty to children, feticide, incest, statutory rape, criminal attempt to murder, bus hijacking, vehicular homicide (while DUI or habitual violator), involuntary manslaughter, aggravated stalking, and residential burglary. Offenders released under the 90-percent policy will serve the remainder of their sentence under parole supervision so they can be reintegrated into the community with structure and surveillance. . . .

Parole Decision Guidelines assist the State Board of Pardons and Paroles in making consistent, soundly based, and understandable parole decisions on inmates serving non-life sentences. Guidelines help the Board decide on a Tentative Parole Month (TPM) for the inmate or that he will complete his sentence without parole.

A Board hearing examiner identifies an inmate's Crime Severity Level from a table of offenses ranked in seven levels. The higher the severity, the longer the inmate is recommended to serve. Then the hearing examiner calculates the inmate's Parole Success Likelihood Score by adding weighted factors with proven predictive value from the inmate's criminal and social history, . . . such as a juvenile record, prior imprisonment, parole or probation failure, heroin or cocaine use or possession, and joblessness. . . . The hearing examiner cross-refers the inmate's Crime Severity Level and Parole Success Likelihood Factor Score on the Guidelines Grid [to obtain] a months-to-serve recommendation for the Board's discretionary consideration.

The Board votes to accept or reject the months-to-serve recommendation. If the Board votes to reject the recommendation, the Board then makes a fully discretionary clemency determination which may or may not permit parole for the inmate. [Any] TPM is conditioned on good conduct in prison and sometimes also on successful completion of a drug, alcohol, sex-offender counseling program, or other pre-condition. . . . Parole Guidelines help keep the Board on track toward its goal of seeing that inmates serving for similar offenses with similar histories are treated the same. . . .

Board members select the lowest-risk offenders for parole, acknowledging that a certain number of inmates must be paroled to allow room for newly sentenced, incoming prisoners. The "least risky" offender is therefore correlated to the characteristics of an ever-changing prison population, with its steady influx of both violent and non-violent, first-time and serial felons. One of Georgia Parole's strengths, in addition to its careful parole-selection process, is its ability to tailor parole community supervision strategies to the risk and needs presented by each offender.[*]

### Georgia's Correctional Population — FY 2001

| Crime Type | Probation | | Inmate | | Parole | | Total |
|---|---|---|---|---|---|---|---|
| Violent personal | 17,960 | 44% | 19,813 | 48% | 3,321 | 8% | 41,094 |
| Sex offense | 5,189 | 47% | 5,730 | 52% | 207 | 2% | 11,126 |
| Property | 46,587 | 74% | 10,058 | 16% | 6,694 | 11% | 63,330 |
| Drug sales | 8,525 | 50% | 4,198 | 25% | 4,260 | 25% | 16,983 |
| Drug possession | 34,448 | 82% | 3,454 | 8% | 4,084 | 10% | 41,986 |
| Habitual violator, DUI | 5,684 | 81% | 588 | 8% | 787 | 11% | 7,059 |
| Other | 8,556 | 76% | 1,662 | 15% | 972 | 9% | 11,190 |
| TOTAL | 126,940 | 66% | 45,503 | 24% | 20,325 | 10% | 192,768 |

## PROBLEM 2-3.   SAVINGS PLAN

The state of Georgia is experiencing a budget crisis, and the governor's office has instructed various state agencies to trim their budgets. The Department of Corrections and the Board of Pardons and Paroles have been told that the state needs to reduce the number of corrections officers on staff and therefore needs to reduce the prison population by a significant amount.

You are a staff member working for the Board of Pardons and Paroles. What strategies would you recommend for increasing the number of prison inmates released on parole? Would you ask the board to restrict its "90 percent policy" to a shorter list of crimes? Perhaps you would recommend abandoning the policy altogether. Alternatively, you might concentrate on the method used to select prisoners to parole from among the groups that are currently eligible. Should the board amend its Parole Decision Guidelines or abandon those guidelines in favor of a case-by-case approach? Should the board lobby the legislature to change the two-strikes law, which makes offenders convicted of specified crimes ineligible for parole? Cf. Daniel F. Wilhelm & Nicholas R. Turner, Is the Budget Crisis Changing the Way We Look at Sentencing and Incarceration?, 15 Fed. Sent'g Rep. 41 (2002).

### NOTES

1. *Parole and sentencing purposes.*   When parole first appeared in this country, it embodied the rehabilitative ideal. Prisoners received longer prison terms to allow the criminal sanctions plenty of time to do their rehabilitative work, and parole marked the successful completion of the process. Parole also served an incapacitative purpose, because it was unfair to society to release prisoners before they were rehabilitated. In theory, the parole board assessed whether rehabilitation had taken place, but in practice this determination was

---

[*] This paragraph, along with the chart for 2001, derive from the board's 2001 Annual Report. — EDS.

far from precise. A staff member for Pennsylvania's parole commission described in 1927 the process for selecting prisoners for parole release:

> [Parole boards] must attempt to separate the sheep from the goats; to liberate certain prisoners and hold others. There are certain factors which generally influence this decision. Of these, prison conduct is usually given the greatest weight. . . . Another factor generally considered is the nature of the crime for which the prisoner was committed. . . . A third item which generally has weight with paroling authorities is the prior criminal record of the applicant for parole. . . . The only other factor generally entering into parole decisions is the appearance, personality, or general demeanor of the applicant. Truthfulness, square shoulders, a good voice, or a steady eye may go far toward winning a scoundrel his freedom in more than one State. Members of parole boards are human, like the rest of us, and are often inclined to congratulate themselves on their ability to read character at a glance. And so, shrewd but experimental guesswork, prejudices, and hunches many times decide whether a boy is to spend another two or three years behind prison walls or to be allowed to circulate among us.

National Commission on Law Observance and Enforcement (Wickersham Commission), Report on Penal Institutions, Probation and Parole (Report No. 9) at 133 (1931). Does the Georgia Board of Pardons and Paroles still purport to serve both rehabilitation and incapacitation purposes?

2. *Parole and parole guidelines.*  Even with rehabilitation becoming less important and convincing as a purpose of criminal sentencing, states find it necessary to give parole or corrections authorities the power to review sentences. This later review imposes a centralized perspective on the decisions of judges or juries from all over the state, and it coordinates the sentences with the amount of correctional resources available. Parole boards decide on the actual time an offender will serve *after* the judge has announced a sentence. Some parole boards decide cases according to formal parole guidelines, while others make more ad hoc decisions, considering prison capacity and other factors. What are the advantages and disadvantages of setting the release date later in the process through a parole board as opposed to a judge applying up-front sentencing rules? We examine parole boards and parole guidelines in more detail in Chapter 11.

Parole today is less instrumental to sentencing in the United States than it was in the middle of the twentieth century. More than a dozen states have abolished parole, and the law in other states restricts parole to certain classes of cases or gives judges more power to set the minimum prison term to be served, leaving the parole authority with less to decide. The movement to restrict parole authority is part of the broader shift to more determinate sentencing laws, a topic we consider more fully in Chapter 3.

3. *Parole and the Constitution.*  Several procedural due process rulings affect the way parole boards decide whether to grant parole to inmates and whether to revoke the parole granted at some earlier time. In Morrissey v. Brewer, 408 U.S. 471 (1972), the Supreme Court held that due process requires that an informal hearing be held before a parole board can revoke an earlier grant of parole. The hearing must be conducted by an impartial hearing officer, and the parolee

must receive written notice of the claimed violations and be given an opportunity to respond to the evidence. A discretionary decision to *grant or deny* parole requires a less formal hearing. Under Greenholtz v. Inmates of Nebraska Penal and Correctional Complex, 442 U.S. 1 (1979), the parole authority must simply review the prisoner's file, give the prisoner an opportunity to be heard, and inform the inmate who is denied parole the reasons that he or she falls short.

4. *Good-time reductions to prison terms.*   Prison officials also have some influence over the length of a prison sentence served. In most states, corrections officials have the power to reduce the sentence by up to one-third the maximum set by the judge or the parole authority. Prison authorities use this discretion to reward good behavior by inmates: the reductions are known as "good time." In the federal system, the maximum such reduction is 15%. The federal government encourages states to keep their good-time discounts below 15% by offering prison funding to states that comply with federal "truth in sentencing" guidelines. Jim Jacobs has pointed out the anomaly of placing legal controls on other sentencing decisions while leaving good-time decisions unregulated. Jacobs, Sentencing by Prison Personnel: Good Time, 30 UCLA L. Rev. 217 (1982). Which institutions would be best suited to create legal constraints on good-time decisions?

## 2.   Sentencing Juries

Juries play a central role in most capital sentencing systems. In a half-dozen states—Arkansas, Kentucky, Missouri, Oklahoma, Texas, and Virginia—juries in some noncapital cases not only rule on guilt or innocence but also decide the sentence to impose. If sentencing is a community judgment, should the community's representatives decide the sentence? Is a judge or legislature or sentencing commission as representative as a sentencing jury? Consider these questions in light of the following Arkansas statutes and the special and intriguing jury sentencing provisions for courts-martial under the Code of Military Justice.

### Arkansas Code §16-97-101 Felony Jury Trials; Guilt and Sentencing Phases

The following procedure shall govern jury trials which include any felony charges:

(1) The jury shall first hear all evidence relevant to every charge on which a defendant is being tried and shall retire to reach a verdict on each charge;

(2) If the defendant is found guilty of one or more charges, the jury shall then hear additional evidence relevant to sentencing on those charges. Evidence introduced in the guilt phase may be considered, but need not be reintroduced at the sentencing phase;

(3) Following the introduction of additional evidence relevant to sentencing, if any, instruction on the law, and argument, the jury shall again retire and determine a sentence within the statutory range;

(4) The court, in its discretion, may also instruct the jury that counsel may argue as to alternative sentences for which the defendant may qualify. The jury, in its discretion, may make a recommendation as to an alternative sentence. However, this recommendation shall not be binding on the court;

(5) After a jury finds guilt, the defendant, with the agreement of the prosecution and the consent of the court, may waive jury sentencing, in which case the court shall impose sentence; and

(6) After a plea of guilty, the defendant, with the agreement of the prosecution and the consent of the court, may be sentenced by a jury impaneled for purposes of sentencing only.

## Arkansas Code §16-97-103
### Relevant Evidence

Evidence relevant to sentencing by either the court or a jury may include, but is not limited to, the following, provided no evidence shall be construed under this section as overriding the rape shield statute . . . :

(1) The law applicable to parole, meritorious good time, or transfer;

(2) Prior convictions of the defendant, both felony and misdemeanor. The jury may be advised as to the nature of the previous convictions, the date and place thereof, the sentence received, and the date of release from confinement or supervision from all prior offenses;

(3) Prior judicial determinations of delinquency in juvenile court, subject to the following limitations:

(i) That prior delinquency adjudications be subject to a judicial determination that the relevant value of the prior juvenile adjudication outweigh its prejudicial value;

(ii) That consideration only be given to juvenile delinquency adjudications for crimes for which the juvenile could have been tried as an adult; and

(iii) That in no event shall delinquency adjudications for acts occurring more than ten (10) years prior to the commission of the offense charged be considered;

(4) Victim impact evidence or statements;

(5) Relevant character evidence;

(6) Evidence of aggravating and mitigating circumstances. The criteria for departure from the sentencing standards may serve as examples of this type of evidence;

(7) Evidence relevant to guilt presented in the first stage;

(8) Evidence held inadmissible in the first stage may be resubmitted for consideration in the second stage if the basis for exclusion did not apply to sentencing; and

(9) Rebuttal evidence.

## Arkansas Code §16-90-107 Punishment; Juries and Courts

(a) When a jury finds a verdict of guilty and fails to agree on the punishment to be inflicted, or does not declare the punishment in its verdict, or if it assesses a punishment not authorized by law, and in all cases of a judgment on confession, the court shall assess and declare the punishment and render judgment accordingly.

(b) (1) Juries and courts shall have the power to assess the punishment of one convicted of a felony at a general sentence to the penitentiary. The sentence shall not be less than the minimum nor greater than the maximum time provided by law.

(2) At any time after the expiration of the minimum time, upon the recommendation of the superintendent and it appearing that a prisoner has a good record as a convict, his sentence may be terminated by the [parole] board.

(c) If the jury in any case assesses a greater punishment, whether of fine or imprisonment, than the highest limit declared by law for the offense for which they convict the defendant, the court shall disregard the excess and enter judgment and pronounce sentence according to the highest limit prescribed by law in the particular case.

(d) If the jury in any case assesses a punishment, whether of fine or imprisonment, below the limit prescribed by law for offenses of which the defendant is convicted, the court shall render judgment and pronounce sentence according to the lowest limit prescribed by law in such cases.

(e) The court shall have power in all cases of conviction to reduce the extent or duration of the punishment assessed by a jury so that the punishment is not in any case reduced below the limit prescribed by law in such cases if the conviction is proper and the punishment assessed is greater than ought to be inflicted under the circumstances of the case.

## Manual for Courts-Martial, United States Exec. Order No. 12,473, 49 Fed. Reg. 17,152 (Apr. 13, 1984)

### RULE 1002. SENTENCE DETERMINATION

Subject to limitations in this Manual, the sentence to be adjudged is a matter within the discretion of the court-martial; except when a mandatory minimum sentence is prescribed by the code, a court-martial may adjudge any punishment authorized in this Manual, including the maximum punishment or any lesser punishment, or may adjudge a sentence of no punishment. . . .

### RULE 1006. DELIBERATIONS AND VOTING ON SENTENCE

(a) *In general.* The members shall deliberate and vote after the military judge instructs the members on sentence. Only the members shall be present during deliberations and voting. Superiority in rank shall not be used in any manner to control the independence of members in the exercise of their judgment.

(b) *Deliberations.* Deliberations may properly include full and free discussion of the sentence to be imposed in the case. Unless otherwise directed by the military judge, members may take with them in deliberations their notes, if any, any exhibits admitted in evidence, and any written instructions. Members may request that the court-martial be reopened and that portions of the record be read to them or additional evidence introduced. The military judge may, in the exercise of discretion, grant such requests.

(c) *Proposal of sentences.* Any member may propose a sentence. Each proposal shall be in writing and shall contain the complete sentence proposed. The junior member shall collect the proposed sentences and submit them to the president.

(d) *Voting.*

(1) *Duty of members.* Each member has the duty to vote for a proper sentence for the offenses of which the court-martial found the accused guilty, regardless of the member's vote or opinion as to the guilt of the accused.

(2) *Secret ballot.* Proposed sentences shall be voted on by secret written ballot.

(3) *Procedure.*

(A) *Order.* All members shall vote on each proposed sentence in its entirety beginning with the least severe and continuing, as necessary, with the next least severe, until a sentence is adopted by the concurrence of the number of members required under subsection (d)(4) of this rule. The process of proposing sentences and voting on them may be repeated as necessary until a sentence is adopted.

(B) *Counting votes.* The junior member shall collect the ballots and count the votes. The president shall check the count and inform the other members of the result.

(4) *Number of votes required.*

(A) *Death.* A sentence which includes death may be adjudged only if all members present vote for that sentence.

(B) *Confinement for life, with or without eligibility for parole, or more than 10 years.* A sentence which includes confinement for life, with or without eligibility for parole, or more than 10 years may be adjudged only if at least three-fourths of the members present vote for that sentence.

(C) *Other.* A sentence other than those described in subsection (d)(4)(A) or (B) of this rule may be adjudged only if at least two-thirds of the members present vote for that sentence.

(5) *Mandatory sentence.* When a mandatory minimum is prescribed under Article 118 the members shall vote on a sentence in accordance with this rule.

(6) *Effect of failure to agree.* If the required number of members do not agree on a sentence after a reasonable effort to do so, a mistrial may be declared as to the sentence and the case shall be returned to the convening authority, who may order a rehearing on sentence only or order that a sentence of no punishment be imposed. . . .

## NOTES

1. *Sentencing juries.*   As mentioned above, in a half-dozen states juries not only rule on guilt or innocence but can also decide the sentence to impose, even in noncapital cases. In some of these states, the jury's choice is binding. Va. Code Ann. §29.2-295.1 (jury sentences unless "jury cannot agree on a punishment" and defendant, prosecutor, and court agree that the court should determine punishment). In other states, such as Kentucky, "the judge can modify a jury sentence if the jury penalty is unduly harsh." Ky. Rev. Stat. §532.070. In Missouri, the sentencing jury recommends a range for sentencing. Mo. Rev. Stat. §557.036. See also Tex. Crim. Proc. Code Ann. §37.07 (judge can assess punishment if defendant does not request probation or jury sentence; jury must be instructed about parole and other devices for reducing actual amount of prison time offender must serve).

The ABA Standards for Criminal Justice, Sentencing 18-1.4 (3d ed. 1994), calls for the abolition of jury sentencing in noncapital cases. Earlier versions of the ABA standards took the same position, leading to the abolition of jury sentencing in Alabama (in 1977), Indiana (1976), and Montana (1967). Why do the ABA standards, along with the strong majority of the states, give sentencing responsibilities to the judge and not the jury, the representatives of the community? For a proposal to expand the use of jury sentencing, see Jenia Iontcheva, Jury Sentencing as Democratic Practice, 88 Va. L. Rev. 311 (2003); but cf. Nancy J. King & Rosevelt L. Noble, Felony Jury Sentencing in Practice: A Three-State Study, 57 Vand. L. Rev. 885 (2004) (expressing reservations about jury sentencing based on relative severity of sentences they impose).

Even in a system that gives no formal sentencing power to juries, the jury might consider likely punishments as it deliberates on the verdict in the case, and jurors might acquit if they believe the sanction is too severe. See Paul Butler, Racially Based Jury Nullification: Black Power in the Criminal Justice System, 105 Yale L.J. 677 (1995). As defense counsel, would you recommend that your client choose jury sentencing? If so, for what types of cases?

Interestingly, although sentencing juries are the exception in noncapital cases, they are the norm in death penalty cases. Is there a principled reason for juries to have a central role in capital sentencing systems but little or no role in noncapital sentencing systems? The role of the jury in sentencing systems is explored more fully in Chapters 3 and 6.

2. *Jury sentencing and expertise.*   One of the most significant concerns about jury sentencing is that different juries might impose significantly different sentences in similar cases. Another source of potential disparity is the difference between judge and jury sentencing choices in states that give the defendant the

option of jury or judge sentencing. Very little is known about whether jury sentencing in fact produces greater disparity.

Effectively allocating scarce punishment resources, another systematic concern of modern reformers, may also be difficult for juries to assess. Perhaps the several states that allow judges to reduce (but not increase) jury sentences, or that allow juries to recommend sentencing ranges, accommodate both the virtues of a jury's sentencing judgment and more systematic concerns.

Is sentencing an "expert" function? Is the expertise the product of sentencing experience, or life experience, or something else? See Nancy J. King & Rosevelt L. Noble, Felony Jury Sentencing in Practice: A Three-State Study, 57 Vand. L. Rev. 885 (2004) (arguing that juries cannot properly reflect community sentiment about the severity of sentences because juries do not have the range of information and sentencing options available to sentencing judges). If sentencing is appropriately a judicial function, does that function have constitutional foundations? See Mistretta v. United States, 488 U.S. 361 (1989).

3. *Jury sentencing and severity.* Do jurors tend to sentence defendants more or less severely than judges in a discretionary sentencing system? Do guideline sentences tend to embody the levels of severity for crimes that a jury would impose on a given defendant? In one famous child pornography case, the sentencing judge asked jurors to recommend anonymously what sentence the defendant should receive. After imposing a sentencing at the high end of the designated guideline range, the judge learned that his sentence was almost five times higher than the average recommendation of the jurors. The judge enlisted colleagues to conduct similar polls of juror sentencing recommendations: across all types of cases, the median juror recommendation was only 19% of the median range in the relevant sentencing guideline. See James S. Gwin, Juror Sentiment on Just Punishment: Do the Federal Sentencing Guidelines Reflect Community Values? 4 Harv. L. & Pol'y Rev. 173 (2010). On the other hand, studies in state court have found that sentencing juries tend to impose more severe sentences than judges. See Nancy J. King & Rosevelt L. Noble, Jury Sentencing in Noncapital Cases: Comparing Severity and Variance with Judicial Sentences in Two States, 2 J. Empirical Legal Studies 331 (2005) (for most crimes, jury sentences were both more varied and more severe than judicial sentences).

4. *Code of Military Justice and non-unanimous sentences.* Should the sentencing jury be required to vote unanimously for a particular sentence? Should its voting rules be the same as the rules for its vote on guilt versus innocence? Recall that in the Manual for Courts-Martial, Rule 1006(c) and (d), members of the court-martial panel propose sentences, and the panel must consider each proposed sentence from least severe to most severe, with the necessary voting requirements turning on the nature of the sentence. How much less protection is provided to defendants by allowing for confinement for more than ten years subject to approval by three-fourths of the jury members? What aspects of the military, if any, might justify the use of sentencing juries in courts-martial as distinguished from regular state felony juries?

# B. LEGISLATURES AND COMMISSIONS

Although indeterminate sentencing was the norm in this country for most of the twentieth century, new arrangements have emerged over the past generation. Some of those alternative approaches put the legislature more firmly in control of sentencing. Legislators have decided for themselves the precise sentences that will attach to various types of offenses; other sentencing institutions such as courts are supposed to carry out the instructions of the legislature without adding any meaningful input of their own. For instance, under 18 U.S.C. §924(c), any person who "uses or carries" a firearm during any federal drug trafficking crime "shall, in addition to the punishment provided for [the] drug trafficking crime . . . be sentenced to a term of imprisonment of not less than 5 years [and] if the firearm is brandished, be sentenced to a term of imprisonment of not less than 7 years; and . . . if the firearm is discharged, be sentenced to a term of imprisonment of not less than 10 years."

Sentences dominated by legislative choices go back to some of the earliest recorded sources of law, including the Code of Hammurabi, excerpted below. This code reflects a society very different from our own; would a review of our current statutes on criminal punishments create a fairly accurate portrait of our own times?

## Code of Hammurabi
### (C. H. W. Johns trans., 1911)

§1: If a man weave a spell and put a ban upon a man, and has not justified himself, he that wove the spell upon him shall be put to death.

§8: If a man has stolen ox or sheep or ass, or pig, or ship, whether from the temple or the palace, he shall pay thirtyfold. If he be a poor man, he shall render tenfold. If the thief has naught to pay, he shall be put to death.

§195: If a man has struck his father, his hands one shall cut off.

§196: If a man has caused the loss of a gentleman's eye, his eye one shall cause to be lost.

§197: If he has shattered a gentleman's limb, one shall shatter his limb.

§198: If he has caused a poor man to lose his eye or shattered a poor man's limb, he shall pay one mina of silver.

§209: If a man has struck a gentleman's daughter and caused her to drop what is in her womb, he shall pay ten shekels of silver for what was in her womb.

§210: If that woman has died, one shall put to death his daughter.

§211: If the daughter of a poor man through his blows he has caused to drop that which is in her womb, he shall pay five shekels of silver.

§212: If that woman has died, he shall pay half a mina of silver.

## Mandatory Minimum Penalties in the Federal Criminal Justice System
### U.S. Sentencing Commission, pp. 7, 22-26, 29-30, 85-103, 115-117 (2011)

Congress has used mandatory minimum penalties since it enacted the first federal penal laws in the late 18th century. [Beginning in 1951, however], Congress changed how it used mandatory minimum penalties in three significant ways. First, Congress enacted more mandatory minimum penalties. Second, Congress expanded its use of mandatory minimum penalties to offenses not traditionally covered by such penalties. Before 1951, mandatory minimum penalties typically punished offenses concerning treason, murder, piracy, rape, slave trafficking, internal revenue collection, and counterfeiting. Today, the majority of convictions under statutes carrying mandatory minimum penalties relate to controlled substances, firearms, identity theft, and child sex offenses. Third, the mandatory minimum penalties most commonly used today are generally lengthier than mandatory minimum penalties in earlier eras. . . .

The Anti-Drug Abuse Act of 1986 established the basic framework of mandatory minimum penalties currently applicable to federal drug trafficking offenses. The quantities triggering those mandatory minimum penalties, which ranged from five years to life imprisonment, differed for various drugs and, in some cases, including cocaine, for different forms of the same drug. . . . The 1986 Act distinguished between powder cocaine and cocaine base (also known as crack cocaine), by treating quantities of cocaine base differently than similar quantities of powder cocaine. Under the so-called "100-to-1" ratio, the 1986 Act established a mandatory minimum penalty of five years of imprisonment for trafficking offenses involving at least five grams of crack cocaine, whereas trafficking offenses involving powder cocaine required at least 500 grams of the substance to trigger the same mandatory minimum. . . .

Congress repealed and amended mandatory minimum penalties for crack cocaine offenses in the Fair Sentencing Act of 2010. These mandatory minimum penalties had drawn widespread criticism since their enactment in the 1980s. . . . The Act altered the mandatory minimum penalties established by the 1986 and 1988 Acts by repealing the mandatory minimum penalty for simple possession of crack cocaine and by increasing the quantities required to trigger the five- and ten-year mandatory minimum penalties for crack cocaine trafficking offenses from five to 28 grams and 50 to 280 grams, respectively. There was broad bipartisan support for these changes among members of Congress. . . .

### POLICY VIEWS IN FAVOR OF MANDATORY MINIMUM PENALTIES

#### 1. Promotion of Uniformity in Sentencing and Avoidance of Unwarranted Disparity

Some view mandatory minimum penalties as promoting uniformity and reducing unwarranted disparities because such penalties require courts to impose similar sentences for similar offenses.... Congress enacted many mandatory minimum penalties, together with the then-mandatory guidelines system, as part of its effort in the 1980s to narrow judicial sentencing discretion and curb what it viewed as unduly disparate and lenient sentences. ...

### 2. Protection of the Public through Certainty in Punishment, Deterrence, and Incapacitation

Another policy rationale in favor of mandatory minimum penalties is that they protect the public. [Law] enforcement officials have historically urged the enactment of mandatory minimum penalties.

According to those who hold this view, mandatory minimum penalties deter crime by imposing certain, predictable, and generally severe punishment. Because mandatory minimum penalties require a certain term of incarceration, they are viewed as an effective means of alerting would-be offenders to the consequences of certain illegal conduct. According to the Department of Justice, sentencing reforms in the 1980s, including the enactment and enhancement of many mandatory minimum penalties, helped reduce crime rates. ... Furthermore, some scholars believe that the severity of mandatory minimum penalties increases their deterrent effect by raising the "cost" of committing crime to would-be offenders.

In addition to their deterrent effect, some policymakers assert that mandatory minimum penalties reduce crime by incapacitating criminals and protecting the public from their potential future offenses. For example, law enforcement officers have reported to the Commission that incapacitation through mandatory minimum penalties has reduced methamphetamine- and firearm-related crime. ...

### 3. Retribution

Some view mandatory minimum penalties as an important means of expressing society's disdain for an offense. Congressman Asa Hutchinson argued that the "strongest justification" for mandatory minimum penalties is that they give society the "means of expressing its outrage toward certain offenses that are so harmful to the public." ...

### 4. Effective Law Enforcement Tool that Induces Pleas and Cooperation

Many in the law enforcement community view mandatory minimum penalties as an important investigative tool. The threat of a mandatory minimum penalty gives law enforcement leverage over defendants, who may be encouraged to cooperate in exchange for lesser charges or safety valve and substantial-assistance benefits. ...

### 5. Assistance to State and Local Law Enforcement

Another justification for federal mandatory minimum penalties relates to the relationship between state and federal law enforcement. Then-Assistant Attorney General Mueller stated that because of the substantial concurrent state and federal jurisdiction in many drug and firearm cases, if "a state sentence for one of these crimes is inappropriately low, the existence of a substantially higher, federal mandatory minimum ensures a sentence that protects the public." . . .

## POLICY VIEWS AGAINST MANDATORY MINIMUM PENALTIES

### 1. Contribution to Excessive Uniformity and Unwarranted Disparity

One of the policy views advanced against mandatory minimum penalties is that they result in excessive uniformity by requiring similar sentences for dissimilar offenders. . . . In the American Bar Association's view, treating unlike offenders identically "is as much a blow to rational sentencing policy as is treating similar offenders differently."

Many believe that mandatory minimum penalties result in arbitrary and disparate sentences because they rely on certain specified triggering facts to the exclusion of all others. . . . For example, so-called "sentencing cliffs" occur when an offender's conduct just barely brings him within the terms of the mandatory minimum. In such a case, the offender is subject to a significantly higher sentence than an offender whose conduct fell just outside the scope of the mandatory minimum penalty, even though his or her conduct was only marginally different . . . .

A majority of judges believe that mandatory minimum penalties contribute to sentencing disparity. In a 2010 Commission survey of United States District Judges on a range of sentencing issues, 52 percent of judges ranked mandatory minimum penalties among the top three factors contributing to sentencing disparity. . . .

### 2. Excessive Severity and Disproportionality

Many view current federal mandatory minimum penalties as producing sentences that are excessively harsh relative to the gravity of the offense committed, in part because all sentences for a mandatory minimum offense must be at the floor or above regardless of the circumstances of the crime. [Many] sentences seem disproportionate to the offense because Congress did not link the minimum sentence to its picture of the least serious version of an offense, but rather to an especially serious offender, and chooses as the "minimum" a sentence that it considers appropriate for him. . . .

The Department of Justice has stated that "there are real and significant excesses in terms of the imprisonment meted out for some offenders under existing mandatory sentencing laws, especially for some non-violent offenders."

The Department of Justice explained that "mandatory minimum sentencing statutes in the federal system now apply to a significant array of serious crimes; and they also, by and large, mandate very severe imprisonment terms." This, in turn, has produced exponential growth in the federal prison population since the 1980s . . . .

Many judges also believe mandatory minimum penalties are too severe overall, with about 62 percent of judges responding to the 2010 Commission survey stating that such penalties across all offenses were "too high." The judges' opinions were more nuanced, however, with regard to specific offenses. More than 50 percent of judges surveyed believed that the mandatory minimum penalties were appropriate in drug trafficking offenses involving heroin (55%), powder cocaine (52%), and methamphetamine (53%), while most of the surveyed judges described the penalties for crack cocaine (76%) and marijuana (54%) offenses as "too high."

In firearms cases, approximately 60 percent of judges who responded in the 2010 Commission survey believed that the mandatory minimum sentences were appropriate for firearm offenders convicted of 18 U.S.C. §924(c) and (e). . . .

### 3.   Lack of Individualized Sentencing

Critics often argue that mandatory minimum penalties conflict with the goal of individualized sentencing. . . . Because mandatory minimum penalties may prevent a judge from considering all (or even most) of the pertinent facts and circumstances of the case (such as offender characteristics), the resulting sentence may be unfair or irrational. . . .

### 4.   Transfer of Sentencing Discretion from Judges to Prosecutors

Mandatory minimum penalties are often viewed as effectively transferring discretion from judges to prosecutors. This transfer of discretion is of concern to some because it both constrains judges' discretion and shifts that discretion to prosecutors, who do not have the incentive, training, or even the appropriate information to properly consider a defendant's mitigating circumstances at the initial charging stage of a case. . . .

This shift in discretion is especially problematic, according to some, because prosecutorial decisions are made outside of public view and in an uncertain and inconsistent manner." Justice Anthony Kennedy has observed that even though a prosecutor may act in good faith, the "trial judge is the one actor in the system most experienced with exercising discretion in a transparent, open, and reasoned way." . . .

Moreover, some argue that mandatory minimum penalties can also be used to coerce defendants to plead guilty and waive constitutional rights. . . . Finally, some believe that the threat of mandatory minimum penalties might cause offenders to give false information, to plead guilty to charges of which they may actually be innocent, or to forfeit a strong defense.

### 5. *Ineffectiveness as a Deterrent or as a Law Enforcement Tool to Induce Pleas and Cooperation*

Some scholars counter the claims made by proponents of mandatory minimum penalties that these penalties serve as an effective deterrent to crime. They note that the research conducted by social scientists and public policy analysts has found little evidence to support the argument that mandatory minimums prevent crime. In fact, many assert it is an increase in the certainty of punishment through the prosecution of more offenders that is the more cost-effective deterrent compared to the severity of punishment that mandatory minimum penalties or longer sentences provide.

Some also dispute the claims that mandatory minimum penalties are a useful law enforcement tool for the investigation and prosecution of criminals by inducing pleas and cooperation. [Many] observe that the exchange of reduced sentences for information results in "inverted sentencing," in which offenders with valuable information — kingpins, organizers, and other highly culpable defendants — can avoid mandatory minimum penalties through charge-bargaining and substantial assistance motions while low-level offenders cannot because they lack such valuable information. . . . Some further believe that mandatory minimum penalties cause a "cooperation backlash" that occurs when sentencing practices are viewed as overly severe and many citizens become reluctant to assist the law enforcement effort. . . .

### 6. *Interference with State Law Enforcement*

Some view federal mandatory minimum penalties as indicative of the "over- federalization" of criminal justice policy and as upsetting the proper allocation of responsibility between the states and federal government. The late Chief Justice Rehnquist noted that mandatory minimum penalties "fueled the trend toward federalizing crimes" because law enforcement elects to pursue charges in federal rather than state courts because of the severe mandatory minimum penalties available under federal law.

### 7. *Impact Across Demographic Groups*

Some express concerns that mandatory minimum penalties unfairly impact racial minorities and the economically disadvantaged. This may be attributed in part to the fact that the most frequently applied mandatory minimum penalties are for drug offenses, which according to some disproportionately impacts certain racial or ethnic groups. . . .

Some also view legally relevant factors, such as criminal history and prosecutorial discretion in charging decisions or plea agreements, as contributors to the demographically disparate impact of mandatory minimum penalties. Studies show that racial minorities are more likely than whites to have a prior record, which may result from disproportionate processing by the criminal justice system. Research likewise indicates that offenders in certain racial groups may be less likely to get the benefit of prosecutorial discretion in charging decisions or plea agreements. Some have also expressed the view that disparate results may occur based on an individual's socio-economic status. . . .

### THE USE OF MANDATORY MINIMUM PENALTIES IN SELECTED DISTRICTS

[The Commission staff selected 13 judicial districts for in-depth research. In these districts, Commission staff interviewed federal prosecutors, full-time federal public defenders, and private defense attorneys.] During the interviews, the Commission asked a series of questions designed to obtain information about whether the practices in the districts concerning mandatory minimum penalties provided support for any of the policy arguments . . .

### 1. *Defendants' Prior Knowledge about Mandatory Minimum Penalties*

The Commission asked defense attorneys whether their clients were aware of mandatory minimum penalties. Most defense attorneys categorically stated that their clients had no knowledge of the possible mandatory minimum penalties applicable to their crime prior to its commission. One defense attorney noted that the occasional client in an urban area might have some awareness of mandatory minimum penalties, and another mentioned possible awareness of crack cocaine penalties. Others described their clients' awareness of penalties as infrequent.

Only recidivist offenders with previous experience in federal court were identified as a category of offenders who might be aware of mandatory minimum penalties. . . .

### 2. *Incentive to Plead Guilty*

The Commission asked prosecutors and defense attorneys to identify the best incentive that the government could offer an offender to induce a guilty plea. Most prosecutors did not identify the mandatory minimum penalty as the best incentive to induce a plea. Rather, the strength of the evidence or a sentence reduction were the two incentives most frequently identified by prosecutors. The defense attorneys agreed that the strength of the evidence and a sentence reduction were among the best incentives offered by the government to induce a guilty plea. . . .

### 3. *Trial Rates Driven by Mandatory Minimum Penalties*

The Commission asked defense attorneys whether some clients chose to go to trial because of charges carrying mandatory minimum penalties. The overwhelming majority said that this was the case. . . .

#### 4. *Impact on Willingness to Provide Substantial Assistance*

The Commission asked prosecutors and defense attorneys whether being charged with a mandatory minimum penalty influenced an offender's willingness to cooperate [with a government investigation of other suspects]. The majority of prosecutors thought that being charged with a mandatory minimum penalty did influence an offender's willingness to cooperate. . . .

The [public defenders] disagreed about the impact of mandatory minimum penalties on their clients' willingness to provide substantial assistance. Most thought that other factors drove the decision and those factors varied for each individual client. Most also thought that a mandatory minimum penalty and the guidelines factored equally into their clients' decision to provide substantial assistance to the government.

Most of the [private defense attorneys] thought that being charged with a mandatory minimum penalty had an influence on their clients' willingness to cooperate. Most also agreed that a mandatory minimum penalty and the guidelines factored equally into their clients' decision to provide substantial assistance. Many also related that others factors also drove the decision and that the weight of any particular factor varied by client.

### PROBLEM 2-4. LETTER FROM A CONGRESSMAN

A panel of the U.S. Court of Appeals for the Seventh Circuit issued an opinion stating that a 97-month sentence imposed on a drug dealer was contrary to statute, because the defendant was convicted under a statute calling for a 120-month mandatory minimum sentence. Nevertheless, the panel allowed the sentence to stand because the government did not appeal this aspect of the sentence.

News of this judicial opinion reached Rep. James Sensenbrenner, the chair of the House Judiciary Committee. Sensenbrenner immediately wrote letters about the case to the chief judge of the Seventh Circuit and to the attorney general. In his letter to attorney general, Sensenbrenner demanded that the Department of Justice file any available appeals in the case. In the letter to the chief judge, Sensenbrenner demanded "a prompt response" about what steps the judge would take "to rectify the panel's actions" in the case. He believed that the government's failure to appeal was not a sufficient reason to allow the reduced sentence to stand, and asked "that all necessary and appropriate measures be taken, whether by members of the panel and/or by the other judges of the court" to ensure that the higher sentence would be imposed in this case. See Maurice Possley, Lawmaker Prods Court, Raises Brows, Chi. Trib., July 10, 2005.

Does this letter qualify as legitimate "oversight" of the judiciary by a committee of Congress? Does it violate separation of powers principles? If there is a problem with sending a letter of this sort to judges, what can a member of Congress do about cases that appear to misapply a mandatory minimum sentencing law?

*NOTES*

1. *Judicial discretion and mandatory penalties.*    Many criticisms of mandatory minimum statutes focus on the loss of judicial discretion in sentencing. Consider, for example, the 1970 statement of then Representative George H.W. Bush:

> Federal judges are almost unanimously opposed to mandatory minimums, because they remove a great deal of the court's discretion. In the vast majority of cases which reach the sanctioning stage today, the bare minimum sentence is levied — and in some cases, less than the minimum mandatory is given. . . . Probations and outright dismissals often result. Philosophical differences aside, practicality requires a sentence structure which is generally acceptable to the courts, to prosecutors, and to the general public.

116 Cong. Rec. H33314, Sept. 23, 1970. Many state and federal judges share these views and believe that mandatory minimum statutes too often force them to impose a fundamentally unjust sentence. In a 2010 survey of federal judges, most of the judges believed that mandatory minimum penalty statutes required them to impose sentences that were generally not appropriate for the offenses in specific cases. On the other hand, a majority of judges felt that the mandatory minimum penalties for some specific crimes (trafficking in heroin, powder cocaine, and methamphetimine; firearms offenses; production and distribution of child pornography) were appropriate.

Are all mandatory minimums subject to the criticisms about uneven enforcement and loss of judicial discretion? Could a legislature address these problems by narrowly defining the offenses and offenders eligible for a mandatory sentence?

Can any decision maker other than a judge — who decides many individual cases — appreciate the facts about an offender's past that should lead to a lighter sentence? Why might judges impose sentences lighter than those set by the legislature? Do judges generally share a different political view on crime control? Do they see too many individual cases?

2. *Mandatory mandatories.*    Most mandatory minimum statutes instruct the judge to impose a particular sentence for a particular charge, but they do not require the prosecutor to file a given charge when adequate facts are present. Thus, typical mandatory sentencing statutes give prosecutors considerable bargaining power during plea negotiations; they also offer prosecutors opportunities to avoid mandatory minimum sentences when they believe that such sentences would be unjust or a poor use of resources. Stephen Schulhofer and Ilene Nagel surveyed charging practices and concluded that prosecutors' concerns about mandatory minimum sentences led them in a substantial number of cases to charge some lesser crime even though the evidence was available to charge for the mandatory minimum crime. Schulhofer & Nagel, A Tale of Three Cities: An Empirical Study of Charging and Bargaining Practices Under the Federal Sentencing Guidelines, 66 S. Cal. L. Rev. 501 (1992).

Legislatures sometimes constrain this prosecutorial power by passing statutes that prevent plea bargaining and require the prosecutor to file charges whenever adequate evidence is available. For instance, in 1973 New York passed a "Rockefeller drug law" imposing severe mandatory minimums and restricting plea bargaining. After passage of this law, there were fewer arrests, indictments, and convictions for drug offenses, but those convicted served longer terms. Jacqueline Cohen & Michael Tonry, Sentencing Reforms and the Impacts, in Research on Sentencing: The Search for Reform 348-349 (Alfred Blumstein et al. eds., 1983). Decades later, the New York legislature eliminated the mandatory minimum penalties.

This sort of "mandatory mandatory" statute is rare. Why do legislators hesitate to pass statutes that remove the prosecutor's discretion to decline charges or to select a charge not subject to the minimum penalty?

3. *Net effects of mandatory minimum penalties on sentencing patterns.* Studies of mandatory minimum penalties have reached different conclusions about the effect of these laws on the crime rates for the targeted offenses. Some studies have found a deterrent effect for gun crimes and homicides, but other studies have found no effect on the commission of drug crimes or violent crimes generally. The effects of mandatory minimum penalties on the criminal justice system are clearer. These laws consistently lead to fewer arrests for the designated crimes, fewer charges filed, more dismissals of charges, more trials rather than guilty pleas, and longer sentences imposed and served. See Michael Tonry, The Mostly Unintended Effects of Mandatory Penalties: Two Centuries of Consistent Findings, 38 Crime and Justice: A Review of Research 65 (2009).

4. *Self-correcting democratic process.* If mandatory minimum sentences truly produced the ill effects described by critics, wouldn't the democratically elected legislature recognize these flaws after a time and abandon the experiment? This has happened in a few states. In 2001 the Connecticut legislature granted judges authority to depart from mandatory minimum sentences for certain drug crimes, such as first-time sales or possession within 1,500 feet of a school. Also that year, Indiana eliminated mandatory 20-year sentences for cocaine dealers (anyone caught with more than three grams of powder cocaine), and Louisiana repealed mandatory sentences for some simple possession and other nonviolent drug offenses. Meanwhile, other jurisdictions have debated for years about changing mandatory minimum drug sentences, without ever taking significant action. See Ronald F. Wright, Are the Drug Wars De-escalating? Where to Look for Evidence, 14 Fed. Sent'g Rep. 141 (2002). What might prevent the legislature from rethinking self-destructive legislation? Who brings information to the legislators' attention as they debate proposals or create an agenda? Is the problem a lack of information, a lack of time, or something else?

---

Legislatures in just under half of the states have empowered permanent "sentencing commissions" to create rules to guide judges as they select sentences within the statutory range. These guidelines (some embodied in statutes and others in administrative rules) are different from statutory maximum and minimum punishments because they allow judges, under some circumstances, to go above or below the recommended range so long as the final sentence remains within the statutorily authorized range.

Legislatures typically create sentencing commissions after other institutions fail. Judges, executive branch officials, and legislators have failed in predictable patterns over the years when they have tried to change or administer sentencing policy. You might think of these patterns of institutional failure as "pathologies," or deviations from the more ordinary and effective functions of these governmental institutions.

*Judicial Pathologies.* Judges create two sorts of difficulties in the sentencing system, both arising because judges sentence individually rather than as a coordinated group. First, different judges sometimes give disparate sentences to offenders who, in every relevant way, seem to be alike. Second, sentencing judges do not conserve corrections resources. There are a fixed number of prison beds and slots in corrections programs, yet a judge has little incentive to use only her proportional share of this "public good."

A sentencing commission is one potential solution to both problems. A commission could reduce disparity by designating, within narrow boundaries, the "ordinary" sentences for particular types of offenses and offenders. A commission could also designate ordinary sentences at a level not likely to over-burden the corrections system.

*Executive Pathologies.*   Some executive branch pathologies in sentencing are made possible because parole release decisions are not easily visible to the public. The parole decision receives less attention than the sentence itself, and it is made by an executive official who, unlike many state court judges, is not directly accountable to the voters.

The difficulties with low-visibility release decisions correspond to the classic objections to all low-visibility discretionary decisions: they may not be based on consistent or proper reasons. The release date may depend on no articulable principles at all, or it may depend on the personal views of the executive officer involved rather than on principles endorsed by the public. Sentencing commissions offer one way to make release decisions more visible and consistent. Under a guideline system, the release date turns on principles adopted through a public process, as applied and announced by a publicly accountable government official, the judge.

*Legislative Pathologies.* Legislators make their own pathological contributions to sentencing policy. But the accounts of exactly how the legislature does so are not altogether consistent. According to some accounts, legislatures need to delegate sentencing authority to a permanent commission because they do not have enough time or expertise to make proper changes in sentencing laws. The complexity of sentencing issues makes it difficult, during the limited time available, for the legislators and their staffs to acquire the necessary information to make wise choices.

Other critics of the legislative role in sentencing argue that the legislature spends far too *much* time dealing with sentencing. Legislators, according to this view, pander to the perceived passions and frustrations of their constituents about crime; they pass laws that prove later to be expensive, ineffectual, and cruel. Periodic tinkering by the legislature creates an inconsistent sentencing scheme, riddled with exceptions. According to these critics, the legislature has more difficulty dealing rationally with crime than with most other subjects.

Just as the descriptions of legislative pathologies are not entirely consistent, the prescriptions for a commission's proper response to the legislative pathologies are in some tension with each other. Under one model, the ideal commission strategy is to minimize legislative involvement in criminal punishment issues. A successful system, in this view, will reduce the legislators' opportunities to interfere with the judgment of the expert members and staff of the commission. The commission will anticipate and deal with any criminal justice crises that could provoke the legislature to take action. Under a second model, the sentencing commission merely attempts to improve legislative deliberation about criminal legislation. The commission can inform the legislators about the consequences (especially the fiscal consequences) of different bills, and it can advocate consistency and rationality in sentencing.

The following materials highlight the different roles that sentencing commissions and sentencing guidelines play in a jurisdiction. They also point out how commissions, when they arrive on the scene, can change the established roles among the existing sentencing institutions in the jurisdiction.

## *ABA Standards for Criminal Justice, Sentencing 18-4.1*
### (3d ed. 1994)

(a) Implementation of legislative policy determinations within the statutory framework of the criminal code requires a state-wide agency to develop a more specific set of provisions that guide sentencing courts to presumptive sentences and in the appropriate use of aggravating and mitigating factors, offenders' criminal history, and offenders' personal characteristics. . . .

(b) The agency performing the intermediate function should be the information center for all elements of the criminal justice system. The agency should collect, analyze and disseminate information on the nature and effects of sentences imposed and carried out. The agency should develop means to monitor, evaluate, and predict patterns of sentencing, including levels of severity of sentences imposed and relative use of each type of sanction. . . .

*Commentary.* This standard gives definition to the concept of the "intermediate function" in sentencing systems. This term [describes] the work done "in between" the legislature's statutory commands and the case-by-case decisions of sentencing judges. Every jurisdiction should create a permanently chartered agency to perform the intermediate function, either in the form of a sentencing commission or an equivalent body in the legislative or judicial branch. . . .

Typically, statutory maxima are set at high levels so that the range of statutorily authorized penalties is wide indeed. One critical function of the sentencing agency, as intermediary between legislature and the courts, is to give structure to the decision-making process for selecting particular sentences within the expansive range allowed by the code.

The agency performs this role through the creation of presumptive sentences and other provisions for the guidance of sentencing judges, including provisions relating to aggravating and mitigating circumstances, and the effect of offenders' prior criminal histories and personal characteristics. Through such measures, courts across the jurisdiction can approach sentencing decisions from a common baseline and can employ similar steps of logic and analysis in adjusting sentences away from the presumptive baseline when required. . . .

## Modeling Discretion in American Sentencing Systems, Kevin Reitz
### 20 Law & Pol'y 389 (1998)

... I have found it helpful to think in pictorial terms about an array of actors in sentencing systems who potentially have sentencing discretion. A generic "discretion diagram," such as that reproduced in Figure 1, can be used to visualize many of the important relationships in existing punishment systems.

[One] function of Figure 1 is to recognize that some discretionary actors operate primarily on the "systemic level" while others discharge their authorities primarily on the "case-specific level." . . . Systemic actors make discretionary decisions intended to influence whole categories of cases; case-specific actors make discretionary judgments that, for the most part, operate on the individual cases before them. . . .

### Indeterminate Sentencing Systems

... Indeterminate schemes, still in effect in roughly half of the American states, are represented . . . in Figure 3. . . .

A number of the distinctive features of indeterminacy jump out from Figure 3. . . . First, the shrunken compartment for the legislature in Figure 3 indicates the very loose statutory boundaries upon punishment outcomes that generally exist in the traditional systems. It would not be unusual in an indeterminate jurisdiction, for example, to find that the legislatively authorized sanction for a crime such as aggravated assault reaches as low as a suspended sentence without conditions, up to a term of incarceration in the ballpark of thirty-two years. . . .

### FIGURE 1
**A Discretion Diagram for Sentencing Systems**

Systemic Level

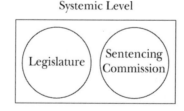

Case-Specific Level

**FIGURE 3**
**A Discretion Diagram of Indeterminate Sentencing**

Systemic Level

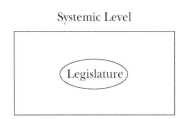

Case-Specific Level

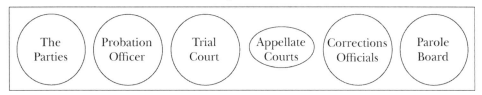

The second defining characteristic of indeterminate structures is their diffusion of meaningful sentencing discretion across numerous actors at the case-specific level. Prosecutors most of the time enjoy unregulated charging discretion; plea bargains between the parties (sometimes including sentence bargains) can have sizable impact on punishment; probation officers, at least in some jurisdictions, make sentence recommendations that are highly influential with judges; the judges themselves usually have a boggling array of choices remaining open to them on the day of sentencing; and following a judicially pronounced prison sentence, correctional officials and parole boards hold impressive powers to fix actual release dates — which can sometimes be set after only a small fraction of the court's sentence has been served.

The only case-specific actor without meaningful sentencing discretion in traditional indeterminate systems, as it turns out, is the appellate judiciary. For reasons of historical practice, deference to trial courts, and caseload pressures, appellate courts almost universally have resisted responsibility to participate in sentencing outcomes. . . .

THE FEDERAL SYSTEM

The most salient discretionary feature of the U.S. sentencing system, especially in comparison with its state counterparts, is the federal system's attempt to concentrate discretionary authority at the systemic level and to constrain such authority at the case-specific level. . . . In comparison with the weak legislative presence in indeterminate sentencing structures, Congress made itself an important discretionary actor in the new federal scheme. Through its many mandatory sentencing laws, and through oversight of the U.S. Sentencing Commission, Congress has assumed and held a major role in the ongoing determination of sentencing outcomes.

More distinctive than the enlargement of the legislative role, however, has been the great measure of authority granted to or assumed by the U.S. Sentencing Commission vis-à-vis downstream players in the sentencing system. [The] federal commission was introduced as a new and authoritative actor, absorbing important discretions that formerly were exercised by other decision makers. . . .

The systemic power wielded by the U.S. commission was compounded by the fact that, when creating the federal guidelines system, Congress abolished parole release and imposed sharp limits on the amount of good-time credit that may be awarded federal prisoners. . . . Thus, the commission's discretion to say what a sentence should be in a particular case could be overruled infrequently by a trial judge, and was subject only to minor adjustment at the "back door" of the incarceration process. . . .

## PENNSYLVANIA

While the federal sentencing system may be seen primarily as an attempt to concentrate authority at the systemic level, the Pennsylvania guidelines structure is distinguished by its very weak exertions of systemwide control over punishment decisions. . . . In comparison with the detailed legislative mandate enacted by Congress for the new federal structure, the Pennsylvania legislature authored a cryptic and open-ended scheme. Notably, the state legislature described the guidelines to be created by the commission as one factor among many, or as merely "considerations," for trial courts to weigh when imposing sentences. . . .

**FIGURE 5A**
**Discretionary Diagram of the Pennsylvania System**

Systemic Level

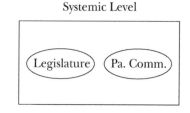

Case-Specific Level

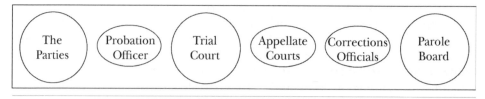

In Pennsylvania, as it turned out, the most important structural decisions about the apportionment of sentencing discretion were made by the state's appellate courts. . . . By the late 1980s, the state supreme court ruled that the new guidelines were only "advisory," that the legislature had required no more than that trial courts "take notice of " the commission's work before choosing a sentence, and that reviewing courts had no power to hear appeals based on the claim that the guidelines had not been followed, except in "exceptional cases." The discretionary implications of these decisions are pictured in Figure 5. . . .

The result, in Pennsylvania, has been to privilege trial court discretion while leaving the parties' plea negotiation powers unregulated. In these terms, Figure 5 still resembles the traditional indeterminate sentencing structure that preceded the Pennsylvania guidelines. No one is in charge at the systemic level; nearly all meaningful sentencing authority has settled down to the case-specific level. [The] discretionary patterns of the Pennsylvania system [reminds us that] not all guideline structures are created equal. With respect to one critical variable — the degree of systemwide control attempted in each structure — the [federal and Pennsylvania guidelines] could hardly be more different. . . .

## NOTES

1. *Where's the jury?*  One of the notable aspects of Professor Reitz's sentencing diagrams is the absence of any "bubbles" for juries. Professor Reitz's article was authored in the late 1990s, before the Supreme Court started to give attention to the jury's role in sentencing determinations through the *Apprendi-Blakely* line of cases (which is discussed fully in Chapter 6).

2. *Reasons to create sentencing commissions and guidelines.*  Almost half the states use sentencing guidelines created by sentencing commissions. The federal system also operates under sentencing guidelines, created in 1987 by the U.S. Sentencing Commission. A state sentencing commission typically drafts the initial set of guidelines on behalf of the legislature, which then enacts an integrated package of sentencing reforms. In states without a commission, the state judiciary adopts a package of guidelines as procedural rules or as informal guidance to judges.

Why would a legislature ask a commission to create a set of sentencing guidelines? Does a commission have any advantages over a legislature in setting specific sentencing ranges for particular types of offenses and offenders? Legislatures turn to commissions when the legislators recognize that they do not have enough time or expertise themselves to do the job well. Political theory also suggests some less noble motives that might lead legislators to deal with criminal sentencing through a commission. When it comes to statutes involving criminal punishments, legislators often have political incentives to advocate severe punishment so that they can be seen as tough on crime. Stiff penalties may be appropriate for the extreme cases that dominate legislative debates; a wide definition of the crime will include both the imagined and the as-yet-unimagined evils.

At the same time, legislators want to avoid blame for the costs of criminal punishments. They would rather leave it to prosecutors to weigh the human costs of unnecessarily strong punishments, since prosecutors can decline prosecution when justice requires it. And they might prefer some other institution, such as a sentencing commission, to make the hard decisions about how to economize on the limited prison and corrections resources available.

Very few jurisdictions outside the United States have created bodies such as sentencing commissions to serve an intermediate function between the legislature and the judges. If sentencing commissions are a good idea, why do we not see them in other places in the world?

3. *Research instead of rules.*   Most guidelines created by commissions are, to some degree or another, presumptive. That is, a judge who sentences outside the presumed range for sentences risks reversal. Are presumptive sentencing rules, created by commissions and approved by legislatures, subject to the same criticisms leveled against legislatively determined sentences? Would sentencing commissions be more valuable if they limited their recommendations to the most commonly encountered "paradigm" cases for sentencing and conducted research into the effects of various types of sanctions? Is lack of knowledge a more pressing concern than lack of uniformity among sentencing judges? See Albert Alschuler, The Failure of Sentencing Guidelines: A Plea for Less Aggregation, 58 U. Chi. L. Rev. 901 (1991).

4. *Sentencing commissions coming and going.*   Sentencing commissions (along with parole boards) are one of the few sentencing actors that can come and go. A number of states have never established sentencing commissions, and a few states eliminated or restructured their sentencing commissions after they were in operation only a short period of time. The current draft of the sentencing provisions in the American Law Institute's Model Penal Code call for states to create and maintain a permanent administrative body to monitor and improve sentencing practices.

5. *Sentencing information systems.*   Are there ways of achieving the goal of reasonable uniformity other than the issuance of detailed rules, whether by courts or sentencing commissions? One idea that has been explored in Scotland and South Australia—but has yet to be applied in the United States—is the creation of "information systems" that will let judges and lawyers know what sentences were imposed in "similar" cases (with great attention to what makes a case "similar"). See Marc Miller, A Map of Sentencing and a Compass for Judges: Sentencing Information Systems, Transparency, and the Next Generation of Reform, 105 Colum. L. Rev. 1351 (2005).

# C.   PROSECUTORS

Just as they are central to most other aspects of criminal justice, prosecutors are central to sentencing. Prosecutors select the charges that define the outer statutory boundaries for the sentence. Because criminal codes in the United

States are typically stuffed with different crimes covering similar conduct, and specific crimes are often defined with broad terms that could cover a wide range of behavior, the prosecutor normally has a number of legal options that could plausibly fit the facts as alleged. Some crimes include mandatory sentences, and in some systems prosecutors can specify particular aggravating factors with dramatic sentencing implications.

The prosecutor also can negotiate a plea agreement with the defendant. Defendants pleading guilty tend to receive substantially lower sentences than defendants who go to trial (in some studies the "plea discount" has been one-third or more off post-trial sentences), but judges tend to sentence based on the original charges filed rather than the charges forming the basis of the guilty plea. And the prosecutor often recommends a particular sentence to the judge — a recommendation that carries great weight, especially in high-volume courtrooms, where the judges and probation officers must depend heavily on the parties to inform them about each case.

Under these conditions, prosecutors have substantial and often determinative sentencing power. Do effective controls exist to prevent an individual prosecutor from misusing this power? As the materials below indicate, such controls are not likely to come from the judiciary, because judges are extremely reluctant to review the merits of prosecutorial charging decisions. The study of the prosecutor's office in New Orleans excerpted below raises the possibility of effective controls over individual prosecutors originating internally, from the prosecutor's office itself.

## People v. Wayne Robert Stewart
### 55 P.3d 107 (Colo. 2002)

MULLARKEY, C.J.

. . . The crimes occurred on a Sunday evening in March 1997 when Wayne Stewart left the bar of a restaurant located in a suburban shopping center. As Stewart began to drive his sports utility vehicle out of the shopping center parking lot, he encountered three pedestrians — Richard Ehrmann, Christine Castro, and Jeffrey Pippenger, in that order — walking abreast in the middle of the driving lane. The pedestrians had just left a video rental store and, as they walked to their vehicle, they were looking up at the Hale Bopp comet streaking across the sky. The testimony of disinterested bystanders established that Stewart veered toward the pedestrians at an angle; Ehrmann, who was closest to the traffic lane, was brushed by Stewart's vehicle. A verbal altercation ensued, after which Stewart began driving back and forth at an angle and in an aggressive manner. [Stewart's car hit Ehrmann, and when the car abruptly stopped, Ehrmann rolled off the hood and landed hard on the ground next to the driver's side. The SUV continued to roll forward, and the rear wheel on the driver's side ran over Ehrmann's head.] Stewart left the scene without stopping. As a result of the incident, Ehrmann suffered massive brain injury and lay comatose for approximately two and one-half years. Ultimately, the victim died.

The state charged Stewart with one count of first degree assault against Ehrmann, a class 3 felony in violation of section 18-3-202(1)(a); one count of reckless second degree assault against Ehrmann, a class 4 felony, in violation of §18-3-203(1)(d); four counts of violent crime, pursuant to §16-11-309; one count of vehicular assault against Ehrmann, a class 5 felony, in violation of §18-3-205(1)(a); and four counts of reckless endangerment against the other two pedestrians and two bystanders, a class 3 misdemeanor, in violation of §18-3-208. Stewart pleaded not guilty to the charges.

At trial, the People contended that Stewart intentionally hit Ehrmann or, in the alternative, that Stewart used his vehicle to scare and intimidate Ehrmann. Stewart took the position ... that Ehrmann jumped onto [the hood of] Stewart's vehicle and that he was unaware that he ran over Ehrmann. . . .

A jury convicted Stewart of reckless second degree assault of Ehrmann and two counts of reckless endangerment against the other two pedestrians. At the sentencing hearing, the trial court found that Stewart "did drive his car at Mr. Ehrmann in an act of anger," and sentenced Stewart to five years in the Department of Corrections for the second degree assault conviction. . . .

Stewart argues that his conviction for reckless second degree assault with a deadly weapon violates his right to equal protection because the statutes governing vehicular assault and reckless second degree assault with a deadly weapon proscribe the same conduct but mete out disparate punishments. He asserts that there is no rational distinction between second degree reckless assault, a class 4 felony requiring mandatory sentencing for a term of five to sixteen years, and vehicular assault, a class 5 felony that is punishable by one to three years of imprisonment in the presumptive range and two to six years in the aggravated range, and which neither requires a mandatory sentence nor precludes probation. The lack of any rational basis for distinguishing the two offenses, he maintains, coupled with the significant difference in penalty, renders his conviction of second degree assault violative of equal protection by penalizing him more severely for the identical criminal conduct proscribed by the lesser offense of vehicular assault. We disagree.

The Fourteenth Amendment to the United States Constitution provides in part that no state "shall deny to any person within its jurisdiction the equal protection of the laws." A similar guarantee is implicit in the due process clause of the Colorado Constitution. Colo. Const., art. II, §25. Colorado, however, has taken a stricter view of the protections afforded by our equal protection guarantee than has the United States Supreme Court in interpreting the federal Constitution. The Supreme Court has held that equal protection is not offended when statutes proscribe identical conduct but authorize different penalties. United States v. Batchelder, 442 U.S. 114 (1979).

By contrast, we have consistently held that if a criminal statute proscribes different penalties for identical conduct, a person convicted under the harsher penalty is denied equal protection unless there are reasonable differences or distinctions between the proscribed behavior. The statutory classification of crimes must be based on differences that are both real in fact and also reasonably related to the general purposes of the criminal legislation.

Equally well established is the principle that a single act may violate more than one criminal statute. We have emphasized that equal protection is offended only when two statutes forbid *identical* conduct. . . . To determine whether two statutes proscribe identical conduct, we analyze the elements of each. We emphasize that this task requires a facial examination of the elements comprising each crime. . . . The crime of reckless second degree assault with a deadly weapon is defined in §18-3-203(1)(d), as follows: "(1) A person commits the crime of assault in the second degree if . . . (d) He recklessly causes serious bodily injury to another person by means of a deadly weapon." . . . Vehicular assault is defined in §18-3-205(1)(a), as follows: "If a person operates or drives a motor vehicle in a reckless manner, and this conduct is the proximate cause of serious bodily injury to another, such person commits vehicular assault." . . .

The language of the statutes differs in [several] ways. First, second degree assault applies to a range of unspecified conduct; the defendant can "recklessly cause" injury in a multitude of ways. The conduct specified in the vehicular assault statute, on the other hand, is strictly limited to "driving or operating" a motor vehicle. . . . An elemental comparison thus illustrates that the two statutes, by their terms, target different conduct. To achieve a conviction under the vehicular assault statute, the prosecution must demonstrate that the defendant drove or operated a motor vehicle. Accordingly, one who causes serious bodily injury by dint of a motor vehicle that is used as a weapon, but that is not driven or operated, could be convicted of reckless second degree assault with a deadly weapon but not vehicular assault. For example, if an adult locks a child in a car on a sweltering summer day to punish or intimidate the child, the adult obviously is not driving or operating the car. Assuming that the other elements of the crime are met, however, the adult could be charged with reckless second degree assault but not vehicular assault.

[Another] difference between second degree assault and vehicular assault lies in the means by which the defendant allegedly caused serious bodily injury. The vehicular assault statute provides that, to be convicted, the defendant's reckless driving or operation of a "motor vehicle" must have proximately caused serious bodily injury. The second degree assault statute requires that the defendant use a "deadly weapon." . . . Section 18-1-901(3)(e), provides the statutory definition of deadly weapon:

> "Deadly weapon" means any of the following which in the manner it is used or intended to be used is capable of producing death or serious bodily injury: (I) A firearm, whether loaded or unloaded; (II) A knife; (III) A bludgeon; or (IV) Any other weapon, device, instrument, material, or substance, whether animate or inanimate. . . .

We have consistently held that whether an object is a deadly weapon for the purposes of section 18-1-903(e)(IV) depends on the manner in which the object is used. People v. Ross, 831 P.2d 1310 (Colo. 1992) (holding that a fist can be a deadly weapon). . . . Any object can be a deadly weapon if it is used in a manner capable of producing death or serious bodily injury. . . . The same is true of a motor vehicle. It is not always a deadly weapon under the statutory definition. A motor vehicle may be a deadly weapon, however, depending on how it is used in a particular situation.

The difference between the "deadly weapon" requirement of the second degree assault statute and the "motor vehicle" element of vehicular assault justifies the disparate penalties established by the General Assembly. The legislature could rationally decide that "road rage" or the use of a car as a deadly weapon justifies an increased penalty. At the same time, it could rationally determine that it is less reprehensible for one to cause serious bodily injury by mere reckless driving of a vehicle as a vehicle. This court cannot hold that the General Assembly has constitutionally erred in providing a more severe penalty for an act which it believes to be of greater social consequence. . . .

Stewart argues that even if the statutes are not identical, he can be convicted only of the more specific crime, motor vehicle assault, and not of the more general crime, second degree assault. Generally, the prosecution has discretion to determine what charges to file when a defendant's conduct violates more than one statute. See §18-1-408(7) ["If the same conduct is defined as criminal in different enactments or in different sections of this code, the offender may be prosecuted under any one or all of the sections or enactments"]. There are certain circumstances in which this general rule does not apply. See, e.g., People v. Smith, 938 P.2d 111, 115-116 (Colo. 1997) [General Assembly can supplant the more general offense by creating a specific offense supported by clear legislative intent to limit prosecution to that statute; in adopting the comprehensive Liquor Code, the General Assembly intended to require the offense of falsely filling out a liquor application to be prosecuted under the Liquor Code and not under the general felony offense of offering a false instrument for recording].

Stewart has failed to show that his crimes fall into this category. He simply asserts that the General Assembly intended to punish motor vehicle offenses pursuant to the motor vehicle statutes. He cites no authority such as statutory language or legislative history to support his theory and we reject it. The prosecution had discretion to charge second degree assault in this case and the jury verdict convicting Stewart on that charge stands. . . .

## The Screening/Bargaining Tradeoff, Ronald Wright and Marc Miller
### 55 Stan. L. Rev. 29 (2002)

[All] prosecutors "screen" when they make any charging decision. By prosecutorial screening we mean a far more structured and reasoned charge selection process than is typical in most prosecutors' offices in this country. The prosecutorial screening system we describe has four interrelated features, all internal to the prosecutor's office: early assessment, reasoned selection, barriers to bargains, and enforcement.

First, the prosecutor's office must make an early and careful assessment of each case, and demand that police and investigators provide sufficient information before the initial charge is filed. Second, the prosecutor's office must file only appropriate charges. Which charges are "appropriate" is determined by several factors. A prosecutor should only file charges that the office would generally want to result in a criminal conviction and sanction. In addition, appropriate charges must reflect reasonably accurately what actually occurred. They are charges that the prosecutor can very likely prove in court. Third, and critically, the office must severely restrict all plea bargaining, and most especially charge bargains. Prosecutors should also recognize explicitly that the screening process is the mechanism that makes such restrictions possible. Fourth, the kind of prosecutorial screening we advocate must include sufficient training, oversight, and other internal enforcement mechanisms to ensure reasonable uniformity in charging and relatively few changes to charges after they have been filed. If prosecutors treat hard screening decisions as the primary alternative to plea bargaining, they can produce changes in current criminal practice that would be fundamental, attractive, and viable. . . .

### THE SCREENING/BARGAINING TRADEOFF IN PRACTICE: NODA DATA

. . . Harry Connick was elected as the District Attorney for Orleans Parish in 1974. He has remained in that office for the past twenty-eight years. Connick first ran for office in 1969 against incumbent Jim Garrison, the flamboyant District Attorney made famous in the film *JFK*. His first unsuccessful campaign did not focus on plea bargaining. He promised faster prosecution and better tracking of defendants who failed to appear for trial. His 1973 campaign began with a similar emphasis on swift prosecution. As the campaign wore on, however, Connick's speeches began to feature attacks on plea bargaining. . . .

Connick told voters that widespread plea bargaining was wrong; years later, he explained that victims were right to resent it when cases were bargained away simply because of a "lazy" prosecutor. He promised to eliminate "baseless" plea bargaining and to hire full-time prosecutors who would not use plea bargains just to move cases from the docket.

As in other American cities, the criminal courts in New Orleans deal with enormous volume. In the face of this large urban caseload, Connick needed a strategy to carry out his campaign statements about plea bargaining. During the weeks between his election victory and taking office, he started speaking publicly about a plan with two central components. First, Connick planned to devote expertise and resources to screening. He proposed a screening procedure that "would weed out those cases really not worthy of being on the criminal docket, so more courtroom emphasis can be devoted to the violent offender." Second, he instructed his prosecutors not to engage in plea bargaining — particularly charge bargaining — except under very limited circumstances. . . .

The distinctiveness of the screening process in the NODA office is apparent from a closer examination of the path each new case takes through the system. Police officers develop a case folder after they complete an investigation and file charges with the magistrate. The first stop for the case folder in the NODA office is the Magistrate Section, where the least experienced assistants work. They typically have logged six months or fewer on the job. The ADA from the Magistrate Section appears for the state at the first appearance and bail hearing before the magistrate. A public defender is also present for the first appearance, but the case is reassigned immediately after the hearing and there is typically no further defense presence or participation in the case until after the DA files an information or obtains an indictment.

After any proceedings in the Magistrate Division, the folder moves to the Screening Section of the NODA office. Connick devotes extraordinary resources to this operation. For instance, in the late 1990s, about fifteen of the eighty-five attorneys in the office worked in Screening. . . . All attorneys in the Screening

Section served previously (usually a couple of years) in the Trial Section. This level of experience comes at a premium in New Orleans, where the turnover among prosecuting attorneys is quite high. The average tenure of an ADA in the NODA office is around two years. . . .

The screener reviews the investigation file, speaks to all the key witnesses and the victims (often by telephone, but sometimes in person), and generally gauges the strength of the case. If the police report neglects to mention a factual issue that is likely to arise at trial, the screening attorney will speak directly with the police officer to resolve it. There is a powerful office expectation that the Screening Attorney will make a decision within ten days of receiving the folder.

NODA instituted a variety of measures to ensure reasonable uniformity in screening decisions. Connick committed his screening principles to writing in an office policy manual. The general office policy is to charge the most serious crime the facts will support at trial. The policy does not, on its face, allow individual prosecutors to consider for themselves the equities in the case when selecting the charge. By the same token, however, Connick insists that overcharging is unacceptable, because the charges chosen for the information will stay in place through the trial. If screening prosecutors overcharge cases too often, the Chief of the Trial Section might send the screening attorney back into the courtroom on at least one of those overcharged matters to "get his teeth kicked in." Supervisors review all refusals to charge. . . .

Neither Connick nor any attorneys in his office claim to have abolished plea bargaining entirely from the New Orleans system. Prosecutors in the office acknowledge that sometimes new information appears and changes the value of a case. Witnesses leave town, victims decide not to testify, new witnesses appear, and investigators find new evidence. On occasion, the screening attorney makes a bad judgment and overcharges, and a plea could save the case.

Nevertheless, office policy tries to keep these changes in charges to a minimum. A supervisor must approve any decision to drop or change charges after the information is filed. The attorney requesting the change must complete a special form naming the screening and trial attorneys, and explaining the reason for the decision, drawing from a list of acceptable reasons. The ADAs believe there is a "stigma" involved in reducing charges, however strong the reasons for a reduction might be.

Attorneys from the NODA office believe that they decline to prosecute an exceptional number of cases. They view this as a necessary part of training police officers to investigate more thoroughly. The relatively high rate of declination also created a political challenge for Connick over the years. During each of his reelection campaigns — in 1978, 1984, 1990, and 1996 — Connick's challengers criticized the number of cases that the NODA office declined to prosecute. As his opponent Morris Reed put it in many public debates, "the PD arrests them and the DA turns them loose." Connick had several replies. Poor police work made declinations necessary. Further, he pointed to specific examples of how his office dealt severely with defendants once they were charged. Connick also explicitly linked his screening policies to his plea bargaining policies: Tough screening, he said, made it possible to keep plea bargaining at low levels.

Connick drew on case data to make specific claims about low rates of plea bargaining in the office: He asserted that plea bargaining in Jim Garrison's day reached 60 to 70%, but fell to 7 or 8% of all cases filed under his office policy. He also routinely mentioned the high number of trials in New Orleans compared to other Louisiana jurisdictions. In addition, Connick pointed to his routine use of the habitual felon law to enhance sentences. By the end of each of the four reelection campaigns, Connick convinced the voters that it was possible both to decline many cases and to run a tough prosecutor's office at the same time. . . .

## NOTES

1. *Prosecutorial "sentencing" through selection of charges.* Prosecutorial selection of charges can have an immense impact on sentencing decisions. Scholars concerned about the exercise of prosecutorial discretion often call for judicial regulation of prosecutors, but as the decision in People v. Stewart illustrates, courts have yet to hear their call, refusing to review prosecutorial decisions except in extraordinarily limited circumstances. See, e.g., James Vorenberg, Decent Restraint of Prosecutorial Power, 94 Harv. L. Rev. 1521 (1981). The experience described above in the New Orleans District Attorney's office under Harry Connick raises the question whether "decent restraint" might come from within prosecutor's offices rather than from external sources.

Prosecutorial control of sentences raises particular issues for guideline sentencing systems that claim to provide legislative or administrative guidance to sentencing judges but not to prosecutors. Guidelines or highly structured criminal codes may provide prosecutors with even greater authority to "specify" the effect at sentencing of the concessions offered in a plea bargain. When the price of a trial becomes this clear, few defendants will ever risk going to trial. In such systems, for all the apparent involvement of multiple actors and rule-based equality, to a considerable extent the true sentencer becomes the prosecutor. See George Fisher, Plea Bargaining's Triumph 205-230 (2003).

2. *Prosecutorial accountability to community priorities.* Should prosecutors also be able to make charging decisions on the basis of local needs? Should prosecutorial needs and resources then be allowed to affect sentences? An important illustration of these questions arises in the courts in southern California. The U.S. Attorney's office in San Diego receives far more immigration cases than it can prosecute. Of the 565,581 illegal aliens apprehended in fiscal year 1992, the U.S. Attorney prosecuted 245 felony immigration cases and another 5,000 misdemeanors. Because the San Diego district attorney, as a matter of policy, will not prosecute any cases related to the border, these cases must be prosecuted in federal court or not at all. William Braniff, Local Discretion, Prosecutorial Choices and the Sentencing Guidelines, 5 Fed. Sent'g Rep. 309 (1993). If every alien apprehended at the border were prosecuted for felony reentry (most are reentering), the size of the entire federal prison system would need to quadruple in a single year based on cases in this one district alone. Of course, the local U.S. Attorney's office has the resources to prosecute only a fraction of these cases — as the numbers indicate. How should a sentencing judge respond to the limited prosecutorial resources that sometimes force unpleasant choices on prosecutors? Should the judge enhance a sentence when she knows that an unusually large number of offenders are going unpunished? Or should the judge reduce the sentence out of concern for selective and

discriminatory treatment or ignore prosecutorial priorities entirely? See United States v. Banuelos-Rodriguez, 215 F.3d 969 (9th Cir. 2000) (rejecting sentencing disparities arising from different charging and plea bargaining policies of different U.S. Attorneys as a basis for departure from presumptive sentencing range).

3. *Prosecutorial punishment: critical yet hidden.* The regulation (or lack thereof) of prosecutorial discretion is one of the great puzzles of the criminal justice system. The puzzle is hidden beneath the surface whenever analysts study whether offenders *convicted* of the same offense are treated similarly: These analyses ignore whether similar offenders were not charged at all or were charged or convicted of a different offense. The impact of a prosecutor's sorting decisions may also be felt when prosecutorial office policy assigns a case to one of two or more possible screening or trial attorneys. Although these kinds of decisions are hard to study, any full assessment of sentencing or the equal treatment of individuals must address these preconviction sorting decisions.

## PROBLEM 2-5.   LOW-HANGING FRUIT

The purposes of prosecution take on additional levels of complexity when multiple jurisdictions might prosecute for the offense, whether those jurisdictions are the federal and one state government, or multiple state governments. In a speech to law enforcement officers on May 13, 2003, U.S. Attorney General John Ashcroft asserted that the Department of Justice was "taking gun-toting thugs off the streets." The next day, the Justice Department echoed his assertion with the following statement:

> This Justice Department has made the aggressive prosecution of those who violate our nation's gun laws a priority, and the 38% increase in prosecutions demonstrates we have been very busy taking criminals who misuse guns off the streets. Last year, the Department had the largest recorded increase in prosecuting and convicting defendants for violating our nation's gun laws. [We have] seen increases in prosecutions of many firearms crimes over the last year, including a 100% increase in gun trafficking prosecutions, [and] a 25% increase in obliterated serial number cases. . . .
> There should be no doubt: the Justice Department is working hard to enforce all federal firearms laws and lock up those who criminally misuse guns. We are also working in very close coordination with our state and local partners, who are also prosecuting gun crimes at higher rates. Our message is clear: gun crime means hard time. . . .

In the same week, a policy group seeking more federal prosecutions, Americans for Gun Safety, released a study with more uneven findings:

**Conclusion #1 — There is a vast enforcement gap between the level of federal gun crimes and the number of federal prosecutions.**

Over the past three fiscal years, prosecutors have filed 25,002 federal gun crime cases. During the same period:

- More than 330,000 guns used in violent gun crimes showed telltale signs of black market trafficking;
- 420,000 firearms were stolen;

- 450,000 individuals lied on the federal background check form used to determine eligibility for a gun;
- 93,000 gun crimes were committed by those under the age of 18; and
- Thousands of guns with obliterated serial numbers were recovered by law enforcement.

It is a violation of federal law to traffic in firearms, steal guns, lie on the background check form, sell to minors, and obliterate serial numbers. This translates into well over a million crimes where it is likely or certain that a federal law was broken. The 25,002 prosecutions represent a ratio of about 2 federal prosecutions for every 100 federal gun crimes.

**Conclusion #2 — Twenty of twenty-two of the major federal gun statutes are rarely enforced.**

Of the 25,002 federal firearms cases over the past three years, 85% of the prosecutions were for violations of just two federal statutes: the illegal possession of a firearm by a felon or other prohibited buyer, and the possession of a firearm while in the commission of a violent or drug-related federal crime. During both the Clinton and Bush Administrations, the other twenty statutes went virtually unenforced. For example, only 2% of prosecutions were for crimes associated with illegal gun trafficking and less than 1% for illegally selling a gun to a minor. . . . [T]he paucity of prosecutions under the other twenty statutes mean[s] that the federal government is doing little or nothing to break up the vast black market in illegal guns.

The Enforcement Gap: Federal Gun Laws Ignored (May 2003). Can you determine whether the federal government is prosecuting too much gun crime, too little gun crime, or the wrong gun crimes? Criminologist Alfred Blumstein described gun prosecutions as aimed at the "low-hanging fruit." See Eric Lichtblau, Justice Dept. Plans to Step Up Gun-Crime Prosecutions, N.Y. Times, May 14, 2003. Given the very large number of crimes that might be prosecuted under firearms statutes and that typically can be prosecuted by federal or state authorities, how can the federal government or a state government decide how best to allocate prosecutorial gun crime resources? What priority should gun crimes take compared with violent offenses against the person, drug crimes, stock fraud, environmental crimes, or immigration offenses? Should Congress authorize and fund new prosecutorial lines solely to prosecute gun crimes? In general, who should make the policy judgments about which crimes to prosecute, how should those policies be articulated, and what institution should see that the policies are consistently applied?

## D. APPELLATE COURT GUIDANCE

In indeterminate sentencing systems, appellate courts play almost no role, and appellate sentencing law before 1980 is almost impossible to find. Appellate courts typically have the simple task of determining whether the sentence of the trial court falls between the statutory minimum and maximum for the charged crime — a very limited notion of legality. In some states, statutes affirmatively limit appellate courts to this measly role. In states that do not explicitly constrain appellate sentencing authority, appellate judges avoid developing sentencing rules, perhaps because they believe that there is little "law" for them to apply. But this explanation is inadequate: in other areas with little law to apply, courts have exercised either interpretive or common law powers and developed rules to guide important discretionary decisions. Why have appellate courts shied away from developing a common law of sentencing?

In a more modern trend in the United States, especially in structured sentencing systems, legislatures provide for more searching appellate review of sentences. In such a system, the appellate court confirms both the legality and the "reasonableness" or "proportionality" of the sentence. An illustration comes from section 244.11 of the Minnesota statutes:

> An appeal to the court of appeals may be taken by the defendant or the state from any sentence imposed or stayed by the district court. . . . On an appeal pursuant to this section, the court may review the sentence imposed or stayed to determine whether the sentence is inconsistent with statutory requirements, unreasonable, inappropriate, excessive, unjustifiably disparate, or not warranted by the findings of fact issued by the district court. . . .

When appellate courts have broader authority to review sentences, they are more likely to come up with sentencing guidance as part of statutory interpretation (an entire legal regime can be created by allowing review for "reasonableness" of sentences) or as part of a common law of sentencing.

In addition to sentencing individuals, there are other ways that judges in general, and appellate judges in particular, might help set the sentencing rules. Judges might be called to testify before a legislature or sentencing commission, or a judge might serve on a sentencing commission. Judges might gather together formally (in a judicial conference) or informally (say, over lunch) and issue nonbinding sentencing recommendations.

Another approach, with its strongest illustration in England, finds appellate courts issuing "guideline judgments" that are announced in specific cases. English appellate courts have become one of the main institutions for developing sentencing policy, because those courts establish benchmark sentences and sentencing principles to operate within broad statutory ranges.

In R. v. Aramah, 76 Crim. App. R. 190 (1983), the Court of Appeal, Criminal Division, first set out a framework for sentencing in drug cases. Aramah was convicted of importing 59 kilograms of cannabis valued between £100,000 and £135,000. The defendant was a 50-year-old man of Nigerian origin who had two previous convictions for drug offenses, one involving the importation of 88 kilograms of cannabis in 1972, for which he had been sentenced to three years' imprisonment. He was sentenced in this most recent case to six years' imprisonment. After stating the facts, the court began its decision by making "some general observations about the level of sentences for drug offences, since our list, as will have been observed, is entirely composed of such crimes." The court then gave the following guidelines:

### Class "A" Drugs and Particularly Heroin and Morphine

It is common knowledge that these are the most dangerous of all the addictive drugs for a number of reasons: first of all, they are easy to handle.

Small parcels can be made up into huge numbers of doses. Secondly, the profits are so enormous that they attract the worst type of criminal. Many of such criminals may think, and indeed do think, that it is less dangerous and more profitable to traffic in heroin or morphine than it is to rob a bank. [The] heroin taker, once addicted[, may require] anything up to hundreds of pounds a week to buy enough heroin to satisfy the craving, depending upon the degree of addiction of the person involved. The [person might obtain these sums by] trafficking in the drug itself and disseminating accordingly its use still further.

[Lastly], and we have purposely left it for the last, because it is the most horrifying aspect, comes the degradation and suffering and not infrequently the death which the drug brings to the addict. It is not difficult to understand why in some parts of the world traffickers in heroin in any substantial quantity are sentenced to death and executed. Consequently anything which the courts of this country can do by way of deterrent sentences on those found guilty of crimes involving these class "A" drugs should be done.

[With large-scale importation of heroin, morphine, and so on], where the street value of the consignment is in the order of £100,000 or more, sentences of seven years and upwards are appropriate. There will be cases where the values are of the order of £1 million or more, in which case the offence should be visited by sentences of 12 to 14 years. It will seldom be that an importer of any appreciable amount of the drug will deserve less than four years.

This, however, is one area in which it is particularly important that offenders should be encouraged to give information to the police, and a confession of guilt, coupled with considerable assistance to the police, can properly be marked by a substantial reduction in what would otherwise be the proper sentence.

Next, supplying heroin, morphine, etc.: it goes without saying that the sentence will largely depend on the degree of involvement, the amount of trafficking and the value of the drug being handled. It is seldom that a sentence of less than three years will be justified and the nearer the source of supply the defendant is shown to be, the heavier will be the sentence. There may well be cases where sentences similar to those appropriate to large scale importers may be necessary. It is, however, unhappily all too seldom that those big fish amongst the suppliers get caught.

Possession of heroin, morphine, etc. (simple possession): it is at this level that the circumstances of the individual offender become of much greater importance. Indeed the possible variety of considerations is so wide, including often those of a medical nature, that we feel it impossible to lay down any practical guidelines. On the other hand the maximum penalty for simple possession of class "A" drugs is seven years' imprisonment and/or a fine, and there will be very many cases where deprivation of liberty is both proper and expedient.

### Class "B" Drugs, Particularly Cannabis

[Importation] of very small amounts [of cannabis] for personal use can be dealt with as if it were simple possession, with which we will deal later. Otherwise importation of amounts up to about 20 kilograms of herbal cannabis, or the equivalent in cannabis resin or cannabis oil, will, save in the most exceptional cases, attract sentences of between 18 months and three years, with the lowest ranges reserved for pleas of guilty in cases where there has been small profit to the offender. The good character of the courier (as he usually is) is of less importance than the good character of the defendant in other cases. The reason for this is, it is well known that the large scale operator looks for couriers of good character and for people of a sort which is likely to exercise the sympathy of the court if they are detected and arrested. . . . There are few, if any, occasions when anything other than an immediate custodial sentence is proper in this type of importation.

Medium quantities over 20 kilograms will attract sentences of three to six years' imprisonment, depending upon the amount involved, and all the other circumstances of the case. Large scale or wholesale importation of massive quantities will justify sentences in the region of 10 years' imprisonment for those playing other than a subordinate role.

Supply of cannabis: here again the supply of massive quantities will justify sentences in the region of 10 years for those playing anything more than a subordinate role. Otherwise the bracket should be between one to four years' imprisonment, depending upon the scale of the operation. Supplying a number of small sellers — wholesaling if you like — comes at the top of the bracket. At the lower end will be the retailer of a small amount to a consumer. Where there is no commercial motive (for example, where cannabis is supplied at a party), the offence may well be serious enough to justify a custodial sentence.

Possession of cannabis: when only small amounts are involved being for personal use, the offence can often be met by a fine. If the history shows, however, a persisting flouting of the law, imprisonment may become necessary.

The court then applied its own guidelines to the case before it and upheld the six-year sentence, finding that there was a "very large quantity of cannabis" and no "mitigating feature," including the absence of a plea of guilty, and prior convictions for drug offenses.

Four years later, the same court reconsidered its *Aramah* guidelines in light of subsequent developments.

## R. v. Edward Bilinski
### 86 Crim. App. R. 146 (1987)

THE LORD CHIEF JUSTICE

On February 20, 1987 in the Crown Court at Chelmsford the appellant pleaded guilty to importing 3.036 kilograms of heroin into the United Kingdom. He was sentenced to 12 years' imprisonment. Against that sentence he now appeals by leave of the single judge.

The material facts are as follows. On November 7, 1986 the M.V. *Gdansk II* was searched at Tilbury by Customs officers. They discovered three packages containing white powder subsequently found to be heroin hidden behind a wiring duct 30 feet above the deck. Suspicion fell on the appellant who was a senior member of the crew. He was questioned in Polish through an interpreter. He denied all knowledge of the packages. However, his fingerprints were found on the sticky side of adhesive tape binding the packages. At first he said that he did not know "by what miracle" his prints had been placed there. The following day on further questioning, however, he admitted that he was responsible for the packages being on board. He had been approached by two Polish men at a time when his finances were at a low ebb. They had suggested he should assist them in transporting drugs from Hamburg to Sydney via Tilbury. He was to be paid the equivalent of some £3,500 in U.S. dollars. The size of the reward, he said, clouded his judgment. He was given the packages in Hamburg. According to his story, he was told that the drugs were cannabis. When they were handed to him the packages were malleable and wrapped in transparent plastic. He could see a white powder inside. He had later wrapped and secured them in further plastic material (hence the fingerprints) in order to protect the contents from the damp, because he had been told to be careful to prevent them from coming to any harm. He said he did not recognize the powder as heroin; he had never seen heroin before; the two men had told him the drug had come from the Far East, but even then he did not realize it might be heroin. Amongst other items found in the appellant's cabin was a book entitled "Heroina," which we are told is the Polish for heroin. Surprisingly this volume had come from the ship's library.

The heroin was of very high purity—90 per cent. Its street value in this country was in the region of £600,000. The mitigation was in essence based on four matters:

1. The appellant thought he was smuggling cannabis not heroin.
2. He had pleaded guilty and given what assistance he could to the authorities in the shape of the names of his suppliers.
3. He was only a courier whose reward as it transpires was to be a minute fraction of the value of the drugs.
4. He was of hitherto good character.

Steyn J., in the course of passing sentence, said this: . . . "It is said that you did not know that it was heroin. I regard that (and I make that clear) as irrelevant. . . . If it had been relevant, I would have directed an issue to be tried on it, but I find that it is irrelevant." [Defense counsel] makes two submissions to this Court: (1) That the judge was in error in regarding the appellant's belief as to the nature of the drug as irrelevant so far as sentence was concerned. (2) That the sentence of 12 years was in any event too long. . . .

Is it relevant? On the one hand is the argument that anyone who chooses to engage in smuggling prohibited drugs must accept the risk that the drug is of a kind different from that which he believes or has been told it is. . . . On the other hand, submits [defense counsel], if a defendant genuinely has been misled as to the type of drug, then in light of the fact that the maximum sentence for importing heroin is imprisonment for life as against the 12 years maximum for importation of cannabis, it would be unjust not to allow some mitigation at least of the punishment. . . .

We are of the view that the defendant's belief in these circumstances is relevant to punishment and that the man who believes he is importing cannabis is indeed less culpable than he who knows it to be heroin. . . . To what extent the punishment should be mitigated by this factor will obviously depend upon all the circumstances, amongst them being the degree of care exercised by the defendant.

How should the issue be determined? In some cases no doubt it will be necessary for the judge to hear evidence. . . . If that procedure had been adopted in the present case . . . the appellant would probably have been the only witness, apart perhaps from someone to speak as to the street value of these packages had they contained cannabis rather than heroin. It is difficult to see what the appellant could have said other than that which he had already stated in his interviews with the Customs officers. If so, it is scarcely likely that the judge would have been in any doubt but that the appellant must have known that the substance was heroin. . . . Where the defendant's story is manifestly false the judge is entitled to reject it out of hand without hearing evidence. Whether that is so or not, we take the view that the exercise of only a small degree of curiosity, enquiry or care would have revealed the true nature of the drug in this case and that accordingly the mitigating effect of the belief, if held, was small.

The next question is what the proper sentence should be for the carrier/importer of this quantity of 90 per cent pure heroin. The guidelines in *Aramah* . . . must be updated to take account of the fact that the maximum sentence for the importation of Class A drugs has now been increased by the Controlled Drugs (Penalties) Act 1985, from 14 years to life imprisonment. It was suggested in *Aramah* that where the street value of the consignment is in the order of £100,000 or more, sentences of seven years and upwards are appropriate, and that 12 to 14 years' imprisonment is appropriate where the value of the drugs involved is £1 million or more. The former figure should now be increased to 10 years and upwards and the latter to 14 years and upwards.

Thus a term of 12 years or thereabouts would have been appropriate for this level of importation in the absence of any mitigating features. There are, however, these matters to be taken into account in mitigation of the penalty. First, the plea of guilty. Secondly, the fact that the appellant gave all the help which he could to the authorities by naming his suppliers and, thirdly, for what it is worth, the possibility (in the absence of a finding to the contrary by the judge) that the appellant may have believed the drugs to be cannabis. We think that in the light of those factors, and taking into account all the circumstances of the case a term of 8 years' imprisonment would have been appropriate. . . .

### NOTES

1. *Appellate court guideline sentencing rules.*   The English experiment with appellate guideline judgments has been under way for over 30 years. The guideline judgments have not kept Parliament from enacting additional sentencing legislation, including harsher punishments for drug offenses. See Aaron Rappaport, Sentencing in England: The Rise of Populist Punishment, 10 Fed. Sent'g Rep. 247 (1998). What sorts of reasons might persuade an appellate court to change its own sentencing guidelines? Based on the drug guidelines in *Aramah* as modified by *Bilinski*, what advantages do you think appellate judges have over legislators in developing sentencing rules? Over sentencing experts such as sentencing commission members? Over trial judges?

In R. v. Barrick, 81 Crim. App. R. 78 (1985), the English Court of Appeal set out guidelines for fraud cases. The defendant in *Barrick* was convicted on four counts of false accounting, four counts of obtaining by deception, and two counts of theft. He was sentenced to two years' imprisonment on each count, to run concurrently. The defendant handled the accounting for a small finance company, and in that capacity he created imaginary borrowers and stole around £9,000. The court used the case as "an opportunity to make some observations upon the proper sentence to be passed in respect of certain types of theft and fraud":

> The type of case with which we are concerned is where a person in a position of trust, for example, an accountant, solicitor, bank employee or postman, has

used that privileged and trusted position to defraud his partners or clients or employers or the general public of sizeable sums of money. He will usually, as in this case, be a person of hitherto impeccable character. It is practically certain, again as in this case, that he will never offend again. . . . It was not long ago that this type of offender might expect to receive a term of imprisonment of three or four years, and indeed a great deal more if the sums involved were substantial. More recently, however, the sentencing climate in this area has changed. . . .

In *Jacob* (1981), . . . a solicitor who had over a period of some three years stolen money from clients and his partners to the tune of between £40,000 and £57,000 had his sentence of four years' imprisonment reduced by this Court to eighteen months. . . . On the other hand postmen do not seem to have fared quite so well. In *Eagleton* (1982), a postman had been sentenced to five years' imprisonment for three offences of theft of packets in transit by mail with 80 offences taken into consideration. A sentence of thirty months' imprisonment was substituted. *Briggs* (1982) was another postman case. The defendant had stolen from the mail goods worth about £1,300, most of which were recovered. On appeal a term of two years' imprisonment was substituted for the three years which had been imposed by the trial judge. We can see no proper basis for distinguishing between cases of this kind simply on the basis of the defendant's occupation. . . .

It is, we appreciate, dangerous to generalize where the circumstances of the offender and the offence may vary so widely from case to case. In the hope that they may be helpful to sentencers generally, and may lead to a little more uniformity, we make the following suggestions.

In general a term of immediate imprisonment is inevitable, save in very exceptional circumstances or where the amount of money obtained is small. Despite the great punishment that offenders of this sort bring upon themselves, the Court should nevertheless pass a sufficiently substantial term of imprisonment to mark publicly the gravity of the offence. The sum involved is obviously not the only factor to be considered, but it may in many cases provide a useful guide. Where the amounts involved cannot be described as small but are less than £10,000 or thereabouts, terms of imprisonment ranging from the very short up to about eighteen months are appropriate. Cases involving sums of between about £10,000 and £50,000 will merit a term of about two to three years' imprisonment. Where greater sums are involved, for example those over £100,000, then a term of three and a half years to four and a half years would be justified. . . .

The following are some of the matters to which the Court will no doubt wish to pay regard in determining what the proper level of sentence should be: (i) the quality and degree of trust reposed in the offender including his rank; (ii) the period over which the fraud or the thefts have been perpetrated; (iii) the use to which the money or property dishonestly taken was put; (iv) the effect upon the victim; (v) the impact of the offences on the public and public confidence; (vi) the effect on fellow-employees or partners; (vii) the effect on the offender himself; (viii) his own history; (ix) those matters of mitigation special to himself such as illness; being placed under great strain by excessive responsibility or the like; where, as sometimes happens, there has been a long delay, say over two years, between his being confronted with his dishonesty by his professional body or the police and the start of his trial; finally, any help given by him to the police.

The court found that Barrick had committed "mean offences" from people of modest means and had given "no help to the police," so the court upheld the two-year sentence. See also R. v. Billam, 8 Crim. App. R. (S.) 48 (1986) (guidelines for sexual assault); D. A. Thomas, Sentencing Sex Offenders—English Law, 10 Fed. Sent'g Rep. 74 (1997) (reviewing interaction of legislation and English guideline decisions); Andrew Ashworth, Three

Techniques for Reducing Sentencing Disparity, in Principled Sentencing 282 (Andrew von Hirsch and Andrew Ashworth eds., 1992).

2. *Judges and rule making in the United States.*   Could appellate courts make rules for sentencing in the United States? Or would this violate the separation of powers, because rule making would be either a legislative or executive function? See State v. Wentz, 805 P.2d 962 (Alaska 1991) (limiting use of judicially created "benchmark" sentence for assault). Appellate courts play a more substantial role in modern U.S. structured sentencing systems, such as the federal and many state guideline systems. Sentencing issues generate lots of work for appellate courts. In the federal system in 2001, 51% of the appeals in criminal cases raised sentencing issues alone, and another 22% challenged the sentence along with the conviction.

Given that judges see so many individual cases and develop such expertise in sentencing, shouldn't judges develop sentencing rules rather than just apply rules that others create? Statutes establishing sentencing commissions often reserve some commission posts for judges. Are there other ways to involve judges in the creation of general sentencing rules? Under the federal guidelines and in many structured state systems, courts that sentence outside the recommended range must explain the decision. The sentencing commission collects data on these sentences and in theory uses the feedback to amend the sentencing rules. We consider the judicial power to depart from sentencing guidelines more thoroughly in Chapter 3.

3. *Regional appellate tribunals.*   National criminal courts traditionally handle criminal trials and sentencing, even if the offenses involve foreign nationals who committed crimes on their territory. While criminal jurisdiction is primarily territorial (the territoriality principle), countries also have the right to try their nationals who commit crimes abroad (the nationality principle), offenders who commit crimes against their territory or political and judicial structure (the protective principle), and offenders who run afoul of universal prohibitions (the universality principle). Some courts have also exercised jurisdiction if the victim was one of its nationals (the passive personality principle). As regional human rights organizations evolved in Europe and the Americas, regional tribunals, such as the European Court of Human Rights (ECHR) and the Inter-American Court of Human Rights, acquired limited appellate jurisdiction over criminal cases tried in the courts of the member nations.

Sentencing appeals have come to the ECHR under Article 3 of the European Convention on Human Rights, which protects individuals against inhuman or degrading treatment or punishment, and Article 5, which guarantees the right to liberty and security of persons. The ECHR has decided what practices constitute torture and whether discretionary decisions as to the release of life prisoners must be subject to judicial control.

4. *The ICTR and the ICTY.*   In the wake of the conflicts in Yugoslavia and Rwanda, the U.N. Security Council established two ad hoc tribunals in 1993 and 1994, respectively: the International Criminal Tribunal for Yugoslavia (ICTY), with its seat in The Hague, Netherlands, and the International Criminal Tribunal for Rwanda (ICTR), located in Arusha, Tanzania. Both courts have jurisdiction over genocide, crimes against humanity, war crimes, and select breaches of

the Geneva Conventions. Their jurisdiction is complementary to that of national courts, but they have the primary right to prosecute and try war criminals. Those convicted in the ICTR include Jean Kambanda, the prime minister of Rwanda during the genocide, who was the first head of government to be indicted and subsequently convicted for genocide. See www.un.org/icty or www.ictr.org.

The maximum sentence either tribunal can hand down is life imprisonment, with the sentence to be served in countries that have entered into agreements with the ad hoc tribunals. The jurisprudence developed by the two tribunals will shape the definition and prosecution of international crimes and has already affected the decision making of national courts. See Mark Drumbl & Kenneth S. Gallant, Sentencing Policies and Practices in the International Criminal Tribunals, 15 Fed. Sent'g Rep. 140 (2002).

5. *Sentencing in the International Criminal Court.* Even though attempts were made immediately after World War II to establish an international criminal tribunal, it took more than 50 years to become a reality. The International Criminal Court (ICC) came into existence in 2002 under the Statute of Rome and opened for business in 2003. The United States withdrew its signature in May 2002, because of concerns about the treaty's applicability to its military personnel, and has since negotiated a number of bilateral treaties intended to shield U.S. nationals from prosecution by the ICC.

The ICC has jurisdiction over genocide, crimes against humanity, war crimes, and the yet undefined crime of aggression. The ICC's jurisdiction complements that of national courts, with trials occurring only if national courts are unwilling or unable to prosecute suspects. The maximum sentence is a life term "when justified by the extreme gravity of the crime and the individual circumstances of the convicted person," with a 30-year maximum for all other offenders (Art. 77, Statute of Rome). A list of aggravating and mitigating circumstances is set out in the Rules of Procedure and Evidence. In addition to imprisonment, the ICC may order a fine, restitution, and forfeiture of property and proceeds received from the crime committed. See www.icc-cpi.int.

# =3=
## ‖ *Regulating Discretion* ‖

Prior to a conviction, discretion plays a key role in the criminal justice system. Victims and witnesses exercise discretion in reporting crimes, police exercise discretion on the street and in investigations, and prosecutors exercise discretion in charging (or declining to charge), plea bargaining, and at trial. While all of these discretions are controversial, it is the sentencing discretion of judges and parole commissions that has been the greatest force for systematic reform.

Sentencing discretion can be portrayed in both positive and negative terms. Because, in the words of the Supreme Court, "every convicted person [is] an individual and every case [is] a unique study in human failings," Koon v. United States, 518 U.S. 81, 113 (1996), it has long been thought essential that sentencers possess some discretion to fine-tune punishments to fit the specific circumstances of particular cases. Yet discretion exercised across a set of cases can result in sentencing disparity: different judges and juries applying the same law in the same jurisdiction on the same facts may reach substantially different sentencing judgments. And sentencing disparity may reflect unwarranted discrimination if irrelevant or illegitimate factors influence the outcomes.

Sentencing discretion can in theory be regulated by many different institutions. This chapter presents two case studies of efforts to regulate sentencing discretion. First is the emergence of guideline systems to structure the exercise of noncapital sentencing discretion. Second is the development of constitutional rules to structure the exercise of capital sentencing discretion.

# A.   SENTENCING GUIDELINE STRUCTURES: REGULATING DISCRETION THROUGH ADMINISTRATIVE RULES

## 1.   Origins and Foundation

Beginning in the late nineteenth and continuing through most of the twentieth century, a highly discretionary, rehabilitative "medical" model dominated criminal sentencing. Trial judges in federal and state systems had nearly unfettered discretion to impose on defendants any sentence selected from wide statutory ranges. Such broad judicial discretion — magnified by similar discretion of parole officials concerning prison release dates—was viewed as necessary to ensure that sentences were tailored to the rehabilitative prospects and progress of each offender.

By the 1970s criminal justice researchers and scholars had become concerned about the unpredictable and widely disparate sentences that indeterminate sentencing systems produced. Empirical and anecdotal evidence revealed that sentencing judges' discretionary choices created substantial and undue differences in both the lengths and types of sentences meted out to similar defendants. Even more worrisome, some studies found that purportedly irrelevant personal factors such as an offender's race, gender, or socioeconomic status were affecting sentencing outcomes.

Troubled by the disparity and discrimination resulting from highly discretionary sentencing practices—and fueled by concerns over increasing crime rates and powerful criticisms from multiple philosophical perspectives of the entire rehabilitative model of punishment and corrections—many criminal justice experts proposed reforms to bring greater consistency and certainty to the sentencing enterprise. Perhaps the most powerful and influential criticism of then prevailing sentencing practices was delivered by Marvin Frankel, who drew on his personal experiences as a federal district judge in New York to author one of the most influential books in American criminal justice.

## Criminal Sentences: Law Without Order, Marvin E. Frankel
### Pages 3-10, 16-19, 39-41, 47, 89-123 (1973)

We boast that ours is a "government of laws, not of men." We do not mean . . . that men make no difference in the administration of law. Among the basic things we do mean is that all of us, governors and governed alike, are or ought to be bound by laws of general and equal application. We mean, too, that in a just legal order, the laws should be knowable and intelligible so that, to the fullest extent possible, a person meaning to obey the law may know his obligations and predict within decent limits the legal consequences of his conduct. . . .

As to the penalty that may be imposed, our laws characteristically leave to the sentencing judge a range of choice that should be unthinkable in a "government of laws, not of men." . . . The almost wholly unchecked and sweeping powers we give to judges in the fashioning of sentences are terrifying and intolerable for a society that professes devotion to the rule of law.

For examples of such unbounded "discretion" [consider that] the federal kidnapping law authorizes "imprisonment for any term of years or for life." To take some of our most common federal crimes — driving a stolen car across state lines may result in a term of "not more than five years," robbing a federally insured bank "not more than twenty-five years." [Federal] trial judges, answerable only to their varieties of consciences, may and do send people to prison for terms that may vary in any given case from none at all up to five, ten, thirty, or more years. . . .

The result . . . is a wild array of sentencing judgments without any semblance of the consistency demanded by the ideal of equal justice. . . . The broad statutory ranges might approach a degree of ordered rationality if there were prescribed any standards for locating a particular case within any range. But neither our federal law nor that of any state I know contains meaningful criteria for this purpose. [Our] legislators have not done the most rudimentary job of enacting meaningful sentencing "laws" when they have neglected even to sketch democratically determined statements of basic purpose. Left at large, wandering in deserts of uncharted discretion, the judges suit their own value systems insofar as they think about the problem at all. . . .

The prevalent thesis of the last hundred years or so has been that the treatment of criminals must be "individualized." [But] we ought to recall that individualized justice is prima facie at war with such concepts, at least as fundamental, as equality, objectivity, and consistency in the law. It is not self-evident that the flesh-and-blood judge coming (say) from among the white middle classes will inevitably achieve admirable results when he individualizes the narcotics sentences of the suburban college youth and the street-wise ghetto hustler.

[Judges] have expressed misgivings — about their own and (perhaps more strongly) about their colleagues' handling of [sentencing] powers so huge and so undefined over the lives of their fellow men. . . . Everyone connected with this grim business has his own favorite atrocity stories. . . . One story concerns a casual anecdote over cocktails in a rare conversation among judges touching the subject of sentencing. Judge *X*, to designate him in a lawyerlike way, told of a defendant for whom the judge, after reading the presentence report, had decided tentatively upon a sentence of four years' imprisonment. At the sentencing hearing in the courtroom, after hearing counsel, Judge *X* invited the defendant to exercise his right to address the court in his own behalf. The defendant [read] from a sheaf of papers . . . excoriating the judge, the "kangaroo court" in which he'd been tried, and the legal establishment in general. Completing the story, Judge *X* said, "I listened without interrupting. Finally, when he said he was through, I simply gave the son of a bitch five years instead of the four." None of the three judges listening to that (including me) tendered a whisper of dissent, let alone a scream of outrage. But think about it. . . . A year in prison for speaking disrespectfully to a judge. . . . Would we tolerate an act of Congress penalizing such an outburst by a year in prison? The question, however rhetorical, misses one truly exquisite note of agony: that the wretch sentenced by Judge *X* never knew, because he was never told, how the fifth year of his sentence came to be added. . . .

## WALLS OF SILENCE

[The] swift ukase, without explanation, is the tyrant's way. The despot is not bound by rules. He need not justify or account for what he does. Criminal sentences, as our judges commonly pronounce them, are in these vital respects tyrannical. Largely unfettered by limiting standards, and thus having neither occasion nor meaningful terms for explaining, the judge usually supplies nothing in the way of a coherent and rational judgment when he informs the defendant of his fate.

[The] parties (especially the loser) are, on deep principles, not merely entitled to a decision; they are entitled to an explanation. . . . The duty to give an account of the decision is to promote thought by the decider, to compel him to cover the relevant points, to help him eschew irrelevancies — and, finally, to make him show that these necessities have been served. The requirement of reasons expressly stated is not a guarantee of fairness. The judge or other official may give good reasons while he acts upon outrageous ones. However, given decision-makers who are both tolerably honest and normally fallible, the requirement of stated reasons is a powerful safeguard against rash and arbitrary decisions. Knowing this to be so, we apply it to affairs of lesser consequence, yet we place no burden of explanation upon the judge who decides that the defendant before him must be locked up for ten years rather than five or one or none. . . .

Improvements in communications are less perceptible — they are practically nonexistent — when we move on to the parole stage. [Parole] boards, like judges and prison officials, for the most part neglect altogether to supply information or explanations. . . . Parole boards don't explain. They confer miracles or they refuse. . . . The general fact [is] that most parole boards, subject to no precise rules of any kind, decree secretly and silently how tens and hundreds of thousands of convict-years shall be passed.

## INDETERMINATE SENTENCES

The case for the indeterminate sentence rests, initially, upon a laudable concern for each unique individual, coupled with a frequently baseless assumption that we are able effectively to understand and uniquely to "treat" the individual. The offender is "sick," runs the humane thought, and/or dangerous. He needs to be helped and "cured." Nobody, certainly not the sentencing judge, can know when he will be well and no more dangerous than the masses of us who are lucky enough not to have been convicted. Hence, those charged with "treatment" must be left to decide the time for release.

This "rehabilitative ideal" [is based on] the fallacious — or, at least, far too broad — assumption that criminals are "sick" in some way that calls for "treatment." . . . We sentence many people every day who are not "sick" in any identifiable respect and are certainly not candidates for any form of therapy or "rehabilitation" known thus far. Many convicted criminals . . . are not driven by, or "acting out," neurotic or psychotic impulses. Instead, they have coldly and deliberately figured the odds, risked punishment for rewards large enough (in their view) to justify the risk, but then had the misfortune to be caught. It seems likely that many of those in organized crime fall within this category. The same is true for large numbers (though by no means all) of those who scheme to defraud, to evade taxes, to counterfeit the currency, or to commit other varieties of acquisitive crime. . . .

The apostles of rehabilitation and indeterminate sentences posit "sickness" without identifying its character and then urge "treatment" no better defined or specified. The absence of treatment or facilities is by itself a fatal defect [as] there is no justification for a regime of rehabilitation through indeterminate sentences unless we have some substantial hope or prospect of rehabilitating. Our subject is, after all, the confinement of people for long and uncertain periods of time. It is an evil to lock people up. There may be compensating goods that warrant it. But a mythical goal of rehabilitation is no good at all. . . .

Believing, then, that there is need for broad and drastic reform of the law, I [offer these] legislative proposals. . . . To begin at the elementary beginning, we have an almost entire absence in the United States of legislative determinations — of "law" — governing the basic questions as to the purposes and justifications of criminal sanctions. Without binding guides on such questions, it is inevitable that individual sentencers will strike out on a multiplicity of courses chosen by each decision-maker for himself. The result is chaos. . . .

Along with the declaration of sentencing purposes, the legislature would — certainly it should — provide that the judge (or sentencing tribunal) must state which among the allowable purposes were the supposed bases for each particular sentence. The simple requirement would compel the judge to think connectedly about his reasons and to justify explicitly decisions now taken on unarticulated hunches. . . . And it would open the way for intelligent scrutiny on appeal since an appellate court can function usefully only when it knows the grounds of the decision brought to it for review. . . .

### TOWARD CODIFIED WEIGHTS AND MEASURES

[We allow the sentencing judge] not merely to "weigh" the various elements that go into a sentence [but also] leave to his unfettered (and usually unspoken) preferences the determination as to what factors ought to be considered at all, and in what direction. . . . We do not allow each judge to make up the law for himself on other questions. We should not allow it with respect to sentencing. . . .

Beyond codifying the numerous factors affecting the length or severity of sentences, an acceptable code of penal law should, in my judgment, prescribe guidelines for the application and assessment of these factors. While it may seem dry, technical, unromantic, and "mechanical," I have in mind the creation eventually of a detailed chart or calculus — to be used (1) by the sentencing judge in weighing the many elements that go into the sentence; (2) by lawyers, probation officers, and others undertaking to persuade or enlighten the judge; and (3) by appellate courts in reviewing what the judge has done.

[The sentencing judge] will presumably consider a host of factors in the case: the relative seriousness of the particular offense — the degree of danger threatened, cruelty, premeditation; the prior record of the defendant;

situational factors — health, family disturbance, drug use; the defendant's work history, skills, potential; etc. In the existing mode of handling the sentence, the judge is under no pressure — and is without guidelines — toward systematic, exhaustive, detailed appraisal of such things one by one. He probably does not list them even for himself. He certainly does not record or announce the analysis. Probably, in most cases, he broods in a diffuse way toward a hunch that becomes a sentence. . . .

The partial remedy I propose is a kind of detailed profile or checklist of factors that would include, wherever possible, some form of numerical or other objective grading. Still being crude and cursory, I suggest that "gravity of offense" could be graded along a scale from, perhaps, 1 to 5. Other factors could be handled in the same way. The overall result might be a score — or, possibly, an individual profile of sentencing elements — that would make it feasible to follow the sentencer's estimates, criticize them, and compare the sentence in the given case with others.

The justification for such a technique does not require that we accept delusions of precision. Admittedly, "gravity of offense" does not lend itself to weighing with the mechanical simplicity of grocery or jewelers' scales. But we know from sufficiently analogous fields that numerical statements may serve, for obviously non-quantifiable subjects, as useful implements for clarification of thought, comparisons, and criticism. . . . The physician who speaks of a grade-three heart murmur may not be reporting a measurement as precise as the number of feet in a yard. But he says a meaningful thing that informs and guides others professionally trained. . . . It is not necessary, or desirable, to imagine that sentencing can be completely computerized. . . .

## A COMMISSION ON SENTENCING

Using the jargon of our time, entirely apt in this instance, there are huge needs for organized research and development in the field of sentencing. . . . There must be a commitment to change, to application of the learning as it is acquired. . . . Since we deal with the law, the normal agency of change is, increasingly, the legislature. But the subject of sentencing is not steadily exhilarating to elected officials. There are no powerful lobbies of prisoners, jailers, or, indeed, judges, to goad and reward. Thus, accounting in good part for our plight, legislative action tends to be sporadic and impassioned, responding in haste to momentary crises, lapsing then into the accustomed state of inattention. . . .

These thoughts . . . lead to my proposed "Commission on Sentencing" [which] would be a permanent agency responsible for (1) the study of sentencing, corrections, and parole; (2) the formulation of laws and rules to which the studies pointed; and (3) *the actual enactment of rules*, subject to traditional checks by Congress and the courts. . . . The commission would require prestige and credibility. It would be necessary to find for it people of stature, competence, devotion, and eloquence. The kinds of people . . . could include lawyers, judges, penologists, and criminologists. They should also include sociologists, psychologists, business people, artists, and, lastly for emphasis, former or present prison inmates.

[The] commission would have the function of actually enacting rules—i.e., making law. This suggestion would presumably generate controversy; legislators do not (and should not) lightly delegate their authority. Nevertheless, there is both precedent and good reason for delegating in this instance. As I have said, the subjects of sentencing, corrections, and parole are going to need ongoing study and an indefinite course of revision. Sweeping changes of policy, touching basic principles and institutions, will naturally remain for the legislature to determine from time to time. But relative details, numerous and cumulatively important, neither require nor are likely to receive from the legislature the necessary measure of steady attention. Thinking along such lines, Congress has delegated in a variety of fields—e.g., securities, transportation, communications—rulemaking powers with substantial day-to-day impact upon the affected areas. The suggestion here contemplates an analogous arrangement. . . .

The uses of a commission, if one is created, will warrant volumes of debate and analysis. For this moment and this writer, the main thing is to plead for an instrumentality, whatever its name or detailed form, to marshal full-time wisdom and power against the ignorance and the barbarities that characterize sentencing for crimes today. . . .

### NOTES

1. *Rise and fall of the rehabilitative ideal.*   As highlighted by Judge Frankel, the grant of broad discretion to sentencing judges and parole officials was linked to a rehabilitative "medical" model of sentencing and corrections in which authority to individualize punishments seemed essential. This model of punishment emerged in the United States from the early development of the modern penitentiary in the late 1800s. See David Rothman, Perfecting the Prison, in The Oxford History of the Prison 111-129 (Norval Morris & David Rothman eds., 1995). The rehabilitative model grew in prominence throughout the 1900s, finding expression in state statutes and model codes, Supreme Court opinions, and major governmental reports. See, e.g., Model Penal Code §6.10 ("An offender sentenced to an indefinite term of imprisonment in excess of one year . . . shall be released conditionally on parole at or before the expiration of the maximum of such term."); §7.04 ("The Court may sentence a person who has been convicted of a misdemeanor or petty misdemeanor to an extended term of imprisonment if it finds [that the defendant] is a chronic alcoholic, narcotic addict, prostitute or person of abnormal mental condition who requires rehabilitative treatment for a substantial period of time.")

President's Commission on Law Enforcement and Administration of Justice, The Challenge of Crime in a Free Society 159-166, 171-177 (1967) (discussing the new "reform model" in which an offender is a "patient" and the system follows "a new maxim—'Let the treatment fit the needs of the individual offender'").

Perhaps the apotheosis of the indeterminate model came in 1949, in the U.S. Supreme Court decision in Williams v. New York, 337 U.S. 241 (1949). Williams was convicted of murder and a jury unanimously recommended life imprisonment. The trial judge imposed a death sentence, relying on information obtained through the court's "Probation Department, and through other sources." This information was not subject to challenge by the defendant and would not have been admissible at trial. Justice Black, writing for the court, affirmed the death sentence. Justice Black summarized the basis for the judge's decision:

> He narrated the shocking details of the crime as shown by the trial evidence, expressing his own complete belief in appellant's guilt. He stated that the pre-sentence investigation revealed many material facts concerning appellant's background which, though relevant to the question of punishment, could not properly have been brought to the attention of the jury in its consideration of the question of guilt. He referred to the experience appellant "had had on thirty other burglaries in and about the same vicinity" where the murder had been committed. The appellant had not been convicted of these burglaries, although the judge had information that he had confessed to some and had been identified as the perpetrator of some of the others. The judge also referred to certain activities of appellant as shown by the probation report that indicated appellant possessed "a morbid sexuality," and classified him as a "menace to society." The accuracy of the statements made by the judge as to appellant's background and past practices were not challenged by appellant or his counsel, nor was the judge asked to disregard any of them or to afford appellant a chance to refute or discredit any of them by cross-examination or otherwise.

In the face of a challenge that the New York law allowing such post-conviction evidence to be considered in sentencing, Justice Black wrote:

> But both before and since the American colonies became a nation, courts in this country and in England practiced a policy under which a sentencing judge could exercise a wide discretion in the sources and types of evidence used to assist him in determining the kind the extent of punishment to be imposed within limits fixed by law. . . .
> A sentencing judge, however, is not confined to the narrow issue of guilt. His task, within fixed statutory or constitutional limits, is to determine the type and extent of punishment after the issue of guilt has been determined. Highly relevant — if not essential — to his selection of an appropriate sentence is the possession of the fullest information possible concerning the defendant's life and characteristics. And modern concepts individualizing punishment have made it all the more necessary that a sentencing judge not be denied an oppor-tunity to obtain pertinent information by a requirement of rigid adherence to restrictive rules of evidence properly applicable to the trial.
> Undoubtedly, the New York statutes emphasize a prevalent modern phi-losophy of penology that the punishment should fit the offender, and not merely the crime. The belief no longer prevails that every offense in a like legal category calls for an identical punishment without regard to the past life and habits of a particular offender. This whole country has traveled far from the period in which the death sentence was an automatic and commonplace result of convictions — even for offenses today deemed triv-ial. . . . Indeterminate sentences the ultimate termination of which are sometimes decided by nonjudicial agencies have, to a large extent, taken the place of the old rigidly fixed punishments. The practice of probation which relies heavily on nonjudicial implementation has been accepted as a wise policy. . . . Retribution is no longer the dominant objective of the criminal law. Reformation and rehabilitation of offenders have become important goals of criminal jurisprudence. . . .
> [We] do not think the Federal Constitution restricts the view of the sentencing judge to the information received in open court. The due process

clause should not be treated as a device for freezing the evidential procedure of sentencing in the mold of trial procedure. So to treat the due process clause would hinder, if not preclude, all courts — state and federal — from making progressive efforts to improve the administration of criminal justice.

While "in general, these modern changes have not resulted in making the lot of offenders harder," and while probation workers were "trained to . . . aid . . . offenders," for Williams the willingness to allow information without adversarial testing or other limitations justified the "harder" outcome of death.

Judge Frankel questioned both the effectiveness and the appropriateness of a purely rehabilitative model of corrections within his broader criticisms of discretionary sentencing practices. Writing around the same time, many other commentators across the political spectrum — liberals stressing concerns about inequitable and uncertain treatment of offenders, and conservatives highlighting increased crime rates and the apparent ineffectiveness of rehabilitative efforts — developed similar criticisms about indeterminate sentencing and the "rehabilitative ideal." See American Friends Service Committee, Struggle for Justice (1971); James Q. Wilson, Thinking About Crime (1975); Francis A. Allen, The Decline of the Rehabilitative Ideal 3-20 (1981) (discussing the "dominance" of the rehabilitative ideal through the late 1960s and the subsequent "wide and precipitous decline of penal rehabilitationism" as a foundational theory for the criminal justice system); Norval Morris, The Future of Imprisonment (1974).

2. *Evidence of disparity and other calls for reform.*   Judge Frankel was not alone in identifying the problem of sentencing disparity and the consequent need for sentencing reform. An influential 1976 report of the Twentieth Century Fund Task Force on Criminal Sentencing lamented that discretionary sentencing schemes were creating "unexplained and seemingly inexplicable sentencing disparity," and it marshaled some of the evidence of this disparity:

> One recent study . . . of felony sentences imposed by judges in one Ohio county [showed that] one judge granted probation to 26% of convicted offenders; another judge imposed probationary terms upon 51% of convicted offenders. . . . One judge imprisoned 56% of black defendants but only 35% of white defendants. . . . A South Carolina sample of sentencing [showed] in two marijuana cases, the same judge sentenced a white youth to one year's probation and a $400 fine; a black male received a two-year sentence. . . . A recent study commissioned by the judges of the U.S. Court of Appeals for the Second Circuit involved 50 federal judges who were given 20 identical files drawn from actual cases and asked what sentence they would impose on each defendant. In [an extortion case], one judge proposed a sentence of 20 years' imprisonment plus a $65,000 fine [while] another judge proposed a 3-year sentence with no fine.

Fair and Certain Punishment: Report of the Twentieth Century Fund Task Force on Criminal Sentencing 3-29 (1976). For similar expressions of concern about sentencing disparity and uncertainty in discretionary sentencing systems, see National Conference of Commissioners on Uniform State Laws, Model Sentencing and Corrections Act (1979); David Fogel, "We Are the Living Proof": The Justice Model for Corrections (1976).

3. *Frankel's impact on federal and state reforms.*   Because Judge Frankel provided a provocative blueprint for change, his book served as a major catalyst

for modern sentencing reforms. Most tangibly, Judge Frankel's work became the centerpiece of a series of policy workshops at Yale Law School, which culminated in a book proposing federal legislation for sentencing reform. See Pierce O'Donnell et al., Toward a Just and Effective Sentencing System (1977). The findings of the Yale workshops and accompanying book in turn provided the foundation for a federal sentencing reform bill introduced by Senator Edward Kennedy of Massachusetts in 1976. In addition, many states looked directly to Judge Frankel's suggestions when embarking on their own sentencing reform efforts. Professor Kevin Reitz has effectively summarized the importance and impact of Judge Frankel's work:

> Judge Frankel's *Criminal Sentences* may be the single most influential work of criminal justice scholarship in the last 20 years. It stands as the best indictment of traditional, indeterminate sentencing practices in the literature. Its proposals have charted the general outline of sentencing reform through the 1980s and into the 1990s [and] the ABA adopted a new edition of its Sentencing Standards modeled largely on Judge Frankel's early plan for commission-based regulation of sentencing discretion.

Kevin R. Reitz, Sentencing Reform in the States: An Overview of the Colorado Law Review Symposium, 64 U. Colo. L. Rev. 645, 650 n.21 (1993). Current drafts of the American Law Institute's project to revise the sentencing provisions of the Model Penal Code also endorse the use of sentencing commissions to develop coherent sentencing policy.

## 2.   Development and Structure of State Guideline Systems

Through the late 1970s and early 1980s, legislatures in a few states — most notably California and North Carolina — passed determinate sentencing statutes that abolished parole and created presumptive sentencing ranges for various classes of offenses. Minnesota became the first state to turn Judge Frankel's ideas into a full-fledged reality when in 1978 the state legislature established the Minnesota Sentencing Guidelines Commission to develop comprehensive sentencing guidelines. Pennsylvania (1978) and Washington State (1981) soon thereafter created their own distinctive forms of sentencing commissions and sentencing guidelines, and the federal government followed suit through the passage of the Sentencing Reform Act of 1984, which created the U.S. Sentencing Commission to develop guidelines for federal sentencing.

As of 2012 about half of U.S. states had adopted a system that fits broadly within the modern sentencing guidelines framework. See, e.g., National Center for State Courts, State Sentencing Guidelines: Profiles and Continuum (July 2008) (providing a brief overview of 20 states and the District of Columbia); National Association of Sentencing Commissions, www.thenasc.org/about-nasc.html (as of September 2012 listing 21 state sentencing commissions, plus the District of Columbia Sentencing and Criminal Code Revision Commission and the United States Sentencing Commission).

A full picture of state sentencing systems, however, is vastly more complicated. Some officials in states with legislatively mandated sentencing ranges, such as Arizona and California, assert that they have guideline systems, though policy analysts do not agree. Indeed, most states since 1980 have adopted a variety of reforms that increase the legislative guidance for sentencers and therefore provide greater "structure" to the sentencing system. These reforms include mandatory minimum sentences and career offender provisions.

Scholars and policy advocates know very little about the sentencing systems in states that have retained a largely indeterminate sentencing framework with an overlay of mandatory and career offender provisions. How much has the modern language of sentencing reform and the principles that have motivated these reforms had an impact on lawyers, judges, legislators, and parole commissions in these "old" system states? And just as important, why have so many states resisted the guidelines reform movement after guidelines achieved considerable success at rationalizing systems and controlling costs, across a wide range of states?

Even within the 20 or so states that have adopted some form of sentencing guidelines there is considerable variation in institutional roles, procedures, and sanctions. Indeed, it would obscure more relevant policy information than it would add to try to summarize the development and fundamental characteristics of all state guideline systems. Among the states that have received the most commentary are the leaders in the guidelines movement—Minnesota, Washington State and Pennsylvania—and more recently North Carolina, Kansas, and Virginia.

Minnesota was not only the first state to create comprehensive sentencing guidelines through the work of a sentencing commission, but it has also enjoyed a quarter-century of success with its reforms and stands as a trailblazer for state guideline systems. The following discussion details some of the choices involved in creating a new guidelines system.

## Structuring Criminal Sentencing, Dale Parent
### Pages 51-53, 57-60 (1988)

In at least three major respects, Minnesota's venture altered traditional institutions and concepts in the realm of criminal sentencing:

- It substituted a new system—guided discretion—for the more extreme methods of dividing authority over the punishment process between legislatures and courts.
- It inserted a new governmental entity—the sentencing commission— between the legislature and the judiciary, and authorized the commission to monitor and continuously adjust criminal sentences.
- And it established an unprecedented conceptual connection— known as capacity constraint—between the degree of severity with which guidelines could specify prison sentences and the extent to which state prison resources were available to carry such sentences into effect. . . .

Minnesota's innovation [conferred] on guidelines the force of law. The former system of indeterminate prison sentences set by a judge, subject to the possibility of early release in the discretion of a parole board, was abolished.

In its place came a system of determinate sentences, set by the judge under guidance from the sentencing commission, with review by an appellate court. Five key elements were incorporated into this plan:

- First, sentences would be scaled to take account of differences both in the gravity of crimes and the prior records of offenders. Guidance would be specified in the form of sentencing ranges, rather than precise sentences.
- Second, factors relevant to the individualization process would be standardized and weighted in advance. Clear rules would encourage similar outcomes in similar cases. Proportionality among different cases would be facilitated by a carefully constructed hierarchy of offense seriousness.
- Third, a set of departure principles would define the circumstances under which judges could deviate from the guideline sentencing range with good reasons. Judges would thus retain discretion to set the actual sentence, to do justice on a case-by-case basis.
- Fourth, sentencing judges would be required to state reasons for each sentence that differed from the applicable guideline, to assure accountability and reviewability.
- Fifth, all sentences would be subject to review by an appellate court whose written opinions could, over time, evolve finely tuned principles to guide future sentencers. . . .

The [1978 Minnesota] law created a nine-member Sentencing Guidelines Commission, consisting of the chief justice or his designee, two district court judges appointed by the chief justice, the Commission of Corrections, the chairman of the Minnesota Corrections Board, and four gubernatorial appointees—a prosecutor, a public defender, and two citizens. . . . The [Commission's] guidelines . . . were to recommend when state imprisonment was appropriate and to recommend presumptive sentencing durations. . . . Judges had to give written reasons for sentences that departed from the guidelines recommendation. The state or the defense could appeal any sentence. . . . The Commission sought to assure that guideline punishments would be proportional to the seriousness of offenders' crimes. To achieve that proportionality, it was necessary for the Commission to rank crimes in the order of their seriousness. The seriousness of a crime varies according to the gravity of the offense and the blameworthiness of the offender. Gravity is determined by the harm caused, directly or as a consequence of the crime. Blameworthiness is determined by the offender's motivation, intent, and behavior in the crime and is enhanced if the offender previously has been convicted of and sentenced for criminal acts. . . .

Although most of us have an intuitive sense of offense seriousness, the concept is highly complex. [Judgments] about the seriousness of criminal events may involve facts about offenders, victims, and criminal acts. Some factors can be dismissed because all would agree they are irrelevant to assessing gravity or ascribing blame—for example, that the victim was a Mason or the offender was a Methodist. Some facts are both irrelevant and invidious—such as that the offender and the victim were of the same or different races. But there is a long list of factors that some would consider relevant to assessing harm or ascribing blame.

The victim may be a normal healthy adult or a person who may be especially vulnerable due to age or infirmity. In violent crimes the extent of physical injury may vary from a scratch to death. Some victims may recover fully from physical injuries, while others suffer permanent damage or impairment. In property crimes, the victim's loss could range from a small amount to a fortune. The consequences of property loss may vary greatly with the economic status of the victim. The crime may involve one victim or many. A crime might involve an offender acting alone or in concert with others. . . .

Given events as complex and diverse as criminal acts, how was the Commission to go about judging their seriousness? [The Commission created a subcommittee to divide the task into more manageable components. The subcommittee grouped] crimes into 6 categories—violent, arson, sex, drug, property, and miscellaneous—5 of which contained 20 or fewer crimes. . . . The subcommittee instructed the Commission to focus on the usual or typical case in [a] ranking exercise. . . . In phase one, individual Commission members ranked crimes within each of the six categories. . . . Phases two, three, and four relied on identification of differences among members, on the articulation of reasons for those differences, and on debate about those reasons. . . . When differences existed it assured that the basis of the differences would be discovered and scrutinized and that the final rankings would reflect a majority opinion. [The Commission divided the overall ranking into ten seriousness levels. The accompanying table] shows the most common types of offenses within each of the ten seriousness levels.

### Most Frequent Offenses in Seriousness Scale

| Seriousness Level | Most Frequent Offenses |
|---|---|
| 1. | Aggravated forgery, less than $100 |
| | Possession of marijuana (more than 1.5 ounces) |
| | Unauthorized use of a motor vehicle |
| 2. | Aggravated forgery, $150 to $2,500 |
| | Sale of marijuana . . . |
| 3. | Aggravated forgery, over $2,500 |
| | Arson, third-degree . . . |
| | Theft crimes, $150 to $2,500 |
| | Sale of cocaine, |
| | Possession of LSD, PCP |
| 4. | Burglary, non-dwellings and unoccupied dwellings |
| | Theft crimes, over $2,500 |
| | Receiving stolen goods, $150 to $2,500 |
| | Criminal sexual assault, fourth-degree |
| | Assault, third-degree (injury) |
| 5. | Criminal negligence (resulting in death) |
| | Criminal sexual conduct, third-degree |
| | Manslaughter, second-degree . . . |
| | Witness tampering |
| | Simple (unarmed) robbery . . . |

**Most Frequent Offenses in Seriousness Scale** *(Cont'd)*

| Seriousness Level | Most Frequent Offenses |
|---|---|
| 6. | Assault, second-degree (weapon) |
| | Burglary (occupied dwelling) |
| | Criminal sexual conduct, second-degree . . . |
| | Kidnapping (released in a safe place) |
| | Sale, LSD or PCP |
| | Sale, heroin and remaining hard narcotics |
| | Receiving stolen goods, over $2,500 |
| 7. | Aggravated (armed) robbery |
| | Arson, first-degree |
| | Burglary (victim injured) . . . |
| | Kidnapping (not released in a safe place) |
| | Manslaughter, first-degree . . . |
| 8. | Assault, first-degree (great bodily harm) |
| | Kidnapping (great bodily harm) |
| | Criminal sexual conduct, first-degree |
| 9. | Murder, third-degree |
| 10. | Murder, second-degree |

## NOTES

1. *Voluntary and presumptive sentencing guidelines in the states.* Though the federal sentencing guidelines garner the most attention from commentators and from courts in non-guidelines states, nearly half the states regulate their sentencing judges' discretion through their own guidelines. In most of these states, a sentencing commission drafts an initial set of guidelines on behalf of the state legislature, which then enacts it as an integrated package of sentencing reforms. Some states, such as Alabama, place the guidelines commission within the judicial branch but include executive, legislative, and citizen members.

Some guidelines are only voluntary: there is no review of a judge's application of the guidelines or decision to sentence outside the range recommended in the guidelines so long as the judge remains within the statutory maximum and minimum for the crime. Other guidelines are presumptive: a judge who misapplies the guidelines or sentences outside the presumed range for sentences without an adequate justification can be overturned on appeal.

If you were a legislator in a state considering the adoption of sentencing guidelines, would you create a sentencing commission or instead look for mechanisms through which the judiciary might develop sentencing structures on its own? Regardless of the institution used to develop guidelines, would you prefer a voluntary or a presumptive approach? What do you see as the potential benefits and drawbacks of each approach to the development of sentencing guidelines?

The Supreme Court's interpretation of the Sixth Amendment in Blakely v. Washington (2004) and United States v. Booker (2005) appears to endow juries with an expanded factfinding role in presumptive guidelines systems, but it also permits judges to engage in factfinding within voluntary guideline systems. As a result of these blockbuster cases, both the federal system and many state systems, either through judicial rulings or legislative changes, have adjusted their systems away from presumptive guidelines systems toward voluntary guideline systems.

Do you think judges operating within a presumptive guideline system are likely to follow the guidelines with the same rigor if a judicial decision or new legislation suddenly converts the system to a voluntary one?

2. *Policy authority given to sentencing commissions.* As highlighted above, the Minnesota Sentencing Commission was given broad authority to assess the seriousness of various offenses when developing sentencing guidelines. Indeed, as Professor Michael Tonry has noted, the Minnesota Sentencing Commission initially made many "bold policy decisions":

> First, it decided to be "prescriptive" and to establish its own explicit sentencing priorities [rather than] to be "descriptive," to attempt to replicate existing sentencing patterns. Second, the commission decided to de-emphasize imprisonment as a punishment for property offenders and to emphasize imprisonment for violent offenders. . . . Third, in order to attack sentencing disparities, the commission decided to establish narrow sentencing ranges (for example, 30 to 34 months, or 50 to 58 months) and to authorize departures from guideline ranges only when "substantial and compelling" reasons were present. Fourth, the commission elected to adopt "just deserts" as the governing premise of its policies concerning who receives prison sentences. Fifth, the commission chose to interpret an ambiguous statutory injunction that it take correctional resources into "substantial consideration" as a mandate that its guidelines not increase prison populations beyond existing capacity constraints. . . . Sixth, the commission forbade consideration at sentencing of many personal factors — such as education, employment, marital status, living arrangements — that many judges believed to be legitimate. This decision resulted from a policy that sentencing decisions not be based on factors that might directly or indirectly discriminate against minorities, women, or low-income groups. . . .

Michael Tonry, Sentencing Guidelines and Their Effects 16-20 (1987). If you were a legislator who had voted in favor of (or against) establishing the Minnesota Sentencing Commission, would you override any of the commission's important policy decisions? How and to what extent should legislatures and sentencing commissions interact in making key policy decisions about the structure and content of guideline systems? Should certain policy decisions be made only by elected legislatures as opposed to appointed commissions?

3. *Discretion within ranges and departure authority.* Even in guideline systems that are presumptive, judges typically retain a measure of sentencing discretion through their power to select a specific sentence within the ranges set forth in the guidelines, as well as through their more limited authority to depart from those ranges. In a few states, guidelines provide fairly broad ranges from which judges make their sentencing decisions, although these states tend to be more restrictive concerning departures from the ranges. Representing the most extreme example, North Carolina's guidelines establish ranges in which the longest available sentence is often twice the shortest available sentence, but they do not permit departures from these ranges for any reason. In most states, the ranges provided in the guidelines are fairly narrow, but authority to depart is given to sentencing judges. In Kansas, for example, the longest sentence within a prescribed range is usually no more than 20% higher than the shortest sentence, but judges can depart from these ranges on numerous grounds.

Departures may affect either the disposition of the sentence (active prison term or nonprison sanctions) or the duration of the sentence (the number of months to be served), and statutes generally require the judge to explain in writing

any departure. In most jurisdictions, the selection of a particular sentence from
the applicable guidelines sentencing range is not subject to appeal, but departure
decisions are appealable, and reliance on improper grounds or inadequate
explanations for a departure can lead to reversal. Although appellate courts in
many jurisdictions have developed extensive case law approving or disapproving
various grounds for departure, state appellate courts have been less inclined to
examine a sentencing judge's decision not to depart. Should defendants' and
prosecutors' opportunities to appeal a decision *not* to depart be equivalent to
their opportunities to appeal a decision to depart from the guidelines?

4. *Amending the rules.*   States with sentencing guidelines sometimes need to
amend those guidelines over time, in response to the passage of new criminal
prohibitions or to problematic judicial interpretations of certain guidelines, or
when particular guidelines provisions do not work well. States typically give the
leading role in the amendment process to a permanent sentencing commission,
although the commission's power to amend the guidelines varies. In the largest
group of states, the commission only recommends changes to the guidelines,
and the legislature (and sometimes the state supreme court) must approve the
changes before they become law. See Kan. Stat. Ann. §74-9101(b)(2), (6), (7);
N.C. Gen. Stat. §§164-36, 164-43. Elsewhere, amendments to the guidelines take
effect at the end of the commission's administrative rule-making process or after
a waiting period to give the legislature a chance to pass a statute disapproving of
the changes. See Minn. Stat. Ann. §244.09(11); 42 Pa. Cons. Stat. §2153(a)(1).
Would you expect these procedural variations to make any difference in the
content of sentencing guidelines?

## PROBLEM 3-1.   THE MINNESOTA MACHINE

Clayton James Hanks broke into a home outside Minneapolis one night
and stole some stereo equipment, worth about $1,000. He also went into the
backyard of the home and took some tools. The prosecutor charged Hanks with
residential burglary and theft; Hanks pled guilty to both charges. Hanks has no
prior arrests or convictions on his record.

At sentencing, the trial court calculated the outcome prescribed under the
Minnesota sentencing guidelines. The presumptive sentence for any felon is
determined by locating the appropriate cell of the Sentencing Guidelines
Grid, reprinted below. The vertical axis of the grid represents the severity
level of the offense of conviction. When an offender is convicted of two or
more felonies, the severity level is determined by the most severe offense of
conviction. The most frequently occurring offenses within a severity level are
listed on the vertical axis of the grid.

The horizontal axis of the grid looks to the offender's criminal history. The
offender is assigned a particular score for every prior criminal or juvenile
sentence, with the more severe prior crimes assigned a larger number of points.

The guidelines remind judges that "the capacities of state and local correctional facilities are finite" and that "incarcerative sanctions should be limited
to those convicted of more serious offenses or those who have longer criminal
histories." In general, the "sanctions used in sentencing convicted felons should
be the least restrictive necessary to achieve the purposes of the sentence."

**Sentencing Guidelines Grid**

*Presumptive Sentence Lengths in Months*

Italicized numbers within the grid denote the range within which a judge may sentence without the sentence being deemed a departure. Offenders with non-imprisonment felony sentences are subject to jail time according to law.

| SEVERITY LEVEL OF CONVICTION OFFENSE (Common offenses listed in italics) | | CRIMINAL HISTORY SCORE | | | | | | |
|---|---|---|---|---|---|---|---|---|
| | | 0 | 1 | 2 | 3 | 4 | 5 | 6 or more |
| *Murder, 2nd Degree (intentional murder; drive-by-shootings)* | XI | 306 *299-313* | 326 *319-333* | 346 *339-353* | 366 *359-373* | 386 *379-393* | 406 *399-413* | 426 *419-433* |
| *Murder, 3rd Degree Murder, 2nd Degree (unintentional murder)* | X | 150 *144-156* | 165 *159-171* | 180 *174-186* | 195 *189-201* | 210 *204-216* | 225 *219-231* | 240 *234-246* |
| *Criminal Sexual Conduct, 1st Degree[2] Assault, 1st Degree* | IX | 86 *81-91* | 98 *93-103* | 110 *105-115* | 122 *117-127* | 134 *129-139* | 146 *141-151* | 158 *153-163* |
| *Aggravated Robbery 1st Degree* | VIII | 48 *44-52* | 58 *54-62* | 68 *64-72* | 78 *74-82* | 88 *84-92* | 98 *94-102* | 108 *104-112* |
| *Felony DWI* | VII | 36 | 42 | 48 | 54 *51-57* | 60 *57-63* | 66 *63-69* | 72 *69-75* |
| *Criminal Sexual Conduct, 2nd Degree (a) & (b)* | VI | 21 | 27 | 33 | 39 *37-41* | 45 *43-47* | 51 *49-53* | 57 *55-59* |
| *Residential Burglary Simple Robbery* | V | 18 | 23 | 28 | 33 *31-35* | 38 *36-40* | 43 *41-45* | 48 *46-50* |
| *Nonresidential Burglary* | IV | 12[1] | 15 | 18 | 21 | 24 *23-25* | 27 *26-28* | 30 *29-31* |
| *Theft Crimes (Over $2,500)* | III | 12[1] | 13 | 15 | 17 | 19 *18-20* | 21 *20-22* | 23 *22-24* |
| *Theft Crimes ($2,500 or less) Check Forgery ($200-$2,500)* | II | 12[1] | 12[1] | 13 | 15 | 17 | 19 | 21 *20-22* |
| *Sale of Simulated Controlled Substance* | I | 12[1] | 12[1] | 12[1] | 13 | 15 | 17 | 19 *18-20* |

☐ Presumptive commitment to state imprisonment. First Degree Murder is excluded from the guidelines by law and continues to have a mandatory life sentence. See section II.E. **Mandatory Sentences** for policy regarding those sentences controlled by law, including minimum periods of supervision for sex offenders released from prison.

 Presumptive stayed sentence; at the discretion of the judge, up to a year in jail and/or other non-jail sanctions can be imposed as conditions of probation. However, certain offenses in this section of the grid always carry a presumptive commitment to state prison. These offenses include Third Degree Controlled Substance Crimes when the offender has a prior felony drug conviction, Burglary of an Occupied Dwelling when the offender has a prior felony burglary conviction, second and subsequent Criminal Sexual Conduct offenses and offenses carrying a mandatory minimum prison term due to the use of a dangerous weapon (e.g., Second Degree Assault). See sections II.C. **Presumptive Sentence** and II.E. **Mandatory Sentences**.

The Minnesota guidelines are presumptive, meaning that any sentence selected from outside the designated range is subject to appeal. The guidelines say that departures from the presumptive sentences established in the guidelines "should be made only when substantial and compelling circumstances exist."

As a judge, what arguments from the prosecution or the defense might be persuasive as you decide whether to depart from the presumptive outcome under the guidelines? What facts would be important to you?

||   *Sentencing Guidelines in Minnesota, Other*   ||
||   *States, and the Federal Courts: A Twenty-Year*   ||
||   *Retrospective, Richard S. Frase*   ||
||   12 Fed. Sent'g Rep. 69 (1999)   ||

[Guidelines] systems are not all alike. . . . Although state guidelines systems are very diverse, they have a couple of things in common which distinguish them from the federal guidelines. Without exception, state systems are more flexible than the federal guidelines. There is a range; some state systems are so flexible that they are hardly "guidelines" at all, others are much more restrictive. . . .

Another thing that distinguishes state guidelines is that they are relatively simple to apply. The federal guidelines are quite ambitious; they try to regulate every decision. This is related to the flexibility point, but it goes beyond that. State guidelines are generally relatively short documents; sometimes very short. [It] is important to keep guidelines relatively easy to apply and easy for courts, defendants, and the public to understand. That is an important point which was lost in the federal system.

[There are some] important structural differences among guidelines systems. . . . For instance, Delaware, Florida, and Ohio don't use a grid (although their "narrative" or "point-system" guidelines could be translated into a grid). State and federal grids vary considerably in such things as: whether certain offenses have a separate grid; the number of grid cells; the breadth of cell ranges; and whether the ranges of adjoining cells overlap. Guidelines systems also differ in the number of disposition options permitted for a given case (e.g., prison, jail, restrictive intermediate sanctions, etc.); whether any guidance is offered as to the choice among sentencing purposes; how criminal history is defined; how multiple offenses are sentenced; and the extent to which the sentencing commission has made independent judgments about appropriate sentences (so-called "prescriptive" rules), rather than simply compiling guidelines which are descriptive of past judicial and paroling practices. . . .

### THE CHANGING PURPOSES OF SENTENCING GUIDELINES

The original goals of sentencing guidelines reforms were two-fold. First, to reduce sentencing discretion and its resulting disparities; and second, to promote more rational sentencing policy developed and monitored by a specialized sentencing commission. . . . Since Minnesota's Guidelines first became effective, sentencing goals and values in Minnesota and other guidelines jurisdictions have evolved considerably. [It] appears that the goal of disparity reduction has become somewhat less important, while other goals have become more important. . . . Almost every guidelines system which was adopted or revised since the mid-1980s has included resource-impact assessments, in an attempt to avoid prison overcrowding and control the growth of prison populations. More recent guideline reforms are also more likely to regulate and attempt to encourage the use of intermediate sanctions. Broader use of such sanctions is intended to reduce unnecessary prison use — thus avoiding prison overcrowding and reducing prison costs — and also to better promote public safety. . . .

### WHAT HAVE GUIDELINES ACCOMPLISHED?

How well have state guidelines [worked]? Any such assessment must begin with a frank admission: no "expert" on sentencing guidelines can say very much about how most state guidelines systems have worked in practice. In some cases, this is because a state's system is too new to have generated enough data for evaluation. In other cases, the guidelines commission has not published or commissioned any evaluations, nor is there some professor or other outside researcher who takes a special interest in that state's guidelines. So much of what follows is based on a few, well-documented systems, and some "educated guesswork" about the rest.

*Disparity Reduction.*   Since most guidelines systems have abolished parole, they have eliminated that form of disparity. Judicial sentencing disparities have also been reduced, at least in the states which have been evaluated. Minnesota is the only system to have been subjected to extensive outside evaluation, but data reported by sentencing commissions or their staff suggest that disparity has also been reduced in Delaware, Oregon, Pennsylvania and Washington. Two of these five jurisdictions do not have legally-binding guidelines (Delaware's are formally voluntary, and Pennsylvania's lack effective appellate review). . . .

*More Rational Sentencing Policy.*   [Most] guidelines systems include a permanent sentencing commission. Although some are more active than others, all of these commissions have begun to develop useful sentencing policy expertise, a comprehensive state-wide view of punishment priorities, better management of resources, and a long-term perspective. Even in states with fairly weak guidelines, sentencing commissions can play an important role, not just in drafting guidelines but also by advising the legislature as to various sentencing policy matters of current concern.

As for the increasingly important goal of resource-impact assessment, there is considerable evidence that sentencing guidelines can help to avoid prison overcrowding and the kinds of dramatic (and very expensive) escalation in prison populations which has occurred in many non-guidelines states in the past 20 years. Minnesota pioneered this concept, and has successfully avoided major prison overcrowding problems for almost two decades — a period in which most non-guidelines states experienced both overcrowding and court intervention. Although Minnesota's prison population has increased substantially since 1979, the average annual rate of growth (about 5 percent per year) has only been about two-thirds the rate for the nation as a whole (8 percent per year). Other guidelines jurisdictions which emphasized resource-management goals have also had low average annual growth rates. . . .

*Truth in Sentencing.*   Any system which has abolished parole release discretion — as the majority of guidelines systems have done — has achieved a greater degree of "truth in sentencing." Of course, this goal has also been achieved in a number of states which abolished parole without adopting judicial sentencing guidelines. However, there is reason to believe that the abolition of parole works much better in a system with such guidelines. [Systems] with judicial guidelines have less need to rely on state-wide parole standards as a means of reducing disparity in the sentences imposed by local judges. [Further,] systems with guidelines and a permanent sentencing commission are in a better position to predict the effects abolition of parole will have on prison populations; such systems can then either build more prisons, modify the guidelines to lower prison commitment or duration rates, or pursue a combination of these strategies. In contrast, the abolition of parole, in a system without judicial guidelines, eliminates a means of counteracting judicial disparity and prison overcrowding at the "back end" of the sentencing process, without providing any means of controlling these problems from the "front end."

*Public Safety.*   States with sentencing guidelines have generally had stable or falling crime rates since their guidelines became effective. However, crime rates have recently been stable or falling in most states, with or without guidelines. And, of course, crime rates depend on many social and economic factors in addition to sentencing policy; a thorough examination of the relationship between guidelines and public safety would thus be very complex (and has not been attempted by quantitative criminologists). But the stable or falling pattern of crime rates, noted above, at least suggests that sentencing guidelines do not threaten public safety. . . .

### Two Persistent Challenges

Despite the accomplishments of many state guidelines, there are a number of legitimate criticisms which can be leveled at even the best of these systems. Two of the most important problems are the failure to effectively regulate prosecutorial discretion and plea bargaining; and the limited efforts to regulate and encourage the use of non-custodial ("intermediate") sanctions. Although each of these "gaps" in guidelines coverage is a problem, neither is a major problem in well-designed systems; indeed they may even be strengths, helping these systems accommodate important contemporary sentencing goals and values.

*Prosecutorial Discretion and Plea Bargaining.*   . . . Since guidelines limit the range of sentences available for a given offense, the power to drop or not drop charges is the power to select the sentence range available to the court (that is, what "box" on the grid the case ends up in). Thus, any disparity in charging translates into disparity in sentencing. Unregulated charging and plea bargaining also make it more difficult for the sentencing commission to predict future resource needs. Yet no guidelines system has come up with an effective way of structuring prosecutorial sentencing power, and its potential for disparity and unpredictability. Washington has state-wide charging guidelines, but they are not legally enforceable. The federal Guidelines tried to mitigate this problem by requiring trial courts to consider certain alleged criminal acts ("relevant conduct") whether or not such acts were included in any conviction offense. But this essentially lawless approach goes too far in the opposite direction—allowing sentences to be based on weak charges which were properly dismissed, resulted in acquittal, or were never even filed.

What should be done? Clearly efforts to structure prosecutorial discretion and plea bargaining should continue, especially by means of internal, administrative measures within prosecutor's offices, such as written policies and review of decisions by supervising staff. [But it will be very difficult to enforce controls,] especially to impose lower limits on charge and recommended-sentence severity (since, in most cases, neither prosecutors nor defendants will appeal cases of prosecution leniency).

However, I believe that most state guidelines systems are valuable reforms even if prosecutorial decisions remain substantially unregulated. I have two reasons for this belief. First, the absence of widespread complaints about prosecutorial dominance in state guidelines systems is an important sign, suggesting that closer regulation may not be needed. Specifically, I am suggesting that, in a properly balanced guidelines system—that is, one with reasonable sentence severity levels and few mandatory minimum statutes, in which courts retain substantial sentencing discretion for any given offense (due to broad guidelines ranges, limited appellate scrutiny, and/or flexible departure powers)—it is rare that prosecutorial decisions will produce sentences which judges strongly disapprove, yet are powerless to prevent (as often seems to occur in federal courts). Second, prosecutorial charging and plea bargaining are valuable sources of flexibility and moderation in sentencing. These discretionary powers permit systems to consider individual offense and offender factors which may not fit squarely within formal statutory and guidelines rules. And of course, prosecutorial discretion also allows systems to tailor sentencing severity to the available resources and evidence.

*Intermediate Sanctions.*   Only a few guidelines jurisdictions have attempted to regulate the conditions of non-custodial sanctions, or even to encourage broader use of such sanctions. Even the few jurisdictions which have attempted to address these issues have not gone very far. Several systems authorize judges, in certain cases, to substitute specified amounts of certain intermediate sanctions for custody; for example, sixteen hours of community service, or a day of home detention, might be substituted for a day of custody. Two states, Pennsylvania and North Carolina, have attempted to define large groups of offenders for whom various kinds of intermediate sanctions are appropriate. These guidelines first classify penalties into three types: incarceration (prison or jail), severe intermediate sanctions (such as residential treatment), and mild intermediate sanctions (such as community service). . . . But the Pennsylvania and North Carolina Guidelines provide no guidance as to the choice to be made, when more than one sanction type is allowed in a given cell, or (when a non-custodial option is chosen), how much of that option to impose (for instance, what length of home detention or community service). . . .

CONCLUSION

After two decades of guidelines reforms, what have we learned? Here is a short list of the most important lessons which a review of this experience teaches:

*First:* guidelines in a number of states have succeeded in improving sentencing policy and practice — reducing bias and disparity in sentencing; avoiding serious prison overcrowding; and ensuring that adequate prison space is available for the most serious offenders. State guidelines regulate but do not eliminate discretion. . . . Most state guidelines systems have abolished parole release discretion, which serves to achieve Truth in Sentencing; offenders serve most of the sentence imposed by the trial court, and there is no pretense that sentences are longer than they really are. State guidelines have achieved more rational sentencing policy because they are developed and monitored by an independent, non-partisan agency charged with the responsibility of collecting detailed data on sentencing practices and resources, evaluating sentencing policy from a long-term perspective, setting priorities for use of limited resources, and developing a comprehensive approach to the sentencing of all crimes, thereby avoiding the problems of piecemeal reforms. [Yet] other major public and private stakeholders . . . have significant input into the development and implementation of state sentencing policy. The Legislature maintains oversight and ultimate control over major policy issues, and important roles are also played by trial and appellate judges, the defense and prosecution, victims, community representatives, and correctional officials. And yet — most state guidelines systems remain relatively simple to understand and apply.

*Second:* the best state guidelines work better, in all of the ways described above, than any other sentencing system which has yet been tried or even proposed. Quite simply, there is no realistic alternative as a means of accommodating all of the many important values and principles which we want sentences to serve. The prior indeterminate sentencing system permitted intolerable extremes of disparity; the unpredictable nature of indeterminate sentencing also prevented effective resource-management, and violated the public's desire for Truth in Sentencing. . . .

*Third:* state sentencing guidelines are politically viable. They have been successfully implemented in many states, and have survived — in some cases for almost 20 years, which is a very long time, given the extreme political salience and volatility of sentencing issues in recent years. These systems have survived because they work. . . .

*Fourth:* state guidelines continue to evolve and improve. Newer systems are more likely to take advantage of the potential which guidelines provide for resource-management and the promotion and structuring of intermediate sanctions. Most older systems are better today than when they began, not only because they have added desirable features (a permanent commission; resource-management; intermediate sanctions) which they originally lacked, but also because these system[s] now openly recognize and incorporate a wide variety of sentencing goals and values. . . .

*Fifth:* the development of sentencing guidelines remains an area of state, not federal, leadership. This reform began in the states; state guidelines have improved over time more than the federal version. [The] great diversity of guidelines systems provides a rich menu of reform options and experience to guide sentencing reformers in other states — and in the federal system — in their efforts to design, implement, improve, and preserve guidelines systems.

## NOTES

1. *Evolving goals for state guideline system.*   The principal goal of early sentencing reforms was to regulate sentencing discretion and thereby limit sentencing disparities. As Professor Frase explains, however, the goals of sentencing reform in many states transformed over time to emphasize controlling the growth of prison populations, making effective and efficient use of expensive punishment resources, and encouraging the use of intermediate sanctions. What forces do you think prompted this evolution in the goals of modern sentencing reform? Do you think a sentencing guideline system managed by a sentencing commission is better suited to effectuate these changed goals than the legislature?

2. *Developing guidelines in the shadow of the federal system.*   Though Minnesota and a few other states adopted guideline systems before the creation of the federal sentencing guidelines, most states with guidelines began their reform efforts afterward. All of the states that have adopted guideline reforms have expressly rejected the federal sentencing guidelines as a model for their own reforms. Professor Michael Tonry has noted that in numerous states considering sentencing reforms, "commissions at early meetings adopted resolutions expressly repudiating the federal guidelines as a model for anything they might develop." Michael Tonry, Sentencing Matters 134 (1996); see Paul J. Hofer, Immediate and Long-Term Effects of United States v. Booker: More Discretion, More Disparity, or Better Reasoned Sentences?, 38 Ariz. St. L.J. 425, 463 (2006) (ALI's review of Model Penal Code sentencing provisions "takes pain to distance itself from the pre-*Booker* federal guidelines"); Kevin R. Reitz & Curtis R. Reitz, Building a Sentencing Reform Agenda: The ABA's New Sentencing Standards, 78 Judicature 189, 189-192 (1995) (explaining that during the American Bar Association's drafting of model standards, "the federal system was held out repeatedly as a bad example," requiring the proposed standards "to be defended as very different than the federal guidelines").

## 3.   Development and Structure of the Federal Sentencing Guidelines

### a.   Statutory Foundations

Though Judge Marvin Frankel's ideas were the catalyst for many reforms, Senator Edward Kennedy was the central political figure who turned Judge Frankel's ideas into a specific proposal for federal sentencing reform. Throughout the 1970s, Senator Kennedy championed Judge Frankel's ideas, as shown in the following excerpt:

> The absence in the federal criminal code of any articulated purposes or goals of sentencing has led to a situation where different judges often mete out different sentences to similar defendants convicted of similar crimes, depending on the sentencing attitudes of the particular judge. [Some] convicted offenders (including repeat offenders) escape jail altogether while others — convicted of the same crime — go to jail for excessively long periods. . . .
>
> An important prerequisite of any effective crime-fighting program — certainty of punishment — is absent. In addition, the criminal justice system

appears arbitrary and unjust, a game of chance in which the offender may
"gamble" on receiving not just a lenient term of imprisonment but no jail
sentence at all. . . . Sentencing disparity also strikingly demonstrates the fallacy
of fighting crime by increasing maximum sentences which can be imposed.
Counterfeiting carries a maximum penalty of fifteen years imprisonment; not
only is the average sentence actually imposed less than five years, but almost
50% of convicted counterfeiters receive no imprisonment at all. Simply increasing maximum penalties is an exercise in futility. . . .

   What can be done? I have introduced legislation in the U.S. Senate, [enti-
tled] the Sentencing Guidelines bill, [which] would bring welcome uniformity to
the sentencing process by articulating for the first time the general purposes and
goals of sentencing that a judge should consider before imposing a sentence of
imprisonment. The bill also provides for appellate review of sentences and creates a United States Commission on Sentencing to establish specific, fixed sentencing ranges for similar defendants who commit similar crimes. . . .

Edward M. Kennedy, Criminal Sentencing: A Game of Chance, 60 Judicature
208, 210-212 (1976).

   Despite the force of Senator Kennedy's advocacy, it took nearly a decade
before a version of his reform bill was passed into law as the Sentencing Reform
Act of 1984 (SRA). In an account of the SRA's legislative history, Kate Stith and
Steve Koh observed that the "legislative history of federal sentencing reform
[reveals a] subtle transformation of sentencing reform legislation: conceived by
liberal reformers as an anti-imprisonment and antidiscrimination measure, but
finally born as part of a more conservative law-and-order crime control measure." Kate Stith & Steve Koh, The Politics of Sentencing Reform: The Legislative History of the Federal Sentencing Guidelines, 28 Wake Forest L. Rev. 223,
226 (1993). Cf. Marc L. Miller & Ronald F. Wright, Your Cheatin' Heart(land):
The Long Search for Administrative Sentencing Justice, 2 Buff. Crim. L. Rev. 723
(1999) (providing different account of the SRA's legislative history, with greater
emphasis on more liberal views of House members). What might appeal to a
political conservative, such as Senator Orrin Hatch, about presumptive sentencing guidelines?

   Though the passage of the SRA in 1984 created the U.S. Sentencing
Commission and provided the statutory foundation for federal sentencing
guidelines, the commission struggled to fulfill the SRA's mandates, and its initial
set of mandatory guidelines did not become effective until November 1987. In a
decision challenging the constitutionality of the guidelines on separation of
powers grounds, Justice Blackmun described the new legislation:

The Act, as adopted, revises the old sentencing process in several ways:

1. It rejects imprisonment as a means of promoting rehabilitation, and it states
   that punishment should serve retributive, educational, deterrent, and incapacitative goals.
2. It consolidates the power that had been exercised by the sentencing judge
   and the Parole Commission to decide what punishment an offender should
   suffer. This is done by creating the United States Sentencing Commission,
   directing that Commission to devise guidelines to be used for sentencing,
   and prospectively abolishing the Parole Commission.
3. It makes all sentences basically determinate. A prisoner is to be released at
   the completion of his sentence reduced only by any credit earned by good
   behavior while in custody.

4.  It makes the Sentencing Commission's guidelines binding on the courts, although it preserves for the judge the discretion to depart from the guideline applicable to a particular case if the judge finds an aggravating or mitigating factor present that the Commission did not adequately consider when formulating guidelines. The Act also requires the court to state its reasons for the sentence imposed and to give "the specific reason" for imposing a sentence different from that described in the guideline.
5.  It authorizes limited appellate review of the sentence. It permits a defendant to appeal a sentence that is above the defined range, and it permits the Government to appeal a sentence that is below that range. It also permits either side to appeal an incorrect application of the guideline. . . .

Mistretta v. United States, 488 U.S. 361, 367-68 (1989).

The guidelines did not become fully operational until 1989 because many of the first guideline cases focused primarily on constitutional challenges to the SRA's entire approach to sentencing reform. In *Mistretta* the Court addressed the question of whether the creation of the U.S. Sentencing Commission, as "an independent commission in the judicial branch of the United States," was constitutional. The commission, as set out in the SRA, has seven voting members who are appointed by the president with the advice of the Senate. They serve for six years and may not serve more than two full terms. Initially, at least three of its members had to be federal judges, selected by the president from a list of six judges recommended by the Judicial Conference. The members of the commission are subject to removal by the president "only for neglect of duty or malfeasance in office or for other good cause shown."

Initially the commission had to promulgate determinate sentencing guidelines. Congress had charged it with meeting the purposes of sentencing set out in the SRA, to provide "certainty and fairness in meeting the purposes of sentencing, avoiding unwarranted sentencing disparities among defendants with similar records . . . while maintaining sufficient flexibility to permit individualized sentences," where appropriate; and to "reflect, to the extent practicable, advancement in knowledge of human behavior as it relates to the criminal justice process." Congress further specified four "purposes" of sentencing that the commission was required to pursue in carrying out its mandate: "to reflect the seriousness of the offense, to promote respect for the law, and to provide just punishment for the offense"; "to afford adequate deterrence to criminal conduct"; "to protect the public from further crimes of the defendant"; and "to provide the defendant with needed . . . correctional treatment." In describing the desired guidelines, Congress directed the commission to develop a system of "sentencing ranges" applicable "for each category of offense involving each category of defendant." For imprisonment sentences, Congress mandated that "the maximum of the range established for such a term shall not exceed the minimum of that range by more than the greater of 25 percent or 6 months." Moreover, it directed the commission to use current average sentences "as a starting point" for structuring the sentencing ranges.

To guide the commission in its formulation of offense categories, Congress directed it to consider seven factors: the grade of the offense; the aggravating and mitigating circumstances of the crime; the nature and degree of the harm caused by the crime; the community view of the gravity of the offense; the public concern generated by the crime; the deterrent effect that a particular sentence may have on others; and the current incidence of the offense. Congress also set forth 11 factors for the commission to consider in establishing categories of defendants. These include the offender's age, education, vocational skills, mental and emotional condition, physical condition (including drug dependence), previous employment record, family ties and responsibilities, community ties, role in the offense, criminal history, and degree of dependence on crime for a livelihood. Congress also prohibited the commission from considering the "race, sex, national origin, creed, and socioeconomic status of offenders" and instructed that the guidelines should reflect the "general inappropriateness" of considering certain other factors, such as current unemployment, that might serve as proxies for forbidden criteria.

The Sentencing Reform Act laid out even more detailed guidance for the commission concerning categories of offenses and offender characteristics. Congress directed that guidelines specify a term of confinement at or near the statutory maximum for certain crimes and ensure a substantial term of imprisonment for various other offenses. On the other hand, Congress directed that guidelines reflect the general inappropriateness of imposing a sentence of imprisonment for certain first-time offenders.

Following promulgation of the guidelines, the statute called for the commission to continually review and revise them and report to Congress any amendments; the commission must also provide an annual analysis of the operation of the guidelines and issue "general policy statements" regarding their application.

In *Mistretta* the Court was asked to address the question of whether Congress granted the commission excessive legislative discretion, in violation of the nondelegation doctrine. Because Congress had provided detailed direction to the commission, the Court found no such violation. The Court also addressed the issue of whether the commission, which was placed in the judicial branch, violated the principles of separation of powers by undermining the independence of the judiciary. It likened the commission's role to that of the Supreme Court

> in establishing rules of procedure under the various enabling Acts. . . . Just as the rules of procedure bind judges and courts in the proper management of the cases before them, so the Guidelines bind judges and courts in the exercise of their uncontested responsibility to pass sentence in criminal cases. In other words, the Commission's functions, like this Court's function in promulgating procedural rules, are clearly attendant to a central element of the historically acknowledged mission of the Judicial Branch. . . .

Justice Scalia dissented, referring to the commission as a "junior-varsity Congress," an expert body with the right to make laws.

> I dissent from today's decision because I can find no place within our constitutional system for an agency created by Congress to exercise no governmental power other than the making of laws. . . .
> There is no doubt that the Sentencing Commission has established significant, legally binding prescriptions governing application of governmental power against private individuals — indeed, application of the ultimate governmental power, short of capital punishment. . . . [T]he decisions made by the Commission are far from technical, but are heavily laden (or ought to be) with value judgments and policy assessments. . . .

[This] case is . . . about the creation of a new Branch altogether, a sort of junior-varsity Congress. It may well be that in some circumstances such a Branch would be desirable; perhaps the agency before us here will prove to be so. But there are many desirable dispositions that do not accord with the constitutional structure we live under. And in the long run the improvisation of a constitutional structure on the basis of currently perceived utility will be disastrous.

## *NOTES*

1. *Judicial resistance to federal sentencing reform.*   Though *Mistretta* ultimately found the constitutional challenges to be unavailing, more than 200 district judges and one circuit court had ruled the SRA unconstitutional on various grounds. Commentators have suggested that federal judges' apparent eagerness to strike down the SRA regime revealed their distaste for the entire agenda of guideline sentencing. See Michael Tonry, Sentencing Matters 73-74 (1996). More tellingly, federal judges were among the most vocal critics of the federal sentencing guidelines following their enactment. See, e.g., Jose A. Cabranes, Sentencing Guidelines: A Dismal Failure, N.Y. L.J. 2 (February 11, 1992); Marc Miller, Rehabilitating the Federal Sentencing Guidelines, 78 Judicature 180, 180-183 (1995) (detailing widespread judicial hostility to the federal guidelines). Some commentators and members of the commission suggested that these complaints simply represented judges' displeasure over losing some of their broad sentencing powers. Others, however, believed that these judicial criticisms were sound indicators of serious problems with the SRA's overall approach to sentencing reform. See Kate Stith & Jose A. Cabranes, Fear of Judging: Sentencing Guidelines in the Federal Courts (1998).

2. *Congress's mandatory sentencing provisions and their impact on the guidelines.* In the very same legislative session in which it enacted the SRA, Congress began relying on mandatory sentencing laws to restrict judicial sentencing discretion. In 1984 Congress created a set of general minimum sentences for certain felonies and enacted a mandatory five-year sentence increase for crimes of violence involving a gun. Additional sentencing mandates followed nearly every two years — synchronized, not coincidentally, with the federal election cycle. Of most consequence, in 1986 Congress enacted a five-year mandatory enhancement for use of a firearm in a drug crime and created a broad set of mandatory minimum penalties for drug trafficking that linked the minimum sentence to the amount of drugs involved in the offense.

Though mandatory sentencing statutes have proved consistently popular with Congress, they have been assailed by judges, researchers, and commentators. In a speech about federal sentencing reform, Justice Stephen Breyer, a member of the original U.S. Sentencing Commission, effectively summarized the many criticisms of mandatory sentencing provisions:

> [Statutory] mandatory sentences prevent the Commission from carrying out its basic, congressionally mandated task: the development, in part through research, of a rational, coherent set of punishments. Mandatory minimums will sometimes make it impossible for the Commission to adjust sentences in light of factors that its research shows to be directly relevant. . . . They will

sometimes prevent the application of Guidelines that would reduce a sentence in light of, for example, a minimal role in a drug offense, thereby sentencing similarly offenders who are very different, perhaps like a drug lord and a mule. Most seriously, they skew the entire set of criminal punishments, for Congress rarely considers more than the criminal behavior directly at issue when it writes these provisions. . . .

Moreover, mandatory minimums . . . may permit the prosecutor, not the judge, to select the sentence by choosing . . . to charge, or not to charge, a violation of a statute that carries a mandatory prison term. [A] 1991 Commission study indicates that in nearly 40% of the cases involving conduct to which a mandatory minimum attached, the offender received a sentence lower than the minimum, perhaps because the prosecutor charged a different crime. . . . In sum, Congress, in simultaneously requiring Guideline sentencing and mandatory minimum sentencing, is riding two different horses. And those horses, in terms of coherence, fairness, and effectiveness, are traveling in opposite directions.

Speech of Associate Justice Stephen Breyer, University of Nebraska College of Law (November 18, 1998), 11 Fed. Sent'g Rep. 180, 184-185 (1999).

In addition to their direct consequences, the mandatory sentencing laws enacted in 1984 and 1986 skewed the initial development of the federal sentencing guidelines. Especially in the creation of the guidelines' drug sentencing provisions, the U.S. Sentencing Commission felt it had to alter its standard approach to guideline development to harmonize its provisions with Congress's sentencing mandates, which focused almost exclusively on drug quantities. See William W. Wilkins Jr. et al., Competing Sentencing Policies in a "War on Drugs" Era, 28 Wake Forest L. Rev. 305, 319-321 (1993).

3. *Composition of a sentencing commission.* Recall that Judge Frankel encouraged broad-based membership in a sentencing commission to ensure the establishment of a well-rounded and knowledgeable group that could insulate sentencing rules from political pressures. In many states, the formation of sentencing commissions lived up to Frankel's ideals. In the words of Professor Michael Tonry, "sentencing commissions in [many states] have operated much as Judge Frankel hoped they would[; they] have achieved and sustained specialized institutional competence, insulated sentencing policy from short-term 'crime of the week' political pressures, and maintained a focus on comprehensive system-wide policymaking." Michael Tonry, The Success of Judge Frankel's Sentencing Commission, 64 U. Colo. L. Rev. 713, 713 (1993).

In the federal system, however, the U.S. Sentencing Commission has, more often than not, reflected the "tough on crime" stance of appointing presidents and confirming Congresses, and commentators have noted that commission deliberations generally reflect a prosecutorial orientation. See Douglas A. Berman, Common Law for This Age of Federal Sentencing: The Opportunity and Need for Judicial Lawmaking, 11 Stan. L. & Pol'y Rev. 93, 108-109 (1999). The statutory structure might explain this turn of events: the SRA provides for a designee of the attorney general to be an ex officio member of the commission, but provides no equivalent representation to a member of the defense bar. See 28 U.S.C. §991(a). And in 2003, apparently in response to concerns that the U.S. Sentencing Commission was not controlling judicial sentencing tightly enough, Congress altered the commission's judicial representation. The SRA's initial mandate that "at least three" of the commission's seven voting members be federal judges was changed to provide that the commission is to be composed of "not more than three" federal judges. Pub. L. 108-21, 117 Stat. 650, §401(n). It is now possible for the commission to have no judicial representation at all.

### b. Basic Guideline Structure

Though the SRA in 1984 created a basic statutory framework as well as a general direction for the development of federal sentencing guidelines, it still left the U.S. Sentencing Commission with sweeping authority and many difficult decisions about how best to regulate judicial discretion through sentencing guidelines. After three years of deliberation and drafting in which the U.S. Sentencing Commission considered a range of approaches to reform, in 1987 the commission finally produced the initial sentencing guidelines.

The following excerpt from the introduction to the Guidelines Manual gives important background on many of the structural and policy choices the commission made in forming its first guidelines. The text from the introduction has changed in subtle ways since the 1987 manual. The following text is from the 2011 guidelines manual — the most recent version available at the time of publication. The current version of the federal guidelines manual, along with prior versions, can be found at http://www.ussc.gov.

> ## Federal Sentencing Guidelines Manual, Chapter One — Introduction, Authority, and General Application Principles
> ### U.S. Sentencing Commission (2011)

. . . The initial sentencing guidelines and policy statements were developed after extensive hearings, deliberation, and consideration of substantial public comment. The Commission emphasizes, however, that it views the guideline-writing process as evolutionary. It expects, and the governing statute anticipates, that continuing research, experience, and analysis will result in modifications and revisions to the guidelines through submission of amendments to Congress. To this end, the Commission is established as a permanent agency to monitor sentencing practices in the federal courts.

#### THE BASIC APPROACH (POLICY STATEMENT)

To understand the guidelines and their underlying rationale, it is important to focus on the three objectives that Congress sought to achieve in enacting the Sentencing Reform Act of 1984. The Act's basic objective was to enhance the ability of the criminal justice system to combat crime through an effective, fair sentencing system. To achieve this end, Congress first sought honesty in sentencing. It sought to avoid the confusion and implicit deception that arose out of the pre-guidelines sentencing system, which required the court to impose an indeterminate sentence of imprisonment and empowered the parole commission to determine how much of the sentence an offender actually would serve in prison. . . .

Second, Congress sought reasonable uniformity in sentencing by narrowing the wide disparity in sentences imposed for similar criminal offenses committed by similar offenders. Third, Congress sought proportionality in sentencing through a system that imposes appropriately different sentences for criminal conduct of differing severity.

Honesty is easy to achieve: the abolition of parole makes the sentence imposed by the court the sentence the offender will serve, less approximately 15 percent for good behavior. There is a tension, however, between the mandate of uniformity and the mandate of proportionality. Simple uniformity — sentencing every offender to five years — destroys proportionality. Having only a few simple categories of crimes would make the guidelines uniform and easy to administer, but might lump together offenses that are different in important respects. . . . [But] a sentencing system tailored to fit every conceivable wrinkle of each case would quickly become unworkable and seriously compromise the certainty of punishment and its deterrent effect. For example: a bank robber with (or without) a gun, which the robber kept hidden (or brandished), might have frightened (or merely warned), injured seriously (or less seriously), tied up (or simply pushed) a guard, teller, or customer, at night (or at noon), in an effort to obtain money for other crimes (or for other purposes), in the company of a few (or many) other robbers, for the first (or fourth) time. . . .

The larger the number of subcategories of offense and offender characteristics included in the guidelines, the greater the complexity and the less workable the system. [Probation] officers and courts, in applying a complex system having numerous subcategories, would be required to make a host of decisions regarding whether the underlying facts were sufficient to bring the case within a particular subcategory. The greater the number of decisions required and the greater their complexity, the greater the risk that different courts would apply the guidelines differently to situations that, in fact, are similar, thereby reintroducing the very disparity that the guidelines were designed to reduce. . . .

In the end, there was no completely satisfying solution to this problem. The Commission had to balance the comparative virtues and vices of broad, simple categorization and detailed, complex subcategorization, and within the constraints established by that balance, minimize the discretionary powers of the sentencing court. Any system will, to a degree, enjoy the benefits and suffer from the drawbacks of each approach.

A philosophical problem arose when the Commission attempted to reconcile the differing perceptions of the purposes of criminal punishment. Most observers of the criminal law agree that the ultimate aim of the law itself, and of punishment in particular, is the control of crime. Beyond this point, however, the consensus seems to break down. Some argue that appropriate punishment should be defined primarily on the basis of the principle of "just deserts." Under this principle, punishment should be scaled to the offender's culpability and the resulting harms. Others argue that punishment should be imposed primarily on the basis of practical "crime control" considerations. This theory calls for sentences that most effectively lessen the likelihood of future crime, either by deterring others or incapacitating the defendant.

Adherents of each of these points of view urged the Commission to choose between them and accord one primacy over the other. As a practical matter, however, this choice was unnecessary because in most sentencing decisions the application of either philosophy will produce the same or similar results.

In its initial set of guidelines, the Commission sought to solve both the practical and philosophical problems of developing a coherent sentencing system by taking an empirical approach that used as a starting point data estimating pre-guidelines sentencing practice. It analyzed data drawn from 10,000 presentence investigations, the differing elements of various crimes as distinguished in substantive criminal statutes, the United States Parole Commission's guidelines and statistics, and data from other relevant sources in order to determine which distinctions were important in pre-guidelines practice. After consideration, the Commission accepted, modified, or rationalized these distinctions. . . .

The Commission did not simply copy estimates of pre-guidelines practice as revealed by the data. . . . Rather, it departed from the data at different points for various important reasons. Congressional statutes, for example, suggested or required departure, as in the case of the Anti-Drug Abuse Act of 1986 that imposed increased and mandatory minimum sentences. In addition, the data revealed inconsistencies in treatment, such as punishing economic crime less severely than other apparently equivalent behavior.

Despite these policy-oriented departures from pre-guidelines practice, the guidelines represent an approach that begins with, and builds upon, empirical data. The guidelines will not please those who wish the Commission to adopt a single philosophical theory and then work deductively to establish a simple and perfect set of categorizations and distinctions. The guidelines may prove acceptable, however, to those who seek more modest, incremental improvements in the status quo, who believe the best is often the enemy of the good, and who recognize that these guidelines are, as the Act contemplates, but the first step in an evolutionary process. . . .

### DEPARTURES

The sentencing statute permits a court to depart from a guideline-specified sentence only when it finds "an aggravating or mitigating circumstance of a kind, or to a degree, not adequately taken into consideration by the Sentencing Commission in formulating the guidelines that should result in a sentence different from that described." 18 U.S.C. §3553(b). The Commission intends the sentencing courts to treat each guideline as carving out a "heartland," a set of typical cases embodying the conduct that each guideline describes. When a court finds an atypical case, one to which a particular guideline linguistically applies but where conduct significantly differs from the norm, the court may consider whether a departure is warranted. Section 5H1.10 (Race, Sex, National Origin, Creed, Religion, and Socio-Economic Status), §5H1.12 (Lack of Guidance as a Youth and Similar Circumstances), the third sentence of §5H1.4 (Physical Condition, Including Drug or Alcohol Dependence or Abuse), and the last sentence of §5K2.12 (Coercion and Duress), and §5K2.19 (Post-Sentencing Rehabilitative Efforts) list several factors that the court cannot take into account as grounds for departure. With those specific exceptions, however, the Commission does not intend to limit the kinds of factors, whether or not mentioned anywhere else in the guidelines, that could constitute grounds for departure in an unusual case.

The Commission has adopted this departure policy for two reasons. First, it is difficult to prescribe a single set of guidelines that encompasses the vast range of human conduct potentially relevant to a sentencing decision. The Commission also recognizes that the initial set of guidelines need not do so. The Commission is a permanent body, empowered by law to write and rewrite guidelines, with progressive changes, over many years. By monitoring when courts depart from the guidelines and by analyzing their stated reasons for doing so and court decisions with references thereto, the Commission, over time, will be able to refine the guidelines to specify more precisely when departures should and should not be permitted.

Second, the Commission believes that despite the courts' legal freedom to depart from the guidelines, they will not do so very often. This is because the guidelines, offense by offense, seek to take account of those factors that the Commission's data indicate made a significant difference in pre-guidelines sentencing practice. Thus, for example, where the presence of physical injury made an important difference in pre-guidelines sentencing practice (as in the case of robbery or assault), the guidelines specifically include this factor to enhance the sentence. . . .

### SENTENCING RANGES

. . . While the Commission has not considered itself bound by pre-guidelines sentencing practice, it has not attempted to develop an entirely new system of sentencing on the basis of theory alone. Guideline sentences, in many instances, will approximate average pre-guidelines practice and adherence to the guidelines will help to eliminate wide disparity. . . . In some instances, short sentences of incarceration for all offenders in a category have been substituted for a pre-guidelines sentencing practice of very wide variability in which some defendants received probation while others received several years in prison for the same offense. Moreover, inasmuch as those who pleaded guilty under pre-guidelines practice often received lesser sentences, the guidelines permit the court to impose lesser sentences on those defendants who accept responsibility for their misconduct. For defendants who provide substantial assistance to the government in the investigation or prosecution of others, a downward departure may be warranted. . . .

The Commission has also examined its sentencing ranges in light of their likely impact upon prison population. Specific legislation, such as the Anti-Drug Abuse Act of 1986 and the career offender provisions of the Sentencing Reform Act of 1984, required the Commission to promulgate guidelines that will lead to substantial prison population increases. These increases will occur irrespective of the guidelines. The guidelines themselves, insofar as they reflect policy decisions made by the Commission (rather than legislated mandatory minimum or career offender sentences), are projected to lead to an increase in prison population . . . estimated at approximately 10 percent over a period of ten years. . . .

THE SENTENCING TABLE

The Commission has established a sentencing table that for technical and practical reasons contains 43 levels. Each level in the table prescribes ranges that overlap with the ranges in the preceding and succeeding levels. By overlapping the ranges, the table should discourage unnecessary litigation. Both prosecution and defense will realize that the difference between one level and another will not necessarily make a difference in the sentence that the court imposes. Thus, little purpose will be served in protracted litigation trying to determine, for example, whether $10,000 or $11,000 was obtained as a result of a fraud. At the same time, the levels work to increase a sentence proportionately. A change of six levels roughly doubles the sentence irrespective of the level at which one starts. The guidelines, in keeping with the statutory requirement that the maximum of any range cannot exceed the minimum by more than the greater of 25 percent or six months (28 U.S.C. §994(b)(2)), permit courts to exercise the greatest permissible range of sentencing discretion. . . .

### A CONCLUDING NOTE

The Commission emphasizes that it drafted the initial guidelines with considerable caution. It examined the many hundreds of criminal statutes in the United States Code. It began with those that were the basis for a significant number of prosecutions and sought to place them in a rational order. It developed additional distinctions relevant to the application of these provisions, and it applied sentencing ranges to each resulting category. In doing so, it relied upon pre-guidelines sentencing practice as revealed by its own statistical analyses based on summary reports of some 40,000 convictions, a sample of 10,000 augmented presentence reports, the parole guidelines, and policy judgments.

The Commission recognizes that some will criticize this approach as overly cautious, as representing too little a departure from pre-guidelines sentencing practice. Yet, it will cure wide disparity. The Commission is a permanent body that can amend the guidelines each year. Although the data available to it, like all data, are imperfect, experience with the guidelines will lead to additional information and provide a firm empirical basis for consideration of revisions.

### NOTES

1. *Theoretical choices (or lack thereof).*   Many of the early calls for sentencing reform urged that reforms be driven by a specific theoretical commitment to a "just deserts" or "limiting retributivism" philosophy. See Andrew von Hirsch, Doing Justice: The Choice of Punishments (1976); Norval Morris, The Future of Imprisonment (1974). As noted before, Minnesota's sentencing commission heeded this recommendation when it adopted just deserts as the governing premise of its policies concerning who receives prison sentences. The American Law Institute (ALI) in its current redrafting of the sentencing provisions in the Model Penal Code has focused on utilitarian goals but mandates that these be

pursued within proportionality constraints. As explained in the introduction to the federal sentencing guidelines, however, the U.S. Sentencing Commission concluded that as a "practical matter" any choice between crime control and retributivist philosophies of punishment in the construction of the guidelines "was unnecessary because in most sentencing decisions the application of either philosophy will produce the same or similar results." Do you agree with this assertion?

2. *Training exercises.* One of the functions of the U.S. Sentencing Commission is to train the judges, probation officers, and attorneys who work with the guidelines daily. The extensive website for the commission, at http://www.ussc.gov, includes training exercises and detailed study papers on how to apply the guidelines in various situations. It is easier to appreciate the design choices the commission made in constructing the guidelines machine after having at least glimpsed that machine in operation. Now, or after reviewing the following overview of the federal guidelines in operation, would be a good time to use the worksheets at the commission's website and step through one or more of the training exercises (perhaps the Robbery Exercise, available at http://www.ussc.gov/Education_and_Training/Guidelines_Educational_Materials/WS_Ex_rob.pdf (hypothetical facts) and http://www.ussc.gov/Education_and_Training/Guidelines_Educational_Materials/sent_ex_rob.pdf (completed worksheet)). The worksheets are helpful in pointing the way through the tangles of the guidelines.

## Overview of the Federal Sentencing Guidelines
### U.S. Sentencing Commission[*]

### HOW THE SENTENCING GUIDELINES WORK

The sentencing guidelines take into account both the seriousness of the offense and the offender's criminal history.

*Offense Seriousness.* The sentencing guidelines provide 43 levels of offense seriousness — the more serious the crime, the higher the offense level

*Base Offense Level.* Each type of crime is assigned a base offense level, which is the starting point for determining the seriousness of a particular offense. More serious types of crimes have higher base offense levels (for example, a trespass has a base offense level of 4, while kidnapping has a base offense level of 32).

*Specific Offense Characteristics.* In addition to base offense levels, each offense type typically carries with it a number of specific offense characteristics. These are factors that vary from offense to offense, but that

___
* Undated. Document available at http://www.ussc.gov/About_the_Commission/Overview_of_the_USSC/Overview_Federal_Sentencing_Guidelines.pdf.

can increase or decrease the base offense level and, ultimately, the sentence an offender receives. Some examples:

- One of the specific base offense characteristics for fraud (which has a base offense level of 7 if the statutory maximum is 20 years or more) increases the offense level based on the amount of loss involved in the offense. If a fraud involved a $6,000 loss, there is to be a 2-level increase to the base offense level, bringing the level up to 9. If a fraud involved a $50,000 loss, there is to be a 6-level increase, bringing the total to 13.
- One of the specific offense characteristics for robbery (which has a base offense level of 20) involves the use of a firearm. If a firearm was displayed during the robbery, there is to be a 5-level increase, bringing the level to 25; if a firearm was actually discharged during the robbery, there is to be a 7-level increase, bringing the level to 27.

*Adjustments.* Adjustments are factors that can apply to any offense. Like specific offense characteristics, they increase or decrease the offense level. Categories of adjustments include: victim-related adjustments, the offender's role in the crime, and obstruction of justice. Examples of adjustments are as follows:

- If the offender was a minimal participant in the offense, the offense level is decreased by 4 levels.
- If the offender knew that the victim was unusually vulnerable due to age or physical or mental condition, the offense level is increased by 2 levels.
- If the offender obstructed justice, the offense level is increased by 2 levels. . . .

*Multiple Count Adjustments.* When there are multiple counts of conviction, the sentencing guidelines provide instructions on how to achieve a "combined offense level." These rules provide incremental punishment for significant additional criminal conduct. The most serious offense is used as a starting point. The other counts determine whether to and how much to increase the offense level. . . .

*Acceptance of Responsibility.* . . . The judge may decrease the offense level by two levels if, in the judge's opinion, the offender accepted responsibility for his offense. In deciding whether to grant this reduction, judges can consider such factors as:

- whether the offender truthfully admitted his or her role in the crime,
- whether the offender made restitution before there was a guilty verdict, and
- whether the offender pled guilty.

Offenders who qualify for the 2-level reduction and whose offense levels are greater than 15 may, upon motion of the government, be granted an additional 1-level reduction if, in a timely manner, they declare their intention to plead guilty.

*Criminal History.* The guidelines assign each offender to one of six criminal history categories based upon the extent of an offender's past misconduct and how recently these crimes took place. Criminal History Category I is assigned to the least serious criminal record and includes many first-time offenders. Criminal History Category VI is the most serious category and includes offenders with lengthy criminal records.

*Determining the Guideline Range.* The final offense level is determined by taking the base offense level and then adding or subtracting from it any specific offense characteristics and adjustments that apply. The point at which the final offense level and the criminal history category intersect on the Commission's sentencing table determines the defendant's sentencing guideline range. [An] offender with a Criminal History Category of I and a final offense level of 20 would have a guideline range of 33 to 41 months. . . .

*Sentences Outside the Guideline Range.* After the guideline range is determined, if an atypical aggravating or mitigating circumstance exists, the court may "depart" from the guideline range. That is, the judge may sentence the offender above or below the range. When departing, the judge must state the reason for the departure.

In January 2005, the U.S. Supreme Court decided United States v. Booker, 543 U.S. 220 (2005). [The] Court held that the Sixth Amendment applies to the sentencing guidelines. In its remedial *Booker* opinion, the Court severed and excised two statutory provisions, 18 U.S.C. §3553(b)(1), which made the federal guidelines mandatory, and 18 U.S.C. §3742(e), an appeals provision.

Under the approach set forth by the Court, "district courts, while not bound to apply the Guidelines, must consult those Guidelines and take them into account when sentencing," subject to review by the courts of appeal for "unreasonableness." . . .

## NOTES

1. *Guideline commentary.* In addition to the detailed instructions set forth in guideline provisions, most guidelines are accompanied by official commentary from the U.S. Sentencing Commission in the form of "application notes" and "background." This commentary is designed to aid courts in applying specific provisions by defining key terms or providing insights into the development and purpose of the provision. In Stinson v. United States, 508 U.S. 36 (1993), the Supreme Court unanimously ruled that "commentary in the *Guidelines Manual* that interprets or explains a guideline is authoritative unless it violates the Constitution or a federal statute, or is inconsistent with, or a plainly erroneous reading of, that guideline." In other words, courts and others interpreting and applying the guidelines must generally treat the commentary as binding and having the same force as the actual guideline provisions.

**Sentencing Table**
*(in months of imprisonment)*

| | Offense Level | Criminal History Category (Criminal History Points) | | | | | |
|---|---|---|---|---|---|---|---|
| | | I (0 or 1) | II (2 or 3) | III (4, 5, 6) | IV (7, 8, 9) | V (10, 11, 12) | VI (13 or more) |
| Zone A | 1 | 0-6 | 0-6 | 0-6 | 0-6 | 0-6 | 0-6 |
| | 2 | 0-6 | 0-6 | 0-6 | 0-6 | 0-6 | 1-7 |
| | 3 | 0-6 | 0-6 | 0-6 | 0-6 | 2-8 | 3-9 |
| | 4 | 0-6 | 0-6 | 0-6 | 2-8 | 4-10 | 6-12 |
| | 5 | 0-6 | 0-6 | 1-7 | 4-10 | 6-12 | 9-15 |
| | 6 | 0-6 | 1-7 | 2-8 | 6-12 | 9-15 | 12-18 |
| | 7 | 0-6 | 2-8 | 4-10 | 8-14 | 12-18 | 15-21 |
| | 8 | 0-6 | 4-10 | 6-12 | 10-16 | 15-21 | 18-24 |
| Zone B | 9 | 4-10 | 6-12 | 8-14 | 12-18 | 18-24 | 21-27 |
| | 10 | 6-12 | 8-14 | 10-16 | 15-21 | 21-27 | 24-30 |
| Zone C | 11 | 8-14 | 10-16 | 12-18 | 18-24 | 24-30 | 27-33 |
| | 12 | 10-16 | 12-18 | 15-21 | 21-27 | 27-33 | 30-37 |
| | 13 | 12-18 | 15-21 | 18-24 | 24-30 | 30-37 | 33-41 |
| | 14 | 15-21 | 18-24 | 21-27 | 27-33 | 33-41 | 37-46 |
| | 15 | 18-24 | 21-27 | 24-30 | 30-37 | 37-46 | 41-51 |
| | 16 | 21-27 | 24-30 | 27-33 | 33-41 | 41-51 | 46-57 |
| | 17 | 24-30 | 27-33 | 30-37 | 37-46 | 46-57 | 51-63 |
| | 18 | 27-33 | 30-37 | 33-41 | 41-51 | 51-63 | 57-71 |
| | 19 | 30-37 | 33-41 | 37-46 | 46-57 | 57-71 | 63-78 |
| | 20 | 33-41 | 37-46 | 41-51 | 51-63 | 63-78 | 70-87 |
| | 21 | 37-46 | 41-51 | 46-57 | 57-71 | 70-87 | 77-96 |
| | 22 | 41-51 | 46-57 | 51-63 | 63-78 | 77-96 | 84-105 |
| | 23 | 46-57 | 51-63 | 57-71 | 70-87 | 84-105 | 92-115 |
| | 24 | 51-63 | 57-71 | 63-78 | 77-96 | 92-115 | 100-125 |
| | 25 | 57-71 | 63-78 | 70-87 | 84-105 | 100-125 | 110-137 |
| | 26 | 63-78 | 70-87 | 78-97 | 92-115 | 110-137 | 120-150 |
| | 27 | 70-87 | 78-97 | 87-108 | 100-125 | 120-150 | 130-162 |
| Zone D | 28 | 78-97 | 87-108 | 97-121 | 110-137 | 130-162 | 140-175 |
| | 29 | 87-108 | 97-121 | 108-135 | 121-151 | 140-175 | 151-188 |
| | 30 | 97-121 | 108-135 | 121-151 | 135-168 | 151-188 | 168-210 |
| | 31 | 108-135 | 121-151 | 135-168 | 151-188 | 168-210 | 188-235 |
| | 32 | 121-151 | 135-168 | 151-188 | 168-210 | 188-235 | 210-262 |
| | 33 | 135-168 | 151-188 | 168-210 | 188-235 | 210-262 | 235-293 |
| | 34 | 151-188 | 168-210 | 188-235 | 210-262 | 235-293 | 262-327 |
| | 35 | 168-210 | 188-235 | 210-262 | 235-293 | 262-327 | 292-365 |
| | 36 | 188-235 | 210-262 | 235-293 | 262-327 | 292-365 | 324-405 |
| | 37 | 210-262 | 235-293 | 262-327 | 292-365 | 324-405 | 360-life |
| | 38 | 235-293 | 262-327 | 292-365 | 324-405 | 360-life | 360-life |
| | 39 | 262-327 | 292-365 | 324-405 | 360-life | 360-life | 360-life |
| | 40 | 292-365 | 324-405 | 360-life | 360-life | 360-life | 360-life |
| | 41 | 324-405 | 360-life | 360-life | 360-life | 360-life | 360-life |
| | 42 | 360-life | 360-life | 360-life | 360-life | 360-life | 360-life |
| | 43 | life | life | life | life | life | life |

The Offense Level (1-43) forms the vertical axis of the Sentencing Table. The Criminal History Category (I-VI) forms the horizontal axis of the Table. The intersection of the Offense Level and Criminal History Category displays the Guideline Range in months of imprisonment. "Life" means life imprisonment. For example, the guideline range applicable to a defendant with an Offense Level of 15 and a Criminal History Category of III is 24-30 months of imprisonment.

2. *Conflicting judicial interpretations of guideline provisions.*   As with any other intricate set of legal rules, the federal sentencing guidelines are often interpreted in conflicting ways by different judges. In Braxton v. United States, 500 U.S. 344 (1991), the Supreme Court unanimously ruled that the U.S. Sentencing Commission is to have the initial and primary responsibility of responding to circuit conflicts over guideline interpretations. According to the Court in *Braxton,* "in charging the Commission 'periodically [to] review and revise' the guidelines, Congress necessarily contemplated that the Commission would periodically review the work of the courts, and would make whatever clarifying revisions to the guidelines conflicting judicial decisions might suggest." Though the Supreme Court in *Braxton* said that it should be more "restrained and circumspect" in using its certiorari power to resolve circuit conflicts for guidelines issues, the Court has still played a role in the development of federal sentencing law by deciding more than two dozen significant sentencing cases in the past decade. The most important of these decisions was United States v. Booker in which the Court declared the federal guidelines advisory only.

3. *Guideline complexity.*   Though the summary above implies that the application of the federal guidelines is relatively simple, in actual practice the federal sentencing guidelines are quite complex. The complexity of the federal guideline system has been a concern since the U.S. Sentencing Commission promulgated its initial guidelines in 1987: there were more than 100 multi-section guidelines filling more than 200 pages in the first Guidelines Manual, and they included an intricate nine-step process for determining a defendant's applicable sentencing range using a 258-box grid known as the "sentencing table." Judicial decisions have since increased the corpus of federal sentencing law and thus complicated an already intricate sentencing process: confronted with numerous interpretive questions in applying the guidelines, district and circuit courts issue hundreds of guideline sentencing opinions each year. Meanwhile, the U.S. Sentencing Commission, honoring its statutory obligation to review and revise the guidelines, has passed almost 700 amendments to the guidelines over the past 18 years. The U.S. Sentencing Guidelines Manual now runs more than 650 pages and has an even lengthier, separate appendix that chronicles the amendments. Tens of thousands of federal court opinions have interpreted these guidelines.

Many judges, practitioners, and commentators have lamented the system's complexity, in part because complex guidelines increase the risk that the sentencing rules will be misunderstood or misapplied. Thus, complexity undercuts the goals of sentencing predictability and certainty. Justice Stephen Breyer, a member of the original Sentencing Commission, identifies a link between complexity and judicial discretion:

> The original 1987 Guidelines draft was just over 200 pages long, and many criticized that draft as too lengthy and too complex. The Guidelines are now twice as long[, and] the greatest obstacle to [simplification] is, I believe, the legal mind itself. We judges and lawyers love to make distinctions. For sentencing purposes, distinctions about how a crime was carried out are important in order to assure sentencing proportionality. . . . But it is important to know when to stop. [The] Commission should review the present Guidelines, acting forcefully to diminish significantly the number of offense characteristics

attached to individual crimes. The characteristics that remain should be justified for the most part by data that shows their use by practicing judges to change sentences. . . . The Commission originally stated that each Guideline was to cover only the "heartland" of the offense at issue. That concept—the "heartland"—should remain our guiding principle. Less typical cases may be left to departures imposed by the sentencing judge, and perhaps guided, though not directly mandated, by the Commission. . . . The result would be an increase in the discretionary authority of the sentencing judge.

Speech of Associate Justice Stephen Breyer, 11 Fed. Sent'g Rep. at 185-186 (1999). The U.S. Sentencing Commission has often indicated that simplifying the guidelines is an institutional goal, but it has failed so far to engineer such simplification. See Marc L. Miller, True Grid: Revealing Sentencing Policy, 25 U.C. Davis L. Rev. 587 (1992). In addition to other impacts, the guidelines' complexity also creates serious problems for the defense bar in providing effective representation for federal defendants. See Alan J. Chaset, A Teacher at the Top: Another Reason to Have a Representative of the Criminal Defense Bar on the Sentencing Commission, 11 Fed. Sent'g Rep. 309, 309-310 (1999) (suggesting that guidelines may "involve too much law for the average practitioner to keep current with"); Douglas A. Berman, From Lawlessness to Too Much Law? Exploring the Risk of Disparity from Differences in Defense Counsel Under Guidelines Sentencing, 87 Iowa L. Rev. 435 (2002).

4. *imbalance between offense and offender characteristics.* Although the characteristics of an *offense* play a central role in establishing applicable sentencing ranges under the federal sentencing guidelines, characteristics of an *offender* (other than past criminal history) play almost no role in the determination of applicable guideline ranges. Such matters are addressed in the federal guidelines only through policy statements that seek to regulate departures, and these provisions state that many such offender characteristics are "not relevant" or "not ordinarily relevant" to a departure decision. See, e.g., U.S. Sentencing Guidelines Manual §5H1.12 ("Lack of guidance as a youth and similar circumstances indicating a disadvantaged upbringing are not relevant grounds in determining whether a departure is warranted."); §5H1.2 ("Education and vocational skills are not ordinarily relevant in determining whether a sentence should be outside the applicable guideline range."); §5H1.4 ("Drug or alcohol dependence or abuse is not a reason for imposing a sentence below the guidelines."); §5H1.6 ("Family ties and responsibilities and community ties are not ordinarily relevant in determining whether a sentence should be outside the applicable guideline range.").

Many judges and commentators have been especially critical of the guidelines' failure to account for offender characteristics, such as disadvantaged background or family circumstances, that judges often used as mitigating considerations in pre-guidelines sentencing practice. See, e.g., Kate Stith & Jose A. Cabranes, Judging Under the Federal Sentencing Guidelines, 91 Nw. U. L. Rev. 1247 (1997); Daniel J. Freed, Federal Sentencing in the Wake of Guidelines: Unacceptable Limits on the Discretion of Sentencers, 101 Yale L.J. 1681 (1992); Charles J. Ogletree, The Death of Discretion? Reflections on the Federal Sentencing Guidelines, 101 Harv. L. Rev. 1938 (1988). Congress and the U.S. Sentencing Commission have not generally heeded these criticisms. In fact,

Congress in 2003 passed legislation that further curtailed the ability of sentencing judges in certain cases to depart from the guidelines based on offender characteristics, and it also directed the commission to review critically how judges were using their departure authority to take into account offender characteristics.

### c.   Departures and Discretion

Although the Sentencing Reform Act significantly altered the judicial role in sentencing, it did not remove the judge's discretion entirely from the federal sentencing process. Despite the strictures of mandatory sentencing laws and complex guidelines, the SRA and the guidelines guaranteed an important role for the sentencing judge.

First and foremost, the guidelines preserve a judicial role simply through the adoption of sentencing ranges. Like most state guideline systems, the federal guidelines do not specify an exact sentence for each offense and offender; they establish a range from which sentencing judges select a specific sentence. Notably, Congress specifically mandated in the SRA that sentencing ranges in the federal guidelines be fairly narrow by providing that "the maximum of the range established for [any imprisonment] term shall not exceed the minimum of that range by more than the greater of 25 percent or 6 months." 28 U.S.C. §994(b)(2). Because district judges have complete discretion to select a sentence from within this range, and because this decision is not subject to appeal, the independent determination and judgment of district judges still, in effect, controls at least one-quarter of every federal guideline sentence.

The SRA also gives judges express authority to depart from the guidelines whenever there is a "circumstance of a kind, or to a degree, not adequately taken into consideration by the Sentencing Commission in formulating the guidelines that should result in a sentence different from that described." 18 U.S.C. §3553(b). How the U.S. Sentencing Commission and courts should interpret this provision has been intensely debated since the guidelines' inception, and for good reason. The rules governing departures are the focal point of the guideline system's efforts to achieve greater sentencing consistency without sacrificing necessary flexibility. If departure authority too readily allows judges to deviate from the guidelines' presumptive sentences, then the system will be too pliant and unwarranted sentencing disparity may persist. Yet if departure authority too rarely allows judges to depart from the guidelines' presumptive sentences, then the system will be too rigid, judicial discretion will be overly limited, and unwarranted sentencing uniformity may occur.

Departure authority technically takes two different forms in the federal guideline system. The commission used the departure mechanism in U.S.S.G. §5K1.1 to implement Congress's directive that judges generally impose lower sentences "to take into account a defendant's substantial assistance in the investigation and prosecution" of others. 28 U.S.C. §994(n). This provision for departures based on a prosecutor's motion plays a critical role not only in the sentence imposed but also in plea negotiations, in which prosecutors use their authority to recommend departures as a way to persuade defendants to cooperate in further criminal investigations. Commentators have noted that section 5K1.1 and other guideline provisions enhance the sentencing discretion of prosecutors; the uneven application of section 5K1.1 and prosecutorial discretion more generally is discussed below.

Even more fundamental to the operation of the guidelines and the preservation of judicial discretion is the district judge's distinct power to depart from the guidelines without a motion from the prosecutor. According to the Guidelines Manual, a sentencing court may depart if the case at issue is "atypical," which means that certain factors differ significantly from the norm and were therefore not considered by the drafters of the guidelines. While some factors, such as race, sex, national origin, creed, religion, socioeconomic status, lack of guidance as a youth, drug or alcohol dependence, and economic hardship, may never serve as reasons for downward departures, the Guidelines Manual sets out some factors as encouraged or discouraged bases for departure — with the latter to be used to justify a departure only "in exceptional cases." If a factor is not mentioned in the guidelines, the sentencing court must determine whether the factor takes the case out of the "heartland" of other cases, after considering the structure and theory of both relevant individual guidelines and the guidelines taken as a whole.

In Koon v. United States, 518 U.S. 81 (1993), the Supreme Court addressed the level of appellate review that was appropriate for assessing a sentencing court's decision to depart. The Court, in an opinion by Justice Kennedy, held that a district court judge's decision to depart from the guidelines

> will in most cases be due substantial deference, for it embodies the traditional exercise of discretion by a sentencing court. . . . Whether a given factor is present to a degree not adequately considered by the Commission, or whether a discouraged factor nonetheless justifies departure because it is present in some unusual or exceptional way, are matters determined in large part by comparison with the facts of other Guidelines cases. District courts have an institutional advantage over appellate courts in making these sorts of determinations, especially as they see so many more Guidelines cases than appellate courts do. In 1994, for example, 93.9% of Guidelines cases were not appealed. . . .
>
> This does not mean that district courts do not confront questions of law in deciding whether to depart. . . . The Government is quite correct that whether a factor is a permissible basis for departure under any circumstances is a question of law, and the court of appeals need not defer to the district court's resolution of the point. . . .

As the Court applied this holding to the facts of the case, it found that the district court had abused its discretion by considering the defendants' collateral employment consequences in granting a downward departure. It found that career loss "is not unusual for a public official who is convicted of using his governmental authority to violate a person's rights to lose his or her job and to be barred from future work in that field." In addition, the Court held that "the low likelihood of petitioners' recidivism was not an appropriate basis for departure," as criminal history category I already indicates a low likelihood of repeat offending. On the other hand, the Court determined that the sentencing court acted within its discretion in considering susceptibility to abuse in prison and successive prosecutions as grounds for a downward departure.

## NOTES

1. *Departure patterns before and after.*    Prior to the Supreme Court's decision in *Koon*, federal district judges used their departure authority rather sparingly, perhaps because many circuit courts reviewed decisions to depart de novo while refusing to review any discretionary decision *not* to depart from the guidelines. Before *Koon*, district judges exercised their independent authority to depart from the guidelines in only about 10% of cases (although, during the same period, prosecutors requested and judges granted departures based on defendants' substantial assistance in about twice as many cases). The *Koon* decision, perhaps responding to judicial and academic complaints about guideline rigidity, seemed designed through its adoption of an "abuse of discretion" review standard to enhance sentencing courts' departure authority. If this was indeed the Supreme Court's goal, *Koon* has proved to be a very effective ruling. The total number of departures has increased steady following the *Koon* decision, and by 2001 there were roughly twice as many departures as in 1995.

Notably, almost all departures involve decisions by sentencing judges to impose a sentence *below* the applicable guideline range. Since the start of guideline sentencing, upward departures have never constituted much more than 1% of all sentenced cases, and in 2001 there were 30 times more downward departures than upward departures. By 2006 the number of upward departures had slightly increased, as had the number of downward departures. Did these trends occur because federal sentencing judges generally disapprove of the severity of sentences under the guidelines, or is some other dynamic at work?

Though consistent in direction, judicial departure rates have not been uniform across federal districts and circuits. The U.S. Sentencing Commission reported in 2011 that the Second Circuit had the highest rate of sentences below the guidelines range (not sponsored by the government), at 38.5%, while the Ninth Circuit had the lowest, at 11.7%. See United States Sentencing Commission, 2011 Sourcebook. A high rate of government sponsored non-guideline sentences in certain southwestern border districts, such as Southern California and Arizona, can be traced in part to "fast track" departure programs adopted in districts with a high volume of immigration cases; these programs were designed to encourage the prompt disposition of cases in which a defendant would ultimately be deported following any term of imprisonment. Should statistics revealing significant regional variations in the use of departure authority be a source of particular concern?

2. *Congressional reaction to* Koon: *the Feeney Amendment.*    Despite the occasional expression of concerns by the Department of Justice and a few commentators over the increased use of downward departure authority after *Koon*, many judges and most commentators welcomed the increased sentencing flexibility that *Koon* seemed to endorse through its expanded view of departure authority. In 2003, however, Congress decreed through a provision known as the Feeney Amendment that the use of departure authority had to be reined in. The statute required circuit courts to apply de novo review of departures (effectively overruling the *Koon* decision) and directed the commission to amend the guidelines to "substantially reduce" the number of downward departures. Pub. L. 108-21, 117 Stat. 650, §401(m). Congress provided no specific guidance to the commission on how to interpret or effectuate this directive.

3. *Extent of departures.* Throughout the history of the federal guidelines, an issue that has been debated and litigated is what the standard should be for assessing the extent of departures. In comparison, the Minnesota Supreme Court, early in the history of the Minnesota sentencing guidelines, held that any upward departure duration should generally not exceed twice the presumptive duration. See State v. Evans, 311 N.W.2d 481 (Minn. 1981).

4. *State approaches to departure authority.* As in the federal system, most state guidelines allow the judge to depart from the sentence range designated in the guidelines. In some states, the departures are categorized according to whether they affect either the disposition of the sentence or the duration of the sentence. Departure standards in most states are generally not as detailed or restrictive as in the federal system: state systems providing for departures typically permit the sentencing court to depart for any "substantial" or "compelling" reasons, or they set forth nonexclusive lists of reasons for departures. The departure statutes generally require the judge to explain any departure, and an inadequate explanation can lead to reversal on appeal. Appellate courts in these jurisdictions have developed extensive case law approving or disapproving various grounds for departure. The case law in some states, such as Pennsylvania, gives the trial judge much wider latitude than that in other states, such as Minnesota.

Despite more permissive departure standards, the number of departures in state systems has remained well below the number of cases sentenced within the state guidelines. For instance, in Minnesota dispositional departures have occurred in around 10% of total cases sentenced, while durational departures have occurred in about 25% of cases involving an active prison term. See Richard Frase, Implementing Commission-Based Sentencing Guidelines: The Lessons of the First Ten Years in Minnesota, 2 Cornell J.L. & Pub. Pol'y 279 (1993). By what criteria could a sentencing commission decide how many departures are too many? Too few?

> ## *Substantial Assistance: An Empirical Yardstick Gauging Equity in Current Federal Policy and Practice, Linda Drazga Maxfield and John H. Kramer*
> ### Pages 2-4, 19-21 (1999)

### THE UNDEFINED SUBSTANCE OF SUBSTANTIAL ASSISTANCE

Congress directed the Commission to create [a method to] decrease sentences below the guideline range for offenders who assist in the investigation or prosecution of another person committing a criminal offense. The Sentencing Commission's response to this congressional mandate took the form of guideline policy statement 5K1.1 — Substantial Assistance to Authorities:

> Upon motion of the government stating that the defendant has provided substantial assistance in the investigation or prosecution of another person who has committed an offense, the court may depart from the guidelines. . . .

Issues raised in the substantial assistance policy statement, but left unanswered elsewhere . . . include [several] that are cited below.

*First,* the factors to be used by the prosecutor prior to sentencing to determine whether the cooperation of a given defendant is "substantial" — and therefore warrants a substantial assistance departure motion — are unaddressed. . . . What objective and equitable parameters distinguish between "substantial" assistance and "non-substantial" assistance?

*Second,* the authority to move for a §5K1.1 departure is limited to the prosecution. This exclusivity has resulted in spirited debate in the criminal justice community. Government prosecutors defend the appropriateness of their substantial assistance monopoly by citing the government's unique capability to judge accurately the benefit obtained from the type and extent of assistance provided. The critical response is that predicating a substantial assistance departure on a government motion is a potential source of disparity because the unilateral government decision whether to make the substantial assistance motion is not subject to challenge by the defense and is not reviewable by the court (unless constitutional grounds are cited). . . .

*Finally,* apparently not all substantial assistance is equal. The policy statement places no conditions on the magnitude of the sentence reduction to be given. Consequently, extensive cooperation theoretically would deserve a larger sentence reduction than less extensive (but still substantial) cooperation. What is the link between assessing the value of a defendant's substantial assistance and deciding on the magnitude of the sentence reduction? . . . Achieving equity in the substantial assistance process has major ramifications for the overall equity of the guidelines system; 19 percent of federal criminal convictions — roughly 7,500 cases per year — were granted downward departures under §5K1.1 over the past three fiscal years (1994 through 1996). . . .

### SUMMARY AND IMPLICATIONS

[A] working group was established to explore the policies and procedures across the judicial districts, and to study the factors associated with §5K1.1 sentence reductions and the magnitudes of the departures [through] a diversity of research methodologies. . . . The data reported were not able to find direct correlations between type of cooperation provided, type of benefit or result received by the government, the making of a §5K1.1 motion, and the extent of the substantial assistance departure received. [The] consistency of the findings across methodologies reveals . . . an equity problem requiring subsequent research.

*First,* this analysis uncovered that the definition of "substantial assistance" was not being consistently applied across the federal districts. Not only were some districts considering cooperation that was not being considered by other districts, but the components of a given behavior that classified it as "substantial" were unclear.

*Second,* while the U.S. attorney offices are required to record the reason for making a substantial assistance motion, there is no provision that this information be made available for review. It is exactly such a lack of review, inherent in preguideline judicial discretion, that led to charges of unwarranted sentencing disparity and passage of the SRA. Under the SRA, the court is now compelled to report a reason for the sentence imposed and a reason for a departure. . . . A comparable §5K1.1 "statement of reasons" appears appropriate for a guideline process affecting nearly one in every five federal defendants. DOJ information on district charging practices, plea bargaining practices, degree and type of cooperation, and usefulness of information to the prosecution is crucial in an assessment of §5K1.1. . . .

*Third*, the evidence consistently indicated that factors that were associated with either the making of a §5K1.1 motion and/or the magnitude of the departure were not consistent with principles of equity. Expected factors (e.g., type of cooperation, benefit of cooperation, defendant culpability or function, relevant conduct, offense type) generally were found to be inadequate in explaining §5K1.1 departures. Even more worrisome, legally irrelevant factors (e.g., gender, race, ethnicity, citizenship) were found to be statistically significant in explaining §5K1.1 departures. . . .

Data indicate that currently judges relate the magnitude of departure to the length of the predeparture sentence: higher predeparture guideline ranges bring more absolute months of departure. However, no evidence supports the conclusion that defendants facing higher sentences, in fact, provide absolutely more cooperation, or absolutely more beneficial cooperation, to warrant a larger relative departure. The issue is whether the magnitude of a substantial assistance departure should be an absolute amount (all defendants who cooperate at a given substantial assistance level receive a set and absolute number of months reduction in sentence) or a relative amount (all defendants who cooperate at a given substantial assistance level receive a proportional . . . reduction in sentence). The philosophical debate that addresses the assumptions and ramifications of the absolute versus proportional approach is long overdue.

## NOTES

1. *Prosecutorial discretion under the guidelines.*   In part because §5K1.1 of the federal guidelines requires a government motion before the court can reduce the sentence based on the defendant's cooperation (and because 18 U.S.C. §3553(e) requires the same before a court can reduce a sentence below a statutory mandatory minimum), many commentators lament that prosecutors ultimately possess more sentencing discretion than judges within the federal sentencing system. For instance, Professor Kate Stith and Judge Jose Cabranes contend that mandatory sentencing schemes "inevitably shift power toward prosecutors":

> Because the sentencing rules are known in advance, prosecutors may greatly influence the ultimate sentence through their decisions on charges, plea agreements, and motions to depart for substantial assistance to law enforcement authorities. Although prosecutors have always had significant discretion in charging and plea bargaining, the prosecutor's decisions on these matters have far greater significance for sentencing in the Guidelines regime; they determine not only the maximum term of a sentence (as provided in the statute prohibiting the conduct), but, in many cases, the precise sentence range that a sentencing court may consider. . . .

Kate Stith & Jose A. Cabranes, To Fear Judging No More: Recommendations for the Federal Sentencing Guidelines, 11 Fed. Sent'g Rep. 187-188 (1999). Though few dispute that prosecutors possess considerable power and discretion within the federal system, some question whether the guidelines themselves are responsible for shifting power to the prosecutors. For example, Justice Stephen Breyer has argued that the guidelines have actually "shifted the power to determine sentences away from prosecutors in at least some ways":

> Prosecutors should find it more difficult than under pre-Guideline practice to control the sentence by manipulating the charge. For, within broad limits, the offender's actual conduct, not the charge, will determine the sentence. For this same reason plea bargaining over charges should have diminished, because again within broad limits, a defendant's promise to plead guilty to a particular, perhaps less serious, charge likely will not affect the sentence. . . . This is not to deny the prosecutor's considerable bargaining power. The prosecutor still may choose to charge an offense that carries a lower statutory maximum penalty (and statutory maximum penalties trump the Guidelines). He may enter into a plea agreement for a fixed sentence, an agreement that will carry significant weight with the judge. He can simply ignore certain conduct, believing that the probation officer will not discover it. And he can ask the judge to depart from a Guideline sentence. But the prosecutor possessed all these powers before the Guidelines as well—and to a greater extent. . . .
>
> I recognize, however, other sources of special prosecutor power. Upon recommendation of the prosecutor, a court may depart downward from a Guideline sentence, and below even a statutory mandatory minimum, where there is "substantial assistance in the investigation or prosecution of another person who has committed an offense." U.S.S.G. §5K1.1. Moreover, statutory mandatory minimum sentences and Guideline sentences written to reflect those mandatory minimums—particularly in respect to drug crimes—may increase the pressure upon a defendant to provide "substantial assistance" in order to obtain a downward departure, or to plead guilty to an offense with a low statutory maximum (e.g., simple possession).
>
> Both factors—"substantial assistance" and "mandatory minimum"—rest upon special provisions in the Guideline statute. Moreover, those two factors play a particularly important role in federal drug prosecutions, which account for about 40% of all federal sentencing. Viewed in light of Guideline history, however, these two special "power-shifting" factors are nonessential, peripheral features of the Guidelines. And, for that reason, I believe it promotes accuracy in analysis, and leads to more constructive recommendations, to point to these two special statutory provisions, rather than the Guidelines themselves, as having increased prosecutorial power. . . .

Speech of Associate Justice Stephen Breyer, 11 Fed. Sent'g Rep. at 182-183 (1999). See also Frank O. Bowman, III, Mr. Madison Meets A Time Machine: The Political Science of Federal Sentencing Reform, 58 Stan. L. Rev. 235, 247 (2005).

2. *Departures, disparity, and discrimination.* Although departure authority provides judges with an opportunity to adjust sentences in light of unique circumstances in particular cases, it also provides a means for disparity and even discrimination to work their way back into a guideline system. Consider again the U.S. Sentencing Commission report on substantial-assistance departures, which stated that "legally irrelevant factors (e.g., gender, race, ethnicity, citizenship) were found to be statistically significant in explaining §5K1.1 departures."

Does this conclusion, and data that show significant circuit-by-circuit discrepancies in the use of departure authority, suggest that guideline systems must more carefully circumscribe and more closely monitor any retained areas of discretion? What roles should Congress, the U.S. Sentencing Commission, and appellate courts play in response to such evidence of disparity in the application of departure authority? May disparity between districts perhaps reflect different charging patterns that ultimately lead to similar sentences? See Laura Storto, Getting Behind the Numbers: A Report on Four Districts and What They Do "Below the Radar Screen," 15 Fed. Sent'g Rep. 204 (2003).

3. *Unavoidable tensions between equal justice and individual justice?*   One could summarize the entire guideline sentencing movement as just another chapter in an endless struggle to calibrate the unavoidable tension between efforts to achieve equal justice across cases and those to achieve individual justice in specific cases. Kate Stith and Jose Cabranes, leading critics of the federal sentencing guidelines, argue that in the federal system this effort has inappropriately prioritized equal justice over individual justice:

> Grounded in a fear of judging, the Guidelines seek not to channel the exercise of informed judicial discretion, but to repress judgment and replace it with a calculus of justice. . . . This structure ignores the most important capacity that judges bring to criminal sentencing: the ability to pronounce moral judgment that takes into account all aspects of the crime and the offender. . . . It is not that the idea of equal treatment is unworthy; rather, this ideal cannot be, and should not be, pursued through complex, mandatory guidelines. . . . Uniform treatment ought to be one objective of sentencing, to be sure, but not the sole or overriding objective.
>
> In the traditional ritual of sentencing, the judge pronounced not only a sentence but society's condemnation as well. . . . The sentencing ritual was predicated on the fundamental understanding that only a person can pass moral judgment, and only a person can be morally judged. In emphasizing the human face of justice, we are not blind to the limitations of the traditional sentencing hearing. Human judgment is fallible. Unfortunately, this is a fact of our existence for which there can be no easy technological solution. By replacing the case-by-case exercise of human judgment with a mechanical calculus, we do not judge better or more objectively, nor do we judge worse. Instead, we cease to judge at all. We process individuals according to a variety of purportedly objective criteria. But genuine judgment, in the sense of moral reckoning, cannot be inscribed in a table of offense levels and criminal history categories. . . .

Stith & Cabranes, 11 Fed. Sent'g Rep. at 187-188 (1999). Compare Vincent Chiao, Ex Ante Fairness in Criminal Law and Procedure, 15 New Crim. L. Rev. 277 (2012), with Dan Markel, Luck or Law? The Constitutional Case Against Indeterminate Sentencing, www.ssrn.com/abstract=1412888 (2009).

## d.  *Advisory Guidelines: The Aftermath of* Booker

From a long-range perspective, it is very helpful to think about the evolution of the federal sentencing guidelines from the broad perspective of the allocation of power and discretion. From this perspective the lessons about how power can be allocated — and discretion constrained — should be universal and important for any state system, or for a future federal system. From this viewpoint, the particular battles and tools of the moment fade with time.

Sentencing is fascinating because there are always big principles and specific people involved in sentencing decisions, because of the number of institutions involved in most sentencing systems, because of the complexity of sentencing judgments, and as this chapter is intended to highlight, because of the discretion inherent in all systems — even those that seek to strictly constrain or eliminate it. One actor that always lurks in the wings is the United States Supreme Court, which can wield its constitutional tools to reshape the federal guidelines system. Within somewhat different jurisdictional limits, it can do so for states as well.

After affirming the constitutional validity of the United States Sentencing Commission in Mistretta v. United States, for the next 11 years the U.S. Supreme Court demonstrated little interest in the federal guidelines system, with the interesting but modest exception of Koon v. United States. Then in 2000, 2004, and 2005, the court took the field again. It changed the superstructure of federal (and state) sentencing in three cases: Apprendi v. New Jersey, 530 U.S. 466 (2000); Blakely v. Washington, 542 U.S. 296 (2004), and United States v. Booker, 543 U.S. 220 (2005).

In *Blakely*, applying *Apprendi*, the Supreme Court held that a jury rather than a judge must find any fact that becomes necessary to authorize a new sentence. Although *Blakely* was a state case that formally addressed only one state sentencing system, its broad statement of the constitutional principles safeguarded by the Sixth Amendment raised questions about any guideline sentencing system that relied on judicial factfinding. Because the federal system relies heavily on judicial factfinding for guideline calculations, litigation began immediately after *Blakely* to determine whether the federal sentencing guidelines could possibly stand after the Court's decision. The Supreme Court gave its answer in *Booker*, in January 2005.

## United States v. Freddie J. Booker
### 543 U.S. 220 (2005)

Stevens, J., delivered the opinion of the Court in part.

The question presented in each of these cases is whether an application of the Federal Sentencing Guidelines violated the Sixth Amendment. . . . In both cases the courts rejected, on the basis of our decision in Blakely v. Washington, 542 U.S. 296 (2004), the Government's recommended application of the Sentencing Guidelines because the proposed sentences were based on additional facts that the sentencing judge found by a preponderance of the evidence. We hold that both courts correctly concluded that the Sixth Amendment as construed in *Blakely* does apply to the Sentencing Guidelines. In a separate opinion authored by Justice Breyer, the Court concludes that in light of this holding, two provisions of the Sentencing Reform Act of 1984 (SRA) that have the effect of making the Guidelines mandatory must be invalidated in order to allow the statute to operate in a manner consistent with congressional intent.

Respondent Booker was charged with possession with intent to distribute at least 50 grams of cocaine base (crack). . . . Based upon Booker's criminal history and the quantity of drugs found by the jury, the Sentencing Guidelines required the District Court Judge to select a "base" sentence of not less than 210 nor more than 262 months in prison. See USSG §§2D1.1(c)(4), 4A1.1. The judge, however, held a post-trial sentencing proceeding and concluded by a preponderance of the evidence that Booker had possessed an additional 566 grams of crack and that he was guilty of obstructing justice. Those findings mandated that the judge select a sentence between 360 months and life imprisonment; the judge imposed a sentence at the low end of the range. Thus, instead of the sentence of 21 years and 10 months that the judge could have imposed on the basis of the facts proved to the jury beyond a reasonable doubt, Booker received a 30-year sentence. . . .

It has been settled throughout our history that the Constitution protects every criminal defendant against conviction except upon proof beyond a reasonable doubt of every fact necessary to constitute the crime with which he is charged. It is equally clear that the Constitution gives a criminal defendant the right to demand that a jury find him guilty of all the elements of the crime with which he is charged. These basic precepts, firmly rooted in the common law, have provided the basis for recent decisions interpreting modern criminal statutes and sentencing procedures. . . .

In Blakely v. Washington, 542 U.S. 296 (2004), we dealt with a determinate sentencing scheme similar to the Federal Sentencing Guidelines. There the defendant pleaded guilty to kidnaping, a class B felony punishable by a term of not more than 10 years. Other provisions of Washington law, comparable to the Federal Sentencing Guidelines, mandated a "standard" sentence of 49 to 53 months, unless the judge found aggravating facts justifying an exceptional sentence. Although the prosecutor recommended a sentence in the standard range, the judge found that the defendant had acted with "deliberate cruelty" and sentenced him to 90 months. . . .

The application of Washington's sentencing scheme violated the defendant's right to have the jury find the existence of "any particular fact" that the law makes essential to his punishment. That right is implicated whenever a judge seeks to impose a sentence that is not solely based on "facts reflected in the jury verdict or admitted by the defendant." . . . The determination that the defendant acted with deliberate cruelty . . . increased the sentence that the defendant could have otherwise received. Since this fact was found by a judge using a preponderance of the evidence standard, the sentence violated Blakely's Sixth Amendment rights.

[There] is no distinction of constitutional significance between the Federal Sentencing Guidelines and the Washington procedures at issue in that case. This conclusion rests on the premise, common to both systems, that the relevant sentencing rules are mandatory and impose binding requirements on all sentencing judges.

If the Guidelines as currently written could be read as merely advisory provisions that recommended, rather than required, the selection of particular sentences in response to differing sets of facts, their use would not implicate the Sixth Amendment. We have never doubted the authority of a judge to exercise broad discretion in imposing a sentence within a statutory range. See Williams v. New York, 337 U.S. 241 (1949). . . . For when a trial judge exercises his discretion to select a specific sentence within a defined range, the defendant has no right to a jury determination of the facts that the judge deems relevant.

The Guidelines as written, however, are not advisory; they are mandatory and binding on all judges. [Subsection (b) of §3553] directs that the court "shall impose a sentence of the kind, and within the range" established by the Guidelines, subject to departures in specific, limited cases. [Departures] are not available in every case, and in fact are unavailable in most. In most cases, as a matter of law, the Commission will have adequately taken all relevant factors into account, and no departure will be legally permissible. In those instances, the judge is bound to impose a sentence within the Guidelines range. . . .

Booker's case illustrates the mandatory nature of the Guidelines. The jury convicted him of possessing at least 50 grams of crack in violation of 21 U.S.C. §841(b)(1)(A)(iii) based on evidence that he had 92.5 grams of crack in his duffel bag. Under these facts, the Guidelines specified an offense level of 32, which, given the defendant's criminal history category, authorized a sentence of 210 to 262 months. See USSG §2D1.1(c)(4). Booker's is a run-of-the-mill drug case, and does not present any factors that were inadequately considered by the Commission. The sentencing judge would therefore have been reversed had he not imposed a sentence within the level 32 Guidelines range. . . .

We recognize . . . that in some cases jury factfinding may impair the most expedient and efficient sentencing of defendants. But the interest in fairness and reliability protected by the right to a jury trial — a common-law right that defendants enjoyed for centuries and that is now enshrined in the Sixth Amendment — has always outweighed the interest in concluding trials swiftly. As Blackstone put it:

> However convenient these [new methods of trial] may appear at first (as doubtless all arbitrary powers, well executed, are the most convenient) yet let it be again remembered, that delays, and little inconveniences in the forms of justice, are the price that all free nations must pay for their liberty in more substantial matters; that these inroads upon this sacred bulwark of the nation are fundamentally opposite to the spirit of our constitution; and that, though begun in trifles, the precedent may gradually increase and spread, to the utter disuse of juries in questions of the most momentous concerns. 4 Commentaries on the Laws of England 343-344 (1769).

Accordingly, [any] fact (other than a prior conviction) which is necessary to support a sentence exceeding the maximum authorized by the facts established by a plea of guilty or a jury verdict must be admitted by the defendant or proved to a jury beyond a reasonable doubt.

BREYER, J., delivered the opinion of the Court in part.

. . . We answer the question of remedy by finding the provision of the federal sentencing statute that makes the Guidelines mandatory, 18 U.S.C. §3553(b)(1), incompatible with today's constitutional holding. We conclude that this provision must be severed and excised, as must one other statutory section, §3742(e), which depends upon the Guidelines' mandatory nature. So modified, the Federal Sentencing Act makes the Guidelines effectively advisory. It requires a sentencing court to consider Guidelines ranges, but it permits the court to tailor the sentence in light of other statutory concerns as well.

## I

We answer the remedial question by looking to legislative intent. We seek to determine what "Congress would have intended" in light of the Court's constitutional holding. Denver Area Ed. Telecommunications Consortium, Inc. v. FCC, 518 U.S. 727, 767 (1996) (plurality opinion) ("Would Congress still have passed" the valid sections had it known about the constitutional invalidity of the other portions of the statute?). In this instance, we must determine which of the two following remedial approaches is the more compatible with the legislature's intent as embodied in the 1984 Sentencing Act.

One approach, that of Justice Stevens' dissent, would retain the Sentencing Act (and the Guidelines) as written, but would engraft onto the existing system today's Sixth Amendment "jury trial" requirement. The addition would change the Guidelines by preventing the sentencing court from increasing a sentence on the basis of a fact that the jury did not find (or that the offender did not admit).

The other approach, which we now adopt, would (through severance and excision of two provisions) make the Guidelines system advisory while maintaining a strong connection between the sentence imposed and the offender's real conduct — a connection important to the increased uniformity of sentencing that Congress intended its Guidelines system to achieve. . . .

In today's context — a highly complex statute, interrelated provisions, and a constitutional requirement that creates fundamental change — we cannot assume that Congress, if faced with the statute's invalidity in key applications, would have preferred to apply the statute in as many other instances as possible. . . . It is, of course, true that the numbers show that the constitutional jury trial requirement would lead to additional decisionmaking by juries in only a minority of cases. Prosecutors and defense attorneys would still resolve the lion's share of criminal matters through plea bargaining, and plea bargaining takes place without a jury. Many of the rest involve only simple issues calling for no upward Guidelines adjustment. And in at least some of the remainder, a judge may find adequate room to adjust a sentence within the single Guidelines range to which the jury verdict points, or within the overlap between that range and the next highest.

But the constitutional jury trial requirement would nonetheless affect every case. It would affect decisions about whether to go to trial. It would affect the content of plea negotiations. It would alter the judge's role in sentencing. Thus we must determine likely intent not by counting proceedings, but by evaluating the consequences of the Court's constitutional requirement in light of the Act's language, its history, and its basic purposes. While reasonable minds can, and do, differ about the outcome, we conclude that the constitutional jury trial requirement is not compatible with the Act as written and that some severance and excision are necessary.

## II

Several considerations convince us that, were the Court's constitutional requirement added onto the Sentencing Act as currently written, the requirement would so transform the scheme that Congress created that Congress likely would not have intended the Act as so modified to stand. First, the statute's text states that "the court" when sentencing will consider "the nature and circumstances of the offense and the history and characteristics of the defendant." 18 U.S.C. §3553(a)(1). In context, the words "the court" mean "the judge without the jury," not "the judge working together with the jury." The Act's history confirms it. See, e.g., S. Rep. No. 98-225, p. 51 (1983) (the Guidelines system "will guide the judge in making" sentencing decisions). . . .

This provision makes it difficult to justify Justice Stevens' approach, for that approach requires reading the words "the court" as if they meant "the judge working together with the jury." Unlike Justice Stevens, we do not believe we can interpret the statute's language to save its constitutionality, because we believe that any such reinterpretation, even if limited to instances in which a Sixth Amendment problem arises, would be plainly contrary to the intent of Congress. . . .

Second, Congress' basic statutory goal — a system that diminishes sentencing disparity — depends for its success upon judicial efforts to determine, and to base punishment upon, the real conduct that underlies the crime of conviction. That determination is particularly important in the federal system where crimes defined as, for example, "obstructing, delaying, or affecting commerce or the movement of any article or commodity in commerce, by . . . extortion," 18 U.S.C. §1951(a), or, say, using the mail "for the purpose of executing" a "scheme or artifice to defraud," §1341, can encompass a vast range of very different kinds of underlying conduct. But it is also important even in respect to ordinary crimes, such as robbery, where an act that meets the statutory definition can be committed in a host of different ways. Judges have long looked to real conduct when sentencing. Federal judges have long relied upon a presentence report, prepared by a probation officer, for information (often unavailable until after the trial) relevant to the manner in which the convicted offender committed the crime of conviction. . . .

To engraft the Court's constitutional requirement onto the sentencing statutes, however, would destroy the system. It would prevent a judge from relying upon a presentence report for factual information, relevant to sentencing, uncovered after the trial. In doing so, it would, even compared to pre-Guidelines sentencing, weaken the tie between a sentence and an offender's real conduct. It would thereby undermine the sentencing statute's basic aim of ensuring similar sentences for those who have committed similar crimes in similar ways.

[An example can] illustrate the point. Imagine Smith and Jones, each of whom violates the Hobbs Act in very different ways. See 18 U.S.C. §1951(a) (forbidding "obstructing, delaying, or affecting commerce or the movement of any article or commodity in commerce, by . . . extortion"). Smith threatens to injure a co-worker unless the co-worker advances him a few dollars from the interstate company's till; Jones, after similarly threatening the co-worker, causes far more harm by seeking far more money, by making certain that the co-worker's family is aware of the threat, by arranging for deliveries of dead animals to the co-worker's home to show he is serious, and so forth. The offenders' behavior is very different; the known harmful consequences of their actions are different; their punishments both before, and after, the Guidelines would have been different. But, under the dissenters' approach, unless prosecutors decide to charge more than the elements of the crime, the judge would have to impose similar punishments. . . .

This point is critically important. Congress' basic goal in passing the Sentencing Act was to move the sentencing system in the direction of increased uniformity. See 28 U.S.C. §991(b)(1)(B); see also §994(f). That uniformity does not consist simply of similar sentences for those convicted of violations of the same statute — a uniformity consistent with the dissenters' remedial approach. It consists, more importantly, of similar relationships between sentences and real conduct, relationships that Congress' sentencing statutes helped to advance and that Justice Stevens' approach would undermine. In significant part, it is the weakening of this real-conduct/uniformity-in-sentencing relationship . . . that leads us to conclude that Congress would have preferred no mandatory system to the system the dissenters envisage.

Third, the sentencing statutes, read to include the Court's Sixth Amendment requirement, would create a system far more complex than Congress could have intended. How would courts and counsel work with an indictment and a jury trial that involved not just whether a defendant robbed a bank but also how? Would the indictment have to allege, in addition to the elements of robbery, whether the defendant possessed a firearm, whether he brandished or discharged it, whether he threatened death, whether he caused bodily injury, whether any such injury was ordinary, serious, permanent or life threatening, whether he abducted or physically restrained anyone, whether any victim was unusually vulnerable, how much money was taken, and whether he was an organizer, leader, manager, or supervisor in a robbery gang? See USSG §§2B3.1, 3B1.1. If so, how could a defendant mount a defense against some or all such specific claims should he also try simultaneously to maintain that the Government's evidence failed to place him at the scene of the crime? . . . How would the court take account, for punishment purposes, of a defendant's contemptuous behavior at trial — a matter that the Government could not have charged in the indictment? See §3C1.1.

Fourth, plea bargaining would not significantly diminish the consequences of the Court's constitutional holding for the operation of the Guidelines. Rather, plea bargaining would make matters worse. Congress enacted the sentencing statutes in major part to achieve greater uniformity in sentencing, i.e., to increase the likelihood that offenders who engage in similar real conduct would receive similar sentences. The statutes reasonably assume that their efforts to move the trial-based sentencing process in the direction of greater sentencing uniformity would have a similar positive impact upon plea-bargained sentences, for plea bargaining takes place in the shadow of (i.e., with an eye towards the hypothetical result of) a potential trial. . . .

The Court's constitutional jury trial requirement, however, if patched onto the present Sentencing Act, would move the system backwards in respect both to tried and to plea-bargained cases. In respect to tried cases, it would effectively deprive the judge of the ability to use post-verdict-acquired real-conduct information; it would prohibit the judge from basing a sentence upon any conduct other than the conduct the prosecutor chose to charge; and it would put a defendant to a set of difficult strategic choices as to which prosecutorial claims he would contest. The sentence that would emerge in a case tried under such a system would likely reflect real conduct less completely, less accurately, and less often than did a pre-Guidelines, as well as a Guidelines, trial.

Because plea bargaining inevitably reflects estimates of what would happen at trial, plea bargaining too under such a system would move in the wrong direction. That is to say, in a sentencing system modified by the Court's constitutional requirement, plea bargaining would likely lead to sentences that gave greater weight, not to real conduct, but rather to the skill of counsel, the policies of the prosecutor, the caseload, and other factors that vary from place to place, defendant to defendant, and crime to crime. Compared to pre-Guidelines plea bargaining, plea bargaining of this kind would necessarily move federal sentencing in the direction of diminished, not increased, uniformity in sentencing. It would tend to defeat, not to further, Congress' basic statutory goal.

Such a system would have particularly troubling consequences with respect to prosecutorial power. Until now, sentencing factors have come before the judge in the presentence report. But in a sentencing system with the Court's constitutional requirement engrafted onto it, any factor that a prosecutor chose not to charge at the plea negotiation would be placed beyond the reach of the judge entirely. Prosecutors would thus exercise a power the Sentencing Act vested in judges: the power to decide, based on relevant information about the offense and the offender, which defendants merit heavier punishment.

In respondent Booker's case, for example, the jury heard evidence that the crime had involved 92.5 grams of crack cocaine, and convicted Booker of possessing more than 50 grams. But the judge, at sentencing, found that the crime had involved an additional 566 grams, for a total of 658.5 grams. A system that would require the jury, not the judge, to make the additional "566 grams" finding is a system in which the prosecutor, not the judge, would control the sentence. That is because it is the prosecutor who would have to decide what drug amount to charge. He could choose to charge 658.5 grams, or 92.5, or less. It is the prosecutor who, through such a charging decision, would control the sentencing range. . . .

For all these reasons, Congress, had it been faced with the constitutional jury trial requirement, likely would not have passed the same Sentencing Act. It likely would have found the requirement incompatible with the Act as written. Hence the Act cannot remain valid in its entirety. Severance and excision are necessary.

## III

We now turn to the question of which portions of the sentencing statute we must sever and excise as inconsistent with the Court's constitutional requirement. [We] do not believe that the entire statute must be invalidated. Most of the statute is perfectly valid. See, e.g., 18 U.S.C. §3551 (describing authorized sentences as probation, fine, or imprisonment); §3552 (presentence reports); §3554 (forfeiture); §3555 (notification to the victims); §3583 (supervised release). And we must refrain from invalidating more of the statute than is necessary.

[We] must sever and excise two specific statutory provisions: the provision that requires sentencing courts to impose a sentence within the applicable Guidelines range (in the absence of circumstances that justify a departure), see 18 U.S.C. §3553(b)(1), and the provision that sets forth standards of review on appeal, including de novo review of departures from the applicable

Guidelines range, see §3742(e). With these two sections excised (and statutory cross-references to the two sections consequently invalidated), the remainder of the Act satisfies the Court's constitutional requirements.

The remainder of the Act functions independently. Without the "mandatory" provision, the Act nonetheless requires judges to take account of the Guidelines together with other sentencing goals. See 18 U.S.C. §3553(a). The Act nonetheless requires judges to consider the Guidelines "sentencing range established for . . . the applicable category of offense committed by the applicable category of defendant,"§3553(a)(4), the pertinent Sentencing Commission policy statements, the need to avoid unwarranted sentencing disparities, and the need to provide restitution to victims, §§3553(a)(1), (3), (5)-(7). And the Act nonetheless requires judges to impose sentences that reflect the seriousness of the offense, promote respect for the law, provide just punishment, afford adequate deterrence, protect the public, and effectively provide the defendant with needed educational or vocational training and medical care. §3553(a)(2).

Moreover, despite the absence of §3553(b)(1), the Act continues to provide for appeals from sentencing decisions (irrespective of whether the trial judge sentences within or outside the Guidelines range in the exercise of his discretionary power under §3553(a)). See §3742(a) (appeal by defendant); §3742(b) (appeal by Government). We concede that the excision of §3553(b)(1) requires the excision of a different, appeals-related section, namely §3742(e), which sets forth standards of review on appeal. That section contains critical cross-references to the (now-excised) §3553(b)(1) and consequently must be severed and excised for similar reasons.

Excision of §3742(e), however, does not pose a critical problem for the handling of appeals. That is because . . . a statute that does not explicitly set forth a standard of review may nonetheless do so implicitly. We infer appropriate review standards from related statutory language, the structure of the statute, and the sound administration of justice. And in this instance those factors, in addition to the past two decades of appellate practice in cases involving departures, imply a practical standard of review already familiar to appellate courts: review for "unreasonableness." 18 U.S.C. §3742(e)(3).

Until 2003, §3742(e) explicitly set forth that standard. In 2003, Congress modified the pre-existing text, adding a de novo standard of review for departures. . . . Prosecutorial Remedies and Other Tools to End the Exploitation of Children Today Act of 2003, Pub. L. 108-21, §401(d)(1), 117 Stat. 670. In light of today's holding, the reasons for these revisions—to make Guidelines sentencing even more mandatory than it had been—have ceased to be relevant. [The text of §3742(e)(3) in effect before 2003 directed appellate courts to review sentences outside the guidelines range to determine whether the sentence was] "unreasonable, having regard for . . . the factors to be considered in imposing a sentence, as set forth in [§3553(a)]." Section 3553(a) remains in effect, and sets forth numerous factors that guide sentencing. Those factors in turn will guide appellate courts, as they have in the past, in determining whether a sentence is unreasonable. . . .

Nor do we share the dissenters' doubts about the practicality of a "reasonableness" standard of review. "Reasonableness" standards are not foreign to sentencing law. The Act has long required their use in important sentencing circumstances — both on review of departures, see 18 U.S.C. §3742(e)(3), and on review of sentences imposed where there was no applicable Guideline, see §§3742(a)(4), (b)(4), (e)(4). Together, these cases account for about 16.7% of sentencing appeals. That is why we think it fair . . . to assume judicial familiarity with a "reasonableness" standard. And that is why we believe that appellate judges will prove capable of . . . applying such a standard across the board.

[The] remedial question we must ask here (as we did in respect to §3553(b)(1)) is, which alternative adheres more closely to Congress' original objective: (1) retention of sentencing appeals, or (2) invalidation of the entire Act, including its appellate provisions? The former, by providing appellate review, would tend to iron out sentencing differences; the latter would not. Hence we believe Congress would have preferred the former to the latter — even if the former means that some provisions will apply differently from the way Congress had originally expected.

[The] Sentencing Commission remains in place, writing Guidelines, collecting information about actual district court sentencing decisions, undertaking research, and revising the Guidelines accordingly. See 28 U.S.C. §994. The district courts, while not bound to apply the Guidelines, must consult those Guidelines and take them into account when sentencing. See 18 U.S.C. §§3553(a)(4), (5). The courts of appeals review sentencing decisions for unreasonableness. These features of the remaining system, while not the system Congress enacted, nonetheless continue to move sentencing in Congress' preferred direction, helping to avoid excessive sentencing disparities while maintaining flexibility sufficient to individualize sentences where necessary. We can find no feature of the remaining system that tends to hinder, rather than to further, these basic objectives. Under these circumstances, why would Congress not have preferred excision of the "mandatory" provision to a system that engrafts today's constitutional requirement onto the unchanged pre-existing statute — a system that, in terms of Congress' basic objectives, is counterproductive? . . .

Ours, of course, is not the last word: The ball now lies in Congress' court. The National Legislature is equipped to devise and install, long-term, the sentencing system, compatible with the Constitution, that Congress judges best for the federal system of justice. . . .

STEVENS, J., dissenting in part.
[Neither] 18 U.S.C. §3553(b)(1), which makes application of the Guidelines mandatory, nor §3742(e), which authorizes appellate review of departures from the Guidelines, is even arguably unconstitutional. . . . While it is perfectly clear that Congress has ample power to repeal these two statutory provisions if it so desires, this Court should not make that choice on Congress' behalf. . . .

When one pauses to note that over 95% of all federal criminal prosecutions are terminated by a plea bargain, and the further fact that in almost half of the cases that go to trial there are no sentencing enhancements, the extraordinary overbreadth of the Court's unprecedented remedy is manifest. . . .

It is a fundamental premise of judicial review that all Acts of Congress are presumptively valid. [It] is abundantly clear that the fact that a statute, or any provision of a statute, is unconstitutional in a portion of its applications does not render the statute or provision invalid, and no party suggests otherwise. The Government conceded at oral argument that 45% of federal sentences involve no enhancements. And, according to two U.S. Sentencing Commissioners who testified before Congress shortly after we handed down our decision in *Blakely*, the number of enhancements that would actually implicate a defendant's Sixth Amendment rights is even smaller. Simply stated, the Government's submissions to this Court and to Congress demonstrate that the Guidelines could be constitutionally applied in their entirety, without any modifications, in the majority of the cases sentenced under the federal guidelines. On the basis of these submissions alone, this Court should have declined to find the Guidelines, or any particular provisions of the Guidelines, facially invalid. . . .

Rather than engage in a wholesale rewriting of the SRA, I would simply allow the Government to continue doing what it has done since this Court handed down *Blakely*—prove any fact that is required to increase a defendant's sentence under the Guidelines to a jury beyond a reasonable doubt. [A] requirement of jury factfinding for certain issues can be implemented without difficulty in the vast majority of cases.

Indeed, this already appears to be the case. The Department of Justice already has instituted procedures which would protect the overwhelming majority of future cases from *Blakely* infirmity. The Department of Justice has issued detailed guidance for every stage of the prosecution from indictment to final sentencing, including alleging facts that would support sentencing enhancements and requiring defendants to waive any potential *Blakely* rights in plea agreements. Given this experience, I think the Court dramatically overstates the difficulty of implementing this solution. . . .

The majority's remedy was not the inevitable result of the Court's holding that *Blakely* applies to the Guidelines. [*Blakely* did not render] determinate sentencing unconstitutional.[17] . . . No judicial remedy is proper if it is "not commensurate with the constitutional violation to be repaired." Hills v. Gautreaux, 425 U.S. 284, 294 (1976). The Court's system fails that test, frustrates Congress' principal goal in enacting the SRA, and violates the tradition of judicial restraint that has heretofore limited our power to overturn validly enacted statutes. I respectfully dissent.

Scalia, J., dissenting in part.

The remedial majority takes as the North Star of its analysis the fact that Congress enacted a "judge-based sentencing system." That seems to me quite misguided. Congress did indeed expect judges to make the factual determinations to which the Guidelines apply, just as it expected the Guidelines to be mandatory. But which of those expectations was central to the congressional purpose is not hard to determine. No headline describing the Sentencing Reform Act of 1984 would have read "Congress reaffirms judge-based sentencing" rather than "Congress prescribes standardized sentences." Justice Breyer's

---

17. Moreover, even if the change to an indeterminate system were necessary, the Court could have minimized the consequences to the system by limiting the application of its holding to those defendants on direct review who actually suffered a Sixth Amendment violation. Griffith v. Kentucky, 479 U.S. 314 (1987), does not require blind application of every part of this Court's holdings to all pending cases, but rather, requires that we apply any new "rule to all similar cases pending on direct review." For obvious reasons, not all pending cases are made similar to Booker and Fanfan's merely because they involved an application of the Guidelines.

opinion for the Court repeatedly acknowledges that the primary objective of the Act was to reduce sentencing disparity. Inexplicably, however, the opinion concludes that the manner of achieving uniform sentences was more important to Congress than actually achieving uniformity—that Congress was so attached to having judges determine "real conduct" on the basis of bureaucratically prepared, hearsay-riddled presentence reports that it would rather lose the binding nature of the Guidelines than adhere to the old-fashioned process of having juries find the facts that expose a defendant to increased prison time. The majority's remedial choice is thus wonderfully ironic: In order to rescue from nullification a statutory scheme designed to eliminate discretionary sentencing, it discards the provisions that eliminate discretionary sentencing. . . .

As frustrating as this conclusion is to the Act's purpose of uniform sentencing, it at least establishes a clear and comprehensible regime—essentially the regime that existed before the Act became effective. That clarity is eliminated, however, by the remedial majority's surgery on 18 U.S.C. §3742, the provision governing appellate review of sentences. Even the most casual reading of this section discloses that its purpose—its only purpose—is to enable courts of appeals to enforce conformity with the Guidelines. All of the provisions of that section that impose a review obligation beyond what existed under prior law are related to the district judge's obligations under the Guidelines. If the Guidelines are no longer binding, one would think that the provision designed to ensure compliance with them would, in its totality, be inoperative. The Court holds otherwise. Like a black-robed Alexander cutting the Gordian knot, it simply severs the purpose of the review provisions from their text, holding that only subsection (e), which sets forth the determinations that the court of appeals must make, is inoperative, whereas all the rest of §3742 subsists. . . . This is rather like deleting the ingredients portion of a recipe and telling the cook to proceed with the preparation portion.

[The Court] announces that the standard of review for all [sentencing] appeals is "unreasonableness." This conflates different and distinct statutory authorizations of appeal and elides crucial differences in the statutory scope of review. Section 3742 specifies four different kinds of appeal,[7] [and it creates] no one-size-fits-all "unreasonableness" review. The power to review a sentence for reasonableness arises only when the sentencing court has departed from "the applicable guideline range." §3742(f)(2).

[Thus, we] have before us a statute that does explicitly set forth a standard of review. The question is, when the Court has severed that standard of review (contained in §3742(e)), does it make any sense to look for some congressional "implication" of a different standard of review in the remnants of the statute that the Court has left standing? Only in Wonderland. . . .

The worst feature of the scheme is that no one knows—and perhaps no one is meant to know—how advisory Guidelines and "unreasonableness" review will function in practice. . . . What I anticipate will happen is that

---

7. The four kinds of appeal arise when, respectively, (1) the sentence is "imposed in violation of law," §§3742(a)(1), (b)(1), (e)(1), (f)(1); (2) the sentence is "imposed as a result of an incorrect application of the sentencing guidelines," §§3742(a)(2), (b)(2), (e)(2), (f)(1); (3) the sentence is either above or below "the applicable guideline range," §§3742(a)(3), (b)(3), (e)(3), (f)(2); and (4) no guideline is applicable and the sentence is "plainly unreasonable," §§3742(a)(4), (b)(4), (e)(4), (f)(2).

"unreasonableness" review will produce a discordant symphony of different standards, varying from court to court and judge to judge. . . .

BREYER, J., dissenting in part.

. . . I find nothing in the Sixth Amendment that forbids a sentencing judge to determine (as judges at sentencing have traditionally determined) the manner or way in which the offender carried out the crime of which he was convicted. . . . I continue to disagree with the constitutional analysis the Court set forth . . . in *Blakely*. But even were I to accept that analysis as valid, I would disagree with the way in which the Court applies it here.

[The] Court's opinion today illustrates the historical mistake upon which its conclusions rest. The Court reiterates its view that the right of "trial by jury has been understood to require" a jury trial for determination of "the truth of every accusation." This claim makes historical sense insofar as an "accusation" encompasses each factual element of the crime of which a defendant is accused. But the key question here is whether that word also encompasses sentencing facts — facts about the offender (say, recidivism) or about the way in which the offender committed the crime (say, the seriousness of the injury or the amount stolen) that help a sentencing judge determine a convicted offender's specific sentence.

History does not support a "right to jury trial" in respect to sentencing facts. Traditionally, the law has distinguished between facts that are elements of crimes and facts that are relevant only to sentencing. Traditionally, federal law has looked to judges, not to juries, to resolve disputes about sentencing facts. Traditionally, those familiar with the criminal justice system have found separate, postconviction judge-run sentencing procedures sensible given the difficulty of obtaining relevant sentencing information before the moment of conviction. They have found those proceedings practical given the impracticality of the alternatives, say, two-stage (guilt, sentence) jury procedures. And, despite the absence of jury determinations, they have found those proceedings fair as long as the convicted offender has the opportunity to contest a claimed fact before the judge, and as long as the sentence falls within the maximum of the range that a congressional statute specifically sets forth. . . .

The upshot is that the Court's Sixth Amendment decisions . . . deprive Congress and state legislatures of authority that is constitutionally theirs. The sentencing function long has been a peculiarly shared responsibility among the Branches of Government. Congress' share of this joint responsibility has long included not only the power to define crimes (by enacting statutes setting forth their factual elements) but also the power to specify sentences, whether by setting forth a range of individual-crime-related sentences (say, 0 to 10 years' imprisonment for bank robbery) or by identifying sentencing factors that permit or require a judge to impose higher or lower sentences in particular circumstances. . . .

## NOTES

1. *Understanding the essence of* Booker.   The decisions in *Booker* run 118 pages, and the unique "split" majority opinion, which can be separated in a "merits" and a "remedial" majority, defies neat summarization. One group of

five Justices — the same five Justices that composed the majority in *Blakely* —
declared that the federal sentencing guidelines violate the Sixth Amendment
because they rely on judicial fact-finding to enhance sentences; another
group of five Justices — the *Blakely* dissenters plus Justice Ginsburg — declared
the guidelines advisory, and in so doing sought to ensure that the guidelines
system would continue to operate in a manner as close to the old system as
possible.

The remedy in *Booker* strikes down only two parts of the Sentencing Reform
Act — 18 U.S.C. §3553(b)(1), the provision that requires trial courts to impose a
sentence within the applicable Guidelines range (in the absence of circumstances that justify a departure), and §3742(e), the provision that sets forth
standards of appellate review, including de novo review of departures from
the applicable guideline range — and stresses that other parts of the Act are
still to play a central role in federal sentencing. The remedial majority requires
judges "to take account of the Guidelines together with other sentencing goals."
This means that they must consider the sentencing ranges set out in the Guidelines, Sentencing Commission policy statements, and other provisions, such as
those governing victim restitution. On the other hand, courts are to consider
general sentencing goals, such as proportionality, just punishment, deterrence,
protection of the public, respect for the law, and rehabilitation, all of which are
set out in §3553(a)(2), in fashioning a sentence.

To ensure that judges follow these requirements, the remedial majority
reinforced the availability of appellate review for "unreasonable" sentences in
all cases. The standard of review, even though no longer explicitly set out in the
statute, could be inferred, according to the remedial majority.

However surprising the remedy in *Booker*, what is the real effect of converting the federal sentencing guidelines from mandatory to advisory sentencing
rules for the 1,200 cases sentenced in federal court each week? What is the real
meaning and likely impact of Justice Breyer's assertion in *Booker* that "district
courts, while not bound to apply the Guidelines, must consult those Guidelines
and take them into account when sentencing"?

2. *Defining a remedy.*   In their remedial opinion five Justices concluded that
the best response to the constitutional problem flowing from *Blakely*'s application to the federal guidelines would be to make the system advisory. Nevertheless, Justice Breyer stressed that the Sentencing Reform Act still "requires judges
to consider the Guidelines" and that "district courts, while not bound to apply
the Guidelines, must consult those Guidelines and take them into account when
sentencing." Moreover, the Court stressed that federal judges imposing sentences after *Booker* remain fully bound by the dictates of 18 U.S.C. §3553(a),
which "sets forth numerous factors that guide sentencing," including the need
to avoid disparities and traditional purposes of punishment.

3. *Rule by judges?*   According to the merits majority opinion by Justice
Stevens, the *Booker* decision is designed to "preserve Sixth Amendment substance" so as to guarantee "in a meaningful way . . . that the jury would still
stand between the individual and the power of the government under the
new sentencing regime." And yet, because of the remedy crafted by the remedial
majority opinion of Justice Breyer, judges may still make all sentencing

determinations under the federal sentencing system. How are lower courts to decipher and give effect to a seemingly inconsistent ruling concerning the roles of judges and juries in sentencing factfinding?

4. *Section 5K1.1 motions in the wake of* Booker. Before *Booker,* §5K1.1 motions were the primary avenue for defendants to obtain below-guideline sentences. Such a motion is no longer required for a *Booker* variance. Some courts have held that a defendant may receive credit for cooperation where the government does not file a motion for substantial assistance. Such cooperation might shed light on the defendant's "history and circumstances." United States v. Fernandez, 443 F.3d 19 (2d Cir. 2006). Will *Booker* break the influence of §5K1.1 motions? As a criminal defense lawyer, how would you explain the role of cooperation in sentencing to your client post-*Booker*?

---

As with any blockbuster decision, the full meaning of *Booker* cannot be understood on the face of that opinion alone. The impact of *Booker* on the federal system can be viewed through a variety of lenses: subsequent Supreme Court cases; published appellate and trial court decisions; sentencing patterns for within guidelines sentences and departures reflected in United States Sentencing Commission data; and detailed (and methodologically varied) studies of charging, plea, and sentencing practices in particular districts.

One of the essential questions following *Booker* is what standards federal appellate courts would use for "reasonableness review" to determine when a sentence was "unreasonable." In June of 2007, two years after *Booker,* the court decided Rita v. United States, 551 U.S. 338 (2007). In an opinion by Justice Breyer, the court held that an appellate court could apply a presumption of reasonableness to sentences within a properly calculated guidelines range.

> [T]he presumption is not binding. It does not, like a trial-related evidentiary presumption, insist that one side, or the other, shoulder a particular burden of persuasion or proof lest they lose their case. Nor does the presumption reflect strong judicial deference of the kind that leads appeals courts to grant greater factfinding leeway to an expert agency than to a district judge. Rather, the presumption reflects the fact that, by the time an appeals court is considering a within-Guidelines sentence on review, *both* the sentencing judge and the Sentencing Commission will have reached the *same* conclusion as to the proper sentence in the particular case. That double determination significantly increases the likelihood that the sentence is a reasonable one. . . .
>
> An individual judge who imposes a sentence within the range recommended by the Guidelines thus makes a decision that is fully consistent with the Commission's judgment in general. [T]he courts of appeals' "reasonableness" presumption, rather than having independent legal effect, simply recognizes the real-world circumstance that when the judge's discretionary decision accords with the Commission's view of the appropriate application of §3553(a) in the mine run of cases, it is probable that the sentence is reasonable. . . .
>
> We repeat that the presumption before us is an *appellate* court presumption. Given our explanation in *Booker* that appellate "reasonableness" review merely asks whether the trial court abused its discretion, the presumption applies only on appellate review. The sentencing judge, as a matter of process, will normally begin by considering the presentence report and its interpretation of the Guidelines. 18 U.S.C. §3552(a); Fed. Rule Crim. Proc. 32. He may hear

arguments by prosecution or defense that the Guidelines sentence should not apply, perhaps because (as the Guidelines themselves foresee) the case at hand falls outside the "heartland" to which the Commission intends individual Guidelines to apply, USSG §5K2.O, perhaps because the Guidelines sentence itself fails properly to reflect §3553(a) considerations, or perhaps because the case warrants a different sentence regardless. See Rule 32(f). Thus, the sentencing court subjects the defendant's sentence to the thorough adversarial testing contemplated by federal sentencing procedure. In determining the merits of these arguments, the sentencing court does not enjoy the benefit of a legal presumption that the Guidelines sentence should apply. *Booker*, 543 U.S., at 259-260.

How much did *Rita* restrict the potential post-*Booker* degree of "freedom" of discretion for sentencing judges? On the one hand, the majority focused at length on the institutional roles of Congress and the Commission. Perhaps reflecting Justice Breyer's own role as one of the key drafters of the federal sentencing guidelines when he served on the United States Sentencing Commission, the *Rita* majority reflected respect for the Commission's guidelines and emphasized that the Commission, following the statutory direction of Congress in the Sentencing Reform Act, considered the purposes of punishment and other factors that are also assessed by sentencing judges.

On the other hand, the court emphasized that no such presumption of reasonableness attached to a trial judge's sentencing determination, and said nothing about whether a sentence imposed outside the guideline range could be considered presumptively unreasonable by appellate courts — the inverse of the question raised directly in *Rita*.

Only six months later, in December 2007, the Supreme Court provided further illumination of the meaning of *Booker* in a pair of decisions. In Gall v. United States, reprinted in Chapter 5, the court, in an opinion by Justice Stevens, reversed an appellate panel that had found unreasonable a downward departure from a 30-37 month prison sentence to 36 months probation where Brian Gall had withdrawn from a college drug conspiracy years before he was prosecuted, had sold no illegal drugs since, and had used no illegal drugs and worked steadily since graduating from college. The court held:

> It is also clear that a district judge must give serious consideration to the extent of any departure from the Guidelines and must explain his conclusion that an unusually lenient or an unusually harsh sentence is appropriate in a particular case with sufficient justifications. For even though the Guidelines are advisory rather than mandatory, they are, as we pointed out in *Rita*, the product of careful study based on extensive empirical evidence derived from the review of thousands of individual sentencing decisions.
>
> In reviewing the reasonableness of a sentence outside the Guidelines range, appellate courts may therefore take the degree of variance into account and consider the extent of a deviation from the Guidelines. We reject, however, an appellate rule that requires "extraordinary" circumstances to justify a sentence outside the Guidelines range. We also reject the use of a rigid mathematical formula that uses the percentage of a departure as the standard for determining the strength of the justifications required for a specific sentence.

An illustration of the discretion granted by *Booker* to federal sentencing courts comes in the following case, decided the same day as *Gall*.

## Derrick Kimbrough v. United States
### 552 U.S. 85 (2007)

GINSBURG, J.[*]

This Court's remedial opinion in United States v. Booker, 543 U.S. 220 (2005), instructed district courts to read the United States Sentencing Guidelines as "effectively advisory." In accord with 18 U.S.C. §3553(a), the Guidelines, formerly mandatory, now serve as one factor among several courts must consider in determining an appropriate sentence. *Booker* further instructed that "reasonableness" is the standard controlling appellate review of the sentences district courts impose.

Under the statute criminalizing the manufacture and distribution of crack cocaine, 21 U.S.C. §841, and the relevant Guidelines prescription, §2D1.1, a drug trafficker dealing in crack cocaine is subject to the same sentence as one dealing in 100 times more powder cocaine. The question here presented is whether, as the Court of Appeals held in this case, "a sentence . . . outside the guidelines range is per se unreasonable when it is based on a disagreement with the sentencing disparity for crack and powder cocaine offenses." We hold that, under *Booker*, the cocaine Guidelines, like all other Guidelines, are advisory only, and that the Court of Appeals erred in holding the crack/powder disparity effectively mandatory. A district judge must include the Guidelines range in the array of factors warranting consideration. The judge may determine, however, that, in the particular case, a within-Guidelines sentence is "greater than necessary" to serve the objectives of sentencing. 18 U.S.C. §3553(a). In making that determination, the judge may consider the disparity between the Guidelines' treatment of crack and powder cocaine offenses.

## I

In September 2004, petitioner Derrick Kimbrough was indicted in the United States District Court for the Eastern District of Virginia and charged with four offenses: conspiracy to distribute crack and powder cocaine; possession with intent to distribute more than 50 grams of crack cocaine; possession with intent to distribute powder cocaine; and possession of a firearm in furtherance of a drug-trafficking offense. Kimbrough pleaded guilty to all four charges.

Under the relevant statutes, Kimbrough's plea subjected him to an aggregate sentence of 15 years to life in prison: 10 years to life for the three drug offenses, plus a consecutive term of 5 years to life for the firearm offense.[1] In

---

[*] [Chief Justice Roberts, and Justices Stevens, Scalia, Kennedy, Souter and Breyer joined this opinion].

1. The statutory range for possession with intent to distribute more than 50 grams of crack is ten years to life. The same range applies to the conspiracy offense. The statutory range for possession with intent to distribute powder cocaine is 0 to 20 years. Finally, the statutory range for possession of a firearm in furtherance of a drug-trafficking offense is five years to life. The sentences for the three drug crimes may run concurrently, see §3584(a), but the sentence for the firearm offense must be consecutive, see §924(c)(1)(A).

order to determine the appropriate sentence within this statutory range, the District Court first calculated Kimbrough's sentence under the advisory Sentencing Guidelines. Kimbrough's guilty plea acknowledged that he was accountable for 56 grams of crack cocaine and 92.1 grams of powder cocaine. This quantity of drugs yielded a base offense level of 32 for the three drug charges. See United States Sentencing Commission, Guidelines Manual §2D1.1(c) (Nov.2004) (USSG). Finding that Kimbrough, by asserting sole culpability for the crime, had testified falsely at his codefendant's trial, the District Court increased his offense level to 34. See §3C1.1. In accord with the presentence report, the court determined that Kimbrough's criminal history category was II. An offense level of 34 and a criminal history category of II yielded a Guidelines range of 168 to 210 months for the three drug charges. The Guidelines sentence for the firearm offense was the statutory minimum, 60 months. See USSG §2K2.4(b). Kimbrough's final advisory Guidelines range was thus 228 to 270 months, or 19 to 22.5 years.

A sentence in this range, in the District Court's judgment, would have been "greater than necessary" to accomplish the purposes of sentencing set forth in 18 U.S.C. §3553(a). As required by §3553(a), the court took into account the "nature and circumstances" of the offense and Kimbrough's "history and characteristics." The court also commented that the case exemplified the "disproportionate and unjust effect that crack cocaine guidelines have in sentencing." In this regard, the court contrasted Kimbrough's Guidelines range of 228 to 270 months with the range that would have applied had he been accountable for an equivalent amount of powder cocaine: 97 to 106 months, inclusive of the 5-year mandatory minimum for the firearm charge. Concluding that the statutory minimum sentence was "clearly long enough" to accomplish the objectives listed in §3553(a), the court sentenced Kimbrough to 15 years, or 180 months, in prison plus 5 years of supervised release.[3]

In an unpublished *per curiam* opinion, the Fourth Circuit vacated the sentence. Under Circuit precedent, the Court of Appeals observed, a sentence "outside the guidelines range is per se unreasonable when it is based on a disagreement with the sentencing disparity for crack and powder cocaine offenses."

We granted certiorari to determine whether the crack/powder disparity adopted in the United States Sentencing Guidelines has been rendered "advisory" by our decision in *Booker*.[4]

---

3. The prison sentence consisted of 120 months on each of the three drug counts, to be served concurrently, plus 60 months on the firearm count, to be served consecutively.

4. This question has divided the Courts of Appeals. [The Court cited opinions from the District of Columbia and the Third Circuit allowing crack/powder disparity departures, and decisions from the First, Second, Fourth, Fifth, Eighth and Eleventh Circuit forbidding sentences outside the guideline range based on the crack/powder cocaine disparity].

# II

We begin with some background on the different treatment of crack and powder cocaine under the federal sentencing laws. Crack and powder cocaine are two forms of the same drug. Powder cocaine, or cocaine hydrochloride, is generally inhaled through the nose; it may also be mixed with water and injected. See United States Sentencing Commission, Special Report to Congress: Cocaine and Federal Sentencing Policy 5, 12 (Feb.1995), available at http://www.ussc.gov/crack/exec.htm (hereinafter 1995 Report). Crack cocaine, a type of cocaine base, is formed by dissolving powder cocaine and baking soda in boiling water. The resulting solid is divided into single-dose "rocks" that users smoke. The active ingredient in powder and crack cocaine is the same. The two forms of the drug also have the same physiological and psychotropic effects, but smoking crack cocaine allows the body to absorb the drug much faster than inhaling powder cocaine, and thus produces a shorter, more intense high.

Although chemically similar, crack and powder cocaine are handled very differently for sentencing purposes. The 100-to-1 ratio yields sentences for crack offenses three to six times longer than those for powder offenses involving equal amounts of drugs. See United States Sentencing Commission, Report to Congress: Cocaine and Federal Sentencing Policy iv (May 2002), available at http://www.ussc.gov/r_congress/02crack/2002crackrpt.pdf (hereinafter 2002 Report). This disparity means that a major supplier of powder cocaine may receive a shorter sentence than a low-level dealer who buys powder from the supplier but then converts it to crack.

## A

The crack/powder disparity originated in the Anti-Drug Abuse Act of 1986. The 1986 Act created a two-tiered scheme of five- and ten-year mandatory minimum sentences for drug manufacturing and distribution offenses. Congress sought "to link the ten-year mandatory minimum trafficking prison term to major drug dealers and to link the five-year minimum term to serious traffickers." The 1986 Act uses the weight of the drugs involved in the offense as the sole proxy to identify "major" and "serious" dealers. For example, any defendant responsible for 100 grams of heroin is subject to the five-year mandatory minimum, and any defendant responsible for 1,000 grams of heroin is subject to the ten-year mandatory minimum.

Crack cocaine was a relatively new drug when the 1986 Act was signed into law, but it was already a matter of great public concern: "Drug abuse in general, and crack cocaine in particular, had become in public opinion and in members' minds a problem of overwhelming dimensions." Congress apparently believed that crack was significantly more dangerous than powder cocaine in that: (1) crack was highly addictive; (2) crack users and dealers were more likely to be violent than users and dealers of other drugs; (3) crack was more harmful to users than powder, particularly for children who had been exposed by their mothers' drug use during pregnancy; (4) crack use was especially prevalent among teenagers; and (5) crack's potency and low cost were making it increasingly popular.

Based on these assumptions, the 1986 Act adopted a "100-to-1 ratio" that treated every gram of crack cocaine as the equivalent of 100 grams of powder cocaine. The Act's five-year mandatory minimum applies to any defendant accountable for 5 grams of crack or 500 grams of powder; its ten-year mandatory minimum applies to any defendant accountable for 50 grams of crack or 5,000 grams of powder.

While Congress was considering adoption of the 1986 Act, the Sentencing Commission was engaged in formulating the Sentencing Guidelines. In the main, the Commission developed Guidelines sentences using an empirical approach based on data about past sentencing practices, including 10,000 pre-sentence investigation reports. The Commission "modif[ied] and adjust[ed] past practice in the interests of greater rationality, avoiding inconsistency, complying with congressional instructions, and the like." Rita v. United States, 551 U.S. 338 (2007).

The Commission did not use this empirical approach in developing the Guidelines sentences for drug-trafficking offenses. Instead, it employed the 1986 Act's weight-driven scheme. The Guidelines use a drug quantity table based on drug type and weight to set base offense levels for drug-trafficking offenses. In setting offense levels for crack and powder cocaine, the Commission, in line with the 1986 Act, adopted the 100-to-1 ratio. The statute itself specifies only two quantities of each drug, but the Guidelines "go further and set sentences for the full range of possible drug quantities using the same 100-to-1 quantity ratio." The Guidelines' drug quantity table sets base offense levels ranging from 12, for offenses involving less than 250 milligrams of crack (or 25 grams of powder), to 38, for offenses involving more than 1.5 kilograms of crack (or 150 kilograms of powder).

### B

Although the Commission immediately used the 100-to-1 ratio to define base offense levels for all crack and powder offenses, it later determined that the crack/powder sentencing disparity is generally unwarranted. Based on additional research and experience with the 100-to-1 ratio, the Commission concluded that the disparity "fails to meet the sentencing objectives set forth by Congress in both the Sentencing Reform Act and the 1986 Act." 2002 Report 91. In a series of reports, the Commission identified three problems with the crack/powder disparity.

First, the Commission reported, the 100-to-1 ratio rested on assumptions about "the relative harmfulness of the two drugs and the relative prevalence of certain harmful conduct associated with their use and distribution that more recent research and data no longer support." For example, the Commission found that crack is associated with "significantly less trafficking-related violence . . . than previously assumed." It also observed that "the negative effects of prenatal crack cocaine exposure are identical to the negative effects of prenatal powder cocaine exposure." The Commission furthermore noted that "the epidemic of crack cocaine use by youth never materialized to the extent feared."

Second, the Commission concluded that the crack/powder disparity is inconsistent with the 1986 Act's goal of punishing major drug traffickers more severely than low-level dealers. Drug importers and major traffickers generally deal in powder cocaine, which is then converted into crack by street-level sellers. But the 100-to-1 ratio can lead to the "anomalous" result that "retail crack dealers get longer sentences than the wholesale drug distributors who supply them the powder cocaine from which their crack is produced."

Finally, the Commission stated that the crack/powder sentencing differential "fosters disrespect for and lack of confidence in the criminal justice system" because of a "widely-held perception" that it "promotes unwarranted disparity based on race." Approximately 85 percent of defendants convicted of crack offenses in federal court are black; thus the severe sentences required by the 100-to-1 ratio are imposed "primarily upon black offenders."

Despite these observations, the Commission's most recent reports do not urge identical treatment of crack and powder cocaine. In the Commission's view, "some differential in the quantity-based penalties" for the two drugs is warranted because crack is more addictive than powder, crack offenses are more likely to involve weapons or bodily injury, and crack distribution is associated with higher levels of crime. But the 100-to-1 crack/powder ratio, the Commission concluded, significantly overstates the differences between the two forms of the drug. Accordingly, the Commission recommended that the ratio be "substantially" reduced.

### C

The Commission has several times sought to achieve a reduction in the crack/powder ratio. In 1995, it proposed amendments to the Guidelines that would have replaced the 100-to-1 ratio with a 1-to-1 ratio. Complementing that change, the Commission would have installed special enhancements for trafficking offenses involving weapons or bodily injury. Congress, acting pursuant to 28 U.S.C. §994(p),[9] rejected the amendments. Simultaneously, however, Congress directed the Commission to "propose revision of the drug quantity ratio of crack cocaine to powder cocaine under the relevant statutes and guidelines."

In response to this directive, the Commission issued reports in 1997 and 2002 recommending that Congress change the 100-to-1 ratio prescribed in the 1986 Act. The 1997 Report proposed a 5-to-1 ratio. The 2002 Report recommended lowering the ratio "at least" to 20 to 1. Neither proposal prompted congressional action.

The Commission's most recent report, issued in 2007, again urged Congress to amend the 1986 Act to reduce the 100-to-1 ratio. This time, however, the Commission did not simply await congressional action. Instead, the Commission adopted an ameliorating change in the Guidelines. The alteration, which became effective on November 1, 2007, reduces the base offense level associated with each quantity of crack by two levels. See Amendments to the Sentencing

---

9. Subsection 994(p) requires the Commission to submit Guidelines amendments to Congress and provides that such amendments become effective unless "modified or disapproved by Act of Congress."

Guidelines for United States Courts, 72 Fed.Reg. 28571-28572 (2007).[10] This modest amendment yields sentences for crack offenses between two and five times longer than sentences for equal amounts of powder. Describing the amendment as "only . . . a partial remedy" for the problems generated by the crack/powder disparity, the Commission noted that any "comprehensive solution requires appropriate legislative action by Congress."

## III

With this history of the crack/powder sentencing ratio in mind, we next consider the status of the Guidelines tied to the ratio after our decision in United States v. Booker. In *Booker*, the Court held that the mandatory Sentencing Guidelines system violated the Sixth Amendment. The *Booker* remedial opinion determined that the appropriate cure was to sever and excise the provision of the statute that rendered the Guidelines mandatory.[12] This modification of the federal sentencing statute, we explained, "makes the Guidelines effectively advisory."

The statute, as modified by *Booker*, contains an overarching provision instructing district courts to "impose a sentence sufficient, but not greater than necessary" to accomplish the goals of sentencing, including "to reflect the seriousness of the offense," "to promote respect for the law," "to provide just punishment for the offense," "to afford adequate deterrence to criminal conduct," and "to protect the public from further crimes of the defendant." 18 U.S.C. §3553(a). The statute further provides that, in determining the appropriate sentence, the court should consider a number of factors, including "the nature and circumstances of the offense," "the history and characteristics of the defendant," "the sentencing range established" by the Guidelines, "any pertinent policy statement" issued by the Sentencing Commission pursuant to its statutory authority, and "the need to avoid unwarranted sentence disparities among defendants with similar records who have been found guilty of similar conduct." In sum, while the statute still requires a court to give respectful consideration to the Guidelines, *Booker* "permits the court to tailor the sentence in light of other statutory concerns as well."

The Government acknowledges that the Guidelines "are now advisory" and that, as a general matter, "courts may vary [from Guidelines ranges] based solely on policy considerations, including disagreements with the Guidelines." But the Government contends that the Guidelines adopting the 100-to-1 ratio are an exception to the "general freedom that sentencing courts have to apply the [§3553(a)] factors." That is so, according to the Government, because

---

10. The amended Guidelines still produce sentencing ranges keyed to the mandatory minimums in the 1986 Act. Under the pre-2007 Guidelines, the 5- and 50-gram quantities that trigger the statutory minimums produced sentencing ranges that slightly *exceeded* those statutory minimums. Under the amended Guidelines, in contrast, the 5- and 50-gram quantities produce "base offense levels corresponding to guideline ranges that *include* the statutory mandatory minimum penalties." 2007 Report 9.

12. The remedial opinion also severed and excised the provision of the statute requiring *de novo* review of departures from the Guidelines, 18 U.S.C. §3742(e), because that provision depended on the Guidelines' mandatory status.

the ratio is a "specific policy determination that Congress has directed sentencing courts to observe." The Government offers three arguments in support of this position. We consider each in turn.

### A

As its first and most heavily pressed argument, the Government urges that the 1986 Act itself prohibits the Sentencing Commission and sentencing courts from disagreeing with the 100-to-1 ratio.[13] The Government acknowledges that the "Congress did not *expressly* direct the Sentencing Commission to incorporate the 100:1 ratio in the Guidelines." Nevertheless, it asserts that the Act "implicitly" requires the Commission and sentencing courts to apply the 100-to-1 ratio. Any deviation, the Government urges, would be "logically incoherent" when combined with mandatory minimum sentences based on the 100-to-1 ratio.

This argument encounters a formidable obstacle: It lacks grounding in the text of the 1986 Act. The statute, by its terms, mandates only maximum and minimum sentences: A person convicted of possession with intent to distribute 5 grams or more of crack cocaine must be sentenced to a minimum of 5 years and the maximum term is 40 years. A person with 50 grams or more of crack cocaine must be sentenced to a minimum of 10 years and the maximum term is life. The statute says nothing about the appropriate sentences within these brackets, and we decline to read any implicit directive into that congressional silence. Drawing meaning from silence is particularly inappropriate here, for Congress has shown that it knows how to direct sentencing practices in express terms. For example, Congress has specifically required the Sentencing Commission to set Guidelines sentences for serious recidivist offenders "at or near" the statutory maximum.

Our cautious reading of the 1986 Act draws force from Neal v. United States, 516 U.S. 284 (1996). That case involved different methods of calculating lysergic acid diethylamide (LSD) weights, one applicable in determining statutory minimum sentences, the other controlling the calculation of Guidelines ranges. The 1986 Act sets mandatory minimum sentences based on the weight of "a mixture or substance containing a detectable amount" of LSD. Prior to *Neal*, we had interpreted that language to include the weight of the carrier medium (usually blotter paper) on which LSD is absorbed even though the carrier is usually far heavier than the LSD itself. See Chapman v. United States, 500 U.S. 453 (1991). Until 1993, the Sentencing Commission had interpreted the relevant Guidelines in the same way. That year, however, the Commission changed its approach and "instructed courts to give each dose of LSD on a carrier medium a constructive or presumed weight of 0.4 milligrams." The Commission's change significantly lowered the Guidelines range applicable to most LSD offenses, but defendants remained subject to higher statutory minimum sentences based on the combined weight of the pure drug and its carrier medium. The defendant in *Neal* argued that the revised Guidelines and the statute should

---

13. The Government concedes that a district court may vary from the 100-to-1 ratio if it does so "based on the individualized circumstances" of a particular case. But the Government maintains that the 100-to-1 ratio is binding in the sense that a court may not give any weight to its own view that the ratio itself is inconsistent with the §3553(a) factors.

be interpreted consistently and that the "presumptive-weight method of the Guidelines should also control the mandatory minimum calculation." We rejected that argument, emphasizing that the Commission had not purported to interpret the statute and could not in any event overrule our decision in *Chapman.*

If the Government's current position were correct, then the Guidelines involved in *Neal* would be in serious jeopardy. We have just recounted the reasons alleged to justify reading into the 1986 Act an implicit command to the Commission and sentencing courts to apply the 100-to-1 ratio to all quantities of crack cocaine. Those same reasons could be urged in support of an argument that the 1986 Act requires the Commission to include the full weight of the carrier medium in calculating the weight of LSD for Guidelines purposes. Yet our opinion in *Neal* never questioned the validity of the altered Guidelines. To the contrary, we stated: "Entrusted within its sphere to make policy judgments, the Commission may abandon its old methods in favor of what it has deemed a more desirable 'approach' to calculating LSD quantities." If the 1986 Act does not require the Commission to adhere to the Act's method for determining LSD weights, it does not require the Commission — or, after *Booker,* sentencing courts — to adhere to the 100-to-1 ratio for crack cocaine quantities other than those that trigger the statutory mandatory minimum sentences.

### B

In addition to the 1986 Act, the Government relies on Congress' disapproval of the Guidelines amendment that the Sentencing Commission proposed in 1995. Congress "not only disapproved of the 1:1 ratio," the Government urges; it also made clear "that the 1986 Act required the Commission (and sentencing courts) to take drug quantities into account, and to do so in a manner that respects the 100:1 ratio."

It is true that Congress rejected the Commission's 1995 proposal to place a 1-to-1 ratio in the Guidelines, and that Congress also expressed the view that "the sentence imposed for trafficking in a quantity of crack cocaine should generally exceed the sentence imposed for trafficking in a like quantity of powder cocaine." But nothing in Congress' 1995 reaction to the Commission-proposed 1-to-1 ratio suggested that crack sentences must exceed powder sentences by a ratio of 100 to 1. To the contrary, Congress' 1995 action required the Commission to recommend a "revision of the drug quantity ratio of crack cocaine to powder cocaine."

The Government emphasizes that Congress required the Commission to propose changes to the 100-to-1 ratio in *both* the 1986 Act and the Guidelines. This requirement, the Government contends, implicitly foreclosed any deviation from the 100-to-1 ratio in the Guidelines (or by sentencing courts) in the absence of a corresponding change in the statute. But it does not follow as the night follows the day that, by calling for recommendations to change the statute, Congress meant to bar any Guidelines alteration in advance of congressional action. The more likely reading is that Congress sought proposals to amend both the statute and the Guidelines because the Commission's criticisms of the 100-to-1 ratio concerned the exorbitance of the crack/powder disparity in both contexts.

Moreover, as a result of the 2007 amendment the Guidelines now advance a crack/powder ratio that varies (at different offense levels) between 25 to 1 and 80 to 1. Adopting the Government's analysis, the amended Guidelines would conflict with Congress' 1995 action, and with the 1986 Act, because the current Guidelines ratios deviate from the 100-to-1 statutory ratio. Congress, however, did not disapprove or modify the Commission-initiated 2007 amendment. Ordinarily, we resist reading congressional intent into congressional inaction. But in this case, Congress failed to act on a proposed amendment to the Guidelines in a high-profile area in which it had previously exercised its disapproval authority under 28 U.S.C. §994(p). If nothing else, this tacit acceptance of the 2007 amendment undermines the Government's position, which is itself based on implications drawn from congressional silence.

## C

Finally, the Government argues that if district courts are free to deviate from the Guidelines based on disagreements with the crack/powder ratio, unwarranted disparities of two kinds will ensue. First, because sentencing courts remain bound by the mandatory minimum sentences prescribed in the 1986 Act, deviations from the 100-to-1 ratio could result in sentencing "cliffs" around quantities that trigger the mandatory minimums. For example, a district court could grant a sizable downward variance to a defendant convicted of distributing 49 grams of crack but would be required by the statutory minimum to impose a much higher sentence on a defendant responsible for only 1 additional gram. Second, the Government maintains that, if district courts are permitted to vary from the Guidelines based on their disagreement with the crack/powder disparity, "defendants with identical real conduct will receive markedly different sentences, depending on nothing more than the particular judge drawn for sentencing."

Neither of these arguments persuades us to hold the crack/powder ratio untouchable by sentencing courts. As to the first, the LSD Guidelines we approved in *Neal* create a similar risk of sentencing "cliffs." An offender who possesses LSD on a carrier medium weighing ten grams is subject to the ten-year mandatory minimum, but an offender whose carrier medium weighs slightly less may receive a considerably lower sentence based on the Guidelines' presumptive-weight methodology. Concerning the second disparity, it is unquestioned that uniformity remains an important goal of sentencing. As we explained in *Booker*, however, advisory Guidelines combined with appellate review for reasonableness and ongoing revision of the Guidelines in response to sentencing practices will help to "avoid excessive sentencing disparities." These measures will not eliminate variations between district courts, but our opinion in *Booker* recognized that some departures from uniformity were a necessary cost of the remedy we adopted. And as to crack cocaine sentences in particular, we note a congressional control on disparities: possible variations among district courts are constrained by the mandatory minimums Congress prescribed in the 1986 Act.

Moreover, to the extent that the Government correctly identifies risks of "unwarranted sentence disparities" within the meaning of 18 U.S.C. §3553(a)(6), the proper solution is not to treat the crack/powder ratio as mandatory. Section 3553(a)(6) directs *district courts* to consider the need to avoid unwarranted disparities—along with other §3553(a) factors—when imposing sentences. Under this instruction, district courts must take account of sentencing practices in other courts and the "cliffs" resulting from the statutory mandatory minimum sentences. To reach an appropriate sentence, these disparities must be weighed against the other §3553(a) factors and any unwarranted disparity created by the crack/powder ratio itself.

## IV

While rendering the Sentencing Guidelines advisory we have nevertheless preserved a key role for the Sentencing Commission. As explained in *Rita* and *Gall*, district courts must treat the Guidelines as the "starting point and the initial benchmark." Congress established the Commission to formulate and constantly refine national sentencing standards. See *Rita v. United States*, 551 U.S. 338 (2007). Carrying out its charge, the Commission fills an important institutional role: It has the capacity courts lack to "base its determinations on empirical data and national experience, guided by a professional staff with appropriate expertise."

We have accordingly recognized that, in the ordinary case, the Commission's recommendation of a sentencing range will "reflect a rough approximation of sentences that might achieve §3553(a)'s objectives." The sentencing judge, on the other hand, has "greater familiarity with . . . the individual case and the individual defendant before him than the Commission or the appeals court." He is therefore "in a superior position to find facts and judge their import under §3353(a)" in each particular case. In light of these discrete institutional strengths, a district court's decision to vary from the advisory Guidelines may attract greatest respect when the sentencing judge finds a particular case "outside the 'heartland' to which the Commission intends individual Guidelines to apply." On the other hand, while the Guidelines are no longer binding, closer review may be in order when the sentencing judge varies from the Guidelines based solely on the judge's view that the Guidelines range "fails properly to reflect §3553(a) considerations" even in a mine-run case.

The crack cocaine Guidelines, however, present no occasion for elaborative discussion of this matter because those Guidelines do not exemplify the Commission's exercise of its characteristic institutional role. In formulating Guidelines ranges for crack cocaine offenses, as we earlier noted, the Commission looked to the mandatory minimum sentences set in the 1986 Act, and did not take account of "empirical data and national experience." Indeed, the Commission itself has reported that the crack/powder disparity produces disproportionately harsh sanctions, *i.e.*, sentences for crack cocaine offenses "greater than necessary" in light of the purposes of sentencing set forth in §3553(a). Given all this, it would not be an abuse of discretion for a district court to conclude when sentencing a particular defendant that the crack/powder disparity yields a sentence "greater than necessary" to achieve §3553(a)'s purposes, even in a mine-run case.

## V

Taking account of the foregoing discussion in appraising the District Court's disposition in this case, we conclude that the 180-month sentence imposed on Kimbrough should survive appellate inspection. The District Court began by properly calculating and considering the advisory Guidelines range. It then addressed the relevant §3553(a) factors. First, the court considered "the nature and circumstances" of the crime, which was an unremarkable drug-trafficking offense. ("[This] defendant and another defendant were caught sitting in a car with some crack cocaine and powder by two police officers — that's the sum and substance of it — [and they also had] a firearm."). Second, the court considered Kimbrough's "history and characteristics." The court noted that Kimbrough had no prior felony convictions, that he had served in combat during Operation Desert Storm and received an honorable discharge from the Marine Corps, and that he had a steady history of employment.

Furthermore, the court alluded to the Sentencing Commission's reports criticizing the 100-to-1 ratio, noting that the Commission "recognizes that crack cocaine has not caused the damage that the Justice Department alleges it has." Comparing the Guidelines range to the range that would have applied if Kimbrough had possessed an equal amount of powder, the court suggested that the 100-to-1 ratio itself created an unwarranted disparity within the meaning of §3553(a). Finally, the court did not purport to establish a ratio of its own. Rather, it appropriately framed its final determination in line with §3553(a)'s overarching instruction to "impose a sentence sufficient, but not greater than necessary" to accomplish the sentencing goals advanced in §3553(a)(2). Concluding that "the crack cocaine guidelines [drove] the offense level to a point higher than is necessary to do justice in this case," the District Court thus rested its sentence on the appropriate considerations and "committed no procedural error."

The ultimate question in Kimbrough's case is "whether the sentence was reasonable — *i.e.*, whether the District Judge abused his discretion in determining that the §3553(a) factors supported a sentence of [15 years] and justified a substantial deviation from the Guidelines range." The sentence the District Court imposed on Kimbrough was 4.5 years below the bottom of the Guidelines range. But in determining that 15 years was the appropriate prison term, the District Court properly homed in on the particular circumstances of Kimbrough's case and accorded weight to the Sentencing Commission's consistent and emphatic position that the crack/powder disparity is at odds with §3553(a). Indeed, aside from its claim that the 100-to-1 ratio is mandatory, the Government did not attack the District Court's downward variance as unsupported by §3553(a). Giving due respect to the District Court's reasoned appraisal, a reviewing court could not rationally conclude that the 4.5-year sentence reduction Kimbrough received qualified as an abuse of discretion. . . .

For the reasons stated, the judgment of the United States Court of Appeals for the Fourth Circuit is reversed, and the case is remanded for further proceedings consistent with this opinion. . . .

THOMAS, J., dissenting.

I continue to disagree with the remedy fashioned in *United States v. Booker*. The Court's post-*Booker* sentencing cases illustrate why the remedial majority in *Booker* was mistaken to craft a remedy far broader than necessary to correct constitutional error. The Court is now confronted with a host of questions about how to administer a sentencing scheme that has no basis in the statute. Because the Court's decisions in this area are necessarily grounded in policy considerations rather than law, I respectfully dissent . . . .

. . . Congress did not mandate a reasonableness standard of appellate review—that was a standard the remedial majority in *Booker* fashioned out of whole cloth. The Court must now give content to that standard, but in so doing it does not and cannot rely on any statutory language or congressional intent. We are asked here to determine whether, under the new advisory Guidelines regime, district courts may impose sentences based in part on their disagreement with a categorical policy judgment reflected in the Guidelines. But the Court's answer to that question necessarily derives from something other than the statutory language or congressional intent because Congress, by making the Guidelines mandatory, quite clearly intended to bind district courts to the Sentencing Commission's categorical policy judgments. By rejecting this statutory approach, the *Booker* remedial majority has left the Court with no law to apply and forced it to assume the legislative role of devising a new sentencing scheme. . . .

## NOTES

1. *Reasonableness review.* The scope of reasonableness review after *Booker* has been one of the central questions of the "Booker era" of federal sentencing reform. Skeptics feared that the flexibility of reasonableness review might allow appellate courts to continue as "guardians" of the guidelines. Optimists hoped that *Booker* would signal a deeper respect and deference towards the decisions of sentencing courts—a respect that some sentencing judges and commentators had been searching for since the Sentencing Reform Act was enacted. Reasonableness plays a central role in so many parts of the law that it comes to haunt the dreams of many first year law students. When appellate courts apply a reasonableness standard, do its virtues outweigh its costs?

Two per curiam decisions in 2009 emphasized that trial courts cannot themselves use a presumption of reasonableness for guideline sentences. See Spears v. United States, 555 U.S. 261 (2009) (reiterating *Kimbrough* standard and stating that "district courts are entitled to reject and vary categorically from the crack-cocaine Guidelines based on a policy disagreement with those Guidelines). See also Nelson v. United States, 555 U.S. 350 (2009):

> Our cases do not allow a sentencing court to presume that a sentence within the applicable Guidelines range is reasonable. In *Rita* we said as much, in fairly explicit terms: "We repeat that the presumption before us is an *appellate* court presumption. [The] sentencing court does not enjoy the benefit of a legal presumption that the Guidelines sentence should apply." And in *Gall* we reiterated that district judges, in considering how the various statutory sentencing factors apply to an individual defendant, "may not presume that the Guidelines range is reasonable."

> In this case, the Court of Appeals quoted the above language from *Rita* but affirmed the sentence anyway after finding that the District Judge did not treat the Guidelines as mandatory. That is true, but beside the point. The Guidelines are not only *not mandatory* on sentencing courts; they are also not to be *presumed* reasonable. We think it plain from the comments of the sentencing judge that he did apply a presumption of reasonableness to Nelson's Guidelines range. Under our recent precedents, that constitutes error.

The most recent extensive application of *Booker* in the Supreme Court came in Pepper v. United States, 562 U.S. ____ (2011). Pepper took a convoluted path to the Supreme Court. Pepper was sentenced to 24 months imprisonment on drug charges, a nearly 75 percent downward department from the low end of the guidelines range, based in part on his substantial assistance to authorities. The Eighth Circuit reversed and remanded for resentencing in light of *Booker* (Pepper I). The sentencing court again sentenced Pepper to 24 months, relying this time on his post-sentencing rehabilitation and low risk of recidivism. The Eighth Circuit again reversed (Pepper II), holding that the sentencing court could not rely on post-sentencing rehabilitation, and mandating that a new judge resentence Pepper. The Supreme Court vacated the Eight Circuit's *Pepper II* judgment in light of *Gall.* The Eighth Circuit reversed and remanded the case again (Pepper III). A new trial judge imposed a 65-month prison term based on substantial assistance and post-sentence rehabilitation. In a case of déjà vu all over again, the Eight Circuit again rejected the post-sentence rehabilitation argument (Pepper IV).

While the wheels of justice may turn slowly, Pepper makes clear that at times they also grind very fine. This time, the Supreme Court held that a district court at resentencing "may consider evidence of the defendant's postsentencing rehabilitation and that such evidence may, in appropriate cases, support a downward variance from the now advisory Federal Sentencing Guidelines range."

The court expressly invalidated a statutory provision, 18 U.S.C. 3742(g)(2), which limited the range and effectively the kind of information a district court could consider at resentencing. And to emphasize the breadth of information that a district could can consider, the court cited a statute — 18 U.S.C. 3661 — and, of all things, *Williams v. New York*—the 1949 decision that allowed a judge to overrule a jury's unanimous sentencing recommendation of a life sentence and instead to impose the death penalty under the then dominant indeterminate sentencing regime based on post-conviction information provided to the judges.

2. *The intersection of §3553(a) and reasonableness review.* Since all of the elements of §3553(a) now govern sentencing decisions in federal courts, these same elements ought to play a central role in appellate determinations of reasonableness. What is the role of appellate courts after *Booker, Rita, Gall, Kimbrough,* and *Pepper* in developing an appellate "law" about each of the §3553(a) sentencing factors?

3. *Sentencing court's duty to explain.* What obligations do sentencing courts have to explain and justify their choices to the defendant, the appellate court, and the Sentencing Commission? Is it better for all concerned when sentencing courts provide more detailed analysis? Should appellate deference — or

Commission respect when they consider changes in the guidelines—be different for sentencing opinions that are explained with great care? See United States v. Irey, 612 F.3d 1160 (11th Cir. 2010) (below-guideline sentence was unreasonable where sentencing judge gave so little consideration to guidelines that it amounted to no real weight); United States v. Irey, 746 F. Supp.2d 1232 (M.D. Fla. 2010) (sentencing judge on remand arguing that appellate court took his remarks in sentencing hearing out of context and imposed sentence based on facts about uncharged conduct never presented to him).

4. *Departures for policy: the uncertain reach of* Kimbrough. *Kimbrough* is a particularly striking decision because the underlying policy and legal issues deal with the gap between sentences for crack cocaine and the sentences for powder cocaine cases, and the racial disparity in such cases. Note the interplay of judicial sentencing discretion, Commission action (even unsuccessful action), and Congressional inaction. Congress did ultimately reform the crack/powder cocaine ratio to 18 to 1 in the Fair Sentencing Act of 2010—three years after the *Kimbrough* decision, and 24 years after the 100:1 crack/powder cocaine ratio was created in a 1986 statute.

Will *Kimbrough* extend to policy decisions other than the crack/powder cocaine penalties? The Supreme Court's opinion in *Kimbrough* emphasized, based on the Commission's own criticisms, that the crack guidelines did "not exemplify the Commission's exercise of its characteristic institutional role" because these guidelines did not take account of "empirical data and national experience." In arguing that other guidelines should still be given significant weight after *Booker*, the Government asserts in many other settings that other guidelines consistently do reflect the Commission's exercise of its characteristic institutional role. In contrast, federal defendants have repeatedly argued that many guidelines, not just those for crack offenses, fail to reflect the Commission's expertise in assessing "empirical data and national experience."

How should a district court assess after *Booker* whether certain guidelines "exemplify the Commission's exercise of its characteristic institutional role"? Because the Commission, other than in the crack setting, has produced very few in-depth reports or public analyses about the soundness of particular guidelines, advocates have often pointed to snippets of legislative history and public Commission materials to bolster their arguments. After *Kimbrough*, may district courts conduct their own investigations—perhaps even a sentencing hearing to receive arguments or even testimony about the background and development of a particular guideline—when deciding how much weight to afford a particular guideline? Should they? Cf. United States v. Grober, 595 F. Supp. 2d 382 (D.N.J. 2008) (discussing at length the evidentiary hearing held by a district judge in an effort to assess whether to give significant or reduced weight to the guidelines for sentencing in child pornography cases involving downloading and trading illegal picture on the Internet).

---

How can lawyers and scholars understand the impact of major structural changes in the guideline system? It is impossible to look at a single case—even a transformative case like *Booker*—and know what impact it will have on actual sentencing decisions. Instead, it is necessary to look at patterns in the roughly 75,000-85,000 cases sentenced under the guidelines in the federal system each year. Since the federal guidelines were first implemented, the United States Sentencing Commission has produced reports and databases reflecting patterns in federal sentencing. Consider the following national "overview" data from 2011.

### National Comparison of Sentence Imposed and Position Relative to the Guideline Range[1]
### Fiscal Year 2011

|  | N | % |
|---|---|---|
| TOTAL CASES | 84,744 | 100.0 |
| CASES SENTENCED WITHIN GUIDELINE RANGE | 46,160 | 54.5 |
| CASES SENTENCED ABOVE GUIDELINE RANGE | 1,527 | 1.8 |
| DEPARTURE ABOVE GUIDELINE RANGE | 488 | 0.6 |
| Upward Departure From Guideline Range[2] | 379 | 0.4 |
| Upward Departure With *Booker*/18 U.S.C. § 3553[3] | 109 | 0.1 |
| OTHERWISE ABOVE GUIDELINE RANGE | 1,039 | 1.2 |
| Above Guideline Range With *Booker*/18 U.S.C. § 3553[4] | 947 | 1.1 |
| All Remaining Cases Above Guideline Range[5] | 92 | 0.1 |
| GOVERNMENT SPONSORED BELOW RANGE[6] | 22,295 | 26.3 |
| §5K1.1 Substantial Assistance Departure | 9,522 | 11.2 |
| §5K3.1 Early Disposition Program Departure | 9,057 | 10.7 |
| Other Government Sponsored Below Range | 3,716 | 4.4 |
| NON-GOVERNMENT SPONSORED BELOW RANGE | 14,762 | 17.4 |
| DEPARTURE BELOW GUIDELINE RANGE | 2,893 | 3.4 |
| Downward Departure From Guideline Range[2] | 1,976 | 2.3 |
| Downward Departure With *Booker*/18 U.S.C. § 3553[3] | 917 | 1.1 |
| OTHERWISE BELOW GUIDELINE RANGE | 11,869 | 14.0 |
| Below Guideline Range With *Booker*/18 U.S.C. § 3553[4] | 11,371 | 13.4 |
| All Remaining Cases Below Guideline Range[5] | 498 | 0.6 |

[1]  This table reflects the 86,201 cases sentenced in Fiscal Year 2011. Of these, 1,457 cases were excluded because information was missing from the submitted documents that prevented the comparison of the sentence and the guideline range. Descriptions of variables used in this table are provided in Appendix A.

[2]  All cases with departures in which the court did not indicate as a reason either *United States v. Booker*, 18 U.S.C. § 3553, or a factor or reason specifically prohibited in the provisions, policy statements, or commentary of the *Guidelines Manual.*

[3]  All cases sentenced outside of the guideline range in which the court indicated both a departure (see footnote 2) and a reference to either *United States v. Booker*, 18 U.S.C. § 3553, or related factors as a reason for sentencing outside of the guideline system.

[4]  All cases sentenced outside of the guideline range in which no departure was indicated and in which the court cited *United States v. Booker*, 18 U.S.C. § 3553, or related factors as one of the reasons for sentencing outside of the guideline system.

[5]  All cases sentenced outside of the guideline range that could not be classified into any of the three previous outside of the range categories. This category includes cases in which no reason was provided for a sentence outside of the guideline range.

[6]  Cases in which a reason for the sentence indicated that the prosecution initiated, proposed, or stipulated to a sentence outside of the guideline range, either pursuant to a plea agreement or as part of a non-plea negotiation with the defendant.

SOURCE: U.S. Sentencing Commission, 2011 Datafile, USSCFY11.

How does this 2011 snapshot compare with sentence patterns since *Booker*? Since *Apprendi*? Since *Koon*? Since the guidelines were first implemented across the country following the Supreme Court's decision in *Mistretta* in 1989?

The United States Sentencing Commission provides annual reports on sentencing data, including circuit-by-circuit and district-by-district assessments. It also produces reports that occasionally show sentencing patterns over time. We encourage anyone interested in sentencing data to look at the most recent reports, and then to consider patterns over time and comparisons across jurisdictions, and, where possible, across judges. To get a sense of how patterns can change, contrast the following FY 2001-FY 2006 sentencing patterns to the 2011 data reported above.

## U.S. Sentencing Commission, Special Post-*Booker* Coding Project: Cases Sentenced Subsequent to United States v. Booker (July 6, 2006)

**National Guideline Application Trends**

| Position of Sentence Relative to Guideline Range | FY2001 | FY2002 | FY2003 | FY2004 (Pre-Blakely) | FY 2005 (Post-Booker) | FY 2006 |
|---|---|---|---|---|---|---|
| Within range | 64.0% | 65.0% | 69.4% | 72.2% | 61.6% | 61.9% |
| Upward departures | 0.6% | 0.8% | 0.8% | 0.8% | 0.3% | 0.9% |
| Otherwise above range | — | — | — | — | 1.4% | 0.8% |
| Substantial assistance departures | 17.1% | 17.4% | 15.9% | 15.5% | 14.7% | 14.3% |
| Other gov't sponsored departures | — | — | 6.3% | 6.4% | 9.1% | 9.9% |
| Other departures downward | 18.3% | 16.8% | 7.5% | 5.2% | 3.2% | 5.2% |
| Departures otherwise below range | — | — | — | — | 9.7% | 7.2% |

## NOTES

1. *Sentences within the guidelines.* The yearly comparison data reveals a downturn in the number of within-guidelines sentences shortly after *Booker*, which follows a notable increase in the number of within-guidelines sentences before *Blakely* and *Booker*. By 2011, the within-guidelines sentences dropped to 54.5%.

How should policymakers in Congress, in the Sentencing Commission, and in the Department of Justice respond to this information? Are the guidelines still "working well" after *Booker* and its progeny? Do these statistics suggest a continuing "stickiness" to the guidelines for trial judges, despite the long-standing criticism of the guidelines before *Booker* and the new and serious constitutional issues raised in *Booker*? What factors may account for the continuing judicial faithfulness to the guideline system?

2. *Sentences outside the guidelines.*  As the data indicate, as of 2011 just under half of all sentences are outside the guidelines, and the majority of those are the result of a motion by the prosecution. Does this suggest that the entire guidelines movement is too focused on the regulation of judicial discretion and not sufficiently concerned with the exercise of prosecutorial discretion? See Honorable John Gleeson, The Sentencing Commission and Prosecutorial Discretion: The Role of the Courts in Policing Sentence Bargains, 36 Hofstra L. Rev. 639, 648 (2008); Wes R. Porter, The Pendulum in Federal Sentencing Can Also Swing Toward Predictability: A Renewed Role for Binding Plea Agreements Post-Booker, 37 Wm. Mitchell L. Rev. 469, 514 (2011).

One issue that has been robustly debated in the wake of *Booker* is whether judges ought to sentence outside the guideline range on grounds such as the defendant's cooperation with authorities or agreement to a rapid guilty plea disposition when the prosecutor does not recommend a sentence below the guidelines on these grounds. See Testimony of James E. Felman, Esq., before the Subcommittee on Crime, Terrorism, and Homeland Security of the Judiciary Committee of the United States House of Representatives, March 16, 2006, Oversight Hearing, United States v. Booker: One Year Later—Chaos or Status Quo?, 19-21 (available at sentencing.typepad.com/sentencing_law_and_policy/files/felman_ testimony.pdf).

Replicating patterns that have developed since the origins of the federal sentencing guidelines, judges, even after *Booker*, are nearly ten times more likely to exercise their discretion to sentence outside the applicable guideline range in order to impose a below-guideline sentence rather than to go above the applicable guideline range. What do these numbers suggest about the overall severity of the sentences set forth in the guidelines? Should the U.S. Sentencing Commission consider lowering guideline sentencing ranges in an effort to achieve greater parity between above- and below-guideline sentences? Should it matter in what types of cases the courts sentence below the guidelines? Whose decision is more democratic, that of the judiciary or that of the commission? Whose is fairer?

3. *Sentence length.*  Even though post-*Booker* data reveals a downturn in the number of sentences within the guideline range, other data released by the Sentencing Commission indicated that average and median sentence lengths appeared at first to be stable (or even rising a bit) post-*Booker*. More recent data suggest a gradual decrease in average sentences. See http://www.ussc.gov/Data_and_Statistics/Federal_Sentencing_Statistics/Quarterly_Sentencing_Updates/USSC_2012_2nd_Quarter_Report.pdf.

4. *Increased disparity?*  The circuit-by-circuit data indicates that the rates of judicial variation from the guidelines are distinctly different in different circuits.

In the Second Circuit, for example, judges sentence within the guideline range in 39 percent of cases — more than 15 percent below the national norm — and judges depart downward in non-government sponsored departures in 38.5 percent — more than twice the national norm. In contrast, in the Fifth Circuit, judges sentence within the guidelines range in 70.6 percent of cases — more than 15 percent above the national norm — and have non-government sponsored downward departures in only 13.7 percent of cases. District variation is even greater. U.S. Sentencing Commission, 2011 Sourcebook of Federal Sentencing Statistics.

5. *How to assess a new sentencing system.*    Should the distribution of sentences reflected in the data be a central concern in assessing the changes *Booker* made to the federal sentencing system? More generally, can data patterns ever serve as a measure of the justice of any individual sentence, or of any sentencing system? Do broad trends in sentencing offer insights about which institutions are best situated to establish general rules for the system? Craig Green, Booker and Fanfan: The Untimely Death (and Rebirth?) of the Federal Sentencing Guidelines, 93 Geo. L.J. 395, 422-424 (2005) (arguing that either reasonableness review will establish new factors to which constitutional protections may attach, or Congress will reestablish mandatory sentencing, raising additional constitutional questions).

## PROBLEM 3-2.   ASYMMETRICAL GUIDELINES

In the aftermath of the *Blakely* decision, staff working for the Sentencing Commission and for various members of Congress began exploring options for a revised federal sentencing system that could overcome those Sixth Amendment violations described in *Blakely*.

One leading option, first conceived by Professor Frank Bowman, a former prosecutor, defense attorney, and staff attorney for the Sentencing Commission, called for asymmetrical guidelines. The proposal asked Congress to pass a statute redefining the "guideline maximum" to be the current statutory maximum for the crime of conviction. However, the existing sentencing guidelines would remain in place for the bottom of the range. Any guideline adjustments that raise the bottom of the guideline range would continue to bind the sentencing judge. Bowman described the justification for and likely effect of this revision as follows:

> The practical effect of such an amendment would be to preserve current federal practice almost unchanged. Guidelines factors would not be elements. They could still constitutionally be determined by post-conviction judicial findings of fact. No modifications of pleading or trial practice would be required. The only theoretical difference would be that judges could sentence defendants above the top of the current guideline ranges without the formality of an upward departure. However, given that the current rate of upward departures is 0.6%, and that judges sentence the majority of all offenders at or below the midpoint of existing sentencing ranges, the likelihood that judges would use their newly granted discretion to increase the sentences of very many defendants above now-prevailing levels seems, at best, remote.
>
> This proposal could not be effected without an amendment of the SRA because it would fall afoul of the so-called "25% rule," 28 U.S.C. §994(b)(2),

which mandates that the top of any guideline range be no more than six months or 25% greater than its bottom. The ranges produced by this proposal would ordinarily violate that provision. . . .

In addition, if such a statute were passed, the Commission might think it proper to enact a policy statement recommending that courts not impose sentences more than 25% higher than the guideline minimum in the absence of one or more of the factors now specified in the Guidelines as potential grounds for upward departure. Failure to adhere to this recommendation would not be appealable, and thus such a provision would not fall foul of *Blakely*. A few modifications to the Guidelines themselves would also be required to bring them into conformity with *Blakely* and the new statute. . . . But otherwise, very little would have to change. . . .

Frank Bowman, Memorandum Presenting a Proposal for Bringing the Federal Sentencing Guidelines into Conformity with Blakely v. Washington, 16 Fed. Sent'g Rep. 364 (2004).

You serve on the staff of a member of Congress, and you specialize in criminal justice issues. Your boss wants to know how various groups are likely to respond to the "asymmetrical guidelines" proposal, both as a response to *Booker* and as a longer-term restructuring of the system. What is the likely reaction from the leadership of the Department of Justice? See Federal Sentencing Guidelines Speech by Attorney General Alberto Gonzalez, 17 Fed. Sent'g Rep. 324 (2005). What about the National Association of Federal Defenders, and the federal judges as represented by the Judicial Conference of the United States?

What suggestions do you have for any longer-term solutions for the federal sentencing system? Here are several options:

- Congress picks some high-priority crimes and designates mandatory minimum sentences for those crimes.
- Congress leaves judges the discretion to impose a sentence anywhere between the statutory minimum and maximum, perhaps relying on guidelines for voluntary guidance (and eliminating any appellate review of sentences based on application of the guidelines).
- Congress creates "inverted guidelines" that designate the presumptive sentence as the statutory maximum and use guideline factors (and judicial factfinding) to justify any downward movement from that statutory maximum.
- Congress designates a few critical "enhancement factors," such as use of a weapon, and authorizes prosecutors to allege such factors in the indictment and prove them to a jury, either during the trial or in a bifurcated sentencing proceeding.

For details on legislative proposals issued in response to *Blakely* and *Booker*, see Defending America's Most Vulnerable: Safe Access to Drug Treatment and Child Protection Act of 2005, H.R 1528, 109th Cong. 12 (2005); Albert W. Alschuler, To Sever or Not to Sever? Why *Blakely* Requires Action by Congress, 17 Fed. Sent'g Rep. 11 (2004); Rachel E. Barkow, The Devil You Know: Federal Sentencing After *Blakely*, 17 Fed. Sent'g Rep. 312 (2004); Stephanos Bibas, *Blakely*'s Federal Aftermath, 16 Fed. Sent'g Rep. 333 (2004); James Felman, How Should the Congress Respond If the Supreme Court Strikes Down the Federal

Sentencing Guidelines? 17 Fed. Sent'g Rep. 97 (2004); Nancy J. King & Susan R. Klein, Beyond *Blakely*, 16 Fed. Sent'g Rep. 316 (2004); Mark Osler, The *Blakely* Problem and the 3x Solution, 16 Fed. Sent'g Rep. 344 (2004); Kevin R. Reitz, The Enforceability of Sentencing Guidelines, 58 Stan. L. Rev. 155 (2005); Ian Weinstein & Nathaniel Z. Marmur, Federal Sentencing During the Interregnum: Defense Practice as the *Blakely* Dust Settles, 17 Fed. Sent'g Rep. 51 (2004).

Sentencing law and policy has emerged as a highly active area of scholarship and practice; most of that literature focuses on the federal guidelines and constitutional regulation of sentencing, despite the huge variety of systems and greater support for guidelines in many states. We encourage anyone interested in this area to search for the most current literature on particular subjects of interest. A sampling of recent articles include: Lynn Adelman & Jon Deitrich, Improving the Guidelines Through Critical Evaluation: An Important New Role for District Courts, 57 Drake L. Rev. 575 (2009); W. David Ball, Heinous, Atrocious, and Cruel: Apprendi, Indeterminate Sentencing, and the Meaning of Punishment, 109 Colum. L. Rev. 893 (2009); Douglas A. Berman, Rita, Reasoned Sentencing, and Resistance to Change, 85 Denv. U. L. Rev. 7 (2007); Stephanos Bibas & Susan Klein, The Sixth Amendment and Criminal Sentencing, 30 Cardozo L. Rev. 775 (2008); Stephanos Bibas et al., Policing Politics at Sentencing, 103 Nw. U. L. Rev. 1371 (2009); Mark Chenoweth, Using Its Sixth Sense: The Roberts Court Revamps the Rights of the Accused, 2009 Cato Sup. Ct. Rev. 223, 225-246; D. Michael Fisher, Striking a Balance: The Need to Temper Judicial Discretion Against a Background of Legislative Interest in Federal Sentencing, 46 Duq. L. Rev. 65 (2007); Bradley R. Hall, Mandatory Sentencing Guidelines By Any Other Name: When "Indeterminate Structured Sentencing" Violates Blakely v. Washington, 57 Drake L. Rev. 643 (2009); Carissa Byrne Hessick & F. Andrew Hessick, Appellate Review of Sentencing Decisions, 60 Ala. L. Rev. 1 (2008); Susan R. Klein & Sandra Guerra Thompson, DOJ's Attack on Federal Judicial "Leniency," the Supreme Court's Response, and the Future of Criminal Sentencing, 44 Tulsa L. Rev. 519 (2009); Susan F. Mandiberg, Why Sentencing by a Judge Satisfies the Right to Jury Trial: A Comparative Law Look at Blakely and Booker, 40 McGeorge L. Rev. 107 (2009); Michael M. O'Hear, Explaining Sentences, 36 Fla. St. U. L. Rev. 459 (2009); Mary Kreiner Ramirez, Into the Twilight Zone: Informing Judicial Discretion in Federal Sentencing, 57 Drake L. Rev. 591 (2009); Kate Stith, The Arc of the Pendulum: Judges, Prosecutors, and the Exercise of Discretion, 117 Yale L.J. 1420 (2008); Benjamin J. Priester, Apprendi Land Becomes Bizarro World: "Policy Nullification" and Other Surreal Doctrines in the New Constitutional Law of Sentencing, 51 Santa Clara L. Rev. 1, 78 (2011).

## B.   CAPITAL PUNISHMENT: REGULATING DISCRETION THROUGH CONSTITUTIONAL RULES

Though many view capital punishment as markedly distinct from other types of sentencing, the regulation of sentencing *discretion* in the modern death penalty closely parallels its regulation in modern noncapital sentencing.

As detailed throughout this section, the modern administration of the death penalty has been centrally concerned with the limitation of sentencing discretion. Two features differentiate the death penalty from other sentencing: the actors targeted for regulation are usually jurors, and the catalyst of reform has been the U.S. Supreme Court. In nondeath sentencing it has been sentencing commissions that have operated as the main innovators in structuring the exercise of judges' discretion.

## 1.   Origins and Foundations

The death penalty once occupied the center of attention in criminal justice; it was the penalty most commonly authorized and imposed under English law before the American colonial period. In part because prison systems did not develop fully until the end of the nineteenth century, the death penalty was a central component of the American criminal justice system during the colonial period and through the eighteenth and early nineteenth centuries. By some counts, there were as many as 15,000 authorized executions (and perhaps as many lynchings) during this period, many of which took place in Southern states and disproportionately involved African Americans. An abolitionist movement took root soon after the nation's founding and gained force through the nineteenth century. This movement combined with the creation of penitentiaries to diminish the reliance on capital punishment, although 100 to 150 executions still took place each year between the Civil War and World War II.

As explained in the following excerpt, discretion claimed a central role long ago in the American story of the death penalty. The late nineteenth and early twentieth centuries saw most states move away from statutes mandating death as the punishment for certain crimes toward new laws that gave juries discretion to choose which defendants would be sentenced to die.

### The Death Penalty in America,
### Hugo Adam Bedau
**Pages 9-12 (3d ed. 1982)**

Traditionally, under English law, death penalties were mandatory; once the defendant was found guilty of a capital offense, the court had no alternative but a death sentence. Thus the jury could avoid a death penalty in a capital case only by acquitting the defendant or by a finding of guilt on a lesser offense (e.g., manslaughter rather than murder). Remission of the death sentence in favor of transportation to the colonies, or some lesser punishment . . . remained a prerogative of the Crown. But as long as the death penalty was a mandatory punishment, there was always the possibility of acquitting a clearly guilty defendant in order to avoid a death sentence, especially in rare cases where the defendant was unusually pitiable or his conduct was thought to be morally excusable. This threat of "jury nullification," as it has come to be called, on the one side, and the undemocratic character of unbridled executive power to pardon, on the other, encouraged the American colonies to reject the traditional mandatory death penalty in favor of some alternative. What eventually developed was the charac-teristically American practice that divided murder into degrees and gave the court some sentencing discretion in capital cases. . . .

The first of the [Massachusetts] Bay Colony's capital statutes to authorize an alternative penalty to the death sentence was for the crime of rape. Under a law enacted in 1642, rape was punishable by death or by some "other grievous punishment," at the discretion of the court. A severe whipping and the humil-iation of standing on the gallows with a rope around one's neck quickly became the most common punishment for the convicted rapist (unless he was a Negro or an Indian, in which case his punishment was likely to be sale into slavery). The heritage of sentencing discretion did not carry over into the post-Revolutionary period, however. [By] 1780 Massachusetts's seven capital felonies (including rape) were subject to a mandatory death penalty. . . .

Elsewhere in the nation, discretionary capital laws slowly replaced mandatory death penalties. . . . In Maryland, where the jury already had the power to fix degrees of murder, the death penalty became optional in 1809 for treason, rape, and arson, but not for homicide. Tennessee (1838) and Ala-bama (1841) were the first to authorize a discretionary death sentence for murder, and Louisiana (1846) appears to have been the first jurisdiction to make all its capital crimes optionally punishable by life imprisonment. Between 1886 and 1900, twenty states and the federal government followed suit; by 1926, the practice had been adopted in 33 jurisdictions[, and] seven more . . . intro-duced this procedure for the punishment of murder [by 1963].

No doubt the development of jury sentencing-discretion in capital cases was seen in part in some jurisdictions as an effective compromise with forces that might otherwise continue to press for complete abolition. . . . In other jurisdic-tions, however, a very different motivation prevailed. In the postbellum South, research has shown that where the number of capital statutes increased dramat-ically, as they did in Virginia, they tended to be enacted in a discretionary rather than a mandatory form. With black Americans newly freed from slavery, but disqualified from testifying against whites, excluded by law from serving on juries, and lacking in trained counsel of their own race, the dominant white class could comfortably place their trust in the judgment of white judges and white juries to administer these discretionary death penalty statutes in the desired manner.

### NOTES

1. *Legislative control of the death penalty.*    Before the U.S. Supreme Court's significant involvement in capital punishment administration starting in the 1970s, America's history with the death penalty had been primarily about sta-tutes and legislative debate. State legislatures were responsible for the evolution (and even sometimes the abandonment) of capital punishment in the American criminal justice system from the colonial era through the twentieth century. A number of colonial legislative enactments, though influenced by England's embrace of the death penalty, defined for themselves a subset of crimes that

were to be subject to capital punishment. State legislatures further narrowed the reach of the death penalty through the early nineteenth century as states, led by developments in Pennsylvania, divided the offense of murder into degrees and provided that only the most aggravated murderers would be subject to punishment of death. And, as highlighted above, this period also saw a slow but steady evolution in the death penalty from a mandatory punishment to a discretionary one. As Hugo Adam Bedau further explained, these legislative developments reflect "the struggle between abolitionists and retentionists, as well as larger social forces shaping the pattern and institutions of criminal justice." Hugo Adam Bedau, The Death Penalty in America 4 (3d ed. 1982).

2. *Parallel paths in Europe and the United States.*   The path followed by the death penalty in Europe paralleled that in the United States. Although a few countries abolished it during the nineteenth and early twentieth centuries, capital punishment saw a resurgence during and after World War I. With the end of World War II, however, a number of European countries abolished the death penalty in their constitutions, largely as a reaction to the abuse of capital punishment during the war. Others accomplished the same result judicially or through legislation. Most countries gradually reduced the use of the death penalty, and by the late 1960s it was virtually no longer employed. In England, for example, though all first-degree murders remained subject to the death penalty until the 1960s, executive clemency commuted most death sentences to life imprisonment until Parliament changed the law.

3. *Constitutional text and capital punishment.*   Capital punishment was a well-established and well-accepted practice during the nation's founding, and the drafters of the Constitution apparently contemplated that it would be a lawful practice in the United States. For instance, the Fifth Amendment says that "[n]o person shall be held to answer for a capital, or otherwise infamous crime, unless on a presentment or indictment of a Grand Jury. . . ." The Amendment's double jeopardy clause provides that no person shall "be twice put in jeopardy of life or limb," and its due process clause declares that no person shall be "deprived of life . . . without due process of law." Do you think this text conclusively establishes the constitutionality of capital punishment so long as appropriate procedural rules are followed? Does the Eighth Amendment's prohibition of "cruel and unusual punishments" change the textual analysis in any way?

---

Despite the U.S. Constitution's apparent acceptance of capital punishment, the seemingly arbitrary use of discretion in capital cases led lawyers in the 1950s to start questioning the constitutionality of the penalty. Legal challenges to the death penalty took many forms in lower courts through the 1960s, and this litigation helped produce a de facto moratorium on the death penalty as courts stayed executions while they considered various constitutional objections. Broad constitutional challenges to the death penalty first came before the Supreme Court in cases from California and Ohio in which defendants challenged as a violation of due process the discretionary systems under which they were sentenced to death.

## Dennis McGautha v. California
### 402 U.S. 183 (1971)

Harlan, J.

... McGautha and his codefendant Wilkinson were charged with committing two armed robberies and a murder. ... In accordance with California procedure in capital cases, the trial was in two stages, a guilt stage and a punishment stage. [Based on testimonial and physical evidence, the jury found both defendants guilty at the guilt stage.] At the penalty trial, which took place on the following day but before the same jury, the State ... presented evidence of McGautha's prior felony convictions and sentences, and then rested. [Wilkinson and McGautha thereafter both testified, each claiming that his accomplice fired the fatal shot. Wilkinson also called character witnesses, who testified that he had] a good reputation and was honest and peaceable. The jury was instructed in the following language:

> In this part of the trial the law does not forbid you from being influenced by pity for the defendants and you may be governed by mere sentiment and sympathy for the defendants in arriving at a proper penalty in this case; however, the law does forbid you from being governed by mere conjecture, prejudice, public opinion or public feeling.
>
> [You] should consider all of the evidence received here in court presented by the People and defendants throughout the trial before this jury. You may also consider all of the evidence of the circumstances surrounding the crime, of each defendant's background and history, and of the facts in aggravation or mitigation of the penalty which have been received here in court. However, it is not essential to your decision that you find mitigating circumstances on the one hand or evidence in aggravation of the offense on the other hand. ... Notwithstanding facts, if any, proved in mitigation or aggravation, in determining which punishment shall be inflicted, you are entirely free to act according to your own judgment, conscience, and absolute discretion. ...
>
> Now, beyond prescribing the two alternative penalties [of death or life imprisonment], the law itself provides no standard for the guidance of the jury in the selection of the penalty, but, rather, commits the whole matter of determining which of the two penalties shall be fixed to the judgment, conscience, and absolute discretion of the jury. In the determination of that matter, if the jury does agree, it must be unanimous as to which of the two penalties is imposed.

The jury returned verdicts fixing Wilkinson's punishment at life imprisonment and McGautha's punishment at death.

[In a companion case on this appeal, John] Crampton was indicted for the murder of his wife. ... He pleaded not guilty and not guilty by reason of insanity. [Physical evidence linked Crampton to his wife's killing, although his attorney submitted evidence suggesting her shooting was accidental.] In accordance with the Ohio practice which Crampton challenges, his guilt and punishment were determined in a single unitary proceeding. The jury was instructed that: "If you find the defendant guilty of murder in the first degree, the punishment is death, unless you recommend mercy, in which event the punishment is imprisonment in the penitentiary during life." The jury was given no other instructions specifically addressed to the decision whether to recommend mercy, but was told in connection with its verdict generally:

> You must not be influenced by any consideration of sympathy or prejudice. It is your duty to carefully weigh the evidence, to decide all disputed questions of fact, to apply the instructions of the court to your findings and to render your verdict accordingly. In fulfilling your duty, your efforts must be to arrive at a just verdict.
>
> Consider all the evidence and make your finding with intelligence and impartiality, and without bias, sympathy, or prejudice, so that the State of Ohio and the defendant will feel that their case was fairly and impartially tried.

The jury deliberated for over four hours and returned a verdict of guilty, with no recommendation for mercy.

[McGautha and Crampton both] claim that the absence of standards to guide the jury's discretion on the punishment issue is constitutionally intolerable. [They] contend that to leave the jury completely at large to impose or withhold the death penalty as it sees fit is fundamentally lawless and therefore violates the basic command of the Fourteenth Amendment that no State shall deprive a person of his life without due process of law. Despite the undeniable surface appeal of the proposition, we conclude that the courts below correctly rejected it. . . .

The history of capital punishment . . . reveals continual efforts, uniformly unsuccessful, to identify before the fact those homicides for which the slayer should die. [Jurors on occasion took the law into their own hands when facing cases that seemed] clearly inappropriate for the death penalty. In such cases they simply refused to convict of the capital offense. [To] meet the problem of jury nullification, legislatures . . . adopted the method of forthrightly granting juries the discretion which they had been exercising in fact. [Our precedents have consistently suggested the lawfulness of] standardless jury sentencing in capital cases, [stressing that juries] express the conscience of the community on the ultimate question of life or death. . . .

In recent years academic and professional sources have suggested that jury sentencing discretion should be controlled by standards of some sort. The American Law Institute first published such a recommendation in 1959. Several States have enacted new criminal codes in the intervening 12 years, some adopting features of the Model Penal Code. Other States have modified their laws with respect to murder and the death penalty in other ways. None of these States have followed the Model Penal Code and adopted statutory criteria for imposition of the death penalty. In recent years, challenges to standardless jury sentencing have been presented to many state and federal appellate courts. No court has held the challenge good. . . .

Those who have come to grips with the hard task of actually attempting to draft means of channeling capital sentencing discretion have confirmed the lesson taught by the history recounted above. To identify before the fact those characteristics of criminal homicides and their perpetrators which call for the death penalty, and to express these characteristics in language which can be fairly understood and applied by the sentencing authority, appear to be tasks which are beyond present human ability.

Thus the British Home Office, which [selected] the cases from England and Wales which should receive the benefit of the Royal Prerogative of Mercy, observed: "No simple formula can take account of the innumerable degrees of culpability, and no formula which fails to do so can claim to be just or satisfy public opinion. . . . Discretionary judgment on the facts of each case is the only way in which they can be equitably distinguished." . . .

The draftsmen of the Model Penal Code [declared] "that it is within the realm of possibility to point to the main circumstances of aggravation and of mitigation that should be weighed and weighed against each other when they are presented in a concrete case." The circumstances the draftsmen selected . . . were not intended to be exclusive. The Code provides simply that the sentencing authority should "take into account the aggravating and mitigating circumstances enumerated . . . and any other facts that it deems relevant," and that the court should so instruct when the issue was submitted to the jury.

It is apparent that such criteria do not purport to provide more than the most minimal control over the sentencing authority's exercise of discretion. They do not purport to give an exhaustive list of the relevant considerations or the way in which they may be affected by the presence or absence of other circumstances. They do not even undertake to exclude constitutionally impermissible considerations. And, of course, they provide no protection against the jury determined to decide on whimsy or caprice. In short, they do no more than suggest some subjects for the jury to consider during its deliberations, and they bear witness to the intractable nature of the problem of "standards" which the history of capital punishment has from the beginning reflected. Thus, they indeed caution against this Court's undertaking to establish such standards itself, or to pronounce at large that standards in this realm are constitutionally required.

In light of history, experience, and the present limitations of human knowledge, we find it quite impossible to say that committing to the untrammeled discretion of the jury the power to pronounce life or death in a capital case is offensive to anything in the Constitution. The States are entitled to assume that jurors confronted with the truly awesome responsibility of decreeing death for a fellow human will act with due regard for the consequences of their decision and will consider a variety of factors, many of which will have been suggested by the evidence or by the arguments of defense counsel. For a court to attempt to catalog the appropriate factors in this elusive area could inhibit rather than expand the scope of consideration, for no list of circumstances would ever be really complete. The infinite variety of cases and facets to each case would make general standards either meaningless "boiler-plate" or a statement of the obvious that no jury would need. . . .

It may well be, as the American Law Institute and the National Commission on Reform of Federal Criminal Laws have concluded, that bifurcated trials and criteria for jury sentencing discretion are superior means of dealing with capital cases if the death penalty is to be retained at all. But the Federal Constitution, which marks the limits of our authority in these cases, does not guarantee trial procedures that are the best of all worlds, or that accord with the most enlightened ideas of students of the infant science of criminology, or even those that measure up to the individual predilections of members of this Court. The Constitution requires no more than that trials be fairly conducted and that guaranteed rights of defendants be scrupulously respected. . . .

## NOTES

1. *Meaning of due process.* Dennis McGautha and John Crampton based their constitutional objection to standardless jury sentencing in capital cases on the Fourteenth Amendment's guarantee that no state shall "deprive any person of life . . . without due process of law." Do you agree with Justice Harlan's core conclusion that the jury instructions used in the trials of McGautha and Crampton provided due process? Do you think the requirements concerning what process is "due" should be heightened in death penalty cases?

2. *Establishing jury standards and the institutions for reform.* Do you concur with Justice Harlan's assertion in *McGautha* that to "identify before the fact those characteristics of criminal homicides and their perpetrators which call for the death penalty, and to express these characteristics in language which can be fairly understood and applied by the sentencing authority, appear to be tasks which are beyond present human ability"? Notably, the drafters of the Model Penal Code, though they took "no position on the desirability of the death penalty," developed a detailed set of possible aggravating and mitigating circumstances that could be used by states adopting the death penalty to guide juries in deciding whether to sentence a particular offender to death. See Model Penal Code §210.6(3) and (4). Justice Harlan's opinion does seem on firmer ground when he states that the history of capital reforms "caution against this Court's undertaking to establish [death penalty] standards itself, or to pronounce at large that standards in this realm are constitutionally required." In other words, though Justice Harlan's assertion about the impossibility of developing jury standards seems questionable, his apparent unwillingness for the Supreme Court to constitutionally mandate such standards seems much more sound.

## 2. Constitutional Regulation of Capital Sentencing Systems

Right after its decision in *McGautha*, the Supreme Court revisited the constitutionality of the death penalty through three cases posing challenges based on the Eighth Amendment's prohibition of "cruel and unusual punishments." This strategy seemed unlikely to succeed since, in Trop v. Dulles, 356 U.S. 86 (1958), a noncapital case in which the defendant raised an Eighth Amendment claim, Chief Justice Warren suggested in dicta that the death penalty, by dint of tradition, must be a constitutionally permissible punishment:

> Whatever the arguments may be against capital punishment, both on moral grounds and in terms of accomplishing the purposes of punishment—and they are forceful—the death penalty has been employed throughout our history, and, in a day when it is still widely accepted, it cannot be said to violate the constitutional concept of cruelty.

In the same opinion, however, Chief Justice Warren further elaborated on how courts should interpret the Eighth Amendment's vague restriction on government power, suggesting that even historically accepted punishments could be subjected to renewed constitutional scrutiny. In an oft-quoted passage, Chief

Justice Warren stressed: "The basic concept underlying the Eighth Amendment is nothing less than the dignity of man. [T]he words of the Amendment are not precise, and their scope is not static. The Amendment must draw its meaning from the evolving standards of decency that mark the progress of a maturing society."

In Furman v. Georgia and companion cases, Justices Potter Stewart and Byron White joined three of the dissenters in *McGautha* to hold that existing capital punishment statutes were applied in a manner that violated the Eighth Amendment's prohibition on "cruel and unusual punishments." There was no majority opinion in *Furman,* just the per curiam order set forth below, and each Justice authored a separate — and lengthy — opinion. (*Furman* still ranks among the longest decisions in U.S. Supreme Court history, occupying 233 pages in the Supreme Court Reporter.)

How can the outcome in *Furman* be explained in light of *McGautha*? Did McGautha and Crampton merely stake their claims on the wrong amendment?

## *William Henry Furman v. Georgia*
### 408 U.S. 238 (1972)

Per Curiam

[Appeals were consolidated here from convictions in three cases. Furman was convicted of murder in Georgia; Jackson was convicted of rape in Georgia; Branch was convicted of rape in Texas. All three were sentenced to death.] Certiorari was granted limited to the following question: "Does the imposition and carrying out of the death penalty in [these cases] constitute cruel and unusual punishment in violation of the Eighth and Fourteenth Amendments?" The Court holds that the imposition and carrying out of the death penalty in these cases constitute cruel and unusual punishment in violation of the Eighth and Fourteenth Amendments. The judgment in each case is therefore reversed insofar as it leaves undisturbed the death sentence imposed, and the cases are remanded for further proceedings. So ordered. . . .

Stewart, J., concurring.

The constitutionality of capital punishment in the abstract is not . . . before us in these cases. . . . Instead, the death sentences now before us are the product of a legal system that brings them, I believe, within the very core of the Eighth Amendment's guarantee against cruel and unusual punishments, a guarantee applicable against the States through the Fourteenth Amendment. In the first place, it is clear that these sentences are "cruel" in the sense that they excessively go beyond, not in degree but in kind, the punishments that the state legislatures have determined to be necessary. In the second place, it is equally clear that these sentences are "unusual" in the sense that the penalty of death is infrequently imposed for murder, and that its imposition for rape is extraordinarily rare. But I do not rest my conclusion upon these two propositions alone.

These death sentences are cruel and unusual in the same way that being struck by lightning is cruel and unusual. For, of all the people convicted of rapes and murders in 1967 and 1968, many just as reprehensible as these, the petitioners are among a capriciously selected random handful upon whom the sentence of death has in fact been imposed. My concurring Brothers have demonstrated that, if any basis can be discerned for the selection of these few to be sentenced to die, it is the constitutionally impermissible basis of race. But racial discrimination has not been proved, and I put it to one side. I simply conclude that the Eighth and Fourteenth Amendments cannot tolerate the infliction of a sentence of death under legal systems that permit this unique penalty to be so wantonly and so freakishly imposed. . . .

WHITE, J., concurring.

The narrower question to which I address myself concerns the constitutionality of capital punishment statutes under which (1) the legislature authorizes the imposition of the death penalty for murder or rape; (2) the legislature does not itself mandate the penalty in any particular class or kind of case (that is, legislative will is not frustrated if the penalty is never imposed), but delegates to judges or juries the decisions as to those cases, if any, in which the penalty will be utilized; and (3) judges and juries have ordered the death penalty with such infrequency that the odds are now very much against imposition and execution of the penalty with respect to any convicted murderer or rapist. . . .

The [death] penalty has not been considered cruel and unusual punishment in the constitutional sense because it was thought justified by the social ends it was deemed to serve. At the moment that it ceases realistically to further these purposes, [it] would violate the Eighth Amendment . . . for its imposition would then be the pointless and needless extinction of life with only marginal contributions to any discernible social or public purposes. A penalty with such negligible returns to the State would be patently excessive and cruel and unusual punishment violative of the Eighth Amendment.

It is also my judgment that this point has been reached with respect to capital punishment as it is presently administered under the statutes involved in these cases. . . . I cannot avoid the conclusion that as the statutes before us are now administered, the penalty is so infrequently imposed that the threat of execution is too attenuated to be of substantial service to criminal justice. [It is clear that] the death penalty is exacted with great infrequency even for the most atrocious crimes and that there is no meaningful basis for distinguishing the few cases in which it is imposed from the many cases in which it is not. . . .

DOUGLAS, J., concurring.

. . . Juries (or judges, as the case may be) have practically untrammeled discretion to let an accused live or insist that he die. . . . Former Attorney General Ramsey Clark has said, "It is the poor, the sick, the ignorant, the powerless and the hated who are executed." One searches our chronicles in vain for the execution of any member of the affluent strata of this society. . . .

Jackson, a black, convicted of the rape of a white woman, was 21 years old. . . . Furman, a black, killed a householder while seeking to enter the home at night. . . . Branch, a black, entered the rural home of a 65-year-old widow, a white, while she slept and raped her, holding his arm against her throat. . . . We cannot say from facts disclosed in these records that these defendants were sentenced to death because they were black. Yet our task is not restricted to an effort to divine what motives impelled these death penalties.

Rather, we deal with a system of law and of justice that leaves to the uncontrolled discretion of judges or juries the determination whether defendants committing these crimes should die or be imprisoned. Under these laws no standards govern the selection of the penalty. People live or die, dependent on the whim of one man or of 12. . . .

The high service rendered by the "cruel and unusual" punishment clause of the Eighth Amendment is to require legislatures to write penal laws that are evenhanded, nonselective, and nonarbitrary, and to require judges to see to it that general laws are not applied sparsely, selectively, and spottily to unpopular groups. A law that stated that anyone making more than $50,000 would be exempt from the death penalty would plainly fall, as would a law that in terms said that blacks, those who never went beyond the fifth grade in school, those who made less than $3,000 a year, or those who were unpopular or unstable should be the only people executed. A law which in the overall view reaches that result in practice has no more sanctity than a law which in terms provides the same. . . .

Thus, these discretionary statutes are unconstitutional in their operation. They are pregnant with discrimination and discrimination is an ingredient not compatible with the idea of equal protection of the laws that is implicit in the ban on "cruel and unusual" punishments. . . .

BRENNAN, J., concurring.

[The] Cruel and Unusual Punishments Clause prohibits the infliction of uncivilized and inhuman punishments. The State, even as it punishes, must treat its members with respect for their intrinsic worth as human beings. A punishment is "cruel and unusual," therefore, if it does not comport with human dignity. . . .

The primary principle is that a punishment must not be so severe as to be degrading to the dignity of human beings. Pain, certainly, may be a factor in the judgment. . . . More than the presence of pain, however, is comprehended in the judgment that the extreme severity of a punishment makes it degrading to the dignity of human beings. The barbaric punishments condemned by history, "punishments which inflict torture, such as the rack, the thumbscrew, the iron boot, the stretching of limbs and the like," . . . have been condemned [because] they treat members of the human race as nonhumans, as objects to be toyed with and discarded. They are thus inconsistent with the fundamental premise of the Clause that even the vilest criminal remains a human being possessed of common human dignity.

[A] second principle inherent in the Clause [is] that the State must not arbitrarily inflict a severe punishment [because] the State does not respect human dignity when, without reason, it inflicts upon some people a severe punishment that it does not inflict upon others. Indeed, the very words "cruel and unusual punishments" imply condemnation of the arbitrary infliction of severe punishments. [W]hen a severe punishment is inflicted in the great majority of cases in which it is legally available, there is little likelihood that the State is inflicting it arbitrarily. If, however, the infliction of a severe punishment is something different from that which is generally done in such cases, there is a substantial likelihood that the State, contrary to the requirements of regularity and fairness embodied in the Clause, is inflicting the punishment arbitrarily.

This principle is especially important today. There is scant danger, given the political processes in an enlightened democracy such as ours, that extremely severe punishments will be widely applied. The more significant function of the Clause, therefore, is to protect against the danger of their arbitrary infliction.

A third principle inherent in the Clause is that a severe punishment must not be unacceptable to contemporary society. Rejection by society, of course, is a strong indication that a severe punishment does not comport with human dignity. In applying this principle, however, we must make certain that the judicial determination is as objective as possible. Thus, for example, . . . one factor that may be considered is the existence of the punishment in jurisdictions other than those before the Court. [Another] factor to be considered is the historic usage of the punishment. . . . Accordingly, the judicial task is to review the history of a challenged punishment and to examine society's present practices with respect to its use. Legislative authorization, of course, does not establish acceptance. The acceptability of a severe punishment is measured, not by its availability, for it might become so offensive to society as never to be inflicted, but by its use.

The final principle inherent in the Clause is that a severe punishment must not be excessive. A punishment is excessive under this principle if it is unnecessary: The infliction of a severe punishment by the State cannot comport with human dignity when it is nothing more than the pointless infliction of suffering. If there is a significantly less severe punishment adequate to achieve the purposes for which the punishment is inflicted, the punishment inflicted is unnecessary and therefore excessive. . . .

The outstanding characteristic of our present practice of punishing criminals by death is the infrequency with which we resort to it. . . . There has been a steady decline in the infliction of this punishment in every decade since the 1930's, the earliest period for which accurate statistics are available. In the 1930's, executions averaged 167 per year; in the 1940's, the average was 128; in the 1950's, it was 72; and in the years 1960-1962, it was 48. There have been a total of 46 executions since then, 36 of them in 1963-1964. Yet our population and the number of capital crimes committed have increased greatly over the past four decades. The contemporary rarity of the infliction of this punishment is thus the end result of a long-continued decline. . . . When the punishment of death is inflicted in a trivial number of the cases in which it is legally available, the conclusion is virtually inescapable that it is being inflicted arbitrarily. Indeed, it smacks of little more than a lottery system.

[The] punishment of death is inconsistent with all four principles: Death is an unusually severe and degrading punishment; there is a strong probability that it is inflicted arbitrarily; its rejection by contemporary society is virtually total; and there is no reason to believe it serves any penal purpose more effectively than the less severe punishment of imprisonment. The function of these principles is to enable a court to determine whether a punishment comports with human dignity. Death, quite simply, does not. . . .

MARSHALL, J., concurring.

[A] penalty may be cruel and unusual because it is excessive and serves no valid legislative purpose. [There are several] purposes conceivably served by capital punishment: retribution, deterrence, prevention of repetitive criminal acts . . . and economy. . . .

The fact that the State may seek retribution against those who have broken its laws does not mean that retribution may then become the State's sole end in punishing. . . . If retribution alone could serve as a justification for any particular penalty, then all penalties selected by the legislature would by definition be acceptable means for designating society's moral approbation of a particular act. . . .

The most hotly contested issue regarding capital punishment is whether it is better than life imprisonment as a deterrent to crime. [Thorsten Sellin, one of the leading authorities on capital punishment, compiled statistics to] demonstrate that there is no correlation between the murder rate and the presence or absence of the capital sanction. He compares States that have similar characteristics and finds that irrespective of their position on capital punishment, they have similar murder rates. . . . Sellin also concludes that abolition and/or reintroduction of the death penalty had no effect on the homicide rates of the various States involved. This conclusion is borne out by others who have made similar inquiries and by the experience of other countries. . . .

Much of what must be said about the death penalty as a device to prevent recidivism is obvious — if a murderer is executed, he cannot possibly commit another offense. The fact is, however, that murderers are extremely unlikely to commit other crimes either in prison or upon their release. For the most part, they are first offenders, and when released from prison they are known to become model citizens. Furthermore, most persons who commit capital crimes are not executed. With respect to those who are sentenced to die, it is critical to note that the jury is never asked to determine whether they are likely to be recidivists. In light of these facts, if capital punishment were justified purely on the basis of preventing recidivism, it would have to be considered to be excessive; no general need to obliterate all capital offenders could have been demonstrated, nor any specific need in individual cases. . . .

As for the argument that it is cheaper to execute a capital offender than to imprison him for life, even assuming that such an argument, if true, would support a capital sanction, it is simply incorrect. A disproportionate amount of money spent on prisons is attributable to death row. Condemned men are not productive members of the prison community, although they could be, and executions are expensive. Appeals are often automatic, and courts admittedly spend more time with death cases. . . . When all is said and done, there can be no doubt that it costs more to execute a man than to keep him in prison for life.

[Even] if capital punishment is not excessive, it nonetheless violates the Eighth Amendment because it is morally unacceptable to the people of the United States at this time in their history. In judging whether or not a given penalty is morally acceptable, most courts have said that the punishment is valid unless "it shocks the conscience and sense of justice of the people." [But] whether or not a punishment is cruel and unusual depends, not on whether its mere mention shocks the conscience and sense of justice of the people, but on whether people who were fully informed as to the purposes of the penalty and its liabilities would find the penalty shocking, unjust, and unacceptable. . . . In other words, the question with which we must deal is not whether a substantial proportion of American citizens would today, if polled, opine that capital punishment is barbarously cruel, but whether they would find it to be so in the light of all information presently available. . . .

It has often been noted that American citizens know almost nothing about capital punishment [and much that I have propounded in this opinion is] critical to an informed judgment on the morality of the death penalty: e.g., that the death penalty is no more effective a deterrent than life imprisonment, that convicted murderers are rarely executed, but are usually sentenced to a term in prison; that convicted murderers usually are model prisoners, and that they almost always become law-abiding citizens upon their release from prison; that the costs of executing a capital offender exceed the costs of imprisoning him for life; that while in prison, a convict under sentence of death performs none of the useful functions that life prisoners perform; that no attempt is made in the sentencing process to ferret out likely recidivists for execution; and that the death penalty may actually stimulate criminal activity.

This information would almost surely convince the average citizen that the death penalty was unwise, but [the] desire for retribution . . . might influence the citizenry's view of the morality of capital punishment. [Yet] no one has ever seriously advanced retribution as a legitimate goal of our society. Defenses of capital punishment are always mounted on deterrent or other similar theories. This should not be surprising. It is the people of this country who have urged in the past that prisons rehabilitate as well as isolate offenders, and it is the people who have injected a sense of purpose into our penology. I cannot believe that at this stage in our history, the American people would ever knowingly support purposeless vengeance. Thus, I believe that the great mass of citizens would conclude on the basis of the material already considered that the death penalty is immoral and therefore unconstitutional.

But, if this information needs supplementing, I believe that the following facts would serve to convince even the most hesitant of citizens to condemn death as a sanction: capital punishment is imposed discriminatorily against certain identifiable classes of people; there is evidence that innocent people have been executed before their innocence can be proved; and the death penalty wreaks havoc with our entire criminal justice system. . . .

Regarding discrimination, it . . . is usually the poor, the illiterate, the underprivileged, the member of the minority group — the man who, because he is without means, and is defended by a court-appointed attorney — who becomes society's sacrificial lamb. . . . Indeed, a look at the bare statistics regarding executions is enough to betray much of the discrimination. A total of 3,859 persons have been executed since 1930, of whom 1,751 were white and 2,066 were Negro. . . .

Assuming knowledge of all the facts presently available regarding capital punishment, the average citizen would, in my opinion, find it shocking to his conscience and sense of justice. For this reason alone capital punishment cannot stand.

BURGER, C.J., dissenting.
. . . Counsel for petitioners properly concede that capital punishment was not impermissibly cruel at the time of the adoption of the Eighth Amendment. Not only do the records of the debates indicate that the Founding Fathers were limited in their concern to the prevention of torture, but it is also clear from the language of the Constitution itself that there was no thought whatever of the elimination of capital punishment. . . .

In the 181 years since the enactment of the Eighth Amendment, not a single decision of this Court has cast the slightest shadow of a doubt on the constitutionality of capital punishment. . . . Today the Court has not ruled that capital punishment is per se violative of the Eighth Amendment; nor has it ruled that the punishment is barred for any particular class or classes of crimes. The substantially similar concurring opinions of Mr. Justice Stewart and Mr. Justice White, which are necessary to support the judgment setting aside petitioners' sentences, stop short of reaching the ultimate question. The actual scope of the Court's ruling, which I take to be embodied in these concurring opinions, is not entirely clear. This much, however, seems apparent: if the legislatures are to continue to authorize capital punishment for some crimes, juries and judges can no longer be permitted to make the sentencing determination in the same manner they have in the past. . . .

Real change could clearly be brought about if legislatures provided mandatory death sentences in such a way as to deny juries the opportunity to bring in a verdict on a lesser charge; under such a system, the death sentence could only be avoided by a verdict of acquittal. If this is the only alternative that the legislatures can safely pursue under today's ruling, I would have preferred that the Court opt for total abolition.

It seems remarkable to me that with our basic trust in lay jurors as the keystone in our system of criminal justice, it should now be suggested that we take the most sensitive and important of all decisions away from them. I could more easily be persuaded that mandatory sentences of death, without the intervening and ameliorating impact of lay jurors, are so arbitrary and doctrinaire that they violate the Constitution. The very infrequency of death penalties imposed by jurors attests their cautious and discriminating reservation of that penalty for the most extreme cases. I had thought that nothing was clearer in history, as we noted in *McGautha* one year ago, than the American abhorrence of "the common-law rule imposing a mandatory death sentence on all convicted murderers." 402 U.S. at 198. [The] nineteenth century movement away from mandatory death sentences marked an enlightened introduction of flexibility into the sentencing process. It recognized that individual culpability is not always measured by the category of the crime committed. I do not see how this history can be ignored and how it can be suggested that the Eighth Amendment demands the elimination of the most sensitive feature of the sentencing system. . . .

BLACKMUN, J., dissenting.

. . . Cases such as these provide for me an excruciating agony of the spirit. I yield to no one in the depth of my distaste, antipathy, and, indeed, abhorrence, for the death penalty, with all its aspects of physical distress and fear and of moral judgment exercised by finite minds. . . . Were I a legislator, I would do all I could to sponsor and to vote for legislation abolishing the death penalty. [However, as judges we] should not allow our personal preferences as to the wisdom of legislative and congressional action, or our distaste for such action, to guide our judicial decision in cases such as these. . . . Although personally I may rejoice at the Court's result, I find it difficult to accept or to justify as a matter of history, of law, or of constitutional pronouncement. I fear the Court has overstepped. It has sought and has achieved an end.

POWELL, J., dissenting.

[A] comment on the racial discrimination problem seems appropriate. The possibility of racial bias in the trial and sentencing process has diminished in recent years. The segregation of our society in decades past, which contributed substantially to the severity of punishment for interracial crimes, is now no longer prevalent in this country. Likewise, the day is past when juries do not represent the minority group elements of the community. The assurance of fair trials for all citizens is greater today than at any previous time in our history. Because standards of criminal justice have "evolved" in a manner favorable to the accused, discriminatory imposition of capital punishment is far less likely today than in the past.

. . . It is important to keep in focus the enormity of the step undertaken by the Court today. Not only does it invalidate hundreds of state and federal laws, it deprives those jurisdictions of the power to legislate with respect to capital punishment in the future, except in a manner consistent with the cloudily outlined views of those Justices who do not purport to undertake total abolition. Nothing short of an amendment to the United States Constitution can reverse the Court's judgments. Meanwhile, all flexibility is foreclosed. The normal democratic process, as well as the opportunities for the several States to respond to the will of their people expressed through ballot referenda . . . is now shut off. . . .

REHNQUIST, J., dissenting.

The Court's judgments today strike down a penalty that our Nation's legislators have thought necessary since our country was founded. My Brothers Douglas, Brennan, and Marshall would at one fell swoop invalidate laws enacted by Congress and 40 of the 50 state legislatures, and would consign to the limbo of unconstitutionality under a single rubric penalties for offenses as varied and unique as murder, piracy, mutiny, highjacking, and desertion in the face of the enemy. My Brothers Stewart and White, asserting reliance on a more limited rationale — the reluctance of judges and juries actually to impose the death penalty in the majority of capital cases, join in the judgments in these cases. Whatever its precise rationale, today's holding necessarily brings into sharp relief the fundamental question of the role of judicial review in a democratic society. . . .

The task of judging constitutional cases [cannot] be avoided, but it must surely be approached with the deepest humility and genuine deference to legislative judgment. Today's decision to invalidate capital punishment is, I respectfully submit, significantly lacking in those attributes. . . . I conclude that this decision holding unconstitutional capital punishment is not an act of judgment, but rather an act of will.

## NOTES

1. *Meaning of "cruel and unusual."* Do you agree with the *Furman* majority's core holding that William Furman's punishment was cruel and unusual? Does your answer hinge, as it did for the Court, on the fact that Furman was sentenced through a system of standardless jury discretion that allowed, in the words of Justice Stewart, "this unique penalty to be so wantonly and so freakishly imposed"?

Considering these issues more generally, by what standards should a judge or other official assess whether a punishment inflicted is cruel and unusual? Or, drawing on Chief Justice Warren's famous discussion of the Eighth Amendment in Trop v. Dulles quoted earlier, how should judges or other officials assess "the evolving standards of decency that mark the progress of a maturing society"?

What impact, if any, should international developments — such as the abolition of capital punishment in Great Britain or the European Union — have on the interpretation of the Eighth Amendment's prohibition of cruel and unusual punishments? Notably, when the European Convention for the Protection of Human Rights and Fundamental Freedoms was adopted in the early 1950s, the death penalty was still widely in use. Therefore, its prohibition on "torture or . . . inhuman or degrading treatment or punishment" in Article 3 did not apply to capital punishment. Protocol 6, in force since 1988, however, explicitly abolishes the death penalty in peacetime. Signature of this protocol has become a virtual prerequisite for membership in the European human rights regime. Consequently, when considered against the backdrop of the near universal abolition of the death penalty in other Western nations, the use of capital punishment in the United States is now unusual. When and how should international human rights norms influence interpretations of U.S. constitutional provisions that implicate human rights concerns?

2. *Discretion, disparity, and discrimination.* What seems to have been the central concern of the Justices voting in the majority in *Furman?* Was it the fact that the juries exercised discretion without having any standards to guide life-and-death decisions? Was it the disparity in outcomes (that is, who was sentenced to die) that resulted from the exercise of standardless jury discretion? Was it the discriminatory judgments seemingly reflected by the results of standardless jury discretion in capital cases? Justice Douglas's opinion makes clear that the potentially discriminatory application of standardless jury discretion was his chief concern, suggesting that the constitutional provision transgressed was actually the Fourteenth Amendment's equal protection clause rather than the Eighth Amendment: "The [discretionary statutes] are pregnant with discrimination and discrimination is an ingredient not compatible with the idea of equal protection of the laws."

3. *The Marshall hypothesis.* In one of the more famous passages from the *Furman* opinions, Justice Marshall argues that the more fully informed people become about the operation of the death penalty, the less likely they are to support its use. (Indeed, Justice Marshall justified his vote in *Furman* by contending that the average citizen, with "knowledge of all the facts presently available regarding capital punishment, would . . . find it shocking to his conscience and sense of justice.") This argument has come to be known as "the Marshall hypothesis." Is it appropriate (or even sensible) for legislators or executive branch officials to defer especially to the judgment of those with the most knowledge or expertise in an area? Is there anything in the role of a judge that should prevent reliance on such arguments? As you work through the remainder of the materials in this chapter and throughout this book, watch for other examples of this argument at work and try to gauge whether your own (or others') opinions about the death penalty change as you become more informed about its application.

4. *State responses to* Furman. The Supreme Court's holding in *Furman* effectively declared unconstitutional the death penalty statutes then in place in 40 states and commuted the sentences of 629 death row inmates around the country.

Because only Justices Brennan and Marshall asserted that the death penalty was per se unconstitutional, the opinions of Justices Stewart, White, and Douglas suggested that states could rewrite their death penalty statutes to remedy the constitutional problems. Led by Florida, which enacted a new death penalty statute five months after *Furman*, 35 states reacted to the decision by passing new death penalty statutes: ten states addressed the unconstitutionality of standardless jury discretion by making the death penalty mandatory for all offenders convicted of certain capital crimes; 25 other states sought to limit discretion by setting forth aggravating and mitigating factors for judge and jury to consider.

5. *The tide turns in 1976.* The nation wide ban on capital punishment that the Court created in 1972 with its opinion in *Furman* did not last long. In 1976 the Court decided a set of five cases testing the constitutionality of various state death penalty statutes passed in reaction to *Furman*. In the lead case, Gregg v. Georgia, 428 U.S. 153 (1976), Justice Stewart authored the opinion of the Court, which held that "the punishment of death does not invariably violate the Constitution." First the Court took note of the widespread debate about capital punishment in state legislatures:

> Despite the continuing debate, dating back to the nineteenth century, over the morality and utility of capital punishment, it is now evident that a large proportion of American society continues to regard it as an appropriate and necessary criminal sanction.
>
> The most marked indication of society's endorsement of the death penalty for murder is the legislative response to *Furman*. The legislatures of at least 35 States have enacted new statutes that provide for the death penalty for at least some crimes that result in the death of another person. And the Congress of the United States, in 1974, enacted a statute providing the death penalty for aircraft piracy that results in death. [The] post-*Furman* statutes make clear that capital punishment itself has not been rejected by the elected representatives of the people.
>
> [The] actions of juries in many States since *Furman* are fully compatible with the legislative judgments, reflected in the new statutes, as to the continued utility and necessity of capital punishment in appropriate cases. At the close of 1974 at least 254 persons had been sentenced to death since *Furman*, and by the end of March 1976, more than 460 persons were subject to death sentences.

428 U.S. at 179-182.

The Court also accepted both deterrence and retribution as appropriate social purposes justifying the use of the death penalty:

> In part, capital punishment is an expression of society's moral outrage at particularly offensive conduct. This function may be unappealing to many, but it is essential in an ordered society that asks its citizens to rely on legal processes rather than self-help to vindicate their wrongs. . . . Retribution is no longer the dominant objective of the criminal law, but neither is it a forbidden objective nor one inconsistent with our respect for the dignity of men. . . . Indeed, the decision that capital punishment may be the appropriate sanction in extreme cases is an expression of the community's belief that certain crimes are

themselves so grievous an affront to humanity that the only adequate response may be the penalty of death.

Statistical attempts to evaluate the worth of the death penalty as a deterrent to crimes by potential offenders have occasioned a great deal of debate. The results simply have been inconclusive. Although some of the studies suggest that the death penalty may not function as a significantly greater deterrent than lesser penalties, there is no convincing empirical evidence either supporting or refuting this view. We may nevertheless assume safely that there are murderers, such as those who act in passion, for whom the threat of death has little or no deterrent effect. But for many others, the death penalty undoubtedly is a significant deterrent. There are carefully contemplated murders, such as murder for hire, where the possible penalty of death may well enter into the cold calculus that precedes the decision to act. . . . The value of capital punishment as a deterrent of crime is a complex factual issue the resolution of which properly rests with the legislatures, which can evaluate the results of statistical studies in terms of their own local conditions and with a flexibility of approach that is not available to the courts.

Id. at 183-186.

Finally, the Court considered the procedural devices that the Georgia statute used to guide the discretion of the sentencing jury:

Jury sentencing has been considered desirable in capital cases in order "to maintain a link between contemporary community values and the penal system. . . ." But it creates special problems. Much of the information that is relevant to the sentencing decision may have no relevance to the question of guilt, or may even be extremely prejudicial to a fair determination of that question. This problem, however, is scarcely insurmountable. Those who have studied the question suggest that a bifurcated procedure, one in which the question of sentence is not considered until the determination of guilt has been made, is the best answer. [And though] members of a jury will have had little, if any, previous experience in sentencing, [this] problem will be alleviated if the jury is given guidance regarding the factors about the crime and the defendant that the State, representing organized society, deems particularly relevant to the sentencing decision. . . .

While some have suggested that standards to guide a capital jury's sentencing deliberations are impossible to formulate, the fact is that such standards have been developed. When the drafters of the Model Penal Code faced this problem, they concluded "that it is within the realm of possibility to point to the main circumstances of aggravation and of mitigation that should be weighed and *weighed against each other* when they are presented in a concrete case." While such standards are by necessity somewhat general, they do provide guidance to sentencing authority and thereby reduce the likelihood that it will impose a sentence that fairly can be called capricious or arbitrary. Where the sentencing authority is required to specify the factors it relied upon in reaching its decision, the further safeguard of meaningful appellate review is available to ensure that death sentences are not imposed capriciously or in a freakish manner.

[To] guard further against a situation comparable to that presented in *Furman*, the Supreme Court of Georgia compares each death sentence with the sentences imposed on similarly situated defendants to ensure that the sentence of death in a particular case is not disproportionate. On their face these procedures seem to satisfy the concerns of *Furman*. No longer should there be "no meaningful basis for distinguishing the few cases in which [the death penalty] is imposed from the many cases in which it is not."

The basic concern of *Furman* centered on those defendants who were being condemned to death capriciously and arbitrarily. Under the procedures before the Court in that case, sentencing authorities were not directed to give attention to the nature or circumstances of the crime committed or to the character or record of the defendant. Left unguided, juries imposed the death sentence in a way that could only be called freakish. The new Georgia sentencing procedures, by contrast, focus the jury's attention on the particularized nature of the crime and the particularized characteristics of the individual defendant. While the jury is permitted to consider any aggravating or mitigating circumstances, it must find and identify at least one statutory aggravating factor before it may impose a penalty of death. In this way the jury's discretion is channeled. No longer can a jury wantonly and freakishly impose the death sentence; it is always circumscribed by the legislative guidelines. In addition, the review function of the Supreme Court of Georgia affords additional assurance that the concerns that prompted our decision in *Furman* are not present to any significant degree in the Georgia procedure applied here. [The] statutory system under which Gregg was sentenced to death does not violate the Constitution.

Id. at 190-198, 206-207.

6. *Key features of approved death penalty schemes.*   Two of the other cases decided the same day as *Gregg* also upheld newly revised statutory schemes to impose the death penalty for some murders. See Jurek v. Texas, 428 U.S. 262 (1976); Proffitt v. Florida, 428 U.S. 242 (1976). The statutes involved in these three cases shared some important features. Each called for bifurcated proceedings, with a jury hearing the evidence relevant to the choice of punishment only after deliberating and delivering a guilty verdict after trial. The statutes also specified aggravating factors for the jury to find as a prerequisite to the death penalty and provided for automatic review of the case in the state's appellate courts. While the Court stopped short of saying that any of these features was absolutely essential to the judgment that they satisfied the Eighth Amendment, each feature drew positive comment in the opinions. Ultimately, the Court's language in *Gregg* about the importance of "a carefully drafted statute that ensures that the sentencing authority is given adequate information and guidance," combined with the Court's rejection of a mandatory death sentencing scheme (detailed below), made it clear that a state's development of a system of "guided discretion" was central to the constitutionality of its use of the death penalty.

7. *Strategic litigation.*   Numerous commentators expected *Furman* to end the death penalty in the United States. Instead, the opposite occurred: the Court's decision reinvigorated capital punishment. To what extent is this a cautionary tale about using the Court to bring about social change? Compare Brown v. Board of Education, 349 U.S. 294 (1954) (striking down the existence of segregated elementary schools), and Roe v. Wade, 410 U.S. 113 (1973) (striking down Texas's absolute prohibition of abortions in cases where the mother's life was not at stake).

## *James Tyrone Woodson v. North Carolina*
### 428 U.S. 280 (1976)

STEWART, J.

The question in this case is whether the imposition of a death sentence for the crime of first-degree murder under the law of North Carolina violates the Eighth and Fourteenth Amendments.

The petitioners, James Tyrone Woodson and Luby Waxton, were convicted of first-degree murder as the result of their participation in an armed robbery of a convenience food store, in the course of which the cashier was killed and a customer was seriously wounded. There were four participants in the robbery: the petitioners Woodson and Waxton and two others, Leonard Tucker and Johnnie Lee Carroll. At the petitioners' trial Tucker and Carroll testified for the prosecution after having been permitted to plead guilty to lesser offenses. . . . The petitioners were found guilty on all charges, and, as was required by statute, sentenced to death.

The North Carolina General Assembly in 1974 [after the invalidation of its death penalty statute in the wake of *Furman*] enacted a new statute that was essentially unchanged from the old one except that it made the death penalty mandatory. . . . It was under this statute that the petitioners were tried, convicted, and sentenced to death.

North Carolina, unlike Florida, Georgia, and Texas, has thus responded to the *Furman* decision by making death the mandatory sentence for all persons convicted of first-degree murder. . . . Although it seems beyond dispute that, at the time of the *Furman* decision in 1972, mandatory death penalty statutes had been renounced by American juries and legislatures, there remains the question whether the mandatory statutes adopted by North Carolina and a number of other States following *Furman* evince a sudden reversal of societal values regarding the imposition of capital punishment. In view of the persistent and unswerving legislative rejection of mandatory death penalty statutes beginning in 1838 and continuing for more than 130 years until *Furman*, it seems evident that the post-*Furman* enactments reflect attempts by the States to retain the death penalty in a form consistent with the Constitution, rather than a renewed societal acceptance of mandatory death sentencing. The fact that some States have adopted mandatory measures following *Furman* while others have legislated standards to guide jury discretion appears attributable to diverse readings of this Court's multi-opinioned decision in that case. . . .

It is now well established that the Eighth Amendment draws much of its meaning from "the evolving standards of decency that mark the progress of a maturing society." [One] of the most significant developments in our society's treatment of capital punishment has been the rejection of the common-law practice of inexorably imposing a death sentence upon every person convicted of a specified offense. North Carolina's mandatory death penalty statute for first-degree murder departs markedly from contemporary standards respecting the imposition of the punishment of death and thus cannot be applied consistently with the Eighth and Fourteenth Amendments' requirement that the State's power to punish "be exercised within the limits of civilized standards."

A separate deficiency of North Carolina's mandatory death sentence statute is its failure to provide a constitutionally tolerable response to *Furman*'s rejection of unbridled jury discretion in the imposition of capital sentences. Central to the limited holding in *Furman* was the conviction that the vesting of standardless sentencing power in the jury violated the Eighth and Fourteenth Amendments.

It is argued that North Carolina has remedied the inadequacies of the death penalty statutes held unconstitutional in *Furman* by withdrawing all sentencing discretion from juries in capital cases. But when one considers the long and consistent American experience with the death penalty in first-degree murder cases, it becomes evident that mandatory statutes enacted in response to *Furman* have simply papered over the problem of unguided and unchecked jury discretion. . . .

Instead of rationalizing the sentencing process, a mandatory scheme may well exacerbate the problem identified in *Furman* by resting the penalty determination on the particular jury's willingness to act lawlessly. While a mandatory death penalty statute may reasonably be expected to increase the number of persons sentenced to death, it does not fulfill *Furman*'s basic requirement by replacing arbitrary and wanton jury discretion with objective standards to guide, regularize, and make rationally reviewable the process for imposing a sentence of death.

A third constitutional shortcoming of the North Carolina statute is its failure to allow the particularized consideration of relevant aspects of the character and record of each convicted defendant before the imposition upon him of a sentence of death. In *Furman*, members of the Court acknowledged what cannot fairly be denied — that death is a punishment different from all other sanctions in kind rather than degree. A process that accords no significance to relevant facets of the character and record of the individual offender or the circumstances of the particular offense excludes from consideration in fixing the ultimate punishment of death the possibility of compassionate or mitigating factors stemming from the diverse frailties of humankind. It treats all persons convicted of a designated offense not as uniquely individual human beings, but as members of a faceless, undifferentiated mass to be subjected to the blind infliction of the penalty of death. . . .

Consideration of both the offender and the offense in order to arrive at a just and appropriate sentence has been viewed as a progressive and humanizing development. While the prevailing practice of individualizing sentencing determinations generally reflects simply enlightened policy rather than a constitutional imperative, we believe that in capital cases the fundamental respect for humanity underlying the Eighth Amendment requires consideration of the character and record of the individual offender and the circumstances of the particular offense as a constitutionally indispensable part of the process of inflicting the penalty of death.

This conclusion rests squarely on the predicate that the penalty of death is qualitatively different from a sentence of imprisonment, however long. Death, in its finality, differs more from life imprisonment than a 100-year prison term differs from one of only a year or two. Because of that qualitative difference, there is a corresponding difference in the need for reliability in the determination that death is the appropriate punishment in a specific case.

For the reasons stated, we conclude that the death sentences imposed upon the petitioners under North Carolina's mandatory death sentence statute violated the Eighth and Fourteenth Amendments and therefore must be set aside. . . .

REHNQUIST, J., dissenting.

[The plurality's holding] will result in the invalidation of a death sentence imposed upon a defendant convicted of first-degree murder under the North Carolina system, and the upholding of the same sentence imposed on an identical defendant convicted on identical evidence of first-degree murder under the Florida, Georgia, or Texas systems, a result surely as "freakish" as that condemned in the separate opinions in *Furman.* . . .

In any event, while the imposition of such unlimited consideration of mitigating factors may conform to the plurality's novel constitutional doctrine that a "jury must be allowed to consider on the basis of all relevant evidence not only why a death sentence should be imposed, but also why it should not be imposed," the resulting system seems as likely as any to produce the unbridled discretion which was condemned by the separate opinions in *Furman.* The plurality seems to believe that provision for appellate review will afford a check upon the instances of juror arbitrariness in a discretionary system. But it is not at all apparent that appellate review of death sentences, through a process of comparing the facts of one case in which a death sentence was imposed with the facts of another in which such a sentence was not imposed, will afford any meaningful protection against whatever arbitrariness results from jury discretion. . . .

The plurality's insistence on "standards" to "guide the jury in its inevitable exercise of the power to determine which . . . murderers shall live and which shall die" is squarely contrary to the Court's opinion in *McGautha.* . . . So is the plurality's latter-day recognition . . . that *Furman* requires "objective standards to guide, regularize, and make rationally reviewable the process for imposing a sentence of death." . . . The plurality's insistence on individualized consideration of the sentencing . . . does not depend upon any traditional application of the prohibition against cruel and unusual punishment contained in the Eighth Amendment. . . . What the plurality opinion has actually done is to import into the Due Process Clause of the Fourteenth Amendment what it conceives to be desirable procedural guarantees where the punishment of death, concededly not cruel and unusual for the crime of which the defendant was convicted, is to be imposed. . . .

## NOTES

1. *Mandatory death penalty.*   In Louisiana v. Roberts, 428 U.S. 325 (1976), a. companion case decided the same day as *Woodson* and *Gregg,* the Court struck down another capital sentencing statute that made the death penalty mandatory for five narrowly defined categories of first-degree murder (and also required juries to be instructed on manslaughter and second-degree murder even if there was no evidence to support such a verdict). Together, *Woodson* and *Roberts* established that the Supreme Court would not let states respond to *Furman*'s concerns about standardless jury discretion by creating mandatory death penalty systems that simply eliminated jury discretion. In subsequent cases, the Supreme Court ultimately ruled that no form of mandatory death penalty could be constitutional. See Sumner v. Shuman, 483 U.S. 66 (1987) (invalidating a mandatory death penalty statute for life-term inmates convicted of murder).

Isn't a mandatory sentencing system the best way to deal with *Furman*'s concerns about arbitrary and potentially discriminatory exercise of juries' capital sentencing discretion? Is the requirement of individualization propounded in *Woodson* and *Roberts* really a constitutional necessity, or just a good idea? Compare the decision of the Judicial Committee of the English Privy Council upholding Singapore's mandatory death penalty statute for certain drug offenses, in which it distinguished legal guilt and moral guilt. The Privy Council did not find Singapore in violation of its equality and due process provisions because "the Constitution is not concerned with equal punitive treatment for equal moral blameworthiness; it is concerned with equal punitive treatment for similar legal guilt." Ong Ah Chuan v. Public Prosecutor, [1981] A.C. 648, 674 (P.C.). Subsequent Privy Council decisions, however, superseded that case. By 2006 the Privy Council had rejected the mandatory death sentence for murder in almost all the cases that came before it, so that it is now outlawed in all the English-speaking countries in the Caribbean, with the exception of two.

2. *Categorical exclusion of certain offenses*   In Coker v. Georgia, 433 U.S. 584 (1977), the Supreme Court struck down the death penalty as a sentencing option in the rape of an adult woman; as in *Furman*, the constitutional basis for the decision was the Eighth Amendment's prohibition of cruel and unusual punishments. Since then only murder convictions have led to death sentences. In addition, through a series of cases culminating in Tison v. Arizona, 481 U.S. 137 (1987), the Supreme Court held that only killers with a mens rea of reckless indifference to human life or worse are sufficiently culpable to be constitutionally subject to the death penalty.

If no crime can trigger a mandatory death sentence, on what basis should a court hold categorically that certain crimes can never be eligible for the death penalty? By what yardstick can and should the Supreme Court determine whether a particularly heinous crime, such as the rape of a young child or attempted murder of a police officer, can justify the death penalty? Some states believe there are offenses other than murder for which death might be the appropriate sanction; at present five states, for example, permit death as punishment for the rape of a minor. See La. Rev. Stat. §14:42(D)(2)(a). The Supreme Court upheld the statute in Kennedy v. Louisiana, 554 U.S. 407 (2008). Should such proportionality determinations be the province of the legislature? Do you see any link between the concerns expressed in *Furman* about the arbitrary imposition of the death penalty and the categorical exclusion of certain offenses from capital punishment?

The federal system allows for the death penalty in cases of treason and terrorism, as do some of the states. During wartime the death penalty may be imposed in cases of desertion. Many European states that have otherwise abolished capital punishment have retained the death penalty during times of war. Almost 40 countries, however, have already ratified Protocol 13 of the European Convention of Human Rights (effective in 2002), which outlaws capital punishment even during wartime. Why should there be an exception to the prohibition on capital punishment during wartime?

3. *Categorical exclusion of certain offenders*   In 2002 the Supreme Court outlawed execution of the mentally retarded because it violates the Eighth Amendment's prohibition of cruel and unusual punishments. The decision in Atkins v. Virginia, 536 U.S. 304 (2002), reversed the Court's prior decision in Penry v. Lynaugh, 492 U.S. 302 (1989), which had held that the Constitution did allow the execution of mentally retarded individuals. The Court's reversal in *Atkins*

reflected the shift in legislative thinking since the *Penry* decision in 1989: during those years, nearly half the states that authorize capital punishment had removed offenders with mental retardation from the reach of the death penalty. Researchers estimate that since the death penalty was reinstated in 1976, at least 35 people with mental retardation had been executed in the United States before the Supreme Court declared this punishment unconstitutional in *Atkins*. The *Atkins* Court found mentally retarded offenders categorically less culpable than others, and therefore ineligible for capital punishment.

Do you see any link between the concerns expressed in *Furman* about the arbitrary imposition of the death penalty and the categorical exclusion of certain offenders from capital punishment? Is there any risk that the definition of "mental retardation" could lead to further inequities in the application of capital punishment? The Supreme Court in *Atkins* left it to states to define which individuals are mentally retarded and thus exempt from capital punishment. As a legislator, how might you draft a definition of mental retardation to minimize disparate application of the death penalty? See People v. Superior Court (Vidal), 155 P.3d 259 (Cal. 2007).

Through another pair of cases in the late 1980s, the Supreme Court held that the Constitution does not permit the execution of an offender who was age 15 or younger at the time of his or her crime, but that it does allow the execution of an offender who was 16 or older at the time of the crime. See Stanford v. Kentucky, 492 U.S. 362 (1989) (allowing execution of 16- and 17-year-old killers); Thompson v. Oklahoma, 487 U.S. 815 (1988) (prohibiting execution of killers age 15 or younger). Between 1976 and the beginning of 2003, 22 men were executed for crimes committed as juveniles; by 2004 there were 80 inmates on death row (all male) who were sentenced as juveniles, constituting about 2% of the total death row population. At that point the United States was one of the few countries in the world that still executed juvenile offenders. Article 6(5) of the International Covenant on Civil and Political Rights — which the United States ratified with a reservation to Article 6(5) — requires that a sentence of death "not be imposed for crimes committed by persons below eighteen years of age."

In its decision in Roper v. Simmons, 543 U.S. 551 (2005), discussed more fully in Chapter 5, the Supreme Court overruled *Stanford* and declared unconstitutional the execution of those who committed capital offenses while under the age of 18. The Court found, as it had in *Atkins*, that for juveniles the death penalty "is a disproportionate punishment" and that a national consensus, supported by international law, had developed against such executions.

Does the categorical exclusion of 17-year-olds not deprive juries of the individualized decision making that the Court demands in its case law? Why should juries not be permitted to decide whether individual offenders who were under 18 at the time they committed their crimes are sufficiently culpable and depraved to deserve the death penalty? Is the difference between a 17- and an 18-year-old sufficient to justify such differential treatment?

In 2008, in Kennedy v. Louisiana, 554 U.S. 407 (2008), the court held that the Eighth Amendment's Cruel and Unusual Punishment Clause did not permit a state to punish the crime of rape of a child with the death penalty. 554 U.S. 407 (2008). The power of the state to impose the death penalty against an individual for committing a crime that did not result in the death of the victim is now limited to crimes against the state (i.e., espionage, treason).

In Graham v. Florida, 130 S.Ct. 2011 (2010), the court held that states must give a juvenile non-homicide offender sentenced to life without parole a meaningful opportunity to obtain release. The "Eighth Amendment prohibits imposition of life without parole sentence on juvenile offender who did not commit homicide." In Miller v. Alabama, 132 S.Ct. 1733 (2012), the court, in an opinion by Justice Kagan, extended *Graham* and held that "mandatory life without parole for those under the age of 18 at the time of their crimes violates the Eighth Amendment's prohibition on 'cruel and unusual punishments.'"

---

Much of the jurisprudence of capital punishment relates not to the availability of the death penalty for entire categories of offenses or offenders, but instead to the guidance offered to the capital jury. One of the cornerstones of that guidance is the idea that the jury must hear a broad range of mitigating evidence.

## Sandra Lockett v. Ohio
### 438 U.S. 586 (1978)

BURGER, C.J.

We granted certiorari in this case to consider, among other questions, whether Ohio violated the Eighth and Fourteenth Amendments by sentencing Sandra Lockett to death pursuant to a statute that narrowly limits the sentencer's discretion to consider the circumstances of the crime and the record and character of the offender as mitigating factors. . . .

Lockett [suggested to acquaintances Al Parker and Nathan Earl Dew] that they could get some money by robbing a grocery store and a furniture store in the area[, and she] also volunteered to get a gun from her father's basement to aid in carrying out the robberies. . . . Lockett's brother [later] suggested a plan for robbing a pawnshop. . . . No one planned to kill the pawnshop operator in the course of the robbery. Because she knew the owner, Lockett was not . . . among those entering the pawnshop, though she did guide the others to the shop that night. The robbery proceeded according to plan until the pawnbroker grabbed the gun when Parker announced the "stickup." The gun went off . . . firing a fatal shot into the pawnbroker, and Parker went back to the car where Lockett waited with the engine running. . . .

Parker was subsequently apprehended and charged with aggravated murder with specifications, an offense punishable by death, and aggravated robbery. Prior to trial, he pleaded guilty to the murder charge and agreed to testify against Lockett, her brother, and Dew. In return, the prosecutor dropped the aggravated robbery charge and the specifications to the murder charge, thereby eliminating the possibility that Parker could receive the death penalty. . . . Two weeks before Lockett's separate trial, the prosecutor offered to permit her to plead guilty to voluntary manslaughter and aggravated robbery (offenses which each carried a maximum penalty of 25 years' imprisonment and a maximum fine of $10,000) if she would cooperate with the State, but she rejected the offer. . . .

Once a verdict of aggravated murder with specifications had been returned, the Ohio death penalty statute required the trial judge to impose a death sentence unless, after "considering the nature and circumstances of the offense" and Lockett's "history, character, and condition," he found by a preponderance of the evidence that (1) the victim had induced or facilitated the offense, (2) it was unlikely that Lockett would have committed the offense but for the fact that she "was under duress, coercion, or strong provocation," or (3) the offense was "primarily the product of [Lockett's] psychosis or mental deficiency." . . . After considering the reports and hearing argument on the penalty issue, the trial judge concluded that the offense had not been primarily the product of psychosis or mental deficiency. Without specifically addressing the other two statutory mitigating factors, the judge said that he had "no alternative, whether [he liked] the law or not" but to impose the death penalty. He then sentenced Lockett to death. . . .

Lockett challenges the constitutionality of Ohio's death penalty statute [based on the fact that it] did not permit the sentencing judge to consider, as mitigating factors, her character, prior record, age, lack of specific intent to cause death, and her relatively minor part in the crime. . . .

Prior to Furman v. Georgia, 408 U.S. 238 (1972), every State that authorized capital punishment had abandoned mandatory death penalties, and instead permitted the jury unguided and unrestrained discretion regarding the imposition of the death penalty in a particular capital case. . . . The constitutional status of discretionary sentencing in capital cases changed abruptly, however, as a result of the separate opinions supporting the judgment in *Furman*. . . . In the last decade, many of the States have been obliged to revise their death penalty statutes in response to the various opinions supporting the judgments in *Furman* and *Gregg* and its companion cases. The signals from this Court have not, however, always been easy to decipher. The States now deserve the clearest guidance that the Court can provide; we have an obligation to reconcile previously differing views in order to provide that guidance. With that obligation in mind we turn to Lockett's attack on the Ohio statute. Essentially she contends that the Eighth and Fourteenth Amendments require that the sentencer be given a full opportunity to consider mitigating circumstances in capital cases and that the Ohio statute does not comply with that requirement. She relies, in large part, on the plurality opinions in *Woodson*. . . .

Although legislatures remain free to decide how much discretion in sentencing should be reposed in the judge or jury in noncapital cases, the plurality opinion in *Woodson*, after reviewing the historical repudiation of mandatory sentencing in capital cases, concluded that "in capital cases the fundamental respect for humanity underlying the Eighth Amendment . . . requires consideration of the character and record of the individual offender and the circumstances of the particular offense as a constitutionally indispensable part of the process of inflicting the penalty of death." That declaration rested "on the predicate that the penalty of death is qualitatively different" from any other sentence. We are satisfied that this qualitative difference between death and other penalties calls for a greater degree of reliability when the death sentence is imposed. The mandatory death penalty statute in *Woodson* was held invalid because it permitted *no* consideration of "relevant facets of the character and record of the individual offender or the circumstances of the particular offense." The plurality did not attempt to indicate, however, which facets of an offender or his offense it deemed "relevant" in capital sentencing or what degree of consideration of "relevant facets" it would require.

We are now faced with those questions and we conclude that the Eighth and Fourteenth Amendments require that the sentencer, in all but the rarest kind of capital case, not be precluded from considering, *as a mitigating factor*, any aspect of a defendant's character or record and any of the circumstances of the offense that the defendant proffers as a basis for a sentence less than death. We recognize that, in noncapital cases, the established practice of individualized sentences rests not on constitutional commands, but on public policy enacted into statutes. The considerations that account for the wide acceptance of individualization of sentences in noncapital cases surely cannot be thought less important in capital cases. Given that the imposition of death by public authority is so profoundly different from all other penalties, we cannot avoid the conclusion that an individualized decision is essential in capital cases. The need for treating each defendant in a capital case with that degree of respect due the uniqueness of the individual is far more important than in noncapital cases. A variety of flexible techniques — probation, parole, work furloughs, to name a few — and various postconviction remedies may be available to modify an initial sentence of confinement in noncapital cases. The nonavailability of corrective or modifying mechanisms with respect to an executed capital sentence underscores the need for individualized consideration as a constitutional requirement in imposing the death sentence.

There is no perfect procedure for deciding in which cases governmental authority should be used to impose death. But a statute that prevents the sentencer in all capital cases from giving independent mitigating weight to aspects of the defendant's character and record and to circumstances of the offense proffered in mitigation creates the risk that the death penalty will be imposed in spite of factors which may call for a less severe penalty. When the choice is between life and death, that risk is unacceptable and incompatible with the commands of the Eighth and Fourteenth Amendments. . . .

## NOTES

1. *Access to mitigating evidence.*   In a series of cases, the Court elaborated on the basic holding of *Lockett*, that a capital jury must have access to a wide range of information about the crime and the offender's character and background. Just as the statutory language at issue in *Lockett* unduly limited access, jury instructions or evidentiary rulings could create the same problem. See Eddings v. Oklahoma, 455 U.S. 104 (1982) (court's instructions wrongly told jury to ignore nonstatutory mitigating evidence); Skipper v. South Carolina, 476 U.S. 1 (1986) (defendant can put in evidence of good behavior in prison to demonstrate nondangerousness). Defense counsel must also have access to the aggravating evidence that the prosecutor plans to present, to prepare for cross-examination or other testing of its accuracy. See Gardner v. Florida, 430 U.S. 349 (1977) (defense counsel must have access to all information in the presentence investigation report provided to the sentencer, based on right to confrontation).

2. *Instructions to underscore mitigating evidence.*   Some Supreme Court rulings have required the trial judge not only to give the jury access to mitigating evidence but also to instruct the jury to take special care in considering certain kinds of mitigating evidence, such as the youth of the offender. See Penry v. Lynaugh, 492 U.S. 302 (1989) (stressing the necessity of instructions that inform the jury how to "consider and give effect" to mitigating evidence so that the jury is "provided with a vehicle for expressing its reasoned moral response to that evidence"); Abdul-Kabir v. Quarterman, 127 S. Ct. 1654 (2007) (special instructions to jury necessary when defendant's mitigation evidence may have meaningful relevance to defendant's moral culpability and jury could not otherwise give meaningful effect to such evidence). Another series of cases provides that trial judges in capital cases have a special obligation to instruct the jury on lesser included offenses. See Beck v. Alabama, 447 U.S. 625 (1980) (court must instruct on lesser included offense whenever a jury issue as to that offense is present); Schad v. Arizona, 501 U.S. 624 (1991) (enough to instruct on second-degree murder but not theft; jury not faced with all-or-nothing choice).

3. *Access to aggravating evidence.*   After having established that defendants have a. broad right to present all sorts of mitigating evidence to the capital sentencing decision maker, the Supreme Court faced cases in which prosecutors argued that they should have similarly broad rights to present all sorts of aggravating evidence. These dynamics had perhaps their greatest impact in Payne v. Tennessee, 501 U.S. 808 (1991), in which the Supreme Court overruled two prior holdings that had limited victim impact evidence in capital cases. Following *Payne*, capital sentencing juries are allowed to receive victim impact evidence relating to the personal characteristics of the murder victim and the emotional impact of the death on the victim's family, and prosecutors are allowed to make statements about the personal qualities of the victim.

4. *Impact of individualization on women.*   Capital prosecutions involving women are extremely rare, and the execution of women rarer still. Though women account for about 1 in 10 murder arrests, they account for only 1 in 52 death sentences imposed at the trial level; of more than 850 persons executed since *Furman*, only 10 have been women. See Victor L. Streib, Gendering the Death Penalty: Countering Sex Bias in a Masculine Sanctuary, 63 Ohio St. L.J. 433 (2002); Victor Streib, Death Penalty for Female Offenders, January 1, 1973, through December 31, 2011 (2012). http://www.deathpenaltyinfo.org/documents/FemDeathDec2011.pdf (in modern death penalty era through 2011 women account for 2.1% (174/8,392) of death sentences imposed at the trial level; 1.8% (58/3,250) of people on death row; 0.9% (12/1,277) of persons actually executed). Usually, such capital cases involve women who killed their children or who are serial killers. The execution in Texas in 1999 of Karla Faye Tucker—who was involved in a brutal double murder when under the influence of a drug addiction, but then became a model prisoner after more than a decade on death row—led to widespread national and international protests. Though it usually does not join international agreements that restrict the use of the death penalty, the United States has signed on to the global ban on executing pregnant women.

What factors may account for the apparent gender disparity in executions? Are female offenders presumed to be less threatening? Is the execution of a woman viewed as particularly repulsive? Or does the execution of women perhaps pose different issues compared with the execution of men, differences that might come to light when we consider the battered-spouse syndrome or the presence of young children?

5. *Inevitability of failure?*  Many observers have noted a tension in the Supreme Court's capital punishment cases decided under the Eighth Amendment. On one hand, cases such as *Furman* and *Gregg* emphasize the importance of guiding or structuring the sentencing jury's discretion through the use of statutory aggravating factors, bifurcated proceedings, appellate review, and other legal controls. On the other hand, cases such as *Woodson* and *Lockett* insist that the decision to impose the death penalty must be individualized, and legal rules must not unduly restrict the information the jury receives about the case or the ability of individual jurors to act on that information. Does the current Eighth Amendment jurisprudence reconcile these competing ambitions? If such a goal is beyond reach, how should judges and other decision makers in the legal system respond? Justices Blackmun and Scalia debated this question in Callins v. Collins, 510 U.S. 1141 (1994). Although the Court denied the petition for writ of certiorari in the case, Justice Blackmun dissented and explained the dilemma he faced in death cases:

> [The] problems that were pursued down one hole with procedural rules and verbal formulas have come to the surface somewhere else, just as virulent and pernicious as they were in their original form. Experience has taught us that the constitutional goal of eliminating arbitrariness and discrimination from the administration of death can never be achieved without compromising an equally essential component of fundamental fairness — individualized sentencing.

Blackmun returned to themes explored in the "partly prophetic" opinion of Justice Harlan in *McGautha*, agreeing that to "identify before the fact those characteristics of criminal homicides and their perpetrators which call for the death penalty" appears to be a task "beyond human ability." Blackmun noted the varying efforts states made to address *Furman*'s constitutional barrier by guiding jury discretion but found that none could balance "fairness to the individual . . . without sacrificing the consistency and rationality promised in *Furman*." Although *Furman, Gregg,* and *Lockett* attempted to strike a balance between consistent sentencing and individualized sentencing in the capital context, Blackmun declared that effort a failure:

> In the first stage of capital sentencing, the demands of *Furman* are met by "narrowing" the class of death-eligible offenders according to objective, factbound characteristics of the defendant or the circumstances of the offense. Once the pool of death-eligible defendants has been reduced, the sentencer retains the discretion to consider whatever relevant mitigating evidence the defendant chooses to offer.
>     Over time, I have come to conclude that even this approach is unacceptable: It simply reduces, rather than eliminates, the number of people subject to arbitrary sentencing. It is the decision to sentence a defendant to death — not merely the decision to make a defendant eligible for death — that may not be arbitrary. While one might hope that providing the sentencer with as much relevant mitigating evidence as possible will lead to more rational and

consistent sentences, experience has taught otherwise. It seems that the decision whether a human being should live or die is so inherently subjective — rife with all of life's understandings, experiences, prejudices, and passions — that it inevitably defies the rationality and consistency required by the Constitution.

Summarizing his views, Blackmun explained that experience has shown that "the consistency and rationality promised in *Furman* are inversely related to the fairness owed the individual when considering a sentence of death. A step toward consistency is a step away from fairness." And this failure to reconcile the requirements of consistency and individualized fairness, in Blackmun's view, caused the Court to "retreat" from its earlier ambitious efforts to regulate discretion, "allowing relevant mitigating evidence to be discarded, vague aggravating circumstances to be employed, and providing no indication that the problem of race in the administration of death will ever be addressed." Blackmun declared himself unwilling to continue to play a part in this enterprise:

> From this day forward, I no longer shall tinker with the machinery of death. For more than 20 years I have endeavored — indeed, I have struggled — along with a majority of this Court, to develop procedural and substantive rules that would lend more than the mere appearance of fairness to the death penalty endeavor. Rather than continue to coddle the Court's delusion that the desired level of fairness has been achieved and the need for regulation eviscerated, I feel morally and intellectually obligated simply to concede that the death penalty experiment has failed. . . .

Justice Scalia agreed with Justice Blackmun that the competing aspirations of the Court's Eighth Amendment jurisprudence could not be reconciled, but he argued for a different response to this dilemma. Because the text of the Constitution, in the Fifth and Eighth Amendments, indicates that the use of the death penalty is a legitimate criminal punishment, he argued that the Court had no business blocking the government from using this sanction. Instead of declaring that the death penalty cannot be administered in accord with the Constitution, Scalia urged the Court to reach a different conclusion:

> Though Justice Blackmun joins those of us who have acknowledged the incompatibility of the Court's *Furman* and *Lockett* lines of jurisprudence, he unfortunately draws the wrong conclusion for the acknowledgment. [At] least one of these judicially announced irreconcilable commands which cause the Constitution to prohibit what its text explicitly permits must be wrong. Convictions in opposition to the death penalty are often passionate and deeply held. That would be no excuse for reading them into a Constitution that does not contain them, even if they represented the convictions of a majority of Americans. . . . If the people conclude that . . . brutal deaths may be deterred by capital punishment — indeed, if they merely conclude that justice requires such brutal deaths to be avenged by capital punishment — the creation of false, untexual, and unhistorical contradictions within "the Court's Eighth Amendment jurisprudence" should not prevent them.

Do you agree with Justice Blackmun's reasoning, or is Justice Scalia's resolution of this conundrum more satisfactory? Or are both Justices wrong to conclude that the competing aspirations of consistency and individualized sentencing cannot be balanced in an acceptable way? Does not much, if not all, of what Justice Blackmun says about the tensions between consistency and individualized fairness in the application of the death penalty also apply to other sanctions?

## 3.  Capital Discretion in Operation

There is often a profound gap between the law on paper and the law in practice. The same is true of capital punishment, for two important reasons: (1) the constitutional rules established by the Supreme Court provide only broad parameters for the structure of capital sentencing, so particular capital statutes in individual states determine the rules under which death penalty systems actually operate; and (2) although statutory provisions structure how states apply the death penalty, the way these provisions are understood and applied by prosecutors, defense counsel, juries, and judges determine the day-to-day operation of the death penalty.

Both legal and social factors have significantly affected the operation of the death penalty since the Supreme Court's 1976 decision in *Gregg*. Most tangibly, 17 states (mostly in the northeastern United States) and the District of Columbia do not authorize capital punishment, and thus the law precludes the operation of the death penalty in these jurisdictions. In the 33 other states (and in the federal system), the use of capital punishment varies dramatically in terms of both the number of persons sentenced to death and the number of executions carried out. Applying either metric, Southern states — particularly Texas and Florida — have been national leaders. Between 1976 and mid-2007, Texas executed almost 400 persons, almost four times more than any other state, and had another 400 defendants on death row. Some states, notably California, Pennsylvania, and Ohio, have sentenced many offenders to death but have carried out relatively few executions. Other states, such as Virginia and Missouri, have carried out a large number of executions but have relatively small death row populations. Overall, the number of death sentences imposed has been declining over the last few years in every state, including Texas.

The impact of appellate review in capital cases can explain some of the differences among states in the number of death sentences imposed and the number of executions carried out. As detailed more fully in Chapter 11, typically both state and federal courts review every death sentence imposed, although the rigor of this review varies greatly by court and region. In total, since *Gregg*, over 8,000 death sentences have been imposed, and more than half of these sentences have been reversed on appeal. Since 1999 the number of death sentences imposed has declined dramatically every year. As of January 2007, 3,350 defendants were on death row and almost 1,100 persons have been executed since 1976. See Death Penalty Information Center, The Death Penalty in 2011: Year End Report (Dec. 2011) (http://www.deathpenaltyinfo.org/documents/2011_Year_End.pdf).

When state legislatures during the years after 1976 created acceptable systems of capital punishment, they based their decisions on some speculation about how prosecutors, jurors, defense lawyers, defendants, judges, and the public would respond. In other words, efforts by courts and legislatures to regulate capital sentencing discretion often relied on a variety of assumptions about how this discretion is exercised. As you review the material in the rest of this chapter, consider whether the capital sentencing structures that emerged as a result of the Supreme Court's regulatory efforts have effectively addressed the problems of arbitrariness that the Court identified in *Furman.*

### a.   Statutory Schemes

State legislatures responded to the various opinions in *Furman* with different strategies for limiting the sentencer's discretion to choose a lengthy prison term or death. As detailed above, the Supreme Court ultimately ruled unconstitutional the efforts by some states to make the death penalty mandatory for certain crimes, and it also required states to allow the consideration of nearly all mitigating circumstances. Other than these basic requirements, however, states have fairly broad latitude in deciding how to structure death penalty decisions. Some states reserve the decision exclusively to a jury, while others allow the judge to make the choice after the jury renders an advisory verdict. Some statutes provide lengthy lists of aggravating and mitigating factors, while others set forth much shorter lists or none at all.

The statutes in operation throughout the various states generally adopt two or three distinct strategies to guide sentencing discretion. Some states, including Georgia, are known as "threshold" states. Their statutes require jurors to find beyond a reasonable doubt at least one aggravating factor from the list included in the statute; after crossing that threshold, the jurors are free to impose life or death without further instructions. The largest group of states, including Florida, use "balancing" statutes. These laws require jurors to determine the presence or absence of aggravating and mitigating factors specified in the statute, and then to balance the aggravating factors against the mitigating factors. In some of these states, the jury is instructed to impose a death penalty if the aggravating factors outweigh the mitigating factors; in others, the jury remains free to impose a life term even if the aggravating factors weigh more heavily than the mitigating factors. Finally, a third group of "directive" or "limiting" states, including Texas, give further structure to the jury's decision by presenting a sequence of special questions to the jury (often related to the future dangerousness of the offender) that supposedly determine the jury's decision on death or life.

The following problem provides an opportunity to observe how different capital sentencing statutes operate in the context of a specific case. As you work through the problem, consider whether these death penalty statutes sufficiently address the problems and other issues that lay behind the Supreme Court's decisions and reasoning in *Furman, Gregg,* and the other early constitutional cases.

### PROBLEM 3-3.   CHOOSE YOUR POISON

During the 1980s and 1990s, Theodore Kaczynski sent a series of bombs through the mail, and a number of them exploded and killed the recipients of the packages. Kaczynski selected as his victims key figures in universities and in transportation, advertising, and high-technology firms because he believed that the reliance on computers and other technological devices was a disastrous trend for modern society, a trend he hoped his bombs would reverse. Kaczynski became known as the "Unabomber." Using this name, he wrote lengthy letters to major newspapers from time to time, explaining his views on the evils of technology and modern life and his reasons for sending the bombs. After years of investigation, authorities found the Unabomber in a small cabin in Montana, and the federal government charged him with several counts of murder. As the proceedings moved along, it became clear that there was some question about Kaczynski's sanity, and prosecutors decided to accept a guilty plea in exchange for a sentence of life in prison without possibility of parole.

This outcome proved unsatisfactory to some prosecutors in states where victims were killed; they still want a piece of the action. Imagine now that prosecutors from Texas and Florida can establish jurisdiction in their states and have contacted the U.S. Attorney General, asking for custody of Kaczynski to try him for murder in their states. (The law of double jeopardy allows states to prosecute a person for a crime even after the federal government has obtained a conviction for that same crime, but the state authorities must have physical custody of Kaczynski before proceeding with a murder trial.)

Lawyers serving on Kaczynski's appointed defense team have asked for your advice about which jurisdiction they should choose to assume custody. (The team has explained to you that the Attorney General feels obliged to allow one state to try Kaczynski but is eager to minimize legal battles over this case now that the federal charges have been resolved. Consequently, the Attorney General wants a transfer decision to have defense counsel's acquiescence in order to avoid any legal challenges.) Read the two statutes that follow, then give the defense lawyers your best advice about the prospects for the government in obtaining a death sentence under each statute. Do the different statutes impact aggravating and mitigating evidence that will be considered or emphasized at trial?

## ‖ *Texas Code of Criminal Procedure, Art. 37.071* ‖

*Section 1.* If a defendant is found guilty in a capital felony case in which the state does not seek the death penalty, the judge shall sentence the defendant to life imprisonment without parole.

*Section 2.* (a) (1) If a defendant is tried for a capital offense in which the state seeks the death penalty, on a finding that the defendant is guilty of a capital offense, the court shall conduct a separate sentencing proceeding to determine whether the defendant shall be sentenced to death or life imprisonment without parole. The proceeding shall be conducted in the trial court and . . . before the trial jury as soon as practicable. In the proceeding, evidence may be presented by the state and the defendant or the defendant's counsel as to any matter that the court deems relevant to sentence, including evidence of the defendant's background or character or the circumstances of the offense that mitigates against the imposition of the death penalty. This subdivision shall not be construed to authorize the introduction of any evidence secured in violation of the Constitution of the United States or of the State of Texas. The state and the defendant or the defendant's counsel shall be permitted to present argument for or against sentence of death. . . . The court, the attorney representing the state, the defendant, or the defendant's counsel may not inform a juror or a prospective juror of the effect of a failure of a jury to agree on issues submitted under Subsection (c) or (e). . . .

(b) On conclusion of the presentation of the evidence, the court shall submit the following issues to the jury:

(1) whether there is a probability that the defendant would commit criminal acts of violence that would constitute a continuing threat to society; and

(2) in cases in which the jury charge at the guilt or innocence stage permitted the jury to find the defendant guilty as [an accomplice], whether the defendant actually caused the death of the deceased or did not actually cause the death of the deceased but intended to kill the deceased or another or anticipated that a human life would be taken.

(c) The state must prove each issue submitted under Subsection (b) of this article beyond a reasonable doubt, and the jury shall return a special verdict of "yes" or "no" on each issue submitted under Subsection (b) of this Article.

(d) The court shall charge the jury that:

(1) in deliberating on the issues submitted under Subsection (b) of this article, it shall consider all evidence admitted at the guilt or innocence stage and the punishment stage, including evidence of the defendant's background or character or the circumstances of the offense that militates for or mitigates against the imposition of the death penalty;

(2) it may not answer any issue submitted under Subsection (b) of this article "yes" unless it agrees unanimously and it may not answer any issue "no" unless 10 or more jurors agree; and

(3) members of the jury need not agree on what particular evidence supports a negative answer to any issue submitted under Subsection (b) of this article.

(e)(1) The court shall instruct the jury that if the jury returns an affirmative finding to each issue submitted under Subsection (b), it shall answer the following issue:

Whether, taking into consideration all of the evidence, including the circumstances of the offense, the defendant's character and background, and the personal moral culpability of the defendant, there is a sufficient mitigating circumstance or circumstances to warrant that a sentence of life imprisonment rather than a death sentence be imposed. . . .

(2) The court shall:

(A) instruct the jury that if the jury answers that a circumstance or circumstances warrant that a sentence of life imprisonment without parole rather than a death sentence be imposed, the court will sentence the defendant to imprisonment . . . for life without parole; and

(B) charge the jury that a defendant sentenced to confinement for life without parole under this article is ineligible for release. . . .

(f) The court shall charge the jury that in answering the issue submitted under Subsection (e) of this article, the jury:

(1) shall answer the issue "yes" or "no";

(2) may not answer the issue "no" unless it agrees unanimously and may not answer the issue "yes" unless 10 or more jurors agree;

(3) need not agree on what particular evidence supports an affirmative finding on the issue; and

(4) shall consider mitigating evidence to be evidence that a juror might regard as reducing the defendant's moral blameworthiness.

(g) If the jury returns an affirmative finding on each issue submitted under Subsection (b) of this article and a negative finding on an issue submitted under Subsection (e)(1) of this article, the court shall sentence the defendant to death. If the jury returns a negative finding on any issue submitted under Subsection (b) of this article or an affirmative finding on an issue submitted under Subsection (e)(1) or is unable to answer any issue submitted under Subsection (b) or (e), the court shall sentence the defendant to confinement in the institutional division of the Texas Department of Criminal Justice for life imprisonment without parole.

(h) The judgment of conviction and sentence of death shall be subject to automatic review by the Court of Criminal Appeals.

## ‖ *Florida Statutes Annotated §921.141* ‖

(1) *Separate proceedings on issue of penalty.* Upon conviction or adjudication of. guilt of a defendant of a capital felony, the court shall conduct a separate sentencing proceeding to determine whether the defendant should be sentenced to death or life imprisonment. . . . The proceeding shall be conducted by the trial judge before the trial jury as soon as practicable. . . . If the trial jury has been waived, or if the defendant pleaded guilty, the sentencing proceeding shall be conducted before a jury impaneled for that purpose, unless waived by the defendant. In the proceeding, evidence may be presented as to any matter that the court deems relevant to the nature of the crime and the character of the defendant and shall include matters relating to any of the aggravating or mitigating circumstances enumerated in subsections (5) and (6). Any such evidence which the court deems to have probative value may be received, regardless of its admissibility under the exclusionary rules of evidence, provided the defendant is accorded a fair opportunity to rebut any hearsay statements. However, this subsection shall not be construed to authorize the introduction of any evidence secured in violation of the Constitution of the United States or the Constitution of the State of Florida. The state and the defendant or the defendant's counsel shall be permitted to present argument for or against sentence of death.

(2) *Advisory sentence by the jury.* After hearing all the evidence, the jury shall deliberate and render an advisory sentence to the court, based upon the following matters:

(a) Whether sufficient aggravating circumstances exist as enumerated in subsection (5);

(b) Whether sufficient mitigating circumstances exist which outweigh the aggravating circumstances found to exist; and

(c) Based on these considerations, whether the defendant should be sentenced to life imprisonment or death.

(3) *Findings in support of sentence of death.* Notwithstanding the recommendation. of a majority of the jury, the court, after weighing the aggravating and mitigating circumstances, shall enter a sentence of life imprisonment or death, but if the court imposes a sentence of death, it shall set forth in writing its findings upon which the sentence of death is based as to the facts:

(a) That sufficient aggravating circumstances exist as enumerated in subsection (5), and

(b) That there are insufficient mitigating circumstances to outweigh the aggravating circumstances.

In each case in which the court imposes the death sentence, the determination of the court shall be supported by specific written findings of fact based upon the circumstances in subsections (5) and (6) and upon the records of the trial and the sentencing proceedings. If the court does not make the findings requiring the death sentence within 30 days after the rendition of the judgment and sentence, the court shall impose sentence of life imprisonment. . . .

(4) *Review of judgment and sentence.* The judgment of. conviction and sentence of death shall be subject to automatic review by the Supreme Court of Florida and disposition rendered within 2 years after the filing of a notice of appeal. Such review by the Supreme Court shall have priority over all other cases and shall be heard in accordance with rules promulgated by the Supreme Court.

(5) *Aggravating circumstances.* Aggravating circumstances. shall be limited to the following:

(a) The capital felony was committed by a person previously convicted of a felony and under sentence of imprisonment or placed on community control or on felony probation.

(b) The defendant was previously convicted of another capital felony or of a felony involving the use or threat of violence to the person.

(c) The defendant knowingly created a great risk of death to many persons.

(d) The capital felony was committed while the defendant was engaged, or was an accomplice, in the commission of, or an attempt to commit, or flight after committing or attempting to commit, any: robbery; sexual battery; aggravated child abuse; abuse of an elderly person or disabled adult resulting in great bodily harm, permanent disability, or permanent disfigurement; arson; burglary; kidnapping; aircraft piracy; or unlawful throwing, placing, or discharging of a destructive device or bomb.

(e) The capital felony was committed for the purpose of avoiding or preventing a lawful arrest or effecting an escape from custody.

(f) The capital felony was committed for pecuniary gain.

(g) The capital felony was committed to disrupt or hinder the lawful exercise of any governmental function or the enforcement of laws.

(h) The capital felony was especially heinous, atrocious, or cruel.

(i) The capital felony was a homicide and was committed in a cold, calculated, and premeditated manner without any pretense of moral or legal justification.

(j) The victim of the capital felony was a law enforcement officer engaged in the performance of his or her official duties.

(k) The victim of the capital felony was an elected or appointed public official engaged in the performance of his or her official duties if the motive for the capital felony was related, in whole or in part, to the victim's official capacity.

(l) The victim of the capital felony was a person less than 12 years of age.

(m) The victim of the capital felony was particularly vulnerable due to advanced age or disability, or because the defendant stood in a position of familial or custodial authority over the victim.

(n) The capital felony was committed by a criminal street gang member. . . .

(o) The capital felony was committed by a person designated as a sexual predator . . . or a person previously designated as a sexual predator who had the sexual predator designation removed.

(p) The capital felony was committed by a person subject to an injunction issued pursuant to §741.30 or §784.046, or a foreign protection order accorded full faith and credit pursuant to §741.315, and was committed against the petitioner who obtained the injunction or protection order or any spouse, child, sibling, or parent of the petitioner.

(6) *Mitigating circumstances.* Mitigating circumstances shall be the following:

(a) The defendant has no significant history of prior criminal activity.

(b) The capital felony was committed while the defendant was under the influence of extreme mental or emotional disturbance.

(c) The victim was a participant in the defendant's conduct or consented to the act.

(d) The defendant was an accomplice in the capital felony committed by another person and his or her participation was relatively minor.

(e) The defendant acted under extreme duress or under the substantial domination of another person.

(f) The capacity of the defendant to appreciate the criminality of his or her conduct or to conform his or her conduct to the requirements of law was substantially impaired.

(g) The age of the defendant at the time of the crime.

(h) The existence of any other factors in the defendant's background that would mitigate against imposition of the death penalty.

(7) *Victim impact evidence.* Once the prosecution has provided evidence of the. existence of one or more aggravating circumstances as described in subsection (5), the prosecution may introduce, and subsequently argue, victim impact evidence to the jury. Such evidence shall be designed to demonstrate the victim's uniqueness as an individual human being and the resultant loss to the community's members by the victim's death. Characterizations and opinions about the crime, the defendant, and the appropriate sentence shall not be permitted as a part of victim impact evidence.

## NOTES

1. *Impact of legal standards.*   In terms of the decision whether to sentence a defendant to death, do the standards that the sentencing jury employs make a

difference? Consider the likely outcome for two infamous defendants. Would Timothy McVeigh, the Oklahoma City bomber who killed 168 people in 1995, have received a death sentence under either or both of these statutes? How about John Allen Mohammad, one of the two Washington-area sniper suspects apprehended in 2002?

To prevent the execution of an innocent person, some have proposed that the jury be required at the sentencing stage to find "no doubt" as to the defendant's guilt. Massachusetts Governor's Council on Capital Punishment, at www.lawlib.state.ma.us/5-3-04Governorsreportcapitalpunishment.pdf. Do you find this helpful? See Erik Lillquist, Absolute Certainty and the Death Penalty, 42 Am. Crim. L. Rev. 45 (2005); Robert Hardaway, Beyond A Conceivable Doubt: The Quest for A Fair and Constitutional Standard of Proof in Death Penalty Cases, 34 New Eng. J. on Crim. & Civ. Confinement 221, 289 (2008).

2. *Impact of procedural rules.*   Can and should the procedures used at a standard criminal trial apply during a capital sentencing hearing? Consider, for example, the traditional rules of evidence, and the possibility that strict adherence to them might significantly limit the ability of prosecutors and defense counsel to present all the evidence they might consider important at a sentencing hearing. How, if at all, might these rules or other traditional trial procedures influence the outcome of a capital sentencing hearing?

3. *Weighing aggravating and mitigating circumstances.*   Both of the preceding statutes stipulate that the jury weigh specific aggravating and mitigating circumstances. How should the jury decide when aggravating and mitigating factors are in equipoise? In Kansas v. Marsh, 548 U.S. 163 (2006), the Supreme Court held that a state statute may direct imposition of the death penalty "when the State has proved beyond a reasonable doubt that mitigators do not outweigh aggravators, including where [they] are in equipoise." In its decision, the Court relied on Walton v. Arizona, 497 U.S. 639 (1990), where it held that a state death penalty statute may place the burden on the defendant to prove that mitigating circumstances outweigh aggravators. In addition, the Court found the Kansas statute to "rationally narrow the class of death-eligible defendants" and to allow the jury to "render a reasoned, individualized sentencing determination," which is required under *Furman* and *Gregg.*

4. *The availability of "life without parole" as a sentencing option.*   Every state except Alaska provides life without parole as a sentencing option. Public opinion polls have indicated that a slightly larger proportion of the American public would chose life without parole rather than the death penalty as the appropriate punishment for murder. May this sanction give jurors who are concerned about public safety the opportunity to avoid imposing a death sentence? Might the decrease in the number of death sentences be connected to the availability of this sanction? The New Jersey Death Penalty Study Commission recommended that the death penalty be abolished in New Jersey since "life without parole" provides sufficient guarantees of public safety and also addresses other penological concerns. New Jersey Death Penalty Study Commission Report 1-2 (January 2007), at www.njleg.state.nj.us/committees/dpsc_final.pdf. The United States Supreme Court has held that "life without parole" for those under the age of 18 violates the Eight Amendment. Miller v. Alabama, 132 S. Ct. 1733 (2012).

## b.   Jury Selection and Decision Making

Although very few states rely on juries for noncapital sentencing decisions, nearly all states that authorize the death penalty give juries a central role in capital sentencing. This raises a number of important and interesting questions: Why do states believe that juries are the appropriate decision makers in capital cases where life and death are at stake, but exclude juries from other sentencing decisions? Should the jury determining a defendant's guilt also decide whether the defendant receives the death penalty, or should two different juries make these respective decisions? Can we be confident that any system of jury decision making in capital cases will be free of the problems that prompted the Supreme Court's decision in *Furman*?

Beyond these broad questions, the reliance on juries to make capital punishment decisions raises a host of more intricate legal and practical issues that can greatly influence the operation of death penalty systems. For example, should a jury have to render a unanimous verdict to impose a death sentence? What standard of proof should a jury apply when making a death penalty decision? Should a defendant have a right to request that a judge instead of a jury make the death sentencing decision? Can we be confident that jurors will understand and follow the detailed instructions in a death penalty statute?

As we have seen, the thrust of the constitutional rules that regulate capital punishment is to channel and preserve the discretion of the sentencing authority, usually a jury. Whenever the law assigns discretion to someone, it becomes critical to know *who* will exercise that discretion. Thus, the method of selecting the jury members in a capital case is a crucial element of this system, which depends so much on guided discretion. When life is at stake, both prosecutors and defense counsel are very concerned about the jury's composition, especially since determining whether to sentence a person to death is fundamentally a moral decision rather than a factual one. As the following case highlights, there is good reason to fear that in the operation of capital sentencing systems, the very processes used in jury selection may prompt some of the same concerns that troubled the Supreme Court in *Furman*.

## *Thomas Joe Miller-El v. Janie Cockrell*
### 537 U.S. 322 (2003)

KENNEDY, J.

In 1986 two Dallas County assistant district attorneys used peremptory strikes to exclude 10 of the 11 African-Americans eligible to serve on the jury which tried Thomas Joe Miller-El. During the ensuing 17 years, petitioner has been unsuccessful in establishing, in either state or federal court, that his conviction and death sentence must be vacated because the jury selection procedures violated the Equal Protection Clause and our holding in Batson v. Kentucky, 476 U.S. 79 (1986). The claim now arises in a federal petition for writ of habeas corpus [and we consider whether the federal habeas corpus statute precludes further consideration of Miller-El's claim].

Petitioner, his wife Dorothy Miller-El, and one Kenneth Flowers robbed a Holiday Inn in Dallas, Texas. They emptied the cash drawers and ordered two employees, Doug Walker and Donald Hall, to lie on the floor. Walker and Hall were gagged with strips of fabric, and their hands and feet were bound. Petitioner asked Flowers if he was going to kill Walker and Hall. When Flowers hesitated or refused, petitioner shot Walker twice in the back and shot Hall in the side. Walker died from his wounds.

The State indicted petitioner for capital murder. He pleaded not guilty, and jury selection took place during five weeks in February and March 1986. When voir dire had been concluded, petitioner moved to strike the jury on the grounds that the prosecution had violated the Equal Protection Clause of the Fourteenth Amendment by excluding African-Americans through the use of peremptory challenges. . . .

A comparative analysis of the venire members demonstrates that African-Americans were excluded from petitioner's jury in a ratio significantly higher than Caucasians were. Of the 108 possible jurors reviewed by the prosecution and defense, 20 were African-American. Nine of them were excused for cause or by agreement of the parties. Of the 11 African-American jurors remaining, however, all but 1 were excluded by peremptory strikes exercised by the prosecutors. On this basis 91% of the eligible black jurors were removed by peremptory strikes. In contrast the prosecutors used their peremptory strikes against just 13% (4 out of 31) of the eligible nonblack prospective jurors qualified to serve on petitioner's jury.

These numbers, while relevant, are not petitioner's whole case. During voir dire, the prosecution questioned venire members as to their views concerning the death penalty and their willingness to serve on a capital case. Responses that disclosed reluctance or hesitation to impose capital punishment were cited as a justification for striking a potential juror for cause or by peremptory challenge [based upon this Court's decision in] Wainwright v. Witt, 469 U.S. 412 (1985). The evidence suggests, however, that the manner in which members of the venire were questioned varied by race. . . .

Most African-Americans (53%, or 8 out of 15) were first given a detailed description of the mechanics of an execution in Texas:

> If those three [sentencing] questions are answered yes, at some point Thomas Joe Miller-El will be taken to Huntsville, Texas. He will be placed on death row and at some time will be taken to the death house where he will be strapped on a gurney, an IV put into his arm and he will be injected with a substance that will cause his death . . . as the result of the verdict in this case if those three questions are answered yes.

Only then were these African-American venire members asked whether they could render a decision leading to a sentence of death. Very few prospective white jurors (6%, or 3 out of 49) were given this preface prior to being asked for their views on capital punishment. Rather, all but three were questioned in vague terms: "Would you share with us . . . your personal feelings, if you could, in your own words how you do feel about the death penalty and capital punishment and secondly, do you feel you could serve on this type of a jury and actually render a decision that would result in the death of the Defendant in this case based on the evidence?"

There was an even more pronounced difference, on the apparent basis of race, in the manner the prosecutors questioned members of the venire about their willingness to impose the minimum sentence for murder. Under Texas law at the time of petitioner's trial, an unwillingness to do so warranted removal for cause. This strategy normally is used by the defense to weed out pro-state members of the venire, but, ironically, the prosecution employed it here. The prosecutors first identified the statutory minimum sentence of five years' imprisonment to 34 out of 36 (94%) white venire members, and only then asked: "If you hear a case, to your way of thinking [that] calls for and warrants and justifies five years, you'll give it?" In contrast, only 1 out of 8 (12.5%) African-American prospective jurors were informed of the statutory minimum before being asked what minimum sentence they would impose. The typical questioning of the other seven black jurors was as follows:

> [Prosecutor]: Now, the maximum sentence for [murder] . . . is life under the law. Can you give me an idea of just your personal feelings what you feel a minimum sentence should be for the offense of murder the way I've set it out for you?
> [Juror]: Well, to me that's almost like it's premeditated. But you said they don't have a premeditated statute here in Texas. . . .
> [Prosecutor]: Again, we're not talking about self-defense or accident or insanity or killing in the heat of passion or anything like that. We're talking about the knowing —
> [Juror]: I know you said the minimum. The minimum amount that I would say would be at least twenty years.

Furthermore, petitioner points to the prosecution's use of a Texas criminal procedure practice known as jury shuffling. This practice permits parties to rearrange the order in which members of the venire are examined so as to increase the likelihood that visually preferable venire members will be moved forward and empaneled. With no information about the prospective jurors other than their appearance, the party requesting the procedure literally shuffles the juror cards, and the venire members are then reseated in the new order. Tex. Code Crim. Proc. Ann., Art. 35.11. Shuffling affects jury composition because any prospective jurors not questioned during voir dire are dismissed at the end of the week, and a new panel of jurors appears the following week. So jurors who are shuffled to the back of the panel are less likely to be questioned or to serve.

On at least two occasions the prosecution requested shuffles when there were a predominate number of African-Americans in the front of the panel. On yet another occasion the prosecutors complained about the purported inadequacy of the card shuffle by a defense lawyer but lodged a formal objection only after the postshuffle panel composition revealed that African-American prospective jurors had been moved forward.

[As additional evidence to support his claims,] petitioner subpoenaed a number of current and former Dallas County assistant district attorneys, judges, and others who had observed firsthand the prosecution's conduct during jury selection over a number of years. Although most of the witnesses denied the existence of a systematic policy to exclude African-Americans, others disagreed.

A Dallas County district judge testified that, when he had served in the District Attorney's Office from the late 1950s to early 1960s, his superior warned him that he would be fired if he permitted any African-Americans to serve on a jury. Similarly, another Dallas County district judge and former assistant district attorney from 1976 to 1978 testified that he believed the office had a systematic policy of excluding African-Americans from juries.

Of more importance, the defense presented evidence that the District Attorney's Office had adopted a formal policy to exclude minorities from jury service. A 1963 circular by the District Attorney's Office instructed its prosecutors to exercise peremptory strikes against minorities: "Do not take Jews, Negroes, Dagos, Mexicans or a member of any minority race on a jury, no matter how rich or how well educated." A manual entitled "Jury Selection in a Criminal Case" was distributed to prosecutors. It contained an article authored by a former prosecutor (and later a judge) under the direction of his superiors in the District Attorney's Office, outlining the reasoning for excluding minorities from jury service. Although the manual was written in 1968, it remained in circulation until 1976, if not later, and was available at least to one of the prosecutors in Miller-El's trial.

Some testimony casts doubt on the State's claim that these practices had been discontinued before petitioner's trial. For example, a judge testified that, in 1985, he had to exclude a prosecutor from trying cases in his courtroom for race-based discrimination in jury selection. Other testimony indicated that the State, by its own admission, once requested a jury shuffle in order to reduce the number of African-Americans in the venire. Concerns over the exclusion of African-Americans by the District Attorney's Office were echoed by Dallas County's Chief Public Defender.

[The] State now concedes that petitioner satisfied step one [under the standards established in Batson v. Kentucky, 476 U.S. 79 (1986)]: "There is no dispute that Miller-El presented a prima facie claim" that prosecutors used their peremptory challenges to exclude venire members on the basis of race. Petitioner, for his part, acknowledges that the State proceeded through step two [of the *Batson* analysis] by proffering facially race-neutral explanations for these strikes. Under *Batson*, then, the question remaining is step three: whether Miller-El "has carried his burden of proving purposeful discrimination." . . .

In this case, the statistical evidence alone raises some debate as to whether the prosecution acted with a race-based reason when striking prospective jurors. The prosecutors used their peremptory strikes to exclude 91% of the eligible African-American venire members, and only one served on petitioner's jury. In total, 10 of the prosecutors' 14 peremptory strikes were used against African-Americans. Happenstance is unlikely to produce this disparity. . . .

In this case, three of the State's proffered race-neutral rationales for striking African-American jurors pertained just as well to some white jurors who were not challenged and who did serve on the jury. The prosecutors explained that their peremptory challenges against six African-American potential jurors were based on ambivalence about the death penalty; hesitancy to vote to execute defendants capable of being rehabilitated; and the jurors' own family history of criminality. In rebuttal of the prosecution's explanation, petitioner identified two empaneled white jurors who expressed ambivalence about the death penalty in a manner similar to their African-American counterparts who were the subject of prosecutorial peremptory challenges. One indicated that capital punishment was not appropriate for a first offense, and another stated that it would be "difficult" to impose a death sentence. Similarly, two white jurors expressed hesitation in sentencing to death a defendant who might be rehabilitated; and four white jurors had family members with criminal histories. As a consequence, even though the prosecution's reasons for striking African-American members of the venire appear race neutral, the application of these rationales to the venire might have been selective and based on racial considerations. Whether a comparative juror analysis would demonstrate the prosecutors' rationales to have been pretexts for discrimination is an unnecessary determination at this stage, but the evidence does make debatable the District Court's conclusion that no purposeful discrimination occurred.

We question the Court of Appeals' and state trial court's dismissive and strained interpretation of petitioner's evidence of disparate questioning. . . . Disparate questioning did occur. Petitioner submits that disparate questioning created the appearance of divergent opinions even though the venire members' views on the relevant subject might have been the same. It follows that, if the use of disparate questioning is determined by race at the outset, it is likely a justification for a strike based on the resulting divergent views would be pretextual. In this context the differences in the questions posed by the prosecutors are some evidence of purposeful discrimination. . . .

We agree with petitioner that the prosecution's decision to seek a jury shuffle when a predominate number of African-Americans were seated in the front of the panel, along with its decision to delay a formal objection to the defense's shuffle until after the new racial composition was revealed, raise a suspicion that the State sought to exclude African-Americans from the jury. Our concerns are amplified by the fact that the state court also had before it, and apparently ignored, testimony demonstrating that the Dallas County District Attorney's Office had, by its own admission, used this process to manipulate the racial composition of the jury in the past. Even though the practice of jury shuffling might not be denominated as a *Batson* claim because it does not involve a peremptory challenge, the use of the practice here tends to erode the credibility of the prosecution's assertion that race was not a motivating factor in the jury selection. . . .

Finally, in our threshold examination, we accord some weight to petitioner's historical evidence of racial discrimination by the District Attorney's Office. . . . Irrespective of whether the evidence could prove sufficient to support a charge of systematic exclusion of African-Americans, it reveals that the culture of the District Attorney's Office in the past was suffused with bias against African-Americans in jury selection. Both prosecutors [in Miller-El's case] joined the District Attorney's Office when assistant district attorneys received formal training in excluding minorities from juries. The supposition that race was a factor could be reinforced by the fact that the prosecutors marked the race of each prospective juror on their juror cards. . . .

To secure habeas relief, petitioner must demonstrate that a state court's finding of the absence of purposeful discrimination was incorrect by clear and convincing evidence, 28 U.S.C. §2254(e)(1), and that the corresponding factual determination was "objectively unreasonable" in light of the record before the court. The State represents to us that petitioner will not be able to satisfy his burden. That may or may not be the case. It is not, however, the question before us [as we are considering only whether his claim may proceed under the federal habeas statute, and that] inquiry asks only if the District Court's decision was debatable. Our threshold examination convinces us that it was.

## NOTES

1. *Death qualification and life qualification of jurors.*   As briefly mentioned. in the *Miller-El* decision, the Supreme Court developed special rules to govern the selection and exclusion of jurors in death penalty cases. Through its decisions in Witherspoon v. Illinois, 391 U.S. 510 (1968), and Wainwright v. Witt, 469 U.S. 412 (1985), the Supreme Court established that jurors may be excused for cause when they indicate they are so opposed to capital punishment that they would not find the defendant guilty regardless of the evidence, or would not consider death as a possible sentence regardless of the circumstances of the crime. In Uttecht v. Brown, 558 U.S. I (2007), the Supreme Court held that a juror may be excused for cause if he indicates during voir dire that a death sanction was an option for him only if the defendant could be released to re-offend. A contrary decision would substantially impact the state's ability to impose the death penalty.

Many commentators have assailed the practice of excluding jurors who express sincere misgivings about capital punishment—a process known as "death qualifying" a juror—arguing that it biases the decision making of capital juries and denies capital defendants their constitutional rights to an impartial jury and to a jury drawn from a fair cross-section of the community. See Craig Haney, Aida Hurtado & Luis Vega, Modern Death Qualification: New Data on Its Biasing Effects, 18 Law & Hum. Behav. 619, 624-631 (1994); Stephen Gillers, Deciding Who Dies, 129 U. Pa. L. Rev. 1 (1980); G. Ben Cohen & Robert J. Smith, The Death of Death-Qualification, 59 Case W. Res. L. Rev. 87, 124 (2008).

Following the same principles it applied in *Witt*, the Supreme Court subsequently held in Morgan v. Illinois, 504 U.S. 719 (1992), that a defendant could seek to "life qualify" a capital jury by excluding for cause any juror who indicates he or she will automatically vote for the death penalty regardless of any presented mitigating circumstances. The efficacy of the Supreme Court's rules regulating the selection of capital jurors has been repeatedly questioned, with a number of commentators raising serious concerns based on data collected by the Capital Jury Project (see below) about the decisions of actual capital jurors. See John H. Blume et al., Probing "Life Qualification" Through Expanded Voir Dire, 29 Hofstra L. Rev. 1209 (2001); William J. Bowers et al., Foreclosed Impartiality in Capital Sentencing: Jurors' Predispositions, Guilt-Trial Experience, and Premature Decision Making, 83 Cornell L. Rev. 1476 (1998); Marla Sandys, Adam Trahan, Life Qualification, Automatic Death Penalty Voter Status, and Juror Decision Making in Capital Cases, 29 Just. Sys. J. 385 (2008).

2. *Review of death sentencing procedures.*   The Supreme Court in *Miller-El* was not asked to resolve the merits of the defendant's constitutional claim because the case was enmeshed in the complicated procedural issues that surround federal habeas review of state death sentences. Because state courts rejected Miller-El's claims on their merits, and because the federal district court denied relief, the specific question before the Supreme Court was whether Miller-El's claim was sufficiently "debatable" to permit further appellate review in the federal courts. Given the force of the factual evidence presented by Miller-El, why do you think the state courts rejected his claims of equal protection violation? Given the concerns expressed by the Supreme Court in *Furman*, do you think capital cases warrant a higher standard of appellate review?

On remand from the Supreme Court after its initial ruling in *Miller-El*, the Fifth Circuit held that defendant Miller-El failed to show by clear and convincing evidence that the state court's finding of no discrimination was wrong. In June 2005, through a 6-3 decision, the Supreme Court once again reversed the Fifth Circuit and ruled that Miller-El was entitled to a new trial in light of strong evidence of racial bias during jury selection at his original trial and general historical evidence of the racially biased policies of the Dallas County District Attorney's office. Miller-El v. Dretke, 545 U.S. 231 (2005). The Supreme Court said the prosecutors' supposedly race-neutral reasons for the strikes were so far at odds with the evidence that pretext is the fair conclusion. The Court stated that the Texas court's finding of no discrimination "blinks reality," and was both unreasonable and erroneous.

3. *Potential sources of racial bias.*   As highlighted earlier, a clear concern for certain justices who voted in the majority in *Furman* was not just the possibility of arbitrary death sentencing but the real potential for discriminatory decisions in capital cases. Do the racial realities revealed in the *Miller-El* case suggest that unique safeguards against racial bias are needed in capital cases? The Supreme Court's struggles with racial discrimination in the administration of the death penalty are covered more fully in Chapter 9.

> ## The Capital Jury Project: Rationale, Design, and Preview of Early Findings, William J. Bowers
> ### 70 Ind. L.J. 1043 (1995)

Now underway in fourteen states, the Capital Jury Project ("CJP") is a multidisciplinary study of how jurors make their life or death sentencing decisions. Drawing upon three-to-four-hour interviews with 80 to 120 capital jurors in each of the participating states, the CJP is examining the extent to which jurors' exercise of capital sentencing discretion is still infected with, or now cured of, the arbitrariness which the United States Supreme Court condemned in Furman v. Georgia, and the extent to which the principal kinds of post-*Furman* guided discretion statutes are curbing arbitrary decision-making — as the Court said they would in Gregg v. Georgia and its companion cases. . . .

### The Guilt Phase

Jurors' responses to questions about the guilt phase of the trial suggest that many of them began considering aggravation and punishment while they were still deciding on the defendant's guilt, and indeed, that many began to take a stand on what the defendant's punishment should be well before being exposed to the statutory guidelines for this decision. We see these indications in their responses to questions about topics they discussed during the jury's guilt deliberations and in their answers to a question about what they thought the punishment should be prior to the punishment phase of the trial.

#### *Considerations of Aggravation and Punishment*

When the questioning turned to the jury's deliberations at the guilt phase of the trial, we asked jurors about a number of specific topics they might have discussed, including some that are legally irrelevant or impermissible in determining guilt, such as the defendant's likely future dangerousness and jurors' feelings about the appropriate punishment — considerations explicitly reserved for the later punishment phase of the trial. . . .

Jurors were evidently concerned with the defendant's future dangerousness and the punishment to be imposed during their deliberation on the defendant's guilt. More than six out of ten said the jury's guilt deliberations focused on each of these topics a "great deal" or a "fair amount." One-half of the jurors said that there was a great deal of discussion about the "right punishment."

Conscious that jurors might not clearly distinguish between the guilt and punishment deliberations in response to this question, and that some topics discussed during guilt deliberations might not have actually figured in the decision-making about guilt, we asked a further question explicitly worded to focus the juror's attention exclusively on the defendant's punishment as a relevant consideration in the jury's decision about the defendant's guilt. [We asked]: In deciding guilt, did jurors talk about whether or not the defendant would, or should, get the death penalty? Here, too, a sizable number (over 30%) of jurors recall that in deciding guilt, there was explicit discussion of what the defendant's punishment would or should be.

#### *Timing of the Punishment Decision*

In addition to these questions about what the jury did as a group, CJP investigators also asked the individual jurors about their own personal thinking and decision-making with respect to the defendant's punishment prior to the sentencing phase of the trial. In particular, we asked whether they had come to a decision on punishment, what they thought the punishment should be, and how convinced they were of their decision. . . .

One-half of the jurors were undecided, but the other one-half said that they had chosen (more or less firmly) between a life or death sentence at the guilt stage of the trial. A second follow-up question, addressed only to those who, at this stage, thought that the defendant should be given a life or death sentence, asked: How strongly did you think so? [Most] of the jurors who had decided what the punishment should be before the sentencing phase of the trial were "absolutely convinced" of their punishment decision, and nearly all the rest were at least "pretty sure." In effect, it appears that three out of ten jurors had essentially made up their minds, and another two in ten were leaning one way or the other, before hearing from the judge about the standards that should guide their sentencing decisions.

### The Punishment Phase

#### Guidelines and Instructions

If statutory standards are to guide the exercise of sentencing discretion, they must, of course, be understood and applied in the course of actually making the sentencing decision. Among the various questions we asked to tap jurors' understanding of sentencing guidelines, the responses to the question regarding the substance of the statutory standards were unsettling. . . .

Contrary to the laws of their states, four out of ten capital jurors believed that they were required to impose the death penalty if they found that the crime was heinous, vile, or depraved, and three out of ten thought that the death penalty was required if they found that the defendant would be dangerous in the future. . . .

Three out of four participating jurors said that the evidence proved that the crime was heinous, vile, or depraved, and that the defendant would be dangerous in the future. In combination with the percentages of those who believed that the death penalty was required if these factors were proved, it appears that between 21% and 33% of the jurors mistakenly believed that the state's proof of heinousness required them to vote for the death penalty. In addition, between 8% and 24% of jurors wrongly believed that evidence of the defendant's dangerousness required them to vote in favor of death. . . .

#### Responsibility for the Punishment

One criticism of guided discretion capital statutes is that they tend to allay jurors' sense of responsibility for their life or death sentencing decisions by appearing to provide them with an authoritative formula that yields the "correct" or "required" punishment. . . . To see where capital jurors located responsibility for punishment, we asked them to: *Rank the following from "most" through "least" responsible for [the defendant's] punishment.*

Unmistakably, jurors placed responsibility for the defendant's punishment elsewhere. Eight out of ten jurors feel that the defendant or the law is the most responsible for the defendant's punishment. More jurors believe that the greatest responsibility lies with the defendant rather than with the law. . . .

### Conclusion

The early indications in our research . . . sketch out a picture of the exercise of capital sentencing discretion that differs from that found in current

Supreme Court precedent. [The] emerging picture is noteworthy for the questions it raises concerning the Supreme Court's presumptions about the exercise of capital sentencing discretion. . . .

[We] find that many jurors appear to make their decisions apart from, and indeed prior to, sentencing instructions on the bases of their unguided feelings or reactions to the crime. The findings also show that sentencing guidelines provide "legal cover" to many who have already made up their minds, and "legal leverage" for persuading the undecided. In either case, the guidelines appear to lessen the sense of responsibility for imposing an awful punishment. Yet, these are still early soundings of what the jurors have to tell us about how they think about the crimes, the defendants, the victims, and how they decide what the defendant's punishment should be. The yet unanswered critical questions, of course, are how standardless is this decision-making process; how widespread is such standardless decision-making; and—for the Court to answer—does it represent a constitutionally unacceptable level or risk of arbitrariness?

## NOTES

1. *Challenges to jurors' life-or-death decision.*   Is it surprising that jurors. typically do not fully understand or adhere to the instructions that are designed to guide their decisions? After comparing the modern capital sentencing statutes used in Texas and Florida (reprinted above) with the instructions used in pre-*Furman* cases in California and Ohio (discussed in *McGautha* above), it is easy to appreciate how the detailed instructions to jurors in capital cases today recast capital sentencing as a legal issue rather than a moral issue for the jury to decide. Should a death sentencing decision be recast in these terms? Whether it is a legal or a moral decision, are you confident that juries are the best sentencers in capital cases? For a dynamic discussion of the psychology surrounding capital jury decision making, see Craig Haney, Violence and the Capital Jury: Mechanisms of Moral Disengagement and the Impulse to Condemn to Death, 49 Stan. L. Rev. 1447 (1997).

Justice John Paul Stevens, in an August 2005 speech to the American Bar Association, made some pointedly critical remarks about the abilities of jurors to make appropriate decisions in capital cases: "In many of these cases the outrageously brutal facts cry out for retribution. . . . Gruesome facts pose a danger that emotion will play a larger role in the decisional process than dispassionate analysis." For the full text of Justice Stevens' address, see http://www.supremecourtus.gov/publicinfo/speeches/sp_08-06-05.html.

2. *Judicial decisions to impose death sentences.*   A few jurisdictions have given some sentencing discretion to judges in capital cases. In some states, this discretion is secondary to the discretion exercised by a capital jury; in Ohio, for example, the trial judge may decide that a defendant does not deserve to die even if the jury recommends death, but the judge may not impose a death sentence if a jury does not so recommend. See Ohio Rev. Code §2929.03. In other states (such as Florida, whose statute is reprinted above), judges can "override" a jury recommendation of either death or life.

The Supreme Court's decision in Ring v. Arizona, 536 U.S. 584 (2002), which partially overruled its prior decision in Walton v. Arizona, 497 U.S. 639 (1990), threw into question the constitutionality of capital sentencing systems in which judges exercise substantial sentencing authority. In *Ring* the Court held that the Sixth Amendment's right to trial by jury in criminal prosecutions requires a jury to determine the presence of those aggravating factors necessary for a sentence of death. Though *Ring* still allows the judge to be the final decision maker as to whether to impose a death sentence, it precludes judges from finding those facts that can form the basis for a death sentence under a state's statutory scheme.

## c.   Executive Discretion

Although the discretion exercised by a jury deciding whether to sentence a defendant to death is the most tangible and visible discretionary decision in capital cases, many other actors make discretionary judgments about the availability and imposition of a death sentence. Prosecutors possess wide (and essentially unreviewable) discretion when initially deciding whether to charge certain murders as capital crimes and whether to reduce capital charges as part of a plea agreement. In addition, nearly every state grants its governor or board of pardons, or both, the authority to commute death sentences. As you review the following materials, think about whether these sorts of discretionary decisions are likely to aggravate or ameliorate the concerns expressed by the Supreme Court in *Furman.*

> ## *Speech at Northwestern University College of Law, Illinois Governor George Ryan*
> ### January 11, 2003

Four years ago I was sworn in as the 39th Governor of Illinois. That was just four short years ago; that's when I was a firm believer in the American System of Justice and the death penalty. I believed that the ultimate penalty for the taking of a life was administrated in a just and fair manner. Today, three days before I end my term as Governor, I stand before you to explain my frustrations and deep concerns about both the administration and the penalty of death. . . .

During my time in public office I have always reserved my right to change my mind if I believed it to be in the best public interest, whether it be about taxes, abortions or the death penalty. But I must confess that the debate with myself has been the toughest concerning the death penalty. I suppose the reason the death penalty has been the toughest is because it is so final — the only public policy that determines who lives and who dies. In addition it is the only issue that attracts most of the legal minds across the country. I have received more advice on this issue than any other policy issue I have dealt with in my 35 years of public service. I have kept an open mind on both sides of the issues of commutation for life or death. . . .

The other day, I received a call from former South African President Nelson Mandela, who reminded me that the United States sets the example for justice and fairness for the rest of the world. Today the United States is not in league with most of our major allies: Europe, Canada, Mexico, most of South and Central America. These countries rejected the death penalty. We are partners in death with several third world countries. Even Russia has called a moratorium. . . .

I never intended to be an activist on this issue. I watched in surprise as freed death row inmate Anthony Porter was released from jail. A free man, he ran into the arms of Northwestern University Professor Dave Protess, who poured his heart and soul into proving Porter's innocence with his journalism students. He was 48 hours away from being wheeled into the execution chamber where the state would kill him. It would all be so antiseptic and most of us would not have even paused, except that Anthony Porter was innocent of the double murder for which he had been condemned to die.

After Mr. Porter's case there was the report by *Chicago Tribune* reporters Steve Mills and Ken Armstrong documenting the systemic failures of our capital punishment system. Half of the nearly 300 capital cases in Illinois had been reversed for a new trial or resentencing. Nearly Half! Thirty-three of the death row inmates were represented at trial by an attorney who had later been disbarred or at some point suspended from practicing law.

Of the more than 160 death row inmates, 35 were African American defendants who had been convicted or condemned to die by all-white juries. More than two-thirds of the inmates on death row were African American. Forty-six inmates were convicted on the basis of testimony from jailhouse informants. . . .

Then over the next few months, there were three more exonerated men, freed because their sentence hinged on a jailhouse informant or new DNA technology proved beyond a shadow of doubt their innocence. We then had the dubious distinction of exonerating more men than we had executed: 13 men found innocent, 12 executed. As I reported yesterday, there is not a doubt in my mind that the number of innocent men freed from our Death Row stands at 17, with the pardons of Aaron Patterson, Madison Hobley, Stanley Howard and Leroy Orange. That is an absolute embarrassment. Seventeen exonerated death row inmates is nothing short of a catastrophic failure. But the 13, now 17 men, is just the beginning of our sad arithmetic in prosecuting murder cases. During the time we have had capital punishment in Illinois, there were at least 33 other people wrongly convicted on murder charges and exonerated. Since we reinstated the death penalty there are also 93 people — 93 — where our criminal justice system imposed the most severe sanction and later rescinded the sentence or even released them from custody because they were innocent. How many more cases of wrongful conviction have to occur before we can all agree that the system is broken?

In the United States the overwhelming majority of those executed are psychotic, alcoholic, drug addicted or mentally unstable. They frequently are raised in an impoverished and abusive environment. Seldom are people with money or prestige convicted of capital offenses, even more seldom are they executed. . . .

At stake throughout the clemency process was whether some, all or none of these inmates on death row would have their sentences commuted from death to life without the possibility of parole. One of the things discussed with family members was [that] life without parole was seen as a life filled with perks and benefits. Some inmates on death row don't want a sentence of life without parole. Danny Edwards wrote me and told me not to do him any favors because he didn't want to face a prospect of a life in prison without parole. They will be confined in a cell that is about 5-feet-by-12 feet, usually double-bunked. Our prisons have no air conditioning, except at our supermax facility, where inmates are kept in their cell 23 hours a day. In summer months, temperatures in these prisons exceed one hundred degrees. It is a stark and dreary existence. They can think about their crimes. Life without parole has even, at times, been described by prosecutors as a fate worse than death. . . .

I started with this issue concerned about innocence. But once I studied, once I pondered what had become of our justice system, I came to care above all about fairness. Fairness is fundamental to the American system of justice and our way of life. The facts I have seen in reviewing each and every one of these cases raised questions not only about the innocence of people on death row, but about the fairness of the death penalty system as a whole. If the system was making so many errors in determining whether someone was guilty in the first place, how fairly and accurately was it determining which guilty defendants deserved to live and which deserved to die? What effect was race having? What effect was poverty having?

And in almost every one of the exonerated 17, we not only have breakdowns in the system with police, prosecutors and judges, we have terrible cases of shabby defense lawyers. There is just no way to sugar coat it. There are defense attorneys that did not consult with their clients, did not investigate the case and were completely unqualified to handle complex death penalty cases. They often didn't put much effort into fighting a death sentence. If your life is on the line, your lawyer ought to be fighting for you. As I have said before, there is more than enough blame to go around.

In Illinois, I have learned, we have 102 decision makers. Each of them [is] politically elected, each beholden to the demands of their community and, in some cases, to the media or especially vocal victims' families. In cases that have the attention of the media and the public, are decisions to seek the death penalty more likely to occur? What standards are these prosecutors using?

Some people have assailed my power to commute sentences. . . . But prosecutors in Illinois have the ultimate commutation power, a power that is exercised every day. They decide who will be subject to the death penalty, who will get a plea deal or even who may get a complete pass on prosecution. By what objective standards do they make these decisions? We do not know, they are not public. There were more than 1,000 murders last year in Illinois. There is no doubt that all murders are horrific and cruel. Yet, less than 2 percent of those murder defendants will receive the death penalty. . . . Moreover, if you look at the cases, as I have done — both individually and collectively — a killing with the same circumstances might get 40 years in one county and death in another county. [You are five times more likely to get a death sentence for first-degree murder in the rural area of Illinois than you are in Cook County.] I have also seen where co-defendants who are equally or even more culpable get sentenced to a term of years, while another less culpable defendant ends up on death row.

In my case-by-case review, I found three people that fell into this category: Mario Flores, Montel Johnson and William Franklin. Today I have commuted their sentences to a term of 40 years to bring their sentences into line with their co-defendants and to reflect the other extraordinary circumstances of these cases.

Supreme Court Justice Potter Stewart has said that the imposition of the death penalty on defendants in this country is as freakish and arbitrary as who gets hit by a bolt of lightning. . . . What are we to make of the studies that showed that more than 50% of Illinois jurors could not understand the confusing and obscure sentencing instructions that were being used? What effect did that problem have on the trustworthiness of death sentences? A review of the cases shows that often even the lawyers and judges are confused about the instructions—let alone the jurors sitting in judgment. Cases still come before the Supreme Court with arguments about whether the jury instructions were proper. . . .

As I prepare to leave office, I had to ask myself whether I could really live with the prospect of knowing that I had the opportunity to act, but that I failed to do so because I might be criticized. Could I take the chance that our capital punishment system might be reformed, that wrongful convictions might not occur, that enterprising journalism students might free more men from death row? . . . Our own study showed that juries were more likely to sentence to death if the victim were white than if the victim were black—three-and-a-half times more likely to be exact. . . . Is our system fair to all? Is justice blind? These are important human rights issues. . . .

In 1994, near the end of his distinguished career on the Supreme Court of the United States, Justice Harry Blackmun wrote an influential dissent in the body of law on capital punishment. Twenty years earlier he was part of the court that issued the landmark *Furman* decision. . . . But 20 years later, after affirming hundreds of death penalty decisions, Justice Blackmun came to the realization, in the twilight of his distinguished career, that the death penalty remains "fraught with arbitrariness, discrimination, caprice and mistake." He expressed frustration with a 20-year struggle to develop procedural and substantive safeguards. In a now famous dissent he wrote in 1994, "From this day forward, I no longer shall tinker with the machinery of death." . . . The Governor has the constitutional role in our state of acting in the interest of justice and fairness. Our state constitution provides broad power to the Governor to issue reprieves, pardons and commutations. Our Supreme Court has reminded inmates petitioning them that the last resort for relief is the governor.

At times the executive clemency power has perhaps been a crutch for courts to avoid making the kind of major change that I believe our system needs. Our systemic case-by-case review has found more cases of innocent men wrongfully sentenced to death row. Because our three year study has found only more questions about the fairness of the sentencing; because of the spectacular failure to reform the system; because we have seen justice delayed for countless death row inmates with potentially meritorious claims; because the Illinois death penalty system is arbitrary and capricious—and therefore immoral—I no longer shall tinker with the machinery of death. I cannot say it more eloquently than Justice Blackmun.

The legislature couldn't reform it. Lawmakers won't repeal it. But I will not stand for it. I must act. Our capital system is haunted by the demon of error, error in determining guilt, and error in determining who among the guilty deserves to die. Because of all of these reasons today I am commuting the sentences of all death row inmates. . . .

## NOTES

1. *Executive clemency.*   Although it was common early in the twentieth century for governors to pardon offenders and to commute many death sentences to life terms, most governors have not used this discretionary power extensively since the courts became actively involved in constitutional regulation and review of capital sentencing. From 1955 to 1965, more than 200 death sentences were commuted and roughly the same number of executions were carried out; from 1985 to 1995, about 20 death sentences were commuted and roughly *ten times* as many executions were carried out.

As detailed in the excerpt above, in January 2003 Governor George Ryan of Illinois followed up his 2000 decision to impose a moratorium on executions in his state with the decision, as one of his last acts in office, to empty death row by pardoning four persons and commuting the sentences of the remaining 156 to life imprisonment.

Anti–death penalty advocates hailed Governor Ryan's decision. Those opposed to his decision accused him of a cheap political ploy designed to divert attention away from his own legal problems stemming from a large-scale corruption investigation. Governor Ryan's action again brought to light cases in which factually innocent prisoners were held on death row, some for decades. See generally Dan Markel, State Be Not Proud: A Retributivist Defense of the Commutation of Death Row and the Abolition of the Death Penalty, 40 Harv. C.R.-C.L. L. Rev. 407 (2005).

Since 1976 there have been five categorical grants of clemency including the 2003 decision of Governor Ryan. The others were by Governor Toney Anaya in New Mexico (1986, all inmates); Governor Richard Celeste in Ohio (1991, 8 inmates); Government Jon Corzine in New Jersey (2007, all inmates); and Governor Pat Quinn in Illinois (2011, all inmates). Short descriptions of the grounds for clemency in death penalty cases after 1976 can be found at http://www.deathpenaltyinfo.org/clemency.

In fifteen states, the Governor has sole authority to grant clemency. In eight states, including Florida and Texas, the Governor must have the recommendation of clemency from a Board; and in 10 states, the Governor may receive a nonbinding recommendation of clemency from a Board. In the final five states, the Board determines clemency. http://www.deathpenaltyinfo.org/clemency. Clemency procedures are discussed in more detail in Chapter 11.

2. *Abolition and the innocence movement.*   As of January 2012, 140 people on death row have been exonerated since 1973. A list of the people who have been exonerated and a brief description of the case can be found at http://www.deathpenaltyinfo.org/innocence-list-those-freed-death-row. Two leading books on the innocence movement are Brandon Garrett, Convincing the Innocent: Where Criminal Prosecutions Go Wrong (2011), and Barry Scheck, Peter Neufedl, & Jim Dwyer, Actual Innocence: When Justice Goes Wrong and How to Make It Right (2003).

Is the innocence movement a sufficient strategy for death penalty opponents to achieve abolition? If the state can develop a system virtually guaranteeing that the death penalty will be imposed only on the guilty, how can one defend the abolition of the death penalty entirely? Might the innocence movement not ensure that the death penalty is reserved for the truly heinous, and thus strengthen the argument of the retentionist?

3. *Abolition and the mode of execution.*   One abolishonist strategy in anti-death penalty litigation is to attack the mode of execution. In some states appellate courts have questioned the constitutionality of procedures used. In Baze v. Rees, 553 U.S. 35 (2008), a plurality of the court held Kentucky's lethal injection protocol satisfies the Eighth Amendment, and that Kentucky was not under a constitutional obligation to adopt a more humane method of execution. Does *Baze* remove the issue of the method of execution as a factor in the debate over the wisdom of the death penalty?

4. *European involvement in capital sanctions.*   Increasingly, European countries have waged a multi-front battle against capital punishment in the United States and Japan. One prong of their strategy had been to support the litigation efforts of those who aimed to exempt juveniles and the mentally retarded from execution. With the Court's decisions in *Atkins* and *Roper*, they have successfully concluded that phase. Europe's opposition to the death penalty has caused serious problems for U.S. diplomats in conducting foreign policy. See Nora V. Demleitner, The Death Penalty in the United States: Following the European Lead?, 81 Or. L. Rev. 131 (2002). To what extent should the determination of common standards of decency depend on international developments? Should a traditionally domestic issue, such as criminal sanctions, be influenced by international bodies or concerns? Elizabeth M. Sher, Death Penalty Sentencing in Japan Under the Lay Assessor System: Avoiding the Avoidable Through Unanimity, 20 P. Rim L. & Policy J. 635, 658 (2011).

5. *The death row phenomenon.*   Many death row inmates spend a decade or more awaiting their execution. Although inmate appeals are frequently the source of this delay, a number of foreign countries have declared the so-called death row phenomenon — years spent under the restrictive conditions imposed by death row confinement — an unjust punishment in its own right. See, e.g., Soering v. United Kingdom, 11 Eur. H.R. Rep. 439 (Eur. Ct. H.R. 1989); Pratt v. Attorney General for Jamaica, Privy Council Appeal No. 10 of 1993 (1993); United States v. Burns [2001] 1 S.C.R. 283, 2001 SCC 7. Countries operating under the European human rights system as well as Canada no longer extradite individuals to the United States unless they are given explicit guarantees that the prosecution will not request a death sentence at trial. Any defendant who is successful in escaping to one of these countries effectively insulates herself from the death penalty. Should a prosecutor promise not to seek a death sentence so that the defendant can be tried in the United States? Or is it preferable to avoid entering into such agreements?

6. *Consular notification.*   Foreign nationals in the United States have the right to have their consulate notified of their arrest. Some foreign countries provide counsel free of charge to their nationals. With many foreign countries willing and able to furnish excellent capital counsel, the foreign-national defendant whose home country is not notified of the need for trial counsel is at a severe disadvantage. Because U.S. law enforcement officials frequently fail to notify the representatives of foreign governments of such arrests, a number of such countries, including Paraguay, Germany, and Mexico, have filed suit before

the International Court of Justice (ICJ) against the United States for violation of the consular convention.

In the case of the LaGrand brothers, two German nationals, the ICJ found that by not informing them of their convention rights and subsequently by not permitting review and reconsideration of their convictions and sentences, the United States violated their rights as well as Germany's rights. It also held the United States in breach for failing to take all measures to prevent Walter LaGrand's execution after the ICJ issued a stay order. The court accepted the United States' assurance that it would implement specific measures to comply with its obligations under the convention. Nevertheless, the ICJ required that should German nationals be sentenced to "severe penalties, without their rights under Article 36, paragraph 1(b), of the Convention having been respected, the United States, by means of its own choosing, shall allow the review and reconsideration of the conviction and sentence by taking account of the violation of the rights set forth in that Convention." LaGrand Case (Germany v. United States of America), 40 I.L.M. 1069 (I.C.J. 2001).

In the later *Avena* case, the ICJ again held the United States in breach of its treaty obligations and asked that the United States provide judicial review and reconsideration of the convictions and sentences of 51 Mexicans who were being held on death row. Case Concerning Avena and Other Mexican Nationals (Mexico v. U.S.) I.C.J (2004). The United States subsequently withdrew from the Optional Protocol to the Convention, which had provided the United States' consent to ICJ jurisdiction over cases arising under the Consular Convention. At the same time the president issued a memorandum to the attorney general indicating that the United States would discharge its obligations under the *Avena* decision. The cases of the 51 Mexicans on death row continue to engage state and federal court systems. In Sanchez-Llamas v. Oregon, 126 S. Ct. 2669 (2006), the Supreme Court held that a violation of the Consular Convention does not automatically require suppression of a defendant's statements and that a state may apply standard procedural default rules to that claim.

The Texas Court of Criminal Appeals, in Ex parte Medellin, 223 S.W.3d 315 (2007), aff'd, 552 U.S. 491(2008) decided not to provide the defendant with the review he sought following the *Avena* decision. The decision stated that neither the ICJ's decision nor the president's memorandum constituted binding federal law that could preempt a state statute limiting habeas relief. The decision has set the stage for a clash between state and federal powers, in particular between presidential authority and the power of the state judiciary.

In Garcia v. Texas, 131 S.Ct. 2866 (2011), the Supreme Court issued a per curiam opinion for five justices refusing to grant a stay in the case of one of the 51 Mexican nationals on death row. The per curiam opinion said:

> Petitioner Humberto Leal Garcia (Leal) is a Mexican national who has lived in the United States since before the age of two. In 1994, he kidnaped 16-year-old AdriaSauceda, raped her with a large stick, and bludgeoned her to death with a piece of asphalt. He was convicted of murder and sentenced to death by a Texas court. He now seeks a stay of execution on the ground that his conviction was obtained in violation of the Vienna Convention on Consular Relations (Vienna Convention), Apr. 24, 1963, 21 U. S. T. 77, T. I. A. S. No. 6820. He relies on *Case Concerning Avena and Other Mexican Nationals*

(*Mex.* v. *U. S.*), 2004 I. C. J. 12 (Judgment of Mar. 31), in which the International Court of Justice (ICJ) held that the United States had violated the Vienna Convention by failing to notify him of his right to consular assistance. His argument is foreclosed by *Medellín* v. *Texas*, 552 U. S. 491 (2008) (*Medellín I*), in which we held that neither the *Avena* decision nor the President's Memorandum purporting to implement that decision constituted directly enforceable federal law. 552 U. S., at 498-499.

Leal and the United States ask us to stay the execution so that Congress may consider whether to enact legislation implementing the *Avena* decision. Leal contends that the Due Process Clause prohibits Texas from executing him while such legislation is under consideration. This argument is meritless. The Due Process Clause does not prohibit a State from carrying out a lawful judgment in light of unenacted legislation that might someday authorize a collateral attack on that judgment.

# PROBLEM 3-4.   MORATORIUM

You are the state governor's chief advisor on criminal justice issues. She has asked for your opinion about whether she should declare a moratorium on the use of capital punishment in the state. She raised the question with you after hearing about the actions of Illinois Governor George Ryan and then receiving a copy of a report from the American Bar Association about the administration of capital punishment. In 1997 the ABA recommended that states not carry out the death penalty "until the jurisdiction implements policies and procedures that are consistent with . . . longstanding American Bar Association policies intended to (1) ensure that death penalty cases are administered fairly and impartially, in accordance with due process, and (2) minimize the risk that innocent persons may be executed. . . ."

The ABA pointed to inadequate defense counsel (and insufficient funding for those lawyers) as one of the central flaws in the system:

> Jurisdictions that employ the death penalty have proven unwilling to establish the kind of legal services system that is necessary to ensure that defendants charged with capital offenses receive the defense they require. Many death penalty states have no working public defender programs, relying instead upon scattershot methods for selecting and supporting defense counsel in capital cases. For example, some states simply assign lawyers at random from a general list—a scheme destined to identify attorneys who lack the necessary qualifications and, worse still, regard their assignments as a burden. Other jurisdictions employ "contract" systems, which typically channel indigent defense business to attorneys who offer the lowest bids. Other states use public defender schemes that appear on the surface to be more promising, but prove in practice to be just as ineffective.
>
> It is scarcely surprising that the results of poor lawyering are often literally fatal for capital defendants. Systematic studies reveal . . . the inexperience of lawyers appointed to represent capital clients. In [many instances, state trial courts have] assigned capital cases to young lawyers who had passed the bar only a few months earlier; [to] a lawyer who had never finished a criminal trial of any kind; and [even] allowed a third-year law student to handle most of a capital trial. . . . Even when experienced and competent counsel are available in capital cases, they often are unable to render adequate service for want of essential funding to pay the costs of investigations and expert witnesses. In

some rural counties in Texas, an appointed attorney receives no more than $800 to represent a capital defendant. Similar limits are in place in other states. In Virginia, the hourly rate for capital defense services works out to about $13. In an Alabama case, the lawyer appointed to represent a capital defendant in a widely publicized case was allowed a total of $500 to finance his work, including any investigations and expert services needed. With that budget, it is hardly surprising that the attorney conducted no investigation at all. . . .

Another systematic problem cited by the ABA was more recent: restrictions on the procedures available for capital defendants to obtain judicial review of legal and factual errors in their trials. The report noted that in 1996 Congress amended the federal habeas corpus statutes to make it "even more difficult for the federal courts to adjudicate federal claims in capital cases."

Finally, the ABA report pointed to race discrimination in the administration of capital punishment:

Numerous studies have demonstrated that defendants are more likely to be sentenced to death if their victims were white rather than black. Other studies have shown that in some jurisdictions African Americans tend to receive the death penalty more often than do white defendants. And in countless cases, the poor legal services that capital clients receive are rendered worse still by racist attitudes of defense counsel. . . .

As you formulate your advice to the governor, what sources will you consult? What sorts of arguments or evidence will be relevant to her decision? Which of the issues raised are solvable, and at what cost?

# =4=

## Sentencing Inputs: The Crime and Its Effects

Chapter 1 introduced the social purposes of punishment, Chapter 2 surveyed the groups and individuals who create sentencing rules and impose sentences, and Chapter 3 offered case studies of sentencing systems designed to control discretion in the hope of ensuring sentencing outcomes are fair and reasonably consistent system-wide. Along the way, you became familiar with the basic contours of sentencing guidelines and the capital punishment system. Building on this foundation, we now turn to the substantive components of sentencing decisions, starting in this chapter with the relevance of the crime and its effects. In Chapter 5 we consider the background and characteristics of the criminal offender. Together, these two chapters address the raw materials of the sentencing decision, what we call "sentencing inputs."

Sentencing practice always informs sentencing theory. Hence, our discussion of the crime and its effects begins with an introductory sentencing exercise. The exercise calls on you to sentence a mythical criminal offender, Rob Anon, and introduces you to the difficulties of selecting a criminal punishment, even in this seemingly simple case. Throughout the next two chapters, we return to Rob's case periodically to see whether our detailed study of sentencing systems changes your initial perspective on Rob's status.

### PROBLEM 4-1. ROB ANON

A jury found Rob Anon guilty of one count of armed bank robbery. The evidence at trial proved that Rob planned the robbery and then recruited his two co-defendants to participate. According to the testimony of co-defendant Zweite (who pled guilty to the charge pursuant to a plea agreement with the government), Rob gave each participant in the robbery a firearm and a ski mask. Rob also provided a getaway car, although the origins and current location of the car remain unknown.

According to the testimony at trial, the activities of the three defendants inside the bank were as follows: Rob disabled the surveillance cameras and alarms; co-defendant Tercero kept his firearm pointed at the teller while Zweite vaulted the counter and collected more than $200,000 in cash. As the threesome hurried out of the bank, Tercero pushed to the ground an elderly man who walked into the bank during the robbery. The man broke his hip when he fell. In dividing the loot, Rob gave Zweite and Tercero one-fourth of the proceeds each, keeping half for himself.

The government's evidence at Rob's trial included surveillance photos, eyewitness accounts, physical evidence, and testimony by Zweite and Tercero. From the moment of his indictment and throughout his prosecution, Rob denied responsibility for the robbery and claimed he was "set up."

Rob is 22 years old and has produced a spotty employment record since dropping out of high school at age 16. Rob was last employed in a series of construction projects with a local landscaping company; he previously worked for a shoe store as a salesman on a part-time basis. Reared by a single mother in an economically depressed urban area and the second youngest of five children, Rob seems to have few friends and mostly keeps to himself. Rob's mother recalls that Rob's siblings taunted and teased him because of his small stature. She believes that Rob became addicted to cocaine in the past year.

Rob's criminal record includes two prior offenses. Six years ago, a juvenile court convicted Rob for shoplifting and sentenced him to 100 hours of community service. Two years ago, Rob was convicted of receipt of stolen goods and sentenced to three years' probation. Rob was still serving that term of probation at the time of the bank robbery. Armed bank robbery carries a maximum penalty of 25 years in prison or a fine of $250,000 or both. Compare http://www.ussc.gov/training/ws_ex_rob.pdf.

1. Assume you are the sentencing judge for Rob in a jurisdiction that places no limits on your discretion to choose a sentence ranging anywhere from probation to the statutory maximum. What sentence would you impose? If you feel you need more information before choosing a sentence, what additional information would you seek?
2. If the robbers had taken less money (say, only $500), would your sentencing decision change?
3. If the elderly man had not been injured, would your sentencing decision change?
4. If you knew that Zweite received a sentence of 5 years' probation as a result of a plea agreement, would your sentencing decision change?

## A.   WHICH CRIME?

It is often said that the punishment must fit the crime. This is a true statement, but radically incomplete. Sentencing judges consider more than the crime; they also consider other wrongdoing by the offender, some of it proven during the criminal trial and some of it not mentioned until the presentence investigation or the sentencing hearing. Some conduct constitutes a separate crime, while some of the wrongdoing is not criminal at all. What guidance does the law give to the sentencing judge, who must sort out the defendant's various forms of wrongdoing?

## 1. Real Offense Versus Conviction Offense

It might seem obvious (to lawyers, at any rate) that defendants can be punished only for the crimes of which they have been *convicted*. Obvious, perhaps, but that is not the law in most jurisdictions. To varying degrees, sentencing laws allow judges to impose punishments based on the "real offense" and not just for the offense of conviction.

### Uses for Uncharged Conduct

How can defendants be punished for acts that are not the basis for a conviction? Under an indeterminate sentencing system, the sentencing judge can consider any evidence of the offender's wrongdoing, regardless of whether the conduct formed the basis of the criminal charges. The statutory floor and ceiling for punishing the crime of conviction leave the judge with plenty of latitude to set a punishment, even if it is based in part on uncharged conduct. It is difficult to define offenses in sufficient detail to capture all the offense-related facts that intuition suggests should affect the sentence. According to the Supreme Court in Williams v. New York, 337 U.S. 241 (1949) (reprinted in Chapter 2), the importance of "individualizing punishments" supports the "age-old practice of seeking information from out-of-court sources" and means that sentencing judges should "not be denied an opportunity to obtain pertinent information by a requirement of rigid adherence to restrictive rules of evidence properly applicable to the trial."

Even structured sentencing systems tend to allow a *range* of presumptive sentences, and when choosing a sentence within that range, a judge may account for circumstances that the elements of the crime cannot cover. Structured systems also usually allow judges to depart up or down from the range of preferred sentences based on various facts and may call for adjustments in the recommended sentencing range based on specified details of the crime such as the use of a weapon or the amount of loss or harm inflicted. In death penalty cases, facts about the "real offense" can determine life or death, as capital statutes make murderers eligible for the death penalty only if the killing involved specific "aggravating circumstances."

### Types of Uncharged Conduct

Judges receive information about conduct beyond the offense itself from several sources: in plea agreements or during trial, in presentence investigation reports, and from prosecutors during the sentencing hearing. Even if a prosecutor ignores or is unaware of some wrongdoing, a probation officer or other presentence investigator may discover this conduct and the judge may still take it into account.

The defendant's uncharged conduct might be an *element* of an offense other than the one charged. For instance, the defendant may have used a gun during the robbery, even though the charge was robbery and not armed robbery. Other facts about the offense, such as the defendant's role in a multi-party offense, may receive no mention in the statutory framework. The extra information could involve criminal conduct that is *conceptually connected* to the charged crime, such as uncharged criminal conduct that happened during the same time period as the charged crime, or uncharged conduct that was part of the same overarching criminal scheme. Finally, the court might rely on the defendant's past *noncriminal* conduct that is nevertheless blameworthy.

When a judge looks at the defendant's behavior beyond the facts necessary to prove the offense of conviction, the judge is said to be considering (to use the vernacular of the federal sentencing guidelines) "relevant conduct." Under indeterminate sentencing, it has always been possible for a judge to consider all this information, though judges could reject some of it as irrelevant or unreliable. Structured sentencing brought the issue of relevant conduct to a more formal and visible level. Legislatures, sentencing commissions, and judges must now decide explicitly which additional facts a sentencing judge may or may not consider and how much impact the uncharged relevant conduct should have. The sentencing laws that allow the judge to consider uncharged conduct are sometimes called "real offense" systems (as opposed to "charge offense" systems) because the judge sentences based on the "real" criminal behavior, independent of the prosecutor's charging decisions.

## Practical Impact of Limiting Use of Uncharged Conduct

The key fact to remember about relevant conduct is the difference in methods of proof at trial and at sentencing. At trial, the prosecution must prove all elements of the crime to a jury, beyond a reasonable doubt. At a noncapital sentencing hearing, the prosecution proves any additional relevant facts to the sentencing judge typically by a preponderance of the evidence. Thus, any decision to restrict the judge's consideration of relevant conduct for sentencing also makes it harder for the prosecutor to use facts proven by a preponderance of evidence at the sentencing hearing. At the same time, rules that limit the use of uncharged conduct make the charges that the prosecutor selects all the more important; such rules make it more difficult for the judge to "correct" any perceived problems with the prosecutor's selection of charges. As you consider the material below sketching various approaches to the problem of uncharged conduct, keep in mind the effects of the rules on prosecutors, in a world where the law places few limits on the prosecutor's choice among potential criminal charges.

## ‖ *U.S. Sentencing Guidelines Manual* ‖

### §1B1.3(a)   Relevant Conduct (Factors that Determine the Guideline Range)

[The seriousness of the offense] shall be determined on the basis of the following:

(1) (A) all acts and omissions committed, aided, abetted, counseled, commanded, induced, procured, or willfully caused by the defendant; and

(B) in the case of a jointly undertaken criminal activity (a criminal plan ... undertaken by the defendant in concert with others, whether or not charged as a conspiracy), all reasonably foreseeable acts and omissions of others in furtherance of the jointly undertaken criminal activity,

that occurred during the commission of the offense of conviction, in preparation for that offense, or in the course of attempting to avoid detection or responsibility for that offense. . . .

(3) all harm that resulted from the acts and omissions specified in [subsection (a)(1)], and all harm that was the object of such acts and omissions. . . .

## United States v. Vernon Watts
### 519 U.S. 148 (1997)

PER CURIAM

[The] Court of Appeals for the Ninth Circuit held that sentencing courts could not consider conduct of the defendants underlying charges of which they had been acquitted. Every other Court of Appeals has held that a sentencing court may do so, if the Government establishes that conduct by a preponderance of the evidence. [Because the Ninth Circuit's holding conflicts with] the clear implications of 18 U.S.C. §3661, the Sentencing Guidelines, and this Court's decisions, particularly Witte v. United States, 515 U.S. 389 (1995), we grant the petition and reverse.

[Police] discovered cocaine base in a kitchen cabinet and two loaded guns and ammunition hidden in a bedroom closet of Watts' house. A jury convicted Watts of possessing cocaine base with intent to distribute, in violation of 21 U.S.C. §841(a)(1), but acquitted him of using a firearm in relation to a drug offense, in violation of 18 U.S.C. §924(c). Despite Watts' acquittal on the firearms count, the District Court found by a preponderance of the evidence that Watts had possessed the guns in connection with the drug offense. In calculating Watts' sentence, the court therefore added two points to his base offense level under [the federal sentencing guidelines. The court of appeals held that a sentencing judge may not, under any standard of proof, rely on facts of which the defendant was acquitted].

We begin our analysis with 18 U.S.C. §3661, which codifies the longstanding principle that sentencing courts have broad discretion to consider various kinds of information. The statute states: "No limitation shall be placed on the information concerning the background, character, and conduct of a person convicted of an offense which a court of the United States may receive and consider for the purpose of imposing an appropriate sentence."

We reiterated this principle in Williams v. New York, 337 U.S. 241 (1949), in which a defendant convicted of murder and sentenced to death challenged the sentencing court's reliance on information that the defendant had been involved in 30 burglaries of which he had not been convicted. We contrasted the different limitations on presentation of evidence at trial and at sentencing: "Highly relevant — if not essential — to [the judge's] selection of an appropriate sentence is the possession of the fullest information possible concerning the defendant's life and characteristics." Neither the broad language of §3661 nor our holding in *Williams* suggests any basis for the courts to invent a blanket prohibition against considering certain types of evidence at sentencing. Indeed, under the pre-Guidelines sentencing regime, it was well established that a sentencing judge may take into account facts introduced at trial relating to other charges, even ones of which the defendant has been acquitted.

The Guidelines did not alter this aspect of the sentencing court's discretion. Very roughly speaking, relevant conduct corresponds to those actions and circumstances that courts typically took into account when sentencing prior to the Guidelines' enactment. Section 1B1.4 of the Guidelines reflects the policy set forth in 18 U.S.C. §3661: "In determining the sentence to impose within the guideline range, or whether a departure from the guidelines is warranted, the court may consider, without limitation, any information concerning the background, character and conduct of the defendant, unless otherwise prohibited by law."

Section 1B1.3, in turn, describes in sweeping language the conduct that a sentencing court may consider in determining the applicable guideline range. The commentary to that section states: "Conduct that is not formally charged or is not an element of the offense of conviction may enter into the determination of the applicable guideline sentencing range." With respect to certain offenses, . . . USSG §1B1.3(a)(2) requires the sentencing court to consider "all acts and omissions . . . that were part of the same course of conduct or common scheme or plan as the offense of conviction." Application Note 3 . . . gives the following example: "Where the defendant engaged in three drug sales of 10, 15, and 20 grams of cocaine, as part of the same course of conduct or common scheme or plan, subsection (a)(2) provides that the total quantity of cocaine involved (45 grams) is to be used to determine the offense level even if the defendant is convicted of a single count charging only one of the sales." Accordingly, the Guidelines conclude that "relying on the entire range of conduct, regardless of the number of counts that are alleged *or on which a conviction is obtained*, appears to be the most reasonable approach to writing workable guidelines for these offenses."

Although the dissent concedes that a district court may properly consider "evidence adduced in a trial that resulted in an acquittal" when choosing a particular sentence within a guideline range, it argues that the court must close its eyes to acquitted conduct at earlier stages of the sentencing process because the "broadly inclusive language of §3661" is incorporated only into §1B1.4 of the Guidelines. This argument ignores §1B1.3 which, as we have noted, directs sentencing courts to consider all other related conduct, whether or not it resulted in a conviction. The dissent also contends that because Congress instructed the Sentencing Commission, in 28 U.S.C. §994(l), to ensure that the Guidelines provide incremental punishment for a defendant who is convicted of multiple offenses, it could not have meant for the Guidelines to increase a sentence based on offenses of which a defendant has been acquitted. The statute is not, however, cast in restrictive or exclusive terms. Far from limiting a sentencing court's power to consider uncharged or acquitted conduct, §994(l) simply ensures that, at a minimum, the Guidelines provide additional penalties when defendants are convicted of multiple offenses. . . . In short, we are convinced that a sentencing court may consider conduct of which a defendant has been acquitted.

As we explained in Witte v. United States, 515 U.S. 389 (1995), . . . sentencing enhancements do not punish a defendant for crimes of which he was not convicted, but rather increase his sentence because of the manner in which he committed the crime of conviction. In *Witte*, we held that a sentencing court could, consistent with the Double Jeopardy Clause, consider uncharged cocaine importation in imposing a sentence on marijuana charges that was within the statutory range, without precluding the defendant's subsequent prosecution for the cocaine offense. We concluded that "consideration of information about the defendant's character and conduct at sentencing does not result in 'punishment' for any offense other than the one of which the defendant was convicted." Rather, the defendant is "punished only for the fact that the *present* offense was carried out in a manner that warrants increased punishment."

The Court of Appeals failed to appreciate the significance of the different standards of proof that govern at trial and sentencing. [Acquittal] on criminal charges does not prove that the defendant is innocent; it merely proves the existence of a reasonable doubt as to his guilt. [It] is impossible to know exactly why a jury found a defendant not guilty on a certain charge. Thus, contrary to the Court of Appeals' assertion . . . , the jury cannot be said to have "necessarily rejected" any facts when it returns a general verdict of not guilty.

For these reasons, an acquittal in a criminal case does not preclude the Government from relitigating an issue when it is presented in a subsequent action governed by a lower standard of proof. The Guidelines state that it is "appropriate" that facts relevant to sentencing be proved by a preponderance of the evidence, USSG §6A1.3 commentary, and we have held that application of the preponderance standard at sentencing generally satisfies due process. McMillan v. Pennsylvania, 477 U.S. 79, 91-92 (1986). . . . We therefore hold that a jury's verdict of acquittal does not prevent the sentencing court from considering conduct underlying the acquitted charge, so long as that conduct has been proved by a preponderance of the evidence.

[In this case], the jury acquitted the defendant of using or carrying a firearm during or in relation to the drug offense. That verdict does not preclude a finding by a preponderance of the evidence that the defendant did, in fact, use or carry such a weapon, much less that he simply *possessed* the weapon in connection with a drug offense.

STEVENS J., dissenting.

The Sentencing Reform Act of 1984 revolutionized the manner in which district courts sentence persons convicted of federal crimes. . . . Strict mandatory rules have dramatically confined the exercise of judgment based on a totality of the circumstances. . . .

In 1970, during the era of individualized sentencing, Congress enacted the statute now codified as 18 U.S.C. §3661 to make it clear that otherwise inadmissible evidence could be considered by judges in the exercise of their sentencing discretion. The statute, however, did not tell the judge how to weigh the significance of any of that evidence. The judge was free to rely on any information that might shed light on a decision to grant probation, to impose the statutory maximum, or to determine the precise sentence within those extremes. Wisdom and experience enabled the judge to give appropriate weight to uncorroborated hearsay or to evidence of criminal conduct that had not resulted in a conviction. . . . Like a jury in a capital case, the judge could exercise discretion to dispense mercy on the basis of factors too intangible to write into a statute.

Although the Sentencing Reform Act of 1984 has cabined the discretion of sentencing judges, the 1970 statute remains on the books. As was true when it was enacted, §3661 does not speak to questions concerning the relevance or the weight of any item of evidence. That statute is not offended by provisions in the Guidelines that proscribe reliance on evidence of economic hardship, drug or alcohol dependence, or lack of guidance as a youth, in making certain sentencing decisions. Conversely, that statute does not command that any particular weight—or indeed that any weight at all—be given to evidence that a defendant may have committed an offense that the prosecutor failed to prove beyond a reasonable doubt. . . .

A closer examination of the interaction among §3661, the other provisions of the Sentencing Reform Act, and the Guidelines demonstrates that the role played by §3661 is of a narrower scope than the Court's opinion suggests. The Sentencing Reform Act was enacted primarily to address Congress' concern that similar offenders convicted of similar offenses were receiving an unjustifiably wide range of sentences. . . . The [statute requires] that for any sentence of imprisonment in the Guidelines, "the maximum of the range established for such a term shall not exceed the minimum of that range by more than the greater of 25 percent or 6 months," 28 U.S.C. §994(b)(2). The determination of which of these narrow ranges a particular sentence should fall into is made by operation of mandatory rules, but within the particular range, the judge retains broad discretion to set a particular sentence.

By their own terms, the Guidelines incorporate the broadly inclusive language of §3661 only into those portions of the sentencing decision in which the judge retains discretion. [The] Guidelines Manual §1B1.4 provides: "In determining the sentence to impose within the guideline range, or whether a departure from the guidelines is warranted, the court may consider, without limitation, any information concerning the background, character and conduct of the defendant, unless otherwise prohibited by law. See 18 U.S.C. §3661."

Thus, as in the pre-Guidelines sentencing regime, it is in the area in which the judge exercises discretion that §3661 authorizes unlimited access to information concerning the background, character, and conduct of the defendant. When the judge is exercising such discretion, I agree that he may consider otherwise inadmissible evidence, including evidence adduced in a trial that resulted in an acquittal. But that practice, enshrined in §3661 and USSG §1B1.4, sheds little, if any, light on the appropriateness of the District Courts' application of USSG §1B1.3, which defines relevant conduct for the purposes of determining the Guidelines range within which a sentence can be imposed. . . .

In 28 U.S.C. §994(l) Congress specifically directed the Commission to ensure that the Guidelines included incremental sentences for multiple offenses. That subsection provides: "The Commission shall insure that the Guidelines promulgated [reflect] the appropriateness of imposing an incremental penalty for each offense in a case in which a defendant is convicted of (A) multiple offenses committed in the same course of conduct . . . and (B) multiple offenses committed at different times. . . ." It is difficult to square this explicit statutory command to impose incremental punishment for each of the "multiple offenses" of which a defendant "is convicted" with the conclusion that Congress intended incremental punishment for each offense of which the defendant has been acquitted. . . .

In my opinion the statute should be construed in the light of the traditional requirement that criminal charges must be sustained by proof beyond a reasonable doubt. That requirement has always applied to charges involving multiple offenses as well as a single offense. Whether an allegation of criminal conduct is the sole basis for punishment or merely one of several bases for punishment, we should presume that Congress intended the new sentencing Guidelines that it authorized in 1984 to adhere to longstanding procedural requirements enshrined in our constitutional jurisprudence. The notion that a charge that cannot be sustained by proof beyond a reasonable doubt may give rise to the same punishment as if it had been so proved is repugnant to that jurisprudence. I respectfully dissent.

## *Charles Frederick Barr v. State*
### 674 So. 2d 628 (Fla. 1996)

HARDING, J.

. . . Charles Frederick Barr stole a car at gunpoint. Thereafter, when a police officer spotted the stolen car and attempted to pull the car over, Barr fled. A high speed chase followed in heavy traffic, nearly causing several accidents. Barr was charged with armed robbery and possession of a firearm by a convicted felon.

A jury convicted Barr of armed robbery. He was sentenced to twenty-five years in prison, which was an upward departure from Barr's recommended guideline sentence of seven to nine years, with a permitted range of five and one-half to twelve years. The trial court entered a written departure order, reasoning that Barr displayed a flagrant disregard for the safety of others by recklessly driving during the chase with the police and endangering the lives of numerous innocent citizens. . . .

Barr argues that Florida Rule of Criminal Procedure 3.701(d)(11) . . . prohibits upward departure sentences when the conduct can be separately charged as another crime. Barr further argues that a contrary holding would eliminate a defendant's constitutional right to a trial as it would permit sentencing for a crime for which the defendant has not been convicted. Thus, he contends, a defendant must be charged and convicted for each instance of criminal conduct.

The State argues, however, that Florida Statutes §921.0016, which includes endangering the lives of many persons as a valid reason for upward departure sentences, controls the instant case instead of Rule 3.701(d)(11). Section 921.0016 addresses recommended sentences and departure sentences. [The statute lists a number of aggravating circumstances that reasonably justify departure from the sentencing guidelines, such as the creation of a "substantial risk of death or great bodily harm to many persons."]

We find that §921.0016 is not applicable to the instant case as it only applies to offenses committed on or after January 1, 1994. Barr was arrested and charged on November 24, 1993. Instead, we look to the language of Rule 3.701(d)(11) to determine whether departure was proper in this case. Rule 3.701(d)(11) provides that "[r]easons for deviating from the guidelines shall not include factors relating to . . . the instant offenses for which convictions have not been obtained."

As this Court explained in State v. Tyner, 506 So. 2d 405 (Fla. 1987), the language of Rule 3.701(d)(11) is "plain" and specifically provides that judges "may consider only that conduct of the defendant relating to an element of the offense for which he has been convicted." *Tyner* involved a defendant originally charged with two counts of first-degree murder and one count of armed burglary. After the murder counts were dismissed, the defendant was convicted of armed burglary. The defendant's departure sentence was invalidated because it was based upon the murders for which Tyner had not yet been found guilty. We concluded that "[to] hold otherwise would effectively circumvent the basic requirement of obtaining a conviction before meting out punishment."

We adhered to this position in State v. Varner, 616 So. 2d 988 (Fla. 1993), and specifically held that "departure may not be based on conduct that could have, but has not yet, resulted in criminal conviction." Varner was convicted of shooting into a building, shooting into a vehicle, and aggravated assault. Prior to his trial, Varner allegedly threatened a witness and the trial court entered a departure sentence based in part upon that threat. On appeal, the district court found this to be an invalid reason for departure. In our review of the case, we approved the district court's decision and explained that "[if] the State wishes to punish such collateral misconduct, the proper method is to separately charge and convict." . . .

Relying upon the reasoning in . . . *Tyner* and *Varner*, a departure sentence based on flagrant disregard for the safety of others is not valid where the conduct at issue could be separately charged and convicted. See, e.g., Felts v. State, 537 So. 2d 995 (Fla. App. 1988) (finding that high speed chase and resulting fatal accident were not valid basis for departure because they involved circumstances surrounding the offense for which convictions were not obtained). However, where the conduct evincing such disregard involves a situation where the conduct could not be separately charged as another crime it can be a valid reason for departure. See, e.g., *Felts* (finding that gun battle with Georgia police officers which posed unnecessary risk of harm was valid basis for departure where the subsequent Georgia convictions for aggravated assault could not be factored into scoresheet); Burgess v. State, 524 So. 2d 1132 (Fla. App. 1988) (upholding departure based on flagrant disregard for safety of others where defendant shot two victims who were standing in an alley while three bystanders stood nearby).

In the instant case, the auto chase that ensued after the officer attempted to stop Barr constituted criminal conduct. Barr could have been charged either with fleeing or attempting to elude a law enforcement officer pursuant to Florida Statutes §316.1935(1), or with reckless driving pursuant to Florida Statutes §316.192(1). Thus, this criminal conduct for which Barr was neither charged nor convicted cannot be a valid reason for a departure sentence. Moreover, while it is not determinative of our conclusion here, we note that Barr's departure sentence far exceeds any sentence that could have been imposed if he had been convicted of the uncharged offenses of eluding a police officer or reckless driving. [At the time of Barr's arrest, fleeing or attempting to elude an officer was punishable by imprisonment for a period not to exceed one year. Reckless driving is punishable for up to 90 days' imprisonment for a first offense and up to six months' imprisonment for a second offense.] Accordingly, we quash the decision below and remand for imposition of an appropriate guideline sentence. . . . It is so ordered.

## NOTES

1. *Relevant conduct in state sentencing: majority position.* Sentencing judges in indeterminate sentencing systems have the power (but not the obligation) to consider any conduct of the defendant, whether charged or uncharged. This conduct might influence the judge's choice of a maximum or minimum sentence from within the broad statutory range. See State v. O'Donnell, 495 A.2d 798, 803 (Me. 1985) ("we find nothing objectionable in treating trial evidence of a defendant's uncharged conduct regarding other victims as relevant information for sentencing purposes on the ground that it indicates a continuing course of conduct over a substantial period of time"); Anderson v. People, 337 P.2d 10 (Colo. 1959) (conviction for forgery; evidence at sentencing of forgeries submitted to six additional victims); see also Williams v. New York, 337 U.S. 961 (1949) (death sentence imposed by judge based on presentence report suggesting defendant had been involved in "30 other burglaries" in area of murder).

States with more structured sentencing systems place more restrictions on the use of the defendant's uncharged conduct. Formally, the structured state systems adopt charge offense rather than real offense sentencing. The charged offense determines a fairly small range of options available to the judge in the normal case. But real and charge offense concepts define the ends of a spectrum, and all systems allow some amount of real offense conduct to affect the sentencing determination. At a minimum, the uncharged conduct is available to influence the judge's selection of a sentence *within* the narrow range that the guidelines designate for typical cases. Some states go further and allow judges to use uncharged conduct as a basis for a departure from the designated normal range of sentences. Other structured sentencing states (such as Florida) prevent the judge from using some types of uncharged conduct to depart from the guideline sentence. Commentary to the Minnesota sentencing guidelines states that "departures from the guidelines should not be permitted for elements of alleged offender behavior not within the definition of the offense of conviction." Minn. Stat. Ann. §244 cmt. II.D.103. The ABA Standards for Criminal Justice, Sentencing 18-3.6 (3d ed. 1994), also opts for an offense-of-conviction model.

2. *Relevant conduct in federal sentencing.* In contrast to the states, the federal guidelines create a modified real offense system. In a 1995 self-study report, the U.S. Sentencing Commission described the trade-offs at stake in framing a relevant conduct provision:

> If uncharged misconduct is considered, punishment is based on facts proven outside procedural protections constitutionally defined for proving criminal charges, introducing an argument of unfairness. . . . The scope of conduct considered at sentencing will also affect, at least to some extent, the complexity of a sentencing system. The scope can be as limited as the conduct defined by the elements of the offense or as broad as any wrongdoing ever committed by the

defendant or the defendant's partners in crime. All things being equal, a large scope of considered conduct will require more fact-finding than a more limited scope. . . . Besides fairness and complexity, the scope of conduct considered at sentencing may have serious implications for the balance between prosecutorial and judicial power in sentencing. For example, if the scope of considered conduct is confined to the offense of conviction, many argue that the sentencing system will provide relatively more power to prosecutors to control sentences. . . . Finding the right balance among fairness, complexity, and the role of the prosecutor has been a struggle for sentencing commissions generally. . . .

Discussion Paper, Relevant Conduct and Real Offense Sentencing (1995) (available at http://www.ussc.gov/simple/relevant.htm). The federal system uses the offense of conviction as a starting point for guideline calculations but then requires many adjustments (and permits a few discretionary adjustments) to the offense level based on other relevant conduct.

The commission explained its support for real-offense factors on several grounds. First, such a system mirrored prior practices in the indeterminate system. It also gave judges a means to refine and rationalize the chaotic federal criminal code. Finally, the real-offense features of the system gave judges a way to check the prosecutor's power to dictate a sentence based on the selection of charges. When the rules allow the trial judge to look behind the charged offense to select a sentence based on the real-offense conduct, the judge serves as a counterweight to the prosecutor. See Julie R. O'sullivan, In Defense of the U.S. Sentencing Guidelines' Modified Real-Offense System, 91 Nw. U. L. Rev. 1342 (1997).

The use of relevant conduct to enhance sentences in the federal system has come under sharp attack from scholars. See Kate Stith & Jose A. Cabranes, Fear of Judging: Sentencing Guidelines in the Federal Courts 66-77 (1998); Elizabeth Lear, Is Conviction Irrelevant?, 40 UCLA L. Rev. 1179 (1993); David Yellen, Illusion, Illogic and Injustice: Real-Offense Sentencing and the Federal Sentencing Guidelines, 78 Minn. L. Rev. 403 (1993). Critics have attacked the uses of uncharged or dismissed conduct as bad policy because of the uncertain proof of the uncharged conduct during the sentencing hearing. They also point out the difficulty of remaining consistent from case to case in deciding how much uncharged conduct is relevant. They also have raised constitutional questions about whether reliance on such information violates due process (by punishing a person for conduct that is not proven beyond a reasonable doubt) or undermines the investigative and charging functions of the grand jury.

3. *Acquitted conduct versus uncharged conduct.*    Although indeterminate sentencing systems typically allow judges to consider prior misconduct when setting a sentence, many states make an exception for acquitted conduct—conduct that formed the basis for a charge resulting in an acquittal at trial. Judges in many states have developed common law rules preventing the use of acquitted conduct at sentencing. See State v. Cobb, 732 A.2d 425 (N.H. 1999); Bishop v. State, 486 S.E.2d 887 (Ga. 1997); Anderson v. State, 448 N.E.2d 1180 (Ind. 1983). On the other hand, a roughly equal number of states approve the use of acquitted conduct. State v. Huey, 505 A.2d 1242 (Conn. 1986); State v. Woodlief, 90 S.E. 137 (N.C. 1916); State v. Leiter, 646 N.W.2d 341 (Wis. 2002). Why do so many states limit the use of acquitted conduct but permit sentencing judges to consider prior convictions and prior uncharged conduct more generally?

The Supreme Court in *Watts* confirmed that neither the Constitution nor the federal sentencing statutes or guidelines bar a judge from using acquitted conduct. See also Edwards v. United States, 523 U.S. 511 (1998) (sentencing judge can determine that defendants were trafficking in both crack and powder, even if jury believed defendants were trafficking only in powder). But the Court did not resolve the policy issue of whether the guidelines *should* limit the use of acquitted conduct. Justices Breyer and Scalia, in separate opinions in *Watts* not reprinted above, disagreed about whether 18 U.S.C. §3661 blocks the U.S. Sentencing Commission from creating such a rule. The statute says that "no limitation shall be placed on the information concerning the background, character, and conduct of a person convicted" that the sentencing judge may "receive and consider." Can the U.S. Sentencing Commission limit the use of acquitted conduct, consistent with this statute?

Just before the Court decided *Watts,* the U.S. Sentencing Commission did in fact consider several options for limiting the use of acquitted conduct. One option would have excluded "the use of acquitted conduct as a basis for determining the guideline range" but would have allowed upward departures based on acquitted conduct. Another option would have allowed acquitted conduct only if it was proved at sentencing by clear and convincing evidence (rather than the usual preponderance standard). A third option would have allowed judges to use acquitted conduct in setting the guideline range but also would have authorized downward departures from the range to avoid fundamental unfairness. 62 Fed. Reg. 151, 161 (Jan. 2, 1997). In the end, the commission did not adopt any of these options. Why do you suppose the commission kept the status quo? Are sentencing commissions better situated than judges to create limits on the use of acquitted conduct?

As discussed fully in Chapter 6, not long after the *Watts* decision, the Supreme Court started to give new attention to the jury's role in sentencing determinations through a revised interpretation of the Sixth Amendment in the *Apprendi-Blakely-Booker* line of cases. Many defendants have argued to lower courts that the Supreme Court's recent Sixth Amendment rulings essentially abrogate *Watts.* The federal circuit courts have so far generally rejected this claim and have consistently ruled that *Watts* remains good law. See, e.g., United States v. Gobbi, 471 F.3d 302 (1st Cir. 2006); United States v. Farias, 469 F.3d 393 (5th Cir. 2006); United States v. White, 551 F.3d 381 (6th Cir. 2008); United States v. Mercado, 474 F.3d 654 (9th Cir. 2007); United States v. Dorcely, 454 F.3d 366, 371 (D.C. Cir. 2006). Some district courts have, however, relied on the Supreme Court's new Sixth Amendment jurisprudence to resist consideration of acquitted conduct at sentencing. See United States v. Wendelsdorf, 423 F. Supp. 2d 927, 937-938 (N.D. Iowa 2006) (rejecting as "an abomination" the government's proposed sentence increase based on acquitted conduct "for two, distinct and separate, criminal acts from the offense of conviction"); United States v. Pimental, 367 F. Supp. 2d 143 (D. Mass. 2005) ("It makes absolutely no sense to conclude that the Sixth Amendment is violated whenever facts essential to sentencing have been determined by a judge rather than a jury, and also conclude that the fruits of the jury's efforts can be ignored with impunity by the judge in sentencing.").

4. *Criminal elements versus noncriminal wrongdoing.*  As *Barr* shows, some states prevent sentencing judges from considering the defendant's wrongdoing

if that conduct could form the basis for additional criminal charges or more serious criminal charges. Other conduct, while blameworthy, does not affect the charging options available to the prosecutor. For example, under the federal criminal code, a mail fraud that nets $10,000 is eligible for the same punishment as a mail fraud that nets $100,000. Should it matter to a sentencing judge (or to a sentencing commission creating sentencing guidelines) whether the conduct in question is an element of some crime for which the defendant was not charged? Consider this approach to the problem in Kan. Stat. §21-4716(b)(3): "If a factual aspect of a crime is a statutory element of the crime . . . that aspect of the current crime of conviction may be used as an aggravating or mitigating factor only if [it] is significantly different from the usual criminal conduct captured by the aspect of the crime."

Review again the provisions of Fla. R. Crim. Proc. 3.701(d)(11) and Fla. Stat. §921.0016, discussed in the *Barr* case. Why did Florida lawmakers generally prohibit sentencing judges from increasing the sentence above the normal guideline range based on "factors relating to . . . the instant offenses for which convictions have not been obtained"? Did the Florida legislature meaningfully change the system when it passed §921.0016(3)(i), which authorizes a departure to a more serious sentence when the offense of conviction "created a substantial risk of death or great bodily harm to many persons"? Should it matter to a sentencing judge whether the defendant's relevant (but uncharged) conduct is recent? What should Florida judges do in cases involving uncharged criminal conduct that is not part of the same transaction or series of events as the crime of conviction?

5. *Conduct after charging.*   Sometimes the defendant's relevant conduct occurs after the government files charges, perhaps during or after the trial. For instance, the law in about 30 states authorizes the sentencing judge to select a higher sentence from within the authorized range if the judge believes the defendant committed perjury at trial. See People v. Redmond, 633 P.2d 976 (Cal. 1981); see also People v. Stewart, 473 N.E.2d 840 (Ill. 1984) (allowing consideration of conduct in jail awaiting trial); Alabama v. Smith, 490 U.S. 794 (1989) (allowing judge who imposes sentence after guilty plea to impose higher sentence on same defendant after appeal and retrial based on information about crime and postconviction conduct). In the federal system, U.S. Sentencing Guidelines Manual §3C1.1 increases the offense level when a defendant obstructs the administration of justice during the prosecution of the offense; this rule can be applied whenever a court finds that the defendant committed perjury at trial. The Supreme Court in United States v. Dunnigan, 507 U.S. 87 (1993), upheld the constitutionality of this provision against a claim that it undermines a defendant's right to testify on his own behalf. But compare Mitchell v. United States, 526 U.S. 314 (1999) (Fifth Amendment privilege against self-incrimination bars judge from drawing inferences about details of crime from defendant's silence at sentencing).

6. *Double jeopardy for enhancing sentences based on prior crimes.*   When criminal conduct gives a sentencing judge the basis for increasing a sentence against a defendant charged with some separate crime, would a later sentence for the original crime constitute multiple punishment for double jeopardy purposes?

In Witte v. United States, 515 U.S. 389 (1995), the defendant raised such a claim. Witte was involved in two illegal drug transactions, one in 1990 and the other in 1991. The judge sentencing Witte for the 1991 sale increased the sentence based on the amount of drugs involved in the 1990 sale, because the judge considered the two sales to be part of a single continuing conspiracy. Later, a grand jury indicted Witte for the 1990 sale, and Witte raised a double jeopardy objection because the judge in the earlier proceeding had already punished him for that conduct. The Supreme Court rejected the challenge, noting that sentencing courts have traditionally "considered a defendant's past criminal behavior, even if no conviction resulted from that behavior." The opinion also concluded that the same practice is acceptable under the federal sentencing guidelines: "Regardless of whether particular conduct is taken into account by rule or as an act of discretion, the defendant is still being punished only for the offense of conviction." The state high courts that have addressed a double jeopardy challenge on similar facts have reached the same result. See, e.g., Traylor v. State, 801 S.W.2d 267 (Ark. 1990).

In capital punishment cases, extensive appeals and habeas corpus proceedings lead to the reversal of many convictions. A retrial on the charges can raise some double jeopardy issues. If the jury in the first capital trial imposes a life sentence rather than the death penalty, double jeopardy prevents the prosecutor from seeking a death penalty in the later retrial. But if the jury in the first trial deadlocks on the question of the proper penalty and the judge imposes a life term, the prosecutor remains free to seek the death penalty during a later retrial after the conviction is reversed on appeal. See Sattazahn v. Pennsylvania, 537 U.S. 101 (2003).

7. *Checks on prosecutorial power at sentencing.* Criminal codes typically give prosecutors several options when deciding which (if any) charges to file based on a given set of acts. As the Supreme Court explained in Bordenkircher v. Hayes, 434 U.S. 357, 364 (1978), other institutions generally do not review the prosecutor's choices: "In our system, so long as the prosecutor has probable cause to believe that the accused committed an offense defined by statute, the decision whether or not to prosecute, and what charge to file or bring before a grand jury, generally rests entirely in his discretion." While courts might overturn charging decisions based on racial or other invidious discrimination, the decision in United States v. Armstrong, 517 U.S. 456 (1996), established that defendants face a heavy burden in obtaining pretrial discovery to prove that their prosecutions were racially motivated.

Sentencing rules, at least in theory, can expand the effects of the prosecutor's charging decisions. Guidelines that instruct judges to set the sentence based largely on charge of conviction give the prosecutor more power to influence the sentence, especially since the vast majority of convictions are secured through plea bargains. Do real-offense elements in a sentencing system offer sentencing judges a realistic method of reviewing the prosecutor's charging and plea bargaining decisions after conviction? Can a real-offense system constrain prosecutorial discretion if it authorizes the prosecutor to prove some conduct at the sentencing hearing under a lower standard of proof? The workloads of prosecutors may affect their willingness to manipulate charges to obtain different sentencing results, since prosecutors with heavy dockets might simply carry forward traditional charging patterns.

8. *The importance of presentence investigations.*   Judges often rely heavily on the investigatory work of probation officers or other court personnel, embodied in a presentence report. Historically, in indeterminate sentencing systems that expressly pursued rehabilitative goals, such presentence investigations and reports focused on defendants' character and background to assess their amenability to various rehabilitative possibilities. With structured sentencing systems now considering real-offense conduct more formally, these presentence investigations sometimes have been transformed into initial evaluations of defendants' relevant conduct. Especially in the federal system, commentators have expressed concerns about the role of probation officers' efforts in guidelines calculations. See, e.g., Kate Stith & Jose A. Cabranes, Fear of Judging: Sentencing Guidelines in the Federal Courts 87-91 (1998). Some defense attorneys have complained that probation officers often act as a sort of "second prosecutor" by uncovering aggravating facts or additional wrongdoing by defendants that did not come to light at trial or in plea negotiations. See, e.g., Felicia Sarner, "Fact Bargaining" Under the Sentencing Guidelines: The Role of the Probation Department, 8 Fed. Sent'g Rep. 328 (1996).

## PROBLEM 4-2.   ROB ANON REVISITED

Recall the case of Rob Anon, described in Problem 4-1. As a probation officer assigned to prepare a presentence report before Rob's sentencing, would you spend any time investigating the background and status of the getaway car used in the robbery? As a sentencing judge in an indeterminate sentencing jurisdiction, would evidence that the getaway car had been reported stolen influence the sentence you select? Suppose this evidence comes to light right before sentencing, when the prosecutor reports that the car had just been recovered. Should a sentencing judge in such a situation hold an evidentiary hearing to give Rob and his lawyer a chance to respond to the car theft allegation? As a member of a state sentencing commission, would you want to draft guidelines that instruct judges to consider (or not to consider) facts such as these? Should such a commission also draft procedural rules to govern this sort of factfinding?

## 2.   *Multiple Convictions*

Many defendants are convicted of more than one crime at trial, and the judge imposes sentences for the multiple convictions during a single sentencing hearing. The judge might impose sentences on the different convictions to run concurrently (all the terms begin at the same time) or consecutively (a second sentence starts after the first one ends). Even if the judge imposes concurrent sentences, he might increase the sentence for the most serious charge to reflect the fact that the defendant committed multiple crimes. States have created a variety of rules to guide sentencing judges as they account for multiple convictions.

Justice (then Judge) Stephen Breyer used the following example to illustrate traditional practices involving multiple convictions:

| Column A | Column B |
| --- | --- |
| 1. *D*, in a brawl, injures one person seriously. | 1. *D*, in a brawl, injures six persons seriously. |
| 2. *D* sells 100 grams of cocaine. | 2. *D* sells 600 grams of cocaine. |
| 3. *D* robs one bank. | 3. *D* robs six banks. |

Most persons react to these examples in accordance with two principles: [First, the] behavior in Column B warrants more severe punishment with respect to each example than the behavior in . . . Column A. [Second, the] punishment for behavior in Column B . . . should not be six times as severe as that in Column A. . . . These two widely held principles, or perceptions, make it difficult to write rules that properly treat "multiple counts."

Some state commissions have dealt with this problem by giving the trial judge considerable discretion as to whether to sentence defendants convicted of several counts consecutively or concurrently. A moment's thought suggests, however, that this approach leaves the prosecutor and the judge free to construct almost any sentence whatsoever. . . .

Other guidelines have distinguished among types of crimes, requiring, for example, concurrent sentences for multiple counts charging property crimes but consecutive sentences for crimes against the person. This approach, however, violates both principles. It violates the first principle with respect to property crimes, since it would treat the Column B defendants no more severely than the Column A defendants; it violates the second principle with respect to crimes against the person, because it is too severe. The federal Commission has tried to satisfy both principles through a system that treats additional counts as warranting additional punishment but in progressively diminishing amounts. . . . The upshot is that a bank robber who robs six banks will receive roughly twice as much (not six times as much punishment) as the robber who robs one bank.

The Federal Sentencing Guidelines and the Key Compromises upon Which They Rest, 17 Hofstra L. Rev. 1, 25-28 (1988). Read the statutes below carefully, and consider how they would guide a sentencing judge in Problem 4-3. Each statute offers judges distinctive guidance in choosing between consecutive and concurrent sentences. The North Carolina statute leaves the decision entirely in the judge's hands. The Indiana statute directs the judge's attention to particular considerations that are relevant to this choice, while the Kansas statute offers no substantive guidance but caps the possible impact of consecutive sentences.

## PROBLEM 4-3.   TAKE TWO

Review the facts of Problem 4-1. In addition to the bank robbery (which occurred in early December), Rob Anon and his co-defendants pled guilty to two other armed robberies. The first, committed on November 12, involved an evening holdup of Joru's Tavern. When Anon, Zweite, and Tercero entered the tavern about 9:00 p.m., Anon acted as lookout while the others took $240 from the tavern cash register. Tercero was armed with a shotgun, and the robbers took wallets and jewelry from three tavern patrons. The proceeds totaled $600.

The second robbery occurred on November 26. It involved the late evening holdup of Mike and Ginny's Tap. Anon, Zweite, and Tercero entered the tavern at 11:20 p.m. Anon was armed with a long-bladed knife, which he held to the throat of tavern owner Virginia Brown, stating, "Where's the money? Give me all of it or I'll slit your throat." Brown sustained a small cut on her right hand when she tried to push the knife away from her throat. One of the other robbers pointed a handgun at tavern patrons. The proceeds this time totaled $225.

Recall that armed robbery is punishable by a prison term of up to 25 years or a fine of up to $250,000 or both. The judge will impose sentences for the bank robbery and the two other robberies at the same time. What sentences are available to a judge applying each of the statutes below?

## ‖ *North Carolina General Statutes §15A-1340.15* ‖

(a) *Consecutive Sentences.* This Article [setting penalty ranges for particular crimes] does not prohibit the imposition of consecutive sentences. Unless otherwise specified by the court, all sentences of imprisonment run concurrently with any other sentences of imprisonment.

(b) *Consolidation of Sentences.* If an offender is convicted of more than one offense at the same time, the court may consolidate the offenses for judgment and impose a single judgment for the consolidated offenses. The judgment shall contain a sentence disposition specified for the class of offense and prior record level of the most serious offense, and its minimum sentence of imprisonment shall be within the ranges specified for that class of offense and prior record level, unless applicable statutes require or authorize another minimum sentence of imprisonment.

## ‖ *Indiana Code §35-38-1-7.1(b)* ‖

The court may consider the following factors as aggravating circumstances or as favoring imposing consecutive terms of imprisonment:

(1) The person has recently violated the conditions of any probation, parole, or pardon granted to the person.

(2) The person has a history of criminal or delinquent activity.

(3) The person is in need of correctional or rehabilitative treatment that can best be provided by commitment of the person to a penal facility.

(4) Imposition of a reduced sentence or suspension of the sentence and imposition of probation would depreciate the seriousness of the crime.

(5) The victim of the crime was less than twelve years of age or at least sixty-five years of age.

(6) The victim of the crime was mentally or physically infirm. . . .

(14) The person committed the offense in the presence or within hearing of a person who is less than eighteen years of age who was not the victim of the offense.

## ‖ *Kansas Statutes §21-4720* ‖

(b) The sentencing judge shall . . . have discretion to impose concurrent or consecutive sentences in multiple conviction cases. . . . In cases where consecutive sentences may be imposed by the sentencing judge, the following shall apply: . . .

(2) The sentencing judge must establish a base sentence for the primary crime. The primary crime is the crime with the highest crime severity ranking. . . .

(4) The total prison sentence imposed in a case involving multiple convictions arising from multiple counts within an information, complaint or indictment cannot exceed twice the base sentence. . . .

(c) The following shall apply for a departure from the presumptive sentence based on aggravating factors within the context of consecutive sentences:

(1) The court may depart from the presumptive limits for consecutive sentences only if the judge finds substantial and compelling reasons to impose a departure sentence for any of the individual crimes being sentenced consecutively.

(2) When a departure sentence is imposed for any of the individual crimes sentenced consecutively, the imprisonment term of that departure sentence shall not exceed twice the maximum presumptive imprisonment term that may be imposed for that crime.

(3) The total imprisonment term of the consecutive sentences, including the imprisonment term for the departure crime, shall not exceed twice the maximum presumptive imprisonment term of the departure sentence following aggravation.

### PROBLEM 4-4.  PREDISPOSED TO PRISON

Anthony Soto met an informant and a police officer who was working undercover. The informant asked Soto about drugs, but Soto replied that he was not involved in the sale of drugs at that time. After this conversation, the informant called Soto three times to discuss a purchase of cocaine. Soto finally agreed to locate some cocaine for the informant because Soto was in bad financial shape.

Soto later agreed to meet the informant and the undercover police officer in a parking lot on February 8, where the undercover officer informed Soto that he had $1,300 for an ounce of cocaine. Soto left the area for five minutes and returned with a bag containing 27 grams of cocaine, which he exchanged with the officer for the money. At that meeting, the officer asked Soto if he could buy two or three more ounces of cocaine from him at a later time. Soto responded that it would be no problem. On February 11 Soto again met with the informant and the undercover police officer in the same parking lot to sell two ounces of cocaine for $2,600. Once again, the officer asked Soto at this meeting if he could buy a larger amount later, and Soto again replied that it was no problem.

After the February 11 sale, the informant and the undercover police officer called Soto at least three times a week to arrange a larger sale of cocaine. On March 11 the officer met Soto and asked to buy eight ounces of cocaine. The officer agreed to buy ten ounces for $1,150 per ounce and they arranged a time to meet later in the day. When the officer arrived at a shopping center to meet with Soto, he was wired with a body microphone and had several officers in the area monitoring him. Soto arrived and gave the officer ten ounces of cocaine in exchange for $11,500. After the exchange was completed, Soto was arrested by the backup officers.

Soto was charged with one count of sale of cocaine in the first degree, and the state offered not to charge him with two additional counts if he would testify against two of his accomplices. Soto declined the offer, and the prosecutors amended their complaint by adding two counts. At trial, Soto asserted the defense of entrapment, but the jury found him guilty of three counts of sale of cocaine in the first degree. The sentencing judge imposed concurrent sentences on the three convictions, with the most serious sentence attached to the March 11 sale, count 3, because of the large amount of drugs involved. The judge also increased the sentence for count 3 based on the fact that Soto engaged in multiple sales.

Soto argues on appeal that the sentencing court should not use the fact that the government charged multiple counts of drug violations as a reason to enhance the guideline sentence for some of the counts. He says that such a sentencing rule would permit police officers and prosecutors to manipulate investigative or charging procedures to achieve a specific sentence. For instance, Soto argues that police officers could manipulate the amount of drugs or the number of sales involved, while prosecutors could separate the drug sales into multiple charges to ensure that a higher sentence would be imposed. Soto further argues that permitting police officers and prosecutors to have such discretion creates the potential for racially biased decisions and perpetuates racial disparities in the prosecution of drug crimes. How would you rule? Compare State v. Soto, 562 N.W.2d 299 (Minn. 1997).

### NOTES

1. *Multiple counts, indeterminate systems.*   Defendants are often convicted of multiple offenses arising from the same transaction or course of conduct. The sentencing judge in an indeterminate system typically has the discretion to impose separate sentences for the multiple convictions and to decide whether those sentences will be served concurrently or consecutively. The sentencing judge faces such a choice if the defendant was convicted of multiple crimes at one trial, or if the defendant is serving some other criminal sentence at the time of sentencing for the current conviction. As the Indiana Supreme Court put it in Williams v. State, 690 N.E.2d 162, 172 (Ind. 1997), "[i]t is within the trial court's discretion to determine . . . whether multiple sentences are to be concurrent or consecutive. The trial court will be reversed only upon a showing of a manifest abuse of discretion." Judges with complete power over the concurrent or consecutive nature of sentences have tended to give what might be termed a "volume discount." Additional convictions will increase the total sentence

served, but in decreasing amounts for each extra conviction. Is there any reason to favor either consecutive or concurrent sentences as the presumptive or normal outcome? Cf. ABA Standards Relating to Sentencing Alternatives and Procedures 18-6.5 (3d ed. 1994) (sentencing court "ordinarily should designate" sentences to be served concurrently).

2. *Multiple counts, structured systems.* Some state systems limit the judge's ability to adjust a sentence based on multiple convictions. The Kansas statute above offers one example. The grouping rules of the federal sentencing guidelines, designed to address this issue, are particularly complex. The basic strategy of the grouping rules of Chapter 3D of the federal guidelines is to increase the sentence for the most serious crime by diminishing amounts for each extra conviction. You might want to practice using the federal grouping rules; try completing Worksheet B at http://www.ussc.gov/training/worksheets01.pdf and the online exercise at http://www.ussc.gov/training/quizmc.pdf.

But controls over sentences for multiple counts are not a necessary part of sentencing guidelines. Some states start with a presumption of concurrent sentences but direct the sentencing judge to consider specific factors that might lead to a consecutive sentence instead. See Utah Code §76-3-401(1). North Carolina has adopted a highly structured sentencing system, yet judges retain all of their traditional authority to choose between consecutive and concurrent sentences. Does a rule such as North Carolina's undermine the predictability and uniformity of sentences, which are the underlying purposes of many guideline sentencing systems?

In sentencing systems that require the finding of some predicate fact before a consecutive sentence is allowed to replace the presumptive concurrent sentence, defendants have recently argued that Blakely v. Washington, 542 U.S. 296 (2004), requires a jury to find the relevant fact before a judge may order the sentences to run consecutively. Most lower courts addressing this issue in *Blakely*'s wake, however, had concluded that *Blakely* applies to the selection of the proper sentence for each crime of conviction, but not to the interaction among those sentences. See, e.g., Smylie v. State, 823 N.E.2d 679 (Ind. 2005); State v. Cubias, 120 P.3d 929 (Wash. 2005). But see State v. Foster, 845 N.E.2d 470 (Ohio 2006) (finding *Blakely* applicable to factfinding required for consecutive sentencing). In early 2008, the Supreme Court took up a case from Oregon presenting the issue of whether *Blakely* requires that those facts which permit a judge to impose consecutive sentences under state law must be proven to a jury. In a 5-4 decision authored by Justice Ginsburg, Oregon v. Ice, 555 U.S. 160 (2009), the Supreme Court declared that the Sixth Amendment, as construed in *Apprendi* and *Blakely*, should not be extended to preclude states from allowing judges to find those fact necessary to the imposition of consecutive sentences.

3. *Special rules for special crimes.* From time to time, a legislature specifies in a criminal statute that any sentence imposed under the statute must be consecutive rather than concurrent. For instance, under Idaho Code §18-2502(1), a sentence for escape by a prisoner "shall commence at the time [the prisoner] would otherwise have been discharged." Similarly, the Supreme Court in United States v. Gonzales, 520 U.S. 1 (1997), interpreted 18 U.S.C. §924(c) to prevent the federal firearm enhancement from being imposed concurrently with an existing state or federal sentence. Are there general criteria that legislatures might follow in selecting crimes to receive consecutive sentences automatically?

See also 11 Del. C. §1447(c). Should sentencing courts set consecutive or concurrent sentences based on what they believe was the legislative intent of the criminal statute violated by the defendant?

4. *Multiplicity and sentencing.*   The rules growing out of the constitutional bar on double jeopardy for the same offense help determine whether the prosecutor can charge multiple crimes based on a single set of related acts. In most states, so long as two crimes each require proof of an element that the other does not require, the prosecutor can file distinct charges, even if they are based on essentially the same conduct. Blockburger v. United States, 284 U.S. 299 (1932). Indeed, so long as the legislature intended to create separate criminal statutes punishing the same conduct, multiple convictions and punishments do not create double jeopardy problems. Missouri v. Hunter, 459 U.S. 359 (1983). Does the law guiding the sentencing judge's choice of consecutive or concurrent sentences supplement these minimal double jeopardy rules aimed at preventing multiple punishments?

The International Criminal Tribunal for Yugoslavia (ICTY) and the International Criminal Tribunal for Rwanda (ICTR) have both addressed the double jeopardy question in connection with multiple charges. The ICTR held that under national and international law "it is acceptable to convict the accused of two offences in relation to the same set of facts in the following circumstances: (1) where the offences have different elements; or (2) where the provisions creating the offences protect different interests; or (3) where it is necessary to record a conviction for both offences in order fully to describe what the accused did." The Prosecutor v. Akayesu, Case No. ICTR-96-4-T, Judgement of Sept. 2, 1998, at para. 468. The court found genocide, crimes against humanity, and war crimes to have different elements and to protect different interests so as to justify multiple convictions arising from the same underlying conduct.

5. *Sentence entrapment and manipulation: majority position.*   Entrapment, like other complete criminal defenses, is an all-or-nothing doctrine, allowing no subtlety or gradation in the analysis of government behavior or its effect. Sentencing, defendants claim, is an appropriate time to make more carefully graded judgments about both the offender's relative culpability (compared with offenders not subject to government encouragement) and the harms more properly attributed to government actions. Claims of sentencing entrapment or sentencing manipulation often arise in drug cases, in which the amount of drugs in a transaction can have a major impact on the likely sentence.

Indeterminate sentencing statutes do not tell a judge whether to take corrective action if she believes that government agents attempted to manipulate a sentence. Likewise, most sentencing guidelines do not address the issue of sentencing entrapment or manipulation. A few courts have refused to recognize government behavior as a potential factor at sentencing. See Commonwealth v. Garcia, 659 N.E.2d 741 (Mass. 1996).

More courts have recognized the possibility of accounting for government behavior but have not found facts that support a departure in a particular case. See United States v. Barth, 990 F.2d 422 (8th Cir. 1993); Leech v. State, 66 P.3d 987 (Okla. Crim. App. 2003). A few lower state courts in structured sentencing systems have altered sentences because of investigators' choices. For instance, in State v. Sanchez, 848 P.2d 208 (Wash. Ct. App. 1993), the government arranged a series of three small drug transactions between the defendant and one confidential informant, and the trial court departed downward to a sentence greater than the norm for one buy but less than the norm for three independent buys. Compare Graham v. State, 608 So. 2d 123 (Fla. Dist. Ct. App. 1992) (undercover officer selects location for drug sale at night within 650 feet of school, increasing penalties).

6. *Developing rules for sentence manipulation.*   "Reverse buys" — in which the government agent sells to the target of the investigation and can choose the amount and price to offer — highlight claims about sentencing manipulation, especially in the federal system, where the type and amount of drugs involved in the offense have a significant and specified impact on final sentencing ranges. The federal sentencing guidelines instruct judges facing this situation: "If, in a reverse sting operation . . . , the court finds that the government agent set a price for the controlled substance that was substantially below the market value of the controlled substance, thereby leading to the defendant's purchase of a significantly greater quantity of the controlled substance than his available resources would have allowed him to purchase . . . a downward departure may be warranted." U.S. Sentencing Guidelines Manual §2D1.1, cmt. n.17. Is this policy an adequate response to potential government manipulation of the sentence? Perhaps government agents could be required to arrest a suspect whenever they have enough proof to make conviction at trial likely. A court might require the government to state its reasons for continuing its investigation after obtaining enough evidence for a conviction. What reasons might the government give?

7. *Inadequate self-defense and other "partial" substantive criminal law defenses.* Should courts develop refined or modified versions of substantive criminal law defenses other than entrapment, such as self-defense or duress? For instance, a defendant's self-defense argument may not result in an acquittal, but the court may nevertheless rely on the argument to reduce a sentence. Some state sentencing statutes explicitly recognize "partial" or "near-miss" defenses at sentencing: In Tennessee, the court may reduce a sentence if "substantial grounds exist tending to excuse or justify the defendant's criminal conduct, though failing to establish a defense." Tenn. Code §40-35-113(3); see also United States v. Whitetail, 956 F.2d 857 (8th Cir. 1992) (battered woman defense); United States v. Cheape, 889 F.2d 477 (3d Cir. 1989) (duress; defendant participated in robbery at gunpoint). Does the lack of a more refined set of "partial" defenses undermine the purposes of punishment?

8. *Pro-defendant sentencing manipulation and plea bargaining.*   How should a sentencing judge respond if the terms of a plea agreement suggest that the prosecution and defense have not fully disclosed to the court all of the defendant's relevant conduct? See U.S. Sentencing Guidelines Manual §5K2.21 (court may increase sentence above the guideline range to reflect "actual seriousness of the offense" based on conduct underlying a dismissed charge or a charge not pursued, if that conduct did not enter into the selection of the applicable guideline range). Especially in the federal system, there is evidence to suggest that, in perhaps as many as one-third of all cases, prosecutors underreport offense facts that could aggravate a defendant's guideline sentence in order to secure a guilty plea. See Stephen J. Schulhofer & Ilene H. Nagel, Plea Negotiations Under the Federal Sentencing Guidelines: Guidelines Circumvention and Its Dynamics in the Post-*Mistretta* Period, 91 Nw. U. L. Rev. 1284 (1997); see also, e.g., United States

v. Mercer, 472 F. Supp. 2d 1319 (D. Utah 2007) (discussing concerns with sentencing recommendation by prosecutors seeking to prevent application of proper guideline enhancement as part of plea deal). Should such pro-defendant manipulation of sentencing outcomes concern us as much as (or perhaps even more than) manipulation of offense facts that potentially harm defendants?

## 3.   Role in a Group Offense

The language of crime recognizes that the pecking order in a group crime matters. We often speak of kingpins and bosses, henchmen and mules. To what extent should a sentencing judge consider the relative blameworthiness of defendants who have different roles in the same offense?

## ‖ U.S. Sentencing Guidelines Manual ‖

### §3B1.1   AGGRAVATING ROLE

Based on the defendant's role in the offense, increase the offense level as follows:

(a) If the defendant was an organizer or leader of a criminal activity that involved five or more participants or was otherwise extensive, increase by 4 levels.

(b) If the defendant was a manager or supervisor (but not an organizer or leader) and the criminal activity involved five or more participants or was otherwise extensive, increase by 3 levels.

(c) If the defendant was an organizer, leader, manager, or supervisor in any criminal activity other than described in (a) or (b), increase by 2 levels.

### §3B1.2   MITIGATING ROLE

Based on the defendant's role in the offense, decrease the offense level as follows:

(a) If the defendant was a minimal participant in any criminal activity, decrease by 4 levels.

(b) If the defendant was a minor participant in any criminal activity, decrease by 2 levels.

In cases falling between (a) and (b), decrease by 3 levels.

## ‖ United States v. Donald Carpenter ‖
### 252 F.3d 230 (2d Cir. 2001)

MESKILL, J.

This appeal arises out of defendant-appellee Donald Carpenter's plea of guilty to conspiring to steal firearms from two Dick's Clothing and Sporting

Goods (Dick's) stores located near Syracuse, New York. . . . The mechanics of the conspiracy's firearm theft and resale scheme are not complicated. [Marty Wise, a sales associate at Dick's,] initially approached Carpenter with the plan to steal firearms from Dick's. As part of their scheme, Wise would contact Carpenter and inform him when a specific theft should occur. When Carpenter arrived at Dick's, Wise handed Carpenter a pre-selected firearm. Carpenter then completed the Alcohol, Tobacco and Firearms (ATF) Form 4473 transferring the firearm from Dick's to himself, and Wise signaled to the cashier that Carpenter "was all set" and could leave without paying for the firearm. . . . Carpenter was in charge of disposing of the firearms stolen from Dick's. As a partner in a business named "The Gun Room," which possessed a federal firearms license, Carpenter was able regularly to acquire firearms and subsequently resell them to Dick's and other businesses. . . .

The thefts were discovered by David Murano, the store manager at Dick's, after Carpenter was unable to produce the sales receipt for one of the firearms he allegedly purchased from Dick's. After being confronted by Murano, Carpenter confessed to his and Wise's involvement in numerous firearm thefts from Dick's. A few months later, Carpenter and Wise made a similar confession to ATF agents. [An] ATF audit revealed that between October 1993 and March 1997, the period the conspiracy was active, Carpenter and Wise engaged in fifty separate firearm thefts from Dick's. . . . Wise kept the proceeds from nineteen guns; Carpenter kept the proceeds from nineteen guns; Wise and Carpenter split the proceeds from three guns; and one firearm actually was purchased by Carpenter.

On July 2, 1998, Carpenter pleaded guilty to an information charging him with one count of conspiring to steal firearms from a licensed firearms dealer. . . . At sentencing, the district court heard extensive argument from both parties on the issue of whether Carpenter was entitled to a mitigating role adjustment. The district court then reduced Carpenter's base offense level by three levels pursuant to U.S.S.G. §3B1.2 for his role in the firearm theft conspiracy. . . .

The base offense level for Carpenter's offense was twelve. Because the offense involved 25-49 firearms, the offense level was increased by five levels. The district court then departed downward three levels for a mitigating role adjustment, and two levels for acceptance of responsibility. This resulted in a total offense level of twelve. This offense level, combined with a criminal history category of I, resulted in a guideline imprisonment range of 10 to 16 months. [T]he district court sentenced Carpenter at the lowest end of that range, and ordered him to serve a term of imprisonment of five months, followed by five months in home detention. The district court also ordered Carpenter to pay restitution in the amount of $17,975.04. . . . Wise, who also pleaded guilty to one count of conspiracy to steal firearms from a licensed firearms dealer, was sentenced to a term of imprisonment of fifteen months and ordered to pay restitution in the amount of $18,975.04. . . .

On appeal, the government argues that the district court misapplied U.S.S.G. §3B1.2 as a matter of law when it held that Carpenter was entitled to a mitigating role adjustment on the ground that his conduct was less culpable than that of Wise, his co-conspirator. We agree that the district court erred. . . . We review factual findings underlying the district court's application of the Sentencing Guidelines for clear error, giving due deference to the district court's application of the guidelines to the facts. In applying [this standard], we are mindful that a sentencing court's assessment of the defendant's role in criminal activity is highly fact-specific and depends upon the nature of the defendant's relationship to other participants, the importance of the defendant's actions to the success of the venture, and the defendant's awareness of the nature and scope of the criminal enterprise. . . .

Section 3B1.2 of the Sentencing Guidelines provides for a four-level downward adjustment if the defendant was a "minimal participant" in criminal activity, and a two-level downward adjustment where the defendant was a "minor participant." The commentary to the Guidelines provides that a "minimal role" adjustment applies to a defendant who is "plainly among the least culpable of those involved in the conduct of a group." U.S.S.G. §3B1.2, commentary (n.1). "Under this provision, the defendant's lack of knowledge or understanding of the scope and structure of the enterprise and of the activities of others is indicative of a role as minimal participant." The Guidelines make clear that the "minimal role" adjustment should be used "infrequently." In comparison, a "minor role" adjustment applies to "any participant who is less culpable than most other participants, but whose role could not be described as minimal." U.S.S.G. §3B1.2, commentary (n.3). The Guidelines further provide that a mitigating role adjustment is appropriate if the defendant is "substantially less culpable than the *average participant*." . . .

On numerous occasions we have reiterated that a reduction pursuant to U.S.S.G. §3B1.2 will not be available simply because the defendant played a lesser role than his co-conspirators; to be eligible for a reduction, the defendant's conduct must be "minor" or "minimal" as compared to the average participant in such a crime. Accordingly, the fact that a defendant played a minimal or minor role in his offense vis-à-vis the role of his co-conspirators is insufficient, in and of itself, to justify a mitigating role reduction.

The rationale for such a rule is self-evident. [If] participation in the offense were measured solely in relation to the co-defendants, the anomaly would arise that a deeply involved participant would be rewarded with a downward adjustment, just because his co-defendants were even more culpable. Further, such a result runs contrary to the statutory purposes of sentencing, which are aimed at reducing unwarranted sentencing disparities among defendants with similar records who have been found guilty of similar criminal conduct. . . .

In ruling that Carpenter's base offense level should be reduced by three levels pursuant to §3B1.2 for his role in the conspiracy, the district court found that

> Carpenter's role in the offense is much less culpable than that of Marty Wise, the co-defendant. It's clear from the record that Wise initiated the offense and recruited Carpenter to take part in the thefts and that [Wise] was the one that had unlimited access to the guns, decided which guns would be stolen, when the thefts would take place, et cetera. Wise used Carpenter and four other individuals to accomplish these thefts and reaped the most from the crimes. . . .

Because the district court compared Carpenter's role to that of Wise, rather than to the *average* participant in a similar firearm theft conspiracy, the sentence imposed by the district court must be vacated.

The government next argues that Carpenter's role in the conspiracy and his knowledge of the scope and structure of the conspiracy render him ineligible as a matter of law for a mitigating role adjustment under U.S.S.G. §3B1.2. . . . Because the relevant facts on this issue are clear from the record, we choose to decide the question of Carpenter's entitlement to a mitigating role adjustment in the first instance, rather than remand that determination to the district court for additional factfinding.

Carpenter's active involvement in stealing the firearms from Dick's and reselling them to various third parties confirms that he played an important and significant part in the conspiracy to violate federal firearms laws to which he pleaded guilty. . . . As a partner in a business that was a federally licensed dealer, Carpenter was able to regularly purchase and transfer firearms without drawing suspicion. This fact was critical to the success of the conspiracy. Further, Carpenter falsely executed the ATF forms that were designed to conceal the thefts of the firearms. Given these facts, we conclude that Carpenter possessed an intimate "knowledge or understanding of the scope and structure of the enterprise" for which he pleaded guilty. U.S.S.G. §3B1.2, commentary (n.1).

The fact that Wise recruited Carpenter for the *first* of fifty firearm thefts does not render Carpenter an unwitting participant in the two and one-half year conspiracy during which he actively and systematically stole firearms and illegally resold them for personal profit. This is not a situation involving the isolated theft of a single firearm; instead, this case involved a scheme designed to deal in stolen firearms. The continuing nature of the conspiracy, coupled with Carpenter's repeated involvement in the firearm thefts and resales, further render Carpenter ineligible for a mitigating role adjustment. . . .

Finally, Carpenter argues . . . that he is entitled to a mitigating role adjustment because the firearms were not used for unlawful purposes. Specifically, Carpenter contends that "the firearms Carpenter obtained were used primarily by him for hunting and target shooting. . . . Unlike many, if not most people involved in gun thefts, Carpenter did not knowingly act as a conduit for supplying weapons in reckless disregard of whether they were to be used in the commission of other illegal acts." Even accepting Carpenter's facts as true, they are irrelevant to our determination of whether Carpenter is entitled to a mitigating role adjustment and, specifically, to the issue of Carpenter's knowledge of the scope and structure of the conspiracy and the scope of his role within that conspiracy. . . .

The judgment imposed by the district court is vacated as to the sentence only and the matter is remanded to the district court with instructions to resentence Carpenter at a base offense level of 15 and a criminal history category of I, which carries a sentencing range of 18-24 months. . . .

## NOTES

1. *Impact of role in offense.* As we saw in the *Carpenter* case, the federal sentencing guidelines decrease the sentence by specific amounts for those who take relatively small roles in an offense carried out by a group. In an indeterminate sentencing system, the judge also traditionally considers the defendant's relative

culpability in the group offense. The extent of any decrease or increase based on this factor is impossible to judge. More structured guideline systems in some states may mention the offender's relative culpability in a group offense as one possible reason to depart from the ordinary sentence range. See Md. Sentencing Guidelines §9.2 (departure below guideline range allowed based on "offender's minor role in the offense"); N.C. Gen. Stat. §15A-1340.16(d)(1), (e)(2) (listing as an aggravating factor the fact that defendant "occupied a position of leadership or dominance over other participants" and listing as a mitigating factor the fact that defendant "was a passive participant or played a minor role in the commission of the offense"). Under the capital punishment statutes in some states, the defendant's role in the offense can mean the difference between life and death. Ohio and Florida, among others, include the defendant's relatively minor role as a mitigating factor that could lead a jury to recommend a life sentence rather than capital punishment. See Ohio Rev. Code §2929.04(B)(6); Fla. Stat. Ann. §921.141(6)(d).

The federal provision flushes out several questions that are not explicitly addressed in the typical state system (either indeterminate or guideline). What is the proper amount to decrease or increase a sentence based on this factor? In judging the relative culpability of a defendant, what is the proper comparison point: others involved in the current crime, or those involved in similar crimes around the country? Note that your answer to these questions might change depending on the size of the group involved or the seriousness of the crime committed. See United States v. Almanza, 225 F.3d 845 (7th Cir. 2000) (Posner, J.) ("The 'mule' who transports one kilogram of cocaine is a more minor participant in a conspiracy to distribute 1,000 kilograms of cocaine than in a conspiracy to distribute 10 kilograms of cocaine, because the potential punishment of a member of the first conspiracy is so much greater, even though his conduct is identical.").

2. *Co-defendant's sentence as a basis for departure.* How should a judge respond when the sentencing rules indicate a sentence for one defendant that is higher than the sentence already imposed on a more culpable co-defendant? In the federal system, courts have usually refused to depart from the sentencing guidelines in an effort to give comparable sentences to co-defendants in the same crime. See United States v. Joyner, 924 F.2d 454, 460-461 (2d Cir. 1991) (consideration of the sentences given to co-defendants "creates a new and entirely unwarranted disparity between the defendant's sentence and that of all similarly situated defendants throughout the country"). The sentencing judge could impose a sentence out of line with the sentence already received by other participants in the present crime, or a sentence out of line with the lesser participants in similar crimes from other districts. Which is the greater (and more visible) threat to the principle of equal treatment at sentencing?

The Supreme Court has never directly ruled upon whether a co-defendant's sentence might provide the basis for a traditional guidelines departure. In Gall v. United States, 552 U.S. 32 (2007), however, the Court indirectly suggested it was appropriate for a district judge to impose a sentence below the guidelines after considering "the need to avoid unwarranted *similarities* among other co-conspirators who were not similarly situated." Id. at 55-56. In addition, both prosecutors and defense attorneys in their sentencing advocacy frequently make mention — and sometimes expressly emphasis — a particular defendant's distinctive role within the broader criminal activity in which he was engaged. Practically speaking, is it all but inevitable that a defendant's relative importance and role within one localized criminal conspiracy will impact sentencing judgments made by local judges as much or more than that defendant's importance and role as compared to "all similarly situated defendants throughout the country"?

3. *Relative culpability and cooperation with the government.*   Conspirators who plead guilty and cooperate with the government in prosecutions against other members of the conspiracy often receive sentence discounts, both in federal and state systems. Recall U.S. Sentencing Guidelines Manual §5K1.1 (allowing departure for substantial assistance). This often means that some higher-ranking conspiracy members — those who know the most about the operation — receive lesser sentences than some lower-ranking conspiracy members who have less to offer the government. Especially in the federal system, in which a substantial assistance departure is authorized only upon a motion by the prosecutor, defendants who cooperate on a similar basis could receive different sentences because of different practices of prosecutors in different districts. Can a sentencing judge counteract these sources of unequal sentences? If a judge learns that prosecutors in the local district deal with some co-conspirators differently than prosecutors in other districts (for instance, by offering immunity under U.S. Sentencing Guidelines Manual §1B1.8 in exchange for information about the conspiracy), should the judge adjust the sentence to equalize outcomes in different districts? See United States v. Buckendahl, 251 F.3d 753 (8th Cir. 2001).

## PROBLEM 4-5.   ROB ANON REVISITED

Look again at §3B1.1 of the federal guidelines, reprinted above. The application notes to this guideline do not define the key terms such as "leader" or "manager." How would these provisions apply to the sentence of Rob Anon, based on the facts described in Problem 4-1? Was this enterprise "otherwise extensive" within the meaning of §3B1.1(a)? The commentary offers some hope for the prosecution here: "In assessing whether an organization is 'otherwise extensive,' all persons involved during the course of the entire offense are to be considered. Thus, a fraud that involved only three participants but used the unknowing services of many outsiders could be considered extensive." Where might the prosecutor find evidence about other "persons involved"?

As explained in Chapter 3, the Supreme Court's decision in United States v. Booker, 543 U.S. 220 (2005), made the federal sentencing guidelines "effectively advisory." In the context of Rob Anon's case, does §3B1.1 provide sound advice that you would likely follow when considering Rob's role in the offense at his sentencing? Do the categories and labels used in §3B1 provide a helpful framework for the consideration of these issues? Can you conceive of another means or a distinct approach to assessing and distinctly weighing a defendant's aggravating or mitigating role?

## B.   ASSESSING OFFENSE SERIOUSNESS

Deciding the scope of behavior that will form the basis for a sentence is only one step in choosing an appropriate sentence. Sentencing authorities must also judge the *seriousness* of the defendant's offense.

In all sentencing systems, legislatures make initial judgments about offense seriousness through the grading of offenses. They decide which crimes to label as felonies or misdemeanors and further subdivide these broad categories by using degrees or classes to specify appropriate punishment ranges. These decisions can sometimes raise constitutional concerns, because the Supreme Court has interpreted the Eighth Amendment's prohibition of cruel and unusual punishments to preclude grossly disproportionate punishments (see Chapter 7). More fundamentally, these legislative decisions always implicate policy choices, because legislatures must decide which aspects of an offense should be categorized as more or less serious.

Basic legislative grading choices are only one component of the many judgments made about the seriousness of offense behavior in the sentencing process. Legislatures also authorize or require specific sentencing enhancements based on particular aspects of offense behavior, such as gun possession. And other sentencing decision makers — including sentencing commissions, prosecutors, judges, and parole officials — measure the seriousness of offense behavior in ways that change final sentencing outcomes.

The following excerpt from the Senate report supporting the Sentencing Reform Act of 1984 instructs the U.S. Sentencing Commission how to establish sentencing rules for different categories of offenses. The report mentions the numerous offense-related elements that become relevant in passing judgment on the overall seriousness of criminal behaviors.

|| *U.S. Senate Report No. 98-225* ||
|| **Pages 169-171 (1984)** ||

[Title 28 U.S.C. §994(c) of the Sentencing Reform Act] lists a number of offense characteristics that the sentencing commission is required to examine [in the establishment of sentencing guidelines. This provision] specifies that the commission consider the degree of relevance of the grade of the offense to the sentencing decision. [All] offenses are graded according to their relative seriousness. [The grading provides] some guide as to the congressional view of the relative seriousness of similar offenses. The rough approximations practical for statutory purposes are expected . . . to be refined considerably by the sentencing guidelines.

[This provision further] specifies that the commission consider the relevance to the sentencing decision of the circumstances under which the offense was committed that might aggravate or mitigate the seriousness of the offense. Among the considerations the commission might examine under this factor are whether the offense was particularly heinous; whether the offense was committed on the spur of the moment or after substantial planning; whether the offense was committed in reckless disregard of the safety of others; whether the offense involved a threat with a weapon or use of a weapon; whether the offense was committed in a manner plainly designed to limit the danger to the victims; whether the defendant was acting under a form of duress not rising to the level of a defense; etc.

[This provision further] specifies that the commission consider the relevance to the sentencing decision of the nature and degree of the harm caused by the offense, including whether it involved property, irreplaceable property, a person, a number of persons, or a breach of public trust. The commission might include in this consideration, or in policy statements, an evaluation of the role that unusual vulnerability of the victim that is known to the defendant should play in the sentencing decision.

[This provision further] specifies that the commission consider the relevance of the community view of the gravity of the offense to the sentencing decision, . . . public concern generated by an offense, . . . the deterrent effect a particular sentence may have on the commission of the offense by others [, and] the current incidence of the offense in the community and in the nation as a whole.

## NOTES

1. *The centrality of harm and culpability on legislative grading of offenses.* Most criminal codes state that the fundamental requirements for criminal liability are a voluntary act (the objective component) and a mens rea, or culpable mental state (the subjective component). See, e.g., N.Y. Penal Code §15.10; Ohio Rev. Code §2901.21; Tex. Penal Code §§6.01-6.04. Similarly, the initial grading of a criminal offense by the legislature typically depends on the objective seriousness of the harm or threat of harm resulting from the defendant's behavior and on the defendant's subjective culpability. Certain classes of crimes share a common objective harm, leading to offense grades that turn entirely on the defendant's subjective mental state. For instance, homicides are usually defined in terms of causing another person's death; the grade of offense depends on whether the killing was intentional, provoked, unintentional, or accidental. See, e.g., Cal. Penal Code §§187-192; Kan. Stat. Ann. §§21-3401B to 21-3404. Other crimes share a common subjective mental state, leading to offense grades that depend on the objective harm inflicted. For example, most forms of theft require the intent to deprive others of property; the grade principally depends on the value of the property stolen.

2. *Institutional roles in judging offense seriousness.* Historically, legislatures made only general assessments of offense seriousness through grading choices, juries applied offense grades to the facts of specific cases, and sentencing judges made more particularized judgments about the seriousness of the defendant's crime when ascribing specific sentences. Professor Paul Robinson has suggested that this traditional allocation of responsibility is fundamentally sound:

> The amount of punishment to be imposed is in large measure a function of the value of the interest injured or threatened and the culpability of the act. In a democracy, . . . the relative value of the interest is a judgment uniquely within the authority of a legislative body[, and] the actor's culpability, which necessarily requires an inferential judgment, is a judgment within the expertise of a jury

of peers. [Because] a criminal code cannot take account of every factor that contributes to the amount of punishment a defendant deserves . . . codes generally give only an approximation of the amount of punishment that should be imposed. The judge must determine the exact amount on the facts of the particular case, which requires exercise of judicial discretion to refine the code's "first cut," or to account for relevant factors not taken into account by the code.

Paul H. Robinson, Are Criminal Codes Irrelevant?, 68 S. Cal. L. Rev. 159, 183 (1994). How should a sentencing commission fit into Professor Robinson's taxonomy of institutional roles? Should the work of sentencing commissions be conceived primarily in traditional legislative terms, focusing on developing sentencing rules that provide only a "first cut" as to the amount of punishment a court ought to impose? Or should the work of sentencing commissions be conceived instead in traditional judicial terms, focusing on developing sentencing rules to account for factors appearing less often in individual cases?

## 1.    *Qualitative Assessments of Harm*

The harm or threat of harm that arises from a defendant's behavior profoundly influences final sentencing choices, perhaps even more than it affects legislative grading of criminal offenses. Various legal structures and rules translate judgments about the seriousness of harm into final sentencing outcomes.

When legislatures, sentencing commissions, and judges think about the seriousness of offenses, they sometimes consider the *type* of harm the crime causes or threatens rather than the *amount* of harm. Which types of harm deserve the most serious punishments? As you read the following cases and materials, think about the inherent challenge of making qualitative judgments about the relative seriousness of violent crimes versus drug crimes versus sex crimes versus economic crimes. Consider also how judges, legislatures, and commissions make these rankings.

|| **Ehrlich Anthony Coker v. Georgia** ||
|| **433 U.S. 584 (1977)** ||

WHITE, J.

Georgia Code §26-2001 provides that "(a) person convicted of rape shall be punished by death or by imprisonment for life, or by imprisonment for not less than one nor more than 20 years." Petitioner Coker was convicted of rape and sentenced to death. Coker [contends] that the punishment of death for rape violates the Eighth Amendment.

While serving various sentences for murder, rape, kidnaping, and aggravated assault, petitioner escaped from [prison. Petitioner] entered the house of Allen and Elnita Carver through an unlocked kitchen door. Threatening the couple with a "board," he tied up Mr. Carver in the bathroom, obtained a knife from the kitchen, and took Mr. Carver's money and the keys to the family car. Brandishing the knife and saying "you know what's going to happen to you if you try anything, don't you," Coker then raped Mrs. Carver. Soon thereafter, petitioner drove away in the Carver car, taking Mrs. Carver with him. Mr. Carver, freeing himself, notified the police; and not long thereafter petitioner was apprehended. Mrs. Carver was unharmed.

Petitioner was charged with [various offenses, including] rape. . . . The jury returned a verdict of guilty, rejecting his general plea of insanity. A sentencing hearing was then conducted in accordance with [our decision in] Gregg v. Georgia, 428 U.S. 153 (1976), where this Court sustained the death penalty for murder when imposed pursuant to [certain] procedures. . . . The jury's verdict on the rape count was death by electrocution.

Furman v. Georgia, 408 U.S. 238 (1972), and the Court's decisions last Term in Gregg v. Georgia, 428 U.S. 153 (1976) [and companion cases] settled that the death penalty is not invariably cruel and unusual punishment within the meaning of the Eighth Amendment; it is not inherently barbaric or an unacceptable mode of punishment for crime; neither is it always disproportionate to the crime for which it is imposed. In sustaining the imposition of the death penalty in *Gregg*, however, the Court firmly embraced the holdings and dicta from prior cases to the effect that the Eighth Amendment bars not only those punishments that are "barbaric" but also those that are "excessive" in relation to the crime committed. Under *Gregg*, a punishment is "excessive" and unconstitutional if it (1) makes no measurable contribution to acceptable goals of punishment and hence is nothing more than the purposeless and needless imposition of pain and suffering; or (2) is grossly out of proportion to the severity of the crime. . . . We have concluded that a sentence of death is grossly disproportionate and excessive punishment for the crime of rape and is therefore forbidden by the Eighth Amendment as cruel and unusual punishment.

[We] seek guidance in history and from the objective evidence of the country's present judgment concerning the acceptability of death as a penalty for rape of an adult woman. At no time in the last 50 years have a majority of the States authorized death as a punishment for rape. In 1925, 18 States, the District of Columbia, and the Federal Government authorized capital punishment for the rape of an adult female. By 1971 just prior to the decision in *Furman*, that number had declined, but not substantially, to 16 States plus the Federal Government. *Furman* then invalidated most of the capital punishment statutes in this country, including the rape statutes. . . .

In reviving death penalty laws to satisfy *Furman*'s mandate, none of the States that had not previously authorized death for rape chose to include rape among capital felonies. Of the 16 States in which rape had been a capital offense, only three provided the death penalty for rape of an adult woman in their revised statutes, Georgia, North Carolina, and Louisiana. . . . It should be noted that Florida, Mississippi, and Tennessee also authorized the death penalty in some rape cases, but only where the victim was a child and the rapist an adult. . . . The current judgment with respect to the death penalty for rape is not wholly unanimous among state legislatures, but it obviously weighs very heavily on the side of rejecting capital punishment as a suitable penalty for raping an adult woman.

It was also observed in *Gregg* that "the jury . . . is a significant and reliable objective index of contemporary values because it is so directly involved," and that it is thus important to look to the sentencing decisions that juries have made in the course of assessing whether capital punishment is an appropriate penalty for the crime being tried. [Out] of all rape convictions in Georgia since 1973, . . . 63 cases had been reviewed by the Georgia Supreme Court as of the time of oral argument; and of these, 6 involved a death sentence. [Recent] experience surely does not prove that jurors consider the death penalty to be a disproportionate punishment for every conceivable instance of rape, no matter how aggravated. Nevertheless, it is true that in the vast majority of cases, at least 9 out of 10, juries have not imposed the death sentence.

These recent events evidencing the attitude of state legislatures and sentencing juries do not wholly determine this controversy, for the Constitution contemplates that in the end our own judgment will be brought to bear on the question of the acceptability of the death penalty under the Eighth Amendment. . . .

We do not discount the seriousness of rape as a crime. It is highly reprehensible, both in a moral sense and in its almost total contempt for the personal integrity and autonomy of the female victim and for the latter's privilege of choosing those with whom intimate relationships are to be established. Short of homicide, it is the "ultimate violation of self." It is also a violent crime because it normally involves force, or the threat of force or intimidation, to overcome the will and the capacity of the victim to resist. Rape is very often accompanied by physical injury to the female and can also inflict psychological damage. Because it undermines the community's sense of security, there is public injury as well.

Rape is without doubt deserving of serious punishment; but in terms of moral depravity and of the injury to the person and to the public, it does not compare with murder, which does involve the unjustified taking of human life. Although it may be accompanied by another crime, rape by definition does not include the death of or even the serious injury to another person. The murderer kills; the rapist, if no more than that, does not. Life is over for the victim of the murderer; for the rape victim, life may not be nearly so happy as it was, but it is not over and normally is not beyond repair. We have the abiding conviction that the death penalty, which is unique in its severity and irrevocability, is an excessive penalty for the rapist who, as such, does not take human life. . . .

POWELL, J., concurring in the judgment in part and dissenting in part.

I concur in the judgment of the Court on the facts of this case, and also in the plurality's reasoning supporting the view that ordinarily death is disproportionate punishment for the crime of raping an adult woman. Although rape invariably is a reprehensible crime, there is no indication that petitioner's offense was committed with excessive brutality or that the victim sustained serious or lasting injury.

[However], the plurality draws a bright line between murder and all rapes regardless of the degree of brutality of the rape or the effect upon the victim. I dissent because I am not persuaded that such a bright line is appropriate. [T]here is extreme variation in the degree of culpability of rapists. The deliberate viciousness of the rapist may be greater than that of the murderer. Rape is never an act committed accidentally. Rarely can it be said to be unpremeditated. There also is wide variation in the effect on the victim. . . . Some victims are so grievously injured physically or psychologically that life is beyond repair. . . .

BURGER, C.J., dissenting.

. . . On December 5, 1971 Ehrlich Anthony Coker raped and then stabbed to death a young woman. Less than eight months later Coker kidnaped and raped a second young woman. After twice raping this 16-year-old victim, he stripped her, severely beat her with a club, and dragged her into a wooded area where he left her for dead. He was apprehended and pleaded guilty to offenses stemming from these incidents. He was sentenced by three separate courts to three life terms, two 20-year terms, and one 8-year term of imprisonment. Each judgment specified that the sentences it imposed were to run consecutively rather than concurrently. Approximately one and a half years later, on September 2, 1974, petitioner escaped from the state prison where he was serving these sentences. He promptly raped another 16-year-old woman in the presence of her husband, abducted her from her home, and threatened her with death and serious bodily harm. It is this crime for which the sentence now under review was imposed.

The Court today holds that Georgia may not impose the death penalty on Coker. In so doing, it prevents the State from imposing any effective punishment upon Coker for his latest rape. The Court's holding, moreover, bars Georgia from guaranteeing its citizens that they will suffer no further attacks by this habitual rapist . . . who has shown total and repeated disregard for the welfare, safety, personal integrity, and human worth of others, and who seemingly cannot be deterred from continuing such conduct. . . .

A rapist not only violates a victim's privacy and personal integrity, but inevitably causes serious psychological as well as physical harm in the process. The long-range effect upon the victim's life and health is likely to be irreparable; it is impossible to measure the harm which results. Volumes have been written by victims, physicians, and psychiatric specialists on the lasting injury suffered by rape victims. Rape is not a mere physical attack, it is destructive of the human personality. The remainder of the victim's life may be gravely affected, and this in turn may have a serious detrimental effect upon her husband and any children she may have. . . . Victims may recover from the physical damage of knife or bullet wounds, or a beating with fists or a club, but recovery from such a gross assault on the human personality is not healed by medicine or surgery. To speak blandly . . . of rape victims who are "unharmed," or to classify the human outrage of rape . . . in terms of "excessively brutal," versus "moderately brutal," takes too little account of the profound suffering the crime imposes upon the victims and their loved ones.

The question of whether the death penalty is an appropriate punishment for rape is surely an open one. It is arguable that many prospective rapists would be deterred by the possibility that they could suffer death for their offense; it is also arguable that the death penalty would have only minimal deterrent effect. It may well be that rape victims would become more willing to report the crime and aid in the apprehension of the criminals if they knew that community disapproval of rapists was sufficiently strong to inflict the extreme penalty; or perhaps they would be reluctant to cooperate in the prosecution of rapists if they knew that a conviction might result in the imposition of the death penalty. Quite possibly, the occasional, well-publicized execution of egregious rapists may cause citizens to feel greater security in their daily lives; or, on the contrary, it may be that members of a civilized community will suffer the pangs of a heavy conscience because such punishment will be perceived as excessive. We cannot know which among this range of possibilities is correct, but today's holding forecloses the very exploration we have said federalism was intended to foster.

[Rape] is not a crime "light years" removed from murder in the degree of its heinousness; it certainly poses a serious potential danger to the life and safety of innocent victims apart from the devastating psychic consequences. . . . Whatever our individual views as to the wisdom of capital punishment, I cannot agree that it is constitutionally impermissible for a state legislature to make the "solemn judgment" to impose such penalty for the crime of rape. Accordingly, I would leave to the States the task of legislating in this area of the law.

### *NOTES*

1. *Constitutional proportionality between harm and severity of punishment.* As *Coker* reveals, the Supreme Court has placed some substantive constitutional limitations on the use of capital punishment for certain crimes. In addition to *Coker*'s preclusion of capital punishment for the crime of adult rape, the Supreme Court has held through a line of decisions culminating in Tison v. Arizona, 481 U.S. 137 (1987), that the death penalty is permissible in homicide cases only for offenders who acted at least with the culpable mental state of reckless indifference to human life. As detailed in Chapter 7, the Supreme Court has also held that noncapital sentences can be unconstitutional if they are "grossly disproportionate" to the offender's crime.

Consider all the people who had to agree that Ehrlich Anthony Coker should die for his crime: the Georgia legislature had to authorize the death penalty for certain rapes; the local prosecutor (influenced perhaps by the victim's input) had to charge and pursue Coker's case as a capital crime; the sentencing jury had to conclude not only that Coker was guilty but also that he deserved to die for his crime; the Georgia state courts had to decide, pursuant to their own state laws, that Coker's sentence was proportionate to the crime. Does the U.S. Supreme Court bring something to the job of measuring the seriousness of Coker's crime that the other actors were missing?

2. *Child rape as a capital offense.* Coker precluded the use of capital punishment only in cases of adult rape. After the decision, at least a few states left on their books laws allowing for the death penalty for rape of a child, and a few states subsequently amended laws to make child rape a potential capital offense. In Louisiana a statute provides that defendants convicted of "aggravated rape" can be subject to the death penalty if "the victim was under the age of twelve years." La. Rev. Stat. §14:42. In State v Wilson, 685 So. 2d 1063 (La. 1996), the Louisiana Supreme Court upheld the facial constitutionality of this statute, and in 2003 defendant Patrick Kennedy was sentenced to death under this statute for raping an eight-year-old girl. His sentence was affirmed by the Louisiana Supreme Court in State v. Kennedy, 957 So. 2d 757 (La. 2007), and the issue was finally taken up and resolved by the U.S. Supreme Court through the following opinion:

## *Patrick Kennedy v. Louisiana*
### 554 U.S. 407 (2008)

KENNEDY, J.

Patrick Kennedy . . . seeks to set aside his death sentence under the Eighth Amendment. He was charged . . . with the aggravated rape of his then- 8-year-old stepdaughter. After a jury trial petitioner was convicted and sentenced to death under a state statute authorizing capital punishment for the rape of a child under 12 years of age. See La. Stat. Ann. §14:42 (West 1997 and Supp.1998). This case presents the question whether the Constitution bars respondent from imposing the death penalty for the rape of a child where the crime did not result, and was not intended to result, in death of the victim. We hold the Eighth Amendment prohibits the death penalty for this offense. The Louisiana statute is unconstitutional.

Petitioner's crime was one that cannot be recounted in these pages in a way sufficient to capture in full the hurt and horror inflicted on his victim or to convey the revulsion society, and the jury that represents it, sought to express by sentencing petitioner to death. At 9:18 a.m. on March 2, 1998, petitioner called 911 to report that his stepdaughter, referred to here as L. H., had been raped. . . .

L.H. was transported to the Children's Hospital. An expert in pediatric forensic medicine testified that L.H.'s injuries were the most severe he had seen from a sexual assault in his four years of practice. A laceration to the left wall of the vagina had separated her cervix from the back of her vagina, causing her rectum to protrude into the vaginal structure. Her entire perineum was torn from the posterior fourchette to the anus. The injuries required emergency surgery . . . .

The trial began in August 2003. L.H. was then 13 years old. She testified that she "'woke up one morning and [petitioner] was on top of [her].'" She remembered petitioner bringing her "[a] cup of orange juice and pills chopped up in it" after the rape and overhearing him on the telephone saying she had become a "young lady." . . .

The jury unanimously determined that petitioner should be sentenced to death. The Supreme Court of Louisiana affirmed. . . .

[W]hen the law punishes by death, it risks its own sudden descent into brutality, transgressing the constitutional commitment to decency and restraint. For these reasons we have explained that capital punishment must be limited to those offenders who commit a narrow category of the most serious crimes and whose extreme culpability makes them the most deserving of execution. Though the death penalty is not invariably unconstitutional, see Gregg v. Georgia, 428 U.S. 153 (1976), the Court insists upon confining the instances in which the punishment can be imposed . . .

In [Eighth Amendment] cases the Court has been guided by objective indicia of society's standards, as expressed in legislative enactments and state practice with respect to executions. . . . The inquiry does not end there, however. Consensus is not dispositive. Whether the death penalty is disproportionate to the crime committed depends as well upon the standards elaborated by controlling precedents and by the Court's own understanding and interpretation of the Eighth Amendment's text, history, meaning, and purpose. . . .

Louisiana reintroduced the death penalty for rape of a child in 1995. See La. Stat. Ann. §14:42 (West Supp.1996). . . . Mistake of age is not a defense, so the statute imposes strict liability in this regard. Five States have since followed Louisiana's lead: Georgia, see Ga. Code Ann. §16- 6-1 (2007) (enacted 1999); Montana, see Mont. Code Ann. §45-5-503 (2007) (enacted 1997); Oklahoma, see Okla. Stat., Tit. 10, §7115(K) (West 2007 Supp.) (enacted 2006); South Carolina, see S.C. Code Ann. §16-3-655(C)(1) (Supp. 2007) (enacted 2006); and Texas, see Tex. Penal Code Ann. §12.42(c)(3) (West Supp. 2007) (enacted 2007); see also Tex. Penal Code Ann. §22.021(a) (West Supp. 2007). . . .

By contrast, 44 States have not made child rape a capital offense. As for federal law, Congress in the Federal Death Penalty Act of 1994 expanded the number of federal crimes for which the death penalty is a permissible sentence, including certain nonhomicide offenses; but it did not do the same for child rape or abuse. . . .

Respondent insists that the six States where child rape is a capital offense, along with the States that have proposed but not yet enacted applicable death penalty legislation, reflect a consistent direction of change in support of the death penalty for child rape. Consistent change might counterbalance an otherwise weak demonstration of consensus. But whatever the significance of consistent change where it is cited to show emerging support for expanding the scope of the death penalty, no showing of consistent change has been made in this case. Respondent and its amici identify five States where, in their view, legislation authorizing capital punishment for child rape is pending. It is not our practice, nor is it sound, to find contemporary norms based upon state legislation that has been proposed but not yet enacted. . . .

Aside from pending legislation, it is true that in the last 13 years there has been change towards making child rape a capital offense. This is evidenced by six new death penalty statutes, three enacted in the last two years. But this showing is not as significant as the [legislative developments grounding rulings in other Eighth Amendment cases. Moreover,] no individual has been executed for the rape of an adult or child since 1964, and no execution for any other nonhomicide offense has been conducted since 1963. . . .

Louisiana is the only State since 1964 that has sentenced an individual to death for the crime of child rape; and petitioner and Richard Davis, who was convicted and sentenced to death for the aggravated rape of a 5-year-old child by a Louisiana jury in December 2007[,] are the only two individuals now on death row in the United States for a nonhomicide offense. After reviewing the authorities informed by contemporary norms, including the history of the death penalty for this and other nonhomicide crimes, current state statutes and new enactments, and the number of executions since 1964, we conclude there is a national consensus against capital punishment for the crime of child rape . . .

As we have said in other Eighth Amendment cases, objective evidence of contemporary values as it relates to punishment for child rape is entitled to great weight, but it does not end our inquiry. The Constitution contemplates that in the end our own judgment will be brought to bear on the question of the acceptability of the death penalty under the Eighth Amendment. . . .

It must be acknowledged that there are moral grounds to question a rule barring capital punishment for a crime against an individual that did not result in death. These facts illustrate the point. Here the victim's fright, the sense of betrayal, and the nature of her injuries caused more prolonged physical and mental suffering than, say, a sudden killing by an unseen assassin. The attack was not just on her but on her childhood. For this reason, we should be most reluctant to rely upon the language of the plurality in *Coker*, which posited that, for the victim of rape, "life may not be nearly so happy as it was" but it is not beyond repair. 433 U.S. at 598. Rape has a permanent psychological, emotional, and sometimes physical impact on the child. We cannot dismiss the years of long anguish that must be endured by the victim of child rape.

It does not follow, though, that capital punishment is a proportionate penalty for the crime. The constitutional prohibition against excessive or cruel and unusual punishments mandates that the State's power to punish "be exercised within the limits of civilized standards." *Trop*, 356 U.S., at 99, 100 (plurality opinion). Evolving standards of decency that mark the progress of a maturing society counsel us to be most hesitant before interpreting the Eighth Amendment to allow the extension of the death penalty, a hesitation that has special force where no life was taken in the commission of the crime. It is an established principle that decency, in its essence, presumes respect for the individual and thus moderation or restraint in the application of capital punishment . . . .

Our concern here is limited to crimes against individual persons. We do not address, for example, crimes defining and punishing treason, espionage, terrorism, and drug kingpin activity, which are offenses against the State. As it relates to crimes against individuals, though, the death penalty should not be expanded to instances where the victim's life was not taken. . . .

Consistent with evolving standards of decency and the teachings of our precedents we conclude that, in determining whether the death penalty is excessive, there is a distinction between intentional first-degree murder on the one hand and nonhomicide crimes against individual persons, even including child rape, on the other. The latter crimes may be devastating in their harm, as here, but "in terms of moral depravity and of the injury to the person and to the public," *Coker*, 433 U.S., at 598 (plurality opinion), they cannot be compared to murder in their "severity and irrevocability."

In reaching our conclusion we find significant the number of executions that would be allowed under respondent's approach. The crime of child rape, considering its reported incidents, occurs more often than first-degree murder. Approximately 5,702 incidents of vaginal, anal, or oral rape of a child under the age of 12 were reported nationwide in 2005; this is almost twice the total incidents of intentional murder for victims of all ages (3,405) reported during the same period. . . . [U]nder respondent's approach, the 36 States that permit the death penalty could sentence to death all persons convicted of raping a child less than 12 years of age. This could not be reconciled with our evolving standards of decency and the necessity to constrain the use of the death penalty.

It might be said that narrowing aggravators could be used in this context, as with murder offenses, to ensure the death penalty's restrained application. We find it difficult to identify standards that would guide the decisionmaker so the penalty is reserved for the most severe cases of child rape and yet not imposed in an arbitrary way. . . . [And i]t is not a solution simply to apply to this context the aggravating factors developed for capital murder. . . . All of these standards have the potential to result in some inconsistency of application. . . . Our concerns are all the more pronounced where, as here, the death penalty for this crime has been most infrequent. . . .

Our decision is consistent with the justifications offered for the death penalty. *Gregg* instructs that capital punishment is excessive when it is grossly out of proportion to the crime or it does not fulfill the two distinct social purposes served by the death penalty: retribution and deterrence of capital crimes.

As in *Coker*, here it cannot be said with any certainty that the death penalty for child rape serves no deterrent or retributive function. This argument does not overcome other objections, however. The incongruity between the crime of child rape and the harshness of the death penalty poses risks of overpunishment and counsels against a constitutional ruling that the death penalty can be expanded to include this offense.

The goal of retribution, which reflects society's and the victim's interests in seeing that the offender is repaid for the hurt he caused, does not justify the harshness of the death penalty here. In measuring retribution, as well as other objectives of criminal law, it is appropriate to distinguish between a particularly depraved murder that merits death as a form of retribution and the crime of child rape.

There is an additional reason for our conclusion that imposing the death penalty for child rape would not further retributive purposes. In considering whether retribution is served, among other factors we have looked to whether capital punishment has the potential to allow the community as a whole, including the surviving family and friends of the victim, to affirm its own judgment that the culpability of the prisoner is so serious that the ultimate penalty must be sought and imposed. In considering the death penalty for nonhomicide offenses this inquiry necessarily also must include the question whether the death penalty balances the wrong to the victim.

It is not at all evident that the child rape victim's hurt is lessened when the law permits the death of the perpetrator. Capital cases require a long-term commitment by those who testify for the prosecution, especially when guilt and sentencing determinations are in multiple proceedings. In cases like this the key testimony is not just from the family but from the victim herself. During formative years of her adolescence, made all the more daunting for having to come to terms with the brutality of her experience, L. H. was required to discuss the case at length with law enforcement personnel. In a public trial she was required to recount once more all the details of the crime to a jury as the State pursued the death of her stepfather. And in the end the State made L.H. a central figure in its decision to seek the death penalty, telling the jury in closing statements: "[L.H.] is asking you, asking you to set up a time and place when he dies." Tr. 121 (Aug. 26, 2003).

Society's desire to inflict the death penalty for child rape by enlisting the child victim to assist it over the course of years in asking for capital punishment forces a moral choice on the child, who is not of mature age to make that choice. The way the death penalty here involves the child victim in its enforcement can compromise a decent legal system; and this is but a subset of fundamental difficulties capital punishment can cause in the administration and enforcement of laws proscribing child rape.

There are, moreover, serious systemic concerns in prosecuting the crime of child rape that are relevant to the constitutionality of making it a capital offense. The problem of unreliable, induced, and even imagined child testimony means there is a "special risk of wrongful execution" in some child rape cases. This undermines, at least to some degree, the meaningful contribution of the death penalty to legitimate goals of punishment. Studies conclude that children are highly susceptible to suggestive questioning techniques like repetition, guided imagery, and selective reinforcement.

Similar criticisms pertain to other cases involving child witnesses; but child rape cases present heightened concerns because the central narrative and account of the crime often comes from the child herself. She and the accused are, in most instances, the only ones present when the crime was committed. And the question in a capital case is not just the fact of the crime, including, say, proof of rape as distinct from abuse short of rape, but details bearing upon brutality in its commission. These matters are subject to fabrication or exaggeration, or both. Although capital punishment does bring retribution, and the legislature here has chosen to use it for this end, its judgment must be weighed, in deciding the constitutional question, against the special risks of unreliable testimony with respect to this crime.

With respect to deterrence, if the death penalty adds to the risk of non-reporting, that, too, diminishes the penalty's objectives. Underreporting is a common problem with respect to child sexual abuse. See Hanson, Resnick, Saunders, Kilpatrick, & Best, Factors Related to the Reporting of Childhood Rape, 23 Child Abuse & Neglect 559, 564 (1999) (finding that about 88% of female rape victims under the age of 18 did not disclose their abuse to authorities); Smith et al., Delay in Disclosure of Childhood Rape: Results From A National Survey, 24 Child Abuse & Neglect 273, 278-279 (2000) (finding that 72% of women raped as children disclosed their abuse to someone, but that only 12% of the victims reported the rape to authorities). Although we know little about what differentiates those who report from those who do not report, one of the most commonly cited reasons for nondisclosure is fear of negative consequences for the perpetrator, a concern that has special force where the abuser is a family member. The experience of the amici who work with child victims indicates that, when the punishment is death, both the victim and the victim's family members may be more likely to shield the perpetrator from discovery, thus increasing underreporting. See Brief for National Association of Social Workers et al. as Amici Curiae 11-13. As a result, punishment by death may not result in more deterrence or more effective enforcement.

In addition, by in effect making the punishment for child rape and murder equivalent, a State that punishes child rape by death may remove a strong incentive for the rapist not to kill the victim. Assuming the offender behaves in a rational way, as one must to justify the penalty on grounds of deterrence, the penalty in some respects gives less protection, not more, to the victim, who is often the sole witness to the crime. See Rayburn, Better Dead Than R(ap)ed?: The Patriarchal Rhetoric Driving Capital Rape Statutes, 78 St. John's L. Rev. 1119, 1159-1160 (2004). It might be argued that, even if the death penalty results in a marginal increase in the incentive to kill, this is counterbalanced by a marginally increased deterrent to commit the crime at all. Whatever balance the legislature strikes, however, uncertainty on the point makes the argument for the penalty less compelling than for homicide crimes.

Each of these propositions, standing alone, might not establish the unconstitutionality of the death penalty for the crime of child rape. Taken in sum, however, they demonstrate the serious negative consequences of making child rape a capital offense. These considerations lead us to conclude, in our independent judgment, that the death penalty is not a proportional punishment for the rape of a child.

Our determination that there is a consensus against the death penalty for child rape raises the question whether the Court's own institutional position and its holding will have the effect of blocking further or later consensus in favor of the penalty from developing. The Court, it will be argued, by the act of addressing the constitutionality of the death penalty, intrudes upon the consensus-making process. By imposing a negative restraint, the argument runs, the Court makes it more difficult for consensus to change or emerge. The Court, according to the criticism, itself becomes enmeshed in the process, part judge and part the maker of that which it judges.

These concerns overlook the meaning and full substance of the established proposition that the Eighth Amendment is defined by "the evolving standards of decency that mark the progress of a maturing society." . . . The rule of evolving standards of decency with specific marks on the way to full progress and mature judgment means that resort to the penalty must be reserved for the worst of crimes and limited in its instances of application. In most cases justice is not better served by terminating the life of the perpetrator rather than confining him and preserving the possibility that he and the system will find ways to allow him to understand the enormity of his offense. Difficulties in administering the penalty to ensure against its arbitrary and capricious application require adherence to a rule reserving its use, at this stage of evolving standards and in cases of crimes against individuals, for crimes that take the life of the victim. The judgment of the Supreme Court of Louisiana upholding the capital sentence is reversed. . . .

ALITO, J., dissenting.

The Court is willing to block the potential emergence of a national consensus in favor of permitting the death penalty for child rape because, in the end, what matters is the Court's "own judgment" regarding "the acceptability of the death penalty." Although the Court has much to say on this issue, most of the Court's discussion is not pertinent to the Eighth Amendment question at hand. And once all of the Court's irrelevant arguments are put aside, it is apparent that the Court has provided no coherent explanation for today's decision. . . .

A major theme of the Court's opinion is that permitting the death penalty in child-rape cases is not in the best interests of the victims of these crimes and society at large. In this vein, the Court suggests that it is more painful for child-rape victims to testify when the prosecution is seeking the death penalty. The Court also argues that "a State that punishes child rape by death may remove a strong incentive for the rapist not to kill the victim," and may discourage the reporting of child rape.

These policy arguments, whatever their merits, are simply not pertinent to the question whether the death penalty is "cruel and unusual" punishment. The Eighth Amendment protects the right of an accused. It does not authorize this Court to strike down federal or state criminal laws on the ground that they are not in the best interests of crime victims or the broader society. The Court's policy arguments concern matters that legislators should — and presumably do — take into account in deciding whether to enact a capital child-rape statute, but these arguments are irrelevant to the question that is before us in this case. Our cases have cautioned against using "the aegis of the Cruel and Unusual Punishment Clause to cut off the normal democratic processes," Atkins v. Virginia, 536 U.S. 304, 323 (2002) (Rehnquist, C. J., dissenting), but the Court forgets that warning here.

The Court also contends that laws permitting the death penalty for the rape of a child create serious procedural problems. Specifically, the Court maintains that it is not feasible to channel the exercise of sentencing discretion in child-rape cases, and that the unreliability of the testimony of child victims creates a danger that innocent defendants will be convicted and executed. Neither of these contentions provides a basis for striking down all capital child-rape laws no matter how carefully and narrowly they are crafted.

The Court's argument regarding the structuring of sentencing discretion is hard to comprehend. The Court finds it "difficult to identify standards that would guide the decisionmaker so the penalty is reserved for the most severe cases of child rape and yet not imposed in an arbitrary way." Even assuming that the age of a child is not alone a sufficient factor for limiting sentencing discretion, the Court need only examine the child-rape laws recently enacted in Texas, Oklahoma, Montana, and South Carolina, all of which use a concrete factor to limit quite drastically the number of cases in which the death penalty may be imposed. In those States, a defendant convicted of the rape of a child may be sentenced to death only if the defendant has a prior conviction for a specified felony sex offense.

Moreover, it takes little imagination to envision other limiting factors that a State could use to structure sentencing discretion in child rape cases. Some of these might be: whether the victim was kidnapped, whether the defendant inflicted severe physical injury on the victim, whether the victim was raped multiple times, whether the rapes occurred over a specified extended period, and whether there were multiple victims.

The Court refers to limiting standards that are "indefinite and obscure," but there is nothing indefinite or obscure about any of the above-listed aggravating factors. Indeed, they are far more definite and clear-cut than aggravating factors that we have found to be adequate in murder cases. For these reasons, concerns about limiting sentencing discretion provide no support for the Court's blanket condemnation of all capital child-rape statutes.

That sweeping holding is also not justified by the Court's concerns about the reliability of the testimony of child victims. First, the Eighth Amendment provides a poor vehicle for addressing problems regarding the admissibility or reliability of evidence, and problems presented by the testimony of child victims are not unique to capital cases. Second, concerns about the reliability of the testimony of child witnesses are not present in every child-rape case. In the case before us, for example, there was undisputed medical evidence that the victim was brutally raped, as well as strong independent evidence that petitioner was the perpetrator. Third, if the Court's evidentiary concerns have Eighth Amendment relevance, they could be addressed by allowing the death penalty in only those child-rape cases in which the independent evidence is sufficient to prove all the elements needed for conviction and imposition of a death sentence. There is precedent for requiring special corroboration in certain criminal cases. For example, some jurisdictions do not allow a conviction based on the uncorroborated testimony of an accomplice. A State wishing to permit the death penalty in child-rape cases could impose an analogous corroboration requirement.

After all the arguments noted above are put aside, what is left? What remaining grounds does the Court provide to justify its independent judgment that the death penalty for child rape is categorically unacceptable? I see two. The first is the proposition that we should be "most hesitant before interpreting the Eighth Amendment to allow the extension of the death penalty." But holding that the Eighth Amendment does not categorically prohibit the death penalty for the rape of a young child would not "extend" or "expand" the death penalty. Laws enacted by the state legislatures are presumptively constitutional, and until today, this Court has not held that capital child rape laws are unconstitutional. Consequently, upholding the constitutionality of such a law would not "extend" or "expand" the death penalty; rather, it would confirm the status of presumptive constitutionality that such laws have enjoyed up to this point. And in any event, this Court has previously made it clear that "[t]he Eighth Amendment is not a ratchet, whereby a temporary consensus on leniency for a particular crime fixes a permanent constitutional maximum, disabling States from giving effect to altered beliefs and responding to changed social conditions." Harmelin v. Michigan, 501 U.S. 957, 990 (1991).

The Court's final — and, it appears, principal — justification for its holding is that murder, the only crime for which defendants have been executed since this Court's 1976 death penalty decisions, is unique in its moral depravity and in the severity of the injury that it inflicts on the victim and the public. But the Court makes little attempt to defend these conclusions. With respect to the question of moral depravity, is it really true that every person who is convicted of capital murder and sentenced to death is more morally depraved than every child rapist? Consider the following two cases. In the first, a defendant robs a convenience store and watches as his accomplice shoots the store owner. The defendant acts recklessly, but was not the triggerman and did not intend the killing. In the second case, a previously convicted child rapist kidnaps, repeatedly rapes, and tortures multiple child victims. Is it clear that the first defendant is more morally depraved than the second? . . .

Indeed, I have little doubt that, in the eyes of ordinary Americans, the very worst child rapists — predators who seek out and inflict serious physical and emotional injury on defenseless young children — are the epitome of moral depravity.

With respect to the question of the harm caused by the rape of child in relation to the harm caused by murder, it is certainly true that the loss of human life represents a unique harm, but that does not explain why other grievous harms are insufficient to permit a death sentence. And the Court does not take the position that no harm other than the loss of life is sufficient. The

Court takes pains to limit its holding to "crimes against individual persons" and to exclude "offenses against the State," a category that the Court stretches — without explanation — to include "drug kingpin activity." But the Court makes no effort to explain why the harm caused by such crimes is necessarily greater than the harm caused by the rape of young children. This is puzzling in light of the Court's acknowledgment that "[r]ape has a permanent psychological, emotional, and sometimes physical impact on the child." As the Court aptly recognizes, "[w]e cannot dismiss the years of long anguish that must be endured by the victim of child rape."

The rape of any victim inflicts great injury, and "[s]ome victims are so grievously injured physically or psychologically that life is beyond repair." Coker, 433 U.S., at 603 (opinion of Powell, J.). "The immaturity and vulnerability of a child, both physically and psychologically, adds a devastating dimension to rape that is not present when an adult is raped." Meister, Murdering Innocence: The Constitutionality of Capital Child Rape Statutes, 45 Ariz. L. Rev. 197, 208-209 (2003). . . . It has been estimated that as many as 40% of 7- to 13-year-old sexual assault victims are considered "seriously disturbed." A. Lurigio, M. Jones, & B. Smith, Child Sexual Abuse: Its Causes, Consequences, and Implications for Probation Practice, 59 Fed. Probation 69, 70 (1995). Psychological problems include sudden school failure, unprovoked crying, dissociation, depression, insomnia, sleep disturbances, nightmares, feelings of guilt and inferiority, and self-destructive behavior, including an increased incidence of suicide.

The deep problems that afflict child-rape victims often become society's problems as well. Commentators have noted correlations between childhood sexual abuse and later problems such as substance abuse, dangerous sexual behaviors or dysfunction, inability to relate to others on an interpersonal level, and psychiatric illness. Victims of child rape are nearly 5 times more likely than nonvictims to be arrested for sex crimes and nearly 30 times more likely to be arrested for prostitution.

The harm that is caused to the victims and to society at large by the worst child rapists is grave. It is the judgment of the Louisiana lawmakers and those in an increasing number of other States that these harms justify the death penalty. The Court provides no cogent explanation why this legislative judgment should be overridden. Conclusory references to "decency," "moderation," "restraint," "full progress," and "moral judgment" are not enough.

### NOTES

1. *Constitutional judgments about punishment purposes and process.* The *Kennedy* ruling included extensive discussion of not only traditional *purposes* of punishment, but also ways in which the *process* of punishment can impact the achievement of these purposes. Do you find the majority's or the dissent's discussion of sentencing purposes and practices more compelling in *Kennedy*? Do you think the Eighth Amendment necessarily demands that judges make constitutional judgments about these matters, or do you agree with the dissent that these considerations are fundamentally policy matters that ought only be considered and assessed by state legislators and ought not be central to judicial

constitutional judgments? The Supreme Court has given extended consideration to punishment purposes, processes and practices principally when defendants are challenging state application of the death penalty; but is there a strong basis in either the text or purposes of the Eighth Amendment which calls for a unique constitutional jurisprudence for the unique punishment of death? Cf. Rachel Barkow, The Court of Life and Death: The Two Tracks of Constitutional Sentencing Law and the Case for Uniformity, 107 Michigan Law Review 1145 (2009).

2. *States as laboratories for extreme (but rare) punishments.* As the majority opinion notes, not long prior to the Supreme Court's ruling in *Kennedy* six states had made child rape a capital offense, and a number of other states had been considering but had not yet enacted similar death penalty legislation. This clear pattern of "change towards making child rape a capital offense" prior to the *Kennedy* ruling clearly reflected growing concerns about extreme sexual offenses against ever younger children, although in most states this concern was focused particularly on repeat offenders: in every state except Louisiana that had enacted or was seriously considering enacting capital child rape laws, only defendants with a prior sex offense conviction would be eligible for the death penalty based on a new conviction for child rape. Despite an Eighth Amendment jurisprudence concerning prison sentencing terms that has sometimes stressed the legitimacy of imposing more severe punishment on repeat offenders (as discussed more fully in Chapter 7), the *Kennedy* ruling did not indicate or even seem open to the possibility that statutes which made only repeat child rapists eligible for the death penalty could be constitutionally sound. Especially with states still in the process of experimenting with whether and how to make extreme forms of child rape subject to the extreme punishment of death, should the Supreme Court in *Kennedy* have tried to set forth its ruling in much narrower terms in order to give states more room to experiment with refined approaches to making some child rapists eligible for the death penalty? Or do you think that the bright-line Eighth Amendment rule prohibiting all forms of child rape from even being the basis for a death sentence has the virtue of directly and conclusively removing all uncertainty concerning the permissibility of this punishment for states, litigants and defendants?

3. *Nonjudicial assessments of harm and severity of punishment.* Distinct from any constitutional questions about permissible punishments are the policy questions concerning appropriate punishments. As to the death penalty, 32 states along with the federal government permit the imposition of capital punishment for certain aggravated homicides, although there is some notable variation in these jurisdictions as to exactly which sorts of aggravating factors make a particular killer eligible for capital punishment. See Death Penalty Information Center website at http://www.deathpenaltyinfo.org/capitaloffenses.html; Va. Code §18.2-31(12) ("killing of a person under the age of fourteen by a person age twenty-one or older"); Ala. Code §13A-5-40(a)(11) ("when the victim is a state or federal public official or former public official and the murder stems from or is caused by or is related to his official position"); Ind. Code §35-50-2-9(b) ("killing the victim while committing or attempting to commit any of the following [crimes]: arson, burglary, child molesting, criminal deviate conduct,

kidnapping, rape, robbery, carjacking, criminal gang activity, dealing in cocaine or a narcotic drug"). Do these aggravating factors speak to the same basic types of harm?

Although varying in their use and application of the death penalty, nearly all jurisdictions deem aggravated forms of homicide to be the most serious of crimes. In states without the death penalty, this means the crime is punished by life imprisonment without the possibility of parole. Similarly, though *Coker* and *Kennedy* make the death penalty unavailable for the crimes of rape, most jurisdictions still provide severe sanctions for serious sexual offenses, especially when these crimes include additional physical harm to the victim or when the victim is young or especially vulnerable. See Ohio Rev. Code §2907.02.

How do legislatures and commissions make judgments about the relative seriousness of offenses less obvious than murder or rape? Consider again Dale Parent's description, reprinted in Chapter 3, of the efforts of the Minnesota Sentencing Commission to rank different offenses. What other methods might you recommend?

Although legislatures and commissions must grade offenses in comparison with other offenses, they also guide sentencing judges in how to distinguish among offenders convicted of the same crime. The following materials highlight two ways that sentencing rules can specifically respond to various harms and threats of harms.

|| *State v. Stanley Royster* ||
|| **590 N.W.2d 82 (Minn. 1999)** ||

STRINGER, J.

On February 12, 1997, the Minneapolis Police executed a search warrant at Royster's residence [searching for illegal drugs]. Police found Royster and another man inside. Items recovered in Royster's search included cash in his pocket and some pre-recorded buy money from the Minneapolis Narcotics Unit. In the premises search, specifically of Royster's bedroom, the police recovered additional pre-recorded buy money, a bag of crack-cocaine in a boot, and a fully-loaded .22 revolver from underneath his mattress located approximately three feet from the boot containing the crack-cocaine. After his arrest Royster admitted to the police that he was selling cocaine out of his home and claimed that his father had given him the revolver for protection because he lived in a dangerous neighborhood. . . .

When Minnesota Statute §609.11, subdivision 5, was enacted in 1981, it originally provided in relevant part [that any defendant convicted of specified offenses] in which "the defendant or an accomplice, at the time of the offense, used, whether by brandishing, displaying, threatening with, or otherwise employing, a firearm"[must receive a minimum prison term of at least three years.] Another subdivision pertaining to commission of a predicate offense while "in possession of a firearm," mandated a minimum sentence of one year. . . . In 1994 the Minnesota Legislature [consolidated these subdivisions to provide that] both *possession* and *use* while committing a predicate felony offense triggered the three-year mandatory minimum sentence.

Royster argues that [the "possession" term in the 1994 amendment] must be read in conjunction with "brandishing, displaying, threatening with, or otherwise employing"[the firearm] to trigger the mandatory minimum sentence and because his firearm was not so employed but rather lay dormant under his mattress, he did not have the "possession" contemplated by the legislature. Clearly the statute cannot be read to reach such a conclusion however, for it is obvious that in 1994 the legislature intended to increase the sentence for those who possess a firearm while committing a crime even though they do not actually use a firearm. To conclude that "possession" must be accompanied by some kind of "brandishing" would render the 1994 amendment meaningless. . . . We hold that "brandishing" is not required as an element of proof of possession to trigger the [three-year] mandatory minimum sentence. . . .

Finally, we consider what should be the test for determining when constructive possession while committing the predicate offense should trigger the mandatory minimum sentence. The sentence enhancement amendment reflects the obvious reality that possession of a firearm while committing a predicate felony offense substantially increases the risk of violence, whether or not the offender actually uses the firearm. The firearm in possession was recognized by the legislature as an "insurance policy . . . to be used to further the crime if need be" and clearly raises the stakes of severe injury or death as a result of the commission of the predicate offenses. It seems reasonable then to examine all aspects of the firearm in possession to determine whether it was reasonable to assume that its presence increased the risk of violence and to what degree the risk is increased: the nature, type and condition of the firearm, its ownership, whether it was loaded, its ease of accessibility, its proximity to the drugs, why the firearm was present and whether the nature of the predicate offense is frequently or typically accompanied by use of a firearm, to name a few of the considerations.

Applying these standards to the present case, we hold that the state presented sufficient evidence to prove beyond a reasonable doubt that Royster's possession of a firearm while committing the predicate felony offense met the requisites of section 609.11, subdivision 5. Because Royster's .22 caliber pistol, fully loaded, was found under Royster's mattress within 3 feet of 2.9 grams of crack-cocaine, the trial court could reasonably infer that possession of the firearm substantially increased the risk of violence related to his drug trafficking.

## ‖ *U.S. Sentencing Guidelines Manual* ‖

### §2B3.1   ROBBERY

(a) Base Offense Level: 20
(b) Specific Offense Characteristics
   (1) If the property of a financial institution or post office was taken, or if the taking of such property was an object of the offense, increase by 2 levels.
   (2) (A) If a firearm was discharged, increase by 7 levels; (B) if a firearm was otherwise used, increase by 6 levels; (C) if a firearm was brandished or possessed, increase by 5 levels; (D) if a dangerous weapon was otherwise used,

increase by 4 levels; (E) if a dangerous weapon was brandished or possessed, increase by 3 levels; or (F) if a threat of death was made, increase by 2 levels.

(3) If any victim sustained bodily injury, increase the offense level according to the seriousness of the injury:

| *Degree of Bodily Injury* | *Increase in Level* |
|---|---|
| (A) Bodily Injury | add 2 |
| (B) Serious Bodily Injury | add 4 |
| (C) Permanent or Life-Threatening Bodily Injury | add 6 |
| (D) If the degree of injury is between that specified in subdivisions (A) and (B), add 3 levels; or | |
| (E) If the degree of injury is between that specified in subdivisions (B) and (C), add 5 levels. | |

*Provided*, however, that the cumulative adjustments from (2) and (3) shall not exceed 11 levels.

## NOTES

1. *Legislative and commission roles in defining offense seriousness.*  Sometimes legislative bodies decide for themselves the specific increases in sentences that must occur when particular harms or threats are present. The *Royster* case gives one example of legislatively enacted mandatory sentencing laws that have proven popular at both the federal and state levels, especially in the context of narcotics and weapons offenses. In the federal system, more than 75 statutes now establish fixed prison terms or minimum sentences that judges must impose based on certain offense factors. Over the past two decades, nearly every state has also adopted some form of mandatory sentencing provisions. See, e.g., Dale Parent et al., National Institute of Justice, Mandatory Sentencing (January 1997). As we saw in Chapter 2, legislators often embrace mandatory sentencing laws primarily for immediate political benefits, even though studies have generally shown that these laws are not applied uniformly and thus have limited deterrent impact and produce sentencing disparities. Indeed, the consensus within the criminal justice community is that, in practice, mandatory sentencing laws are ineffectual and often produce unjust outcomes. See, e.g., Jonathan P. Caulkins et al., Rand Corporation, Mandatory Minimum Drug Sentences: Throwing Away the Key or the Taxpayer's Money (1997); Barbara S. Vincent & Paul J. Hofer, Federal Judicial Center, The Consequences of Mandatory Minimum Prison Terms: A Summary of Recent Findings (1994); Gary T. Lowenthal, Mandatory Sentencing Laws: Undermining the Effectiveness of Determinate Sentencing Reform, 81 Cal. L. Rev. 61 (1993).

Judges also tend to have a low regard for mandatory minimum sentences set by legislatures. In August 2003 Justice Anthony Kennedy delivered a speech to the American Bar Association that was frankly critical of mandatory sentencing laws in the federal system: "Our resources are being misspent. Our punishments are too severe. Our sentences are too long." He urged the ABA to tell Congress, "Don't take discretion away from the courts. . . . Let judges be judges." Although he agreed with the need for federal sentencing guidelines to set uniform sentences, he contrasted guidelines with mandatory minimum sentences: "I can accept neither the wisdom, the justice nor the necessity of mandatory minimums. . . . In all too many cases, they are unjust. . . . A country which is secure in its institutions and confident in its laws should not be ashamed of the concept of mercy."

Section 2B3.1 of the federal sentencing guidelines illustrates an important alternative to mandatory minimum sentences. Structured sentencing jurisdictions can employ a more refined approach to assessing offense seriousness. In the federal system, determinations of an offense's overall seriousness can be highly detailed; for example, in addition to the portion reprinted above, §2B3.1 has four additional subsections and incorporates three pages of application notes. In state guideline systems, the computation is less complex but the idea is similar. The guidelines list particularly serious harms or threats as grounds for increasing the presumptive sentence. See N.C. Gen. Stat. §15A-1340.16(d)(8), (13) (aggravating factor if the defendant "knowingly created a great risk of death to more than one person" or "involved a person under the age of 16 in the commission of the crime").

2. *Sentencing enhancements based on "use" of firearm or weapon.* Federal criminal law and the laws of many states increase criminal penalties and sometimes mandate certain minimum sentences when the offense behavior involves use of a firearm or other weapon. See, e.g., 18 U.S.C. §924(c) (mandating five years' imprisonment consecutive to the sentence for the underlying offense whenever a defendant "uses or carries" a firearm "during and in relation to" any crime of violence or drug trafficking offense); 42 Pa. Cons. Stat. Ann. §9712 (mandating five-year minimum sentence for "visibly possessing a firearm or a replica of a firearm during the commission of a crime of violence").

As *Royster* highlights, statutes that include such weapons enhancements often raise legal questions about the "use" or "possession" that is sufficient to trigger the special sanctions. For example, in Bailey v. United States, 516 U.S. 137 (1995), the Supreme Court narrowed application of the "uses" provision in the federal firearms enhancement, overturning a conviction of a defendant who possessed a loaded pistol that police found inside a bag in his locked car trunk after they arrested him for possession of cocaine that they found in the passenger compartment. Congress soon amended the statute to cover all forms of possession of a firearm "in furtherance of" the crime and also introduced even higher mandatory penalties for brandishing or discharging a weapon, for repeat offenders, and for using certain types of dangerous guns. As a legislator, would you attach use of a weapon to particular crimes, or would you use it as a sentence enhancement for any crime? Are certain kinds of crimes categorically more blameworthy or more harmful by the presence or use of a gun?

In June 2008, the Supreme Court in Heller v. District of Columbia, 554 U.S. 570 (2008), held that the Second Amendment protects an individual right to possess a firearm in the home for self-protection, though the Court left unclear the exact scope of this right or the level of constitutional scrutiny that must now

be given to firearm prohibitions. Before *Heller*, federal sentencing enhancements for possessing a firearm in furtherance of a drug crime have been broadly
applied — e.g., defendants would regularly be subject to such an enhancement
based on the presence of a gun in an upstairs bedroom closet even if all the
evidence of drug dealing was confined to a basement location. In the wake of
*Heller*, should a defendant be able to challenge the application of any sentencing
enhancement based on possession of a gun in the home if the defendant can
make a credible claim that the gun was only kept for personal self-protection and
was never used or brandished in connection with any criminal activity taking
place in the home?

3. *Bodily harm and other aggravating factors.*  Federal criminal law and the
laws of many states increase criminal penalties or mandate certain minimum
sentences, or both, when offenses result in bodily harm. Sometimes these
enhancements are codified as elements of other crimes. For example, many
kidnapping statutes increase the penalty when the offender harms the seized
victims. See, e.g., 18 U.S.C. §1201; Cal. Penal Code §209. Especially in states with
guidelines, it is common to place such enhancements in general sentencing
instructions. See, e.g., Fla. Stat. Ann. §921.0016(3)(l) (allowing departure
from guideline sentence if the victim "suffered extraordinary physical or emotional
trauma or permanent physical injury"). Courts have addressed many issues under
these statutes, including whether certain injuries are severe enough to constitute
harm within the statutory meaning and whether harm inflicted by an accomplice or
accessory can be attributed to the defendant for sentencing purposes.

Many other indicators of serious harms or threats can operate just like use
of a firearm or bodily injury. Legislatures or sentencing commissions designate
these factors as a basis for increased sentences. Sometimes the increase is
defined, and in other instances the judge is allowed to increase the sentence
in her discretion. See, e.g., U.S. Sentencing Guidelines Manual §3B1.4 (increasing offense level by 2 if defendant used a minor to commit crime); Utah Sentencing Guidelines Form 4 (listing as an aggravating sentencing factor the fact
that the "offense was characterized by extreme cruelty or depravity").

## PROBLEM 4-6.  ROB ANON REVISITED

Recall again Rob Anon, described in Problem 4-1, and then reexamine the
specifics of §2B3.1 of the federal guidelines. Based on that provision, how many
offense levels should be added to the base offense level of 20? Though it appears
that at least 9 levels must be added, interpretation of the provision's key terms
might suggest that as many as 13 levels should be added; the difference between
adding 9 and adding 13 levels could mean a sentencing range for Rob as low as 8
to 10 years or as high as 12 to 15 years.

## 2.  *Quantitative Assessments of Harm*

Certain types of offenses — particularly drug crimes and economic crimes —
lend themselves to quantitative measures of offense seriousness. For drug

crimes, offense harms are defined in terms of the type and quantity of the drugs involved. For economic crimes, offense harms are defined in terms of the quantity of money taken. Larger quantities of drugs or a larger amount of money mean a more severe sentence.

As the following case highlights, the amount of "quantified harm," especially in drug cases under federal law, can have a dramatic impact on sentence length, eclipsing the impact of all other sentencing factors. For example, even for a first-time offender, the amount of drugs involved in a drug distribution offense could mean the difference between a sentence of life imprisonment (for very large quantities) and a sentence of probation (for very small quantities). See U.S. Sentencing Guidelines Manual §2D1.1(c). As you read the following case, consider why jurisdictions rely so heavily on quantifiable measures of offense seriousness in drug crimes and financial crimes, and also consider whether there can and should be other ways to judge offense seriousness in these settings.

## Richard Chapman v. United States
### 500 U.S. 453 (1991)

REHNQUIST, C.J.

Section 841(b)(1)(B)(v) of Title 21 of the United States Code calls for a mandatory minimum sentence of five years for the offense of distributing more than one gram of a "mixture or substance containing a detectable amount of lysergic acid diethylamide (LSD)." We hold that it is the weight of the blotter paper containing LSD, and not the weight of the pure LSD, which determines eligibility for the minimum sentence.

Petitioner Richard L. Chapman [was] convicted of selling 10 sheets (1,000 doses) of blotter paper containing LSD. The District Court included the total weight of the paper and LSD in determining the weight of the drug to be used in calculating petitioners' sentences. . . . [Chapman and his co-petitioner claim] that the blotter paper is only a carrier medium, and that its weight should not be included in the weight of the drug for sentencing purposes. Alternatively, [they argue] that, if the statute and Sentencing Guidelines were construed so as to require inclusion of the blotter paper or other carrier medium when calculating the weight of the drug, this would violate the right to equal protection incorporated in the Due Process Clause of the Fifth Amendment. . . .

Title 21 U.S.C. §841(b)(1)(B) provides that [a person who distributes one gram or more of a "mixture or substance containing a detectable amount" of LSD must be sentenced to a prison term of at least five years; §841(b)(1)(A)(v) calls for a mandatory minimum of ten years' imprisonment for a violation involving ten grams or more]. Section 2D1.1(c) of the Sentencing Guidelines parallels the statutory language and requires the base offense level to be determined based upon the weight of a "mixture or substance containing a detectable amount of" LSD.

According to the Sentencing Commission, the LSD in an average dose weighs 0.05 milligrams; there are therefore 20,000 pure doses in a gram. The pure dose is such an infinitesimal amount that it must be sold to retail customers in a "carrier" [such as] paper or gel . . . cut into "one-dose" squares and sold by the dose. . . . Although gelatin and paper are light, they weigh much more than the LSD. The ten sheets of blotter paper carrying the 1,000 doses sold by petitioners weighed 5.7 grams; the LSD by itself weighed only about 50 milligrams, not even close to the one gram necessary to trigger the 5-year mandatory minimum.

Petitioners argue that §841(b) should not require that the weight of the carrier be included when computing the appropriate sentence for LSD distribution, for the words "mixture or substance" are ambiguous, and should not be construed to reach an illogical result. Because LSD is sold by dose, rather than by weight, the weight of the LSD carrier should not be included when determining a defendant's sentence, because it is irrelevant to culpability. They argue that including the weight of the carrier leads to anomalous results, viz: a major wholesaler caught with 19,999 doses of pure LSD would not be subject to the five-year mandatory minimum sentence, while a minor pusher with 200 doses on blotter paper, or even one dose on a sugar cube, would be subject to the mandatory minimum sentence. Thus, they contend, the weight of the carrier should be excluded, the weight of the pure LSD should be determined, and that weight should be used to set the appropriate sentence.

We think that petitioners' reading of the statute — a reading that makes the penalty turn on the net weight of the drug, rather than the gross weight of the carrier and drug together — is not a plausible one. The statute refers to a "mixture or substance containing a detectable amount." So long as it contains a detectable amount, the entire mixture or substance is to be weighed when calculating the sentence.

This reading is confirmed by the structure of the statute. With respect to various drugs, including heroin, cocaine, and LSD, it provides for mandatory minimum sentences for crimes involving certain weights of a "mixture or substance containing a detectable amount" of the drugs. With respect to other drugs, however, namely phencyclidine (PCP) or methamphetamine, it provides for a mandatory minimum sentence based either on the weight of a mixture or substance containing a detectable amount of the drug, or on lower weights of pure PCP or methamphetamine. . . . Thus, with respect to these two drugs, Congress clearly distinguished between the pure drug and a "mixture or substance containing a detectable amount of" the pure drug. But with respect to drugs such as LSD, which petitioners distributed, Congress declared that sentences should be based exclusively on the weight of the "mixture or substance." Congress knew how to indicate that the weight of the pure drug was to be used to determine the sentence, and did not make that distinction with respect to LSD. . . .

The history of Congress's attempts to control illegal drug distribution shows why Congress chose the course that it did with respect to sentencing. The Comprehensive Drug Abuse Prevention and Control Act of 1970 . . . did not link penalties to the quantity of the drug possessed; penalties instead depended upon whether the drug was classified as a narcotic or not. The Controlled Substances Penalties Amendments Act of 1984 . . . first made punishment dependent upon the quantity of the controlled substance involved [and was] intended "to provide a more rational penalty structure for the major drug trafficking offenses," by eliminating sentencing disparities caused by classifying drugs as narcotic and non-narcotic. Penalties were based instead upon the weight of the pure drug involved.

The current penalties for LSD distribution originated in the Anti–Drug Abuse Act of 1986. Congress adopted a "market-oriented" approach to punishing drug trafficking, under which the total quantity of what is distributed, rather than the amount of pure drug involved, is used to determine the length of the sentence. To implement that principle, Congress set mandatory minimum sentences corresponding to the weight of a "mixture or substance containing a detectable amount of" the various controlled substances, including LSD. It intended the penalties for drug trafficking to be graduated according to the weight of the drugs in whatever form they were found—cut or uncut, pure or impure, ready for wholesale or ready for distribution at the retail level. Congress did not want to punish retail traffickers less severely, even though they deal in smaller quantities of the pure drug, because such traffickers keep the street markets going. . . .

Petitioners argue that the due process of law guaranteed them by the Fifth Amendment is violated by determining the lengths of their sentences in accordance with the weight of the LSD "carrier," a factor which they insist is arbitrary. . . . We find that Congress had a rational basis for its choice of penalties for LSD distribution. The penalty scheme set out in the Anti-Drug Abuse Act of 1986 is intended to punish severely large-volume drug traffickers at any level. . . . That is a rational sentencing scheme.

This is as true with respect to LSD as it is with respect to other drugs. Although LSD is not sold by weight, but by dose, and a carrier medium is not, strictly speaking, used to "dilute" the drug, that medium is used to facilitate the distribution of the drug. Blotter paper makes LSD easier to transport, store, conceal, and sell. It is a tool of the trade for those who traffic in the drug, and therefore it was rational for Congress to set penalties based on this chosen tool. Congress was also justified in seeking to avoid arguments about the accurate weight of pure drugs which might have been extracted from blotter paper had it chosen to calibrate sentences according to that weight. . . .

Petitioners argue that those selling different numbers of doses, and, therefore, with different degrees of culpability, will be subject to the same minimum sentence because of choosing different carriers. The same objection could be made to a statute that imposed a fixed sentence for distributing any quantity of LSD, in any form, with any carrier. Such a sentencing scheme—not considering individual degrees of culpability—would clearly be constitutional. Congress has the power to define criminal punishments without giving the courts any sentencing discretion. Determinate sentences were found in this country's penal codes from its inception, and some have remained until the present. . . . That distributors of varying degrees of culpability might be subject to the same sentence does not mean that the penalty system for LSD distribution is unconstitutional. . . .

STEVENS, J., dissenting.

The consequences of the majority's construction of 21 U.S.C. §841 are so bizarre that I cannot believe they were intended by Congress. [There] is no evidence that Congress intended the weight of the carrier to be considered in the sentence determination in LSD cases, and that there is good reason to believe Congress was unaware of the inequitable consequences of the Court's interpretation of the statute. . . .

In light of the ambiguity of the phrase "mixture or substance" and the lack of legislative history to guide us, it is necessary to examine the congressional purpose behind the statute. [The] majority's construction will lead to anomalous sentences that are contrary to one of the central purposes of the Sentencing Guidelines, which was to eliminate disparity in sentencing. [Widely] divergent sentences may be imposed for the sale of identical amounts of a controlled substance simply because of the nature of the carrier. If 100 doses of LSD were sold on sugar cubes, the sentence would range from 188-235 months, whereas if the same dosage were sold in its pure liquid form, the sentence would range only from 10-16 months. The absurdity and inequity of this result is emphasized in Judge Posner's dissent:

> . . . A person who sells five doses of LSD on sugar cubes is not a worse person than a manufacturer of LSD who is caught with 19,999 doses in pure form, but the former is subject to a ten-year mandatory minimum no-parole sentence, while the latter is not even subject to the five-year minimum. If defendant Chapman, who received five years for selling a thousand doses of LSD on blotter paper, had sold the same number of doses in pure form, his Guidelines sentence would have been fourteen months. . . . In none of these computations, by the way, does the weight of the LSD itself make a difference — so slight is its weight relative to that of the carrier — except of course when it is sold in pure form. Congress might as well have said: if there is a carrier, weigh the carrier and forget the LSD. . . .

Sentencing disparities that have been described as "crazy" and "loony" could well be avoided if the majority did not insist upon stretching the definition of "mixture" to include the carrier along with the LSD. It does not make sense to include a carrier in calculating the weight of the LSD because LSD, unlike drugs such as cocaine or marijuana, is sold by dosage, rather than by weight. Thus, whether one dose of LSD is added to a glass of orange juice or to a pitcher of orange juice, it is still only one dose that has been added. But if the weight of the orange juice is to be added to the calculation, then the person who sells the single dose of LSD in a pitcher, rather than in a glass, will receive a substantially higher sentence. If the weight of the carrier is included in the calculation, not only does it lead to huge disparities in sentences among LSD offenders, but also it leads to disparities when LSD sentences are compared to sentences for other drugs. [The severity of the sentences in LSD cases would be comparable with those in other drug cases only if the weight of the LSD carrier were disregarded. Congress] did not express any intention to treat those who sell LSD differently from those who sell other dangerous drugs. . . .

## NOTES

1. *Quantity-based measures of harm in drug offenses.* Federal statutes and guidelines make sentences for most drug convictions depend primarily on the type and amount of drugs involved in the offense. Section 2D1.1(c) of the federal guidelines provides that the base offense level for most drug

convictions depends on the type and amount of drugs involved. Much of the wrangling at sentencing hearings in drug cases (the largest single category of crimes now charged in the federal system) revolves around the amount of drugs actually involved in the sale or the amount "reasonably foreseeable" to the defendant. Courts must determine how to calculate specific drug quantities and the requisite mens rea for attributing drug amounts to particular offenders so as to quantify the harm created by a particular offender.

As intimated in *Chapman*, federal drug sentencing has not always relied on drug quantities. In 1956 Congress mandated minimum sentences for drug importation and distribution offenses through the Narcotic Control Act, but in the Comprehensive Drug Abuse Prevention and Control Act of 1970 Congress repealed these mandates and returned significant discretion to judges in setting drug sentences. Through a series of statutory enactments in the mid-1980s, however, Congress directly linked mandatory minimum penalties and sentencing ranges to the type and quantity of drugs involved in the offense. When it first created the federal sentencing guidelines, the U.S. Sentencing Commission also adopted a quantity-based scheme for drug sentencing in an effort to harmonize its guidelines with Congress's sentencing mandates. See William W. Wilkins Jr. et al., Competing Sentencing Policies in a "War on Drugs" Era, 28 Wake Forest L. Rev. 305 (1993).

Many state jurisdictions in the 1970s and 1980s joined the trend of using quantity-based measures of culpability and mandatory sentencing terms for drug crimes. New York began this trend in 1973 with the passage of the "Rockefeller drug laws" (named for Governor Nelson Rockefeller) requiring mandatory 15-year prison sentences for possession or sales of relatively small amounts of narcotics. The New York Court of Appeals interpreted the statute to require proof that a defendant knew about the amount of drugs involved, but the state legislature later eliminated this requirement. See People v. Ryan, 626 N.E.2d 51 (N.Y. 1993). In 1978 Michigan enacted the so-called 650 lifer law, which required mandatory life imprisonment for possession or sale of 650 grams of cocaine or heroin. See Harmelin v. Michigan, 501 U.S. 957 (1991) (upholding this sanction against a constitutional challenge). A number of states that have adopted guideline systems (including Virginia and Kansas) have separate sentencing grids for drug offenses, and these systems also rely heavily on drug types and quantities.

In more recent years, some states have reduced sentence lengths based on drug quantity triggers. In Michigan, for example, legislation that became effective in 2003 eliminated mandatory minimum sentences for certain controlled-substance violations. Similarly, in December 2004 the New York legislature made some modest amendments to the Rockefeller drug laws. Some first-time drug offenders who were eligible for sentences ranging from 15 years to life under the prior law now face reduced terms of 8 to 20 years in prison. Though these sorts of legislative changes can often ameliorate the sentencing consequences of particular drug quantities, the type and weight of illegal narcotics involved in an offense will still frequently play a central role in sentencing outcomes in many jurisdictions.

2. *Quantity-based measures of harm for economic offenses.*   Under the federal sentencing guidelines, sentence severity for economic offenses such as fraud increases with the value of the property involved. For losses greater than $5,000,

§2B1.1 calls for incremental increases in the offense level as the amount of loss rises. The sentencing judge adds two levels for losses over $5,000, four levels for losses over $10,000, and so on, to the top of the scale: 26 levels added for losses of more than $100 million. Because the U.S. Sentencing Commission made the concept of "loss" the centerpiece for setting sentence length in fraud and theft cases, loss calculations have generated lots of litigation and numerous doctrinal splits within the federal circuits. As a result, the commission in 2001 made a considered effort to reform the guidelines' "loss table" to create a doctrinally coherent, easy-to-apply set of rules. The old rules defined "loss" to mean "the value of the property taken, damaged or destroyed." The current, amended rules give more specific guidance on the question of causation. The sentence turns on the actual or intended loss, whichever is greater, and actual loss is defined as "the reasonably foreseeable pecuniary harm that resulted from the offense." This definition requires, at a minimum, that the defendant's offense be a cause-in-fact of the economic harm. But it also limits losses to those foreseeable by a reasonable person. See Frank O. Bowman III, The 2001 Economic Crime Sentencing Reform: An Analysis and Legislative History, 35 Ind. L. Rev. 5 (2001).

In the federal system, all fraud and theft offenses use the same loss table, and the amount of loss determines the bulk of the punishment (for fraud, the base offense is 6 and the loss could add up to 26 levels to that base). Robbery, under §2B3.1, uses a separate loss table and the loss determines a smaller proportion of the sentence: the base offense is 20, and the amount of loss could add only 7 further levels. Why does loss account for relatively more of the sentence in fraud or theft than in robbery cases? Are there recurring features of frauds or thefts that should figure more heavily in the sentence? Think again about the robberies described in Problems 4-1 and 4-3. To what extent does the amount of money lost in each robbery determine in your mind the seriousness of the crime?

3. *Quantity-based measures of harm for child pornography offenses.* The growth of online technology has been accompanied by the growth of online pornography and of new sentencing laws targeting illegal child pornography disseminated or accessed via the Internet. Federal sentencing guidelines and some state sentencing laws rely heavily on the number of images of child pornography distributed or downloaded. See, e.g., U.S. Sentencing Guidelines §2G2.2(b)(7) (providing progressively enhanced punishment if the offense involves more than 10 images, more than 150 images, more than 300 images, or more than 600 images). In Arizona, which treats the possession of each image of child pornography as a separate offense with a 10-year mandatory minimum sentencing term that must be imposed consecutively, the state Supreme Court affirmed over an Eighth Amendment objection a 200-year sentence imposed on a high school teacher convicted of possessing 20 images of child pornography. See State v. Berger, 134 P.3d 378 (Ariz. 2006), *cert. denied*, 549 U.S. 1252 (2007).

Especially in a modern digital world in which hundreds of illegal images can be downloaded in seconds based on simply the click of a button, do the number of images involved in a child pornography offense serve as a sensible and sound metric of a defendant's culpability? In recent testimony to the U.S. Sentencing Commission concerning potential reforms to the child pornography guidelines, representatives of the U.S. Department of Justice expressly urged significant reform of the existing child pornography guideline in part because the guideline "has not keep pace with technological developments" and "does not adequately differentiate among offenders given the severity of their conduct." Written Statement of James M. Fottrell, Steve Debrota, and Francey Hakes on Behalf of U.S. Department of Justice Before U.S. Sentencing Commission at pp. 7-8, 16-17 (Feb. 15, 2012), available at http://www.ussc.gov/Legislative_and_Public_Affairs/Public_Hearings_and_Meetings/20120215-16/Testimony_15_Hakes_DeBrota_Fottrell.pdf. Through this testimony, the Justice Department asserted that reform of guidelines enhancements based on illegal images "are worth examining in light of technological advances and patterns among offenders to determine whether the overall emphasis on the content and number of the images comes at the expense of other criteria that can measure the degree of an offender's conduct." Id. What kinds of "other criteria" might you urge a sentencing commission to consider as mitigating or aggravating factors for the sentencing of child pornography offenders to ensure its sentencing guidelines "adequately differentiate among offenders given the severity of their conduct"?

4. *Statutory interpretation: absurd results.*   As the dissenting opinion in *Chapman* argues, the LSD punishment scheme based on weight of the carrier can produce absurd results. How can judges best respond to such a statute? Two distinguished federal judges, Frank Easterbrook and Richard Posner, debated this question in the lower court opinions in this case. Judge Easterbrook suggested that judges ordinarily must enforce what they believe to be an unwise sentencing scheme:

> A preference for giving statutes a constitutional meaning is a reason to construe, not to rewrite or "improve." Canons are doubt-resolvers, useful when the language is ambiguous and a construction of the statute is fairly possible by which the question may be avoided. "Substance or mixture containing a detectable quantity" is not ambiguous. . . . The canon about avoiding constitutional decisions, in particular, must be used with care, for it is a closer cousin to invalidation than to interpretation. It is a way to enforce the constitutional penumbra, and therefore an aspect of constitutional law proper. Constitutional decisions breed penumbras, which multiply questions. Treating each as justification to construe laws out of existence too greatly enlarges the judicial power.

United States v. Marshall, 908 F.2d 1312, 1318 (7th Cir. 1990). Judge Posner's dissent described a more active form of statutory interpretation for judges:

> Well, what if anything can we judges do about this mess? The answer lies in the shadow of a jurisprudential disagreement . . . between the severely positivistic view that the content of law is exhausted in clear, explicit, and definite enactments . . . from legislatures, and the natural lawyer's or legal pragmatist's view that the practice of interpretation and the general terms of the Constitution (such as "equal protection of the laws") authorize judges to enrich positive law with the moral values and practical concerns of civilized society. Judges who in other respects have seemed quite similar, such as Holmes and Cardozo, have taken opposite sides of this issue. Neither approach is entirely satisfactory. The first buys political neutrality and a type of objectivity at the price of substantive injustice, while the second buys justice in the individual case at the price of considerable uncertainty and, not infrequently, judicial willfulness. It is no wonder that our legal system oscillates between the approaches. The positivist view, applied unflinchingly to this case, commands the affirmance of prison sentences that are exceptionally harsh by the standards of the modern Western

world, dictated by an accidental, unintended scheme of punishment nevertheless implied by the words (taken one by one) of the relevant enactments. The
natural law or pragmatist view leads to a freer interpretation, one influenced by
norms of equal treatment.

908 F.2d at 1334-1335. Is it possible to generalize as to when judges should use
each of these approaches to statutory interpretation?

   5. *Quantification of crack versus powder cocaine.*   The use of quantity measures
for assessing the seriousness of drug offenses has proved most controversial in
the context of cocaine, especially in the federal system. At the inception of
modern sentencing reforms in the mid-1980s, federal statutes and guidelines
incorporated a "100-to-1 ratio" between powder cocaine and crack — that is, an
offense must involve 500 grams of powder cocaine, but only 5 grams of crack, to
trigger a five-year minimum penalty. As discussed more fully in Chapter 9, this
100-to-1 ratio had long been the subject of heated debate, primarily because of
its disparate impact on minority defendants, and in 2010 Congress finally passed
legislation, titled the Fair Sentencing Act, which required a greater amount of
crack to trigger certain sentencing terms (though under the law it remained the
case than 18 times more powder cocaine was needed to trigger the same sentences for a quantity of crack). Even before this statutory change, but after the
Supreme Court in United States v. Booker, 543 U.S. 220 (2005), made the
federal sentencing guidelines "effectively advisory," lower courts struggled to
determine whether and when the severe crack guidelines should be followed.
The Supreme Court addressed these matters through its ruling in Kimbrough v.
United States, 552 U.S. 85 (2007), which is reprinted in Chapter 3. In *Kimbrough*,
the Supreme Court provided this review of the U.S. Sentencing Commission's
approach to setting guidelines for crack and powder cocaine offenses:

   The Commission did not use [an] empirical approach in developing the Guidelines sentences for drug-trafficking offenses. Instead, it employed the 1986 Act's
   weight-driven scheme. The Guidelines use a drug quantity table based on drug
   type and weight to set base offense levels for drug trafficking offenses. See USSG
   §2D1.1(c). In setting offense levels for crack and powder cocaine, the
   Commission, in line with the 1986 Act, adopted the 100-to-1 ratio. The statute
   itself specifies only two quantities of each drug, but the Guidelines go further
   and set sentences for the full range of possible drug quantities using the same
   100-to-1 quantity ratio. The Guidelines' drug quantity table sets base offense
   levels ranging from 12, for offenses involving less than 250 milligrams of crack
   (or 25 grams of powder), to 38, for offenses involving more than 1.5 kilograms
   of crack (or 150 kilograms of powder).
       Although the Commission immediately used the 100-to-1 ratio to define
   base offense levels for all crack and powder offenses, it later determined that the
   crack/powder sentencing disparity is generally unwarranted. Based on additional research and experience with the 100- to-1 ratio, the Commission concluded that the disparity fails to meet the sentencing objectives set forth by
   Congress in both the Sentencing Reform Act and the 1986 Act. In a series of
   reports, the Commission identified three problems with the crack/powder disparity. First, the Commission reported, the 100-to-1 ratio rested on assumptions
   about the relative harmfulness of the two drugs and the relative prevalence of
   certain harmful conduct associated with their use and distribution that more
   recent research and data no longer support. . . .
       Second, the Commission concluded that the crack/powder disparity is
   inconsistent with the 1986 Act's goal of punishing major drug traffickers more

severely than low-level dealers. Drug importers and major traffickers generally
deal in powder cocaine, which is then converted into crack by street-level sellers.
But the 100-to-1 ratio can lead to the "anomalous" result that "retail crack
dealers get longer sentences than the wholesale drug distributors who supply
them the powder cocaine from which their crack is produced."

Finally, the Commission stated that the crack/powder sentencing
differential "fosters disrespect for and lack of confidence in the criminal justice
system" because of a "widely-held perception" that it "promotes unwarranted
disparity based on race." Approximately 85 percent of defendants convicted of
crack offenses in federal court are black; thus the severe sentences required by
the 100-to-1 ratio are imposed "primarily upon black offenders."

Despite these observations, the Commission's most recent reports do not
urge identical treatment of crack and powder cocaine. In the Commission's
view, "some differential in the quantity-based penalties" for the two drugs is
warranted, because crack is more addictive than powder, crack offenses are
more likely to involve weapons or bodily injury, and crack distribution is associated with higher levels of crime. But the 100-to-1 crack/powder ratio, the
Commission concluded, significantly overstates the differences between the
two forms of the drug. Accordingly, the Commission recommended that
the ratio be "substantially" reduced.

The Commission has several times sought to achieve a reduction in the
crack/powder ratio. In 1995, it proposed amendments to the Guidelines that
would have replaced the 100-to-1 ratio with a 1-to-1 ratio. Complementing
that change, the Commission would have installed special enhancements for
trafficking offenses involving weapons or bodily injury. See Amendments to the
Sentencing Guidelines for United States Courts, 60 Fed. Reg. 25075-25077
(1995). Congress, acting pursuant to 28 U.S.C. §994(p), rejected the amendments. Simultaneously, however, Congress directed the Commission to "propose revision of the drug quantity ratio of crack cocaine to powder cocaine
under the relevant statutes and guidelines."

In response to this directive, the Commission issued reports in 1997 and
2002 recommending that Congress change the 100-to-1 ratio prescribed in the
1986 Act. The 1997 Report proposed a 5-to-1 ratio. See United States Sentencing Commission, Special Report to Congress: 25 Cocaine and Federal Sentencing Policy 2 (Apr. 1997), http://www.ussc.gov/r_congress/newcrack.pdf. The
2002 Report recommended lowering the ratio "at least" to 20 to 1. Neither
proposal prompted congressional action.

The Commission's most recent report, issued in 2007, again urged Congress to amend the 1986 Act to reduce the 100-to-1 ratio. This time, however, the
Commission did not simply await congressional action. Instead, the
Commission adopted an ameliorating change in the Guidelines. The alteration,
which became effective on November 1, 2007, reduces the base offense level
associated with each quantity of crack by two levels. See Amendments to the
Sentencing Guidelines for United States Courts, 72 Fed. Reg. 28571-28572
(2007). This modest amendment yields sentences for crack offenses between
two and five times longer than sentences for equal amounts of powder. Describing the amendment as "only . . . a partial remedy" for the problems generated
by the crack/powder disparity, the Commission noted that any "comprehensive
solution requires appropriate legislative action by Congress." . . .

As the *Kimbrough* decision details, the differential treatment of crack and
powder cocaine offenses has long been a source of significant controversy and
dynamic interbranch debate in the federal sentencing system. Given this long-
standing debate, it was not surprising that some district courts utilized the new
discretion afforded by the *Booker* decision to impose sentences below applicable
guideline ranges in crack cases. Before the ruling in *Kimbrough*, however, most
circuit courts declared unreasonable any decision to impose a sentence below

the crack guidelines based simply on a policy disagreement with the severity levels established by the crack guidelines incorporating the 100-to-1 ratio. The ruling in *Kimbrough* has been especially important to the operation of the advisory guidelines after *Booker* (even in non-drug cases) in part because the Government conceded that courts are generally authorized after *Booker* to vary from guidelines ranges "based solely on policy considerations, including disagreements with the guidelines," and because the Supreme Court rejected the Government's claims that this post-*Booker* sentencing authority did not extend to cases involving the crack guidelines (hundreds of which are sentenced in federal courts every month).

6. *The Fair Sentencing Act of 2010 and new (improved?) crack/powder ratios.*   In summer 2010, Congress finally responded to the long-standing criticisms of the unfairness of the 100-to-1 ratio incorporated into the triggering quantities for statutory mandatory minimum sentencing terms for powder and crack cocaine. Through the Fair Sentencing Act of 2010 (FSA), which was signed into law by President Barack Obama on August 3, 2010, Congress adjusted upward the amount of crack needed to trigger mandatory minimum prison terms. Though President Obama's Department of Justice and many public policy groups urged Congress to completely equalize the sentencing provisions for powder and crack cocaine, Congress settled on a compromise proposal that produced a new 18-to-1 ratio for powder and crack sentences by raising from 5 to 28 grams and from 50 to 280 grams the amount of crack needed to trigger 5- and 10-year minimum prison terms. (The Fair Sentencing Act also completely eliminated the unique mandatory minimum prison term for simple possession of crack cocaine.) In addition to changing the trigger amounts for applicable minimum prison terms, the Fair Sentencing Act of 2010 ordered the U.S. Sentencing Commission to promulgate new emergency guidelines in accord with the statutory changes made by Congress. The Act's instructions to the U.S. Sentencing Commission also included a list of aggravating and mitigating factors that Congress wished to have reflected in revised crack sentencing guidelines.

The Commission in 2011 completed the task of producing revised drug sentencing guidelines, and it fully incorporated the new 18-1 crack/powder drug quantity ratio that the FSA built into the revised statutory mandatory minimum sentencing statutes that trigger 5- and 10-year minimum prison terms. Notably, some public policy groups and commentators urged the Commission to seize the passage of the Fair Sentencing Act as an opportunity to significantly revise the entire structure for drug sentencing under the guidelines to give far less significance to the weight of the drugs involved in the offense and far more significance to other relevant sentencing factors like role in the offense. In the wake of the long history of problems and controversy in the federal sentencing system that flowed from Congress's initial decision to adopt the 100-1 crack/powder ratio and then its subsequent 2010 decision to retain a significant difference in the treatment of crack and powder cocaine for statutory purposes, do you think the Commission was wise to continue to structure its revised sentencing guidelines in lock-step with the mandatory minimum sentencing statutes? Given that the original crack/powder sentencing differential was, as the *Kimbrough* opinion highlights, seen to "fosters disrespect for and lack of confidence in the criminal justice system because of a widely-held perception that it promotes unwarranted disparity based on race," is there reason to be concerned that the new 18-1 ratio will be merely viewed as just a little less racist?

In light of the *Kimbrough* decision, which clearly authorized district judges after *Booker* to refuse to follow the severe pre-FSA guidelines for crack offenses in even typical cases based on the long-standing and well-justified criticisms of their severity and unfairness, can and should district judges continue to refuse to follow the post-FSA crack guidelines because they still reflect a considerable sentencing disparity with powder cocaine guidelines, even though this disparity has been reduced? Consider these concluding thoughts by U.S. District Judge Mark Bennett in a lengthy opinion in which he explained why he still was not going to follow the new crack guidelines:

> I believe that the replacement of the 100:1 crack-to-powder ratio of the 1986 Act and associated Sentencing Guidelines with the 18:1 crack-to-powder ratio of the 2010 FSA and the November 1, 2010, amendments to the Sentencing Guidelines was a huge improvement, in terms of fairness to crack defendants. While such incremental improvement is often the nature of political progress on difficult social justice issues — and, in this instance, the increment is perhaps unusually large — an incremental improvement is not enough to make me abdicate my duty to critically evaluate the crack/cocaine ratio in terms of its fealty to the purposes of the Sentencing Reform Act.
>
> Performing that duty here, I must reject the Sentencing Guidelines using the "new" 18:1 ratio, just as I rejected the Sentencing Guidelines using the "old" 100:1 ratio, based on a policy disagreement with those guidelines, even in "mine-run" cases, such as this one. I must do so, because I find that the "new" 18:1 guidelines still suffer from most or all of the same injustices that plagued the 100:1 guidelines, including the failure of the Sentencing Commission to exercise its characteristic institutional role in developing the guidelines, the lack of support for most of the assumptions that crack cocaine involves greater harms than powder cocaine, the improper use of the quantity ratio as a "proxy" for the perceived greater harms of crack cocaine, and the disparate impact of the ratio on black offenders. I also find that the "new" guidelines suffer from some additional concerns, in that they now create a "double whammy" on crack defendants, penalizing them once for the assumed presence of aggravating circumstances in crack cocaine cases and again for the actual presence of such aggravating circumstances in a particular case.
>
> In one respect the "new" 18:1 guideline ratio is more irrational and pernicious than the original 100:1. When the 100:1 ratio was enacted, Congress and the Sentencing Commission did not have access to the overwhelming scientific evidence that they now have. This overwhelming scientific evidence now demonstrates that the difference between crack and powder is like the difference between ice and water — or beer and wine. Can anyone imagine a sentence that is many times harsher for becoming legally intoxicated by drinking wine rather than beer? Of course not.

United States v. Williams, 788 F. Supp. 2d 847, 891-92 (N.D. Iowa 2011).


## PROBLEM 4-7.   GETTING TOUGH ON DRUNK DRIVERS

The National Commission Against Drunk Driving reports that state laws "frequently fail to reflect the seriousness" of driving while intoxicated. "Courts frequently impose lenient sentences without regard for the offender's driving and criminal record, alcohol problems, or the damage caused to the victims. This undercuts any general deterrent effect of the laws regulating the drinking driver."

You are a senator in a state where a number of serious, well-publicized accidents have occurred recently involving intoxicated drivers with a history of drinking and driving. Your state law currently provides for a maximum sentence of six months' imprisonment for a first drunk-driving offense and a three-year maximum for a repeat offender. Bills are circulating to increase the statutory penalties for driving while intoxicated.

One bill — entitled Responding to Inebriated Drivers (RID) — increases the range of available punishment for driving under the influence. The RID bill proposes raising the maximum sentence for a first offense to 5 years and the maximum sentence for repeat offenders to 20 years. The bill gives sentencing judges broad discretion to individualize punishments while suggesting that higher sentences are more fitting for offenders with high blood-alcohol content at the time of arrest.

Another bill — entitled Taking on Utterly Grotesque Harmers (TOUGH) — mandates minimum sentences for those who cause property or bodily harm while drinking and driving. Specifically, the TOUGH bill requires at least a 1-year imprisonment term for anyone who causes more than $500 of property damage, at least 5 years' imprisonment for anyone who causes serious physical harm, and 20 years' imprisonment for anyone who causes a death while driving under the influence.

Which bill would you support? Why?

## 3.   The Role of Mens Rea and Motive

### a.   Strict Liability Sentencing Factors

Legal philosopher H. L. A. Hart, in his renowned text on criminal law and punishment theory *Punishment and Responsibility*, referred to this fundamental principle of just punishment: "causing harm intentionally must be punished more severely than causing the same harm unintentionally." Though legislatures have usually taken this advice to heart when grading offenses, they do not give mens rea concepts so much weight at sentencing.

## United States v. Ana Marin de Velasquez
### 28 F.3d 2 (2d Cir. 1994)

McLAUGHLIN, J.

Ana Marin de Velasquez arrived at New York's John F. Kennedy International Airport from Colombia. During a customs inspection, she appeared to be extremely nervous and was sweating profusely. A search of the soles of the shoes she was wearing revealed that the shoes contained 167.8 grams of heroin. Customs agents also determined that she was transporting 636.3 grams of heroin internally, for a total of 804.1 grams.

After her arrest, the defendant admitted to agents that she was transporting drugs internally, but disclaimed all knowledge of the drugs found in the soles of her shoes. She claimed that Colombian drug traffickers gave her a pair of shoes that would identify her to her New York contact but she never knew the shoes contained heroin. Eventually, defendant pled guilty to importing heroin. During the plea allocution, defendant stated that she knew she was importing narcotics, although she did not know what kind. . . . In calculating the total quantity of heroin defendant possessed for sentencing purposes, the court included the heroin in defendant's shoes.

Defendant argues that the mens rea doctrine and considerations of due process required the district court to exclude the heroin in her shoes when calculating the total amount of drugs she possessed for sentencing purposes. In the alternative, she argues that the heroin in her shoes should have been included only if it was reasonably foreseeable that her shoes contained heroin.

[We have previously] held that neither due process nor the doctrine of mens rea requires that a defendant actually know the total quantity of drugs in his possession to be sentenced for the full amount under the Sentencing Guidelines. We reaffirm that holding here. We now [also] hold that in a possession case the sentence should be based on the total amount of drugs in the defendant's possession, without regard to foreseeability. [Federal law] makes it a crime to "knowingly" import certain illicit drugs into the United States [and] makes it a crime to "knowingly" manufacture, distribute, or otherwise possess illicit drugs. Quantity is not part of the corpus delicti, i.e., forms no part of the substantive offense under any of these statutes. Conviction rests solely on the knowing possession of some quantity, however large or small, of illicit drugs.

Quantity comes into play only at the sentencing stage, where it determines the minimum or maximum penalty the defendant may receive. It is settled that the minimum and maximum sentences are to be strictly imposed, regardless of the defendant's state of mind concerning the total quantity of drugs in his possession. Mens rea and due process concerns are fully satisfied at the conviction stage, where the defendant must be found guilty of, or plead to, "knowingly" possessing some amount of drugs. . . .

Particularly in drug offense cases, it is by no means unusual to peg the sentence to factors that were not known — or even foreseeable — to the defendant at the time the crime was committed. For example, a defendant who distributes drugs within 1000 feet of a school is subject to twice the maximum penalties for drug distribution. This is true, regardless of whether he knew or could foresee that he was within the proscribed distance. Similarly, a defendant who distributes drugs to a minor is subject to twice the maximum penalty, regardless of whether he knew or could foresee that the buyer was a minor. Thus, there is nothing startling, or even notable, in the conclusion that a defendant who knows she is carrying some quantity of illicit drugs should be sentenced for the full amount on her person. This remains true even where, as here, defendant claims she did not know she was carrying an additional quantity of drugs — additional to the packet she agreed to carry.

A fertile imagination can conjure bizarre situations where the defendant's possession is tenuous and fleeting. The statute has yet to be drafted that could not be unconstitutionally applied in some extraordinary case, and these cases will have to be dealt with if they arise. Here, however, the defendant was wearing the very shoes that contained the heroin. Clearly, her possession was not ephemeral, and the statute properly applied to her. . . .

There is no requirement under the Guidelines that the defendant know or foresee the total quantity of drugs in his possession to be sentenced for the full amount — just as there is no such requirement under the statutes. [The] Guidelines provide that defendants are accountable for "all quantities" of drugs with which they are "directly involved."

The Guidelines contain two enlightening illustrations. In the first, a hypothetical defendant is arrested while assisting in offloading a ship containing a large amount of marijuana. In the second, a defendant transports a suitcase knowing that it contains some quantity of drugs. In both cases, the Guidelines conclude, the defendant's sentence should be based on the full amount of drugs involved, "without regard to the issue of reasonable foreseeability" and "regardless of his knowledge or lack of knowledge." Thus, the Guidelines make clear that a defendant who knowingly possesses some quantity of illicit drugs cannot disclaim "direct involvement" with the full amount on the ground that the full amount was not foreseeable. . . .

In a possession case, . . . we see no reason why a defendant who knowingly traffics in drugs should not bear the risk that his conduct may be more harmful to society than he intends or foresees. We decline to fashion a rule that would permit a defendant to avoid the consequences of that risk because of a fortuitous lack of knowledge or foreseeability — fortuities which apparently occur with some frequency. See United States v. Ekwunoh, 12 F.3d 368, 369 (2d Cir. 1993) (defendant thought she possessed 400 grams of heroin instead of one kilogram); United States v. Obi, 947 F.2d 1031, 1032 (2d Cir. 1991) (defendant thought he was importing cocaine rather than heroin). In the drug trade, there is always the chance, as is alleged in most of these cases, that the supplier will not recognize "the punctilio of an honor the most sensitive." Meinhard v. Salmon, 164 N.E. 545, 546 (N.Y. 1928) (Cardozo, J.). . . .

It is certainly possible, of course, to imagine a situation where the gap between belief and actuality was so great as to make the Guideline grossly unfair in application. In such cases, a downward departure may be appropriate. The Guidelines, however, were designed to apply to the ordinary mine-run case. This is such a case. Applying the foregoing principles, we believe Ana Marin de Velasquez was properly sentenced for the total amount of heroin in her possession, without regard to whether she knew or could foresee the heroin concealed in her shoes.

## NOTES

1. *The role (or lack thereof) of mens rea at sentencing.* Though mens rea concepts are usually integral to legislative grading of offenses, mens rea issues are secondary or altogether ignored at sentencing. In the federal system, drug type and quantity (along with a number of other increases to the offense level) apply as a matter of strict liability. See United States v. Litchfield, 986 F.2d 21 (2d Cir. 1993) (guideline increasing sentence for possession of stolen firearm did not require knowledge that firearm was stolen); United States v. Lewin, 900 F.2d 145

(8th Cir. 1990) (upholding penalty enhancement for distribution of drugs when sale occurs within 1,000 feet of school, regardless of defendant's knowledge of proximity); United States v. Schnell, 982 F.2d 216 (7th Cir. 1992) (upholding enhancement for possession of firearm with an altered or obliterated serial number regardless of knowledge about obliteration). Jack B. Weinstein, a federal district court judge, laments the lowly place of mens rea in federal sentencing:

> Mens rea, a principle central to our criminal law, is crucial in linking punishment to individual culpability. It is the bridge between morality and law. Yet, in the guidelines era, mens rea has been all but eliminated from the sentencing of drug offenders. This development is a disastrous departure from the great traditions of Anglo-American law. . . .
>
> Courts have defended the absence of mens rea protections in sentencing as not "in any way criminaliz[ing] otherwise innocent activity." Is this really so? In *de Velasquez*, the defendant effectively committed a second crime of which she had no knowledge. Had the drugs in her shoes been the only contraband on her, mens rea principles dictate that she could not have been convicted.

Jack B. Weinstein & Fred A. Bernstein, The Denigration of Mens Rea in Drug Sentencing, 7 Fed. Sent'g Rep. 121, 121-122 (1994). The authors illustrate their point with a "simple hypothetical":

> Your daughter is packing up her car to return home after her first year of college. A friend who is helping her pack asks her to carry a parcel home to a mutual friend, Steven. To your daughter's query, "What's in it?" her friend answers, "Some Stephen King novels and a couple of joints." In fact, there is more than a kilogram of cocaine in the box, which is discovered when your daughter is pulled over for a traffic violation. Your daughter is properly charged with possession with intent to distribute (to Steven). Her intent related to two marijuana cigarettes, yet the government contends that she should be punished for transporting a kilogram of cocaine. The sentence? Years in prison. Despite this frightening prospect, the government insists that your daughter's contention — that she was unaware that she was carrying cocaine — is irrelevant "at the sentencing stage."

Weinstein & Bernstein, 7 Fed. Sent'g Rep. at 123. Is the government's argument in this hypothetical case a necessary logical consequence of the holding in *de Velasquez*?

2. *Reasonable foreseeability in conspiracy cases.*   Though mens rea does not have a guaranteed place in sentencing determinations, the federal sentencing guidelines do provide in commentary to the relevant conduct rules that a defendant charged with conspiracy will be sentenced only for conduct that was reasonably foreseeable by the individual defendant. See U.S. Sentencing Guidelines Manual §1B1.3, cmt. n.1 ("In the case of criminal activity undertaken in concert with others . . . the conduct for which the defendant 'would be otherwise accountable' also includes conduct of others in furtherance of the execution of the jointly-undertaken criminal activity that was reasonably foreseeable by the defendant."). Though it is akin to a test of a defendant's subjective mens rea, federal courts in sentencing cases have stressed that the "test as to whether conduct is reasonably foreseeable is an objective one." United States v. Cochran, 14 F.3d 1128, 1133 (6th Cir. 1994).

### b.   Hate Crimes and the Relevance of Motive

Whereas mens rea matters *less* at sentencing than for the substantive crime, a defendant's motives (that is, her reasons for committing the crime) tend to matter *more* at sentencing. Sentencing statutes and rules allow judges to consider motives. Indeed, for some particular motives, the rules call for mandatory increases in the sentence.

> ## *Wisconsin v. Todd Mitchell*
> ### 508 U.S. 476 (1993)

REHNQUIST, C.J.

Respondent Todd Mitchell's sentence for aggravated battery was enhanced because he intentionally selected his victim on account of the victim's race. The question presented in this case is whether this penalty enhancement is prohibited by the First and Fourteenth Amendments. We hold that it is not.

On the evening of October 7, 1989, a group of young black men and boys, including Mitchell, gathered at an apartment complex in Kenosha, Wisconsin. Several members of the group discussed a scene from the motion picture "Mississippi Burning," in which a white man beat a young black boy who was praying. The group moved outside and Mitchell asked them: "Do you all feel hyped up to move on some white people?" Shortly thereafter, a young white boy approached the group on the opposite side of the street where they were standing. As the boy walked by, Mitchell said: "You all want to fuck somebody up? There goes a white boy; go get him." Mitchell counted to three and pointed in the boy's direction. The group ran toward the boy, beat him severely, and stole his tennis shoes. The boy was rendered unconscious and remained in a coma for four days.

After a jury trial in the Circuit Court for Kenosha County, Mitchell was convicted of aggravated battery. That offense ordinarily carries a maximum sentence of two years' imprisonment. But because the jury found that Mitchell had intentionally selected his victim because of the boy's race, the maximum sentence for Mitchell's offense was increased to seven years under [a Wisconsin statutory provision that] enhances the maximum penalty for an offense whenever the defendant "[i]ntentionally selects the person against whom the crime . . . is committed . . . because of the race, religion, color, disability, sexual orientation, national origin or ancestry of that person. . . ." The Circuit Court sentenced Mitchell to four years' imprisonment for the aggravated battery. Mitchell . . . appealed his conviction and sentence, challenging the constitutionality of Wisconsin's penalty-enhancement provision on First Amendment grounds. The Wisconsin . . . Supreme Court held that the statute "violates the First Amendment directly by punishing what the legislature has deemed to be offensive thought." . . .

The State argues that the statute does not punish bigoted thought, as the Supreme Court of Wisconsin said, but instead punishes only [the conduct of intentional selection of a victim]. While this argument is literally correct, it does not dispose of Mitchell's First Amendment challenge. To be sure, . . . a physical assault is not by any stretch of the imagination expressive conduct protected by the First Amendment. But the fact remains that under the Wisconsin statute the same criminal conduct may be more heavily punished if the victim is selected because of his race or other protected status than if no such motive obtained. . . . Because the only reason for the enhancement is the defendant's discriminatory motive for selecting his victim, Mitchell argues (and the Wisconsin Supreme Court held) that the statute violates the First Amendment by punishing offenders' bigoted beliefs.

Traditionally, sentencing judges have considered a wide variety of factors in addition to evidence bearing on guilt in determining what sentence to impose on a convicted defendant. The defendant's motive for committing the offense is one important factor. See 1 W. LaFave & A. Scott, Substantive Criminal Law §3.6(b) (1986) ("Motives are most relevant when the trial judge sets the defendant's sentence, and it is not uncommon for a defendant to receive a minimum sentence because he was acting with good motives, or a rather high sentence because of his bad motives"). Thus, in many States the commission of a murder, or other capital offense, for pecuniary gain is a separate aggravating circumstance under the capital sentencing statute.

[M]otive plays the same role under the Wisconsin statute as it does under federal and state antidiscrimination laws, which we have previously upheld against constitutional challenge. Title VII of the Civil Rights Act of 1964, for example, makes it unlawful for an employer to discriminate against an employee "*because of* such individual's race, color, religion, sex, or national origin." 42 U.S.C. §2000e-2(a)(1) (emphasis added). [We have] rejected the argument that Title VII infringed employers' First Amendment rights. . . .

Nothing in our decision last Term in R.A.V. v. St. Paul, 505 U.S. 377 (1992), compels a different result here. That case involved a First Amendment challenge to a municipal ordinance prohibiting the use of "fighting words" that insult, or provoke violence, "on the basis of race, color, creed, religion or gender." Because the ordinance only proscribed a class of "fighting words" deemed particularly offensive by the city—i.e., those "that contain . . . messages of bias-motivated hatred," we held that it violated the rule against content-based discrimination. But whereas the ordinance struck down in *R.A.V.* was explicitly directed at expression (i.e., "speech" or "messages"), the statute in this case is aimed at conduct unprotected by the First Amendment.

Moreover, the Wisconsin statute singles out for enhancement bias-inspired conduct because this conduct is thought to inflict greater individual and societal harm. For example, according to the State and its amici, bias-motivated crimes are more likely to provoke retaliatory crimes, inflict distinct emotional harms on their victims, and incite community unrest. The State's desire to redress these perceived harms provides an adequate explanation for its penalty-enhancement provision over and above mere disagreement with offenders' beliefs or biases. As Blackstone said long ago, "it is but reasonable that among crimes of different natures those should be most severely punished, which are the most destructive of the public safety and happiness." 4 W. Blackstone, Commentaries.

Finally, there remains to be considered Mitchell's argument that the Wisconsin statute is unconstitutionally overbroad because of its "chilling effect" on free speech. Mitchell argues (and the Wisconsin Supreme Court agreed) that the statute is "overbroad" because evidence of the defendant's prior speech or associations may be used to prove that the defendant intentionally selected his victim on account of the victim's protected status. . . .

The sort of chill envisioned here is far more attenuated and unlikely than that contemplated in traditional "overbreadth" cases. [T]he prospect of a citizen suppressing his bigoted beliefs for fear that evidence of such beliefs will be introduced against him at trial if he commits a more serious offense against person or property . . . is simply too speculative a hypothesis to support Mitchell's overbreadth claim. . . .

## NOTES

1. *Hate crimes legislation.*   States have passed an array of hate crimes laws that either create new crimes based on the offender's motives or enhance penalties for existing crimes if the government proves that the offender committed the crime because of characteristics of the victim. See, e.g., Fla. Stat. Ann. §921.0016(3); Haw. Rev. Stat. §706-662(6). In addition to statutes prohibiting violence or intimidation toward persons based on certain characteristics, some state laws prohibit vandalism of religious sites, the wearing of masks, and the burning of crosses. States still differ as to the size of the penalty enhancement, the types of biases that trigger these sentence enhancements, and the predicate offenses that may qualify as hate crimes. Congress has often debated but never passed federal hate crimes legislation. It did in 1994 enact the Hate Crime Statistics Act, 28 U.S.C. §534, which requires the federal government to collect and publish information concerning crimes that "manifest evidence of prejudice based on race, religion, disability, sexual orientation, or ethnicity."

Following the lead of Wisconsin v. Mitchell, most state courts hold that sentencing enhancements for hate crimes are consistent with their state constitutions. See, e.g., In re M.S., 896 P.2d 1365 (Cal. 1995); State v. McKnight, 511 N.W.2d 389 (Iowa 1994); State v. Wyant, 624 N.E.2d 722 (Ohio 1994). Though broad consensus exists concerning the constitutionality of most hate crimes legislation, considerable dispute remains over the soundness of these politically popular provisions. Scholarly commentary on the functioning of hate crimes has been dynamic and varied. See James B. Jacobs & Kimberly Potter, Hate Crimes: Criminal Law and Identity Politics 4 (1998). Apart from worries about the free speech and association rights of a defendant, can you think of any potential negative effects of a sentencing enhancement for offenders who select their victims based on race? On religion? On sex? On sexual orientation?

2. *Economic motives as an aggravating factor.*   As the *Mitchell* Court notes, sentencing judges and juries have a long tradition of considering various motives at sentencing. In capital cases in particular, many jurisdictions have statutes that call for the judge or jury to consider whether a murder was committed for "pecuniary gain." See, e.g., 18 U.S.C. §3952(c)(8); Ariz. Rev. Stat. Ann. §13-703(F)(5). In addition, a number of sentencing guideline states provide that an economic motivation aggravates the offense in ways calling for an enhanced sentence. See N.C. Gen. Stat. §15A-1340.16(d)(4) (aggravating factor present when "defendant was hired or paid to commit the offense").

3. *Making motives matter more.*   In a recent article, Motive's Role in Criminal Punishment, 80 S. Cal. L. Rev. 89 (2006), Professor Carissa Byrne Hessick has argued that motive should play a more prominent and formal role in sentencing determinations. Her article's conclusion sums up her main contentions:

> Motive plays an important role in criminal law. But its present role does not reflect its centrality to the relative culpability of different defendants. Because our system of criminal punishment is predicated on the moral assessment of a defendant and her actions, motive should play an expanded role in criminal punishment. The most efficient and effective method to accomplish this integration is to identify and classify various motives *ex ante* and then incorporate an individual defendant's reasons for committing a crime into the amount of her punishment. Accounting for motives at sentencing will help to ensure that a defendant receives the punishment she deserves and that criminal punishment accurately expresses the appropriate amount of moral condemnation for the defendant's actions. Because a punishment system that reflects shared values is more effective at deterring crime, and because motives are perceived as relevant to a defendant's blameworthiness, a punishment system that accounts for motives may also result in less crime.

In her article, Hessick recognizes "the challenge of classifying motives" but asserts that this challenge "should not prevent motive from playing a larger role in criminal punishment." If you were a legislator or a member of a sentencing commission convinced by Hessick's arguments, what first steps would you pursue to give motives a larger and more formal role in sentencing determinations? Are motives best assessed ex ante by legislatures and sentencing commissions or ex post by individual judges deciding particular sentences?

## PROBLEM 4-8.   ROB ANON (aka JEAN VALJEAN?) REVISITED

Although it is common for statutes or guidelines to provide expressly that certain "bad" motives will increase a sentence, rarely are there provisions expressly stating that "good" motives can reduce a sentence. An exception might be provisions that encourage a mitigated sentence when a defendant commits an offense because of serious coercion, blackmail, or duress. These rules might well be understood as reducing the defendant's sentence because his reason for doing wrong was not so bad. The provision of the federal sentencing guidelines that encourages a reduced sentence based on coercion or duress, U.S. Sentencing Guidelines Manual §5K2.12, goes on to state that "personal financial difficulties and economic pressures upon a trade or business do not warrant a decrease in sentence."

Do you agree with the U.S. Sentencing Commission that personal financial pressures should not warrant a decrease in sentence? Consider again the case of Rob Anon, described in Problem 4-1, and now imagine that he had a profound personal motivation for his crime: his fiancée was in a car accident and lacked medical insurance or the personal funds needed to pay for a life-saving operation. In light of this "personal financial difficulty," would you be willing to decrease his sentence? Cf. *John Q.* (New Line Cinema 2002).

## C.   THE ROLE OF VICTIMS AND THE COMMUNITY

One key source of information about the harm that a crime causes is the victim of the crime. In a traditional indeterminate sentencing system, victims do not formally address the sentencing court. Of course, the prosecutor attempts in many cases to bring the victim's concerns or information to the court's attention, and the judge may account for this in imposing a sentence. But until recently, the victim had little opportunity to speak directly to the sentencing court.

In recent decades, most jurisdictions have created a formal role for victims at sentencing. But what impact should victims have on individual sentences? Should the victim's personal or family circumstances matter? Will these factors, if considered, become a cover for invidious factors such as wealth and race?

|| *State v. Rasheed Muhammad*  ||
678 A.2d 164 (N.J. 1996)

GARIBALDI, J.

Defendant is charged with the kidnapping, rape, and murder of an eight-year-old child, Jakiyah McClain. On the afternoon of April 1, 1995, Jakiyah received permission from her mother to visit a friend, Ah-Tavia Maxey, who lived only a few blocks away. Jakiyah arrived at her friend's apartment between 4:00 p.m. and 5:00 p.m. . . .

While Jakiyah and Ah-Tavia were talking, defendant entered the apartment building. He volunteered to walk Jakiyah upstairs. He knew Jakiyah's mother. Ah-Tavia watched defendant take Jakiyah's hand and lead her upstairs. Ah-Tavia apparently remained on the ground floor. Shortly after, Ah-Tavia heard kicking, banging, and the sound of Jakiyah's screams. [The next day, the] police found Jakiyah's body, curled in a fetal position with her underpants around one ankle, under a pile of clothes in the bedroom closet [of Muhammad's apartment]. Ah-Tavia Maxey identified defendant as the man she saw the day before with Jakiyah.

Defendant was taken into custody. He gave a statement to the police in which he admitted to kidnapping, sexually assaulting, and murdering Jakiyah. An autopsy of the victim indicated that the cause of death was asphyxiation and that the victim was sexually assaulted. On June 27, 1995, an Essex County Grand Jury indicted defendant for the capital murder of Jakiyah McClain. . . . Defendant brought a pretrial motion, challenging the constitutionality of the victim impact statute under both the New Jersey and United States Constitutions. The trial court granted defendant's motion and declared the statute unconstitutional under both Constitutions. . . .

In 1985, the Legislature enacted the Crime Victim's Bill of Rights, which granted crime victims and witnesses certain rights, including the right to be treated with dignity, the right to be informed about the criminal justice process, and the right to be told about available remedies and social services. The following year, the Legislature [allowed] family members of murder victims to include a written statement in the defendant's presentence report. In 1991, the Legislature amended the Crime Victim's Bill of Rights to provide victims with the opportunity to submit to a representative of the county prosecutor's office a written statement about the impact of the crime on the family and to allow victims to make in-person victim impact statements in non-capital cases directly to the sentencing court.

Finally, on November 5, 1991, the New Jersey electorate overwhelmingly approved Article I, paragraph 22 of the New Jersey Constitution, which is better known as the Victim's Rights Amendment. . . . The Victim's Rights Amendment explicitly authorizes the Legislature to provide victims with "those rights and remedies" that are deemed appropriate to effectuate the purpose of that amendment. On the basis of that constitutional authority . . . the New Jersey Legislature enacted the victim impact statute [in 1995].

The various victims' statutory rights enacted in this State are the product of a "victims' rights" movement that has swept through this nation over the last two decades. Historically, the legal system did not view crime victims as having any rights. Because criminal attacks were viewed as attacks and threats on the entire community, and were prosecuted by the state on behalf of "the people," the actual victim was treated as merely another piece of evidence. Although victims were expected to cooperate with authorities and to testify as part of the state's case-in-chief, little attention was paid to the financial, physical, and emotional needs of victims. [Crime] victims are largely excluded from the criminal justice system, and . . . those who are able to participate suffer a "second victimization" at the hands of the system. That feeling of isolation from the system causes many victims and their families to report widespread dissatisfaction with the criminal system. . . .

The victim impact statute provides that if the defendant presents evidence of his character or record pursuant to [a "catch-all" statutory provision allowing introduction of any mitigating evidence during his capital sentencing trial], the State may present evidence of the murder victim's character and background and of the impact of the murder on the victim's survivors. . . . Defendant alleges that the admission of victim impact statements in a capital case is likely to confuse and impassion the jury, and thus creates an impermissible risk that the penalty decision will be made in an arbitrary and capricious manner rather than on the basis of the relevant evidence. . . . The State contends that victim impact evidence is relevant to the sentencing decision because it illustrates each victim's uniqueness as a human being and the nature of the harm caused by the defendant's criminal conduct. . . .

The victim impact statute does not violate the United States Constitution. [In Payne v. Tennessee, 501 U.S. 808 (1991), the] Supreme Court overruled the prior holdings of Booth v. Maryland, 482 U.S. 496 (1987), in which the Court held that the Eighth Amendment prohibits a capital sentencing jury from receiving victim impact evidence relating to the personal characteristics of the murder victim and the emotional impact of the death on the victim's family, and South Carolina v. Gathers, 490 U.S. 805 (1989), in which the Supreme Court extended the rule adopted in *Booth* to statements made by the prosecutor about the personal qualities of the victim.

In reevaluating the exclusion of victim impact evidence, the Court [in *Payne*] rejected two of the premises underlying *Booth* and *Gathers:* first, that evidence of the personal characteristics of the victim and of the emotional impact of the crimes on the family does not in general reflect on the defendant's blameworthiness, and second, that only evidence of moral culpability is relevant to a capital sentencing decision. . . . The Court opined that . . . *Booth* had "unfairly weighted the scales in a capital trial" because it allowed the defendant to introduce virtually all mitigating evidence concerning his own circumstance, but barred the State from offering any victim impact evidence. . . .

The *Payne* Court thus held that if a "State chooses to permit the admission of victim impact evidence and prosecutorial argument on that subject, the Eighth Amendment erects no per se bar." The majority opined that "[v]ictim impact evidence is simply another form or method of informing the sentencing authority about the specific harm caused by the crime in question, evidence of a general type long considered by sentencing authorities." *Payne* left undisturbed the holding in *Booth* that the admission of a victim's family members' characterizations and opinions about the crime, the defendant, and the appropriate sentence violates the Eighth Amendment.

[Our] State Constitution explicitly provides victims of crimes with more rights than the Federal Constitution. The Victim's Rights Amendment expressly authorizes the Legislature to provide crime victims with "those rights and remedies" as it determines are necessary. Even if we were inclined to diverge from the holding in *Payne* and interpret the Cruel and Unusual Punishment Clause of our State Constitution as providing greater protections against the arbitrary imposition of the death penalty, the text of the New Jersey Constitution demands that we not pursue such an independent course. . . . To hold the victim impact statute unconstitutional would require us to ignore the Victim's Rights Amendment and the will of the electorate that overwhelmingly approved the constitutional amendment. . . .

Defendant asserts that, to the extent that a victim impact statement presents evidence about conditions that the defendant was unaware [of] when he committed the criminal act, such as the victim's occupation and marital status, the statement is irrelevant and impermissibly diverts the jury from making its sentencing decision on the character of the defendant and the circumstances of the crime. However, [while] it is clear that a defendant's foreknowledge of the specific consequences that his acts are likely to have is relevant to sentencing, the foreseeable consequences of a defendant's actions are equally relevant. Murder has foreseeable consequences. . . . Defendants who intentionally choose to kill know that their actions will destroy a unique individual who is likely to be a parent, child, spouse, brother, or sister.

While a defendant might be unaware of the specific characteristics of his victim or of the particular survivors that the victim will leave behind, it is completely foreseeable that the killing will eliminate a unique person and destroy a web of familial relationships. That conclusion is buttressed by the facts of this case. When the killer brutally attacked eight-year-old Jakiyah, it was completely foreseeable that the homicidal behavior would eliminate a uniquely individual human being and cause great harm to the survivors of the little girl. Although the killer might have been ignorant of the details about Jakiyah and her family, it does not violate the Constitution if the jury is permitted to take into account such obviously foreseeable consequences.

Although victim impact evidence when offered to rebut a defendant's presentation of catch-all mitigation evidence is not prohibited by the New Jersey Constitution, it must nevertheless be relevant and reliable. The admission of evidence relating to the victim's character or the impact of the murder on the victim's family requires a balancing of the probative value of the proffered evidence against the risk that its admission may pose the danger of undue prejudice or confusion to the jury. . . .

Although the decision to admit specific victim impact statements will typically be in the discretion of the trial court, certain statements are clearly impermissible. For example, the State will not be permitted to elicit testimony concerning the victim's family members' characterizations and opinions about the defendant, the crime, or the appropriate sentence. . . . Victim impact evidence should be limited to statements designed to show the impact of the crime on the victim's family and to statements that demonstrate that the victim was not a faceless stranger, but was a unique individual human being. There is no place in a capital case for unduly inflammatory commentary. . . .

The Legislature has taken appropriate steps to reduce the possibility that jurors will misuse victim impact evidence. Under the victim impact statute, the admission of victim impact evidence is limited to a clearly delineated course. Only if the jury finds that the State has proven at least one aggravating factor beyond a reasonable doubt and the jury finds the existence of a [catch-all] mitigating factor may the jury consider victim impact evidence. Even if these requirements are met, the victim impact statements can be used solely for the purpose of determining how much weight to attach to the catch-all mitigating factor. Victim impact testimony may not be used as a general aggravating factor or as a means of weighing the worth of the defendant against the worth of the victim. Our law does not regard a crime committed against a particularly virtuous person as more heinous than one committed against a victim whose moral qualities are perhaps less noteworthy or apparent. . . . While legislatures in other states have enacted statutes that allow victim impact evidence to be admitted for any purpose, . . . the New Jersey Legislature was very careful not to allow victim impact evidence to be used as a general aggravating factor. . . .

To harmonize the victim impact statute with the due process clauses of the Federal and State Constitutions, the Attorney General and County Prosecutors Association have both urged us to devise additional procedural safeguards to reduce the possibility that victim impact evidence is admitted for improper purposes or is used inappropriately. As a matter of fairness, we hold that certain additional procedures must be followed before victim impact statements can be entered into evidence. The defendant should be notified prior to the commencement of the penalty phase that the State plans to introduce victim impact evidence if the defendant asserts the catch-all factor. The State shall also provide the defendant with the names of the victim impact witnesses that it plans to call so that defense counsel will have an opportunity to interview the witnesses prior to their testimony. The greater the number of survivors who are permitted to present victim impact evidence, the greater the potential for the victim impact evidence to unduly prejudice the jury against the defendant. Thus, absent special circumstances, we expect that the victim impact testimony of one survivor will be adequate to provide the jury with a glimpse of each victim's uniqueness as a human being and to help the jurors make an informed assessment of the defendant's moral culpability and blameworthiness. Further, minors should not be permitted to present victim impact evidence except under circumstances where there are no suitable adult survivors and thus the child is the closest living relative.

Before a family member is allowed to make a victim impact statement, the trial court should ordinarily conduct a hearing, outside the presence of the jury, to make a preliminary determination as to the admissibility of the State's proffered victim impact evidence. The witness's testimony should be reduced to writing to enable the trial court to review the proposed statement to avoid any prejudicial content. The testimony can provide a general factual profile of the victim, including information about the victim's family, employment, education, and interests. The testimony can describe generally the impact of the victim's death on his or her immediate family. The testimony should be factual, not emotional, and should be free of inflammatory comments or references.

The trial court should weigh each specific point of the proffered testimony to ensure that its probative value is not substantially outweighed by the risk of undue prejudice or misleading the jury. N.J.R.E. 403. Determining the relevance of the proffered testimony is particularly important because of the potential for prejudice and improper influence that is inherent in the presentation of victim impact evidence. However, in making that determination, there is a strong presumption that victim impact evidence that demonstrates that the victim was a unique human being is admissible. During the preliminary hearing, the trial court should inform the victim's family that the court will not allow a witness to testify if the person is unable to control his or her emotions. That concern should be alleviated by our requirement that the witness be permitted only to read his or her previously approved testimony. . . . Finally, the trial court should inform the prosecutor that any comments about victim impact evidence in his or her summation should be strictly limited to the previously approved testimony of the witness. . . .

Even though we hold that the introduction of victim impact statements during the sentencing phase of a capital case does not violate the New Jersey Constitution, we recognize that under certain circumstances victim impact statements could render a defendant's sentencing fundamentally unfair and could lead to the arbitrary imposition of the death penalty. . . . We have confidence in the ability of the courts to determine whether a defendant has been impermissibly prejudiced by the admission of unduly inflammatory victim impact evidence. . . .

HANDLER, J., dissenting.
[Expanding] "relevant evidence" to include victim-impact evidence will effectively prevent a jury from rendering a death penalty verdict based on the defendant's character and the circumstances of the crime. Evidence about the crime victim has always been admissible in a capital prosecution when it is relevant to guilt or innocence. Victim-impact evidence, as now authorized, however, is not relevant to criminal guilt or innocence. A death sentence must be based on a determination of the defendant's deathworthiness in terms of his or her character and the circumstances of the case. The constitutionality of the death penalty based on that determination hinges on the requirement that clear standards guide jury discretion. A jury's consideration of victim-impact evidence, as now

authorized by the Court, cannot be controlled by any standards. Jurors will not be capable of disregarding victim-impact evidence's extreme prejudicial effects or avoiding its distorting and devastating impact. Thus, victim-impact evidence will inevitably derail the jury's function and purpose, resulting in the unconstitutional imposition of the death penalty. . . .

The introduction of victim-impact evidence unacceptably exacerbates the racial disparities evident in capital sentencing. Victim-impact evidence encourages jurors to examine and use, both consciously and unconsciously, the comparative worth of the defendant and the victim. Race unquestionably influences our perceptions. . . . Jurors will utilize their unconscious impressions of the victim's worth when considering whether the credibility of the victim-impact evidence and the degree to which the survivors' suffering will counter the weight of the [general mitigating] evidence. First, jurors will consider whether the victim-impact evidence correlates to what the jurors believe is the appropriate impact for the victim's death. Second, jurors will make a moral determination of the gravity of the victim's death. Such steps accentuate disparate capital sentencing on the basis of the victim's race. For these reasons, victim-impact evidence raises the foreboding possibility that death-penalty sentencing decisions influenced by victim-impact evidence will be based on the same invidious motives as race-based discrimination. . . .

### NOTES

1. *Victim input at sentencing.*   Over the past 20 years nearly every state has increased victim involvement at sentencing. See generally National Victim Center, The 1996 Victims' Rights Sourcebook: A Compilation and Comparison of Victims' Rights Laws (1996). Almost all states now permit victim input through the presentence report. Many state laws allow victims a separate opportunity to make a written or oral statement regarding sentencing, often detailing the kinds of information victims may offer. A few states have retained sharper limits, such as those allowing judges to choose whether to admit or refuse victim impact information; Texas allows a victim to make a personal statement in court only *after* sentencing, Tex. Code Crim. Proc. art. 42.03. The Victim and Witness Protection Act of 1982 amended the Federal Rules of Criminal Procedure to require the inclusion of a victim impact statement as a part of the presentence investigation report in federal court. See Fed. R. Crim. P. 32 (presentence report must contain "verified information, stated in a nonargumentative style, containing an assessment of the financial, social, psychological, and medical impact on any individual against whom the offense has been committed"). Why do some jurisdictions (such as New Jersey) accept the victim's statements about the impact of the crime but not the victim's opinion about an appropriate sentence? Cf. Fryer v. State, 68 S.W.2d 628 (Tex. 2002) (law allows sentencing court to consider victim's opinion about proper punishment, as recorded in presentence report; here, victim recommends that defendant in sexual assault case not receive probation).

Victim impact information is supposed to influence the judge; indeed, many statutes require the judge to take account of victim information. The rich variety of statutes has not produced detailed case law regarding victim impact statements outside the capital sentencing context. Is victim impact evidence a less difficult issue in the noncapital setting because a judge rather than a jury selects the sentence? Is a judge more likely to ignore any "emotional" aspects of the victim's testimony? Is it even *possible* to distinguish, as the *Muhammad* court attempted to do, between emotional and informational statements from victims?

2. *Sentencing provisions in federal victim rights legislation.*   In October 2004 Congress enacted a comprehensive Crime Victims Rights Act (CVRA), codified at 18 U.S.C. §3771. Among its comprehensive list of rights, the act gives victims "the right to be reasonably heard at any public proceeding in the district court involving . . . sentencing." This act thus seems to codify in federal law the right of crime victims to provide what is known as a "victim impact statement" to the court. This new act does not, however, limit the right of victims to providing just impact information. The rights conferred by the act are designed to be broad and to allow victims to be "reasonably heard" at all sentencing proceedings.

In the first major test of the sentencing reach of the CVRA, the Ninth Circuit in Kenna v. U.S. District Court for the Central District of California, 435 F.3d 1011 (9th Cir. 2006), indicated that Congress sought to confer broad rights on victims and granted a writ of mandamus to ensure that victims could speak at a defendant's sentencing hearing. In a subsequent ruling, however, the Ninth Circuit summarily rejected a crime victim's claim that the CVRA provided victims the right to obtain disclosure of a full presentence report. See Kenna v. U.S. District Court for the Central District of California, 453 F.3d 1136 (9th Cir. 2006).

The particulars of working victims into the sentencing process presents various challenges, and requires preliminary resolution of who exactly qualifies as a victim under applicable laws. In the context of some offenses, the victims as so defined will be obvious; but are there any "victims" in drug and firearm possession offenses, and are there not hundreds of thousands of victims in large corporate frauds that impact financial markets? Though many policy-makers embrace the basic idea of granting victims rights in the criminal justice system, in practice victims can sometimes disrupt the traditional operation of the system. For a fuller review of these and related issues, see generally Victim Impact Evidence, the Crime Victims' Rights Act and *Kenna*, 19 Fed. Sent'g Rep. no. 1 (October 2006).

3. *Support services for victims.*   Although the law in many jurisdictions now allows a victim to provide formal input to the sentencer (whether jury or judge), most victims in noncapital cases do not take advantage of the opportunity. What practical hurdles might block the routine participation of victims at sentencing? What support services might a prosecutor's office (or some other government agency) offer to victims that could increase the number of victims who take an active role at sentencing? Do prosecutors have incentives to provide such services?

4. *Vulnerable victims.*   Structured sentencing rules often instruct a judge to enhance a sentence if the victim of the crime was vulnerable or otherwise worthy of exceptional protection. The Minnesota sentencing guidelines authorize the

judge to decrease a sentence if "the victim was an aggressor in the incident" and to increase the sentence if the "victim was particularly vulnerable due to age, infirmity, or reduced physical or mental capacity, which was known or should have been known to the offender" or if the "victim was treated with particular cruelty for which the individual offender should be held responsible." Minn. Sentencing Guidelines II.D.2.a.1, II.D.2.b.1 to II.D.2.b.2. The federal guidelines contain a similar provision for enhancement of the sentence by a designated amount if "the defendant knew or should have known that a victim of the offense was unusually vulnerable due to age, physical or mental condition, or that a victim was otherwise particularly susceptible to criminal conduct." U.S. Sentencing Guidelines Manual §3A1.1. A specified increase is also required when the victim is "a government officer or employee" or a law enforcement officer.

5. *Community perspectives at sentencing.*   Crimes rarely have only one victim. Indeed, many crimes affect an entire community. How can the sentencing judge learn about such wide-ranging effects? The Sentencing Reform Act requires the U.S. Sentencing Commission to consider, when creating the federal sentencing guidelines, "the community view of the gravity of the offense." 28 U.S.C. §944(c)(4). Should the commission interpret that instruction to require polls on the views of the national "community" to create one set of guidelines, or does it instead call for the creation of guideline provisions that are uniquely attentive to the various communities that make up the United States? Since the commission chose to create uniform federal guidelines, would it be appropriate for judges in different federal jurisdictions to weigh community impact differently? Federal judge Reena Raggi argues that federal guidelines should allow local variation among federal districts because particular crimes may create special harms in some localities and because the judges in that area develop special expertise on certain topics:

> I first began to question [the nationally uniform approach of the sentencing guidelines] when I had to impose sentences on a number of defendants who had unlawfully transported firearms into New York from other states. Almost daily my fellow New Yorkers and I would read in the press of the senseless shooting of young children, on the streets, even in their own homes, all victims of random gun fire. . . . Almost invariably the guns used in these crimes, as well as most others unlawfully possessed in this area, had come from out of state.
>
> This sort of interstate transportation of guns into the New York area is big business. In the two years between 1990 and 1992, a joint federal-state task force operating in New York arrested 260 people for such trafficking. And yet, when it came time for me to impose sentences in my cases that summer of 1990, I was confronted by a guideline range that rarely exceeded six months' incarceration. When I voiced my concern to the Sentencing Commission about these guidelines for gun trafficking as they applied in New York, I was told that other parts of the country viewed gun crimes differently and that the guidelines were meant to reflect an average. . . .
>
> The insight judges have about crimes in their particular districts goes beyond simply recognizing which conduct is more destructive to a community. It also reaches the question of how different levels of conduct contribute to an area's crime problems. For example, . . . few judges have as broad an experience dealing with drug importation and large-scale distribution as my colleagues in the Eastern District of New York. The piers and airports of the district make it . . . the entry point for a large percentage of the contraband

entering this country. . . . The fact that a sentencing factor . . . does not pertain nationwide, indeed, the fact that it may be unique to the case at hand, does not make the factor irrelevant to the imposition of a just sentence. District judges should enjoy more discretion — indeed they should be encouraged — to depart from the guidelines to reflect specific local concerns.

Reena Raggi, Local Concerns, Local Insights, 5 Fed. Sent'g Rep. 306-308 (1993). As a member of the U.S. Sentencing Commission, how might you respond?

   6. *Limits on the manner or means of victim and community input at sentencing?* In our electronic age, there are a variety of manners and means through which victim and community input might be presented to a sentencing judge or jury. Especially in murder cases, the family of the victim may have a personal archive of pictures, songs, videos, websites, and other materials that might be presented to showcase the best features and best moments of the person killed. Should there be any limit on what kinds of visual materials can be presented at sentencing? If a community is struggling with the effects of a certain crime in a particular neighborhood, should prosecutors consider creating a neighborhood video to show to judges at the sentencing of any and all persons convicted on this crime?

   In November 2008, the U.S. Supreme Court denied cert in a pair of cases from California in which defendants objected to the admission of videos during the sentencing phase of their capital trials. Justice John Paul Stevens authored a separate statement in which he detailed the nature of these video's and explained his view that the Justices had an obligation to place legal limits on how victim impact evidence could be presented:

> These two capital cases raise questions concerning the admissibility of so-called "victim impact evidence" during the penalty phase of a capital trial. The term is a misnomer in capital cases because the evidence does not describe the impact of the crime on the victim — his or her death is always an element of the offense itself. Rather, it describes the impact of the victim's death on third parties, usually members of the victim's family. In the first of these cases, petitioner Douglas Kelly was convicted of murdering 19-year-old Sara Weir. The prosecution played a 20-minute video consisting of a montage of still photographs and video footage documenting Weir's life from her infancy until shortly before she was killed. The video was narrated by the victim's mother with soft music playing in the background, and it showed scenes of her swimming, horseback riding, and attending school and social functions with her family and friends. The video ended with a view of her grave marker and footage of people riding horseback in Alberta, Canada — the "kind of heaven" in which her mother said she belonged. In the second case, petitioner Samuel Zamudio was convicted of robbing and murdering Elmer and Gladys Benson. Two of the victims' daughters and two of their grandchildren testified about the effects of the murders on themselves and their families. During one daughter's testimony the prosecution played a video containing 118 photographs of the victims at various stages of their lives, including their childhood and early years of marriage. The photographs showed the couple raising their children, serving in the military, hunting, fishing, vacationing, bowling, celebrating holidays and family events, and attending recognition dinners for Gladys's community service. The last three photographs in the montage showed, in order, Gladys' grave marker with the inscription readable, Elmer's grave marker with the inscription readable, and both grave markers from a distance, each accompanied by a vase of flowers.
>
>    In both cases the California Supreme Court upheld the admissibility of the videos. The court explained that the video admitted during Kelly's

sentencing "expressed no outrage" and contained no "clarion call for vengeance," but "just implied sadness." 42 Cal. 4th, at 797, 171 P. 3d, at 558.
Similarly, the court held that the video shown during Zamudio's penalty
phase proceedings was "not unduly emotional." 43 Cal. 4th, at 367, 181 P.
3d, at 137. Only one dissenting justice expressed any concern that the evidence
had the potential to "imbue the proceedings with 'a legally impermissible level
of emotion." 42 Cal. 4th, at 803, 171 P. 3d, at 575 (Moreno, J., concurring and
dissenting). No member of the court suggested that the evidence shed any light
on the character of the offense, the character of the offender, or the defendant's moral culpability. . . .

Victim impact evidence is powerful in any form. But in each of these cases,
the evidence was especially prejudicial. Although the video shown to each jury
was emotionally evocative, it was not probative of the culpability or character of
the offender or the circumstances of the offense. Nor was the evidence particularly probative of the impact of the crimes on the victims' family members: The
pictures and video footage shown to the juries portrayed events that occurred
long before the respective crimes were committed and that bore no direct
relation to the effect of crime on the victims' family members. Equally troubling
is the form in which the evidence was presented. As these cases demonstrate,
when victim impact evidence is enhanced with music, photographs, or video
footage, the risk of unfair prejudice quickly becomes overwhelming. While the
video tributes at issue in these cases contained moving portrayals of the lives of
the victims, their primary, if not sole, effect was to rouse jurors' sympathy for the
victims and increase jurors' antipathy for the capital defendants. The videos
added nothing relevant to the jury's deliberations and invited a verdict based on
sentiment, rather than reasoned judgment. . . .

These videos are a far cry from the written victim impact evidence at issue
in [our prior cases]. In their form, length, and scope, they vastly exceed the
"quick glimpse" the Court's majority contemplated when it [approved victim
impact testimony in capital cases]. At the very least, the petitions now before us
invite the Court to apply the standard announced in Payne, and to provide the
lower courts with long-overdue guidance on the scope of admissible victim
impact evidence. Having decided to tolerate the introduction of evidence
that puts a heavy thumb on the prosecutor's side of the scale in death cases,
the Court has a duty to consider what reasonable limits should be placed on its
use. Kelly v. California, 129 S. Ct, 564, 564-67 (2008).

Do you agree with Justice Stevens that the Supreme Court "has a duty to
consider" limits should be place on the use of a modern new form of victim-
related evidence in capital cases? From what constitutional provision does this
duty stem? Does this duty only apply in capital cases where evidence is typically
being presented to a sentencing jury, or should there be constitutional limits on
the victim-related information that can be presented to a judge considering noncapital sentencing options? And what exactly should those limits be?

# = 5 =

## *Sentencing Inputs: The Offender's Record and Background*

In Chapter 4 we reviewed how various features of the crime can affect sentencing outcomes. But that review covered only one side of the substantive components of sentencing decisions — the offense. In this chapter we turn to another major sentencing input, the background and characteristics of the criminal offender. A prior criminal record, cooperation with the government in other investigations, and other aspects of the offender's personal history and prospects can all play a role in the sentencing decision. The foundational question to consider throughout this chapter is why sentence determinations should turn on *who* the offender is in addition to *what* the offender did.

As we stressed at the outset of Chapter 4, sentencing practice always informs sentencing theory, and thus it is again appropriate to begin our discussion of offender characteristics with an introductory sentencing exercise — indeed, the same basic exercise that started Chapter 4. Below we supplement the facts relating to the fictitious offender Rob Anon. The questions following the facts highlight the relevance of Rob's personal characteristics rather than his crime. As before, you should be prepared to return to Rob's case periodically to see whether our detailed study of sentencing systems changes your initial perspective on Rob's status.

### PROBLEM 5-1. ROB ANON

A jury found Rob Anon guilty of one count of armed bank robbery. The evidence at trial proved that Rob planned the robbery and then recruited his two co-defendants to participate. According to the testimony of co-defendant Zweite (who pled guilty to the charge pursuant to a plea agreement with the government), Rob gave each participant in the robbery a firearm and a ski mask. Rob also provided a getaway car, although the origins and current location of the car remain unknown.

According to the testimony at trial, the activities of the three defendants inside the bank were as follows: Rob disabled the surveillance cameras and alarms; co-defendant Tercero kept his firearm pointed at the teller while Zweite vaulted the counter and collected more than $200,000 in cash. As the threesome hurried out of the bank, Tercero pushed to the ground an elderly man who walked into the bank during the robbery. The man broke his hip when he fell. In dividing the loot, Rob gave Zweite and Tercero one-fourth of the proceeds each, keeping half for himself.

The government's evidence at Rob's trial included surveillance photos, eyewitnesses, physical evidence, and testimony by Zweite and Tercero. From the moment of his indictment and throughout his prosecution, Rob denied responsibility for the robbery and claimed he was "set up."

Rob is 22 years old and has produced a spotty employment record since dropping out of high school at age 16. Rob was last employed in a series of construction projects with a local landscaping company; he previously worked for a shoe store as a salesman on a part-time basis. Reared by a single mother in an economically depressed urban area and the second youngest of five children, Rob seems to have few friends and mostly keeps to himself. Rob's mother recalls that Rob's siblings taunted and teased him because of his small stature. She believes that Rob became addicted to cocaine in the past year.

Rob's criminal record includes two prior offenses. Six years ago, a juvenile court convicted Rob of one count of shoplifting and sentenced him to 100 hours of community service. Two years ago, Rob was convicted of receipt of stolen goods and sentenced to three years' probation. Rob was still serving that term of probation at the time of the bank robbery. In the federal system, armed bank robbery carries a maximum penalty of 25 years in prison or a fine of $250,000 or both.  Compare  http://www.ussc.gov/Education_and_Training/Guidelines_ Educational_Materials/WS_Ex_rob.pdf.

1. You are the sentencing judge for Rob in a jurisdiction that places no limits on your discretion to choose a sentence from probation to the statutory maximum of 25 years. What sentence would you impose? If you need more information before choosing a sentence, what additional information would you seek?
2. If this had been Rob's first offense rather than his third, would your sentencing decision change?
3. If Rob accepted responsibility for his action, pled guilty to the charged offense, and agreed to testify against his co-conspirators, would your sentencing decision change?
4. If Rob was 45 years old with a Ph.D. and had been raised in an affluent home, would your sentencing decision change?
5. If Rob (and an expert testifying on his behalf) claimed that his criminal behavior was the product of his cocaine addiction and Rob was now voluntarily enrolled in an intensive drug treatment program, would your sentencing decision change?

# A.  PRIOR CRIMINAL RECORD

At sentencing, the court learns about the defendant's life before the crime of conviction took place. Probation officers collect some of this information; attorneys for either the prosecution or the defense present facts about the offender's personal background and history as well. Often the offender's past includes prior convictions or other encounters with the criminal justice system. In an unstructured sentencing system, the judge gives the prior criminal record whatever weight she thinks appropriate. Sentencing statutes and guidelines, however, instruct judges in some systems more precisely about the effect that a prior criminal record must have on a sentence.

## 1.  *"Strikes" Laws and Other Mandatory Rules*

|| ***People v. Jerry Garcia*** ||
|| 976 P.2d 831 (Cal. 1999) ||

CHIN, J.

In this case, we consider whether a trial court, when applying the "Three Strikes" law, Penal Code §§667(b)-(i), 1170.12(a)-(d), may exercise its discretion under Penal Code §1385(a), so as to dismiss a prior conviction allegation with respect to one count but not another. We conclude that a court may exercise its discretion in this way and that the trial court did not abuse its discretion in doing so here. . . .

On June 19, 1996, Barbara Gantt left her home suddenly to go to the hospital and inadvertently left a window open. She returned home less than two hours later and found the place ransacked. Various items were missing, including a translating machine, jewelry, and a videocassette recorder. As she was cleaning up, she found a wallet with defendant's driver's license on the floor among some of her papers.

On September 4, 1996, Grace Kobel returned home to find defendant bicycling out of her driveway. A window was broken, the screen was lying on the ground, and her front door was open. Kobel called the police, who arrived a few minutes later. She entered the house with the police and found various items missing, including a telephone, jewelry, and a toy airplane. About the same time, police officers spotted defendant riding a bicycle several blocks away and stopped him. Defendant was holding two plastic bags that contained many of the items missing from Kobel's home. He also had jewelry in his pockets. . . .

The court found defendant guilty on [two counts of burglary]. The court also found true an allegation that defendant had five prior serious felony convictions qualifying as "strikes" for purposes of the Three Strikes law.[1] These

---

1. Penal Code §667(e)(2) provides:

(A) If a defendant has two or more prior felony convictions [qualifying as serious or violent felonies under this law], the term for the current felony conviction shall be an indeterminate term of life imprisonment with a minimum term of the indeterminate

convictions, all on July 17, 1991, were for five burglaries that took place on separate occasions during a short crime spree. The court also found that the same five burglary convictions qualified as one prior serious felony conviction for purposes of the five-year enhancement set forth in §667(a)(1).[2] Finally, for purposes of the one-year enhancement set forth in §667.5(b),[3] the court found true an allegation that defendant had served three prior prison terms. The first of these terms was for a January 10, 1985, conviction for receiving stolen property, the second for a February 19, 1987, conviction for possession of heroin, and the third for the five 1991 burglary convictions already mentioned.

At the sentencing hearing, the court considered a probation report indicating defendant had a history of burglarizing homes and then trading stolen property for drugs. Barbara Gantt and Grace Kobel then described the impact defendant's crimes had on them and asked the court to give defendant the maximum sentence. Next, defendant's girlfriend described defendant's difficult life, saying he grew up in foster homes and was addicted to heroin by age 12. Finally, defendant expressed remorse about the burglaries and asked for forgiveness.

Defense counsel then asked the court to exercise its discretion under §1385(a),[4] and dismiss, or "strike," four of the five prior conviction allegations as to both counts, thereby making the case a "second strike" case and reducing defendant's sentence to a term of twenty-two years and eight months. The court responded that "the interests of justice would not be served by striking four strikes in this case," and to do so "would be for the sole purpose of avoiding the sentence I'm required to hand down by law." The court noted that defendant

---

sentence calculated as the greater of [three] times the term otherwise provided as punishment for each current felony conviction subsequent to the two or more prior felony convictions [or] imprisonment in the state prison for 25 years. . . .

(B) The indeterminate term described in subparagraph (A) shall be served consecutive to any other term of imprisonment for which a consecutive term may be imposed by law. Any other term imposed subsequent to any indeterminate term described in subparagraph (A) shall not be merged therein but shall commence at the time the person would otherwise have been released from prison. — Eds.

2. Penal Code §667(a)(1) provides as follows: "[Any] person convicted of a serious felony who previously has been convicted of a serious felony in this state or of any offense committed in another jurisdiction which includes all of the elements of any serious felony, shall receive, in addition to the sentence imposed by the court for the present offense, a five-year enhancement for each such prior conviction on charges brought and tried separately. The terms of the present offense and each enhancement shall run consecutively." — Eds.

3. Penal Code §667.5(b) provides: "[Where] the new offense is any felony for which a prison sentence is imposed, in addition and consecutive to any other prison terms therefor, the court shall impose a one-year term for each prior separate prison term served for any felony; provided that no additional term shall be imposed under this subdivision for any prison term served prior to a period of five years in which the defendant remained free of both prison custody and the commission of an offense which results in a felony conviction." — Eds.

4. Penal Code §1385(a) provides: "The judge or magistrate may, either of his or her own motion or upon the application of the prosecuting attorney, and in furtherance of justice, order an action to be dismissed. The reasons for the dismissal must be set forth in an order entered upon the minutes. . . ." — Eds.

committed five separate residential burglaries, went to state prison, and then, shortly after his release and while still on parole, committed two more residential burglaries. "[If] the Three Strikes law was meant for anyone it was meant for Mr. Garcia," the court said. [The] court agreed that defendant's drug addiction was "a factor in mitigation." The court also noted that all defendant's prior serious felony convictions arose from a single period of aberrant behavior for which he served a single prison term. The court commented that defendant had cooperated with police both in 1991 and when they arrested him for the current offenses. Finally, the court stated that defendant had no record of violence.

As to the Kobel burglary, the court sentenced defendant to a term of 30 years to life in state prison. This sentence included 25 years to life under the Three Strikes law plus the mandatory 5-year enhancement under §667(a)(1). The court initially imposed three 1-year enhancements under §667.5(b), for the prior prison terms, but then exercised its discretion under §1385(a), and struck these enhancements. As to the Gantt burglary, the court exercised its discretion under §1385(a), and struck all the prior conviction allegations. In a minute order, the court stated it was striking the prior conviction allegations because they "all refer [to] one case, defendant has cooperated with police in both cases, is addicted to drugs and has not suffered any violent priors." The court calculated a sentence of 16 months, which was one-third the middle term of 4 years. The court ordered that this sentence be served consecutive to the sentence on the Kobel burglary, because the two counts reflected "two separate incidents on two separate dates." Nevertheless, the court stated that a sentence of 30 years to life was "appropriate" and that, but for the constraints of the Three Strikes law, it would have ordered that the 16-month sentence on the Gantt burglary be served concurrently. Defendant's total sentence on both counts was 31 years and 4 months to life. The court imposed a $200 restitution fine, and also ordered $400 restitution to Grace Kobel and $20,000 restitution to Barbara Gantt, less the value of any property returned.

[On appeal, the Attorney General] asserted that the trial court lacked authority under §1385(a) to strike the prior conviction allegations as to the Gantt burglary while not striking them as to the Kobel burglary, claiming that therefore defendant's sentence was unauthorized. [He argued] that striking prior conviction allegations as to some, but not all, current counts was inconsistent with the requirement in the Three Strikes law that sentences be consecutive for current felonies relating to separate criminal episodes. . . .

Section 1385(a) authorizes a trial court to act on its own motion to dismiss a criminal action "in furtherance of justice." We have long held that this power includes the ability to strike prior conviction allegations that would otherwise increase a defendant's sentence. People v. Burke, 301 P.2d 241 (Cal. 1956). Our reasoning in *Burke* is particularly relevant to the issue in this case. In *Burke*, the defendant had been convicted of possession of marijuana . . . , and he admitted a prior conviction for the same offense. At that time, Health and Safety Code former §11712 provided: "Any person convicted . . . for having in possession any narcotic [if] such a person has been previously convicted [of the same offense] shall be imprisoned in the state prison for not less than two years. . . ." Nevertheless, the trial court struck the prior conviction allegation and sentenced the defendant to county jail. . . . We concluded that this power to strike a sentencing allegation fell within the broader power to dismiss an entire action under section

1385. More importantly, however, we also concluded that "[the] striking or dismissal of a charge of prior conviction . . . is not the equivalent of a determination that defendant did not in fact suffer the conviction [citations]; such judicial action is taken . . . for the purpose of sentencing only and any dismissal of charges of prior convictions . . . does not wipe out such prior convictions or prevent them from being considered in connection with later convictions." Thus, we acknowledged that a court might strike a prior conviction allegation in one context, but use it in another.

In People v. Superior Court (Romero), 928 P.2d 1171 (Cal. 1996), we held that the Three Strikes law did not remove or limit this §1385 power to strike sentencing allegations. The defendant in *Romero* pleaded guilty to possession of 0.13 grams of cocaine base. . . . The information also alleged five prior felony convictions, two of which—attempted burglary and first degree burglary of an inhabited dwelling—qualified as strikes for purposes of the Three Strikes law. The trial court struck the prior conviction allegations and imposed a sentence of six years in state prison. This sentence represented three years (the upper term) for possession of a controlled substance plus three consecutive one-year enhancements for prior prison terms. [We] concluded that, in a Three Strikes case, the trial court can, on its own motion and over the prosecutor's objection, strike a prior conviction allegation in furtherance of justice.

Our holding in *Romero* flowed directly from the plain language of the Three Strikes law, which expressly authorizes prosecutors to move to strike prior conviction allegations "pursuant to"§1385(a). We reasoned that, because the Three Strikes law makes express reference to §1385 and does not anywhere bar courts from acting pursuant to that section, the drafters of the law must have intended that section to apply without limitation in Three Strikes cases. . . .

Nevertheless, we stressed that "[a] court's discretion to strike prior felony conviction allegations in furtherance of justice is limited."[A] court may not strike a sentencing allegation solely "to accommodate judicial convenience or because of court congestion." Nor may a court strike a sentencing allegation "simply because a defendant pleads guilty." Finally, we stated that a court may not strike a sentencing allegation "guided solely by a personal antipathy for the effect that the three strikes law would have on [a] defendant," while ignoring defendant's background, the nature of his present offenses, and other individualized considerations.

In People v. Williams, 948 P.2d 429 (Cal. 1998), we further delineated the parameters that govern a trial court's discretion under §1385(a), to strike prior conviction allegations in a Three Strikes case. *Williams* involved a defendant who pleaded guilty to driving a vehicle under the influence of phencyclidine (PCP). . . . The defendant had a 19-year criminal history, including convictions for attempted robbery, rape, and spousal battery, and a series of convictions for firearm possession and driving under the influence. The attempted robbery and rape convictions, which the defendant admitted, qualified as strikes for purposes of the Three Strikes law. However, because those convictions were about 13 years old and because of "the lack of any kind of violence related crimes from then until now," the trial court vacated its finding with respect to the prior attempted robbery conviction, leaving only the prior rape conviction. [We] concluded that the trial court had abused its discretion by vacating one of its prior conviction findings [and] discussed the factors a trial court may legitimately consider when exercising its §1385 discretion in a Three Strikes case. We said that the trial court could give "no weight whatsoever . . . to factors extrinsic to the [Three Strikes] scheme." On the other hand, the court must accord "preponderant weight . . . to factors intrinsic to the scheme, such as the nature and circumstances of the defendant's present felonies and prior serious and/or violent felony convictions, and the particulars of his background, character, and prospects." Ultimately, a court must determine whether "the defendant may be deemed outside the scheme's spirit, in whole or in part."

The reasoning of *Romero* and the standards we enunciated in *Williams* logically support the trial court's action in this case. In *Romero*, we concluded that, by referencing §1385, the Three Strikes law incorporated that section without limitation. [The] standards we enunciated in *Williams* indicate that a trial court has discretion in a Three Strikes case to strike prior conviction allegations on a count-by-count basis. In *Williams*, we instructed trial courts to consider among other things, "individualized considerations" such as the nature and circumstances of the defendant's present felonies and his "prospects." In many cases, "the nature and circumstances" of the various felonies described in different counts will differ considerably. A court might therefore be justified in striking prior conviction allegations with respect to a relatively minor current felony, while considering those prior convictions with respect to a serious or violent current felony.

The Attorney General argues, however, that in a case such as this one, where both current felonies are for the same or similar crimes, the "individualized considerations" we enumerated in *Williams* do not provide a "principled basis" for treating the felonies differently. We disagree. Even if the current offenses are virtually identical, a defendant's "prospects" will differ greatly from one count to another because a Three Strikes sentence on one count will itself radically alter those prospects. Here, for example, once the trial court had sentenced defendant to a term of 30 years to life for the Kobel burglary, his "prospects" for committing future burglaries diminished significantly. [A] defendant's sentence is . . . a relevant consideration when deciding whether to strike a prior conviction allegation; in fact, it is the overarching consideration because the underlying purpose of striking prior conviction allegations is the avoidance of unjust sentences. . . .

The Attorney General, however, points to the requirement in the Three Strikes law that sentencing on distinct current offenses be consecutive, §§667(c)(6)-(8), 1170.12(a)(6)-(8), and without any aggregate term limitation, §§667(c)(1), 1170.12(a)(1). The Attorney General argues that striking prior conviction allegations with respect to one count, but not with respect to another, undermines this principle of consecutive Three Strikes sentences. Again, we disagree. A requirement that a defendant serve the individual sentences for different current felonies consecutively does not indicate how the trial court should determine the lengths of those individual sentences. Here, for example, the trial court conformed to the consecutive sentencing requirement by ordering that the 16-month sentence for the Gantt burglary be served consecutively to the 30-year-to-life sentence for the Kobel burglary. . . .

The Attorney General also argues that the trial court here "eviscerated" the Three Strikes law, the purpose of which was to restrict the discretion of "soft-on-crime judges" and "ensure longer prison sentences." We agree with the

Attorney General that a primary purpose of the Three Strikes law was to restrict judicial discretion, but the Attorney General's argument merely begs the question of *how* judicial discretion was to be restricted. The answer to that question can be found only by examining the language of the act. The Three Strikes law expressly incorporates the power to strike prior conviction allegations under §1385(a). Therefore, rather than eviscerating the Three Strikes law, the trial court in this case *applied* that law, which expressly contemplates the trial court's action.

[Appellate] review of a trial court's §1385 decision is not de novo. [The abuse of discretion] standard is deferential. But it is not empty. Although variously phrased in various decisions, it asks in substance whether the ruling in question falls outside the bounds of reason under the applicable law and the relevant facts. Here, we cannot say that the trial court's decision to strike the prior conviction allegations as to count 3 "falls outside the bounds of reason." The court sentenced defendant to 31 years and 4 months to life in state prison. This sentence is not lenient. . . . Moreover, as the trial court noted, defendant's prior convictions all arose from a single period of aberrant behavior for which he served a single prison term. Defendant cooperated with police, his crimes were related to drug addiction, and his criminal history does not include any actual violence. Cumulatively, all these circumstances indicate that "defendant may be deemed outside the [Three Strikes] scheme's spirit," at least in part, and that the trial court acted within the limits of its §1385 discretion. . . .

BROWN, J., dissenting.

I respectfully dissent. This case asks the age-old question: does judicial commitment to principle matter? The majority gives the modern answer. Not if it gets in the way of expediency.

The "Three Strikes" law reflects the public's long-simmering frustration with perceived laxity in a criminal justice system that allowed repeatedly convicted felons to be released after serving modest sentences with time off for good behavior. All too often, this revolving door led to more crimes, new victims, and greater tragedies. The public saw "soft on crime" judges who were more solicitous of criminal defendants than public safety as the problem; they viewed Three Strikes as the solution. . . .

Under our precedents, the trial court retains discretion under Penal Code §1385 or §17(b), to remove a case from the reach of the law. But, until today, in choosing to rely upon these latter statutes, a trial court had to make a principled determination that the defendant did not come within the spirit of the Three Strikes law and therefore should not be subject to its letter. Thus, I disagree that a court can dismiss prior convictions on a count-by-count basis. Moreover, even if in rare cases a court has that power, the principles we articulated in our recent precedents bar the trial court from doing so here.

[Unless] carefully circumscribed, the power to strike prior felony conviction allegations "in furtherance of justice" . . . carries with it the real potential for undermining the intent of the Three Strikes law itself—namely, to restrict courts' discretion in sentencing repeat offenders. In *Williams*, we . . . undertook to "render §1385(a)'s concept of 'furtherance of justice' somewhat more determinate." We concluded that "in ruling whether to strike or vacate a prior serious and/or violent felony conviction allegation or finding under the Three Strikes law, on its own motion, 'in furtherance of justice' pursuant to §1385(a), or in reviewing such a ruling, the court in question must consider whether, in light of the nature and circumstances of his present felonies and prior serious and/or violent felony convictions, and the particulars of his background, character, and prospects, the defendant may be deemed outside the scheme's spirit, in whole or in part, and hence should be treated as though he had not previously been convicted of one or more serious and/or violent felonies. If it is striking or vacating an allegation or finding, it must set forth its reasons in an order entered on the minutes, and if it is reviewing the striking or vacating of such allegation or finding, it must pass on the reasons so set forth." We emphasized that "no weight whatsoever may be given to factors extrinsic to the [Three Strikes] scheme, such as the mere desire to ease court congestion or, a fortiori, bare antipathy to the consequences for any given defendant."

While professing to follow *Williams*, in reality, the majority tosses aside its carefully crafted limits on judicial discretion. [Notwithstanding] *Williams's* unequivocal holding that "bare antipathy to the consequences for any given defendant" should be given "no weight whatsoever," the majority now concludes that the "overarching consideration" in determining whether to strike prior felony conviction allegations with respect to some, but not all, counts is the total length of a defendant's sentence "because the underlying purpose of striking prior conviction allegations is the avoidance of unjust sentences." In other words, the "overarching consideration" in determining whether to strike prior felony conviction allegations "in furtherance of justice" under §1385(a) is the trial court's antipathy to the sentence the law would otherwise require. . . .

One need only compare the facts of this case to the facts of *Williams* to see how standardless things have become. In *Williams*, in concluding that the trial court had abused its discretion in striking one of Williams's prior felony convictions, we pointed to his failure to "follow through in efforts to bring his substance abuse problem under control." Here, in upholding the trial court's decision to strike, the majority points to the fact defendant's crimes were related to drug addiction. In *Williams*, in concluding that the trial court had abused its discretion in striking one of Williams's prior felony convictions, we noted that "as to his present felony: It is a conviction of driving under the influence that followed three other convictions of driving under the influence; the existence of such convictions reveals that he had been taught, through the application of formal sanction, that such criminal conduct was unacceptable — but had failed or refused to learn his lesson." Here, in upholding the trial court's decision to strike, the majority glosses over the fact defendant's two present convictions for burglary followed quickly on the heels of five previous convictions for exactly the same offense. . . .

The real effect of today's decision is to make the defendant's eligibility for punishment under Three Strikes a factor in mitigation. When a defendant receives a lengthy Three Strikes term on the first of multiple counts, the trial court may disregard the law as to all other counts. . . . *Romero* is no longer reserved for the rare case involving a particularly harsh sentence for a relatively minor offense. Courts may now routinely apply *Romero* to the benefit of recidivists for whom such solicitude is not appropriate. That is not what I heard the voters demand when they enacted the Three Strikes law. Three Strikes was not about judicial discretion; it was about accountability. It was not about "just" sentences; it was about swift, certain, and harsh retribution. Moreover, by encouraging courts to impose only a single Three Strikes sentence regardless of the circumstances, the majority's decision rewards the industrious career criminal — after the first count, the rest are virtually free. . . .

The sentence imposed here was lengthy. But that is beside the point. It was still less than the law required. When the Legislature enacted, and the voters passed, the Three Strikes law, they intended to restrict trial courts' discretion in sentencing. The trial court here had it right when it initially observed that striking defendant's prior felony convictions "would be for the sole purpose of avoiding the sentence I'm required to hand down by law" and that "if the Three Strikes law was meant for anyone it was meant for Mr. Garcia." Today's holding eviscerates the intent of the Three Strikes law. . . .

## *NOTES*

1. *Habitual-offender statutes: the three-strikes variety.* The provision under which Garcia was sentenced, California Penal Code §667, is an example of a habitual-offender law popularly known as "three strikes and you're out." Almost all states have habitual-felon statutes, which increase sentences by designated amounts for offenders with a particular prior felony record. The three-strikes variety is distinctive for the type of prior record necessary and the amount of increase in the sentence. California's three-strikes law is the most severe in the nation for several reasons: many types of prior convictions qualify as "serious" or "violent" and thus count as a strike, a third felony results in a minimum sentence of 25 years to life even if the third felony is neither violent nor serious, and sentences are doubled even for offenders with only one strike. The U.S. Supreme Court in 2003 upheld the application of California's three-strikes law to two shoplifters with extended criminal histories who claimed that their lengthy imprisonment terms violated the Eighth Amendment's prohibition of cruel and unusual punishments. See Ewing v. California, 538 U.S. 11 (2003); Lockyer v. Andrade, 538 U.S. 63 (2003).

About half the states have enacted three-strikes laws, but they vary considerably in reach and impact. A few states have two-strikes provisions for particularly serious felonies, while others have adopted four-strikes provisions. See, e.g., Ga. Code Ann. §17-10-7 (providing a sentence of life without parole for two serious violent felonies); Fla. Stat. Ann. §775.084 (requiring three prior felonies to trigger sentence of life imprisonment). The federal three-strikes law imposes a mandatory sentence of life imprisonment on defendants convicted of a serious federal violent felony if they have been previously convicted in state or federal court of two or more serious violent felonies or one serious violent felony and one serious drug offense. See 18 U.S.C. §3559.

2. *Impact of three-strikes law in California and elsewhere.* Because of its broad reach, California's three-strikes law has had the biggest impact of any jurisdiction's, although that impact is certain only with respect to increased prison rolls. There is a robust debate over whether decreases in crime rates in California through the 1990s and 2000s could be attributed to the deterrent or incapacitation effects of California's three-strikes law. Critics of the law note that some

states with no comparable three-strikes law had crime drops equal to or greater than California's. While the deterrent effect of three-strikes is a disputed question, there is no doubt that the law is responsible for major growth in California's prison system. Other states, which enacted three-strikes laws that reached fewer prior felonies and fewer offenders, did not see a meaningful impact on their prison population.

3. *Prosecutors and habitual felons.* Although habitual-felon laws in California and elsewhere empower the prosecutor to file additional charges that result automatically in increased sentences, the laws usually do not *require* the prosecutor to file the habitual-felon charge for every qualifying defendant. Not many California citizens appreciate how much prosecutorial discretion remains in this law and how much its use varies around the state. Steve Cooley won election in 2000 as the new district attorney in Los Angeles on a platform of increasing screening of three-strikes cases by focusing on those who have committed serious or violent felonies. Cooley appealed both to the public's perception that the law was creating unjust outcomes and to the need to concentrate resources on truly serious offenses. Limits such as those employed by Cooley in Los Angeles County ultimately became the basis for statewide reform. In 2012, California voters approved Proposition 36, restricting life sentences to those cases where the new felony conviction is "serious or violent."

Habitual-felon laws in other states (not just the three-strikes variety) also give prosecutors the critical power to choose which among the eligible defendants will be charged as habitual felons. If you were the chief prosecutor for a county, what instructions would you give your trial attorneys about which defendants to charge under the habitual-felon law?

4. *Politics surrounding passage of three-strikes laws.*   A high-profile crime by a repeat offender often serves as the catalyst for the enactment of three-strikes laws. In California, the drive for a three-strikes ballot initiative was instigated by Mike Reynolds, a Fresno photographer whose 18-year-old daughter was murdered in 1992 by a parolee. Though headline-making crimes gave the public the impression that tougher criminal sanctions were needed for repeat offenders, most jurisdictions already had laws in place that provided lengthy terms of imprisonment for serious recidivists. When California restricted the reach of its three-strikes law in 2012, the reform campaign relied heavily on stories of perceived injustices when the law required life sentences for relatively minor crimes. One typical story involved Norman Williams, whose third "strike" was the theft of a floor jack from a tow truck when he was homeless and addicted to drugs.

Of course, the distorting influences of politics and symbolism in the criminal justice system are not new. As discussed in Chapter 2, the development of sentencing commissions was driven in large part by the hope that this sort of institution — consisting of knowledgeable experts, insulated from short-term political pressures, who would have the time and opportunity to study sentencing — would avoid these influences while developing sound criminal justice laws and policies. But in the face of politicians and the public clamoring for tough habitual-offender laws, most sentencing commissions have been unsuccessful in limiting the impact of this legislation. See Ronald F. Wright, Three Strikes Legislation and Sentencing Commission Objectives, 20 Law & Pol'y 429, 437 (1998).

What features of a three-strikes law might create special problems for a sentencing commission advocating cautious changes in sentencing laws?

## 2.  Long Records

An offender's criminal past played a central role in sentencing well before the enactment of modern three-strikes laws. The law rarely mandated a particular sentence based on an offender's criminal history in the era of indeterminate sentencing, but judges still used their discretion to impose longer sentences on defendants who had a lengthy criminal record. Modern sentencing reforms have focused on systematizing the effect that a criminal record has on the sentence imposed.

‖ *United States v. Anthony Croom* ‖
50 F.3d 433 (7th Cir. 1995)

EASTERBROOK, J.

Anthony Croom is a punk who grew up to be a thug. His first juvenile conviction was for battery. Next came a conviction for child molestation: when 13 years old, Croom had sexual intercourse with an 11 year old girl. Later Croom was convicted of burglary and other offenses. The burglary conviction disqualified Croom from possessing guns, but he thumbed his nose at the law. One day, while attired like a refugee from a gangster movie, with gloves and a hat pulled down to cover his face, Croom bolted from a meal into the arms of police, who recovered a semi-automatic weapon. He was charged with violating 18 U.S.C. §922(g)(1) and released pending trial. Ten days later Croom invaded a fast food restaurant, drew a gun, ordered the staff into the meat locker (threatening them with death if they did not cooperate), and emptied the till. He did not get far, and his capture led to another federal weapons charge. Croom pleaded guilty to both; another, similar charge was dismissed as part of a plea bargain. His sentence of 160 months' imprisonment exceeds the guideline range of 110-137 months for a level 28 offense by someone with a criminal history category of IV, and he appeals from the upward departure.

A district judge may give a sentence exceeding the range specified by the Sentencing Guidelines only on account of circumstances "not adequately taken into consideration" by the Sentencing Commission. 18 U.S.C. §3553(b). The district judge gave this explanation of his decision:

> [Considering] the offenses which did not count for criminal history score points [as well as the] short period of time which elapsed between the defendant's last incarceration and the first of these offenses and [the fast food robbery committed after the initial gun arrest], and considering the nature of the offenses reflected in [the presentence investigation report plus the charges to which Croom pleaded guilty, I find] that the criminal history category IV does not adequately reflect the seriousness of the defendant's past criminal conduct, and perhaps more so the likelihood that the defendant will commit other crimes. I think there is a clearly ascertainable and projectable pattern here by this defendant of ever increasing in ever more dangerous offenses as he proceeds through life. . . . So I will depart upward to a criminal history category of VI. . . .

The judge did not reveal which of these factors he believed the Sentencing Commission has "not adequately taken into consideration" or why he increased the criminal history category from IV to VI rather than V. Croom has earned a substantial sentence, but 137 months' imprisonment—more than 11 years without possibility of parole—is stern punishment. The stated rationale for tacking on two years is problematic under §3553(b).

The judge's explanation starts with the observation that the Guidelines did not count two of Croom's juvenile convictions. Under U.S.S.G. §4A1.2(d)(2) juvenile convictions the sentences for which ended more than five years before the commission of the latest offense do not contribute any criminal history points. Far from representing an aspect of criminal history that the Sentencing Commission overlooked or did not consider adequately, this exclusion is a conscious decision, one a district judge may not override by the mechanism of an upward departure. The Sentencing Commission believed that old juvenile convictions should be "forgiven" in assigning criminal history points; that the district judge is less forgiving than the Commission does not authorize him to strike out on a different path. To forgive is not necessarily to forget, however; as we explain below the judge may consider the juvenile convictions as part of the larger picture when deciding whether to depart under the criteria of U.S.S.G. §4A1.3.

After remarking on the juvenile convictions, the judge observed that Croom committed the first federal gun offense shortly after release from his most recent state imprisonment, then committed the second gun offense while on pretrial release from the first. These are surely grounds for increasing a sentence—but the Sentencing Commission took them into consideration. Croom received two criminal history points under §4A1.1(d) for committing the first gun offense while on parole from a state sentence, and one point under §4A1.1(e) for committing that offense within two years after leaving prison. He paid for the close relation between the first and second gun offenses by forfeiting the three-level reduction for acceptance of responsibility that otherwise would have been available to one who entered a prompt plea of guilty. The judge did not explain why these adjustments are an insufficient recognition of the circumstances.

The district court's final observation—that Croom has led a life of essentially continual crime, of increasing violence—is a sound reason for a departure. Croom not only has a long record but also admitted that he possessed guns all the time between 1991 and 1993. That amounts to many additional offenses under §922(g). He scarcely gets out of the jail's shadow before committing another crime. The Guidelines are designed for normal cases; a defendant who has demonstrated criminal propensities that make him more dangerous than the ordinary person with the same criminal history score may receive a higher sentence. So the Commission said in §4A1.3, describing some situations that it has not fully considered and that therefore authorize departures. Thus, for example, the fact that Croom committed his second gun offense while on release from the first led to the denial of a reduction for acceptance of responsibility; but the fact that he committed the second, more serious, gun offense swiftly after release on the first also shows that he is incorrigible—an armed career criminal in fact if not technically one under 18 U.S.C. §924(e)(1). His juvenile convictions may not be counted directly, but they may be considered as part of the pattern of recidivism. U.S.S.G. §4A1.2 Application Note 8. Meeting most of the criteria for designation as an armed career criminal (or "career offender" under the Guidelines) does not permit the judge to impose the penalties designed for those who meet all of the criteria, but it does permit a departure in the *direction* of those penalties.

What we have, then, is a good reason for departure coupled with two bad ones. The district court must reconsider Croom's sentence but need not necessarily lower it. On remand the court should hew to the considerations approved in §4A1.3 and choose the offense level that best approximates the seriousness of Croom's record and the threat of future crimes it portends. How much to increase the sentence is a judgment call, which if thoughtfully explained will not be disturbed on any later appeal. . . .

ROVNER, J., concurring.

Although I concur in the result and rationale of the majority, I believe that the appropriate exercise of our judicial function requires restraint in the language we use to describe the people who come before us, regardless of how dreadful their transgressions.

## NOTES

1. *Considering prior convictions at sentencing.*    In all U.S. sentencing systems, the offender's prior convictions are among the most important determinants of the sentence imposed. Most sentencing guideline systems place onto a severity scale the number and seriousness of prior convictions. The federal sentencing guidelines, for example, convert prior offenses into criminal history points, which are then grouped into criminal history categories ranging from I (for first offenders) to VI (for offenders with lengthy records); these categories are then used to determine the offender's applicable sentencing range. In most sentencing guideline systems, more-serious prior offenses increase the sentence more than less-serious prior offenses; prior convictions for the same type of crime as the current offense often increase a sentence more than prior convictions for unrelated wrongdoing. Minnesota, for example, assigns prior felony offenses from 1/2 to 2 points depending on the offense's "severity level." Similarly, Pennsylvania assigns 4 criminal history points, the maximum amount available, for the most serious prior convictions such as murder, voluntary manslaughter, kidnapping, rape, involuntary deviate intercourse, arson, and robbery.

2. *Theoretical foundations for considering criminal history.*    Why increase a defendant's sentence for the current offense based on *past* criminal behavior? Are such enhanced sentences designed to deter the offender, or other offenders, from committing future crimes? Are they designed to select a sentence proportionate to the crime committed (that is, to give the offender her just deserts)? Consider this excerpt from a U.S. Sentencing Commission report

discussing the philosophy behind using criminal history to help determine sentencing outcomes:

> Those who argue that retribution is a key principle in sentencing [contend] that criminal history is inappropriate to consider at sentencing because the defendant has already been punished for the previous offense [and] that a defendant has no greater culpability (blameworthiness) because of having committed the prior offense; nor is victimization greater in the current offense as a result of the prior offense. . . . A contrary theory of the role of criminal justice is incapacitation. This approach advocates the expanded use of imprisonment to incapacitate offenders[, assuming] that while offenders are incarcerated they will not be able to engage in additional criminal behavior. [Selective] incapacitation seeks to prevent crime by using certain criteria to identify for restraint a smaller number of offenders who are predicted to commit more crime and/or serious crime. . . . Society and its elected representatives have reached a level of frustration with crime so that current policies more frequently tend to reflect the selective incapacitation philosophy in sentencing practices in general and criminal history in particular.

U.S. Sentencing Commission, Simplification Draft Paper (1995) (see http://www.ussc.gov/simple/crimhist.htm); see also Youngjae Lee, Recidivism as Omission: A Relational Account, 87 Tex. L. Rev. 571 (2009). What role would criminal records play for those who emphasize the rehabilitative power of criminal sentences? Consider, in this regard, the fictional character Jean Valjean from Victor Hugo's 1862 novel Les Misérables. Should his past criminal conduct and punishment mean that he deserves a blank slate? If the state treats him differently from other citizens based on his criminal past, is that warranted by virtue of desert, or dangerousness, or general deterrence, or something else?

3. *Intricacies and complexities in assessing criminal history.* As the decision in *Croom* suggests, the federal guidelines that quantify a defendant's criminal history are complex, in large part because the U.S. Sentencing Commission decided to base its criminal history points on the *length* of prior sentences imposed. Consequently, the federal guidelines include intricate application notes and commentary that address the myriad of possible state court dispositions and instruct judges how to assess each prior sentence, including the custodial component, sentence type, and length. State sentencing rules typically group prior convictions into only a few categories (such as felonies and misdemeanors), which simplifies the criminal history calculation. Nevertheless, quantifying the variations in offenders' criminal records is always intricate. In Maryland, for example, calculation of the offender score has four primary components (relationship to criminal justice system when instant offense occurred, juvenile delinquency, prior adult criminal record, and prior adult criminal justice violation), each of which has multiple subparts with detailed application instructions. See Md. Sentencing Guidelines §7.1.

4. *Stale offenses.* Older convictions tell us less about an offender than more recent ones. Should older convictions have less of an impact (or no impact at all) on the sentence for the current crime? Guideline systems often consider the time period of a prior conviction when assessing criminal history. The federal guidelines use five different time periods for calculating criminal history points, based on the length of the sentence imposed and the age of the defendant when the prior offense was committed. State rules that discount or ignore older convictions

generally set one applicable expiration date for all offenses (say, all convictions more than ten years old). Instead of setting an expiration date for older crimes, some states allow defendants to benefit from "crime free" periods. In these states, if the defendant was conviction free for a certain length of time (usually 10 or 15 years, not including periods of imprisonment, probation, or parole) prior to the instant offense, the sentencing judge does not count any convictions prior to that period. Other states leave this item as a departure consideration.

5. *Unreliable prior convictions.*   The use of prior convictions to enhance the sentence for the current offense becomes more controversial when there are reasons to question the accuracy of the earlier conviction. This is true especially when the earlier conviction occurred without the involvement of defense counsel. The Constitution bars the use at sentencing of some uncounseled prior convictions, but only if the government obtained the prior conviction by violating the defendant's constitutional right to counsel. See Nichols v. United States, 511 U.S. 738 (1994) (sentencing court may consider defendant's previous uncounseled misdemeanor conviction in sentencing him for subsequent offense); United States v. Tucker, 404 U.S. 443 (1972) (conviction obtained in violation of Sixth Amendment rights cannot enhance later sentence). These questions often arise when the prior conviction took place in the juvenile system or when the earlier case dealt with charges of driving while intoxicated. See Thompson v. State, 583 S.E.2d 14 (Ga. 2003) (explaining that prior uncounseled DUI convictions could not be used to enhance a sentence for a later offense). Compare United States v. Huggins, 467 F.3d 359 (2006) (adjudication as a delinquent under Pennsylvania law not a "prior conviction" for purposes of a sentencing enhancement under federal law, as "an adjudication of delinquency is not the same as an adult conviction") with State v. LaMunyon, 911 P.2d 151 (Kan. 1996) (finding no constitutional or statutory bar to using juvenile adjudication in calculating criminal history status).

6. *Prior criminal record exception.*   As a result of the decision in Almendarez-Torres v. United States, 523 U.S. 224 (1998), a "prior conviction" exception has been built into the Sixth Amendment's application of the jury trial right to sentence enhancements in *Apprendi* and *Blakely*. Both *Apprendi* and *Blakely* state that its rule requiring sentence-enhancing facts to be proven to a jury beyond a reasonable doubt or admitted by the defendant applies only to facts "other than the fact of a prior conviction." The theoretical soundness of this exception has been widely questioned, and there is some question how a majority of the current Court would vote on this question. In the wake of *Blakely*, lower state and federal courts have split over the scope and application of the "prior conviction" exception, debating whether only the fact of a prior conviction or other, related facts (such as a defendant's status on probation) fall within the exception.

7. *Federal violent crime enhancements.*   A number of different federal statutes and guidelines provide for significantly enhanced federal sentences when a defendant's prior offenses include a "crime of violence," an "aggravated felony," or a "violent felony." Lower courts have struggled to apply these terms, especially in the context of the federal Armed Career Criminal Act, which provides for a mandatory minimum prison term of 15 years. The Supreme Court has gotten involved in trying to sort out which prior state offenses should be

considered a "violent felony." See Sykes v. United States, 131 S. Ct. 2267 (2011) (vehicle flight under Indiana law is a violent felony); Chambers v. United States, 555 U.S. 122 (2009) (failure to report to prison under Illinois law does not qualify as a "violent felony"). For a debate about the federalism implications of constructing criminal history, compare Wayne A. Logan, Horizontal Federalism in an Age of Criminal Justice Interconnectedness, 154 U. Pa. L. Rev. 257 (2005) with Dan Markel, Connectedness and Its Discontents: The Difficulties of Federalism and Criminal Law, 4 Ohio St. Crim. L. Rev. 573 (2007).

### 3. The First-Time Offender

Since all sentencing systems increase punishment levels for repeat offenders, they conversely and necessarily provide lesser sentences for first-time offenders. But is there something special about first-time offenders compared with those with a limited previous criminal record? Should special rules be in place to further mitigate the sentences of first-time offenders?

## ‖ Washington Revised Code §9.94A.650 ‖

### FIRST-TIME OFFENDER WAIVER

(1) This section applies to offenders who have never been previously convicted of a felony in this state, federal court, or another state, and who have never participated in a program of deferred prosecution for a felony, and who are convicted of a felony that is not:

(a) Classified as a violent offense or a sex offense under this chapter;

(b) Manufacture, delivery, [sale] or possession with intent to manufacture or deliver [various controlled substances]. . . .

(2) In sentencing a first-time offender the court may waive the imposition of a sentence within the standard sentence range and impose a sentence which may include up to ninety days of confinement in a [local jail] facility and a requirement that the offender refrain from committing new offenses.

(3) The court may impose up to six months of community custody unless treatment is ordered, in which case the period of community custody may include up to the period of treatment, but shall not exceed one year.

(4) As a condition of community custody . . . the court may order the offender to pay all court-ordered legal financial obligations and/or perform community restitution work.

## ‖ State v. Joshua Fowler ‖
### 38 P.3d 335 (Wash. 2002)

ALEXANDER, C.J.

On October 30, 1997, Joshua Fowler joined friends . . . at "Fast Freddy's Tavern" in Kent. Fowler, who had gone without sleep for three days while drinking alcohol and using methamphetamine, ingested additional alcohol and methamphetamine at the tavern. Fowler [later] departed the tavern [with companions] to collect a debt he believed [Ken] Carroll owed to him, . . . armed with a handgun and knife. Once inside [Carroll's] apartment, an argument ensued between Fowler and Carroll. This led to Fowler hitting Carroll in the head with the gun that Fowler was carrying. Carroll was then taken to a back bedroom where . . . he was threatened and beaten by Fowler. As Fowler administered the beating, he told Carroll that he would "cut him" in order to "teach him a lesson." Carroll's roommate, Thomas Gochanour . . . was struck in the face by Fowler with the flat side of the knife that Fowler was carrying. Fowler also threatened to cut Gochanour's throat with the knife. After engaging in this activity, Fowler and his accomplices fled taking some videotapes, a cellular phone, a wallet, and some money from the apartment.

Eighteen months after the above-described incident, Fowler turned himself in to the police. He was thereafter charged with and pleaded guilty to first degree robbery. At sentencing, the trial court determined that because Fowler had no prior criminal history, the standard sentencing range for the offense was 31 to 41 months, plus a mandatory 60 month firearm enhancement penalty. Fowler sought an exceptional sentence of six months, exclusive of the firearm enhancement, basing his request on what he claimed was the presence of three statutory mitigating factors. Although the trial court did not find any of those factors present, it nevertheless imposed a 15 month exceptional sentence based on its determination that Fowler: (1) had no history of violent behavior and no pertinent criminal history; (2) was experiencing symptoms of extreme sleep deprivation at the time of the offense; (3) exhibited behavior at the time of the offense that was aberrational and represented an isolated incident of violence; (4) had strong family support; and (5) was a low to moderate risk to reoffend. . . .

A court must generally impose a sentence within the standard sentence range. It may, however, impose a sentence above or below the standard range for reasons that are "substantial and compelling." [Washington's Sentencing Reform Act] contains a list of aggravating and mitigating factors "which the court may consider in the exercise of its discretion to impose an exceptional sentence." Although this list is not exclusive, any such reasons must relate to the crime and make it more, or less, egregious. . . . A sentencing court may not, in imposing an exceptional sentence, take into account the defendant's criminal history and the seriousness level of the offense because those are considered in computing the presumptive range for the offense. . . .

The first factor the sentencing court relied on in imposing an exceptional sentence was that the "defendant [had] no history of violent behavior and no pertinent criminal history." Although Fowler concedes that a defendant's lack of criminal history alone is an insufficient ground for a sentence below the standard range, he asserts that a clean record combined with a complete absence of police contacts may be a substantial and compelling reason for imposing an exceptional sentence.

This argument is without merit. Saying that the defendant had no history of violent behavior and no pertinent criminal history is essentially equivalent to saying that he has no criminal record. [A] lack of a criminal history is not a mitigating factor because criminal history is already encompassed in the sentencing guidelines. The only exception to this general rule is that a lack of criminal history may be considered "in combination with the finding that the defendant was 'induced' to commit the crime" or lacked a predisposition to commit the crime. State v. Ha'mim, 132 Wash. 2d 834, 842-843 (1997). Here, the trial court rejected a finding that Fowler was either induced by others to commit the crime or that he lacked a predisposition to commit the crime. . . .

The trial court also found that a downward exceptional sentence was justified on the basis that Fowler's behavior during the commission of the crime was aberrational and represented an isolated incident of violence. Specifically the trial court stated:

> I have absolutely no trouble believing the defendant when he said and his family said that the behavior that occurred on the night of this incident was an aberration. It was unusual. It was out of character for him. . . . I believe the defendant when he says that his behavior was fueled by some form of chemical imbalance, whether it was chronic depression I can't say. I certainly think there is every indication that it was fueled by sleep deprivation, ingestion of methamphetamines, ingestion of alcohol. . . .

Fowler argues here that federal case law supports the proposition that aberrant behavior is a valid mitigating factor. [However, the] fact that a defendant's criminal conduct is exceptional or aberrant does not distinguish the defendant's crime from others in the same category. Furthermore, to say that conduct is an aberration is tantamount to saying that the defendant "has not done anything like this before." That, in our view, is yet another way of saying that the defendant has little or no history of criminal behavior. . . .

Even if we were inclined to follow the lead of the federal circuit courts that have recognized that aberrational behavior may justify a departure from the standard range, Fowler's conduct does not resemble the type of conduct that those courts have found to be aberrational. The act Fowler committed was not committed without forethought and planning, and thus fails the spontaneity test enunciated in [federal cases on this subject]. Indeed, the record shows that Fowler's motivation in going to Ken Carroll's house was to collect a debt. To aid himself in that endeavor he armed himself with a handgun and knife, items that he subsequently used in the commission of the robbery. This was hardly a spontaneous act. Neither can it be said that any of the factors [are present] evidencing aberrational behavior under the "totality of the circumstance test," . . . i.e., that the defendant suffered from a psychological disorder, that he was under external pressure, that his motivation was other than pecuniary gain, or that he took steps to mitigate the effects of his acts. In short, Fowler's conduct was not aberrational, even under the case law or federal guidelines. . . .

Fowler also contends that . . . what the trial court described as his low to moderate risk to reoffend is . . . a substantial and compelling reason for imposing an exceptional sentence. Specifically, he argues that a low risk of reoffense is a valid factor when a court finds by clear and convincing evidence that a standard range disposition would be detrimental to the goal of rehabilitating the offender. . . . The sentencing court's finding that Fowler was a low to moderate risk to reoffend was based upon an evaluation and report of the Washington State Department of Corrections. [However, our prior cases establish] that the risk of reoffense is not a substantial and compelling reason for an exceptional sentence. State v. Estrella, 798 P.2d 289 (Wash. 1990). [Protection] of the public has already been considered by the legislature in computing the presumptive sentencing range.

MADSEN, J., dissenting.

. . . The defendant, Joshua Fowler, urges the court to follow federal cases recognizing aberrant behavior as a mitigating factor in sentencing. The majority summarily concludes that calling a defendant's criminal conduct aberrational is simply another way of saying that the defendant has little or no history of criminal behavior. . . . Federal courts agree that a lack of criminal history is not a basis for a downward sentence under the federal scheme. They conclude, however, that "aberrational behavior" is not equivalent to a lack of criminal history. . . . All of the federal circuits have recognized aberrational behavior as a factor that may, in the appropriate case, justify an exceptional sentence downward. A split developed in the circuits, however, as to what constitutes aberrational behavior. Some courts concluded that "a spontaneous and seemingly thoughtless act, rather than one which was the result of substantial planning" was a single act of aberrant behavior. Others applied a totality of circumstances approach, considering a number of factors. . . . In November 2000, the federal sentencing commission added §5K2.20 to the guidelines, defining "aberrant behavior" as "a single criminal occurrence or single criminal transaction that (A) was committed without significant planning; (B) was of limited duration; and (C) represents a marked deviation by the defendant from an otherwise law-abiding life." The commission directed that in deciding whether to depart from the guideline sentences on the basis of aberrant behavior, a court could consider the defendant's "(A) mental and emotional conditions; (B) employment record; (C) record of prior good works; (D) motivation for committing the offense; and (E) efforts to mitigate the effects of the offense."

[Some] crimes represent the truly unusual behavior of individuals who are generally nonviolent, law-abiding citizens [and were committed] under unusual circumstances. Similar to the federal approach, this court should hold that a trial court may, in its discretion, impose an exceptional sentence downward based upon aberrant behavior. . . .

The majority also rejects the trial court's reliance on a low to moderate risk of reoffending as supporting a downward sentence. [The sentencing statutes do not currently account for this factor.] A presumptive sentencing range is based upon the seriousness level of the current offense and the defendant's offender score. Whether the individual defendant has a low, moderate, or high risk of reoffending is not part of the calculation. . . . Further, this court has in the past accepted the premise that future dangerousness is an appropriate nonstatutory aggravating factor under certain circumstances involving offenders convicted of sex offenses. If future dangerousness can justify an upward sentence, albeit in limited cases, why should a low risk of reoffending be rejected as a mitigating factor? At least two of the goals of the SRA favor allowing sentencing discretion to impose a downward sentence where there is a low risk of reoffending: the promotion of respect for the law by provision of just punishment, and making frugal use of the state's resources. . . .

## NOTES

1. *Treatment of first-time offenders at sentencing.* With the exception of the most serious and violent offenses, most first-time offenders can expect a sentencing judge to impose a relatively brief sentence of imprisonment or suspend any incarceration and place the offender on probation. As the statute from Washington highlights, this tendency to cut first-time offenders a break has been codified in many structured sentencing systems. The Sentencing Reform Act requires the U.S. Sentencing Commission to "insure that the [federal] guidelines reflect the general appropriateness of imposing a sentence other than imprisonment in cases in which the defendant is a first offender who has not been convicted of a crime of violence or an otherwise serious offense. . . ." 28 U.S.C. §994(j).

More generally, all structured sentencing systems provide for first-time offenders to receive no criminal history points or the lowest possible offender score, which in turn limits the upper level of the sentencing range designated for the offense. Many of these systems, however, group the true first-time offender with other offenders who have some minor criminal history. In the federal system, for example, criminal history category I treats a wide range of defendants the same; defendants who have no prior record (no prior arrests, no pending charges, no dismissed charges, no prior convictions) fall into category I, along with defendants who have one prior conviction and received a sentence of imprisonment of up to 60 days. This category also includes defendants who may have had contact with the criminal justice system, such as arrests or dismissed charges, and defendants with convictions not counted under the guidelines for a variety of reasons, such as the "age" of the conviction, the locality where the conviction occurred, or the minor nature of the offense. What reasons might support such a structure for considering criminal history, which seems to allow defendants "one free bite at the apple"?

In a 2004 research report on "Recidivism and the 'First Offender,'?" the U.S. Sentencing Commission's staff found different recidivism rates for those with no prior arrests, those with prior arrests but no prior convictions, and those with prior convictions that do not count toward criminal history under the federal guidelines. See http://www.ussc.gov/Research/Research_Publications/Recidivism/200405_Recidivism_ First_Offender.pdf. Is there any explanation as to why the group with prior arrests but no prior convictions has the highest recidivism rate, almost twice as high as that of offenders with prior but uncounted convictions? What would be the impact — in terms of information collection and length of sentence by offender and offense categories — if Congress approved the creation of a "no prior connection with the criminal justice system" category?

2. *Departures for first-time offenders and "aberrant behavior."* In part because many guideline systems group true first-time offenders with other offenders who have some minor criminal history, cases like *Fowler* arise when a sentencing judge departs below the applicable guideline sentence because the offender's wrongdoing seems truly exceptional and the judge believes the offender is unlikely to engage in criminal activity again. Most appellate courts rule that first-time offender status and related concerns have already been considered in the guideline

scheme and thus cannot serve as the basis for a departure. See, e.g., Koon v. United States, 518 U.S. 81, 110-112 (1996) (holding that district court could not depart based on defendant's "low likelihood of recidivism" because the U.S. Sentencing Commission took that factor into account in formulating the lowest criminal history category); cf. State v. Grady, 258 Kan. 72, 87-88 (1995) ("While generally criminal history is an improper departure factor because criminal history has already been used to set the presumptive sentence, we believe the legislature intended in the interest of justice that a trial court have discretion to impose a downward dispositional departure where a defendant has no prior criminal history and has a failed common-law or statutory defense that is not meritless.").

As noted in *Fowler*, the federal system developed a way to reduce sentences in exceptional cases based on the concept of "aberrational behavior." A federal sentencing judge may depart downward when the defendant's background and the nature of the offense show that the offense grew out of peculiar circumstances not likely to be repeated. The rationale has been common among downward departures. As noted in the *Fowler* dissent, the federal courts of appeals were initially divided over when to allow an aberrant behavior departure. Some required the offense to be a single "spontaneous and seemingly thoughtless act"; others allowed sentencing judges more latitude under a "totality of the circumstances" approach. The U.S. Sentencing Commission's policy statement in §5K2.20 adopted a compromise view of what constitutes aberrant behavior, going beyond a "single act" to include "a single criminal *occurrence* or single criminal *transaction* that (1) was committed without significant planning; (2) was of limited duration; and (3) represents a marked deviation by the defendant from an otherwise law-abiding life" (emphasis added). The policy statement also barred departures on this basis for certain crimes, including serious drug trafficking offenses, those that cause "serious bodily injury or death," and crimes in which the defendant uses a dangerous weapon. Does the fact that a defendant used a gun make a crime any less aberrational?

3. *Safety valve to ameliorate mandatory sentences.* One common complaint lodged against mandatory sentencing statutes is that by requiring a particular sentence based only on the offense, the provisions fail to allow for mitigated sentences for first-time offenders. Congress responded to these concerns in the context of federal mandatory minimum drug sentences by enacting a "safety valve" provision as part of the Violent Crime Control and Law Enforcement Act of 1994. This provision instructs judges to apply the federal guidelines, rather than the often harsher mandatory minimum drug sentencing statutes, when five criteria are satisfied: "(1) the defendant does not have more than one criminal history point, as determined under the [federal] sentencing guidelines; (2) the defendant did not use violence ... or possess ... a dangerous weapon ... in connection with the offense; (3) the offense did not result in death or serious bodily injury ... ; (4) the defendant was not an organizer, leader, manager, or supervisor of others in the offense ... ; and (5) ... the defendant ... truthfully provided to the Government all information and evidence the defendant has concerning the offense or offenses that were part of the same course of conduct or of a common scheme or plan, but the fact that the defendant has no relevant or useful other information to provide or that the Government is already aware

of the information shall not preclude a determination by the court that the defendant has complied with this requirement." 18 U.S.C. §3553(f).

## B.  THE COOPERATIVE DEFENDANT

By the time a convicted defendant faces a sentencing judge, several months or even years may have passed since the crime occurred. During that time, the defendant performs many acts that can have some bearing on the sentence. For a sentencing judge who emphasizes retributive purposes of a criminal sentence, with a focus on the harm created by the crime, this postcrime behavior might have little effect. But for a sentencing judge (or a sentencing system) placing more weight on utilitarian goals such as incapacitation or rehabilitation, post-crime behavior plays a significant role. This recent conduct offers important clues about how the defendant will act in the near future. In this section, we explore postcrime conduct that signals the defendant's willingness to cooperate with the authorities, both in her own case and in other cases.

### 1.  Acceptance of Responsibility and Plea Bargains

Most courtroom veterans believe that a guilty plea produces big advantages at sentencing, and empirical research confirms this belief. Defendants pleading guilty tend to receive substantially lower sentences than defendants who go to trial (in some studies the "plea discount" is more than one-third off post-trial sentences).

In structured sentencing systems, the rules give sentencing judges different instructions about the impact of a plea agreement. Some rules say that plea agreements should not change the sentence at all; other rules allow the judge to accept the parties' recommendations within certain broad limits. For instance, under the Minnesota sentencing guidelines, judges must impose the sentence indicated in the guideline grid unless there is a valid ground for departure. A plea agreement, standing alone, is not a sufficient reason to depart from the guidelines. In Washington state, statutory guidelines tell the judge to "determine if the agreement is consistent with the interests of justice and with the [statutory] prosecuting standards" and to reject the agreement if it is not. Wash. Rev. Code §9.94A.431(1). The federal sentencing guidelines also advise judges to limit the impact of a guilty plea at sentencing. The court may accept sentencing recommendations offered in a plea agreement "if the court is satisfied either that (1) the recommended sentence is within the applicable guideline range; or (2) (A) the recommended sentence departs from the applicable guideline range for justifiable reasons; and (B) those reasons are specifically set forth in writing in the statement of reasons or judgment and commitment order." U.S. Sentencing Guidelines Manual §6B1.2(b).

If it is true that sentencing judges in most systems reward defendants who plead guilty, does that mean that sentencing judges punish a defendant for exercising the right to a trial? Do sentencing rules discourage judges from honestly explaining what they are doing?

|| ***State v. David Tiernan***
|| **645 A.2d 482 (R.I. 1994)**

WEISBERGER, Acting C.J.

... The precise issue we confront in this appeal is the question of whether the trial justice improperly considered either defendant's exercise of his privilege against self-incrimination under the Fifth Amendment to the United States Constitution or his exercise of his right to a public trial guaranteed by the Sixth Amendment to the United States Constitution and article 1, section 10, of the Rhode Island Constitution. We answer this question in the negative. ...

In November 1990 defendant was convicted of two counts of second-degree child molestation after a trial by jury in Superior Court. At the sentencing hearing defendant argued that in light of his background, the absence of any prior record, and the nature of the crime involved, he should be given a sentence involving only treatment and counseling rather than imprisonment. The prosecutor disagreed, arguing that such treatment would not be effective unless defendant acknowledged his wrongdoing, which defendant refused to do. As a matter of deterrence and punishment, the prosecutor urged the court to impose a lengthy jail sentence.

The trial justice agreed with the prosecutor, citing five factors that were considered in formulating his decision — "the nature of the offense and the offender, punishment, rehabilitation and deterrence." The trial justice explained that "some program of counseling could be effective if culpability is accepted, but the problem is defendant's continued protestations of innocence." The trial justice explained this comment, stating that "it is my understanding from everybody knowledgeable in this area that treatment is not effective unless and until the person being treated, the defendant, acknowledges guilt, and the defendant still protests his innocence, and has done so here in court." Therefore, the trial justice reasoned that since rehabilitation was improbable, ... "punishment and deterrence are most important to the Court in this case when determining an appropriate sentence." In light of the aforementioned factors, the trial justice sentenced defendant to two terms of twenty years, eight years to serve and twelve years suspended on each count, to be served concurrently.

[The] defendant filed a timely Rule 35 motion to reduce sentence. At the hearing on the motion, defendant presented the court with an admission of guilt and a profession of remorse — the key ingredients that the trial justice had found lacking at the time of the original sentencing with respect to defendant's potential for rehabilitation. The defendant attempted to justify his delayed acknowledgment of his crime by explaining that at the time of the sentencing hearing he had not yet come to terms with the sexual molestation that, he revealed to the court, he himself had endured in his own childhood. After hearing from defendant, the trial justice was presented with testimony from the victim's mother who painfully recounted the traumatic effect that the molestation and the trial had had upon her daughter.

After considering the testimony presented, the trial justice denied defendant's motion to reduce sentence and made the following observations:

> [I observed] that little girl testify. The defendant sat there and required her to testify. She did, and although she was a little girl, she was believed by the jury and by me; and yet he stood up and indicated to me that he intended to pursue all of his rights of appeal, again, which I believe he had his right to do, everybody does. He did that knowing full well that what that little girl said from the stand was absolutely true and he let her go through it. While I am somewhat moved by defense counsel's argument and even the defendant's own statements, I am not persuaded by them, not in the least. . . .

On appeal defendant challenges his sentence on the grounds that at both the sentencing hearing and the Rule 35 hearing the trial justice violated defendant's constitutional rights by considering improper factors. First, defendant claims that at the sentencing hearing the trial justice's decision was tainted by his consideration of the fact that defendant invoked his Fifth Amendment privilege against self-incrimination and he used that fact to justify the imposition of a lengthy sentence upon defendant. Then at the Rule 35 hearing, when defendant waived his Fifth Amendment right and admitted his guilt, defendant claims that the trial justice justified defendant's lengthy sentence with an alternative, but equally objectionable, fact—that defendant had exercised his right to stand trial and thereby forced his child victim to endure a painful court experience. The defendant cites to us in support of his assertions a plethora of cases from other jurisdictions. . . .

A motion to reduce sentence under Rule 35 is basically a plea by a defendant for leniency and, as such, is addressed to the sound discretion of the trial justice. Because of our strong policy against interfering with a trial justice's exercise of discretion with respect to such motions, we shall interfere with the lower court's decision only in the rarest of cases. With this deferential standard of review in mind, we now turn to the applicable substantive law.

A judge has no more difficult duty nor awesome responsibility than the pronouncement of sentence in a criminal case. To guide trial justices in carrying out this responsibility, we have identified the following factors as falling within the scope of constitutionally permissible sentencing considerations: (1) the severity of the crime, (2) the defendant's personal, educational, and employment background, (3) the potential for rehabilitation, (4) the element of societal deterrence, and (5) the appropriateness of the punishment. State v. Bertoldi, 495 A.2d 247 (R.I. 1985); State v. Upham, 439 A.2d 912 (R.I. 1982).

Most of these factors are multidimensional and require a trial justice to reflect upon a variety of subsidiary factors. For example, with respect to the element of rehabilitation, a trial justice may consider a defendant's attitude toward society, his sense of remorse, as well as his inclination and capacity to take his place as an honest and useful member of society. Likewise, a defendant's giving of false testimony may be probative of his attitude toward society and consequently his prospects for rehabilitation.

In addition to the above five factors, a trial justice may also take into consideration a corollary factor to justify reducing a sentence—that a defendant exhibited contrition and consideration for the victims of his or her criminal activity and pled guilty to the crime charged. See Brady v. United States,

397 U.S. 742 (1970) ("encouraging a guilty plea by opportunity or promise of leniency" does not violate Fifth Amendment). We are mindful that a defendant, by pleading guilty, waives a broad array of rights, including the right to trial by jury, the presumption of innocence, the state's burden to prove one guilty beyond a reasonable doubt, the privilege against self-incrimination, the right to confront and cross-examine one's accusers, the right to testify and call witnesses in one's defense, and the right to appeal one's conviction to this court. By waiving these rights, a defendant, first, has spared the state from expending considerable time, money and other precious judicial and law enforcement resources and, second, has prevented the public scrutiny of and embarrassment to the victim that derives from recounting his or her victimization in a public forum. In exchange therefor a defendant may properly be extended a certain amount of leniency in sentencing.

Although we have recognized the propriety of extending leniency when a defendant pleads guilty, we have specifically prohibited the lengthening of a sentence on the basis of a defendant's refusal to plead guilty or his or her insistence on holding the state to its burden of proving guilt beyond a reasonable doubt at trial. State v. Rollins, 359 A.2d 315, 320 (R.I. 1976). [The] rights implicated when a defendant chooses to stand trial . . . are some of the most jealously guarded and deeply embedded rights of our criminal justice jurisprudence, rights that both the Federal and our State Constitutions unconditionally extend to criminal defendants. To exact a price or impose a penalty upon a defendant in the form of an enhanced sentence for invoking such rights would amount to a deprivation of due process of law, and that we shall not condone. . . .

### FIFTH AMENDMENT PRIVILEGE AGAINST SELF-INCRIMINATION CLAIM

Reviewing the transcript of the original sentencing hearing, we cannot say that the trial justice improperly considered in his sentencing decision defendant's exercise of his Fifth Amendment privilege against self-incrimination. In making the sentencing determination, the trial justice articulated and applied the very five factors we condoned in *Upham* and *Bertoldi*: the nature of the offense and of the offender, punishment, rehabilitation, and deterrence. [The trial justice] considered defendant's refusal to acknowledge guilt for the limited purpose of assessing defendant's potential for rehabilitation. Underlying rehabilitation is the thesis that the offender needs assistance in making behavioral and/or psychological changes. In order for that assistance to be effective, a defendant must be open and receptive to the proffered treatment. A defendant's adamant denial of engaging in any wrongful conduct — the very conduct that necessitates the treatment — cannot be said to be indicative of any receptiveness to rehabilitation. Accordingly we hold that the trial justice properly considered defendant's refusal to admit perpetrating the molestation in his assessment of defendant's rehabilitative potential. Other courts have similarly recognized the probative value of a defendant's refusal to acknowledge wrongdoing with respect to assessing the element of rehabilitative capacity. See Gallucci v. State, 371 So. 2d 148, 150 (Fla. App. 1979). . . .

After evaluating defendant's questionable potential for rehabilitation, the trial justice properly determined that "example type" sentencing was demanded. [Defendant] was not penalized for refusing to waive his Fifth Amendment right; rather he was simply not extended a benefit which he might have enjoyed had he waived his rights and pled either guilty or nolo to the charges.

### THE RIGHT TO STAND TRIAL

... In considering defendant's motion to reduce his sentence, the trial justice remarked that defendant had "required" the child to testify by exercising his right to stand trial, after which defendant indicated his intention to appeal while "knowing full well that what that little girl said from the stand was absolutely true." The defendant claims that these remarks evidence an intent to penalize him for standing trial. We cannot agree.

At the outset we are compelled to point out that the right guaranteed to defendant by the Sixth Amendment to the United States Constitution and article 1, section 10, of the Rhode Island Constitution is the right to stand trial and *truthfully* testify in his own behalf. This defendant did not do. Rather defendant exercised his right and took the opportunity to present false testimony to the court in the hopes of escaping conviction and punishment.

The trial justice's remarks clearly related to the fact that defendant had, while under a solemn oath and in a court of law, knowingly and intentionally perpetrated a falsehood. The trial justice proceeded to identify the impact upon the victim of defendant's decision to stand trial and tell a falsehood — namely, that she was forced to endure the trauma of testifying about embarrassing and intimate sexual details and to undergo an intense cross-examination.

[The] trial justice's consideration of defendant's false testimony and the impact of the trial upon the victim was proper as these factors related to his prospects for rehabilitation. With respect to defendant's falsehood, we stated in *Bertoldi* that a defendant's willingness to take the stand and lie "not only demonstrates a disrespect for the law and the judicial system, but also evidences an important character trait. It reveals that the defendant is perfectly willing to commit a crime in an attempt to conceal an earlier crime...." The fact that defendant claimed to have lied because of an event he endured in his childhood does not cast a different light onto his falsehood or justify in any way, shape, or form his decision to give false testimony while under a solemn judicial oath to tell the truth.

Likewise, consideration of the impact of the trial upon the child victim, especially in the face of a posttrial confession, is proper as it reflects a defendant's attitude toward his victim and society. In State v. Farnham, 479 A.2d 887 (Me. 1984), the Supreme Judicial Court of Maine upheld consideration of this factor in circumstances very similar to those in the case at hand. [As the court noted, although the defendant] "had an absolute right to a trial and to conduct vigorous cross-examination in connection with a crime for which he soon after admitted his guilt, he cannot escape the fact that his exercise of those rights are probative of his attitude towards the victim and society." ...

We note that this was not a case in which the trial justice threatened pretrial to impose a harsher sentence if defendant opted to stand trial, see United States v. Stockwell, 472 F.2d 1186 (9th Cir. 1973), or one in which the trial justice stated posttrial that a more severe sentence was warranted because defendant wasted time, public funds, and resources by insisting on a trial, see United States v. Hutchings, 757 F.2d 11 (2d Cir. 1985). . . .

The length of the sentence imposed was well within the parameters set forth by the Legislature in G.L. 1956 (1981 Reenactment) §11-37-8.4 ("every person who shall commit second degree child molestation sexual assault shall be imprisoned for not less than six years nor more than thirty years"). Given our limited scope of review, we hold that the trial justice remained soundly within the bounds of his discretion. . . .

## Charles Hynes v. Albert Tomei
### 706 N.E. 2d 1202 (N.Y. 1991)

KAYE, C.J.

Thirty years ago, the United States Supreme Court struck down the death penalty provision of the Federal Kidnaping Act, which allowed a defendant to be sentenced to death only after a jury trial. The Supreme Court invalidated the provision because, by needlessly encouraging guilty pleas and jury waivers to avoid death sentences, it impermissibly burdened defendants' Fifth Amendment right against self-incrimination and Sixth Amendment right to a jury trial. United States v. Jackson, 390 U.S. 570 (1968). Despite the passage of three decades, a plethora of decisions involving the death penalty and a sea change in plea bargaining, the Supreme Court has never overruled *Jackson*, which binds this Court. Indeed, every other death penalty State has fit its capital murder plea-bargaining procedures within the rationale of *Jackson*.

Three years ago, the New York State Legislature enacted a capital punishment statute that—like the Federal Kidnaping Act—allows a defendant to be sentenced to death only after a jury trial. Bench trials are not permitted in capital cases, N.Y. Const., art. I, §2, and the statute bars imposition of a death sentence upon a guilty plea. The New York law thus explicitly provides two levels of penalty for the same offense, imposing death only on those who assert innocence and proceed to trial. . . . We are convinced that *Jackson* compels [us to] declare CPL §§220.10(5)(e) and 220.30(3)(b)(vii) unconstitutional. . . .

The Federal Kidnaping Act considered in *Jackson* provided [that whoever knowingly transports in interstate commerce a kidnaped person] "shall be punished (1) by death if the kidnaped person has not been liberated unharmed, and if the verdict of the jury shall so recommend, or (2) by imprisonment for any term of years or for life, if the death penalty is not imposed." Because the Act authorized the death penalty only on the recommendation of a jury, while a defendant convicted of the same offense on a guilty plea or by a Judge escaped the threat of capital punishment, the Supreme Court concluded that the Act "needlessly" encouraged guilty pleas and jury waivers. The Court acknowledged that restricting the death penalty to cases in which a jury recommends it is a legitimate goal, and that such a restriction would likely decrease the frequency of capital punishment. However, the Court concluded these considerations did not save the Act from constitutional infirmity. While the Act's chilling effect on a defendant's exercise of the Fifth Amendment right against self-incrimination and Sixth Amendment right to a jury trial may have been incidental, the effect was also "unnecessary and therefore excessive," since Congress could have achieved its goals by allowing juries to sentence defendants to the full range of punishments regardless of how guilt was determined.

Shortly after *Jackson*, this Court invalidated two provisions of the former Code of Criminal Procedure that required waiver of a jury trial in order to receive the benefit of youthful offender treatment. See People v. Michael A.C., 261 N.E.2d 620 (N.Y. 1970). Although respondents who refused to waive a jury trial were not subject to the death penalty, they were exposed to longer prison sentences than those prosecuted as youthful offenders. Drawing a parallel to *Jackson*, this Court held that "a procedure which offers an individual a reward for waiving a fundamental constitutional right, or imposes a harsher penalty for asserting it, may not be sustained."

New York's death penalty statute authorizes a District Attorney to file a notice of intent to seek the death penalty against a defendant charged with murder in the first degree. Upon conviction by a jury, a capital defendant faces a separate sentencing proceeding before a jury to determine whether the penalty imposed will be death or life imprisonment without parole. The statute affords a defendant the opportunity to ensure a maximum sentence of life without parole by pleading guilty pursuant to the following provisions:

> A defendant may not enter a plea of guilty to the crime of murder in the first degree . . . ; provided, however, that a defendant may enter such a plea with both the permission of the court and the consent of the people when the agreed upon sentence is either life imprisonment without parole or a term of imprisonment for . . . murder in the first degree other than a sentence of life imprisonment without parole. CPL §§220.10(5)(e); 220.30(3)(b)(vii).
>
> A defendant who has entered a plea of not guilty to an indictment may, with both the permission of the court and the consent of the people, withdraw such plea at any time before the rendition of a verdict and enter . . . a plea of guilty to part of the indictment . . . but subject to the limitation in subdivision five of section 220.10. CPL §220.60(2)(a). . . .

Thus, like the invalidated Federal Kidnaping Act provision, New York's death penalty statute explicitly provides for the imposition of the death penalty only upon a jury verdict. As a result, under the New York statute, only those defendants who exercise the Fifth Amendment right against self-incrimination and Sixth Amendment right to a jury trial put themselves at risk of death.

[Respondents] argue that the challenged New York provisions are distinguishable from the Federal Kidnaping Act because they merely codify permissible plea bargaining, which was not at issue in *Jackson*. Subsequent to *Jackson*, both the Supreme Court and this Court have acknowledged the legitimacy and desirability—indeed, the necessity—of plea bargaining. See Santobello v. New York, 404 U.S. 257 (1971); People v. Selikoff, 318 N.E.2d 784 (N.Y. 1974). Plea bargaining serves important functions for both prosecutors and defendants, such as individualized justice, leniency and economy. A State clearly may encourage guilty pleas by offering benefits to defendants in return for a guilty plea. Furthermore, plea bargaining becomes no less lawful or desirable when it is codified in statutory form.

While plea bargaining is permissible, the Supreme Court in *Jackson* prohibited statutes that "needlessly" encourage guilty pleas, which are not constitutionally protected, by impermissibly burdening constitutional rights. Given the availability of alternatives that do not impermissibly burden defendants' constitutional rights, the plea provisions of the statute before us cannot be justified by an ostensible purpose such as the facilitation of plea bargaining.

Respondents rely heavily on Corbitt v. New Jersey, 439 U.S. 212 (1978), in which the Supreme Court held that it is constitutionally permissible to offer a defendant the possibility of escaping the most severe penalty by pleading guilty. The New Jersey statute at issue in *Corbitt,* however, provided for the same maximum sentence — life imprisonment — regardless of a defendant's plea. While a lesser sentence was permitted for those defendants who pleaded guilty, it was not guaranteed. Thus, the statute survived constitutional scrutiny because it did "not reserve the maximum punishment for murder for those who insist on a jury trial." This situation is readily distinguishable from the challenged New York provisions, which indeed prescribe a lesser agreed-upon sentence for those who plead guilty. . . .

In sum, respondents' attempts to distinguish New York's death penalty statute from the death penalty invalidated by the Supreme Court in *Jackson* fail. [By] statutory mandate, the death penalty hangs over only those who exercise their constitutional rights to maintain innocence and demand a jury trial. Thus, *Jackson* compels us to invalidate these provisions, just as it has compelled other State high courts to invalidate their capital plea provisions with the same constitutional infirmity. See State v. Johnson, 595 A.2d 498 (N.H. 1991); Commonwealth v. Colon-Cruz, 470 N.E.2d 116 (Mass. 1984); State v. Frampton, 627 P.2d 922 (Wash. 1981); State v. Funicello, 286 A.2d 55 (N.J. 1972). By contrast, the death penalty statutes of States that have rejected a *Jackson* challenge, with one exception, provide for the possibility of a death sentence upon a guilty plea. See State v. Mann, 959 S.W.2d 503 (Tenn. 1996); Conger v. Warden, 510 P.2d 1359 (Nev. 1973). The exception, Arkansas, avoided a *Jackson* problem because the Trial Judge, not the jury, made the final determination of whether the death penalty would be imposed, and because guilty pleas were permitted only after the prosecutor waived the death penalty. See Ruiz v. State, 630 S.W.2d 44 (Ark. 1982).

[Invalidation of the death penalty is not] necessary to obviate the *Jackson* problem: excision of the capital pleading provisions eliminates the burden on constitutional rights prohibited by *Jackson*, since without those provisions there is only one maximum penalty for first degree murder. [While] CPL §§221.10(5)(e) and 220.30(3)(b)(vii) relate exclusively to pleas in first degree murder cases and "needlessly" encourage guilty pleas in violation of *Jackson*, CPL §220.60(2)(a) is not limited to first degree murder cases, nor does it, in the absence of CPL §220.10(5)(e), violate *Jackson*. Therefore, only CPL §§220.10(5)(e) and 220.30(3)(b)(vii) must be stricken. Under the resulting statute, a defendant may not plead guilty to first degree murder while a notice of intent to seek the death penalty is pending.

We realize this result will reduce the flexibility of both prosecutors and defendants who wish to plea bargain in capital cases. Indeed, our reversal in these cases may well have an ironic twist in that capital defendants will have fewer opportunities to avoid the possibility of the death penalty. . . . While reducing the flexibility of plea bargaining in capital cases, excision of the unconstitutional provisions does not prevent pleas of guilty to first degree murder when no notice of intent to seek the death penalty is pending, since defendants in that situation face the same maximum sentence regardless of how they are convicted. Nor does the resulting statute prevent a defendant from pleading guilty to another offense not punishable by death, even when a notice of intent to seek the death penalty is pending, since nothing in *Jackson* prohibits imposing different penalties for different crimes. . . . Thus, while a defendant may not plead guilty to first degree murder while a notice of intent to seek the death penalty is pending, plea bargaining to lesser offenses even when a notice of intent is pending, or to first degree murder in the absence of a notice of intent, remains unaffected. . . .

## ‖ *U.S. Sentencing Guidelines Manual* ‖

### §3E1.1 Acceptance of Responsibility

(a) If the defendant clearly demonstrates acceptance of responsibility for his offense, decrease the offense level by 2 levels.

(b) If the defendant qualifies for a decrease under subsection (a), the offense level determined prior to the operation of subsection (a) is level 16 or greater, and upon motion of the government stating that the defendant has assisted authorities in the investigation or prosecution of his own misconduct by timely notifying authorities of his intention to enter a plea of guilty, thereby permitting the government to avoid preparing for trial and permitting the government and the court to allocate their resources efficiently, decrease the offense level by 1 additional level.

## ‖ *Powers of Criminal Courts (Sentencing) Act* 2000 (United Kingdom), Ch. 6, Pt. VIII, §152 ‖

(1) In determining what sentence to pass on an offender who has pleaded guilty to an offence in proceedings before that or another court, a court shall take into account—

(a) the stage in the proceedings for the offence at which the offender indicated his intention to plead guilty; and

(b) the circumstances in which this indication was given.

(2) If, as a result of taking into account any matter referred to in subsection (1) above, the court imposes a punishment on the offender which is less severe than the punishment it would otherwise have imposed, it shall state in open court that it has done so.

(3) In the case of an offence the sentence for which falls to be imposed under subsection (2) of section 110 or 111 above [dealing with minimum sentences for drug and burglary crimes], nothing in that subsection shall prevent the court, after taking into account any matter referred to in subsection (1)

above, from imposing any sentence which is not less than 80 per cent of that specified in that subsection.

## NOTES

1. *The guilty plea discount and the trial penalty at sentencing.* Courts walk a fine line when talking about the effect of a guilty plea on a sentence. On the one hand, they routinely say that a sentencing court may not penalize a defendant for exercising the constitutional rights that go along with a criminal trial. On the other hand, courts declare that a sentencing judge may reward a defendant for pleading guilty. State v. Balfour, 637 A.2d 1249 (N.J. 1994) (defendant's agreement to plead guilty can appropriately be weighed in the decision to downgrade an offense to a lower degree at sentencing). The defendant who pleads guilty saves the resources of the system for other cases; the administrative reasons for rewarding this choice are obvious. Is there a meaningful difference between penalizing a defendant and refusing to reward a defendant who insists on a trial? Do these rules encourage judges to do anything more than choose their words carefully?

The sentencing judge often reasons that a defendant's decision to go to trial reveals a lack of remorse or a refusal to accept responsibility for the crime. These facts have some bearing on the defendant's prospects for rehabilitation, or perhaps on the chances that the offender will commit crimes in the future. Cf. Ohio Rev. Code §2929.12(D)(5) (providing that judges should consider the fact that "offender shows no genuine remorse for the offense" as a factor indicating a greater likelihood of recidivism). Thus, the judges say, an enhanced penalty after trial merely responds to this relevant information and does not directly punish the exercise of rights. Jennings v. State, 664 A.2d 903 (Md. 1995). Similarly, the judge might believe that the impact of a trial on a victim (particularly a vulnerable victim who must testify at trial) justifies a more severe sentence. Does this reasoning apply to most (or all) defendants who go to trial? See Michael O'Hear, Remorse, Cooperation and "Acceptance of Responsibility": The Structure, Implementation and Reform of Section 3E1.1 of the Federal Sentencing Guidelines, 91 Nw. U. L. Rev. 1507 (1997).

2. *Legislative and commission rules on the guilty plea discount.* The New York court in the *Tomei* case discussed the constitutional limits on the use of incentives to plead guilty in death penalty cases. The court looked for guidance in United States v. Jackson, 312 U.S. 275 (1968), but distinguished another case, Corbitt v. New Jersey, 439 U.S. 212 (1978). In *Corbitt* a statute required the sentencing judge in first-degree murder cases to impose a life sentence when the defendant was convicted after trial. Should the defendant plead guilty, however, the judge could choose either a life term or a 30-year term (the punishment for second-degree murder). How do you explain the difference in the outcomes in *Jackson* and *Corbitt*?

Many jurisdictions with structured sentencing rules provide for some form of guilty plea discount, either directly or indirectly. The Massachusetts sentencing guidelines list the plea agreement as a mitigating factor for a court to consider at sentencing. Section 3E1.1 of the federal sentencing guidelines (reprinted above) allows courts to reduce a sentence for a defendant who accepts responsibility. The application notes indicate that pleading guilty operates as a close proxy for accepting responsibility:

> This adjustment is not intended to apply to a defendant who puts the government to its burden of proof at trial by denying the essential factual elements of guilt, is convicted, and only then admits guilt and expresses remorse. Conviction by trial, however, does not automatically preclude a defendant from consideration for such a reduction. In rare situations a defendant may clearly demonstrate an acceptance of responsibility for his criminal conduct even though he exercises his constitutional right to a trial. This may occur, for example, where a defendant goes to trial to assert and preserve issues that do not relate to factual guilt. . . .

The commentary goes on to remind courts that pleading guilty will not necessarily lead to a lower sentence: "A defendant who enters a guilty plea is not entitled to an adjustment under this section as a matter of right." Yet historically, well over 90% of offenders who plead guilty get this reduction. Is section 3E1.1 significantly different from a sentencing guideline provision that sets a uniform discount for the sentences of all defendants who plead guilty? Does it reward cooperation that produces administrative savings or remorse for the crime or both?

3. *Prevalence and size of the discount.* In discretionary sentencing systems, judges give different discounts to defendants for pleading guilty (or for accepting responsibility or expressing remorse, if you prefer). Those studying sentences in the aggregate have estimated that a guilty plea can reduce a sentence by 15-40%. Under the federal guidelines section 3E1.1, if a defendant "clearly demonstrates acceptance of responsibility," her "offense level" can be reduced by two or three levels. A three-level discount could mean a reduction of as much as 50% of the sentence for lesser crimes or as little as 20% for more serious offenses. The three-level discount is conditioned on a motion by the prosecution stating that the defendant's early plea or cooperation was beneficial to the government. What was Congress's goal in specifying a motion by the government as a prerequisite to an increased reduction for acceptance of responsibility?

The structured sentencing rules in most states do not specify how much the judge should discount the sentence of a defendant who pleads guilty. Compare this with the cap specified in the legislation from the United Kingdom, reprinted above. It does appear that early guilty pleas in the Crown Court lead to more nonprison sentences and to shorter prison terms. See Ralph J. Henham, Sentence Discounts and the Criminal Process (2001). If a state were to pass a statute identical to the UK legislation, would it survive constitutional challenge? Some state statutes in the United States do specify the maximum discount that a court may grant for pleading guilty. See Iowa Code §901.10(3) (in sentencing certain drug defendants otherwise subject to a mandatory minimum sentence, "the court may, at its discretion, reduce the maximum sentence by up to one-third" for a defendant who pleads guilty).

In a world where more than 90% of all felony defendants plead guilty, how many defendants fail to receive a discount? In only 7% of cases did offenders fail to receive some discount for acceptance of responsibility in 2006 (with almost

65% receiving three-level discounts and 28% receiving two-level discounts). Only 4.3% of the defendants convicted in federal court in 2006 actually went to trial. Does this pattern undermine the claim that courts are not punishing defendants who exercise their trial rights?

4. *Silence, perjury, and sentencing.* As the Rhode Island court in *Tiernan* mentioned, defendants have a right to trial, but they have no right to perjury. A defendant who testifies at trial might receive a stiffer punishment if the judge believes that the testimony was not truthful. See United States v. Dunnigan, 507 U.S. 87, 97 (1993) (sentencing court can enhance defendant's sentence by designated amount under federal guidelines if the court finds that the defendant committed perjury at trial; court must make "findings to support all the elements of a perjury violation in the specific case").

But the trial is not the only setting in which it is dangerous for the defendant to speak. The probation officer who prepares a presentence investigation report might ask to interview the defendant. If the officer believes that the defendant lied during the interview, she might recommend against any discount for acceptance of responsibility. Cf. People v. Hicks, N.E.2d 205 (N.Y. 2002) (approving imposition of an enhanced sentence after defender lied about crime to probation officer). At the same time, the Fifth Amendment's privilege against self-incrimination limits the consequences of a defendant's decision to remain silent. In Mitchell v. United States, 526 U.S. 314 (1999), the defendant faced a sentence of anywhere from one year to life depending on the quantity of drugs involved in her offense. Mitchell did not testify at the sentencing hearing, but contended that the evidence established the presence of only a small amount of cocaine. The Supreme Court held that the trial court could not consider Mitchell's silence as a basis for a factual finding that higher amounts of drugs were involved in the case. Drawing such inferences from her silence impermissibly burdened her exercise of the constitutional right against compelled self-incrimination. Would the same reasoning apply to a defendant who declines a probation officer's invitation to discuss the case? Consider this application note to section 3E1.1: "[A] defendant is not required to volunteer, or affirmatively admit, relevant conduct beyond the offense of conviction in order to obtain a reduction. . . ."

5. *"Vindictive" sentencing after retrial.* Just as courts insist that a sentence may not be increased to punish a defendant for exercising the right to trial, federal and state courts say that a trial judge may not punish a defendant for exercising the statutory right to appeal. If a defendant successfully appeals a conviction and is convicted again after retrial, a sentence higher than the original sentence imposed is presumed to be a product of vindictiveness by the sentencing judge. A sentence motivated by such vindictiveness violates federal due process. The judge must rebut this presumption by placing on the record her reasons for increasing the sentence after the second conviction. See North Carolina v. Pearce, 395 U.S. 711, 726 (1969). A trial judge could rebut the presumption of vindictiveness by pointing to any "objective information" that the judge did not consider during the first sentencing proceeding. See Texas v. McCullough, 475 U.S. 134 (1986).

## 2.  *Substantial Assistance*

Sometimes it takes a crook to catch a crook. A defendant can tell investigators about crimes that others committed in the past or can agree to take part in future sting operations. In the federal system, substantial assistance to the government is by far the most common single reason judges give for departing downward from the sentencing range specified in the guidelines. Judges relied on substantial-assistance departures in more than 11% of all federal cases in 2010.

It is clear that all sentencing systems allow trial judges to reduce a defendant's sentence based on cooperation. What is less clear is exactly *who* can determine whether the defendant should benefit from an effort to cooperate and how large the benefit should be.

|| *United States v. Amanda Williams*
474 F.3d 1130 (8th Cir. 2007) ||

COLLOTON, J.

The Sentencing Reform Act provides that a district court has "limited authority to impose a sentence below a statutory minimum," upon motion of the government, "so as to reflect a defendant's substantial assistance in the investigation or prosecution of another person who has committed an offense." 18 U.S.C. §3553(e). This case presents the question whether a district court, after reducing a sentence based on substantial assistance pursuant to §3553(e), may reduce the sentence further based on factors, other than assistance, set forth in 18 U.S.C. §3553(a). We hold that it may not. Where a court has authority to sentence below a statutory minimum only by virtue of a government motion under §3553(e), the reduction below the statutory minimum must be based exclusively on assistance-related considerations.

Amanda Williams pled guilty to conspiracy to distribute more than 500 grams of methamphetamine within 1000 feet of a protected location. At sentencing, the government filed motions under USSG §5K1.1 and 18 U.S.C. §3553(e) to reduce her sentence based on the provision of substantial assistance to authorities in the investigation or prosecution of other persons. A motion under §5K1.1 authorizes the sentencing court to depart below the applicable advisory guideline range in determining the advisory guideline sentence, and a §3553(e) motion permits the court to sentence below a statutory minimum. See Melendez v. United States, 518 U.S. 120 (1996).

Prior to any reduction for assistance, the advisory guideline sentence for Williams was 120-121 months' imprisonment, and the applicable statutory minimum was 120 months. The district court granted the substantial-assistance motions and announced that it would reduce the term of imprisonment to 78 months based on Williams's assistance. The court then invoked §3553(a) to reduce the sentence further, to a final term of 60 months' imprisonment, based on Williams's young age, medical history, drug use, and limited criminal history. The government does not challenge the district court's reduction of the sentence to 78 months based on substantial assistance, but argues that the additional reduction to 60 months was legally impermissible, because the court relied on factors other than substantial assistance. This is a legal question that we review *de novo*.

We have said that a reduction in sentence based on §3553(e) may be based only on assistance-related considerations, but we have twice reserved deciding whether, in light of United States v. Booker, 543 U.S. 220 (2005), a district court may also rely on §3553(a) to reduce a sentence further below the statutory minimum once the government has filed a motion under §3553(e). In [an earlier case], we implied strongly — if we did not explicitly hold — that a district court in that situation is limited to assistance-related considerations. . . . The clear implication of [that case] is that factors unrelated to assistance were not "permissible" considerations in determining the extent of a reduction below the statutory minimum.

To the extent the question remains open . . . , we conclude that the text of §3553(e) provides a clear answer, and that *Booker* does not expand the district court's authority to impose a sentence below a statutory minimum. Section 3553(e) provides:

> *(e) Limited authority to impose a sentence below a statutory minimum.* — Upon motion of the Government, the court shall have the authority to impose a sentence below a level established by statute as a minimum sentence so as to reflect a defendant's substantial assistance in the investigation or prosecution of another person who has committed an offense. Such sentence shall be imposed in accordance with the guidelines and policy statements issued by the Sentencing Commission pursuant to section 994 of title 28, United States Code.

Two aspects of the text are particularly instructive. First is the title, which states that the section provides only "limited authority" to impose a sentence below the statutory minimum. Congress evidently wanted statutory minimum sentences to be firmly enforced, subject only to carefully "limited" exceptions. The body of §3553(e) specifies precisely how a sentencing court's authority is limited. It may impose a sentence below the statutory minimum only "*so as to reflect a defendant's substantial assistance.*" 18 U.S.C. §3553(e) (emphasis added). If a district court imposes a sentence below the statutory minimum in part so as to reflect the history and characteristics of the defendant, see §3553(a)(1), then the court exceeds the limited authority granted by §3553(e). The second textual sentence of §3553(e) refers back to the penal sentence contemplated in the first textual sentence, and thus "restricts the court's reference to those guidelines and policy statements that bear directly upon the desirability and extent of a substantial assistance departure." United States v. Ahlers, 305 F.3d 54, 61 (1st Cir. 2002).

Nothing in the reasoning of *Booker* expands the authority of a district court to sentence below a statutory minimum. The Court's remedial holding provided that to cure the constitutional infirmity of the mandatory guidelines system, a district court is authorized to consider the factors set forth in §3553(a), and to vary from the sentence otherwise indicated by the sentencing guidelines. But *Booker* did not question the constitutionality of statutory minimum sentences, and while the Court excised §§3553(b)(1) and 3742(e) from the Code, §3553(e) was unmentioned in the opinion. The Court deviated from the mandatory guidelines system adopted by Congress only insofar as the deviation was necessary to make the remaining advisory system consistent with the Sixth Amendment. Because statutory minimum sentences remain constitutional, and it is constitutional for Congress to limit a court's authority to sentence below such minimums, the remedial holding of *Booker* does not impact the pre-existing limitations embodied in §3553(e).

In this case, the district court reduced Williams's sentence below the statutory minimum in two increments — one based on substantial assistance and one based on other factors. Because the second increment was impermissible for the reasons explained above, we vacate the sentence and remand for resentencing consistent with this opinion.

## ‖ *Nevada Revised Statutes §453.3405(2)* ‖

The court, upon an appropriate motion, may reduce or suspend the sentence of any person convicted of violating any of the [code provisions dealing with trafficking in controlled substances] if the court finds that the convicted person rendered substantial assistance in the investigation or prosecution of any offense. The arresting agency must be given an opportunity to be heard before the motion is granted. Upon good cause shown, the motion may be heard in camera.

### PROBLEM 5-2.   HELPING OTHERS

The County Police Department of Nassau, New York, and the U.S. Bureau of Alcohol, Tobacco and Firearms (BATF) conducted a joint investigation of Lancelotte Kaye's illegal trafficking in narcotics and firearms. During this investigation, Kaye sold both marijuana and illegal firearms to an undercover Nassau County detective. The state authorities arrested Kaye for selling marijuana; the federal authorities arrested him for illegal possession of firearms. Soon after his indictments on these charges, Kaye agreed to cooperate with both state and federal authorities in the identification and conviction of other wrongdoers.

His efforts for the state investigators proved fruitful. Kaye covertly recorded conversations with various individuals, at some personal risk. As a result of these recordings, the Nassau P.D. arrested two individuals, one of whom pleaded guilty to a misdemeanor. In Nassau County Court, Kaye pleaded guilty to a lesser drug felony and was sentenced to time served. Unfortunately, Kaye's efforts on behalf of the federal authorities were unproductive. Kaye recorded phone conversations with the individual who sold him weapons. He also met with that individual and provided the BATF with his first name, telephone number, and home address. Nevertheless, the BATF made no arrests.

In federal district court, Kaye pleaded guilty to possession of firearms with obliterated serial numbers. The prosecutor declined to move for a downward departure pursuant to section 5K1.1. In a letter to the court, the prosecutor acknowledged that Kaye had cooperated in Nassau County but noted that he had received the benefit of a light sentence in return. The letter went on: "The federal effort was ultimately unsuccessful. As such, the government cannot certify that the defendant has provided substantial assistance."

As defense counsel for Kaye in federal court, how might you construct arguments for a downward departure based on Kaye's cooperation in the state and federal investigations? How is Kaye's case different from the typical refusal by federal prosecutors to request a departure under section 5K1.1? How might you use section 5K2.0, which empowers a sentencing judge to depart downward from a sentence designated under the guidelines if the case presents a factor that the U.S. Sentencing Commission did not "adequately consider" as it formulated the guidelines? Compare United States v. Kaye, 140 F.3d 86 (2d Cir. 1998).

## PROBLEM 5-3.   EARNED TIME

Return your attention to the robbery case involving Rob Anon and his accomplices. Suppose that during pretrial negotiations, the prosecutor made the same plea offer to Anon, Zweite, and Tercero: the government would move for a downward departure from the presumptive sentence under the sentencing guidelines, based on substantial assistance to the government, if one of the defendants would plead guilty and testify against the other defendants. The prosecutor told all three defendants that he did not care which of them received the downward departure motion, but that the government would make the motion for only one defendant.

Several weeks passed. Tercero finally accepted the offer and entered a plea agreement. He pled guilty and testified at the trial of Anon and Zweite; the jury convicted the two defendants on all charges. At the sentencing hearing, the prosecutor recommended a sentence of 12 months for Tercero, which was a downward departure from the presumptive sentence under the guidelines. The government recommended sentences within the relevant guideline range for Anon and Zweite, 108-135 months. The sentencing guidelines in the jurisdiction would make it difficult for the sentencing judge to depart downward (below 108 months) for Anon or Zweite.

As a law clerk to the sentencing judge, what sentence would you recommend for the three defendants? As a member of a sentencing commission, would you draft rules placing any limits on the use of substantial assistance as a basis for a departure? Any limits on the size of such a departure? Compare United States v. Maddox, 48 F.3d 791 (4th Cir. 1995).

## *NOTES*

1. *Assisting in other investigations.*   In the unstructured sentencing states, cooperation with the government in investigating and trying other criminal cases is generally believed to have some positive effect both on the sentencing court's disposition of the case and on the duration of the sentence imposed. See State v. Johnson, 630 N.W.2d 583 (Iowa 2001). The states with more structured sentencing systems follow the same route, instructing the judge that cooperation with the government can scrve as a basis for departing from the guideline range and imposing some lesser sentence. See Or. ADC 213-008-0002(1)(a)(F).

Is this reduction of the sentence a necessary evil, the price that prosecutors pay for creating additional criminal cases? Or would courts adjust a sentence in light of a defendant's cooperation even in an ideal world? Michael Simons argues that "cooperating" defendants are ostracized from their communities, so they have already been punished to some extent, and the criminal sanction should be reduced accordingly. He also suggests that cooperation encourages the defendant's atonement, increasing the odds that she will eventually reintegrate into the community. See Michael Simons, Retribution for Rats: Cooperation, Punishment, and Atonement, 56 Vand. L. Rev. 1 (2003). Should prosecutors consider the defendant's prospects for atonement through cooperation when recommending a reduced sentence for that defendant, or should the recommendation simply turn on the value of the help the defendant provided? If the latter, consider this irony: the "biggest fish" in any criminal organization is likely to know the most and to offer the most value to the government's investigators. Thus, the largest sentence reductions might go to the most important (and most culpable) defendants.

2. *Substantial in whose eyes?* There is some variation in the amount of control the prosecution has over the use of the "substantial assistance" sentencing factor. If the prosecution refuses to accept a defendant's offer of cooperation, then the sentence usually will not be affected. See Matos v. State, 878 P.2d 288 (Nev. 1994). But what happens if the government accepts the cooperation and later determines that it was not valuable or complete?

According to the U.S. Supreme Court in Wade v. United States, 504 U.S. 181 (1992), the Constitution places some boundaries on the prosecutor's power to refuse to request a reduced sentence based on a defendant's substantial assistance. But only when the defendant makes a "substantial threshold showing" of a prosecutor's unconstitutional motive (such as a refusal based on race or religion) can the trial judge adjust the sentence without a government motion.

The real debate over limiting prosecutorial power in this sphere takes place at the nonconstitutional level. Legislatures and sentencing commissions must decide whether to make a prosecutor's motion a necessary precondition to this sort of sentence reduction. The concern, of course, is that an unsupervised prosecutor's grounds for making or refusing to make the recommendations may be arbitrary or inconsistent. State legislatures and courts have debated this issue for years, although the state debate has not figured in the federal discussions of this question. See State v. Sarabia, 875 P.2d 227 (Idaho 1994) (declaring unconstitutional on state grounds a statute allowing sentence below mandatory minimum only when prosecutor moves for reduction based on substantial assistance).

With the ruling in *Booker*, federal courts may impose a non-guideline sentence based on substantial assistance even without a governmental motion; the same does not hold for sentences below a mandatory minimum, for which a governmental motion is still required. Are other institutions, such as sentencing courts, able to evaluate the prosecutor's decisions about which defendants provided substantial assistance?

In the federal system, prosecutors have attempted to regulate themselves by creating written policies concerning which defendants should receive a reduced sentence for substantial assistance. About 80% of the federal districts have adopted written guidelines on the subject, and their content is fairly consistent. A study sponsored by the U.S. Sentencing Commission (known as the Maxfield-Kramer Study), however, found great variety among the 94 federal districts in their granting of substantial assistance motions. See Linda Drazga Maxfield & John Kramer, Substantial Assistance: Empirical Yardstick Gauging Equity in Federal Policy and Practice (1998). The study found that the demographic characteristics of defendants had some influence on whether they received a motion: defendants who were male, black, Hispanic, non-citizens, and older were all less likely to receive a discount.

4. *Magnitude and type of discount.*   The federal guidelines do not instruct the sentencing judge on how much of a departure to grant to a cooperating defendant, but section 5K1.1 does list a few factors to consider: the "usefulness of the defendant's assistance," the "truthfulness, completeness, and reliability of any information or testimony provided," and "any injury suffered, or any danger or risk of injury to the defendant or his family resulting from his assistance." The Maxfield-Kramer Study found that judges gave larger departures in the cases involving the highest sentences, not necessarily for the defendants who provided the most valuable cooperation or who cooperated under the most dangerous circumstances. It also found that demographic features of defendants affected the size of the discount awarded. After controlling for various features of the crime and the type of cooperation, "female defendants received departures that were nine percentage points higher than did similar male defendants. Smaller, but still significant, differences were measured for ethnicity and citizenship (five percentage points), age (four percentage points), and race and education (two percentage points)." As a U.S. Sentencing Commission member, would you favor the imposition of limits on the magnitude of a departure expressed in absolute terms (say, two years or two offense levels) or in relative terms (say, 20% of the sentence)?

Defendants can receive not just different amounts of discounts but different *types* of benefits other than sentence adjustments for their cooperation with government investigations. These include a reduction of charges during plea negotiations or favorable treatment for immigration purposes. See Nora V. Demleitner, Immigration Threats and Rewards: Effective Law Enforcement Tools in the War on Terrorism?, 51 Emory L.J. 1059 (2002).

## C.   THE OFFENDER'S CHARACTER AND CIRCUMSTANCES

A criminal defendant is not merely the sum of his or her contacts with the criminal justice system; there is, of course, much more to every offender than simply a criminal record and some post-offense behavior. Indeed, many people think that personal characteristics — ethnicity, gender, age, family context, educational background, and social and economic history — define not only who we are but also how we ought to be judged by others. Sentencing judges usually learn facts about an offender's personal background and circumstances, and historically they have adjusted sentences in light of the offender's overall character, often giving particular attention to facts relating to the offender's family, physical or mental health, and prospects for rehabilitation. A persistent challenge in modern sentencing reform efforts has been to identify and regulate the appropriate role of so-called offender characteristics.

## PROBLEM 5-4.  TURNING GUIDANCE INTO GUIDELINES

It is 1985 and you have been appointed as one of the U.S. Sentencing Commission's first seven commissioners. Your institution has the enormous task of turning all the mandates of the recently passed Sentencing Reform Act (SRA) into sentencing guidelines for use by federal courts. The commissioners agreed to subdivide the work ahead, with each taking responsibility for drafting one part of the guidelines. You are assigned the section dealing with offender characteristics, and your work is guided by the following provisions of 28 U.S.C. §994, part of the SRA:

> (d) The U.S. Sentencing Commission in establishing [sentencing guidelines for federal offenses] shall consider whether the following matters, among others with respect to a defendant, have any relevance to the nature, extent, place of service, or other incidents of an appropriate sentence . . . : (1) age; (2) education; (3) vocational skills; (4) mental and emotional condition . . . ; (5) physical condition, including drug dependence; (6) previous employment record; (7) family ties and responsibilities; (8) community ties; . . . .
>     The Commission shall assure that the guidelines and policy statements are entirely neutral as to the race, sex, national origin, creed, and socioeconomic status of offenders.
>     (e) The Commission shall assure that the guidelines and policy statements, in recommending a term of imprisonment or length of a term of imprisonment, reflect the general inappropriateness of considering the education, vocational skills, employment record, family ties and responsibilities, and community ties of the defendant.

How will you turn the SRA's guidance into specific guidelines for courts to follow in sentencing individual offenders? Will you leave all these questions to the sentencing judge, or will you instead try to encourage or require judges to adjust a sentence up or down in light of some of these factors? Is it a good idea to specify the amount of adjustment that the judge should use in a normal case? Cf. U.S. Sentencing Guidelines Manual §5H1.1 (age), §5H1.2 (education and vocational skills), §5H1.3 (mental and emotional conditions), §5H1.4 (physical condition, including drug or alcohol dependence or abuse), §5H1.5 (employment record), §5H1.6 (family ties and responsibilities).

## NOTES

1. *Offender characteristics at sentencing: majority rule.*  Every U.S. jurisdiction allows judges at sentencing to consider various aspects of the defendant's life, including events occurring far before the offense, matters that do not bear directly on guilt or innocence, and post-offense activities. In unstructured sentencing systems, it is difficult to establish or measure just how much an offender's personal

background and characteristics influence the sentence, although anecdotal reports suggest that the influence can be sizable. Most structured systems do not directly integrate personal characteristics into the calculation of offenders' presumptive guideline sentences; instead, they often allow or encourage sentencing judges to depart from the guidelines to raise or lower the sentence based on these factors. In addition, legislatures as well as sentencing commissions sometimes instruct judges *not* to consider certain offender characteristics. The Minnesota sentencing guidelines, for example, state in section 2.D.04 that the following factors "should not be used as reasons for departing from the presumptive sentences" provided in guidelines:

(a)   Race
(b)   Sex
(c)   Employment factors, including: (1) occupation or impact of sentence on profession or occupation; (2) employment history; (3) employment at time of offense; (4) employment at time of sentencing
(d)   Social factors, including: (1) educational attainment; (2) living arrangements at time of offense or sentencing; (3) length of residence; (4) marital status
(e)   The exercise of constitutional rights by the defendant during the adjudication process

2. *Theory and concerns behind considering offender characteristics.*   What is the theoretical justification for altering a defendant's sentence based on certain personal characteristics? Could one argue from a retributivist perspective that certain personal characteristics, such as mental condition, education, and drug dependence, are not only relevant but fundamental to determining what sentence is needed to give an offender his just deserts? Could one argue from a utilitarian perspective that certain other personal characteristics, such as age, employment circumstances, and family background, are not only relevant but fundamental to determining what sentence is needed to effectively incapacitate, deter, or rehabilitate an offender?

Many modern structured-sentencing reforms were prompted by concerns that personal factors such as an offender's ethnicity, gender, and socioeconomic status were influencing judges' exercise of their broad sentencing discretion, resulting in unwarranted sentencing disparities. As detailed in Problem 5-4 above, Congress addressed this concern in federal sentencing reform by mandating that the federal sentencing guidelines be "entirely neutral as to the race, sex, national origin, creed, and socioeconomic status of offenders." Do you think this mandate is realistic or merely aspirational — that is, is it truly possible for a sentencing system to be "entirely neutral" with respect to all these factors? Can a principled argument be made that at least some of these listed factors ought to be considered at sentencing?

A number of other personal factors are closely associated with these forbidden factors. Employment and education, for example, are highly correlated with socioeconomic class; pregnancy is associated with gender, as can be some child-rearing realities. To the extent that gender and socioeconomic status are deemed per se illegitimate as sentencing considerations, should rules also bar any consideration of these related factors at sentencing? Consider the commentary to the Minnesota guidelines provision discussed above in note 1:

> [The] Commission has listed several factors which should not be used as reasons for departure from the presumptive sentence, because these factors are highly correlated with sex, race, or income levels. Employment is excluded as a reason for departure not only because of its correlation with race and income levels, but also because this factor is manipulable — offenders could lessen the severity of the sentence by obtaining employment between arrest and sentencing.

Minn. Sentencing Guidelines comment 2.D.101. Do you agree that consideration of employment history and status should be prohibited at sentencing?

## 1.   Immutable Characteristics

Should the treatment of certain personal characteristics at sentencing depend on whether they are within the offender's control? The immutability of certain factors that seem irrelevant to an offender's culpability and future prospects — factors such as race or creed — might suggest firm rules forbidding their consideration at sentencing. However, the immutability of other factors that seem quite relevant to an offender's culpability and future prospects — factors such as mental or physical condition — might suggest the need for rules requiring judges to consider them at sentencing.

‖ *ABA Standards for Criminal Justice,* ‖
‖ *Sentencing 18-3.4(d)* ‖
‖ **(3d ed. 1994)** ‖

The legislature should specify that the following personal characteristics shall not, in and of themselves, be used for [any] purpose with regard to sentencing: (i) Race, (ii) Gender or sexual orientation, (iii) National origin, (iv) Religion or creed, (v) Marital status, (vi) Political affiliation or belief.

‖ *Evan Miller v. Alabama* ‖
‖ **132 S. Ct. 2455 (2012)** ‖

KAGAN, J.[*]

The two 14-year-old offenders in these cases were convicted of murder and sentenced to life imprisonment without the possibility of parole. In neither case did the sentencing authority have any discretion to impose a different punishment. State law mandated that each juvenile die in prison even if a judge or jury would have thought that his youth and its attendant characteristics, along with the nature of his crime, made a lesser sentence (for example, life *with* the possibility of parole) more appropriate. Such a scheme prevents those meting out punishment from considering a juvenile's lessened culpability and greater

---

[*] Justices Kennedy, Ginsburg, Breyer and Sotomayor joined this opinion.

capacity for change, Graham v. Florida, 130 S. Ct. 2011 (2010), and runs afoul of our cases' requirement of individualized sentencing for defendants facing the most serious penalties. We therefore hold that mandatory life without parole for those under the age of 18 at the time of their crimes violates the Eighth Amendment's prohibition on "cruel and unusual punishments."

# I

## A

In November 1999, petitioner Kuntrell Jackson, then 14 years old, and two other boys decided to rob a video store. En route to the store, Jackson learned that one of the boys, Derrick Shields, was carrying a sawed-off shotgun in his coat sleeve. Jackson decided to stay outside when the two other boys entered the store. Inside, Shields pointed the gun at the store clerk, Laurie Troup, and demanded that she give up the money. Troup refused. A few moments later, Jackson went into the store to find Shields continuing to demand money. At trial, the parties disputed whether Jackson warned Troup that "we ain't playin'," or instead told his friends, "I thought you all was playin'." When Troup threatened to call the police, Shields shot and killed her. The three boys fled empty-handed.

Arkansas law gives prosecutors discretion to charge 14-year-olds as adults when they are alleged to have committed certain serious offenses. The prosecutor here exercised that authority by charging Jackson with capital felony murder and aggravated robbery. Jackson moved to transfer the case to juvenile court, but after considering the alleged facts of the crime, a psychiatrist's examination, and Jackson's juvenile arrest history (shoplifting and several incidents of car theft), the trial court denied the motion, and an appellate court affirmed. A jury later convicted Jackson of both crimes. Noting that "in view of the verdict, there's only one possible punishment," the judge sentenced Jackson to life without parole. . . .

Following Roper v. Simmons, 543 U.S. 551 (2005), in which this Court invalidated the death penalty for all juvenile offenders under the age of 18, Jackson filed a state petition for habeas corpus. He argued, based on *Roper*'s reasoning, that a mandatory sentence of life without parole for a 14-year-old also violates the Eighth Amendment. The circuit court rejected that argument and granted the State's motion to dismiss. While that ruling was on appeal, this Court held in Graham v. Florida that life without parole violates the Eighth Amendment when imposed on juvenile nonhomicide offenders. . . .

## B

Like Jackson, petitioner Evan Miller was 14 years old at the time of his crime. Miller had by then been in and out of foster care because his mother suffered from alcoholism and drug addiction and his stepfather abused him.

Miller, too, regularly used drugs and alcohol; and he had attempted suicide four times, the first when he was six years old.

One night in 2003, Miller was at home with a friend, Colby Smith, when a neighbor, Cole Cannon, came to make a drug deal with Miller's mother. The two boys followed Cannon back to his trailer, where all three smoked marijuana and played drinking games. When Cannon passed out, Miller stole his wallet, splitting about $300 with Smith. Miller then tried to put the wallet back in Cannon's pocket, but Cannon awoke and grabbed Miller by the throat. Smith hit Cannon with a nearby baseball bat, and once released, Miller grabbed the bat and repeatedly struck Cannon with it. Miller placed a sheet over Cannon's head, told him "I am God, I've come to take your life," and delivered one more blow. The boys then retreated to Miller's trailer, but soon decided to return to Cannon's to cover up evidence of their crime. Once there, they lit two fires. Cannon eventually died from his injuries and smoke inhalation.

Alabama law required that Miller initially be charged as a juvenile, but allowed the District Attorney to seek removal of the case to adult court. The D.A. did so, and the juvenile court agreed to the transfer after a hearing. Citing the nature of the crime, Miller's "mental maturity," and his prior juvenile offenses (truancy and "criminal mischief"), the Alabama Court of Criminal Appeals affirmed. The State accordingly charged Miller as an adult with murder in the course of arson. That crime (like capital murder in Arkansas) carries a mandatory minimum punishment of life without parole. Relying in significant part on testimony from Smith, who had pleaded to a lesser offense, a jury found Miller guilty. He was therefore sentenced to life without the possibility of parole. . . . We granted certiorari in both cases and now reverse.

## II

The Eighth Amendment's prohibition of cruel and unusual punishment guarantees individuals the right not to be subjected to excessive sanctions. That right, we have explained, flows from the basic precept of justice that punishment for crime should be graduated and proportioned to both the offender and the offense. [We view the concept of proportionality] less through a historical prism than according to "the evolving standards of decency that mark the progress of a maturing society." Trop v. Dulles, 356 U.S. 86, 101 (1958) (plurality opinion).

The cases before us implicate two strands of precedent reflecting our concern with proportionate punishment. The first has adopted categorical bans on sentencing practices based on mismatches between the culpability of a class of offenders and the severity of a penalty. So, for example, we have held that imposing the death penalty for nonhomicide crimes against individuals, or imposing it on mentally retarded defendants, violates the Eighth Amendment. See Kennedy v. Louisiana, 554 U.S. 407 (2008); Atkins v. Virginia, 536 U.S. 304 (2002). Several of the cases in this group have specially focused on juvenile offenders, because of their lesser culpability. Thus, *Roper* held that the Eighth Amendment bars capital punishment for children, and *Graham* concluded that the Amendment also prohibits a sentence of life without the possibility of parole for a child who committed a nonhomicide offense. *Graham* further likened life without parole for juveniles to the death penalty itself, thereby evoking a second line of our precedents. In those cases, we have prohibited mandatory imposition of capital punishment, requiring that sentencing authorities consider the characteristics of a defendant and the details of his offense before sentencing him to death. See Woodson v. North Carolina, 428 U.S. 280 (1976) (plurality opinion); Lockett v. Ohio, 438 U.S. 586 (1978). Here, the confluence of these two lines of precedent leads to the conclusion that mandatory life-without-parole sentences for juveniles violate the Eighth Amendment.

To start with the first set of cases: *Roper* and *Graham* establish that children are constitutionally different from adults for purposes of sentencing. Because juveniles have diminished culpability and greater prospects for reform, we explained, they are less deserving of the most severe punishments. Those cases relied on three significant gaps between juveniles and adults. First, children have a "lack of maturity and an underdeveloped sense of responsibility," leading to recklessness, impulsivity, and heedless risk-taking. Second, children "are more vulnerable . . . to negative influences and outside pressures," including from their family and peers; they have limited "control over their own environment" and lack the ability to extricate themselves from horrific, crime-producing settings. And third, a child's character is not as "well formed" as an adult's; his traits are "less fixed" and his actions less likely to be "evidence of irretrievable depravity."

Our decisions rested not only on common sense—on what "any parent knows"—but on science and social science as well. In *Roper*, we cited studies showing that only a relatively small proportion of adolescents who engage in illegal activity develop entrenched patterns of problem behavior. And in *Graham*, we noted that developments in psychology and brain science "continue to show fundamental differences between juvenile and adult minds"—for example, in "parts of the brain involved in behavior control." We reasoned that those findings—of transient rashness, proclivity for risk, and inability to assess consequences—both lessened a child's moral culpability and enhanced the prospect that, as the years go by and neurological development occurs, his "deficiencies will be reformed."

*Roper* and *Graham* emphasized that the distinctive attributes of youth diminish the penological justifications for imposing the harshest sentences on juvenile offenders, even when they commit terrible crimes. Because the heart of the retribution rationale relates to an offender's blameworthiness, the case for retribution is not as strong with a minor as with an adult. Nor can deterrence do the work in this context, because the same characteristics that render juveniles less culpable than adults—their immaturity, recklessness, and impetuosity—make them less likely to consider potential punishment. Similarly, incapacitation could not support the life-without-parole sentence in *Graham*: Deciding that a juvenile offender forever will be a danger to society would require making a "judgment that he is incorrigible"—but "incorrigibility is inconsistent with youth." 130 S. Ct., at 2029 (quoting Workman v. Commonwealth, 429 S.W.2d 374, 378 (Ky. App. 1968)). And for the same reason, rehabilitation could not justify that sentence. Life without parole forswears altogether the rehabilitative ideal. It reflects "an irrevocable judgment" about an offender's value and place in society, at odds with a child's capacity for change.

*Graham* concluded from this analysis that life-without-parole sentences, like capital punishment, may violate the Eighth Amendment when imposed on children. To be sure, *Graham*'s flat ban on life without parole applied only to nonhomicide crimes, and the Court took care to distinguish those offenses from murder, based on both moral culpability and consequential harm. But none of what it said about children—about their distinctive (and transitory) mental traits and environmental vulnerabilities—is crime-specific. Those features are evident in the same way, and to the same degree, when (as in both cases here) a botched robbery turns into a killing. So *Graham*'s reasoning implicates any life-without-parole sentence imposed on a juvenile, even as its categorical bar relates only to nonhomicide offenses.

Most fundamentally, *Graham* insists that youth matters in determining the appropriateness of a lifetime of incarceration without the possibility of parole. . . . But the mandatory penalty schemes at issue here prevent the sentencer from taking account of these central considerations. By removing youth from the balance—by subjecting a juvenile to the same life-without-parole sentence applicable to an adult—these laws prohibit a sentencing authority from assessing whether the law's harshest term of imprisonment proportionately punishes a juvenile offender. That contravenes *Graham*'s (and also *Roper*'s) foundational principle: that imposition of a State's most severe penalties on juvenile offenders cannot proceed as though they were not children.

And *Graham* makes plain these mandatory schemes' defects in another way: by likening life-without-parole sentences imposed on juveniles to the death penalty itself. Life-without-parole terms, the Court wrote, "share some characteristics with death sentences that are shared by no other sentences." Imprisoning an offender until he dies alters the remainder of his life "by a forfeiture that is irrevocable." And this lengthiest possible incarceration is an "especially harsh punishment for a juvenile," because he will almost inevitably serve "more years and a greater percentage of his life in prison than an adult offender." . . .

That correspondence—*Graham*'s treatment of juvenile life sentences as analogous to capital punishment—makes relevant here a second line of our precedents, demanding individualized sentencing when imposing the death penalty. In *Woodson*, 428 U.S. 280, we held that a statute mandating a death sentence for first-degree murder violated the Eighth Amendment. We thought the mandatory scheme flawed because it gave no significance to "the character and record of the individual offender or the circumstances" of the offense, and excluded from consideration "the possibility of compassionate or mitigating factors." Subsequent decisions have elaborated on the requirement that capital defendants have an opportunity to advance, and the judge or jury a chance to assess, any mitigating factors, so that the death penalty is reserved only for the most culpable defendants committing the most serious offenses.

Of special pertinence here, we insisted in these rulings that a sentencer have the ability to consider the "mitigating qualities of youth." Johnson v. Texas, 509 U.S. 350, 367 (1993). Everything we said in *Roper* and *Graham* about that stage of life also appears in these decisions. As we observed, "youth is more than a chronological fact." It is a time of immaturity, irresponsibility, impetuousness, and recklessness. It is a moment and condition of life when a person may be most susceptible to influence and to psychological damage. And its signature qualities are all transient. Eddings v. Oklahoma, 455 U.S. 104 (1982) is especially on point. There, a 16-year-old shot a police officer point-blank and killed him. We invalidated his death sentence because the judge did not consider evidence of his neglectful and violent family background (including his mother's drug abuse and his father's physical abuse) and his emotional disturbance. We found that evidence particularly relevant—more so than it would have been in the case of an adult offender. We held: "Just as the chronological age of a minor is itself a relevant mitigating factor of great weight, so must the background and mental and emotional development of a youthful defendant be duly considered" in assessing his culpability. . . .

So *Graham* and *Roper* and our individualized sentencing cases alike teach that in imposing a State's harshest penalties, a sentencer misses too much if he treats every child as an adult. To recap: Mandatory life without parole for a juvenile precludes consideration of his chronological age and its hallmark features—among them, immaturity, impetuosity, and failure to appreciate risks and consequences. It prevents taking into account the family and home environment that surrounds him—and from which he cannot usually extricate himself—no matter how brutal or dysfunctional. It neglects the circumstances of the homicide offense, including the extent of his participation in the conduct and the way familial and peer pressures may have affected him. Indeed, it ignores that he might have been charged and convicted of a lesser offense if not for incompetencies associated with youth—for example, his inability to deal with police officers or prosecutors (including on a plea agreement) or his incapacity to assist his own attorneys. And finally, this mandatory punishment disregards the possibility of rehabilitation even when the circumstances most suggest it.

Both cases before us illustrate the problem. Take Jackson's first. As noted earlier, Jackson did not fire the bullet that killed Laurie Troup; nor did the State argue that he intended her death. Jackson's conviction was instead based on an aiding-and-abetting theory; and the appellate court affirmed the verdict only because the jury could have believed that when Jackson entered the store, he warned Troup that "we ain't playin'," rather than told his friends that "I thought you all was playin'." To be sure, Jackson learned on the way to the video store that his friend Shields was carrying a gun, but his age could well have affected his calculation of the risk that posed, as well as his willingness to walk away at that point. All these circumstances go to Jackson's culpability for the offense. And so too does Jackson's family background and immersion in violence: Both his mother and his grandmother had previously shot other individuals. At the least, a sentencer should look at such facts before depriving a 14-year-old of any prospect of release from prison.

That is true also in Miller's case. No one can doubt that he and Smith committed a vicious murder. But they did it when high on drugs and alcohol consumed with the adult victim. And if ever a pathological background might have contributed to a 14-year-old's commission of a crime, it is here. Miller's stepfather physically abused him; his alcoholic and drug-addicted mother neglected him; he had been in and out of foster care as a result; and he had tried to kill himself four times, the first when he should have been in kindergarten. Nonetheless, Miller's past criminal history was limited—two instances of truancy and one of "second-degree criminal mischief." That Miller deserved severe punishment for killing Cole Cannon is beyond question. But once again, a sentencer needed to examine all these circumstances before concluding that life without any possibility of parole was the appropriate penalty.

We therefore hold that the Eighth Amendment forbids a sentencing scheme that mandates life in prison without possibility of parole for juvenile offenders. By making youth (and all that accompanies it) irrelevant to imposition of that harshest prison sentence, such a scheme poses too great a risk of disproportionate punishment. Because that holding is sufficient to decide these cases, we do not consider Jackson's and Miller's alternative argument that the Eighth Amendment requires a categorical bar on life without parole for juveniles, or at least for those 14 and younger. But given all we have said in *Roper, Graham,* and this decision about children's diminished culpability and heightened capacity for change, we think appropriate occasions for sentencing juveniles to this harshest possible penalty will be uncommon. That is especially so because of the great difficulty we noted in *Roper* and *Graham* of distinguishing at this early age between the juvenile offender whose crime reflects unfortunate yet transient immaturity, and the rare juvenile offender whose crime reflects irreparable corruption. Although we do not foreclose a sentencer's ability to make that judgment in homicide cases, we require it to take into account how children are different, and how those differences counsel against irrevocably sentencing them to a lifetime in prison. . . .

## III

### A

The States . . . claim that Harmelin v. Michigan, 501 U.S. 957 (1991), precludes our holding. The defendant in *Harmelin* was sentenced to a mandatory life-without-parole term for possessing more than 650 grams of cocaine. The Court upheld that penalty, reasoning that "a sentence which is not otherwise cruel and unusual" does not become so simply because it is mandatory. We recognized that a different rule, requiring individualized sentencing, applied in the death penalty context. But we refused to extend that command to noncapital cases "because of the qualitative difference between death and all other penalties." According to Alabama, invalidating the mandatory imposition of life-without-parole terms on juveniles would effectively overrule *Harmelin.*

We think that argument myopic. *Harmelin* had nothing to do with children and did not purport to apply its holding to the sentencing of juvenile offenders. We have by now held on multiple occasions that a sentencing rule permissible for adults may not be so for children. Capital punishment, our decisions hold, generally comports with the Eighth Amendment — except it cannot be imposed on children. So too, life without parole is permissible for nonhomicide offenses — except, once again, for children. . . . So if (as *Harmelin* recognized) "death is different," children are different too. Indeed, it is the odd legal rule that does *not* have some form of exception for children. In that context, it is no surprise that the law relating to society's harshest punishments recognizes such a distinction. Our ruling thus neither overrules nor undermines nor conflicts with *Harmelin.*

Alabama and Arkansas . . . next contend that because many States impose mandatory life-without-parole sentences on juveniles, we may not hold the practice unconstitutional. In considering categorical bars to the death penalty and life without parole, we ask as part of the analysis whether objective indicia of society's standards, as expressed in legislative enactments and state practice, show a national consensus against a sentence for a particular class of offenders. By our count, 29 jurisdictions (28 States and the Federal Government) make a life-without-parole term mandatory for some juveniles convicted of murder in adult court. The States argue that this number precludes our holding.

We do not agree; indeed, we think the States' argument on this score *weaker* than the one we rejected in *Graham*. For starters, the cases here are different from the typical one in which we have tallied legislative enactments. Our decision does not categorically bar a penalty for a class of offenders or type of crime — as, for example, we did in *Roper* or *Graham*. Instead, it mandates only that a sentencer follow a certain process — considering an offender's youth and attendant characteristics — before imposing a particular penalty. And in so requiring, our decision flows straightforwardly from our precedents: specifically, the principle of *Roper, Graham,* and our individualized sentencing cases that youth matters for purposes of meting out the law's most serious punishments. When both of those circumstances have obtained in the past, we have not scrutinized or relied in the same way on legislative enactments. We see no difference here. . . .

Almost all jurisdictions allow some juveniles to be tried in adult court for some kinds of homicide. But most States do not have separate penalty provisions for those juvenile offenders. Of the 29 jurisdictions mandating life without parole for children, more than half do so by virtue of generally applicable penalty provisions, imposing the sentence without regard to age. And indeed, some of those States set no minimum age for who may be transferred to adult court in the first instance, thus applying life-without-parole mandates to children of any age — be it 17 or 14 or 10 or 6. [Under these circumstances, we think] that the statutory eligibility of a juvenile offender for life without parole does not indicate that the penalty has been endorsed through deliberate, express, and full legislative consideration. That Alabama and Arkansas can count to 29 by including these possibly (or probably) inadvertent legislative outcomes does not preclude our determination that mandatory life without parole for juveniles violates the Eighth Amendment.

### B

Nor does the presence of discretion in some jurisdictions' transfer statutes aid the States here. Alabama and Arkansas initially ignore that many States use mandatory transfer systems: A juvenile of a certain age who has committed a specified offense will be tried in adult court, regardless of any individualized circumstances. Of the 29 relevant jurisdictions, about half place at least some juvenile homicide offenders in adult court automatically, with no apparent opportunity to seek transfer to juvenile court. Moreover, several States at times lodge this decision exclusively in the hands of prosecutors, again with no statutory mechanism for judicial reevaluation. And those prosecutorial discretion laws are usually silent regarding standards, protocols, or appropriate considerations for decisionmaking.

Even when States give transfer-stage discretion to judges, it has limited utility. First, the decisionmaker typically will have only partial information at this early, pretrial stage about either the child or the circumstances of his offense. Miller's case provides an example. [The] juvenile court denied Miller's request for his own mental-health expert at the transfer hearing, and the appeals court affirmed on the ground that Miller was not then entitled to the protections and services he would receive at trial. But by then, of course, the expert's testimony could not change the sentence; whatever she said in mitigation, the mandatory life-without-parole prison term would kick in. The key moment for the exercise of discretion is the transfer — and as Miller's case shows, the judge often does not know then what she will learn, about the offender or the offense, over the course of the proceedings.

Second and still more important, the question at transfer hearings may differ dramatically from the issue at a post-trial sentencing. Because many juvenile systems require that the offender be released at a particular age or after a certain number of years, transfer decisions often present a choice between extremes: light punishment as a child or standard sentencing as an adult (here, life without parole). In many States, for example, a child convicted in juvenile court must be released from custody by the age of 21. Discretionary sentencing in adult court would provide different options: There, a judge or jury could choose, rather than a life-without-parole sentence, a lifetime prison term *with* the possibility of parole or a lengthy term of years. It is easy to imagine a judge deciding that a minor deserves a (much) harsher sentence than he would receive in juvenile court, while still not thinking life-without-parole appropriate. For that reason, the discretion available to a judge at the transfer stage cannot substitute for discretion at post-trial sentencing in adult court — and so cannot satisfy the Eighth Amendment.

## IV

*Graham, Roper,* and our individualized sentencing decisions make clear that a judge or jury must have the opportunity to consider mitigating circumstances before imposing the harshest possible penalty for juveniles. By requiring that all children convicted of homicide receive lifetime incarceration without possibility of parole, regardless of their age and age-related characteristics and the nature of their crimes, the mandatory sentencing schemes before us violate this principle of proportionality, and so the Eighth Amendment's ban on cruel and unusual punishment. . . .

ROBERTS, C.J., dissenting.[*]

Determining the appropriate sentence for a teenager convicted of murder presents grave and challenging questions of morality and social policy. Our role, however, is to apply the law, not to answer such questions. The pertinent law

---

\* Justices Scalia, Thomas, and Alito joined this opinion.

here is the Eighth Amendment to the Constitution, which prohibits "cruel and unusual punishments." Today, the Court invokes that Amendment to ban a punishment that the Court does not itself characterize as unusual, and that could not plausibly be described as such. I therefore dissent.

The parties agree that nearly 2,500 prisoners are presently serving life sentences without the possibility of parole for murders they committed before the age of 18. The Court accepts that over 2,000 of those prisoners received that sentence because it was mandated by a legislature. And it recognizes that the Federal Government and most States impose such mandatory sentences. Put simply, if a 17-year-old is convicted of deliberately murdering an innocent victim, it is not "unusual" for the murderer to receive a mandatory sentence of life without parole. That reality should preclude finding that mandatory life imprisonment for juvenile killers violates the Eighth Amendment.

Our precedent supports this conclusion. When determining whether a punishment is cruel and unusual, this Court typically begins with "objective indicia of society's standards, as expressed in legislative enactments and state practice." We look to these objective indicia to ensure that we are not simply following our own subjective values or beliefs. Such tangible evidence of societal standards enables us to determine whether there is a consensus against a given sentencing practice. If there is, the punishment may be regarded as "unusual." But when, as here, most States formally require and frequently impose the punishment in question, there is no objective basis for that conclusion.

Our Eighth Amendment cases have also said that we should take guidance from "evolving standards of decency that mark the progress of a maturing society." Mercy toward the guilty can be a form of decency, and a maturing society may abandon harsh punishments that it comes to view as unnecessary or unjust. But decency is not the same as leniency. A decent society protects the innocent from violence. A mature society may determine that this requires removing those guilty of the most heinous murders from its midst, both as protection for its other members and as a concrete expression of its standards of decency. As judges we have no basis for deciding that progress toward greater decency can move only in the direction of easing sanctions on the guilty.

In this case, there is little doubt about the direction of society's evolution: For most of the 20th century, American sentencing practices emphasized rehabilitation of the offender and the availability of parole. But by the 1980's, outcry against repeat offenders, broad disaffection with the rehabilitative model, and other factors led many legislatures to reduce or eliminate the possibility of parole, imposing longer sentences in order to punish criminals and prevent them from committing more crimes. Statutes establishing life without parole sentences in particular became more common in the past quarter century. And the parties agree that most States have changed their laws relatively recently to expose teenage murderers to mandatory life without parole. . . .

[The] Court's opinion suggests that it is merely a way station on the path to further judicial displacement of the legislative role in prescribing appropriate punishment for crime. The Court's analysis focuses on the mandatory nature of the sentences in this case. But then — although doing so is entirely unnecessary to the rule it announces — the Court states that even when a life without parole sentence is not mandatory, "we think appropriate occasions for sentencing juveniles to this harshest possible penalty will be uncommon." Today's holding may be limited to mandatory sentences, but the Court has already announced that discretionary life without parole for juveniles should be "uncommon" — or, to use a common synonym, "unusual."

Indeed, the Court's gratuitous prediction appears to be nothing other than an invitation to overturn life without parole sentences imposed by juries and trial judges. If that invitation is widely accepted and such sentences for juvenile offenders do in fact become "uncommon," the Court will have boot-strapped its way to declaring that the Eighth Amendment absolutely prohibits them.

This process has no discernible end point — or at least none consistent with our Nation's legal traditions. . . . The principle behind today's decision seems to be only that because juveniles are different from adults, they must be sentenced differently. There is no clear reason that principle would not bar all mandatory sentences for juveniles, or any juvenile sentence as harsh as what a similarly situated adult would receive. Unless confined, the only stopping point for the Court's analysis would be never permitting juvenile offenders to be tried as adults. Learning that an Amendment that bars only "unusual" punishments requires the abolition of this uniformly established practice would be startling indeed. . . .

THOMAS, J., dissenting.[*]

. . . As I have previously explained, the Cruel and Unusual Punishments Clause was originally understood as prohibiting torturous *methods* of punishment — specifically methods akin to those that had been considered cruel and unusual at the time the Bill of Rights was adopted. The clause does not contain a "proportionality principle." In short, it does not authorize courts to invalidate any punishment they deem disproportionate to the severity of the crime or to a particular class of offenders. Instead, the clause leaves the unavoidably moral question of who "deserves" a particular nonprohibited method of punishment to the judgment of the legislatures that authorize the penalty. [This] Court's cases prohibiting mandatory capital sentencing schemes have no basis in the original understanding of the Eighth Amendment, and, thus, cannot justify a prohibition of sentencing schemes that mandate life-without-parole sentences for juveniles. . . .

ALITO, J., dissenting.[**]

The Court now holds that Congress and the legislatures of the 50 States are prohibited by the Constitution from identifying any category of murderers under the age of 18 who must be sentenced to life imprisonment without parole. Even a 17 1/2-year-old who sets off a bomb in a crowded mall or guns down a dozen students and teachers is a "child" and must be given a chance to persuade a judge to permit his release into society. Nothing in the Constitution supports this arrogation of legislative authority.

The Court long ago abandoned the original meaning of the Eighth Amendment, holding instead that the prohibition of "cruel and unusual punishment" embodies the "evolving standards of decency that mark the progress

---

[*] Justice Scalia joined this opinion.
[**] Justice Scalia joined this opinion.

of a maturing society." Both the provenance and philosophical basis for this
standard were problematic from the start. (Is it true that our society is inexorably evolving in the direction of greater and greater decency? Who says so,
and how did this particular philosophy of history find its way into our
fundamental law? And in any event, aren't elected representatives more likely
than unaccountable judges to reflect changing societal standards?) But at least at
the start, the Court insisted that these "evolving standards" represented something
other than the personal views of five Justices. Instead, the Court looked for
objective indicia of our society's moral standards and the trajectory of our
moral "evolution." [The] staple of this inquiry was the tallying of the positions
taken by state legislatures. . . .

Today, that [limiting] principle is entirely put to rest. . . . The two (carefully selected) cases before us concern very young defendants, and despite the
brutality and evident depravity exhibited by at least one of the petitioners, it is
hard not to feel sympathy for a 14-year-old sentenced to life without the possibility of release. But no one should be confused by the particulars of the two
cases before us. The category of murderers that the Court delicately calls "children" (murderers under the age of 18) consists overwhelmingly of young men
who are fast approaching the legal age of adulthood. Evan Miller and Kuntrell
Jackson are anomalies; much more typical are murderers like Donald Roper,
who committed a brutal thrill-killing just nine months shy of his 18th birthday.

Seventeen-year-olds commit a significant number of murders every year,
and some of these crimes are incredibly brutal. Many of these murderers are at
least as mature as the average 18-year-old. Congress and the legislatures of 43
States have concluded that at least some of these murderers should be sentenced
to prison without parole, and 28 States and the Federal Government have
decided that for some of these offenders life without parole should be
mandatory. . . .

The Eighth Amendment imposes certain limits on the sentences that
may be imposed in criminal cases, but for the most part it leaves questions of
sentencing policy to be determined by Congress and the state legislatures —
and with good reason. Determining the length of imprisonment that is
appropriate for a particular offense and a particular offender inevitably
involves a balancing of interests. If imprisonment does nothing else, it
removes the criminal from the general population and prevents him from
committing additional crimes in the outside world. When a legislature prescribes that a category of killers must be sentenced to life imprisonment, the
legislature, which presumably reflects the views of the electorate, is taking the
position that the risk that these offenders will kill again outweighs any countervailing consideration, including reduced culpability due to immaturity or
the possibility of rehabilitation. When the majority of this Court counter-
mands that democratic decision, what the majority is saying is that members
of society must be exposed to the risk that these convicted murderers, if
released from custody, will murder again.

Unless our cases change course, we will continue to march toward some
vision of evolutionary culmination that the Court has not yet disclosed. The
Constitution does not authorize us to take the country on this journey.

## NOTES

1. *Treatment of immutable characteristics: majority position.* Driven by constitutional concerns and also policy considerations, every jurisdiction has either expressly or implicitly adopted the ABA's recommendation to bar the consideration at sentencing of factors such as race, gender, religion, and national origin. But as Chapter 9 details, many sentencing practices have a disproportionate impact on these groups despite the formal legal rules.

Statutory and guideline provisions take different approaches when it comes to certain other immutable personal factors such as mental condition, physical disability, and age. See, e.g., U.S. Sentencing Guidelines Manual §§5H1.1, 5H1.3, 5H1.4 (stating that age, mental condition, and physical condition "may be relevant" at sentencing if "present to an unusual degree and distinguish the case from the typical cases covered by the guidelines"); N.C. Gen. Stat. §15A-1340.16(e)(3), (4) (providing that defendant's "mental or physical condition" and defendant's "age, immaturity, or limited mental capacity" can serve as the basis for a mitigated sentence).

2. *Age as mitigating (aggravating?) factor.* Under common law rules and throughout modern times, very young children have generally been exempted from all criminal responsibility. And because of the view that even older children are less responsible for their actions and have more potential to be redeemed even after doing wrong, every jurisdiction has special courts and legal rules for juvenile offenders. Because the punishments imposed under these special rules tend to be less severe than those imposed under the rules for adults, age serves as a mitigating factor at sentencing for young offenders who are eligible for specialized juvenile systems. Jurisdictions vary considerably in defining the exact age and circumstances when an offender will be handled as a juvenile rather than as an adult.

The Supreme Court's opinion in *Miller* includes much interesting discussion of the "diminished culpability of juveniles" and the "immaturity" and "vulnerability" of juveniles. Based on a similar set of reasons, the Court in Graham v. Florida, 130 S. Ct. 2011 (2010), held that the Eighth Amendment categorically prohibits a state from sentencing a juvenile offender to life without possibility of parole. While a state might confine an individual offender for life based on a crime committed before age 18, it must give defendants "some meaningful opportunity to obtain release based on demonstrated maturity and rehabilitation." The *Graham* opinion is reprinted in Chapter 7, anchoring a discussion of the Supreme Court's "proportionality" jurisprudence under the Eighth Amendment.

Once an offender comes within the jurisdiction of the adult criminal justice system, her age rarely serves as a definitive or formal criterion for a reduced sentence. Social science data reveals, however, that recidivism rates for older offenders are much lower than for offenders in their teens and 20s. Consequently, a sentencing system or sentencing judge concerned particularly with incapacitation goals might reasonably assign longer sentences to younger offenders and shorter sentences to older offenders. Indeed, anecdotal evidence suggests that in unstructured systems, judges and parole officials do grant a "senior sentencing discount." Structured-sentencing systems, however, have not consistently codified such sentencing discounts based on the offender's age.

3. *Mental impairments in noncapital sentencing.*    The Supreme Court in Atkins v. Virginia, 536 U.S. 304 (2002), declared the execution of the mentally retarded unconstitutional. If a mental impairment justifies a categorical reduction in the available sentence in capital cases, does it likewise justify an automatic sentence reduction in noncapital cases? The Supreme Court's opinion in *Atkins* viewed the decision by many states to exempt mentally retarded persons from the death penalty as "powerful evidence that today our society views mentally retarded offenders as categorically less culpable than the average criminal." Does this suggest that mentally retarded offenders also ought to be exempt from the strictures of mandatory sentencing provisions or guideline sentencing systems altogether? Cf. Mont. Code Ann. §46-18-222(2) (mandatory minimum sentences do not apply if "the offender's mental capacity at the time of the commission of the offense for which the offender is to be sentenced, was significantly impaired, although not so impaired as to constitute a defense to the prosecution").

At common law those with severe mental impairments could be excused from guilt altogether, but offenders with lesser impairments would usually be subject to the same punishments as mentally sound offenders. In more recent times, judges in unstructured-sentencing jurisdictions have had discretion to consider the defendant's mental condition in setting the sentence, while judges in structured-sentencing systems face varying instructions concerning the way mental retardation or mental condition ought to be considered at sentencing. See, e.g., Or. Sentencing Guidelines §213-008-0002(1)(a)(C) (providing that a mitigating departure factor can be that the "defendant's mental capacity was diminished").

In the federal system, section 5H1.3 of the federal sentencing guidelines provides that mental and emotional conditions "are not ordinarily relevant in determining whether a sentence should be outside the applicable guideline range [but] may be relevant in determining the conditions of probation or supervised release; e.g., participation in a mental health program." But another federal guidelines provision, section 5K2.13, states that a "sentence below the applicable guideline range may be warranted if the defendant committed the offense while suffering from a significantly reduced mental capacity." While making diminished capacity an "encouraged" basis for a departure, the federal guidelines further state that a court may not depart if "(1) the significantly reduced mental capacity was caused by the voluntary use of drugs or other intoxicants; (2) the facts and circumstances of the defendant's offense indicate a need to protect the public because the offense involved actual violence or a serious threat of violence; or (3) the defendant's criminal history indicates a need to incarcerate the defendant to protect the public." Similarly, the Oregon sentencing guidelines provide that a mitigating departure factor can be that the "defendant's mental capacity was diminished," but this provision expressly excludes "diminished capacity due to voluntary drug or alcohol abuse." Or. Sentencing Guidelines §213-008-0002(1)(a)(C).

4. *Procedures to determine mental retardation in capital cases.*    The unique severity of capital punishment explains in large part why many jurisdictions have statutes prohibiting the execution of the mentally retarded, and why *Atkins* drew from these legislative decisions to find in the Eighth Amendment a constitutional ban against applying the death penalty to the mentally retarded. In *Atkins* the Supreme Court did not suggest specific procedures for

determining which offenders are mentally retarded and thus exempt from the death penalty. The Court left to individual states "the task of developing appropriate ways to enforce" the rule announced in *Atkins*. If you were a legislator or a sentencing commissioner or a judge in a state that had not previously addressed this issue, what sorts of procedures would you propose? Should it be for a judge or for a jury to decide whether an offender is mentally retarded? Should an offender have the burden of proving mental retardation by a preponderance of the evidence to avoid execution, or should a prosecutor have to disprove any claim of retardation beyond a reasonable doubt? Should an inquiry about an offender's mental status occur before any indictment on a capital charge, or only after an offender has been convicted of a crime that qualifies for the death penalty?

5. *Does immutability matter?*   Is the immutability of certain personal characteristics a significant consideration in whether that characteristic should play a role at sentencing, or is the only relevant question whether the factor is related to the offender's culpability and future prospects? If immutability is an important consideration, should certain conditions such as drug dependency, treatable mental illness, or socioeconomic class be deemed immutable?

## 2.   *Circumstances Within the Defendant's Control*

A criminal conviction holds a defendant responsible for the criminal act; the criminal sentence carries the ideal of responsibility one step further. Sentencing allows the judge to fine-tune the clumsy notions of responsibility, such as those embodied in the insanity defense. A defendant who is guilty, but who is less clearly responsible than some other defendants convicted of similar crimes, will often receive a lesser sentence.

Moreover, the concept of responsibility at sentencing extends to events that happen after the crime. Some defendants take actions after their crime or even after their arrest — such as enrolling in treatment programs or making restitution to victims — to show they are amenable to rehabilitation and will not present a danger in the future. Do sentencing rules and sentencing judges treat these notions of responsibility during the crime and after the crime similarly? Do they react consistently to the various ways that defendants signal their prospects for rehabilitation?

‖   *Brian Michael Gall v. United States*   ‖
**552 U.S. 38 (2007)**

STEVENS, J.

### . . . I

In February or March 2000, petitioner Brian Gall, a second-year college student at the University of Iowa, was invited by Luke Rinderknecht to join an ongoing enterprise distributing a controlled substance popularly known as "ecstasy." Gall—who was then a user of ecstasy, cocaine, and marijuana—accepted the invitation. During the ensuing seven months, Gall delivered ecstasy pills, which he received from Rinderknecht, to other conspirators, who then sold them to consumers. He netted over $30,000.

A month or two after joining the conspiracy, Gall stopped using ecstasy. A few months after that, in September 2000, he advised Rinderknecht and other co-conspirators that he was withdrawing from the conspiracy. He has not sold illegal drugs of any kind since. He has, in the words of the District Court, "self-rehabilitated." He graduated from the University of Iowa in 2002, and moved first to Arizona, where he obtained a job in the construction industry, and later to Colorado, where he earned $18 per hour as a master carpenter. He has not used any illegal drugs since graduating from college.

After Gall moved to Arizona, he was approached by federal law enforcement agents who questioned him about his involvement in the ecstasy distribution conspiracy. Gall admitted his limited participation in the distribution of ecstasy, and the agents took no further action at that time. On April 28, 2004—approximately a year and a half after this initial interview, and three and a half years after Gall withdrew from the conspiracy—an indictment was returned in the Southern District of Iowa charging him and seven other defendants with participating in a conspiracy to distribute ecstasy, cocaine, and marijuana, that began in or about May 1996 and continued through October 30, 2002. The Government has never questioned the truthfulness of any of Gall's earlier statements or contended that he played any role in, or had any knowledge of, other aspects of the conspiracy described in the indictment. When he received notice of the indictment, Gall moved back to Iowa and surrendered to the authorities. While free on his own recognizance, Gall started his own business in the construction industry, primarily engaged in subcontracting for the installation of windows and doors. In his first year, his profits were over $2,000 per month.

Gall entered into a plea agreement with the Government, stipulating that he was "responsible for, but did not necessarily distribute himself, at least 2,500 grams of [ecstasy], or the equivalent of at least 87.5 kilograms of marijuana." In the agreement, the Government acknowledged that by "on or about September of 2000," Gall had communicated his intent to stop distributing ecstasy to Rinderknecht and other members of the conspiracy. . . .

In her presentence report, the probation officer concluded that Gall had no significant criminal history; that he was not an organizer, leader, or manager; and that his offense did not involve the use of any weapons. The report stated that Gall had truthfully provided the Government with all of the evidence he had concerning the alleged offenses, but that his evidence was not useful because he provided no new information to the agents. The report also described Gall's substantial use of drugs prior to his offense and the absence of any such use in recent years. The report recommended a sentencing range of 30 to 37 months of imprisonment.

The record of the sentencing hearing held on May 27, 2005, includes a "small flood" of letters from Gall's parents and other relatives, his fiance, neighbors, and representatives of firms doing business with him, uniformly praising his character and work ethic. . . . The AUSA did not contest any of the evidence concerning Gall's law-abiding life during the preceding five years, but . . . requested that the court impose a prison sentence within the Guidelines range.

He mentioned that two of Gall's co-conspirators had been sentenced to 30 and 35 months, respectively, but upon further questioning by the District Court, he acknowledged that neither of them had voluntarily withdrawn from the conspiracy.

The District Judge sentenced Gall to probation for a term of 36 months. In addition to making a lengthy statement on the record, the judge filed a detailed sentencing memorandum explaining his decision, and provided the following statement of reasons in his written judgment:

> The Court determined that, considering all the factors under 18 U.S.C. 3553(a), the Defendant's explicit withdrawal from the conspiracy almost four years before the filing of the Indictment, the Defendant's post-offense conduct, especially obtaining a college degree and the start of his own successful business, the support of family and friends, lack of criminal history, and his age at the time of the offense conduct, all warrant the sentence imposed, which was sufficient, but not greater than necessary to serve the purposes of sentencing. [Gall] will not be able to change or make decisions about significant circumstances in his life, such as where to live or work, which are prized liberty interests, without first seeking authorization from his Probation Officer or, perhaps, even the Court. . . .
>
> The Defendant's post-offense conduct indicates neither that he will return to criminal behavior nor that the Defendant is a danger to society. In fact, the Defendant's post-offense conduct was not motivated by a desire to please the Court or any other governmental agency, but was the pre-Indictment product of the Defendant's own desire to lead a better life.

## II

The Court of Appeals reversed and remanded for resentencing. [It] held that a sentence outside of the Guidelines range must be supported by a justification that "is proportional to the extent of the difference between the advisory range and the sentence imposed." Characterizing the difference between a sentence of probation and the bottom of Gall's advisory Guidelines range of 30 months as "extraordinary" because it amounted to "a 100% downward variance," the Court of Appeals held that such a variance must be–and here was not–supported by extraordinary circumstances.

Rather than making an attempt to quantify the value of the justifications provided by the District Judge, the Court of Appeals identified what it regarded as five separate errors in the District Judge's reasoning: (1) He gave "too much weight to Gall's withdrawal from the conspiracy"; (2) given that Gall was 21 at the time of his offense, the District Judge erroneously gave "significant weight" to studies showing impetuous behavior by persons under the age of 18; (3) he did not "properly weigh" the seriousness of Gall's offense; (4) he failed to consider whether a sentence of probation would result in "unwarranted" disparities; and (5) he placed "too much emphasis on Gall's post-offense rehabilitation." As we shall explain, we are not persuaded that these factors, whether viewed separately or in the aggregate, are sufficient to support the conclusion that the District Judge abused his discretion. . . .

## III

In United States v. Booker, 543 U.S. 220 (2005), we invalidated both the statutory provision, 18 U.S.C. §3553(b)(1), which made the Sentencing Guidelines mandatory, and §3742(e), which directed appellate courts to apply a de novo standard of review to departures from the Guidelines. As a result of our decision, the Guidelines are now advisory, and appellate review of sentencing decisions is limited to determining whether they are "reasonable." Our explanation of "reasonableness" review in the *Booker* opinion made it pellucidly clear that the familiar abuse-of-discretion standard of review now applies to appellate review of sentencing decisions.

It is also clear that a district judge must give serious consideration to the extent of any departure from the Guidelines and must explain his conclusion that an unusually lenient or an unusually harsh sentence is appropriate in a particular case with sufficient justifications. . . . In reviewing the reasonableness of a sentence outside the Guidelines range, appellate courts may therefore take the degree of variance into account and consider the extent of a deviation from the Guidelines. We reject, however, an appellate rule that requires "extraordinary" circumstances to justify a sentence outside the Guidelines range. We also reject the use of a rigid mathematical formula that uses the percentage of a departure as the standard for determining the strength of the justifications required for a specific sentence.

[Deviations] from the Guidelines range will always appear more extreme — in percentage terms — when the range itself is low, and a sentence of probation will always be a 100% departure regardless of whether the Guidelines range is 1 month or 100 years. Moreover, quantifying the variance as a certain percentage of the maximum, minimum, or median prison sentence recommended by the Guidelines gives no weight to the "substantial restriction of freedom" involved in a term of supervised release or probation. . . .

On the other side of the equation, the mathematical approach assumes the existence of some ascertainable method of assigning percentages to various justifications. Does withdrawal from a conspiracy justify more or less than, say, a 30% reduction? Does it matter that the withdrawal occurred several years ago? Is it relevant that the withdrawal was motivated by a decision to discontinue the use of drugs and to lead a better life? What percentage, if any, should be assigned to evidence that a defendant poses no future threat to society, or to evidence that innocent third parties are dependent on him? The formula is a classic example of attempting to measure an inventory of apples by counting oranges.

[A] district court should begin all sentencing proceedings by correctly calculating the applicable Guidelines range. As a matter of administration and to secure nationwide consistency, the Guidelines should be the starting point and the initial benchmark. The Guidelines are not the only consideration, however. Accordingly, after giving both parties an opportunity to argue for whatever sentence they deem appropriate, the district judge should then consider all of the §3553(a) factors to determine whether they support the sentence requested by a party. In so doing, he may not presume that the Guidelines range is reasonable. He must make an individualized assessment based on the facts presented. If he decides that an outside-Guidelines sentence is warranted, he must consider the extent of the deviation and ensure that the justification is sufficiently compelling to support the degree of the variance. We find it uncontroversial that a major departure should be supported by a more significant justification than a minor one. After settling on the appropriate sentence, he must adequately explain the chosen sentence to allow for meaningful appellate review and to promote the perception of fair sentencing.

Regardless of whether the sentence imposed is inside or outside the Guidelines range, the appellate court must review the sentence under an abuse-of-discretion standard. . . . Assuming that the district court's sentencing decision is procedurally sound, the appellate court should then consider the substantive reasonableness of the sentence imposed under an abuse-of-discretion standard. . . . If the sentence is within the Guidelines range, the appellate court may, but is not required to, apply a presumption of reasonableness. But if the sentence is outside the Guidelines range, the court may not apply a presumption of unreasonableness. It may consider the extent of the deviation, but must give due deference to the district court's decision that the §3553(a) factors, on a whole, justify the extent of the variance. The fact that the appellate court might reasonably have concluded that a different sentence was appropriate is insufficient to justify reversal of the district court.

Practical considerations also underlie this legal principle. The sentencing judge is in a superior position to find facts and judge their import under §3553(a) in the individual case. The judge sees and hears the evidence, makes credibility determinations, has full knowledge of the facts and gains insights not conveyed by the record. . . . Moreover, district courts have an institutional advantage over appellate courts in making these sorts of determinations, especially as they see so many more Guidelines sentences than appellate courts do.

It has been uniform and constant in the federal judicial tradition for the sentencing judge to consider every convicted person as an individual and every case as a unique study in the human failings that sometimes mitigate, sometimes magnify, the crime and the punishment to ensue. The . . . opinion of the Court of Appeals in this case does not reflect the requisite deference and does not support the conclusion that the District Court abused its discretion.


## IV

As an initial matter, we note that the District Judge committed no significant procedural error. He correctly calculated the applicable Guidelines range, allowed both parties to present arguments as to what they believed the appropriate sentence should be, considered all of the §3553(a) factors, and thoroughly documented his reasoning. The Court of Appeals found that the District Judge erred in failing to give proper weight to the seriousness of the offense, as required by §3553(a)(2)(A), and failing to consider whether a sentence of probation would create unwarranted disparities, as required by §3553(a)(6). We disagree. . . .

The Court of Appeals concluded that "the district court did not properly weigh the seriousness of Gall's offense" because it "ignored the serious health risks ecstasy poses." Contrary to the Court of Appeals' conclusion, the District Judge plainly did consider the seriousness of the offense. It is true that the District Judge did not make specific reference to the (unquestionably significant) health risks posed by ecstasy, but the prosecutor did not raise ecstasy's effects at the sentencing hearing. [It] was not incumbent on the District Judge to raise every conceivably relevant issue on his own initiative.

The Government's legitimate concern that a lenient sentence for a serious offense threatens to promote disrespect for the law is at least to some extent offset by the fact that seven of the eight defendants in this case have been sentenced to significant prison terms. Moreover, the unique facts of Gall's situation provide support for the District Judge's conclusion that, in Gall's case, "a sentence of imprisonment may work to promote not respect, but derision, of the law if the law is viewed as merely a means to dispense harsh punishment without taking into account the real conduct and circumstances involved in sentencing."

Section 3553(a)(6) requires judges to consider "the need to avoid unwarranted sentence disparities among defendants with similar records who have been found guilty of similar conduct." [It] is perfectly clear that the District Judge considered the need to avoid unwarranted disparities, but also considered the need to avoid unwarranted similarities among other co-conspirators who were not similarly situated. The District Judge regarded Gall's voluntary withdrawal as a reasonable basis for giving him a less severe sentence than the three codefendants discussed with the AUSA, who neither withdrew from the conspiracy nor rehabilitated themselves as Gall had done. . . . Since the District Court committed no procedural error, the only question for the Court of Appeals was whether the sentence was reasonable — i.e., whether the District Judge abused his discretion in determining that the §3553(a) factors supported a sentence of probation and justified a substantial deviation from the Guidelines range. . . .

### V

The Court of Appeals gave virtually no deference to the District Court's decision that the §3553(a) factors justified a significant variance in this case. Although the Court of Appeals correctly stated that the appropriate standard of review was abuse of discretion, it engaged in an analysis that more closely resembled de novo review of the facts presented and determined that, in its view, the degree of variance was not warranted.

The Court of Appeals thought that the District Court "gave too much weight to Gall's withdrawal from the conspiracy because the court failed to acknowledge the significant benefit Gall received" from being subject [to sentencing guidelines less severe than an amended version that would have applied to later conduct]. This criticism is flawed in that it ignores the critical relevance of Gall's voluntary withdrawal, a circumstance that distinguished his conduct not only from that of all his codefendants, but from the vast majority of defendants convicted of conspiracy in federal court. The District Court quite reasonably attached great weight to the fact that Gall voluntarily withdrew from the conspiracy after deciding, on his own initiative, to change his life. This lends strong support to the District Court's conclusion that Gall is not going to return to criminal behavior and is not a danger to society. Compared to a case where the offender's rehabilitation occurred after he was charged with a crime, the District Court here had greater justification for believing Gall's turnaround was genuine, as distinct from a transparent attempt to build a mitigation case.

The Court of Appeals thought the District Judge "gave significant weight to an improper factor" when he compared Gall's sale of ecstasy when he was a 21-year-old adult to the "impetuous and ill-considered" actions of persons under the age of 18. . . . In that portion of his sentencing memorandum, however, the judge was discussing the "character of the defendant," not the nature of his offense. He noted that Gall's criminal history included a ticket for underage drinking when he was 18 years old and possession of marijuana that was contemporaneous with his offense in this case. In summary, the District Judge observed that all of Gall's criminal history "including the present offense, occurred when he was twenty-one-years old or younger" and appeared "to stem from his addictions to drugs and alcohol." The District Judge [explained the relevance of a defendant's immaturity as follows]:

> Immaturity at the time of the offense conduct is not an inconsequential consideration. Recent studies on the development of the human brain conclude that human brain development may not become complete until the age of twenty-five. [The recent National Institute of Health] report confirms that there is no bold line demarcating at what age a person reaches full maturity. While age does not excuse behavior, a sentencing court should account for age when inquiring into the conduct of a defendant.

Given the dramatic contrast between Gall's behavior before he joined the conspiracy and his conduct after withdrawing, it was not unreasonable for the District Judge to view Gall's immaturity at the time of the offense as a mitigating factor, and his later behavior as a sign that he had matured and would not engage in such impetuous and ill-considered conduct in the future. . . .

The Court of Appeals clearly disagreed with the District Judge's conclusion that consideration of the §3553(a) factors justified a sentence of probation. . . . But it is not for the Court of Appeals to decide de novo whether the justification for a variance is sufficient or the sentence reasonable. On abuse-of-discretion review, the Court of Appeals should have given due deference to the District Court's reasoned and reasonable decision that the §3553(a) factors, on the whole, justified the sentence. . . .

ALITO, J., dissenting.

[According to *Booker*, the federal courts must treat the sentencing guidelines] as "effectively advisory," and . . . individual sentencing decisions are subject to appellate review for "reasonableness." The *Booker* remedial opinion did not explain exactly what it meant by a system of "advisory" guidelines or by "reasonableness" review, and the opinion is open to different interpretations. [The best] reading is that sentencing judges must still give the Guidelines' policy decisions some significant weight and that the courts of appeals must still police compliance. . . .

Read fairly, the opinion of the Court of Appeals holds that the District Court did not properly exercise its sentencing discretion because it did not give sufficient weight to the policy decisions reflected in the Guidelines.

Petitioner was convicted of a serious crime, conspiracy to distribute "ecstasy." He distributed thousands of pills and made between $30,000 and $40,000 in profit. Although he eventually left the conspiracy, he did so because he was worried about apprehension. The Sentencing Guidelines called for a term of imprisonment of 30 to 37 months, but the District Court imposed a term of probation. . . .

If the question before us was whether a reasonable jurist could conclude that a sentence of probation was sufficient in this case to serve the purposes of punishment set out in 18 U.S.C. §3553(a)(2), the District Court's decision could not be disturbed. But because I believe that sentencing judges must still give some significant weight to the Guidelines sentencing range, the Commission's policy statements, and the need to avoid unwarranted sentencing disparities, I agree with the Eighth Circuit that the District Court did not properly exercise its discretion.

Appellate review for abuse of discretion is not an empty formality. [When] a trial court is required by statute to take specified factors into account in making a discretionary decision, the trial court must be reversed if it ignored or slighted a factor that Congress has deemed pertinent. Here, the District Court "slighted" the factors set out in 18 U.S.C. §§3553(a)(3), (4), and (5) — namely, the Guidelines sentencing range, the Commission's policy statements, and the need to avoid unwarranted sentencing disparities. . . .

The court listed five considerations as justification for a sentence of probation: (1) petitioner's "voluntary and explicit withdrawal from the conspiracy," (2) his "exemplary behavior while on bond," (3) "the support manifested by family and friends," (4) "the lack of criminal history, especially a complete lack of any violent criminal history," (5) and his age at the time of the offense, 21.

Two of the considerations that the District Court cited — "the support manifested by family and friends" and his age — amounted to a direct rejection of the Sentencing Commission's authority to decide the most basic issues of sentencing policy. In the Sentencing Reform Act, Congress required the Sentencing Commission to consider and decide whether certain specified factors — including "age," "education," "previous employment record," "physical condition," "family ties and responsibilities," and "community ties" — "have any relevance to the nature [and] extent . . . of an appropriate sentence." 28 U.S.C. §994(d). These factors come up with great frequency, and judges in the pre-Sentencing Reform Act era disagreed regarding their relevance. Indeed, some of these factors were viewed by some judges as reasons for increasing a sentence and by others as reasons for decreasing a sentence. For example, if a defendant had a job, a supportive family, and friends, those factors were sometimes viewed as justifying a harsher sentence on the ground that the defendant had squandered the opportunity to lead a law-abiding life. Alternatively, those same factors were sometimes viewed as justifications for a more lenient sentence on the ground that a defendant with a job and a network of support would be less likely to return to crime. If each judge is free to implement his or her personal views on such matters, sentencing disparities are inevitable.

In response to Congress' direction to establish uniform national sentencing policies regarding these common sentencing factors, the Sentencing Commission issued policy statements concluding that "age," "family ties," and "community ties" are relevant to sentencing only in unusual cases. See United States Sentencing Commission, Guidelines Manual §§5H1.1 (age),

5H1.6 (family and community ties). The District Court in this case did not claim that there was anything particularly unusual about petitioner's family or community ties or his age, but the court cited these factors as justifications for a sentence of probation. Although the District Court was obligated to take into account the Commission's policy statements and the need to avoid sentencing disparities, the District Court rejected Commission policy statements that are critical to the effort to reduce such disparities.

The District Court relied on petitioner's lack of criminal history, but criminal history (or the lack thereof) is a central factor in the calculation of the Guidelines range. Petitioner was given credit for his lack of criminal history in the calculation of his Guidelines sentence. Consequently, giving petitioner additional credit for this factor was nothing more than an expression of disagreement with the policy determination reflected in the Guidelines range.

The District Court mentioned petitioner's "exemplary behavior while on bond," but this surely cannot be regarded as a weighty factor.

Finally, the District Court was plainly impressed by petitioner's "voluntary and explicit withdrawal from the conspiracy." As the Government argues, the legitimate strength of this factor is diminished by petitioner's motivation in withdrawing. He did not leave the conspiracy for reasons of conscience, and he made no effort to stop the others in the ring. He withdrew because he had become afraid of apprehension. While the District Court was within its rights in regarding this factor and petitioner's self-rehabilitation as positive considerations, they are not enough, in light of the Guidelines' call for a 30- to 37-month prison term, to warrant a sentence of probation. . . .

## PROBLEM 5-5. TREATMENT AND TIMING

Review again the facts from State v. Joshua Fowler, reprinted earlier in this chapter. Suppose that Fowler's abuse of alcohol and methamphetamines during the three days before the crime was typical. The day after he committed the crime, Fowler realized that his addictions had become a major problem, and he sought help by enrolling in a treatment program. During the 18 months between the crime and the time he turned himself in to authorities, Fowler made real progress in the program.

You are the judge who must sentence Fowler for first-degree armed robbery. In Washington, the standard sentencing range for the offense is 31 to 41 months, plus a mandatory 60-month firearm enhancement penalty. Fowler asks for an exceptional sentence of 6 months, given that he voluntarily enrolled in a treatment program before his arrest and has nearly completed the program. If the relevant law leaves you with discretion on this question, would you impose a sentence below the standard range based on this factor?

Now suppose that federal authorities charged Fowler with illegal possession of a weapon, and the guidelines produce an adjusted offense level of 9, resulting in a presumptive prison term of 4 to 10 months for somebody with no prior criminal history. As a federal judge, would you depart below the guideline range and grant a probationary sentence based on Fowler's enrollment in the treatment program?

Finally, let us consider the timing of Fowler's decision to undertake treatment. As a sentencing judge, would you still consider Fowler's treatment in setting the criminal sentence if he began his treatment after arrest but before prosecution? After conviction but before sentencing? Would you grant a motion to reconsider the sentence if he began treatment after you imposed the original sentence?

A policy statement in the federal guidelines addresses the last question. Section 5K2.19 provides that "post-sentencing rehabilitative efforts, even if exceptional" are not an appropriate basis for a downward departure when resentencing the defendant for the original offense. But post-sentencing rehabilitation can give corrections authorities reason to shorten the defendant's period of "supervised release" to be served at the end of a prison term. Note also that the federal policy statement does not restrict departures based on extraordinary post-offense rehabilitation that occurs *before* the original sentencing, even if it begins after arrest or after conviction. Appellate courts often view post-offense rehabilitative efforts as part of acceptance of responsibility under §3E1.1. In post-*Booker* cases courts may deem post-offense rehabilitation a §3553(a) factor in sentencing below the otherwise applicable guideline range. See United States v. Clay, 483 F.3d 739 (11th Cir. 2007). Should the federal guidelines discourage or prohibit judges from reducing sentences based on any post-arrest rehabilitation efforts?

## PROBLEM 5-6.   RESTITUTION AND REHABILITATION

Cattle rancher William Oligmueller misrepresented the number of cattle he owned in an application for a loan from First State Bank. The bank discovered the fraud when bank officers arrived at the ranch to inspect the collateral. At the time the officers discovered the fraud, Oligmueller owed the bank approximately $894,000 on the loan, which was secured by livestock, feed, and machinery.

Oligmueller began liquidating his assets in September 1997 to initiate repayment to the bank. He tended the crops until harvest, and the livestock until sale, increasing the price that the bank ultimately received through the sales. He often worked 16-hour days. He loaded the hay trucks for the bank. Oligmueller pledged assets not previously pledged to the bank, including his ranch. He turned over to the bank his life insurance policy and his wife's certificate of deposit, and he and his wife sold their home and moved in with their daughter. Oligmueller also took a job with a farm supply company and set up a lawn mower repair business. In addition, he sent to the bank approximately half of his Social Security check each month to pay his debts.

By October 1998, through asset liquidation, Oligmueller had repaid the bank approximately $808,000. The bank also received $28,000 in cash payments directly from Oligmueller. This brought the bank's loss down to approximately $58,000.

A federal grand jury indicted Oligmueller in August 1998 for making false statements to the bank. He pled guilty. You are the district court judge who will preside at the upcoming sentencing hearing.

Under section 2F1.1 of the U.S. Sentencing Guidelines, the amount of loss used to determine a sentence for a fraudulent loan application is the greater of the actual loss to the victim or the intended loss. In determining the amount of actual loss, the application notes to the guidelines say that a sentencing court cannot consider payments made to the bank after the fraud is discovered unless the payments are the result of the sale of pledged assets. Of the $808,000 paid to the bank from the sale of assets, only $65,000 resulted from the sale of pledged assets. The sentencing guidelines also allow either a downward or an upward departure if the amount of loss significantly overstates or understates the risk to the lending institution. See U.S. Sentencing Guidelines Manual §2F1.1, cmt. n.8(b).

Oligmueller argues that his offense level should be reduced based on his "acceptance of responsibility." Commentary to the sentencing guidelines lists "post-offense efforts to rehabilitate" and "voluntary payment of restitution before adjudication of guilt" as two factors that tend to show when a defendant qualifies for a two-level reduction for "acceptance of responsibility." U.S. Sentencing Guidelines Manual §3E1.1, cmt. n.1. Oligmueller also requests a downward departure from the guideline sentence based on his extraordinary efforts at rehabilitation.

As a sentencing judge, how will you calculate the amount of loss (and thus the initial offense level) involved in this fraud? Will you reduce the offense level based on Oligmueller's acceptance of responsibility? Will you grant any further downward departure? How much restitution will you order him to pay? Cf. United States v. Oligmueller, 198 F.3d 669 (8th Cir. 1999). Would you deem Oligmueller's conduct sufficient to lead to a sentence outside the guidelines in light of §3553(a)?

## NOTES

1. *Post-arrest efforts at rehabilitation.*  The opinions in *Gall* note that the defendant's "self-rehabilitation" efforts were unusual because they occurred before he was arrested. Defendants with substance abuse problems more commonly enroll themselves in treatment programs after arrest, but before the time of conviction or sentencing. Does this action suggest an effort to manipulate the sentence or a genuine willingness to fix the root problem behind the crime? In the federal courts, it is clear that truly "extraordinary" rehabilitation efforts could create a basis for a downward departure and may now be considered as a possible justification for a sentence outside the guidelines. See United States v. Clay, 483 F.3d 739 (11th Cir. 2007) (district court's consideration of extraordinary post-offense rehabilitation from drug addiction found reasonable). A number of state systems also allow drug treatment or even amenability to treatment as a basis for a mitigated sentence. See Md. Sentencing Guidelines §13.2(7) (providing as a reason for a departure an "offender's commitment to substance abuse treatment or other therapeutic program"); Or. Sentencing Guidelines §213-008-0002(I) (providing for a mitigated sentence when "offender is amenable to treatment and an appropriate treatment program is available to which the offender can be admitted within a reasonable period of time; the

treatment program is likely to be more effective than the presumptive prison term in reducing the risk of offender recidivism; and the probation sentence will serve community safety interests by promoting offender reformation"). As a sentencing judge, how would you respond during a resentencing hearing to evidence of an offender's post-*sentencing* rehabilitation? See Pepper v. United States, 131 S. Ct. 1229 (2011) (judge may consider post-sentencing rehabilitation when resentencing a defendant after his initial sentence was set aside on appeal).

2. *Addiction at sentencing.*   The fact that a defendant was extremely intoxicated at the time of the crime can, in some states and for some crimes, lead to an acquittal because the intoxication may have prevented the defendant from forming a criminal intent. But this argument rarely succeeds as a complete defense to criminal charges. Cf. Montana v. Egelhoff, 518 U.S. 37 (1996) (finding constitutionally permissible Montana's statute barring consideration of intoxication as a defense). Intoxication or addiction at the time of an offense matters more often at the sentencing stage. In unstructured sentencing jurisdictions, the judge usually has discretion (and little direction) concerning how to consider the defendant's addiction in setting the sentence. Does substance abuse share any features with mental impairments such as those considered in the previous section? Should the law insist on the same sentence for two defendants, one whose addiction contributed to the crime and another who faced no substance abuse problems?

In most jurisdictions with more structured sentencing rules, the law instructs a sentencing judge to give limited or no consideration to substance abuse. Under the federal guidelines, section 5H1.4 states that drug or alcohol dependence or abuse "ordinarily is not a reason for imposing a sentence below the guidelines. Substance abuse is highly correlated to an increased propensity to commit crime." Substance abuse can lead a judge to order treatment during a prison term or a period of supervised release. See U.S. Sentencing Guidelines Manual §5D1.3(d)(4). In other jurisdictions, this result has been reached through case law. See, e.g., State v. Gaines, 859 P.2d 36, 42 (Wash. 1993) (holding that "drug addiction and its casual role in an addict's criminal offense may not properly serve as justification for a durational departure from the standard range").

Can an argument be made that sentencing rules should authorize (or even require) judges to treat addiction as an aggravating factor that can (or must) increase a sentence? See Ariz. Stat. §41-1604.15 ("Notwithstanding any law to the contrary, any person who is convicted of a violent crime . . . that is committed while the person is under the influence of marijuana, a dangerous drug or a narcotic drug . . . is not eligible for probation or release on any basis until the entire sentence has been served"; statute passed by voter initiative also providing for nonprison treatment sanctions for drug possession offenses).

3. *Education and employment.*   There is an obvious correlation between employment and crime. A person with a steady job is less likely to commit a crime. Further, education can create skills that make a person easier to employ. Should a sentencing judge consider the defendant's education, vocational skills, and employment record as a basis for choosing a lower sentence? As a sentencing

judge, would you find post-arrest *changes* in education or employment status to be more significant than education or employment at the time of the crime?

In the federal system, sections 5H1.2 and 5H1.5 of the sentencing guidelines provide that education, vocational skills, and employment record are "not ordinarily relevant in determining whether a sentence should be outside the applicable guideline range," but they can be relevant in selecting appropriate conditions for probation or community service activities. What reasons could explain the reluctance to consider education, vocational skills, and employment record in the federal system?

The consideration of these factors in state systems varies considerably. Compare Minn. Sentencing Guidelines II.D.1 (precluding departures based on "employment factors" or "educational attainment") with Delaware Sentencing Accountability Commission, Benchbook 2006 (providing for an exceptional sentence below the presumptive range if the "offender is gainfully employed and will more than likely lose his/her job if the sentencing standard is imposed") and Brian Netter, Using Group Statistics to Sentence Individual Criminals: An Ethical and Statistical Critique of the Virginia Risk Assessment Program, 97 J. Crim. L. & Criminology 699 (2007) (criticizing Virginia state guidelines that treat lack of employment at time of crime as a risk factor in deciding whether offender qualifies for shorter sentence).

4. *Voluntary restitution before sentencing.*   Most state systems allow the judge to consider voluntary restitution as a basis for reducing a sentence. See Wash. Code §9.94A.535(1)(b) (mitigating circumstance present if "[b]efore detection, the defendant compensated, or made a good faith effort to compensate, the victim of the criminal conduct for any damage or injury sustained"); Fla. Stat. Ann. §921.0016(4)(h) (authorizing a departure if "[b]efore the identity of the defendant was determined, the victim was substantially compensated"). Is it realistic, as many of these statutes require, to expect an offender to make restitution before his crime is detected? As Problem 5-6 indicates, the federal system allows a judge to consider voluntary restitution in several contexts. What features does voluntary restitution share with post-offense addiction treatment as a mitigating factor? Does voluntary restitution give more affluent defendants a chance to "buy" a lower sentence?

5. *Federal policy change on offender circumstances.*   Perhaps in part in response to *Gall* and to an increasing number of district judges referencing offender circumstances when deciding to sentence below applicable guideline ranges after *Booker*, the U.S. Sentencing Commission revised the policy statements in Chapter Five, Part H, addressing specific offender characteristics. The policy statements originally deemed age, mental and emotional conditions, physical condition, and military service "not ordinarily relevant" to deciding whether a sentence should include a departure outside the guidelines. The new proposed guidelines policy statements now state that age, mental and emotional conditions, physical condition, and military service "may be relevant" in determining whether a departure is warranted if these factors are "present to an unusual degree and distinguish the case from the typical cases." The policy statements for other commonly discussed offender circumstances, factors such as family circumstances and community service, were not amended and they remain

subject to the Sentencing Commission's admonition that such factors are "not ordinarily relevant" in determining whether a departure is warranted.

Does it make sense to change policy for age, mental and emotional conditions, physical conditions, and military service, but not for family circumstances and employment? Do you think there are certain types of offenders who will be especially likely to press arguments for departures based on these new guidelines? Is there a risk that those defendants with the resources to hire psychologists to produce a report asserting the defendant suffers from mental and emotional conditions will benefit disproportionately from these new guidelines?

## 3.   Social Context of the Offender

Even offenders who might be described as loners have a lifetime of social history and interpersonal connections. Should such social contexts play a role in sentencing decision making? Consider what theoretical grounds might support consideration or exclusion of such factors at sentencing.

|| **United States v. Fadya Husein** ||
|| 478 F.3d 318 (6th Cir. 2007) ||

GILMAN, J.

Fadya Husein pled guilty to federal charges relating to her role in the distribution of 763 pills of ecstasy, a controlled substance. A probation officer calculated her advisory Guidelines range to be between 37 and 46 months in prison. Prior to sentencing, Husein moved the district court to grant a downward departure based on extraordinary family circumstances. Husein alleged that her father was totally incapacitated due to the effects of several strokes that he had recently suffered, and that the round-the-clock care that she provided both to him and to her three younger minor siblings was "irreplaceable." A court-ordered home visit by Husein's probation officer subsequently confirmed these allegations.

Acting pursuant to United States Sentencing Guidelines (U.S.S.G.) §§5H1.6 and 5K2.0, as well as 18 U.S.C. §3553(a), the district court concluded that Husein's family circumstances were in fact extraordinary, and therefore granted her motion for a downward departure. The result was a noncustodial sentence of 3 years' supervised release, which included an initial term of 270 days of home confinement. As a formality, the district court also imposed a one-day term of custodial imprisonment, but Husein was given credit for already having served that time.

The government argues on appeal that certain post-sentencing . . . developments undermine the basis for Husein's sentence and, in the alternative, that even based on the facts in the record alone, the departure granted by the district court was an abuse of discretion and/or unreasonable in light of *Booker*. For the reasons set forth below, we affirm the judgment of the district court.

## I. BACKGROUND

### A. *Factual Background*

In August and September of 2004, Fadya Husein participated in two transactions involving the sale of ecstasy near her home in Dearborn, Michigan. She was physically present for both transactions, which took place in or around the cars of the other individuals who were indicted along with her. Husein was neither a buyer nor a seller in either transaction, and she was not the source of the ecstasy pills exchanged. But she did help to arrange the meetings by putting Mohammed Nasser, "the number one Defendant in this case" according to the government, in contact with the other indicted individuals. In her guilty plea, Husein admitted these basic facts.

Husein is 25 years of age and the oldest of five children. She has three brothers and one sister, who were 21, 15, 11, and 17 years of age, respectively, at the time of sentencing. All of the siblings live together in Dearborn, Michigan, with the exception of Husein's eldest brother Fady, who resides in Florida. Husein married Tarek Hussein in 2001, but they separated in 2003 and have had no contact since. She stayed in school through the eleventh grade and is currently pursuing a GED. Husein works as a packager at a factory in Sterling Heights, Michigan. Until her father's death in February of 2006, she and her 46-year-old mother had alternated shifts at the factory to ensure that at all times an adult would be at home to attend to her father.

This appeal principally concerns the healthcare needs of Husein's father, as well as the overall financial condition of the Husein household, at the time of sentencing. The district court provided a thorough summary of the relevant facts during the October 2005 sentencing hearing:

> The Defendant's father suffered a stroke seven years ago, after which various organs began to fail. He was placed on dialysis to treat chronic kidney failure. Mr. Husein also suffers from coronary artery disease, diabetes, hypertension and cardiomyopathy. Several weeks ago he suffered another stroke. He was taken to the hospital on September 14th due to complications from renal failure, dementia and fluid on the brain. These conditions, according to Mr. Weidemeyer's [Husein's probation officer] visit to the family on September 15th, 2005, have left Mr. Husein paralyzed on his right side, unable to use the restroom without assistance, unable to walk, barely able to talk. . . .
>
> Mr. Husein does not receive financial assistance from Social Security. Therefore, Defendant says that she and her mother provide for all of the family's financial and other needs. . . .
>
> Additionally, Defendant Husein is the only member of the household with a valid driver's license and says that she is responsible for transporting her siblings as necessary and performing all other functions that require an automobile. Defendant also says that she helps the youngest child with homework and assists in cooking, cleaning and shopping. . . .
>
> Miss Husein's day begins as early as six a.m. and ends at 11 p.m. each day. At six [a.m.], she and her mother work or depart for work at [Volt] Services in Sterling Heights. At 10 a.m., Miss Husein drives home everyday to administer her father's medicine and feed him through his feeding tube. I believe she returns to work at 2:30 [p.m.], picks up her younger siblings from middle school, drives them home and returns to work again. At 4:30 [p.m.], the Defendant drives her mother home from work and then returns to work

until 11 p.m. She reports that she works approximately 65 hours per week and that she's responsible for 50% of the family income; that all of her income is used to pay the home mortgage and the mortgage is in her name. . . .

### B.   Procedural Background

. . . Husein pled guilty to [conspiracy to possess and distribute ecstasy and two counts of unlawfully aiding and abetting in the distribution of ecstasy]. Prior to sentencing, she filed a motion requesting that the district court grant a downward departure in light of Husein's extraordinary family circumstances, specifically the condition of her dying father. The government opposed the motion, arguing, among other things, that Husein and the care that she provided to her father were not "irreplaceable."

[The] district court concluded that Husein "has presented sufficient facts to warrant a departure under U.S.S.G. §5H1.6, and the Court will grant the [defendant's] motion." The court based this conclusion in large part on its earlier finding that Husein was irreplaceable to her family: . . . "It appears that there is no one else available to fill Defendant's role if she were incarcerated."

The district court then imposed a noncustodial sentence of 3 years' supervised release, which included an initial 270-day term of home confinement. . . . At the conclusion of the sentencing hearing, the district court offered Husein the following words of advice:

> Miss Husein, the sentence is imposed in large part because the Court has reviewed the Presentence Investigation Report and believes that . . . your family is going to benefit more by your presence than society is going to benefit from your incarceration. But the sentence in no way is meant to minimize what you did and your participation in this crime, and we hope that this is an adequate enough deterrent to you so that you don't engage in criminal activity in the future.
>
> You have a family that obviously depends on you a great deal and if you do anything that is violative of the conditions that are set on you, you could find yourself back here or in front of some other Court and another Judge may not give you this break that you are asking for and that we granted today.

The government timely appealed the district court's ruling in regard to Husein's sentence.

### II.   ANALYSIS

We read the government's briefs as presenting two distinct arguments: (1) that certain facts discovered by the government after sentencing would have necessarily altered the district court's conclusion that Husein's family circumstances were extraordinary, and (2) that, even ignoring these new facts, the lengthy downward departure granted by the court on account of extraordinary family circumstances was still an abuse of discretion and/or unreasonable in light of 18 U.S.C. §3553(a). These arguments will be addressed in reverse order. . . .

## B. Husein's Family Circumstances

### 1. The District Court Did Not Abuse Its Discretion

The government correctly notes that even though the Guidelines are no longer mandatory, sentencing courts still must consider "any pertinent policy statement" contained therein. See 18 U.S.C. §3553(a)(5). And, to be sure, §5H1.6 is one such statement. It provides in pertinent part that "family ties and responsibilities are not ordinarily relevant in determining whether a departure may be warranted." This, in turn, makes family circumstances a "discouraged" factor under the Guidelines. . . .

But this policy statement alone does not render the district court's decision to grant Husein a downward departure based on family circumstances an abuse of discretion. [When] a district court departs downward on the basis of a discouraged factor such as family circumstances, those circumstances must be "exceptional." U.S.S.G. §5K2.0(a)(4) ("An offender characteristic or other circumstance identified in . . . the guidelines as not ordinarily relevant in determining whether a departure is warranted may be relevant to this determination only if such offender characteristic or other circumstance is present to an exceptional degree.").

This court has not yet articulated a set of factors to consider in determining what constitutes "exceptional" or "extraordinary" family circumstances. It has instead resorted to a less structured comparative approach that takes the facts of a given case and compares them to the facts and holdings of other cases also involving departures for family circumstances. Fortunately, the recent commentary added to §5H1.6 offers substantial guidance by requiring the presence of the following four "circumstances" before a determination of extraordinariness may be made:

> (i) The defendant's service of a sentence within the applicable guideline range will cause a substantial, direct, and specific loss of essential caretaking, or essential financial support, to the defendant's family.
> (ii) The loss of caretaking or financial support substantially exceeds the harm ordinarily incident to incarceration for a similarly situated defendant. For example, the fact that the defendant's family might incur some degree of financial hardship or suffer to some extent from the absence of a parent through incarceration is not in itself sufficient as a basis for departure because such hardship or suffering is of a sort ordinarily incident to incarceration.
> (iii) *The loss of caretaking or financial support is one for which no effective remedial or ameliorative programs reasonably are available, making the defendant's caretaking or financial support irreplaceable to the defendant's family.*
> (iv) The departure effectively will address the loss of caretaking or financial support.

U.S.S.G. §5H1.6, ct. 1(B) (emphasis added). . . .

The government argues [on appeal] that because "there were untapped resources available to the family," Husein was not irreplaceable. Specifically, the government refers to Husein's oldest sister Shadya, Husein's mother Fizan, Husein's oldest brother Fady, and unnamed "friends, other extended family members, or neighbors [who] *might have been* able to render assistance in Mr. Husein's care." (Emphasis added.) But the mere existence of potential alternative sources of assistance or care is not sufficient to undermine a claim of irreplaceability. Instead, as the wording of the Guidelines makes clear, the alternatives must also be "reasonably available," which has been understood to mean "feasible" and "relatively comparable" to the defendant.

None of the alternatives suggested by the government meets this standard. Although the government is correct in noting that Shadya Husein "was only three months shy of her eighteenth birthday at the time of sentencing," she was also a full-time high-school student at the time. Fizan Husein was an even less feasible option. She alternated shifts with Fadya at the factory in Sterling Heights in order to ensure that one adult would be home at all times to attend to Husein's father. If the district court had sent Fadya to jail, her mother Fizan would have been forced to quit her job and stay home. But Fizan was the family's only source of income aside from Fadya, because Fadya's father was not receiving any Social Security benefits. Jailing Fadya, in other words, not only would have forced her mother to remain at home, but would have put the entire family on welfare. This fact alone strongly suggests infeasibility.

Finally, Fady Husein lived in Florida, did not have a job, and was unwilling to "step up to the plate" to help his family in Michigan. Fizan herself said that her son "does not help the family in any way. He visits us on occasion, but he doesn't have a job. *He will not come back to live here no matter what happens to Fadya.*" (Emphasis added.) In any event, the district court's conclusion that Fady was not a feasible alternative "financially or otherwise" was based not only on the evidence offered by Husein, but also on the court's own investigation.

The one obvious nonfamilial alternative that neither party mentions—and that the district court failed to consider at sentencing—was for Husein's father to have gone to a hospital for professional care. [The Husein family, however,] would not have been able to afford the hospital bills. We recognize that the options of Medicaid and/or hospice treatment might have been available, but the government never suggested them as alternatives.

[In United States v. Reed, 264 F.3d 640 (6th Cir. 2001), the appellate] court held that the district court had in fact abused its discretion in departing downward 13 levels to account in part for the money-laundering defendant's role in helping to care for her sister's five children. A psychiatrist-prepared assessment had deemed *Reed* "the glue that holds this family together" for her role in supervising her "dysfunctional" sister and raising her sister's children. But *Reed* . . . is distinguishable from the present case because Reed, unlike Husein, was not living with or financially supporting the nieces and nephews there in question, and in fact took extended, sometimes several-months-long vacations to Jamaica every year. . . .

We therefore conclude that the district court did not abuse its discretion by departing downward under §5H1.6. As noted, however, we must still review the resulting one-day prison sentence for reasonableness within the meaning of *Booker* and 18 U.S.C. §3553(a).

### 2. Husein's Sentence Was Both Procedurally and Substantively Reasonable

In the sentencing memorandum that she submitted to the district court, Husein argued that she was entitled to the noncustodial sentence that she ultimately received with or "even without a downward departure from the guidelines" under §5H1.6. Post-*Booker* caselaw confirms Husein's understanding that family circumstances can form the basis of either a Guidelines-authorized departure or a non-Guidelines, §3553(a)-based departure, also known as a variance. . . .

*a. Procedural Reasonableness* We review sentences post-*Booker* for reasonableness. Under the law of this circuit, reasonableness has both procedural and substantive components. A sentence is procedurally unreasonable if the district judge fails to "consider" the applicable Guidelines range or neglects to "consider" the other factors listed in 18 U.S.C. §3553(a), and instead simply selects what the judge deems an appropriate sentence without such required consideration. . . .

A review of the record in the present case compels the conclusion that Husein's one-day sentence was procedurally reasonable. In arriving at this sentence, the district court considered facts that correspond to five of the seven §3553(a) factors. And the seventh §3553(a) factor — "the need to provide restitution to any victims of the offense" — was inapplicable to Husein's case because, as the PSR makes clear, "there is no identifiable victim."

Regarding the first factor, the district court amply considered the "nature and circumstances" of Husein's offense as well as her "history and characteristics." At various points during the sentencing hearing, the court addressed the degree of Husein's participation in the ecstasy transactions, the nature of her relationship with the relevant buyers and sellers, and the amount of ecstasy involved. The district court also considered Husein's background, including her financial and employment record, her lack of a criminal record, and, obviously, her family circumstances.

Despite the government's argument to the contrary, the district court also considered the second §3553(a) factor, which directs the sentencing court to consider, among other things, "the seriousness of the offense" and the need "to afford adequate deterrence to criminal conduct," including "further crimes of the defendant." The court explicitly determined that the sentence . . . would act as a sufficient deterrent to Husein despite the seriousness of her crime. . . .

Regarding the third, fourth, and fifth factors, the district court considered the availability of both custodial and noncustodial sentencing options, the applicable Guidelines range of 37 to 46 months in prison, and also, as noted above, the Sentencing Commission's stated policy of discouraging the invocation of family circumstances as a ground for a downward departure.

The only applicable factor that the district court appears not to have considered is the sixth factor, which references "the need to avoid unwarranted sentence disparities among defendants with similar records who have been found guilty of similar conduct." To be sure, as this court recently emphasized in United States v. Davis, 458 F.3d 491, 499 (6th Cir. 2006), drastic departures from the applicable Guidelines range typically leave "no room to make reasoned distinctions" between the fortunate defendant and others who might be more deserving. But, as discussed in the substantive-reasonableness analysis below, affirming Husein's sentence in the present case would not be contrary to the goal of allowing for "reasoned distinctions" that §3553(a)(6) codifies. . . .

*b. Substantive Reasonableness*   Even if a sentence is calculated properly, i.e., the Guidelines were properly applied and the district court clearly considered the §3553(a) factors and explained its reasoning, a sentence can yet be unreasonable. A sentence is substantively unreasonable if the district court selects the sentence arbitrarily, bases the sentence on impermissible factors, fails to consider pertinent §3553(a) factors or gives an unreasonable amount of weight to any pertinent factor.

Although within-Guidelines sentences receive a presumption of reasonableness in this circuit, a sentence outside of the Guidelines range — either higher or lower — is not presumptively *un*reasonable. . . . Rather, our reasonableness review is in light of the §3553(a) factors which the district court felt justified such a variance. In reviewing outside-the-Guidelines sentences such as the one imposed in the present case, accordingly, we apply a form of proportionality review: the farther the judge's sentence departs from the guidelines sentence, the more compelling the justification based on factors in section 3553(a) must be. . . .

As an initial matter, the offense to which Husein pled guilty, 21 U.S.C. §841(b)(1)(C), does not mandate a minimum sentence. (The statutory range is 0 to 20 years in prison.) Congress thus not only envisioned, but accepted, the possibility that some defendants found guilty of that subsection of the statute would receive no jail time at all. This is especially significant in the area of drug-related crimes, where mandatory-minimum sentences . . . are most common. . . .

Sentences must nonetheless comport with prevailing standards of reasonableness, of course, and we recognize that Husein's one-day sentence in the present case represents an exponentially large departure from the applicable advisory Guidelines range of 37 to 46 months in prison. Expressed as a percentage, the departure is 99.91% below the low end of the range. This makes it even more extraordinary than the 99.89% variance (from a 30-to-37-month range to a one-day sentence) held to be unreasonably and unjustifiably low under the "proportionality" standard of review first articulated and employed by this court in *Davis*. But in judging the extent of the departure granted by the district court in this case, we bear in mind the departure's primary purpose of allowing Husein to provide the assistance that her father needed to survive. Any time that Husein would have spent in jail necessarily would have defeated this purpose. This distinguishes the present case from *Davis*, which instead dealt with a multifactor-based variance whose only discernible purpose was, and generally is, leniency. . . .

Husein's one-day sentence in the present case, [unlike the sentence in *Davis*,] leaves fairly ample "room to make reasoned distinctions" between Husein's Guidelines departure and what other defendants with extraordinary family circumstances might receive. These distinctions will be based not only on the exigency or seriousness of the family circumstances in each individual case, but also on the relative "worthiness" of each individual defendant. No judge, for example, would likely reduce the sentence of a convicted mass murderer due to family circumstances, and we do not intend to suggest otherwise. The extent of a downward departure or variance, in other words, should bear an inversely proportional relationship to the "evilness" of the crime, and criminal, at issue.

In *Davis,* the court belabored the defendant's considerable unworthiness: "The record shows that the fraud [perpetrated by Davis] caused over $900,000 in loss; Davis did not repay the lost money; he did not accept responsibility for the crimes; and he has yet to show remorse for the crimes." If such a defendant received what amounted to the lowest sentence possible, the court worried, how could sentencing courts confronted with far more worthy defendants possibly grant greater, more deserved departures? . . .

In the present case, however, "more worthy defendants" than Husein are difficult to imagine, short of those found to be not guilty. Her actions — namely, helping to arrange the sale of ecstasy between several of her acquaintances — caused no immediate harm to the individuals involved, much less the type of harm for which restitution was available as in *Davis.* In addition, Husein fully accepted responsibility for her actions. . . . She further appears to have expressed remorse for her actions, as several handwritten letters from family members and coworkers attest. Husein was also found to have no prior criminal history. [In] the world of convicted and guilty defendants . . . Husein appears to be precisely the type of defendant most worthy of the one-day sentence that she received. . . .  For all of the reasons set forth above, we conclude that Husein's sentence is substantively reasonable under the proportionality test of *Davis.*

## C.   *The Effect of the Post-Sentencing Discoveries and Developments . . .*

### 2.   Death of Husein's Father

Finally, the government argues that because of the death of Husein's father four months after sentencing, Husein is currently enjoying a "windfall" by remaining at home as opposed to being in prison. . . .

The finality of judgments is a key element of the American system of justice. This is especially true for defendants in criminal cases, where the enhancement of a sentence in a subsequent proceeding can violate the defendant's rights to the due process of law. As the Supreme Court has held, "when the Government has already imposed a criminal penalty and seeks to impose additional punishment in a second proceeding, the Double Jeopardy Clause protects against the possibility that the Government is seeking the second punishment because it is dissatisfied with the sanction obtained in the first proceeding." United States v. Halper, 490 U.S. 435, 451 n.10 (1989).

The relevant question is whether the additional sentence upsets the defendant's legitimate expectation of finality in the original sentence. If a defendant has a legitimate expectation of finality, then an increase in that sentence is prohibited. A defendant has a legitimate expectation in the finality of a sentence unless he is or should be aware at sentencing that the sentence may permissibly be increased.

In the present case, nothing in the record indicates that Husein was aware at the time of sentencing that her sentence could "permissibly be increased" or otherwise transformed from noncustodial to imprisonment. The district court, to be sure, did warn Husein that "if you do anything that is violative of the conditions [of home confinement and supervised release] that are set on you, you could find yourself back here or in front of some other Court and another Judge may not give you this break that you are asking for and that we granted today." But the court did not mention that a change in Husein's family circumstances, the relevant issue here, also might result in an increased sentence. . . .

The government further argues that as "events unfolded, a mere four-month delay in the defendant's sentencing or her report date would have obviated the need for any departure whatsoever." [Given the fact that the defendant's father suffered from multiple and worsening ailments, the government submits] that the district court could, and should, have at least considered the possibility of either delaying sentencing or granting a delayed report date as part of the sentencing equation. But the fact remains that the district court did not do so, and that the government, more tellingly, never asked the court to do so. . . .

Finally, although the health of Husein's father was the primary family circumstance on which the district court based its downward departure, it was not the only circumstance. The court also took note of Husein's "significant" responsibilities to her siblings and mother. Accordingly, the likelihood that waiting for Husein's father to die would have resulted in the district court's imposing an entirely different sentence is not as certain as the government seems to imply. Several of the extraordinary circumstances would still have existed, and Husein presumably would have had the added responsibility of helping her mother and siblings cope with the loss of their husband and father.

For all of these reasons, the government's windfall argument is without merit. It is also shortsighted. What if, instead of "getting better," Husein's family situation had actually become worse? Suppose, for example, that both Husein's father and mother had died in the several months after sentencing, leaving Husein alone to care for her three younger siblings. Also suppose that Husein had timely appealed on other grounds and, upon learning of this unfortunate news, argued for the first time that even her term of home confinement and supervised release was too harsh of a punishment. Would this court have accepted her argument and further reduced her sentence? Almost certainly not. . . . To hold to the contrary, after all, would mainly harm the government by subjecting it to a flood of post-sentencing litigation brought by unforeseeably worse-off defendants. . . .

## NOTES

1. *Consideration of social context factors: majority position.* Historically, in indeterminate sentencing systems, social context factors such as family history and situation, educational background, and employment record have been of great importance to sentencing judges (and parole officials) when exercising their discretion to individualize sentences with the offender's rehabilitation in mind. Presentence reports have often provided considerable detail on each offender's social history, education, and employment, and they have suggested how these background factors might affect the offender's rehabilitative prospects and progress.

Anecdotal and empirical research suggests that undue sentencing disparity, and the apparent disfavoring of certain minority offenders, can be traced back to the emphasis on these sorts of social context factors. As a result, many modern sentencing reforms have precluded or greatly restricted the consideration of these factors. The U.S. Sentencing Commission has excluded these social context factors from sentencing calculations for the most part and has further declared most social context matters "not ordinarily relevant" to a departure determination. See, e.g., U.S. Sentencing Guidelines Manual §§5H1.2 (education and vocational skills), 5H1.5 (employment record), 5H1.6 (family ties and responsibilities and community ties), and 5H1.11 (military, civic, charitable, or public service). Federal case law has interpreted these instructions to mean that social context factors can be the basis for a departure in "extraordinary" cases. In the advisory guideline system, courts may also consider such factors in fashioning a reasonable sentence. Likewise, in many state structured sentencing systems, social context factors are not directly incorporated into most sentencing determinations, but they can on occasion serve as a basis for a departure. See, e.g., Utah 2007 Adult Sentencing and Release Guidelines Form 2 (providing that a mitigating factor to be considered at sentencing is that "offender has exceptionally good employment and/or family relationships").

2. *Connection between culpability and the offenders' social context.*   In some cases, certain social context factors might directly bear on the offender's culpability; an offender with many children who steals in order to feed his family, for example, seems less culpable than a thief who lacks any such family needs. Such factors might seem important considerations in light of the traditional purposes of sentencing. But should consideration of such social context factors be permitted at sentencing when they do not directly bear on an offender's culpability or future prospects? Consider ABA Standard for Criminal Justice, Sentencing 18-3.4 (3d ed. 1994), which suggests the following approach for allowing limited consideration of the offender's personal characteristics at sentencing:

> (a) The legislature and [sentencing commission] should authorize sentencing courts, sentencing individual offenders, to consider their physical, mental, social and economic characteristics, even though not material to their culpability for the offense, only as provided in this Standard.
> (b) The legislature and [sentencing commission] should permit sentencing courts to use information about offenders' financial circumstances for the purpose of determination of the amount or terms of fines or other economic sanctions.
> (c) Except as provided in (b), the legislature and the agency should provide that sentencing courts may take into account personal characteristics of offenders not material to their culpability to determine the appropriate types of sanctions to impose or, if the characteristics are indicative of circumstances of hardship, deprivation, or handicap, to lessen the severity of sentences that would have been imposed.

What uses of personal history are permitted and not permitted under this standard? Why, if an offender's "physical, mental, social and economic characteristics" are "not material" to his or her culpability for the offense, should these characteristics be considered at all at sentencing? The commentary to the standards explains its compromise position:

> Many determinate jurisdictions have sought to restrict or prohibit the sentencing consideration of personal characteristics unrelated to culpability on the theory that such consideration can act to preserve or exacerbate preexisting class and race disparities in sentencing patterns. At least in the federal system such restrictions have prompted criticism that the sentencing process has been dehumanized, that the life history of defendants can no longer be argued to show extenuating circumstances, and that desirable individualization of sentences cannot occur. The Standards attempt to find a balance between the need to avoid class and race disparities and the need to preserve a meaningful level of individualization in sentences.

3. *Family circumstances.* Especially because offenders at sentencing will often highlight family situations when pleading for leniency, sentencing judges are frequently asked to consider the impact of a proposed sentence on the defendant's family. As detailed in *Husein,* the federal sentencing guidelines attempt to limit this practice by declaring that "family ties and responsibilities" are "not ordinarily relevant" to a sentence, and appellate courts have upheld departure sentences based on such circumstances only when they are present to an "extraordinary" degree. The federal circuits are less than perfectly consistent in assessing what sorts of family situations qualify as extraordinary.

Because of the huge number of cases and families affected, this is a high-stakes decision for every sentencing system. More than half of all female prisoners and more than one-quarter of all male prisoners are caring for minor children at the time they enter prison. Other prisoners have primary responsibility for the care of parents, siblings, spouses, or grandchildren. As Judge Patricia Wald framed the issue, the precedent is conflicting because the guidelines assign to judges a "frustrating and counterintuitive" task: "where on the spectrum we should draw the line between 'ordinary' and 'extraordinary' family tragedies?" United States v. Dyce, 91 F.3d 1462, 1472-78 (D.C. Cir. 1996) (dissenting).

In your view, what are extraordinary family circumstances? If you were a judicial clerk, how would you help your judge develop a principled but individualized approach to determining in which cases a sentence outside the guidelines is appropriate based on family circumstances? If you were a member of the U.S. Sentencing Commission, do you think a more structured approach to this issue — for example, one that depends on the number of children affected or the likely home for the children if the parent is incarcerated — would provide for more sensible and consistent results than the current prescription of not ordinarily considering family circumstances? Do you think the ABA approach would be an improvement? For a general framework for considering both the benefits and burdens that flow from various types of family relationships during criminal enforcement and punishment, see Dan Markel, Jennifer M. Collins, and Ethan J. Leib, Privilege or Punish: Criminal Justice and the Challenge of Family Ties (2009).

## PROBLEM 5-7.  PILLAR OF THE COMMUNITY

John Morken owned and operated a cattle brokerage business based in a small town in Minnesota. When the company's cash flow began to suffer, Morken began "kiting" checks (shifting funds to create the illusion of larger bank accounts), thus inflating his purchasing power in the cattle market. He used the nonexistent funds to buy more cattle, and then cattle prices fell. Ultimately, Morken put the business into bankruptcy. A federal grand jury indicted Morken for bank fraud and making false statements to a financial institution. He pled guilty to one count of bank fraud, and the government dropped the remaining charges. The applicable provisions of the U.S. Sentencing Guidelines call for a prison term of between 63 and 78 months.

Many citizens of Morken's hometown (with a population just over 1,000) wrote to the sentencing judge, asking him to impose a lenient sentence. The letters portrayed Morken as a hard-working and honest businessman, the owner of a once-thriving operation. Morken's father started the business in the 1930s. Morken joined it in 1964 and assumed leadership of the company in 1992. The letters to the judge also praised Morken for his community service. They spoke of him as an accommodating neighbor and a good friend. He advised local business owners, hired young people, served on his church council, and raised money for charity.

In addition to the family cattle brokerage business, Morken owned and operated the All Phase Arena, which hosted horse shows, farm and home shows, and the like. This operation provided dozens of jobs for local workers and generated revenue for local businesses. The All Phase Arena was unaffected by the bankruptcy of Morken's cattle operation, but it likely would not survive if Morken were to serve a lengthy prison term.

The federal sentencing guidelines advise judges that "community ties are not ordinarily relevant in determining whether a sentence should be outside the applicable guideline range." U.S. Sentencing Guidelines Manual §5H1.6. They also say that "military, charitable, or public service; employment-related contributions; and similar prior good works are not ordinarily relevant in determining whether a sentence should be outside the applicable guideline range." U.S. Sentencing Guidelines Manual §5H1.11. As the district court judge in this case, what sentence would you impose? How would you explain your decision? Cf. United States v. Morken, 133 F.3d 628 (8th Cir. 1998).

### NOTES

1. *The significance of prior good works.*  As noted earlier in this chapter, every jurisdiction views an offender's criminal history as an aggravating factor justifying an enhanced sentence for the current offense. Because these criminal history rules essentially mandate an increased sentence based on the defendant's past *bad* acts, logic would seem to dictate that jurisdictions should also have sentencing rules that mandate a reduced sentence based on the defendant's past *good* works. In other words, if defendants are to be penalized for prior bad behavior, shouldn't they also be rewarded for prior good behavior? A few

jurisdictions follow this logic. North Carolina, for example, provides that a mitigated sentence could be appropriate when the defendant "has been a person of good character or has had a good reputation in the community" or when the defendant "has been honorably discharged from the United States armed services." N.C. Gen. Stat. §15A-1340.16(e)(12), (14). As noted in Problem 5-7, however, the federal sentencing guidelines provide that "[m]ilitary, charitable, or public service; employment-related contributions; and similar prior good works are not ordinarily relevant in determining whether a sentence should be outside the applicable guideline range." U.S. Sentencing Guidelines Manual §5H1.11. Why do you think the U.S. Sentencing Commission deemed these factors inappropriate as the basis for a departure in the ordinary case? Should service to the country through participation in the military merit some consideration in sentencing? See United States v. Lett, 483 F.3d 782 (11th Cir. 2007).

2. *The significance of third-party impact.* The criminal conviction and potential incarceration of an offender almost always affect various third parties — most commonly the offender's immediate family and dependents, but often also the offender's employer or employees. As part of a plea for leniency, sentencing judges will almost invariably hear from the defendant or defense counsel about the hardships that third parties may suffer if the defendant is incarcerated. Should sentencing judges reduce sentences to try to minimize the harm to third parties, or does that unfairly reward defendants who are fortunate enough to have others depend on them? Professor Darryl Brown has noted that both prosecutors and judges have historically considered third-party interests in their charging and sentencing decisions, even though traditional criminal law theories do not suggest the consideration of such interests. See Darryl K. Brown, Third-Party Interests in Criminal Law, 80 Tex. L. Rev. 1383 (2002). However, not all agree that family ties are appropriate for consideration at sentencing. Dan Markel et al., Criminal Justice and the Challenge of Family Ties, 2007 U. Ill. L. Rev. 1147 (acknowledging that in cases of nondangerous irreplaceable caregivers, deferred incarceration might be appropriate).

At least a few states have codified in their structured-sentencing reforms the idea that judges should consider third-party concerns at sentencing. See Utah 2007 Adult Sentencing and Release Guidelines Form 2 (providing that a mitigating factor to be considered at sentencing is that "imprisonment would entail excessive hardship on offender or dependents"). In the federal system, the appropriateness of considering third-party interests is less clear although a number of commentators have asked federal courts to consider family interests. See Myrna S. Raeder, Rethinking Sentencing Post-*Booker:* Gender-Related Issues in a Post-*Booker* Federal Guidelines World, 37 McGeorge L. Rev. 691 (2006).

3. *The significance of upbringing and social environment.* Criminologists, psychologists, and other social scientists trace the roots of much crime to deep social causes relating to the offender's childhood social environment and upbringing. Recognizing that a poor childhood environment is not the offender's fault, should sentencing judges consider reducing an offender's sentence when her wrongdoing can be linked to childhood abuse or an otherwise unfortunate early social history? Not long after the federal sentencing guidelines were enacted, one federal circuit held that a downward departure was permissible based on the defendant's "youthful lack of guidance." United States v.

Floyd, 945 F.2d 1096 (9th Cir. 1991). Fearing the potentially expansive reach of this ground for departing from the guidelines, the U.S. Sentencing Commission amended the sentencing guidelines to provide that "lack of guidance as a youth and similar circumstances indicating a disadvantaged upbringing are not relevant grounds for imposing a sentence outside the applicable guideline range." U.S. Sentencing Guidelines Manual §5H1.12. If you had been a commissioner during this period, would you have favored or opposed this amendment? For a more general discussion of social environment theories and criminal law, see Patricia J. Falk, Novel Theories of Criminal Defense Based upon the Toxicity of the Social Environment: Urban Psychosis, Television Intoxication, and Black Rage, 74 N.C. L. Rev. 731 (1996). The defendant's unsupportive or abusive family of origin often figures into capital murder trials as defendants attempt to establish mitigating circumstances for the crime.

# =6=

## ‖ *Procedure and Proof at Sentencing* ‖

Chapter 1 explored *why* society punishes, Chapters 2 and 3 focused on *who* holds the power and discretion to set sentences, and Chapters 4 and 5 together examined *what* elements factor into sentencing decisions (offense and offender characteristics). This chapter looks at *how* sentencing and punishment decisions are made.

The possible application of trial rights at sentencing is the focus of the first half of this chapter. The Fifth and Sixth Amendments to the United States Constitution lay down some foundational rules for the prosecution of criminal offenses. These provisions include both relatively specific commands (for example, "presentment or indictment" is required for "capital, or otherwise infamous" crimes) and some that are notoriously abstract (no person shall be "deprived of life, liberty, or property, without due process of law"). The constitutional amendments are conspicuously silent on the subject of sentencing.

Until relatively recently, procedural rights at sentencing had been the subject of an interesting but largely academic discussion. No longer. The Supreme Court's consequential decisions in *Apprendi* and *Blakely* have made the issue of procedural rights in the sentencing process one of the most debated topic in modern sentencing law.

While the constitutional doctrine has changed the procedures used in the courtroom to determine sentences, procedural realities that affect sentencing outcomes still take place mostly outside the courtroom. Criminal justice is far more commonly negotiated than adjudicated; defendants and their attorneys often need to be more concerned about the charging and plea bargaining practices of prosecutors and the presentence investigations of probation offices than they do about the sentencing procedures of judges or juries. The second part of this chapter explores these less visible presentence practices and policies.

# A.  CONSTITUTIONAL SENTENCING PROCEDURES: TRIAL VERSUS SENTENCING

The substantive distinction between criminal trials and criminal sentencing is fairly obvious: trials determine a defendant's legal guilt and sentencing determines how a guilty defendant will be treated. Far less obvious is what this substantive distinction means in procedural terms. Should the rights typically afforded criminal defendants at a trial also apply at sentencing? Should the answer to this question be influenced by the reality that very few criminal defendants ever experience trial procedures because so many defendants plead guilty?

If you believe that different procedures are appropriate (or inevitable) at a criminal trial and at a criminal sentencing, who gets to decide which issues and facts are resolved at trial and which will be considered only at sentencing? Should legislatures — the institutions typically responsible for defining crimes and for authorizing punishments — have sole authority to define what "elements" are subject to resolution at trial and what "sentencing factors" are subject to consideration only at sentencing?

## 1.  Formal Trial, Informal Sentencing

The Fifth and Sixth Amendments to the Constitution provide rules for the prosecution and trial of criminal offenses. Read the text of the amendments closely. Do you find these commands specific or abstract compared with other rights specified in the Bill of Rights?

### U.S. Const. Amend. V

No person shall be held to answer for a capital, or otherwise infamous crime, unless on a presentment or indictment of a grand jury . . . ; nor shall any person be subject for the same offense to be twice put in jeopardy of life or limb, nor shall be compelled in any criminal case to be a witness against himself, nor be deprived of life, liberty, or property, without due process of law. . . .

### U.S. Const. Amend. VI

In all criminal prosecutions, the accused shall enjoy the right to a speedy and public trial, by an impartial jury . . . , and to be informed of the nature and cause of the accusation; to be confronted with the witnesses against him; to have compulsory process for obtaining witnesses in his favor, and to have the assistance of counsel for his defense.

Noticeably absent from these amendments are explicit procedural rights at sentencing. When the Constitution speaks of punishment, it mentions the legislative obligation to define crimes before they occur and to give them general application (the ex post facto and bill of attainder clauses), or it limits the available sanctions (the Eighth Amendment's prohibition of "excessive fines" and "cruel and unusual punishments"), or it recognizes that convicted criminals have qualified civil rights (the Thirteenth Amendment's decree that "[n]either slavery nor involuntary servitude, except as a punishment for crime whereof the party shall have been duly convicted, shall exist within the United States").

The silence on sentencing process is perhaps not surprising given the sentencing dynamics at the time of the founding. Following English traditions, during the founding era each particular criminal offense typically had a distinct sentencing consequence, and thus the substantive results of a criminal trial conclusively determined an offender's sentence. See Report of the Twentieth Century Fund Task Force on Criminal Sentencing, Fair and Certain Punishment 83-85 (1976). The Constitution's failure to regulate procedures at sentencing simply reflects the fact that at the time of the founding there were no distinct sentencing procedures to be regulated.

But with the emergence of the penitentiary and a shift in punishment theory toward a rehabilitative model in the late nineteenth century, the direct connection between the criminal verdict and the sentence was severed and distinct sentencing proceedings emerged. Trial judges were given discretion to impose on defendants any sentence among the broad statutory ranges and were permitted to consider any and all evidence when crafting a sentence. Judge and commentator Nancy Gertner summarized this evolution:

> [In] colonial times verdict and sentencing were closely linked. Felony conviction led to a definite punishment, often death, unless the defendant could offer a legal reason to excuse it. The jury's verdict was the pivotal event. Pronouncement of the sentence by the judge was an essentially ministerial task.
>
> By the nineteenth century, tradition and changes in penology dramatically altered the function of sentencing, while the jury's functions changed little. The sentencing model was now a therapeutic one, seeking to rehabilitate the offender. Each offense carried a very broad range of potential sentences; the judge had the discretion to pick any sentence within the range.

Nancy Gertner, *Apprendi* and the Return of the Criminal Code, 37 Crim. L. Bull. 553, 557 (2001).

The emergence of a distinct sentencing proceeding raised questions about whether traditional trial rights ought to apply at sentencing. These questions came before the Supreme Court most dramatically in Williams v. New York, 337 U.S. 241 (1949), after the progressive rehabilitative model of sentencing had already been operating for nearly half a century. As we saw in Chapter 2, the trial judge in *Williams* sentenced to death a defendant convicted of first-degree murder, despite a jury recommendation of life imprisonment, relying on allegations in the presentence report about illegal and unsavory activities by the defendant. Williams appealed and claimed that he had a right at sentencing — just as he did at trial — to confront and cross-examine the witnesses against him.

The Supreme Court in *Williams* approved the reliance on informal procedures at sentencing. The Court stressed rehabilitation of offenders as an important goal of criminal jurisprudence and spoke approvingly of the "prevalent modern philosophy of penology that the punishment should fit the offender and not merely the crime." To deprive sentencing judges of "the fullest information possible concerning the defendant's life and characteristics" would undermine "modern penological procedural policies." In other words, the rehabilitative ideal not only justified entrusting judges with enormous sentencing discretion, but it also freed sentencing judges from any procedural trial rules that might limit the sound exercise of their discretion.

*Williams* was decided before the Supreme Court began "revolutionizing" criminal procedure by interpreting the Constitution expansively to provide criminal defendants with an array of procedural rights. Nevertheless, throughout the 1960s and 1970s, as the Supreme Court established numerous pretrial and trial rights for defendants, the Court continued to cite *Williams* favorably and continued to suggest that sentencing was to be treated differently — and should be far less procedurally regulated — than a traditional criminal trial. See North Carolina v. Pearce, 395 U.S. 711, 723 (1969) (favorably citing *Williams* while stressing "the freedom of a sentencing judge" to consider a defendant's postconviction conduct in imposing a sentence).

The Supreme Court did hold that defendants had a right to an attorney at sentencing hearings in Mempa v. Rhay, 389 U.S. 128 (1967), and suggested that defendants also had a right to discovery of evidence that could affect a sentence in Brady v. Maryland, 373 U.S. 83 (1963). Nevertheless, even as the Supreme Court expanded defendants' procedural rights in many other criminal justices arenas, the Court did not formally extend other Bill of Rights protections to the sentencing process.

As the Supreme Court continued to cite *Williams* favorably and to sanction informal sentencing procedures, the theory supporting the rehabilitative model of sentencing itself came under attack. Through the 1960s and 1970s, criminal justice researchers and scholars grew increasingly concerned about the unpredictable and disparate sentences produced by highly discretionary sentencing systems. During the last quarter of the twentieth century, jurisdictions started to adopt more structured sentencing laws. Some states tried determinate sentencing statutes, which abolished parole and created presumptive sentencing ranges, while others created full-fledged sentencing guideline systems.

These new sentencing laws attached specific sentencing effects to particular factual findings. Conspicuously absent from modern sentencing reform, however, has been a concern for factfinding procedures at sentencing. From the start of the modern structured sentencing reform era and continuing through today, lawmakers and sentencing commissions have largely ignored fundamental procedural issues such as notice to parties, burdens of proof, appropriate factfinders, evidentiary rules, and hearing processes while they have been creating a huge body of modern substantive sentencing law. Some critics of lax sentencing procedures blame this neglect on the Supreme Court's decision in McMillan v. Pennsylvania, litigated during the early development of structured sentencing reforms.

‖ *Dynel McMillan v. Pennsylvania* ‖
477 U.S. 79 (1986)

Rehnquist, J.

Pennsylvania's Mandatory Minimum Sentencing Act, 42 Pa. Cons. Stat. 9712, . . . was adopted in 1982. It provides that anyone convicted of certain enumerated felonies is subject to a mandatory minimum sentence of five years' imprisonment if the sentencing judge finds, by a preponderance of the evidence, that the person "visibly possessed a firearm" during the commission of the offense. At the sentencing hearing, the judge is directed to consider the evidence introduced at trial and any additional evidence offered by either the defendant or the Commonwealth. The Act operates to divest the judge of discretion to impose any sentence of less than five years for the underlying felony; it does not authorize a sentence in excess of that otherwise allowed for that offense. . . .

McMillan, who shot his victim in the right buttock after an argument over a debt, was convicted by a jury of aggravated assault. [The Commonwealth sought an enhanced sentence under the Act, but McMillan and his co-defendants argued] that visible possession of a firearm is an element of the crimes for which they were being sentenced and thus must be proved beyond a reasonable doubt under In re Winship, 397 U.S. 358 (1970). . . . Petitioners also contended that even if visible possession is not an element of the offense, due process requires more than proof by a preponderance of the evidence. . . .

*Winship* held that "the Due Process Clause protects the accused against conviction except upon proof beyond a reasonable doubt of every fact necessary to constitute the crime with which he is charged." In Mullaney v. Wilbur, 421 U.S. 684 (1975), we held that the Due Process Clause "requires the prosecution to prove beyond a reasonable doubt the absence of the heat of passion on sudden provocation when the issue is properly presented in a homicide case." But in Patterson v. New York, 432 U.S. 197 (1977), we rejected the claim that whenever a State links the "severity of punishment" to "the presence or absence of an identified fact" the State must prove that fact beyond a reasonable doubt. In particular, we upheld against a due process challenge New York's law placing on defendants charged with murder the burden of proving the affirmative defense of extreme emotional disturbance. *Patterson* stressed that in determining what facts must be proved beyond a reasonable doubt the state legislature's definition of the elements of the offense is usually dispositive. [The] Pennsylvania Legislature has expressly provided that visible possession of a firearm is not an element of the crimes enumerated in the mandatory sentencing statute, but instead is a sentencing factor that comes into play only after the defendant has been found guilty of one of those crimes beyond a reasonable doubt. . . .

As *Patterson* recognized, of course, there are constitutional limits to the State's power in this regard; in certain limited circumstances *Winship*'s reasonable-doubt requirement applies to facts not formally identified as elements of the offense charged. Petitioners argue that Pennsylvania has gone beyond those limits and that its formal provision that visible possession is not an element of the crime is therefore of no effect. We do not think so. While we have never attempted to define precisely the constitutional limits [on] the extent to which due process forbids the reallocation or reduction of burdens of proof in criminal cases, and do not do so today, we are persuaded by several factors that Pennsylvania's Mandatory Minimum Sentencing Act does not exceed those limits.

We note first that the Act plainly does not . . . discard the presumption of innocence [nor] relieve the prosecution of its burden of proving guilt; §9712 only becomes applicable after a defendant has been duly convicted of the crime for which he is to be punished. [Further], §9712 neither alters the maximum penalty for the crime committed nor creates a separate offense calling for a separate penalty; it operates solely to limit the sentencing court's discretion in selecting a penalty within the range already available to it without the special finding of visible possession of a firearm. Section 9712 "ups the ante" for the defendant only by raising to five years the minimum sentence which may be imposed within the statutory plan. The statute gives no impression of having been tailored to permit the visible possession finding to be a tail which wags the dog of the substantive offense. . . .

Finally, we note that the specter raised by petitioners of States restructuring existing crimes in order to "evade" the commands of *Winship* just does not appear in this case. As noted above, §9712's enumerated felonies retain the same elements they had before the Mandatory Minimum Sentencing Act was passed. The Pennsylvania Legislature did not change the definition of any existing offense. It simply took one factor that has always been considered by sentencing courts to bear on punishment — the instrumentality used in committing a violent felony — and dictated the precise weight to be given that factor if the instrumentality is a firearm. Pennsylvania's decision to do so has not transformed against its will a sentencing factor into an "element" of some hypothetical "offense." . . .

Having concluded that States may treat "visible possession of a firearm" as a sentencing consideration rather than an element of a particular offense, we now turn to petitioners' subsidiary claim that due process nonetheless requires that visible possession be proved by at least clear and convincing evidence. Like the court below, we have little difficulty concluding that in this case the preponderance standard satisfies due process. [Petitioners] do not and could not claim that a sentencing court may never rely on a particular fact in passing sentence without finding that fact by "clear and convincing evidence." Sentencing courts have traditionally heard evidence and found facts without any prescribed burden of proof at all. See Williams v. New York, 337 U.S. 241 (1949). . . .

Petitioners apparently concede that Pennsylvania's scheme would pass constitutional muster if only it did not remove the sentencing court's discretion, i.e., if the legislature had simply directed the court to consider visible possession in passing sentence. We have some difficulty fathoming why the due process calculus would change simply because the legislature has seen fit to provide sentencing courts with additional guidance. Nor is there merit to the claim that a heightened burden of proof is required because visible possession is a fact concerning the crime committed rather than the background or character of the defendant. Sentencing courts necessarily consider the circumstances of an offense in selecting the appropriate punishment, and we have consistently approved sentencing schemes that mandate consideration of facts related to the crime, without suggesting that those facts must be proved beyond a reasonable doubt.

In light of the foregoing, petitioners' final claim — that the Act denies them their Sixth Amendment right to a trial by jury — merits little discussion. Petitioners again argue that the jury must determine all ultimate facts concerning the offense committed. Having concluded that Pennsylvania may properly treat visible possession as a sentencing consideration and not an element of any offense, we need only note that there is no Sixth Amendment right to jury sentencing, even where the sentence turns on specific findings of fact. . . .

STEVENS, J., dissenting.

. . . In my view, a state legislature may not dispense with the requirement of proof beyond a reasonable doubt for conduct that it targets for severe criminal penalties. Because the Pennsylvania statute challenged in this case describes conduct that the Pennsylvania Legislature obviously intended to prohibit, and because it mandates lengthy incarceration for the same, I believe that the conduct so described is an element of the criminal offense to which the proof beyond a reasonable doubt requirement applies.

Once a State defines a criminal offense, the Due Process Clause requires it to prove any component of the prohibited transaction that gives rise to both a special stigma and a special punishment beyond a reasonable doubt. . . . Nothing in *Patterson* or any of its predecessors authorizes a State to decide for itself which of the ingredients of the prohibited transaction are "elements" that it must prove beyond a reasonable doubt at trial. . . .

A legislative definition of an offense named "assault" could be broad enough to encompass every intentional infliction of harm by one person upon another, but surely the legislature could not provide that only that fact must be proved beyond a reasonable doubt and then specify a range of increased punishments if the prosecution could show by a preponderance of the evidence that the defendant robbed, raped, or killed his victim "during the commission of the offense." . . .

It is true, as the Court points out, that the enhanced punishment is within the range that was authorized for any aggravated assault. That fact does not, however, minimize the significance of a finding of visible possession of a firearm whether attention is focused on the stigmatizing or punitive consequences of that finding. The finding identifies conduct that the legislature specifically intended to prohibit and to punish by a special sanction. . . .

## NOTES

1. *Standard of proof at sentencing.*    In *McMillan*, the Court noted that sentencing courts "have traditionally heard evidence and found facts without any prescribed burden of proof at all." What does it mean to have no prescribed burden of proof? Can sentencing judges rely on whatever facts tickle their fancy? A more plausible reading of the *McMillan* holding is that the Constitution's due process clause allows states to treat some facts relevant to the sentence as "sentencing factors" subject only to proof by a preponderance of the evidence at sentencing. Only when an extreme increase in punishment attaches to a sentencing factor — or, to use the Court's terms, when the "tail" of the sentencing factor "wags the dog" of the substantive offense — will a federal court overturn the legislature's choices.

Virtually all states use the preponderance standard for facts to be proven at sentencing, although this issue has not been litigated (or even expressly considered) as often as one might expect. When the question does arise, most state courts have held that their state constitutions allow the prosecution to prove certain facts to increase a sentence using the lower standard of proof at sentencing. See, e.g., People v. Williams, 599 N.E.2d 913 (Ill. 1992). In a discretionary sentencing system, when judges pronounce sentences from the bench without any written opinion, how can a defendant know what standard of proof the judge applied? Are the judges making *factual* determinations that can be regulated through standards of proof or are they making legal judgments?

Structured sentencing systems, which distinctly define the factual determinations that can have an impact on sentencing outcomes, often expressly establish preponderance of the evidence as the standard of proof at sentencing. In the federal system, the U.S. Sentencing Commission, in commentary to a policy statement on resolution of disputed factors, stated that "use of a preponderance of the evidence standard is appropriate to meet due process requirements and policy concerns in resolving disputes regarding application of the guidelines to the facts of a case." U.S. Sentencing Guidelines Manual §6A1.3. Why shouldn't the traditional standard of proof beyond a reasonable doubt apply at sentencing? How about some other heightened standard, such as clear and convincing evidence?

In guideline systems, not only can certain aggravating factors lead to an increase in the applicable sentence, but certain mitigating factors can lead to a decrease in the applicable sentence. For example, in the federal system, the sentencing guidelines provide that a defendant's sentence will be less severe if the defendant establishes that her role in a large criminal enterprise was minor or minimal. Should the Constitution require different standards of proof depending on whether a fact is raised by prosecutors seeking an increase in the applicable sentence or by defendants seeking a decrease in the applicable sentence? Should legislatures and sentencing commissions develop different procedural rules and evidence standards for aggravating and mitigating facts?

2. *Formative doctrinal legacy of* McMillan.   It is important to remember that in 1986, when *McMillan* was decided, only a few states had guideline systems in place and the federal guideline system was in its developmental stages. Since then, as many more jurisdictions have adopted forms of structured sentencing, two contrasting developments have emerged. State courts and lower federal courts, citing *McMillan* and *Williams* as controlling authority, have consistently rejected constitutional challenges to structured sentencing systems that impose punishment without affording defendants at sentencing the procedural protections of a criminal trial. See, e.g., State v. Rettinghaus, 591 N.W.2d 15 (Iowa 1999); Farris v. McKune, 911 P.2d 177 (Kan. 1996); United States v. Mergerson, 995 F.2d 1285 (5th Cir. 1993). At the same time, individual judges and academic commentators have regularly lamented the continued adherence to *McMillan* and *Williams* as controlling authority, citing the unfairness of subjecting defendants to fact-driven guideline sentencing determinations without significant procedural rights. See, e.g., United States v. Concepcion, 983 F.2d 369, 389, 396 (2d Cir. 1992) (Newman, C.J., concurring); Sara Sun Beale, Procedural Issues Raised by Guidelines Sentencing: The Constitutional Significance of the "Elements of the Sentence," 35 Wm. & Mary L. Rev. 147 (1993).

3. *Tails wagging dogs.*   Most state courts have upheld legislative decisions that allow the government to prove some facts as "sentencing enhancements" at the sentencing hearing. See Vega v. People, 893 P.2d 107 (Colo. 1995). Only rarely have courts found that a fact introduced at sentencing was so important that it required proof by some standard higher than a preponderance. In United States v. Kikumura, 918 F.2d 1084 (3d Cir. 1990), the federal sentencing

guidelines prescribed a sentence between 27 and 33 months for explosives and passport violations. The sentencing court, however, departed from this range to impose a 30-year sentence based on evidence that the defendant was engaged in terrorist activities for the Japanese Red Army. Although the appeals court acknowledged that most sentencing facts could be proven under a preponderance standard, it held that a clear and convincing standard should apply to this case: "[Here] we are dealing with findings that would increase Kikumura's sentence from about 30 months to 30 years. . . . This is perhaps the most dramatic example imaginable of a sentencing hearing that functions as 'a tail which wags the dog of the substantive offense.' "

4. *Informal procedures and rules of evidence at sentencing.*   Most states allow sentencing judges to consider evidence inadmissible under the rules of evidence. See Tex. Crim. Proc. Code Ann. §37.07(3). Particularly in states with an indeterminate sentencing system, the informal presentation of evidence supposedly enables to judge to make an individualized (perhaps even clinical) decision about the best response to the case and the offender at hand. More than half of the states use such an indeterminate sentencing system for large groups of cases, although many of these same states use more narrowly circumscribed sentencing rules for some crimes.

Most states indicate that evidence presented at sentencing must be relevant and reliable. According to one court, the Constitution prohibits sentencing only on "materially untrue information." State v. Ramsay, 499 A.2d 15, 20 (Vt. 1985). Reliable hearsay is often allowed, and many sentences are based mostly or entirely on hearsay. The federal courts do not apply the rules of evidence at sentencing: "the rules (other than with respect to privileges) do not apply in . . . sentencing." Fed. R. Evid. 1101(d)(3). The federal sentencing guidelines adopt the following standard: "any information may be considered, so long as it has sufficient indicia of reliability to support its probable accuracy." U.S. Sentencing Guidelines Manual §6A1.3(a). Is the federal guideline standard higher or lower than the New York practice challenged in *Williams*?

Those who argue in favor of the current federal position (and a similar position in many states) explain that rules of evidence do not apply because of the burden they would place on sentencing judges, converting the sentencing hearing into a second trial. Should Congress or the U.S. Sentencing Commission change positions and apply the rules of evidence to sentencing hearings? Professor Deborah Young favors use of the rules of evidence over other methods of increasing the reliability of factfinding at sentencing because it corrects both potential errors that benefit the prosecution and those that benefit the defense. She argues that evenhanded factfinding rules make sense at sentencing since an offender has already been convicted and should no longer be given the benefit of the presumption of innocence. Deborah Young, Fact-Finding at Federal Sentencing: Why the Guidelines Should Meet the Rules, 79 Cornell L. Rev. 299 (1994).

5. *Confrontation of witnesses.*   Although the evidentiary rules governing hearsay do not apply to sentencing hearings in federal or state courts, the overlapping protections of the Sixth Amendment's confrontation clause (and the equivalent provisions of a state constitution) still might require that a defendant be allowed to cross-examine witnesses at the sentencing hearing. The Supreme Court interpreted the confrontation clause in Crawford v. Washington, 541 U.S.

36 (2004), to bar admission during trial of "testimonial" hearsay unless the declarant is unavailable and the defendant had a prior opportunity for cross-examination of the declarant. Would the same reasoning apply to the testimony and evidence used at sentencing?

Before *Crawford*, courts mostly concluded that the confrontation clause did not apply to the evidence presented during a sentencing hearing. See United States v. Wise, 976 F.2d 393 (8th Cir. 1992); State v. DeSalvo, 903 P.2d 202 (Mont. 1995). After *Crawford*, the lower federal courts and state courts reopened the question of whether the use of testimonial hearsay during noncapital sentencing proceedings violates the defendant's confrontation rights. Most concluded that it does not. See Summers v. State, 148 P.3d 778 (Nev. 2006).

Might the courts rule differently in capital sentencing proceedings? The imposition of a death sentence based on information that a defendant does not have the opportunity to deny or explain may run afoul of the confrontation clause, but this does not necessarily require full confrontation rights. See Gardner v. Florida, 430 U.S. 349 (1977); United States v. Brown, 441 F.3d 1330, 1361 n.12 (11th Cir. 2006) (applying *Crawford* to capital sentencing); United States v. Fields, 483 F.3d 313 (5th Cir. 2007) (declining to apply *Crawford*); State v. McGill, 140 P.3d 930 (Ariz. 2006) (full confrontation rights do not apply to rebuttal testimony at capital sentencing hearing).

It is clear that the sentencing hearing is part of the "criminal proceedings" and that the right to counsel applies at that stage of the proceedings. Mempa v. Rhay, 389 U.S. 128 (1967) (establishing right to counsel at sentencing). If the Sixth Amendment's right to counsel (granted to "the accused") applies at sentencing, why doesn't the same conclusion apply to the Sixth Amendment's right to confront witnesses?

6. *Right to remain silent.* In Mitchell v. United States, 526 U.S. 314 (1999), the Supreme Court held that a defendant, after pleading guilty to a specific offense, can assert her Fifth Amendment privilege against self-incrimination at the sentencing hearing and not have a judge draw an adverse inference from the defendant's silence. Mitchell refused to testify at a sentencing hearing about her involvement in a cocaine conspiracy. The sentencing judge drew a negative inference from the defendant's refusal to discuss the amount of drugs involved in the offense and sentenced her to ten years' imprisonment. The Supreme Court reversed, holding that neither the defendant's guilty plea nor her statements at a plea colloquy functioned as a waiver of her right to remain silent at sentencing. Furthermore, relying on Griffin v. California, 380 U.S. 609 (1995), which held that it is constitutionally impermissible for the prosecutor or judge to comment at trial on a criminal defendant's refusal to testify, the Court concluded that the defendant should have been allowed to remain silent without paying the price of a longer sentence.

7. *Other rights at sentencing.* Although many academic commentators focus on (and lament) the courts' refusal to extend to sentencing traditional trial rights and procedures relating to proof and evidence standards, Professor Alan Michaels has pointed out that many more trial rights apply at sentencing than one might expect. Michaels systematically examined judicial decisions regarding the applicability of constitutional trial rights to sentencing proceedings and produced a comprehensive taxonomy of sentencing rights.

Summarizing the cases relating to 25 trial rights "from employing an attorney to not having inferences drawn from one's silence, from bail and *Brady* to presence and proceeding pro se," Michaels concluded that that the Supreme Court "has found roughly one quarter apply at sentencing and one quarter do not" and has not ruled definitively on the other half. The lower federal courts have reached a similar pattern of outcomes. Alan C. Michaels, Trial Rights at Sentencing, 81 N.C. L. Rev. 1771, 1775 (2003). According to Michaels, the Court's decisions tend to follow what he calls a "best estimate" principle: trial rights that are "directed primarily at determining the correct result apply at sentencing, whereas those rights designed to offer special protection to a defendant's liberty or autonomy interests do not." Id. at 1771.

## 2.  *The Resurgent Jury Trial Right*

When jurisdictions began to develop structured reforms in which sentencing determinations turned on particular facts, sentencing became a more trial-like enterprise and the justification for having limited procedural rights at sentencing lost a key foundation. Yet legislators and sentencing commissions enacting structured sentencing reforms paid little attention to procedural rules and generally failed to justify their continued use of lax procedures. As a result, the soundness and stability of *Williams* and *McMillan* became ever more questionable.

After offering a series of clues pointing in different directions, the Supreme Court in 2004 finally laid out a new vision of constitutional limits on sentencing procedures. The following opinion represents an alternative to the model of informal sentencing procedures, creating stronger constitutional limits on the power of legislatures to sort factual issues into a formal trial process and an informal sentencing process.

## ‖ *Ralph Blakely, Jr. v. Washington* ‖
### 542 U.S. 296 (2004)

SCALIA, J.

Petitioner Ralph Howard Blakely, Jr., pleaded guilty to the kidnaping of his estranged wife. The facts admitted in his plea, standing alone, supported a maximum sentence of 53 months. Pursuant to state law, the court imposed an "exceptional" sentence of 90 months after making a judicial determination that he had acted with "deliberate cruelty." We consider whether this violated petitioner's Sixth Amendment right to trial by jury.

## I

Petitioner married his wife Yolanda in 1973. He was evidently a difficult man to live with, having been diagnosed at various times with psychological and personality disorders including paranoid schizophrenia. His wife ultimately filed for divorce. In 1998, he abducted her from their orchard home in Grant County, Washington, binding her with duct tape and forcing her at knifepoint into a wooden box in the bed of his pickup truck. In the process, he implored her to dismiss the divorce suit and related trust proceedings.

When the couple's 13-year-old son Ralphy returned home from school, petitioner ordered him to follow in another car, threatening to harm Yolanda with a shotgun if he did not do so. Ralphy escaped and sought help when they stopped at a gas station, but petitioner continued on with Yolanda to a friend's house in Montana. He was finally arrested after the friend called the police.

The State charged petitioner with first-degree kidnaping. Upon reaching a plea agreement, however, it reduced the charge to second-degree kidnaping involving domestic violence and use of a firearm. Petitioner entered a guilty plea admitting the elements of second-degree kidnaping and the domestic-violence and firearm allegations, but no other relevant facts.

The case then proceeded to sentencing. In Washington, second-degree kidnaping is a class B felony. State law provides that [a person convicted of a class B felony faces a maximum punishment of ten years confinement]. Other provisions of state law, however, further limit the range of sentences a judge may impose. Washington's Sentencing Reform Act specifies, for petitioner's offense of second-degree kidnaping with a firearm, a "standard range" of 49 to 53 months. A judge may impose a sentence above the standard range if he finds "substantial and compelling reasons justifying an exceptional senten-ce."§9.94A.120(2). The Act lists aggravating factors that justify such a departure, which it recites to be illustrative rather than exhaustive. . . . When a judge imposes an exceptional sentence, he must set forth findings of fact and conclusions of law supporting it. A reviewing court will reverse the sentence if it finds that under a clearly erroneous standard there is insufficient evidence in the record to support the reasons for imposing an exceptional sentence.

Pursuant to the plea agreement, the State recommended a sentence within the standard range of 49 to 53 months. After hearing Yolanda's description of the kidnaping, however, the judge rejected the State's recommendation and imposed an exceptional sentence of 90 months — 37 months beyond the standard maximum. He justified the sentence on the ground that petitioner had acted with "deliberate cruelty," a statutorily enumerated ground for depar-ture in domestic-violence cases.

Faced with an unexpected increase of more than three years in his sentence, petitioner objected. The judge accordingly conducted a 3-day bench hearing featuring testimony from petitioner, Yolanda, Ralphy, a police officer, and medical experts. After the hearing, he issued 32 findings of fact, [reaffirming] his initial determination of deliberate cruelty. Petitioner appealed, arguing that this sentencing procedure deprived him of his federal constitutional right to have a jury determine beyond a reasonable doubt all facts legally essential to his sentence.

## II

This case requires us to apply the rule we expressed in Apprendi v. New Jersey, 530 U.S. 466, 490 (2000): "Other than the fact of a prior conviction, any fact that increases the penalty for a crime beyond the prescribed statutory maximum must be submitted to a jury, and proved beyond a reasonable doubt." This rule reflects two longstanding tenets of common-law criminal juris-prudence: that the "truth of every accusation" against a defendant "should afterwards be confirmed by the unanimous suffrage of twelve of his equals and neighbours," 4 W. Blackstone, Commentaries on the Laws of England 343 (1769), and that "an accusation which lacks any particular fact which the law makes essential to the punishment is . . . no accusation within the requirements of the common law, and it is no accusation in reason," 1 J. Bishop, Criminal Procedure §87, p. 55 (2d ed. 1872). These principles have been acknowledged by courts and treatises since the earliest days of graduated sentencing. . . .

*Apprendi* involved a New Jersey hate-crime statute that authorized a 20-year sentence, despite the usual 10-year maximum, if the judge found the crime to have been committed "with a purpose to intimidate . . . because of race, color, gender, handicap, religion, sexual orientation or ethnicity." . . .

In this case, petitioner was sentenced to more than three years above the 53-month statutory maximum of the standard range because he had acted with "deliberate cruelty." The facts supporting that finding were neither admitted by petitioner nor found by a jury. The State nevertheless contends that there was no *Apprendi* violation because the relevant "statutory maximum" is not 53 months, but the 10-year maximum for class B felonies in §9A.20.021(1)(b). . . . Our pre-cedents make clear, however, that the "statutory maximum" for *Apprendi* pur-poses is the maximum sentence a judge may impose solely on the basis of the facts reflected in the jury verdict or admitted by the defendant. In other words, the relevant "statutory maximum" is not the maximum sentence a judge may impose after finding additional facts, but the maximum he may impose without any additional findings. When a judge inflicts punishment that the jury's verdict alone does not allow, the jury has not found all the facts "which the law makes essential to the punishment," Bishop, *supra*, §87, at 55, and the judge exceeds his proper authority.

The judge in this case could not have imposed the exceptional 90-month sentence solely on the basis of the facts admitted in the guilty plea. Those facts alone were insufficient because, as the Washington Supreme Court has explained, "[a] reason offered to justify an exceptional sentence can be con-sidered only if it takes into account factors other than those which are used in computing the standard range sentence for the offense," State v. Gore, 21 P.3d 262, 277 (Wash. 2001), which in this case included the elements of second-degree kidnaping and the use of a firearm. Had the judge imposed the 90-month sentence solely on the basis of the plea, he would have been reversed. . . .

The State defends the sentence by drawing an analogy to those we upheld in McMillan v. Pennsylvania, 477 U.S. 79 (1986), and Williams v. New York, 337 U.S. 241 (1949). Neither case is on point. *McMillan* involved a sentencing scheme that imposed a statutory minimum if a judge found a particular fact. We specifically noted that the statute "does not authorize a sentence in excess of that otherwise allowed for [the underlying] offense." *Williams* involved an inde-terminate-sentencing regime that allowed a judge (but did not compel him) to rely on facts outside the trial record in determining whether to sentence a defendant to death. The judge could have sentenced the defendant to death giving no reason at all. Thus, neither case involved a sentence greater than what state law authorized on the basis of the verdict alone. . . .

## III

Our commitment to *Apprendi* in this context reflects not just respect for longstanding precedent, but the need to give intelligible content to the right of jury trial. That right is no mere procedural formality, but a fundamental reservation of power in our constitutional structure. Just as suffrage ensures the people's ultimate control in the legislative and executive branches, jury trial is meant to ensure their control in the judiciary. *Apprendi* carries out this design by ensuring that the judge's authority to sentence derives wholly from the jury's verdict. Without that restriction, the jury would not exercise the control that the Framers intended.

Those who would reject *Apprendi* are resigned to one of two alternatives. The first is that the jury need only find whatever facts the legislature chooses to label elements of the crime, and that those it labels sentencing factors—no matter how much they may increase the punishment—may be found by the judge. This would mean, for example, that a judge could sentence a man for committing murder even if the jury convicted him only of illegally possessing the firearm used to commit it—or of making an illegal lane change while fleeing the death scene. Not even *Apprendi*'s critics would advocate this absurd result. The jury could not function as circuit-breaker in the State's machinery of justice if it were relegated to making a determination that the defendant at some point did something wrong, a mere preliminary to a judicial inquisition into the facts of the crime the State actually seeks to punish.

The second alternative is that legislatures may establish legally essential sentencing factors within limits—limits crossed when, perhaps, the sentencing factor is a "tail which wags the dog of the substantive offense." *McMillan*, 477 U.S., at 88. What this means in operation is that the law must not go too far—it must not exceed the judicial estimation of the proper role of the judge.

The subjectivity of this standard is obvious. Petitioner argued below that second-degree kidnaping with deliberate cruelty was essentially the same as first-degree kidnaping, the very charge he had avoided by pleading to a lesser offense. . . . Petitioner's 90-month sentence exceeded the 53-month standard maximum by almost 70 percent; the Washington Supreme Court in other cases has upheld exceptional sentences 15 times the standard maximum. Did the court go too far in any of these cases? There is no answer that legal analysis can provide. . . .

Whether the Sixth Amendment incorporates this manipulable standard rather than *Apprendi*'s bright-line rule depends on the plausibility of the claim that the Framers would have left definition of the scope of jury power up to judges' intuitive sense of how far is too far. We think that claim not plausible at all, because the very reason the Framers put a jury-trial guarantee in the Constitution is that they were unwilling to trust government to mark out the role of the jury.

## IV

. . . This case is not about whether determinate sentencing is constitutional, only about how it can be implemented in a way that respects the Sixth Amendment. . . .

Justice O'Connor argues that, because determinate sentencing schemes involving judicial factfinding entail less judicial discretion than indeterminate schemes, the constitutionality of the latter implies the constitutionality of the former. This argument is flawed on a number of levels. First, the Sixth Amendment by its terms is not a limitation on judicial power, but a reservation of jury power. It limits judicial power only to the extent that the claimed judicial power infringes on the province of the jury. Indeterminate sentencing does not do so. It increases judicial discretion, to be sure, but not at the expense of the jury's traditional function of finding the facts essential to lawful imposition of the penalty. . . . In a system that says the judge may punish burglary with 10 to 40 years, every burglar knows he is risking 40 years in jail. In a system that punishes burglary with a 10-year sentence, with another 30 added for use of a gun, the burglar who enters a home unarmed is entitled to no more than a 10-year sentence — and by reason of the Sixth Amendment the facts bearing upon that entitlement must be found by a jury.

But even assuming that restraint of judicial power unrelated to the jury's role is a Sixth Amendment objective, it is far from clear that *Apprendi* disserves that goal. Determinate judicial-factfinding schemes entail less judicial power than indeterminate schemes, but more judicial power than determinate jury-factfinding schemes. Whether *Apprendi* increases judicial power overall depends on what States with determinate judicial-factfinding schemes would do, given the choice between the two alternatives. Justice O'Connor simply assumes that the net effect will favor judges, but she has no empirical basis for that prediction. Indeed, what evidence we have points exactly the other way: When the Kansas Supreme Court found *Apprendi* infirmities in that State's determinate-sentencing regime in State v. Gould, 23 P.3d 801, 809-814 (Kan. 2001), the legislature responded not by reestablishing indeterminate sentencing but by applying *Apprendi*'s requirements to its current regime. The result was less, not more, judicial power.

Justice Breyer argues that *Apprendi* works to the detriment of criminal defendants who plead guilty by depriving them of the opportunity to argue sentencing factors to a judge. But nothing prevents a defendant from waiving his *Apprendi* rights. When a defendant pleads guilty, the State is free to seek judicial sentence enhancements so long as the defendant either stipulates to the relevant facts or consents to judicial factfinding. . . . Even a defendant who stands trial may consent to judicial factfinding as to sentence enhancements, which may well be in his interest if relevant evidence would prejudice him at trial. We do not understand how *Apprendi* can possibly work to the detriment of those who are free, if they think its costs outweigh its benefits, to render it inapplicable.

Nor do we see any merit to Justice Breyer's contention that *Apprendi* is unfair to criminal defendants because, if States respond by enacting "17-element robbery crimes," prosecutors will have more elements with which to bargain. Bargaining already exists with regard to sentencing factors because defendants can either stipulate or contest the facts that make them applicable. If there is any difference between bargaining over sentencing factors and bargaining over elements, the latter probably favors the defendant. Every new element that a prosecutor can threaten to charge is also an element that a defendant can threaten to contest at trial and make the prosecutor prove beyond a reasonable doubt. Moreover, given the sprawling scope of most criminal codes, and the power to affect sentences by making (even nonbinding) sentencing recommendations, there is already no shortage of in terrorem tools at prosecutors' disposal.

Any evaluation of *Apprendi*'s "fairness" to criminal defendants must compare it with the regime it replaced, in which a defendant, with no warning in either his indictment or plea, would routinely see his maximum potential sentence balloon from as little as five years to as much as life imprisonment . . . based not on facts proved to his peers beyond a reasonable doubt, but on facts extracted after trial from a report compiled by a probation officer who the judge thinks more likely got it right than got it wrong. . . .

Justice Breyer's more general argument — that *Apprendi* undermines alternatives to adversarial factfinding — is not so much a criticism of *Apprendi* as an assault on jury trial generally. . . . Ultimately, our decision cannot turn on whether or to what degree trial by jury impairs the efficiency or fairness of criminal justice. One can certainly argue that both these values would be better served by leaving justice entirely in the hands of professionals; many nations of the world, particularly those following civil-law traditions, take just that course. There is not one shred of doubt, however, about the Framers' paradigm for criminal justice: not the civil-law ideal of administrative perfection, but the common-law ideal of limited state power accomplished by strict division of authority between judge and jury. . . .

Petitioner was sentenced to prison for more than three years beyond what the law allowed for the crime to which he confessed, on the basis of a disputed finding that he had acted with "deliberate cruelty." The Framers would not have thought it too much to demand that, before depriving a man of three more years of his liberty, the State should suffer the modest inconvenience of submitting its accusation to "the unanimous suffrage of twelve of his equals and neighbours," 4 Blackstone, Commentaries, at 343, rather than a lone employee of the State. . . .

O'CONNOR, J., dissenting.

The legacy of today's opinion, whether intended or not, will be the consolidation of sentencing power in the State and Federal Judiciaries. The Court says to Congress and state legislatures: If you want to constrain the sentencing discretion of judges and bring some uniformity to sentencing, it will cost you — dearly. Congress and States, faced with the burdens imposed by the extension of *Apprendi* to the present context, will either trim or eliminate altogether their sentencing guidelines schemes and, with them, 20 years of sentencing reform. . . .

## I

. . . Prior to 1981, Washington, like most other States and the Federal Government, employed an indeterminate sentencing scheme. . . . This system of unguided discretion inevitably resulted in severe disparities in sentences received and served by defendants committing the same offense and having similar criminal histories. . . . To counteract these trends, the state legislature passed the Sentencing Reform Act of 1981. The Act had the laudable purposes of making the criminal justice system "accountable to the public," and ensuring that "the punishment for a criminal offense is proportionate to the seriousness of the offense [and] commensurate with the punishment imposed on others committing similar offenses." Wash. Rev. Code Ann. §9.94A.010. The Act neither increased any of the statutory sentencing ranges for the three types of felonies . . . nor reclassified any substantive offenses. It merely placed meaningful constraints on discretion to sentence offenders within the statutory ranges, and eliminated parole. There is thus no evidence that the legislature was attempting to manipulate the statutory elements of criminal offenses or to circumvent the procedural protections of the Bill of Rights. . . .

## II

Far from disregarding principles of due process and the jury trial right, as the majority today suggests, Washington's reform has served them. Before passage of the Act, a defendant charged with second degree kidnaping, like petitioner, had no idea whether he would receive a 10-year sentence or probation. The ultimate sentencing determination could turn as much on the idiosyncrasies of a particular judge as on the specifics of the defendant's crime or background. A defendant did not know what facts, if any, about his offense or his history would be considered relevant by the sentencing judge or by the parole board. After passage of the Act, a defendant charged with second degree kidnaping knows what his presumptive sentence will be; he has a good idea of the types of factors that a sentencing judge can and will consider when deciding whether to sentence him outside that range; he is guaranteed meaningful appellate review to protect against an arbitrary sentence. . . .

While not a constitutional prohibition on guidelines schemes, the majority's decision today exacts a substantial constitutional tax. [Facts] that historically have been taken into account by sentencing judges to assess a sentence within a broad range — such as drug quantity, role in the offense, risk of bodily harm — all must now be charged in an indictment and submitted to a jury simply because it is the legislature, rather than the judge, that constrains the extent to which such facts may be used to impose a sentence within a pre-existing statutory range. . . . The majority may be correct that States and the Federal Government will be willing to bear some of these costs. But simple economics dictate that they will not, and cannot, bear them all. To the extent that they do not, there will be an inevitable increase in judicial discretion with all of its attendant failings.

[The] guidelines served due process by providing notice to petitioner of the consequences of his acts; they vindicated his jury trial right by informing him of the stakes of risking trial; they served equal protection by ensuring petitioner that invidious characteristics such as race would not impact his sentence. Given these observations, it is difficult for me to discern what principle besides doctrinaire formalism actually motivates today's decision. . . .

The consequences of today's decision will be as far reaching as they are disturbing. Washington's sentencing system is by no means unique. Numerous other States have enacted guidelines systems, as has the Federal Government.

Today's decision casts constitutional doubt over them all and, in so doing, threatens an untold number of criminal judgments. Every sentence imposed under such guidelines in cases currently pending on direct appeal is in jeopardy. . . . What I have feared most has now come to pass: Over 20 years of sentencing reform are all but lost, and tens of thousands of criminal judgments are in jeopardy. I respectfully dissent.

KENNEDY, J., dissenting.
. . . The Court, in my respectful submission, disregards the fundamental principle under our constitutional system that different branches of government converse with each other on matters of vital common interest. . . . Case-by-case judicial determinations often yield intelligible patterns that can be refined by legislatures and codified into statutes or rules as general standards. As these legislative enactments are followed by incremental judicial interpretation, the legislatures may respond again, and the cycle repeats. This recurring dialogue, an essential source for the elaboration and the evolution of the law, is basic constitutional theory in action.

Sentencing guidelines are a prime example of this collaborative process. Dissatisfied with the wide disparity in sentencing, participants in the criminal justice system, including judges, pressed for legislative reforms. In response, legislators drew from these participants' shared experiences and enacted measures to correct the problems. [Because] the Constitution does not prohibit the dynamic and fruitful dialogue between the judicial and legislative branches of government that has marked sentencing reform on both the state and the federal levels for more than 20 years, I dissent.

BREYER, J., dissenting.
[The] difference between a traditional sentencing factor and an element of a greater offense often comes down to a legislative choice about which label to affix. [One might ask why it should matter for jury trial purposes whether the statute (or guideline) labels a fact as a sentencing factor or a crime element. But] the conclusion that the Sixth Amendment always requires identical treatment of the two scenarios [carries] consequences that threaten the fairness of our traditional criminal justice system; it distorts historical sentencing or criminal trial practices; and it upsets settled law on which legislatures have relied in designing punishment systems. . . .

As a result of the majority's rule, sentencing must now take one of three forms, each of which risks either impracticality, unfairness, or harm to the jury trial right the majority purports to strengthen. This circumstance shows that the majority's Sixth Amendment interpretation cannot be right.

### A

A first option for legislators is to create a simple, pure or nearly pure "charge offense" or "determinate" sentencing system. In such a system, an indictment would charge a few facts which, taken together, constitute a crime, such as robbery. Robbery would carry a single sentence, say, five years' imprisonment. . . .

Such a system assures uniformity, but at intolerable costs. First, simple determinate sentencing systems impose identical punishments on people who committed their crimes in very different ways. When dramatically different conduct ends up being punished the same way, an injustice has taken place. Simple determinate sentencing has the virtue of treating like cases alike, but it simultaneously fails to treat different cases differently. . . .

Second, in a world of statutorily fixed mandatory sentences for many crimes, determinate sentencing gives tremendous power to prosecutors to manipulate sentences through their choice of charges. Prosecutors can simply charge, or threaten to charge, defendants with crimes bearing higher mandatory sentences. Defendants, knowing that they will not have a chance to argue for a lower sentence in front of a judge, may plead to charges that they might otherwise contest. . . .

## B

A second option for legislators is to return to a system of indeterminate sentencing. . . . When such systems were in vogue, they were criticized, and rightly so, for producing unfair disparities, including race-based disparities, in the punishment of similarly situated defendants. [Under] such a system, the judge could vary the sentence greatly based upon his findings about how the defendant had committed the crime — findings that might not have been made by a "preponderance of the evidence," much less "beyond a reasonable doubt." Returning to such a system would . . . do little to ensure the control of what the majority calls "the people," i.e., the jury, "in the judiciary," since "the people" would only decide the defendant's guilt, a finding with no effect on the duration of the sentence. . . .

## C

A third option is that which the Court seems to believe legislators will in fact take. That is the option of retaining structured schemes that attempt to punish similar conduct similarly and different conduct differently, but modifying them to conform to *Apprendi*'s dictates. Judges would be able to depart downward from presumptive sentences upon finding that mitigating factors were present, but would not be able to depart upward unless the prosecutor charged the aggravating fact to a jury and proved it beyond a reasonable doubt. . . .

This option can be implemented in one of two ways. The first way would be for legislatures to subdivide each crime into a list of complex crimes, each of which would be defined to include commonly found sentencing factors such as drug quantity, type of victim, presence of violence, degree of injury, use of gun, and so on. A legislature, for example, might enact a robbery statute, modeled on robbery sentencing guidelines, that increases punishment depending upon (1) the nature of the institution robbed, (2) the (a) presence of, (b) brandishing of, (c) other use of, a firearm, (3) making of a death threat, (4) presence of (a) ordinary, (b) serious, (c) permanent or life threatening, bodily injury,

(5) abduction, (6) physical restraint, (7) taking of a firearm, (8) taking of drugs, (9) value of property loss, etc.

[Under this option, the] prosecutor, through control of the precise charge, controls the punishment, thereby marching the sentencing system directly away from, not toward, one important guideline goal: rough uniformity of punishment for those who engage in roughly the same real criminal conduct. . . .

This "complex charge offense" system . . . prejudices defendants who seek trial, for it can put them in the untenable position of contesting material aggravating facts in the guilt phases of their trials. Consider a defendant who is charged, not with mere possession of cocaine, but with the specific offense of possession of more than 500 grams of cocaine. Or consider a defendant charged, not with murder, but with the new crime of murder using a machete. Or consider a defendant whom the prosecution wants to claim was a "supervisor," rather than an ordinary gang member. How can a Constitution that guarantees due process put these defendants, as a matter of course, in the position of arguing, "I did not sell drugs, and if I did, I did not sell more than 500 grams" or, "I did not kill him, and if I did, I did not use a machete," or "I did not engage in gang activity, and certainly not as a supervisor" to a single jury? . . .

The majority announces that there really is no problem here because "States may continue to offer judicial factfinding as a matter of course to all defendants who plead guilty" and defendants may stipulate to the relevant facts or consent to judicial factfinding. [The] fairness problem arises because States may very well decide that they will not permit defendants to carve subsets of facts out of the new, *Apprendi*-required 17-element robbery crime, seeking a judicial determination as to some of those facts and a jury determination as to others. . . .

The second way to make sentencing guidelines *Apprendi*-compliant would be to require at least two juries for each defendant whenever aggravating facts are present: one jury to determine guilt of the crime charged, and an additional jury to try the disputed facts that, if found, would aggravate the sentence. Our experience with bifurcated trials in the capital punishment context suggests that requiring them for run-of-the-mill sentences would be costly, both in money and in judicial time and resources. . . . The Court can announce that the Constitution requires at least two jury trials for each criminal defendant — one for guilt, another for sentencing — but only because it knows full well that more than 90% of defendants will not go to trial even once, much less insist on two or more trials.

What will be the consequences of the Court's holding for the 90% of defendants who do not go to trial? The truthful answer is that we do not know. . . . At the least, the greater expense attached to trials and their greater complexity, taken together in the context of an overworked criminal justice system, will likely mean, other things being equal, fewer trials and a greater reliance upon plea bargaining — a system in which punishment is set not by judges or juries but by advocates acting under bargaining constraints. At the same time, the greater power of the prosecutor to control the punishment through the charge would likely weaken the relation between real conduct and real punishment as well. . . .

For more than a century, questions of punishment (not those of guilt or innocence) have reflected determinations made, not only by juries, but also by judges, probation officers, and executive parole boards. Such truth-seeking determinations have rested upon both adversarial and non-adversarial processes. The Court's holding undermines efforts to reform these processes, for it means that legislatures cannot both permit judges to base sentencing upon real conduct and seek, through guidelines, to make the results more uniform. . . .

Now, let us return to the question I posed at the outset. Why does the Sixth Amendment permit a jury trial right (in respect to a particular fact) to depend upon a legislative labeling decision, namely, the legislative decision to label the fact a sentencing fact, instead of an element of the crime? The answer is that the fairness and effectiveness of a sentencing system, and the related fairness and effectiveness of the criminal justice system itself, depend upon the legislature's possessing the constitutional authority (within due process limits) to make that labeling decision. To restrict radically the legislature's power in this respect, as the majority interprets the Sixth Amendment to do, prevents the legislature from seeking sentencing systems that are consistent with, and indeed may help to advance, the Constitution's greater fairness goals. . . . Whatever the faults of guidelines systems—and there are many—they are more likely to find their cure in legislation emerging from the experience of, and discussion among, all elements of the criminal justice community, than in a virtually unchangeable constitutional decision of this Court. . . .

## NOTES

1. Blakely *and sentencing guideline systems.*  The sweeping language that Justice Scalia used in *Blakely* suggested to most readers that many nondiscretionary sentencing procedures were constitutionally suspect. Most immediately, the *Blakely* decision cast doubt on the constitutionality of the federal sentencing guidelines. As we saw in Chapter 3, the second shoe did drop for the federal system: a few months after *Blakely,* the Supreme Court ruled in United States v. Booker, 543 U.S. 220 (2005), that the presumptive guideline system in the federal courts violated the Sixth Amendment jury trial guarantee. The Court remedied this constitutional error in a surprising way, by excising only those portions of the federal statutes that gave the guidelines binding force on the sentencing judge.

In the states, the courts responded to *Blakely* in a variety of ways. Some declared that their determinate sentencing systems violated jury trial rights as described in *Blakely.* See Smylie v. State, 823 N.E.2d 679 (Ind. 2005); State v. Natale, 878 A.2d 724 (N.J. 2005). Others labored to demonstrate that their statutes governing sentencing leave enough discretion to the trial judge to avoid any *Blakely* problems. See People v. Black, 113 P.3d 534, 543, 548 (Cal. 2005); State v. Lopez, 123 P.3d 754, 768 (N.M. 2005).

The Supreme Court reaffirmed the impact of the *Blakely* rule on a variety of structured sentencing laws in Cunningham v. California, 127 S. Ct. 856 (2007). The California sentencing laws gave judges a choice among three sentencing outcomes in many cases, and designated the "middle term" as the presumptively correct sentence, but allowed the judge to select the upper term after finding "circumstances in aggravation" of the offense. Justice Ginsburg's opinion declared that the California determinate sentencing law violated the "bright-line rule" of *Apprendi*: "Except for a prior conviction, any fact that increases the penalty for a crime beyond the prescribed statutory maximum must be submitted to a jury, and proved beyond a reasonable doubt."

To what extent do the *Blakely* and *Apprendi* cases cast doubt on earlier holdings about sentencing procedure? In Nichols v. United States, 511 U.S. 738 (1994), the Court held that a sentencing court may consider a defendant's previous uncounseled misdemeanor conviction when sentencing him for a subsequent offense, and it cited both *Williams* and *McMillan* when stressing that the "traditional understanding of the sentencing process [is] less exacting than the process of establishing guilt." Recall also from Chapter 5 the decision in Witte v. United States, 515 U.S. 389 (1995), where the Court held that there was no double jeopardy violation when a prior conviction increased punishment through sentence calculations under the federal sentencing guidelines. In United States v. Watts, 519 U.S. 148 (1997), the Court stressed the "significance of the different standards of proof that govern at trial and sentencing" in holding that courts sentencing under the federal guidelines could consider conduct relating to charges of which defendants had been acquitted. Do any of these decisions survive *Blakely*?

2. *Glimpses of broader jury rights before* Apprendi.   Though now overshadowed by the *Apprendi* and *Blakely* decisions, the Supreme Court's decisions in Almendarez-Torres v. United States, 523 U.S. 224 (1998), and Jones v. United States, 526 U.S. 227 (1999), showed that the traditional approach to sentencing procedures was near the breaking point. In *Almendarez-Torres*, the Supreme Court interpreted the federal alien reentry statute, which imposed punishment of up to two years in prison if a deported alien reentered the United States without permission, but raised the maximum sentence to 20 years if the alien had been convicted of an aggravated felony before deportation. Although the government asked for the enhanced sentence for Almendarez-Torres, prosecutors did not allege his prior felony in the indictment or prove it at trial but instead submitted proof of his record at sentencing. On appeal, Almendarez-Torres argued that the recidivism issue could not be treated as a mere sentencing enhancement but rather constituted an element of the separate aggravated felony authorizing the 20-year sentence. In a 5-4 decision, the Supreme Court interpreted the reentry statute to provide for a recidivism enhancement only as a sentencing factor, and thus the facts about his prior record were not subject to the procedural rules of proof at trial. The majority opinion, authored by Justice Breyer, emphasized that recidivism long has been a sentencing factor not needed to be proven to the jury.

When a similar issue arose the following term in Jones v. United States, there were five votes to recast what looked like a sentencing factor into a traditional element of an offense. The majority in *Jones* concluded that the federal carjacking statute created distinct crimes with distinct elements, because several related subsections defined increasing maximum penalty levels if the offense resulted in serious bodily injury or death. In a revealing footnote, the *Jones* Court suggested an emerging due process principle that "any fact (other than prior conviction) that increases the maximum penalty for a crime must be charged in an indictment, submitted to a jury, and proven beyond a reasonable doubt." The majority reinterpreted *Almendarez-Torres* to create a recidivism "exception" to this rule.

Despite these early clues in the cases, the decisions in *Apprendi* and *Blakely* took most observers by surprise. Even after the Court decided *Apprendi*, most observers believed that the decision was limited to factual findings that moved a sentence higher than the original statutory maximum, not findings that changed the relevant maximum under the sentencing guidelines. Among the persistent critiques of the federal sentencing system over the years, almost nobody claimed that the key problem was its failure to rely on juries for factual findings.

3. *The Swiss cheese* Blakely *holding.*   Despite the breadth of *Blakely's* holding and dicta, the ruling still allows judicial factfinding in an array of sentencing settings. The *Blakely* decision formally distinguished United States v. Harris, 536 U.S. 545 (2002), which permits judges to find those facts that increase *minimum* sentences. The *Blakely* decision also formally distinguished Williams v. New York, 337 U.S. 241 (1949), which permits judges to find facts in the course of making discretionary sentencing determinations. In addition, the *Apprendi* and *Blakely* rulings apply only to those facts that *increase* sentences; judges may still find those facts that the law provides as the basis for decreasing sentences. As we have seen, the decision in Almendarez-Torres v. United States, 523 U.S. 224 (1998), built a "prior conviction" exception into the Sixth Amendment's jury requirements for sentencing facts. Both *Apprendi* and *Blakely* stated that the jury must find sentence-enhancing facts "other than the fact of a prior conviction." See generally Kevin Reitz, The New Sentencing Conundrum: Policy and Constitutional Law at Cross-Purposes, 105 Colum. L. Rev. 1082 (2005) ("As things stand, there are so many exceptions to the new safeguards announced in *Apprendi* and *Blakely*—and many of them are important exceptions—that we are left with a kind of constitutional 'Swiss cheese.' "). Could a jurisdiction, drawing on these gaps in the reach of the *Blakely* rule, construct a sound sentencing system that is still administered principally through judicial factfinding?

4. *Jury rights and plea bargaining.*   Because the *Apprendi* and *Blakely* decisions established that defendants are entitled to a fuller set of trial procedures for facts that raise the applicable maximum sentence, the cases appear to give a big victory to defendants. It is worth asking, however, how this grant of trial rights will play out in a world that only rarely sees criminal cases go to trial. Professor Stephanos Bibas argued that the trial right protected by *Apprendi* does little good and much harm for most defendants, because the rule gave prosecutors an incentive to pressure defendants into admitting as part of a plea agreement those facts that would support a higher sentence. See Stephanos Bibas, Judicial Fact-Finding and Sentence Enhancements in a World of Guilty Pleas, 110 Yale L.J. 1097, 1100 (2001). Professors Nancy King and Susan Klein, responded, however, that prosecutors have no more leverage over defendants after *Apprendi* than they did before, while defendants have the additional bargaining chip of forcing a prosecutor to prove certain facts to a jury beyond a reasonable doubt. Nancy J. King & Susan R. Klein, *Apprendi* and Plea Bargaining, 54 Stan. L. Rev. 295, 297 (2001). How might you resolve such conflicting claims about bargaining behavior? Is there a practical empirical test you might perform? A relevant theoretical model that makes one account more plausible than the other?

5. *Retroactivity and cases in the pipeline.* The *Blakely* holding arguably called into question the validity of hundreds of thousands of existing sentences that were imposed without input from a jury. In Teague v. Lane, 489 U.S. 288 (1989), the Supreme Court set out the modern ground rules for the retroactive application of its constitutional pronouncements. Reduced to their essence, these rules suggest that *Blakely* applies to all cases that were not yet "final" (meaning that direct appeals were still pending) on the date the decision was rendered (June 24, 2004), but that *Blakely* would not apply to any cases that were final on that date.

Despite viable arguments about *Blakely*'s retroactivity, most commentators took the (slightly cynical) view that courts will seek to limit retroactivity simply because the consequences of giving *Blakely* retroactive effect could be so extreme. (Justice O'Connor's dissent in *Blakely* suggested, in a footnote, that well over 200,000 cases in the federal system alone could be impacted if *Blakely* were to be made retroactive to the date *Apprendi* was decided in 2000.) From a legal realist perspective, it seems quite unsurprising that courts have not applied *Blakely* retroactively. In United States v. Cotton, 536 U.S. 625 (2002), the Supreme Court effectively limited the retroactive impact of *Apprendi* by ruling that indictments rendered defective by the *Apprendi* rule should be reviewed only for plain error and do not require automatic reversal of a conviction or sentence.

As for cases pending at the time of the *Blakely* decision, the Supreme Court gave lower courts the means to sustain most sentences despite any errors. The Court declared in Washington v. Recuenco, 548 U.S. 212 (2006), that the failure to submit a sentencing factor to a jury does not qualify as "structural error" requiring the automatic reversal of an enhanced sentence. Instead, explained the Court, *Blakely* errors should be reviewed on appeal and can be excused as "harmless error."

Do other branches of government bear some responsibility for devising a remedy for those prisoners who may be serving decades of additional jail time based on a judicial factfinding that the Supreme Court has now deemed unconstitutional? Should the clemency power be reinvigorated to address this situation?

6. *Principle versus pragmatism.* Do the *Blakely* dissenters provide any strong constitutional arguments against the majority's interpretation of the Sixth Amendment, or might it be fair to characterize their complaints as providing only pragmatic arguments against the Court's holding? An old Roman maxim, "Let justice be done though the heavens fall," is meant to suggest that a decision's adverse practical consequences should not keep a court from rendering justice. Can this maxim, though inspiring, really be practiced?

## PROBLEM 6-1. MOVING VIOLATIONS OF *BLAKELY*

Responding to concerns expressed by the National Commission Against Drunk Driving and to a recent rise in alcohol-related accidents, the state legislature passed a bipartisan package of bills amending the Penal Code. The new laws include the following provisions:

- Operating a motor vehicle with a Blood Alcohol Concentration (BAC) greater than .08% constitutes the offense of Driving Under the Influence (DUI), requiring, in addition to license revocation and other administrative sanctions, a mandatory minimum sentence of no less than $5,000 fine and a maximum sentence of no more than 1 year's imprisonment and a $50,000 fine.
- Operating a motor vehicle with a BAC greater than .15% constitutes the offense of Driving While Intoxicated (DWI), requiring, in addition to administrative sanctions, a mandatory minimum sentence of no less than 3 months and a $10,000 fine and a maximum sentence of no more than 2 years and $100,000 fine.
- Operating a motor vehicle with a BAC greater than .25% constitutes the offense of Aggravated Driving While Intoxicated (ADWI), requiring, in addition to administrative sanctions, a mandatory minimum sentence of no less than 2 years and a maximum sentence of no more than 5 years.
- If a defendant has previously been convicted of one drunk-driving–related charge, the required minimum and allowed maximum sentences for these crimes shall be doubled. If the defendant has previously been convicted of two or more drunk-driving–related charges, the required minimum and allowed maximum sentences shall be multiplied by a factor of 10.
- A sentencing judge may sentence a defendant below the applicable mandatory minimum sentence if the defendant shows, by clear and convincing evidence, that the incident of drunk driving involved a completely aberrant act or was the result of an unavoidable and compelling necessity.
- A sentencing judge may sentence a defendant above the otherwise applicable maximum if the prosecution shows, by clear and convincing evidence, that the incident of drunk driving resulted in serious physical harm or death to any innocent persons.

Adam Even, the first person prosecuted under the state's new drunk-driving laws, comes to you for legal advice. This past weekend he drove to a friend's house (which was only two miles from his home) to watch a big football game on television. After drinking beer throughout the evening, Adam realized he was not fit to drive home after the game ended.

Upon calling his wife to tell her he planned to stay at his friend's house until the morning, Adam learned that his young daughter was ill and that he was needed at home as soon as possible. Unable to secure a ride from his friends (who themselves were intoxicated), Adam quickly downed a few cups of coffee and convinced himself that he would now be able to navigate the ride home.

Adam managed to drive safely and without incident until he reached the traffic light at the entrance to his subdivision. Feeling sleepy from the alcohol in his system, Adam momentarily dozed off while waiting for the light to turn from red to green. He awoke to the sound of car horns and breaking glass, and saw that two cars had collided in the intersection in front of him. (Adam's car remained untouched, idling in front of the traffic light.) Before Adam could take in what was going on, the police and an ambulance arrived at the scene. The ambulance quickly drove away with a passenger from one of the smashed cars, who appeared to have a broken leg.

Adam and the other motorists on the scene were given Breathalyzer tests. To Adam's surprise, he registered a BAC of .254%, while the other drivers tested fully sober. The police interviewed the drivers involved in the collision. One driver told the police that, after sitting a while behind Adam's car at the green light, she tried to navigate her car around his vehicle, but apparently did not get through the intersection before the light changed, and a car coming the other way drove into hers. After hearing this story, the police arrested Adam for Aggravated DWI; he was processed that night and released on bail.

The district attorney has now informed Adam that he plans to prosecute fully. This DA told Adam that he planned to introduce evidence establishing that Adam had pled guilty to two prior DUIs: one 15 years ago, when Adam was a high school junior, and another 10 years ago, when Adam was a college senior.

What would be the longest sentence Adam could face under the new drunk-driving laws? What procedural rights might Adam have if he pleads guilty to DWI but wants to contest some of the facts that seem to be the basis for an enhanced sentence? What procedure should the prosecutor follow to make sure the new law complies with *Apprendi* and *Blakely*?

## PROBLEM 6-2.   THE CAPITAL JURY

Timothy Ring was convicted of felony murder in the course of an armed robbery but acquitted of premeditated murder. As required by Arizona law, the trial judge then held "a separate sentencing hearing to determine the existence or nonexistence" of certain enumerated circumstances "for the purpose of determining the sentence to be imposed." According to Arizona law, the "court alone shall make all factual determinations required by this section or the constitution of the United States or this state." The statute authorized the judge to sentence the defendant to death only if there was at least one aggravating circumstance and there were "no mitigating circumstances sufficiently substantial to call for leniency." The trial judge sentenced Ring to death.

Because Ring was convicted of felony murder, not premeditated murder, the judge recognized that Ring was eligible for the death penalty only if he was the victim's actual killer or if he was "a major participant in the armed robbery that led to the killing and exhibited a reckless disregard or indifference for human life." Based on evidence at the sentencing hearing, the judge concluded that Ring "is the one who shot and killed Mr. Magoch" and then found two aggravating factors: (1) Ring committed the offense in expectation of receiving something of "pecuniary value," and (2) the offense was committed "in an especially heinous, cruel or depraved manner."

On appeal, Ring argued that Arizona's capital sentencing scheme violated the Sixth and Fourteenth Amendments to the U.S. Constitution because it entrusted to a judge the finding of a fact raising the defendant's maximum penalty. If *Apprendi* were the most recent relevant authority, how would you rule on Ring's argument? What if *Blakely* were the most recent case?

## NOTES

1. *The* Harris *retreat.*    There was a serious tension between *Apprendi*'s "elements" rule for facts that raise maximum sentences and *McMillan*'s holding that facts triggering mandatory minimum sentences can be found by a judge based on a preponderance standard of proof. In Harris v. United States, 536 U.S. 545 (2002), the Court addressed this tension and came down on the side of *McMillan.* The opinion significantly restricted the reach of *Apprendi,* holding that facts that increase mandatory minimum penalties can still be treated as sentencing factors and thus do not require submission to a jury or proof beyond a reasonable doubt. The holding seemed, at the time, to endorse a narrow reading of *Apprendi*; it remains a puzzling (and perhaps unstable) limit on the broader *Blakely* rule.

On a regular basis after *Blakely,* defendants subject to significant mandatory minimum sentencing terms based on judicial factfinding filed petitions with the Supreme Court urging reversal of *Harris.* For nearly a decade, the Justices repeatedly denied cert on these petitions. But in Fall 2012, the Supreme Court granted review in Alleyne v. United States, a federal case in which the defendant received an additional seven-year prison term based upon a finding by a judge that he likely knew a partner in a robbery planned to "brandish" a gun. In the *Alleyne* case, the defendant was convicted at trial of robbery, but was not convicted by the jury of having brandished a firearm during the robbery. During the subsequent sentencing hearing, the district court stated that "I think it's fair to say [the jurors] didn't find brandishing beyond a reasonable doubt because they were told they had to find it beyond a reasonable doubt if they were going to do it." The court further stated, "I don't like the role of being the reverser of juries," but then went on to conclude that it was bound by *Harris* to make its own factual determination concerning the applicability of mandatory minimum sentencing terms. The court found, by a preponderance of the evidence, that Mr. Alleyne reasonably foresaw that his criminal partner would brandish a firearm during the robbery. As a result, the court imposed a required additional 84-month sentence, consecutive to a 46-month sentence imposed for the robbery conviction. Many court-watchers have expressed the view that the Supreme Court finally accepted review of this kind of case because newly appointed Justices are now eager to overrule *Harris.*

2. *Capital sentencing procedures and the Sixth Amendment.*    The constitutional and statutory sentencing procedures that apply in death penalty cases have filled many textbooks and treatises. The Supreme Court's landmark decisions in Furman v. Georgia, 408 U.S. 238 (1972), and Gregg v. Georgia, 428 U.S. 153 (1976), initiated a series of reforms that transformed capital sentencing into perhaps the most procedurally intricate and complicated area of any legal field. To what extent does the *Apprendi-Blakely* vision of the jury's functions for sentencing facts influence capital sentencing?

On the same day the U.S. Supreme Court significantly restricted the reach of *Apprendi* through Harris v. United States, 536 U.S. 545 (2002), the Court also significantly expanded *Apprendi* through its opinion in Ring v. Arizona, 536 U.S. 584 (2002). The Court held that facts establishing eligibility for the death penalty must be treated as "elements" and thus require submission to a jury and proof beyond a reasonable doubt. Although the Court had upheld Arizona's system in the past, that outcome was no longer tenable. Writing for the majority, Justice Ginsberg explained:

> In Walton v. Arizona, 497 U.S. 639 (1990), we upheld Arizona's scheme against a charge that it violated the Sixth Amendment. [We now] overrule *Walton* to the extent that it allows a sentencing judge, sitting without a jury, to find an aggravating circumstance necessary for imposition of the death penalty. Because Arizona's enumerated aggravating factors operate as "the functional equivalent of an element of a greater offense," the Sixth Amendment requires that they be found by a jury. . . .
>
> The right to trial by jury guaranteed by the Sixth Amendment would be senselessly diminished if it encompassed the factfinding necessary to increase a defendant's sentence by two years, but not the factfinding necessary to put him to death. We hold that the Sixth Amendment applies to both.

Justice Scalia (joined by Justice Thomas) concurred. While disagreeing with the capital jurisprudence that requires findings of aggravating factors to justify a capital sentence, he stated that "the fundamental meaning of the jury-trial guarantee of the Sixth Amendment is that all facts essential to imposition of the level of punishment that the defendant receives — whether the statute calls them elements of the offense, sentencing factors, or Mary Jane — must be found by the jury beyond a reasonable doubt."

Justice O'Connor and Chief Justice Rehnquist dissented. While they agreed that *Apprendi* and *Walton* were inconsistent, the experience of two years suggested to them that *Apprendi* should be reversed. Justice O'Connor wrote:

> Not only was the decision in *Apprendi* unjustified in my view, but it has also had a severely destabilizing effect on our criminal justice system. I predicted in my dissent that the decision would "unleash a flood of petitions by convicted defendants seeking to invalidate their sentences in whole or in part on the authority of [*Apprendi*]." As of May 31, 2002, less than two years after *Apprendi* was announced, the United States Courts of Appeals had decided approximately 1,802 criminal appeals in which defendants challenged their sentences, and in some cases even their convictions, under *Apprendi*. These federal appeals are likely only the tip of the iceberg, as federal criminal prosecutions represent a tiny fraction of the total number of criminal prosecutions nationwide. The number of second or successive habeas corpus petitions filed in the federal courts also increased by 77% in 2001, a phenomenon the Administrative Office of the United States Courts attributes to prisoners bringing *Apprendi* claims. . . .
>
> The decision today is only going to add to these already serious effects. The Court effectively declares five States' capital sentencing schemes unconstitutional [by] identifying Colorado, Idaho, Montana, and Nebraska as having sentencing schemes like Arizona's. There are 168 prisoners on death row in these States, each of whom is now likely to challenge his or her death sentence. . . . In addition, I fear that the prisoners on death row in Alabama, Delaware, Florida, and Indiana, which the Court identifies as having hybrid sentencing schemes in which the jury renders an advisory verdict but the judge makes the ultimate sentencing determination, may also seize on today's decision to challenge their sentences. There are 529 prisoners on death row in these States. By expanding on *Apprendi*, the Court today exacerbates the harm done in that case.

3. *Non-prison punishments and the Sixth Amendment.*   For more than a decade, nearly all lower court disputes and all Supreme Court rulings concerning the reach and application of *Apprendi* and *Blakely* dealt with judicial factfinding for the imposition of the death penalty or terms of imprisonment. Significantly, the rulings in *Apprendi* and *Blakely* speak generally about factfinding concerning "any fact that increases the penalty for a crime" and "facts legally essential to the punishment" without any clear limit on the kinds of criminal "penalty" or "punishment" subject to the Sixth Amendment rules set forth in these landmark rulings. In turn, defendants facing a range of non-prison punishments based on judicial factfinding were quick to claim that they were due the Sixth Amendment right to jury determination of key facta established in *Apprendi* and *Blakely*. But some lower courts concluded that judges were still permitted to make factual findings necessary for fines, forfeitures and restitution awards, often based on the theory that *Apprendi* does not apply to factfinding in determining, for example, fine amounts or forfeiture or restitution awards when the applicable statutes does not create a fixed penalty ceiling.

In June 2012, the Supreme Court addresses the application of *Apprendi* to criminal fines in Southern Union Co. v. United States, 132 S. Ct. 2344 (2012). In *Southern Union*, the defendant corporation had been convicted by a jury of a single count of a federal statute which criminalizes certain conduct that adversely affects the environment, and the jury was not asked to find the number of days of violation. The statute provided for a $50,000 fine for each day of a violation, and the trial judge decided to impose (and the First Circuit affirmed) a fine of over $6 million based on judical findings that the violation extended 762 days. In reversing the First Circuit, the Supreme Court declared without reservation that *Apprendi* applies to the imposition of criminal fines. The Court explained that it had never distinguished one form of penal sanction from another, so that *Apprendi* applies to all forms of criminal sanctions. The Court in *Southern Union* found that there is "no principled basis under *Apprendi* for treating criminal fines differently" from other forms of punishment. The Court explained that: "In stating *Apprendi*'s rule, we have never distinguished one form of punishment from another. Instead, our decisions broadly prohibit judicial factfinding that increases maximum criminal 'sentence[s],' 'penalties,' or 'punishment[s]' — terms that each undeniably embrace fines." Id. at 2351.

In light of Southern Union's ruling as to *Apprendi*'s applicability to criminal fines, is it now perfectly clear that *Apprendi* and *Blakely* now also require juries to find beyond a reasonable doubt any and all facts legally necessary to orders of criminal forfeiture and restitution awards? Can you think of principled or practical reasons why lower court judges would still resist applying the Sixth Amendment limit on judicial factfinding to forfeitures and restitution awards?

4. *The implications of juries for other trial procedures.*   The Sixth Amendment jury trial right now requires jury involvement in finding the facts that authorize certain sentence increases. Based on passing statements in the *Apprendi* and *Blakely* opinions, it appears that the standard of proof for the criminal trial — beyond a reasonable doubt — also applies to those facts that are relevant to sentencing.

What other aspects of trial procedure are implicated in the finding of these facts? Does *Blakely* mean that defendants now have a constitutional right to testify in their own behalf at a sentencing hearing? To present favorable witnesses or other evidence at sentencing? To cross-examine witnesses at the sentencing hearing? Procedural rules already provide many of these opportunities, but will practices change once these procedures gain constitutional status?

### 3.  Rebuilding Guideline Procedures

The Supreme Court's new vision of the role of juries in sentencing disrupted the operation of many sentencing procedures. The cases have required legislators, judges, prosecutors, defense attorneys, sentencing commissioners, and many other criminal justice players to think creatively and to rebuild systems in light of the new requirements. The following materials — a state appellate opinion and a report from a state sentencing commission — show this creative rebuilding at work.

|| **State v. Abdul Abdullah** ||
|| 878 A.2d 746 (N.J. 2005) ||

ALBIN, J.

The Sixth Amendment's jury trial guarantee forbids a judge from imposing a sentence beyond the range authorized by either a jury's verdict or a defendant's admissions at a plea hearing. To conform the Code of Criminal Justice to that constitutional principle, today, in State v. Natale, we struck down the Code's system of presumptive term sentencing. 878 A.2d 724 (N.J. 2005) (*Natale II*).

Under the Code, the maximum sentence that a judge may impose based on a jury verdict alone is the statutory presumptive term. Without being bound by the verdict, however, the judge is empowered by the Code to sentence a defendant above the presumptive term based on a finding of one or more aggravating factors listed in N.J.S.A. 2C:44-1(a). It is the delegation of that authority to a judge to impose a sentence above the presumptive based on judicial factfinding that runs afoul of the Sixth Amendment. In *Natale II* we removed the presumptive terms from N.J.S.A. 2C:44-1(f) to bring the Code into compliance with the Sixth Amendment.

We now must decide whether other sentencing procedures under the Code intrude on the authority reserved to the jury under the Constitution. In this case, we conclude that the powers given to a judge by the Code to sentence a defendant to a period of life imprisonment for murder, to a period of parole disqualification pursuant to N.J.S.A. 2C:43-6(b), and to consecutive sentences for multiple convictions do not run counter to the Sixth Amendment.

[Catrina Lark and Abdul Aleem Abdullah] were involved in a two-year romantic relationship that ended in December 1998. During that period, defendant spent daytime hours with Lark and his evenings with his girlfriend Joan Robinson, the mother of his two children. Around January 1999, while incarcerated in the Atlantic County jail for a parole violation, defendant learned that Lark was involved in a relationship with his cousin, Robert Boswell, who also was detained in that jail facility. . . .

In April 1999, defendant was released from jail. On May 2, 1999, [a neighbor discovered Lark's body on the kitchen floor of her apartment.] Upon arriving in Lark's apartment, the police observed blood on the walls and the scene in total disarray. Lark was found lying naked from the waist down in a pool of her own blood on the kitchen floor. She had no pulse and had suffered "multiple lacerations, contusions, and cutting wounds" and "blunt force injuries" over her entire upper body and head. . . .

The police retrieved from the area near Lark's body a bloody rolling pin, a broken clothes iron, an electric skillet, a cast-iron frying pan, and a ceramic lamp. The police also recovered a variety of broken, bent, and blood-stained knives scattered throughout the apartment, and a bloody weightlifting glove. The physical evidence pointed to defendant as the killer. Defendant's fingerprints were discovered on the skillet's broken handle.

[The] police arrested defendant at his home. At the time of his arrest, defendant was bleeding from a cut on his hand that he claimed occurred when he fell from his bicycle the previous day. In response to questioning, defendant maintained that he had been home with his girlfriend, Robinson, on the morning of the killing. However, Robinson testified that defendant got up and left their apartment at around 2:40 A.M., and returned sometime between 3:00 and 3:30 A.M., making "a lot of noise when he came in." . . .

The jury found defendant guilty of all counts in the indictment, [including murder, second-degree burglary, third-degree possession of a weapon for an unlawful purpose, and fourth-degree unlawful possession of a weapon]. At sentencing, the trial court identified four aggravating factors: "the nature and circumstances of the offense . . . including whether or not it was committed in an especially heinous, cruel, or depraved manner"; "the risk that . . . defendant will commit another offense"; the extent and seriousness of defendant's prior criminal record; and the need to deter defendant and others from violating the law. Finding the aggravating factors to be "overwhelming" and no mitigating factors, the court sentenced defendant to life imprisonment with a thirty-year parole disqualifier on the murder conviction and to a consecutive ten-year prison term with a five-year parole disqualifier on one of the second-degree burglary convictions. The remaining charges were merged into the murder conviction.

The court detailed its reasons for imposing sentence:

> This is the most brutal murder the court has seen in over 23 years on the bench. Defendant stabbed and bludgeoned the victim. Six knives were either bent or broken. A cast iron frying pan, an electric frying pan, a wooden rolling pin, an electric iron and a ceramic lamp were also smashed and broken over the victim's head and body. Defendant has a prior history of domestic violence. He has previously violated parole. This is a vicious dangerous defendant. Society needs to be protected from him. . . . An 18-year prison term imposed on a prior offense did not deter defendant. He violated parole on that offense and committed this murder shortly after being released when he "maxed out." . . . [He] is the same man who laughed and smirked at the victim's family during trial. His sympathy at sentencing rings hollow.

On appeal, defendant argued that because the jury did not determine the essential facts necessary for the imposition of maximum terms for murder and second-degree burglary, for the burglary parole disqualifier, and for consecutive sentences, defendant was denied his Sixth Amendment jury trial right as articulated in Blakely v. Washington. . . .

We first consider the constitutionality of defendant's sentence for second-degree burglary. . . . Under the Code of Criminal Justice, a second-degree crime is punishable by a term of imprisonment between five and ten years, with a presumptive term of seven years. In *Natale II* we held that the maximum sentence that can be imposed based on a jury verdict alone is the presumptive term. [A] sentence *above the presumptive term* premised on a judge's finding of aggravating factors, other than the fact of a prior criminal conviction, is incompatible with the holdings in *Apprendi* [and] *Blakely*. . . .

In this case, the trial court imposed a ten-year sentence for second-degree burglary based on its finding four aggravating factors in N.J.S.A. 2C:44-1(a): (1) nature of the offense, (3) risk of recidivism, (6) prior criminal record, and (9) need to deter. Apparently, based on facts not found by the jury, defendant received a sentence three years above the presumptive term for second-degree burglary. . . . On the spare record before us, it appears that the sentencing court used the "especially heinous, cruel, or depraved nature of the crime" — a fact not specifically found by the jury — as a basis for increasing the burglary sentence above its presumptive term. Moreover, we cannot tell from the record whether the court used that factfinding to support only aggravating factor (1) or whether it also was used to support aggravating factors (3) and (9). In other words, the sentencing court may have concluded that the "especially heinous, cruel, or depraved manner" of the killing indicated a risk of recidivism and a need to deter. In light of *Blakely* and our decision in *Natale II* only a jury finding of that fact would justify increasing a sentence above the presumptive. Accordingly, we are compelled to remand for resentencing on the burglary conviction.[2]

[On] remand, without the presumptive term as the required starting point, the court will consider all applicable aggravating and mitigating factors in determining the appropriate sentence within the range for second-degree burglary. Unlike almost every crime enumerated in the Code, murder has no presumptive term. N.J.S.A. 2C:11-3(b)(1) provides in relevant part:

> Murder is a crime of the first degree but a person convicted of murder shall be sentenced . . . by the court to a term of 30 years, during which the person shall not be eligible for parole, or be sentenced to a specific term of years *which shall be between 30 years and life imprisonment* of which the person shall serve 30 years before being eligible for parole. [Emphasis added.]

The provision of the Code that implements presumptive term sentencing specifically exempts murder from its sweep: "*Except for the crime of murder,* unless

---

2. We note that had the trial court specifically found that aggravating factors (3), (6), and (9) related to defendant's prior convictions as the basis for increasing defendant's sentence above the presumptive, we might have come to a different result. "[T]he fact of a prior conviction" may be used to increase the "penalty for a crime beyond the prescribed statutory maximum." *Apprendi,* 530 U.S. at 490; see also Almendarez-Torres v. United States, 523 U.S. 224, 243 (1998) ("[Recidivism] is a traditional, if not the most traditional, basis for a sentencing court's increasing an offender's sentence"). Aggravating factors (3), (6), and (9), *arguably,* are inextricably linked to the recidivism exception. . . .

the preponderance of aggravating or mitigating factors . . . weighs in favor of a higher or lower term" within the sentencing ranges for the four degrees of crimes, the court "shall impose" the presumptive term. N.J.S.A. 2C:44-1(f)(1) (emphasis added). Accordingly, the standard range for murder is a sentence between thirty years and life imprisonment. In contrast with defendant's burglary conviction, in which the upper sentencing limit based on the jury's verdict alone was the presumptive term, defendant's murder conviction did not impose a *de facto* ceiling below life imprisonment. Therefore, the trial court had discretion to impose a sentence within the statutory range of thirty years to life based on its consideration of the applicable sentencing factors. This state's sentencing scheme for murder is almost identical to the example of an indeterminate sentencing scheme depicted with approval in *Blakely*. . . .

Based on its finding of four aggravating factors and no mitigating factors, the trial court imposed the maximum parole disqualifier—five years—on the ten-year burglary sentence in accordance with N.J.S.A. 2C:43-6(b). That statute provides sentencing judges with the authority to impose a period of parole ineligibility on the four graded crimes enumerated in the Code:

> As part of a sentence for any crime, *where the court is clearly convinced that the aggravating factors substantially outweigh the mitigating factors,* as set forth in subsections a. and b. of N.J.S.A. 2C:44-1, *the court may fix a minimum term not to exceed one-half of the term set pursuant to subsection a.,* or one-half of the term set pursuant to a maximum period of incarceration for a crime set forth in any statute other than this code, during which the defendant shall not be eligible for parole. . . .

In making the discretionary decision whether to impose a parole disqualifier, the court balances the same aggravating and mitigating factors used to determine the length of the sentence, but applies a stricter standard that reflects the serious impact that a parole disqualifier will have on the "real time" a defendant serves on his sentence.

Both the United States Supreme Court and this Court have upheld the constitutionality of statutes that allow judges to impose mandatory-minimum parole ineligibility terms within the sentencing range authorized by the jury verdict. See, e.g., Harris v. United States, 536 U.S. 545, 568 (2002); McMillan v. Pennsylvania, 477 U.S. 79, 84-86 (1986); State v. Stanton, 820 A.2d 637 (N.J. 2003). [For] Sixth Amendment purposes, facts used to extend the sentence beyond the statutory maximum are deemed different from facts used to set the minimum sentence. Within the range authorized by the jury's verdict, . . . the political system may channel judicial discretion—and rely upon judicial expertise—by requiring defendants to serve minimum terms after judges make certain factual findings. . . .

[The aggravating and mitigating factors that the judge weighs under N.J.S.A. 2C:43-6(b)] are the traditional factors that courts always have considered in determining an appropriate sentence. They were neither intended by the Legislature to constitute elements of a crime nor were they transformed into constitutional elements when the judge used them to justify imposing a parole disqualifier. . . .

Last, defendant claims that *Blakely* requires that the jury, not the judge, make the findings of fact necessary for the imposition of consecutive sentences.

On that basis, he challenges the judicially-imposed consecutive sentences that he received for murder and burglary. We find no constitutional impediment to a judge's deciding whether a defendant should serve consecutive sentences under the standards governing sentencing in this state. N.J.S.A. 2C:44-5(a) provides in relevant part that when "multiple sentences of imprisonment are imposed on a defendant for more than one offense, . . . such multiple sentences shall run concurrently or consecutively as the court determines at the time of sentence." The discretion given to sentencing courts to impose consecutive sentences by the Code of Criminal Justice was the continuation of a long-standing common-law principle. The Code, however, does not set forth any standards to guide the court's discretion in deciding whether to impose consecutive or concurrent sentences when a defendant is convicted of multiple offenses. To bring rationality to the process and to further the goal of sentencing uniformity, this Court, in State v. Yarbough, 498 A.2d 1239 (N.J. 1985), developed criteria to be applied by the courts in making those decisions. The *Yarbough* criteria are:

(1)  there can be no free crimes in a system for which the punishment shall fit the crime;
(2)  the reasons for imposing either a consecutive or concurrent sentence should be separately stated in the sentencing decision;
(3)  some reasons to be considered by the sentencing court should include facts relating to the crimes, including whether or not:
   (a)  the crimes and their objectives were predominantly independent of each other;
   (b)  the crimes involved separate acts of violence or threats of violence;
   (c)  the crimes were committed at different times or separate places, rather than being committed so closely in time and place as to indicate a single period of aberrant behavior;
   (d)  any of the crimes involved multiple victims;
   (e)  the convictions for which the sentences are to be imposed are numerous;
(4)  there should be no double counting of aggravating factors;
(5)  successive terms for the same offense should not ordinarily be equal to the punishment for the first offense; and
(6)  there should be an overall outer limit on the cumulation of consecutive sentences for multiple offenses not to exceed the sum of the longest terms (including an extended term, if eligible) that could be imposed for the two most serious offenses.

In 1993, the Legislature eliminated the cap on the number of consecutive sentences that could be imposed pursuant to the sixth factor by amending N.J.S.A. 2C:44-5(a)(2) to provide that "[t]here shall be no overall outer limit on the cumulation of consecutive sentences for multiple offenses." The amendment granted greater discretion to judges in determining the overall length of a sentence.

Under our sentencing scheme, there is no presumption in favor of concurrent sentences and therefore the maximum potential sentence authorized by the jury verdict is the aggregate of sentences for multiple convictions. See N.J.S.A. 2C:44-5(a). In other words, the sentencing range is the maximum sentence for each offense added to every other offense. The *Yarbough* factors serve much the same purpose that aggravating and mitigating factors do in guiding the court toward a sentence within the statutory range. . . .

In that vein, consecutive sentences do not invoke the same concerns that troubled the Supreme Court in *Apprendi* [and] *Blakely*. . . . As in any indeterminate sentencing scheme, the jury verdict in this case allowed the judge to impose a consecutive or concurrent sentence within the maximum range based on the sentencing court's discretionary findings. Unlike a trial court that engages in factfinding as the basis for exceeding the sentence authorized by a jury's verdict, the court here imposed consecutive sentences that were supported by the jury's separate guilty verdicts for each offense. With the exception of merged offenses, defendant knew that he potentially could be sentenced to the sum of the maximum sentences for all of the offenses combined.

We therefore conclude that imposing a consecutive sentence for murder and burglary in this case did not exceed the statutory maximum for *Blakely* or *Apprendi* purposes. However, because the trial court did not explain why it imposed consecutive sentences, we are compelled to remand for the court to place its reasons on the record. We remind our courts that when imposing either consecutive or concurrent sentences, the focus should be on "the fairness of the overall sentence," and that they should articulate the reasons for their decisions with specific reference to the *Yarbough* factors. . . .

## PROBLEM 6-3.   PRIOR JUVENILE ADJUDICATIONS

Charles Weber was at a friend's apartment with several people drinking beer, when Weber started to argue with Gabriel Manzo. During the argument, Weber pulled a gun on Manzo, who escaped the apartment by jumping out of a bedroom window and running to his motorcycle. Weber followed Manzo outside and fired multiple shots at Manzo. One of the bullets grazed Manzo's side, causing a slight injury. When the police investigated the incident, Manzo told them that a man he knew as "Guero Loco" (or "crazy white guy") shot him. He identified Weber from a photo lineup.

The prosecuting attorney charged Weber with first-degree attempted murder with a firearm, first-degree assault with a firearm, first-degree unlawful possession of a firearm, and possession of cocaine with intent to manufacture or deliver. Weber pleaded guilty to possession of cocaine with intent to deliver. A jury acquitted Weber of first-degree attempted murder and instead found him guilty of second-degree attempted murder with a firearm, as well as first-degree assault with a firearm and first-degree unlawful possession of a firearm.

At sentencing, the trial court declined to count a prior juvenile adjudication for first-degree attempted robbery against Weber in his offender score. The judge reasoned that enough years had passed since the juvenile adjudication that it now "washed out" under the state's sentencing guideline rules. The trial court also noted that Weber's second juvenile adjudication, for taking a motor vehicle without permission, only counted half a point and therefore did not factor into his offender score.

The state appealed the trial court's finding that Weber's juvenile attempted robbery adjudication "washed out." Weber replied that the inclusion of his prior juvenile adjudications in his offender score would violate his due process rights under the Fifth and Fourteenth Amendments and his right to a jury trial under the Sixth Amendment.

Assume that you serve as a judge on the state's intermediate appellate court. You are convinced that the sentencing guidelines, correctly interpreted, do not prevent the sentencing judge from considering Weber's two prior juvenile adjudications because they happened too long ago. In other words, they do not "wash out."

Inclusion of Weber's juvenile adjudications in his offender score would increase his maximum sentence above the sentence supported by the jury's verdict. Weber argues, therefore, that the Sixth Amendment blocks the judge from considering his juvenile adjudications as part of the guidelines calculation.

The U.S. Supreme Court has suggested in a few cases that an offender's prior criminal record is one aggravating factor at sentencing that need not be proven to a jury beyond a reasonable doubt. It described the basis for this exception to the *Apprendi* rule as follows: "One basis for that possible constitutional distinctiveness is not hard to see: unlike virtually any other consideration used to enlarge the possible penalty for an offense, . . . a prior conviction must itself have been established through procedures satisfying the fair notice, reasonable doubt, and jury trial guarantees." Jones v. United States, 526 U.S. 227, 249 (1999).

Because juvenile adjudications do not carry the right to a jury trial, Weber argues that they do not fall within the prior-conviction exception. Weber further points out that juvenile adjudications are not convictions. The focus of the juvenile justice system is on rehabilitation and individualized treatment of the juvenile rather than assigning criminal responsibility and punishment. The state argues that juvenile adjudications carry sufficient procedural safeguards to qualify them as prior convictions under the *Apprendi* exception.

What would you need to know about Weber's juvenile adjudications, and about the state's juvenile system more generally, to decide this case? Compare State v. Weber, 149 P.3d 646 (Wash. 2006) with State v. Harris, 118 P.3d 236 (Oregon 2005).

## NOTES

1. *State* Blakely *challenges.*   As many as 20 states had statutory or guideline structured sentencing systems or provisions that were subject to new constitutional questions in the wake of *Blakely.* The amount of *Blakely* litigation in which took place in states soon after the Supreme Court ruled was staggering: within a year of the *Blakely* decision, there were more than 2500 state judicial opinions appearing in online databases grappling with the impact of *Blakely,* and these opinions likely represent the proverbial tip of the *Blakely* iceberg. Interestingly, the pace of *Blakely* litigation in the states has been varied even in those jurisdictions in which structured sentencing rules clearly needed reexamination in light of *Blakely:* In a few states (such as Minnesota and Oregon), litigation over

*Blakely* issues produced a major state supreme court ruling less than six months after the *Blakely* decision was handed down by the Supreme Court; in other states (such as New Jersey and Ohio), over a year passed before the state's highest court addressed *Blakely*'s local impact.

2. *Judicial determination of concurrent versus consecutive sentences.*   In systems that require the finding of some predicate fact before a consecutive sentence can replace the presumptive concurrent sentence, judicial determination of the facts supporting the application of consecutive sentencing has the functional impact of extending a defendant's sentence. Don't such factual determinations to support the application of consecutive sentences necessarily implicate the Sixth Amendment concerns raised in *Blakely*? Most lower courts addressing this question had held, like the New Jersey Supreme Court in *Abdullah*, that *Blakely* applied only to the selection of the proper sentence for each crime of conviction, and not to the interaction among those sentences. In early 2008, the Supreme Court took up a case from Oregon presenting the issue of whether *Blakely* requires facts that permit a judge to impose consecutive sentences under state law must be proven to a jury. In a 5-4 decision authored by Justice Ginsburg, Oregon v. Ice, 550 S. Ct. 160 (2009), the Court declared that the Sixth Amendment, as construed in *Apprendi* and *Blakely*, should not be extended to preclude states from allowing judges to find those fact necessary to the imposition of consecutive sentences.

Intriguingly, two of the five Justices voting to limit the reach of *Apprendi* and *Blakely* in Oregon v. Ice were two of the Justices who were in the majority in those earlier cases: Justices Ginsburg and Stevens. This fact, and Court's emphasis in *Ice* on the traditional role of judges in finding certain types of sentencing facts, led some observers to conclude that a majority of justices were at that time prepared and perhaps even eager to restrict the reach of *Apprendi* and *Blakely*. But by 2012 when the Court heard its next big Sixth Amendment case concerning *Apprendi*'s application to criminal fines, Southern Union Co. v. United States, two new Justices had come on the Court (Justices Kagan and Sotomayor) and both voted to extend the reach of *Apprendi* and *Blakely* to a new form of punishment.

3. *Reach of the prior-conviction exception.*   Many sentencing laws call for the sentencing judge to consider some aspects of the defendant's past dealings with the criminal justice system, and yet the consideration involves something more than the mere "fact" of a prior conviction. For instance, the state of Washington asks the sentencing judge to consider whether the defendant was serving a "community placement" sentence at the time he committed the new crime. See State v. Jones, 149 P.3d 636 (Wash. 2006) (community placement status included within prior-conviction exception). North Carolina law increases the sentence if the defendant committed the current offense while serving probation for a previous crime. N.C.G.S. §15A-1340.14(b)(7). Can you resolve these issues through a functional assessment of the types of facts that juries and judges are well suited to find?

4. *Juveniles and prior convictions.*   There is a split on the issue of whether a juvenile adjudication is "the functional equivalent" of a prior conviction for purposes of *Apprendi*. The legal debate about whether juvenile adjudications

fall within the prior-conviction exception is fascinating for a number of reasons. First, the exception itself is both doctrinally and theoretically shaky. Second, because juveniles are not afforded the right to a jury trial, juvenile proceedings do not employ the sorts of safeguards that may give adult prior convictions the added reliability justifying an exception to the *Apprendi-Blakely* rule. The lower federal courts and the state courts are split on this issue. Compare United States v. Smalley, 294 F.3d 1030 (8th Cir. 2002), and State v. McFee, 721 N.W.2d 607 (Minn. 2006), with United States v. Tighe, 266 F.3d 1187 (9th Cir. 2001), and State v. Brown, 879 So. 2d 1276 (La. 2004). See also Colleen P. Murphy, The Use of Prior Convictions after *Apprendi*, 37 U.C. Davis L. Rev. 973 (2004).

5. *Jury rights and back-end punishments.* Think about Justice Scalia's breathtakingly bold assertion in *Blakely* that "every defendant has the right to insist that the prosecutor prove to a jury all facts legally essential to the punishment." Could this apply to decisions other than the judge's selection of the length of a prison term, and decisions that took place after the initial sentencing hearing? For instance, what if the judge orders a suspended sentence, and then some months (or years) later is asked to revoke the probation and send the offender back to prison, will jury findings be necessary to establish the probation violation conditions that are the necessary precursor to a revocation? See Laura Appleman, Retributive Justice and Hidden Sentencing After *Blakely*, 68 Ohio St. L.J. 1307 (2007).

---

## The Impact of Blakely v. Washington on Sentencing in Minnesota: Short Term Recommendations
### Minnesota Sentencing Guidelines Commission
### (August 6, 2004)

. . . The recent *Blakely v. Washington* decision directly impacts neither the constitutionality nor the structure of the Minnesota Sentencing Guidelines. However, the decision does affect certain sentencing procedures pertaining to aggravated departures and specific sentence enhancements that will need to be modified to meet the constitutionality issues identified under *Blakely*. . . .

Aggravated departures resulting in enhanced sentences under the Minnesota Sentencing Guidelines are outside the structure of the guidelines. Unlike the federal guidelines, there are no points assigned for aggravating factors, nor are judges mandated by the guidelines to impose an aggravated departure or enhanced sentence. The sentencing guidelines determine presumptive sentences for offenses on the sentencing grid. Departures are viewed as sentences outside or apart from presumptive sentences set forth on the sentencing grid and are available for judges to use when deciding a case that is atypical or when the factors surrounding a specific case sets it apart from the norm. A departure/enhanced sentence is not controlled by the guidelines regarding the length of the enhancement other than not exceeding the statutory maximum for a specific offense. . . .

The Sentencing Guidelines Commission strongly believes that preserving aggravated departures is necessary to ensure public safety and provide for appropriate sentencing when aggravating factors related to an offense are present and an enhanced sentence is in the interest of justice. . . . In Minnesota, aggravated departures accounted for approximately 7.7% (1,002) of a total of 12,978 felony sentences in 2002. Aggravated departures can occur in two ways under sentencing guidelines. The first type of aggravated departure is an aggravated dispositional departure in which the defendant should have received a presumptive stayed sentence under the guidelines but the court instead imposes a prison sentence. The second type of aggravated departure is an aggravated durational departure that occurs when the offender receives a sentence length that is longer than the sentence recommended by the sentencing grid, regardless of whether the sentence is a presumptive stay or a presumptive prison sentence. Listed below is the distribution of aggravated departures for 2002.

| Total Aggravated Departures For 2002 | | |
|---|---|---|
| *Type of Departure* | *# Cases* | *% Overall Cases* |
| Aggravated Disposition | 481 | 3.7% |
| Agg. Disposition and Agg. Duration | 50 | 0.4% |
| Aggravated Duration — Prison | 224 | 1.7% |
| Aggravated Duration — Probation | 247 | 1.9% |
| Total | 1,002 | 7.7% (of 12,978) |

From the data available, approximately 1,000 cases per year involve aggravated departures and would be subject to the constitutional issues raised in *Blakely*. When this data is further examined by method of conviction, approximately 92% (923) of the cases involved a guilty plea and only 8% (79) of the cases involved a trial. The data would indicate that a very small number of cases resulting in aggravated departures actually involve a criminal trial. [The largest number of trials occurred for defendants who received an aggravated duration in a prison term: 46 of 224 (21%) of those cases were resolved by trial rather than guilty plea.]

It would be reasonable to assume that there will be a slight increase in the number of trials in the future since a certain percentage of offenders who currently plead guilty may request a jury trial in the future to have the aggravating factors determined by a jury. There would be corresponding costs to the courts for these additional trials. However, it should be noted that 67% of the offenders who pled guilty in 2002, either agreed to the departure in the guilty plea or the defendant requested the aggravated dispositional departure. . . .

There are four potential situations that could result when pursuing aggravated departures:

(1)   the defendant pleads not guilty to the offense and does not admit to any of the aggravating factors;

(2)   the defendant pleads not guilty to the offense but admits to the aggravating factors;

(3)   the defendant pleads guilty to the offense but does not admit the aggravating factors; and

(4)   multiple offenses involve any combination of the above.

The issue of whether a defendant can waive a jury trial on guilt or innocence but request a jury to determine the presence of aggravating factors is an issue that will have to be addressed. The Kansas statute relevant to bifurcated trials states that if a defendant waives the right to a jury trial he also waives the right to have a jury determine the presence of aggravating factors. This is an issue that will need further legislative or judicial consideration. . . .

Although the plea bargaining process is permitted when aggravated departures are involved, the defendant must stipulate to the aggravating factors or consent to judicial fact finding. Neither of these options is currently being required in pleas involving aggravated departures, thus, our current plea process would need to be modified to bring the state into compliance with the *Blakely v. Washington* ruling.

### RECOMMENDATIONS:

(1)  Notice Procedures should be modified when there is an intent to seek an aggravated departure . . .

(3)  Procedures will need to be developed to permit juries to determine aggravating factors

    a.  Develop bifurcated trial policies and procedures . . .

    b.  Develop special jury verdict forms to be used in bifurcated jury trial situations . . .

    c.  Incorporate Special Interrogatories on the jury verdict form

In Minnesota, there are several specific statutory enhancements for certain offenses that result in an aggravated departure or an enhanced sentence above the presumptive sentence for the offense due to the determination of one or more aggravating factors, other than prior convictions. Currently, the court makes the determination of additional factors that increase the length of sentence for a conviction under these statutes. They include sentencing enhancements for heinous crimes; certain pattern and predatory sex offenders; mandatory sentences for repeat sex offenders; dangerous offenders; career offenders; and depriving of custodial or parental rights. . . .

A very small number of offenders are sentenced under these statutes per year. The number averages 50 to 60 offenders per year, with only a total of 420 offenders sentenced since 1991.

### RECOMMENDATION:

Due to the public safety issues and seriousness of the offenses in this category, bifurcated trials should be used when sentencing under these specific statutes. . . .

. . . The commission recommends that the state move cautiously and thoughtfully as it explores potential changes to the current sentencing system.

It may be counter productive to begin developing solutions before the nature of the problem is fully understood. Before embarking on a series of statutory responses to the *Blakely* decision, it may be more prudent for the judiciary, prosecutors and defense attorneys to develop temporary interim policies and procedures that are advisory in nature for conducting bifurcated jury trials, plea negotiations, and sentencing procedures that impact the areas of sentencing that have previously been identified as most likely be affected by this decision. . . .

Although advisory policies and procedures will carry no legal force, they will provide for some consistency in sentencing throughout the state as the legal issues work their way through the courts at both the state and federal levels. In addition, they will help to limit the number of future of appeals that could result from every judicial district interpreting and responding to *Blakely* in a different manner. . . .

## PROBLEM 6-4.  INDICTING *BLAKELY*

Kevin Badoni was initially charged in 1998 with one count of murder, two counts of attempted murder "by any of the means with which death may be caused," aggravated battery, and tampering with evidence for disposing of a .380 handgun. All the charges resulted from a confrontation between two groups of young men during which one man was killed and two men were seriously wounded by gunshots. Badoni was convicted of second-degree murder and aggravated battery.

Through a special verdict, the jury found that Badoni used a firearm in the commission of these offenses. Badoni's attorney had opposed the use of the special verdict because the use of a firearm was not pled in the murder and attempted murder charges. Badoni was sentenced to 15 years in prison for the murder conviction, three years for aggravated battery, and 18 months for tampering with evidence. The murder and aggravated battery sentences were each enhanced by one year because of the application of an enhancement statute based on the use of a firearm.

Badoni argues that, under *Apprendi* and *Blakely*, the state must give formal notice in the criminal information or indictment that Badoni used a firearm in the commission of the offense before the state may seek to enhance Badoni's sentence under the statute.

As an appellate court judge, how would you rule? See State v. Badoni, 62 P.3d 348 (N.M. Ct. App. 2002).

As a prosecutor, would you encourage the use of indictments even if you had no constitutional obligation to include the enhancement factor in the indictment? Assuming that you would oppose a constitutional requirement of indictment, would you take a different posture toward a proposed amendment to the state rules of criminal procedure to require notice of enhancement facts before trial?

### NOTES

1. *Number of cases affected.*  The central claim of the report from the Minnesota Sentencing Commission is that *Blakely* does not require a fundamental restructuring of the sentencing guidelines because it affects so

few "contested" enhancement cases. As the commission put it, "The impact of *Blakely* on sentencing in Minnesota, while temporarily disruptive, is limited in scope and can be addressed within the current sentencing guidelines scheme." This limited impact applies to most state systems because the number of enhancement-related factual findings to be made at sentencing is small. In contrast with the federal system's use of "relevant conduct" to increase the upper available guideline boundary, most state systems rely more heavily on "charge offense conduct" — that is, conduct already alleged in the indictment and proven at trial (or admitted in the guilty plea).

Are courts or sentencing commissions best suited to estimate the number of cases affected by the new Sixth Amendment jurisprudence? Does the commission have an incentive to minimize its estimate of the impact? The Minnesota Commission report mentions only in passing two loudly ticking time bombs that could lead to an explosion in the number of cases affected. First, *Blakely* might affect all cases involving a "custody status point" (an additional criminal history point added if the current offense was committed while the defendant was still on probation or parole status from a previous crime). Second, *Blakely* could affect all probation revocations. These two categories could overwhelm the small number of cases with *Blakely* effects noted elsewhere in the report.

2. *Guilty pleas and the scope of waiver.*    When a defendant pleads guilty, she waives the right to a jury trial. As *Blakely* makes clear, this waiver does not necessarily include the right to a jury determination of sentencing factors. Does the use of a jury for sentencing factors undermine the value of the defendant's guilty plea? In People v. Lopez, 148 P.3d 121 (Colo. 2006), the defendant pled guilty to vehicular homicide and vehicular assault. The trial court impaneled a jury solely to determine the facts surrounding the commission of the crime, which the court then considered to be aggravating circumstances justifying an enhanced sentence. The Colorado Supreme Court held that the trial court erred in impaneling a jury at sentencing, because the defendant's guilty plea set a statutory maximum, and the jury findings created the "functional equivalent of elements of a greater offense." The state must abide by the plea, and courts must enforce the state's concessions. As the lead prosecutor in a jurisdiction that views guilty pleas in this way, how would you adjust office policy to allow enhanced sentencing based on aggravating circumstances?

3. *Minimum and maximum starting points.*    If only the facts that increase the penalty for a crime beyond the prescribed statutory maximum must be submitted to a jury and proved beyond a reasonable doubt, legislatures could avoid procedural safeguards by raising the statutory maximum sentences for all crimes and then listing facts that could authorize *reduced* sentences. Justice O'Connor's dissent in *Apprendi* assailed this apparent formalism and suggested that it rendered the constitutional rule "meaningless." Yet at least a few academic commentators have suggested that there is value in even such a formalistic reading of *Apprendi*. See Benjamin J. Priester, Constitutional Formalism and the Meaning of *Apprendi v. New Jersey*, 38 Am. Crim. L. Rev. 281 (2001); Alan C. Michaels, Truth in Convicting: Understanding and Evaluating *Apprendi*, 12 Fed. Sent'g Rep. 320 (2000).

In footnote 16 of his opinion for the Court, Justice Stevens responded to the formalism charge:

> [Structural] democratic constraints exist to discourage legislatures from enacting penal statutes that expose *every* defendant convicted of, for example, weapons possession, to a maximum sentence exceeding that which is, in the legislature's judgment, generally proportional to the crime. This is as it should be. Our rule ensures that a State is obliged to make its choices concerning the substantive content of its criminal laws with full awareness of the consequence, unable to mask substantive policy choices of exposing all who are convicted to the maximum sentence it provides. So exposed, the political check on potentially harsh legislative action is then more likely to operate.
>
> In all events, if such an extensive revision of the State's entire criminal code were enacted for the purpose the dissent suggests, or if New Jersey simply reversed the burden of the hate crime finding (effectively assuming a crime was performed with a purpose to intimidate and then requiring a defendant to prove that it was not), we would be required to question whether the revision was constitutional under this Court's prior decisions.
>
> Finally, the principal dissent ignores the distinction the Court has often recognized between facts in aggravation of punishment and facts in mitigation. If facts found by a jury support a guilty verdict of murder, the judge is authorized by that jury verdict to sentence the defendant to the maximum sentence provided by the murder statute. If the defendant can escape the statutory maximum by showing, for example, that he is a war veteran, then a judge that finds the fact of veteran status is neither exposing the defendant to a deprivation of liberty greater than that authorized by the verdict according to statute, nor is the Judge imposing upon the defendant a greater stigma than that accompanying the jury verdict alone. Core concerns animating the jury and burden-of-proof requirements are thus absent from such a scheme.

530 U.S. at 490 n.16.

4. *Translation of jury functions to a new context.*   The criminal justice system changed enormously between the eighteenth and twenty-first centuries. Consider, for example, the increased role of guilty pleas and the enormous innovations in sentencing rules. How can courts in the twenty-first century give meaning to the constitutional vision of a criminal adjudication process that gives juries the real power to apply the criminal law reasonably? Judge Jack Weinstein offered the following long-term historical perspective on the subject:

> [In the eighteenth century], the discretionary function in sentencing was shared by judge and jury. . . . Juries decided questions of law and fact in criminal and civil cases. . . . The authors known to the founders had a high respect for the wide powers of the jury over law, fact and punishment. In a sense, the jury was, and remains, the direct voice of the sovereign, in a collaborative effort with the judge. It expresses the view of a sometimes compassionate free people faced with an individual miscreant in all of his or her tainted humanity, as opposed to the abstract cruelties of a more theoretical and doctrinaire distant representative government. . . . Clemency was widespread. The jury could exercise its charity. . . .
>
> [The use of advisory juries for sentencing questions] cannot be said to be out of character for a colonial judge faced with the kind of sentencing dilemmas a federal judge now confronts under the Guidelines. It is not aberrational to suggest that use of a jury on sentencing issues of fact—and perhaps on severity—is consistent with history, practice and the inherent role of federal courts and juries.

Reliance on the jury represents a reflection of our government's dependence on the ultimate and residual sovereignty of the people. That foundation for all power — executive, legislative and judicial — is reflected in the preamble to the Constitution beginning, "We the People . . . do ordain and establish this Constitution."

United States v. Khan, 325 F. Supp. 2d 218 (E.D.N.Y. 2004).

5. *Possible structures for jury involvement in sentencing.*   Despite its broad language, *Blakely* technically mandates that juries have a role in factfinding only to support sentence enhancements. Especially in light of Judge Weinstein's comments in *Khan* noted above, we might want to think more dynamically about how to construct a new sentencing world with significant jury participation. Consider just some of the ways juries might be involved in sentencing decision making that go beyond *Blakely*'s mandate:

> *Juries as comprehensive fact finders.* We might require juries to be the finders of all (or at least all significant) sentencing facts. Notably, *Blakely* requires juries to be finders only of aggravating facts, allowing judges still to find mitigating facts. But though the Constitution apparently permits this distinction, a sounder system might be one in which juries decide all these facts.
>
> *Juries as fact finders and sentence advisors.* We might prefer that juries not only find facts, but also advise judges on appropriate punishments. Though the Constitution may not require juries to do anything more than find (aggravating) sentencing facts, we might still envision a sounder system to be one where juries also recommend sentences based on these facts.
>
> *Juries as fact finders and sentencers.* We might want juries not only to find facts, but also to impose specific punishments. Again, though the Constitution may not require juries to do anything more than find (aggravating) sentencing facts, we might still think a sounder system would have juries impose specific sentences based on these facts.

In this context, it is worth remembering that jury participation in death penalty sentencing is the norm; in that setting, juries typically find and weigh aggravating and mitigating facts and also recommend or impose the ultimate sentence. In addition, six states allow jury sentencing in noncapital cases. See Ronald F. Wright, Rules for Sentencing Revolutions, 108 Yale L.J. 1355 (1999). In foreign countries professional judges often sit with lay jurors, and together they decide on guilt and the appropriate sentence.

6. *Jury findings and the purposes of sentencing.*   Is there a natural fit between the functions of a jury and particular purposes of sentencing? Consider the possibility that the *Blakely* line of cases is an outgrowth of shifting purposes for sentencing. In an era of indeterminate sentencing, when rehabilitation and other consequentialist theories dominated our thinking, the jury was not especially well suited to the clinical determinations necessary to impose a successful sentence. On the other hand, in an era when limited retributivism has become the leading rationale for determinate sentencing laws, the jury's

findings about historical facts have become more important to the enterprise. Cf. Laura Appleman, Retributive Justice and Hidden Sentencing After *Blakely*, 68 Ohio St. L.J. 1307 (2007).

7. *Indictments and negotiating strength.* While the Sixth Amendment cases address the right to a jury trial, there are related rights that require the government to begin proving its facts before the time of sentencing. Must the government allege any aggravating facts that affect the authorized sentence in the indictment before trial? See State v. Davis, 141 S.W.3d 600 (Tenn. 2004) (*Apprendi* and *Blakely* do not require aggravating circumstances that enhance first-degree murder punishment to be alleged in the indictment; primary function of indictment is to offer defendant notice of issues, and current procedural rules provide notice of issues in other formats). Some states have resolved this question through statute or procedural rule, requiring the state to notify the defendant about the issues before trial, but not necessarily in the indictment. How will the relevant state rules on indictments and other disclosure of aggravating facts influence the timing and outcome of plea negotiations?

## B. PROCEDURAL REALITIES

Defendants' concerns about the sentence they may receive shape the entire criminal process. Sentencing "process" might reach back to include each stage of criminal proceedings that has a distinct impact on the sentence determination. While in some situations, constitutional rights (including any developing rights under *Apprendi* and *Blakely*) may be an essential part of sentencing process, in most cases the principal procedures will be nonconstitutional, guided by statute and, to an even greater extent, by rules of procedure, prosecutorial policies, defense normal and local judicial and legal culture.

The dominant procedural reality for all defendants is this: the overwhelming majority of cases in both state and federal systems are resolved by guilty pleas, and those pleas generally reflect bargaining between prosecution and defense. The contents of guilty pleas, going well beyond simply the offense of conviction, are likely to have a significant effect on the sentence.

After an exploration of the connection between plea negotiations and sentencing, the latter part of this chapter considers two procedures unique to sentencing—sentencing hearings and the creation of presentence investigation (PSI) reports—along with the special institutional role of probation officers who write the PSI reports.

### 1. Plea Practices and Sentencing

Given the importance of guilty pleas and the underlying plea bargains, it might seem that there should be a constitutional jurisprudence to match. There is not;

indeed, there has historically been relatively little case law or constitutional doctrines governing the use of guilty pleas or the negotiation of plea bargains. There has long been, however, quite a bit of relevant law governing plea bargains and guilty pleas in statutes and rules. These statutes and rules have typically found expression as part of a jurisdiction's rules of criminal procedure with specific directions to judges for the acceptance of guilty pleas.

In addition, decisions whether to offer or accept plea bargains are also governed by executive branch policies. These policies vary in their level of detail; in many smaller offices, prosecutors follow consistent plea practices that may reflect unwritten (but explicit) guidelines, or they may simply reflect shared office culture and experience. Sometimes prosecutors develop formal plea review standards, describing substantively the types of bargains that are acceptable. Other times they create procedural review mechanisms, such as supervisory review or committee review of possible plea bargains.

Federal prosecutors, under the central control of the attorney general, have developed a detailed set of written plea bargaining policies. In addition to the nationwide guidelines set out below, many of the U.S. Attorneys' offices in the federal districts around the country have developed guidance to reflect the distinctive caseloads, resources, and other factors in each district.

The following policies require slow and careful reading. Note that some reverse earlier policies, while others add new standards or procedures. The following questions applied to each policy may help to reveal the dynamics at work.

- What are the goals of the policy, and are they explicitly stated? Do the goals relate to authorizing statutes, general principles of justice (such as sentencing purposes), or internal administrative aims?
- Is the link between plea bargains and sentencing explicitly stated?
- Does the policy use substantive limitations (rules about the content of acceptable agreements) or procedures (written decisions, internal review and approval) to achieve its goals?

The first policy below was promulgated before the legislation that created the federal guidelines, when the federal system (and most state systems) still operated under an indeterminate sentencing model. To what extent were these original principles (developed in 1980) concerned with sentencing?

## Federal Rule of Criminal Procedure 11, Pleas

**(a) Entering a Plea.**

(1) *In General.* A defendant may plead guilty, not guilty, or (with the court's consent) nolo contendere. . . .

**(b) Considering and Accepting a Guilty or Nolo Contendere Plea.**

(1) *Advising and Questioning the Defendant.* Before the court accepts a plea of guilty or *nolo* contendere, the defendant may be placed under oath, and the court must address the defendant personally in open court. During this

address, the court must inform the defendant of, and determine that the defendant understands, the following:

(A) the government's right, in a prosecution for perjury or false statement, to use against the defendant any statement that the defendant gives under oath;

(B) the right to plead not guilty, or having already so pleaded, to persist in that plea;

(C) the right to a jury trial;

(D) the right to be represented by counsel — and if necessary have the court appoint counsel — at trial and at every other stage of the proceeding;

(E) the right at trial to confront and cross-examine adverse witnesses, to be protected from compelled self-incrimination, to testify and present evidence, and to compel the attendance of witnesses;

(F) the defendant's waiver of these trial rights if the court accepts a plea of guilty or nolo contendere;

(G) the nature of each charge to which the defendant is pleading;

(H) any maximum possible penalty, including imprisonment, fine, and term of supervised release;

(I) any mandatory minimum penalty;

(J) any applicable forfeiture;

(K) the court's authority to order restitution;

(L) the court's obligation to impose a special assessment;

(M) the court's obligation to apply the Sentencing Guidelines, and the court's discretion to depart from those guidelines under some circumstances; and

(N) the terms of any plea-agreement provision waiving the right to appeal or to collaterally attack the sentence.

**(2)** *Ensuring that a Plea Is Voluntary.* Before accepting a plea of guilty or nolo contendere, the court must address the defendant personally in open court and determine that the plea is voluntary and did not result from force, threats, or promises (other than promises in a plea agreement).

**(3)** *Determining the Factual Basis for a Plea.* Before entering judgment on a guilty plea, the *court* must determine that there is a factual basis for the plea.

**(c) Plea Agreement Procedure.**

**(1)** *In General.* An attorney for the government and the defendant's attorney, or the defendant when proceeding pro se, may discuss and reach a plea agreement. The court must not participate in these discussions. If the defendant pleads guilty or nolo contendere to either a charged offense or a lesser or related offense, the plea agreement may specify that an attorney for the government will:

(A) not bring, or will move to dismiss other charges;

(B) recommend, or agree not to oppose the defendant's request, that a particular sentence or sentencing range is appropriate or that a particular provision of the Sentencing Guidelines, or policy statement, or sentencing factor does or does not apply (such a recommendation or request does not bind the court); or

(C) agree that a specific sentence or sentencing range is the appropriate disposition of the case, or that a particular provision of the Sentencing Guidelines, or policy statement, or sentencing factor does or does not apply (such a recommendation or request binds the court once the court accepts the plea agreement).

(2) *Disclosing a Plea Agreement.* The parties must disclose the plea agreement in open court when the plea is offered, unless the court for good cause allows the parties to disclose the plea agreement in camera.

(3) *Judicial Consideration of a Plea Agreement.*

(A) To the extent the plea agreement is of the type specified in Rule 11(c)(1)(A) or (C), the court may accept the agreement, reject it, or defer a decision until the court has reviewed the presentence report.

(B) To the extent the plea agreement is of the type specified in Rule 11(c)(1)(B), the court must advise the defendant that the defendant has no right to withdraw the plea if the court does not follow the recommendation or request.

(4) *Accepting a Plea Agreement.* If the court accepts the plea agreement, it must inform the defendant that to the extent the plea agreement is of the type specified in Rule 11(c)(1)(A) or (C), the agreed disposition will be included in the judgment.

(5) *Rejecting a Plea Agreement.* If the court rejects a plea agreement containing provisions of the type specified in Rule 11(c)(1)(A) or (C), the court must do the following on the record and in open court (or, for good cause, in camera):

(A) inform the parties that the court rejects the plea agreement;

(B) advise the defendant personally that the court is not required to follow the plea agreement and give the defendant the opportunity to withdraw the plea; and

(C) advise the defendant personally that if the plea is not withdrawn, the court may dispose of the case less favorably toward the defendant than the plea agreement contemplated.

**(d) Withdrawing a Guilty or Nolo Contendere Plea.** A defendant may withdraw a plea of guilty or nolo contendere:

(1) before the court accepts the plea, for any reason or no reason; or

(2) after the court accepts the plea, but before it imposes sentence if:

(A) the court rejects a plea agreement under Rule 11(c)(5); or

(B) the defendant can show a fair and just reason for requesting the withdrawal.

**(e) Finality of a Guilty or Nolo Contendere Plea.** After the court imposes sentence, the defendant may not withdraw a plea of guilty or nolo contendere, and the plea may be set aside only on direct appeal or collateral attack.

## *U.S. Department of Justice, Principles of Federal Prosecution* (1980)

ENTERING INTO PLEA AGREEMENTS

1. The attorney for the government may, in an appropriate case, enter into an agreement with a defendant that, upon the defendant's plea of guilty or nolo

contendere to a charged offense or to a lesser or related offense, he will move for dismissal of other charges, take a certain position with respect to the sentence to be imposed, or take other action.

2. In determining whether it would be appropriate to enter into a plea agreement, the attorney for the government should weigh all relevant considerations, including:

(a) the defendant's willingness to cooperate in the investigation or prosecution of others;

(b) the defendant's history with respect to criminal activity;

(c) the nature and seriousness of the offense or offenses charged;

(d) the defendant's remorse or contrition and his willingness to assume responsibility for his conduct;

(e) the desirability of prompt and certain disposition of the case;

(f) the likelihood of obtaining a conviction at trial;

(g) the probable effect on witnesses;

(h) the probable sentence or other consequences if the defendant is convicted;

(i) the public interest in having the case tried rather than disposed of by a guilty plea;

(j) the expense of trial and appeal; and

(k) the need to avoid delay in the disposition of other pending cases.

*Comment:* . . . The provision is not intended to suggest the desirability or lack of desirability of a plea agreement in any particular case or to be construed as a reflection on the merits of any plea agreement that actually may be reached; its purpose is solely to assist attorneys for the government in exercising their judgment as to whether some sort of plea agreement would be appropriate in a particular case. Government attorneys should consult the investigating agency involved in any case in which it would be helpful to have its views concerning the relevance of particular factors or the weight they deserve. . . .

A plea disposition in one case may facilitate the prompt disposition of other cases, including cases in which prosecution might otherwise be declined. This may occur simply because prosecutorial, judicial, or defense resources will become available for use in other cases, or because a plea by one of several defendants may have a "domino effect," leading to pleas by other defendants. In weighing the importance of these possible consequences, the attorney for the government should consider the state of the criminal docket and the speedy trial requirements in the district, the desirability of handling a larger volume of criminal cases, and the workloads of prosecutors, judges, and defense attorneys in the district.

3. If a prosecution is to be concluded pursuant to a plea agreement, the defendant should be required to plead to a charge or charges:

(a) that bears a reasonable relationship to the nature and extent of his criminal conduct;

(b) that has an adequate factual basis;

(c) that makes likely the imposition of an appropriate sentence under all the circumstances of the case; and

(d) that does not adversely affect the investigation or prosecution of others.

*Comment:* [T]he considerations that should be taken into account in selecting the charge or charges to which a defendant should be required to plead guilty . . . are essentially the same as those governing the selection of charges to be included in the original indictment or information.

(a) Relationship to criminal conduct — The charge or charges to which a defendant pleads guilty should bear a reasonable relationship to the defendant's criminal conduct, both in nature and in scope. . . . In many cases, this will probably require that the defendant plead to the most serious offense charged. . . . The requirement that a defendant plead to a charge that bears a reasonable relationship to the nature and extent of his criminal conduct is not inflexible. There may be situations involving cooperating defendants in which [lesser charges may be appropriate].

(b) Factual basis — The attorney for the government should also bear in mind the legal requirement that there be a factual basis for the charge or charges to which a guilty plea is entered. This requirement is intended to assure against conviction after a guilty plea of a person who is not in fact guilty. . . .

(c) Basis for sentencing — [T]he prosecutor should take care to avoid a "charge agreement" that would unduly restrict the court's sentencing authority. [I]f restitution is appropriate under the circumstances of the case, a sufficient number of counts should be retained under the agreement to provide a basis for an adequate restitution order. . . .

(d) Effect on other cases — . . . Among the possible adverse consequences to be avoided are the negative jury appeal that may result when relatively less culpable defendants are tried in the absence of a more culpable defendant or when a principal prosecution witness appears to be equally culpable as the defendants but has been permitted to plead to a significantly less serious offense. . . .

5. If a prosecution is to be terminated pursuant to a plea agreement, the attorney for the government should ensure that the case file contains a record of the agreed disposition, signed or initialed by the defendant or his attorney. . . .

## NOTES

1. *Plea procedures and sentencing.* Federal Rule of Criminal Procedure 11 has been a model for many states. The types of pleas in Rule 11 were identified before the implementation of the federal guideline system; one of those types allows for plea agreements to particular sentences. Such binding sentence pleas are quite rare — most prosecutors refuse to make such pleas and some courts refuse to accept them.

Rule 11 was amended and reorganized effective December 1, 2002. Most of the cases and literature before that date and some (by force of habit) afterward use a reference to the prior rule — with "(e)(1)(A)" pleas being the prior form of current "(c)(1)(A)" (charge bargains), "(e)(1)(B)" pleas the earlier form of "(c)(1)(B)" (sentence recommendation bargains), and "(e)(1)(C)" the earlier form of "(c)(1)(C)" (binding pleas to a specific sentence).

2. *Federal sentencing reforms, sentencing guidelines and plea agreements.* When Congress transformed federal sentencing through the Sentencing Reform Act of 1984, it had precious little to say about guilty pleas and plea bargaining practices. Reprinted below is the single statutory provision of the SRA which directed the U.S. Sentencing Commission to promulgate "general policy statements" concerning whether and how federal judges should accept or reject plea agreements. Given the lack of constitutional doctrines and the limited statutory rules controlling the plea process, should the Sentencing Commission have developed an elaborate set of regulations concerning plea bargains and how district courts should review plea agreements? With pleas having always accounted for more than 80% of all convictions in the federal system and with plea bargains often being a basis for the parties to impact (and sometimes mandate) sentencing outcomes, should the Sentencing Commission have considered the regulation of plea practices as a central part of its mission to bring greater fairness, consistency and honesty to the federal sentencing system?

When the Sentencing Commission created its initial set of guidelines, it included a "policy statement" about plea agreements, which is reprinted below. At the time, it was generally assumed that policy statements had less binding effect than the guidelines themselves, although later events have all but erased this distinction. What was the commission trying to accomplish with regard to plea agreements?

‖ *28 U.S.C. §994(a)(2)(E)* ‖

The Commission . . . shall promulgate . . . general policy statements regarding application of the guidelines or any other aspect of sentencing or sentence implementation . . . including the appropriate use of . . . the authority granted under Rule 11(c)(2) of the Federal Rules of Criminal Procedure to accept or reject a plea agreement. . . .

‖ *U.S. Sentencing Guidelines §§6B1.2, 6B1.4 (Policy Statements)* ‖

**§6B1.2** STANDARDS FOR ACCEPTANCE OF PLEA AGREEMENTS

(a) In the case of a plea agreement that includes the dismissal of any charges or an agreement not to pursue potential charges [under Rule 11(c)(1)(A)], the court may accept the agreement if the court determines, for reasons stated on the record, that the remaining charges adequately reflect the seriousness of the actual offense behavior and that accepting the agreement will not undermine the statutory purposes of sentencing or the sentencing guidelines. Provided, that a plea agreement that includes the dismissal of a charge or a plea agreement not to pursue a potential charge shall not preclude the conduct underlying such charge from being considered under the provisions of §1B1.3 (Relevant Conduct) in connection with the count(s) of which the defendant is convicted.

(b) In the case of a plea agreement that includes a nonbinding recommendation [under Rule 11(c)(1)(B)], the court may accept the recommendation if the court is satisfied either that: (1) the recommended sentence is within the applicable guideline range; or (2) the recommended sentence departs from the applicable guideline range for justifiable reasons.

(c) In the case of a plea agreement that includes a specific sentence [under Rule 11(c)(1)(C)], the court may accept the agreement if the court is satisfied either that: (1) the agreed sentence is within the applicable guideline range; or (2) the agreed sentence departs from the applicable guideline range for justifiable reasons.

### §6B1.4    Stipulations

(a) A plea agreement may be accompanied by a written stipulation of facts relevant to sentencing. [S]tipulations shall: (1) set forth the relevant facts and circumstances of the actual offense conduct and offender characteristics; (2) not contain misleading facts; and (3) set forth with meaningful specificity the reasons why the sentencing range resulting from the proposed agreement is appropriate.

(b) To the extent that the parties disagree about any facts relevant to sentencing, the stipulation shall identify the facts that are in dispute. . . .

(d) The court is not bound by the stipulation, but may with the aid of the presentence report, determine the facts relevant to sentencing.

### A.    Modern Guidance for Federal Prosecutors in Guideline Sentencing Era

The U.S. Department of Justice soon realized that the new federal system of guideline sentencing was complicated and greatly impacted the import and impact of prosecutorial charging and bargaining discretion. Consequently, the Department issued special guidance to prosecutors that appeared simultaneously with the guidelines. Excerpts from the 1987 "Redbook" are reprinted below. Is this internal guidance to prosecutors consistent with the statute and with the policy statements? What changes does it make to the 1980 Principles of Federal Prosecution?

After the first few months of practice under the new sentencing and plea bargaining rules, officials in the Department of Justice believed that federal prosecutors in the field were not adhering closely enough to the Department's plea bargaining policies. Consequently, the leadership of the Department (housed in "Main Justice" in Washington, D.C.) revised the 1987 Redbook by issuing the 1989 "Thornburgh Bluesheet," also reprinted below. The revision of the policy was aimed at increasing compliance with the plea practices that the leadership of the department wanted. What elements of the policy did the revisers focus on? What were the likely effects of the revisions?

After the 1992 elections, the incoming Clinton Administration appointed new leadership to the Department of Justice. The new attorney general, Janet

Reno, reviewed plea bargaining policies and issued a "Bluesheet" of her own. It too is reprinted below. In most districts, this policy was carried out by newly appointed U.S. Attorneys, along with many career attorneys who had also served under the previous administration. What prior statements does the Reno Bluesheet hark back to? What, if anything, is new in the policy?

---

### *Prosecutors' Handbook on Sentencing Guidelines ("The Redbook")*
#### William Weld, Assistant Attorney General (1987)

---

[T]he validity and use of the Commission's policy statements by prosecutors should depend upon whether the agreement reflects charge bargaining or sentence bargaining under [Rule 11(c)].

#### SENTENCE BARGAINING

A significant problem with the Commission's policy statements on plea bargains which include a specific sentence under [Rule 11(c)(1)(B) and (C)], §6B1.2(b) and (c), is that the standard they set forth for acceptance or rejection of a sentence that departs from the guidelines appears to be of doubtful validity under the Sentencing Reform Act (SRA). The standard for departure from the guidelines is set forth in the Act and requires a finding that an aggravating or mitigating circumstance exists that was not adequately taken into consideration by the Commission in formulating the guidelines. Yet the Commission's policy statements relating to sentence bargains authorize departure "for justifiable reasons." We do not believe it is possible to argue that the Commission has not adequately taken into consideration the value of a plea agreement as a mitigating factor so as to support a departure. . . . We recognize, nonetheless, that many judges might be tempted to take a realistic approach; a sentence outside the guidelines in the context of a plea agreement is unlikely to result in an appeal of the sentence. Therefore, if urged to accept a plea agreement that departs from the guidelines, they will follow the policy statements despite their questionable basis.

Nevertheless, the Criminal Division has concluded that the apparent authority for a judge to depart from the guidelines pursuant to the Commission's policy statements, §6B1.2(b) and (c), for plea agreements involving a particular sentence under [Rule 11(c)(1)(B) and (C)] is at variance with the more restrictive departure language of [the statute] and that, consequently, these policy statements should not be used as a basis for recommending a sentence that departs from the guidelines. [P]rosecutors should not recommend or agree to a lower-than-guideline sentence merely on the basis of a plea agreement. They may, however, recommend or agree to a sentence at the low end of an applicable sentencing range [within the guidelines].

In addition to the above-described legitimate guideline reductions that may be used in sentence-type negotiations, a departure from the guidelines may be warranted and may be included in the recommended or agreed-upon sentence if the [statutory] standard . . . is met. That is, a mitigating circumstance must exist (other than the reaching of a plea agreement) that was not adequately taken into consideration by the Commission in formulating the guidelines and that should result in a sentence different from that described. Moreover, a departure from the guidelines may also be reflected in a plea agreement if the defendant provided substantial assistance in the investigation or prosecution of another person who has committed an offense. . . . Therefore, even though plea-bargained sentences must accord with the law and the guidelines, there is considerable room for negotiating.

The basic reason for rejecting the Commission's policy statements on sentence bargains and treating sentences which are the subject of a sentence bargain in the same manner as sentences which result from conviction after trial is that any other result could seriously thwart the purpose of the SRA to reduce unwarranted disparity in sentencing [among defendants with similar records who have been found guilty of similar criminal conduct]. Congress could not have expressed the concerns reflected in the SRA and the legislative history with unwarranted disparity and uncertainty in sentencing but have intended the reforms enacted to be limited to the small percentage of cases that go to trial. The legislative history of the SRA indeed indicates that Congress was concerned with the potential shift of discretion in sentencing from the court to the prosecutor through plea agreements and the unwarranted disparity that could result. . . .

### CHARGE BARGAINING

The policy statement on charge bargaining addresses agreements that include the dismissal of any charges under [Rule 11(c)(1)(A)] or an agreement not to pursue potential charges. It authorizes the court to accept such an agreement if it determines, "for reasons stated on the record, that the remaining charges adequately reflect the seriousness of the actual offense behavior and that accepting the agreement will not undermine the statutory purposes of sentencing."§6B1.2(a). The requirement that the "remaining charges adequately reflect the seriousness of the actual offense behavior" in charge bargaining is important since the charge of conviction itself is the most significant factor in establishing the guideline sentence. . . .

Although Congress intended that courts exercise "meaningful" review of charge reduction plea agreements, it is our view that moderately greater flexibility legally can and does attach to charge bargains than to sentence bargains. While, as indicated previously, the Commission's quite liberal policy statements on sentence bargaining appear to be inconsistent with the controlling (and stricter) statutory departure standard, the statutory departure standard is not applicable in the charge-bargain context. . . .

Nevertheless, in order to fulfill the objectives of the Sentencing Reform Act prosecutors should conduct charge bargaining in a manner consistent with the direction in the applicable policy statement, §6B1.2(a), i.e., subject to the policy statement's instruction that the "remaining charges [should] adequately reflect the seriousness of the actual offense behavior" and that the agreement not undermine the statutory purposes of sentencing. In our view, this translates into a requirement that readily provable serious charges should not be bargained away. The sole legitimate ground for agreeing not to pursue a charge that is relevant under the guidelines to assure that the sentence will reflect the seriousness of the defendant's "offense behavior" is the existence of real doubt as to the ultimate provability of the charge.

Concomitantly, however, the prosecutor is in the best position to assess the strength of the government's case and enjoys broad discretion in making judgments as to which charges are most likely to result in conviction on the basis of the available evidence. For this reason, the prosecutor entering into a charge bargain may enjoy a degree of latitude that is not present when the plea bargain addresses only sentencing aspects. . . .

It is appropriate that the sentence for an offender who agrees to plead guilty to relatively few charges should be different from the sentence for an offender convicted of many charges since guilt has not been determined as to the dismissed charges. At the same time, however, sentence bargaining should not result in a vastly different sentence as compared to a sentence following trial. . . .

The overriding principle governing the conduct of plea negotiations is that plea agreements should not be used to circumvent the guidelines. This principle is in accordance with the policies set forth in the Principles of Federal Prosecution. . . . For example, charges should not be filed simply to exert leverage to induce a plea. Rather, the prosecutor should charge the most serious offense consistent with the defendant's provable conduct. . . .

A subsidiary but nonetheless important issue concerns so-called "fact" bargaining or stipulations. [The policy statement §6B1.4] attaches certain conditions to such stipulations. The most important condition, with which the Department concurs, is that stipulations shall "not contain misleading facts." Otherwise, the basic purpose of the SRA to reduce unwarranted sentence disparity will be undermined. Thus, if the defendant can clearly be proved to have used a weapon or committed an assault in the course of the offense, the prosecutor may not stipulate, as part of a plea agreement designed to produce a lower sentence, that no weapon was used or assault committed. If, on the other hand, certain facts surrounding the offense are not clear, e.g., the extent of the loss or injury resulting from the defendant's fraud, the prosecutor is at liberty to stipulate that no loss or injury beyond that clearly provable existed. Prosecutors may not, however, instruct investigators not to pursue leads, or make less than ordinary efforts to ascertain facts, simply to be in a position to say that they are unable clearly to prove a sentencing fact and thereby increase the latitude for bargaining. . . . Subject to the above constraints, however, the Department encourages the use of stipulations accompanying plea agreements to the extent practicable. . . .

## Plea Policy for Federal Prosecutors ("Thornburgh Bluesheet")
### Richard Thornburgh, Attorney General (1989)

. . . Should a prosecutor determine in good faith after indictment that, as a result of a change in the evidence or for another reason (e.g., a need has arisen to protect the identity of a particular witness until he testifies against a more significant defendant), a charge is not readily provable or that an indictment exaggerates the seriousness of an offense or offenses, a plea bargain may reflect the prosecutor's reassessment. There should be a record, however, in a case in which charges originally brought are dropped. . . .

Department policy requires honesty in sentencing; federal prosecutors are expected to identify for U.S. District Courts departures when they agree to support them. For example, it would be improper for a prosecutor to agree that a departure is in order, but to conceal the agreement in a charge bargain that is presented to a court as a fait accompli so that there is neither a record of nor judicial review of the departure. . . .

The basic policy is that charges are not to be bargained away or dropped, unless the prosecutor has a good faith doubt as to the government's ability readily to prove a charge for legal or evidentiary reasons. It would serve no purpose here to seek to further define "readily provable." The policy is to bring cases that the government should win if there were a trial. There are, however, two exceptions.

First, if the applicable guideline range from which a sentence may be imposed would be unaffected, readily provable charges may be dismissed or dropped as part of a plea bargain. . . . Second, federal prosecutors may drop readily provable charges with the specific approval of the United States Attorney or designated supervisory level official for reasons set forth in the file of the case. This exception recognizes that the aims of the Sentencing Reform Act must be sought without ignoring other, critical aspects of the federal criminal justice system. For example, approval to drop charges in a particular case might be given because the United States Attorney's office is particularly overburdened, the case would be time-consuming to try, and proceeding to trial would significantly reduce the total number of cases disposed of by the office. . . .

The Department's policy is only to stipulate to facts that accurately represent the defendant's conduct. If a prosecutor wishes to support a departure from the guidelines, he or she should candidly do so and not stipulate to facts that are untrue. Stipulations to untrue facts are unethical. If a prosecutor has insufficient facts to contest a defendant's effort to seek a downward departure or to claim an adjustment, the prosecutor can say so. If the presentence report states facts that are inconsistent with a stipulation in which a prosecutor has joined, it is desirable for the prosecutor to object to the report or to add a statement explaining the prosecutor's understanding of the facts or the reason for the stipulation. . . .

## Charging and Plea Decisions ("Reno Bluesheet")
### Janet Reno, Attorney General (1993)

As first stated in the preface to the original 1980 edition of the Principles of Federal Prosecution, "they have been cast in general terms with a view to providing guidance rather than to mandating results. The intent is to assure regularity without regimentation, to prevent unwarranted disparity without sacrificing flexibility."

It should be emphasized that charging decisions and plea agreements should reflect adherence to the Sentencing Guidelines. However, a faithful and honest application of the Sentencing Guidelines is not incompatible with selecting charges or entering into plea agreements on the basis of an individualized assessment of the extent to which particular charges fit the specific circumstances of the case, are consistent with the purposes of the federal criminal code, and maximize the impact of federal resources on crime. Thus, for example, in determining "the most serious offense that is consistent with the nature of the defendant's conduct, that is likely to result in a sustainable conviction," it is appropriate that the attorney for the government consider, inter alia, such factors as the sentencing guideline range yielded by the charge, whether the penalty yielded by such sentencing range (or potential mandatory minimum charge, if applicable) is proportional to the seriousness of the defendant's conduct, and whether the charge achieves such purposes of the criminal law as punishment, protection of the public, specific and general deterrence, and rehabilitation. Note that these factors may also be considered by the attorney for the government when entering into the plea agreements.

To ensure consistency and accountability, charging and plea agreement decisions must be made at an appropriate level of responsibility and documented with an appropriate record of the factors applied.

## NOTES

1. *The 1992 Terwilliger Bluesheet.* After a few years of experience with the new system, officials in the Department of Justice remained dissatisfied with the plea bargaining practices of its attorneys in the field. In a 1992 revision of the plea bargaining policy, known as the "Terwilliger Bluesheet," the department moved away from an emphasis on describing the types of bargains that are acceptable. Instead, the revised policy strengthened the procedural review process for plea agreements:

> All negotiated plea agreements to felonies or misdemeanors negotiated from felonies shall be in writing and filed with the court. . . . There shall be within each office a formal system for approval of negotiated pleas. The approval authority shall be vested in at least a supervisory criminal Assistant United States Attorney . . . who will have the responsibility of assessing the appropriateness of the plea agreement under the policies of the Department of Justice pertaining to pleas, including those set forth in the Thornburgh Memo.

The 1992 policy allowed for categorical review of certain plea bargains. Fact situations that "arise with great frequency and are given identical treatment" could be handled through a "written instruction" that "describes with particularity the standard plea procedure to be followed, so long as that procedure is otherwise within Departmental guidelines." The policy listed as an example "a border district which routinely deals with a high volume of illegal alien cases daily." What do you suppose were the effects of these 1992 policy changes?

2. *Prosecutorial discretion and control.* How would you describe these DOJ policies in terms of the degree of control each policy exerted over federal

prosecutorial plea practices? Did all of these policies move toward increasing control over individual prosecutorial decisions? For further background on the creation of these federal policies, see David Robinson, The Decline and Potential Collapse of Federal Guideline Sentencing, 74 Wash. U. L.Q. 881 (1996). Are executive plea bargaining policies a good idea? What problems could they solve? What problems might they create?

3. *Policies and political accountability.*   In response to the Reno Bluesheet, on January 13, 1994, Senator Orrin Hatch (R-Utah), the ranking minority member on the Judiciary Committee, sent Attorney General Janet Reno a letter strongly opposing her directive:

> The Department's new policy now permits prosecutors to make independent decisions about whether a prescribed guideline sentence or mandatory minimum charge is not "proportional to the seriousness of the defendant's conduct." In other words, this new policy increases the potential for the unwarranted softening of sentences for violent offenders. . . .
>
>    I do not support the Department's announcement to drug traffickers and violent criminals that certain illegal conduct may not be charged because a Department employee may find the prescribed punishment too severe. If the Administration believes that existing sentences for drug cases and violent criminals are too severe, then it should seek to change the law or the relevant sentencing guidelines—not ignore them. I strongly urge you to reconsider your action in this matter.

Reno responded on March 8, 1994:

> Let me reiterate, as set forth in the clarifying bluesheet to which you allude, that it remains the directive of the Department of Justice that prosecutors charge the most serious offense that is consistent with the nature of the defendant's conduct, that is likely to result in a sustainable conviction; that prosecutors adhere to the Sentencing Guidelines; and that charging and plea agreements be made at an appropriate level of responsibility with appropriate documentation. In short, contrary to what you suggest, individual prosecutors are not free to follow their own lights or to ignore legislative directives. . . . We are steadfast in our opposition to unwarranted softening of sentences for violent offenders or drug traffickers. . . .

4. *Congress reasserts control over federal sentencing.*   In 2003 Congress enacted the PROTECT Act, Public Law 108-21, 117 Stat. 650. Although the statute dealt primarily with crimes involving child abuse, it also changed several features of federal sentencing law more generally, making downward departures from the sentencing prescribed by the federal guidelines more difficult for judges to invoke. Congress also asked the attorney general to submit a report to the House and Senate judiciary committees, detailing the policies the department would follow to discourage downward departures.

5. *The Ashcroft and Holder Memos.*   The PROTECT Act requested a report from the Department of Justice within 90 days of the statute's passage. If such a report did not appear by that deadline, the law imposed a more onerous set of reporting requirements for the attorney general to follow. The statute was

signed into law on April 30, 2003. On July 28, Attorney General John Ashcroft issued a set of policies concerning "sentencing recommendations and sentencing appeals." The policies emphasized "honesty in sentencing, both with respect to the facts and the law." A prosecutor's sentencing recommendations to the court "must honestly reflect the totality and seriousness of the defendant's conduct and must be fully consistent with the Guidelines," regardless of whether the individual prosecutor agrees with the policy embodied in the sentencing guidelines. Under the policy, prosecutors may not agree to "stand silent" while a defendant requests a downward adjustment to a sentence, "unless the prosecutor determines in good faith that the adjustment is supported by facts and the law."

Two months later, Attorney General Ashcroft issued a second policy statement, this one dealing with selection of charges and plea agreements. The policy is reprinted below. The most significant and most widely discussed element of what became known as the Ashcroft Memo was the emphatic statement that "in all federal criminal cases, federal prosecutors must charge and pursue the most serious, readily provable offense or offenses that are supported by the facts of the case." Seven years later, with a change in administrations and with a number of years of experience with the post-Booker advisory federal sentencing guidelines, Attorney General Eric Holder in May 2010 issued a new memorandum to all federal prosecutors concerning "Department Policy on Charging and Sentencing." This document, which came to be known as the Holder memo, is also reprinted below and expressly states that it replaces the Ashcroft memo concerning how federal prosecutors are supposed to make basic charging, plea bargaining, and sentencing decisions. Distilled to its essence, the Holder memo asserts that federal prosecutors "ordinarily should" charge and pursue the most serious offense and "should generally" continue to advocate a within-guideline sentence.

How do the policies appearing in the Ashcroft and Holder memos compare with those of prior Justice Department officials Reno, Terwilliger, Thornburgh, and Weld?

## *Department Policy Concerning Charging Criminal Offenses, Disposition of Charges, and Sentencing*
### ("Ashcroft Memo") John Ashcroft, Attorney General (September 2003)

. . . The fairness Congress sought to achieve by the Sentencing Reform Act and the PROTECT Act can be attained only if there are fair and reasonably consistent policies with respect to the Department's decisions concerning what charges to bring and how cases should be disposed. Just as the sentence a defendant receives should not depend upon which particular judge presides over the case, so too the charges a defendant faces should not depend upon the particular prosecutor assigned to handle the case. . . .

## I.   DEPARTMENT POLICY CONCERNING CHARGING AND PROSECUTION OF CRIMINAL OFFENSES

### A.   General Duty to Charge and to Pursue the Most Serious, Readily Provable Offense in All Federal Prosecutions

It is the policy of the Department of Justice that, in all federal criminal cases, federal prosecutors must charge and pursue the most serious, readily provable offense or offenses that are supported by the facts of the case, except as authorized by an Assistant Attorney General, United States Attorney, or designated supervisory attorney in the limited circumstances described below. The most serious offense or offenses are those that generate the most substantial sentence under the Sentencing Guidelines, unless a mandatory minimum sentence or count requiring a consecutive sentence would generate a longer sentence. A charge is not "readily provable" if the prosecutor has a good faith doubt, for legal or evidentiary reasons, as to the Government's ability readily to prove a charge at trial. Thus, charges should not be filed simply to exert leverage to induce a plea. Once filed, the most serious readily provable charges may not be dismissed except to the extent permitted in Section B.

### B.   Limited Exceptions

The basic policy set forth above requires federal prosecutors to charge and to pursue all charges that are determined to be readily provable and that, under the applicable statutes and Sentencing Guidelines, would yield the most substantial sentence. There are, however, certain limited exceptions to this requirement:

1. *Sentence would not be affected.*   First, if the applicable guideline range from which a sentence may be imposed would be unaffected, prosecutors may decline to charge or to pursue readily provable charges. However, if the most serious readily provable charge involves a mandatory minimum sentence that exceeds the applicable guideline range, counts essential to establish a mandatory minimum sentence must be charged and may not be dismissed, except to the extent provided elsewhere below.

2. *"Fast-track" programs.*   With the passage of the PROTECT Act, Congress recognized the importance of early disposition or "fast-track" programs [to handle the high volume of cases (particularly immigration cases) in some districts. As a matter of Department policy, Attorney General authorization is necessary for] any fast-track program that relies on "charge bargaining" — *i.e.,* an expedited disposition program whereby the Government agrees to charge less than the most serious, readily provable offense. Such programs are intended to be exceptional and will be authorized only when clearly warranted by local conditions within a district. . . .

3. *Post-indictment reassessment.*   In cases where post-indictment circumstances cause a prosecutor to determine in good faith that the most serious offense is not readily provable, because of a change in the evidence or some other justifiable reason (*e.g.,* the unavailability of a witness or the need to protect

the identity of a witness until he testifies against a more significant defendant), the prosecutor may dismiss the charge(s) with the written or otherwise documented approval of an Assistant Attorney General, United States Attorney, or designated supervisory attorney.

4. *Substantial assistance.* The preferred means to recognize a defendant's substantial assistance in the investigation or prosecution of another person is to charge the most serious readily provable offense and then to file an appropriate motion or motions under U.S.S.G. §5K1.1, 18 U.S.C. §3553(e), or Federal Rule of Criminal Procedure 35(b). However, in rare circumstances, where necessary to obtain substantial assistance in an important investigation or prosecution, and with the written or otherwise documented approval of an Assistant Attorney General, United States Attorney, or designated supervisory attorney, a federal prosecutor may decline to charge or to pursue a readily provable charge as part of plea agreement that properly reflects the substantial assistance provided by the defendant in the investigation or prosecution of another person.

5. *Statutory enhancements.* The use of statutory enhancements is strongly encouraged, and federal prosecutors must therefore take affirmative steps to ensure that the increased penalties resulting from specific statutory enhancements [such as use of a weapon] are sought in all appropriate cases. . . . In many cases, however, the filing of such enhancements will mean that the statutory sentence exceeds the applicable Sentencing Guidelines range, thereby ensuring that the defendant will not receive any credit for acceptance of responsibility and will have no incentive to plead guilty. Requiring the pursuit of such enhancements to trial in every case could therefore have a significant effect on the allocation of prosecutorial resources within a given district. Accordingly, an Assistant Attorney General, United States Attorney, or designated supervisory attorney may authorize a prosecutor to forgo the filing of a statutory enhancement, but *only* in the context of a negotiated plea agreement. . . .

6. *Other exceptional circumstances.* Prosecutors may decline to pursue or may dismiss readily provable charges in other exceptional circumstances with the written or otherwise documented approval of an Assistant Attorney General, United States Attorney, or designated supervisory attorney. This exception recognizes that the aims of the Sentencing Reform Act must be sought without ignoring the practical limitations of the federal criminal justice system. For example, a case-specific approval to dismiss charges in a particular case might be given because the United States Attorney's Office is particularly overburdened, the duration of the trial would be exceptionally long, and proceeding to trial would significantly reduce the total number of cases disposed of by the office. However, such case-by-case exceptions should be rare; otherwise the goals of fairness and equity will be jeopardized.

## II. DEPARTMENT POLICY CONCERNING PLEA AGREEMENTS

[It] remains Department policy that the sentencing court should be informed if a plea agreement involves a "charge bargain." Accordingly, a negotiated plea that uses any of the options described in Section I(B)(2), (4), (5), or (6) must be made known to the court at the time of the plea hearing and at the time of sentencing, *i.e.*, the court must be informed that a more serious, readily provable offense was not charged or that an applicable statutory enhancement was not filed. . . . Charges may be declined or dismissed pursuant to a plea agreement only to the extent consistent with the principles set forth in Section I of this Memorandum.

[As for sentence bargains], prosecutors may enter into a plea agreement for a sentence that is within the specified guideline range. For example, when the Sentencing Guidelines range is 18-24 months, a prosecutor may agree to recommend a sentence of 18 or 20 months rather than to argue for a sentence at the top of the range. Similarly, a prosecutor may agree to recommend a downward adjustment for acceptance of responsibility under U.S.S.G. §3E1.1 if the prosecutor concludes in good faith that the defendant is entitled to the adjustment. . . .

In passing the PROTECT Act, Congress has made clear its view that there have been too many downward departures from the Sentencing Guidelines, and it has instructed the Commission to take measures "to ensure that the incidence of downward departures [is] substantially reduced." The Department has a duty to ensure that the circumstances in which it will request or accede to downward departures in the future are properly circumscribed.

Accordingly, federal prosecutors must not request or accede to a downward departure except in the limited circumstances specified in this memorandum and with authorization from an Assistant Attorney General, United States Attorney, or designated supervisory attorney. . . .

Federal criminal law and procedure apply equally throughout the United States. As the sole federal prosecuting entity, the Department of Justice has a unique obligation to ensure that all federal criminal cases are prosecuted according to the same standards. . . .

## Department Policy on Charging and Sentencing ("Holder Memo")
### Eric Holder, Attorney General (May 2010)

The reasoned exercise of prosecutorial discretion is essential to the fair, effective, and even-handed administration of the federal criminal laws. Decisions about whether to initiate charges, what charges and enhancements to pursue, when to accept a negotiated plea, and how to advocate at sentencing, are among the most fundamental duties of federal prosecutors. For nearly three decades, the Principles of Federal Prosecution, as reflected in Title 9 of the U.S. Attorneys' Manual, Chapter 27, have guided federal prosecutors in the discharge of these duties in particular and in their responsibility to seek justice in the enforcement of the federal criminal laws in general. The purpose of this memorandum is to reaffirm the guidance provided by those Principles.

Persons who commit similar crimes and have similar culpability should, to the extent possible, be treated similarly. Unwarranted disparities may result from disregard for this fundamental principle. They can also result, however, from a failure to analyze carefully and distinguish the specific facts and circumstances of each particular case. Indeed, equal justice depends on individualized justice, and smart law enforcement demands it. Accordingly, decisions regarding charging, plea agreements, and advocacy at sentencing must be made on the merits of each case, taking into account an individualized assessment of the defendant's conduct and criminal history and the circumstances relating to commission of the offense (including the impact of the crime on victims), the needs of the communities we serve, and federal resources and priorities. Prosecutors must always be mindful of our duty to ensure that these decisions are made without unwarranted consideration of such factors as race, gender, ethnicity, or sexual orientation.

*Charging Decisions*: Charging decisions should be informed by reason and by the general purposes of criminal law enforcement: punishment, public safety, deterrence, and rehabilitation. These decisions should also reflect the priorities of the Department and of each district. Charges should ordinarily be brought if there is probable cause to believe that a person has committed a federal offense and there is sufficient admissible evidence to obtain and sustain a conviction, unless "no substantial Federal interest" would be served, the person is subject to U.S. Department of Justice "effective prosecution" elsewhere, or there is "an adequate non-criminal alternative to prosecution" [USAM 9-27.200 et seq.].

Moreover, in accordance with long-standing principle, a federal prosecutor should ordinarily charge "the most serious offense that is consistent with the nature of the defendant's conduct, and that is likely to result in a sustainable conviction" [USAM 9-27.300]. This determination, however, must always be made in the context of "an individualized assessment of the extent to which particular charges fit the specific circumstances of the case, are consistent with the purpose of the Federal criminal code, and maximize the impact of Federal resources on crime" [USAM 9-27.300]. In all cases, the charges should fairly represent the defendant's criminal conduct, and due consideration should be given to the defendant's substantial assistance in an investigation or prosecution. As a general matter, the decision whether to seek a statutory sentencing enhancement should be guided by these same principles.

All charging decisions must be reviewed by a supervisory attorney. All but the most routine indictments should be accompanied by a prosecution memorandum that identifies the charging options supported by the evidence and the law and explains the charging decision therein. Each office shall promulgate written guidance describing its internal indictment review process.

*Plea Agreements*: Plea agreements should reflect the totality of a defendant's conduct. These agreements are governed by the same fundamental principle as charging decisions: prosecutors should seek a plea to the most serious offense that is consistent with the nature of the defendant's conduct and likely to result in a sustainable conviction, informed by an individualized assessment of the specific facts and circumstances of each particular case. Charges should not be filed simply to exert leverage to induce a plea, nor should charges be abandoned to arrive at a plea bargain that does not reflect the seriousness of the defendant's conduct. All plea agreements should be consistent with the Principles of Federal Prosecution and must be reviewed by a supervisory attorney. Each office shall promulgate written guidance regarding the standard elements required in its plea agreements, including the waivers of a defendant's rights.

*Advocacy at Sentencing* :   As the Supreme Court has recognized, Congress has identified the factors for courts to consider when imposing sentences pursuant to 18 U.S.C. §3553. Consistent with the statute and with the advisory sentencing guidelines as the touchstone, prosecutors should seek sentences that reflect the seriousness of the offense, promote respect for the law, provide just punishment, afford deterrence, protect the public, and offer defendants an opportunity for effective rehabilitation. In the typical case, the appropriate balance among these purposes will continue to be reflected by the applicable guidelines range, and prosecutors should generally continue to advocate for a sentence within that range. The advisory guidelines remain important in furthering the goal of national uniformity throughout the federal system. But consistent with the Principles of Federal Prosecution and given the advisory nature of the guidelines, advocacy at sentencing — like charging decisions and plea agreements — must also follow from an individualized assessment of the facts and circumstances of each particular case. All prosecutorial requests for departures or variances — upward or downward — must be based upon specific and articulable factors, and require supervisory approval. Each office shall provide training for effective advocacy at sentencing.

With respect to charging decisions, plea agreements, and advocacy at sentencing, the mechanisms established for obtaining supervisory approval should be designed to ensure, as much as possible, adherence to the Principles of Federal Prosecution and the guidance provided by this memorandum, as well as district-wide consistency. Supervisory attorneys selected to review exercises of discretion should be skilled, experienced, and thoroughly familiar with Department and district-specific policies, priorities, and practices. All guidance described above must be shared with the Executive Office for U.S. Attorneys upon promulgation.

## NOTES

1. *Prosecutor plea policies and legislative oversight.*   In what ways do the Ashcroft and Holder Memos reflect responses to Congress's request to push sentencing practices in a particular direction? Do you think it appropriate to equate the criteria for initial selection of charges (Section I of the Ashcroft Memo) and the criteria for evaluating charge bargains (Section II of the Ashcroft Memo)?

2. *Policies and practice.*   Do "line" attorneys follow directives from their boss? The most complete studies of federal plea practices during the early implementation of the guidelines concluded that prosecutors manipulated the guidelines in 20-35% of all cases. Stephen Schulhofer & Ilene Nagel, A Tale of Three Cities: An Empirical Study of Charging and Bargaining Practice Under the Federal Sentencing Guidelines, 66 S. Cal. L. Rev. 501 (1992). Sentencing Commission studies found charge manipulation in 17% of all cases and 26% of drug cases. U.S. Sentencing Commission, The Federal Sentencing Guidelines: A Report on the Operation of the Guidelines System and Short-Term Impacts on Disparity in Sentencing, Use of Incarceration, and Prosecutorial Discretion and Plea Bargaining, Executive Summary 31-54 (December 1991). Why might line attorneys not follow plea guidelines? Why might different U.S. Attorneys' offices develop different patterns of plea bargaining?

3. *Written and unwritten guidance.*   A striking feature of the plea bargaining policies in the federal system is the fact that they are written. Many other prosecutors' offices in state systems have pursued goals similar to those of the Department of Justice in creating its plea policies. They hope to maintain adequate control over prosecutors in the field and to send appropriate public signals about sentencing and plea bargaining. Nonetheless, within the state systems, such policies are rarely written, even when they are explicit. Why might a supervising prosecutor choose to keep such a critical office policy unwritten? See William Pizzi, Understanding Prosecutorial Discretion in the United States: The Limits of Comparative Criminal Procedure as an Instrument of Reform, 54 Ohio St. L.J. 1325 (1993) (discussing reasons that offices keep their plea bargaining policies informal and unwritten, including ill effects on deterrent value of criminal law, unfavorable public impressions related to policies perceived as lenient, need for flexibility in unusual cases, need to avoid judicial review of prosecutorial decisions); but compare Kim Banks Mayer, Applying Open Records Policy to Wisconsin District Attorneys: Can Charging Guidelines Promote Public Awareness? 1996 Wis. L. Rev. 295 (giving examples of prosecutorial charging and plea bargaining guidelines made public with no apparent ill effects, and arguing generally for public availability of policies). Is there any reason not to create a written office policy, given that all plea agreements in individual cases will become a matter of public record?

4. *Sentencing guidelines and the shift to charge bargains.*   A large number of states have changed their sentencing laws over the past few decades to reduce the discretion of judges in selecting a sentence and to restrict the discretion of corrections or parole officials in releasing offenders before the end of their announced sentences. These more "determinate" sentencing systems make the selection of the criminal charge more important than it was under more discretionary sentencing systems. Unlike the federal system, state guideline systems reject the use of uncharged conduct when setting a sentence. As a result, prosecutors and defendants in these jurisdictions have shifted away from sentence bargains toward charge bargains and "fact" bargains. In Minnesota, which adopted a more determinate sentencing guideline system in 1980, studies focusing on the first few years of practice under the new laws revealed an increase in charge negotiations and a decrease in sentence negotiations. Terance Miethe, Charging and Plea Bargaining Practices Under Determinate Sentencing: An Investigation of the Hydraulic Displacement of Discretion, 78 J. Crim. L. & Criminology 155 (1987) (describing earlier studies).

5. *Uniformity within a jurisdiction.*   The federal plea bargaining policies reprinted above apply to U.S. Attorneys' offices throughout the country. While these offices still have a great deal of independence and vary from one another in their plea bargaining practices, they are still subject to more centralized control than the various prosecutors' offices located throughout a given state. Since prosecutors often create plea bargaining policies for their own offices, shouldn't there be great variety in plea bargaining practices among the different prosecutors within a state? Or are there institutions or incentives that produce similar prosecutorial plea policies throughout a state or even across different states?

6. *Waivers of the right to appeal: federal policy.*   One question about potential limits on the substantive content of pleas is whether defendants may waive the right to appeal or collaterally attack their sentences. This is an especially significant issue because of the importance of appellate decisions in providing law and norms for some structured sentencing systems, including the federal system. At the same time, sentencing appeals have made up a very significant proportion of criminal appeals, and indeed of all appeals in the federal system.

In 1995 the Department of Justice circulated a memo to all U.S. Attorneys to provide guidance on the drafting and use of sentencing appeal waivers in plea agreements. Though each of the U.S. Attorneys' offices sets its own policies — with some refusing to make use of these waivers and others using them regularly — the memorandum made a determined argument for waivers. The "Keeney memo" stated that the use of appeal waivers is "helpful in reducing the burden of appellate and collateral litigation involving sentencing issues," though it also cautions that the use of broad sentencing appeal waivers "could result in guideline-free sentencing of defendants in guilty plea cases, and it could encourage a lawless district court to impose sentences in violation of the guidelines."

Noting the increased use of appeal waivers in plea agreements, the Committee on Criminal Law of the Judicial Conference of the United States issued a memorandum in July 1996 to aid district judges and probation officers in their consideration of such provisions. This memo noted that "waivers have been consistently upheld as legal, primarily because it is well established that a defendant can waive any right, even a constitutional right, as long as the waiver is knowing and voluntary." The committee suggested that courts provide all defendants with a "qualified, yet informative, advisement of the right to appeal at sentencing," followed by a specific oral colloquy about the terms of any appeal waiver provision to which a defendant has agreed.

As the use of appeal waivers has become more common in the federal system, judges have expressed concerns that such waivers, especially in their broadest forms, can be unlawful, inappropriate, and dangerous. A number of circuit courts have expressed concerns about broad appeal waivers that eliminate all appellate rights concerning any guideline sentence that is imposed. These courts have indicated that they would look closely at the particular facts of each case to ensure that a defendant fully understood and voluntarily accepted such a waiver. See United States v. Rosa, 123 F.2d 94 (2d Cir. 1997) (affirming appeal waiver while observing that a broad waiver "presents grave dangers and implicates both constitutional questions and ordinary principles of fairness and justice"). More dramatically, a number of district judges have refused to accept pleas that include broad appeal waivers. Will such positions by district judges lead to different outcomes in their courts? Will it create disparities in substance and sentence, or only in process?

7. *Waivers of the right to appeal: state practices.*   Prosecutors in many systems will try to include explicit waivers of the right to appeal a conviction or sentence as part of the plea agreement. Most state courts have concluded that a defendant may explicitly waive the right to appeal a conviction as part of a plea agreement. See State v. Hinners, 471 N.W.2d 841 (Iowa 1991); People v. Seaberg, 541 N.E.2d 1022 (N.Y. 1989). A few courts maintain that public policy forbids prosecutors

from insulating themselves from review by bargaining away a defendant's appeal rights. Cf. State v. Ethington, 592 P.2d 768 (Ariz. 1979) (defendant can appeal conviction, notwithstanding agreement not to appeal).

Is it necessary for a defendant to waive the right to appeal explicitly, or does it go without saying that a defendant who pleads guilty will not attack the conviction on appeal? If a defendant wants to appeal some aspect of a conviction based on a guilty plea, should she explicitly condition the guilty plea on the outcome of the planned appeal? How might we decide what must be explicit in a plea agreement and what will be implied? Does this depend on what the parties are likely to have contemplated, even if they did not address the issue specifically? See Peter Westen, Away from Waiver: A Rationale for the Forfeiture of Constitutional Rights in Criminal Procedure, 75 Mich. L. Rev. 1214 (1977).

8. *Substantive limits on bargains.*    There are a few types of legal challenges to a conviction that some courts say a defendant may not waive, even if the waiver appears explicitly in a plea agreement. Courts have taken this position on constitutional speedy trial rights, see People v. Callahan, 604 N.E.2d 108 (N.Y. 1992), and for sentences more severe than the statutory maximum allowable sentence, see Lanier v. State, 635 So. 2d 813 (Miss. 1994). Courts are split on whether the parties can agree to a sentence outside the statutorily authorized range of punishments; often they enforce illegal sentences falling below the authorized range of punishments but not illegal sentences set above the authorized range. See Ex parte Johnson, 669 So. 2d 205 (Ala. 1995) (enforces prosecutor's agreement to two-year prison term, even though prosecutor failed to account for sentencing enhancements requiring additional minimum sentences); but see Patterson v. State, 660 So. 2d 966 (Miss. 1995) (holding plea bargain to life without possibility of parole invalid because no statute authorizes such a sentence for murder).

When defendants attempt to raise challenges that they waived in plea agreements, claiming that the agreement is unenforceable, it is far more common for courts to refuse to hear the challenge. Courts allow defendants to bargain away rights of all sorts. See United States v. Mezzanatto, 513 U.S. 196 (1995) (allowing defendant to waive protections of Rule 11(e)(6), which prevented later introduction into evidence of statements made during plea negotiations); People v. Stevens, 610 N.W.2d 881 (Mich. 2000) (statements made during plea negotiations are admissible in prosecution's case-in-chief); Cowan v. Superior Court, 926 P.2d 438 (Cal. 1996) (allowing waiver of statute of limitations); People v. Allen, 658 N.E.2d 1012 (N.Y. 1995) (allowing waiver of double jeopardy); Joseph A. Colquitt, Ad Hoc Plea Bargaining, 75 Tul. L. Rev. 695 (2001). Is there a pattern that separates the waivable from the nonwaivable rights? Are the waivable rights the lesser ones? Professor Nancy King notes the increasing willingness of courts to allow waivers. She favors keeping as nonwaivable rights only constitutional claims that have an impact on third parties, since legislatures can decide whether to protect statutory rights from waiver. See Nancy J. King, Priceless Process, 47 UCLA L. Rev. 113 (1999). Should courts allow defendants to waive their right to effective assistance of counsel?

9. *Waiving discovery.*    If defendants must know about the nature of the charges and the direct consequences of a guilty plea, must they also know about the basic facts the prosecutor could present against them at trial? In

United States v. Ruiz, 536 U.S. 622 (2002), the Court held that the Fifth and Sixth Amendments did not "require federal prosecutors, before entering into a binding plea agreement with a criminal defendant, to disclose 'impeachment information relating to any informants or other witnesses.'" The Supreme Court's decision in *Ruiz* is typical in its refusal to declare a per se rule against bargaining away discovery rights. A few courts, however, have concluded that in some cases, accepting a guilty plea based on a plea agreement that prevents the defendant from engaging in discovery violates due process. See State v. Draper, 784 P.2d 259 (Ariz. 1989) (due process and right to counsel sometimes may prohibit plea agreement conditioned on defendant not interviewing victim of alleged crime; remand to determine defendant's access to state's evidence through other witnesses). Can you identify circumstances in which a defendant could make a knowing waiver of the right to a jury trial without discovery? The *Ruiz* Court found it significant that the condition relating to discovery was non-mandatory—the defendant could choose to go forward with discovery and forgo the plea agreement. Are there any terms that prosecutors simply may not offer because they prevent the defendant from making a knowing waiver?

10. *Are plea bargains contracts?* Some scholars have accepted the essentially contractual nature of plea bargaining—a position that largely supports the right of defendants to bargain for whatever they want. Critics of plea bargaining, such as Professor Stephen Schulhofer, have rejected the notion that plea bargains are fair simply because the defendant agreed to the terms and because the agreement puts the defendant in a better position than if the defendant had gone to trial. Stephen Schulhofer, Plea Bargaining as Disaster, 101 Yale L.J. 1979 (1992). Schulhofer and other critics focus on the public interest in criminal justice that the contract model obscures. Does plea bargaining undermine public confidence in the criminal justice system? See Stanley Cohen & Anthony Doob, Public Attitudes to Plea Bargaining, 32 Crim. L.Q. 85 (1989-1990) (1988 survey found that more than two-thirds of Canadians disapprove of plea bargaining). What other public interests are at stake in plea bargains? In sentences?

### B. Modern Review of Defense Representation in Plea Bargaining

As noted before, there has historically been precious little case law or constitutional doctrines governing the use of guilty pleas or the negotiation of plea bargains. The Supreme Court did not seriously discuss plea practices until 1971 when, in Santobello v. New York, 404 U.S. 257 (1971), the Court favorably discussed plea bargaining practices in these terms:

> Disposition of charges after plea discussions is not only an essential part of the process but a highly desirable part for many reasons. It leads to prompt and largely final disposition of most criminal cases; it avoids much of the corrosive impact of enforced idleness during pre-trial confinement for those who are denied release pending trial; it protects the public from those accused persons who are prone to continue criminal conduct even while on pretrial release; and, by shortening the time between charge and disposition, it enhances whatever may be the rehabilitative prospects of the guilty when they are ultimately imprisoned.

> [A]ll of these considerations presuppose fairness in securing agreement between an accused and a prosecutor. It is now clear, for example, that the accused pleading guilty must be counseled, absent a waiver. . . . The plea must, of course, be voluntary and knowing and if it was induced by promises, the essence of those promises must in some way be made known. There is, of course, no absolute right to have a guilty plea accepted. A court may reject a plea in exercise of sound judicial discretion.
>
> This phase of the process of criminal justice, and the adjudicative element inherent in accepting a plea of guilty, must be attended by safeguards to insure the defendant what is reasonably due in the circumstances. Those circumstances will vary, but a constant factor is that when a plea rests in any significant degree on a promise or agreement of the prosecutor, so that it can be said to be part of the inducement or consideration, such promise must be fulfilled.

The Supreme Court thereafter had precious little to say about the plea process after *Santobello*, and lower courts generally read this ruling to mean that plea agreements should be interpreted and enforced based roughly on traditional contract principles. Moreover, and perhaps most importantly, the statement in *Santobello* that a defendant has "no absolute right to have a guilty plea accepted" led lower courts to reject consistently varied claims by defendants in various settings that their constitutional rights were violated by some facet of the plea bargaining process.

As structured sentencing reforms and other new criminal justice sanctions became increasingly popular during the last decades of the 20th century, commentators and some lower courts began to appreciate ever more fully (and sometimes complain ever more loudly) how consequential the plea bargaining process could be to the fair and just disposition of criminal charges. See, e.g., George Fisher, Plea Bargaining's Triumph: A History of Plea Bargaining in America (2003); Stephanos Bibas, Plea Bargaining Outside the Shadow of Trial, 117 Harv. L. Rev. 2463 (2004). In the federal system, the advent of sentencing guidelines and mandatory minimum sentencing statutes had the (somewhat unexpected) consequence of further increasing the percentage of guilty verdicts resulting from plea bargaining to over 90%, largely because the these reforms made sentences more predictably harsh and limited the authority of judges to reduce sentencing terms after a trial conviction. Perhaps as a result of these developments and enduring concerns about the historically lax regulations surrounding the plea bargaining process, the Supreme Court in the last few years has handed down a set of consequential Sixth Amendment rulings addressing the enforceable constitutional responsibilities of defense attorneys in the process.

## *Jose Padilla v. Kentucky*
### 130 S. Ct. 1473 (2010)

STEVENS, J.

Petitioner Jose Padilla, a native of Honduras, has been a lawful permanent resident of the United States for more than 40 years. Padilla served this Nation with honor as a member of the U.S. Armed Forces during the Vietnam War. He now faces deportation after pleading guilty to the transportation of a large amount of marijuana in his tractor-trailer in the Commonwealth of Kentucky. In this postconviction proceeding, Padilla claims that his counsel not only failed to advise him of this consequence prior to his entering the plea, but also told him that he "did not have to worry about immigration status since he had been in the country so long." Padilla relied on his counsel's erroneous advice when he pleaded guilty to the drug charges that made his deportation virtually mandatory. He alleges that he would have insisted on going to trial if he had not received incorrect advice from his attorney. Assuming the truth of his allegations, the Supreme Court of Kentucky denied Padilla postconviction relief without the benefit of an evidentiary hearing. The court held that the Sixth Amendment's guarantee of effective assistance of counsel does not protect a criminal defendant from erroneous advice about deportation because it is merely a "collateral" consequence of his conviction. . . . We agree with Padilla that constitutionally competent counsel would have advised him that his conviction for drug distribution made him subject to automatic deportation. Whether he is entitled to relief depends on whether he has been prejudiced, a matter that we do not address.

The landscape of federal immigration law has changed dramatically over the last 90 years. While once there was only a narrow class of deportable offenses and judges wielded broad discretionary authority to prevent deportation, immigration reforms over time have expanded the class of deportable offenses and limited the authority of judges to alleviate the harsh consequences of deportation. [Deportation] or removal is now virtually inevitable for a vast number of noncitizens. . . .

Under contemporary law, if a noncitizen has committed a removable offense . . . his removal is practically inevitable but for the possible exercise of limited remnants of equitable discretion vested in the Attorney General to cancel removal for noncitizens convicted of particular classes of offenses. Subject to limited exceptions, this discretionary relief is not available for an offense related to trafficking in a controlled substance. These changes to our immigration law have dramatically raised the stakes of a noncitizen's criminal conviction. The importance of accurate legal advice for noncitizens accused of crimes has never been more important. These changes confirm our view that, as a matter of federal law, deportation is an integral part — indeed, sometimes the most important part — of the penalty that may be imposed on noncitizen defendants who plead guilty to specified crimes.

Before deciding whether to plead guilty, a defendant is entitled to the effective assistance of competent counsel. The Supreme Court of Kentucky rejected Padilla's ineffectiveness claim on the ground that the advice he sought about the risk of deportation concerned only collateral matters, i.e., those matters not within the sentencing authority of the state trial court. . . . We, however, have never applied a distinction between direct and collateral consequences to define the scope of constitutionally "reasonable professional assistance" required under Strickland v. Washington, 466 U.S. 668 (1984). Whether that distinction is appropriate is a question we need not consider in this case because of the unique nature of deportation. We have long recognized that deportation is a particularly severe "penalty," Fong Yue Ting v. United States, 149 U.S. 698 (1893); but it is not, in a strict sense, a criminal sanction. Although removal proceedings are civil in nature, deportation is nevertheless intimately related to the criminal process. Our law has enmeshed criminal convictions and the penalty of deportation for nearly a century. And, importantly, recent changes in our immigration law have made removal nearly an automatic result for a broad class of noncitizen offenders. Thus, we find it most difficult to divorce the penalty from the conviction in the deportation context. Moreover, we are quite confident that noncitizen defendants facing a risk of deportation for a particular offense find it even more difficult. Deportation as a consequence of a criminal conviction is, because of its close connection to the criminal process, uniquely difficult to classify as either a direct or a collateral consequence. The collateral versus direct distinction is thus ill-suited to evaluating a *Strickland* claim concerning the specific risk of deportation. We conclude that advice regarding deportation is not categorically removed from the ambit of the Sixth Amendment right to counsel. *Strickland* applies to Padilla's claim.

Under *Strickland*, we first determine whether counsel's representation fell below an objective standard of reasonableness. Then we ask whether there is a reasonable probability that, but for counsel's unprofessional errors, the result of the proceeding would have been different. The first prong—constitutional deficiency—is necessarily linked to the practice and expectations of the legal community: the proper measure of attorney performance remains simply reasonableness under prevailing professional norms. We long have recognized that prevailing norms of practice as reflected in American Bar Association standards and the like are guides to determining what is reasonable. Although they are only guides, and not inexorable commands, these standards may be valuable measures of the prevailing professional norms of effective representation, especially as these standards have been adapted to deal with the intersection of modern criminal prosecutions and immigration law. The weight of prevailing professional norms supports the view that counsel must advise her client regarding the risk of deportation. National Legal Aid and Defender Assn., Performance Guidelines for Criminal Representation §6.2 (1995); Chin & Holmes, Effective Assistance of Counsel and the Consequences of Guilty Pleas, 87 Cornell L. Rev. 697, 713-718 (2002); ABA Standards for Criminal Justice, Prosecution Function and Defense Function 4-5.1(a), p. 197 (3d ed. 1993). . . . We too have previously recognized that preserving the client's right to remain in the United States may be more important to the client than any potential jail sentence. . . .

Padilla's counsel could have easily determined that his plea would make him eligible for deportation simply from reading the text of the statute, which addresses not some broad classification of crimes but specifically commands removal for all controlled substances convictions except for the most trivial of marijuana possession offenses. Instead, Padilla's counsel provided him false assurance that his conviction would not result in his removal from this country. This is not a hard case in which to find deficiency: The consequences of Padilla's plea could easily be determined from reading the removal statute, his deportation was presumptively mandatory, and his counsel's advice was incorrect. Immigration law can be complex, and it is a legal specialty of its own. Some members of the bar who represent clients facing criminal charges, in either state or federal court or both, may not be well versed in it. There will, therefore, undoubtedly be numerous situations in which the deportation consequences of a particular plea are unclear or uncertain. The duty of the private practitioner in such cases is more limited. When the law is not succinct and straightforward (as it is in many of the scenarios posited by Justice Alito), a criminal defense attorney need do no more than advise a noncitizen client that pending criminal charges may carry a risk of adverse immigration consequences. But when the deportation consequence is truly clear, as it was in this case, the duty to give correct advice is equally clear.

Accepting his allegations as true, Padilla has sufficiently alleged constitutional deficiency to satisfy the first prong of *Strickland*. Whether Padilla is entitled to relief on his claim will depend on whether he can satisfy *Strickland*'s second prong, prejudice, a matter we leave to the Kentucky courts to consider in the first instance.

The Solicitor General has urged us to conclude that *Strickland* applies to Padilla's claim only to the extent that he has alleged affirmative misadvice. In the United States' view, counsel is not constitutionally required to provide advice on matters that will not be decided in the criminal case, though counsel is required to provide accurate advice if she chooses to discusses these matters. Respondent and Padilla both find the Solicitor General's proposed rule unpersuasive, although it has support among the lower courts. [We believe, however, that] that there is no relevant difference between an act of commission and an act of omission in this context. A holding limited to affirmative misadvice would invite two absurd results. First, it would give counsel an incentive to remain silent on matters of great importance, even when answers are readily available. Silence under these circumstances would be fundamentally at odds with the critical obligation of counsel to advise the client of "the advantages and disadvantages of a plea agreement." Libretti v. United States, 516 U.S. 29, 50-51 (1995). When attorneys know that their clients face possible exile from this country and separation from their families, they should not be encouraged to say nothing at all. Second, it would deny a class of clients least able to represent themselves the most rudimentary advice on deportation even when it is readily available. It is quintessentially the duty of counsel to provide her client with available advice about an issue like deportation and the failure to do so clearly satisfies the first prong of the Strickland analysis. . . .

There is no reason to doubt that lower courts — now quite experienced with applying Strickland — can effectively and efficiently use its framework to separate specious claims from those with substantial merit. It seems unlikely that our decision today will have a significant effect on those convictions already obtained as the result of plea bargains. For at least the past 15 years, professional norms have generally imposed an obligation on counsel to provide advice on the deportation consequences of a client's plea. We should, therefore, presume that counsel satisfied their obligation to render competent advice at the time their clients considered pleading guilty. Likewise, although we must be especially careful about recognizing new grounds for attacking the validity of guilty pleas, in the 25 years since we first applied Strickland to claims of ineffective assistance at the plea stage, practice has shown that pleas are less frequently the subject of collateral challenges than convictions obtained after a trial. Pleas account for nearly 95% of all criminal convictions. But they account for only approximately 30% of the habeas petitions filed. The nature of relief secured by a successful collateral challenge to a guilty plea — an opportunity to withdraw the plea and proceed to trial — imposes its own significant limiting principle:

Those who collaterally attack their guilty pleas lose the benefit of the bargain obtained as a result of the plea. Thus, a different calculus informs whether it is wise to challenge a guilty plea in a habeas proceeding because, ultimately, the challenge may result in a less favorable outcome for the defendant, whereas a collateral challenge to a conviction obtained after a jury trial has no similar downside potential. Finally, informed consideration of possible deportation can only benefit both the State and noncitizen defendants during the pleabargaining process. By bringing deportation consequences into this process, the defense and prosecution may well be able to reach agreements that better satisfy the interests of both parties. As in this case, a criminal episode may provide the basis for multiple charges, of which only a subset mandate deportation following conviction. Counsel who possess the most rudimentary understanding of the deportation consequences of a particular criminal offense may be able to plea bargain creatively with the prosecutor in order to craft a conviction and sentence that reduce the likelihood of deportation, as by avoiding a conviction for an offense that automatically triggers the removal consequence. At the same time, the threat of deportation may provide the defendant with a powerful incentive to plead guilty to an offense that does not mandate that penalty in exchange for a dismissal of a charge that does.

In sum, we have long recognized that the negotiation of a plea bargain is a critical phase of litigation for purposes of the Sixth Amendment right to effective assistance of counsel. The severity of deportation — the equivalent of banishment or exile — only underscores how critical it is for counsel to inform her noncitizen client that he faces a risk of deportation.

It is our responsibility under the Constitution to ensure that no criminal defendant — whether a citizen or not — is left to the mercies of incompetent counsel. To satisfy this responsibility, we now hold that counsel must inform her client whether his plea carries a risk of deportation. Our longstanding Sixth Amendment precedents, the seriousness of deportation as a consequence of a criminal plea, and the concomitant impact of deportation on families living lawfully in this country demand no less. Taking as true the basis for his motion for postconviction relief, we have little difficulty concluding that Padilla has sufficiently alleged that his counsel was constitutionally deficient. . . .

ALITO, J., concurring in the judgment.

I concur in the judgment because a criminal defense attorney fails to provide effective assistance within the meaning of Strickland v. Washington, 466 U.S. 668 (1984), if the attorney misleads a noncitizen client regarding the removal consequences of a conviction. In my view, such an attorney must (1) refrain from unreasonably providing incorrect advice and (2) advise the defendant that a criminal conviction may have adverse immigration consequences and that, if the alien wants advice on this issue, the alien should consult an immigration attorney. I do not agree with the Court that the attorney must attempt to explain what those consequences may be. As the Court concedes, immigration law can be complex; it is a legal specialty of its own; and some members of the bar who represent clients facing criminal charges, in either state or federal court or both, may not be well versed in it. The Court nevertheless holds that a criminal defense attorney must provide advice in this specialized area in those cases in which the law is "succinct and straightforward" — but not, perhaps, in other situations. This vague, halfway test will lead to much confusion and needless litigation. . . .

Under *Strickland*, an attorney provides ineffective assistance if the attorney's representation does not meet reasonable professional standards. Until today, the longstanding and unanimous position of the federal courts was that reasonable defense counsel generally need only advise a client about the direct consequences of a criminal conviction. While the line between "direct" and "collateral" consequences is not always clear, the collateral-consequences rule expresses an important truth: Criminal defense attorneys have expertise regarding the conduct of criminal proceedings. They are not expected to possess — and very often do not possess — expertise in other areas of the law, and it is unrealistic to expect them to provide expert advice on matters that lie outside their area of training and experience. This case happens to involve removal, but criminal convictions can carry a wide variety of consequences other than conviction and sentencing, including civil commitment, civil forfeiture, the loss of the right to vote, disqualification from public benefits, ineligibility to possess firearms, dishonorable discharge from the Armed Forces, and loss of business or professional licenses. A criminal conviction may also severely damage a defendant's reputation and thus impair the defendant's ability to obtain future employment or business opportunities. All of those consequences are serious, but this Court has never held that a criminal defense attorney's Sixth Amendment duties extend to providing advice about such matters. . . .

Because many criminal defense attorneys have little understanding of immigration law, it should follow that a criminal defense attorney who refrains from providing immigration advice does not violate prevailing professional norms. But the Court's opinion would not just require defense counsel to warn the client of a general risk of removal; it would also require counsel in at least some cases, to specify what the removal consequences of a conviction would be. The Court's new approach is particularly problematic because providing advice on whether a conviction for a particular offense will make an alien removable is often quite complex. . . .

[T]he conclusion that affirmative misadvice regarding the removal consequences of a conviction can give rise to ineffective assistance would, unlike the Court's approach, not require any upheaval in the law. [The] vast majority of the lower courts considering claims of ineffective assistance in the plea context have distinguished between defense counsel who remain silent and defense counsel who give affirmative misadvice. . . . In concluding that affirmative misadvice regarding the removal consequences of a criminal conviction may constitute ineffective assistance, I do not mean to suggest that the Sixth Amendment does no more than require defense counsel to avoid misinformation. When a criminal defense attorney is aware that a client is an alien, the attorney should advise the client that a criminal conviction may have adverse consequences under the immigration laws and that the client should consult an immigration specialist if the client wants advice on that subject. By putting the client on notice of the danger of removal, such advice would significantly reduce the chance that the client would plead guilty under a mistaken premise.

In sum, a criminal defense attorney should not be required to provide advice on immigration law, a complex specialty that generally lies outside the scope of a criminal defense attorney's expertise. On the other hand, any competent criminal defense attorney should appreciate the extraordinary importance that the risk of removal might have in the client's determination whether to enter a guilty plea. Accordingly, unreasonable and incorrect information concerning the risk of removal can give rise to an ineffectiveness claim. In addition, silence alone is not enough to satisfy counsel's duty to assist the client. Instead, an alien defendant's Sixth Amendment right to counsel is satisfied if defense counsel advises the client that a conviction may have immigration consequences, that immigration law is a specialized field, that the attorney is not an immigration lawyer, and that the client should consult an immigration specialist if the client wants advice on that subject. . . .

SCALIA, J, dissenting.

In the best of all possible worlds, criminal defendants contemplating a guilty plea ought to be advised of all serious collateral consequences of conviction, and surely ought not to be misadvised. The Constitution, however, is not an all-purpose tool for judicial construction of a perfect world; and when we ignore its text in order to make it that, we often find ourselves swinging a sledge where a tack hammer is needed. The Sixth Amendment guarantees the accused a lawyer "for his defense" against a criminal prosecution–not for sound advice about the collateral consequences of conviction. For that reason, and for the practical reasons set forth in Part I of Justice Alito's concurrence, I dissent from the Court's conclusion that the Sixth Amendment requires counsel to provide accurate advice concerning the potential removal consequences of a guilty plea. For the same reasons, but unlike the concurrence, I do not believe that affirmative misadvice about those consequences renders an attorney's assistance in defending against the prosecution constitutionally inadequate; or that the Sixth Amendment requires counsel to warn immigrant defendants that a conviction may render them removable. Statutory provisions can remedy these concerns in a more targeted fashion, and without producing permanent, and legislatively irreparable, overkill. The Sixth Amendment as originally understood and ratified meant only that a defendant had a right to employ counsel, or to use volunteered services of counsel. We have held, however, that the Sixth Amendment requires the provision of counsel to indigent defendants at government expense, and that the right to "the assistance of counsel" includes the right to effective assistance. Even assuming the validity of these holdings, I reject the significant further extension that the Court, and to a lesser extent the concurrence, would create. We have until today at least retained the Sixth Amendment's textual limitation to criminal prosecutions. . . . Because the subject of the misadvice here was not the prosecution for which Jose Padilla was entitled to effective assistance of counsel, the Sixth Amendment has no application.

Adding to counsel's duties an obligation to advise about a conviction's collateral consequences has no logical stopping-point. [It] seems to me that the concurrence suffers from the same defect. The same indeterminacy, the same inability to know what areas of advice are relevant, attaches to misadvice. And the concurrence's suggestion that counsel must warn defendants of potential removal consequences—what would come to be known as the "Padilla warning"—cannot be limited to those consequences except by judicial caprice. It is difficult to believe that the warning requirement would not be extended, for example, to the risk of heightened sentences in later federal prosecutions pursuant to the Armed Career Criminal Act, 18 U.S.C. §924(e). . . .

The Court's holding prevents legislation that could solve the problems addressed by today's opinions in a more precise and targeted fashion. If the subject had not been constitutionalized, legislation could specify which categories of misadvice about matters ancillary to the prosecution invalidate plea agreements, what collateral consequences counsel must bring to a defendant's attention, and what warnings must be given. Moreover, legislation could provide consequences for the misadvice, nonadvice, or failure to warn, other than nullification of a criminal conviction after the witnesses and evidence needed for retrial have disappeared. Federal immigration law might provide, for example, that the near-automatic removal which follows from certain criminal convictions will not apply where the conviction rested upon a guilty plea induced by counsel's misadvice regarding removal consequences. Or legislation might put the government to a choice in such circumstances: Either retry the defendant or forgo the removal. But all that has been precluded in favor of today's sledge hammer. In sum, the Sixth Amendment guarantees adequate assistance of counsel in defending against a pending criminal prosecution. We should limit both the constitutional obligation to provide advice and the consequences of bad advice to that well defined area.

## *Missouri v. Galin Frye*
## 132 S. Ct. 1399 (2012)

KENNEDY, J., delivered the opinion of the Court.

The Sixth Amendment, applicable to the States by the terms of the Fourteenth Amendment, provides that the accused shall have the assistance of counsel in all criminal prosecutions. The right to counsel is the right to effective assistance of counsel. See Strickland v. Washington, 466 U.S. 668, 686 (1984). This case arises in the context of claimed ineffective assistance that led to the lapse of a prosecution offer of a plea bargain, a proposal that offered terms more lenient than the terms of the guilty plea entered later. The initial question is whether the constitutional right to counsel extends to the negotiation and consideration of plea offers that lapse or are rejected. If there is a right to effective assistance with respect to those offers, a further question is what a defendant must demonstrate in order to show that prejudice resulted from counsel's deficient performance. Other questions relating to ineffective assistance with respect to plea offers, including the question of proper remedies, are considered in a second case decided today. See Lafler v. Cooper, [132 S. Ct. 1376 (2012)].

In August 2007, respondent Galin Frye was charged with driving with a revoked license. Frye had been convicted for that offense on three other occasions, so the State of Missouri charged him with a class D felony, which carries a maximum term of imprisonment of four years. On November 15, the prosecutor sent a letter to Frye's counsel offering a choice of two plea bargains. The prosecutor first offered to recommend a 3-year sentence if there was a guilty plea to the felony charge, without a recommendation regarding probation but with a recommendation that Frye serve 10 days in jail as so called "shock" time. The second offer was to reduce the charge to a misdemeanor and, if Frye pleaded guilty to it, to recommend a 90-day sentence. The misdemeanor charge of driving with a revoked license carries a maximum term of imprisonment of one year. The letter stated both offers would expire on December 28. Frye's attorney did not advise Frye that the offers had been made. The offers expired.

Frye's preliminary hearing was scheduled for January 4, 2008. On December 30, 2007, less than a week before the hearing, Frye was again arrested for driving with a revoked license. At the January 4 hearing, Frye waived his right to a preliminary hearing on the charge arising from the August 2007 arrest. He pleaded not guilty at a subsequent arraignment but then changed his plea to guilty. There was no underlying plea agreement. App. 5, 13, 16. The state trial-court accepted Frye's guilty plea. Id., at 21. The prosecutor recommended a 3-year sentence, made no recommendation regarding probation, and requested 10 days shock time in jail. Id., at 22. The trial judge sentenced Frye to three years in prison. . . .

It is well settled that the right to the effective assistance of counsel applies to certain steps before trial. The "Sixth Amendment guarantees a defendant the right to have counsel present at all 'critical' stages of the criminal proceedings." Montejo v. Louisiana, 556 U. S. 778, 786 (2009) (quoting United States v. Wade, 388 U. S. 218, 227-228 (1967)). Critical stages include arraignments, postindictment interrogations, postindictment lineups, and the entry of a guilty plea.

With respect to the right to effective counsel in plea negotiations, a proper beginning point is to discuss two cases from this Court considering the role of counsel in advising a client about a plea offer and an ensuing guilty plea: Hill v. Lockhart, 474 U. S. 52 (1985); and Padilla v. Kentucky, 559 U. S. 356 (2010). *Hill* established that claims of ineffective assistance of counsel in the plea bargain context are governed by the two-part test set forth in *Strickland*. [I]n Frye's case, the Missouri Court of Appeals, applying the two-part test of *Strickland*, determined first that defense counsel had been ineffective and second that there was resulting prejudice. In *Hill*, the decision turned on the second part of the Strickland test. There, a defendant who had entered a guilty plea claimed his counsel had misinformed him of the amount of time he would have to serve before he became eligible for parole. But the defendant had not alleged that, even if adequate advice and assistance had been given, he would have elected to plead not guilty and proceed to trial. Thus, the Court found that no prejudice from the inadequate advice had been shown or alleged.

In *Padilla*, the Court again discussed the duties of counsel in advising a client with respect to a plea offer that leads to a guilty plea. *Padilla* held that a guilty plea, based on a plea offer, should be set aside because counsel misinformed the defendant of the immigration consequences of the conviction. The Court made clear that "the negotiation of a plea bargain is a critical phase of litigation for purposes of the Sixth Amendment right to effective assistance of counsel." It also rejected the argument made by petitioner in this case that a knowing and voluntary plea supersedes errors by defense counsel.

In the case now before the Court the State, as petitioner, points out that the legal question presented is different from that in *Hill* and *Padilla*. In those cases the claim was that the prisoner's plea of guilty was invalid because counsel had provided incorrect advice pertinent to the plea. In the instant case, by contrast, the guilty plea that was accepted, and the plea proceedings concerning it in court, were all based on accurate advice and information from counsel. The challenge is not to the advice pertaining to the plea that was accepted but rather to the course of legal representation that preceded it with respect to other potential pleas and plea offers.

To give further support to its contention that the instant case is in a category different from what the Court considered in *Hill* and *Padilla*, the State urges that there is no right to a plea offer or a plea bargain in any event. It claims Frye therefore was not deprived of any legal benefit to which he was entitled. Under this view, any wrongful or mistaken action of counsel with respect to earlier plea offers is beside the point. The State is correct to point out that *Hill* and *Padilla* concerned whether there was ineffective assistance leading to acceptance of a plea offer, a process involving a formal court appearance with the defendant and all counsel present. Before a guilty plea is entered the defendant's understanding of the plea and its consequences can be established on the record. This affords the State substantial protection against later claims that the plea was the result of inadequate advice. At the plea entry proceedings the trial court and all counsel have the opportunity to establish on the record that the defendant understands the process that led to any offer, the advantages and disadvantages of accepting it, and the sentencing consequences or possibilities that will ensue once a conviction is entered based upon the plea.

*Hill* and *Padilla* both illustrate that, nevertheless, there may be instances when claims of ineffective assistance can arise after the conviction is entered. Still, the State, and the trial court itself, have had a substantial opportunity to guard against this contingency by establishing at the plea entry proceeding that the defendant has been given proper advice or, if the advice received appears to have been inadequate, to remedy that deficiency before the plea is accepted and the conviction entered.

When a plea offer has lapsed or been rejected, however, no formal court proceedings are involved. This underscores that the plea-bargaining process is often in flux, with no clear standards or timelines and with no judicial supervision of the discussions between prosecution and defense. Indeed, discussions between client and defense counsel are privileged. So the prosecution has little or no notice if something may be amiss and perhaps no capacity to intervene in any event. And, as noted, the State insists there is no right to receive a plea offer. For all these reasons, the State contends, it is unfair to subject it to the consequences of defense counsel's inadequacies, especially when the opportunities for a full and fair trial, or, as here, for a later guilty plea albeit on less favorable terms, are preserved.

The State's contentions are neither illogical nor without some persuasive force, yet they do not suffice to overcome a simple reality. Ninety-seven percent of federal convictions and ninety-four percent of state convictions are the result of guilty pleas. See Dept. of Justice, Bureau of Justice Statistics, Sourcebook of Criminal Justice Statistics Online, Table 5.22.2009, http://www.albany.edu/sourcebook/pdf/t5222009.pdf; Dept. of Justice, Bureau of Justice Statistics, S. Rosenmerkel, M. Durose, & D. Farole, Felony Sentences in State Courts, 2006-Statistical Tables, p. 1 (NCJ226846, rev. Nov. 2010), http://bjs.ojp.usdoj.gov/content/pub/pdf/ fssc06st.pdf; The reality is that plea bargains have become so central to the administration of the criminal justice system that defense counsel have responsibilities in the plea bargain process, responsibilities that must be met to render the adequate assistance of counsel that the Sixth Amendment requires in the criminal process at critical stages. Because ours "is for the most part a system of pleas, not a system of trials," *Lafler*, post, at 11, it is insufficient simply to point to the guarantee of a fair trial as a backstop that inoculates any errors in the pretrial process. "To a large extent . . . horse trading [between prosecutor and defense counsel] determines who goes to jail and for how long. That is what plea bargaining is. It is not some adjunct to the criminal justice system; it is the criminal justice system." Scott & Stuntz, Plea Bargaining as Contract, 101 Yale L. J. 1909, 1912 (1992).

In today's criminal justice system, therefore, the negotiation of a plea bargain, rather than the unfolding of a trial, is almost always the critical point for a defendant. To note the prevalence of plea bargaining is not to criticize it. The potential to conserve valuable prosecutorial resources and for defendants to admit their crimes and receive more favorable terms at sentencing means that a plea agreement can benefit both parties. In order that these benefits can be realized, however, criminal defendants require effective counsel during plea negotiations. "Anything less . . . might deny a defendant 'effective representation by counsel at the only stage when legal aid and advice would help him.'" *Massiah*, 377 U. S., at 204 (quoting Spano v. New York, 360 U. S. 315, 326 (1959) (Douglas, J., concurring)).

The inquiry then becomes how to define the duty and responsibilities of defense counsel in the plea bargain process. This is a difficult question. "The art of negotiation is at least as nuanced as the art of trial advocacy and it presents questions farther removed from immediate judicial supervision." Premo v. Moore, 562 U. S. ____, ____ (2011) (slip op., at 8–9). Bargaining is, by its nature, defined to a substantial degree by personal style. The alternative courses and tactics in negotiation are so individual that it may be neither prudent nor practicable to try to elaborate or define detailed standards for the proper discharge of defense counsel's participation in the process.

This case presents neither the necessity nor the occasion to define the duties of defense counsel in those respects, however. Here the question is whether defense counsel has the duty to communicate the terms of a formal offer to accept a plea on terms and conditions that may result in a lesser sentence, a conviction on lesser charges, or both. This Court now holds that, as a general rule, defense counsel has the duty to communicate formal offers from the prosecution to accept a plea on terms and conditions that may be favorable to the accused. Any exceptions to that rule need not be explored here, for the offer was a formal one with a fixed expiration date. When defense counsel allowed the offer to expire without advising the defendant or allowing him to consider it, defense counsel did not render the effective assistance the Constitution requires. Though the standard for counsel's performance is not determined solely by reference to codified standards of professional practice, these standards can be important guides. The American Bar Association recommends defense counsel "promptly communicate and explain to the defendant all plea offers made by the prosecuting attorney," ABA Standards for Criminal Justice, Pleas of Guilty 14-3.2(a) (3d ed. 1999), and this standard has been adopted by numerous state and federal courts over the last 30 years. . . . The standard for prompt communication and consultation is also set out in state bar professional standards for attorneys. See, e.g., Fla. Rule Regulating Bar 4-1.4 (2008); Ill. Rule Prof. Conduct 1.4 (2011);Kan. Rule Prof. Conduct 1.4 (2010); Ky. Sup. Ct. Rule 3.130, Rule Prof. Conduct 1.4 (2011); Mass. Rule Prof.Conduct 1.4 (2011-2012); Mich. Rule Prof. Conduct 1.4(2011).

The prosecution and the trial courts may adopt some measures to help ensure against late, frivolous, or fabricated claims after a later, less advantageous plea offer has been accepted or after a trial leading to conviction with resulting harsh consequences. First, the fact of a formal offer means that its terms and its processing can be documented so that what took place in the negotiation process becomes more clear if some later inquiry turns on the conduct of earlier pretrial negotiations. Second, States may elect to follow rules that all offers must be in writing, again to ensure against later misunderstandings or fabricated charges. See N. J. Ct. Rule 3:9-1(b) (2012) ("Any plea offer to be made by the prosecutor shall be in writing and forwarded to the defendant's attorney"). Third, formal offers can be made part of the record at any subsequent plea proceeding or before a trial on the merits, all to ensure that a defendant has been fully advised before those further proceedings commence. At least one State often follows a similar procedure before trial. See Brief for National Association of Criminal Defense Lawyers et al. as Amici Curiae 20 (discussing hearings in Arizona conducted pursuant to State v. Donald, 198 Ariz. 406, 10 P. 3d 1193 (App. 2000)); see also N. J. Ct. Rules 3:9-1(b), (c) (requiring the prosecutor and defense counsel to discuss the case prior to the arraignment/status conference including any plea offers and to report on these discussions in open court with the defendant present); In re Alvernaz, 2 Cal. 4th 924, 938, n. 7, 830 P. 2d 747, 756, n. 7 (1992) (encouraging parties to "memorialize in some fashion prior to trial (1) the fact that a plea bargain offer was made, and (2) that the defendant was advised of the offer [and] its precise terms, . . . and (3) the defendant's response to the plea bargain offer").

Here defense counsel did not communicate the formal offers to the defendant. As a result of that deficient performance, the offers lapsed. Under *Strickland*, the question then becomes what, if any, prejudice resulted from the breach of duty.

To show prejudice from ineffective assistance of counsel where a plea offer has lapsed or been rejected because of counsel's deficient performance, defendants must demonstrate a reasonable probability they would have accepted the earlier plea offer had they been afforded effective assistance of counsel. Defendants must also demonstrate a reasonable probability the plea would have been entered without the prosecution canceling it or the trial court refusing to accept it, if they had the authority to exercise that discretion under state law. To establish prejudice in this instance, it is necessary to show a reasonable probability that the end result of the criminal process would have been more favorable by reason of a plea to a lesser charge or a sentence of less prison time. Cf. Glover v. United States, 531 U. S. 198, 203 (2001) ("[A]ny amount of [additional] jail time has Sixth Amendment significance"). . . .

In a case, such as this, where a defendant pleads guilty to less favorable terms and claims that ineffective assistance of counsel caused him to miss out on a more favorable earlier plea offer, *Strickland's* inquiry into whether "the result of the proceeding would have been different," 466 U. S., at 694, requires looking not at whether the defendant would have proceeded to trial absent ineffective assistance but whether he would have accepted the offer to plead pursuant to the terms earlier proposed.

In order to complete a showing of *Strickland* prejudice, defendants who have shown a reasonable probability they would have accepted the earlier plea offer must also show that, if the prosecution had the discretion to cancel it or if the trial court had the discretion to refuse to accept it, there is a reasonable probability neither the prosecution nor the trial court would have prevented the offer from being accepted or implemented. This further showing is of particular importance because a defendant has no right to be offered a plea, see Weatherford, 429 U. S., at 561, nor a federal right that the judge accept it, Santobello v. New York, 404 U. S. 257, 262 (1971). In at least some States, including Missouri, it appears the prosecution has some discretion to cancel a plea agreement to which the defendant has agreed, see, e.g., 311 S. W. 3d, at 359 (case below); Ariz. Rule Crim. Proc. 17.4(b) (Supp. 2011). The Federal Rules, some state rules including in Missouri, and this Court's precedents give trial courts some leeway to accept or reject plea agreements, see Fed. Rule Crim. Proc. 11(c)(3); see Mo. Sup. Ct. Rule 24.02(d)(4); Boykin v. Alabama, 395 U. S. 238, 243-244 (1969). It can be assumed that in most jurisdictions prosecutors and judges are familiar with the boundaries of acceptable plea bargains and sentences. So in most instances it should not be difficult to make an objective assessment as to whether or not a particular fact or intervening circumstance would suffice, in the normal course, to cause prosecutorial withdrawal or judicial nonapproval of a plea bargain. The determination that there is or is not a reasonable probability that the outcome of the proceeding would have been different absent counsel's errors can be conducted within that framework.

These standards must be applied to the instant case. As regards the deficient performance prong of Strickland, the Court of Appeals found the "record is void of any evidence of any effort by trial counsel to communicate the [formal] Offer to Frye during the Offer window, let alone any evidence that Frye's conduct interfered with trial counsel's ability to do so." 311 S. W. 3d, at 356. On this record, it is evident that Frye's attorney did not make a meaningful attempt to inform the defendant of a written plea offer before the offer expired. The Missouri Court of Appeals was correct that "counsel's representation fell below an objective standard of reasonableness." *Strickland,* supra, at 688. The Court of Appeals erred, however, in articulating the precise standard for prejudice in this context. As noted, a defendant in Frye's position must show not only a reasonable probability that he would have accepted the lapsed plea but also a reasonable probability that the prosecution would have adhered to the agreement and that it would have been accepted by the trial court. Frye can show he would have accepted the offer, but there is strong reason to doubt the prosecution and the trial court would have permitted the plea bargain to become final. There appears to be a reasonable probability Frye would have accepted the prosecutor's original offer of a plea bargain if the offer had been communicated to him, because he pleaded guilty to a more serious charge, with no promise of a sentencing recommendation from the prosecutor. It may be that in some cases defendants must show more than just a guilty plea to a charge or sentence harsher than the original offer. For example, revelations between plea offers about the strength of the prosecution's case may make a late decision to plead guilty insufficient to demonstrate, without further evidence, that the defendant would have pleaded guilty to an earlier, more generous plea offer if his counsel had reported it to him. Here, however, that is not the case. The Court of Appeals did not err in finding Frye's acceptance of the less favorable plea offer indicated that he would have accepted the earlier (and more favorable) offer had he been apprised of it; and there is no need to address here the showings that might be required in other cases. The Court of Appeals failed, however, to require Frye to show that the first plea offer, if accepted by Frye, would have been adhered to by the prosecution and accepted by the trial court. Whether the prosecution and trial court are required to do so is a matter of state law, and it is not the place of this Court to settle those matters. The Court has established the minimum requirements of the Sixth Amendment as interpreted in Strickland, and States have the discretion to add procedural protections under state law if they choose. A State may choose to preclude the prosecution from withdrawing a plea offer once it has been accepted or perhaps to preclude a trial court from rejecting a plea bargain. In Missouri, it appears "a plea offer once accepted by the defendant can be withdrawn without recourse" by the prosecution. 311 S. W. 3d, at 359. The ex-tent of the trial court's discretion in Missouri to reject a plea agreement appears to be in some doubt. Compare id., at 360, with Mo. Sup. Ct. Rule 24.02(d)(4).

We remand for the Missouri Court of Appeals to consider these state-law questions, because they bear on the federal question of *Strickland* prejudice. If, as the Missouri court stated here, the prosecutor could have canceledthe plea agreement, and if Frye fails to show a reasonable probability the prosecutor would have adhered to the agreement, there is no *Strickland* prejudice. Likewise, if the trial court could have refused to accept the plea agreement, and if Frye fails to show a reasonable probability the trial court would have accepted the plea, there is no *Strickland* prejudice. In this case, given Frye's new offense for driving without a license on December 30, 2007, there is reason to doubt that the prosecution would have adhered to the agreement or that the trial court would have accepted it at the January 4, 2008, hearing, unless they were required by state law to do so. It is appropriate to allow the Missouri Court of Appeals to address this question in the first instance.

SCALIA, J., with whom THOMAS, C.J., and ALITO, J., join, dissenting.

This is a companion case to Lafler v. Cooper, post. The principal difference between the cases is that the fairness of the defendant's conviction in Lafler was established by a full trial and jury verdict, whereas Frye's conviction here was established by his own admission of guilt, received by the court after the usual colloquy thatassured it was voluntary and truthful. In Lafler all that could be said (and as I discuss there it was quite enough) is that the fairness of the conviction was clear, though a unanimous jury finding beyond a reasonable doubt can sometimes be wrong. Here it can be said not only that the process was fair, but that the defendant acknowledged the correctness of his conviction. . . .

Galin Frye's attorney failed to inform him about a plea offer, and Frye ultimately pleaded guilty without the benefit of a deal. Counsel's mistake did not deprive Frye of any substantive or procedural right; only of the opportunity to accept a plea bargain to which he had no entitlement in the first place. So little entitlement that, had he known of and accepted the bargain, the prose-cution would have been able to withdraw it right up to the point that his guilty plea pursuant to the bargain was accepted. The Court acknowledges, moreover, that Frye's conviction was untainted by attorney error: "[T]he guilty plea that was accepted, and the plea proceedings concerning it in court, were all based on accurate advice and information from counsel." Ante, at 5. Given the "ultimate focus" of our ineffective-assistance cases on "the fundamental fairness of the proceeding whose result is being challenged," Strickland v. Washington, 466 U. S. 668, 696 (1984), that should be the end of the matter. Instead, here, as in Lafler, the Court mechanically applies an outcome-based test for prejudice, and mistakes the possibility of a different result for constitutional injustice.

[T]hat approach is contrary to our precedents on the right to effective counsel, and for good reason. The Court announces its holding that "as a general rule, defense counsel has the duty to communicate formal offers from the prosecution" as though that resolves a disputed point; in reality, however, neither the State nor the Solicitor General argued that counsel's performance here was adequate. The only issue was whether the in-adequacy deprived Frye of his constitutional right to a fair trial. In other cases, however, it will not be so clear that counsel's plea-bargaining skills, which must now meet a constitutional minimum, are adequate. "[H]ow to define the duty and responsibilities of defense counsel in the plea bargain process," the Court acknowledges, "is a difficult question," since "[b]argaining is, by its nature, defined to a substantial degree by personal style." Ante, at 8. Indeed. What if an attorney's "personal style" is to establish a reputation as a hard bargainer by, for example, advising clients to proceed to trial rather than accept anything but the most favorable plea offers? It seems inconceivable that a lawyer could compromise his client's constitutional rights so that he can secure better deals for other clients in the future; does a hard-bargaining "personal style" now violate the Sixth Amendment? The Court ignores such difficulties, however, since "[t]his case presents neither the necessity nor the occasion to define the duties of defense counsel in those respects." Ante, at 8. Perhaps not. But it does present the necessity of confronting the serious difficulties that will be created by constitutionalization of the plea-bargaining process. It will not do simply to announce that they will be solved in the sweet by-and-by. While the inadequacy of counsel's performance in this case is clear enough, whether it was prejudicial (in the sense that the Court's new version of *Strickland* requires) is not. The Court's description of how that question is to be answered on remand is alone enough to show how unwise it is to constitutionalize the plea-bargaining process.

Prejudice is to be determined, the Court tells us, by a process of retrospective crystal-ball gazing posing as legal analysis. First of all, of course, we must estimate whether the defendant would have accepted the earlier plea bargain. Here that seems an easy question, but as the Court acknowledges, it will not always be. Next, since Missouri, like other States, permits accepted plea offers to be withdrawn by the prosecution (a reality which alone should suffice, one would think, to demonstrate that Frye had no entitlement to the plea bargain), we must estimate whether the prosecution would have withdrawn the plea offer. And finally, we must estimate whether the trial court would have approved the plea agreement. These last two estimations may seem easy in the present case, since Frye committed a new infraction before the hearing at which the agreement would have been presented; but they assuredly will not be easy in the mine run of cases. The Court says "[i]t can be assumed that in most jurisdictions prosecutors and judges are familiar with the boundaries of acceptable plea bargains and sentences." Ante, at 13. Assuredly it can, just as it can be assumed that the sun rises in the west; but I know of no basis for the assumption. Virtually no cases deal with the standards for a prosecutor's withdrawal from a plea agreement beyond stating the general rule that a prosecutor may withdraw any time prior to, but not after, the entry of a guilty plea or other action constituting detrimental reliance on the defendant's part. And cases addressing trial courts' authority to accept or reject plea agreements almost universally observe that a trial court enjoys broad discretion in this regard.

Of course after today's opinions there will be cases galore, so the Court's assumption would better be cast as an optimistic prediction of the certainty that will emerge, many years hence, from our newly created constitutional field of plea bargaining law. Whatever the "boundaries" ultimately devised (if that were possible), a vast amount of discretion will still remain, and it is extraordinary to make a defendant's constitutional rights depend upon a series of retrospective mind-readings as to how that discretion, in prosecutors and trial judges, would have been exercised. The plea-bargaining process is a subject worthy of regulation, since it is the means by which most criminal convictions are obtained. It happens not to be, however, a subject covered by the Sixth Amendment, which is concerned not with the fairness of bargaining but with the fairness of conviction. "The Constitution . . . is not an all purpose tool for judicial construction of a perfect world; and when we ignore its text in order to make it that, we often find ourselves swinging a sledge where a tack hammer is needed." Padilla v. Kentucky, 559 U. S. ____, ____ (2010) (Scalia, J., dissenting) (slip op., at 1). In this case and its companion, the Court's sledge may require the reversal of perfectly valid, eminently just, convictions. A legislature could solve the problems presented by these cases in a much more precise and efficient manner. It might begin, for example, by penalizing the attorneys who made such grievous errors. That type of subconstitutional remedy is not available to the Court, which is limited to penalizing (almost) everyone else by reversing valid convictions or sentences. Because that result is inconsistent with the Sixth Amendment and decades of our precedent, I respectfully dissent.

### NOTES

1. *Why now?*   After four decades of leaving plea bargaining largely unregulated in any significant way by constitutional doctrines, the Supreme Court in Padilla v. Kentucky and Missouri v. Frye (and the *Frye* companion case Lafler v. Cooper) concluded that the Sixth Amendment's right to the assistance of counsel serves to regulate plea bargaining practices through the responsibilities of defense attorneys to the accused. What formal or informal legal developments do you think has prompted the Court in these cases to, in the derisive words of Justice Scalia's dissent, "open a whole new boutique of constitutional jurisprudence ('plea-bargaining law')"? In his dissents to these cases, Justice Scalia contends "that legislature could solve the problems presented by these cases in a much more precise and efficient manner." This may well be true, but there is very little history to suggest that legislatures are eager to view plea bargaining processes as problematic and in need of statutory fixes. Is it appropriate, and

perhaps even essential, for the Supreme Court and lower courts to develop and expand constitutional doctrines to remedy clear problems in the practical administration of criminal justice systems once it is clear that other branches of government are unwilling or unable to address these problems?

2. *Why the Sixth Amendment?*   Is it likely to be efficient or effective to seek to regulate plea processes by developing rules for what *defense attorneys* must do under the Sixth Amendment in the course of plea bargaining? Wouldn't it likely be much more efficient or effective for plea process regulations to be focused on what *prosecutors* must do as part of proposing a plea bargain and what judges must do before they accept a guilty plea or embrace the provisions of any formal plea agreement? Doesn't the Fifth Amendment's expression of the constitutional command that no person "be deprived of life, liberty, or property, without due process of law" provide an appropriate and potentially more direct and effective means for developing a constitutional jurisprudence that would regulate the terms and procedures of modern plea bargaining?

3. *Remedies for plea process and Sixth Amendment violations.*   In his dissents in *Padilla* and *Frye*, Justice Scalia stressed that fashioning a remedy for ineffective lawyering in plea-bargaining cases is necessarily challenging. Justice Kennedy's majority opinion acknowledges these difficulties in *Lafler*: "Today's decision leaves open to the trial court how best to exercise that discretion in all the circumstances of the case." The Supreme Court thus left it to lower courts to experiment with remedies when a defendant can establishes a Sixth Amendment violation during the plea process. Is this an area in which legislatures can sensibly step in with a set of statutory rules for how courts should try to respond to these kinds of constitutional violations? Are legislatures permitted to define and restrict the kinds of remedies courts may craft for constitutional violations?

## 2.   Presentence Reports and the Role of Probation Officers

Sentencing systems for the most part encourage judges to consider additional information that was not presented at trial. The defense might want to provide additional information about the defendant. The prosecution might want to illuminate aspects of the crime or criminal record. A victim might want to speak about the harm the crime inflicted. As noted in Chapters 4 and 5, the scope of information that might be considered at sentencing can be extremely wide, especially in the federal system, which constructed its guidelines in reliance on the availability of additional facts about the defendant's "real offense" and "relevant conduct" (uncharged acts). 18 U.S.C. §3661, promulgated before the guidelines, remains in effect:

> No limitation shall be placed on the information concerning the background, character, and conduct of a person convicted of an offense which a court of the United States may receive and consider for the purpose of imposing an appropriate sentence.

Where do judges get the additional information that might inform their sentencing judgments? Who gathers the information?

The short answer in most sentencing systems is twofold. First, the parties may present additional evidence, and second, the judge will receive a presentence investigation report, typically prepared by a probation officer who works for the court. In the federal system, the presentence investigation report includes the probation officer's assessment of the applicable guidelines and a sentence recommendation to the judge.

Many issues are generated by these odd procedures, documents, and actors — odd, at least, in comparison with the model of an adversarial system in which advocates present and challenge information and arguments to a neutral judge. The issues surrounding presentence reports include the following:

- What will be included in the report?
- Do the attorneys have access to the report?
- Is there an opportunity to challenge the report?
- What deference or independent assessment does the judge bring to the report?

The first part of this section considers rules on the content and access to presentence investigation reports. The second part considers the role of the probation officer, with a focus on the federal system.

### a.   Presentence Investigation Reports

How are the purposes of presentence reports (or of the sentencing system as a whole) served by the procedures used to produce and contest those reports? Consider the following rules.

## Federal Rules of Criminal Procedure 32(c)-(h), Sentencing and Judgment

**(c) Presentence Investigation.**

**(1) *Required Investigation.***

(A) *In General.* The probation officer must conduct a presentence investigation and submit a report to the court before it imposes sentence unless: . . .

(ii) the court finds that the information in the record enables it to meaningfully exercise its sentencing authority under 18 U.S.C. §3553, and the court explains its finding on the record.

(B) *Restitution.* If the law requires restitution, the probation officer must conduct an investigation and submit a report that contains sufficient information for the court to order restitution.

**(2) *Interviewing the Defendant.*** The probation officer who interviews a defendant as part of a presentence investigation must, on request, give the defendant's attorney notice and a reasonable opportunity to attend the interview.

**(d) Presentence Report.**

(1) *Applying the Sentencing Guidelines.* The presentence report must:

(A) identify all applicable guidelines and policy statements of the Sentencing Commission;

(B) calculate the defendant's offense level and criminal history category;

(C) state the resulting sentencing range and kinds of sentences available;

(D) identify any factor relevant to:

(i) the appropriate kind of sentence, or

(ii) the appropriate sentence within the applicable sentencing range; and

(E) identify any basis for departing from the applicable sentencing range.

(2) *Additional Information.* The presentence report must also contain the following information:

(A) the defendant's history and characteristics, including:

(i) any prior criminal record;

(ii) the defendant's financial condition; and

(iii) any circumstances affecting the defendant's behavior that may be helpful in imposing sentence or in correctional treatment;

(B) verified information, stated in a nonargumentative style, that assesses the financial, social, psychological, and medical impact on any individual against whom the offense has been committed;

(C) when appropriate, the nature and extent of nonprison programs and resources available to the defendant;

(D) when the law provides for restitution, information sufficient for a restitution order; . . .

(F) any other information that the court requires.

(3) *Exclusions.* The presentence report must exclude the following:

(A) any diagnoses that, if disclosed, might seriously disrupt a rehabilitation program;

(B) any sources of information obtained upon a promise of confidentiality; and

(C) any other information that, if disclosed, might result in physical or other harm to the defendant or others.

**(e) Disclosing the Report and Recommendation.**

(1) *Time to Disclose.* Unless the defendant has consented in writing, the probation officer must not submit a presentence report to the court or disclose its contents to anyone until the defendant has pleaded guilty or nolo contendere, or has been found guilty.

(2) *Minimum Required Notice.* The probation officer must give the presentence report to the defendant, the defendant's attorney, and an attorney for the government at least 35 days before sentencing unless the defendant waives this minimum period.

(3) *Sentence Recommendation.* By local rule or by order in a case, the court may direct the probation officer not to disclose to anyone other than the court the officer's recommendation on the sentence.

**(f) Objecting to the Report.**

(1) *Time to Object.* Within 14 days after receiving the presentence report, the parties must state in writing any objections, including objections to material information, sentencing guideline ranges, and policy statements contained in or omitted from the report.

**(2)** *Serving Objections.* An objecting party must provide a copy of its objections to the opposing party and to the probation officer.

**(3)** *Action on Objections.* After receiving objections, the probation officer may meet with the parties to discuss the objections. The probation officer may then investigate further and revise the presentence report as appropriate.

**(g) Submitting the Report.** At least 7 days before sentencing, the probation officer must submit to the court and to the parties the presentence report and an addendum containing any unresolved objections, the grounds for those objections, and the probation officer's comments on them.

**(h) Notice of Possible Departure from Sentencing Guidelines.** Before the court may depart from the applicable sentencing range on a ground not identified for departure either in the presentence report or in a party's prehearing submission, the court must give the parties reasonable notice that it is contemplating such a departure. The notice must specify any ground on which the court is contemplating a departure.

---

### U.S. Sentencing Guidelines Manual
### §§6A1.1, 6A1.2 (Policy Statements)

#### §6A1.1   PRESENTENCE REPORT

A probation officer shall conduct a presentence investigation and report to the court before the imposition of sentence unless the court finds that there is information in the record sufficient to enable the meaningful exercise of sentencing authority pursuant to 18 U.S.C. §3553, and the court explains this finding on the record. Rule 32(b)(1), Fed. R. Crim. P. The defendant may not waive preparation of the presentence report.

#### §6A1.2   DISCLOSURE OF PRESENTENCE REPORT; ISSUES IN DISPUTE

Courts should adopt procedures to provide for the timely disclosure of the presentence report; the narrowing and resolution, where feasible, of issues in dispute in advance of the sentencing hearing; and the identification for the court of issues remaining in dispute. Rule 32(b)(6), Fed. R. Crim. P.

---

### Pennsylvania Rules of Criminal Procedure 702, 703

#### RULE 702. AIDS IN IMPOSING SENTENCE

(A) Pre-sentence investigation report.

1. The sentencing judge may, in the judge's discretion, order a pre-sentence investigation report in any case.

2. The sentencing judge shall place on the record the reasons for dispensing with the pre-sentence investigation report if the judge fails to order a pre-sentence report in any of the following instances:

(a) where incarceration for one year or more is a possible disposition under the applicable sentencing statutes;

(b) where the defendant is less than twenty-one years old at the time of conviction or entry of a plea of guilty; or

(c) where a defendant is a first offender in that he or she has not heretofore been sentenced as an adult.

3. The pre-sentence investigation report shall include information regarding the circumstances of the offense and the character of the defendant sufficient to assist the judge in determining sentence.

4. The pre-sentence investigation report shall also include a victim impact statement as provided by law. . . .

### RULE 703. DISCLOSURE OF PRE-SENTENCE REPORTS

(A) All pre-sentence reports and related psychiatric and psychological reports shall be confidential, and not of public record. They shall be available to the sentencing judge, and to:

1. an examining professional or facility appointed to assist the court in sentencing . . . ;

2. the attorney for the Commonwealth and counsel for the defendant, for inspection and copying, unless the sentencing judge orders that they be available for inspection only.

(B) If the defendant or the Commonwealth alleges any factual inaccuracy in a report under this rule, the sentencing judge shall, as to each inaccuracy found, order that the record be corrected accordingly. . . .

> ## *Use of Pre-sentence Investigations in Maryland Circuit Courts, January 1999-June 2002,*
> ## *Jill Farrell*
> ### Sentencing Fax (Maryland State Commission on Criminal Sentencing Policy), Mar. 28, 2003

In Maryland, pre-sentence investigation reports (PSIs) are prepared by the Division of Parole and Probation in an effort to provide background information on defendant and case characteristics. The information contained within PSIs is designed to assist the courts in the sentencing process. According to the Maryland statute, a PSI may be requested in, but not limited to, cases in which the defendant is (1) convicted of a felony or misdemeanor that resulted in serious physical injury or death to the victim or (2) being referred to Patuxent Institution.[*] Between January 1999 and June 2002, 26% of all valid cases sentenced in Maryland circuit courts indicated the existence of a PSI report. PSIs were nearly three times more likely to be completed for felony offenses (72%) than for misdemeanors (28%). With respect to offense types (Fig. 1), PSI reports were most likely completed for property offenses (68%), followed closely by

---

[*] The Patuxent Institution is a facility in the Maryland system that focuses on offender remediation and treatment, and includes mental health and substance abuse populations. — EDS.

person offenses (62%). Drug offenses were the least likely offense type (16%) to have a PSI report submitted.

As indicated in Figure 2, there was substantial variation between circuits. Eighty percent of cases in Circuit 2 had PSI reports submitted, while only 6% of cases submitted reports in Circuit 8. This may be due in part to a disproportionate number of drug cases in Circuit 8, thus minimizing the necessity for a PSI

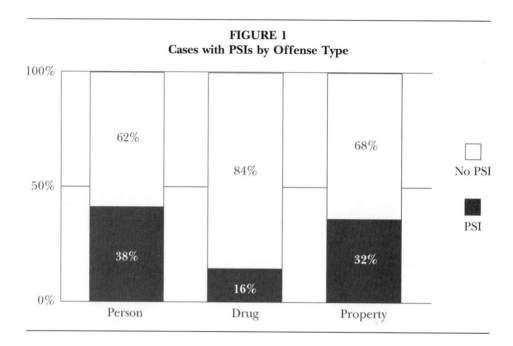

FIGURE 1
Cases with PSIs by Offense Type

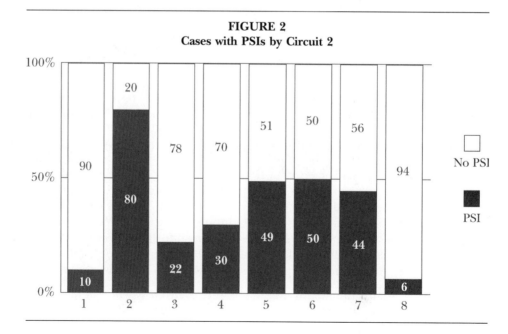

FIGURE 2
Cases with PSIs by Circuit 2

**FIGURE 3**
**Cases with PSIs by Victim Injury Status**

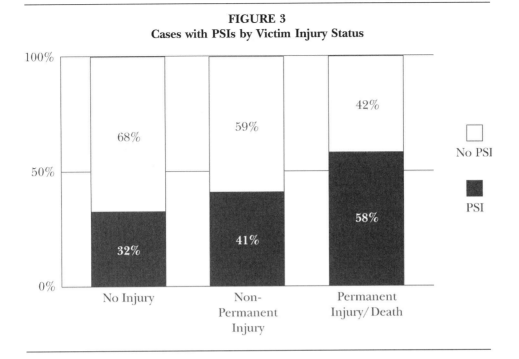

report. On average, 25% of circuit court cases in Maryland included PSI reports (75% did not).

With regard to victim injury, Figure 3 shows a gradual increase in the presence of PSI reports. In cases where there was a victim, a PSI was more likely to be completed when the offense resulted in serious injury or death (58%) than when the injury was non-permanent (41%) or when there was no injury (32%).

## NOTES

1. *Presentence investigation reports.* Presentence investigation reports are the focal point of the many kinds of information that may be relevant to sentencing. Traditionally, probation officers expended much effort on offender facts that had no bearing on the determination of the offender's guilt or innocence. Now in the federal system probation officers include in their reports a wide range of offense information (beyond the offense of conviction), offender information, and information impacting sentencing guideline application.

2. *Presentence reports and secrecy.* One of the critical issues involving presentence reports is who gets to see them and when. Confidentiality in presentence reports is generally considered important to allow for a full exploration of the defendant's situation. For many years, however, rules kept not only the public but also defense counsel and the defendant from seeing the report. Questions about the processes for challenging reports and the standards of proof at sentencing fade in importance when such critical information is hidden.

The modern view is that the presentence report should (indeed, must) be shared with the defendant and defense counsel. But not all information in presentence reports is shared as a matter of course. For example, Federal Rule 32(e)(3) leaves the decision whether to share the sentencing recommendation with local federal courts and individual judges. This extraordinary variation in practice (and the interesting question of why a probation officer's sentence recommendation ought or ought not to be shared) has gone largely without remark in the case law and literature.

3. *Presentence reports and plea bargains.*   Rule 32 prohibits the probation officer from submitting the presentence report to the judge before guilty pleas (or a finding of guilt by a jury), unless the defendant consents in writing. The idea behind this limitation is that the judge should not be biased in accepting or rejecting the plea based on what is in the report. But without first seeing the report, how can the judge know when accepting a plea that includes dismissal of charges whether "the remaining charges adequately reflect the seriousness of the actual offense behavior and that accepting the agreement will not undermine the statutory purposes of sentencing or the sentencing guidelines"? U.S. Sentencing Guidelines Manual §6B1.2 (policy statement). And if a judge accepts a plea but then relies (as instructed by the sentencing guidelines) on relevant conduct revealed in the presentence report, how can it be said that the defendant's plea was "knowing" and "voluntary"? It is not hard to argue around these questions: The defendant knows what the presentence report is likely to say, and therefore what the judge might rely on, so the defendant takes the risks of sentence calculations, departures, and possible ranges into account in deciding whether to plea. But this technical answer leaves the deeper issue unaddressed: Either pleas are made with a full understanding of the consequences, or they are not; either the pleas are accepted with a full picture of the offense and offender, or they are not.

4. *Challenging presentence reports.*   Notice the timing requirements in Rule 32. The probation officer must give the presentence report to the defendant and both attorneys at least 35 days before sentencing unless the defendant waives this minimum period. The defendant then has 14 days to assess and challenge the report in writing. Is 14 days enough time? Should the same strict time frame apply to objections by the government? Compare United States v. Young, 140 F.3d 453 (2d Cir. 1998) (allowing untimely objections to presentence report by the government if defendant is given the opportunity to respond), with United States v. Chung, 261 F.3d 536 (5th Cir. 2001) (upholding refusal to consider supplemental objections by defendant to presentence report filed after 14-day limit). Rule 32 suggests that defendants and their counsel may object to information relevant to sentencing guideline application. As noted above, however, courts are left with the decision whether to share the probation officer's sentencing recommendation with the defendant. Can defendants fully appreciate the calculus of federal sentencing and judgment that underlies guilty pleas when they do not know what recommendation the judge will receive?

## b.   The Special Role of Probation Officers

In 1989 federal defender Judy Clarke foresaw the important role that probation officers would play in the federal guideline sentencing era:

The federal probation officer has emerged as the guardian of the guidelines. The probation officer not only collects the factual data important to the sentencing decisions but also makes recommendations regarding application of the guidelines. The Sentencing Commission has one or more federal probation officers on assignment to provide training for probation officers. There is a Commission staffed hotline for probation officers to call for help with application problems. Federal probation officers send to the Commission copies of presentence reports which reflect the officer's application decisions as well as how the court imposed sentence. In a practical sense, federal probation officers have become guardians, a role which results from the probation officer being closely connected with the Commission's training efforts and becoming well versed in the Commission's view of the guidelines. Whether the prosecutor, defense attorney or sentencing court agree with the guardian's conclusion is insignificant — the guardian reports the result to the Commission and moves on to the next presentence report. All's well that ends.

Judy Clarke, Ruminations on Restrepo, 2 Fed. Sent'g Rep. 131 (1989). The phrase "guardians of the guidelines" and the ideas raised by Clarke caught on. Chief probation officer Charlie Varnon, however, begged to differ:

I find it very interesting that some members of the defense bar are so hostile to the role of the probation officer in the guideline sentencing process. The probation officer's report to the court has no impact on the defendant whatsoever unless the judge adopts the recommended findings and guideline calculations. The defense and the prosecution have the opportunity to present their own recommended findings and calculations to the court. Under these circumstances, I might assume the real complaint is that the court too often adopts the recommendations of the probation officers and not those of the lawyers. It is more politic, I assume, to criticize the probation officer for making the recommendation than to criticize the court for adopting the recommendation.

Charlie E. Varnon, Response to Judy Clarke, 2 Fed. Sent'g Rep. 202, 202 (1990).

Probation officers may act below the radar of most scholars and many policymakers, but careful observers and participants agree that they are a central part of the guideline sentencing process. Consider the account of the probation officer's role — central or supportive, heroic or tragic — in the following report, written by a member of the U.S. Sentencing Commission, as well as in the subsequent commentary, written by a former supervising probation officer.

## The Independent Role of the Probation Officer at Sentencing and in Applying
### Koon v. United States,
### *Catharine M. Goodwin*
#### 60 Fed. Probation 71 (Sept. 1996)

The question of the nature of the role of the probation officer in federal guidelines sentencing is a fundamental and recurring one. . . .

There are various ways the independent role of the probation officer at sentencing is challenged or impeded. The probation officer is sometimes impeded from doing a complete investigation by the parties' withholding information, and, for various reasons, plea agreements do not always accurately reflect the facts of the case. Critics of the guideline system have periodically complained about probation officer "advocacy" and called for restricting probation officers to computing the "matrix calculations" or restricting them from making recommendations on "discretionary decisions" such as departures. In addition, a court will sometimes ask the probation office to restrict its investigation to the parties' stipulations, and others may be tempted to do so, in order to avoid objections to the presentence report and disputed issues.

As an initial matter, it must be noted that the probation officer is an officer of the court. Ultimately, the court determines the scope of the probation officer's role in sentencing in any particular district or courtroom. . . .

## I.   THE ROLE OF THE PROBATION OFFICER IN GUIDELINE SENTENCING

The legal authorities which define the role of the probation officer in federal guideline sentencing consistently define it as an integral, independent function, apart from party stipulations.

*A. Rule 32.*   Rule 32, Federal Rules of Criminal Procedure (F.R.Cr.P.), indicates that the presentence report must contain:

> (B) the classification of the offense and of the defendant under the categories established by the Sentencing Commission under 28 U.S.C. §994(a), as the probation officer believes to be applicable to the defendant's case; the kinds of sentence and the sentencing range suggested for such a category of defendant as set forth in the guidelines issued by the Sentencing Commission under 28 U.S.C. §994(a)(1); and the probation officer's explanation of any factors that may suggest a different sentence — within or without the applicable guideline — that would be more appropriate, given all the circumstances.

Rule 32(b)(4)(B). Thus, the probation officer has a duty directed by the federal rules to compute and describe what the officer believes to be the appropriate sentence under the guidelines, as well as what, if any, departure the officer believes is appropriate. . . .

*B. Sentencing Reform Act, Its Legislative History, and the Guidelines.*   The Sentencing Reform Act provided that the probation officer would conduct an "investigation" of the defendant, pursuant to Rule 32 F.R.Cr.P. and report that investigation to the court. In addition, it is clear that Congress intended sentencing courts to actively exercise their discretion to accept or reject plea agreements to ensure that the resulting sentences meet the purposes of sentencing.

However, Congress recognized that the potential for prosecutorial charging and plea practices to effectively determine the sentence "could well reduce the benefits otherwise to be expected from the bill's guideline sentencing system." It directed the Sentencing Commission to promulgate policy statements for district courts to use in determining whether to accept plea agreements, in order "to provide an opportunity for meaningful judicial review of proposed charge-reduction plea agreements, as well as other forms of plea agreements, while at the same time to guard against improper judicial intrusion upon the responsibilities of the Executive Branch."

Accordingly, the Commission promulgated the Chapter Six Policy Statements to guide courts in accepting plea agreements. Those Policy Statements describe an active, independent role for the probation officer because, "[a] thorough presentence investigation is essential in determining the facts relevant to sentencing." . . . While the guidelines provide for "stipulations," which are points upon which the parties agree or disagree, "[the] court is not bound by the stipulation, but may with the aid of the presentence report, determine the facts relevant to sentencing." Further: Even though stipulations are expected to be accurate and complete, the court cannot rely exclusively upon stipulations in ascertaining the factors relevant to the determination of the sentence. Rather, in determining the factual basis for the sentence, the court will consider the stipulation, together with the results of the presentence investigation, and any other relevant information. . . .

Clearly, the presentence report prepared by the probation officer is the only source of information outside the stipulations of the parties which the court can use to decide whether or not to accept those stipulations in fashioning the sentence. . . . This is also true regarding the court's determination whether to accept a plea agreement. For example, where the plea agreement includes a dismissal of charges or an agreement not to pursue potential charges, the court is asked to evaluate whether the remaining charges "adequately reflect the seriousness of the actual offense behavior," and whether the agreement will support the statutory purposes of sentencing or the sentencing guidelines. Therefore, it is easy to see that Congress intended that "[t]he probation officers will be a crucial link in the effectiveness of both sentencing guidelines and policy statement."

*C. Publication 107.* There are numerous provisions to support the independent role of the probation officer in Publication 107. For example:

> A primary role of the probation officer is to prepare a presentence report of the highest quality for the court that will assist in sentencing a defendant. Under guideline sentencing, the probation officer's role as *the court's independent investigator* is critical, although the scope of the investigation may be determined by the court. . . . [In determining a tentative guideline range, the officer must]-*thoroughly explore and analyze the circumstances of the offense and the offender.* (emphasis added)

The officer is to provide the court ". . . with relevant, objective, and verifiable information that will assist in the selection of a proper sentence"; and ". . . it is crucial that a probation officer exercise independence as an agent of the court by developing factual and rule-related assertions."

To underscore the fact that the monograph envisions the probation officer doing more than providing sentence calculations based on the parties' stipulations, it says that where the parties' stipulations differ from the results of the officer's investigation, the officer should "display the range that would have resulted if there had been no plea agreement" under the "Impact of the Plea Agreement" section of the PSR, to assist "the court in evaluating the impact of the plea agreement on the ultimate sentence." Finally, to further underscore the independent nature of the probation officer's investigation, the monograph also envisions that the probation officer will discuss any potential bases for departure, and possibly make a recommendation on departure in the "Factors That May Warrant Departure" section of the presentence report. . . .

*D. Case Law.* Not surprisingly, the courts have uniformly endorsed and upheld the independent role of the probation officer in federal guideline sentencing. . . .

*E. The Officer's Investigation in the Presentence Report.* The "Impact of the Plea Agreement" section of the presentence report should provide a comparison of the sentencing range which results from the independent investigation, where different, with that which results from the parties' stipulations. . . . The most important thing is that the court is provided with the maximum amount of information upon which to make the sentencing determination.

*F. Practical and Logical Necessity for Independent Investigation.* Realistically, the court has the ultimate authority to determine the "scope" of the probation officer's role at sentencing. And, to the extent that the officer's role is limited, the potential for objections to the presentence report is admittedly minimized. . . .

There are strong practical and logical needs for an independent probation officer at sentencing. The reason the court needs "objective" information, which may go beyond and differ from the stipulation of the parties, is that the court has the discretion, and, indeed, the responsibility, to determine whether to accept the plea agreement, pursuant to Rule 11(c)(1)(A) and (C), and whether to impose a sentence in accord with any non-binding recommendations ("stipulations") of the parties, pursuant to Rule 11(c)(1)(B). [The] sentencing process must provide the court with the information necessary to perform its duty to supervise the plea process and to make a sentence determination.

To the extent that the court relies on stipulations and agreements, practical problems and concerns arise. The court is denied information on sentencing factors which the parties may not have anticipated or agreed upon. Stipulations sometimes omit, either intentionally or inadvertently, key facts necessary to apply the guidelines. Familiarity with the guidelines varies considerably among practitioners and prosecutors, and the parties cannot always identify and adequately address all pertinent sentencing factors or bases for departure at the plea stage. For example, if the parties do not stipulate to adequate facts to determine role, or do not anticipate what ultimately appears to be a meritorious basis for departure, a court that does not receive such information, or limits itself to the stipulations of the parties, loses the ability to employ its sentencing discretion in a fully knowledgeable manner.

Aside from such practical problems, larger, institutional concerns arise if the role of the probation officer in sentencing is limited. . . . Without the "check" on the system that the probation officer provides, we would still have a complicated, resource intensive guideline system, but without the measure of proportionality and uniformity in sentencing which the guidelines were created to achieve. This would primarily be because the court's ability to supervise the plea bargaining process and to sentence based on all the relevant information would be significantly diluted. . . .

> *G. Procedural Suggestions to Narrow the Gap and to Enhance Fact Finding and Dispute Resolution at Sentencing.* Critics periodically complain that the probation officer's independent investigation results in the probation officer recommending a sentence different than that recommended by the parties, thereby converting the officer into a "third advocate." There are many reasons that the officer may arrive at a different calculation than the parties, including the fact that the officer is not subject to the same negotiation pressures of the parties, and the fact that the officer does not always have the same perspective of the strength of some of the evidence as, for example, the government may have, given that the officer often receives merely a written summary of that evidence.

While some of these differences can be minimized with better communication . . . , wherever differences exist between the sentence calculations of the officer and the parties, the existence of an independent probation investigation does not eliminate nor diminish the opportunity for advocacy by the parties. On the contrary, it highlights and enhances the need for advocacy of the parties, and enriches the information given the court, thereby helping to ensure the best sentence determination possible by the court. Parties still have the opportunity to convince the court of the validity of their positions. The courts have denied any claim that the role of the probation officer improperly influences the court, finding that, in spite of recommendations made by probation officers on sentencing factors, the court is still required to resolve any and all disputes, and that the court has the ability to read a presentence report without being improperly influenced. . . .

1. Some districts have found it beneficial to require, or offer as a possibility, some form of pre-plea advisory conference with a probation officer for a non-binding computation of guidelines relevant to computing at least the offense level, or sometimes even an estimated range (with appropriate waivers that it is non-binding and subject to change upon preparation of a full presentence report). A few districts provide for a Magistrate, or non-sentencing district court judge, to conduct the conference, which becomes in essence a settlement conference. All pre-plea computations or conferences, if they are to be meaningful, depend on full discovery from the government, which is perhaps their primary value, which in turn assists plea negotiations and presentencing disclosure.

2. Some districts require that the government (and defense, optionally) submit within so many days after a plea or trial, an early statement of the facts, disputed issues, and applicable sentencing and guideline factors, in order to focus attention early on sentencing factors and to assist the probation officer.

3. Rule 32(6)(B) F.R.Cr.P. suggests, after the parties submit objections to the presentence report, that the probation officer "may meet with the defendant, the defendant's counsel, and the attorney for the government to discuss those objections." While this is no doubt helpful, some districts find it useful, in addition to this requirement, to require or urge both counsel to meet with the probation officer earlier, during the preparation of the draft

presence report, in order to provide maximum assistance to the officer, to avoid misunderstandings regarding the evidence, and to focus the parties' attention on sentencing factors early in the process.

4. Rule 32 F.R.Cr.P. directs that objections, if any, to the draft presentence report be submitted to the probation officer. It does not specify what form the objection should take. . . .

5. [U.S. Court of Appeals Judge Edward R.] Becker suggests that courts provide an opportunity for a presentence conference with the court (at least in more complicated cases) in order to narrow issues, plan evidence, minimize delay and avoid last-minute submissions.

Obviously, most of these measures require court initiation, but probation officers can implement some on their own, such as requesting early conferences with the parties and asking parties to submit their sentencing positions (and legal authorities for those positions) prior to the issuance of the draft presentence report. Some probation offices may wish to . . . seek the court's endorsement of their requests for meetings and early submissions.

## Looking at the Federal Sentencing Process One Judge at a Time, One Probation Officer at a Time, Leslie A. Cory
### 51 Emory L.J. 379 (2002)

Probation officers are employees of the court, hired and fired by the sentencing judges for whom they write presentence reports. While 18 U.S.C. §3603 sets out the duties of the probation officer in regard to the court, 28 U.S.C. §995(a) authorizes the Sentencing Commission to "monitor the performance of probation officers with regard to sentencing recommendations, including application of the Sentencing Commission guidelines and policy statements"; and to "issue instructions to probation officers concerning the application of Commission guidelines and policy statements. . . ." If the instructions of the Sentencing Commission and the judge for whom the probation officer works diverge, the officer will be forced to choose whose instructions take precedence.

[How] do probation officers view their role? One study found that probation officers' perceptions of their role varied from one district to another. Some officers viewed their role as enforcers of the sentencing guidelines. Others viewed themselves as employees of the court, gathering whatever information on sentencing factors, including offender characteristics, the judges will want to evaluate at sentencing. In that study, neither group of officers acknowledged that the particular officer writing the presentence report might have a significant impact on the sentencing outcome. The officers did comment upon an informal policy in each district, set by the judges, of either giving offender characteristics significant consideration in sentencing decisions or of disregarding offender characteristics as a sentencing consideration.

Because the probation officer stands between the sentencing judge and the other parties, the other parties may regard the officer as an obstacle to the achievement of their purposes. From some officers' perspective, the source of the conflict is that, unlike defense attorneys and prosecutors, the probation officer is required to make an "impartial" determination of the guidelines. And unlike the judge, the probation officer is not insulated from ex parte communications. The officer is required to meet with the parties and to develop relationships with them. The positive implication of the probation officer's availability is that the parties have far more of an opportunity to persuade the officer than they do the judge.

The parties involved in the sentencing process often consider the probation officer the sentencing expert. Probation officers ought to be sentencing experts. However, because they have so much discretion in interpreting and applying the guidelines, probation officer error can have a powerful impact upon sentences. A study conducted by the Federal Judicial Center . . . demonstrated the possible impact on sentencing of probation officer error in interpreting the guidelines.[78] In this study, forty-seven probation officers were given the same crime scenario, dealing with three defendants involved in a drug conspiracy. The officers' assignment was to determine the quantity of drugs attributable to each defendant. Based upon the same set of facts, the officers came up with widely varying offense levels, depending upon how the officers interpreted the provisions of the Relevant Conduct guideline. Over-reliance on probation officer expertise, by defense attorneys, prosecutors, or judges, can be disastrous for defendants.

How a judge uses a presentence report varies according to the judge's assessment of the Sentencing Commission and its sentencing guidelines, and according to how much control the judge chooses to exercise over the sentencing process. . . .

The use a judge makes of the presentence report will also vary according to the judge's attitude toward plea agreements. A judge who believes sentencing outcomes should be determined by the parties (defendant, defense attorney, and prosecutor) may forego inquiry into whether the plea agreement adequately reflects the statutory purposes of sentencing. . . .

When a probation officer presents to a judge the facts that the officer believes are relevant to sentencing, the officer exercises great informal discretion — it is the officer alone who decides which facts are relevant. Policy may guide, but the officer decides. When a judge disregards facts that are arguably relevant under the guidelines, to achieve a lower offense level, the judge is exercising her discretion. Whether that exercise is legitimate depends upon the judge's motivation. Whether it appears legitimate depends upon the care with which she frames her explanation. Each participant in the sentencing process exercises the discretion accorded to him or her in a unique manner. A passive prosecutor may defer to an aggressive defense attorney. A laissez-faire judge may defer to whatever compromises the prosecution and defense are prepared to accept. An inexperienced probation officer may rely heavily on the input of the prosecutor. . . .

The study suggests the following conclusions . . . :

3. Some probation officers are more inclined to recommend sentences that cover the entire spectrum of the guideline range. Others are more inclined to recommend sentences toward the bottom. Judges frequently rely on these

---

78. Pamela B. Lawrence & Paul J. Hofer, An Empirical Study of the Application of the Relevant Conduct Guideline 1B1.3, 10 Fed. Sent'g Rep. 16 (1997).

recommendations, with the result that where within the guideline range a defendant's sentence is imposed will depend in part upon who the probation officer is. . . .

5. Although judges depart [less often than probation officers recommend], judges do rely on the information supplied by probation officers for making the departure decision. Some probation officers are more inclined than others to suggest possible grounds for departure.

6. Defendants who object to the presentence report experience no adverse consequences, and have a relatively good record of success. . . .

## NOTES

1. *Probation officers as officers of the court.*   As these readings indicate, the role of the probation officer in the federal system, while long important to the administration of justice, has taken on a more central and contested role under the sentencing guidelines. The probation officer, when drafting the presentence investigation report for the judge, does not simply serve as a conduit for the competing claims of the parties. The officer makes preliminary factual findings and recommendations to the judge.

> Criminal procedures are adversarial in the pretrial and trial phases with the two sides guarding the interests of the client or the government by introducing information for the court's consideration and debating whether it is admissible. At sentencing, on the other hand, the primary source of information is the presentence investigation report, a document submitted from the vantage of a third party. The notion is that the investigation should be conducted by one who has not been a party to the case prior to conviction, is theoretically neutral, and is strictly responsible to the court. In this role, the probation officer acts as an "arm" of the court. . . .
>
> In the past, an officer could collect facts from several sources and present various renditions of the facts of the offense (the prosecution version, the defendant's version, and the victim's version). Under the guidelines, however, the officer is required to sort out and analyze the facts with the goal of determining, on the best available information, what happened during the course of the offense. This investigation is necessary in order to apply the facts to the guideline provisions. Because a specific fact, such as the presence of a gun, or the dimension of a fact, such as the amount of drugs, may translate to a difference in exposure to a prison term, effective advocates will challenge the officer's guideline application in order to protect the interest of the defendant or government. This process may bring the officer into conflict with the attorneys. Although the officer does not have an adversarial role in the sentencing process, he may find himself in the gunsight of one attorney or be caught in the crossfire of both. . . .

Magdeline E. Jensen, Has the Role of the U.S. Probation Officer Really Changed?, 4 Fed. Sent'g Rep. 94 (1991).

2. *Probation officers as advocates.*   Once the probation officer makes preliminary judgments about various guideline calculations, the parties inevitably agree, and the officer is drawn into an advocacy role, defending the conclusions of the report in court. As one supervising probation officer put it:

[As] a group we generally abhor being placed in an adversarial position. Probation officers traditionally were attracted to the job to have personal contact with the clients — to get into their lives. We are, by profession, nosey. We get into the client's home, figure out what went wrong and then are paid to fix it. The way it is fixed can vary from pure social work to investigation and surveillance. But it all amounts to the same thing — access to other people's lives. Our mindset, therefore, differs substantially from that of lawyers, who are always ready for a good fight, and from judges, who have left the good fight and now do referee work.

With the adoption of the guidelines, we found ourselves thrown into the fight with the professional heavyweights. At first we objected, but as we found ourselves sparring, the great American competitive spirit prevailed and it turned out to be not only interesting, but challenging — even fun. To the government, we have become a thorny contender; to the defense, we are accused of being more cutthroat than the government. For our part, it is all done in the name of being true to the guidelines. And we have been scrupulous.

Francesca D. Bowman, The Greening of Probation Officers in Their New Role, 4 Fed. Sent'g Rep. 99 (1991).

3. *Probation officers as deal busters.*   The role of the probation officer is especially precarious when he or she disagrees with the stipulations of both parties about the proper resolution of various guideline findings and calculations.

In applying the guidelines, particularly to cases in which the parties have agreed to certain facts or guideline applications which are at odds with the officer's perception of the matter at hand, does the officer strictly adhere to his guideline manual and cause a further independent and time-consuming investigation, provoke argument, create the need to prepare a presentence addendum in defense of his position, and ultimately find that no one will argue his view at the time of the sentencing hearing? Or, will the officer pursue the path of least resistance and prepare the computations based upon the parties' agreement? While one might hope that this never occurs, a perfunctory understanding of human behavior suggests otherwise.

At the time of the sentencing hearing, the court is frequently faced with an agreement between the parties which produces a much different guideline computation than the one presented by the probation officer. This situation poses the potential for lengthy fact-finding hearings. Not infrequently, the prosecutor may take the position that the government cannot prove those facts contained in the probation officer's report by a preponderance of evidence standard. How is an already overburdened court — inundated by increasing numbers of drug related crimes — to respond?

Frank S. Gilbert, A Probation Officer's Perception of the Allocation of Discretion, 4 Fed. Sent'g Rep. 109 (1991).

## 3.   Sentencing Hearings

After prosecutors and defense counsel strike a plea bargain (or after the jury returns a guilty verdict in those rare cases that go to trial), and after a probation officer has completed a presentencing investigation report, the sentencing drama moves to its most public setting, the courtroom, for a sentencing hearing.

Do sentencing hearings resemble trials? What is the standard for admission of evidence? What rules and procedures are used to test evidence? Should the sentencing hearing be a minitrial?

> ### Federal Rule of Criminal Procedure 32(i), Sentencing and Judgment

**(i) Sentencing.**

(1) *In General.* At sentencing, the court:

(A) must verify that the defendant and the defendant's attorney have read and discussed the presentence report and any addendum to the report;

(B) must give to the defendant and an attorney for the government a written summary of—or summarize in camera—any information excluded from the presentence report . . . on which the court will rely in sentencing, and give them a reasonable opportunity to comment on that information;

(C) must allow the parties' attorneys to comment on the probation officer's determinations and other matters relating to an appropriate sentence; and

(D) may, for good cause, allow a party to make a new objection at any time before sentence is imposed.

(2) *Introducing Evidence; Producing a Statement.* The court may permit the parties to introduce evidence on the objections. . . .

(3) *Court Determinations.* At sentencing, the court:

(A) may accept any undisputed portion of the presentence report as a finding of fact;

(B) must—for any disputed portion of the presentence report or other controverted matter—rule on the dispute or determine that a ruling is unnecessary either because the matter will not affect sentencing, or because the court will not consider the matter in sentencing; . . .

(4) *Opportunity to Speak.*

(A) *By a Party.* Before imposing sentence, the court must:

(i) provide the defendant's attorney an opportunity to speak on the defendant's behalf;

(ii) address the defendant personally in order to permit the defendant to speak or present any information to mitigate the sentence; and

(iii) provide an attorney for the government an opportunity to speak equivalent to that of the defendant's attorney.

(B) *By a Victim.* Before imposing sentence, the court must address any victim of a crime of violence or sexual abuse who is present at sentencing and must permit the victim to speak or submit any information about the sentence. Whether or not the victim is present, a victim's right to address the court may be exercised by the following persons if present:

(i) a parent or legal guardian, if the victim is younger than 18 years or is incompetent; or

(ii) one or more family members or relatives the court designates, if the victim is deceased or incapacitated.

(C) *In Camera Proceedings.* Upon a party's motion and for good cause, the court may hear in camera any statement made under Rule 32(i)(4).

---

|| *U.S. Sentencing Guidelines Manual* ||
|| §6A1.3 (Policy Statement) ||

## §6A1.3  RESOLUTION OF DISPUTED FACTORS

(a) When any factor important to the sentencing determination is reasonably in dispute, the parties shall be given an adequate opportunity to present information to the court regarding that factor. In resolving any dispute concerning a factor important to the sentencing determination, the court may consider relevant information without regard to its admissibility under the rules of evidence applicable at trial, provided that the information has sufficient indicia of reliability to support its probable accuracy.

(b) The court shall resolve disputed sentencing factors at a sentencing hearing in accordance with Rule 32(c)(1), Fed. R. Crim. P.

### COMMENTARY

In pre-guidelines practice, factors relevant to sentencing were often determined in an informal fashion. The informality was to some extent explained by the fact that particular offense and offender characteristics rarely had a highly specific or required sentencing consequence. This situation no longer exists under sentencing guidelines. The court's resolution of disputed sentencing factors usually has a measurable effect on the applicable punishment. More formality is therefore unavoidable if the sentencing process is to be accurate and fair.

Although lengthy sentencing hearings seldom should be necessary, disputes about sentencing factors must be resolved with care. When a dispute exists about any factor important to the sentencing determination, the court must ensure that the parties have an adequate opportunity to present relevant information. Written statements of counsel or affidavits of witnesses may be adequate under many circumstances. An evidentiary hearing may sometimes be the only reliable way to resolve disputed issues. The sentencing court must determine the appropriate procedure in light of the nature of the dispute, its relevance to the sentencing determination, and applicable case law.

In determining the relevant facts, sentencing judges are not restricted to information that would be admissible at trial. See 18 U.S.C. §3661; see also United States v. Watts, 117 S. Ct. 633, 635 (1997) (holding that lower evidentiary standard at sentencing permits sentencing court's consideration of acquitted conduct); Witte v. United States, 515 U.S. 389 (1995) (noting that sentencing courts have traditionally considered wide range of information without the procedural protections of a criminal trial, including information concerning criminal conduct that may be the subject of a subsequent prosecution); Nichols v. United States, 511 U.S. 738 (1994) (noting that district courts have traditionally considered defendant's prior criminal conduct even when the conduct did not result in a conviction). Any information may be considered, so long as it has sufficient indicia of reliability to support its probable accuracy. Out-of-court declarations by an unidentified informant may be considered where there is good cause for the non-disclosure of the informant's identity and there is sufficient corroboration by other means.

The Commission believes that use of a preponderance of the evidence standard is appropriate to meet due process requirements and policy concerns in resolving disputes regarding application of the guidelines to the facts of a case.

## NOTES

1. *Sentencing hearings.* How much do the federal sentencing guidelines have to say about the procedures that should govern sentencing hearings? What are the key procedural questions that should be determined by statute or rule? For example, do the federal rules determine what proof and procedure will be allowed at sentencing hearings? Questions raised by the constitutional debate over *Apprendi* arise again in the context of sentencing hearings. What does it mean for a judge to accept testimony with "sufficient indicia of reliability"? How does that standard relate to the more familiar standards and evidentiary rules at trial? See Susan N. Herman, The Tail that Wagged the Dog: Bifurcated Fact-Finding and the Limits of Due Process Under the Federal Sentencing Guidelines, 66 S. Cal. L. Rev. 289 (1992); Deborah Young, Fact-Finding at Federal Sentencing: Why the Guidelines Should Meet the Rules, 79 Cornell L. Rev. 299 (1994); David Adair, House Built on Weak Foundation — Sentencing Guidelines and the Preponderance Standard of Proof, 10 Fed. Sent'g Rep. 41 (1997).

2. *Exclusionary rule at the sentencing hearing.* Most jurisdictions allow sentencing judges to consider evidence obtained in violation of a defendant's constitutional rights, even when that evidence is suppressed at trial. See Elson v. State, 659 P.2d 1195 (Alaska 1983) (allowing evidence obtained illegally at sentencing unless violation was for purpose of obtaining facts to enhance sentencing); Smith v. State, 517 A.2d 1081 (Md. 1986). The federal courts are split on whether the exclusionary rule applies in sentencing proceedings. The U.S. Supreme Court held in Estelle v. Smith, 451 U.S. 454 (1981), that a sentencing judge in a capital case could not consider a statement obtained in violation of the Fifth Amendment, but the Court has never addressed whether the exclusionary rule applies in noncapital sentencing proceedings. Some state statutes and cases allow the introduction of illegally obtained evidence in capital cases, at least within the boundaries of Estelle v. Smith. See, e.g., Utah Code §76-3-207(2) ("Any evidence the court deems to have probative force may be received regardless of its admissibility under the exclusionary rules of evidence."); Stewart v. State, 549 So. 2d 171 (Fla. 1989). Most lower federal courts have decided that the exclusionary rule does not apply at sentencing in noncapital

proceedings. See, e.g., United States v. Torres, 926 F.2d 321 (D.C. Cir. 1991). A smaller group apply the exclusionary rule at sentencing. See Pens v. Bail, 902 F.2d 1464 (9th Cir. 1991).

3. *The right of allocution.* Federal Rule of Criminal Procedure 32 gives the defendant the right to speak at sentencing, which is often known as a right of allocution. As *Black's Law Dictionary* explains, an allocution is "an unsworn statement from a convicted defendant to the sentencing judge or jury in which the defendant can ask for mercy, explain his or her conduct, apologize for the crime, or say anything else in an effort to lessen the impending sentence. This statement is not subject to cross-examination." *Black's Law Dictionary* 75 (7th ed. 1999).

Perhaps in part because most states, like the federal system, expressly grant defendants the right to speak at sentencing, the Supreme Court has never squarely addressed whether the constitution protects the right of allocution. The Court has, however, spoken grandly of the history and importance of this right:

> [Rule 32's] legal provenance was the common-law right of allocution. As early as 1689, it was recognized that the court's failure to ask the defendant if he had anything to say before sentence was imposed required reversal. . . . Taken in the context of its history, there can be little doubt that the drafters of Rule 32 intended that the defendant be personally afforded the opportunity to speak before imposition of sentence. We are not unmindful of the relevant major changes that have evolved in criminal procedure since the seventeenth century—the sharp decrease in the number of crimes which were punishable by death, the right of the defendant to testify on his own behalf, and the right to counsel. But we see no reason why a procedural rule should be limited to the circumstances under which it arose if reasons for the right it protects remain. None of these modern innovations lessens the need for the defendant, personally, to have the opportunity to present to the court his plea in mitigation. The most persuasive counsel may not be able to speak for a defendant as the defendant might, with halting eloquence, speak for himself.

Green v. United States, 365 U.S. 301, 303 (1961). And yet, in Hill v. United States, 368 U.S. 424 (1962), the Court held that a trial judge's failure to expressly ask a defendant represented by counsel whether he wished to make a statement at sentencing was not an error of constitutional dimension and therefore provided no basis for a collateral attack.

Lower state and federal courts split over whether a right of allocution is constitutionally protected, although most of these cases turn on whether defendants were fully afforded their statutory right to speak at sentencing and what the appropriate remedy should be for statutory violations. See, e.g., Michigan v. Petit, 648 N.W.2d 193 (Mich. 2002); In re Personal Restraint of Echeverria, 6 P.3d 573 (Wash. 2000).

The practical importance of the right of allocution may be as debatable as its legal standing. Especially in sentencing systems with structured sentencing rules, it is far more likely for a defendant's statement to have symbolic value than to present information directly relevant to a judge's or jury's sentencing determination. Even if allocution is likely to be only symbolic most of the time, is there anything wrong with symbolic rights? Allocution can have tangible costs for a defendant: an admission made during an allocution might be used against the defendant at retrial or re-sentencing. If concerns about the possible future use of an allocution statement might chill the practice, should jurisdictions adopt rules limiting the later use of allocution statements against defendants?

4. *Victims' right to speak at sentencing.*   Is the right of victims or their representatives to speak also merely symbolic? The inclusion of victim statements is now widespread throughout the United States in response to the victims' rights movement that emerged in the 1980s. The Victim and Witness Protection Act of 1982 amended the Federal Rules of Criminal Procedure to require the inclusion of a victim impact statement as part of the presentence report in federal court..

Over the past 20 years, nearly every state has decided to allow victim involvement at sentencing. See generally National Victim Center, The 1996 Victims' Rights Sourcebook: A Compilation and Comparison of Victims' Rights Laws (1996). It is difficult to capture the depth, range, and impact of this dramatic change in sentencing practice. Almost all states allow victim input through the presentence report. Many allow victims a separate opportunity to make a written or oral statement regarding sentencing, often specifying the kinds of information victims may offer. A few states have retained sharper limits: several allow judges to choose whether to admit or refuse victim impact information; Texas allows victim to make a statement only after sentencing, Tex. Code Crim. Proc. art. 42.03.

The rich variety of statutes has not produced a substantial case law in the states regarding victim impact statements in the noncapital context. Challenges to such statements often assert that the judge was biased or unduly influenced by the information. Should judges rely on their own sense of the unique nature of harm imposed in particular cases? Does victim impact information differ in kind from other types of new information, such as information about the offender?

In the federal arena, victims' advocates initially pushed for the adoption of a federal constitutional amendment which would have extended a series of rights to crime victims, including the right for victims to be heard at any and all public release, plea, sentencing, reprieve, and pardon proceedings. When that effort stalled, the victims' rights movement pressed for federal statute and in 2004 the Crime Victims' Rights Act was enacted. 18 U.S.C. §3771. The CVRA expressly guarantees crime victims the right "to be reasonably heard at any public proceeding in district court involving release, plea, sentencing, or any parole proceeding." And, providing a means to enforce these rights, the CVRA authorizes crime victims to petition circuit courts for a writ of mandamus if a district court does not respect victims' rights to allocution. As a result of the passage of the CVRA, federal courts and academic commentators have begun more broadly considering the import and impact of victim allocutions at sentencing. See, e.g., See Jayne W. Barnard, Listening to Victims, 79 Fordham L. Rev. 1479, 1488-89 (2011); Julie Kaster, Note, The Voices of Victims: Debating the Appropriate Role of Fraud Victim Allocution Under the Crime Victims' Rights Act, 94 Minn. L. Rev. 1682 (2010).

# ═7═

## Sentencing Outcomes: The Scale of Imprisonment

We have reviewed the typical "inputs" that influence the choice of sentences in a particular case and the procedural setting for the sentencing decision. Now we turn to the typical outcomes of the sentencing decision, beginning with imprisonment.

We start with prison, although it is not the most common sentencing outcome. Very few misdemeanors result in a prison term, and many of the least serious felonies (which account for the greatest number of felonies) also result in a nonprison punishment. Yet prison is the sentence that occupies a large place in public debates and the largest place in public budgets despite ongoing attempts to curb state corrections budgets. In the United States, it is the expected sentence for the most serious felonies. Gustave du Beaumont and Alexis de Tocqueville, who toured prisons in the United States on behalf of the French government in 1831, noted the emphasis that Americans placed on the prison early in its history: "they have caught the monomania of the penitentiary system, which to them seems the remedy for all the evils of society." Gustave de Beaumont & Alexis de Tocqueville, On the Penitentiary System in the United States and Its Application in France 80 (Francis Lieber trans., 1833).

In this chapter we consider why criminal justice in the United States relies as much as it does on the prison sanction. What do governments hope to accomplish when they use prison rather than other punishments for crimes? Which of the limits on the use of prison are legal, and which are political or cultural?

## A. INCARCERATION TRENDS

Prison began as a distinctly American contribution to criminal justice, and today the United States is unmatched in its use of prison as a criminal punishment. But our reliance on prison has changed in interesting ways over time. In the following passage, Norval Morris briefly summarizes the history of prison as a sanction for crimes, emphasizing its American origins. He then evokes a moment that is now difficult to reconstruct: a time in the 1960s and 1970s when a serious debate occurred in the United States about whether to abolish or seriously limit the use of prison.

That moment has passed. Since the early 1980s, governments in the United States have embraced prison as never before. The tables following the Morris excerpt track the increasing rate of imprisonment in the United States since 1970; of particular significance are the differences among various regions and states. Note that at present many states see their prison populations plateau or even decrease.

## The Future of Imprisonment, Norval Morris
### Pages 3-9 (1974)

[Until] quite recently the serious offender, other than the political criminal, was not imprisoned as a penal sanction. He may have been penned for other purposes but not imprisoned as a punishment. Felons were dealt with by exile, banishment, transportation, and a diversity of demeaning and painful corporal punishments—the "cat," the ear and nose cropper, the branding iron, and that reliable standby, capital punishment. Prisons for felons arose as a reaction to the excesses and barbarisms of earlier punishments; imprisonment was one of the early "diversions" from traditional criminal sanctions.

The jail, the workhouse, the almshouse, the reformatory, and the convict ship all antedate the prison. The castle keep for the political personage out of favor or office and the church's cell for retreat and penance were part of the genesis of the prison, but they were established for different social classes and different political purposes. What is sometimes forgotten . . . is that the prison is an American invention, an invention of the Pennsylvania Quakers of the last decade of the eighteenth century, though one might also note the confining "People Pen" put up by the Massachusetts Pilgrims nearly two centuries earlier. In their "penitentiary" the Quakers planned to substitute the correctional specifics of isolation, repentance, and the uplifting effects of scriptural injunctions and solitary Bible reading for the brutality and inutility of capital and corporal punishments. These three treatments—removal from corrupting peers, time for reflection and self-examination, the guidance of biblical precepts—would no doubt have been helpful to the reflective Quakers who devised the prison, but relatively few of them ever became prisoners. The suitability of these remedies for the great mass of those who subsequently found their way to the penitentiary is more questionable. . . .

At all events, in 1790 a cell block was opened in the Walnut Street Jail of Philadelphia as the "penitentiary" for the Commonwealth of Pennsylvania. In 1796, Newgate began service as the penitentiary for the State of New York, modeled on the Walnut Street Jail but taking its name from an earlier English institution serving a different clientele (civil and criminal debtors and those awaiting trial or punishment).

Prisons grew and flourished throughout America and later throughout the world; they are a pervasive American export, like tobacco in their international acceptance and perhaps also in their adverse consequences. The Pennsylvania Quakers must be praised or blamed for the invention or reinvention of the prison. Their vision and initiative gave us our hulking penal institutions, our "edifice complex." It was a gift born of benevolence not malevolence, of philanthropy not punitiveness, so that the most important contemporary lesson of this historical sketch may well be a deeper appreciation of the truth that benevolent intentions do not necessarily produce beneficent results.

### ABOLITION OR ABATEMENT OF IMPRISONMENT

Contemporary Quakers in the American Friends Service Committee's book, *Struggle for Justice*, recognize that "the horror that is the American prison system grew out of an eighteenth century reform" proposed by their ideological forebears. [T]hey are by no means alone in their castigation of imprisonment. . . . Both national crime commissions of the past decade recommended the swift abatement of imprisonment, and the 1973 commission urged a moratorium on the construction of all new institutions for adult or juvenile offenders, a position also adopted by the National Council on Crime and Delinquency. Judge James E. Doyle, a federal district judge of the Western District of Wisconsin, was formidably direct in the matter. In Morales v. Schmidt, 340 F. Supp. 544, 548-549 (W.D. Wis. 1972), a prison mail censorship case, he said: "I am persuaded that the institution of prison probably must end. In many respects it is as intolerable within the United States as was the institution of slavery, equally brutalizing to all involved, equally toxic to the social system, equally subversive of the brotherhood of man, even more costly by some standard, and probably less rational."

The 1973 national commission, the National Advisory Commission on Criminal Justice Standards and Goals, recommended that "the institution should be the last resort for correctional problems," gave their reasons—failure to reduce crime, success in punishing but not in deterring, providing only temporary protection to the community, changing the offender but mostly for the worse—and concluded that "the prison . . . has persisted, partly because a civilized nation could neither turn back to the barbarism of an earlier time nor find a satisfactory alternative." . . .

Imprisonment has been too much used, it has discriminated against races and classes, sentences imposed have been too long, and too many of them have been served in degrading and brutalizing circumstances. There is widespread advocacy of the swift abatement if not an abolition of imprisonment. How is this to be achieved?

### THE PATHS TO ABATEMENT OF IMPRISONMENT

[Several] paths are believed to lead to the abatement of imprisonment. First, the "overreach" of the criminal law is to be reduced. . . . Regulatory systems, backed by the criminal sanctions if regulations are flouted, should be substituted for the mass of prohibitory propositions at present brought to bear on a wide swath of behavior. Though much of what now busies the criminal justice system may be immoral or troublesome or distasteful or unseemly or injurious to the actor and those who love him or depend on him, it does not represent a serious threat to the physical safety of others nor a major depredation to property nor a serious challenge to governmental authority. . . .

Just as there has been an overemphasis on the use of the prohibitory sanctions of the criminal law, so there has been an overemphasis on custody. It is widely recognized that we have locked up too many social nuisances who are not social threats, too many petty offenders and minor thieves, severing such few social ties as they have and pushing them further toward more serious criminal behavior. This excessive use of incarceration, the prison and the jail, the reformatory and the detention center, has been expensive, criminogenic, and unkind. Hence, increasingly we try to "divert" different categories of offenders from the criminal justice system and from penal institutions.

Diversions from the criminal justice system and from prisons grow apace at the police, prosecutorial, and judicial levels. Police diversions to mental health, social welfare, and addiction treatment units reduce the flow to prison as do judicial and prosecutorial diversions to probationary and similar supervisory and supportive services. There is also support for increased reliance on the fine and on restitution and compensation payments to the victims of crime as an alternative to imprisonment. . . .

Despite these movements, the prison population remains stable at about the 200,000 mark (I do not count the jails), though an increased proportion of convicted offenders are on probation, in "halfway" houses and probation hostels, and in other community-based treatments. . . .

As Norval Morris noted, for much of the 20th century the total U.S. prison population was stable. So too were the prison populations of the federal system, and of some of the biggest states, such as California. Starting in the mid 1970s that stability unraveled, and the U.S. prison population has now reached well over 2 million.

**U.S. Incarceration Rate, 1925-2008 Prisoners per 100,000 Population**

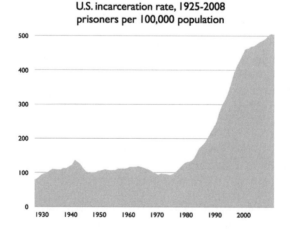

*Data Source:* Sourcebook of Criminal Justice Statistics. (Graph: Prison Policy Initiative, 2010)

**Prisoners Under State and Federal Jurisdiction at Yearend, 2000-2011**

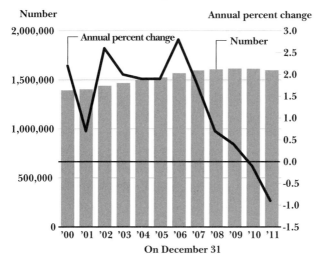

On December 31

Note: Jurisdiction refers to the legal authority of state or federal correctional officials over a prisoner regardless of where the prisoner is held.

*Source:* Bureau of Justice Statistics, National Prisoner Statistics Program, 2000-2011.

For the first time in 38 years, in 2010 the total prison population declined. See The Pew Center on the States, Prison Count 2010 (rev. Apr. 2010), at http:// www.pewtrusts.org/uploadedFiles/wwwpewtrustsorg/Reports/sentencing_and_ corrections/Prison_Count_2010.pdf. This decline continued in 2011, with approximately half the states showing a decreased imprisonment rate. California accounted for more than half the decrease in prisoner headcount numbers, while the federal prison led the increases.

Consider the increase and now the decrease in state prison use over the past decade.

## NOTES

1. *Origins of the prison.*   The prison has especially strong historical ties to the rehabilitative ideal. As prisons became the predominant criminal punishment in the late eighteenth and early nineteenth centuries, the legal system relied heavily on the hope or assumption that the penitentiary would create genuine penitence and change among the offenders living within its walls. See Edgardo Rotman, The Failure of Reform, in The Oxford History of the Prison 169-197 (Norval Morris & David Rothman eds., 1995); David J. Rothman, The Discovery of the Asylum: Social Order and Disorder in the New Republic (1971).

Prison began as an alternative to the death penalty and to various types of corporal punishment, such as the public stockade. Prison was also believed to be a humane alternative to banishment, which is still used on a limited (and often informal) basis in the United States. A sentencing judge "banishes" an offender by prohibiting him from entering the jurisdiction. See State v. Collett, 208 S.E.2d 472 (Ga. 1974) (banishment of the defendant from seven counties in Georgia, imposed as condition for suspension of 12-month sentence for drug offense, was not unconstitutional or violative of public policy); but see McCreary v. State, 582 So. 2d 425 (Miss. 1991) (banishment from state does not serve a rehabilitative function and dumps offenders on other states). Today deportation, though a non-criminal sanction imposed solely by the federal government and available only for non-citizens, fulfills the purpose of banishment. *See* Chapter 8.

2. *Types of prisons.*    Prisons are not interchangeable. Prisons run with different levels of security, meaning different types of restrictions on liberty and different levels of staffing. For instance, the Bureau of Prisons in the federal system gives the following description of security levels:

> The Bureau operates institutions at four security levels (minimum, low, medium, and high) to meet the various security needs of its diverse inmate population and has one maximum-security prison for the less than 1 percent of the inmates who require that level of security. It also has administrative facilities, such as pretrial detention centers and medical referral centers, that have specialized missions and confine offenders of all security levels. The characteristics that help define the security level of an institution are perimeter security measures (such as fences, patrol officers, and towers), the level of staffing, the internal controls for inmate movement and accountability, and the type of inmate living quarters (for example, cells or open dormitories). The Bureau's graduated security [] classification scheme[] allow[s] staff to assign an inmate to an institution in accordance with the inmate's individual needs. Thus, inmates who are able to function with relatively less supervision, without disrupting institution operations or threatening the safety of staff, other inmates, or the public, can be housed in lower security level institutions.

U.S. Department of Justice, About the Federal Bureau of Prisons (Jan. 2011). The maximum-security prisons cost the most both to build and to operate. Keep in mind that prisons are not the only secure facilities that governments operate: other institutions serving similar functions include secure mental health facilities, immigration detention facilities, and the Guantanamo Detention Center. Research indicates that in the middle of the twentieth century total confinement rates — counting inmates in mental institutions and those in prisons — are similar to those today, except that the number of prison inmates has increased substantially while mental institutions are comparatively empty. Bernard E. Harcourt, From the Asylum to the Prison: Rethinking the Incarceration Revolution, 84 Texas L. Rev. 1751 (2006).

Recent prison classifications include the "supermax" prison, in which the emphasis lies on incapacitation rather than rehabilitation. Supermax prisons have provoked international objections on human rights grounds because of their reliance on long-term solitary confinement. In a recent report, the U.N. Special Rapporteur on torture asked for a total ban on solitary confinement. For a comprehensive study of supermax prisons, see New York City Bar Association, Committee on International Human Rights, Supermax Confinement in U.S.

Prisons (Sept. 2011). The report finds supermax confinement to violate international human rights norms and the Eighth Amendment. The European Court of Human Rights, however, rejected a recent challenge to an extradition to the United States on the grounds that confinement in a supermax facility would amount to a violation of article 3 of the European Convention which prohibits torture as well as inhuman or degrading treatment or punishment. Case of Babar Ahmad and Others v. The United Kingdom (Application nos. 24027/07, 11949/08, 36742/08, 66911/09 and 67354/09) (10 Apr. 2012, final 24/09/2012).

3. *Prison capacity and overcrowding.* Prisons in the United States are routinely said to operate above capacity, but the concept of capacity has several layers. Rated capacity is the maximum number of beds assigned to a particular facility by corrections accrediting bodies. Operational capacity is set by state officials based on the facility's staff and programs. Design capacity represents the number of inmates that the designers of the facility intended for it to hold. Overcrowding is a perennial complaint recorded by those who survey criminal justice systems in the United States, dating back to when prison populations were much lower. See National Commission on Law Observance and Enforcement (Wickersham Commission), Report on Penal Institutions, Probation and Parole 211, 231-238 (1931); President's Commission on Criminal Justice and the Administration of Justice, The Challenge of Crime in a Free Society 45 (1967). Federal courts have occasionally ruled in favor of prison inmates who allege that overcrowded prisons violate the Eighth Amendment's prohibition of cruel and unusual punishments. Some, such as the legendary federal judge Frank Johnson in Alabama, took over entire systems, sometimes for decades, and managed them through special masters, ongoing hearings, and personal visits to prison facilities. See Malcolm Feeley & Edward Rubin, Judicial Policy Making And The Modern State: How The Courts Reformed America's Prisons (1998); see also Marc Miller, Wise Masters, 51 Stan. L. Rev. 1751 (1999). The most recent prison overcrowding decision is Brown v. Plata, 131 S. Ct. 1910 (2011), which confirms the impact constitutional law doctrine can have on the definition of a prison's capacity.

4. *The* Plata *(California Prison Healthcare) Case.* Through a series of judicial and legislative rulings, including a significant narrowing of federal habeas corpus relief through the Antiterrorism and Effective Death Penalty Act of 1996 (Chapter 11) and restrictions on prisoner lawsuits through the Prison Litigation Reform Act (PLRA), the opportunity to challenge prison conditions through litigation and the power of courts to grant "structural" relief have been significantly narrowed, if not eviscerated. Pub. L. No. 104-134, 110 Stat. 1321. See, e.g., Brian J. Ostrom, Roger A. Hanson & Fred L. Cheesman, II, Congress, Courts and Corrections: An Empirical Perspective on the Prison Litigation Reform Act, 78 Notre Dame L. Rev. 1525 (2002-2003); Margo Schlanger & Giovanna E. Shay, Preserving the Rule of Law in America's Jails and Prisons: The Case for Amending the Prison Litigation Reform Act, 11 Penn. J. Con. Law 1 (2009).

Among the many barriers to prison litigation in the PRLA are requirements that claimants exhaust administrative review and that a court "shall not grant or approve any prospective relief unless the court finds that such relief is narrowly drawn, extends no further than necessary to correct the violation of the Federal right, and is the least intrusive means necessary to correct the violation of the Federal right." 18 U.S.C. §3626(a)(1)(A).

Against this legal and policy background, a special three-judge court, empaneled under the PLRA, issued an 184-page opinion after 14 days of testimony in a case, which had its roots in a lawsuit filed in 1990 — before the PLRA — and focused on both the mental and physical health of inmates. As the court determined substantial prison overcrowding to have been the underlying reasons for the failure of California's prison system to attend to prisoners' basic health needs, it ordered the State to reduce its prison population to 137.5% of the prisons' design capacity within two years. Assuming the State does not increase capacity through new construction, the order requires a population reduction of 38,000 to 46,000 persons.

The court did not order the State to achieve this reduction in any particular manner. Instead, it required the State to formulate a plan for compliance and submit its plan for approval by the court. Because it appears all but certain that the State cannot complete sufficient construction to comply fully with the order, the prison population will have to be reduced to at least some extent.

In Brown v. Plata, 131 S. Ct. 1910 (2011), the Supreme Court, in a 5-4 decision, upheld the order of the three-judge panel. Justice Kennedy's opinion for the Court noted:

> For years the medical and mental health care provided by California's prisons has fallen short of minimum constitutional requirements and has failed to meet prisoners' basic health needs. Needless suffering and death have been the well-documented result. . . .
>
> As a consequence of their own actions, prisoners may be deprived of rights that are fundamental to liberty. Yet the law and the Constitution demand recognition of certain other rights. Prisoners retain the essence of human dignity inherent in all persons. Respect for that dignity animates the Eighth Amendment prohibition against cruel and unusual punishment. The basic concept underlying the Eighth Amendment is nothing less than the dignity of man. . . .

Justice SCALIA dissented:

> Today the Court affirms what is perhaps the most radical injunction issued by a court in our Nation's history: an order requiring California to release the staggering number of 46,000 convicted criminals.
>
>     . . . . One would think that, before allowing the decree of a federal district court to release 46,000 convicted felons, this Court would bend every effort to read the law in such a way as to avoid that outrageous result. Today, quite to the contrary, the Court disregards stringently drawn provisions of the governing statute, and traditional constitutional limitations upon the power of a federal judge, in order to uphold the absurd.
>
>     The proceedings that led to this result were a judicial travesty. I dissent because the institutional reform the District Court has undertaken violates the terms of the governing statute, ignores bedrock limitations on the power of Article III judges, and takes federal courts wildly beyond their institutional capacity.

Justice ALITO's dissent also aimed at the policy implications of the order and the legal authority on which it was built:

The decree in this case is a perfect example of what the Prison Litigation Reform Act was enacted to prevent.

The Constitution does not give federal judges the authority to run state penal systems. Decisions regarding state prisons have profound public safety and financial implications, and the States are generally free to make these decisions as they choose.

The Eighth Amendment imposes an important — but limited — restraint on state authority in this field. The Eighth Amendment prohibits prison officials from depriving inmates of "the minimal civilized measure of life's necessities." Federal courts have the responsibility to ensure that this constitutional standard is met, but undesirable prison conditions that do not violate the Constitution are beyond the federal courts' reach.

In this case, a three-judge court exceeded its authority under the Constitution and the PLRA. The court ordered a radical reduction in the California prison population without finding that the current population level violates the Constitution. . . .

The prisoner release ordered in this case is unprecedented, improvident, and contrary to the PLRA. In largely sustaining the decision below, the majority is gambling with the safety of the people of California. Before putting public safety at risk, every reasonable precaution should be taken. The decision below should be reversed, and the case should be remanded for this to be done.

I fear that today's decision, like prior prisoner release orders, will lead to a grim roster of victims. I hope that I am wrong. In a few years, we will see.

California remains the most important state not to have implemented any type of modern guideline sentencing reform, though the topic has reemerged on state policy-maker's radars. See State of Emergency: The California Correctional Crisis, Fed. Sent'g Rep., Vol. 22, No. 3 (Feb. 2010). Will *Brown v. Plata* stand as a fascinating but unique echo of past reforms, or signal the beginning of a new era of punishment reforms, with the judicial role yet to be determined? Does the case indict the entire system of mass imprisonment as a violation of human dignity? Will researchers take up the implicit challenge issued by the Supreme Court dissenters and evaluate the impact of significant reductions in the California state prison population to counter or confirm the fears expressed by the dissenters? And if they do, will the public or anyone in a policy-making setting (including courts) care?

5. *Demographic impact of incarceration rates.* Many prisoners in the United States have committed nonviolent crimes, such as low-level drug trafficking. Over time, their sentences affect the demographic makeup of the prison population. For instance, the prison population now includes more black inmates than it once did, because blacks are arrested and convicted more often for the drug crimes that receive the longest prison terms. Blacks account for about three-fourths of all those sentenced to prison for drug offenses, although only about 11% of regular drug users in the United States are black.

The prison population today also includes a larger number of inmates over 55 because for several decades prison terms have been getting longer and older people are being sentenced to prison. Between 1995 and 2010 the number of these prisoners quadrupled, while those over 65 increased by 63% between 2007 and 2010 alone. These inmates create management challenges, as they succumb to mobility problems, hearing and vision loss, dementia and Alzheimer's, and put other pressures on prisons in light of their increased health need. Medical expenditures can run between three and nine times those of other prisoners.

The Human Rights Watch report *Old Behind Bars: The Aging Prison Population in the United States* (2012), available at www.hrw.org/reports/2012/01/27/old-behind-bars, argues for earlier release of the elderly because of insufficient funding for age-appropriate housing and medical care for the elderly. It also demands a review of institutional rules, largely written for a much younger population.

While the male prison population substantially surpasses the number of female inmates, the latter grew dramatically faster during the 1990s. We explore further the distribution of sentencing outcomes across race, class, and gender in Chapter 9.

*6. Life without parole (LWOP).*   Slightly over 40,000 prison inmates in the United States are currently serving LWOP sentences. Such sentences have experienced a dramatic increase, in part because of an expansion of the offenses triggering this sanction, because of habitual offender laws that make ever more offenders with a prior criminal record eligible for this sanction, and because of the expansion of prison terms that far extend beyond an offender's expected life span. Distrust in the criminal justice system and an extensive desire for retribution appear to drive this increased availability and imposition of LWOP. See Ashley Nellis, Throwing Way the Key: The Expansion of Life Without Parole Sentences in the United States, 23 Fed. Sentencing Rep. 27 (2010). The permanent exclusion of such inmates from society imposes high costs on the criminal justice system. It is also frequently overinclusive, and in many ways may become a similar challenge to society as the death penalty currently presents. See generally Life Without Parole: America's New Death Penalty (Charles J. Ogletree, Jr. & Austin Sarat eds., 2012).

Even though most European and Latin American countries do not impose LWOP sentences, a chamber of the European Court of Human Rights, in a recent decision, held that a mandatory life term which allowed only for release at the discretion of an executive branch official on compassionate grounds did not amount to inhuman and degrading treatment under article 3 of the European Convention on Human Rights in light of the continued penological justification of the sentence. As the ongoing imprisonment remained grounded in punishment and deterrence, the Court saw no reason to intervene. Vinter and Others v. The United Kingdom, application nos. 66069/09 and 130/10 and 3896/10), 17 Jan. 2012, referred to Grand Chamber, 09/07/2012.

# B.   IS THE U.S. STORY UNIQUE?

Some scholars have made the claim that United States rates of imprisonment are "exceptional" and the factors that have driven the massive use of imprisonment are unique to United States culture and politics. A competing view has been expressed most prominently by legal sociologist David Garland in his 2001 book *The Culture of Control.* Garland identifies the following 12 factors as central and common "currents of change" across the United States and Britain: (1) the decline of the rehabilitative ideal; (2) the reemergence of punitive sanctions and expressive justice; (3) changes in the emotional tone of crime policy; (4) the return of the victim; (5) public protection as a predominant purpose of punishment; (6) politicization and a "new populism" in punishment policy (e.g., "three strikes and you're out," "truth in sentencing," "zero tolerance"); (7) the reinvention of prison; (8) the transformation of criminological thought from multifaceted theories of behavior and reform to "control theories"; (9) the expanding infrastructure of crime prevention and community safety; (10) civil society and the commercialization of crime control; (11) new management styles and working practices of major criminal justice organizations; and (12) a perpetual sense of crisis. See David Garland, The Culture of Control: Crime and Social Order in Contemporary Society (2001). Historical scholarship, however, indicates that U.S. sentences may have been longer than those in England, France, and Germany even in the early years of the penitentiary. See Ashley T. Aubuchon, The Origin of Long Prison Sentences in America: A Case Study of Pennsylvania, 1829-1865.

Consider the following descriptions of Canadian imprisonment rates and imprisonment rates around the world. Does the Canadian experience reinforce or undermine the claim of American exceptionalism? Does it provide lessons for other countries? If so, what are those lessons?

> ## Countering Punitiveness: Understanding Stability in Canada's Imprisonment Rate, Anthony N. Doob and Cheryl Marie Webster

Canada's imprisonment rate has not changed appreciably since 1960. . . . Canada's anomalous imprisonment trend provides a contrast to patterns in nations generally considered to be similar in nature to Canada. The most obvious examples are England and Wales — to which Canada is historically and institutionally tied — and the United States — to which Canada is geographically, culturally, and economically linked. Despite these close affinities, Canadian criminal justice policies as they relate to imprisonment have diverged from those of these two comparators.[3]

### INCREASING PUNITIVENESS: CANADA AMONG OTHER NATIONS

. . . [T]he similarities among Canada, the United States, and England are not only historical, cultural, economic, or geographic in nature. They are also criminological. Canada has experienced a crime culture similar to that found in the United States and England since the 1960s. [B]oth the (police-recorded)

---

3. The irony of the Canadian reality would not be lost on those familiar with Blumstein and Cohen (1973). They proposed that stable incarceration rates in the United States and Norway in the half-century preceding the writing of their article reflected the natural state of equilibrium maintained by modern societies. Blumstein et alia (1977) extended this analysis by including Canadian data. Ironically, it would seem that unlike Americans, Canadians (and Norwegians; Lappi-Seppälä 2005) took this "stability hypothesis" to heart, providing unexpected support for a theory whose ability to fit U.S. data ended almost simultaneous to its publication.

total and the violent crime rates for Canada from 1962 to 2003[8] [show] a substantial increase in reported crime beginning in the early 1960s and only leveling off in the early 1990s. This pattern is similar to that found in the United States and — at least until the mid-1990s — the trend in England.

Even more convincing are the data on Canadian and U.S. homicide rates. . . . Although Canada's homicide rate (in absolute terms) is approximately one-third of that of the United States during this period, the shapes of the curves across time in the two countries are similar. . . .

Given these similarities, one might assume that the criminal justice responses of these countries would also be similar. . . . [S]cholars have been content simply to note that Canada's imprisonment rate (e.g., 103 per 100,000 in the general population in 2002) is comparable to that in some European countries (e.g., 101 in the Netherlands, and 92 in an unweighted average of the European Union countries) and English-speaking nations (e.g., 116 in Australia), while it is lower than that found in other countries (e.g., 137 in England and Wales, 126 in Scotland, 144 in New Zealand, and [the most obvious difference] 702 in the United States) for the same year.

Indeed, the focus of recent discussions surrounding levels of incarceration has been on the dramatic increase in the United States over the past 30 years, as well as a similar — albeit less dramatic — rise in England. While the recent increase in imprisonment rates in the Netherlands, the contrasting decreases in certain periods in other countries such as Germany and Finland, and the relative stability — at least until very recently — in such nations as Denmark, Norway, and Sweden have received sporadic attention, the United States and England continue to hold a near monopoly on scholarly inquiry in the English language academic literature.

[T]he increase . . . in American imprisonment rates since the mid-1970s justifies this focus. In striking contrast to the remarkable stability described by Blumstein and Cohen (1973) between 1930 and 1970, combined state and federal prison incarceration rates increased almost fivefold between 1970 and 2002. When the jail populations are included, the 2003 U.S. rate was 714 per 100,000 in the general population.

In contrast, Canadian imprisonment rates (comprising sentenced and all other — largely pretrial remand — prisoners) over the same period look quite different. The level of incarceration in Canada has been relatively stable since 1960. While there has been some fluctuation — with a low of 83 per 100,000 residents in 1974 to a high of 116 in 1995 — there is no consistent upward trend in Canada's imprisonment rate. . . .

Clearly, the data depict Canadian blandness: imprisonment rates have not changed dramatically since 1960. . . .

---

8. Unless otherwise noted, all Canadian statistics reported in this article are from publications of the Canadian Centre for Justice Statistics, Statistics Canada (previously the Dominion Bureau of Statistics), or from Statistics Canada's Web site, http://www.statcan.ca. Statistics Canada typically publishes annual reports on such matters as *Canadian Crime Statistics* or *Adult Correctional Services in Canada*. Rather than list each year that we accessed, we have listed a single illustrative instance of each series in the references.

### Canadian Punitiveness: Talk Tough—Act Softly

[I]t would be misguided to conclude from these data that Canada has been immune to pressure to adopt more punitive policies. On the contrary, an examination of several of the changes introduced in Canadian policy and legislation suggests that many of the forces behind higher incarceration rates in other countries have also impacted Canada.

Most obviously, Canada witnessed the introduction, in 1996, of mandatory minimum sentences for offenders found guilty of any of 10 serious violent crimes with a firearm. Similarly, the maximum sanctions for certain offenses were increased during the 1990s. Paralleling, to some extent, these changes in the adult criminal justice system, the maximum sentences for youths convicted of murder in youth court were increased both in 1992 (from three years to a total sentence length of five years less a day) and again in 1996 (to 10 years). This change in the youth system was also accompanied by changes in the rules governing the transfer of young offenders charged with serious crimes to adult court, rendering this process easier to accomplish by creating "presumptive transfers" to adult court of those over 16 years old charged with a serious violent offense. . . .

Clearly, Canada has not escaped many of the broader forces propelling countries toward more punitive responses to criminal behavior. The difference—it would seem—resides in the extent to which harsher policies and practices have been allowed to affect the level of punitiveness. Indeed, while the mandatory minimum sentence for violent crimes carried out with a firearm (four years in prison) did, in fact, increase the sentences that *some* offenders received, it is likely that the "new" sanction would not significantly differ from that which would have been handed down under the prior legislation for most offenders. Given the seriousness of the offense and the fact that those offenders falling under these new mandatory minimum sentences would frequently have criminal records—often serious in nature—it is probable that they would already have received a four-year sentence. Hence the legislation almost certainly contributed little to prison populations.

It is also noteworthy that previously legislated mandatory minimum sentences disappeared for drug offenses—a type of criminal activity responsible for a disproportionate proportion of the increase in the U.S. prison population during the 1980-1990s. Until 1987, Canada had a mandatory minimum sanction of seven years for importing narcotics. In that year, the Supreme Court of Canada ruled in *R. v. Smith* (34 C.C.C. (3d) 97) that this mandatory minimum penalty constituted cruel and unusual punishment under Section 12 of the Charter of Rights and Freedoms. . . . [Effective November 2012, Canadian law reinstituted mandatory minimum sanctions of one and two years for certain "serious drug crime[s]," though an exemption is included for addicted, non-violent offenders who agree to treatment.]

The pattern depicted in these examples is one of muted or limited expression of wider punitive trends. While Canada has obviously not been immune to the broader forces that compel other nations toward harsher responses to crime, it has been largely able to restrict or contain their impact. . . . Borrowing from the language of developmental psychology, it would seem that Canada has not only been able to escape several of the forces — or "risk factors" — producing higher imprisonment rates in other nations. Rather, there also appear to be certain "protective factors" that have restricted the extent to which Canada has adopted the punitive policies at the root of the U.S. and English levels of incarceration. . . .

### RESISTING PUNITIVE TRENDS: REDUCED RISK FACTORS

In contrast with the United States and England, Canada has never given primacy to any one specific sentencing purpose. Rather, Canadian sentencing policies have historically been guided by the notion that multiple (and presumably equally acceptable) purposes of sentencing exist and that judges are responsible for choosing the most relevant purposes for each case (*R. v. Morrissette and two others*, 1 C.C.C. (2d) 307 [1970]). Indeed, Canadian judges have had — for the most part — wide discretion to sentence within a range determined largely by practice and by guidance from appeals courts. In fact, courts of appeal have not only developed the notion that judges should choose among all of the standard purposes of sentencing (i.e., denunciation, individual and general deterrence, incapacitation, and rehabilitation), but they have also reined in individual outliers.

Even when Parliament gave sentencing a legislated purpose and a set of principles in the Criminal Code in 1996, these provisions did not challenge the guiding notions in place for decades as a result of judicial decisions. The legislation stated that sentences were supposed to

> contribute, along with crime prevention initiatives, to respect for the law and the maintenance of a just, peaceful and safe society by imposing just sanctions that have one or more of the following objectives: [denunciation, general and individual deterrence, incapacitation, rehabilitation, reparations to victim and community, promoting a sense of responsibility and acknowledgment of harm by offenders] (Criminal Code, Section 718). While there was also a new requirement that "[a] sentence [be] proportionate to the gravity of the offence and the degree of responsibility of the offender" (Criminal Code, Section 718.1), we can find no important discernible changes or shifts in sentencing *practices* in Canada as reflected in imprisonment levels since 1996.

Within this context, Canada — unlike the United States — has never experienced a crisis of principles in sentencing whereby disillusionment with one predominant objective leads to the wholesale adoption of another. Hence, the radical shift in American courts from an indeterminate model based on a rehabilitative paradigm to one of determinate sentencing rooted in principles of denunciation, deterrence, and incapacitation was averted. . . .

Second, Canada has lacked the enthusiasm of the United States and England (primarily since the 1990s) toward harsher sanctions. Indeed, the tough-on-crime movement adopted by the United States and England appears to have permeated and propelled a number of key players — the general public, the media, the politicians, and the judiciary — toward support for increased punitiveness. While the causal relationships among these groups are unclear, the introduction of more punitive practices and policies has gone largely unchallenged in these countries. Indeed, politicians from the two main political parties in the United States and England have positioned themselves as tough on crime, neither wanting to be associated with "softer" responses. Similarly, judges — either voluntarily or through increasingly punitive sentencing guidelines — have begun showing a greater propensity to send more people to prison and for longer periods of time. Coupled with the "institutionalization" of the experience of crime through the mass media and an increasingly punitive public mood, these countries have lacked powerful inhibiting forces that would challenge or moderate punitive enthusiasm.

In contrast, the tough-on-crime movement has not caught on to the same extent within the Canadian imagination. While the media and the general public have not been immune to calls for tougher policies and practices, recent research shows that most Canadians do not strongly support "get tough" strategies as a solution to crime (Public Safety and Emergency Preparedness Canada 2001). More important, the government and the opposition rarely make crime issues a central part of their political platform. Rather, the role of the governing party tends to be one of quiet acceptance of a more balanced response to crime. As an illustration, the federal ministry responsible for federal penitentiaries recently concluded on its official Web site that

> [m]ost Canadians feel safe in their communities. Conveying these findings to the public is important to counter-balance media portrayals of crime as a pervasive problem. Compared to other issues, the majority of Canadians do not view crime as a priority issue for the government. This information is helpful in ensuring that the government's response to the crime problem is kept in perspective (Public Safety and Emergency Preparedness Canada 2001:2). Canadian judges have also demonstrated a lack of enthusiasm for more punitive responses to crime. Despite legislative freedom to increase the punitiveness of sentences, there was no notable change in the proportion of convicted cases sentenced to prison or in the overall mean prison sentence length handed down over the most recent 10-year period of available national data, from 1994-1995 to 2003-2004. Further, court decisions — like legislation more generally — have resisted many of the exclusionary practices adopted by other countries toward offenders. . . .

Canada's response to issues of race and sentencing also differs from that of the Americans. In the United States, the "war on drugs" arguably reflected a period of intolerance toward African Americans who were labeled as "bad people" — a view rooted in the individual rather than in social forces that may have produced the original criminal behavior. While Canada — and its justice system — have certainly not been immune to racist attitudes, with disadvantaged groups such as African Americans and Aboriginal Canadians continuing to be overrepresented in Canada's prisons (*Report of the Commission on Systemic Racism in the Ontario Criminal Justice System* 1995), its response — at least in terms of its expression through laws related to imprisonment — has clearly been different. Indeed, the government of Canada has attempted, through targeted legislation, to *reduce* the incarceration level of its most disadvantaged and imprisoned group: Aboriginal Canadians. In particular, a sentencing principle was included in the 1996 Criminal Code amendments requiring that "[a]ll available sanctions other than imprisonment that are reasonable in the circumstances should be considered for all offenders, with particular attention to the circumstances of aboriginal offenders" (Section 718.2[e]). Further, the constitutionality of this section was challenged and upheld by the Supreme Court of Canada (*R. v. Gladue*, 1 S.C.R. 688 [1999]). [See Chapter 9] In fact, specialized courts in some locations deal exclusively with Aboriginal people in an attempt to give meaning to this provision.

## HISTORICAL PROTECTIVE FACTORS

In striking contrast with the United States and England, Canada has shown deep skepticism about imprisonment as an appropriate response to crime.

Canada's caution in the use of imprisonment was written into legislation in 1996. Section 718.2 of Canada's Criminal Code states that "[a]n offender should not be deprived of liberty, if less restrictive sanctions may be appropriate in the circumstances," and "All available sanctions other than imprisonment that are reasonable in the circumstances should be considered for all offenders. . . ."

However, these statements constitute only part of a long history of recognition by the government and government-appointed commissions of the overuse of incarceration. . . . [The omitted paragraphs contain references to various government committees, commissions, and policy papers all of which took strong positions in favor of non-prison alternatives and a smaller inmate population.]

[T]here is no empirical evidence demonstrating any appreciable *reduction* in Canadian incarceration rates since 1960. Rather, this official culture of restraint would seem to be important in protecting Canada from some of the broader forces that have propelled other nations toward more punitive policies. Certainly in comparison with the United States or England, the simple maintenance of the status quo in imprisonment rates may be seen as an accomplishment.

## STRUCTURAL-POLITICAL PROTECTIVE FACTORS

This politicization of crime policy has been identified as a powerful force in the trend toward more punitive approaches to criminal behavior. Hence, it is noteworthy that Canada has largely escaped this phenomenon. . . .

Unlike England with its unitary criminal justice jurisdiction and the United States with its 51 separate criminal justice jurisdictions, the Canadian federal government is responsible for criminal law while the provinces have responsibility for the administration of criminal justice. Therefore, Canadian provincial governments have no direct power to modify the criminal law despite the fact that they play the largest role in the administration of justice. This distinction is crucial in creating and maintaining a two-tiered political structure that distances the federal government—with the power to increase punitiveness within the criminal justice realm—from provincial and public demands.

Indeed, provincial governments, which tend to be susceptible to populist punitive talk, have no legislative power over sentencing. The federal government appoints all appeals court judges. Hence, no structural mechanism is available for local (grassroots) citizens' groups to create laws that have a direct impact on imprisonment policies, as has been the case in some U.S. states (e.g., California's three-strikes legislation). . . .

This division of responsibility between the federal and provincial/ territorial governments also ensures that changes to the criminal law require extensive consultation between the two "partners." . . . Not surprisingly, this process is typically time-consuming, virtually (albeit not entirely) eliminating the possibility of introducing quick-fix, politically motivated legislation in response to unusual circumstances that arise from isolated cases. . . .

Beyond these structural benefits of the two-tiered political system whereby the federal government is both insulated from public petitions for harsher sentences and strategically positioned to moderate provincial demands, many of the key players in the decisionmaking processes involving criminal justice issues also have the advantage of being insulated—to some degree—from swings in public opinion. Potentially most important is the fact that Canadian judges are appointed rather than elected, with no need for them to be confirmed or examined by any formal process. . . .

Further, criminal justice reforms in Canada are typically written by non-elected bureaucrats, civil servants, and nongovernmental experts—not politicians—who are less susceptible to public pressure, as they almost always remain in their positions independent of changes in government. Unlike citizens of the United States and England, Tonry notes that Canadians continue to demonstrate considerable confidence "in both the appropriateness and the competence of professionals to determine policy," entrusting these nonpartisan, non-elected authorities with significant power to guide criminal justice policy in Canada. Indeed, while the Minister of Justice and the federal cabinet ultimately determine any modifications of criminal law introduced into Parliament, specialists tend to define the need for changes, the nature of those changes, and the specific means of accomplishing them. . . .

In contrast with the American and English power struggles during the 1990s between sentencing judges on the one hand and governments and prosecutors on the other, sentencing power has always remained firmly in the hands of Canadian judges. Even when the Canadian Sentencing Commission recommended that the government of Canada adopt a system of very permissive presumptive guidelines that would be established by a permanent sentencing commission and confirmed by Parliament, the proposal was rejected—in part because guidelines of any kind were seen as a radical departure from traditional policy. Indeed, despite the fact that these presumptive guidelines would have left enormous power to sentence with the sentencing judge in particular, and with judges (including appeals judges) more generally, the historically entrenched model in which judges are given almost complete responsibility for sentencing prevailed. . . .

### PROTECTIVE FACTORS: CULTURAL VALUES

. . . . Canadians appear to lack the moral taste for harshness—on an individual level—and faith—at the political level—regarding the effectiveness of more-punitive sanctions in solving the crime problem.

Unlike Canada, the United States and England (since the 1990s) have shown a belief in the possibility of legislating away the crime problem. The history of crime control in the United States reflects characteristically American optimism in the ability of the state to reduce crime rates through sentencing. Whether the solution resides in the belief that rehabilitation works or — more currently — that deterrence and incapacitation are effective in solving crime, the United States has been continually lured by the utilitarian purposes of sentencing. . . .

In contrast, Canadian politicians have shown skepticism about the effectiveness of criminal punishment in reducing criminal activity. The federal government's 1982 policy statement sets the tone of Canadian political culture related to sentencing by affirming that "[i]t is now generally agreed that the [criminal justice] system cannot realistically be expected to eliminate or even significantly reduce crime . . ." (Government of Canada 1982:28). . . .

This rejection of the "punishment stops crime" argument was reiterated a decade later in the political realm. The Canadian Minister of Justice affirmed publicly that just as "war is too important to be left to the generals . . . [c]rime prevention is too important to be left to the lawyers, or the justice ministers, or even the judges. . . . In the final analysis, crime prevention has as much to do with the [Minister of] . . . Finance, [the Minister of] . . . Industry, and [the Minister of] . . . Human Resources Development, as it does with [the Minister of] Justice" (Rock 1996:191-2). While this message has not always been expressed in such clear terms — as Canadian politicians have always had highly developed abilities to support both sides of a criminal justice policy issue — the lack of general endorsement from politicians of the notion that judges are well-placed to solve the problem of crime seems to have ensured ambivalence within Canadian political culture vis-à-vis tough-on-crime measures. . . .

Indeed, some have suggested that Canadian identity is often constructed in opposition to its American neighbor. . . . Many Canadian policy makers have shown a desire to shun an Americanized approach to criminal justice. In particular, Canada has been especially vocal in its rejection of U.S. imprisonment policies and practices. As a Conservative-dominated 1993 Parliamentary committee noted, "[i]f locking up those who violate the law contributed to safer societies, then the United States should be the safest country in the world. In fact, the United States affords a glaring example of the limited impact that criminal justice responses may have on crime" (Standing Committee on Justice and the Solicitor General 1993:2). . . .

## *Incarceration Rates Across the World,* *Andre Kuhn* **10 Overcrowded Times, no. 2 (April 1999)**

[The number of prison inmates per 100,000 inhabitants in different countries] varies today from about 20 in Indonesia to about 685 in the Russian Federation. In Western Europe it varies between 35 (Cyprus) and 145 (Portugal) and in the United States there were at midyear 1998 about 668 inmates per 100,000 population. [This] article tries to show national trends in prison population rather than to analyze differences between countries. A number of generalizations emerge from examination of penal patterns in the countries discussed. First, though crime rates increased substantially in most industrialized countries in the 1970s and 1980s, there is no standard of incarceration rate patterns. Finland and Japan have experienced declining rates for several decades, the U.S. has experienced unbroken increases since 1973, and other countries' patterns vary between those extremes. Second, . . . prison population trends are powerfully shaped by countries' cultures and histories and by contemporary politics and ideologies; whether imprisonment-use changes inevitably must follow or can themselves lead penal attitudes, remains to be seen.

The Netherlands illustrates the recent increase in incarceration rates in many European countries. Although the Netherlands is well known for its low incarceration rate, its prison population increased from 28 prisoners per 100,000 population in 1983 to about 74 in 1997, an increase of 164 percent. The increase is attributable largely to longer sentences for sentenced offenders rather than to growth in the numbers of sentenced or pretrial inmates.

[The] Swiss incarceration rate fell by half between the 1930s and 1980s, suggesting that the contemporary criminal justice system is less severe than formerly. Between 1982 and 1997, however, the average length of sentences increased by 132 percent, from 74 to 172 days, while the median term increased by only 50 percent, from 28 to 42 days. This suggests that [most] sentences stayed short but that longer ones became substantially longer.

[In Italy between] 1991 and 1997, the total incarceration rate increased significantly, from 56 to 86 per 100,000. This seems to be an effect of illegal Albanian immigration, enlargement of the anti-Mafia fight after the assassination of judges, and anticorruption operations led by the magistrates. . . .

Between 1983 and 1991, the German incarceration rate fell significantly from 93.3 to 69.2 per 100,000. This phenomenon has not been fully explained by criminal policy specialists, although it may be attributable, in part, to change in judges' and prosecutors' attitudes. Nonetheless, . . . the German incarceration rate increased between 1990 and 1997 by 15.7 percent [to reach] ninety prisoners per 100,000 inhabitants. This remains, however, below the 1983 level. . . .

Finland, unlike any other European country discussed here, has long had a decreasing incarceration rate. . . . Twenty years ago, the Finnish incarceration rate was one of the highest in Europe. Today, with about 60 inmates per 100,000 population, Finland has one of the lowest. . . . Finland has moved gradually toward a criminal justice system based on general prevention, which holds that it is important that criminals are caught and punished, but that the severity of the sanction is, in comparison, a minor issue. The Finnish criminal justice system therefore emphasizes the *certainty* of the sanction rather than its *severity*. That philosophy, according to which it is not useful to sentence an offender to several months of deprivation of liberty if several weeks will equally effectively demonstrate society's condemnation, has affected incarceration rates.

[Japan] has experienced decreasing incarceration rates since 1950 and has one of the lowest incarceration rates (37 per 100,000 in 1995) among the industrialized countries. . . . Notions of a hierarchical social order remain important in Japan today: knowing one's place in the societal scheme, fulfilling the Confucian obligations that the ruler be benevolent and the ruled be obedient, and holding the respect of others by maintaining social harmony, even at the expense of self-interest, remain widely held norms. The law breaker is expected to be repentant and to undertake self correction. It is therefore understandable that the criminal justice system is "lenient" toward offenders who express repentance and show willingness and capacity for self correction. Legal standards and procedures permit diversion extensively of defendants from trials and suspended prison sentences. . . . Japan decreased its prison population principally by reducing the number of entries into prison from 64,112 in 1951 to 31,122 in 1989. The incarceration rate dropped despite growth in the mean length of sentence from 17.5 months in 1970 to 20.9 months in 1990 and despite a rising crime rate. . . .

The differences [in incarceration rates] between Europe and the United States are largely ideological. Americans tend to accept the proposition that human beings are possessed of free will and are capable of making rational choices. They are generally receptive to the idea that people succeed or fail as a result of their own initiative. That ideology views crimes as the moral failure of individuals who freely elect to commit crimes, and who can therefore be held to account for their behavior. In this light, punishment ought to be designed to increase the costs of crime to such an extent that rationally acting individuals will no longer have incentives to commit crimes. Europeans more often view human behavior as more than just a function of free will. Human behavior is influenced by social circumstances such as education, peer relationships, and many other variables. All are important factors in the progression of events that lead to crime. Viewing crime as the product of both social and individual circumstances inclines Europeans more readily to accept responses to crime that include rehabilitative measures. That reflects the moral understanding that if individuals cannot be held solely responsible for what they become and what they do, society has an obligation to try to correct the influences or the conditions which may have led an individual into crime.

## NOTES

1.*Imprisonment rates abroad.*   Imprisonment rates in the United States are on average much higher than those in most other industrialized countries. There is some question as to whether that difference derives from shorter prison terms in other countries or a lower rate of imprisonment or some combination of the two. Transnational Institute, Systems Overload: Drug Laws and Prisons in Latin America (Mar. 2011), available at www.wola.org/sites/default/files/downloadable/Drug%20Policy/2011/TNIWOLA-Systems_Overload-def.pdf (focusing on increasing severity of drug sanctions as source of overcrowding in Latin American prisons); Sheryl Van Horne & Graham Farrell, Drug Offenders in the Global Criminal Justice System (European Institute for Crime Prevention and Control affiliated with the United Nations, HEUNI Paper No. 13, 1999, available at www.heuni.fi/uploads/jh0bv0x.pdf) (larger number of drug prosecutions rather than severity of drug sentences is the primary contributor to the difference between United States and Western Europe); Michael Tonry, Prisons and Imprisonment, in 18 International Encyclopedia of the Social and Behavioral Sciences 12,062 (2001). Do any of the differences in prison trends in industrialized nations surprise you? Are you convinced by the explanation provide by Doob and Webster for the striking difference in imprisonment rates in Canada compared with the United States — in the face of similar crime trends? In the end does the Canadian story undermine or reinforce the theory of exceptionalism (unique circumstances) for the United States? For Canada? Are you surprised to hear that the current Canadian government has moved to expand the list of offenses that carry mandatory minimum sentences, largely in light of public fear about crime despite a low crime rate? Looking farther abroad, can you explain why imprisonment rates in Finland fell over time while rates in Italy increased? For more detailed accounts of the evolution of sentencing policies in other nations, see Michael Tonry & Richard Frase, Sentencing and Sanctions in Western Countries (2001); James Q. Whitman, Harsh Justice: Criminal Punishment and the Widening Divide Between America and Europe (2003).

Might the difference in the imprisonment rates be related to a differing understanding of "evil"? At least one commentator charges that the United States is too facile in who it labels truly evil and tends to categorize those whose crimes may be due as much to deprivation or passion with those few who are evil. On the other hand, he argues that the German system in its denial of the existence of true evil goes too far and therefore begins to develop fictions that allow for lifelong imprisonment without acknowledging the evil character of the crime committed and of the offender. Joshua Kleinfeld, The Concept of Evil in American and German Criminal Punishment, available at papers.ssrn.com/sol3/papers.cfm?abstract_id=1667093.

2. *An imaginary future.*   Imagine a world without prison. Such a world did exist, and in historical perspective it was not so long ago — only a few hundred years. The Norval Morris passage reprinted above appears as part of a larger effort to consider whether modern society could get along without prisons. Could such a world be established again today? What would it look like? Cf. John Braithwaite, A Future Where Punishment Is Marginalized: Realistic or Utopian?, 46 UCLA L. Rev. 1727 (1999).

### PROBLEM 7-1.   THE COMPANY WE KEEP

The Centre for Prison Studies at King's College, London, reports that as of late 2010 the United States boasts the highest imprisonment rates in the world (reported at 730 per 100,000), followed by St Kitts–Nevis (649, estimated as of late 2011), the Seychelles (estimated at 641 as of mid-2012), the U.S. Virgin Islands (estimated at 539 as of early 2011), Rwanda (around 527 as of late 2011), Georgia (514 in mid-2012), Cuba (510 as of mid-2012), the Russian Federation (estimated at 498 as of 2012), Anguilla (UK) (480 as of fall 2011), the Virgin Islands (U.K.) (around 460), Belarus (438, estimated as of 2009), El Salvador (425 as of summer 2012), Bermuda (U.K.) (417 as of mid-2012), Azerbaijan and Belize (both at 407 as of September 2010 and summer 2012, respectively), and Grenada (402 as of February 2012). See Centre for Prison Studies, Entire world — Prison Population Rates per 100,000 of the national population. Current U.S. imprisonment rates appear to exceed rates from apartheid-era South Africa — 368 per 100,000 population in 1993 but 851 per 100,000 black males — the former Soviet Union, and China. Comparison of the imprisonment rate of black males between apartheid-era South Africa and the United States today makes the discrepancy even more stark. But are such comparisons useful? In what way may they be helpful in public and in legal discourse? In what way misleading?

## C.   COMPETING EXPLANATIONS FOR GROWTH

A massive change in practice such as the enormous increase in American incarceration rates over the last 30 years begs for some explanation. There is likely no single reason, but many criminologists, political scientists, and criminal law scholars have offered theories. The materials that follow begin with one of the more straightforward theories: prison rates go up as a rational governmental response to increases in crime (or increases in certain serious crimes). The later materials point out some difficulties in linking crime rates and imprisonment rates, and explain our increased use of prison as a product of our national politics and our social psyche.

> ### The Social Benefits of Confining Habitual Criminals, Kent Scheidegger and Michael Rushford
> #### 11 Stan. L. & Pol'y Rev. 59 (1999)

. . . The cycle of rising and dropping crime rates appears to correspond to the level of public and political resolve to aggressively capture and incapacitate criminal offenders. In periods when crime rates and public concern about crime have been relatively low, the premium on aggressive law enforcement appears to diminish, while programs attempting to socialize rather than punish offenders enjoy popularity in political and academic circles. Later, as crime rates and public concern about crime increase, such increases are accompanied by political pressure for a return to aggressive law enforcement and the incapacitation of criminals.

The simple truth is that imprisonment works. Locking up more criminals for longer periods reduces the level of crime. The benefits of doing so far offset the costs.

### THE CURRENT CYCLE

The national reduction in crime over the past eight years (1990-1998) is rooted in a crime policy cycle that began in the mid-1970s, with the public's response to a doubling of the rate of serious crimes between 1965 and 1975. The initial indicators in California, which played a leading role in this cycle, included a ballot initiative to reinstate capital punishment in 1972, the Legislature's adoption of the "Use a Gun, Go to Prison" law in 1975, the override of the Governor's veto of another death penalty law in 1977, and the adoption of strict sentencing increases for habitual criminals as part of the "Victims' Bill of Rights" initiative in 1982.

The sentence increases in the 1982 initiative represented a major statewide policy shift toward lengthened incarceration of habitual felons. In accordance with the new law, a California judge could sentence a convicted felon to an additional five years in prison for each prior felony conviction. A 1995 study led by Berkeley law professor Franklin Zimring, a well-known opponent of tough sentencing, credited increased incarceration with a marked drop in burglary and larceny crimes between 1980 and 1991, but found the evidence more ambiguous for violent offenses. . . .

In the early 1990s, several states began to adopt sentence increases for habitual criminals. . . . California's "Three Strikes and You're Out" law . . . provid[ed for] increased sentences for all repeat felons and a top term of 25 years to life for those convicted of any felony if they had two prior convictions for violent or serious felonies. While California's earlier sentencing and procedural reforms corresponded with a 10 percent reduction in the crime rate between 1991 and 1994, after adoption of the Three Strikes in 1994 the crime rate plummeted over 21 percent during the next 3 years. . . .

During the 15-year period between 1982 and 1997, as the state more than tripled its prison commitment rate with a focus on incarcerating habitual felons, the number of California victims of serious crime dropped from 4,777.1 per 100,000 in 1982 to 2,381.4 per 100,000 in 1997, less than half the previous figure. . . . The increase of young males in the population may well have contributed to the growth in the rate of incarceration, especially over the past 7 years, but it appears that the correct criminal justice policies were in place to prevent the predicted rise in crime.

### COMMON SENSE AND EMPIRICAL EVIDENCE

The idea that increased incarceration of criminals will reduce the rate of crime has two bases in common sense. First, incentives matter. When the incentives to engage in or refrain from a particular behavior change, the number of people who choose to engage in that behavior also changes. In criminology, this effect is called deterrence. Second, the crime rate is determined by the number of criminals, not by the availability of victims, and removing a criminal from the street to prison prevents him from committing crimes against the general public. Reducing crime by direct restraint is called incapacitation.

The anti-incarceration hypothesis that neither effect is significant, i.e., that prison neither deters nor incapacitates, is extremely difficult to swallow. There will always be some people who cannot be deterred because they act without thinking. There will always be some who do not need to be deterred because their character and conscience would prevent them from committing crimes even if they could do so with impunity. Between the wild beasts and the saints, though, there will always be a large segment of the population that refrains from crime out of fear of the consequences, i.e., that is deterrable, and the size of that segment naturally depends on the severity of the consequences. For incapacitation, the often-heard notion that if we incarcerate one criminal another will take his place assumes that there are a fixed number of places. This assumption makes no sense. As high as the rates of burglary and robbery are, there are still far more targets than crimes each year.

The anti-incarceration hypothesis is so strongly contrary to common sense that it would take powerful empirical evidence to support it. In fact, there is substantial empirical reason to believe that imprisonment works.

For an initial, admittedly simplistic overview, Figure 1 plots incarceration versus crime. The solid line represents the FBI crime index per 100,000 population. The dotted line represents prisoners in custody per 1000 index crimes. As imprisonment fell sharply in the 1960s, the crime rate more than doubled. As imprisonment remained low in the 1970s, the crime rate continued its rise. As imprisonment rose in the 1980s, the crime rate fluctuated, dropping in the early part of the decade then rising during the crack epidemic of 1985-1990. Finally, as imprisonment rose sharply in the 1990s, the crime rate went steadily down, although the rate still remains far above where it was in 1960.

These time-line data provide an indication, but not proof. There is a possibility that other changes occurring in society could account for the crime rate changes. The claim is often made, for example, that the sharp increase in crime in the 1960s was due primarily, if not entirely, to the young males of the "baby boom" reaching their peak crime-prone years. There can be no doubt that punishment is only one of many factors affecting crime rates. The simple time-line data need to be confirmed by other methods that control, at least partially, for these other variables. . . .

A more sophisticated cross-jurisdictional comparison was done by University of Chicago economist Steven Levitt. See Steven D. Levitt, The Effect of Prison Population Size on Crime Rates: Evidence from Prison Overcrowding Litigation, 109 Q. J. Econ. 319 (1996). Levitt grappled with the problem of separating cause from effect in the connection between crime rates and incarceration rates. "Increased incarceration is likely to reduce the amount of crime, but there is also little question that increases in crime will translate into larger prison populations." This creates a measurement problem called "simultaneity bias." To control this effect, Levitt compared states where statewide prison overcrowding litigation had capped the use of incarceration with states not subject to such caps.

Levitt found that an adverse decision in prison overcrowding litigation slowed the growth of the prison population by 13.7-19.7 percent. This caused an increase in violent crime of 7.9-8.3 percent, and an increase in property crime of 5.7-6.2 percent. Applying the rates derived from this study to the 272 percent increase in per capita incarceration in the United States from 1971 to 1993, Levitt concluded that violent crime would be 70 percent higher and property crime would be 50 percent higher without that increase. . . .

### COSTS AND BENEFITS

Is the benefit of reducing crime through tough sentencing worth the cost? The answer, we believe, is quite clearly yes. In 1994, during the debate over

Three Strikes, RAND Corporation produced a study predicting a 22-34 percent reduction in crime at a cost of $4.5-6.5 billion. The law appears to have a much lower cost than predicted.

RAND's cost figures were based on prison population projections showing, for example, about 250,000 prisoners by 1999 under Three Strikes, compared with about 120,000 under prior law. The actual prison population at present is 159,706, closer to RAND's "prior law" figure than its Three Strikes figure. In part, the lower cost is the result of court decisions implementing Three Strikes less severely than RAND anticipated. It is also likely, though, that tougher sentencing is simply more effective than anticipated at bringing down the crime rate and thus reducing the number of repeat felons who need to be imprisoned. RAND's projections were based on an assumption of a zero deterrent effect, a highly doubtful assumption. . . .

Tough sentencing is effective and economically efficient. We can and should investigate crime prevention and operate pilot programs to find out what works on the front end of criminal careers. We should not, however, turn career criminals loose on the streets to prey upon innocent people.

## Why Are U.S. Incarceration Rates So High?, Michael Tonry
### 45 Crime & Delinq. 419 (1999)

American imprisonment rates, 668 per 100,000 residents behind bars in mid-1998, have reached unprecedented levels compared with other times in United States history or with current times in other Western democracies. . . . Only in the United States are prison sentences longer than 1 or 2 years common; in most countries, fewer than 5 percent of sentences are for a year or longer. In the United States, in 1994, the average sentence among people sent to state prisons for felonies was 71 months. Among those in prison, more than half were serving terms exceeding 10 years.

All of this is a drastic change from earlier times. In the 1930s, for example, the United States had incarceration rates comparable to or lower than European countries such as England, France, Switzerland, and Finland. More recently, in the 1960s, the United States was in the mainstream. The death penalty was withering away, the incarceration rate was dropping and comparable to those in other Western countries, the courts were establishing and refining defendants' procedural protections, and crime control was not generally viewed as a partisan or ideological issue.

Now, of course, the United States is unique. The aim of this article is to offer and assess alternate explanations for why American policies have diverged so far from our own past practices and from the practices of other Western countries. . . .

### CRUDE EMPIRICISM

The first explanation for why so many Americans are in prison, that our crime rates are higher or faster rising than other countries', has virtually no validity. Crime rates in the United States in the 1990s are, for the most part, no higher than in other Western countries. . . . For property crimes, the United States is in the middle of the pack. Chances of being burglarized, having your pocket picked, or having your car stolen are considerably higher in England and several other European countries. For most violent crimes, American rates are among the highest, along with Australia, Canada, Spain, and France, but not the highest. Chances of being robbed, being assaulted, or being a victim of a stranger rape are higher in several other Western countries.

[Trends] in American imprisonment, homicide, and violent crime rates from 1960 to 1993 . . . suggest that violent crime and imprisonment at least initially rose together (more recently, however, imprisonment rates have continued their steep climb whereas violence rates have dropped sharply). However, . . . data for Finland and Germany during the same period indicate that there is no [necessary connection between crime rates and imprisonment rates]. Although the homicide and violent crime curves in Finland and Germany rose as steeply as the U.S. curves . . . the imprisonment rate in Germany fell throughout the 1960s and remained roughly level thereafter, and the incarceration rate in Finland fell sharply and steadily throughout the entire period. The reasons for those two countries' patterns are somewhat different, but the important point is that they reflect policy decisions that are based on the belief that increased incarceration is neither an appropriate nor an effective response to rising crime rates. American politicians decided otherwise. American imprisonment rates did not rise simply because crime rates rose. They rose because American politicians wanted them to rise.

Something was not working, and deterrence and incapacitation were chosen as strategies to lower crime rates. The only problem with this is that the most drastic such strategies were adopted long after crime rates began to fall. [Crime] rates for most crimes peaked around 1980, fell through the mid-1980s, rose for awhile for reasons largely associated with the crack cocaine epidemic, and have since fallen sharply. However, the first three-strikes law was enacted in 1993, and the federal truth-in-sentencing law, which authorized $8 billion for state prison construction, was passed in 1994. The meanings of these data are complex, but whatever else they show, they do not show any simple interaction between crime trends and imprisonment patterns.

### PUBLIC OPINION

The second explanation for the high imprisonment rate is that public opinion survey results sometimes show that crime and drugs come in first as America's most pressing problem, that large majorities often express the view that sentencing is too lenient, and that people demand that criminal punishment be made tougher. On this account, elected officials have merely respected the public will, and imprisonment rates have risen as a result.

There are two serious deficiencies in this story. [First,] ordinary citizens base their opinions on what they know about crime from the mass media. Consequently, they regard heinous crimes and bizarre sentences as the norms, they believe sentences are much softer than they are, and they believe crime rates are rising when they are falling. As a result, majorities nearly always report that judges' sentences are too lenient; yet, when they are asked to propose sentences appropriate for individual cases, they generally propose sentences that are shorter than those actually imposed. . . .

The second point is more important. Public nomination of crime as the nation's most pressing problem and public support for harsh laws typically follow, not precede, media and political preoccupation with crime. Although politicians who attempt to win favor by demonstrating their toughness nearly always say that they are honoring citizens' wishes, the evidence is that harping by politicians and the media on crime issues is what causes citizens to become concerned. . . .

### PARTISAN POLITICS

Crime and punishment have been high on American political agendas since the late 1960s. Before Republican presidential candidate Barry Goldwater raised crime in the streets as a partisan issue in his unsuccessful 1964 campaign, public safety was generally seen as one among several important, but unglamorous, core functions of government, like public health, public transit, and public education. Public officials were expected to do their work conscientiously and well. . . . Reasonable people differed over the best approaches for addressing particular problems, but the debates were seldom partisan or ideological. Criminal justice policy was a subject for practitioners and technocrats, and sentencing was the specialized case-by-case business of judges and corrections officials.

In recent decades, however, crime control has been at the center of partisan politics, and policies have been shaped more by symbols and rhetoric than by substance and knowledge. [During the 1960s, a fissure developed] within the Democratic Party between racial and social policy liberals and racial and social policy conservatives. This occurred initially in the South, and eventually nationwide. Republican strategists seized the opportunity to appeal to Nixon (later Reagan) Democrats by defining sharp differences between the parties on three wedge issues: crime control, welfare, and affirmative action. On crime control, conservatives blamed rising crime rates on lenient judges and soft punishments, and demanded toughness. . . .

Crime's role as a wedge issue has had important consequences. Issues that are debated on television and examined in 15- and 30-second commercials necessarily are presented in simplistic and emotional terms. Matters judges and prosecutors agonize over in individual cases are addressed in slogans and symbols, which often leads to the adoption of ham-fisted and poorly considered policies. Notable recent examples include widespread adoption of broadly defined three-strikes laws, mandatory minimum-sentence laws, sexual psychopath laws, and the federal sentencing guidelines. . . . When issues are defined in polar terms of morality and immorality, or responsibility and irresponsibility, few elected officials are prepared to be found at the wrong pole. . . .

What is needed is an explanation for why crime and punishment served so nicely as a wedge issue, and why so many elected officials were prepared, in recent decades, to behave in ways that their opponents and many observers often perceived as demagogic. [One such explanation] comes from the work of historian David Musto, which suggests that crime policies, political sensibilities, and the nature of public attitudes about crime are determined by cyclical trends in criminality and responses to it. David Musto, The American Disease: Origins of Narcotic Control (1987).

### HISTORICAL CYCLES

Historians have long known that crime rates rise and fall over extended periods for reasons that have little to do with crime control policies. The three most influential scholars of the subject — historian Roger Lane and political scientists Ted Robert Gurr and James Q. Wilson — concur in the view that crime rates in the United States, England, Germany, France, and other Western countries have followed a U-shaped or a backwards J-shaped curve, falling from the second quarter of the nineteenth century through the middle of the twentieth century and rising until late in the twentieth century. . . .

More recently, there is evidence that crime rates in Western countries may be in another long-term decline. In the United States, for example, data from the National Crime Victimization Survey show that rates for many crimes fell steadily from 1973 to the 1980s, after which, they increased or stabilized for a few years and resumed a downward path. Police data from the Federal Bureau of Investigation's Uniform Crime Reports show a somewhat different (but reconcilable) pattern of crime rates that rose through 1981, fell through 1986, rose again through 1991, and have plummeted since then to levels that, for some crimes, have not been seen since the 1960s. English, Dutch, Swedish, and Norwegian data likewise show significant victimization-rate declines in the 1990s. . . .

Yale historian David Musto has shown that antidrug policies interact in predictable ways with patterns of drug use. Seemingly perverse but, on reflection understandable, the harshest policies are adopted and the most vigorous prosecutions are carried out after drug use has begun to decline. In our era, for example, self-reported use of marijuana, heroin, and amphetamines peaked for every age group in 1979 to 1980 (for cocaine, in 1984 to 1985) and fell steadily thereafter, but the harshest federal antidrug laws were not enacted until 1986 and 1988, and the first federal drug czar was not named until 1989. If reduced drug use was its aim, the war was being won a decade before it was declared.

The reason all this is understandable is that recreational drug use during prohibitionistic periods is widely seen as immoral and socially destructive. Such attitudes explain why an increasing number of people stop using and experimenting with drugs and why, after drug use begins falling, comparatively few voices are raised in opposition to harsh policies. Few people, especially elected public officials, are comfortable speaking out on behalf of immorality. . . . In more tolerant periods, by contrast, many more people celebrate Enlightenment ideals of moral autonomy and individuals' rights to make choices about their own lives, and comfortably oppose harsh laws and policies on those grounds.

I mention the recurrent interaction between drug-use patterns and drug abuse policy because similar patterns may characterize interactions between contemporary crime patterns and crime-control policies. [The] harshest crime control policies—three-strikes laws; lengthy mandatory minimum sentence laws; truth-in-sentencing laws; and increased use of the death penalty—date from the early and mid-1990s, long after crime rates began their steep decline.

[Enhancing] people's predisposition to believe that harsh measures work, harsh laws are often enacted when crime rates are already falling. People who want to make year-to-year comparisons can easily show that the new, tougher policies have worked, because crime rates have fallen in the years immediately after the change when compared with the year immediately before. This happened in relation to New York City's adoption in the early 1990s of zero-tolerance policing, California's adoption in 1994 of a broadly defined three-strikes law, and many states' passage in the mid-1990s of truth-in-sentencing laws. These may be plausible claims on the part of people who are unaware of long-term crime trends, but for people who are, they are disingenuous. The year-to-year crime-rate declines are at least as likely merely to be a continuation of long-term trends as they are to be effects of policy changes. . . .

As a hypothesis, Musto's paradigm provides a richer account of American exceptionalism in the past quarter century than do any of the other accounts that I have attempted. It explains why public attitudes are harsher when crime rates are falling than when they are rising and, consequently, why law-and-order appeals fell on fertile electoral ground. It explains why politicians feel comfortable appealing to base instincts and proposing policies that, in other times, would have seemed demagogic and cruel. It explains not only why so few voices were raised in opposition to those policies but also why few people felt a need to speak out in opposition. It explains why people were inclined to believe that declining crime and drug-use rates showed that harsh policies worked. . . .

America's unprecedented and unmatched taste for imprisonment and harsh criminal justice policies has little to do with them—the offenders who get dealt with one way or another—and everything to do with us. If we took the historical lessons to heart, we might be less quick to adopt harsh crime policies. . . .

## NOTES

1. *Crime control through deterrence.*   The most straightforward way to explain why U.S. legal systems rely so heavily on prison relates to crime control. Prison, the argument goes, both deters crimes and incapacitates criminals better than the alternatives, so the heavy use of prison in the United States is a rational effort to reduce crime. There are powerful theoretical reasons to believe that at least some use of prison can deter crime. For instance, one could analogize potential criminals to rational economic actors, who weigh the benefits of crime against the likelihood of conviction and the severity of the punishment. Longer prison terms, in this model, increase the cost of crime and encourage more people to avoid it. See Gary S. Becker, Crime and Punishment: An Economic Approach, 76 J. Pol. Econ. 169 (1968).

The difficulty arises in the gap between theory and experience. While many agree that at least some use of prison deters crime, there is intense debate over whether marginal increases in the use of prison translate into marginal increases in deterrence. See David S. Lee & Justin McCrary, The Deterrence Effect of Prison: Dynamic Theory and Evidence (July 2009), available at www.princeton.edu/ceps/workingpapers/189lee.pdf (deterrent effect of imprisonment is very limited, at least for those around 18); Cassia Spohn & David Holleran, The Effect of Imprisonment on Recidivism Rates of Felony Offenders: A Focus on Drug Offenders, 40 Criminology 329 (2002) (comparison of drug offenders in Missouri sentenced to prison and probation; prison increases rather than reduces likelihood of recidivism); Richard A. Wright, The Evidence in Favor of Prisons, in Crime and Criminals (Frank R. Scarpitti & Amiel Nelsen eds., 1999). What specific claims do Scheidegger and Rushford make about deterrence, and what specific evidence do they use? Does Tonry address their evidence?

2. *Crime control through incapacitation.*   There is no question that prison incapacitates some offenders from committing new crimes during their prison term. Given the number of career criminals and the short span of years that constitutes the criminal "career" for many offenders, it should be possible in theory to reduce crime through heavier use of prison. One practical difficulty is deciding how to target the offenders who are most likely to commit new crimes, a practice known as "selective incapacitation." See James Q. Wilson, Thinking About Crime 193-194 (1977); Shlomo Shinnar & Reuel Shinnar, The Effects of the Criminal Justice System on the Control of Crime: A Quantitative Approach, 9 Law & Soc'y Rev. 581 (1975). In limited circumstances such targeting might be successful, as lengthened sentences for repeat property offenders in the Netherlands showed. Ben Vollaard, Preventing crime through selective incapacitation (Jan. 2011), available at ssrn.com/abstract=1738900. Given the difficulty of predicting which offenders are the best targets, some argue for general incapacitation, claiming that higher levels of incapacitation will generally reduce crime even if we cannot know which offenders would have committed the extra crimes. Apart from the costs of this approach (both in human and in economic terms), it is doubtful that it works across all categories of crimes. For some crimes (perhaps narcotics sales), new criminals may simply step forward to fill the positions vacated by those sentenced to prison.

To some extent (long-term) incapacitation reflects resignation and abdication of confidence in rehabilitative measures. "The peculiar pattern of mid-1990s legislation was produced not because imprisonment for incapacitation had become the dominant method of crime control in America but because it had for the most part been recognized as the *only* method of controlling crime that fit the notion of persistent high-rate offenders." Franklin E. Zimring, The City That Became Safe 180 (2012). Some studies have indicated that prison growth has not been due to longer sentences but rather to increased admissions. Those, in turn, appear to be governed largely by prosecutorial decisions to file felony charges. John F. Pfaff, The Causes of Growth in Prison Admissions and Populations, available at papers.ssrn.com/sol3/papers.cfm?abstract_id=1990508 (posted Jan. 23, 2012); John F. Pfaff, The Myths and Realities of Correctional Severity: Evidence from the National Corrections Reporting Program on Sentencing Practices, 13

Am. L. & Econ. Rev. 491 (2011); John F. Pfaff, The Durability of Prison Populations, 2010 U. Chi. Legal F. 72 (2010).

New York City's dramatic drop in crime rates throughout the last two decades has confounded many researchers. While its precise causes are still subject to debate, they are not solely (if at all) tied to incapacitation but at least to some extent to policing measures. In 2007 the incarcerated population in New York City was smaller than in 1990, an especially startling number in light of the growth in prison population around the country in those years. Franklin E. Zimring, The City That Became Safe, Appendix B (2012). Some have argued that the wide availability of cell phones has been at least partially responsible for the drop in crime, as they facilitate crime reporting and detection of the offender. Other studies have indicated that the drop in leaded gasoline may have positively impacted brain development, which in turn affected crime rates.

3. *Economics and demographics.* We could also explain imprisonment rates not as a product of deliberate policy but as a natural outcome of a slowdown in the economy and a corresponding increase in crime. Similarly, demographics (such as the number of young males in the population at a given time) may drive levels of imprisonment. How would you go about testing these hypotheses? See Franklin E. Zimring & Gordon J. Hawkins, The Scale of Imprisonment 119-136 (1991) (reviewing potential explanations for prison rates in the United States, including crime rates, public opinion, demographics, economics, and drug use).

4. *Politics and public opinion.* Michael Tonry and others have argued that U.S. politics is uniquely pathological when it comes to crime. The political rhetoric in the United States has remained partisan and "tough on crime" for several generations. Some of it can be called "paranoid," often driven by intolerance and religious fundamentalism. The debate over crime has marginalized rehabilitation as a purpose of criminal sanctions and has suggested that prison is the only "real" sanction. What in particular about the U.S. political system produces these results? Sara Sun Beale traces the influence to the news media's focus on crime for purposes of attracting high ratings: the coverage affects public perceptions of the level of serious crime, and it shapes the political agenda that gets a positive response from the public. Sara Sun Beale, What's Law Got to Do with It? The Political, Social, Psychological and Other Non-legal Factors Influencing the Development of (Federal) Criminal Law, 1 Buff. Crim. L. Rev. 23 (1997). See also Katherine Beckett, Making Crime Pay: Law and Order in Contemporary American Politics (1997); Michael Tonry, Explanations of American punishment policies, 11 Punishment & Soc'y 377 (2009); Bert Useem, Raymond V. Liedka & Anne Morrison Piehl, Popular Support for the Prison Build-up, 5 Punishment & Soc'y 5 (2003) (finding that people supported prison built-up because of their concern about crime and belief that increased imprisonment would be responsive).

Inclusive decision-making structures and the involvement of criminal justice experts may also impact the rate of imprisonment. A study indicates that such "populist deliberative democracy" increases happiness, which enhances empathy. In turn such structures lead to less retributive, prison-focused sentencing strategies and greater acceptance of therapeutic and alternative models of sentencing. Andrew E. Taslitz, The Criminal Republic: Democratic Breakdown as a Cause of Mass Incarceration, 9 Ohio St. J. Crim. L. 133 (2011).

5. *Social control or social cohesion.*   Some accounts of prison look beyond the instrumental reasons such as deterrence or incapacitation and emphasize the prison's place in struggles among social groups or in creating social solidarity. Some of these "social control" arguments draw generally on Marxist theory. For instance, Georg Rusche and Otto Kirchheimer, in Punishment and Social Structure (1939), suggest that the demands of the labor market shape the penal system and determine its transformation over time. In years of high employment, prisons must shrink to provide more workers for society, while in years of lower employment, prisons expand to maintain control over the unemployed. Cf. Christian Parenti, Lockdown America: Police and Prisons in the Age of Crisis (1998). The recent American experience, however, provides little support for this theory. Social theorist Michel Foucault's famous work, Discipline and Punish: The Birth of the Prison (1977) (excerpted in Chapter 1), describes the prison as one among many tools used in modern societies to exert more minute control over the human body as a way of making the masses more useful and docile.

The fact that many released offenders return to prison regularly either because of parole violations or the commission of new offenses may lend credence to the social control approach. In California, for example, the so-called "back-end sentencing," which occurs through parole board revocations, reflects the offenders' demographic status (gender and race/ethnicity) as well as the types of crimes committed. Prison overcrowding also contributes to the likelihood of re-imprisonment as does a community's political punitiveness under certain circumstances. Jeffrey Lin, Ryken Grattet & Joan Petersilia, "Back-end Sentencing" and Reimprisonment: Individual, Organizational, and Community Predictors of Parole Sanctioning Decisions, 48 Criminology 759 (2010).

"Social cohesion" theories, in contrast, stress the role of prison in creating agreement and shared ideologies across social groups rather than in controlling unruly social orders. Sociologist Émile Durkheim pointed to criminal law and punishment as a method of expressing and creating social consensus. As traditional communities give way to complex economic arrangements and societies that celebrate individual freedom, criminal law becomes an especially important source of social solidarity. See Émile Durkheim, The Division of Labor (1933); cf. Joseph Kennedy, Monstrous Offenders and the Search for Solidarity Through Modern Punishment, 51 Hastings L.J. 829 (2000). For an overview of the different perspectives that social theory brings to questions of punishment, see Jonathan Simon, Sanctioning Government: Explaining America's Severity Revolution, 56 U. Miami L. Rev. 217 (2001).

Earlier we considered social and political forces that could explain the remarkable growth in U.S. prisons over the past quarter-century. Now we examine the other side of the coin: what political forces or institutions might operate to *check* the growth of prisons?

One of those limiting forces might be money. Prisons are more expensive to build and operate than any other criminal sanction. In difficult economic times, as Marc Miller explains, budgetary considerations become especially powerful at the state and local levels of government:

> Criminal justice expenditures, and spending on corrections in particular, increasingly occupy a noticeable chunk of total state budgets. The growth of corrections budgets is so great that they have come to threaten other major

categories of government expenditure. In California, for example, the corrections budget equaled 85 percent of the higher education budget in 1994, and by 1995 corrections had surpassed higher education. (A few years earlier, in the late 1980s, corrections cost only one-half the total spent on higher education.) [State] governments spend almost all of their funds on a handful of areas — education, health and welfare, transportation, housing, and crime. When criminal justice expenditures go up, they compete with these other basic services, not with the purchase of aircraft carriers or with foreign aid.

[Policy] and budget changes are much harder to hide at the local government level. [The] smaller size of the budgets and political playing fields makes the budget [effect] more likely to be noticed for all budget expenditures. It is more likely that a county hospital or city clinic or board of education (in states where local funds support primary education) will feel that dollars put into corrections are dollars out of their pockets than will health care or educational representatives at state and federal levels. At higher levels of government, with bigger budgets and more abstract debates, a decision about prisons will rarely seem like a choice about schools or hospitals. At local levels, even modest proposed expenditures will be seen to compete with the full range of social services provided by local government. . . .

Marc Miller, Cells vs. Cops vs. Classrooms, in The Crime Conundrum 127 (Lawrence M. Friedman & George Fisher eds., 1997). The corrections budget alone may not capture the full cost of incarceration in many states as other state entities often fund part of the prison system. Those may include capital expenses, hospital care for inmates, and health care benefits and pensions for correctional staff. See Christian Henrichson & Ruth Delaney, Vera Institute of Justice, Center on Sentencing and Corrections, The Price of Prisons: What Incarceration Costs Taxpayers (updated July 20, 2012).

The following two statutes build on the observation that prison growth can be slowed if the relevant decision makers are forced to consider long-term budgets when making choices that would expand the use of prisons. Note the differences between the budgetary mechanisms at work in these two statutes. Can you devise similar strategies that might apply to other sentencing actors, such as judges or prosecutors? The subsequent statistical study by David Greenberg and Valerie West examines the larger political and social context to identify factors limiting prison growth.

## ‖ *North Carolina General Statutes* ‖
### *§120-36.7(d)*

Every bill and resolution introduced in the General Assembly proposing any change in the law that could cause a net increase in the length of time for which persons are incarcerated or the number of persons incarcerated, whether by increasing penalties for violating existing laws, by criminalizing behavior, or by any other means, shall have attached to it at the time of its consideration by the General Assembly a fiscal note prepared by the Fiscal Research Division. The fiscal note shall be prepared in consultation with the Sentencing Policy and Advisory Commission and shall identify and estimate, for the first five fiscal years the proposed change would be in effect, all costs of the proposed net increase in incarceration, including capital outlay costs if the legislation would require increased cell space. . . . No comment or opinion shall be included in the fiscal note with regard to the merits of the measure for which the note is prepared. . . .

The sponsor of each bill or resolution to which this subsection applies shall present a copy of the bill or resolution with the request for a fiscal note to the Fiscal Research Division. . . . The Fiscal Research Division shall prepare the fiscal note and transmit it to the sponsor within two weeks after the request is made, unless the sponsor agrees to an extension of time. . . .

## ‖ Kansas Statutes §74-9101(b) ‖

(1) . . . In developing its recommended sentencing guidelines, the [Kansas sentencing] commission shall take into substantial consideration current sentencing and release practices and correctional resources, including but not limited to the capacities of local and state correctional facilities. . . .

(6) [The commission shall] advise and consult with the secretary of corrections and members of the legislature in developing a mechanism to link guidelines sentence practices with correctional resources and policies, including but not limited to the capacities of local and state correctional facilities. Such linkage shall include a review and determination of the impact of the sentencing guidelines on the state's prison population. . . .

(15) [The commission shall] produce official inmate population projections annually on or before six weeks following the date of receipt of the data from the department of corrections. When the commission's projections indicate that the inmate population will exceed available prison capacity within two years of the date of the projection, the commission shall identify and analyze the impact of specific options for (A) reducing the number of prison admissions; or (B) adjusting sentence lengths for specific groups of offenders. . . .

## ‖ State Prison Populations and Their Growth, 1971-1991, David F. Greenberg and Valerie West ‖
### 39 Criminology 615 (2001)

. . . Between 1970 and midyear 2000, the federal and state imprisonment rate increased by a factor of almost five, from 98 per 100,000 to 476 per 100,000. These national figures disguise much variation among states in the rates of growth. In Oklahoma, for example, the imprisonment rate in 1981 was just 17% higher than it had been ten years earlier, whereas in Montana, it was 196% higher. . . .

Previous research on state differences in imprisonment rates . . . has focused on a small number of explanatory variables—state crime rates, racial composition, and economic conditions (unemployment or labor force participation, income level). . . . Our work extends the theoretical scope of this body of research by [examining] the importance of a state's culture and political arrangements to policy outcomes in a number of different domains, such as welfare. . . .

|| *Theorizing Imprisonment Rates* ||

[We expect] institutional responses to law violations to be determined at least in part by the volume of crime in that state, but only in part. We expect a state's responses to be conditioned by its ability to finance their cost, and by its political culture. The anxieties and fears that lead residents and politicians to support the expanded use of imprisonment can be heightened or moderated by factors other than crime. . . .

*Crime Rates.*   If imprisonment is a strategy for coping with crime, one would expect states with more crime to make more extensive use of imprisonment. We expect imprisonment to be more strongly related to violent crime than to property crime because violent crimes are considered more serious than are nonviolent crimes of acquisition. Defendants convicted of violent crimes are more likely to be sentenced to prison terms than are those convicted of stealing. Nevertheless, substantial numbers of prisoners are serving sentences for property offenses. . . . We thus consider the violent crime rate and the property crime rate as two measures of the "problem" to which the prison is supposedly a response. . . .

Drug law violations are expected to influence imprisonment rates because publicity about arrests contributes to public perceptions about the seriousness of crime as a social problem and thus influences public punitiveness. Drug arrestees also represent a caseload burden: if convicted, many drug arrestees will be sentenced to a term of imprisonment. . . .

*Fiscal Constraint.*   Prison construction and maintenance are expensive. Costs of prison construction have been estimated at $23,000 to $54,000 per bed, and operating costs from $9500 to $39,000 per prisoner each year. . . . Less affluent states may have to restrict spending on criminal justice in order to repair potholes, plant trees, pay teachers, and shelter the homeless. For this reason, we predict a positive relationship between imprisonment rates and the state's capacity to tax its citizens and business enterprises.

*Perceived Threat.*   Students of penality have argued that imprisonment can be a response to anxiety-provoking conditions other than crime. In particular, it may be targeted at "the dangerous classes" — populations perceived as threatening because of their economic circumstances, race, or ethnicity, independently of their involvement in crime. . . . We introduce the percentage of families below the poverty line as an alternative measure of the population that might be seen as having little to lose and who must, therefore, be dealt with through imprisonment.

The numerical overrepresentation of blacks in prison is high. Even though blacks make up about 12 percent of the population, slightly more than half of all new court commitments to prison are black, a rate that is approximately 6.5 times as high as that of whites. . . . By looking at the effect of a state's racial composition on the prison population controlling for crime rates, we should be able to clarify the relationship between race and imprisonment. . . .

*Cultural Influences.*    . . . Social structural theories of social control suggest that urbanized polities will make greater use of formal methods of control, such as courts and prisons, to make up for deficiencies in informal social control. The anonymity and heterogeneity of large urban populations linked by impersonal market transactions supposedly impair informal social control, leading to the compensatory strengthening of governmental control. Rural regions, on the other hand, are presumed to require less vigorous formal social control because they can rely on personal ties based on kinship and multiplex patterns of informal association. On this basis, one would expect imprisonment rates to be higher in states whose populations are highly urbanized. On the other hand, urban criminal courts may face especially heavy caseloads, necessitating more generous concessions in plea bargaining to induce guilty pleas. This should slow prison growth. Moreover, urban populations, exposed as they are to greater cultural diversity, should be more tolerant of rule breakers and, thus, less punitive. . . .

Historically, welfare benefits were instituted as alternatives to human institutions for poor and marginalized populations. . . . If imprisonment indeed reflects an exclusionary stance toward those who have broken the law, . . . it should be used with greater reluctance in those states that are relatively generous toward the poor by providing greater welfare benefits, [and] cuts in welfare should be accompanied by increases in imprisonment. . . .

*Political Factors.*    . . . We examine the influence of officeholders' party affiliation at the state level. We focus on the governor because it is the governor who prepares budgets, making decisions about prison construction that should ultimately impact on prison populations. It is also the governor who appoints parole board members. . . .

A number of policy analysts have attributed growth in prison populations to determinate sentencing legislation that severely restricts judicial discretion to impose a sentence and eliminates release on parole for prison inmates. [Ten] states adopted fixed sentencing legislation ending release on parole between the mid-1970s and mid-1980s. Because the adoption of determinate sentencing legislation was often accompanied by "get tough" rhetoric, one might expect that states with determinate sentencing legislation will have higher prison populations and experience more rapid growth in these rates. . . .

## METHODS AND RESULTS

[We used a statistical technique known as regression analysis to measure the impact of each of these variables on a state's imprisonment rate between 1971 and 1991. We used a second model to estimate the impact of these variables on the *changes* in rates of imprisonment that each state experienced during these two decades.]

Consistent with public choice theory, states with high violent crime rates have higher levels of imprisonment. An increase in the violent crime rate of 1 per 100,000 is associated with an increase of .12 per 100,000 in the imprisonment rate, whereas the increase associated with the property crime rate is smaller and not statistically significant. An increase in the narcotics arrest rate of 1 per 100,000 increases the imprisonment rate by about .11 per 100,000.

As expected, states with higher revenues have higher prison populations. Although economic inequality and urbanization are unrelated to imprisonment, there are more people in prison in states with higher unemployment rates and where there is a higher percentage of blacks in the population. Other things being equal, an increase in the unemployment rate of 5% corresponds to an imprisonment rate that is higher by about 16.5 per 100,000. A state with a population that is 10% black will have an imprisonment rate higher than that of a state that has no blacks by . . . 91 per 100,000, a substantial amount. The presence of Latinos, however, does not raise imprisonment rates. . . .

Several measures of a state's political culture are related to its imprisonment rate. States that are more generous with welfare payments had lower prison populations. An increase of $30 per person in welfare spending is associated with an imprisonment rate that is smaller by about 19 per 100,000. . . .

In states where there were more conservatives, imprisonment rates were not only higher, but also grew more rapidly. . . . If cultural differences are associated with the South, they did not contribute to high rates of imprisonment growth; quite the contrary, growth rates were significantly slower in the South than elsewhere, so that by 1991, regional disparities in imprisonment rates were substantially smaller than in 1971. In other words, in recent years regions outside the South have been catching up to the South in imprisonment. . . .

Contrary to popular opinion, the adoption of determinate sentencing legislation did not increase imprisonment rates; it moderately reduced them. The adoption of these laws may have helped to placate a punitive public, reducing pressure on state officials to impose harsh sentences. [Perhaps] these laws were carefully crafted to be largely symbolic and, in many states, had little effect because prosecutors and judges took steps to minimize their impact.

Some of the most striking findings concern state economic and demographic characteristics. Unemployment was associated with higher rates of prison population growth, as was change in unemployment. Economic inequality was not. Growth in imprisonment rates was also related to the size of the black population and its increase. It cannot be stressed too strongly that the coefficients for unemployment and race are direct effects, with crime rates controlled, and so they cannot be explained away by claims that crime rates are higher where there is more unemployment or where more blacks live.

Consistent with much research showing that party control of state government has little or no impact on state policy and is unrelated to the liberalism or conservatism of the state's voters, the political party of a state's governor failed to make a significant contribution to prison populations or their growth. It appears that the political incentives for an expansive prison policy transcend party affiliations. States governed by Democrats responded to the crime issue no differently from states governed by Republicans. . . .

Our results are equally consistent with the presence and absence of racial discrimination. [A] positive relationship between percent black in a state and the state's imprisonment rate could occur in the absence of racial discrimination. [At the same time, our] results are consistent with the "racial threat" hypothesis. Blacks — black males in particular — appear to have become "symbolic assailants" whose presence in a city evokes fear of crime independently of the actual level of crime. . . . That the presence of Latinos is not associated with imprisonment rate growth indicates that it is not minorities in general, but blacks in particular, who are perceived as threatening. Our results also point to unemployment as a separate, distinct source of threat or anxiety. . . . We think that welfare is important to imprisonment not because it directly restrains legislators, prosecutors, and judges; rather, we see the comparative leniency in high-welfare states as reflecting a more general policy of avoiding excessively harsh treatment of the poor, who make up the bulk of criminal court defendants. . . .

### NOTES

1.*Prisons and state budget cycles.*   Sentencing commissions are considered one of the most important institutions in state government to highlight the connection between corrections budgets and sentencing rules. According to a 2003 survey by the National Association of Sentencing Commissions, 12 of the 19 responding states gave their commissions responsibility to create impact statements for at least some criminal justice bills after their introduction in the state legislature. Note the distinction, however, between a commission advocating a smaller prison system and a commission advocating a fully funded prison system.

In 2009 the number of people held in state prisons had decreased for the first time in four decades. The small decline, however, did not occur across the entire country. An almost equal number of states witnessed an increase in prison inmates as saw a decline. The Pew Center on the States, Prison Count 2010: State Population Declines for the First Time in 38 Years (Apr. 1, 2010). This trend continued in 2011. E. Ann Carson & William J. Sabol, Bureau of Justice Statistics, Prisoners in 2011, NCJ 23988 (Dec. 2012).

The severe national economic downturn that started in 2008 forced nearly every state to find ways to reduce the growing fiscal costs of large prison systems and has prompted many states to enact or consider new sentencing rules designed to reduce these costs. A report from the Center on Sentencing and Corrections at the Vera Institute of Justice entitled "The Continuing Fiscal Crisis in Corrections: Rethinking Policies and Practices" (updated Oct. 2010) documented that the 2008 recession forced a majority of states to cut budgets in ways that impacted sentencing and prison policies and practices. Among policy changes are increased good-time and enhanced parole and early release mechanisms; the re-assessment of expensive approaches to prison management, such as segregation of nonviolent offenders, and a general increase in operational efficiencies; decriminalization or non-prosecution of select offenses and the abolition of mandatory minimum sentences; or diversion of offenders. How do these policy approaches differ with respect to the philosophy underlying them? What impact may they have on individual offenders and communities? In light of overall political ideologies, especially with respect to governmental power and expenditures, what arguments do you expect the two sides of the political spectrum to make as they come together to advocate for smaller prison budgets?

The federal system has not been impacted by budget cuts in the way the state systems have. As of 2009 the rate at which federal offenders were being sentenced to prison had increased substantially over time, perhaps in part due to the increase of non-citizen offenders on the federal docket.

2. *More on costs and benefits of prison.*   The balance between the costs and benefits of longer prison terms could shift if one considers as a benefit the crimes prevented through detention. Economists have employed statistical techniques to estimate the number of crimes prevented and the monetary value of the harm that would have occurred if those crimes had happened. See Edwin W. Zedlewski, Making Confinement Decisions (National Institute of Justice, Research in Brief, 1987); Joanna Mehlhop Shepherd, Police, Prosecutors, Criminals, and Determinate Sentencing: The Truth About Truth-in-Sentencing Laws, 45 J.L. & Econ. 509 (2002) (estimating that sentencing laws requiring violent offenders to serve at least 85% of their prison sentences decrease murders by 16%, aggravated assaults by 12%, robberies by 24%, rapes by 12%, and larcenies by 3%; however, violent offenders shift to property crimes, meaning that burglaries increase by 20% and auto thefts by 15%). What types of data are used to make estimates of these sorts? What uncertainties are involved in constructing the estimates?

## D.   THE HUMAN EXPERIENCE OF PRISON

Part of understanding the nature of prison is to recognize the size of the institution and its functions over the years. The statistics and trends we have discussed thus far address these aspects, but they miss the profound human experience of prison. The offenders who fill prisons in large numbers, for long periods of time, experience the daily routines, the boredom and restrictions of life in prison. Their families and communities may experience their absence — and their return — in different ways. The victims of their crimes may remain aware of their stay in prison and (sometimes) of the moment of their release. The officers who run the prisons work under extraordinarily tough conditions.

The law surrounding conditions in prison is complex and deserves far more attention than we can offer here. See Michael B. Mushlin, Rights of Prisoners (4th ed. 2009, last updated 2011). Instead, we aim for a more personal glimpse into prison life as a way to place the law of sentencing in context. In the following excerpt, Norval Morris presents a rewritten version of a diary, recording the mundane events in the day of an inmate, Sam Gutierrez, incarcerated in Stateville Prison in Illinois.

*The Contemporary Prison, 1965-Present,*
*Norval Morris*
**The Oxford History of the Prison: The Practice**
**of Punishment in Western Society**
**202, 203-211 (1998)**

. . . It is not easy to describe a day of monotony and boredom other than as monotonous and boring. Before I start on the diary, let me say this: if you expect the usual prison tale of constant violence, brutal guards, gang rapes, daily escape efforts, turmoil, and fearsome adventures, you will be deeply disappointed. . . .

6:00 A.M.:

. . . As F House came to life, the noise began — radios, TVs, shouting from cell to cell — and so it would go on till night, with an occasional scream of rage or fear through the night. Tyrone and I did our best to keep out of each other's way in the space of nine feet by six in our cell while we used our toilet and washed and dressed and pulled up the blankets on our steel bunks. We change our outer clothes sometimes twice a week, sometimes once a week, and our socks and underwear every other day. If you have money, or influence, or a friend in the laundry, you can do better than this. Our dress in summer is blue jeans and a blue shirt or a white T-shirt; in winter we wear blue jeans, a blue shirt, and one of those heavy, lined, blue jackets. Our sartorial flourish is our sneakers, with Nike outranking Reebok and so on down the line; they cost a lot, but in this place they are worth it. . . .

6:30 A.M.:

F House began to be unlocked, with the loudspeaker from the tower guards bellowing, "Three and four galleries: in the tunnel for chow." I turned off the radio and flipped the light switch at the back of the cell, on and off, on and off, the flickering light being my request to the tower guard to open the door to this cell, which he does. . . .

Food is served cafeteria style. We pick up our trays and wait in line. The food is either waiting in bowls for us to pick up, as we file by, or is served onto our plates by the kitchen detail. Knives and forks and spoons are of plastic, not particularly useful for making weapons, though they are sometimes smuggled back to the cells and narrowed and sharpened for this purpose. . . .

They serve meals here, three times a day, to over two thousand prisoners each meal, 365 times a year, on a twelve-day repeating menu. I calculate that this comes to more than two million meals a year. I suppose I should expect it to be dull and lifeless food — and it is. But guys mostly tend to put on weight in prison; I know I do. The meals are not light on carbohydrates. The cartons of milk cannot be spoiled by our prison cooks, and I usually manage to collect two of them with whatever else is handed to me. I did this today.

After you get your food you walk back to the seating area, metal tables with six metal seats fixed to them. You have to be careful where you sit; there are "regulars" who sit together and expect this to be known. And, of course, the blacks and Hispanics don't welcome a white guy joining their tables. The prison is more than 90 percent black and Hispanic, but this causes no great problem — the whites tend to congregate with one another in the mess hall and in the yard. . . .

8:30 A.M.:

[I went to the yard to] get a workout, bench-pressing some weights. . . . The yard is of playing-field size and of rounded, triangular shape, with a rough baseball diamond, with other areas of grass and of packed earth, surrounded by a running track and a fence. Some sparse outdoor gym equipment is in one corner. There are two telephones, protected a little from the weather by steel surrounds; a small line formed. Guys ran around the track or walked around in twos or small groups. Five or six of us worked out on the equipment.

The telephones here and in F House are monitored, and every few minutes a voice interrupts telling you and whomever you are speaking to that this is a call from a "state correctional facility." And the time you are allowed for any one call is limited, depending on whatever the prison authorities have arranged with the telephone company. Of course, only collect calls can be made, so that no one outside has to talk to a prisoner on the telephone, and this makes the telephone expensive for the person you are calling, particularly long-distance calls.

10:30 A.M.:

[I showered after my workout.] The showers are dangerous places; gangs tend to shower together as a protective measure; only a very few prisoners shower alone and without security, as I do. I am known as a loner and dangerous to cross and tend therefore to be left alone. . . .

When you come to prison it is wise to leave all shyness behind. But I am not anxious for myself in the showers. Here in Stateville there aren't gang rapes or even rapes that I hear about, though they are reputed to take place occasionally, and they are certainly more frequent in the jails. . . . Prisoners taking showers need security from gang attacks, not from sexual attacks. Still, I suppose I am always a little anxious in the showers; I avoid being alone in the showers with any one or more who might have some particular reason to dislike me. Even if violence is not all that common, still there is often tension and anxiety and, I suppose, fear.

11:30 A.M.:

I looked for some semi-clean socks, got dressed, and started typing a letter. I was waiting for the call to lunch, though I hate the mess hall at lunchtime. It is chaos at lunch; the prisoners refuse to act "orderly," and the guards do not take the trouble to enforce order. The gang element is definitely in control. Nevertheless, to the sound of "Chow going out the door," I joined the mass of prisoners heading for the tunnel. . . .

1:00 P.M.:

I joined the "school" detail and with six others from F House went off to a course on computers run in the school area. Unlike all but a few prisoners in Stateville, I am a genuine high school graduate. [The] majority of my fellow prisoners in Stateville are functionally illiterate, and only a handful have any sort of a record of high school academic achievement. In earlier years in Stateville I worked in the furniture factory and in the tailor shop, earning more than I can earn at school; but the computer course interested me, and I applied for it and got it. I have now been in it for three months and am beginning to be able to write programs. The course is taught by an Indian who speaks strangely but knows what he is doing. It fills my afternoons, three days a week, two hours each day.

The better-educated have the pick of the jobs in Stateville. Though it is poorly paid, the library, particularly the law library, is probably the best job, passing prison time more swiftly than other prison jobs, having influence in the prison, and being left alone by the guards; but the computer class seems to me in some ways even better. In the distant years when I am free I may be able to use what I am learning about computer programming, but I doubt it; the point is that it helps to keep me alive here. . . .

3:30 P.M.:

Two guards escorted the school detail back to F House. I went back to my cell. Tyrone was showering, his work in the tailor shop finished. While he was away I turned on the TV. It is my set, but I cannot control what we watch, since his friends outside could afford to give him a set if he wanted it. So, if we are to share this cell, we have to strike some bargain about what we watch. I am fortunate; he mostly falls in with my preferences, and when he doesn't, I yield.

I've never watched so much TV as I do here. My set is a thirteen-inch RCA color TV. . . . The TV is on a little table we have rigged up beside the toilet; it is best watched by lying on one's bunk. Tyrone came in and lay down on his bunk without speaking. It's the best way; avoid useless chatter. I got sleepy and dozed. I was awakened by the mailman rapping on the bars of our cell and giving a small package of mail to Tyrone. Nothing for me; after a year or two in prison, incoming mail dries up to a trickle, even if you write regularly. . . .

7:00 P.M.:

[After dinner at 5:25, the evening count of inmates] went smoothly. Most everyone was by now back in the cell houses, and there were fewer places — schoolroom, gym, yard, industry, barbershop, kitchen, and so on — to be counted.

It was F House's turn for evening gym. Many, including Tyrone, went to throw basketballs around. I stayed in the cell and followed a batch of my favorite TV programs — they passed the time well for me, and I had had my exercise for that day.

And so the evening went: TV, reading a little in my computer training manual, TV again, and by nine o'clock Tyrone was back in the cell, and I got out of my clothes, except my undershorts, and got into my bunk. The central lights in F House stay on through the night. I wondered if perhaps we should put up some sort of curtains, and with that thought the day ended for me.

[Let me comment a bit on my diary.] Yesterday was unusually uneventful. Often in prison something happens to disturb the dull flow of the day. . . . There are times to go to the library and to the law library for those of us still appealing our convictions or pursuing prisoners' rights litigation, which they tell me is a good way to "do time" but rarely produces any success in the courts. And then there are the hard-to-avoid confrontations with some of the guards — leading to tickets and segregation and loss of "good time." Even worse are the collective punishments of the "lockdown," when cells are locked for all twenty-four hours, sometimes for months, with only one shower a week out of the cell; time moves even slower then.

Neither Tyrone nor I use prison hooch [alcohol] or drugs to get through the days and nights, but many prisoners do, and the disorder of prison, the frequency of punishments and of lockdowns, is increased because of it. Drugs, all drugs, are readily available at about twice their street price, payable inside or outside the prison. . . .

There are regular and intermittent shakedowns of all the cells and other areas for shanks and other contraband. It is a violent place, but most prisoners do their time without being victimized physically unless they are looking to prove something to themselves or unless they get into trouble with betting, or hooch, or drugs, or with the gangs.

[This diary] fails to capture the constant unhappiness of prison life and the constant sense of danger. [It] misses the relentless, slow-moving routine, the dull repetitiveness, the tension mixed with occasional flashes of fear and rage; it misses the consuming stupidity of living this way. I am sorry; it is not easy. . . .

## NOTES

*1. The pains of imprisonment.*   Have we reached a Foucoult level of punishment? Conceptually, one can think of the deprivations of imprisonment as centered around three areas: those that are inherent to imprisonment; those that result from deliberate abuse; and those that flow from systemic policies and institutional rules and practices. Psychological assessments, deprivation of control over one's life, combined with the indeterminacy of punishment, and increased supervision upon release amount to a tight, psychologically based punishment structure. See Ben Crewe, Depth, Weight, Tightness: Revisiting the Pains of Imprisonment, 13(5) Punishment & Soc'y 509 (2011).

*2. Prisoners and correctional officers.*   The officers who maintain order in a prison have a complex relationship with the inmates they monitor every day. The stereotype of the brutal prison guard is a staple of literature and movies such as *Cool Hand Luke* (1967) and *The Shawshank Redemption* (1994). The following passage from a prison memoir (written by a former middle manager at a telephone company, convicted in Nevada for manslaughter) summarizes the nature of this relationship from the vantage point of the inmate:

> The sergeant glared down at the benches till the dawgs hushed. "Rule number one," he continued, "y'all got *nothin'* coming! Rules number two to two thousand — see rule number one." The sergeant paused to let us bask in this bit of penological cleverness.
> "My name is Sergeant Grafter. I am a correctional officer — not a fucking prison guard and not a cop. You will address me as 'C.O.' or 'Sergeant.' . . . cause you're *convicts!* Your job here is to lie, cheat, steal, extort, get tattoos, take drugs, sell drugs, shank, sock, fuck, and suck each other. Just don't let us catch you — that's *our* job." . . .
> "The warden and prison medical director have asked me to pass along a . . . health advisory. This prison has a combined HIV and hepatitis C infection rate of 60 percent. If you choose to just say yes, and use drugs, and you will — that's your job — then snort them, smoke them, or swallow them, but don't shoot them." Grafter irritably perused the rest of the memo before crushing it into a ball and tossing it over the rail. . . .
> "Finally, don't cross the red lines unless you like getting shot. Above all, *don't get caught!* We catch you, you got nothin' comin'."

Jimmy A. Lerner, You Got Nothing Coming: Notes from a Prison Fish 37-38 (2002).

The relationship looks different from the perspective of the correctional officer. Writer Ted Conover worked for a year as a correctional officer in New York's legendary Sing Sing prison; his account of that year emphasizes the combination of boredom and danger in the atmosphere: "I always thought of an assembly line in a poorly run explosives factory. Tedium, tedium, tedium, then — *bang* — you'd be missing your hands." Conover describes the tension between inmates and officers in these terms:

> A consequence of putting men in cells and controlling their movements is that they can do almost nothing for themselves. For their various needs they are dependent on one person, their gallery officer. Instead of feeling like a big, tough guard, the gallery officer at the end of the day often feels like a waiter serving a hundred tables or like the mother of a nightmarishly large brood of sullen, dangerous, and demanding children. When grown men are infantilized, most don't take to it nicely.
>
> That morning, I decided to count the number of times I said no before lunch. . . .
>
> — CO, can you find out when my disciplinary hearing is?
> — CO, can you call to see why my laundry bag didn't come back? . . .
> — CO, do all you guys get your hair cut in the same place? (a joke) . . .
> — CO, do you got any more state soap?
> — CO, can I go on the W side and borrow a belt from my homey?
> I got a visit. . . .
>
> Not all of these were improper requests; but the others were mainly favors, to be done when I had spare time, which was seldom. You had to get good at saying no. . . .

Ted Conover, Newjack: Guarding Sing Sing 234-235, 250 (2000).

3. *Violence, gangs, and race in prison.* One constant in the fictional and nonfictional accounts of prison life is violence and — more commonly — the threat of violence. In 2003 Congress passed the Prison Rape Elimination Act, which includes an ongoing reporting requirement of sexual assaults in prisons and funds preventive programs. The Department of Justice promulgated the mandated Prison Rape Elimination Act National Standards in spring 2011. http://www.ojp.usdoj.gov/programs/pdfs/prea_nprm.pdf. They were widely criticized as insufficient and too driven by cost considerations. See David Kaiser & Lovisa Stannow, Prison Rape and the Government, N.Y. Rev. of Books (Feb. 23, 2011). In a recent sexual victimization study involving former state prisoners, almost 10% of them reported one or more incidents of such victimization during their most recent period of incarceration, with most of these events occurring in state prisons. The percentage of inmates reporting incidents with other prisoners or with prison staff was almost identical, though many more former prisoners indicated that nonconsensual sex with another inmate was more likely forced or pressured and involved physical injuries. Homosexual and bisexual men were at almost ten times greater risk of victimization than heterosexual men; women were at three times greater risk than all males. Allen J. Beck & Candace Johnson, Bureau of Justice Statistics, National Former Prisoner Survey, 2008, Sexual Victimization Reported by Former State Prisoners, 2008, NCJ 237363 (May 2012).

The impact gender masculinities in prison may have in the community and on families upon inmate release remains largely unexplored. SpearIt, Gender Violence in Prison & Hyper-masculinities in the 'Hood: Cycles of Destructive Masculinity, 37 J. Law & Pol'y 89 (2011).

Many inmates, including female inmates, join gangs in prison for a sense of security, and the gangs tend to break down along racial lines and to deepen racial tensions in prisons. See American History X (1998). Jimmy Lerner's prison memoirs chronicle the racial tension at the center of prison life, observing that the correctional officers assigned cell mates on the basis of race: "Following some unwritten rule, he scrupulously placed blacks with the blacks, the white dawgs with the white dawgs."

The California prison system used to racially segregate inmates when they arrived in prison because of concerns about racially based gang violence. In *Johnson v. California*, 543 U.S. 499 (2005), the Supreme Court responded to an equal protection challenge by holding such race-based policies subject to strict scrutiny analysis.

Racial injustice in society spills over into the views of inmates about the legitimacy of their own punishment. Consider this classic passage from Eldridge Cleaver:

> One thing that the judges, policemen, and administrators of prisons seem never to have understood, and for which they certainly do not make any allowances, is that Negro convicts, basically, rather than see themselves as criminals and perpetrators of misdeeds, look upon themselves as prisoners of war, the victims of a vicious, dog-eat-dog social system that is so heinous as to cancel out their own malefactions: in the jungle there is no right or wrong.
>
> Rather than owing and paying a debt to society, Negro prisoners feel that they are being abused, that their imprisonment is simply another form of the oppression which they have known all their lives. Negro inmates feel that they are being robbed, that it is "society" that owes them, that should be paying them, a debt. America's penology does not take this into account. . . .

Eldridge Cleaver, Soul on Ice 58-59 (1968).

4. *Women in prison.*   The United States imprisons at least three times as many women as the next following country. The female prison population differs from the male in several respects. Women tend to be incarcerated for non-violent offenses, such as prostitution and theft, or for drug crimes. Women tend to be economically worse off than male offenders. Drug usage of women admitted into state prisons is substantially higher than that of men. Women pose different health challenges than men: pregnancy and a possibly higher percentage of women than men with positive HIV-tests upon admission, usually because of intravenous drug use or work in the sex industry. Some may also contract the infection while imprisoned. Almost 60% of female state prisoners have a history of physical or sexual abuse or both. See generally A Jailhouse Laywer's Manual, Chapter 41: Special Issues of Women Prisoners, Colum. Hum. Rts. L. Rev. (9th ed. 2011), available at www3.law.columbia.edu/hrlr/jlm/toc/.

> One late afternoon as we sit in [Delia's] room, she tells me that her stepfather had sexually molested her at the age of eleven. She hoped that by telling her mother the man would be thrown out of the house. Instead she was sent from her home to live with an aunt. At twelve, she had her first child. From that point on, her life revolved around a series of violent relationships with men.

Andi Rierden, The Farm: Life Inside a Women's Prison 81 (1997). Often the abuse continues in prison, as male correctional officers and other prison employees sexually assault female prisoners or coerce them into sexual relationships. See Kim Shayo Buchanan, Impunity: Sexual Abuse in Women's Prisons, 42 Harv. Civ. Rts. — Civ. Liberties L. Rev. 45 (2007).

The most important differences between female and male inmates are related to reproduction and parenting. Five to 10% of women who enter prisons are pregnant, but only three prisons in the country permit women to spend time with their newborns. Despite a federal policy against shackling during labor and childbirth, many state prison systems continue the practice. For an assessment of state and federal policies with respect to prenatal care, shackling, family-based treatment programs as alternatives to prison, and the availability of prison nurseries, see The Rebecca Project for Human Rights & National Women's Law Center, Mothers Behind Bars (2010); Michal Gilad & Tat Gat, U.S. v. My Mommy: Evaluation of Prison Nurseries as a Solution for Children of Incarcerated Women, 36 N.Y.U. Rev. L. & Soc. Change (forthcoming 2013) (discussing reasons for increasing number of prison nursery programs).

Sixty-four percent of state inmates lived with their minor children prior to incarceration. In contrast to the children of male prisoners, the children of female inmates do not usually end up living with their other parent but with other close family members. Because of the smaller number of female prisons, women are often incarcerated far from their families. Not seeing their children during incarceration is difficult, but seeing them can be equally excruciating. The excerpt below is taken from the 1995 inmate handbook of the Edna Mahon Correctional Facility for Women:

> All visits will be conducted in a quiet, orderly and dignified manner. Handshaking, embracing and kissing by the immediate family members and close friends are permitted within the bounds of good taste at the beginning and at the end of the visit only. Hand holding, in full view, is the only body contact allowed between a visitor and their inmate during a visit. Visitors and inmates must sit facing each other. Visiting children must remain under the inmate's supervision. Failure to properly supervise visiting children will be cause to terminate the visit.

Kathryn Watterson, Women in Prison: Inside the Concrete Womb 215 (rev. ed. 1996). Visiting with children is particularly difficult:

> Two weeks in segregation, with no visitors, nothing but stone-cold walls, a window to a parking lot, a pot to pee in, and thoughts, thoughts, thoughts. . . . Two weeks later [BeBe] emerges from segregation, from the cell block of her mind, raw, humiliated, shamed. Her two children visit. They are very young, under ten. They still think they are visiting their mommy in the hospital. It is the lie a lot of inmates spin. BeBe prays they never learn the truth. "When will you be better, mommy?" they ask her. Soon babies, soon.

Rierden, The Farm at 125. For a realistic account written by an educated inmate of a federal women's prison that details the difficulties of adjusting to imprisonment and then of re-integration for many of the inmates, see Piper Kerman, Orange is the New Black: My Year in a Women's Prison (2009).

5. *Release.*   Especially for inmates who have served long sentences, release is both joyful and stressful, according to an inmate:

You just come out *bam.* . . . And you don't know how to deal with it. You don't have a family to go to, half the time. You don't have a home or a job. All this time you've been fantasizing about the way things are and the way things are going to be when you really have no way of knowing how they are. You can imagine the shock. A lot of times the only thing left for a person to do is commit a new crime.

Besides that, prisons really help produce crime. You take away any human being and put them out of contact and take away all their responsibility and you're denying them an opportunity to grow. So to expect a person to leave here being grown and responsible, you're making an impossible demand, because all her sense of responsibility and her ability to interact has been brutalized.

To deal with society you have to interact with society. We only know how to interact with one society — and that's prison society.

Watterson, Women in Prison at 311. For the special problems women face in re-entry and how to accommodate them more effectively, see Anthony C. Thompson, Releasing Prisoners, Redeeming Communities 45-67 (2008).

One of the most challenging problems is the lack of preparedness for release, as the skills needed to succeed in prison tend to be counter to those making a released offender stay crime-free and reintegrating successful. The Arizona prison system has begun to address this issue through its "Getting Ready" program, which is designed to "remak[e] [] prison life to resemble life in the community. . . ." Dora Schriro, Getting Ready: How Arizona Has Created a 'Parallel Universe' for Inmates, 263 Nat'l Inst. Justice 2, 3 (June 2009).

How effective prior incarceration is in deterring offenders from future offenses remains an open question. One study of federal inmates indicates that "harsher prison conditions do not reduce post-release criminal behavior, and may even increase it." M. Keith Chen & Jesse M. Shapiro, Do Harsher Prison Conditions Reduce Recidivism? A Discontinuity-based Approach, 9 Am. L. & Econ. Rev. 1 (2007).

## E.   LIMITING IMPRISONMENT UNDER THE EIGHTH AMENDMENT

The language of the Eighth Amendment and similar provisions in state constitutions goes back to the English Bill of Rights of 1689, which prohibited "cruel and unusual punishments." This provision arose from concerns about the unwarranted infliction of pain through unlimited state power. The Supreme Court and lower courts have spent much effort explicating the meaning of the Eighth Amendment to guide states in imposing the death penalty. To a lesser extent, courts interpreting the Eighth Amendment have also restricted the imposition of other sentences, especially imprisonment.

The Supreme Court's proportionality analysis in imprisonment situations has been limited. The truncated review of prison sentences may indicate the degree to which the death penalty drives the entire sentencing structure in the United States. After all, if death is available as the ultimate sanction, how can life without parole be disproportionate?

Two sets of imprisonment cases have raised Eighth Amendment concerns: first, those involving habitual offenders whose current conviction would not justify the sentence imposed but where the sentence has to be assessed in light of the prior criminal record; second, those where it is questionable arises whether the gravity of the offense itself can justify the sentence imposed. Graham v. Florida, 130 S. Ct. 2011 (2010) (excerpted below), summarizes the cases in this area, including the three-part test in Solem v. Helm, 463 U.S. 277 (1983), the modified version of that test developed by Justice Kennedy in Harmelin v. Michigan, 501 U.S. 957 (1991), and its application in Ewing v. California, 538 U.S. (2003).

Justice Breyer, in his dissent in *Ewing*, summarizes Justice Kennedy's test as follows:

> [C]ourts faced with a "gross disproportionality" claim must first make "a threshold comparison of the crime committed and the sentence imposed." If a claim crosses that threshold–itself a *rare* occurrence–then the court should compare the sentence at issue to other sentences "imposed on other criminals" in the same, or in other, jurisdictions. The comparative analysis will "validate" or invalidate "an initial judgment that a sentence is grossly disproportionate to a crime." *Harmelin* (Kennedy, J., concurring in part and concurring in judgment).

The *Ewing* plurality, however, applied only the first prong:

> We first address the gravity of the offense compared to the harshness of the penalty. . . . In weighing the gravity of Ewing's offense, we must place on the scales not only his current felony, but also his long history of felony recidivism. . . . Ewing's sentence is justified by the State's public-safety interest in incapacitating and deterring recidivist felons, and amply supported by his own long, serious criminal record. . . . To be sure, Ewing's sentence is a long one. But it reflects a rational legislative judgment, entitled to deference, that offenders who have committed serious or violent felonies and who continue to commit felonies must be incapacitated.

In a companion case to *Ewing*, Lockyer v. Andrade, 538 U.S. 63 (2003), the defendant stole videotapes worth $154 from two Kmart stores. Andrade also had a criminal record with several convictions for misdemeanor theft, residential burglary, and transportation of marijuana. Although Andrade was sentenced under California's three-strikes law to a life term lasting at least 50 years, the Court upheld the sentence. How can the Court assess the first prong of its test — the gravity of the offense and the harshness of the penalty — other than by relying on prongs 2 and 3 to provide an answer?

## PROBLEM 7-2.  LOOKOUT

Arthur Beckom and Kentrell Stoutmire believed people walking through their neighborhood to belong to a rival gang. They approached Leon Miller, a fifteen-year-old, who was standing on a street corner, and asked him to stand as a lookout. Miller saw that the two were armed and agreed to act as a lookout. Miller himself never handled or touched the guns. Shortly thereafter, Beckom and Stoutmire fired gunshots in the direction of two young men, who both died as a result of their injuries. Once the shooting began, Miller ran to his girl-friend's house.

Miller gets charged with two counts of first-degree murder, based on accomplice liability. Section 5-4(6)(a) of the Juvenile Court Act of 1987 mandates that all 15- or 16-year-old offenders charged with murder be automatically transferred and prosecuted as adults in criminal court. The accountability statute bars courts from considering the offender's degree of participation in the crime by making all persons who participate in a common criminal design equally responsible. The multiple-murder sentencing statute provides:

> [For] first degree murder . . . the court shall sentence the defendant to a term of natural life imprisonment when the death penalty is not imposed if the defendant . . . is a person who, at the time of the commission of the murder, had attained the age of 17 or more and is found guilty of murdering an individual under 12 years of age; or, irrespective of the defendant's age at the time of the commission of the offense, is found guilty of murdering more than one victim.

The proportionate penalties clause of the Illinois Constitution declares that "all penalties shall be determined . . . according to the seriousness of the offense." Ill. Const. 1970, art. I, §11.

Miller challenges a mandatory life term as violative of the Illinois and the federal Constitution. How could he convince the judge to rule in his favor?

Assume the judge accepts his argument and instead imposes a 50-year sentence. What arguments should he present to defeat the sentence? Could he prevail on a federal constitutional argument alone? Compare People v. Leon Miller, 781 N.E.2d 300 (Ill. 2002).

## PROBLEM 7-3.   FAMILY BUSINESS

Angela Thompson was reared in Jamaica by her grandmother and then lived with a variety of family members in Jamaica and later in the United States. Her uncle, Norman Little, ran a major drug-selling operation in Harlem, and he employed Thompson in his illegal enterprise when she was 17 years old. One summer afternoon, an undercover police officer bought 200 vials of cocaine from her for $2,000 on the street outside Little's residence. The officer claimed that it was customary in a sale of this size for him to receive a bonus of 20 additional vials. Thompson, however, gave him only 14 extra vials and promised to "take care" of him personally the next time he made a purchase.

On that same day, officers also made five separate purchases from Little, and one purchase from another of Little's employees, a young woman known as "Shorty." Uniformed officers later arrested Thompson and Little. They decided, however, not to arrest Shorty because they were afraid that an arrest would reveal the identity of an undercover officer. Thompson had no previous encounters with law enforcement officials.

Thompson was indicted for the sale of 2.13 ounces of cocaine, a class A-I felony that carries a mandatory prison sentence. Under the New York statute, the judge must impose a minimum prison term of between 15 and 25 years and a maximum term of life. If Thompson had not awarded the bonus vials to the undercover officer, the government could have charged her only with an A-II sale (less than two ounces), whose mandatory minimum sentence is three years.

Little was indicted for five criminal sales of a controlled substance in the first degree. He had three prior felony and seven prior misdemeanor convictions; Little pleaded guilty to one illicit sale in exchange for dismissal of the remaining four counts and a sentence of 15 years to life imprisonment. The prosecutor offered Thompson a plea bargain carrying a sentence of three years to life, but she rejected the offer and went to trial. The jury convicted her of the A-I felony.

As defense counsel, how would you convince the sentencing judge that a minimum sentence of 15 years for Angela Thompson is cruel and unusual punishment, under either the federal or state constitution? Compare People v. Thompson, 633 N.E.2d 1074 (N.Y. 1994).

## PROBLEM 7-4.   ENOUGH IS ENOUGH

Chris Crosby was a drug addict who displayed little interest in drug treatment but much greater interest in petty offending. A trial judge finally reached his limit and imposed a 45-year sentence on Crosby, under a habitual offender statute, after convicting him of forgery in the second degree and criminal impersonation. Crosby had given a false name to the police officer who had arrested him on several misdemeanor drug offenses. The prosecution had asked for a sentence close to ten years in prison. In this jurisdiction felonies of the second degree are the lowest category of felony-level offenses, carrying a maximum of two years of incarceration.

The conviction and sentence followed upon five previous felonies, incurred over a fifteen-year timespan, which consisted of burglary in the third degree, forgery in the second degree, possession of a deadly weapon by a person prohibited, possession with intent to deliver, and burglary in the second degree. In addition, Crosby had a fair number of probation violations and misdemeanor convictions to his credit. He was still on probation when sentenced for the new offenses. His prognosis for future law-abiding conduct is poor and has been that way for years, in part because he refuses to address his underlying drug addiction.

As defense counsel, how would you attack Crosby's sentence in light of existing case law? See Crosby v. State, 824 A.2d 894 (Del. 2003).

## NOTES

1. *Non-U.S. courts' limits on legislative choice of sanctions.* The Canadian Supreme Court's proportionality test requires an assessment of the circumstances of the particular conduct involved in an individual case and the defendant's personal characteristics. A sentence would have to fall if it either "outraged decency" or was grossly disproportionate in some reasonably imaginable hypothetical situation. R. v. Goltz, [1991] S.C.R. 485.

In the International Criminal Court (ICC), the maximum penalties under the Statute of Rome are a term of 30 years or a life sentence; the latter must be justified in light of the "extreme gravity of the crime" and the personal circumstances of the defendant. The ICC's governing statute explicitly grants prosecutors and the convicted person the right to appeal "on the ground of disproportion between the crime and the sentence." Statute of Rome, Art. 81(2)(a). Should the Appeals Chamber find the sentence disproportionate, it may vary the sentence. Art. 83(3). What test, if any, should the ICC adopt in determining whether a sentence is disproportionate? For a critique of such proportionality analysis in one international tribunal, see Jens David Ohlin, Proportional Sentences at the ICTY, *in* The Legacy of the International Criminal Tribunal for the Former Yugoslavia (Bert Swart et al. eds., 2011), available at http://papers.ssrn.com/sol3/papers.cfm?abstract_id=1726411.

2. *Deference to the legislature.*   In a number of the Supreme Court proportionality opinions, the Justices have emphasized their deference to legislative decisions. In *Ewing* Justices Scalia and Thomas concluded that federal courts should never inquire into the proportionality of noncapital offenses because this concern is purely a legislative issue. Nevertheless, state and federal courts still insist that they can engage in an abbreviated proportionality review. Is it appropriate for courts to defer substantially to the legislature in defining the Eighth Amendment? Would such deference be more justified if a sentencing commission developed the sentence range? Or is it more — or less — justified when particular offender populations, such as juveniles, are the convicted?

3. *Multiple charges and the Eighth Amendment.*   In Close v. People, 48 P.3d 528 (Colo. 2002), the Colorado court upheld a 60-year term for a teenager charged with multiple offenses arising from a single incident. In its review of consecutive sentences, the Colorado court relied on O'Neil v. Vermont, 144 U.S. 323 (1892), in which the Supreme Court analyzed the severity of a defendant's sentence in light of the number of crimes he had committed. The *Close* court concluded that a proportionality review can be applied only to each conviction, not to the sum of the consecutive prison terms imposed. This approach gives prosecutors room to increase the maximum available sentence by adding counts to the indictment, without running into Eighth Amendment problems. Typically, judges counter this prosecutorial power by imposing concurrent rather than consecutive sentences. Is it possible to craft a constitutional rule here that would still ordinarily allow a defendant who commits more offenses to receive a more severe punishment?

4. *Life is different?*   In *Solem, Harmelin,* and Miller v. Alabama, 567 U.S. _____ (2012), the defendants received life-without-parole terms. The *Solem* Court contrasted the sentence facing the defendant with the life sentence in *Rummel,* which allowed for parole after 12 years. In *Miller* the Supreme Court rejected a mandatory life sentence because Miller had been a juvenile when committing his crime. Should a life-without-parole term change the parameters of the proportionality review employed? In proportionality decisions, the courts frequently refer to the more searching proportionality review used in death

cases, under the notion that "death is different." Does the impact of a life-without-parole sanction also justify a different approach?

Many countries in Latin America and Europe, including Portugal and Mexico which bar all life sentences, prohibit the imposition of life-without-parole sentences. They view such a penalty as violating human dignity and as inherently inhumane because it denies an individual the opportunity to rehabilitate herself. What purpose does the life-without-parole sentence serve? What may it tell us about a society's attitude toward its population and its government and judicial officials? Has the recent European Court of Human Rights' decision in Vinter and Others v. The United Kingdom, application nos. 66069/09 and 130/10 and 3896/10), 17 Jan. 2012, referred to Grand Chamber, 09/07/2012, changed Europe's attitude toward LWOP sentences? In that case, the Court's Chamber upheld an irreducible life term as long as penological justifications continue to exist for the ongoing incarceration. For an in-depth discussion of life imprisonment around the world, see Dirk van Zyl Smit, Taking Life Imprisonment Seriously in National and International Law (2002).

5. *Juveniles and proportionality.*   In State v. Green, 502 S.E.2d 819, 833-834 (N.C. 1998), the Supreme Court of North Carolina upheld a life sentence imposed on a 13-year-old repeat offender convicted of first-degree sexual offense, attempted first-degree rape, and first-degree burglary. It considered the sentence to comport with "evolving standards of decency" in light of public and legislative concern about violent juvenile crime. In addition, it found the sentence not excessive in the constitutional sense in light of the violent nature of the crime, the defendant's culpability, his prior record, and the potential maximum sentence of 4 years that could have been imposed under the juvenile system. Finally, the court addressed the question whether the sentence was "unusual," as the defendant was the only 13-year-old offender who was convicted and sentenced under the legislative scheme that mandated a life term under similar circumstances:

> The fact that a particular punishment is "unusual," in the sense that few defendants fall within its purview, is largely irrelevant to our inquiry. . . . This Court and the United States Supreme Court traditionally have not afforded separate treatment to the words "cruel" and "unusual," but have looked only to whether a particular punishment involves basic inhuman treatment. . . . The suggestion that an equally applicable punishment is rendered unconstitutional by virtue of the fact that few choose to commit the crime underlying it, or that only one of many who commit such crime is the one caught and convicted, does not fall within the bounds of any reasonable constitutional discourse.

A 1998 study indicated that most U.S. courts refuse to consider a defendant's age when engaging in a proportionality analysis under the Eighth Amendment. See Wayne A. Logan, Proportionality and Punishment: Imposing Life Without Parole on Juveniles, 33 Wake Forest L. Rev. 681 (1998). To what extent will *Graham* impact the judicial approach to the assessment of disproportionality in a juvenile's sentence?

## Terrance Jamar Graham v. Florida
### 130 S. Ct. 2011 (2010)

Kennedy, J.

The issue before the Court is whether the Constitution permits a juvenile offender to be sentenced to life in prison without parole for a nonhomicide crime. The sentence was imposed by the State of Florida. Petitioner challenges the sentence under the Eighth Amendment's Cruel and Unusual Punishments Clause....

## I

Petitioner is Terrance Jamar Graham. He was born on January 6, 1987. Graham's parents were addicted to crack cocaine, and their drug use persisted in his early years. Graham was diagnosed with attention deficit hyperactivity disorder in elementary school. He began drinking alcohol and using tobacco at age 9 and smoked marijuana at age 13.

In July 2003, when Graham was age 16, he and three other school-age youths attempted to rob a barbeque restaurant in Jacksonville, Florida. One youth, who worked at the restaurant, left the back door unlocked just before closing time. Graham and another youth, wearing masks, entered through the unlocked door. Graham's masked accomplice twice struck the restaurant manager in the back of the head with a metal bar. When the manager started yelling at the assailant and Graham, the two youths ran out and escaped in a car driven by the third accomplice. The restaurant manager required stitches for his head injury. No money was taken.

Graham was arrested for the robbery attempt. Under Florida law, it is within a prosecutor's discretion whether to charge 16- and 17-year-olds as adults or juveniles for most felony crimes. Graham's prosecutor elected to charge Graham as an adult. The charges against Graham were armed burglary with assault or battery, a first-degree felony carrying a maximum penalty of life imprisonment without the possibility of parole, and attempted armed-robbery, a second-degree felony carrying a maximum penalty of 15 years' imprisonment

On December 18, 2003, Graham pleaded guilty to both charges under a plea agreement.... The court withheld adjudication of guilt as to both charges and sentenced Graham to concurrent 3-year terms of probation. Graham was required to spend the first 12 months of his probation in the county jail, but he received credit for the time he had served awaiting trial and was released on June 24, 2004.

[O]n the night of December 2, 2004, Graham again was arrested, ... [for participating] in a home invasion robbery ... [and an attempted robbery].... [H]e was 34 days short of his 18th birthday.... The trial court held hearings on Graham's violations about a year later.... The trial court ... found that Graham had violated his probation by committing a home invasion robbery, by possessing a firearm, . . . by associating with persons engaged in criminal activity [and avoiding arrest]. . . . [At sentencing the] trial court found Graham guilty of the earlier armed burglary and attempted armed robbery charges. It sentenced him to the maximum sentence authorized by law on each charge: life imprisonment for the armed burglary and 15 years for the attempted armed robbery. Because Florida has abolished its parole system, a life sentence gives a defendant no possibility of release unless he is granted executive clemency.

Graham filed a motion in the trial court challenging his sentence under the Eighth Amendment[, which was] denied. . . . The First District Court of Appeal of Florida affirmed, concluding that Graham's sentence was not grossly disproportionate to his crimes. The court took note of the seriousness of Graham's offenses and their violent nature, as well as the fact that they "were not committed by a pre-teen, but a seventeen-year-old who was ultimately sentenced at the age of nineteen." The court concluded further that Graham was incapable of rehabilitation. Although Graham "was given an unheard of probationary sentence for a life felony . . . wrote a letter expressing his remorse and promising to refrain from the commission of further crime, and . . . had a strong family structure to support him," the court noted, he "rejected his second chance and chose to continue committing crimes at an escalating pace." The Florida Supreme Court denied review. We granted certiorari.

## II

The Eighth Amendment states: "Excessive bail shall not be required, nor excessive fines imposed, nor cruel and unusual punishments inflicted." To determine whether a punishment is cruel and unusual, courts must look beyond historical conceptions to "'the evolving standards of decency that mark the progress of a maturing society.'" Estelle v. Gamble, 429 U.S. 97 (1976) (quoting Trop v. Dulles, 356 U.S. 86, 101 (1958) (plurality opinion)). . . .

The Cruel and Unusual Punishments Clause prohibits the imposition of inherently barbaric punishments under all circumstances. . . . For the most part, however, the Court's precedents consider punishments challenged not as inherently barbaric but as disproportionate to the crime. . . .

The Court's cases addressing the proportionality of sentences fall within two general classifications. The first involves challenges to the length of term-of-years sentences given all the circumstances in a particular case. The second comprises cases in which the Court implements the proportionality standard by certain categorical restrictions on the death penalty.

In the first classification the Court considers all of the circumstances of the case to determine whether the sentence is unconstitutionally excessive. Under this approach, the Court has held unconstitutional a life without parole sentence for the defendant's seventh nonviolent felony, the crime of passing a worthless check. Solem v. Helm, 463 U.S. 277 (1983). In other cases, however, it has been difficult for the challenger to establish a lack of proportionality. A leading case is Harmelin v. Michigan, 501 U.S. 957 (1991), in which the offender was sentenced under state law to life without parole for possessing a large quantity of cocaine. A closely divided Court upheld the sentence. The controlling opinion concluded that the Eighth Amendment contains a "narrow proportionality principle," that "does not require strict proportionality between crime and sentence" but rather "forbids only extreme sentences that are 'grossly disproportionate' to the crime." . . .

The controlling opinion in *Harmelin* explained its approach for determining whether a sentence for a term of years is grossly disproportionate for a particular defendant's crime. A court must begin by comparing the gravity of the offense and the severity of the sentence. 501 U.S., at 1005 (opinion of Kennedy, J.). "[I]n the rare case in which [this] threshold comparison . . . leads to an inference of gross disproportionality" the court should then compare the defendant's sentence with the sentences received by other offenders in the same jurisdiction and with the sentences imposed for the same crime in other jurisdictions. . . . If this comparative analysis "validate[s] an initial judgment that [the] sentence is grossly disproportionate," the sentence is cruel and unusual.

The second classification of cases has used categorical rules to define Eighth Amendment standards. The previous cases in this classification involved the death penalty. The classification in turn consists of two subsets, one considering the nature of the offense, the other considering the characteristics of the offender. With respect to the nature of the offense, the Court has concluded that capital punishment is impermissible for nonhomicide crimes against individuals. . . . In cases turning on the characteristics of the offender, the Court has adopted categorical rules prohibiting the death penalty for defendants who committed their crimes before the age of 18, Roper v. Simmons, 543 U.S. 551 (2005), or whose intellectual functioning is in a low range, Atkins v. Virginia, 536 U.S. 304 (2002). . . .

In the cases adopting categorical rules the Court has taken the following approach. The Court first considers "objective indicia of society's standards, as expressed in legislative enactments and state practice" to determine whether there is a national consensus against the sentencing practice at issue. Next, guided by "the standards elaborated by controlling precedents and by the Court's own understanding and interpretation of the Eighth Amendment's text, history, meaning, and purpose," Kennedy v. Louisiana, 554 U.S., at 407, 128 S. Ct. 2641 (2008) the Court must determine in the exercise of its own independent judgment whether the punishment in question violates the Constitution.

The present case involves an issue the Court has not considered previously: a categorical challenge to a term-of-years sentence. . . . This case implicates a particular type of sentence as it applies to an entire class of offenders who have committed a range of crimes. As a result, a threshold comparison between the severity of the penalty and the gravity of the crime does not advance the analysis. Here, in addressing the question presented, the appropriate analysis is the one used in cases that involved the categorical approach, specifically *Atkins, Roper,* and *Kennedy*.

## III

### A

The analysis begins with objective indicia of national consensus. . . . Six jurisdictions do not allow life without parole sentences for any juvenile offenders. Seven jurisdictions permit life without parole for juvenile offenders, but only for homicide crimes. Thirty-seven States as well as the District of Columbia permit sentences of life without parole for a juvenile nonhomicide offender in some circumstances. Federal law also allows for the possibility of life without parole for offenders as young as 13. Relying on this metric, the State and its *amici* argue that there is no national consensus against the sentencing practice at issue.

This argument is incomplete and unavailing. . . . Actual sentencing practices are an important part of the Court's inquiry into consensus. Here, an examination of actual sentencing practices in jurisdictions where the sentence in question is permitted by statute discloses a consensus against its use. Although these statutory schemes contain no explicit prohibition on sentences of life without parole for juvenile nonhomicide offenders, those sentences are most infrequent. . . . [There appear to be] 129 juvenile nonhomicide offenders serving life without parole sentences. A significant majority of those, 77 in total, are serving sentences imposed in Florida. The other 52 are imprisoned in just 10 States — California, Delaware, Iowa, Louisiana, Mississippi, Nebraska, Nevada, Oklahoma, South Carolina, and Virginia — and in the federal system. . . . Thus, only 12 jurisdictions nationwide in fact impose life without parole sentences on juvenile nonhomicide offenders — and most of those impose the sentence quite rarely — while 26 States as well as the District of Columbia do not impose them despite apparent statutory authorization. . . .

It must be acknowledged that in terms of absolute numbers juvenile life without parole sentences for nonhomicides are more common than the sentencing practices at issue in some of this Court's other Eighth Amendment cases. This contrast can be instructive, however, if attention is first given to the base number of certain types of offenses. For example, in the year 2007 . . . a total of 13,480 persons, adult and juvenile, were arrested for homicide crimes. That same year, 57,600 juveniles were arrested for aggravated assault; 3,580 for forcible rape; 34,500 for robbery; 81,900 for burglary; 195,700 for drug offenses; and 7,200 for arson. . . . [T]he comparison suggests that in proportion to the opportunities for its imposition, life without parole sentences for juveniles convicted of nonhomicide crimes is as rare as other sentencing practices found to be cruel and unusual. . . .

The sentencing practice now under consideration is exceedingly rare. And it is fair to say that a national consensus has developed against it.

### B

Community consensus, while "entitled to great weight," is not itself determinative of whether a punishment is cruel and unusual. In accordance with the constitutional design, "the task of interpreting the Eighth Amendment remains our responsibility." *Roper*, 543 U.S., at 575. The judicial exercise of independent judgment requires consideration of the culpability of the offenders at issue in light of their crimes and characteristics, along with the severity of the punishment in question. In this inquiry the Court also considers whether the challenged sentencing practice serves legitimate penological goals.

*Roper* established that because juveniles have lessened culpability they are less deserving of the most severe punishments. As compared to adults, juveniles have a "'lack of maturity and an underdeveloped sense of responsibility'"; they "are more vulnerable or susceptible to negative influences and outside pressures, including peer pressure"; and their characters are "not as well formed." These salient characteristics mean that "[i]t is difficult even for expert psychologists to differentiate between the juvenile offender whose crime reflects unfortunate yet transient immaturity, and the rare juvenile offender whose crime reflects irreparable corruption." Accordingly, "juvenile offenders cannot with reliability be classified among the worst offenders." Juveniles are more capable of change than are adults, and their actions are less likely to be evidence of "irretrievably depraved character" than are the actions of adults. It remains true that "[f]rom a moral standpoint it would be misguided to equate the failings of a minor with those of an adult, for a greater possibility exists that a minor's character deficiencies will be reformed." These matters relate to the status of the offenders in question; and it is relevant to consider next the nature of the offenses to which this harsh penalty might apply. . . .

There is a line "between homicide and other serious violent offenses against the individual." *Kennedy*, 128 S. Ct. 2641, 2660. Serious nonhomicide crimes "may be devastating in their harm . . . but 'in terms of moral depravity and of the injury to the person and to the public,' . . . they cannot be compared to murder in their 'severity and irrevocability.'" This is because "[l]ife is over for the victim of the murderer," but for the victim of even a very serious nonhomicide crime, "life . . . is not over and normally is not beyond repair."

It follows that, when compared to an adult murderer, a juvenile offender who did not kill or intend to kill has a twice diminished moral culpability. The age of the offender and the nature of the crime each bear on the analysis.

As for the punishment, life without parole is "the second most severe penalty permitted by law." *Harmelin*, 501 U.S., at 1001. . . . [L]ife without parole sentences share some characteristics with death sentences that are shared by no other sentences. [The] sentence alters the offender's life by a forfeiture that is irrevocable. It deprives the convict of the most basic liberties without giving hope of restoration, except perhaps by executive clemency. . . .

The Court has recognized the severity of sentences that deny convicts the possibility of parole. . . . [I]n *Solem*, the only previous case striking down a sentence for a term of years as grossly disproportionate, the defendant's sentence was deemed "far more severe than the life sentence we considered in *Rummel*," because it did not give the defendant the possibility of parole. Life without parole is an especially harsh punishment for a juvenile. Under this sentence a juvenile offender will on average serve more years and a greater percentage of his life in prison than an adult offender. A 16-year-old and a 75-year-old each sentenced to life without parole receive the same punishment in name only. . . .

The penological justifications for the sentencing practice are also relevant to the analysis. Criminal punishment can have different goals, and choosing among them is within a legislature's discretion. It does not follow, however, that the purposes and effects of penal sanctions are irrelevant to the determination of Eighth Amendment restrictions. A sentence lacking any legitimate penological justification is by its nature disproportionate to the offense. With respect to life without parole for juvenile nonhomicide offenders, none of the goals of penal sanctions that have been recognized as legitimate — retribution, deterrence, incapacitation, and rehabilitation — provides an adequate justification.

Retribution is a legitimate reason to punish, but it cannot support the sentence at issue here. Society is entitled to impose severe sanctions on a juvenile nonhomicide offender to express its condemnation of the crime and to seek restoration of the moral imbalance caused by the offense. But "[t]he heart of the retribution rationale is that a criminal sentence must be directly related to the personal culpability of the criminal offender." Tison v. Arizona, 481 U.S. 137, 149 (1987). And as *Roper* observed, "[w]hether viewed as an attempt to express the community's moral outrage or as an attempt to right the balance for the wrong to the victim, the case for retribution is not as strong with a minor as with an adult."

Deterrence does not suffice to justify the sentence either. *Roper* noted that "the same characteristics that render juveniles less culpable than adults suggest . . . that juveniles will be less susceptible to deterrence." Because juveniles' lack of maturity and underdeveloped sense of responsibility . . . often result in impetuous and ill-considered actions and decisions, they are less likely to take a possible punishment into consideration when making decisions. This is particularly so when that punishment is rarely imposed. . . . Even if the punishment has some connection to a valid penological goal, it must be shown that the punishment is not grossly disproportionate in light of the justification offered. Here, in light of juvenile nonhomicide offenders' diminished moral responsibility, any limited deterrent effect provided by life without parole is not enough to justify the sentence.

Incapacitation, a third legitimate reason for imprisonment, does not justify the life without parole sentence in question here. Recidivism is a serious risk to public safety, and so incapacitation is an important goal. But while incapacitation may be a legitimate penological goal sufficient to justify life without parole in other contexts, it is inadequate to justify that punishment for juveniles who did not commit homicide. To justify life without parole on the assumption that the juvenile offender forever will be a danger to society requires the sentencer to make a judgment that the juvenile is incorrigible. The characteristics of juveniles make that judgment questionable. . . .

Here one cannot dispute that this defendant posed an immediate risk, for he had committed, we can assume, serious crimes early in his term of supervised release and despite his own assurances of reform. Graham deserved to be separated from society for some time in order to prevent what the trial court described as an "escalating pattern of criminal conduct," but it does not follow that he would be a risk to society for the rest of his life. . . . A life without parole sentence improperly denies the juvenile offender a chance to demonstrate growth and maturity. Incapacitation cannot override all other considerations, lest the Eighth Amendment's rule against disproportionate sentences be a nullity.

Finally there is rehabilitation, a penological goal that forms the basis of parole systems. The concept of rehabilitation is imprecise; and its utility and proper implementation are the subject of a substantial, dynamic field of inquiry and dialogue. . . . It is for legislatures to determine what rehabilitative techniques are appropriate and effective.

A sentence of life imprisonment without parole, however, cannot be justified by the goal of rehabilitation. The penalty forswears altogether the rehabilitative ideal. By denying the defendant the right to reenter the community, the State makes an irrevocable judgment about that person's value and place in society. This judgment is not appropriate in light of a juvenile nonhomicide offender's capacity for change and limited moral culpability. A State's rejection of rehabilitation, moreover, goes beyond a mere expressive judgment. As one *amicus* notes, defendants serving life without parole sentences are often denied access to vocational training and other rehabilitative services that are available to other inmates. For juvenile offenders, who are most in need of and receptive to rehabilitation, the absence of rehabilitative opportunities or treatment makes the disproportionality of the sentence all the more evident.

In sum, penological theory is not adequate to justify life without parole for juvenile nonhomicide offenders. This determination; the limited culpability of juvenile nonhomicide offenders; and the severity of life without parole sentences all lead to the conclusion that the sentencing practice under consideration is cruel and unusual. This Court now holds that for a juvenile offender who did not commit homicide the Eighth Amendment forbids the sentence of life without parole. . . . [T]hose who were below . . . [18] when the offense was committed may not be sentenced to life without parole for a nonhomicide crime.

A State is not required to guarantee eventual freedom to a juvenile offender convicted of a nonhomicide crime. What the State must do, however, is give defendants like Graham some meaningful opportunity to obtain release based on demonstrated maturity and rehabilitation. . . . The Eighth Amendment does not foreclose the possibility that persons convicted of nonhomicide crimes committed before adulthood will remain behind bars for life. It does forbid States from making the judgment at the outset that those offenders never will be fit to reenter society. . . .

## D

There is support for our conclusion in the fact that, in continuing to impose life without parole sentences on juveniles who did not commit homicide, the United States adheres to a sentencing practice rejected the world over. This observation does not control our decision. The judgments of other nations and the international community are not dispositive as to the meaning of the Eighth Amendment. But "'[t]he climate of international opinion concerning the acceptability of a particular punishment'" is also "'not irrelevant.'" *Enmund,* 458 U.S., at 796, n. 22. The Court has looked beyond our Nation's borders for support for its independent conclusion that a particular punishment is cruel and unusual. Today we continue that longstanding practice in noting the global consensus against the sentencing practice in question. A recent study concluded that only 11 nations authorize life without parole for juvenile offenders under any circumstances; and only 2 of them, the United States and Israel, ever impose the punishment in practice. See M. Leighton & C. de la Vega, Sentencing Our Children to Die in Prison: Global Law and Practice 4 (2007). An updated version of the study concluded that Israel's "laws allow for parole review of juvenile offenders serving life terms," but expressed reservations about how that parole review is implemented. De la Vega & Leighton, Sentencing Our Children to Die in Prison: Global Law and Practice, 42 U.S.F.L. Rev. 983, 1002-1003 (2008). But even if Israel is counted as allowing life without parole for juvenile offenders, that nation does not appear to impose that sentence for nonhomicide crimes; all of the seven Israeli prisoners whom commentators have identified as serving life sentences for juvenile crimes were convicted of homicide or attempted homicide. See Amnesty International, Human Rights Watch, The Rest of Their Lives: Life without Parole for Child Offenders in the United States 106, n. 322 (2005); Memorandum and Attachment from Ruth Levush, Law Library of Congress, to Supreme Court Library (Feb. 16, 2010) (available in Clerk of Court's case file).

Thus, as petitioner contends and respondent does not contest, the United States is the only Nation that imposes life without parole sentences on juvenile nonhomicide offenders. We also note, as petitioner and his *amici* emphasize, that Article 37(a) of the United Nations Convention on the Rights of the Child, Nov. 20, 1989, 1577 U. N. T. S. 3 (entered into force Sept. 2, 1990), ratified by every nation except the United States and Somalia, prohibits the imposition of "life imprisonment without possibility of release . . . for offences committed by persons below eighteen years of age." Brief for Petitioner 66; Brief for Amnesty International et al. as *Amici Curiae* 15-17. As we concluded in *Roper* with respect to the juvenile death penalty, "the United States now stands alone in a world that has turned its face against" life without parole for juvenile nonhomicide offenders.

The State's *amici* stress that no international legal agreement that is binding on the United States prohibits life without parole for juvenile offenders and thus urge us to ignore the international consensus. . . . These arguments miss the mark. The question before us is not whether international law prohibits the United States from imposing the sentence at issue in this case. The question is whether that punishment is cruel and unusual. In that inquiry, "the overwhelming weight of international opinion against" life without parole for nonhomicide offenses committed by juveniles "provide[s] respected and significant confirmation for our own conclusions." *Roper, supra,* at 578. . . .

The Constitution prohibits the imposition of a life without parole sentence on a juvenile offender who did not commit homicide. A State need not guarantee the offender eventual release, but if it imposes a sentence of life it must provide him or her with some realistic opportunity to obtain release before the end of that term. . . .

Roberts, C.J., concurring in the judgment.

I agree with the Court that Terrance Graham's sentence of life without parole violates the Eighth Amendment's prohibition on "cruel and unusual punishments." Unlike the majority, however, I see no need to invent a new constitutional rule of dubious provenance in reaching that conclusion. Instead, my analysis is based on an application of this Court's precedents, in particular

(1) our cases requiring "narrow proportionality" review of noncapital sentences and (2) our conclusion in Roper v. Simmons, 543 U.S. 551 (2005), that juvenile offenders are generally less culpable than adults who commit the same crimes.

These cases expressly allow courts addressing allegations that a noncapital sentence violates the Eighth Amendment to consider the particular defendant and particular crime at issue.... [H]ere Graham's juvenile status — together with the nature of his criminal conduct and the extraordinarily severe punishment imposed — lead me to conclude that his sentence of life without parole is unconstitutional....

Graham's case arises at the intersection of two lines of Eighth Amendment precedent. The first consists of decisions holding that the Cruel and Unusual Punishments Clause embraces a "narrow proportionality principle" that we apply, on a case-by-case basis, when asked to review noncapital sentences....

Our cases indicate that courts conducting "narrow proportionality" review should begin with a threshold inquiry that compares the gravity of the offense and the harshness of the penalty. This analysis can consider a particular offender's mental state and motive in committing the crime, the actual harm caused to his victim or to society by his conduct, and any prior criminal history....

Only in the rare case in which a threshold comparison of the crime committed and the sentence imposed leads to an inference of gross disproportionality, should courts proceed to an "intrajurisdictional comparison of the sentence at issue with those imposed on other criminals in the same jurisdiction, and an "inter-jurisdictional" comparison with sentences imposed for the same crime in other jurisdictions. If these subsequent comparisons confirm the inference of gross disproportionality, courts should invalidate the sentence as a violation of the Eighth Amendment.

The second line of precedent relevant to assessing Graham's sentence consists of our cases acknowledging that juvenile offenders are generally — though not necessarily in every case — less morally culpable than adults who commit the same crimes....

Today, the Court views *Roper* as providing the basis for a new categorical rule that juveniles may never receive a sentence of life without parole for non-homicide crimes. I disagree....

... A life sentence is of course far less severe than a death sentence, and we have never required that it be imposed only on the very worst offenders, as we have with capital punishment. Treating juvenile life sentences as analogous to capital punishment is at odds with our longstanding view that the death penalty is different from other punishments in kind rather than degree. It is also at odds with *Roper* itself.... Indeed, *Roper* explicitly relied on the possible imposition of life without parole on some juvenile offenders.

But the fact that *Roper* does not support a categorical rule barring life sentences for all juveniles does not mean that a criminal defendant's age is irrelevant to those sentences. On the contrary, our cases establish that the "narrow proportionality" review applicable to noncapital cases itself takes the personal "culpability of the offender" into account in examining whether a given punishment is proportionate to the crime. There is no reason why an offender's juvenile status should be excluded from the analysis. Indeed, given

*Roper*'s conclusion that juveniles are typically less blameworthy than adults, an offender's juvenile status can play a central role in the inquiry. . . .

In short, our existing precedent already provides a sufficient framework for assessing the concerns outlined by the majority. Not every juvenile receiving a life sentence will prevail under this approach. Not every juvenile should. But all will receive the protection that the Eighth Amendment requires.

Applying the "narrow proportionality" framework to the particular facts of this case, I conclude that Graham's sentence of life without parole violates the Eighth Amendment.

. . . . There is no question that the crime for which Graham received his life sentence — armed burglary of a nondomicil with an assault or battery — is a serious crime deserving serious punishment. So too is the home invasion robbery that was the basis of Graham's probation violation. But these crimes are certainly less serious than other crimes, such as murder or rape.

As for Graham's degree of personal culpability, he committed the relevant offenses when he was a juvenile — a stage at which, *Roper* emphasized, one's "culpability or blameworthiness is diminished, to a substantial degree, by reason of youth and immaturity." . . . . There is no reason to believe that Graham should be denied the general presumption of diminished culpability that *Roper* indicates should apply to juvenile offenders. If anything, Graham's in-court statements — including his request for a second chance so that he could "do whatever it takes to get to the NFL" — underscore his immaturity.

The fact that Graham committed the crimes that he did proves that he was dangerous and deserved to be punished. But it does not establish that he was particularly dangerous — at least relative to the murderers and rapists for whom the sentence of life without parole is typically reserved. On the contrary, his lack of prior criminal convictions, his youth and immaturity, and the difficult circumstances of his upbringing noted by the majority, all suggest that he was markedly less culpable than a typical adult who commits the same offenses.

Despite these considerations, the trial court sentenced Graham to life in prison without the possibility of parole. This is the second-harshest sentence available under our precedents for any crime, and the most severe sanction available for a nonhomicide offense. Indeed, as the majority notes, Graham's sentence far exceeded the punishment proposed by the Florida Department of Corrections (which suggested a sentence of four years), and the state prosecutors (who asked that he be sentenced to 30 years in prison for the armed burglary). No one in Graham's case other than the sentencing judge appears to have believed that Graham deserved to go to prison for life.

Both intrajurisdictional and interjurisdictional comparisons of Graham's sentence confirm the threshold inference of disproportionality. Graham's sentence was far more severe than that imposed for similar violations of Florida law, even without taking juvenile status into account. For example, individuals who commit burglary or robbery offenses in Florida receive average sentences of less than 5 years and less than 10 years, respectively. Florida Dept. of Corrections, Annual Report FY 2007-2008: The Guidebook to Corrections in Florida 35. Unsurprisingly, Florida's juvenile criminals receive similarly low sentences — typically less than five years for burglary and less than seven years for robbery.

Graham's life without parole sentence was far more severe than the average sentence imposed on those convicted of murder or manslaughter, who typically receive under 25 years in prison. . . .

Finally, the inference that Graham's sentence is disproportionate is further validated by comparison to the sentences imposed in other domestic jurisdictions. . . .

. . . The fact that Graham cannot be sentenced to life without parole for his conduct says nothing whatever about [other] offenders [] who commit nonhomicide crimes far more reprehensible than the conduct at issue here. The Court uses Graham's case as a vehicle to proclaim a new constitutional rule — applicable well beyond the particular facts of Graham's case — that a sentence of life without parole imposed on any juvenile for any nonhomicide offense is unconstitutional. This categorical conclusion is as unnecessary as it is unwise . . . .

[T]here is nothing inherently unconstitutional about imposing sentences of life without parole on juvenile offenders; rather, the constitutionality of such sentences depends on the particular crimes for which they are imposed. But if the constitutionality of the sentence turns on the particular crime being punished, then the Court should limit its holding to the particular offenses that Graham committed here, and should decline to consider other hypothetical crimes not presented by this case.

In any event, the Court's categorical conclusion is also unwise. Most importantly, it ignores the fact that some nonhomicide crimes . . . are especially heinous or grotesque, and thus may be deserving of more severe punishment. . . .

Our system depends upon sentencing judges applying their reasoned judgment to each case that comes before them.

THOMAS, J., dissenting.

. . . Although the text of the Constitution is silent regarding the permissibility of [a life without parole sentence imposed on a juvenile for a non-homicide] and although it would not have offended the standards that prevailed at the founding, the Court insists that the standards of American society have evolved such that the Constitution now requires its prohibition.

The news of this evolution will, I think, come as a surprise to the American people. Congress, the District of Columbia, and 37 States allow judges and juries to consider this sentencing practice in juvenile nonhomicide cases, and those judges and juries have decided to use it in the very worst cases they have encountered.

The Court does not conclude that life without parole itself is a cruel and unusual punishment. It instead rejects the judgments of those legislatures, judges, and juries regarding what the Court describes as the "moral" question of whether this sentence can ever be "proportionat[e]" when applied to the category of offenders at issue here.

I am unwilling to assume that we, as members of this Court, are any more capable of making such moral judgments than our fellow citizens. Nothing in our training as judges qualifies us for that task, and nothing in Article III gives us that authority.

I respectfully dissent. . . .

## NOTES

1. *The debate over categorical or case-by-case approaches to the Eighth Amendment.* While the five Justices in the majority and the Chief Justice all agree that Terrance Graham's LWOP sentence violated the Eighth Amendment, they dispute whether to reach this result through application of a categorical rule or case-by-case analysis. Does the express text of the Eighth Amendment's prohibition of "cruel and unusual punishments" provide support for one approach or the other? Taking an originalist perspective, would the Framers likely favored one approach or the other?

Would defendants serving life sentences or very long prison terms have preferred the majority had adopted the case-by-case approach to the Eighth Amendment advocated by Chief Justice Roberts?

Does the decision in *Graham* reflect merely the predilections of the majority of the Court rather than a principled assessment of the sentence? Would it have been more honest for the Court to decline proportionality review in imprisonment cases generally?

2. *When and how can juvenile offenders like Terrance Graham seek parole?* The *Graham* opinion indicates that juvenile offenders who commit nonhomicide offenses can still be subject to life sentences, but they must be given "some meaningful opportunity to obtain release based on demonstrated maturity and rehabilitation" which the Court later describes as "some realistic opportunity to obtain release before the end of that term." Can (and should) executive branch officials in Florida now declare that they will not consider any request for parole from Terrance Graham until he reaches at least age 75? If that were the case, can (and should) Terrance Graham challenge in federal court the state's failure to provide him with an earlier opportunity for parole?

3. Graham's *impact on other sentences for other crimes and other offenders.* Will the holding and opinions in *Graham* likely impact any sentences other than life without parole for juvenile nonhomicide offenders? Could a state insulate its punishment from constitutional attack by providing that the most severe sentence for juvenile offenders in non-homicide cases will be a term of 75 years of imprisonment? In People v. Caballero, 282 P.3d 291 (Cal. 2012), the California Supreme Court struck down a sentence of 110 years imposed on an 16-year-old who had been convicted of three counts of attempted murder. The court held unconstitutional a "term-of-years sentence that amounts to a functional equivalent" of LWOP.

Could any adult nonhomicide offender subject to an LWOP sentence press an effective Eighth Amendment challenge in the wake of *Graham*? See, e.g., State v. Oliver, 812 N.W.2d 636 (Iowa 2012) (affirming, under state and federal constitutions, LWOP imposed on adult recidivist offender for second conviction of third-degree sexual abuse).

4. *The jurisprudence of state courts.* State courts have applied the *Harmelin* test under the Eighth Amendment to bar some disproportionate sentences. See Crosby v. State, 824 A.2d 894 (Del. 2003) (life sentence amounting to a 45-year fixed term for second-degree forgery was excessive, even for defendant with prior felony convictions). It is more common for state courts to uphold a

legislative choice of sanctions in the case at hand, even if they recognize that a proportionality challenge might succeed in theory. State v. Moss-Dwyer, 686 N.E.2d 109 (Ind. 1997) (recognizing possible proportionality challenges under state constitution, but refusing to declare a sentence disproportionate where statute made misinformation on a handgun permit application a greater crime than carrying a handgun without a license).

A few state courts have been willing to insist, under various provisions of their state constitutions, that the legislature select a punishment that is proportionate to the crime. The *Miller* court, for example, rested its decision solely on the Illinois constitution, without reaching the federal constitutional question. Whose standards — those of a state, of the nation, of a local community — should apply in determining what shocks the conscience?

Nonconstitutional limitations on imprisonment provide more meaningful day-to-day controls than do constitutional limitations. Sentencing guidelines, for example, set out presumptive sentencing ranges for specific offenses. While guideline regimes allow for departures, they require detailed justifications and are open to appellate challenges. Another statutory limitation on imprisonment is the federal safety valve program, which allows for the sentencing of low-level, nonviolent drug offenders to prison terms below the mandatory minimum. Other limitations may be imposed by state statutes mandating that certain offenders not be sentenced to prison. Among such legislation is the 2002 California referendum requiring drug treatment rather than imprisonment for first-time, nonviolent drug offenders. For discussion of a similar statute, see State v. DePiano, 926 P.2d 494 (Ariz. 1996) (despondent mother's unsuccessful attempt to commit suicide and infanticide by asphyxiation was punished by 34-year prison term; court reduced sentence under statute allowing reduction if "the punishment imposed is greater than under the circumstances of the case ought to be inflicted").

5. *Internal consistency: similar statutes, similar safety threats.* In People v. Walden, 769 N.E.2d 928 (Ill. 2002), the court struck down a 15-year sentencing enhancement for the carrying of a firearm during an armed robbery as violating the proportionate penalties clause of the Illinois constitution. David Walden was charged with one count of armed robbery while in possession of a firearm. He challenged his sentence as disproportionate under the state constitution, because it punished him more severely than a related crime in the state code, armed violence predicated upon aggravated robbery. The appellate court reviewed the legislative history of the two provisions and concluded that they share a statutory purpose — the more severe punishment of violent crimes when committed with firearms:

> Having concluded that the two offenses share an identical statutory purpose, we next must determine whether one offense is more serious than the other. This is not a difficult inquiry, as armed violence predicated upon aggravated robbery is clearly the more serious offense. [Armed] violence predicated upon aggravated robbery . . . requires that the offender, while using or threatening the imminent use of force, inform the victim that he or she is presently armed with a firearm. Thus, armed robbery while in possession of a firearm may be committed while carrying a concealed firearm that is neither revealed nor even mentioned to the victim. . . .

Our final inquiry, then, is whether armed robbery while in possession of a firearm is punished more or less severely than armed violence predicated upon aggravated robbery. [Armed] robbery while in possession of a firearm is punishable by 21 to 45 years in prison. Armed violence predicated upon aggravated robbery is a Class X felony punishable by either 10 to 30 or 15 to 30 years in prison, depending upon the type of firearm used in the offense. Thus, it is the less serious offense — armed robbery while in possession of a firearm — that is punished more severely. The 15-year enhancement for armed robbery while in possession of a firearm therefore violates the proportionate penalties clause of the Illinois Constitution and is unenforceable.

769 N.E.2d at 931-932. *Walden* is reminiscent of People v. Stewart (reprinted in Chapter 2), in which the Colorado court addressed an equal protection challenge to Stewart's conviction of reckless second-degree assault rather than vehicular assault, which carried a lesser sentence. The court denied the claim since it found a sufficient rational basis for distinguishing the offenses so as to justify the different penalties attached to them.

Should courts engage in a proportionality review of the internal consistency of state sentencing laws? How would you expect a state legislator to react to the *Walden* decision?

6. *Expanding on the prohibition of cruel and unusual punishments.*   Human rights law has borrowed heavily from U.S. legal principles, but the Eighth Amendment analogues have been drawn more broadly in the international arena. The International Covenant for Civil and Political Rights, which the United States has ratified, prohibits "cruel, inhuman or degrading treatment or punishment." The United States has taken a reservation to Article 7, interpreting this provision to reach no further than the Fifth, Eighth, and Fourteenth Amendments. Article 3 of the European Convention on Human Rights prohibits "inhuman or degrading treatment or punishment." On their face, do these provisions differ with regard to proportionality of prison terms? How important should the drafters' intent be in reviewing sentences under these provisions?

7. *Recent academic perspectives.*   There is a significant array of new academic commentary on how the Constitution's prohibition on Cruel and Unusual Punishments should be interpreted and applied. See, e.g., John Stinneford, Rethinking Proportionality under the Cruel and Unusual Punishments Clause, 97 Va. L. Rev. 899 (2011) (proposing a reconsideration of the term "unusual" to consider recent, often popularly inspired dramatic sentence increases as unusual); Rachel E. Barkow, The Court of Life and Death: the Two Tracks of Constitutional Sentencing Law and the Case for Uniformity, 107 Mich. L. Rev. 1145 (2009); Joshua L. Shapiro, And Unusual: Examining the Forgotten Prong of the Eighth Amendment, 38 U. Mem. L. Rev. 465 (2008); Eva S. Nilsen, Decency, Dignity, and Desert: Restoring Ideals of Humane Punishment to Constitutional Discourse, 41 U.C. Davis L. Rev. 111 (2007); Laurence Claus, Methodology, Proportionality, Equality: Which Moral Question Does the Eighth Amendment Pose?, 31 Harv. J.L. & Pub. Pol'y 35 (2007); Bradford R. Clark, Constitutional Structure, Judicial Discretion, and the Eighth Amendment, 81 Notre Dame L. Rev. 1149 (2006); Tom Stacy, Cleaning Up the Eighth Amendment Mess, 14 Wm. & Mary Bill Rts. J. 475, 475 (2005); Youngjae Lee, The

Constitutional Right Against Excessive Punishment, 91 Va. L. Rev. 677 (2005); Richard S. Frase, Excessive Prison Sentences, Punishment Goals, and the Eighth Amendment: "Proportionality" Relative to What?, 89 Minn. L. Rev. 571 (2005); Erwin Chemerinsky, The Constitution and Punishment, 56 Stan. L. Rev. 1049, 1063-65 (2004).

8. *Proportionality analysis in extraditions.* National courts have employed proportionality analysis to assess the penalty threatening an individual upon extradition. In 2002 the German courts, for example, rejected a Turkish extradition request based on a 1996 conviction for trafficking of .05 gram of heroin. The alleged offender was threatened with a sentence of three years and four months, which could be reduced to one year and four months upon good behavior. The court considered the penalty inappropriate because the defendant was a first offender and the Turkish authorities had waited five years to request extradition. If required to assess the proportionality of the penalty in extradition cases, courts frequently attempt to determine possible justifications for a particular sentence under the laws of the country requesting the extradition and then compare the sentence with penalties for comparable offenses in their home countries.

In 2002 the Mexican Supreme Court rejected extradition to the United States in cases in which the alleged offenders faced life-without-parole terms. Such sentences are prohibited under the Mexican constitution and therefore constitute a total barrier to extradition.

In a recent decision, the European Court of Human Rights affirmed an extradition request even though the alleged offenders were threatened with LWOP sentences in the United States. The court declared them not grossly disproportionate, even though it indicated that it would carefully scrutinize especially mandatory LWOP terms to ascertain whether the continued imprisonment accorded with penological justifications. Cases of Harkins and Edwards v. United Kingdom, Application nos. 9146/07 and 32650/07 (17 January 2012, final 09/07/2012).

How can U.S. prosecutors make successful extradition requests in cases in which the indictment charges offenses that carry life without parole as a sentencing option or as a mandatory sentence? Is it appropriate for national courts to hold the potential sentences of foreign countries as disproportionate under their own laws and therefore as grounds for refusal to extradite?

9. *The* Plata *(California Healthcare Prison) Case.* Does the Supreme Court's decision in this case (discussed earlier in this Chapter) portend more active use of the Eighth Amendment in prisoner rights litigation? Is this use of the Eighth Amendment more amenable to judicial decision making than an assessment of the proportionality of a sentence?

## F.   RECONSIDERING MASS INCARCERATION

Is the trend toward mass incarceration likely to continue? What are the consequences if it does? Is there any idea, fact, or policy that might change the trend toward mass incarceration? Or, when change comes, will it be the result of some long-term "natural" cycle or perhaps of some subtle, complex, and possibly unpredictable combination of factors? Is the strongest argument against mass imprisonment that it may fail to achieve a meaningful social benefit while entailing a great cost? Would a shift from "purposes of punishment" to "principles of public safety" lead to a significant reduction in the use of imprisonment as a tool by either the criminal justice system or society in general?

## *Reconsidering Incarceration: New Directions for Reducing Crime, Don Stemen*
### Vera Institute of Justice (Jan. 2007)

Research has consistently shown crime rates to be affected by many factors, including economics, social and demographic characteristics, culture, politics, and incarceration rates. . . . [T]hanks to rapid increases in crime and imprisonment through the 1970s and 1980s, followed by a sharp decrease in crime in the 1990s, we now have a large body of recent empirical work on the effects of incarceration to draw on as well. . . .

[R]esearchers have found that a 10 percent higher incarceration rate is associated with anywhere from a 9 percent to a 22 percent lower crime rate. In contrast, analyses using state-level data found a weaker association, concluding that a 10 percent increase in incarceration is associated with a crime rate that is anywhere from 0.11 percent to 4 percent lower. Similar estimates have been generated from studies using county-level data, ranging from a 2 percent to a 4 percent crime-rate difference. Moreover, several studies have found no relationship between incarceration rates and crime rates. One study even found that higher incarceration rates were associated with *higher* crime rates in states with already high incarceration rates (incarceration rates above 325 inmates per 100,000 population).

As these disparate findings suggest, the impact of incarceration on crime is inconsistent from one study to the next. . . .

### APPLYING THE RESEARCH FINDINGS: PERILS FOR POLICY

. . . Research only provides an estimate of *average* relationships between incarceration and crime rates across jurisdictions. Thus, such findings are a blunt instrument whose applicability to any specific jurisdiction is dubious.

Research, therefore, cannot predict the impact of future prison increases in a given state. . . .

### THE SIZE OF STATE PRISON POPULATIONS

The size of a state's prison population and crime rate will influence the impact of increases in incarceration rates. . . . [F]or a state with an already high incarceration rate the costs of increasing incarceration by 10 percent to achieve a 2 to 4 percent reduction in crime could be tremendous. For example, California and Nebraska had very similar crime rates in 2003 of approximately 4,000 index offenses per 100,000 people in the population. To achieve a 2 to 4 percent reduction, California, with a prison population of 162,678 inmates, would have to incarcerate an additional 16,089 inmates. To achieve the same rate of reduction, Nebraska, with a prison population of 3,976, would have to incarcerate just 400 additional inmates. If the average cost to incarcerate an offender for one year is $22,650, California would spend $355 million *more* than Nebraska to achieve the same level of public safety. . . . Thus, increases in incarceration rates are associated with lower crime rates at low levels of imprisonment, but the size of that association shrinks as incarceration rates get bigger. Eventually, they say, there is an "inflection point" where increases in incarceration rates are associated with *higher* crime rates. This inflection point occurs when a state's incarceration rate reaches some point between 325 and 492 inmates per 100,000 people. In other words, states with incarceration rates above this range can expect to experience higher crime rates with future increases in incarceration rates. . . .

## THE CONTENT OF PUNISHMENT

Incarceration is not the only punishment that may reduce crime rates. Other types of punishment, including fines, probation, community service, drug treatment, or other sanctions, have also been shown to suppress crime. These alternative sanctions are not considered in the crime control studies noted above, however. Had they increased at the same time as the expansion of imprisonment, these sanctions may have contributed — in part or even completely — to the effects found in those studies. Similarly, the content of incarceration — the quality of inmates' experience in prison — may matter greatly as well. Studies so far have only considered how the size of prison populations affects crime rates. . . .

## THE TYPES OF OFFENDERS IN PRISON

The type of offenders a state decides to incarcerate may also be a relevant factor. . . . By 2004, 419,000 drug possessors were incarcerated in state prisons or local jails at a cost of nearly $8.3 billion annually. Ilyana Kuziemko and Steven D. Levitt argue that the continued increase in the number of drug offenders in prisons may lead to a "crowding out" effect, in which the high number of incarcerated drug offenders prevents the incarceration of offenders prone to more serious crime, thereby reducing the effectiveness of incarceration to reduce crime. Analysts agree with apparent unanimity that future increases in incarceration rates for such offenders will do less and cost more. Washington State, for example, . . . concluded that while incarcerating violent and high-volume property offenders continued to generate more benefits than costs, in the future each additional person incarcerated will result in fewer prevented crimes. Washington even found that increasing the incarceration rate for drug offenders in the 1990s actually had a negative impact overall, as it now costs more to incarcerate additional drug offenders than the average value of the crimes prevented by the imprisonment. . . .

### ESTIMATING THE IMPACT OF OTHER FACTORS ON CRIME

Between 1990 and 2005, the crime rate in the United States fell dramatically to its lowest point in 30 years. However, . . . according to Spelman only 25 percent of this crime drop through the 1990s could be explained by increasing incarceration rates. The remaining 75 percent, therefore, must be due to factors other than incarceration. Indeed, researchers have identified a number of such factors including, for example, fewer young persons in the population, smaller urban populations, decreases in crack cocaine markets, lower unemployment rates, higher wages, more education and high school graduates, more police per capita, and more arrests for public order offenses. An examination of just a few of these indicates that future investment in other policy areas may be not only more effective but also more cost effective than continued investment in increased prison populations. . . .

*Policing.*    Several authors have found an association between increases in the number of police per capita and lower crime rates. For example, using city-level data, Levitt found that a 10 percent increase in the size of a city's police force was associated with an 11 percent lower violent crime rate and a 3 percent lower property crime rate. . . . [W]e can imagine how a crime reduction policy focusing on policing might operate in, say, New York City, where the 2004 index crime rate was 2,800 offenses per 100,000 people in the population. To achieve a 3 percent reduction in the crime rate by increasing incarceration, New York City—with a prison population of 33,564 inmates—would have to incarcerate an additional 3,300 inmates at a cost of approximately $121.5 million per year. With a police force of 39,110 sworn police officers, the city could achieve the same reduction in crime by hiring 3,911 more police officers at a cost of $97.2 million per year. Compared to policing, then, incarceration would cost the city $24.3 million more to achieve the same level of public safety. . . .

*Unemployment and Wages.*    . . . Research has shown that men with criminal records experience no growth in earnings and, therefore, have few choices other than day labor. At the community level, neighborhoods with high incarceration rates may be shunned by employers. Further, as John Hagan argues, incarceration can generate social connections to illegal rather than legal employment, thus, potentially increasing crime. . . .

Using state-level data, Steven Raphael and Rudolf Winter-Ebmer found that a 10 percent decrease in a state's unemployment rate corresponded with a 16 percent reduction in property crime rates; the researchers concluded that, between 1992 and 1997, "slightly more than 40 percent of the decline [in the

overall property crime rate] can be attributed to the decline in unemployment." . . .

Research has also considered the relationship between real wages and
crime. Using national-level data, Gould, Weinberg, and Mustard determined
that a 10 percent increase in real wages saw a 13 percent lower index crime
rate—specifically, a 12 percent lower property crime rate and a 25 percent
lower violent crime rate. . . .

*Education.*   . . . Lance Lochner and Enrico Moretti . . . have shown an
increase in citizens' education levels to be associated with lower crime rates:
specifically, a one-year increase in the average education of citizens results in a
1.7 percent lower index crime rate. In addition, they associated a 10 percent
increase in graduation rates with a 9.4 percent lower index crime rate.
Combined with Gould and his colleagues' findings on the link between
wages and crime, Lochner and Moretti argue that "a 10 percent increase in
high school graduation rates should reduce arrest rates by 5 to 10 percent
through increased wages alone." "[A] 1 percent increase in male high
school graduation rates would save as much as $1.4 billion" nationally
through crime reduction, they conclude. Moreover, prison-based education
programs have been found to significantly reduce recidivism rates for
offenders after release. . . .

### BEYOND INCARCERATION

. . . As William Spelman has cautioned, "It is no longer sufficient, if it ever
was, to demonstrate that prisons are better than nothing. Instead, they must be
better than the next-best use of the money."

Yet, in the past two decades, spending on these other factors has been cut.
Corrections expenditures were the only state budget category other than Medicaid to increase as a percentage of total state spending over the past 20 years.
Between 1985 and 2004, states increased corrections spending by 202 percent.
By comparison, spending on higher education grew by just 3 percent, Medicaid
by 47 percent, and secondary and elementary education by 55 percent; spending
on public assistance decreased by more than 60 percent during the same period
(see Figure 1). . . .

. . . But a broader approach would require a shift in criminal justice policy
away from reactive responses to criminal offending and toward a proactive
attempt to address the underlying causes of criminal offending. . . .

Moreover, the public favors a policy that addresses the underlying causes of
crime rather than simply responds to crime after it occurs. Polling by Peter D.
Hart Research Associates, for example, shows the public questioning whether
incarceration is the best crime control policy. In 1994, 42 percent of Americans
favored responding to crime with stricter sentencing; by 2001, this had
decreased to just 32 percent. Conversely, in 1994, only 48 percent of Americans
said they favored addressing the underlying causes of crime; by 2001, this had
increased to 65 percent.

## Percent Change in State Spending, 1985-2004

Incarceration Rates (2005)—10 Highest & 10 Lowest States (and the Federal system)
Rate Per 100,000 People

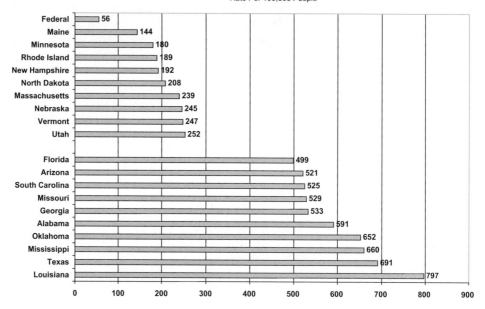

*Source:* National Association of State Budget Officers. State Expenditure Reports annual series.

## TOWARD A NEW APPROACH TO PUBLIC SAFETY

After 15 years of declining crime rates, many analysts are claiming that "prison works." But, as Elliot Currie notes, "if 'prison works' is the answer, what was the question?" If the question is whether it is possible to prevent individuals from committing crimes by putting them in prison, then prison certainly works; it works to punish and incapacitate those who have committed crimes. But if the question is what is the best way to reduce crime, "prison works" may not be the most helpful response. Does a five-year prison sentence "work" better to reduce crime than a two-year prison sentence? Does a two-year prison sentence for nonviolent offenders "work" as well as a two-year prison sentence for violent offenders?

The most salient question of all may be, Do the resources devoted to prison "work" better to ensure public safety than if those resources were devoted to something else? Prisons are not the only way to fight crime. Policymakers could spend money on more judges, better staffed or equipped law enforcement, or better-trained probation and parole officers. They could invest, as this paper indicates, in other, non-criminal-justice areas shown to affect crime: education, employment, economic development, etc. The impact of incarceration on crime is limited and diminishing. The public's support for reactive crime control is also in decline. It is therefore fitting that we reconsider the continued emphasis on and dedication of resources to incarceration.

Public safety cannot be achieved only by responding to crime after it occurs; research shows that it may also depend on protecting people against those factors that have been shown to be associated with high crime rates, such as unemployment, poverty, and illiteracy. By pursuing crime reduction chiefly through incarceration, states are forgoing the opportunity to invest in these other important areas. As state policymakers continue to feel pressure to introduce measures to keep crime rates low, they would therefore do well to look beyond incarceration for alternative policies that not only may be able to accomplish the important task of protecting public safety, but may do so more efficiently and more effectively.

## NOTES

1. *Slowing growth as a victory.*   The rate of incarceration has begun to stabilize in state systems, and even decline in some, though the federal system continues to grow. How far will the decline go? Will there come a time when the United States is no longer the unqualified leader in world imprisonment rates? When will the decrease be reflected in federal inmate numbers? A return to a time like the early 1970s, when many scholars and policy actors believed imprisonment was fading as a social tool, is unlikely on any short or moderate time horizon. Perhaps the increasing attention by state actors and voters to the substantial social and economic costs of mass imprisonment may together signal a turning point in United States punishment policy. As a policymaker, what strategies might you suggest to speed or magnify this change? Should responsibility for criminal justice policy be shifted more to local levels? Professor Marc Miller suggests that in a time of central and abstract punitiveness, liberals ought to reconsider their fears of control at the local level, where resources are more limited and choices among competing social policies often more stark. See Marc Miller, Cells vs. Cops vs. Classrooms, in The Crime Conundrum: Essays on Criminal Justice 127 (Lawrence Friedman & George Fisher eds., 1997).

2. *The possible shift to public safety.*   Don Stemen identifies a possible shift from crime control (or some mix of current purposes) to public safety as the governing rationale for the criminal justice system. Of course, such a shift would necessarily involve more than the criminal justice system; the system would become more emphatically a part of a larger enterprise (public safety). But what would such a shift mean if it were taken seriously and made the defining justification for criminal justice actors? How would police act in a system defined by public safety? How would prosecutors act? How is a shift to public safety as a governing rationale related to policies of "community prosecution" and "problem-oriented prosecution"? See Mark A.R. Kleiman, When Brute Force Fails: How to Have Less Crime and Less Punishment (2010); Walter Dickey & Peggy McGarry, The Search for Justice and Safety Through Community Engagement: Community Justice and Community Prosecution, 42 Idaho L. Rev. 313 (2006). What would a shift to public safety mean for sentencing systems and sentencing purposes?

3. *Does mass incarceration obscure consistent mass social control?*  Professor Bernard Harcourt makes the claim that a focus on dramatically increasing imprisonment rates in the United States obscures a longer and more consistent level of mass social control. He points to the deinstitutionalization of mental health institutions in the 1960s and 1970s and claims that when populations of psychiatric institutions and prisons are combined, the United States' level of incarceration has remained relatively stable.

> [T]he empirical data on mental hospitalization reflect extraordinarily high rates of institutionalization at mid-century. Simply put, when the data on mental hospitalization rates are combined with the data on prison rates for the years 1928 through 2000, the incarceration revolution of the late twentieth century barely reaches the level of aggregated institutionalization that the United States experienced at mid-century. The highest rate of aggregated institutionalization during the entire twentieth century occurred in 1955 when almost 640 persons per 100,000 adults over age fifteen were institutionalized in asylums, mental hospitals, and state and federal prisons. Throughout almost the entire period from 1938 to 1960, the U.S. population experienced rates of institutionalization in excess of 600 inmates per 100,000 adults. . . .
>
> Aggregating mental hospitalization and imprisonment rates into a combined institutionalization rate significantly changes the trend line for confinement over the twentieth century. We are used to thinking of confinement through the lens of incarceration only, and to referring to the period prior to the mid-1970s as one of "relative stability" followed by an exponential rise. . . . As a literal matter, this is of course right. If all we are describing is the specific variable in our study and the source of the data, then indeed the observations are relatively stable over the five decades. But the truth is, what we are trying to capture when we use the variable of imprisonment is something about confinement in an institutional setting — confinement that renders the population in question incapacitated or unable to work, pursue educational opportunities, and so forth. And from this larger perspective, the period before 1970 — in fact, the entire twentieth century — reflects remarkable instability.

Bernard Harcourt, From the Asylum to the Prison: Rethinking the Incarceration Revolution, 84 Tex. L. Rev. 1751, 1754-1755 (2006). Harcourt describes a relationship between the rate of homicides and total social control. But his work also forces scholars and policy advocates to step back and ask what "real" social forces and phenomena explain the use of incarceration in the United States. If Harcourt's analysis is correct, what impact should this have on the law and politics of incarceration? Does Harcourt's analysis encourage the proposed shift to a central goal of public safety, or should it lead to concern that under various rubrics the United States may favor very high levels of confinement and that deeper forces are at work?

Mass incarceration may reverberate far beyond mass social control on the entire political system in light of its impact on political participation, community cohesion, and the meaning of citizenship. Marie Gottschalk, The Long Reach of the Carceral State: The Politics of Crime, Mass Imprisonment, and Penal Reform in the United States and Abroad, 34 L. & Soc. Inquiry 439 (2009).

4. *Structural reforms.*    While economic pressures and a declining crime rate have slowed the growth in incarceration and given states the ability to focus more on rehabilitation and re-entry, those developments may not suffice to assure a continued decline in imprisonment. David Cole has argued that

empathy will be a necessary ingredient to avoid fear of crime from overwhelming public debate, especially once state coffers become fuller again. The innocence movement constitutes an effective beginning. What other measures might build empathy toward those imprisoned or in the criminal justice system? See David Cole, Turning the Corner on Mass Incarceration?, 9 Ohio St. J. Crim. L. 27 (2011).

# =8=

## Sentencing Outcomes: Nonprison Punishments

In the United States, the dominant criminal sanction appears to be imprisonment (see Chapter 7), but appearances can be deceiving: In reality, the majority of criminal defendants receive nonprison sentences. Nevertheless, policymakers typically speak as if prison were the only penalty worth discussing, and much of the criminal justice system operates in an imprisonment mindset. Other countries and some U.S. jurisdictions, however, seek other options or operate under different punishment presumptions.

The terms "nonprison sanctions" and "alternatives to imprisonment" are revealing. Since imprisonment is frequently viewed as the default option, the implication is that such sanctions are acceptable only if they resemble prison in some way. Excellent examples are boot camp, which mimics the conditions of prison, and home confinement.

The United Nations Global Report on Crime and Justice distinguishes countries by the primary form of punishment they use. Some countries focus on imprisonment, others on fines, and still others on a combination of deprivation of liberty and probation. In most of the countries that responded to the U.N. survey, a fine is the most common noncustodial sentence. For example, more than 95% of Japanese offenders are assessed a fine. Noncustodial sanctions are little used in Latin America, Africa, and Asia—with the exception of Japan and South Korea—but are popular in Europe and North America.

The prevalence of noncustodial sanctions does not necessarily indicate a systematically low use of imprisonment. It may reflect a shift away from custody or an increase in the proportion of the population being criminally sanctioned. It may also be a response to other developments in the criminal justice arena, such as a focus on the risk certain offenders pose, increased opportunities to combine criminal with administrative sanctions, the development of new sentencing options, and the prosecution of new criminal actors such as organizations.

Noncustodial sanctions can serve a variety of purposes. Some sanctions, such as probation and annulment of licenses, are intended to provide some degree of control and supervision over offenders, if less than imprisonment. Other sanctions, such as fines and confiscation, are meant to punish without individual corporal control.

This chapter outlines the use of noncustodial sanctions in the United States. The first part addresses the dominant nonprison sanctions of probation and fines. The second part discusses modern alternative sanctions that have received much public attention but relatively little use. The third section considers a set of punishments labeled "collateral sanctions" that are applied in addition to other sanctions, including imprisonment.

## A.    TRADITIONAL ALTERNATIVES

The most common and best-established nonprison sanctions are fines and probation. Much of the public debate over punishment turns on the little-used but severe and highly symbolic imposition of capital punishment and the dominant coin of the realm — imprisonment. Yet most criminal sentences use some combination of fines and probation. The use of fines, both alone and especially in conjunction with prison or other sanctions, is far more prevalent than public debate and, indeed, much of the scholarly literature would suggest. Even among felons, straight probation (with no time in jail or prison) is used in about one-third of all cases.

Sanctions often have several components, but the public takes note of only the most severe aspects of the punishment. Among all felons sentenced in 2006 to either incarceration or probation, a fine was imposed on 38%, restitution on 18%, community service on 11%, and treatment on 11%. See Bureau of Justice Statistics, Felony Sentences in State Courts, 2006 (NCJ 226846, December 2009).

For all sanctions, one key but often implicit issue is the purpose of punishment that the sanction is intended to fulfill. When can fines and probation serve purposes similar to those served by prison — that is, when can they "replace" imprisonment? How do constitutional and political considerations limit the use of nonprison sanctions?

### 1.   Fines

Fines have been used extensively in some European countries, where the amount of the penalty is keyed to the type of offense and the offender's income. This approach has not caught on in the United States, but the use of fines here has been increasing generally, even though judges often express reluctance to levy them. Like many European countries, the United States has also seen a steady increase in statutory or guideline requirements for restitution by criminal offenders to their victims. Only in the United States are offenders asked to pay for some or all of the costs of punishment, though it is not clear how often such fines are in fact imposed or paid.

Some of the recurring issues with fines are whether they are fair to the poor and whether they impose a proportional punishment on either the poor or the rich. In the following case, the Mississippi Supreme Court addresses one of these issues.

|| *Mary Ann Moody v. State*  ||
|| **716 So. 2d 562 (Miss. 1998)** ||

BANKS, J.

Here we consider the question of whether a standard practice of extracting a set fine from persons accused of writing bad checks on the pain of suffering a full criminal prosecution for failure to do so comports with the Equal Protection Clause of the Fourteenth Amendment to the Constitution of the United States. We answer that it does not. . . .

On or about October 12, 1991, Mary Ann Moody wrote a check to the order of City Salvage for $123.89. The check was written in exchange for two doors for Moody's mother's house. The check was returned to City Salvage for "non-sufficient funds." On February 24, 1993, she was indicted by a Jones County Grand Jury, for the crime of False Pretense. Moody was appointed counsel as an indigent defendant. After indictment the district attorney's office assessed a levy of $500 plus restitution. Moody was given the option of paying a $500 fine plus restitution and having the case nolle prossed, or not paying the fine and being subjected to prosecution. Jeanne Jefcoat of the district attorney's office testified that this fine is imposed automatically once a defendant is indicted. . . . Moody testified that she could not pay all the fine, restitution and other costs at one time. Moody's motion to dismiss the action was denied and the case proceeded to trial.

. . . She was subsequently convicted of the crime of false pretense [and sentenced to three years in the Mississippi Department of Corrections and fined $1,000, which was ordered one year suspended and $500 suspended] and appeals, raising a violation of the Fourteenth Amendment to the Constitution of the United States as her sole ground on appeal.

Moody claims that the district attorney's office lacks statutory or constitutional authority to automatically impose a set fine of $500 on all defendants indicted under the Mississippi Bad Check Law. Furthermore, she claims that such a fine violates an indigent's right to equal protection under the Fourteenth Amendment. The State argues that the fine is merely a plea bargain, and as such is in the discretion of the district attorney. This is a case of first impression before this Court. We are unable to find any cases directly on point in any other jurisdiction. . . .

In Bearden v. Georgia, 461 U.S. 660 (1983), the United States Supreme Court considered whether a sentencing court can revoke a defendant's probation for failure to pay the imposed fine and restitution. The *Bearden* Court stated:

This Court has long been sensitive to the treatment of indigents in our criminal justice system. Over a quarter-century ago, Justice Black declared that "[t]here can be no equal justice where the kind of trial a man gets depends on the amount of money he has."

*Bearden*, 461 U.S. at 664 (quoting Griffin v. Illinois, 351 U.S. 12 (1956) (plurality opinion)). The Court held that before revocation of an indigent's probation, the court must inquire into the reasons for failure to pay. In holding such, the Court opined:

> If the probationer willfully refused to pay or failed to make sufficient bona fide efforts legally to acquire the resources to pay, the court may revoke probation and sentence the defendant to imprisonment within the authorized range of its sentencing authority. If the probationer could not pay despite sufficient bona fide efforts to acquire the resources to do so, the court must consider alternative measures of punishment other than imprisonment. Only if alternative measures are not adequate to meet the State's interests in punishment and deterrence may the court imprison a probationer who has made sufficient bona fide efforts to pay. To do otherwise would deprive the probationer of his conditional freedom simply because, through no fault of his own, he cannot pay the fine. Such a deprivation would be contrary to the fundamental fairness required by the Fourteenth Amendment.

See also Tate v. Short, 401 U.S. 395 (1971) (holding that a State cannot convert a fine imposed under a fine-only statute into a jail term solely because the defendant is indigent and cannot immediately pay the fine in full).

Moody cites Cassibry v. State, 453 So. 2d 1298 (Miss. 1984), where this Court held that an indigent may not be incarcerated because he is financially unable to comply with an otherwise lawfully imposed sentence of a fine. *Cassibry* is distinguishable in that, the defendant had failed to pay a fine and was subsequently imprisoned for failure to pay the fine while in this case, Moody was sentenced to an appropriate statutory prison term for her crime. But see Lee v. State, 457 So. 2d 920 (Miss. 1984) (stating *Cassibry* requires consideration of statutory alternatives to imprisonment for indigents financially unable to pay a fine). . . .

In a case similar to this one, the Oklahoma Criminal Court of Appeals considered whether a defendant was deprived of equal protection in plea bargaining. Gray v. State, 650 P.2d 880 (Okla. Crim. App. 1982). In *Gray* the defendant claimed that he was denied an opportunity to plea bargain because he was unable to contribute to a special community relations fund. The *Gray* court opined:

> The recognition of plea bargaining as an essential component of the administration of justice, however, does not elevate it to a constitutional right. That is not to say, that a prosecutor can accept or refuse plea negotiations in a way that discriminates against defendants on account of their race, religion, economic status or other arbitrary classification.

The court found that there was no violation of the defendant's equal protection rights, because he did not attempt to seek a plea bargain.

The State argues that Moody is confusing this fine with a plea bargain. There is no constitutional right to a plea bargain. Allman v. State, 571 So. 2d 244, 254 (Miss. 1990). The State argues that since there is no constitutional right to a plea bargain there can be no violation in this case. Furthermore, the State claims that since the fine or plea offer is offered to everyone who is indicted, there can be no equal protection violation, because it is treating everyone the same.

The record clearly indicates that after a defendant is indicted under the Bad Check Law, an automatic $500 plus restitution is charged to drop the prosecution. The amount is due immediately. The defendant then has the option of paying the $500 and have the indictment nolle prossed or proceeding to trial. Thus, one who is unable to pay will always be in a position of facing a felony conviction and jail time, while those with adequate resources will not. The automatic nature of the fine is what makes it discriminating to the poor, in that only the poor will face jail time. We hold that an indigent's equal protection rights are violated when all potential defendants are offered one way to avoid prosecution and that one way is to pay a fine, and there is no determination as to an individual's ability to pay such a fine. Subjecting one to a jail term merely because he cannot afford to pay a fine, due to no fault of his own, is unconstitutional.

Additionally, we note that this procedure does not involve a plea bargain at all because the only charge is nolle prosequi. There is no plea at all. What and all that happens is that a $500 fee is extracted in order to avoid prosecution. Thus the scheme is both procedurally and constitutionally flawed.

[W]e conclude that the only way to put Moody on a footing roughly equivalent to those able to purchase a nolle prosequi is to remand for new sentencing in which the trial court can withhold adjudication and place her on probation requiring restitution plus reasonable efforts to pay a reasonable fine and costs. This remedy does not restrict the trial judges where one complains of indigency. There are methods in use today which allow for indigent status where the penalty to be imposed is a fine. These include working out a payment schedule which is appropriate to the means of the offender. It is a proper solution for this case, granting Moody relief from an improper and unconstitutional practice subjecting her to disparate treatment based upon her indigency. In the future, it is to be hoped that this unconstitutional scheme will be abandoned and the matter of plea bargains will be handled in a proper manner which comports with the right to equal protection of the laws.

For the foregoing reasons, this matter is reversed and remanded to the circuit court for re-sentencing.

McRae, J., concurring in part and dissenting in part.

The Jones County District Attorney's approach to enforcing the Mississippi Worthless Check Law by charging a fine to avoid prosecution and incarcerating those who cannot pay discriminates against the poor in violation of the equal protection provisions of the United States Constitution and the Mississippi Constitution and offends the prohibition against imprisonment for civil debt found in art. 3, §30 of the Mississippi Constitution. It further allows the District Attorney's office to exercise powers well in excess of those afforded it by statute pursuant to the directive of art. 6, §174 of the Mississippi Constitution. The root of the problem, however, lies in our statutory framework that subjects one who "bounces" a check to criminal penalties. To remand Mrs. Moody's case for resentencing and merely "hope" that the practices used in her situation will be abandoned does nothing to remedy the larger problem.

Miss. Code Ann. §97-19-67(1)(d)(1994) sets the penalty for writing a bad check in excess of $100, regardless of whether a first or second offense, *upon conviction*, at a fine of not less than $100 and not more than $1000, *or* imprisonment for not more than three years *or* both, *in the discretion of the court.* Jeanne Jefcoat, the Worthless Check Director for the Jones County District Attorney's Office, however, testified that once an individual has been indicted by the grand jury for writing a bad check, he must immediately pay a set $500 fine, the amount of the check and a variety of fees, or else face trial. She stated that Mrs. Moody was told that to avoid prosecution, she would have to pay more than $800: the $123.89 check, the $500 fine, $163.50 court costs, a $40 processing fee levied by the District Attorney's Office and a $10 returned check fee. Thus, Mrs. Moody was fined before she was convicted and in essence, promised that if she paid the fine and costs, she wouldn't be convicted. Contrary to the State's argument, this cannot be construed as a "standard" plea bargain in any sense merely because Mrs. Moody was offered the opportunity to pay. . . .

Imprisonment may be an appropriate remedy for a defendant who refuses or neglects to pay a fine he can afford, or even when collection is unsuccessful despite the defendant's reasonable efforts to make payment. However, the imprisonment of an indigent defendant who cannot pay a fine imposed to avoid conviction is a violation of the fourteenth amendment to the United States Constitution as well as to art. 3, §30 of the Mississippi Constitution. . . .

Debtor's prison was abolished long ago. Our statutory system, nevertheless, allows for imprisonment of one who cannot pay all of the fines that may arise from "bouncing" a check. Further, while they may pursue actions for false pretenses, District Attorneys do not have the authority under our State Constitution or . . . Code . . . either to collect civil debts or to use criminal statutes to coerce payment of those debts and any fees and penalties which also might accrue. Moreover, the power to render fines and judgments belongs with the courts and not the District Attorney's Office. Accordingly, I do not think that the majority has gone far enough by recognizing only the fourteenth amendment problems or "hoping" that problematic debt collection practices are abandoned.

## NOTES

1. *The use of fines.*   Straight fines (fines in the absence of other sanctions) are used most often for misdemeanants and other more minor offenders. Some states prohibit the use of fines for certain types of offenses. Little data appear available on fines generally, though it is obvious that fines are rarely used as the only or primary punishment for serious crimes. Of all those convicted of felonies, only 3% received a sanction solely other than prison, jail, or probation. Straight fines are also relatively uncommon in the federal system. In federal court 7.9% of all offenders sentenced during fiscal year 2011 received a sentence that either included a fine as part of or as the sole component of a criminal justice sanction. This number has decreased over time. The federal sentencing guidelines mandate that the court impose a fine unless the offender shows that he is unable to pay a fine and it is unlikely that that situation will change.

Collection of fines remains challenging unless resources are committed to track payment and implement follow-up punishments, including incarceration. Only for traffic and parking violations are collection rates high. How should criminal fines be prioritized if the offender also owes, for example, child support?

Fines may not be as efficient as may appear because their collection can be expensive and require a substantial back-up system, including sanctions. Can their use nevertheless be defended on efficiency grounds? What kind of backup system needs to be constructed to make fines credible and effective? Anne Morrison Piehl & Geoffrey Williams, Institutional Requirements for Effective Imposition of Fines (2010), available at www.nber.org/papers/w16476.

2. *Who gets fined?* Men are more likely to be fined than women; whites are more likely to be fined than blacks or Hispanics; employed offenders are significantly more likely to be fined than unemployed offenders; older offenders are more likely to be fined than younger offenders; nondrug offenders are more likely to be fined than drug offenders. In urban settings fines are imposed less frequently than in rural or suburban communities. In sum, fines are more likely to be used for low-level offenses and low-risk offenders, with judges considering the defendant's actual or perceived wealth and income.

3. *Fines in white-collar and corporate cases.* The largest fines are generally imposed in healthcare fraud and antitrust prosecutions. Often companies reach agreements with the prosecution designed to settle criminal charges and civil liabilities arising from the same nucleus of facts. Such fines are paid into the federal Crime Victims Fund and are available for disbursement to crime victims and to fund training programs during the following year.

4. *Restitution.* In more than one-third of the states, courts are statutorily required to order restitution unless there are compelling or extraordinary circumstances to the contrary. In about half the states with crime victims' rights constitutional amendments, victims have a right to restitution. Some states allow broad exceptions to restitution requirements. More than a dozen states require courts to state on the record the reasons for failing to order restitution or for ordering only partial restitution. Some states — and the federal government — have enacted specific directives to order restitution to victims of particular offenses.

Restitution is awarded for crime-related expenses incurred by the victim or, in homicide cases, the victim's family; it includes medical and counseling expenses, lost wages, and costs for lost or damaged property. Some states permit the award of future damages. Nevertheless, victims only infrequently receive restitution. The reasons for this include failure to request restitution, inability to demonstrate or calculate loss, the court's opinion that restitution is inappropriate in light of other penalties, and the defendant's inability to pay. Most states require courts to consider the defendant's financial resources and obligations when awarding restitution. Some states are beginning to move away from this requirement, instead merely considering the defendant's ability to pay when setting the payment schedule.

In 1996 Congress enacted the Mandatory Victims Restitution Act (MVRA), which mandates that restitution be ordered in full in certain cases to each victim, regardless of the offender's economic situation. In contrast to fines, restitution is not meant to be punitive but rather to make the victim whole. Despite the MVRA's mandate, of 86,000 individual federal offenders in fiscal year 2011, only about 13.3% were ordered to pay restitution. Factors that appear to have influenced courts in ordering an offender to pay restitution included the offense of conviction, length and type of sentence imposed, and offender characteristics such as sex, race, education, and citizenship. Historically, the most important factor was the judicial district or circuit in which the offender was sentenced. General Accounting Office, Federal Courts: Differences Exist in Ordering Fines and Restitution (May 1999).

Should victims of child pornography receive restitution from those who possessed the images but did not create them? *Compare* United States v. Aumais, 656 F.3d 147 (2d Cir. 2011) *with In re:* Amy Unknown, 701 F.3d 749 (5th cir 2012) (ex base).

The use of fines as the sole or primary sanction for offenses, both violent and nonviolent, raises two central questions. First, when can fines satisfy a sufficient mix of purposes to substitute for or improve on the use of imprisonment, and second, can fines be made relatively similar in impact for offenders with widely varying wealth? A related concern is whether people with more access to legitimate funds through family and friends will just "pay their way" out of a sanction, while poorer offenders may be induced to commit further crimes to pay their fines. Consider whether these issues are addressed in the following materials.

## *Day Fines, Sally T. Hillsman*
### Intermediate Sanctions in Overcrowded Times (Michael Tonry and Kate Hamilton eds., 1995)

Day fines — fine sentences in which the amount is set in proportion to both the seriousness of the offense and the financial resources of the offender — have long been the sentence of choice in northern Europe for most offenses. The name derives from the practice of using the offender's daily income as the base for setting the fine amount.

Systematic day-fine systems typically rely upon flexible, written guidelines. They are increasingly attractive to American judges, prosecutors, and other criminal justice policymakers who look for a wider range of intermediate penalties that can be scaled to provide appropriate punishment for offenses of varying gravity, while reserving imprisonment for violent and predatory offenses.

The fine has always been an attractive sentence in American courts, and it is used more widely than is generally recognized. The fine's advantages are well known. Fines are unmistakably punitive; they deprive offenders of ill-gotten gain; they are inexpensive to administer; and they provide revenue to cover such things as the cost of collection or compensation to victims. Recent research has supported their deterrent impact: fines are associated with lower rates of recidivism than probation or jail for offenders with equivalent criminal records and current offenses.

Fines have not been used in the United States, particularly as a sole penalty, as frequently or for as wide a range of offenses as in European countries, which share many of our sentencing principles. In Germany, for example, 81 percent of adult offenses and 73 percent of crimes of violence are punished solely by fines. In England, 38 percent of offenses equivalent to our felonies and 39 percent of violent offenses result in fines. [Those numbers have declined for England and Wales over the last decade.]

A major impediment in American courts has been the widespread view that poor offenders cannot pay fines and that affluent offenders who do so are buying their way out of more punitive sanctions. Whatever truth there is in this view, however, stems largely from American use of "tariff" systems to set fine amounts. Tariff systems use informal "going rates" to guide judges in setting amounts. Because tariff systems tend to equate equity with consistency, they generally result in fines keyed to the lowest common economic denominator. This tends to limit judges' ability to adjust fines to an individual offender's financial means and to restrict their use of fines to less serious crimes or first offenders.

In contrast, day fines provide courts with greater capacity to vary fine amounts in a systematic and principled way. Day-fine systems accomplish this by a two-step process. First, the judge sentences an offender to a given number of fine units (e.g., 10, 15, or 90), which reflects the appropriate degree of punishment. Courts that rely on day fines have developed informal guidelines or benchmarks that suggest what number (or range) of units is appropriate for crimes of differing gravity.

The second step is to determine the monetary value of these units. Courts typically develop a rough but standardized method for calculating the proportion of a defendant's daily income that they view to be a "fair share" for the purposes of fining.

Using information routinely available from the police, a pretrial agency, probation, or (most often) the defendant, the judge will estimate the defendant's daily income and calculate the day-fine unit value. Multiplication of the number of units by this unit value produces the fine amount.

Since 1988, a day-fine system has been operating successfully in the Criminal Court of Richmond County, Staten Island, New York. A day-fine program has also been running successfully for over a year in the Maricopa Superior Court in Phoenix, Arizona. In Milwaukee, the day fine was introduced with considerable success as a strategy to reduce high levels of default among low-income offenders. Day-fine projects are under way in Oregon, Iowa, and Connecticut as part of a national demonstration project on "structured fines" sponsored by the Bureau of Justice Assistance. Numerous other jurisdictions are beginning to experiment with the concept, sometimes with encouragement from their state legislatures. In California, for example, legislation authorizes implementation of day-fine pilots.

## Fines Reduce Use of Prison Sentences in Germany, Thomas Weigend
### Intermediate Sanctions in Overcrowded Times (Michael Tonry and Kate Hamilton eds., 1995)

Between 1968 and 1989, the former West Germany greatly reduced the proportion of convicted offenders sentenced to prison. In 1968, roughly a quarter of convicted offenders were sentenced to imprisonment. Two years later, the size of that group had dropped from 136,000 to 42,000, and the percentage of convicted offenders who were imprisoned had fallen from 24 percent to 7 percent. In 1989 (the latest year for which data are available), only 33,000 persons, less than 6 percent of adults convicted in West Germany, were sent directly to prison. . . . [The percentage data remains accurate even after German unification. Overall, however, imprisonment has increased substantially in Europe over the last decade. See Hans-Joerg Albrecht, Sanction Policies and Alternative Measures to Incarceration: European Experiences with Intermediate and Alternative Criminal Penalties, available at www.unafel.or.jp/english/pdf/RS_No80/No80_07VE_Albrecht.pdf.]

The remarkable decline in prison use is due to a determined assault on use of short-term imprisonment. At the [start of the twentieth century], more than 50 percent of offenders received prison sentences of three months' duration or less. Legislation passed in 1921 obliged the courts to impose fines instead of short prison terms whenever the purpose of punishment could as well be achieved by a fine. Even so, the portion of short prison sentences among all prison sentences remained high; 83 percent of offenders sentenced to imprisonment in 1968 received sentences of six months or less. By that time, the German legislature had embraced the idea that short-term imprisonment does more harm than good: it disrupts the offender's ties with his family, job, and friends, introduces him into the prison subculture, and stigmatizes him for the rest of his life, but does not allow sufficient time for promising rehabilitative measures. Moreover, the data on the deterrent effectiveness of short-term imprisonment were inconclusive at best.

As a consequence, the German legislature in 1970 enacted section 47, sub. 1 of the Penal Code: "The court shall impose imprisonment below six months only if special circumstances concerning the offense or the offender's personality make the imposition of a prison sentence indispensable for reforming the offender or for defending the legal order." That amendment meant, in effect, that prison sentences below six months could be imposed only under exceptional circumstances for purposes of rehabilitation or general prevention. The number of such sentences dropped dramatically from 184,000 (1968) to 56,000 (1970); after some ups and downs, that figure reached a low of 48,000 in 1989 (and many of these were suspended).

At the same time, the German legislature extended the possibility of suspending short-term prison sentences (suspension being the German equivalent of probation). . . .

The court can combine suspension with various conditions and restrictions, including the duty to make restitution to the victim or to pay a sum of money to the state or to a charitable organization. . . .

German courts have made use of the suspension option with consistently increasing frequency. In 1968, the year before the reform, only 36 percent of

**FIGURE 1**
**Criminal Sanctions, 1968 and 1989**

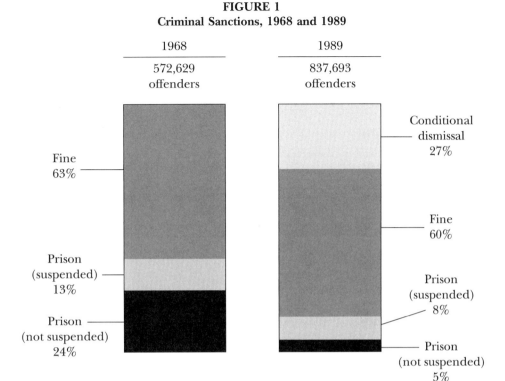

*Sources:* Statistisches Bundesamt, Fachserie A., Reihe 9: Rechtspflege 1968, p. 120; Statistisches Bundesamt, Fachserie 10, Reihe 3: Strafverfolgung 1989, p. 42; Statistisches Bundesamt Staatsanwaltschaften 1989, p. 14.

prison sentences were suspended. By 1979, that portion had climbed to 65 percent, and it has not significantly changed since then (1989 — 67 percent). Prison sentences of six months or less have been suspended even more liberally (1989 — 77 percent). Revocations of suspension have diminished despite the more generous use of suspension. Whereas 46 percent of suspensions were revoked in 1986, less than a third (29 percent) were revoked in 1989.

For minor offenses, German law since 1975 offers an additional option of informal sanctioning. According to section 153a of the Code of Criminal Procedure, either the public prosecutor or the court can "invite" a suspect to pay a sum of money to the state, the victim, or a charitable organization in exchange for dismissal of the criminal prosecution. The theory of this quasi-sanction is that the suspect, by making the payment, eliminates the public interest in prosecuting the minor offense. The payment neither requires a formal admission of guilt nor implies a criminal conviction, but the (presumed) offender must pay an amount of money roughly equivalent to the fine that might be imposed if he were convicted. The use of this procedural option has greatly increased since its inception; prosecutors and courts employ it not only in petty cases but also for sanctioning fairly serious, especially economic, offenses without trial. Taking the quasi-sanction of section 153a into account, the distribution of criminal sanctions in Germany before and after the reforms of 1970 and 1975 is shown in figure 1.

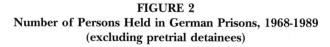

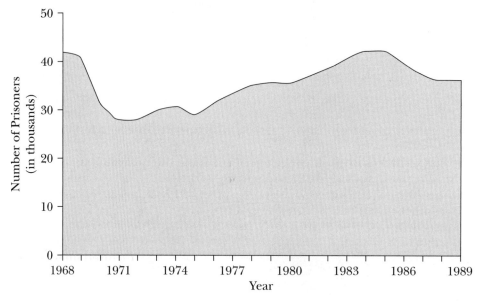

**FIGURE 2**
**Number of Persons Held in German Prisons, 1968-1989**
**(excluding pretrial detainees)**

*Sources:* Statistisches Bundesamt, Fachserie A. Reihe 9: Rechtspflege 1968, 1971, 1973; Statistisches Bundesamt, Fachserie 10, Reihe 1: Ausgewählte Zahlen für die Rechtspflege 1984, 1988, 1989.

The de-emphasis of nonsuspended short prison sentences and the introduction of conditional dismissal produced a marked shift from custodial sentences (which, even in 1968, had a comparatively low incidence) to monetary sanctions. One might expect this shift to have led to a proportional depletion of German prisons. Curiously, that has failed to occur. Figure 2 shows the numbers of persons (excluding pretrial detainees) held in German prisons on March 31 of selected years.

[T]here are rational explanations for this development. First, the overall number of convicted offenders has increased, though not dramatically, from 573,000 (1968) to 609,000 (1989). More important, those who receive nonsuspended prison sentences tend to receive longer sentences than before: within fifteen years, the share of lengthy sentences (two to fifteen years) among all nonsuspended prison sentences increased from 9 percent (1974) to 15 percent. This change may be due to the increase in drug-related offenses, which tend to draw heavy sentences.

Moreover, the initial imposition of a noncustodial sentence does not necessarily mean that the offender can avoid prison, since about one third of suspended sentences are revoked (usually due to the commission of a new offense). Offenders who receive fines can be sent to prison for nonpayment. Under German law, nonpayment can transform a fine into a prison term; the state need not show that the offender willfully refused to pay although he had the means to do so (section 43, Penal Code). Although only 6-7 percent of fined offenders eventually serve a prison term because of nonpayment, this group, due to the large absolute numbers involved, imposes a heavy burden on the corrections system: each year approximately 30,000 such persons enter prison.

In recent years, the German states have increasingly attempted to reduce that number by offering destitute offenders an alternative to prison. They can enter community service programs and thereby work off the fine instead of "sitting it off." These programs, though reaching only a limited number of offenders, have been described as fairly successful, especially when they are adequately staffed and organized. . . .

## NOTES

1. *Day fines.* The underlying concept of day fines is that "punishment by a fine should be proportionate to the seriousness of the offense and should have roughly similar impact (in terms of economic sting) on persons with differing financial resources who are convicted of the same offense." Bureau of Justice Assistance, How to Use Structured Fines (Day Fines) as an Intermediate Sanction (NCJ 156242, 1996). The concept was introduced in Sweden in the 1920s and then adopted in other Scandinavian and European countries. In Germany structured fines are used as the sole sanction for three-quarters of all offenders convicted of property crimes and two-thirds of offenders convicted of assaults. In the United States the first experiment with structured fines began on Staten Island, New York, in 1988. Fewer than a dozen U.S. jurisdictions have tried structured fine systems experimentally since that time. Why has the concept not (yet) taken off nationally?

In 2009 three states passed legislation that allowed day fines to be imposed at least for some select offenses. Why might the concept be of more interest now? How might day fines become more attractive? Edwin W. Zedlewski, National Institute of Justice, Alternatives to Custodial Supervision: The Day Fine, (NCJ 230401, 111) (May 2010).

2. *Structuring day fines.* Day fines present structural and policy challenges. First the court must determine the number of fine units for each offense, based on offense seriousness. Then the court sets the dollar amount by multiplying the number of fine units by a portion of the defendant's daily income, subject to adjustment for taxes, dependents, and special circumstances. Both determinations — the relative seriousness of an offense and relative ability to pay — involve multiple policy choices. How should courts treat unemployed offenders? How should they calculate day fines on offenders working in the shadow economy, engaged in legal but untaxed activity?

3. *Constitutional limitations on fines.* The Eighth Amendment to the Constitution prohibits "excessive fines." The provision's history can be traced back to the English Magna Carta, which gave judges the opportunity to overrule excessive penalties. In recent years the clause has been used most frequently to challenge punitive damage awards in civil cases as well as civil and criminal forfeitures, as discussed in more detail in Chapter 10. See, e.g., United States v. Bajakajian, 524 U.S. 321 (1998) (amount forfeited must be proportionate to the criminal offense); Austin v. United States, 509 U.S. 602 (1993). Might fines in criminal cases raise less of an Eighth Amendment question of absolute proportionality than an equal protection issue, given their disparate impact depending on a person's resources?

4. *Nonprison sanctions and crime rates.*   Do countries adopt nonprison sanctions only at times of decreasing crime (or decreasing fear of crime)? Note that
the emphasis on fines described by Weigend occurred during a time of increasing crime rates.

> [O]fficial sentencing policy in Germany has responded in an anticyclical
> fashion by discouraging the imposition of prison sentences in the face of a
> growing crime rate. . . . German policies, and the faithful implementation of
> their directives by prosecutors and courts, . . . led to a "cushioning" of the
> crime wave of the 1970s. A greater percentage of offenses than before were
> resolved without conviction, and potential overcrowding of prisons was avoided
> by increased use of fines and suspended sentences. The crime wave ebbed after
> 1983, independent of any action or inaction on the part of criminal justice
> policymakers.

To what extent have concerns about the negative impact of short-term
prison sentences (less than six months) driven the introduction of day fines
in Germany? Current social science research in Europe indicates that such
short prison terms do not have the feared negative impact, and some countries
are moving back toward the imposition of short prison sentences.

May fines be viewed as categorically insufficient for some types of offenders
and offenses? The Department of Justice, for example, has indicated that for
high-level corporate officials involved in white-collar crime, prison is an appropriate sanction because of its deterrent value, stigmatizing effect, and ability to
highlight the seriousness of the offense. Such individual accountability will
make it also unlikely that offenders consider a corporate fine merely a function
of doing business. See, e.g., Scott D. Hammond, Department of Justice, The
Evolution of Criminal Antitrust Enforcement Over the Last Two Decades, Presentation at the 24th Annual National Institute on White Collar Crime (Feb. 25,
2010), at www.justice.gov/atr/public/speeches/255515.pdf; James B. Comey
Jr., The Genesis of the Sentencing Provisions of the Sarbanes-Oxley Act, "Are
We Getting Really Tough on White-Collar Crime?," Hearing Before the Sub-
comm. on Crime and Drugs, S. Judiciary Comm. (June 19, 2002), pt. 1, reprinted
in,15 Fed. Sent'g Rep. 234 (2002).


## 2.   Probation

Probation, an outgrowth of the belief in rehabilitation, emerged during the
second half of the nineteenth century. Probationary sentences typically release
the offender into the community after sentencing but restrict the offender's
freedom and actions. Usually a probation officer is assigned to supervise the
offender. Probationary sentences are by far the most common type of criminal
sanction imposed. At the end of 2010, almost 4.9 million adults were on probation in the United States. Half of them had been convicted of a felony, the others
of misdemeanors and infractions. More than a quarter of them were drug offenders; 15% of them had been convicted of driving while intoxicated, and another
12% had been convicted of some form of larceny or theft offense. See Bureau of
Justice Statistics, Probation and Parole in the United States, 2010 (NCJ 236019,
November 2011).

Probationary sentences involve two closely related issues: first, what are acceptable conditions of probation, and second, what are the procedures and consequences for violation of those conditions?

### a.  Probationary Conditions

The following case explores the foundations and limits of probationary conditions. Consider whether each judge's gender might have affected his or her view of the condition at issue.

|| *State v. David Oakley* ||
|| **629 N.W.2d 200 (Wis. 2001)** ||

WILCOX, J.

[W]e must decide whether as a condition of probation, a father of nine children, who has intentionally refused to pay child support, can be required to avoid having another child, unless he shows that he can support that child and his current children. We conclude that in light of Oakley's ongoing victimization of his nine children and extraordinarily troubling record manifesting his disregard for the law, this anomalous condition — imposed on a convicted felon facing the far more restrictive and punitive sanction of prison — is not overly broad and is reasonably related to Oakley's rehabilitation. Simply put, because Oakley was convicted of intentionally refusing to pay child support — a felony in Wisconsin — and could have been imprisoned for six years, which would have eliminated his right to procreate altogether during those six years, this probation condition, which infringes on his right to procreate during his term of probation, is not invalid under these facts. Accordingly, we hold that the circuit court did not erroneously exercise its discretion. . . .

David Oakley (Oakley), the petitioner, was initially charged with intentionally refusing to pay child support for his nine children he has fathered with four different women. The State subsequently charged Oakley with seven counts of intentionally refusing to provide child support as a repeat offender. His repeat offender status stemmed from intimidating two witnesses in a child abuse case — where one of the victims was his own child. . . .

Oakley . . . entered into [a] plea agreement in which he agreed to enter a no contest plea to three counts of intentionally refusing to support his children and have the other four counts read-in for sentencing. . . . The State, in turn, agreed that in exchange for his no contest plea, it would cap its sentencing recommendation to a total of six years on all counts. Oakley, however, was free to argue for a different sentence.

Oakley had paid no child support and there were arrears in excess of $25,000. Highlighting Oakley's consistent and willful disregard for the law and his obligations to his children, the State argued that Oakley should be sentenced to six years in prison. . . . Oakley, in turn, asked for the opportunity to maintain full-time employment, provide for his children, and make serious payment towards his arrears.

After taking into account Oakley's ability to work and his consistent disregard of the law and his obligations to his children, Judge Hazlewood observed that "if Mr. Oakley had paid something, had made an earnest effort to pay anything within his remote ability to pay, we wouldn't be sitting here," nor would the State argue for six years in prison. But Judge Hazlewood also recognized that "if Mr. Oakley goes to prison, he's not going to be in a position to pay any meaningful support for these children." Therefore, even though Judge Hazlewood acknowledged that Oakley's "defaults, are obvious, consistent, and inexcusable," he decided against sentencing Oakley to six years in prison . . . , as the State had advocated. Instead, Judge Hazlewood sentenced Oakley to three years in prison on the first count, imposed and stayed an eight-year term on the two other counts, and imposed a five-year term of probation consecutive to his incarceration. Judge Hazlewood then imposed the condition at issue here: while on probation, Oakley cannot have any more children unless he demonstrates that he has the ability to support them and that he is supporting the children he already has. After sentencing, Oakley filed for postconviction relief contesting this condition. . . .

Refusal to pay child support by so-called "deadbeat parents" has fostered a crisis with devastating implications for our children. Of those single parent households with established child support awards or orders, approximately one-third did not receive any payment while another one-third received only partial payment. For example, in 1997, out of $26,400,000,000 awarded by a court order to custodial mothers, only $15,800,000,000 was actually paid, amounting to a deficit of $10,600,000,000. These figures represent only a portion of the child support obligations that could be collected if every custodial parent had a support order established. Single mothers disproportionately bear the burden of nonpayment as the custodial parent. On top of the stress of being a single parent, the nonpayment of child support frequently presses single mothers below the poverty line. In fact, 32.1% of custodial mothers were below the poverty line in 1997, in comparison to only 10.7% of custodial fathers. . . .

The effects of the nonpayment of child support on our children are particularly troubling. In addition to engendering long-term consequences such as poor health, behavioral problems, delinquency and low educational attainment, inadequate child support is a direct contributor to childhood poverty. And childhood poverty is all too pervasive in our society. Over 12 million or about one out of every six children in our country lives in poverty. . . . Child support — when paid — on average amounts to over one-quarter of a poor child's family income. There is little doubt that the payment of child support benefits poverty-stricken children the most. Enforcing child support orders thus has surfaced as a major policy directive in our society.

In view of the suffering children must endure when their noncustodial parent intentionally refuses to pay child support, it is not surprising that the legislature has attached severe sanctions to this crime. . . . The legislature has amended this statute so that intentionally refusing to pay child support is now punishable by up to five years in prison.

But Wisconsin law is not so rigid as to mandate the severe sanction of incarceration as the only means of addressing a violation of §948.22(2). In sentencing, a Wisconsin judge can take into account a broad array of factors, including the gravity of the offense and need for protection of the public and potential victims. Other factors — concerning the convicted individual — that a judge can consider include:

> the past record of criminal offenses; any history of undesirable behavior patterns; the defendant's personality, character and social traits; the results of a presentence investigation; the vicious or aggravated nature of the crime; the degree of defendant's culpability; the defendant's demeanor at trial; the defendant's age, educational background and employment record; the defendant's remorse, repentance and cooperativeness; the defendant's need for close rehabilitative control; the rights of the public; and the length of pretrial detention.

After considering all these factors, a judge may decide to forgo the severe punitive sanction of incarceration and address the violation with the less restrictive alternative of probation coupled with specific conditions. Wisconsin Stat. §973.09(1)(a) provides:

> [I]f a person is convicted of a crime, the court, by order, may withhold sentence or impose sentence under s. 973.15 and stay its execution, and in either case place the person on probation to the department for a stated period, stating in the order the reasons therefor. The court may impose any conditions which appear to be reasonable and appropriate.

The statute, then, grants a circuit court judge broad discretion in fashioning a convicted individual's conditions of probation. As we have previously observed, "[t]he theory of the probation statute is to rehabilitate the defendant and protect society without placing the defendant in prison. To accomplish this theory, the circuit court is empowered by Wis. Stat. §973.09(1)(a) to fashion the terms of probation to meet the rehabilitative needs of the defendant." While rehabilitation is the goal of probation, judges must also concern themselves with the imperative of protecting society and potential victims. On this score, we have explained:

> [Probation] involves a prediction by the sentencing court society will not be endangered by the convicted person not being incarcerated. This is risk that the legislature has empowered the courts to take in the exercise of their discretion. . . .
>     If the convicted criminal is thus to escape the more severe punishment of imprisonment for his wrongdoing, society and the potential victims of his anti-social tendencies must be protected.

State v. Evans, 252 N.W.2d 664, 666 (Wis. 1977). Thus, when a judge allows a convicted individual to escape a prison sentence and enjoy the relative freedom of probation, he or she must take reasonable judicial measures to protect society and potential victims from future wrongdoing. To that end — along with the goal of rehabilitation — the legislature has seen fit to grant circuit court judges broad discretion in setting the terms of probation. . . .

In the present case, the record indicates that Judge Hazlewood was familiar with Oakley's abysmal history prior to sentencing. The record reveals that Judge Hazlewood knew that Oakley had a number of support orders entered for his nine children, but he nevertheless continually refused to support them. He was aware that Oakley's probation for intimidating two witnesses in a child abuse case — where one of the witnesses was his own child and the victim — was in the process of being revoked. Judge Hazlewood was also apprised that Oakley had promised in the past to support his children, but those promises had failed to translate into the needed support. Moreover, he knew that Oakley had been employed and had no impediment preventing him from working. . . .

Judge Hazlewood asserted that some prison time coupled with conditional probation might convince Oakley to stop victimizing his children. With probation, Judge Hazlewood sought to rehabilitate Oakley while protecting society and potential victims — Oakley's own children — from future wrongdoing. The conditions were designed to assist Oakley in conforming his conduct to the law. . . . At the same time, Judge Hazlewood sought to protect the victims of Oakley's crimes — Oakley's nine children.

But Oakley argues that the condition imposed by Judge Hazlewood violates his constitutional right to procreate. This court, in accord with the United States Supreme Court, has previously recognized the fundamental liberty interest of a citizen to choose whether or not to procreate. Eberhardy v. Circuit Court for Wood County, 307 N.W.2d 881 (Wis. 1981); Skinner v. Oklahoma ex rel. Williamson, 316 U.S. 535 (1942) (recognizing the right to procreate as "one of the basic civil rights of man"). Accordingly, Oakley argues that the condition here warrants strict scrutiny. That is, it must be narrowly tailored to serve a compelling state interest. Although Oakley concedes, as he must, that the State's interest in requiring parents to support their children is compelling, he argues that the means employed here is not narrowly tailored to serve that compelling interest because Oakley's "right to procreate is not restricted but in fact eliminated." . . . While Oakley's argument might well carry the day if he had not intentionally refused to pay child support, it is well-established that convicted individuals do not enjoy the same degree of liberty as citizens who have not violated the law. We emphatically reject the novel idea that Oakley, who was convicted of intentionally failing to pay child support, has an absolute right to refuse to support his current nine children and any future children that he procreates, thereby adding more child victims to the list. In an analogous case, Oregon upheld a similar probation condition to protect child victims from their father's abusive behavior in State v. Kline, 963 P.2d 697, 699 (Or. App. 1998). . . .

Oakley fails to note that incarceration, by its very nature, deprives a convicted individual of the fundamental right to be free from physical restraint, which in turn encompasses and restricts other fundamental rights, such as the right to procreate. Therefore, given that a convicted felon does not stand in the same position as someone who has not been convicted of a crime, we have previously stated that "conditions of probation may impinge upon constitutional rights as long as they are not overly broad and are reasonably related to the person's rehabilitation." Edwards v. State, 246 N.W.2d 109 (Wis. 1976). In Krebs v. State, 568 N.W.2d 26 (Wis. Ct. App. 1997), the court of appeals recently applied this established standard to uphold a condition of probation that required a defendant who sexually assaulted his own daughter to obtain his probation agent's approval before entering into an intimate or sexual relationship. The court found that although the condition infringed upon a constitutional right, it was reasonable and not overly broad.

Applying the relevant standard here, we find that the condition is not overly broad because it does not eliminate Oakley's ability to exercise his constitutional right to procreate. He can satisfy the condition of probation by making efforts to support his children as required by law. . . . If Oakley decides to continue his present course of conduct—intentionally refusing to pay child support—he will face eight years in prison regardless of how many children he has. Furthermore, this condition will expire at the end of his term of probation. He may then decide to have more children, but of course, if he continues to intentionally refuse to support his children, the State could charge him again under §948.22(2). Rather, because Oakley can satisfy this condition by not intentionally refusing to support his current nine children and any future children as required by the law, we find that the condition is narrowly tailored to serve the State's compelling interest of having parents support their children. It is also narrowly tailored to serve the State's compelling interest in rehabilitating Oakley through probation rather than prison. The alternative to probation with conditions—incarceration for eight years—would have further victimized his children. And it is undoubtedly much broader than this conditional impingement on his procreative freedom for it would deprive him of his fundamental right to be free from physical restraint. Simply stated, Judge Hazlewood preserved much of Oakley's liberty by imposing probation with conditions rather than the more punitive option of imprisonment.

Moreover, the condition is reasonably related to the goal of rehabilitation. A condition is reasonably related to the goal of rehabilitation if it assists the convicted individual in conforming his or her conduct to the law. See State v. Miller, 499 N.W.2d 215 (Wis. Ct. App. 1993) (ruling that condition on probationer convicted of making obscene telephone calls forbidding him to make calls to any woman other than a family member was reasonably related to his rehabilitation). Here, Oakley was convicted of intentionally refusing to support his children. The condition at bar . . . is narrowly tailored to serve the compelling state interest of requiring parents to support their children as well as rehabilitating those convicted of crimes. . . .

BABLITCH, J., concurring. . . .

The two dissents frame the issue in such a way that Oakley's intentional refusal to pay support evolves into an inability to pay support. This case is not at all about an inability to pay support; it is about the intentional refusal to pay support. . . .

The dissents conclude that the majority's means of advancing the state's interest is not narrowly tailored to advance the state's interest. The dissents fail to advance any realistic alternative solution to what they concede is a compelling state interest. As long as the defendant continues to intentionally refuse to pay support, the alternatives posed by the dissents will end up with incarceration—which of course accomplishes indirectly what the dissents say the state cannot do directly. . . .

I conclude that the harm to others who cannot protect themselves is so overwhelmingly apparent and egregious here that there is no room for question. Here is a man who has shown himself time and again to be totally and completely irresponsible. He lives only for himself and the moment, with no regard to the consequences of his actions and taking no responsibility for them. He intentionally refuses to pay support and has been convicted of that felony. The harm that he has done to his nine living children by failing to support them is patent and egregious. . . . Under certain conditions, it is overwhelmingly obvious that any child he fathers in the future is doomed to a future of neglect, abuse, or worse. That as yet unborn child is a victim from the day it is born.

I am not happy with this result, but can discern no other. And the dissents provide none. Accordingly, I join the majority opinion. . . .

BRADLEY, J., dissenting.

I begin by emphasizing the right that is at issue: the right to have children. The majority acknowledges this right, but certainly does not convey its significance and preeminence. The right to have children is a basic human right and an aspect of the fundamental liberty which the Constitution jealously guards for all Americans. See Skinner v. Oklahoma ex rel. Williamson, 316 U.S. 535 (1942).

Thus, the stakes are high in this case. The majority's decision allows, for the first time in our state's history, the birth of a child to carry criminal sanctions. Today's decision makes this court the only court in the country to declare constitutional a condition that limits a probationer's right to procreate based on his financial ability to support his children. Ultimately, the majority's decision may affect the rights of every citizen of this state, man or woman, rich or poor.

I wholeheartedly agree with the majority that the governmental interest at stake in this case is of great magnitude. . . . However, when fundamental rights are at issue, the end does not necessarily justify the means. The majority concludes that the means of effecting the state's interest are sufficiently narrow in light of this governmental interest. I disagree. . . .

The circuit court order forbids Oakley from fathering another child until he can first establish the financial ability to support his children. Oakley is not prohibited from having intercourse, either indiscriminately or irresponsibly. Rather, the condition of probation is not triggered until Oakley's next child is born. . . .

While on its face the order leaves room for the slight possibility that Oakley may establish the financial means to support his children, the order is essentially a prohibition on the right to have children. Oakley readily admits that unless he wins the lottery, he will likely never be able to establish that ability. The circuit court understood the impossibility of Oakley satisfying this financial requirement when it imposed the condition. . . . Stressing the realities of Oakley's situation, the circuit court explained:

> [Y]ou know and I know you're probably never going to make 75 or 100 thousand dollars a year. You're going to struggle to make 25 or 30. And by the time you take care of your taxes and your social security, there isn't a whole lot to go around, and then you've got to ship it out to various children.

In light of the circuit court's recognition of Oakley's inability to meet the condition of probation, the prohibition cannot be considered a narrowly drawn means of advancing the state's interest in ensuring support for Oakley's children. . . .

Let there be no question that I agree with the majority that David Oakley's conduct cannot be condoned. It is irresponsible and criminal. However, we must keep in mind what is really at stake in this case. The fundamental right to have children, shared by us all, is damaged by today's decision. Because I will not join in the majority's disregard of that right, I dissent.

SYKES, J., dissenting.

Can the State criminalize the birth of a child to a convicted felon who is likely to be unwilling or unable to adequately support the child financially? That is essentially the crux of the circuit court order in this case, or at least its apparent practical effect. . . .

Oakley must seek the court's permission and obtain the court's approval before bringing another child into the world. He is subject to probation revocation and imprisonment if he fathers a child without prior court approval.

While I sympathize with the circuit court's understandable exasperation with this chronic "deadbeat dad," I cannot agree that this probation condition survives constitutional scrutiny. It is basically a compulsory, state-sponsored, court-enforced financial test for future parenthood. . . .

## NOTES

1. *Probation: the most common U.S. sanction.*   At the end of 2010, almost 4.9 million adults were on probation in the United States. About half of them had been convicted of a felony offense. See Bureau of Justice Statistics, Probation and Parole in the United States, 2010 (NCJ 236019, November 2011). Of those sentenced to probation, the mean sentence length was 33.6 months, the median 36 months. The United States has the highest probation rate in the world, with 536 per 100,000 population, followed by Canada (269) and England and Wales (217).

In federal court 7.1% of all offenders sentenced between October 1, 2010, and September 30, 2011, received a probation-only sentence. Among felons a large disparity existed: only 2.1% of those convicted of drug trafficking received straight probation, but almost 60% of those convicted of food and drug or environmental and wildlife offenses received a probation sentence. Should certain types of offenders presumptively receive probationary sentences?

2. *Probationary conditions.*   While the specific condition in *Oakley* may be unusual, another court imposed a ten-year probationary sentence on a twenty-year-old woman with the "reasonable condition" not to conceive or bear any more children during that time, after conviction for failure to provide protection and medical treatment for her 19-month-old daughter. Is this sentence more or less constitutional or defensible than the one in *Oakley?*

The more general question these sentences raise is: what conditions may or should be imposed as part of probationary sentences? Are no-Internet or no-computer probation conditions, for example, permissible? Probationary sentences are inherently more varied than imprisonment, and idiosyncratic probation conditions, such as the one in *Oakley*, are often challenged on appeal. For further examples and a critical review of such conditions, see Andrew Horwitz,

Coercion, Pop-Psychology, and Judicial Moralizing: Some Proposals for Curbing Judicial Abuse of Probation Conditions, 57 Wash. & Lee L. Rev. 75 (2000). Is this flexibility always a virtue? Should lists of conditions be standardized? If so, by whom? See Demarce v. Willrich, 56 P.3d 76 (Ariz. Ct. App. 2002) (upholding lifetime probation for sex offender); People v. Kimbrell, 684 N.E.2d 443 (Ill. App. Ct. 1997) (upholding probation condition for theft offense forbidding contact with defendant's son's father); *But see* Commonwealth v. Hall, 994 A.2d 1141 (Pa. Super. Ct. 2010) (striking down child support payment for victim's children as condition of probation), *appeal granted*, 6 A.3d 1287 (Pa. 2010) State v. V.D., 951 A.2d 1088 (N.J. Super. Ct. App. Div. 2008), (striking special probation condition that defendant notify ICE of her convictions for possessing a false document, as defendant could not have reasonably anticipated imposition of this condition).

3. *The nature and evolution of probationary sanctions.* Probationary sanctions are beginning to focus on the idea of "responsibilization," shifting more responsibility to offenders to solve their own problems. Is probation a privilege? What obligations flow from it? Some newer probationary sanctions have tended to emphasize greater control than regular probation. Among them are intensive supervised probation and house arrest, which often includes electronic monitoring. Would it be more effective to move a smaller number of higher-risk offenders to increased supervision and decrease supervision for those considered a lesser or intermediate risk? Do the parallel trends of increasing "self-rescue" on the one hand and increasing intensive control on the other suggest differing conceptions of probation in general, or do they reflect the notion that probation may be structured to achieve different purposes for different offenders?

4. *The efficacy of probation.* Research on the effectiveness of probation indicates that a high percentage of probationers either violate the conditions of probation or commit another offense while on probation. During 1990 17% of all persons arrested for felonies in large, urban counties were on probation. Nevertheless, risky behavior as well as criminal activity go down during supervision. When the intensity of supervision increases, probation revocations also increase, largely because of technical violations. Increased reliance on probation as an alternative to more expensive prison sentences attracts some support from political conservatives, who approach the issue as one of fiscal responsibility. Studies have indicated that at least a few states have kept increases in the number of prison inmates steady and costs down through expansion of probation as a sentencing option. In Texas, probation has become a safe and cheap alternative to imprisonment: "for every $10.00 spent in prison, probation departments only spend $1.00." American Bar Association, Criminal Justice Section, State Policy Implementation Project Texas & Mississippi: Reducing Prison Populations, Saving Money, and Reducing Recidivism.

### b.  Probation Violations

Probation is violated when the offender acts contrary to the conditions of supervision established by the court or the probation department. The violation may be criminal, as in the commission of a new offense, or technical, as in the failure to meet a specific probation condition. Not all violations lead to automatic revocation of probation. While protection of the community is the guiding principle, after a violation other strategies to monitor and control offender behavior may be used.

Do the probation rules give probationers too many chances? Should all probation violations lead to immediate termination of probation?

Because probationary sentences involve substantially lower levels of social control than prison sentences and are served in the community, not only the specified conditions but also the processes for review and revocation reflect the essential qualities and purposes of such sentences. Consider the following policies and procedures in North Carolina.

> ## *Violations Policies — Procedures, North Carolina Department of Correction Division of Community Corrections*
> ### March 1, 2002

### GENERAL PROVISIONS

A *violation* is any action by the offender that is contrary to the conditions of supervision established by the Court or Post-Release Supervision and Parole Commission. Violations may be criminal (involving the commission of a new offense) or technical (involving a failure to meet one or more specific conditions of the probation judgment or parole or post-release supervision agreement).

### 1.  *Violation Philosophy.*

All responses to violation behavior will be considered in light of the Department's mission and objectives, as well as the goals of the supervision process. While protection of the community must always be the primary consideration, it does not follow that revocation is always, or even usually, the most effective or efficient way of achieving this goal. The goal of community supervision is to selectively and proactively intervene with offenders to reduce the likelihood of future criminal activity and promote compliance with the supervision strategy. Strategies involve holding offenders accountable for their actions, monitoring and controlling offender behavior, and referring to rehabilitation programs specific to offender needs. Another significant piece of the supervision strategy is ensuring an appropriate and proportionate response to all violations of the conditions of probation, taking into account offender risk, the nature of the violation, and the objective of offender accountability.

The purpose of this policy is to provide a framework to guide officer decision-making when a violation of probation has occurred. . . . Technical violations of the conditions of probation are inevitable. It is unrealistic to believe offenders, even if they sincerely desire to develop drug-free, pro-social lifestyles, will immediately have the skills or abilities to do so. The issues and forces that brought them into the system will most likely continue to impact their behavior to some extent until they learn new skills and methods of dealing with these forces.

The basic expectations underlying the Division's policy regarding probation violations are:

- There will be a response to every detected violation;
- Responses to violations will be proportional to the risk to the community posed by the particular offender, the severity of the violation, and the current situational risk;
- The least restrictive response necessary to respond to the behavior will be used;
- There will be consistency in handling similar violation behavior given similar risk factors;
- Responses to violations will hold some potential for long-term positive outcomes in the context of the supervision strategy;
- While response to violation behavior is determined by considering both risk and needs, risk to the community is the overriding consideration; *and*
- Probationers who demonstrate a habitual unwillingness to abide by supervision requirements or who pose undue risk to the community will be subject to revocation of probation.

### 2.  *Violation Response Procedures*

When a violation occurs the supervising officer will assess the type of violation (emergency or nonemergency) and take appropriate action.

### A.  Emergency Violations

Emergency violations involve behavior that *requires the immediate arrest of the offender* in order to ensure public safety. Emergency violations include, but are not limited to, the following:

- An imminent threat by the offender of physical harm to self or others;
- Electronic House Arrest violations such as equipment tampering;
- For probation cases only, possession of contraband necessitating an arrest incidental to search and/or seizure;
- Willful violations of residential facility rules; and/or
- For sex offenders, violations of specific conditions directly related to the crime. . . .

### B.  Non-emergency Violations

Non-emergency violations involve behavior that does not indicate the need for immediate arrest of the offender in order to ensure public safety. Non-emergency violations . . . include:

- A new conviction for any felony or a Class A1, 1 or 2 [or 3] misdemeanor;
- A new conviction for the same offense for which currently being supervised;
- Pending charges on a case about to expire;
- Being charged with a new offense in addition to [or without] one or more technical violations;
- Absconding;
- Financial arrearage of greater than six months for probation . . . cases . . . ;
- Lesser Electronic House Arrest violations that do not require immediate arrest;
- Possession of a weapon;
- Unwanted contact with the victim;
- Any violation related to substance abuse or any driving violation for DWI Level I or II cases;
- Pending technical violations at the expiration of the term of probation;
- Failure to comply with treatment;
- Notification of non-compliance with the rules of a Day Reporting Center, residential program, or the DART Program;
- Failure to report for jail time; . . .
- Non-compliance with community service requirement[;] . . .
- Verbal refusal to participate in substance abuse screening, not necessitating a Violation Report;
- Non-reporting for supervision; . . .
- Financial arrearage of less than six months for probation . . . cases . . . ; the Probation/Parole Officer may consider this violation an "A" violation for cases in which victim restitution is ordered;
- Curfew violation;
- Positive substance abuse screening;
- Unemployment, not seeking employment as ordered, or failure to notify the Probation [] Officer of employment loss;
- GED/school non-attendance;
- Leaving the jurisdiction or changing residence without permission;
- Going to restricted areas;
- Violating an order not to possess pagers or cellular phones;
- Failure to attend a prison tour; and
- Reporting in an unreasonable manner. . . .

Probation/Parole Officer will respond to non-emergency violations according to the Non-Emergency Violation Response Guidelines. The purpose for the Non-Emergency Violation Response Guidelines is to insure swift and certain response to every violation and to utilize the full continuum of sanctions prior to revocation. The Non-Emergency Response Guidelines apply to all technical violations except substance abuse testing violations. . . .

### C.   Non-emergency Violation Response Guidelines

a.   Level I Violationa. Response — Officer Response

Upon detection of the offender's first violation(s), the supervising officer will warn the offender either verbally or in writing or seek the assistance of the Chief Probation [] Officer in warning the offender either verbally or in writing. The Probation [] Officer may also require the offender to report more frequently. Subsequent violation(s) may be addressed at Level I or Level II Response.

b.   Level II Violationb. Response — Officer/Chief Response

If the supervising Probation [] Officer determines a Level II Response is needed, the officer will staff the case with the Chief Probation [] Officer. Level II Response includes override of supervision level and use of delegated authority sanctions available within community or intermediate punishment. . . .

c.   Level III Violationc. Response — Court/Hearing Response

A Level III Violation Response may be initiated only after options from Level I and Level II have been used. Level III options, which may be pursued after staffing the case with the Chief Probation [] Officer, include a recommendation for an Intermediate Punishment, extending/modifying probation or contempt of court. . . .

d.   Level IV Violationd. Response — Revocation

Revocation may be recommended only after staffing the case with the Chief Probation [] Officer and a Level III response has been used.

### 3.   Non-emergency Violation Response Charts

The following [chart gives] non-emergency violation response guidelines for probation . . . cases.

### 4.   Positive Substance Abuse Screening Guidelines

Following confirmation of the first positive screen result, the Probation [] Officer will confront the offender with the positive screen result within ten (10) days:

### A.   Procedure for First Positive Drug Screen Result

1.   Offender Admits Illegal Drug Use

   a.   If the offender agrees to seek treatment, make a referral to TASC where available for assessment and referral to treatment or to any licensed treatment program where TASC is unavailable.

**Non-Emergency Violation Response Chart — Probation**

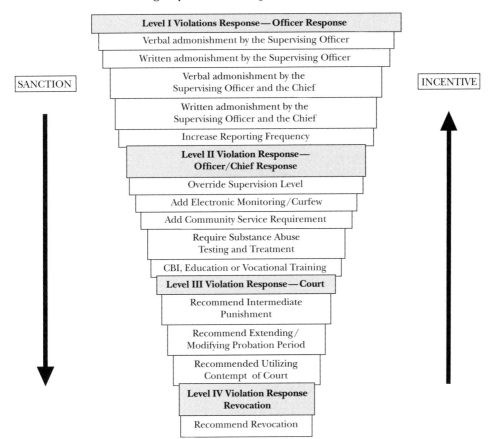

b.  If the offender refuses to submit to assessment and/or treatment, the officer will staff the case with the Chief Probation [] Officer and will use delegated authority to have the offender submit to assessment and treatment. If delegated authority is not available issue a . . . Violation Report or . . . [a] Non-Compliance Report and recommend a modification to the conditions of supervision requiring substance abuse assessment and compliance with the results.

2.  Offender Denies Illegal Drug Use

a.  If the offender refuses to submit to a treatment assessment, . . . obtain a confirmation test of the positive drug screen from the substance abuse screening lab and forward with a . . . Violation Report to the court of conviction or . . . to the Post-Release Supervision and Parole Commission; and,

b.  During the violation hearing, recommend a modification to the conditions of supervision requiring substance abuse assessment and compliance with the results.

### B.   Procedure for Second or Subsequent Positive Result

Following receipt of the second or subsequent positive screen result, the Probation [] Officer will review the case with the Chief Probation [] Officer and treatment provider, if applicable, to evaluate the offender's treatment needs and determine an appropriate course of action, including but not limited to therapeutic sanctions. . . .

### VIOLATION HEARINGS

Violation hearings may be held in the District Court or Superior Court having original jurisdiction, the judicial district in which the offender resides, or the judicial district in which he/she is alleged to have violated probation. . . .

### NOTES

1. *Probation violations.*   The structure, purpose, and efficacy of probationary sentences turn as much on the procedures and consequences of violations as on the terms of the sentence itself. One of the puzzles of probationary sentences is that more aggressive enforcement and more rigid responses to conditions such as drug screens can lead to very high rates of violation. Yet nonenforcement may undermine the purposes and goals of the particular sentences. Does the structured and graduated system in North Carolina respond to these concerns? How would you define success in the North Carolina system? Why does it matter whether the court or the agency has the authority to impose sanctions? Should other states adopt a similar system? For a panoply of state responses to probation violators, see Alison Lawrence, National Conference of State Legislatures, Probation and Parole Violations — State Responses (Nov. 2008).

2. *Probation violators.*   The most recent statistics on probation violators in state prisons are from 1991. They show a steady increase since the 1970s in the incarceration of probation violators. As of 1991, almost one-quarter of probationers were incarcerated for probation violations. One-quarter of these had probation revocation hearings because they had committed a new crime, 10% had failed a drug test, 36% did not report to their probation officer, and 12% percent had failed to pay fines or restitution or to comply with other financial commitments. See Robyn L. Cohen, Probation and Parole Violators in State Prison, 1991 (NCJ 149076, August 1995). Is revocation of probation appropriate for any, or all, of these violations?

3. *Probation violations and modern social media.*   May courts use evidence from social media sites, such as Facebook, in probation revocation hearings as a basis for revocation? *See* State v. Altajir, 33 A.3d 193 (Conn. 2012).

## B.  MODERN ALTERNATIVE SANCTIONS

Appearing in the news much more often than probation and fines, but in reality much less common, are a range of new sentences — some creations of the postmodern mind and some resurrections of sentences long defunct (and perhaps justly so). The most significant of these are boot camp, home confinement, shaming sanctions, and community service.

While modern alternative sanctions are relatively rare, they appear to have captured the imagination of the public, politicians, and a fair number of legal scholars. They deserve attention here because of the public attention paid to them and because of the extent to which they reveal deeper symbolic aspects and needs of punishment (a point that may be made about capital sentences as well). Perhaps these unusual but dramatic sanctions highlight a demand for an "expressive" purpose distinct from (or perhaps a component of) the more traditional purposes of retribution and reinforcement of community norms. See Joel Feinberg, The Expressive Function of Punishment, reprinted in Joel Feinberg, Doing and Deserving 98 (1970).

These new sanctions also raise further concern about "net widening." Will they be applied to offenders who otherwise would go to prison? Or will they instead be imposed on those who would receive probationary sanctions, or even those whose cases would be dismissed? In the latter cases, intermediate sanctions have become supplements rather than alternatives to more traditional criminal justice sanctions.

In thinking about these new kinds of sentences, a useful distinction can be drawn between those that include some degree of physical detention, and that therefore either replace or mimic imprisonment, and those that do not.

### 1.  Nonprison Detention: Boot Camp and Home Confinement

Boot camps were initially considered a promising alternative to detention-based sentences but fell out of favor upon shocking findings of abuse and documented failure of accomplishing their purpose. In the mid-1990s, there were about 75 boot camps for adult offenders in more than 30 states and about 30 for juveniles; since then the number of boot camps has declined precipitously. Many states have closed their boot camps or retained them only for juveniles. In 2005, the federal government eliminated its boot camp program, which had been termed Intensive Confinement Centers (ICCs) because of the view of federal prison officials that the program was neither cost-effective nor successful in preventing people from becoming repeat offenders.

The first boot camps — originally designed for adult men — were developed in 1983 in Georgia and Oklahoma to contain rising confinement costs and alleviate prison overcrowding. Over the next decade boot camps began to serve women and juvenile offenders as well. The average age of state boot camp inmates is between 19 and 20.

Because boot camps are considered an intermediate sanction, only offenders convicted of less serious, nonviolent offenses are usually admitted, and for relatively short periods of time. While the first boot camps were modeled after military boot camps, they came to emphasize education, therapeutic and treatment services, and community aftercare, with the goal of reducing recidivism. Despite initially promising results and wide adoption, in recent years boot camps have fallen out of favor.

From reading the following study of boot camps, do you think they should become (or remain) part of the array of available sanctions in your state? If so, for which offenders? Could a regime be developed that would allow boot camps to reach their goals of decreasing recidivism and reducing cost, or are the two inextricably conflicting purposes?

> ## *Correctional Boot Camps: Lessons from a Decade of Research, Dale G. Parent*
> **(National Institute of Justice, NCJ 197018, July 2003)**

### WHY BOOT CAMPS?

As the name implies, correctional boot camps are in-prison programs that resemble military basic training. . . .

*Three Generations of Camps.*    Boot camps proliferated in the late 1980s and early 1990s. By 1995, State correctional agencies operated 75 boot camps for adults, State and local agencies operated 30 juvenile boot camps, and larger counties operated 18 boot camps in local jails.

The camps evolved over time. . . . Although first-generation camps stressed military discipline, physical training, and hard work, second-generation camps emphasized rehabilitation by adding such components as alcohol and drug treatment and prosocial skills training. Some also added intensive postrelease supervision that may include electronic monitoring, home confinement, and random urine tests. A few camps admitted females, but this proved somewhat controversial. [S]ome boot camps, particularly those for juveniles, have substituted an emphasis on educational and vocational skills for the military components to provide comparable structure and discipline.

After the mid-1990s, the number of boot camps declined. By 2000, nearly one-third of State prison boot camps had closed — only 51 camps remained. The average daily population in State boot camps also dropped more than 30 percent.

*Boot Camps' Goals.*    Boot camps had three main goals: reducing recidivism, reducing prison populations, and reducing costs.

Camps were expected to reduce recidivism by changing inmates' attitudes, values, and behaviors and by addressing factors that increase the likelihood of returning to prison (such as lack of job skills, addiction, and inability to control anger). Camps were expected to reduce prison populations by shortening time served. Reduced length of stay was expected to reduce costs.

*Reducing Recidivism — An Unmet Goal.*   NIJ evaluation studies consistently showed that boot camps did not reduce recidivism regardless of whether the camps were for adults or juveniles or whether they were first-generation programs with a heavy military emphasis or later programs with more emphasis on treatment. Most of the research suggested that the limitations of boot camps prevented them from reducing recidivism or prison populations, even as they achieved other goals. These limitations mostly resulted from —

- Low "dosage" effects. The length of stay in boot camps — usually from 90 to 120 days — was too brief to realistically affect recidivism.
- Insufficient preparation of boot camp inmates for reentry into the community. Many boot camps provided little or no postrelease programming to prepare graduates to lead productive lives. In addition, the intensive supervision common to later generations of boot camps meant heightened surveillance levels for boot camp graduates. These factors combined to magnify the high rates of return for technical parole violations.
- Conflicting or unrealistic goals or mandates set by State legislatures. For example, most boot camp programs sought to reduce prison populations. Shorter programs more effectively meet this goal, but they also lower dosage effects and reduce the likelihood that treatment programs will work, thereby potentially increasing recidivism.
- The absence of a strong underlying treatment model. Pragmatism and local politics often affected boot camp structure more than theory and research results. . . .

*Improving Behavior — A Success Story.*   Boot camps were almost universally successful in improving inmates' attitudes and behavior during the course of the program; they also produced safer environments for staff and residents, presumably due to their highly structured atmosphere and activities.

Several studies indicated that adult boot camp participants had better attitudes about their confinement experiences and had improved their prosocial attitudes more than comparison group members. One study concluded that inmates in adult boot camps had increased self-esteem, reduced antisocial attitudes, increased problem-solving skills, improved coping skills, and improved social support. In other studies, boot camp inmates improved their self-esteem and standardized education scores in reading and math more than comparison group members.

Anxiety and depression declined to a greater degree among juveniles in boot camps than among those in comparison facilities. Dysfunctional impulsivity (the inability to control one's impulses) increased among youths in comparison facilities but decreased among boot camp participants. Social attitudes improved among youths in boot camps, but worsened among those in comparison facilities.

*Reducing Prison Population — Mixed Results.*   NIJ-sponsored boot camp researchers agree that correctional boot camps might achieve small relative[14] reductions in prison populations. Boot camps could reduce the number of prison beds needed in a jurisdiction, which would lead to modest reductions in correctional costs. . . .

However, restrictive entry criteria for boot camp participants often made it impossible to reduce prison populations. For example, some jurisdictions required that boot camp inmates be nonviolent offenders convicted of their first felony. This small pool of eligible candidates typically serves short prison terms before parole. These inmates had little incentive to volunteer for boot camps that would not shorten their terms. When inmates sentenced to longer prison terms were recruited, however, a reduction in time served became a compelling incentive.

Efforts to meet the recidivism goal may work against meeting population and cost reduction goals. For example, lengthening a boot camp term to add more treatment programs in order to reduce the chances of recidivism would shorten the discount in time served and, thus, not reduce the population or prison bed costs.

## NOTES

1. *Boot camps.*   Has the 30-year experiment with boot camps failed? What lessons can be drawn about creative or modern sanctions more generally? Does the problem with boot camps lie in their conception? Their operation? Will there be any boot camps in operation in ten years? How could boot camps be reconfigured to fulfill their goals more effectively?

2. *Home confinement.*   While it is relatively rare, many jurisdictions make some use of home confinement as a sanction, especially for short periods of time. For example, in the federal system in 1999 about 16,000 defendants and offenders had home confinement orders. The majority of home confinements, however, occur before trial. Home confinement does not necessarily mean 24-hour confinement: it can allow for specific periods of work or other reasons to leave the home. What purpose does home confinement serve? Do its goals differ from those of imprisonment? Home confinement orders have led to lower recidivism rates and cost-savings. Development Services Group, Inc., U.S. Department of Justice, Home Confinement/Electronic Monitoring: Literature Review (Oct. 15, 2009). In light of such findings, why are home confinement orders not more actively used? May home confinement orders re-create socio-economic distinctions between offenders?

3. *Electronic monitoring.*   Electronic monitoring may be combined with, or replace different aspects of a criminal justice sanction. It is often combined with home confinement, though the two concepts are distinct. Electronic monitoring adds a high-tech gloss by tracking the presence or absence of the offender at required locations (home, office, car). Is electronic monitoring efficient? Does

---

14. Boot camps were unlikely to lower absolute prison population levels. The camps opened during a time when major changes in sentencing policies and practices caused prison populations to soar. Even at the height of their popularity, the total capacity of boot camps was minuscule compared to the total prison population.

it serve primarily an incapacitative function? How cost-effective is it? Development Services Group, Inc., U.S. Department of Justice, Home Confinement/ Electronic Monitoring: Literature Review (Oct. 15, 2009). What impact will constant supervision outside of prison have on the individual probationer and on society? See Graeme Wood, Prison Without Walls, the Atlantic (Sept. 2010), at www.theatlantic.com/magazine/archive/2010/09/prison-without-walls/8195/.

Many states are adopting or considering global positioning system (GPS) tracking for serious offenders, and especially for sex offenders, after their release from prison, including well beyond parole or supervised release. California and a few other states currently require life-long tracking of certain convicted sex offenders. A recent California study has indicated that GPSs tracking is successfully decreasing recidivism and the violation of parole conditions but is more expensive than manual monitoring. Stephen V. Gies et al., U.S. Department of Justice, Monitoring High-Risk Sex Offenders With GPS Technology: An Evaluation of the California Supervision Program, Final Report (Apr. 2012). Other studies, however, have been more cautious in evaluating GPS technology, especially as the technology itself may lead to false alarms, ultimately creating a sense of complacency — rather than urgency — in those monitoring it. See Gaylene S. Armstrong & Beth C. Freeman, Examining GPS monitoring alerts triggered by sex offenders: The divergence of legislative goals and practical application in community corrections, 39(2) J. Crim. Justice 175 (2011).

Although GPS monitoring is discussed mostly as a supplement to a period of incarceration, should jurisdictions start seriously exploring techno-tracking as an alternative to incarceration for certain types of offenders?

### 2. Nondetention Sanctions: Shaming and Community Service

During the past two decades, shame has emerged as an explicit and independent sanction. Many criminal sentences may convey or carry some shame for the convicted offender. Indeed, the shame associated with the fact of conviction alone for some offenders may, from their perspective or the perspective of friends, family, or fellow workers, be a substantial punishment in itself.

Academics have led the call for officially shaming offenders. John Braithwaite, an Australian scholar, called for greater use of shame in criminal penalties in his 1989 book Crime, Shame and Reintegration. Braithwaite distinguished "reintegrative" shaming, which reaffirms "the morality of the offender by expressing personal disappointment that the offender should do something so out of character" and invites the offender to rejoin the community, from "disintegrative" shaming, which further pushes the offender into outcast status. A leading academic proponent in the United States has been Professor Dan Kahan. A major critic of proposals to sanction through shame is Professor Toni Massaro, who questions the existence of the kind of societies and norms that would make social sanctions such as shame fair, consistent, and effective. See generally Note, Shame, Stigma and Crime: Evaluating the Efficacy of Shaming Sanctions in Criminal Law, 116 Harv. L. Rev. 2186 (2003).

While rare, shaming sanctions are starting to appear more often in statutes and in individual cases. Consider the purposes and wisdom of the shaming sanctions in the following statute and case. Should shaming sanctions become more widely used? If so, for what offenses and offenders? And which institutions should design, implement, and test such sanctions?

> ## Ohio Revised Code §4503.231, Special Plates for Vehicles Registered to Persons Whose Registration Certificates and License Plates Have Been Impounded

No motor vehicle registered in the name of a person whose certificate of registration and identification license plates have been impounded . . . shall be operated or driven on any highway in this state unless it displays identification license plates which are a different color from those regularly issued and carry a special serial number that may be readily identified by law enforcement officers. The registrar of motor vehicles shall designate the color and serial number to be used on such license plates, which shall remain the same from year to year and shall not be displayed on any other motor vehicles. . . .

> ## People v. Glenn Meyer
> ### 680 N.E.2d 315 (Ill. 1997)

McMorrow, J.

The sole question presented for our review in the instant case is whether section 5-6-3(b) of the Unified Code of Corrections (Code) (730 ILCS 5/5-6-3(b) (West 1994)) authorizes a trial court to order, as a condition of probation, that the defendant post a large sign at all entrances to his family farm which reads "Warning! A Violent Felon lives here. Enter at your own risk!" The appellate court affirmed the trial court's imposition of this condition. . . . We reverse, and hold that the trial court exceeded the scope of its sentencing authority because posting a sign of this type is not a reasonable condition of probation under section 5-6-3(b) of the Code. Therefore, we vacate the order of the circuit court in part.

Following a jury trial, the defendant, Glenn Meyer, was convicted of the aggravated battery of Gary Mason. The trial testimony showed that on February 25, 1995, Gary Mason visited the defendant's farm in order to return some vehicle parts that he purchased from the defendant. Mason and the defendant began to quarrel over whether the parts were functioning properly. During the argument the defendant swung one of the parts at Mason, striking him in the nose and eye, causing several injuries.

At the defendant's sentencing hearing, evidence was presented in aggravation and mitigation. On behalf of the State, Tim Belford testified that in September 1986, he went to the defendant's farm in order to collect monies for two insufficient fund checks issued by defendant to Belford's employer, the First National Bank of Pittsfield. Belford stated that the defendant eventually gave him the money, but then kicked him and ordered him off the farm. Belford acknowledged that a jury acquitted the defendant of aggravated battery charges stemming from this incident.

Next, Harry Dyel testified that in May of 1990, he went to the defendant's farm on behalf of his employer, Shelter Insurance Company, in order to investigate a claim filed by the defendant. Dyel testified that the defendant became hostile because he was annoyed by the company's failure to process his claim promptly. Dyel stated that after he attempted to comply with the defendant's demands for payment, the defendant pushed him down and kicked him several times, causing injuries to his torso, arms, face and head. The defendant was convicted of the aggravated battery of Dyel. Finally, Gary Mason, the victim in the present case, testified regarding the defendant's actions on February 25, 1995.

Several witnesses testified in mitigation. Kenwood Foster testified that he is a licensed clinical social worker who operates a private counselling service. The defendant began seeing Foster in the fall of 1991. Foster testified that doctors at several different clinics have diagnosed the defendant as having "major depressive disorder" or clinical depression. Foster further stated that he believes that the defendant may also suffer from a condition similar to a type of post-traumatic stress disorder. He indicated that the defendant has been taking prescription medication known as Zoloft, to control his illness.

Foster further testified that certain stresses, such as a perceived threat to the defendant or his family, could trigger a change in the defendant's behavior. Foster acknowledged that the defendant may perceive certain behavior as threatening, even if the average individual would not feel threatened under similar circumstances.

Friends of the defendant, Gregg Smith, David Gratton and Bruce Lightle, also testified. All three described the defendant's good character and reputation within the community.

Mary Meyer, the defendant's wife of 36 years, testified that the defendant's elderly mother relies on the defendant, her only child, for care and assistance. Mrs. Meyer stated that she teaches high school, and has always relied on the defendant to manage the farm. She indicated that her family would suffer great hardship if the defendant were incarcerated. Mrs. Meyer also testified regarding the defendant's prolonged psychological illness and his efforts to control his sickness with medication.

In addition to the testimony of the witnesses, 20 letters were submitted by individuals from throughout the defendant's community. These letters chronicle examples of the defendant's generosity and willingness to assist friends and neighbors in need. The letters contain many descriptions of the defendant's good character and reputation.

Additionally, the presentence investigation report contains a detailed description of the defendant's mental health history. Several psychological evaluations of the defendant, dating from 1989, show that he suffers from major depressive disorder and possibly an additional psychological malady.

Upon evaluating all of the evidence in mitigation and aggravation, the trial court sentenced the defendant to 30 months' probation. The court considered the defendant's family members and the adverse impact that incarceration would have upon them. The court stated that it considered that the defendant was 62 years old, his mother's age and ill-health, and Mary Meyer's need to have the defendant care for the farm, in deciding to sentence the defendant to probation instead of prison.

The court conditioned defendant's probation on the following: (1) payment of $9,615.95 in restitution, (2) payment of a $7,500 fine, (3) payment of a $25 monthly probation services fee, (4) psychological psychiatric evaluation and treatment, (5) one-year home confinement and (6) the placement of a "violent felon" warning sign at each entrance to the defendant's property for the duration of the probation period. With respect to the sign requirement, the court stated that it believed that "maybe [the sign] will protect society." The court's supplemental order regarding the sign provides:

> As a condition of probation defendant shall erect and maintain at each entrance of his property a $4' \times 8'$ sign with clearly readable lettering at least 8″ in height reading: "Warning! A Violent Felon lives here. Enter at your own Risk!" To be erected by 8-11-95. . . .

The sole issue presented to us for review is whether the trial court was authorized to order the violent felon warning sign as a condition of probation. The defendant maintains that the trial court acted outside of the scope of its sentencing authority because the sign is not a reasonable condition of probation within the meaning of the Unified Code of Corrections. Section 5-6-3(b) of the Code lists 16 permissible probation conditions that the trial court may impose "in addition to other *reasonable conditions* relating to the nature of the offense or the rehabilitation of the defendant as determined for each defendant in the proper discretion of the Court." (Emphasis added.) The defendant maintains that the warning sign is not a reasonable condition of probation because it does not comport with traditional notions of punishment or probation in Illinois, and instead is an unauthorized "shaming penalty" or a scarlet letter type of punishment. The defendant argues that nothing in the Code supports the subjection of probationers to public ridicule as a goal of probation.

The State responds that while the sign may embarrass the defendant, it is not intended to subject him to public ridicule. Rather, the State and the amicus curiae, the American Alliance for Rights and Responsibilities, contend that this condition of probation furthers the goals of probation because it protects the public and serves to rehabilitate the defendant.

The State maintains that the sign protects the public by warning against provoking the defendant and by reducing the number of guests or business invitees who visit the farm. The State and the amicus argue that the goal of rehabilitation is fostered by the sign because it reminds the defendant that society disapproves of his criminal conduct. The amicus further argues that because the sign reminds the defendant of his offense, the defendant will modify his behavior and will be less likely to commit acts of violence in the future. Finally, both the State and the amicus argue that the trial court acted within its discretion by carefully fashioning the conditions of probation to correspond to the needs of the defendant and the public.

Generally, the trial court is afforded wide discretion in fashioning the conditions of probation for a particular defendant. However, while the trial court has discretion to impose probation conditions which will foster rehabilitation and protect the public, the exercise of this discretion is not without limitation.

Section 5-6-3(b) of the Code contains 16 permitted conditions of probation which may be imposed "in addition to other *reasonable* conditions." (Emphasis added.) Requiring the defendant to erect a sign on his property, proclaiming his status as a violent convicted felon, is not statutorily identified as one of the conditions of probation. The statute gives the trial court the discretion to impose additional conditions of probation provided that they are reasonable. In People v. Ferrell 659 N.E.2d 992 (Ill. App. 1995), the court determined that a probation condition not expressly enumerated in the statute may be imposed as long as it is (1) reasonable and (2) relates to (a) the nature of the offense or (b) the rehabilitation of the defendant as determined by the trial court. We must, therefore, determine whether compelling defendant to post a 4-foot by 8-foot sign in front of his residence which, in 8-inch-high letters, states that defendant is a violent felon is a reasonable condition under section 5-6-3 of the Code.

Section 1-1-2 of the Unified Code of Corrections provides:

The purposes of this Code of Corrections are to:
(a) prescribe sanctions proportionate to the seriousness of the offenses and permit the recognition of differences in rehabilitation possibilities among individual offenders;
(b) forbid and prevent the commission of offenses;
(c) prevent arbitrary or oppressive treatment of persons adjudicated offenders or delinquents; and
(d) restore offenders to useful citizenship. 730 ILCS 5/1-1-2 (West 1994).

Consistent with this legislative intent, this court has recognized repeatedly that the purpose of probation is to benefit society by restoring a defendant to useful citizenship, rather than allowing a defendant to become a burden as an habitual offender. Probation simultaneously serves as a form of punishment and as a method for rehabilitating an offender. Protection of the public from the type of conduct that led to a defendant's conviction is one of the goals of probation. . . .

Although the sign may foster the goals of probation to the extent that it punishes the defendant and protects the public, furtherance of these two goals alone does not render the condition reasonable. Indeed, we are persuaded by defendant's contention that the sign, in fact, may hamper the goal of rehabilitation, and that the erection of the sign is inconsistent with the conditions of probation listed in section 5-6-3(b). We recognize that the trial court labored arduously and sincerely to develop a sentence which would serve the needs of society and simultaneously avoid incarceration of the defendant. Nonetheless, we hold the sign condition of probation imposed in this case was unreasonable and did not serve the purposes of section 5-6-3(b).

The Tennessee Supreme Court in State v. Burdin, 924 S.W.2d 82 (Tenn. 1996), considered and rejected a comparable "shaming sign," finding that it was unreasonable. The Tennessee court held that the Tennessee statute at issue there did not authorize a condition of probation which required the defendant to erect a sign in the front yard of his residence which read, "Warning, all children. [Defendant] is an admitted and convicted child molester. Parents beware."

In *Burdin*, the defendant pleaded guilty to sexual battery of a 16-year-old victim. As a condition of probation, the court ordered the defendant to place the warning sign in front of his residence where he lived with his mother. . . .

The *Burdin* court stated:

> The consequences of imposing such a condition without the normal safeguards of legislative study and debate are uncertain. Posting a sign in the defendant's yard would dramatically affect persons other than the defendant and those charged with his supervision. . . . [C]ompliance with the condition would have consequences in the community perhaps beneficial, perhaps detrimental, but in any event unforeseen and unpredictable.

Similarly, in People v. Johnson, 528 N.E.2d 1360 (Ill. App. 1988), the court cautioned against allowing trial courts to impose unconventional conditions of supervision, which may have unknown consequences. The defendant in *Johnson* was convicted of driving under the influence of alcohol. As a condition of supervision, the trial court in *Johnson* ordered the defendant to place an advertisement in the local daily newspaper, which contained her booking picture and an apology. The appellate court vacated this condition, finding it to be inconsistent with the overall intent of section 5-3-6.1. . . .

We are mindful of the distinctions in the case sub judice and the *Burdin* and *Johnson* cases. However, we agree with the specially concurring opinion in *Johnson*, which observed:

> [T]o uphold the condition imposed here would encourage other courts to impose other unusual, dramatic conditions, and the proliferation of these types of conditions would cause problems of a greater magnitude than their propensity to rehabilitate.

See also People v. Harris, 606 N.E.2d 392 (Ill. App. 1992) (banishing the defendant from the state of Illinois as a condition of probation was unreasonable because no valid purpose would be served); People v. Letterlough, 655 N.E.2d 146 (N.Y. 1995) (condition of probation requiring the defendant to affix a fluorescent sign reading "convicted dwi" to the license plate of any vehicle he drove was not authorized); People v. Hackler, 16 Cal. Rptr. 2d 681 (Cal. App. 1993) (court not authorized to require probationer to wear a T-shirt bearing bold printed statement proclaiming his felony status); but see Lindsay v. State, 606 So. 2d 652 (Fla. App. 1992) (condition of probation requiring defendant to place a newspaper advertisement showing a mug shot, name and caption "DUI-convicted" upheld under Florida statute); Goldschmitt v. State, 490 So. 2d 123 (Fla. App. 1986) (bumper sticker reading "CONVICTED D.U.I. — RESTRICTED LICENSE" upheld); Ballenger v. State, 436 S.E.2d 793 (Ga. App. 1993) (court had the authority to require the defendant to wear a pink fluorescent bracelet reading "D.U.I. CONVICT").

We hold that section 5-6-3(b) of the Code did not authorize the trial court to require the sign as a condition of the defendant's probation. The sign contains a strong element of public humiliation or ridicule because it serves as a formal, public announcement of the defendant's crime. Thus, the sign is inconsistent with the conditions of probation listed in section 5-6-3(b), none of which identify public notification or humiliation as a permissible condition. Further, we determine that the sign may have unpredictable or unintended consequences which may be inconsistent with the rehabilitative purpose of probation.

Finally, the nature and location of the sign are likely to have an adverse effect on innocent individuals who may happen to reside with the defendant. At the time of sentencing in this case, the defendant's wife was living on the premises where the violent felon sign was to be displayed. The defendant's elderly mother also intended to live there. The record shows that the defendant has two adult children who visit the farm, as well as young grandchildren. We believe that the manner in which the sign affects others also renders it an impermissible condition of probation.

Conditions which label a defendant's person or property have a stigmatizing effect and are considered shaming penalties. D. Kahan, What Do Alternative Sanctions Mean? 63 U. Chi. L. Rev. 591 (1996). Although a probationer may experience a certain degree of shame from a statutorily identified condition of probation, shame is not the primary purpose of the enumerated conditions.

The judicially developed condition in the case at bar does not reflect present penological policies of this state as evidenced by our Unified Code of Corrections. The authority to define and fix punishment is a matter for the legislature. The drastic departure from traditional sentencing concepts utilized in this case is not contemplated by our Code. Therefore, we determine that the erection of the sign as a condition of probation was unreasonable, and may be counterproductive to defendant's rehabilitative potential. . . .

## NOTES

1. *Shaming.*   Shaming has been big news in academic circles since John Braithwaite's pioneering work in the late 1980s. Occasional shaming sanctions make news — sometimes national news — highly disproportionate to their modest character and infrequent use. Shaming sanctions raise many issues. As is so often the habit of lawyers and legal scholars, among the first questions to be addressed is whether shaming sanctions are "legal" or, in the more common and often distorting reaction, whether they are constitutional. The much more difficult and important questions, however, have received less attention. Are shaming sanctions moral? Effective? To what purpose? Which institutions should authorize, design, impose, and review them? See James Q. Whitman, What Is Wrong with Inflicting Shame Sanctions?, 107 Yale L.J. 1055 (1998). In People v. Letterlough, 631 N.Y.S.2d 105 (N.Y. 1995), the court rejected a condition of probation for a DUI offender that he affix to any car he drove a fluorescent sign stating "convicted DWI." In response to *Letterlough* and People v. McNair, 642 N.Y.S.2d 597 (N.Y. 1996) (rejecting a one-year electronic monitoring sentence as beyond statutory authority), the New York legislature amended the relevant statute in 1996 to expand the authorized purposes of probation:

New York Penal Law §65.10. When imposing a sentence of probation the court may, in addition to any conditions imposed pursuant to [existing authority], require that the defendant comply with any other reasonable condition as the court shall determine to be necessary or appropriate to ameliorate the conduct which gave rise to the offense or to prevent the incarceration of the defendant.

Based on this statutory mandate, what review powers, if any, do New York appellate courts have over probation conditions? How could the court interpret the "reasonableness" requirement?

   2. *Community service sanctions.*   A more common alternative to detention is the community service order, either as a stand-alone sentence or in conjunction with fines or shorter periods of incarceration. Community service sanctions seem to be used most often for low-level offenders, perhaps as a more intensive substitute for straight probation. New York instituted a community service sentence program designed both to broaden the base of offenders punished and to reduce the number of offenders serving short jail terms. See Douglas Corry McDonald, Punishment Without Walls: Community Service Sentences in New York City (1986). Community service sentences are usually imposed under the general authority of probationary sanctions. It is very hard to determine how many community service sentences are imposed in the United States, whether they are stand-alone sentences, and how many are successful.


## 3.   Alternative Courts

Sometimes alternative sentences have different purposes from those of traditional sanctions and call for different adjudicative or sentencing institutions. One prominent example of an alternative court that appears to seek traditional goals is drug court. The growth of drug courts has been dramatic. The first self-identified drug court was created in 1989 at the urging of Judge Herbert Klein in Miami. See Peter Finn and Andrew Newlyn, Miami's Drug Court: A Different Approach (NCJ 142412, 1996). As of December 2011 there were 1,435 reported drug courts for adult offenders in operation and more than 1,100 more specialized courts dealing with sub-categories of drug offenders. At least 200 drug courts are in the planning stages. See National Institute of Justice, Office of Justice Programs, Drug Courts (2012), at http://www.nij.gov/topics/courts/drug-courts/welcome.htm. Part of this growth may be attributed to the federal Drug Courts Program Office (created and funded by the Violent Crime Control and Law Enforcement Act of 1994), which spent $56 million to support the creation of drug courts between 1995 and 1997. Today the Bureau of Justice Assistance provides grants for the creation of drug courts. For a comprehensive overview, see Celinda Franco, Congressional Research Service, Drug Courts: Background, Effectiveness, and Policy Issues for Congress (Oct. 12, 2010).

   Judges and reformers created drug courts in response to both the limited range of sentencing options in traditional criminal courts for drug users and concerns about the effectiveness and cost of punishment instead of — or at least in the absence of — drug treatment. Drug courts typically use a less adversarial approach that is aimed at ensuring public safety. In some states drug courts amount to a diversionary program, where offenders must perform successfully to prevent a criminal conviction. Increasingly, however, drug court programs form part of a probationary sentence or follow a guilty plea while sentencing is being deferred. For a discussion and comparison of different drug court models, see Shelli B. Rossman et al., The Urban Institute, The Multi-Site Adult Drug Court Evaluation: The Drug Court Experience — Final Report (Nov. 2011).

Drug courts have not only spread like wildfire, they have offered a model for breaking the heavily regimented and restricted punishment settings of traditional courts and the erosion of rehabilitation. For drug offenders and others the rehabilitative ideal remains, or is again vibrant as, a goal of "punishment" (though perhaps the goal of rehabilitation is in some important way different from punishment). The broader philosophical and practical labels used to describe this larger movement are "restorative justice" and "therapeutic courts." For a comprehensive review of the literature and a discussion of the advantages and disadvantages of restorative justice concepts and models, see Carrie Menkel-Meadow, Restorative Justice: What Is It and Does It Work?, 3 Annu. Rev. Law & Soc. Sci. 161 (2007). We already saw one illustration of restorative purposes in the sentencing circle examined in Chapter 1.

## *Therapeutic Justice in Alaska's Courts,* *Teresa Carns, Michael Hotchkin,* *and Elaine Andrews* ### 19 Alaska L. Rev. 1 (2002)

### I. THERAPEUTIC COURTS IN ALASKA: HISTORY, DEVELOPMENT AND PRESENT STRUCTURES

Wellness Court . . . Anchorage Felony Drug Court . . . Mental Health Court . . . Therapeutic Justice Courts. . . . Underlying these new projects is a growing change in the justice system's response to the difficult problems presented by defendants whose substance abuse or mental disabilities appear to be related inextricably to repeated criminal behavior. Justice professionals describe this approach as "therapeutic justice." . . .

Therapeutic justice emphasizes the need to address the root causes of a specific offender's criminality, to treat the offender to remove the problems and to return the offender to the community as a responsible citizen. Restorative justice emphasizes repair of the relationships between the victim, community and offender. Retributive justice, the model on which much of the United States' criminal justice system is based, emphasizes fairness and punishment as more important values than rehabilitation or other interests. Each model seeks to express community condemnation in order to protect public safety and deter or dissuade the specific offender and others from similar behavior in the future. . . .

### C. *Therapeutic Courts: Assets and Liabilities*

[P]olicymakers and justice system professionals have identified a wide range of benefits and concerns based on their experiences [with therapeutic courts].

*1. The Views of Judges and Court Administrators.* Judges and court administrators differ strongly in their beliefs about the benefits of the therapeutic justice approach. Proponents of therapeutic justice courts believe that the therapeutic justice model has reduced recidivism and increased the chances that defendants can return to their communities as productive individuals. Judges are willing to see a defendant repeatedly in a structured setting for months if they believe that in the end they will not see that defendant back before them for sentencing on repeated offenses. . . . Some judges see the situation as particularly troublesome for misdemeanor offenders who receive at best minimal supervision and often little or no treatment. . . .

Some court administrators and other judges express concerns that the therapeutic courts will be of limited benefit to a few defendants while consuming scarce resources at a rapid rate. In the short term, the projects require extra time to (1) facilitate the frequent meetings among the professionals and court staff involved in each case, (2) hold regular hearings and (3) administer the network of services, sanctions and incentives required to make the therapeutic process work. . . . [J]ustice system professionals are [] concerned about the lack of resources for the added work involved in each therapeutic justice project case.

Other concerns include worries that therapeutic courts may be coercive, may become more paternalistic and repressive than the existing system and may be "net-widening," i.e., they may impose harsher penalties or expectations on relatively less serious offenders rather than targeting more serious offenders. . . .

Perhaps the most serious concern is that courts will be unable to apply therapeutic justice concepts to more than a select few defendants. In a climate where all courts struggle for resources to address their caseloads' demands, resource-intensive therapeutic processes appear out of reach for most cases. Therapeutic courts typically serve only a fraction of potentially eligible defendants. . . . [Some o]bservers . . . believe that drug court procedures eventually may become abbreviated and perfunctory if they "go to scale" to serve a majority of the defendants with substance abuse problems. Under such a system, defendants will lose the benefits of individualized attention and therapeutic justice approaches will devolve into pro forma applications that would be no more effective than the court procedures they replaced.

*2. The Views of Defendants.* One stated purpose of therapeutic justice projects is to provide defendants with the structure, resources and incentives to end their addictions or help them resolve the problems that prevent them from leading satisfying and productive lives. Some defendants in therapeutic projects participate because they share the belief that rehabilitation is possible. Other defendants may participate because they believe that the projects are a less onerous choice than incarceration.

Proponents of therapeutic justice cite substantial evidence that coercing treatment through structures such as drug courts may result in better outcomes. Evidence suggests that people in coerced or mandated treatment (as distinct from voluntary treatment) are more likely to complete the treatment. Completion of treatment is critical to significant reduction in the likelihood of relapse.

Conversely, defendants may assess the difficulties of therapeutic justice projects and decide that incarceration is preferable. They may believe that they would fail in any case and would prefer to serve time in custody and be done with it. Some do not believe that they have a problem that needs treatment or that is amenable to the treatment offered, and they may decline to participate on those grounds. Additionally, defense attorneys perceive incarceration as less damaging for some defendants than participation in programs in which the defendant can be repeatedly incarcerated for violations of program guidelines.

***3. The Views of Prosecutors.*** Prosecutors who favor drug courts tend to believe that their role is to "represent[] the community's interest in public order." Other prosecutors question that "broader vision" and suggest instead that the goal of the criminal justice system is for prosecutors to "put bad guys in jail" by winning individual cases. Supporters of the therapeutic approach suggest that prosecutors working in therapeutic courts are as zealous as those working in regular courts, but more accountable. . . .

Some prosecutors may object to specific ways of administering therapeutic justice programs. For example, many oppose pre-plea programs that preserve defendants' options for going back to trial. "As time passes I am in a weaker position as to my case and my expenditure of resources." For this reason, many prosecutors insist on a plea from the defendant as a condition of entry into a therapeutic justice project. Other prosecutors perceive therapeutic justice's collaborative, non-adversarial approach as incompatible with "the public safety- and punishment-oriented goals of the prosecution[.]" They may reserve use of this approach for specific types of defendants and consider it inappropriate for others.

***4. Other Justice System Perspectives.*** Departments of Corrections and the public have responded favorably to therapeutic justice projects in their current form and scope. They favor the projects' potential for reducing incarceration costs and for successfully treating addictions. . . .

Many treatment providers also are supportive, although some individuals believe that the process may be too coercive and that coerced treatment does not work. Thorny confidentiality issues may arise with therapeutic justice projects because the projects require agencies to share and discuss information that is otherwise protected by complex confidentiality laws and regulations. Another concern is the change in the role of treatment providers from serving "exclusively as the gatekeepers to treatment, as they have been accustomed to doing," to having "courts . . . decide who will be sent to treatment and when treatment can be terminated for poor performance."

## D.  *Effectiveness of Therapeutic Courts*

. . . Although fewer than one hundred evaluations of therapeutic courts have been published in the last ten years, many are underway. A number of preliminary or partial evaluations have been completed and researchers have considered the effectiveness of many of the separate components of drug courts, particularly the use of monitoring and supervision, completion of treatment programs and use of coerced treatment.

*1. Treatment of Addiction/Disease.*   Various researchers have demonstrated that treatment, if completed, reduces recidivism. Partial completion of treatment often appears to be better than no treatment in reducing recidivism, but length of time in treatment generally predicts the addict's post-treatment success. Other studies have shown that some types of treatment correlate more significantly with reduced recidivism than others. . . .

Other components of drug or therapeutic courts also have proven effective when used separately or outside the context of the therapeutic court. In a Washington, D.C. study, monitoring and closely supervising offenders on probation by itself reduced the incidence of positive drug tests. A Florida program uses intensive supervision of probationers for DWI offenders . . . and has shown significant reduction in recidivism.

The combination of these separate effective elements into therapeutic justice courts has proven successful in many, though not all, instances. Published research shows that many drug courts have reduced recidivism during their existence. However, a few projects have not been able to demonstrate that the drug court population fared any better in terms of post-program recidivism rates than the control or comparison groups.

*2. Recidivism.*   Researchers have conducted very few follow-up evaluations analyzing re-arrest rates and experiences of participants and controls in drug court programs over the months or years after completion of the program. The difficulties posed by long-term evaluations include the added costs of more evaluations, the problem of finding former participants and control group subjects and the management of confidentiality issues. Since most drug court programs are relatively new, insufficient time has elapsed to make realistic follow-up evaluations possible. A similar situation exists for mental health courts and other therapeutic justice projects. . . .

### E.  Costs of Therapeutic Justice

Therapeutic justice projects are resource intensive. Even the projects that have functioned for some period of time without outside funding have managed only by using substantial time volunteered by judges, attorneys and other persons and organizations in the community. . . . The resources needed for therapeutic justice projects include added time for judges, attorneys and clerical staff, increased treatment resources, increased monitoring and drug testing of defendants, and expenses (in most programs) for case managers and coordinators. . . .

A [] realistic analysis would compare the costs for a drug court to the costs of incarcerating the same defendant for at least a year (the typical length of many drug court programs) and the costs of releasing the defendant untreated (the typical situation for most defendants). In Alaska, the cost for an Anchorage Felony Drug Court participant is estimated at $16,950 annually, as compared to the cost of more than $40,000 per year for incarceration. One observer suggests that because many of the defendants are repeat offenders who face presumptive sentences of two years or more, the actual costs of incarceration usually would be double the $40,000. The cost of incarceration does not include any of the costs associated with investigating the crimes charged, the costs of court processing (clerical and judge time, prosecution and defense costs) or costs of pretrial incarceration or pre-sentence report preparation for felony defendants. The cost for the Anchorage Felony Drug Court does include some attorney time, but neither judge time nor clerical time for any of the participants.

Depending on the program, defendants bear some of the costs. . . .

These differences in practices highlight different philosophies underlying similar projects. Proponents of having defendants pay argue that even if some defendants cannot participate due to very limited resources, those defendants who can should participate. Others contend that requiring any payment unfairly limits the program to those who have the economic resources to participate. . . .

## II.  THERAPEUTIC JURISPRUDENCE: LEGAL ISSUES

[T]he therapeutic justice projects discussed in this Article describe a well-defined approach that differs significantly from that embodied in the traditional American adversarial system. Most of the legal issues that therapeutic justice approaches raise have not been resolved by the courts, although a few courts have issued opinions addressing them. . . .

### A.  Constitutional Issues

Courts that have considered cases involving drug courts have dealt with a fairly limited range of the possible constitutional issues that could arise. . . .

*1. Separation of Powers.* Many drug court-related cases deal with the defendant's rights in plea bargaining situations and the balance of powers between the executive and judicial branches in determining who is eligible for drug court programs and who makes the final decisions on admission to them. Most of the courts deciding cases related to plea bargains appear to treat drug court agreements as any other plea bargain. . . .

The other major separation of powers issue focuses on the prosecutor's exclusive right to decide initial eligibility for drug court admission versus the judge's right to make the final decision about admission to the drug court. Several state courts, including those in Oklahoma and Florida, have held that separation of powers requires that prosecutors be permitted to make the first determination of admission to drug courts. Judges are not allowed to admit defendants to drug courts over the objections of prosecutors. On the other hand, Iowa and Louisiana courts have held that judges have the power to make the final decision about admission to drug court and are under no obligation to accept the prosecutor's recommendation.

*2. Due Process.*   A few cases address due process issues that have arisen in drug courts. For example, a Washington case held that the defendant must have a meaningful opportunity to respond to allegations of non-compliance before being terminated from the program. An Oklahoma case held that the court must give written reasons for termination of a defendant. This opinion also held that the court must state why the program sanctions were inadequate or inappropriate for the defendant.

*3. Equal Access to Courts (Equal Protection).*   Several courts have decided that defendants have no right to be admitted to drug courts and that they can be excluded on a variety of grounds. Prior felonies often are mentioned as grounds for ineligibility. A Florida case held that a defendant does not have a constitutional right to participate in a drug court if one had not been established in the circuit in which he was charged. . . . One author has warned that therapeutic justice projects "need to be sensitive to class and race bias, real or apparent. Unless care is taken, diversion courts may tend disproportionately to work with white and middle-class substance abusers."

Several authors have discussed the question of equal access to drug courts when programs do not have enough slots to serve all of the eligible defendants, as well as the question of whether the costs of programs where defendants pay all or part of the costs prohibit indigent defendants from using them. These problems have often been addressed in the context of "going to scale" or expanding the programs to serve the estimated seventy to eighty percent of defendants who have substance abuse problems. One court commentator noted: "We must address the fact that we are providing more resources for a misdemeanor drug offense than we are for a non-capital murder offense or a rape offense. Most states can't afford to continue to do this—politically and fiscally—if problem-solving courts go to scale." . . .

## NOTES

1. *Therapeutic courts and restorative justice.*   The concepts of therapeutic courts and restorative justice exploded in policy and scholarly debates in the 1990s, but these ideas, and the closely linked traditional purpose of rehabilitation, have deep historic roots.

The restorative justice movement has become very popular in developed countries in recent years, though it has existed for decades in African countries in the form of informal customary practices. The goal of restorative justice is to restore the victim and the community that has been harmed. While it has only recently become popular for street offenses, it has been used for decades to address business regulatory challenges. Business regulatory practices focus on restitution, victim empowerment, and the restoration of trust and relationships. Restorative justice can be viewed as an extension of the victim-offender mediation and restorative justice conferences used in business disputes.

2. *Judicial and prosecutorial discretion and power sharing.*   Legislatures have limited judicial discretion in recent years through the establishment of mandatory sentences and sentencing guidelines. As judicial discretion has

narrowed, prosecutorial discretion has broadened. How has the tension between prosecutorial and judicial discretion been resolved in therapeutic courts? To what extent are legislative actions necessary to institute therapeutic courts? In what areas would legislative action be helpful in facilitating the work of therapeutic courts? See Daniel Van Ness & Pat Nolan, Legislating for Restorative Justice, 10 Regent U. L. Rev. 53 (1998).

Tensions and contradictory goals and missions may also plague the different players in alternative courts. In mental health courts the criminal justice system and the mental health system often seem to pursue incompatible aims that impact communication negatively and hinder true collaboration. See Michelle Manasse, The Dilemmas and Opportunities of Collaboration: Drawing Lessons from One Mental Health Court, 2:1 J. Court Innovation 157 (2009).

3. *Drug courts.* Drug courts have emerged as the most common example of therapeutic courts. They provide intensive, long-term treatment services to offenders with long histories of drug use and criminal justice contacts and high rates of health and social problems. Most drug court participants are men with poor employment and educational records, fairly extensive criminal histories, and prior treatment failures. Usually drug courts target offenders who constitute a medium risk to the community. Hallmarks of the program are access to treatment and rehabilitation services as well as frequent alcohol and drug testing, all under ongoing judicial supervision and interaction with each participant. Treatment programs generally run for one year and are outpatient services. A team of social workers and substance abuse counselors assists the drug court judge. Occasional lapses are expected, and sanctions and rewards are built into the program. The penalty is designed to enforce the prescribed treatment regime rather than solely to punish. Drug courts enjoy widespread popularity and substantial funding. Recent empirical studies indicate that support is justified as they have found recidivism reduced and indicia of long-term rehabilitation, at least in certain locales and court configurations. See Michael W. Finigan, Shannon M. Carey & Anton Cox, Impact of a Mature Drug Court Over 10 Years of Operation: Recidivism and Costs (Final Report) (July 2007).

The graduation rate for drug court enrollees ranges between a quarter and two-thirds. This result is better than for many other community-based offender treatment programs. During drug court enrollment, criminal activity and drug use are reduced, but the duration of such success following enrollment remains undetermined. Some program-specific studies have found beneficial longer-term results, notably a decrease in recidivism and a greater likelihood of employment. See, e.g., Shelli B. Rossman et al., The Multi-site Adult Drug Court Evaluation (Urban Institute 2011), available at www.urban.org/justice/abuse.cfm; Denise C. Gottfredson & M. Lyn Exum, The Baltimore City Drug Treatment Court: One-Year Results from a Randomized Study, 39 J. Res. Crime & Delinq. 337 (2002); National Center on Addiction and Substance Abuse at Columbia University, Crossing the Bridge: An Evaluation of the Drug Treatment Alternative-to-Prison (DTAP) Program, A CASA White Paper (March 2003).

Some critics of drug courts believe the courts undermine the adversarial system, since offenders must waive some of their rights in order to be enrolled: courts have a right of access to all treatment records and are permitted ex parte communications with the prosecution. Judicial power changes dramatically in drug courts as the judges become activist problem-solvers, who have refocused the aims of sentencing from retribution to therapy. Another concern, documented in some individual studies, is that drug court participants receive harsher sentences than other offenders. On the other hand, netwidening is a potential problem, as those otherwise sentenced to probation may now be subject to heightened supervision. Finally, some non-addicts choose drug court to avoid criminal conviction, and therefore deplete limited resources unnecessarily.

The drug court model has been exported. In 2001 Glasgow established the first drug court in Scotland. Canada and Ireland also have similar programs as do Australia, New Zealand, Norway, and increasingly countries in Latin America. While the U.S. programs are based on abstinence, this is not always true of drug courts in other countries.

4. *Drug courts and prosecutorial discretion.*   Should the imposition of a drug court probation sentence depend on the prosecutor's recommendation? In Louisiana v. Taylor, 769 So. 2d 535 (La. 2000), the Louisiana Supreme Court held that a trial court is not authorized to place a defendant in a drug court program absent the prosecutor's recommendation. How can such a limitation on judicial discretion be justified in this context?

5. *Confidentiality concerns.*   Therapeutic justice courts raise difficult confidentiality concerns, as Carns, Hotchkin, and Andrews observe:

> Drug and alcohol courts require access to participants' drug and alcohol abuse treatment records. . . . The program's treatment assessor uses this information in determining whether the defendant is diagnostically appropriate for inclusion in the program and in designing an appropriate case plan. Once a program has accepted a defendant, the drug or alcohol court team uses reports of that person's ongoing treatment compliance and prognosis to assess the person's progress. The judge uses the reports to award incentives, impose sanctions and determine whether the participant should graduate, continue in the program or be terminated from the program. . . .
>
> Drug and alcohol courts face two significant issues created by [the] federal regulatory scheme [protecting information about an individual's participation in drug or alcohol abuse treatment programs]. First, . . . [p]articipants consent to release treatment information, both past and future, when they first apply for the programs. . . .
>
> The second issue facing drug and alcohol courts stems from the fact that the regulatory definition of "program" encompasses virtually all of these courts. This subjects them to the regulatory restrictions on disclosure of information that might identify a patient as an alcohol or drug abuser. A problem arises because the courts conduct public proceedings. Although most interactions among judges, attorneys and offenders in drug court do not go into significant detail about a participant's treatment, the mere fact that a person is participating in a drug or alcohol court program indicates that the person has abused alcohol or drugs. One author notes that part of drug court procedure is for the judge to "hold[] the offender publicly accountable for the results of the [drug use] test and the treatment progress." The regulations thus create a conflict between public access to court proceedings and the court's duty not to identify or discuss drug and alcohol court participants in a public setting. . . .
>
> . . . Drug court team members are permitted to use such information for their "official duties with regard to the patient's conditional release or other action in connection with which the consent was given." One authority states that the federal regulations have been interpreted to allow team members to mention confidential information in court. . . . The authority goes on to say

that drug court officials should be mindful that consent has not been given to disclose confidential information to unnamed third party bystanders in the courtroom (e.g., public, press and law enforcement). Therefore, courtroom discussions should avoid specific, confidential details of a person's treatment experience and, instead, focus on more general concerns such as the participant's progress.

The same authority notes that the question of whether confidentiality rules apply to drug courts has not been fully resolved. . . .

19 Alaska L. Rev. at 48-49. Should there be more concern about confidentiality in other areas of sentencing?

In light of the uneasy fit of drug courts in the criminal system, should drug courts instead be civil courts? See Alex Kreit, The Decriminalization Option: Should States Consider Moving From a Criminal to a Civil Drug Court Model?, 2010 U. Chi. Legal F. 299 (2010).

*6. Beyond drug courts.* Drug courts have spearheaded the movement toward therapeutic justice. They have been supplemented by a host of other types of courts, some of which are focused on particular types of offenders — mental health courts and veterans' courts — or particular types of offenses, such as felony DWI courts and wellness courts.

# C. COLLATERAL SANCTIONS

Collateral sanctions, or "collateral consequences," as they are often called, have been part of the U.S. criminal justice system for centuries, and in recent years they have received renewed support from legislatures and policymakers. The origin of collateral sanctions can be found in so-called civil death provisions, prevalent in the nineteenth century and earlier in the United States and Europe. Civil death, the deprivation of an offender's civil rights, made it impossible for convicted felons to enter into contracts, arranged for automatic divorce from their spouses, prevented them from making a will, and imposed a host of other sanctions on them that amounted to legal death. While many of the most offensive of these restrictions have been eliminated, others remain. Some modern collateral sanctions are particularly restrictive in a regulatory welfare state and, for some offenders, may have more dramatic and longer-term consequences than the sentence imposed in court.

The offenders released from U.S. prisons every year — over 675,000 in 2009 — do not again become "free" citizens. To the contrary, they often face such a large number of restrictions that some have called the postrelease period a time of "invisible punishment." Offenders can be barred from a large number of jobs, from bartender to barber, from securities trader to bail bondsperson, from nurse to beautician. They may be automatically disqualified from such positions by their felony conviction, the specific offense they committed, or restrictions on necessary licenses or mobility. Ironically, in some prisons, inmates continue to be trained for jobs they cannot hold after release.

With the expansion of the welfare state, limitations or outright bans on public benefits have become a new form of collateral sanction. Drug and sex offenders are not eligible for public housing; drug offenders are barred from welfare benefits and student loans. Political rights are also restricted. In many states offenders are barred from the voting booth, the jury box, and political office — sometimes forever.

For a general discussion of collateral consequences, see Nora V. Demleitner, Preventing Internal Exile: The Need for Restrictions on Collateral Sentencing Consequences, 11 Stan. L. & Pol'y Rev. 153 (1999); Invisible Punishment: The Collateral Consequences of Mass Incarceration (Marc Mauer & Meda Chesney-Lind eds., 2002). For a review of collateral sanctions imposed on drug offenders, see Nora V. Demleitner, "Collateral Damage": No Re-entry for Drug Offenders, 47 Vill. L. Rev. 1027 (2002).

There are so many collateral sanctions that judges, prosecutors, and criminal defense attorneys are unable to inform most defendants of all the sanctions that will apply to them. For that reason, the American Bar Association has demanded that such sanctions be cataloged and that defendants be informed of them before they plead guilty. American Bar Association, Criminal Justice Standards, ch. 19 (2003).

Courts have generally declared collateral sanctions civil rather than criminal sanctions. They are assumed to protect the public against risk rather than constituting further punishment of the offender. Because they are civil sanctions, they are typically applied and enforced without the traditional procedural protections that apply in criminal cases. In light of the panoply of collateral sanctions and their impact on the offender, should potential collateral sanctions be included in the pre-sentence report, especially as they may impact compliance with probation and other sentence conditions because they affect the offender's employment and financial status? See Gabriel J. Chin, Taking Plea Bargaining Seriously: Reforming Pre-Sentence Reports After *Padilla v. Kentucky*, 31 St. Louis U. Pub. L. Rev. 61 (2011).

## 1. Automatic Disabilities

### a. Disenfranchisement

All but two states — Maine and Vermont — prohibit prison inmates from voting. Most states also prevent offenders from voting while under a criminal justice sentence: 35 states prohibit felons from voting while they are on parole, and of those 30 also exclude felony probationers from the voting process. Some states prohibit only those who have committed certain crimes from voting; others do so for all felonies. Offenders automatically regain the right to vote in most states upon completion of their sentence. In a small number of states, a felon must apply for a pardon or undergo another burdensome restoration process to be permitted to vote.

Currently more than 5,8 million U.S. citizens are denied the right to vote because of criminal convictions, and more than 1 million of these have completed their sentences but live in states that deny voting rights to anyone who has been convicted of a felony and has not received a gubernatorial pardon or undergone the restoration process. State rather than federal law governs voting rights, including the right to vote in presidential and congressional elections.

In recent years, the issue of felon disenfranchisement has received more public policy attention, and a few states have acted to ease restrictions on voting rights. In 2007, for example, Maryland's legislature repealed all provisions of the state's lifetime voting ban, including the three-year waiting period after sentence completion for certain categories of offenses, and instituted an automatic restoration policy for all persons upon completion of sentence. In Florida, the state's Office of Executive Clemency voted to amend the state's voting rights restoration procedure to automatically approve the reinstatement of rights for many persons who have been convicted of nonviolent offenses. In 2011, however, Florida's governor imposed a five-year waiting period before an offender can apply for restoration of voting rights.

In 1974 the Supreme Court confronted the question whether denial of the right to vote for felons who had served their sentences violated the equal protection clause. Richardson v. Ramirez, 418 U.S. 24 (1974). In its decision the Court stated that the drafting history, historic practice, and language of section 2 of the Fourteenth Amendment, the apportionment clause, justified state disenfranchisement of felons. The clause reads in part:

> [W]hen the right to vote at any election . . . is denied to any of the male inhabitants of such State, being twenty-one years of age, and citizens of the United States, or in any way abridged, *except for participation in rebellion, or other crime*, the basis of representation therein shall be reduced in the proportion which the number of such male citizens shall bear to the whole number of male citizens twenty-one years of age in such State. [Emphasis added.]

In his dissent, Justice Marshall questioned the majority's analysis of section 2 and advocated addressing the disenfranchisement question under section 1 of the Fourteenth Amendment. He considered the state as having failed its burden of justifying felon disenfranchisement under the compelling interest standard. The state had advocated felon voting restrictions because it wished to prevent voting fraud and because the "likely voting pattern [of felons] might be subversive of the interests of an orderly society." Are these grounds valid?

About a decade later the Court revisited the issue of felon disenfranchisement in Hunter v. Underwood, 471 U.S. 222 (1985). There the Court struck down Alabama's constitutional provision barring felons convicted of "any crime [felony and misdemeanor] . . . involving moral turpitude" from voting. The Court found a violation of the equal protection clause because the state constitutional provision had been passed with a racially discriminatory motive — the exclusion of blacks (and poor whites) from the ballot box.

State courts and lower federal courts have heard numerous challenges on constitutional and statutory grounds to felon disenfranchisement provisions. So far, none of them have been successful. The most frequently cited objections to inmate voting are practical difficulties in arranging for in-prison voting and philosophical objections to granting those who have violated society's laws the right to participate in the making of laws. Even the ABA's Criminal Justice Standards in their latest chapter on collateral sanctions allow for disenfranchisement during incarceration while generally condemning it as a collateral sanction. Standard 19-2.6. In the 1968 version of this chapter, the Standards rejected all disenfranchisement based on a criminal conviction. For a different perspective, one more characteristic of other Western democracies, consider the following case.

## Richard Sauvé v. Canada (Chief Electoral Officer)
### [2002] 3 S.C.R. 519, 2002 SCC 68

McLachlin, C.J.

1. The right of every citizen to vote, guaranteed by s. 3 of the *Canadian Charter of Rights and Freedoms,* lies at the heart of Canadian democracy. The law at stake in this appeal denies the right to vote to a certain class of people — those serving sentences of two years or more in a correctional institution. The question is whether the government has established that this denial of the right to vote is allowed under s. 1 of the Charter as a "reasonable limit . . . demonstrably justified in a free and democratic society." I conclude that it is not. The right to vote, which lies at the heart of Canadian democracy, can only be trammeled for good reason. Here, the reasons offered do not suffice.

2. The predecessor to s. 51(e) of the Canada Elections Act, R.S.C. 1985, c. E-2, prohibited all prison inmates from voting in federal elections, regardless of the length of their sentences. This section was held unconstitutional as an unjustified denial of the right to vote guaranteed by s. 3 of the Charter. Parliament responded to this litigation by replacing this section with a new s. 51(e), which denies the right to vote to all inmates serving sentences of two years or more. . . .

7. To justify the infringement of a Charter right, the government must show that the infringement achieves a constitutionally valid purpose or objective, and that the chosen means are reasonable and demonstrably justified. This two-part inquiry — the legitimacy of the objective and the proportionality of the means — ensures that a reviewing court examine rigorously all aspects of justification. Throughout the justification process, the government bears the burden of proving a valid objective and showing that the rights violation is warranted — that is, that it is rationally connected, causes minimal impairment, and is proportionate to the benefit achieved. . . .

20. The objectives' analysis entails a two-step inquiry. First, we must ask what the objectives are of denying penitentiary inmates the right to vote. This involves interpretation and construction, and calls for a contextual approach. Second, we must evaluate whether the objectives as found are capable of justifying limitations on Charter rights. The objectives must not be "trivial," and they must not be "discordant with the principles integral to a free and democratic society." . . .

21. Section 51(e) denying penitentiary inmates the right to vote was not directed at a specific problem or concern. Prisoners have long voted, here and abroad, in a variety of situations without apparent adverse effects to the political process, the prison population, or society as a whole. In the absence of a specific

problem, the government asserts two broad objectives as the reason for this denial of the right to vote: (1) to enhance civic responsibility and respect for the rule of law; and (2) to provide additional punishment, or "enhance the general purposes of the criminal sanction." . . .

22. This leaves the question of whether the objectives of enhancing respect for law and appropriate punishment are constitutionally valid and sufficiently significant to warrant a rights violation. . . . However, precisely because they leave so little room for argument, vague and symbolic objectives make the justification analysis more difficult. Their terms carry many meanings, yet tell us little about why the limitation on the right is necessary, and what it is expected to achieve in concrete terms. The broader and more abstract the objective, the more susceptible it is to different meanings in different contexts, and hence to distortion and manipulation. . . .

26. Quite simply, the government has failed to identify particular problems that require denying the right to vote, making it hard to say that the denial is directed at a pressing and substantial purpose. Nevertheless, despite the abstract nature of the government's objectives and the rather thin basis upon which they rest, prudence suggests that we proceed to the proportionality analysis, rather than dismissing the government's objectives outright. The proportionality inquiry allows us to determine whether the government's asserted objectives are in fact capable of justifying its denial of the right to vote. At that stage, as we shall see, the difficulties inherent in the government's stated objectives become manifest.

27. At this stage the government must show that the denial of the right to vote will promote the asserted objectives (the rational connection test); that the denial does not go further than reasonably necessary to achieve its objectives (the minimal impairment test); and that the overall benefits of the measure outweigh its negative impact (the proportionate effect test). . . .

28. Will denying the right to vote to penitentiary inmates enhance respect for the law and impose legitimate punishment? The government must show that this is likely, either by evidence or in reason and logic.

29. The government advances three theories to demonstrate rational connection between its limitation and the objective of enhancing respect for law. First, it submits that depriving penitentiary inmates of the vote sends an "educative message" about the importance of respect for the law to inmates and to the citizenry at large. Second, it asserts that allowing penitentiary inmates to vote "demeans" the political system. Finally, it takes the position that disenfranchisement is a legitimate form of punishment, regardless of the specific nature of the offence or the circumstances of the individual offender. . . .

30. The first asserted connector with enhancing respect for the law is the "educative message" or "moral statement" theory. The problem here, quite simply, is that denying penitentiary inmates the right to vote is bad pedagogy. . . .

31. Denying penitentiary inmates the right to vote misrepresents the nature of our rights and obligations under the law and consequently undermines them. In a democracy such as ours, . . . the legitimacy of the law and the obligation to obey the law flow directly from the right of every citizen to vote. As a practical matter, we require all within our country's boundaries to obey its laws, whether or not they vote. But this does not negate the vital symbolic,

theoretical and practical connection between having a voice in making the law and being obliged to obey it. This connection, inherited from social contract theory and enshrined in the Charter, stands at the heart of our system of constitutional democracy.

32. The government gets this connection exactly backwards when it attempts to argue that depriving people of a voice in government teaches them to obey the law. The "educative message" that the government purports to send by disenfranchising inmates is both anti-democratic and internally self-contradictory. Denying a citizen the right to vote denies the basis of democratic legitimacy. It says that delegates elected by the citizens can then bar those very citizens, or a portion of them, from participating in future elections. But if we accept that governmental power in a democracy flows from the citizens, it is difficult to see how that power can legitimately be used to disenfranchise the very citizens from whom the government's power flows. . . .

38. The theoretical and constitutional links between the right to vote and respect for the rule of law are reflected in the practical realities of the prison population and the need to bolster, rather than to undermine, the feeling of connection between prisoners and society as a whole. The government argues that disenfranchisement will "educate" and rehabilitate inmates. However, disenfranchisement is more likely to become a self-fulfilling prophecy than a spur to reintegration. Depriving at-risk individuals of their sense of collective identity and membership in the community is unlikely to instill a sense of responsibility and community identity, while the right to participate in voting helps teach democratic values and social responsibility. . . .

To deny prisoners the right to vote is to lose an important means of teaching them democratic values and social responsibility.

39. Even if these difficulties could be overcome, it is not apparent that denying penitentiary inmates the right to vote actually sends the intended message to prisoners, or to the rest of society. People may be sentenced to imprisonment for two years or more for a wide variety of crimes, ranging from motor vehicle and regulatory offences to the most serious cases of murder. The variety of offences and offenders covered by the prohibition suggest that the educative message is, at best, a mixed and diffuse one.

40. It is a message sullied, moreover, by negative and unacceptable messages likely to undermine civic responsibility and respect for the rule of law. Denying citizen law-breakers the right to vote sends the message that those who commit serious breaches are no longer valued as members of the community, but instead are temporary outcasts from our system of rights and democracy. More profoundly, it sends the unacceptable message that democratic values are less important than punitive measures ostensibly designed to promote order. If modern democratic history has one lesson to teach it is this: enforced conformity to the law should not come at the cost of our core democratic values. . . .

42. The government also argues that denying penitentiary inmates the vote will enhance respect for law because allowing people who flaunt the law to vote demeans the political system. The same untenable premises we have been discussing resurface here — that voting is a privilege the government can suspend and that the commission of a serious crime signals that the offender has chosen to "opt out" of community membership. But beyond this, the argument that

only those who respect the law should participate in the political process is a variant on the age-old unworthiness rationale for denying the vote.

43. . . . Until recently, large classes of people, prisoners among them, were excluded from the franchise. The assumption that they were not fit or "worthy" of voting — whether by reason of class, race, gender or conduct — played a large role in this exclusion. We should reject the retrograde notion that "worthiness" qualifications for voters may be logically viewed as enhancing the political process and respect for the rule of law. . . .

45. This brings us to the government's final argument for rational connection — that disenfranchisement is a legitimate weapon in the state's punitive arsenal against the individual lawbreaker. Again, the argument cannot succeed. The first reason is that using the denial of rights as punishment is suspect. The second reason is that denying the right to vote does not comply with the requirements for legitimate punishment established by our jurisprudence.

46. . . . I do not doubt that Parliament may limit constitutional rights in the name of punishment, provided that it can justify the limitation. But it is another thing to say that a particular class of people for a particular period of time will completely lose a particular constitutional right. This is tantamount to saying that the affected class is outside the full protection of the Charter. It is doubtful that such an unmodulated deprivation, particularly of a right as basic as the right to vote, is capable of justification under s. 1. Could Parliament justifiably pass a law removing the right of all penitentiary prisoners to be protected from cruel and unusual punishment? I think not. What of freedom of expression or religion? Why, one asks, is the right to vote different? The government offers no credible theory about why it should be allowed to deny this fundamental democratic right as a form of state punishment.

47. The social compact requires the citizen to obey the laws created by the democratic process. But it does not follow that failure to do so nullifies the citizen's continued membership in the self-governing polity. Indeed, the remedy of imprisonment for a term rather than permanent exile implies our acceptance of continued membership in the social order. Certain rights are justifiably limited for penal reasons, including aspects of the right to liberty, security of the person, mobility, and security against search and seizure. But whether a right is justifiably limited cannot be determined by observing that an offender has, by his or her actions, withdrawn from the social compact. Indeed, the right of the state to punish and the obligation of the criminal to accept punishment is tied to society's acceptance of the criminal as a person with rights and responsibilities. . . .

52. When the facade of rhetoric is stripped away, little is left of the government's claim about punishment other than that criminals are people who have broken society's norms and may therefore be denounced and punished as the government sees fit, even to the point of removing fundamental constitutional rights. Yet, the right to punish and to denounce, however important, is constitutionally constrained. It cannot be used to write entire rights out of the Constitution, it cannot be arbitrary, and it must serve the constitutionally recognized goals of sentencing. On all counts, the case that s. 51(e) furthers lawful punishment objectives fails. . . .

60. The negative effects of s. 51(e) upon prisoners have a disproportionate impact on Canada's already disadvantaged Aboriginal population, whose

over-representation in prisons reflects "a crisis in the Canadian criminal justice system." To the extent that the disproportionate number of Aboriginal people in penitentiaries reflects factors such as higher rates of poverty and institutionalized alienation from mainstream society, penitentiary imprisonment may not be a fair or appropriate marker of the degree of individual culpability. . . . Aboriginal people in prison have unique perspectives and needs. Yet, s. 51(e) denies them a voice at the ballot box and, by proxy, in Parliament. That these costs are confined to the term of imprisonment does not diminish their reality. The silenced messages cannot be retrieved, and the prospect of someday participating in the political system is cold comfort to those whose rights are denied in the present. . . .

62. . . . I leave for another day whether some political activities, like standing for office, could be justifiably denied to prisoners under s. 1. It may be that practical problems might serve to justify some limitations on the exercise of derivative democratic rights. Democratic participation is not only a matter of theory but also of practice, and legislatures retain the power to limit the modalities of its exercise where this can be justified. Suffice it to say that the wholesale disenfranchisement of all penitentiary inmates, even with a two-year minimum sentence requirement, is not demonstrably justified in our free and democratic society.

GONTHIER, J., dissenting.

67. . . . If the social or political philosophy advanced by Parliament reasonably justifies a limitation of the right in the context of a free and democratic society, then it ought to be upheld as constitutional. I conclude that this is so in the case at bar.

68. I am of the view that by enacting s. 51(e) of the Act, Parliament has chosen to assert and enhance the importance and value of the right to vote by temporarily disenfranchising serious criminal offenders for the duration of their incarceration. . . . The Chief Justice and I are in agreement that the right to vote is profoundly important, and ought not to be demeaned. Our differences lie principally in the fact that she subscribes to a philosophy whereby the temporary disenfranchising of criminals does injury to the rule of law, democracy and the right to vote, while I prefer deference to Parliament's reasonable view that it strengthens these same features of Canadian society. . . .

70. . . . While there is little logical correlation between maintaining a "decent and responsible citizenry" and any of the past discriminatory exclusions (such as land-ownership, religion, gender, ethnic background), there clearly is such a logical connection in the case of distinguishing persons who have committed serious criminal offences. "*Responsible* citizenship" does not relate to what gender, race, or religion a person belongs to, but is logically related to whether or not a person engages in serious criminal activity.

71. [S]erious criminal offenders are excluded from the vote for the reason that they are the *subjects of punishment*. The disenfranchisement only lasts as long as the period of incarceration. Thus, disenfranchisement, as a dimension of punishment, is attached to and mirrors the fact of incarceration. This fact makes the Canadian experience significantly different from the situation in some American states which disenfranchise ex-offenders for life.

72. It is important to look at prisoner disenfranchisement from the perspective of each serious criminal offender rather than perceive it as a form of targeted group treatment. Disenfranchised prisoners can be characterized loosely as a group, but what is important to realize is that each of these prisoners has been convicted of a serious criminal offence and is therefore serving a personalized sentence which is proportionate to the act or acts committed. Punishment is guided by the goals of denunciation, deterrence, rehabilitation and retribution and is intended to be morally educative for incarcerated serious criminal offenders. Each prisoner's sentence is a temporary measure aimed at meeting these goals, while also being aimed at the long-term objective of reintegration into the community. . . .

116. Permitting the exercise of the franchise by offenders incarcerated for serious offences undermines the rule of law and civic responsibility because such persons have demonstrated a great disrespect for the community in their committing serious crimes: such persons have attacked the stability and order within our community. Society therefore may choose to curtail temporarily the availability of the vote to serious criminals both to punish those criminals and to insist that civic responsibility and respect for the rule of law, as goals worthy of pursuit, are prerequisites to democratic participation. . . .

119. . . . The disenfranchisement of serious criminal offenders serves to deliver a message to both the community and the offenders themselves that serious criminal activity will not be tolerated by the community. In making such a choice, Parliament is projecting a view of Canadian society which Canadian society has of itself. The commission of serious crimes gives rise to a temporary suspension of this nexus: on the physical level, this is reflected in incarceration and the deprivation of a range of liberties normally exercised by citizens and, at the symbolic level, this is reflected in temporary disenfranchisement. The symbolic dimension is thus a further manifestation of community disapproval of the serious criminal conduct.

120. From the perspective of the person whose criminal activity has resulted in their temporary disenfranchisement, their benefiting from society brought with it the responsibility to be subjected to the sanctions which the state decides will be attached to serious criminal activity such as they have chosen to undertake. This understanding is complemented by the rehabilitative view that those who are in jail will hope and expect to regain the exercise of the vote on their release from incarceration, just like they hope and expect to regain the exercise of the fullest expressions of their liberty. Once released from prison, they are on the road to reintegration into the community. Obtaining the vote once released or paroled is a recognition of regaining the nexus with the community that was temporarily suspended during the incarceration. . . .

159. [G]iven that, the objectives are largely symbolic, common sense dictates that social condemnation of criminal activity and a desire to promote civic responsibility are reflected in disenfranchisement of those who have committed serious crimes. This justification is rooted in a reasonable and rational social and political philosophy which has been adopted by Parliament. Further, it can

hardly be seen as "novel." . . . The view of the courts below is that generally supported by democratic countries. Countries including the United States, the United Kingdom, Australia, New Zealand, and many European countries such as France and Germany, have, by virtue of choosing some form of prisoner disenfranchisement, also identified a connection between objectives similar to those advanced in the case at bar and the means of prisoner disenfranchisement. . . .

## NOTES

1. *Voting restrictions on felons in the United States.*   In the United States voting restrictions based on a prior criminal record go back to the beginning of the Republic. They did not begin to play a prominent role until after the Civil War, when Southern legislatures in particular used them to prevent blacks from voting. See Hunter v. Underwood, 471 U.S. 222 (1985) (striking down Alabama voting restriction because it was motivated by racial animus). Even though in recent years states have cut back on voting restrictions on those with criminal convictions, currently 48 states prevent inmates from voting. See generally Felony Disenfranchisement, The Sentencing Project, at www.sentencingproject.org.

2. *Justifications for felon disenfranchisement.*   Felon disenfranchisement has been justified on a number of grounds. Some have claimed that felons violate the implicit social contract and should therefore be excluded from voting. Others have stated that civic virtues are necessary for participation in political decision making; in their absence, individuals should be excluded from the polity. Among the more practical and frequently raised arguments are potential election fraud by convicted felons (the "purity of the ballot box" argument), potential problems of arranging for voting in prisons, and in the past, racial arguments defending felon disenfranchisement as a way of excluding blacks (and sometimes also poor whites) from voting. For a discussion of the political philosophies underlying criminal disenfranchisement, see Alec Ewald, "Civil Death": The Ideological Paradox of Criminal Disenfranchisement Law in the United States, 2002 Wis. L. Rev. 1045. In light of the Canadian high court's decision, are there certain justifications that you consider particularly valid (or invalid)?

3. *Race and felon disenfranchisement.*   Despite challenges to disenfranchisement provisions on equal protection grounds, the Supreme Court has upheld state laws disenfranchising felons generally. See Richardson v. Ramirez, 418 U.S. 24 (1974). In a handful of subsequent cases, however, courts have struck down disenfranchisement provisions that were animated by racial bias, in violation of the equal protection clause.
    A 1998 study published by Human Rights Watch and the Sentencing Project illuminated the racially disproportionate impact of the exclusion of felons from voting. The Sentencing Project & Human Rights Watch, Losing the Vote: The Impact of Felony Disenfranchisement in the United States (October 1998) (available at www.sentencingproject.org/pdfs/9080.pdf). Because of their

overrepresentation among convicted felons and their large numbers in states that continue disenfranchisement after an offender's sentence has been served, 1.8 million African Americans are excluded from the franchise. Should the disproportionate racial impact on a fundamental constitutional right — the franchise — be a reason for striking down such legislation on equal protection grounds? How could a legislator use the study to argue for the abolition or at least the restriction of felon disenfranchisement?

4. *The impact of felon disenfranchisement in elections.*  The 2000 presidential election, whose outcome hinged on the result in the state of Florida, focused national attention in part on felon disenfranchisement. The state, with its large inmate population, disenfranchises not only prison inmates but also ex-offenders released from any criminal justice sanction unless they have their civil rights restored which remains a difficult and protracted process despite some recent changes. Many argued that felon disenfranchisement changed the outcome of the presidential election in Florida. For some empirical support for the possible impact of felon disenfranchisement on election outcomes, see Christopher Uggen & Jeff Manza, Democratic Contraction? The Political Consequences of Felon Disenfranchisement in the United States, 67 Am. Soc. Rev. 777 (2002). For an account of how a new movement to restore voting rights to felons may significantly influence the electoral map, see Emily Bazelon, The Secret Weapon of 2008: Felons Are Getting the Vote Back — and Republicans Aren't Stopping Them, Slate (April 27, 2007).

5. *Restoration of voting rights.*  Most states automatically restore voting rights to all offenders after they have served their criminal justice sentence. Some, however, restrict automatic restoration provisions to first-time or nonviolent offenders. States that do not have automatic restoration provisions offer administrative, judicial, or legislative relief. The difficulty and cost of obtaining relief varies based on the procedure and the state. See Margaret Colgate Love, Relief from the Collateral Consequences of a Criminal Conviction: A State-by-State Resource Guide (2008).

When a criminal justice sanction ends may also be disputed. In Johnson v. Bredesen, 624 F.3d 742 (6th Cir. 2010), the court upheld Tennessee's disenfranchisement law, which conditioned restoration of voting rights on payment of court-ordered victim restitution and child support obligations.

6. *Felon disenfranchisement — uniquely American?*  In most other Western democracies, voting restrictions on convicted felons are very limited. Germany, for example, allows disenfranchisement only upon conviction of one of a very small number of offenses, including treason and voting fraud, for a maximum period of five years, and only if imposed by a judge at sentencing in open court. See Nora V. Demleitner, Continuing Payment on One's Debt to Society: The German Model of Felon Disenfranchisement as an Alternative, 84 Minn. L. Rev. 753 (2000). In Scoppola v. Italy (No. 3), App. No. 126/05, Eur. Ct. H.R. (May 22, 2012), the European Court of Human Rights reviewed international law and comparative developments:

### III. RELEVANT INTERNATIONAL AND EUROPEAN DOCUMENTS

### A. International Covenant on Civil and Political Rights (adopted by the General Assembly of the United Nations on 16 December 1966)

40. . . .

### Article 10

. . .

3. The penitentiary system shall comprise treatment of prisoners the essential aim of which shall be their reformation and social rehabilitation . . ."

### Article 25

"Every citizen shall have the right and the opportunity, without any of the distinctions mentioned in article 2 [race, colour, sex, language, religion, political or other opinion, national or social origin, property, birth or other status] and without unreasonable restrictions:

(a) To take part in the conduct of public affairs, directly or through freely chosen representatives;

(b) To vote and to be elected at genuine periodic elections which shall be by universal and equal suffrage and shall be held by secret ballot, guaranteeing the free expression of the will of the electors; . . . .

### B. United Nations Human Rights Committee

41. In its General Comment no. 25 (1996) on Article 25 of the International Covenant on Civil and Political Rights, the Human Rights Committee expressed the following view:

"14. In their reports, States parties should indicate and explain the legislative provisions which would deprive citizens of their right to vote. The grounds for such deprivation should be objective and reasonable. If conviction for an offence is a basis for suspending the right to vote, the period of such suspension should be proportionate to the offence and the sentence. Persons who are deprived of liberty but who have not been convicted should not be excluded from exercising the right to vote." . . .

### C. American Convention on Human Rights of 22 November 1969

43. Article 23 of the American Convention, under the heading "Right to Participate in Government", provides:

"1. Every citizen shall enjoy the following rights and opportunities:

a. to take part in the conduct of public affairs, directly or through freely chosen representatives;

b.   to vote and to be elected in genuine periodic elections, which shall be by universal and equal suffrage and by secret ballot that guarantees the free expression of the will of the voters; . . . .

2. The law may regulate the exercise of the rights and opportunities referred to in the preceding paragraph only on the basis of age, nationality, residence, language, education, civil and mental capacity, or sentencing by a competent court in criminal proceedings."

### D.   *Venice Commission Code of Good Practice in Electoral Matters*

44. This document, adopted by the European Commission for Democracy through Law ("the Venice Commission") at its 51st plenary session (5-6 July 2002) and submitted to the Parliamentary Assembly of the Council of Europe on 6 November 2002, lays out the guidelines developed by the Commission concerning the circumstances in which people may be deprived of the right to vote or to stand for election. The relevant passages read as follows:

i. provision may be made for depriving individuals of their right to vote and to be elected, but only subject to the following cumulative conditions:
ii. it must be provided for by law;
iii. the proportionality principle must be observed; conditions for depriving individuals of the right to stand for election may be less strict than for disenfranchising them;
iv. the deprivation must be based on mental incapacity or a criminal conviction for a serious offence;
v. Furthermore, the withdrawal of political rights or finding of mental incapacity may only be imposed by express decision of a court of law.

### IV.   Comparative Law

### A.   *The legislative framework in the Contracting States*

45. Nineteen of the forty-three Contracting States examined in a comparative law study place no restrictions on the right of convicted prisoners to vote: Albania, Azerbaijan, Croatia, Cyprus, Czech Republic, Denmark, Finland, Ireland, Latvia, Lithuania, Moldova, Montenegro, Serbia, Slovenia, Spain, Sweden, Switzerland, "the former Yugoslav Republic of Macedonia" and Ukraine.

46. Seven Contracting States (Armenia, Bulgaria, Estonia, Georgia, Hungary, Russia and the United Kingdom) automatically deprive all convicted prisoners serving prison sentences of the right to vote.

47. The remaining sixteen member States (Austria, Belgium, Bosnia and Herzegovina, France, Germany, Greece, Luxembourg, Malta, Monaco, Netherlands, Poland, Portugal, Romania, San Marino, Slovakia and Turkey) have adopted an intermediate approach: disenfranchisement of prisoners depends on the type of offence and/or the length of the custodial sentence. Italy's legislation on the subject resembles that of this group of countries.

48. In some of the States in this category the decision to deprive convicted prisoners of the right to vote is left to the discretion of the criminal court (Austria, Belgium, France, Germany, Greece, Luxembourg, Netherlands, Poland, Portugal, Romania and San Marino). In Greece and Luxembourg, in the event of particularly serious offences disenfranchisement is applied independently of any court decision.

### B.   Other relevant case-law
### 1.   Canada

[discussion of *Sauve supra*]

### 2.   South Africa

### (a) *August and Another v. Electoral Commission and Others* (CCT8/99:1999 (3) SA 1)

52. On 1 April 1999 the Constitutional Court of South Africa considered the application of prisoners for a declaration and orders that the Electoral Commission take measures enabling them and other prisoners to register and vote while in prison. It noted that, under the South African Constitution, the right of every adult citizen to vote in elections for legislative bodies was set out in unqualified terms, and it underlined the importance of that right:

> "The universality of the franchise is important not only for nationhood and democracy. The vote of each and every citizen is a badge of dignity and personhood. Quite literally, it says that everybody counts."

53. The Constitutional Court found that the right to vote by its very nature imposed positive obligations upon the legislature and the executive and that the Electoral Act must be interpreted in a way that gave effect to constitutional declarations, guarantees and responsibilities. It noted that many democratic societies imposed voting disabilities on some categories of prisoners. Although there were no comparable provisions in the Constitution, it recognised that limitations might be imposed upon the exercise of fundamental rights, provided they were, *inter alia*, reasonable and justifiable.

54. The question whether legislation barring prisoners would be justified under the Constitution was not raised in the proceedings and the court emphasised that the judgment was not to be read as preventing Parliament from disenfranchising certain categories of prisoners. In the absence of such legislation, prisoners had the constitutional right to vote and neither the Electoral Commission nor the Constitutional Court had the power to disenfranchise them. It concluded that the Commission was under the obligation to make reasonable arrangements for prisoners to vote.

**(b)** *Minister of Home Affairs v. National Institute for Crime Prevention and the Reintegration of Offenders (NICRO)* **(no. 3/04 of 3 March 2004)**

55. The Constitutional Court of South Africa examined whether the 2003 amendment to the Electoral Act, depriving of the right to vote those prisoners serving sentences of imprisonment without the option of a fine, was compatible with the Constitution.

56. The Constitutional Court found the measure unconstitutional, by nine votes to two, and ordered the Electoral Commission to take the necessary steps to allow prisoners to vote in elections.

57. Chaskalson CJ, for the majority, . . . . noted that this was a blanket exclusion aimed at every prisoner sentenced to imprisonment without the option of a fine, and that there was no information about the sort of offences concerned, the sort of persons likely to be affected and the number of persons who might lose their vote for a minor offence.

58. Madala J, for the minority, considered that the temporary removal of the vote and its restoration upon the prisoner's release was in line with the Government's objective of balancing individual rights and the values of society, particularly in a country like South Africa with its very high crime rate.

### 3. *Australia*

59. The High Court of Australia found by four votes to two against the general voting ban that had been introduced in the place of the previous legislation, which had provided for the loss of the right to vote only in connection with prison sentences of three years or more (see *Roach v. Electoral Commissioner* [2007] HCA 43 (26 September 2007)).

60. The High Court noted, *inter alia*, that the earlier legislation took into account the seriousness of the offence committed as an indicium of culpability and temporary unfitness to participate in the electoral process, beyond the bare fact of imprisonment.

In *Hirst* the European Court of Human Rights (ECHR) declared the British disenfranchisement practice regarding inmates in violation of the European Convention of Human Rights. Hirst v. United Kingdom, App. No. 40787/98, Eur. Ct. H.R. (July 24, 2001). Despite repeated promises of reviewing the ECHR decision, the British parliament has made no changes to the indiscriminate and automatic denial of voting rights upon imposition of a prison sentence. The Court has notified Great Britain that it is in violation of its treaty obligations. Hirst v. United Kingdom (No. 2), App. No. 74025/01, Eur. Ct. H.R. (Oct. 6, 2005). In a recent decision, the ECHR has declared that not all lifetime disenfranchisement of a prisoner violates the Convention. Disenfranchisement, however, must be closely tied to the offense and the sentence imposed, as under Italian law lifetime disenfranchisement follows only upon imposition of a sentence of at least five years imprisonment. Scoppola v. Italy (No. 3), App. No. 126/05, Eur. Ct. H.R. (May 22, 2012).

## b.   Notification, Registration, and Residency Restrictions

In recent years sanctions have increased dramatically against sex offenders as a class. State and federal legislatures and sentencing commissions have lengthened prison sentences; numerous states have passed civil confinement statutes that allow judges to commit sex offenders civilly after their release from prison, a development sanctioned by the Supreme Court in Kansas v. Hendricks, 521 U.S. 346 (1996), and discussed in Chapter 11.

These harsher sanctions came in response to assessments that sentences for sex offenses were disproportionately low compared to other violent and nonviolent crimes and in light of beliefs about the future danger such offenders pose. Incapacitative goals animate sex offender civil commitment statutes, which are based on risk assessments derived from the offender's prior criminal record and assumptions about whether he is likely to reoffend. In addition to civil commitment laws, registration statutes enacted in the mid-1990s require that sex offenders register with local police upon release so that their names can be entered into a database. Notification statutes also require police to alert neighbors, schools, and certain other institutions when a sex offender moves into the area. A new wave of state and local laws has placed formal restrictions on where sex offenders may reside after their release. As you review the next two cases, discussing constitutional challenges to registration rules and residency restrictions for sex offenders, consider more broadly whether these laws are sound from a policy perspective. If you think these types of collateral sanctions are potentially effective, should jurisdictions consider expanding their reach to cover other criminal offenders, such as drug dealers and thieves?

|| *Delbert Smith v. John Doe I* ||
538 U.S. 84 (2003)

KENNEDY, J.

The Alaska Sex Offender Registration Act requires convicted sex offenders to register with law enforcement authorities, and much of the information is made public. We must decide whether the registration requirement is a retroactive punishment prohibited by the Ex Post Facto clause.

The State of Alaska enacted the Alaska Sex Offender Registration Act (Act) on May 12, 1994. Like its counterparts in other States, the Act is termed a "Megan's Law." Megan Kanka was a 7-year-old New Jersey girl who was sexually assaulted and murdered in 1994 by a neighbor who, unknown to the victim's family, had prior convictions for sex offenses against children. The crime gave impetus to laws for mandatory registration of sex offenders and corresponding community notification. In 1994, Congress passed the Jacob Wetterling Crimes Against Children and Sexually Violent Offender Registration Act, 42 U.S.C. §14071, which conditions certain federal law enforcement funding on the States' adoption of sex offender registration laws and sets minimum standards for state programs. By 1996, every State, the District of Columbia, and the Federal Government had enacted some variation of Megan's Law.

The Alaska law . . . contains two components: a registration requirement and a notification system. Both are retroactive. The Act requires any "sex offender or child kidnapper who is physically present in the state" to register, either with the Department of Corrections (if the individual is incarcerated) or with the local law enforcement authorities (if the individual is at liberty). Prompt registration is mandated. . . . The sex offender must provide his name, aliases, identifying features, address, place of employment, date of birth, conviction information, driver's license number, information about vehicles to which he has access, and postconviction treatment history. He must permit the authorities to photograph and fingerprint him.

If the offender was convicted of a single, nonaggravated sex crime, he must provide annual verification of the submitted information for 15 years. If he was convicted of an aggravated sex offense or of two or more sex offenses, he must register for life and verify the information quarterly. The offender must notify his local police department if he moves. A sex offender who knowingly fails to comply with the Act is subject to criminal prosecution.

The information is forwarded to the Alaska Department of Public Safety, which maintains a central registry of sex offenders. Some of the data . . . is kept confidential. The following information is made available to the public: "the sex offender's or child kidnapper's name, aliases, address, photograph, physical description, description[,] license [and] identification numbers of motor vehicles, place of employment, date of birth, crime for which convicted, date of conviction, place and court of conviction, length and conditions of sentence, and a statement as to whether the offender or kidnapper is in compliance with [the update] requirements . . . or cannot be located." . . . Alaska has chosen to make most of the nonconfidential information available on the Internet.

Respondents John Doe I and John Doe II were convicted of sexual abuse of a minor, an aggravated sex offense. . . . Both were released from prison in 1990 and completed rehabilitative programs for sex offenders. Although convicted before the passage of the Act, respondents are covered by it. After the initial registration, they are required to submit quarterly verifications and notify the authorities of any changes. Both respondents, along with respondent Jane Doe, wife of John Doe I, brought an action . . . seeking to declare the Act void as to them under the Ex Post Facto Clause of Article I, §10, cl. 1, of the Constitution and the Due Process Clause of §1 of the Fourteenth Amendment. . . .

This is the first time we have considered a claim that a sex offender registration and notification law constitutes retroactive punishment forbidden by the Ex Post Facto Clause. The framework for our inquiry, however, is well established. We must "ascertain whether the legislature meant the statute to establish 'civil' proceedings." Kansas v. Hendricks, 521 U.S. 346, 361 (1997). If the intention of the legislature was to impose punishment, that ends the inquiry. If, however, the intention was to enact a regulatory scheme that is civil and nonpunitive, we must further examine whether the statutory scheme is "'so punitive either in purpose or effect as to negate [the State's] intention' to deem it 'civil.'" Because we "ordinarily defer to the legislature's stated intent," "'only the clearest proof' will suffice to override legislative intent and transform what has been denominated a civil remedy into a criminal penalty," Hudson v. United States, 522 U.S. 93, 100 (1997); United States v. One Assortment of 89 Firearms, 465 U.S. 354 (1984). . . .

Whether a statutory scheme is civil or criminal "is first of all a question of statutory construction." We consider the statute's text and its structure to determine the legislative objective. Flemming v. Nestor, 363 U.S. 603 (1960). A conclusion that the legislature intended to punish would satisfy an ex post facto challenge without further inquiry into its effects, so considerable deference must be accorded to the intent as the legislature has stated it.

The courts "must first ask whether the legislature, in establishing the penalizing mechanism, indicated either expressly or impliedly a preference for one label or the other." Here, the Alaska Legislature expressed the objective of the law in the statutory text itself. The legislature found that "sex offenders pose a high risk of reoffending," and identified "protecting the public from sex offenders" as the "primary governmental interest" of the law. The legislature further determined that "release of certain information about sex offenders to public agencies and the general public will assist in protecting the public safety." As we observed in *Hendricks*, where we examined an ex post facto challenge to a post-incarceration confinement of sex offenders, an imposition of restrictive measures on sex offenders adjudged to be dangerous is "a legitimate nonpunitive governmental objective and has been historically so regarded." In this case, as in *Hendricks*, "nothing on the face of the statute suggests that the legislature sought to create anything other than a civil . . . scheme designed to protect the public from harm."

Respondents seek to cast doubt upon the nonpunitive nature of the law's declared objective by pointing out that the Alaska Constitution lists the need for protecting the public as one of the purposes of criminal administration. As the Court stated in Flemming v. Nestor, rejecting an ex post facto challenge to a law terminating benefits to deported aliens, where a legislative restriction "is an incident of the State's power to protect the health and safety of its citizens," it will be considered "as evidencing an intent to exercise that regulatory power, and not a purpose to add to the punishment." [P]recedents instruct us that even if the objective of the Act is consistent with the purposes of the Alaska criminal justice system, the State's pursuit of it in a regulatory scheme does not make the objective punitive. . . .

The procedural mechanisms to implement the Act do not alter our conclusion. After the Act's adoption Alaska amended its Rules of Criminal Procedure concerning the acceptance of pleas and the entering of criminal judgments. The rule[s] on pleas [and written judgments for sex offenses and child kidnapping] now require[] the court to "inform the defendant in writing of the requirements of [the Act] and, if it can be determined by the court, the period of registration required." . . .

The policy to alert convicted offenders to the civil consequences of their criminal conduct does not render the consequences themselves punitive. When a State sets up a regulatory scheme, it is logical to provide those persons subject to it with clear and unambiguous notice of the requirements and the penalties for noncompliance. . . . Although other methods of notification may be available, it is effective to make it part of the plea colloquy or the judgment of conviction. Invoking the criminal process in aid of a statutory regime does not render the statutory scheme itself punitive.

Our conclusion is strengthened by the fact that, aside from the duty to register, the statute itself mandates no procedures. Instead, it vests the authority to promulgate implementing regulations with the Alaska Department of Public Safety—an agency charged with enforcement of both criminal *and* civil regulatory laws. The Act itself does not require the procedures adopted to contain any safeguards associated with the criminal process. That leads us to infer that the legislature envisioned the Act's implementation to be civil and administrative. . . .

We conclude . . . that the intent of the Alaska Legislature was to create a civil, nonpunitive regime.

In analyzing the effects of the Act we refer to the seven factors noted in Kennedy v. Mendoza-Martinez, 372 U.S. 144 (1963), as a useful framework. These factors, which migrated into our ex post facto case law from double jeopardy jurisprudence, have their earlier origins in cases under the Sixth and Eight Amendments, as well as the Bill of Attainder and the Ex Post Facto Clauses. . . . The factors most relevant to our analysis are whether, in its necessary operation, the regulatory scheme: has been regarded in our history and traditions as a punishment; imposes an affirmative disability or restraint; promotes the traditional aims of punishment; has a rational connection to a nonpunitive purpose; or is excessive with respect to this purpose.

A historical survey can be useful because a State that decides to punish an individual is likely to select a means deemed punitive in our tradition, so that the public will recognize it as such. . . . Respondents argue [] that the Act—and, in particular, its notification provisions—resemble shaming punishments of the colonial period.

Some colonial punishments indeed were meant to inflict public disgrace. Humiliated offenders were required "to stand in public with signs cataloguing their offenses." Hirsh, From Pillory to Penitentiary: The Rise of Criminal Incarceration in Early Massachusetts, 80 Mich. L. Rev. 1179 (1982); see also L. Friedman, Crime and Punishment in American History 38 (1993). At times the labeling would be permanent: A murderer might be branded with an "M," and a thief with a "T." R. Semmes, Crime and Punishment in Early Maryland 35 (1938); see also Massaro, Shame, Culture, and American Criminal Law, 89 Mich. L. Rev. 1880 (1991). The aim was to make these offenders suffer "permanent stigmas, which in effect cast the person out of the community." The most serious offenders were banished, after which they could neither return to their original community nor, reputation tarnished, be admitted easily into a new one. . . .

Any initial resemblance to early punishments is, however, misleading. Punishments such as whipping, pillory, and branding inflicted physical pain and staged a direct confrontation between the offender and the public. Even punishments that lacked the corporal component, such as public shaming, humiliation, and banishment, . . . either held the person up before his fellow citizens for face-to-face shaming or expelled him from the community. By contrast, the stigma of Alaska's Megan's Law results not from public display for ridicule and shaming but from the dissemination of accurate information about a criminal record, most of which is already public. Our system does not treat dissemination of truthful information in furtherance of a legitimate governmental objective as punishment. . . . In contrast to the colonial shaming punishments, however, the State does not make the publicity and the resulting stigma an integral part of the objective of the regulatory scheme.

The fact that Alaska posts the information on the Internet does not alter our conclusion. . . . Widespread public access is necessary for the efficacy of the scheme, and the attendant humiliation is but a collateral consequence of a valid regulation.

The State's Web site does not provide the public with means to shame the offender by, say, posting comments underneath his record. An individual seeking the information must take the initial step of going to the Department of Public Safety's Web site, proceed to the sex offender registry, and then look up the desired information. The process is more analogous to a visit to an official archive of criminal records than it is to a scheme forcing an offender to appear in public with some visible badge of past criminality. The Internet makes the document search more efficient, cost effective, and convenient for Alaska's citizenry.

We next consider whether the Act subjects respondents to an "affirmative disability or restraint." Here, we inquire how the effects of the Act are felt by those subject to it. If the disability or restraint is minor and indirect, its effects are unlikely to be punitive.

The Act imposes no physical restraint, and so does not resemble the punishment of imprisonment, which is the paradigmatic affirmative disability or restraint. The Act's obligations are less harsh than the sanctions of occupational debarment, which we have held to be nonpunitive. See [*Hudson*] (forbidding further participation in the banking industry); De Veau v. Braisted, 363 U.S. 144 (1960) (forbidding work as a union official); Hawker v. New York, 170 U.S. 189 (1898) (revocation of a medical license). The Act does not restrain activities sex offenders may pursue but leaves them free to change jobs or residences. . . .

Although the public availability of the information may have a lasting and painful impact on the convicted sex offender, these consequences flow not from the Act's registration and dissemination provisions, but from the fact of conviction, already a matter of public record. The State makes the facts underlying the offenses and the resulting convictions accessible so members of the public can take the precautions they deem necessary before dealing with the registrant.

. . . The Court of Appeals held that the registration system is parallel to probation or supervised release in terms of the restraint imposed. This argument has some force, but, after due consideration, we reject it. Probation and supervised release entail a series of mandatory conditions and allow the supervising officer to seek the revocation of probation or release in case of infraction. By contrast, offenders subject to the Alaska statute are free to move where they wish and to live and work as other citizens, with no supervision. Although registrants must inform the authorities after they change their facial features (such as growing a beard), borrow a car, or seek psychiatric treatment, they are not required to seek permission to do so. A sex offender who fails to comply with the reporting requirement may be subjected to a criminal prosecution for that failure, but any prosecution is a proceeding separate from the individual's original offense. [T]he registration requirements make a valid regulatory program effective and do not impose punitive restraints in violation of the Ex Post Facto Clause.

The State concedes that the statute might deter future crimes. Respondents seize on this proposition to argue that the law is punitive, because deterrence is one purpose of punishment. This proves too much. Any number of governmental programs might deter crime without imposing punishment. "To hold that the mere presence of a deterrent purpose renders such sanctions 'criminal' . . . would severely undermine the Government's ability to engage in effective regulation."

The Court of Appeals was incorrect to conclude that the Act's registration obligations were retributive because "the length of the reporting requirement appears to be measured by the extent of the wrongdoing, not by the extent of the risk posed." The Act, it is true, differentiates between individuals convicted of aggravated or multiple offenses and those convicted of a single nonaggravated offense. The broad categories, however, and the corresponding length of the reporting requirement, are reasonably related to the danger of recidivism, and this is consistent with the regulatory objective.

The Act's rational connection to a nonpunitive purpose is a "most significant" factor in our determination that the statute's effects are not punitive. . . . A statute is not deemed punitive simply because it lacks a close or perfect fit with the nonpunitive aims it seeks to advance. The imprecision respondents rely upon does not suggest that the Act's nonpunitive purpose is a "sham or mere pretext."

. . . Alaska could conclude that a conviction for a sex offense provides evidence of substantial risk of recidivism. The legislature's findings are consistent with grave concerns over the high rate of recidivism among convicted sex offenders and their dangerousness as a class. The risk of recidivism posed by sex offenders is "frightening and high." McKune v. Lile, 536 U.S. 24, 33 (2002) ("When convicted sex offenders reenter society, they are much more likely than any other type of offender to be rearrested for a new rape or sexual assault") (citing U.S. Dept. of Justice, Bureau of Justice Statistics, Sex Offenses and Offenders 27 (1997); U.S. Dept. of Justice, Bureau of Justice Statistics, Recidivism of Prisoners Released in 1983, p. 6 (1997)).

The Ex Post Facto Clause does not preclude a State from making reasonable categorical judgments that conviction of specified crimes should entail particular regulatory consequences. We have upheld against ex post facto challenges laws imposing regulatory burdens on individuals convicted of crimes without any corresponding risk assessment. . . . The State's determination to legislate with respect to convicted sex offenders as a class, rather than require individual determination of their dangerousness, does not make the statute a punishment under the Ex Post Facto Clause.

. . . Our examination of the Act's effects leads to the determination that respondents cannot show, much less by the clearest proof, that the effects of the law negate Alaska's intention to establish a civil regulatory scheme. The Act is nonpunitive, and its retroactive application does not violate the Ex Post Facto Clause. . . .

STEVENS, J., dissenting.

. . . The Court's opinion[] fail[s] to decide whether the statutes deprive the registrants of a constitutionally protected interest in liberty. . . .

The statutes impose significant affirmative obligations and a severe stigma on every person to whom they apply. . . .

The registration and reporting duties imposed on convicted sex offenders are comparable to the duties imposed on other convicted criminals during periods of supervised release or parole. And there can be no doubt that the "widespread public access," to this personal and constantly updated information has a severe stigmatizing effect. In my judgment, these statutes unquestionably affect a constitutionally protected interest in liberty.

It is also clear beyond peradventure that these unique consequences of conviction of a sex offense are punitive. They share three characteristics, which in the aggregate are not present in any civil sanction. The sanctions (1) constitute a severe deprivation of the offender's liberty, (2) are imposed on everyone who is convicted of a relevant criminal offense, and (3) are imposed only on those criminals. Unlike any of the cases that the Court has cited, a criminal conviction under these statutes provides both a *sufficient* and a *necessary* condition for the sanction.

[T]he Constitution prohibits the addition of these sanctions to the punishment of persons who were tried and convicted before the legislation was enacted. As the Court recognizes, "recidivism is the statutory concern" that provides the supposed justification for the imposition of such retroactive punishment. . . . Reliance on that rationale here highlights the conclusion that the retroactive application of these statutes constitutes a flagrant violation of the protections afforded by the Double Jeopardy and Ex Post Facto Clauses of the Constitution.

[T]he State may impose registration duties and may publish registration information as a part of its punishment of this category of defendants. Looking to the future, these aspects of their punishment are adequately justified by two of the traditional aims of punishment — retribution and deterrence. Moreover, as a matter of procedural fairness, Alaska requires its judges to include notice of the registration requirements in judgments imposing sentences on convicted sex offenders and in the colloquy preceding the acceptance of a plea of guilty to such an offense. Thus, I agree with the Court that these statutes are constitutional as applied to postenactment offenses. . . .

GINSBURG, J., dissenting.

[I]n resolving whether the Act ranks as penal for ex post facto purposes, I would not demand "the clearest proof" that the statute is in effect criminal rather than civil. Instead, guided by Kennedy v. Mendoza-Martinez, 372 U.S. 144 (1963), I would neutrally evaluate the Act's purpose and effects.

. . . What ultimately tips the balance for me is the Act's excessiveness in relation to its nonpunitive purpose. . . . The Act applies to all convicted sex offenders, without regard to their future dangerousness. And the duration of the reporting requirement is keyed not to any determination of a particular offender's risk of reoffending, but to whether the offense of conviction qualified as aggravated. The reporting requirements themselves are exorbitant: The Act requires aggravated offenders to engage in perpetual quarterly reporting, even if their personal information has not changed. And meriting heaviest weight in my judgment, the Act makes no provision whatever for the possibility of rehabilitation: Offenders cannot shorten their registration or notification period, even on the clearest demonstration of rehabilitation or conclusive proof of physical incapacitation. However plain it may be that a former sex offender currently poses no threat of recidivism, he will remain subject to long-term monitoring and inescapable humiliation.

John Doe I, for example, pleaded nolo contendere to a charge of sexual abuse of a minor nine years before the Alaska Act was enacted. He successfully completed a treatment program, and gained early release on supervised probation in part because of his compliance with the program's requirements and his apparent low risk of re-offense. He subsequently remarried, established a business, and was reunited with his family. He was also granted custody of a minor daughter, based on a court's determination that he had been successfully rehabilitated. The court's determination rested in part on psychiatric evaluations concluding that Doe had "a very low risk of re-offending" and is "not a pedophile." Notwithstanding this strong evidence of rehabilitation, the Alaska Act requires Doe to report personal information to the State four times per year, and permits the State publicly to label him a "Registered Sex Offender" for the rest of his life.

Satisfied that the Act is ambiguous in intent and punitive in effect, I would hold its retroactive application incompatible with the Ex Post Facto Clause, and would therefore affirm the judgment of the Court of Appeals.

## *John Doe v. Tom Miller*
### 405 F.3d 700 (8th Cir. 2005)

COLLOTON, C.J.

In 2002, in an effort to protect children in Iowa from the risk that convicted sex offenders may reoffend in locations close to their residences, the Iowa General Assembly passed, and the Governor of Iowa signed, a bill that prohibits a person convicted of certain sex offenses involving minors from residing within 2000 feet of a school or a registered child care facility. The district court declared the statute unconstitutional on several grounds . . . .

Because we conclude that the Constitution of the United States does not prevent the State of Iowa from regulating the residency of sex offenders in this manner in order to protect the health and safety of the citizens of Iowa, we reverse the judgment of the district court. We hold unanimously that the residency restriction is not unconstitutional on its face. . . .

## I

Iowa Senate File 2197, now codified at Iowa Code §692A.2A, took effect on July 1, 2002. It provides that persons who have been convicted of certain criminal offenses against a minor, including numerous sexual offenses involving a minor, shall not reside within 2000 feet of a school or registered child care facility. The law does not apply to persons who established a residence prior to July 1, 2002, or to schools or child care facilities that are newly located after July 1, 2002. . . .

Almost immediately after the law took effect, three named plaintiffs — sex offenders with convictions that predate the law's effective date — filed suit asserting that the statute is unconstitutional on its face. . . . The named plaintiffs, identified as various "John Does," had committed a range of sexual crimes, including indecent exposure, "indecent liberties with a child," sexual exploitation of a minor, assault with intent to commit sexual abuse, lascivious acts with a child, and second and third degree sexual abuse, all of which brought them within the provisions of the residency restriction. A defendant class, including all of Iowa's county attorneys, also was certified.

During a two-day bench trial, plaintiffs presented evidence concerning the enforcement of §692A.2A, including maps that had been produced by several cities and counties identifying schools and child care facilities and their corresponding restricted areas. After viewing these maps and hearing testimony from a county attorney, the district court found that the restricted areas in many cities encompass the majority of the available housing in the city, thus leaving only limited areas within city limits available for sex offenders to establish a residence. In smaller towns, a single school or child care facility can cause all of the incorporated areas of the town to be off limits to sex offenders. The court found that unincorporated areas, small towns with no school or child care facility, and rural areas remained unrestricted, but that available housing in these areas is "not necessarily readily available." Doe v. Miller, 298 F. Supp. 2d 844, 851 (S.D. Iowa 2004).

Plaintiffs also presented evidence of their individual experiences in seeking to obtain housing that complies with the 2000-foot restriction. Several of the plaintiffs . . . have friends or relatives with whom they would like to live, but whose homes are within 2000 feet of a school or child care facility. Many . . . live in homes that are currently compliant, either because they were established prior to July 1, 2002, or because the homes are outside the 2000-foot restricted areas. These plaintiffs, however, testified that they would like to be able to move into a restricted area. Still others . . . are living in noncompliant residences that they wish to maintain.

. . .

In addition to evidence regarding the burden that §692A.2A places on sex offenders, both plaintiffs and defendants presented expert testimony about the potential effectiveness of a residency restriction in preventing offenses against minors. The State presented the testimony of Mr. Allison, a parole and probation officer who specialized in sex offender supervision. Allison described the process of treating sex offenders and his efforts at preventing recidivism by identifying the triggers for the original offense, and then imposing restrictions on the residences or activities of the offender. According to Allison, restrictions on the proximity of sex offenders to schools or other facilities that might create temptation to reoffend are one way to minimize the risk of recidivism. In the parole and probation context, Allison also has authority to limit offenders' activities in more specific ways, and he testified that he attempts to remove temptation by preventing offenders from working in jobs where they would have contact with potential victims or from living near parks or other areas where children might spend time unsupervised. In addition to the limits that he imposes on offenders under his supervision, Allison also testified that there is "a legitimate public safety concern" in where unsupervised sex offenders reside. In Allison's view, reoffense is "a potential danger forever." . . .

The plaintiffs offered the testimony of Dr. Luis Rosell, a psychologist with experience in sex offender treatment. Dr. Rosell estimated that the recidivism rate for sex offenders is between 20 and 25 percent, and like Allison . . . stated his belief that the key to reducing the risk of recidivism is identifying the factors that led to the offender's original offense and then helping the offender to deal with or avoid those factors in the future. Dr. Rosell testified that reducing a specific sex offender's access to children was a good idea, and that "if you remove the opportunity, then the likelihood of reoffense is decreased." He did not believe, however, that "residential proximity makes that big of a difference." Moreover, Dr. Rosell thought that a 2000-foot limit was "extreme." [He] worried that the law might be counterproductive to the offender's treatment goals by causing depression and potentially removing the offender from his "support system."

After hearing the testimony of all three experts and of the individual plaintiffs, the district court declared that §692A.2A was unconstitutional. . . . Having found the statute unconstitutional, the district court issued a permanent injunction against enforcement.

## II

We first address the contention that §692A.2A violates the rights of the covered sex offenders to due process of law under the Fourteenth Amendment. The appellees (to whom we will refer as "the Does") argue that the statute is unconstitutional because it fails to provide adequate notice of what conduct is prohibited, and because it does not require an individualized determination whether each person covered by the statute is dangerous. This claim relies on what is known as "procedural due process."

. . . The Does contend that they are deprived of notice required by the Constitution because some cities in Iowa are unable to provide sex offenders with information about the location of all schools and registered child care facilities, and because it is difficult to measure the restricted areas, which are measured "as the crow flies" from a school or child care facility. We disagree that these potential problems render the statute unconstitutional on its face. A criminal statute is not vague on its face unless it is impermissibly vague in all of its applications, and the possibility that an individual might be prosecuted in a particular case in a particular community despite his best efforts to comply with the restriction is not a sufficient reason to invalidate the entire statute. . . . Due process does not require that independently elected county attorneys enforce each criminal statute with equal vigor, and the existence of different priorities or prosecution decisions among jurisdictions does not violate the Constitution.

The Does also argue that §692A.2A unconstitutionally forecloses an "opportunity to be heard" because the statute provides no process for individual determinations of dangerousness. . . .

We . . . conclude that the Iowa residency restriction does not contravene principles of procedural due process under the Constitution. The restriction applies to all offenders who have been convicted of certain crimes against minors, regardless of what estimates of future dangerousness might be proved in individualized hearings. Once such a legislative classification has been drawn, additional procedures are unnecessary, because the statute does not provide a potential exemption for individuals. . . . Thus, the absence of an individualized hearing in connection with a statute that offers no exemptions does not offend principles of procedural due process.

## III

The Does also assert that the residency restriction is unconstitutional under the doctrine of substantive due process. . . . The Does argue that several "fundamental rights" are infringed by Iowa's residency restriction, including the "right to privacy and choice in family matters," the right to travel, and "the fundamental right to live where you want." The district court agreed that §692A.2A infringed upon liberty interests that constitute fundamental rights, applied strict scrutiny to the legislative classifications, and concluded that the statute was unconstitutional.

The Does first invoke "the right to personal choice regarding the family." . . .

We do not believe that the residency restriction of §692A.2A implicates any fundamental right of the Does that would trigger strict scrutiny of the statute. . . . The Does' characterization of a fundamental right to "personal choice regarding the family" is so general that it would trigger strict scrutiny of innumerable laws and ordinances that influence "personal choices" made by families on a daily basis. . . .

Unlike the precedents cited by the Does, the Iowa statute does not operate directly on the family relationship. Although the law restricts where a residence may be located, nothing in the statute limits who may live with the Does in their residences. . . .

While there was evidence that one adult sex offender in Iowa would not reside with his parents as a result of the residency restriction, that another sex offender and his wife moved 45 miles away from their preferred location due to the statute, and that a third sex offender could not reside with his adult child in a restricted zone, the statute does not directly regulate the family relationship or prevent any family member from residing with a sex offender in a residence that is consistent with the statute. We therefore hold that §692A.2A does not infringe upon a constitutional liberty interest relating to matters of marriage and family in a fashion that requires heightened scrutiny.

The Does also assert that the residency restrictions interfere with their constitutional right to travel. The modern Supreme Court has recognized a right to interstate travel in several decisions [and has] explained that the federal guarantee of interstate travel "protects interstate travelers against two sets of burdens: 'the erection of actual barriers to interstate movement' and 'being treated differently' from intrastate travelers." Bray v. Alexandria Women's Health Clinic, 506 U.S. 263, 277 (1993). . . .

The Does argue that §692A.2A violates this right to interstate travel by substantially limiting the ability of sex offenders to establish residences in any town or urban area in Iowa. They contend that the constitutional right to travel is implicated because the Iowa law deters previously convicted sex offenders from migrating from other States to Iowa. The district court agreed, reasoning that the statute "effectively bans sex offenders from residing in large sections of Iowa's towns and cities."

We respectfully disagree with this analysis. The Iowa statute imposes no obstacle to a sex offender's entry into Iowa, and it does not erect an "actual barrier to interstate movement." *Bray*, 506 U.S. at 277 (internal quotation omitted). There is "free ingress and regress to and from" Iowa for sex offenders, and the statute thus does not "directly impair the exercise of the right to free interstate movement." Saenz v. Roe, 526, U.S. 489, 501 (1999). Nor does the Iowa statute violate principles of equality by treating nonresidents who visit Iowa any differently than current residents, or by discriminating against citizens of other States who wish to establish residence in Iowa. We think that to recognize a fundamental right to interstate travel in a situation that does not involve any of these circumstances would extend the doctrine beyond the Supreme Court's pronouncements in this area. That the statute may deter some out-of-state residents from traveling to Iowa because the prospects for a convenient and affordable residence are less promising than elsewhere does not implicate a fundamental right recognized by the Court's right to travel jurisprudence.

The Does also urge that we recognize a fundamental right "to live where you want." ... Some thirty years ago, our court said "we cannot agree that the right to choose one's place of residence is necessarily a fundamental right," Prostrollo v. Univ. of S.D., 507 F.2d 775, 781 (8th Cir. 1974), and we see no basis to conclude that the contention has gained strength in the intervening years. ... The Does have not developed any argument that the right to "live where you want" is "deeply rooted in this Nation's history and tradition," Washington v. Glucksberg, 521 U.S. 702, 721 (1997) (quoting *Moore*, 431 U.S. at 503 (plurality opinion)). ... We are thus not persuaded that the Constitution establishes a right to "live where you want" that requires strict scrutiny of a State's residency restrictions.

Because §692A.2A does not implicate a constitutional liberty interest that has been elevated to the status of "fundamental right," we review the statute to determine whether it meets the standard of "rationally advancing some legitimate governmental purpose." Reno v. Flores, 507 U.S. 292, 306 (1993). ... The Does contend ... that the statute is irrational because there is no scientific study that supports the legislature's conclusion that excluding sex offenders from residing within 2000 feet of a school or child care facility is likely to enhance the safety of children.

We reject this contention because we think it understates the authority of a state legislature to make judgments about the best means to protect the health and welfare of its citizens in an area where precise statistical data is unavailable and human behavior is necessarily unpredictable. ...

We think the decision whether to set a limit on proximity of "across the street" (as appellees suggest), or 500 feet or 3000 feet (as the Iowa Senate considered and rejected, *see* S. Journal 79, 2d Sess., at 521 (Iowa 2002)), or 2000 feet (as the Iowa General Assembly and the Governor eventually adopted) is the sort of task for which the elected policymaking officials of a State, and not the federal courts, are properly suited. ...

The record does not support a conclusion that the Iowa General Assembly and the Governor acted based merely on negative attitudes toward, fear of, or a bare desire to harm a politically unpopular group [and] ... we are not persuaded that the means selected to pursue the State's legitimate interest are without rational basis.

## IV

The Does next argue that the residency restriction, "in combination with" the sex offender registration requirements of §692A.2, unconstitutionally compels sex offenders to incriminate themselves in violation of the Fifth and Fourteenth Amendments. The district court concluded that a sex offender who establishes residence in a prohibited area must either register his current address, thereby "explicitly admitting the facts necessary to prove the criminal act," or "refuse to register and be similarly prosecuted." 298 F. Supp. 2d at 879. The court then held that §692A.2A "unconstitutionally requires sex offenders to provide incriminating evidence against themselves," and enjoined enforcement of the residency restriction on this basis as well.

We disagree that the Self-Incrimination Clause of the Fifth Amendment renders the residency restriction of §692A.2A unconstitutional. Our reason is straightforward: the residency restriction does not compel a sex offender to be a witness against himself or a witness of any kind. The statute regulates only where the sex offender may reside; it does not require him to provide any information that might be used against him in a criminal case. A separate section of the Iowa Code, §692A.2, requires a sex offender to register his address with the county sheriff. The Does have not challenged the constitutionality of the registration requirement, or sought an injunction against its enforcement, and whatever constitutional problem may be posed by the registration provision does not justify invalidating the residency restriction. . . .

## V

A final, and narrower, challenge advanced by the Does is that §692A.2A is an unconstitutional ex post facto law because it imposes retroactive punishment on those who committed a sex offense prior to July 1, 2002. . . . In determining whether a state statute violates the Ex Post Facto Clause by imposing such punishment, we apply the framework outlined in Smith v. Doe, 538 U.S. 84, 92 (2003). . . .

The district court found that in passing the residency restriction of §692A.2A, the Iowa General Assembly intended to create "a civil, non-punitive statutory scheme to protect the public.". The Does do not dispute this conclusion on appeal, and we agree that the legislature's intent was not punitive. . . .

We must next consider whether the Does have established that the law was nonetheless so punitive in effect as to negate the legislature's intent to create a civil, nonpunitive regulatory scheme. In this inquiry, we refer to what the Supreme Court described in Smith v. Doe as "useful guideposts" . . . [F]ive factors drawn from Kennedy v. Mendoza-Martinez, 372 U.S. 144, 168-69, (1963), as particularly relevant: whether the law has been regarded in our history and traditions as punishment, whether it promotes the traditional aims of punishment, whether it imposes an affirmative disability or restraint, whether it has a rational connection to a nonpunitive purpose, and whether it is excessive with respect to that purpose. These factors are "neither exhaustive nor dispositive," Smith, 538 U.S. at 97. (quotation omitted). . . .

Turning first to any historical tradition regarding residency restrictions, the Does argue that §692A.2A is the effective equivalent of banishment, which has been regarded historically as a punishment. . . .

While banishment of course involves an extreme form of residency restriction, we ultimately do not accept the analogy between the traditional means of punishment and the Iowa statute. Unlike banishment, §692A.2A restricts only where offenders may reside. It does not "expel" the offenders from their communities or prohibit them from accessing areas near schools or child care facilities for employment, to conduct commercial transactions, or for any purpose other than establishing a residence. With respect to many offenders, the statute does not even require a change of residence: the Iowa General Assembly included a grandfather provision that permits sex offenders to maintain a residence that was established prior to July 1, 2002, even if that residence is within 2000 feet of a school or child care facility. Iowa Code §692A.2A(4)(c). . . . We thus conclude that this law is unlike banishment in important respects, and we do not believe it is of a type that is traditionally punitive.

The second factor that we consider is whether the law promotes the traditional aims of punishment — deterrence and retribution. Smith v. Doe, 538 U.S. at 102. . . . The primary purpose of the law is not to alter the offender's incentive structure by demonstrating the negative consequences that will flow from committing a sex offense. The Iowa statute is designed to reduce the likelihood of reoffense by limiting the offender's temptation and reducing the opportunity to commit a new crime. . . .

The statute's "retributive" effect is similarly difficult to evaluate. . . . The Supreme Court . . . emphasized that the reporting requirements were "reasonably related to the danger of recidivism" in a way that was "consistent with the regulatory objective." *Smith* at 102. While any restraint or requirement imposed on those who commit crimes is at least potentially retributive in effect, we believe that §692A.2A, like the registration requirement in Smith v. Doe, is consistent with the legislature's regulatory objective of protecting the health and safety of children.

The next factor we consider is whether the law "imposes an affirmative disability or restraint." Imprisonment is the "paradigmatic" affirmative disability or restraint, *Smith* at 100, but other restraints, such as probation or occupational debarment, also can impose some restriction on a person's activities. Id. at 100-01. While restrictive laws are not necessarily punitive, they are more likely to be so; by contrast, "if the disability or restraint is minor and indirect, its effects are unlikely to be punitive." Id. at 100. For example, sex offender registration laws, requiring only periodic reporting and updating of personal information, do not have a punitive restraining effect. At the same time, civil commitment of the mentally ill, though extremely restrictive and disabling to those who are committed, does not necessarily impose punishment because it bears a reasonable relationship to a "legitimate nonpunitive objective," namely protecting the public from mentally unstable individuals. Kansas v. Hendricks, 521 U.S. 346, 363 (1997).

Iowa Code §692A.2A is more disabling than the sex offender registration law at issue in Smith v. Doe. . . . The residency restriction is certainly less disabling, however, than the civil commitment scheme at issue in *Hendricks*, which permitted complete confinement of affected persons. In both *Smith* and

*Hendricks*, the Court considered the degree of the restraint involved in light of the legislature's countervailing nonpunitive purpose, and the Court in *Hendricks* emphasized that the imposition of an affirmative restraint "does not inexorably lead to the conclusion that the government has imposed punishment." 521 U.S. at 363 (internal quotation omitted). Likewise here, while we agree with the Does that §692A.2A does impose an element of affirmative disability or restraint, we believe this factor ultimately points us to the importance of the next inquiry: whether the law is rationally connected to a nonpunitive purpose, and whether it is excessive in relation to that purpose.

This final factor — whether the regulatory scheme has a "rational connection to a nonpunitive purpose" — is the "most significant factor" in the ex post facto analysis. *Smith* at 102. The requirement of a "rational connection" is not demanding: A "statute is not deemed punitive simply because it lacks a close or perfect fit with the nonpunitive aims it seeks to advance." Id. at 103. The district court found "no doubt" that §692A.2A has a purpose other than punishing sex offenders, 298 F. Supp. 2d at 870, and we agree. In light of the high risk of recidivism posed by sex offenders, see Smith v. Doe, 538 U.S. at 103, the legislature reasonably could conclude that §692A.2A would protect society by minimizing the risk of repeated sex offenses against minors.

. . .

The Does also urge that the law is excessive in relation to its regulatory purpose because there is no scientific evidence that a 2000-foot residency restriction is effective at preventing sex offender recidivism. "The excessiveness inquiry of our ex post facto jurisprudence is not an exercise in determining whether the legislature has made the best choice possible to address the problem it seeks to remedy," but rather an inquiry into "whether the regulatory means chosen are reasonable in light of the nonpunitive objective." *Smith* at 105. In this case, there was expert testimony that reducing the frequency of contact between sex offenders and children is likely to reduce temptation and opportunity, which in turn is important to reducing the risk of reoffense. None of the witnesses was able to articulate a precise distance that optimally balanced the benefit of reducing risk to children with the burden of the residency restrictions on sex offenders, and the Does' expert acknowledged that "there is nothing in the literature that has addressed proximity".

We believe the legislature's decision to select a 2000-foot restriction, as opposed to the other distances that were considered and rejected, is reasonably related to its regulatory purpose. . . .

\*\*\*

The judgment of the district court is reversed, and the case is remanded with directions to enter judgment in favor of the defendants.

MELLOY, C.J., concurring and dissenting.

I join in the majority's opinion, sections I through IV. However, I dissent as to section V because I believe section 692A.2A is an unconstitutional ex post facto law.

. . . I agree with the majority that the purpose of section 692A.2A is to protect the public. This purpose is nonpunitive, so we must determine if the statute is so punitive either in purpose or effect as to negate the State's intention to deem it civil. . . .

Though I believe a rational connection exists between the residency restriction and a nonpunitive purpose, I would find that the restriction is excessive in relation to that purpose. The statute limits the housing choices of all offenders identically, regardless of their type of crime, type of victim, or risk of re-offending. The effect of the requirement is quite dramatic: many offenders cannot live with their families and/or cannot live in their home communities because the whole community is a restricted area. This leaves offenders to live in the country or in small, prescribed areas of towns and cities that might offer no appropriate, available housing. In addition, there is no time limit to the restrictions.

. . . The severity of residency restriction, the fact that it is applied to all offenders identically, and the fact that it will be enforced for the rest of the offenders' lives, makes the residency restriction excessive. . . . Because the imposition of the residency requirement "'changes the punishment, and inflicts a greater punishment, than the law annexed to the crime, when committed,'" Stogner v. California, 539 U.S. 607, 612 (2003) (quoting Calder v. Bull, 3 U.S. 386, 390 (1798), I would find section 692A.2A is an unconstitutional ex post facto law that cannot be applied to persons who committed their offenses before the law was enacted.

## NOTES

1. *An array of constitutional challenges.*   As detailed in Smith v. Doe and Doe v. Miller, sex offenders subject to new registration requirements and residency restrictions have attacked these laws in many state and federal courts by bringing constitutional challenges based on an array of different theories and constitutional provisions. Especially when the laws are applied to offenders originally convicted before the registration requirement or restriction was enacted, the most common challenge is based on the ex post facto clause. Notably, ex post fact challenges address only when, and not whether, these laws can be applied. Some of them will be resolved on constitutional grounds, others based on statutory interpretation. See, e.g., Reynolds v. United States, 132 S. Ct. 975 (2012); Carr v. United States 130 S. Ct. 2229 (2010). Other, broader challenges to these laws include claims based on due process, both procedural and substantive, equal protection, cruel and unusual punishment, double jeopardy, and self-incrimination. Most registration and residency restrictions are upheld against these challenges, validated as civil provisions that are generally justified by the state's interest in protecting public safety.

2. *Are registration and residency restrictions sound policy?*   Registration and residency laws are enacted purportedly to protect the health and safety of the public. In theory, knowing where sex offenders live helps law enforcement solve sex crimes and enables the public to protect themselves against known registered offenders. In theory, residency restrictions reduce the contacts offenders have with children, which may in turn reduce offenders' ability and temptation to commit offenses. However, critics of these laws have developed arguments and evidence suggesting that registration and residency restrictions are not as beneficial as legislators may hope.

First, 80-90% of sex offenders' victims are family members or people known to the offender despite high-profile cases that imply the contrary and heighten public fears of sexual abuse by strangers. While registration and residency restrictions may help curb random sex offenses and in fact deter non-registered potential sex offenders, they are unlikely to operate in a manner that can effectively curtail the vast majority of sex offenses, including those committed by registered offenders.

Second, registration and residency restrictions are in tension with each other. If an offender lives within a restricted zone, he may choose not to register his address for fear that he will be told to move. Consequently, neither law enforcement nor neighbors will know where the sex offender resides, a situation that will undermine the interests of public safety.

Third, all of these sex offender restrictions drain law enforcement resources. Police departments must choose between hiring more people to enforce and administer the restrictions or requiring the personnel they have to take time away from other enforcement priorities to enforce sex offender-related laws.

Fourth, the registration and residency restrictions have negative effects on sex offenders. The laws hinder the offender's rehabilitation when he is unable to find employment, a place to live, and to establish beneficial relationships with friends and neighbors. Often, offenders reoffend because they fail to develop a social environment that supports them in preventing a relapse. This is especially true when such restrictions last for the duration of an offender's life, as no tangible benefit exists to engage with counseling and complete rehabilitation efforts. The benefits of a crime-free life appear minuscule.

Fifth, the laws not only harm the offender's ability to rehabilitate, but they also affect offenders' families. Children may be pulled out of school and spouses may have to quit their jobs because an offender is required to relocate; family members may be shunned once an ex-offender's prior conviction becomes public knowledge. See J.J. Prescott & Jonah E. Rockoff, Do Sex Offender Registration and Notification Laws Affect Criminal Behavior? 54 J. L. & Economics 161 (2011).

Sixth, the restrictions affect law enforcement on the front end. When charged with a sex offense, defendants may be less likely to plead guilty or into enter a plea agreement, knowing that they will be subject to registration and residency restrictions. With a reduction in the number of guilty pleas, trial dockets will become more crowded and child—and adult—victims of sex offenses will have to endure the trauma of a trial. Rose Corrigan, When is a Rapist a Sex Offender? Prosecuting Sex Crimes After Megan's Law, Western Political Science Association Annual Meeting Paper (Apr. 17, 2011), at http://papers.ssrn.com/sol3/papers.cfm?abstract_id=1766831. Sex abuse cases have a higher trial rate than most other types of cases, with the exception of other serious violent and civil rights charges. A South Carolina study has indicated that sex offenders are increasingly more likely to be permitted to plead to non-sex offenses or even be acquitted, which ultimately will decrease public safety. Elizabeth Letourneau et al., Evaluating the Effectiveness of Sex Offender Registration and Notification Policies for Reducing Sexual Violence Against Women, Grant 231989 (Sept. 2010), available at https://www.ncjrs.gov/pdffiles1/nij/grants/231989.pdf. Perhaps in response to such developments, a number of state courts permit registration of persons for non-sex offenses, including kidnapping of a minor.

Emphasizing all of the concerns set out above, the Iowa County Attorneys Association issued a Statement on Sex Offender Residency Restrictions in Iowa (February 14, 2006) urging legislators to rework the broad restrictions under Iowa law. This important statement originating from law enforcement officials has led some jurisdictions, though not all, to question whether the benefits of these laws really outweigh the undesirable consequences. If you were a legislator in a state considering a sex offender residency restriction bill, how might you gather information about the costs and benefits of such legislation and weight these data.

3. *Risk assessment.*   The Supreme Court held that individual risk assessments were not needed for entry into sex offender databases. Thus, states can continue to classify offenders broadly based on the offense of conviction. Different states take different offenses as predicate crimes for entry into the database. Recent research indicates that the prediction of whether an offender will commit another serious sex-based violent crime in the short term is most effective when it combines an actuarial risk assessment, based on prior record, type of sex offense, and similar factors, with a clinical prediction model. Eric S. Janus & Robert A. Prentky, Forensic Use of Actuarial Risk Assessment with Sex Offenders: Accuracy, Admissibility and Accountability, 40 Am. Crim. L. Rev. 1443 (2003).

4. *Recidivism and sex offenses.*   The Smith v. Doe Court relies in part on the substantial risk that convicted sex offenders pose to the public. It cites a study indicating that sex offenders are much more likely than other offenders to commit a sex crime. But the same holds true for other types of criminals, such as drug and property offenders, with respect to their general crime of conviction. Moreover, reconviction rates for sex offenders are the second lowest among all offenders. Does this indicate that the Court's analysis is incorrect? Or does it support a more limited sex offender registry?

Many sex offender registries include the personal information of those convicted of possession of child pornography based on the assumption that such possession offenses make it more likely that the offender will commit a sexual crime against a child. How should the public assess knowledge of a convicted sex offender, defined broadly, living in its community?

5. *Conduct-based ban.*   May sanctions or limits be imposed on offenders based on noncriminal conduct after sentencing? In Doe v. City of Lafayette, Ind., 377 F.3d 757 (7th Cir. 2004), the Seventh Circuit, sitting en banc, upheld the city's decision to ban a sex offender from all park property for life after he had visited a park and admitted to having had sexual urges while observing the children playing there. In this case the offender's prior criminal record combined with his later conduct (or thoughts?) caused the city to act. Administrative agencies and courts may also impose sanctions based on criminal conduct, even if no criminal conviction occurs. See Department of Housing and Urban Development v. Rucker, 535 U.S. 125 (2002) (eviction from public housing upheld when a member of the household or a guest engaged in drug-related criminal activity, regardless of whether the tenant knew, or should have known, of the drug-related activity).

6. *Federal involvement in sex offender registration and tracking.* In 2006 Congress enacted the Adam Walsh Child Protection and Safety Act which created a national sex offender registry and encouraged states to adopt a uniform three-tier system for sex offender registration. This Act followed a number of prior federal acts, all named after the victims of sex offenders, which required states to establish notification and registration regimes and provided federal funding. The Adam Walsh Act also created a new federal crime for failing to register and update information as required by state or federal law. Though subject to various legal challenges, most lower courts have upheld the authority of Congress to require sex offender registration and to criminalize a failure to register.

## PROBLEM 8-1.   DON'T WORK IN MY BACKYARD

As detailed on the city's official website, the City of Upper Arlington, Ohio, has enacted a sex offender ordinance that "bars convicted sexual offenders from living *or working* within 1,000 feet of any school premises, licensed daycare facility, preschool, public park, swimming pool, library, or playground." In light of Smith v. Doe and Doe v. Miller, what kinds of constitutional arguments might you be able to make against this legislation if you were representing a person who, after having pled guilty to a sex offense while in college, has been working for over a decade as a real estate agent in a professional office building in Upper Arlington that happens to be 950 feet from a licensed daycare facility?

### c.   Firearms

For convicted felons, the most common collateral sanction (sometimes called a disability), which may be imposed for a term or for life, is the state and federal prohibition of the possession of firearms. Some statutes single out certain types of felony offenses or classes of offenses to trigger a firearms ban. Typically, drug offenses are included in this category. What rationale justifies this collateral sanction?

Given the broad applicability of such prohibitions, the wide availability of firearms, and the strong legal, cultural, and social traditions surrounding gun ownership, it is not surprising that the desire to own firearms is among the most common reasons former offenders request relief from collateral sanctions.

> ## Ohio Revised Code §2923.13, Having
> ## Weapons While Under Disability

(A) [N]o person shall knowingly acquire, have, carry, or use any firearm or dangerous ordnance, if any of the following apply:

    (1) The person is a fugitive from justice.

    (2) The person is under indictment for or has been convicted of any felony offense of violence. . . .

(3) The person is under indictment for or has been convicted of any offense involving the illegal possession, use, sale, administration, distribution, or trafficking in any drug of abuse. . . .

(4) The person is drug dependent, in danger of drug dependence, or a chronic alcoholic.

(5) The person is under adjudication of mental incompetence.

(B) No person who has been convicted of a felony of the first or second degree shall violate division (A) of this section within five years of the date of the person's release from imprisonment or from post-release control that is imposed for the commission of a felony of the first or second degree.

(C) Whoever violates this section is guilty of having weapons while under disability. A violation of division (A) of this section is a felony of the fifth degree [punishable by six, seven, eight, nine, ten, eleven, or twelve months]. A violation of division (B) of this section is a felony of the third degree [punishable by one, two, three, four, or five years].

## Ohio Revised Code §2923.14, Relief from Disability

(A) Any person who, solely by reason of the person's disability under division (A)(2) or (3) of section 2923.13 of the Revised Code, is prohibited from acquiring, having, carrying, or using firearms, may apply to the court of common pleas in the county in which the person resides for relief from such prohibition.

(B) The application shall recite the following:

(1) All indictments, convictions, or adjudications upon which the applicant's disability is based, the sentence imposed and served, and any release granted under a community control sanction, post-release control sanction, or parole, any partial or conditional pardon granted, or other disposition of each case;

(2) Facts showing the applicant to be a fit subject for relief under this section.

(C) A copy of the application shall be served on the county prosecutor. . . .

(D) Upon hearing, the court may grant the applicant relief pursuant to this section, if all of the following apply:

(1) The applicant has been fully discharged from imprisonment, community control, post-release control, and parole, or, if the applicant is under indictment, has been released on bail or recognizance.

(2) The applicant has led a law-abiding life since discharge or release, and appears likely to continue to do so.

(3) The applicant is not otherwise prohibited by law from acquiring, having, or using firearms. . . .

### NOTES

1. *Felon-in-possession statutes.*   State and federal law prohibits some convicted felons from owning and using firearms. Federal law prohibits a convicted

felon whose crime was "punishable by a term exceeding one year" from posses-sing firearms. Do you believe felon-in-possession statutes are effective as law-enforcement tools? Are statutes such as Ohio's over- or underinclusive? As a state legislator, would you support such legislation? Why?

2. *Removal of firearms disabilities.* Most states provide judicial or adminis-trative relief from firearms disabilities, but no equivalent procedure exists at the federal level. A part of the federal felon-in-possession statute grants the secretary of the treasury the right to reinstate a former felon's firearms privileges if past good conduct indicates that the disability should be removed. Since 1992, however, Congress has failed to fund this portion of the secretary's work. The U.S. Supreme Court declared that a lack of review amounted to inaction rather than denial—and the Bureau of Alcohol, Tobacco and Firearms had to act for judicial review to apply. United States v. Bean, 537 U.S. 71 (2002). The sole avenue of relief from a federal firearms bar, therefore, is a presidential pardon.

3. *The domestic violence firearms ban.* Federal law prohibits all persons con-victed of a domestic violence misdemeanor from possessing firearms. This may be particularly problematic for police officers and members of the military who lose not only their right to possess a firearm but consequently also their employ-ment. What consequences may such a law have for prosecutorial and judicial decision-making?

## 2. Administrative Sanctions

While many collateral sanctions befall the offender automatically upon convic-tion, others are imposed in regulatory hearings. One of the most important and pervasive illustrations of such a collateral sanction is deportation, which is declared by an immigration judge or the immigration agency rather than by the criminal court. For a proposal to allow the criminal sanctioning and the deportation decisions to be made by the sentencing judge, see Margaret Taylor & Ronald Wright, The Sentencing Judge as Immigration Judge, 51 Emory L.J. 1131 (2002).

Since the 1996 immigration acts, the deportation of criminal offenders has expanded dramatically. In 1986 not quite 2,000 noncitizens were removed for criminal violations; in fiscal year 2010 the figure had risen to almost 217,000, with approximately 45,000 of the convictions underlying the deportations based on drug offenses and 36,000 on driving under the influence. Removal is now mandatory for all noncitizens convicted of "aggravated felonies," a large cate-gory of offenses that includes more than just the most heinous crimes that the term implies. Moreover, deportation can occur upon conviction of "crimes of moral turpitude." Not surprisingly, lower courts sometimes disagree on the definitions of some these terms.

Immediately upon the passage of the 1996 legislation, the Immigration and Naturalization Service enforced the deportation provisions retroactively. This means that individuals who had pled guilty to offenses many years, and often decades, in the past were detained and deported without having available to them the more generous discretionary relief provisions they had relied on in earlier legislation. In its 2001 decision in INS v. St. Cyr, 533 U.S. 289 (2001), the

Supreme Court held that such discretionary relief remained available to these individuals since they had relied on them in working out plea bargains.

Whether criminal defendants need to be informed of the immigration consequences of a guilty plea by the court, the prosecutor, or their counsel has been an important question, with far-reaching consequences for other, albeit less dramatic, collateral sanctions. Either through legislative or judicial mandate, a number of states have required courts to inform defendants that immigration consequences may attach to a conviction if the defendant is not a U.S. citizen.

## Jose Padilla v. Kentucky
### 130 S. Ct. 1473 (2010)

STEVENS, J.

Petitioner Jose Padilla, a native of Honduras, has been a lawful permanent resident of the United States for more than 40 years. Padilla served this Nation with honor as a member of the U. S. Armed Forces during the Vietnam War. He now faces deportation after pleading guilty to the transportation of a large amount of marijuana in his tractor-trailer in the Commonwealth of Kentucky.[1]

In this postconviction proceeding, Padilla claims that his counsel not only failed to advise him of this consequence prior to his entering the plea, but also told him that he "'did not have to worry about immigration status since he had been in the country so long.'" 253 S. W. 3d 482, 483 (Ky. 2008). Padilla relied on his counsel's erroneous advice when he pleaded guilty to the drug charges that made his deportation virtually mandatory. He alleges that he would have insisted on going to trial if he had not received incorrect advice from his attorney.

Assuming the truth of his allegations, the Supreme Court of Kentucky denied Padilla postconviction relief . . . . The court held that the Sixth Amendment's guarantee of effective assistance of counsel does not protect a criminal defendant from erroneous advice about deportation because it is merely a "collateral" consequence of his conviction. In its view, neither counsel's failure to advise petitioner about the possibility of removal, nor counsel's incorrect advice, could provide a basis for relief.

We granted certiorari to decide whether, as a matter of federal law, Padilla's counsel had an obligation to advise him that the offense to which he was pleading guilty would result in his removal from this country. We agree with Padilla that constitutionally competent counsel would have advised him that his conviction for drug distribution made him subject to automatic deportation. Whether he is entitled to relief depends on whether he has been prejudiced, a matter that we do not address.

## I

The landscape of federal immigration law has changed dramatically over the last 90 years. While once there was only a narrow class of deportable offenses

---

1. Padilla's crime, like virtually every drug offense except for only the most insignificant marijuana offenses, is a deportable offense under 8 U.S.C. §1227(a)(2)(B)(i).

and judges wielded broad discretionary authority to prevent deportation, immigration reforms over time have expanded the class of deportable offenses and limited the authority of judges to alleviate the harsh consequences of deportation. . . .

The Nation's first 100 years was "a period of unimpeded immigration." C. Gordon & H. Rosenfield, Immigration Law and Procedure §1.(2)(a), p. 5 (1959). . . .

The Immigration and Nationality Act of 1917 (1917 Act) brought "radical changes" to our law. S. Rep. No. 1515, 81st Cong., 2d Sess., pp. 54-55 (1950). For the first time in our history, Congress made classes of noncitizens deportable based on conduct committed on American soil. . . .

While the 1917 Act was "radical" because it authorized deportation as a consequence of certain convictions, the Act also included a critically important procedural protection to minimize the risk of unjust deportation: At the time of sentencing or within 30 days thereafter, the sentencing judge in both state and federal prosecutions had the power to make a recommendation "that such alien shall not be deported." This procedure, known as a judicial recommendation against deportation, or JRAD, had the effect of binding the Executive to prevent deportation. . . . Thus, from 1917 forward, there was no such creature as an automatically deportable offense. Even as the class of deportable offenses expanded, judges retained discretion to ameliorate unjust results on a case-by-case basis.

However, the JRAD procedure is no longer part of our law. . . . in 1990 Congress entirely eliminated it. In 1996, Congress also eliminated the Attorney General's authority to grant discretionary relief from deportation. . . . Under contemporary law, if a noncitizen has committed a removable offense after the 1996 effective date of these amendments, his removal is practically inevitable but for the possible exercise of limited remnants of equitable discretion vested in the Attorney General to cancel removal for noncitizens convicted of particular classes of offenses.[6] Subject to limited exceptions, this discretionary relief is not available for an offense related to trafficking in a controlled substance.

These changes to our immigration law have dramatically raised the stakes of a noncitizen's criminal conviction. The importance of accurate legal advice for noncitizens accused of crimes has never been more important. These changes confirm our view that, as a matter of federal law, deportation is an integral part—indeed, sometimes the most important part—of the penalty that may be imposed on noncitizen defendants who plead guilty to specified crimes.

## II

Before deciding whether to plead guilty, a defendant is entitled to "the effective assistance of competent counsel." McMann v. Richardson, 97 U.S. 759, 771 (1970); Strickland v. Washington, 466 U.S. 668 (1984). The Supreme Court of Kentucky rejected Padilla's ineffectiveness claim on the ground that the

---

6. The changes to our immigration law have also involved a change in nomenclature; the statutory text now uses the term "removal" rather than "deportation."

advice he sought about the risk of deportation concerned only collateral matters, *i.e.*, those matters not within the sentencing authority of the state trial court. In its view, "collateral consequences are outside the scope of representation required by the Sixth Amendment," and, therefore, the "failure of defense counsel to advise the defendant of possible deportation consequences is not cognizable as a claim for ineffective assistance of counsel." The Kentucky high court is far from alone in this view.

We, however, have never applied a distinction between direct and collateral consequences to define the scope of constitutionally "reasonable professional assistance" required under *Strickland*, 466 U.S., at 689. Whether that distinction is appropriate is a question we need not consider in this case because of the unique nature of deportation.

We have long recognized that deportation is a particularly severe "penalty;" but it is not, in a strict sense, a criminal sanction. Although removal proceedings are civil in nature, see INS v. Lopez-Mendoza, 468 U.S. 1032, 1038 (1984), deportation is nevertheless intimately related to the criminal process. Our law has enmeshed criminal convictions and the penalty of deportation for nearly a century. And, importantly, recent changes in our immigration law have made removal nearly an automatic result for a broad class of noncitizen offenders. Thus, we find it "most difficult" to divorce the penalty from the conviction in the deportation context. United States v. Russell, 686 F. 2d 35, 38 (D.C Cir. 1982). Moreover, we are quite confident that noncitizen defendants facing a risk of deportation for a particular offense find it even more difficult.

Deportation as a consequence of a criminal conviction is, because of its close connection to the criminal process, uniquely difficult to classify as either a direct or a collateral consequence. The collateral versus direct distinction is thus ill-suited to evaluating a *Strickland* claim concerning the specific risk of deportation. We conclude that advice regarding deportation is not categorically removed from the ambit of the Sixth Amendment right to counsel. *Strickland* applies to Padilla's claim.

## III

Under *Strickland*, we first determine whether counsel's representation "fell below an objective standard of reasonableness." Then we ask whether "there is a reasonable probability that, but for counsel's unprofessional errors, the result of the proceeding would have been different." The first prong—constitutional deficiency—is necessarily linked to the practice and expectations of the legal community: "The proper measure of attorney performance remains simply reasonableness under prevailing professional norms." We long have recognized that "[p]revailing norms of practice as reflected in American Bar Association standards and the like ... are guides to determining what is reasonable. ..." Although they are "only guides," and not "inexorable commands," Bobby v. Van Hook, 558 U. S. 4, 130 S. Ct. 13 (slip op., at 5) (2009) (per curiam), these standards may be valuable measures of the prevailing professional norms of effective representation, especially as these standards have been adapted to deal with the intersection of modern criminal prosecutions and immigration law.

The weight of prevailing professional norms supports the view that counsel must advise her client regarding the risk of deportation. ... "[A]uthorities of every stripe — including the American Bar Association, criminal defense and public defender organizations, authoritative treatises, and state and city bar publications — universally require defense attorneys to advise as to the risk of deportation consequences for non-citizen clients. . . ." Brief for Legal Ethics, Criminal Procedure, and Criminal Law Professors as *Amici Curiae* 12–14 (footnotes omitted) (citing, *inter alia*, National Legal Aid and Defender Assn., Guidelines, §§6.2-6.4 (1997); S. Bratton & E. Kelley, Practice Points: Representing a Noncitizen in a Criminal Case, 31 The Champion 61 (Jan./Feb. 2007); N. Tooby, Criminal Defense of Immigrants §1.3 (3d ed. 2003); 2 Criminal Practice Manual §§45:3, 45:15 (2009)). . . .

In the instant case, the terms of the relevant immigration statute are succinct, clear, and explicit in defining the removal consequence for Padilla's conviction. See 8 U.S.C. ¶1227(a)(2)(B)(i) ("Any alien who at any time after admission has been convicted of a violation of (or a conspiracy or attempt to violate) any law or regulation of a State, the United States or a foreign country relating to a controlled substance . . . , other than a single offense involving possession for one's own use of 30 grams or less of marijuana, is deportable"). Padilla's counsel could have easily determined that his plea would make him eligible for deportation simply from reading the text of the statute, which addresses not some broad classification of crimes but specifically commands removal for all controlled substances convictions except for the most trivial of marijuana possession offenses. Instead, Padilla's counsel provided him false assurance that his conviction would not result in his removal from this country. This is not a hard case in which to find deficiency: The consequences of Padilla's plea could easily be determined from reading the removal statute, his deportation was presumptively mandatory, and his counsel's advice was incorrect.

Immigration law can be complex, and it is a legal specialty of its own. Some members of the bar who represent clients facing criminal charges, in either state or federal court or both, may not be well versed in it. There will, therefore, undoubtedly be numerous situations in which the deportation consequences of a particular plea are unclear or uncertain. The duty of the private practitioner in such cases is more limited. When the law is not succinct and straightforward (as it is in many of the scenarios posited by Justice Alito), a criminal defense attorney need do no more than advise a noncitizen client that pending criminal charges may carry a risk of adverse immigration consequences. But when the deportation consequence is truly clear, as it was in this case, the duty to give correct advice is equally clear.

Accepting his allegations as true, Padilla has sufficiently alleged constitutional deficiency to satisfy the first prong of *Strickland*. Whether Padilla is entitled to relief on his claim will depend on whether he can satisfy *Strickland*'s second prong, prejudice, a matter we leave to the Kentucky courts to consider in the first instance.

## IV

The Solicitor General has urged us to conclude that *Strickland* applies to Padilla's claim only to the extent that he has alleged affirmative misadvice. In the United States' view, "counsel is not constitutionally required to provide advice on matters that will not be decided in the criminal case . . . ," though counsel is required to provide accurate advice if she chooses to discusses these matters.

[T]here is no relevant difference "between an act of commission and an act of omission" in this context.

A holding limited to affirmative misadvice would invite two absurd results. First, it would give counsel an incentive to remain silent on matters of great importance, even when answers are readily available. Silence under these circumstances would be fundamentally at odds with the critical obligation of counsel to advise the client of "the advantages and disadvantages of a plea agreement." Libretti v. United States, 516 U.S. 29, 50-51 (1995). When attorneys know that their clients face possible exile from this country and separation from their families, they should not be encouraged to say nothing at all. Second, it would deny a class of clients least able to represent themselves the most rudimentary advice on deportation even when it is readily available. It is quintessentially the duty of counsel to provide her client with available advice about an issue like deportation and the failure to do so "clearly satisfies the first prong of the *Strickland* analysis." Hill v. Lockhart, 474 U.S. 52, 62 (1985) (White, J., concurring in judgment).

We have given serious consideration to the concerns that the Solicitor General, respondent, and *amici* have stressed regarding the importance of protecting the finality of convictions obtained through guilty pleas. We confronted a similar "floodgates" concern in *Hill*, but nevertheless applied *Strickland* to a claim that counsel had failed to advise the client regarding his parole eligibility before he pleaded guilty.[12]

A flood did not follow in that decision's wake. Surmounting *Strickland*'s high bar is never an easy task. Moreover, to obtain relief on this type of claim, a petitioner must convince the court that a decision to reject the plea bargain would have been rational under the circumstances. There is no reason to doubt that lower courts — now quite experienced with applying *Strickland* — can effectively and efficiently use its framework to separate specious claims from those with substantial merit.

It seems unlikely that our decision today will have a significant effect on those convictions already obtained as the result of plea bargains. For at least the past 15 years, professional norms have generally imposed an obligation on counsel to provide advice on the deportation consequences of a client's plea. We should, therefore, presume that counsel satisfied their obligation to render competent advice at the time their clients considered pleading guilty.

Likewise, although we must be especially careful about recognizing new grounds for attacking the validity of guilty pleas, in the 25 years since we first applied *Strickland* to claims of ineffective assistance at the plea stage, practice has shown that pleas are less frequently the subject of collateral challenges than convictions obtained after a trial. . . . Those who collaterally attack their guilty

---

12. However, we concluded that, even though *Strickland* applied to petitioner's claim, he had not sufficiently alleged prejudice to satisfy Strickland's second prong. This disposition further underscores the fact that it is often quite difficult for petitioners who have acknowledged their guilt to satisfy *Strickland*'s prejudice prong. . . . *Hill* does not control the question before us. But its import is nevertheless clear. Whether *Strickland* applies to Padilla's claim follows from *Hill*, regardless of the fact that the *Hill* Court did not resolve the particular question respecting misadvice that was before it.

pleas lose the benefit of the bargain obtained as a result of the plea. Thus, [ ] the challenge may result in a *less favorable* outcome for the defendant, whereas a collateral challenge to a conviction obtained after a jury trial has no similar downside potential. . . .

Finally, informed consideration of possible deportation can only benefit both the State and noncitizen defendants during the plea-bargaining process. By bringing deportation consequences into this process, the defense and prosecution may well be able to reach agreements that better satisfy the interests of both parties. As in this case, a criminal episode may provide the basis for multiple charges, of which only a subset mandate deportation following conviction. Counsel who possess the most rudimentary understanding of the deportation consequences of a particular criminal offense may be able to plea bargain creatively with the prosecutor in order to craft a conviction and sentence that reduce the likelihood of deportation, as by avoiding a conviction for an offense that automatically triggers the removal consequence. At the same time, the threat of deportation may provide the defendant with a powerful incentive to plead guilty to an offense that does not mandate that penalty in exchange for a dismissal of a charge that does. . . .

## V

It is our responsibility under the Constitution to ensure that no criminal defendant—whether a citizen or not—is left to the "mercies of incompetent counsel." *Richardson*, 397 U.S., at 771. To satisfy this responsibility, we now hold that counsel must inform her client whether his plea carries a risk of deportation. Our longstanding Sixth Amendment precedents, the seriousness of deportation as a consequence of a criminal plea, and the concomitant impact of deportation on families living lawfully in this country demand no less.

Taking as true the basis for his motion for postconviction relief, we have little difficulty concluding that Padilla has sufficiently alleged that his counsel was constitutionally deficient. Whether Padilla is entitled to relief will depend on whether he can demonstrate prejudice as a result thereof, a question we do not reach because it was not passed on below. . . .

ALITO, J., concurring.

I concur in the judgment because a criminal defense attorney fails to provide effective assistance within the meaning of Strickland v. Washington, 466 U.S. 668 (1984), if the attorney misleads a noncitizen client regarding the removal consequences of a conviction. In my view, such an attorney must (1) refrain from unreasonably providing incorrect advice and (2) advise the defendant that a criminal conviction may have adverse immigration consequences and that, if the alien wants advice on this issue, the alien should consult an immigration attorney. I do not agree with the Court that the attorney must attempt to explain what those consequences may be. As the Court concedes, "[i]mmigration law can be complex"; "it is a legal specialty of its own"; and "[s]ome members of the bar who represent clients facing criminal charges, in either state or federal court or both, may not be well versed in it." The Court nevertheless holds that a criminal defense attorney must provide advice in this specialized area in those cases in which the law is "succinct and straightforward" — but not, perhaps, in other situations. This vague, halfway test will lead to much confusion and needless litigation.

## I

Under *Strickland*, an attorney provides ineffective assistance if the attorney's representation does not meet reasonable professional standards. Until today, the longstanding and unanimous position of the federal courts was that reasonable defense counsel generally need only advise a client about the *direct* consequences of a criminal conviction. While the line between "direct" and "collateral" consequences is not always clear, the collateral-consequences rule expresses an important truth: Criminal defense attorneys have expertise regarding the conduct of criminal proceedings. They are not expected to possess — and very often do not possess — expertise in other areas of the law, and it is unrealistic to expect them to provide expert advice on matters that lie outside their area of training and experience.

This case happens to involve removal, but criminal convictions can carry a wide variety of consequences other than conviction and sentencing, including civil commitment, civil forfeiture, the loss of the right to vote, disqualification from public benefits, ineligibility to possess firearms, dishonorable discharge from the Armed Forces, and loss of business or professional licenses. A criminal conviction may also severely damage a defendant's reputation and thus impair the defendant's ability to obtain future employment or business opportunities. All of those consequences are "seriou[s]," but this Court has never held that a criminal defense attorney's Sixth Amendment duties extend to providing advice about such matters.

The Court tries to justify its dramatic departure from precedent by pointing to the views of various professional organizations. However, ascertaining the level of professional competence required by the Sixth Amendment is ultimately a task for the courts. Although we may appropriately consult standards promulgated by private bar groups, we cannot delegate to these groups our task of determining what the Constitution commands. And we must recognize that such standards may represent only the aspirations of a bar group rather than an empirical assessment of actual practice.

Even if the only relevant consideration were "prevailing professional norms," it is hard to see how those norms can support the duty the Court today imposes on defense counsel. Because many criminal defense attorneys have little understanding of immigration law, it should follow that a criminal defense attorney who refrains from providing immigration advice does not violate prevailing professional norms. But the Court's opinion would not just require defense counsel to warn the client of a general *risk* of removal; it would also require counsel in at least some cases, to specify what the removal *consequences* of a conviction would be.

The Court's new approach is particularly problematic because providing advice on whether a conviction for a particular offense will make an alien removable is often quite complex. "Most crimes affecting immigration status are not specifically mentioned by the [Immigration and Nationality Act (INA)], but instead fall under a broad category of crimes, such as crimes involving moral turpitude or *aggravated felonies.*" M. Garcia & L. Eig, CRS Report for Congress, Immigration Consequences of Criminal Activity (Sept. 20, 2006) (summary) (emphasis in original). As has been widely acknowledged, determining whether a particular crime is an "aggravated felony" or a "crime involving moral turpitude [(CIMT)]" is not an easy task. See R. McWhirter, ABA, The Criminal Lawyer's Guide to Immigration Law: Questions and Answers 128 (2d ed. 2006) (hereinafter ABA Guidebook) ("Because of the increased complexity of aggravated felony law, this edition devotes a new [30-page] chapter to the subject"); *id.,* §5.2, at 146 (stating that the aggravated felony list at 8 U.S.C. §1101(a)(43) is not clear with respect to several of the listed categories, that "the term 'aggravated felonies' can include misdemeanors," and that the determination of whether a crime is an "aggravated felony" is made "even more difficult" because "several agencies and courts interpret the statute," including Immigration and Customs Enforcement, the Board of Immigration Appeals (BIA), and Federal Circuit and district courts considering immigration-law and criminal-law issues); . . . .

Many other terms of the INA are similarly ambiguous or may be confusing to practitioners not versed in the intricacies of immigration law. To take just a few examples, it may be hard, in some cases, for defense counsel even to determine whether a client is an alien, or whether a particular state disposition will result in a "conviction" for purposes of federal immigration law. The task of offering advice about the immigration consequences of a criminal conviction is further complicated by other problems, including significant variations among Circuit interpretations of federal immigration statutes; the frequency with which immigration law changes; different rules governing the immigration consequences of juvenile, first-offender, and foreign convictions; and the relationship between the "length and type of sentence" and the determination "whether [an alien] is subject to removal, eligible for relief from removal, or qualified to become a naturalized citizen," Immigration Law and Crimes §2:1, at 2-2 to 2-3.

. . . . I therefore cannot agree with the Court's apparent view that the Sixth Amendment requires criminal defense attorneys to provide immigration advice.

The Court tries to downplay the severity of the burden it imposes on defense counsel by suggesting that the scope of counsel's duty to offer advice concerning deportation consequences may turn on how hard it is to determine those consequences. Where "the terms of the relevant immigration statute are succinct, clear, and explicit in defining the removal consequence[s]" of a conviction, the Court says, counsel has an affirmative duty to advise the client that he will be subject to deportation as a result of the plea. But "[w]hen the law is not succinct and straightforward . . . , a criminal defense attorney need do no more than advise a noncitizen client that pending criminal charges may carry a risk of adverse immigration consequences." This approach is problematic for at least four reasons.

First, it will not always be easy to tell whether a particular statutory provision is "succinct, clear, and explicit." How can an attorney who lacks general immigration law expertise be sure that a seemingly clear statutory provision actually means what it seems to say when read in isolation? What if the application of the provision to a particular case is not clear but a cursory examination of case law or administrative decisions would provide a definitive answer?

Second, if defense counsel must provide advice regarding only one of the many collateral consequences of a criminal conviction, many defendants are likely to be misled. To take just one example, a conviction for a particular offense may render an alien excludable but not removable. If an alien charged with such an offense is advised only that pleading guilty to such an offense will not result in removal, the alien may be induced to enter a guilty plea without realizing that a consequence of the plea is that the alien will be unable to reenter the United States if the alien returns to his or her home country for any reason, such as to visit an elderly parent or to attend a funeral. Incomplete legal advice may be worse than no advice at all because it may mislead and may dissuade the client from seeking advice from a more knowledgeable source.

Third, the Court's rigid constitutional rule could inadvertently head off more promising ways of addressing the underlying problem — such as statutory or administrative reforms requiring trial judges to inform a defendant on the record that a guilty plea may carry adverse immigration consequences. . . . A nonconstitutional rule requiring trial judges to inform defendants on the record of the risk of adverse immigration consequences can ensure that a defendant receives needed information without putting a large number of criminal convictions at risk; and because such a warning would be given on the record, courts would not later have to determine whether the defendant was misrepresenting the advice of counsel. Likewise, flexible statutory procedures for withdrawing guilty pleas might give courts appropriate discretion to determine whether the interests of justice would be served by allowing a particular defendant to withdraw a plea entered into on the basis of incomplete information.

Fourth, the Court's decision marks a major upheaval in Sixth Amendment law. . . . The majority appropriately acknowledges that the lower courts are "now quite experienced with applying *Strickland*," but it casually dismisses the long-standing and unanimous position of the lower federal courts with respect to the scope of criminal defense counsel's duty to advise on collateral consequences. . . .


# II

While mastery of immigration law is not required by *Strickland*, several considerations support the conclusion that affirmative misadvice regarding the removal consequences of a conviction may constitute ineffective assistance.

First, a rule prohibiting affirmative misadvice regarding a matter as crucial to the defendant's plea decision as deportation appears faithful to the scope and nature of the Sixth Amendment duty this Court has recognized in its past cases. . . . [R]easonably competent attorneys should know that it is not appropriate or responsible to hold themselves out as authorities on a difficult and complicated subject matter with which they are not familiar. Candor concerning the limits of one's professional expertise, in other words, is within the range of duties reasonably expected of defense attorneys in criminal cases. . . .

Second, incompetent advice distorts the defendant's decision making process and seems to call the fairness and integrity of the criminal proceeding itself into question. . . . [W]hen a defendant bases the decision to plead guilty on counsel's express misrepresentation that the defendant will not be removable[,] it seems hard to say that the plea was entered with the advice of constitutionally competent counsel — or that it embodies a voluntary and intelligent decision to forsake constitutional rights.

Third, a rule prohibiting unreasonable misadvice regarding exceptionally important collateral matters would not deter or interfere with ongoing political and administrative efforts to devise fair and reasonable solutions to the difficult problem posed by defendants who plead guilty without knowing of certain important collateral consequences.

Finally, the conclusion that affirmative misadvice regarding the removal consequences of a conviction can give rise to ineffective assistance would, unlike the Court's approach, not require any upheaval in the law. . . .

## III

In sum, a criminal defense attorney should not be required to provide advice on immigration law, a complex specialty that generally lies outside the scope of a criminal defense attorney's expertise. On the other hand, any competent criminal defense attorney should appreciate the extraordinary importance that the risk of removal might have in the client's determination whether to enter a guilty plea. Accordingly, unreasonable and incorrect information concerning the risk of removal can give rise to an ineffectiveness claim. In addition, silence alone is not enough to satisfy counsel's duty to assist the client. Instead, an alien defendant's Sixth Amendment right to counsel is satisfied if defense counsel advises the client that a conviction may have immigration consequences, that immigration law is a specialized field, that the attorney is not an immigration lawyer, and that the client should consult an immigration specialist if the client wants advice on that subject.

SCALIA, J., dissenting.

In the best of all possible worlds, criminal defendants contemplating a guilty plea ought to be advised of all serious collateral consequences of conviction, and surely ought not to be misadvised. The Constitution, however, is not an all-purpose tool for judicial construction of a perfect world; and when we ignore its text in order to make it that, we often find ourselves swinging a sledge where a tack hammer is needed.

The Sixth Amendment guarantees the accused a lawyer "for his defense" against a "criminal prosecutio[n]" — not for sound advice about the collateral consequences of conviction. For that reason, and for the practical reasons set forth in Part I of Justice Alito's concurrence, I dissent from the Court's conclusion that the Sixth Amendment requires counsel to provide accurate advice concerning the potential removal consequences of a guilty plea. For the same reasons, but unlike the concurrence, I do not believe that affirmative misadvice about those consequences renders an attorney's assistance in defending against the prosecution constitutionally inadequate; or that the Sixth Amendment requires counsel to warn immigrant defendants that a conviction may render them removable. Statutory provisions can remedy these concerns in a more targeted fashion, and without producing permanent, and legislatively irreparable, overkill.

\* \* \*

The Sixth Amendment as originally understood and ratified meant only that a defendant had a right to employ counsel, or to use volunteered services of counsel. We have held, however, that the Sixth Amendment requires the provision of counsel to indigent defendants at government expense, Gideon v. Wainwright, 372 U.S. 335, 344-345 (1963), and that the right to "the assistance of counsel" includes the right to *effective* assistance, Strickland v. Washington, 466 U.S. 668, 686 (1984). Even assuming the validity of these holdings, I reject the significant further extension that the Court, and to a lesser extent the concurrence, would create. We have until today at least retained the Sixth Amendment's textual limitation to criminal prosecutions. . . . We have limited the Sixth Amendment to legal advice directly related to defense against prosecution of the charged offense — advice at trial, of course, but also advice at postindictment interrogations and lineups, and in general advice at all phases of the prosecution where the defendant would be at a disadvantage when pitted alone against the legally trained agents of the state. . . .

There is no basis in text or in principle to extend the constitutionally required advice regarding guilty pleas beyond those matters germane to the criminal prosecution at hand — to wit, the sentence that the plea will produce, the higher sentence that conviction after trial might entail, and the chances of such a conviction. Such matters fall within "the range of competence demanded of attorneys in criminal cases," McMann v. Richardson, 397 U.S. 759, 771 (1970). We have never held, as the logic of the Court's opinion assumes, that once counsel is appointed all professional responsibilities of counsel — even those extending beyond defense against the prosecution — become constitutional commands. Because the subject of the misadvice here was not the prosecution for which Jose Padilla was entitled to effective assistance of counsel, the Sixth Amendment has no application.

Adding to counsel's duties an obligation to advise about a conviction's collateral consequences has no logical stopping-point. . . . But it seems to me that the concurrence suffers from the same defect. The same indeterminacy, the same inability to know what areas of advice are relevant, attaches to misadvice. And the concurrence's suggestion that counsel must warn defendants of potential removal consequences — what would come to be known as the "*Padilla* warning" — cannot be limited to those consequences except by judicial caprice. It is difficult to believe that the warning requirement would not be extended, for example, to the risk of heightened sentences in later federal prosecutions pursuant to the Armed Career Criminal Act. We could expect years of elaboration upon these new issues in the lower courts, prompted by the defense bar's devising of ever-expanding categories of plea-invalidating misadvice and failures to warn — not to mention innumerable evidentiary hearings to determine whether misadvice really occurred or whether the warning was really given. . . .

The Court's holding prevents legislation that could solve the problems addressed by today's opinions in a more precise and targeted fashion. If the subject had not been constitutionalized, legislation could specify which categories of misadvice about matters ancillary to the prosecution invalidate plea agreements, what collateral consequences counsel must bring to a defendant's attention, and what warnings must be given. Moreover, legislation could provide consequences for the misadvice, nonadvice, or failure to warn, other than nullification of a criminal conviction after the witnesses and evidence needed for retrial have disappeared. Federal immigration law might provide, for example, that the near-automatic removal which follows from certain criminal convictions will not apply where the conviction rested upon a guilty plea induced by counsel's misadvice regarding removal consequences. Or legislation might put the government to a choice in such circumstances: Either retry the defendant or forgo the removal. But all that has been precluded in favor of today's sledge hammer.

In sum, the Sixth Amendment guarantees adequate assistance of counsel in defending against a pending criminal prosecution. We should limit both the constitutional obligation to provide advice and the consequences of bad advice to that well-defined area.

## PROBLEM 8-2.   WHAT'S WORSE?

Juan Nico, a permanent resident alien who entered the United States at age three and has lived here since then, got caught up in a bar brawl. He admits to having been drunk when his sister's ex-boyfriend, Bob Friendly, came into the bar. His sister had told him about the abuse Bob had inflicted on her, and he decided to show Bob what it would be like to be beaten up. Bob had not fully sat down when Juan threw a beer mug at him but missed. Juan and Bob got into a fight, which ended when other patrons separated them. Both had minor injuries, largely scrapes and bruises.

The district attorney suggests that Nico plead guilty to assault with a one-year suspended sentence. It is the local district attorney's policy to offer such pleas to noncitizens. Had Nico been a citizen, the district attorney would have insisted on some jail time.

If he accepts the plea, Nico will become automatically deportable as an aggravated felon since he committed a crime of violence. As Nico's attorney, what options do you have at your disposal? Could you attack the district attorney's policy offering different pleas to citizens and noncitizens?

Assume Nico accepted the plea but neither the district attorney nor his attorney discussed with him the resulting immigration consequences. What opportunities, if any, may he have to avoid removal from the United States?

## NOTES

1. *Deportation as a civil sanction.*   A long line of cases defines deportation as a civil rather than a criminal sanction. The distinction has traditionally been that collateral sanctions are indirect, and in the case of deportation they are imposed by an agency outside the criminal justice system. None of the procedural

protections that attach in criminal cases, therefore, applied in deportation hearings, even though deportation for a criminal offense includes a long-term ban on reentry and often requires the offender to uproot his entire life and be separated from his family. See INS v. Lopez-Mendoza, 468 U.S. 1032 (1984). *Padilla*, however, changes this framework by recognizing the harsh sanction of removal. Now failure to advise a client of potential adverse immigration consequences can constitute ineffective assistance of counsel in a criminal case, subject to the test set forth in *Strickland*.

2. *Defense counsel's role.*  After the 1996 immigration legislation substantially expanded the category of crimes making aliens deportable, some state legislatures mandated that courts inform noncitizen criminal defendants of potential immigration consequences. In some other states, courts have ruled to that effect. Chapter 19 of the ABA Standards on Collateral Sanctions (2003) recommends that judges inform criminal defendants before the guilty plea of the whole panoply of potential collateral sanctions. This would necessitate that courts compile a list of existing sanctions, many of which are currently unknown to judges, prosecutors, and defense counsel. How likely is the expansion of *Padilla* to other collateral sanctions, such as civil commitment, sex offender notification or disenfranchisement?

3. *Prosecutorial manipulation of collateral sanctions.*  Prosecutors are able to influence the imposition of collateral consequences through charging decisions and plea offers. If a defendant refuses to accept an apparently generous plea offer because of a collateral consequence, and the judge agrees with the defendant's decision because she considers the collateral sanction too harsh, what options does she have?

4. *Representation outside the criminal context.*  While an alien has a right to counsel in immigration proceedings, no right to governmentally funded counsel exists. How could *Padilla* be used to expand *Gideon* outside the strictly criminal process?

5. *Retroactivity.*  One of the questions that remains open after *Padilla* is whether it applies to criminal cases decided before the Court issued its opinion. State and lower federal courts have split over the question whether the decision is a new rule of constitutional law or merely an application of *Strickland*, the existing precedent. Under the Supreme Court's method of analysis set out in *Teague*, the answer determines in part whether the rule will be applied retroactively. Chaidez v. United States, 655 F.3d 684 (7th Cir. 2011), *cert. granted*, 132 S. Ct. 2101 (2012)(mem.).

6. *Welfare and financial aid benefits.*  Federal law gives sentencing courts discretion to bar drug offenders temporarily from access to benefits. 21 U.S.C. §862(a). Studies have shown that neither state nor federal courts take advantage of this provision. See Robert Musser Jr., Denial of Federal Benefits to Drug Traffickers and Drug Possessors: A Broad-Reaching but Seldom Used Sanction, 12 Fed. Sent'g Rep. 252 (2000). Upon a third conviction for sale of illegal narcotics, the ban becomes mandatory. 21 U.S.C. §862a requires that states permanently deny certain welfare benefits and food stamps to people convicted of state or federal felony drug possession, use, or sale offenses, unless

the state explicitly opts out of such a ban. Currently, less than a dozen states retain the ban, with many having loosened or entirely abandoned it over the last few years. The denial of welfare benefits has been found to have a particularly devastating impact on women released from prison, who are more likely to suffer a relapse as they find it more difficult to establish a life for themselves without support and as their families are more likely to dissolve without financial assistance. See Amy E. Hirsch, Parents with Criminal Records and Public Benefits: "Welfare Helps Us Stay in Touch with Society," in Every Door Closed: Barriers Facing Parents with Criminal Records 27, 31 (Community Legal Services 2002). The first conviction for a drug possession or sale offense also carries with it a temporary denial of financial aid benefits for students applying to or enrolled in institutions of higher learning. The sponsor of the legislation wanted the provision to apply only for convictions occurring while the student receives such benefits, but currently it is being implemented to apply to anyone with a drug offense conviction, however far in the past. The third possession or second sale offense results in indefinite suspension of financial aid. Students may restore their eligibility if they complete a drug rehabilitation program that complies with certain criteria. See 20 U.S.C. §1091(r).

Even though courts have generally held individual collateral sanctions to be civil and therefore not subject to protections under the criminal procedural system, could the sheer amount of collateral sanctions and their impact in the modern world suffice for such protections to apply? After all, the fact of a criminal conviction changes an individual's status permanently and makes her subject to the imposition of collateral sanctions at any point. See Gabriel J. Chin, The New Civil Death, Rethinking Punishment in the Era of Mass Conviction, 160 U. Penn. L. Rev. 1789 (2012).

7. *Administrative sanctions based on criminal conduct.*   Collateral sanctions depend on a criminal conviction. Some administrative restrictions, however, are based not on a criminal conviction but rather on criminal conduct. For example, involvement in drug activity carries with it a ban from public housing, irrespective of whether the renter was convicted of a drug offense. Although criminal conduct is most easily proven through a criminal record, a formal conviction is not required. See, e.g., HUD v. Rucker, 545 U.S. 125 (2002) (housing authority may evict tenant even if tenant had given neither consent nor had knowledge of family member's or guest's illicit drug activities).

8. *Extralegal collateral sanctions.*   Employers such as schools, long-term care facilities, and security services are statutorily obligated to investigate the criminal record of a job applicant. In addition to governmental restrictions imposed on offenders after they have served their criminal justice sentences, nongovernmental (private) disabilities apply as well. Many employers voluntarily check criminal records and refuse to hire ex-offenders. Licensing boards frequently deny ex-offenders licenses for employment positions ranging from attorney to beautician. Ex-offenders are also finding it increasingly difficult to rent apartments and homes. This is particularly problematic for sex offenders, but many other offenders are also denied housing by rental agencies and homeowners. Should the government protect the civil rights of ex-offenders who have served their sentences? Would an ex-offender nondiscrimination act have any chance of being enacted?

Notably, in his 2004 State of the Union address, President George W. Bush spoke passionately about the importance of showing compassion (and providing job training and placement services) to convicted offenders because "America is the land of second chance." In April 2008 the president signed the "Second Chance Act" into law. It provides federal grants to government agencies and not-for-profit organizations with the goal of decreasing recidivism of those returning back to their communities. Despite recent budget cuts, the program remains funded, albeit at a lower level than in preceding years.

# 9

## ‖ Race, Class, and Gender ‖

Fundamental constitutional and moral principles of equal treatment tell us that people should not be punished more or less severely because of their race (or ethnicity), social or economic class, or gender. These abstract principles quickly confront a dramatic reality of American criminal justice: criminal defendants, as a group, are overwhelmingly male and poor. Equally striking, African Americans and Native Americans are convicted of crimes at highly disproportionate levels. These unsettling facts of the American criminal justice system — disproportions shared in varying degrees by other countries — raise a profound question: why are men, members of (some) racial minority groups, and the poor convicted more frequently than others?

For a good part of U.S. history, state laws explicitly justified differential treatment on the basis of race and gender. But such laws have for some time been anathema to the U.S. legal system. See, e.g., Commonwealth v. Butler, 328 A.2d 851 (Pa. 1974) (statute requiring mandatory minimum sentence for men but not women declared unconstitutional). Now, the issue of whether people are sentenced more severely on the basis of their race, ethnicity, wealth, or gender has become more subtle and difficult to answer.

Studies conducted in the United States find little difference between races in their formal treatment by the criminal justice system after controlling for other differences among cases. Some of the racial disproportionality in prison sentences appears to be largely contextual: African American defendants are more likely to go to prison in areas of high unemployment, in places where blacks constitute a larger percentage of the population, and in the South. For other racial groups the data are more ambiguous and more difficult to explain. The few empirical studies done on inmate populations indicate that those sentenced to custodial terms are poorer than the rest of the population. The gender data are clear: despite rising imprisonment rates for women, they are dramatically underrepresented, and the offenses of which they are convicted tend to be less violent than those of male offenders.

This chapter considers the charge that racism, classism, and sexism are an inherent part of the criminal justice process and that their end product is highly disproportionate punishment. The chapter also raises the question whether the criminal justice system in general, and sentencing law in particular, is an appropriate place to remedy bias that may stem from more pervasive societal and historical forces.

## A.   AFRICAN AMERICANS IN THE CRIMINAL JUSTICE SYSTEM

> There is nothing more painful to me at this stage in my life than to walk down the street and hear footsteps and start thinking about robbery—then look around and see somebody white and feel relieved.
> *Jesse Jackson, 1993*

Race is an unavoidable issue in modern American criminal procedure. Difficult questions arise at all stages of the criminal process: What is the role of race in police stops and investigations? When might racial disparities justify challenges to charging practices? How may race affect the setting of bail, which has an impact on the likelihood of a conviction? What role should race play in jury selection? In arguments at trial? But perhaps the most common and visible questions about race arise at the end of the process, in the form of claims that black Americans and other minorities are punished more severely than whites. In some situations, the responsible decision makers may be identifiable; in other situations, the source of racial disparity may be hard to specify even when it clearly exists.

The first section of this chapter sets the stage by identifying the aggregate racial disparities in sanctioning and by presenting some preliminary arguments about the source of those disparities. The next part examines the 1987 decision of the U.S. Supreme Court in McCleskey v. Kemp, one of the most difficult and contentious racial cases of the past half century. *McCleskey* addresses a claim that the state of Georgia discriminates on the basis of the *victim's* race when it imposes the death penalty. The last section considers the link between early decisions made in investigations or charging and the later pattern of sentencing outcomes. Sometimes early decisions by police and by prosecutors become de facto decisions about punishment, and the entire criminal justice process can be said to be racially skewed. In what circumstances—and in what legal institutions—should challenges to entire systems be allowed based on claims of racial bias? Does the criminal justice system exacerbate or mitigate larger social problems? Can criminal justice systems respond to intentional or unintentional racial bias in society?

### 1.   An American Dilemma

It seems obvious to many that there is a relationship between race and punishment, but it is difficult to study or discuss. Problems with studying racial disparities include difficulties in defining race, the propriety and cost of collecting useful data, and the difficulties in knowing what conclusions to draw from the information. Does the very pervasiveness of racial tension, and the difficulty of frank discussion about race in the United States, make it impossible to explain the numbers satisfactorily? Much of the racial focus in the United States has been on the black-white disparity. In December 2010 black men were incarcerated about 7 times more than white non-Hispanic men. Bureau of Justice Statistics, Prisoners in 2010 (NCJ 236096, 2011). When the number of young men on probation or parole are combined with the number in prison or jail, almost one-third of young black men are under criminal justice supervision on any given day. Imprisonment rates vary dramatically by state: In some states 10-15% of the black male population are in prison. The black-to-white ratio also differs substantially, from a high of 13.6-to-1 to a low of 1.9-to-1, with the highest ratio found disproportionately in the Northeast and Midwest. Drug offenses have contributed more than any other crime to the rapid growth in the imprisonment rate for African Americans.

## Malign Neglect: Race, Crime and Punishment in America, Michael Tonry
### Pages 4, 29-30, 49-52 (1995)

Crime by blacks is not getting worse. The proportions of serious violent crimes committed by blacks have been level for more than a decade. Since the mid-1970s, approximately 45 percent of those arrested for murder, rape, robbery, and aggravated assault have been black (the trend is slightly downward). Disproportionate punishment of blacks, however, [has] been getting worse, especially since Ronald Reagan became president. Since 1980, the number of blacks in prison has tripled. . . .

Black Americans are far more likely than whites to be in prison or jail. [At the end of 2010 3,074 black men per 100,000 were in prison; among white non-Hispanic men, 459 per 100,000 were imprisoned. For women the comparable figures were 133 and 47.]

Another even more remarkable pattern of black-white disparities has been revealed by a series of studies attempting to determine the proportions of blacks under the control of the criminal justice system on a given day. Of all the people in prison or jail, on probation or parole, or released on bail or recognizance pending trial, what percentage are black? . . .

Three findings about race, crime, and punishment stand out concerning blacks. First, at every criminal justice stage from arrest through incarceration, blacks are present in numbers greatly out of proportion to their presence in the general population. . . . Second, although black disproportions in the front of the system — as offenders and arrestees — are essentially stable, since the early 1980s they have steadily grown worse at the back [in sentencing and in prison populations]. Third, perhaps surprisingly, for nearly a decade there has been a near consensus among scholars and policy analysts that most of the black disproportions result not from racial bias or discrimination within the system but from patterns of black offending and of blacks' criminal records. Drug law enforcement is the conspicuous exception. . . .

Do not misunderstand. A conclusion that black overrepresentation among prisoners is not primarily the result of racial bias does not mean that there is no racism in the system. Virtually no one believes that racial bias and enmity are absent, that no police, prosecutors, or judges are bigots, or that some local courts or bureaucracies are not systematically discriminatory. The overwhelming weight of evidence, however, is that invidious bias explains much less of racial disparities than does offending by black offenders. Much offending is intraracial, which means that a failure by the state to take crimes by blacks seriously depreciates the importance of victimization of blacks — discrimination little less objectionable than bias against black offenders. Virtually every sophisticated review of social science evidence on criminal justice decision making has concluded, overall, that the apparent influence of the offender's race on official decisions concerning individual defendants is slight. . . .

How is it possible that black participation in serious crime has not increased while rising numbers and proportions of blacks are in prison or jail, and yet racial bias does not pervade the system? . . . There is an answer, and it lies not in the criminal justice system but in the . . . aggressive promotion of punitive crime control policies and a "War on Drugs." [These policies have] caused the ever harsher treatment of blacks by the criminal justice system, and it was foreseeable that they would do so. Just as the tripling of the American prison population between 1980 and 1993 was the result of conscious policy decisions, so also was the greater burden of punishment borne by blacks. Crime control politicians wanted more people in prison and knew that a larger proportion of them would be black.

## NOTES

1. *Data and knowledge about race.*   Surprisingly little race data is available in the criminal justice system. In most states,

> race data are virtually nonexistent with regard to victims; information on the race of the offender is limited. Race data on offenders are collected by law enforcement at arrest and maintained in the criminal history record for felons and gross misdemeanants. Race data on offenders are also collected by probation officers on sentencing worksheets. . . . There are no race data anywhere on misdemeanants.
>
> Debra Dailey, Minnesota's Continuing Efforts to Address Racial Disparities in Sentencing, 8 Fed. Sent'g Rep. 89, 89 (1995) (describing the situation in Minnesota as typical for most states).

The absence of race data also hampers analysis in other states, including an assessment whether disparity amounts to discrimination. See Governor Jim Doyle's Commission on Reducing Racial Disparities in the Wisconsin Justice System, Final Report (Feb. 2008). For a thorough discussion of the limited available data on the racial impact of the federal sentencing guidelines, see United States Sentencing Commission, Fifteen Years of Guidelines Sentencing, 113-135 (2004) (available at http://www.ussc.gov/15_year/chap4.pdf). Some studies have indicated relatively little contribution of offender's race to sentencing disparities.

Are the social and financial costs of collecting additional race data likely to be worth the benefits? Should the United States follow the model of many European states that do not collect racial data on offenders, or does its history make this impossible? Dailey provides this cautionary note:

> One reason for the paucity of data is ambivalence as to whether the race of individuals ought to be recorded at all. In 1993, for instance, the mayor of Minneapolis declared that "the use of race in crime statistics is an abomination and an outrage." The mayor questioned the purpose of reporting arrest data by race and expressed concern that such data can lead to improper inferences about the relationship between crime and race. . . .
> Racial or ethnic data must be treated with caution because [this data] may be recorded from observation or from self-identification. . . . Moreover, existing research on crime has generally shown that racial or ethnic identity is not predictive of crime behavior within data which has been controlled for social or economic factors such as education levels, family status, income, housing density, and residential mobility.

Dailey at 89. Is race merely a proxy for other factors? One study's findings seems to indicate that race does not explain disparities at sentencing but instead racial stereotyping occurs based on the perceived Afrocentric facial appearance of the offender. William T. Pizzi, Irene V. Blair & Charles M. Judd, Discrimination in Sentencing on the Basis of Afrocentric Features, 10 Mich. J. of Race & L. 7 (2005). With increasing rates of intermarriage and offspring with multiple racial identities, will collections of racial data become misleading or even irrelevant?

2. *Who takes action?*   Even if we do understand the sources of some racial disparities in the criminal justice system, how can we best implement changes? In 1993 the Minnesota legislature created the Criminal and Juvenile Justice Information Policy Group to provide leadership and support for improving criminal justice. Made up of representatives from the state's sentencing commission, the judiciary, and other governmental bodies, the group was expected to recommend a framework for integrating criminal justice information, including information about race and ethnicity. Was the Minnesota legislature likely to defer to the group's recommendations? What institutions are most likely to make changes in law that will reduce disparate racial effects throughout the criminal justice system? Are courts the best avenue to bring about such changes? Sentencing commissions? If none of these institutions is the answer, then what should we do? Wait for society to improve?

## 2.   Whose Race?

Our exploration of the influence of race on punishment begins where the issue has received the most sustained attention: in the context of capital punishment. On the morning of May 13, 1978, Warren McCleskey and three other men planned to rob a furniture store. McCleskey had a .38 caliber Rossi nickel-plated revolver, which he had stolen in an armed robbery of a grocery store a month earlier. The others carried a sawed-off shotgun and pistols. McCleskey, who was black, entered the front of the store, and the other three came through the rear. While the robbers tied up all the employees, Officer Frank Schlatt, who was white, answered a silent alarm and entered the store, where he was fatally shot. The robbers fled but, some time later McCleskey was arrested in Cobb County in connection with another armed robbery. He confessed to the furniture store robbery but denied the shooting. Ballistics showed that Schlatt had been shot by a .38 caliber Rossi revolver. The weapon was never recovered.

McCleskey was convicted in 1978. The jury found two aggravating circumstances that authorized the use of the death penalty: (1) the murder was committed while the offender was committing another capital felony (armed robbery), and (2) the murder was committed against a police officer engaged in the performance of his official duties. The jury sentenced McCleskey to death for murder. One co-defendant was sentenced to life imprisonment, while another received a 20-year sentence.

On direct appeal in the Georgia courts, McCleskey first raised the claim that the death penalty violates the due process and equal protection provisions of the federal and state constitutions because prosecutorial discretion permits the government to apply the penalty in a racially discriminatory way. The Georgia Supreme Court rejected this claim as follows: "Appellant's argument is without merit. Gregg v. Georgia, 428 U.S. 153 (1976); Moore v. State, 243 S.E.2d 1 (Ga. 1978)." McCleskey v. State, 263 S.E.2d 146, 148 (Ga. 1980). After his direct appeals were exhausted, McCleskey began to file a series of state and federal habeas challenges to his conviction and sentence, which culminated in a decision by the U.S. Supreme Court.

## Warren McCleskey v. Ralph Kemp
### 481 U.S. 279 (1987)

POWELL, J.

This case presents the question whether a complex statistical study that indicates a risk that racial considerations enter into capital sentencing determinations proves that petitioner McCleskey's capital sentence is unconstitutional under the Eighth or Fourteenth Amendment.

### THE BALDUS STUDY

[In support of his habeas claim], McCleskey proffered a statistical study performed by Professors David Baldus, Charles Pulaski, and George Woodworth (the Baldus study) that purports to show a disparity in the imposition of the death sentence in Georgia based on the race of the murder victim and, to a lesser extent, the race of the defendant. The Baldus study is actually two sophisticated statistical studies that examine over 2,000 murder cases that occurred in Georgia during the 1970's. The raw numbers collected by Professor Baldus indicate that defendants charged with killing white persons received the death penalty in 11% of the cases, but defendants charged with killing blacks received the death penalty in only 1% of the cases. . . . Baldus also divided the cases according to the combination of the race of the defendant and the race of the victim. He found that the death penalty was assessed in 22% of the cases involving black defendants and white victims; 8% of the cases involving white defendants and white victims; 1% of the cases involving black defendants and black victims; and 3% of the cases involving white defendants and black victims. . . .

Baldus subjected his data to an extensive analysis, taking account of 230 variables that could have explained the disparities on nonracial grounds. One of his models concludes that, even after taking account of 39 nonracial variables, defendants charged with killing white victims were 4.3 times as likely to receive a death sentence as defendants charged with killing blacks. According to this model, black defendants were 1.1 times as likely to receive a death sentence as other defendants. Thus, the Baldus study indicates that black defendants, such as McCleskey, who kill white victims have the greatest likelihood of receiving the death penalty. . . .

### DISCRIMINATORY INTENT AND STATISTICS

McCleskey's first claim is that the Georgia capital punishment statute violates the Equal Protection Clause of the Fourteenth Amendment. He argues that race has infected the administration of Georgia's statute. . . . McCleskey's claim of discrimination extends to every actor in the Georgia capital sentencing process, from the prosecutor who sought the death penalty and the jury that imposed the sentence, to the State itself that enacted the capital punishment statute and allows it to remain in effect despite its allegedly discriminatory application. [This] claim must fail.

[To] prevail under the Equal Protection Clause, McCleskey must prove that the decisionmakers in his case acted with discriminatory purpose. He offers no evidence specific to his own case that would support an inference that racial considerations played a part in his sentence. Instead, he . . . argues that the Baldus study compels an inference that his sentence rests on purposeful discrimination. McCleskey's claim that these statistics are sufficient proof of discrimination, without regard to the facts of a particular case, would extend to all capital cases in Georgia, at least where the victim was white and the defendant is black.

The Court has accepted statistics as proof of intent to discriminate in certain limited contexts. First, this Court has accepted statistical disparities as proof of an equal protection violation in the selection of the jury venire in a particular district. Although statistical proof normally must present a "stark" pattern to be accepted as the sole proof of discriminatory intent under the Constitution, because of the nature of the jury-selection task, we have permitted a finding of constitutional violation even when the statistical pattern does not approach such extremes. Second, this Court has accepted statistics in the form of multiple-regression analysis to prove statutory violations under Title VII of the Civil Rights Act of 1964.

But the nature of the capital sentencing decision, and the relationship of the statistics to that decision, are fundamentally different from the corresponding elements in the venire-selection or Title VII cases. Most importantly, each particular decision to impose the death penalty is made by a petit jury selected from a properly constituted venire. Each jury is unique in its composition, and the Constitution requires that its decision rest on consideration of innumerable factors that vary according to the characteristics of the individual defendant and the facts of the particular capital offense. Thus, the application of an inference drawn from the general statistics to a specific decision in a trial and sentencing simply is not comparable to the application of an inference drawn from general statistics to a specific venire-selection or Title VII case. In those cases, the statistics relate to fewer entities, and fewer variables are relevant to the challenged decisions.

Another important difference between the cases in which we have accepted statistics as proof of discriminatory intent and this case is that, in the venire-selection and Title VII contexts, the decisionmaker has an opportunity to explain the statistical disparity. Here, the State has no practical opportunity to rebut the Baldus study. Controlling considerations of public policy dictate that jurors cannot be called to testify to the motives and influences that led to their verdict. Similarly, the policy considerations behind a prosecutor's traditionally wide discretion suggest the impropriety of our requiring prosecutors to defend their decisions to seek death penalties, often years after they were made. Moreover, absent far stronger proof, it is unnecessary to seek such a rebuttal, because a legitimate and unchallenged explanation for the decision is apparent from the record: McCleskey committed an act for which the United States Constitution and Georgia laws permit imposition of the death penalty.

Finally, McCleskey's statistical proffer must be viewed in the context of his challenge. McCleskey challenges decisions at the heart of the State's criminal justice system. "[One] of society's most basic tasks is that of protecting the lives of its citizens and one of the most basic ways in which it achieves the task is through criminal laws against murder." Gregg v. Georgia, 428 U.S. 153, 226 (1976) (White, J., concurring). Implementation of these laws necessarily requires discretionary judgments. Because discretion is essential to the criminal justice process, we would demand exceptionally clear proof before we would infer that the discretion has been abused. . . . Accordingly, we hold that the Baldus study is clearly insufficient to support an inference that any of the decisionmakers in McCleskey's case acted with discriminatory purpose. . . .

### ARBITRARY AND CAPRICIOUS

[McCleskey also] contends that the Georgia capital punishment system is arbitrary and capricious in application, and therefore his sentence is excessive [and contrary to the Eighth Amendment], because racial considerations may influence capital sentencing decisions in Georgia. . . .

To evaluate McCleskey's challenge, we must examine exactly what the Baldus study may show. Even Professor Baldus does not contend that his statistics prove that race enters into any capital sentencing decisions or that race was a factor in McCleskey's particular case. Statistics at most may show only a likelihood that a particular factor entered into some decisions. There is, of course, some risk of racial prejudice influencing a jury's decision in a criminal case.

There are similar risks that other kinds of prejudice will influence other criminal trials. The question is at what point that risk becomes constitutionally unacceptable. McCleskey asks us to accept the likelihood allegedly shown by the Baldus study as the constitutional measure of an unacceptable risk of racial prejudice influencing capital sentencing decisions. This we decline to do.

Because of the risk that the factor of race may enter the criminal justice process, we have engaged in "unceasing efforts" to eradicate racial prejudice from our criminal justice system. Our efforts have been guided by our recognition that "the inestimable privilege of trial by jury . . . is a vital principle, underlying the whole administration of criminal justice," Ex parte Milligan, 4 Wall. 2, 123 (1866). . . .

Individual jurors bring to their deliberations qualities of human nature and varieties of human experience, the range of which is unknown and perhaps unknowable. The capital sentencing decision requires the individual jurors to focus their collective judgment on the unique characteristics of a particular criminal defendant. It is not surprising that such collective judgments often are difficult to explain. But the inherent lack of predictability of jury decisions does not justify their condemnation. On the contrary, it is the jury's function to make the difficult and uniquely human judgments that defy codification and that build discretion, equity, and flexibility into a legal system.

McCleskey's argument that the Constitution condemns the discretion allowed decisionmakers in the Georgia capital sentencing system is antithetical to the fundamental role of discretion in our criminal justice system. Discretion in the criminal justice system offers substantial benefits to the criminal defendant. Not only can a jury decline to impose the death sentence, it can decline to convict or choose to convict of a lesser offense. Whereas decisions against a defendant's interest may be reversed by the trial judge or on appeal, these discretionary exercises of leniency are final and unreviewable. Similarly, the capacity of prosecutorial discretion to provide individualized justice is firmly entrenched in American law. As we have noted, a prosecutor can decline to charge, offer a plea bargain, or decline to seek a death sentence in any particular case. Of course, the power to be lenient also is the power to discriminate, but a capital punishment system that did not allow for discretionary acts of leniency would be totally alien to our notions of criminal justice. . . .

At most, the Baldus study indicates a discrepancy that appears to correlate with race. Apparent disparities in sentencing are an inevitable part of our criminal justice system. The discrepancy indicated by the Baldus study is a far cry from the major systemic defects identified in Furman v. Georgia, 408 U.S. 238 (1972), [which struck down existing capital punishment statutes because they imposed the punishment arbitrarily and capriciously. There] can be no perfect procedure for deciding in which cases governmental authority should be used to impose death. Despite these imperfections, our consistent rule has been that constitutional guarantees are met when the mode for determining guilt or punishment itself has been surrounded with safeguards to make it as fair as possible. Where the discretion that is fundamental to our criminal process is involved, we decline to assume that what is unexplained is invidious. In light of the safeguards designed to minimize racial bias in the process, the fundamental value of jury trial in our criminal justice system, and the benefits that discretion provides to criminal defendants, we hold that the Baldus study does not demonstrate a constitutionally significant risk of racial bias affecting the Georgia capital sentencing process.

Two additional concerns inform our decision in this case. First, McCleskey's claim, taken to its logical conclusion, throws into serious question the principles that underlie our entire criminal justice system. The Eighth Amendment is not limited in application to capital punishment, but applies to all penalties. Thus, if we accepted McCleskey's claim that racial bias has impermissibly tainted the capital sentencing decision, we could soon be faced with similar claims as to other types of penalty. Moreover, the claim that his sentence rests on the irrelevant factor of race easily could be extended to apply to claims based on unexplained discrepancies that correlate to membership in other minority groups, and even to gender. Similarly, since McCleskey's claim relates to the race of his victim, other claims could apply with equally logical force to statistical disparities that correlate with the race or sex of other actors in the criminal justice system, such as defense attorneys or judges. Also, there is no logical reason that such a claim need be limited to racial or sexual bias. If arbitrary and capricious punishment is the touchstone under the Eighth Amendment, such a claim could — at least in theory — be based upon any arbitrary variable, such as the defendant's facial characteristics, or the physical attractiveness of the defendant or the victim, that some statistical study indicates may be influential in jury decisionmaking. As these examples illustrate, there is no limiting principle to the type of challenge brought by McCleskey. The Constitution does not require that a State eliminate any demonstrable disparity that correlates with a potentially irrelevant factor in order to operate a criminal justice system that includes capital punishment. . . .

Second, McCleskey's arguments are best presented to the legislative bodies. It is not the responsibility — or indeed even the right — of this Court to determine the appropriate punishment for particular crimes. It is the legislatures, the elected representatives of the people, that are constituted to respond to the will and consequently the moral values of the people. Legislatures also are better qualified to weigh and evaluate the results of statistical studies in terms of their own local conditions and with a flexibility of approach that is not available to the courts. Capital punishment is now the law in more than two-thirds of our States. It is the ultimate duty of courts to determine on a case-by-case basis whether these laws are applied consistently with the Constitution. Despite McCleskey's wide-ranging arguments that basically challenge the validity of capital punishment in our multiracial society, the only question before us is whether in his case the law of Georgia was properly applied. [T]his was carefully and correctly done in this case. . . .

BRENNAN, J., dissenting.

At some point in this case, Warren McCleskey doubtless asked his lawyer whether a jury was likely to sentence him to die. A candid reply to this question would have been disturbing. First, counsel would have to tell McCleskey that few of the details of the crime or of McCleskey's past criminal conduct were more important than the fact that his victim was white. Furthermore, counsel would feel bound to tell McCleskey that defendants charged with killing white victims in Georgia are 4.3 times as likely to be sentenced to death as defendants charged with killing blacks. In addition, frankness would compel the disclosure that it was more likely than not that the race of McCleskey's victim would determine whether he received a death sentence: 6 of every 11 defendants convicted of killing a white person would not have received the death penalty if their victims had been black, while, among defendants with aggravating and mitigating factors comparable to McCleskey's, 20 of every 34 would not have been sentenced to die if their victims had been black. Finally, the assessment would not be complete without the information that cases involving black defendants and white victims are more likely to result in a death sentence than cases featuring any other racial combination of defendant and victim. The story could be told in a variety of ways, but McCleskey could not fail to grasp its essential narrative line: there was a significant chance that race would play a prominent role in determining if he lived or died. . . .

Georgia's legacy of a race-conscious criminal justice system, as well as this Court's own recognition of the persistent danger that racial attitudes may affect criminal proceedings, indicates that McCleskey's claim is not a fanciful product of mere statistical artifice.

For many years, Georgia operated openly and formally precisely the type of dual system the evidence shows is still effectively in place. The criminal law expressly differentiated between crimes committed by and against blacks and whites, distinctions whose lineage traced back to the time of slavery. During the colonial period, black slaves who killed whites in Georgia, regardless of whether in self-defense or in defense of another, were automatically executed. A. Higginbotham, In the Matter of Color: Race in the American Legal Process 256 (1978).

By the time of the Civil War, a dual system of crime and punishment was well established in Georgia. See Ga. Penal Code (1861). The state criminal code contained separate sections for "Slaves and Free Persons of Color," and for all other persons. The code provided, for instance, for an automatic death sentence for murder committed by blacks, but declared that anyone else convicted of murder might receive life imprisonment if the conviction were founded solely on circumstantial testimony or simply if the jury so recommended. The code established that the rape of a free white female by a black "shall be" punishable by death. However, rape by anyone else of a free white female was punishable by a prison term not less than 2 nor more than 20 years. The rape of blacks was punishable "by fine and imprisonment, at the discretion of the court." . . .

Citation of past practices does not justify the automatic condemnation of current ones. But it would be unrealistic to ignore the influence of history in assessing the plausible implications of McCleskey's evidence. . . .

The Court . . . states that its unwillingness to regard petitioner's evidence as sufficient is based in part on the fear that recognition of McCleskey's claim would open the door to widespread challenges to all aspects of criminal sentencing. Taken on its face, such a statement seems to suggest a fear of too much justice. Yet surely the majority would acknowledge that if striking evidence indicated that other minority groups, or women, or even persons with blond hair, were disproportionately sentenced to death, such a state of affairs would be repugnant to deeply rooted conceptions of fairness. The prospect that there may be more widespread abuse than McCleskey documents may be dismaying, but it does not justify complete abdication of our judicial role.

[To] reject McCleskey's powerful evidence . . . is to ignore both the qualitatively different character of the death penalty and the particular repugnance of racial discrimination, considerations which may properly be taken into account in determining whether various punishments are "cruel and unusual." Furthermore, it fails to take account of the unprecedented refinement and strength of the Baldus study. . . .

Warren McCleskey's evidence confronts us with the subtle and persistent influence of the past. His message is a disturbing one to a society that has formally repudiated racism, and a frustrating one to a Nation accustomed to regarding its destiny as the product of its own will. Nonetheless, we ignore him at our peril, for we remain imprisoned by the past as long as we deny its influence in the present. . . .

The destinies of the two races in this country are indissolubly linked together, and the way in which we choose those who will die reveals the depth of moral commitment among the living. . . .

## PROBLEM 9-1.   OFFENDER'S RACE AND RECORD

You represent Gerald Lane, a black man who is accused of murder. Lane claims that the Washoe County, Nevada, district attorney's office seeks the death penalty much more frequently when the defendant in a murder case is black. "If a person is accused of murder in Washoe County," Lane asserts, "it is better to be a white felon than a black with no prior felony convictions."

In support of this charge, you evaluate the 86 murder cases prosecuted by the Washoe County district attorney's office since Nevada's death penalty law took effect. In approximately 80% of cases involving a white defendant with at least one prior felony conviction, the district attorney did not seek the death penalty. By contrast, in approximately 80% of cases involving a black defendant without prior felony convictions, the district attorney did seek the death penalty. In other words, Lane argues that the Washoe County district attorney's office seeks the death penalty for only one out of five white murderers with past felonies and seeks the death penalty for four out of five black murderers without prior felonies.

In what legal terms will you frame the claim that might bar the use of the death penalty against Lane? How would you distinguish *McCleskey*? How would you use it? Compare Lane v. State, 881 P.2d 1358 (Nev. 1994).

### *NOTES*

1. *Compelling evidence of intent.*   What sort of statistical study might provide the circumstantial evidence necessary to convince a court that arbitrary racial discrimination plays a large enough role in a sentencing system to invalidate the outcome in a particular case? Is such a statistical study possible? If racial discrimination does influence some decision makers in some cases, how might one demonstrate that fact in a court of law? In *McCleskey* both the court of appeals and the Supreme Court concluded that a stronger statistical showing would be

necessary for racial influences in sentencing to amount to a constitutional problem. What sort of evidence did the courts have in mind?

2. *Whose race, victim's or defendant's?* Note that the Baldus study found that the race of the *defendant* had no statistically significant effect on the use of capital punishment. In Furman v. Georgia, 408 U.S. 238 (1972), the Supreme Court struck down several capital punishment statutes, declaring that the death penalty (as administered at that time) was a "cruel and unusual punishment" in violation of the Eighth Amendment. Several of the Justices argued that capital punishment could not stand because it was imposed disproportionately against the poor and racial minorities. Would the Supreme Court have reached a different outcome in *McCleskey* if the Baldus study had pointed to racial discrimination based on the defendant's race rather than the victim's race? Can a punishment be racially discriminatory if the government imposes it equally on defendants of all races?

A recent study indicates the African-Americans are underrepresented on death row as compared with the number of black murders. This disproportion stems from a reluctance to seek or impose the death penalty on black defendants when the victim is also black. On the other hand, black murders are more likely to be sentenced to death if the victim is white. John Blume, Theodore Eisenberg & Martin T. Wells, Explaining Death Row's Population and Racial Composition, 1 J. Empirical Legal Studies 165 (2004). Would a white defendant be able to argue this finding in a capital case?

To complicate the situation further, not all members of the same racial group may be perceived or treated alike. One study has indicated that more pronounced Afrocentric facial features may lead to longer sentences and that judges are less sensitized to control for discrimination within the same racial group. William T. Pizzi, Irene V. Blair & Charles M. Judd, Discrimination in Sentencing on the Basis of Afrocentric Features, 10 Mich. J. of Race & L. 7 (2005).

3. *Other venues.* Suppose that on the day after the Supreme Court issues its decision, the NAACP sends a copy of the Baldus study to a member of the Georgia legislature, and that member distributes copies. As the chair of the Senate's committee on criminal justice matters, would you hold hearings? If so, what would be the topic of the hearings — the validity of the study or the most appropriate response to the study? If the Supreme Court had concluded instead that the influence of race in Georgia's capital punishment system rendered McCleskey's sentence unconstitutional, how would you advise Georgia legislators and prosecutors to respond? Would a victory for McCleskey mean abolition of the death penalty in Georgia? Would it necessitate any other changes or inquiries into Georgia's sentencing system?

4. *Statistical studies of capital punishment after* McCleskey. The "race of the victim" effect that appeared in the Baldus study in Georgia has also appeared in statistical studies of other states. See, e.g., Glenn L. Pierce & Michael L. Radelet, Race, Region, and Death Sentencing in Illinois, 1988-1997, 81 Or. L. Rev. 39 (2002); Glenn L. Pierce & Michael L. Radelet, The Impact of Legally Inappropriate Factors on Death Sentencing for California Homicides, 1990-99, 46 Santa Clara L. Rev. 1-47 (2005); Michael L. Radelet & Glenn L. Pierce, Race and Death Sentencing in North Carolina, 1980-2007, 89 N.C.L. Rev. 2119 (2011);

Glenn L. Pierce & Michael L. Radelet, Death Sentencing in East Baton Rouge Parish, 1990-2008, 71 Louisiana L. Rev. 647 (2011). These claims have received little serious attention from courts; many simply cite *McCleskey* and refuse to consider the studies as relevant evidence of racial discrimination in the use of capital punishment. See People v. Davis, 518 N.E.2d 78 (Ill. 1987). The Supreme Court of New Jersey indicated that evidence along the lines of that presented in *McCleskey* could be sufficient to establish a prima facie case of a violation of the state constitution. The court also indicated, however, that New Jersey had not yet executed enough people to form the basis for a convincing statistical study. See State v. Bey, 645 A.2d 685, 712 (N.J. 1994) ("Our abiding problem with analyzing the effect of race is that the case universe still contains too few cases to prove that the race of a defendant improperly influences death sentencing."). New Jersey abolished the death penalty legislatively in 2007.

5. *The Kentucky Racial Justice Act.*   In 1998 Kentucky's governor signed into law "An Act relating to the fair and reliable imposition of capital sentences":

(1) No person shall be subject to or given a sentence of death that was sought on the basis of race.

(2) A finding that race was the basis of the decision to seek a death sentence may be established if the court finds that race was a significant factor in decisions to seek the sentence of death in the Commonwealth at the time the death sentence was sought.

(3) Evidence relevant to establish a finding that race was the basis of the decision to seek a death sentence may include statistical evidence or other evidence, or both, that death sentences were sought significantly more frequently:

(a) Upon persons of one race than upon persons of another race; or

(b) As punishment for capital offenses against persons of one race than as punishment for capital offenses against persons of another race.

(4) The defendant shall state with particularity how the evidence supports a claim that racial considerations played a significant part in the decision to seek a death sentence in his/her case. The claim shall be raised by the defendant at the pre-trial conference. The court shall schedule a hearing on the claim and shall prescribe a time for the submission of evidence by both parties. If the court finds that race was the basis of the decision to seek the death sentence, the court shall order that a death sentence shall not be sought.

(5) The defendant has the burden of proving by clear and convincing evidence that race was the basis of the decision to seek the death penalty. The Commonwealth may offer evidence in rebuttal of the claims or evidence of the defendant.

Is this law an appropriate response to the Baldus study and other evidence concerning the impact of race on the application of the death penalty? Would a capital defendant in Kentucky armed with a Kentucky version of the Baldus study be able to prevail on a claim based on this act? Would it surprise you that no defendant has yet been able to make a case under the statute?

As a legislator in a death penalty state, would you advocate the adoption of such a law? Does this legislation go far enough to address racial disparities in the application of the death penalty? Or does it go too far by providing all capital defendants with an additional set of arguments to delay appropriate and otherwise lawful executions?

In August 2009 North Carolina enacted its Racial Justice Act, which provides that pre-trial defendants and death-row inmates can challenge racial bias in the death penalty system, ranging from the county to the state level, through the use of statistical studies and/or other evidence. A sufficient showing of race being a significant factor in the request or imposition of the death penalty requires prosecutors to rebut the claim that the disparities indicate racial bias in the application of the death penalty in the defendant's case. If they are unable to make such a showing, the court may grant relief from the death sentence.

In July 2010, Michael Radelet, a professor of sociology at the University of Colorado, and Glenn Pierce, a criminologist at Northeastern University, published a study of over 15,000 North Carolina homicides between 1980 and 2008. The study concluded that a convicted killer is three times more likely to receive a death sentence if the victim is white rather than black, a finding consistent with studies of capital punishment in other states. The study attempted to control for additional crimes committed by the offender at the time of the murder, but it did not control for the offender's prior criminal record. Another study by Barbara O'Brien and Catherine Grosso indicated that across the state prosecutors remove a substantially larger number of African-Americans than whites from juries.

Almost all of the 159 inmates on death row filed claims under the Act. In 2012 a North Carolina court converted the death sentence of Marcus Robinson to life without parole upon a finding, based on statistical analysis combined with individual testimony in this case, that intentional racial bias against African-Americans tainted jury selection.

In July 2012 the North Carolina legislature overrode a gubernatorial veto and amended the Racial Justice Act to limit statistical proof to the county or prosecutorial district where the crime occurred rather than the entire state or region. In addition, statistical findings with respect to the race of the victim are no longer acceptable, and statistics alone are insufficient to prove bias.

6. *The federal death penalty.*   The federal death penalty, which had been defunct for many decades before the early 1990s, has been the focus of much recent race-based debate. More than 80% of the federal death row inmates are nonwhite. The first individual executed since the reinstitution of the federal death penalty — Timothy McVeigh — was white, however. See, e.g., U.S. Department of Justice, The Federal Death Penalty System: A Statistical Survey (1988-2000), 14 Fed. Sent'g Rep. 35 (2002); U.S. Department of Justice, The Federal Death Penalty System: Supplementary Data, Analysis and Revised Protocols for Capital Case Review, 14 Fed. Sent'g Rep. 40 (2002). Nevertheless, criticism of the racial makeup on federal death row continues. How should this debate affect prosecutorial discretion? As a federal prosecutor, would you be more inclined to ask for capital punishment in the case of a white defendant since you know about the existing disparity? Federal death penalty decisions appear to be centralized in the hands of the attorney general. Will a centralized decision-making structure protect better against racial disparity across the country? See, e.g., G. Ben Cohen & Robert J. Smith, The Racial Geography of the Federal Death Penalty, 85 Wash. L. Rev. 425 (2010).

## 3.   Discretionary Decisions and Race

Racial disparities at sentencing can result from decisions, such as the selection of charges, made at various earlier stages of the criminal justice process. If prosecutors discriminate on the basis of race (or gender or other objectionable grounds), the U.S. Supreme Court has stated that it is possible, at least in theory, to overturn a prosecutor's charging decision. A defendant who makes such a claim must establish that the prosecutor (1) made different charging decisions for similarly situated suspects (a discriminatory effect) and (2) intentionally made the decision on the basis of an "arbitrary" classification (a discriminatory intent). Arbitrary classifications would include "suspect classes" under equal protection doctrine or those defendants exercising their constitutional liberties such as freedom of speech or religion. See Oyler v. Boles, 368 U.S. 448 (1962); Wayte v. United States, 470 U.S. 598 (1985).

The *Wayte* decision made it clear that a criminal defendant claiming discrimination must demonstrate that the prosecutor chose the defendant for criminal charges "because of" and not "despite" the protected conduct or status of the defendant. This basic federal framework for analyzing constitutional challenges to discriminatory charging policies has also been influential in state courts. See, e.g., State v. Muetze, 534 N.W.2d 55 (S.D. 1995) (no proof that non–Native Americans who were not charged were similarly situated).

In 1996 the U.S. Supreme Court considered the claim of Christopher Armstrong, who was indicted in 1992 for crack distribution. He responded by filing a motion for discovery or for dismissal of the indictment, alleging that he had been selected for federal prosecution because he was black. The issue in the case was not whether Armstrong was able to show selective prosecution, but what burden he had to carry to obtain discovery on a selective prosecution claim. Armstrong based his initial motion on evidence that the defendant was black in all 24 narcotics cases closed in 1991 by the U.S. Attorney's office that had prosecuted him.

The Supreme Court rejected Armstrong's claim, holding that a court hearing a claim of selective prosecution may grant discovery to the defendant only if there is "some evidence" to support each of the elements of the claim, and finding that the "study" presented by Armstrong "failed to identify individuals who were not black, could have been prosecuted for the offenses for which respondents were charged, but were not so prosecuted." The Court did not explain how Armstrong or other claimants should obtain information about the pool of nonprosecuted suspects. Armstrong v. United States, 517 U.S. 456 (1996). Very few courts have reversed convictions on selective prosecution grounds, and no U.S. Supreme Court decisions have done so on racial grounds since Yick Wo v. Hopkins, 118 U.S. 356 (1886). In United States v. Bass, 536 U.S. 862 (2002), the Supreme Court held that national charging and plea bargaining statistics on the race of offenders in federal death penalty cases were insufficient under *Armstrong*'s credible evidence requirement to trigger a discovery order.

Claims of selective prosecution are difficult to pursue successfully, not only because of the difficult proof requirements under federal law, but also because so many actors are involved, including prosecutors, police, judges, probation officers, and decision makers in a variety of other institutions, such as schools. A strong bias in investigations or arrests may be concealed by studies showing unbiased decision making at a later stage of the process. For example, if whites and blacks who are convicted of a particular offense are punished identically, but members of one race are disproportionately investigated, then the sanction will appear neutral but will in fact be highly disparate, at least to the extent that the investigatory practices do not accurately reflect underlying behavior.

Much of the racial disparity in the criminal justice system can be explained through the offender's criminal record. As detailed in Chapter 5, offenders with prior convictions are typically punished more harshly; many minority offenders have such records. Studies indicate that one of the most discriminatory elements of the criminal justice system is the juvenile system. African American boys, in particular, are more likely to come under its supervision than white youngsters who commit similar offenses. Our Children, Their Children: Confronting Racial and Ethnic Differences in American Juvenile Justice (Kimberly Kempt-Leonard & Darnell F. Hawkins, eds. (University of Chicago Press 2005); Perry L. Moriearty, Combating the Color-Coded Confinement of Kids: An Equal Protection Remedy, 32 N.Y.U. Rev. L. & Soc. Change 285, 315 (2008); Barry C. Feld, Juvenile and Criminal Justice Systems' Responses to Juvenile Violence, 24 Crime & Just. 189, 231-232 (1998). The juvenile case becomes the stepping-stone into the adult criminal justice system.

In states that allow transfer of juveniles into the adult system, racial disparity also occurs. Missouri's state law mandates consideration of racial disparity when making a transfer. Nevertheless, racial disparity continues and has even widened in recent years. What type of data does a court need to have to decide on the impact of racial disparity? What forms of racial disparity should the court consider—systemic or individual?

This section highlights the difficulty of proving the source of discrimination in large, complicated systems with many participants. Discrimination may be especially hard to unearth when it is the product of ongoing, low-level behavior of a large group of criminal justice officials and, perhaps, the result of unconscious influences on decision making. This section also raises questions about the law's capacity to change group behavior.

## Freddie Stephens v. State
### 456 S.E.2d 560 (Ga. 1995)

FLETCHER, J.

Freddie Stephens challenges the constitutionality of OCGA §16-13-30(d), which provides for life imprisonment on the second conviction of the sale or possession with intent to distribute a controlled substance. He contends that the provision as applied is irrational and racially discriminatory in violation of the United States and Georgia Constitutions. . . . The challenged statute states:

> [Any] person who violates subsection (b) of this Code section with respect to a controlled substance in Schedule I or a narcotic drug in Schedule II shall be guilty of a felony and, upon conviction thereof, shall be punished by imprisonment for not less than five years nor more than 30 years. Upon conviction of a second or subsequent offense, he shall be imprisoned for life.

Subsection (b) makes it unlawful to "manufacture, deliver, distribute, dispense, administer, sell, or possess with intent to distribute any controlled substance." For a defendant to receive a life sentence for a second conviction, the state must notify the defendant prior to trial that it intends to seek the enhanced punishment based on past convictions.

Stephens contends that the statute as applied discriminates on the basis of race. He argues that this court should infer discriminatory intent from statewide and county-wide statistical data on sentences for drug offenders. In Hall County, where Stephens was convicted, the trial court found that one hundred percent (14 of 14) of the persons serving a life sentence under OCGA §16-13-30(d) are African-American, although African-Americans make up less than ten percent of the county population and approximately fifty to sixty percent of the persons arrested in drug investigations. Relying on evidence provided by the State Board of Pardons and Paroles, the trial court also found that 98.4 percent (369 of 375) of the persons serving life sentences for drug offenses as of May 1, 1994 were African-American, although African-Americans comprise only 27 percent of the state's population. Finally, a 1994 Georgia Department of Corrections study on the persons eligible for a life sentence under subsection (d) shows that less than one percent (1 of 168) of the whites sentenced for two or more convictions for drug sales are serving a life sentence, compared to 16.6 percent (202 of 1219) of the blacks.

In an earlier challenge to death penalty sentencing in Georgia based on statistics showing that persons who murder whites are more likely to be sentenced to death than persons who murder blacks, the United States Supreme Court held that the defendant had the burden of proving the existence of purposeful discrimination and that the purposeful discrimination had a discriminatory effect on him. McCleskey v. Kemp, 481 U.S. 279 (1987). . . .

Stephens concedes that he cannot prove any discriminatory intent by the Georgia General Assembly in enacting the law or by the Hall County district attorney in choosing to seek life imprisonment in this case. . . . These concessions preclude this court from finding an equal protection violation under the United States Constitution.

We also conclude that the statistical evidence Stephens presents is insufficient evidence to support his claim of an equal protection violation under the Georgia Constitution. Stephens fails to present the critical evidence by race concerning the number of persons eligible for life sentences under OCGA §16-13-30(d) in Hall County, but against whom the district attorney has failed to seek the aggravated sentence. Because the district attorney in each judicial circuit exercises discretion in determining when to seek a sentence of life imprisonment, a defendant must present some evidence addressing whether the prosecutor handling a particular case engaged in selective prosecution to prove a state equal protection violation. . . .

Stephens's argument about inferring intent from the statistical evidence also ignores that other factors besides race may explain the sentencing disparity. Absent from the statistical analysis is a consideration of relevant factors such as the charges brought, concurrent offenses, prior offenses and sentences, representation by retained or appointed counsel, existence of a guilty plea, circuit where convicted, and the defendant's legal status on probation, in prison, or on parole. Without more adequate information about what is happening both statewide and in Hall County, we defer deciding whether statistical evidence alone can ever be sufficient to prove an allegation of discriminatory intent in sentencing under the Georgia Constitution.

The dissent argues that McCleskey v. Kemp is not the controlling precedent, instead relying on the United States Supreme Court decision on peremptory challenges in jury selections in Batson v. Kentucky, 476 U.S. 79 (1986). We must look to *McCleskey* for a proper analysis of the substantive issue before us, rather than *Batson*, because *McCleskey* dealt with the use of statistical evidence to challenge racial disparity in sentencing, as does this case.

The Supreme Court in *McCleskey* pointed out several problems in requiring a prosecutor to explain the reasons for the statistical disparity in capital sentencing decisions. Many of these same problems exist in requiring district attorneys to justify their decisions in seeking a life sentence for drug offenses based on statewide, and even county-wide, statistics of persons serving life sentences in state prisons for drug offenses.

First, "requiring a prosecutor to rebut a study that analyzes the past conduct of scores of prosecutors is quite different from requiring a prosecutor to rebut a contemporaneous challenge to his own acts. See Batson v. Kentucky, 476 U.S. 79 (1986)." *McCleskey*, 481 U.S. at 296. Second, statewide statistics are not reliable in determining the policy of a particular district attorney. Finally, the Court stated that the policy considerations behind a prosecutor's discretion argue against requiring district attorneys to defend their decisions to seek the death penalty. Since district attorneys are elected to represent the state in all criminal cases, it is important that they be able to exercise their discretion in determining who to prosecute, what charges to bring, which sentence to seek, and when to appeal without having to account for each decision in every case. . . .

Stephens also argues that the statute violates due process and equal protection by creating an irrational sentencing scheme. Seeking to deter repeated drug sales by the same person is not irrational. Therefore, we adhere to our previous decision that there is a rational basis for the sentencing scheme in OCGA §16-13-30(d) and that it does not deprive persons of due process or equal protection under the law. . . .

THOMPSON, J., concurring.

[We] are presented once again with the claim that OGCA §16-13-30(d) is being used in a discriminatory fashion. This time, we are introduced to statewide statistical information which must give us pause: From 1990 to 1994, OCGA §16-13-30(d) was used to put 202 out of 1,107 eligible African-Americans in prison for life. During that same period, the statute was used to put 1 out of 167 eligible whites in prison for life. A life eligible African-American had a 1 in 6 chance of receiving a life sentence. A life eligible white had a 1 in 167 chance of receiving a life sentence. An African-American was 2,700 percent more likely to receive a life sentence than a white. . . . These statistics are no doubt as much a surprise to those who work and practice within the judicial system as to those who do not.

Statistical information can inform, not explain. It can tell what has happened, not why. However, only a true cynic can look at these statistics and not be impressed that something is amiss. That something lies in the fact that OCGA §16-13-30(d) has been converted from a mandatory life sentence statute into a statute which imposes a life sentence only in those cases in which a district attorney, in the exercise of his or her discretion, informs a defendant that the State is seeking enhanced punishment. . . .

McCleskey v. Kemp, 481 U.S. 279 (1987), should continue to be applied in death penalty cases where there is a system of checks and balances to ensure that death sentences are not sought and imposed autocratically. Likewise *McCleskey* should be applied in other cases where the courts have discretion to determine the length of time to be served. However, *McCleskey* probably should not be applied where a district attorney has the power to decide whether a defendant is sentenced to life, or a term of years. . . .

I am persuaded that Batson v. Kentucky, 476 U.S. 79 (1986), could be used to supply a general framework in analyzing cases of this kind. . . . Nevertheless, it is my considered view that the judgment in this case must be affirmed because the defendant has failed to meet his burden even under a *Batson*-type analysis.

In order to establish a prima facie case under *Batson*, a defendant must prove systematic discrimination in his particular jurisdiction. Although the statistics presented by defendant are indicative of a statewide pattern of discrimination in the use of OCGA §16-13-30(d), the Hall County statistics are insufficient to make such a case. They simply show that all the persons in Hall County serving a life sentence under OCGA §16-13-30(d) are African-Americans. They do not show how many African-Americans were eligible to receive a life sentence under the statute; nor do they show how many whites were eligible. Moreover, they offer no information concerning the record of the district attorney in this case. Thus, upon careful review, I must conclude that this defendant, in this case and on this record, failed to prove a pattern of systematic discrimination in his jurisdiction. . . .

Statewide, approximately 15 percent of eligible offenders receive a life sentence under OCGA §16-13-30(d). The statistical evidence presented in this case serves as notice to the General Assembly of Georgia that the mandatory life sentence provision of OCGA §16-13-30(d) has been repealed de facto. With such notice, there are at least three courses of action the legislature might now choose to pursue.

One. The General Assembly could choose to leave the mandatory life sentence on the books realizing that it is being used in a small percentage of the eligible cases. Militating against this course of action is the fact that all laws passed by the legislature should be followed. Contempt for and failure to follow any law breeds contempt for and failure to follow other laws.

Two. The General Assembly could reaffirm its commitment to a mandatory life sentence by requiring district attorneys to inform all defendants of prior convictions and thus enforce OCGA §16-13-30(d) with respect to all life eligible offenders. Militating against this course of action is the fact that mandatory life sentences are not favored by the prosecuting bar or by the defense bar. That is evidenced by the fact that from 1990 to 1994 only 203 out of 1,274 life eligible defendants actually received a life sentence under OCGA §16-13-30(d). . . .

Three. The General Assembly could choose to change the mandatory life sentence penalty to one of several sentencing options which the court could impose. For example, the penalty for a second or subsequent sale could be imprisonment for not less than 5 nor more than 30 years, or life. . . .

It is my concern that these problems be resolved in whatever way the General Assembly deems best and that, thereafter, the prosecutors and the courts carry out that legislative will.

BENHAM, P.J., dissenting.

Of those persons from Hall County serving life sentences pursuant to OCGA §16-13-30(d), which mandates a life sentence for the second conviction for sale of or possession with intent to distribute certain narcotics, 100 percent are African-American, although African-Americans comprise only approximately 10 percent of Hall County's population. In our state prison system, African-Americans represent 98.4 percent of the 375 persons serving life sentences for violating OCGA §16-13-30(d). These statistics were part of the finding of the trial court in this case. In the face of such numbing and paralyzing statistics, the majority say there is no need for inquiry. It is with this determination that I take issue and from which I respectfully dissent. . . .

[In Batson v. Kentucky, 476 U.S. 79 (1986), the Supreme Court] installed a system that shifted the burden to the prosecutor to give race-neutral reasons for the peremptory challenges once the defendant established facts supporting an inference that the prosecutor's use of peremptory challenges was racially motivated. [The] court in *Batson* stated that an inference of discriminatory intent could be drawn from certain conduct or statistical data. Beyond its effect on peremptory challenges, the importance of *Batson* was that it significantly reduced the burden on one claiming discrimination, recognizing that under certain circumstances, the crucial information about an allegedly discriminatory decision could only come from the one who made the decision.

This is the course of reasoning we need to follow in analyzing the issue in this case rather than the more restrictive course taken in McCleskey v. Kemp and applied by the majority. . . .

I am not unmindful or unappreciative of the vital and taxing role district attorneys are called upon to undertake in the ongoing battle against the blight of illicit drug trafficking. Throughout this state, they shoulder an enormous burden of responsibility for advancing the fight against drugs, and to do so successfully, they must be invested with considerable discretion in making decisions about ongoing prosecutions. However, it is the very breadth of that discretion, concentrated in a single decision-maker, which makes it necessary that the one exercising the discretion be the one, when confronted with facts supporting an inference of discriminatory application, to bear the burden of establishing that the discretion was exercised without racial influence. This case is more like *Batson* than *McCleskey* because all the discretion in the sentencing scheme involved in this case resides in the district attorney, to the exclusion of the trial court, whereas in death penalty cases such as *McCleskey*, the spread of discretion among the prosecutor, the trial court, and the jurors introduces variables which call for more rigorous statistical analysis. In addition, the complexity of the death penalty procedure, with its many safeguards and the recurring necessity of specific findings at every stage from the grand jury to the sentencing jury, differentiates it from the relative simplicity of the sentencing scheme applicable to this case.

[The] U.S. Supreme Court recognized in *McCleskey* itself that statistical proof which presents a "stark pattern" may be accepted as the sole proof of discriminatory intent. In distinguishing *McCleskey* from such a case, the Supreme Court mentioned in a footnote two cases in which "a statistical pattern of discriminatory impact demonstrated a constitutional violation." . . . The statistics in those cases presented a "stark pattern," but no more stark than the pattern presented in this case. In the present case, based on evidence from law enforcement officers who testified as to arrest rates and other relevant statistics, the trial court found that 100% of the people from that county who were serving life sentences pursuant to OCGA §16-13-30(d) were African-Americans and that statewide, 98.4% of all the persons serving life sentences pursuant to OCGA §16-13-30(d) were African-Americans. . . .

I believe it is necessary that we adopt a procedure which will make it possible to address the issue openly and honestly in the trial courts. . . . I would hold, therefore, as a matter purely of state constitutional law, that equal protection of the law in the context of OCGA §16-13-30(d) requires that the prosecution be required, when a defendant has made a prima facie showing sufficient to raise an inference of unequal application of the statute, to "demonstrate that permissible racially neutral selection criteria and procedures have produced the monochromatic result." *Batson*, 476 U.S. at 94. . . .

Because appellant has made a sufficient showing of discriminatory application of OCGA §16-13-30(d) that the State should be required to give race-neutral reasons for the "monochromatic" application of that statute in Hall County, this court should vacate the life sentences and remand this case to the trial court for a hearing. At such a hearing, should the trial court find that the prosecution could not provide race-neutral reasons for the "monochromatic result" of the application of OCGA §16-13-30(d) in Hall County, sentencing for the offenses involved would still be permissible, but not with the aggravation of punishment authorized by OCGA §16-13-30(d). On the other hand, should the trial court find that the State has provided appropriate race-neutral reasons, the life sentences would be reimposed, whereupon appellant would be entitled to a new appeal.

Just as the prosecution was reined in by *Batson*, it must also be reined in here and called upon to give an account of itself. The statistics offered in this case show an enormous potential for injustice, and those statistics are just like the tip of an iceberg, with the bulk lying below the surface, yet to be realized. . . .

## PROBLEM 9-2.   TOWN AND COUNTRY

Darryl Pierre Wooden, an African American man sentenced to ten years in prison for selling illegal narcotics, believes that an Alabama law is racially discriminatory and asks for your help. His sentence was the product of the following two statutes, each of which mandates a five-year term:

• §13A-12-250. In addition to any penalties . . . provided by law for any person convicted of an unlawful sale of a controlled substance, there is hereby imposed a penalty of five years' incarceration in a state corrections facility with no provision for probation if the situs of such unlawful sale was on the campus or within a three-mile radius of the campus boundaries of any public or private school . . . or other educational institution in this state.

- §13A-12-270. In addition to any penalties . . . provided by law for any person convicted of an unlawful sale of a controlled substance, there is hereby imposed a penalty of five years' incarceration in a state corrections facility with no provision for probation if the situs of such unlawful sale was within a three-mile radius of a public housing project owned by a housing authority.

Wooden's conviction and ten-year mandatory sentence resulted from his sale to an undercover police officer of one tablet of "hydromorphone." Indisputably, this $50 transaction, which occurred on the 100 block of Fourth Avenue North in Birmingham, occurred within a three-mile radius both of a school and of a housing project. Wooden claims these statutes disproportionately impose a heavier sentence on black defendants in Jefferson County than on similar defendants in other Alabama counties because the conditions described in the statute ordinarily are present in an urban setting rather than a rural setting, and the overwhelming majority of citizens living in the city of Birmingham are black.

You gather the following evidence: Birmingham Police Officer B. H. Butler reports that of 150 persons he arrested for the "unlawful sale of a controlled substance," 145 were black and were subject to the enhanced sentence provisions of §13A-12-250 and 13A-12-270. Officer Eric Benson asserts that of approximately 100 persons he arrested for the "unlawful sale of a controlled substance" in the preceding year, 70 were black. He also states that "any sale of a controlled substance within the city limits of Birmingham would be within three miles of both a school and a housing project, and that 98% to 99% of those living in these housing projects are black."

Alabama Administrative Office of Courts official Larry Forston provides computer data gleaned from circuit court clerks' offices throughout the state. He tells you that from 1989, when the three-mile-radius provisions were adopted, through 1994, only three black defendants and one white defendant were sentenced in Jefferson County under either statute, compared with 267 black defendants and 90 white defendants sentenced elsewhere in the state.

Is Wooden right to focus on the application of the law to his county? How would you frame that claim? What other information would you try to obtain? Whose actions are suspect? Compare Ex parte Wooden, 670 So. 2d 892 (Ala. 1995).

## NOTES

1. *Who discriminates against whom?* What discrimination does Freddie Stephens claim? Other than the fact that both McCleskey and Stephens asserted that race was the basis for discrimination, were these similar claims? A controversial case at all stages, *Stephens* garnered additional attention when, 13 days before issuing the above opinion, the Georgia justices issued a slip opinion with a majority written by Justice Hugh Thompson announcing the "watershed" conclusion that under the equal protection clauses of both the federal and

state constitutions these statistics required a prosecutor to provide a race-neutral explanation for the decision to apply the statute to Stephens. The slip opinion was bitterly attacked by the Georgia attorney general and the 46 state district attorneys, who together filed a brief asking that it be reversed. Attorney General Michael Bowers asserted that it was the worst decision from the Georgia Supreme Court in more than 20 years and that it "sets up sentencing quotas."

2. *Competing analogies.* Did the majority in Stephens v. State think that Stephens's claim was the same as McCleskey's? Did the concurrence think so? The dissent? Were you convinced by the competing analogy to discriminatory jury selection in Batson v. Kentucky? Did you find convincing Justice Thompson's application of *Batson* in the concurring opinion? Justice Robert Benham, dissenting in *Stephens*, argued that sentencing under the Georgia drug statute was different from capital punishment because it concentrates the decision in the hands of the district attorney. Do you agree? Are there ways a police officer might influence who receives a life sentence under the statute? Does the judge have some control over this question? The defense counsel? The state attorney general? Voters in the county or in the state?

3. *The federalization of drug law enforcement.* In many criminal cases, state and federal prosecutors both have jurisdiction. Sometimes they investigate cases together and then allocate prosecutorial responsibilities; sometimes state prosecutors call in federal investigatory assistance; and sometimes federal prosecutors refer cases, especially those of a minor nature, to the state for trial. The different penalty structures in state and federal courts, together with procedural differences, may provide an incentive for state and federal prosecutors to send cases to federal court. This is true particularly when higher penalties exist under the federal sentencing guidelines or congressional mandatory sentences. While the so-called federalization of crime has been thoroughly criticized, it provides prosecutors with substantial additional discretion. See American Bar Association, Criminal Justice Section, Task Force on the Federalization of Criminal Law, Report on the Federalization of Criminal Law (1998).

Some of the results of the federalization may be startling. Hispanics, for example, make up about 15% of the inmates in state prisons but almost one third of the inmates in federal prisons. This substantial difference likely reflects Hispanics' higher rate of federal drug and especially immigration convictions. In FY 2011 50% of those sentenced under the federal guidelines were Hispanic; about 47% of all drug trafficking offenders and almost 90% of all immigration offenders were Hispanic.

In a study of charging for crack cocaine offenses in Los Angeles, Richard Berk and Alex Campbell found that black defendants are more likely than white or Latino defendants to be charged in federal court with sale of crack cocaine (which translates into more severe punishments than for comparable charges in state court). While black defendants represented 58% of those arrested by the Los Angeles Sheriff's Department for sale of crack cocaine between 1990 and 1992, they made up 83% of the defendants charged with that crime in federal court. White and Latino defendants arrested for this crime were more likely to be prosecuted in state court. Richard Berk & Alex Campbell, Preliminary Data on Race and Crack Charging Practices in Los Angeles, 6 Fed. Sent'g Rep. 36

(1993). What might explain the racially disparate federal crack prosecutions reported by Berk and Campbell?

4. *Racial patterns in charging.* Racial minorities are charged with crimes in a number disproportionate to their percentage in the population. But are minorities charged with crimes at a higher rate, once one accounts for different levels of participation in crime? Criminologists addressing this question have studied records of large numbers of cases, using statistical techniques (especially regression analysis) to compare similar cases and to sort out racial and nonracial influences over charging decisions. These charging decision also seem to be impacted by the availability of mandatory minimums. See, e.g., M. Marit Rehavi & Sonja B. Starr, Racial Disparity in Federal Criminal Charging and Its Sentencing Consequences (2012) (black males face more severe charges than others, with the disparity increasing when charges with mandatory minimums are available), available at papers.ssrn.com/sol3/papers.cfm?abstract_id=1985377##; Jeffery T. Ulmer, Megan C. Kurlycheck & John H. Kramer, Prosecutorial Discretion and the Imposition of Mandatory Minimum Sentences, 44 J. Res. in Crime & Delinq. 427 (2007) (in Pennsylvania prosecutors exercise their charging decisions when mandatory minimums are available primarily against young Hispanic men). See also Cassia Spohn, John Gruhl & Susan Welch, The Impact of the Ethnicity and Gender of Defendants on the Decision to Reject or Dismiss Felony Charges, 25 Criminology 175 (1987) (study of 33,000 felony cases between 1977 and 1980 to determine whether racial bias influenced prosecutors' decisions to decline felony charges; declinations occurred more frequently for white suspects after controlling for age, criminal record, and seriousness of offense). If racial discrimination in charging is indeed widespread, is it unrealistic to ask a defendant to make a prediscovery showing? Or is it necessary to limit litigation to the most egregious cases of racial discrimination in prosecutorial decision making? How egregious must the disparity be?

A factor that overlaps with race is neighborhood. As indicated in Problem 9-2, some laws that increase punishment for drug sales based on the proximity to school grounds have markedly different effects between urban and rural counties. In New Jersey, the legislature increased judicial discretion with respect to the application of such laws in response to a state sentencing commission report which found that only a miniscule percentage of the drug sales in such areas were made to juveniles and that the law largely impacted only Hispanics and Blacks, many of whom were non-violent offenders.

5. *Race and intermediate sanctions.* In Chapter 7, we indicated the depth of state budget problems and increasing state interest in intermediate sanctions in lieu of imprisonment. Recent studies, however, have indicated that minority offenders are less likely to receive such sanctions. Whether this is the case because judges consider them less suitable for such sanctions or because they view such sanctions as too onerous and therefore decide against them remains an open question. Brian D. Johnson & Stephanie M. DiPietro, The Power of Diversion: Intermediate Sanctions and Sentencing Disparity under Presumptive Guidelines, 50 Criminology 811 (2012).

6. *Influence of race on sentencing in the United Kingdom.* The United States is not the only nation in which the influence of race on sentencing has

ignited controversy. In a study of the English crown courts of Birmingham, Wolverhampton, Coventry, Warwick, and Stafford in 1989, Roger Hood noted that blacks were given prison sentences rather than a nonprison alternative more often than whites (56.6% of blacks sentenced, compared with 48.4% of whites). After attempting to account statistically for differences in cases based on arguably nonracial factors such as the seriousness of the offense or past criminal record, Hood concluded that race still had a minor influence on the custody decision: There was a "5 percent greater probability of a male black defendant being sentenced to custody than a white male." Race seemed to have more influence in cases of "medium seriousness": black defendants had a 13% higher probability of receiving custody in these cases. Roger Hood, Race and Sentencing: A Study in the Crown Court 198 (1992). A recent governmental set of data indicates that these racial disparities continue, if not widen, though the data set was not robust enough to indicate whether this was due to discrimination. Why is the specific racial difference Hood found of particular concern?

## PROBLEM 9-3.  THE CRACK-POWDER DIFFERENTIAL

By 1989 the Minnesota legislature was debating the sentencing of crack offenses. The legislators considered a bill that would make a person who possessed three or more grams of crack cocaine guilty of a third-degree offense. Under the same statute, a person who possessed ten or more grams of cocaine powder would be guilty of the same offense; someone who possessed fewer than ten grams of cocaine powder would be guilty of a fifth-degree offense. The bill became known as the "10-to-3 ratio" law.

The sponsors of the bill argued that this structure facilitated prosecution of street-level drug dealers. Law enforcement officers who testified at legislative hearings suggested that three grams of crack and ten grams of powder indicated a level at which dealing, not merely using, took place. A person convicted of selling 100 grams of crack may often be characterized as a midlevel dealer (someone who provides the drug to street-level retailers). By comparison, 100 grams of powder usually typifies a low-level retailer; 500 grams is more indicative of a midlevel dealer. But witnesses from the Department of Public Safety Office of Drug Policy contradicted these estimates for the typical amount of drugs carried by dealers, suggesting that most cocaine powder users are dealers as well.

The customary units of sales for the two drugs are also different. The typical unit of crack is a rock weighing .1 gram, which at the time sold for $20 to $25. The customary unit of powder is the 8-ball, one-eighth of an ounce or about 3.5 grams, which sold for about $350. Ten grams of powder cocaine could be easily converted into more than three grams of crack.

Sponsors of the bill echoed Congress's argument that crack is more addictive and dangerous than cocaine powder, and witnesses at the hearings supported this contention. But other witnesses pointed out that crack and powder cocaine have the same active ingredient and produce the same type of pharmacological effects. The difference in effect between the two drugs stems from the fact that cocaine powder is sniffed through the nostrils while crack cocaine is smoked. If powder cocaine is dissolved and injected, it is just as addictive as crack.

As a member of the Minnesota legislature, would you have supported the 10-to-3 ratio bill? What else would you like to have known before you vote? Compare State v. Russell, 477 N.W.2d 886 (Minn. 1991).

## NOTES

1. *Constitutional challenges to punishment differentials: majority position.* Racial disparities in the application of death penalty laws highlight several distinct forms of discrimination. A law can be discriminatory in intent, either at the point of creation or when it is applied. Some laws have racially discriminatory effects, even though the people who create and enforce the law do not intend to burden one racial group more than another and even though they apply the law with complete evenhandedness. These effects occur when the criminal sanctions apply to behavior that people of one race engage in more often than people of other races. Would it ever be unconstitutional for a legislature to criminalize conduct when one racial group is more likely to engage in it?

A number of defendants convicted of trafficking in crack cocaine have argued for a downward departure from the guideline sentence (or an invalidation of the relevant guidelines and statutes) based on an equal protection claim. Federal courts have uniformly rejected this assertion, reasoning that any disparate racial impact of the crack cocaine statutes and guidelines on African Americans was unintentional. See, e.g., United States v. Reece, 994 F.2d 277 (6th Cir. 1993) (per curiam); United States v. Thomas, 900 F.2d 37 (4th Cir. 1990). While not often addressing such claims, high state courts have also usually rejected the constitutional challenges.

2. *Legislative response.* The Minnesota Supreme Court struck down the legislation described in Problem 9-3 based on the state's equal protection clause in State v. Russell, 477 N.W.2d 886 (Minn. 1991). The legislature responded by increasing the penalties for powder to equal the former penalties for crack. Minn. Stat. §152.021-023. The crack-powder differential has received attention in other states as well. In 2005 the Connecticut legislature equalized powder and crack cocaine sentences. So did South Carolina. Nicole D. Porter & Valerie Wright, The Sentencing Project, Cracked Justice (Mar. 2011).

3. *Crack and cocaine sentences in the federal system.* In 1986 Congress passed the Anti-Drug Abuse Act to increase the penalties for various drug crimes. The new law imposed heavier penalties on cocaine base (crack) than on cocaine powder, a relationship later known as the "100-to-1 ratio." An offense involving mixtures weighing 5 grams or more containing cocaine base was subject to the same punishment as an offense involving mixtures weighing 500 grams or more containing cocaine powder.

Congress considered crack cocaine to be more dangerous than cocaine powder because of crack's potency, its more highly addictive nature, and its greater accessibility because of its relatively low cost. Some of the impetus for the federal law came from the news media. Stories associated the use of crack cocaine with social maladies such as gang violence and parental neglect among user groups. Critics of the federal law, however, argued that these social problems resulted not from the drug itself but from the disadvantaged social and economic environment in places where the drug is often used.

The increased penalties for crack meant that African American defendants received heavier penalties than whites for possession and sale of cocaine. More than 90% of all people arrested for sale or possession of crack were African American; roughly 80% of all people arrested for sale or possession of powder cocaine were white.

Proposals to reduce this ratio flared into combustible debates several times over the years. In 1994 Congress ordered the U.S. Sentencing Commission to report on cocaine punishment policies in the federal system. The following year the commission issued a report attacking the 100-to-1 quantity ratio and recommending instead a 1-to-1 crack-powder quantity ratio, to be achieved by lowering the penalties for crack while punishing behavior associated with crack offenses more severely.

The commission's proposed ratio came under attack from legislators across the political spectrum. In 1995 Congress, for the first time in the history of the commission, voted to override a proposed amendment to the sentencing guidelines.

In May 2007, the commission unanimously adopted an amendment that abandoned the 100-to-1 ratio and modestly reduced crack cocaine guideline levels across the board, even though mandatory minimum penalty statutes remained in place to trump the guideline sentences in some cases. In the original guidelines, the commission established guideline ranges that were set above applicable mandatory minimum penalties for crack set by Congress. The 2007 amendment reduced the base offense level for crack cocaine offenses so that the sentencing range includes, rather than exceeds, any applicable statutory mandatory minimum.

After reviewing the statutory purposes of sentencing under 18 U.S.C. §3553(a), the scientific and medical literature, and its own extensive research into sentencing patterns in drug cases, the commission found that the existing crack penalties failed in several respects:

(1)   The current quantity-based penalties overstate the relative harmfulness of crack cocaine compared to powder cocaine.

(2)   The current quantity-based penalties sweep too broadly and apply most often to lower level offenders.

(3)   The current quantity-based penalties overstate the seriousness of most crack cocaine offenses and fail to provide adequate proportionality.

(4)   The current severity of crack cocaine penalties mostly impacts minorities.

Report to the Congress: Cocaine and Federal Sentencing Policy 8 (2007) (available at http://www.ussc.gov/r_congress/cocaine2007.pdf). The revised guidelines use different ratios at different offense levels, with higher powder-to-crack ratios operating at higher offense levels. The commission estimated that its modifications to the guidelines would affect 69.7% of crack cocaine offenses and would reduce the average sentence for all crack cocaine offenses from 121 months to 106 months. The commission also urged Congress to revise the mandatory minimum penalties for crack cocaine to "focus the penalties more closely on serious and major traffickers" and to exclude simple possession of crack from the reach of any mandatory penalty.

This amendment attracted relatively little congressional attention, and took effect on November 1, 2007. Thereafter in December 2007, the Sentencing Commission voted unanimously to give retroactive effect to this amendment, effective on March 3, 2008. As a result of these actions, approximately 1500 inmates became eligible for immediate release and approximately 16,000 received a sentence reduction of two years on average in the following years.

What explains the different political outcomes in 1995 and 2007? Did the commission manage the 2007 process more effectively, or did an overall change in the political atmosphere or practical experience with drug sentencing make the difference? As for the merits of the proposal, what might explain the use of a ratio between powder and crack that varies depending on the seriousness of the offense?

In August 2010, the Fair Sentencing Act of 2010 became law. The federal statute reduced the disparity between mandatory minimums applying to crack and powder cocaine sentencing. The new statutory law reduces the crack-powder sentencing disparity from 100-to-1 under the former law to about 18-to-1 by raising the amounts of crack needed to trigger applicable mandatory minimum sentencing terms. As a result of the legislation, the U.S. Sentencing Commission promulgated new guidelines that applied the lower sentencing threshold but also included a list of aggravating and mitigating factors Congress wished to have reflected in revised crack sentencing guidelines. In a recent decision, the U.S. Supreme Court found the new law to apply when the crime had been committed before its passage but the defendant was to be sentenced after adoption. Dorsey v. United States, 567 U.S. ____ (2012).

4. *Crack sentencing after* Booker. As we saw in Chapter 3, the Supreme Court in United States v. Booker, 543 U.S. 220 (2005), ruled that the federal sentencing guidelines could not compel federal sentencing judges to impose the sentences that were indicated as "presumptive" under the guidelines. On the other hand, appellate courts were still allowed to review sentences for "reasonableness." In Kimbrough v. United States, 552 U.S. 85 (2007), the Court upheld a district court's decision to go outside the applicable guideline range in crack cocaine cases if it found the sentence to be imposed "greater than necessary, to comply with" the statutory purposes of sentencing.

5. *Race and crack.* Are racial differentials the central issue in the crack-powder punishment debate, or are they rather a by-product of social structure? Do different parts of the criminal world just happen to be controlled by groups of a particular race or ethnicity, as the analogy to the use of racketeering laws against the Mafia suggests? Or do you find convincing the position that, in effect, racially disproportionate effects (but not intent) justify reworking the system to start with a 1-to-1 quantity ratio?

In an excerpt reprinted in the first part of this section, Michael Tonry asserted that politicians pursued the war on drugs with full knowledge that "the greater burden of punishment [would be] borne by blacks. Crime control politicians wanted more people in prison and knew that a larger proportion of them would be black." Is this the sort of discriminatory intent that could form the basis for an equal protection challenge? Does this argument create a politically viable basis for revising penalties for drug offenses?

## B.  NATIVE PEOPLES

The concept of race is being undermined by the growing diversity of racialized identities. The most prominent example is professional golfer Tiger Woods. Nevertheless, race remains a powerful concept in U.S. legal discourse. Equality is constitutionally guaranteed, and limits on unequal treatment are reinforced in statutes and rules. Congress required the U.S. Sentencing Commission to "assure that the guidelines and policy statements are entirely neutral as to the race, sex, national origin, creed, and socioeconomic status of offenders." 28 U.S.C. §994(d). In accordance with this mandate, the guidelines state unequivocally that race, sex, national origin, creed, religion, and socioeconomic status "are not relevant in the determination of a sentence." U.S. Sentencing Guidelines Manual §5H1.10. Should national origin never be relevant in a sentence determination?

The strong statements of equal treatment, grounded in constitutional principle, contrast sharply with the social realities of Native Americans. This contrast generates dilemmas for courts trying to balance the defendants they see with the constitutional, statutory, and guideline nondiscrimination provisions that seem to prohibit the recognition of racial and ethnic differences.

> ## *Native Americans in South Dakota: An Erosion of Confidence in the Justice System*
> ### South Dakota Advisory Committee to the United States Civil Rights Commission, Mar. 2000

*South Dakota Demographics.*   . . . The estimated white population in South Dakota is 669,007, or 90.6 percent. American Indians are by far the largest minority group, making up 8 percent (59,292) of the population. Only Alaska and New Mexico have larger percentages of American Indian residents. . . .

*Native Americans in South Dakota.*   Nationwide, American Indians number approximately 1.2 million, with 900,000 living on or near Indian reservations. . . . South Dakota's nine reservations vary in size from Lower Brule, with about 1,200 residents, to Pine Ridge, with more than 30,000, making it the second largest reservation in the United States.

*Economic Conditions.*   Despite a booming economy, nationwide half of the potential work force in Indian Country is unemployed. For American Indians in

South Dakota the statistics are even worse. More than 50 percent of the labor force was unemployed in 1997 on 8 of the 9 reservations in the state, with unemployment reaching as high as 85 percent at Yankton and 80 percent at Cheyenne River.

Of the 10 poorest counties in the United States in 1990, 4 were on Indian reservations in South Dakota. The poorest county in the Nation is Shannon County, which includes much of Pine Ridge Reservation: 63.1 percent of county residents have incomes that fall below the poverty line. The average annual income for families living on Pine Ridge is just $3,700.

The effects of poverty are far reaching. According to the director of [the Bureau of Indian Affairs' (BIA's)] Great Plains Regional Office, on South Dakota's reservations "economic depression has manifested itself in the form of suicides, alcohol and drug abuse, juvenile gangs, and dropping out of school, to physical abuse, sexual abuse, and child abuse."

*Health.* On average, men in Bangladesh can expect to live longer than Native American men in South Dakota. A study by the Harvard School of Health in conjunction with health statisticians from the Centers for Disease Control found that Native American men living in six South Dakota counties had the shortest life expectancy in the Nation. . . . Indian men in South Dakota . . . usually live only into their mid-50s. . . .

In 1993, age-adjusted death rates for the following causes were considerably higher for American Indians [than for the general population]: alcoholism, 579 percent greater; tuberculosis, 475 percent; diabetes mellitus, 231 percent; accidents, 212 percent; suicide, 70 percent; pneumonia and influenza, 61 percent; and homicide, 41 percent. Further, infant mortality in Indian Country is double the national average, and Pine Ridge Reservation has the highest infant mortality rate in the Nation.

*Crime.* In an October 1997 report, the Justice Department's Criminal Division concluded "there is a public safety crisis in Indian Country." While most of the Nation has witnessed a drastic reduction in serious crime over the past 7 years, on Indian reservations crime is spiraling upwards. Between 1992 and 1996, the overall crime rate dropped about 17 percent, and homicides were down 22 percent. For the same period, however, the Bureau of Indian Affairs reported that murders on America's Indian reservations rose sharply. Some tribes, the Justice Department report says, "have murder rates that far exceed those of urban areas known for their struggles against violent crime." And other violent crimes parallel the rise in homicide.

Tribal law enforcement agencies do not have the resources to meet their growing caseloads. The Criminal Division's report concluded, "The single most glaring problem is a lack of adequate resources in Indian Country. Any solution requires a substantial infusion of new money in addition to existing funds." A chronic shortage of personnel plagues most agencies. For example, in 1996 Indian Country residents were served by less than one-half the number of officers provided to small non-Indian communities. Tribal officers are also in dire need of training. According to the BIA, no reservation in South Dakota has a fully staffed, adequately trained law enforcement program.

[A 1999 study by the Bureau of Justice Statistics found] that American Indians experience per capita rates of violence which are more than twice those of the U.S. population. From 1992 through 1996 the average annual rate of violent victimizations among Indians 12 years and older was 124 per 1,000 residents, compared with 61 for blacks, 49 for whites, and 29 for Asians. The rate of violent crime experienced by American Indian women is nearly 50 percent higher than that reported by black males.

**Annual Average Rate of Violent Victimization by Race of Victim, 1992-96**
*Number of victimizations per 1,000 persons age 12 or older in each racial group*

|                        | All Races | American Indian | White | Black | Asian |
|------------------------|-----------|-----------------|-------|-------|-------|
| Violent victimizations | 50        | 124             | 49    | 61    | 29    |
| Rape/ sexual assault   | 2         | 7               | 2     | 3     | 1     |
| Robbery                | 6         | 12              | 5     | 13    | 7     |
| Aggravated assault     | 11        | 35              | 10    | 16    | 6     |
| Simple assault         | 31        | 70              | 32    | 30    | 15    |

The report also found that in 7 out of 10 violent victimizations of American Indians the assailant was someone of a different race, a substantially higher incidence of interracial violence than experienced by white or black victims. Among white victims, 69 percent of the offenders were white; similarly, black victims are most likely to be victimized by a black assailant (81 percent). For American Indian victims of rape/sexual assault, the offender is described as white in 82 percent of the cases.

Alcohol is more often a factor in crimes committed by and against American Indians than for other races. Seventy percent of Indians in local jails for violent crimes had been drinking when they committed the offense, nearly double the rate for the general population. In 55 percent of violent crimes against American Indians, the victim said the offender was under the influence of alcohol and/or drugs. The offender's use of alcohol is less likely for white and black victims (44 and 35 percent, respectively). Other important findings of the study are as follows:

- The arrest rate for alcohol-related offenses among American Indians (drunken driving, liquor law violations and public drunkenness) was more than double that for the total population during 1996. However the drug arrest rate was lower than for other races.
- Almost four in 10 American Indians held in local jails had been charged with a public order offense—most commonly driving while intoxicated.
- During 1996 the American Indian arrest rate for youth violence was about the same as that for white youths.
- On any given day an estimated one in 25 American Indians 18 years old and older is under the jurisdiction of the nation's criminal justice

system. This is 2.4 times the rate for whites and 9.3 times the per capita rate for Asians but about half the rate for blacks.

- The number of American Indians per capita confined in the state and federal prisons is about 38 percent above the national average. However, the rate of confinement in local jails is estimated to be nearly 4 times the national average.


MAJOR CONCERNS AND CONCLUSIONS

1. Many Native Americans in South Dakota have little or no confidence in the criminal justice system and believe that the administration of justice at the Federal and State levels is permeated by racism. There is a strongly held perception among Native Americans that there is a dual system of justice and that race is a critical factor in determining how law enforcement and justice functions are carried out. This perception includes a belief that violent crimes involving Native Americans are dealt with differently from those involving whites. It is believed that crimes perpetrated by whites against Indians are investigated and prosecuted with less vigor than those committed by Indians against whites. . . . Information was received by the Advisory Committee suggesting disparities in many aspects of the criminal justice system, including law enforcement stops and racial profiling, arrests, prosecutions, legal representation, and sentencing. . . .

6. The Advisory Committee heard many complaints concerning Federal sentencing guidelines. It was alleged that crimes prosecuted in the Federal system require harsher sentences than similar offenses prosecuted in State courts. Because of the much broader Federal jurisdiction applicable to crimes committed by Native Americans in Indian Country, disparate sentencing — with more severe punishment for Native Americans — may result. This serves to reinforce and strengthen the perception of unequal justice for American Indians. . . .

8. Native Americans are underrepresented in the employment of all institutions involved in the administration of justice, at the Federal, State, and local levels. They are also largely excluded from elected positions and other decision-making positions that govern the administration of justice. . . .

13. There appear to be limited legal resources available for Native Americans in South Dakota. Victims of discrimination often find it difficult to secure legal representation. Court-appointed defense attorney systems and local public defender programs have been described as inadequate, due to inexperience, lack of funding, and potential conflicts of interest. There are also few Native Americans in the legal professions. National civil rights legal organizations are not easily accessible, and there are few such programs at the State level. . . .

While some have overcome the obstacles and achieved great success, most American Indians have been left behind. For the most part, Native Americans are very much separate and unequal members of society. Thus, it is not surprising that they are underrepresented in terms of economic status and overrepresented in the population of the State's jails, juvenile facilities, and prisons. Systemic, institutionalized, and historic discrimination disadvantage Native Americans in many ways, and therefore the problems they encounter when caught up in the criminal justice system are wholly consistent with other forms of discrimination.

Despair is not too strong a word to characterize the emotional feelings of many Native Americans who believe they live in a hostile environment. . . .

## PROBLEM 9-4.  HARD WORKER

Following an evening of heavy drinking, David Big Crow and his wife, Margaret, returned from a dance to their trailer home near Porcupine, South Dakota, on the Pine Ridge Indian Reservation. They were met there by Donald Twiss and several other friends who had attended the same dance and who also had been drinking. The group gathered in the kitchen and began playing a drinking game called quarter pitch.

Some time later, David left the kitchen. When he returned, he fell on Donald, who had been asleep on the floor. Donald awoke feeling a sharp pain above his eye and bleeding from his forehead. David stood next to him with a piece of firewood in his hand, making derogatory remarks about the Twiss family. The two of them fought until Donald left the room. At that point, David hit Margaret with a folding chair. She was taken to the hospital and remained unconscious until noon the next day.

Big Crow was convicted of assault with a dangerous weapon and assault resulting in serious bodily injury. Under the Guidelines, aggravated assault has a base offense level of 15. Use of a dangerous weapon and the infliction of serious bodily injury increase the offense level by 8 levels for a total of 23. U.S.S.G. §2A2.2(b)(2)(B), 2A2.2(b)(3)(B). Big Crow had no criminal record, and this gave him a criminal history category of I. The United States Probation Officer's presentence investigation report recommended that Big Crow receive 2 points for acceptance of responsibility, and suggested that a departure from the Guideline range might be warranted because Big Crow's offense was out of character and he had been a decent citizen living in a difficult environment. An offense level of 21 carries a range of 37-46 months.

As the sentencing judge in this case, you have received letters written on Big Crow's behalf by community leaders and a Bureau of Indian Affairs official. The letter writers include a local school principal, the president of the Oglala Sioux Tribe, and the agency safety officer of the Bureau of Indian Affairs. The presentence investigation report also noted that Big Crow has a positive reputation in his community and is well liked by his employers and area law enforcement personnel.

Big Crow, who was 23 at the time of his offense, has worked steadily since the age of 17. With his wife's help, he provides more than adequately for the needs of their family, which includes two children. During the three years before this offense, Big Crow worked as a forestry aid and firefighter for the Bureau of Indian Affairs. His employer indicated that Big Crow was "a hard worker in what is not too pleasant a job." He expressed willingness to hold Big Crow's job for him until he is released from custody. The unemployment rate on the Pine Ridge Indian Reservation is 72%. Per-capita annual income on the reservation is estimated at $1,042.

In your experience, extreme intoxication appears to play a role in a large number of crimes committed in the Indian country. Will the role of alcohol in Big Crow's offense affect the sentence you impose? Is his lack of a prior criminal record a basis for imposing a sentence below the Guideline range? Does his employment history, in the context of this community, convince you to sentence outside the Guideline range?

Guideline policy statements indicate that previous employment record, family ties and responsibilities, and community ties are "not ordinarily relevant in determining whether a sentence should be outside the guidelines." U.S.S.G. §5H1.5, 5H1.6 (policy statements). A policy statement in the Guidelines states that race, national origin, and socioeconomic status are not relevant in the determination of a sentence. U.S.S.G. §5H1.10 (policy statement). On the other hand, the legislative history of the Sentencing Reform Act notes that the "requirement of neutrality . . . is not a requirement of blindness." S. Rep. No. 225, 98th Cong., 1st Sess. 171 n.409 (1983). Cf. United States v. David Big Crow, 898 F.2d 1326 (8th Cir. 1990).

Perhaps it is the principle of equality itself that should be moderated to take account of racial, ethnic, biological, social, or historical circumstances. The Canadian Charter, for example, mandates consideration of the disadvantaged circumstances in which Native Americans find themselves at sentencing. Does this make for fairer sentences in light of the extreme economic disadvantage of aborigines? Should all those who are defined as aborigines benefit from such special consideration, or is it designed only for those on reservations? Is the differentiating characteristic race or race "plus" some other feature(s)? Consider the solution offered by the legislature and high court in Canada. Alternatively, should we move away from equality of punishment and instead consider equality as a pre-conviction matter, i.e., as an "equal threat of investigation and prosecution" rather than an "equal threat of punishment"? James Q. Whitman, Equality in Criminal Law: The Two Divergent Western Roads, 1 J. Leg. Analysis 119 (Winter 2009).

## *Jamie Tanis Gladue v. R.*
### [1999] S.C.R. 688

Cory and Iacobucci, JJ.

[Criminal Code §718.2(e)] provides that all available sanctions other than imprisonment that are reasonable in the circumstances should be considered for all offenders, with particular attention to the circumstances of aboriginal offenders. This appeal must consider how this provision should be interpreted and applied.

### Factual and Procedural Background

. . . The appellant and the victim Reuben Beaver started to live together in 1993, when the appellant was 17 years old. Thereafter they had a daughter, Tanita. . . . By September 1995, the appellant and Beaver were engaged to be married, and the appellant was five months pregnant with their second child. . . .

In the early evening of September 16, 1995, the appellant was celebrating her 19th birthday. She and Reuben Beaver, who was then 20, were drinking beer with some friends and family members in the townhouse complex. The appellant suspected that Beaver was having an affair with her older sister, Tara. During the course of the evening she voiced those suspicions to her friends. The appellant was obviously angry with Beaver. She said, "the next time he fools around on me, I'll kill him." . . .

The appellant and Beaver returned separately to their townhouse and they started to quarrel. During the argument, the appellant confronted him with his infidelity and he told her that she was fat and ugly and not as good as the others. . . .

Mr. Gretchin, [a neighbor,] saw the appellant run toward Beaver with a large knife in her hand and, as she approached him, she told him that he had better run. Mr. Gretchin heard Beaver shriek in pain and saw him collapse in a pool of blood. The appellant had stabbed Beaver once in the left chest, and the knife had penetrated his heart. As the appellant went by on her return to her apartment, Mr. Gretchin heard her say, "I got you, you fucking bastard." The appellant was described as jumping up and down as if she had tagged someone. Mr. Gretchin said she did not appear to realize what she had done. At the time of the stabbing, the appellant had a blood-alcohol content of between 155 and 165 milligrams of alcohol in 100 millilitres of blood.

[After] a jury had been selected, the appellant entered a plea of guilty to manslaughter. [The government had evidence] that Beaver had subjected the appellant to some physical abuse in June 1994, while the appellant was pregnant with their daughter Tanita. Beaver was convicted of assault, and was given a 15-day intermittent sentence with one year's probation. The neighbour, Mr. Gretchin, told police that the noises emanating from the appellant's and Beaver's apartment suggested a fight. . . . Bruises later observed on the appellant's arm and in the collarbone area were consistent with her having been in a physical altercation on the night of the stabbing. However, the trial judge found that the facts as presented before him did not warrant a finding that the appellant was a "battered or fearful wife."

The appellant's sentencing took place 17 months after the stabbing. Pending her trial [she] took counselling for alcohol and drug abuse at Tillicum Haus Native Friendship Centre in Nanaimo, and completed Grade 10 and was about to start Grade 11. After the stabbing, the appellant was diagnosed as suffering from a hyperthyroid condition, which was said to produce an exaggerated reaction to any emotional situation. . . .

In his submissions on sentence at trial, the appellant's counsel did not raise the fact that the appellant was an aboriginal offender but, when asked by the trial judge whether in fact the appellant was an aboriginal person, replied that she was Cree. When asked by the trial judge whether the town of McLennan, Alberta, where the appellant grew up, was an aboriginal community, defence counsel responded: "it's just a regular community." No other submissions were made at the sentencing hearing on the issue of the appellant's aboriginal heritage. Defence counsel requested a suspended sentence or a conditional sentence of imprisonment. Crown counsel argued in favour of a sentence of between three and five years' imprisonment. The appellant was sentenced to three years' imprisonment and to a ten-year weapons prohibition. . . .

The trial judge noted that both the appellant and the deceased were aboriginal, but stated that they were living in an urban area off-reserve and not "within the aboriginal community as such." He found that there were not any special circumstances arising from their aboriginal status that he should take into consideration. He stated that the offence was a very serious one, for which the appropriate sentence was three years' imprisonment with a ten-year weapons prohibition.

The appellant appealed her sentence of three years' imprisonment [on the ground that] the trial judge failed to give appropriate consideration to the appellant's circumstances as an aboriginal offender. The appellant also sought to adduce fresh evidence at her appeal regarding her efforts since the killing to maintain links with her aboriginal heritage. . . .

### INTERPRETATION OF SENTENCING PROVISION

The issue in this appeal is the proper interpretation and application to be given to §718.2(e) of the Criminal Code. The provision reads as follows:

> A court that imposes a sentence shall also take into consideration the following principles: . . . (e) available sanctions other than imprisonment that are reasonable in the circumstances should be considered for all offenders, with particular attention to the circumstances of aboriginal offenders. . . .

As a general principle, §718.2(e) applies to all offenders, and states that imprisonment should be the penal sanction of last resort. Prison is to be used only where no other sanction or combination of sanctions is appropriate to the offence and the offender.

The next question is the meaning to be attributed to the words "with particular attention to the circumstances of aboriginal offenders." The phrase cannot be an instruction for judges to pay "more" attention when sentencing aboriginal offenders. It would be unreasonable to assume that Parliament intended sentencing judges to prefer certain categories of offenders over others. Neither can the phrase be merely an instruction to a sentencing judge to consider the circumstances of aboriginal offenders just as she or he would consider the circumstances of any other offender. There would be no point in adding a special reference to aboriginal offenders if this was the case. Rather, the logical meaning to be derived from the special reference to the circumstances of aboriginal offenders, juxtaposed as it is against a general direction to consider "the circumstances" for all offenders, is that sentencing judges should pay particular attention to the circumstances of aboriginal offenders *because those circumstances are unique*, and different from those of non-aboriginal offenders. The fact that the reference to aboriginal offenders is contained in §718.2(e) . . . dealing with restraint in the use of imprisonment, suggests that there is something different about aboriginal offenders which may specifically make imprisonment a less appropriate or less useful sanction. . . .

Section 718 now sets out the purpose of sentencing in the following terms:

The fundamental purpose of sentencing is to contribute, along with crime prevention initiatives, to respect for the law and the maintenance of a just, peaceful and safe society by imposing just sanctions that have one or more of the following objectives:

(a)  to denounce unlawful conduct;
(b)  to deter the offender and other persons from committing offences;
(c)  to separate offenders from society, where necessary;
(d)  to assist in rehabilitating offenders;
(e)  *to provide reparations for harm done to victims or to the community;* and
(f)  *to promote a sense of responsibility in offenders, and acknowledgment of the harm done to victims and to the community.*[Emphasis added.]

Clearly, §718 is, in part, a restatement of the basic sentencing aims, which are listed in paras. (a) through (d). What are new, though, are paras. (e) and (f), which along with para. (d) focus upon the restorative goals of repairing the harms suffered by individual victims and by the community as a whole, promoting a sense of responsibility and an acknowledgment of the harm caused on the part of the offender, and attempting to rehabilitate or heal the offender. [As] a general matter restorative justice involves some form of restitution and reintegration into the community. The need for offenders to take responsibility for their actions is central to the sentencing process. Restorative sentencing goals do not usually correlate with the use of prison as a sanction. In our view, Parliament's choice to include (e) and (f) alongside the traditional sentencing goals must be understood as evidencing an intention to expand the parameters of the sentencing analysis for all offenders. . . .

The parties and interveners agree that the purpose of §718.2(e) is to respond to the problem of overincarceration in Canada, and to respond, in particular, to the more acute problem of the disproportionate incarceration of aboriginal peoples. They also agree that one of the roles of §718.2(e) . . . is to encourage sentencing judges to apply principles of restorative justice alongside or in the place of other, more traditional sentencing principles when making sentencing determinations. . . .

Although the United States has by far the highest rate of incarceration among industrialized democracies, at over 600 inmates per 100,000 population, Canada's rate of approximately 130 inmates per 100,000 population places it second or third highest. Moreover, the rate at which Canadian courts have been imprisoning offenders has risen sharply in recent years, although there has been a slight decline of late. This record of incarceration rates obviously cannot instil a sense of pride. . . .

If overreliance upon incarceration is a problem with the general population, it is of much greater concern in the sentencing of aboriginal Canadians. In the mid-1980s, aboriginal people were about 2 percent of the population of Canada, yet they made up 10 percent of the penitentiary population. In Manitoba and Saskatchewan, aboriginal people constituted something between 6 and 7 percent of the population, yet in Manitoba they represented 46 percent of the provincial admissions and in Saskatchewan 60 percent. The situation has not improved in recent years. By 1997, aboriginal peoples constituted closer to 3 percent of the population of Canada and amounted to 12 percent of all federal inmates. The situation continues to be particularly worrisome in Manitoba, where in 1995-96 they made up 55 percent of admissions to provincial correctional facilities, and in Saskatchewan, where they made up 72 percent of admissions. A similar, albeit less drastic situation prevails in Alberta and British Columbia. . . .

Not surprisingly, the excessive imprisonment of aboriginal people is only the tip of the iceberg insofar as the estrangement of the aboriginal peoples from the Canadian criminal justice system is concerned. Aboriginal people are over-represented in virtually all aspects of the system. As this Court recently noted in R. v. Williams, [1998] 1 S.C.R. 1128, at para. 58, there is widespread bias against aboriginal people within Canada, and "[there] is evidence that this widespread racism has translated into systemic discrimination in the criminal justice system." . . . The figures are stark and reflect what may fairly be termed a crisis in the Canadian criminal justice system. [Section 718.2(e)] may properly be seen as Parliament's direction to members of the judiciary to inquire into the causes of the problem and to endeavour to remedy it, to the extent that a remedy is possible through the sentencing process.

It is clear that sentencing innovation by itself cannot remove the causes of aboriginal offending and the greater problem of aboriginal alienation from the criminal justice system. The unbalanced ratio of imprisonment for aboriginal offenders flows from a number of sources, including poverty, substance abuse, lack of education, and the lack of employment opportunities for aboriginal people. It arises also from bias against aboriginal people and from an unfortunate institutional approach that is more inclined to refuse bail and to impose more and longer prison terms for aboriginal offenders. There are many aspects of this sad situation which cannot be addressed in these reasons. What can and must be addressed, though, is the limited role that sentencing judges will play in remedying injustice against aboriginal peoples in Canada. Sentencing judges are among those decision-makers who have the power to influence the treatment of aboriginal offenders in the justice system. They determine most directly whether an aboriginal offender will go to jail, or whether other sentencing options may be employed which will play perhaps a stronger role in restoring a sense of balance to the offender, victim, and community, and in preventing future crime.

How are sentencing judges to play their remedial role? The words of §718.2(e) instruct the sentencing judge to pay particular attention to the circumstances of aboriginal offenders, with the implication that those circumstances are significantly different from those of non-aboriginal offenders. . . . The background factors which figure prominently in the causation of crime by aboriginal offenders are by now well known. Years of dislocation and economic development have translated, for many aboriginal peoples, into low incomes, high unemployment, lack of opportunities and options, lack or irrelevance of education, substance abuse, loneliness, and community fragmentation. These and other factors contribute to a higher incidence of crime and incarceration.

[The] circumstances of aboriginal offenders differ from those of the majority because many aboriginal people are victims of systemic and direct discrimination, many suffer the legacy of dislocation, and many are substantially affected by poor social and economic conditions. Moreover, as has been emphasized repeatedly in studies and commission reports, aboriginal offenders are, as a result of these unique systemic and background factors, more adversely affected by incarceration and less likely to be "rehabilitated" thereby, because the internment milieu is often culturally inappropriate and regrettably discrimination towards them is so often rampant in penal institutions. . . .

In cases where [unique background and systemic] factors have played a significant role [in bringing the particular offender before the courts], it is incumbent upon the sentencing judge to consider these factors in evaluating whether imprisonment would actually serve to deter, or to denounce crime in a sense that would be meaningful to the community of which the offender is a member. In many instances, more restorative sentencing principles will gain primary relevance precisely because the prevention of crime as well as individual and social healing cannot occur through other means.

Closely related to the background and systemic factors which have contributed to an excessive aboriginal incarceration rate are the different conceptions of appropriate sentencing procedures and sanctions held by aboriginal people. A significant problem experienced by aboriginal people who come into contact with the criminal justice system is that the traditional sentencing ideals of deterrence, separation, and denunciation are often far removed from the understanding of sentencing held by these offenders and their community. [Most] traditional aboriginal conceptions of sentencing place a *primary* emphasis upon the ideals of restorative justice. This tradition is extremely important to the analysis under §718.2(e).

[Restorative] justice may be described as an approach to remedying crime in which it is understood that all things are interrelated and that crime disrupts the harmony which existed prior to its occurrence, or at least which it is felt should exist. The appropriateness of a particular sanction is largely determined by the needs of the victims, and the community, as well as the offender. The focus is on the human beings closely affected by the crime.

The existing overemphasis on incarceration in Canada may be partly due to the perception that a restorative approach is a more lenient approach to crime and that imprisonment constitutes the ultimate punishment. Yet in our view a sentence focussed on restorative justice is not necessarily a "lighter" punishment. . . .

In describing the effect of §718.2(e) in this way, we do not mean to suggest that, as a general practice, aboriginal offenders must always be sentenced in a manner which gives greatest weight to the principles of restorative justice, and less weight to goals such as deterrence, denunciation, and separation. It is unreasonable to assume that aboriginal peoples themselves do not believe in the importance of these latter goals, and even if they do not, that such goals must not predominate in appropriate cases. Clearly there are some serious offences and some offenders for which and for whom separation, denunciation, and deterrence are fundamentally relevant.

Yet, even where an offence is considered serious, the length of the term of imprisonment must be considered. In some circumstances the length of the sentence of an aboriginal offender may be less and in others the same as that of any other offender. Generally, the more violent and serious the offence the more likely it is as a practical reality that the terms of imprisonment for aboriginals and non-aboriginals will be close to each other or the same, even taking into account their different concepts of sentencing. . . .

How then is the consideration of §718.2(e) to proceed in the daily functioning of the courts? The manner in which the sentencing judge will carry out his or her statutory duty may vary from case to case. In all instances it will be necessary for the judge to take judicial notice of the systemic or background factors and the approach to sentencing which is relevant to aboriginal offenders. However, for each particular offence and offender it may be that some evidence will be required in order to assist the sentencing judge in arriving at a fit sentence. Where a particular offender does not wish such evidence to be adduced, the right to have particular attention paid to his or her circumstances as an aboriginal offender may be waived. Where there is no such waiver, it will be extremely helpful to the sentencing judge for counsel on both sides to adduce relevant evidence. . . .

However, even where counsel do not adduce this evidence, where for example the offender is unrepresented, it is incumbent upon the sentencing judge to attempt to acquire information regarding the circumstances of the offender as an aboriginal person. Whether the offender resides in a rural area, on a reserve or in an urban centre the sentencing judge must be made aware of alternatives to incarceration that exist whether inside or outside the aboriginal community of the particular offender. The alternatives existing in metropolitan areas must, as a matter of course, also be explored. Clearly the presence of an aboriginal offender will require special attention in pre-sentence reports. Beyond the use of the pre-sentence report, the sentencing judge may and should in appropriate circumstances and where practicable request that witnesses be called who may testify as to reasonable alternatives.

Similarly, where a sentencing judge at the trial level has not engaged in the duty imposed by §718.2(e) as fully as required, it is incumbent upon a court of appeal in considering an appeal against sentence on this basis to consider any fresh evidence which is relevant and admissible on sentencing. [Although] §718.2(e) does not impose a statutory duty upon the sentencing judge to provide reasons, it will be much easier for a reviewing court to determine whether and how attention was paid to the circumstances of the offender as an aboriginal person if at least brief reasons are given. . . .

The fact that a court is called upon to take into consideration the unique circumstances surrounding these different parties is not unfair to non-aboriginal people. Rather, the fundamental purpose of §718.2(e) is to treat aboriginal offenders fairly by taking into account their difference. . . .

Section 718.2(e) applies to all aboriginal offenders wherever they reside, whether on- or off-reserve, in a large city or a rural area. Indeed it has been observed that many aboriginals living in urban areas are closely attached to their culture. . . .

Based on the foregoing, the jail term for an aboriginal offender may in some circumstances be less than the term imposed on a non-aboriginal offender for the same offence. . . .

### APPLICATION OF PRINCIPLES

In most cases, errors such as those in the courts below would be sufficient to justify sending the matter back for a new sentencing hearing. It is difficult for this Court to determine a fit sentence for the appellant according to the suggested guidelines set out herein on the basis of the very limited evidence before us regarding the appellant's aboriginal background. However, as both the trial judge and all members of the Court of Appeal acknowledged, the offence in question is a most serious one, properly described . . . as a "near murder." Moreover, the offence involved domestic violence and a breach of the trust inherent in a spousal relationship. That aggravating factor must be taken into account in the sentencing of the aboriginal appellant as it would be for any offender. For that offence by this offender a sentence of three years' imprisonment was not unreasonable.

More importantly, the appellant was granted day parole on August 13, 1997, after she had served six months in the Burnaby Correctional Centre for Women. She was directed to reside with her father, to take alcohol and substance abuse counselling and to comply with the requirements of the Electronic Monitoring Program. On February 25, 1998, the appellant was granted full parole with the same conditions as the ones applicable to her original release on day parole.

In this case, the results of the sentence with incarceration for six months and the subsequent controlled release were in the interests of both the appellant and society. In these circumstances, we do not consider that it would be in the interests of justice to order a new sentencing hearing in order to canvass the appellant's circumstances as an aboriginal offender. . . .

## NOTES

1. *Aboriginal offenders in prison.*   The *Gladue* court recognized the disproportionate imprisonment of aboriginal offenders in Canada. In response to the problem, Parliament added Criminal Code §718.2(e). In Australia aborigines are also overrepresented in prisons. In fact, the racial disparities in Canada and Australia between aborigines and non-aborigines are worse than those between blacks and whites in the United States. What factors account for the high imprisonment rates of natives? Much of Australia's high aboriginal imprisonment rate has been blamed on mandatory sentencing laws for relatively minor property offenses. Why would mandatory sentences not lead to *greater* ethnic equality? Should the disparate impact on minority groups be a reason for abolishing such legislation?

2. *Aboriginal sentencing practices.*   In a later decision, Canada's highest court emphasized that in cases of aboriginal offenders sentencing judges must consider

> the types of sentencing procedures and sanctions which may be appropriate in the circumstances for the offender because of his or her particular Aboriginal heritage or connection. In particular, given that most traditional Aboriginal approaches place a primary emphasis on the goal of restorative justice, the alternative of community-based sanctions must be explored.
> R. v. Wells, [2000] S.C.R. 207, para. 53.

To what extent can and should U.S. courts consider the punishment practices of native courts? While some aboriginal groups have focused on restorative justice, others have used punishment practices that many today would consider torture. How should the courts accommodate considerations of traditional practice and modern human rights concerns? See, e.g., Barbara Creel, Tribal Court Convictions and the Federal Sentencing Guidelines: Respect for Tribal Courts and Tribal People in Federal Sentencing, 46 U.S.F. L. Rev. 37 (2011).

3. *Native Americans, blacks, and other minority offenders.* Data from the United States indicate that at least in some areas Native Americans appear to be treated unequally with respect to length of sentence and time served. See Richard Braunstein & Steve Feimer, South Dakota Criminal Justice: A Study of Racial Disparities, 48 South Dakota L. Rev. 171 (2003). In many countries with native populations, natives are not the only ones overrepresented in prison. Should the situation of native offenders be any more disconcerting than the situation of offenders from other racial groups? Why? To what extent can sentencing judges be expected to "fix" racial disparity at individualized sentencing hearings? Will such attempts not merely lead to other forms of injustice?

4. *Ethnicity.* Ethnicity has become an alternative to race in describing human diversity, but the term also carries deep ambiguities. Ethnicity focuses on the cultural distinctiveness of a group: country of origin, language, religion, food, and values all create a particular ethnic identity. Which of these characteristics are relevant and the extent to which one should be allowed to self-classify as a member of a particular ethnic group remain ambiguous. Ethnicity allows for distinctions within racial groups (blacks emigrating from the Caribbean, for example, differ from those hailing from the African continent), but it may also conceal racial differences (blacks and whites from Brazil are both considered Hispanics). Often ethnicity appears to be a substitute for national origin, but in fact the latter is usually limited to first- and possibly second-generation immigrant populations, though such categorization is likely to vary between countries.

5. *Culture and sentencing.* Offenders from some ethnic groups may be culturally conditioned or socialized not to enter guilty pleas. Since guilty pleas often result in a sentence reduction, offenders who insist on their right to trial may receive longer sentences. In imposing a sentence, should a court consider whether the choice of trial may be characteristic of the offender's ethnic group? If not, is the offender being punished for a cultural value that differs from that of mainstream society rather than for offense-relevant conduct? Australia's Crimes Act requires courts to consider the "cultural background" of an offender, including "ethnic, environmental and cultural matters." Would the insistence on going to trial be a cultural factor?

6. *Culture and victims.* Most crime is committed *within* a given racial or ethnic group. Sentencing patterns based on the offender's culture, therefore, often parallel the victims' ethnicity and culture. Do lower sentences based on offenders' cultural background devalue the suffering of their victims or indicate that the victims deserve less state protection?

7. *Principles of equality.*   U.S. law is based on principles of equality. All individuals, independent of their race, ethnicity, or national origin, should be treated the same. The federal sentencing guidelines as well as state sentencing regimes reflect this mantra. Such neutrality can lead to injustice, however, when the situations of individuals are so different that equal treatment in the criminal justice system merely magnifies the unequal treatment in other aspects of life.

As the preceding materials indicate, many Native Americans who commit offenses on reservations are tried in federal court and sentenced under the federal guidelines. Historically, the guarantee of criminal trials in federal courts was designed to protect Native Americans from discriminatory state courts. Today, however, when federal sentences are perceived as harsher than those in many states, Native Americans tend to consider themselves as being treated unfairly. While the guidelines appear to have decreased racial disparity within the federal system, federal courts have refused to undertake state-federal comparisons to determine whether a sentence is too harsh.

8. *Inequality and the state.*   In contrast to the current approach to race equality, an alternative sentencing system might deliberately take group differences into account. But considering group status at sentencing could undermine the concept of "one nation" and the fundamental equality of the victims of crime. It could also excuse the state's inability or unwillingness to equalize the social and economic starting points for all members of society.

## PROBLEM 9-5.   ALIEN STATUS

Peter Onwuemene, a Nigerian citizen, and other Nigerians participated in a nationwide automobile insurance fraud scheme that caused losses of about $1 million to several insurance companies. A member of the group would obtain liability insurance on an old car from 10 to 15 insurance companies. Subsequently, the policy owner would report a collision with an expensive, late-model car owned by another member of the group, who would claim damage to his car.

Onwuemene was charged with four counts of mail fraud. He pled guilty to one of the counts in return for the government's agreement to recommend dismissal of the others. Onwuemene faced a sentencing range under the federal sentencing guidelines of 6 to 12 months. The presentence investigation report recommended 6 months' incarceration and a work release program. At sentencing, Onwuemene agreed to pay restitution of $3,723.

The district court sentenced him to 12 months' imprisonment, the top of the sentencing range, because the crime was serious and could have resulted in a much greater loss if the victims had failed to discover it and because Onwuemene "failed or refused" to identify the other participants in the fraud. The court added:

> The other thing that I feel that warrants imposition at the high end of the guideline range: You are not a citizen of this country. This country was good enough to allow you to come in here and to confer upon you . . . a number of the benefits of this society, form of government, and its opportunities, and you repay that kindness by committing a crime like this. We have got enough criminals in the United States without importing any.

Onwuemene appeals. How should the appellate court rule? See United States v. Onwuemene, 933 F.2d 650 (8th Cir. 1991).

## NOTES

1. *Immigration status and sentencing.* Large-scale immigration into North America and Western Europe has caused an ever-increasing number of immigrants to become involved in the criminal justice system. May a court consider an offender's immigration status at sentencing? Because of the possibility (or even likelihood) of deportation, a court could impose a lesser sentence than it would on a citizen offender. Federal courts, however, have generally rejected downward departures based on a noncitizen's deportability. See, e.g., United States v. Restrepo, 999 F.2d 640 (2nd Cir. 1993); United States v. Lopez-Salas, 266 F.3d 842 (8th Cir. 2001). But see United States v. Gallo-Vasquez, 284 F.3d 780, 784 (7th Cir. 2002) (district court may depart downward when "defendant's status as a deportable alien . . . may lead to conditions of confinement, or other incidents of punishment, that are substantially more onerous than the framers of the guidelines contemplated in fixing the punishment range for the defendant's offense.").

Alternatively, a court may view an immigrant's offense as more heinous because he abused his guest status, as did the trial court in Problem 9-5. When judges explicitly refer to alien status, some federal courts have held that they are violating the Constitution by sentencing an offender on the basis of factors such as race, national origin, or alienage. See United States v. Onwuemene, 933 F.2d 650 (8th Cir. 1991) (consideration of defendant's alien status violates his constitutional rights); United States v. Borrero-Isaza, 887 F.2d 1349, 1352 (9th Cir. 1989) (imposing stricter sentence on defendant because of his national origin and alienage violated right to due process). One state court tried to impose a higher sentence on a member of an ethnic community:

> [S]ometimes it is necessary in sentencing to send a message to the community, and I am sending a message by this sentence to a small segment of the Albanian community that they now live in the United States and they are governed by our laws, and we are not going to tolerate whatever the customs may be in Albania, and that includes the customs of dealing with family members as well as the use of guns.

The appellate court considered this justification an impermissible consideration of defendant's national origin. People v. Gjidoda, 364 N.W.2d 698 (Mich. 1985). See also United States v. Trujillo-Castillon, 692 F.3d 575 (2012).

Courts have denied probation sentences to undocumented offenders who would be deported upon completion of their sentence because they are deemed a flight risk and cannot work legally in the United States. See, e.g., People v. Hernandez-Clavel, 186 P.3d 96 (2008), cert. granted, June 30, 2008, 2008 Colo. LEXIS 700. On the other hand, state courts have considered an offender's immigration status in crafting a sentence. See, e.g., State v. Svay, 828 A.2d 790, 791 (Me. 2003) ("immigration status and the effect that criminal convictions and criminal sentences can have on deportation are factors that a sentencing court can consider"); State v. Quintero Morelos, 137 P.3d 114 (Wash. Ct. App. 2006) (affirming reduction of sentence to less than a year to prevent deportation). Should immigration status generally be considered at sentencing in light of other consequences that may befall a non-citizen either directly or indirectly, such as denial of intermediate sanctions, restrictions on prison-based programming, and deportation. See Francesca Brody, Extracting Compassion from Confusion: Sentencing Noncitizens after *United States v. Booker*, 79 Fordham L. Rev. 2129 (2011).

2. *Noncitizen offenses.*   A number of immigration offenses, such as reentry of a convicted felon, can be committed only by noncitizens. Do such statutes not discriminate based on national origin? Because of increases in congressional funding and changes in law enforcement priorities and federal sentencing, between 2000 and 2010 the percentage of noncitizens sentenced in federal court increased by almost 15%, with the largest percentage of non-citizens convicted of immigration offenses or drug trafficking. About 85% of the offenders prosecuted for unlawfully entering or reentering the United States are Mexican nationals, and 78% of all federal immigration offenders hail from Mexico, according to U.S. Sentencing Commission data.

Felony re-entry offenders are now nationally able to benefit from the "fast-track" program, which allows them to receive a decreased sentence if they plead guilty and waive certain procedural rights. Before the expansion to all federal districts, the availability of this program only in border districts caused substantial sentencing disparity nationally.

3. *Immigrants and crime.*   With the growth of immigration, new groups add to the existing racial and ethnic diversity in the United States and Europe. Overall first-generation immigrants have lower crime rates than the native population. Nevertheless, in Western Europe and North America crime and incarceration rates for members of some minority groups greatly exceed those for the majority population. The same minority groups are also socially and economically disadvantaged (but not all disadvantaged groups are also high-crime groups). While some discrimination may be present, the principal cause of the disparities appears to be differences in offending patterns rather than official bias. How should the criminal justice system react to such increasing diversity and disparity?

One approach would be to exempt certain immigrant groups from the coverage of select substantive criminal law provisions that are legally and culturally foreign to them. So far, no one has seriously considered this idea. Another notion is to consider an offender's ethnicity at the sentencing stage. For example, when a recent immigrant from a country that allows the marriage of adult men to teenage girls is convicted of statutory rape, the sentencing court may consider as a mitigating circumstance that the immigrant and his teen "wife" viewed the marriage as legitimate. Feminists, however, have objected that such exemptions generally come at the expense of women's rights, as in many societies around the world women and girls have fewer legal rights than is the case in the United States. Can a color-blind society permit courts and prosecutors to consider ethnicity when it prohibits them from basing their sentences on race or national origin? Should the court be allowed to consider the laws prevalent in the defendants' home countries and their cultural immersion in such values? How should home and host country values and laws be reconciled? Should such special treatment exist for all first-generation immigrants? For all members of an ethnic group? For all members of an ethnic group growing up in a distinctly ethnic environment?

4. *What sentencing practices and values?*   Some have argued that immigrant offenders should be punished based on the sentence that would be appropriate in their home countries. The reason given is that the sentencing regime in the United States is too lenient to deter offenders from countries where the death penalty is available for more offenses, where physical punishments such as flogging are practiced, and where longer prison terms may be imposed for select offenses.

In a number of federal cases, courts have departed from the applicable guideline range because of the offender's adoption of American values. See, e.g., United States v. Melendez-Torres, 420 F.3d 43 (1st Cir. 2005) (cultural assimilation generally recognized as proper basis for downward departure in certain illegal reentry cases); United States v. Rodriguez-Montelongo, 263 F.3d 429, 432-434 (5th Cir. 2001) (cultural assimilation considered a mitigating factor). Under the federal guidelines such a departure is now explicitly permitted. U.S. Sentencing Guidelines Manual 2L1.2 cmt. n.8 (2012). Is this an appropriate ground for departure from the guidelines?

# C.   CLASS

In the United States legal scholars, sociologists, political scientists, and public commentators tend to pay less attention to class differences than do those in other Western countries. Race-based analysis has replaced much of the focus on class. While racial distinctions and poverty do not go hand in hand, they do overlap.

Class is relatively difficult to define. If a person's class is determined by annual income, some members of the Rockefeller family may be categorized as poor. If it is based on educational attainment or status of employment, to what economic class do the stay-at-home spouses of executives of major corporations belong? The intellectual tradition in the United States combined with these definitional difficulties and related challenges in data collection make it difficult to find empirical studies on class.

Courts are also reluctant to identify "class." White-collar offenses are often associated with high-class defendants, while blue-collar defendants are generally viewed as lower-class. The relationship between class and type of crime is not perfect; many embezzlers are members of the middle class, for example. To the extent that courts do discuss class, they focus on high-status offenders. A prosecutor may request a higher sentence for "someone who had choices," or a defense lawyer may argue that "family" or "community" contributions and good works justify a lower sentence. Consider the relevance of class in the following case.

|| *United States v. Frank Serafini* ||
|| 233 F.3d 758 (3d Cir. 2000) ||

RENDELL, J.

In this appeal, Frank Serafini challenges his conviction and sentence for one count of perjury in violation of 18 U.S.C. §1623. Serafini, a popular state legislator in northeastern Pennsylvania, was convicted based on his false testimony before a federal grand jury; the grand jury was investigating a scheme wherein corporate political contributions were funneled through third-party conduits in violation of federal election laws. In his grand jury testimony, Serafini had denied that he was reimbursed for a contribution he had made to Senator Bob Dole's presidential campaign. [The government appeals] Serafini's sentence, contesting . . . the District Court's three-level downward departure for exceptional civic or charitable contributions pursuant to U.S.S.G. §5H1.11. [We conclude that the District Court's downward departure was] not an abuse of its discretion. . . .

Serafini was subpoenaed to testify before a grand jury that was investigating possible violations of the Federal Election Campaign Act (FECA).[5] The principal targets of the probe were Renato Mariani, president of Empire Sanitary Landfill, Inc. (Empire), and Serafini's nephew, Michael Serafini. The apparent violations were that Michael Serafini and his secretary had solicited numerous employees, business associates, and family members to make $1,000 contributions to Senator Bob Dole's presidential campaign, and that Michael reimbursed them for these contributions; the resulting transactions between Michael and these "conduits" therefore allegedly violated FECA. . . .

Serafini was called before the grand jury to answer questions about Michael's having solicited Serafini for a $1,000 contribution and allegedly having reimbursed him for that contribution. . . . The [government] sought and received an order immunizing Serafini so that the government could compel his testimony before the grand jury; the resulting subpoena ordered him to produce "[all] documents relative to political contributions you were reimbursed for." During Serafini's appearance before the grand jury, the Assistant U.S. Attorney informed him that he could be prosecuted if he provided false testimony. Although Serafini did acknowledge that Michael had solicited and obtained from him a $1,000 contribution to Dole, he denied that a $2,000 check given to him by Michael that same week was in part a reimbursement for that contribution. Instead, Serafini maintained that the $2,000 probably represented Michael's reimbursing Serafini for payments that Serafini made to a mechanic who had fixed Michael's Porsche. [Serafini repeatedly asserted that he was not reimbursed for any contributions.]

The jury convicted Serafini of perjury.] . . . . [The] adjusted offense level resulted in a guideline range of 18 to 24 months' imprisonment. However, the

---

5. FECA prohibits corporations from making contributions in connection with any federal election. FECA also makes it unlawful for any person to make a contribution in the name of another person (referred to in this opinion as a "conduit"), or for any person to permit his or her name to be used as a conduit. FECA limits individual contributions to federal candidates to $1,000 per election per candidate. [This law has been changed substantially through recent Supreme Court rulings.]

District Court granted a three-level downward departure for Serafini's community and charitable activities. The government argues that the District Court's departure is an abuse of discretion. . . .

The District Court . . . correctly determined that departing on the basis of civic and charitable good works was discouraged, but not forbidden, by the Guidelines. U.S.S.G. §5H1.11 ("Military, civic, charitable, or public service; employment-related contributions; and similar prior good works are not ordinarily relevant in determining whether a sentence should be outside the applicable guideline range"). The District Court recognized that, in order to depart downward on this basis, it must find that this factor existed "to an exceptional degree or, in some way, that makes the case different from the ordinary case in which the factor is present." The District Court made a finding that Serafini's civic and charitable contributions did exist to such an exceptional degree, or in an extraordinary manner. . . .

At the sentencing hearing, the District Court was presented with several character witnesses, and more than 150 letters. The letters submitted to the Court fall into three categories: (i) the first category presents Serafini as a good person; (ii) the second category refers to his activities as a state legislator; and (iii) the third category refers to his assistance, in time and money, to individuals and local organizations.

As to the first category, these can be quickly dismissed with the observation that being a "good person," a quality indeed to be admired, does not qualify as extraordinary or exceptional civic or charitable conduct.

As to Serafini's activities as a state legislator, they are work-related and political in character. For example, a letter from the Fire Chief of Greenfield Township Volunteer Fire Company stated that he "had worked tirelessly to obtain grant monies to help the community afford the lifesaving equipment they need." . . . Conceptually, if a public servant performs civic and charitable work as part of his daily functions, these should not be considered in his sentencing because we expect such work from our public servants. [To] the extent this second group of letters does not evidence extraordinary community service under Guideline §5H1.11, but instead, reflects merely the political duties ordinarily performed by public servants, we are of the view that they cannot form the basis of a departure.

However, unlike the first and second categories of letters the Court received, the third category of letters provided an adequate basis for the District Court's conclusion that Serafini's community service warranted a downward departure. Many of the letters that fall within this last group contain substantive descriptions of Serafini's generosity with his time as well as his money. Several constituents and friends described situations in which Serafini extended himself to them in unique and meaningful ways during times of serious need. In particular, three letters are especially noteworthy.

William Drazdowski, an accountant and "a close personal friend" of the defendant, explains Serafini's role in providing a $300,000 guarantee to Dr. Edward Zaloga so that he could secure new cutting edge data from certain Tokyo physicians for the treatment of his brother's brain tumor. Dr. Zaloga testified at the sentencing hearing that he telephoned Serafini at 1:00 A.M. seeking his assistance in raising the money. Just thirty minutes later, Serafini called back and informed Dr. Zaloga "that everything was in place." . . . In reading the

Zaloga letter, both Serafini's readiness to help and his reluctance to seek gratitude make a strong impression. Such behavior is hardly part of the normal duties of a local politician.

Another letter came from George E. Seig, who also testified at the sentencing hearing. He sustained a serious injury as a result of an accident while he was a college student. The physicians' prognosis was that he would never be able to carry on any form of normal social functioning. After a year of frustrating physical therapy, Seig lost all ambition to return to school. Then, he was contacted by Serafini's office who told him that Serafini had heard of the tragic incident and wanted Seig to come work for him. The record reflects that Serafini's offer of employment went far beyond just hiring a young person on his staff. Serafini took Seig under his wing, mentored him, and strongly encouraged him to attend college. He even loaned him money until Seig could repay it. The letter from Seig — now an attorney — reflects his immense gratitude and his feeling that Serafini is responsible for turning his life around.

A third letter came from a widow who approached Serafini in tears because she was about to lose her house. He wrote her a personal check for $750 to forestall foreclosure. She expressed doubt about her future ability to repay him, but Serafini insisted that she need not do so unless she could afford it.

The remaining letters, taken as a whole, depict Serafini as an exceptionally giving person. . . . For example, the letters describe Serafini's volunteer work as an usher at St. Mary's Church; at the Abington Heights School District; and at Lackawanna Trail High School. In addition, he helped to establish a fund to defray the cost of a bone marrow transplant for a man suffering from leukemia. Several letters note that Serafini was generous with his time even with people who lived outside his district. The letters also describe Serafini's financial contributions to organizations such as The Arc (a nonprofit agency serving people with mental retardation and their families); the Rotary Run Against Drugs; the Scranton Lackawanna Human Development Agency; the Little League; the Boy Scouts; St. Francis of Assisi Kitchen; the Abington Heights School District; and the leukemia sufferer's fund mentioned above. A letter from an official at the University of Scranton refers to Serafini's financial assistance to college students, and a letter from a high school social studies teacher describes Serafini's contributions to a scholarship for graduating seniors. . . .

The District Court concluded that the letters and testimony demonstrated that Serafini had distinguished himself, "not by the amount of money [he has] given, but by the amount of time that [he has] devoted." The District Court found that these efforts made Serafini's community and charitable activities "exceptional" when compared to what an average person in Serafini's circumstances would have done:

> Those weren't acts of just giving money, they were acts of giving time, of giving one's self. That distinguishes Mr. Serafini, I think, from the ordinary public servant, from the ordinary elected official, and I had ample testimony, today, that says that Mr. Serafini distinguishes himself, that these are acts not just undertaken to assure his re-election, but are taken because of the type of person he is. . . .

We realize, as did the District Court, that Serafini's largesse was in part financial, and in part, devotion of himself and his time. Since he is a wealthy individual, we must ensure that a district court does not run afoul of the prohibition against considering socioeconomic differences in relying on financial contributions as a basis for a departure. See U.S.S.G. §5H1.11. However, the District Court here recognized this particular aspect of Serafini's situation, but nonetheless found *all* his contributions, not merely monetary ones, exceptional.

It is not our role to decide in the first instance whether Serafini's civic and charitable contributions were exceptional given Serafini's role as a public servant and his apparent wealth. Our review is far more deferential. We conclude that the District Court had an adequate basis for its factual finding, and that the District Court's decision was not clearly out of line with other reported cases. See, e.g., United States v. Woods, 159 F.3d 1132, 1136 (8th Cir. 1998) (upholding defendant's downward departure for charitable activities, which included bringing two troubled young women into her home and paying for them to attend a private high school, as well as helping to care for an elderly friend, where the court found no basis to overturn the district court's finding that these efforts were exceptional). . . .

ROSENN, J., dissenting.
. . . I believe that when it came to sentencing, the voluminous letters from the defendant's political constituents, colleagues, and other friends misled the Court to depart downward from the Guidelines. . . .

The Sentencing Guidelines are clear that a defendant's record of charitable work and community service are a discouraged justification for a sentencing departure. The historical note to the Civic and Charitable Amendment to the Guidelines (§5H1.11) "expresses the Commission's intent that the factors set forth in this part are not ordinarily relevant in determining whether a sentence should be outside the applicable guideline range. . . ." This appears to be a recognition that in our culture and society, every person is expected reasonably to contribute charity to the poor and to non-profit organizations dedicated to educational, health, and religious purposes.[1] . . .

The defendant is not only a wealthy individual, but his federal income tax returns show substantial income from sources other than his salary as a state official. Included are substantial royalties from the Empire Landfill. A financial analysis of his pertinent income returns for the period 1991 through 1996 reveals the following undisputed evidence.

| Year | $ Total Income | $ Charitable Deductions | Charity as % of Income |
|------|------|------|------|
| 1991 | 724,019 | 13,407 | 1.8 |
| 1993 | 857,000 | 22,604 | 2.6 |
| 1994 | 855,000 | 16,620 | 1.9 |
| 1995 | 908,172 | 17,385 | 1.9 |
| 1996 | 1,101,276 | 20,310 | 1.8 |

---

1. According to a national survey by Independent Sector on "Giving and Volunteering in the United States," approximately 69% of all households in the United States made voluntary contributions to charity in 1995. See Statistical Abstract of the United States 404 (1999).

Except for 1993, in which his contributions exceeded 2%, all of his contributions are less than 2% per annum. Donating less than 2% of one's income to charity—even 2.6%—is lackluster and pedestrian by any measure; it is not exceptional. It is far below the average measure of giving in the United States by people in the defendant's socioeconomic status.[2] . . .

As noted, the majority and the District Court were persuaded by Serafini's non-financial charitable acts. But much of Serafini's civic participation was either honorary or obligatory because of his job as a Representative. Numerous letters submitted on his behalf were written by constituents or other beneficiaries of his public position. . . . Neither Drazdowski, an accountant, nor Dr. Zaloga claim that Serafini personally made the guarantee; nor does the defendant. There is no information how the guarantee was accomplished, to whom it was made, who made it, and the substance of the guarantee, or the relationship between Dr. Zaloga and the defendant. [The] entirely obscure and mysterious incident may very well have its genesis in defendant's political agenda. In any event, it hardly rises to the level of significant community service.

The Seig letter attests to Serafini's offer to employ Seig, a young friend of the family, on the defendant's legislative staff, a loan to him of an unstated sum of money, and encouragement to Seig to attend college. The third letter reports a personal check of $750 from the defendant to a widow who was about to lose her home through foreclosure. The widow expressed doubt about her ability to repay and defendant insisted she need not do so unless able.

These three "noteworthy" letters do reflect commendable action by the defendant, but neither they, nor the other letters, show community service to an exceptional or extraordinary degree. A few acts of personal kindness to individual friends do not add up to community service; they do not fulfill the purpose of the Guidelines. The District Court relied considerably on the defendant's gift "of time." I can find no evidence of the amount of time given to community service, as distinguished from some personal favors to friends and political constituents. . . .

The 1999 Statistical Abstract of the United States reveals that in the year 1995, persons in the United States with income of $100,000 or more contributed an average of 4.4 hours per week to volunteer work without monetary pay. In this case, although Serafini earned many times more than $100,000 in 1994 and 1995, we have no record that he gave any amount of time to volunteer work, whether it was for one or more weeks during the year, or for fifty-two weeks.

The cases support the foregoing analysis. Courts may not leniently interpret the requirement of extraordinary circumstances to grant a downward departure. See, e.g., United States v. Rybicki, 96 F.3d 754, 758 (4th Cir. 1996) (defendant was a highly-decorated Vietnam veteran, had saved an innocent civilian during the My Lai massacre, and had served with the Secret Service; these deeds did not warrant a departure); United States v. McHan, 920 F.2d 244, 247 (4th Cir. 1990) (defendant's work history, family ties and

---

2. According to the Statistical Abstract of the United States, the average American household contributed 2.2% of its income to charity in 1991. . . . In 1995, households with greater than $100,000 income contributed 3.4% of their household income to charity. . . .

responsibilities, and extensive contribution to the town's economic well-being could not justify downward departure). . . .

Measured by any reasonable standard, whether it be tithing to his church and community, or other charitable contributions of money or community time, Serafini's charitable and community service was far from exceptional or extraordinary. . . . I therefore conclude that it was impermissible under the Guidelines for the District Court to depart from the Sentencing Guidelines.

## NOTES

1. *Higher class status and sentencing advantage.* Is membership in a privileged class a basis for increased or decreased sentencing, or should it be irrelevant? Should monetary charity ever be considered a basis for adjusting a sentence downward? If money is a poor indicator of anything other than class, are there aspects of social or community behavior not tied to class that should nonetheless be relevant to sentencing? For a different perspective on a downward departure in the case of a wealthy white-collar defendant based on charitable giving and good deeds, see United States v. Thurston, 338 F.3d 50 (1st Cir. 2003) (review of downward departure de novo).

2. *Lower class status and sentencing disadvantage.* The striking reality of the U.S. criminal justice system is the disproportionate presence of members of the lower class. Should the disproportionate presence of the poor in U.S. courts, prisons, and jails prompt changes in our sentencing systems or our social systems? In a survey of federal judges conducted in 2002, only 54-60% of them believed that there was "almost always" neutrality with regard to the offender's socioeconomic status, in contrast to 62-68% who believed the same with regard to race and almost 90% who shared that belief with regard to religion or creed.

3. *White-collar v. street-crime.* Many so-called white-collar offenses are being committed by offenders at the lower end of the socio-economic strata, who often resemble street–level property offenders more than the upper echelon of white-collar offenders. A recent study has indicated that white-collar offenders continue to be treated more leniently than street-level property offenders, with those at the upper end of the socio-economic spectrum continually protected by a "status shield." Nevertheless, recent corporate scandals have had an impact on sentences. How long that effect will last is an open question. Shanna Van Slyke & William D. Bales, A contemporary study of the decision to incarcerate white-collar and street property offenders, 14(2) Punishment & Soc'y 217 (2012).

## D.  GENDER

Criminal laws used to distinguish explicitly between men and women. Some, such as rape laws, made it impossible for women to commit the crime; others relegated women automatically to victimhood. See, e.g., M. v. Superior

Court of Sonoma County, 450 U.S. 464 (1981) (state statute criminalizing only the male's conduct in sexual intercourse with an underage woman did not violate the equal protection clause); People v. Liberta, 474 N.E.2d 567 (N.Y. 1984) (statute that prohibited only forcible rape of women by men violated the equal protection clause; conviction could stand as court extended coverage to rape of men by women). Because such legislation treated women differently, often in a manner appropriate to a child, feminists urged their abolition. Ultimately these arguments succeeded; the few gender-based distinctions that remain mostly revolve around the childbearing functions of women. For example, until recently Ohio mandated the imposition of nonprison sentences involving prenatal care and drug rehabilitation for pregnant drug abusers who were willing to enter treatment.

Although gender equality has become the nominal hallmark of our criminal justice system, issues of differential treatment continue to rear their head in substantive criminal law and sentencing. Most common are charges of preferential sentencing. Traditionally, women have benefited from the paternalism and chivalry of a largely male judiciary. Women often receive lesser sentences because men believe they need protection and help.

While some of this discrimination may be due to gender stereotypes, judges may implicitly recognize the reality of the lives of many female offenders. They are dominated or abused by fathers, husbands, or boyfriends who involve them in criminal activities; their offenses are designed to benefit their families; and, perhaps most significant, their incarceration sends children into foster homes.

But prosecutors and judges do not favor all women. Rather, they distinguish between "good" and "bad" women. As crime victims the former—or their male representatives—are taken seriously; as offenders the former group appear to receive substantially lower sentences than men convicted of the same offenses. The criminal justice system, however, is often not so generous to women who violate social norms—prostitutes, for example, or women who assault and kill their children or mates—by engaging in behavior that is considered "unnatural." Minority and poor women also tend to be included among those who receive harsher sentences.

Whether anecdotal evidence of differential treatment amounts to gender-based discrimination is more difficult to determine. The number of women committing crimes (especially violent crimes) is small. Possible sentencing discrimination remains hidden behind a process that makes it difficult to determine whether similar offenders receive similar sentences. Consider the following case, in which the defendant challenged a blatantly gender-based policy.

|| *Virginia Salaiscooper v. Eighth* ||
|| *Judicial District* ||
|| 34 P.3d 509 (Nev. 2001) ||

PER CURIAM

Petitioner Virginia Anchond Salaiscooper contends that, in prosecuting her for solicitation of prostitution, Clark County District Attorney Stewart Bell is engaging in impermissible unconstitutional selective prosecution that violates her right to equal protection under the law. More specifically, Salaiscooper contends that the district attorney intended to discriminate against females by implementing a policy that prohibited his deputies from entering into plea negotiations with female defendants charged with solicitation of prostitution, thereby foreclosing any possibility that they could attend a diversion class in order to avoid solicitation convictions. . . .

The policy at issue was summarized in a December 1999 memo from Clark County District Attorney Stewart Bell to his deputies. The memo provided:

> In light of some changes in policy at the Las Vegas Metropolitan Police Department with regard to work card licensing for exotic dancers charged with prostitution, it has been agreed . . . that (*except in cases of first time male offenders who opt for the diversion program*) we will not negotiate the nature of cases of soliciting prostitution, nor will we agree that they may be in the future dismissed for any reason.

The policy was implemented due to the American Civil Liberties Union's (ACLU) objection to the fact that the Las Vegas Metropolitan Police Department (Metro) was revoking adult entertainment industry employees' work cards based merely on an arrest for solicitation of prostitution. The ACLU contended that revoking a work card needed to work in the entertainment industry without an underlying conviction violated due process. In response to the ACLU's objection, the district attorney implemented a no-plea-bargain policy that prohibited his deputies from entering into a plea agreement with a defendant charged with solicitation of prostitution allowing a plea to a lesser charge. The plain language of the policy prohibiting plea bargains excepted first time male defendants.

Because the justice court was concerned with the gender-specific language used in the policy, it ordered an evidentiary hearing where both sides could present evidence to support or refute a specific finding of discriminatory purpose. . . .

The State called . . . Dr. Roxanne Clark Murphy, a clinical psychologist and the Program Coordinator for the First Offender Program for Men in Las Vegas. Murphy testified that she developed the First Offender Program in collaboration with Metro and that it boasted an extremely low recidivism rate of less than one percent. Murphy explained that the diversionary program was designed for buyers of sex that are statistically almost always male. Murphy also described the requisite for entrance into the program was that a defendant must be a first-time offender charged with soliciting a prostitute.

Murphy testified that the vast majority of sellers of sex are females. Murphy also stated that it would take a minimum of a year to successfully rehabilitate a seller of sex. Murphy explained that, in order for a diversion program to be an effective deterrent, it would need to be a residential program that would protect women from their pimps, teach them job skills, and provide substance abuse and psychological counseling. Murphy further explained that more effort is required to rehabilitate and deter sex sellers than buyers because many prostitutes have been sexually abused, selling sex since the age of 13 to 14, disassociated from their actions through the use of drugs and alcohol, and/or controlled by a violent pimp or procurer. . . .

Judge Togliatti issued a lengthy order stating that the Las Vegas Justice Court had unanimously found that the policy did not discriminate on the basis of gender and that its distinction based on buyers of sex and sellers of sex was constitutionally permissible. In so finding, Judge Togliatti qualified this conclusion by stating that the judges were relying on the district attorney's representations that his policy applied to all sellers of sex regardless of gender, and consequently ordered Mr. Bell to clarify this fact in writing to his deputies within ten days.

In response to the court's order, Mr. Bell filed a clarification of policy in the justice court, affirming that he had distributed a memo clarifying that the First Offender Program for Men was available only to buyers of sex regardless of whether they were male or female. Accordingly, under the clarified policy, if a female buyer of sex was charged with solicitation of prostitution, she, like a male buyer of sex, would have the option of attending the First Offender Program, thereby avoiding a solicitation conviction. . . .

Salaiscooper argues that, in enacting the policy, the district attorney engaged in impermissible and unconstitutional selective prosecution that violated her right to equal protection under the law. Specifically, Salaiscooper argues that the policy's distinction between buyers and sellers of sex is "nothing more than a facade" concealing "conscious, intentional discrimination" against women, and thereby violates the Equal Protection Clauses of the United States and Nevada Constitutions. We conclude that Salaiscooper's argument lacks merit.

The government's decision to deny an arrestee admission into a diversion program is a decision to prosecute and [on review is treated] as a claim of selective prosecution. A defendant alleging unconstitutional selective prosecution has an onerous burden. Indeed, a district attorney is vested with immense discretion in deciding whether to prosecute a particular defendant that "necessarily involves a degree of selectivity." In exercising this discretion, the district attorney is clothed with the presumption that he acted in good faith and properly discharged his duty to enforce the laws. Although the district attorney's prosecutorial discretion is broad, it is not without limitation. The Equal Protection Clause constrains the district attorney from basing a decision to prosecute upon an unjustifiable classification, such as race, religion or gender.

The requisite analysis for a claim of unconstitutional selective prosecution is two-fold. First, the defendant has the burden to prove a prima facie case of discriminatory prosecution. To establish a prima facie case, the defendant must show that a public officer enforced a law or policy in a manner that had a discriminatory effect, and that such enforcement was motivated by a discriminatory purpose. A discriminatory effect is proven where a defendant shows that other persons similarly situated "are generally not prosecuted for the same conduct." A discriminatory purpose or "evil eye" is established where a defendant shows that a public administrator chose a particular course of action, at least in part, because of its adverse effects upon a particular group. If a defendant proves a prima facie case, the burden then shifts to the State to establish that there was a reasonable basis to justify the unequal classification. Where the classification is based on gender, the court applies an intermediate standard of scrutiny; in other words, the court must conclude the unequal classification in the policy is "reasonable, not arbitrary, and [rests] upon some ground of difference having a fair and substantial relation to the object of the legislation."

In the instant case, the justice court found that the district attorney had a valid, gender-neutral motivation for creating the policy classification — to draw a distinction between buyers and sellers of sex in order to deter acts of prostitution. More specifically, the justice court found that it was reasonable for the district attorney to prohibit sellers of sex from attending the one-day diversion program because it would have no deterrent effect. The justice court opined that the classification was therefore necessary because buyers of sex should not be precluded from participating in a successful diversion program merely because such treatment would be ineffective in rehabilitating the sellers. Finally, the justice court found that there was "nothing sinister" about the district attorney's primary goal of obtaining solicitation of prostitution convictions against sellers of sex so that he could revoke their work cards and, ultimately, stop prostitutes from working in the adult entertainment industry.

The lower court's findings with respect to the district attorney's motivation and intent underlying the policy are findings of fact to be given deference, and they should not be reversed if supported by substantial evidence. The district court correctly concluded that there is substantial evidence in support of the justice court's factual findings. In particular, Dr. Murphy testified that the diversion class would not be an effective deterrent for sex sellers because they would need a one-year rehabilitation program in light of the deeply-entrenched culture of drug abuse, psychological abuse, and violence associated with prostitution. Moreover, [there was testimony] that the district attorney needed solicitation convictions against sellers of sex so that Metro could revoke their work cards and eradicate prostitution from the strip clubs. Because the State presented evidence that the purpose of the policy's buyer/seller distinction was to deter acts of prostitution, the justice court's findings that the policy did not run afoul of the Equal Protection Clause is supported by substantial evidence.

Other jurisdictions have reached an analogous conclusion, holding that it is constitutionally permissible to treat prostitutes differently than the customers who patronize them. In People v. Superior Court of Alameda County, 562 P.2d 1315, 1320 (Cal. 1977), the Supreme Court of California, sitting en banc, held that it was permissible for law enforcement officials to target sellers of sex, because the "sexually unbiased policy of concentrating its enforcement effort on the profiteer" was not initiated by an intent to discriminate. The court reasoned that the policy was created because of the belief that focusing criminal prosecution on the sellers of sex had the most deterrent effect: "Prostitutes, the municipal court found, average five customers per night; the average customer does not patronize prostitutes five times a year. Because of an effective grapevine, arrest of one prostitute by an undercover officer will deter others, at least for a time."

Like the law enforcement officials in *Alameda*, [the] State presented evidence in support of its belief that a one-day class would not stop a prostitute from selling sex. . . . In light of our conclusion that the policy does not violate the Equal Protection Clauses of the United States and Nevada Constitutions, we conclude that extraordinary relief is not warranted in this matter. The legislature has vested the district attorney with prosecutorial discretion, and we conclude it is within the purview of the district attorney's prosecution powers to treat buyers of sex differently than sellers of sex. After all, the decision to prosecute, including the offer of a plea bargain, is a complex decision involving multiple considerations, including prior criminal history, the gravity of the offense, the need to punish, the possibility of rehabilitation, and the goal to deter future crime. Unless a defendant can prove that a district attorney's decision to prosecute arose from an impermissible desire to discriminate on the basis of race, gender or other protected class, our federal and state constitutions do not compel our intervention. Because there is no evidence of a discriminatory motive in the case before us, we deny Salaiscooper's petition.

## PROBLEM 9-6.   SENTENCING AND MOTHERHOOD

Amrhu Dyce, an immigrant in her twenties, pled guilty in federal court to conspiracy to commit possession with intent to distribute crack cocaine. She had carried drugs from New York City to North Carolina, largely to increase her limited household budget. Under the federal sentencing guidelines, Dyce faced an imprisonment range of 121 to 151 months. At sentencing she argued for a substantial downward departure based on her "extraordinary" family responsibilities, claiming that her case fell outside the heartland of cases for which the U.S. Sentencing Commission had declared family responsibilities "not ordinarily relevant." At the time of the sentencing hearing, Dyce had three small children. She breastfed the youngest, a newborn (a practice the U.S. government recommends at least for the first year of a baby's life while the World Health Organization suggests two years). The other two children were one and three years old. Dyce's boyfriend, the father of her children, was not involved in her criminal activities but seemed incapable of raising one, let alone all three, of his children. Dyce's mother and sister, who live in England, were willing and able to take in only the middle child.

Because of the father's inability to bring up two children, the youngest and the eldest may have to be placed in foster care should Dyce be sentenced to prison. Should the court consider her family circumstances extraordinary so as to allow for a nonprison sentence? Should it matter whether residential treatment facilities are available that would allow Dyce to live in a restrictive environment but keep at least the infant, and possibly even the other two children, with her? May the court consider the separation of the family and the impossibility of visitation should one of the children be removed from the United States? See United States v. Amrhu Dyce, 91 F.3d 1462 (D.C. Cir. 1996).

### NOTES

1. *Backfiring.*   Much feminist criticism of law enforcement has centered on gender-specific offenses such as prostitution, domestic violence, and rape. Substantive law and enforcement practices have changed in all three, but the impact of the changes is often imperceptible or ambiguous.

Consider prostitution. As *Salaiscooper* indicates, much of the enforcement of gender-neutral statutes still centers on the providers of the service — largely women. What justifies this enforcement focus? Who is in the best position to ascertain the information to make this decision?

Imagine a reverse world in which legislation criminalizes only the purchasing of sexual services. What could justify the sole prosecution and sentencing of the largely male customers? Prostitution is frequently deemed particularly harmful to the female providers, many of whom were abused as children, are drug addicts, suffer from low self-esteem, and do not view themselves as having other employment options. Would such legislation, if adopted in a U.S. jurisdiction, run afoul of the equal protection clause? See Vermont v. George, 602 A.2d 953 (Vt. 1991). What effect do you expect such a change in enforcement practice to have on the supply of and demand for prostitution services? Sweden has adopted this model to protect women's dignity. Many consider it successful despite — or perhaps because of — few prosecutions of male customers.

2. *Criminal law defenses and sentencing.* Feminists have charged that substantive criminal law, and especially the area of criminal defenses, focuses on men. This issue has been publicized most frequently with regard to abused women who kill their batterers. The women often argue that they acted in self-defense, and they frequently introduce the battered spouse syndrome to bolster their claim. Juries usually either reject the defense outright or find liability for a lesser, included offense. Once the defense has been fully or partially rejected, the lesser culpability of the defendant can be recognized merely through the sentence. See United States v. Whitetail, 956 F.2d 857 (8th Cir. 1992) (federal sentencing guidelines allow for consideration of battered spouse syndrome through downward departures).

The same situation occurs when a female defendant raises a duress defense. The defendant's emotional, psychological, or sexual dependence on a male partner who abused the defendant may fail as a defense at the guilt phase, but still might allow the court to impose a lesser sentence. See United States v. Gaviria, 804 F. Supp. 476 (E.D.N.Y. 1992). On the other hand, some juries may want to acquit of the primary offense but then assure some albeit limited sentence by convicting of a secondary charge.

3. *More female offenders?* The number of women in state and federal prison rose by 757% between 1977 and 2004. Women's Prison Association, The Punitiveness Report — Hard Hit: The Growth in Imprisonment of Women, 1977-2004 (2005) (available at http://www.wpaonline.org/institute/hardhit/index.htm). During this period the number of women imprisoned increased at almost twice the male rate. Drug offenses accounted for almost half of the rise in women's incarceration, and federal prisons outpaced state facilities in the growth of female admissions. African American and, to a lesser extent, Hispanic women bore the brunt of this development. Curiously, in the last few years the number of African-American women in prison has dropped substantially even though the number of Hispanic and white women in prison has continued to increase.

What explains the explosion in female imprisonment? Some blame a change in enforcement strategies; some point to enforcement and sentencing practices, stemming largely from the war on drugs, that no longer discriminate in favor of women; some see a rise of women in the drug underworld, paralleling their rise in the legitimate business world; some blame the feminization of poverty. See Phyllis Goldfarb, Counting the Drug War's Female Casualties, 6 J. Gender, Race & Just. 277 (2002).

Despite the increase in female convicts, the gender differences in incarceration rates remain striking. At year-end 2010, about 1.5 million men (943 per 100,000 residents) were incarcerated in state and federal prisons, but only about 113,000 women (67 per 100,000) were incarcerated. Why are so few women imprisoned, comparatively speaking? Victimization studies indicate that men commit more offenses, especially more violent crimes. In 1996 women accounted for 16% of all felons convicted in state courts: They made up almost one-quarter of property offenders but less than one-tenth of violent criminals. However, the number of women who commit violent crimes has been rising steadily, especially among adolescents. In 2009 over a third of female offenders sentenced to more than 1 year were incarcerated for a violent offense. Slightly over a quarter of women offenders are now serving time for a drug offense and around 30% are imprisoned for a property crime. Even if these numbers underestimate female offending somewhat, they raise the issue of whether biological differences or socialization, or both, explain why men are more violent and more likely to engage in crime generally.

4. *Women are different.* In contrast to people of different races, men and women truly differ. Some of these differences are clearly biological; others may or may not be. To what extent should the criminal justice system consider a woman's ability to bear children? There is an international consensus that pregnant women should not be executed, but beyond that, criminal justice systems differ on whether and to what extent biological differences should be considered.

In imposing a 20-year prison sentence on a 25-year-old woman and a 25-year-old man, should a court consider that this makes it virtually impossible for the woman to bear a child (putting aside expensive modern reproductive technologies) but not for the man to father a child? Cf. Gerber v. Hickman, 291 F.3d 617, 623 (9th Cir. 2002) ("[T]he right to procreate while in prison is fundamentally inconsistent with incarceration."); Goodwin v. Turner, 908 F.2d 1395, 1396 (8th Cir. 1990) (Bureau of Prisons' restriction on allowing inmate to ejaculate into a clean container so that his semen could be used to artificially inseminate his wife "is reasonably related to legitimate penological interest of treating all prisoners equally"). Since 2007 the British Home Office has granted one inmate access to "artificial insemination facilities." Five more petitions are under consideration, 16 have been rejected. The prisoners most likely to benefit are those with long prison sentences, whose spouses would likely be too old to conceive a child upon their release. The policy extends also to female inmates, but it is unclear whether any of them have requested access to artificial insemination.

Concerned that women will become pregnant to avoid incarcerative sentences, courts have declined to consider pregnancy, childbirth, and the presence of a young child as mitigating sentencing factors. If courts should not and cannot consider such biological differences in their sentencing, is there a societal responsibility to create institutional facilities that would allow female offenders to keep their children with them?

5. *Pregnancy and drugs.* In 19 states and the District of Columbia, pregnant women have been prosecuted for substance abuse. Some prosecutors have

argued that the small amount of drugs that travels from the mother to the child either during the pregnancy or through the umbilical cord at birth constitutes drug trafficking—and a more severe form at that, since the drugs are delivered to a minor. In South Carolina, Charleston prosecutors filed child neglect charges against women who had just given birth in a state hospital. The U.S. Supreme Court struck down this policy because the hospital's practice of collecting urine samples, without the patient's consent, to obtain evidence of the patient's criminal conduct constituted an unreasonable search. It reached this result even though the state's interest in deterring pregnant women from using cocaine is high. See Ferguson v. City of Charleston, 532 U.S. 67 (2001). In other cases prosecutors have charged "exposure of a child to controlled substances" or various types of homicide if the child was stillborn. Particularly disturbing is the fact that the vast majority of such drug prosecutions are aimed at poor African American women, generally because they frequent public hospitals and because of the allegedly more destructive impact of crack on a fetus. Seema Mohapatra, Unshackling Addiction: A Public Health Approach to Drug Use During Pregnancy, 26 Wisc. J. L., Gender & Soc'y 242 (2011).

6. *Gender equality redux.* Gender equality is writ large in the legal system. Does it make sense if there is no such equality in the larger society? While many male inmates are also fathers, data on state prisoners indicate that 90% of fathers who were incarcerated had wives who cared for their children. For female offenders, less than one-quarter had husbands who cared for their children. Because of changes in foster care and adoption laws, a likely consequence of long-term imprisonment for single parents who cannot find another caregiver for their children is loss of parental rights. While differences in caregiving may not be solely biological, should a court consider them? Such consideration would also benefit men who are not able to find stable caregiving arrangements for their minor children during imprisonment. Alternatively, should the large numbers of single parents in the criminal justice system (and society at large) counsel against consideration of single-parent status at sentencing?

Federal courts that consider family circumstance in their departure jurisprudence frequently note the defendant's financial contribution to the family. Women who do not appear to be gainfully employed, even if they are the sole caregiver for minor children, are thus at a disadvantage. Does such an approach not privilege one type of parenting over another? May it not also discriminate against minority groups in which the mother is expected to stay at home with her children?

In light of the known consequences of imprisonment on children, should parental status be considered at sentencing? Even if the result may be gender inequity?

7. *The numbers disadvantage in imprisonment.* Because there are substantially fewer prisons for women than for men, often the conditions of incarceration differ by gender. In the federal system especially, the small number of female offenders and the location of women's prisons often necessitate incarceration far from family and friends. This is particularly difficult for women with young children and women whose families cannot afford lengthy trips, for financial or other reasons. Should courts consider such well-known facts in deciding whether to impose a prison sentence?

786 Chapter 9. Race, Class, and Gender

Female prisons also offer different conditions than all-male institutions. Many have fewer or different educational programs, and most have only limited employment options. This may further disadvantage women who entered the system with educational and vocational deficits. Nevertheless, courts have not found equal protection violations based on different prison conditions. See Klinger v. Department of Corrections, 31 F.3d 727, 731 (8th Cir. 1994) (substantial differences between men's and women's prisons did not constitute an equal protection violation because male and female prisoners "were not similarly situated for purposes of prison programs and services"). At the same time, women often enjoy better prison facilities and more privacy than men. In those cases, courts, relying on *Klinger,* have also found no constitutional violations. See Oliver v. Scott, 276 F.3d 736 (5th Cir. 2002).

8. *Female recidivism and risk-based sentencing.* Women commit fewer violent offenses and have lower recidivism rates than men. If the risk of future offending were the focus of sentencing, most women would receive lesser sentences than most men for a similar offense. Does risk-based sentencing violate the equal protection clause? Without risk-based sentencing, doesn't equal treatment put women at a disadvantage?

9. *Women on death row.* Women constitute only about two percent of the death row population in 2012. As a group they were more likely to escape execution and benefit from sentence commutation than men. Why women are sentenced to death less frequently and less likely to be executed remains subject to debate. See Laura M. Argys & H. Naci Mocan, Who Shall Live and Who Shall Die? An Analysis of Prisoners on Death Row in the United States, 33 J. Legal Stud. 255 (2004).

10. *Women as crime victims.* Men are disproportionately the victims of crime. While this finding may contradict public perception, it holds true for most offenses. Women make up the majority of domestic violence and rape victims, however — both destructive, usually violent offenses that are vastly underreported. Normatively, the victimization of women is considered substantially more heinous than that of men. Why?

Women are often the targets of crime because offenders consider them more vulnerable. Imagine, for example, a young man choosing a robbery victim: The 5'2", 90-pound woman is a more attractive target than most men, possibly barring Woody Allen. Should offenders who pick vulnerable female targets be subject to sentence enhancements? Or is a new substantive criminal law provision more appropriate? Consider one proposed definition for hate crime: "a crime in which the defendant intentionally selects a victim, or in the case of a property crime, the property that is the object of the crime, because of the actual or perceived ... gender ... of any person."

## PROBLEM 9-7. SAUCE FOR THE GANDER

Gilberto Redondo-Lemos was charged in Arizona federal court for acting as a drug courier. He alleged that prosecutors in the U.S. Attorney's office violated his right to equal protection by offering more favorable plea bargains to female couriers.

The district court held an evidentiary hearing. At the hearing, the assistant U.S. Attorney (AUSA) handling the Redondo-Lemos prosecution said that she offered, in exchange for a guilty plea, to recommend the lowest sentence allowed by the federal sentencing guidelines and the mandatory minimum. She testified that she assessed the strength of her case, followed the factors set out in departmental memos dealing with plea bargains generally, was not motivated by defendant's gender, and knew of no office policy of plea bargaining on the basis of gender.

Another AUSA's testimony concerned a case against a couple where the evidence was actually stronger against the woman. The AUSA nonetheless agreed to let the husband plead guilty to a lesser charge in exchange for allowing the wife to go free and take care of their three children. The AUSA noted that, after 25 years of experience, he'd observed that it was "usually the Mexican men that will stand up and take responsibility," and he'd come to expect it. The AUSA noted that when couples are faced with a choice, they usually select the woman to care for the children and that allowing this choice reflects no government policy of gender discrimination. The government argued that it was the private party, not the government, who made the decision and "discriminated." The government simply practiced compassion when it allowed parents to decide which parent would be the better caregiver for children who otherwise would be effectively orphaned.

In ten additional cases that concerned the district judge, the responsible AUSAs testified that they based their plea bargaining decisions on the strength of the evidence, the legality of the stops and searches, the defendant's cooperation, the level of the defendant's involvement, and special circumstances of particular defendants. In one case, the AUSA allowed a woman who was overdue in her pregnancy to plead guilty to a misdemeanor. Because the Marshal's Service indicated it couldn't give her proper medical care, she was sentenced to time served, while her male partner, who had a record, pleaded guilty and was sentenced to 90 months in prison. The AUSA explained that she would have responded the same way had the Marshal's Service expressed concern about medical care for a male defendant.

The court considered two sets of statistics to show intentional discrimination in plea bargaining with male "mules" in the District of Arizona. Statistics from the local probation office showed that male drug offenders in the District of Arizona were sentenced to an average of 36 months compared to 32 months for females and that only 11% of all males received probation compared with 35% of females. A U.S. Sentencing Commission report showed that nationwide, 61.5% of men who committed crimes subject to mandatory minimum sentences received them, while only 50% of women did.

The district court rejected the explanations by the AUSAs as "mere general assertions that the AUSAs did not discriminate." In the case of the couple, the court found the discriminatory plea to be unjustified. Based on that case and the two sets of statistics, the district court found intentional invidious discrimination and sentenced Redondo-Lemos below the statutory minimums for the offenses of which he was convicted.

Suppose the government appeals the finding of invidious discrimination and the remedy of ordering sentences below the statutory minimum. How should the appellate court rule? See United States v. Redondo-Lemos, 27 F.3d 439 (9th Cir. 1994).

## NOTES

1. *Male claims of bias.* A striking feature of gender bias claims is that they are often raised by men rather than women. Why? Claims of gender bias face the problems of definition and proof confronted by Warren McCleskey and others making claims of bias based on race and other factors.

2. *The centrality of plea bargaining.* Defendants who plea bargain face two obstacles in challenging bias in their prosecution and sentence. First, by plea bargaining they may have waived some right to challenge any bias in treatment and sentence; second, bias challenges to charges and pleas are almost always based on claims of systematic rather than individual bias. Are the doctrines of equality able to make the leap from individual to collective treatment, from individual bias to disparate outcome, which may or may not be based on biased judgments and rules by the decision maker whose actions are challenged?

3. *Information on sentencing disparities.* Does the focus on legally compelling claims of bias obscure important policy issues with respect to equal treatment? How should policymakers, scholars, or judges concerned with issues of bias in sentencing or the criminal justice system address or illuminate those issues?

4. *The interplay of various forms of discrimination.* In United States v. Guzman, 236 F.3d 830 (7h Cir. 2001), the court vacated a sentence because the district court had held that the Mexican immigrant's gender and "cultural heritage" made it more likely that she had supported her boyfriend's criminal activity. As women benefit from such stereotypes in some cases, why should they present a cause of action in others? Why may the use of gender stereotypes not ever be appropriate? See Deborah W. Denno, Gender, Crime, and the Criminal Law Defenses, 85 J. Crim L. & Criminology 80 (1994). Can the same be said for race- and ethnicity-based stereotypes?

# = 10 =
## ‖ *Alternatives to Criminal Sentences* ‖

Criminal punishments presuppose a criminal conviction, and the collateral consequences discussed in Chapter 8 occur only after a criminal conviction. But there are alternatives to criminal punishment that create many of the effects of a criminal sanction without a criminal conviction being entered. As you read about the alternative sanctions surveyed in this chapter, ask yourself whether they differ in meaningful ways from true criminal sanctions. When might the lack of a criminal conviction make it improper or difficult to impose some of these alternatives?

## A. DIVERSION PROGRAMS

Diversion threatens an offender but does not use the criminal process. Its goal is to protect the offender from the sanctions and stigma arising from a criminal conviction while preserving criminal justice resources. Precharge diversion is emphatically within the broad general bounds of prosecutorial discretion. Diversion programs started with juvenile cases and expanded to include adult drug offenses in the 1960s; more formalized programs exist today in both state and federal systems.

Diversion programs can take several forms, attaching at different points in the criminal process. Pre-arrest diversion allows the police or the prosecutors to divert offenders at the earliest stage, without ever starting the criminal process. Its informality may open the process to possible abuse and prevent structured oversight of the offender's subsequent actions. But it spares the offender the stigma of an arrest record.

Pre-arraignment diversion directs individual offenders out of the system after their arrest but prior to the formal filing of charges. This process ensures prosecutorial control over the diversion process and allows for more screening to remove unsuitable offenders from the program. In this way it saves the criminal justice system the costs of prosecution without saddling the offender with a criminal record.

Diversion may occur at later stages in the process, after formal charges have been filed but before a judgment has been rendered. Pretrial diversion, for example, allows charges to be dismissed after a defendant has successfully fulfilled the conditions the prosecutor imposed. In some cases defendants may plead guilty conditionally with the understanding that the judge will vacate the plea after the offender has met all of the required conditions.

Prosecutors and judges use diversion programs especially often in drug cases. Minor, nonviolent drug users in particular benefit from programs that move them into drug treatment. Diversion can be used for defendants ranging from juveniles to corporations. A corporation might escape potentially damaging publicity in exchange for monetary payment. The juvenile might perform community service or pay a fine. Among the more imaginative diversion programs are those using offender-victim mediation.

The prosecutor typically controls access to these diversion programs (also known as "deferred prosecution" programs). But given their functional similarity to criminal sentences, should judges also have a role in selecting who gets diverted and what conditions the defendant must meet?

|| *State v. Carolyn Curry* ||
|| **988 S.W.2d 153 (Tenn. 1999)** ||

ANDERSON, C.J.

... The defendant, Carolyn C. Curry, worked as an assistant clerk for the City of McKenzie, Tennessee, from 1985 to 1995. Over a two-year period from July of 1993 to July of 1995, Curry embezzled over $27,000 from the City. She later was indicted for theft of property valued between $10,000 and $60,000.

Curry applied for pretrial diversion. According to her application, she was a divorced, 34-year-old mother of three children, ages 19, 13, and 8. Curry had graduated from college with honors in 1983, and she served in the Tennessee National Guard from 1983 to 1990, when she was honorably discharged. She was an active member of her church and numerous charitable and community organizations including the United Way, United Neighbors, Concerned Citizens, and youth softball. Numerous letters included with her application attested to her charitable and community involvement. Curry had no prior arrests or convictions. She cooperated with authorities in this case when her actions were discovered, admitting that she took money for family and living expenses and proposing a restitution program. She stated that: "I sincerely regret my actions and regret the shame that my actions have brought to bear on myself and my family."

In denying the application for pretrial diversion, the prosecutor, in a written response, gave the following reasons:

> . . . We have carefully reviewed the application and the attached letters. . . . We have considered the defendant's past history and her conduct for two years in defrauding the City of McKenzie. This was a calculated criminal scheme that took planning and thought. It manifests a criminal intent for a long period of time and not something that happened at once. We cannot believe that it would be in the best interests of the public, the defendant, and justice to overlook a criminal scheme of this proportion and grant pre-trial diversion. . . .

Curry sought review of the prosecutor's decision by filing a petition for writ of certiorari in the trial court. After hearing argument of counsel, the trial court found that diversion had been denied solely based upon the circumstances of the offense, specifically, the two-year duration, and ruled [that the district attorney's office had "abused its discretion in denying pretrial diversion" and that Curry should be placed on pretrial diversion].

The pretrial diversion program, drafted and enacted by the Legislature, allows the District Attorney General to suspend a prosecution against a qualified defendant for a period of up to two years. Tenn. Code Ann. §40-15-105(a)(1)(A). A qualified defendant pursuant to the statute is one who has not previously been granted diversion and does not have a prior misdemeanor conviction for which confinement was served or a prior felony conviction within a five year period after completing the sentence or probationary period for the conviction. The offense for which diversion is sought may *not* be a class A felony, a class B felony, a sexual offense, driving under the influence, or vehicular assault. Tenn. Code Ann. §40-15-105(a)(1)(B)(i)(c).

Any grant of diversion must be conditioned on one or more of the following conditions: that the defendant not commit any criminal offense; that the defendant refrain from activities, conduct, or associations related to the charge; that the defendant receive rehabilitative treatment, counseling, and education; that the defendant make restitution to the victim; that the defendant pay court costs and the costs of the diversion; and that the defendant abide by any other terms or conditions as may be agreed upon. Tenn. Code Ann. §40-15-105(a)(2)(A)-(H). If the defendant violates a term or condition, the prosecution may terminate diversion and resume the criminal prosecution.

One who is statutorily eligible is not presumptively entitled to diversion. Instead, whether to grant pretrial diversion to a qualified defendant who is statutorily eligible is a determination that lies in the discretion of the district attorney general. The relevant considerations for the prosecutor are as follows:

> When deciding whether to enter into a memorandum of understanding under the pretrial diversion statute a prosecutor should focus on the defendant's amenability to correction. Any factors which tend to accurately reflect whether a particular defendant will or will not become a repeat offender should be considered. . . . Among the factors to be considered in addition to the circumstances of the offense are the defendant's criminal record, social history, the physical and mental condition of a defendant where appropriate, and the likelihood that pretrial diversion will serve the ends of justice and the best interest of both the public and the defendant.

State v. Pinkham, 955 S.W.2d 956, 959-960 (Tenn. 1997).

If the district attorney general denies pretrial diversion, the denial must be in writing and must include an enumeration of the evidence that was considered and a discussion of the factors considered and weight accorded each. This requirement entails more than an abstract statement in the record that the district attorney general has considered these factors. Instead, the factors considered must be clearly articulable and stated in the record. . . .

The prosecutor's response must be in writing. [The written statement compels] the prosecutor to think about and justify his denial in terms of the applicable standards. [The] statement of reasons [also restricts] the prosecutor to a particular rationale and insure[s] that the prosecutor would offer no new reasons at the evidentiary hearing. The prosecutor's written response must also identify any factual disputes between the evidence relied upon and the application filed by the defendant.

If the application for pretrial diversion is denied, the defendant may appeal by petitioning the trial court for a writ of certiorari. Tenn. Code Ann. §40-15-105(b)(3). The only evidence that may be considered by the trial court is the evidence that was considered by the district attorney general. The trial court may conduct a hearing only to resolve any factual disputes raised by the prosecutor or the defendant concerning the application, but not to hear additional evidence that was not considered by the prosecutor. The action of the prosecutor is presumptively correct, and it is subject to review by the trial court only for an abuse of discretion.

[In this case,] the prosecutor's primary consideration in the written denial of diversion was the circumstances of the offense, specifically, the amount of money taken and the duration of the criminal activity. The denial letter stated that diversion was not "in the best interest of the public," which, although imprecise, arguably includes deterrence. Although the prosecutor asserts that he had "carefully reviewed the application and the attached letters," the denial does not discuss the defendant's favorable social history, lack of a criminal record, and potential for rehabilitation. Moreover, assuming these essential factors were, in fact, considered, there is no explanation as to how much weight they were afforded and no rationale as to why they were outweighed by the other factors in denying diversion.

The State argues, and the dissent writes, that the seriousness of the offense itself may justify a denial of diversion. A review of the case law reveals, however, that the circumstances of the offense and the need for deterrence may alone justify a denial of diversion, *but only if all of the relevant factors have been considered as well.* See State v. Washington, 866 S.W.2d 950, 951 (Tenn. 1993) ("circumstances of the case and the need for deterrence may be considered as two of the many factors, [but] they cannot be given controlling weight unless they are of such overwhelming significance that they . . . outweigh all other factors"). The facts and circumstances of nearly all criminal offenses are by definition serious; only by analyzing all of the relevant factors, including those favorable to the defendant, can appropriate candidates for this legislative largess be identified in a manner consistent with the purpose of the pretrial diversion act.

In *Pinkham,* for instance, the defendant was charged with falsely representing himself as a lawyer, impersonating a licensed professional, and aggravated perjury. The denial of diversion emphasized the circumstances of the offense, the losses sustained by the victim, and the "systematic and continuing criminal activity," but also gave extensive consideration to the other relevant factors:

> In making this decision to reject the defendant's diversion application, I have considered that [the defendant] is a 50 year old man with no criminal record. I have considered his exemplary social history. I have considered that [the defendant] appears to be a leader in his community, as evidenced by the character and reference letters from lawyers, teachers, professors, ministers, doctors, et al. I have considered all of the parameters of [the defendant's] social, family, personal, educational and professional background. . . . Since [the defendant] is a highly educated person who holds a law degree, [the defendant] knew that his conduct was unlawful and unethical. . . .

955 S.W.2d at 959.

In contrast, the defendant in State v. Herron, 767 S.W.2d 151, 155 (Tenn. 1989), a 24-year-old woman with no prior criminal record, was charged with two counts of larceny by trick, one offense involving $5000 and the other involving $6000. The prosecutor's denial of pretrial diversion was based primarily on the circumstances of the "contrived, deliberate" offenses and the need to deter such offenses. Although the trial court denied the defendant's petition for certiorari, [this court held that] both the prosecutor and the trial court failed to consider "that defendant did not have any criminal record, her social history, her physical and mental condition, including her educational background, her employment history as well as the stability and continued support of her family."

[The] dissent strains to conclude that the evidence regarding the defendant's background was unfavorable and that her potential for rehabilitation was minimal simply by looking only to the circumstances and time span of the offense. Under such an analysis, in which the facts and circumstances are given conclusive weight against a defendant's potential for correction, rare is the defendant who would qualify for pretrial diversion. . . .

HOLDER, J., dissenting.

. . . Pretrial diversion is a legislative largess as well as extraordinary relief. Pretrial diversion relieves criminal defendants of the burden of being tried for or convicted of a crime for which they are guilty. Once defendants have completed a diversion program, they are under no legal obligation to disclose their offenses to prospective employers, and their public records are expunged. Mere eligibility for diversion should not provide a presumption for program suitability.[1] Defendants, therefore, should at all times carry the burden of establishing suitability given the extraordinary nature of diversionary relief. . . .

The pretrial diversion statute does not enumerate specific criteria that a prosecuting attorney should use when making pretrial diversion determinations. The legislature apparently recognized the extraordinary relief provided by the pretrial diversion statute and intended to provide prosecuting attorneys substantial discretion in making pretrial diversion decisions. This grant of discretion would presumptively include the broad discretion to determine

---

1. Pursuant to Tenn. Code Ann. §40-15-105, defendants committing extremely serious offenses such as aggravated assault, voluntary manslaughter, vehicular homicide (not involving intoxication), kidnapping, robbery, arson, and aggravated burglary may be eligible for pretrial diversion.

not only the relevant criteria and considerations of each case but also the weight to be afforded the relevant considerations of each diversionary decision. Courts, however, have judicially imposed general considerations to guide a prosecuting attorney's decision.

... In the case now before us, the prosecuting attorney set out the following reasons in support of the pretrial diversion denial: (1) the long-term and continuing nature of the offense; (2) the fact that the circumstances of the offense reveal a systematic scheme to commit crimes which "manifest a criminal intent for a long period of time" and not a crime of impulse; (3) the magnitude of the offense, noting the amount of money ($27,368.73) embezzled during a period from July 1, 1993 to July 11, 1995; (4) the deceitful nature of the criminal violations; and (5) the deterrent effect of crimes to defraud city or municipal organizations ("[w]e cannot believe that it would be in the best interests of the public, the defendant and justice to overlook a criminal scheme of this proportion and grant pre-trial diversion to the defendant").

The reasons cited by the prosecutor are well-supported by the record and have been held sufficient for denials of pretrial diversion in numerous published opinions involving similar crimes and crimes of a less serious nature. . . . In State v. Carr, 861 S.W.2d 850, 854 (Tenn. App. 1993), the defendant's crimes were very similar to the crimes in the case now before us. Pretrial diversion was denied based on the following factors:

(1) The circumstances show "a systematic scheme to defraud . . . not a crime of impulse," involving considerable planning which would have continued absent discovery.

(2) The magnitude of the offense, noting the amount of money ($23,370.85). . . .

(3) The number of individual claims and continuing nature of the offense.

(4) The particular need for deterrence because of the considerable opportunity for Medicaid fraud, which is serious and prevalent.

(5) The defendant's statements indicate little remorse and failure to accept responsibility.

The appellate court stated that . . . in a close case, the courts should defer to the prosecutor's decision. The appellate court held that substantial evidence in the record supported the denial based on the circumstances of the crime and the need for deterrence. . . .

In the case now before us, I believe that the record is replete with substantial evidence supporting the district attorney's reasons for denying pretrial diversion. . . . I would hold that the district attorney's letter denying diversion more than adequately addressed the criteria set forth in Pinkham, even though the letter could have been more detailed. . . . The circumstances of the defendant's offense and the need to deter fraud as well as thefts of large sums of money are sufficiently overwhelming to justify denial of pretrial diversion in this case. . . .

I disagree with the majority's finding that the defendant has a "favorable" social history and background. I believe that someone who continually commits serious crimes involving deception, planning, and fraud over a two-year period of time has a less than favorable social history, has an extensive criminal background, and is a poor candidate for rehabilitation. Moreover, the defendant ceased her criminal activity only when she was caught, and her criminal activity would likely have continued had she not been caught.

I disagree with the majority's decision that an abuse of discretion occurred merely due to a district attorney's failure to specifically or explicitly address non-statutory criteria. . . . The majority's holding could effectively allow defendants committing serious offenses such as manslaughter, kidnapping, and vehicular homicide to avoid prosecution merely because a district attorney commits a non-prejudicial omission affecting neither a constitutional nor a statutory right.

## PROBLEM 10-1.   CURRY RECIPES

Imagine that you are a trial judge in Tennessee. Consider whether a prosecutor in Tennessee abused discretion under the statutory provisions described in the *Curry* case by refusing to allow diversion in the following two cases.

*Case #1.*   On the morning of August 9, 2004, Stephen McKim was running late for a meeting with his co-workers at Central North Church, where he serves as a Minister to Students. Before leaving his home for work, he placed his seven-month-old daughter Mia in a car seat in the back seat of his car. Mia attended a daycare center next door to the church where Stephen worked. By the time Stephen arrived at his workplace, Mia had fallen asleep. Forgetting that his daughter was in the car, Stephen rushed into his meeting. When Stephen remembered that he had not removed his daughter from his car, he hurried to retrieve her. Although she was still alive at that time, Mia died a short time later from hyperthermia as a result of the high temperature in the vehicle. Stephen was later indicted for criminally negligent homicide.

In response to his indictment, the defendant applied for pretrial diversion. The defendant's application indicates that he has no prior criminal record; holds a college degree and is seeking a Masters of Divinity degree; taught in the public school system from 2001 to 2003, leaving to take his current position; is in excellent physical health; is married and emotionally stable with significant support from his extended family and community; has an "excellent reputation within the community"; and is "amenable to any conditions imposed during the diversion period." The defendant's application was accompanied by nineteen letters of support from family, friends, co-workers, and students, including an eloquent letter of support from his wife, Mia's mother.

The district attorney general's office denied the defendant's application for pretrial diversion. The written denial sets forth without discussion four factors favoring diversion: the defendant's employment "at the same job for seven years," the defendant's college degree, his lack of a prior criminal record, and the "numerous letters of support." The denial also sets forth four factors supporting denial of pretrial diversion: the defendant's negligence in failing to remove his daughter from his car on a hot summer day, thereby causing her death; the seriousness of the offense; the "need to deter crimes such as these," citing the deaths of almost one hundred children across the nation from being left in "hot vehicles"; and that the grant of diversion to the defendant would "lead the public to believe that crimes that involve death are treated lightly by the criminal justice system." Significantly, in assessing the seriousness of the offense, the assistant district attorney general who authored the written denial wrote,

> Even though this class of crime is divertible, it appears to be an aberration of the law. Other crimes involving death that were once divertible have been removed by legislation from consideration. These are voluntary manslaughter and vehicular homicide involving intoxication. Also, Aggravated Assault involving serious bodily injury has been removed from consideration for pretrial diversion by legislation. Certainly, the type of crime and the fact that it involved a death weigh heavily against the defendant's application for pretrial diversion.

The written denial concludes:

> After weighing and considering all the factors both for and against the defendant's application for pretrial diversion as outlined above, this office has reached the following conclusion. The positive aspects of the defendant's application for pretrial diversion when weighed against the negative aspects of this application indicate that this office should not grant the defendant's application for pretrial diversion. Having considered and weighed all of the aspects of this application, both positive and negative, this office must respectfully deny the defendant's application for pretrial diversion.

Upon the denial of his request for pretrial diversion, the defendant petitioned the trial court for a writ of certiorari. As the judge, would you agree with the defendant that the prosecutor abused his discretion in refusing to grant this application for pretrial diversion? Cf. Tennessee v. McKim, 215 S.W.3d 781 (2007).

*Case #2.* A Smyrna Police Department detective saw Heather Richardson make a drug sale in a grocery store parking lot on February 17, 2009. After police arrested and searched her, they found an ounce of marijuana, a set of drug scales, and eighty-seven pills. In a statement given to the police, Richardson admitted to selling a small amount of marijuana for thirty dollars and selling five prescription pills for thirty-five dollars. She said she sold the drugs "to get ahead" on her bills because she was a waitress, business was slow, and her rent was $1000 a month. The Rutherford County Grand Jury indicted Richardson for possession of .5 ounces or more of a Schedule VI controlled substance with the intent to deliver or sell; possession of a Schedule III controlled substance with the intent to deliver or sell; and possession of drug paraphernalia.

According to the defendant's application for pretrial diversion, she was a twenty-five-year-old, unmarried mother of two young children. She had no prior criminal record, had obtained a general equivalency diploma (GED), and had been steadily employed since 2001. As to the offense, the defendant stated that she had a prescription for Lortab, was desperate for some cash, and sold five Lortabs to a friend. She said that she had a small amount of marijuana with her and a set of scales but that they were for her personal use only. She admitted that her conduct was "very wrong and it was out of my character. I was only trying to make ends meet. I have definitely learned my lesson, and feel very stupid. I will never do this again in my life." She also provided favorable letters from eight people. The Tennessee Bureau of Investigation certified that the defendant was eligible for pretrial diversion.

The Rutherford County District Attorney General denied the defendant's application. The prosecutor listed several factors that were potentially favorable to the granting of pretrial diversion, including the defendant's lack of previous criminal convictions, her GED, her "good physical and mental health," her lack of history of illegal drug use, and her nine-year history of steady employment. The prosecutor further noted that favorable letters were submitted indicating that the defendant was "a loving mother, dependable, hard-working and sorry for her actions." The prosecutor observed that she was responsible for taking care of her two young children and stated that she "may be amenable to correction."

In enumerating several negative factors, the prosecutor stated that "trafficking in narcotics has long been a problem in this jurisdiction" and that to deter others from participating in this offense, "it is necessary that a punishment harsher than diversion be imposed." The prosecutor also noted that the defendant had declined to assist law enforcement in prosecuting other drug dealers in the area, had failed to mention in her application that she had sold some marijuana before she sold the Lortabs, was refusing to accept responsibility for her actions, and had brought her two young children with her to the drug transaction. Based on these considerations, the prosecutor denied the application for pretrial diversion. As a judge, how would you rule on a challenge to this decision? Cf. State v. Richardson, 357 S.W.3d 620 (Tenn. 2012).

## U.S. Attorneys' Manual, Pretrial Diversion Program
### U.S. Department of Justice (April 2011)

### 9-22.100 ELIGIBILITY CRITERIA

The U.S. Attorney, in his/her discretion, may divert any individual against whom a prosecutable case exists and who is not:

1. Accused of an offense which, under existing Department guidelines, should be diverted to the State for prosecution;
2. A person with two or more prior felony convictions;
3. A public official or former public official accused of an offense arising out of an alleged violation of a public trust; or
4. Accused of an offense related to national security or foreign affairs.

## Criminal Resource Manual, 715 USA
## Form 186 — Pretrial Diversion Agreement
### U.S. Department of Justice

. . . Upon accepting responsibility for your behavior and by your signature on this Agreement, it appearing, after an investigation of the offense, and your background, that the interest of the United States and your own interest and the interest of justice will be served by the following procedure; therefore

On the authority of the Attorney General of the United States, by _____, United States Attorney for the _____ District of _____, prosecution in this District for this offense shall be deferred for the period of _____ months from this date, provided you abide by the following conditions and the requirements of this Agreement set out below.

Should you violate the conditions of this Agreement, the United States Attorney may revoke or modify any conditions of this pretrial diversion program or change the period of supervision, which shall in no case exceed eighteen months. The United States Attorney may release you from supervision at any time. The United States Attorney may at any time within the period of your supervision initiate prosecution for this offense should you violate the conditions of this Agreement. In this case [he/she] will furnish you with notice specifying the conditions of the Agreement which you have violated.

After successfully completing your diversion program and fulfilling all the terms and conditions of the Agreement, no prosecution for the offense . . . will be instituted in this District, and the charges against you, if any, will be dismissed.

Neither this Agreement nor any other document filed with the United States Attorney as a result of your participation in the Pretrial Diversion Program will be used against you, except for impeachment purposes, in connection with any prosecution for the above-described offense.

### GENERAL CONDITIONS OF PRETRIAL DIVERSION

1. You shall not violate any law (Federal/State/Local). You shall immediately contact your pretrial diversion supervisor if arrested and/or questioned by any law enforcement officer.
2. You shall attend school or work regularly at a lawful occupation or otherwise comply with the terms of the special program described below. If you lose your job or are unable to attend school, you shall notify your pretrial diversion supervisor at once. You shall consult him/her prior to job or school changes.
3. You shall report to your supervisor as directed and keep him/her informed of your whereabouts.
4. You shall follow the program and such special conditions as may be described below. . . .

I hereby state that the above has been read and explained to me. I understand the conditions of my pretrial diversion program and agree that I will comply with them.

[Name of Divertee] _____
Defense Attorney _____
United States Attorney _____
Chief Pretrial Services Officer (or Chief Probation Officer) _____

## PROBLEM 10-2.   IN NEED OF TREATMENT?

Melissa has abused legal and illegal narcotics for years. One day she asks her best friend, Claire, to pick up a package for her in a neighborhood with a reputation for drug trafficking. Melissa's husband no longer allows her to leave the house without their driver, so she has no other way of getting drugs. Claire feels uncomfortable about this errand, but she owes Melissa a major favor and agrees.

Claire picks up the package and is arrested shortly after leaving the drug house. A police officer arrests Claire with about three ounces of cocaine in her pocket and informs her of her *Miranda* rights. On her way to the station house, she overhears two police officers discuss the severe sentences that apply to drug crimes. Upon arrival there, the police begin to interrogate Claire. They tell her that she has the right to an attorney but that if she cooperates with them and admits her guilt, they might be able to keep her from "going to court." Her interrogator suggests that with a quick admission of guilt, the case would basically be over for her. Surely, he intimates, she would prefer that over seeing her name and picture in the newspaper and having a criminal record. When she mentions her children, he tells her that only her agreement to go through a diversion program would guarantee that she could keep her children. Claire also speaks quickly to a harried assistant district attorney. She then agrees to enroll in a drug treatment program and to complete it successfully in exchange for the prosecutor's agreement not to file charges against her. Is Claire an appropriate candidate for diversion? What purpose(s) would the prosecutor serve by diverting her case?

### NOTES

1. *Purposes of diversion.*   According to the U.S. Attorneys' Manual, the purposes of diversion are to prevent future criminal activity, to save prosecutorial and judicial resources for major cases, and to provide restitution to communities and victims. Section 712 of the Criminal Resource Manual for U.S. Attorneys states that a pretrial diversion program "should be tailored to the offender's needs and may include employment, counseling, education, job training, psychiatric care," and so forth. The provision also endorses restitution and community service and strongly encourages "innovative approaches." Which of the traditional purposes of the criminal law does this provision emphasize? How successfully were any of these accomplished in Claire's case (Problem 10-1)?

2. *Prevalence of diversion.*   Diversion of arrestees is less common than the outright rejection of criminal charges. Prosecutors are most likely to offer diversion to suspects who face misdemeanor charges. About 8% of all felony arrestees in the largest urban counties in 2006 took part in diversion or "deferred adjudication" programs; 15% of less serious drug offenses were handled by diversion or deferred adjudication. Bureau of Justice Statistics, Felony Defendants in Large Urban Counties, 2006 at 24 (NCJ 2289-44, February 2010); see http://bjs.ojp.usdoj.gov/content/pub/pdf/fdluc06.pdf. Federal diversion programs are even smaller: just over 1,100 suspects were handled through pretrial

diversion in 2004 (compared with more than 116,000 cases prosecuted and almost 32,000 cases declined). Why do diversion programs remain relatively rare? National Association of Pretrial Services Agencies (NAPSA), Pretrial Diversion in the 21st Century (2009) (see http://www.napsa.org/publications/NAPSA PretrialPracticeSurvey.pdf); National Association of Pretrial Services Agencies, Promising Practices in Pretrial Diversion (2009) (see http://www.pretrial.org/ Docs/Documents/PromisingPracticeFinal.pdf). What resource limitations might restrict their availability? See Steven Belenko, The Challenges of Integrating Drug Treatment into the Criminal Justice Process, 63 Alb. L. Rev. 833 (2000).

Are the considerations that affect the decision to defer prosecution meaningfully different when the criminal defendant is a corporate entity? Under a 2003 Department of Justice memorandum (written after the collapse of Arthur Andersen following the accounting firm's indictment), the federal government's policy is to permit a corporate defendant to enter into a "deferred prosecution agreement." After the corporation is indicted, it agrees to pay a fine and restitution to victims, to cooperate with ongoing investigations of its officers, and to institute governance reforms that will be verified by some form of external monitoring. Between 18 months and two years later, the prosecutor will dismiss the indictment if the corporation has complied with all of these conditions. What might motivate a corporation to enter such an agreement? What variations would you expect to find among such agreements in different cases? See Lawrence D. Finder & Ryan D. McConnell, Devolution of Authority: The Department of Justice's Corporate Charging Policies, 51 St. Louis L.J. 1 (2006); John C. Coffee Jr., Deferred Prosecution: Has It Gone Too Far?, Nat'l L.J. (July 25, 2005). P.J. Meitl, Who's the Boss? Prosecutorial Involvement in Corporate America, 34 N. Ky. L. Rev. 1 (2007); Rachel Delaney, Congressional Legislation: The Next Step for Corporate Deferred Prosecution Agreements, 93 Marq. L. Rev. 875 (2009)

3. *Prosecutors and judges as gatekeepers.*   Prosecutors retain complete control over precharge diversion programs but often share authority with judges over diversion programs that begin after charges are filed. State statutes dealing with postcharge diversion programs ordinarily empower the judge to approve the prosecutor's recommendations for offenders to enter the program. See Mont. Code Ann. §46-16-130(3) ("After a charge has been filed, a deferral of prosecution may be entered into only with the approval of the court"). Consider this discussion of institutional roles in Polikov v. Neth, 699 N.W.2d 802 (Neb. 2005):

> [The] formalization of pretrial diversion programs is the type of broad restructuring of the goals of the criminal justice system that is entrusted to the Legislature rather than to the executive branch. [Although] the power to design formal pretrial diversion programs is a legislative function, the use of informal diversion is included in the executive power of prosecutorial discretion. Thus, the Legislature cannot use its power to design formal pretrial diversion programs in a way so as to limit the prosecutor's power to engage in the informal diversion process . . . Second, although the power to design a pretrial diversion program is a legislative one, the power to determine whether to divert a particular person to an established formal pretrial diversion program, at least before the accused is charged, is an executive power, encompassed within the charging function.

See also Clayton v. Lacey, 589 N.W.2d 529 (Neb. 1999) (court has no jurisdiction to consider refusal to divert because it is an exercise of prosecutorial discretion and not "a decision made by a tribunal, board, or officer exercising judicial functions").

The Tennessee court in *Curry* recognized that it is usually the prosecutor who decides which defendants or suspects enter a pretrial diversion program, and that courts are hesitant to interfere with the prosecutor's decision. Indeed, courts in many states refuse to review the prosecutor's decision whether to offer diversion to a suspect unless the prosecutor relies on unconstitutional grounds, such as racial discrimination. See Cleveland v. State, 417 So. 2d 653 (Fla. 1982) (decision on pretrial intervention is prosecutorial, rather than judicial, in nature and is not subject to judicial review; review of arbitrary decisions allowed in other jurisdictions because statutes explicitly authorize review). But some trial and appellate courts, including those in Tennessee, have been more willing to review prosecutorial refusals to allow pretrial diversion as an abuse of discretion, sometimes based on statutory authority either setting standards for review or requiring written reasons for refusals. See State v. Caliguiri, 726 A.2d 912, 916 (N.J. 1999) (If prosecutor refuses application for admission to pretrial intervention program, written statement of reasons must be provided; this clear statement of reasons fosters effective judicial review and allows the offender a meaningful opportunity to challenge the rejection; therefore, "the written rejection may not simply 'parrot' the language of relevant statutes.").

Courts have also rejected challenges to pretrial diversion statutes and programs as an unconstitutional burden on those who choose to exercise their right to trial. See, e.g, Aguilar-Raygoza v. State, 255 P.3d 262 (Nev. 2011) ("the possibility of entering an alcohol treatment program provided in NRS 484C.340 is a form of leniency that is available in exchange for a plea of guilty or nolo contendere and is not an unconstitutional penalty for refusing to enter such a plea or a burden on the exercise of constitutional rights.") Statutes in about a dozen states give prosecutors complete control over who may enter pretrial diversion programs.

Prosecutors' offices sometimes create uniform policies to govern eligibility for diversion, at least for some types of cases. Are the guidelines provided in the U.S. Attorneys' Manual sufficiently precise to limit prosecutorial discretion? Why does the manual exclude drug addicts from access to the diversion program?

In many Continental European countries, such as Germany, where prosecutors have traditionally not been assumed to have any discretion, diversion programs may indicate an increase in prosecutorial power. Is that also true for the United States, or do diversion programs tend to circumscribe prosecutorial discretion by allowing judicial supervision over the prosecutor's choices?

4. *Other gatekeepers.*   Pre-arrest diversion programs tend to shift the police function from law enforcement to social work without providing guidance as to which offenders are well suited to a diversion program. What role should experts such as probation officers play in the initial recommendation process? In the federal system, prosecutors are instructed to refer potential candidates for pretrial diversion to the chief pretrial services officer or the chief probation officer

for the district. See Criminal Resources Manual 712D. What can the probation officer add that the prosecutor does not know or see?

Should the victim have any input in deciding whether an offender may enter a diversion program? The German Juvenile Justice Act permits prosecutors to dismiss cases after the juvenile offender has tried to reach a settlement with the victim.

Legislatures also create some preconditions for defendants or suspects to participate in pretrial diversion programs. See, e.g., S.C. Code §17-22-50 (no pretrial intervention for offenses including repeated domestic violence, blackmail, DUI, a crime of violence); Utah Code §77-36-2.7 (court may not approve diversion for domestic violence defendants but may hold guilty plea in abeyance during treatment program). If the prosecutor and the suspect disagree about the statutory eligibility requirements, should a court be able to review the prosecutor's decision based on its independent interpretation of the statute?

5. *Who decides if the defendant has completed the program?*  Suppose a defendant believes that she has fulfilled all the conditions of the diversion program but the prosecutor disagrees and files criminal charges. Will a court review the prosecutor's conclusion that the defendant failed to complete the program? Is there any reason to treat this question differently from the question of who will enter a diversion program? Among states with statutes addressing judicial review, the majority require some sort of court approval for a decision to remove an offender from a diversion program; others (fewer than ten) grant this decision exclusively to the prosecutor. See Fla. Stat. §948.08; State v. Hancich, 513 A.2d 638 (Conn. 1986) (once defendant was admitted to pretrial alcohol education program following her first arrest for driving under the influence, she could not be removed unless court independently determined that she had lost her eligibility or that she had failed to complete the program successfully). What circumstances might make a court more willing to judge the defendant's success or failure in the program?

6. *Admission of guilt and involvement of counsel.*  The existence of a diversion program may be used to pressure individuals to waive their rights and admit guilt in order to gain entrance. How could a precharge diversion program be structured to avoid such problems? The federal system requires the involvement of a defense attorney. If a suspect or defendant cannot afford counsel, one is appointed. The Canadian statute governing diversion involving juveniles requires that the juvenile, before consenting to participate in a diversion program, be "advised of his or her right to be represented by counsel and [be] given a reasonable opportunity to consult with counsel." Youth Criminal Justice Act, Part 1, 10(2)(d) (2002, c. 1) (Can.). Why does the U.S. Attorneys' Manual mandate that counsel be involved rather than simply require that defendants be informed of their right to counsel?

7. *Widening the net.*  The beginning of formal diversion programs can be traced back to juvenile courts in the early twentieth century. Diversion was formally extended to narcotics cases in the 1960s. Since then concerns have existed about "widening the net" of such programs. The fear is that individuals who would have previously been released without any action are now being diverted

into programs while the cases of more serious offenders, who would not be eligible for diversion, are dismissed. Does diversion amount to decriminalization of certain offenses or offender groups? Or does it instead increase the level of social control over offenders, as community service and drug treatment complement the traditional prison sanctions?

8. *Female offenders and diversion.* Might diversion programs be particularly suitable for and attractive to female defendants? See e.g., 57 Okl. St. Ann. §510.8b (authorizing "Women in Recovery" Program). Many of these offenders commit nonviolent crimes and have dependent children. Lengthy pretrial detention or incarceration forcibly separates mothers from their children, whereas diversion programs allow them to remain together. Should such family considerations help determine which offenders qualify for admission into diversion programs? If not, should offense type be the sole determining factor?

9. *Therapeutic courts and the criminal/civil divide.* Drug courts, domestic violence courts, and some other specialty courts sit uncomfortably in the zone between criminal and civil justice systems. These courts were discussed in Chapter 8, as sources of alternative (non-prison) sanctions. The goals of therapeutic courts sound like civil and social objectives more than any of the traditional goals of the criminal justice system. The discomfort — the demilitarized zone of justice — exists because therapeutic courts use the power (and threat) of the criminal justice system to move (or force) people to change their behavior. See Alex Kreit, The Decriminalization Option: Should States Consider Moving from A Criminal to A Civil Drug Court Model?, 2010 U. Chi. Leg. Forum 299 (2010) ("The best way to treat drug addiction as a public health problem is to end the criminalization of drug use and addiction entirely and enact a civil drug court system similar to Portugal's.").

There are positive ways to think about this complex interplay of criminal and civil justice goals. Specialty courts may create the political space needed to reconsider the goals and efficiency of existing justice models. Judges in specialty courts may mediate the immense power of prosecutors to offer (or refuse to offer) diversion or alternative sanctions. Yet such courts also risk widening the net and further confusing the relationship between criminal and civil justice and therefore the relationship between state and citizen. See Max Deitchler, You Can't Manage What You Don't Measure: An Evaluation of Arkansas's Drug Courts, 64 Ark. L. Rev. 715, 745-46 (2011):

> Drug courts' benefits to the State of Arkansas are significant — reducing prison populations, saving tax dollars versus incarceration, reintegrating drug offenders into society, and providing a path to substance-abuse treatment for those who are addicted. Many of the justifications for drug courts are utilitarian in nature, and these effects should be maximized by encouraging drug courts in Arkansas to trend toward a pre-adjudication model — in order to minimize employment opportunity hurdles and successfully reintegrate offenders into their local communities. Most critically, Arkansas must adopt a more detailed set of performance measures and require all Arkansas drug courts to collect, report, and maintain a comprehensive set of data elements.

## PROBLEM 10-3:    VETERANS COURTS

Unemployment among veterans who have served since 2001 is higher than for non-veterans. Veterans make up 20% of all suicides. Nearly a fifth of the homeless population in the United States are veterans. Substance abuse is pervasive, and many veterans have mental-health problems. These characteristics lead some veterans to commit criminal acts. In 2008 Robert Russell, a judge in Buffalo, New York, after noticing an increasing number of veterans on his docket, created the first specialized court adapted to meet the needs of veterans. Two judges have written about veterans courts. See Michael Daly Hawkins, Coming Home: Accommodating the Special Needs of Military Veterans to the Criminal Justice System, 7 Ohio St. J. Crim. L. 563, 565 (2010); Wendy S. Lindley, The Promise of Veterans Court, 51 Orange County Lawyer 29 (November 2009). See also "Leave No Veteran Behind: A Special Court Tries to Keep Troubled Veterans Out of Prison," The Economist, June 2, 2011. Veterans courts have spread more slowly than drug courts, but about 100 have been created between 2008 and 2012. Justice for Vets is an organization that supports and follows veterans courts. http://www.justiceforvets.org/about.

As with other therapeutic courts, good intentions and an innovative spirit often drive the reforms; evaluation and understanding of the benefits and costs, both for the parties, the justice system, and for broader society, tend to come later. For a description of one veterans court, in Tucson, Arizona, see http://cms3.tucsonaz.gov/courts/veterans-court.

You are a member of the state legislature in a state that does not have explicit statutory authorization for veterans courts. Constituents have asked for a bill that would authorize misdemeanor and felony trial courts in the state to create separate veterans courts. What information will you request from the proponents? What individuals, institutions, and groups will you reach out to for advice and support? If you propose veterans court legislation, what guidelines and limitations would you create?

# B.   DOMESTIC VIOLENCE PROTECTION ORDERS

Crime victimization surveys show a decline in nonfatal intimate-partner violence since 1993. Nevertheless, between 1998 and 2002, almost 700,000 non-fatal violent incidents occurred annually between intimate partners in the United States. These included rapes and sexual assaults, robberies, aggravated assaults, and (most commonly) simple assaults. Eighty-five percent of that violence was directed at women.

In domestic violence cases, the state may file criminal charges against the perpetrator. But other avenues are available: in all states, a family member who is the victim of domestic violence can get a so-called civil protection or restraining order. Survey data indicate that about 17% of women and 3.5% of men who are physically assaulted by an intimate obtain such an order. Over 1.1 million victims of intimate violence obtain protective or restraining orders annually. At the end of the last decade there were an estimated 2 million active restraining orders. Patricia Tjaden & Nancy Thoennes, Extent, Nature and Consequences of Intimate Partner Violence: Findings from the National Violence Against Women Survey 52-54 (National Institute of Justice 2000); U.S. Department of Justice, Office for Victims of Crime, Legal Series Bulletin No. 4, Enforcement of Protective Orders (January 2002).

Protection orders are designed to empower the victim, allowing her to act when the state is unwilling to file a criminal complaint against the batterer. In this sense, civil protection orders create an alternative to the criminal justice process. The goal of such an order is to break the cycle of violence by removing the perpetrator from the abusive relationship without immediately involving the criminal justice system. A civil protection order prohibits a named person from harassing, stalking, or threatening an intimate partner. In addition, a protection order may forbid the person from contacting the victim, require the person to vacate a joint household, or set conditions for child visitation and financial support.

Protection orders are relatively easy to obtain, allowing a victim to proceed without an attorney. Frequently, victims get help from non-attorney domestic violence advocates. A judge issues a preliminary order after an ex parte hearing, and a final protection order follows a hearing at which both sides appear and present evidence.

Protection orders, while technically the product of a civil process, lie between the civil and criminal arenas. Those who violate a protection order can be sanctioned for disobeying the court, through misdemeanor charges, contempt charges, or both. This civil process, therefore, carries a criminal sanction if its target fails to comply with the civil order. Of course, the state may file a criminal complaint if the violation of the protection order also amounts to a substantive offense, such as assault or attempted murder. Despite these sanctions, about 60% of restraining orders are violated.

## PROBLEM 10-4.   RESTRAINT

John and Miriam lived in Louisville, Kentucky, and were having marital difficulties. Even though they hoped to reconcile, they agreed that it would be best if John moved out. One night John came over to pick up their son for a walk. When John asked his son to get ready, five-year-old Ben said, "Get out of my face." John then began to shout at Miriam for failing to teach Ben respect for his father. She responded, also in a raised voice, that Ben's attitude might be John's fault because he was not a good father or husband. John lost his temper and slapped Miriam. She then yelled, "I'll divorce you." John yelled back that he would "bury" her if she filed for divorce, and he stormed off.

Based on this exchange, Miriam filed for an emergency protective order requiring John to keep his distance from her and Ben. The court granted the protective order and sent notice to John immediately after granting the order.

A week later, Miriam's car broke down on the highway. She called John at work and asked him whether he could pick her up and fix the car. John arrived immediately. While he was driving Miriam home, they began to quarrel again.

After they arrived at home and got out of the car, John screamed at Miriam so loudly that her neighbor came out to see what was going on. At that point, John raised his hand as if he were about to hit Miriam, but he then thought better of it and instead continued berating her. Miriam asked the neighbor to call the police. Within minutes the police arrived and arrested John for violating the protective order.

At his trial for violation of the protective order and attempted assault, John challenges the validity of the initial protective order. He argues that the court violated the Constitution when it issued the protective order without hearing from him, and he contends that the government has not established the statutory requirements to convict him of violating the restraining order and attempted assault.

As prosecuting counsel, how would you respond? Before you answer this question, consult the following Kentucky statutes describing the relevant procedures for protective orders.

## ‖ *Kentucky Statutes §403.720 to 403.760* ‖

### §403.720  DEFINITIONS

As used in [this chapter], (1) "Domestic violence and abuse" means physical injury, serious physical injury, sexual abuse, assault, or the infliction of fear of imminent physical injury, serious physical injury, sexual abuse, or assault between family members or members of an unmarried couple; (2) "Family member" means a spouse, including a former spouse, a parent, a child, a stepchild, or any other person related by consanguinity or affinity within the second degree . . . (4) "Member of an unmarried couple" means each member of an unmarried couple which allegedly has a child in common, any children of that couple, or a member of an unmarried couple who are living together or have formerly lived together.

### §403.740  EMERGENCY PROTECTIVE ORDER

(1) If, upon review of the petition, . . . the court determines that the allegations contained therein indicate the presence of an immediate and present danger of domestic violence and abuse, the court shall issue, upon proper motion, ex parte, an emergency protective order:

(a) Restraining the adverse party from any contact or communication with the petitioner except as directed by the court;

(b) Restraining the adverse party from committing further acts of domestic violence and abuse;

(c) Restraining the adverse party from disposing of or damaging any of the property of the parties;

(d) Restraining the adverse party from going to or within a specified distance of a specifically described residence, school, or place of employment of the petitioner, minor child of the petitioner, family member, or member of an unmarried couple protected in the order;

(e) Directing the adverse party to vacate the residence shared by the parties to the action;

(f) [Granting] temporary custody;

(g) Restraining the adverse party from approaching the petitioner or a minor child of the petitioner within a distance specified in the order, not to exceed five hundred (500) feet; or

(h) [Entering] other orders the court believes will be of assistance in eliminating future acts of domestic violence and abuse; or any combination thereof.

(2) [If] the court issues an emergency protective order pursuant to subsection (1) of this section, the court shall not order or refer the parties to mediation for resolution of the issues alleged in the petition [unless the victim of the alleged domestic abuse voluntarily requests it and mediation is a realistic and viable alternative to or adjunct to a protective order].

(3) An emergency protective order issued in accordance with this section shall be issued without bond being required of the petitioner.

(4) An emergency protective order issued in accordance with this section shall be effective for a period of time fixed in the order, but not to exceed fourteen days. Upon the issuance of an emergency protective order, a date for a full hearing . . . shall be fixed not later than the expiration date of the emergency protective order. An emergency protective order shall be reissued for a period not to exceed fourteen days if service has not been made on the adverse party by the fixed court date and time or as the court determines is necessary for the protection of the petitioner. . . .

### §403.745  HEARING

(1) If, upon review of the petition . . . , the court determines that the allegations contained therein do not indicate the presence of an immediate and present danger of domestic violence and abuse, the court shall fix a date, time, and place for a hearing and shall cause a summons to be issued for the adverse party. . . . The hearing shall be fixed not later than fourteen days following the issuance of the summons. . . .

### §403.750

(1) Following the hearing provided for under §403.740 and 403.745, the court, if it finds from a preponderance of the evidence that an act or acts of domestic violence and abuse have occurred and may again occur, may:

(a-e) [take any actions described in §403.740(1a-e)];

(f) award temporary support;

(g) direct that either or both parties receive counseling services available in the community, except that the court shall not order or refer the parties to participate in mediation for resolution of the issues alleged in the petition filed pursuant to [the provisions on domestic violence protective orders].

(2) Any order entered pursuant to this section shall be effective for a period of time, fixed by the court, not to exceed three years and may be reissued upon expiration for an additional period of up to three years. The number of times an order may be reissued shall not be limited. With respect to whether an order should be reissued, any party may present to the court testimony relating to the importance of the fact that acts of domestic violence or abuse have not occurred during the pendency of the order. . . .

### §403.760    CONTEMPT OF COURT

(1) Violation of the terms or conditions of an order issued under the provisions of §403.740 or 403.750, whether an emergency protective order, or an order following hearing, after service of the order on the respondent, or notice of the order to the respondent, shall constitute contempt of court.

(2) Any peace officer having probable cause to believe a violation has occurred of an order issued under the provisions of §403.740 or 403.750 . . . shall arrest the respondent without a warrant for violation of a protective order. . . . Following a hearing the District Court in the county in which the peace officer made the arrest for the violation may punish the violation of a protective order. . . .

(4) Nothing in this section shall preclude the Commonwealth from prosecuting and convicting the respondent of criminal offenses other than violation of a protective order.

(5) Civil proceedings and criminal proceedings for violation of a protective order . . . shall be mutually exclusive. Once either proceeding has been initiated the other shall not be undertaken regardless of the outcome of the original proceeding.

## NOTES

1. *Goals of civil protection orders.*   What goals are civil protection orders intended to achieve? Why can these not be accomplished with criminal actions? Civil protection orders appear to be a valuable alternative to the criminal justice process when the criminal justice system either does not act or does not act quickly enough. Such orders also serve important symbolic ends by allowing the victim to demonstrate her ability to act, her strength, and her independent decision-making skills. They constitute a direct action by the victim against the abuser.

Despite the support of the justice system, however, restraining orders may not reduce domestic violence. See Elaine Chiu, Confronting the Agency in Battered Mothers, 74 S. Cal. L. Rev. 1223 (2001). Is a civil process insufficiently stigmatizing to keep the offender from battering again? Many abusers in domestic violence situations have criminal records that resemble those of other violent criminals. Should restraining orders be utilized only for first-time domestic violence offenders or for individuals without a criminal record?

Some have argued that restraining orders may be unsuccessful because batterers do not perceive the process as fair. Often they do not understand the difference between the civil and criminal systems and are left alone to navigate the judicial system. Should batterers be provided with more process, such as information about the system or even the right to counsel? May such services be advisable only if it is shown that they increase compliance? See Deborah Epstein, Procedural Justice: Tempering the State's Response to Domestic Violence, 43 Wm. & Mary L. Rev. 1843 (2002).

In some counties in Kentucky, domestic violence orders have earned the nickname "the poor man's [and woman's] divorce." Domestic violence orders may be used to accomplish some of the goals of divorce, but much more quickly. How could such abuses of the system be prevented without limiting access for abused persons?

2. *Ex parte civil proceedings.*   Emergency protection orders are granted without a hearing and without notice being provided to the respondent. They often stay in place for about two weeks. Many states provide extensive self-help manuals for battered spouses, explaining how to obtain a restraining order. Shortly before the emergency protection order runs out, the court holds a hearing in which both sides are present. Because the grant of civil protection orders takes place in a civil proceeding, the petitioner (note the civil terminology) has to establish the occurrence of domestic violence merely by a preponderance of the evidence.

There is no right to publicly funded counsel in civil proceedings, including hearings on civil protection orders. Petitioners, however, are frequently represented by women's advocates or law school clinics in their requests for emergency protection orders. These advocates become regular players in the process, with the respondents remaining largely unrepresented until a protection order is violated. Once criminal proceedings are under way, the alleged batterer has the right to an attorney.

3. *Specialized domestic violence courts or judges.*   In some states, specially designated domestic violence judges grant civil protection orders, sit on domestic violence cases, and deal with violations of civil protection orders. What reasons are there for the institution of such "one-stop shopping"? What advantages and disadvantages flow from subject matter–focused judging? See Dag MacLeod & Julia F. Weber, Judicial Council of California, Administrative Office of the Courts, Domestic Violence Courts: A Descriptive Study (May 2000); Randal B. Fritzler & Leonore M. J. Simon, The Development of a Specialized Domestic Violence Court in Vancouver, Washington: Utilizing Innovative Judicial Paradigms, 69 UMKC L. Rev. 139 (2000); Susan Keilitz, Specialization of Domestic Violence Case Management in the Courts: A National Survey (2004, NCJ 199724).

4. *Double jeopardy and domestic violence orders.*   The violation of a civil protection order may lead to a panoply of actions against the batterer. Breach of the court's order could lead to a contempt citation or a criminal prosecution for the violation; an assault and battery could also lead to a separate criminal action. In

United States v. Dixon, 509 U.S. 688 (1993), the Supreme Court addressed whether charges of assault and threats were nullified by the double jeopardy clause because they were filed after a misdemeanor contempt conviction based on the same conduct. The Court, in a splintered opinion, held that the misdemeanor assault prosecution was barred, but the prosecutions for assault with intent to kill and felony threats could go forward because misdemeanor contempt and each of the latter crimes required proof of an element that the other did not. See Blockburger v. United States, 284 U.S. 299 (1932) (describing traditional "same elements" test to determine which crimes qualify as the same offense and thus are barred by double jeopardy). Does this decision deter prosecutors from filing criminal assault charges after the courts have issued contempt citations? See David M. Zlotnick, Battered Women and Justice Scalia, 41 Ariz. L. Rev. 847 (1999).

5. *Weapon possession and protection orders.*   The federal Violence Against Women Act, enacted in 1994, prohibits anyone under a civil protection order from possessing firearms or ammunition. See 18 U.S.C. §922(g)(8) and (g)(9) (extending the firearm prohibition to anyone "who has been convicted in any court of a misdemeanor crime of domestic violence"). Federal law and most state statutes, however, prohibit possession of weapons only upon a finding of abuse after an evidentiary hearing that gives the defendant an opportunity to be heard. This means that in many states an emergency protective order will not place the respondent under the coverage of the gun ban. Some commentators argue that without an immediate confiscation of weapons when the court issues the emergency order, the threat to the victim continues until the hearing. See Carrie Chew, Domestic Violence, Guns, and Minnesota Women: Responding to New Law, Correcting Old Legislative Need, and Taking Cues from Other Jurisdictions, 25 Hamline J. Pub. L. & Pol'y 115 (2003).

6. *Control of litigation.*   In situations in which physical harm is inflicted or threatened, the state asserts its interest as a representative of the people, not merely of the victim of the alleged crime. This means that the decision whether to prosecute is made by a state agent rather than the victim. In many jurisdictions, mandatory prosecution in domestic violence cases (sometimes required by statute, more often by prosecutorial office policy) does not leave the victim any option. Should she refuse to testify or choose to testify falsely, the criminal justice system can sanction her. Because the victim and the offender in a domestic violence situation have a relationship — and sometimes try to preserve that relationship — the traditional adversarial criminal justice model may break down.

In what other situations may civil actions be preferable over criminal actions? Are there other types of criminal offenses in which the victim's interests may not be adequately represented by the state? In corporate embezzlement and similar types of business crimes, businesses often choose to settle with the offenders, under the threat of reporting them to the criminal justice system, without ever involving the official system. This is possible because the victimized business is in a more advantageous bargaining position than the offender — and its sole interest is recouping its financial loss rather than vindicating a greater goal. In fraud crimes committed against the government, prosecutors often threaten to file criminal suits while also proceeding civilly. The threat of criminal litigation can lead to more advantageous civil settlements for the government. Should there be constitutional or statutory limits on the use of such dual threats?

7. *Confrontation clause and domestic violence.*   Prosecution of domestic violence cases has become more difficult, and taken a strong constitutional regulatory turn, with the line of United States Supreme Court cases starting with Crawford v. Washington, 541 U.S. 36 (2004). Those cases revitalize the confrontation clause and the need for cross-examination with regard to hearsay in a broad range of circumstances. See, e.g., Deborah Tuerkheimer, Forfeiture After Giles: The Relevance of "Domestic Violence Context," 13 Lewis & Clark L. Rev. 711 (2009); Eleanor Simon, Confrontation and Domestic Violence Post-Davis: Is There and Should There Be A Doctrinal Exception?, 17 Mich. J. Gender & L. 175 (2011); John M. Leventhal, Liberty Aldrich, The Admission of Evidence in Domestic Violence Cases After Crawford v. Washington: A National Survey, 11 Berkeley J. Crim. L. 77 (2006); Myrna S. Raeder, Domestic Violence Cases After Davis: Is the Glass Half Empty or Half Full?, 15 J.L. & Policy 759 (2007)

# C.  ASSET FORFEITURE

While the alternatives to criminal sentences we have considered so far all emphasize restrictions on liberty, other alternative remedies depend on taking the property of a suspected wrongdoer. Asset forfeiture is among the most important of these sanctions. Technically, most asset forfeiture occurs through civil proceedings, with no necessary connection to criminal charges. In practice, asset forfeiture is tightly integrated with criminal enforcement. Asset forfeiture has become an important part of prosecution and punishment, especially for crimes with an economic motive, such as drug offenses, money laundering, and racketeering. Forfeiture is said to "take the profit out of crime."

The effectiveness of asset forfeiture lies partly in the procedural edge it gives the prosecution. Civil asset forfeiture gives the prosecution a more favorable standard of proof, extensive discovery, and summary judgment, among other advantages. Forfeiture can also take place during proceedings following on the heels of a criminal conviction, essentially as part of the criminal sentencing. Such "criminal forfeitures" are less common than civil forfeitures, however, because of the relative procedural difficulties they present to the government.

The destination of forfeited property also makes forfeiture an attractive device for law enforcement. Federal statutes and executive policies, along with most state statutes, assign forfeited property directly to the budgets of law enforcement agencies. See John Burnett, National Public Radio Morning Edition, Seized Drug Assets Pad Police Budgets (2008) (http://www.npr.org/templates/story/story.php?storyId=91490480). Funds from forfeitures carried out under state law generally go to local police and sheriff's offices, after reimbursement of prosecutors for the costs of processing the forfeiture. When federal agents complete a forfeiture, the proceeds go to the participating federal agencies. Moreover, the federal government can "adopt" the forfeitures of state or local authorities. If state or local police seize property that is forfeitable under federal law, and federal prosecutors obtain the final forfeiture order in federal court, they split the proceeds.

Because the police and prosecutors who select property for forfeiture directly benefit from the forfeitures, property owners have argued that the police have an incentive to abuse the practice. Alleged abuses in spending forfeited funds often make the headlines. For instance, news reports widely noted a small-town sheriff who seized a Rolls-Royce from a drug dealer and used it as his personal car.

In this section, we examine the asset forfeiture procedures that operate in tandem with the criminal justice system. Consider the ways in which civil forfeiture proceedings differ from criminal proceedings, and determine whether those differences are justified by the different purposes of these systems or by the different consequences flowing from them.

## 1.   Property Subject to Forfeiture

The forfeiture laws target only property with some defined connection to a crime. It is ordinarily not enough that an accused felon owns the property; the suspect must use it to commit a crime or acquire it as a result of the crime. The materials below describe the property that the law targets for forfeiture and the property it exempts from forfeiture. Consider what these categories reveal about the objectives of the forfeiture laws and their imperfect overlap with the objectives of criminal law enforcement.

In the federal system, roughly 200 criminal statutes provide for forfeiture. Many of these statutes deal with violations of customs laws or food and drug laws. Most federal forfeitures, however, are exercised under the laws against money laundering, racketeering, and illicit drugs. The same pattern holds for most state forfeiture laws: they apply primarily to violations of drug, gambling, liquor, and racketeering laws. In a few states, any felony can serve as the basis for a forfeiture. The following case discusses the necessary connection between the crime and the forfeited property under an early federal statute.

## United States v. Cargo of the Brig Malek Adhel
### 43 U.S. 210 (1844)

STORY, J.

[The information in this case alleged that the brig *Malek Adhel* was used to commit "piratical aggression and restraint upon the high seas" against five vessels. The government pursued forfeiture proceedings against the ship and its cargo after it arrived in Maryland. The firm of Peter Harmony and Co. of New York claimed the ship and cargo as its property and attempted to prevent the forfeiture. At the hearing in district court, the vessel was condemned and the cargo acquitted. Peter Harmony and Co. brought this appeal.]

It was fully admitted in the court below, that the owners of the brig and cargo never contemplated or authorized the acts complained of; that the brig was bound on an innocent commercial voyage from New York to Guayamas, in

California; and that the equipments on board were the usual equipments for such a voyage. It appears from the evidence that the brig sailed from the port of New York on the 30th of June, 1840, under the command of one Joseph Nunez, armed with a cannon and ammunition, and with pistols and daggers on board. The acts of aggression complained of, were committed at different times under false pretences, and wantonly and wilfully without provocation or justification, between the 6th of July, 1840, and the 20th of August, 1840, when the brig arrived at Bahia; where, in consequence of the information given to the American consul by the crew, the brig was seized by the United States ship *Enterprize*, then at that port, and carried to Rio Janeiro, and from thence brought to the United States. . . . Now upon this posture of the case, it has been contended [that] neither the brig nor the cargo are liable to condemnation, because the owners neither participated in nor authorized the piratical acts, but are entirely innocent thereof. . . .

The [first] question is, whether the innocence of the owners can withdraw the ship from the penalty of confiscation under the act of Congress. Here, . . . it may be remarked that the act makes no exception whatsoever, whether the aggression be with or without the co-operation of the owners. The vessel which commits the aggression is treated as the offender, as the guilty instrument or thing to which the forfeiture attaches, without any reference whatsoever to the character or conduct of the owner. The vessel or boat (says the act of Congress) from which such piratical aggression, &c., shall have been first attempted or made shall be condemned. . . . And this is done from the necessity of the case, as the only adequate means of suppressing the offence or wrong, or insuring an indemnity to the injured party. The doctrine also is familiarly applied to cases of smuggling and other misconduct under our revenue laws. . . . In short, the acts of the master and crew, in cases of this sort, bind the interest of the owner of the ship, whether he be innocent or guilty; and he impliedly submits to whatever the law denounces as a forfeiture attached to the ship by reason of their unlawful or wanton wrongs. . . .

The ship is also by the general maritime law held responsible for the torts and misconduct of the master and crew thereof, whether arising from negligence or a wilful disregard of duty; as, for example, in cases of collision and other wrongs done upon the high seas or elsewhere within the admiralty and maritime jurisdiction, upon the general policy of that law, which looks to the instrument itself, used as the means of the mischief, as the best and surest pledge for the compensation and indemnity to the injured party. The act of Congress has therefore done nothing more on this point than to affirm and enforce the general principles of the maritime law and of the law of nations.

The remaining question is, whether the cargo is involved in the same fate as the ship. In respect to the forfeiture under the act of 1819,[*] it is plain that the cargo stands upon a very different ground from that of the ship. Nothing is said in relation to the condemnation of the cargo in the fourth section of the act; and

---

[*] The act of 1819 provides as follows: "[Whenever] any vessel or boat from which any piratical aggression . . . shall have been first attempted or made, shall be captured and brought into any port of the United States, the same shall and may be adjudged and condemned to their use and that of the captors, after due process and trial in any court have admiralty jurisdiction, . . . and the same court shall thereupon order a sale and distribution thereof accordingly, and at their discretion." — EDS.

in the silence of any expression of the legislature, in the case of provisions confessedly penal, it ought not to be presumed that their intention exceeded their language. . . .

So far as the general maritime law applies to torts or injuries committed on the high seas and within the admiralty jurisdiction, the general rule is, not forfeiture of the offending property; but compensation to the full extent of all damages sustained or reasonably allowable, to be enforced by a proceeding therefor in rem or in personam. It is true that the law of nations goes in many cases much farther, and inflicts the penalty of confiscation for very gross and wanton violations of duty. But, then, it limits the penalty to cases of extraordinary turpitude or violence. For petty misconduct, or petty plunderage, or petty neglect of duty, it contents itself with the mitigated rule of compensation in damages. . . .

The present case seems to us fairly to fall within the general principle of exempting the cargo. The owners are confessedly innocent of all intentional or meditated wrong. They are free from any imputation of guilt, and every suspicion of connivance with the master in his hostile acts and wanton misconduct. [The act of Congress limits] the penalty of confiscation to the vessel alone, [showing] that the public policy of our government in cases of this nature is not intended to embrace the cargo. It is satisfied by attaching the penalty to the offending vessel, as all that public justice and a just regard to private rights require. For these reasons, we are of opinion that the decrees condemning the vessel and restoring the cargo, rendered in both the courts below, ought to be affirmed. . . .

## NOTES

1. *Objectives of forfeiture.* Why did the government seek forfeiture of the ship and its cargo? The statute in question called for the forfeiture proceeds to become government property and did not mention use of the property to compensate victims of wrongdoing. Was the forfeiture done to prevent future criminal uses of the property? Won't future pirates be able to use some other ordinary vessel just as readily? Did Peter Harmony and Co. do anything wrong? Does it matter in forfeiture proceedings whether the firm was responsible for the piracy?

2. *Statutory connection to vessel and cargo.* Why did the Court in *Malek Adhel* interpret the statute to allow forfeiture of the vessel but not the cargo? Would the Court have enforced a statute that clearly provided for the forfeiture of the cargo, or could the law of admiralty and the law of nations actually trump the statute? Why do the law of admiralty and the law of nations require gross and wanton acts before allowing forfeiture of cargo? Consider whether this is an early indication of a need for proportionality between the crime committed and the assets forfeited.

3. *The expanding statutory connection.* Legislatures have steadily increased the categories of property subject to forfeiture. Take, for instance, the evolution of one of the primary federal forfeiture statutes, 21 U.S.C. §881. The original

1970 version of the statute applied to (1) all controlled substances; (2) all raw materials, products, and equipment used or intended to be used to manufacture or deliver controlled substances; (3) all containers for property described in the first two categories; (4) all conveyances (including aircraft, vehicles, and vessels) used or intended to be used to facilitate the transportation, sale, receipt, possession, or concealment of property described in the first two categories; and (5) all books, records, and research used in violation of controlled substances laws. Law enforcement officers were not able to seize much property meeting these criteria — only $30 million during the first nine years following passage of the law. A 1978 amendment expanded forfeiture to reach (1) all money, securities, and other "things of value furnished or intended to be furnished" in exchange for a controlled substance; (2) all proceeds traceable to such an exchange; and (3) all money, negotiable instruments, and securities used or intended to facilitate a violation of the drug laws. In 1984 the statute was expanded further to allow forfeiture of all real property used or intended "to commit, or to facilitate" a violation of drug laws. For a discussion of the "widening net" of property subject to forfeiture under federal laws, see Jimmy Gurulé, Sandra Guerra Thompson & Michael O'Hear, The Law of Asset Forfeiture ch. 5 (2004). Asset forfeiture has also become an important tool in punishing and preventing financial crimes in many European nations. See Laura Donohue, Anti-Terrorist Finance in the United Kingdom and the United States, 27 Mich. J. Int'l L. 303 (2006) (discussing forfeiture in the United Kingdom and the United States).

4. *Forfeiture of estate.* None of the major forfeiture statutes attempts to subject to forfeiture *all* of the property of a person suspected, accused, or convicted of a crime. Is there anything stopping Congress and the state legislatures from adopting a statute along these lines? In eighteenth-century English practice, felons and traitors forfeited all their property. As William Blackstone explained it, allowing forfeitures of an entire estate "will help to restrain a man, not only by the sense of his duty, and dread of personal punishment, but also by his passions and natural affections; and will interest every dependent and relation he has, to keep him from offending." 4 William Blackstone, Commentaries on the Laws of England *375. The U.S. Constitution forbids forfeiture of estate as a punishment for treason, although it is allowed "during the Life of the Person attainted." U.S. Const. art. III, §3, cl. 2. The First Congress passed a law prohibiting federal forfeiture of estate as a punishment for other felonies. Could a state pass a statute providing for forfeiture of estate? What abuses might have occurred under English law to create such a reaction among early American lawmakers?

## PROBLEM 10-5.  WEAPONS ON WHEELS

In 1999 New York City introduced a "Zero Tolerance Drinking and Driving Initiative." Under this policy, police officers who arrest someone for driving while intoxicated (registering .10 or higher on a Breathalyzer test) may seize the automobile. The policy prevents the police from seizing a vehicle in cases where drivers are arrested for the lesser offense of "driving while impaired" (registering between .06 and .10 on a Breathalyzer test). The seized car is searched and stored in a city facility. If the driver is either the owner or principal user of the car, the city will begin a civil forfeiture proceeding to take the car away. If the owner of the car knew that someone else would use it to commit a crime (including driving while intoxicated), the car is also declared subject to forfeiture. Before the city adopted this new policy, the police held the car of someone arrested for drunken driving until some other person arrived at the station to pick up the car. The city sometimes asked for forfeiture of the car, but only after a criminal conviction.

The change in policy was based on an existing provision of the Administrative Code of the City of New York. Section 14-140 provides that the Police Property Clerk may take possession of all property "suspected of having been used as a means of committing crime." A person who uses property in furtherance of a crime "or suffers the same to be used . . . shall not be deemed to be the lawful claimant."

The mayor explained the new policy as follows: "It isn't punishment. It's remedial. The car is seized to protect society against this car being driven around in the communities of New York City because it's been demonstrated that this car will be operated unsafely." The forfeiture action is "a way of preventing the use of what, in fact, is a weapon when driven while intoxicated against the public." There were 6,368 arrests of drunken drivers in New York City in 1998, and 31 fatalities attributed to driving while intoxicated.

Francisco Almote, one of the first motorists whose vehicle was seized under the new policy, had been convicted five times previously on charges that he drove while intoxicated. Police seized his 1987 Toyota when they arrested him. A second driver whose car was seized was Pavel Grinberg, who was driving with his wife in Brooklyn one night when he was pulled over for not wearing a seat belt. Police officers said that a Breathalyzer test showed a blood alcohol level of .11 percent, so the officers arrested Grinberg and seized his 1988 Acura Integra (with a book value of about $1,650). "I was at my good friend's daughter's first birthday party and I had one beer — that was it," Grinberg said.

You are an attorney in the office of the Corporation Counsel for New York City. What difficulties (if any) do you foresee in enforcing this policy? How should the city respond in cases where the defendant charged with driving while intoxicated is willing to plead guilty to the lesser charge of driving while impaired (a charge that is not a basis for seizing the car under the city's policy)? What if the defendant is willing to "settle" the forfeiture proceeding by paying one-quarter of the car's value?

## Richard Austin v. United States
### 509 U.S. 602 (1993)

BLACKMUN, J.

In this case, we are asked to decide whether the Excessive Fines Clause of the Eighth Amendment applies to forfeitures of property under 21 U.S.C. §881(a)(4) and (a)(7). We hold that it does and therefore remand the case for consideration of the question whether the forfeiture at issue here was excessive.

On August 2, 1990, petitioner Richard Lyle Austin was indicted on four counts of violating South Dakota's drug laws. Austin ultimately pleaded guilty to one count of possessing cocaine with intent to distribute and was sentenced by the state court to seven years' imprisonment. On September 7, the United States filed an in rem action in the United States District Court for the District of South Dakota seeking forfeiture of Austin's mobile home and auto body shop under 21 U.S.C. §881(a)(4) and (a)(7). Austin filed a claim and an answer to the complaint.

[According to affidavits supporting a government motion for summary judgment], Austin met Keith Engebretson at Austin's body shop on June 13, 1990, and agreed to sell cocaine to Engebretson. Austin left the shop, went to his mobile home, and returned to the shop with two grams of cocaine which he sold to Engebretson. State authorities executed a search warrant on the body shop and mobile home the following day. They discovered small amounts of marijuana and cocaine, a .22 caliber revolver, drug paraphernalia, and approximately $4,700 in cash. [The district court granted summary judgment to the government, and the Eighth Circuit affirmed.]

Austin contends that the Eighth Amendment's Excessive Fines Clause applies to in rem civil forfeiture proceedings. . . . The United States now argues that "any claim that the government's conduct in a civil proceeding is limited by the Eighth Amendment generally, or by the Excessive Fines Clause in particular, must fail unless the challenged governmental action, despite its label, would have been recognized as a criminal punishment at the time the Eighth Amendment was adopted." It further suggests that the Eighth Amendment cannot apply to a civil proceeding unless that proceeding is so punitive that it must be considered criminal under [our prior cases]. We disagree. . . .

The purpose of the Eighth Amendment, putting the Bail Clause to one side, was to limit the government's power to punish. The Cruel and Unusual Punishments Clause is self-evidently concerned with punishment. The Excessive Fines Clause limits the Government's power to extract payments, whether in cash or in kind, as punishment for some offense. The notion of punishment, as we commonly understand it, cuts across the division between the civil and the criminal law. It is commonly understood that civil proceedings may advance punitive and remedial goals, and, conversely, that both punitive and remedial goals may be served by criminal penalties. Thus, the question is not, as the United States would have it, whether forfeiture under §881(a)(4) and (a)(7) is civil or criminal, but rather whether it is punishment. . . . We turn, then, to consider whether, at the time the Eighth Amendment was ratified, forfeiture was understood at least in part as punishment and whether forfeiture under §881(a)(4) and (a)(7) should be so understood today.

Three kinds of forfeiture were established in England at the time the Eighth Amendment was ratified in the United States: deodand, forfeiture upon conviction for a felony or treason, and statutory forfeiture [for violations of the customs and revenue laws]. Each was understood, at least in part, as imposing punishment. At common law the value of an inanimate object directly or indirectly causing the accidental death of a King's subject was forfeited to the Crown as a deodand. . . . The value of the instrument was forfeited to the King, in the belief that the King would provide the money for Masses to be said for the good of the dead man's soul, or insure that the deodand was put to charitable uses. When application of the deodand to religious or eleemosynary purposes ceased, and the deodand became a source of Crown revenue, the institution was justified as a penalty for carelessness. . . .

Of England's three kinds of forfeiture, only the third took hold in the United States. [The] common law courts in the Colonies—and later in the states during the period of Confederation—were exercising jurisdiction in rem in the enforcement of English and local forfeiture statutes. The First Congress passed laws subjecting ships and cargos involved in customs offenses to forfeiture. . . .

Our cases also have recognized that statutory in rem forfeiture imposes punishment. [This] understanding of forfeiture as punishment runs through our cases rejecting the "innocence" of the owner as a common-law defense to forfeiture. In these cases, forfeiture has been justified on two theories—that the property itself is "guilty" of the offense, and that the owner may be held accountable for the wrongs of others to whom he entrusts his property. . . . In *Brig Malek Adhel*, it reasoned that "the acts of the master and crew, in cases of this sort, bind the interest of the owner of the ship, whether he be innocent or guilty; and he impliedly submits to whatever the law denounces as a forfeiture attached to the ship by reason of their unlawful or wanton wrongs." . . . Like the guilty-property fiction, this theory of vicarious liability is premised on the idea that the owner has been negligent. . . . We conclude, therefore, that forfeiture generally and statutory in rem forfeiture in particular historically have been understood, at least in part, as punishment.

We turn next to consider whether forfeitures under 21 U.S.C. §881(a)(4) and (a)(7) are properly considered punishment today. We find nothing in these provisions or their legislative history to contradict the historical understanding of forfeiture as punishment. Unlike traditional forfeiture statutes, §881(a)(4) and (a)(7) expressly provide an "innocent owner" defense. . . . These exemptions serve to focus the provisions on the culpability of the owner in a way that makes them look more like punishment, not less. . . .

The legislative history of §881 confirms the punitive nature of these provisions. When it added subsection (a)(7) to §881 in 1984, Congress recognized "that the traditional criminal sanctions of fine and imprisonment are inadequate to deter or punish the enormously profitable trade in dangerous drugs." It characterized the forfeiture of real property as "a powerful deterrent." . . .

The Government argues that §881(a)(4) and (a)(7) are not punitive but, rather, should be considered remedial in two respects. First, they remove the "instruments" of the drug trade "thereby protecting the community from the threat of continued drug dealing." Second, the forfeited assets serve to compensate the Government for the expense of law enforcement activity and for its expenditure on societal problems such as urban blight, drug addiction, and other health concerns resulting from the drug trade.

In our view, neither argument withstands scrutiny. Concededly, we have recognized that the forfeiture of contraband itself may be characterized as remedial because it removes dangerous or illegal items from society. The Court, however, previously has rejected government's attempt to extend that reasoning to conveyances used to transport illegal liquor, [because there] is nothing even remotely criminal in possessing an automobile. The same, without question, is true of the properties involved here, and the Government's attempt to characterize these properties as "instruments" of the drug trade must meet the same fate.

The Government's second argument about the remedial nature of this forfeiture is no more persuasive. We previously have upheld the forfeiture of goods involved in customs violations as a reasonable form of liquidated damages. But the dramatic variations in the value of conveyances and real property forfeitable under §881(a)(4) and (a)(7) undercut any similar argument with respect to those provisions. . . .

Fundamentally, even assuming that §881(a)(4) and (a)(7) serve some remedial purpose, the Government's argument must fail. A civil sanction that cannot fairly be said solely to serve a remedial purpose, but rather can only be explained as also serving either retributive or deterrent purposes, is punishment, as we have come to understand the term. In light of the historical understanding of forfeiture as punishment, the clear focus of §881(a)(4) and (a)(7) on the culpability of the owner, and the evidence that Congress understood those provisions as serving to deter and to punish, we cannot conclude that forfeiture under §881(a)(4) and (a)(7) serves solely a remedial purpose. We therefore conclude that forfeiture under these provisions constitutes payment to a sovereign as punishment for some offense, and, as such, is subject to the limitations of the Eighth Amendment's Excessive Fines Clause.

Austin asks that we establish a multifactor test for determining whether a forfeiture is constitutionally "excessive." We decline that invitation. . . . Prudence dictates that we allow the lower courts to consider that question in the first instance. . . . The judgment of the Court of Appeals is reversed and the case is remanded to that court for further proceedings consistent with this opinion. It is so ordered.

SCALIA, J., concurring.

. . . However the theory may be expressed, it seems to me that this taking of lawful property must be considered, in whole or in part, punitive. Its purpose is not compensatory, to make someone whole for injury caused by unlawful use of the property. Punishment is being imposed, whether one quaintly considers its object to be the property itself, or more realistically regards its object to be the property's owner. . . . The Court apparently believes, however, that only actual culpability of the affected property owner can establish that a forfeiture provision is punitive, and sets out to establish that such culpability exists in the case of in rem forfeitures. [But we] have never held that the Constitution requires negligence, or any other degree of culpability, to support such forfeitures. . . .

That this forfeiture works as a fine raises the excessiveness issue, on which the Court remands. I agree that a remand is in order, but think it worth pointing out that on remand the excessiveness analysis must be different from that applicable to monetary fines and, perhaps, to in personam forfeitures. In the case of a monetary fine, the Eighth Amendment's origins in the English Bill of Rights, intended to limit the abusive penalties assessed against the king's opponents, demonstrate that the touchstone is value of the fine in relation to the offense. [The] same is true for in personam forfeiture. . . .

Unlike monetary fines, statutory in rem forfeitures have traditionally been fixed, not by determining the appropriate value of the penalty in relation to the committed offense, but by determining what property has been "tainted" by unlawful use, to which issue the value of the property is irrelevant. Scales used to measure out unlawful drug sales, for example, are confiscable whether made of the purest gold or the basest metal. But an in rem forfeiture goes beyond the traditional limits that the Eighth Amendment permits if it applies to property that cannot properly be regarded as an instrumentality of the offense — the building, for example, in which an isolated drug sale happens to occur. Such a confiscation would be an excessive fine. The question is not how much the confiscated property is worth, but whether the confiscated property has a close enough relationship to the offense. . . .

## Kansas Constitution Art. 15, §9

A homestead to the extent of . . . one acre within the limits of an incorporated town or city, occupied as a residence by the family of the owner, together with all improvements on the same, shall be exempted from forced sale under any process of law, and shall not be alienated without the joint consent of husband and wife. . . .

## Philadelphia Police Department Directive 102

. . . The Police Department has established the following minimal value guidelines for seizure under Drug Forfeiture Laws:

| | | | |
|---|---|---|---|
| Currency | $1,000 | Vehicles | $2,500 |
| Jewelry | $5,000 | Aircraft, Vessels | $5,000 |
| Real Estate | $10,000 | Other Property | $1,000 |

## United States Attorneys Manual
### 9-111.120. Net Equity Values

The following guidelines set minimum net equity levels that generally must be met before federal forfeiture actions are instituted. The net equity values are intended to decrease the number of federal seizures, thereby enhancing efforts to improve case quality and to expedite processing of the cases we do initiate. The thresholds are also intended to encourage state and local law enforcement agencies to use state forfeiture laws. . . . In general, the minimum net equity requirements are:

- Residential Property and vacant land — minimum net equity must be at least 20 percent of the appraised value, or $20,000, whichever is greater. As a general rule, the Department of Justice does not seize or adopt contaminated real properties.

- Vehicles — minimum net equity must be at least $5,000. The value of multiple vehicles seized at the same time may be aggregated for purposes of meeting the minimum net equity. . . . This restriction does not apply in the case of seizures by the United States Immigration and Customs Enforcement of vehicles used in the smuggling of aliens or in the case of vehicles modified or customized to facilitate illegal activity.
- Cash — minimum amount must be at least $5,000, unless the person from whom the cash was taken was criminally prosecuted or is being prosecuted by state or federal authorities for criminal activities related to the property, in which case, the amount must be at least $1,000.
- Aircraft — minimum net equity must be at least $10,000. Note that failure to obtain the log books for the aircraft will reduce the aircraft's value significantly.
- Vessels — minimum net equity must be at least $10,000.
- All Other Personal Property — minimum net equity must be at least $1,000 in the aggregate. Exceptions from the minimum net equity requirement should not be made for any individual item if it has a value of less than $1,000. Such exceptions can be made if practical considerations support the seizure (e.g., 20 items of jewelry, each valued at $500, might be seized, as the total value of the items is $10,000 and the cost of storing 20 small items of jewelry is not excessive).

Heads of investigative agencies may continue to establish higher thresholds for seizures made by their agencies. . . . Each United States Attorney may institute higher district-wide thresholds for judicial forfeiture cases. In doing so, United States Attorneys should confer with the seizing agencies affected by the change and develop, in concert with those agencies, written district-wide guidelines for implementation. . . .

It is understood that in some circumstances the overriding law enforcement benefit will require the seizure of an asset that does not meet these criteria. In individual cases, these thresholds may be waived where forfeiture will serve a compelling law enforcement interest (e.g., forfeiture of a "crack house," a conveyance with hidden compartments, a computer or Internet domain name seized to disrupt a major fraud scheme, or assets connected to a child pornography ring or a terrorist organization). Any downward variations from the above thresholds must be approved in writing by a supervisory-level official and an explanation of the reason for the departure noted in the case file. A copy of this approval, in either a written memorandum or an e-mail, must be provided to the United States Marshals Service district office that will take custody of the assets(s).

## PROBLEM 10-6.   HIGH ROLLERS

The government seeks forfeiture of the $150,000 Miami residence of Emilio and Yolanda Delio because it was used in an illegal gambling operation. Emilio Delio is an 80-year-old wheelchair-bound man residing at the property with his 66-year-old wife, Yolanda. Emilio and Yolanda own the property jointly. Their adult children also reside at the house.

Mr. Delio conducted a poker game at his home, involving some of his relatives and associates, on Wednesday nights. Government agents observed poker games at the house on five occasions between September 12 and October 10. Witnesses later said that the poker games were held at the house on a regular basis. The government charged Delio and other members of the family with directing a gambling operation and obtained criminal convictions against Emilio and three other participants (including one of Emilio's sons). The statute applied only to gambling businesses (1) owned or directed by five or more persons, (2) remaining in "substantially continuous operation" for more than 30 days, (3) with a gross revenue of $2,000 in any single day. In the separate civil forfeiture proceedings, the government seeks summary judgment.

Will the government obtain forfeiture of this property? How should the "excessiveness" of this fine be measured? Compare United States v. One Single Family Residence at 18755 North Bay Road, Miami, 13 F.3d 1493 (11th Cir. 1994).

## NOTES

1. *Excessive fines and forfeitures: majority position.*   The *Austin* opinion left for other courts the task of deciding how to measure the excessiveness of a forfeiture under the Eighth Amendment. The lower federal courts developed a proportionality test that weighs the severity of the offense, the harshness of the sanction, and the culpability of the claimant. Then the Supreme Court returned to the question of what standard to use in measuring the excessiveness of a forfeiture in United States v. Bajakajian, 524 U.S. 321 (1998).

Bajakajian was waiting in the Los Angeles airport to board an international flight when a customs inspector approached him and told him that he was required to report all cash in excess of $10,000 in his possession or baggage. Bajakajian lied about the amount of cash he was holding; cash-sniffing dogs indicated the presence of currency in his luggage, and customs inspectors found $357,144. Bajakajian pled guilty to the currency reporting offense and elected to have a bench trial on the forfeiture. The trial judge found that the funds were not connected to any other crime and that Bajakajian was transporting the money to repay a lawful debt; he held that forfeiture of the entire amount was constitutionally excessive and reduced the forfeiture to $15,000.

The Supreme Court held that the forfeiture was a punishment for purposes of the excessive fines clause because the statute authorized an in personam forfeiture that applied only to the property of a person who willfully fails to report the cash. The Court then described the proper method for a court to use in determining whether a forfeiture is excessive:

> [There are two considerations] that we find particularly relevant. The first . . . is that judgments about the appropriate punishment for an offense belong in the first instance to the legislature. The second is that any judicial determination regarding the gravity of a particular criminal offense will be inherently imprecise. Both of these principles counsel against requiring strict proportionality between the amount of a punitive forfeiture and the gravity of a criminal offense, and we therefore adopt the standard of gross disproportionality

articulated in our Cruel and Unusual Punishments Clause precedents. See Solem v. Helm, 463 U.S. 277 (1983); Rummel v. Estelle, 445 U.S. 263 (1980).

In applying this standard, the district courts in the first instance, and the courts of appeals, reviewing the proportionality determination de novo, must compare the amount of the forfeiture to the gravity of the defendant's offense. If the amount of the forfeiture is grossly disproportional to the gravity of the defendant's offense, it is unconstitutional.

Under this standard, the forfeiture of respondent's entire $357,144 would violate the Excessive Fines Clause. Respondent's crime was solely a reporting offense. It was permissible to transport the currency out of the country so long as he reported it. . . . Furthermore, as the District Court found, respondent's violation was unrelated to any other illegal activities. The money was the proceeds of legal activity and was to be used to repay a lawful debt. Whatever his other vices, respondent does not fit into the class of persons for whom the statute was principally designed: He is not a money launderer, a drug trafficker, or a tax evader. And under the Sentencing Guidelines, the maximum sentence that could have been imposed on respondent was six months, while the maximum fine was $5,000. . . .

The harm that respondent caused was also minimal. Failure to report his currency affected only one party, the Government, and in a relatively minor way. There was no fraud on the United States, and respondent caused no loss to the public fisc. Had his crime gone undetected, the Government would have been deprived only of the information that $357,144 had left the country. . . . Comparing the gravity of respondent's crime with the $357,144 forfeiture the Government seeks, we conclude that such a forfeiture would be grossly disproportional to the gravity of his offense.

After the Supreme Court's decision in *Bajakajian*, Congress enacted 31 U.S.C. §5332, which declares bulk cash smuggling into and out of the United States a criminal offense. The provision, a part of the U.S. PATRIOT Act, mandates criminal forfeiture and allows for civil forfeiture of the entire amount of money smuggled. The only case that has addressed the issue so far found *Bajakajian* applicable, and therefore subjected the civil forfeiture to the excessive fines clause. United States of America v. $293,316 in U.S. Currency, 349 F. Supp. 2d 638 (E.D.N.Y. 2004).

The states have assumed that the excessive fines clause of the Eighth Amendment applies to them. Like the lower federal courts, many high state courts seem content for now to ask trial judges to consider a range of factors in judging the excessiveness of fines, including the value of the property, the amount of the illicit transaction, and the physical and temporal extent of involvement between the property and the crime. Commonwealth v. Fint, 940 S.W.2d 896 (Ky. 1997); State v. Hill, 635 N.E.2d 1248 (Ohio 1994).

2. *Instrumentalities versus proceeds.* Should the proceeds of crimes be subject to a proportionality test at all? What about the property offered in exchange for illicit drugs? See United States v. 15,538 Panulirus Argus Lobster Tails, 834 F. Supp. 385 (S.D. Fla. 1993) (contraband forfeited will always be proportional to crime committed). Suppose that a government agent posing as a buyer had first approached Austin in a public park and had proposed that they complete their transaction in the privacy of Austin's shop. If the government influences the choice of property that will facilitate a crime, should the property still be forfeited?

3. *"Punitive" versus "remedial" label.*    Why was Justice Blackmun so intent on demonstrating that the forfeiture in *Austin* was individual punishment? Justice Scalia and three other justices did not agree that all forfeitures involve some type of punishment. What is at stake in this argument over the label "punishment"? Will the holding in this case apply also to statutes containing no "innocent owner" defense?

4. *Forfeiture and criminal sentencing.*    Civil forfeiture sometimes takes place after the owner has been convicted and sentenced for a crime in a separate proceeding. If the offender was fined or otherwise suffered a loss of property during the criminal process, should this reduce the amount of property subject to civil forfeiture? In other words, should proportionality analysis account for related criminal sanctions? See Sandra Guerra, Reconciling Federal Asset Forfeitures and Drug Offense Sentencing, 78 Minn. L. Rev. 805 (1994) (urging Congress and courts to factor amount of forfeited property into criminal sentence).

5. *Exempt property.*    Residences seem to create the most difficult forfeiture cases for the government. Homestead property is exempt from forfeiture under some state constitutions and statutes, even if it has a clear connection to the commission of a crime and even if its forfeiture would be proportional to the crime. State courts have vigorously enforced exceptions for homestead property.

> The purpose of the homestead exemption has been described broadly as being to protect the family, and to provide for it a refuge from misfortune, without any requirement that the misfortune arise from a financial debt. [The homestead protections] create no personal qualifications touching the moral character of the resident nor do they undertake to exclude the vicious, the criminal, or the immoral from the benefits so provided.

Butterworth v. Caggiano, 605 So. 2d 56, 60 (Fla. 1992). Does the exemption of a home used to commit a crime further the objective of family security that the drafters of the homestead exemptions hoped to achieve? Cf. Unif. Controlled Substances Act §505(c)(3), (d) (1994) (homestead exemptions). Should a homestead exemption apply to any home, regardless of size and value? Would the same logic apply to a residence purchased with assets obtained through criminal activity? The federal government is not bound by such limitations in state law, even when seeking forfeiture of property within the state. Furthermore, the federal government offers to adopt the property seized during investigations by state law enforcers. In light of the federal adoption alternative, are the homestead exemptions under state law now dead letters?

The United States Attorneys Manual and the Philadelphia Police Department directive indicate that there is some forfeitable property that police and prosecutors will not bother to obtain. Although covered by the statute, as a practical matter such property is immune from forfeiture. Why would law enforcement agencies decline to pursue a small amount of property even when it is clearly within the coverage of the forfeiture statute? Some state statutes also exempt certain property from forfeiture if the criminal activity is relatively insignificant. For instance, a South Carolina statute exempts vehicles from forfeiture if they transport less than ten grams of cocaine or one pound of marijuana. S.C. Code §44-53-520(a)(6). Some police department rules require higher levels of certainty among officers as to the forfeitability of property when the property value is small.

## 2.  *Procedures for Resolving Forfeitures*

The government may begin forfeiture proceedings in several ways. It might simply file a civil complaint against either the property (in rem) or the owner (in personam). The government might also choose criminal forfeiture proceedings, which begin as part of the criminal action and with the final forfeiture hearing occurring after conviction. In criminal forfeiture cases the government must prove beyond a reasonable doubt that the defendant committed the crime (or it must obtain a guilty plea reflecting such a conclusion). Further findings are also necessary to show the relationship between the property at issue and the crime of conviction. In most states, civil forfeiture is far more common than criminal forfeiture.

Judges and juries do not often resolve civil forfeitures; instead, most forfeitures are handled administratively. After a government attorney sends notice to all interested parties, the property owners might choose not to contest the forfeiture. For forfeitures below a designated dollar amount, the government can then take possession of the property through an uncontested administrative forfeiture without any judicial proceedings at all.

Because the property owner might attempt to dispose of the disputed property before the government can take possession, the government often seizes or arrests the property at the beginning of the civil proceedings. The government may take physical possession of a movable asset such as a vehicle; it may ask a financial institution to freeze an account. For real property, the government often files a notice of lis pendens against the property; in a few cases, it takes actual possession of the property and renegotiates the rental arrangements with residents on the property. For some ongoing businesses seized, the government continues to operate the business and collect the revenue pending the final forfeiture determination.

No property may be seized or arrested for purposes of forfeiture unless the government has probable cause to believe it is subject to forfeiture. Probable cause can be demonstrated in different ways. Most often, the government arrests the property after obtaining a warrant in an ex parte hearing. An adversarial probable cause hearing takes place after the seizure. Before real property can be seized, however, the person with a claim to the property must be given notice and an opportunity to be heard. United States v. James Daniel Good Real Property, 510 U.S. 43, 44, 58, 62 (1993) ("Because real property cannot abscond, the court's jurisdiction can be preserved without prior seizure. . . . Sale of the property can be prevented by filing a notice of lis pendens. [Based] upon the importance of the private interests at risk and the absence of countervailing Government needs, we hold that the seizure of real property . . . is not one of those extraordinary instances that justify the postponement of notice and hearing.").

Once the government has frozen the property it seeks to obtain through forfeiture, any claimant may file a bond, hire an attorney, and contest the validity of the forfeiture. If the claimant loses the judicial challenge, she forfeits the value of the bond along with the property in dispute. The stated purpose of the bond is to reimburse the government for expenses incurred in litigating a "frivolous" forfeiture action. Does the bond requirement explain why the great majority of forfeiture cases are never challenged in court? Or do most forfeitures go unchallenged because the owners have no realistic prospect of prevailing in court? One of the most important features of the Civil Asset Forfeiture Reform Act of 2000, P.L. 106-185 (codified at 18 U.S.C. §983(a)(2)(E)), was its elimination of the bond requirement for parties challenging a forfeiture in federal court. The Act does not change the procedure in state court.

Forfeiture statutes take various positions on the relevant burden of proof and standard of proof. Consider the following constitutional decision on the subject.

## Department of Law Enforcement v. Real Property
### 588 So. 2d 957 (Fla. 1991)

BARKETT, J.

[We hold today that the Florida Contraband Forfeiture Act] is facially constitutional provided that it is applied consistent with the minimal due process requirements of the Florida Constitution as set forth in this opinion. Charles DeCarlo was arrested on drug trafficking charges on May 15, 1990, stemming from a reverse sting operation conducted by [the] Florida Department of Law Enforcement (FDLE) and the Levy County Sheriff's Department. On May 16, the state initiated forfeiture proceedings in circuit court against [a 60-acre tract of land, part of which includes an extension of an airstrip; 420 acres subdivided for mobile home sites and 300 permanent residences; and a personal residence and property, including garages and sheds].

Based solely on an affidavit executed by an FDLE special agent, the circuit court on May 16 issued warrants to seize the aforementioned properties. The state that day also filed a notice of lis pendens against those properties and petitioned for a rule to show cause why the properties should not be forfeited. . . . The claimants moved to dismiss the petitions on constitutional grounds. . . .

The basic due process guarantee of the Florida Constitution provides that "[n]o person shall be deprived of life, liberty or property without due process of law." Art. I, §9, Fla. Const. . . . Procedural due process serves as a vehicle to ensure fair treatment through the proper administration of justice where substantive rights are at issue. Procedural due process under the Florida Constitution guarantees to every citizen the right to have that course of legal procedure which has been established in our judicial system for the protection and enforcement of private rights. It contemplates that the defendant shall be given fair notice and afforded a real opportunity to be heard and defend in an orderly procedure, before judgment is rendered against him. . . .

The process provided in the Act [as amended in 1989] enables the state to seize property — whether real or personal — "which has been or is being used" to commit one of the enumerated offenses, or "in, upon or by means of which" any enumerated violation "has taken or is taking place." . . . After seizure, the state must "promptly proceed" against the property "by rule to show cause in the circuit court," and may have the property forfeited "upon producing due proof" that the property was being used in violation of the Act. If the state does not initiate proceedings within 90 days after the seizure, the claimant may maintain an action to recover the property. . . . Owners may raise a defense only after the property has been seized, and they must bear the burden in forfeiture proceedings of proving that they neither knew, nor should have known after a reasonable inquiry, that the property was being used or was likely to be used to commit an enumerated crime. Lienholders who can establish their perfected interests also may raise a defense only after seizure, and they bear the same burden as property owners plus an additional burden of proving that they did not consent to having the property used to commit a crime. At some point, the court is to issue a "final order of forfeiture" perfecting title in the seizing agency relating back to the date of seizure. Legal title to the property, or proceeds derived from the property after satisfaction of bona fide liens, are then transferred to [a specified agency or fund].

The Act raises numerous constitutional concerns that touch upon many substantive and procedural rights protected by the Florida Constitution. In construing the Act, we note that forfeitures are considered harsh exactions, and as a general rule they are not favored either in law or equity. Therefore, this Court has long followed a policy that it must strictly construe forfeiture statutes. Strict construction, however, may clash with the traditional judicial policy that all doubts as to the validity of a statute are to be resolved in favor of constitutionality where reasonably possible. . . .

The Act provides that after the property is first seized, the state must file a petition for a rule to show cause in the circuit court, and upon producing due proof that the property was used in violation of the Act, the court shall issue a final order of forfeiture vesting legal title in the appropriate agency under the Act. However, that is the sum total of direction given by the Act. The Act does not set out any procedures for filing the petition or issuing the rule to show cause, except that a rule shall issue upon the showing of "due proof." The Act does not address any requirements for filing the petition; which procedural rules should apply to control the litigation; what standard and burden of proof is "due" for issuance of the rule; whether a trial — with or without a jury — is required to decide the merits of the action once the rule has been issued; what standard and burden of proof apply in deciding the ultimate issue, including defenses; and whether and how property is to be divided or partitioned to ensure that only the "guilty" property is forfeited. . . .

It is now well settled that the ultimate issue of forfeiture must be decided by jury trial unless claimants waive that right. That substantive right is also subsumed within article I, section 9 of the Florida Constitution. However, the issue of standard and burden of proof has not been previously addressed by this Court. The state argues that the agency seeking forfeiture need establish its case by at most a preponderance of the evidence, whereas the claimants argue that the constitution requires proof beyond a reasonable doubt, or alternatively, by clear and convincing evidence. Case law reflects no uniformity in this state as to the appropriate burden and standard of proof.

We conclude that the state has the burden of proof at trial, which should be by no less than clear and convincing evidence. The state and the decisions on which it relies fail to recognize the significance of the constitutionally protected rights at issue and the impact forfeiture has on those rights. In forfeiture proceedings the state impinges on basic constitutional rights of individuals who may never have been formally charged with any civil or criminal wrongdoing. This Court has consistently held that the constitution requires substantial burdens of proof where state action may deprive individuals of basic rights. For example, when an individual is charged with a crime, the government cannot deprive that person of life, liberty, or property unless it carries the burden of proof beyond every reasonable doubt as to each essential element. In noncriminal contexts [such as termination of parental rights, termination of an incompetent patient's life support, defamation suits brought by public figures, or establishment of land ownership through adverse possession], this Court has held that constitutionally protected individual rights may not be impinged with a showing of less than clear and convincing evidence.

Accordingly, "due proof" under the Act constitutionally means that the government may not take an individual's property in forfeiture proceedings unless it proves, by no less than clear and convincing evidence, that the property being forfeited was used in the commission of a crime. Lack of knowledge of the holder of an interest in the property that the property was being employed in criminal activity is a defense to forfeiture, which, if established by a preponderance of the evidence, defeats the forfeiture action as to that property interest. . . .

This Court is obliged and authorized to establish rules to enforce the Florida Constitution and to administer the courts of this state. Although we are concerned with the multitude of procedural deficiencies in the Act, the procedures described above are required to satisfy due process and are not inconsistent with the language and intent of the Act. We conclude that the Act can be reasonably construed as constitutional provided that it is applied consistent with the due process requirements summarized in this opinion.

Turning to the facts of this case, it is clear that the state did not comply with due process: It seized real property, including residential property, prior to giving the claimants any notice or opportunity to be heard. Accordingly, we affirm the result reached by the [lower] court in dismissing the forfeiture action. . . .

## NOTES

1. *Burden of proof: majority position.*   It is most common for civil forfeiture statutes to place the burden of proof on the state to demonstrate that the property is forfeitable; the claimant then has the burden of proof to demonstrate that any exemptions or exceptions apply. The federal government and more than 30 states allocate the burden in this way. Roughly a dozen other states follow a different approach to the burden of proof: After the prosecution establishes probable cause to believe that property is forfeitable, the claimant carries the

burden of persuasion and must show that the property is not forfeitable. Court challenges to the constitutionality of this burden of proof have mostly failed.

In the federal system, the Civil Asset Forfeiture Reform Act of 2000 changed the burden of proof in civil forfeiture. Before this amendment to the federal statutes, the burden of proof on the question of forfeitability shifted to a claimant after the government showed probable cause to believe that the property was forfeitable. Would you expect this statutory amendment to lead to a different outcome in many cases? Will this amendment change more outcomes than the elimination of the bond requirement (also a part of the Civil Asset Forfeiture Reform Act)? See Eric Moores, Reforming the Civil Asset Forfeiture Reform Act, 51 Ariz. L. Rev. 777, 782 (2009).

Civil forfeiture statutes commonly include a provision creating a "presumption of forfeitability" for certain property, such as large amounts of currency found near narcotics. This presumption effectively shifts the burden of proof back to the claimant. Is this feature of the asset forfeiture laws likely to survive a court ruling that requires the government to carry the burden of proof in forfeiture proceedings?

2. *Standard of proof: majority position.* In more than 30 states, civil forfeiture statutes require a party to establish facts by a preponderance of the evidence. For *criminal* forfeiture actions, which are resolved after a criminal conviction for the underlying crime, the government must prove the elements of the crime beyond a reasonable doubt. But after conviction, in the sentencing phase, the government usually must establish the forfeitability of the property only by a preponderance of the evidence rather than beyond a reasonable doubt. Clear and convincing evidence is the government's standard of proof in the civil forfeiture statutes of about a half-dozen states. See Minn. Stat. §609.531(6a)(a). A handful require proof beyond a reasonable doubt for some civil forfeitures. Why would a prosecutor ever use a civil forfeiture statute that requires proof beyond a reasonable doubt?

The Florida decision in the *Real Property* case was unusual in requiring a particular burden of proof and standard of proof as a matter of constitutional law. The Florida constitution forbids one of the branches of government from invading the province of another. Did the court invade the province of the legislature with its decision in *Real Property*? Or did it instead create law within its area of special expertise — procedural fairness — at the implicit invitation of the legislature? The Florida legislature later amended the statute dealing with civil forfeiture actions — without changing the "due proof" language relating to the procedure at trial.

3. *Juries.* Most state courts have concluded that their state statutes or constitutions require a jury trial for civil asset forfeiture proceedings. The relevant constitutional provision often protects the right to jury trial in any action recognized at common law at the time the state first adopted a constitution. Since civil in rem forfeitures were common law actions available during the relevant time period, jury trial is still available. See, e.g., Idaho Department of Law Enforcement v. Real Property, 885 P.2d 381 (Idaho 1994). About a dozen states, however, have reached the opposite conclusion. Federal courts have concluded that the Seventh Amendment requires jury trial for in rem forfeitures on the question of forfeitability. In practice, juries do not hear many civil asset

forfeiture cases, in part because claimants rarely exercise their right to a jury trial and because the rules of civil procedure allow the government to move for summary judgment. When these motions succeed, as they often do, the court disposes of the case before it reaches a jury.

4. *Counsel fees from frozen assets.* In civil forfeiture proceedings, there is no federal constitutional right to appointed counsel. The U.S. Supreme Court in Caplin and Drysdale, Chartered v. United States, 491 U.S. 617 (1989), concluded that the right to counsel does not prevent the government from freezing assets necessary to hire criminal defense counsel so long as the assets are potentially subject to forfeiture. Most state courts agree. See State v. Nine Thousand One Hundred Ninety-Nine Dollars, 791 P.2d 213 (Utah 1990).

Constitutions are not the only source of law that determines whether forfeitable funds may be used for attorneys' fees. Some state forfeiture statutes explicitly allow a court to order the release of some frozen assets to permit a defendant to hire an attorney. New York statutes allow the release of such funds to hire an attorney for representation during civil forfeiture proceedings, criminal forfeiture proceedings, or related criminal proceedings. See N.Y. C.P.L.R. 1312(4); N.Y. Crim. Proc. Law §480.05(3) (allows payment for "bona fide fees" for legal services).

The Civil Asset Forfeiture Reform Act of 2000 expands access to attorneys for claimants of property being subject to civil asset forfeiture proceedings in federal court. The federal government now provides legal counsel for indigent claimants of property that the government is attempting to seize, along with attorneys' fees for winning claimants. Would expanded access to fees in civil proceedings be enough to convince private defense counsel to accept a forfeiture case?

## PROBLEM 10-7.   JOINT OWNERS

Tina and John Bennis jointly owned an 11-year-old Pontiac. Detroit police arrested John after observing him engaged in a sexual act with a prostitute in the automobile while it was parked on a Detroit city street. He was convicted of gross indecency. The state then filed a civil action to have the car declared a public nuisance (and therefore forfeited) under Michigan statutes.

Tina defended against the forfeiture of her interest in the car on the ground that she did not know her husband would use the car to violate Michigan's indecency law. The circuit court rejected this argument and declared the car a public nuisance. Even though the statute gave the judge the authority to award half of the sale proceeds to Tina (as an innocent titleholder) and the other half to the state, the judge refused to divide the proceeds. The judge noted that the couple owned another automobile and that the Pontiac was worth only $600. Is there any constitutional bar to the forfeiture of the car under these circumstances? Compare Bennis v. Michigan, 516 U.S. 442 (1996).

## NOTES

1. *Innocent owners under federal statutes.*   Under 18 U.S.C. §983(d)(2)(A), an innocent property owner can reclaim property that might otherwise be forfeited if the owner can show that he "did not know of the conduct giving rise to forfeiture [or] upon learning of the conduct giving rise to the forfeiture, did all that reasonably could be expected under the circumstances to terminate such use of the property." The property owner may establish his "innocence" even if he obtains the property after the previous owner commits a crime that makes the property forfeitable. The U.S. Supreme Court, in United States v. 92 Buena Vista Avenue, Rumson, New Jersey, 507 U.S. 111 (1993), decided that the unqualified language of the "innocent owner" provision (it applies to any "owner") precludes any per se bar against using the defense, even for persons who obtain the property after it becomes forfeitable. Under what circumstances can persons who were paid with illegal proceeds for providing goods or services to drug traffickers claim to be innocent owners?

2. *Innocent owners under state statutes.*   While most state forfeiture statutes do provide "innocent owner" defenses, a few statutes without such a defense remain in place. The elements of the defense vary from state to state. Compare the two major model statutes, the Forfeiture Reform Act (FRA) of the President's Commission on Model State Drug Laws, and the Uniform Controlled Substances Act (UCSA) of the National Conference of Commissioners on Uniform State Laws. When it comes to an owner who acquires property interests before the property becomes forfeitable, the FRA requires that the owner either "did not and could not reasonably have known" about the likelihood of conduct making the property forfeitable or "acted reasonably to prevent the conduct." Section 8(a). The UCSA requires that the owner either "did not know the conduct would occur" or acted "in a manner the owner reasonably believed appropriate to prevent" the wrongful conduct. Sections 505(b), (c). On which drafting commission do you think prosecutors had more influence? Would Tina Bennis have been able to meet either test? See Kasey L. Higgins, "Shiver Me Timbers!" Civil Asset Forfeiture: Crime Deterrent or Incentive for the Government to Pillage and Plunder Property?, 4 Phoenix L. Rev. 771, 789 (2011).

3. *Constitutions and innocent owners.*   There is no federal constitutional bar to the forfeiture of an innocent owner's property when the forfeiture is allowed by state or federal statute. In Bennis v. Michigan, 516 U.S. 442 (1996), the basis for Problem 10-5, the Supreme Court decided that due process was not violated by the forfeiture of an innocent owner's property without compensation: A "long and unbroken line of cases holds that an owner's interest in property may be forfeited by reason of the use to which the property is put even though the owner did not know that it was to be put to such use." The Court said that forfeiture of property — even an innocent owner's property — serves a deterrent purpose by preventing further illicit use of the property and by making illegal behavior unprofitable.

In an oft-cited case, State v. Richards, 301 S.W.2d 597 (Tex. 1957), the Texas Supreme Court upheld the forfeiture of a pickup truck when the owner lent it to an acquaintance who (unbeknownst to the truck's owner) was carrying two Dolophine pills in his shirt pocket. A dissenting justice declared that the "right to acquire and own property" is a "natural right" and that forfeiture interferes with this right. Many critics of forfeiture argue that the practice should remain limited because forfeiture is based on the "legal fiction" that the property reverts to the government as soon as the crime is committed. What is a legal fiction? Aren't all property rights recognized and enforced through a fiction of sorts? Is there a difference between a government declaration that a private party owns certain property and a government declaration that property used to commit a crime automatically belongs to the government? Does your answer to these questions depend on your views of the source of individual rights?

4. *Multiple owners.*  Often the criminal offender's interest in the property is less valuable than the innocent owner's interest, such as when the offender borrows or leases the property. In other cases, the innocent owner and the offender are equal co-owners of the property in question. In that situation, should the property become forfeitable even if the innocent owner qualifies in every respect for the statutory defense? If so, what is the proper remedy? Forced sale of the property followed by an equal split of the proceeds? Should the innocent owner have to pay her share of the litigation costs? A number of statutes provide special protection to spouses who own forfeitable property jointly with wrongdoers. See Wash. Rev. Code §69.50.505(d) (innocent spouse with community property interest can block forfeiture). Should a formal property interest be necessary before this protection applies? See Sandra Guerra, Family Values? The Family as an Innocent Victim of Civil Drug Asset Forfeiture, 81 Cornell L. Rev. 343 (1996).

5. *The innocent tenant.*  Under section 715 of New York's Real Property Actions and Proceedings Law, the owner of any real property "used or occupied in whole or in part . . . for any illegal trade, business or manufacture" may bring expedited civil proceedings to evict the tenant. If the landlord refuses to evict the tenant, the district attorney may bring a civil action against the tenant and recover litigation expenses from the landlord. See Peter Finn, The Manhattan District Attorney's Narcotics Eviction Program (National Institute of Justice, NCJ 153146, May 1995). If the statute itself contains no provision for an innocent co-tenant, what charging limitations (if any) should the district attorney employ? Should the D.A. evict any tenant (say, a grandmother) who "knew or should have known" about illegal activity of another tenant (say, a grandson)? If "reasonable efforts" to stop the illegal activity are enough to avoid eviction, how much effort is considered reasonable? Pleading with the grandson to stop the illegal activity? Reporting it to the police? Cf. Department of Housing and Urban Development v. Rucker, 535 U.S. 125 (2002) (Anti-Drug Abuse Act required lease terms that gave local public housing authorities discretion to terminate lease when any member of household or guest engaged in drug-related activity).

6. *Bypassing the criminal process.*  One of the virtues of asset forfeiture from the perspective of law enforcement is its efficiency. It allows the government to remove dangerous or illicit goods from circulation quickly, and as a practical matter it allows for some punishment of guilty property owners without having to clear the hurdles of the criminal process. Elsewhere in this chapter we have

considered other legal procedures that accomplish some of the objectives of criminal sentences without going through the criminal process. Do these procedures differ from one another in important ways? Do some present greater potential for abuse by prosecutors or other law enforcement officials?

7. *Standing to challenge forfeitures.*   In Alvarez v. Smith, 130 S. Ct. 576 (2009), the Supreme Court held moot the claims of six individuals in Illinois who claimed that Illinois law failed to provide a sufficiently speedy opportunity for an individual, whose car or cash police have seized without a warrant, to contest the lawfulness of the seizure. The Court decided the case without addressing the merits. Because all the plaintiffs either received their property or conceded that it was properly confiscated, "there was no longer any dispute about ownership or possession of the relevant property." In light of this, the court held that the appeal was an "abstract dispute about the law, unlikely to affect these plaintiffs any more than it affects other Illinois citizens." *Alvarez* limited the circumstances where forfeiture claims can be challenged. See Nicholas A. Loyal, Bills to Pay and Mouths to Feed: Forfeiture and Due Process Concerns After Alvarez v. Smith, 55 St. Louis U. L.J. 1143, 1162 (2011).

## D.   CIVIL AND ADMINISTRATIVE REMEDIES

Rather than pursuing criminal charges against wrongdoers, government enforcers sometimes go to court to obtain civil sanctions such as fines or injunctions. Or they make their claims against the wrongdoer in administrative proceedings, without involving the judicial branch at all. Under what circumstances do government enforcers tend to ask for civil or administrative remedies rather than filing criminal charges? What are the risks for potential targets who face criminal and civil proceedings simultaneously?

|| *John Hudson v. United States* ||
   522 U.S. 93 (1997)

REHNQUIST, C.J.
The Government administratively imposed monetary penalties and occupational debarment on petitioners for violation of federal banking statutes, and later criminally indicted them for essentially the same conduct. We hold that the Double Jeopardy Clause of the Fifth Amendment is not a bar to the later criminal prosecution because the administrative proceedings were civil, not criminal. . . .

During the early and mid-1980's, petitioner John Hudson was the chairman and controlling shareholder of the First National Bank of Tipton and the First National Bank of Hammon. During the same period, petitioner Jack Rackley was president of Tipton and a member of the board of directors of Hammon, and petitioner Larry Baresel was a member of the board of directors of both Tipton and Hammon. An examination of Tipton and Hammon led the Office of the Comptroller of the Currency to conclude that petitioners had used their bank positions to arrange a series of loans to third parties in violation of various federal banking statutes and regulations. According to the OCC, those loans, while nominally made to third parties, were in reality made to Hudson in order to enable him to redeem bank stock that he had pledged as collateral on defaulted loans.

On February 13, 1989, OCC issued a "Notice of Assessment of Civil Money Penalty." The notice alleged that petitioners had violated 12 U.S.C. §84(a)(1) and 375b and 12 CFR §31.2(b) and 215.4(b) by causing the banks with which they were associated to make loans to nominee borrowers in a manner that unlawfully allowed Hudson to receive the benefit of the loans. The notice also alleged that the illegal loans resulted in losses to Tipton and Hammon of almost $900,000 and contributed to the failure of those banks. However, the notice contained no allegation of any harm to the Government as a result of petitioners' conduct. After taking into account the size of the financial resources and the good faith of petitioners, the gravity of the violations, the history of previous violations and other matters . . . OCC assessed penalties of $100,000 against Hudson and $50,000 each against Rackley and Baresel. On August 31, 1989, OCC also issued a "Notice of Intention to Prohibit Further Participation" against each petitioner. These notices, which were premised on the identical allegations that formed the basis for the previous notices, informed petitioners that OCC intended to bar them from further participation in the conduct of any insured depository institution.

In October 1989, petitioners resolved the OCC proceedings against them by each entering into a "Stipulation and Consent Order." These consent orders provided that Hudson, Baresel, and Rackley would pay assessments of $16,500, $15,000, and $12,500 respectively. In addition, each petitioner agreed not to participate in any manner in the affairs of any banking institution without the written authorization of the OCC and all other relevant regulatory agencies.

In August 1992, petitioners were indicted in the Western District of Oklahoma in a 22-count indictment on charges of conspiracy, misapplication of bank funds, and making false bank entries. The violations charged in the indictment rested on the same lending transactions that formed the basis for the prior administrative actions brought by OCC. Petitioners moved to dismiss the indictment on double jeopardy grounds [and the trial court granted the motion].

The Double Jeopardy Clause provides that no "person [shall] be subject for the same offence to be twice put in jeopardy of life or limb." We have long recognized that the Double Jeopardy Clause does not prohibit the imposition of all additional sanctions that could, in common parlance, be described as punishment. The Clause protects only against the imposition of multiple *criminal* punishments for the same offense, and then only when such occurs in successive proceedings.

Whether a particular punishment is criminal or civil is, at least initially, a matter of statutory construction. A court must first ask whether the legislature, in establishing the penalizing mechanism, indicated either expressly or impliedly a preference for one label or the other. Even in those cases where the legislature has indicated an intention to establish a civil penalty, we have inquired further whether the statutory scheme was so punitive either in purpose or effect as to transform what was clearly intended as a civil remedy into a criminal penalty.

In making this latter determination, the factors listed in Kennedy v. Mendoza-Martinez, 372 U.S. 144, 168-169 (1963), provide useful guideposts, including: (1) whether the sanction involves an affirmative disability or restraint; (2) whether it has historically been regarded as a punishment; (3) whether it comes into play only on a finding of scienter; (4) whether its operation will promote the traditional aims of punishment—retribution and deterrence; (5) whether the behavior to which it applies is already a crime; (6) whether an alternative purpose to which it may rationally be connected is assignable for it; and (7) whether it appears excessive in relation to the alternative purpose assigned. It is important to note, however, that these factors must be considered in relation to the statute on its face, and "only the clearest proof" will suffice to override legislative intent and transform what has been denominated a civil remedy into a criminal penalty.

Our opinion in United States v. Halper, 490 U.S. 435 (1989), marked the first time we applied the Double Jeopardy Clause to a sanction without first determining that it was criminal in nature. In that case, Irwin Halper was convicted of violating the criminal false claims statute based on his submission of 65 inflated Medicare claims each of which overcharged the Government by $9. He was sentenced to two years' imprisonment and fined $5,000. The Government then brought an action against Halper under the civil False Claims Act, 31 U.S.C. §3729-3731. The remedial provisions of the False Claims Act provided that a violation of the Act rendered one "liable to the United States Government for a civil penalty of $2,000, an amount equal to 2 times the amount of damages the Government sustains because of the act of that person, and costs of the civil action." Given Halper's 65 separate violations of the Act, he appeared to be liable for a penalty of $130,000, despite the fact he actually defrauded the Government of less than $600.

[This Court held that a penalty of this magnitude would violate the Double Jeopardy Clause in light of Halper's previous criminal conviction. As the *Halper* Court saw it, any] sanction that was so overwhelmingly disproportionate to the injury caused that it could not "fairly be said *solely* to serve the remedial purpose" of compensating the Government for its loss, was thought to be explainable only as "serving either retributive or deterrent purposes."

The analysis applied by the *Halper* Court deviated from our traditional double jeopardy doctrine in two key respects. First, the *Halper* Court bypassed the threshold question: whether the successive punishment at issue is a "criminal" punishment. Instead, it focused on whether the sanction, regardless of whether it was civil or criminal, was so grossly disproportionate to the harm caused as to constitute "punishment." In so doing, the Court elevated a single *Kennedy* factor—whether the sanction appeared excessive in relation to its non-punitive purposes—to dispositive status. But as we emphasized in *Kennedy* itself, no one factor should be considered controlling as they may often point in differing directions. The second significant departure in *Halper* was the Court's decision to assess the "character of the actual sanctions imposed," rather than, as *Kennedy* demanded, evaluating the "statute on its face" to determine whether it provided for what amounted to a criminal sanction. . . .

As subsequent cases have demonstrated, *Halper*'s test for determining whether a particular sanction is "punitive," and thus subject to the strictures of the Double Jeopardy Clause, has proved unworkable. We have since recognized that all civil penalties have some deterrent effect. See Department of Revenue of Montana v. Kurth Ranch, 511 U.S. 767, 777 n.14 (1994) [applying a *Kennedy*-like test before concluding that Montana's dangerous drug tax was "the functional equivalent of a successive criminal prosecution"]; United States v. Ursery, 518 U.S. 267, 284-285 (1996) [civil in rem forfeitures do not violate the Double Jeopardy Clause]. If a sanction must be "solely" remedial (i.e., entirely nondeterrent) to avoid implicating the Double Jeopardy Clause, then no civil penalties are beyond the scope of the Clause.

[It] should be noted that some of the ills at which *Halper* was directed are addressed by other constitutional provisions. The Due Process and Equal Protection Clauses already protect individuals from sanctions which are downright irrational. The Eighth Amendment protects against excessive civil fines, including forfeitures. The additional protection afforded by extending double jeopardy protections to proceedings heretofore thought to be civil is more than offset by the confusion created by attempting to distinguish between "punitive" and "nonpunitive" penalties.

Applying traditional double jeopardy principles to the facts of this case, it is clear that the criminal prosecution of these petitioners would not violate the Double Jeopardy Clause. It is evident that Congress intended the OCC money penalties and debarment sanctions imposed for violations of 12 U.S.C. §84 and 375b to be civil in nature. As for the money penalties, both §93(b)(1) and 504(a), which authorize the imposition of monetary penalties for violations of §84 and 375b respectively, expressly provide that such penalties are "civil." While the provision authorizing debarment contains no language explicitly denominating the sanction as civil, we think it significant that the authority to issue debarment orders is conferred upon the appropriate Federal banking agencies. That such authority was conferred upon administrative agencies is prima facie evidence that Congress intended to provide for a civil sanction.

[There] is little evidence, much less the clearest proof that we require, suggesting that either OCC money penalties or debarment sanctions are so punitive in form and effect as to render them criminal despite Congress' intent to the contrary. First, neither money penalties nor debarment has historically been viewed as punishment. We have long recognized that revocation of a privilege voluntarily granted, such as a debarment, "is characteristically free of the punitive criminal element." Helvering v. Mitchell, 303 U.S. 391, 399 (1938). . . .

Second, the sanctions imposed do not involve an "affirmative disability or restraint," as that term is normally understood. While petitioners have been prohibited from further participating in the banking industry, this is certainly nothing approaching the "infamous" punishment of imprisonment. Third, neither sanction comes into play "only" on a finding of scienter. The provisions under which the money penalties were imposed, 12 U.S.C. §93(b) and 504, allow for the assessment of a penalty against any person "who violates" any of the underlying banking statutes, without regard to the violator's state of mind. "Good faith" is considered by OCC in determining the amount of the penalty to be imposed, but a penalty can be imposed even in the absence of bad faith. The fact that petitioners' "good faith" was considered in determining the amount of the penalty to be imposed in this case is irrelevant, as we look only to "the statute on its face" to determine whether a penalty is criminal in nature.

Similarly, while debarment may be imposed for a "willful" disregard for the safety or soundness of an insured depository institution, willfulness is not a prerequisite to debarment; it is sufficient that the disregard for the safety and soundness of the institution was "continuing."§1818(e)(1)(C)(ii).

Fourth, the conduct for which OCC sanctions are imposed may also be criminal (and in this case formed the basis for petitioners' indictments). This fact is insufficient to render the money penalties and debarment sanctions criminally punitive, particularly in the double jeopardy context. See United States v. Dixon, 509 U.S. 688 (1993) (rejecting "same-conduct" test for double jeopardy purposes).

Finally, we recognize that the imposition of both money penalties and debarment sanctions will deter others from emulating petitioners' conduct, a traditional goal of criminal punishment. But the mere presence of this purpose is insufficient to render a sanction criminal, as deterrence may serve civil as well as criminal goals. For example, the sanctions at issue here, while intended to deter future wrongdoing, also serve to promote the stability of the banking industry. To hold that the mere presence of a deterrent purpose renders such sanctions "criminal" for double jeopardy purposes would severely undermine the Government's ability to engage in effective regulation of institutions such as banks.

In sum, there simply is very little showing . . . that OCC money penalties and debarment sanctions are criminal. The Double Jeopardy Clause is therefore no obstacle to their trial on the pending indictments, and it may proceed. . . .

STEVENS, J., concurring.

. . . As is evident from the first sentence of the Court's opinion, this is an extremely easy case. It has been settled since the decision in Blockburger v. United States, 284 U.S. 299 (1932), that the Double Jeopardy Clause is not implicated simply because a criminal charge involves "essentially the same conduct" for which a defendant has previously been punished. Unless a second proceeding involves the "same offense" as the first, there is no double jeopardy. The two proceedings at issue here involved different offenses that were not even arguably the same under *Blockburger*.

Under *Blockburger*'s "same-elements" test, two provisions are not the "same offense" if each contains an element not included in the other. The penalties imposed on the petitioners in 1989 were based on violations of 12 U.S.C. §84(a)(1) and 375b and 12 CFR §31.2(b) and 215.4(b). Each of these provisions required proof that extensions of credit exceeding certain limits were made, but did not require proof of an intent to defraud or the making of any false entries in bank records. The 1992 indictment charged violations of 18 U.S.C. §371, 656, and 1005 and alleged a conspiracy to willfully misapply bank funds and to make false banking entries, as well as the making of such entries; none of those charges required proof that any lending limit had been exceeded. Thus, I think it would be difficult to find a case raising a double jeopardy claim that would be any easier to decide than this one. . . .

Despite my disagreement with the Court's decision to use this case as a rather lame excuse for writing a gratuitous essay about punishment, I do agree with its reaffirmation of the central holding of *Halper*,[which held] that sanctions imposed in civil proceedings constituted "punishment" barred by the

Double Jeopardy Clause. Those holdings reconfirmed the settled proposition that the Government cannot use the "civil" label to escape entirely the Double Jeopardy Clause's command, as we have recognized for at least six decades. That proposition is extremely important because the States and the Federal Government have an enormous array of civil administrative sanctions at their disposal that are capable of being used to punish persons repeatedly for the same offense, violating the bedrock double jeopardy principle of finality. . . .

BREYER, J. concurring.

. . . I would not decide now that a court should evaluate a statute only "on its face," rather than assessing the character of the actual sanctions imposed. *Halper* involved an ordinary civil-fine statute that as normally applied would not have created any "double jeopardy" problem. It was not the statute itself, but rather the disproportionate relation between fine and conduct as the statute was applied in the individual case that led this Court, unanimously, to find that the "civil penalty" was, in those circumstances, a second "punishment" that constituted double jeopardy. . . . It seems to me quite possible that a statute that provides for a punishment that normally is civil in nature could nonetheless amount to a criminal punishment as applied in special circumstances. And I would not now hold to the contrary. . . .

## NOTES

1. *Double jeopardy and civil sanctions: majority position.*    If the government seeks a penalty in a civil proceeding, it can be instituted after a criminal conviction, before a criminal conviction, or indeed in the absence of any criminal conviction or criminal charges. The possibility of facing two separate proceedings raises the concern that the government will pursue a second "punishment" for a crime if it is dissatisfied with the punishment after the first set of proceedings. Nevertheless, in *Hudson* the U.S. Supreme Court decided that civil penalties usually do not constitute "punishment" for purposes of the double jeopardy clause of the Eighth Amendment. As a result, there is no double jeopardy bar to the government's bringing both criminal charges and civil forfeiture proceedings based on the same conduct or transaction. See also United States v. Ursery, 518 U.S. 267 (1996) (civil in rem forfeiture proceedings are not punishment for double jeopardy purposes).

2. *Choice of proceedings.*    While the government's ability to pursue both criminal and civil sanctions (or criminal fines and civil money penalties) is now clearly accepted, this was not always the case. For an early survey of the issues, see Walter Gellhorn, Administrative Prescription and Imposition of Penalties, 1970 Wash. L.Q. 265. Defendants might worry that the government will use civil proceedings as an insurance policy against an unfavorable outcome in the criminal process. For instance, if the government fails to obtain a conviction or the court imposes a sentence unsatisfactory to the prosecutor, the government could try to obtain a more favorable outcome by pursuing civil charges. Can courts prevent this sort of manipulation by insisting that the civil proceedings commence before the verdict or sentence in the criminal case? See Mary M.

Cheh, Constitutional Limits on Using Civil Remedies to Achieve Criminal Law Objectives: Understanding and Transcending the Criminal-Civil Law Distinction, 42 Hastings L.J. 1325 (1991); Kenneth Mann, Punitive Civil Sanctions: The Middleground Between Criminal and Civil Law, 101 Yale L.J. 1795 (1992). The government also might use the relatively broad discovery devices of civil litigation to get around the barriers built into discovery for criminal proceedings.

In the corporate context, the federal government may be inclined to threaten an entity with criminal prosecution in an attempt to leverage large civil payments. This is the case when similar statutes allow for criminal and civil fines. Whether a criminal or a civil proceeding is preferable against a corporation may be debatable, especially if the wrongdoing is limited to a handful of employees rather than being indicative of widespread corruption. See Elizabeth K. Ainslie, Indicting Corporations Revisited: Lessons from the Arthur Andersen Prosecution, 43 Am. Crim. L. Rev. 107 (2006).

3. *The publicity alternative.* Consider this alternative to criminal proceedings: After the end of apartheid in South Africa, the government established the Truth and Reconciliation Commission to create some accountability and public disclosure for many acts of public wrongdoing during the earlier era. The commission did not impose criminal sanctions, but its proceedings and findings received intense public attention. Perpetrators of apartheid crimes who did not appear before the commission could end up in front of a criminal court — and all perpetrators could still face criminal charges before an international or non-national tribunal. In what situations is intense public scrutiny and debate an acceptable alternative to criminal punishments? To what extent should a country be allowed to opt for forgiveness instead of criminal sanctions for serious offenses, such as apartheid, torture, or crimes against humanity? See Eric Blumenson, The Challenge of a Global Standard of Justice: Peace, Pluralism, and Punishment at the International Criminal Court, 44 Colum. J. Transnat'l L. 801 (2006).

4. *Drug taxes.* A majority of states impose taxes on illegal drugs or on those who distribute them. The statutes typically require any possessor of a controlled substance to purchase "tax stamps" for each ounce of the controlled substance. Some of the drug tax statutes apply regardless of whether the owner of the controlled substance was ever arrested or convicted. In Department of Revenue of Montana v. Kurth Ranch, 511 U.S. 767 (1994), the Supreme Court held that such a drug tax might qualify as an additional "punishment" for conduct; the double jeopardy bar means that the tax cannot be used in conjunction with a criminal prosecution. The Court described the statute and its reasons as follows:

> Montana's Dangerous Drug Tax Act . . . imposes a tax "on the possession and storage of dangerous drugs," and expressly provides that the tax is to be "collected only after any state or federal fines or forfeitures have been satisfied." The tax is either 10 percent of the assessed market value of the drugs . . . or a specified amount depending on the drug ($100 per ounce for marijuana, for example, and $250 per ounce for hashish), whichever is greater. [At] the time of arrest law enforcement personnel shall complete the dangerous drug information report as required by the department and afford the taxpayer an opportunity to sign it. If the taxpayer refuses to do so, the law enforcement officer is

required to file the form within 72 hours of the arrest. . . . The taxpayer has no obligation to file a return or to pay any tax unless and until he is arrested. . . .

Whereas fines, penalties, and forfeitures are readily characterized as sanctions, taxes are typically different because they are usually motivated by revenue-raising rather than punitive purposes. Yet at some point, an exaction labeled as a tax approaches punishment, and our task is to determine whether Montana's drug tax crosses that line.

We begin by noting that neither a high rate of taxation nor an obvious deterrent purpose automatically marks this tax a form of punishment. . . . A significant part of the assessment was more than eight times the drug's market value — a remarkably high tax. That the Montana legislature intended the tax to deter people from possessing marijuana is beyond question. . . .

Other unusual features . . . set the Montana statute apart from most taxes. First, this so-called tax is conditioned on the commission of a crime. [The] assessment not only hinges on the commission of a crime, it also is exacted only after the taxpayer has been arrested for the precise conduct that gives rise to the tax obligation in the first place. . . . The Montana tax is exceptional for an additional reason. Although it purports to be a species of property tax — that is, a "tax on the possession and storage of dangerous drugs" — it is levied on goods that the taxpayer neither owns nor possesses when the tax is imposed. Indeed, the State presumably destroyed the contraband goods in this case before the tax on them was assessed.

Id. at 770, 778-783. The Court concluded that the imposition of the drug tax in Montana constituted "punishment" and therefore created a double jeopardy bar that prevented the state from bringing criminal charges for possession of drugs.

State tax provisions have withstood some, but not all, challenges under various provisions of state constitutions. The state courts have split when deciding whether their statutes violated the state or federal rules against double jeopardy. The statutes surviving a double jeopardy challenge are usually different from the Montana statute in *Kurth Ranch* because they provide for collection of the tax and punishment of violators even when there is no prosecution or conviction for other narcotics violations. See Covelli v. Commissioner of Revenue Services, 668 A.2d 699 (Conn. 1995).

5. *Driver's license.* Persons who are arrested for driving while intoxicated often lose their driver's licenses in administrative hearings and are convicted of a crime in separate criminal proceedings. The defendants sometimes claim that the two proceedings amount to double jeopardy. Such arguments have failed in about 30 states and have succeeded in almost 20 (mostly in the intermediate appellate courts). Compare State v. Young, 544 N.W.2d 808 (Neb. 1996) (no double jeopardy violation) with State v. Gustafson, 668 N.E.2d 435 (Ohio 1996) (double jeopardy violation). How might you argue that the loss of a driver's license is different from civil in rem forfeiture of assets? Should the legal analysis change if the government is threatening to remove some other form of license, such as a license to practice medicine or law?

# =11=
## ‖ *Sentences Reconsidered* ‖

As discussed in Chapter 2, many institutions and individuals have input into the sentences imposed on convicted offenders. We often think of this input as culminating in the decision of a sentencing judge. Many different players, however, have the opportunity to reconsider sentencing choices made by others.

Some of the legal structures through which sentences are reconsidered involve the judiciary, as detailed in the first half of this chapter; others involve executive branch officials, as discussed in the second half. Some review structures are unique to death sentences, while others apply to all sentences. In all settings, the officials may reconsider not only specific sentencing outcomes but also some of the theoretical, policy-based, and legal arguments that influenced initial sentencing decisions.

## A.  JUDICIAL RECONSIDERATION OF SENTENCES

Judges are commonly viewed as central figures in sentencing. Yet we have seen that other institutions often divert or impose sanctions that either sidestep or substitute for conviction and formal sentencing. We have also seen throughout the book that even where judges do impose a sentence after conviction — the archetype of what it means to sentence — many other institutions and individuals, including legislatures, sentencing commissions, prosecutors, and probation officers, influence the types of sentences that judges can impose. Indeed, when a legislature enacts a mandatory sentencing provision, or when a sentencing commission establishes strict sentencing guidelines, the judiciary's role in determining initial sentences can seem more ministerial than substantive.

Many structured sentencing reforms have allowed institutions other than courts to play a larger part in initial sentencing decisions, and one of the explicit purposes of structured reform is to constrain or guide the discretion of judges. But other legal developments have increased the judiciary's role in the reconsideration of initial sentencing decisions.

The judicial role in sentence reconsideration, especially through appeals and collateral review, is relatively new. Review of convictions and sentences were historically part of an appeal made to the sovereign — the governor or president. But no longer is such an appeal to the sovereign an offender's only avenue for relief. There are now elaborate legal structures and rules that give offenders a way to obtain judicial review of their convictions and sentences. Indeed, there are now far greater opportunities for judicial than for executive review.

## 1.   Sentencing Judge

The sentencing choices of legislatures, sentencing commissions, and prosecutors are inevitably reexamined and reassessed by a sentencing judge when she decides what specific sentence to impose on a particular offender. As the following case highlights, modern systems with defined sentencing rules present sentencing judges with opportunities to reconsider the appropriateness and the application of general sentencing rules in individual cases.

## California v. Superior Court of San Diego County (Jesus Romero, Real Party in Interest)
### 917 P.2d 628 (Cal. 1996)

WERDEGAR, J.

Penal Code section 1385, subdivision (a), authorizes a trial court to dismiss a criminal action "in furtherance of justice" on its own motion. . . . This case raises the question whether a court may, on its own motion, strike prior felony conviction allegations in cases arising under the law known as "Three Strikes and You're Out." . . .

### I.   BACKGROUND

#### A.   The Three Strikes Law

The Three Strikes law consists of two, nearly identical statutory schemes designed to increase the prison terms of repeat felons. . . . In summary, both statutes have this effect: When a defendant is convicted of a felony, and it is pleaded and proved that he has committed one or more prior felonies defined as "violent" or "serious," sentencing proceeds under the Three Strikes law. Prior felonies qualifying as "serious" or "violent" are taken into account regardless of their age. The current felony need not be "violent" or "serious."

If the defendant has only one qualifying prior felony conviction, the prescribed term of imprisonment . . . is twice the term otherwise provided as punishment for the current felony conviction. If the defendant has two or more prior qualifying felonies, the prescribed sentence is an indeterminate term of life imprisonment [with a minimum term before parole eligibility of] the greater of: (a) three times the term otherwise provided for the current conviction; (b) twenty-five years; or (c) the term required [under other statutes]. In sentencing, the court may not grant probation, suspend execution or imposition of sentence, divert the defendant, or commit the defendant to any facility other than state prison.

## B. Facts

On June 3, 1994, the District Attorney of San Diego County filed an information in the superior court charging defendant Jesus Romero with possession of a controlled substance, namely 0.13 grams of cocaine base. The information also alleged defendant had previously been convicted of the following felonies on the dates indicated: second degree burglary on June 25, 1980; attempted burglary of an inhabited dwelling on November 16, 1984; first degree burglary of an inhabited dwelling on September 2, 1986; and possession of a controlled substance on April 6, 1992, and June 8, 1993.

Defendant's two prior serious felonies, namely burglary and attempted burglary of inhabited dwellings, made him eligible for a life sentence under the Three Strikes law. Without the prior felony conviction allegations, defendant's sentence would fall between one and six years. . . . Defendant pled not guilty. At a subsequent hearing, the court indicated its willingness to consider striking the prior felony conviction allegations if defendant changed his plea to guilty as charged on all counts. The prosecutor objected to that procedure, arguing the court had no power to dismiss prior felony allegations in a Three Strikes case unless the prosecutor asked the court to do so. The court disagreed [and] permitted defendant to change his plea and struck the prior felony conviction allegations. [The court] imposed a sentence of six years in state prison. . . .

## II. Discussion

The ultimate question before us is whether a trial court may dismiss prior felony conviction allegations in furtherance of justice on its own motion in a case brought under the Three Strikes law. In answering this question, two statutes are of central importance. The first is section 1385. It provides as follows:

> (a) The judge or magistrate may, either of his or her own motion or upon the application of the prosecuting attorney, and in the furtherance of justice, order an action to be dismissed. The reasons for the dismissal must be set forth in an order entered upon the minutes. . . .
> (b) This section does not authorize a judge to strike any prior conviction of a serious felony for purposes of enhancement of a sentence under Section 667.

[We] have construed section 1385(a) as permitting a judge to dismiss not only an entire case, but also a part thereof, including the allegation that a defendant has previously been convicted of a felony. When a court strikes prior felony conviction allegations in this way, it does not wipe out such prior convictions or prevent them from being considered in connection with later convictions. Instead, the order striking such allegations simply embodies the court's determination that, in the interest of justice, defendant should not be required to undergo a statutorily increased penalty which would follow from judicial determination of the alleged fact.

The other statute of central importance to this case is section 667, subdivision (f). A part of the Three Strikes law, the statute provides as follows:

> (f) (1) Notwithstanding any other law, subdivisions (b) to (i), inclusive, shall be applied in every case in which a defendant has a prior felony conviction as defined in subdivision (d). The prosecuting attorney shall plead and prove each prior felony conviction except as provided in paragraph (2).
>
> (2) The prosecuting attorney may move to dismiss or strike a prior felony conviction allegation in the furtherance of justice pursuant to Section 1385, or if there is insufficient evidence to prove the prior conviction. If upon the satisfaction of the court that there is insufficient evidence to prove the prior felony conviction, the court may dismiss or strike the allegation.

Defendant argues that the Three Strikes law, if interpreted to permit a court to strike a prior felony conviction allegation *only* on the prosecutor's motion, violates the doctrine of separation of powers. [In People v. Tenorio, we held] unconstitutional a statute purporting to empower a prosecutor to veto a court's decision to dismiss a prior conviction allegation. . . . One may fairly summarize the court's reasoning in this way: [Conceding] the Legislature's power to bar a court from dismissing certain charges altogether, when the Legislature does permit a charge to be dismissed the ultimate decision whether to dismiss is a judicial, rather than a prosecutorial or executive, function; to require the prosecutor's consent to the disposition of a criminal charge pending before the court unacceptably compromises judicial independence. In subsequent cases, the court relied on People v. Tenorio to hold unconstitutional other statutes purporting to give prosecutors the power to veto similar judicial decisions related to the sentencing or other disposition of criminal charges. . . .

The Attorney General suggests the Three Strikes law serves the purpose of the separation of powers doctrine by making the decision to dismiss under section 1385 a "joint" decision, in the sense that the court and the prosecutor each may veto the other's preferred disposition. [But] interference with the traditional prerogatives of the executive cannot justify interference with the independence of the judiciary. . . . That the Legislature and the electorate may eliminate the courts' power to make certain sentencing choices may be conceded. Subject to the constitutional prohibition against cruel and unusual punishment, the power to define crimes and fix penalties is vested exclusively in the legislative branch. It does not follow, however, that having given the court the power to dismiss, the Legislature may therefore condition its exercise upon the approval of the district attorney. This court has not upheld any law purporting to subject to prosecutorial approval the court's discretion to dispose of a criminal charge. Instead, we have consistently held such laws unconstitutional. . . .

We thus arrive at this question: Does the Three Strikes law contain a "clear legislative direction" that courts may not strike sentencing allegations in furtherance of justice under section 1385 without the prosecutor's approval? [It is] self-evident that the Legislature assumed a court would at least have the power to grant the prosecutor's motion to strike a prior felony allegation in the furtherance of justice. The question then becomes: Does the court also have the power to strike such an allegation on its own motion?

[Defendant] contends, the Three Strikes law confirms that the court retains its powers under section 1385: Because section 667(f)(2) permits the prosecuting attorney to "move to dismiss or strike a prior felony conviction allegation in the furtherance of justice *pursuant to Section 1385* "(italics added), a fortiori the court must have power to grant the motion *pursuant to section 1385.* . . .

[There] is a long history of dispute among the various branches of state government over the application of section 1385 to sentencing allegations [, and] the lesson of section 1385's controversial history is that references to the section in sentencing statutes are not lightly or thoughtlessly made. The drafter's express invocation of section 1385 in the Three Strikes law, together with the absence of any language purporting to bar courts from acting pursuant to it, virtually compels the conclusion no such prohibition was intended. . . .

The district attorney . . . argues that section 1385(b) independently bars a court from striking prior felony allegations in Three Strikes cases [because it] qualifies the general power to dismiss granted to courts in section 1385(a), in these words: "This section does not authorize a judge to strike any prior conviction of a serious felony for purposes of enhancement of a sentence under Section 667." The Three Strikes law, the district attorney contends, was codified as part of section 667 and articulates a sentence "enhancement" within the meaning of section 1385(b). . . . Defendant's [main response is] that section 1385(b) cannot fairly be read as referring to the Three Strikes law [because it was enacted first and because it is not an "enhancement" under the terms of section 1385(b). Legislative] intent is the governing consideration. [The] Legislature's decision to place the Three Strikes law within section 667 falls short of a "clear legislative direction" to eliminate courts' power to strike prior felony allegations sua sponte. . . .

The district attorney [further argues that the] Three Strikes initiative was motivated by the voters' desire for longer sentences and by a mistrust of judges. The proponents of the initiative argued in its favor that "soft-on-crime judges, politicians, defense lawyers and probation officers care more about violent felons than they do victims. They spend all of their time looking for loopholes to get rapists, child molesters and murderers out on probation, early parole, or off the hook altogether."

Plainly the Three Strikes initiative, as well as the legislative act embodying its terms, was intended to restrict courts' discretion in sentencing repeat offenders. . . . Both versions of the Three Strikes law expressly declare that a court, in sentencing, may not grant probation, suspend execution or imposition of sentence, divert the defendant, or commit the defendant to any facility other than state prison. But to say the intent of a law was to restrict judicial discretion begs the question of *how* judicial discretion was to be restricted. The answer to that question can be found only by examining the language of the act. In it, one finds the express restrictions on the courts' power mentioned above, but no others. . . .

For these reasons, we conclude that section 1385(a) does permit a court acting on its own motion to strike prior felony conviction allegations in cases brought under the Three Strikes law. Our holding respects the principle that legislative acts are construed, if at all possible, to be constitutional. Our holding also avoids conflict with the principle that ambiguous penal statutes are construed to favor the defendant.

To guide the lower courts in the exercise of their discretion under section 1385(a), whether acting on their own motion or on motion of the prosecuting attorney, we emphasize the following: A court's discretion to strike prior felony conviction allegations in furtherance of justice is limited . . . and is subject to review for abuse. We reviewed the applicable principles in People v. Orin, 533 P.2d 193 (Cal. 1975):

> The trial court's power to dismiss an action under section 1385 . . . is limited by the amorphous concept which requires that the dismissal be "in furtherance of justice." . . . From the case law, several general principles emerge. Paramount among them is the rule that the language of [section 1385], "in furtherance of justice," requires consideration "both of the constitutional rights of the defendant, and *the interests of society represented by the People,* in determining whether there should be a dismissal." At the very least, the reason for dismissal must be "that which would motivate a reasonable judge." . . .

From these general principles it follows that a court abuses its discretion if it dismisses a case, or strikes a sentencing allegation, solely to accommodate judicial convenience or because of court congestion. A court also abuses its discretion by dismissing a case, or a sentencing allegation, simply because a defendant pleads guilty. Nor would a court act properly if guided solely by a personal antipathy for the effect that the Three Strikes law would have on a defendant, while ignoring defendant's background, the nature of his present offenses, and other individualized considerations.

. . . Section 1385 anticipates, and facilitates, appellate review with the requirement that "[t]he reasons for the dismissal must be set forth in an order entered upon the minutes." The statement of reasons is not merely directory, and neither trial nor appellate courts have authority to disregard the requirement. It is not enough that on review the reporter's transcript may show the trial court's motivation; the *minutes* must reflect the reason so that all may know why this great power was exercised.

Having decided that section 1385(a) applies to this case, we must determine the appropriate disposition. [Here] the record does not contain all of the material a reviewing court should consider . . . because the trial court did not set forth its reasons for striking the prior felony conviction allegations in the relevant minute order, as required by section 1385(a). . . . Under these circumstances, the appropriate remedy is to vacate the judgment, to permit defendant to withdraw his plea, and otherwise to proceed in conformity with this opinion. . . .

## NOTES

1. *Means for judicial sentencing reconsideration: constitutional review.*  Though the decision in *Romero* is based ultimately on an interpretation of a California statute, the court's discussion reveals that judges always have an opportunity — indeed, an obligation — to reexamine sentencing decisions made by legislatures and others in light of prevailing state and federal constitutional rules. The federal Constitution's mandates of due process and separation of powers, and its prohibition of cruel and unusual punishments create procedural and substantive limits on sentencing structures and outcomes that judges can and do enforce. Many states also have additional constitutional provisions and precedents that enable judges to reconsider the sentencing decisions of legislatures, sentencing commissions, and others.

Because constitutional provisions are usually vague and subject to interpretation, there has been a robust debate concerning how judges should review sentencing determinations in light of constitutional norms. See Ewing v. California, 538 U.S. 11 (2003) (explaining that the Supreme Court has a long-standing tradition of deferring to state legislatures in making and implementing important policy decisions regarding sentencing); Harmelin v. Michigan, 501 U.S. 957 (1991) (developing arguments for why the Supreme Court should not rigorously review state sentencing choices on constitutional grounds). Do you think the standards for constitutional review ought to differ depending on the nature and severity of the sentence at issue — that is, should constitutional review of death sentences or lengthy prison terms be more exhaustive than review of shorter terms of imprisonment or alternative sanctions? See Gregory Schneider, Sentencing Proportionality in the States, 54 Ariz. L. Rev. 241 (2012); Richard S. Frase, Limiting Excessive Prison Sentences Under Federal and State Constitutions, 11 U. Pa.. J. Const. L. 39 (2008).

2. *Means for judicial sentencing reconsideration: statutory authority.*  Though influenced by constitutional concerns, the decision in *Romero* makes clear that statutes give sentencing judges in California the power to strike prior felony allegations (and thereby avoid application of the three-strikes law). The decision details inappropriate grounds for striking prior felony allegations, but it does not indicate what grounds may be appropriate. What types of reasons for striking prior felony allegations would be "in the furtherance of justice"?

Though relatively few jurisdictions give sentencing judges direct means to avoid the application of mandatory sentencing statutes, nearly all jurisdictions that employ guideline sentencing systems have granted sentencing judges some express statutory authority to depart from these guidelines. In the state of Washington, a sentencing judge may depart from the presumptive guideline sentence and impose a more or less severe sentence only when the case presents "substantial and compelling reasons justifying an exceptional sentence." Wash. Rev. Code Ann. §9.94A.535. Departures from the presumptive sentences established in the guidelines are authorized when the sentencing judges find "substantial and compelling circumstances." Like the provisions at issue in *Romero*, departure statutes generally require judges to explain the basis for any departure, and an inadequate explanation can lead to reversal on appeal.

3. *Means for judicial sentencing reconsideration: circumvention.*   In any taxonomy of the ways sentences get reconsidered, one should not overlook the extralegal "authority" judges possess to circumvent the application of sentencing rules established by legislatures and sentencing commissions. A sentencing judge who is disconcerted by the application of a mandatory sentencing provision in a particular case might condone (and even encourage) a plea bargain in which the offender pleads to a lesser offense. See U.S. Sentencing Commission, Special Report to Congress: Mandatory Minimum Penalties in the Federal Criminal Justice System 56-58 (August 1991). In a series of articles based on empirical research into the operation of the federal sentencing guidelines, Professors Stephen Schulhofer and Ilene Nagel concluded that the guidelines were circumvented in up to one-third of all federal cases during the period studied. See Schulhofer & Nagel, Plea Negotiations Under the Federal Sentencing Guidelines: Guideline Circumvention and Its Dynamics in the Post-*Mistretta* Period, 91 Nw. U. L. Rev. 1284, 1305 (1997); Schulhofer & Nagel, Negotiated Pleas Under the Federal Sentencing Guidelines: The First Fifteen Months, 27 Am. Crim. L. Rev. 232, 272-278 (1989).

4. *Judicial override in death sentencing systems.*   Most of the 38 states that authorize capital punishment rely on juries to decide whether an offender should be sentenced to die and give the trial judge authority to reconsider a jury's capital sentencing decision. In many states, a judge has the authority to override a jury's recommendation only by imposing a life sentence after the jury has recommended death. See, e.g., Ohio Rev. Code §2727.16. But four states — Alabama, Delaware, Florida, and Indiana — use "advisory" juries in their capital sentencing process, which means that the trial judge has the authority to override a jury's recommendation in either direction: The judge might impose a life sentence when the jury voted for death or might impose a death sentence even when a jury has recommended life. See Ala. Stat. §13A-5-46; Del. Code tit. 11, §4209; Fla. Stat. §921.141; Ind. Code Ann. §35-50-2-9. The constitutionality of permitting judges to impose a death sentence has been thrown into question by the Supreme Court's decision in Ring v. Arizona, 536 U.S. 584 (2002), which held that a jury must make any factual findings that allow a sentence of death under the applicable state statute. The ruling in Blakely v. Washington, 542 U.S. 296 (2004), deepened the questions about these advisory jury jurisdictions. Most courts, however, have upheld the review of jury capital decision making by trial judges after *Ring* and *Blakely* so long as juries play a central role in finding the facts on which a death sentence is based. See Stephanos Bibas, *Apprendi* in the States, 94 J. Crim. L. & Criminology 1 (2003).

How would you expect judges and juries to view aggravating and mitigating circumstances differently? William J. Bowers et al., The Decision Maker Matters: An Empirical Examination of the Way the Role of the Judge and the Jury Influence Death Penalty Decision-Making, 63 Wash. & Lee L. Rev. 931 (2006).

## 2.   *Direct Appeal of Sentences*

The modern history of appellate review of criminal *convictions* extends nearly a century, with a rich set of doctrines governing when and how trial error can be corrected. The important doctrine does not come from constitutional law; the Supreme Court held in McKane v. Durston, 153 U.S. 684 (1894), that there is no federal constitutional right to appeal, and most state constitutions lack express provisions guaranteeing appeals in criminal cases. Nevertheless, all American jurisdictions have long provided for appellate review of convictions, and statutes and rules of appellate procedure establish who can file an appeal and what issues the parties can raise.

The modern history of appellate review of criminal *sentences* is far more abbreviated and much less evolved. Frequent appellate review of the outcome of capital cases did not begin until the 1970s, following the Supreme Court's decision in Furman v. Georgia, 408 U.S. 238 (1972), which struck down existing capital sentencing schemes. And, as Professor Kevin Reitz notes, serious appellate review of noncapital sentencing did not begin until a decade later, when jurisdictions started adopting guideline systems and other structured sentencing reforms:

> Prior to the guideline innovations of the 1980s, little meaningful appellate review of sentencing decisions had ever occurred in the United States, in federal or state courts. Those few appellate decisions that existed did not, for the most part, focus on substantive issues of the appropriate principles for punishment decisions, or the application of those principles to particular factual scenarios. Instead, the cases dealt primarily with constitutional issues. . . . Even in those states where a power of sentence review existed, it was used sparingly. Appellate courts refrained from interference with a sentence below unless it could be characterized as clearly excessive or as a clear abuse of discretion. . . .
>
> The absence, or near absence, of appellate input into the law of criminal punishment was due in part to the embarrassment that there was no substantive law of sentencing to be applied at the trial level. [There] were effectively no legal principles against which a sentence could be tested on review. Another disablement of appellate review was the widespread rule that trial courts were not obliged to explain the reasons for their sentencing decisions on the record, [which provided] little practical way for an appeals court to discover what thought process a trial judge had followed in a given case.

Kevin R. Reitz, Sentencing Guideline Systems and Sentence Appeals: A Comparison of Federal and State Experiences, 91 Nw. U. L. Rev. 1441, 1443-1446 (1997).

As this excerpt suggests, modern sentencing reforms radically changed the dynamics surrounding appellate review of noncapital sentencing. By creating defined sentencing law through mandatory sentencing provisions and guideline sentencing rules, structured sentencing reforms established a corpus of legal rules that sentencing judges had to apply and appellate judges could review. The following statute establishes the authority and the role of appellate courts in reviewing sentences in a typical guideline state.

## ‖ *42 Pennsylvania Consolidated Statutes §9781* ‖

(a) *Right to appeal.* The defendant or the Commonwealth may appeal as of right the legality of the sentence.

(b) *Allowance of appeal.* The defendant or the Commonwealth may file a petition for allowance of appeal of the discretionary aspects of a sentence for a felony or a misdemeanor to the appellate court that has initial jurisdiction for such appeals. Allowance of appeal may be granted at the discretion of the appellate court where it appears that there is a substantial question that the sentence imposed is not appropriate under this chapter.

(c) *Determination on appeal.* The appellate court shall vacate the sentence and remand the case to the sentencing court with instructions if it finds:

(1) the sentencing court purported to sentence within the sentencing guidelines but applied the guidelines erroneously;

(2) the sentencing court sentenced within the sentencing guidelines but the case involves circumstances where the application of the guidelines would be clearly unreasonable; or

(3) the sentencing court sentenced outside the sentencing guidelines and the sentence is unreasonable.

In all other cases the appellate court shall affirm the sentence imposed by the sentencing court.

(d) *Review of record.* In reviewing the record the appellate court shall have regard for:

(1) The nature and circumstances of the offense and the history and characteristics of the defendant.

(2) The opportunity of the sentencing court to observe the defendant, including any presentence investigation.

(3) The findings upon which the sentence was based.

(4) The guidelines promulgated by the commission. . . .

(f) Limitation on additional appellate review.—No appeal of the discretionary aspects of the sentence shall be permitted beyond the appellate court that has initial jurisdiction for such appeals.

## PROBLEM 11-1.   HOW APPEALING?

Corrine Marie Denardi was convicted on an indictment charging conspiracy to distribute cocaine. At the time of sentencing, her attorney argued for a departure from the sentencing guidelines, citing mitigating factors such as the defendant's cooperation with the government, the absence of a prior criminal record, an exemplary work history, and a lifetime of love and devotion to friends and family. Ms. Denardi's attorney stressed that the imposition of a sentence within the recommended guideline range would cause extreme hardship on Ms. Denardi's family because she was the sole caretaker of three young children, one of whom was developmentally disabled. The relevant provision of the Pennsylvania Sentencing Guidelines states that nonguideline sentences may be imposed if the trial court determines that an aggravating or mitigating factor "is present." Such factors should be "sufficiently important to warrant a sentence" above or below the standard range."

The trial court refused to depart from the guidelines, and sentenced Ms. Denardi to 24 months' imprisonment. In so doing, the judge stated:

> I find nothing here that permits me to depart from the guidelines, and I am very much guided by them. I recognize all of the favorable points that the defendant has produced, and the best that I can do with those is to apply them to my choice

of where within the guidelines the sentence would fall. I have been asking and trying to get some factor that would justify a deviation, and I haven't found any.

Based on the appellate review provisions of the Pennsylvania code, reprinted above, does Ms. Denardi have the right to appeal the trial court's decision not to depart from the sentencing guidelines? Does the answer to this question depend on whether the trial court believed it lacked the legal authority to depart or instead simply made a discretionary decision not to exercise its departure authority? Cf. United States v. Denardi, 892 F.2d 269 (3d Cir. 1989); see also David Yellen, Appellate Review of Refusals to Depart, 1 Fed. Sent'g Rep. 264 (1988).

## PROBLEM 11-2. WAIVING GOOD-BYE TO AN APPEAL?

In December 2001, Walter Grange's house was burglarized. During the course of the investigation, police seized from Grange's home a microwave oven, which contained 6.44 grams of crack cocaine residue coated on the inside, and a bag containing nearly $12,000 in cash. Pursuant to a plea agreement, Grange pleaded guilty to possessing crack cocaine in violation of 21 U.S.C. §844(a). The plea agreement stated that the government and the defendant agreed that the total amount of drugs possessed was just over six grams of crack cocaine. The agreement also included the following statement:

> Defendant knowingly waives the right to appeal any sentence within the guideline range applicable to the statute of conviction as determined by the Court after resolution of any objections by either party to the presentence report to be prepared in this case, and defendant specifically agrees not to appeal the determination of the Court in resolving any contested sentencing factor. In other words, Defendant waives the right to appeal the sentence imposed in this case except to the extent, if any, that the Court may depart upwards from the applicable sentencing guideline range as determined by the Court. The defendant also waives his right to challenge his sentence or the manner in which it was determined in any collateral attack.

The probation officer investigating the offense and writing the presentence report for the sentencing court concluded that the $12,000 in cash should be converted into crack cocaine when computing the base offense level under the federal sentencing guidelines. At the sentencing hearing the prosecutor, when asked about the probation officer's computation, stated:

> On the $12,000, your Honor, I have nothing to add. I think the Probation Department set out the facts. Also, I'm in a little bit of a difficult position because I signed a plea agreement agreeing to the 6.44 grams. To be honest with the Court, it doesn't take a genius to know if you have that much residue in the facility that was cooking it, there's a little bit more involved there; but on the other hand, that was the extent of our evidence at that point.

The trial judge accepted the probation office's determination and sentenced Grange to 78 months in prison.

Under the terms of the plea agreement, can Grange appeal directly or file for a writ of habeas corpus? Can he attack the validity of the plea agreement, arguing that the government failed to live up to its promise? Can Grange assert that he received ineffective assistance of counsel as a means to try to void the plea agreement? See United States v. Brown, 328 F.3d 767 (5th Cir. 2003).

## PROBLEM 11-3.   BEGGING FOR PRESUMPTIONS

On October 12, 2011, the Chair of the U.S. Sentencing Commission, Judge Patti Saris, gave detailed testimony before the House Subcommittee on Crime, Terrorism, and Homeland Security — part of the Committee on the Judiciary. Judge Saris reviewed trends in guideline application, particularly the impact of "blockbuster" decisions, such as *Koon*, *Apprendi*, and *Booker*. Recognizing that post-*Booker* sentencing was popular with district judges and defense attorneys, but less so with prosecutors, Judge Saris testified as follows:

> While sentencing data and case law demonstrate that the federal sentencing guidelines continue to provide gravitational pull in federal sentencing, the Commission has observed an increase in the numbers of variances from the guidelines in the wake of the Supreme Court's recent jurisprudence. There are troubling trends in sentencing, including growing disparities among circuits and districts and demographic disparities which the Commission has been evaluating.
>
> The Commission believes that a strong and effective guidelines system is an essential component of the flexible, certain, and fair sentencing scheme envisioned by Congress when it passed the SRA. To improve sentencing in light of *Booker* and its progeny, the Commission has the following statutory suggestions: First, Congress should enact a more robust appellate review standard that requires appellate courts to apply a presumption of reasonableness to sentences within the properly calculated guidelines range. The Commission also believes that Congress should require that the greater the variance from a guideline, the greater should be the sentencing court's justification for the variance. Congress also should create a heightened standard of review for sentences imposed as a result of a "policy disagreement" with the guidelines. Second, the Commission recommends that Congress clarify statutory directives to the sentencing courts and Commission that are currently in tension. Section 994 of title 28, United States Code, instructs *the Commission* to assure the guidelines reflect the general inappropriateness of considering certain offender characteristics (for example "family ties and responsibilities") in the guidelines, but 18 U.S.C. §3553(a) can be read to direct the *sentencing courts* to consider those same characteristics. Accordingly, judges often determine that the guidelines have not sufficiently addressed offender characteristics and impose a sentence outside the guidelines.

Would the Commission's proposals for more "robust" appellate review be wise? Would they be constitutional under *Rita* and *Gall*? Judge Saris' detailed testimony is worth reading for those interested in trends in guideline application and the Commission's perspective on those trends. See http://www.ussc.gov/Legislative_and_Public_Affairs/Congressional_Testimony_and_Reports/Testimony/20111012_Saris_Testimony.pdf.

## NOTES

1. *Whose right to appeal?*   Under U.S. law in every jurisdiction, the prosecution cannot appeal from an acquittal, while in civil law countries such an appeal is possible. In the United States, such appeals are considered a violation of double jeopardy prohibitions; civil law countries consider the trial and appeal to be part of one proceeding, and therefore a direct appeal does not constitute double jeopardy.

As revealed by the Pennsylvania appeals provision reprinted above, this American imbalance in appellate rights has generally not carried over to sentencing; in nearly all jurisdictions, prosecutors as well as defendants may appeal after a guilty verdict and the sentence. Why should the prosecution have the right to appeal from a sentence, especially since it controls charging and has unique power during plea negotiations? Should it matter whether the case is adjudicated in a guideline or a nonguideline jurisdiction?

2. *Dual functions of error correction and lawmaking.*   Appellate courts are often said to have the dual functions of correcting trial errors and expounding legal rules that control future cases through the force of precedent. Is one role more important than the other when it comes to sentencing?

Many early advocates of modern sentencing reforms urged the more active role for appellate courts, hoping that appellate review would foster an "evolutionary and principled development of a common law of sentencing." Norval Morris, Towards Principled Sentencing, 37 Md. L. Rev. 267, 284 (1977); see also Marvin E. Frankel, Sentencing Guidelines: A Need for Creative Collaboration, 101 Yale L.J. 2043, 2050 (1992). But in a thorough assessment of appellate review in three guideline jurisdictions, Professor Kevin Reitz documented that in practice, reviewing courts have favored the task of error correction over substantive lawmaking. In "hundreds of appellate decisions across different guideline jurisdictions," he notes, "one seldom encounters thoughtful opinions that advance our understanding of the substantive problems of punishment. Instead, guideline appeals lean toward technical, even technocratic, analyses." Kevin R. Reitz, Sentencing Guideline Systems and Sentence Appeals: A Comparison of Federal and State Experiences, 91 Nw. U. L. Rev. 1441, 1450 (1997). Can you imagine why the reformist vision of developing a "common law of sentencing" has proven hard to achieve in practice?

3. *Standards for review in federal sentencing.*   The influence and impact of appellate review will often hinge on the standard of review employed by the court. In most appellate review settings, factual findings are reviewed for clear error, legal rulings are reviewed de novo, and discretionary judgments are reviewed for an abuse of discretion. Would you describe sentencing decisions made under guideline systems as factual findings, legal rulings, or discretionary judgments?

The original version of the appellate review portion of the federal Sentencing Reform Act stated simply in 18 U.S.C. §3742(e) that circuit courts should "give due deference to the district court's application of the guidelines to the facts." This somewhat oblique instruction led the circuit courts to develop a range of approaches to reviewing certain guideline determinations, particularly decisions to depart from the guidelines. In Koon v. United States, 518 U.S. 81, 97 (1996), the U.S. Supreme Court, interpreting section 3742(e), stated that the deference to be given on appeal depends on the nature of the guideline question presented, and that a departure decision will in most cases be "due substantial deference" because "it embodies the sentencing court's traditional exercise of discretion." The Court thus concluded that circuit courts should apply an abuse of discretion standard when reviewing departures. See Douglas A. Berman, Balanced and Purposeful Departures: Fixing a Jurisprudence that Undermines the Federal Sentencing Guidelines, 76 Notre Dame L. Rev. 21 (2000); Ian Weinstein, The Discontinuous Tradition of Sentencing Discretion: *Koon*'s Failure to Recognize the Reshaping of Judicial Discretion Under the Guidelines, 79 B.U. L. Rev. 493 (1999); Barry L. Johnson, Discretion and the Rule of Law in Federal Guidelines Sentencing: Developing Departure Jurisprudence in the Wake of *Koon v. United States*, 58 Ohio St. L.J. 1697 (1998).

Data from the U.S. Sentencing Commission show that the number of downward departures granted by district courts increased steadily between 1996 and 2003. The total number of downward departures granted for reasons other than a defendant's assistance to prosecutors nearly doubled. Concerns about the number of departures ultimately led Congress in 2003, as part of a package of reforms designed to decrease the number of downward departures, to modify the language of 18 U.S.C. §3742(e) to provide that when considering "determinations [to depart from the guidelines], the court of appeals shall review de novo the district court's application of the guidelines to the facts." Through this alteration of the appellate review standard from "abuse of discretion" to "de novo," Congress apparently intended not only that circuit judges more rigorously review questionable downward departures on appeal, but also that district judges feel more restrained in granting departures in the first instance.

As we saw in Chapter 3, the Supreme Court held in Booker v. United States, 543 U.S. 220 (2005), that the "presumptive" federal sentencing guidelines violated the Sixth Amendment because they authorized judges to impose higher sentences only after finding certain facts that had not been found by a jury. Nonetheless, the Court retained the guidelines on a voluntary basis, while instructing appellate courts to review the sentences imposed in the district court for "reasonableness." In the aftermath of *Booker*, federal appellate courts started to embrace two devices that the Department of Justice urged on them: (a) the "presumption" on appeal that a guideline sentence was "reasonable" and (b) the "proportionality" principle, stating that larger variances from the guidelines require stronger justifications on appeal. The Supreme Court upheld a presumption by appellate courts that the district court sentence was reasonable in Rita v. United States, 551 U.S. 338 (2007), reprinted in chapter 3. However, the presumption was at best a weak one. The Court noted that "the presumption is not binding," did not place the burden of persuasion or proof on either party, and did not allow appellate courts to favor the Commission's fact-finding over that of trial judges. In Gall v. United States, 552 U.S. 38 (2007), the Court rejected the proposition that a sentence falling outside the guideline range was presumptively unreasonable.

4. *Waivers of the right to appeal.* Prosecutors in some federal districts routinely seek waivers of defendants' appeal rights in plea agreements. In 1995 the

Department of Justice issued a memorandum to all U.S. Attorneys' offices (discussed in Chapter 6) providing guidance on the drafting and use of appeal waivers. That memo recognized that the use of appeal waivers is "helpful in reducing the burden of appellate and collateral litigation involving sentencing issues" but also cautioned that it "could result in guideline-free sentencing of defendants in guilty plea cases, and it could encourage a lawless district court to impose sentences in violation of the guidelines." In July 1996 the Judicial Conference of the United States, in a memorandum to aid district judges and probation officers in their consideration of appeal waiver provisions, noted "that waivers have been consistently upheld as legal . . . as long as the waiver is knowing and voluntary." It also suggested that courts provide all defendants with a "qualified, yet informative, advisement of the right to appeal at sentencing," followed by a specific oral colloquy about the terms of any appeal waiver provision to which a defendant has agreed.

The federal courts have endorsed the validity of appeal waivers, while adopting a few exemptions for certain sorts of claims. Some courts exempt from the waivers any claims that a sentence is based on race discrimination, United States v. Baramdyka, 95 F.3d 840, 843 (9th Cir. 1996), is the product of ineffective assistance of counsel, United States v. Attar, 38 F.3d 727, 732-733 (4th Cir. 1994), or amounts to a "miscarriage of justice," United States v. Khattak, 273 F.3d 557, 563 (3d Cir. 2001).

A 2005 empirical analysis of appeal waivers found that defendants entered such waiver agreements in almost two-thirds of the cases settled by plea agreement. The government provides some sentencing concessions more frequently to defendants who sign waivers, such as downward departures, safety valve credits, and factual stipulations. The waivers are used more frequently in some circuits than in others. Nancy J. King & Michael E. O'Neill, Appeal Waivers and the Future of Sentencing Policy, 55 Duke L.J. 209 (2005). See also Jesse Davis, Texas Law Rides to the Rescue: A Lone Star Solution for Dubious Federal Presentence Appeal Waivers, 63 Baylor L. Rev. 250 (2011); Kristine Karnezis, Validity and Effect of Criminal Defendant's Express Waiver of Right to Appeal as Part of Negotiated Plea Agreement, 89 A.L.R.3d 864.

5. *Appeal rights under international law.*  Article 14(5) of the International Covenant on Civil and Political Rights, which the United States has ratified, grants every defendant the right to have the conviction and sentence reviewed by a higher tribunal. Similar rights are granted in the American and European Human Rights Conventions. Exceptions apply to minor offenses and cases tried in front of the nations' highest tribunals. Notably, there was no appeal from the decisions of the two post–World War II tribunals in Nuremberg and Tokyo. Because of the evolution of international human rights law as a part of the due process norm, however, appeals are explicitly mentioned in the procedural rules for the ad hoc tribunals trying offenders for atrocities committed in the former Yugoslavia and in Rwanda as well as for the International Criminal Court. The ad hoc tribunals have allowed for sentence appeals, even in the case of guilty pleas.

In contrast to noncapital sentencing, in which appellate review is relatively new and still somewhat novel, death sentences have been subject to appellate scrutiny since the early 1900s. The severity and finality of the penalty not only have prompted capital defendants to appeal in greater numbers and with greater urgency, but also have led appellate courts to examine more closely the legality and appropriateness of death sentences in individual cases. As the case below highlights, when states enacted new death penalty statutes after the Supreme Court struck down existing capital sentencing schemes in Furman v. Georgia, 408 U.S. 238 (1972), appellate review became a central tool in efforts to ensure that the death penalty was administered in a more consistent and reasoned way.

## Reginald Pulley v. Robert Alton Harris
### 465 U.S. 37 (1984)

WHITE, J.

[Robert Alton] Harris was convicted of a capital crime in a California court and was sentenced to death. Along with many other challenges to the conviction and sentence, Harris claimed on appeal that the California capital punishment statute was invalid under the United States Constitution because it failed to require the California Supreme Court to compare Harris' sentence with the sentences imposed in similar capital cases and thereby to determine whether they were proportionate. . . .

The proportionality review sought by Harris . . . and provided for in numerous state statutes[1] [inquires whether a death sentence is] unacceptable in a particular case because disproportionate to the punishment imposed on others convicted of the same crime. The issue in this case, therefore, is whether the Eighth Amendment, applicable to the States through the Fourteenth Amendment, requires a state appellate court, before it affirms a death sentence, to compare the sentence in the case before it with the penalties imposed in similar cases if requested to do so by the prisoner. Harris insists that it does and that this is the invariable rule in every case. . . . We do not agree.

Harris' submission is rooted in Furman v. Georgia, 408 U.S. 238 (1972). In *Furman*, the Court concluded that capital punishment, as then administered under statutes vesting unguided sentencing discretion in juries and trial judges, had become unconstitutionally cruel and unusual punishment. The death penalty was being imposed so discriminatorily, so wantonly and freakishly, and so infrequently that any given death sentence was cruel and unusual. In response to that decision, roughly two-thirds of the States promptly redrafted their capital sentencing statutes in an effort to limit jury discretion and avoid arbitrary and inconsistent results. All of the new statutes provide for automatic appeal of death sentences. Most, such as Georgia's, require the reviewing court, to some extent at least, to determine whether, considering both the crime and the defendant, the sentence is disproportionate to that imposed in similar cases.

---

1. Under the much-copied Georgia scheme, for example, the Supreme Court is required in every case to determine "[whether] the sentence of death is excessive or disproportionate to the penalty imposed in similar cases, considering both the crime and the defendant." Ga. Code Ann. §17-10-35(c)(3)(1982). If the court affirms the death sentence, it is to include in its decision reference to similar cases that it has taken into consideration. The court is required to maintain records of all capital felony cases in which the death penalty was imposed since 1970.

Not every State has adopted such a procedure. In some States, such as Florida, the appellate court performs proportionality review despite the absence of a statutory requirement; in others, such as California and Texas, it does not.

Four years after *Furman*, this Court examined several of the new state statutes. We upheld one of each of the three sorts mentioned above. See Gregg v. Georgia, 428 U.S. 153 (1976); Proffitt v. Florida, 428 U.S. 242 (1976); Jurek v. Texas, 428 U.S. 262 (1976). Needless to say, that some schemes providing proportionality review are constitutional does not mean that such review is indispensable. . . .

Assuming that there could be a capital sentencing system so lacking in other checks on arbitrariness that it would not pass constitutional muster without comparative proportionality review, the 1977 California statute is not of that sort. Under this scheme, a person convicted of first-degree murder is sentenced to life imprisonment unless one or more "special circumstances" are found, in which case the punishment is either death or life imprisonment without parole. Special circumstances are alleged in the charging paper and tried with the issue of guilt at the initial phase of the trial [and] must be proved beyond a reasonable doubt. If the jury finds the defendant guilty of first-degree murder and finds at least one special circumstance, the trial proceeds to a second phase to determine the appropriate penalty. Additional evidence may be offered and the jury is given a list of relevant factors [and,] guided by the aggravating and mitigating circumstances referred to in this section, [determines] whether the penalty shall be death or life imprisonment without the possibility of parole. If the jury returns a verdict of death, the . . . trial judge then reviews the evidence and, in light of the statutory factors, makes an independent determination as to whether the weight of the evidence supports the jury's findings and verdicts. The judge is required to state on the record the reasons for his findings. If the trial judge denies the motion for modification, there is an automatic appeal. The statute does not require comparative proportionality review or otherwise describe the nature of the appeal. It does state that the trial judge's refusal to modify the sentence "shall be reviewed." . . . As the California Supreme Court has said, "the statutory requirements that the jury specify the special circumstances which permit imposition of the death penalty, and that the trial judge specify his reasons for denying modification of the death penalty, serve to assure thoughtful and effective appellate review, focusing upon the circumstances present in each particular case."

By requiring the jury to find at least one special circumstance beyond a reasonable doubt, the statute limits the death sentence to a small subclass of capital-eligible cases. The statutory list of relevant factors, applied to defendants within this subclass, provides jury guidance and lessens the chance of arbitrary application of the death penalty, guaranteeing that the jury's discretion will be guided and its consideration deliberate. The jury's "discretion must be suitably directed and limited so as to minimize the risk of wholly arbitrary and capricious action." *Gregg*, 428 U.S., at 189. Its decision is reviewed by the trial judge and the State Supreme Court. On its face, this system, without any requirement or practice of comparative proportionality review, cannot be successfully challenged under *Furman* and our subsequent cases. . . .

STEVENS, J., concurring in part and concurring in the judgment.

. . . The systemic arbitrariness and capriciousness in the imposition of capital punishment under statutory schemes invalidated by Furman v. Georgia, 408 U.S. 238 (1972), resulted from two basic defects in those schemes. First, the systems were permitting the imposition of capital punishment in broad classes of offenses for which the penalty would always constitute cruel and unusual punishment. Second, even among those types of homicides for which the death penalty could be constitutionally imposed as punishment, the schemes vested essentially unfettered discretion in juries and trial judges to impose the death sentence. Given these defects, arbitrariness and capriciousness in the imposition of the punishment were inevitable, and given the extreme nature of the punishment, constitutionally intolerable. The statutes we have approved in *Gregg, Proffitt,* and *Jurek* were designed to eliminate each of these defects. Each scheme provided an effective mechanism for categorically narrowing the class of offenses for which the death penalty could be imposed and provided special procedural safeguards including appellate review of the sentencing authority's decision to impose the death penalty.

In *Gregg,* the [plurality opinion] indicated that some form of meaningful appellate review is required, and . . . focused on the proportionality review component of the Georgia statute because it was a prominent, innovative, and noteworthy feature that had been specifically designed to combat effectively the systemic problems in capital sentencing which had invalidated the prior Georgia capital sentencing scheme. But observations that this innovation is an effective safeguard do not mean that it is the only method of ensuring that death sentences are not imposed capriciously or that it is the only acceptable form of appellate review. [I]n each of the statutory schemes approved in our prior cases, as in the scheme we review today, meaningful appellate review is an indispensable component of the Court's determination that the State's capital sentencing procedure is valid. Like the Court, however, I am not persuaded that the particular form of review prescribed by statute in Georgia—comparative proportionality review—is the only method by which an appellate court can avoid the danger that the imposition of the death sentence in a particular case, or a particular class of cases, will be so extraordinary as to violate the Eighth Amendment.

BRENNAN, J., dissenting.

[In 1976, when considering challenges to] new death penalty statutes enacted by the States of Georgia, Florida, and Texas, a majority of the Court concluded that the procedural mechanisms included in those statutes provided sufficient protection to ensure their constitutional application. Thus began a series of decisions from this Court in which, with some exceptions, it has been assumed that the death penalty is being imposed by the various States in a rational and non-discriminatory way. Upon the available evidence, however, I am convinced that the Court is simply deluding itself, and also the American public, when it insists that those defendants who have already been executed or are today condemned to death have been selected on a basis that is neither arbitrary nor capricious, under any meaningful definition of those terms. . . .

Disproportionality among sentences given different defendants can only be eliminated after sentencing disparities are identified. And the most logical way to identify such sentencing disparities is for a court of statewide jurisdiction to conduct comparisons between death sentences imposed by different judges or juries within the State. This is what the Court labels comparative proportionality review. Although clearly no panacea, such review often serves to identify the most extreme examples of disproportionality among similarly situated defendants. At least to this extent, this form of appellate review serves to eliminate some of the irrationality that currently surrounds imposition of a death sentence. If only to further this limited purpose, therefore, I believe that the Constitution's prohibition on the irrational imposition of the death penalty requires that this procedural safeguard be provided.

Indeed, despite the Court's insistence that such review is not compelled by the Federal Constitution, over 30 States now require, either by statute or judicial decision, some form of comparative proportionality review before any death sentence may be carried out. By itself, this should weigh heavily on the side of requiring such appellate review. In addition, these current practices establish beyond dispute that such review can be administered without much difficulty by a court of statewide jurisdiction in each State. Perhaps the best evidence of the value of proportionality review can be gathered by examining the actual results obtained in those States which now require such review. For example, since 1973, . . . the Georgia Supreme Court has vacated at least seven death sentences because it was convinced that they were comparatively disproportionate. . . .

What these cases clearly demonstrate, in my view, is that comparative proportionality review serves to eliminate some, if only a small part, of the irrationality that currently infects imposition of the death penalty by the various States. Before any execution is carried out, therefore, a State should be required under the Eighth and Fourteenth Amendments to conduct such appellate review.

## NOTES

1. *Proportionality review of death sentences.*  As suggested in Pulley v. Harris, most states with the death penalty require their appellate courts to review the proportionality of any death sentence. In a few states, notably Florida, many death sentences have been reversed on the basis of a finding of disproportionality. See Cooper v. State, 739 So. 2d 82 (Fla. 1999). Commentators have noticed, however, that the rigor and significance of proportionality review of death sentences seems to have waned after the Supreme Court held in *Pulley* that such review was not constitutionally mandated. Professor Penny White explains the trend:

> Rather than conducting a meaningful comparison between similar cases, courts all too often simply state that a particular death sentence is proportionate and cite previous decisions without analyzing their similarities and differences, or the appropriateness of the death sentence. . . .
> Examples of cases in which codefendants are treated disproportionately with the least culpable receiving the death sentence are not rare. Similarly, there are many cases in which almost identical defendants commit almost identical crimes, but are sentenced differently. . . . On occasion before *Pulley*, the appellate courts in most states (when their statutes mandated) would step in and correct what would otherwise have been a tragic injustice by reducing a disproportionate death sentence to life imprisonment. However, *Pulley*'s removal of

what was believed to be proportionality's constitutional underpinning, coupled with the politically charged climate that surrounds most capital cases are undermining *Furman*'s mandate for nonarbitrary, nondiscriminatory death penalty schemes.

Penny J. White, Can Lightning Strike Twice? Obligations of State Courts after Pulley v. Harris, 70 U. Colo. L. Rev. 813, 816-817, 841-842 (1999). Since the decision in *Pulley*, eight states have repealed statutory provisions calling for proportionality review while three other states have established proportionality review. (Tennessee repealed and then reenacted its proportionality requirement after *Pulley*.) See Barry Latzer, The Failure of Comparative Proportionality Review of Capital Cases (with Lessons from New Jersey), 64 Alb. L. Rev. 1161, 1168 n.31 (2001); Kristen Nugent, Proportionality and Prosecutorial Discretion: Challenges to the Constitutionality of Georgia's Death Penalty Laws and Procedures Amidst The Deficiencies in of the State's Mandatory Appellate Review Structure, 64 U. Miami L. Rev. 175 (2009). What is it about death penalty cases that justifies proportionality review, a procedure that seems to entitle a defendant to a reduced sentence because of a failure to impose the same harsh sentence on other, similarly situated defendants? Should all sentences, or at least all serious sentences (such as sentences of 25 or more years of imprisonment), be subject to proportionality review, or is the entire concept of substantive sentencing review unsound? Compare Latzer, 64 Alb. L. Rev. 1161 (suggesting that proportionality review in death penalty cases has been largely a waste of time and money) with Evan J. Mandery, In Defense of Specific Proportionality Review, 65 Alb. L. Rev. 883 (2002) (arguing that proportionality review with the right focus could be valuable).

2. *Automatic appellate review of death sentences.* Another unique feature of appellate review in capital cases is its automatic nature. Most states with the death penalty provide for automatic review of every death sentence, and some jurisdictions provide for expedited review by the state's highest court. See, e.g., Ala. Code §12-22-150; Del. Code tit. 11, §4209(g); Neb. Const. art. 1, §23 ("In all capital cases, appeal directly to the Supreme Court shall be as a matter of right.").

Suggesting that automatic appellate review provisions are in some ways akin to trial courts' review of negotiated plea agreements, Professor Richard Bonnie has explained that such procedures are fundamentally based in society's interest "in the integrity of its institutions of criminal punishment and in the dignity of the processes through which these punishments are carried out." Richard J. Bonnie, The Dignity of the Condemned, 74 Va. L. Rev. 1363, 1369 (1988). But Professor Bonnie has also noted that these interests have been given particularly broad application in the appellate review of death sentences:

> The practice of requiring automatic appeal of death sentences . . . would not represent a significant expansion of integrity-protecting procedures if it were limited to a review of the sufficiency of the substantive predicates for the sentence under state and federal law. The actual scope of appellate review, however, appears to be seldom so restricted. The prevailing practice appears to be to review all claims of error in automatic appeals in the same manner as they would have been reviewed had the appeal been brought at the defendant's

own request. . . . In death cases—and only in death cases—state appellate courts have assumed the responsibility of assuring that the death sentence is not tainted by any legal error.

Id. at 1372-1373.

## PROBLEM 11-4.   VOLUNTEERING TO DIE

On October 7, 1976, Gary Mark Gilmore was convicted of murder and sentenced to death in a Utah court for killing a motel clerk and a gas station attendant. Gilmore's death sentence was imposed before any court had conclusively ruled on the constitutionality of Utah's capital sentencing procedures. Gilmore admitted to the murders throughout his trial and demanded that his attorneys not file an appeal or seek a stay of execution on his behalf, even though he was informed about possible grounds for challenging the constitutionality of Utah's death penalty statute.

The state court in Utah, relying on psychiatric reports and other evidence, held that Gilmore was competent and legally entitled to waive his rights of appeal. Gilmore's efforts to accelerate his execution troubled his family as well as prosecutors, though Gilmore seemed to enjoy the frenzy and attention he had created. Gilmore's mother petitioned the U.S. Supreme Court for "next friend" standing to claim that her son was incompetent to waive his right to state appellate review. Her petition also raised the claim that given the importance of settling the constitutional validity of Gilmore's sentence, her son should be unable as a matter of law to waive the right to state appellate review.

Should the U.S. Supreme Court examine the state court's conclusion that Gilmore was competent to waive his appeals? Do the principles underlying automatic appellate review of all death sentences also support a claim that such review cannot be waived by the defendant? Would your answer to these questions change if the procedures through which Utah sentenced Gilmore to death were clearly constitutionally flawed? See Gilmore v. Utah, 429 U.S. 1012 (1978); see also Franklin ex rel. Berry v. Francis, 144 F.3d 429 (6th Cir. 1998) (considering efforts by family members to intervene on behalf of a death row defendant with a history of mental illness who sought to waive appeal rights).

## 3.   *Habeas Corpus and Other Collateral Review of Sentences*

A conviction and direct appeal are not the end of the line for the criminal defendant. Even after the direct appeal is complete, the offender can still challenge the validity of the conviction and sentence in court. These postconviction review procedures take a variety of names and have somewhat different historical roots: the best-known form, mentioned in both federal and state constitutions, is the writ of habeas corpus, though some states structure postconviction processes around the writ of error coram nobis.

Other jurisdictions have supplanted the traditional (and often quite limited) postconviction remedies with broader statutes, typically labeled postconviction review acts. These various postconviction review procedures are known as "collateral review" because they are nominally civil proceedings, distinct from the direct appeal in criminal proceedings. Convicted offenders file a petition in trial court against a state official, alleging that their convictions or sentences are illegal or unconstitutional in some way. A judge typically has the power to grant relief by overturning the conviction or sentence.

In this section, we briefly review the doctrines and dynamics surrounding collateral review of sentences. The following case involves a direct appeal, but it provides considerable background about the nature of collateral review and its relationship to direct review of convictions and sentences. In so doing, the case provides some preliminary insights into the two central questions that arise in this arena: What distinguishes collateral review procedures from direct appeals, and to what extent are such procedures necessary at all?

|| *Commonwealth v. Robert Freeman* ||
827 A.2d 385 (Pa. 2003)

CASTILLE, J.

On June 18, 1998, a jury sitting in the Court of Common Pleas of Philadelphia County convicted appellant of two counts of first-degree murder. . . . At the penalty hearing, the jury found one aggravating circumstance — that appellant had been convicted of another murder at the time of the current offense — and no mitigating circumstances; accordingly, the jury imposed a sentence of death. Trial counsel subsequently withdrew from the matter and present counsel entered the case. This direct appeal followed.

Before turning to . . . substantive issues . . . , we note this Court's recent decision in Commonwealth v. Grant, 813 A.2d 726 (Pa. 2002). *Grant* overruled the procedural rule announced in Commonwealth v. Hubbard, 372 A.2d 687 (Pa. 1977), which required new counsel to raise claims of previous counsel's ineffectiveness at the first opportunity, even if that first opportunity is on direct appeal and the claims of ineffectiveness were not raised in the trial court. The new general rule announced in *Grant* is that a defendant "should wait to raise claims of ineffective assistance of trial counsel until collateral review." . . .

*Grant* affects the appeal sub judice in two ways. First, it affects the case directly because appellant is represented by new counsel on appeal and appellant raises numerous claims sounding in the ineffective assistance of trial counsel which were not raised below. Second, *Grant* affects this case indirectly because there are a number of additional claims raised in this appeal which, though they do not sound in the alleged ineffective assistance of trial counsel, nevertheless were not raised below. These waived claims of trial court error are reviewable here, if at all, only under this Court's direct capital appeal relaxed waiver doctrine. For reasons explicated below, we believe that many of the same considerations powering our decision in *Grant* require a similar ree-valuation of the viability of the capital case relaxed waiver doctrine. . . .

## I.   INEFFECTIVE ASSISTANCE OF TRIAL COUNSEL

Appellant raises eight primary claims of ineffective assistance of trial counsel involving both the guilt and penalty phases of trial. None of these claims were raised below. Consistently with *Grant*, we dismiss the claims without prejudice to appellant's right to pursue these claims, and any other available claims, via a petition for relief under the Post Conviction Relief Act (PCRA), 42 Pa. C.S. §9541 et seq.

## II. Relaxed Waiver

Appellant also raises nine claims of trial court error. Many of these claims are waived because appellant failed to raise them in the trial court. Pa. R. A. P. 302 ("Issues not raised in the lower court are waived and cannot be raised for the first time on appeal."). However, since this is a direct appeal in a capital case, consistently with this Court's long-standing precedent, we have the discretion to reach claims of trial court error which, though waived, are resolvable from the record. . . . Nevertheless, [we find in this case] many of the same difficulties that prompted this Court . . . in *Grant*[to hold] that new claims of trial counsel ineffectiveness are generally better suited for review on collateral attack. We think a similar general rule should govern consideration of claims of trial court error in capital cases that were not raised before the trial court.

*Grant* noted that, as reflected in Appellate Rule 302(a), appellate courts generally will not entertain claims raised for the first time on appeal. We explained that:

> [Such] a prohibition is preferred because the absence of a trial court opinion can pose a substantial impediment to meaningful and effective appellate review. Further, . . . appellate courts do not act as fact finders, since to do so would require an assessment of the credibility of the testimony and that is clearly not our function.

[Also in *Grant*,] we noted that the general preference in the overwhelming majority of jurisdictions was to defer review of counsel ineffectiveness claims until collateral review. We also noted the difficult task facing appellate counsel . . . in attempting to uncover and develop extra-record claims of counsel ineffectiveness in the truncated time frame available on direct appeal review, a task further complicated by the fact that counsel's duty in this regard is not entirely clear, at least as a constitutional matter. . . .

Some of the same difficulties . . . also arise when this Court employs relaxed waiver in capital cases to address issues of trial error not raised below. This Court often is required to decide such issues without the benefit of a trial court opinion or other indication of the trial judge's view. We observed in *Grant* that "the trial court is in the best position to review claims related to trial counsel's error in the first instance as that is the court that observed first hand counsel's allegedly deficient performance." This is no less true for claims of alleged trial court error—and particularly where discretionary decisions, such as the admission or exclusion of evidence, which often depend upon trial context, are involved. . . .

Similarly, the uncabined availability of relaxed waiver to resurrect unpreserved claims degrades the importance of the trial itself by providing an incentive not to raise contemporaneous objections so as to build in claims for appeal. [There] are multiple, salutary reasons for this Court to encourage practices by which trial judges are given the initial opportunity to timely address claims of error, thereby ensuring prompt resolution at the most important stage of a case, and forestalling the necessity for appellate review and after-the-fact relief. . . .

In light of these difficulties with the relaxed waiver doctrine, it is worth reexamining its history, purpose, and contours to see whether there is a compelling reason to retain this broad and unique exception to the basic requirement of contemporaneous objection and issue preservation. As this Court noted in Commonwealth v. Albrecht, 720 A.2d 693 (Pa. 1998), the operating principle behind the relaxed waiver doctrine, as originally formulated, was to prevent this court from being instrumental in an unconstitutional execution. The doctrine has its genesis in [a time of uncertainty about the structure of appellate review in death penalty cases] after the United States Supreme Court issued its landmark decision in Furman v. Georgia, 408 U.S. 238 (1972). [This Court] provided the following rationale for the Court's determination not to adhere strictly to its normal rules of waiver in capital appeals:

> [Because] this Court has an independent, statutory obligation to determine whether a sentence of death was the product of passion, prejudice or some other arbitrary factor, whether the sentence is excessive or disproportionate to that imposed in similar cases, and to review the record for sufficiency of the evidence to support aggravating circumstances, we will not adhere strictly to our normal rules of waiver. The primary reason for this limited relaxation of waiver rules is that, due to the final and irrevocable nature of the death penalty, the appellant will have no opportunity for post-conviction relief wherein he could raise, say, an assertion of ineffectiveness of counsel for failure to preserve an issue or some other reason that might qualify as an extraordinary circumstance for failure to raise an issue. 19 P.S. §1180-4(2). Accordingly, significant issues perceived sua sponte by this Court, or raised by the parties, will be addressed and, if possible from the record, resolved. . . .

Commonwealth v. Zettlemoyer, 454 A.2d 937, 955 n.19 (Pa. 1982).

[Since these early cases], this Court has had extensive experience with state post-conviction review in capital cases. This experience has proven with absolute certainty that [a] fear of an absence of collateral review, the primary basis for the [expanded] relaxed waiver doctrine, is erroneous. Death-sentenced prisoners in Pennsylvania have an opportunity for full post-conviction review, via the PCRA, where they can, and do, pursue waived claims through assertions of ineffective assistance of trial counsel. . . .

In addition to deriving from a faulty "primary" rationale, the [expanded] relaxed waiver rule has evolved in a way [that sets it] adrift from its unconstitutional execution moorings, [which] envisioned only a "limited" relaxation of waiver rules to address "significant issues." In practice, the rule has become such a matter of routine that it is invoked to capture a myriad of claims, no matter how comparatively minor or routine, [and has] been routinely employed to reach claims that were not merely "technically" waived, but which in fact were not raised at all in the trial court.

It is notable that, even when applying the rule, this Court in recent years has expressed its increasing unease and concern that the doctrine [is being] employed by counsel as a litigation tool. . . .

In Commonwealth v. Brown, 711 A.2d 444, 455 (Pa. 1998), we further noted that we shared the concerns advanced by the Commonwealth in that case that the doctrine "'sabotages' the trial court's efforts to correct errors" and "encourages defense attorneys to withhold objections during trial for tactical reasons, and by that create an error upon which this Court may later grant relief."

We are also troubled by the potential equal protection implications arising from the near-indiscriminate availability of relaxed waiver to invigorate claims never pursued below. Assume a joint capital trial of two defendants, each convicted of first-degree murder, but one receives a sentence of life imprisonment while the other receives the death penalty. Upon their appeals, these appellants perceive an identical claim, which both failed to raise below. If it is a claim premised upon a new constitutional rule that came into existence after the trial, the life-sentenced appellant will not be able to pursue it at all in the Superior Court, while the capital appellant will receive review in this Court and, possibly, relief. Even if it is not a claim based upon a new rule, the capital appellant will have the much easier road of having his claim reviewed as if it were a preserved claim of trial error (even though it was not), subject to a mere showing of error and harmfulness, while the otherwise identically-situated life-sentenced appellant will be required to make the more difficult showing required under the three-part standard applicable to ineffective assistance of counsel. Commonwealth v. Howard, 645 A.2d 1300, 1307 (Pa. 1994). Since the claims subject to capital case relaxed waiver are not limited to the penalty phase, the fact of the death sentence cannot rationally justify such a preferential, substantive treatment of a claim available to otherwise identically-situated defendants.

In light of these multiple concerns, and the unquestionable availability of the PCRA as a vehicle to consider waived claims of trial court error through the guise of claims of trial counsel ineffectiveness, we are convinced that the time has come to return the relaxed waiver doctrine to its roots. . . . Having created the rule, this Court is certainly empowered to modify or eliminate the doctrine if jurisprudential concerns warrant a change from our current practice.

We hold that, as a general rule on capital direct appeals, claims that were not properly raised and preserved in the trial court are waived and unreviewable. Such claims may be pursued under the PCRA, as claims sounding in trial counsel's ineffectiveness or, if applicable, a statutory exception to the PCRA's waiver provision. This general rule, like the rule announced in Commonwealth v. Grant, reaffirms this Court's general approach to the requirements of issue preservation. Since [our early cases] an assumption has arisen that all waived claims are available for review in the first instance on direct appeal. The general rule shall now be that they are not. In adopting the new rule, we do not foreclose the possibility that a capital appellant may be able to describe why a particular waived claim is of such primary constitutional magnitude that it should be reached on appeal. Indeed, nothing we say today shall be construed as calling into question the bedrock principles . . . concerning the necessity of reaching fundamental and plainly meritorious constitutional issues irrespective, even, of the litigation preferences of the parties. . . .

In reformulating this Court's approach to claims not raised below, we have not lost sight of the undeniable fact that a death penalty appeal is different in quality and kind because of the final and irrevocable nature of the penalty. But our abrogation of relaxed waiver does not eliminate or diminish other substantial safeguards ... which already serve to prevent this Court from being instrumental in an unconstitutional execution. These protections, not available in other criminal matters, serve a function similar to the relaxed waiver rule. First, this Court performs a self-imposed duty to review the sufficiency of the evidence underlying the first-degree murder conviction in all capital direct appeals, regardless of whether the appellant has raised the issue. The Court is also required to conduct a statutory review of the death sentence itself to determine whether it was the product of passion, prejudice or any other arbitrary factor, and to determine whether the evidence adduced at trial was sufficient to support the aggravating circumstance(s) found by the jury. ... In addition to these special protections afforded capital appellants, the PCRA exists for them, as for other criminal defendants, as a vehicle for a full and fair, counseled proceeding through which they may challenge the stewardship of trial counsel and pursue other appropriate collateral claims.

This new general rule will be applied prospectively, beginning with those capital direct appeals in which the appellant's brief has not yet been filed in this Court, and is not due for thirty days or more after today's decision. It will then apply to all future capital appeals. ... Prospective application of our new approach will avoid upsetting the expectations of capital appellants and their direct appeal counsel who have already briefed, or are in the process of briefing, their appeals in reliance upon the prospect that this Court, in its discretion, might reach the merits of some of their otherwise waived claims of trial error. ...

## NOTES

1. *Means and methods of collateral review.*   As the *Freeman* decision highlights, in addition to providing criminal defendants opportunities for "direct review" of convictions and sentences through traditional appellate mechanisms, jurisdictions also provide defendants with opportunities for "collateral review" through various procedural systems. The most common, and most commonly discussed, method of collateral review is the writ of habeas corpus, and defendants in some cases will have access to both state and federal habeas corpus review. Indeed, particularly in state death penalty cases (where defendants have the greatest interest and opportunity to seek every possible appellate review), it is not uncommon for a conviction and sentence to be reviewed in seven distinct stages:

(1)   direct review by a state intermediate court,
(2)   direct review by the state supreme court,
(3)   collateral state habeas corpus review by a state trial court,
(4)   appellate review of the state habeas corpus decision by a state appellate court,
(5)   collateral federal habeas corpus review by a federal district court,

(6) appellate review of the federal habeas corpus decision by a federal circuit court, and

(7) final appellate review by the U.S. Supreme Court.

Though many of these layers of review are available in all criminal cases, they are disproportionately invoked in death penalty cases. In capital cases, where the stakes are high and the consequences of an unlawful execution cannot be reversed, do you think these multiple layers of review are justified, or are capital defendants given too many "bites at the apple" of appellate review?

2. *Relationship between direct and collateral review.* As the *Freeman* case reveals, appellate courts reviewing convictions and sentences are often aware of the various other opportunities for review that a defendant might invoke, and there is an unavoidable (though not often expressly discussed) tendency for reviewing courts to alter their decisions in light of these realities. *Freeman* provides an interesting, but somewhat rare, example of a court limiting its approach to direct review because of the availability (and perceived appropriateness) of collateral review for certain claims. It is far more common to see courts that conduct collateral review limiting their examination of certain issues or claims because such matters were already decided (or preclusively waived) during a defendant's pursuit of direct review. See, e.g., 28 U.S.C. §2254(b)-(e), (i) (setting forth various limits on when a federal court can grant a writ of habeas corpus on behalf of a person in custody following a state conviction). Is it a sound practice for reviewing courts to avoid duplicated effort by coordinating when and how certain legal claims will be examined? Or is a significant point of collateral review to give defendants a chance to have decisions made on direct review double-checked?

3. *The British Criminal Cases Review Commission.* The United Kingdom has a very limited appellate review system in criminal cases, and many defendants forgo the right to appeal. In the wake of a number of high-profile miscarriages of justice in the mid-1990s, however, the British government created the Criminal Cases Review Commission to review the applications of criminal defendants who claim to be wrongfully convicted. If the commission considers it "a real possibility that the conviction, verdict, finding or sentence would not be upheld," it refers the case to the court of appeal. As of October 2000, the Commission had referred 4.3% of the cases reviewed, and the court of appeal had overturned more than three-quarters of these convictions.

Especially in light of recent evidence that many innocent persons were wrongly convicted and were able to establish their innocence only with the help of public interest organizations that donated time and money to conduct DNA testing and other forms of investigation, do you think such a commission should be created in the United States? What might be some of the benefits of using a commission, rather than a traditional court, to review the lawfulness and appropriateness of criminal convictions and sentences? Should such a commission provide an additional means of review in criminal cases, or should it operate in place of certain levels of direct or collateral review? How would you try to structure its membership and operation to protect it from undue political influence?

4. *Political debates over federal habeas corpus review.*   A highly political debate about federalism arises when federal courts review and invalidate convictions obtained in state court through collateral review. Although the federal writ of habeas corpus has a constitutional foundation and a long history, debates over postconviction judicial review began to heat up following modern expansions of habeas corpus review of state court convictions in federal court. Expanded federal habeas review began in the mid-1960s after a few groundbreaking U.S. Supreme Court decisions, although there was some significant retrenchment in the methods of review in the 1980s and 1990s. See generally Jordan Steiker, Restructuring Post-conviction Review of Federal Constitutional Claims Raised by State Prisoners: Confronting the New Face of Excessive Proceduralism, 1998 U. Chi. Legal F. 315 (discussing history and controversies over federal habeas review and suggesting ways to redesign federal habeas review of state convictions in capital cases).

The impact of politics on federal habeas corpus review was reflected in Congress's passage of the Antiterrorism and Effective Death Penalty Act (AEDPA) in 1996 after the Oklahoma City bombing of the Murrah Federal Building by Timothy McVeigh. The AEDPA dramatically altered federal habeas corpus practice in many ways, establishing restrictions on the filing of federal habeas corpus petitions, new procedures for treating unexhausted claims and for appealing the denial or dismissal of a petition, and new standards for reviewing state court rulings. See generally Bryan A. Stevenson, The Politics of Fear and Death: Successive Problems in Capital Federal Habeas Corpus Cases, 77 N.Y.U. L. Rev. 699 (2002).

## A Broken System: Error Rates in Capital Cases, 1973-1995, James S. Liebman et al. (2000)

### SUMMARY OF CENTRAL FINDINGS

[We] undertook a painstaking search, beginning in 1991 and accelerating in 1995, of all published state and federal judicial opinions in the U.S. conducting direct and habeas review of state capital judgments, and many of the available opinions conducting state post-conviction review of those judgments. We then (1) checked and catalogued all the cases the opinions revealed, and (2) collected hundreds of items of information about each case from the published decisions and the NAACP Legal Defense Fund's quarterly death row census, and (3) tabulated the results. Nine years in the making, our central findings thus far are [set forth below.]

- Between 1973 and 1995, approximately 5,760 death sentences were imposed in the U.S. Only 313 (5.4%; one in 19) of those resulted in an execution during the period.
- Of the 5,760 death sentences imposed in the study period, 4,578 (79%) were finally reviewed on "direct appeal" by a state high court. Of those, 1,885 (41%; over two out of five) were thrown out because of "serious error," i.e., error that the reviewing court

concludes has seriously undermined the reliability of the outcome or otherwise "harmed" the defendant.

- Nearly all of the remaining death sentences were then inspected by state post-conviction courts. Our data reveal that state post-conviction review is an important source of review in states such as Florida, Georgia, Indiana, Maryland, Mississippi, North Carolina, and Tennessee. In Maryland, at least 52 percent of capital judgments reviewed on state post-conviction during the study period were overturned due to serious error; the same was true of at least 25 percent of the capital judgments that were similarly reviewed in Indiana, and at least 20 percent of those reviewed in Mississippi.

- Of the death sentences that survived state direct and post-conviction review, 599 were finally reviewed in a first habeas corpus petition during the 23-year study period. Of those 599, 237 (40%; two out of five) were overturned due to serious error. . . .

- The "overall error-rate" is . . . the proportion of fully reviewed capital judgments that were overturned at one of the three stages due to serious error. Nationally, over the entire 1973-1995 period, the overall error-rate in our capital punishment system was 68 percent. . . .

- The most common errors are (1) egregiously incompetent defense lawyering (accounting for 37 percent of the state post-conviction reversals), and (2) prosecutorial suppression of evidence that the defendant is innocent or does not deserve the death penalty (accounting for another 16%–19%, when all forms of law enforcement misconduct are considered). . . .

- The seriousness of these errors is . . . revealed by what happens on retrial, when the errors are cured. In our state post-conviction study, an astonishing 82 percent (247 out of 301) of the capital judgments that were reversed were replaced on retrial with a sentence less than death, or no sentence at all. In the latter regard, 7 percent (22/301) of the reversals for serious error resulted in a determination on retrial that the defendant was not guilty of the capital offense.

- The result of very high rates of serious, reversible error among capital convictions and sentences, and very low rates of capital reconviction and resentencing, is the severe attrition of capital judgments. As is illustrated by the flow chart . . . , [for] every 100 death sentences imposed and reviewed during the study period, 41 were turned back at the state direct appeal phase because of serious error. Of the 59 that got through that phase to the second, state post-conviction stage, at least 10 percent—meaning 6 more of the original 100—were turned back due to serious flaws. And, of the 53 that got through that stage to the third, federal habeas checkpoint, 40 percent—an additional 21 of the original 100—were turned back because of serious error. All told, at least 68 of the original 100 were thrown out because of serious flaws, compared to only 32 (or less) that were found to have passed muster—after an average of 9-10 years had passed. . . .

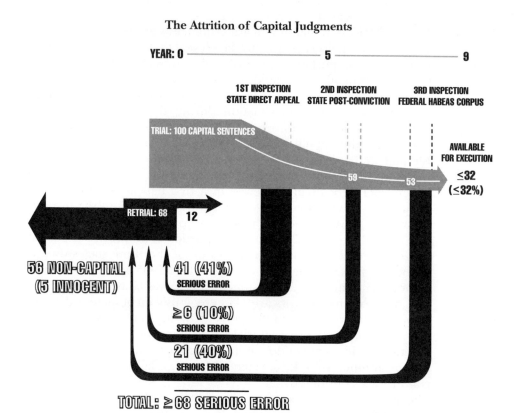

The Attrition of Capital Judgments

- The 68 percent rate of capital error found by the three stage inspection process is much higher than the error rate of less than 15 percent found by those same three inspections in noncapital criminal cases.
- Appointed federal judges are sometimes thought to be more likely to overturn capital sentences than state judges, who almost always are elected in capital-sentencing states. In fact, state judges are the first and most important line of defense against erroneous death sentences. They found serious error in and reversed 90 percent of the capital sentences that were overturned during the study period. . . .
- Finding all this error takes time. . . . It took an average of 7.6 years after the defendant was sentenced to die to complete federal habeas consideration in the 40 percent of habeas cases in which reversible error was found. . . . In the cases in which no error was detected at the third inspection stage and an execution occurred, the average time between sentence and execution was 9 years. Matters did not improve over time. In the last 7 study years (1989-95), the average time between sentence and execution rose to 10.6 years.

FIGURE 1

**Overall Error Rate and Percent of Death Sentences Carried Out, 1973-95**

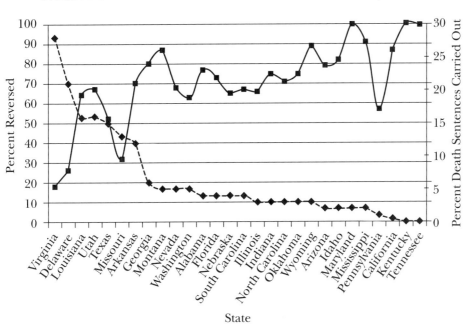

—■—Overall Error Rate    --◆-- Percent of Death Sentences Carried Out

- High rates of error, and the time consequently needed to filter out all that error, frustrate the goals of the death penalty system. [As Figure 1 shows], where the rate of serious reversible error in a state's capital judgments reaches 55 percent or above (as is true for the vast majority of states), the state's capital punishment system is effectively stymied—with its proportion of death sentences carried out falling below 7 percent.

The recent rise in the number of executions is not inconsistent with these findings. Instead of reflecting improvement in the quality of death sentences under review, the rising number of executions may simply reflect how many more sentences have piled up for review. If the error-induced pile-up of cases is the cause of rising executions, their rise provides no proof that a cure has been found for disturbingly high error rates. To see why, consider a factory that produces 100 toasters, only 32 of which work. The factory's problem would not be solved if the next year it made 200 toasters (or added 100 new toasters to 100 old ones previously backlogged at the inspection stage), thus doubling its output of working products to 64. With, now, 136 duds to go with the 64 keepers, the increase in the latter would simply mask the persistence of crushing error rates. The decisive question, therefore, is not the number of death sentences carried out each year, but the proportion. . . .

FIGURE 2

**Persons on Death Row and Percent and Number Executed, 1974-99**

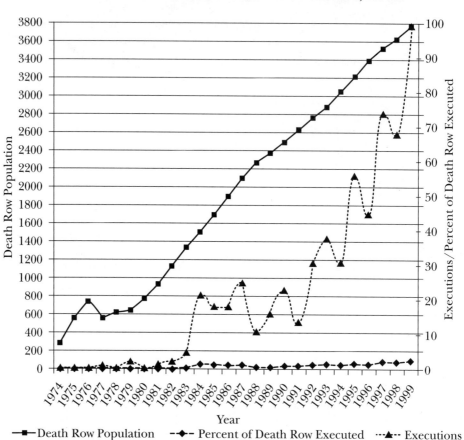

━■━Death Row Population     ━◆━ Percent of Death Row Executed     ┉▲┉ Executions

- [As Figure 2 shows, in] contrast to the annual number of executions (the middle line in the chart), the proportion of death row inmates executed each year (the bottom line) has remained remarkably stable — and extremely low. Since post-*Furman* executions began in earnest in 1984, the nation has executed an average of about 1.3 percent of its death row inmates each year; in no year has it ever carried out more than 2.6 percent — or 1 in 39 — of those on death row. . . .

### NOTES

1. *Success or failure?* Though the title of the groundbreaking report by Professor James Liebman and his colleagues speaks of "a broken system," can one rely on some of this data to claim that the system works? From 1973 to 1995,

two of every three death sentences were reversed at some point in the many layers of capital case reviews. Does this show that appellate courts have appropriately invested time and energy to instill greater confidence in the lawfulness and appropriateness of the death sentences that have been carried out? For an illuminating debate over the meaning and significance of the data in the Liebman study, see Joseph L. Hoffmann, Violence and the Truth, 76 Ind. L.J. 939 (2001); Valerie West, Jeffrey Fagan & James S. Liebman, Look Who's Extrapolating: A Reply to Hoffmann, 76 Ind. L.J. 951 (2001); Joseph L. Hoffmann, A Brief Response to Liebman, Fagan, and West, 76 Ind. L.J. 957 (2001).

One way we might consider what conclusions to draw from the Liebman data is to reflect on the finding that the "68 percent rate of capital error found by the three stage inspection process is much higher than the error rate of less than 15 percent found by those same three inspections in noncapital criminal cases." Why do you think the "error rate" is so much higher in capital than in noncapital cases? Does this finding suggest that more fundamental mistakes are made in capital cases, or does it instead reveal that there are more legal regulations that apply in death penalty cases and thus many more possible bases for committing error? More provocatively, does this finding suggest that courts in capital cases review verdicts and sentences more seriously and therefore that the only major difference between capital and noncapital cases is the rate at which error is detected?

2. *The time and costs of review.* The Liebman study details not only the results of appellate review in death penalty cases, but also the considerable time it takes to conduct this review. Specifically, the study reports that "in the cases in which no error was detected at the third inspection stage and an execution occurred, the average time between sentence and execution was 9 years," and that the time needed for all the layers of appellate review has grown longer, not shorter, over time. This timeline of appellate review is significant not only for the defendant sitting on death row and his family, but also for the family members of the victim. In addition, though not specifically calculated in the Liebman study, the economic costs of all this review of capital verdicts is considerable (some rough estimates suggest that just the appellate review stages of a fully appealed capital case may cost up to $1 million). Not to be overlooked are the lost opportunities: the time that courts, state lawyers, and defense attorneys spend on death penalty appeals that could be devoted instead to other important aspects of the criminal justice system.

In short, although it would be impossible to calculate precisely the economic and noneconomic costs of appellate review of capital cases, no one could reasonably question the conclusion that the costs are enormous in many respects. But like the data in the Liebman study, that determination does not suggest an obvious legal response. Should the enormity of the time and resources spent on appellate review in capital cases lead us to conclude that opportunities for review should be more sharply limited or that more money needs to be invested in ensuring that errors are not committed in capital cases in the first place? Or does the data suggest that we ought to abolish the death penalty altogether? See generally James Liebman, The Overproduction of Death, 100 Colum. L. Rev. 2030 (2000).

3. *Geographic and court variations in "error" data.*   What conclusions can and should we draw from the fact that Professor Liebman's data reveals many variations in reversal rates based on geography and reviewing courts? This variation is most apparent in Figure 1 of the excerpt, which shows, for example, that less than 20% of all capital cases in Virginia are reversed on appeal, whereas nearly 100% of all capital cases in Tennessee are reversed on appeal. Do these numbers indicate that Tennessee is more "error-prone" in operating its capital sentencing system, or rather that the courts reviewing Tennessee death sentences detect more errors on appeal? More generally, do you need to know the reasons for reversals rather than just the cumulative numbers in order to assess what the Liebman study establishes?

4. *Appellate review and punishment purposes.*   The authors of the Liebman study assert that high rates of error "and the time consequently needed to filter out all that error frustrate the goals of the death penalty system." Is that the conclusion you would draw? Does a "successful" death penalty system really depend on executing offenders efficiently and at a low cost, or should success be measured more in terms of whether defendants who deserve to die, and only those who deserve to die, are executed? More generally, can one effectively assess the success of appellate review in capital cases or of other sentencing outcomes without first reaching some conclusions about the purposes of punishment canvassed in Chapter 1?

5. *"Error" in non-death cases.*   With some notable exceptions, the focus on errors in criminal convictions and sentences has been almost exclusively on death penalty cases. Perhaps this is due to the irreversibility of death sentences. Perhaps it is a reflection of the anti–capital punishment agenda of some scholars and lawyers. But is a system that is error-prone in death cases likely to function more accurately in other cases? How may the pressures vary between death and non-death cases? In countries without the death penalty, such as the United Kingdom, concern about error in criminal cases has focused almost exclusively on cases involving imprisonment.

---

In contrast to the Liebman study of collateral review in death penalty cases, consider the following study by Professors Joseph Hoffmann and Nancy King.

## Rethinking the Federal Role in State Criminal Justice
**Joseph L. Hoffmann & Nancy J. King**
**84 N.Y.U. L. Rev. 791-797, 805-809, 815-818, 826-828, 848-849 (2009)**

For almost half a century the federal courts have sought to ensure that state criminal defendants are convicted and sentenced in accordance with the Constitution. As a means to this end, federal courts and Congress have opted for case-by-case review of individual state criminal judgments. State compliance with federal procedural standards is tested through a repetitive combination of certiorari petitions to the United States Supreme Court from state appellate and post-conviction proceedings, followed by federal habeas corpus petitions in federal district courts after state court review has been completed.

It is time to rethink the federal role in state criminal justice. The present approach is a failure because it wastes federal resources, spending them in the wrong places, and because it does not effectively address the most serious constitutional deficiency in state criminal justice today — inadequate assistance of counsel. We need a new federal approach that focuses on avoiding constitutional errors instead of trying to fix them after they have occurred.

Post-conviction litigation in the federal courts to enforce the Constitution may have made sense as a response to the particular structural and systemic problems that plagued state criminal justice in the 1960s and 1970s. But as a means of correcting or deterring routine, case-specific constitutional errors, habeas is completely ineffectual in all but capital cases.

A recently completed empirical study,[1] conducted by [Nancy King] along with a team of researchers from the National Center for State Courts, has exposed the futility of habeas review. In 99.99% of all state felony cases — excluding those cases in which the defendant is sentenced to death[2] — the time, money, and energy spent on federal habeas litigation is wasted, generating virtually no benefit for anyone. Noncapital federal habeas is, in essence, a lottery, funded at great expense by taxpayers, open almost exclusively to the small group of state inmates who are sentenced to the longest prison terms, and producing almost no marginal increase in the enforcement of constitutional rights.

At the same time, state and local governments in fiscal crisis are struggling to provide minimal representation to indigent persons accused of crime. In the past two years alone, courts or government commissions have condemned underfunding of defense services in Michigan, Nevada, New York, Oklahoma, and Wisconsin. Defender offices in Arizona, Florida, Kentucky, Maryland, Minnesota, Missouri, and Tennessee have taken the drastic step of refusing to take new cases, citing crushing caseloads, far in excess of the maximum set by the U.S. Department of Justice's National Advisory Commission on Criminal Justice Standards. The promise of Gideon, almost fifty years later, remains unfulfilled. . . .

Although there were important reasons to support a system of duplicative post-conviction litigation during the incorporation controversies of the 1960s and 1970s, those justifications are no longer compelling. The need for habeas review to force defiant state courts to obey federal constitutional law has diminished. Moreover, since the 1960s, all states have developed appellate and collateral review procedures that provide defendants an opportunity to litigate their constitutional claims and that today result in the reversal of a significant percentage of convictions and sentences.

---

1.  Nancy J. King, Fred L. Cheesman II & Brian J. Ostrom, Final Technical Report: Habeas Litigation in U.S. District Courts (2007), available at http://www.ncjrs.gov/pdffiles1/nij/grants/219559.pdf. The study was funded by Vanderbilt University Law School and the National Institute of Justice.

2.  Of the approximately 1.1 million people convicted and sentenced for felonies in state court in 2004, only 115 were sentenced to death. Matthew R. Durose & Patrick A. Langan, Felony Sentences in State Courts, 2004, Bureau of Just. Stat. Bull. (U.S. Dep't of Justice, Washington, D.C.), July 2007, at 2, 3, available at http://www.ojp.usdoj.gov/bjs/pub/pdf/fssc04.pdf.

The particular structural and systemic problems in state criminal justice that led to widespread deprivations of federal rights and the Court's corresponding expansion of the scope of federal habeas in the 1960s have largely dissipated. In light of this fundamental change, we should no longer support a wasteful system that relies on duplicative post-trial litigation of individual state criminal cases, in both state and federal court, to pursue case-by-case compliance with the Constitution. Indeed, habeas review has never been capable — even during the Warren Court era — of effectively performing that kind of case-specific, error-correcting role.

Habeas is decidedly not the best place to invest federal resources today to ensure that individual state criminal cases comply with the Constitution. Most people convicted of crimes in state court never even get the chance to file a habeas petition because they are not in custody long enough to reach that stage of the litigation process. Others waive their rights in plea proceedings. Finally, habeas is ill-suited to address the longstanding and fundamental problem of inadequate defense counsel because the very nature of that inadequacy ensures that habeas courts usually will not have the ability to provide a meaningful remedy.

It is time for Congress to end this fifty-year experiment in post hoc federal court enforcement of constitutional criminal procedure. By clinging to habeas review while ignoring the continuing crisis in indigent defense, Congress is pouring tax dollars down the drain and overlooking a more effective way to enforce the Constitution: helping states to provide competent representation in criminal cases. Posttrial review of individual state criminal convictions and noncapital sentences for federal constitutional error should be left largely to the state courts. The federal role in criminal justice should focus instead on how best to help the states avoid constitutional error in the first place.

Lack of resources, lack of political will, or both deprive far too many state criminal defendants of the vigorous lawyering that is essential to the effective protection of their rights. Until now, Congress and the Court have responded to the problem of defense representation by creating and maintaining the opportunity for convicted defendants to complain in federal court, after the fact and case by case, that they received ineffective assistance of counsel in violation of the Sixth Amendment. Such claims are almost always unsuccessful. Even the very rare new trial or sentencing order does nothing to force a change in the local system of defense representation, nor does it prevent future defendants from suffering exactly the same fate, sometimes even with the same lawyer. As a society, we can, and should, do better.

If the federal government is serious about enforcing the Constitution in state criminal cases, including the right to counsel, using federal resources to spur serious reform of state and local defense representation systems is a better way to do it. . . . We should replace the doomed strategy of post hoc, case-by-case federal litigation with funding incentives already proven effective in prompting system-wide reforms at the local level.

In this way, Congress could direct federal dollars toward the benefit of all criminal defendants, not just the vanishingly small number of prisoners who manage to win the habeas lottery. In political terms, our proposal creates opportunities for coalition by offering the kind of tradeoff that has facilitated criminal justice reform in the past. In institutional terms, our proposal defines a new federal role that not only allocates resources more efficiently but is also more likely, over time, to protect the constitutional rights of state criminal defendants. . . .

### *The Cold, Hard Reality of Federal Habeas Litigation Today*

Even including the Warren Court's heyday, habeas relief has always been extremely rare outside of the capital context. Recent reforms have only hobbled it further. Two decades of legislative proposals to reverse the Warren Court's habeas expansions, based on criticisms that these expansions undermined finality in state criminal justice, culminated in the passage of the 1996 Antiterrorism and Effective Death Penalty Act (AEDPA). AEDPA restricted habeas by creating a series of new procedural obstacles: a first-ever time limit for filing a first habeas petition; stricter barriers to review of second and successive petitions; and a new, tougher standard of review that precludes habeas courts from granting relief unless the state court's prior decision was "contrary to, or involved an unreasonable application of, clearly established federal law" as declared by the Court.

An empirical study of federal habeas litigation completed in 2007, the first comprehensive look at habeas since its substantial revision by AEDPA, found that between 1992 and 2006 both the average amount of time that elapses from conviction to filing and the median amount of time it takes federal courts to resolve habeas petitions once filed have increased, while by contrast the likelihood of obtaining habeas relief has decreased. The study's findings suggest that federal habeas provides little meaningful relief for prisoners and little deterrence against constitutional violations in state criminal proceedings. Except in capital cases, where federal habeas continues to operate as a vital forum for litigation over the scope of the Constitution's commands, habeas is an expensive but almost completely ineffectual remedy that is no longer worth preserving in its current form. . . .

The prolonged time required to satisfy the prerequisites for filing a habeas petition, and then to obtain a decision on that petition from a habeas court, dramatically skews the distribution of habeas cases among the overall population of state prison inmates. The Vanderbilt-NCSC Study found that almost 30% of all noncapital habeas petitions were filed by inmates serving life sentences, even though only 1% of all prison sentences are for life. On the other hand, only 12% of all noncapital habeas petitions were filed by those serving sentences of five years or less, even though that group represents the majority of all those who are sent to prison. Because most federal habeas cases will not be resolved until years after the original conviction and sentencing, only inmates who receive life or other very long prison sentences will be in custody long enough even to file. For the vast majority of the more than two million people now incarcerated in America, the Great Writ is a pipe dream.

Moreover, except in capital cases, those inmates who do manage to obtain federal habeas review can expect to lose. Although federal judges are taking longer to resolve petitions, they ultimately reject almost all of them. The chances that a petitioner will obtain any relief are even more miniscule now than they were before AEDPA. The grant rate for noncapital cases has dropped from 1% in the early 1990s to only 0.34% today. Only eight of the 2384 noncapital habeas filings the study examined resulted in a grant of habeas relief, and one of those eight grants was later reversed on appeal. At this rate, we estimate that fewer than sixty-five of the more than 18,000 petitions filed each year by noncapital petitioners will eventually be granted by district courts. Efforts to improve the efficiency of habeas litigation only appear to have exacerbated this trend.

Today, the necessary prelude in the state courts to a first federal habeas filing is so lengthy, the habeas review process itself so prolonged, and habeas relief so unlikely that post-AEDPA federal habeas in noncapital cases is approaching a lottery for lifers.

The Vanderbilt-NCSC study suggests that habeas review represents a substantial commitment of societal resources for very little practical gain. The study cannot tell us, of course, whether the incredibly low rate of habeas grants reflects a comparably low frequency of meritorious claims, or whether there are many more habeas petitioners who deserve relief but do not obtain it. But both possibilities ultimately lead to the same conclusion: Habeas review, at least as a means for case-by-case correction and deterrence of constitutional errors, is a failure, either because it is wasteful or because it is ineffectual. . . .

Despite the fact that federal habeas provides little meaningful relief to prisoners and little deterrence of constitutional violations by state courts, these cases entail a significant investment of resources by federal courts and states' attorneys. Today, one out of every fourteen civil cases filed in federal district court is a habeas challenge by a state prisoner. Most of these cases are not summarily dismissed. Instead, noncapital habeas cases average eighteen docket entries per case, more than a third of the average number of docket entries in the capital cases included in the study. Almost six in ten noncapital cases included at least one responsive motion and brief by the state, and nearly seven in ten of those cases included a reply by petitioner. On average, prisoners raised four claims per petition. More than one of every eight cases included an amended petition, and amended petitions generally require an additional responsive pleading.

In half of the cases, the judge did not decide the case on the petition and responsive pleading alone but first referred the petition to a magistrate judge for disposition. A referral often generates a report and recommendation to the district judge, which affords the petitioner an opportunity to file a pleading objecting to the magistrate's report and often requires yet another response from the state. Not surprisingly, the study found that the presence of a report and recommendation lengthened the case.

In addition to the merits of these claims, courts and parties addressed many procedural issues along the way, including statute of limitations and procedural default, as well as substitution of counsel and motions for in forma pauperis status (filed in 56% of cases; granted 62% of the time). Litigation in these cases often involved motions filed by the petitioner (with replies by the state) even after the initial final order of dismissal or denial had been entered, including motions for reconsideration or for a certificate of appealability.

Addressing the procedural and substantive questions raised in these petitions takes not only the time of the district and circuit judges and their clerks but in many districts the time of magistrate judges, their clerks, and pro se attorney staff as well. And unlike other civil and criminal cases in which documents are filed and distributed electronically, prisoner cases are exempted from e-government rules, requiring clerks to scan, print, copy, and mail documents by hand.

To the states, these cases may appear to be less complex or demanding than other civil cases that states may litigate in federal court. Discovery and evidentiary hearings, for example, are rarely granted. But with more than 18,000 habeas petitions filed each year, the cost for the states adds up as well, particularly for those states with the largest prison populations. States can count on winning almost every one of these cases, but they can also count on a significant expenditure of state dollars to defend them.

Any system of justice that expends so much effort and produces so little benefit deserves reconsideration. Whatever we may think in theory about the importance of providing convicted state defendants an opportunity to vindicate their federal constitutional rights in a federal judicial forum, the opportunity provided today is a charade. For noncapital defendants, it may never have been much more. Ever since the Warren Court began its expansion of habeas, critics have condemned the result as a "debilitating, . . . court-clogging hydra.". . .

After four decades of habeas reform by the Court and Congress, prisoners today cannot claim access even to this. The new procedural barriers to review and relief imposed by Congress in AEDPA have failed to reduce either the number of filings or the time expended on each case, while the hope that habeas will correct, much less deter, any constitutional error that persists in state criminal proceedings has even less foundation than before.

In light of the empirical evidence, it is time for Congress to consider whether this multilayered system of post-conviction review in criminal cases represents a justifiable use of societal resources. The unavoidable answer is that except in capital cases, federal habeas is not a judicial remedy worth preserving. . . .

We believe that the time has come for Congress to acknowledge not only that effective criminal defense at the trial and appellate levels is a far better means of guaranteeing constitutional rights in criminal cases than post hoc habeas litigation but also that state criminal defense systems are in crisis and require federal support. Our adversarial system relies on defense counsel to protect individual rights in criminal cases. Yet case-by-case litigation under Strickland v. Washington has failed, and will continue to fail, as a means of ensuring the right to counsel in noncapital cases. Systematic underfunding of criminal defense representation in the state courts persists, resulting in repeated and widespread breakdowns in defense representation in many states. As a chorus of commentators has observed, the scant post-conviction reversals under Strickland have had little or no impact on the pervasive pressures on state and county legislative bodies to limit funding for defense services. This is a systemic problem that habeas is woefully inadequate to address.

Lawsuits seeking injunctive relief from these constitutional deficiencies, combined with political coalition-building and public awareness campaigns, have prompted some reform in a handful of states. Faced with the prospect of a court order commanding compliance with the Sixth Amendment, policy makers in Connecticut, Georgia, Louisiana, Massachusetts, Montana, New York, Oklahoma, Oregon, Pennsylvania, and Washington have responded with reforms and increased resources. These scattered efforts have produced a growing body of research into successful (and failed) practices in the provision of defender services. They have also promoted wider acceptance of minimum standards in areas such as caseload, case assignment, and client contact, and have contributed to a growing consensus that state-level funding and oversight is crucial in states that leave the administration of defense representation to the uneven fiscal capability of county authorities.

What is needed now is a comprehensive national plan to encourage state and local legislative bodies to provide adequate funding for representation services. Only the federal government possesses the power and the resources to provide the necessary encouragement. . . .

It is time to start over and ask again: What is the best way—the most effective and most efficient way—for the federal government to ensure that federal constitutional rights are observed in state criminal proceedings? In our view, the current system cannot possibly be the right answer. Instead, it is time to implement a new paradigm, one that relies on state courts to do the heavy lifting of case-by-case judicial review but uses the leadership and financial strength of the federal government to bring about a sea change in state systems of defense representation.

## NOTES

1. *Is non-death different?*   Does the study by Hoffmann and King change your judgment about whether death is different—whether the line between the death penalty and all other sanctions so different that it can explain active collateral review for death sentences and virtually non-existent collateral review for non-death sentences?

2. *Grand bargains.*   Hoffmann and King suggest a significant tradeoff between resources spent on appellate and collateral review, and resources spent in the adjudicative process—at the front end (with greater effect) rather than the back end (with little impact beyond watching the wheels of justice grind in non-death cases). What are the political, historical, and institutional elements that might make such a grand bargain possible? If you had a job for the next three years with a non-profit funded to make this grand bargain a reality, how would you spend your time? Would you focus on policy-makers, and if so, which ones? Actors in the system—and which actors? The general public?

## 4.   Supranational Review of Sentences

While the U.S. Supreme Court is the highest binding authority in direct appeals and collateral review in the United States, U.S. citizens and residents may bring complaints about their sentences before the Inter-American Human Rights Commission and the United Nations Human Rights Committee. Both of these institutions can issue recommendations to the U.S. government, though their decisions are not binding on any U.S. official.

In other countries, however, supranational courts may review sentences and issue decisions that can bind national governments and courts. Among such institutions are the European Court of Human Rights (ECHR) and the Judicial Committee of the Privy Council, the highest court for former Commonwealth countries that continue to accept its jurisdiction. In recent years the Judicial Committee has heard a large number of death penalty appeals. The most famous may be the one set out below.

## Earl Pratt and Ivan Morgan v. The Attorney General for Jamaica
### (Appeal No. 10 of 1993)

JUDGMENT OF THE LORDS OF THE JUDICIAL COMMITTEE OF THE PRIVY COUNCIL

LORD GRIFFITHS.

The appellants, Earl Pratt and Ivan Morgan, were arrested 16 years ago for a murder committed on 6th October 1977 and have been held in custody ever since. On 15th January 1979 they were convicted of murder and sentenced to death. Since that date they have been in prison in that part of Saint Catherine's prison set aside to hold prisoners under sentence of death and commonly known as death row. On three occasions the death warrant has been read to them and they have been removed to the condemned cells immediately adjacent to the gallows. . . . The statement of these bare facts is sufficient to bring home to the mind of any person of normal sensitivity and compassion the agony of mind that these men must have suffered as they have alternated between hope and despair in the 14 years that they have been in prison facing the gallows. It is unnecessary to refer to the evidence describing the restrictive conditions of imprisonment and the emotional and psychological impact of this experience, for it only reveals that which it is to be expected. These men are not alone in their suffering for there are now 23 prisoners in death row who have been awaiting execution for more than ten years and 82 prisoners who have been awaiting execution for more than five years. It is against this disturbing background that their Lordships must now determine this constitutional appeal. . . .

The death penalty in the United Kingdom has always been carried out expeditiously after sentence, within a matter of weeks or in the event of an appeal even to the House of Lords within a matter of months. Delays in terms of years are unheard of. . . . The Report of the Royal Commission on Capital Punishment 1949-53 (Cmd. 8932) gave the average delay in 1950 as six weeks if there was an appeal and three weeks if there was not. In 1947 there was great public disquiet that men convicted of a murder on the Gold Coast had been under sentence of death for two years. . . .

The murder was committed on 6th October 1977 and the appellants were sentenced to death on 15th January 1979. Their application for leave to appeal was dismissed by the Court of Appeal on 5th December 1980 who said that they would hand down their reasons later. Although notice of application for leave to appeal was given within three days of the conviction on 18th January 1979, it took almost two years to arrange a hearing by the Court of Appeal. Making every allowance for the pressure of work on the Jamaican courts this does seem a long time to arrange a hearing in a capital case which one would have expected to have been expedited.

[In the meantime, the defendants could not pursue their appeals in the Jamaican Privy Council. On 16th August 1984, Pratt] wrote to the Registrar of the Court of Appeal asking for the reasons why his application for leave to appeal was dismissed. It then transpired that no reasons had yet been prepared by the judge to whom the writing of the judgment had been assigned. The papers had apparently been put in the wrong bundle and forgotten. This was a serious oversight by the judge and by those in the office of the Court of Appeal who should have reminded him that reasons had not been provided in accordance with the practice of the Court of Appeal, which is to provide a reserved judgment or reasons within three months of a hearing. Prompted by Pratt's request reasons were quickly prepared and handed down on 24th September 1984. No immediate steps were, however, taken to petition the Judicial Committee of the Privy Council.

On 3rd October the [Inter-American Commission on Human Rights (IACHR), which Pratt had petitioned, rejected his] submission that his trial was unfair; but recommended that his sentence be commuted for humanitarian reasons. . . . On 28th January 1986 Pratt petitioned the United Nations Human Rights Committee [UNHRC] under the International Covenant on Civil and Political Rights.

On 13th March 1986 the appellants lodged notice of intention to petition for special leave to appeal to the Judicial Committee of the Privy Council. The application for special leave was heard with reasonable dispatch and special leave to appeal was refused by the Judicial Committee of the Privy Council on 17th July 1986. . . . In dismissing the application Lord Templeman expressed the concern of the Judicial Committee that three years and nine months had elapsed between the dismissal of the appeal and the delivery of the reasons. . . .

On 21st July 1986 the UNHRC requested Jamaica not to carry out the death sentence on Pratt and Morgan before it had an opportunity to consider the admissibility of the complaint. On 18th November 1986 the [Jamaican Privy Council (JPC)], apparently for the first time, considered the appellants' case. They did not accede to the request of the UNHRC to stay the execution and the first warrant of execution was issued on 12th February 1987 for execution on 24th February.

On 23rd February the Governor-General issued a stay of execution. The reasons for the stay are not entirely clear but may have been the result of a telegram from the UNHRC urging a stay of execution and a letter from Mr. Noel Edwards Q.C., to the Governor-General informing him that the case of the appellants was due to be considered by the UNHRC on 23rd March 1987 and the IACHR on 26th March 1987. . . .

On 9th July 1987 the IACHR pursuant to further representations of Pratt and Morgan informed the Jamaican government of the following findings:

> Pratt and Morgan suffered a denial of justice during the period 1980-1984 violative of Article 5(2) of the American Convention on Human Rights. The

Commission found that the fact that the Jamaican Court of Appeal issued its decision on December 5, 1980 but did not issue the reasons for that decision until four years later, September 24, 1984, was tantamount to cruel, inhuman and degrading treatment because during that four year delay the petitioners could not appeal to the Privy Council and had to suffer four years on death row awaiting execution. The Inter-American Commission on Human Rights... requests that the execution of Messrs. Pratt and Morgan be commuted for humanitarian reasons.

... On 13th October 1987 the JPC reconsidered the appellants' case. They did not accede to the request of the IACHR and on their advice the second warrant of execution was issued on 18th February 1988 for execution on 1st March.

On 29th February 1988 the second stay of execution was issued by the Governor-General. This time it appears to have been as a result of a further request from the UNHRC not to execute the men until the Committee had completed their review of the case. . . .

On 6th April 1989 the UNHRC gave their decision on the merits. They held that the failure of the Court of Appeal to deliver reasons for 45 months was a violation of Article 14 para. 3(c) and Article 14 para. 5 of the International Covenant on Civil and Political Rights and Optional Protocol which [states that everyone "shall be entitled to... be tried without undue delay" and "shall have the right to his conviction and sentence being reviewed by a higher tribunal according to law."].

The Committee gave the following reasons for their decision [and made the following recommendation]:

> ... The Committee considers that the responsibility for the delay of 45 months lies with the judicial authorities of Jamaica. This responsibility is neither dependent on a request for production by the accused in a trial nor is non-fulfilment of this responsibility excused by the absence of a request from the accused. . . .
>
> In the absence of a written judgement of the Court of Appeal, the authors were not able to proceed to appeal before the Privy Council. [It] matters not that in the event the Privy Council affirmed the conviction of the authors. The Committee notes that in all cases, and especially in capital cases, accused persons are entitled to trial and appeal without undue delay, whatever the outcome of those judicial proceedings turns out to be.
>
> [Although] capital punishment is not per se unlawful under the Covenant, it should not be imposed in circumstances where there have been violations by the State party of any of its obligations under the Covenant. The Committee is of the view that the victims of the violations of articles 14, paragraph 3(c)... are entitled to a remedy; the necessary prerequisite in the particular circumstances is the commutation of the sentence.

Eighteen months then passed before a decision was taken by the JPC on this recommendation of the UNHRC. Press reports of parliamentary proceedings show that in June 1990 the question of the death penalty was under review by the Cabinet but that no conclusions had yet been reached on commuting sentences.

On 17th September 1990 the JPC again reconsidered the appellants' case. They rejected the recommendations made eighteen months earlier by the UNHRC. On 18th February 1991 the warrant of execution was issued for execution on 7th March 1991, the delay in issuing the warrant of execution from 17th September 1990 to 18th February 1991 apparently being accounted for by the wish of the Governor-General to obtain the Attorney-General's advice on the legal status of decisions of human rights bodies. This is advice which it would have been appropriate to place before the members of the JPC at a much earlier date, and before they considered any recommendations of such bodies. Their Lordships have not seen the Attorney-General's advice but do not doubt that it correctly advised that, Jamaica being a signatory to the International Covenant on Civil and Political Rights and to the Optional Protocol, the views of the UNHRC should be afforded weight and respect but were not of legally binding effect; and that the like considerations applied to the IACHR.

On 28th February 1991 the appellants commenced these proceedings. . . .

The primary submission of the appellants is that to hang them after they have been held in prison under sentence of death for so many years would be inhuman punishment or other treatment and thus in breach of section 17(1) of the Constitution. Section 17 of the Constitution provides [that] "No person shall be subjected to torture or to inhuman or degrading punishment or other treatment.". . .

There is an instinctive revulsion against the prospect of hanging a man after he has been held under sentence of death for many years. What gives rise to this instinctive revulsion? The answer can only be our humanity; we regard it as an inhuman act to keep a man facing the agony of execution over a long extended period of time. But before their Lordships condemn the act of execution as "inhuman or degrading punishment or other treatment" within the meaning of section 17(1) there are a number of factors that have to be balanced in weighing the delay. If delay is due entirely to the fault of the accused such as an escape from custody or frivolous and time wasting resort to legal procedures which amount to an abuse of process the accused cannot be allowed to take advantage of that delay for to do so would be to permit the accused to use illegitimate means to escape the punishment inflicted upon him in the interest of protecting society against crime.

A much more difficult question is whether the delay occasioned by the legitimate resort of the accused to all available appellate procedures should be taken into account, or whether it is only delay that can be attributed to the shortcomings of the State that should be taken into account.

There is a powerful argument that it cannot be inhuman or degrading to allow an accused every opportunity to prolong his life by resort to appellate procedures however extended may be the eventual time between sentence and execution. This is the view that currently prevails in some States in the United States of America and has resulted in what has become known as the death row phenomenon where men are held under sentence of death for many years while their lawyers pursue a multiplicity of appellate procedures. . . . Support for this view is also to be found in previous decisions of the Privy Council. . . . There are other authorities which do not accept that delay occasioned by use of appeal procedures is to be disregarded. In Catholic Commission for Justice and Peace in Zimbabwe v. Attorney-General [Judgment No. S.C. 73/93, unreported, delivered on June 24, 1993] Gubbay C.J. said:

> It seems to me highly artificial and unrealistic to discount the mental agony and torment experienced on death row on the basis that by not making the

maximum use of the judicial process available the condemned prisoner would have shortened and not lengthened his suffering. The situation could be otherwise if he had resorted to a series of untenable and vexatious proceedings which, in consequence, had the effect of delaying the ends of justice. . . .

In Soering v. United Kingdom (1989) 11 E.H.R.R. 439 the applicant, a West German national, alleged that the decision by the Secretary of State for the Home Department to extradite him to the United States of America to face trial in Virginia on a charge of capital murder would, if implemented, give rise to a breach by the United Kingdom of Article 3 of the European Convention for the Protection of Human Rights and Fundamental Freedoms (Cmd. 8969) which provides that no one should be subjected to torture or to inhuman or degrading treatment or punishment. . . . The European Court of Human Rights recognised that the death row phenomenon in Virginia where prisoners were held for a period of six to eight years before execution arose from repeated applications by the prisoner for a stay of execution but nevertheless held that such a long period of delay might go beyond the threshold set by Article 3. . . .

In their Lordships' view a State that wishes to retain capital punishment must accept the responsibility of ensuring that execution follows as swiftly as practicable after sentence, allowing a reasonable time for appeal and consideration of reprieve. It is part of the human condition that a condemned man will take every opportunity to save his life through use of the appellate procedure. If the appellate procedure enables the prisoner to prolong the appellate hearings over a period of years, the fault is to be attributed to the appellate system that permits such delay and not to the prisoner who takes advantage of it. Appellate procedures that echo down the years are not compatible with capital punishment. The death row phenomenon must not become established as a part of our jurisprudence.

The application of the appellants to appeal to the Judicial Committee of the Privy Council and their petitions to the two human rights bodies do not fall within the category of frivolous procedures disentitling them to ask the Board to look at the whole period of delay in this case. The total period of delay is shocking and now amounts to almost fourteen years. It is double the time that the European Court of Human Rights considered would be an infringement of Article 3 of the European Convention and their Lordships can have no doubt that an execution would now be an infringement of section 17(1) of the Jamaican Constitution. . . .

Their Lordships are very conscious that many other prisoners under sentence of death are awaiting the outcome of this appeal. In an attempt to assist the Jamaican authorities who may be faced with a large number of appeals their Lordships wish to make some general observations. . . .

There may of course be circumstances which will lead the JPC to recommend a respite in the carrying out of a death sentence, such as a political moratorium on the death sentence, or a petition on behalf of the appellants to IACHR or UNHRC or a constitutional appeal to the Supreme Court. But if these respites cumulatively result in delay running into several years an execution will be likely to infringe section 17(1) and call for commutation of the death sentence to life imprisonment.

Their Lordships are very conscious that the Jamaican government faces great difficulties with a disturbing murder rate and limited financial resources at their disposal to administer the legal system. Nevertheless, if capital punishment is to be retained it must be carried out with all possible expedition. Capital appeals must be expedited and legal aid allocated to an appellant at an early stage. The aim should be to hear a capital appeal within twelve months of conviction. [It] should be possible to complete the entire domestic appeal process within approximately two years. Their Lordships do not purport to set down any rigid timetable but to indicate what appear to them to be realistic targets which, if achieved, would entail very much shorter delay than has occurred in recent cases and could not be considered to involve inhuman or degrading punishment or other treatment.

The final question concerns applications by prisoners to IACHR and UNHRC. Their Lordships wish to say nothing to discourage Jamaica from continuing its membership of these bodies and from benefiting from the wisdom of their deliberations. It is reasonable to allow some period of delay for the decisions of these bodies in individual cases but it should not be very prolonged. The UNHRC does not accept the complaint unless the author "has exhausted all available domestic remedies.". . . A complainant [can] lodge a complaint immediately after his case has been disposed of by the Judicial Committee of the Privy Council. If, however, Jamaica is able to revise its domestic procedures so that they are carried out with reasonable expedition no grounds will exist to make a complaint based upon delay. And it is to be remembered that the UNHRC does not consider its role to be that of a further appellate court.

It therefore appears to their Lordships that provided there is in future no unacceptable delay in the domestic proceedings complaints to the UNHRC from Jamaica should be infrequent and when they do occur it should be possible for the Committee to dispose of them with reasonable dispatch and at most within eighteen months.

These considerations lead their Lordships to the conclusion that in any case in which execution is to take place more than five years after sentence there will be strong grounds for believing that the delay is such as to constitute "inhuman or degrading punishment or other treatment." If, therefore, rather than waiting for all those prisoners who have been in death row under sentence of death for five years or more to commence proceedings pursuant to section 25 of the Constitution, the Governor-General now refers all such cases to the JPC who, in accordance with the guidance contained in this advice, recommend commutation to life imprisonment, substantial justice will be achieved swiftly and without provoking a flood of applications to the Supreme Court for constitutional relief pursuant to section 17(1). . . .

Their Lordships will accordingly humbly advise Her Majesty that this appeal ought to be allowed, and the sentences of the appellants be commuted to life imprisonment.

## NOTES

1. *The Privy Council and its death penalty jurisprudence.*   With the expansion of the British Empire during the nineteenth century, courts in the colonies

increasingly gained the right to appeal to the Privy Council and, later, its Judicial Committee. The Judicial Committee is an independent court composed of members of the high English judiciary and that of Commonwealth countries. Today it continues to hear appeals from British territories and the former English colonies that recognize it as their highest court. The modern line of death penalty jurisprudence in the Judicial Committee began with *Pratt.* In later cases, the Judicial Committee found a delay of less than five years unconstitutional. Moreover, the Judicial Committee found that not only delay but also unreasonable speed could lead to sentence commutation, since a defendant deserved reasonable notice of his execution.

As a consequence of these decisions, in the Caribbean countries scores of death sentences were commuted to life, and new appellate procedures were instituted to shorten the delay. What problems do such changes entail? For the U.S. Supreme Court's view of delay in capital cases (as well as a discussion of the value of foreign opinions on such issues), see Knight v. Florida, 528 U.S. 990 (1999) (concurrence and dissent from denial of certiorari).

2. *The Inter-American Human Rights system and the ECHR.* The Inter-American Human Rights system consists of two organs, a commission and a court. While not all countries have accepted the court's jurisdiction, their citizens and residents have the right to petition the commission unless expressly excluded. For signatories of the American Declaration of Human Rights only, such as the United States, the commission may issue a recommendation at the end of a factual investigation; if a country signed the American Convention on Human Rights, the commission can refer a complaint to the court.

In past cases, the commission has held the United States in violation of the international prohibition of the execution of juveniles and has chastised it for the disparate application of the death penalty. The Inter-American court, while not outlawing the death penalty, has applied strict scrutiny in capital cases.

The European Human Rights system, with the European Court of Human Rights (ECHR), has only rarely had the opportunity to consider the death penalty. In a seminal decision, the court ruled that Great Britain could not extradite a German national to Virginia because of the so-called death row phenomenon — the delay between sentence imposition and execution and the conditions on death row — unless it received guarantees that the German would not be sentenced to death. Soering v. United Kingdom, 11 Eur. H.R. Rep. 439 (Eur. Ct. H.R. 1989). This opinion has had a lasting impact on other national and supranational tribunals around the world. For details on the recent European reaction to the death penalty in the United States, see Nora V. Demleitner, The Death Penalty in the United States: Following the European Lead?, 81 Or. L. Rev. 131 (2002).

3. *The U.N. Human Rights Committee.* The U.N. Human Rights Committee is a treaty body under the International Covenant on Civil and Political Rights and under the Convention Against Torture and Other Cruel, Inhuman or Degrading Treatment or Punishment. In that capacity it can hear a complaint once an individual has exhausted domestic remedies. In 1994 the Human Rights Committee found the use of gas chambers in select U.S. states to be a violation of the International Covenant on Civil and Political Rights. Other subcommittees and U.N. rapporteurs have focused on the question of juvenile executions.

Should a governor be influenced by pronouncements of the U.N. Human Rights Committee or other U.N. institutions in individual petitions or on larger questions pertaining to the application of the death penalty?

4. *The International Court of Justice (ICJ).*   The ICJ can hear only state-to-state complaints, some of them lodged by countries on behalf of individual citizens. In 1999 Germany asked the ICJ to issue a stay of execution in the case of a German citizen sentenced to death in Arizona. It alleged that the United States had violated the Vienna Convention on Consular Rights by failing to inform him and his brother, who had already been executed, that they had the right to contact the German embassy, which would have paid for their defense attorneys. The state of Arizona proceeded to execute the German, in violation of the ICJ's stay order. The ICJ held that it had the power to issue such provisional measures and stated that in future cases in which the United States failed to live up to its treaty obligations and sentenced someone severely, a sentence commutation and monetary compensation to the German government were in order. LaGrand Case (Germany v. United States of America), 40 I.L.M. 1069 (I.C.J. 2001). The case was styled not as a death penalty case but rather as a case involving the violation of an important treaty. The Mexican government filed a similar case against the United States before the ICJ. Case Concerning Avena and other Mexican Nationals (Mex. v. U.S.), 2004 I.C.J. No. 128 (Judgment of Mar. 31). Are Germany and Mexico merely trying to protect the right to consular notification, or are they attempting to change U.S. law on the death penalty? If the latter, is such action legitimate?

# B.   EXECUTIVE RECONSIDERATION OF SENTENCES

Even after trial, sentencing, appeals, and judicial postconviction challenges have ended and a convict begins to serve a sentence, the criminal justice process is not complete. A variety of mechanisms under the control of executive branch agencies determine whether, at some point before the sentence expires, an offender should be released from prison and what continuing controls are to be placed on an offender after release.

The most common mechanism for early prison release decisions and for supervising offenders after release is parole, a period of conditional supervised release following a prison term. Parole was once a fundamental component of nearly every American sentencing system, but the past quarter-century has seen dramatic reforms. The purpose, structure, and operation of parole (and parole boards) have changed in significant ways over the past several decades, and in some jurisdictions, including the federal system, parole has been technically eliminated. Nevertheless, parole remains a key aspect of most state sentencing systems, and as of year-end 2005 more than 780,000 people were on parole.

Another form of executive review takes place when a governor or president issues a pardon or commutation. The pardon power typically has a constitutional foundation; like the role of parole, however, the role of pardons in modern sentencing systems has evolved considerably. In recent times, an executive decision to grant a pardon or commutation has become both rare and often controversial. These two fundamental forms of executive sentence review will occupy the second part of this chapter.

## 1.  Parole

At the start of the twentieth century, reformers introduced parole as a cornerstone of a new approach to sentencing and corrections, and by 1950 all of the states, the federal system, and the District of Columbia relied heavily on the parole function as part of an indeterminate sentence system. In indeterminate sentencing, judges could impose both maximum and minimum sentences, choosing a range as broad as "zero to life" (though most sentences were imposed in a narrower range). Parole boards were authorized to consider offenders for release starting at a designated point within the broad sentencing ranges. Inherent in this system, and in the function of parole boards, was the belief that the primary purpose of imprisonment was to rehabilitate offenders. The prevailing belief was that experts in the social and psychological sciences would be able to determine when an individual was rehabilitated and therefore ready for release.

In the 1970s many began to doubt the ability of the criminal justice system to rehabilitate offenders. The discretion of both judges and parole boards in indeterminate sentencing systems was criticized on various grounds, and an array of reforms led to a movement in many jurisdictions toward more determinate sentencing, in which offenders know their release date (subject to a slight decrease for good institutional behavior, so-called good time) on the day they are sentenced. Nevertheless, the model of indeterminate sentencing that dominated American sentencing systems for most of the twentieth century can still be found in more than half of the states, and thus parole continues to be critical in many jurisdictions.

As researchers Jeremy Travis and Sarah Lawrence have explained, parole and parole boards play three critical roles:

> First, parole boards determine the actual length of a prison sentence. With indeterminate sentencing, judges sentence an offender to a prison term, specifying a minimum and a maximum length of prison stay. The parole board, an executive branch agency, then decides on a case-by-case basis whether a prisoner is ready to be released to the community.
>
> Second, parole agencies supervise recently released individuals in the community for the remainder of their sentence. In the classic indeterminate sentencing model, a prisoner released on parole is not free. Rather, he or she is still serving a criminal sentence, in the community rather than in prison, and must abide by a number of conditions established by the parole board at the time of release. Thus, parole agencies are expected to play a critical role in overseeing the reintegration of returning prisoners.
>
> Third, parole officers and parole boards are authorized to revoke a parolee's conditional liberty and return him or her to prison. If a parole officer (also referred to as a parole agent) determines that the parolee has failed to observe a condition of his release — for example, has committed a new crime, failed to maintain employment, or failed a drug test — the officer can recommend that parole be revoked. The parole board, or in some states a judicial officer, then decides whether to send the parolee back to prison for some or all of the remainder of the prison sentence.

Jeremy Travis & Sarah Lawrence, Beyond the Prison Gates: The State of Parole in America 2 (Urban Institute, Nov. 2002).

In the sections that follow, we first examine the composition and authority of parole commissions, the key decision makers in parole systems. We then turn to an examination of the three major functions of parole commissions: (1) determining when inmates will be released from prison, (2) supervising offenders on parole, and (3) creating rules for parole revocation. As you read these materials, it is worthwhile to review some of the doctrines and issues concerning probation covered in Chapter 8, since probation and parole both involve conditional releases into the community. They differ, however, in that probation is imposed at sentencing by a judge whereas parole is imposed by a parole board after an offender has already served a prison term.

### a.   Parole Commissions and Guidelines

Early in their history parole boards had nearly unfettered discretion in making parole release decisions. One distinct feature of modern parole decision making is that boards are now typically governed by guidelines of varying detail. Usually those guidelines have been issued by the parole board itself, although they are sometimes produced under legislative direction. Some guidelines state principles to guide the parole board's release decisions; others specify particular parole terms for a given offender committing a specific offense. Some guidelines are based on an unweighted list of factors related to the underlying offense: the offender's threat to the community or to individuals, or the inmate's likelihood of reoffending. Other guidelines create a scoring system based on social science data reflecting risk factors and favor release of individuals who, based on their similarity to prior offenders, are designated as least likely to commit serious offenses in the near future.

## ‖  *Iowa Code §§904A.1, 904A.2*  ‖

The board of parole is created to consist of five members. Each member, except the chairperson, shall be compensated on a day-to-day basis. Each member shall serve a term of four years. . . . The terms shall be staggered. The chairperson of the board shall be a full-time, salaried member of the board. A majority of the members of the board constitutes a quorum to transact business.

The membership of the board shall be of good character and judicious background, shall include a member of a minority group, may include a person ordained or designated as a regular leader of a religious community and who is knowledgeable in correctional procedures and issues, and shall meet at least two of the following three requirements:

1.   Contain one member who is a disinterested layperson.
2.   Contain one member who is an attorney licensed to practice law in this state and who is knowledgeable in correctional procedures and issues.
3.   Contain one member who is a person holding at least a master's degree in social work or counseling and guidance and who is knowledgeable in correctional procedures and issues.

## Colorado Revised Statutes §17-22.5-404(1),(2)

(1) As to any person. . . who is eligible for parole. . . , the board may consider all applications for parole, . . . and may parole any person who is sentenced or committed to a correctional facility when the board determines, by using the guidelines established by this section, that there is a strong and reasonable probability that the person will not thereafter violate the law and that his release from institutional custody is compatible with the welfare of society. The board shall first consider the risk of violence to the public in every release decision it makes.

(2) (a) In considering offenders for parole, the board shall consider, but need not be limited to, the following factors:

(I) The testimony of the victim of the crime or a relative of the victim, if the victim has died. . . ;

(II) The offender's conduct which would indicate whether he has substantially observed all of the rules and regulations of the institution or facility in which he has been confined and has faithfully performed the duties assigned to him;

(III) The offender's demonstration of good faith efforts to make restitution to the victim of his conduct for the actual damages that were sustained. . . ;

(IV) The offender's demonstration of good faith efforts to pay reasonable costs of parole supervision. . . ;

(V) The offender's demonstration of good faith efforts to devote time to a specific employment or occupation;

(VI) The offender's good faith efforts to enroll in a school, college, university, or course of vocational or technical training designed to fit the student for gainful employment;

(VII) Whether the offender has diligently attempted but has been unable to obtain employment that provides the offender sufficient income, whether the offender has an employment disability, or whether the offender's age prevents him or her from obtaining employment;

(VIII) The offender's demonstration of good faith efforts to remain within prescribed geographical boundaries and notify the court or the parole officer of any change in the offender's address or employment;

(IX) The offender's demonstration of good faith efforts to report as directed to the parole officer;

(X) The offender's demonstration of good faith efforts to participate in some type of community service work;

(XI) The offender has not harassed the victim either verbally or in writing;

(XII) The offender's demonstration of good faith efforts to provide support, including any court-ordered child support, for any minor children;

(XIII) The offender's participation in the literacy corrections programs.

(b) Nothing in this subsection . . . shall preclude the board from considering factors other than those stated in paragraph (a). . . when considering applicants for parole.

## *Michael McDermott v. James McDonald*
### 24 P.3d 200 (Mont. 2001)

Petitioner Michael McDermott (McDermott) is serving a thirty-year sentence for assault and felony bail jumping in the Crossroads Correctional Center. The Board of Pardons and Parole (Board) has denied his application for parole, based in part on his failure to participate in a sexual offender program (SOP). He petitions this Court for a writ of habeas corpus, alleging that the Board has illegally denied him parole. We deny his petition.

### BACKGROUND

In May 1989, McDermott was charged by information with four counts of assault and four counts of incest against his two stepsons, then aged five and six. The information alleged that, between June 1985 and January 1986, McDermott assaulted his stepsons physically and sexually by burning their arms on the stove, knocking out their teeth, beating them on their legs, buttocks and penis with a wooden spoon and forcing them to engage in anal and oral intercourse. After being charged and released on bond, McDermott fled the jurisdiction. Eventually recaptured, he was extradited back to Montana and charged with an additional count of felony bail jumping.

McDermott pled guilty to the assault and bail jumping charges in exchange for dismissal of the four incest counts. The District Court sentenced him to five years on each assault charge and ten years on the bail jumping charge, for a total sentence of thirty years. Because of the violent nature of the assaults, because he committed them against young victims and because the court found that he represents a substantial danger to society, McDermott was designated a dangerous offender for purposes of parole.

McDermott began serving his sentence in May 1992. At that time, an initial needs assessment concluded that he suffers from "severe sexual problems" and recommended that he participate in the prison's treatment program for sexual offenders. McDermott elected not to participate in the SOP, and the Board later considered this fact during evaluations for placement in a prerelease center, for parole and for inmate classification purposes.

McDermott first applied for parole in September 1998. After notice and a hearing, the Board denied his application, citing McDermott's multiple offenses as well as their nature and severity. It noted that participation in the SOP would "enhance success on parole and further ensure that the applicant is willing and able to fulfill the obligations of a law-abiding citizen." McDermott again chose not to participate. As a result, he had four points added to his classification status for noncompliance with the Board's SOP recommendation. In September 1999, the Board again denied McDermott's parole application, citing the nature and severity of his offenses as well as his failure to comply with the Board's previous SOP recommendation.

McDermott contends that by requiring him to complete an SOP as a condition to early release on parole, the Board infringed upon his liberty interest in parole without due process of law. He petitions this Court for a writ of habeas corpus ordering his immediate release and rescinding the four points added to his classification status.

## DISCUSSION

Our due process analysis requires us to determine whether McDermott has a protected liberty interest in parole, and, if so, what process he is due and whether he received that process.

### A. McDermott's Liberty Interest in Parole

As a general rule, inmates have no liberty interest in parole. Greenholtz v. Inmates of the Nebraska Penal and Correctional Complex, 442 U.S. 1, 7 (1979). We have, however, recognized an exception to this general rule for inmates who committed their offenses prior to 1989. Before that year, Montana's parole eligibility statute stated: "the board *shall* release on parole . . . any person confined in the Montana state prison. . . when in its opinion there is reasonable probability that the prisoner can be released without detriment to the prisoner or to the community." Section 46-23-201, MCA (emphasis added). The United States Supreme Court held that the mandatory language of this provision created a liberty interest in parole that is protected by the due process clause of the federal constitution. Board of Pardons v. Allen, 482 U.S. 369, 377 (1987). . . .

### B. The Process Due McDermott

There is no absolute standard for what constitutes due process. Rather, the requirements of due process are flexible, so that they may be adapted to meet the procedural protections demanded by a particular situation. Thus, the process due in any given case varies according to the factual circumstances of the case, the nature of the interests at stake, and the risk of making an erroneous decision.

It is well established that a parole release determination is not subject to all the due process protections required to convict or confine. Nor must a parole release determination provide the same due process protections as are required in a parole revocation hearing. These situations present a much greater risk of error than a parole release determination because incarceration, whether as a result of conviction or parole revocation, involves a loss of liberty. Denial of parole, on the other hand, involves the loss of the mere anticipation of freedom — freedom to which the lawfully-convicted inmate is otherwise not entitled. As a consequence, the United States Supreme Court has held that due process is satisfied when the prisoner seeking parole is, at a minimum, provided with an opportunity to be heard and a written statement explaining why he was denied parole. *Greenholtz*, 442 U.S. at 16.

## C.  The Board's Authority to Consider McDermott's Participation in the SOP

McDermott does not contend that he was denied an opportunity to come before the Board or that he did not receive a statement of the reasons his parole was denied. Rather, he argues that the Board does not have authority to consider his lack of participation in an SOP as a basis for denying him early release on parole. For support, he relies on two of this Court's recent decisions: State v. Ommundson, 974 P.2d 620 (Mont. 1999), in which we held that a district court could not force an offender to complete a sexual offender program that had no correlation or connection to the underlying offense, and State v. Field, 11 P.3d 1203 (Mont. 2000), in which we held that the Board had no authority to impose conditions on a probationer that were not a part of his original sentence. We conclude, however, that neither of these cases limit the Board's authority to consider McDermott's failure to participate in the recommended SOP.

In *Ommundson*, the defendant pled guilty to driving under the influence of alcohol (DUI). After a presentence investigation revealed that he had more than ten previous convictions for indecent exposure, the district court conditioned suspension of the defendant's DUI sentence on his participation in an SOP. On appeal, we struck down the SOP condition, holding that "a sentencing limitation or condition must have . . . some correlation or connection to the underlying offense for which the defendant is being sentenced." We based our decision on the requirement of MCA §46-18-202(1)(e), that a sentence be "reasonably related to the objectives of rehabilitation and protection of the victim and society." . . . Since he was not convicted of a sex offense, McDermott contends that the Board has no authority to condition his parole on his participation in an SOP. We find this argument without merit. . . .

McDermott's argument fails to recognize the fundamental difference between imposition of a sentence — as in *Ommundson* — and release on parole. A sentence, or condition included in that sentence, is a *limitation on liberty*. A condition on parole is not. The district court's authority is properly restrained when it acts to limit an individual's freedom. Once lawfully sentenced, however, a prisoner is not entitled to release prior to the completion of his full sentence. Parole, therefore, is a *grant of liberty*. A condition on parole only limits freedom to which the inmate is otherwise not entitled. As a general proposition, then, it is invalid to assume, as McDermott does, that the Board's authority to set conditions precedent to parole is necessarily limited by a court's sentencing authority. . . .

Under both Montana and federal precedent, parole is a privilege and not a right. Since parole is granted as a matter of grace, rather than right, the state may offer such grace under and subject to such conditions as it considers most conducive to accomplish the desired purpose. In Montana, that grace is offered only when, in the Board's opinion, three conditions have been satisfied: "there is a reasonable probability that the prisoner can be released without detriment to the prisoner or to the community," MCA §46-23-201(1); when it is in "the best interests of society"; and when the prisoner "is able and willing to fulfill the obligations of a law-abiding citizen." MCA §46-23-201(2). Rather than restricting the authority of the Board to set conditions precedent to parole, these provisions obligate the Board to ensure that no prisoner is released on parole who cannot meet these three criteria.

As a complement to its broad discretion to grant, deny, or condition parole, the Board is authorized to consider factors that may not be considered by the district court at trial and sentencing. For instance, parole authorities are not limited to consideration of formally adjudicated cases when determining the likelihood of a prisoner's success on parole. Christopher v. U.S. Board of Parole, 589 F.2d 924 (7th Cir. 1978). Moreover, they may consider evidence of offenses which were charged in dismissed counts. Robinson v. Hadden, 723 F.2d 59 (10th Cir. 1983). A parole board may even hear and consider evidence excluded at trial under the exclusionary rule. In re Martinez, 463 P.2d 734 (Cal. 1970). In Montana, the Board is specifically required to "consider all pertinent information regarding each prisoner, including the circumstances of his offense, his previous social history and criminal record, his conduct, employment and attitude in prison, and the reports of any physical and mental examinations which have been made." MCA §46-23-202.

We conclude that the Board's authority to condition parole is not limited by our holding in *Ommundson*. Furthermore, the Board's statutory authority is broad enough to permit its consideration of McDermott's dismissed incest counts, the results of his initial needs assessment showing severe sexual problems and his refusal to participate in an SOP when determining whether to grant him an early release on parole.

McDermott's second argument is based on this Court's recent holding in *Field*. In that case, we held that the Board could not impose a condition on a probationer's postrelease conduct that was not specifically authorized by his sentence. *Field* dealt with a prisoner who had served the full term of his unsuspended sentence and was released on probation. Prior to release, the Board imposed the condition that he have no unsupervised contact with minors. Violation of this condition was later used to rescind the probation and return Field to prison. On appeal, this Court applied MCA §46-18-801, which provides that no "offender may be *deprived of a civil or constitutional right* except as provided in the Montana Constitution or as specifically enumerated by the sentencing judge as a necessary condition of the sentence. . . ." We reversed recision of the suspended sentence after determining that the condition that Field have no unsupervised contact with minors was a violation of his constitutional right to freedom of association and that it was not specifically included as a condition of his sentence.

McDermott argues that the Board's authority to impose conditions on his *parole* can be no greater than its authority to impose postsentence conditions on Field. He contends that, even if the District Court had the authority to impose a condition that he participate in an SOP as part of his sentence, no such condition was included. Therefore, he asserts, as in *Field*, the Board cannot now impose it as a condition of his release. We disagree.

In applying this Court's holding in *Field*, it is important to distinguish release on *parole* and release on *probation*. Parole, as stated above, is a discretionary grant of freedom from incarceration. Probation is an original condition of sentence that, for some period of time, the offender will not be incarcerated. . . . Under *Field*, the Board has no authority to impose conditions on *probation* that were not part of the original sentence because, under the terms of the sentence,

Field was entitled to be released at the time and under the conditions set by the court. But *Field* does not limit the Board's authority to place conditions on *parole*. The Board's placement of a condition on *probation* is a restriction on someone who would otherwise be free. A condition on *parole* is a limited grant of freedom to someone who would otherwise be incarcerated. We conclude that our holding in *Field* does not limit the Board's authority to impose conditions on parole and is not relevant to McDermott's case.

### CONCLUSION

Under MCA §46-23-201, . . . the Board must consider "all pertinent information regarding the prisoner." McDermott, while not a convicted sex offender, had four counts of incest dismissed pursuant to a plea bargain. He has been identified as having severe sexual problems. His completion — or lack of completion — of the SOP is pertinent to his ability to be released without "detriment to the. . . community" and "to fulfill the obligations of a law-abiding citizen." Therefore, the Board was well within its authority to consider McDermott's refusal to enroll in the recommended SOP when it denied his application for an early release.

## PROBLEM 11-5.   BEING UNDER THE WEATHER

On October 20, 1981, Kathy Boudin was arrested in conjunction with the robbery of an armored car during which the driver, Peter Paige, had been killed. Boudin had not participated in the planning of the robbery of $1.6 million, and was unarmed at the time of her arrest. She belonged to a radical group, the Weather Underground, that was willing to use violence to support its goals. After the robbery Boudin was riding in a U-Haul truck with those who had participated in the robbery. When the U-Haul was stopped at a roadblock, Boudin immediately surrendered to the police. Shortly thereafter, as police attempted to open the back of the truck, shooting erupted, and two police officers were killed.

Boudin pled guilty under New York's felony murder statute. She was sentenced to 20 years to life in prison for her role in the robbery. No charges were filed against her in connection with the death of the officers since she had already surrendered at the time they were killed. At sentencing, Judge Ritter imposed what he characterized as a "minimal" but "just" sentence. He explained his reasons for doing so: "In my judgment there is evidence of honest contrition and remorse, and abhorrence of violence as a technique to further goals, however noble." He concluded that Boudin's role in the tragedy was a "secondary one," and stated that there was no evidence to believe she was guilty of "any form of terrorist activity." Finally, Judge Ritter stated, "I see no reason in the world why Miss Boudin should not be paroled at the expiration of the twenty years."

In prison Boudin was a model inmate. At Bedford Hills, New York's prison for women, she established a program for women inmates with HIV that served as the model for such programs nationwide. In addition, she set up programs in adult literacy and for incarcerated women with children. In that capacity she organized workshops and developed curricula. She also completed a master's degree in adult education while in prison and published widely on HIV, literacy, mother-child relationships, and higher education.

At her first parole hearing in August 2001, Boudin was denied parole; the parole board stated that "due to the violent nature and circumstances of the instant offenses," Boudin's release "would be incompatible with the welfare of society and would serve to deprecate the seriousness of the criminal behavior herein so as to undermine respect for the law." At her second parole hearing in May 2003, the board again refused to grant her parole, because of the seriousness of the crimes and the fact that three individuals died in the crime spree.

After the second parole hearing, a New York judge ordered a new hearing because the parole board had failed to consider adequately Judge Ritter's remarks at sentencing and Boudin's remarkable record while in prison. At her third hearing in the summer of 2003, the board granted Boudin parole, effective October 1, 2003.

To what extent should Judge Ritter's remarks influence the parole board's decision? Should it have mattered to the parole board that some but not all of the victims' family members opposed the grant of parole? Would the parole decision for Boudin have been different under Colorado's parole guidelines (reprinted above)? Under Montana's parole rules (discussed in the *McDermott* case above)?


## NOTES

1. *Representation requirements and expertise.* Parole board members are usually appointed by the governor for fixed terms. Traditional membership requirements include backgrounds in psychology and social work to assess the likely behavior and rehabilitation of inmates. More modern membership requirements focus on diverse representation, sometimes including specific allocation of spots to members of different political parties. The assumptions underlying the representation requirements on parole boards have changed over time. Why do statutes like the Iowa provisions now require membership of community members, religious leaders, and members of minority groups? What influence can a "disinterested layperson" have if the other members of the parole board appear to be more knowledgeable in criminal justice matters?

2. *Political insulation.* The structure and composition of parole boards can determine to what extent politics influences parole decision making. For instance, Colorado has two separate institutions to address parole issues: the parole board, which makes individual parole decisions, and the commission to review and approve parole guidelines. The commission membership includes the attorney general, the executive director of the department of public safety, the executive director of the department of corrections, the chairperson of the state board of parole, the chairperson of a community corrections board, a parole officer, a law enforcement officer, and a private citizen. Why would Colorado create a separate body to set parole policy? Should a jurisdiction

seek to maximize the political insulation of parole decision makers or instead create structures that ensure political accountability in parole decisions?

3. *Right to parole.*    As noted in *McDermott,* in Greenholtz v. Inmates of the Nebraska Penal and Correctional Complex, 442 U.S. 1 (1979), the Supreme Court held that state prisoners do not have a constitutional right to parole and that there is no constitutionally protected interest in receiving parole unless a state's parole statute contains mandatory language restricting the parole board's discretion. In such a case, the prisoner develops a legitimate expectation of parole that cannot be denied without due process. In *Greenholtz,* the Supreme Court held that the due process requirement was satisfied through an informal hearing in which the inmate had an opportunity to present letters and statements on his behalf.

4. *Parole procedures.*    Parole hearings are typically open to the public, and the offender as well as the victim or the victim's family are allowed to make statements. The members of the parole board are furnished information about the offense committed, the offender's behavior while incarcerated, and reports from prison psychiatrists, if applicable. Although the precise contours of prisoners' due process rights in parole proceedings have not been definitively established, most jurisdictions tend to provide a hearing (with prior notice provided), a defined opportunity for the presentation of information by the inmate, notice of the criteria used to make the parole decision, and notice of the decision together with reasons for denial. See Victoria J. Palacios, Go and Sin No More: Rationality and Release Decisions by Parole Boards, 45 S.C. L. Rev. 567 (1994).

5. *Discretionary and mandatory parole releases and good time.*    Parole release schemes in which parole boards have nearly unfettered discretion to determine a release date have fallen out of favor over the past few years. Parole decision making has become increasingly structured, and mandatory releases to parole supervision are much more common now than in the past. To reflect the increase in mandatory supervised released from prison—which defines 98 percent of prisoners released from the federal system, and a smaller proportion in the states—federal crime statisticians have changed the categories around which they monitor parole trends. See Lauren E. Glaze & Thomas E. Bonczar, Probation and Parole in the United States, 2010 (NCJ 236019, Nov. 2011). Mandatory release occurs largely in determinate sentencing systems, in which inmates are conditionally released from prison after serving a portion of their original sentence minus any good time earned. In the report on 2010 data, Glaze and Bonczar noted a several year decline in the total number of people on parole, after decades of growth. They note that "Declines in California, Florida, Minnesota, Texas, and Maryland accounted for 54% of the total decrease among states whose probation population declined during 2010. California (down 18,854 probationers) and Florida (down 11,228) accounted for almost a third of the decrease."

Inmates earn so-called good-time credit for obeying prison rules. The ceiling on good-time credits varies by jurisdiction. In the past, inmates in some systems earned a day (or more) of good time for every day served. This led to heavy criticism, as inmates were released substantially earlier than the community and the victims expected.

Many systems now cap good time at 15% of the total sentence imposed, and they have been encouraged to do so by federal funding criteria for prison construction grants. Under the federal prison-building "truth-in-sentencing" grants, states received building grants only if they kept violent offenders incarcerated for 85% of the prison time imposed. See generally Paula Ditton & Doris James Wilson, Truth in Sentencing in State Prisons (Bureau of Justice Statistics, NCJ 170032, 1999). The Minnesota system began with a good-time provision allowing credits of up to 33% of the pronounced term, but legislation later cut back on that authorization. See Minn. Stat. ch. 244. Why would a legislature decrease good-time credits inmates can earn? What advantages are there in an increase of good-time credits? Consider these questions from the perspective of a warden, a state legislator, and a member of a crime-ridden community.

6. *Elimination of parole and other changes in parole rules.*   More than a dozen states have abolished early release by a parole board for all offenders, and several others have significantly restricted parole either through formal legal limits on eligibility or through the evolving decision making by parole boards. Even in states that have retained parole, parole boards have become more hesitant to grant it. In Texas, for example, 57% of all cases considered for parole release in 1988 were approved; by 1998 that figure had dropped to 20%. See Joan Petersilia, Parole and Prisoner Reentry in the United States, 26 Crime & Just. 479 (1999).

Defendants sometimes claim that formal changes in the rules governing parole eligibility can transgress the U.S. Constitution's ex post facto clause. In Johnson v. Commissioner of Corrections, 786 A.2d 1091 (Conn. 2002), the Connecticut Supreme Court cited such constitutional concerns when interpreting a state change in release rules (the new rules made violent offenders eligible for parole release only after serving 85% rather than 50% of their sentences) to apply only prospectively. In a similar vein, but reaching a different sort of result, the Supreme Court in Garner v. Jones, 529 U.S. 244 (2000), examined whether the retroactive application of a Georgia law permitting the extension of intervals between parole considerations violated the ex post facto clause. Defining the inquiry in terms of whether Georgia's change in parole rules created "a sufficient risk of increasing the measure of punishment attached to the covered crimes," the Court sent the case back to the court of appeals to determine whether the change in Georgia's parole board rules did create a significant risk of increased punishment for inmate Jones.

7. *Supervised release under the federal sentencing guidelines.*   As part of the Sentencing Reform Act of 1984, federal law formally eliminated parole and recast post-incarceration supervision in terms of "supervised release." Federal judges must impose a term of supervised release if the offender is sentenced to at least one year in prison. The length of supervised release depends on the seriousness of the felony committed, ranging from a minimum of one year for minor felonies and the most serious misdemeanors to five years for the most serious felonies. Select offenses allow for the imposition of a life term of supervised release.

In addition, the district court may impose a specific condition of supervision so long as the condition meets four criteria: (1) it must be reasonably related to specified sentencing factors, namely the nature and circumstances of the offense and the history and characteristics of the defendant; (2) it must be reasonably related to the need to afford adequate deterrence, to protect the public from further crimes of the defendant, and to provide the defendant with necessary educational or vocational training, medical care, or other correctional treatment in the most effective manner; (3) it must involve no greater deprivation of liberty than is reasonably necessary to achieve these goals; and (4) it must be consistent with any pertinent policy statements issued by the U.S. Sentencing Commission. See 18 U.S.C. §§3583(d), 3563(d), 3553.

To what extent do parole and supervised release differ? How are they similar? Suppose a person who runs a credit repair business is convicted of conspiracy to distribute methamphetamine and has a prior conviction for passing counterfeit notes. In light of the provisions for supervised release, would it be appropriate for a court to impose on the defendant an occupational restriction demanding that he inform his clients of the conviction? See United States v. Britt, 332 F.3d 1229 (9th Cir. 2003).

8. *International tribunals.*   Under the Statute of the International Criminal Court, the court reviews a sentence after the offender has served two-thirds of the sentence imposed. At that point the sentence may be reduced and the individual may qualify for early release. The statute contemplates that early release is to be granted only to individuals who have cooperated with prosecutors, have made attempts at reparation, and appear capable of benefiting from early release. The gravity of the offense also matters. How parole is to work in practice, however, remains unresolved. It is unclear, for example, to what country the offender should be released on parole — the country of imprisonment, the home state, or possibly a third country close to the home state.

## b.   Parole Conditions

Like sentencing courts, which establish conditions of probation (see Chapter 8), parole boards often establish conditions of parole. Some parole conditions are mandated by statute, but others are imposed as individualized requirements. As you review the following materials, consider what sorts of parole conditions should be mandated in all cases, and which should be applied on a case-by-case basis or never applied at all.

## ‖ *Alaska Statutes §33.16.150* ‖

(a) As a condition of parole, a prisoner released on special medical, discretionary, or mandatory parole

(1) shall obey all state, federal, or local laws or ordinances, and any court orders applicable to the parolee;

(2) shall make diligent efforts to maintain steady employment or meet family obligations;

(3) shall, if involved in education, counseling, training, or treatment, continue in the program unless granted permission from the parole officer assigned to the parolee to discontinue the program;

(4) shall report (A) upon release to the parole officer assigned to the parolee; (B) at other times, and in the manner, prescribed by the board or the parole officer assigned to the parolee;

(5) shall reside at a stated place and not change that residence without notifying, and receiving permission from, the parole officer assigned to the parolee;

(6) shall remain within stated geographic limits unless written permission to depart from the stated limits is granted the parolee;

(7) may not use, possess, handle, purchase, give, distribute, or administer a controlled substance. . . or a drug for which a prescription is required under state or federal law without a prescription from a licensed medical professional to the parolee;

(8) may not possess or control a firearm. . . ;

(9) may not enter into an agreement or other arrangement with a law enforcement agency or officer that will place the parolee in the position of violating a law or parole condition without the prior approval of the board;

(10) may not contact or correspond with anyone confined in a correctional facility of any type serving any term of imprisonment or a felon without the permission of the parole officer assigned to a parolee;

(11) shall agree to waive extradition from any state or territory of the United States and to not contest efforts to return the parolee to the state;

(12) shall provide a blood sample, an oral sample, or both, when requested by a health care professional acting on behalf of the state to provide the sample or samples, or an oral sample when requested by a juvenile or adult correctional, probation, or parole officer, or a peace officer, if the prisoner is being released after a conviction of an offense requiring the state to collect the sample or samples for the deoxyribonucleic acid identification system under AS 44.41.035.

(13) from a conviction for a sex offense shall submit to regular periodic polygraph examinations. . . .

(b) The board may require as a condition of special medical, discretionary, or mandatory parole, or a member of the board acting for the board under (e) of this section may require as a condition of mandatory parole, that a prisoner released on parole

(1) not possess or control a defensive weapon, a deadly weapon other than an ordinary pocket knife with a blade three inches or less in length, or ammunition for a firearm, or reside in a residence where there is a firearm capable of being concealed on one's person or a prohibited weapon. . . ;

(2) refrain from possessing or consuming alcoholic beverages;

(3) submit to reasonable searches and seizures by a parole officer, or a peace officer acting under the direction of a parole officer;

(4) submit to appropriate medical, mental health, or controlled substance or alcohol examination, treatment, or counseling;

(5) submit to periodic examinations designed to detect the use of alcohol or controlled substances;

(6) make restitution ordered by the court according to a schedule established by the board;

(7) refrain from opening, maintaining, or using a checking account or charge account;

(8) refrain from entering into a contract other than a prenuptial contract or a marriage contract;

(9) refrain from operating a motor vehicle;

(10) refrain from entering an establishment where alcoholic beverages are served, sold, or otherwise dispensed;

(11) refrain from participating in any other activity or conduct reasonably related to the parolee's offense, prior record, behavior or prior behavior, current circumstances, or perceived risk to the community, or from associating with any other person that the board determines is reasonably likely to diminish the rehabilitative goals of parole, or that may endanger the public; in the case of special medical parole, for a prisoner diagnosed with a communicable disease, comply with conditions set by the board designed to prevent the transmission of the disease. . . .

(f) In addition to other conditions of parole imposed under this section, the board may impose as a condition of special medical, discretionary, or mandatory parole for a prisoner serving a term for a crime involving domestic violence (1) any of the terms of protective orders. . . ; (2) a requirement that, at the prisoner's expense, the prisoner participate in and complete, to the satisfaction of the board, a program for the rehabilitation of perpetrators of domestic violence that meets the standards set by, and that is approved by, the department. . . ; and (3) any other condition necessary to rehabilitate the prisoner. . . .

## ‖ *Colorado Revised Statutes §16-11.7-105(2)* ‖

Each sex offender placed on parole by the state board of parole . . . shall be required, as a condition of such parole, to undergo treatment to the extent appropriate to such offender. . . . Any such treatment shall be at a facility or with a person certified or approved by the board and at such offender's expense, based upon such offender's ability to pay for such treatment.

### PROBLEM 11-6.  BANISHMENT

John Beavers was paroled from prison after serving 7 years of a 30-year sentence. As one of the special conditions of his parole, he was barred from Houston County, Alabama, where he and his family had lived prior to his incarceration. When he returned to Houston County without permission to see his two young daughters, he was arrested, and his parole was revoked. On appeal, what arguments should Beavers's counsel make to attack the revocation? Is the underlying parole condition constitutional? What purpose does the condition serve? See Beavers v. State, 666 So. 2d 868 (Ala. Crim. App. 1995).

### PROBLEM 11-7.  COMPUTER CONDITION

Gregory Sofsky received on his home computer via the Internet more than 1,000 images of child pornography in the form of both still and moving pictures.

He did not produce any of the images but transferred some of them to CD-ROM disks. In addition, he used the Internet to exchange images of child pornography with other (apparently like-minded) individuals. He is prosecuted for receiving child pornography, a federal offense.

The presentence report recommended that the judge impose a three-year period of supervised release. In addition to the standard conditions of supervised release, the report suggested that the court impose three special conditions: (1) the defendant must participate in mental health treatment, including a program for sexual disorders; (2) the defendant must permit a search of his premises at any time on reasonable suspicion that contraband or evidence of a violation of a condition of supervision may be found; and (3) the defendant must not view, purchase, or possess child pornography. The court followed the report's recommendations and added a fourth condition: the defendant must not "access a computer, the Internet, or bulletin board systems at any time, unless approved by the probation officer."

On appeal Sofsky challenges the conditions of his supervised release. What standard of review should the appellate court apply? How should it assess the validity of the four conditions? For different answers, see United States v. Sofsky, 287 F.3d 122 (2d Cir. 2002); United States v. Paul, 274 F.3d 155 (5th Cir. 2002); United States v. White, 244 F.3d 1199 (10th Cir. 2001); United States v. Crandon, 173 F.3d 122 (3d Cir. 1999).

## NOTES

1. *Parole conditions.*   Paroled inmates are released before their maximum sentence has expired, but usually they must report regularly to a parole officer and comply with a host of conditions, such as finding a job, abstaining from alcohol and illegal drugs, and not associating with convicted felons. In what settings do such apparently benign conditions become more onerous? Consider the predicament of a parolee who, having returned from prison to live with his parents, is visited one afternoon by his elder brother, a convicted felon.

At year-end 2005, about 70% of all parolees were under active parole supervision, which meant they were required to maintain regular contact with their parole officers. About 10% of parolees could not be located. Lauren E. Glaze & Thomas E. Bonczar, Probation and Parole in the United States, 2005 at 6 (NCJ 215091, November 2006). In 2010, about 82% were on active status. Lauren E. Glaze & Thomas E. Bonczar, Probation and Parole in the United States, 2010 (NCJ 236019, Nov. 2011).

2. *Evolving nature of parole supervision and services.*   The rise of determinate sentences and the corresponding reduced reliance on parole mechanisms have significantly changed the nature of postrelease supervision. Professor Joan Petersilia has observed an evolution in parole supervision toward controlling the offender at the expense of providing social services necessary for reentry into society:

> Historically, parole agents were viewed as paternalistic figures who mixed authority with help. Officers provided direct services (e.g., counseling) and

also knew the community and brokered services (e.g., job training) to needy offenders. Parole was originally designed to make the transition from prison to the community more gradual, and, during this time, parole officers were to assist the offender in addressing personal problems and searching for employment and a place to live. Many parole agencies still do assist in these "service" activities. Increasingly, however, parole supervision has shifted away from providing services to parolees and more toward monitoring and surveillance (e.g., drug testing, monitoring curfews, and collecting restitution). . . .

There are a number of reasons for this. For one, a greater number of parole conditions are being assigned to released prisoners. In the federal system, for example, between 1987 and 1996 the proportion of offenders required to comply with at least one special supervision condition increased from 67 percent of entrants to 91 percent. . . .

It is also true that the fiscal crises experienced in most states in recent years reduced the number of treatment and job-training programs in the community at large, and given the fear and suspicion surrounding ex-convicts, these persons are usually placed at the end of the waiting lists. . . . If there is one common complaint among parole officers in the United States, it is the lack of available treatment and job programs for parolees. . . .

The main reason, however, that "services" are not delivered to most parolees is that parole supervision has been transformed ideologically from a social service to a law enforcement system.

Joan Petersilia, Parole and Prisoner Reentry in the United States, 26 Crime & Just. 479, 506-508 (1999).

### c.   Parole Revocation

Should parolees be returned to prison for committing *any* infraction of the terms of parole? What procedures should be used to determine whether an offender has violated parole?

Consider the statistics described in the following study of prisoners. What accounts for the dramatic increase in reincarcerated parole violators? Should violation of a reporting condition, a geographic restriction, a work requirement, or a drug screen be cause for automatic parole revocation? If not, when is revocation called for?

> *Trends in Parole Supervision, 1990-2000,*
> *Timothy A. Hughes, Doris James Wilson,*
> *and Allen J. Beck*
> **Bureau of Justice Statistics (Sept. 2001)**

#### RE-RELEASES AN INCREASING PORTION OF STATE PAROLE ENTRIES

Among parole entries, the percentage who had been re-released rose between 1990 and 1999. Re-releases are persons leaving prison after having served time either for a violation of parole or other conditional release or for a new offense committed while under parole supervision. In 1990, 27% of entries to parole were re-releases; in 1999, 45% were re-releases. . . .

After having been returned to prison for a parole or conditional release violation, re-releases served on average 13 months in prison in 1999. From 1990 to 1999 their average time served in prison following re-admission increased by 2 months. In both years about 7 in 10 re-releases had served less than 12 months in prison. . . .

### PAROLE SUCCESS RATES UNCHANGED SINCE 1990

Of the 410,613 discharges from State parole in 1999, 42% successfully completed their term of supervision, 43% were returned to prison or jail, and 10% absconded. In 1990, 45% of State parole discharges were successful. Between 1990 and 1999 the percent successful among State parole discharges has ranged from 42% to 49%, without any distinct trend.

States differed in their rate of success among parole discharges. States with the highest rates of success in 1999 were Massachusetts and Mississippi (at 83% each), followed by North Carolina (80%) and North Dakota (79%). Utah (18%) and California (21%) had the lowest rates of success in 1999.

When comparing State success rates for parole discharges, differences may be due to variations in parole populations, such as age at prison release, criminal history, and most serious offense. Success rates may also differ based on the intensity of supervision and the parole agency policies related to revocation of technical violators.

### SUCCESS RATES HIGHEST AMONG FIRST RELEASES AND DISCRETIONARY PAROLE RELEASES

In every year during the 1990's, first releases to State parole were more likely to have been successful than re-releases. Among State parole discharges in 1990, 56% of first releases successfully completed their supervision, compared to 15% of re-releases. Of all those exiting parole in 1999, 63% of first releases were successful, compared to 21% of re-releases.

Success rates also varied by method of release. In every year between 1990 and 1999, State prisoners released by a parole board had higher success rates than those released through mandatory parole. Among parole discharges in 1999, 54% of discretionary parolees were successful compared to 33% of those who had received mandatory parole. . . .

### AMONG PAROLE DISCHARGES, SUCCESS RATES ROSE FOR BLACKS AND HISPANICS; DROPPED FOR WHITES

Between 1990 and 1999 the success rates among State parole discharges increased from 33% to 39% among blacks and increased from 31% to 51% among Hispanics, but dropped from 44% to 41% among whites. The 11 percentage-point difference in success rates between white and black parole discharges in 1990 narrowed to less than 2 percentage points in 1999. . . .

For female parole discharges, the rate of success rose over 10 percentage points (from 37% in 1990 to 48% in 1999). The success rate among male parole discharges increased from 36% to 39%.

Older parole discharges had the highest rates of success in both years. Accounting for 2.1% of discharges in 1999, parolees age 55 or older had the highest rate of successful completion (55%). Among parole discharges in other age groups, success rates fluctuated between 36% and 43%. . . .

### NUMBER OF PAROLE VIOLATORS RETURNED TO PRISON CONTINUED TO RISE DURING THE 1990's

In 1999, 197,606 parole violators were returned to State prison, up from 27,177 in 1980 and 131,502 in 1990. As a percentage of all admissions to State prison, parole violators more than doubled from 17% in 1980 to 35% in 1999. Between 1990 and 1999 the number of parole violators rose 50%, while the number of new court commitments rose 7%. . . .

In 1999 parole violators accounted for more than 50% of State prison admission in California (67%), Utah (55%), Montana (53%), and Louisiana (53%). In five States — Florida (7%), Alabama (9%), Indiana (10%), Mississippi (10%) and West Virginia (10%) — parole violators comprised 10% or less of all admissions. . . .

Based on personal interviews of State inmates, an estimated 24% of prisoners in 1997 said they were on parole at the time of the offense for which they were serving time in prison (up from 22% in 1991). . . .

### 70% OF PAROLE VIOLATORS IN PRISON IN 1997 RETURNED FOR A NEW OFFENSE

Among parole violators in State prison in 1997, 215,964 (85%) reported that their parole had been revoked or taken away for violating the conditions of their release. Of that number, 70% said that their parole had been revoked because of an arrest or conviction for a new offense; 22% said they had absconded or otherwise failed to report to a parole officer; 16% said they had a drug-related violation; and 18% reported other reasons such as possession of a gun, maintaining contact with known felons, or failure to maintain employment.

### HALF OF PAROLE VIOLATORS INCARCERATED IN 3 STATES

The three largest State prison systems (California, Texas, and New York) held over half of all parole violators in prison in 1997. California held 22% of all parole violators in prison, Texas, 21%, and New York, 8%. Within each of these States, the percentage of prisoners who were parole violators was higher than the national level: 39% in Texas, 38% in California, and 28% in New York, compared to 24% nationally.

Among parole violators returned to prison, those held in California (60%) were the least likely to have been arrested or convicted for a new offense and the most likely to have been returned for a drug violation (23%). About 11% of parole violators in New York and Texas reported a drug violation as a reason for their return to prison. . . .

New York had the highest percentage of parole violators in prison who were black (54%), followed by Texas (50%) and California (33%). In New York, 11% of parole violators were white; in Texas, 23%; in California, 31%. The percent Hispanic among parole violators ranged from 26% to 33% in the three States.

New York had the highest percentage of parole violators convicted of a violent offense (41%), compared to 33% in Texas and 24% in California. New York also had the highest percentage of parole violators returned for a drug offense (34%), compared to 27% in California and 21% in Texas. . . .

## NOTES

1. *The purposes of parole.* Traditionally, parole was supposed to help an offender reenter society successfully. Parole officers often had a background in social work. In recent years, the function of parole and the background of parole officers have changed dramatically. Parole is increasingly viewed as a way to control offenders once they are back in the community. Parole officers more often have a criminal justice background and see themselves as enforcers of rules rather than as assistants in the reintegration project. Parole violators thus tend to be returned to prison. In some jurisdictions, however, parole may be revoked but then immediately reinstated, often with new conditions added or following a warning that continued infractions will result in imprisonment. Do such differences in the enforcement culture account for the nationally disparate numbers of parole violators who return to prison?

2. *Types of violations.* Data on parole violations tends to distinguish technical violations from new offenses. Technical violations may include failing to meet with the parole officer, testing positive for drugs, or leaving the jurisdiction without informing the parole officer. Why should technical violations lead to reincarceration? What other sanctions are available? A recent study of juvenile parolees indicated that young parolees who test positive for drugs during their first three months on parole are more likely to commit offenses while on parole than are other parolees. How can such findings be used to prevent later parole violations?

3. *Revocation procedures.* The rights of parolees at revocation proceedings are limited since such proceedings are not part of a criminal prosecution and the liberty of parolees is considered only conditional. In Pennsylvania Board of Probation and Parole v. Scott, 524 U.S. 357 (1998), for example, the Supreme Court held that the exclusionary rule does not apply to parole revocation hearings. In Morrissey v. Brewer, 408 U.S. 470 (1972), however, the Supreme Court set out the necessary due process protections in parole revocation hearings, including written notice of the claimed violations of parole, disclosure to the

parolee of the evidence against him, opportunity to be heard in person and to present witnesses and documentary evidence, the right in general to confront and cross-examine adverse witnesses, the right to be heard by a "neutral and detached" body whose members need not be judicial officers, and a written statement by the factfinders as to the evidence relied on and reasons for revoking parole. In some states the proceeding is heard by the parole board, in others by an administrative law judge. Many states allow for appeals from an adverse decision.

4. *Reentry courts.*   Because of the large number of parole violators who return to prison and the concomitant expense, criminal justice professionals and politicians have renewed their focus on the reentry of prisoners into the community. Some federally funded projects have established reentry courts that follow the model of drug courts (discussed in Chapter 8). A judge regularly sees a parolee and monitors her progress. Successive violations carry sanctions of increasing magnitude, and successful program participation carries small rewards. The goal is to allow for occasional violations of parole rules but to prevent future crime while assisting the offender in her reintegration.

## 2.   Civil Commitment

Parole provides a certain check on released offenders, largely by requiring that they report regularly to their parole officers, but it does not prevent all crime. Offenders who are considered very dangerous may be released from prison at their mandatory release date. What should society do in that situation? One possibility is an enhanced level of parole in which released offenders are monitored through electronic bracelets or are subject to unannounced visits by parole officers.

In the highly charged cases of sexual offenders, however, state legislators may not be willing to risk another offense. Therefore, a number of states have adopted special civil commitment statutes for sexual offenders. In most such cases, civil commitment appears to equate to life imprisonment. Is civil commitment for sex offenders constitutional? What types of safeguards have to be in place?

### Kansas v. Leroy Hendricks
### 521 U.S. 346 (1997)

THOMAS, J.

In 1994, Kansas enacted the Sexually Violent Predator Act, which establishes procedures for the civil commitment of persons who, due to a "mental abnormality" or a "personality disorder," are likely to engage in "predatory acts of sexual violence." Kan. Stat. Ann. §59-29a01 et seq. The State invoked the Act for the first time to commit Leroy Hendricks, an inmate who had a long history of sexually molesting children, and who was scheduled for release from prison shortly after the Act became law. Hendricks challenged his commitment on, inter alia, "substantive" due process, double jeopardy, and ex post facto grounds. . . .

## I. BACKGROUND

### A. Sexually Violent Predator Act

The Kansas Legislature enacted the Sexually Violent Predator Act (Act) in 1994 to grapple with the problem of managing repeat sexual offenders. [The] legislature determined that existing civil commitment procedures were inadequate to confront the risks presented by "sexually violent predators." In the Act's preamble, the legislature explained:

> [Sexually] violent predators' likelihood of engaging in repeat acts of predatory sexual violence is high. The existing involuntary commitment procedure. . . is inadequate to address the risk these sexually violent predators pose to society. The legislature further finds that the prognosis for rehabilitating sexually violent predators in a prison setting is poor, the treatment needs of this population are very long term and the treatment modalities for this population are very different than the traditional treatment modalities for people appropriate for commitment under the [general involuntary civil commitment statute].

Kan. Stat. Ann. §59-29a01.

As a result, the Legislature found it necessary to establish "a civil commitment procedure for the long-term care and treatment of the sexually violent predator." The Act defined a "sexually violent predator" as: "any person who has been convicted of or charged with a sexually violent offense and who suffers from a mental abnormality or personality disorder which makes the person likely to engage in the predatory acts of sexual violence."§59-29a02(a). A "mental abnormality" was defined, in turn, as a "congenital or acquired condition affecting the emotional or volitional capacity which predisposes the person to commit sexually violent offenses in a degree constituting such person a menace to the health and safety of others."

As originally structured, the Act's civil commitment procedures pertained to: (1) a presently confined person who, like Hendricks, "has been convicted of a sexually violent offense" and is scheduled for release; (2) a person who has been "charged with a sexually violent offense" but has been found incompetent to stand trial; (3) a person who has been found "not guilty by reason of insanity of a sexually violent offense"; and (4) a person found "not guilty" of a sexually violent offense because of a mental disease or defect.

The initial version of the Act, as applied to a currently confined person such as Hendricks, was designed to initiate a specific series of procedures. The custodial agency was required to notify the local prosecutor 60 days before the anticipated release of a person who might have met the Act's criteria. The prosecutor was then obligated, within 45 days, to decide whether to file a petition in state court seeking the person's involuntary commitment. If such a petition were filed, the court was to determine whether "probable cause" existed to support a finding that the person was a "sexually violent predator" and thus eligible for civil commitment. Upon such a determination, transfer of the individual to a secure facility for professional evaluation would occur. After that evaluation, a trial would be held to determine beyond a reasonable doubt whether the individual was a sexually violent predator. If that determination were made, the person would then be transferred to the custody of the Secretary of Social and Rehabilitation Services (Secretary) for "control, care and treatment until such time as the person's mental abnormality or personality disorder has so changed that the person is safe to be at large."

In addition to placing the burden of proof upon the State, the Act afforded the individual a number of other procedural safeguards. In the case of an indigent person, the State was required to provide, at public expense, the assistance of counsel and an examination by mental health care professionals. The individual also received the right to present and cross-examine witnesses, and the opportunity to review documentary evidence presented by the State.

Once an individual was confined, the Act required that "the involuntary detention or commitment . . . shall conform to constitutional requirements for care and treatment." Confined persons were afforded three different avenues of review: First, the committing court was obligated to conduct an annual review to determine whether continued detention was warranted. Second, the Secretary was permitted, at any time, to decide that the confined individual's condition had so changed that release was appropriate, and could then authorize the person to petition for release. Finally, even without the Secretary's permission, the confined person could at any time file a release petition. If the court found that the State could no longer satisfy its burden under the initial commitment standard, the individual would be freed from confinement.

### B.  Leroy Hendricks

In 1984, Hendricks was convicted of taking "indecent liberties" with two 13-year-old boys. After serving nearly 10 years of his sentence, he was slated for release to a halfway house. Shortly before his scheduled release, however, the State filed a petition in state court seeking Hendricks' civil confinement as a sexually violent predator. . . .

Hendricks . . . requested a jury trial to determine whether he qualified as a sexually violent predator. During that trial, Hendricks' own testimony revealed a chilling history of repeated child sexual molestation and abuse, beginning in 1955. . . . He testified that despite having received professional help for his pedophilia, he continued to harbor sexual desires for children. . . .

Hendricks admitted that he had repeatedly abused children whenever he was not confined. He explained that when he "gets stressed out," he "can't control the urge" to molest children. Although Hendricks recognized that his behavior harms children, and he hoped he would not sexually molest children again, he stated that the only sure way he could keep from sexually abusing children in the future was "to die." Hendricks readily agreed with the state physician's diagnosis that he suffers from pedophilia and that he is not cured of the condition; indeed, he told the physician that "treatment is bull — ." The jury unanimously found beyond a reasonable doubt that Hendricks was a sexually violent predator. The trial court subsequently determined, as a matter of state law, that pedophilia qualifies as a "mental abnormality" as defined by the Act, and thus ordered Hendricks committed to the Secretary's custody. . . .

## II.  DISCUSSION

### A.  *Prerequisites of Civil Confinement: Dangerousness and Mental Abnormality*

Kansas argues that the Act's definition of "mental abnormality" satisfies "substantive" due process requirements. We agree. Although freedom from physical restraint "has always been at the core of the liberty protected by the Due Process Clause from arbitrary governmental action," Foucha v. Louisiana, 504 U.S. 71, 80 (1992), that liberty interest is not absolute. The Court has recognized that an individual's constitutionally protected interest in avoiding physical restraint may be overridden even in the civil context.

Accordingly, States have in certain narrow circumstances provided for the forcible civil detainment of people who are unable to control their behavior and who thereby pose a danger to the public health and safety. We have consistently upheld such involuntary commitment statutes provided the confinement takes place pursuant to proper procedures and evidentiary standards. It thus cannot be said that the involuntary civil confinement of a limited subclass of dangerous persons is contrary to our understanding of ordered liberty.

The challenged Act unambiguously requires a finding of dangerousness either to one's self or to others as a prerequisite to involuntary confinement. Commitment proceedings can be initiated only when a person "has been convicted of or charged with a sexually violent offense," and "suffers from a mental abnormality or personality disorder which makes the person likely to engage in the predatory acts of sexual violence." The statute thus requires proof of more than a mere predisposition to violence; rather, it requires evidence of past sexually violent behavior and a present mental condition that creates a likelihood of such conduct in the future if the person is not incapacitated. As we have recognized, "previous instances of violent behavior are an important indicator of future violent tendencies." Heller v. Doe, 509 U.S. 312, 323 (1993). A finding of dangerousness, standing alone, is ordinarily not a sufficient ground upon which to justify indefinite involuntary commitment. We have sustained civil commitment statutes when they have coupled proof of dangerousness with the proof of some additional factor, such as a "mental illness" or "mental abnormality." These added statutory requirements serve to limit involuntary civil confinement to those who suffer from a volitional impairment rendering them dangerous beyond their control. The Kansas Act is plainly of a kind with these other civil commitment statutes: It requires a finding of future dangerousness, and then links that finding to the existence of a "mental abnormality" or "personality disorder" that makes it difficult, if not impossible, for the person to control his dangerous behavior. . . .

The mental health professionals who evaluated Hendricks diagnosed him as suffering from pedophilia, a condition the psychiatric profession itself classifies as a serious mental disorder. Hendricks even conceded that, when he becomes "stressed out," he cannot "control the urge" to molest children. This admitted lack of volitional control, coupled with a prediction of future dangerousness, adequately distinguishes Hendricks from other dangerous persons who are perhaps more properly dealt with exclusively through criminal proceedings. Hendricks' diagnosis as a pedophile, which qualifies as a "mental abnormality" under the Act, thus plainly suffices for due process purposes.


### B.   Civil v. Criminal Proceedings

[Hendricks argues] that the Act establishes criminal proceedings; hence confinement under it necessarily constitutes punishment. He contends that where, as here, newly enacted "punishment" is predicated upon past conduct for which he has already been convicted and forced to serve a prison sentence, the Constitution's Double Jeopardy and Ex Post Facto Clauses are violated. We are unpersuaded by Hendricks' argument that Kansas has established criminal proceedings.

The categorization of a particular proceeding as civil or criminal is first of all a question of statutory construction. We must initially ascertain whether the legislature meant the statute to establish "civil" proceedings. If so, we ordinarily defer to the legislature's stated intent. Here, Kansas' objective to create a civil proceeding is evidenced by its placement of the Sexually Violent Predator Act within the Kansas probate code, instead of the criminal code, as well as its description of the Act as creating a "civil commitment procedure." Nothing on the face of the statute suggests that the legislature sought to create anything other than a civil commitment scheme designed to protect the public from harm.

Although we recognize that a civil label is not always dispositive, we will reject the legislature's manifest intent only where a party challenging the statute provides the clearest proof that the statutory scheme [is] so punitive either in purpose or effect as to negate [the State's] intention to deem it civil. . . .

As a threshold matter, commitment under the Act does not implicate either of the two primary objectives of criminal punishment: retribution or deterrence. The Act's purpose is not retributive because it does not affix culpability for prior criminal conduct. Instead, such conduct is used solely for evidentiary purposes, either to demonstrate that a "mental abnormality" exists or to support a finding of future dangerousness. . . . In addition, the Kansas Act does not make a criminal conviction a prerequisite for commitment—persons absolved of criminal responsibility may nonetheless be subject to confinement under the Act. An absence of the necessary criminal responsibility suggests that the State is not seeking retribution for a past misdeed. Thus, the fact that the Act may be tied to criminal activity is insufficient to render the statute punitive.

Moreover, unlike a criminal statute, no finding of scienter is required to commit an individual who is found to be a sexually violent predator; instead, the commitment determination is made based on a "mental abnormality" or "personality disorder" rather than on one's criminal intent. The existence of a scienter requirement is customarily an important element in distinguishing criminal from civil statutes. The absence of such a requirement here is evidence that confinement under the statute is not intended to be retributive.

Nor can it be said that the legislature intended the Act to function as a deterrent. Those persons committed under the Act are, by definition, suffering from a "mental abnormality" or a "personality disorder" that prevents them from exercising adequate control over their behavior. Such persons are therefore unlikely to be deterred by the threat of confinement. . . . The State has represented that an individual confined under the Act is not subject to the more restrictive conditions placed on state prisoners, but instead experiences essentially the same conditions as any involuntarily committed patient in the state mental institution. Because none of the parties argues that people institutionalized under the Kansas general civil commitment statute are subject to punitive conditions, even though they may be involuntarily confined, it is difficult to conclude that persons confined under this Act are being "punished."

Although the civil commitment scheme at issue here does involve an affirmative restraint, "the mere fact that a person is detained does not inexorably lead to the conclusion that the government has imposed punishment." United States v. Salerno, 481 U.S. 739, 746 (1987). The State may take measures to restrict the freedom of the dangerously mentally ill. This is a legitimate nonpunitive governmental objective and has been historically so regarded. . . .

Hendricks focuses on his confinement's potentially indefinite duration as evidence of the State's punitive intent. That focus, however, is misplaced. Far from any punitive objective, the confinement's duration is instead linked to the stated purposes of the commitment, namely, to hold the person until his mental abnormality no longer causes him to be a threat to others. If, at any time, the confined person is adjudged "safe to be at large," he is statutorily entitled to immediate release.

Furthermore, commitment under the Act is only *potentially* indefinite. The maximum amount of time an individual can be incapacitated pursuant to a single judicial proceeding is one year. If Kansas seeks to continue the detention beyond that year, a court must once again determine beyond a reasonable doubt that the detainee satisfies the same standards as required for the initial confinement. This requirement again demonstrates that Kansas does not intend an individual committed pursuant to the Act to remain confined any longer than he suffers from a mental abnormality rendering him unable to control his dangerousness. . . .

Finally, Hendricks argues that the Act is necessarily punitive because it fails to offer any legitimate "treatment." Without such treatment, Hendricks asserts, confinement under the Act amounts to little more than disguised punishment. Hendricks' argument assumes that treatment for his condition is available, but that the State has failed (or refused) to provide it.

[Under] the appropriate circumstances and when accompanied by proper procedures, incapacitation may be a legitimate end of the civil law. . . . While we have upheld state civil commitment statutes that aim both to incapacitate and to treat, we have never held that the Constitution prevents a State from civilly detaining those for whom no treatment is available, but who nevertheless pose a danger to others. A State could hardly be seen as furthering a "punitive" purpose by involuntarily confining persons afflicted with an untreatable, highly contagious disease. Similarly, it would be of little value to require treatment as a precondition for civil confinement of the dangerously insane when no acceptable treatment existed. To conclude otherwise would obligate a State to release certain confined individuals who were both mentally ill and dangerous simply because they could not be successfully treated for their afflictions. . . .

Although the treatment program initially offered Hendricks may have seemed somewhat meager, it must be remembered that he was the first person committed under the Act. That the State did not have all of its treatment procedures in place is thus not surprising. What is significant, however, is that Hendricks was placed under the supervision of the Kansas Department of Health and Social and Rehabilitative Services, housed in a unit segregated from the general prison population and operated not by employees of the Department of Corrections, but by other trained individuals. And, before this Court, Kansas declared "absolutely" that persons committed under the Act are now receiving in the neighborhood of 31.5 hours of treatment per week.

Where the State has "disavowed any punitive intent"; limited confinement to a small segment of particularly dangerous individuals; provided strict procedural safeguards; directed that confined persons be segregated from the general prison population and afforded the same status as others who have been civilly committed; recommended treatment if such is possible; and permitted immediate release upon a showing that the individual is no longer dangerous or mentally impaired, we cannot say that it acted with punitive intent. We therefore hold that the Act does not establish criminal proceedings and that involuntary confinement pursuant to the Act is not punitive. Our conclusion that the Act is nonpunitive thus removes an essential prerequisite for both Hendricks' double jeopardy and ex post facto claims. . . .

Because we have determined that the Kansas Act is civil in nature, initiation of its commitment proceedings does not constitute a second prosecution. Moreover, as commitment under the Act is not tantamount to "punishment," Hendricks' involuntary detention does not violate the Double Jeopardy Clause, even though that confinement may follow a prison term. . . . The Ex Post Facto Clause, which forbids the application of any new punitive measure to a crime already consummated, has been interpreted to pertain exclusively to penal statutes. . . . Because the Act does not criminalize conduct legal before its enactment, nor deprive Hendricks of any defense that was available to him at the time of his crimes, the Act does not violate the Ex Post Facto Clause. . . .

KENNEDY, J., concurring.

[I write] to caution against dangers inherent when a civil confinement law is used in conjunction with the criminal process, whether or not the law is given retroactive application. [The] power of the state to confine persons who, by reason of a mental disease or mental abnormality, constitute a real, continuing, and serious danger to society is well established. . . . The Kansas law, with its attendant protections, including yearly review and review at any time at the instance of the person confined, is within this pattern and tradition of civil confinement.

Notwithstanding its civil attributes, the practical effect of the Kansas law may be to impose confinement for life. At this stage of medical knowledge, although future treatments cannot be predicted, psychiatrists or other professionals engaged in treating pedophilia may be reluctant to find measurable success in treatment even after a long period and may be unable to predict that no serious danger will come from release of the detainee.

A common response to this may be, "A life term is exactly what the sentence should have been anyway," or, in the words of a Kansas task force member, "So be it." The point, however, is not how long Hendricks and others like him should serve a criminal sentence. With his criminal record, after all, a life term may well have been the only sentence appropriate to protect society and vindicate the wrong. The concern instead is whether it is the criminal system or the civil system which should make the decision in the first place. . . . We should bear in mind that while incapacitation is a goal common to both the criminal and civil systems of confinement, retribution and general deterrence are reserved for the criminal system alone.

On the record before us, the Kansas civil statute conforms to our precedents. If, however, civil confinement were to become a mechanism for retribution or general deterrence, or if it were shown that mental abnormality is too imprecise a category to offer a solid basis for concluding that civil detention is justified, our precedents would not suffice to validate it.

BREYER, J., dissenting.

I agree with the majority that the Kansas Act's definition of mental abnormality satisfies the "substantive" requirements of the Due Process Clause. Kansas, however, concedes that Hendricks' condition is treatable; yet the Act did not provide Hendricks (or others like him) with any treatment until after his release date from prison and only inadequate treatment thereafter. These, and certain other, special features of the Act convince me that it was not simply an effort to commit Hendricks civilly, but rather an effort to inflict further punishment upon him. The Ex Post Facto Clause therefore prohibits the Act's application to Hendricks, who committed his crimes prior to its enactment.

[When] a State believes that treatment does exist, and then couples that admission with a legislatively required delay of such treatment until a person is at the end of his jail term (so that further incapacitation is therefore necessary), such a legislative scheme begins to look punitive. . . . I have found 17 States with laws that seek to protect the public from mentally abnormal, sexually dangerous individuals through civil commitment or other mandatory treatment programs. Ten of those statutes, unlike the Kansas statute, begin treatment of an offender soon after he has been apprehended and charged with a serious sex offense. Only seven, like Kansas, delay "civil" commitment (and treatment) until the offender has served his criminal sentence (and this figure includes the Acts of Minnesota and New Jersey, both of which generally do not delay treatment). Of these seven, however, six (unlike Kansas) require consideration of less restrictive alternatives. Only one State other than Kansas, namely Iowa, both delays civil commitment (and consequent treatment) and does not explicitly consider less restrictive alternatives. But the law of that State applies prospectively only, thereby avoiding ex post facto problems. Thus the practical experience of other States, as revealed by their statutes, confirms . . . that for Ex Post Facto Clause purposes, the purpose of the Kansas Act (as applied to previously convicted offenders) has a punitive, rather than a purely civil, purpose. . . .

To find that the confinement the Act imposes upon Hendricks is "punishment" is to find a violation of the Ex Post Facto Clause. . . . To find a violation of that Clause here, however, is not to hold that the Clause prevents Kansas, or other States, from enacting dangerous sexual offender statutes. A statute that operates prospectively, for example, does not offend the Ex Post Facto Clause. Neither does it offend the Ex Post Facto Clause for a State to sentence offenders to the fully authorized sentence, to seek consecutive, rather than concurrent, sentences, or to invoke recidivism statutes to lengthen imprisonment. Moreover, a statute that operates retroactively, like Kansas' statute, nonetheless does not offend the Clause *if the confinement that it imposes is not punishment*—if, that is to say, the legislature does not simply add a later criminal punishment to an earlier one.

The statutory provisions before us do amount to punishment primarily because, as I have said, the legislature did not tailor the statute to fit the non-punitive civil aim of treatment, which it concedes exists in Hendricks' case. The Clause in these circumstances does not stand as an obstacle to achieving important protections for the public's safety; rather it provides an assurance that, where so significant a restriction of an individual's basic freedoms is at issue, a State cannot cut corners. Rather, the legislature must hew to the Constitution's liberty-protecting line. See The Federalist, No. 78, p. 466 (C. Rossiter ed. 1961) (A. Hamilton).

## NOTES

1. *Civil commitment for sex offenders.*  The Supreme Court's decision in *Hendricks* clearly labeled commitment for sex offenders a civil sanction that can follow a criminal conviction or be imposed instead of one. In Seling v. Young, 531 U.S. 250 (2001), the Court rejected the claim that Washington state's sex offender commitment statute could be found punitive as applied to a particular sex offender. It found the "as applied" determination unworkable and rejected the notion that an "as applied" challenge could lead to release on ex post facto or substantive due process grounds.

2. *Prerequisites for sex offender commitment.*  In *Hendricks*, the Supreme Court held that the statutory requirement of a "mental abnormality or personality disorder" satisfied due process requirements. In Kansas v. Crane, 534 U.S. 407 (2002), the Court required the state to prove that a sex offender had *difficulty* controlling his sexual urges before he could be committed civilly. There is no constitutional requirement, however, that the individual be *unable* to control his urges before commitment. Why does the Court require the existence of a mental abnormality for civil commitment? Why does the continued dangerousness of the offender not suffice?

3. *Treatment during confinement.*  While the *Hendricks* Court showed some concerns about the minimal treatment Hendricks had received, Justice Breyer appeared the most concerned about the absence of treatment during imprisonment, which in turn seemed to imply the state's lack of interest in curing Hendricks. Justice Kennedy, in his concurrence, noted that treatment, as it is currently available, may never be useful to offenders such as Hendricks, leaving them in preventive detention for the rest of their lives. For a discussion of substantive due process considerations during civil commitment, see Eric S. Janus & Wayne A. Logan, Substantive Due Process and the Involuntary Confinement of Sexually Violent Predators, 35 Conn. L. Rev. 319 (2003). Should society's inability to develop successful treatment options be sufficient reason for virtual life imprisonment of offenders after they have served their criminal justice sanctions?

4. *Alternatives to civil commitment.*   Civil commitment statutes for sex offenders have generated much discussion in legal circles, but their practical impact has remained low as other risk control mechanisms have replaced or substituted for them. All states have enacted sex offender notification and registration laws (see Chapter 8), and many have lengthened criminal penalties for sex crimes. Are longer sentences for sex offenders generally desirable, based on a risk analysis? Consider that predictions of recurrent acts of sexual violence have gotten more accurate in the short term, but psychiatrists and psychologists are loath to make long-term predictions. See Eric S. Janus & Robert A. Prentky, Forensic Use of Actuarial Risk Assessment with Sex Offenders: Accuracy, Admissibility and Accountability 40 Am. Crim. L. Rev. 1443 (2003).

## 3.   Sealed Records and Expungements

Many convicted individuals carry their criminal records with them until they die. In some states, however, administrative procedures are available to seal or expunge criminal records. Sealed records, which are common for juveniles, are inaccessible to anyone other than law enforcement agencies and courts, in case of a later conviction. Expungement of records is no longer available to every offender. Some states allow expungement of criminal records only for certain first offenses, others for offenses in which the sentence was suspended or the offender successfully completed probation. In a few jurisdictions courts expunge records; in others administrative agencies fulfill this function.

## *Christopher John Dillingham v. INS*
### 267 F.3d 996 (9th Cir. 2001)

B. FLETCHER, J.

In this case, we consider whether an alien's right to equal protection is violated if, in the course of removal proceedings, the Immigration and Naturalization Service ("INS") refuses to recognize the effects of a British expungement[1] statute on a simple drug possession offense that would have qualified for federal first offender treatment had it occurred in the United States. . . .

### I

Dillingham pled guilty in April 1984 to criminal charges in Great Britain for possessing marijuana and cocaine, paying a £50 fine. As a first-time offender convicted of a minor controlled substance offense, Dillingham's conviction was later expunged pursuant to Great Britain's Rehabilitation of Offenders Act of

---

1. Throughout this opinion, we use the term "expungement" to refer generally to the effect of a rehabilitative statute on a prior conviction — regardless of whether, as a procedural matter, the statute allows for a deferral of the conviction itself, such that no judgment is ever entered (as under the [Federal First Offender Act]), or a judgment of conviction is entered but later removed from the books (as under various state rehabilitative statutes, as well as the British statute at issue in this case).

1974. Under the terms of the Act, a conviction is treated as "spent" if an offender complies with his sentence and is not convicted of a subsequent offense within five years. In such cases, the statute requires that the offender be treated "for all purposes in law as a person who has not committed or been charged with or prosecuted for or convicted of or sentenced for the offense," except that any penalty resulting from the conviction that extends beyond the five-year period is unaffected, and evidence of the conviction may be introduced in a subsequent criminal proceeding.

In September 1991, seven years after his drug conviction (and two years after his rehabilitation), Dillingham married his U.S.-citizen wife. Although his conviction rendered him inadmissible to the United States under [the Immigration and Naturalization Act], he was permitted to enter the country in July 1992 on a six-month nonimmigrant visitor visa, pursuant to the waiver provisions of 8 U.S.C. §1182(d)(3)(A). After his authorized period of stay had expired, Dillingham applied for adjustment of status to legal permanent resident on May 13, 1993, pursuant to an immediate relative visa petition filed by his wife. The INS district director in Portland, Oregon, denied his application on September 14, 1993, on the grounds that the British Rehabilitation of Offenders Act was not a counterpart to the Federal First Offender Act ("FFOA"), and that his prior drug conviction therefore rendered him inadmissible. . . .

At his hearing before an Immigration Judge ("IJ") . . . Dillingham cited the [Board of Immigration Appeals' (BIA's) decision in In re Manrique, Interim Decision 3250 (BIA 1995)], in which the Board established a policy of treating aliens who had been convicted of simple possession and rehabilitated under any state's expungement statute equivalently to those who had been convicted and rehabilitated under the FFOA.[5]

On June 13, 1996, the IJ ruled that *Manrique* did not extend to foreign rehabilitation statutes and denied the application for adjustment of status. . . .

On appeal, the BIA (sitting en banc) . . . affirmed the IJ's decision. . . . Specifically, the Board analogized the expungement of Dillingham's prior drug offense to a foreign pardon and declined to recognize it for U.S. immigration purposes. . . .

## IV . . .

### A

As a general rule, the BIA does not recognize expungements of controlled substance offenses for federal immigration purposes. However, in 1970,

---

5. The BIA's decision in *Manrique* followed our holding in Garberding v. INS, 30 F.3d 1187 (9th Cir. 1994), and constituted a reversal of its former policy of not recognizing, for immigration purposes, the effects of state rehabilitation laws that were not the exact counterparts of the FFOA. Under *Manrique,* the BIA created a four-part test for determining when an expungement pursuant to a state rehabilitative statute should be recognized: (1) the alien is a first offender; (2) the alien has pled to or been found guilty of a simple possession offense; (3) the alien has not been accorded first offender treatment under any law; (4) the court has entered an order pursuant to a state rehabilitative statute either deferring or dismissing the criminal proceedings.

Congress carved out a narrow exception for simple possession offenses when it enacted the Federal First Offender Act ("FFOA"). The FFOA, which applies exclusively to first-time drug offenders who are guilty only of simple possession, serves to expunge such convictions (after the successful completion of a probationary period) and was intended to lessen the harsh consequences of certain drug convictions, including their effects on deportation proceedings. Under the FFOA, no legal consequences may be imposed following expungement as a result of the defendant's former conviction. 18 U.S.C. §3607.

In Garberding v. INS, 30 F.3d 1187 (9th Cir. 1994), we rejected on equal protection grounds the BIA's policy that only expungements under exact state counterparts to the FFOA could be recognized in deportation proceedings. We held that this policy was inconsistent with the Constitution's equal protection guarantee, because there was no rational basis for treating two persons found guilty of the identical conduct differently based on the breadth of the rehabilitation statutes in their respective states, when both persons were eligible for relief under their own state's law and both would have been had the state law been an exact counterpart of the federal Act. . . . The Constitution is concerned with the differential treatment of persons not statutes. [Absent] a rational basis (and as long as the FFOA remains extant), the INS may not discriminate against aliens convicted of simple possession offenses whose subsequent conduct would have qualified them for FFOA rehabilitation, but for the fact that they were convicted and rehabilitated under the laws of another sovereign. . . .

### B

We evaluate Dillingham's constitutional challenge according to the requirements of equal protection law. In order to succeed on his challenge, the petitioner must establish that his treatment differed from that of similarly situated persons. Our prior cases dictate that persons similarly situated to petitioner for equal protection purposes are persons convicted of drug offenses based upon conduct for which they would have been eligible for relief under the FFOA, and whose convictions were ultimately expunged by the sovereign that imposed them.

For this reason, we find that the Board's categorical decision not to recognize foreign expungements for simple drug possession offenses did indeed result in differential treatment between the petitioner and persons whose federal and state expungements of identical crimes were honored by the INS. The BIA erred when it found that "the expungement of [Dillingham]'s conviction is akin to a foreign pardon and is therefore ineffective for immigration purposes.". . . By likening foreign expungements of simple drug possession offenses to foreign pardons of crimes of moral turpitude — a category of crimes for which Congress has not enacted a domestic rehabilitation statute analogous to the FFOA — the Board improperly skirted the constitutional issue of differential treatment in this case. . . .

Thus, having found differential treatment, we turn to the question of whether the Board's decision is supported by a rational basis. The government's chief contention is that its policy of not recognizing foreign expungements is justified because of the added administrative difficulty in verifying that an alien's conviction has indeed been validly expunged, and that he or she in fact complied with the requirements of the foreign expungement statute such that the alien also would have qualified for relief under the FFOA. The Supreme Court has held, however, that in cases where the petitioner's interest is substantial and the government's interest in putting forth the policy in question is unquantifiable or de minimis, such a policy cannot withstand even rational basis review. . . .

The private liberty interests involved in deportation proceedings are indisputably substantial. [Yet the BIA would] establish, by way of its decision in this case, an irrebuttable presumption against the validity of all foreign expungements — irrespective of where the offense in question occurred; how comparable to ours the system of criminal justice (including the operation of the expungement law) may be; and what degree of evidence verifying the expungement the alien may present.

[Although] procedure by presumption is always cheaper and easier than individualized determination, we find that the government's interest in administrative convenience is insufficient to establish a rational basis for its categorical dismissal of foreign expungements. Indeed, we fail to see how the administrative burden of identifying and verifying foreign convictions (which the government already undertakes as a matter of course to determine whether an alien is admissible into the United States) is any different from the incremental burden of verifying foreign expungements — especially in light of the government's failure to provide any evidence in support of this claim in regard to the present case. We accordingly find the government's decision establishing an irrebuttable presumption against the validity of foreign expungements to be unacceptably overbroad, in light of an alien's substantial interest in avoiding deportation, as well as the government's minimal (or nonexistent) incremental burden in verifying that his or her conviction was expunged. Thus, we hold that the government's purported interest in administrative convenience does not constitute a legitimate basis for distinguishing aliens like Dillingham, whose illicit conduct and subsequent rehabilitation occurred on British soil (but who would otherwise have qualified for relief under the FFOA), from aliens whose convictions and expungements took place domestically under state procedures. . . .

FERNANDEZ, J., dissenting.

Dillingham argues that as a matter of constitutional law expungements in all of the countries of the world must be treated in the same manner as expungements within the United States because anything less would violate the principle of equal protection. I disagree.

While Congress could, no doubt, so decree, it is not compelled to do so by the Constitution. As in other equal protection claims, what we must ask is whether there was a rational basis for the choice made here. And in the immigration area [w]e will only overturn a classification if it is "wholly irrational."

I see nothing irrational in a determination that we will not treat aliens who obtain expungement of drug offenses in other countries in the same way that we treat those who obtain expungement of offenses in this country. Of course, under the Federal First Offender Act, 18 U.S.C. §3607, some simple drug possession convictions can be expunged. When they are, they are not used as a predicate for deportation; the Attorney General has so decided. On equal protection grounds, we have extended that to expungements under state laws.

As I see it, that is a far cry from stating that the Attorney General is equally required to treat the expungement statutes from all of the countries of the world in the same manner that he treats the FFOA and, by extension, state expungement statutes. It is no "mere fortuity" that foreign offenders are prosecuted in their own countries and not here. See Paredes-Urrestarazu v. INS, 36 F.3d 801, 812 (9th Cir. 1994). Nor do foreign expungement laws have anything to do with "uniform nationwide application of [our] immigration laws." In fact, foreign countries and their ways are not necessarily, or even particularly, the same as this country and its ways. A much more complex task is placed upon the shoulders of an administrative agency when it is told that it must not only review the varying ways and means of expungements all over the world, but also the full records of aliens who have admittedly committed foreign offenses, not to mention the difficulties that can be encountered in authenticating the accuracy of those records. . . .

That is not to say that it will be impossible to administer a system which requires ranging all over the world in that manner—we know that [people can live] with and administer just about any kind of system, no matter how difficult. But it is to say that it is perfectly rational to decline to undertake that process. . . .

In fine, equal protection does not require the progression we have here: recognition of FFOA expungements, to recognition of similar state statutes, to recognition of all state statutes and, finally, to recognition of enactments all over the world. To say that, does not enisle this country, although it does recognize that we are a separate nation. One world is a fine concept, but it is not a constitutional imperative. Not yet anyway. Thus, I respectfully dissent.


## PROBLEM 11-8.   FIRE WHEN READY

In 1970 a Pennsylvania state court sentenced Philip Rice to probation for a number of felonies involving stolen auto parts. Federal law prohibits a convicted felon whose crime was "punishable by a term exceeding one year" from possessing firearms. Rice would like to get a gun dealer's license, despite this obstacle under federal law.

Another part of the federal felon-in-possession statute grants the Secretary of the Treasury the right to reinstate a former felon's firearms privileges if past good conduct indicates that his disability should be removed. Rice applied for restoration of his firearms privileges, but the Bureau of Alcohol, Tobacco and Firearms refused to consider his application because Congress had not funded that part of its operation since 1992.

Rice decided to petition a federal district court for review since the statute allows him to seek judicial review of the denial of his petition and it empowers the court to hear additional evidence to prevent a miscarriage of justice. What should the court do? See Rice v. United States Dep't of Alcohol, Tobacco and Firearms, 68 F.3d 702 (3d Cir. 1995); but see United States v. McGill, 74 F.3d 64 (5th Cir. 1996).

## NOTES

1. *Expungement and sealing of records.*   While the term "expungement" carries no universally agreed-upon meaning, an expunged criminal record is generally considered to be one that is no longer available to the public. The files documenting the conviction may be physically destroyed or sealed. In the latter case they are frequently available to law enforcement personnel but not to others, such as private employers.

Once a criminal record is expunged, it has limited or no impact on the offender's future prospects. The types of conviction that can be expunged and the ramifications of expungement, however, vary widely by statute. Juvenile records, for example, are automatically expunged in almost all states once the juvenile reaches a particular age. In some states, the ex-offender does not have to reveal expunged convictions on employment applications; in other states, even expunged convictions may limit employment opportunities.

Criminal records may be expunged by administrative or judicial action. Some courts have recognized an inherent judicial power to expunge records, weighing privacy rights against the public's right of access to criminal records.

What purposes do expungement statutes serve? Some argue that ex-offenders should not continually pay for past crimes; others view expungement as a positive reward for a crime-free period. Expungement also restores the offender to the community. Without such statutes, an ever larger number of Americans would have criminal records. See Julian V. Roberts, The Role of Criminal Record in the Sentencing Process, 22 Crime & Just. 303, 356 (1997). Should expungement be available for all offenses? Should some types of crimes — such as drug offenses, sex crimes, and murder — be categorically excluded from expungement? What drawbacks, if any, do you see to expungement of criminal records? Why would Congress create but not fund a provision that would allow for the expungement of a record for a limited purpose, the ability to acquire a gun license?

2. *Prior expunged convictions at sentencing.*   The availability of expungement differs dramatically between the states. As we learned in Chapter 5, an offender's criminal record influences sentencing decisions in both guideline and nonguideline states. Why should a sentencing court not be able to consider the prior conviction of an offender who benefited from a generous expungement statute? Does this scheme provide an inappropriate advantage to this offender? Or does it place at an unfair disadvantage the offender whose prior record could not have been expunged because of a less generous statutory regime?

3. *Foreign convictions and expungement.*   As the *Dillingham* court indicates, foreign countries often have more generous expungement provisions than the United States. Should U.S. courts consider such expungements? Do you see practical problems to such determinations, or are you more concerned about inequities between U.S. and foreign offenders? Should a court be able to consider a foreign expunged conviction at sentencing? Are you more or less concerned about that scenario than about the impact of collateral sanctions (see Chapter 8), as in *Dillingham*?

## 4. *Pardons, Commutations, Clemencies, and Amnesties*

A form of executive review distinct from the parole system takes place when a governor or president considers a pardon or commutation. The history of the pardon power runs quite deep and has constitutional underpinnings. There have been times when the pardon power was a central and functional aspect of criminal justice systems. But the ancient origins of pardons have not insulated them from the same evolutionary developments that have occurred with the parole authority. Indeed, because pardons tend to be more visible, even though they are far less common than grants of parole, they also tend to be far more controversial. Most states give the governor unrestricted clemency power, although a substantial minority give the clemency power to special pardoning boards.

The differences among pardons, commutations, clemencies, and amnesties are slight and more a matter of semantics than of substance. *Clemency* is an umbrella term encompassing pardons, commutations, and amnesties. A *pardon* typically removes all consequences of criminal conviction and may come with strings attached. A *commutation* is a partial pardon, usually reducing a sentence but not erasing such consequences of conviction as voting bars, prohibitions from holding office, and restrictions on future gun ownership. In the United States, *amnesty* is a term often used in the context of war to connote a pardon for a war-related crime.

The number of pardons in states and the federal system has declined dramatically over the past century. Interestingly enough, in death cases more pardons were granted prior to the Supreme Court's decision in *Furman* than after it. In the early to mid-1940s governors pardoned those condemned to death in between one-fifth and one-fourth of all capital cases. In recent years presidents have granted fewer pardons and commutations. President George H. W. Bush granted 38 pardons and 1 commutation during his four-year administration. In contrast, President Ronald Reagan granted 393 pardons and 13 commutations during his eight years in office. Looking back to the 1960s, President Lyndon Johnson granted 960 pardons and 227 commutations in his five years in office. No federal pardons or commutations were granted in 1992 or 1994. In his first term President Obama pardoned only 23 people — a tiny fraction of those who requested pardon review, and an even more infinitesimal fraction of federal offenders. President Obama has probably pardoned more turkeys at Thanksgiving than human beings over four years. Ari Shapiro, Tough Turkey: People Have A Harder Time Getting Pardons Under Obama, National Public Radio (Nov. 20, 2012).

Use of pardons and commutations varies substantially among the states. Pardons are granted for a variety of reasons. They may be granted in cases of miscarriage of justice, including a violation of substantive rules, or in cases in which the accused is proven to be innocent or is deemed highly likely not to have committed the offense. In addition, individuals may be pardoned when the goals of their sentence appear to have been accomplished, such as when they appear to be fully rehabilitated. Pardons are often requested for the purpose of removing certain disabilities that go with a felony conviction, such as loss of voting rights. Occasionally a death sentence is commuted to a life sentence without the possibility of parole, but such commutations have been rare in recent years.

The use of pardons and commutations also reflects changing social perspectives on the seriousness of or justification for various kinds of crimes. Some governors, for example, have pardoned women who killed battering spouses or boyfriends after many years of abuse. At the time the women were convicted, the battered spouse syndrome was not used in their defense, and the governors believed that the women had served enough time for their offenses.

## ‖ U.S. Constitution Art. II, §2, Cl. 1 ‖

The President shall . . . have Power to grant Reprieves and Pardons for Offences against the United States, except in Cases of Impeachment.

## ‖ Alabama Constitution Art. V, §124 ‖

### GOVERNOR; PARDONS AND COMMUTATION OF SENTENCES

The governor shall have power to remit fines and forfeitures, under such rules and regulations as may be prescribed by law; and, after conviction, to grant reprieves, paroles, commutations of sentence, and pardons, except in cases of impeachment. The attorney-general, secretary of state, and state auditor shall constitute a board of pardons, who shall meet on the call of the governor, and before whom shall be laid all recommendations or petitions, for pardon, commutation, or parole, in cases of felony; and the board shall hear them in open session, and give their opinion thereon in writing to the governor, after which or on the failure of the board to advise for more than sixty days, the governor may grant or refuse the commutation, parole, or pardon, as to him seems best for the public interest. He shall communicate to the legislature at each session every remission of fines and forfeitures, and every reprieve, commutation, parole, or pardon, with his reasons therefor, and the opinion of the board of pardons in each case required to be referred, stating the name and crime of the convict, the sentence, its date, and the date of reprieve, commutation, parole, or pardon. Pardons in cases of felony and other offenses involving moral turpitude shall not relieve from civil and political disabilities, unless approved by the board of pardons and specifically expressed in the pardon.

## ‖ Washington Revised Code §9.94A.728 ‖

(5) The governor, upon recommendation from the clemency and pardons board, may grant an extraordinary release for reasons of serious health problems, senility, advanced age, extraordinary meritorious acts, or other extraordinary circumstances; . . .

(7) The governor may pardon any offender; . . .

|| *Ohio Adult Parole Authority v. Eugene Woodard* ||
|| 523 U.S. 272 (1998) ||

REHNQUIST, C.J.

The Ohio Constitution gives the Governor the power to grant clemency upon such conditions as he thinks proper. The Ohio General Assembly cannot curtail this discretionary decision-making power, but it may regulate the application and investigation process. The General Assembly has delegated in large part the conduct of clemency review to petitioner Ohio Adult Parole Authority.

In the case of an inmate under death sentence, the Authority must conduct a clemency hearing within 45 days of the scheduled date of execution. Prior to the hearing, the inmate may request an interview with one or more parole board members. Counsel is not allowed at that interview. The Authority must hold the hearing, complete its clemency review, and make a recommendation to the Governor, even if the inmate subsequently obtains a stay of execution. If additional information later becomes available, the Authority may in its discretion hold another hearing or alter its recommendation.

Respondent Eugene Woodard was sentenced to death for aggravated murder committed in the course of a carjacking. His conviction and sentence were affirmed on appeal. When respondent failed to obtain a stay of execution more than 45 days before his scheduled execution date, the Authority commenced its clemency investigation. It informed respondent that he could have a clemency interview on Sept. 9, 1994, if he wished, and that his clemency hearing would be on Sept. 16, 1994.

Respondent did not request an interview. Instead, he objected to the short notice of the interview and requested assurances that counsel could attend and participate in the interview and hearing. When the Authority failed to respond to these requests, respondent filed suit in United States District Court on September 14, alleging that Ohio's clemency process violated his Fourteenth Amendment right to due process and his Fifth Amendment right to remain silent. . . .

Respondent argues first . . . that there is a life interest in clemency broader in scope than the "original" life interest adjudicated at trial and sentencing. This continuing life interest, it is argued, requires due process protection until respondent is executed. . . .

In Connecticut Bd. of Pardons v. Dumschat, 452 U.S. 458 (1981), an inmate claimed Connecticut's clemency procedure violated due process because the Connecticut Board of Pardons failed to provide an explanation for its denial of his commutation application. The Court held that "an inmate has no constitutional or inherent right to commutation of his sentence." It noted that, unlike probation decisions, "pardon and commutation decisions have not traditionally been the business of courts; as such, they are rarely, if ever, appropriate subjects for judicial review." The Court relied on its prior decision in Greenholtz v. Inmates of Neb. Penal and Correctional Complex, 442 U.S. 1 (1979), where it rejected the claim "that a constitutional entitlement to release [on parole] exists independently of a right explicitly conferred by the State." The individual's interest in release or commutation "is indistinguishable from the initial resistance to being confined," and that interest has already been extinguished by the conviction and sentence. The Court therefore concluded that a petition for commutation, like an appeal for clemency, "is simply a unilateral hope."

Respondent's claim of a broader due process interest in Ohio's clemency proceedings is barred by *Dumschat*. The process respondent seeks would be inconsistent with the heart of executive clemency, which is to grant clemency as a matter of grace, thus allowing the executive to consider a wide range of factors not comprehended by earlier judicial proceedings and sentencing determinations. . . .

The reasoning of *Dumschat* did not depend on the fact that it was not a capital case. The distinctions accorded a life interest to which respondent and the dissent point are primarily relevant to trial. And this Court has generally rejected attempts to expand any distinctions further. . . . The Court's analysis in *Dumschat*, moreover, turned, not on the fact that it was a non-capital case, but on the nature of the benefit sought: "In terms of the Due Process Clause, a Connecticut felon's expectation that a lawfully imposed sentence will be commuted or that he will be pardoned is no more substantial than an inmate's expectation, for example, that he will not be transferred to another prison; it is simply a unilateral hope." A death row inmate's petition for clemency is also a "unilateral hope." The defendant in effect accepts the finality of the death sentence for purposes of adjudication, and appeals for clemency as a matter of grace.

Respondent also asserts that as in *Greenholtz*, Ohio has created protected interests by establishing mandatory clemency application and review procedures. . . . Ohio's clemency procedures do not violate due process. Despite the Authority's mandatory procedures, the ultimate decisionmaker, the Governor, retains broad discretion. Under any analysis, the Governor's executive discretion need not be fettered by the types of procedural protections sought by respondent. There is thus no substantive expectation of clemency. . . .

Respondent also . . . claims that under the rationale of Evitts v. Lucey, 469 U.S. 387 (1985), clemency is an integral part of Ohio's system of adjudicating the guilt or innocence of the defendant and is therefore entitled to due process protection. Clemency, he says, is an integral part of the judicial system because it has historically been available as a significant remedy, its availability impacts earlier stages of the criminal justice system, and it enhances the reliability of convictions and sentences. Respondent further suggests that *Evitts* established a due process continuum across all phases of the judicial process.

In *Evitts*, the Court held that there is a constitutional right to effective assistance of counsel on a first appeal as of right. This holding, however, was expressly based on the combination of two lines of prior decisions [indicating] that a criminal defendant has a right to effective assistance of counsel on a first appeal as of right.

The Court did not thereby purport to create a new "strand" of due process analysis. And it did not rely on the notion of a continuum of due process rights. Instead, the Court evaluated the function and significance of first appeal as of right, in light of prior cases. Related decisions similarly make clear there is no continuum requiring varying levels of process at every conceivable phase of the criminal system. Murray v. Giarratano, 492 U.S. 1, 9-10 (1989) (no right to counsel for capital inmates in state postconviction proceedings).

An examination of the function and significance of the discretionary clemency decision at issue here readily shows it is far different from the first appeal of right at issue in *Evitts*. Clemency proceedings are not part of trial — or even the adjudicatory process. They do not determine the guilt or innocence of the defendant, and are not intended primarily to enhance the reliability of the trial process. They are conducted by the Executive Branch, independent of direct appeal and collateral relief proceedings. . . . And they are usually discretionary, unlike the more structured and limited scope of judicial proceedings. While traditionally available to capital defendants as a final and alternative avenue of relief, clemency has not traditionally been the business of courts. . . .

Thus, clemency proceedings are not "an integral part of the . . . system for finally adjudicating the guilt or innocence of a defendant," *Evitts*, 469 U.S. at 393. Procedures mandated under the Due Process Clause should be consistent with the nature of the governmental power being invoked. Here, the executive's clemency authority would cease to be a matter of grace committed to the executive authority if it were constrained by the sort of procedural requirements that respondent urges. Respondent is already under a sentence of death, determined to have been lawfully imposed. If clemency is granted, he obtains a benefit; if it is denied, he is no worse off than he was before. . . .

Respondent also [argues] that the provision of a voluntary inmate interview, without the benefit of counsel or a grant of immunity for any statements made by the inmate, implicates the inmate's Fifth and Fourteenth Amendment right not to incriminate himself. . . .

The Fifth Amendment protects against compelled self-incrimination. [We] do not think that respondent's testimony at a clemency interview would be "compelled" within the meaning of the Fifth Amendment. It is difficult to see how a voluntary interview could "compel" respondent to speak. . . .

A defendant who takes the stand in his own behalf may be impeached by proof of prior convictions without violation of the Fifth Amendment privilege. A defendant whose motion for acquittal at the close of the Government's case is denied must then elect whether to stand on his motion or to put on a defense, with the accompanying risk that in doing so he will augment the Government's case against him. In each of these situations, there are undoubted pressures — generated by the strength of the Government's case against him — pushing the criminal defendant to testify. But it has never been suggested that such pressures constitute "compulsion" for Fifth Amendment purposes. . . .

Here, respondent has the same choice of providing information to the Authority — at the risk of damaging his case for clemency or for postconviction relief — or of remaining silent. But this pressure to speak in the hope of improving his chance of being granted clemency does not make the interview compelled. We therefore hold that the Ohio clemency interview, even on assumptions most favorable to respondent's claim, does not violate the Fifth Amendment privilege against compelled self-incrimination.

O'CONNOR, J., concurring in part and concurring in the judgment.
. . . When a person has been fairly convicted and sentenced, his liberty interest, in being free from such confinement, has been extinguished. But it is incorrect . . . to say that a prisoner has been deprived of all interest in his life before his execution. Thus, although it is true that pardon and commutation

decisions have not traditionally been the business of courts, and that the decision whether to grant clemency is entrusted to the Governor under Ohio law, I believe that . . . some minimal procedural safeguards apply to clemency proceedings. Judicial intervention might, for example, be warranted in the face of a scheme whereby a state official flipped a coin to determine whether to grant clemency, or in a case where the State arbitrarily denied a prisoner any access to its clemency process.

In my view, however, a remand to permit the District Court to address respondent's specific allegations of due process violations is not required. [Woodard] contends that 3 days' notice of his interview and 10 days' notice of the hearing were inadequate; that he did not have a meaningful opportunity to prepare his clemency application because postconviction proceedings were pending; that his counsel was improperly excluded from the interview and permitted to participate in the hearing only at the discretion of the parole board chair; and that he was precluded from testifying or submitting documentary evidence at the hearing. I do not believe that any of these allegations amounts to a due process violation. The process respondent received, including notice of the hearing and an opportunity to participate in an interview, comports with Ohio's regulations and observes whatever limitations the Due Process Clause may impose on clemency proceedings. . . .

STEVENS, J., concurring in part and dissenting in part.

. . . The text of the Due Process Clause properly directs our attention to state action that may "deprive" a person of life, liberty, or property. When we are evaluating claims that the State has unfairly deprived someone of liberty or property, it is appropriate first to ask whether the state action adversely affected any constitutionally protected interest. [There is] no room for legitimate debate about whether a living person has a constitutionally protected interest in life. He obviously does. . . .

There are valid reasons for concluding that even if due process is required in clemency proceedings, only the most basic elements of fair procedure are required. Presumably a State might eliminate this aspect of capital sentencing entirely, and it unquestionably may allow the executive virtually unfettered discretion in determining the merits of appeals for mercy. Nevertheless, there are equally valid reasons for concluding that these proceedings are not entirely exempt from judicial review. I think, for example, that no one would contend that a governor could ignore the commands of the Equal Protection Clause and use race, religion, or political affiliation as a standard for granting or denying clemency. Our cases also support the conclusion that if a State adopts a clemency procedure as an integral part of its system for finally determining whether to deprive a person of life, that procedure must comport with the Due Process Clause. . . .

The interest in life that is at stake in this case warrants even greater protection than the interests in liberty at stake in [non-capital] cases. For "death is a different kind of punishment from any other which may be imposed in this country. . . . It is of vital importance to the defendant and to the community that any decision to impose the death sentence be, and appear to be, based on reason rather than caprice or emotion." Gardner v. Florida, 430 U.S. 349,

357-358 (1977). Those considerations apply with special force to the final stage of the decisional process that precedes an official deprivation of life. . . .

## NOTES

1. *Due process in clemency procedures?* Though Woodard's claims were rejected, five justices appear to have held that at least some modicum of process is constitutionally required in clemency proceedings. What sorts of "minimum procedural safeguards" do you think are now required? What if a state denies a death row prisoner any hearing and allows its parole board members to vote individually on clemency petitions by fax or phone, without providing any reason for their votes and without even having a meeting to discuss the petition? See Faulder v. Texas Bd. of Pardons and Paroles, 178 F.3d 343, 345 (5th Cir. 1999). What if a lawyer for the state screens information before it reaches the governor so that the ultimate decision maker does not know all the mitigating facts that might justify clemency? See Alan Berlow, The Texas Clemency Memos, Atlantic Monthly (July/August 2003), at 91.

2. *The historical place for clemency.* In Herrera v. Collins, 506 U.S. 390 (1993), a defendant sentenced to death claimed that habeas corpus had to be available as a means of establishing his innocence and thus of obtaining further review of his conviction and sentence after his initial appeals had been exhausted. In the course of rejecting this claim, Chief Justice William Rehnquist discussed the role of clemency in the criminal justice system, particularly as a means to redress wrongful convictions:

> Clemency is deeply rooted in our Anglo-American tradition of law, and is the historic remedy for preventing miscarriages of justice where judicial process has been exhausted.
>
> In England, the clemency power was vested in the Crown and can be traced back to the 700's. Blackstone thought this "one of the great advantages of monarchy in general, above any other form of government; that there is a magistrate, who has it in his power to extend mercy, wherever he thinks it is deserved: holding a court of equity in his own breast, to soften the rigour of the general law, in such criminal cases as merit an exemption from punishment." 4 W. Blackstone, Commentaries *397. Clemency provided the principal avenue of relief for individuals convicted of criminal offenses — most of which were capital — because there was no right of appeal until 1907. It was the only means by which one could challenge his conviction on the ground of innocence.
>
> Our Constitution adopts the British model and gives to the President the "Power to grant Reprieves and Pardons for Offences against the United States." Art. II, §2, cl. 1. . . . The original States were reluctant to vest the clemency power in the executive. And although this power has gravitated toward the executive over time, several States have split the clemency power between the Governor and an advisory board selected by the legislature. Today, all 36 States that authorize capital punishment have constitutional or statutory provisions for clemency.
>
> Executive clemency has provided the "fail safe" in our criminal justice system. It is an unalterable fact that our judicial system, like the human beings who administer it, is fallible. But history is replete with examples of wrongfully convicted persons who have been pardoned in the wake of after-discovered

evidence establishing their innocence. In his classic work, Professor Edwin Borchard compiled 65 cases in which it was later determined that individuals had been wrongfully convicted of crimes. Clemency provided the relief mechanism in 47 of these cases; the remaining cases ended in judgments of acquittals after new trials. Borchard, Convicting the Innocent (1932). Recent authority confirms that over the past century clemency has been exercised frequently in capital cases in which demonstrations of "actual innocence" have been made. See M. Radelet, H. Bedau, and C. Putnam, In Spite of Innocence 282-356 (1992).

In recent years, however, clemency has been granted in substantially fewer cases than was the case prior to the U.S. Supreme Court's 1972 decision declaring the form then used for administering the death penalty unconstitutional. Michael A. G. Korengold et al., And Justice for Few: The Collapse of the Capital Clemency System in the United States, 20 Hamline L. Rev. 349 (1996) (noting that in the United States from 1960 to 1970, 261 people were executed and clemency was granted to 204 death row inmates, whereas from 1985 to 1995, 281 people were executed and only 20 death row inmates were granted clemency). Among the factors accounting for this decline may be a changing political climate that encourages tougher criminal penalties and the erroneous belief that clemency is unnecessary today because death row inmates receive "super due process" in the courts.

3. *Pardon patterns.*   Although many state legislatures require the governor or pardon board to issue reports on pardons every year, there is no readily available information on the number of pardons granted in the states, the basis for particular decisions, or pardon patterns over time. Consider Professor Daniel Kobil's summary of pardons in Ohio:

> At the close of his second term, former Ohio Governor Richard Celeste granted clemency to sixty-eight individuals. Many of the cases were controversial, with Celeste being alternately praised and vilified for reducing the punishments of, among others, twenty-five battered women who had killed or assaulted their purported abusers, eight condemned murderers, a famous country-western singer, and an embezzler of hundreds of thousands of dollars.

Daniel Kobil, Do the Paperwork or Die: Clemency, Ohio Style?, 52 Ohio St. L.J. 655 (1991). The country music star, for fans of such music, was Johnny Paycheck, the creator of the unforgettable song "Take This Job and Shove It." According to a newspaper article, Governor Celeste found the 7-to-9-year sentence for the 1985 shooting of a man in a bar "unbelievably harsh." See Celeste Orders Paycheck Freed, Columbus Dispatch (January 11, 1991), at 5B, col. 1.

4. *Clemency procedures.*   The chief executive traditionally holds the clemency and pardon powers, with little judicial interference. The offender has only limited due process rights, such as the right to notice of the clemency proceeding and the right to be heard at the proceeding.

Nine states require that the governor have a recommendation of clemency from a board or advisory group before granting clemency. In three states the board makes the ultimate decision, and in another three states the governor sits on this board. In the remaining states, the governor is largely responsible for the decisions herself. See generally Death Penalty Information Center, Clemency

Process by State (available at www.deathpenaltyinfo.org/article.php?
did=126&scid=13#process). The setup of clemency procedures influences
the number of clemencies granted. They are more likely to occur when an
administrative board rather than the governor holds clemency authority. Why
do you suppose this is the case?

5. *The effect of a pardon.* Many, and possibly all, nations recognize some
possibility of obtaining a pardon, but the effects of pardons vary. In England, for
example, pardons do not exonerate the accused but merely amount to nonenforcement of the sentence. England also recognizes sentence remissions to
reward prisoners who cooperate with authorities or to release those who are
terminally ill. In the United States a pardon allows a person to hold himself out
as innocent. However, disciplinary boards and professional licensing bodies may
deny professional licenses based on the underlying criminal conduct even after
the offender has received a pardon. See In re William A. Borders, Jr., 797 A.2d
716 (D.C. Ct. App. 2002).

6. *Pardons and politics.* Critics have charged that the number of pardons
and the types of cases in which they are granted depend on the political situation. Governors at the end of their terms seem more inclined to take political
gambles in granting pardons. Charges of influence peddling and outright corruption sometimes crop up in the pardon process. As Helen Prejean recounts,
the former chair of the Louisiana Board of Pardons described some of the
political maneuvering that went on:

> [The governor's chief legal counsel] told me that I knew the governor did not
> like to be confronted with these cases and wanted us to handle it. [This implied
> that the board, out of loyalty to the governor, had to follow the governor's
> decision, independent of their own opinion. Otherwise they would be
> replaced.]
>     [Before] our Board hearings, I'd get the word from the governor's office
> about which deals would go down when the Board met. "The governor wants
> this one or that one," that's what they'd say. [T]here would be cases sometimes,
> where . . . some of the Board members would balk at giving the pardon, and
> [I'd] have to pull them aside and tell them the governor had already committed
> to the pardon and their task was to put it through.

Helen Prejean, Dead Man Walking 171, 173 (1993). Here the pardon board
functioned less to insulate the governor from a difficult decision-making process
than to camouflage the decision already made.

Female governors seem even less inclined than their male counterparts to
issue pardons and commute sentences. How do you account for this disparity?

7. *Women and clemency.* Women receive executive clemency substantially
more often than men. Even though their numbers on death row are already very
small, they benefit disproportionately from gubernatorial commutations of
death sentences. See Michael Heise, Mercy by the Numbers: An Empirical Analysis of Clemency and Its Structure, 89 Va. L. Rev. 239, 275-278 (2003). No longer
is it the case, however, that governors can pardon women or commute their
sentences merely because they are women. Frequently, pardons are granted to
women who killed spouses or boyfriends who allegedly abused them and to
women whose criminal activity stemmed from duress caused by a male figure

in their lives. Nevertheless, governors frequently reserve such pardons and commutations for the very end of their terms in office.

8. *Clemency abroad.* In some western European countries amnesties for entire groups of incarcerated offenders occur regularly. Often they are announced around Christmas. Why do you think such amnesties are not used in the United States?

9. *Compensation after release from wrongful conviction.* In some cases governors have issued pardons when it became clear that an incarcerated offender was innocent of the offense but no judicial recourse remained to overturn his conviction. In such situations most European countries would allow for compensation after release from imprisonment following a wrongful conviction. The same does not hold true in all U.S. states. Moreover, even states that provide for such compensation often strictly limit it. Under New York's Unjust Conviction and Imprisonment Act, for example, the claimant must show by clear and convincing evidence that his conviction was reversed, that he did not commit any of the acts charged, and that he did not by his own conduct cause or bring about his conviction. N.Y. Ct. Cl. Act §8-b (1984). Of the 12 successful claimants in New York — out of 200 claims filed between 1984 and 2002 — the awards ranged from $40,000 to $1.9 million, the latter to compensate for almost 20 years in prison.

---

## Pardon Us: Systematic Presidential Pardons, Charles Shanor and Marc Miller
### 13 Fed. Sent'g Rep. 139 (2001)

Scholars, judges and commentators often emphasize the individualized and mercy-driven nature of the pardon power. . . . We consider whether it is constitutional and appropriate to use the pardon power in a systematic way, applied to a group of offenders selected through consistent criteria and processes, and for reasons that may reflect concerns of justice, equality, and wise policy, rather than mercy.

### 1.   THE CONSTITUTIONALITY OF SYSTEMATIC PARDONS

One constitutional objection might be made to systematic use of the pardon power by a president to further a policy goal. If Congress passes a statute that directs differential penalties for two crimes, and the judiciary implements this law, even upholding its constitutionality in the process, does it violate the separation of powers to allow the president to undo what Congress and the courts have approved?

Of course, the president has an obligation to "take Care that the Laws be faithfully executed." Art. II, §3. However, we do not believe this obligation overrides, much less obliterates, the distinct constitutional power stating that the President "shall have Power to grant Reprieves and Pardons for Offences against the United States, except in Cases of Impeachment." Art II, §2, cl. 1.

Were the "faithful execution" duty extended so far, it would effectively remove the pardon power from the Constitution altogether. This power, explicitly given to the Executive responsible for enforcing the law rather than sharing with Congress, should be viewed as a limited exception to the general duty of the president to faithfully execute the laws. The pardon power qualifies the duty only in connection with enforcement of criminal statutes. It has no bearing on enforcement of regulatory statutes or on private civil actions established by Congress.

Moreover, even as to criminal law statutes, the pardon power operates only as a check on prosecutions or sentences; it in no way alters congressional criminalization of particular behavior. Indeed, because the pardon power is explicit in the Constitution's text, it seems less vulnerable to criticism on separation of powers grounds than the authority of the executive branch, regularly exercised, to decline to prosecute particular cases or to plea bargain for lesser offenses than those recognized by Congress as applicable to particular behaviors. . . .

At least a third of all United States presidents, including many of our greatest presidents, and from the earliest administrations, have used systematic pardons. This long history convinces us that even class-wide pardons, with the potential to dramatically limit the impact of federal criminal laws, are constitutional. . . .

| | | |
|---|---|---|
| 1795 | Washington | Pardoned participants in the Pennsylvania Whiskey Rebellion. . . . |
| 1801 | Jefferson | Pardoned all persons convicted under the Alien and Sedition Acts. . . . |
| 1862-1864 | Lincoln | Granted amnesty to Confederate sympathizers. |
| 1865-1868 | Johnson | Granted amnesty to Confederate soldiers, officials, and sympathizers. . . . |
| 1945 | Truman | Pardoned pre-war convicts who served in the U.S. armed forces during World War II subject to review by presidential board. |
| 1961-1963 | Kennedy | Pardoned offenders sentenced under mandatory minimum penalties of Narcotics Act of 1956. |
| 1974-1975 | Ford | Pardoned Vietnam-era violators of Service Act subject to review by presidential board. |
| 1977 | Carter | Pardoned Vietnam-era violators of the Selective Service Act. |

While a quick review of the historical record makes it difficult to determine the extent to which these were systematic pardons, this review does suggest a history of using the pardon power, not simply as an act of individualized mercy, or as a political tool to reward supporters, but as a tool to reconcile national divisions. . . .

## 2.  Unpardonable and Irregular Pardons

. . . The recent focus on pardon abuse may arise in part from the fact that the federal pardon power has fallen into desuetude. There have been over 20,000 presidential pardons and commutations granted during the twentieth century, and many thousands of additional war-related amnesties falling within the pardon power. However, the vast majority of those pardons occurred before 1980, and the percentage of pardons granted to those sought has been declining steadily for the past 40 years. . . .

| President | Pardons Sought | Pardons Granted | Percent Granted |
| --- | --- | --- | --- |
| Nixon | 2,591 | 923 | 35.6% |
| Ford | 1,527 | 404 | 26.5% |
| Carter | 2,627 | 563 | 21.4% |
| Reagan | 3,404 | 406 | 11.9% |
| Bush | 1,466 | 77 | 5.3% |
| Clinton | 6,622 | 456 | 6.9% |

Looking back even further, around 1300 pardons and commutations were granted in Lyndon Johnson's five years in office (around 31% of requests), and around 600 pardons were granted during John Kennedy's three years (around 36% of requests). . . .

The combination of the recent controversial pardons [at the end of President Clinton's second term] and the highly sporadic use of non-controversial pardons has obscured two important dimensions of the pardon power.

First, when the numbers of pardons are insubstantial, the pardon power offers little possibility for more consistent and substantial executive assessments of sentences. The low and decreasing number of pardons is even more striking in light of [large] size of the federal prison population. . . .

The significance of the small numbers and percentages of pardons in recent years is magnified even further by the fact that, prior to the implementation of the [federal sentencing] guidelines in 1987, all sentences were subject to standardized executive review of the U.S. Parole Commission. It seems that the elimination of the Parole Commission should have led to an increase in the use of presidential pardons, since one of the two major forms of traditional executive post-conviction review and adjustment is no longer available.

Second, the irregular and seemingly random Clinton pardons obscure the possibility of presidents using the pardon power as a principled, systematic policy tool.

### 3. SOME MODERN SYSTEMATIC PARDONS

Presidents have sometimes issued multiple pardons on the same or different dates, and given the same reason for those pardons. Such pardons are not necessarily systematic, unless they are the product of articulated principles applied consistently to an identified group, so that all members of the group who satisfy the principles are pardoned or subject to a standard and reasonably structured process of review.

*Wars.* The most common form of systematic pardons in the twentieth century appear to be amnesty or clemency for those who avoided military service or even opposed the U.S. during a conflict. The most recent illustration of this type of systematic pardon was President Carter's decision to pardon Vietnam-era violators of the Selective Service Act. . . .

*Drugs.*   An example of what may have been systematic, non-wartime, drug offense pardons appears, in brief form, in the Annual Reports of the Attorney General issued during the Kennedy administration. Those reports suggest that there was a large number of pardons or commutations reducing sentences under the Narcotic Control Act of 1956 [which included mandatory minimum sentences of five to thirty years for various drug offenses]. . . .

The 1964 report confirmed that "[as] in the years preceding, the commutations of sentence granted included some long-term narcotics offenders who, by statute, were not eligible for parole but whose sentences were considerably longer than average." The 1964 report also explicitly refers to efforts to make review of pardons and commutations more systematic:

> During the year, the Director of the Bureau of Prisons was called upon to encourage the wardens of the federal prisons to review cases in their institutions and present to the Attorney General selected cases which they considered to be worthy of clemency and whose sentences could be considered disparate. For the first time there is a policy of attempting to systematically review cases which may be deserving of commutation. As a result, a very sizeable increase in commutations has resulted.

While it is not clear whether the Narcotics Act commutations were fully systematic in the sense we suggest, they do combine a statement of principle (disparity) and a suggestion of regularized review to identify similarly situated offenders. . . .

### 4.  WISE USE OF SYSTEMATIC PARDONS

Even if systematic pardons are constitutional, are they a desirable tool for the president compared to other possible strategies available to the executive branch, such as advocating changes in the laws, or changing executive charging, plea, or sentencing policies?

A president might believe that a distinction made by a federal criminal law is unconstitutional. This was the basis for President Jefferson's pardons of those convicted of violating the Alien and Sedition Acts, which Jefferson believed to be unconstitutional. . . . Under the oath of office, the president not only has the power but the duty to apply the commands of the constitution in the exercise of his office.

A president also might use systematic pardons when the constitutionality of the conviction and sentence is abundantly clear. . . . Presidents Truman, Ford, and Carter all believed that a process of amnesty would help to heal the many wounds of war at home. President Kennedy did not suggest that convictions under the mandatory minimum penalties of the Narcotics Act of 1956 were unconstitutional, but he did point to the excessive and unequal sentences imposed under those laws.

As a political matter, a president might hesitate to issue a series of class-wide pardons in the face of Congressional or public criticism. When Lincoln used the pardon power in 1865, he referenced not only his constitutional authority, but also Congressional support for pardoning a large class of southerners "guilty of treason." When Congress had passed laws calling for forfeiture of property by those in rebellion against the Union, it granted the President the authority to grant pardons or amnesty "on such conditions as he may deem expedient for the public welfare." The legislation was perhaps helpful to Lincoln, but it was also unnecessary, for Lincoln could have granted the pardons without it.

Systematic pardons would likely initiate reconsideration of punishment and incarceration policies by Congress. Given the political difficulty of generating rich discussions of criminal justice policy, confident and wise chief executives may be in the best position to generate such debate. Systematic pardons thus offer the chance for a visible and public dialogue about important legal issues. On the other hand, pardons cannot and should not supplant the legislative role on a continuing basis.

## NOTES

1. *Systematic clemencies.*   Perhaps one of the most noteworthy and dramatic examples of the systematic use of the clemency power occurred in January 2003, when outgoing Illinois governor George Ryan granted clemency to all of the 156 death row inmates in Illinois (as well as 11 inmates who were awaiting sentencing or resentencing) in response to the flawed process in Illinois that led to these sentences. (A portion of Governor Ryan's speech announcing his decision is reprinted in Chapter 3.) Note that these grants of clemency did not result in the release of the inmates, since many still faced sentences of life in prison. Governor Ryan also completely pardoned four wrongly convicted death row inmates.

Do you think it is appropriate for governors or presidents to use their pardon and clemency powers systematically? Are such actions an effective way to influence criminal justice or sentencing policy? Should a change in administration and in criminal justice priorities provide a sound basis for considering the systematic use of the pardon power?

2. *Unsystematic pardons.*   Perhaps equally noteworthy and even more controversial than systematic pardons or clemencies are instances in which the pardon power is used in ways that seem particularly unsystematic. Only two hours before surrendering the White House, President Bill Clinton pardoned some persons involved in various scandals that touched the Clinton presidency, along with former Cabinet members, onetime fugitive heiress Patricia Hearst Shaw, and his own brother, Roger Clinton. The number and nature of these pardons not only surpassed the scope of last-minute pardons granted by previous presidents, but also generated widespread public outrage. Both the Senate Judiciary Committee and the House Government Reform Committee scheduled hearings to investigate particularly whether Clinton's pardon of financier Marc Rich was motivated by campaign contributions made by Rich's former wife. For an insightful discussion of these pardons and the lessons to be learned from them, see Margaret Colgate Love, Fear of Forgiving: Rule and Discretion in the Practice

of Pardoning, 13 Fed. Sent'g Rep. 125 (2001). See also Harold Krent, Conditioning the President's Conditional Pardon Power, 89 Cal. L. Rev. 1665 (2001).

3. *The decline in clemency.* The drop in presidential pardons over the past few decades is startling, particularly in view of the dramatic rise in imprisonment rates during the same period (see Chapter 7). How do you explain the decrease in individual pardons? Is the current pardon process fatally flawed, as some have argued? In light of more systematic guideline sentencing, should we increasingly object to unsystematic executive clemency? Have presidents become less courageous? See Margaret Colgate Love, The Twilight of the Pardon Power, 100 Journal Crim. L. & Criminology 1169 (2010). Are there specific and substantive uses of the pardon power that might still be functional and politically defensible? See, e.g., Nora Demleitner, Using the Pardon Power to Prevent Deportation: Legitimate, Desirable, or Neither in a Federal System, 12 Loy. J. Pub. Int. L 365 (2011).

## PROBLEM 11-9.   A CURIOUS COMMUTATION

In July 2007 President George W. Bush exercised his clemency power to commute the 30-month prison term given to former White House aide I. Lewis "Scooter" Libby before he was to start serving this sentence. The prison sentence was imposed in June 2007 after a federal court convicted Libby of perjury, obstruction of justice, and lying to investigators in the course of a special counsel's investigation of possible White House involvement in the leak of the name of a CIA operative. Here is part of the statement made by President Bush in support of his decision:

> From the very beginning of the investigation into the leaking of Valerie Plame's name, I made it clear to the White House staff and anyone serving in my administration that I expected full cooperation with the Justice Department. Dozens of White House staff and administration officials dutifully cooperated.
>
> After the investigation was under way, the Justice Department appointed United States Attorney for the Northern District of Illinois Patrick Fitzgerald as a special counsel in charge of the case. Mr. Fitzgerald is a highly qualified, professional prosecutor who carried out his responsibilities as charged.
>
> This case has generated significant commentary and debate. Critics of the investigation have argued that a special counsel should not have been appointed, nor should the investigation have been pursued after the Justice Department learned who leaked Ms. Plame's name to columnist Robert Novak. Furthermore, the critics point out that neither Mr. Libby nor anyone else has been charged with violating the Intelligence Identities Protection Act or the Espionage Act, which were the original subjects of the investigation. Finally, critics say the punishment does not fit the crime: Mr. Libby was a first-time offender with years of exceptional public service and was handed a harsh sentence based in part on allegations never presented to the jury.
>
> Others point out that a jury of citizens weighed all the evidence and listened to all the testimony and found Mr. Libby guilty of perjury and obstructing justice. They argue, correctly, that our entire system of justice relies on people telling the truth. And if a person does not tell the truth, particularly if he serves in government and holds the public trust, he must be held accountable. They say that had Mr. Libby only told the truth, he would have never been indicted in the first place.

Both critics and defenders of this investigation have made important points. I have made my own evaluation. In preparing for the decision I am announcing today, I have carefully weighed these arguments and the circumstances surrounding this case.

Mr. Libby was sentenced to 30 months of prison, two years of probation and a $250,000 fine. In making the sentencing decision, the district court rejected the advice of the probation office, which recommended a lesser sentence and the consideration of factors that could have led to a sentence of home confinement or probation.

I respect the jury's verdict. But I have concluded that the prison sentence given to Mr. Libby is excessive. Therefore, I am commuting the portion of Mr. Libby's sentence that required him to spend 30 months in prison.

My decision to commute his prison sentence leaves in place a harsh punishment for Mr. Libby. The reputation he gained through his years of public service and professional work in the legal community is forever damaged. His wife and young children have also suffered immensely. He will remain on probation. The significant fines imposed by the judge will remain in effect. The consequences of his felony conviction on his former life as a lawyer, public servant and private citizen will be long-lasting.

The Constitution gives the president the power of clemency to be used when he deems it to be warranted. It is my judgment that a commutation of the prison term in Mr. Libby's case is an appropriate exercise of this power.

Is there something unique (and uniquely troubling) about a president's decision to use his clemency power to mitigate the sentence of an executive branch official convicted of an offense during a criminal investigation into suspect activities taking place within that president's administration? Should Congress have some means (short of initiating the process for a constitutional amendment) to oversee or regulate the use of clemency powers that may appear to be part of an effort to cover up activities of high-ranking executive branch officials?

Also, in light of all the materials in this text, are the president's stated reasons for this commutation in harmony with prevailing modern sentencing doctrines? Are they convincing?

# Table of Cases

# Table of Statutes, Rules, and Guidelines

# Index

Minor participant, 302, 304-307
Multiple counts, 173, 294-302
Multiplicity, 300

Native Peoples, 754-771
Net widening, 653, 666, 672, 802-803, 815

Offender characteristics, 177-178, 326-336
Offense characteristics, 172-173, 177, 398-401,
    415-428, 439-441

Pardons. *See* executive clemency.
Parole
    boards, 81, 83, 85-86, 97, 142, 888-890,
        897-900
    conditions, 900-904
    guidelines, 97, 890-897
    procedures, 898
    revocation, 893, 904, 907-908
Parsimony, 7
Perjury, 292, 392, 489
Plea bargains
    acceptance of responsibility, 381-392, 424, 503,
        504
    functions, 387
    guidelines, 158, 390, 492-493, 507
    influence on sentence, 293, 721
    prosecutorial policies, 487-492
Police, 81-82, 618
Politics, 64-70, 369-370, 575, 579, 616, 931
Presentence investigation/reports, 89, 90, 281,
    528-534, 537, 542
Prior convictions. *See* criminal history.
Prisons and jails
    capacity, 555
    deterrence of crime, 577-578
    non-U.S. imprisonment, 568-569
    origins, 553-554
    race, 592-593
    security levels, 554-555
    stability of punishment hypothesis, 559
    trends in usage, 555-558
    violence, 587
    women, 593-595, 783
Probation, 646-652
Probation officers, 90, 294, 527-543
Probation violations, 646
Procedures, sentencing
    confrontation, 451-452
    hearings, 543-548
    rules of evidence, 87, 451
    standard of proof, 449-450
Proportionality
    constitutional, 314
    extraditions, 615
    fines, 626-631
    foreign jurisdictions, 615
    internal consistency, 613-614
    juveniles, 600
    punishment/sentencing, 56, 150, 627
    state law, 603
Prosecutorial policies, 482-493
Public safety, 158, 480-482, 620-622, 648-649
Public sentiment, 71-78

Purposes of punishment
    choice among, 463-464
    consequentialist, 2
    crime and social policies, 580-584
    deontological, 2
    deterrence, 12-13, 67, 106
    historical development, 7, 33
    implicit purposes, 26
    incapacitation, 2, 14-15, 106, 554, 578-579
    limiting retributivism, 8-9
    multiple purposes, 3, 9
    parsimony, 7
    rehabilitation, 4-5, 16-17, 145-147
    restorative, 18-19, 24-25
    retribution, 2, 8, 15-16
    stated purposes, 3-36

Quantity of drugs, 105, 334, 342, 343

Real offense sentencing, 281-293
Recidivism, 41, 655, 668, 705, 786
Registration of offenders, 688-706
Rehabilitation, 16-17, 145-147
Relevant conduct, 158, 282-294, 344, 484
Religion, 347, 401, 413
Remorse, 383, 390-391
Resource constraints, 68-70
Restitution, 4, 6, 7, 11, 375, 415, 427, 471, 528,
    626, 627, 631-632
Restorative justice, 18-19, 24-25, 665, 670, 762, 764
Retribution, 15-16, 106, 232
Role in group offense, 302-307
    aggravating role, 302
    minimal participant, 173, 302, 304
    minor participant, 302, 304
    mitigating role, 302

Safety valve, 380-381, 613
Sentencing circles, 18-25
Sentencing commission
    composition, 166
    state development, 119-120, 148-154,
        160, 161
Sentencing guidelines
    accomplishments, 158
    amendments, 154, 164, 167, 205-206
    departures, 136, 153-155, 169-170, 178-181,
        188
    federal. *See* federal sentencing guidelines.
    goals, 156-158, 161
Sex offenders
    registration and notification, 688-690
    residency restrictions, 688, 703-705
Shaming sanctions, 653, 657, 663-664
Socioeconomic status, 65, 140, 164, 400-401,
    754-759
Standard of proof, 449-450, 829
Standard of review, 198, 383, 418, 420, 853
State prison population, 582, 616-617
Statistics, 34-36, 553, 652, 731-732, 756-757,
    904-907
Statutory interpretation, 336
Substantial assistance, 109, 111, 170, 181-184, 307,
    393-395, 397-398, 496, 503,

cultural baggage of the first immigrants to cross the Bering Straits. The extremely wide distribution of the concept suggests great time depth, rather than diffusion. Additionally, the ideas are simply and readily adaptable to the further elaborations through time seen in American Indian cosmologies—for example, the four quadrants of the ritual calendar, the four world trees, the four colors of ceremonial corn, and so forth.

While all Mesoamerican Indian groups viewed the world this way, the association of a specific color with a specific direction was regionally variable. Perhaps best known is the Maya scheme, in which east was red, west black, north white, south yellow, and the center blue-green (Marcus 1973); among the Mixtec, the colors red, black (or yellow), white, and blue-green were used, but the directional associations varied (Nowotny 1970).

The sixteenth-century Valley Zapotec resembled the Maya in that the fourfold division of the universe was mirrored in a fourfold division of the 260-day ritual calendar; each quarter of the sacred "year" was a *cocijo* or "lightning." Similarly, there were four *chacs* or "lightnings" among the Maya, each associated with one of the four color-directions. It is very difficult to reconstruct the color associations of the sixteenth-century Zapotec, but fortunately, some vestiges have persisted to the present day. In the Zapotec sierra south of Miahuatlán, several communities studied by Weitlaner and de Cicco (1962) still believe in four "lightnings" that reside on certain hills oriented to the major world directions. These four directions are associated with colors, and these in turn are symbolized during ritual by the use of five kinds of flowers: East—black flower; West—white flower; North—green flower; South—yellow flower; and Midday (center?)—blue flower.[2]

## SUMMARY

Without attempting to be too specific, we would be willing to guess that the Proto-Otomangueans bequeathed to their cultural descendants (1) a view of the world as divided into four quarters, each associated with a color and one of four "lightnings"; (2) a set of directional terms based on the east-west path of the sun; (3) a concept of "vital force" from which the Zapotec *pèe* and Mixtec *ini* developed; (4) a set of great supernatural forces including lightning (or lightning-rain), clouds, thunder, fire, wind, and earthquake, which were not "gods" in our sense; (5) a single word for "day," "time," and possibly "sun"; (6) an animal classifier prefix, and a division into animals walking on four legs, flying, or swimming; (7) a single word for "plant," "wood," and "tree"; (8) classification of plants into "harvestable" or "edible" versus "useless" varieties; (9) a complex technology for plant and animal utilization, including the atlatl, lance, metate, mortar, net, basket, snare, fire-drill, and roasting pit; (10) a language which used tone to distinguish between otherwise similar words; and (11) as discussed more fully in Topic 8, some simple form of bilateral kinship organization. It is on this simple yet amazingly durable legacy that the later Cloud People were to build.

[2]This is obviously an acculturated ritual, since the Precolumbian Zapotec would not have distinguished blue from green. See Marcus and Flannery 1978.

# The Formative Village and the Roots of Divergence

## Editors' Introduction

The establishment of sedentary village life was a crucial period in the divergent evolution of the Cloud People. As we suggested in the preceding chapter, it probably accelerated the separation of various Otomanguean languages by diminishing contacts between some widely scattered peoples, and by increasing some local populations to the point where regional endogamy was possible. This possibility is supported by the extraordinary number of linguistic divisions that are thought to have taken place between 2100 and 1300 B.C. in glottochronological years (1500–995 B.C. in radiocarbon years). Cuicatec is believed to have diverged from Mixtec of the Cuyamecalco region; Amuzgo diverged from the same branch of Mixtec; Trique split off from the Costa Chica dialect of Mixtec; and Mixe is thought to have split off from Zoque (see Topic 2). In archaeological terms, these divergences mean that a great deal of regionalization must have been taking place during the Tierras Largas and San José phases of the Valley of Oaxaca, the Early Cruz phase of the Mixteca Alta, and the Ajalpan phase of the Tehuacán Valley.

One aspect of this process was a great change in territorial organization. Highland Oaxaca was composed of riverine valleys, separated by mountain ranges rich in wild foods. As long as man was a hunter–gatherer, those mountains were one of his main habitats, and he crossed them with frequency to share food and exchange genes with the people in the next valley. As soon as he became a village-based agriculturalist, his main interest focused on the alluvial valleys and their water resources, and the mountains became a barrier between farming areas. This change was only reinforced when

improvements such as permanent houses, storage pits, wells, or irrigation canals were made at certain places in the valley. So far as we can tell from the ethnohistoric and ethnographic records, the Zapotec and Mixtec did not share these improved valley lands with their neighbors, as hunters and gatherers typically share the resources of an oak-forested mountain range. They were prepared to defend them—by force if necessary—and they established their right to them through the burial there of their ancestors, the construction of shrines and temples, and the designation of sacred landmarks.

We will not spend a great deal of time on the early village period in Oaxaca, since it is partially covered in a recent book (Flannery [ed.] 1976). We attempt to outline in this chapter the 1500-year evolution that led up to the origins of the state in Oaxaca. Beginning with an egalitarian society residing in tiny hamlets, Oaxaca saw the growth of ranked societies and a complex settlement system including both hamlets and large villages. Evolution proceeded at different rates in different areas, and the Mixteca and the Valley of Oaxaca diverged in several ways. For the first time in the archaeological sequence, regional differences in ceramic complexes make it possible to draw tentative cultural boundaries between areas which had looked homogenous during the Preceramic period.

The cultural legacy of the Formative was enormous. Almost all the basic skills of village life—weaving, pottery making, adobe manufacture, stone masonry, and so on—were well established during that period. Many aspects of Oaxacan religion described by the sixteenth-century Span-

41

iards—ancestor worship, ritual bloodletting, human sacrifice, and more—had their roots in the Formative period. Most techniques of Otomanguean agriculture, as outlined in Topic 94, originated before the end of the Formative. Moreover, it was during the Formative period that adaptations to

minor environmental differences between the Mixteca Alta and the Valley of Oaxaca first became apparent. These differences were reflected in farming methods, settlement patterns, and population growth, starting the two areas on their long, divergent path.

## TOPIC 10
## The Espiridión Complex and the Origins of the Oaxacan Formative

JOYCE MARCUS

The oldest ceramics thus far recovered from the Valley of Oaxaca come from stratigraphic Zone H in Area C at San José Mogote, in the central Etla Valley. They were associated with the remains of a small wattle-and-daub house (House 20) which was probably one of the first built in Area C, its wall posts having been set in bedrock.

The small sample of sherds, numbering only 262, is entirely without paint, slip, or plastic decoration. It includes a series of jar rims, jar shoulders, and body sherds virtually indistinguishable from those of Purrón Plain (MacNeish, Peterson, and Flannery 1970:22), and hence assigned by us to that type.[1] It also features a previously undescribed type, Espiridión Thin, consisting entirely of hemispherical bowls whose walls are no more than 2–2.5 mm thick (Figure 3.1e). The best-represented type, however, is Tierras Largas Burnished Plain; the collection is made up of undecorated jars and hemispherical bowls. The entire sample of sherds from Zone H is irregularly fired, and grades in color from buff or tan to pinkish or mahogany brown. In addition, there is one small crude figurine head which seems to represent a feline.

Clearly, the Espiridión complex finds its closest ceramic parallels with the Purrón Phase ceramics from levels K and K[1] at Purrón Cave in the Tehuacán Valley (MacNeish, Peterson, and Flannery 1970). Unfortunately, the Purrón Cave collection is even smaller than that from San José Mogote, numbering 127 sherds. Thus it can truthfully be said that this entire ceramic "horizon," if it can be dignified by such a term, is known throughout the Oaxaca–Puebla area from a total of 389 sherds. We have therefore given the Espiridión collection only the status of a ceramic complex, rather than a true archaeological phase.

Our first instinct was simply to call the collection Purrón rather than to invent a new name for it. The Espiridión collection, however, lacks the *tecomate* shape seen at Purrón Cave, while the Purrón collection lacks Espiridión Thin bowls. For this reason we decided to keep the two complexes separate, although they could certainly be combined in the future if larger collections show the present differences to be due only to sampling error. Our strong suspicion, however, is that for this time period it is extremely unlikely that we will find a true stylistic "horizon" of pottery such as oc-

curred at later stages of the Formative. It seems more likely that each valley was experimenting with the techniques of pottery making, that some villages already had ceramics while others did not, and that no two valleys (indeed, perhaps no two sites) will show identical pottery complexes. It also seems unlikely to us that these early potters were trying to make as many "types" as we (and MacNeish) have defined for the period. On one conceptual level Purrón Coarse, Ajalpan Coarse, Purrón Plain, Ajalpan Plain, and Tierras Largas Burnished Plain are just a collection of bowls and jars with minor variations, made from the same kinds of piedmont clays that formed *in situ* above the ancient metamorphic rocks of the Oaxaca–Puebla region.

As for the origins of ceramics in Oaxaca, we have only the

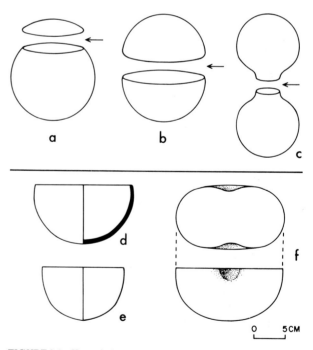

FIGURE 3.1. Vessel shapes of the Purrón and Espiridión complexes: possible prototypes for the (a) *tecomate*, (b) hemispherical bowl, and (c) jar, achieved by cross-sectioning gourds (see text); reconstructions of (d) Purrón Plain bowl and (e) Espiridión Thin bowl, (f) Tierras Largas phase bowl with dimples suggesting gourd stem scars.

---

[1] Richard S. MacNeish examined these sherds in August 1978 and agreed with our assessment.

following observations. We do not see in our material, as some Mesoamericanists have seen in theirs, compelling evidence that pottery making arrived from Asia or South America. Obviously, the technique of making vessels from fired clay may have been introduced from outside Oaxaca, but the shapes need not have been. Every vessel shape known from the Purrón or Espiridión complexes can be seen as one way or another of cross-sectioning a bottle gourd, one of the oldest containers known from Preceramic Oaxaca. Cut off the upper fifth of a spherical gourd, and you have a *tecomate* (Figure 3.1a). Cut one in half, and you have two hemispherical bowls (Figure 3.1b). Cut in half the typical wasp-waisted water-carrying gourd of Oaxaca, and you have a jar (Figure 3.1c). Most early Oaxacan pottery is press-molded (William O. Payne, personal communication, 1970) and there is not a single bowl from the Purrón–Espiridión collections that could not be explained as the result of press-molding a clay vessel inside (or outside) a gourd. Indeed, most Espiridión Thin bowls would, from a distance, appear indistinguishable from a jícara (Figure 3.1b,e). Some hemispherical bowls from the subsequent Tierras Largas phase provide further evidence for this relationship: the bowls have dimples at the rim on opposite sides of the vessel, right where one would expect them if the vessel were press-molded inside a gourd that had been cross-sectioned through the stem scars (Figure 3.1f).

At this writing, no radiocarbon dates are available for the Espiridión complex, so its dating is inferential. No actual Tierras Largas phase date has so far exceeded 1400 B.C. (see Drennan, this volume, Appendix). No actual Purrón phase radiocarbon date has exceeded 1925 B.C. (see Topic 6). The Espiridión complex should thus fall somewhere in the 1900 to 1400 B.C. span, but exactly where is anyone's guess.

# TOPIC 11
## The Tierras Largas Phase and the Analytical Units of the Early Oaxacan Village

KENT V. FLANNERY

## INTRODUCTION

The first period in the prehistory of the Valley of Oaxaca to be characterized by a widespread and universally recognizable ceramic complex is the Tierras Largas phase (1400–1150 B.C.). The principal vessel shapes of the Tierras Largas phase are jars and hemispherical bowls, with *tecomates* and flat-based, outleaned-wall bowls constituting a minor element. While some vessels are undecorated buff to brown (Tierras Largas Burnished Plain), many hemispherical bowls are decorated with a red band at the rim, red parallel stripes, or red chevrons (Avelina Red-on-buff). Some large jars are slipped completely red (Matadamas Red) or completely orange (Matadamas Orange). Another characteristic form of decoration is zoned, dentate rocker-stamping on *tecomates* or outleaned-wall bowls.

Tierras Largas phase sites occur throughout the Valley of Oaxaca, from San Lázaro Etla in the north to Santa Ana Tlapacoyan in the south, and from Zaachila in the west to Mitla in the east. There are currently at least 17 permanent settlements known from survey (Fisch 1978; Feinman and Kowalewski 1979), and the number should eventually rise to more than 20 when intensive surveys are completed. With a single exception—San José Mogote—all those for which population estimates are available were hamlets of 10 households or fewer (cf. Marcus 1976b:Table 3.9). In addition, Tierras Largas phase salt makers evidently visited the saline spring at Fábrica San José, where they broke a few pots, but there is no evidence they actually lived there (Drennan 1976b:74). There are also some Tierras Largas phase sherds from Zone B of Cueva Blanca, a cave near Mitla, suggesting a brief visit by villagers from the latter site.

Of the areas of the valley so far intensively surveyed, the Etla region was the most densely occupied, with six permanent settlements in an area of 200 km² (Feinman and Kowalewski 1979). Five of these were very small hamlets, but San José Mogote was already a small village with lime-plastered public buildings at this time (Topic 13). Surface remains at the latter site consist of 10 discrete scatters of Tierras Largas phase sherds, varying between 0.1 and 1.6 ha each, and totaling 7.8 ha (Fisch 1978). Four of these scatters fall within the area excavated during seven field seasons by Flannery and Marcus, estimated by Fisch at 2.0 ha; five of the six remaining surface scatters lie in areas never excavated. While the area with Tierras Largas phase surface sherds has almost certainly been increased through the use of early fill in later buildings, not all of the remaining scatters can be explained in this way. San José Mogote at this period is therefore reconstructed as a community with an estimated 147 persons (Fisch 1978) occupying 10 small residential areas, strung out over a horseshoe-shaped area of piedmont spur and sharing a public building. Thus, while the residential pattern is "dispersed" at the household level, it shows "clustering" relative to the rest of the valley, and suggests the rise of San José Mogote as a center of regional significance as early as 1150 B.C. Figure 3.2 suggests the centrality of San José Mogote to the other sites in the Etla region, none of which appears to have had any public buildings on the basis of present data.

A total of only 9 to 10 small, dispersed occupations were found in the remaining areas intensively surveyed, the 801-

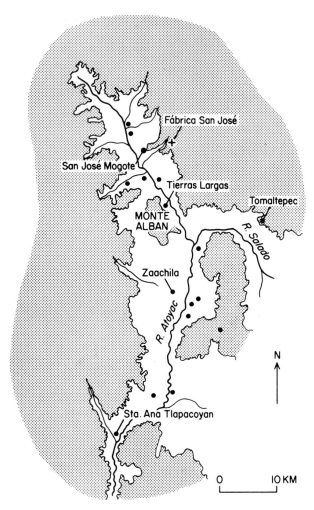

FIGURE 3.2. Tierras Largas phase sites in the Etla, Central, and Zaachila–Zimatlán regions of the Valley of Oaxaca according to Feinman and Kowalewski (1979) and Varner (1974). Black circles are villages or hamlets; plus signs are camps or ephemeral occupations.

km² Central and Zaachila–Zimatlán valleys; it seems likely that these were all hamlets of only 3 to 10 households. Feinman and Kowalewski (1979) have estimated the total population of this area to be approximately 125 persons, giving the Central and Zaachila–Zimatlán regions a population density of 0.16 persons per km². Thus, there may have been more people living at San José Mogote than in the entire central and southwestern regions of the valley. Kowalewski has estimated the total population of the western valley (Etla, Central, and Zaachila–Zimatlán survey areas) at approximately 425 persons.

Wherever excavations have been carried out, the subsistence base of the Tierras Largas phase seems to have involved the growing of maize (accompanied by, and perhaps interplanted with, teosinte); the cultivation of avocados and other domesticates; the collection of wild plants from the piedmont and mountains; and the hunting of deer, cottontail, and other game.

To the north, the earliest known stage of the Cruz phase in the Yanhuitlán–Nochixtlán Valley is very similar to Tierras Largas. Sherds from area K 203 on the site of Yucuita, excavated by Spores (Topic 12), are so similar as to suggest near identity with samples from the Etla region. Farther away, the early Ajalpan phase of the Tehuacán Valley shows strong similarities, although the peak popularity of red-on-buff hemispherical bowls there (Coatepec Red-on-buff) seems to fall later in time; also, tall-necked bottles slipped with specular hematite are more common in Tehuacán than in Oaxaca (MacNeish, Peterson, and Flannery 1970:Fig. 12). These similarities and differences allow us to suggest that the Cañada de Cuicatlán was more closely affiliated to the Tehuacán Valley than the Etla region at that time, for tall-necked, red-slipped bottles occur at Rancho Dolores Ortiz near San Pedro Chicozapotes in the Cañada, a site excavated by Adriana Alaniz of the INAH Centro Regional de Oaxaca (Boletín del Centro Regional 1975). To the south, at Laguna Zope near Juchitán in the Isthmus of Tehuantepec, Robert and Judith Zeitlin have defined a Lagunita phase (R. Zeitlin 1978) with coastal ceramics that are significantly different from those of Tierras Largas, although some of their flat-based, outleaned-wall bowls look almost identical. My conclusion is that the Tehuacán–Cuicatlán area and the Nochixtlán–Valley of Oaxaca area were convincingly related at this time period, while the isthmus had a closer relationship with the Grijalva Depression and the Chiapas Coast. This may, of course, reflect the dichotomy between an emerging Zapotec–Mixtec region to the north and an emerging Zoque–Mixe area to the south.

## ANALYTICAL UNITS OF THE EARLY OAXACAN VILLAGE

In *The Early Mesoamerican Village* (Flannery [ed.] 1976), the early Oaxacan village was characterized as having several units of analysis—the activity area, feature, male or female work area, house, household cluster, residential ward, and community. Houses were 3–4 m wide and 5–6 m long, with pine posts, wattle-and-daub walls, and a stamped earth floor with a coating of sand. They were frequently spaced 20–40 m apart during the Tierras Largas phase, separated by open areas with a lower density of features and activity areas. While I would still hold to most of these analytical units, I would now like to propose a major revision of the unit formerly called "the household cluster," for reasons which will be evident presently.

Early Formative houses in the Valley of Oaxaca are frequently surrounded by an area of some 300 m² containing bell-shaped storage pits, earth ovens, burials, lean-to's, and various outdoor activity areas. Since these clusters of features seem to be archaeologically associated with a specific house—and separated from other houses by 20 meters or more of open space—Winter (1976a:25–31) employed the phrase "household cluster" to refer to the complex of structures, features, activity areas, and burials resulting from a single household. At the time it seemed like a good idea, and I went on to reanalyze some Guatemalan coastal material in these terms (Flannery 1976a:31–34).

Since then, a number of problems with this analytical unit have become apparent. First, a number of colleagues have hastened to point out to us that several Mesoamericanists already used the term *household cluster* to refer not to a cluster of archaeological features surrounding one household, but to a cluster of households (i.e., a *hamlet* or *village* in settlement pattern terms). For example, Borhegyi (1965) applied the terms *cluster, minor aggregate cluster,* and *major aggregate cluster* to hamlets and villages of highland Guatemala. In his northeast Petén survey, Bullard (1960) used the term *cluster* to refer to one of his three main levels of settlement organization, "clusters of about five to twelve [houses] within an area roughly 200 to 300 meters square." There is therefore an immediate danger of confusion between our use of the term and that of Borhegyi, Bullard, and others.

Second, some problems have arisen with the original definition of the term. Based on his excavations at the hamlet of Tierras Largas, Winter (1976a:25) concluded that "pits, burials, and other features generally occur outside but within a few meters of the house structures" and that therefore the household cluster concept could "provide a context in which pits, burials, house remains, and other features can be understood not simply as isolated cultural features, but as manifestations of a specific segment of society." This concept worked reasonably well for the "actual" household clusters, such as Cluster No. 1 of the Late Tierras Largas phase at the type site, which contained a series of postmolds, eight bell-shaped pits, and three burials (Winter 1976a:Fig. 2.8 and p. 31). It became shakier when "probable" or "possible" clusters were identified on the basis of a single burial, a single oven, or a single bell-shaped pit (Winter 1976b:Figs. 8.3–8.5). While many of these features probably do indicate that a house is nearby, others do not.

In particular, burials would seem to be a poor indicator of the presence of a household cluster, because it is now known that isolated burial areas or cemeteries were present in some Formative villages. These areas might vary from small barrio cemeteries of 8 to 15 individuals (such as in Area C at San José Mogote) to larger cemeteries of 60 to 80 individuals such as the one at Tomaltepec (Topic 15). Drennan was the first to make this problem explicit at Fábrica San José when, after identifying two possible household clusters on the basis of burials, he took a hard look at the data and concluded:

> One, and possibly two, of the household clusters of the Rosario Phase seem not to have been the sites of households at all. . . .

Clusters R-9 and perhaps R-10 were used as a cemetery [Drennan 1976b:132].

In short, the variety of contexts in which burials, pits, ovens, and other features occur is much greater than was originally thought.

A third problem has resulted from Winter's own attempts to extend the concept of household cluster much further than is really appropriate. Except for the somewhat infelicitous choice of the word *cluster*, it was a useful way of describing the organization of space around the typical small wattle-and-daub house of Early Formative Oaxaca. Unfortunately, as will be pointed out more fully in Topic 41, in a separate article Winter (1974) has tried to extend the concept of household cluster not only to large adobe residences of the Late Formative and to minor palaces with interior patios of the Classic, but also to structures that may be commemorative buildings erected over the tombs of Zapotec rulers. This overextension not only reduces the utility of the concept for the very period to which it was most suited, but also masks the significant residential changes of Late Formative and Classic times, which deserve terms of their own.

I therefore propose the following changes at the analytical level of the Early Formative household.

1. The term *household cluster* should be dropped, being too easily confused with the *cluster of households* already entered in the literature by Borhegyi, Bullard, and others. It should be replaced by the term *household unit,* which expresses unambiguously the fact that a single household is referred to.[1]

2. The term *household unit* should be used to refer to the complex of structures and features resulting from a typical Early Formative household—usually a wattle-and-daub house, its associated storage pits, ovens, middens, activity areas, and any sheds, lean-to's, or burials occurring with it.

3. The presence of a burial, an isolated bell-shaped pit, or any other feature should not be taken as evidence for a household unit. Only if it can be shown that a house is present—in the form of postmolds, masses of burnt daub, or both—should the term be used.

4. The term *household unit* should be used only to refer to the aforementioned 300-m² area of a wattle-and-daub house and its associated features and activity areas. It should not be extended to large adobe residences, houses with courtyards, or palaces. Such residential units had different modes of storage, different sets of activities, and different personnel, and these differences are only obscured by overextension of the term.

---

[1]Gaxiola (1976) has already anticipated this change by her translation of *household cluster* into *unidad doméstica.*

## TOPIC 12
## Origins of the Village in the Mixteca (Early Cruz Phase)

RONALD SPORES

The lack of systematic investigation of the Preceramic to Early Formative, or semisedentary to sedentary occupational transitions in the Mixteca means little can be stated with certainty relating to the origins of village life in any of the three major regions of that area. Although Early Formative artifacts resembling those of the Tierras Largas phase have been recovered in mixed contexts at Yucuita (site N 203) and Coyotepec (site N 233), no household units or activity areas comparable to those recovered in the Valleys of Oaxaca or Tehuacán have yet been excavated in the Mixteca.

The two earliest Formative sites identified in the Nochixtlán Valley of the Mixteca Alta are located on low lomas rising some 12–15 m (N 203) and 25–30 m (N 233) above the Yucuita River, and 750 m (N 203) and 1200 m (N 233) east of the river (Figure 3.3). The Coyotepec site is located 3.5 km north of the Yucuita site on relatively high but gradually sloping, well-drained, arable terrain. The sites crown the low *lomas* and are only a few minutes' walk from rich bottom lands along the river. The relative positions of the sites, their probable sizes (considered on the basis of surface indicators to be not larger than 100 m on a side), and their ceramic inventories are analogous to most localities of the Tierras Largas phase in the Valley of Oaxaca (see Topic 11). To comment further on settlement at this time, however, would be speculative and premature. Formative architecture so far encountered in excavations at Yucuita (Spores

1974a), Monte Negro (Caso 1938; Acosta n.d.a), or at Huamelulpan (Gaxiola 1976) dates to no earlier than the Middle Formative period and, for the most part, later. Future excavations at Yucuita, Coyotepec, and Etlatongo should substantially clarify the origins of village life in the Mixteca Alta. We hope similar investigations can soon be mounted elsewhere in the Alta, in the Baja, and the Costa.

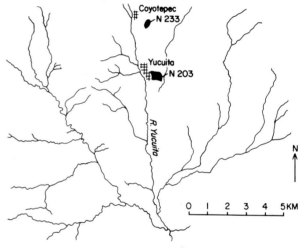

FIGURE 3.3. Early Cruz phase settlements (ca. 1300 B.C.) in the Nochixtlán Valley.

## TOPIC 13
## Ritual and Ceremonial Development at the Early Village Level

ROBERT D. DRENNAN

### THEORETICAL FRAMEWORK

In this topic I will consider ritual and ceremonial developments of the early village period in terms of the sociocultural similarities and differences between the inhabitants of what are today the Zapotec- and Mixtec-speaking regions of the state of Oaxaca.[1] These sociocultural similarities and differences can be divided into two broadly different sorts: those of form and those of content. The distinction between

form and content made here is similar to that made by art historians and estheticians (see, for example, Weitz 1964 and Panofsky 1964), although perhaps sufficiently dissimilar to cause a certain amount of discomfort among them. The term *content* is here used to denote the set of elements of which a sociocultural system is composed: knowledge, beliefs, customs, practices, and so on. The trait lists according to which ethnographic data have often been recorded and used are essentially lists of sociocultural content. In contrast, the term *form* is here used to denote the ways in which these elements are interrelated to form an operating sociocultural system.

The distinction between sociocultural content and form is

---

[1]This focus on regions, rather than on peoples, avoids the problem of having to specify the ethnic makeup of various sites or valleys during the Early Formative.

related, but not identical, to the distinction Rappaport (1968:237–239) has made between *cognized* and *operational* models. Operational models deal with the functioning of a sociocultural system in terms of understandings developed by the analyst of such a system, in contrast to cognized models that deal with the same subject but in terms of the understandings of the participants in the system. Sociocultural systems are formally similar, in the sense in which that term is used here, to the extent that the operational models accurately characterizing them are similar (at least at the most general level). Similarity of content, however, involves more than similarity of cognized models: it includes similarity of behavior patterns as well. Thus, while similarity of form is equivalent to operational similarity, similarity of content involves both cognitional and behavioral similarity.

It is entirely possible for two sociocultural systems of quite similar form to be different in content. Thus, being simplistic for the sake of illustration, one can imagine two hunter–gatherer societies that are formally similar in that their populations remain at a constant size as the result of certain interrelated practices and beliefs. The two may, however, differ in content, one practicing a long postpartum taboo on sexual intercourse because of beliefs about the nature of fertility, the other practicing selective infanticide because of beliefs concerning the effects of birth circumstances on the character of infants. It is also possible, although perhaps less common, for two sociocultural systems to differ in form but to remain quite similar in some aspect of content. Thus, in one society the belief that humans were descended from clouds in the remote past might be related to other elements of a set of beliefs and practices resulting in the legitimization of the higher status of a chief, while a very similar belief in another society might have the effect of strengthening the bonds among equal members of the society and excluding outsiders. In practice, of course, no two sociocultural systems are identical in either content or form; the distinction itself will break down if pushed too far, because sociocultural content and form are not two separate entities but rather two contrasting (but integrally related) aspects of the multifaceted phenomenon that is a cultural system. The distinction, however, has utility in dealing with two contrasting aspects of sociocultural similarities and differences in the present context.

In considerations of ritual behavior and the belief systems that underlie it, the focus is almost always on the content—the nature of the behavior itself and the specific character of the beliefs. Here, however, form and content will both be considered, according to the availability of relevant data. This is essentially the approach followed for the hunter–gatherer level in Topic 7 above, but the greater availability of Formative data makes possible a more complete treatment of this subject for the early village level.

Elsewhere (Drennan 1976a) I have argued that the establishment of sedentary, fully agricultural villages involves at least two kinds of changes which have important formal implications for ritual behavior and the belief systems which support it. These two changes are (1) a considerable loss of social fluidity, and with it a major outlet for intragroup dissension; and (2) a vastly increased dependence on a much smaller number of food procurement systems which the population takes a substantially greater hand in regulating than previously. The resulting more rigidly organized society must make more decisions involving all members as a group and the importance of the acceptance of these decisions by all members is increased. In the Valley of Oaxaca, the principal formal change in ritual behavior that seems to have accompanied this social shift was a substantially increased role for ritual and associated sets of beliefs, particularly religious beliefs, in the process of overall societal integration and in the process of group decision making (Drennan 1976a). This formal change is attested by changes in ceremonial architecture and artifacts.

## PUBLIC BUILDINGS

In Topic 7 we considered the cleared and boulder-lined area of the Preceramic site of Gheo-Shih, and the likelihood that rituals there took place during periods of population aggregation keyed to unpredictable resource abundance. During the transition from the poorly known Espiridión complex (Topic 10) to the early Tierras Largas phase (Topic 11), a feature vaguely similar to the Gheo-Shih cleared area was constructed at San José Mogote, which was then a hamlet or small village:

> The evidence . . . consists of an open area (perhaps 7 m wide from west to east), set apart from the residential areas of the hamlet by a double line of staggered posts. In some places, this double line of posts was reinforced by a row of heavy stone slabs set on edge. The orientation of this enclosure, which contained no architecture and was nearly free of artifacts, was slightly west of true north [Flannery and Marcus 1976a:208].

The pattern of post molds described for this enclosure (see Flannery and Marcus 1976a:Fig. 10.2) is reminiscent of the more substantial structures described and illustrated by Lowie (1915:826) for Great Basin dance grounds.

Very soon after the abandonment of this structure, however, in early Tierras Largas phase times (ca. 1350 B.C.), a different type of "public" construction was built at San José Mogote, which by this time had grown to 1.5–2.0 ha. This was a lime-plastered, one-room public building of which eight examples are known, although there is no evidence that more than one was in use at any time. The best preserved was Structure 6 (Flannery and Marcus 1976a:Fig. 10.3), which was roughly 4.4 by 5.4 m in extent and oriented north–south. The walls had a core of upright pine posts (perhaps 20 in the entire structure) with bundles of canes lashed into the spaces between the posts, and clay daubed over the walls. The floor was of lime stucco over a platform-like foundation of crushed bedrock, clay, lime, and sand;

where preservation was good, the lower 40 cm of the wall appeared to have been expanded into a low bench which ran around the inside of the room.

> Two features occurred in these buildings with stereotyped regularity. Set against the south wall was a low rectangular platform, possibly a step, but more likely an altar of some kind. . . . Directly north of this altar appeared a storage pit, incorporated into the original floor of the room and coated with the same white stucco. In three cases, these pits were filled with powdered lime [Flannery and Marcus 1976a:211].

In their original description of these pits, Flannery and Marcus (1976a:211) described them as "filled with powdered lime of the very type used for the plastering and replastering of the room." This may be true, but the amount of lime that could be stored in these small features seems insufficient for such a task. In response to a suggestion from Michael Coe, Flannery and Marcus (personal communication, 1978), have now changed their interpretation as follows:

> We now prefer Michael Coe's suggestion that these pits may have been used to store powdered lime for ritual purposes, such as mixing with narcotics like tobacco. The use of tobacco was widespread among the Zapotec, being mentioned in the *relaciones* from Macuilxochitl, Miahuatlán, Nejapa, and other places.

Further support for this alternative intepretation has since come from the site of La Coyotera in the Cañada de Cuicatlán, where Spencer and Redmond (Topic 17) discovered a similar lime-filled pit in a Middle Formative public building. In this case, there was no evidence that the building had ever been stuccoed, making it less likely that this was the purpose of the lime.

At any rate, Tierras Largas phase public buildings such as

Structure 6 from San José Mogote (Figure 3.4) suggest differences of both form and content between early village sociocultural systems and those of the hunter–gatherers who preceded them, even though the precise nature of the activities for which the structure was built cannot be determined.

First, this early Tierras Largas phase structure is considerably smaller than the cleared and boulder-lined area already described for Gheo-Shih. This fact suggests that fewer people were involved in the activities performed inside it. Moreover, since the amount of wattle-and-daub debris suggests that Structure 6 had full-height walls (presumably supporting a roof), the activities performed inside were screened from the view of those outside. This suggests the presence of a ritual of more complex content, involving a classification of participants into those allowed to enter the structure and those who remained outside. Such classification is particularly common in religious rituals, in which close contact with the sacred is often allowed to only a restricted number of individuals. In its formal aspect this classification could well be related to the increasingly complex group decision-making structure of sedentary agriculturists through the process of *sanctification*, whereby the privileged access of some people to the sacred renders them particularly effective in influencing the behavior of the social group as a whole.

Second, the presence of such a permanent and substantial community structure right within the village suggests an increased social investment in ritual activity, an increased frequency and regularity of group ritual, and a more continuously present physical reminder of its importance—all very adaptive changes, if religious ritual were carrying a heavier social burden with respect to societal integration and group decision making. The tradition of periodic rebuilding or su-

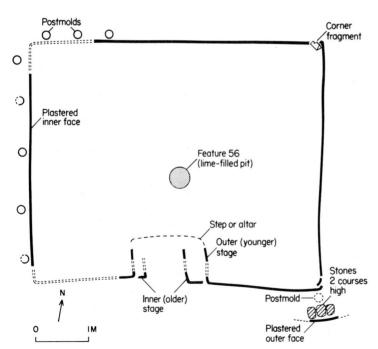

FIGURE 3.4.  Ground plan of Structure 6 at San José Mogote, a Tierras Largas phase public building.

perimposition of such structures (which began with the earliest Tierras Largas phase structure) indicates the continued importance in early village life of the activities for which these structures served.

## FIGURINES

Concurrent with the establishment of the first sedentary villages in the Valley of Oaxaca comes the appearance of the first ceramic figurines, such as the small feline head found in an "Espiridión complex" house at San José Mogote (Topic 10). Admittedly, there are a few antecedent occurrences in the previllage period elsewhere in Mexico: a single clay figurine from Preceramic times comes from Zohapilco (Tlapacoya) in the Valley of Mexico (Niederberger 1969:22, 24), and a possible antecedent for the clay figurine is the carved *Jatropha* seed from an Abejas phase floor of Coxcatlán Cave in the Tehuacán Valley (MacNeish, Nelken-Terner, and Johnson 1967:160). It is only at the early village level, however, that ceramic figurines become a very frequently encountered artifact. I will not repeat here the argument made in Drennan (1976a) for considering figurines ritual artifacts, but will simply consider them so. Whether figurines represented mythical beings, spirits, deities, real persons, ancestors (Flannery and Marcus 1976b), or something else, their presence in virtually all kinds of contexts in rather high frequencies indicates that every household, if not every individual, in an early village in the Valley of Oaxaca participated in the activity involving figurines, and that this activity occurred quite frequently. Ritual with these characteristics would be well suited to the role of societal integration—binding the early villagers together into a more solid social grouping.

## OLMEC SYMBOLISM

During the San José phase (1150–850 B.C.), further changes in ritual activity accompanied the emergence of larger-scale, ranked society in the Valley of Oaxaca. In form, these changes consisted of the support, largely through rituals of sanctification, both of a system of social ranking and of a series of more complex, increasingly hierarchical processes of group decision making (Flannery 1968b; Drennan 1976a). Ritual activities of the period involved possible "household shrines" in some houses at San José Mogote (Flannery 1976b:Fig. 11.3) and a network of interregional contacts through which were transmitted several kinds of ritual objects and materials, together with symbols of probable religious meaning. The symbols concerned, which involve figurines and designs on ceramics (Figure 3.5), have generally been classified as Olmec (Pyne 1976), although it is now clear that the sharing of symbols in this Formative period interaction was more mutual than has often been pictured. The ritual objects and materials exchanged over long distances included magnetite mirrors, marine shell, fish and stingray spines, shark teeth, and lowland turtle shell. The use of Olmec symbols and the intensity of long-distance exchange reached a peak during the San José phase, following which both processes declined (Flannery 1968b:101; Pires-Ferreira 1975:1, 10, 84).

Thus the San José phase in the Valley of Oaxaca saw changes in both form and content of ritual. In form, ritual (and especially religious ritual) came more to emphasize and reinforce institutions of social differentiation. In content, connections with other regions of Mesoamerica were emphasized through the use of certain materials and symbols. Since this interpretation of San José phase ritual activity has already been elaborated (Drennan 1976a), it would be redundant to go into it in detail here. Let it suffice to say that, as usual, form and content were not unrelated. The connection with other regions of Mesoamerica was particularly useful in the formal aspects that came to apply to ritual activity.

The above discussion has focused on the Valley of Oaxaca. Less is known of the Early Cruz phase in the Nochixtlán Valley than of the Tierras Largas and San José phases in the Valley of Oaxaca, which are contemporaneous with it, because of the smaller amount of excavation in Early Cruz

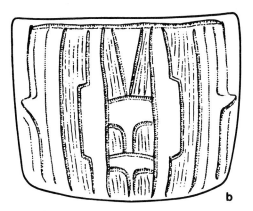

FIGURE 3.5. San José phase ceramics with Olmec motifs: (a) gray cylinder with stylized fire-serpent; (b) white cylinder with stylized were-jaguar.

phase sites (Spores 1974a). There are, however, indications that special buildings, similar to the public buildings of early villages in the Valley of Oaxaca, may have been present in early villages in the Nochixtlán Valley as well (Spores 1972:173–174). Figurines were also made by the Early Cruz phase villagers. There is as yet no indication of substantial differences between Tierras Largas phase ritual and Early Cruz phase ritual, in either form or content, although more excavation will be necessary to document similarities.

The information now available, however, does indicate the presence of differences between the two regions by later in the Early Cruz phase, during times contemporaneous with the San José phase. The figurines and ceramics of the Nochixtlán Valley do not show the degree of participation in the Olmec interregional interaction sphere of the times that those of the Valley of Oaxaca do (Spores 1972:17–75). While both ceramics and figurines of the Nochixtlán Valley show certain similarities to those of the Valley of Oaxaca, the complex of Olmec designs and features is marked only in the Valley of Oaxaca material.

## SUMMARY

More excavation will be necessary before we know if, by the end of the Early Cruz phase, a socially ranked and more hierarchically organized society existed in the Nochixtlán Valley. Present evidence, however, tends to suggest that it did not. The lack of such a society would account for the absence of Olmec features, if the interpretations presented by Flannery (1968b) and Drennan (1976a) are accurate. Thus, some differences between what are today the Zapotec and Mixtec regions emerged at the early village level. Best

documented is a difference in content: ritual in the Nochixtlán Valley did not involve the manipulation of Olmec symbols derived from the intense interregional interaction that marked the latter part of the Early Formative in Mesoamerica. There are indications that this difference in content reflects a difference in form—in the formal social role played by ritual and in the form of social organization itself.

During succeeding time periods, a highly ranked (and eventually stratified) society with a complex hierarchical social organization emerged in the Nochixtlán Valley, just as it had earlier in the Valley of Oaxaca. Similarities and differences during these later periods are the subject of the remainder of this volume. Some questions regarding the genesis of these similarities or differences are raised by the early differences noted above, however. Was the essence of the early differences simply that the Nochixtlán Valley lagged behind the Valley of Oaxaca in the earliest stages of a course of social development which otherwise was parallel in the two regions? Or did the Nochixtlán Valley's delayed start affect the course of development in that region? If the latter, did it encourage divergence because of the different regional social environments in which the earliest stages of the development took place by virtue of their different timing? Or did it encourage similarity through a tendency towards imitation of a more advanced neighbor? Do different considerations in this regard apply to differences and similarities of form and of content? The differences at the early village level noted above are basically differences of form—different forms of social organization and different formal roles of ritual. These formal differences, however, led to differences of content as well. Such differences in content might well have gone on to be erased by subsequent formal convergence. It is even possible that such differences in content could have led to further differences in form.

## TOPIC 14
## San José and Guadalupe Phase Settlement Patterns in the Valley of Oaxaca

STEPHEN KOWALEWSKI
EVA FISCH
KENT V. FLANNERY

The San José phase of the Valley of Oaxaca (1150–850 B.C.) is characterized by a ceramic complex resembling that of Tlatilco in the Valley of Mexico, Las Bocas in southwestern Puebla, Chiapa de Corzo I in Chiapas, and the San Lorenzo phase in southern Veracruz. One dominant type, Leandro Gray, features cylindrical bowls with excised (*raspada*) decoration in the form of the Olmec fire-serpent; another type, Atoyac Yellow-white, features cylindrical bowls with fine-line hachure representations of the Olmec were-jaguar. White bowls with double-line-break incising also occur in low frequency early in the phase, increasing in frequency as the Guadalupe phase approaches. Apart from

these gray and white types, the ceramics may be bichrome red-on-white, white-rim black, specular hematite red, or coarse buff. Common shapes are cylinders, flat-based bowls, necked jars, and *tecomates;* decoration includes incising, excising, rocker stamping (plain, dentate, and "false") in zones, and designs like the St. Andrew's cross and U motif in addition to the aforementioned Olmec motifs. This phase occurs throughout the valley, and when intensive surveys are complete there could be as many as 30 San José phase sites.

The Guadalupe phase (850–700 B.C.) was originally defined at Barrio del Rosario Huitzo and San José Mogote, and it was assumed at that time to be a valley-wide phenomenon like the San José phase (Flannery 1968b, Flannery [ed.] 1970). Subsequent surveys and excavations, however, now suggest that the complex of ceramic horizon markers used to define the Guadalupe phase may not extend far beyond the Etla arm of the Valley of Oaxaca. The most logical conclusion is that some of these diagnostics—Atoyac Yellow-white bowls with a wavy line incised between two straight lines (Plog 1976:Fig. 9.2, designs 35–38), Fidencio Coarse jars with plastic decoration in zones on the shoulder, undecorated Socorro Fine Gray and Josefina Fine Gray composite silhouette bowls—originated at Huitzo and are decidedly rare outside Huitzo's sphere of influence. We can find no concrete evidence, for example, to suggest that the Tlacolula or Zaachila–Zimatlán areas went through a comparable Guadalupe phase. Because those areas do share a very high frequency of Atoyac Yellow-white bowls with Huitzo, it is possible that what takes the place of the Guadalupe ceramic complex elsewhere in the valley is a later version of the San José phase ceramic complex. For this reason, we have included San José and Guadalupe sites all on a single map (Figure 3.6).

## THE SAN JOSÉ PHASE

One of the most striking phenomena of the San José phase is the enormous growth of San José Mogote. The "downtown" area of occupation there (including all public buildings and elite residential areas) covered at least 20 ha (Marcus 1976b: Table 3.10). Flanking this is a strip of annually flooded alluvium from a tributary of the Atoyac, an area which excavations show to have no permanent occupation. Immediately beyond this strip, to the east, are more residential areas which could be considered either separate small hamlets or outlying barrios of San José Mogote. If they are considered outlying barrios and combined with the main area of occupation, "greater" San José Mogote at this time would have covered 70 ha, with a population estimated by Fisch (1978) at 700 persons. This area of occupation would make it one of the largest Early Formative sites in the highlands of Mesoamerica.

The enormous growth of San José Mogote was in marked contrast to virtually every other site of the period; at least 26 other San José phase sites in the intensively surveyed parts of the valley remained in the 0.1–2.0 ha size range. The Tlacolula region has not yet been intensively surveyed, but the known sites there (Tomaltepec, Abasolo, and Mitla) are also small.

San José Mogote also seems to have played a role in keeping the demographic center of gravity in the Etla arm of the valley. There was a net increase of one site in the Zaachila–Zimatlán region, two sites in the Central region, and five sites in the Etla region. This pattern of population growth during the San José phase does not correspond to A. Kirkby's (1973:131, 137) predicted pattern of growth based on the valley's agricultural potential. During the San José phase, an increment in mean corn cob size made possible a doubling of the land in the Valley of Oaxaca which was potentially productive for maize farming (A. Kirkby 1973:131, 137). Since the Zaachila–Zimatlán region would have had twice as much productive land as the Etla region, Kirkby predicted 16 villages for the Zaachila–Zimatlán area and only 9 for Etla.

As Figure 3.6 shows, the Etla region had more sites and a much greater population, despite having half the amount of agricultural land; population grew most rapidly in the vicinity of San José Mogote. This phenomenon suggests that growth was associated more strongly with the organizational differences among the various arms of the valley than with the distribution of arable land. The differential rates of population growth may have been the consequence of increased demands for agricultural labor and/or tribute (and the increased services resulting from them) placed on the local population in the Etla region by the decision makers (or chiefs?) now residing at San José Mogote. It appears, for example, that someone at San José Mogote was pooling and redistributing obsidian from various sources to a whole series of households dependent on him (Winter and Pires-Ferreira 1976).

In addition, some of the tiny San José phase hamlets founded during this phase may have been placed so as to take advantage of specialized resources needed by San José Mogote and other villages. An example would be Las Salinas, a hamlet located at a saline spring in the Etla piedmont whose waters can be boiled to produce table salt.

There are also interesting differences in settlement choice among the various areas of the valley. In the Etla region, major sites are generally located on low piedmont spurs overlooking the main Atoyac River or its major tributary coming from San Juan del Estado; these major sites tend to be spaced about 5 km apart (Flannery 1976c:Fig. 6.9). When sites are located in the piedmont, they seem to be small and at specialized resource localities like salt springs or pottery clay deposits.

This pattern of settlement along the main Atoyac River seems also to characterize the Zaachila–Zimatlán region. In the Tlacolula valley, however, there are major sites on tributary streams in the northern piedmont virtually from the beginning of permanent settlement, which may be because several of the north-bank tributaries of the Río Salado provide more advantages for settlement and agriculture than do some stretches of the main river. Finally, both Zaachila and Abasolo occur in areas where no stream could have been a factor: both are in areas of humid alluvium where water-table farming or well irrigation can be practiced (see Topic 94).

## THE GUADALUPE PHASE

The bulk of the San José phase sites in the Etla region continued to be occupied during the Guadalupe phase. Fá-

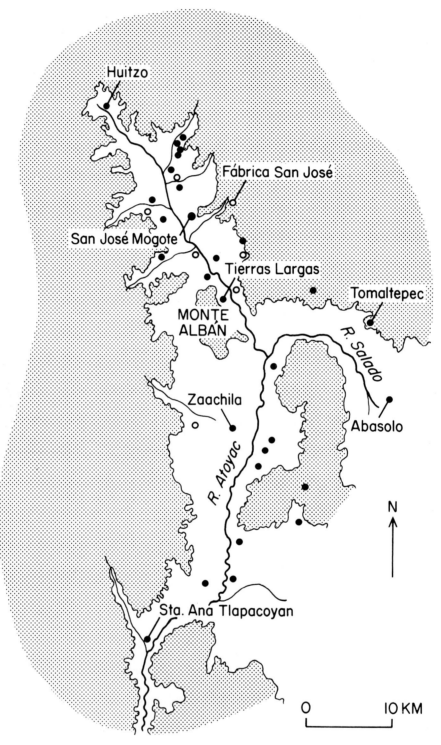

FIGURE 3.6. San José and Guadalupe phase sites in the Etla, Central, and Zaachila–Zimatlán regions of the Valley of Oaxaca, according to Feinman and Kowalewski (1979) and Varner (1974). White circles represent villages or hamlets which appear to have been first founded in the Guadalupe phase; all other villages and hamlets (black circles) were founded prior to that phase.

brica San José was founded during this period, as was a village at Santo Tomás Mazaltepec; both were almost certainly colonized from San José Mogote.

One of the important events of the Guadalupe phase was the growth of Barrio del Rosario Huitzo from a relatively unimportant San José phase hamlet to an important Guadalupe phase civic–ceremonial center with a main residential zone of at least 2.7 ha (exclusive of any outlying barrios) and a ceremonial precinct of at least 3500 m². Design element analyses carried out by S. Plog (1976) suggest that Huitzo and San José Mogote were competing ceremonial centers, interacting less and sharing fewer designs on ceramics than would have been predicted on the basis of their proximity. The settlement pattern studies summarized in Figure 3.6 (which were not available at the time Plog did his study) show this dramatically: Huitzo sits all alone at the headwaters of the upper Atoyac, separated by 10 km from its nearest neighbor, while San José Mogote appears to be part of an impressive string of communities stretching from Santa Marta Etla to Tierras Largas.

# TOPIC 15
## The Growth of Site Hierarchies in the Valley of Oaxaca: Part I

KENT V. FLANNERY
JOYCE MARCUS

There are a number of phenomena which distinguished the San José, Guadalupe, and Rosario phases from the earlier Formative periods in the Valley of Oaxaca. One of these phenomena was a complex pattern of differential community growth which produced a site-size hierarchy.

Most sites of this period remained small, showing little tendency to grow beyond 1 or 2 ha in size; these hamlets seem to have had no public architecture. One site, San José Mogote, grew explosively to cover 70 ha during late San José–Guadalupe times and 61.9 ha during the Rosario phase (Fisch 1978); it featured a series of impressive public buildings of several different kinds. A small number of communities—perhaps fewer than half a dozen—may represent an intermediate settlement type which falls somewhere between the tiny hamlet and the 60–70 ha ceremonial center. These villages, averaging about 3 ha in size, had public buildings of fairly impressive proportions, but lacked the full range of buildings seen at San José Mogote.

The development of this site hierarchy in late Early Formative and Middle Formative Oaxaca is important for theoretical reasons. As will be discussed more fully in Chapter 4, one of the lines of evidence used by some archaeologists to document the rise of the state is the emergence of a site hierarchy with three administrative levels or "tiers" above the level of the hamlet (Wright and Johnson 1975). We do not feel that such a multilevel administrative hierarchy is demonstrable in the Valley of Oaxaca prior to Monte Albán II. The differential community growth of the San José, Guadalupe, and Rosario phases, however, may reflect the setting in motion of some of the processes that led toward the Monte Albán II hierarchy.

One important distinction should nevertheless be made clear at this point: in the San José, Guadalupe, and Rosario phases we are talking about a *size hierarchy*. We cannot demonstrate that a corresponding *administrative hierarchy* existed at that time. In other words, we have constructed a settlement typology that includes (1) one 60–70 ha "first-order" site; (2) several 3-ha "second-order" sites, with perhaps one public building each; and (3) a large number of 1 to 2-ha "third-order" sites, without apparent public architecture. Because this typology takes the presence, absence, and variety of public buildings into account, it is not solely based on size. We cannot demonstrate, however, that the 60–70-ha first-order site was administratively "over" any of the 3-ha sites with public buildings, or that the latter were administratively "over" any of the tiny third-order hamlets. Wright and Johnson (1975) did this in the Near East by showing that "administrative artifacts" (seals, seal impressions, bullae, and other items) occurred from top to bottom in the hierarchy, with increasing variety and complexity toward the top. We cannot do this.

Indeed, there is some reason to believe that the relationship between some second-order sites in Oaxaca and our one first-order site, San José Mogote, was competitive rather than subordinate. S. Plog (1976) compared the decorated Atoyac Yellow-white pottery of five San José–Guadalupe phase villages by means of a gravity model, based on the assumption that the degree of interaction between two communities is directly proportional to their size and inversely proportional to the distance between them. Several third-order sites shared a high frequency of decorative motifs with San José Mogote, suggesting that the latter may have served as a regional civic–ceremonial center for a whole series of hamlets without public architecture of their own. San José Mogote, however, shared many fewer motifs with one second-order site, Barrio del Rosario Huitzo, than would have been predicted on the basis of distance, suggesting that Huitzo, despite its much smaller size and more limited range of public buildings, may have been a competing regional center. If this is the case, then one of the most important problems for future archaeologists will be to find out how this competitive situation at 850 B.C. became restructured as a three-tiered administrative hierarchy by 200 B.C.

In this topic, we examine in detail one example of a first-order center, and two examples of second-order centers in different parts of the Valley of Oaxaca. In Topic 16, Drennan and Flannery consider three examples of third-order sites in different parts of the valley. While our evidence is fragmentary, it is hoped that a comparison of the household units, burials, and public buildings at these various sites will add some substance to the site-size hierarchy.

## SAN JOSÉ MOGOTE

San José Mogote, lying at an elevation of 1610 m in the Etla arm of the valley, is our only excavated example of a first-order center during the periods we are discussing. The site covers the top of a low piedmont spur near the left bank of the main Atoyac River in an area of extremely productive high-water-table alluvium (see Topic 94).

In Topic 13, Drennan has described the Tierras Largas phase public buildings and the San José phase Olmec symbolism which were prominent features in the Early Formative development of San José Mogote. In this topic, we will consider the growth of this large site to its position of prominence in the Middle Formative size hierarchy.

In the Tierras Largas phase, San José Mogote consisted of an estimated 147 persons living in 10 discrete residential areas totaling 7.8 ha, at least 300 m² of which was devoted to small public buildings. During the San José–Guadalupe phases it grew to a large nucleated village of 70 ha with an estimated 700 persons, perhaps 2 ha of which was devoted to public buildings. In the Rosario phase, this same site was a large nucleated village of 61.9 ha with an estimated 1000 persons, and an acropolis of public buildings occupying roughly 1 ha (Fisch 1978).

### San José and Guadalupe Phases

One-room public buildings like Structure 6 of the Tierras Largas phase (see Topic 13) were still constructed during the early San José phase (1150–1000 B.C.), though during this period their stucco was more frequently yellow than white.

They were soon joined, however, by public buildings of other types. Near the eastern limits of San José Mogote, a gentle slope that once had been covered with ordinary residences was converted into a series of stepped terraces, faced with stones set in hard puddled adobe clay. The westernmost terrace rose in two stages to a height of 3 m; the easternmost was lower, but had two small stairways made from stone slabs on its downhill face. This latter terrace, called Structure 2, had a facing of several tiers of heavy volcanic tuff boulders and limestone slabs. Below it were found two carved stones, Monuments 1 and 2, which originally may have been set in an upper tier of the terrace (Figure 3.7). Tentatively, Monument 1 seems to depict the head of a jaguar or other feline, while Monument 2 represents a raptorial bird. Dating to between 1000 and 900 B.C., they are, for the moment, the oldest carved stones from the Valley of Oaxaca.

During the course of the San José phase, public buildings evolved in both size and diversity. While white-plastered wattle-and-daub remained in favor for the buildings themselves, now these structures often were set on platforms of stone and adobe and sometimes were equipped with stairways. The standard adobe of the period was round to oval in plan, and plano-convex, or bun-shaped, in cross section.

Several stone-and-adobe platforms occurred at San José Mogote, the most fully investigated being Structure 8. Dating to terminal San José or earliest Guadalupe times (900–800 B.C.), the building was oriented 8° west of north. The east side (which appeared to be the front) was a wall more than a meter wide, composed of several layers of undressed field stones. Running west from this were retaining walls of plano-convex adobes, which apparently represented the northern and southern limits of the structure. In places, the adobes were preserved to a height of four courses totaling 70 cm and capped with a thick floor of puddled adobe clay. The area between the retaining walls had been filled with hundreds of basketloads of earth. A few postholes were all that remained of the building that had once stood on the platform.

Residential patterns of the San José phase offer some insight into the social organization of that period. The data

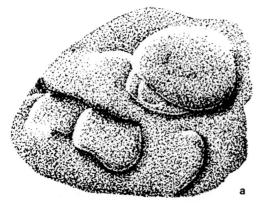

a                                                              b

FIGURE 3.7.  Early Formative stone monuments from San José Mogote: (a) Monument 1; (b) Monument 2. (Drawings by Lois Martin.)

suggest that there were emerging status differences, but that these took the form of a continuum from relatively higher to relatively lower status, without a true division into social classes as took place in later periods. Since several household units of this phase have already been illustrated in *The Early Mesoamerican Village* (Flannery [ed.] 1976), we shall describe the continuum of residences only in general terms.

The simplest and most common type of residence in the San José phase would be the kind represented by House 13 (Flannery [ed.] 1976:Fig. 2.3): a rectangular wattle-and-daub house 3 by 5 to 4 by 6 m in extent, with a stamped clay floor surfaced with river sand, one doorway on the longer side, and a series of upright pine posts 10–15 cm in diameter. A somewhat better-made type of house, also fairly common, is represented by House 2 (Flannery [ed.] 1976:Fig. 2.15). This house had a partial foundation of fieldstones, posts 15–20 cm in diameter (including large corner posts), and a burnished white surface of limey clay or whitewash over the daub. Such houses tend to have a higher concentration of marine shell ornaments, shell debris, mica, and high quality chert from the Rancho Matadamas quarries, suggesting that greater access to exotic raw materials was one of the ways in which relatively higher status was expressed.

Another example of a higher-status household is the House 16–17 complex (Flannery [ed.] 1976:Fig. 2.10). Here the actual whitewashed house (House 17) was accompanied by an additional structure (possibly a kitchen, shed, or outbuilding), forming an L-shaped unit facing onto a small patio. Through the patio (and between the two structures) ran a small drainage or rain-runoff canal which was connected to a large cistern excavated in bedrock. In addition to large quantities of heat-treated high quality chert, this house produced a true stingray spine (one from an actual ray, rather than a whittled deer-bone imitation) and a set of figurines arranged in the form of a scene, buried beneath the floor of the outbuilding (Flannery [ed.] 1976:Fig. 11.9).

Perhaps the highest-status residence found so far in San José phase context is Structure 16 in Area A. While the house itself was not unusual in its size, posthole pattern, or wattle-and-daub construction, it rested on a meter-high platform of puddled abode with a coating of white lime plaster. Although smaller than the platform of Structure 11 at Tomaltepec, this construction showed some similarities to the former. Its associated debris (including a metate and mano), like that from Structure 11 at Tomaltepec, indicated a residence rather than a public building. Area A produced more than 500 fragments of magnetite and related iron ores, plus the bulk of the magnetite mirrors and all the mirror-working areas so far found at the site. Hence, one possible interpretation of Structure 16 would be that it was the residence of the most important family occupying the magnetite-working barrio of the village during the San José phase.

Human burials of the San José phase suggest the same kind of continuum from relatively simple to relatively elaborate reflected in the residences. Most of the burials found so far come from a small area which may represent a barrio

cemetery on the west edge of the site. Like the burials from the much larger Tomaltepec cemetery, both sexes are represented and most skeletons are adults, buried face down and fully extended. Some burials are oriented east–west, others north–south. Almost all have at least a single jade bead in the mouth and one or more pottery vessels; as is the case with burials at Tomaltepec and Tierras Largas, vessels with carved Olmec fire-serpent designs occur only with males.[1] The simplest burials have no beads and no offerings, and some may be stuffed into abandoned storage pits; at the other end of the continuum was Tomb 3, an adult male in a grave lined with stone slabs which suggests a precursor for the later Zapotec tomb. One of the most elegant burials found so far was a middle-aged woman, Burial 18, apparently associated with the House 16–17 complex; she had two fine jade earspools and a jade labret. If it were possible to associate all San José phase burials with particular houses (as we feel can be done in the latter case), we might be able to link burial types and residence types into a single status continuum. Unfortunately, this cannot as yet be done.

### The Rosario Phase

During the Rosario phase (700/650 B.C. to ca. 500 B.C.), San José Mogote grew to be the central place for a network of some 18 to 20 villages in the Etla region, serving as the ceremonial center for a population we would estimate at 1300 to 1400 persons (Stephen Kowalewski, personal communication, 1980). The actual number of villages linked to San José Mogote cannot be specified until we know the limits of influence of Barrio del Rosario Huitzo, a smaller (but possibly competitive) center to the northwest.

As Figure 3.8 shows, the Etla region continued to be the demographic center of gravity for the entire Valley of Oaxaca. There were 25–26 settlements in the 801 km² Central and Zaachila–Zimatlán survey areas, but their total population is estimated by Feinman and Kowalewski (1979) as less than that of San José Mogote alone. The "downtown" area at the latter site had now reached 40 ha, with an estimated population of 100–140 households (Marcus 1976b:Table 3.11), and if all possible outlying barrios are added to this, the total area of Rosario phase occupation is estimated by Fisch (1978) at 61.9 ha with a population of 1000 persons. At the very least, San José Mogote was the largest community in the valley prior to the founding of Monte Albán.

The map of Rosario phase settlements (Figure 3.8) also suggests two concentrations of villages—in the Etla and Zaachila–Zimatlán areas—with the Central region almost devoid of sites. If a third concentration shows up when the Tlacolula area is intensively surveyed, it will support Blanton's (1978) model for the founding of Monte Albán by three previously autonomous polities from different areas of the valley.

---

[1] All aging and sexing of burials at sites discussed in this topic is by Richard G. Wilkinson, State University of New York at Albany.

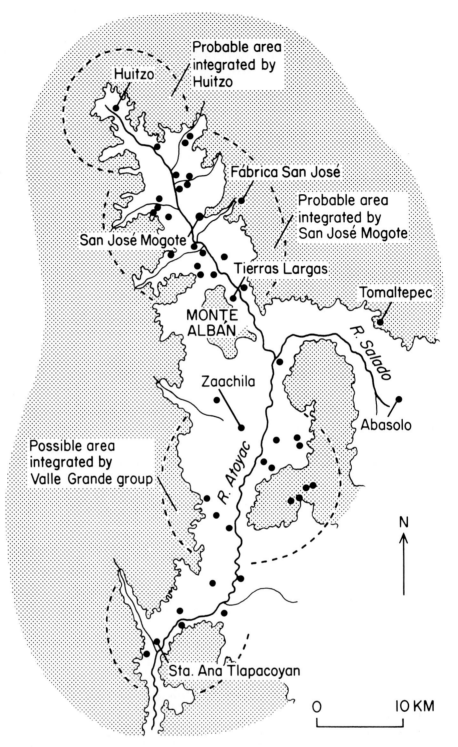

FIGURE 3.8. Rosario phase sites in the Etla, Central, and Zaachila–Zimatlán regions of the Valley of Oaxaca according to Feinman and Kowalewski (1979). Dashed lines indicate the presumed areas of influence of various Rosario phase civic–ceremonial centers that may have integrated subregions of the valley. Boundaries of these areas have deliberately been left vague until further studies of shared design elements can be undertaken.

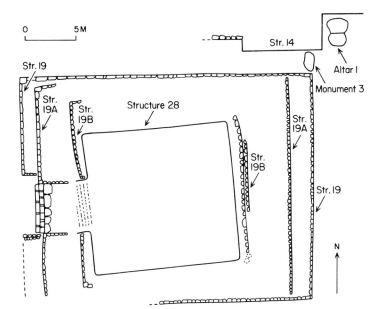

FIGURE 3.9. Complex of Rosario phase public buildings, altar, and stone monument atop Mound 1 at San José Mogote.

During the Rosario phase, the focus of public building at San José Mogote had shifted to the top of Mound 1, a natural hill whose subsequent architectural modification raised its summit to a level 15 m above the rest of the village. At this writing, we have not yet exposed the earliest public buildings atop Mound 1, lying as they do below a long series of superimposed structures. Perhaps the largest Rosario phase building (Figure 3.9) was Structure 19, which is described in more detail in Topic 19. This building, roughly 22 by 28 m in extent and standing up to 2 m high in places, was built of huge limestone blocks many of which weigh more than a ton. These rough-hewn blocks—some containing veins of chert—came from a quarry at Rancho Matadamas, some 5 km to the west of San José Mogote. To reach the area of Structure 19, they had to be brought across 5 km of valley and the Atoyac River, then dragged to the top of a 13-m hill. Structure 19 shares its stairway with a still earlier building, Structure 19A, which represents an earlier and almost equally impressive building stage within Structure 19; both buildings seem to have been the successively enlarged stone-faced platforms which supported a series of buildings made with rectangular adobes and surfaced with lime plaster. The best preserved of these, Structure 28, measures 13.4 by 14.2 m and stands 1.5 m high.

Structure 14, to the north of Structure 19, is also incompletely explored but seems to have had a Rosario phase stage as well; it is made of still better-trimmed limestone blocks, and rises in places to a height of 3 m. In an angle of the south wall of the building is a huge altar (Altar 1) composed of two huge blocks of limestone weighing a total of 5 metric tons.[2]

A narrow corridor separates Structures 14 and 19, and serving as the threshold for this corridor is a large carved stone, Monument 3 (Figure 3.10). The stone was laid flat on a bed of stone slabs so that anyone entering or leaving the corridor would tread on the body of the person depicted: a naked individual shown with his eyes closed and mouth partly open, sprawled awkwardly in the manner of the so-called *danzantes* of Monte Albán (see Topic 22). Elsewhere, Marcus (1974, 1976c) has interpreted this stone as the depiction of a slain or sacrificed captive. A complex scroll covers his chest, possibly depicting blood issuing from an open wound like that made for removal of the heart during sacrifice; a ribbon-like stream extends from this scroll to the edge of the stone, where two motifs wrap around onto the east edge of the monument. These two elements, each composed of a circle and triangle, may represent stylized drops of blood. They are identical to a motif which occurs on shell ornaments of the Guadalupe phase (see Drennan 1976b:Fig. 78d), and are very similar to motifs carved on the stairway stones of some public buildings at Monte Negro (see Topic 26). Finally, carved between the individual's feet are two hieroglyphs which probably represent a name taken from the Zapotec 260-day ritual calendar (see Topic 23). The ornate dot, below, represents the number one; the other glyph, above, is *xoo*, or "earthquake" ("motion"), the seventeenth day in the Zapotec list of 20 day names (Córdova 1578b). At the moment, this inscription, 1 Earthquake, is our oldest evidence for the 260-day calendar and, perhaps, for the Zapotec custom of naming individuals for the day of their birth. It may also indicate that the custom of recording the sacrifices of named individuals had begun by this time. Ethnohistorically, such individuals were usually captives taken in warfare, a fact that may have some significance for the Rosario and subsequent Monte Albán I periods.

---

[2] We are indebted to José Luis Lorenzo for the conversion of limestone volume into tonnage.

FIGURE 3.10.  Monument 3 at San José Mogote, Oaxaca. On the east edge of the stone (left) appear two circle and triangle motifs seen on a shell ornament at Fábrica San José and on stairway risers at Monte Negro. (Drawing by Mark Orsen).

### Elite Residences of the Rosario Phase

During the course of the Rosario phase, an interesting event took place on Mound 1 at San José Mogote. Structure 28 (and presumably also its supporting platform, Structure 19) ceased to function as a public building. Soon afterward, its flat upper surface was chosen as the level on which a series of adobe residences or residential compounds were built. These residences would have been reached by ascending the same monumental stone staircase built for Structure 19A. These are the only Rosario phase residences known from Mound 1. They overlook the village from a height of 15 m and have as their platform a former public building whose construction required considerable corvée labor. These facts

give us reason to suspect we are dealing with families of quite high status within Rosario society.

The best-preserved compound was the second one built on the spot, belonging to stratigraphic Zone B (Figure 3.11). It consisted of a puddled-adobe patio surrounded by remains of adobe residences (Structures 25-east, 25-south, 26, and 30) and including a large tomb (Tomb 10) in the center of the patio.

Structure 26 was the most complete building of the group; the walls are of rectangular adobes over a foundation of field stones and occasional reused metates. Room 2, poorly preserved, measured just over a meter in width. Under one wall of this room was an adult skeleton, Burial 55, apparently incorporated into the building at the time of its founding; it recalled the sacrificed individual buried under the retaining

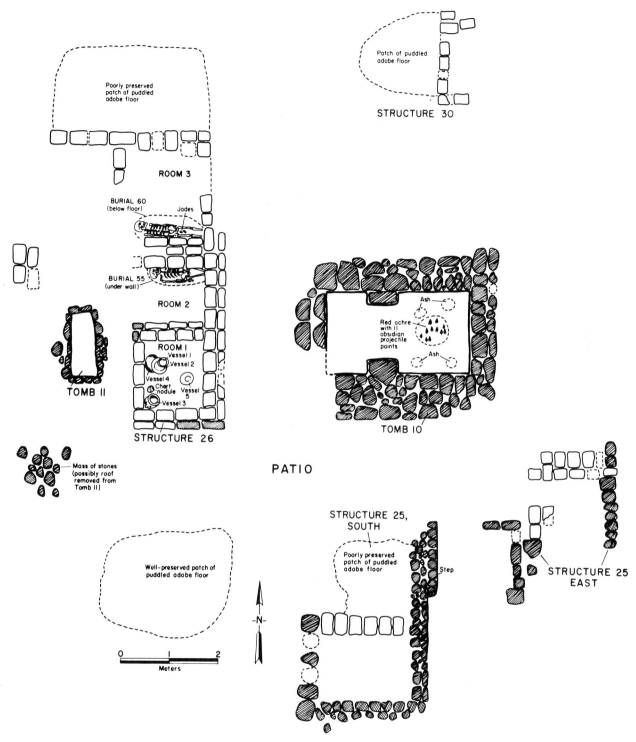

Patch of puddled adobe floor

STRUCTURE 30

Poorly preserved patch of puddled adobe floor

ROOM 3

BURIAL 60
(below floor)    Jades

BURIAL 55
(under wall)

ROOM 2

ROOM I
Vessel I
Vessel 2
Vessel 4
Chert
nodule      Vessel
            5
            Vessel 3

TOMB II

STRUCTURE 26

Mass of stones
(possibly roof
removed from
Tomb II)

Ash

Red ochre
with II
obsidian
projectile
points

Ash

TOMB 10

PATIO

Well-preserved patch of
puddled adobe floor

STRUCTURE 25,
SOUTH

Poorly preserved
patch of puddled
adobe floor

Step

STRUCTURE 25
EAST

0        1        2
Meters

-N-

FIGURE 3.11. Rosario phase elite residential complex with tombs from stratigraphic Zone B (above Structure 19) on Mound 1, San José Mogote.

wall of Platform 2 at Huitzo (see p. 62). Room 1 of Structure 26 (1.2 × 1.4 m) was apparently a storage unit of some kind, for it continued 1.0–1.2 m below the floor of the building and contained five whole vessels.[3] Because we do not know the height of the roof we cannot estimate the storage capacity of Room 1, but its subfloor area alone had a volume of close to 2 m³. Assuming the roof was at least as tall as the average adult skeleton of the period, this room would have had a storage capacity four or five times that of the average bell-shaped pit. Under the floor of Room 3 appeared Burial 60—possibly a relatively high-status Rosario woman—with an artificially deformed skull and three jade ornaments.

Tomb 10, in the center of the patio, is the largest tomb so far known from the pre-Monte Albán era in the Valley of Oaxaca; it was 3 m long and 1.7 m wide, divided by short wall stubs into a main chamber and an antechamber. The construction was of stone masonry, with a floor of flagstones and a layer of mud or adobe plaster on the walls. It appeared to have been emptied in ancient times (prior, in fact, to the Monte Albán I period), with a human patella and a few ribs left behind to indicate the former presence of a skeleton. Also left behind was a large deposit of red ocher with 11 obsidian projectile points, the only remaining vestige of an offering.

Still another tomb of this level had apparently been emptied in Formative times. This is Tomb 11, a smaller masonry sepulcher (50 × 130 cm) close to Structure 26 and probably associated with it. Nearby was a group of stones which may represent the former roof of the tomb, hastily removed and scattered. Since Zone B was the final Rosario phase level overlying Structure 19, it is possible that the skeletons and offerings from this level were taken away by departing residents at the end of the Rosario phase, which was a time of substantial population loss at San José Mogote.

In addition to this relatively high-status residence, several residences of relatively lower-status families were discovered in Area A, to the east of Mound 1 and hence more than a dozen meters lower. While badly robbed of their building stones by later settlers, these Rosario phase residences seemed to be similar to those found by Drennan (1976b) at Fábrica San José. All were apparently of rectangular adobes over a foundation of fieldstones and occasional reused metates.

From the standpoint of political evolution, it is interesting to note that even the most elaborate Rosario phase residences so far discovered could have been built by the members of one family; they required no corvée labor, such as was required by the later palaces of Monte Albán II (see Chapter 4). The compound which included Structures 25, 26, and 30 (and Tombs 10 and 11) at San José Mogote is reminiscent in some ways of the elite residential compound found by Spencer and Redmond at La Coyotera in the Cañada de Cuicatlán (Topic 17). The latter, which is broadly contemporary with the Rosario and/or Monte Albán I phases, has the same pattern of a relatively large residence with a large tomb in the patio; it also would have been within the construction capabilities of a single family. Both elite residences are in close proximity to public buildings, a pattern which continues at the later site of Monte Negro (Topic 26). We might tentatively conclude from the evidence at San José Mogote that the highest-ranking family of a Rosario phase community had sufficient power to direct the construction of a huge public building by corvée labor—and even to preempt that platform as a site for his personal residence once the building's public function had ceased—but did not yet have the power to use that same corvée labor in the construction of an elaborate residence (i.e., palace) for himself. Such leadership would be consistent with a society that was ranked but not yet stratified—a "chiefdom" rather than a "state," in Service's (1962) terms.

## BARRIO DEL ROSARIO, HUITZO

Excavations in the Barrio del Rosario of San Pablo Huitzo by Flannery ([ed.] 1970:27–37) shed some light on the development of a second-order center in the Etla arm of the valley. The site runs north–south along an intermittent tributary stream some 250 m from its confluence with the Atoyac River, at 1696 m elevation. The Formative village appears to have covered at least 2.7 ha, of which 3500 m² (about 13%) consist of an artificial mound that contains the remains of a sequence of superimposed public buildings (Flannery [ed.] 1976:Fig. 3.6).

While materials of the late San José phase are present at Huitzo, they are so covered by later structures that it is impossible to describe the site during that period. We estimate that it was a hamlet of 5 to 10 households.

### Guadalupe Phase

During the early Guadalupe phase Huitzo became a civic–ceremonial center of some importance, serving the northern end of the Etla valley. A study of ceramic design elements undertaken by S. Plog (1976) showed that Huitzo and San José Mogote shared fewer design preferences than would be predicted from the small distance (about 15 km) that separated them; if this is an accurate reflection of their degree of interaction, one could advance the hypothesis that "Huitzo and San José Mogote were competing ceremonial-civic centers and hence had less interaction than would be predicted by the gravity model" (Plog 1976:270).

*Platform 4* in stratigraphic Zone F was a structure 2 m high and more than 15 m wide, built of earth and faced with stone in the same manner as Platform 8 at San José Mogote. The structure at Huitzo rose in tiers, with a sloping outer

---

[3]These were a bowl, a large *apaxtle,* a cooking *olla,* a shallow dish, and a white-slipped anthropomorphic brasero or charcoal brazier.

wall, and was oriented 8° west of true north. Although the outside presented a boulder or cobble facing set in hard clay, the interior was of earthen fill containing predominantly San José phase sherds. Retaining the earthen fill were walls made of plano-convex or bun-shaped adobes, about 25–30 cm in diameter. Included in the structure were two carbonized pine posts 30 cm in diameter, one of which gave a radiocarbon date of 850 B.C. Judging by the burned remains we found, the fill included debris from an earlier building of wattle-and-daub, with a very thick outer coating of clay but no stucco or whitewash. Platform 4 appears to have been built at the end of the San José phase and perhaps enlarged early in the subsequent Guadalupe phase. Unfortunately, because it underlay modern houses, Platform 4 could not be fully investigated, and we do not know its precise shape or dimensions.

Above Platform 4, in stratigraphic Zone E, we found traces of a building that might once have stood on the platform. These remains included part of a plastered patio floor and the lower part of a lime-plastered stairway leading up from it; the stairway ran 8° west of true north. It was clear that we were dealing with a structure similar to Platform 3 (see below), except that this one had fronted on the east side of a patio. The upper part of the stairway (which was reinforced with plano-convex adobes) had been truncated by later construction activity.

*Platform 3* (Figure 3.12) in stratigraphic Zone C was the best-preserved Guadalupe phase public building found at Huitzo (Flannery and Marcus 1976a:Fig. 10.6). This was a platform roughly 1.3 m high and 11.5 m long east–west. The north–south width could not be determined because so much of the platform had been removed by modern adobe makers; what remained was the northernmost 3.5 m, which included a stairway 7.6 m wide. There were three steps to the stairway, and all of them, as well as the northern façade of the platform, were heavily plastered with lime plaster. The whole platform was oriented 8° west of true north, and faced onto a white-plastered patio. To the east and west, attached to Platform 3 by low benches perhaps 1 m long, were remnants of what appear to be other structures running north into the unexcavated part of the mound.

Because of the partial destruction by adobe makers, we could see a good deal of the internal structure of Platform 3. It had retaining walls of plano-convex (bun-shaped) adobes, between which there were layers of black clay and gritty yellow loam. The steps of the stairway were built of rows of such adobes, capped with hard clay. The collapsed remains of the building above the platform indicated that it was a

FIGURE 3.12.  Artist's reconstruction of Platform 3, a Guadalupe phase public building at Barrio del Rosario, Huitzo. (Drawing by N. Hansen.)

heavy, square-cornered structure of wattle-and-daub with a thick coating of adobe clay, also surfaced with white plaster.

### Rosario Phase

*Platform 2* in stratigraphic Zone B was yet another super-imposed public building, this time from late in the Rosario phase. This was a large earthen platform with retaining walls of stone and adobe, and a possible stairway on the extreme west side. Because it had been badly truncated by modern adobe makers, we could not determine the actual dimensions, but it was more than 20 m long. Most of the fill was earth with redeposited Guadalupe phase sherds, but in a few places nearly complete vessels of very late Rosario type were found. The retaining walls were oriented roughly 8° west of true north, and showed the first use of rectangular adobes in the Huitzo sequence. Under one of the adobe re-taining walls in this earthen platform we found the skeleton of an adult male 35–40 years old, head pointing north, body oriented with the long axis of the wall, and mashed flat by the weight of the adobe bricks. Called Burial 3, this indi-vidual may represent a dedication or sacrifice as part of the construction of the platform, as in the case of Burial 55 in Structure 26 at San José Mogote.

### The Late Rosario–Early Monte Albán Ia Transition

*Platform 1* in stratigraphic Zone A was the final major building found at Huitzo. It seemed to fall right at the transi-tion from the Rosario phase to Monte Albán Ia, when some of the Period Ia pottery types of Caso, Bernal, and Acosta (1967) had begun to appear, but before the final disap-pearance of three crucial Rosario phase diagnostic at-tributes—pennant incising, zoned toning, and negative white-on-gray technique (see Topic 19).

Platform 1 was composed of stone masonry walls several courses high, running east–west for at least 20 m. The main north wall was flanked by a series of curious smaller walls which may constitute either supports for a porch of some kind, or a row of small (1.5 × 1.5 m) storage rooms. The whole platform was oriented 8° west of true north. A super-imposed series of white plaster floors extended north from the main wall and passed under the small rooms; none of the debris on these floors suggested that the building had a cere-monial function. Thus, Platform 1 may have been a large residential unit of some kind, but it was so badly destroyed we may never know its exact function. In the course of our work, we found a nearly identical structure exposed in the bank of the arroyo flowing to the east of the mound, which suggests that there may have been several such buildings at Huitzo during the Rosario–Monte Albán Ia transition. The approximate distance between the two we discovered was 100 m.

### Household Units and Burials at Huitzo

Most work at Huitzo was stratigraphic and dealt with the sequence of public buildings, but fragments of at least four Guadalupe phase houses were exposed in the course of ex-cavation. Most of these had been built on the slopes of the mound not far from public buildings, a location which might indicate that the occupants were of higher-than-average status.

*House 6*, the earliest, seemed to have been built on the same land surface as Platfrom 3 and only about 2 or 3 m away from it. This house had a red or orange clay floor; four postholes were seen in cross section in the profile before work began, and a fifth was found from above during ex-cavation. Like some other house floors, the one in House 6 was slighly basin-shaped, with a clear lip or slight "bench" running along the edge.

*House 3* was a house lens with an actual basin-shaped floor, coated with clean sand. A small posthole occurred just inside the bench which rimmed the floor. House 3 had been built after the abandonment of Platform 3, and contained a few reused plano-convex adobes which probably had been "robbed" from that structure. Sherds, obsidian, and cut mica platelets were found on the floor.

*House 1*, the uppermost, also dated to the Guadalupe phase. It, too, had a basin-shaped floor coated with clean sand, and one possible posthole just inside the bench. Abun-dant chunks of burnt daub with finger-sized pole impres-sions had fallen to the floor, and a charcoal brazier was found on the floor. Elsewhere, this house produced a figu-rine, bits of Gulf Coast mussel shell, and some animal bone.

One double burial—a young man and a young woman, perhaps constituting a marital pair—was found downslope from the houses and produced no offerings.

An important midden area was found not far from the Guadalupe phase public buildings, stratigraphically inter-mediate between the white plastered stairway of Zone E and Platform 3. This midden contained a fragment of conch shell (possibly a trumpet fragment) and a broken stingray spine of the type used in ritual bloodletting (Flannery [ed.] 1976:Fig. 11.7b). The midden debris, almost certainly traceable to the nearby civic–ceremonial structures and/or elite residences, included the carbonized remains of maize, beans, cucurbits, chiles, avocados, prickly pear and organ cactus fruit, acorns, hackberries, and seeds of acacia and *cuajilote (Parmentiera)*.

## SANTO DOMINGO TOMALTEPEC

Excavations at Santo Domingo Tomaltepec by Michael E. Whalen (1976a, 1976b, 1981) revealed the history of a sec-ond-order center in the Tlacolula arm of the valley. The site lies in the piedmont zone at an elevation of 1630 m, near the point where a tributary stream emerges from a mountain canyon and flows south through the lower piedmont toward the valley floor. This is a typical location for the Tlacolula area, where piedmont tributary areas sometimes have more agricultural potential than the main Río Salado floodplain.

In the late Tierras Largas phase, Tomaltepec was a hamlet of at least two, and perhaps as many as five household units, with wattle-and-daub houses and bell-shaped storage pits. During the early San José phase it grew to an estimated five to eight household units, including both higher-status and lower-status households, plus a cemetery located beyond the limits of the site as defined by surface sherds and artifacts (Whalen 1976a:Fig. 3.8).

## Early San José Phase

The most elaborate building from the early San José phase was Structure 11, a platform roughly 4 by 8 m in extent and 1 m high (see Figure 3.13), resembling in some of its details Structure 16 at San José Mogote. It was built on large foundation stones, above which the construction was of puddled adobe, fist-size stones, and plano-convex (bun-shaped) adobes. No stairway was found, but the structure did have one unusual feature: beneath its floor was an adobe-plastered storage cell with a volume of 9 m³, approximately six times the capacity of the average bell-shaped pit of that period. Although the building had an orientation of about 8° west of north, the debris in the storage cell (and the refuse associated with the rest of Structure 11) suggested a residence rather than a public building; there was also no associated lime plaster. The debris included large numbers of deer and rabbit bones; quantities of pine charcoal; abundant mica and marine shell, including some evidence for shell-

working; carbonized maize, teosinte, and avocado; and more than 50% of the total Early Formative obsidian recovered on the site.

This relatively higher-status residence may be contrasted with House 4 in Early San José phase Household Unit 2 (Flannery [ed.] 1976:20 and Fig. 2.5), a relatively lower-status household. This ordinary wattle-and-daub house had no platform, much less animal bone, much less obsidian, virtually no marine shell, and a chipped-stone sample composed mostly of locally available chert. Thus, as at San José Mogote, relatively higher status seems to have been reflected in greater access to nonlocal products, relatively greater access to deer meat, greater involvement in ornament production, and a residence more elaborate than the average, although not beyond the construction capacity of a single family.

The cemetery outside the residential limits of the village was an unexpected and exciting discovery: more than 60 burials, amounting to the remains of some 80 individuals, 55 of whom could be aged and sexed by physical anthropologist Richard G. Wilkinson (Whalen 1981). There were no infants in the cemetery (babies apparently were buried near the house, as at San Sebastián Abasolo), and only one child. All the remaining burials were those of adults or of adolescents old enough to have passed through puberty, that is, the initiated members of the community; the oldest were over 50 years.

There were virtually equal numbers of males and females in the cemetery, but most females had died at 20 to 29 years and most males had survived until 30 to 39 years of age. All burials were face down, and almost all had their heads to the east; a few males were flexed, but most burials were fully extended. Most of the secondary burials at the site occurred with the flexed group, that is, they had been added to the burial of a flexed male.

Although the flexed males constituted only 12.7% of the cemetery, they received 50% of the burial vessels with carved fire-serpent designs and 88% of the jade beads; 66% of the burials covered by stone slabs also fell in this flexed-male group. As at Tierras Largas (Topic 16) and San José Mogote, vessels with fire-serpents occurred exclusively with males. One 20 to 29-year-old male with a cylindrical fire-serpent vessel was accompanied by a 20–29-year-old female with a magnetite ornament in the shape of an Olmec U motif; this couple may represent a husband and wife pair.

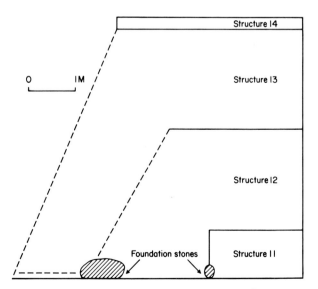

FIGURE 3.13. Schematic representation of stratigraphic relationship of Structures 11–14 at Santo Domingo Tomaltepec. (After Whalen 1976a.)

## Late San José and Guadalupe Phases

These phases are poorly represented at Tomaltepec. As noted in Topic 14, pottery diagnostics of the Guadalupe phase, as originally defined at Huitzo, are rare to absent everywhere in the Tlacolula region. Thus, their absence at Tomaltepec may represent regional stylistic variation rather than chronological discontinuity.

## Rosario Phase

It was during the Rosario phase that Tomaltepec became a second-order site in our tentative Middle Formative hierarchy—smaller and less elaborate than San José Mogote, yet larger and more elaborate than Tierras Largas and Fábrica San José. Rosario phase Tomaltepec was a community of 10 to 15 household units, with at least one public building of modest proportions.

*Structure 12,* an adobe platform, was more than 3 m high. It was founded on a series of stone slabs up to a meter long, and its fill was earth and rock rubble. As in the case of Platform 2 at Huitzo, there were burials included in the fill—one adult male of 40 years, and three females aged approximately 14, 30, and 40 years. Unfortunately, the full dimensions of this public building could not be investigated, but it seems to have continued in use into the Monte Albán Ia period, at which time some new floors were laid down on its surface.

It is doubtful that Whalen's excavations exposed the full range of residences at Rosario phase Tomaltepec. One pair of houses (Numbers 5 and 7) formed an L-shaped unit, partially framing a patio or work area. Each house had roughly 10.5 m² of floor area and was built of adobes over a stone foundation. Associated features included an oven or roasting pit, a hearth, two infant burials beneath the patio, and a fragment of what may be a turtle-shell drum. This unit may represent the residences of an extended family or two closely related nuclear families.

## GENERAL OBSERVATIONS

At this writing, first- and second-order sites of the Early and Middle Formative have produced more than three dozen household units and over 100 burials. It is hoped that future excavations will substantially increase this sample; some tentative observations can be advanced at this point.

The larger Early and Middle Formative communities in the Valley of Oaxaca seem to reflect a society with steadily increasing differences in status. In the Early Formative, all residences seem to have been wattle-and-daub nuclear family houses. The simplest had no whitewash and only a modest range of primarily utilitarian artifacts; others had a burnished and whitewashed surface and more diversified debris, including mica, *Spondylus* and pearl oyster shell, iron ores, and imported fish and stingray spines. At least one residence (in a magnetite mirror-producing residential ward) was on a meter-high platform. By the Middle Formative, the most important residences consisted of groups of adobe-walled rooms flanking a common courtyard, and may have housed extended families.

One way in which relatively high Early Formative status was expressed was through differential access to exotic raw materials and the objects made from them, especially objects used in sacred ritual or personal ornamentation. In the case of obsidian, there is some evidence that higher-status families at San José Mogote may have acted as a central agency which received, pooled, and later redistributed this product to other families (Pires-Ferreira 1975). By the Middle Formative, another way in which relatively high status was expressed was in the location of residences near public buildings. In two Rosario phase cases, at Huitzo and San José Mogote, elite families seem to have preempted localities formerly occupied by public buildings. This phenomenon was particularly striking at San José Mogote, where the locality was on a 15-m high mound with no other Rosario phase residences on it, and human sacrifice may have accompanied the construction of the building.

Burials in the Early Formative show a similar continuum from simple (individuals buried with no offerings) to more elaborate (individuals buried with jade labrets and earspools, well-made pottery, shell or magnetite ornaments). The tendency for gray or white vessels bearing Olmec designs to occur with male burials suggests that some men belonged to descent lines with the fire-serpent or were-jaguar as apical ancestor. Most Early Formative burials were individual, but through time there were increases in double burials involving a man and a woman (perhaps a marital pair) and of cases where secondary burials were added to the primary burial of an adult male (perhaps a household head). From the San José phase onward, some skulls (most often those of women) show the tabular deformation that was considered a sign of beauty and high status in later periods. We still do not know why some individuals were buried near the house, while others (primarily adults) were buried in cemeteries set apart from the residences; nor do we know why certain individuals were accompanied by dog burials. Finally, certain Early Formative adults were buried in graves lined with stone slabs; by the Middle Formative, at least a few were in actual masonry tombs, one of which (associated with a Rosario phase elite residence) had two chambers.

Formative ritual is reflected in burials, in households, and in public buildings. Small, solid figurines were arranged to form ritual scenes, one of which was buried under the floor of a relatively high-status Early Formative household (Flannery [ed.] 1976:Fig. 11.9); large, hollow figurines were occasionally included with Middle Formative burials. Pottery masks, dance costume parts, and turtle-shell drums were found in household units, conch-shell trumpets near public buildings. Ritual bloodletting with fish or stingray spines was carried out in the Early Formative; human sacrifice, perhaps on large stone altars, was carried out by the Rosario phase. Some probable sacrificial victims were included in the foundations of Rosario phase buildings, and at least one named victim may have been represented on a carved stone monument. It would be interesting to know whether this particular victim was a captive taken in combat, for this would be our first evidence suggesting that armed conflict was an important aspect of Middle Formative culture.

## TOPIC 16
# The Growth of Site Hierarchies in the Valley of Oaxaca: Part II

ROBERT D. DRENNAN
KENT V. FLANNERY

In this topic, we discuss the third tier in the site-size hierarchy for the San José, Guadalupe, and Rosario phases in the Valley of Oaxaca. The sites in this tier were primarily hamlets of 1 to 3 ha in size, consisting of an estimated 5 to 15 households and a population somewhere between 25 and 75 persons. None has produced conclusive evidence for public architecture.

A number of observations have already been made about these hamlets in earlier publications (e.g. Flannery [ed.] 1976). For one thing, sites in the third tier showed little tendency to grow; Tierras Largas remained at 8 to 10 households throughout most of its history, and Fábrica San José seems never to have grown beyond 10 to 12 families. For another thing, many institutions seen at large sites during the Early Formative appear at small sites during the Middle Formative. For example, at Middle Formative Tierras Largas, Winter and Pires-Ferreira (1976) found the same evidence for pooling of obsidian by a central agency which had appeared during the Early Formative at San José Mogote. And Middle Formative Tierras Largas and Fábrica San José show some evidence of burial grounds segregated from residential areas, a phenomenon already seen in the Early Formative at San José Mogote and Tomaltepec.

Let us now examine in detail three hamlets in the third tier of the size hierarchy, in order to see what other general observations can be made.

## FÁBRICA SAN JOSÉ

Fábrica San José (Drennan 1976b) is a small Formative hamlet in the lower piedmont 5 km east of San José Mogote. It overlooks a perennial tributary stream which is used for canal irrigation today, and may have been so used in the past, although there is no direct evidence in the form of Precolumbian canals. The site adjoins a series of mineral springs which constitute one of the best sources for edible salt in the Valley of Oaxaca; ancient spring activity in the area has also produced massive travertine deposits of fine-grained commercial quality.[1] Studies by S. Plog (1976) show Fábrica San José to have shared a high percentage of ceramic design preferences with San José Mogote, as might be predicted from their close proximity. Fábrica San José may thus serve as an example of a third-order site in the Etla region—one that, lacking any public buildings of its own, presumably used (and participated in the maintenance of) those at San José Mogote. Indeed, large slabs of Fábrica San José travertine were found in Structure 19A at San José Mogote.

### Subsistence at Fábrica San José

Fábrica San José's piedmont and salt-spring location presented it with a different set of subsistence possibilities when contrasted with San José Mogote. When a circle of 2.5-km radius is drawn around the latter site, it contains 76% alluvium and 24% piedmont. A similar circle drawn around Fábrica San José would include 73% piedmont, 15% mountains, and 12% alluvium. This proximity to the forested mountain zone seems to have affected hunting at Fábrica San José: bones of white-tail deer represent 30–67% of the animal remains at various proveniences there, as contrasted with 18–21% of the bones at sites like Huitzo and San José Mogote. Cottontail rabbit was more common at Huitzo and San José Mogote, however, and mud turtle was particularly common at the latter site (presumably because of its riverine location). The game hunted by the villagers at Fábrica San José showed high species diversity, including peccary, jackrabbit, gray fox, raccoon, coatimundi, ringtail cat, skunk, weasel, tree squirrel, quail, raven, owl, hawk, and falcon.

Apparently the mountains provided Fábrica San José with a greater variety of fuels than San José Mogote; pine dominates in charcoal samples from the latter site, but oak was as common as pine at Fábrica San José, and manzanita, acacia, and mesquite were also used. Fábrica San José also seems to have grown more avocados, perhaps in the humid tributary canyons behind the site. The maize at Fábrica San José was grown with teosinte, and kernels of both occurred in the carbonized remains (Ford 1976). So did maguey, beans, white zapotes (*Casimiroa*), and *chipil* (*Crotalaria*), a field weed whose leaves are still eaten by the Zapotec as greens.

Finally, it appears that most households at Fábrica San José engaged in a little salt production; the salt was evidently rendered down in ollas, which still retain a carbonate crust from the local water. It should be stressed that there is no evidence that this was either a commercial specialization or a full-time craft. The occupants of Fábrica San José were basically farmers, but taking advantage of the nearby spring they may well have produced enough salt to supply neighboring villages. This seems to have been a village activity, not restricted to higher status households but generally widespread.

---

[1] This fine-grained travertine ($CaCO_3$) is the stone referred to erroneously in some site reports as "Oaxaca onyx" or "marble"; it is the type of stone used, for example, in the famous Lápida de Bazán (see Topic 53).

## Early Guadalupe Phase

Fábrica San José seems to have been founded first by a single household (Early Guadalupe-1), followed by a second (E.G.-3), then a third (E.G.-2) which may be an expansion of E.G.-1. Households 1 and 2 occur near each other, more than 100 m upslope from E.G.-3.

## Late Guadalupe Phase

During the Late Guadalupe phase, the hamlet expanded to about 11 households. These were divided into two groups: two households (Late Guadalupe-1 and -2) were upslope in the area formerly occupied by E.G.-1 and -2, and 9 households (L.G.-3 to L.G.-11) were downslope in the area formerly occupied by E.G.-3. Within each of these spatially defined groups 1 household (L.G.-1 in the upslope group and L.G.-6 in the downslope group) seems to reflect families of higher status than the others in its group; however, the differences are of degree rather than kind, and do not suggest a division into social strata. These higher-status households have higher percentages of bowls and of decorated white-slipped bowls, more artifacts of exotic raw material, and more children buried with numerous offerings. Associated with the higher-status household in the downslope group was an area (called L.G.-7 although it may actually have been part of the same household as L.G.-6) where people engaged in the working of craft items. Included were fragments of a possible turtle-shell drum and a shell ornament whose shape virtually duplicates a motif on Monument 3 from San José Mogote (compare Drennan 1976b:Fig. 78d with Figure 3.10, this volume).

One possible interpretation of this community pattern is that the sites of the original founding households at Fábrica San José remained relatively high-status residential areas throughout the Guadalupe phase; the higher-status Late Guadalupe households (L.G.-1 and -6) were in the same locations as the first two households founded at the site (E.G.-1 and -3). A similar pattern has been noted at Tomaltepec (see Topic 15). Late Guadalupe-1, perhaps the most elaborate household unit, featured a house with a partial stone foundation and as many as five superimposed sand floors, each perhaps representing a refurbishing of the house. Associated with the house were several hearths, some midden debris, at least one jar sherd with a calcareous crust suggesting the rendering of salt, six human burials, and a buried dog. One of the human burials was a woman of about 60 years,[2] laid to rest face down with 53 jade beads, a jade pendant, and a brown stone bead, all in her mouth. She was accompanied by a Delia White cylinder beneath her chest, two Atoyac Yellow-white bowls, and a Fidencio Coarse jar. The other burials were those of children between the ages of

2 and 5 years, each with 1 to 5 greenstone (jade-like) beads; two of them were accompanied by Atoyac Yellow-white vessels. These would be relatively elaborate burials by the standards of our present Guadalupe phase sample.

## Rosario Phase

The Rosario phase community is estimated at about 10 to 16 households. During this phase, the area of relatively higher-status households shifted. Rosario-1, the most elaborate, appeared in an area of the site that had formerly been occupied by a relatively lower-status household; the next most elaborate, Rosario-3, emerged in an area where no one had previously lived. At the same time the area previously occupied by the relatively high-status household Late Guadalupe-1 was converted to a Rosario phase cemetery, segregated from the residential areas of the community. This development may be compared with that of Area C at San José Mogote, where an area previously occupied by Tierras Largas phase public buildings was turned into a small San José phase cemetery (see Topic 15).

Rosario-1, perhaps the most interesting of the higher-status households of this phase, included a house whose stone foundation had been partially removed for use in later structures. Associated were a hearth, several middens, two burials, and a bell-shaped pit filled with fire-cracked rocks that had evidently been used as an earth oven. One burial was that of an adult (probably female) under 40 years of age, accompanied by a fine gray vessel, a burnished brown bowl, and a large obsidian flake. The other was a young woman of about 15 years of age with an artificially deformed skull; her burial offerings included a marine shell, six fine gray vessels, and a large hollow ceramic doll (Drennan 1976b:Fig. 89). While these are relatively elaborate burials by the standards of our Rosario phase sample they are clearly of a different order of complexity from the broadly contemporary "chief's tomb" at La Coyotera (see Topic 17). Other Rosario phase discoveries, such as Tomb 10 at San José Mogote (Topic 15), make it appear that the continuum of rank now had greater extremes than at any previous period in Oaxaca prehistory.

Partial exploration of the Rosario phase cemetery at Fábrica San José yielded at least 10 burials, some of them multiple interments. All ages and both sexes seem to be represented; most burials have at least one vessel, and some have as many as three. If one can judge from the offerings, these would appear to be individuals of modest social status.

1. *Adult males*
   Burial 38:   accompanied by two infants and one fine gray vessel
   Burial 45:   accompanied by three secondary burials, at least one male and one female
   Burial 50:   grave has stone slabs, pearl oyster offering
   Burial 52:   skull artifically deformed; accompanied by three fine gray vessels (one of them an animal effigy), a figurine, and a "greenstone" bead

---

[2]All aging and sexing of burials at sites discussed in this topic is by Richard G. Wilkinson, State University of New York at Albany.

2. *Teenage males*
   Burial 44:  accompanied by one fine gray bowl, one pot rest
3. *Adult females*
   Burial 19:  accompanied by one fine gray effigy vessel
   Burial 27:  accompanied by one coarse jar, one fine gray bowl
   Burial 36:  possibly accompanied by a stone celt
4. *Infants*
   Burial 37:  accompanied by one fine gray miniature vessel
   Burial 53:  no offerings

## SAN SEBASTIÁN ABASOLO

San Sebastián Abasolo (Flannery [ed.] 1970:70–78) serves as an example of an Early and Middle Formative hamlet in the western part of the Valley of Tlacolula. Lying 15 km east–southeast of Oaxaca City, Abasolo today is a small, relatively prosperous village surrounded on all sides by an extremely productive, broad alluvial plain. Individual fields around Abasolo produce three crops of vegetables (maize, garlic, and chiles) in a single year. This is made possible by a high water table which allows irrigation from shallow wells three times a week, regardless of season.

The main church at Abasolo rests on an almost imperceptible rise of higher ground which does not flood during the summer rains; this area also seems to have been the main locus of prehistoric settlement. The altitude here is about 1600 m; frosts are not unknown, so farmers protect the seed beds of their winter-grown chiles with covers of straw, thatch, or burlap.

A kilometer and a half south of Abasolo, the Río Salado is joined by a tributary coming from San Juan Teitipac. A kilometer to the east, another tributary enters from the region of Teotitlán del Valle. The latter stream, now dry for the greater part of the year, flows through the important archaeological zone of Macuilxochitl and past the newly explored ruins of Dainzú (Topic 33). Still other sites occur on the limestone and volcanic tuff hills rising out of the plain 2 km to the north and east. At this writing, it seems likely that the population whose massive architectural works grew to line that tributary, from Tlacochahuaya and Dainzú through Macuilxochitl and Teotitlán, had its beginnings in the Early Formative settlement at Abasolo.

### San José Phase

The San José phase component at Abasolo probably covers no more than 1–2 hectares (5–10 households) and lies buried beneath 2 m of recent alluvium and Postclassic deposits. Stratigraphic Zone D in Test A was a midden of this phase, associated with two apparent wells, Features 3 and 6.

Both were "walk-in" wells (in Southwest United States terminology), wide and funnel-shaped at the top and tapering to a narrow tube-like shaft farther down. While the purpose of the wells cannot be proven, the excavators suspect that both were used for the kind of hand irrigation (*riego a brazo*) employed at Abasolo, Zaachila, and other high-water-table localities in the Valley of Oaxaca (see Topic 94). Both wells were filled with trash and organic debris, which on being subjected to flotation in the laboratory produced a quantity of identifiable carbonized seeds. In the bottom of each well was a smashed *cántaro*, made of pottery but otherwise analogous in form to the jars used today for drawing water from wells for *riego a brazo*.

A clay house floor and a thin lens of San José phase debris overlay Zone D and sealed it off from above. Zone C, stratigraphically higher, was another midden layer of the San José phase. Included in this midden, which may be associated with the patio area of a household unit, were three infant burials of the San José phase. It seemed to the excavators that these three infants (all too young to be identified as to age or sex) might have belonged to the same household, but were buried at different times.

Offerings with these infant burials were more elegant than those of many adult burials of the period. One (Burial 4) was accompanied by three Leandro Gray cylinders, two of which had carved decoration in the form of the Olmec fire-serpent. A second (Burial 1) had three more carved gray cylinders with fire-serpent designs done in a different style. The third (Burial 2) had two small *tecomates* or neckless jars, one of them a cucurbit effigy. The sex of the infants is unknown, but San José phase adult burials receiving such *tecomates* are frequently female and adults receiving cylinders with fire-serpent designs have so far always been male. What the Abasolo burials show is that such offerings could occur even with infants or children too young to have gone through initiation or to have "acquired" status through their accomplishments.

One other San José phase burial at Abasolo—Burial 3—was an adult stuffed into a bell-shaped pit and unaccompanied by any offerings. He was not associated with the infants, having come from another household on a different stratigraphic level.

Two other interesting features of the San José phase occurred in Test C. Feature 9 was a maguey-roasting oven; Feature 11 was a very large San José phase bell-shaped pit (not a well) with a maximum diameter of 2 m, probably originally a storage facility but ending up as a refuse pit. Included in the fill were masses of burnt daub with house pole or cane impressions, stones, charcoal, and ash; based on findings at other sites, we can reasonably suspect the presence of a nearby San José phase house whose walls had been destroyed and thrown in the pit. There were definite whitewashed-wall clay fragments present, and the occupants of the house had apparently eaten quite a bit of deer (killed in the dry season, to judge by its antlers), some dog and jackrabbit, and evidently human flesh as well. A roasted and butchered fragment of human fibula found in this area suggests that at Abasolo, as at many other Formative sites in the Valley of Oaxaca and the Mixteca, ritual cannibalism was practiced.

Finally, it should be noted that S. Plog's (1976) study of Atoyac Yellow-white pottery motifs showed Abasolo to have shared more design frequencies with San José Mogote than would have been predicted on the basis of distance, and to have shared fewer with Huitzo. Assuming this situation reflects rates of interaction, one could conclude that San José Mogote was a far more important regional civic–ceremonial center for the people of Abasolo than was Huitzo. Plog's study, however, was done before the excavation of Tomaltepec, a small civic–ceremonial center even closer to Abasolo. Future design studies should be aimed at establishing the degree of similarity between these two sites before any final conclusions are drawn.

### Rosario Phase

Little is known of the Rosario phase component at Abasolo, but it appears to have been not much larger than the San José phase component. Feature 8 in Test B was either a bell-shaped pit or a collapsed "walk-in" well, found badly deteriorated below the present-day water table. Despite erosion and subsequent caving in, it was evident that the upper part of this feature had originally been lined with stone slabs. After abandonment, it had been filled with mixed San José phase and early Rosario phase trash, including carbonized maize kernels and cob fragments, beans, chiles, maguey quids, and nearly 100 avocado pits. In addition, the muck at the bottom of the feature contained a special vessel that may have been designed for drawing water from a well by means of a rope. Superficially shaped like a large *tecomate*, the vessel has a loop handle for easy pouring and an off-center mouth which permits it to flop over on its side and fill easily when lowered into water.

### Summary

Settlement at San Sebastián Abasolo began in the Early Formative, apparently on a gentle slope which rose imperceptibly above the humid flood plain of the Río Salado. Farming may have been intensified with shallow wells that reached water table after only 2.5–3.0 meters of digging; maize, avocados, beans, and chile peppers were grown. Although the settlement may have been no more than 1–2 ha in extent during the San José phase, it included households whose infant children were buried with gray cylinders bearing excised glyphs of the Olmec fire-serpent. Ritual cannibalism evidently occurred at Abasolo, but no "public" ritual or ceremonial buildings have come to light there; the overall impression is of a hamlet of 5 to 10 household units, each of which might have had a few bell-shaped pits, 1–2 walk-in wells, and perhaps a maguey-roasting oven.

## TIERRAS LARGAS

The site of Tierras Largas (Winter 1972, 1976c) is a small Formative hamlet on the tip of a piedmont spur below the ruins of Atzompa. This spur is surrounded on three sides by the flat alluvial deposits of a former stage of the Atoyac River. Fully a kilometer wide, this belt of alluvium is partly planted in alfalfa, indicating the presence of a high water table and good clay soil.

The area studied by Winter was apparently a hamlet whose size fluctuated between 0.95 and 3.0 ha and whose occupation varied between 5 and 10 households during seven consecutive subphases (Early Tierras Largas through Rosario). No clear evidence for public buildings was ever established for this time span. An artificial mound not far to the west (and upslope from Winter's study area) was later found by Kowalewski (personal communication, 1976) to display surface sherds of many of these same periods; however, it is not known whether this discovery reflects a second Formative residential ward or a later mound built with Formative fill. We therefore tentatively consider Tierras Largas to be another example of a small third-order community in the Etla region. Ceramic design studies by S. Plog (1976) show enough shared motifs between Tierras Largas and San José Mogote to suggest that the latter site was probably the local civic–ceremonial center serving the former.

### Tierras Largas Phase

During this period, Tierras Largas consisted of about 10 households, covering an area of 1.58 to 2.24 ha. No evidence of status differentiation was found in the sample of houses, burials, or features. One of the most fully exposed household units was L.T.L.-1 of the Late Tierras Largas phase (Winter 1976a:Fig. 2.8 and p. 31). The house itself was of whitewashed wattle-and-daub, covering about 4 by 6 m; to the west, and presumably associated, were eight bell-shaped pits with an average storage capacity of 1.5 m³. Members of this household had engaged in agriculture (as indicated by carbonized maize kernels and avocado seeds), food preparation (as indicated by 14 fragments of metates and manos), hunting and trapping (as indicated by the bones of deer, cottontail, jackrabbit, gopher, and mud turtle), and sewing (as indicated by a bone needle). The bell-shaped pits also yielded fragments of turtleshell drum, and some wing bones of the blue-green macaw which had been cut as if to remove the feathers.

Several adult members of this household had died during the occupation. One woman, 20–30 years of age, had been buried in an open area west of the house; another adult female had been buried in a bell-shaped pit. Finally, a man over 40 years of age had been buried fully extended (face up) in a large bell-shaped pit near the house. Since the fill of that pit included more than 70 fragments of burnt daub with cane impressions, it is possible that the house had been abandoned and destroyed—and its remains buried—following the death of that middle-aged male individual.

## San José Phase

During this period, Tierras Largas was a hamlet estimated at 5 to 8 households covering an area of between 0.95 and 1.59 ha. Household unit L.S.J.-1 of the Late San José phase includes one of the more complete houses found (Flannery and Winter 1976:Fig. 2.17). The house was approximately 3.4 by 7 m in extent, but part of its longer dimension included a raised bench with *petate* (mat) impressions, which might have been a sleeping area. Most chert cores, scrapers, areas of retouch flakes, and at least one biface lay in front or to the left of the door as one would enter. All bone needles, deer-bone cornhuskers, and pierced-sherd discs, which may be spindle whorls, lay in front or to the right of the door as one would enter; this part of the house also included a gray ash deposit from cooking activity, containing another bone needle and deer-bone cornhusker. These findings raised the possibility that the house had been conceptually divided into male and female work areas.

Like other San José phase samples, the burials from Tierras Largas show a continuum from what may be relatively lower-status individuals to what may be relatively higher-status individuals. Individuals with relatively few offerings include Burials 40 and 42 in Area C, possibly in the vicinity of a lower-status household. Burial 40 was an adult, possibly female, buried in the seated position within an abandoned oven. Burial 42 was a 35–40-year-old man stuffed head first into an abandoned bell-shaped pit.

Two somewhat more elaborate burials came from Area A, possibly in the vicinity of a somewhat higher-status household. Burial 11 was a male over 40 years of age with a jade or greenstone gorget near his face and a small, burnished gray jar at his left shoulder. Burial 4, an adult whose skeleton had been plowed away except for the lower legs, was accompanied by three Atoyac Yellow-white cylinders, a burnished jar, and a dog burial.

Finally, Burial 20, a male over 40 years of age, was accompanied by two obsidian blades and a Leandro Gray bowl with carved Olmec fire-serpent motifs. Although badly decomposed, Burial 20 appeared to be oriented east–west in the flexed position, his arms folded on his chest, like so many of the presumed higher-status males in the Tomaltepec cemetery (see Topic 15). Thus the sample of burials from Tierras Largas, while too small to draw any meaningful conclusions from in its own right, reinforces some of the patterns seen at sites with larger samples of San José phase burials.

## Guadalupe Phase

During this period, Tierras Largas remained at an estimated 9 to 10 households, though these were now scattered over an area of about 3 ha. Its size and population, therefore, approximated those of Fábrica San José during the same period. While the sample of structures excavated is not large, Winter (1972:99) has assumed on the basis of the available evidence that a "typical" household unit included at least one house, two burials, four bell-shaped pits, and two ovens. It is possible that some of the larger units consisted of an extended family occupying two adjacent houses fronting on the same courtyard or open work area.

The Guadalupe phase sample includes the first dual or multiple burials at Tierras Largas. It will be remembered that some multiple burials were already present in the San José phase cemetery at Tomaltepec, and that some interments of that period at San José Mogote (e.g., Tomb 3 and Burial 16) may represent a husband and wife buried side by side; Burials 1 and 2 at Huitzo may be Guadalupe phase examples of the same pattern. The evidence from Tierras Largas confirms the strength of this trend toward dual or multiple burials during the Middle Formative.

Each of the Guadalupe phase multiple burials at Tierras Largas involved an adult male, possibly a household head. Burial 46 consisted of a 35–40-year-old male, an adult female, and a child less than one year old; they were accompanied by two white-slipped vessels. Burial 36 consisted of a 25–35-year-old male, another adult tentatively identified as a female, and a child of 9 years; all had been buried in an abandoned oven, unaccompanied by grave goods. Burial 18 consisted of an adult male and a female less than 40 years of age accompanied by a small coarse jar.

In addition, Winter (1972:239) found one skeleton (Burial 24) eroding out of a small arroyo 200 m northwest of the main occupation area as defined by surface ceramics. This 30–40-year-old female was fully extended face down (like the burials in the Tomaltepec cemetery), covered by stone slabs, and possibly associated with an Atoyac Yellow-white vessel nearby. This burial raises the question of whether Tierras Largas might have had a segregated cemetery area away from the household units like the one at Tomaltepec.

## Rosario Phase

Tierras Largas remained a hamlet of 3 ha with an estimated nine households during the Rosario phase. It is possible that during that phase there was an increase in status differentiation

> with the appearance of a high-status residence in the center of the occupation area [see Winter 1976b:Fig. 8.5]. More excavation will be necessary to confirm this possibility, but we did find a prepared earth floor, a concentration of [33] postholes, three large ovens, and a number of artifacts that may indicate the presence of a high-status residence. . . . Common or low-status Rosario phase households are dispersed around the center of the site where the probable high-status residence is located [Winter 1976b:229].

We would hasten to add here that, however elaborate this household may have seemed in the context of Tierras

Largas, there is no evidence to suggest that it was more elaborate than the large, stone-founded houses of relatively higher-status families at Fábrica San José or the adobe residential compound (Structures 25, 26, and 30) atop Mound 1 at San José Mogote. Rather, the households at Tierras Largas fit within an apparent continuum of Rosario phase structures, from relatively humble to relatively elaborate.

The evidence for a cemetery area, segregated from the residences at Tierras Largas, becomes stronger during the Rosario phase. Two poorly preserved burials (30 and 31) were discovered far to the southwest of the known residential area, in a locality that apparently served as a cemetery in Late Formative times. Burial 30 consisted of two adults of indeterminate sex, apparently extended in a common grave. Burial 31 consisted of an adult male and an individual of undetermined sex and age, also apparently extended. Two other burials (one of them a child of 6 to 8 years) were found in the residential area of the site.

In short, despite the relative diversity of structures at Rosario phase Tierras Largas and its relatively high number of ovens when contrasted with earlier periods (Winter 1976b:Fig. 8.5), it seems never to have been more than a hamlet in the third tier of our proposed size hierarchy.

### General Observations on Third-Order Sites

While considerably more work is needed before we fully understand the hamlets or "third-order" sites of this period, a few observations can be made. The nuclear family seems to have been the basic unit of residence during San José and Guadalupe times, with some evidence for extended families appearing during the Guadalupe and Rosario phases. In some cases, as at Tierras Largas, it appears that houses may have been destroyed after the death of a male household head.

Some evidence for economic specialization on the hamlet level comes from Fábrica San José, where salt was produced from saline springs at the site. The salt thus produced was presumably used at other communities in the valley, as well as at Fábrica San José. At the same time, salt production seems to have been a part-time specialty engaged in by households that were also agricultural; it represents the focusing of productive effort by many (or all) households in a single hamlet on a product that could be produced particularly advantageously at that locality.

During the Middle Formative at Tierras Largas, there is evidence for the pooling of obsidian from various sources by some central agency, for later distribution to households. This pooling continues a trend seen already in the Early Formative at large villages like San José Mogote. The same kinds of ritual paraphernalia reaching large villages—conch-shell trumpets, turtle-shell drums, pottery masks, macaw feathers, and fish spines—also reached the hamlets, but perhaps in smaller quantities. Some status differences between residents of first-order and third-order sites may also be reflected in the ritual debris: "true" stingray spines

are rare in the hamlets, and both Tierras Largas and Fábrica San José yielded imitation stringray spines whittled from bone splinters (Flannery [ed.] 1976:Table 11.4).

Residents at hamlets exhibit the already-mentioned continuum of statuses from relatively low to relatively high, without a clear division into social classes. They may lack examples of the relatively highest-status families seen at large sites like San José Mogote, however, just as they apparently lack public buildings. Better-made and/or larger houses, with more evidence of exotic materials obtained through interregional exchange, also have a higher proportion of fine gray or white serving bowls to cooking jars—perhaps reflecting the feeding of more persons, or persons of more importance. Some burials show the deliberate tabular skull deformation which we know was a symbol of higher status in later periods. The association of pottery vessels bearing Olmec fire-serpent or were-jaguar motifs with male burials, already seen at first-order and second-order sites, appears also at hamlets. Moreover, burials at Abasolo suggest that the association may have been there from infancy.

While most burials of the Tierras Largas phase were single individuals, the pattern became more complex at San José phase sites like San José Mogote and Tomaltepec; this complexity reached the hamlet level during Guadalupe and Rosario times. Although some individuals were buried near the house (or in a convenient bell-shaped pit nearby), small cemeteries kept apart from the residential areas became more common during the Middle Formative. Double burials—usually an adult male and an adult female, with one of the pair having been added later—increase in frequency. There are also multiple burials, including one or more primary individuals accompanied by secondary interments as well; because at least one primary adult male is usually present in these multiple burials, they may represent family members reburied with a male household head. The fact that females received some of the richest offerings at Fábrica San José could mean that women from higher-ranking families at sites like San José Mogote occasionally married into somewhat less-important families at neighboring hamlets, but this is only one possible explanation.

The Middle Formative trend toward "husband-and-wife" or "family" burials was to increase with time, and to supplant the pattern of male burials with fire-serpent and were-jaguar vessels. It may therefore reflect an important sociopolitical trend, in which the elite family became a more and more important institution while descent from a mythological Olmec ancestor became a less and less important one.

One can follow the history of several relatively higher-status households at Fábrica San José. The site was founded during the Early Guadalupe phase by a single household, soon followed by a second. By the Late Guadalupe phase, when the hamlet had grown to 11 households, it was the families occupying the same locations as the original founders that seem to have occupied the two positions of highest status in the community. This phenomenon is consistent with the later Zapotec-Mixtec system of ranking, in which the more ancient, "founding" descent lines were of higher rank than the "cadet" descent lines that branched off from them. It would take a much more extensive program of excavation, however, to expose the sociopolitical organization of the Middle Formative in any detail.

One reason this more extensive program is needed is that Valley-wide developments undoubtedly affected the organization of even the smallest hamlets. For example, a shift in the locus of higher-status households took place during the Rosario phase at Fábrica San José, suggesting that the traditional pattern of rank ascription was disrupted. Such a disruption may have been connected to the Rosario phase reorganization of San José Mogote, which we are only beginning to investigate.

Finally, during the Late Guadalupe phase, one area of Fábrica San José seems to have been occupied by part-time specialists in the production of ornaments from a variety of raw materials. This area was spatially associated with one of the higher-status households of the community, raising the possibilities that the higher-status household was composed of a larger number of individuals than other households and that some of these extra individuals specialized in the production of ornaments serving as insignia of status. An alternative interpretation is that a separate household, including part-time craft specialists, was attached to the higher-status household.

# TOPIC 17
# A Middle Formative Elite Residence and Associated Structures at La Coyotera, Oaxaca

CHARLES S. SPENCER
ELSA M. REDMOND

From November 1977 to April 1978, excavations were carried out at the site of La Coyotera, near Dominguillo in the Cañada de Cuicatlán (see Figure 4.23). One of the goals of our excavation program was the partial exposure of a village contemporary with the Rosario and Monte Albán I phases in the Valley of Oaxaca (600–300 B.C.). Largely because of the shallowness of the site, we were able to open up more than 1600 m² of excavated area. In the course of this work we recovered the remains of nearly two dozen complete houses, along with associated features and burials. The result is a revealing picture of the anatomy of a Middle Formative village.

We found that the village was organized into a series of large residential compounds, each measuring about 30–40 m on a side and separated from the others by at least 25 to 35 meters of unoccupied space. We were able to excavate one compound completely and extensively test one of the others. The compound we exposed completely consisted of 18 structures arranged around three patios. The westernmost of these patio groups appears to have been where the highest-ranking family of the village resided. This patio group will be the focus of this brief report.

On the south side of the patio in question we located a structure we called House 4. As we began to excavate House 4, we quickly realized that it was not a house in the normal sense, but rather a mausoleum. Laid to rest in this elaborate tomb was an adult male individual[1] in an extended supine position with his head to the north. The body had been painted with red pigment prior to interment, and was accompanied by 30 whole ceramic vessels and several shell ornaments, including a shell necklace. By comparison, no other burial we excavated had more than 3 associated ceramic vessels, and two burials had no burial accompaniments at all. Clearly, the burial in House 4 represents an extremely high-status individual, probably *the* highest-ranking member of the community: in a word, the chief.

If House 4 was the chief's tomb, where was his house? Immediately adjacent to House 4, on the west side of the same patio, we found a large (56 m²) house—the largest residence, in fact, found anywhere at the site. This structure, House 7 (see Figure 3.14), was apparently built by placing rectangular adobe bricks on a foundation of pebbles brought from the nearby Río de Las Vueltas. The foundation stones, of course, most clearly survived, but we also found many chunks of preserved adobe bricks scattered amidst the domestic debris above the house floor itself. The southeast corner of House 7 was walled off to create a small room within the larger house. Interestingly, this room has the same interior dimensions (3.0 × 2.4 m) as House 4, the chief's mausoleum. Might both the room in House 7 and House 4 represent resting places for the chief—the former during his lifetime, the latter following his demise?

House 6 is located on the north side of the patio, adjacent to House 7 and facing House 4. This structure was apparently a low platform, standing at least a meter above the patio floor. One ascended to the top of the platform by way of a staircase on the patio side of the building. Unfortunately, the top of the platform was even higher than the present-day ground surface, so the preservation is not quite complete. Nevertheless, two levels of the staircase were well pre-

---

[1] Aging and sexing of all skeletons was by Richard G. Wilkinson, State University of New York at Albany.

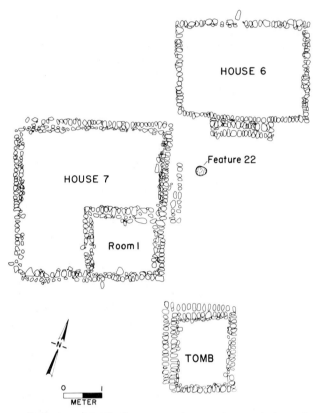

FIGURE 3.14. Middle Formative elite residence, tomb, and public building at La Coyotera, Oaxaca.

served, and the interior of the platform (not shown in Figure 3.14) contained the honeycomb pattern of internal reinforcing walls commonly used by Formative Oaxacan Indians in building such platforms.

The morphology of House 6 and the apparent paucity of associated domestic debris suggest that its function was nonresidential in nature. Perhaps House 6 was a platform on which certain ceremonial activities occurred. We did find a number of artifacts associated with House 6 that probably had ritual functions. Furthermore, in the patio just south of the staircase to House 6, we located Feature 22, a small circular depression in the patio floor containing powdered lime. This feature is similar to the lime-filled pits found by Flannery and Marcus (1976a) in several Tierras Largas phase public buildings in the Valley of Oaxaca (Topic 13). Such lime, they suggest, may have been stored for rituals or for mixing with narcotics such as tobacco. Feature 22 seems to be another example of this kind of feature, and lends support to our interpretation of House 6 as a focus of ritual activity.

Perhaps the central point of this brief report is that we have evidence at La Coyotera for the physical association of a Middle Formative chief's house, his tomb, and a building that served in some sort of ceremonial capacity. It thus seems likely that the high social status enjoyed by this individual was functionally related to his position and participation in certain ceremonial activities. This evidence would support Spores's view (Topic 70) that religion and ritual may well have played an important part in the establishment and maintenance of emerging social status in Oaxaca.

# TOPIC 18
## Middle and Late Formative Settlement Patterns in the Mixteca Alta

RONALD SPORES

In the Nochixtlán Valley, the two Early Formative sites identified to date (N 203, Yucuita, and N 233, Coyotepec) continued to be occupied in Middle Formative times; in addition, known occupations increased to 17 for the Middle and Late Formative (Late Cruz phase), with eight sites having been intensively utilized. All but four of these sites continued to be occupied into the succeeding Ramos phase, and all the sites were reutilized at least once again before the Spanish Conquest.

Locations for Middle and Late Formative sites continued the pattern seen during Early Formative times, with strong preference given to low ridges and piedmont spurs rising above the valley floor and adjacent to, but not directly upon, valley bottom lands (see Figure 3.15). Individual sites did not increase in size, and, despite the eightfold increase in number of occupations, ample spacing continued to exist between sites. On survey, sites appear quite uniform in size, location, and in observable artifact complexes and architec-

tural features. No large structures or extensive features or artifact complexes (other than pottery) have yet been found associated with Formative sites.

Cruz phase sites are small, always being totally dwarfed by later settlements. Three major locations are found: (1) on the lower ends of piedmont spurs reaching down from the mountains to the river's edge (N 012, N 035), (2) at stream confluences (N 810), or (3) on low rises in the central portions of the valley or along its margins (N 233, N 203, N 240, N 419). Although Cruz phase sites could be concealed under later alluvial deposits, great care has been taken to examine the numerous erosional channels cutting through the alluvium, and it seems probable that the number of sites so concealed are few rather than many.

Portions of structures consisting of adobe-block and adobe-block-and-boulder foundations have been excavated at Yucuita (N 203 B, N 203 K) and at Initiyu (N 233 A–B). These remains are associated with packed yellow or red clay floors, often showing signs of having been burned and polished either through use or by design. There is always evidence of fire and cooking activity, indicating the domestic nature of excavated localities. One probable elite residence, a multiple-floored mound measuring 25 m square at the base, has been partially excavated at Initiyu; portions of four domestic structures have been excavated at Yucuita (N 203 B and N 203 K), but to date no complete structures have been revealed.

An earthen platform, the extent of which is presently unknown, was built during Cruz phase times (and greatly expanded during Ramos times) in the V at the confluence of the Yucuita and Yanhuitlán rivers at Etlatongo (N 810). This structure is buried under at least 5 m of Ramos phase earthworks and is observable only along the rivers and in manmade cuts into the deposit. This is probably the largest and most impressive Cruz phase site in the Nochixtlán Valley, and one of the largest single constructions undertaken in Formative Mesoamerica. Middle to Late Formative remains (mounds, alignments, and artifacts) cover an area measuring some 300 by 200 m. Further work at the site, probably the largest and most important of the Middle and Late Formative sites in the Nochixtlán Valley, is imperative.

Excavations conducted in 1970 indicated that the Cruz phase is more complex than anticipated and that it will be necessary to delineate two, probably three, subphases or phases within the period. The existence of at least two complexes is already clear: an earlier manifestation corresponding to the late Tierras Largas and San José phases of the Valley of Oaxaca, and one, or perhaps two, phases contemporaneous with the Guadalupe, Rosario, and Monte Albán I phases in Oaxaca.

At the present stage of analysis, delineation of Early and Late Cruz manifestations can be made on the basis of distinctions in ceramic complexes. While some information on settlement location, architecture, and artifact assemblages is available, it is not yet possible to differentiate clearly subphases in the several Cruz phase sites that have been located in the Nochixtlán Valley. They are grouped into one phase until further analyses can be undertaken.

The ceramic complex pertaining to the earlier Cruz phase, as encountered in the basal portions of stratigraphic tests at Yucuita (N 203 K) and radiocarbon dated at 1300 B.C. (GX 2187), consists of several equivalents of wares recovered in the Oaxaca Valley. Etlatongo Buff Wares approximate Tierras Largas phase Red-on-buff bowls of the Oaxaca series. Jazmín Red and White Ware: Reyes White Variety, as presently constituted, would correspond to Atoyac Yellowwhite. Yucuita Thin Tan: Francisca Variety is similar to Tierras Largas Burnished Plain jars. The Early Cruz phase will ultimately be defined in terms of high frequencies of these ceramic classes. Cruz phase figurines resemble types encountered in Santa María phase deposits in the Tehuacán Valley. Nochixtlán Gray Ware: Pablito Variety includes specimens that are very similar to Leandro Gray of the San José phase in the Oaxaca Valley.

The indicated ceramic complex is found in association with block adobe walls (20 × 10 cm blocks); undressed stone alignments—foundations; hard packed—and sometimes charred—red, yellow, orange, and/or black clay, or

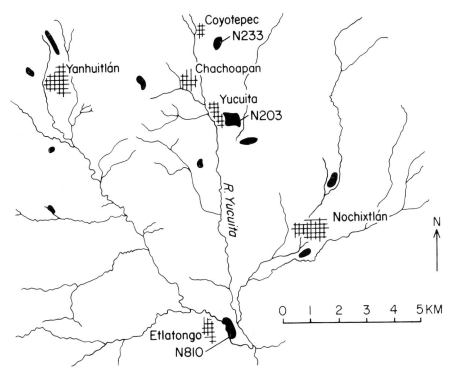

FIGURE 3.15.  Late Cruz phase settlements in the Nochixtlán Valley.

powdered *endeque* (caliche) floors. Structural size and configurations are not as yet determined. Complete exposure of Early Cruz structures at Yucuita would require the removal of from 2 to 3 m of natural and cultural overburden, and probably Early Cruz remains at Etlatongo would necessitate the removal of 5 m of deposit.

Late Cruz remains consist of earthen, stone, and plastered platforms, houses with rough stone foundations, wattle-and-daub, adobe, or unfinished stone walls, tamped-earth or stone-paved house floors with associated hearths, and rubbish accumulations. These features are associated with low frequencies of the earlier Cruz ceramic complex and with relatively high frequencies of Nochixtlán Gray Ware: Pablito and Juanito varieties, Yucuita Red-on-tan, Yucuita Thin Tan ollas, Yucuita Tan Wares, Jazmín Red and White, Etlatongo Buff Ware, and Polished Brown Ware (see Spores 1972, 1974a). Numerous similarities (e.g., double- and tri-ple-line-break rims on gray-white, yellow-white, tan, and brown wares, zoned incising and punctation, and a few Olmec design elements) occur between elements of the Cruz phase ceramic complex and other Early, Middle, and Late Formative manifestations found in an area extending from Chiapas through Oaxaca and Veracruz to Puebla and beyond. Also present in Nochixtlán Valley sites are Formative figurines of types found in the Late San José, Guadalupe, Rosario, and Monte Albán I phases in the Oaxaca Valley, in the Early and Late Santa María phase in the Tehuacán Valley, in deposits at Chiapa de Corzo and other sites in Chiapas, and in Veracruz, Morelos, Guerrero, and the Valley of Mexico. These similarities support the view that in terms of pottery and figurine styles, the Cruz phase is linked to Formative stage manifestations distributed widely over central Mesoamerica.

## TOPIC 19
## The Rosario Phase and the Origins of Monte Albán I

KENT V. FLANNERY
JOYCE MARCUS

The Rosario phase, which may have begun as early as 700 or 650 B.C. and ended some time around 550 or 500 B.C., represents the final stage of the "early village" period in the Valley of Oaxaca. Following the Rosario phase came the founding of Monte Albán, the great urban center described in the next section of this volume—a city that dominated the Valley of Oaxaca for more than 1000 years. Even in its earliest period, called Monte Albán I, the city covered a square kilometer, and it figures prominently in any model for the origins of the Zapotec state (see Chapter 4).

As recently as 1966, it was still very much in doubt whether Monte Albán I was an *in situ* development in the Valley of Oaxaca or the result of an immigration from some other area, such as the Mixteca Alta or the Olmec region (Paddock 1966a:90). By 1967, it was clear that Monte Albán I was an *in situ* development that showed enormous continuity from the earlier Formative periods of the Valley of Oaxaca and owed little (if anything) to diffusion. The roots of Monte Albán I pottery, architecture, art, and even hieroglyphic writing can all be found in the preceding Rosario phase. The major difference between the two periods occurs in settlement patterns, reflecting a major change in sociopolitical organization which is described by Blanton in Topic 21.

The Rosario phase takes its name from the Barrio del Rosario of San Pablo Huitzo, where it was first recovered (Flannery et al. 1970:27–37). It is now much better known, however, through larger samples from San José Mogote and its satellite community, Fábrica San José (Drennan 1976b). In this topic we will outline the ways in which Rosario ce-ramics and architecture evolve into those of the earliest sub-phase of Monte Albán I, called Ia (see Topic 22), leaving the advances in sociopolitical organization for a later section.

## THE EVOLUTION IN CERAMICS

To begin with, the pottery of the Rosario phase evolves directly into Monte Albán Ia pottery through a series of gradual, quantifiable steps, many of which have already been outlined by Drennan (1976b:56–57). For example, the Socorro Fine Gray pottery of the Rosario phase is the direct ancestor of the Monte Albán Ia Types G3, G5, G15, G16, and G17 (see Topic 22); Guadalupe Burnished Brown pottery of the Rosario phase evolves into Monte Albán Ia type K3; and Fidencio Coarse jars of the Rosario phase, with their drab red wash, become the C2 jars of Monte Albán Ia (Caso, Bernal, and Acosta 1967).

One of the most common vessels of the Rosario phase is a flat-based Socorro Fine Gray bowl with a wall that leans or flares outward, its rim varying from gently to widely everted. Drennan (1976b:Fig. 28) has divided this continuum into 12 bowl rim forms, 4 of which are restricted to the Rosario phase and 8 of which carry over into Monte Albán Ia gray ware. He has further defined 7 forms of rim eccentricities, of which 5 are restricted to the Rosario phase and 2 carry over (in modified form) into Monte Albán Ia gray ware. Incised designs on the rims of these bowls show a similar series of gradual changes. Early in the Rosario phase, the designs include crescents, double-line-breaks, and a curious motif like a pennant or naval flag (Figure 3.16). By the end of the Rosario phase pennants are virtually absent, and during the transition to Monte Albán Ia bands of fine-line crosshatching and complex scallops come to the fore. During Ia, crescents and pennants are absent; only the most elaborate versions of the double-line break survive, and swirling clouds, sine curves, and triangular areas of opposed hachure come to dominate. These are the classic G15s and G16s of the Caso, Bernal, and Acosta (1967) typology.

Two other attributes on Socorro Fine Gray bowls are restricted to the Rosario phase. One is a form of pattern burnishing between incised lines, called "zoned toning," in the Tehuacán Valley (MacNeish, Peterson, and Flannery 1970). The other is the use of negative or resist white painting to produce crescents, double-line-breaks, or even pennants on gray bowl rims. In over 100 pits made to bedrock at Monte Albán, Caso, Bernal, and Acosta failed to find a single example of negative white painting, pennant incising, or Tehuacán-style zoned toning. Thus it appears that these three attributes died out before Monte Albán was founded, and we have therefore used their disappearance as the dividing line between Rosario and Monte Albán Ia.

Still another vessel whose evolution documents the transition to Monte Albán I is a shallow dish with three solid, stubby supports. Early in the Rosario phase it is entirely undecorated and may occur in unburnished (Lupita Heavy Plain) or burnished (Guadalupe Burnished Brown) wares. Toward the end of Rosario a few examples with a red band at the rim appear; these vessels increase during the transition to Period Ia, after which the undecorated variety dies out completely. In Monte Albán Ia, these tripod dishes always have a red rim (C2 or C4 in the Caso–Bernal–Acosta sys-

tem), and may even be decorated with a fillet band. The latter vessels have been nicknamed "Suchilquitongo tripod dishes"[1] in reference to a large collection which was looted from tombs at Suchilquitongo in the 1950s and sold to the Museo Frissell de Arte Zapoteca in Mitla.

In addition, during Monte Albán Ia, the Caso–Bernal–Acosta types G16, G17, G18, G30, C1, C3, C5, C6, C20, K1, K8, A4, A6, A12, and A17 become common (see Topic 22). All these types are either totally absent or insignificant in Rosario times, even late in the phase.

We have dwelt (perhaps to the point of tedium) on these ceramic details for one reason: we regard the founding of Monte Albán as one of the two or three most important political events in the history of the Valley of Oaxaca. It is, therefore, an event that needs to be fixed in time. From the point of view of settlement patterns and political development, it makes a great deal of difference whether a civic–ceremonial center like San José Mogote or Huitzo was abandoned before, during, or after the founding of Monte Albán. As we have seen, that founding occurred not at the point when the first identifiable G15 or G16 incising appeared on the rims of burnished gray bowls, but at the point when the last negative white painting, zoned toning, and pennant incising had vanished from those rims. By using this point as our dividing line between Rosario and Ia, we can make the following observations:

1. Construction of Structure 19 at San José Mogote was begun well before the founding of Monte Albán.

2. Structure 19 ceased to function as a public building, and came to be used as the platform to support an elite residence, during late Rosario times.

3. Platform 1 at Huitzo was built during the transition from Rosario to Monte Albán Ia, when the first G16s and G30s had already appeared, but before the last of the negative white painting and zoned toning had died out.

4. At the end of the Rosario phase, several excavated sites in the Etla region suffered a striking population loss (almost approaching abandonment in some cases) in the following order: Tierras Largas, then San José Mogote, then Fábrica San José, then Huitzo.

5. This population loss coincided with the founding of Monte Albán, suggesting that the villages just named had participated in that founding.

## THE EVOLUTION IN ARCHITECTURE

The stone masonry architecture of the Rosario phase also leads directly into the architecture of Monte Albán I. Perhaps the strongest similarities can be seen between Structures 19 and 19A at San José Mogote, Building L and an

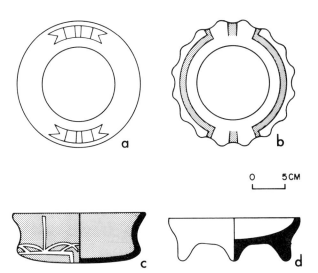

FIGURE 3.16. Diagnostic ceramics of the Rosario phase: (a) fine gray bowl with incised pennant motif, top view; (b) fine gray bowl with zoned toning indicated by stipple, top view. Note eccentric rim; (c) fine gray bowl with negative or resist white decoration, side view, (d) undecorated tripod bowl of Suchilquitongo type.

O     5 CM

---

[1]Drennan (1976b:26) refers to these as "Suchilquitongo footed plates," which may be considered a synonym.

unnamed Period I building under Mound IV at Monte Albán, Temples T and X at Monte Negro near Tilantongo (see Topic 26).

Structure 19 at San José Mogote, built atop Mound 1 during the Rosario phase, measures 21.7 by 28.5 m. It represents the final enlargement of an earlier building, Structure 19A, which also dates to the Rosario phase but is incompletely explored at this writing. The architects of Structure 19 reused the stairway of Structure 19A, simply turning their later (and larger) west wall back to meet the earlier (and less impressive) west wall of 19A on both sides of the staircase (see Figure 3.17).

The outer wall of Structure 19 features a series of huge slabs of chert-bearing limestone, up to a meter high and 40 cm thick, set vertically in the manner which Robertson (Topic 28) has called "orthostatic". The irregular gaps between these orthostats are filled with smaller, rectangular limestone blocks which are set one above the other in ladder fashion. This Rosario phase construction is strikingly similar to that of Building L (the so-called Building of the Danzantes) at Monte Albán, which dates to Period Ia. The orthostats on Structure 19 are plain, while those on Building L are carved; however, there is a carved stone—Monument 3, just outside the northeast corner of Structure 19

FIGURE 3.17. Limestone block stairways of Middle and Late Formative public buildings in highland Oaxaca: (a) stairway of Structure 19A, San José Mogote (from a photo by J. Marcus); (b) stairway of Temple T at Monte Negro (from a photo by Acosta 1965). (Drawings by Margaret Van Bolt.)

(Topic 15)—which is stylistically similar to those on Building L.

The Structure 19–19A stairway from San José Mogote shows similarities with Period I stairways at both Monte Albán and Monte Negro: all are internal stairways without balustrades, composed of huge, irregular blocks of limestone. In both wall construction and stairway construction, the intent is clearly to impress the viewer with the immensity of the stones used, rather than with the workmanship; most are undressed, uncut, and far from symmetrical, and some weigh more than a ton.

Finally, an early structure found beneath Mound IV at Monte Albán and assigned by Acosta to Period I (see Topic 22) shows the same orthostatic construction: huge slabs are set vertically in rows 1 and 2, while another series are set horizontally in rows 3 and 4, much like the Building of the Danzantes. The original height of the building was at least 6 m (see Paddock 1966a:111, Figure 48).

# TOPIC 20
## Divergence of the Mixteca and the Valley of Oaxaca, 1330–500 B.C.

RONALD SPORES

Although the locations selected and the artifact complexes recovered at some 17 sites in the Nochixtlán Valley, as well as at Monte Negro near Tilantongo and Yatachío near Tamazulapan (Paddock 1953), bear striking resemblances to manifestations in the Valley of Oaxaca, there were divergent developments. The Nochixtlán Valley provides only a pale reflection of the more advanced Early and Middle Formative developments in Oaxaca. While it is probable that one or two village sites like Tierras Largas may be found in the Mixteca, surface remains suggest nothing comparable in size or complexity to San José Mogote (Topic 15). Clearly, Oaxaca was proceeding more rapidly toward higher levels of social and political development than the Mixteca.

The functional differentiation among sites that occurred in Oaxaca during Middle Formative times did not, as far as we can now determine, occur until Terminal Formative–Early Classic times. Monte Negro emerges as a relatively small but functionally complex center late in the Formative and (I believe) continues into the Early Classic. Thus far it would appear that the site developed in relative isolation from other Late Formative–Early Classic sites. Monte Negro does, in fact, have the appearance of an outpost, albeit a relatively large and impressive one, situated in a high, rugged, isolated region—a placement quite unusual for the time (Topic 26). The site was occupied for a relatively short time, apparently being abandoned in the Early Classic period and never reoccupied.

Yucuita arose at the beginning of the Ramos phase as a multiplex urban center surrounded by other kinds of settlements, two or three medium-sized towns, and roughly two dozen settlements of about the size, shape, and placement of the earlier Formative villages (Topic 36). Other sites—such as Yatachío near Tamazulapan, Diquiyu near

Tezoatlán in the Mixteca Baja, and other sites containing Middle and/or Late Formative remains—are likely to be investigated in the near future, but for the present no firm inferences regarding Formative development in the area should be made. With the exception of the aberrant Monte Negro, Formative sites are located near naturally well-watered agricultural lands. While it is too early to tell, it is likely that important Formative occupations will be found in and around such relatively well-watered areas as Tecomastlahuaca, Juxtlahuaca, Acatlán, Chila, Teposcolula, Silacayoapan, Putla, and along the streams of the Mixteca Costa.

The Mixteca appears to have lagged behind the Valley of Oaxaca in its Formative development, both in the density of occupation and in the level of cultural complexity. Striking similarities in settlement patterns, artifact inventories, and decorative styles, however, indicate that the Mixteca and the Valley of Oaxaca were related, and that they were in turn involved in the Formative *oikoumene* extending from Guatemala to upper central Mexico. Much effort must be expended to explain the observable ties that existed among the areas, as well as the differential rate of development between Oaxaca and the various parts of the Mixteca. Are the ties economic, social, political–hierarchical, and/or ideological? We must proceed with studies that will not only yield needed information about developments within the areas, but also allow us to explain in cultural–anthropological terms the relationships that existed among the areas. Contrasting technoenvironmental adaptations certainly figured in the distinctive patterns of development in the various Mixtecas and the Valley of Oaxaca, but ecological strategems alone will explain few of the more significant parallels, relationships, and divergences among the areas.

# The Origins of the State in Oaxaca

## Editors' Introduction

To explain the origin of primary states—those which arise in a context of interacting prestate societies—has remained an objective of anthropologists since the publication of [Lewis H.] Morgan's *Ancient Society* 100 years ago. It is a fundamental problem which, though it cannot have an ultimate solution, serves as a measure against which to evaluate the effectiveness of new perspectives and new methods. [Reproduced, with permission, from the Annual Review of Anthropology, Volume 6. © 1977 by Annual Reviews Inc.].

H. T. Wright 1977:379

As the above quotation from Henry T. Wright suggests, the origin of the state is a problem that has been with us since anthropology began. It is also an area of research in which Oaxaca archaeology potentially has a contribution to make. The Valley of Oaxaca, for example, is surely one region where the state arose "in a context of interacting prestate societies." It is even possible—although we will not press the point here—that the Cloud People were the first of Mesoamerica's Indian groups to achieve true statehood.

## THE CHRONOLOGY OF STATE FORMATION

The relevant periods involved are the Rosario, Monte Albán I, and Monte Albán II phases in the Valley of Oaxaca, and the Ramos phase in the Mixteca Alta. In Topic 19 we discussed the relationships and ceramic horizon markers of the Rosario phase (700–500 B.C.) and Monte Albán Ia (500–400 B.C.), but the boundary between the two is significant only as a founding date for the site of Monte Albán. No such boundary can be drawn for the origin of the state; indeed, it is a process that must have taken centuries.

## THE GLOTTOCHRONOLOGICAL EVENTS OF THE PERIOD

There are only a few events of glottochronological significance during the period in question, and none seems to relate to the rise of statehood. Between 500 and 300 B.C., Mazatec is thought to have split off from Chocho–Popoloca; this split would date to 450 to 250 B.C. in radiocarbon years, falling within the Late Santa María phase of the Tehuacán Valley. Around A.D. 100 (in glottochronological terms), Chatino is thought to have separated from the Zapotec of the Miahuatlán area. This process may have something to do with the incorporation of the Miahuatlán area into the Zapotec state centered at Monte Albán in Period II (see below), but so little is known of the prehistory of the Chatino that we have no idea when they entered the area they occupy today.

## A DEFINITION OF THE STATE

Flannery (1972c:403) has previously defined the state as "a type of very strong, usually highly centralized government, with a professional ruling class, largely divorced from

79

the bonds of kinship which characterize simpler societies."
The state also can wage war and "draft soldiers, levy taxes,
and exact tribute" (Flannery 1972c:404). States "have public buildings, works, and services of various sorts, usually
implemented through professional architects, engineers and
bureaucrats. Among these will usually appear public works
of a religious nature, attended by full-time specialists maintaining a state religion" (Flannery 1972c:404). States also
have a multitiered administrative hierarchy, with the uppermost level effecting the panregional integration of previously autonomous local centers. Wright and Johnson
(1975:270–274) have argued that in Mesopotamia, for example, there were four levels of settlement hierarchy in
which large centers successively dominated small centers,
large villages, and small villages by 3150 B.C.; administrative
artifacts (stamp seals, stampings themselves, and counting
devices) occurred in sites of all levels. In the Maya lowlands,
Marcus (1976a) has suggested that a four-tiered hierarchy of
primary, secondary, tertiary, and quaternary centers
emerged early in Cycle 9 (by A.D. 534); administrative artifacts (in this case, hieroglyphic inscriptions on stone monuments) occurred in centers of all levels.

Based on the above definition, we would phrase the chronology of state formation in Oaxaca as follows. For the
Rosario phase (700–500 B.C.), there is no archaeological
evidence for state institutions. For Monte Albán II (200
B.C.–A.D. 100), we consider the evidence for statehood clear
and unmistakable, which throws the spotlight on Monte
Albán I (500–200 B.C.) as the crucial 300-year period for
our understanding of state origins. And as so often happens,
the evidence from Monte Albán I is so fragmentary as to be
ambiguous.

## THE EVIDENCE FOR STATEHOOD
## IN MONTE ALBÁN II

If, for the sake of simplicity, we consider only the limited
definition given above, we can list the following questions
about the state for which Oaxaca archaeology can provide
partial answers.

1. *When did a highly centralized government with a professional ruling class first appear?* We have seen that even the
San José phase society in the Valley of Oaxaca displayed
some evidence of hereditary social ranking, and that ranking
must have been strong in the Guadalupe and Rosario phases
as well. Nevertheless, we see in these earlier societies a continuum of statuses, without a sharp division into classes.
William T. Sanders has provided us with an important observation on one difference between *ranked* societies with
"chiefs," and *stratified* societies with "kings":

> In a seminar at Pennsylvania State University, which I have con-
> ducted over the past three years, we have attempted to relate
> material culture to levels of political organization, based upon
> an ethnographic sample of at least 100 contemporary or recent

societies. One of the things that stands out very clearly, in the
survey of this literature, is the fact that although chiefs frequently can summon considerable numbers of workers for sustained periods of time for the construction of such public buildings as tombs and temples, they cannot amass such levels of
manpower for the construction of residences for themselves
[Sanders 1974:109].

While Sanders's observations would have to be rephrased
somewhat for our purposes (for example, most Oaxacan
tombs would not qualify as public buildings), they provide a
framework for some of our data. The earlier Formative elite
do seem to have lived in relatively modest houses, even
though their people built relatively elaborate public buildings. Classic period Oaxacan societies, however, built monumental palaces for their rulers, perhaps because the Classic
period palace was more than a dwelling. The palace was also
a structure for conducting the affairs of state and for receiving distinguished guests, and in time it may have become an
institutional structure that far outlasted any one occupant.

Following Sanders, one archaeological clue to the rise of a
professional ruling class should be the appearance of the true
palace—a monumental structure consisting of both habitation areas and audience halls and requiring corvée labor
beyond the capabilities of even an extended family. As we
will see in this section of the book, such palaces are as yet
unknown from the Middle Formative; they are clearly present in Monte Albán II, perhaps as early as 200–100 B.C.
This fact focuses attention on the Monte Albán I period,
whose elite residential architecture has never been discovered at Monte Albán itself. Only at Monte Negro, in the
Tilantongo region of what is now the Mixteca Alta, do we
get a clear look at Monte Albán Ic elite residences, and those
do not qualify as palaces (see Topic 26). They are, however,
connected to nearby public buildings by roofed passage-
ways, suggesting that social status in the Late Formative was
still characterized by differential levels of involvement in the
ritual life of the community.

Significantly, the elite residences at Monte Negro usually
have burials below the floor, whereas the larger palaces at
Monte Albán usually do not. Apparently, as Caso was fond
of pointing out, important Zapotec rulers were buried in
special places where commemorative buildings shaped like
miniature palaces could be erected over their tombs.[1] The
palace itself probably outlived many rulers, and stood more
for the institution of kingship than for any one king.

The sixteenth-century Zapotec royalty and nobility were
class-endogamous; their former kinship ties to the common
people had been severed, and by the time of the Conquest
they were more likely to marry a Mixtec or Aztec noble than
a Zapotec commoner. This kind of social gulf is certainly
reflected in the differences between Monte Albán Tombs
104 and 105 and the graves of commoners of the same period (see Topic 40). Our suspicion is that the withering of kin
ties between nobility and commoners began with the found-

---

[1]This is one case in which a tomb might be part of a "public building" in
Sanders's sense (see above).

ing of Monte Albán around 500 B.C. and was complete by the start of Period II 300 years later.

Monte Albán, a mountain rising 400 m above the plain at the point where all three arms of the Valley of Oaxaca intersect, shows no signs of occupation during the Rosario phase. At this time, there is also no evidence for an overall integration of the Valley of Oaxaca. A population estimated by Kowalewski at perhaps 1300 to 1400 persons occupying a series of 18 to 20 villages in the Etla region was integrated by the 62-ha center of San José Mogote; in all probability, the Tlacolula and Zaachila–Zimatlán regions were occupied by separate polities with their own regional centers. Whoever the paramount chief of San José Mogote was, it is unlikely his authority extended beyond the Etla region.

In Blanton's model for the founding of Monte Albán (Topic 21), the site was selected as an administrative center precisely because it was on unoccupied, politically neutral (though possibly sacred) ground in the no man's land between the various arms of the valley. Its founding, around 500 B.C., might therefore be seen as the result of a confederacy among previously autonomous (perhaps even competitive) chiefdoms from various parts of the valley. This model is supported by an apparent cessation of monumental construction at places like San José Mogote and Huitzo at roughly the time that Monte Albán was founded. It is also supported by continuities between the architecture of the Rosario phase and the architecture of Monte Albán I, between the monument carving of the Rosario phase and the stone monuments of Monte Albán I, and between the ceramics of the Rosario phase and the ceramics of Monte Albán Ia. It is also supported by the fact that Monte Albán, in its first stage, seems to have consisted of three discrete areas of settlement, possibly reflecting populations from three major areas of the valley.

Consider, for a moment, the implications of such a confederacy. At first the founding elite would have consisted of chiefly individuals (for the sake of argument, let us say from Etla or Zaachila) whose kin ties to their areas of origin would have been strong. But Monte Albán was the first administrative center of valley-wide significance, considerably extending the authority of such an elite. Perhaps during the 300 years of the Monte Albán I period the status of the Etla elite and the Zaachila elite escalated to that of the lords of Monte Albán. While it is doubtful that *political* ties to their respective regions ever vanished completely, 300 years of prestigious intermarriage at Monte Albán might eventually have converted them into a class-endogamous stratum of professional rulers by severing their *kin* ties to the commoners of those regions.

In our opinion, the available evidence supports most of the scheme for the founding of Monte Albán proposed by Blanton (1978 and Topic 21). Since it is always useful to consider alternative hypotheses, however, we should perhaps comment on the different interpretation offered by Sanders and Santley (1978). They have suggested that "subsistence requirements were a major consideration" in the location of Monte Albán, and that "a polity controlling the nearby alluvial plain" with its "ample prime cultivable land" was able to dominate "lesser polities in the valley" and eventually to unify them. They would thus see Monte Albán as the work of one of the valley's polities, and its walls as defense against competing groups within the valley. As evidence they cite "a central palace many times larger than any other residence on the site," implying that one polity (not a confederacy) had risen to dominance.

We are not sure what palace Sanders and Santley are referring to. Monte Albán was founded around 500 B.C.; its largest palaces date to A.D. 300 to 700 (Topic 41), by which time there had been some 800 years of political evolution, perhaps including the escalation in status suggested above. There is no evidence that the founders of Monte Albán had large palaces, and since less than one percent of the site has been excavated, we can hardly know how large the unexcavated residences in the remaining 99% were.

It also seems unlikely that Monte Albán was the work of a single polity—for example, the large one centered at San José Mogote in the Etla arm of the valley. While this was the most populous area of the valley in the Rosario phase, Blanton's estimated population for Monte Albán in Period I is larger than the estimated population of the entire Etla arm in the Rosario phase (Kowalewski 1976), and not all sites in the Etla region were abandoned at the end of the Rosario phase. Hence, in order to account for the large Period I population of Monte Albán, we must propose that its founders came from several parts of the valley, rather than just one. This suggestion would account for the three Period I barrios at Monte Albán, which are discrete both spatially and in ceramic style preferences (Blanton 1978:Table 2.1).

Finally, we are a bit surprised by Sanders and Santley's attempt to explain Monte Albán in terms of prime agricultural land. Here is a city on a fortified, nearly waterless mountaintop, 400 m above the valley in one of its narrowest areas. Some of its earliest major constructions reflect militarism, and the Main Plaza is dominated by temples. It is not located on the best farmland in the valley—such as San José Mogote, Zaachila, or Santa Ana Tlapacoyan—but on a hill that had never before been occupied, yet is central to all three arms of the valley. We agree with Blanton that its unique location and nature must be explained, and they are certainly not explained very fully by agricultural considerations.

If there is a point where our interpretation differs from Blanton's—and it is a minor point—it would be in the purpose of Monte Albán's early fortifications. Blanton has interpreted them as essentially defensive, but as Sanders and Santley have pointed out, it is hard to imagine that any of the small surrounding valleys posed a threat to the Valley of Oaxaca. We suspect the Zapotec stance was essentially offensive, and our evidence would be the conquest slabs of Building J (Topic 29) and the Period Ic–II takeover of the Cañada de Cuicatlán by Monte Albán (Topic 35). We would tend to see the occupants of Monte Albán as the aggressors against a whole range of weaker neighbors outside the valley, preferably in regions where a different range of products could be produced.

2. *When do the "public buildings, works, and services" of the state appear, including "public works of a religious nature" with "full-time specialists maintaining a state religion?"* We have already seen that the public building had a long history in the Valley of Oaxaca. For the most part, however, the public buildings of Early and Middle Formative times were architecturally "generalized": one cannot specify their functions, or assign them to categories such as "temple," "men's house," "ceremonial lodge," or the like. Not until the start of Monte Albán II can one point to public buildings with the stereotyped ground plan and features of the Zapotec temple—a ground plan that was preserved, with only minor changes, from 200 B.C. to the sixteenth century A.D.

The Zapotec temple, according to ethnohistoric documents, was a two-room structure. In the slightly higher inner chamber, to which laymen never penetrated, lived the Zapotec "priests". Although it may be an exaggeration, some documents state that the *bigaña* or minor priests "never left the temple" (Espíndola 1580:139); at the very least, a great deal of their behavior was hidden from view. To the slightly lower outer chamber came worshipers with quail, dogs, turkeys, or other creatures to be sacrificed at the temple. These they delivered to the *bigaña* "through whose hands everything passed" (Espíndola 1580:138). These full-time religious functionaries performed the actual sacrifices, sometimes filling a basin (set in the floor) with sacrificial blood into which colored feathers were dipped. Church and state were united to the extent that priests were recruited from the sons of the nobility, and the Zapotec lord himself underwent a year of religious training before he took office. After all, his royal ancestors were semidivine interceders between his community and the great supernatural forces whose favor the Zapotec sought to incur (Topic 97).

The appearance of the standard two-room temple is our first archaeological clue to the origins of state religion. By the time it appears—almost simultaneously with the palace—it is fairly certain that the Zapotec possessed full-time priests who had, in effect, taken a great deal of religion out of the hands of the common man. Men who could have sacrificed their own quail at 1000 B.C. probably had to bring it to the temple for professional sacrifice at 100 B.C. It is also probably no accident that the small handmade figurines used for the construction of ritual scenes in households of the Early and Middle Formative had totally disappeared by Monte Albán II. The evolution of state religion presumably involves a mechanism called *linearization* (Flannery 1972c:413), in which a special-purpose arm (the priesthood) of a higher-order system (the state) takes over an activity (certain rituals) that had formerly been performed by a lower-order system (the individual, family, or sodality).

One of the first discovered (and best preserved) temples of the Monte Albán II period was the one found by Caso (1935) within Mound X, northeast of the Main Plaza at Monte Albán. This structure, built atop a platform with a stairway on the south side, measures 10 by 8 m. The doorway to the outer chamber or vestibule is 4 m wide and flanked by single columns. To reach the inner chamber, one would have to cross 2 m of vestibule and step up 25 to 30 cm through a second doorway flanked by single columns. This second doorway is narrower (2 m) and the inner sanctum measures only 8 by 3 m. Such a temple plan is typical not only of Monte Albán but of secondary civic-ceremonial centers like San José Mogote (see Topic 27).

The two-room temple was not the only public building to appear during Monte Albán II. Ballcourts in the shape of a capital I appear both at Monte Albán and at secondary centers at about the same time. While little is known about the Precolumbian ballgame in the Valley of Oaxaca, it is known to have had ritual significance. Presumably it was an institution with its own personnel, separate from the temple staff.

Still another, more enigmatic feature of Monte Albán II was an arrowhead-shaped structure, represented by Building J at Monte Albán and Building O at Caballito Blanco (see Topics 29, 34). Unless more of these unusual structures are discovered, we may never know their original function. They constitute, however, additional evidence for the explosive diversity of public buildings—and presumably of state institutions—in Monte Albán II.

3. *When did a four-tiered administrative hierarchy first appear?* Because of the ambiguity of the relationship between a site-size hierarchy and an administrative hierarchy, this question is difficult to answer. We can say that not until the founding of Monte Albán were there as many as four tiers in the Valley of Oaxaca site-size hierarchy. By 200 B.C., Monte Albán covered more than a square kilometer and exhibited great diversity in public buildings. It stood at the top of the site-size hierarchy and was, presumably, the only administrative center of valley-wide significance.

One apparent Period II secondary center, San José Mogote, had a palace, several temples, a ballcourt, and a main plaza in imitation of Monte Albán's; if its outlying settlements are considered satellite barrios rather than separate hamlets, its maximum size may have been over 70 ha. Its significance may have extended throughout the Etla arm of the valley (Topic 32).

Fábrica San José, a possible tertiary center, covered about 2 ha during Monte Albán II. In the center of the community is a single large artificial mound whose lower levels contain a plaster-floored structure that may be either a public building or an elite residence of Period II (Drennan 1976b:269). Santo Domingo Tomaltepec was a probable tertiary center of roughly the same size, also with a plaster-floored temple of the Monte Albán II period, in this case perched atop the highest artificial mound on the site (Whalen 1981). Presumably these smaller sites were only of local significance.

The fourth level in the hierarchy consists of small sites in the 1- to 3-ha range for which there is no evidence of large-scale architecture at all (Kowalewski 1976).

4. *When did the Zapotec state begin to "wage war, draft soldiers, levy taxes, and exact tribute"?* This question raises a more general one, that of the role played by warfare in the rise of the state. David Webster (1975) has suggested a way in which warfare could be used by the paramount chief in a ranked society to support a specialized administration, in spite of demands upon him for redistribution to his own

supporters. Webster suggests that successful rulers who could gain control of local populations *outside their own kin networks* would be able to extract tribute from these marginal populations while redistributing to them nothing in return. While we would not support a "universal" warfare-based model for the origins of the state, Webster's idea could certainly find support in the specific case of the Valley of Oaxaca.

If we have correctly interpreted both Monument 3 at San José Mogote and the more than 300 *danzantes* at Monte Albán as slain or sacrificed captives (Marcus 1974, 1976d), evidence for local conflict may go back at least to the Rosario–Monte Albán Ia phases. The selection of a 400-m-high mountain for Monte Albán may imply defense as a consideration. Most significantly, Blanton's work (see Topic 21) has shown that Monte Albán was fortified by several kilometers of defensive walls as early as Periods Ic–II. Depictions of bound captives in the monumental art of the city continue well into Period III (Marcus 1976d).

During Monte Albán II, more than 50 "town conquest" slabs were carved on Building J in the Main Plaza at Monte Albán. As explained by Marcus in Topic 29, those that can be matched to later hieroglyphic toponyms seem to refer to places outside the Valley of Oaxaca—in fact, they may represent the frontiers of Zapotec conquest or influence. From the standpoint of Webster's model, they might constitute a list of the marginal areas conquered by Monte Albán during Period II, whose tribute made possible the elaboration of the Zapotec state despite the redistributive demands of the valley's lesser nobility.

If such is the case, we would expect all those marginal areas to show evidence of Monte Albán occupation. Three of them—Miahuatlán, Tututepec, and Cuicatlán—certainly do. And of all these, the most exciting data relevant to this model may soon emerge from the Cuicatec Cañada. There Charles Spencer and Elsa Redmond have, at this writing, discovered what may be a fortified Zapotec center guarding the main pass between the Cañada and the Tehuacán Valley. To the south, sites have Monte Albán pottery; to the north, sites have Tehuacán Valley ceramics. Two sites, Quiotepec and La Coyotera, may provide evidence for Zapotec tribute extraction from the region recorded on Monte Albán's Building J as "the Place of Song" [= Cuicatlán] (Spencer and Redmond, Topic 35).

5. *When did the state arise in the Mixteca?* When all the facts are in, several valleys in the Mixteca Alta may prove to have undergone an evolution of statehood much like the Valley of Oaxaca. Spores (Topic 36), drawing on archaeological data from the Nochixtlán–Yanhuitlán Valley, dates the inception of the state to his Ramos phase—broadly contemporary with Monte Albán II and IIIa in the Valley of Oaxaca.

During this period, political and economic power became centralized at Yucuita, a complex urban center covering 2 km$^2$ and presumably serving the same valley-wide integrative functions as Monte Albán. Located on a series of hills which rise from the center of the Nochixtlán plain, Yucuita had at least 10 major complexes of public buildings and magnificent stone and adobe residences for the elite. It stood at the top of a multitiered administrative hierarchy which included 10 towns (or secondary centers) and 20 sites in the village (tertiary), rancho, and *sujeto* size ranges. The development of this hierarchy was accompanied by a doubling of population when compared with the preceding Cruz phase. In this case, the Late Cruz phase (like its contemporary, the Monte Albán I phase) becomes crucial to our understanding of state origins, and once again the available archaeological data are so fragmentary as to be ambiguous.

## ORGANIZATION OF THIS CHAPTER

We begin this chapter with Blanton's description of the founding of Monte Albán and follow that city through Period II, discussing its early public buildings, writing, and calendrics. Kowalewski examines the valley-floor settlement patterns that accompanied early urbanism, and we discuss related sites like Monte Negro and Yagul. Spores introduces us to early urbanism in the Mixteca. We examine the state institutions of Monte Albán II, the conquest slabs of Monte Albán, and the frontier areas it may have conquered. Finally, we examine secondary Period II centers in the Zapotec area such as San José Mogote, Caballito Blanco, and Dainzú, as well as contemporary Mixtec centers like Yucuita and Huamelulpan.

## TOPIC 21
## The Founding of Monte Albán[1]

RICHARD E. BLANTON

The group of hills on which the archaeological site of Monte Albán lies was not occupied until the period called

---

[1]Since much of the data presented here has now been published in detail this paper has been kept brief, and the reader is referred to *Monte Albán: Settlement Patterns at the Ancient Zapotec Capital* (Blanton 1978) for fuller treatment.

Monte Albán Ia, around 500 B.C. In all cases where excavations there reached sterile soil, the earliest pottery found pertains to this or later periods (Bernal 1965:797; Caso, Bernal, and Acosta 1967 passim). During the course of our urban survey (see Blanton 1978 for details), we located only one pre-Monte Albán Ia artifact, a Guadalupe phase figurine.

A number of other new communities were founded in the valley during Period Ia, but what makes Monte Albán stand out from the rest is that even during this initial phase of occupation it was a key regional center or "central place" (Blanton 1976b). Its importance in Period Ia is reflected in two ways. First, it was the valley's largest community, according to our survey data and the data collected by Flannery and his associates from their preliminary reconnaissance of Formative sites. We found dense concentrations of Period Ia sherds over an area of roughly 65 ha at Monte Albán, and scattered sherds of this period over an additional 300 ha. A second indicator of Monte Albán's immediate rise to regional prominence is its large corpus of carved stone monuments, over 300 pertaining to Period Ia (Topic 22). No other contemporary site in the Valley of Oaxaca or elsewhere in the southern highlands of Mexico has nearly this number of monuments.

At first glance it seems enigmatic that a region's major center should so suddenly appear, without precedents in its locality, and that it should have located in such a remote place. True, the location of Monte Albán is central to the valley's three major arms (Etla, Zaachila, and Tlacolula), but its access is restricted due to its setting atop a steep-sided mountain, as high as 400 m above the valley floor. There is no extractable resource on that series of ridges that would have attracted so large a population, and based on Anne Kirkby's work (1973:Figure 51, passim), we may infer that the adjacent slopes were not particularly suitable for maize cultivation, especially as early as Period Ia. The spot chosen for the new Period Ia site was near to and on the top of the major ridge, and Monte Albán "proper" was in the least accessible locality.

Because such a spot was chosen for settlement, Monte Albán's location would not have been advantageous from the viewpoint of exchange of goods. In fact, we must conclude that the site was chosen for the new capital without consideration of practical economic matters, or of subsistence. I have suggested previously (Blanton 1976a) that one genre of human communities typically displays this pattern of locating in marginal or "neutral" localities, and that Monte Albán was a member of this genre. I have termed such centers *disembedded capitals* in reference to the fact that they are special-function administrative centers, spatially separated from the remainder of their region's central place hierarchy (Blanton 1976b). Because these centers have as their only major function decision making on a regional level and are supported through taxes or tribute, their locations need not be predictable in economic terms. In fact, marginal locations are often chosen purposely, to avoid "distortion" of the existing central place hierarchy, and/or to avoid competition between the administrative center and existing communities for land or other valuable resources.

One of the situations favoring the formation of a disembedded capital is where several autonomous societies join in a league or confederacy to take advantage of their mutual strength in matters of offense and defense (Blanton 1976b). The center of confederacy decision making is likely to be separated from any of the existing centers in order to avoid increasing the influence of any one of these centers at the expense of the others. Washington, D.C. is a good example of this. It was founded in a muddy, malaria-ridden swamp, away from the existing major centers, and midway between the southern and northern states (see, for example, Morison 1965:360). I suggest that about 500 B.C. a panregional confederacy was formed in the Valley of Oaxaca, and that the formation of this new polity was manifested by the construction of a capital center on the top of Monte Albán. That one major function of this confederacy was military (either defensive or expansionistic) seems clear, as evidenced by the concentration there of 300 carved *danzantes*, figures which seem best interpreted as depictions of slain or sacrificed captives (see Topic 22).

This model for the foundation of Monte Albán not only has the advantage of explaining its unusual location and the fact that it appeared practically overnight, but also may account for the strange distributional pattern of Monte Albán Ia sherds on the surface of the site. Figure 4.1 shows this pattern, based on our surface collections and plotted on our grid system (see Blanton 1978:12–15) in sherds per hectare collected. The distribution of Monte Albán Ia sherds seems to indicate three major areas of settlement (1) in the vicinity of grid squares 0111 and 0010; (2) around squares 0410, 0310, and 0411; and (3) around squares 0407, 0408 and 0308, as well as two minor areas near the base of the hill to the north and northwest at square 0606 and at squares 0609 and 0610.[2] The presence of these three major concentrations of sherds may indicate three barrios or neighborhoods (Blanton 1978:37–39).

Such a pattern would make sense in terms of a model in which Monte Albán was the center of a confederacy, and a place where representatives from various previously separate valley polities may have resided. Discrete barrios, closely situated, could have promoted communication while at the same time preserving some of the autonomy of the members of the confederacy. Of further interest is the presence of three apparently isolated public buildings on the very top of the hill, in an apparently nonresidential area between the three sherd clusters—the very area which was later transformed into the Main Plaza (Figure 4.1). The building to the south bears the *danzantes* gallery; the building to the northwest was discovered during the course of excavations in Mound K of System IV (Acosta n.d.b); and the building to the northeast is the one encountered in the deep test into the southeast corner of the North Platform (the P.S.A. excavation: see Caso, Bernal, and Acosta 1967:95–96; see also Topic 22). The locations of these public buildings also make sense in terms of the model presented. They are not located in the residential zones, but rather in a "neutral" (and possibly "sacred") precinct between three barrios. This location

---

[2]For clarification in this and the other such distributional maps in this volume, sherd density values are not indicated for those grid squares containing only a few collected terraces. Squares eliminated in this way are 0803, 0809, 0208, 0109, 0209, 0311, and 0309.

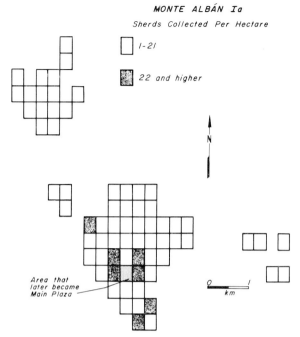

MONTE ALBÁN Ia

Sherds Collected Per Hectare

☐ 1-21

▨ 22 and higher

FIGURE 4.1. Distribution of Period Ia sherds on the surface of Monte Albán, showing three major areas of settlement. (Redrawn, with modifications, from Blanton 1978.)

might be expected if the buildings functioned for the confederacy as a whole, and did not pertain to activities in any one of the residential zones. Very little is known about the functions of these buildings, except that the Building of the Danzantes may have been a symbolic display of military power.

## MONTE ALBÁN IN PERIODS IC AND II

As far as we know now, Monte Albán continued as the major central place for the Valley of Oaxaca from its founding in Period Ia through the remainder of the Formative period. Although we have no means at this time of discovering the details of population fluctuations at the center, a few inferences can be drawn based on the distributions of sherds pertaining to Periods Ic and II. During Period Ic, the community expanded to cover the total occupied ridge of Monte Albán proper, and the nearby ridge called El Gallo was colonized. While scattered Period Ia pottery was found over much of this same area, the density of Ic sherds suggests that much filling in of the gaps between the Ia barrios had occurred. While the Period Ia population was probably roughly 3600–7200, by Period Ic Monte Albán contained an estimated 10,200–20,400, and during Period II roughly 9650–19,300 persons. (Methods of estimating population from hectares of residential area are given in Blanton 1978:29–30.)

Monte Albán not only expanded in size following the period of its original founding, but was also the scene of new large-scale construction. Apparently during Period Ic or Period II the site's major defensive wall was constructed; a Period II tomb (Tomb 177) postdates the wall (Kuttruff and Autry 1978). This defensive wall extends along the north, northwest, and part of the western limits of Monte Albán proper (Figure 4.2). It is roughly 3 km in length, and averages 3–4 m in height. Where it crosses a large barranca in the northern section of the city, Neely (1972) believes it to have dammed up a reservoir some 2.25 ha in surface area, which would have held an estimated maximum 67,500 m³ of water.

Another, smaller dam has been located to the east of the Main Plaza area, also probably dating to Periods I and II. This dam collected water for an irrigation system that fed a series of agricultural terraces above the modern town of Xoxocotlán. On the basis of work there by Neely and his students, we feel that the beginnings of construction on the system began in Period I, that the major extension of the system occurred during Period Ic, and that it was largely abandoned during Period II (Mason et al. 1977; see Topic 94). Even at the system's maximum extent, however, only about 50 ha of terraces could have been irrigated. Thus it could have produced food for only an estimated 250 persons (Mason et al. 1977), and cannot therefore be considered to have been an important source of subsistence for the city's population as a whole, although it might have contributed to the subsistence of the smaller elite segment of the population.

Excavations in the Main Plaza area have revealed Period Ic or Period II pottery in construction fill located on sterile soil in several localities (Caso, Bernal, and Acosta 1967), indicating considerable new construction there after Period Ia. The exact configuration of the Main Plaza during these periods will not be known until the publication of the excavations, but apparently much of the leveling and plastering of the Main Plaza was carried out during Period II (Acosta 1965:818; Bernal 1965:801; see Topic 27). Similarly, given the paucity of excavations and reports on excavations outside the Main Plaza area, it will be difficult to describe the remainder of the city during these periods, except to note its maximum extent.

In Topic 39, I infer certain features of the city's organization in Period IIIb, on the basis of a spatial analysis of mounded buildings. I am not sure to what extent this organizational model can be pushed back into Periods Ic and II. It seems, however, that many of the platform mounds in the area occupied during Period II have early building stages going back to those times. Whether or not this is true, of course, can only be determined by excavation, but it is my impression—based on a superficial examination of the cores of many of these buildings where they have been exposed by erosion, excavation, or pot hunting—that much original construction pertains to the Late or Terminal Formative. If this interpretation is correct, then, although the spatially discrete barrios of Period Ia were no longer present, the city

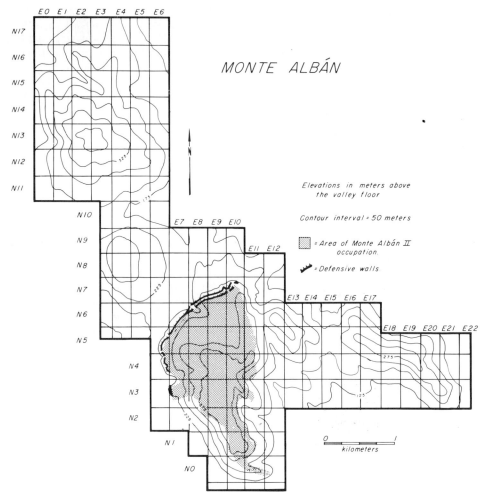

FIGURE 4.2.  Period II settlement at Monte Albán, showing defensive walls constructed during Period Ic or II. (Redrawn, with modifications, from Blanton 1978.)

may still have been made up of discrete units, each focused on a cluster of civic–ceremonial buildings and elite residences. In Topic 39 I explain how I arrived at this interpretation and offer an explanation for it.

## THE SANDERS–SANTLEY MODEL:
## A BRIEF RESPONSE

W. T. Sanders and R. Santley (1978), in a review of my Monte Albán volume (Blanton 1978), present an alternative model for the founding of Monte Albán. First, they argue that I failed to account for how, "if the center was founded by a group of autonomous polities, roughly comparable in size and power, one of them evolved into the dominant polity, as is suggested by the presence of a central palace many times larger than any other residence on the site" (p. 303). Second, they argue that, contrary to my suggestions, the location of the site can be explained in terms of the agri-

cultural advantages of the valley's central area. According to them, Monte Albán's location "strongly implies that subsistence requirements were a major consideration in its positioning," and "a polity controlling the nearby alluvial plain, because of a demographic advantage, was successful in competition with lesser polities in the valley and unified the valley politically and economically" (Sanders and Santley 1978:303).

Sanders and Santley's first criticism results from an unfortunate misunderstanding of my argument. I argued that a *new institution* evolved during Period Ia—a regional confederacy—and that this new institution was located at Monte Albán. I did not argue that one valley polity was able to dominate others, but that several small polities were able to join in the creation of a larger unit of greater regional significance. As a result, no "central palace" is known during Monte Albán I.

Regarding their second criticism, it is true that if one quickly scans a 1:1,000,000 map of the Valley of Oaxaca, such as A. Kirkby's (1973) Figure 18, it does appear that the central part of the valley is a reasonable location for a large center. There is a large area of good floodwater land southeast of contemporary Oaxaca City; and, some kilometers farther south, there is an area of even more valuable high-water-table land. Such a superficial scanning, however, is misleading for two reasons: at least two areas in the Valley of Oaxaca are considerably more productive agriculturally than this central zone (and would therefore, it seems, have had the "demographic advantage"). The northern (or Etla) arm, according to Kirkby, has an advantage in agricultural production in the region because of the greater availability of water for canal irrigation (A. Kirkby 1973:50, passim). The southern (or Zaachila) arm has three advantages over the central area: (1) less likelihood of frost, (2) the largest area of low alluvium and hence of high-water-table farming, and (3) higher rainfall than the remainder of the valley (A. Kirkby 1973:50, Figure 8, passim).

A second problem for any agricultural argument is that Monte Albán was not founded adjacent to the alluvium of the central part of the valley. The hilltop location of the Period Ia center is 400 m up, and all of the land adjacent to the site and downslope in every direction is piedmont which would not have been very productive with Period I maize (A.

Kirkby 1973:Fig. 51). The nearest usable alluvium is not only far downhill, but is also at least 4 km from where the capital was located. Farmers in nonindustrial societies normally avoid having to walk this far to fields, according to the cross-cultural study by Chisholm (1962), because of the energy and time costs of movement and the difficulties in protecting distant fields. Our Period Ia secondary central place Site 2-33 is located adjacent to the Central Valley alluvium, and the population there undoubtedly exploited it (Blanton, et al. 1982). As I stated in the Monte Albán volume, if agricultural productivity had been an important consideration for the founders of Monte Albán, the long ridge to the east of the main hill (Monte Albán Chico) would have been chosen, providing as it does both a defensible location and direct access to alluvium. This ridge, however, was not even colonized until the Classic period, hundreds of years later.

I do not wish to belabor these points here, for I feel the various positions have been summarized adequately in Santley (1980), Blanton (1980), and Kowalewski (1980). I thank Sanders and Santley for their interest in our Valley of Oaxaca work, and while I have given their suggestions careful thought, in the present volume I have adhered to the model I feel best accounts for all our survey data.

## TOPIC 22
## The Earliest Public Buildings, Tombs, and Monuments at Monte Albán, with Notes on the Internal Chronology of Period I

KENT V. FLANNERY
JOYCE MARCUS

Monte Albán shows dense Period Ia settlement over 65 ha, with lighter sherd cover on another 300 ha; its estimated population was 3600–7200 persons, apparently distributed through three residential wards. By the end of Period Ic the estimated population had grown to 10,200–20,400 persons, filling in the gaps between the previously separate residential areas (Blanton, Topic 21). Our purpose in this section is to examine the fragmentary evidence for public buildings and elite burials during Period I (Bernal 1946; Marquina 1951; Acosta 1965; Caso, Bernal, and Acosta 1967; Bernal, personal communication, 1975).

As it happens, the public architecture of Monte Albán I is very poorly known because of the massive overburden of later constructions. It would appear that there was no Main Plaza, as we know it today, during Period I. Isolated remnants of Period I architecture, however, have been found under later buildings in and around the Main Plaza.

### THE *PATIO AL SUR DE MONTÍCULO A*

An apparent Monte Albán Ia public building was discovered underneath the southeast corner of the North Plat-

form, at a place called "the patio south of Mound A" (abbreviated P.S.A. in several publications). During the 1942–1944 excavations, Caso placed pits 10, 12–15, 17, and 18 in the North Platform, which became the type locality for defining phases a, b, and c within Period I (Figure 4.3). In his master's thesis, Bernal (1946) described Monte Albán I pottery on the basis of 47,000 sherds from the P.S.A. and Mound Y, combined with 303 whole vessels from features and tombs.

Far below the surface of the North Platform lies a partly destroyed structure, apparently a public building, with a vertical *tablero* covered with "serpentine motifs modeled in stucco" (Acosta 1965:816 and Figure 4). Barely exposed in the deep stratigraphic pit, this structure, which apparently dates to Monte Albán Ic (ca. 300 B.C.?), could not be fully investigated. Below its floor were three more levels which produced the sherds used to define phases Ia, Ib, and Ic. Resting on bedrock at the base of the pit, and hence presumably dating to Ia, was a sloping wall (*muro en talud*) from an earlier building—perhaps one of the first public buildings erected at Monte Albán.

Because these three lowest stratigraphic levels below the P.S.A. section of the North Platform produced the type collections on the basis of which the internal chronology of

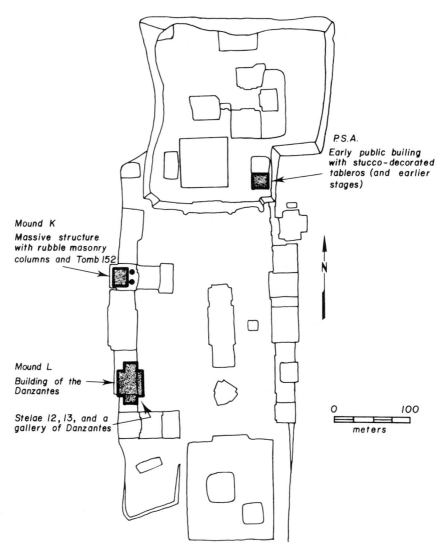

*P.S.A.*
*Early public builing with stucco-decorated tableros (and earlier stages)*

*Mound K*
*Massive structure with rubble masonry columns and Tomb 152*

N

*Mound L*
*Building of the Danzantes*

*Stelae 12, 13, and a gallery of Danzantes*

0                    100
meters

FIGURE 4.3.  The earliest public buildings at Monte Albán, superimposed on an outline of the later Main Plaza (see Figure 4.12).

Monte Albán I has been defined, let us examine them in detail. After the 1942–1944 excavations, Caso and Acosta divided all Monte Albán pottery into four categories, based on the postfiring color of the clay: Gris (G), Crema (C), Amarillo (A), and Café (K). Bernal (1946) further subdivided the categories into numbered "types" such as G-1, A-2, and so on. Actually, most of these "types" correspond to what other archaeologists have called "modes" or "attributes"; once that correspondence is understood, the Monte Albán chronology works extraordinarily well everywhere in the Valley of Oaxaca. It should be remembered, however, that the sequence, by definition, reflects a succession of architectural levels in the Main Plaza of Monte Albán. It is unlikely that excavations elsewhere will match it exactly; for this reason, most recent attempts to redefine it or to slice it up differently have been futile, and are likely to remain so. During the settlement pattern survey, Monte Albán Ia and Ic have proven to be easily recognizable when

surface collections are substantial, but Ib has not (see also comments by Drennan 1976b:18). For the purpose of this volume, we will refer only to Ia and Ic, regarding Ib as a transition between those two phases.

Table 4.1 gives the order in which various of Caso, Bernal, and Acosta's types appear in Bernal's (1946) analysis of the P.S.A. material. Each type is listed in the phase in which it first appears; most types continue for a phase or two after their initial appearance, although redeposition could have strengthened this phenomenon.

It is, of course, the gray ware of Monte Albán I that one most often sees illustrated because it displays the greatest diversity and artistic expression. In ordinary Period I refuse at Monte Albán, gray pottery constitutes only 25% of the sherds; among whole vessels from tombs and features, it is 76% (Bernal 1946:31). Monte Albán Ia gray ware is highly burnished and often feels smooth and waxy to the touch. There are flat-based bowls, hemispherical bowls, jars with

TABLE 4.1
Initial Appearance of Various Pottery Types in Basal Stratigraphic Levels of
the P.S.A., North Platform, Monte Albán[a]

| | |
|---|---|
| Already appearing in Level 1 (phase Ia) | G-1, G-3, G-5, G-15, G-16, G-17, G-18, G-24, G-30<br>C-1, C-2, C-3, C-4, C-5, C-6, C-20<br>K-1, K-3, K-3a, K-8<br>A-4, A-6, A-12, A-17 |
| Not appearing until Level 2 (phase Ib) | G-2, G-6, G-10, G-12, G-13, G-14, G-19, G-32, G-33<br>C-7<br>K-2, K-6, K-13, K-19<br>A-1, A-10, A-13, A-18 |
| Not appearing until Level 3 (phase Ic) | G-7, G-25, G-26<br>C-13, C-14<br>K-5<br>A-2, A-5 |

[a] After Bernal 1946:29.

tall necks, bottles, even fish-effigy dishes. Bowls frequently have outcurved or wide everted rims, decorated with a variety of incised geometric designs (G-15, G-16). Significantly, three diagnostics of the preceding Rosario phase—negative or resist white-on-gray, pennant incising, and "zoned toning"—did not appear in Bernal's sample from the P.S.A. or in any of the other 100 pits made to bedrock at Monte Albán (see Topic 19).

During Monte Albán Ic, one of the most significant stylistic markers was the flat-based bowl with two incised lines on its outcurved rim and fine multitoothed, parallel ("combed") incisions made on the inside of the base. These gray combed-bottom bowls ("type G-12" of Caso, Bernal, and Acosta 1967) occur throughout the Valley of Oaxaca and appear in the Mixteca as well, although they last somewhat longer in the latter region (Spores 1974a).

## THE BUILDING OF THE DANZANTES

Another of the earliest public buildings at Monte Albán was the Edificio de los Danzantes. Its full dimensions may never be known, as it is currently submerged under the southeast portion of Mound L, below a much later building that has been consolidated; a few "tunnels" allow parts of the Building of the Danzantes to be viewed. It is a pyramidal platform with a core of rubble and an outer shell of what Donald Robertson (Topic 28) calls "orthostats"—huge rectangular slabs of pre-Cambrian gneiss set upright so that the greatest dimension is vertical rather than horizontal.

The 1806 expedition of Guillermo Dupaix was the first to record the danzantes at Monte Albán; his artist, Castañeda, illustrated five slabs that were set into the east side of the southern section of the platform of the original building, or Mound L (Dupaix 1969: Vol. II, Lám. 20 [41], Fig. 66 [A–E]). Other early explorers such as Sologuren and Belmar (ca. 1900), Batres (1902), and Seler (1904) uncovered additional danzantes or illustrated some of the known visible danzantes (see Marcus 1976d:125).

The majority of the danzante carvings, however, which now number over 300, were discovered during the 18 field seasons (1931–1958) of the Monte Albán project directed by Caso. Many carvings had remained in situ in Mound L but additional danzantes were found reused as construction material in numerous other Main Plaza structures. Although Agustín Villagra drew the stones for Caso as they were discovered, they were, for the most part, never published (Caso 1947, 1965b; Scott 1971).

Although today the danzantes occur scattered and reused throughout the area of the Main Plaza, all the evidence at our disposal (from old photos, drawings, and surviving remnants in Mound L) suggest that all of the more than 300 carvings were once displayed as a huge gallery on the east face of Building L (Marcus 1974:Fig. 26). Each danzante represents a single, naked, grotesquely sprawled figure, eyes closed, scrolls occasionally issuing from one or more parts of the body (Figure 4.4). Those in the lowest row are set vertically as orthostats, facing to the right (their left). Presumably because this row would be the easiest to see and read, it contains the most elaborate danzantes, often accompanied by necklaces, earplugs, complicated hairdos, and hieroglyphic names; those in the uppermost row are the simplest. Above the Row 1 orthostats is a second row of figures lying horizontally with heads pointing north. A third row consists of vertical orthostats with less elaborate danzantes, facing to the viewer's left (their right). Above this is a fourth row of monuments with horizontal figures similar to those in the second row. Building L also had a massive staircase without balustrades, composed of huge stone blocks laid horizontally; many danzante figures are carved on the stairway risers. Paddock (1966a:Fig. 38) considers some of these to belong to the original building.

While the danzantes have been subjected to every conceivable interpretation (dancers, swimmers, ecstatic priests, medical anomalies), in our opinion the only interpretation consistent with iconographic conventions elsewhere in Mesoamerica is Michael Coe's (1962:95). Coe points out that nudity was "scandalous" in Mesoamerica; it was used to humiliate captives, as in the case of the famous prisoner

FIGURE 4.4. Surviving remnant of the earliest stage of Building L at Monte Albán, showing the original arrangement of the so-called *danzantes*. (Drawing by Margaret Van Bolt.)

galleries or prisoner staircases in the Maya region (Morley and Morley 1938:13). Important personages were never shown naked, or in awkward, distorted, sprawling positions, but such depictions were standard for captives; thus we feel that Coe is correct in interpreting the *danzantes* as the corpses of captives slain or sacrificed by the rulers of Monte Albán. The figures carved on the stairway risers are analogous to those on prisoner staircases in the Maya region, where anyone ascending the stairway would tread on their bodies.

It is perhaps significant that this gallery of more than 300 monuments, dating to the first period of occupation, represents 80% of the effort expended on monument carving at Monte Albán. Marcus (1974:90) has suggested that it represents a symbolic display of power which coincided with the time when Monte Albán's rulers would have felt the greatest need for propaganda to intimidate their enemies and reassure their supporters, that is, before they had achieved true statehood and really effective political power.

## A STRUCTURE INSIDE SYSTEM IV

System IV is a complex of buildings and courtyards on the west side of the Main Plaza. Inside Mound K, the largest component of System IV, lie the buried remains of a much earlier structure which may be a Monte Albán I public building. The structure has a 6-m-high sloping wall (*muro en talud*) of huge stones and a pair of rubble masonry columns. These columns are round on the front but flat on the back surface, with a small recess in the back as well. Both the platform construction and the flat-backed rubble columns

are strongly reminiscent of the public buildings at the site of Monte Negro near Tilantongo, another Late Formative site (see Topic 26).

## OTHER PERIOD I STRUCTURES

The lower fill of Mound Y (outside the Main Plaza) has what may be the remains of a Late Monte Albán I structure. There is also a Period I building of some kind under Ballcourt Number 2.

## TOMBS OF MONTE ALBÁN I

Caso, Bernal, and Acosta found a half-dozen tombs of this period, most of them from phase Ic; all are described as of "plain rectangular construction, doorless and roofed with slabs of stone laid horizontally" (Acosta 1965:817). Even the poorest tombs may have as many as 4 pottery vessels, and the richest so far known (Tomb 43) had 72 vessels, including at least 10 conch shell effigies, a duck effigy, frog effigies, and other elaborate vessels. Tomb 43 may be from early in phase I, and because the conch shell trumpet among the Zapotec was associated with public office, such a large number of effigies may indicate a person of some importance.

Tomb 111 had 51 vessels, including a duck effigy, "ashtray" incensarios, and several combed-bottom G-12 bowls. Tombs 33 and 94 also had fish or duck effigy vessels. Such effigies were not restricted to tombs, however, occurring with tombless burials (such as Burial V-19) as well. Nor were they restricted to adult burials; Tomb 152 in Mound K of System IV had a 2-year-old child accompanied by conchshell effigies.

Caso, Bernal, and Acosta also found more than a dozen burials (without tombs) from Period I. Some had as little as one pottery vessel, while Burial VI-12 had 29 vessels, including phase Ic style "ashtray" incensarios and what have been

called Cocijo urns.[1] Combed-bottom G-12 bowls are other common offerings, as are vessels with bridge spouts, duck effigies, and bowls with mammiform feet. Perhaps the earliest burial is V-2, whose offerings appear to be in phase Ia style.

---

[1]These are probably not really urns, but effigy vessels depicting a person costumed to represent *Cocijo* or "lightning."

# TOPIC 23
## The First Appearance of Zapotec Writing and Calendrics

JOYCE MARCUS

We have seen that the first known Zapotec hieroglyphs occur on Monument 3 at San José Mogote, dating to the Rosario phase. The two-glyph phrase, "One Earthquake," is presumably a date (or a name drawn from a date) derived from the Zapotec 260-day ritual calendar. Such dates occur with greater frequency on the monuments of Monte Albán during Period I. This group of monuments would include Stelae 12, 13, 14, 15, and 17 (Caso 1928, 1947).

Before describing some of these monuments, let us first consider the Zapotec calendar and numerical system as they were known at the time of the Spanish Conquest, which in turn provides the framework by which the hieroglyphic texts of Monte Albán I can be described.

## THE CALENDAR

The Precolumbian Zapotec, like many other Mesoamerican peoples, had two calendars, one secular and one ritual. In the sixteenth century, the 365-day secular calendar was called *yza*. Although the Zapotec did count months or "moons" (*pèo*), the essential subdivision of the *yza* was the season, called *cocij*, "lightning" (Córdova 1578b). In Juchitán, these words have remained very similar to their ancient counterparts—*iza* for year, *beeu* for month or moon, *gusi* for season (Pickett 1959).

The sixteenth-century year could be divided several ways, perhaps the most common being the contrast between a dry season, *cocijcobàa*, and a rainy season, *cocijquije* (from *niçaquie* or *niçaquije*, "rain"). These terms survive in Juchitán as *gusi ba* and *gusi guie* (Pickett 1959), while in Mitla, where the Spanish word *tiempo* has been adopted, the only vestige of the ancient system is the term *tiemp gusgih* for "rainy season" (Messer 1978).

The 260-day ritual calendar was called *pije* or *piye*,[1] a term whose initial phoneme suggests that it had *pèe;* ritual or sacred time was alive, it moved, and its calculations were in the hands of a group of ritual specialists called *colanij*,

---

[1]Since the *j* used by Córdova was the Latin *j*, the pronunciation would have been *pi-ye* regardless of spelling.

"diviners" (Marcus 1978). The term *cocijo* was also used for units of the *pije*, but in this case the division was into 4 *cocijo* of 65 days each. In turn, each 65-day *cocijo* was divided into five units, called *cocii*, of 13 days each (Córdova 1578b:202). Each "day" (*chij*) of the *pije* had its own number and name, usually an animal or a natural force; a *chij* began at midday and ran until the next midday (Córdova 1578b:212). Figure 4.5 depicts the *pije* with its 260 *chij*, 20 *cocii*, and 4 *cocijo*.

The four *cocijo* were also called *pitào* ("great spirits"), perhaps a reference to the four lightnings which resided in the four quadrants of the Zapotec world. The *cocijo* or *pitào* were said to cause all events (Córdova 1578b:202). To these *cocijo* the Zapotec offered sacrifices, including blood from various parts of their own bodies (ears, thighs, tip of the tongue, and so forth). Each of the 260 *chij* had its own corresponding fortune, benevolent or malevolent. The day names and numbers were used to name newborn children, as well as to determine the feasibility of marriage for a particular couple; the *colanij* decided whether the combination of names and numbers augured well for a wedding.

Most 260-day ritual calendars in Mesoamerica had 20 different day names which combined with the numbers 1–13 (Marcus 1976c). There are interesting differences, however, between the Zapotec *pije* and the Maya 260-day

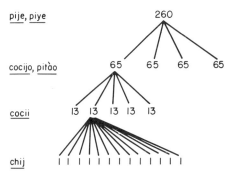

FIGURE 4.5. The Zapotec *pije*, or 260-day ritual calendar, with its division into *cocijo*, *cocii*, and *chij*. (Redrawn from Marcus and Flannery 1978.)

ritual calendar. For the Maya (as recorded in the codices Dresden and Madrid), the 260 days were usually divided into five units of 52 days; these 52-day units were in turn divided into "irregular intervals" (Thompson 1950:101). By contrast, the Zapotec division into four 65-day units, each subdivided into five 13-day units, was more uniform.

Each *cocijo* or *pitào* contained 65 days; an example of one of the four *cocijo* is given in Table 4.2, divided up into five *cocii*. Each term is a combination of the number and day name, fused together in a style that suggests great antiquity for the Zapotec *pije*. The four *cocijo* were called by the days on which they began: (1) *quiachilla*, (2) *quialana*, (3) *quiagoloo*, and (4) *quiaguilloo*.

The 20 day names of the *pije* were originally given by Córdova (1578b:204–212). Caso (1965c:944, 1967:84a) and Seler (1904) attempted to translate the Zapotec sixteenth-century terms into Spanish. These are given in Table 4.3, where I have compared them to the day names of the Mixtec (Caso 1967), the Maya (Thompson 1950), and the Aztec (Caso 1965c, 1967; M. E. Smith 1973a). I find several of these translations dubious—frequently, one has the feel-

ing the author tried to impose more similarity on the calendars than is really there—but I have decided to leave them for now because it will require a great deal of future work to develop convincing alternative translations. Note that, at least superficially, there are notable Zapotec–Maya similarities and Mixtec–Aztec similarities. The latter may be of Postclassic origin (see Chapter 8).

## NUMERATION

The Zapotec system of counting was vigesimal, as were other Mesoamerican systems. Córdova (1578b:176–186) gives the cardinal numbers as follows:

| | |
|---|---|
| 1 | *tobi, chaga* |
| 2 | *topa, cato* |
| 3 | *chona, cayo* |
| 4 | *tapa, taa* |
| 5 | *caayo* |
| 6 | *xopa* |
| 7 | *caache* |
| 8 | *xoono* |
| 9 | *caa, gaa* |
| 10 | *chij* |
| 11 | *chijbitobi* (10 + 1) |
| 12 | *chijbitopa, chibicato* (10 + 2) |
| 13 | *chijño, chijbichona* (10 + 3) |
| 14 | *chijtaa* (10 + 4) |
| 15 | *chino* |
| 16 | *chinobitobi* (15 + 1) |
| 17 | *chinobitopa, chinobicato* (15 + 2) |
| 18 | *chinobichona* (15 + 3); *cetopa calle* (20 − 2 = 18) |
| 19 | *chinobitapa* (15 + 4); *cetobicalle* (20 − 1 = 19) |
| 20 | *calle* |
| 30 | *callebichij* (20 + 10) |
| 40 | *tova* (2 (×20) ?) |
| 50 | *tovabichij* (40 + 10) |
| 60 | *cayona* (3 × (20) ) |
| 70 | *cayobabichij* (60 + 10) |
| 80 | *taa* (4 (×20) ) |
| 90 | *taabichij* (80 + 10) |
| 100 | *cayoa* (5 (×20) ) |
| 110 | *cayoabichij* (100 + 10) |
| 120 | *xopalalle* (6 × 20) |
| 140 | *caachelalle* (7 × 20) |
| 150 | *caachelal lebichij* (7 × 20 + 10) |
| 160 | *xoonolalle* (8 × 20) |
| 170 | *xoonolallebichij* (8 × 20 + 10) |
| 180 | *Caalal le* (9 × 20) |
| 200 | *chija* (10 (×20) ) |
| 300 | *chinoua* (15 (×20) ?) |
| 400 | *tobiela, chagael la* (1 *ela* = 400) |
| 500 | *tobiela cayoa* (1 *ela* + 5 (×20) ) |
| 600 | *tobiela chija* (1 *ela* + 200) |
| 700 | *chagaela chinoua* (1 *ela* + 300) |
| 800 | *topael, catoela* (2 *ela*: 2 × 400) |

TABLE 4.2
The Five Cocii of the Cocijo Named *Quiachilla* (Sixteenth Century A.D.)

| The first Cocii | | The third Cocii (continued) | |
|---|---|---|---|
| (1) | Quiachilla | (8) | Lache |
| (2) | Pillaa | (9) | Pelannaa |
| (3) | Pelaala | (10) | Neloo |
| (4) | Nelachi | (11) | Nixoo |
| (5) | Peciguij | (12) | Piñopa |
| (6) | Quelana | (13) | Pizaape |
| (7) | Pillachina | | |
| (8) | Nelaba | **The fourth Cocii** | |
| (9) | Pelaqueça | (1) | Quialao |
| (10) | Pillatela | (2) | Pichijlla |
| (11) | Neloo | (3) | Peolaa |
| (12) | Piñopija | (4) | Laala |
| (13) | Piciguij | (5) | Peolache |
| | | (6) | Qualaze |
| **The second Cocii** | | (7) | Pillalaana |
| (1) | Quiagueche | (8) | Nichina |
| (2) | Palannaa | (9) | Peolapa |
| (3) | Peoloo | (10) | Pillanica |
| (4) | Calaxoo | (11) | Netel |
| (5) | Pellopa | (12) | Peñeloo |
| (6) | Qualappe | (13) | Pizopija |
| (7) | Pillalao | | |
| (8) | Nichijlla | **The fifth Cocii** | |
| (9) | Peolaa | (1) | Quiaguij |
| (10) | Pillaala | (2) | Pelache |
| (11) | Lachi | (3) | Pelaana |
| (12) | Piñaze | (4) | Calaloo |
| (13) | Pecelana | (5) | Pexoo |
| | | (6) | Qualopa |
| **The third Cocii** | | (7) | Pillape |
| (1) | Quiachina | (8) | Neloo |
| (2) | Pelapa | (9) | Pichijlla |
| (3) | Peolaqueça | (10) | Pillaa |
| (4) | Calatella | (11) | Laala |
| (5) | Pelloo | (12) | Pinijchi |
| (6) | Qualapija | (13) | Picici |
| (7) | Pillaa | | |

TABLE 4.3
The 20 Day Names of the 260-Day Ritual Calendar: A Comparison of the Maya, Zapotec, Mixtec, and Aztec (Sixteenth Century A.D.)

| Maya | Zapotec | Mixtec | Aztec |
|---|---|---|---|
| Imix (Earth Surface, Crocodile) | Chilla, Chijlla (Crocodile, Divination Bean) | Quehui (Day) | Cipactli (Crocodile) |
| Ik (Wind) | Laa, Quij, Guij (Fire?, Live Coal?) | Chi (Wind) | Ehecatl (Wind) |
| Akbal (Night) | Guela, Ela (Night) | Cuau, Huahi (House) | Calli (House) |
| Kan (Yellow, Maize) | Gueche, Quichi, Achi (Iguana, Toad) | Q, Cuu (?) | Cuetzpallin (Lizard) |
| Chicchan (Snake) | Zee, Zij, Cee, Zije (Snake?, Evil?, Young Corn?) | Yo, Yococo (Serpent) | Coatl (Serpent) |
| Cimi (Death) | Lana, Laana (Rabbit?, Soot) | Mahua (?) | Miquiztli (Death) |
| Manik (?) | China, Chijña (Deer) | Cuaa (Deer) | Mazatl (Deer) |
| Lamat (Venus?) | Lapa, Laba (Crown?) | Xayu (Rabbit) | Tochtli (Rabbit) |
| Muluc (Water, Jade?) | Niça, Queça (Water) | Duta (Water) | Atl (Water) |
| Oc (Dog?) | Tela, Tella (Face Down?, Dog?) | Ua (Coyote) | Itzcuintli (Dog) |
| Chuen (Craftsman, Monkey?) | Loo, Goloo (Monkey?) | Ñuu (?) | Ozomatli (Monkey) |
| Eb (Mist, Dew) | Pija (Twisted?) | Cuañe (Yerba) | Malinalli (Yerba) |
| Ben (Reed?) | Quij, Laa, Nij (Reed?) | Huiyo (Reed?) | Acatl (Reed) |
| Ix (Jaguar?) | Gueche, Eche, Ache (Tigre, Fierce Animal) | Vidzu (Tigre) | Ocelotl (Tigre) |
| Men (Old Moon Goddess) | Naa, Na, Ñaa (Mother?) | Xayacu (Eagle) | Cuauhtli (Eagle) |
| Cib (Wax) | Guiloo, Loo (Raven?, Eye?) | Cuij (Turkey) | Cozcacuauhtli (Vulture) |
| Caban (Earth) | Xoo (Earthquake) | Qhi (?) | Ollin (Earthquake) |
| Etz'nab (Sacrificial Knife?) | Opa, Gopa, Oppa (Vapor from the earth) | Cuxi (Flint) | Tecpatl (Flint Knife) |
| Cauac (Lightning, Thunderbolt) | Appe, Ape (Cloudy?) | Dzahui (Rain) | Quiauitl (Rain) |
| Ahau (Lord, Chief) | Lao, Loo (Face) | Uaco (?) | Xochitl (Flower) |

| | |
|---|---|
| 1,000 | *catoel la chija* (2 *ela* + 200) |
| 1,200 | *chonaela, cayoela* (3 *ela*) |
| 1,600 | *tapaela* (4 *ela*) |
| 2,000 | *caayoela, gaayoela* (5 *ela*) |
| 8,000 | *chagaçoti, tobiçoti* (1 *çoti*); *cal leela* (20 *ela*) |
| 16,000 | *topaçoti, catoçoti* (2 *çoti*) |
| 24,000 | *chonaçoti, cayoçoti* (3 *çoti*) |

The Zapotec evidently used the same conventions for writing numbers as did the Maya: the dot stood for 1, while a bar stood for 5. In this respect the Zapotec differed from the later Mixtec, who used five dots to represent a 5. During the early centuries of Zapotec writing (Monte Albán I and II phases), when dates or calendric names were given, the bars and dots were positioned beneath the associated hieroglyphs with the bars below the dots. During the Monte Albán IIIa period, however, the bars and dots could appear to the left of the associated hieroglyph (e.g., on Stelae 1 and 3)—which is comparable to the Maya convention—or below the hieroglyphs, with the bars above the dots (e.g., on Stelae 1, 2, 3, 4, 5, 6, 7, and 9). These changes in the positioning of the numerical coefficients can aid the researcher in assigning various texts to their archaeological period.

A finger or digit also was employed in the early inscriptions at Monte Albán. In the Maya system, a thumb or finger stood for 1 (Thompson 1950:137), but for the ancient Zapotec it may have stood for an ordinal number. According to Córdova (1578b:213), the Zapotec used a similar set of ordinal numbers to refer to the fingers of their right and

left hands and the birth order of their sons. As will be clear from the list below, the Zapotec referred to their sons with terms which ran from "right thumb" to "right fourth finger" and then from "left thumb" to "left third finger."

| Right hand | Left hand | Birth order, sons |
|---|---|---|
| *yobi* ("thumb") | *yobijye* ("thumb") | *yobi* ("first") |
| *tini* ("index finger") | *teije* ("index finger") | *tini* ("second") |
| *texi* ("third finger") | *texije* ("third finger") | *tixi* ("third") |
| *payo* ("fourth finger") | *xayoyye* ("fourth finger") | *payo* ("fourth") |
| *yee* ("fifth finger") | *pijye* ("fifth finger") | *yopije* ("fifth")<br>*teyye* ("sixth")<br>*texiye* ("seventh") |

## A SAMPLE OF MONTE ALBÁN I INSCRIPTIONS

*Stelae 12 and 13* At the southern extreme of the Building L *danzantes* gallery are two carved stones, Stelae 12 and 13, which contain one of the oldest hieroglyphic "texts" from Monte Albán (Figure 4.6). Their exact relationship to the four rows of *danzantes* has never been spelled out, but early photos and drawings (e.g., Batres 1902) show the two stelae once fit so closely together there can be no question that they

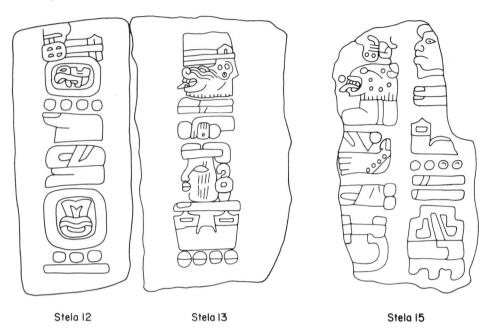

Stela 12                    Stela 13                              Stela 15

FIGURE 4.6. Period I monuments from Monte Albán. Left, Stelae 12 and 13; right, Stela 15.

constitute a single text. Both calendric and noncalendric hieroglyphs occur. Of the four calendric glyphs, some appear to be day signs and others are apparently month signs; one is Caso's year sign indicator with the year bearer housed within its cartouche.

For an example of a possible month sign glyph, we can turn to the last glyph in column B.[2] This glyph occurs on other monuments at Monte Albán with numbers greater than 13, which no day sign in the 260-day calendar can. Months, however, can be associated with numbers as high as 19. The noncalendric glyphs are sandwiched between the calendric ones; thus, noncalendric glyphs A3 and B3 seem to be the subjects of the phrases or clauses. Note that A2 and B2 are parts of hands or hand compounds, some of which may represent verbs. There are several other Mesoamerican writing systems (e.g., Maya and Aztec) in which hands are commonly used as verbs or parts of verbs. (This usage is in addition to the possibility that some "thumb" or "finger" glyphs represent ordinal numbers; see above.)

While Stelae 12 and 13 constitute a single text, the order of reading is still not agreed upon. According to one view, Column A (1–4) should be read first, then Column B (1–4). This reading would give us two parallel texts, as follows:

A1   Year sign (with day beginning that year inside the cartouche), 4 Serpent
A2   Hand with thumb prominent (possible verb)
A3   Noncalendric glyph; meaning unknown

A4   Possible day sign, 8 Water
B1   Jaguar glyph with possible coefficient of 10 (2 bars); this could be a month sign or a personal name
B2   Hand grasping an object, a possible verb
B3   Profile head with subfix of a digit or finger; a possible personal name and probable subject of the column
B4   Calendric glyph; in other texts it is associated with numbers greater than 13, making this glyph an excellent candidate for a month

If, however, the text were intended to be read as paired columns, (A1–B1, then A2–B2, and so on), the result would be as follows:

Year name, month (A1–B1, calendric glyphs)
Four event glyphs (noncalendric glyphs, verbs, and nouns)
Day, followed by month (calendric glyphs)

More work needs to be done before we can "prove" which order of reading is correct—left to right, top to bottom, bottom to top, paired columns, single columns—a fact which clearly indicates that the study of Zapotec writing is still in its infancy.

*Stela 14* (Caso 1947:Fig. 20) was also found between Mounds L and M, but somewhat to the east of Stelae 12 and 13, and apparently not *in situ* as part of the gallery of the *danzantes*. This stela is really just a fragment which includes four separate hieroglyphs. The clearest glyph is the last one, possibly a bowl or vase of water.

*Stela 15* (Figure 4.6) (Caso 1947:Fig. 14) is an important fragment, bearing two columns. The last glyph in Column A is very similar to the final glyph on Stela 14 (see Caso 1928:Fig. 60). Stela 15 has an incomplete glyph at A1 and at

---

[2]In this and all subsequent discussions of hieroglyphs, we use the standard Mesoamerican system for designating glyphs. Columns receive letters (A, B, C) beginning on the left, while glyphs within a column (rows) receive numbers (1, 2, 3) beginning at the top. Thus, for example, the second glyph from the top in the second column is B2.

A2 there is a jaguar compound; at A3 there is a hand out-stretched, cradling a glyph; at A4 there is a glyph somewhat similar to the one at A3 on Stela 12; and finally, at A5 we have the "closed bag" or vessel glyph which will be discussed further below. At B1 there is a profile human subfixed by two fingers; at B2 we have Caso's Glyph W with a subfix of 14 (2 bars and 4 dots). As this numerical coefficient is greater than 13 (which is the highest number that can be employed in the 260-day calendar), it seems possible that Glyph W represents a month sign, since those can be associated with numbers greater than 13. This Glyph W or "castle glyph" is very similar to that represented on Stela 13 (at B4). Finally, at B3 on Stela 15 we have the earliest example of a "hill sign" (see Topic 29) with various subfixes.

*Stela 17* is another early and very important fragment (Figure 4.7; Caso 1947:Fig. 15), which also bears two columns. At A1 we have a head in profile facing downward; at A2 we have an apparent day sign, possibly a water sign inside a cartouche, with the numerical coefficient of 10. At A3 we have an apparent year sign, with a day sign enclosed within a cartouche serving as the year bearer; in Caso's system it would be called Glyph E or "precious stone." This year sign and Glyph E carry the subfix of 12. At B1 we have a profile head with a subfix of two fingers; at B2 we have an unusual glyph with a numerical coefficient of 18 (another possible month sign); at B3 we have what may be a down-facing head; at B4 there is a possible skull fragment; finally, at B5 we have a head glyph with an unusual hat, a prominent circular earplug, a long nose, and a protruding lip (perhaps indicating a mask). This head is nearly identical to the one appearing inside the body of Danzante 55 (Caso 1947:Fig. 16).

*Danzante 55* (Figure 4.7) is another important Period I

monument in that it has quite an extensive text. At A3 we have the "closed bag" or vessel glyph already seen on Stelae 15 (at A5) and 14 (final glyph). Although Caso argues that this glyph carries a superfix of 7, I interpret it merely as a strap closing the bag. In Monte Albán I times, numerical coefficients appear below the signs, and it would be unusual if any glyph always appeared with a superfix of 7.

The close links between the glyphs on Stelae 14, 15, and 17 and Danzante 55 seem clear. Assigning all these stones to Monte Albán I thus seems equally secure. One further suggestion appears worthwhile: during Monte Albán I, the closed bag or vessel glyph just discussed may be an early version of the glyph Caso calls *la bolsa* on Stela 1 in the South Platform, dating to Monte Albán IIIa (Caso 1928:Fig. 26). On Stela 1, the bolsa glyph ends both Columns A and B. It also ends the inscriptions on the right side of Stela 2 and the front of Stela 8 (Caso 1928:Fig. 46), both IIIa monuments in the South Platform. The exact meaning of this "tied bag" glyph, according to Caso, was "end"; alternatively, it might be read "thus it has been written." This same argument has been made for an analogous Maya compound (*Imix-comb-Imix*) glyph, because it also was used to close inscriptions (Thompson 1962:96).

## ADDITIONAL COMMENTS

As Caso noted (1947:9), the writing of Monte Albán I is the most ancient that has appeared in Mesoamerica. Its antiquity is demonstrated principally by its connection with the earliest ceramics in the deepest stratigraphic excavations. The difficulty with its origins is that the writing system

 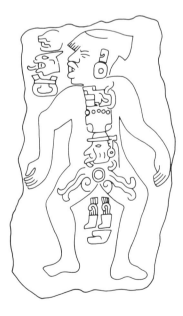

FIGURE 4.7. Period I monuments from Monte Albán. Left, Stela 17; right, Danzante 55.

appears fully developed— with single and double columns, day signs, possible month signs, and noncalendric signs. Many later Zapotec glyphs seem to appear in an early form in Period I, as do some Mesoamerican conventions such as the use of hands or hand gestures as verbs.

In the preceding Rosario phase (i.e., on Monument 3, San José Mogote) there is evidence for the 260-day Zapotec ritual calendar, but it is not until the Monte Albán I period that we have examples of pure texts, such as Stelae 12, 13, 14, 15, and 17. This clear development in both the number of glyphs employed, and the variety of glyphs, apparently took place at Monte Albán. No Period I site other than Monte Albán itself employed such a writing system, and this fact indicates the new and special role Monte Albán was able to fill—the valley's controller, manipulator, and disseminator of political information, propaganda, and decisions. It appears that the confederacy at Monte Albán served as an impetus for the explosive evolution of Zapotec writing, because its major development evidently took place sometime between the late Rosario phase and Monte Albán Ic. We should keep in mind, however, that we are comparing one monument from the Rosario phase with more than 20 with texts from Period I at Monte Albán.

## TOPIC 24
## Valley-Floor Settlement Patterns during Monte Albán I

STEPHEN KOWALEWSKI

### THE ETLA AND CENTRAL REGIONS OF THE VALLEY OF OAXACA

A striking growth in the number and size of sites began in the early part of Monte Albán I and continued until the end of the period. Rosario phase and Monte Albán Ia sites in the Etla arm of the Valley of Oaxaca numbered 48, with a total occupied area of 215 ha. The number of settlements declined to 44 in Monte Albán Ic, but the population may have been somewhat higher, as many of the sites were larger and more densely occupied in Period Ic (Varner 1974:111–115).

The expansion in site numbers and sizes, as well as in population, continued throughout Monte Albán I in the Central Valley survey area (number of sites: Rosario phase, 5; Monte Albán Ia, 36; Monte Albán Ic, 154; occupied area: Rosario phase, 6.2 ha.; Monte Albán Ia, 61.6 ha.; Monte Albán Ic, 402.8 ha.).

Total population for those areas intensively surveyed, including the site of Monte Albán itself, probably ranged between 7,070 and 14,474 in phase Ia, and between 28,563 and 58,397 in phase Ic. To quantify this population growth, it is possible to calculate average annual rates of increase from the archaeological population estimates, with the understanding that the figure (r) is only a gross measure of change, not an indicator of actual demographic processes. For the time period between 1400 B.C. and 500 B.C. (Tierras Largas through Rosario phase), the average annual rate of increase is estimated to have been between 0.1 and 0.4%; the rate was apparently much higher—0.5 to 1.0%—during Monte Albán I.

This period also saw an extension of the range of environmental zones occupied by permanent settlements. Monte Albán I communities were located not only along the Río Atoyac, but also up major and even very small tributaries, back into the steeply sloping piedmont. In the Etla survey area, half the Monte Albán Ia population lived in the upper piedmont, and there are a number of Monte Albán Ic settlements in the Central Valley area that are located beyond the margins of optimum maize production. While canal irrigation was probably known and practiced during earlier periods, two canal systems for which we have good surface evidence (one at the base of Monte Albán, the other in the western Tlacolula Valley) were constructed and used primarily during Monte Albán I.

A clear difference between the settlement system of earlier periods and that of Monte Albán I was the emergence of a new class of communities, larger than the hamlet but smaller than the leading regional center. Thirteen settlements in the Etla survey area and eight in the Central Valley area had minimum populations of 100 or more (the largest probably had fewer than 1000 people). Many of these sites have artificial mounds. Our surface surveys suggest that at the beginning of Monte Albán I there was a major reorganization of the settlement hierarchy, with the eclipse of San José Mogote; the establishment of a new, larger, and more centrally located administrative and ceremonial center at Monte Albán; and the emergence of a series of second-order communities between the regional center and the smallest villages. Thus, there were at least two administrative levels above the hamlet in Period I.

Another important aspect of the population expansion of Monte Albán I was the proliferation of very small settlements. Isolated residences, hamlets, and tiny villages account for 89% of the settlements in the Etla and Central Valley areas. It seems reasonable to infer from this pattern that the individual household was still an important unit of agricultural production in Monte Albán I, despite the changes taking place on a higher sociopolitical level. But in Monte Albán Ia, roughly half the people in the intensively surveyed areas of the valley resided at Monte Albán, and many of the latter may not have been engaged in agricultural production. By Monte Albán Ic, the proportion of urban dwellers had increased to 77% of the total. Anne Kirkby (1973:134) predicted from her agricultural reconstruction a maximum population of 21,000 for these areas at 300 to 100 B.C.; our archaeological estimates of 28,563 to 58,397 are much higher. The rural population, considered alone, seems to be closer to Kirkby's predictions; the city of Monte Albán accounts for the difference between predicted and observed population.

The urban center must have relied for its provisioning on a system of production and distribution much wider than just the Etla and Central sections of the valley. The new system established in Monte Albán I would have entailed more intensive demands for energy in the form of agricultural production. Possible ways of meeting these demands would have been ideological changes encouraging population growth, thus increasing the number of productive units (households), the opening up of previously uncultivated lands, and the use of the small-scale irrigation techniques archaeologically documented for Period I. Control over constituent households may have been exercised by Monte Albán through outlying secondary centers, although this is not yet clear for Period I.

Monte Albán's influence seems to have been most strongly felt in the Central section of the valley, and less so in Etla, judging by the following figures. Figure 4.8 shows the increased density of rural population in the Central survey area that followed the decline of San José Mogote and the rise of Monte Albán. By Period Ic, the Central region accounted for 47% of the rural population in our intensive survey area as opposed to only 9% at the apogee of San José Mogote during the Rosario phase, representing a 38% shift to the vicinity of Monte Albán.

## THE TLACOLULA REGION

The Tlacolula region has not yet been intensively surveyed, but preliminary surveys indicate a substantial population increase there as well. Mitla, Yagul, Abasolo, Yegüih, and Tomaltepec are all possible candidates for second-order communities like those described for the Etla and Central regions. All have artificial mounds, and Whalen's (1981) excavations at Tomaltepec have revealed an apparent public building dating to Monte Albán I.

## SUMMARY

In summary, Monte Albán I was a period which witnessed both the founding of a 365-ha city and an increase in rural population growth. During the course of the period, this rural population was shifted toward the urban center, and there may have been a three-tiered settlement hierarchy whose upper two tiers were administrative.

FIGURE 4.8.  Monte Albán Ic settlements in the Central District of the Valley of Oaxaca. Stippled area shows the extent of Period Ic occupation at Monte Albán itself according to Blanton 1978. (Redrawn from Kowalewski 1976.)

# TOPIC 25
## Yagul during Monte Albán I

JOHN PADDOCK

The ruins of Yagul cover a kilometer-long volcanic tuff mesa which rises from the floor of the Valley of Oaxaca, some 3 km to the east of Tlacolula. At various points in its history, Yagul was probably a "second-order" administrative center in the sense that Kowalewski (Topics 24, 30) uses the term. This may have been the case during Monte Albán I, but remains of that period at Yagul have been either so disturbed or so covered by later materials that the evidence is ambiguous. Two occupational terraces, C and F, have provided Monte Albán I remains.

The finds of the 1960 season at Yagul, supervised by Charles Wicke, have been published by Chadwick (1966), except for rather minor details. The 1958 work on Terrace C at Yagul, however, is unpublished and provides several interesting inferences.

This work, done in a residential area rather remote from the city center, showed indications of a significant Period I occupation at Yagul; the Terrace F work of Chadwick et al. resoundingly confirmed it. There is no indication that it was a populous occupation, and except for the Terrace F adobe tombs, no architecture has been discovered dating from Period I; however, the quality of the ceramic remains found is, to say the least, astonishing. These remains are almost all associated with either tombs or open burials, and hence were probably selected precisely for quality (though in later periods extremely ordinary pottery went into even the luxurious tombs).

A few traits at Yagul are somewhat different from those of Monte Albán, perhaps because the reported Monte Albán excavations (Caso, Bernal, and Acosta 1967) were virtually limited to the central part of the city, whereas the Yagul excavations were mainly in habitation areas. Nevertheless, much of the Monte Albán material of Period I comes from tombs, as does much of that at Yagul; therefore, this explanation of their differences is of limited utility.

Caso and Bernal (1952:180–184, 326–336) describe two types of early braziers: a cylindrical one that has a face on the front, often with Olmec features, and a biconical or hourglass-shaped one that also may have effigies. The cylindrical ones are found at Monte Albán and a number of Valley of Oaxaca sites, as well as at Monte Negro in the Mixteca Alta (Topic 26), but the most beautiful of all is the small, exquisitely made one from Terrace F at Yagul (Chadwick 1966:Fig. 2); usually these objects are of rather coarse workmanship.

Large portions of the faces from two other braseros of this type came from Terrace C excavations. They are extremely similar, though not identical. Surviving portions of one include only the lower part up to the eyes, while the other, overlapping slightly, consists of the nose, eyes, and forehead. Both are of "Olmec" style, though the pottery is a coarse red-brown classed as K-ware at Monte Albán.

It is worth noting that all three of these pieces from Yagul belong to a class of objects unknown on the Gulf Coast, the area that is usually considered to be somehow central to Olmec culture or style. Thus, somebody in the Valley of Oaxaca had a total understanding of Olmec style in a cultural setting that in most respects was no longer identifiably Olmec.

Braseros of this type are sometimes made with a clay prevalent before the foundation of Monte Albán (a yellow paste, usually showing traces of a white wash), and the general form continues until Transición II–III (Caso and Bernal 1952:Fig. 312b).

A note on stratigraphy will be welcome. Its content will not, for there is no stratigraphy as such on Terrace C. Rather, the deposit ranges from 30 cm to somewhat over 1 m in depth; adjacent areas, only a few steps apart, consist of Period I burials, Period V tombs, Period IV or V houses, and Period IV burials. The spatial differentiation makes it easy to keep the several classes of remains separate, but if these classes had not been previously dated, the Yagul deposits would have done little to establish a chronology. Fortunately, the nature of the remains allows for an almost totally clean separation with no mixing—a situation not common at Yagul where, at least in the central city, every spoonful of earth from a Monte Albán V building is likely to have been used in several previous periods.

In the Frissell Museum of Zapotec Art at Mitla, there are a number of braziers of the biconical shape from various localities in the Valley of Oaxaca. It should be noted that the cones may be fairly equal, but often the brazier consists of a dish or plate on a high conical pedestal; the terms *biconical* or *hourglass* are rather misleading in such cases. In dating these for display, I discovered that Caso and Bernal (1952) had shown some fairly similar objects and had attributed them to Period I; none of the similar ones came from Monte Albán itself, however, and the only very similar ones I knew of were from the Terrace C explorations at Yagul.

The biconical or hourglass braziers very often have an effigy on the front, but this effigy is extremely variable; in the case of the two Terrace C pedestal braziers, it is reduced to three perforations of the pedestal to suggest a face, reinforced in one of them with appliqué ears. The Yagul ones thus represent a type not known from Monte Albán or Monte Negro, and most resembling reported pieces from places outside Monte Albán.

Dating the Terrace C pedestal braziers to Monte Albán I would be rather tenuous in view of the stratigraphic situation, except for their plain and intimate association with a number of other ceramic offerings, all of which are Period I diagnostics, and for the absence of mixing with the adjacent, much later deposits. The fact that the adjoining deposits are not of chronologically adjacent periods is also a great help; the contrasts between Monte Albán I and IV or V are striking and instructive.

In the Monte Albán excavations a single combination *cajete–ollita* was reported (Caso, Bernal, and Acosta 1967:195, Fig. 165a). Its occurrence in Tomb 111, however, places it firmly in Period I. The small burial area of Period I on Terrace C at Yagul yielded three of these curious objects. The shape of the *cajete* is typical of the period, with near-vertical walls forming a right angle at the base, wide and perfectly flat bottoms, and thin walls, all contrasting with the G-35 and other conical *cajetes* of later times. The little globular *ollita* attached on one side to, but not opening into, the *cajete* might be of any period. The clay and the finish of the whole are not typical of Period I, and if the pieces had not been found in such clear context, one would be hard put to place them stylistically. The sloppy polish is, in fact, highly characteristic of much later times and uncharacteristic of Period I. (This shape occurred at the nearby site of Caballito Blanco in Period II, but was not reported for these later times at Monte Albán. The carry-over of utilitarian types from I into II was common, however.) Though all the above examples are gray, there is a cream or yellow one, highly polished, in the Frissell Museum.

Other Period I pieces from the Yagul Terrace C excavations include polished bottles, hemispherical *cajetes,* and small animal effigies as well as figurine fragments, all indicative of Period I as distinguished from II.

In the area that was the central part of Yagul during Periods IV and V, Period I sherds are not rare. Nevertheless, a number of pits followed to bedrock failed to reveal anything *in situ* earlier than Monte Albán IV, with a single Period IIIa exception. Apparently, then, the later central city was unoccupied in Period I, and there was no foreshadowing of the later central area, such as occurred in Period I at Monte Albán, by the placement of major buildings. Unless the Yagul pits mentioned simply failed by chance to touch some existing Period I deposit, which is quite possible if it is as small as those of Terraces C and F, the later central area was indeed bare in Period I; the occurrence of something parallel to what was found on the outlying terraces would still not indicate anything that could reasonably be classed as urban.

That is to be expected; if Monte Albán was the first place to reach urban status in the Valley of Oaxaca, which seems overwhelmingly likely, then by definition it was for some time the only urban center.

# TOPIC 26
## Monte Negro: A Reinterpretation

KENT V. FLANNERY

Few sites have been conceded as much mystery and speculation as Monte Negro, a mountaintop center in the rolling mountains near Tilantongo. It was discovered in 1936 by Alfonso Caso on a trip through the Mixteca Alta. During 1937–1940, Caso excavated there for two field seasons; Jorge Acosta and Alberto Ruz took over for a third season. Caso was intrigued that Monte Negro, like Monte Albán, was located on a mountaintop 400 m above the valley floor—a mountaintop covered with artificial terraces, and just as lacking in obvious water sources as Monte Albán[1]—while the entire site seemed to fall within the Monte Albán I period (Caso 1942). At that time, nothing earlier than Monte Albán I had been found in the Valley of Oaxaca, and Monte Negro held out the fascinating possibility that the origins of Monte Albán were to be found in this rugged area of the high Mixteca. Indeed, as recently as 1965, most textbooks informed us that Monte Albán I culture had spent centuries forming at Monte Negro, then swept down out of the mountains around 500 B.C. when the mythical lake in the Valley of Oaxaca went dry.

Today it seems clear that the origins of Monte Albán are to be found in the Valley of Oaxaca, where permanent vil-

lages with public buildings had existed for hundreds of years before Monte Negro was built. Moreover, the ceramics of Monte Negro have their closest ties with Monte Albán Ic, rather than Ia. Despite its radiocarbon date of 649 B.C. ± 170 (C−424)—an old, Libby-era solid-carbon determination—Monte Negro's ceramic ties to the very late Cruz or earliest Ramos phases of the Nochixtlán Valley (Spores, personal communication) would place it more in the realm of 200 B.C. (see Appendix). No longer a likely ancestor for Monte Albán, Monte Negro looks more like an outpost from the northwesterly expansion of Monte Albán's influence during the Late or Terminal Formative, and an abortive outpost at that—one that did not survive into the Classic period. Precisely because of its lack of Classic overburden, however, Monte Negro presents us with something we cannot see clearly at Monte Albán: the layout and architecture of a Late Formative civic–ceremonial center.

## THE SITE LAYOUT

Tilantongo, with an approximate elevation of 1740 m, lies in a zone that would once have been rolling, oak-forested mountains with the bright red soil characteristic of parts of

---

[1]The recent discovery of dams and possible reservoirs at Monte Albán (see Topic 21) suggests that early views on its lack of water supply were unduly pessimistic.

the Mixteca Alta. A limestone range, fog-shrouded during parts of the rainy season, towers above the river on the opposite side from the town; on its summit, in the *tierra fría* above 2000 m, the ruins of Monte Negro can be reached after a steep climb through dark green oaks and scattered white limestone outcrops (Acosta n.d.a).

Few tourists who see the scale-model reconstruction of Monte Negro in the Mexican National Museum of Anthropology realize how small the site is: the entire civic–ceremonial complex of Monte Negro would fit inside the Main Plaza at San José Mogote or Monte Albán. It consists of an L-shaped alignment of two groups of buildings, the longer (140 × 50 m) running east–west, the shorter (60 × 35 m) north–south (Figure 4.9). Beyond the area of public buildings is a zone of low mounds, presumably residential, some of which are on artificial terraces reminiscent of Monte Albán's.

The buildings at Monte Negro have platform-like foundations of huge stone blocks with earthen fill, and the construction is simple and vertical, with no cornices or other decoration. Exterior walls are of huge white limestone blocks almost as hard as marble, located in irregular rows because they are of different sizes and not well trimmed. These simple, solid platforms were never larger than 20 by 20 m and rarely over 2 m high; most were smaller. The stairways are set into the building and also composed of huge blocks, lacking balustrades and rarely more than six steps high. The

buildings above the platforms were of adobe or wattle-and-daub except where stone columns were present, and when mortar was used it was local red clay.

Most public buildings are rectangular, a few having a "plus-sign" shape. They are arranged fairly symmetrically around patios which are sometimes paved with flagstones, and occasionally these flagstones surround circular stone discs which may be column bases. Drum-like stone column sections occurred in the debris, and some were found *in situ* serving as the solid core for a rubble column.

None of the buildings at Monte Negro are covered with later constructions, although some have several superimposed floors. These successive floors all seem to date to roughly the same period, and none changes the original shape of the building. The ceramics from the floors, as well as from burials in the fill of the platforms, include gray ware with some affinities to Monte Albán Ic. Some of the shapes are incense burners with the so-called young god effigy (see Paddock, Topic 25), bowls with the G-12 "combed-bottom" design typical of Monte Albán Ic in the Valley of Oaxaca (but known to have lasted longer at Nochixtlán), plates with an eccentric rim depicting a fish, tall-necked bottles, composite silhouette bowls, and shoe-shaped vessels. Spores (personal communication) estimates that Monte Albán style gray diagnostics are roughly 10 times as common at Monte Negro as at Yucuita. The bulk of the Monte Negro pottery, however, is brown or buff, and includes some jars with a red

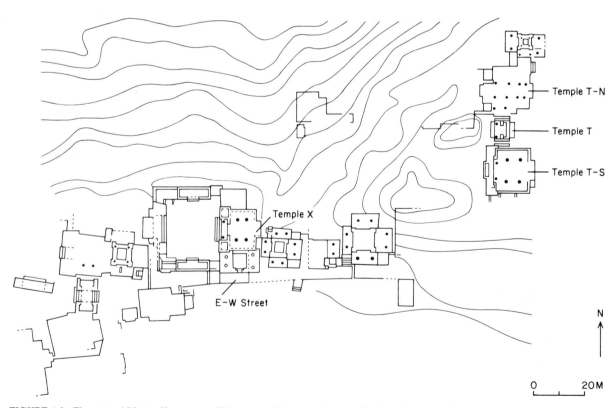

FIGURE 4.9. The site of Monte Negro near Tilantongo, Oaxaca, showing L-shaped layout. (Redrawn from Marquina 1950.)

wash that occur in the late Cruz or Ramos phases in Nochix-tlán, as well as specimens like C2 Red-on-buff from Monte Albán I.

## Public Buildings

*Temple T* at Monte Negro is 8.8 by 6.4 m and rectangular, with a 2-m-high platform; it has two stairways of large stone blocks which project out 1.6 m from the building (Acosta n.d.a, 1965:Fig. 28). Carved onto the risers of some of the steps is the same circle-and-triangle motif seen on Monument 3 at San José Mogote and in shell ornaments at Fábrica San José (Figure 3.10). The building on top is very simple—two vestibules open to the front, one of which had two columns—but it shares some features with the later temples of Monte Albán II (see Topic 27).

*Temple X*, except for its heavily reinforced stairway, has the plus-sign shape already mentioned. Its platform is 15 by 10 m wide and 2 m high, and a portico above the stairway has two columns. The roof was supported by four more columns, and in the back (in one arm of the plus sign) are two *tlecuiles* or offering basins (Figure 4.10).

*Temple T-South* is similar in plan to Temple X, but it has two superimposed stucco floors 75 cm apart. A burial with 21 vessels (Burial VIII-3) occurred in a niche in the south wall of the building. In the basal fill of the platform were two adobe tombs (Tombs 1 and 2), one with a roof of wooden beams and one with a roof of stone slabs. One tomb had two adults, one above the other, the uppermost evidently having been added later. Acosta interpreted this as a high-status husband–wife pair with abundant offerings, and it is clear their tomb was incorporated into the original foundation of the building, not added later. The other tomb had a pair of male skeletons.

*Temple T-North* has a very irregular and asymmetrical ground plan, with many entrances, many exits, and a roof supported by at least 10 columns. Below the floor was Tomb 4, containing one skeleton with seven vessels.

## Elite Residences

Elite residences occur near the temples, sometimes connected to them by a *pasillo techado* or roofed corridor.[1] They consist of open patios with a column in each corner, surrounded by three or four rooms situated at the cardinal points (Figure 4.11). Columns supported the roof of each house, and walls were of adobe or wattle-and-daub over a stone foundation two courses high. Courtyards were paved with flat stones, and there were drains below some buildings which Acosta felt might lead to a ceramic drain system. He compared the Monte Negro houses to the Roman *impluvium* residence, in which an inner paved court traps rain runoff from roofs and channels it to reservoirs which could

[2]Spores (personal communication, 1975) reports similar roofed passage-ways from Yucuita, dating to the Ramos phase.

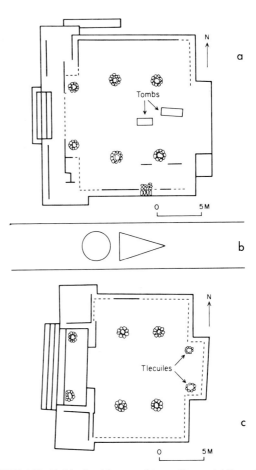

FIGURE 4.10. Public buildings at Monte Negro: (a) Temple T; (b) circle-and-triangle motif from stairway riser of Temple T; (c) Temple X. (Redrawn from Acosta n.d.a.)

alleviate the shortage of water. If Acosta's comparisons are valid, Monte Negro would therefore provide an exception to Kubler's observation that the *impluvium* residence never developed in Mesoamerica (Kubler 1964).

While more standardized and elegant than residences from earlier periods in Oaxaca, these houses fall short of the palaces that appear in Monte Albán II. Their floors are of

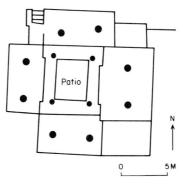

FIGURE 4.11. Elite residence at Monte Negro. Black circles are column bases. (Redrawn from Acosta n.d.a.)

stamped earth, in contrast to the public buildings whose floors are stucco. Perhaps most noteworthy are their location (which frequently permitted elite individuals to enter public buildings by means of their own covered passageways) and the relative privacy created by all rooms facing in on the courtyard.

### Other Features

An apparent street occurs at Monte Negro. It measures 100 m long by 4 to 6 m wide, running east–west and lined on both sides by buildings. The street is not level, but steps down in a series of stages.

Twenty burials were discovered at Monte Negro, some in simple graves and some in adobe tombs. Usually these were fully extended east–west or north–south, supine, with the arms down at the sides, although two females were in the fetal position; two "burials" were simply skulls from decapitated males. The offerings varied from nothing to 21 pottery vessels, and both jade and shell earspools were found.

Physical anthropological studies suggested that the Monte Negro people were taller, on the average, than the people of Monte Albán (Acosta n.d.a). Ten of 13 skulls show artificial deformation of the annular type. One adult male had a trephination; another adult male had circular inlays of pyrite in both upper canines. Both the deformation and the pyrite inlays were probably high-status characteristics.

## CONCLUSIONS

While Monte Negro is an important site and is far from being well understood, discoveries over the more than 40 years since its excavation have removed at least some of the mystery. Certainly we can lay to rest the idea that Monte Negro has anything to do with the origins of Monte Albán. Drennan's work in the Mountain Survey zone between Huitzo and Nochixtlán (Topic 31) suggests that Monte Albán I was a period of expansion for Valley of Oaxaca people, with many new settlements founded in the northern mountains. Tilantongo lies only 50 km west of Huitzo, and the gray ware from Monte Negro shows far stronger Monte Albán Ic affinities than do the ceramics of Huamelulpan

(Topic 37) or Yucuita (Topic 36). For example, during Period I approximately 25% of Monte Albán household sherds were gray (Bernal 1946). The comparable figure for Monte Negro is 14% (Acosta n.d.a), and for Yucuita, no more than 1% (Spores, personal communication).

Monte Negro's architecture finds some parallels with Rosario phase San José Mogote: the two sites share stone-faced platforms shaped like a plus sign, stairways of rough-hewn blocks with no balustrades, stone columns made from drum-like sections, circular column bases set among courtyard paving stones, use of the circle-and-triangle motif in and around public buildings, and vertical walls of poorly trimmed limestone blocks set in irregular rows. Furthermore, Monte Negro has an L-shaped layout, which may also have characterized Monte Albán's public buildings in Period I. Thus, while Tilantongo was the seat of an important Mixtec *cacicazgo* during the Postclassic (Topic 73), its major ties in the Late Formative seem to have been with the Valley of Oaxaca. Obviously, my discussion ignores the question of whether Monte Negro was ethnically Zapotec or Mixtec—a question I do not believe can be answered on the basis of present evidence. It is enough to say that Monte Negro tells us more about the influence of the early Zapotec state than about the origins of the Mixtec state.

Significantly, Monte Negro has no palace. High status was expressed in cranial deformation, jade earspools, pyrite tooth inlays, residence near a public building, household privacy, and burial in adobe tombs within the platforms of religious structures, accompanied by up to 20 vessels. Leaders, however, did not yet occupy a monumental building, partly civic and partly residential, whose construction required the same level of corvée labor seen in the public buildings. That evolutionary advance is not documented until Monte Albán II.

The Monte Negro elite residences, with their *impluvium* layout, their reduced accessibility, and their private corridors to public buildings, may reflect the prototype from which the Terminal Formative palace evolved. Beyond that, they remind us how ignorant we are of the pattern of elite residence around the Period I public buildings at Monte Albán itself. As for the Monte Negro temples, they already have the vertical stone platform, stairway, rubble columns, adobe walls, and offering basins of their Monte Albán II counterparts, lacking only the stereotyped division into an outer vestibule and an inner sanctum.

## TOPIC 27
### The Development of Monte Albán's Main Plaza in Period II

KENT V. FLANNERY

We have already described the scattered, poorly known remains of Period I public architecture at Monte Albán (Topic 22). This series of early constructions, possibly

strung out like an east–west, north–south letter L, was considerably enlarged upon during Period II. Perhaps most significantly, the Main Plaza as we know it was laid out and paved during Monte Albán II (Figure 4.12). Other important Period II constructions include Building J and the early stages of Buildings G, H, and I, the adoratory and tunnel between Buildings P and I, an early stage of the ballcourt and several of the other buildings on the east side of the plaza, Mound "g" in the North Platform, an important series of temples in Mound X, just off the northeast corner of the

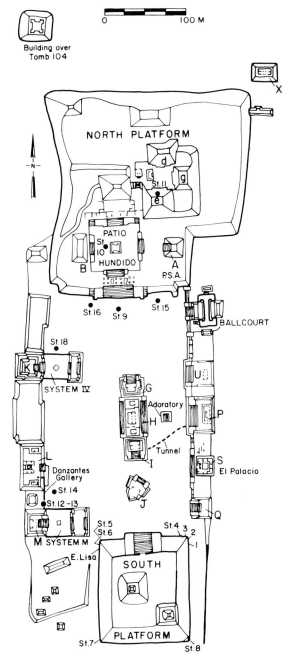

FIGURE 4.12. The Main Plaza at Monte Albán. (A synthesis based on the work of several investigators, including Blanton's most recent mapping; original locations of stelae according to Caso 1928).

North Platform, and numerous tombs with distinctive vaulted roofs. Let us examine some of these structures.

## THE MAIN PLAZA

During Period II, the architects of Monte Albán leveled off a huge area (at least 300 m north–south) and paved it with white stucco. In places where natural outcrops of bedrock projected too high above the surface to be leveled, they were used as the nuclei for buildings, including an eastern line of buildings whose later stages run from the main ballcourt to Building Q, a central spine of outcrops on which Buildings G, H, I, and J were built, and a western series whose extremes are Systems M and IV. Some of the buildings in this latter series already contained Period I structures, such as those inside Building L (the *Danzante* Building) and Building K (in System IV).

Because the natural rock outcrops that formed the cores of these buildings were not equidistant from each other, an initial asymmetry resulted: the central row of buildings was only 60 m or so from the eastern row, and roughly 120 m from Buildings K, L, and M. In Bernal's words, the buildings of Monte Albán eventually corrected this asymmetry "with a solution worthy of a Le Corbusier" (Bernal 1946:8). In front of the western Buildings K and M, and united to the latter by walled courtyards, they constructed small temples which were roughly equidistant between the K–M row and the central or G–J row. These complexes have been called System IV (K and its extension) and System M (M and its extension).

### Buildings G, H, and I

Exactly what the original Period II stages of buildings G, H, and I looked like is hard to say. The upper stages now visible are standard two-room temples which face to the north (G), east (H), and south (I), and it is possible the earlier stages were temples as well.

At a depth of 9.5 m inside Building I was discovered Offering 2, which contained Monte Albán II pottery. It also contained a necklace of marine shell, flower-shaped jade earspools, two mosaic masks (one of jade and turquoise, the other of pyrite and shell), and a bone carved in the shape of a chess pawn (Acosta n.d.b). These objects were found in a typical Monte Albán style offering box, and there were many bird bones below and around the box. These bones may well be the remains of sacrificed birds, such as quail, doves, or macaws, but they apparently remain unidentified.

### The Building H Adoratory

In the Main Plaza between Buildings P and H, and directly in front of the east stairway of the latter building, lies a sunken adoratory. This multilevel, altar-like construction is set in a large, rectangular recessed area, so that its upper surface is roughly level with the plaza (see Paddock 1966a:Fig. 167).

During the fourteenth field season at Monte Albán, excavators discovered an important multiple burial (Burial XIV-10) near the base and east side of the Building H adoratory. At least five adults (Skeletons A–E) lay on a flagstone floor which runs partly under the adoratory; they were provided with multiple jade necklaces, flower-shaped jade earspools, masks and pectorals of jade, pearls, conchs, and other marine shell (Acosta n.d.b). Most of the skeletons, which were in poor condition, were of young people. Skeleton E wore as its pectoral the incredible bat mask that has become famous as a masterpiece of Zapotec art (cf. Paddock 1966a:Fig. 155)—25 individual pieces of jade fitted together to form the face of a man disguised as a bat, with eyes and teeth of marine shell. Typical Monte Albán II tetrapod vessels accompanied Skeletons A and E.

It is interesting that this multiple burial, in spite of the richness of its offering, did not have a tomb. This unusual set of skeletons and offerings, so close to the adoratory, remains enigmatic and raises many questions about the status of the various individuals. Were they honored dead, sacrificial victims, or both?

### The Subplaza Tunnel

During Period II the architects of Monte Albán constructed a tunnel below the Main Plaza in the area of the Building H adoratory. The tunnel links Building P with the central spine of buildings to the west; four offerings found inside during the fourteenth field season are of Monte Albán II date (Acosta n.d.b). Acosta feels that the tunnel was built early in Period II (perhaps simultaneously with the paving of the plaza), then destroyed and filled in during late II. It would have connected several important buildings much as the covered passages of Monte Negro and Yucuita did (see Topic 26).[1]

### Building J

The southernmost building of the "central spine" of the Main Plaza was Building J, a unique Period II structure whose ground plan resembles an arrowhead. Its most distinctive feature is a series of more than 50 carved slabs which are believed to list places subjugated by Monte Albán. This building is described in detail by Marcus in Topic 29.

## MOUND "g," NORTH PLATFORM

During the seventeenth season at Monte Albán (1949), excavators discovered a multiple burial in Mound "g," situ-

ated in the northeast area of the North Platform. Two skeletons, probably both female, were associated with the remains of a mother-of-pearl mosaic, two necklaces of greenstone and shell, and six Monte Albán II vessels, including waxy red-on-orange C-7 ware (Acosta n.d.b). This offering may have been a dedication within the fill of a limited-access temple.

## MONTE ALBÁN II TEMPLE, MOUND X

During the fourteenth field season at Monte Albán (1945–1946), excavators uncovered another Period II temple in Mound X, below the one illustrated by Caso in 1935 (see Editors' Introduction, p. 82). Mound X, located just northeast of the North Platform, was peripheral to the major public buildings of the Main Plaza. Acosta (n.d.b) describes the temple as 12.8 by 11.2 m in extent and preserved to a height of 2.7 m; it was reached by a stairway of 7 steps covered with stucco, which ran the length of the south side of the building. As is typical of these structures, the building was divided into two rooms on different levels, each reached by openings between rubble columns. The inner (higher) room has a *tlecuil* or basin buried flush with the stucco floor and an offering box in the back of the room at the midline of the temple. These features presumably relate to the placement of offerings, or the washing or bloodletting of sacrificial items such as birds, dogs, infants, or captives.

There were other enigmatic features in the temple, such as a tubular vase set in the floor before a red-painted triangular rock. In the core of a column was found an offering consisting of a small jade figurine, three conch shells, one smaller shell, and a disc of yellow-green paint. Some fallen stones with low relief carving may once have been part of a frieze on the upper interior of the temple.

## SUMMARY

While all the details are not known, the civic–ceremonial center of the city of Monte Albán during Period II (200 B.C.–A.D. 100) included a paved Main Plaza, several rows of public buildings built over bedrock outcrops, altars or adoratories, and a subplaza tunnel. Included among the public buildings were a ballcourt, an arrowhead-shaped building with carved "conquest slabs," and several two-room temples with rubble columns. In addition to the elaborate burials already mentioned, there were stone masonry tombs with vaulted or "corbelled" roofs like Tomb 77 (Marquina 1951:Lám. 94). Finally, this "ceremonial core" lay in an area protected by several kilometers of defensive wall (Topic 21).

---

[1]In 1958, James Neely and I attempted to traverse this tunnel on hands and knees. Our efforts were terminated halfway through when we came upon the very recently shed skin of a rattlesnake.

# TOPIC 28
## An Analysis of Monte Albán II Architecture

DONALD ROBERTSON

Architecture from Monte Albán II includes Building J (aberrant in plan from other Mesoamerican architecture with one exception), the building under Mound X (suggesting parallels with a standard form at Teotihuacán), the use of orthostatic construction in low-relief architectural sculpture, and tombs with ceilings showing the lost opportunity to develop the true arch in the New World.

Building J, with its arrow-shaped plan, is paralleled by Mound O at Caballito Blanco (see Topic 34). Both exhibit evidence of having been added to in later times. They show such strikingly unique plans as to imply a function not known at other sites and other times. But Building J seems to have existed and functioned from Period II of Monte Albán until much later periods, and thus its specialized function must have been of equally long duration. If either functioned as an observatory (as the popular literature sometimes suggests), it is odd that their orientations are so different.

Mound X at Monte Albán, at its lowest level, presents us with an architectural form similar to certain architectural structural types at Teotihuacán. A rectangular room with one entrance flanked by large round columns is raised one step above an outer vestibule or porch almost the same size with a wide opening reaching almost from side wall to side wall. The entrance to this vestibule or porch is between another pair of large columns placed inside the lateral extensions of the side walls, creating something quite close to what we would call in the study of ancient European architecture a pair of columns *in antis.* This form of the room and porch or vestibule echoes the formal type known in Greek antiquity as the *megaron* and is the architectural form of the largest rooms or units in the palaces or apartment complexes of Teotihuacán. This example seems to have existed in isolation, however, whereas the examples from Teotihuacán appear in groups of two, three, or four fronting upon a courtyard or patio whose space they create and define. Other differences from the Teotihuacán buildings include columns that are round, not square, and columns that appear flanking the entrance to the rear room as well as the porch or vestibule. Aside from these relatively minor differences, the two buildings are remarkably similar. This type of building has been identified by Flannery and Marcus (Editors' Introduction) as a temple.

Building J, the wall of the *danzantes,* and the wall of a pyramid within the present main pyramid of System IV are all examples of orthostatic construction, which is not common in later periods in the history of the architecture of Mesoamerica. It does call to mind structural techniques of the ancient Near East in the Old World, where it is often used to protect what we would call adobe walls and serves as a surface for rich surface relief sculpture. This use of relatively thin slabs of stone placed with their greatest surface dimension from top to bottom, rather than from side to side, suggests the function of a retaining wall rather than a proper masonry bearing wall. It is appropriate for the outer skin of pyramids, perhaps functionally more secure than the rubble walls used in later buildings, to retain the form of the earth core so that slump does not cause the pyramid to collapse or to lose its geometric shape.

Relief sculpture at Monte Albán seems to be associated with what we have called orthostatic construction. In other words, individual figures or groups of hieroglyphs are carved on individual slabs of stone. The design and the field of sculpture are coterminous. The design does not continue from one stone to the next, again suggesting the Near East in the Old World where large compositions are carved on single slabs. For architectural sculpture, the combination of relief with flat slabs has advantages which probably led to the combination of both. The thin slab reduces the amount of weight, so that if the stone is carved first and then put into place it can be more easily moved than if the stone were larger and heavier. If the design is limited to a single stone, then assembling the stones on the building can be done with less precision than if the precut designs on more than one stone had to be fitted together. This practice in itself suggests an answer to the problem of whether the stones were cut *in situ* or elsewhere and moved to their present locations already cut.

Tombs with flat-slab stone ceilings represent a simple constructional technique, where stability is assured as long as the weight of the superior mass is not sufficient to crack the stone ceiling stones which act essentially as simple lintels. More sophisticated in technique are the ceilings of tombs such as Tombs 155 or 118 at Monte Albán, where the ceiling is, in effect, vaulted by two flat slabs (suggesting in their dimensions the orthostatic slabs of other Monte Albán II buildings) butting against each other. This construction depends upon a solid resistance to the outward thrust of the slabs where they rest upon the wall, a counterthrust which is achieved both by the solidity of a heavy masonry wall, and, in turn, the resistance of the surrounding earth which supports the wall. By the use of two inclined slabs, one leaning upon the other, the builders created the thrust of a vault. As they increased the span of the space covered, the builders also decreased the weight upon the individual ceiling slabs so that thinner slabs could be used than in the simpler lintel ceiling. Within the limitations of this technology, they created what is in effect an arch of two voussoirs. By increasing the number of voussoirs considerably, they could have created the true arch. But I think their experience with the great lateral thrust of a two-voussoir arch of relatively low pitch would have discouraged them from the further experiments that would have led to the evolution of the true arch; to use it above ground for a simple walled building would have required tremendously heavy abutting walls in contrast with the relatively lower amount of thrust developed by the Old World round arch and the almost minimal thrust of the Maya corbelled arch. (As Roys [1934] has pointed out, ultimately, after the mortar has set, the Maya arch is, in effect, a monolith exerting no thrust.) The vault, or two-voussoir arch, of Monte Albán II remains a functioning, dynamic arch. The vault of Tomb 77 with a central voussoir supported by two lateral ones amounts to three voussoirs and carries the technical proficiency of the Monte Albán mason

even further, presenting us with the phenomenon of an even closer approach to the principle of the European arch. The basic and fundamental principle of the true European arch, however, still eluded the builders. They did not cut the edges of the individual stones or slabs to an oblique abutting surface; thus the stability of the Monte Albán vault was not assured, because slippage of one rough stone face against the other was more possible than with true voussoirs.

The use of slab masonry seems to be a technical device of Monte Albán II with great possibilities both in terms of architectural techniques and for providing greater facility for architectural sculptural embellishment. One wonders why the technique of slab masonry seems to have disappeared and not been continued and further exploited for its greater flexibility than rubble or even ashlar masonry.

## TOPIC 29
## The Conquest Slabs of Building J, Monte Albán

JOYCE MARCUS

One of the major public buildings erected in the Main Plaza at Monte Albán during Period II was Building J, an unusual structure with an arrowhead-shaped ground plan (Figure 4.13). In addition to its unusual plan, Building J's stairway faces northeast, an orientation which differs from all other structures in the Main Plaza. These two characteristics have suggested to scholars that Building J was a special-purpose building of some kind; it has frequently been described as an astronomical observatory, although no one has yet been able to link its orientation to a specific star, planet,

constellation, or other astronomical landmark (see Aveni and Linsley 1972). Three observations could be made in this regard. First, I can see no specific evidence to suggest an astronomical function for the building. Second, its lack of alignment vis-à-vis known temples in the Main Plaza might indicate that its functions were secular, not religious. Third, the astronomical interpretation does not take into account one of Building J's most distinctive characteristics, a series of more than 50 carved stones which Caso (1938, 1947) believed to depict localities conquered by Monte Albán.

As of 1937, some 51 of these carved stones had been located, and since that time additional examples have come to light. Most were found *in situ* and have been consolidated in the second or third tiers of the building; others were found in the rubble at the base of its walls. Of the latter group, some remain on the ground today, while others were "reset" in the building (Caso 1947:20), not necessarily in their original positions. There are some *danzantes* in the lowest tier of the walls, but these were apparently reused simply as construction stones, and there is some evidence to indicate that they were covered over with stucco. Building J went through several construction phases, but the original building and the "conquest slabs" apparently date to Monte Albán II. This series of carved slabs, all set as orthostats, shows thematic and stylistic homogeneity, and most contain the following elements (see Figure 4.14):

1. A "hill" glyph signifying "the place of" or "the hill of," which is a constant feature on each stone.
2. A glyph (or combination of glyphs) that varies from stone to stone and represents the name of the place or hill below it.

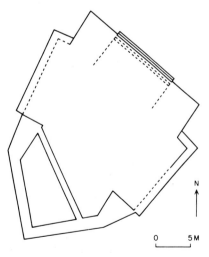

FIGURE 4.13. Ground plan of Building J, Monte Albán. (Redrawn, with modifications, from Caso 1938.)

FIGURE 4.14. Conquest slab from Building J, Monte Albán, showing place name, hill glyph, upside-down head, and hieroglyphic inscription.

3. A human head, upside down, below the hill glyph, its headdress varying from stone to stone. Caso regarded these as the dead rulers of subjugated places, with the headdress perhaps regionally distinct and therefore serving to reinforce the place-name data.
4. Occasionally, a hieroglyphic text which in its most complete form includes a year, month, and day, plus noncalendric glyphs—perhaps relating to the date when certain places were subjugated.

As Caso (1947) has noted, all of the inverted heads below the hill element are facing the same direction and are drawn to the same scale. The majority of these heads have a specific pattern of lines crossing the face or eye, which may indicate facial painting or tattoos; in addition, all the heads are shown wearing distinctive headdresses. The eyes of some are closed, while others lack a pupil; on the basis of these two characteristics, Caso (1947) concluded that these humans were depictions of dead rulers of the named places. Far more uniform is the element that Batres (1902) and Caso (1947) have interpreted as the hill glyph, in whose central part are transverse bands or lines that begin at the top and slant

down from right to left. To either side are projections that rise up in the manner of organ cactus arms.

I feel that Caso's interpretation of these slabs is essentially correct, particularly when one considers how analogous they are to the Zapotec depiction of place names in the sixteenth-century Lienzo de Guevea (see Topics 89, 90). Following this analogy, one could suggest that the Building J stones represent 50-odd landmarks—"Hill of the Rabbit," "Hill of the Bird," and "Hill of the Chile Plants" are a few examples—that constituted the limits of Monte Albán's tribute territory in Period II. In the Lienzo de Guevea, as will be discussed in Topic 89, the Zapotec town of Santiago Guevea lies encircled by named hills and rivers that were landmarks on the limits of its territory.

While Caso's interpretation of the hill signs and dead rulers' heads is reasonable, he declined to take the next logical step—the identification of the specific place names involved. In 1976, I suggested that a few of them might be identified by comparison with the Matrícula de Tributos or Codex Mendoza, a sixteenth-century Aztec document listing 11 places in Oaxaca that paid tribute to the Aztec (Marcus 1976d, 1980). First of all, the Aztec scribes of the Codex Mendoza also used the *tepetl* or hill sign to indicate place names, and in several cases it is clear that the Aztec place name was simply a translation of the former Zapotec place name. Second, the Aztec used a burning temple structure to indicate the conquest of a town, perhaps an analogy to the inverted, closed-eye heads of the Building J glyphs. If all or most of the place names in the Codex Mendoza were Aztec translations of Zapotec names, might there be some which matched the hieroglyphs on Building J?

Obviously, I was initially quite doubtful that very many of the places could be reliably identified. After all, it would require that some places retained the same name for 1500 years, and then were hieroglyphically depicted in the Codex Mendoza in much the same way they had been in Monte Albán II. I felt it was worth the attempt, however, because of the potential payoff in political and historical information. So far, I have found at least four hieroglyphic place names on Building J that closely resemble hieroglyphic place names from Oaxaca in the Codex Mendoza.

In the Codex Mendoza, 11 towns were assigned to the tributary province of Coyolapan (now Cuilapan), an important *cabecera* in the heart of Oaxaca (Barlow 1949:118–119). Eleven place signs are depicted on the page of the Codex Mendoza devoted to that jurisdiction (Marcus 1976d). Another 24 were reconstructed by Robert Barlow (1949) from other sources, primarily the 1579–1581 series of *Relaciones Geográficas*. The conquest slabs from Building J whose glyphs resemble place names in the Codex Mendoza are as follows:

1. *Lápida 43* on Building J seems to show the cross-section of an irrigation canal with maize tassels growing out of it (Figure 4.15). It is remarkably similar to the glyph for Miahuapan (from the Nahuatl *miahuatl,* "maize tassel,"

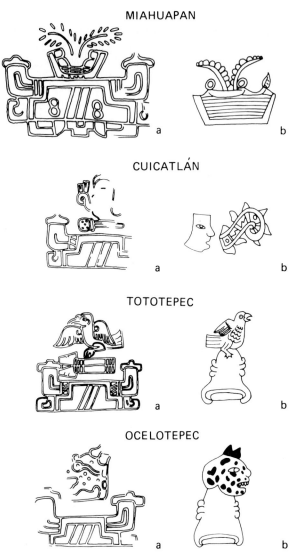

MIAHUAPAN

a                                          b

CUICATLÁN

a                                          b

TOTOTEPEC

a                                          b

OCELOTEPEC

a                                          b

FIGURE 4.15. Comparisons of four place-glyphs from Building J, Monte Albán, with place-glyphs from the Codex Mendoza: (a) glyphs from Building J; (b) glyphs from the Codex Mendoza.

and *apan*, "*acequia*" or "irrigation canal") from the Codex Mendoza (Barlow and MacAfee 1949:10, 25). Miahuapan may have been an alternative name for Miahuatlán, a town some 85 km south of Oaxaca City.

2. *Lápida 47* on Building J shows a human head with a feathered speech scroll emanating from its mouth (Figure 4.15). It is similar to the glyph for Cuicatlán (Nahuatl for "The Place of Song") in the Codex Mendoza (Fol. 43r, Peñafiel 1885:101). The Cuicatlán Cañada runs north from the Valley of Oaxaca toward Tehuacán, and the present town of Cuicatlán lies 85 km northeast of Oaxaca City.

3. *Lápida 57* on Building J shows a bird perched atop a hill sign; a lower element of the place sign was originally identified by Caso (1947:27) as two bound arrows (Figure

4.15). It is similar to the glyph for Tototepec (Nahuatl for "Hill of the Bird"), an alternative name for the important town of Tututepec on the Oaxaca Coast, in the Codex Mendoza (Barlow and MacAfee 1949:39). Tututepec lies roughly 140 km southwest of Oaxaca City.

4. *Lápida 23* on Building J shows a spotted feline, either a jaguar or an ocelot, above a hill sign (Figure 4.15). It is similar to the glyph for Ocelotepec (Nahuatl for "Hill of the Jaguar") in the Codex Mendoza. Ocelotepec is a district in the mountains beyond Miahuatlán, perhaps 140 km southeast of Oaxaca City; its ancient Zapotec name, Quiebeche (incorrectly translated by Espíndola 1580), also meant "Hill of the Jaguar" (*quie*, "rock, hill"; *peche*, "jaguar, fierce animal").

Several other conquest slabs on Building J have very clear hieroglyphic names, such as "Hill of the Grasshopper" or "Hill of the Rabbit," but they do not match specific places listed in the Codex Mendoza for tribute-paying localities in the Oaxaca area. Countless other conquest slabs remain untranslated, however, and it will require a different methodology to translate them. Indeed, it may be unlikely we will be able to locate even a third of them.

Because all four of the places discussed above lie well outside the Valley of Oaxaca, my suggestion is that the "conquered places" listed on Building J reflect the limits or frontiers of Zapotec territory in Monte Albán II. Note that this is also the case with the places listed in the Lienzo de Guevea, which indicate the limits of Guevea's territory, rather than nearby places (Topic 89). Thus, Miahuatlán, Cuicatlán, Tututepec, and Ocelotepec might have been at or near the frontiers of Zapotec influence.

Obviously, this approach can only be considered a hypothesis to be confirmed or rejected by future work. It might be rejected if Miahuatlán, Cuicatlán, Tututepec, and Ocelotepec show no evidence of Monte Albán II occupation. It might be confirmed if they all have important Period II sites, especially if those sites are fortified, or if there is striking evidence for a Zapotec takeover in Period II.

Ocelotepec is virtually unknown archaeologically, but both Miahuatlán (Topic 30) and Tututepec (Topic 75) are already known to have important Monte Albán II occupations. Perhaps the best support for the hypothesis, however, comes from the Cuicatlán area, and is reported in Topic 35 by Spencer and Redmond. In that previously autonomous region, there seems to have been a clear military takeover by the Zapotec around the end of Monte Albán I or the beginning of Monte Albán II. At one small settlement, the conquerors erected a *tzompantli*-style skull rack; farther to the north, they fortified a mountaintop which closed off the main route to the neighboring Tehuacán Valley. Monte Albán II pottery ends at this fort, and beyond it to the north one finds only sites with ceramics in clear Tehuacán style. Should future work show a similar expansion of "Zapotec influence" at places like Tututepec, we would have to conclude that Building J records the Period II subjugation of an area with a radius of 80 to 150 km from Monte Albán.

## TOPIC 30
## Valley-Floor Settlement Patterns in Monte Albán II

STEPHEN KOWALEWSKI

### THE ETLA AND CENTRAL REGIONS
### OF THE VALLEY OF OAXACA

Our population estimates for the intensively surveyed Etla and Central portions of the Valley of Oaxaca remain remarkably stable from Monte Albán Ic through the Early Classic (Period IIIa). There were, however, major changes in the *distribution* of population during Monte Albán II and IIIa. Monte Albán itself grew: the urban center's share of the population increased from 77% in Late Period I, to 80% in Period II, and eventually to 91% in Period IIIa. The outlying areas experienced more drastic fluctuations, with the total

rural population divided about equally between the Etla and Central Valley areas during Late Period I, but splitting in favor of the Etla Valley by 96 to 4% in Monte Albán II. Population shifted again in Period IIIa to 43% in the Etla region and 57% in the Central survey area.

In the Etla region the total hectarage of occupation increased from 231 in Late Monte Albán I to 303 in Period II, with a proportionate increase in population (Varner 1974:117). The slight trend toward nucleation detected between Early and Late Period I continued during Monte Albán II. The fact that the Etla region contained most of the population in the Central and Etla survey areas during Period II (Figure 4.16) may be related to the revitalization of San

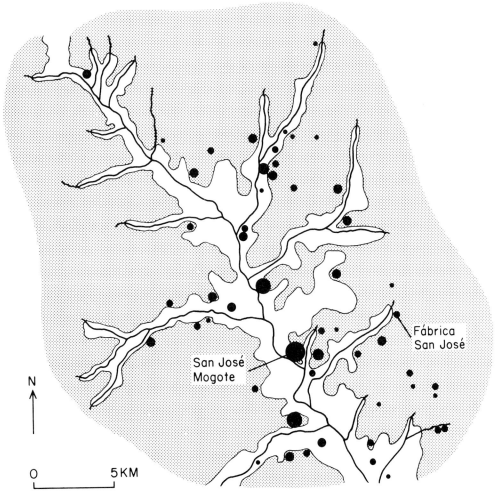

FIGURE 4.16. The Etla region of the Valley of Oaxaca, showing Monte Albán II settlements according to Varner (1974). Sizes of black circles suggest relative sizes of sites.

José Mogote as an important secondary center during this period (see Topic 32).

Population in the Central area surrounding Monte Albán, however, was severely reduced at this time. Only 23 Monte Albán II occupations were located, and most covered less than 1 ha. Many of these sites were remnant occupations found near the centers of important Late Period I sites. There is some evidence for a more substantial Period II community at Xoxocotlán, on the valley floor about 4 km southeast of Monte Albán.

## THE TLACOLULA REGION

The Tlacolula region has not yet been intensively surveyed, but substantial Monte Albán II settlements are already known in that area. Dainzú (Topic 33) was a major Period II center, and nearby Abasolo has related material. San Juan Teitipac, in the southwestern corner of the Tlacolula plain, was large in Period II. To the east lies a complex of Monte Albán II settlements including Brawbehl, Caballito Blanco, Loma Larga, and Mitla (Topic 34). Marcus (personal communication, 1975), points out that during Period II, the Dainzú–Macuilxochitl–Teotitlán del Valle area had its own regional monumental carving style, distinct from that of Monte Albán itself.

## THE MIAHUATLÁN VALLEY

Monte Albán II was a period of some importance in the Miahuatlán Valley, with at least 10 sites reported by Brockington (1973). All sites are near the river, with 7 clustered in a 1-km$^2$ area south of the present city of Miahuatlán (Figure 4.17). The largest site of this cluster is Brockington's site 1A, described as "the largest and most impressive site" in the area, "the center that dominated the region" (Brockington 1973:10). A "relatively heavy concentration of Period II sherds" was also found at site 5A (Brockington 1973:15); most of the other sites in the central cluster were small.

About 3 km upstream from Miahuatlán is site 10, whose most northerly mound yielded a surface collection which

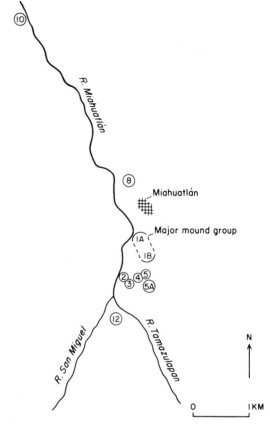

FIGURE 4.17. Monte Albán II settlements in the Miahuatlán Valley. (Redrawn from Brockington 1973.)

was 30% Period II and III sherds (Brockington 1973:17). This site may have been a "ceremonial and habitation zone" of some importance, with half a dozen significant mounds.

One might surmise that Period II settlement at Miahuatlán was supported by irrigation agriculture along the river. The explosion of Period II population is interesting in view of how little Period I material Brockington discovered. Marcus (Topic 29) believes she has found a place glyph for Miahuatlán on Building J at Monte Albán. If so, Miahuatlán may well have been an important tribute-paying region on the southern frontier of the Zapotec state.

## TOPIC 31
## Monte Albán I and II Settlement in the Mountain Survey Zone between the Valleys of Oaxaca and Nochixtlán

ROBERT D. DRENNAN

During 1971, I conducted an archaeological survey in the zone of forested mountains that separate the Nochixtlán Valley of the Mixteca Alta from the Etla, or northern, arm of the Valley of Oaxaca. I suspected that this Mountain Survey would shed some light on the changing relationships of these two valleys through time. In particular, I felt that the mountain zone might provide information on the movement of Zapotec peoples out of the Valley of Oaxaca during the expansion of the Monte Albán state, and on the suspected movement of Mixtec peoples into the Valley of Oaxaca during Postclassic times. In this section I will comment only on the pattern of Monte Albán I and II sites; later periods will be discussed in subsequent chapters.

The zone covered by the Mountain Survey includes some 650 km² to the north of the Etla arm of the Valley of Oaxaca. It includes land from the *municipios* of San Juan del Estado, San Francisco Telixtlahuaca, Santiago Tenango, San Jerónimo Sosola, and San Juan Bautista Jayacatlán (Figure 4.18). It was not surveyed intensively on a field-by-field basis; rather, visits to sites were made on the basis of informants' knowledge of the region. A number of small sites were undoubtedly missed, but the fact that such sites were rarely encountered on the way to other places indicates that this number was not excessive. Virtually all sites of substantial size were certainly recorded. The ground cover rendered phase-by-phase site-size estimates impossible, but attempts were made to estimate the maximum extent of each site. Even these estimates remain very approximate. For that reason, only numbers of sites are given below.

The earliest occupation encountered in the region dates to Monte Albán Ia, with certain occupation at eight sites and possible occupation at two others. During Monte Albán Ic and II (combined for lack of enough diagnostic sherds to distinguish them consistently) five sites showed certain occupations and two others possible occupations. About half of these were continuations of Monte Albán Ia sites. Ceramic affinities at this time period (Late and Terminal For-

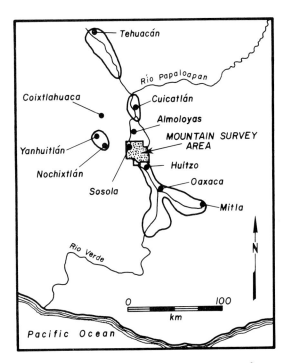

FIGURE 4.18. Location of the Mountain Survey area between the Valley of Oaxaca, the Cuicatlán Cañda, and the Valley of Yanhuitlán–Nochixtlán.

mative) are clearly with the Valley of Oaxaca rather than with Nochixtlán, and suggest Zapotec expansion. This conclusion is supported by the evidence from Monte Negro (see Topic 26).

## TOPIC 32
## San José Mogote in Monte Albán II: A Secondary Administrative Center

KENT V. FLANNERY
JOYCE MARCUS

Surveys in the Valley of Oaxaca have suggested a four-tiered hierarchy for Monte Albán II settlements, with three tiers of administrative centers above the hamlet level. Monte Albán itself constitutes the top level of the hierarchy; San José Mogote would be an example of a second-order administrative center; Fábrica San José in Period II might be an example of a third-order center.

In this topic, we examine the Period II remains from San José Mogote, which was probably the most important secondary center in the Etla region, north of Monte Albán. After an apparent hiatus in public construction during Monte Albán I, San José Mogote seems to have been deliberately selected for development as a regional administrative center during Period II. Not only did the site enjoy a kind of renaissance, but as pointed out by Kowalewski (Topic 30) its rural hinterland seems to have enjoyed a significant popula-

tion growth, perhaps drawing actual settlers out of the Central region that surrounded Monte Albán. Perhaps most significantly, during Period II San José Mogote was made to look like a local carbon copy of Monte Albán (Figure 4.19).

### THE MAIN PLAZA

The Main Plaza at San José Mogote, laid out north–south, has almost the same dimensions as the Main Plaza at Monte Albán: 300 m north–south, roughly 150 m east–west. Mound 1 on its southern border, like the South Platform at Monte Albán, supported a series of temples. Mound 8 on its northern border, like the North Platform at Monte Albán, supported a palace. Like Monte Albán, it had a ballcourt on one side. The ballcourt at San José Mogote, however, is on the west side of the Main Plaza, while the

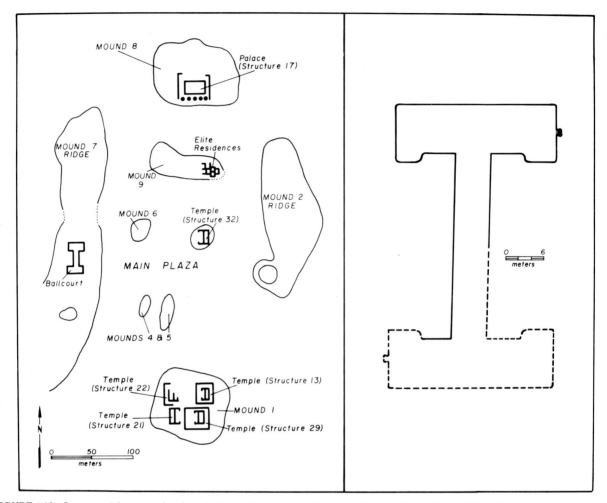

FIGURE 4.19. Aspects of the second-order administrative center at San José Mogote during Monte Albán II. Left, the layout of the Main Plaza (compare with that of Monte Albán, Figure 4.12). Right, the ballcourt in Mound 7 south.

ballcourt at Monte Albán is on the east. Also like Monte Albán, San José Mogote has important structures built over bedrock outcrops inside its Main Plaza.

## THE TEMPLES ON MOUND 1

The Period II temples on Mound 1 at San José Mogote, like the temples in Mound X at Monte Albán, are rectangular two-room structures with a main chamber, a lower vestibule, and columns to either side of the doorways. Structures 13 and 21 can serve as examples. Although poorly preserved, Structure 13 appears to be half again as large as its Mound X counterpart—perhaps because it was a major temple at San José, while Mound X was peripheral to the main temples at Monte Albán. Assuming that Structure 13 was symmetrical and had roughly the same proportions as the Mound X temple, it would have been at least 15 by 8 m in size. In addition to its greater size, Structure 13 had pairs of

columns to either side of the vestibule doorway. Like the temple on Mound X at Monte Albán, it was oriented to the cardinal points. Structure 21, even more poorly preserved than 13, is similar in plan (Figure 4.20).

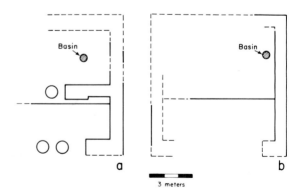

FIGURE 4.20. Monte Albán II temples from San José Mogote: (a) Structure 13; (b) Structure 21.

## THE BALLCOURT IN MOUND 7 SOUTH

An early stage of the ballcourt in Mound 7 south (Mound 7s) at San José Mogote dates to Monte Albán II, and was excavated by Chris Moser in 1974 (Moser n.d.). Ballcourts of equivalent age were present at Monte Albán, but their remains are incompletely known because of superimposed later constructions (Acosta 1965:824). The upper stage of the ballcourt in the Main Plaza at Monte Albán, presently reconstructed for viewing by tourists, dates to Period III.

Oaxacan ballcourts generally have the shape of a Roman numeral I (Figure 4.19), with great sloping *taludes* or inclined surfaces rising from the central axis. The courts have a north–south orientation, and lack the rings seen in Maya ballcourts. The examples from Mound 7s at San José Mogote and the Main Plaza at Monte Albán are so similar in size as to suggest the use of a standard plan, as follows:

|  | Mound 7s, San José Mogote (m) | Main Plaza, Monte Albán (m) |
|---|---|---|
| Maximum length | 41.5 | 41 |
| Maximum width | 24.2 | 24 |
| Central court, between *taludes* | 27.2 | 26 |

## THE PALACE ON MOUND 8

The earliest construction stage of the palace on Mound 8 at San José Mogote seems also to be Period II. This building,

Structure 17, resembles the palaces at Monte Albán but its exact dimensions cannot be recovered because of subsequent destruction and erosion. It was greater than 30 m on its longest side, and its façade included huge limestone blocks weighing a ton or more. On its south side, facing the Main Plaza, was a porch of some kind with massive columns. The rooms inside had plaster floors, and there was at least one sunken patio.

## MULTIFAMILY (?) APARTMENT DWELLINGS

Adjacent to the Main Plaza on the southwest corner at San José Mogote were a series of large, multiroomed Monte Albán II buildings which appear to be residential. The foundations were of stone, the upper walls of adobe, and the floors plastered. Small tombs or slab-lined graves occur beneath the floors of some rooms; ash, broken domestic pottery, animal bones, and habitation refuse cover the floors in several cases. The buildings are large (more than 20 m on a side) but the individual rooms are small, sometimes opening onto narrow corridors. No two room floors are on the same level; whenever one passed from one room to another within the complex, he stepped up or down. What these structures most suggest is a simpler version of the multifamily apartment compounds known from Teotihuacán (R. Millon 1973).

## TOPIC 33
## Monte Albán II in the Macuilxochitl Area

JOYCE MARCUS

Some of the most important Precolumbian settlements in the Tlacolula arm of the Valley of Oaxaca were established along an intermittent tributary which runs south from Teotitlán del Valle toward the Río Salado. From the point where it leaves the mountains until it enters the seasonally swampy central Tlacolula arm, this tributary passes near five great centers of ancient population—Teotitlán, Macuilxochitl, Dainzú, Tlacochahuaya, and Abasolo. It also passes through three different agricultural zones—those featuring canal irrigation (Teotitlán), floodwater farming (Macuilxochitl), and well irrigation (Abasolo). Apart from Bernal's work at Dainzú (see below), very little is known of the Monte Albán II occupation of this area. These five localities between them have produced nearly 100 carved stone monuments, however, many of which date to the general Monte Albán II range, and perhaps another 20 from

later times. This is the largest body of stone monuments in the Valley of Oaxaca, except for the corpus from Monte Albán itself.

Perhaps even more significant is the fact that this body of stone monuments is somewhat distinct from that of Monte Albán both in style and in subject matter. While the Period II carvings of Monte Albán deal with dates, places, conquests, and other militaristic themes, those from the Macuilxochitl area deal with important personages (each one with a stone reserved for the individual), ballplayers, and jaguar figures (Figure 4.21). Each site's monuments are internally homogeneous, differing somewhat from those of neighboring sites in the Macuilxochitl area, and differing even more from the carvings of Monte Albán although their contemporaneity seems clear. The diversity of themes and styles is impressive and serves as a contrast to Period II Monte Albán.

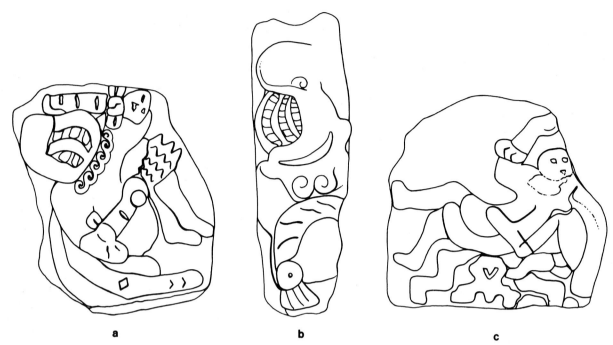

**a**          **b**          **c**

FIGURE 4.21.  Period II carved stones of the Macuilxochitl area: (a) ballplayer from Dainzú (redrawn from Bernal 1968); (b) Stone No. 4 from Macuilxochitl; (c) Stone No. 3 from Tlacochahuaya (redrawn from Bernal and Seuffert 1973).

Because this was not the case in later periods—for example, Period IIIb–IV monuments from the Tlacolula region conform to valley-wide thematic and stylistic canons (Topic 57)—one could suggest the following hypothesis: as late as Monte Albán II, the Tlacolula arm of the Valley of Oaxaca was still relatively independent of Monte Albán when compared with the regions of Etla, Zaachila, and the Central Valley.

## DAINZÚ

The site of Dainzú lies approximately 20 km southeast of Oaxaca City, and about the same distance west of Mitla. In order to avoid confusion with nearby sites, such as Macuilxochitl and Teotitlán del Valle, the name Dainzú was selected by Bernal in a manner similar to the one he employed for selecting the name of Yagul—by polling his Zapotec workmen and recording the most frequent response (Bernal 1968a:10). The name reflects the local pronunciation of *Dan Zun,* "hill of Tlacochahuaya."

At the base of the hill at Dainzú one large stone lay partially exposed, revealing traces of carving, and this carved stone led Bernal to begin excavations at the site in 1966–1967. The exposed monument proved to be the huge cornerstone of a structure; to the north of the cornerstone, Bernal found a series of carved stones *in situ* along the wall. Additionally, there were other stones that had apparently fallen from the upper part of the wall.

This major structure faces west, measuring 45.7 m along

its north–south axis and 7.6 m in height. In all, Bernal located some 27 carved stones *in situ,* all to the south of the center line of the structure. All of these carved stones are somewhat irregular in shape and size. The wall itself is vertical, and Bernal suggests that the building may have had three "bodies" or levels; he notes that this is exactly the form followed in the construction of the Building of the Danzantes at Monte Albán. In other words, the *talud–tablero* or slope-and-panel style of architecture associated with Classic Monte Albán IIIa and with Teotihuacán had not yet appeared (Bernal 1968a:18). The lowest level of the building was composed of at least two rows of slabs, each depicting a single figure or man. Bernal (1968b:247) classified the slabs into three groups according to the subject depicted: Group 1, human figure with large headdress; Group 2, humanized jaguars; and Group 3, contorted human beings with "baseball catcher's" masks. Group 1 consists of but one example, the second group includes two stones, and the third group is the largest by far.

Actually, one could simplify Bernal's classification by combining Groups 1 and 2. Although the Group 1 stone depicts a seated human with an elaborate headdress, its seated position is shared with the "humanized" jaguars of Group 2. Thus, it is possible that all are performing the same action, differing only in that those in Group 2 are masked and dressed as jaguars, and the Group 1 stone lacks the jaguar mask and tail.

Each of the Group 3 stones depicts a human wearing a mask and holding a small ball in his right hand. The figures wear long gloves, short pants, and padding. Additionally, their unnatural or contorted positions suggested activity or motion to Bernal. Given all these characteristics, Bernal concludes that these figures are ballplayers. In addition to the carvings on this building, there is a series of small "ballplayer's masks" carved on a rock atop the hill which overlooks the site (Bernal 1973:Fig. 9).

Stratigraphic pits help to place in time the building with the Group 1–3 monuments. The main pit behind Stone 24 contained Monte Albán Ic sherds in great number, as well as Monte Albán II sherds, although the latter constituted less than 2% of the total. Thus the building might well have been constructed at the very start of Period II, when many Period I sherds (and only a few Period II sherds) would be likely to show up in the fill.

These Group 3 ballplayers from Dainzú, more than 47 in number, cannot readily be compared to other Oaxacan carved stones, because they display a distinctive theme and style. Caso's North Platform excavations at Monte Albán, however, did produce one small slab that is very similar to the elaborate masked heads carved on the rock atop the Dainzú hill (Caso 1969:24, Fig. 8; 1932a:499, top stone). Additionally, at least one stone at Macuilxochitl (Stone 4) and one at Tlacochahuaya (Stone 3) show traces of the distinctive ballplayer style (Bernal and Seuffert 1973).

Although Bernal cites similarities among the Dainzú monuments, the *danzantes* of Monte Albán, and the stone monuments of the Gulf Coast Olmec, I am even more impressed by the differences. In many ways, the Dainzú monuments reveal a unique subject matter and a distinctive style which characterizes the central Tlacolula Valley during Monte Albán II.

## MACUILXOCHITL, TLACOCHAHUAYA, AND TEOTITLÁN DEL VALLE

Over the years, a large number of carved stone monuments have been unearthed by the residents of Macuilxochitl, Tlacochahuaya, and Teotitlán del Valle. The exact number of monuments is impossible to determine because the process of discovery has been continuous, with previously discovered stones disappearing almost as fast as new ones appear. For example, Bernal and Seuffert (1973) recently published some 36 of these monuments, 11 from Tlacochahuaya and 25 from Macuilxochitl. Bernal was unable to locate two carved stones previously reported, however, one from Macuilxochitl (Rickards 1910:Fig. 26) and one from Tlacochahuaya (Berlin 1951:17). Seler (1904) also illustrated 5 stones from Macuilxochitl and Teotitlán, some of which have since been moved to different localities. Two of the stones in the original Oaxaca Museum he describes as coming from Macuilxochitl (Seler 1904:Fig. 70 b,c), while two others (Seler 1904:Figs. 69, 70a) are set in the wall of the church in Teotitlán. In addition, both Bernal and I have found new stones in recent years which would bring the total for all three villages to more than 60 monuments. The earliest of these appear to be contemporary with Monte Albán II and IIIa, but with important thematic and stylistic differences that have already been mentioned; the latest are in true Monte Albán IIIb–IV style. Unfortunately, none of the relevant sites has received the archaeological attention it deserves.

# TOPIC 34
# Monte Albán II in the Yagul–Caballito Blanco Area

JOHN PADDOCK

The site of Caballito Blanco, situated on a volcanic mesa only 300 m from Yagul, cannot be considered apart from the latter site. Unfortunately, what can be said of Yagul at this period is negligible. Not even a small group of burials, such as we have from Period I, is known. Nevertheless, the diagnostic sherds of Period II are common enough to suggest an occupation on the scale of a hamlet at least, and somewhat more would be easy to believe. Had there been one or more groups of buildings at Yagul like those at Caballito Blanco in Period II, the intense construction activity of Periods IV and V at Yagul might well have wiped them out without a trace—except for the telltale sherds we find in the fill of the later buildings.

In the absence of urns, it is difficult to distinguish Period II from Transición II–III, and Loma Larga is the only site in the area where the Transición urns have turned up. There does seem to exist a network of sites at this time in the eastern extreme of the Tlacolula Valley, however, placed at

intervals of around 5 km. For example, about 5 km north of Yagul–Caballito Blanco is Díaz Ordaz, which seems to have been occupied. At the same distance, roughly, to the west is Yegüih–Brawbehl. To the east lies Loma Larga, and at another 5 km east from there is Mitla, with a well-established (though almost unexplored) Period II occupation at a subarea called La Playa. It would not be surprising if Matatlán could be added to the list.

## RELEVANT CERAMICS

For Caballito Blanco, Loma Larga, and Mitla we can identify a highly interesting shared characteristic (to what extent it occurs at the other sites named it is not possible now to say). This is a type of pottery that seems to occur only very rarely, if at all, in Monte Albán, but to have reached a considerable elaboration in the east extreme of the valley.

There are several examples of White-rimmed Black vessels at Monte Albán, and they belong in Period II. Nevertheless, they differ noticeably from those of Caballito Blanco–Loma Larga–Mitla; the paste is entirely different, the surface finish is not the same, the Monte Albán ones show some incised decoration absent on the others.

But much more striking is the development that seems to have occurred from the Mitla area Black and White base. As is well known, White-rimmed Black may be all white, all black, all gray, or clouded irregularly with combinations of these colors, depending on how it is fired.

If the surface is oxidized to white, it can be decorated by painting, as occurred in the Caballito Blanco area. Some vessels are completely, though unevenly, covered with an orange-red paint; flat-bottomed *cajetes* ("bowls") with slightly convex walls may get a line of red on the rim and a red disk in the bottom.

These vessels, whatever their shape and color and decoration, are notable for a dense black, porous paste with only a thin layer (if any) oxidized on the surface. The surface is polished, but is neither very even nor visibly lustrous. In addition to the *cajetes* mentioned, there are cylindrical *cajetes* and boxes with lids; so far no other shapes have been noted. (Examples of this ware, found in the La Playa area at Mitla, are on display in the Mitla case at the Frissell Museum of Zapotec Art.)

The Black and White complex described is rare at Yagul, common at Caballito Blanco, common at Loma Larga, and common at the La Playa area at Mitla—suggesting that it might be a mark of Transición II–IIIa and that during Transición, Yagul might have been nearly replaced in its area by Caballito Blanco. This interpretation makes much of just a few data, however.

The truth is that we have no real evidence for occupation at Caballito Blanco except in Period II. While any residential occupation of Period II leaves remains of certain ceramic types, especially domestic ones, that are holdovers from Period I, at Caballito Blanco there are no known remains that are diagnostic of I and absent from II. Likewise, there is no conclusive evidence of Transición, though the absence of Transición urns, IIIa types, and Teotihuacanoid types is far from a proof that the place was not inhabited at that time. From Period III there are only a couple of urn fragments; from IV, nothing. In Period V, evidently the remains of Period II buildings were known even though not used, for somebody placed a considerable offering of miniature vessels (like those of Yagul and of Mound B, Monte Albán) against one of the walls, just under the surface of the debris.

## CABALLITO BLANCO

The known buildings (other than houses) of Caballito Blanco consist of three small, low platforms with vertical

walls that define a central plaza, open to the north (looking toward Yagul). A few meters away to the southwest is an arrowhead-shaped structure (Building O) which resembles Building J at Monte Albán (Figure 4.22). To the south we located a tiny structure interpreted as the foundation of a *temascal* (or sweathouse). A few meters to the southeast was a rectangle of very large stones—not megaliths, but noticeably large just the same—that was never explored. Before we got to it, a Tlacolula farmer had used an ox team to haul them off to the edge of the mesa. (This destruction probably parallels what happened to Period II buildings at Yagul, though the motivation and the means 'were different.)

Except for the ancient reconstruction of a couple of buildings, there is little stratigraphy at Caballito Blanco. The top of the mesa is, more than anything else, an expanse of bare rock with tiny pockets of thin soil. Even on the south tip of the mesa, where the occupation left the thickest deposits, they are never even a meter deep except in and immediately around the remains of buildings. Since there was only one rebuilding, and the structures were small even after enlargement, there are no sherd samples of significant size that might show change. All radiocarbon dates from Caballito Blanco are therefore considered to be associated with remains of Monte Albán II (and possibly Transición II–IIIa) time.

On the basis of all known Monte Albán II dates, Drennan (see Appendix) has chosen 200 B.C.–A.D. 200 as the most likely limits of that period. The excavations of Monte Albán revealed Period II to be relatively short, but on the basis of surveys and excavations elsewhere in the valley, Blanton and Flannery consider the period long and complex.

It is important to note that the three late dates from Caballito Blanco—40 B.C., A.D. 100, and A.D. 190—may all have come from the same layer; the latter two definitely did. Mound 1-S at Caballito Blanco had a stairway on the

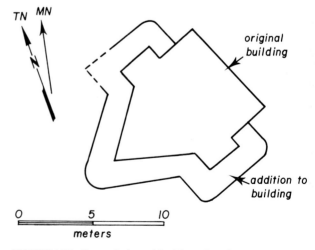

FIGURE 4.22. Ground plan of Building O at Caballito Blanco (compare with Figure 4.13). (Redrawn from Paddock 1966e.)

west in its first construction stage. When it was enlarged, this stairway, which had rather large but not abnormal steps, was covered with adobe blocks; a new stairway, of almost megalithic dimensions, was then built farther out to the west over the adobe. The 40 B.C. date came from the foot of the stairs on the first-stage building; the dates of A.D. 100 and 190 both came from the adobe fill between the two stairways. Thus the 40 B.C. date might be associated either with the construction of the first stairway at whose foot it lay, or with the enlargement of the building. Since it was placed below the level of the bottom of the steps, I judge it more likely to be associated with the first construction, even though the date itself seems to me much more satisfactory for something late at Caballito Blanco.

Because it is so widespread—it is found in the Mixteca Alta and Baja and at Teotihuacán's Oaxaca barrio—perhaps a note on type G-12 (the "combed-bottom" gray bowl) at Caballito Blanco is not out of order. The type appears first in Phase Ib, and Bernal says it continues until early IIIa. There is only one place where I have ever seen it in what might be called "abundance," however—Caballito Blanco. A Period II peak for a type that begins in Late I and ends in Early III is natural enough, but I think the rise and fall of this type have not before been noted.

## THE SITE OF BRAWBEHL

A note on Brawbehl may also be helpful. There is some doubt as to whether it should be considered a separate community from the site of Yegüih (see Topic 60). It is about a kilometer west from Lambityeco, and slightly less from the nearest section of Yegüih that has Period II remains. The salt-producing area on the south edge of Yegüih and Lambityeco, however, links Brawbehl to them, for it too lies just north of the salt deposits. Today Brawbehl shows no mounds. But during the middle 1950s, accompanying Bernal on one of his surveys, I visited the ranch of Don Jaime, an elderly Tlacolula man who had papers accrediting him as inspector of archaeological remains in the Tlacolula area for the government of Porfirio Díaz. At his ranch he affably agreed that indeed there were a lot of surface sherds around, and added that there used to be a group of mounds too, until he leveled them. When we did our very small study of Brawbehl, I realized we were very near Don Jaime's ranch, but I couldn't find the house. Such remains as a water tank, however, suggest that the area we dug in may well have been right where he leveled a group of mounds. The house had just disappeared.

# TOPIC 35
# The Cuicatlán Cañada and the Period II Frontier of the Zapotec State

ELSA M. REDMOND
CHARLES S. SPENCER

An intriguing research problem in Oaxaca archaeology concerns the political and military frontier of the Zapotec state centered at Monte Albán. On Building J in the Main Plaza of Monte Albán is a series of carved slabs which Caso (1947) and Marcus (1976d) have interpreted as a list of places subdued by Monte Albán during Period II. Marcus is presently attempting to identify the places to which the glyphs refer, and in Topic 29 has suggested that Tututepec, Miahuatlán, and the Cuicatlán Cañada are among the areas mentioned.

During 1975–1976, the authors visited a number of archaeological sites in the Cuicatlán Cañada, which constitutes the major Precolumbian route between the Valleys of Oaxaca and Tehuacán. What we observed tended to support the proposition that the Cañada was subjugated by Monte Albán during the very Late or Terminal Formative and became, for a time, a frontier region of the Zapotec state. In 1977, we began a two-phase research project in the Cañada, aimed at clarifying its relationship to Monte Albán. The first phase was an intensive survey of the region between the present towns of Tecomavaca and Dominguillo (see Figure 4.23). Directed by Redmond, this survey concentrated on sites with Formative and Classic occupa-

tion; Postclassic sites have already been covered by E. Hunt (1972) and Hopkins (1974 and Topic 77). All sites with Formative or Classic occupation were located on aerial photographs and then intensively mapped and surface collected. The second phase of the project, directed by Spencer, involved excavations at the site of La Coyotera near Dominguillo. While conclusions are still tentative and considerable analysis remains to be done, preliminary results support the hypothesis of a Zapotec takeover of the Cañada by Monte Albán II. In this brief report, we will mention only the economic potential of the region, the fortress of Quiotepec, and the site of La Coyotera.

## THE REGION

The Cañada is a long, north–south river canyon located strategically between the Valleys of Tehuacán and Oaxaca. Here the Río Salado, flowing south from Tehuacán, and the Río Grande, flowing north from the mountains on the border of the Valley of Oaxaca, join to form the Papaloapan River. In contrast to the 1500–1700-m elevations of the Valley of Oaxaca, the floor of the Cañada varies between

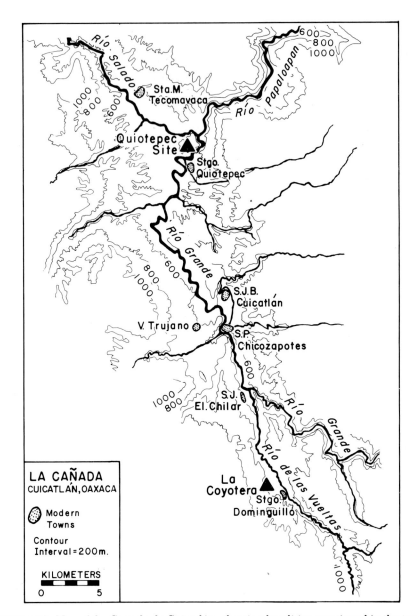

FIGURE 4.23. Map of the Cañada de Cuicatlán, showing localities mentioned in the text.

500 and 700 m above sea level. As a consequence, the Caña-da is a frost-free area with much higher temperatures than Oaxaca. For example, the mean annual temperature of Cuicatlán, in the center of the Cañada, is 24.5° C (Hopkins 1974:48), compared to 20.6° C for Oaxaca (Kirkby 1973:7). Recordings of 40° C or more are not uncommon in the Cañada, especially during the months of April and May. The Cañada is, in effect, a pocket of *tierra caliente* sur-rounded on all sides by the *tierra templada* and *tierra fría* of the southern highlands.

Although there is too little rainfall in the Cañada for suc-cessful dry farming (Hunt and Hunt 1974:137), the al-luvium of the Río Grande can be irrigated with water from its tributaries, and simple floodwater farming (Kirkby 1973)

is possible on some stretches of low alluvium. The alluvium thus improved is extremely productive land; it can yield up to 2000 kg of maize per hectare per planting, and more than one planting is possible because of the unlikelihood of frost. Today much of the alluvium is used for growing much-de-sired tropical fruits which cannot be successfully cultivated in the higher Oaxaca Valley.

The distribution of this alluvium, however, is not uniform in the Cañada. "Habitation in the Cañada is found only in association with broad alluvial fans formed where major tributaries join the Río Grande, in locations where the can-yon opens out into a relatively wide valley floor. Elsewhere the terrain is rough, non-irrigable, and uninhabitable" (Hunt and Hunt 1974:135–136). Four major alluvial fans (and hence important loci for settlement) are situated near Quiotepec, Cuicatlán, El Chilar, and Dominguillo. Hopkins (Topic 77) discusses the Postclassic irrigation which the ethnohistoric Cuicatec developed at Cuicatlán; we will discuss Formative and Classic developments on the alluvial fans.

What aspect of the Cañada might have so interested the Zapotec that they would have expended the effort necessary to subjugate and control the region? One very likely possibility is the productive capabilities of the Cañada with respect to frost-free agriculture. By taking over the Cañada the Zapotec could regulate the production of *tierra caliente* agricultural goods according to their own needs, rather than relying upon exchange relationships with the Cañada to provide them with the desired products.

## QUIOTEPEC

The site of Quiotepec is located at a natural pass through a mountain ridge that otherwise seals off the northern Cañada from the Tehuacán Valley; immediately south of the site is a major ford on the Río Grande which is still in use today. Virtually all traffic passing between Tehuacán and Oaxaca would have had to use this pass and ford, making it a crucial control point.

At a time equivalent to Monte Albán Ia,[1] occupation in this area consisted of a 2-ha site on a spur overlooking a small alluvial fan. Between Monte Albán Ic times and the end of Monte Albán II, settlement expanded to more than 40 ha distributed through five occupational areas. The largest of these is a 15-ha settlement covering both sides of the mountain pass and protected by a defensive wall on its west side; to the east are plazas, artificial platforms, and a 75-m-long ballcourt. Immediately to the south of the river ford is an extremely large plaza with elongated earthen mounds, through which any traveler using the ford would have to pass. Additional areas of settlement, apparently residential, occur farther to the south (upstream). On all these settlements we found abundant pottery showing close stylistic affinity to that of Monte Albán II in the Valley of Oaxaca. Prior to our work, Pareyón (1960) had discovered an elaborate tomb painted in what he interpreted as Monte Albán III style at Quiotepec, and Hunt (1972:182) had declared the site a military installation.

The significance of the Quiotepec pottery is made even clearer by our reconnaissance at Tecomavaca, a contemporaneous site only 7 km north of the pass. Here the surface collections yielded mainly sherds of the Palo Blanco phase—a purely Tehuacán manifestation—and the story is the same at other sites extending north to Coxcatlán and the Tehuacán Valley. Clearly, the fortified site at Quiotepec

in some way marks the northern limits of Monte Albán II expansion. By controlling the pass, the Zapotec may have laid claim to the hot-country products of the larger alluvial fans to the south, at Cuicatlán, El Chilar, and Dominguillo.

## LA COYOTERA

The site of La Coyotera is situated 2 km northwest of Dominguillo near the banks of the Río de las Vueltas, a major tributary of the Río Grande in the southern Cañada. The site lies still closer to the Valley of Oaxaca than does Quiotepec, and was clearly affected by the expansionistic activities of the Zapotec during Monte Albán II.

The sequence of events at La Coyotera between Periods I and II typifies the changes in settlement patterns and local economy that occurred throughout the Cañada south of Quiotepec. At a time equivalent to the Rosario and Monte Albán Ia phases of the Valley of Oaxaca, occupation at La Coyotera covered about 2.5 ha on a high alluvial terrace overlooking the low alluvium of the Río de las Vueltas. Cultivation of this low alluvium would have been possible using the techniques of simple diversionary canal and floodwater farming (see A. Kirkby 1973). We have found no evidence for canal irrigation facilities associated with this earlier community on the high alluvium, however.

Then, beginning at a time equivalent to Monte Albán Ic, a decisive settlement shift occurred at La Coyotera. The community on the high alluvium was abandoned and a new settlement, just over 3 ha in size, was established immediately to the west, on a piedmont ridge rising above the alluvium. Associated with this later settlement is a large and well-built aqueduct which brought water down from a tributary barranca behind the site to the expanse of high alluvium below.

Elsewhere in the central and southern Cañada, we find a similar shift off the high alluvium contemporary with Periods Ic and II, accompanied by the appearance of sophisticated irrigation technology. It seems clear that much more land in the Cañada was brought under cultivation by Monte Albán II times than had been the case during the local equivalent of Period Ia.

Why was agricultural production so drastically expanded during Late Period I and Period II? Was it to support a growing local population, or was production increased to meet demands of a different sort? At La Coyotera, our Period Ic–II deposits contain a much higher density of tropical fruit and nut remains than do our Rosario–Ia deposits. Furthermore, we detect very little, if any, population increase between the earlier settlement on the alluvium and the later settlement on the adjacent ridge. We thus feel that the extra land was brought under cultivation during Late Period I–Period II for the primary purpose of increasing the production of tropical fruits and nuts. This increase, in turn, may have been in response to demands by the Zapotec state for tribute in the form of *tierra caliente* agricultural produce.

---

[1]The ceramics of the Middle and Late Formative in the Cañada are not identical to those of the Rosario, Monte Albán Ia, and Monte Albán Ic phases in the Valley of Oaxaca. There are enough ceramic cross-ties, however, to establish their contemporaneity with those phases.

A further discovery at La Coyotera leads us to believe that the Zapotec domination of the Cañada was far from benevolent. In front of the major pyramidal mound in the Period Ic–II occupation we found a concentration of 61 human skulls, roughly aligned in rows, which we interpret as the remains of a toppled-over skullrack—what the Aztec in the Late Postclassic termed a *tzompantli*. This skull rack probably served as a symbol of Zapotec imperial power, designed to terrorize the local population and help keep them submissive as well as productive. A failure to produce enough tribute or an attempt at insurrection may well have landed the malefactor's head on the rack.

Continuing analyses of the La Coyotera excavations and the Cañada survey will further clarify the Cañada's role as a frontier region of the early Zapotec state. We hope that this work will lead ultimately to an improved understanding of the relationship between the Period Ic–II Zapotec expansion and the origins and development of the Monte Albán state itself.

# TOPIC 36
## Ramos Phase Urbanization in the Mixteca Alta

RONALD SPORES

The urban transformation of Mixtec society occurred in the Nochixtlán Valley during the Ramos phase, roughly from 200 B.C. to about A.D. 300 (Figure 4.24). Qualitative as well as quantitative changes accompany the transition from village-based Formative society to urbanized Classic civilization. The number and size of sites increase, and the settlement system becomes organically complex. One large, functionally diversified center deserving the designation "urban" emerged at Yucuita (localities N 203, N 204, N 217, N 218, N 225). Whereas occupation during the Cruz phase at Yucuita apparently was restricted to an area approximately 150 m square, the Ramos phase settlement covered nearly 2 km². There were, in addition, at least five adjacent "satellites" (sites N 208, N 220, N 226, N 227, N 229) in the Yucuita sector.

Yucuita consisted of a concentrated center containing several hundred structures situated on a *loma–cerro* system just east of the center of the present community. Included were at least 10 major mound complexes containing floors and alignments of quartered stone, standing megalithic walls, patios and plazas, a subterranean vault-roof tunnel system, quarries, terraces, adobe and stone-slab tombs, and single-cell and multiroomed structures with block masonry foundations and walls. Deep refuse containing remains of deer, rabbit, dog and cannibalized human bone, corn, beans, avocados, zapotes, and chili was associated with Yucuita Tan Ware bowls, jars, and braziers, Yucuita Red-on-tan Ware jars, and Yucuita Thin Tan jars, as well as lesser quantities of Nochixtlán Gray Wares: Juanito variety, Nochixtlán Rust Ware jars and bowls, and Yucuita Polished Brown Ware. Specific horizon markers found at Yucuita and in surface deposits at other sites include incision-decorated flat-bottom bowls in Tan and Gray wares and distinctive Ramos phase figurines in seated, kneeling, standing, acrobatic, and "pregnant" poses.

Other artifacts recovered in stratigraphic tests include small siliceous gray chert and quartz tools and flakes, and black and gray-black obsidian blades, sheet mica, shell objects, and carved bone spindle whorls, awls, beads, and pendants. Block adobe tombs containing extended burials, grouped reburials (one tomb at locality N 203 E contained remains of seven individuals, while an adjoining unit contained the extended remains of a single individual), and individual skull burials have been recovered in excavations at Yucuita (Spores 1972, 1974a).

In all, 35 sites are assigned to the Ramos phase, and 31 of these localities were intensively utilized for perhaps 500 years. This pattern represents, at the very least, a doubling of population since Cruz phase times (17 sites, 8 intensively utilized during a span of perhaps 1000 years). Sites are also much larger and more complex; low *lomas* and the ends of high ridge spurs were preferred site locations, and other locations were less frequently chosen (Spores 1972).

In addition to the one Ramos phase urban center of Yucuita, there were 10 town-size settlements (N 208, N 209, N 220, N 226, N 227, N 229, N 419, N 605, N 801, N 810) and some 20 sites of hamlet, rancho, or *sujeto* type. The major clustering of sites is in the immediate area of Yucuita (Yucuita, 15 Ramos phase sites; Yanhuitlán, 7; Nochixtlán, 4; Etlatongo–Jaltepec, 9), suggesting localized power, control, or expansion favoring that area over the other sectors. It is certainly more than coincidental that the site of Yucuita rises immediately adjacent to some of the most fertile alluvial deposits in the Nochixtlán Valley, an area where good agricultural yields can be obtained with simple technology and only moderate rainfall. A second relatively high representation of Ramos phase sites is in the Etlatongo–Jaltepec sector, where 9 of 23 total sites show utilization. It is important to note that Etlatongo is the second most fertile and productive area of the valley in modern times. Ramos remains are poorly represented in the Yanhuitlán (7 of 72 known sites) and Nochixtlán (4 of 42 sites) sectors.

I believe that insofar as the Nochixtlán Valley is concerned, primary political and economic power was concentrated in Yucuita during the Ramos phase. This Ramos site is

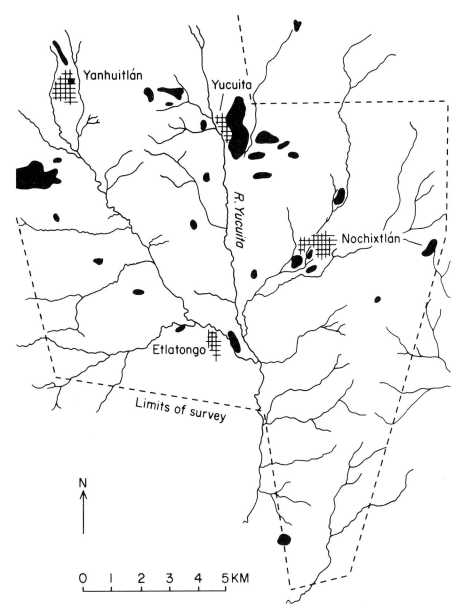

FIGURE 4.24. Ramos phase settlements in the Nochixtlán Valley.

by far the largest and most complex in the valley. It is also the oldest excavated site, with remains dating to both Early and Late Formative times. Continuity is inferred from Cruz to Ramos times, a pattern that will probably be established in future excavations at Etlatongo, but is rarely observed in other valley sites.

The majority of intensively utilized Ramos sites, most of them newly founded during this phase, occur in the Yucuita sector, and most of the larger "town" sites cluster in satellite fashion around Yucuita. Deposits are deeper, architecture and material goods more heavily concentrated, diverse, and complex; more "elite" goods, more ambitious architecture and planning, and more exotic goods (sea shell, chert and obsidian, sheet mica, Monte Albán-like braziers, and type

G-12 "combed-bottom" bowls) are found in Yucuita than elsewhere in the valley. The site is enormous for its time and by comparison with earlier settlements. In fact, during any period only one site in the entire valley approaches it in size—Yucuñudahui—and no site is more complex or richer in its content and organization.

## SOCIOPOLITICAL IMPLICATIONS OF RAMOS PHASE URBANIZATION

While direct ethnohistoric and ethnographic models (coupled with an absence of hard archaeological evidence to the contrary) lead me to doubt that full-time occupational specialization was at this, or at any other, time a feature of native culture in the Nochixtlán Valley, I am finally convinced that Yucuita must be considered an urban center. It was the original urban keystone in a city–town–rancho interdependent settlement system that was to typify life in the valley from Ramos times to the present.

As the principal link in the valley's internal socioeconomic network and (assuming that a high degree of political, as well as economic, control was centered here) as the main channel of contact with the world outside the valley, Yucuita became the primary generator of a pattern that I believe characterized life in this region from Ramos times to the Spanish conquest. A special kind of urban behavior emerged. Urbanism in the classic sense normally implies, among other things, the functional integration of diverse activities into a complex, organic whole within a densely settled and concentrated center, a city. In order for an archaeological site to be urban it should be large for its time and place, internally complex, and reflect not only monumental cultural achievement but functional and occupational (nonagricultural) specialization (Sjoberg 1960:11–37). If we are to bring Yucuita into the urban category, however, we must reconsider and liberalize the concept of urbanism.

With reference to the important behavioral transformation that took place in the early Classic period in the Nochixtlán Valley, urbanism should be seen as extending beyond the resources, specializations, and physical confines of any particular settlement to incorporate by socioeconomic means organically interdependent components. Relatively complex settlements like Yucuita were linked with settlements that were internally relatively undifferentiated. The large centers depended not only on their own resources but also on the goods and resources produced by smaller neighboring settlements. Undifferentiated settlements depended on the large centers for market exchange activities, ceremonialism, and probably protection. The many settlements were linked into a system of functionally interdependent units. This multiloci organic whole was composed of settlements that were relatively undifferentiated internally, but which served specialized functions in the macrostructural sense in terms of access to local resources, specific local adaptations, part-time occupational specialization, varieties of products, demographic configuration, and probably social ranking.

Towns and cities, according to Doxiadis (1968:91) contain 2,000 to 20,000 people (sometimes 50,000 to 100,000) and density varies from 150 to 350 inhabitants per hectare (60 to 140 inhabitants per acre). "In towns and cities Man and Society are both urban and almost all the economy is urban; the rural population, if there is any, is comparatively very small. . . . Like the urban-agricultural settlements, towns and cities usually have one continuously developed center, in most cases much more densely built than the rest" (Doxiadis 1968:91).

Yucuita, the first urban center in the Nochixtlán Valley, lacks the absolute size, density, and degree of specialization for central placement in the towns-and-cities class but may be somewhat marginal to both categories. I doubt that population ever exceeded 8000. Large-scale (full-time) craft specialization certainly cannot be inferred from site placement, structural configurations, ceramic distributions, or activity areas thus far identified. Dwellings, even those placed on steep slopes, appear to be exclusively one-floored and rather well spaced, with no suggestion of congestion in any one area of the site. Much of the deepest midden deposit seems to have been associated with ceremonialism and laid down quickly as a result of intensive but short-term utilization. Possibly much of it was attributable to visiting celebrants who were not themselves residents of the city. Numerous test trenches, areal excavations, road cuts, and *barro* pits in the approximately 1.0 to 1.5 km² area composed of the lower southern slopes of Cerro Las Flores and the south extending loma reveal that nearly the entire area was covered by structures. Probably ceremonial structures are prominent but by no means abundant or tightly clustered. At present, however, it cannot be claimed with certainty that all units were occupied or utilized simultaneously, which leaves serious doubts as to the precise demographic situation in Yucuita and prompts us to be somewhat conservative in our population estimates.

Yucuita served as a "mother site," a major evolutionary and functional landmark in the emergence of the Mixtec cultural tradition in the Nochixtlán Valley. The transformation to the urban stage that occurred there 2000 years ago, important in itself, was functionally correlated with the establishment of a new configuration of intercommunity relations, a settlement system that was to continue to function and evolve until modern times. While forms of suprasettlement socioeconomic integration may have been present on a low level during the Cruz phase, these mechanisms are clearly and intensively operative during the Ramos phase. This situation parallels the emergence of Teotihuacán in the Valley of Mexico, both in terms of the rise of a great urban center and with reference to correlated changes in socioeconomic and demographic patterns in the Teotihuacán–Texcoco area in Formative, Classic, and Postclassic times (Sanders 1965; J. R. Parsons 1968).

The Nochixtlán Valley diverges from its Formative base in Ramos times. It is identifiable as an "ekistic region," a geographically delimited area which over the years has "developed a particular system of organized life within these natural boundaries expressed as a system of interrelated human settlements" (Doxiadis 1968:132). Yucuita was the first center where sufficient demographic, technological, economic, and political power was concentrated to the point that urban life and an unprecedented level of both functional divergence in settlement and regional socioeconomic integration could be achieved.

Absence of sharp discontinuities in the archaeological record of settlement patterns during the Ramos, Las Flores, and Natividad phases encourages the utilization of the protohistoric and historic model of the Mixtec kingdom (described in Topics 70 and 75) as an appropriate interpretive framework for developments during the period under consideration. First, I would postulate the existence of a ruling family at Yucuita composed of a ruler descended in a direct line from ruling highest-status individuals, a spouse of equal rank probably from another community, their equally high-ranked offspring, and other close relatives. The ruling couple exercised political control over Yucuita, its lands, waters, and resources, and received personal services and tribute from the residents of the center. They also probably ruled one or more dependencies administered by lower-ranking members or descendants of the royal family placed in those settlements by royal direction.

The ruling family, while serving an internally integrative function within the kingdom, stood in a position of reciprocal dependency with similar elite families located in other centers in the Nochixtlán Valley, in the Mixteca, or conceivably in other areas of Mesoamerica. Reciprocal ties were based on two primary requirements, one social, one economic: the necessity of arranging appropriate marriages for elite ruling class and noble children, and economic interdependency stemming from increasing demands of a growing population and needs of ruling families and their supporting nobility to accumulate high status goods and to maintain an increasingly demanding redistributive economic network. These requirements led to the establishment of alliance networks that linked Yucuita and other communities in the valley to a broad socioeconomic macrocosm that extended across the valley and beyond, to other regions of Mesoamerica. I believe that such a model helps explain the structure of the Nochixtlán Valley settlement system as it emerged during the early Classic period, and as it continued to evolve during the ensuing 1500 years.

# TOPIC 37
## San Martín Huamelulpan, Periods I and II

ADDED BY THE EDITORS

San Martín Huamelulpan is an important hilltop civic–ceremonial center discovered by Alfonso Caso's explorations in the 1930s. Huamelulpan is in a chain of narrow valleys along an upper Río Mixteco tributary between Tlaxiaco and Teposcolula in the Mixteca Alta, and the site is composed of five major mound groups running east–west for approximately 1.5 km along a series of hills. The linear layout, lacking the Main Plaza form of Monte Albán or San José Mogote, is more reminiscent of Monte Negro or Yucuñudahui (Topic 47).

Early work at Huamelulpan was sporadic. Lorenzo Gamio (1957) worked there for one field season, and Caso and Gamio (1961) for a second season. Numerous carved stones had previously been found by the villagers, and Caso and Gamio discovered more, some of which were published by Caso in *El Calendario Mixteco* (1956). One of these, the so-called Huamelulpan monolith, is also published in the *Handbook of Middle American Indians* (Caso 1965b; see also Paddock 1966a:Fig. 2). In the same volume of the *Handbook*, Bernal (1965:800) calls Huamelulpan an important Monte Albán II site, and refers to Caso and Gamio's discovery of "a stairway bounded by enormous rectangular stones on whose outer faces are hieroglyphs and numerals in the Monte Albán II style. The pottery of this building appears to belong to the same period or to the end of Period I." Caso (1956) also dated the hieroglyphs to Monte Albán II, noting their similarity to the Building J hieroglyphs at Monte Albán, and pronounced them Zapotec, as far as style is concerned.

In 1974, after repeated requests from the villagers of Huamelulpan, the Oaxaca Regional Center of the Instituto Nacional de Antropología e Historia carried out an additional five months of work at the site. The archaeological results have now been published in an excellent monograph by Margarita Gaxiola (1976), and the ethnohistory will be reported by María de los Angeles Romero (in preparation). Manuel Esparza, director of the Oaxaca Regional Center, is to be commended for responding with such sensitivity to the needs and aspirations of the local villagers, who chose to have the site professionally excavated rather than looted.

The five mound groups of Huamelulpan are divided by Gaxiola into Cerro Volado (large), the Panteón Group (small), the Iglesia Vieja Group (small), the Grupo de las Lápidas (large), and the Iglesia Group (large). Gaxiola's efforts were concentrated in and around the Grupo de las Lápidas, which includes four elongated platforms on various levels. One of these, Building C, includes the stairway with carved stones found by Caso and Gamio; another, Building G, yielded a new series of carved stones. Most seem to be calendric, with the day sign enclosed in a cartouche and the numbers written in typical Monte Albán II style (see below).

## HUAMELULPAN I (400–100 B.C.)

The Huamelulpan I period, as defined by Gaxiola, shows at least a few ceramic cross-ties with Monte Albán Ic and Monte Negro. Bowls with G-12 style combed-bottom designs, vessels with G-14 rim decoration, and fish-effigy plates all occur in gray ware, though there are also abundant overlaps with the Cruz phase of the Nochixtlán Valley. This seems to be the initial period of occupation, and during Huamelulpan I a series of houses were built to the north of Building G. The early stages of the latter building—a huge platform 50 m on its south side, composed of giant limestone blocks reminiscent of Monte Negro—were built toward the end of Period I, as was the early stage of an altar to be described below.

A relatively high-status residence of this period excavated by Gaxiola had two to four rooms on a low platform, three hearths, and the burial of a child of 3 years accompanied by one pottery vessel. The domestic refuse included abundant deer bone, as well as remains of dog and cottontail.

## HUAMELULPAN II (100 B.C.–A.D. 200)

The Huamelulpan II period has ties with the Ramos phase in Nochixtlán and with Monte Albán II in the Valley of Oaxaca, including the use of G-21 gray bowls with coarse, swirled incising on the interior base. During this phase—evidently the major period of occupation at Huamelulpan—Building G was remodeled and enlarged, and some carved stones were placed in its southeast corner. Building C, the platform with the two immense monoliths originally discovered by Caso and Gamio (1961), was also erected during this period.

Another interesting construction of the Huamelulpan II phase was the Altar de los Craneos, a 36-m² stone-walled altar located 17 m from the southeast corner of Building C. Above the plaster floor of the altar were found three apparent trophy skulls, all with postmortem holes drilled in the frontal bone from both sides, perhaps for suspension; a fourth skull, found nearby, was incompletely drilled. Since the mandibles were found still articulated to the cranium, the drilling may have been done while the skin was still present. Physical anthropologist Richard G. Wilkinson has identified the skulls as belonging to a female between 20 and 25 years; a male of 18 to 20 years; a male of 20 to 30 years with filed teeth; and a male over 40 (Gaxiola 1976:123–125). Associated were five urns (all showing a small seated figure with a buccal mask in Monte Albán II style) as well as shell objects, a greenstone celt, and other items. Significantly, there were also some huge cooking vessels, charcoal braziers, storage jars, and stone manos associated with the altar.

West of Building G was a Huamelulpan II house, located near the public buildings and described by Gaxiola as the highest-status residence found during her excavations. This was a large, stone-founded house covering more than 64 m² (see Figure 4.25) and divided into several rooms. Beneath the floor was a stone tomb (Tomb 4) containing two skeletons (a male of about 70, a female of about 40) who may constitute

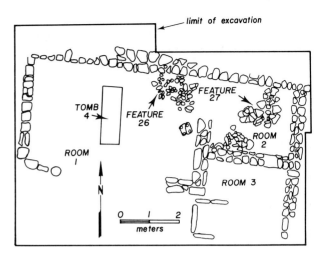

FIGURE 4.25. Period II residence from San Martín Huamelulpan, Oaxaca. (Redrawn from Gaxiola 1976.)

a marital pair; although the tomb had been looted, nine vessels remained. In two places, groups of ceramics had been broken over the floor of the house in such density as to receive feature numbers from the archaeologists. Feature 26 had broken vessels mixed with hearth charcoal and carbonized bones, primarily from humans and deer; Feature 27 included bowls whose huge size "suggests they were used for the distribution of food for a considerable group of people" (Gaxiola 1976:161).

## CONCLUSIONS

Huamelulpan is another Late and Terminal Formative center on a defensible mountaintop in what is today the Mixteca. While its ceramics can be cross-dated with the Valley of Oaxaca, its ties with Monte Albán are weaker than Monte Negro's, and Spores (personal communication) sees numerous ties with the Nochixtlán sequence. Huamelulpan's hieroglyphs, however, follow the Valley of Oaxaca canon (see Topic 38).

Huamelulpan has the linear layout characteristic of Classic Mixtec centers. While impressive, its known Period I–II elite residences are not palaces by our definition (see Editors' Introduction), but they are located significantly near public buildings. Interestingly, Period II Huamelulpan yields evidence suggestive of the preparation of trophy skulls, the cooking and eating of humans around altars, and perhaps the distribution of substantial cannibalistic meals at the nearby residences of community leaders. This evidence parallels that from Ramos phase Yucuita (see Spores, Topic 36), and suggests a very long history for ritual cannibalism in the Mixteca. The sixteenth-century *relaciones* make it clear that both the Zapotec and the Mixtec sacrificed, cooked, and ate prisoners taken in war, as well as condemned criminals, both male and female.

TOPIC 38
## The Style of the Huamelulpan Stone Monuments

JOYCE MARCUS

Perhaps the most interesting aspect of the stone monuments from Huamelulpan is the fact that, despite the site's location in what is today the Mixteca, all the hieroglyphs are done in Monte Albán II style. This does not in any sense imply that the site was Zapotec. It merely suggests that at the time the Mixteca did not have its own distinct writing system, separate from that of the Valley of Oaxaca.

This phenomenon is perhaps best seen in the carvings of Building C, the structure reported in 1961 by Caso and Gamio. Set in the southeast corner of the building are two immense monoliths which display hieroglyphs set in cartouches (Gaxiola 1976:145; Moser 1977:239). The south face of the monolith (corresponding to the front of the building) reveals a lizard[1] carved in high relief, below which are two square cartouches with rounded corners, subfixed with bars and dots. Glyph 1 would be 9J in Caso's system, which assigned each Zapotec glyph a letter of the alphabet (Caso 1928). Glyph 2 is 13 Monkey. Note that the numbers are done in the Monte Albán style, where 5 is represented by a bar, rather than in the Postclassic Mixtec system, where 5 is represented by five dots (Figure 4.26).

---

[1]The iconographic significance of this lizard is unknown, but it is significant to note that for the Zapotec the small lizard or *chintete* was a form sometimes taken by certain kinds of lightning (Cruz 1946:33; see Topic 97).

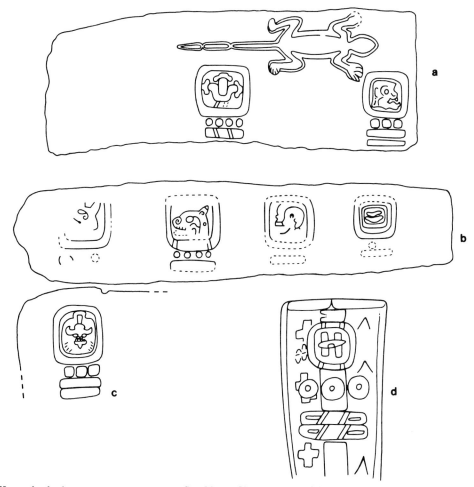

FIGURE 4.26. Hieroglyphs from stone monuments at San Martín Huamelulpan: (a) lizard and glyphs from south face of monolith in the southeast corner of Building C; (b) glyphs from east face of monolith in the southeast corner of Building C; (c) glyphs on the east face of a stone set immediately below the monolith mentioned in (a) and (b); (d) carved stone removed from its original context and set in the wall of the *municipio*.

If we return now to the east face of the same monolith, we see a string of four cartouches all subfixed with numerals. Glyph 3 is quite eroded, reading 2 (indistinct). Glyph 4 may be 9 Tiger. This is followed by Glyph 5—5 Death—and Glyph 6, which appears to be 1 (or 6) Water. The cartouches on the east side of the monolith contain animal heads, all shown facing south (to the left), while the monkey head in Glyph 2 on the south side faces east (to the right). All six glyphs may record dates in the 260-day ritual calendar, or perhaps six persons named for the days of their births.

Immediately below the monolith just described is another stone, which is only carved on its east face. This stone provides a single name, 13 Bat (?). These two stones set in the southeast corner of Structure C show great uniformity in style, and conform well to similar cartouches, numbers, and day names at Monte Albán during Period II. The seven glyphs are all set within cartouches with the numbers below them, and the dots appear above the bars, which is also characteristic of Monte Albán II.

There are two more stone monuments which have been removed from their original context and are set in the wall of the *municipio* office at Huamelulpan. The first of these, to the left of the doorway, gives a single name (or 260-day calendric position), 13 Flint Knife. Caso (1928:42–43) classifies the latter as his Glyph Q, and he illustrates a very similar compound glyph—13 Flint Knife—taken from the chest of the famous Monte Albán II ceramic sculpture known as The Scribe of Cuilapan (Caso 1928:Fig. 20). In both cases, the two bars forming the number 13 have bands binding them together or transecting them; additionally, the dots in both cases are circular, with inner circles. Two curious aspects of this Huamelulpan stone are the series of St. George's crosses running down the left side of the stone, and the series of chevrons running down the right side.

Also set in the wall of the municipal office is another stone, in some respects similar to the one just described. The stone is only a fragment, bearing an 11 (?), but the numbers are executed in a very similar style to the 13 Flint Knife carving. A small photo of this stone can be seen in Paddock (1966a:Fig. 2, left, behind the famous Huamelulpan monolith).

The aforementioned "monolith"—a freestanding sculpture whose original context has long since been lost—is perhaps the best-known monument from Huamelulpan. Depicting a human figure, the carving is quite simple, although the sculptor devoted most of his attention to the head. The eyes are almond-shaped and the mouth large, showing an expanse of gums; the head tapers to a cone, perhaps wearing a headband or cap. In 1971, Charles Wicke compared this monolith to a seriation of "Olmec" votive axes employing a Guttman Scale analysis. The monolith seriated at one end of the scale, and was eventually pronounced by Wicke (1971) to be the earliest Olmec monument. There is nothing iconographically Olmec about the monolith, however—no cleft skull, no flame brows, no crossed bands, no U elements, or related motifs. And Gaxiola's recent stratigraphic excavations indicate that the Huamelulpan site was not even occupied prior to 400 B.C., some 500–800 years later than the colossal Olmec heads of San Lorenzo, Veracruz (Coe 1968). Given the lack of provenience data, one can only guess that the Huamelulpan monolith dates between 400 B.C. and A.D. 200, which seems to be the case with the other carved stones at the site.

There are at least three other carved stones from the site of Huamelulpan, all appearing to be contemporaneous with late Monte Albán II (or perhaps IIIa) on stylistic grounds.

# The Early Urban Period

## Editors' Introduction

The period A.D. 100–600 saw the maximum development of the largest cities ever to exist in the Oaxaca region. Hilltop centers like Monte Albán in the Valley of Oaxaca and Yucuñudahui in the Nochixtlán Valley were urban in the usual sense of the word, for each seems to have had a large nucleated population (including both upper and lower-status residents), a variety of public buildings (including both political and religious types), and a rural hinterland with which they appear to have been integrated. Each city seems to have been on the upper tier of a hierarchy of sites, with communities in the second tier also displaying some administrative functions, though not as many as the primary center. This period also seems to have been when regions like Nochixtlán and the Valley of Oaxaca displayed the highest degree of centralization and unification (in political and religious terms) in all of their history.

It used to be fashionable to refer to this period as the *Classic,* and we have sometimes resorted to that term in the course of this voiume. An alternative term is *Early Urban,* suggested by John Paddock (1966a:111–112) in order to describe the "first-generation civilizations" of Oaxaca without conjuring up some of the undesired implications of the term *Classic.* We prefer the term *Early Urban,* but would hasten to point out that early cities did not arise synchronously all over Oaxaca. While urbanism was widespread during A.D. 100–600, some centers, like Monte Albán, had already been urban for hundreds of years.

The archaeological periods discussed in this chapter are Monte Albán III in the Valley of Oaxaca and the Las Flores phase in the Valley of Nochixtlán. Monte Albán III has been divided into phases IIIa (A.D. 100–400?) and IIIb (A.D. 400–600?), but there are some problems involved with these subdivisions. Monte Albán IIIa has a number of very distinct pottery types associated with it, but some of these diagnostics occur primarily in tombs or in elite residences, and show up less frequently in surface collections. Monte Albán IIIb

pottery, however, is so similar to Monte Albán IV pottery that Caso, Bernal, and Acosta (1967) treat both periods in a single chapter entitled "Época IIIb–IV." The result is that for some purposes it is most convenient to treat Period III as a unit (as in Topic 39); for others, it is most convenient to treat IIIa as a unit separate from IIIb–IV (as in Topic 44). The Las Flores phase has radiocarbon dates running from as early as A.D. 300 to later than A.D. 1000, although the very latest dates could be in error (see Appendix).

A further complication in the chronology is provided by the transition from Monte Albán II to IIIa. Although some Oaxaca archaeologists regard this simply as a gradual change in ceramic styles such as might take place between any two periods, other Oaxaca archaeologists regard it as a separate period in itself, called "Transición II–IIIa" or simply "Transición" (cf. Paddock 1966a:Fig. 1). Even those archaeologists who regard it as a distinct period, however, rarely attempt to define it except in terms of anthropomorphic urns or whole vessels; no radiocarbon dates can as yet be assigned to it, nor can it be detected in surface collections. In this volume, most authors have not emphasized it any more than they would the transition from Period I to II, or from Period III to IV.

Perhaps because Monte Albán III was a period of great regional unification, there are very few glottochronological separations assigned to it. The separation of Chatino from Zapotec (18–20 minimum centuries) is probably too ancient to be relevant here; however, the separation of Miahuatlán Zapotec and Sierra Zapotec from the dialects of the Valley of Oaxaca is so recent (A.D. 500–1000) that it might reflect the eventual decline of Monte Albán's integrative power (see Chapter 7), rather than the events of the Early Urban period we discuss here.

Because the Early Urban period provides a very complex and lengthy series of problems, we have divided our discussion into two chapters. Chapter 5 deals with the nature of

Monte Albán III and the Las Flores phase as Oaxacan phenomena. Chapter 6 deals with the relationship between Monte Albán and Teotihuacán, two great cities of the Early Urban period. The latter chapter gives us our first real glimpse at how developments in Oaxaca differed from, yet were related to, the rise of civilization elsewhere in Mesoamerica.

## TOPIC 39
## Urban Monte Albán during Period III

RICHARD E. BLANTON

During Period III, Monte Albán expanded to achieve its maximum population size and was the scene of abundant monumental construction, especially in the Main Plaza area. The hills of Atzompa and Monte Albán Chico were first colonized in Period IIIa, and by Period IIIb, as far as we can tell, every terrace visible on the surface of the site was occupied (Figure 5.1). A strong argument can be made, in my opinion, that for the most part the general morphology of Monte Albán in Period IIIb is essentially what we see at the site today. Although Monte Albán continued to be occupied during Periods IV and V, it was much reduced in population relative to IIIb levels, and there is little evidence for new monumental construction. In fact, public buildings in the Main Plaza area were left to deteriorate after Period IIIb (Caso, Bernal, and Acosta 1967:89). By assuming that most of what we see on the ground today pertains to Period IIIb, I can use the surface data to derive a maximum population estimate for the site; also, based on the distribution of platform mounds, ancient roads, and evidence for workshops, I can make certain inferences concerning Monte Albán's organization and functions during IIIb.

## THE POPULATION ESTIMATE

Archaeological features at Monte Albán extend over an area of about 6.5 km². although in some portions of the site these features are widely scattered. Features occur densely packed over an area of about 3.6 km². Of the 2100 archaeological features we located, mapped, and described, 2004 were identified as probably residential terraces. Of these 2004 terraces, 35 support rooms elevated on platform mounds. We identified these as "elaborate residences." Of the remaining 1969 terraces (those lacking mounds), 19 had residential buildings preserved to such an extent that I was able to calculate the terrace area taken by each house. Fortunately, these terraces occurred in a variety of contexts, and do not appear to be biased in terms of socioeconomic level, or any other variable (although this would be very difficult to prove since we do not know the full range of variation in the total sample). In spite of the small size of this sample, the mean figure derived seems to make sense. The value, 311.9 m² per house, is probably not unreasonably low or high. This value is consistent with Winter's discovery, in his recent excavations in the Terrace 634–636 area at Monte Albán, that scatters of debris and features from Late Formative households extended over an area with a radius of about 10 m (Winter 1974).

Elaborate residences cover much larger areas. The mean terrace surface area per elaborate residence from our sample is 2473.3 m², based on 19 well-preserved examples. Terraces lacking elaborate residences have a total surface area of 902,947 m², which should represent space for roughly 2899 houses at 311.9 m² of terrace area per house. Similarly, there should have been roughly 57 elaborate residences on the 140,100 m² of terrace surface area supporting these structures. The total estimated population for Period IIIb can be derived if we assume 5–10 persons per nonelaborate household (Sanders 1965:134). Elaborate residences probably housed more people. Carrasco, for example, found this assertion to be true based on sixteenth-century data from Morelos (Carrasco 1964). What average figure should be used for Period IIIb at Monte Albán, however, is unknown.

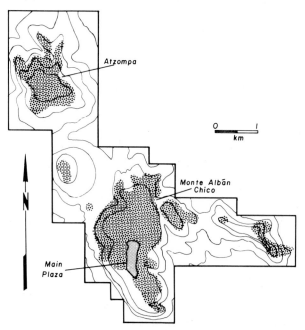

FIGURE 5.1. The extent of occupation at Monte Albán in Period IIIb. (Redrawn, with modifications, from Blanton 1978.)

If we assume 10–20 persons as an average for these large households—probably an underestimate—then the total population of Monte Albán at its height would have been about 15,000 to 30,000.

The population estimates given for earlier periods were based on the area of occupation of each period as a proportion of the total area occupied during IIIb. This method requires the possibly shaky assumption that population density in all periods was equivalent to that of Period IIIb. For Periods Ia and V, during which there were concentrations of dense settlements surrounded by less-dense settlement, I assumed that sparsely occupied zones had one-third the density of nucleated areas.

## SPATIAL ORGANIZATION

Platform mound groups at Monte Albán typically consist of two to four mounds facing a patio, although occasional isolated mounds do occur. These mound groups and single mounds are not randomly distributed within the boundaries of the site. Instead, they tend to occur in clusters. Using the nearest-neighbor statistic (Clark and Evans 1954), a value for mound-group spacing of 0.6 was derived, indicating a high degree of clustering (where 0 = perfectly clustered and 2.15 = evenly spaced).

Figure 5.2 shows the locations of the mound clusters. Clearly, the largest such cluster consists of the Main Plaza area and a series of adjacent mound groups that appear to be

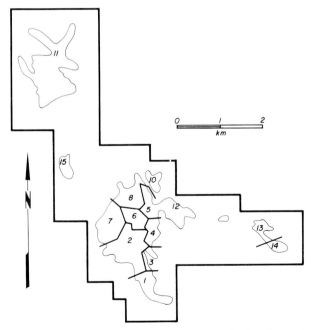

FIGURE 5.2. Thiessen polygons suggesting the localities of 14 "neighborhoods" associated with mound-group clusters at Monte Albán during Period IIIb. (Redrawn, with modifications, from Blanton 1978.)

elite residences. The other, smaller clusters are distributed throughout the site's residential areas. Each of these smaller mound-group clusters has the same composition. Specifically, each cluster consists of one or two "closed" mound groups that I infer were elite residences (insofar as the enclosed patios and inward-facing staircases and doorways would have assured familial privacy), plus one mound or mound group with an "open" patio, and therefore easily accessible to the general population. These latter features were probably civic buildings, ritual areas, or some comparable public, general-access buildings.

I suggest that each of the mound-group clusters served as the civic–ceremonial focus for the group of people living on the set of adjacent terraces. This suggestion would imply that the residential portion of the site away from the Main Plaza area (which is obviously distinct) was divided into a series of units, perhaps corporate groups analogous to the sixteenth-century Zapotec barrio headed by a *golaba* (see Topic 41). In order to discover the composition and function of these units, I attempted to identify those terraces associated with each mound cluster using the method of drawing Thiessen polygons around the mound-group clusters (Bogue 1949) (Figure 5.2). Fourteen such neighborhood subdivisions of Monte Albán were present during Period IIIb (apart from the Main Plaza). Clearly the site subdivision dominated by the Main Plaza cannot be considered comparable to the other site subdivisions. This subdivision contains a much higher ratio of total mound volume to terrace area, and it contains over 95% of all carved stone monuments on the site. The Main Plaza undoubtedly served as the locus of regional decision making and religious ritual. It is interesting to note that there are 14 so-called commemorative buildings facing the Main Plaza. Perhaps each site subdivision had a representative building there.

I interpret the spatial organization of Monte Albán in Period IIIb to imply that the barrio organization that seems to have characterized the site during Period Ia, as manifested by three discrete areas of sherd scatter, persisted into the Classic period. Of course, by Period IIIb it is possible to postulate 14 such barrios, rather than three; and these units, at least in Monte Albán proper, were no longer spatially separated but had expanded to become spatially contiguous. The Main Plaza area, with its three Period Ia buildings, including the danzantes gallery, continued until Period IIIb to be a special place, probably the focus of regional decision making. The model I presented earlier, which argued, in other words, that Monte Albán may have been the center for decision making in the context of a confederacy, still might be applicable to the city during Period IIIb.

The differences between the Late Formative and Early Classic city, at any rate, seem to be differences of degree rather than of kind. According to this model, Monte Albán was still "disembedded" from the remainder of the region's central place hierarchy, serving as a special-function governmental center more analogous to Washington, D.C. than to modern Mexico City. The archaeological evidence we collected during the course of the Monte Albán survey tends to support this interpretation of the function of the city during Period IIIb. The monumentality of public and elite residential architecture on the site as a whole (over 1,000,000 m³ of platform mounds) attests to its regional, political, and religious importance.

Such special-function governmental centers, however, do not have important roles to play in regional marketing or production. We located 142 artifact scatters at Monte Albán that might have been "workshops" (the bulk of which were small concentrations of local Valley of Oaxaca chert). René Millon (1973) located roughly 500 such deposits at Monte Albán's commercially oriented contemporary, Teotihuacán. Even the nature of many of these supposed workshops at Monte Albán, however, is equivocal. For example, most of the obsidian concentrations we found are near elite residences, perhaps reflecting differential consumption rather than production (obsidian would have been a relatively valuable commodity at Monte Albán, since it is not locally

available). Another problem is that, as I discuss in Topic 81, the city seems to have become more commercially oriented during Period V than it was during the Classic; the evidence suggests that many of the possible workshops visible on the surface pertain to that period, rather than to earlier periods.

Monte Albán's road system, insofar as we were able to reconstruct it from fragmentary evidence on the surface, is also suggestive of the lack of commercial orientation of the city in Period IIIb. No large market-like feature is serviced by major roads, in contrast to typical preindustrial marketing centers. This contrast is clear if one examines maps of, for example, Yoruba cities (Krapf-Askari 1969), medieval cities (e.g., Saalman 1968), or Teotihuacán (R. Millon 1973). Figure 5.3 shows Monte Albán's most important ancient roads. None of these leads directly to the Main Plaza area, as far as we can tell. Access to the Main Plaza seems to have been by way of three small entrances (at least during Period IIIb)— one near the southwest corner of the North Platform, and

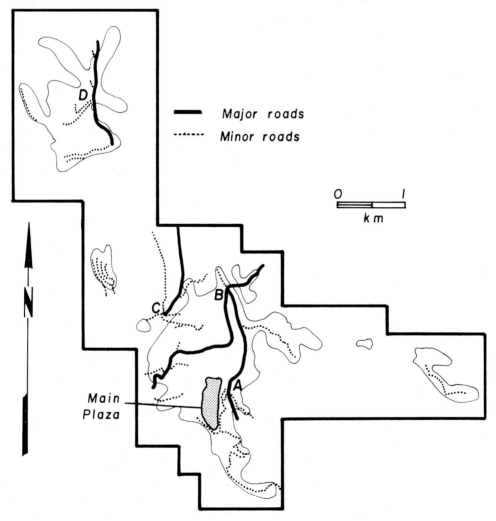

FIGURE 5.3. The network of roads at Monte Albán during Period IIIb, showing nodes of high accessibility. (Redrawn, with modifications, from Blanton 1978.)

two near the northern corners of the South Platform. Not one of these is near a major road. It seems likely, therefore, that the Main Plaza was a largely closed area, access to which could have been easily regulated.

Three localities in the site (A, B, and C in Figure 5.3) were "nodes" in the city's road system where several roads join, implying a high degree of accessibility at that point. Points A and C are lesser nodes, where one or two major roads join one or two minor roads. Node B is the point of highest accessibility at Monte Albán, where three major roads and

one minor road join. Again, in contrast to the predictions one would make concerning the road network of a market center, Node B is not near the city's center, adjacent to a market-like feature. Instead, it is located near the very edge of the city, in an area that is not even particularly densely occupied. The nature of the road network, in combination with the relatively little evidence for specialized production, tends to support the hypothesis that Monte Albán was a center of regional decision making and religious ritual, but not a commercial center.

# TOPIC 40
## Functional Analysis of Architecture at Monte Albán

DONALD ROBERTSON

In contrast to the fragmentary data from earlier periods, during Monte Albán III one can see the evolution of a hierarchy of architectural form (Figure 4.12). The danzantes wall today seems to link two buildings as a retaining wall for a low platform of earth, although it was originally a wall with a series of façade sculptures for the original Building of the Danzantes, now partly buried within the present-day danzantes pyramid structure and only partly visible. At a later time, front platforms linked to the main pyramid behind by two parallel walls were added to both Building M and System IV. The front lines of these two addenda are still linked by what we call the "Second Wall." This second wall marks a change in level of the great plaza at Monte Albán, since it separates the slightly lower Main Plaza from the somewhat higher surface on which Building M, the danzantes pyramid, and System IV now rest. It serves the formal function of separating a subarea of the Main Plaza from the west side of the plaza and probably fulfilled this function even more efficiently originally when it was stuccoed over (and possibly painted in contrasting colors).

The wall also fulfilled the function of narrowing the space between the western edge of the plaza and the central spine of buildings. An overall reason for this narrowing of the west side is that it gives the whole plaza, when seen from the North or South Platforms, a greater degree of symmetry by visually pulling the west side in closer to the center, which is implicit in the "spine" group of buildings. The deviation of the central axis where it cuts the North Platform is concealed from the sunken plaza of the North Platform by the great portico. The jog in the center line of the two stairs entering it is an indication that such a compositional device was a consideration in the later rebuilding of the site.

The foreplatforms or mounds for Building M and System IV with the walls connecting them to the existing pyramids create not only a closure of space in the Main Plaza but also enclose plazas of their own which give the effect of being sunken plazas; the low platforms in each, reflecting the adoratory of the North Platform, give to these "sunken plazas" the effect of enclosed spaces—almost outdoor antechambers

or vestibules of enormous size, if that is what their role is—with a central focal point. Each pyramid, then, is the towering raison d'être for its sunken plaza revolving around a low platform.

Where and how were rites performed? On the basis of later Aztec-period accounts, sacrifice took place on the main platform in front of the temple proper. Other sequential rites were performed within the temple. Is the low "dance platform," as it is sometimes called, also a place for sacrifice, or is sacrifice limited to the space in front of temple and image, and the low platform the locus of another, additional preparatory state in rite and ritual? In other words, we do not know the function of the low platforms.

At least the hierarchy of architectural form at Classic Monte Albán is quite clear. In terms of architecture, the central spine (Buildings G, H, I, and J) is to the Main Plaza as the central adoratory is to the sunken plaza of the North Platform, and as the central platforms are to the enclosed patios of Systems IV and M. As we look at the site now, we can see this relationship quite clearly as a repetition of a motif either from a small scale to a larger one, or from a larger scale to a smaller one. Probably in terms of the history of the site the second sequence is more likely. A question probably not answerable is whether the Zapotec were conscious of this hierarchy of form; that is, was it planned, or is it merely the consequence of a Zapotec "way of thinking" that in more than one situation arrived at similar solutions to similar architectural problems?

Another possible explanation is that there is a coincidence at work here. The buildings of the central spine function not as platforms in the center of a sunken plaza fronting a major temple, but are placed there for other reasons, such as the rocky ridge underlying them, according to Bernal's master's thesis (1946). The ritual explanation may very well link the architectural program of the sunken plaza of the North Platform and the buildings of Systems M and IV of the west side of the group of buildings.

TOPIC 41

## The Legacy of the Early Urban Period: An Ethnohistoric Approach to Monte Albán's Temples, Residences, and Royal Tombs

KENT V. FLANNERY

In previous chapters we have discussed those aspects of Zapotec culture that may be legacies from the Preceramic and Formative periods. It is now time to consider the legacy of the so-called Classic or Early Urban period in the Valley of Oaxaca.

Judged by any criteria available to the archaeologist, the early Zapotec state was at the height of its power during Monte Albán III. Public construction reached its apogee late in Period III, and most of the reconstructed or consolidated buildings the tourist sees at the site today date from that period. Whether by spectacular internal growth or deliberate urban nucleation, the city achieved its maximum population in Period IIIb. Evidently unassailable because of its increased size, it expanded well beyond the limits of its earlier defensive walls.

It is likely that during Monte Albán III a great many of the trappings of Zapotec statehood became formalized. Such institutions as kingship, state religion, and a professional ruling class—already suggested for Monte Albán II—became unmistakably clear during Period III. In this topic I will briefly discuss a series of Zapotec sociopolitical institutions that were described by the early Spanish ethnohistorians (del Paso y Troncoso 1905; Córdova 1578a, 1578b; Burgoa 1670, 1674). I will then suggest the ways in which such institutions ought to be manifested archaeologically. Finally, I will point to a series of archaeological features from Monte Albán III that probably reflect early versions of those institutions. I should add that I would not even attempt this reconstruction were the archaeological continuity in the Valley of Oaxaca not so remarkable.

## THE TEMPLE AND THE PRIESTHOOD

Among the sixteenth-century Zapotec the temple was known as *yohopèe* (from *yoho*, "house" and *pèe*, "wind, breath, or spirit"). Such temples were manned by full-time "priests" called *copa pitào* or *bigaña*, who spent a great deal of their time in the inner room of the *yohopèe*; in addition, there was a "high priest" called a *uija-tào* (Marcus 1978). Church and state were only partially separated, since priests were recruited from the families of the nobility, and the Zapotec lord himself underwent a year of religious training before taking office.

Since we have already discussed the initial appearance of the standard two-room Zapotec temple (Chapter 4), I will simply note here that it is widespread at Monte Albán during Period III. Among the most striking are the three temples on Buildings G, H, and I in the center of the Main Plaza (Figure 4.12), but there are numerous examples elsewhere on the site. Excavations at Monte Albán also produced a series of earthenware or stone models of Period III temples that show the type of roof used (Acosta 1965:Fig. 25). The models depict a flat roof constructed on a center-beam base supported by large transverse timbers or rafters of wood; the front side of the roof was decorated with a type of panel called a *doble escapulario,* formed by an overlapping set of rectangular *tableros* in two planes.

The largest single pyramidal structure ever destined for the support of a temple at Monte Albán was the South Platform, which is believed to have been built entirely during Monte Albán IIIa (Acosta n.d.b). Poorly preserved remains of two structures on its summit have never been fully investigated, but their shape and steepness suggest temple mounds. In addition, the South Platform has an important series of carved stones and dedicatory caches, described by Marcus (Topic 53). Some of these carvings link Monte Albán and Teotihuacán, a topic which we have chosen to defer until the next section of the book.

One topic that has never been rigorously investigated by Oaxaca archaeologists is exactly how one would distinguish the burial of a "priest" from that of a "lord". There are occasional tombs below the floors of some temples (e.g., Building H); however, we do not have published data on the layout and contents of an adequate sample of such tombs, nor are there enough of them to account for all the *copa pitào* and *bigaña* who staffed the numerous temples. Moreover, the ethnohistoric documents dwell on the burials of the Zapotec lords and on the honoring and curating of their remains, providing little or no comparable data on priests.

## THE MAIN PLAZA

The *copa pitào* and *bigaña* conducted much of the temple business; the Zapotec also held public religious ceremonies that involved fasting, sacrifices, ritual bloodletting, dancing, and the taking of drugs or intoxicating drinks like pulque. These rituals were generally held near the temple, and even if we allow for a certain amount of exaggeration and disapproval from the sixteenth-century chroniclers, they must have been spectacular. The Zapotec of Teotitlán del Valle are described as sacrificing children, drinking, and dancing at night (Asensio 1580b). Inhabitants of Macuilxochitl are described as fasting for periods of 40 or 80 days, while taking tobacco every 4 days; they drew blood from their tongue and ears, danced, and became intoxicated (Asensio 1580a). At Teitipac, sacrifices of dogs and slaves were followed by dances and the eating of hallucinogenic mushrooms "so that they saw many visions and frightful figures" (Pérez de Zamora 1580).

The great concentration of temples in Monte Albán's Main Plaza suggests that it was a likely spot for such ceremonies. Several of the temples have altars or adoratories in front of them where various rituals could have been performed in full view of the public. Blanton's analysis of Monte Albán's road system, however, shows that the Main Plaza was in an area of relatively low accessibility. Furthermore, new construction during Periods IIIa and IIIb reduced entry into the Main Plaza, restricting it to gaps at the four corners. Participants at the Santa Fe seminar did not agree on what this meant. Some felt that Zapotec commoners might seldom have reached the Main Plaza; others argued that there would be little reason to build a 300 by 150 m plaza except to accommodate hundreds of visitors. A compromise position (which fits reasonably well with the ethnohistoric sources) would see the Main Plaza as a place to which access would ordinarily have been restricted, but to which thousands might have been admitted on the day of a formal, state-sanctioned event. As for how many persons might have fit comfortably in the Main Plaza, my estimate would be approximately 15,000.[1]

## RESIDENCES

Winter (1974) has proposed a typology of Period III residences at Monte Albán, based on the size of the patio in square meters; in a sample of 14 "household clusters," he detected three modal patio sizes. Blanton's measurement of a sample of more than 80 residences shows at least six modes, however, suggesting more variation than Winter's sample (Blanton 1978:96–98, Figs. 4.46–4.47).

In fact, there are additional reasons for not using Winter's typology. In Topic 11, we have already suggested that the term *household cluster* be rephrased *household unit* and restricted to the Early and Middle Formative; the term loses its utility when one stretches it so painfully on the Procrustean bed of the Classic, applying it to minor palaces and even to the buildings which the Zapotec erected as memorials over royal tombs. In the second place, to be truly useful such a typology should take into account what is known ethnohistorically about Zapotec residences. An approach based purely on patio size (however appropriate it might be for the discovery of modal sizes in a population of buildings) lacks a perspective based on Zapotec social organization. In this chap-

ter, therefore, we will begin with what was known about Zapotec status and residence at the time of the Conquest.

There were only two class-endogamous social strata in Zapotec society, though each stratum had its subdivisions. The upper stratum, a professional ruling class, might be conceived of as including royalty and hereditary nobility. The lord was referred to as a *coqui,* his lady as *xonaxi.* Augmentative suffixes of various kinds were used to distinguish a *coquitao,* "great lord," "king," or *coquihualao,* "prince". A minor noble might be referred to as a *xoana,* "hidalgo." The lower stratum of society consisted of free commoners, servants, or slaves. Terms of respect among commoners included *peni coxana,* "male household head," and *golaba* or "lord's solicitor," probably to be interpreted as an appointed "barrio head."

Ethnohistoric sources indicate the Zapotec had a graded hierarchy of residences, based on the status of the occupant; these residences should provide the archaeological manifestations of the various statuses. Ordinary Zapotecs lived in a simple house called a *yoho* or *yo'o.* A *coqui* or lord resided in a *quehui* or *yoho quehui,* "casa real," probably to be considered a minor palace. The *coquitao* or supreme ruler lived in a *quihuitao* (quehui + augmentative), "palacio real hermoso" (Córdova 1578a). This major palace was as much a place for conducting the affairs of state as a royal residence. The building went with the office of king, and served for many generations. Hence, the Zapotec king was not buried under the floor of the *quihuitao,* just as the President of the United States is not buried in the White House. As Caso (probably relying on the accounts of Father Burgoa) was fond of pointing out, Zapotec rulers were taken to special places deemed appropriate for burial; there they were laid to rest in tombs already prepared during their lifetimes, possibly even under their own supervision. Major masonry structures were built over these tombs; some were temples, but others took the form of small palaces. The latter have contributed to some confusion over which "palaces" are actual residences, and which are buildings designed to commemorate the ruler.

## THE *QUIHUITAO*

Where, precisely, was the *quihuitao* of the paramount ruler at Monte Albán? The question is not easily answered. We must identify a massive palace with room for conducting the affairs of state, a building whose construction required both architects and corvée labor, and whose location suggests both high status and restricted access. Based on the location of the Period II palace on Mound 8 at San José Mogote, the most likely place to look on Monte Albán is the North Platform.

One possibility that presents itself immediately is the so-called Patio Hundido, a massive sunken patio separated from the Main Plaza by an immense staircase and a hall whose roof was once supported by four pilasters and six

---

[1]This estimate is based on the official statistics for Band Day at the University of Michigan football stadium, October 2, 1976. On that day, 13,000 high-school musicians (some with large tubas) fit comfortably on a football field that is somewhat smaller than Monte Albán's Main Plaza.

pairs of massive columns (Figure 4.12; see also Blanton
1978:Plate 7 and Paddock 1966a:Figs. 154, 165). This patio, which contains a small adoratory, is virtually all that
remains of a very large building whose upper walls (presumably of adobe) have since been destroyed, and which has
since been covered by a few later constructions. Its stairway
and colonnaded hall are reminiscent not only of Structure 17
at San José Mogote, but also of the later "palace" at Mitla,
which the sixteenth-century chroniclers describe as the place
where the local lord conducted his affairs of state (see Topic
88). Almost immediately behind the Patio Hundido is a
smaller patio surrounded by temples,[2] a spot which Blanton's ekistic study suggests was the least accessible single
locality at Monte Albán (Blanton 1978:61–63). The
Zapotec ruler is known to have had a temple (or temples) for
his private ritual activities. This complex of elite residences
and limited-access temples may therefore be the inner sanctum of political and religious authority at Monte Albán, a
place of residence and worship for the *coquitao*.

Hartung (1974:16) gives the dimensions of the great stairway leading to the Patio Hundido as 40 m in width with
balustrades 12 m wide to either side. The sunken patio is
more than 50 m across and so deep (4 m) that no one inside it
could be seen from the Main Plaza. Other residences of relatively limited access occur next to the temple patio already
mentioned and in the nearby Patio al Sur de Montículo A,
where Caso's important stratigraphic excavations were carried out (see Topic 22).

## THE *QUEHUI* OR *CASA REAL*

Far more common at Monte Albán are smaller stone-
masonry "palaces," each representing a single building divided into a series of rooms around a plastered interior patio. Typical features are L-shaped corner rooms with sleeping
benches and a curtain wall behind the doorway that provides privacy by screening the interior of the residence from
view.

One important *casa real* is Building S, on the east side of
the Main Plaza between two temples (Buildings P and Q).
Often referred to simply as El Palacio, it consists of a residence 25 m on a side, divided originally into 10 to 12 rooms
arranged around a central patio (Figure 5.4). The curtain

<hr>

[2]There is some disagreement between Blanton's interpretation of this small
patio (D in Blanton 1978:Fig. 4.3) and mine. He tentatively identifies it as an
elite residence because of its "closed" nature, but I know of no Zapotec elite
residence composed of three small steep-sided pyramids, such as these
(Mounds d, e, and g in Fig. 4.12, this volume). On the other hand, we have
numerous examples of small, "closed" patios with three steep temple pyramids. Furthermore, the buildings atop Mounds d, e, and g have been excavated, and appear to be typical small temples with columns *in antis* (see photo
in Paddock 1966a:Fig. 170); one of them, Mound g, had an important offering in its fill like those in some Cuilapan temples (see Topic 61). I would
therefore interpret Blanton's locality D as the temple group reserved for the
ruler and his family (logically, the area of least accessibility on the site), and
Blanton's locality H (the Patio Hundido) as the surviving remnant of the
ruler's actual palace.

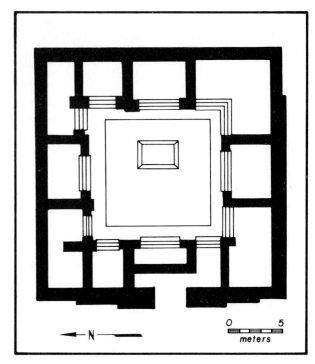

FIGURE 5.4. Building S, a major palace in the Main Plaza at
Monte Albán.

wall, sleeping benches, and L-shaped corner rooms are all
familiar features; some small rooms in palaces of this type
appear to be kitchens, but any functional interpretations are
hampered by the fragmentary nature of the published data.
That Building S went with an "office" (rather than an individual) is suggested by the fact that it has no tomb.

A smaller structure atop Building L, across the Main Plaza
from S, may also be a residence. Flanked as it is by temples, it
raises the question of whether some major priests had houses
adjacent to the temples they used, as seems to have been the
case at Postclassic Mitla (See Topic 88).

## ROYAL TOMBS

The treatment of deceased rulers at Monte Albán invites
comparison with the sixteenth-century descriptions of
Zapotec religion (see Topic 97 and Marcus 1978). The
Zapotec believed that a dead ruler continued to influence the
affairs of his royal descendants as well as his subjects because he became a venerated intermediary between mortal
men and the great supernatural forces on whom they depended. A dead king became not merely a "cloud person,"
but the most influential kind of cloud person. If properly
taken care of by his descendants, he could intercede on their
behalf with the sacred lightning.

One of the favorite localities for royal burial was a series
of ridges and promontories to the north of the Main Plaza at

Monte Albán, including the picturesque settings referred to by Caso and Acosta as "El Cementerio Norte" and "El Patio de las Tumbas." Each of the royal tombs was associated with a building, and Acosta's careful attention to architectural detail revealed that in each case the tomb was constructed first. Frequently excavating into bedrock, the architects laid out a main chamber, an antechamber, and a stairway ascending to the level where the patio was to be; heavy masonry construction ensured that the tomb would not collapse under the weight of the building above.

Over Tomb 7, originally constructed in Period IIIb, the architects built a standard *yohopèe* or two-room Zapotec temple (Acosta 1965:Fig. 24), suggesting that perhaps the temple was intended as a living memorial or shrine to the original Period IIIb tomb occupant(s).[3] Over Tombs 104 and 105, however (see Figure 5.5), the architects constructed small Period III style "palaces" (*quehui*), complete with stuccoed patio, L-shaped corner rooms, and curtain wall (Caso 1938:*Planos* 13, 18). It may be that in this case the descendants of the ruler were to continue to live directly over his tomb and take care of his remains.

In the case of some tombs (e.g., Tomb 104), only a single skeleton was discovered. Other tombs (e.g., Tomb 103) contained two adults, perhaps a conjugal pair. Still others (especially tombs with a cruciform shape) seem to have been veritable ossuaries, the final resting place for dozens of secondary burials. This variability suggests that the burial program at Monte Albán was a complex one, involving stages of burial and reburial which have never been adequately analyzed, and perhaps including not only the ruler but his wives, relatives, servants, and retainers. Moreover, we cannot be sure that the tombs of the most important rulers at Monte Albán have been found. Perhaps a study of qualitative skeletal characters like that carried out by Michael Spence (1976) at Teotihuacán could shed light on family relationships within the population of skeletons.

Some tombs are decorated with mural paintings, and many are accompanied by the typical Zapotec "funerary urn" of the Classic period. While both urns and murals have usually been assumed to depict "gods" (see Caso 1938), this interpretation is now largely abandoned by Marcus (Topic 43). Noting that no known Zapotec "deity" had a name taken from the 260-day calendar, she interprets the personages so named in tomb murals as actual members of the nobility. Much the same can be said of the urns, many of which also have calendric names. The vast majority, although sometimes wearing masks which suggest *Cocijo* or some other supernatural force, appear distinctly human behind the masks; many may well be ancestors of the deceased who were already serving as intermediaries. Finally, the buildings over many tombs have later offerings which suggest that rituals associated with deceased lords continued long after their interment.

Intriguing questions remain to be answered about the

---

[3]Tomb 7 was, of course, later reused during Monte Albán V (see Topic 82).

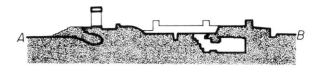

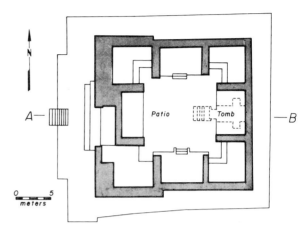

FIGURE 5.5. Tomb 105 and the small "palace" (possibly a commemorative building) above it at Monte Albán: top, cross-section of building and tomb; bottom, plan of building. (Redrawn from Caso 1938.)

buildings over royal tombs such as Tomb 103, 104, and 105. Since we know the tombs were built first, is it possible they were purely commemorative structures which were never lived in at all? Alternatively, did the dead rulers' descendants continue to live in the structure as curators of his remains? Were these the residences of Zapotec lords who ordered their own tombs to be built, as an integral part of the house, long before their death? Or were these "second residences" maintained by Zapotec lords who spent part of their time in the *quihuitao,* in the manner of the later Mixtec kings?

## *YOHO:* ORDINARY RESIDENCES OF PERIOD III

Little is known of the households of Monte Albán's lower-status residents. Winter's excavations in the Terrace 634–636 area, a kilometer northwest of the Main Plaza, revealed three Period IIIb households "spaced about 25 m. apart on separate terraces" (Winter 1974:983). One of these households (Figure 5.6) is reconstructed as a series of four rooms (3–4 m on a side); four burials in slab-lined graves occurred under the floor of one room (Winter 1974:Fig. 3). While some lower-status houses had adobe walls over a boulder foundation, others were evidently of more ephemeral materials like cane or wattle-and-daub.

Two oven-like features also discovered in the Terrace 634–636 area are interpreted as pottery kilns for the manufacture of Period IIIb pottery types G-35 and K-14 (Winter and Payne 1976). The presence of these kilns, coupled with a

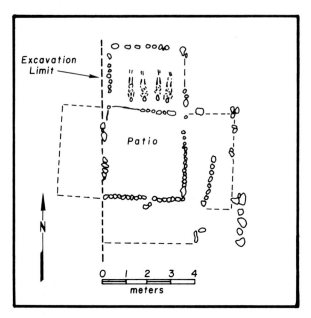

FIGURE 5.6. Monte Albán IIIb residence in Terrace 634–636 area, 1 km from the Main Plaza. (Redrawn from Winter 1974.)

lack of storage facilities for agricultural products, suggests to Winter (1974:986) that some of Monte Albán's lower-status residents were more heavily engaged in craft activities than in food production. If so, it is significant that this craft activity seems to have involved small individual households, rather than the huge industrialized compounds seen at Teotihuacán (R. Millon 1973).

## RELATIVE PROPORTIONS OF ELITE AND COMMONER RESIDENCES

Blanton (Topic 39) has estimated that during Period IIIb, there were approximately 57 "elaborate residences" at Monte Albán as opposed to approximately 2899 "non-elaborate residences". Assuming that Blanton's elaborate residences correspond to the ethnohistoric quehui and his nonelaborate residences to yoho, we might conclude that only 2% of Monte Albán's households belonged to the hereditary nobility. If we accept Blanton's estimates of 5 to 10 persons per nonelaborate household and 10 to 20 persons per elaborate household, however, we might conclude that up to 4% of the city's population belonged to the hereditary nobility. Obviously such figures are only crude estimates, but they are interesting nonetheless.

## THE LEGACY OF MONTE ALBÁN III

To summarize, the cultural legacy of Monte Albán III almost certainly included a society with two class-endo-

gamous strata. The upper stratum, constituting perhaps 2–4% of the population, was the forerunner of the sixteenth-century coqui and xoana. Most resided in stone or adobe palaces equivalent to the sixteenth-century quehui; the supreme ruler conducted the affairs of state in a huge palace (quihuitao). Rulers and major nobles were buried in elegant tombs below buildings in which offerings continued to be made long after their death; some of these buildings were actually two-room temples in the manner of the sixteenth-century yohopèe, while others have a residential layout.

The lower stratum of society, constituting perhaps 96–98% of the population, included the commoners. They lived in smaller houses of adobe or wattle-and-daub which were the forerunners of the sixteenth-century yoho; they were buried not in elegant tombs but in simple pits or slab-lined graves beneath the floor. According to Blanton's surveys, the urban commoners of Monte Albán may have been divided into some 14 residential wards, each with its own small area of ceremonial structures (Blanton 1978:65–93). Future excavators should attempt to determine if those wards were each headed by a golaba as were the barrios of the sixteenth-century Zapotec.

Since this book went to press, Wilkinson and Norelli (1981) have examined 321 skeletons from Monte Albán and could find no significant genetic differences between those they consider high-status and those they consider low-status. From this they conclude that class endogamy was unlikely. While I have the utmost respect for the authors as physical anthropologists (indeed, much of what we know of Formative Oaxaca depends on Wilkinson's aging and sexing of burials), I cannot agree with their "cultural" conclusions because they rest on the questionable assumption that class endogamy will be reflected in two archaeologically detectable, genetically different populations. We know from the ethnohistoric documents that the Zapotec nobility, while class endogamous, were not community endogamous; they married nobility from other towns and other regions, and even Mixtecs and Aztecs (see Chapter 8b). The lower stratum included genetically diverse peoples as well, including slaves taken in combat with other regions. We also know that Zapotec rulers were buried with servants, retainers, even slaves; thus we cannot even guarantee that a given skeleton (or more frequently, fragment of skeleton) from a "royal" tomb is actually that of a royal person. We have already presented evidence that ascribed status existed in Oaxaca even before Monte Albán was founded; I have little doubt that Classic Monte Albán, with its palaces, royal tombs, and genealogical inscriptions, had a two-stratum society like that of all well-known Mesoamerican states. In my opinion, what Wilkinson and Norelli's interesting analysis shows us is that class endogamy is an emic ideal; in etic terms, there was gene flow among classes and among regions. After all, Prince Charles and Princess Diana are class endogamous, but it is doubtful their skeletons would show significant differences from the rest of the British population.

# TOPIC 42
## Stone Monuments and Tomb Murals of Monte Albán IIIa

JOYCE MARCUS

In this topic I will discuss those stone monuments and tomb murals that date to Period III, the peak of urban occupation at Monte Albán. There are a number of ways in which the information contained in these paintings and inscriptions supplements our other data from Monte Albán.

Stone monuments of Period IIIa continue to depict the themes of militarism and conquest seen in Periods I and II, but frequently they contain more hieroglyphic information than the monuments of earlier periods. Tomb murals, however, seem to deal with the royal relatives and ancestors of the tomb occupants. They include our first examples of the element which Caso has called the *fauces del cielo*, the "Jaws of the Sky," which in later periods seems to have been used to indicate noble descent. For example, in the genealogical registers of Period IV (Topic 59), the venerated ancestors of royal marriage partners are shown emerging from the "Jaws of the Sky." Also, the tomb murals include personages whose names are taken from the 260-day calendar; for the reasons given in Topic 97, these figures can be interpreted as actual human beings, presumably ancestors of the tomb occupant(s), because no known Zapotec "deity" had a calendric name.

## STONE MONUMENTS OF PERIOD IIIA

Approximately 15 stone monuments from Monte Albán can be assigned to Period IIIa. By far the majority of these were discovered in and around the South Platform, an immense structure which constitutes the southern border of the Main Plaza. It appears that most of these were set vertically in the building as orthostats. Eight numbered stelae were associated with the four corners of the building, as shown in Figure 4.12. The outer faces of six of these monuments apparently depict bound, high-status captives standing atop "hill glyphs" that presumably indicate their place of origin. The two other numbered stelae portray elegantly dressed persons wielding lances; they are presumably local Zapotec lords, whose portrayal contrasts with that of the six figures with their arms tied behind their backs. A ninth monument, erroneously called the Estela Lisa or "plain (uncarved) stela," accompanies these monuments but has never been given a number.

In this topic, I consider only the faces of these monuments, which apparently depict Period IIIa rulers and their captives and conquests. In Topic 53 I deal with the inscriptions on the edges of these same monuments, which are more appropri-

ately treated in the chapter on Monte Albán and Teotihuacán.

Those monuments displaying bound captives are Stelae 2, 3, 5, 6, 7, and 8 (Caso 1928; Marcus 1976d). Stela 2 (Figure 5.7; also Caso 1928:Figs. 27, 28) depicts an individual dressed as a jaguar, standing on a hill sign which apparently includes the number 3 among other elements. Caso (1928:81) interpreted this figure as a "god" with the name "3 Jaguar;" but an alternative interpretation can be offered. As explained more fully in Topic 43, the Zapotec did not have deities with names taken from the 260-day calendar; such names were for human beings. Second, it seems more likely that the name of a place is to be found set within the hill sign, while the name of the individual is to be found in the adjacent column of hieroglyphs.

The inscription begins with a glyph defined by Caso (1928) as the "year sign," containing the day 13 Turquoise (Caso's "Glyph E"). The appearance of the three dots below the bar in the number 13 is characteristic of Monte Albán IIIa; in Monte Albán I and II, the numerical coefficients had been carved with the dots above the bar. This is, however, only one reason for assigning these monuments to Monte Albán IIIa; the caches of Period IIIa ceramic offerings at the corners of the South Platform (see Topic 53) provide an additional line of evidence for assigning these sculptures to that phase.

The text on Stela 2 continues with the name of the individual enclosed within a three-quarter cartouche, the jaguar glyph replicating the pictorial information. Below the name of the individual we see two footprints, perhaps suggesting the travel of this jaguar-costumed individual to Monte Albán on the day which follows, 3 Knot (Caso's "Glyph A"). The text continues on the right side of the monument with a day of 13 Owl, and ends with the *bolsa* glyph.

Stela 3 (Figure 5.7; see also Caso 1928:Figs. 31, 32) also displays a bound captive dressed as an animal. In this case the identification of the animal is uncertain, but Caso (1928:82) suggests a coyote or opossum. The text begins with a year sign and numerical coefficient of 10; a footprint is also included in this text in conjunction with a conch shell (trumpet?). The similarities of this monument to Stela 2 are interesting to note. Both figures are completely outfitted as animals, with masks, long tails, elaborate headdresses, and with arms bound behind the back with cord; in both cases there is an association with footprints and similar hill signs or place glyphs.

The other monuments that display bound captives (Stelae 5–8) show men with their arms similarly bound behind their back, but not dressed in animal costumes. All stand on different hill signs, none of which matches the places that were

FIGURE 5.7. Stela 2 (left) and Stela 3 (right) from Monte Albán. (Drawings by Mark Orsen.)

subjugated by Monte Albán during Period II (see Topic 29). Thus, the themes of conquest and capture persist, but different places are involved, and the captives appear to be named lords or nobility.

There are other important Monte Albán IIIa monuments that do not display bound captives, however. For example, Stela 1 in the same building may depict a local Zapotec ruler with elaborate headdress, wielding a lance. This lord is shown seated upon a jaguar cushion that rests on a combination throne and place sign. At the base of the throne are two long-nosed profile heads which Caso calls "*rostros de Cocijos*," showing the earplug common to both (Figure 5.8).

The associated double-column text (Caso 1928:Fig. 26) is extremely important not only because it is quite lengthy but also because it includes many new noncalendric glyphs. Both columns of text terminate with the *bolsa* or "tied pouch" glyph, which frequently ends inscriptions; the two texts, therefore, are probably to be read individually, from top to bottom. Column A includes a glyph similar to Caso's Glyph E, which appears to be tied up; the next may be an event glyph including a heart and two flint knives perhaps recording a sacrifice; at A3 we see possibly another small flint

knife; at A4, the day of the event is given as 7 Knot (Caso's "Glyph A"). The next compound glyph at A5–6 combines the sky sign (called *narices del tigre* by Caso) with an ornate speech scroll and an outstretched hand—probably a verb of action.

Column B begins with an 8 Sky sign as a prefix to the year sign; the numerical coefficient 8 is shown as a prefix with the dots to the left of the vertical bar, as the Classic period Maya would have done it. A compound glyph also appears at B2–3 using Caso's Glyph E as the body of an animal; in this case, Caso felt Glyph E was to be interpreted as "the sun." At B4–5 we see two footprints and the expression 12 Jaguar, a possible name for the Zapotec lord depicted to the left. At B6 we see two clasped hands, followed by a year sign with the coefficient 5 (at B7). At B8 we see a temple with (perhaps) an offering in front of it. By B9 we have the day-name 8 Water or Vessel, and as with Column A the text closes with a *bolsa* or tied pouch.

Another apparent portrayal of a local Zapotec ruler is Stela 4 (Caso 1928:Figs. 33, 34). This lord is shown with an elaborate headdress, holding a knife in his right hand and a lance in his left; on the left is the hieroglyphic name 8 Deer.

FIGURE 5.8. Stela 1 from Monte Albán. (Drawing by Mark Orsen.)

Unfortunately, the identity of the place that this lord stands on (or is "conquering") is unknown. The intent may be to show the lance entering the hill sign, perhaps conveying the act of subjugation of a specific place. Below the name 8 Deer[1] there is a footprint, once again suggesting travel.

Stela 11 (Caso 1928:Figs. 56–58) may also show a local Zapotec lord beneath the symbol Caso called the *fauces del cielo;* this lord holds in his left hand a fish or turtle head, which elsewhere forms part of an important hieroglyph (e.g., Stela 6, both in position A2, and the last glyph on the left side). As in Stela 2, the name of the individual seems to appear in a cartouche. Again, the name of the hill sign is uncertain (it encloses a possible face, while to the right of the hill sign a large mandible protrudes). Thus, the place glyphs shown on Stelae 1, 4, and 11 all appear to be different.

One of the important characteristics of these South Platform stelae is their size; for example, Stela 1 is more than 2 m high, in striking contrast to the later "genealogical registers"

of Period IIIb–IV (Topic 59), which are much smaller. Stela 11 shares with these later genealogical registers the *fauces del cielo,* which seems to be associated with persons of royal descent, but in general respects the Period IIIa monuments continue the themes of capture and conquest seen in earlier periods rather than the themes of marriage and descent typical of Periods IIIb–IV.

## TOMB MURALS OF PERIOD III

Although earlier types of tombs continued to be used during Monte Albán III, this period also saw the introduction of a new type of tomb with a cruciform ground plan. Acosta (1965:829) suggests that this cruciform plan may have evolved from a tomb type with large wall recesses or niches which appeared during Monte Albán II. One way in which some of these cruciform tombs stand out from others is by the unusually large numbers of burials they often contain. Both Caso and Acosta have described them as "veritable ossuaries," perhaps family tombs in which many members

---

[1]This individual 8 Deer should not be confused with the Mixtec ruler 8 Deer "Tiger Claw" of the eleventh century (see Chapter 8).

of the same family ultimately were interred, either as primary or secondary burials.

In Topic 41, Flannery suggests that some important Zapotec lords were taken to special places for burial, and interred there in previously prepared tombs over which commemorative buildings were erected. Some of these commemorative buildings have the ground plan of minor palaces or *quehui*, with a large tomb under the floor of one room usually reached by a stairway from the patio. Many of these tombs are cruciform, and all appear to have been constructed (or sometimes excavated into bedrock) before the building above. Presumably the entryway through the patio was left accessible so that relatives could be interred later.

Some of the most elegant of these tombs occur to the northwest of the North Platform, in an area with a high concentration of elite residences and/or commemorative buildings. Two of the most famous are Tombs 104 and 105, both dating to Period III and both containing murals that seem to portray the royal ancestors of the deceased. Evidently such tombs were commissioned prior to the death of a lord or his royal family, for some were never used.

## Tomb 104

The façade of this tomb is very elaborate, including a niche in the center supporting a large urn (Caso 1938:Fig. 92). The figure on the urn has a headdress containing two jaguar heads and feathers, wears huge ear plugs and a large pectoral with shells, and carries a copal bag in one hand; another jaguar forms part of the pedestal beneath.

The tomb door was carved both inside and outside. Caso (1938:76) concluded that the inside carving was contemporaneous with Tomb 104, whereas the carvings on the outside of the door had been carved at an earlier time; therefore, this particular tomb door was reused and recarved. Its interior side (Caso 1938:Fig. 94) shares some of the hieroglyphs with the murals painted on the inside of the tomb.

On the right side of the interior inscription appear the glyph for the year 6 Turquoise, Caso's "Glyph I," and a small "figurine" of stone; on the left side appears the glyph for the year 7 Deer. To the far left we have 6 Serpent; below that is 7 Glyph I, four small cartouches with a postfix (?) of 15 (three bars), and another glyph with the subfix of 7. In the central part of this slab we have a footprint at the very top, below that the abbreviated Sky Symbol, and to the right, 5 Turquoise. Below those two glyphs we have the lower half of a face or mask in profile, and then the important glyph 1 Serpent above a box-like symbol.

There are some five niches inside the tomb, two on the side walls and the other three lined up on the back wall, with one of these in the center and the other two at the corners (Caso 1938:*Plano* 17). Four of these niches contained ceramic offerings, and the famous mural appears on the wall of this chamber. The mural painter began by producing an outline of the design on the wall with diluted red paint (Caso 1965b:862). Later, the areas were filled in with various col-

ors and finished by applying black lines to separate these colored areas (Figure 5.9; also Caso 1938:*Lám.* 1).

At the left (south side) of the mural is a male figure holding a bag in one hand, with the other hand extended; his peaked (possibly cotton) hat and feathered headdress are somewhat unusual. Above the niche is perhaps a box painted in red, white, and green with a parrot standing atop it. Next we encounter two hieroglyphs plus numerical coefficients—2 Serpent (?) and 5 Serpent—over another box. On the back wall, all three niches have red spots in or above them. Along the back wall we also have the glyph 5 Turquoise, which we saw in the center of the carving on the interior side of the tomb door.

At the very center of the mural appear Caso's *fauces del cielo* with the *narices del tigre* above them. The central face is shown frontally, with a subfix of 5 (broken by the central niche). On the right (or north) wall of the tomb there is the calendric name 5 Owl (?); below appears the name 5 (or possibly 7) Thunder (in head form). Over the next niche appears the name 1 Serpent, which was also carved in the lower center on the interior side of the door stone. (Below this glyph is the "treble scroll" discussed in Topic 53 in connection with Stelae 7 and 8 in the South Platform.) Finally, on the far right, we see another figure wearing an elaborate serpent headdress with bifid tongue, holding a bag in his left hand and with his right hand extended. Unlike the mural in Tomb 105, which portrays both men and women in a procession exiting from the tomb, the two human figures shown in the mural of Tomb 104 are both male, and both face inward toward the back wall of the tomb. My suggestion is that both are actual persons, presumably relatives or royal ancestors of the tomb's main occupant.

The repetitions of the date 5 Turquoise (which appears both in the center of the door stone and in the mural on the back wall of the tomb) and the name 1 Serpent (which appears both in the center of the door stone and in the mural over the north niche) are impressive, because this is our only known case where redundancy is introduced into the message by repeating some of the same glyphs on the tomb door as well as in the mural.

## Tomb 105

Tomb 105 is located below a commemorative building at the beginning of the trail leading to the hill called El Plumaje. This building (Figure 5.5) has the classic "small palace" or *quehui* plan, with four large rooms flanking a patio with four rectangular spaces in its corners. Caso (1938) noticed that such buildings were likely to have tombs, and his attention was particularly drawn to the Tomb 105 building because it had an enormous stone lintel and two large stone door jambs which reminded him of the ruins of Mitla.

The four main rooms around the patio were oriented to the four cardinal points. The western room served as the portico which included the huge lintel as its doorway; Tomb 105 was found under the eastern room. Under the floor of

FIGURE 5.9. Mural from Tomb 104, Monte Albán. (Redrawn from Caso 1938:*Lám.* I.)

FIGURE 5.10. Mural from Tomb 105, Monte Albán. (Redrawn from Caso 1938:*Lám.* IV.)

the western room, Caso found a small *Cocijo* urn (see Topic 43) painted red, and other objects including a female figurine of jade in Teotihuacán style (Caso 1938:84).

In the exploration of the patio some offerings were found in the center, placed in a rectangular cavity whose walls were formed by well-dressed stones and which had as its floor the natural bedrock of the hill—an "offering box" not unlike those found beneath the corners of the South Platform (see Topic 53). In this offering were various Monte Albán IIIa vessels called *floreros,* very similar to examples from Teotihuacán (Séjourné 1966b:*Lám.* 2). Caso also found some rectangular vessels, small ollas, and an obsidian knife.

Tomb 105, beneath the eastern room, is a cruciform construction of great dimensions that had, in part, been carved into bedrock. Enormous stones were used to roof it over, forming a flat ceiling. The tomb has a small antechamber which could be entered by a descending stairway of four steps. The tomb had been closed with large stones; its doorway is very low, but once inside, one may stand and walk in the tomb interior, which has a height of 2 m. In the back of the tomb (Caso 1938:Fig. 104) there were two fragments of columns, the partial remains of a human skeleton, and a fragment of worked bone.

With the exception of these skeletal remains, the tomb was practically empty. Initially, it might seem to have been looted; however, Caso argued that the arrangement of the stones that formed the door, their great weight, and the well-preserved stucco over the antechamber made it impossible to believe that the tomb had been opened and looted.

The murals of Tomb 105 (Caso 1938:*Láms.* III, IV), like that of Tomb 104, depict pairs of royal men and women who were presumably related to the occupant. The first royal couple is mentioned over the south jamb, their names given as ♂ 2 Jaguar and ♀ 1 Deer (Caso 1938:*Lám.* II-A). The man is elderly and shown wearing a high turban of jaguar skin, and the woman wears a complicated headdress. Although the north jamb (Caso 1938:*Lám* II-B) is not well preserved, another couple can be seen painted there. Thus, two couples once flanked the entryway into Tomb 105.

Entering the main chamber, one sees that running from the doorway to the rear niche there are, on both sides of the tomb, two more sets of couples shown walking in procession toward the doorway to exit from the tomb. On the north wall, beneath a depiction of the *fauces del cielo,* there are shown (in order, from doorway to niche) (Figure 5.10):

| ♀ 7 Turquoise (Combination of glyphs) | ♂ Glyph J + Glyph E + Turquoise | ♀ 3 Hill (?) Glyph J 1 Water | ♂ Glyph J + Glyph E + 3 (or 8?) Glyph A |
|---|---|---|---|

Note that the two men in this procession have very similar hieroglyphic names composed of "Glyph J" + "Glyph E" + a compound glyph; each carries a lance in his right hand and

a bag in his left. The women wear elaborate headdresses, each one distinctive (as are their names). The men wear sandles, while the women go barefoot.

On the south wall, beneath another depiction of the *fauces del cielo,* we find another series of two royal couples running from doorway to the niche as follows:

| ♂ 3 Monkey + (?) | ♀ 4 Jaguar | ♂ 4 Serpent | ♀ 12 Monkey with serpent tongue |
|---|---|---|---|

As was the case with the north wall, each individual in this procession bears a distinctive hieroglyphic name and headdress. Each male is shown carrying a bag in his right hand; in addition, ♂ 3 Monkey seems to be "divining" with beans or grains, throwing them from his left hand in the manner of some "priests" in the Teotihuacán frescoes (Miller 1973). Since several of the individuals in this procession are shown as elderly, the intent may indeed be to depict ancestors.

The central glyph on the back wall of the tomb may be 13 Death (?); a woman appears to the right of the glyph and a man appears to the left. Thus the back wall provides us with still another couple. The tomb roof is painted red with some black areas, and also displays the ever-present vermilion that Caso (1938:92) associated with funerary symbolism.

## SUMMARY

The royal tombs and tomb murals of Monte Albán III provide us with a number of interesting possibilities. The large numbers of burials in some cruciform tombs, which include both males and females, suggest that in some cases we may be dealing not only with a ruler but a royal marital pair, or several members of a royal family. The *fauces del cielo,* which make their first appearance in Period IIIa, suggest a heightened interest in royal genealogy; the fact that both named men and named women occur beneath the *fauces* suggests that elite descent was bilateral, just as in the case of the sixteenth-century Zapotec. This possibility is reinforced by the high frequency of apparent husband–wife pairs in the mural paintings. In their choice of subject matter (although not in their style), some of these tomb murals anticipate the later Mixtec codices, in which rulers' genealogies were expressed as a series of named ancestors, both male and female. They also anticipate the genealogical registers or marriage slabs of the Monte Albán IIIb–IV period (Topic 59), which represent a real departure from the militaristic themes of the stone monuments of Monte Albán I–IIIa. Possibly, therefore, Period IIIa witnessed a gradual shift of concern from the military exploits of male rulers to a concern with establishing the genealogical credentials of Zapotec royalty, both male and female.

## TOPIC 43
### Rethinking the Zapotec Urn

JOYCE MARCUS

Among the manifestations most frequently cited by scholars as characteristic of Zapotec civilization are the anthropomorphic vessels called Zapotec urns. These urns are distinctive, and are unique within Mesoamerica (Caso and Bernal 1952:9).

During Monte Albán Ia, when small solid figurines were still present but gradually disappearing from the archaeological inventory, there were numerous effigy vessels (Paddock 1966a:Fig. 67), but as yet no true urns. During Periods Ic and early II there were many examples of ollas with effigy faces on one side (Paddock 1966a:Fig. 112) as well as an early form of urn (Fig. 75). During late Monte Albán II, Period IIIa, and Periods IIIb–IV there appeared the "classic" Zapotec urn, which is a cylindrical vessel fronted by a complete human figure (Figure 5.11). I will be concerned with that type of urn in this paper: a vessel with a human effigy of either sex, with variations in such items as (1) headdress, (2) pectoral, (3) mask, (4) object(s) held, and (5) sometimes a calendric name taken from the 260-day calendar.

From the excavations of Saville (1899, 1904), Sologuren (in Saville 1899), Caso (1932a, 1935, 1938), and Caso, Bernal, and Acosta (1967), it is clear that such urns are well represented in tombs. Although for this reason they have been called funerary urns, they occur as offerings in temples and caches as well. Within tombs, urns may be found (1) in the antechamber, (2) in the tomb itself, (3) in the niche above the tomb, or (4) on the floor outside the antechamber; they may frequently be arranged in groups.

Caso and Bernal (1952:10) felt the term *cremation urn* was inadequate or inappropriate, since they never found human bones or ashes within the urns. Usually, they were found empty; occasionally, they were found to contain obsidian knives, beads of greenstone, shells, or animal bones. Caso and Bernal (1952:10) comment that one of the unsolved problems is to find the purpose or function of the urns placed in the tombs, because they so frequently contain nothing. It is possible, they suggest, that they once contained water or organic material which has since disintegrated.

When the urns were used as offerings in temples or caches, they frequently contained the beads and other nonperishables mentioned above. For example, in an offering found in Mound I at Monte Albán, one large urn was full of greenstone figures in Teotihuacán style (Caso 1965a:903).

Although many urns are currently found in museums in Europe, the United States, and Mexico, a much smaller number have been found *in situ* in controlled excavations. When found *in situ* in or around tombs (at places such as Xoxocotlán, Monte Albán, or Cuilapan), there are often several identical urns arranged in a group, frequently appearing to be made from the same mold.

## INTERPRETING THE URNS

The Zapotec urns of Monte Albán III–IV have most frequently been interpreted as "gods." One often hears specific urns referred to as "the rain god," "the maize god," "the goddess 2 J," or "the goddess with a Yalálag headdress." One common type of urn is thought to depict Cocijo ("Lightning"), a powerful Zapotec supernatural.

For various reasons, I would like to present an alternative interpretation, questioning the identification of most urns as "deities." First, the latter is founded on the assumption that the Zapotec had a pantheon of anthropomorphized gods—an assumption I have already questioned (Marcus 1978), and which is more fully explored in Topic 97. Second, I can find no evidence for any Zapotec gods with names taken from the 260-day calendar; such names, according to ethnohistoric sources, were given only to human beings (see following material). In fact, no images were ever made of the Zapotec supreme being, the one supernatural who might be considered a "deity" in our terms. In my opinion, a substantial number of these urns depict humans, probably deceased ancestors of the occupant(s) in the tombs, or persons with masks, showing the attributes associated with great supernatural forces such as lightning.[1] I believe this depiction of deceased ancestors accounts for a third bit of evidence—the fact that the inventory of names varies from period to period and site to site, in a way that would be unlikely if they were indeed deities.

Why have the urns so frequently been interpreted as depicting "gods"? The reasons are historic, and began with the Spanish chroniclers of the sixteenth century. The Spaniards never understood ancestor worship, which was an integral part of Zapotec religion (Topic 97), especially in the case of royal ancestors. The ancestors of royalty were more important than those of ordinary men, for they were thought to have ascended to a position intermediate between man and the supernatural, and had the power to intercede on behalf of the whole Zapotec community. They were commemorated and often sacrificed to (Flannery and Marcus 1976b:381), and their images were frequently kept in temples or other important places. It was the sacred images of deceased rulers which the Spaniards found in so many temples, and which they mistakenly described as "idols" of "gods." Clues to this misidentification can be found in the names they collected for these "deities," which frequently contain garbled versions of the words *coqui* ("male ruler"),

---

[1] It should be borne in mind that while lightning is a "natural" force in our cosmology, it was a great *supernatural* force in the Zapotec cosmos.

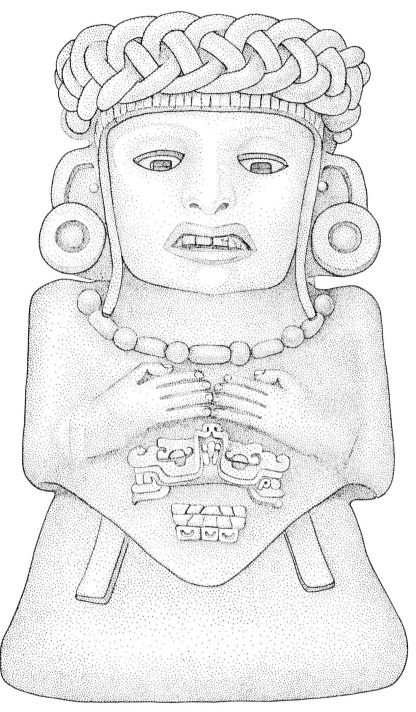

FIGURE 5.11. Classic Zapotec urn from Monte Albán III, showing calendric name. (Drawing by Margaret Van Bolt from a photograph in Caso and Bernal 1952: Fig. 431.)

*coquihualao* ("prince"), or *xonaxi* ("female ruler"). A second clue is that many have names taken from the 260-day calendar, which we know from Córdova (1578b:16) and Burgoa (1674:Chapter 70, 316) were given to human beings. For example, in Macuilxochitl one of the idols was recorded by Asensio (1580a:101) as "Coquebila" (Coqui Vila?). Tlalixtac had an "idol" named "Coqui Huani" (del Río 1580:179); Coatlán had "a married pair of idols" named ♂ Benelaba, "Seven Rabbit" and ♀ Xonaxi Belachina, "3 Deer" (Espíndola 1580:134; although Espíndola's translation of the animal names is accurate, the numbers he provides do not agree with Córdova 1578b). Mitla had a similar husband–wife pair: Xonaxi Quecuya and Coqui Bezelao (Canseco 1580:149). *Coqui* and *xonaxi* were the titles of earthly rulers, as were names such as 3 Deer and 7 Rabbit. Small wonder the names of these "idols" varied from town to town; they were probably often the names of venerated deceased rulers, not patron deities!

The Spanish priests who recorded the names of these idols frequently had a classical education, and assumed they were viewing the Zapotec equivalent of a Greco-Roman pantheon. Interestingly, the list compiled by Fray Juan de Córdova (1578a) includes no gods with names drawn from the 260-day calendar, but rather a set of terms which can be translated as "lightning," "earthquake," and other natural forces and objects. These terms contrast with the lists of gods in the *Relaciones Geográficas*, which feature many names derived from the 260-day calendar (and hence probably those of deceased nobility). These two sixteenth-century sources thus clearly deal with separate phenomena, although both claim to list gods populating the Zapotec cosmos.

It was these lists of Zapotec gods that I feel misled Caso and Bernal (1952) in their classic study *Urnas de Oaxaca*, from which almost all subsequent studies of Zapotec urns follow. Caso and Bernal concluded that the majority of the urns were either gods or priests wearing the costumes of gods. One exception was the type of urn they called the *acompañante*, a more clearly human figure which accompanied the deceased in his or her tomb.

For the classification of gods and associated deities, Caso and Bernal (1952:11) took into account virtually all the urns they knew of from excavations and museum collections. The bulk of these were in the collection of the National Museum of Anthropology in Mexico City or had been recovered in exploration at Monte Albán and other sites in Oaxaca.

Taking Córdova's list of gods they tried to decide which deity was depicted on each urn. As Caso and Bernal express it,

> Al agrupar las urnas, hemos procurado darles los nombres que se señalan para los dioses zapotecas en el Vocabulario de Córdoba, cuando es fácil la identificación, o bien los nombres calendáricos con los que aparecen en algunos ejemplares [1952:11].

One problem they ran into early was that Córdova's list of gods, as we have seen, included none with calendric names that often accompany the urns. This lack of calendric names should have served as a warning that one of their basic assumptions was shaky. Also missing from Córdova's list are such beings as a "goddess with a Yalálag headdress." I can find no evidence that the Zapotec had anthropomorphized female deities, but such hairstyles may well have been worn by royal females who were later venerated.

## URNS WITH *COCIJO*

A great deal of energy has been spent on the analysis of those urns labeled "Cocijo." As we shall see in Topic 97, *cocijo* was the Zapotec term for "lightning"; when one wanted to address or invoke the supernatural, the "great spirit within the lightning," he used the expression *Pitào Cocijo*. There is no reason to believe that the Zapotec ever conceived of lightning in anthropomorphized form, and I suspect that many of these urns actually depict persons wearing masks or headdresses that refer to attributes of *Pitào Cocijo*. Indeed, Caso and Bernal (1952:17–18) single out the mask which surrounds the eyes, nose, and mouth as the most common characteristic of Cocijo. This mask frequently includes nonhuman features such as the bifid tongue of a snake, or fangs. In the headdresses of these Cocijos we frequently find the "Glyph C," which Caso (1928) variously interprets as the mouth of a tiger or as a vessel holding water. At other times an urn bearing a Cocijo mask has corncobs as part of its headdress, and in these cases, Caso and Bernal (1952) interpret the urn as "the God of Harvest of Maize." Rather than interpreting each urn as a depiction of a different god, I would simply suggest that lightning, as a powerful Zapotec supernatural, was conceded the power to bring rain and thereby to contribute to the growth of corn. In other words, we might simply have a system that includes a human figure and a set of attributes (e.g., water, corn, lightning) that define the supernatural force or set of forces depicted in the headdress. In addition to the naturalistic corncobs appearing in some headdresses of Cocijo urns, Caso and Bernal (1952:19) have interpreted Caso's Glyph J as a stylized form of corncob. Thus, some of the urns of human figures which lack calendric names may represent persons associated with animals or great supernatural forces, perhaps after returning to the clouds of their ancestors.

In Monte Albán I and II there are effigy vessels that carry the attributes of Cocijo (Paddock 1966a:Fig. 6); by late Period II or IIIa, the vessels are fronted by a human figure seated cross-legged with hands resting on his knees, wearing a mask with *cocijo* attributes and a headdress that may include Glyph C, or maize, or water (Figure 5.12). Although no Cocijo urns of Monte Albán II date had been found at Monte Albán itself at the time of Caso and Bernal's study, one possible example was found at Cuilapan and assigned to that period on the basis of style (Caso and Bernal 1952:32). In this urn, an old man with a beard displays some of the attributes of Cocijo (including mask and eye ornaments), but he wears no elaborate headdress—no Glyph C, corncobs, water, and so on.

One Cocijo urn of the transitional period between Monte Albán II and IIIa was found in Mound X, on the floor of a

FIGURE 5.12. Monte Albán III urn with mask showing Cocijo attributes and headdress with Glyph C. (Drawing by Margaret Van Bolt from a photograph in Caso and Bernal 1952: Fig. 3.)

temple; this vessel displays undulating lines which Caso and Bernal interpreted as water. The use of a true Glyph C in the headdress, however, apparently does not begin to appear until Monte Albán IIIa (Leigh 1966).

For Caso and Bernal there is one particularly important urn, that pictured in Figure 34 of *Urnas de Oaxaca*. This is the only Cocijo urn that may carry a calendric glyph—a possible Glyph L (*xoo* or "earthquake" in the Zapotec 260-day calendar) with 3 (?) dots. This glyph and number appear below another (undeciphered) symbol in a headdress composed of circles and undulating lines. On the basis of this single example, Caso and Bernal (1952:35) state, "we are able to say that the god Tlaloc or Cocijo was calendrically called 3 L among the Zapotecs." For the reasons given above, I find this interpretation extremely unlikely; it seems

to me further evidence that most urns represent people, not gods.[2] If 3 L was the Zapotec name for Cocijo, why is it then that we have but one questionable association, whereas more than a hundred Cocijo urns occur with no glyphs—and in fact with no calendric information at all?

By Monte Albán IIIa times the human face with Cocijo attributes and a Glyph C in its headdress is commonly attached to spouted vessels or bowls. Some of these Cocijo masks with Glyph C are attached to a cluster of four smaller vessels (frequently ollas) that occur behind them (Caso and Bernal 1952:Figs. 54, 55).[3]

---

[2] I would also recommend that we resist the temptation to equate Zapotec "Cocijo" with Nahuatl "Tlaloc."

[3] For an interpretation of these four vessels, see Topic 97.

Also during Monte Albán IIIa, there are human figures that wear a Cocijo mask covering a small face in their head-dress, rather than wearing a Cocijo mask directly over their own face. These are clearly men, not even Cocijo impersonators. A good example of this type is the urn from the façade of Tomb 104 at Monte Albán: a man seated atop a jaguar place sign (or throne) wears an elaborate headdress which includes the depiction of a human face wearing a Cocijo mask or set of attributes. That this Tomb 104 urn is not a god seems clear; however, Caso and Bernal (1952:50) call this urn the "dios con cabeza de Cocijo en el tocado." This labeling of yet another god only obscures the possibly significant difference between the masked urns and those depicting individuals who wear no mask but who have a smaller figure wearing a Cocijo mask in their headdress. One group might represent ancestors who had taken on supernatural attributes, while the other group might represent contemporary royalty honoring both their ancestors and the supernatural by wearing their likeness in the headdress. To group both together as Cocijo blurs this distinction and precludes what might be an important series of interpretive clues.

## TOPIC 44
## Valley-Floor Settlement Patterns during Monte Albán IIIa

STEPHEN KOWALEWSKI

Several interesting patterns are evident during Monte Albán IIIa in those areas of the Valley of Oaxaca that have been intensively surveyed.

### THE ETLA REGION

The Early Classic settlement pattern in the Etla survey area displays the same reduction in rural population seen earlier in the Central area (see Topic 30). The Etla evidence shows that aside from San José Mogote, which is described as having been reduced to "large village" status, as of 1974 the only other Early Classic settlements were 18 hamlets and one isolated residence (Varner 1974:120).

### THE CENTRAL REGION

In the Central survey area (Figure 5.13), the Early Classic saw a small increase in the number of sites (from 23 to 37), but as in the Etla Valley most of the countryside was virtually unoccupied. This rural abandonment and concentration of population at the urban center of Monte Albán might be compared to similar developments in the Early Dynastic Period in southern Mesopotamia (Adams and Nissen 1972) and during Early Classic times in the Valley of Mexico (J. R. Parsons 1974).

### THE SITE OF XOXOCOTLÁN

In Oaxaca, however, the pattern described above may not have extended far beyond the northern and central parts of the valley. Bernal located a very large Early Classic center in the valley's southern arm at Santa Inés Yatzeche, and another major occupation was situated at the northern end of this arm, within the limits of the Central Valley survey area.

The latter site is known as Los Mogotes de Xoxocotlán, and is located on the high alluvium of the valley floor. Today the visible occupation consists of 15 mounds, widely scattered over an area of more than 1 km². Some of these mounds have been plowed down, but 10 are sizeable (as large as 30 × 70 m, and 16 m high).

Saville's turn-of-the-century excavations at Xoxocotlán showed that the mounds were constructed of adobe and earth fill, and probably served as platforms for elaborate residences. He also demonstrated that lesser house constructions could be found beneath the deposits of alluvium that have covered the site (Saville 1899; field notes in the American Museum of Natural History, New York).

Less than 5 km from Monte Albán, Xoxocotlán was the capital's nearest major site. Several participants at the Santa Fe seminar suggested that it might be regarded as an outlying barrio of Monte Albán, whose major role was to provide food for the urban center. There is an apparent correlation between the location of relatively large Early Classic centers and the present distribution of low alluvium in the valley (see Kirkby 1973:Fig. 3). As Kirkby (1973:15) observes, however, most modern low alluvial deposits date to after A.D. 1500. The precise hydrographic situation in A.D. 400 is unknown, but the co-occurrence mentioned above suggests the possibility of uncommonly favorable agricultural circumstances. The elite residences trenched by Saville might perhaps be the houses of administrators drawn from the ruling families of Monte Albán and appointed to oversee local production as were some *coqui* of the sixteenth century. The latter interpretation would be supported by a text Saville found on a tomb lintel, listing a long line of royal ancestors (Marcus, Topic 45).

Major valley floor centers like Xoxocotlán also may have had important exchange functions. While, as Blanton notes (Topic 39), Monte Albán itself was an unlikely market location, Xoxocotlán was open and easily accessible both from the valley's major Early Classic population centers and from Monte Albán. How much control Monte Albán exerted over

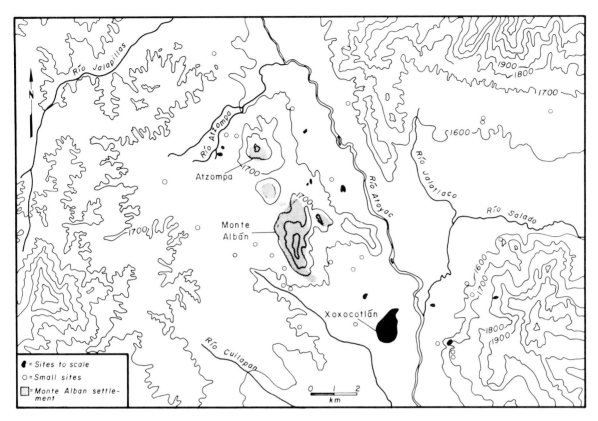

FIGURE 5.13.   Monte Albán IIIa settlements in the Central region of the Valley of Oaxaca. Dark areas refer to sites to scale; shaded areas show extent of settlement at Monte Albán itself. Smallest sites are indicated by circles because they would be almost invisible if drawn to scale. (Redrawn from Kowalewski 1976.)

key administrative, productive, or exchange functions in the valley is still not known, but future surveys may be able to suggest how these functions were distributed within the region's hierarchy of central places.

## CONCLUSIONS FOR THE CENTRAL AND NORTHERN VALLEY

At present it seems clear that patterns in the center of the valley and the Etla arm were most strongly influenced by Monte Albán. The rural abandonment that characterized most of the Central section in Monte Albán II and IIIa occurred later (during IIIa) in the Etla arm. The shift away from the extensive settlement patterns of Monte Albán I implies a major reorganization of political and economic institutions, involving, perhaps, some or all of the following trends.

1. The independent household was no longer the fundamental unit of agricultural production as it had been in earlier periods.

2. As an alternative, labor may have been concentrated in larger work groups, which would have allowed stricter con-

trol over mass labor power. I would speculate that the social bases for such concentrations were corporate groups—perhaps organized under *golaba* who in turn answered to a local member of the nobility as did the sixteenth-century Zapotec—and having territorial affiliations with Monte Albán and/or specific sectors of the valley.

3. When I was surveying some of the broad, high alluvial land in the Central part of the valley (including, interestingly enough, the Xoxocotlán area), it seemed to me that tracts subdivided into small, individual plots were often subject to disappointingly small harvests, while land in the same area controlled by larger enterprises had consistently greater yields. This discrepancy is apparently due to the larger units' ability to amass capital and apply it to irrigation and flood-control works of sufficient scale. It may be inferred then that an emphasis on land and labor-intensive production on a few fertile alluvial areas near population centers may have been a viable alternative to the extensive system of Monte Albán I.

4. To speculate further, such a reorganization might have had a temporarily dampening effect on birth rates, since demands for agricultural production were not being met by increasing the number of households, but by controlling the allocation of the existing labor supply. In some respects, *latifundia* systems of production in which rural populations

are comparatively low and stable due to the relatively low and constant demand for labor might be parallels of interest (see Boserup 1965:95–101).

5. The centralization of population and economic functions in Monte Albán II–IIIa points to the rise to dominance of a strong, state-level administrative apparatus at Monte Albán. I have elsewhere argued (Kowalewski, Blanton, and Varner 1975) that the Monte Albán II–IIIa economic reorganization was a strategy devised by the highest decision-making class to cope with increasing administrative costs and diminishing rates of return from the expansive economic system characteristic of Monte Albán I. Whether these speculations are idle or potentially productive remains to be seen.

## THE TLACOLULA REGION

Although the eastern Valley of Oaxaca has not yet been intensively surveyed at this writing, a number of major Period IIIa sites have been tested or excavated there, including Mitla, Dainzú, and Yegüih. Period III remains have been found at Yagul and Loma Larga, and Teotitlán del Valle has carved stones, some of which might be of that period. The overall importance of the Tlacolula valley prior to the rise of

Lambityeco in Period IV, however, will remain uncertain until surveys are completed.

## THE MIAHUATLÁN REGION

The Miahuatlán plain enjoyed an apparent population increase during Monte Albán III (Brockington 1973). Ten settlements were found near the Miahuatlán River or its tributaries; most occupation centered on the area just south of the present city.

While most of the Period III sites are probably hamlets, Sites 1A and 10 were larger. Largest and most impressive was 1A, where Period III sherds were found both on the surface and in excavations near the pyramidal mounds. Site 10 covers six ha and includes both ceremonial structures and habitation areas.

In addition, Brockington's survey located three looted tombs with associated Period III sherds. All "seem to have been simple box-like constructions, more nearly rectangular holes, with roughly formed limestone *lajas* [flat slabs] for roofing. All were on the upper third of hillslopes overlooking a river and all seem to have been of Period IIIa" (Brockington 1973:21). Another IIIa burial, found in a brickyard near Miahuatlán, brought the number of localities with Classic period remains to 14.

## TOPIC 45
## Lintel 2 at Xoxocotlán

JOYCE MARCUS

Kowalewski (Topic 44) has singled out the Monte Albán IIIa site of Xoxocotlán for special comment because (1) it was the nearest major site to Monte Albán during that period, (2) it covered a square kilometer and had mounds up to 16 m high, and (3) its environmental setting makes it a likely center for intensive agriculture, perhaps forming part of the support base for Monte Albán.

My purpose in writing this topic is to consider the possibility (already raised by Kowalewski in Topic 44) that the occupants of the elaborate residences at Xoxocotlán were hereditary nobility, perhaps descended from one of the ruling lineages at Monte Albán, or appointed by the rulers of Monte Albán to oversee this important community. While it would be difficult to prove this hypothesis at present, there is a tomb lintel from Xoxocotlán which appears to list 15 individuals, perhaps genealogically related to the occupant of the tomb.

### LINTEL 2

Excavating at Xoxocotlán for the American Museum of Natural History in the spring of 1898, Saville (1899) discovered Lintel 2 with Tomb 3 in Mound 9 (Figure 5.14). The

lintel measured 1.77 m in length, 0.67 m in width, and 0.29 m in height, with an indented lower edge. The inscription is composed of 15 compartments; each compartment includes a day name and numerical coefficient taken from the *pije* or 260-day calendar and a bearded human head in profile. The day names and numbers of the inscription can be transcribed as follows, in the sequence of the compartments (as numbered) from left to right:

1. 5 Lizard (?)
2. 5 Monkey
3. 8 Earthquake (?)
4. 8 Reed (Caso's Glyph J)
5. 4 *Narices del Tigre*
6. 6 Earthquake (?)
7. 8 Water (?)
8. 4 Jaguar (Caso's Glyph B)
9. 1 Flower (Caso's Glyph D)
10. 6 Grasshopper (?)
11. 7 Owl (Caso's Glyph F)
12. 2 Jade Jewel (?)
13. 2 Mouth of a Jaguar (Caso's Glyph C)
14. 3 Deer
15. 12 (?) Turquoise (Caso's Glyph E)

FIGURE 5.14. Lintel 2 from Xoxocotlán, Oaxaca. (Drawing by Mark Orsen.)

This text of 15 day names and numbers and its association with wrinkled, bearded men are most significant. Although Caso (1928:107) originally believed that the text presented "a series of day signs," he failed to ask why the "dates" were not in chronological order, why they appeared across a tomb lintel, and why they appeared with elderly profile heads beneath them.

I would offer the alternative interpretation that these day signs and numbers constitute the names of people, presumably ancestors or relatives of the person buried in the tomb. That these are personal names, and not simply day signs with numerical coefficients, is further reinforced by the fact that some of these same glyphs (i.e., same day sign and same number) are employed on monuments at other sites, also in association with the portrayal of a person.

For example, 6 Earthquake appears not only on Lintel 2 at Xoxocotlán, but also on Lápida 1 of the Museo Nacional, reportedly from a Zaachila tomb (see Figure 7.4 in Topic 59). In fact the name 6 Earthquake appears twice on Lápida 1—behind the man being married, as well as in the text accompanying the scene. Since Zaachila lies only 10 km from Xoxocotlán, 6 Earthquake might well have been a hereditary lord important in the royal lineages of both communities.

As for the choice of a tomb lintel for this inscription, it seems quite appropriate that the Zapotec would record the names of important ancestors in association with a high-status tomb. This interpretation would also explain the profile heads associated with each name; one could reasonably argue that all the heads are male because they are bearded, and that they all are "old people" (*binigulaza,* as the Zapotec call them today) because of the lines and wrinkles so clearly delineated.

Thus Lintel 2 at Xoxocotlán may well represent a roll call of the male ancestors of the deceased, who was buried in a tomb that appears, on the basis of ceramic offerings, to be late Monte Albán IIIa (or possibly early IIIb).

It is worth noting the similarities in text between Lintel 2 at Xoxocotlán and Lápida 1 of the Museo Nacional. One important similarity is the linear arrangement of names—13 in the text on Lápida 1 (from Zaachila) and 15 listed on the Xoxocotlán lintel. A second important similarity is that both stones were apparently used in tombs. Lintel 2 is the earlier inscription (late IIIa?) while Lápida 1 is the later (IIIb?), yet both mention a 6 Earthquake who could be a royal ancestor shared by the rulers of Xoxocotlán and Zaachila. As yet, we cannot link this genealogy to any specific lords at Monte Albán, but we cannot rule out the possibility that future discoveries will permit this. At the very least, Lintel 2 from Xoxocotlán offers us an Early Classic prototype out of which the "genealogical registers" of Monte Albán IIIb–IV may have developed (Topic 59), a type of monument of which Lápida 1 is a good example.

# TOPIC 46
## Las Flores Phase Settlement Patterns in the Nochixtlan Valley

RONALD SPORES

Forces of sociopolitical and economic integration set in motion during the Ramos phase persisted into Late Classic times. The Las Flores phase of the Nochixtlán Valley (A.D. 300–1000) was a time of expansion and further ramification of intercommunity linkages. The number and size of sites increased greatly; although larger sites show no greater architectural complexity than was present in Early Classic times and ceramics are, if anything, less distinctive, the number of relatively large, complex, and intensively utilized sites and sheer quantities of ceramics increased greatly. With the exception of Yucuita and a few smaller sites, there is a notable expansion of former Ramos settlements, and a number of new sites are opened. Las Flores phase sites number 113 (as compared with 35 in Ramos times), 74 of which were intensively utilized (Figure 5.15).

One of the new sites, Yucuñudahui—the Late Classic successor to Yucuita in terms of size, complexity, and probably socioeconomic power—emerges full-grown as a planned urban center located at the crest of one of the highest mountains in the valley (see Topic 47). Numerous relatively large, relatively complex sites emerge. Yucuñudahui heads the list, but large civic–ceremonial centers are also found at Cerro Jazmín (N 011), La Palmita (N 238), Etlatongo (N 802), Topiltepec (N 071), Jaltepec (N 602), and Perales (N 224), and along the several ridges north and east of Nochixtlán. Yucuita continues to be occupied, but the Las Flores component is much less pronounced than the Ramos component.

Relatively small quantities of Las Flores phase ceramics are associated with Ramos phase artifact and architectural complexes at Yucuita. Two loci, one on the extreme eastern edge of Yucuita and one on the northern extension of the site, have relatively large concentrations of Las Flores ceramics. My present interpretation (supported by radiocarbon determinations) is that a more or less "pure" Ramos phase complex persisted at Yucuita alongside and concurrent with Las Flores phase complexes at most other sites in the valley. Las Flores phase manifestations are overwhelmingly dominant in the valley after A.D. 500, but it is important to note that the "ancestral" Ramos complex seems to have persisted into Late Classic times in what might be a reflection of a secondary or subordinant manifestation in a community subject to an ascending center like

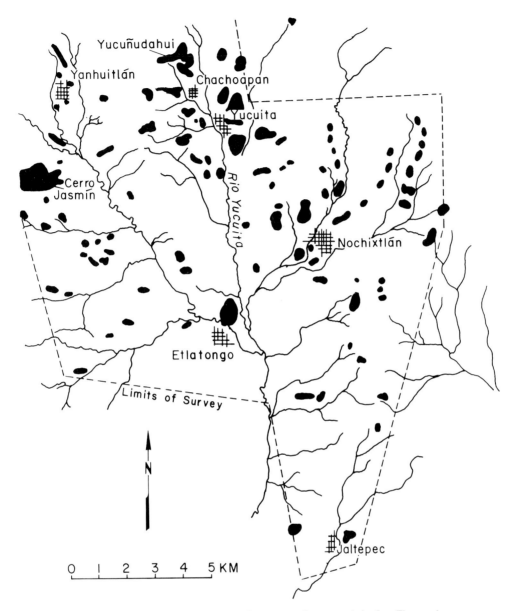

FIGURE 5.15. The Nochixtlán Valley, showing settlements of the Las Flores phase.

Yucuñudahui. The following tabulation provides some indication of the absolute and sectoral growth differential in the valley from Ramos to Las Flores times:

Yanhuitlán Sector: total sites surveyed, 72; Ramos sites, 7; Las Flores sites, 31.
Yucuita Sector: total sites surveyed, 40; Ramos sites, 15; Las Flores sites, 29.
Nochixtlán Sector: total sites surveyed, 42; Ramos sites, 4; Las Flores sites, 36.
Etlatongo–Jaltepec Sector: total sites surveyed, 23; Ramos sites, 9; Las Flores sites, 16.

Pressed to express population in absolute terms, I would estimate that valley population reached 30,000 during Las

Flores times. This estimate is based on size and number of sites, concentration of material remains, and projections from an ethnohistorically inferred population of 50,000 for the valley in A.D. 1520. Clearly, the population was more than double that of the Ramos phase.

The number, size, and apparent intensity of utilization of sites suggest that the valley was beginning to fill up and that there may have been considerable pressure being exerted against its productive resources. Although sites are greater in size and number, there is a significant shift upslope from low-lying lomas that could quite easily be farmed. In terms of proportional increase, the Nochixtlán and Yanhuitlán sectors show the greatest surge of growth. Yucuita and its environs are more conservative, to the point of retaining

Ramos patterns probably after other sites were undergoing substantial, presumably externally induced (i.e., from the valleys of Mexico, Puebla, and Oaxaca) changes in ceramic complexes, architecture, and settlement patterns; the Yucuita urban development appears to contract in physical size and complexity, in population, and in overall importance. Certainly there is a substantial occupation at Yucuita during Las Flores times, but the site declined perceptibly as a civic and ceremonial center relative to developments in other valley sites. Occupational emphasis shifts from the central area to the northern, and western peripheries of the loma portion of the site and to the upper reaches of Cerro de Yucuita.

In addition to differences that may be observed in form, placement, and probably function, Las Flores sites vary greatly in size. Yucuñudahui covers 2 km²; Cerro Jazmín and Etlatongo—like Cerro de Dos Arbolitos and El Fortín in the Teposcolula Valley, and Yatachío in the Tamazulapan Valley—cover approximately 1 km²; Topiltepec and Jaltepec measure some 500–750 m square; dozens of smaller sites range in size from 100 to 500 m square. A second variable is an apparently unequal representation of better-made Gray and Orange ceramics; these appear in relatively high frequencies in such sites as Yucuñudahui, Cerro Jazmín, and Topiltepec, and are scarce in the smaller ridgetop sites to the north and east of Nochixtlán.

Little appears at Yucuñudahui that is not found in comparable contemporaneous sites: planned architectural complexes consisting of stone and adobe structures with plastered floors, rubble-filled flat-topped mounds with crowning structures, architectural terraces, courts, plazas, compartmentalized or multiroomed structures, low-relief stone carving, and similar ceramic and lithic assemblages. The larger, more complex sites reflect preferences for locating all or most structures on high hills, ridges, or mountains. This tendency for sites to be in high (and defensible) positions allows dozens of contemporaneous sites to be seen from any one Las Flores site. Sight contact may well have been an important factor in selecting site locations and may have facilitated intersite communication or figured significantly in ritual behavior.

There are several possible explanations for lofty site placement: (1) the emergence of increasing levels of intersite or interregional conflict; (2) demographic pressure coupled with static technology placing a strain on the tillable lands of the low lomas and valley alluvium; (3) an ideological preference for the "reaching-up-to-heaven" high places; or (4) an emerging proficiency for organizing people committed to providing service and tribute to an elite group, so that large impressive centers could be built and maintained in difficult access locations; this would provide a symbolic manifestation of sacral–political power and authority, heightened ceremonial significance, protection, and/or release of pressure on farmlands.

I would lean strongly toward the latter kind of integrative interpretation and would give primary emphasis to the social mechanism, that is, the ability to organize human groups

for such activities. There is a desire for protection, for increasing productivity, and in a time of increasingly formalized and monumental ritualism, to magnify the material manifestation of the supernatural in those high locations. It is improbable that there would be an economic advantage in placing settlements in such localities, and I would discard this as a motivating factor in placement and orientation of settlements; I can see no obvious ecological explanation for this shift in settlement. But the needs are there, and the social mechanism for responding to those needs are provided in the model of the Mixtec kingdom, or something very like it, that served as an integrative focus for the creative output of thousands of Las Flores phase people living in and around the important centers of the time.

Most Las Flores settlements tend to conform to either of two basic patterns: (1) larger centers composed of several to numerous large multicomponent dwelling complexes (palaces) centrally located, adjacent to civic–ceremonial architectural clusters (ballcourts, steep-gradient mounds crowned by small, probably ceremonial, buildings, platforms, plazas, patios, and stelae) with an enveloping ring of smaller one- or two-celled dwellings on terraces on level or moderately sloping land; or (2) lesser settlements with a small central mound–plaza complex and one or two centrally located multicomponent dwellings surrounded by numerous one- or two-celled structures. Further functionally oriented intrasite study is required to substantiate these models fully, but the contrast has been observed in my own excavations at Yucuñudahui (N 236 Q, S, T) and on the Nochixtlán ridge system (N 423) and is strongly supported by survey (Spores 1972).

The described physical pattern corresponds quite well to the ethnohistoric model which would place the ruling family and supporting nobility in the principal center (places like Yucuñudahui, Topiltepec, or Cerro Jazmín) together with a group of permanent or rotating service–maintenance personnel; the outlying settlements were occupied by subject groups of farmers administered by members of the nobility loyal to the ruler.

It is a common pattern in the Mixteca today for wealthier individuals to maintain two or more residences: a relatively large, complex "modern" house in Nochixtlán; a second house, either complex or simple, in a rancho of Nochixtlán; and in the case of the very wealthy, perhaps a third house in the state capital of Oaxaca or even in Mexico City. I believe that a similar pattern was in operation in prehispanic times. A noble (*principal*) family might, for example, reside in a satellite settlement of Yucuñudahui. On important ceremonial occasions, when business or civic matters needed attention, or when summoned by the ruler, members of the family could move to Yucuñudahui, occupy an appropriate dwelling for the necessary period of time, and then return to their residence in the subject settlement. By the same token, a noble functionary or advisor to the ruler would maintain his principal household in the center but make frequent visits to carry out administrative functions, tend to business, or oversee the working of his fields. The ethnohistoric record renders it quite clear that such movement did occur and that this was an important way of maintaining relations between the principal center and the subject settlements (Spores 1967). I believe that we are well on our way to establishing that this pattern existed at least as early as Las Flores times and that the ethnohistoric and ethnographic models will serve as fully appropriate explanatory models.

Looking beyond the Nochixtlán Valley to other areas of the Mixteca, it is quite clear that the Late Classic period was a time of the grand diffusion of urbanism through the Mixteca. Large centers, most of them on high ridges or buttes above drained valleys, are apparent at such sites as Mogote del Cacique near Tilantongo (Spores 1967), Cerro de Dos Arboles and El Fortín in the environs of Teposcolula, Cerro de la Virgen and Loma de Órganos near Tlaxiaco (Spores 1967:38, 44), Cuquila and Santa Cruz Tayata (Contreras and Rodrigo 1972), Yatachío near Tamazulapan (Paddock 1953), Huajuapan, Tequixtepec, Cerro de Luna de Chazumba, Miltepec, and Silacayoapan in the Mixteca Baja (Moser 1977), and at Piedra Parada, and possibly other sites, in the Jamiltepec–Río Verde area in the Costa (Brockington 1957; de Cicco and Brockington 1956; Jorrín 1974). The Early Classic period was a time of initial and relatively restricted urbanism in the Mixteca Alta, while the Late Classic witnessed the widespread diffusion of urbanism through the greater Alta and Baja and, to an apparently more limited degree, in the Costa.

# TOPIC 47
## Yucuñudahui

RONALD SPORES

Yucuñudahui, located on a high, narrow, ridge 400 m above the valley floor in the Chachoapan–Coyotepec region, was the major civic–ceremonial center in the Nochixtlán Valley during Las Flores times. Following a reconnaissance by Daniel Rubín de la Borbolla and Martín Bazán, Alfonso Caso excavated several major central features at Yucuñudahui in 1937 (Caso 1938). There was no additional work until 1970 when I conducted limited excavations in dwelling complexes located on the western and southern peripheries of the central ceremonial complex.

Yucuñudahui lacks the main central plaza layout of Monte Albán; instead, it is organized in linear fashion as a series of plazas, mounds, alignments and patios running along an L-shaped ridgetop for approximately 1 km west–east, then—less impressively—nearly 3 km south–north. The site measures no more than 250 m in breadth, and in the major "ceremonial" zone (west–east arm) it is no more than 150 m wide.

## THE WEST COMPLEX AND PLATFORM

The western extremity of the west–east ridge contains several unexcavated terraces, patios, and alignments, and two parallel linear mounds. Rising above and to the east of this complex is the leveled West Platform containing a large central mound (Caso's partially excavated Mound A) and a smaller "sentinel" mound (Mound B) in the southeast corner of the platform. While the major development of the West Platform and its structures was in the Las Flores phase, excavations and survey conducted in 1970 revealed that the platform had been resurfaced and utilized during the Natividad phase.

## The Ballcourt

An I-shaped ballcourt is located in a declivity between the West Platform and the Central Plaza (Figure 5.16). Its central patio, 44 m long and 6 m wide, was aligned just to the west of true north; its end-patios were 26 by 12 m. Because of its poor condition, we know only that its side embankments were sloping, its surface was stucco, and it had once been decorated with an ornamental frieze.

## CENTRAL PLAZA

### Mound C

Mound C, to the east of the ballcourt, yielded the remains of a poorly preserved "temple" on a rectangular platform. Because the local Mixtecs referred to Mound C as "the temple of the rain god," Caso (1938) and Marquina (1951) gave this building the ethnically inappropriate title, "el Templo de Tlaloc." Its principal feature was a square pit dressed with stones.

### Mound E

Mound E, "el Mogote Grande," yielded the remains of another "temple" virtually destroyed by treasure-hunters.

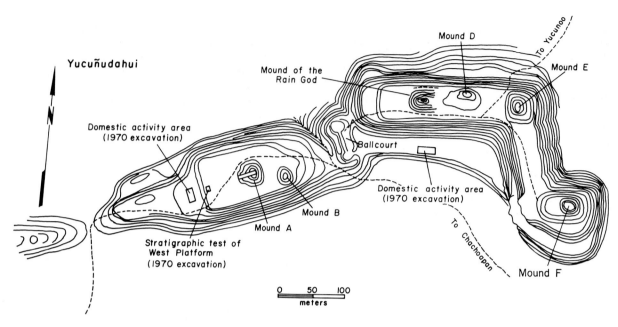

FIGURE 5.16.  The ruins of Yucuñudahui. (Redrawn, with modifications, from Caso 1938.)

Interestingly, neither this building nor the one in Mound C appears to have been a two-room temple like the Zapotec *yohopèe;* they seem to have been one-room buildings, although their location on a raised platform is similar to Monte Albán temples. These Yucuñudahui examples may be forerunners of the Mixtec *huahiñuhu.*

### Mound F

Mound F, at the eastern extremity of the ceremonial complex, was designated "La Forteleza" because of its lofty and commanding view of the eastern and southern slopes of Yucuñudahui mountain and dozens of other Classic period sites distributed along the ridges and valleys of the Nochixtlán Valley. In the rubble that filled the abandoned temple, Bazán discovered an offering formed of animal skulls, which Caso believed were jaguars (although no zoologist has confirmed this); it also contained perforated shells. Nearby was the burial of a child, also in the rubble and therefore postdating the temple.

## YUCUNOO

### The Chert Quarry

Extending northward is the south–north arm of the ridge called Yucunoo. Midway along Yucunoo is an enormous limestone and chert quarry (Figure 5.17). Although the exis-

tence and significance of this major activity area were not acknowledged in Caso's report, recent investigations leave no doubt as to the enormous importance of the quarry as the source of white and gray-black chert used for stone tools at

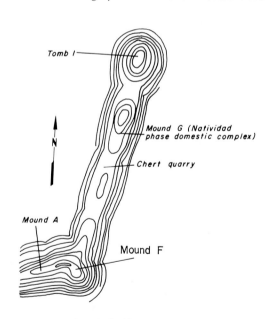

FIGURE 5.17.  The Yucunoo sector of Yucuñudahui. (Redrawn, with modifications, from Caso 1938.)

Yucuñudahui and distributed widely throughout the Nochixtlán Valley, appearing as far away as the Teposcolula and Tamazulapan valleys.

## Mound G

In the principal mound on the ridge of Yucunoo, Caso discovered a small temple with adobe walls whose entrance was flanked by columns. This structure, especially in its style of dressing with stone, was more reminiscent of Monte Albán than the larger temples described above. Investigations conducted in 1970, however, revealed that major structures in this area pertained to the Postclassic rather than the Classic period major occupation of the site.

## Tomb 1

At the terminus of the Yucunoo ridge was the "residence" with Tomb 1. The mound itself was rectangular and 20 by 16 m in size, with the tomb somewhat to the south of center. It was reached by a stairway leading down six steps to a long narrow antechamber which is, significantly, cruciform like some Period III tombs at Monte Albán. The main chamber is square and 3.5 m on a side; where it meets the antechamber there is a smaller square space, like a tomb within a tomb, recessed below the level of the main chamber and having its own roof. The roof of the main chamber was composed of 17 beams of juniper wood, which were miraculously preserved (Acosta 1965:Fig. 29). Caso obtained a radiocarbon date of A.D. 298 from one of these beams; with his approval, I took two more samples in 1966 from a piece of beam set aside in storage since Caso's excavation. These samples were submitted for dating by John Paddock, yielding dates of A.D. 320 and 540 (see Appendix). Some participants at the Santa Fe symposium preferred the earlier dates, some the later; all dates indicate contemporaneity with Monte Albán IIIa for this early Las Flores phase tomb.

## RECENT EXCAVATIONS IN THE RESIDENTIAL ZONE

Below the high ridgetop of Yucuñudahui with its public buildings are the occupational terraces where most of the inhabitants of the urban center must have resided. In 1970, as part of the Vanderbilt Nochixtlán Valley project, two residential areas were excavated in order to relate them to the central ceremonial complexes and to compare them with residences at secondary centers in other areas of the valley.

## Structure N 236 Q

A stone-walled complex was located 15 m downslope (south) from Mound C on the central plaza. Remarkably

well preserved, the house floor was approximately 12 by 4 m in extent, with apparent storage areas in southwest and northeast corners. In the center of the floor was a central warming hearth, and there were traces of partitions which once served to compartmentalize the structure. A masonry extension, apparently a supporting buttress, was attached to the structure's downslope side. A great variety of implements was recovered from the floor of this building: chipped-chert scrapers and gravers, obsidian blades, abraders and grinders, spindle whorls, long-handled incensors, orange and gray dishes and bowls, a stone dog effigy, and three large gray ware storage jars associated with the central hearth.

Two special "house offering" clusters were recovered from under the floor of the western extremities of the residence. One cluster in the northwest corner consisted of a ring-based fine orange bowl inverted over a similarly formed gray ware vessel. Along the southwest edge of the floor was a cluster containing a gray cylindrical tripod, an engraved gray bowl, a *candelero,* and a gray cup. Nearby, although not directly associated with either offering, a movable-arm figurine body was found on the dwelling floor. The ceramics found on the structure floor were overwhelmingly of the orange- and gray-ware traditions considered characteristic and diagnostic of the Late Classic Las Flores phase in the Nochixtlán Valley. Ceramic complexes, including specific forms, show clear relations with Teotihuacán and Monte Albán of Period III.

Human remains consisted of two children under 1 year of age buried under the house floor, a flexed mature female buried outside but immediately adjacent to the north wall of the building, and adult and children's bones scattered on the floor and immediately downslope in refuse deposits. These remains show signs of burning and cutting, obvious indicators of the cannibalistic activities observed for the Ramos phase of Yucuita and in Ramos phase elite residences at Huamelulpan.

## Structure N 236 T

A rather similar structure containing three major cells was excavated on a terrace lying just below and west of the West Platform. The structure was clearly of Las Flores phase residential function, but was in bad repair due to what appeared to have been intentional destruction. Artifact inventories were less diversified than at location 236 Q, no burials were recovered, and biotic remains were much less in evidence. Conceivably the functions of structures 236 Q and 236 T could have been somewhat different.

## COMPARISONS WITH SECONDARY CENTERS

There are numerous Las Flores phase sites in the valley that occupy settings similar to that of Yucuñudahui. In 1970 a residential structure was excavated at ridgetop site N 423, some 8 km southeast of Yucuñudahui in the municipality of Nochixtlán. The site measures 200 by 125 m and contains three major mounds, many floors, patios, and alignments, and a medium concentration of ceramics. A large central mound measures approximately 12 m at the base and is 4 m high. The Las Flores phase settlement contained, in addition to one or two probably elite households at the core of the site, an estimated 50 to 60 households (erosion and destruction make it difficult to be more precise) distributed concentrically around relatively small mounds (Spores 1972:133). The house that was excavated was less than half the size of the one at Yucuñudahui (ca. 4 × 3 m.), and instead of having limestone block walls, its foundations were of caliche blocks and the upper courses of adobe. It had no central warming hearth, very few elegant gray ceramics, no cylindrical tripods, no effigy vessels, no spindle whorls, and very few ring-base bowls; its assemblage was dominated by utilitarian-looking rust-colored pottery. Deer and dog bones were in the food debris, but no evidence of ritual cannibalism was found.

Survey of similar "secondary" sites where surface indicators were plentiful reveal that the patterns found at N 423 can safely be projected to at least 20 other contemporaneous settlements in the valley. Differences between first- and second-order sites go beyond functional divergence. Obviously, our sample of excavated houses is too small to allow weighty conclusions, but it affords a working hypothesis: elite residents of first-order administrative centers lived in larger, better-built houses, used more elegant pottery, participated more fully in ritual and sacrificial activity, and had stronger ties to areas outside the Nochixtlán Valley than did residents of second-order administrative centers. Intersite social stratification was an essential component of life in the Nochixtlán Valley during Late Classic times.

## TOPIC 48
## Huamelulpan during Period III

ADDED BY THE EDITORS

The site of Huamelulpan has already been described in Topic 37. Having reached its peak during Period II (100 B.C.–A.D. 200), Huamelulpan remained an important site during Period III (A.D. 200–600); however, few major public constructions are known from this phase, and the site was eventually abandoned.

*Building G*—a huge platform with walls of large, roughly dressed stones—continued in use during Period III, as did a nearby patio. In addition, Gaxiola (1976) discovered a series of Period III elite residences, each consisting of four or more rooms functionally divided into (1) habitation areas, including subfloor burials and tombs; (2) patios, some perhaps sunken; and (3) kitchens with hearths, grinding stones, animal bones, and other evidence of domestic activity. The tombs had flat roofs and interior niches, but lacked a formal entrance.

*One early Period III house,* northeast of Building G, was an extended-family residence of at least 8 stone-founded rooms. Rooms 1, 2, and 3 are considered "service rooms" because of their small size and abundant deer and dog remains, while Rooms 5, 7, and 8 are considered "habitational"; Room 6 may actually be a sunken patio with an earthen floor. Grinding stones were found in Rooms 2 and 4, while utilitarian pottery was found in Room 1. In one wall of a habitation room was Burial 6, an 18-year-old male accompanied by five vessels. Tomb 3, from the same house, contained three adult females but had also been disturbed by looters.

*A late Period III house* was found on a terrace east of Building G, but its plan was only partially recovered. Below the floor were tombs and burials from perhaps two generations of occupants. The lowest, Tomb 5, contained one primary burial and three secondary burials accompanied by 55 pottery vessels; included were a male over 60, a male over 30, a female over 40, and a fragmentary fourth adult. Above was a later tomb, Tomb 2, containing three burials and 68 pottery vessels including a local imitation of Teotihuacán Thin Orange.[1] The skeletons were those of a male over 40, a female over 40, and a female over 30.

Possibly related to Tomb 2 were Burial 9 (a male over 60, accompanied by one vessel) and Burial 8 (a pair of secondary burials, both females over 40). Yet another interment, Burial 7, was a child of 7 or 8 years accompanied by three elegant vessels.

## CONCLUSIONS

Period III Huamelulpan, a contemporary of Yucuñudahui, was still an important center although its peak of public construction had evidently passed. No "palaces" are yet known, in the sense that we have used the term (see Editors'

---

[1]Acosta (n.d.a) also reports Teotihuacán vessels in the surface debris covering the ruins of Monte Negro.

Introduction to Chapter 4), but the elite residences do have a sunken patio and functionally differentiated rooms. Both men and women from elite families were buried together; and in some cases, when a household head died, it appears that relatives (?) buried previously were reinterred with him as secondary burials. It would be interesting to know why some household members received stone tombs and others were placed in simple graves.

# Monte Albán and Teotihuacán

## Editors' Introduction

Monte Albán and Teotihuacán were two of the greatest urban centers of Precolumbian Mexico. Monte Albán, founded by 500 B.C., grew to 6.5 km² with a population conservatively estimated at 30,000 by A.D. 600 (Blanton 1978). Teotihuacán, founded by 150 B.C., grew to 20 km² with population estimated at 125,000 to 200,000 by A.D. 600 (R. Millon 1976:212). Inevitably, questions have arisen about the relationships, the similarities, and the differences between these two great cities. At the Santa Fe seminar, half a day was devoted to the discussion of such topics.

The traditional view, dating from Caso's work, was to see Classic Teotihuacán as a source of inspiration for Classic Monte Albán. Just as the Olmec were once regarded as the stimulus for Monte Albán I, and the Maya as the foreign elite responsible for Monte Albán II, heavy "Teotihuacán influence" was seen in Monte Albán III. As recently as 1970, a label in the former Regional Museum in Oaxaca—now converted to a tourist assistance office—read: "During Monte Albán IIIa, the Olmec tradition fused with Maya and Teotihuacán influence to produce the Zapotec culture." Poor Zapotecs! They were seen not merely as orphans, but also as cultural hybrids.

Fortunately, the excavations of the last decade have revealed that the Zapotec had an autonomous tradition of their own which goes back some 10,000 years. Excavations at Huitzo in 1967 left no doubt that the Monte Albán I phase was an indigenous development in the Valley of Oaxaca. Long before this excavation, Paddock had pointed out that the monumental stone masonry architecture of Monte Albán could hardly have had its roots in the Olmec region, and

now Marcus has argued that even the *danzantes* of Period I are more Zapotec than Olmec. Moreover, Monte Albán II, despite its corbelled-vault tombs, does not look very "Maya" to us at this point. Rather, it looks like the first clear manifestation of the Zapotec state—a state that was writing in double columns of hieroglyphs before Teotihuacán was founded, and before a single monument had appeared in the Petén.

Finally there came a rethinking of "Teotihuacán influence" at Monte Albán. To be sure, there are *taludes* and *tableros* in the architecture of Monte Albán, and there are Thin Orange vessels with ring bases. On balance, however, the differences between the two cities are more impressive than the similarities, as will be clear from the following discussion. Perhaps the most dramatic case is made by John Paddock, in this chapter; we only briefly summarize his comparisons with Teotihuacán influence at Kaminaljuyú. Monte Albán lies only 350 km from Teotihuacán; Kaminaljuyú lies at a distance of 1050 km, or virtually 3 times as far away. The area excavated at Monte Albán is more than 10 times that at Kaminaljuyú. Despite this difference, the number of Teotihuacán-style vessels found at Kaminaljuyú is easily 10 times greater than at Monte Albán, and Sanders (1974:107,113) has argued that actual Teotihuacanos were resident at Kaminaljuyú. Any Teotihuacán influence at Monte Albán pales by comparison. In the end, Paddock agrees with René Millon (1973:42) that there may have been "a kind of special relationship" between Teotihuacán and Monte Albán, one which was "closer and of a different kind than the relationship of Teotihuacán to other foreign cen-

161

ters." For example, that relationship seems to have involved no militarism, no coercion, no conquest, and no resident colony from Teotihuacán.

Ironically, the very "specialness" of the relationship—in a diplomatic or ambassadorial sense—may be one reason for the fact that Monte Albán shows less blatant Teotihuacán influence than a heavily dominated center like Esperanza phase Kaminaljuyú. In all probability, as Blanton has suggested, Monte Albán was simply too big and too powerful to be dominated; and during Period III the rulers of Monte Albán may have made a conscious effort to increase the size of the city still further for that very reason.

Let us begin by summarizing the ways in which Monte Albán differs from Teotihuacán, as proposed by the various members of the Santa Fe seminar whose topics follow. We then discuss what the actual relationship between Monte Albán and Teotihuacán might have been, based on the few clues at our disposal. Even those few clues suggest that the real relationship was more fascinating than any simplistic model of Teotihuacán influence.

1. *Striking differences in city planning.* Monte Albán is not laid out on a grid, nor is there any readily apparent geometric pattern to its growth. Its main roads wind along the contours of the mountaintop, and do not serve any major public buildings; indeed, Blanton's ekistic studies show that the Main Plaza is in one of the areas of most limited access as far as the road system goes. Teotihuacán was built, if not on an actual grid, at least on a cruciform plan whose major axes are an east–west highway and the north–south Street of the Dead, intersecting near the Ciudadela. René Millon (1976:212) has suggested that "successive additions to a basic cruciform plan . . . may give more of an impression of the realization of a master plan than was actually the case," but Jeffrey Parsons (personal communication, 1975) points to survey evidence for planned growth: early in the city's history, he feels, the Street of the Dead was laid out 5 km north–south, and the main east–west highway was laid out 2–3 km to the west and 6 km to the east, well in advance of additional settlement along those avenues.

2. *Monte Albán was primarily an administrative and religious center, while Teotihuacán was administrative, religious, and commercial.* We have already mentioned the intersection of Teotihuacán's main north–south and east–west avenues at the Ciudadela, which may be the main seat of "government" at the city. On the same intersection lies the Great Compound, an open area which Millon feels may be a marketplace. This interpretation is strengthened by its high accessibility in ekistic terms, since the major arteries of the city would carry people to and from it, literally from as far away as the suburban and rural hinterland.

There is no evidence for a marketplace at Monte Albán, and indeed it would make little sense to place a regional marketplace on a 400-m mountaintop. The largest open area, the Main Plaza, not only lies well off the main road system, but surrounds one set of temples and adoratories and is in turn flanked by more temples, making its function

fairly obvious. And in contrast to the Ciudadela at Teotihuacán, Monte Albán's most likely seat of government—the North Platform—includes the single least accessible spot on the entire site from the standpoint of ekistics (Topics 39, 41).

Equally striking is the difference in craft production at the two cities. René Millon (1976:233) estimates that at least 400 of Teotihuacán's 2200 apartment compounds were occupied primarily by craftsmen, and in addition, "there were perhaps another 200 or 300 apartment compounds, some of whose occupants were engaged in craft activities." Perhaps 25% of the city's population may have lived in such households—there were, in fact, over 300 obsidian workshops alone—and at the city's height "craftsmen and the members of their households may therefore have exceeded 30,000" (R. Millon 1976:233). Both rural and urban surveys suggest that virtually all the artisans in the Valley of Mexico were drawn into the metropolis, where they were organized into huge compounds of 60 to 100 persons. This pattern of urban-based craftsmen, which continued at Tula and Tenochtitlán, might be considered a basic pattern in the Basin of Mexico.

In Oaxaca, then as now, the pattern is for craft specialization by village. For example, during Monte Albán Ic, when Santo Domingo Tomaltepec (see Topic 15) was only a "third-order" administrative center in the Tlacolula arm of the valley, it was apparently a significant producer of fine gray pottery. Two Monte Albán Ic households excavated by Whalen (1976b), Units Ic-1 and Ic-3, had in their courtyards

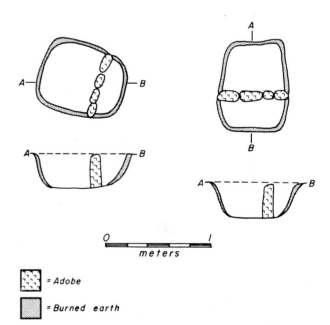

= Adobe

= Burned earth

FIGURE 6.1. Apparent two-chambered pottery kilns from Sto. Domingo Tomaltepec (Monte Albán Ic phase). Left, plan and cross-section of Feature 53, Household Unit Ic-3. Right, plan and cross-section of Feature 51, Household Unit Ic-1. (Redrawn from Whalen 1976a.)

what appear to have been two-chambered kilns. Features 51 (in Unit Ic-1) and 53, 61, and 75 (in Unit Ic-3) were all pits 60–80 cm in diameter divided into two parts by an adobe wall, constituting possible forerunners of the two-chambered Monte Albán V kiln found at Cueva Blanca (Topic 88). In such a kiln, very even firing could be accomplished by placing the vessels in one chamber and the fuel (predominantly oak, according to ethnobotanist Judith E. Smith) in the other; the subterranean reducing atmosphere would produce gray ware (Figure 6.1).

This group of four kilns from Tomaltepec is the largest known so far for this time period in Oaxaca. Small features which may also have been pottery kilns have been found in a Monte Albán IIIb residential area at Monte Albán itself (Winter and Payne 1976), but there is no reason to believe that this craft was pursued any more intensely in the city than in any good-sized village in the valley (Figure 6.2). Obsidian-working areas are also rare at Monte Albán, and Blanton feels most may be Postclassic. Monte Albán also

lacks evidence for large residential compounds of craft specialists such as those that characterized Teotihuacán.

In contrast, Teotihuacán had 100–150 compound-sized ceramic workshops, "many of them spanning the city's entire history, others concentrating on the mass production of a common cooking ware during the height of the city's existence" (R. Millon 1976:232). Such workshops are detectable even from the surface by massive amounts of homogeneous ceramic debris, including kiln wasters; kiln wasters do occur at Valley of Oaxaca sites, but fewer than a dozen were found in Blanton's survey of Monte Albán. Additionally, Teotihuacán has more than 15 compounds in which mold-made figurines were produced; none is known from Monte Albán.

Finally, there is another way in which Teotihuacán's "commercialism" contrasts with Monte Albán. At least some of the obsidian workers at Teotihuacán "spent part of their time making implements of obsidian within a walled precinct west of and attached to the Moon Pyramid" and

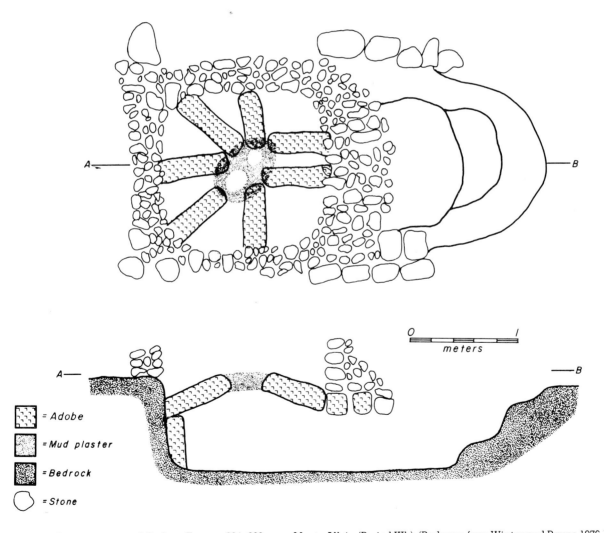

FIGURE 6.2. Apparent pottery kiln from Terrace 634–636 area, Monte Albán (Period IIIb). (Redrawn from Winter and Payne 1976.)

therefore "directly within the jurisdiction of a temple community"; this activity may have been "part of the larger involvement of the state in obsidian working" (R. Millon 1976:231). If we assume, on the basis of strong ethnohistoric evidence, that one of the functions of obsidian blades was for ritual bloodletting, the involvement of the temple makes sense; it also gives religious significance to the possibility that most of the obsidian blades used in the Mexican highlands during the Classic period were funneled through the Great Compound at Teotihuacán. Given the scanty evidence for craft activities at Monte Albán, there is no evidence to suggest that the Zapotec state was heavily involved in commercial craft production, much less involved with craft production for export beyond the Valley of Oaxaca. We find this difference between the two cities highly significant in spite of efforts by Sanders and Santley (1978) to downplay it.

3. *Teotihuacán was a "primate city" with highly skewed rank–size relations with its hinterland; Monte Albán was a "disembedded capital" with a less skewed multilevel hierarchy below it.* Our brief discussion of this point draws not only on Blanton's comments in this chapter, but also on two of his recent theoretical papers—one in a previous Santa Fe seminar (Blanton 1976c) and one in the *Annual Review of Anthropology* (Blanton 1976b). Blanton (1976c) has defined as "primate cities"[1] those first-order centers which are so huge, and have so many functions, that a meaningful hierarchy of second- and third-order centers never develops beneath them. This situation can be displayed as a rank–size graph (see Topic 51) in which the sizes of centers of descending rank in a region deviate strongly from the log–normal slope predicted from the size of the largest center. Blanton's modern example would be Buenos Aires, which is virtually the sole link between the Argentine economy and the outside world, and has grown so vast that there is an enormous drop-off in size between it and the cities that constitute Argentina's secondary centers. In much the same way, Classic Teotihuacán dominated the Valley of Mexico (Blanton 1976c, Fig. 10; Kowalewski, Topic 51). There is an enormous drop-off between Teotihuacán (population 125,000–200,000) and the next largest centers (population 1500–3000), perhaps because larger secondary centers literally would not have been able to compete with the capital. With virtually all the craft specialists drawn into its urban area and organized in apartment compounds, Teotihuacán virtually monopolized all administrative, religious, and commercial functions for the Basin of Mexico.

The situation was quite different with Monte Albán, below which there developed a multitiered hierarchy of secondary and tertiary centers which conforms more closely to the predicted log–normal distribution. Monte Albán had 2500 occupational terraces, but there are secondary centers with over 1000 terraces and tertiary centers with over 500;

lower-level administrative centers might reach 40 ha, and there were villages of 5 ha and hamlets of 1 ha.

Blanton (1976b:257–258) further points out that in cases where the administrative functions of government are "disembedded" from the commercial functions of central places, the capital is frequently located away from the commercial centers, becoming "a permanent but neutrally located special function community involved primarily in decision making at the regional level"; modern examples would include Brasilia and Washington, D.C. Monte Albán, on its 400-m mountaintop at the juncture of all three arms of the Valley of Oaxaca, appears to be just such a disembedded capital.

4. *Monte Albán was fortified; Teotihuacán was not.* As already mentioned, Blanton's surveys have turned up several kilometers of apparent defensive walls on the gentler slopes below the early (Period I–II) limits of Monte Albán; during Period III the city expanded well beyond those walls. At Teotihuacán, no evidence of fortification has ever been found.

Sheer size, of course, is a form of defense; a Mesoamerican city of 125,000 to 200,000 even on an undefended plain was hardly at a disadvantage. Blanton has in fact suggested that part of Monte Albán's enormous growth during Period III may have been designed to make it similarly impregnable. Certainly it would appear that by the time its population reached 30,000 or more it no longer needed the defensive walls built early in its history.

5. *Both cities relied to a certain extent on water control systems.* R. Millon (1976:244–245) points out that "ancient streams within and beyond [Teotihuacán] were canalized, often in accord with Teotihuacán orientations" and adds that while evidence is circumstantial, "it seems probable that the Teotihuacanos irrigated as large an area as the water flow permitted." At Monte Albán, as we have already seen, there were canal irrigation systems in use on the outskirts of the site as early as Period I. We side with Millon, however, in suspecting that the growth of these two great urban centers provided incentives for expanded irrigation, rather than resulting from it. Particularly in the case of Monte Albán, no known water source (or combination of sources) could really have "supported" a city of 30,000. Brumfiel (1976) has presented data to suggest that tribute was already an important part of the support base for Terminal Formative centers in the Basin of Mexico. We suspect that tribute and local agriculture supported Monte Albán, while Teotihuacán relied on a combination of tribute, local agriculture, and commerce.

6. *Writing was an integral part of the operation of the state centered at Monte Albán.* From the very founding of the city, stone monuments were used to display power, to record conquest, to date political events, and to commemorate leaders and places. Hieroglyphic writing in vertical columns, names, and dates from the 260-day calendar appeared on stelae, lintels, and murals. We learn of "The Hill of the Bird," "The Place of the Canal with Maize Tassels,"

---

[1] We confess that when we first heard the term *primate cities* we thought it might be a reference to the film *Planet of the Apes.*

"The Place of Song"—toponyms that may have been places at the limits of Zapotec conquest. We find cups which commemorate the "Lord 1 Jaguar" and his "Lady 2J," who, along with other named persons, may have been an early royal pair at Monte Albán.

The only place within the entire city of Teotihuacán where actual writing occurs is on a tomb jamb in the Oaxaca barrio (Topic 52). The writing is Zapotec, and the name taken from the 260-day ritual calendar—"9 Earthquake" or "9 Motion"—is a typical Zapotec name (see Figure 6.6). Recently, Clara Millon (1973) has searched the art of Teotihuacán for individual glyphs in an effort to see whether Teotihuacán had writing. She certainly encountered complex iconography, but as Marcus (1976c:43) has argued, "complex iconography—whether produced by the Olmec, the Kwakiutl, or the Maori—does not qualify as a writing system." At Teotihuacán, one rarely finds two or three glyphs set together in a column. We do not know the name of a single ruler at Teotihuacán, nor the name of a single place conquered by Teotihuacán. This is no denigration of Teotihuacán, but rather a comment on how different its system of government may have been. Writing was not an important part of their strategy, and the glorification of individual rulers by carving their names and deeds in stone was of no apparent concern.

Let us think for a moment of what this contrast may mean. Both the Zapotec and the Maya displayed the names, exploits, and genealogies of their rulers on permanent monuments in public places. Both were states ruled by hereditary dynasties in which succession was determined by royal blood lines. The Aztec provide an interesting contrast: although rulers were recruited from hereditary nobility, they were in fact selected by a Council of Noble Elders, and rarely were stone monuments erected to individual rulers as the Maya or Zapotec might have done (the Stone of Tizoc is one of the few examples). We might therefore consider the possibility that Teotihuacán had a form of government more oligarchic than either the Zapotec or Maya, one in which the monumental glorification of individual rulers was of low priority—a form of government, in other words, out of which the Toltec and Aztec states could logically have evolved.

7. *The nature of the "special relationship" between Monte Albán and Teotihuacán.* In this introduction we will do no more than prepare the reader for this topic, which is dealt with in detail by Paddock and Marcus later in the chapter. Paddock (Topic 52) covers the apparent barrio of Oaxacan residents at Teotihuacán, which he helped to excavate. Marcus (Topic 53) covers a series of stone monuments which apparently depict important Teotihuacanos who visited Monte Albán during Period IIIa.

The Oaxaca barrio of Teotihuacán covers 1–2 ha on the western outskirts of the city. According to René Millon,

The people of the Oaxaca barrio do not appear to have occupied a high status in the city; rather, they appear to fall in one of the

lower two intermediate levels. They seem to have maintained cultural and other ties with Oaxaca, judging from the fact that in one of the apartment compounds in the barrio, several of them were buried in a Oaxaca-style tomb with a stela made from a reused Teotihuacán building stone and bearing a glyph and number in Oaxaca style. Two funerary urns—both made in Oaxaca—were also found in this apartment compound. The people who lived in the barrio also continued to use domestic objects of Oaxaca style. While adopting many Teotihuacán customs, they seem to have remained an ethnic enclave until the fall of the city. The compounds in which they lived, while not especially well constructed, conformed to Teotihuacán building standards and to the Teotihuacán orientation of walls [1976:234].

Paddock's dating of the Oaxaca barrio differs somewhat from Millon's, and he argues that the carved stone is not a stela but a typical Zapotec tomb jamb.

No comparable Teotihuacán barrio is known from Monte Albán. Persons from Teotihuacán, however, are mentioned on stone monuments at the four corners of the South Platform at Monte Albán, and on the famous Lápida de Bazán from Mound X. These persons can be identified as Teotihuacanos by a distinctive headgear that Clara Millon (1973) has called the Tassel Headdress and that Kidder, Jennings, and Shook (1946) called the Trimountain Symbol; to this, Marcus adds a sandal style which is so distinctive that it can be used as a shorthand glyph for a Teotihuacano. A distinct "treble-scroll element," commonly used at Teotihuacán, occurs within a hill sign in such a way that it may represent the Zapotec name for Teotihuacán; on the Street of the Dead, this treble scroll seems to represent a sacrificed human heart, sometimes shown being eaten by pumas. The Teotihuacán visitors to Monte Albán are also shown departing from a temple, stylized exactly as are temples in the Tetitla murals at Teotihuacán, and carrying copal bags. In contrast to Teotihuacanos depicted at Kaminaljuyú, Tikal, and Yaxhá, the visitors to Monte Albán carry no weapons, a fact already noted by René Millon (1973).

Two columns of text on the Lápida de Bazán apparently deal with what was said and done by a Zapotec lord and a Teotihuacano visitor during a meeting. The stones in the South Platform apparently deal with eight named Teotihuacanos who visited a named Zapotec lord, possibly on the occasion of the platform's dedication. The scenes relating to Teotihuacanos are not carved on the faces but on the edges of the stone monuments; three are accompanied by offerings of shell and jade which resemble contemporary caches at Teotihuacán. It is ironic that these may be the only eight Teotihuacanos whose names we know, and that the Zapotec name for Teotihuacán may be the only name we presently have for that great city.[2]

Certainly the relationship between the two cities seems to have been peaceful, nonmilitary, and "ambassadorial," and

___
[2]It is also ironic that the one resident of Teotihuacán whose name appears on a tomb jamb there is apparently a Zapotec, 9 Earthquake, in the Oaxaca barrio (see the preceding).

some politically important marriage alliances might have been involved (R. Millon 1973:42), although the data are inconclusive on this point. Important Teotihuacanos—perhaps religious functionaries—visited Monte Albán. Zapotecs important enough to be buried in a tomb with a carved jamb lived at Teotihuacán. Moreover, they were not the only Oaxacan visitors to Central Mexico: new surveys by Robert Cobean, reported in Topic 54, have revealed what may be a Oaxacan enclave near Tula,Hidalgo. Although its precise dating and cultural affiliation are unclear, this new discovery raises a host of exciting questions about the relations between the Cloud People and the great cities beyond their northern frontier.

# TOPIC 49
## Some Differences in Urban and Rural Settlement Patterns between Monte Albán and Teotihuacán

RICHARD E. BLANTON

The settlement pattern work by René Millon (1973) at Teotihuacán and by Sanders (1965; Sanders et al. 1975), Parsons (1971a), and myself (Blanton 1972) in the rural portions of the Valley of Mexico has provided data usable for comparison with our Valley of Oaxaca settlement pattern data (see also Wolf [ed.] 1976). The picture emerging there of Teotihuacán and its impact on rural populations in the Valley of Mexico is quite distinct from what our data indicate about the nature of regional organization and the capital center in the Valley of Oaxaca during the Classic period.

Perhaps the most striking feature of Teotihuacán's layout during the Classic is the presence of two large avenues that divide the city into quarters. At the point where these two roads intersect at the city's center, there are two large features—the Ciudadela, probably a governmental center, and the "Great Compound," probably the site's major marketplace (R. Millon 1973). This spatial organization, plus the presence of over 500 workshops, signify Teotihuacán's strong commercial orientation. In addition, Teotihuacán was surely the most important center of government and ritual for a large region, as indicated by the monumentality of public buildings there, not duplicated in scale in any other known site. The fact that Teotihuacán served simultaneously as its region's most important political, ritual, and commercial center explains its large population size: probably well over 125,000 at A.D. 600 (R. Millon 1976). Monte Albán was a smaller center in part because it had fewer regional and extraregional commercial functions. Teotihuacán's sphere of influence seems to have been much broader than Monte Albán's, extending all the way to the Guatemalan Highlands (Sanders and Price 1968).

Regions dominated by centers of the type exemplified by Teotihuacán, which combine the highest-order commercial and decision-making functions in one place, typically have a settlement pattern unlike that predicted by classical Central Place Theory as originally developed by Christaller (1966; Blanton 1976b). In such regions the development of secondary centers is retarded because, in a sense, of their inability to "compete" effectively with the dominant center. This lack of competition produces what geographers refer to as a "primate" settlement distribution, where the major center is much larger than secondary and tertiary centers (see Berry 1961). Regions dominated by such primate centers tend to be strongly "ruralized" and often poor in an economic sense, because of the inability of persons distant from the major center to participate actively in the region's marketing and production network (see C. A. Smith 1975). Our settlement pattern surveys in the rural Valley of Mexico suggest that this was precisely the impact Teotihuacán had on rural areas. Most communities distant from Teotihuacán were small hamlets and villages, and there was overall population decline in rural areas relative to previous periods (Parsons 1971a; Blanton 1972). As far as we know, secondary centers in the valley were only roughly $\frac{1}{20}$ the size of the major center, and there is little evidence for specialized production except in Teotihuacán itself or in directly adjacent communities (Blanton 1976c).

Even though we have only completed the settlement pattern survey in a relatively small portion of the Valley of Oaxaca, it is already becoming clear that Monte Albán had much less impact on rural population densities and the central place hierarchy of the region. In fact, as Monte Albán reached its largest size in Period IIIb, rural populations—at least in the area adjacent to the center—were as high as or higher than had been the case for all prior periods (Varner 1974; Kowalewski 1976); Monte Albán was only about six times the size of the second largest center in those areas we have intensively surveyed so far. While this is a primate distribution, it by no means reached the extreme primacy of the Valley of Mexico.

This situation is one which might have been predicted on theoretical grounds alone. Regions with the "disembedded" capital pattern—the Monte Albán type—typically have a more "normal" settlement distribution (i.e., closer to what would be predicted by Central Place Theory) because the political capital, spatially separated from other communities and with limited functions, does not distort the settlement hierarchy or inhibit the growth of secondary centers, especially commercial centers (Blanton 1976b).

These differences between Monte Albán and Teotihuacán are, in my opinion, some of the most interesting kinds of information to emerge from our work in Oaxaca; they show that there are several pathways to urban civilization. Thus, I am forced to disagree with Sanders and Santley's (1978) attempt to make the two sites sound more similar than they really are. In their review of the Monte Albán volume (Blanton 1978), they state that "the sequences of growth and decay at Monte Albán and Teotihuacán are very comparable, suggesting that similar processes were operative in affecting developments at the two centers" (Sanders and Santley 1978:303). I could not disagree more strongly, for obvious reasons. Clearly the two centers do not have similar histories. Teotihuacán has a long occupational sequence going back well into the Late Formative (R. Millon 1973:51). It developed from a few small villages into the region's dominant central place. Monte Albán has no such extended background. It was founded de novo in Period Ia, and from that time until the end of Period IIIb was the region's capital. It was this singular fact that led me to suggest that it had had a role in the region unlike that of Teotihuacán. Too, I doubt that similar processes were operative in both centers. The evidence seems to indicate that, in large part, the two differed considerably. Not only did the two centers have contrasting growth histories, they also had dramatically different locations relative to agricultural resources, and the evidence indicates the much greater importance of commercial activities at Teotihuacán. As Sanders and Santley themselves indicate in their review, "Teotihuacán was the center of a vast commercial market, a role made possible by the localized nature of obsidian source deposits. Monte Albán was not, in contrast, because the Valley of Oaxaca contained few if any resources whose natural distribution was so sharply circumscribed" (1978:303). I couldn't have stated it better myself.

# TOPIC 50
## Some Differences in Urban Layout between Monte Albán and Teotihuacán

DONALD ROBERTSON

The Teotihuacán settlement pattern or plan is one of strictly organized urban form, where the north–south east–west gridiron pattern which prevails (although not in a rigid checkerboard) dominates the location of individual residential and housing units. The formal importance of the residential part of the city is as great as the central "spine" of the Avenue of the Dead and its associated religious buildings. In other words, city planning, so easily possible on such a scale on a relatively flat valley floor, is pursued to its highest point in Mesoamerica and to its most inclusive degree; the whole city is included in the dominant overall plan, not just the ritual center.

Monte Albán in contrast, precisely because of its majestic setting on a mountain dominating such a valley floor, seems to be limited in its formal planning to the Main Plaza area. On the basis of data presented by Blanton (1978), it would seem that residences were distributed in a "functional," not a formal, way, on the slopes of the hill.

One can think here of the representative Colonial Spanish American city as the analog to Teotihuacán (San Francisco, California is an example of the sort of aberration that can emerge when the "formal" pattern of a rigid checkerboard is applied to a site of precipitous slopes and hills). Some Mexican mining towns, such as Taxco or Guanajuato, are examples of the Colonial functional plan—a plan that develops from the terrain rather than ignoring it, and uses natural rises and falls of land to determine the paths of streets, the location of buildings, and the placing of plazas. If these analogies are justified, then I would think of the residential buildings of Monte Albán as following no set imposed pattern but, like the Colonial mining town, following the demands and dictates of terrain.

This seems to be the case when one looks at the isolated buildings excavated so far away from the central planned Main Plaza. Is it possible that the original Period I city of Monte Albán, and even its center, was closer to the Colonial mining town type of plan than it is now? If the idea of a reorganization of the center during Periods II and III through such devices as the use of the wall and of forecourts to regularize the plaza is accepted, then the disjointed main axis of the Main Plaza and the askew placing of Building J and the slightly off-grid location, as it were, of Systems M and IV, were all to be corrected for. Perhaps we have (1) a somewhat irregular original plan for the plaza and a completely informal and irregular plan for the residential areas on the skirts of the hills, and (2) a later "regularizing" of the main religious concentration—but no parallel regularizing of residential areas, either because this task was too great or because no need was felt for it.

In this case, we could consider the possibility that Classic Monte Albán is an "old town" which grew and developed without a priori planning (cf. medieval plans such as the old parts of Paris, or all of London even today). Teotihuacán would, however, suggest a "new town" such as the late medieval *bastides* of southern France or the Colonial cities of the Spanish world, where a general plan of some sort and a pattern of formal regularity existed before the actual building began—a plan that survived throughout the subsequent development and growth of the city. The "new town" requires for the survival of its original regular plan a central authority with power to protect the plan from encroachments (some few seem to be present even in Teotihuacán). The "old town," on the other hand, requires for its later regularization an even stronger authority to impose on the inhabitants its will and its drive for regularity and unity. The Crown could not do this with the irregular plan of London after the Great Fire, even though plans were drawn up to make London into a magnificently organized Baroque planned city by destroying what little was left and overlaying the ruins with a completely new plan. Louis Napoleon, however, through Baron Haussmann, was able to do this in Paris where the *grandes boulevards* were laid out according to a new plan as though a plow had gone through the city, cutting it into a great spider web of streets intersecting at plazas

round, square, and rectangular, leaving behind the uniform façades of today. Even on the Right Bank, the irregular, tortuous, narrow medieval streets have become the back alleys of the elegant quarters in an "old town" become a "new town."

It is safe to say, thus, that a concentration of urban, or even national, political power is necessary to maintain an ideal plan, and even more political power to change an irregular plan into a regular one. Enough power seems to have been present to preserve the initial regularity of Teotihuacán, and enough was present ultimately to regularize the center of Monte Albán. It would seem that the residential areas of Monte Albán were on such irregular terrain that no attempt was ever mounted to impose a grid plan on them (although regularizing the center was done), in spite of the fact that the lords of Classic Monte Albán must have had knowledge of the regular plan of the residential quarters of Teotihuacán.

## TOPIC 51
## Differences in the Site Hierarchies below Monte Albán and Teotihuacán: A Comparison Based on the Rank–Size Rule

STEPHEN KOWALEWSKI

One of the ways that Monte Albán and Teotihuacán can be compared is by reference to a phenomenon called the *rank–size rule*, which is actually not a "rule" at all, but a description of the population size relationships among the members of a hierarchy of sites.

Both Monte Albán and Teotihuacán were the largest settlements in their respective areas. Each had below it a series of smaller settlements which could be ranked as second, third, fourth, fifth, and so on (in terms of population) for that area. Geographers (see Zipf 1949; Berry 1961, 1967; Haggett 1966) have experimented with various ways of displaying this ranking graphically. One way is to prepare a graph, using full-logarithmic paper, on which the population sizes of the various settlements in a system are plotted against their rank in size. In this format, the rank–size graphs of many modern-day regions take the form of a straight line: the size of the second largest city is half that of the leading center, the third largest city is one-third the size of the leading center, and so on. This straight-line distribution, which is log–normal, occurs when settlement satisfies the rank–size rule $Pn - P1(n)^{-1}$, where "$Pn$ is the population of the $n$th town in the series 1,2,3 . . . $n$ in which all towns in a region are arranged in descending order by population, and $P1$ is the population of the biggest town" (Haggett 1966:101). Although there is room for disagreement about what a log–normal city–size distribution reveals about a settlement system (see the discussion in Johnson 1977), in many cases it may mark a well-integrated system in

which each center is fairly tied to centers of more or less the same size as well as to several higher- and lower-order settlements.

Some settlement systems, however, produce rank–size graphs that depart from the log–normal pattern. If the size of the leading center is much larger than expected, or if the second order site is much smaller, the distribution is termed *primate*. Blanton (1976c) has suggested that in primate systems the leading center monopolizes much of the interaction of all sorts within its region and monopolizes exchange between its region and other regions. In primate systems the size of the largest center might not be explainable by internal factors, but could be accounted for by the city's participation in a wider network. One example used by Blanton (1976c) is Buenos Aires, which virtually monopolizes Argentina's exchange with the outside world and is enormously larger than the second city in its hierarchy.

Using population estimates from Parsons (1971a, 1971b) and Blanton (1972) for rural settlements in the Valley of Mexico, as well as an estimate of 175,000 persons for Teotihuacán (the midpoint of R. Millon's [1973] 150,000–200,000 estimate), Blanton (1976c) has constructed a series of rank–size graphs for the Valley of Mexico. His Figure 10 (republished here as Figure 6.3) shows Classic Teotihuacán as a huge primate center at the top of a series of sites that deviates widely from a log–normal distribution.

In Figure 6.4, I have prepared a similar graph for Monte

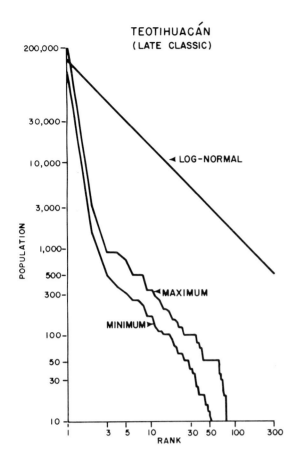

FIGURE 6.3. Rank–size distribution from the Late Classic period in the Valley of Mexico. (Redrawn from Blanton 1976c: Figure 10.)

Albán III in the Valley of Oaxaca, using population estimates for rural sites derived from unpublished surveys by Blanton, Varner, and myself. Monte Albán has been assigned a population of 22,500 (the midpoint of Blanton's [1978] 15,000–30,000 estimate). This graph may be compared with Blanton's for Teotihuacán and its region.

Whereas both Monte Albán and Teotihuacán were clearly the capitals of primate systems, the most striking feature of the rank–size graphs is the fact that Teotihuacán was much more of a primate center than was Monte Albán (compare, for example, the drop from first to second rank centers). This fact makes the whole Valley of Mexico graph seem much more "primate" in its general form. Closer inspection, however, shows that from the second to the *n*th rank the curves are quite similar, and actually would conform rather well to a log–normal line drawn through one of the secondary centers.

Finally, we might speculate a bit on what some of the differences mean. In both areas, sites below the second rank

have a more regular rank–size relationship; the major centers distort the pattern, and Teotihuacán distorts it far more than Monte Albán. As in the case of Buenos Aires, one reason for this distortion may be the fact that virtually all interaction with the outside world takes place through the capital; it could help explain the differences we see in the charts. Judging by the evidence presented in Topic 53, Monte Albán was probably the major point of articulation between the Zapotec and the rest of Mesoamerica. Teotihuacán, however, may have been the major point of articulation between the entire "central Mexican symbiotic area" (Sanders 1956) and the rest of Mesoamerica, thus monopolizing the internal and external relations of a much greater area.

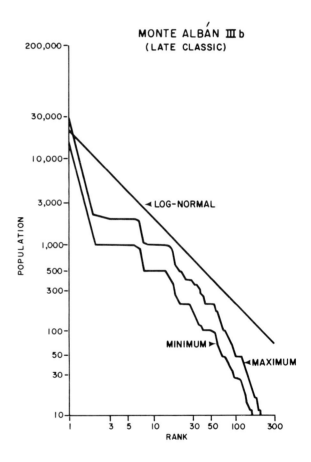

FIGURE 6.4. Rank–size distribution for the Monte Albán IIIb (Late Classic) period in the Etla, Central, and Zaachila–Zimatlán regions of the Valley of Oaxaca. Populations estimated at 10–25 persons per hectare, with settlements of less than 10 persons not counted. Future surveys of the Tlacolula and Ocotlán regions and reanalyses of Etla sites by Gary Feinman may necessitate some changes in this diagram, but are not expected to modify the basic pattern. (Data taken from Blanton 1978, Kowalewski 1976, and Varner 1974.)

# TOPIC 52
## The Oaxaca Barrio at Teotihuacán

JOHN PADDOCK

During the course of René Millon's study of urbanization at Teotihuacán, a zone was found that has since been called the "Oaxaca barrio." This area covers approximately 100 by 150 m and consists of sites 5, 6, and 7 within Square N1W6 (R. Millon 1973, Vol. 1, Part 2, p. 70). Its location is on the western outskirts of the city, roughly 3 km west of the Ciudadela and 2 km southwest of Tetitla.

Sites 5, 6, and 7, probably all building complexes, were characterized by a surface scatter of gray pottery that appeared identical to that found on many sites in the Valley of Oaxaca. At Site 7—a building approximately 20 by 50 meters in extent—I was able to excavate some 11.25 m² to bedrock, and Juan Vidarte later excavated an additional 64 m². The excavations yielded two Zapotec urns, one sealed under a floor and the other apparently associated with a burial; at least one sherd made of Oaxaca clay, and many more sherds made in Valley of Oaxaca style, but with local Teotihuacán clay; and a tomb having a stone jamb with Zapotec hieroglyphs carved on it. The associated building was a standard Teotihuacán apartment complex, very much like Xolalpan.

## DATING OF THE OAXACA BARRIO

As René Millon (1973:xiv) notes in the first volume of his final report on the Teotihuacán Mapping Project, our respective interpretations have been marked from the beginning by disagreements. One day in late 1966, during the excavations I supervised there, he noted that we were finding fragments of some very large Oaxaca-style vessels (*apaxtlis*). Millon proposed that this indicated the social role of the Oaxacans at Teotihuacán: they were servants, and these vessels were their washtubs. My reply was (and still is, though only 78% serious) that, in view of Millon's late dating of the Teotihuacán sequence, the first large constructions took place there when Monte Albán was already a centuries-old city; obviously the Oaxacans had been called in to show the Teotihuacanos how to do masonry construction.

Nevertheless, though we continue to differ, areas of agreement are growing. I think we both have believed from the first that further research would erase, or at least explain, our divergences. That process seems to have begun. There is still plenty to occupy us for a while, though, and the problem remains almost where it was in 1968.

So long as the Teotihuacán chronology remains tied to the Maya and the Goodman–Martínez–Thompson correlation, and the Oaxaca chronology to the Tehuacán Valley radiocarbon sequence, interpretations such as that put forward here [in *American Antiquity*] in July, 1967 are inevitable. However, some recent carbon dates from Oaxaca have been late enough to correspond well with the G–M–T correlation, resolving the difficulty while creating discrepancies with Tehuacán. At the same time, acceptance of the majority of the Teotihuacán radiocarbon dates would also wipe out the Oaxaca–Teotihuacán discrepancy; but so long as Millon rejects them, most others remain at least skeptical of the Teotihuacán radiocarbon dates. The Spinden correlation of the Maya dates is still another alternative that would bring the Teotihuacán and Oaxaca chronologies together. Lack of carbon dates in statistically firm numbers remains the fundamental difficulty in both Oaxaca and Teotihuacán [Paddock 1968a:126].

For some years now, and more than once in this seminar, I have deplored cross-dating from region to region as a proven source of problems. Monte Albán should be dated with materials from Monte Albán, and Teotihuacán with materials from Teotihuacán. Then we can approach the complex matter of the nature and duration of their contacts (not, please, "influences") in a way less imperiled by circularity. As long as we are dating them by cross-relations, our analysis of cross-relations is going to be weakened. We are not yet able to treat any of our regional sequences as finally and independently dated, however, so the obviously important matter of Teotihuacán–Monte Albán relations still cannot get the kind of analysis it deserves. Nevertheless, we know significantly more about Oaxaca than we did in 1967, and that knowledge justifies a careful review of the problem.

Since then, too, I have done an individual attribute analysis on the approximately 850 Oaxaca-style sherds we recovered at Teotihuacán. The results are far from earthshaking, but they will help.

Every sherd of Oaxaca style that I know from the Oaxaca barrio fits without forcing into a Transición II–III date at Monte Albán (though nearly all of them were produced at Teotihuacán from local clay). There are three classes of diagnostics that mark Transición: Period II ceramic types, Transición urns, and Period IIIa ceramic types. The Oaxaca barrio materials include all three, though the IIIa materials consist of exactly one fine urn. Perhaps we could count it as 40 sherds.

Obviously I cannot discard completely the possibility of a Monte Albán II occupation, because the Period II diagnostics are not only indistinguishable from, but identical with, many of those of Transición. I can and do infer that the evidence for a IIIa occupation justifies no more than a slight possibility of a very short one, for there is not a scrap of IIIa material except the urn—which Bernal classed as from the beginning of IIIa and which might, by definition, be a product of Transición. And I resort to Occam's Razor to propose that a short occupation is more likely than a long one. That is, a long one takes more explaining.

## THE ARCHAEOLOGICAL
## MATERIALS

There is one more point to be made regarding the length of the occupation as seen from Oaxaca. We did not dig much at the Oaxaca barrio, nor did Millon. We made 35 pits, 2.25 m², and extended one of them a meter out to one side. Of these, only 5 pits were taken to bedrock. Juan Vidarte, as a member of Millon's staff, then later excavated an 8- by 8-m area in detail. The 30 pits that were excavated only until a structure was exposed were helpful in showing us the nature of the last building at the site, but not much more.

This structure, which resembles the Xolalpan complex in nature and size, is about 20 by 50 m, or 1000 m². We excavated 11.25 m² to bedrock, and Vidarte did 64 more; and we excavated 45 m² down only to the first structure or other feature. The sherds I studied came from our work and from my surface pickup on not only Site 7 (in Millon's square N1W6), but also Sites 5 and 6. Let's assume that my group of Oaxaca-style sherds constitutes 2% of those that existed in the barrio, which would mean there were about 42,500 in all. A single potter, firing once every 5-day "week" and turning out only 20 vessels every 5 days, would produce 1460 vessels in a (solar) year. That is, one lone potter might easily have produced in 2 to 3 years all the sherds we found of Oaxaca style, and all those we left in the ground as well.

That a genuine Valley of Oaxaca potter—or several of them—did the work is beyond dispute. When it was done, and why, and why the product was limited to a small range of domestic types, are questions I do not think we can settle now. We do not know when, but Millon still believes—as he did in 1967—that the occupation lasted for centuries.

He is not just being unreasonable. If we go beyond the evidence of the Oaxaca-style sherds, the picture is complicated by several factors. I do not have the field data, and am not willing to trust memory for details, but I think what Millon means is that some of the crucial Oaxaca pieces were found overlying late Teotihuacán materials. He does not say so exactly, but I hope it is what he means:

> The excavations in the Oaxaca barrio suggest that these ties began in the latter part of the Tlamimilolpa phase (ca. A.D. 400). . . . In many ways our most striking discovery in the Oaxaca barrio was a stone-lined tomb in Oaxaca style. . . . The tomb is very late in Teotihuacán's history, surely dating to the seventh century A.D., whereas the Oaxaqueños had originally come to Teotihuacán in the fourth or early fifth century [1973:41–42].

The Transición urn, which was incomplete but included all the identifying features, was lying in fragments around an extended burial just under the surface. But Millon says that "the urn was evidently an heirloom if associated with the burial, for the other vessels found when the burial was excavated date toward the end of Teotihuacán's history as a city" (1973:41–42).

The other urn was no more helpful. Vidarte found it, broken but virtually complete, "apparently ritually smashed late in the city's history, in a small room attached to the south side of the principal temple" [of the residential complex] (R. Millon 1973:41).

The heirloom interpretation is usually avoided, but it may be inescapable here. The Transición urn definitely was virtually on the surface; no doubt the missing parts had been carried away in past plowing of the field where they lay. Portions of the burial, too, had been cut off by the plow. If there were Xolalpan or Metepec remains under the burial, that urn must have been at least 200 years old when placed there, even by my chronology. But a fine Transición urn— and this was a fine one before it was broken—is an object one can believe would be kept with care and might well last several centuries. (Caso and Bernal [1952] call it the Dios con Máscara Bucal de Serpiente, with a Glyph C in the headdress.)

Regarding the associations of this urn, Millon refers to "a burial" in a way that may be open to more than one interpretation. As I noted (Paddock 1967:426), this burial consisted of at least three skeletons, of which two were (disturbed) primaries in extended posture. The disturbance was considerable, and was obviously the work of a plow whose marks were visible in a nearby stucco floor. The field was fallow at the time of the excavation, but may have been cultivated for centuries. The burials were partially in the plow zone, and thus it is impossible to say what objects found nearby had been burial offerings, if any. But fragments of the urn were in virtual physical contact with the bones.

Extended burials are very rare in Teotihuacán, and thus Millon quite properly infers that these, in a posture normal to Oaxaca and in the area of Oaxaca ceramics, were extended because they were burials of Oaxacans. But there are some important questions left unanswered. If Oaxacans, even as few as one family, lived here for two or three centuries, where are the bodies? One burial and one tomb (much looted) do not go very far toward accounting for the number of people involved. If we make the highly dubious assumption that full excavation of the building would reveal 20 burials and 20 tombs (because we excavated in so little of it), with three persons interred in each burial and each tomb, that would give us 120 bodies. R. Millon (1973:45) estimates a minimum density of one person for each 53 m² in an apartment compound of about 1600 m², and one per 52 m² in a compound of 625 m², but he considers more probable the higher densities of one per 32 and 31 m² respectively. For the Site 7 compound of about 1000 m², then, we may try a minimum density of one person per 50 m² and a more probable figure of one per 30 m², giving us a minimum population of 20 and a more probable one of 33.

If this compound had a mean population of 30 for four generations—about 112 years—and all were buried there, we should have our 120 bodies.

As Millon notes, "the compound was constructed like other apartment compounds at Teotihuacán, though not of the best building materials. There was a good deal of adobe construction in walls, for example" (R. Millon 1973:41). If we accept his apparently reasonable inference that the Oaxacans were not of very high status at Teotihuacán, we should expect them to be more crowded in their living quarters. (Millon suggests on page 43 [1973] that foreign enclaves such as the Oaxaca barrio were kept outside an "inner city," thus accounting for the Oaxacans' location 3 km west of the city center, almost at its edge.)

From the viewpoint of a Oaxacan or a Oaxacanist, however, adobe construction is not inferior. It is preferred at Monte Albán. It is far more resistant to earthquakes, if it is well done, than is the inherently weak Teotihuacán wall structure. At Teotihuacán, where stone is superabundant and clayey earth fit for adobes much less so, adobe construction may even have been more costly.

The social status of the Oaxacans may have been somewhat different with respect to Teotihuacán and to Monte Albán. That they should have had two urns, both notable for quality, suggests that they would not have been lower-class at Monte Albán. But, except for the urns, there is no trace of real wealth in these people's possessions. The tomb might have shown some, but R. Millon (1973:41) says it was looted twice.

The second urn is not only fine; in some respects it is unique (R. Millon 1967b:44, 1973:Figs. 58, 59). Like the Transición one, it represents the Dios con Máscara Bucal de Serpiente, who, Caso and Bernal (1952:155, 162) cautiously suggest, may have been related to Quetzalcoatl. To be sure, he is utterly lacking in feathers or other avian attributes, and they see a number of other connections, especially with Cocijo. Like the Transición urn, it was made in Oaxaca, in Bernal's opinion and in mine; and, again like the other, it is of such quality that it was well worth carrying on foot to Teotihuacán. At 34 cm, it is a large example for its period. The personage wears only a *maxtlatl* and his symbolic and decorative elements, which consist of bracelets, a necklace, the mouth mask, and a large glyphic carving over the forehead. The necklace is unique in having a small shell plaque at each side and a rather large rectangular plaque of smooth, polished green stone, perhaps jade, placed as if it were hanging from the center of the necklace.

Beginning in Transición II–III, this personage is commonly represented with a Glyph C over the forehead (in Periods I and II there is no glyph at all, and often no other decoration, in the headdress). The Teotihuacán specimen is unique again in having not only a day sign but a numeral as well in the headdress, and the day sign is not Glyph C, but D (Flower) or J (Reed?). Glyphs D and J probably are often confused if, for any reason, the diagonal slash across the center element, distinctive of Glyph J, is missing. Removing this slash converts Glyph J, in fact, into a very typical Glyph D, especially if there is a small circle or *chalchihuitl* at bottom center where the three "petals" come together.

Unfortunately for interpretation, the Teotihuacán urn has a day sign I find difficult to assign clearly to one or the other glyph. It lacks the diagonal slash, but the center "petal" where it would be is lower than the rest of the relief, and rough, as if something were missing there. Is it then a Glyph D? There is a small and rounded element right at the point where it should be for a Glyph D, but that element is a

numeral 1, part of the 8 made up by a 5-bar and three units, the other two resting on the points of the 5-bar. Thus interpretation as Glyph D is less than certain, though we should have in mind that use of a numeral there might be a visual pun of a kind ancient Mesoamericans were given to. Thus I am unable to rule out either Glyph D or Glyph J; if the rough area of the center petal had, in shell or jade—as seems fairly likely—a mosaic with a diagonal, the name of the personage would be 8 J; but if the center numeral is simultaneously a *chalchihuitl*, he is 8 D. Unhappily again, 8 D occurs on Stela 9 at Monte Albán (Caso 1928:31), and 8 J on Stela 8 (Caso 1928:36).

Less troublesome by far is the name on a doorjamb of the tomb (R. Millon 1973:Fig. 60). This is 9 L, and there is no doubt about it, even though the eye that usually occurs in the middle is missing here, replaced by a rather faint U-shaped incision.

Less than 2m deep and badly scrambled, the deposits do have some stratigraphy because of the alterations and reconstructions that the buildings underwent. "So far as we know, no major stone-walled, 'concrete'-and-plaster surfaced, residential compounds have been found outside the 'Street of the Dead' area that antedate the Tlamimilolpa phase," says Millon, and the Oaxaca compound is an example he cites of the new kind of construction taking place in that phase.

> The Tlamimilolpa phase (ca. A.D. 200–450) is characterized by an enormous amount of building activity, apparently signaling a revolutionary change in settlement pattern. Permanent stone-walled residential compounds, most consisting of a number of apartments, appear to have been built in all parts of the city, replacing most of the earlier structures built of relatively impermanent materials [R. Millon 1973:56].

"No immediately identifiable Oaxaca remains were found in what could confidently be interpreted as primary deposition. They were all fragmented and mixed with presumably later Teotihuacán materials, some of the latter including whole vessels. The Oaxaca sherds occurred from surface to bedrock in a series of buildings," I reported after our excavations and before Vidarte's (Paddock 1967:426). After Vidarte's work, the picture was slightly altered: "That all the Oaxaca material found was in secondary deposition now seems somewhat less likely. The burials and the two urns argue against it, and the discovery on bedrock of enormous sherds of Oaxaca basins likewise weakens the interpretation. However, that most of the Oaxaca material was in secondary deposition still seems clear" (Paddock 1968a:126). Now we have an explanation, I think.

Millon agrees that Teotihuacán–Monte Albán connections antedate the construction at Site 7:

> Both urns belong . . . to the time . . . when contacts between Teotihuacán and Monte Albán are traditionally thought to have become important. The excavations in the Oaxaca barrio suggest that these ties began in the latter part of the Tlamimilolpa phase (ca. A.D. 400). . . . Interestingly, the ceramic links to Teotihuacán at Monte Albán may begin slightly earlier. The Teotihuacán forms that appear in Monte Albán during the Epoch of Transition there are either forms with a wide time span ('*floreros*') or are forms that appear to coexist in the middle of

the Tlamimilolpa phase at Teotihuacán (ca. A.D. 350) [R. Millon 1973:41].

And, he also agrees, "It is possible that our chronology places Teotihuacán too late, and that the time span represented by the Miccaotli, Tlamimilolpa, Xolalpan, and Metepec phases is shorter than we think, that is shorter than the period from A.D. 150 to A.D. 750" (1973:61).

Further facilitating explanation of the chronological disagreement, even if not doing away with it, are the interesting possibilities of Millon's assertion that little is known of pre-Tlamimilolpa housing, partly because "in building the great residential walled compounds the Teotihuacán builders seem to have deliberately removed the shallow topsoil to expose the underlying hard, dense tepetate, which makes a good foundation for the heavy compound walls. In order to make a reasonably level surface, the tepetate itself was cut down in places, and hollows in it were filled in with tamped earth" (R. Millon 1973:56). The Oaxaca compound of Site 7 was one of those Tlamimilolpa constructions.

Therefore, my field observation on the spot seems to have been fairly close to the mark: "the tentative inference first put forward is that the Oaxaca sherds came to the buildings as fill, taken from a dump probably not far away" (Paddock 1967:427). Now I would propose that the material came, perhaps not from a midden, but from the process of clearing itself, as described by Millon for construction of a Tlamimilolpa-phase building.

Only this kind of operation would account for the high proportion of early Oaxaca sherds on the surface, over remains of relatively late Teotihuacán buildings—they had been incorporated in walls. Those few Oaxaca-style sherds found on the tepetate may have been in primary deposition, left there with earth left to fill in low spots. The IIIa urn was likewise in apparently primary deposition, though, as Millon proposed, it no doubt was already an heirloom by then. After the urn was smashed on a small pyre on a floor of the compound, the building was demolished around it and a new floor laid over it. After that, a temple was built over the room of the urn, and two additions were made to the temple later still (R. Millon 1967b:42).

Because I think all Oaxaca specialists would agree that a date of A.D. 400 for Transición II–III is now out of the question, I should like to propose a rather simple and plausible, though not now demonstrable, way out of the dilemma that does not demand of Millon that he give up his chronology. Let's suppose that during Transición, around A.D. 100 or, perhaps, as late as A.D. 200, a group of Monte Albán people took up residence at Teotihuacán. At that time, hard as it is to imagine, though the city had a highly organized and imposing central area, its outlying residential sections were much less structured and the buildings there were of impermanent types. The time (A.D. 100–200) is, by Millon's chronology, Teotihuacán II or Miccaotli. After several decades, perhaps a couple of generations, the rebuilding begins in residential areas; eventually it reaches the Oaxaca people's area. There is planning, and a new regularity appears in the outer parts of the city. Since the houses have been built of impermanent materials, they have by now been rebuilt several times. There is a fair amount of debris around, and there is a small mound made of the remains of earlier versions of the houses. When the tepetate is cleared for the foundations of the new and more ambitious structure, this debris and the mound are just moved aside while the site is levelled. Then the same debris is incorporated into the walls of the new structure.

During 1974 I prepared a paper on Middle Classic in Monte Albán for a symposium chaired by Esther Pasztory (Paddock 1978). I will here cite a paragraph because it says as well as I can just what needs to be said about why I am so insistent on a Transición date for the Oaxaca-style pottery I have studied.

The "official" statement on the subject of Teotihuacán II–Transición resemblances, of course, can be found in Caso, Bernal, and Acosta (1967:306). As I have summarized it:

> Many years ago, Caso hypothesized that the beginning of Teotihuacán contacts in Transition II–III at Monte Albán had occurred during Teotihuacán II. In pre-radiocarbon days, his bases for this were necessarily stylistic. For example, he noted that the large "lampshade" headdress of the Transition urn (Paddock 1966e:Figs. 91, 93, 95, 97), if flattened from front to back, would result in the sort of broad band headdress (Covarrubias 1957:129 center) typical of many Teotihuacán II figurines (personal communication; he seems not to have published these observations, but see Caso 1965b:856). The surprisingly small number of objects imported from Teotihuacán that turned up in excavations at Monte Albán does in fact include some from Teotihuacán II. And excavations in the 'Oaxaca barrio' at Teotihuacán in 1966–67 showed that occupation there had occurred (in my present opinion, exclusively) during Transition II–III of Monte Albán (R. Millon 1967b; Paddock 1967:426–27, 1968a:125–26). Unhappily, the area had been thoroughly churned up during ancient reconstructions. As a result it is possible to say with confidence only that the associated Teotihuacán materials range from Early Tlamimilolpa (initial III) to Late Xolalpan (final III) or even Metepec (IV) [Evelyn C. Rattray, personal communication, 1974].

The absence of Miccaotli materials in the excavated area might be attributed to scanty excavation and to the tendency of the Oaxacans to use Oaxaca-style ceramics at first. (They became acculturated, as is shown by the development of "hybrid" pieces that seem to be Teotihuacanized Oaxaca types.)

In addition to the headdress of the Transición urns (which reminds me of a lampshade and Caso of a visor), a short cape is an important and frequent element in their costume and in that of the corresponding Teotihuacán II figurines. Obviously such a combination of two traits is much more than twice as strong an argument as would be either one alone.

Illustrations cited (Caso, Bernal, and Acosta 1967:306) include a number in early publications on Teotihuacán by Seler and by Gamio, now so hard to locate that I will not list them. The citation of Veracruz material is mistaken, referring to Medellín Zenil 1962 (*Magia de la Risa*) when what is meant is his 1960 *Cerámicas del Totonacapan*, Láminas (not Figuras) 38 and 39. For Teotihuacán, they cite Covarrubias (1957:Fig. 54). I would add a Veracruz example (Covarrubias 1957:Fig. 85, upper right).

But the Covarrubias illustration of a Teotihuacán II figurine (center of his Fig. 54) reveals, just above it, a fascinating further point. The two figurines at top left, included as examples of Teotihuacán I, have "lampshade" headdresses, and the one at the left has a cape. Showing prudence just this once, I will not offer an opinion on the soundness of attributing these figurines to Teotihuacán I as the caption does; Covarrubias died before having checked the captions in the book, and they include many errors. This same one, for example, says the Classic at Teotihuacán is Periods III and IV.

For clarity, I should like to add some further illustrations of the Monte Albán lampshade headdress and the corresponding Teotihuacán II figurines. For the first, see Caso and Bernal (1952), Figures 33, 71, 229, 262, 263, 266, 416, 417, and 419. For the second, see Séjourné (1966a), dust jacket, Figures 2, 38, 41, 49, 57A top, 106 left, 150, 154, and Láminas 52 and 54.

Caso's own statement in print on the topic is rather glancing, but the documentation will be the better for including it: "We have no sculpture attributable with certainty to the transition period between Periods II and IIIA in Monte Albán. This corresponds to Teotihuacán II and is the time when the influence of the latter city begins to be felt in the valley of Oaxaca" (Caso 1965b:856).

Another pertinent point is made regarding the exceptional urn that was found not to be empty. Perhaps not by coincidence, it too is the Dios con Máscara Bucal de Serpiente. Caso and Bernal (1952:158) tell us that "an urn of this type was found in Mound i at Monte Albán, together with a vase engraved with the glyph 2 or 3 J . . . (Fig. 270). This urn was filled with jade figurines of the Teotihuacán III type." It is of Monte Albán IIIa, and plainly later than the one from Teotihuacán—that is, it lacks the reminiscences of Transición that are so clear in that one. Like almost everything in the data on cross-relations, this interpretation is not quite airtight. Stone figurines last a long time. Still, it does fit.

If we do not adopt some such strategy as this, we may find ourselves being asked to equate Transición temporally with Xolalpan, dated A.D. 450–650 by Millon, or even Metepec, A.D. 650–750. Since we should be hard pressed to accept a date later than A.D. 250 or so for beginning IIIa, in view of its ending by A.D. 400 or earlier, I have tried to make my argument clear even at cost of brevity.

But it is already overlong, and I have not even begun the description of the sherds. Some data on the pottery, and the neutron activation studies that showed I was right about what it was made of, may be found in a paper now in Fowler and Paddock (1973).

Of the 856 sherds brought to Oaxaca for study, 9 were discarded as normal Teotihuacán material on examination. And of the 847 remaining, 464 were fragments from the sides of highly recognizable Monte Albán conical *cajetes*—except that they were made, used, and broken in Teotihuacán. There were 87 olla sherds. Interestingly, the 11 sherds from cylindrical *cajetes* were not copies of Teotihuacán cyl-

inders, but rather were the distinctive Monte Albán kind. All the 15 sahumador fragments were of the Monte Albán II type, a nearly orange ware with subhemispherical bowl. Another striking find was 4 sherds of the apparently "independent" Black-and-White ware of the Caballito–Loma Larga–Mitla area; this ware is virtually unknown in Monte Albán.

The G-12 gray pottery, which is especially important because it turns up in the Mixteca Alta and Baja as well, was represented by 39 sherds, all rims—because not a single sherd with combed bottom was found. The single one that includes the whole side and a bit of bottom has a smooth, plain bottom instead. This trait seems to be associated with wide, shallow grooves on the rim, so wide that the polisher gets into them. There was an unusual proportion of non-gray colors in the Teotihuacán batch. Perhaps the several varieties of G-12 can be seriated.

The G-21 of Monte Albán was identified in 51 bottom sherds, but we have no idea of the vessel form; the enormous proportion of plain gray or black conical *cajete* sides probably represents many sherds from G-12 and G-21 as well as from truly plain *cajetes*.

## THE BURIALS FROM THE OAXACA BARRIO

Michael Spence (1976) studied human skeletal material from the Oaxaca barrio. The sample comprised four adults (two males, one female, and one indeterminate, ranging in age from 25 years to middle age), one child of 5 to 7 years, and an infant, all from the tomb with the carved jamb, and several burials from outside the tomb area, including at least two definite adult males, one probable and one possible female, and some indeterminate adults. Spence examined the material for 21 qualitative genetic traits such as supraorbital foramina, malar tuberosities, bridged supraorbital notches, and so on. He concluded that the homogeneity of the individuals from the tomb suggests close genetic ties, but the burials from outside the tomb "show some genetic distance, indicating little or no intermarriage between the elite [i.e., those in the tomb] and the commoner occupants of the [Oaxaca] *barrio*." He concludes that the commoners were somewhat homogeneous genetically as well, suggesting only limited intermarriage between the people of the Oaxaca barrio and the Teotihuacanos who surrounded them.

## TEOTIHUACÁN, MONTE ALBÁN, AND KAMINALJUYÚ: SOME GENERAL CONSIDERATIONS

Even though much more might, and eventually will, be said, it is time to return to more general considerations. Can we characterize the relations of Teotihuacán and

Monte Albán? We have some small but interesting beginnings. Millon notes that, in contrast to the Maya area, there seem to be few or no representations of armed Teotihuacanos at Monte Albán (see Marcus, Topic 53). "Altogether, the evidence suggests that the relationship . . . may have been closer and of a different kind than the relationship of Teotihuacán to other foreign centers. There may have been a kind of 'special relationship' between Teotihuacán and Monte Albán. This may explain why so far the only unmistakable foreign enclave at Teotihuacán is the *barrio* of Oaxaqueños" (R. Millon 1973:42).

At the 1966 Mesa Redonda on Teotihuacán, Caso and Bernal were present, and so was I; but the discussion of Teotihuacán–Monte Albán relations was limited to the following:

> Let's see what happens if we attempt a first approximation of a comparative quantification of Teotihuacán influence at two important sites. If we compare the excavations in Kaminaljuyú and in Monte Albán, for example, we might suggest that in tons of dirt moved, or in area explored, the Monte Albán work is of over 10 times the magnitude of the Kaminaljuyú work. Conceivably it is 100 times, but that doesn't matter here; let's say 10 times. Now, how many Teotihuacán pieces were found at each of these sites, that is, how many pieces imported from Teotihuacán? Those of Kaminaljuyú surely are more than 10 times as many as those found at Monte Albán. Combining these two conservative figures, we see that the evidence of trade with Teotihuacán in Kaminaljuyú indicates an intensity 100 times that in Monte Albán. A detailed study easily might raise the figure to 1,000 times, or more [Paddock 1972a:232–233].

If we multiply that figure by 3 because Kaminaljuyú is 3 times as far from Teotihuacán, we will perhaps begin to communicate what seems to me so special about the relationship between Teotihuacán and Monte Albán.

If Teotihuacán were less visibly connected with Tikal, and even with Copán, we might perhaps try to shrug off the Kaminaljuyú phenomenon and its contrast with Monte Albán as a weird accident of geography, or war, or temperament, or commerce. Millon is absolutely right in calling the Monte Albán case special, for it is a defiance of relative propinquity. The handful of Teotihuacán objects at Monte Albán is, nevertheless, more than its converse: at Teotihuacán, nobody but Oaxacans has ever been caught dead with a Oaxaca object.

# TOPIC 53
## Teotihuacán Visitors on Monte Albán Monuments and Murals

JOYCE MARCUS

No Teotihuacán barrio, paralleling the Oaxaca barrio at Teotihuacán, has been found at Monte Albán. Persons from Teotihuacán, however, are apparently represented on a number of important monuments at Monte Albán. Most of these occurrences date to Monte Albán IIIa, which (if we gloss over the chronological disagreements between Paddock [Topic 52] and René Millon [1973]) makes them at least broadly contemporary with the Oaxaca barrio at Teotihuacán. Two examples that I discuss include stone monuments of the South Platform in the Main Plaza and the Lápida de Bazán, found on the slope of Mound X. My discussion will support earlier suggestions by Kidder, Jennings, and Shook (1946), as well as Clara Millon's (1973) definition of a specific kind of headgear, the "Tassel Headdress," which is associated with Teotihuacán persons (perhaps of "ambassadorial" status) who traveled to distant parts of Mexico and Guatemala.

## THE SOUTH PLATFORM

The South Platform is one of the most impressive single structures on the Main Plaza at Monte Albán. Its base is more than 100 m on a side, and its flat summit rises more than 15 m above the plaza, serving as a platform for several structures which add further to its height. The building has not been fully explored, but Acosta's (1958–1959) excavations suggest that the South Platform is a huge pyramidal mound built in one stage during Monte Albán IIIa.

At the turn of the century, Leopoldo Batres (1902) visited Monte Albán to obtain carved stones to exhibit at the World's Fair in Mexico City. He removed a number of monuments from the corners of the South Platform. Caso (1928), utilizing Batres's plans and field notes, reports that Stela 1 was removed from the northeast corner (Stelae 2, 3, and 4 were also found in this area); Stela 8 was removed from the southeast corner; and Stela 7 was removed from the southwest corner. In the northwest corner, Batres removed Stelae 5 and 6, but apparently did not notice that one apparently blank cornerstone, the so-called Estela Lisa, was carved on its underside.

During the 1950s, Jorge Acosta (1958–1959) was assigned the task of replacing the monuments in the South Platform. In most cases, however, he was given well-made cement copies of the stelae, and the originals were left in Mexico City. Acosta evidently did not have Batres's original plan, and was uncertain where some of the stones had originally stood. He therefore set several according to "esthetic criteria" alone; his principal mistake was the placement of Stela 8 near the northwest corner, rather than the southeast corner. Acosta, however, in the process of setting the copies of Stelae 5 and 6 in the northwest corner, discovered the hidden carving on the underside of the Estela Lisa. Acosta also, in the process of preparing the northwest corner to receive the stones, discovered a well-made stone box 56 cm below the corner of the building. Inside the box was an offering of 5 large spiny oyster shells, 5 smaller spiny oyster shells, 10 tent olive shells, a necklace of 7 jade beads, and a Monte Albán IIIa spouted olla, all painted with red pigment. Excited by this discovery, Acosta (1958–1959) checked for offerings in the three other corners of the building. The northeast and southwest corners had virtually identical offerings in stone boxes, but the southeast corner did not reveal a stone box. The reasons were probably architectural—because bedrock was so much lower there, the southeast corner of the building had an extra 4.4 m of fill below it compared with the other corners.

Intrigued by these new discoveries, Acosta examined the underside of Stela 1, which previously had never been examined. He was surprised to find that its underside, like that of the Estela Lisa, had a carved inscription that was totally different from the one on its face. Eventually it became clear that all four corners of the South Platform had stones carved on one or two edges with related inscriptions. None of these inscriptions would have been visible to an observer when the stones were in place[1]; probably, however, they dated to the dedication of the building, since three of them were underlain by offerings in stone boxes.

Iconographic details suggest that all four of these "hidden" inscriptions depict named personages from Teotihuacán visiting Monte Albán, and the associated dedicatory offerings suggest this visit might have coincided with the completion of the South Platform. Further, I would argue that even the standardized offerings of *Spondylus* shells can be duplicated at Teotihuacán; the only clearly "Zapotec" elements are the Period IIIa ollas. These ollas correlate well with the appearance of the associated stelae, all of which are carved in Monte Albán IIIa style.

These "hidden" carvings in the corners of the South Platform all seem to relate to the same event: eight persons, wearing typical Teotihuacano headdresses, leave a place with temples decorated in typical Tetitla style, and arrive at a place called "the Hill of 1 Jaguar" where they are greeted by a lord wearing a typical Zapotec headdress. These eight persons can be divided into two groups of four, and each group of four is mentioned on two of the building corners. One group is named on Stelae 7 and 8 (southwest and southeast corners), the other group on Stela 1 and the Estela Lisa (northeast and northwest corners). On Stela 7 and the Estela Lisa, we see the full figures of each group of four; on Stelae 1 and 8, we have only abbreviations of their names. Now let us look at these carvings in detail (Figure 6.5).

[1] The carvings on the *faces* of these stelae, which *would* have been visible, have been discussed in Topic 42.

## STELA 7

On the right edge of Stela 7, which would have been hidden, four individuals in a procession are shown. These four individuals are elegantly dressed; from left to right, the first is wearing a Tlaloc headdress, the second a jaguar headdress, and the third and fourth serpent headdresses. They all carry small copal bags, similar to the one carried by the figure on the left side on the Lápida de Bazán (see p. 179), and to those carried by the figures on the Calpulalpan bowl from Las Colinas in Tlaxcala (Linné 1942:Figures 170–174), a site contemporary with Teotihuacán.

Additionally, the individuals on Stela 7 have a row of feathered tassels as part of their headdresses. Kidder, Jennings, and Shook (1946:234–235) first called attention to this headdress element, calling it the "Tri-mountain Symbol," and noting that such a headdress decoration seemed to be characteristic of Teotihuacán art. The same Tri-mountain Symbol occurred on a polychrome bowl at Kaminaljuyú, and the authors proceeded to compare it to Stelae 7 and 8 and the Lápida de Bazán at Monte Albán as well as to the already-mentioned mold-made bowl from Calpulalpan. In other words, as far back as 1946, Kidder, Jennings, and Shook had already associated the so-called Tri-mountain Symbol with the sites of Teotihuacán and Monte Albán; however, since there were at that time more known occurrences of the symbol at Monte Albán, they were cautious in their designation of site origin.

It is now clear that this type of headdress (more recently designated "Tassel Headdress" by Clara Millon [1973]) is associated with people from Teotihuacán. Clara Millon (1973:303) notes that more fragments similar to the Calpulalpan vessel have now been found within Teotihuacán itself, especially in the Yayahuala compound, and in a test excavation in a structure west of the Street of the Dead. On the Calpulalpan bowl, the Tassel Headdress occurs as a separate glyph and as the headgear of one of the four men in a procession (Séjourné 1966b:Fig. 117).

On Stela 7, the four men in Tassel Headdresses are given hieroglyphic names in the system of Caso (1938:87) as follows. Individual 1: broken off; Individual 2: 7 or 8 Glyph N + 3 calendric hieroglyph?; Individual 3: 5 Glyph D ("Turquoise")[2] + noncalendric hieroglyph; and Individual 4: 12 Glyph H ("Skull") + treble-scroll compound (this last element occurs with great frequency in the iconography of Teotihuacán). Caso believed the other hieroglyphs associated with these "day names" were "months"; however, it seems more reasonable to assume that these accompanying glyphs are additional titles which add specificity to a personal name taken from the 260-day calendar (as in the case of later names such as ♂ 8 Deer "Tiger Claw").

[2] Although Caso (1928:Fig. 7, XVI) classifies this glyph as 5D, it bears a closer resemblance to "Turquoise" than the other "Flower" glyphs designated in Fig. 7 as "D."

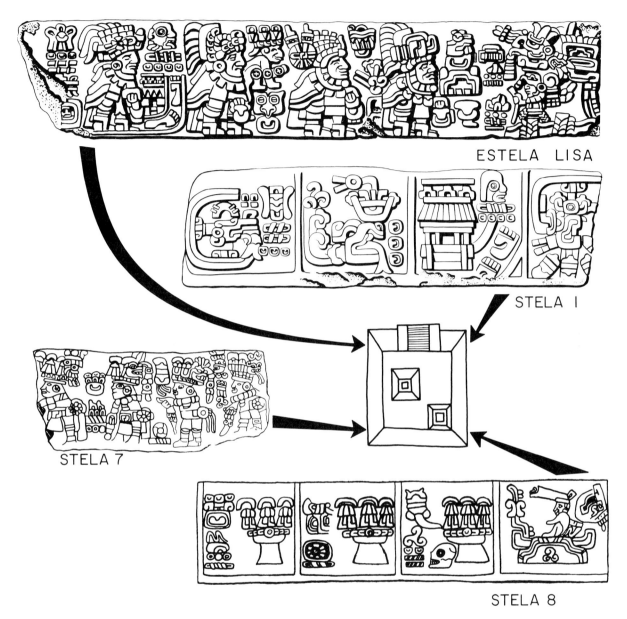

FIGURE 6.5. Carvings on the edges of stelae in the four corners of the South Platform at Monte Albán, showing named visitors from Teotihuacán.

## STELA 8

On the under and upper edges of Stela 8 can be found more hidden carvings of Teotihuacán personages. One is immediately impressed with the similarity between the names on the underside of Stela 8 and the names on the right edge of Stela 7. Stela 8, however, does not reveal the complete portrayals of the persons themselves, but rather a set of abbreviated references consisting of the Tassel Headdress plus the hieroglyphic names. From left to right, these are 7 or 8 Glyph N + 3 calendric hieroglyph(?) + brasero with Tassel Headdress; 5 Glyph D + noncalendric hiero-

glyph + brasero with Tassel Headdress; 12 Glyph H + treble-scroll hieroglyphic compound + brasero with Tassel Headdress. These abbreviations appear to contain three of the same names and hieroglyphs we saw on the right edge of Stela 7; however, the Tassel Headdresses are supported by braseros or incense burners instead of the heads of the individuals as on Stela 7. Following these three abbreviations on Stela 8 comes a place glyph containing the treble-scroll element; above the "hill sign" is a seated person. The identity of this place glyph is unknown, but Teotihuacán looms as one candidate.

On the upper edge of Stela 8 there are two other glyphic

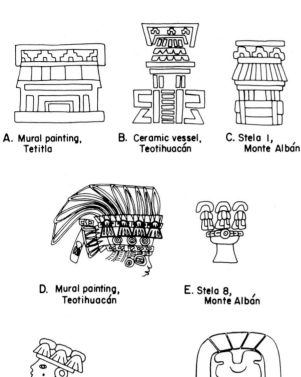

FIGURE 6.6. Hieroglyphs, symbols, and motifs linking Teotihuacán and Monte Albán: (A) temple decorated in Tetitla style from a mural at Teotihuacán; (B) Tetitla-style temple carved on a ceramic vessel from Teotihuacán; (C) Tetitla-style temple shown on Stela 1, Monte Albán; (D) figure with Tassel Headdress from mural at Teotihuacán; (E) stylized Tassel Headdress shown on Stela 8, Monte Albán; (F) figure with Tassel Headdress on polychrome bowl, Kaminaljuyú; (G) stylized Tassel Headdress from Lápida de Bazán, Monte Albán; (H) 9 Earthquake glyph from tomb jamb in Oaxaca Barrio, Teotihuacán.

compartments preserved, containing (among other elements) the same treble-scroll element that formed part of the name of an individual mentioned above (on Stelae 7 and 8) as well as the interior of the place glyph shown on the upper edge of Stela 8.

## THE ESTELA LISA

This stela from the northwest corner of the South Platform has no carving on its face, as its name implies. On its underside, however, is yet another carved "hidden" scene,

showing four men in a procession facing a Zapotec lord. In order to distinguish them from Individuals 1–4 on Stela 7, we call them Individuals A–D. From left to right, the hieroglyphic names with which they are associated are Individual A, 13 Knot + hieroglyph (somewhat eroded); Individual B, 9 Monkey + "Tetitla" temple with footprints; Individual C, 1 Owl + Jaguar hieroglyphic compound; and Individual D, treble-scroll + other glyphs. To the right, the Zapotec lord wears an elaborate headdress with serpent head, as well as a mask covering his eyes and the upper third of his face; his name is given as 8 (?) + unknown hieroglyph. He is associated with a hill sign with the glyph 1 Jaguar above it. The name "Hill of 1 Jaguar" may possibly refer to Monte Albán, or to one of the hills that make up Monte Albán.

## STELA 1

Stela 1, in the northeast corner of the platform, has hidden scenes carved on both its upper and lower edges. On the underside we find abbreviated references to some of the same persons shown in more detail on the Estela Lisa; these references are given in a series of glyphic "compartments" set apart by vertical bands. Moving from left to right, in Compartment 1 we find the same name that appears with Individual A on the Estela Lisa (13 Knot). In Compartment 2 we have a serpent and the number 3 with Glyph C. In Compartment 3 we immediately recognize the name that appeared with Individual B on the Estela Lisa (9 Monkey), associated with footprints leading away from a temple.

This temple structure associated with footprints and the name 9 Monkey are depicted in an identical manner on the underside of the Estela Lisa and Stela 1. This temple is nearly identical with several from the Tetitla compound at Teotihuacán (von Winning 1947; Séjourné 1966c:Figure 26), where they appear frequently in murals (e.g., Room 12 at Tetitla) and on ceramics. The *talud–tablero* architecture, the placement of the jambs, and the characteristic type of roofs are described by Séjourné for Tetitla as follows:

1) Una superficie trapezoidal cuya altura, en Teotihuacán como entre los aztecas, sobrepasa a menudo la de los muros de los aposentos.
2) Una cornisa en la que se empotraban las espigas de las almenas.
3) Un caballete que, al juntarse con la cornisa, enmarcaba las almenas [1966c:126].

Von Winning has also noted, in his description of a Teotihuacán vessel, that this type of temple structure is characteristic of Teotihuacán:

The first example to be considered is a champlevé tripod vase on which has been incised four times a temple construction, alternating with a Tlaloc face. . . . The temple has been depicted in such a way that all its architectural details are clear and unmistakable. The sloping base, as well as the rectangular wall panels, is characteristic of the classical Teotihuacán period. The stairway in the center ascends to the entrance of the temple chamber. Emphasis is given to the elaborate roof, consisting of beams over the doorway, supporting the typical thatched roof, which, in turn, is crowned by three pinnacles. Thus we have a complete picture of a teocalli, and if we compare it with the corresponding designs on the murals at Tetitla [Teotihuacán] of the epoch . . . , we find that the artist followed an established pattern. Also at Tetitla the roof is out of proportion, being larger than the lower part. In both cases the pinnacles are above the thatch [1947:170–171].

It therefore seems reasonable to propose that the individual 9 Monkey came from Teotihuacán, if not from the actual Tetitla precinct, which lies only 2 km from the Oaxaca barrio at Teotihuacán.

## THE OFFERING BOXES

The stone offering boxes associated with Stelae 1 and 7 and the Estela Lisa are also of interest, since similar offerings of jade beads and *Spondylus* shells coated with red ocher were common at Teotihuacán (Séjourné 1966a:*Lám.* 47). The uniformity of each offering, as indicated in Table 6.1, is remarkable.

## THE LÁPIDA DE BAZÁN

The famous Lápida de Bazán is a slab of *tecali* (actually fine-grained Oaxaca travertine) discovered by Martín Bazán in a deposit of fill on the west side of Mound X at Monte Albán (Caso 1938:Fig. 25). Based on the carving style, Caso assigned this stone to Monte Albán IIIa, and I see no reason to question the date.

The slab (Figure 6.7) shows two figures, the one on the left dressed as a Teotihuacano with a copal pouch in one hand, the other dressed as a jaguar in the manner of the lords of Monte Albán. Caso, who was the first to interpret the figure on the left as a Teotihuacano, identified his name as 8 Turquoise, and that of the jaguar-lord as 3 Turquoise, based on the glyphs in the pedestals beneath each individual. (It is possible, however, that their names are in the columns of text rather than the pedestals.)

Each figure is accompanied by a column of text that, because it contains no calendric signs, appears to be essentially narrative (historical and political) in content.

TABLE 6.1
Contents of Three Stone Offering Boxes under the Corners
of the South Platform at Monte Albán[a]

| Location | Spiny oyster (*Spondylus princeps*) | Spiny oyster (*Spondylus calcifer*) | Tent olive (*Oliva porphyria*) | Jade beads | Period IIIa olla |
|---|---|---|---|---|---|
| NW corner | 5 | 5 | 10 | 7 | 1 |
| NE corner | 5 | 5 | 10 | 7 | — |
| SW corner | 5 | 5 | 10 | 7 | 1 |

[a]From Acosta (1958–1959:27).

Teotihuacán is referred to twice, once by a Tassel Headdress used as a glyph (in Column A, glyph 6) and once by a foot in a Teotihuacán-style sandal (Column B, glyph 4). Travel is indicated by the footprints at A7 and B6, and flowery speech by the scrolls issuing from the head at A5 and the "jaguar nose" at B7. At A8 appears an incense burner of the type used in Zapotec rituals (see Caso, Bernal, and Acosta 1967:Fig. 163), and at A4 is a hand holding a single bean. As discussed in Topic 97 (see also Marcus 1978), beans were cast by Zapotec diviners (*colanij*) to help decide important issues, and the single bean may indicate that an "odd number" decided the issue—being the one bean left over after removing beans by twos, threes, fours and so on (see Córdova 1578b). The hieroglyphic text includes a number of hand gestures of the type used as parts of verbs, or verbs of action, in the Maya and Aztec writing systems. Finally, the series of glyphs at A5-A7 might be read "representative from Teotihuacán came to confer."

Pending the complete decipherment of the Lápida de Bazán, I would tentatively regard it as the permanent record in stone of an agreement reached by representatives from Teotihuacán and Monte Albán. These representatives traveled, met, spoke, consulted diviners, and burned incense to establish the seriousness of their agreement by putting it in a sacred context. Probably through diplomatic encounters such as these, Teotihuacán and Monte Albán maintained their social distance, their tribute boundaries, and their "special relationship."

## SUMMARY

It has long been suspected that Monte Albán and Teotihuacán had an important relationship. For the early excavators of Monte Albán, Teotihuacán was seen as a source of architectural, and perhaps cultural, inspiration. The realization that Monte Albán may have existed as an urban center well before Teotihuacán provided some complications for this simple scheme. The discovery of the Oaxaca barrio at Teotihuacán suddenly made the relationship more direct and personal than anyone had suspected. More recently, René Millon (1973) has suggested that Monte Albán and Teotihuacán had a "special relationship."

Kidder, Jennings, and Shook (1946) and Clara Millon (1973) have all pointed to the Tri-mountain Symbol or Tassel Headdress as a distinguishing feature of Teotihuacanos who visited other regions of Mesoamerica. For Clara Millon (1973:305) the Tassel Headdress "seems to be associated with Teotihuacán as a political entity outside its own boundaries, or (and it may add up to the same thing), is associated with a social group of high rank from the city which, in some way, was involved in foreign relations, possibly on a diplomatic level." She goes on to say that this distinctive Tassel Headdress "seems to name the metropolitan center as the point of origin for whatever and whoever was being represented in foreign lands." Such

FIGURE 6.7. The Lápida de Bazán, Monte Albán. Capital letters (A and B) refer to the two columns of hieroglyphs. Numbers (1–8) identify the glyphs within each column. (Drawing by Mark Orsen.)

headdresses are associated with armed Teotihuacanos at Maya centers like Tikal, Yaxhá, and Kaminaljuyú; at Monte Albán, however, René Millon (1973:42) points out that no military weapons are ever shown with persons wearing such headdresses. A good example are the Teotihuacanos on the South Platform stelae and the Lápida de Bazán, who carry "copal bags" instead, suggesting that some kind of ambassadorial relations are involved, without a hint of military activity (Marcus 1980:56, 58).

The association of eight named Teotihuacanos (two groups of four each) with apparent offering caches under the corners of the South Platform suggest that they may have been involved with the dedication of the building. One could interpret the evidence as indicating that during the reign of a Zapotec lord ♂8 (?), a group of Teotihuacán emissaries bearing copal bags visited "the Hill of 1 Jaguar"; offerings of jade and *Spondylus* shell were placed under the corners of the South Platform, and the visit was commemorated by carvings on the edges of four monuments. The specific place of origin of the Teotihuacanos is shown as having temples similar to that on the Room 12 mural of Tetitla, which lies only 2 km from the Oaxaca barrio at Teotihuacán.

The Lápida de Bazán seems to represent a "summit meeting" of the same Period IIIa, involving a Teotihuacano ♂8 Turquoise and a Zapotec lord ♂3 Turquoise. The hieroglyphs in Column A relate what the Teotihuacano said and/or did, while Column B relates what the Zapotec lord said and/or did. Here both the Tassel Headdress and a distinctive Teotihuacán-style sandal are used to identify the visitor's place of origin. Unfortunately, we do not know the original spot where the Lápida de Bazán was displayed, as it was not found *in situ*. Nor do we know why the carved scenes of Teotihuacanos were hidden on the edges of the South Platform stelae rather than being displayed in full view.

# TOPIC 54
## A Possible Oaxacan Enclave near Tula

ADDED BY THE EDITORS

The Oaxaca barrio at Teotihuacán was an exciting discovery, and raised the question: could there be more such ethnic enclaves in other areas of Classic Mesoamerica? Almost immediately the answer came back: maybe. As part of Richard Diehl's archaeological project at Tula, Hidalgo, Robert Cobean (1974) surveyed the area of Tepeji del Río (Edo. de Mexico), not far to the south of Tula. This area has now produced another possible Oaxacan enclave.

Cobean reports that two large sites near Tepeji were surveyed and test-pitted. One, called El Tesoro, contains a small ceremonial precinct with several structures on a plaza; the second is smaller, with one pyramidal mound on a plaza. Cobean goes on to say:

> An additional interesting find at Tepeji del Río is the presence of considerable pottery similar to that of the "Oaxaca Barrio" at Teotihuacán. Little of this pottery was noticed in our test pit excavations, but the surface surveys at both sites (El Tesoro and the one just described) have recovered numerous sherds of several kinds of pottery found in the "Oaxaca Barrio" at Teotihuacán (E. Rattray, personal communication, 1972). (The Oaxaca Barrio at Teotihuacán dates largely to the Tlamimilolpa through the Metepec phases: 350–750 A.D.) The most common kind of pottery in the "Oaxaca" ceramics at Tepeji del Río is gray ware similar in appearance to the "Juanito Decorated Fine Gray" reported by Ronald Spores from the Nochixtlán Valley in northern Oaxaca during the Las Flores Phase (AD 500–1000) (Spores, 1972. Figure 9). The possible presence of a "Oaxacan" community at Tepeji del Río is certainly fascinating [1974:10].

Tepeji del Río lies at one of the major passes between the Valley of Mexico and Tula, "and it may have been a major center for trade between the Valley of Mexico and Northwest Mexico throughout much of Mesoamerica's prehistory" (Cobean 1974:10). Any Oaxacan enclave there will remain enigmatic, however, until the precise affiliation of its pottery becomes clear. The Oaxaca barrio at Teotihuacán appears convincingly Zapotec on the basis of its urns and hieroglyphs, while Juanito Decorated Fine Gray is a pottery type from the Mixteca. It is, however, strongly related to Monte Albán gray ware (Spores 1972:43–45).

Any of the Juanito Fine Gray sherds illustrated by Spores (1972:Figs. 8, 9, 10) could be duplicated in the Valley of Oaxaca, but those in his Figure 9—specifically referred to by Cobean—would be most common in the Late or Terminal Formative (Monte Albán Ic–II); in the Valley of Oaxaca, they would correspond to Caso, Bernal, and Acosta's type G-12. If this is a dominant type in the "Oaxaca barrio" at Teotihuacán, it would tend to support Paddock's chronological placement of that barrio as earlier than Tlamimilolpa (see Topic 52). Spores (personal communication, 1975), however, has evidence to suggest that G-12 lasted longer in Nochixtlán than in the Valley of Oaxaca. Thus, we await future investigations at Tepeji del Río with great interest.

# The Changing Politics of A.D. 600–900

## 7

### Editors' Introduction

We come now to the period A.D. 600–900, a time we have described as one of "changing politics". From the standpoint of the Cloud People, so many processes can be seen at work that it is difficult to know where to start in describing them. Moreover, this period witnessed a number of events outside the Zapotec–Mixtec area that were of pan-Mesoamerican importance and that undoubtedly had an impact on the Cloud People. Indeed, this is one period in which outside influences and interregional political relations may have had even more to do with shaping Zapotec–Mixtec differences than did internal evolutionary processes.

Teotihuacán, the greatest city in Precolumbian Mexico, had for at least 600 years enjoyed an enormous growth and development. Blanton (1978) has in fact suggested that the competitive presence of Teotihuacán was one of the main factors encouraging the massive urban development of Classic Monte Albán. By its very size—30,000–60,000 inhabitants occupying 6.5 km²—Monte Albán may have discouraged the kind of Teotihuacanoid expansion seen at Kaminaljuyú, and encouraged the peaceful "ambassadorial" relations seen in the monuments described by Marcus in Topic 53. Now Teotihuacán inexplicably began to decline, and by A.D. 700 had ceased to exist as a major urban center, a collector of tribute, or a religious and commercial focus in highland Mexico. The decline of Monte Albán took place at about the same time, and by A.D. 700 its Main Plaza was in disrepair and its population greatly reduced. In spite of frequent references in the literature to an "abandonment" of Monte Albán, however, the great mountaintop center was never really deserted; as late as A.D. 1400 it was still a nucleated settlement (Blanton, Topic 81). It did cease to be a metropolis, a "city above other cities," as Pad-

dock called it at the seminar (personal communication, 1975).

Why did Monte Albán decline? Blanton (Topic 55) offers two suggestions, one related to internal pressures, one to external pressures. Population was dense at Monte Albán, which depended on the valley floor for its food. In some parts of the southern or Zaachila–Zimatlán Valley, Late Classic rural population seems to have been higher than today's (Kowalewski, unpublished data). Perhaps this dense population strained relations between the metropolis and the valley-floor secondary centers that provided much of its support. On the external side, the collapse of Teotihuacán may have removed one of the main reasons for maintaining a densely nucleated metropolis at Monte Albán. Perhaps one could combine both of Blanton's suggestions into a single sentence: without the ever-present competitive threat of Teotihuacán, there was one less reason to support what already had become a maladaptive concentration of population on an unproductive 400-m mountaintop.

For several reasons, we prefer the "external" or "combined" explanations to the "internal" one alone. For one thing, Anne Kirkby (1973) has argued that even the current rural population is well below what the Valley of Oaxaca could potentially support. For another, we cannot believe that purely local factors would lead Teotihuacán and Monte Albán into declines that were so suspiciously close in time. It seems more likely that the two are related, although the exact nature of the relationship is undetermined.

One reason it is so hard to determine is our poor chronological control of the decline of Monte Albán. In the case of Teotihuacán, collapse of the city was followed by the replacement of Metepec-phase pottery by ceramics of the Ox-

183

toticpac phase around A.D. 750. In Caso's original scheme, the "abandonment" of Monte Albán's Main Plaza was by definition the boundary between Monte Albán IIIb and Monte Albán IV. Unfortunately, the ceramics of IIIb and IV are so similar that Caso, Bernal, and Acosta (1967) covered them in a single chapter labeled "IIIb–IV," and for years it was standard practice to treat them as if they belonged to a single ceramic horizon. Only recently, with Paddock's work at Lambityeco—a "pure" Monte Albán IV site (see Topic 60)—have any substantial number of criteria for distinguishing IIIb and IV been added to the meager list from Monte Albán itself. Moreover, these criteria (bat-claw vessels, spiked censers, and the like) usually do not appear in the typical surface collection. What dominates such collections is a large, open, flat-based gray bowl that is wiped smooth on the inside and left unsmoothed on the outside—Caso, Bernal, and Acosta's infamous G-35 bowl, which is characteristic of both IIIb and IV. For sheer tackiness, G-35 is the Zapotec equivalent of Mesopotamia's Late Prehistoric "beveled-rim bowl."

Even if we had more criteria to effect a separation of IIIb and IV, we would have no guarantee that the ceramic transition would be synchronized with the end of public building in Monte Albán's Main Plaza. At the Santa Fe seminar, Paddock gave several examples of the problems that can result from Caso's use of the single political event as the boundary between time periods. Occupation continued at Monte Albán in Period IV, and occasional visits to the Main Plaza area were made for the purpose of repairing floors; any Period IV sherds (defined on the basis of ceramic criteria) which were incorporated into these repairs might have been considered "Period IIIb" by Caso's definition. Most seminar participants agreed that in the future IIIb and IV should be defined on the basis of rigorous, valley-wide ceramic criteria, not on isolated political events.

Unfortunately, the currently available radiocarbon dates do little to clarify the boundary between IIIb and IV (see Appendix). Lambityeco has provided us with a set of six consistent Monte Albán IV dates between A.D. 640 and 755; the earliest Monte Albán IIIa date from the Zapotec region is A.D. 350. Drennan has selected A.D. 450–600 as falling within IIIb, but neither the IIIb–IV boundary nor the final important building erected on the Main Plaza at Monte Albán can be dated with any precision. Indeed, the "abandonment" of the Main Plaza may have been such a gradual process that attempts to provide a precise date for it will be futile.

## THE GROWTH OF MONTE ALBÁN IV CENTERS

There are two other processes that appeared simultaneously with, and related to, the decline of Monte Albán. One was the rise of a whole series of valley-floor civic–ceremonial centers that seem to have taken over the political leadership—and perhaps even most of the population—lost by Monte Albán. Few, if any, of these places were newly founded in Monte Albán IV; many of them are among the oldest permanently occupied settlements in the valley. Zaachila and Mitla go back at least to the Early Formative, Cuilapan at least to the Middle Formative, the Teotitlán del Valle and Macuilxochitl areas at least to Monte Albán I. The Lambityeco sector of Yegüih grew enormously in Period IV, but Yegüih also goes back to the Middle Formative (Paddock, Topic 60). All were growing to a degree in Period IIIb, but because of the chronological problems of IIIb–IV we do not know whether their major growth began *before* the decline of Monte Albán, was *synchronous* with the latter, or took place mainly *after* the decline.

The other process was a major shift in the nature of stone monuments in the Valley of Oaxaca. Beginning in Period IIIb and increasing dramatically in IV, a new type of monument, the "genealogical register," makes its appearance (Marcus, Topic 59). Unlike the large stelae set in public buildings of the Classic period, genealogical registers are so small that many examples have been removed from their original context and placed in museums and private collections; a few are known to have come from tombs. These monuments often document the marriages of important royal men and women at places like Cuilapan, Zaachila, Xoxocotlán, Lambityeco, and Matatlán. The most elaborate genealogical registers may trace royal infants through several life-crisis situations, or depict members of the parental and grandparental generations of a royal marriage partner.

In our opinion, it is no accident that this shift in monumental themes accompanied the decline of Monte Albán and the rise of the "second-generation" urban centers in the Valley of Oaxaca: both Precolumbian codices and sixteenth-century documents make it clear that royal marriage alliances were a major source of political clout in Postclassic Oaxaca, and in the scramble for power following the decline of Monte Albán such marriages may have taken on unprecedented importance.

If we assume, as argued by Blanton (1978 and Topic 21), that the founding of Monte Albán was the result of a confederacy among many of the valley's early regional centers, the following model can be suggested for the period A.D. 600–900. With the decline of Teotihuacán, many of the pressures for supporting a large, defensible urban center at Monte Albán dwindled. The original members of the confederacy retained more and more tribute for their home territories and directed less and less to the capital, building up their own regional centers at the expense of the capital. With the eventual decline of Monte Albán, a number of lesser centers on the valley floor rose to prominence by making strategic royal marriages and military alliances, but none ever dominated the region as had Monte Albán. Judging by the ethnohistoric documents, Zaachila eventually became the most powerful center, but it sowed the seeds of its own destruction when it arranged a series of marriage alliances with certain powerful Mixtec neighbors (see the Introduction to Chapter 8).

## THE MIXTECA

We come to the period A.D. 600–900 in the Mixteca, where the processes were somewhat different and apparently not synchronized with those of the Valley of Oaxaca. In the Nochixtlán Valley and in much of the Mixteca Alta, the great Classic-period mountaintop centers seem to have lingered on well after the fall of Teotihuacán and Monte Albán (Spores, Topic 63). When they finally declined—perhaps as late as A.D. 900, or even later—their demise took the form of a functional change rather than an abandonment. Large centers arose on the valley floor, but in contrast to the Valley of Oaxaca they were not civic–ceremonial centers in the Classic tradition. Rather, the valley-floor settlements seem to have been the major residential sites, while the old hilltop localities continued to serve as ritual centers. A "chain reaction" may even have been involved; in much the same way that the decline of Monte Albán followed the collapse of Teotihuacán, the Mixtec may have descended from their defensible mountaintop centers only after the competitive threat of Monte Albán had been removed. In the Nochixtlán–Yanhuitlán Valley, the period involved was the final three centuries of the Las Flores phase.

No genealogical registers accompanied the decline of Yucuñudahui and the other great centers of the Classic Mixteca. The Postclassic Mixtecs developed royal marriage alliance and genealogical reckoning to an art (Spores 1974b), but did not record them in stone. Instead, the Mixtecs painted a series of codices, or screenfold manuscripts on deer hide, which documented their marriages, conquests, rituals, and genealogies. In 1949, Caso was able to show that the Mixtec codices recorded actual history and their genealogies could possibly be tied to persons living at the time of the Conquest. For a time, Caso's correlations between the Mixtec and Christian calendars suggested that one of the persons depicted in Codex Bodley might date back to A.D. 692. Research by Emily Rabin (1974, 1975) has pushed that date three 52-year cycles later to roughly A.D. 848. This date raises the question of the relationship between the Zapotec genealogical registers of Monte Albán IIIb–IV and the later Mixtec codices: both contain royal genealogical data and both, Marcus suspects, were read in zig-zag or boustrophedon style, although the hieroglyphic systems were different.

In the Mixteca Baja, along the Puebla–Oaxaca border, the events of A.D. 600–900 were radically different. Here a whole series of important urban centers rose to prominence following the decline of Teotihuacán and Monte Albán, almost as if political development in the area had been long suppressed by those two great centers. The associated style of the Baja has been christened "Ñuiñe" by Paddock (1966a), and it includes a whole series of elements that may be pan-Mesoamerican in distribution. Paddock (Topic 65) points out that many of the centers sharing these elements—Xochicalco, El Tajín, and the Ñuiñe—flourished in the interregnum between the fall of Teotihuacán and the rise of the

Toltec state. The establishment of Tula as the Toltec capital in A.D. 968 seems to have put a political damper on the Ñuiñe area once again. During their relatively brief florescence, however, the civic–ceremonial centers of the Mixteca Baja—located on mountaintops like the earlier centers of the Alta—developed their own hieroglyphic writing and monumental carving style (Moser, Topic 66), which drew greatly on preexisting Zapotec patterns. This development is perhaps not surprising, as contemporary monuments at Xochicalco also show considerable similarity to Zapotec writing (Saenz 1961).

We end this chapter with a note on the rise of Tula (Topic 69). It is the second "international" event which, like the decline of Teotihuacán, had a profound impact on the Cloud People. During the period of Tula's greatest power, no important center seems to have arisen anywhere in the Valley of Oaxaca, the Mixteca Alta, the Mixteca Baja, or the nearby Tehuacán Valley. Of all those areas, however, the Mixteca was probably the most altered by its relations to the Toltecs. During the heydey of Tula, some Mixtec rulers traveled to the Toltec capital for the insertion of the nose ornament which legitimized their accession to the throne; at least one, the ruler ♂ 8 Deer "Tiger Claw," may have returned with a model for bureaucratic government previously unknown in Oaxaca. Caso also found evidence that in A.D. 983, the Mixtec calendar was deliberately changed to approximate the Toltec version. Finally, the fall of Tula is believed by some to have triggered the great Mixtec expansion, which is the subject of Chapter 8.

## THE GLOTTOCHRONOLOGICAL EVIDENCE

There are only a few glottochronological events which can be cross-tied to the archaeological record for this time period. Between A.D. 500 and 1000, the Miahuatlán Zapotec and Sierra Zapotec dialects are believed to have diverged from Valley Zapotec. This divergence might reflect a situation of reduced contact between the Valley of Oaxaca, the Sierra Juárez, and the Miahuatlán region following the decline of Monte Albán. With the integrative power of the great metropolis gone, each of these three areas of Zapotec power may have gone its own way.

An intriguing (though peripheral) event was the separation of Pochutla Nahuatl from Classical Nahuatl, which is also thought to have taken place during this period. It is known that there were Nahua speakers at Pochutla on the Pacific coast of Oaxaca at the time of the Conquest, but most sources have regarded this as the result of Aztec expansion. This dating implies that the linguistic separation, at least, took place in Toltec times, and raises still unanswered questions about the arrival of Nahua speakers on the Oaxaca coast.

## TOPIC 55
### The Urban Decline of Monte Albán

RICHARD E. BLANTON

In the secondary literature, one frequently hears that Monte Albán was "abandoned" at the end of Period IIIb. This is a misconception, caused in part by the fact that the Main Plaza area fell into disuse after Period IIIb (Caso, Bernal, and Acosta 1967:89, passim), and in part by the fact that surface ceramics from IIIb and IV are virtually indistinguishable unless one has a very good collection. In fact, portions of Monte Albán continued to be occupied in Period IV, but there was a significant drop in population and a virtual cessation of public building.

Acosta (1965:831) refers to a Period IV "enclave" on the north slope of Monte Albán proper where most of the tombs of this period were located. Because of the problem of distinguishing IIIb–IV ceramics, we have been unable to specify the extent or density of occupation of this enclave or its function. The abandonment of the Main Plaza area and the reduction of the extent of the site to include only a small enclave on the north slope indicates that Monte Albán in Period IV was considerably reduced in importance. Important persons were still buried there, however. For example, Laurette Séjourné (1960) undertook an analysis of the 138 tombs at Monte Albán which provided adequate data for an analysis of funerary ritual symbolism. Using Caso's criteria for dating of the tomb offerings (and the fact that whole vessels from IIIb and IV are easier to separate than sherd collections), she provided the following breakdown: 8 tombs from Period I, 22 tombs from Period II, 7 tombs from Transición II–IIIa, 22 tombs from Period IIIa, 33 tombs from Period IIIb, 40 tombs from Period IV, and 6 tombs from Period V (Séjourné 1960:78–79). Ironically, therefore, there were in Séjourné's sample more tombs from Period IV than from any of the periods of Monte Albán's "florescence." This fact may indicate that even after many noble families had pulled out of Monte Albán, it was considered an appropriate place for important Zapotec burials.

At least two factors may have been at work in the decline in the city's fortunes. First, as Kowalewski points out in Topic 57, settlement patterns suggest that Period IIIb saw a rapid population growth expressed mainly as a proliferation of small villages, hamlets, and isolated residences. As this growing population filled up most or all of the usable valley-floor agricultural land, it is likely that the number of disputes over access to productive land could have increased dramatically, both between individual households and between larger territorial units. Disputes would have placed an increasing strain on the adjudicative authorities, including, no doubt, those at Monte Albán. Also, a valley-floor population of the size seen in Period IIIb—larger than today's in some parts of the valley—would have had little, if any, "buffer" between its nutrient demands and those of the city of Monte Albán, leading to the possibility of widespread food shortages in dry years. Shortages, too, could have strained the abilities of administrative institutions, which would have borne the increased costs of food redistribution while experiencing declines in income.

A second set of problems facing the political unit at Monte Albán toward the end of Period IIIb has to do with the demise, after about A.D. 700, of Teotihuacán as a multiregional power. If one of the most important reasons for the maintenance of the polity and nucleated population centered at Monte Albán had been protection of the region from expansionist Teotihuacán, then the decline of the Valley of Mexico center might have removed one of the reasons for supporting such an expensive supraregional authority in Oaxaca. Local elites—especially those at emerging centers like Zaachila or Lambityeco—may have increasingly resisted pressure to support the capital, further diminishing its income at a time when there may have been pressing local problems and increased administrative costs. Such a situation would have been disastrous for the authority based at Monte Albán because, as I pointed out in Topic 21, it was purposely located in a politically neutral area which lacked the agricultural potential for self-support.

Deciding which of these two alternatives (or combination of alternatives) is the more important must await completion of our valley-floor survey, from which we hope to learn more about the history of the centers that took over from Monte Albán.

## TOPIC 56
### Some Thoughts on the Decline of Monte Albán

JOHN PADDOCK

After 17 years of repeated forays into the problem of Monte Albán's decline (see Paddock 1959), I can offer as a minimum a list of errors (some of them my own) that need not be repeated. While it may not be acceptable to anyone else, I can also formulate a scheme that knits together what we know. Of necessity, such a scheme includes definitions.

Having endured long and sterile wrangles over definitions at professional meetings, however, I also offer a defensive strategy: evasion of certain issues in order to avoid protracted semantic struggles.

In agreement with Caso, I concluded long ago that Monte Albán had not been abandoned by a population suddenly fleeing some catastrophe, but rather that it had declined little by little over a considerable length of time. Further, I agreed with Caso that abandonment had never become total, at least for any considerable period; activity of some kind took place in the center of the city even when it was in ruins. The evidence for these inferences is well known and is certainly confirmed by Blanton's urban survey.

In its busiest days, Monte Albán was a regional capital; it also was a metropolis. The terms are closely related; a metropolis is an urban center that holds a dominant place in a complex of other urban centers. Once decline began, Monte Albán at some point lost the status of metropolis because its dominion over the other urban centers of the valley became too inconsequential. It is likely that dominion over some places became an empty form, for example, when real economic contributions to Monte Albán would be reduced to near zero while maintaining a symbolic, nominal, or verbal subordination at some of the secondary centers. Some other places might, less diplomatically, openly break the former dominance–submission relations, and this break might or might not involve physical conflict. In general, places farther from the capital would tend to declare independence (openly or more subtly) first, for obvious reasons.

At some point that we could try to define (if we were more inclined to argue than to reach conclusions), the number of places still subordinate to Monte Albán, or the degree of subordination of the places still outwardly secondary to it, or perhaps the total income from subordination of secondary urban centers in the valley, reaches a level so low that we no longer class Monte Albán as a metropolis dominating a complex of urban centers. Does this constitute abandonment of Monte Albán? Not in any usual sense of the word. Decline, yes; but it is not an abandoned place because it still is an urban center with a considerable population.

Abandonment will not go away, however. In its new status as an urban center and former metropolis, Monte Albán cannot sustain as large a population as it had before, and it is unlikely that normal attrition will have accounted for all the decline in population. That is, a fairly considerable number of people, formerly residents at Monte Albán, probably go elsewhere under the pressure of "economic forces," or, much better, because it has become easier to make a better living elsewhere.

Abandonment, that is, has begun even though it is not a completed process. Abandonment has been going on since early and prosperous times, in fact; some individuals leave the capital for outlying centers because they do better in the secondary places, or because they have personal reasons, but in earlier times the abandonments are outnumbered by the arrivals of new people who want to—and can—"make it" in the capital.

And by this tiresome route we arrive at a definition of abandonment as one of several processes affecting the population of a city (along with birth, death, and arrivals of new people by choice); abandonment seems to be the same thing, here at least, as emigration.

Fortunately we need not review all the disputes over definition of urbanism; as population continues declining and the variety of activities carried out declines along with it, at some point Monte Albán will cease to meet our definition (whatever that may be) of a city. It might not slip from urban into a condition we would define as rural. But we should not fall into the trap of thinking that being unrural necessarily means being urban. We have no name for the condition of a declined formerly urban place because we are so fanatically devoted to growth and the study of growth that we have never seriously considered negative growth. Perhaps we don't really need, for now, a name for the condition of Monte Albán as a former, but still not totally depopulated, city.

Here we come to Caso's definitions. He never specified what he meant by abandonment, but by implication he meant "what ends Monte Albán IIIb and begins Monte Albán IV," and the criterion he uses is, in actual fact, construction of masonry floors. The case of Tomb 125, discussed in Caso, Bernal, and Acosta (1967:440–443), seems clear-cut. Unfortunately, it is a selected illustration that does not clarify all the confusions, as we know to our dismay. What Caso's criterion unfortunately implies is that if new masonry floors are laid down over Monte Albán IV cultural remains, those late remains become—by Caso's definition—Monte Albán IIIb remains.

Caso's use of the cessation of construction at Monte Albán as a rule of thumb for the IIIb–IV boundary—coupled with the frustrating similarity of IIIb and IV ceramics—leads to a number of pitfalls. To be as brief as possible, let us consider the chronological problems posed by Maya-style Fine Orange "trade" sherds which show up in low frequency at Lambityeco in Period IV and at Monte Albán under sealed floors.

For example, Balancán or Z Fine Orange occurs at Lambityeco; the later (Y and X) Fine Oranges do not. But Y Fine Orange does occur at Monte Albán, in offerings that have intact floors over them. That is, some construction went on at Monte Albán after Lambityeco had come and gone. Yet Lambityeco's culture cannot be accommodated in Monte Albán IIIb, for it includes many traits that are not a part of IIIb, and quite a few of these traits had already been identified (before work began at Lambityeco) as marks of Period IV in the Monte Albán excavations. Period IV as a ceramic complex would thus seem to begin well before the end of IIIb as a construction phase at Monte Albán.

Lambityeco strongly suggests that Monte Albán was, by A.D. 700 and probably by quite a few decades before, in process of abandonment. Lambityeco by then was independent in significant degree. Whether that independence indicates loss of regional capital status for Monte Albán cannot be determined by any amount of material from Lambityeco alone, however; we should have a list of Period IV sites, with dates. Lambityeco, like Miahuatlán, is well placed to be an early deserter from the Monte Albán economic and political system. It is not by chance that centers relatively distant from

Monte Albán appear to break away first, and the area immediately around the capital appears to be culturally more conservative.

## TOPIC 57
## Monte Albán IIIb–IV Settlement Patterns in the Valley of Oaxaca

STEPHEN KOWALEWSKI

Any discussion of the Late Classic (Monte Albán IIIb) and Early Postclassic (Monte Albán IV) in Oaxaca must be tempered by the notorious difficulty of distinguishing surface collections of Period IIIb from those of Period IV, and the fact that at this writing so much of the valley has yet to be intensively surveyed.

## THE CENTRAL AND ETLA REGIONS
## OF THE VALLEY OF OAXACA

It seems fairly clear that the trend toward rural abandonment—coupled with population concentration at Monte Albán—was reversed, and an extensive settlement system reestablished in the Late Classic. In this respect, Monte Al-

bán IIIb settlement patterns are very similar to those of Late Period I; the main difference is that IIIb had even more people, living on more sites. Roughly one-third of the IIIb population in the areas intensively surveyed did *not* live at Monte Albán (see Figure 7.1).

In Saville's unpublished field notes and collections, there is some evidence for activities at Xoxocotlán in the earliest part of IIIb, but that large site appears to have declined in the Late Classic. In fact, the whole eastern part of the Central Valley survey area may have had very little IIIb occupation. In the remaining areas of the valley, sites of this period are common. There were 75 IIIb–IV sites in the Etla arm, with a total occupied area of 669 ha and a population estimated between 12,175 and 24,350 (Varner 1974:122); in spite of the already mentioned low populations in the eastern part of the Central Valley, there were 216 IIIb sites with a total

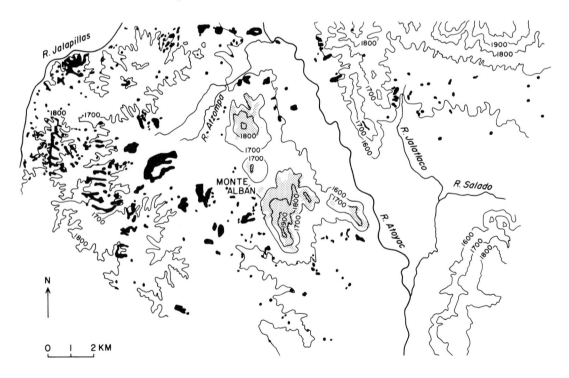

FIGURE 7.1.  The central region of the Valley of Oaxaca, showing settlements of the Monte Albán IIIb period. Stippled area shows extent of occupation at Monte Albán itself.

occupied area of 740.8 ha and a population of 4,625 to 10,807 in the Central Valley as a whole.

The reemergence of both very small settlements and a developed site hierarchy is in marked contrast to the settlement pattern of the Early Classic. Roughly 90% of all IIIb–IV sites were isolated residences, hamlets, or tiny villages with maximum populations of fewer than 290 people; 8% were somewhat larger villages (minimum 180–500, maximum 380–1000 people), and only 2% of the settlements were in the 1000 to 2500 range. The total rural population was fairly evenly divided among these size modes, with the intermediate size having a slight edge. The larger sites, and many of the intermediate communities (e.g., El Mirador, San Pedro Ixtlahuaca, and Reyes Etla) had groups of apparent elite residences, administrative buildings, plazas, and sometimes ballcourts, though few of these have been legally excavated. An interesting, but still unanswered, question is how these secondary and tertiary communities may have been linked to the 15 spatially segregated mound and terrace clusters at Monte Albán (Blanton 1978).

The preceding comments would apply only to the settlement patterns of the Late Classic (Period IIIb). The decline of Monte Albán at the end of this phase was accompanied by a radical restructuring of the entire settlement system, which affected the rural areas as well. The nature of this change is clouded because of the aforementioned difficulty of separating IIIb and IV ceramics, but our recent survey work in the Central Valley area, together with Paddock's excavations in the eastern Tlacolula Valley, may provide a basis for resolving the problem.

During the Central Valley survey we found no sites with Period IV pottery complexes exactly like that of Lambityeco. There were, however, two spatially separate groups of sites that appear to have had Monte Albán IV occupations (Figure 7.2).

In the northern and western parts of the Central Valley areas are a series of Late Classic occupations that appear to have persisted into the Postclassic. Here one might make a case for ceramic continuities between the *gris-cremosa* wares of the Classic (perhaps distributed from a manufacturing center around Atzompa) and the obviously Postclassic sandy-cream complex. The latter consists of utility wares and vessels similar to Yanhuitlán Red-on-cream (see Spores 1972). Sherds of these types are found mainly in the western part of the Central area—often on the same sites with early forms of Monte Albán V "G3M" gray ware (see Chapter 8)—and in many places in the Etla Valley. They are not found at Monte Albán, and are very rare in the Tlacolula Valley. The red-on-cream pottery is very similar to that from the Nochixtlán–Yanhuitlán Valley, but when it was first made and how long it lasted in the Valley of Oaxaca is not known. Tentatively, I would suggest a significant decline in population at the beginning of Monte Albán IV in the northwestern part of the Valley of Oaxaca, with perhaps some persistence in small settlements in the western part of the Central Valley area, and with the concentration of remain-

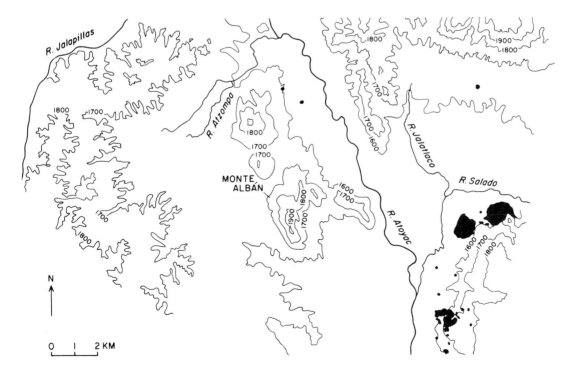

FIGURE 7.2.   The central region of the Valley of Oaxaca, showing valley-floor settlements of the Monte Albán IV period. The extent of Period IV occupation at Monte Albán itself is not shown because it is difficult to determine precisely.

ing populations in the Etla Valley around several fortified hilltop locations.

Another group of apparent Monte Albán IV settlements was located in the hills just east of the confluence of the Río Salado and the Río Atoyac. This group consists of 17 sites on 236.6 ha, with population estimated between 1720 and 4050 people. Fourteen of these settlements were less than 3 ha in extent, but there were larger sites of 38.4, 84.7, and 103.4 ha. The largest is the site of Loma de la Montura, initially described by Bernal (unpublished survey notes). The occupation is spread over the top and sides of a high hill at the edge of the valley floor. There are 133 residential terraces and a separate administrative precinct at the crest of the hill. Examination of the traffic patterns here suggests that limits of access to the crest were directed toward the site's own population, rather than being part of a system of fortifications against military threats from the outside. Loma de la Montura, with its satellites, may be an example of the smaller, localized polities that arose as the result of an Early Postclassic "Balkanization" of the Late Classic Zapotec state (see Chapter 8).

The impressive public buildings at San Luis Beltrán, excavated by Bernal and resurveyed in 1974, are still not adequately dated. If they pertain to Monte Albán IV, as Bernal (1965:807) suggested, then that site might have been linked to this second group. (It might be noted, however, that the same area covered by this proposed Monte Albán IV pattern had a few IIIb sites, suggesting that the occupation had already begun while Monte Albán was still going strong. This is the case with many sites that rose to prominence during Period IV.)

Early Postclassic (Monte Albán IV) components in this area are defined by the preponderance of undecorated gray wares, including examples of types G-35 and early G3M which are stylistically distinct from those of both Monte Albán and Lambityeco, and perhaps different in some respects from the Postclassic materials from Yagul and Cuilapan. All of this indicates the existence of several Period IV ceramic production centers with separate distribution spheres: perhaps one near Atzompa, an early one at Lambityeco, another at Coyotepec, and possibly a few others.

## THE MIAHUATLÁN VALLEY

In Miahuatlán, Brockington (1973) found half a dozen sites dating to Monte Albán IV; four of these occur just to the south of the town of Miahuatlán itself. Period IV seems to have been a time of major occupation at Site 1A, described as the largest in the Miahuatlán area. In addition to a ceramic complex which suggested the growth of Monte Albán V G3M fine gray ware out of Period IV gray ware, Site 1A yielded a sherd of "Z or Balancán Fine Orange" (Brockington 1973:13). This specimen parallels Paddock's discovery of Balancán Fine Orange in Period IV levels at Lambityeco (see Topic 60).

Two interesting phenomena of Period IV are the near absence of sites along the river downstream from Miahuatlán and the small size of most Period IV sites. Sites 7 and 13 are described as having a "thin scatter" of sherds, and Site 5 has "two small mounds, possibly representing a modest ceremonial group or large houses" (Brockington 1973:15). All in all, Brockington's data suggest a decline in number of sites and in public architecture when compared with Monte Albán III.

## TOPIC 58
## Monte Albán IIIb–IV Settlement in the Mountain Survey Zone between the Valleys of Oaxaca and Nochixtlán

ROBERT D. DRENNAN

Enormous population growth occurred in the Mountain Survey zone between the Valleys of Nochixtlán and Oaxaca (see Topic 31) during Monte Albán IIIb–IV. "Certain" occupations appeared at 33 sites and "possible" occupations at 5 more. Many of these sites show evidence of extensive monumental architecture, including rather large plazas surrounded by mounds, and several ballcourts. Restudy of the ceramic collections, aimed at separating Period IIIb from IV, should make it possible to relate the demographic changes of this region more closely with those of the Valley of Oaxaca and especially with those at Monte Albán.

This large number of IIIb–IV sites can be contrasted with the smaller numbers for Monte Albán II (five to seven sites) and IIIa (one diagnostic sherd). The meager Period IIIa evidence, however, may also reflect a scarcity of good ceramic horizon markers.

## TOPIC 59
# Changing Patterns of Stone Monuments after the Fall of Monte Albán, A.D. 600–900

JOYCE MARCUS

## INTRODUCTION

One of the striking innovations of the Monte Albán IIIb–IV period is a new type of stone monument which I have called a "genealogical register." In contrast to the huge carved stones of previous periods, which are obviously meant to be seen from a great distance, the genealogical registers are small and intended to be seen and read from close up. Rather than being set in public buildings like the earlier Zapotec monuments, the IIIb–IV stones were probably originally all placed in tombs (as is known to be the case at Cuilapan, Noriega, and Lambityeco) or in elite residences. These stones do not continue the militaristic themes of Monte Albán I–IIIa; rather, they deal with the ancestry, birth, ritual events, and marriages of the Zapotec lords and nobility of Periods IIIb and IV. They are particularly common in and around the valley-floor centers that rose to prominence during and immediately after the decline of Monte Albán: Zaachila, Cuilapan, Lambityeco, Macuilxochitl, Mitla, and Matatlán (Marcus 1976d).

Particularly common on these stones are scenes of royal marriage, which was one of the principal ways in which the Zapotecs established political alliances between important communities after the collapse of Monte Albán (see Chapter 8). The royal couple is usually shown seated on woven mats or hill signs, usually accompanied by their calendric names, and sometimes burning incense or sharing a cup of hot chocolate or pulque. Above them is an element Caso called "the Jaws of the Sky," associated with a group of iconographic elements indicating royal descent. On more elaborate stones, we may follow a royal individual through a series of events, beginning with the marriage of his parents, continuing with his birth and proceeding through various life crisis events, perhaps ending with his own marriage. These events are arranged in a series of compartments that are usually meant to be read from bottom to top in zig-zag or boustrophedon fashion.

## SCENES OF ROYAL MARRIAGE

Marriage scenes account for a great many IIIb–IV monuments. Some stones, in fact, show only a marital pair and give little further information. I have not considered these a separate category of monument, however, because I feel they are simply at one end of a continuum from simple to complex. The simplest may have only a marriage scene, most also have the *fauces del cielo* that indicate royal descent, many have the names of the marital partners, and they grad-

ually grade into more elaborate depictions of the marital pair, their ancestors, and their children. Therefore I consider them to be part of the broader category of genealogical registers.

All the stones with marriage scenes are thin, squarish slabs or *lápidas* whose small size contrasts with the stelae, monoliths, or immense multiton carved stones that characterized Monte Albán IIIa. All of the marriage-scene stones I have been able to measure are less than 10 cm in thickness, and vary between 40 and 60 cm in height and between 30 and 40 cm in width. Although most of my sample of these stones were not found *in situ*, they were clearly made to be read from up close. By contrast, the carved stones at Monte Albán in periods I–IIIa were set in public buildings or in open galleries, and were meant to be visible from great distances.

There are approximately 20 marriage-scene stones known, and although many are known to have come from a specific town, the majority are unfortunately without archaeological context. Most marriage scenes share the following elements:

1. The couple is shown facing each other; the woman most frequently appears on the left, with the man on the right.

2. Marital partners are often seated on mats or hill signs.

3. Partners are frequently shown holding bowls or bags, burning incense, speaking (?), and/or drinking some beverage (pulque and chocolate are both mentioned ethnohistorically for wedding ceremonies).

4. Above the couple appears what Caso called the *fauces celestiales*, apparently a stylized mandible with teeth often prominently displayed (see also Topic 42). Descending from these "celestial jaws" we see a range of elements—an individual carrying a necklace, for example, or a bird. Above or attached to the sides of the mandible we often see leaves, a "cherub's face," or conch shells. This iconographic combination of elements tends to occur above scenes dealing with dynasties, genealogies, and royal births, and presumably reflects the ideology of divine descent for the royal line.

5. The term *genealogical register* refers (1) to the fact that the most elaborate stones are divided into separate registers (usually two or three) which seem to convey the order or sequence of events that took place at different times in the past, with the events in the top register being the most recent in most cases; and (2) to the fact that these events frequently involve several generations of a royal family.

6. The hieroglyphic names of the marital couple are usually given, as well as the names of their relatives or ancestors. These names are clearly taken from the *pije* or 260-day ritual calendar, and consist of a numerical coefficient and a day

glyph. Some are the same glyphs we saw enclosed by a cartouche when used to refer to a date, but when used as a name they apparently appear without a cartouche.

7. It would appear from the order of depiction in these more complex genealogical registers that they were intended to be read in zig-zag or boustrophedon style (see Robertson, Topic 68). For example, in the case of the Noriega stone shown in Figure 7.5, the reader should probably begin on the right in the lower register, read to the left, go up to the left side of the middle register, read to the right, go up to the right side of the upper register, and so on. This order of reading raises the question of whether those scenes might have served as prototypes for the later Mixtec codices, many of which were also done in boustrophedon style, and some of which also recorded the genealogical history of royal families.

The pictorial conventions for marriage in the Mixtec codices are nicely summarized by M. E. Smith (1973a:29–31). The primary convention for royal Mixtec marriages was the confrontation of a male and female, both appearing in seated positions. The Mixtec man either wears a long gown with tassels or a loincloth, whereas the woman wears a skirt with a very loose *huipil* or overblouse. Many of the Mixtec women wear their hair braided with ribbons, which also clearly distinguishes them from the males.

Smith cites Herrera's (1947:VI, 320) statement that a Mixtec man and woman were not supposed to marry if their calendrical names had the same numerical coefficient, for example, ♀ 8 Serpent and ♂ 8 Deer, because the numerical coefficient of the man's name had to be higher than the woman's calendrical name. As Smith notes, however, this "emic" restriction is not borne out by the actual marriages shown in the Mixtec codices.

In various codices (e.g., Bodley, Selden, and Becker II) a couple is shown seated on a *petate* or woven mat, or on a place sign. Sometimes the bride is shown offering an earthenware vessel containing chocolate or pulque to the bridegroom. Finally, when a man and woman are seated together on a *petate* or place sign and they face the same direction rather than facing each other, they are considered to be already married (M. E. Smith 1973a:29).

There are a number of idioms in the Mixtec language that refer to royal marriages (M. E. Smith 1973a:30). In the Alvarado dictionary of the sixteenth century (Alvarado 1593), two phrases are given for the marriage of a nobleman, one meaning that the nobility join hands and the other meaning that a feast or celebration takes place. From the Reyes grammar of the sixteenth century (Reyes 1593), four additional idiomatic expressions are provided: (1) there is a royal celebration of the *petate;* (2) the nobility join hands; (3) the empire is sanctified; and (4) the noblemen begin to drink pulque. Smith goes on to say that the jar of chocolate held in the woman's hand may constitute part of the woman's dowry, because the sixteenth-century Mixtec word for "royal dowry" (according to Reyes 1593) means "chocolate and tobacco(?)".

The codex scene for marriage—the seated man and woman facing each other—is apparently a pictorial convention that has no direct corollary in the Mixtec language, although various motifs such as the woven mat and the royal earthenware vessel containing pulque or chocolate had counterparts in the sixteenth-century Mixtec phrases for marriages linking noble persons.

## PROVENIENCE OF GENEALOGICAL REGISTERS IN THE VALLEY OF OAXACA

Of the 20 or so monuments of this type, most presently reside in museums. Their provenience in several cases is tentatively given, following the lead of Galindo y Villa (1905), Seler (1902–1923), and Caso (1928, 1965b,c). Five marriage stones can be attributed to Zaachila, two to Cuilapan, two to Matatlán, one to Lambityeco, and one to Macuilxochitl. Less secure are the proveniences of one attributed to Monte Albán, one from Teotitlán del Valle, one from Ayoquesco, and at least four examples in the Frissell Museum which might be from the Mitla area. There are additional marriage scenes in Period IIIb–IV style, without any provenience, that are displayed or stored in the INAH Museums in Oaxaca and Mexico City.

All of the very few marital-pair scenes that have ever been found *in situ* were found in tombs. One of these was discovered by Saville (1904) in Tomb 1 at Cuilapan (see Topic 61), a Period IIIb–IV sepulcher which also had a carved lintel and a series of urns and whole vessels in IIIb–IV style (Bernal 1958b:23).

The marital-pair scene from Cuilapan (Figure 7.3) is now in the American Museum of Natural History. Caso (1928:Fig. 80 and pp. 107–109) comments on the central element at the top of the stone, calling it "*las narices del tigre: una simplificación de las fauces que indican el cielo.*" Small spirals at the top of this element were interpreted by Caso as stylized representations of clouds. Descending from either side of the celestial jaws are what appear to be beads strung on a necklace. Attached to the bottom of the *fauces del cielo* is Caso's Glyph E, which he interprets (1928:32) as signifying "turquoise" or "precious stone," or in more general terms "the sun." Below the Glyph E are a human head, and some burning incense (?) with smoke emanating from it; both the head and burning copal (?) appear on top of a hill sign serving as an altar.

A couple is seated to one side of this central part of the scene; the woman sits behind her husband on a mat. On the other side of the center is a man seated upon a mat. The glyphs associated with the male on the left appear to be either 2 (or 4?) Deer. The male on the right is associated with two glyphs; in front of him appear two distorted bars (10) and a variant of glyph E and behind him are two dots and a Dog or Deer (?). By analogy with the Mixtec codices (see previous section), the couple on the left should be already

FIGURE 7.3. Carved stone from Tomb 1 at Cuilapan, apparently showing named members of a noble family. (Drawing by Margaret Van Bolt, after a photograph in Caso 1928: Figure 80.)

married, because they face the same way; the woman is seated on the mat behind her husband, who is conferring with another man seated on a mat. The entire *lápida* measures some 27.9 by 40.6 cm; in order to read the glyphs naming the individual or to view the scene, one must be very close to it, a point we have already made.

One of the most elaborate and well-known genealogical registers is currently displayed in the Museo Nacional in Mexico City. Caso (1928:Figure 81; 1965b:Vol. 3, 857, Fig. 16) attributes this stone (Lápida 1) to the site of Zaachila and to the period Monte Albán IIIa. Both attributions should be considered tentative. First, the stone is in the IIIb–IV style typical of such monuments. Second, although Caso (1928) says that Spinden (1924) gave Zaachila as the provenience for this Lápida 1, I found no reference to Zaachila or to any other provenience in Spinden's comments.

This *lápida* (measuring 38 × 60 × 8 cm.) is divided into two registers (Figure 7.4). On the left in the upper register we see a woman kneeling without (?) a mat, facing a man who is seated on a mat; she is shown with a speech scroll. Both carry pottery vessels; between them grows a flowering plant. The woman's hieroglyphic name appears behind her head and is 3 Glyph M in Caso's system, which he interprets in this case as 3 Serpent. The name of the man (also given behind his head) is 6 Glyph L (6 *Xoo* or Earthquake), with the bar (5) above the day glyph and the dot (1) below it. Above ♀ 3 M and ♂ 6 L are the *fauces del cielo*, with a personage shown descending out of the jaw grasping a strand of beads. To either side of the *fauces del cielo* we see conch (?) shells.

Above the *fauces del cielo* is Caso's *narices del tigre* element, very similar to the one we saw on the stone from Tomb 1 at Cuilapan. Additionally, there are small spirals to either side of the *narices* which Caso felt were stylized representations of clouds. For reasons which will be discussed, I feel this upper register shows a marriage in the recent past.

In the lower register we find another couple. The woman appears on the left, kneeling on a hill sign; to the right appears a man, with a speech scroll emanating from his mouth. Her name in Caso's system is apparently 11 Glyph 0 (Monkey), while his name is perhaps 6 Glyph D (Flower). Note that if we consider the two dots behind his back as part of his name, the man might be named 8 Flower; this interpretation should be considered tentative, however, since the two dots behind the man are not really directly associated with any glyph.

There are two reasons for believing that this lower register shows a scene in the more distant past than that in the upper register: (1) the man in the lower register is shown as bearded, with a lined, elderly face, and the man in the upper register appears to be younger; (2) the upper register shows the man seated on a woven mat, which is consistent with the scene of a marriage actually taking place. Additionally, in other such monuments it also appears that the lower register relates more distant times and events than the upper register.

On the outer edge of Lápida 1 (Marcus 1980:63) is a long series of day-signs with numerical coefficients. These signs do not occur in the order in which they would appear in the 260-day calendar, however, and should be interpreted not as dates but as a list of personal names. Starting at the bottom,

FIGURE 7.4. Genealogical register (Lápida 1) attributed to Zaachila by Caso. (Drawing by Mark Orsen.)

proceeding to the right, then up the right side and around to the center, we can transcribe the inscription as follows (Caso 1928:110–111): (1) 13 A (Knot), (2) 10 L (Earthquake, Motion), (3) 5 B (Jaguar Head?), (4) 4 E (Precious Stone or Sun?), (5) 4 C (Nose and Mouth of Jaguar?), (6) 4 G (Deer), (7) 1 F (Owl?), (8) 2 Z (Vessel of Water?), (9) 1 N (Cleft Head?), (10) 6 L (Earthquake, Motion), (11) 3 M (Serpent Head), (12) 13 J (Open Mouth of Jaguar?), (13) 10 Y (Serpent) or 10 M (Caso 1928:Fig. 18,IV).

One possible explanation for this sequence of 13 calendric names is that it represents a list of ancestors of one or all of the persons on the stone. It seems significant that the eleventh and tenth glyphs in the list (3M and 6L) are the same ones that occur with the couple in the upper register. I have already proposed that a similar pattern of listing ancestors by their calendric names is found on Lintel 2 from Mound 9 at Xoxocotlán (see Topic 45).

Preceding the list of 13 calendrical names on Lápida 1, we have an open right hand (possibly a verb of action) with a Glyph I immediately above it; on top of the Glyph I appears a bird's head. The meaning of these three glyphs appearing in a vertical phrase is not known. At the beginning of the text, we see Caso's year-sign—but in this situation it appears with a day that is not usually known as a year bearer, the day Glyph N with a subfix of 8. This year sign may document the year of the marriage depicted in the upper register of the *lápida*.

Although Caso (1928:26) recognized that the sequences of calendrical signs on Lápida 1 del Museo Nacional and Lintel 2 from Xoxocotlán were not in the proper order to represent a *trecena* in the 260-day calendar (in contrast to some of the calendric inscriptions on the carved bones from Tomb 7 at Monte Albán; see Topic 82), he felt both inscriptions were too confusing to decipher. Since he must have known from Córdova (1578b:16–17) that the Zapotecs named their children after the day of their birth in the 260-day calendar, it is surprising that it did not occur to him that these might be the listed names of ruling family members. My position is that on Lápida 1 we have the names of some 13 members of a ruling family (including a marital pair), and we recover an additional 15 names on the lintel of Tomb 1 at Xoxocotlán.

## OTHER GENEALOGICAL REGISTERS

In addition to the 20-odd stones dealing with royal marriage, there are other genealogical registers dealing with royal births, life crises, and generational succession during Monte Albán IIIb–IV. One of the most famous comes from Noriega, a site lying between Cuilapan and Zaachila, where it was found in the roof of a tomb (Caso 1965c:942, Fig. 18).

This elaborate *lápida* (Fig. 7.5) is divided into three registers or scenes (Marcus 1980:64). On the left in the bottom register, we see a male with the name 10 Vessel(?); to the right is a female with the name 9M (Serpent) (Caso 1928:Fig. 18). Between these two figures there is a hill sign with two Cipactli[1] heads attached; above we have what appear to be stylized *fauces del cielo*. Both the woman (with speech scroll) and the man (with buccal mask) appear to be kneeling on low platforms which rest on plumes protruding from the noses of the "Cipactlis."

The middle register is evidently to be read from left to right, as it appears to follow a child from birth to later childhood. A woman with an elaborate trapezoidal headdress, braided buccal mask, and speech scroll is shown giving birth to a child named 2 Vessel. Another glyph, 2 Water, appears near the mother's face, and may indicate her name. The child, now sufficiently old enough to be able to sit up, is shown on the far right with a male figure, perhaps his father; the latter wears a distinctive headdress that we will see again in the upper register.

A large male figure with a unique headdress dominates the center of this register; there is a 5 near his waist, and he carries in his hand what may be a skull. In Caso's published drawing (1965c:Fig. 18), it is very clearly shown as a skull. If the 5 can be associated with the skull, and this combination of glyphs proves to be the name of the central male figure, it may aid us in explaining the association of 5 Skull above the carapace of the flying turtle in the upper register.

Moving now to the top register, we see on the right the same woman with the trapezoidal headdress, now holding a staff similar to the "manikin scepter" that appears frequently in Classic Maya art (Marcus 1976a:169). Seated in front of the woman is a smaller figure, perhaps a servant, apparently fixing the headband of the child; assuming once again that this is the same child, he appears still older than in the previous scene. Next, on the far left is a familiar male figure, perhaps the father, with the same headdress he wore on the far right in the middle register.

Dominating the central part of the upper register, however, is a flying turtle with a "Cipactli" head, superfixed by the name 5 Skull. This flying turtle may symbolize the fact that the central figure 5 Skull in the middle register has died and become an ancestor. A similar flying turtle with a human head wearing a Cipactli headdress appears in modeled stucco on the rear wall of the much-later Tomb 1 at Zaachila (see Topic 87 and Caso 1966:324, Fig. 20). It has been pointed out that the sixteenth-century Zapotec conceived of the clouds from which their ancestors had descended as flying turtles. If that is the case, the presence of flying turtles in Postclassic Zapotec tomb art is consistent with the genealogical themes we have already detected. This monument from Noriega is considered by most scholars to date to Monte Albán IV, making it one of the earliest representations of the flying turtle or "cloud ancestor" in Zapotec tomb art.

Finally, in the upper right hand corner of this register is a series of glyphs—9 (?) Dog—not clearly associated with any one individual, and hence possibly a date.

---

[1] I have severe reservations about the application of this Nahuatl term to a Zapotec creature, but it is frequently so used.

FIGURE 7.5. Genealogical register from Noriega. (Drawing by Mark Orsen.)

On ethnohistoric grounds, I would suggest that the Noriega stone shows a series of life-crisis rites in the early history of a ruler named ♂ 2 Vessel. Below are his more distant ancestors, ♂ 10 Vessel (?) and ♀ 9 M. In the middle register, his mother ♀ 2 Water gives birth to him; he is later presented to his father. Then, in a later scene, he is still older and is being dressed for a different ritual. There is much more information in the monument than this brief description would indicate, and I intend to develop it more fully in a later paper; I offer it here merely as a contrast to those stones that depict only marriage scenes.

## SUMMARY

The genealogical registers of Monte Albán IIIb–IV represent a real departure from the militaristic themes (slain cap-

tives, bound elite captives, and conquered place names) of Monte Albán I–IIIa, and contrast with the monumental size of earlier carved stones. They tend to occur with tombs rather than with public buildings, and they are common at valley-floor sites and rare at Monte Albán. They deal with the birth, ancestry, origins, and marriage of royal individuals, and in their boustrophedon layout and their emphasis on genealogy they constitute one possible prototype for some of the later codices. In terms of political history, they suggest less concern with militarism and more concern with the establishment of the royal dynasties that were still functioning when the Spaniards arrived in Oaxaca. This was clearly a major preoccupation of the valley-floor civic–ceremonial centers that took over from Monte Albán between A.D. 600 and 900.

# TOPIC 60
## Lambityeco

JOHN PADDOCK

"Yegüih" is the local Zapotec name for an archaeological zone of over 75 ha recorded by Ignacio Bernal in 1953. The most recent count of visible archaeological mounds at Yegüih, conducted by David Peterson in 1975, is approximately 230. These mounds occur on both sides of the Pan American Highway about 2 km west of Tlacolula in the eastern Valley of Oaxaca. According to one early survey, there are more than 80 mounds of a meter or less in height, more than 90 which vary from 1 to 10 m in height, and at least 2 over 10 m in height. Yegüih shows evidence of many periods from Middle Formative times to Monte Albán V, but not all the mounds were occupied at any one time. The earliest remains are in the southeast quadrant of the site, but the period of greatest occupation was Monte Albán IV, when well over 100 mounds were in use. On the northwestern part of the site there is a concentration of some 70 mounds which were occupied exclusively in Monte Albán IV; this is the area for which we were given the local name, "Lambityeco." Lambityeco is therefore defined as an area of pure Monte Albán IV occupation within a larger archaeological zone known as Yegüih (Paddock, Mogor, and Lind 1968).

The Institute of Oaxacan Studies conducted research intermittently at Lambityeco from 1961 to 1975. This research has included the excavation of two mounds in the 1- to 10-m range and two more in the under-1-m class; several important tombs were found in these explorations. There have also been several intensive surface pickups, aimed at an understanding of the growth and development of Yegüih, and many stratigraphic pits outside the constructions. This part of the Tlacolula Valley, between Lambityeco and San

Juan Guelavía, has areas where salt can be extracted from saline soil. There is evidence that salt was produced at Yegüih as early as Monte Albán Ic, and during Monte Albán IV Lambityeco was producing both salt and pottery in quantity (Peterson 1976).

## THE GROWTH OF YEGÜIH

In order to put the Monte Albán IV occupation of Lambityeco in perspective, we can examine the growth of the Yegüih area in general. I base my comments primarily on the results of our 1973 intensive surface pickup because David Peterson's later ones have been concerned with salt production. Peterson's work raises the total number of mounds from 182 to 230 and adds a considerable salt-working zone to the area, but it only confirms our impression of the overall growth pattern (Peterson 1976).

It is essential here, as elsewhere, to state certain assumptions that underlie the results, as well as other factors that increase or decrease the precision of the deceptively exact-looking figures we present.

1. We assume that all mounds (or sherd scatters included as mounds, if that is the case) having sherds of a given period were occupied throughout the period; or we assume that the proportion of mounds occupied at a given moment during a period is the same for all periods.

2. We assume that the periods are in some way of equal or of equivalent length.

3. We assume that there is no meaningful difference in

density of occupation from mound to mound. One sherd is interpreted for purposes of the map as meaning Mound 999 was occupied in period X; 100 sherds at the same location would result in the same interpretation; and 10,000 sherds at the same spot would still give the same result—the simple indication on the map that the mound was "occupied" in that period.

4. We assume that sherds are in something close to primary deposition, or that they have not been brought in from elsewhere.

5. We assume that occupation of any mound at a particular period is equivalent to occupation of any other mound; the map makes no distinctions except to give a rough idea of mound area.

6. Though the appearance of the map suggests that the site has been surveyed in its entirety, that is not quite true.

Areas subject to alluviation may not have any surface remains visible to give them away, and hence may not be indicated at all. Further, a few areas heavily overgrown with spiny vegetation have not been covered.

7. The number of diagnostic ceramic traits varies from period to period. The map is made, however, as if the number were always the same. This difficulty is countered by trying to search the entire area of each mound for diagnostics, but the success of that effort depends on one's ability to recognize them in the field, which brings up the following point.

8. The visibility of diagnostic sherds varies notably from one period to another, leading to a tendency for some periods to be recognized more easily and more often than others. This problem is partially met by making a total pickup of remains in a defined area, but the sample area may not have

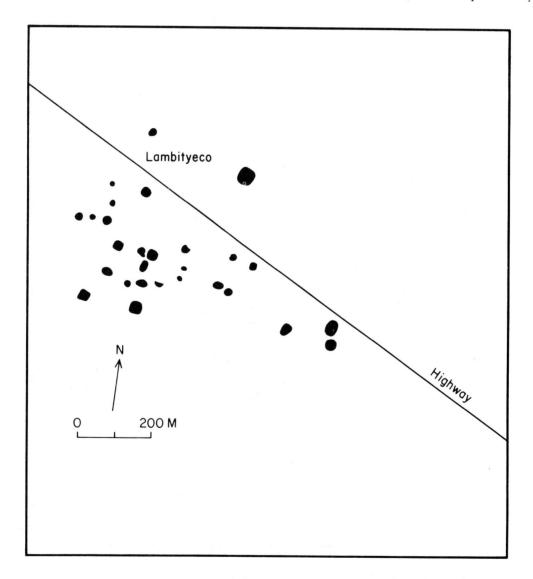

FIGURE 7.6. Yegüih, showing mounds with surface evidence of Monte Albán IIIb occupation. (Courtesy David Peterson.)

remains of all periods during which the mound was occupied.

9. The maps available at present date from 1973. They are based on data from excavations, sporadic surface finds, and several surface surveys carried out by different methods. But subsequent work has resulted in significant revisions upward; for example, the number of mounds is now thought to be well over 230, though the map shows only 182; late Monte Albán I is now known to occur in previously unknown areas of the site, and to some extent all periods are now better represented; some division of periods into shorter intervals will be possible with data now in hand but not yet analyzed.

10. The map does not show the westernmost extension of the site. Since the Monte Albán II site of Brawbehl is only about 1 km to the west of the excavated area, and closer than

that to the western mounds, the question of community form in Period II is not made clear by its map.

Peterson (letter of September 16, 1975) offers some interesting calculations. Though he thinks the occupied area might be as much as 20% higher, he has used the previously estimated area of 740,000 square meters as his base. He has used surface materials from 1038 m² of the site, from which he has classified 93,334 sherds. (John Carroll's ceramic typology is based on nearly 200,000 other sherds.)

Assuming his surface sample to be representative—he covered several different kinds of occupation areas—Peterson then finds that the mean is 89.9 sherds per m², which he reduces to 89.0 for further calculations—giving the rather intimidating figure of 65,860,000 sherds *on the surface* of Yegüih. The maximum density so far noted is of 690 sherds

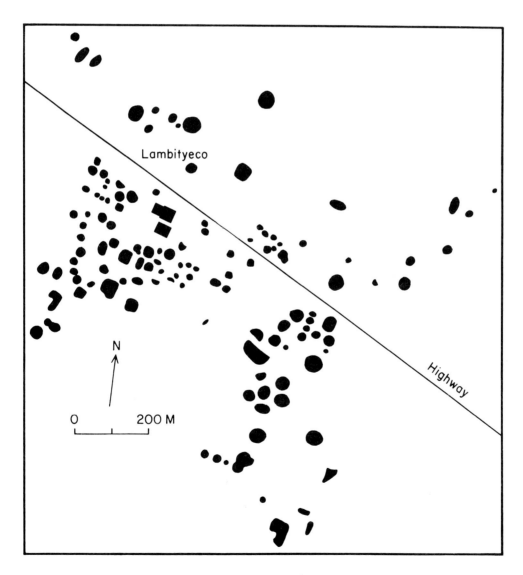

FIGURE 7.7.  Yegüih, showing mounds with surface evidence of Monte Albán IV occupation. (Courtesy David Peterson.)

per m²; densities from 300 to 500 are not rare, though in habitation areas the densities tend to run from 20 to 90, with a mean around 60.

In view of the obvious impossibility of achieving an adequate sample of 65,000,000 surface sherds, to say nothing of the buried ones, Peterson believes (and I agree) that recourse to some kind of guiding principle is essential. The mounds are visible, and they are utterly legitimate data. Therefore they have been used prominently to guide the surveys. The areas not having mounds, however, have also been incorporated, by two methods. In the first surveys, the areas lacking mounds were covered by a grid of total pickup spots; in Peterson's most recent surveys, he used transects to incorporate these areas.

In addition to the exploration of mounds, cited previously, and the surface surveys, data come from a series of 30 pits, 2 by 2 m each, made in 1973 by Bill Fowler in a random scatter of spots within the Lambityeco sector but avoiding mounds. The material from these pits constitutes the principal basis for Carroll's classification.

Still further, Peterson has carried out surface surveys and minor excavations in 1974 and 1975 to provide data for his analysis of salt production and trade. Having drawn on all available data for his new analysis, naturally Peterson feels that the 1973 maps of Yegüih period by period are now outdated. The new analysis, however, will not be done for some time, and the 1973 maps are at hand. They have not been found to overestimate. Remembering, then, that a "mound" may be a pyramid, an elite house, a rather poor house (especially if long occupied and much rebuilt), or an industrial area never inhabited, this is the 1973 count.

Number of Mounds Occupied
in Each Period

| Monte Albán I | 18 |
|---|---|
| Monte Albán II | 53 |
| Monte Albán IIIa | 15 |
| Monte Albán IIIb | 28 |
| Monte Albán IV | 129 |
| Monte Albán V | 21 |

Keeping in mind that the Monte Albán IV occupation appears to be one of the shortest—being restricted to early Period IV—these figures seem to lead to some inferences that will not be shaken by even rather drastic revisions of the mound count. Clearly, the period of greatest growth at Yegüih was between IIIb and IV (see Figures 7.6 and 7.7).

The 70 mounds showing exclusively Period IV occupation are concentrated north of the highway and on the far western edge of the site, though the western ones are liberally interspersed with mounds occupied in other periods as well. The southeast part of Yegüih has little occupation exclusive to Period IV, though it was in use then.

Because periods other than IV show clustering that is distinct for each one, I infer that there was no significant error introduced by carrying fill with sherds in it from one mound to another. Abundant outcrops of sterile gravel, often used for fill, probably account for the apparently slight use of sherd-bearing fill that had been moved significant distances.

According to the 1973 maps, only one mound used in Period IIIb was unused in IV, though the difficulty of distinguishing between the two periods affects the validity of this inference—which is, in any case, an argument from absence (but absence of Period IV, in the heart of the northwest area, is extremely uncommon). Five Period V mounds were unused in Period IV.

## RESIDENTIAL EXCAVATIONS

The two higher mounds explored at Lambityeco (Mounds 195 and 190) were elite residences. Both are highly similar in layout and dimensions to the Palacio on the east side of the Main Plaza at Monte Albán and to the structures above Tombs 103 and 104 at that site. In early versions, the house on Mound 195 had a single patio, but a second one was added in the rebuilding that preceded its conversion (perhaps never finished) into a pyramid. The Mound 190 house may also have been of a single patio in early versions, but they are inaccessibly overlain by rather well-preserved later ones, which have two patios each. Before it was made into a pyramid, Mound 195 was rebuilt at least once; Mound 190 was completely reconstructed at least five times.

One tomb, in Mound 195, had stucco representations of a man and a woman (accompanied by hieroglyphic names); the same woman is also mentioned in a marriage scene on a carved stone (of the type called a "genealogical register" by Marcus, Topic 59) that was in place under the tomb door. This is one of the very few Period IV marriage scenes from the valley whose exact context and provenience is known.

Tomb 2, in Mound 190, had been installed in a building already standing by means of an elliptical cut in a preexisting lime-cement floor (Paddock, Mogor, and Lind 1968). The burials inside were accompanied by Monte Albán IV offerings, including bat-claw vessels, spiked braziers, G-35 bowls, carved bones, numerous bone tools, and unfired clay vessels. William O. Payne (1970) has since shown that a clay source 400 m south of Mound 190 can be used to duplicate the Lambityeco ceramics, as well as the unfired clay vessels from Tomb 2. This readily accessible clay source facilitated a massive, presumably commercial production of G-35 bowls at Lambityeco.

While Lambityeco undoubtedly was supported by Monte Albán IV agricultural products similar to those from nearby Guilá Naquitz Cave (see Flannery and Smith, Topic 62), the residents also collected local wild plants and ate both wild and domestic animals. C. Earle Smith, Jr. has identified both avocado and hackberry from carbonized remains at Lambityeco, and Flannery has identified domestic dog, coyote, pocket gopher, cottontail, and jackrabbit from the Mound 195–190 area. Bird bones include the domestic turkey (presumably eaten), and the American egret and military macaw (probably used for their feathers).

## CRAFT PRODUCTION AT LAMBITYECO

One of the lower mounds explored at Lambityeco is also residential, though smaller and more modest than either Mound 190 or 195. It left only a very low mound, probably because it had not been repeatedly rebuilt rather than because it was of perishable construction. The other low mound explored turned out to be an industrial area. An assembly of huge ollas surrounded and covered a deposit of ash that might be the result of firing pottery in a way similar to that used today in nearby San Marcos Tlapazola. Peterson believes, however, on the basis of considerable analysis, that this was a salt-processing area. It immediately adjoins the remains of another fairly modest house that left no mound.

Well over a hundred of the Yegüih mounds have signs of Period IV occupation, indicating a sizable community, yet the location is notoriously poor for agriculture. Colonial sources do not recognize it as a significant salt producer. Nevertheless, in his dissertation, Peterson (1976) finds it capable of supplying a very large population and a considerable area; and until 30 to 40 years ago, some of its salt production was traded to areas well beyond the Valley of Oaxaca.

That the salt industry was important in Monte Albán IV and V (as Peterson has already learned) and in earlier times as well (as he has reason to suspect) does not exclude pottery production as another source of income. In his analysis (still in manuscript) of the Lambityeco ceramics, John E. Carroll has shown that the proportion of serving dishes (G-35 *cajetes*) is many times what it would be if these were only being consumed at the site; that is, the number of cooking vessels is proportional to the demands of a reasonable population for the area, whereas the number of G-35s is astronomical by comparison.

Likewise, the ample use of sherds, mostly G-35 fragments, in construction indicates that they were in superabundant supply.

In the course of his analysis of salt production, Peterson has made complete surface pickups in over 1000 1-m squares over the site. Although the occupation was short, probably less than 200 years and possibly much less, Peterson has found a variation from 0 to 690 sherds per m². And these are relatively massive sherds; 150–250 of them fill a bag that, in Teotihuacán, easily holds 300–400 of the thinner, smaller Teotihuacán sherds.

Therefore, even though our excavated firing area may belong to the salt and not to the ceramic industry, there is still every reason to believe the latter was important to the local economy (Payne 1970).

In his analysis of the salt trade, Peterson has found that Lambityeco is strategically located with respect to nearby agricultural areas much more productive than its own immediate agricultural surroundings; it is central also with respect to several other communities, and thus may have had a third source of income as a central place.

## LAMBITYECO AND THE DEFINITION OF MONTE ALBÁN IV

One by-product of the excavations at Lambityeco has been an increased understanding of the Monte Albán IV period. This period has proved hard to define because it was poorly known from Monte Albán; Lambityeco was the first "pure" Period IV site to be excavated. Blanton's confirmation that Monte Albán was still occupied in Period IV (except for the Main Plaza) is added support for our impression that Lambityeco was occupied before Monte Albán's Main Plaza was abandoned, and that some occupation at Monte Albán continued after Lambityeco's Period IV people had moved on—perhaps to nearby Yagul. Six of seven radiocarbon dates from Lambityeco cluster between A.D. 640 and 755, giving us what is presumably a reliable estimate; two dates on similar material from Guilá Naquitz Cave are A.D. 620–740 (see Drennan, Appendix).

Assignment of the Lambityeco remains to Period IV was viewed at first as a radical decision. Probably existing publications have explained it adequately, and here I present only the briefest summary of the reasons and some recent and unpublished confirmations.

Definition of Monte Albán IV began long before anything was known of Lambityeco, thus providing a securely noncircular way to begin the characterization. Period IV is defined by

1. positive characterization, that is, traits distinctive of it;
2. negative characterization, that is, by clarifying what it is not:
   a. how it differs from Period V, and
   b. how it differs from Period IIIb.

Any proper definition states what the defined entity includes, and also what is excluded from the defined class. The inclusion has to come first in this case. Caso and his collaborators, in many publications predating the Lambityeco work, referred to three groups of positively defining traits for Period IV: (1) those found in postabandonment contexts at Monte Albán itself; (2) those found in late contexts at other sites but not known at Monte Albán; and (3) those not yet known, but whose discovery was predicted at sites occupied during Period IV, and still to be identified.

All these characterizations, however, are valid not only for Period IV, but potentially for V as well, unless a new Period IV site could be located that would be free of Period V remains.

Yagul provided an abundant sample of Period V. In stratigraphic pits, this sample is heavily mixed with IV; but the many well-stocked Period V tombs gave us a clear and rather complete picture of Period V ceramics free of the admixture that is inevitable in stratigraphy. This pure tomb sample was essential later on to help define what Period IV is not. Because Yagul appears to present a brusque cutoff of IV at a time when it is well defined, to be replaced by an also already well-defined Period V, the situation luckily is much clearer there than it would be at a place where there was a gradual mixture, or even an evolution—as, for example, at Miahuatlán (Brockington 1973) and Abasolo (Flannery, Topic 87).

On the basis of Monte Albán data, ceramic types K-11 and A-7 were assigned to Period IV, as was also a highly polished black ware that was not included in the Monte Albán classification. It was also pointed out that most Period IIIb ceramics continued with no marked or sudden change into Period IV, and that the gradual decline of technical and esthetic quality that had been evident throughout Monte Albán IIIb could be expected to make Period IV ceramics even poorer. Bernal (1965: 806–808) summarizes the pre-Lambityeco idea of Period IV.

Without exception, the Period IV traits known from Monte Albán have been found at Lambityeco; likewise, the traits unknown at Monte Albán but considered as probably of Period IV have been found there, and, as predicted, a number of previously unknown traits also mark the period. Available lists of these traits are now somewhat outdated (Paddock, Mogor, and Lind 1968), so it would be a good idea to present one here. It should be kept in mind that this list almost certainly includes some peculiarities that are local or personal rather than temporal; that is, a given new trait may be a true Period IV marker, but valid only for Lambityeco or even for the work of a single craftsman. Only study of other Period IV sites will tell us which traits are valley-wide Period IV diagnostics and which are local (Hartung 1970; Kowalewski and Truell 1970; Payne 1970; Rabin 1970; Sharp 1970).

■

## LAMBITYECO (EARLY MONTE ALBÁN IV) TRAITS

I. Architecture
   A. Stone veneer (versus stone-on-stone and thick facing)
   B. Use of sherds in place of stone
      1. chinking
      2. areas in walls big enough for small or medium stones
      3. laid vertically as base for stucco floors
   C. Hemispherical adobes, flat side up, in fill
   D. *Grecas* (see Iconography)
   E. Pretentious exteriors over shoddy work in invisible parts
II. Inscriptions
   New style and new kind of content in stone inscriptions: "marriage pairs" and generally smaller, more detailed scenes (see Marcus, Topic 59)
III. Iconography
   A. New elements on portable effigies
      1. flint knife as centerpiece of tiger's necklace
      2. bat-claw beakers
      3. appliqué medallion in form of a hill glyph or bifid tongue with a jade bead at the top, all made with a "worm" of clay
      4. appliqué medallion in which two or three feathers (?) hang from a jade bead
      5. a long list of new traits on urns and a ceramic figure from the lintel offering of Tomb 6, Lambityeco, and an urn from Tomb 8, same site
      6. "hourglass" braseros, braseros made of globular *tecomates* on high pedestals, and braseros in form of large high *cajetes,* all having tiger or bat effigies
      7. hourglass braseros with attributes of urns, but often lacking the face even though earplugs are present
   B. Nonportable sculpture
      1. river with "eyes" flowing from *florero* held in hand of Cocijo
      2. old man holding human femur, distal end cut off square
      3. personages named
         a Lord 4 P
         b. Lady 10 O
         c. Lady 3 E
         d. Lord 8 F
         e. Lord 1 L
         f. Lady 10 J
   C. *Grecas*
      1. repetition of the simple *xicalcoliuhqui*
      2. *xicalcoliuhqui* without triangular notch in base
      3. Use of inverted T forms, presumably related to *grecas,* combined with figures
   D. Various traits of the unbaked clay figurines of Lambityeco Tomb 2
IV. Funerary customs
   A. Offerings on exterior lintels of tombs
   B. Unfired vessels (besides figurines) in tomb offerings
   C. Offering of unbaked clay cones (but cf. Monte Albán I in Caso and Bernal 1952:Fig. 187)
   D. Careless treatment of previous remains in tomb on making a new burial in it
V. Techniques
   A. Use of clay, pebbles, and sherds, covered with a thin coat of stucco, to make sculptures in place of former stone, solid stucco, or baked clay
   B. Revival of hand-modelling in clay sculpture to replace extremely degraded molding techniques
   C. Use of small adobe-walled cells, filled with earth and gravel, as building fill
VI. Ceramics
   (No attempt will be made here to condense Carroll's extremely detailed and exhaustive classification of Lambityeco ceramics. This is a simple listing of what seem to be Period IV markers. The list would be much longer if we did not eliminate all those traits found at Monte Albán and classed as of IIIb–IV.)

A. Gray wares
   1. Glossy black
      a. *tecomate*
      b. conical *cajetes* with large globular feet
      c. conical lids with handles on the sides
   2. *ollotas:* the very large ollas of the salt works
   3. large bell-shaped vessels, medium thick
   4. very large barrel-shaped vessels with flanged rims
B. Orange wares
   1. Balancán (or "Z") Fine Orange, imported or locally made
   2. A-7 of Monte Albán
   3. perforated discs, apparently not *malacates:* wheels?
   4. Puuc Slate (identified by Kowalewski)
C. K-wares
   1. K-11 of Monte Albán: a semifired tan
   2. spiked crude braseros in form of ollas, with perforations in the shape of crosses

The Lambityeco figurines have been classified by Alain Y. Dessaint (manuscript). Because recognizable fragments of Period IV types are so common at Lambityeco, and figurines of all kinds and all periods are uncommon at Monte Albán, they are a very useful diagnostic. Several Period IV types were found in small numbers at Monte Albán, always in late contexts and never inside structures. At Lambityeco, though no whole figurines have been found in offerings, fragments are everywhere.

In Monte Albán I, figurines are fairly common. There is no convincing evidence that they were made at all in Period II. One complete Period I-style figurine, and a few fragments of others, have been found in Period II contexts and are commonly attributed to Monte Albán II, however. The early figurine tradition seems to end with that.

In Period IIIa an entirely different kind of figurine emerges (Caso and Bernal 1952:290–291): mold-made from a flat slab of clay, this is the figurine style that comes down to Lambityeco. The bottom, really almost the whole body below the head, may be distended to make the body of a whistle, but the heads remain the same whether the body is a flat cookie of clay or a hollow whistle. Though rare in Period IIIa, these figurines become more and more common in IIIb.

In early Period IV, that is, at Lambityeco, they seem to be dying out. Workmanship is poorer and poorer; features made in relief are partially replaced by painted ones (in red, over a coat of white); orange clay replaces gray; the figurines become smaller and smaller. One very late kind of female figure is commonly less than 2 cm wide and often only 4 or 5 cm tall, with barely enough relief to make it recognizable (Paddock 1966a:Fig. 277).

As this tradition weakens, a new one arises. The new kind has radically different proportions: whereas the Period III tradition had heads that made up about half their height—like Valley of Oaxaca urns—the Period IV types have much smaller heads, roughly in natural proportion to their body size. The new style is rarely gray, and much more often of tan than of orange clay. Whistles are still a feature, but rather than having their abdomens made into whistles, the Period IV figurines always have flat bodies. A few have small solid supports on the back, but it is much more common for the supports to be little whistles. Some of the personages represented seem to be descended from the ones who appeared in the Period III figurines and urns, but others are new, or at least take on forms we do not recognize. Figurine fragments of this Period IV style occurred in such numbers at Yagul that, even though they were not found in offerings, we believed at first that they were a Period V trait, and it was only when they were found at Lambityeco that it became clear they are much older.

As in the case of the ceramics, I will not attempt here to condense Dessaint's analysis of the nearly endless combinations of traits that occur in the figurines of Period IV. Some accessible illustrations will be helpful. Especially in the cases of drawings, some of my judgments here must be rated as tentative. In many examples, however, the diagnostic traits are so plain that I am fully confident of the dating. All references are to figure numbers in Caso and Bernal (1952), *Urnas de Oaxaca.*

Whistles, IIIa:  294f, 295, 296
     IIIb:  294a–e, g, h; 459; 460a, e, g
     IV:  460b–d, f; 461
Flat figurines, IIIa:  443, 445
        IIIb:  444a, b; 446a, c, d
The Period IV figurine tradition: 135, 136, 141, 304-bis, 411, 412, 444c, 446b, e, 447, 452, 453, 456, 457, 458, 517, 518

Once again with respect to the architecture, a detailed report is finished in manuscript by David F. Potter; and once again, no summary of the length possible here could do other than distort it. Potter has analyzed the evolution of two elite houses that probably span almost the entire occupation of Lambityeco. They did not grow much; both were large from the beginning, by Valley of Oaxaca standards. In dimensions and layout they are much like the Monte Albán elite houses, but their construction is significantly less sturdy.

The house of Mound 190 kept very nearly the same form through half a dozen rebuildings, but that of Mound 195, only a few yards away, was transformed into a pyramid the first time it was fully rebuilt. The pyramid, however, is not necessarily nonresidential. This one is wide in proportion to its height. On its ample top there is a platform across the front. From this platform, several steps descend to a patio that occupies the rear, and the three open sides (the platform closes the fourth) were occupied by small structures that probably constituted a house, though I should mention that Potter disagrees with this interpretation. I believe it is tenable because there are several ethnohistoric mentions of priests who lived in their temples. Thus the residential-style layout is not necessarily incompatible with a temple function.

Both David Peterson and I have long suspected that this complex was never completed. In 1963, on exploring Tomb 1—located under the top patio of the pyramid—Emily Rabin and I found it empty, with only an offering of a few censers around the door. The south building on the pyramid top, if it ever was finished, did not leave any trace. One conspicuous feature of the "system" in front of the pyramid, a complex like Systems IV and M at Monte Albán on a smaller scale, was a mound on the south end of the west platform. I cut completely through it in one direction, and failed to find any evidence that it had ever gotten further than being a mound of earth. Michael D. Lind worked further on it, and found finished pieces of the system platform, but not of the mound. Then Peterson cut through it in the other direction, not having been told of my suspicions, and concluded, as I had, that it probably was left unfinished.

What happened? Whether or not Mound 195 was finished, it was not used long enough for Tomb 1 to be occupied (unless it was looted in a highly peculiar way, cleaning the main chamber perfectly and the access pit not at all). In any case, Lambityeco was abandoned.

At Yagul, many pits to bedrock have revealed, after going through up to 5.5 m of fill, that Monte Albán IV material was placed on bedrock to begin a series of ambitious constructions. Yagul had been a quite modest place in previous periods. There seems clearly to have been a construction boom there, however, in Period IV. The pottery and figurines from this time are utterly indistinguishable from those of Lambityeco. The inference that the Lambityeco population moved to the defensible hill of Yagul from their flat location is supported, I believe, by everything we know, and contradicted by nothing.

# TOPIC 61
## Cuilapan

ADDED BY THE EDITORS

Cuilapan de Guerrero (Figure 7.8), a site extending along both banks of the Río Valiente some 7 km southwest of Monte Albán, was another valley-floor center that rose to prominence during the decline of Monte Albán. And like so many of those great Period IIIb–IV centers—among them Yegüih–Lambityeco, Zaachila, and Mitla—it had been occupied, though on a smaller scale, from Formative times onward. We therefore offer this brief summary of Cuilapan to increase our sample of important centers from the period A.D. 600–900.

### HISTORY OF WORK AT CUILAPAN

During 1902 Marshall Saville excavated at Cuilapan, finding a number of important buildings and tombs which he never fully published. In 1954 Ignacio Bernal, accompanied by John Paddock and Lorenzo Gamio, excavated another series of structures at Cuilapan; Bernal's report, on which we have relied heavily in our summary, synthesizes both his work and Saville's unpublished field notes (Bernal 1958b). Bernal was led to the site by his interest in the Postclassic Mixtec incursions into the Valley of Oaxaca, which are mentioned in the *Relaciones* of Teozapotlan [Zaachila] (Mata 1580) and Cuylapa [Cuilapan] (Salazar 1581). Both Cuilapan and Xoxocotlán were said to have Mixtec speakers as recently as Saville's era (Saville 1899:350), but Bernal's excavations revealed no extensive archaeological remains traceable to the Postclassic or histor-

ic Mixtec (see Editors' Introduction to Chapter 8). In 1967 the University of Michigan mapped and surface-collected the site of Cuilapan, discovering Atoyac Yellow-white pottery of the San José or Guadalupe phase near one of Saville's 1902 backdirt piles; unknowingly, Saville may have been the first archaeologist to recover Early Formative pottery in the Valley of Oaxaca. More recently, the site has been included in the Zaachila Valley surveys of Blanton et al. (1982).

### MOUNDS I AND I-BIS

Mound I, rising 9.5 m above the plain south of the river, was the recipient of one of Saville's huge cruciform trenches; Mound I-bis, only 6 m high, was a northeasterly extension of Mound I. Here Saville exposed a two-room Monte Albán II temple reminiscent of the one from Mound X at Monte Albán and Structures 13 and 21 at San José Mogote (see Figure 7.9). The construction was of huge adobes, with stuccoed columns to either side of the antechamber and inner chamber surviving to a height of 1.22 m. There were three more buildings above this one—probably all rebuildings along the same temple plan—and associated with the third of these (dating to Monte Albán IIIa) was an apparent dedicatory offering including a sacrificed child. The child's body was covered with hematite pigment and accompanied by 17 jade "Teotihuacanoid" figurines, 400 jade beads, 35 marine shells, 2 pottery earspools, and disintegrated mosaics of shell, obsidian, and hematite (Bernal 1958b:25). The con-

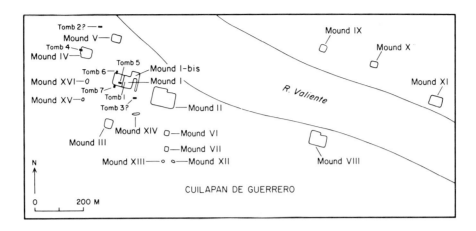

FIGURE 7.8. The ruins of Cuilapan de Guerrero, Oaxaca. (Redrawn, with modifications, from Bernal 1958.)

text of the find, the lack of ceramic vessels or any conventional grave or tomb, and the similarity of the offerings to some found in Mound I at Monte Albán indicate that this was an important offering rather than a high-status burial. Perhaps the sacrifice had been made at the time of the leveling of one temple and the founding of another above it.

In his huge trench in Mound I, Saville passed through many construction layers of adobe, earth, and stone fill before striking Tomb 1. This was a large Monte Albán IIIb–IV tomb with an east–west chamber and a north–south antechamber reached by a stairway of nine steps; Saville reported a "slave" sacrificed in a stone-lined grave near the top step. Inside the tomb were more than two dozen vessels (including a 70-cm "Cocijo" urn with filed teeth). Significantly, this tomb also contained a small carved stone (Caso 1928:Fig. 80) of the type Marcus has called a "genealogical register" (Topic 59). It depicts a man and a woman seated on a *petate* below the *fauces del cielo*, conversing with another individual on a separate *petate*. Tomb 1 at Cuilapan thus joins the tomb from Lambityeco's Mound 195 as having produced one of the few Period IIIb–IV genealogical stones with known provenience.

## TOMBS 3 AND 4

Tombs 3 and 4 of Saville (which Bernal found difficult to relocate) were also reminiscent of Lambityeco; both were Period IIIb–IV masonry tombs with stucco friezes over the lintel. Bernal interprets both friezes as representing bats.

## TOMBS 5, 6, 7

West of Mound I was a typical Period IIIb–IV patio with large ceramic *apaxtles* set in the floor; it was evidently the interior patio of a structure of some kind (perhaps an elite residence), with a *banqueta* running around the edges. Saville found three tombs beneath the *banqueta*. Tomb 5, on the east side, had a niche above the door with three urns representing Lady 2J, an *acompañante* with a Glyph C in his headdress, and a bat. Tomb 6, on the north side, had four skeletons and 50 whole vessels. Tomb 7, on the south side, apparently was not extensively treated in Saville's field notes.

## MOUND III

Mound III was a Monte Albán IIIb–IV stepped pyramid with a stucco floor on top, excavated by Bernal in 1954. The stucco floor was all that remained of a building, perhaps a temple, which had been burned; four *tlecuiles* or floor-level basins and some G-35 vessels remained in association. Inside the adobe fill of the pyramidal mound, Bernal found another massive offering: 71 jade beads, 157 beads of other stones, 2 jade earspools, 3 obsidian blades (of the type used for ritual bloodletting), 8 marine shells, 3 stones, a pearl, and "numerous bones of small animals" including "skull and bones of

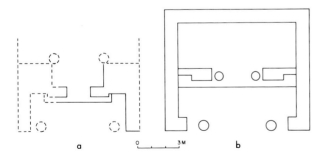

FIGURE 7.9. Monte Albán II temples (a) temple from Mound I at Cuilapan (redrawn from Bernal 1958); (b) temple from Mound X at Monte Albán, shown for comparison (redrawn from Caso 1935).

bird" (Bernal 1958b:79,91–92). We can only speculate that the latter were from quail, doves, or other small birds of the type frequently sacrificed by the Zapotecs (Marcus 1978 and Topic 97).

## MOUND II

Mound II was stratigraphically complex and apparently dated to Period IV, since it contained some incense burner types absent in IIIb deposits at Monte Albán. In the patio east of the mound, Bernal passed through two stucco floors whose pottery dated to the end of Monte Albán IV: as in the case of San Sebastián Abasolo (Topic 87), this Late Period IV pottery contained both the G-35 bowls typical of IIIb–IV and some of the fine gray bowls and jars which were to become dominant in Monte Albán V.

## SUMMARY

Cuilapan de Guerrero was one of the more ancient sedentary communities in the Valley of Oaxaca, founded perhaps as early as San José or Guadalupe times. During Monte Albán II and IIIa it was a local ceremonial–civic center—perhaps in the second tier of the hierarchy below Monte Albán—with important two-room temples, massive offerings, and evidence for human sacrifice. Cuilapan really began to grow in Period IIIb, however, and reached its apogee in IIIb–IV, expanding downstream on both sides of the Río Valiente during the very period when Monte Albán was contracting in size. This later phase of Cuilapan's growth was accompanied by the construction of temples on pyramidal mounds, elite residences with interior patios, and tombs with carved stones establishing the marriages and blood lines of its rulers.

# TOPIC 62
## Monte Albán IV Foodstuffs in Guilá Naquitz Cave

KENT V. FLANNERY
C. EARLE SMITH, JR.

Because the Mitla area included some of our driest caves (Guilá Naquitz, Cueva Redonda, Silvia's Cave, and Cueva de los Afligidos), we know quite a bit about the crops grown and the wild plants collected in the eastern Valley of Oaxaca during the Postclassic. The main crop was a form of Chapalote maize, which, according to Paul Mangelsdorf's preliminary examination, displays a number of drought adaptations in the structure of its roots and leaf sheaths. This corn had been crossed with teosinte (probably another strategy against drought), and some actual teosinte specimens occurred in the same levels. Large black twining beans, short bush beans, pumpkins, yellow chile peppers, white zapotes, avocados, and cotton were among the other cultivars. The roasting of maguey in rock-lined pits was also a common Postclassic activity.

Our most important Monte Albán IV deposit was Zone A at Guilá Naquitz, which had radiocarbon dates of A.D. 620–740 (Flannery 1970:16). This small cave has already been described in Topic 5. Zone A was a thick layer of grass and soft gray ash which overlay the lower deposits in all squares. It was by far the most extensive deposit in the cave, and had the best preservation, presumably because it was much younger than Zones B–E. There were effigy "bat-claw" vessels, frying-pan style *sahumadores* (*incensarios*), and domestic pottery like that from the nearby Monte Albán IV site of Lambityeco (Paddock, Topic 60). The deposit may represent use of the cave as a repository for collected wild plants and harvested domestic plants by a medium-sized group of people, possibly coming either from Mitla or from Lambityeco.

The people who visited the cave during Period IV times made a number of temporary facilities for themselves. A series of very large storage pits were dug into the older deposits near the back wall of the shelter (Features 1a, 1b, 9, 15, and 13). Other storage pits were scattered throughout the site, about a dozen in all. Later, these pits had been used for trash. One of them (Feature 13) contained what may have been the debris from a "new maize" ceremony, including abundant harvested maize, "pulque cups," effigy vessels and bat-claw vessels, *incensarios*, and a possible ball of copal. Harvested wild products were abundant in the zone and included acorns, *susí*, hackberry, maguey, nopal, tuna, mesquite, *guajes*, and wild onions. Piñon nuts do not seem to be as well represented as in the Preceramic layers, and the piñon pine may have been in the process of disappearing from the area (it is a preferred fuel, and may well have been utilized to extinction in the Mitla region). In addition, there were many domestic plants which presumably had been grown on the Río Mitla floodplain below the cave: maize, large black twining beans, small black bush beans, *Canavalia* beans, avocados, pumpkins, bottle gourds, chile peppers, cotton, and white zapotes (*Casimiroa*). The bush bean plants had been pulled up by the roots, just as is the Zapotec custom today at Mitla. The cotton is interesting, because it confirms a statement in the *Relación de Tlacolula y Mitla* (Canseco 1580) that indicates Mitla grew its own cotton before the Conquest (it no longer does so today), and because one boll contained a boll weevil, the oldest known from an archaeological context (Warner and Smith 1968).

## TOPIC 63
### The Mixteca Alta at the End of Las Flores

RONALD SPORES

The pattern in the Mixteca Alta is different from that described for the Valley of Oaxaca by Blanton and Kowalewski (Topics 55, 57). For one thing, there was no giant "primate" center equivalent to Monte Albán. For another, the boundary between the Las Flores phase and the subsequent Natividad phase was not contemporaneous with the Monte Albán IIIb–IV transition. Our radiocarbon dates are few, but they suggest that Las Flores may have lasted until A.D. 900 or even A.D. 1100—that is, up to the time of Tula, Hidalgo.

Rather than an "abandonment" of major hilltop centers, there was a shift in site function and utilization. Many new sites were founded on the valley floor, and the former multiplex urban centers of the Classic—among them Yucuñudahui, Cerro Jasmín, and La Palmita in the Nochixtlán Valley—shrank to half their former size. The major loss seems to be in the habitational area; ceremonial activity continued at these sites, although any new architecture was less impressive than the Classic architecture. Instead of constructing major new ceremonial complexes, the tendency was to use the old centers for ritual purposes while constructing new residential sites that lacked the multiplex functional aspect of the Classic centers. Eventually, Natividad sites came to look very different from Las Flores sites.

In order to test these impressions, which we had derived from settlement pattern survey, we decided to excavate a few strategic areas at Yucuñudahui. Around the occupational zones and the elite residences in the area Caso had excavated, we found only the Las Flores ceramic complex. Test excavations, however, revealed that the West Platform had been repaved with powdered *ndeque* (crushed calcified stone) during the Natividad phase. Additionally, the only important Natividad architecture found at Yucuñudahui is a three-celled patio–dwelling complex (a noble "overseer's" residence?) situated immediately adjacent to the great chert quarry on Yucunoo. Clearly, by the end of the Classic period Yucuñudahui had lost its importance as a complex ceremonial–civic–residential urban center but retained some importance as a ceremonial site and resource procurement locality for a very long time.

The largest of the Mixteca Alta Classic sites became a dependency of some other politically dominant center in Postclassic times. The same fate appears to have befallen other primary and secondary settlements of the Classic period. Classic sites were either abandoned or partially utilized, most probably in quite different ways in Postclassic times. The pattern observed in the Nochixtlán Valley appears to extend to other parts of the Mixteca which have been surveyed, the Teposcolula and Tamazulapan valleys, the Huajuapan area, and Tequixtepec. Although some Classic sites were utilized in Postclassic times, the manner and intensity of use were quite different. There seems to have been a preference for new ground in Postclassic times. Site hierarchies continued but with shifts in size, organization, and location of sites, and a refocusing of power.

## TOPIC 64
### The Tehuacán Valley at the End of the Palo Blanco Phase (A.D. 700)

ROBERT D. DRENNAN

The political events in the Tehuacán Valley between A.D. 600 and 900 were significantly different from those in the Valley of Oaxaca or the Valley of Nochixtlán. Tehuacán did not witness the abandonment of a major, dominant urban center at this time because no such center had existed during the Palo Blanco phase (200 B.C.–A.D. 700). To help understand this situation, let us briefly describe the Palo Blanco phase.

The most obvious settlement pattern difference between Palo Blanco phase Tehuacán and contemporaneous periods in the Valleys of Oaxaca and Nochixtlán is at the highest level of the settlement hierarchy. The latter two were dominated by single centers whose size and internal complexity put each in a class by itself for the valley. Some Palo Blanco phase sites seem to be in the same size range as Yucuita and perhaps approach the size of Yucuñudahui, but the Tehuacán Valley had no population center on the scale of Monte Albán. On the basis of data already collected, no single site overshadows the Tehuacán Valley to the extent seen in Nochixtlán or Oaxaca.

MacNeish et al. (1972:405–447), for example, list as many as 14 "towns" which may have been occupied at the same time during the Palo Blanco phase. They divide the valley into seven or eight hypothetical relatively independent sociopolitical units. While more systematic surface survey with more precise chronological control will provide a firmer basis for conclusions concerning the Palo Blanco phase, it is unlikely that such work will drastically change the overall impression that the Tehuacán Valley was more fragmented into less integrated subdivisions than was the case in the Valleys of Oaxaca or Nochixtlán. These subdivisions may be analogous to subunits within the Valleys of Oaxaca or Nochixtlán centered on secondary centers and thus linked to the primary regional center. The situation in Tehuacán, then, resembles that in Nochixtlán or Oaxaca, only without the highest level of the settlement hierarchy observed in those two regions.

The nature of environmental variability in the Tehuacán Valley is such that the various subdivisions differ more with respect to available natural resources than is the case with subunits in either Nochixtlán or Oaxaca. Whereas a cross section of the Valleys of Nochixtlán or Oaxaca from central drainage to watershed reveals a similar succession of environmental zones regardless of where the section is taken, such a cross section of the Tehuacán Valley would reveal environments of different potentials in different parts of the valley. While rainfall is uniformly low in Tehuacán, available water varies considerably in different sections of the valley because of the locations of springs and the extravalley sources of surface water. Elevation drops from over 1800 m at the head of the valley to less than 600 m. Varying soils and topography combine with these patterns to result in the substantial environmental differences among the areas occupied by the subdivisions. According to some explanatory schemes, such an environment would make centralized organization advantageous to facilitate the exchange of products among the subdivisions. The evidence produced to date, however, indicates that less sociopolitical centralization occurred in Tehuacán than in the Valleys of Oaxaca and Nochixtlán.

Apart from valley-wide organizational considerations, some trends of population distribution seen in the Valleys of Oaxaca and Nochixtlán are also observed in Palo Blanco phase Tehuacán. A general trend towards nucleation of population into larger concentrations than during previous periods applies to all three regions, although the particular form that this takes is different in Tehuacán, as noted previously. A tendency to locate sizable and important population concentrations on hilltops is also seen in all three regions. In Tehuacán this tendency is absent until Early Palo Blanco times and seems to weaken during Late Palo Blanco times. The beginning of this trend in Tehuacán comes after that in the Valley of Oaxaca, where hilltop towns appear in Monte Albán Ia.

The survey results reported by MacNeish et al. (1972:405–447) indicate that the production of salt had become a major industry by Early Palo Blanco times, although more recent research has cast doubt on the interpretation of certain surface features as salt mounds (Drennan 1978:60–62). Extensive irrigation by means of canals also seems to have been widespread in the Tehuacán Valley. Water sources included natural springs in the upstream end of the valley and the reservoir created by the Purrón Dam, whose most impressive building stages fall in this time span.

As for the end of the Palo Blanco phase and the beginning of the Venta Salada phase (A.D. 700), this period for the Tehuacán Valley is even more poorly known than contemporary periods in other valleys. Obviously, it was not characterized by the abandonment of a major Classic urban center like Monte Albán, as there was no major urban center to be abandoned. By existing estimates, the Palo Blanco phase ended with a lower population in the valley than that observed during Early Palo Blanco times. For the first time in the Tehuacán Valley sequence, fortifications came to be built at a number of sites in the Early Venta Salada phase (A.D. 700–900). Also, the first real "cities" of the Tehuacán Valley came into existence at this time, although no one city seems to have dominated the entire valley.

## TOPIC 65
### The Rise of the Ñuiñe Centers in the Mixteca Baja

JOHN PADDOCK

The Mixteca Baja (Figure 7.10)—a series of arid, semitropical, lower-altitude valleys in the headwaters of the Balsas River basin along the Puebla–Oaxaca border—shows a sequence divergent from that of the areas just described. During the period A.D. 600–900, while Monte Albán and the Early Urban centers of the Mixteca Alta declined, urbanism in the Mixteca Baja reached a kind of peak. Interestingly, and perhaps significantly, the urban centers of this region began to grow after the fall of Teotihuacán and did not decline significantly until the rise of Tula. This region, which I have called the Ñuiñe after a sixteenth-century

Mixtec word for "hot lands" (Paddock 1966a:174–200), had its own florescence of writing (see Moser, Topic 66) and its own urban centers—places like Ñuyoo (Huajuapan), Tequixtepec, Miltepec, Acatlán, Chila, and others.

One of the more considerable innovations in this area is that, whereas in 1966 and later I classed the Ñuiñe phenomenon as Early Urban, today I propose a refinement of its chronological placement and a major amplification of its relationships with regions outside Oaxaca. This results in a confession that I have almost nothing to say about Early Urbanism in the area, for the Ñuiñe style is, rather, a man-

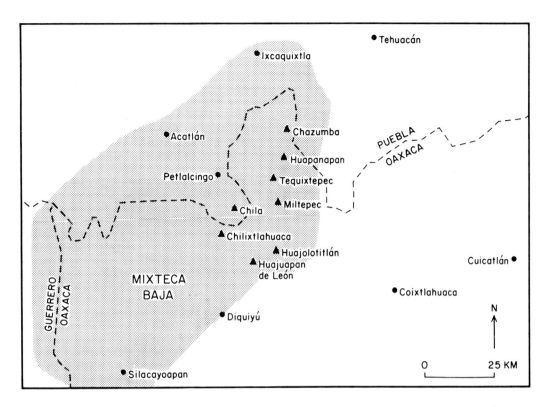

FIGURE 7.10. The Mixteca Baja, showing some of the localities mentioned in Topics 65 and 66. Towns with Ñuiñe-style carved stones indicated by ▲.

ifestation in the Mixteca Baja of a pan-Mesoamerican horizon called Middle Urban.

But first, what about pre-Ñuiñe days in the Mixteca Baja? Bernal, Vaillant, Jiménez Moreno, and others have more than once predicted successfully the discovery of periods and even horizons; I will venture a very small prediction. The Ñuiñe did not grow exclusively out of Monte Albán and Teotihuacán. Its large proportion of local traits will be found to have roots in an Early Urban culture of the area, and that culture may well have a greater resemblance to its neighbors in the Mixteca Alta than does the Ñuiñe to its contemporaries there. Though Diquiyú is close to the border of the two Mixtecas, I suspect it will be a major center of the Baja for Early Urban. No, this is not speculation. Prediction is a normal process in science, some would say an identifying characteristic of it.

Now about that Middle Urban horizon: for reasons having no connection with science, Mesoamerican archaeology was centered for decades on the exploration of two areas, the Maya region and the Valley of Mexico. This narrow focus was nobody's fault, but it led inevitably to a formulation of Mesoamerican culture history based on the events of those two areas that tended to disregard others. One of the greatest contributions Oaxaca studies can make will be the abandonment of the delusion that one can utter generalizations about Mesoamerica on the basis of those two areas alone.

From the viewpoint of the Valley of Mexico, there was indeed a "Classic," followed by a catastrophic depression and then by the rise of a "Postclassic." In the Maya region the *Classic* Classic (first to be discovered, even if not the first to begin) was likewise followed by hard times and the resurgence of an altered culture called Postclassic.

El Tajín, Cholula, Xochicalco, Uxmal were known, but were persistently dismissed by being treated as provincial derivatives of the areas first studied. When necessary, they were jammed by force into the existing categories, the categories drawn from knowledge of the two Mesoamerican poles so sacred to the vested interests. Neither Classic nor Postclassic in time, they were equally awkward in culture and in location, for they represented something like a revolution in Mesoamerica, changing its character and the location of its centers of power. For years, however, they were denied their status and relegated to Epiclassic, Protopostclassic, or some other place below-stairs.

Recent discoveries in Oaxaca and in Guatemala have put an end to all that. On first reading *Ancient Oaxaca*, Eric Thompson wrote to me to point out that stone inscriptions enclosed in circular cartouches occurred not only in the Ñuiñe, but also conspicuously at Cotzumalhuapa. But in some way I was not ready for the data, and not even my participation in the Teotihuacán round table of 1966 (in which I dealt with exterior relations of Teotihuacán) made the light go on.

Struggling to cope with the failure of his Bilbao–Cotzumalhuapa materials to fit into established concepts of the Maya Classic, Lee Parsons in 1969 proposed a remedy in the form of the Middle Classic concept. In his exposition, L. Parsons (1969:151–185) lists 41 traits that he believes link Teotihuacán III–IV, Bilbao, Xochicalco, Ñuiñe, and Chichén–Puuc.

In 1973, not consciously aware of any direct connection with Middle Classic as Parsons had defined it, and in fact embarrassingly ignorant of the details of his work, I participated in a symposium on rise and fall of the non-Maya Classic, and in my contribution was obliged to face up to certain conceptual difficulties. I found them neatly resolved by the simple and obvious device of placing a new Middle between Early Urban and Late Urban.

Anyone working in Oaxaca is sharply aware that a scheme based on Teotihuacán and the Valley of Mexico does not fit Oaxaca developments comfortably. But a view centered on Oaxaca has the same defect as one centered on the Valley of Mexico: it fails to treat Mesoamerica as a whole. When I strove to phrase what happened to the Classic in Mesoamerica as a whole, it was plain that

> the Mesoamerican "Classic" did not "fall." It was not extinguished, and it was not followed by a Dark Age that preceded the rise of the "Postclassic." The "Classic," which I have long preferred to call the Mesoamerican Early Urban, was followed directly and immediately by a pan-Mesoamerican stage that I hereby propose to call Middle Urban. What we used to call "Postclassic" I now think should be simply Late Urban.
>
> What then is Middle Urban? As a time, it is not exactly placed; roughly the second half of the first millennium A.D. As a developmental period, it is closely related to Early Urban, but at the same time transformed. This transformation may be in some degree an adaptation to changed circumstances, for in every case the major centers of Middle Urban are different from those of Early Urban [Paddock 1973:19].

That is, all the power centers of Early Urban are replaced (though surely not all at once), and new capitals define Middle Urban by their rise to dominance. These new capitals are El Tajín, Cholula, Xochicalco, Uxmal, Bilbao–Cotzumalhuapa, and some place or places in the Ñuiñe. After several centuries, these Middle Urban capitals in their turn were replaced by others, those of the Late Urban.

Mesoamerican culture history cannot be written sensibly from the viewpoint of any single place, or even any single region (though Oaxaca is more nearly satisfactory for this purpose than less central regions are). This insight is not without antecedents. In presenting the Epiclassic concept, Jiménez Moreno (1959, 1966) was recognizing the increasing inadequacy of the old Classic–Postclassic scheme, specifically with reference to the Tajín–Cholula–Xochicalco events. Various scholars, in toying with such ideas as a Protopostclassic, were conceding something similar, but without willingness to relinquish the old order. What I propose is, then, no bolt out of the blue, but rather a further step in a more or less orderly progress.

But why complicate our lives with a new term and concept if Parsons had already used the same events (the rises to power of the Middle Urban capitals) to integrate the Middle Classic? Unhappily, Middle Urban is not at all the same as Middle Classic; it is a parallel device, but the problems it deals with are quite different, as are its temporal and spatial limits. The coincidence is limited to names and to some of the raw materials.

Middle Classic is a central division of the span from A.D. 300 to 900, whereas Middle Urban is a central division of the entire span from the first urbanism in Mesoamerica to the Spanish Conquest. Being tied to the same events—the rise of Tajín, Bilbao, and all the new capitals between—obviously the two concepts coincide at one period. L. Parsons dates Middle Classic at approximately A.D. 400 to 700, dividing it into an early and a late phase. The early one might be called the Teotihuacán apogee, the late one the Teotihuacán exodus; the exodus coincides with the major florescence of his Bilbao center. Probably it coincides also with parallel prosperity at the other Middle Urban–Middle Classic centers, for a florescence at A.D. 550–700 fits very well with presently known materials. (Though, of course, Middle Urban does not end with the end of Middle Classic.)

However, just as we now know we cannot proclaim a simultaneous emergence of urbanism in all parts of Mesoamerica (runners from the Maya region used to be imagined as advising authorities at Teotihuacán, Monte Albán, and elsewhere that they would "go urban" at noon on the day of the summer solstice in A.D. 300), we should not expect a simultaneous collapse of the first urban centers and a rush for the exits ("today is Abandonment Day"). Likewise, we should be imprudent to expect simultaneity in the events of Middle Urbanism or Late Urbanism; every innovation must have one beginning, at one time and one place, in one human mind.

This is a very long preface to a very short statement. Ñuiñe has become important to the definition of both Middle Classic and Middle Urban. At the same time, it has been woven into a pan-Mesoamerican fabric of events through the clear signs of cultural borrowings and lendings. I believe that these signs, as well as the utility of the Middle Classic concept, are demonstrated in the symposium edited by Esther Pasztory (1978).

It may seem anomalous for a regional culture that is still almost untouched by archaeological excavations to have such a large role. Since the first publication on the Ñuiñe (Paddock 1965:136), however, much has been added. Two small salvage excavations have taken place in the region, and both of them occurred in deposits of the Ñuiñe period (Paddock 1968a; 1970a,b; Winter, Deraga, and Fernández 1976). Other sources too have brought new materials to attention, with the important result that the proposals I made with some hesitation a decade ago are now abundantly confirmed.

Even so, we remain in painful ignorance of the region for all periods, even for the time of the Ñuiñe style. Thus, we can still date the Ñuiñe style only by reference to other regions, a procedure I have long deplored. We still do not have so much as a thorough surface survey of a single site, though a number of sites have been visited by archaeologists. On the south and west, we cannot even say how far the region and its style extended. Yet a Ñuiñe literature has begun to take shape, with important contributions of data and concept by Moser, L. Parsons, Wilkerson, and Winter, Deraga, and Fernández.

To Moser's materials (manuscript) on the *cabecitas colosales* we may now add the information that at least some of these objects did not represent neckless heads, for two specimens in the Frissell Museum had necks and, apparently, bodies, though the bodies are now missing. In addition, Winter, Deraga, and Fernández recovered an elongated, but otherwise fairly typical, example in their salvage work at the site of Cerro de la Codorniz, near Chilixtlahuaca, northwest of Huajuapan. The crest it wears is the one common to many others (Paddock 1966a:Figs. 201, 203).

For the first time, a Ñuiñe urn has come from a scientific excavation. In a tomb at Cerro de la Codorniz, Winter, Deraga, and Fernández found one that, although it adds some new details to our information about the urns, is an entirely typical example in every respect except the iconographic. It is made of the same orange paste with large flakes of silvery mica that is used in others, and in most pottery vessels of the region as well. It consists of a large vase that sits on a square pedestal and is almost concealed by a figure on the front. The figure is purely illusion—a sketchy assembly of flat mold-made plaques that successfully suggest an animal, or animal-

disguised personage, seated cross-legged with hands on knees. The vase is smoke-blackened on the inside.

New features include the face, apparently that of a wrinkled jaguar (it lacks the forehead horn and disks at the corners of the mouth that would identify a bat). The face seems to be framed by a beard whose edges are adorned with circles, symbols of jade. The "mustache" mask that is worn by the God of Glyph L at Monte Albán hides a part of the mouth area. Below each hand, where the knees ought to be, is a small motif of crossed diagonal bands. The pedestal has *grecas* on the front; these are an unusual part-angular and part-rounded variant, with a cross-hatched design on one area. Smoke or cloud symbols are prominent in several of the ornaments, as is natural in a brazier.

The same tomb produced confirmation of the association of provincial Thin Orange, in the shapes of hemispherical ring-base bowls, spout-handled *ollitas*, and some new shapes, with the urn. Stone inscriptions recovered by Winter, Deraga, and Fernández include a circular one with a date of 1 or 2 Death and a fragment of another that repeats elements known from the first urn of Huajuapan (Paddock 1966a:Fig. 226).

Wilkerson, engaged in a study of inscriptions on one of the Tajín ballcourts, was startled by the virtual identity of relief carvings on an urn (Paddock 1970b:Fig. 1) and some stones (Paddock 1968a:Foto 36; 1970a: Fig. 1) from Huajuapan. This is further indication that many Ñuiñe traits are part of a widespread Middle Classic horizon.

## TOPIC 66
## The Middle Classic Ñuiñe Style of the Mixteca Baja, Oaxaca: A Summary Report

CHRISTOPHER L. MOSER

Ñuiñe, Mixtec for "hot lands," refers to the lower Mixteca region (1000–2000 m above sea level) of northwestern Oaxaca and southern Puebla (Moser 1977:5). In the decade since John Paddock (1966a) first recognized and defined the Middle Classic (or Middle Urban) Ñuiñe art style of the Mixteca Baja, only very limited field research has occurred there. The traits which Paddock (1966a) used to define the Ñuiñe art style include: (1) micaceous schist-tempered Thin Orange pottery, (2) a distinctive glyphic system, (3) *cabecitas colosales* or distinctive ceramic heads, (4) a small spouted olla with a turned-down rim that has the edge cut in steps, and (5) large effigy pottery urns of orange paste.

In 1968 Paddock (1968b, 1970a,b) excavated a partially looted Ñuiñe tomb and made a test pit at Ñuyoo (Cerrito de las Minas), a site on the north edge of Huajuapan de León, Oaxaca. The test pit revealed that occupation in this area can be extended back to the Formative. The only other excavation in the Mixteca Baja was carried out in 1974 by Winter, Deraga, and Fernández (1976) on another Ñuiñe

tomb near Santiago Chilixtlahuaca, Oaxaca. This tomb produced an urn and numerous bowls, all in the Ñuiñe style.

Between 1964 and the summer of 1972 I carried out a series of limited area surveys and data gathering excursions into the Acatlán, Huajuapan, and Tequixtepec areas. In 1970 I was able to trace a number of *cabecitas colosales* of various public and private collections to several Ñuiñe sites in the immediate vicinity of Acatlán, Puebla and was able to show that there are three distinct types and at least one subvariety which I have described as "squat headlets" (Moser 1977b).

By 1974 I had recorded some 49 Mixteca Baja stones bearing Ñuiñe glyphs and nine urns. This material provided the basis for an initial study of Ñuiñe writing and iconography (Moser 1977a). A catalog of more than 139 Ñuiñe motifs have been factored out and several logographic conventions were suggested by the sample. Primarily the writing style shows more similarity with Monte Albán than with any other Mesoamerican area (except perhaps the relatively un-

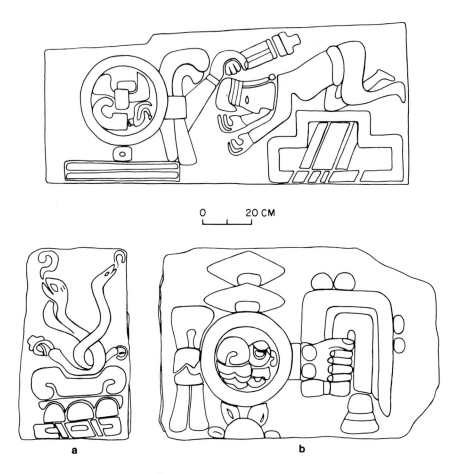

0        20 CM

a                                    b

FIGURE 7.11. Examples of carved stones in the Ñuiñe style. Top, Tequixtepec Stone I. Bottom, Tequixtepec Stone XVIII: (a) left side; (b) face. (Redrawn from Moser 1977a.)

known Mixteca Alta). They share many glyphic motifs including the use of the 5-bar and dots for numerical notations in calendrical dates and personal names. The Ñuiñe calendrical-year sign seems to take several forms ranging from the Monte Albán I–II headband form to the Postclassic Mixtec "A–O" form and occurs with the days Flower, Turquoise, and Flint (or Stone). So far only 13 or 14 of the 20 calendric day signs have been found, though others are hinted at in noncalendric contexts. Another six glyphs (Owl, Bat, Foot, Bars, Heart or Blood, Double Pillared Temple) suggest alternate day names or perhaps month glyphs. The "Crown" sign can alternatively be interpreted as a possible glyph for the 52-year period or Mixtec *Eedziya* (Moser 1972) or perhaps a sign for rank (Moser 1977a:148).

Noncalendric signs include the speech scroll, place glyphs, and the cartouche. Two forms of the cartouche occur: a circular form and a square or rectangular form with rounded corners. The latter nearly always contain a day-sign and are accompanied with a numerical coefficient below it. A square cartouche, then, has only a calendrical date-bearing role. The circular form contains either a known day sign, an alternate month-like sign, or some unrecognizable glyph, and has

the usual numerical subfix; it is always associated with other affixed signs as well. Usually there is a prefix of a folded bow-like element which I have suggested may be a loincloth and represents the Mixtec prefix *ya-* that indicates a masculine name. Other affixed elements include other parts of the person's name, and often there is an arm or hand projecting out from the circle holding a banner or club (Figure 7.11). Other glyphic texts associated with place glyphs are probably place names, perhaps records of conquests.

From the calendric and other glyphic representations it can be suggested that the Ñuiñe pantheon was similar to that of Classic Mesoamerica in general. We can see the Earth Monster Alligator, the Rain God, the Death God, the Serpent, the Wind God, the Jaguar, the Old Man (Fire?) God, and even perhaps Xipe Totec. The Jaguar appears as a full-figure animal, often sitting atop a place glyph on eight or nine stones and as part of the costume of the figures on Ñuiñe urns. The Jaguar may represent a ruling lineage of this area as suggested by page 2 of the Codex Sánchez Solís (Moser 1977a:190).

On the basis of a comparative regional style analysis of the hieroglyphic stones, urns, and surface pottery collections, it appears that the Ñuiñe can definitely be placed during what Lee Parsons (1969) designates as the Middle Classic (A.D. 400–700) and was contemporary with Teotihuacán III and IV as well as Monte Albán IIIb (see also Paddock 1978). Parsons (1969:164) points out that the Middle Classic was a phase when "many eclectic elements were mixed," from Teotihuacán, Monte Albán, and Maya trade systems, "but imperfectly fused" into several new derived regional styles such as the Ñuiñe. It would seem also that the Ñuiñe–Monte Albán relationship extended back into the Protoclassic (100 B.C.–A.D. 100) or at least to the Early Classic (A.D. 100–400), and only began to diverge sometime during the Middle Classic, probably at about the time that Monte Albán and Teotihuacán became fully involved. For example, the early Monte Albán I and II form of placing numerical dots above 5-bars is retained in the Ñuiñe long after it is

reversed at Monte Albán in Period IIIa, when the dots were placed below the 5-bar.

Other surface pottery collections from several sites in the vicinity of Tequixtepec also show a Late Classic and Early Postclassic occupation during which Xochicalco or Puebla and Toltec ceramic influences can be recognized. Still later Late Postclassic Mixteca–Puebla styles of polychrome pottery can be found at several sites near Huajuapan de León and near Acatlán. It is often difficult to distinguish Postclassic Mixtec from Aztec glyphic carved stones. Clearly, the Mixteca Baja–Ñuiñe will provide a great deal of information on regional cultural development as well as an insight to the cultural development in the major nuclear center of Mesoamerica when more intensive archaeological investigations can be carried out there.

# TOPIC 67
## The Earliest Mixtec Dynastic Records

MARY ELIZABETH SMITH

At the present time, it is impossible to discuss with any certainty Mixtec dynastic records of the period A.D. 600–900. Although Alfonso Caso (1949, 1950, 1960, 1964) proposed correlations between the specific year-dates in the Mixtec manuscripts and Christian year-dates, these correlations are currently being reevaluated and will undoubtedly be revised.

H. B. Nicholson (1967) first suggested that such a revision might be necessary, and Emily Rabin has been actively working on some of the problems connected with the date correlations proposed by Caso. Rabin (1974) feels that many of these correlations are too early and has presented convincing arguments that one of the initial dynastic marriages shown in the manuscripts has been dated three 52-year cycles—or 156 years—too early. The date of this marriage was considered by Caso (1950:12; 1960:79) to be A.D. 732; according to the evidence presented by Rabin, the date should be A.D. 888. The marriage in question, between ♂ 4 Alligator "Bleeding Tiger" and ♀ 1 Death "Sun Ornament," is shown toward the beginning of Codex Bodley (1-

III), as the first marriage on the Vienna reverse (I-3), and at the beginning of one of the genealogical segments in Codex Nuttall (21-II). If, as Rabin suggests, this very early dynastic marriage occurs in A.D. 888, then very little is recorded in the Mixtec histories for the period A.D. 600–900.

Undoubtedly, many of Caso's correlations of the later dates in the manuscripts—that is, dates from the period just prior to or soon after the Spanish Conquest—will not be revised. The latest date in any of the Mixtec Preconquest-style screenfolds is a date toward the end of Codex Selden interpreted by Caso (1950; 1964:14, 57, 52) as A.D. 1556. I see no reason to question this correlation, because this date cannot be moved one cycle earlier to equate with the year 1504, nor is it possible to move it one cycle later to the year 1608.

The work on the revision of correlations proposed by Caso for the dates toward the beginning of the manuscripts is still in progress. Nonetheless, it would seem that most of the Mixtec dynastic history depicted in the manuscripts is Postclassic in date.

# TOPIC 68
## Comments on the Earliest Mixtec Dynastic Records

DONALD ROBERTSON

My main question is one posed elsewhere: How far back in time can the Mixtec genealogies be considered historical, that is, factual, and when does the content turn into a series

of mythological persons who are ancestors to historical persons figuring in the manuscripts? If, as Caso (1949) seems to have thought, the genealogical figures are all historical, it indeed gives these historical manuscripts an almost unique historical time depth. More recent studies, however, would indicate that the genealogies of historical persons are, in effect, an addendum to genealogies of earlier mythological persons, or that the mythological sequences act as a prelude to historical genealogies much the way that Colonial Nahuatl written legal documents often begin with an historical preamble.

The present form of the documents, with the figures displayed in boustrophedon fashion, almost surely implies a reediting of older examples into an economical use of space using an older form, now lost, where the sequences of figures would be presented in a single file. One can present, as a focus of discussion, the possibility that Aztec manuscripts, such as the Tira de Tepechpan or even certain passages of the Codex Telleriano Remensis, preserve the older form in the manner of a provincial or regional survival. If so, this possibility would fit in with what we know from the sources. The Aztecs thought the source of their knowledge of writing was the Tlailotlaque or "Those Who Came Back," the people who went to Tlillan–Tlapallan, the Land of the Red and the Black, the land of writing, most surely the Mixteca. If the

art of manuscript writing went in its original form from the Mixtecs to the Tlailotlaque of Texcoco to the Aztecs, the new format, or reediting, of the historical texts in the Mixteca could date from some time after this transfer of a most important item of Oaxacan culture to their northern, somewhat less civilized, neighbors.

The question remains open of when we should date the present manuscripts and thus the texts of the Mixtec histories. There have been previous attempts based on the date of the historical data, a not wholly reliable method because it links the present surviving manuscripts on the basis of content to events that may very well have taken place much earlier than the period when the manuscripts were written—even before the hypothetical reediting of texts into their present boustrophedon pattern. Why should we not suppose that the Spaniards early in the sixteenth century received the most recent edition, as it were, of the historical texts in their modern reediting from the Mixteca, and that we now have these newest editions? The original first editions were probably long gone, in most instances, when the Spaniards first arrived in the land.

# TOPIC 69
## Oaxaca and the Toltecs: A Postscript

KENT V. FLANNERY
JOYCE MARCUS

We cannot leave the period A.D. 600–900 without commenting briefly on one last series of events that had "international" significance for the Cloud People. Those events included the founding of Tula by Ce Acatl Topiltzin and the rise of the Toltec state. We have already suggested that the rise of this state may have been related to the decline of the Ñuiñe centers in the Mixteca Baja, a zone that lies virtually on the border between Mixtec and Nahua speakers. Now we would like to follow up Ignacio Bernal's (1966a:365) suggestion that the collapse of Tula had something to do with the Postclassic Mixtec expansion (documented in the following chapter).

Ce Acatl, son of the Toltec leader Totepeuh (Feldman 1974) is thought to have been born at Tepoztlán, Morelos, in A.D. 935 or 947 (Jiménez Moreno 1941). After searching for, and burying, his deceased father's remains, he moved the Toltec capital to Tula in A.D. 968. Although Ce Acatl himself was eventually driven out of Tula around A.D. 987, the city flourished and the Toltec became the most politically powerful state in highland Mexico. As Coe observes,

At the height of its power, Tula is pictured in the poems as a sort of marvellous never-never land, where ears of maize were as big as *mano* stones, and red, yellow, green, blue and many other colours of cotton grew naturally. There were palaces of jade, of

gold, a turquoise palace, and one made of blue-green quetzal feathers [1962:138].

After exerting tremendous political and artistic influence on Mesoamerica for some 200 years, Tula fell in approximately A.D. 1160; its last ruler, Huemac, moved his capital to Chapultepec in the Valley of Mexico in A.D. 1156 or 1168.

During the florescence of Tula, no neighboring urban center came forth to challenge it. Toltec impact on the Cloud People was so great that even ♂ 8 Deer "Tiger Claw", an important Mixtec ruler described in the next chapter, supposedly traveled to Tula in A.D. 1045 to receive the nose ornament which marked his investiture as a ruler of the Second Dynasty of Tilantongo (Clark 1912). Even after the fall of this great city, its impact continued: "in death, as in life, Tula remained the most potent force in Mesoamerica" (Coe 1962:139). Toltec royalty migrated to other parts of Mexico, penetrating even the northern Maya area, and in central Mexico it became standard practice for important rulers to claim descent from the Toltec. Codex Nuttall shows ♂ 8 Deer "in typical Toltec dress, while those surrounding him are clearly Mixtecs" (Weaver 1972:220). It may well be that some of the Mixtec rulers who originally founded the great *cacicazgos* of the Natividad phase also claimed Toltec ancestry.

We raise this possibility for two reasons; one is timing. The great Classic centers of the Mixteca, obviously influenced by the Zapotec both in their architecture and their writing, declined with the rise of Tula. After the fall of Tula they emerged with different settlement patterns, with *greca-* panelled architecture, with screenfold manuscripts, and with a whole new set of ceramic vessel shapes. When some of these traits appear in the Valley of Oaxaca, they have been singled out as evidence for Mixtec influence on the Zapotec. We, however, are becoming increasingly convinced that they reflect the impact of the Toltec state on both the Mixtec and the Zapotec.

# The Postclassic Balkanization of Oaxaca

### An Introduction to the Late Postclassic

JOYCE MARCUS
KENT V. FLANNERY

> From a broader point of view, I believe that the end of Toltec control (in about 1160) was the event which allowed the Mixtecs to expand. This expansion took the Mixtecs into several areas, one of which was the Valley of Oaxaca.
> Bernal 1966a:365

> If our hypothesis is correct, the Mixtec adopted the Toltec calendar at the end of the tenth century, and from then on the Mixtec glyphs were closely related to the Mexican [glyphs], and years were named Reed, Flint, House, and Rabbit.
> Caso 1956:488

We come now to one of the most fascinating and controversial periods in all of Oaxaca archaeology. For the first time, our data from excavation and settlement pattern survey can be combined with information from the Mixtec and Aztec codices and with ethnohistoric data from the *Relaciones Geográficas* of the sixteenth century, giving us an incomparably richer portrait of the Cloud People. On the one hand, this richness provides a basis for controversy, owing to the innumerable areas of conflict and dispute between ethnohistory, textual analysis, and dirt archaeology. On the other hand, we are presented with a unique opportunity to test hypotheses derived from one subdiscipline against the data derived from another.

Our archaeological data come from the Monte Albán V phase in the Valley of Oaxaca (A.D. 950–1530), the Late Natividad phase in the Nochixtlán Valley (A.D. 1000–1530), the Late Venta Salada phase in the Tehuacán Valley (A.D. 1000–1530), and the Ulam phase in the Isthmus of Tehuantepec (A.D. 900–1530). We would characterize this period as one of Balkanization, a term used by political scientists to refer to the division of a region into numerous small states that are hostile to each other. The archaeological data reveal no single, dominant center that could have integrated either the Zapotec or the Mixtec; in addition, evidence of fortification is widespread. Both the Postclassic codices and the ethnohistoric documents describe frequent military conflicts—often involving members of the same ruling family—interrupted by ephemeral truces brought about through royal marriage or military alliance.

In spite of the constant sparring of these relatively small, competitive states, the Late Postclassic period also had aspects of genuine "internationalism." Ceramic complexes became extremely widespread, with some wares crosscutting many ethnic boundaries. Nobles of most groups ate from polychrome pottery, and the officers of competing armies shared a common technology including quilted cotton armor, cane or wooden shields, wooden broadswords edged with obsidian blades, bows and arrows, slings, and the atl-

217

THE CLOUD PEOPLE

Copyright © 1983 by Academic Press, Inc.
All rights of reproduction in any form reserved.
ISBN 0-12-259860-1

atl. Certain state offices, such as "tribute collector" and "ward boss," were widespread and the terms for these offices occur in several languages. From the standpoint of cultural evolution, these similarities are less the result of *convergence* than of *parallel evolution:* the Aztec, Mixtec, Cuicatec, and Zapotec were in continual contact and conflict, borrowing from each other at an accelerated rate.

## THE MIXTEC EXPANSION

As one of the quotations at the start of this Introduction indicates, Ignacio Bernal suspects that the fall of Tula in A.D. 1160 set in motion many of the processes discussed here. He believes that the collapse of the Toltec permitted a buildup of power in the Mixteca which was to have profound cultural, political, and military consequences for southern Mexico. This is an intriguing suggestion, as many of the Mixtec kings underscored their royalty by claiming descent from the lords of Tula[1] (see Topic 69). The Postclassic Mixtec evolved what may have been the most highly stratified society in Mesoamerica, if we judge by the pattern by which kings were recruited. While other Postclassic states were also characterized by a class-endogamous professional ruling class, few placed as much emphasis on birth order and nearness to the main trunk of elite parentage as did the Mixtec. Aztec rulers were chosen from eligible royal offspring by a council of noble elders; the Zapotec had a notion of primogeniture, but their throne frequently passed to the most competent prince, regardless of birth order. Only the Mixtec valued main trunk descent so highly that rulers occasionally married their full siblings to ensure the high rank of their offspring. Among the descendants of the Mixtec lord ♂ 8 Deer "Tiger Claw" alone, there are four cases of brother–sister marriage (Dahlgren de Jordán 1954). We believe this emphasis on the main trunk is paralleled in an interesting difference in collateral kin terms between Mixtec and Zapotec (see Topic 95).

The aforementioned 8 Deer (A.D. 1011–1063) was significant for another reason: he may have been the first ruler of the Cloud People to establish a truly bureaucratic state, possibly modeled on that of the Toltec. In contrast to the Aztec, most Mixtec and Zapotec states show little bureaucratization. The ruler resided at a capital, and he selected the nobles who were to rule specific subject communities. The sixteenth-century *relaciones* list very few terms that could describe lower-order bureaucrats in such communities, and are almost universal in their statements that there was no law except what the lord directed.

8 Deer "Tiger Claw" was born on the day 8 Deer in the year 12 Reed (A.D. 1011) at Tilantongo, the site of one of the most prestigious royal lineages in the Mixteca Alta. He was the first son of ♀ 11 Water "Blue Jewel Bird," the second

wife of his father ♂ 5 Lizard, and therefore was outranked by an older half-brother who was the son of his father's first wife. Because this older half-brother was the logical heir to the second dynasty of Tilantongo, 8 Deer turned his attention to the Mixtec colony of Tututepec on the tropical Oaxaca coast. There he established an expansionist, militaristic state which wreaked havoc on the Chatino and the southern Zapotec, especially in the area between Miahuatlán and the coast.

8 Deer received more than his share of attention in the Mixtec pictorial manuscripts, and Mary Elizabeth Smith (personal communication) estimates that 75–100 place signs may be attributed to his conquests. In 1912, J. Cooper Clark, inspired by the Codex Colombino, published an entire book on the life of 8 Deer (Clark 1912) which can serve as an example of the adventures that frequently awaited the Mixtec rulers of that period.[2]

### The Life of 8 Deer

Portions and slightly different versions of the life of 8 Deer "Tiger Claw" appear in the codices Nuttall, Bodley, Selden, Reverse of the Vienna, Becker I and II, Sánchez Solís, and Colombino. The Nuttall and other codices present his biography from the perspective of the Mixteca Alta, whereas the Codex Colombino presents the Pacific coastal version of the same story (M. E. Smith 1963:288, 1973a).

In A.D. 1030, when 8 Deer was 19 years old, his father died; because ♂ 5 Lizard had been alive in A.D. 969, he must have been over 60 when he succumbed. Turning his attention to the south coast of Oaxaca, 8 Deer made the site of Tututepec his base of operations for a series of conquests. This fact is interesting because, as we have seen in Topic 29, Tututepec may previously have been one of the "conquered places" listed on Building J at Monte Albán in Period II.

In the codices, 8 Deer's conquests were often depicted by an arrow inserted in the hill or place sign. This pictorial convention has an analog in sixteenth-century Mixtec (Alvarado 1593), inasmuch as one expression for "to conquer," *chihi nduvua ñuhu ñaha,* means "to put an arrow into the lands of another person" (M. E. Smith 1973a:33). One of the important places conquered by 8 Deer in A.D. 1044 (according to the codices Bodley and Colombino) was Acatepec, to the east of Tututepec. 8 Deer is shown in one scene leading the ruler of Acatepec by a rope around his neck and presenting him to the Lord ♂ 4 Tiger "Face of Night."

Apparently the conquest of Acatepec was a major accomplishment for the 33-year-old 8 Deer, for the following year he received an honor recorded in at least four different codices: the placing of an ornament in his nose, signifying he was a great lord (*yya*) or warrior (Clark 1912:20–21). Ac-

---

[1]The Maya nobility in the sixteenth century also occasionally traced their descent from the Toltec lords, even though the majority retained the Maya patronymic.

[2]We are aware that the specific dates proposed for events in the codices by Alfonso Caso are currently undergoing debate and revision (see sections by M. E. Smith [this volume] as well as Rabin [1974, 1976] and Troike [1978]). We have decided to leave such revision to the Mixtec specialists because our purpose here is merely to illustrate the kind of events that characterized the life of a Postclassic ruler.

cording to one version, 8 Deer traveled to Tula to have his nose pierced; if this is so, it suggests a familiarity with the Toltec court that could have served as a model for his Tututepec administration. In one scene, 8 Deer is shown lying on his back on a jaguar pelt while the officiating priest holds his nose with his left hand and a sharpened bone in his right, preparatory to inserting the ornament in his nasal septum.

In A.D. 1051, when 8 Deer was already 40 years old, he married ♀ 13 Serpent "Serpent of Flowers" (Caso 1950:31). In A.D. 1057, he and his wife made an offering in the Temple of the Lizard Serpent on a hill with two points. Caso (1950) suggests that this offering was made by the royal couple for the purpose of asking for descendants, because immediately thereafter, in A.D. 1058 (according to both the Bodley and Nuttall codices), their first son was born, the prince ♂ 4 Dog "Gentle Coyote."

In A.D. 1053, 8 Deer took a second wife, ♀ 6 Eagle "Tiger–String" or "Tiger–Spiderweb." In A.D. 1060 a son was born of this union and named ♂ 6 House "Tiger that Falls from the Sky." ♂ 6 House later became the third ruler of the second dynasty of Tilantongo. According to Caso (1950), 8 Deer "Tiger Claw" married some five times in all and had at least 11 offspring.

There is some evidence that 8 Deer effected an ephemeral Mixtec consolidation by becoming simultaneously the ruler of Tututepec as well as of Tilantongo, the town that had originally been denied him because of his older half-brother. According to M. E. Smith,

> 8-Deer is now known to have ruled Tututepec, the principal town on the Coast, as well as Tilantongo, the most prestigious town of the Mixteca Alta. It thus seems very likely that, at least for a short period in the eleventh century, this ruler effected a temporary consolidation of the Mixtec-speaking people. But the sign of Tututepec as it has been described above appears only within the context of the 8-Deer biography [1973a:68].

Eventually, 8 Deer fell victim to his own ambition and the intrigues of his rivals; he was sacrificed in A.D. 1063 after attempting to subjugate the hometown of his second wife, ♀ 6 Eagle "Tiger–Cobweb." 8 Deer was sacrificed at a place whose name is still untranslated, and his burial was witnessed by his brother-in-law and father-in-law.

8 Deer's son, ♂ 6 House "Tiger that Falls from the Sky," married ♀ 9 Flower "Jewel Heart," daughter of the ruler of Juquila. Through this marriage, ♂ 6 House (who had inherited the throne of Tilantongo) formed a marriage alliance with the coastal town of Juquila, and thus served to perpetuate for a time the consolidation of the coast and the Mixteca Alta that his father 8 Deer had effected (M. E. Smith 1973a:76).

### Events in the Mixteca Alta

Because of their highly stratified society, the Mixtec were able to mobilize manpower for both agriculture and warfare. Spores's work in the Nochixtlán–Yanhuitlán Valley has shown that an enormous population increase in the Natividad phase was accompanied by an equally enormous

expansion of the labor-intensive *lama–bordo* system, which turns agriculturally marginal canyons into terraced cornfields (Topic 73). Hopkins's work in the Cañada occupied by the Cuicatecs—close linguistic relatives of the Mixtecs—shows population increases accompanied by the expansion of irrigation canals (Topic 77). Yanhuitlán was one of the richest kingdoms of the Mixteca Alta, with subject communities as far to the east as Almoloyas, on the edge of the Cañada. Almoloyas, a region poor in level land, exacted tribute from the Cuicatec farmers, and when the Cuicatec balked, Almoloyas called on Yanhuitlán to enforce its demands. If some sixteenth-century *relaciones* are to be believed, Almoloyas may also have had its eye on a 700-km$^2$ expanse of alluvial land not far to the southwest: the Valley of Oaxaca.

As we have seen from the monuments of Monte Albán IIIb–IV, royal marriages had become a common theme in the Valley of Oaxaca during the period A.D. 600–900 (Topic 59). In the politically fragmented situation following the decline of Monte Albán, they were to become one of the principal mechanisms for the temporary integration of normally hostile kingdoms. Spores (1974b) has already documented the importance of marriage alliance among the Mixtec rulers, and the sixteenth-century documents also describe marriages between Zapotec and Mixtec royalty and between Zapotec and Aztec royalty. Through such marriages, Mixtecs entered the Valley of Oaxaca, and a tenuous peace was achieved between the Aztec and Zapotec.

Before considering some specific examples of royal marriage, let us look at Spores's description of the Mixtec "kingdom," or *cacicazgo*, which was the largest stable polity of its time (Topics 70, 75). At its head was a lord, known as *yaa tnuhu* in Mixtec (and referred to by the Spaniards as a cacique, using a borrowed Carib word that has since become common usage). Below the lord came a series of nobles (*tay toho*) who, because of their decreasing proximity to the main line of royal descent, were of lesser rank. This was the upper stratum of Mixtec society, which was class-endogamous but frequently community-exogamous. In the lower stratum came Mixtec commoners (*tay yucu*), who were class-endogamous and usually community-endogamous, and various kinds of servants and slaves. Spores has also identified a group called the *tay situndayu*, roughly translated by the Spaniards as *terrazgueros;* these were landless peasants who worked the fields of the lord and went wherever he told them to go. As Spores has put it, "In return for political, social, and ceremonial leadership, economic security, and protection which were provided by the ruling elites, the citizens of a kingdom were required to pay tribute, to provide labor for the fields and houses of the rulers, to support the religious cult, and to serve in war" (1969:557–558).

### Evolutionary Implications

We would not interpret the Postclassic *cacicazgo* system as a kind of "devolution" from Classic Yucuñudahui and

Monte Albán, as has frequently been suggested. It is true that the kind of centralized panregional integration seen at Monte Albán was generally lacking, but the late Postclassic ruler may actually have enjoyed an escalation of social stratification and political power. We have already suggested in Chapter 4 that the founding of Monte Albán overrode the Zapotec noble's ties to the particular community from which he had come—Etla, Zaachila, and so on—and elevated him to a position of valley-wide significance. We would now suggest that continuing evolution in the Postclassic elevated the Mixtec lord to a level where even his ties to a particular region or valley became almost irrelevant: what mattered most was his lineage. Given sufficiently blue blood lines, a cacique could move from one valley to another, bringing his *tay situndayu* with him to work his lands and to fight whomever he wished. He could move his *cacicazgo*: he could settle in and rule over an area where Mixtec was not even spoken, and he could dislodge any ruler whose strength was not equal to his. He was no longer "the lord of Achiutla (or Tilantongo, or Almoloyas)" but "the Lord ♂ 5 Flower (or ♂ 8 Motion, or ♂ 3 Monkey)," and his power came not solely from the home constituency of his place of birth but also from a group of subjects who owed him allegiance wherever he chose to settle.

Whether this regional flexibility was true of the Zapotec as well is a difficult question to answer, for the *relaciones* speak of "the lord of Teozapotlan" as if regional ties were still primary. Later Zapotec rulers, however, such as Cocijoeza (A.D. 1487–1523), easily moved their base of operations from Zaachila to Tehuantepec, and some gave Zapotec valley lands to their royal Mixtec in-laws as dowries (see following discussion). It therefore seems reasonable to assume that both Mixtec and Zapotec rulers in the Late Postclassic enjoyed a status high enough to free them from regional ties, even from the comparatively broad regional ties of a Yucuñudahui or a Monte Albán.

## Royal Marriage

It is probably the maintenance of this elevated status that made royal marriage such a crucial and carefully considered activity. Just as some Mixtec rulers pointed with pride to their putative Toltec ancestors, there is reason to believe that some Zapotec rulers hoped to raise the status of their offspring by marrying members of important Mixtec dynasties. The somewhat more elite behavior of the Mixtec is expressed metaphorically in the *Relación de Cuylapa* (Salazar 1581), which states that while a Zapotec noblewoman would grind her own corn, a Mixtec noblewoman would not.

It is possible that royal marriages between the Zapotec and Mixtec date back to the period of "genealogical registers" in Monte Albán IIIb–IV. They may even have facilitated the decline of Monte Albán by helping members of the Zapotec confederacy to break away and increase their own power base through strategic alliance. The oldest ethnohistoric evidence for such marriages, however, was collected by the writers of the sixteenth-century *relaciones*, and refers to events that probably took place no more than a few hundred years before the Spanish Conquest. All known cases cite Mixtecs entering the Valley of Oaxaca; none mentions Zapotecs entering the Mixteca. Because these ethnohistoric references have sparked such controversy, we have decided to give the complete quotation from each document here so that the reader (assuming he accepts our translation) can judge for himself.

The *Relación de Teozapotlan* was written by Fray Juan de Mata in 1580 and published by del Paso y Troncoso in 1905. Mata was struck by the fact that while the dominant population of the Teozapotlan or Zaachila region was Zapotec, nearby Cuilapan de Guerrero had Mixtec speakers. When he asked how this situation had come to be, he received the following answer (our editorial comments are in brackets):

> for on being asked how they [the Mixtecs of Cuilapan] came to this Zapotec province, they being Mixtecs, they answer that [it was] by means of a marriage between a Mixtec woman and a lord of Teozapotlan; they came more than 300 years ago [i.e., A.D. 1280], although few came at that time; but a little before the arrival of the Spaniards, there was another marriage involving a lord of Yanhuitlan who married the sister of the wife of the lord and king of Teozapotlan, [and] who lived in Cuilapan because the lord of Teozapotlan gave it to him so he might live there. Then many more [Mixtecs] came than had come before; thus all agree that Teozapotlan was the Zapotec *señorío* [Mata 1580:190–191].

This document, readily accessible to readers since 1905, focused attention on Cuilapan as a possible Mixtec center during Monte Albán V. As we mentioned in Topic 61, Ignacio Bernal excavated there (and reanalyzed the earlier excavations of Marshall Saville) in an effort to learn more about the Mixtec presence in the Valley of Oaxaca (Bernal 1958b). However, Bernal found only meager traces of Monte Albán V at Cuilapan, which had been an impressive site during Period IIIb–IV. In 1945, Robert Barlow published the *Relación de Cuylapa*, written in 1580 by Fray Agustín de Salazar, which helped to explain why Cuilapan had not lived up to its reputation. According to Salazar, who gives what may be a somewhat different version of the same royal marriage, the Mixtecs settled first at the foot of Monte Albán and only later moved to Cuilapan, where their houses were thinly dispersed over the landscape. The Salazar version goes as follows:

> These Indians came from some towns in the Mixteca called the Almoloyas—a very rugged and craggy region—because of certain marriages that took place at various times, up to 300 years ago; they came in great numbers, and because both were members of the nobility and one wedding was with the daughter of Teozapotlan, which lies three-quarters of a league from here, [the ruler of Teozapotlan] gave his son-in-law the site of this town, although when he gave it to him it was a bit farther off . . . it was not then called Ynchaca as it is today, but Sayucu [Sa'a Yucu], which means "at the foot of the mountain," and because those lands were not as good as those [they later gained] through their struggle with the king of Teozapotlan, at the advice of the church the Indians moved to where they are now [Salazar 1581:23].

## The Mixtec Presence in the Valley of Oaxaca

There are several contradictions between the Mata and Salazar accounts, but they may turn out to be superficial. Although Mata states that the groom came from Yanhuitlán, Salazar says that Mixtecs came from Almoloyas; but Almoloyas was, in fact, a *sujeto* or dependency within the Yanhuitlán *cacicazgo*. Salazar states that the bride was a "daughter of Teozapotlan", Mata that she was a sister-in-law of the lord of Teozapotlan; but she could have been simultaneously the daughter of one *coqui* and the sister-in-law of another. Alternatively, two different marriages may be involved. At any rate, the Salazar account directs our attention to Sa'a Yucu, a Mixtec colony at the base of Monte Albán, which may be the site recovered by Kowalewski's Central Valley survey as C-V-132 (see Topic 85).

Site C-V-132 is a community with no evidence of public buildings, apparently consisting of an estimated 980 to 1960 persons dispersed over the valley piedmont in hundreds of individual residences. Throughout this Central Valley of Oaxaca region, as well as the southern part of the Etla valley, small hamlets and isolated residences are typical of the late Postclassic settlement pattern (Kowalewski, Topic 83). This is the pattern we would expect if incoming Mixtec lords were accompanied by low-status *tay situndayu* or *terrazgueros* who worked their land. A lord from Yanhuitlán might well have brought *tay situndayu* with him from his land-poor *sujetos* at Almoloyas, and settled them on the agricultural lands that he received as a dowry.

The fact that C-V-132 seems to be without palaces or temples need not dismay us; Sa'a Yucu may have been viewed only as farmland to be used for the Mixtec lord's support, whereas the lord himself resided at Zaachila with his in-laws. This possibility might account for Tomb 1 at Zaachila, whose occupant Caso (1966) believed to be the descendant of specific Mixtec caciques named in the Codex Nuttall (see Topic 87). Alternatively, the Mixtec lord might have lived neither at Sa'a Yucu nor at Zaachila, but in the substantial Monte Albán V settlement on top of Monte Albán, which Blanton estimates at 4050 to 8100 persons (Topic 81). This alternative might account for Tomb 7 at Monte Albán, whose occupants—along with the greatest treasure in all of Postclassic Mesoamerica—received a series of jaguar (?) bones carved in the style of the Mixtec codices (Topic 82).

Many of the questions raised at the Santa Fe seminar concerned the motivation behind the Zapotec–Mixtec marriage alliances recorded by the *relaciones*. Suggestions varied from the political (to strengthen certain Zapotec valley-floor centers) to the ideological (to raise the status of certain Zapotec royal lineages) or the materialistic (the Almoloyas Mixtecs needed more farmland). One suggestion, made by Blanton, proposed mutual advantages for marital alliances between overpopulated, land-poor areas of the Mixteca Alta and underpopulated, land-rich areas such as the central and Etla regions of the Valley of Oaxaca.

The surprisingly low population densities we see in some western parts of the Valley of Oaxaca during the Postclassic could mean an agricultural labor shortage. In the light of such a shortage (whether real or cognized), Zapotec elites may have increasingly married into elite Mixtec families as a means for bringing these Mixtecs and their *terrazguero* laborers into the valley. This would have been an especially viable strategy for Zapotec as well as Mixtec elites during the Late Postclassic because there may have been population surpluses in the Mixteca at that time, according to Spores [Blanton, verbal comments on seminar tapes].

Obviously, an alternative to Blanton's suggestion would be the notion that some Zapotec lords needed Mixtec military support and were willing to give up some land to get it.

We come now to a second quotation from the Relación de Cuylapa, which we feel touched off one of the most interesting controversies in Oaxaca archaeology: were there a modest number of Mixtecs in the Valley of Oaxaca as the result of strategic marriage alliances with specific Zapotec royal families, or was there an actual "Mixtec invasion" of the valley? Salazar's account, published by Barlow in 1945, is as follows:

> because of a certain injury that they feared might be done to the son of an Indian woman who came from the Mixteca to be married at Teozapotlan, this Indian [the son] went back to his native land [the Mixteca] and there mounted a war and developed it, and finally they declared war on those of Teozapotlan, who, realizing their enemies' advantage, fled to the region of Tehuantepec; and the Mixtecs [of Cuilapan] believe and maintain that they subjugated almost all the Zapotecs of the valleys of Oaxaca, and were paid tribute by them, [including] Mitla and Teitipac [Salazar 1581:25].

We suspect that Barlow's publication of this account, more than any other, reinforced the Mixtec invasion interpretation of Late Postclassic Oaxaca. According to this interpretation, which can also be found in the widely read writings of Francisco de Burgoa (1670, 1674), the Mixtecs achieved virtually total control of the Valley of Oaxaca, forcing the Zapotec rulers of Zaachila to shift their capital to Tehuantepec. Monte Albán V pottery, which occurs throughout the Valley of Oaxaca, was in this view considered to be the ceramic complex of the invading Mixtecs. Indeed, it is not uncommon in the literature to find Monte Albán V referred to as "the Mixtec period," to find its ceramics referred to as "Mixtec pottery," or to find Postclassic tombs described as having "only Mixtec offerings."

A decade ago, Bernal (1966a) divided the Mixtec invaders of the valley into "Western Mixtec" (at places such as Cuilapan, Xoxocotlán, and Zaachila) and "Eastern Mixtec" (at Mitla, Yagul, and Matatlán). The Zapotecs were accounted for by postulating that in areas not conquered by the Mixtecs, Monte Albán IV pottery—considered ethnically "Zapotec"—had lasted until the Spanish Conquest and coexisted with Monte Albán V "Mixtec pottery." Such an overlap, however, is not supported by the available radiocarbon dates (see Drennan, Appendix).

In *Ancient Oaxaca*, Bernal (1966a) and Paddock (1966a) have synthesized much of the evidence in support of the Mixtec invasion framework, and we have asked Paddock to present his view of the situation in Topic 79. Because this is perhaps the subject in which the Santa Fe conferees display the least unanimity, the editors will try to remain neutral in this Introduction, saving our opinion for Topic 80.

## THE AZTEC EXPANSION

Complicating Mixtec–Zapotec relations were the Aztec, who saw the Cuicatec Cañada and the Valley of Oaxaca as the easiest routes toward the isthmus and Soconusco. The Aztec exerted pressure on the Mixtec; the Mixtec exerted pressure on the Zapotec; the Zapotec, in turn, exerted pressure on the Huave and other peoples of the isthmus. The Aztecs subdued some Cañada towns, and captured Huitzo in spite of a military alliance between Zaachila III and the cacique of Tilantongo (Topic 91). The most famous conflict of this era, however, was the battle of Guiengola in the lowlands of Tehuantepec. There the Zapotec, under their ruler Cocijoeza, reportedly having moved their capital from Zaachila to the isthmus because of pressure from the expansionist Cuilapan Mixtec, formed an alliance with other Mixtecs and successfully defeated the Aztec at Guiengola (Topic 91). A tenuous peace was established by a marriage between Cocijoeza and princess "Cotton Flake," a daughter of the Aztec king Ahuitzotl. The Aztec also supposedly established a "friendly" garrison in the Valley of Oaxaca at a place called Acatepec, currently thought to lie on the east slope of Monte Albán (Topic 92).

## MULTIETHNIC RELATIONS

In addition to their accounts of warfare and royal marriage, the sixteenth-century documents paint a picture of incredibly complex multiethnicity. Consider the *Relación de Xuchitepec* (Díez de Miranda 1579), about a Zapotec town with a series of Chontal villages as its dependencies. One of these Chontal villages produced tar that was carried to the Nahuatl-speaking Pacific coast port of Huatulco and exchanged for cacao, which arrived by sea. The villagers paid tribute to their Zapotec overlords, who in turn surrendered cotton mantles and cochineal to Tututepec, 17 leagues to the west. Thus we have a Chontal hamlet, dependent on a Nahuatl-speaking port and subject to a Zapotec town, producing tribute that ultimately reached a *cacicazgo* of the Mixteca Baja.

From the standpoint of adaptive radiation, the sixteenth-century peoples of Oaxaca present an exciting and potentially informative spectrum of sociopolitical complexity. Perhaps the most highly stratified were the Mixtec, whose rulers were so elevated that there was even a special vocabulary for the parts of their body, to distinguish them from the body parts of ordinary men (Table 8.1). The Zapotec, whose noblewomen "were still willing to grind their own corn," ran second to the Mixtec but displayed their own highly

TABLE 8.1
Comparison of Sixteenth-Century Mixtec Terms for the Body Parts of a Common Man and a Hereditary Lord[a]

| Body part | Common man (*tay yucu*) | Hereditary lord or cacique (*yaa tnuhu*) |
|---|---|---|
| Head | dzini | yáyaya |
| Face | nuuu | nanaya |
| Eyes | tenuu | duchiya |
| Nose | dzitni | dutuya |
| Ears | tutnu | tnahaya |
| Mouth | yuhu | diyaya |
| Teeth | noho | yequeya |
| Shoulders | sata | yusaya |
| Chest | dica | yequendi yaya |
| Stomach | nuu ini | nuundiyaya |
| Elbow | sitendaha | catnundaya |
| Hand | daha | dayaya |
| Feet | saha | duhuaya |

[a]After Antonio de los Reyes (1593).

stratified state and their own royal dynasties at Zaachila and (later) Tehuantepec (see Topics 89, 90). Below them on the sociopolitical scale came the Mixe—who may have had no more than a "chiefdom" level of organization by comparison—and the Chontal, whom the Spaniards considered "as brutish as the wild deer in the mountains" (see Díez de Miranda 1579:26). According to the *Relación de Nexapa* (Santamaría and Canseco 1580), the Aztec and Zapotec fought with *macana* and bow-and-arrow, while the Mixe and Chontal had only wooden lances. In other documents, the Zapotec officers emerge as consummate strategists in quilted armor, whereas the Mixe wear cotton garments "like the Moorish aljuba," and the Chontal run naked in the forest. Even if we allow for a great deal of prejudice and ethnocentricity in the *relaciones*, sixteenth-century Oaxaca should be a goldmine of information for comparing different levels of sociopolitical evolution in a relatively small geographical area.

## THE GLOTTOCHRONOLOGICAL EVIDENCE

Drennan (see Appendix) has selected A.D. 950 as the date "most compatible with the overall pattern of radiocarbon dates available at the moment" for the boundary between Monte Albán IV and V. In Drennan's view, the radiocarbon dates do not indicate a persistence of Monte Albán IV ceramics up to the Spanish Conquest, nor do they support "a major deviation from the simple assumption of successive phases," that is, Period V following and replacing IV (Drennan, Appendix). Dates for the Late Natividad phase in the Nochixtlán Valley also fall in this time range.

There are only a few glottochronological events of archaeological relevance to this period. By at least A.D. 1000–1200 there had occurred some internal divisions within Cuicatec,

Mazatec, and Valley Zapotec; also by this period, Chocho had split off from Popoloca. This Chocho– Popoloca split might be represented by a divergence of archaeological materials between the valleys of Tamazulapan, Coixtlahuaca, and Tehuacán, but that possibility has never been investigated.

By somewhere in the neighborhood of A.D. 1200 to 1400 (in glottochronological time), Isthmus Zapotec had split off from Valley Zapotec. This has always been considered a glottochronological event of great archaeological importance because it could have been related to the shifting of the Zapotec royal house from Zaachila to Tehuantepec. However, because a few Monte Albán IV sherds have been discovered at Guiengola (see Topic 93), that legendary Zapotec stronghold on the isthmus may have been occupied as early as A.D. 950–1000 (in radiocarbon years). Both the glottochronological evidence and the Monte Albán IV sherds at Guiengola would suggest that the Zapotec had reached the isthmus centuries before the reign of Cocijoeza (A.D. 1487–1523), and perhaps before any of the events mentioned in the relaciones.

Among other things, Zapotec expansion to Tehuantepec changed several commercial patterns. For example, coastal salt sources were made readily available, and some valley salt production (such as at Lambityeco) declined as a result (Peterson 1976). Also, Tlacolula imported its cotton from Tehuantepec, while Mitla continued to grow its own (Canseco 1580).

The Isthmus Zapotec owed allegiance to the lord of Zaachila, and Cocijoeza reportedly found support there when Mixtec pressure in the valley became too strong. One of the legendary Zapotec battles was fought there at Guiengola, with Cocijoeza winning both a military victory and an Aztec bride while suckering his Mixtec allies into a military alliance that was never adequately compensated. Even today, the Isthmus Zapotec are among the most colorful descendants of the Cloud People, and a small group of Mixteco speakers occupies an enclave near Tehuantepec, farming the second-class lands with which Cocijoeza "rewarded" their ancestors.

## CERAMICS AND ETHNICITY

As long as Monte Albán IV and V could be considered contemporaneous area cotraditions, there seemed to be no problem in distinguishing "Zapotec" and "Mixtec" occupations at Postclassic sites. Now the available radiocarbon dates, coupled with stratigraphic evidence from places such as Abasolo and Miahuatlán (see Topic 87), have convinced some archaeologists that Monte Albán V ceramics succeeded, and ultimately replaced, those of Period IV. This information leads us to a consideration of the Postclassic ceramic evidence and its relevance to the ethnic makeup of late Preconquest Oaxaca.

The dominant pottery of Monte Albán V is a thin, well-fired, hard gray ware, occurring in a wide variety of shapes;

thin gray or black jars and pitchers, shallow two-tone gray dishes, and bowls with serpent-head tripod supports are a few of the most common. When Caso originally found these ceramics in the uppermost levels at Monte Albán, they were sometimes mixed with sherds of polychrome pottery—usually regarded as Mixtec, in spite of the fact that some of it may have been made in Cholula. Caso's discovery of Tomb 7, with its codex-style carved bones (see Topic 82), convinced him even more strongly that the Mixtec were the bearers of Monte Albán V culture. This finding, coupled with the accounts of Mixtec expansion into the Valley of Oaxaca given in the relaciones, Burgoa (1670, 1674), and Gay (1881), led Caso to the conclusion that it was the Mixtecs who had introduced the thin gray pottery into the Zapotec region. This view was undoubtedly strengthened when Bernal (1949b) excavated at Coixtlahuaca in the Mixteca Alta and found gray tripods with serpent-head feet there as well, mixed with even more abundant polychrome. Caso, Bernal, and Acosta (1967) eventually named this gray ware G3M—G3 because of its similarity to the burnished gray type G-3 of Monte Albán I–IV, M to distinguish it as Mixtec.

Because of this resemblance to G-3, and because the Valley of Oaxaca had a 2000-year history of gray ware prior to Monte Albán V, some critics have asked why G3M ought to be Mixtec at all. Could not the Mixtecs, entering the Valley of Oaxaca through marriage alliances, have made use of the locally available gray ceramics produced by Zapotec potters? The most frequent reply is that some G3M vessel shapes do not look Zapotec. Bernal (1966a:Fig. 12) lists a dozen shapes that he believes are Mixtec, some of which do seem to be represented in ritual scenes in the Mixtec codices. However, a great many of those shapes also occur well outside the Oaxaca area, and a few are virtually pan-Mesoamerican. For example, bowls with tripod legs ending in an animal effigy (e.g., eagle or serpent head, deer's hoof) were used by the Aztec, the occupants of Cholula and the Mixteca, the Chinantla, Chiapas, and Soconusco; some critics have argued that to single them out as Mixtec implies more knowledge about their center of origin than we really have. Others have suggested that some of these traits may go back to the Toltecs, whose influence on the Mixtecs has already been suggested by Bernal; for example, many of the shapes listed by Bernal as Mixtec also occurred at Tula (Acosta 1956–1957:Figures 17–20).

To add to the controversy, archaeological surveys and excavations in the past 10 years have brought to light an interesting fact: the distribution of G3M pottery is apparently not coextensive with the areas occupied by speakers of Mixteco in the sixteenth century. In August 1970, Donald Brockington chaired a meeting at which various archaeologists prepared maps summarizing their knowledge of the geographic distribution of Oaxacan pottery types, with the following results:

> It became clear that the [Monte Albán] Period IV and Period V grey ceramic traditions had nearly identical distributions which

agreed nicely with the known distribution of Zapoteco speakers in 1580. An exception was the occurrence of Period V grey ware up the Callejón [Cuicatec Cañada] and toward nearby Coixtlahuaca. Further, the Mixtec [sic] grey pottery was in complementary distribution to the Mixtec red-on-cream (and its variants) which agreed well with the known Mixteco linguistic distribution, other than those within the central parts of the Valley of Oaxaca. Working from these charts one might conclude that the Mixtec [sic] grey pottery was produced by Zapoteco speakers and the Mixtec red-on-cream by Mixteco speakers and therefore that it is erroneous to refer to the grey pottery as "Mixtec" [Brockington 1973:61–62].

To be specific, the conference found that G3M was abundant in the Valley of Oaxaca, the Isthmus of Tehuantepec, the valleys of Ejutla and Miahuatlán, and the southern Cañada as far north as Cuicatlán. Because Cuicatlán had strong market ties with Coixtlahuaca, the presence of G3M at the latter site is not unexpected. G3M is also common around the structures at Mitla which Canseco (1580) attributes to Zapotec rulers and Zapotec priests (see Topic 88), and it is abundant at the ostensibly Zapotec site of Guiengola near Tehuantepec (see previous discussion). Moreover, as Paddock points out in Topic 79, the probable area of major diversity of G3M vessel shapes is the Valley of Oaxaca. In contrast to G3M, the red-on-cream pottery mentioned by Brockington was abundant both in the Mixteca Alta (at Nochixtlán, Tamazulapan, and Coixtlahuaca) and in the area of Tututepec in the Mixteca Baja, but relatively rare in the Valley of Oaxaca.

In spite of the distributional data brought out at Brockington's conference, many respected Oaxacan specialists remain convinced that G3M was a Mixtec product. Brockington himself has continued to refer to it as "Mixtec grey ware," and finds the notion that G3M might be a Zapotec ware to be "partly right and partly wrong" (Brockington 1973:61–62). This view is all the more interesting because Brockington's own work at Miahuatlán (Brockington 1973) strongly suggests that thin, hard, gray pottery of G3M type already occurs in low frequency in the Late Classic, and that it grows out of the earlier gray ware of the Monte Albán tradition. Gradually increasing in frequency, it becomes the dominant ware of the Late Postclassic at Miahuatlán. Some critics feel that this local dominance seriously challenges the notion that G3M is Mixtec-inspired, arguing that there is no known Late Classic assemblage in the Mixteca that looks like a convincing ancestor for Monte Albán V. In the Nochixtlán region, for example, the Classic Las Flores phase is reportedly dominated by Tan, Orange, and Rust wares; there is indeed a gray ware—Juanito Fine Gray—but it seems to be a local version of the Monte Albán gray-ware tradition, "particularly types G1 and G3 in the Monte Albán taxonomy" (Spores 1972:43). Moreover, "Tan and Fine Cream wares tend to dominate over Gray wares in the Nochixtlán ceramic tradition, which is in contrast to the Oaxaca Valley and areas to the south and east, where Monte Albán gray wares tend to dominate ceramic assemblages, particularly in Classic and Postclassic times" (Spores 1972:43).

If one follows through to the Postclassic Natividad phase in the Yanhuitlán area—the very *cacicazgo* from which some of the royal Mixtec marriage partners are said to have come—one sees a ceramic complex that could in no way be confused with that of Monte Albán V. According to Spores (1972:188), the Natividad phase at Yanhuitlán "is characterized by the rise to dominance of Fine Cream Wares and a corresponding decline of Tan, Gray, Orange and Rust Wares." There are bowls with serpent-head tripod feet and tall-necked pitchers in Miguelito Hard Gray which do resemble G3M vessels, but they do not dominate the assemblage and they actually become more common in the early Colonial period (Spores 1972:188). More distinctive of the Natividad phase are Yanhuitlán Red-on-cream bowls, Mixteca Graphite-on-orange bowls, and Mixteca polychrome. It is interesting to speculate that, had Bernal chosen to excavate at Yanhuitlán rather than Coixtlahuaca in 1949, our whole concept of what constitutes Mixtec pottery might very well be different.

Yanhuitlán Red-on-cream and Mixteca Graphite-on-orange did reach the Valley of Oaxaca—although in very low frequency—and in some archaeologists' opinions, they are far better indicators of Mixtec influence than is G3M. Red-on-cream vessels occur at Huitzo (where Mixtecs from Tilantongo joined the Zapotecs in a military alliance), at San José Mogote, and at many sites in the central and Etla regions of the valley. Graphite-on-orange also occurs at such places as Huitzo, San José Mogote, and Yagul. Some archaeologists have argued, however, that the Zapotec nobility may well have regarded polychrome pottery, Red-on-cream, and Graphite-on-orange as exotic luxury wares worth importing.

Still another ceramic element with an interesting distribution during this period is the gray or tan bowl with a stamped or mold-made design on the interior of the base, the so-called *fondo sellado* technique. Such bowls were common in the Tehuacán Valley during the late Venta Salada phase (MacNeish et al. 1970), and occurred with some frequency as far south down the Cañada as Cuicatlán (Hopkins 1973). Spores (personal communication) reports they are far less common at Yanhuitlán than at Coixtlahuaca, suggesting that their frequency drops as one moves farther from the Cañada. Such vessels are virtually absent in the Valley of Oaxaca, but a single *fondo sellado* sherd was found by Susan Lees at San Juan del Estado, where one ancient route from the Cañada enters the valley (unpublished survey data).

We therefore have several choices. We can regard each of these distinctive types as the product of a specific ethnic group, with the Mixtecs bringing their Red-on-cream vessels wherever they go, the Popoloca carrying their *fondo sellado* along through the Cañada, and the conservative Zapotecs continuing to manufacture G-35 bowls long after the arrival of the Mixtec. Even if this interpretation is chosen, however, we could argue that G3M gray pottery should be kept separate from Mixteca polychrome, Yanhuitlán Red-on-cream, and Mixteca Graphite-on-orange because of its very different geographic distribution. Alternatively, we can view the

Postclassic as having a series of specialized pottery-making centers whose products were distributed by a network of regional market systems, actually crosscutting ethnic boundaries. In this view, a Zapotec farmer might use locally made G3M pottery whereas the Zapotec nobility used a mixture of local G3M, imported Yanhuitlán Red-on-cream, and Mixteca or Cholula polychrome. One implication of this latter view would be that widespread types such as G3M could not be used to establish the "ethnicity" of archaeological sites, and that luxury types such as polychrome might only be evidence for the presence of high-status individuals. It is unlikely that this controversy will be resolved in the near future.

## ARCHITECTURE AND ETHNICITY

The architecture of Monte Albán V is another area in which some archaeologists see the presence, or at least the influence, of Mixtecs. The spectacular architecture of Mitla, seemingly so different from that of Monte Albán, is frequently given as an example. Other sites in the Tlacolula valley, such as Yagul, Matatlán, Teotitlán del Valle, and Tlalixtac de Cabrera, show elements of the Mitla style, as does a small site named Santo Domingo in the southern part of the Cuicatec Cañada (Bernal and Gamio 1974). As Bernal has put it:

> The architecture of Mitla is too well-known to need description here. However, I should like to emphasize that as I understand it, the architecture is not a completely new phenomenon in the area; rather it combines elements of an older style, Zapotec, with new elements that we may tentatively call Mixtec. The principal new elements are the elaborate decoration of stone mosaic, the use of enormous monoliths, and the general arrangement of rooms. This last has no direct antecedents in Monte Albán or other valley cities [Bernal 1966a:346].

By "arrangement of rooms" Bernal is referring primarily to the rooms in palaces or elite residences, which are often spectacular in Monte Albán V; he believes that, at least for the Tlacolula region, the temples "are much less grand than their palaces" (Bernal 1966a:363). Bernal also notes a real architectural difference between the western Valley of Oaxaca (Cuilapan, Xoxocotlán, Zaachila) and the eastern valley (Mitla, Yagul, Teotitlán). "More as hypotheses than as conclusions," he presents the notion that "two different Mixtec-influenced groups" existed in the valley during Monte Albán V (Bernal 1966a:363). Only for parts of the valley is there ethnohistoric evidence that actual Mixtec people are involved; hence the use of the term *Mixtec-influenced*.

There are, however, conflicting opinions about the extent to which Mitla's architecture represents a break with Zapotec tradition. One of the men most familiar with Oaxaca architecture was the late Jorge R. Acosta, who did much of the reconstruction and consolidation at Monte Albán (Acosta 1965). As coauthor of the Monte Albán ceramic report (Caso et al. 1967), Acosta was aware that the

*xicalcoliuhqui* or "step-fret" design had already appeared on Monte Albán II pottery. During the fourteenth field season at Monte Albán, he discovered *tableros* on the walls of the patio at Tomb 153 that had *grecas escalonadas*, or step-fret motifs, dating to Monte Albán IIIb, and he commented on a IIIb structure at nearby Atzompa which had a similar *tablero* with *grecas* (Acosta n.d.b). Later in this report, Acosta set down the evolution of the architectural tablero in the Valley of Oaxaca as he saw it:

1. The first *tableros* are flat, stuccoed, and sometimes red painted.
2. In a second stage, they have decorated painted motifs.
3. In the final stages at Monte Albán, they have motifs sculptured in limestone or modeled in stucco, sometimes with color added. (The stucco-modeled *tablero* carried on into the Monte Albán IV architecture of Lambityeco; see Topic 60).
4. These sculptured motifs are representations of gods, calendric dates, or simple geometric figures. Of the simple geometric figures, Acosta says, "the latter were those which the builders of the temples [sic] of Mitla adapted and evolved to [a state of] perfection. It is becoming increasingly clear that the buildings at Mitla received strong influences from Monte Albán, so much so, that one can say they are the direct result of an evolution out of the less refined architecture of the great Zapotec center" (n.d.b:19).

As for why the builders of Monte Albán never used stone mosaics for the *greca* motifs in their *tableros*, one answer has been suggested by Williams and Heizer (1965) and is discussed in Topic 88: the soft volcanic tuffs of which Mitla is made permitted stoneworking techniques that would have been nearly impossible with the hard limestones of Monte Albán.

Thus we are left with two alternatives for the ethnicity of Monte Albán V architecture. In Acosta's view, the ruins of Mitla (and by implication Yagul, Matatlán, and Teotitlán) represent a Postclassic refinement that grows out of the Monte Albán architectural tradition, the different room arrangements simply reflecting Postclassic changes in elite residence. If this alternative is accepted, the builders of Mitla were presumably Valley Zapotecs (although they may well have been Mixtec-influenced as Bernal suggests, given the political climate of Oaxaca). An alternative view would hold that Mitla and Yagul represent such a break with tradition as to have been built by "Eastern Mixtecs." This theory would explain the codex-style paintings in the Church Group at Mitla (see Topic 88), but it also runs into two problems—first, a sixteenth-century *relación* (Canseco 1580) that clearly states that Mitla was Zapotec, both politically and religiously; and second, the fact that so far no buildings found in the Mixteca look very much like prototypes for Mitla. The only site outside the Valley of Oaxaca that has a similar layout is Santo Domingo in the Cuicatec Cañada, but Bernal and Gamio (1974) consider it smaller and less impressive than Yagul, which in turn is smaller and less impressive than Mitla. In this case, a skeptic could consider Santo Domingo to represent Zapotec influence on the Cuicatec, rather than the reverse.

Finally, some archaeologists have suggested that we must take care not to attribute to the Mixtec what may ultimately prove to be Toltec influence in elite architecture. There are more panels of *greca* motifs at Tula (see Marquina 1951:Fot. 51) and at "Toltec-influenced" Chichén Itzá (Marquina 1951:Fot. 415–421) than have been found in the entire Mixteca Alta, and we may not yet fully appreciate the impact of the important eleventh-century Toltec state on the Cloud People. Thus, as in the case of the controversies surrounding G3M pottery, the problems of Monte Albán V architecture are complex and unresolved.

# SECTION 8a
# The Buildup of
# Mixtec Power

## TOPIC 70
## The Origin and Evolution of the Mixtec System of Social Stratification[1]

RONALD SPORES

Social stratification, most scholars would agree, is a primary attribute of states. Several students of political evolution (e.g., Fried 1960, 1967: 224–226, 325; Dumond 1972; Lenski 1966:160, 164–168, 210–219) do, in fact, hold that one condition necessarily implies the other, that state organization and social stratification go together. Fried (1967:235) goes so far as to claim that the state "is a collection of specialized institutions and agencies, some formal and others informal, that maintains an order of stratification." It is, however, one thing to observe the coexistence of social stratification and the state, but quite another to demonstrate the relationship of certain social, political, and economic variables. Several descriptive, problem-oriented, and/or comparative studies of the organization and/or development of specific states have been conducted in recent decades (Nadel 1942; M. G. Smith 1960; Skinner 1964; Fallers 1965; Lloyd 1965; Katz 1972). Additionally, a few anthropologists have contributed theoretical statements relating to the rise of the state as an evolutionary process (e.g., Fried 1960, 1967; Adams 1966; Sanders and Price 1968; Carneiro 1970; Service 1975) and on the variety, origins, and concomitants of social stratification (e.g., Sahlins 1958; Lenski 1966; Gould 1969; Harner 1970).

Despite obvious advances in analyzing, relating, and comparing complex social and political systems, it is clear from recent studies that a satisfactory articulation of sociopolitical theory and analyses of specific developments of class and state has yet to be achieved. Clearly, there is a need for better understanding of social stratification and the state in all areas of the world, Mesoamerica included; setting this as a desirable goal, I wish to consider the class structure of ancient Mixtec society, to consider its political implications, and to grapple with the thorny problem of the origins of social stratification and the development of Mixtec states in western Oaxaca.

Development of social stratification and the state was neither inevitable nor precluded by the relatively restrictive environment of the Mixteca. Similar environments in other areas of Mesoamerica supported autonomous egalitarian communities (northeastern Oaxaca, Hidalgo–Tamaulipas–northern Veracruz), a highly centralized "imperial" state (Tarascan Michoacán), as well as the system of interrelated states in the Mixteca. No single valley or region of the Mixteca was capable of producing the massive surpluses usually associated with large-scale class and state systems in other parts of the world. Mixtec-speaking peoples did, however, develop a social system that allowed effective integration of localized clusters of communities and furnished mechanisms whereby territorial boundaries, distance, and even ethnic frontiers could be overridden. The formulation

[1] I wish to acknowledge a debt of gratitude to the editors and cocontributors to this volume and to Thomas Gregor and David J. Thomas who raised important questions and provided able criticism regarding the subjects treated in this topic.

of appropriate institutions made possible the adaptive radiation of Mixtec society through a system of social differentiation, marital alliance, a marketing network, conquest warfare, concentration of decision-making power in the hands of an elite group capable of controlling natural and human productive resources and their allocation, and a supporting ideological system. Impressive cultural achievements were based on a technoenvironmental adaptation featuring a simple agricultural and supplemental collecting pattern appropriate to existence at the egalitarian village level or, with appropriate sociopolitical and economic mobilization of society, to the level of the state.

Sixteenth-century Spanish documentation, Prehispanic and Colonial manuscripts in native pictographic traditions, and modern anthropological studies often project a view of Mesoamerican societies as if they were composed primarily of elites. Texts more often than not refer to the deeds, traditions, relations, and concerns of the aristocratic elements of native societies, and the Spanish administrative system tended to favor the same groups, with the aristocracy being afforded primary access to Spanish courts and offices.

The several studies of Mixtec society published as of this writing (Jiménez Moreno and Mateos Higuera 1940; Dahlgren 1954; Caso 1949, 1960, 1966; M. E. Smith 1963; Spores 1965, 1967, 1974a) have emphasized the ruling class and have devoted little attention to the overall structure of native society, to lower aristocratic class or group organization, or to interclass or intergroup relations. Aristocratic aspects of native life are, therefore, most easily extracted from the documentation. Perception of broader patterns of social relations requires considerably greater effort.

## CLASS STRUCTURE

Concepts of social stratification permeated Mixtec society, regulating individual and group behavior and intergroup relations and figuring prominently in Mixtec ideology and political organization. It is therefore crucial to confront the problem of social stratification.

I have previously treated the concept and reality of Mixtec social stratification in terms of regulation of access to productive resources; differential privilege, duties, and obligations; and contrasting behavioral complexes in marriage, residence, inheritance, ritual observance, language, and so on, but with particular reference to the royal class. Clearly, a more balanced treatment is required if we are to understand the phenomenon of social stratification and its relationship to environmental adaptation, economic institutions, occupational specialization (or role differentiation), conquest, mobility, ideology, and the political implications of stratification and social mobility.

Class, social hierarchy, and social etiquette receive attention in the chronicles of Herrera (1947:Dec. 3, lib. 3, caps. 12–13), Burgoa (1674:1, 376–396), the *Relaciones Geo-*

*gráficas* of 1579–1581 (Avendaño 1579; Eras 1579; Pacho 1581; RMEH 1:174–178; RMEH 2:131–163; Caso 1949; Bernal [Ed.] 1962), the Alvarado lexicon and the Reyes grammar of the 1590s (Jiménez Moreno [Ed.] 1962), and in the abundant pictographic and conventional administrative, legal, and ecclesiastical documentation of the sixteenth century (Berlin 1947; Dahlgren 1954:127–145; Spores 1967:9–14, 139–141; Spores 1974b). The sources reveal that ancient Mixtec society was organized into two major social strata: (1) the hereditary rulers (*casta linaje, yaa tnuhu*), plus a hereditary noble or *principal* (*tay toho*) group, and (2) a humble or plebian class also known by the Nahuatl derivative *macehuales* or, in Mixteco, *nanday tay ñuu, tay yucu,* or *tay sicaquai* (Spores 1965:977–985; 1967:9–14; 1974b). In the lower stratum was a fourth group composed of landless tenant–servant–tributaries generally designated *terrazgueros* or, in Mixteco, *tay situndayu*, present in at least four of the larger and wealthier kingdoms, Yanhuitlán (AGN Civil 516; AGN Tierras 400; AGN Tierras 985–986) and Achiutla (AJT 9, exp. 7) of the Mixteca Alta, Tecomaxtlahuaca in the Mixteca Baja (AGN Tierras 2692, exp. 16), in Tututepec of the Mixteca de la Costa (AGN Mercedes 6, fol. 404), and quite probably in Teposcolula (AGN Tierras 1433, exp. 1) and Tilantongo (AGN Mercedes 7, fol. 253v) of the Mixteca Alta. Finally, there were the slaves who performed domestic service, functioned as concubines, and became sacrificial victims. Slaves figured in tribute assessments, were captured in battle (*tay nicuvuinduq*), were born in the households of their elite masters (*dzayadzana*), were bought and sold (*dahasaha* or *tay noho yahui*) (AGN *Inquisición* 37; Herrera 1947: Dec. 3, lib. 3, cap. 13), but did not constitute an identifiable social group. Insofar as can presently be determined, no definable slave subculture or social class developed in the Mixteca.

Returning to the upper end of the social order, suggestions by early and more recent writers (Herrera 1947:Dec. 3, lib. 3, cap. 13; Dahlgren 1954:141) that there may have been a privileged merchant or wealthy class (*mercaderes y gente rica*) outside the hereditary aristocracy are not substantiated by available documentation. There is little doubt that merchants and men of wealth did exist in Mixtec society, but significant individual differences in wealth do not seem to have led to the formation of social aggregates beyond the major class groupings previously delineated. Ascribed social status was the crucial criterion of power, wealth, and privilege. Lacking appropriate class affiliation, one would be denied access to productive resources that allowed the acquisition of wealth, economic advantage, or deferential status.

It is axiomatic perhaps that the process of social stratification—the unequal distribution of social, political, and economic power among major identifiable strata of a society—is based on differential access to productive resources. This was clearly the case in the Mixteca where the ruling class controlled the most productive lands and the most important resources. Just as clearly, the land—farming land—was the primary productive resource, and good lands have been in both absolute and relative short supply in the Mixteca since the area has been extensively occupied and intensively utilized by agriculturalists. Information on land tenure, so important an aspect of social stratification in agricultural societies, is by no means abundant for the Mixteca, but several inferences can be drawn from available information.

The royalty and the nobility held private, heritable title to lands, and *terrazgueros* were bound to the privately owned lands of the aristocracy but held no property in their own right. The plebians, however, constitute a special problem for analysis. Members of this worker–farmer–tributary class worked upon and collected tribute from community lands, but their relationship to the land is somewhat unclear. Land claims and suits relative to *macehual* lands are extremely rare during the Colonial period, most certainly during the sixteenth century. It is difficult to determine to what extent this rarity may reflect lack of access to the Spanish legal system, poorly developed concepts of private ownership of lands, or simply a lack of conflict over small private holdings or traditional claims to community held lands. It is not clear whether natives had perpetual or usufructory rights to farmlands or whether rights pertained to individuals, or to kinship or residence groups, or to all categories. Neither do we know the kinds of levels of rights to different kinds of land. The native rulers of Yanhuitlán controlled the best alluvial bottomlands of the Nochixtlán Valley from Yanhuitlán to Yucuita and to Zahuatlán, a gerrymandered strip of the valley's best lands (AGN Civil 516; AGN Tierras 400; Spores 1967:164–171). The Tecomaxtlahuaca rulers' lands were also said to be among the best in the Mixteca. It is known that although the lower stratum of society did have access to community collecting areas and to firewood, wild plant resources, some mineral resources, rodents, small animals, and small birds taken there, only the aristocracy ordinarily had the right to hunt and consume deer and quail and to utilize certain hides, furs, teeth, feathers, and fibers on their wearing apparel. Such important resources as irrigation waters and salt were controlled by the aristocracy.

As in the case of any stratified society, rights to lands and resources must be qualified and carefully scrutinized. It is my present belief that private lands and resources were controlled by the ruling families and the nobility with the consent of their rulers, and that commoners did not hold private title to farmlands. The *macehuales* were traditionally allowed to work relatively less-productive farmlands and collecting preserves—subject to the whim of the ruling aristocracy and only as long as tribute and service were given. In return for the privilege of land use, the maintenance of shrines and temples, and protection provided by the aristocracy, commoners were expected to serve and to pay tribute to the aristocracy and to the state. This differential access to agricultural lands served as the economic base for the Mixtec class system.

In the sixteenth century, land disputes involving *caciques, principales,* and whole communities appeared in profusion from around 1530 (e.g., AGN Indios 101, exp. 1) to the end of the Colonial period (Spores and Saldaña 1973:passim; Spores and Saldaña 1975:passim; AJT, leg. 23, exp. 30), but cases involving private lands held by Indian commoners are quite rare, even in the seventeenth century. It is difficult, at this point, to say just what the status of the Prehispanic commoner relative to land might have been. Neither Taylor (1972:67–100), working in the Valley of Oaxaca, nor I have arrived at definitive opinions regarding Prehispanic *macehual* land tenure. I suggest, however, that private ownership of lands for commoners evolved in the Mixteca gradually during the Colonial period. Large private holdings were held by *caciques* and Spaniards, and when commoners did obtain titles to lands, they were small and usually relatively less-productive plots. While it is clear that *macehuales* were obtaining and holding lands in the latter part of the sixteenth century, their Prehispanic relationship to the land and the precise manner by which they began to acquire it in Colonial times remain uncertain.

The Prehispanic commoner was a citizen participating in the life of his community to the extent allowable for his status. He held usufruct rights to certain community lands but he was required to pay tribute, to respect, obey, and serve his ruler, and to observe special restrictions and rules of etiquette concerning his interaction with other classes, his ritual and subsistence activities, and his dress, diet, professional activity, and movement. Although the ruling aristocracy normally entered into marital alliances that extended beyond the community and the kingdom, the commer observed patterns of local endogamy. Had it not been for marketing activities and religious peregrination, life for the Prehispanic commoner would have been totally restricted to his community.

Reference has been made to the existence of serfdom in at least six of the more important Mixtec communities, including Yanhuitlán, Tututepec, Tecomaxtlahuaca, Teposcolula, and Tilantongo, but it is quite likely that the pattern was more widespread. During the last quarter of the sixteenth century, Spanish administrators attempted to remove this special class of tenant–servants from the traditional custody and control of the rulers of at least two kingdoms in the Mixteca and to place these individuals who had served and paid tribute only to their rulers on regular Crown and encomienda tribute rolls. The caciques of Yanhuitlán (AGN Civil 516; AGN Tierras 200; AGN Tierras 400; AGN Tierras 985–986) and Tecomaxtlahuaca (AGN Tierras 2692, exp. 16) brought suits claiming ancient, traditional, and exclusive rights to the services and tribute of numerous families residing in specified barrios of the affected communities. Elsewhere (Spores 1967:159–160), I have estimated that some 2000 *terrazgueros (tay situndayu)* were in the service of the rulers of Yanhuitlán at the time of the Conquest. By 1580, the number of such individuals had declined by at least half, and native witnesses stated that when the Spaniards came to this New Spain, they removed these from the said caciques, and from other [caciques] and registered them so that they would pay tribute like the rest of the people, notwithstanding the fact . . . that the said barrios and the Indians belonged to the said patrimony [of the cacique of Yanhuitlán] [AGN Civil 516].

In Tecomaxtlahuaca, the number of *terrazgueros* given over to the exclusive use of the ruler was said to have declined from some 800 "indios" at the time of the Conquest to 60 males (or an estimated 240 individuals) in 1578 (AGN Tierras 2692, exp. 16). The *cacica* of Teposcolula, Doña Lucía Cortés y Orozco, still claimed rights to services of *terrazgueros* in 1704 but complained of a serious erosion of her traditional rights to goods and services (AGN Tierras 1433, exp. 1, fs. 113–121).

The *terrazgueros* worked the rulers' private irrigated land (*nuhundoyo*) (said in both Yanhuitlán and Tecomaxtlahuaca to be the best lands in each kingdom), provided services in the households of ruling families, and resided in special, named barrios. The *terrazgueros* appear to have been dependents who were probably excluded from public affairs in their respective communities and kingdoms. There are explicit references in the Tecomaxtlahuaca case to *maceguales terrazgueros* and *esclavos y indios forasteros y venidizos*. The implication is that the *tay situndayu* originated outside the affected kingdoms, or at the very least that they occupied a quite special status relative to the rest of Mixtec society. It would be totally erroneous, however, to equate the statuses of serf and slave.

Although the Prehispanic origins of the *terrazgueros* remain problematic, it is my strong impression that they derived from five sources: (1) captives in the wide-ranging raiding and warfare of the Late Postclassic period; (2) slaves purchased by the rulers; (3) local *macehuales* who placed themselves "in servitude" to the ruler for the privilege of working and deriving some benefit from the rich agricultural lands of the royal patrimony; (4) migrants, or displaced foreigners who either chose or were forced to accept *terrazguero* status for the advantages it provided; and (5) offspring of *terrazgueros*.

The role and function of *terrazgueros* or *mayeques* in Mesoamerica remains uncertain—not only for the Mixteca, but even for areas such as México–Tenochtitlán (Caso 1963:871–874; Katz 1972:144–148, 224–227; Carrasco 1971:355–356; Sanders 1971:12–22). I believe that although upward and downward mobility were possible in this class, the status of *terrazguero* generally placed the individual and his family at an economic advantage. The landless remained landless, but there were fields to be worked and shares to be derived from some of the most fertile lands in the Mixteca. Further, the onus of servitude was offset by the advantages of protection offered by the lord. It is clear that the *tay situndayu* represented a significant socioeconomic component of Mixtec society and that their composition, their origins, and their relationship to other classes and groups must be further analyzed in the ongoing study of Mixtec social structure.

## THE ORIGINS OF SOCIAL STRATIFICATION

Even under ideal circumstances in which historical records are plentiful, it is difficult to explain the origins and early course of development of any system of stratification. In the case of the Mixteca, information can be derived from archaeological and linguistic materials, from patterns observable through the documentary record, and from mythicohistorical accounts. Herrera, Reyes, Torquemada, Burgoa, Orozco y Berra, and Martínez Gracida have given varying interpretations of origin myths. Burgoa, depending on written and oral sources, recounted a mythicohistoric account suggesting conquest-related origins for Mixtec social stratification:

> [Along the Apoala River] were born the trees that produced the first caciques, male and female. . . . And from here by succession they grew and extended to populate an extensive kingdom. Others agree with Father Torquemada that the first men who settled this very rugged and mountainous region came from the west, like the Mexicans. . . . The first settlers were attracted to the lands located in high ramparts and inaccessible mountains . . . , some believing that the original population was in the meadows of the town which the Mexicans called Sosola. . . . Others assert that the first *señores* and *capitanes* came from the northwest, where they originated, after the Mexicans came, and they came guided by their gods and penetrated these mountains and arrived in a rugged site which is between Achiutla and Tilantongo in a spacious plain, formed in the nearby lofty mountains, and that they settled here, making fortresses. They made impregnable walls of such magnitude that for more than six leagues around the people of the garrison went to settle. . . . And all the mountains and barrancas today are marked by stepped and terraced fields from top to bottom and looking like stone-edged stairways. These were the pieces of land that the *señores* gave to the soldiers and macehuales for the sowing of their seed, the size and quality of the land depending on the size of each family. . . .
>
> It can be inferred, then, that the ancient *capitanes* or *señores* were dominated by a greater power and searched for a site which would aid them in their defense, and motivated by this fear they struggled valiantly. They cultivated and worked the steep slopes where they grew and harvested seeds because they did not venture forth to hunt or go beyond the walls where they could remain hidden. This appears to be the most reasonable theory because the greatest *Señorío* of these Mixtecas was preserved from its antiquity up until the light of the gospel shone on Tilantongo (that was the frontier of that settlement) and touched one of the sons of that *Señor;* and the *conquistadores*, in baptizing him, gave him the name of the King, our *Señor*, don Felipe de Austria, thus indicating the royal blood of this great cacique [Burgoa 1674:274–276].

The Burgoa account relies rather heavily on earlier accounts by Reyes and Torquemada, but pictographic accounts in codices Nuttall, Bodley, and Vindobonensis provide important parallel evidence of the widespread acceptability of these conquest–migrational–radiational views. This evidence suggests that conquest and unequal allocation of productive resources according to rank did contribute to social stratification in the Mixteca. While mythicohistorical accounts are difficult to substantiate, conventional documentary and pictographic sources leave little doubt that warfare had been an important aspect of Mixtec culture since Classic times. In the case of the Kingdom of Tututepec, it is quite clear that as political expansion by military conquest occurred, representatives of the Tututepec ruling family were placed in control of conquered communities as governors, administrators, and tribute collectors (Avendaño 1579; Eras 1579; Pacho 1581; RMEH 1:174–178; RMEH 2:131–163; Berlin 1947). In time, such high-status individuals must have coalesced into a significant stratum of society, a self-conscious, identifiable social class. This coalescence can be viewed as an adaptive strategy aimed at expanding and consolidating control over a large ecologically diverse and productive geopolitical sphere to satisfy the needs of an increasingly demanding aristocracy. Conquest and marital alliance, then, were not aimed at meeting basic subsistence needs, but at the maintenance of a social system based on social stratification.

Elsewhere, I have attempted to demonstrate that the Mixtecs attained a significant level of social and political organization without the development of true occupational specialization that is normally found in state societies and which is a frequent concomitant or progenitor of social stratification (Gould 1969). It is true that sixteenth-century documentation does mention specialized endeavor. Herrera (1947:Dec. 3, lib. 3, cap. 12) states that "habia en la tierra muchos capitanes y caballeros, maestros de su Ley; tenían sortílegos y médicos," and the Alvarado lexicon provides terms for physician (*tay tatna*), priest (*ñaha niñe* or *tay saque*), merchant (*mercader: tay cuica*), peddler (*merchante: tay dzata, tay yosai*), artisan (*tay huisi*), and scribe (*tay toatutu*).

It is quite clear that craftsmen, scribes, potters, weaver–tailors, body servants, and domestics were drawn into part-time or periodic service from the common class. Major retainers, advisors, and courtiers, however, were of noble and royal rank. A semblance of full-time specialization may have existed among the priests, but even this is a doubtful assumption. Herrera (1947:Dec. 3, lib. 3, cap. 13) indicates that boys who had reached at least their seventh year were eligible to enter a "monastery" for special religious training. Practitioners, observing celibacy, rose through a series of grades in the monasteries, and after 4 years they left the monasteries, dropped vows of celibacy, and entered the service of the native ruler.

The tenure of the religious practitioner would appear to have been limited, but at least some who had performed as priests continued to serve in ritualistic capacities as royal counsellors. When a priest achieved the status of nonelibate advisor to the ruler, it is likely that his religious advice (ceremonial form, reading of omens, soothsaying, prognostication, etc.) continued to be provided to the royal patron as an important component of the political role of the priestly *pasado*.

Unlike the ascribed statuses of members of the ruling and noble classes and of the ruler's advisory council, priests were drawn from both the plebian and *principal* classes (Avendaño 1579; Eras 1579; Pacho 1581; RMEH 1:174–178; RMEH 2:131–163; Caso 1949; Bernal 1962; AGN Inquisi-

ción 37). Despite such references, there is little compelling evidence to indicate the existence of professional classes of priests, warriors, craftsmen, curers, administrators, scribes, service personnel, or tradesmen, or of full-time commitment to such endeavor. In fact, there is little evidence—historical, archaeological, or ethnographic—to suggest the existence of full-time occupational specialization at any time during the Prehispanic period.

In addition to inferences derived from historic and linguistic sources, it is probable that archaeological investigations may provide insights into origins, movements, and relations of various Mixtec groups. Archaeological researches in the Nochixtlán Valley (Spores 1972:171–194; 1974b) suggest that observable settlement and socioeconomic differentiation evolved in the Ramos phase (approximately 200 B.C.–A.D. 300) when the first large, complex settlement developed at Yucuita. The valley settlement pattern prior to this time, in the Cruz phase, had been characterized by several relatively small, homogeneous, and widely spaced villages. Although knowledge of the Formative period in the valley is relatively limited, there are clearly no sites of the size and complexity of Formative settlements in the Valley of Oaxaca, in the Valley of Mexico, in Guatemala, or on the Gulf Coast. Thus far, indicators of the marked social complexity, elaborate ceremonialism, or extended political integration inferred for Formative developments in other areas are not present in the Nochixtlán Valley. Although ritualism is strongly indicated by the appearance of numerous figurine fragments, decorated ceramics, and brazier fragments, the Nochixtlán Valley appears lacking in unusual ceremonial complexes, elite dwellings, differential distribution of exotic goods, sumptuary burials, or the sculptural–hieroglyphic indicators of either status differentiation or conquest and political integration found in other areas (Sanders and Price 1968:26–29; Coe 1965; Bernal 1965; Flannery 1968b; Marcus 1974).

Expansion of settlement size and complexity occurred during the Ramos phase when a large, complex (functionally diversified) center worthy of the designation "urban" emerged at Yucuita (sites N 203, N 204, N 217, N 218, N 220, N 225). Whereas the main Cruz phase occupation at Yucuita was apparently confined to an area approximately 4 ha, the Ramos-phase settlement covered at least 1.5 km². Nearly continuous structural remains may be observed extending along and across the entire *loma–cerro* system just east of the Yucuita community center, and four adjacent "satellites" (sites N 208, N 226, N 227, N 229) are located within 3 km of Yucuita. Included in the large but highly concentrated Yucuita structural complex are at least 10 major mound complexes containing floors and alignments of quartered stone and associated ritual deposits (such as heavy ash and charcoal, braziers and incensarios, skull burials, and anthropophagic remains), plazas, a subterranean vaulted-roof tunnel system, quarries, terraces, single-celled and multiroomed buildings with masonry block foundations and walls, and adobe-block tombs with stone slab covers. Deep refuse containing culinary remains of deer, rabbit, dog, and human bone, corn, beans, avocados, zapotes and chile are found in association with heavy deposits of Yucuita Tan, Yucuita Red-on-tan, Yucuita Thin Tan and lesser quantities of Gray, Rust, and Brown wares. The ceramic complex is typical of the Ramos phase here and at other Nochixtlán Valley sites such as Nochixtlán Panteón (N 606), Etlatongo (N 810), and Atrás de la Concha (N 009), as well as sites outside the valley such as Huamelulpan (Gaxiola 1976); there are even similarities with Monte Negro in Tilantongo (Caso 1938; Acosta n.d.a). Distinctive Ramos-phase incised-bottom bowls, anthropomorphic and anthropozoomorphic figurines, siliceous gray chert tools and flakes, obsidian blades, sheet mica, marine shell objects, and carved bone beads and pendants are also found in unprecedented abundance at Yucuita. Block-adobe tombs containing extended burials, grouped secondary burials (one at N 203 F containing remains of seven individuals), and individual skull burials recovered in excavations at Yucuita are similar to manifestations at Huamelulpan and Monte Negro.

Of the 35 Ramos-phase sites known thus far in the Nochixtlán Valley, Yucuita is by far the largest and most complex, and I believe that it was the primary center of political and economic power in the valley and probably in the Mixteca Alta. Nearly half of the Ramos-phase sites are located in the Yucuita arm of the valley and most of the larger "town" sites cluster quite near the primary center. Deposits are deeper; architecture and material goods are more heavily concentrated, diverse, and complex; and more "elite" goods, obsidian, sheet mica, Monte Albán-like Type G-12 incised bowls, and braziers are found at Yucuita than elsewhere in the valley. The site is extremely large for its time and by comparison with earlier settlements. In fact, only one site—Late Classic Yucuñudahui—approaches it in size, and no site is richer in content or more complex in organization. Etlatongo (N 810) in the south-central portion of the valley contained massive earthworks and was undoubtedly of substantial importance in the Ramos phase, but it is both smaller and less diversified in its structure than Yucuita. Yucuita became the primary source of a cultural pattern that I believe characterized life in the central Mixteca from Ramos times to the Spanish Conquest. This early urban center served an integrative function as no site had before its time (Spores 1972:177–182), for it was the first center where sufficient demographic, technological, economic, and political power was concentrated to make possible urban life and an unprecedented level of functional divergence in settlement (hamlets, towns, and a city) and regional integration. A principal feature of the new urban orientation of Yucuita was an emphasis on "public" architecture, much of it ceremonial, that completely outstrips such manifestations in the previous period. Formal religion was a dominant theme in the center, suggesting the integration of political and sacred activities.

The Ramos-phase emphasis on ritualism appears in the form of large special-function areas containing dense deposits of ritual waste in association with monumental architecture, adjacent to (but separable from) associated domiciliary

remains. By contrast, goods with probable ritual functions or connotations (figurines, effigy vessels, inscribed ceramics, etc.) from earlier periods are found with household goods in dwellings with boulder-stone foundations and/or stone-and-adobe lower walls. The only Formative "mound" yet explored (at Coyotepec, site N 233) was a multilevel occupational deposit dating to both the Formative and Classic periods, but the complex recovered in and around the mound was quite similar to complexes found associated with dwellings at Yucuita (N 203 B, N 203 K). In contrast, at least some of the mounds, probably the majority, in later centers such as Yucuita, Yucuñudahui, Etlatongo, and Cerro Jasmín, were certainly ritual rather than domiciliary foci (Caso 1938; Spores 1972, 1974a). Although ceremonial activity areas are immediately adjacent to habitational areas in Yucuita, architectural and artifact complexes can be rather easily differentiated for the two types of functional areas.

The emphasis on ceremonialism in Ramos and Las Flores times suggests that urbanism and social stratification emerged in the Mixteca as part of an ideological transformation whereby formalized religion became a central integrative feature of Mixtec society. I suggest that religious practitioners, in effect, created a situation of social inequality and then, in order to reinforce and perpetuate the system, emphasized and strengthened their spiritual, political, and economic hold on the greater society. This is one of several strategies that could have been adopted in an environment allowing various subsistence and sociopolitical adaptations. Such adaptations ranged from scattered extended family homesteads to small economically, socially, and politically independent clusters of comparable egalitarian communities; to a hierarchically integrated cluster of simply organized villages; to a ranked regional complex of differentiated settlements; to an extensively organized interregional sociopolitical system. Late Formative–Early Classic Mixtecs pursued an adaptive strategy that ensured continuation of a system of social stratification and reinforced the decision-making power of the new elite. Religious practitioners of the Formative period became the priests of the Classic period.

It is logical to assume, in the absence of evidence indicating true division of labor or military overthrow, that political power also rested with the religious elite. The status of religious mediator in an expanding society with increasing needs and increasing dependence on ritual manipulation, rather than technological innovation, was of special adaptive significance to the Mixtecs. Survival of mankind and of a cultural system depended on religious power; a demonstrated ability to understand and control the supernatural universe placed great temporal power in the hands of the religious practitioner.

According to our argument, the first special status to emerge was the religious specialist having the ability to control sacred and, increasingly, secular activities. The first large and complex architecture at Yucuita is associated with material remains that suggest, beyond doubt, formalized ritualistic activity. As religious practitioners became priests, they were able to control and direct the effort and output of the members of a formerly egalitarian society. These efforts were directed toward ritual enterprises, including construction of impressive ceremonial complexes and the provision of vast quantities of tribute and services, ostensibly in support of cult activities, but in fact consumed and redirected in large part by the emergent elite. The amount and diversity of exotic goods obtained in and around Ramos-phase remains at Yucuita is impressive (Spores 1972, 1974a) and the pattern is repeated at Las Flores-phase Yucuñudahui. Someone had the ability and power to demand goods and services and to channel them in specified directions.

Observing the archaeology of the Early Classic, it is clear that significant social transformations occurred, but the sources and supportive mechanisms of social inequality are more difficult to ascertain. Although there are ample indications of contact between the Nochixtlán Valley and such outlying areas as the Valley of Mexico, Puebla–Tehuacán, Veracruz, Chiapas, and the Valley of Oaxaca from Formative times to the Spanish Conquest (Spores 1972, 1974a), there is no conclusive evidence of external conquest for the Classic period. The movement of Nochixtlán Valley settlements from valley floor to mountain- and ridgetops, as seen in at least 88 of 113 Las Flores sites (Spores 1973:165–168), may indicate widespread conflict in the Mixteca Alta, but if there was extensive warfare, it is by no means clear who may have been fighting whom. Given only the archaeological evidence, it is difficult to say whether movement to high ground was prompted by military, economic, or primarily ideological determinants. Neither, I must add, is there any material evidence of the fifteenth- and sixteenth-century subordination of the Nochixtlán Valley to the Culhua–Mexica Confederacy (settlement during the Postclassic being divided between low-ground and medium-altitude sites), yet we know from historical sources that numerous towns in the valley were reduced to tributary status by the Aztecs. The Bodley, Nuttall, and Colombino codices certainly do suggest that intercommunity conflict and internal warfare, raiding, and conquest were well established throughout the Mixteca by A.D. 900, and the codices and conventional documentation indicate the persistence of this pattern through the Postclassic period.

So, while the case for a conquest basis for social stratification is quite inconclusive, certainly warfare coexisted with an extensive system of aristocratic marital alliance and underlay, reinforced, and amplified the social status quo in the Mixteca from mid-Classic times to the Spanish Conquest. Further, while there is no convincing evidence for the emergence of full-time occupational specialization in the Mixteca from the Formative period to the Conquest, I do believe that a particular kind of specialization did emerge during the Late Formative–Early Classic transition and that herein may lie at least a partial explanation for the origins of social stratification in the Mixteca.

I would hypothesize that the first "specialists" to emerge in Mixtec society were individuals possessing specialized ritual, magical, or curing knowledge. Such individuals stand out, even in simple egalitarian societies where shamans oc-cupy what may be their societies' only specialized, if not necessarily privileged, status. Latent, if not active, political power *may* accrue to such statuses, and, depending on social, economic, and ideological circumstances and the personal attributes and abilities of the practitioner, latent power *may* be translated into active localized or extended political power.[2] Netting states the case rather well and in a way that I believe is applicable to Mixtec society:

> Let us suggest that political development in many cases takes place internally and voluntarily rather than by imposition or wholesale borrowing from neighboring groups, and that the main lines of development and channels for change are prefigured in existing institutions and patterns of behavior. I would claim that on the road to statehood, society must first seek the spiritual kingdom, that essentially religious modes of focusing power are often primary in overcoming the critical structural weaknesses of stateless societies.
>
> These weaknesses are by definition those of a society based on localized, highly autonomous units. To integrate a number of such units or to allow an existing unit to expand without fission, ways must be found to keep the peace while enlarging personal contacts beyond the range of kin group and locality. . . . The new grouping must be united, not by kinship or territory alone, but by belief, by the infinite extensibility of common symbols, shared cosmology, and the overarching unity of fears and hopes made visible in ritual. A leader who can mobilize these sentiments, who can lend concrete form to an amorphous moral community, is thereby freed from complete identification with his village or section or age group or lineage [1972:233].

To emphasize the point I wish to make, it is advantageous to quote from the continuation of Netting's argument:

> A leader who can simultaneously reassure farmers worried about their harvest, adjudicate their quarrels, and profitably redistribute or promote the exchange of valued goods is obviously not the same as other men. He occupies a central social position. A higher social status is both functionally necessary to his activities and an appropriate reward for his services. . . .
>
> Political chiefship may be dignified by titles and inherited through more rigidly defined kinship links. Regular differences in access to resources, control of services, and possession of valued goods may emerge. Privilege becomes both more overt and increasingly ascribed. Both the powers and the prerequisites of a highly ranked individual or group are justified by ritual status. Such people are singled out fundamentally by their relationship to sacred things and suprahuman potency [1972:236–237; © 1972 by the MIT Press].

I believe that Netting's inferences and conclusions apply specifically to Mixtec society. I would argue that the origins of social stratification—and coincidentally the state—in the Mixteca are attributable to internal processes of social differentiation based on the emergence of religious practi-

---

[2] I have consciously used and emphasized *may,* for I am quite aware that political power does not *necessarily* fall to those holding supernatural or ritual power and that latent power is not *necessarily* translated into active political power. There are too many cases to the contrary. With reference to the Mixteca, however, archaeological and historical evidence converge, suggesting convincingly that the relationships among ritual, social, and political power, power-holders, and institutions evolved as I have hypothesized. On the basis of data presently available, I believe this to be the best explanation of the rise of social stratification in the Mixteca. I make no pretense of attempting to generalize for society at large.

tioners as political powerholders. Power to mediate between man and the supernatural world could be translated into power to demand goods and labor services from believers, to control scarce resources, to divert resources to private as well as public ends, to concentrate decision-making and coercive power in the hands of a small group, and to make possible the expansion of political dominion through warfare, alliance, or by voluntary aggregation. Eventually, wealth in goods and services, privileges, and entitlement to lands and productive resources accumulated to a significant degree in the hands of a few families. Ritual power and authority were transformed into political power and authority. Through religious and economic control and through a combination of alliance, annexation, and conquest, members of the Mixtec elite were able to reinforce their privileged status, to establish their royal charters, to perpetuate supportive mythologies, and to expand their power and influence.

Once such social and political systems had been established, elite status depended on the nearness or directness of relationship to elite ancestors, both real and fictive. In time there arose a gradation of most direct descendants (royal class), collateral or secondary descendants or kinsmen (noble class), and unrelated (common class) status groups. Historic and protohistoric usage suggests that conquered peoples could be assimilated into any one of the three major social categories or attached as *mayeques* (*tay situndayu*) or slaves. Eventually, priestly and political functions became differentiated (again, I do not see these as occupations in the sense of Gould 1969). Architectural manifestations of this changing relationship may be perceived in the archaeological sites. Dwellings in Ramos-phase Yucuita, many of them containing numerous contiguous rooms, were built within and immediately adjacent to ceremonial precincts. There is no clear demarcation of dwelling and monumental ceremonial activity areas. In Las Flores-phase Yucuñudahui, the distinctions between dwelling areas and ceremonial architecture is far clearer; I do not deny the existence of possible domiciliary structures in ceremonial areas, but insofar as the main central complex of ballcourt, plazas, courts, and mounds is concerned, the area at Yucuñudahui is more clearly aligned and set apart as a special activity area as opposed to the adjacent, but separable, dwelling areas. The dozens of smaller Late Classic sites scattered about the peaks and ridges of the Nochixtlán Valley show a similar pattern of a central ritual activity area surrounded concentrically by habitations.

Interesting parallels might be drawn between Ramos-phase Yucuita and Yagul, the Valley of Oaxaca site. Yagul is smaller than Yucuita but comparable in general orientation and complexity. Yucuita and Yagul are squeezed into compact, multifunctional units; they can be contrasted with Classic Yucuñudahui or with Monte Albán or, even though placement is quite different, with Teotihuacán. The latter three centers contain elaborated central ceremonial complexes surrounded by dwellings and service areas. Other early centers in the Mixteca Alta—Monte Negro,

Huamelulpan, and probably Yatachío—share the multiplex core features of Yucuita. The large site of Cerro Jazmín appears to have begun in Ramos times as a relatively small but multiplex center, grew during the Las Flores period as much the same kind of settlement, and continued to be utilized during the Postclassic period as a ceremonial center but only quite marginally as a dwelling area.

In the Postclassic period, there was even greater distinction between civic–ceremonial centers and dwelling areas. Ceremonial sites were often located at some distance from socially differentiated dwelling zones. Many Postclassic sites contained numerous household structures and indications of ceremonial activity (braziers, offering cups, incensors, offering blades, etc.) but very little in the way of obvious ceremonial architecture. Other sites, many of them formerly occupied as dwelling centers, show signs of intensive ceremonial activity in and around mound–plaza complexes but little or no indication of permanent settlement.

It is clear that there were substantial increases in population in the Nochixtlán Valley from the Cruz phase (18 known localities, 8 intensively occupied) to the Ramos phase (35 localities, 27 intensively occupied) (Spores 1972:165–194). There were not only more sites, and more intensively occupied sites, in the Ramos period, but settlements were larger and, at least in several instances, more complex than in the Cruz phase. I would hold to my previous estimate of 12,000 for Ramos (see "Note on Population Estimates" in this topic). One site alone—Yucuita—had a population that must have approached 8000 persons (5 of 35 Ramos localities, all intensively utilized, are now considered to constitute one large complex settlement, Yucuita).[3] By Las Flores times, the number of sites (113), localities intensively occupied (74), and large (approximately 1 km² or larger) centers (e.g., Yucuñudahui, Cerro Jazmín, Jaltepec, Etlatongo) were sufficiently developed to support a population of 35,000. The maximum population for the valley, however, was in the Postclassic Natividad phase when 159 sites were occupied, 113 of them intensively. Many Postclassic sites were quite large, though less "monumental" in plan and construction than Classic sites, and we believe that a population estimate of 50,000 is not out of line with available archaeological and ethnohistoric evidence.

Continuing with archaeological data, there are certain manifestations of cult–state differentiation in that major Postclassic ceremonial precincts are often quite distantly removed from civic centers (Spores 1967:90–108, 1972:175–192). Shrines were constructed in the compact centers, as we have observed in such Postclassic sites as

---

[3] In the case of complex settlements, such as Yucuita, without historical documentation as a basis of inference it is quite difficult to say where the city of Yucuita leaves off and other nearby communities begin. With this point in mind, I have raised an earlier estimate of the population of Ramos-phase Yucuita from 7000 to 8000 because I have decided that I had arbitrarily excluded an adjacent but not totally contiguous site, Tindehuehano (N 220), which lies some 250 m across an irrigated valley from the main site but is culturally directly related. It now seems inconceivable that this 100-by-200-m site could be outside the social, political, and economic realm of Yucuita just because it is separated from the center by a corn patch.

Yucuita, Chachoapan, Nochixtlán, and Loma de Ayuxi in Yanhuitlán. But many ceremonial sites were set apart from the main population centers, in caves, on high mountains, and, in several instances, in old, abandoned, or nearly abandoned Classic sites that continued to be used, not as habitation zones, but as religious centers (Spores 1972:189). This placement tends to confirm ethnohistorically derived inferences that in Postclassic times the religious cult and its practitioners were differentiated from, under control of, and supported by, the ruler (Spores 1967:9, 22–27; 1974b).

During the Postclassic period, males of the ruling class served a 1-year religious "apprenticeship" in a hermitage. Subsequent to assumption of title, rulers served important functions as sponsors of cult activities, but others drawn from both the common and noble classes served as priests in cult activities supported by the ruling family of each kingdom. As far as I am concerned, the combined weight of documentary and archaeological evidence clearly indicates the separation of duties between ruler and priest, even though the ruler, as the primary patron of the religious cult, did from time to time perform ritualistic functions.

Further archaeological and ethnohistorical research will, I believe, reinforce the view that the Mixtec class system began in the terminal Formative or Early Classic period, around A.D. 1. As increasing numbers of people adapted themselves to the Nochixtlán Valley and the surrounding mountains and valleys of the Mixteca, skilled religious practitioners took advantage of their specialized roles in supernatural mediation, exercised increasing control over goods, lands, resources, and the productive services of their followers, and rose to positions of political authority. Special forms of social interaction, marriage, and creation of hereditary charters led to a differentiation of the religious–political sector from the mass of Mixtec society. An ideological reorientation emphasized recognition of and reliance upon a religious elite; complex settlement and cultural systems arose in conjunction with a system of social stratification based not on further differentiation of the labor force or on military conquest but on consanguineal and affinal propinquity to members of the religious–political elite. Ritual and economic power (through the right to demand goods and services for ritual services rendered) were transformed into political power. Localized sociopolitical elites evolved true social groupings (classes), and diversified, multicommunity political networks (Mixtec kingdoms) emerged. During the Classic period, social, political, and economic ties between elite families and communities were further extended and intensified through intermarriage, military conquest, and annexation. Eventually, probably some time in the later Classic or Postclassic periods, the political elite (the ruling families and the *principales*) became differentiated from, and exercised control over, the religious professionals and cult activities.

By Postclassic times, social and political power, initially based on ritual power, transcended this traditional base and became far more secular and oriented toward (1) traditional rights and privileges and a supporting ideology that rein-

forced the social order, (2) control of productive resources and systems of tribute, redistribution, and market exchange, and (3) extension and consolidation of political power and domain through marital alliance, economic control, and conquest–annexation. As population increased (Spores 1969, 1972; Sanders 1972) and perceived needs of the aristocracy and basic needs of the general population changed, institutions underwent adjustments. Adaptation was achieved through extension of spheres of influence and control by sociopolitical means rather than through technological innovation, organized conflict over resources, or interregional migration. Converging ethnohistoric and archaeological data indicate the differentiation of religious and political institutions, but, clearly, formal ritual activities were controlled and sponsored by the political elite. To speak of a "priestly state" in Late Formative and Early Classic times may not be far from the truth, but to ignore the transformation to a secular state in later times would be erroneous. While occupational specialization in the form of the religious practitioner with his specialized knowledge and power may have stood at the base of the stratification process, such an occupation was not subsequently prominent in the rise of the Mixtec class system. Once the social system began to take on its characteristic form and became fully established, secular concerns and secular supports and the weight of tradition furnished the sustaining foundation of the Mixtec social system. Religion and its ritual and ideological extensions (e.g., reflections and justifications for social stratification in creation myths and elite genealogical mythology) provided supernatural validation for the sociocultural system and justification and reinforcement for the political order.

## NOTE ON POPULATION ESTIMATES

A general statement relative to population is in order. Population estimates for the prehistoric period in the Nochixtlán Valley are necessarily based on projections from the historic period of the sixteenth century. On the basis of demographic data taken from Spanish documentation I have estimated that the population of the valley was around 50,000 in A.D. 1520 (Spores 1969).

Even though we now know that there were at least 159 Natividad sites occupied (113 intensively), instead of the 111 sites that were known up to 1969, I am not persuaded that the population of the valley was any greater than 50,000. The population was simply dispersed over more space than we formerly realized. Additionally, we obviously do not know with certainty that all of the Postclassic sites were occupied simultaneously, despite the fact that structures and ceramic and artifact complexes look contemporaneous. The census data from the sixteenth century, difficult to interpret at their best, allow one to arrive at total population for a given community—Yanhuitlán, for example—but seldom is there an indication of precisely where the population was located on the ground (see Borah and Cook [1960] for a detailed treatment of Mixtec population trends since 1520). The "community of Yanhuitlán" may have had a population of 24,000, but it is not clear how the population was dispersed over the landscape. I believe that the political community of Yanhuitlán consisted of as many as 15 settlements or clusters, some contiguous and some located 10 km or farther from the capital.

It is possible to arrive at population figures for various communities at a given point in time, say A.D. 1540, but it is exceedingly difficult to equate community and archaeological sites. It is safe to assume that families lived in certain settlements and that they related to one another somehow, in some way. It is difficult to say how individuals and families within a settlement were related and just as difficult—but just as important—to say how one contiguous cluster of dwellings may have related to others. How many settlements constitute a community? How many communities a kingdom or other sociopolitical unit? How were communities or kingdoms linked into larger socioeconomic networks or systems? How do we correlate settlement units of components with socioeconomic or political communities, or "interaction spheres"?

What I am saying is that the town-by-town census materials for the sixteenth century can provide reasonably reliable community population estimates, but it is quite difficult in many cases to say whether given archaeological localities were associated with one community or another, or whether certain sites were occupied before, during, or after the Conquest, or at all three points in time. We can say that a population of 50,000 in A.D. 1520 is correlated with 159 sites of certain width, length, complexity, and orientation relative to natural and cultural features. In time, I hope, archaeological analysis will become precise enough for us to work out political configurations and socioeconomic relations among sites, particularly *cabeceras* and their political satellites. When and if that can be done, it is at least conceivable that archaeological and ethnohistoric evidence will allow identification of Yanhuitlán's aboriginal center and each, or most, of its subject settlements. Until that time, to imply that demographic precision is possible is counterproductive.

Although villages of about 100 souls can consistently be differentiated from a Tikal or a Monte Albán, I fear that I am chronically skeptical of procedures that yield "exact" population figures for particular prehistoric archaeological sites at particular points in time. There is too much room for distortion of the physical remains, too many complexities of construction—destruction—reconstruction to be dealt with in the usual time available to the archaeologist, too little methodological aptitude, too much left unexcavated, too much leeway in artifact chronologies, too little geochronological precision, too much pseudorigorous statistical manipulation of excavated complexes which may be quite revealing in a collector band's camp site but hardly so for complex sites characteristic of Mesoamerican civilization. The painstaking excavation of two or three foci in

medium or large settlements is simply inadequate to reveal the kind of demographic data that archaeologists care to discuss but are hard put to substantiate. Furthermore, can we ever be quite sure that configurations of sites with comparable cultural complexes were actually occupied simultaneously, or years, decades, or centuries apart? They may appear to be contemporaneous settlements, but are they?

Population figures for prehistoric sites are too inexact to satisfy normal scientific requirements, and this is regrettable. I believe, however, that when we can correlate number, size, and general orientation of a series of sites with known population figures (not to imply that I am by any means satisfied with even the historical demographic data from the Mixteca Alta or that either Borah and Cook or I interpret them properly or adequately), that it will be possible, by exercising some care, to project relative numbers, sizes, and orientations into prehistoric time and arrive at reasonable approximations of population. Until better methodologies are found, I believe not only that the procedure is reasonably sound but that the figures are fair "ballpark" estimates of total population in the valley at various points in time. We must now move forward with better paleodemographic studies for the greater Mixteca and for Mesoamerica as a whole.

## CONCLUSION

A differentiation of religious practitioners qua political leaders is postulated for the Late Formative and the Ramos phase in the Mixteca. (Settlement patterns and sociopolitical organization are diagrammed in Figure 8.1.) While the rise of religious specialists to positions of secular power may have been fundamental to the origins of the Mixtec class system, occupational specialization does not appear to have been a significant causal factor in the rise and maintenance of social stratification. Moreover, conquest of Mixtec communities by outside powers does not appear to have played a significant role in the stratification process. The emergence of religious practitioners as a political elite undoubtedly was associated with a complex of reinforcing marital and political alliances and internal military conquest that promoted exploitation of widespread resources and contributed to the overall integration of the social system.

These factors, coupled with a relatively low population density, the ecology of the Mixteca, the economic system, and the ideology, did not encourage development of a true division of labor and an occupationally based system of stratification. The system was, rather, what could be called traditional patrimonial, whereby once an elite element was established, it maintained social and political dominance as much through ritual and ideological "management" as out of economic necessity. This is not to say that control of land, resources, wealth, and power symbols did not figure in maintenance of the system; they did. But physical or economic coercion do not loom large in this development. The

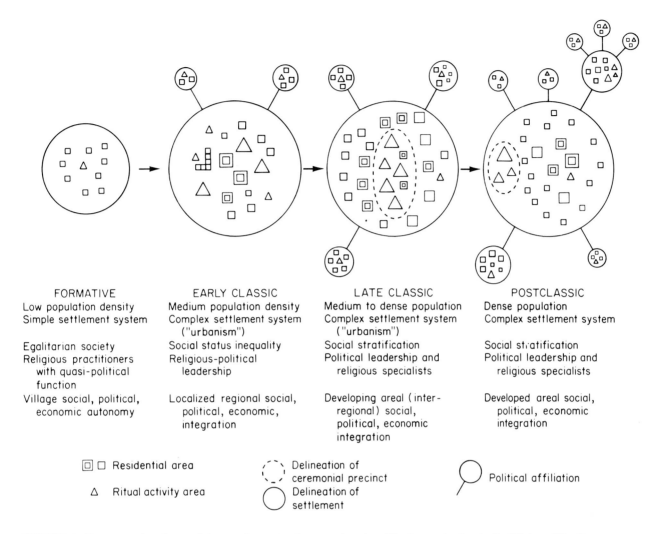

FIGURE 8.1.  Diagrams showing evolving settlement patterns and sociopolitical organization in the Mixteca Alta: time, space, and functional relationships.

force of tradition and sanctified social custom were as pervasive and fundamental to the maintenance of the system as were economic considerations.

In late times, conquest of one kingdom by another seems not to have affected significantly the societal status quo established in Classic and Early Postclassic times. While there were undoubtedly individual differences in wealth, power, and prestige, as far as the class system was concerned, new rulers were the social equals of displaced rulers, *principales* remained *principales,* and commoners remained commoners. Even external control of Mixtec kingdoms by the Culhua–Mexica tripartite confederacy was far more economic than sociopolitical or ideological in its impact on native society and does not seem to have altered the class system, the integration, the "authenticity," and functional–adaptive persistence of the Mixtec social system.

Regarding claims that the Mixtec social system was highly adaptive, I must make it clear that I am emphasizing the sociopolitical, rather than the technoenvironmental, adaptation of an evolving society. The ideological, social, and political aspects of adaptation are primary in the development of the system of stratification, and technoenvironmental adaptation is secondary. The environment of the Mixteca, while somewhat limited in total productive potential, is internally dversified, allowing a variety of adaptations. Similar environments have supported similar and dissimilar social systems. Why, then, did the Mixtec system develop as it did?

The adaptive radiation of Mixtec society from a generalized Oaxacan or Mesoamerican Formative base can be seen as a result of a series of choices made by people both within and outside Mixtec society relative to the assignment of values or emphases to particular aspects of their culture. The power to make things grow, to ensure fertility, to maintain good health, to ensure the continuity of life in the supernatural world, and the power to mediate between supernatural forces and man rested in the hands of religious practitioners who converted their powers to deal with the supernatural world into power to deal with the natural world and to make decisions having a binding effect on increasingly larger numbers of people. Control of resources, the ability to ally, conquer, and control, and, we must not forget, the ability to deal with external threats both supernatural and political, operated in shaping Mixtec society and in the creation and maintenance of the class system. The fact that the rulers of Yanhuitlán and Tecomaxtlahuaca controlled by far the most productive lands in their respective domains was determined not by the existence of certain technoenvironmental relationships but by the existence of a highly evolved set of social mechanisms that allowed those highest-status individuals to take charge of and maintain control of those resources. The environment, so to speak, was adapted to preexisting social institutions rather than those institutions being the product of a special technoenvironmental relationship. The Mixtec sociopolitical system developed in the Classic period and, evolving through the Postclassic and Colonial periods, allowed for adaptations to

diverse environments, cold and dry, temperate and moist, hot and dry, hot and humid, mountaintops and slopes, narrow and broad valleys, and coastal plains. Evolving mechanisms allowed for the bridging and integration of diverse regions and, eventually, ethnic domains consisting of speakers of various Mixtec dialects as well as Chochones, Triques, Amuzgos, Chatinos, Nahuas, coastal Zapotec, and, finally, Zapotec speakers of the western portion of the Valley of Oaxaca.

I believe that we might go far toward a response to the ethnologist's query, Why do some societies endure and hold together while others are changed radically and disintegrate?, by examining carefully the evolution of the Mixtec social system and by observing the sequence of options—including the delegation of power to particular individuals, the creation and maintenance of a system of social stratification, and the development of a flexible but effective and highly integrative political and economic system—which were exercised by Mixtecs between the end of the Formative period and the Spanish Conquest.

## TOPIC 71
## The Mixtec Writing System

MARY ELIZABETH SMITH

The Mixtec writing system is usually described as a "limited" or "partial" writing system because it uses signs principally to record names of persons and places. The remainder of the story is conveyed through symbols and pictorial conventions that appear to have only occasional relationship to language. In addition, as far as can be determined at the present time, the signs utilized to express names are based on whole words in the Mixtec language rather than on syllables or single sounds (phonemes). This type of writing, sometimes called logographic (Gelb 1963:99–107), is considered by historians of writing to be an early or formative stage of writing.

The Mixtec writing system discussed in this topic is that seen in a group of Late Postclassic painted manuscripts, or codices, that set forth genealogical and historical data. Stone monuments and wall paintings from earlier periods and found within the present-day Mixtec-speaking region have been excluded because it is still uncertain which native language is depicted in the writing on these earlier monuments.[1]

Also omitted are such objects as carved bones, goldwork, and polychrome ceramics (Caso et al. 1967; Caso 1969; Ramsey 1975) that exhibit "Mixtec" style and often contain short texts. Here, too, it is still a question whether the texts on these objects reflect the Mixtec or some other language. For the same reason, the wall paintings of Mitla (León 1901; Seler 1904) will not be discussed in detail, although they, as well, are considered to be Mixtec in style. The painted manuscripts, on the other hand, are very definitely based on the Mixtec language, and they form a substantial corpus that amply illustrates the Mixtec system of writing in use at the time of the Spanish Conquest.

Included in the group of Mixtec manuscripts painted in a Preconquest style are Codices Nuttall (Nuttall 1902), Bodley (Caso 1960), Selden (Caso 1964), Colombino (Caso and Smith 1966; Troike 1974), Becker I and II (Nowotny 1961a), Vienna (Nowotny 1948; Caso 1950; Adelhofer 1963), and Sánchez Solís (also called Egerton 2895 [Burland 1965]). From the Mixtec-speaking region, there have also survived numerous Postconquest pictorial manuscripts (listed in Glass 1975:67) that retain elements of Prehispanic style and whose precise provenience is known. In some instances, these Postconquest manuscripts are accompanied by glosses written in European script or can be related to Colonial legal documents, and hence these later manuscripts are invaluable in interpreting the specific motifs found in the Preconquest manuscripts.

[1]Some of the stone sculpture and painting from the Mixtec-speaking region has been discussed briefly by Alfonso Caso (1956, 1965b). A distinctive group of stone monuments from the Mixteca Baja region of northern Oaxaca–southern Puebla, presumably Late Classic in date, has been named Ñuiñe and studied in most detail by Paddock (1966a:174–200, 1970a, 1970b) and Moser (1977). The stone sculpture of the Oaxaca coast (the western section of which is Mixtec speaking) has been treated in depth by María Jorrín (1974).

The origins of the Mixtec writing system are unknown, although this system or adaptations of it seem to have been utilized in other regions of Mesoamerica in the late Postclassic period. It has been suggested, for example, that the system being used by the Aztecs and other groups in and around the Valley of Mexico at the time of the Spanish Conquest is based on the "Mixtec system" (Robertson 1959a:13). In the manuscripts from the Valley of Mexico, however, the writing system is used to express the Nahuatl language, whereas in the Mixtec manuscripts the system reflects the Mixtec langauge.

The Mixtec writing system, as it is exhibited in the genealogical–historical manuscripts, uses three means of conveying information: signs, symbols, and pictorial conventions. Signs—or pictorial motifs that represent one or more words in the Mixtec language—are found principally in the names of persons and places.

Symbols, in my definition, are motifs that do not depend on language for their interpretation and that are often distributed in more than one region of Mesoamerica. For example, I would consider the Mesoamerican "speech scroll" to be a symbol. The speech scroll—a volute usually shown being emitted from the mouth of a human being or animal—represents speech or sound in many regions of Mesoamerica, and, as far as I know, the name of this motif is not known in any native language. What I call a symbol some historians of writing call an ideograph or ideogram.

Pictorial conventions have little relationship to language and, in common with symbols, are found in regions of Mesoamerica where various languages are spoken. Examples of pictorial conventions include a mummy bundle to indicate a dead person, the confrontation of a male and a female figure to indicate marriage, and the grasping of the hair of one person by another to indicate conquest or prisoner-taking.

## SIGNS

Signs are used to express both the names of persons and of places, although the place-name signs seem to be more complex in their composition than personal-name signs. In addition, a more extensive vocabulary of signs is used to depict names of places than is used in the names of persons.

Most of the persons who appear in the Mixtec histories have two types of names: the calendrical name, which indicates the day on which they were born, and the so-called personal name or nickname, which was supposedly given to a child at the age of 7 by a priest (Herrera 1947:321). Utilizing the traditional Mesoamerican calendar system, calendrical names of persons are composed of 20 day-signs which combine with the numbers 1 through 13 for a possible 260 day-names.[2] Personal names usually consist of two motifs,

---

[2]Emily Rabin (1975) has demonstrated that the "lucky" and "unlucky" days seen in the calendrical names in Mixtec manuscripts are very different from the lucky and unlucky day-dates recorded by Sahagún for the Valley of Mexico.

although occasionally as many as three or four or as few as one are used. From glosses in the Mixtec language written on Codices Sánchez Solís and Muro (M. E. Smith 1973b), we know that most personal names are composed of two or three motifs that represent nouns only, such as "Rain Deity–Flint Blade" (Sánchez Solís 23). Occasionally, however, the personal name is a noun–verb–object combination, such as "The Tiger Who Burns the Sky" (Muro 3).

### Deities and Mythological Figures in Personal Names

Although the motifs used in personal names have yet to be studied completely as a system of nomenclature, the vocabulary of signs that appears in these names is very definitely a finite one. For example, very few of the rich variety of deities and mythological figures depicted on the obverse or ritual side of the Codex Vienna are included as motifs in personal names. The deity motif that occurs most frequently in the names of persons who are historical and neither priests nor mythological personages is the rain deity known in Nahuatl as *Tlaloc* and in Mixtec as *Dzavui*. This deity is part of the names of 56 different rulers in the Mixtec genealogies (50 men and 6 women). The prevalence of the rain deity motif in Mixtec names is not surprising because the Mixtec people call themselves in their own language *ñuu dzavui,* or "the people of the rain deity."

A mythological figure that is also a fairly frequent component of personal names is the fire-serpent, whose name is

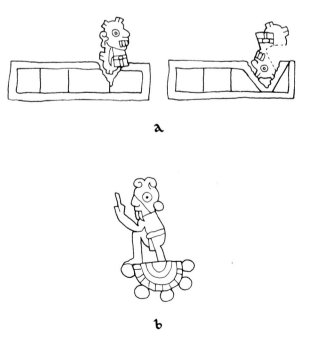

FIGURE 8.2. "Ollin figures," "Xolotls," or "Earth men": (a) Codex Vienna 52; (b) Codex Selden 14-IV. (Drawing prepared by Caren Walt.)

*Xiuhcoatl* in Nahuatl and *Yahui* in Mixtec (M. E. Smith 1973b:60–64). This motif is seen in the names of 47 persons (38 men and 9 women).

The third most prevalent deity or mythological figure (Figure 8.2) is a motif that appears frequently on the obverse or ritual side of Codex Vienna and that Lehmann and Smital (1929) and Nowotny (1948, 1961b) called an "ollin figure." This same figure is referred to as "Xolotl" by Alfonso Caso in his detailed analyses of the Mixtec codices (1950, 1960, 1964, Caso and Smith 1966), although the connection between this figure and the Xolotl deity of the Nahuatl-speaking regions seems tenuous. I have suggested, on the basis of the glosses accompanying these figures in Codices Sánchez Solís and Muro, that the figure is an "earth man," as the earliest group of Mixtecs were characterized (M. E. Smith 1973b:65–71). The "earth men," or "first Mixtecs," supposedly emerged from the center of the earth and were later conquered by a second group of Mixtecs who came from Apoala, a town in the Mixteca Alta reputed to be one of the originating points for the hereditary Mixtec rulers. This figure is part of the personal names of 35 Mixtec rulers (25 women and 10 men). Moreover, it seems to be very much a Mixtec diagnostic. To my knowledge, the only appearance of this figure outside of the Mixtec historical manuscripts and *lienzos* is among a group of nine pulque drinkers on page 72 of Codex Vaticanus B, one of the ritual manuscripts of the so-called Borgia Group and of unknown provenience (Nowotny 1961b:Pl. 38b).

The remaining deities and mythological figures seen in Mixtec personal names occur less frequently. The "earth monster" motif known in Nahuatl as *Tlaltecuhtli* is included in the names of 13 rulers, 8 of whom are men and 5 of whom are women (Baird 1973), whereas the deity known in Nahuatl as *Tlahuizcalpantecuhtli* appears in 10 names (9 men, 1 woman). Caso (1966b) postulated that the features associated with the deity known in Nahuatl as *Xipe-Totec* are part of the personal names of 5 men from the same family shown in Codex Nuttall (33–35, 61), and Jill Furst (1975) has studied how these *Xipe* attributes function as personal names and as costume elements. Another possible deity motif that is part of a Mixtec ruler's name is the so-called Pinocchio nose which may refer to the merchant deity known in Nahuatl as *Yacatecuhtli* (Thompson 1966) and which is seen only in the name of 1 man (Bodley 2-IV) and 1 woman (Bodley 5-III; Nuttall 23-III).

For the most part, the motifs used in personal names are easily recognizable portrayals of animals (such as tigers and coyotes), birds (such as eagles and parrots), serpents, jewels, flowers, blood, flames, ballcourts, sun disks, sky bands, and the like. As indicated above, the number of motifs seen in personal names, though large, is finite; a greater variety of motifs is seen in the signs that represent names of places.

Moreover, as far as can be determined at the present time, place signs seem to utilize more fully the various types of "logograms" or word signs delineated by I. J. Gelb (1963:99–107): primary signs, associative signs, signs that utilize the principle of phonetic transfer, and signs with pho-

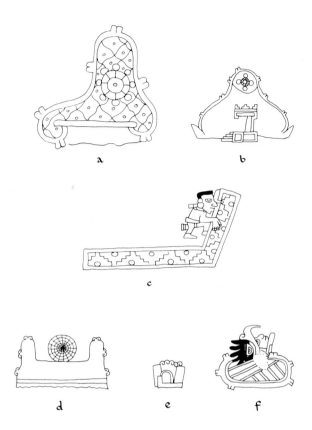

FIGURE 8.3. Place signs from Mixtec manuscripts: (a) the sign of Acatlán (Codex Sánchez Solís 23); (b) the sign of Texupan (1579 *Relación Geográfica* Map of Tejupan); (c) the sign of Teozacoalco (Codex Bodley 15-III); (d) sign with cobweb on plateau flanked by peaks (Codex Vienna 7-II); (e) water and cradle (*Lienzo de Jicayán*, sign 50); (f) the sign of Tututepec (Codex Bodley 9-III). (Drawing prepared by Caren Walt.)

netic indicators. Hence, in the discussion below of these types of signs, all the examples to be considered will be place signs.

## Primary Signs

A primary sign is one in which the pictorial sign represents the word depicted by the sign in a straightforward manner. A typical example of a primary sign in the Mixtec manuscripts is the sign for the town of Acatlán in southern Puebla that appears in Codex Sánchez Solís (M. E. Smith 1973a:61–62). The Mixtec name of Acatlán is *yucu yusi*, which means "hill of the turquoise jewel"; this place name is depicted by a hill sign that contains a turquoise jewel sign (Figure 8.3a).

## Associative Signs

An associative sign is one in which the word represented by a pictorial motif is not the name of the motif itself but of one of the qualities associated with this motif. A good example of an associative sign occurs in the sign of the town of Texupan in the Mixteca Alta, which appears in the 1579 *Relación Geográfica* map of this town (Bailey 1972; del Paso y Troncoso 1905–1906:Vol. IV). The Texupan sign consists of a hill and a turquoise jewel (Figure 8.3b), as does the sign of Acatlán discussed previously. However, we know from the text accompanying the map (Avendaño 1579:53–54) and from the list of Mixtec town names included in the sixteenth-century Mixtec grammar of Fray Antonio de los Reyes (1890:89) that the Mixtec name of Texupan is *ñuu ndaa,* or "blue town." Hence, in this case, the turquoise jewel motif is functioning as an associative sign and represents the word *blue* (*ndaa* in Mixtec), one of the qualities of turquoise, rather than the jewel itself (*yusi* in Mixtec).

### Signs That Utilize the Principle of Phonetic Transfer

In signs that utilize the principle of phonetic transfer, a pictorial sign depicts a word that is the same as or similar to another word, often one that would be difficult to represent in a pictorial fashion. Because Mixtec is a tone language in which each vowel can be pronounced with a high, middle, or low tone, many words in the language are homonymous except for variations in tone. It has been well documented that "tone puns"—substitution of a word with one tonal pattern for one with a different tonal pattern—are a common feature in spoken Mixtec (Pike 1945). Thus it seems natural that pictorial tone puns—or signs that involve the principle of phonetic transfer—would be utilized in the writing that reflects the Mixtec language.

The best-known instance of phonetic transfer in Mixtec writing is one of the signs for the town of Teozacoalco, a sign that Caso (1949) identified in his pioneering study of the 1580 *Relación Geográfica* map of Teozacoalco. The known Mixtec name of Teozacoalco is *chiyo canu,* which means "the large temple platform." The representation of the "large" definition of *canu* as a pictorial sign would be difficult, but the word *canu* with a different pattern of tones means "to break," and hence the sign that represents this place name consists of a small human figure bending or "breaking" a platform (Figure 8.3c).

### Signs with Phonetic Indicators

A phonetic indicator is a sign whose function is to clarify the word or sound being represented by another sign. For example, in a place sign in Codex Vienna, a cobweb motif (*nduhua* in Mixtec) is combined with a sign that consists of twin peaks flanking a plateau (Figure 8.3d). The purpose of the cobweb sign is to indicate that the twin peaks–plateau represents a homonym of the Mixtec word *nduhua,* meaning "gully," rather than the Mixtec *yuvui,* meaning "gully, ravine between two hills" (M. E. Smith 1973a:48–49). Simi-larly, in one of the place signs in the Postconquest Lienzo of Jicayán, a cradle motif (*dzoco* in Mixtec) is included in a sign showing water (Figure 8.3e). The cradle tells the reader that the body of water in question is a spring, also *dzoco* in Mixtec, rather than a river (*yuta*), lake (*mini*), or swamp (*ndoyo*).

Still another example of the use of a phonetic indicator occurs in the place sign of the town of Tututepec in the coastal region of the Mixteca. The Mixtec name of Tututepec is *yucu dzaa,* or "Hill of the Bird," and the *dzaa* element of this name is represented by the head of an eagle whose beak contains a human chin (Figure 8.3f). The human chin (*dzaa* in Mixtec) indicates that the eagle head should be read as *dzaa* or "bird" rather than as *yaha* or *ya'a,* the Mixtec word for "eagle" (M. E. Smith 1973a:67).

My impression is that phonetic indicators are a fairly common feature of Mixtec writing, especially in the composition of place signs. In part, the use of phonetic indicators may be related to the fact that Mixtec is a tone language. That is, because many Mixtec words may have a variety of meanings depending on variations in tone, it is comparatively easy to find two meanings of a word that can be readily represented by pictorial signs, as in the examples given above of *nduhua* ("cobweb, gully"), *dzoco* ("cradle, spring") and *dzaa* ("human chin, bird").

### Widely Distributed Motifs That Function as Signs in Mixtec Writing

In a number of instances, motifs that occur in other regions of Mesoamerica—and which do not seem to function as signs in these other regions—are used as signs in Mixtec manuscripts. Such a motif is the band of chevrons often used in Mesoamerica as an enframing border, as in wall paintings from Teotihuacán (e.g., Miller 1973:Fig. 366) and in Late Classic Maya ceramics (e.g., S. Morley 1956:398). In the examples cited above, it is not known whether the chevron pattern has a specific meaning or whether it is being used decoratively.

In Mixtec manuscripts, however, bands of chevrons have a very specific meaning. When a chevron band appears in a personal or place name, it is functioning as a sign representing the word *yecu,* the Mixtec word for "enemy" (Smith 1973a:33, 1973b:78–79).

A band of chevrons also functions in Mixtec manuscripts in much the same way as does a road, with the chevrons replacing the footprints used in the bands that represent roads. In this case, what is being depicted is a "road to the enemy," or more colloquially, a "warpath," a pictorial convention first identified by Caso (1950:14). In most instances, an armed human figure is shown walking along the band of chevrons, followed by a scene showing the conquest of a specific place. This configuration reflects an idiom in the Mixtec language, one of the phrases in Mixtec for a person who wages war being *tay caca yecu,* or "the man who walks [to] the enemy" (M. E. Smith 1973a:33).

In one instance in Codex Colombino (19-III), the ruler 8 Deer is shown walking along a band of chevrons, and this scene is followed by a series of place signs that are not shown as conquered. Nancy Troike (1974:223) has offered the reasonable explanation that in this case 8 Deer is making a journey into a hostile region—that is, he is taking a "road to the enemy" but one that does not involve conquest of the named towns in enemy territory.

## SYMBOLS

The category of symbols, as distinguished from signs, is based on the function of the motif and on its distribution in regions of Mesoamerica that speak different languages. For example, when a horizontal band containing star motifs represents "the sky"—as it does in the opening mythological-origin scene in Codex Selden and in the wall paintings of Mitla (León 1901) and Santa Rita Corozal in British Honduras (Gann 1900)—then this band of stars is functioning as a symbol of the sky. When the same motif appears in the Mixtec manuscripts as a component of the personal name of a ruler, it is functioning as a sign, depicting *andevui*, the Mixtec word for "sky" (M. E. Smith 1973b:78). Similarly, a repoussé gold sun disk from a tomb at Zaachila (Paddock [ed.] 1966e:328, Fig. 33) seems to function as a symbol of the sun. When the same sun disk appears in a place sign in Codex Mendoza from the Valley of Mexico, it functions as a sign that represents *tonatiuh*, the Nahuatl name of the sun god (Barlow and MacAfee 1949:39); when this motif occurs in personal names of rulers in Mixtec codices, it functions as a sign for the Mixtec word for "sun," *ndicandii* (M. E. Smith 1973b:67, 81–82).

Some historians of writing use the terms *ideograph* or *ideogram* to refer to the type of motif that I call a *symbol*. Unfortunately, the terms *ideograph* or *ideogram* have often not been applied consistently and, at times, these terms have been used to refer to motifs that function as signs or to configurations of motifs that I call *pictorial conventions* (cf. Gelb 1963:35–36). Although the term *symbol* is by no means an ideal substitution for *ideograph* or *ideogram*—because *symbol*, too, has been variously defined—the term does indicate that the function of any motif to which it is applied is different from that of a sign.

Much of the symbolic vocabulary used in Mixtec writing—as well as many of the motifs that appear in signs—is by no means unique to the Mixteca but is characteristic of the Late Postclassic style seen throughout Mesoamerica and sometimes called Mixteca–Puebla or Mixteca–Cholula. This style is delineated by Nicholson:

> Among the most highly distinctive individual symbols are: solar and lunar disks, celestial and terrestrial bands, the Venus or bright star symbols, skulls and skeletons (with double-outlined bones), jade or *chalchihuitl,* water, fire and flame, heart, war (*atl-tlachinolli,* shield, arrows, and banner), mountain or place, "downy feather ball," flower (many variants), stylized eyes as

stars, stepped fret (*xicalcoliuqui*), sliced spiral shell (*ehecacozcatl*), and the twenty *tonalpohualli* signs [1960:614].

Notwithstanding the wide distribution of this symbolic vocabulary, a number of the specific symbols seem to have regional distributions—which may or may not be based on language—and some of the symbols undergo modifications in the various regions of Mesoamerica in which they appear. Indeed, one of the symbols for war listed by Nicholson, the *atl-tlachinolli* or "burning-water" motif, is based on a metaphor in the Nahuatl language and appears to be distributed in areas in which Nahuatl is the principal language spoken. As far as I know, the burning-water motif does not occur at all in manuscripts reflecting the Mixtec language.

Moreover, there is some indication that at least some of the symbolic vocabulary associated with the "Mixteca–Puebla" style may have originated in the Mixteca, since a few of the motifs seem to express the Mixtec—and no other—language. One such motif is the so-called star-eye that is used in Mixtec manuscripts within sky bands, in place signs, and as the eye of rain and other deities. In many dialects of Mixtec, the word for "eye" is the same as that for "star" except for variations in tone (M. E. Smith 1973a:59). The same cannot be said for the star-eye motif in manuscripts that reflect the Nahuatl language because the word in Nahuatl for "eye" is *ixtli* and that for "star" is *citlalli*.

Two additional examples of regional variations or modifications of widely distributed symbols are the "adjectives" that modify speech scrolls, and the types of straw thrones and mats. In both examples, variant forms can be distinguished and seem to reflect Valley of Mexico usage rather than the traditions seen in Mixtec manuscripts.

### Speech Scrolls and Their Adjectives

A scroll or volute being emitted from a human mouth is a symbol of speech in many regions of Mesoamerica. This symbol appears at least as early as the Classic period in wall paintings from Teotihuacán, in stone sculpture and wall paintings from Monte Albán, and in relief sculpture from the Classic Veracruz site of El Tajín. The use of this symbol continues through the Postclassic period and is also seen in Early Colonial manuscripts that still have elements of Preconquest style.

Although the basic speech scroll itself has a wide distribution, the pictorial adjectives that modify speech scrolls seem to show regional variations. In the Valley of Mexico region, from Classic-period Teotihuacán through the Late Postclassic Aztec period, when speech scrolls are modified by flowers, this indicates singing. To my knowledge, flowers never accompany speech scrolls in Mixtec manuscripts; instead, the adjectives used to modify speech scrolls suggest degrees of hardness (flint blades, stones) and softness ("downy feather balls").

In the story of the female ruler 6 Monkey as related in Codex Selden (7-III), she visits two rulers who receive her by emitting speech scrolls with flint blades. Spinden astutely suggested that 6 Monkey is being insulted by these two rulers; as he pointed out, the combination of speech scrolls and flint blades are "a logical ideograph for cutting words" (1935:435).

An instance of the use of a stone to modify a speech scroll occurs in the biography of the famous ruler and warrior 8 Deer "Tiger Claw" as it is narrated in Codex Bodley. On 9-II of Bodley, a prisoner captured by 8 Deer is presented to the ruler or priest 4 Tiger, and appended to the speech scroll of the person making the presentation is a stone motif—again, undoubtedly indicating stern or harsh speech.

In Codex Becker I (7-III), a man who is playing a drum has speech scrolls that are delineated by dots rather than a solid line, and a downy feather ball is placed on top of the configuration of speech scrolls. By contrast to the flint blades and stones that indicate "hard" words, the downy feather ball seems to indicate "soft" or dulcet words and, since they are attached to a musician, this conjunction of speech scrolls and downy feather ball may well indicate that he is singing.

As far as I know, the flint-blade, stone, and downy-feather-ball motifs are not used as adjectives describing speech scrolls in manuscripts from the Valley of Mexico region, nor are they known from other regions of Mesoamerica. Thus these adjectives may be a local Mixtec variation on the widely distributed speech-scroll symbol.

## Straw Thrones and Mats

In his study of pictorial writing that reflects the Nahuatl language, Charles Dibble (1971:324) includes in his list of ideographs the "mat or seat" motif, which symbolizes "authority, rulership, government." Although the mat or seat symbol is one seen in painting and sculpture from several regions of Mesoamerica, specific types of thrones and mats seem to have a regional distribution. For example, a throne that is shown as made of woven straw or *petate* and has a triangular shape in profile (Figure 8.4a) appears only in

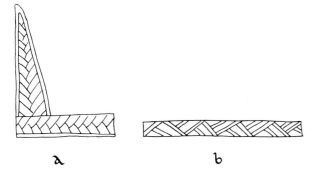

FIGURE 8.4. Straw thrones and mats: (a) throne typical of Valley of Mexico manuscripts; (b) rectangular mat typical of Mixtec manuscripts. (Drawing prepared by Caren Walt.)

those manuscripts that are from the Valley of Mexico or in manuscripts that exhibit considerable stylistic influence from the Valley of Mexico.

When this type of straw throne appears more than once or twice in manuscripts from the Mixtec-speaking region, these manuscripts also have the following three characteristics: a Postconquest date; a provenience within one of the regions of the Mixteca which paid tribute to the Aztecs prior to the Spanish Conquest; and other Valley of Mexico features, as, for example, the so-called Aztec woman's pose (Caso 1960:14; Robertson 1966:302). (In the Aztec woman's pose, seated female figures are shown kneeling with their legs tucked under their torsos; in Mixtec manuscripts, seated female figures usually have their legs placed in front of them.) One example of a manuscript that has all of these characteristics is the *Lienzo of Ihuitlán* (Caso 1961:237–49, 1965d:949). This *lienzo* is one of a group of assuredly Postconquest cloth documents from the Coixtlahuaca Basin (Parmenter 1961:2; M. E. Smith 1973a:182–184)—a region of the Mixteca Alta that paid tribute to the Aztecs prior to the Conquest, according to Codex Mendoza, a mid-sixteenth-century manuscript from the Valley of Mexico (Clark 1938:fol. 43/r). Not only are straw thrones seen in this *lienzo*, but all the female figures are seated in the Aztec woman's pose and all the place signs are identified by glosses in the Nahuatl language.

By way of contrast, the straw or *petate* throne does not occur at all in such Preconquest Mixtec screenfolds as Codices Nuttall, Bodley, Vienna, Colombino–Becker I, and Becker II. A few thrones with a back that is roughly triangular in profile appear in these manuscripts, but they are not shown as made of straw. For the most part, the rulers in the Preconquest Mixtec screenfolds are seated on footstool-like seats and low platforms, cushions (sometimes of jaguar hide), stones, and place signs or rectangular straw mats.

Codices Selden and Sánchez Solís are two Mixtec manuscripts that seem to be transitional between the screenfolds which lack straw thrones and the Postconquest manuscripts in which straw thrones appear frequently. The straw throne occurs once each in Codices Selden and Sánchez Solís: in connection with the death goddess 9 Grass on Selden 7-IV, and in connection with the first male ruler, 1 Alligator, shown on page 3 of Sánchez Solís.

The style of Codex Selden is Preconquest, although the manuscript was actually painted after the Conquest, because the latest date in the codex is A.D. 1556 (Caso 1964:14, 47, 52, 62, 94, 97). As discussed in Topic 74, Selden is probably from the town of Jaltepec in the Mixteca Alta, a town shown in Codex Mendoza as paying tribute to the Aztecs of the Valley of Mexico (Clark 1938:fol. 43/r). In its overall style and iconography, however, Selden is Mixtec, with few indications of Valley of Mexico intrusions.

In common with Codex Selden, Codex Sánchez Solís is basically Preconquest in style. This manuscript appears to deal in part with rulers from the Mixteca Baja region of northern Oaxaca and southern Puebla (M. E. Smith 1973a:18–19), another Mixtec region that paid tribute to the Aztecs prior to the Conquest. Unlike Selden, Sánchez Solís has a number of Valley of Mexico features, such as the Aztec woman's pose and the use within hill signs of a pattern of wavy crisscrossed lines interspersed with dots (e.g., Figure 8.3a), a pattern seen in such Postconquest manuscripts from the Valley of Mexico as Codex Xolotl (Dibble 1951).

In general, then, the straw-throne motif is common in Postconquest manuscripts from the Valley of Mexico region but rare in Preconquest manuscripts from the Mixtec-speaking region. When the motif occurs in Mixtec manuscripts at all, it occurs in those that were painted after, or around the time of, the Spanish Conquest, and it usually appears in conjunction with other Valley of Mexico features.

In some of the Preconquest Mixtec manuscripts, rectangular woven straw mats serve as platforms for seated couples (Figure 8.4b); but even here there is considerable variation that may be due to regional or temporal differences. Woven straw mats are most prevalent in Codices Bodley, Selden, and Becker II—three screenfolds presumed to have been painted around the time of, or soon after, the Spanish Conquest. In manuscripts that may be earlier in date or from regions other than those where Bodley, Selden, and Becker II originated, the straw mat does not appear at all or is comparatively rare. No straw mats are shown in Codex Colombino–Becker I or on the reverse of Codex Vienna; only one straw mat appears in Codex Nuttall (24-II), and on the obverse of Codex Vienna, the straw mat appears only with two pairs of mythological ancestors (35-I, 35-II, 34-I).

When a couple is shown seated on a straw mat or *petate* in the Mixtec manuscripts, this configuration seems to relate as much to their marriage as it does to the mat as a symbol of authority or government. One of the Mixtec idioms for royal marriage recorded in the sixteenth-century Mixtec grammar of Fray Antonio de los Reyes can be translated as "there was a royal celebration of the *petate*" (1890:76). Hence when a straw mat or *petate* is shown as the platform for a marriage pair, the mat is related to this Mixtec idiom.

As can be seen from the examples discussed above, many of the motifs that function as symbols in the Mixtec writing system are also seen in regions of Mesoamerica outside of the Mixteca, but some of these motifs show distinctive variations or adaptations in different regions. Some of these variations may, in part, be related to idioms in a specific native language, as the example of the use of the *petate* for marriage pairs in Mixtec manuscripts and the idiom for royal marriage in the Mixtec language that also contains the *petate* motif. Other variations may, perhaps, be related to local customs or ceremonies. Further studies could—and should—be made of the regional variations in symbols that occur in writing systems reflecting different native languages. Such studies are essential, not merely to determine more precisely the vocabulary of motifs used in any one writing system, but to define the character of the writing system as a whole.

## PICTORIAL CONVENTIONS

Pictorial conventions are, for the most part, relatively straightforward portrayals of a scene or event with little reference to language. They often involve configurations of figures and motifs, for example, the convention for marriage, indicated by the confrontation of a male and a female figure, or the convention for conquest, shown by a place sign pierced with an arrow.

In some histories of writing these pictorial conventions are called *pictographs,* a term that has been used even more vaguely than the terms *ideograph* or *ideogram* discussed previously (page 242). Indeed, any type of pictorial motif or configuration—from a rock carving showing a fairly representational hunting scene to an abstract calendrical sign—has at one time or another been described as a pictograph. As a result, the term has become almost meaningless and I feel that it is best replaced by the phrase *pictorial convention*.

The pictorial conventions have been extensively commented on in earlier studies of the Mixtec history manuscripts (Nuttall 1902; Clark 1912; Long 1926; Spinden 1935; Caso 1949, 1950, 1960:14–19, 1965d; M. E. Smith 1973a:20–35).[3] In part, these conventions are better known than the specific signs that appear in the manuscripts, because the conventions are, by their very nature, more instantly recognizable and do not depend on a knowledge of the Mixtec language for their interpretation. In common with some of the symbols used in Mixtec writing, many of the pictorial conventions are by no means unique to Mixtec manuscripts, but are also seen in stone sculpture and wall painting from other regions of Mesoamerica and—most especially—in Postconquest manuscripts from the Nahuatl-speaking region in and around the Valley of Mexico.

For example, the representation of conquest by a place sign pierced with an arrow is easily comprehensible without reference to language, and this convention also has analogies to the pictorial traditions of other regions. In the historical section of the Postconquest Codex Telleriano Remensis from the Valley of Mexico (Hamy 1899; Robertson 1959a:Pl. 28), the conquest of a town is often indicated by the town's place sign flanked by two armed men, one of whom holds a bow and arrow, with the arrow shown piercing the hill of the place sign. The warriors-attacking place sign seen in Telleriano Remensis is a more prolix and less economical representation than the place-sign-with-arrow seen in Mixtec manuscripts, but it is essentially the same pictorial convention and can be interpreted without reference to either the Mixtec or Nahuatl languages.

Nonetheless, the pictorial representation of conquest seen in the Mixtec manuscripts does have a counterpart in an idiom of the Mixtec language. In the sixteenth-century Span-

---

[3] I am by no means implying in this discussion that all the pictorial conventions used in the Mixtec codices are completely understood. At this writing, for example, Nancy Troike (1975) is working on the meaning of the limited number of postures and gestures seen in these manuscripts.

ish–Mixtec dictionary of Fray Francisco de Alvarado, the first definition given for the verb "to conquer" (*conquistar*) is *chihi nduvua ñuhu ñaha*, which means "to put an arrow into the lands of another," a phrase that described precisely the pictorial convention seen in the painted manuscripts. Thus, in common with some of the symbols used in Mixtec codices, some of the pictorial conventions may have a stronger relationship to language than has previously been suspected.

## CONCLUSIONS

The purpose of this study has been not merely to characterize the Mixtec writing system, but also to demonstrate that any Preconquest Mesoamerican writing system must be related specifically to the language the writing represents. This view holds not only for the system that reflects the Mixtec language, but also for writing that may represent Zapotec, Huastec, Tarascan, or any other New World native language.

To date, the two most extensively studied writing systems are those that express the Nahuatl and Maya languages. Because more is known about these two systems, there has been a tendency (often, perhaps, an unconscious tendency) to relate the lesser-known systems of writing to these better-documented systems, especially if there is a similarity between the forms of the signs, symbols, and pictorial conventions seen in the lesser-known writing systems and those of either Nahuatl or Maya writing. In the case of Mixtec writing, the pictorial conventions and the motifs used in signs and symbols are often similar to those seen in Postconquest manuscripts from the Nahuatl-speaking region of central Mexico, and hence the Mixtec motifs have frequently been given Nahuatl names or interpreted by means of Nahuatl texts. The interpretation of Mixtec motifs by analogies with their Nahuatl counterparts is extremely unsatisfactory and often tends to obscure the meanings of the Mixtec motifs.

Although it cannot be denied that much of the imagery seen in Mixtec writing has a wide distribution throughout Mesoamerica in the Late Postclassic period, regional adaptations of some of these images may well be significant and may well be related to language or to local customs or ceremonies. Usually, only signs show a direct relationship to the language on which a native writing system is based. But, as has been demonstrated above, symbols and pictorial conventions may, at times, reflect metaphors and idioms of a specific native language. Thus I think it is imperative that each native writing system be related to the language it represents rather than to another language with a similar form of writing.

## TOPIC 72
## Differences between Mixtec and Aztec Writing

DONALD ROBERTSON

There are several similarities and differences between the Mixtec and Aztec writing systems that are worthy of mention.

The Aztec writing system seems to be based on a relation between the written form and the sound of the name of the word when pronounced. The pictorial form of the reed called *acatl* is used to represent the day-name in the calendar. In other words, as the pictures are identified or "read," they automatically give the corresponding sound. The same system seems to have been used in Oaxaca, but there a different set of sounds would be triggered by the same sign. That is, as in the case of written Chinese or the Arabic numbers, any Chinese dialect can be used to vocalize the written forms, and any spoken language can do the same for our numbers. The written or painted form is thus common to both the Oaxacan and Aztec systems, but the language it represents can be any dialect of Nahuatl or any Oaxacan language, as well as English, Spanish, German, French, or other modern language.

Except for the numbers, the two systems do not seem, at least on the level of the Late Postclassic manuscripts, to present great differences. In most Mixtec writing, the number 5 is represented by five dots. The main exceptions are certain manuscripts from the Borgia Group in which bars appear for the number 5. This exception is potentially of great importance for separating the manuscripts into groups, and may someday work as an invaluable clue to the locus of origin of those using the bar-equals-5 group. The presence of the bar-equals-5 system in the stelae of Monte Albán makes a link between these manuscripts and Monte Albán very likely because they are surely not Maya on the basis of content and formal comparison with Maya manuscripts, the other group that uses the bar-equals-five system.

The other well-known difference is the presence of the interlocking A–O used in the Mixtec historical manuscripts to indicate that a calendrical date represents a year, not a person's name or a day in the calendar. This useful pointer sign is absent in the Aztec manuscripts so consistently that its presence has been used as a diagnostic of Mixtec manuscripts, and thus its appearance in the Codex Borgia, for instance, links that manuscript to the Mixtecs.

## TOPIC 73
## Postclassic Settlement Patterns in the Nochixtlán Valley

RONALD SPORES

Perhaps no part of the Mixteca Alta shows the Postclassic buildup of population and political power more clearly than the Yanhuitlán–Nochixtlán Valley. This buildup took place during the Natividad phase, to which we have assigned a time span of A.D. 1000 to 1520–1535 (Spores 1972).

The Natividad phase represented the time of maximum

occupation of the Nochixtlán Valley (see Figure 8.5). A total of 159 of the 176 sites in the valley show indications of utilization during this period, and intensive use is indicated in 113 sites occupied at various times during the phase.

Individual sector concentration runs as follows: Yanhuitlán sector, 72 of 72 sites occupied during Natividad

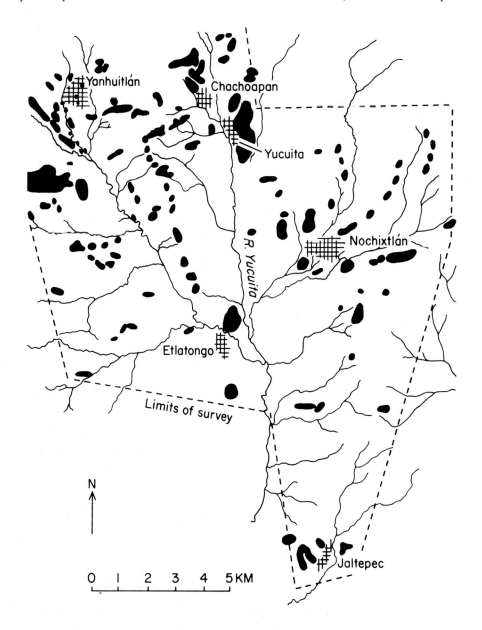

FIGURE 8.5. The Nochixtlán Valley, showing settlements of the Natividad phase.

phase; Yucuita sector, 37 of 39 sites occupied; Nochixtlán sector, 32 of 41 sites occupied; Etlatongo–Jaltepec sector, 18 of 23 sites occupied.

In terms of sites occupied, the above figures represent absolute maximums for all sectors except Nochixtlán (which had 35 of 41 sites occupied during the Las Flores phase). The greatest increase came in the Yanhuitlán sector, where there was an increase from 32 sites in Las Flores times to 72 sites (comparable to or larger than those of the Las Flores phase) in Natividad times. This increase suggests a substantial shift in settlement toward the Yanhuitlán sector. I believe that shift is correlated with a rise to dominance of the kingdom of Yanhuitlán and with intensification of occupation in settlements under its political control.

The Natividad phase was a period of reduction in monumental architecture compared with earlier times. Although tendencies to congregate in relatively large and compact centers persisted, the more monumental material manifestations of urbanization underwent a noticeable decline. Ceremonial structures continued to be built, but they were far less imposing than in earlier times. Ruling elites appear to have lacked either the desire or the necessary power or organizational ability to create impressive architectural complexes on a par with those of the Classic period.

There is a strong "parasitic" tendency evident, whereby centers constructed in earlier times continued to be utilized, not as complex functioning communities, but probably as ritual centers. Dense-to-moderate concentrations of Natividad ceramics are found deposited in and around major mound–plaza–court complexes at such sites as Yucuñudahui, Cerro Jazmín, Jaltepec, and Topiltepec. At former major Las Flores sites, Natividad architecture is sometimes present (e.g., at Area X, Yucuñudahui), but it is peripheral to the main central areas and is relatively insignificant. This archaeological demonstration of the continued utilization of the ancient centers for ceremonial purposes conforms exceedingly well to the pattern inferred from the historical record for the sixteenth century (Spores 1967:96–98).

Generally speaking, houses were smaller and more widely spaced than in Las Flores or Ramos times, but there were clear exceptions. As in earlier times, there was a marked trend toward a dichotomous pattern whereby centers were differentiated internally, and centers also differed from dependencies. Centers such as Pueblo Viejo de Chachoapan (sites N 205 A–G, K, M), Loma de Ayuxi of Yanhuitlán (N 005, N 006, N 007), Pueblo Viejo de Nochixtlán (N 405), Yucuita (N 203 E and J), and Etlatongo (N 802) contained a core of "elite" multicomponent dwelling complexes ("palaces") built of stone and adobe walls, sometimes faced with stone-slab veneering, plaster interior walls and floors, drainage systems, and so forth. Elite clusters were flanked by smaller single- or double-celled structural units that, on the basis of location, appearance of functionally diverse ceramic and lithic assemblages, deep culinary debris, hearths and ash as recovered in excavated units (N 205 M, N; 428 A, B, C, and N 271 H), appear to be dwelling areas for lower-ranking families.

The second type of site is the dependency, rancho, or *sujeto*-type settlement found by the dozens throughout the valley. These may be large or small, but tend to be composed of relatively uniform one- and two-celled structures throughout. Some of the dependency sites contain relatively small mound structures of undetermined function; others have no obvious unusual architectural features. Many of the Natividad dependency sites are thin and have been badly disturbed by stone and adobe collectors, rendering it difficult to determine precise conformations or to conduct meaningful excavations aimed at working out architectural complexes. Numerous sites are well preserved, however, and further work in these localities is imperative.

This was the period of maximum *lama–bordo* terracing, a major technological and adaptive innovation, which we have interpreted as a mechanism for increasing agricultural production in response to increasing needs of an expanding population, growing demands of a tribute-collecting royal–noble elite, and the superimposed tributary demands of the Culhua–Mexica Empire (Spores 1969). New Postclassic settlements appeared far up the tributary valleys of the Nochixtlán Valley in conjunction with *lama–bordo* terraces at Soyaltepec, Pozoltepec, Tonaltepec, and Chicahua, suggesting an adaptive response to pressures to increase agricultural productivity by applying the *lama–bordo* technique to areas not formerly utilized for agricultural purposes.

The crowding and downhill shift in settlement placement are particularly noticeable in the Yanhuitlán arm of the valley, where 26 sites appear on the low lomas and buttes and 9 sites appear on the alluvium of the valley floor. Although some of the downhill shift could reflect Spanish pressure to resettle some of the population (which continued to employ a Natividad ceramic complex), I believe the shift took place long before the Conquest. This tendency toward occupational utilization of the valuable flat alluvial lands had begun in the Yanhuitlán sector as early as Ramos times (2 sites), continued into Las Flores (3 sites) and peaked in Natividad times. Further, only 3 of the 9 valley sites and 8 of 26 loma sites showed Convento (European-influenced) ceramics (Spores 1972). Although Spanish clerics and administrators may have encouraged continuation of the pattern, I believe initial reorientations took place long before the Spanish Conquest and as a result of a combination of internal demographic pressures and internally and externally induced socioeconomic factors.

The high ridges and low lomas preferred in Las Flores times continued to be occupied, but there was a noticeable shift in Postclassic settlement to the tapering ends of ridges, lower piedmonts, and low lomas. Although most sites are near defensible mountains, *cerros*, and ridges to which populations fled when settlements were attacked, there is little other material indication of defensive considerations in settlement placement. The overwhelming majority of sites are in low locations, apparently unprotected and highly vulnerable to attack. Site placement and lack of fortification would imply that the Natividad phase was a time of peace and tranquility in the valley. Neither the historic record nor the archaeological evidence suggest that the Postclassic was a time of high-level intercommunity conflict within the Nochixtlán Valley. The documentation of the sixteenth century (e.g., AGI *Escribanía de Cámara* 162; *relaciones* of 1579–1580) suggests that the kingdom of Yanhuitlán had been quite stable for four to five centuries before the Conquest. Certainly, the web of marital alliances among the ruling families of the various kingdoms located in the valley, as well as economic interdependence (in terms of community specializations), must have served to inhibit intercommunity conflict, at least to some extent.

While internal peace does seem to typify the Natividad period, two points are very clear: (1) there was a very real external threat from the Culhua–Mexica Empire that the valley communities were unable to resist even through interregional alliances. The ease with which the armies of the Empire overwhelmed the hastily assembled Mixtec armies and brought the area under control would suggest a less-than-brilliant military capability; and (2) the ethnohistorical sources (Spores 1965, 1967; *relaciones* of 1579–1580) make it clear that the Postclassic was a time of rather intense intercommunity and interregional conflict in the greater Mixteca. It was a time of expansion not only of Mexico–Texcoco–Tacuba but of the kingdom–empire of Tututepec, whose armies raided from their home base in the Mixteca de la Costa well up into the Mixteca Alta. Other communities and seats of important kingdoms—Tilantongo, Tlaxiaco, Teposcolula, Mitlatongo, Tamazola, and Tejupan—also engaged in raiding and warfare. But the macrocosm does not necessarily reflect internal patterns of intercommunity relations in the Nochixtlán Valley. In fact, external threat may have served to dampen emergent hostilities between communities within the valley and brought them into closer cooperation than might normally have been the case. This community cooperation, added to the probable political dominance of Yanhuitlán, the requirements of economic interdependence, the intercommunity ceremonial cycle, and the social interdependence of the aristocratic families, brought about a period of peaceful coexistence in the valley that lasted from well before the Spanish Conquest until late in the sixteenth century. On this point, historical and archaeological records are in agreement.

The primary focus of sociopolitical power and demographic concentration that had been centered in Yucuita in Ramos times and Yucuñudahui in Las Flores times shifted to Yanhuitlán in Natividad times. Kingdoms were seated at Yanhuitlán, Nochixtlán, Etlatongo, Chachoapan, Soyaltepec, Jaltepec, and Tiltepec. All of the other settlements in the valley were subject to (i.e., socioeconomically integrated into) one of these kingdoms. Clearly the largest and most important of the valley kingdoms was Yanhuitlán, whose ruling lineage controlled at least 20 other settlements, including Añañe, Suchixtlán, Tillo, Yucucui, Tlatayapan, Tlachitongo, Sinaxtla, Sayultepec, Andúa, Chindúa, Yucuita, Amatlán, Zahuatlán, Quilitongo, Zachio, Jaltepetongo, Añuma, Adequez, Tecomatlán, and Pozoltepec (Spores 1967:90–104).

By virtue of the fluid nature of Mixtec kingdoms, which could change in composition and in terms of relative importance from generation to generation, it is difficult to establish at any given time the precise composition of the political entity. This point is, however, less important for present purposes than for understanding the reformulating processes (e.g., community fission and fusion) that were constantly operative as a result of (1) fluctuating patterns of inheritance, marital alliance, accession, and deletion of subject communities by agreement or through conquest and rebellion; (2) colonization of new areas at the direction of rulers of the nuclear kingdoms; (3) rising and declining population; (4) differential ties to the outside; and (5) changing utilization of a relatively stable natural environment with highly persistent forms of resource exploitation. Full delineation of this system requires lengthy treatment that must, for the present, be deferred.

## TOPIC 74
## Codex Selden: A Manuscript from the Valley of Nochixtlán?

MARY ELIZABETH SMITH

Codex Selden is one of a small group of screenfold manuscripts from the Mixtec-speaking region of southern Mexico that delineate the genealogies of some of the hereditary native rulers of this region. The codex is now in the Bodleian Library at Oxford, where it is catalogued as 3135 (A.2).

The earliest publication of Codex Selden was a color lithographic copy included in Volume I of Lord Kingsborough's monumental *Antiquities of Mexico* (1831). More recently, Alfonso Caso (1964) published a color photographic facsimile of the manuscript accompanied by a de-

tailed commentary on its contents. Caso's work also lists and discusses the earlier literature on the codex.

The pictorial narrative of Codex Selden deals principally with the genealogy of one town whose rulers presumably commissioned the painting of the manuscript. The as-yet-unidentified sign of this town was first described in English by Herbert J. Spinden (1935) as "Cloud-Belching Mountain"; in the English translations of Caso's extensive interpretations of the Mixtec histories (1960, 1964; Caso and Smith 1966), the description has been shortened to "Belching Mountain." In the original Spanish text of these same commentaries, Caso himself refers to the place sign as *Montaña que escupe* ("Mountain that spits").

All that is known of the history of Codex Selden prior to its acquisition by the Bodleian Library in the mid-seventeenth century is that the manuscript was formerly in the collection of the English lawyer and scholar John Selden, for whom the codex is now named. Selden purchased many Oriental manuscripts, and in his collection catalogue the Mexican manuscript under discussion is considered to have been an "Oriental book" (Caso 1964:18, 66, n. 16). Shortly after the death of John Selden in 1654, most of his manuscripts and papers were transferred to the Bodleian Library.

As yet, nothing is known of the history of Codex Selden before it left Mexico; the purpose of this topic is to propose a more specific provenience within the Mixteca for this manuscript: the Valley of Nochixtlán in the Mixteca Alta.

## THE GLOSS WRITTEN ON CODEX SELDEN

On the reverse of the first page of Codex Selden is a three-line text written in European script. A transcription of this text made by Philip Dark (1959:526) is as follows:

*petajna*
*don Diego hijo de don Domingo*
*yucha nam. . . .*

The meaning of the word or phrase *petajna*, visible as the first line of the text, is unknown. In all likelihood, part of the inscription on the first line is now missing, because the letters *petajna* appear above the center of the second line of the inscription, probably indicating that the initial letters of the first line are no longer visible.

The second line of the inscription names "Don Diego, son of Don Domingo," and the third line gives a place name in Mixtec. As noted above, Dark has transcribed this Mixtec name as *yucha nam . . . ,* a name which he tentatively suggested is the equivalent of *yucu nama,* the Mixtec name of the town of Santiago Amoltepec in the southern Mixteca Alta. Alfonso Caso (1964:19, 67) objected to Dark's hypothesis that Codex Selden was from Santiago Amoltepec, because the known sign for Amoltepec—a hill with a plant, illustrating both the Mixtec and Nahuatl names of the town, "hill of the *amole* or soap plant"—is very different from the "Belching Mountain" sign, the principal place sign in Codex Selden.[1]

Another reason why I would object to Dark's interpretation of this place name is his equating of *yucha*, the first word on the third line of the inscription, with the Mixtec word *yucu* meaning "hill." Rather, the word *yucha* is a dialect variation of *yuta*, meaning "river." In the standard sixteenth-century sources on the Mixtec language, such as the Spanish–Mixtec dictionary of Fray Francisco de Alvarado (Jiménez Moreno 1962) and the Mixtec grammar of Fray Antonio de los Reyes (1890), the Mixtec word for river is given as *yuta;* but in the sixteenth-century documents from the Valley of Nochixtlán, the word for river is usually written in European script as *yucha* (as, for example, in lists of place names from the Nochixtlán Valley published in Spores 1967:165–167). Moreover, in the 1964 reproduction of Codex Selden, the second section of the place name on the third line of the gloss does not appear to be *nam . . .* as transcribed by Dark, but *ña . . . ,* with a tilde over the *n.*

If the place name on the third line of the inscription on Codex Selden is *yucha ña . . . ,* and the initial word *yucha* means "river," the only known town name in the Mixteca which this gloss could represent is that of Chachoapan in the Valley of Nochixtlán, whose Mixtec name is *yuta ñani* (Reyes 1890:88). This Mixtec name is usually translated as "river of the brother(s)," although *ñani* can mean "mole" (the animal) as well as "brother(s)."

The Mixtec name *yuta ñani* ("river of the mole" or "river of the brothers") does not seem to be represented by any of the place signs in Codex Selden, and there may be two reasons for this: (1) Chachoapan had a second Mixtec name other than *yuta ñani*, a name that has not been recorded in the standard sixteenth-century sources, such as the list of Mixtec town names given at the end of the grammar by Fray Antonio de los Reyes (1890:88–93),[2] or (2) Codex Selden was not commissioned by the native rulers of Chachoapan, but was inherited by these rulers in the early Colonial period.

As to the possible connection between the "Don Diego, son of Don Domingo" mentioned in the gloss on Codex Selden and the known Early Colonial native rulers of Chachoapan, Colonial written documents dealing with Chachoapan (AGN Tierras 3343-12; summarized in Spores 1967:135) indicate that soon after the Spanish Conquest the native ruler of this town was Domingo *Cunquisi* (the last name being the calendrical name 1, 2, or 3 Flint in Mixtec). Domingo *Cunquisi* died without heirs, and the *cacicazgo* of Chachoapan was inherited by his brother Diego *Ñuqh* (the last name being the calendrical name 6 Motion in Mixtec). Unfortunately, the name of the father of Domingo *Cunquisi* and Diego *Ñuqh* is not known so that it is a moot point whether Diego *Ñuqh*'s father as well as his brother were

---

[1] The sign of Santiago Amoltepec appears in the 1580 *Relación Geográfica* map of this town, now in the Latin American Library of the University of Texas at Austin (Robertson 1959b:544, Fig. 3; Caso 1960:18–19). The Mixtec name of Amoltepec is given as *yucu nama* in the text of the 1580 *Relación Geográfica* (RMEH I:177) and in the list of Mixtec town names published by Fray Antonio de los Reyes (1890:89). A second town in the Mixteca Alta whose present-day name is San Pedro Yucunama in the former district of Teposcolula. A drawing of the place sign of Yucunama from an otherwise unpublished *lienzo* from the latter town is included in Caso's Selden commentary (1964:19, Fig. 1).

[2] A well-documented example of a town's having two Mixtec names, one of which supplanted the other, is recorded in the 1581 *Relación Geográfica* of Acatlán in the Mixteca Baja (Vera 1581:58–59). According to the *Relación,* Acatlán was formerly named in Mixtec *yucu yuxi* ("hill of precious stones [turquoise]"), and in the sixteenth century the town was also called in Mixtec *yutta tixaa* ("water filled with ashes"). Only this second name is included in the list of Mixtec place names compiled by Fray Antonio de los Reyes and published in 1593 (1890:90).

both named Domingo. It is possible that if the father died
before the Spanish Conquest of the Mixteca Alta, he was not
baptized with a Christian name.

Another problem is that while Codex Selden provides genealogical information well into the Colonial period—with
its latest date being 1556 according to Alfonso Caso's chronology (1964:52,97)—no male ruler with the calendrical
name 6 Motion appears in the pictorial narrative, and the
only male person named 1, 2, or 3 Flint who appears in
Selden seems not to be Domingo *Cunquisi* of Chachoapan.
The person in question is 2 Flint "Tlaloc Sun," who is shown
on Selden 18-II with his wife 5 Wind "Garland of Cocoa
Flowers" at "Hill of the Yellow Disk." This couple is depicted as the parents of the noblewoman 2 Motion "Earth
Figure (or Xolotl) Emerging from a Butterfly," who married
4 Reed "Tlahuizcalpantecuhtli Sun" of "Belching Mountain" in 1503 (Caso 1964:44,91). Because the nobleman 2
Flint in Codex Selden is shown as a parent of a daughter of
marriageable age, it seems unlikely that he is Domingo *Cunquisi*, who is known to have died without heirs. Moreover,
the "Hill with Yellow Disk" place sign with which 2 Flint is
associated in Selden 18–II does not represent the known
Mixtec name of Chachoapan, although it is possible that the
"Hill with Yellow Disk" may have been ruled by 2 Flint's
wife 5 Wind, rather than by 2 Flint himself.

Thus, the gloss written in the Colonial period on the outside of Codex Selden includes a Mixtec town name which is
assuredly the name of Chachoapan in the Nochixtlán Valley. But, as far as can be determined at the present time,
neither the rulers of Chachoapan nor the place sign of this
town appear in the pictorial narrative of the codex.

## GROUP OF PLACE SIGNS
## ASSOCIATED WITH THE FIRST
## RULER OF "BELCHING
## MOUNTAIN"

Another indication that Codex Selden may be from the
Valley of Nochixtlán is a group of 14 place signs shown on
Selden 3-IV through 4-III as associated with the nobleman
10 Reed "Flames–Eagle," the first ruler of Belching Mountain. Three of these 14 signs can be surely identified, and all
three represent names of towns in the Valley of Nochixtlán.

The scene in question begins on Selden 3-III where 10
Reed is shown facing a group of 20 objects, presumably
offerings. Following the depiction of the 20 objects are the
14 place signs. Associated with the first 12 are named persons; no persons are shown with the last 2 place signs of the
sequence, and in four instances two persons seem to be connected with a single place sign (Frieze with Man who Points
Upward on 4-I and Earth Monster Frieze, White Earth Hill,
Hill with Tigerskin Necklace on 4-II). Several of these persons have only calendrical names and lack personal names,
perhaps indicating that they are *principales*, or secondary

nobility who ruled subject towns, rather than *caciques* who
ruled *cabeceras* or major town units.

Alfonso Caso (1964: 29, 76) has interpreted this sequence
as a pilgrimage made by the ruler 10 Reed to the 14 places
represented by the signs on Selden 3-IV through 4-III, with
the 20 objects shown on page 3, III-IV being taken with him
on this pilgrimage. But there is no evidence—such as bands
of footprints—that 10 Reed is making a pilgrimage, and it
seems to me more likely that the persons from the 14 places
are bringing the 20 objects to the ruler and that these objects
represent tribute given to 10 Reed.

It is also possible that, because 10 Reed is the first ruler of
"Belching Mountain," this entire sequence represents an
"offering of the royal insignia" ceremony of the type depicted in such early Colonial Mixtec manuscripts as the Map
of Teozacoalco (Caso 1949:160, 162) and Lienzo of
Zacatepec 1 (M. E. Smith 1973a:111). However, while an
"offering of the royal insignia" scene usually shows a group
of noblemen making a presentation to one ruler, the noblemen making the offering are usually not shown seated on
place signs as is the case with the noblemen who appear to be
presenting offerings in Selden 3-IV through 4-III.

Still another possibility is that the confrontation of 10
Reed with 14 places involves an alliance, much as that which
is depicted on Nuttall 54–68, where the famous ruler 8 Deer
"Tiger Claw" and his half-brother 12 Motion meet with 112
persons. In the case of this scene in Nuttall, however, no
series of offerings is associated with the person or persons
convening the meeting, as is the case of the group of 20
objects shown in front of 10 Reed in Selden 3, III-IV.

Whether we are dealing with allies, tribute-paying subjects, or neighboring towns who are confirming that they
recognize 10 Reed as ruler of "Belching Mountain," it
would seem that 10 Reed is the authoritative figure in the
scene that begins on Selden 3-III and ends on Selden 4-III
because connected with the figure of 10 Reed are speech
scrolls, a traditional symbol of power or authority. For the
purposes of this topic, only 3 of the 14 place signs that can be
securely identified will be discussed. As mentioned above,
these 3 signs represent names of towns in the Valley of
Nochixtlán, and it seems likely that the majority of the 14
place signs in this group—though most of them are as yet
unidentified—may also represent names of towns in this
region.

### The Sign of Zahuatlán

The third of the 14 place signs associated with the ruler 10
Reed appears on the left side of Selden 3-IV and consists of a
hill containing a small male figure who holds a shield in one
hand and a flower in the other (Figure 8.6a). The person
seated on this sign is 4 Grass "Bleeding Eagle," who does not
appear in any other Mixtec manuscript.

This same place sign also appears on pages 11-II and 13-I
of Codex Selden. In the first instance (Figure 8.6b), the small

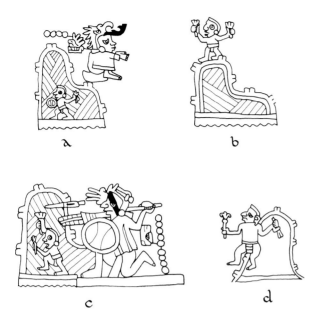

FIGURE 8.6. The sign of Zahuatlán: (a) Codex Selden 3-IV; (b) Codex Selden 11-II; (c) Codex Selden 13-II; (d) Codex Muro 7. (Drawing prepared by Caren Walt.)

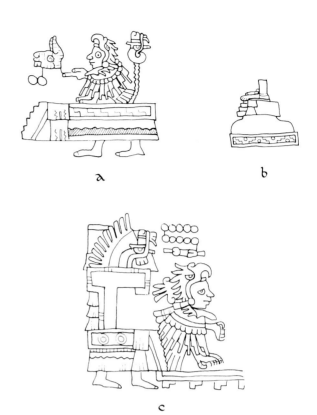

FIGURE 8.7. The sign of Sachio: (a) Codex Selden 4-I; (b) Codex of Yanhuitlán, Pl. VII; (c) Codex Selden 3-II. (Drawing prepared by Caren Walt.)

figure is shown on top of the hill, rather than within it, and he carries flowers in both hands and no weapons. In this case, the place is shown as ruled by the nobleman 5 Dog "Earth Figure (or Xolotl) Wearing a Tigerskin" and the noblewoman 7 Motion "Jewelled Cobweb," the parents of the noblewoman 12 Rain "Bleeding Feathers–Butterfly," who married 13 Wind "Ballcourt with Warbands" of "Belching Mountain." Again, none of these persons appears in any other Mixtec manuscript.

In the second instance, on Selden 13-II (Figure 8.6c), the place is shown being conquered by 9 Lizard "Flaming Face," ruler of "Belching Mountain." Here, the small male figure connected with the place sign is shown within the hill and holds flowers in both hands. He also has one foot raised, almost as though he were fleeing the attacking 9 Lizard.

Outside of Codex Selden, the only other Mixtec manuscript in which this place sign occurs is on page 7 of Codex Muro (Figure 8.6d), a Colonial-period manuscript from San Pedro Cántaros, a town on the eastern edge of the Valley of Nochixtlán. The sign appears in the lower-left corner of page 7, below the figure of the noblewoman 4 Water "Turquoise Jewel within a Fan." In this case, the male figure connected with the place sign is superimposed on the left border of the hill and carries a flower in one hand and an atlatl in the other. The gloss written above the figure of 4 Water in Codex Muro indicates that this place is her birthplace and that the town's Mixtec name is *yucu nicata*, which can be translated as "the hill that danced." (*Yucu* = "hill"; *ni-* is a past-tense prefix; *cata* is a form of the verb *sita*, meaning "to dance, sing"). According to a sixteenth-century

document which lists the Mixtec names of former subjects of Yanhuitlán, *yucu nicata* is the Mixtec name of the town of Magdalena Zahuatlán in the Valley of Nochixtlán, located about 8 km south of Nochixtlán.[3]

## The Sign of Sachio

The fourth of the group of 14 place signs under consideration appears on the left side of Selden 4-I and consists of a temple platform supported by two human feet (Figure 8.7a). Alfonso Caso (1964:30, 77) described this place sign as "The Temple from which the Alligator is Born," considering the umbilical cord attached to an alligator head as part of the temple base. But it seems to me equally likely that the umbilical cord and alligator head may be part of the personal name of the ruler 2 Rabbit, who is seated on the temple base and who wears an eagle costume to which the umbilical cord

---

[3]The Mixtec name of Zahuatlán is given as *yucu nicata* in a 1565 list of subjects and barrios of Yanhuitlán (AGI, *Escribanía de Cámara* 162; published in Spores 1967:194–196). At an unknown time after this list was compiled, the Mixtec name of Zahuatlán was shortened to *yucu cata* (Martínez Gracida 1888b:430–431; present-day Mixtec speaker from neighboring Jaltepetongo).

seems to be attached. Unfortunately, 2 Rabbit is another of the many persons in Codex Selden who does not appear in any other extant Mixtec manuscript, so it cannot be determined by comparing this representation with other depictions of him whether the umbilical cord and alligator head are part of his personal name.

The essential elements of the place sign on Selden 4-I—that is, human feet and a temple platform—are the same as those of a place sign shown with a group of 12 place signs on a page of the Codex of Yanhuitlán that seems to illustrate names of places formerly subject to Yanhuitlán (Jiménez Moreno and Mateos Higuera 1940:Pl. VII; Figure 8.7b of this chapter). The sign in the Yanhuitlán Codex shows a single human foot placed on a temple base that in turn rests on a hill above a frieze with geometric decorations. I have previously identified this sign as representing the name of San Andrés Sachio in the Valley of Nochixtlán, located about 8 km southeast of Nochixtlán (Smith 1973a:50). *Sachio* means "at the foot of the temple platform"; *sa-* is an abbreviated form of *saha,* meaning "foot, at the foot of," and *chiyo* means "temple platform." Thus the place sign on the left side of Selden 4-I undoubtedly represents the name of Sachio.

It is likely that a sign that appears earlier in Codex Selden also represents Sachio. On page 3-II of the manuscript, in the scene prior to the meeting of 10 Reed "Flames–Eagle" with rulers from 14 places, 10 Reed is shown presiding over another offering ceremony. In this scene, he appears in front of a building that rests on a temple platform supported by two human feet (Figure 8.7c), the same elements seen in the place sign of Sachio on Selden 4-I. Caso (1964:28, 76) has described this place sign as the "Temple of the Plumed Serpent" because the roof of the building contains a serpent head with a feathered headdress. These motifs on the roof may well depict a deity or rite connected with a temple within the town of Sachio where the ceremony that 10 Reed is witnessing took place. It is also possible that the building-with-plumed serpent may be united with the platform-with-human-feet to form a compound place sign, indicating that the town or site represented by the building-with-plumed-serpent is allied with or located within the boundaries of Sachio, which is represented by the temple with human feet.

**The Sign of Andúa**

The sixth of the group of 14 place signs associated with 10 Reed appears on Selden 4-I and consists of a hill that contains a human jaw that supports an arrow (Figure 8.8a). The ruler of this place is 10 Vulture "Eagle with Balls of Down" (Caso 1964:30, 77: "Golden Eagle"), another individual who appears only in Codex Selden.

In common with the place sign of Sachio discussed above, the human-jaw-and-arrow sign also appears on the page of the Codex of Yanhuitlán that contains signs representing the names of towns formerly subject to Yanhuitlán (Jiménez Moreno and Mateos Higuera 1940:Pl. VII; Figure 8.8b of

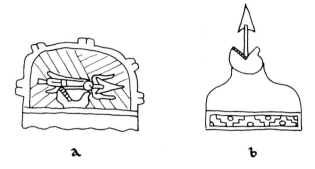

FIGURE 8.8.  The sign of Andúa: (a) Codex Selden 4-I; (b) Codex of Yanhuitlán, Pl. VII. (Drawing prepared by Caren Walt.)

this chapter). I have previously identified this sign as representing the Mixtec name *anduvua*—the name of San Andrés Andúa in the Nochixtlán Valley, located about 10 km west of Nochixtlán (Smith 1973a:42). The human jaw with open mouth represents the locative prefix *a-,* which means "place, place where something exists" and which is usually found only in place names in the Valley of Nochixtlán and vicinity. *Nduvua* means "arrow" in Mixtec, and this section of Andúa's name is represented in the sign in Codex Selden by an arrow that rests horizontally on a human jaw and in the sign in the Yanhuitlán Codex by an arrow that projects vertically from the open mouth of a human jaw.

Thus three of the place signs among the group of 14 signs that are shown in Codex Selden (3-IV through 4-III) in connection with the first ruler of Belching Mountain, and can be surely identified represent names of towns in the Valley of Nochixtlán. It seems to me likely that the remaining 11 place signs in this group may also represent names of towns in the same general vicinity.

## THE BELCHING MOUNTAIN SIGN: A HYPOTHESIS

Certainly, by far the most important place sign in Codex Selden represents the name of the town whose rulers are the principal concern of the manuscript—that is, the place sign usually described in English as Belching Mountain. In Codex Selden itself, the place sign seems to be a compound one: one part consists of a human jaw from which emerges a group of black dots on a white ground; the second part consists of a frieze bordered by the white curlicue motif that usually represents clouds in Mixtec manuscripts (Figure 8.9a). In all cases, these two parts appear in connection with a hill sign.

In Codex Bodley, the only other Mixtec screenfold in which this place sign is depicted, the sign has several variant forms: in three instances (Bodley 2-II; 5–6, III; and 17–18, IV) a hill, a jaw with open mouth, and a group of dots appended to the mouth comprise the sign (Figure 8.9b); in four instances (Bodley 17-I; 19-I; 19-II; 23–24, IV), a frieze with geometric decorations, a jaw with open mouth, and a

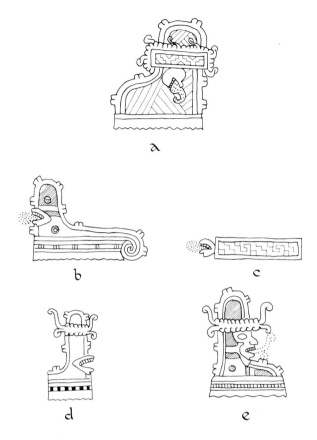

FIGURE 8.9. The Belching Mountain sign (sign of Magdalena Jaltepec?): (a) usual sign in Codex Selden (example from page 6-II); (b–e) variant forms in Codex Bodley; (b) Bodley 17–18, IV; (c) Bodley 17-I; (d) Bodley 12-III; (e) Bodley 36-III. (Drawing prepared by Caren Walt.)

To my knowledge, two previous identifications of the Belching Mountain sign have been proposed. The first was made by Philip Dark (1959:527–528), who suggested that this sign may represent Yucuñudahui, an important archaeological site near Chachoapan in the Valley of Nochixtlán (Caso 1938; Spores 1972). Dark felt that the Belching Mountain sign in Codex Selden was similar to a sign in the Codex of Yanhuitlán that consists of a hill with a cloud containing dots and a human jaw with a bird—a sign interpreted by Jiménez Moreno and Mateos Higuera (1940:64; Pl. XVI) as Yucuñudahui. However, it seems to me unlikely that either the Belching Mountain sign or the cloud/mouth-with-bird sign in the Codex of Yanhuitlán represents the Mixtec name *Yucuñudahui*, which means "hill where there is rain or a rain deity." (*Yucu* = "hill"; *nu* = "place where something exists"; *dahui* or *dzahui* = "rain, rain deity.") Neither rain—usually shown as schematized drops of water—nor a rain deity seems ever to be associated with the Belching Mountain sign, nor is either motif included in the place sign in the Codex of Yanhuitlán.

A second identification of the Belching Mountain sign was proposed by Robert Chadwick (1971:492), who suggested, for reasons he did not delineate, that Belching Mountain represents the town of Atzompan in the Valley of Oaxaca. This interpretation also seems to me unlikely because the Mixtec name of Atzompan (*ozumba*) is given in the 1581 *Relación Geográfica* of Cuilapa as *dzini mini* (Barlow 1945:24), which means "above the lake or declivity." Neither an entire human head to depict the *dzini* section of this Mixtec name nor a body of water to indicate a lake or the *mini* section of the name is part of the Belching Mountain sign.

As an alternative hypothesis, I would like to suggest that the human jaw and dots motifs—which appear to be the two most crucial motifs in the Belching Mountain sign—represent *añute,* the Mixtec name of Magdalena Jaltepec, a town in the southern end of the Nochixtlán Valley.[4] The name *añute* means "place of sand," with the initial *a-* being the locative prefix meaning "place, place where something exists," and *ñute* meaning "sand." As we have seen above in the discussion of the sign of San Andrés Andúa, the locative prefix *a-*, which is common in names of places in and around the Valley of Nochixtlán, is represented by a human jaw with open mouth and, in the logographic writing system used by the Mixtecs and other groups in Central Mexico, dots are often used to represent the word "sand."

Indeed, an example of the use of dots to represent sand in an early Postconquest manuscript from the Valley of Mexico occurs in the sign representing the Nahuatl name of Magdalena Jaltepec in the page of Codex Mendoza which records the tribute paid to the Aztecs by towns in the Mixteca Alta (Figure 8.10a). The Nahuatl name *jaltepec* or *xaltepec*

group of dots appended to the mouth comprise the sign (Figure 8.9c); in one instance (Bodley 12-III), a hill and mouth with no dots appended to the mouth and a band of clouds around the hill, comprise the sign (Figure 8.9d); and in one instance (Bodley 36-III), a hill with a profile face and dots being emitted from the mouth of this face, as well as a band of clouds around the hill, comprise the sign (Figure 8.9e). In both representations of the sign on the Bodley reverse (23–24, IV and 36-III), the dots are arranged in the form of scrolls, suggesting either speech scrolls or, in the case of the sign in Bodley 36-III (Figure 8.9e), an echo of the volute forms that appear on either side of the band of clouds around the hill.

Notwithstanding the variations in these place signs in Bodley, all are known to be the same sign as the Belching Mountain of Codex Selden because in all cases the persons shown as rulers of the signs in Bodley are also shown as rulers of Belching Mountain in Codex Selden. Moreover, with one exception (the sign in Bodley 12-III that lacks the group of dots), the pictorial elements that appear in all the signs in Bodley are a human jaw with open mouth and a group of dots appended to the open mouth.

[4]*Añute* is given as the Mixtec name of Jaltepec in the 1593 list of Mixtec town names compiled by Fray Antonio de los Reyes (1890:89), in the 1579 *Relaciones Geográficas* of Tilantongo (Eras 1579:72) and Tamazola (ibid.:83), and by present-day Mixtec speakers in the Valley of Nochixtlán.

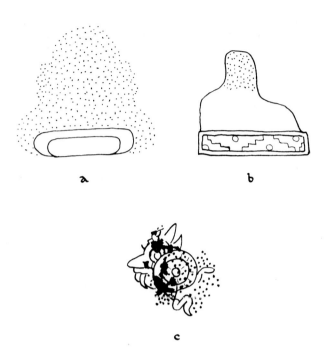

FIGURE 8.10. Signs that include the sand motif: (a) sign for the Nahuatl name *xaltepec* (Codex Mendoza, fol. 43/r); (b) sign for *itnu ñute* ("slope of sand"), the Mixtec name of San Francisco Jaltepetongo (Codex of Yanhuitlán, Pl. VII); (c) personal-name signs of the nobleman 3 Monkey (Codex Muro 7). (Drawing prepared by Caren Walt.)

means "in the hill of sand," and the sign depicting this name consists of a hill formed by the dots that represent sand.

An example of the representation of sand as dots in a manuscript from the Mixteca Alta itself occurs in the page of the Codex of Yanhuitlán that lists twelve former subjects of Yanhuitlán (Jiménez Moreno and Mateos Higuera 1940:Pl. VII). The sign in the lower-left corner of this page is a sloping hill with a group of dots placed within its rounded peak (Figure 8.10b). This sign represents the Mixtec name of San Francisco Jaltepetongo, located about 8 km southwest of Nochixtlán and listed in at least one sixteenth-century document as a subject of Yanhuitlán (AGN Tierras 985). Jaltepetongo's Mixtec name is *itnu ñute,* or "slope of sand"[5] (*itnu* = "slope"; *ñute* = "sand").

Still another use of the sand motif in a manuscript from the Mixtec-speaking region is found in Codex Muro, in the signs that make up the personal name of the nobleman 3 Monkey on page 7 (Figure 8.10c). These signs include a

profile rain deity appended to the circle of dots that represent sand; at the bottom (and top?) edge of the circle of dots are what may be human mouths. These motifs are described in a Mixtec gloss written above the head of 3 Monkey which has been translated (Smith 1973b:85–86) as "a profile rain deity who appeared from the place of sand."[6] The Mixtec word for "place of sand" in this gloss is *añute*, the same as the Mixtec name of Magdalena Jaltepec.

Thus I propose, as a hypothesis, that the Belching Mountain sign in Codices Selden and Bodley represents *añute* ("sand place"), the Mixtec name of Magdalena Jaltepec in the Valley of Nochixtlán, because two of the essential pictorial elements of this place sign—the human jaw and the dots—represent the two components of the name *añute*. But I do think that this interpretation remains hypothetical until it can be confirmed or disproved by other documentary evidence.

One of the most useful kinds of documentary evidence, if it could be found, would be a sixteenth-century document delineating the Mixtec names of the native rulers of Jaltepec in the early Colonial period. If the names of these rulers were the same as those given as the rulers of Belching Mountain in the last two pages of Codex Selden—which provide information on rulers at the time of the Spanish Conquest and into the Early Colonial period—then this document would confirm that the Belching Mountain sign is Jaltepec. Unfortunately, very little Early Colonial documentation has yet been found concerning Jaltepec, in contrast to the copious sixteenth-century documentation known for other Mixtec towns, such as nearby Yanhuitlán (Jiménez Moreno and Mateos Higuera 1940; Caso 1966; Spores 1967, 1974b). Because the genealogical narrative of Codex Selden extends somewhat beyond the time of the Spanish Conquest, however, I believe that it may yet be possible to locate written Colonial documents that help explain the content of the manuscript and, more specifically, help to determine its provenience.

Also, if the human jaw–dots configuration in the Belching Mountain sign represents the Mixtec name of Magdalena Jaltepec, it is still not known what place is represented by the frieze with clouds that usually appears in this place sign in Codex Selden and is occasionally seen in the sign in Codex Bodley. Perhaps the cloud section of the place sign represents a ceremonial site or a subject town that is within the boundaries of Jaltepec. A possible clue to the site represented by the frieze and cloud motifs may be found in the Mixtec name of one of the present-day boundary markers between Jaltepec and Tilantongo, Jaltepec's neighbor to the west.[7] The Mixtec name in question is *ytnu nu vigo*, which means "slope

---

[5]The Mixtec name of San Francisco Jaltepetongo is given as *itnu ñute* in a 1733 land document (AGN Tierras, vol. 986, fol. 14, et passim) and by a present-day Mixtec speaker from Jaltepetongo. Martínez Gracida (1888b:342–43) erroneously reports that *itnu ñute* is the Mixtec name of San Pedro Jaltepetongo, a town about 30 km northeast of Nochixtlán and, in common with San Francisco Jaltepetongo, within the ex-district of Nochixtlán. According to the 1580 *Relación Geográfica* of San Pedro Jaltepetongo (Bernal 1962:10), the Mixtec name of San Pedro Jaltepetongo is *ayagua*; according to a present-day Mixtec speaker from nearby Apoala, it is *yahua*.

[6]The group of dots appended to the rain deity head in this personal name appears to be drawn over or to be underneath a cobweb sign. The Mixtec word for "cobweb" (*duva* in the dialect of the person who wrote the glosses on Codex Muro that set forth names of persons), however, is not part of the gloss that describes this personal name.

[7]Archive of the Departmento de Asuntos Agrarios y Colonización (DAAC), Mexico City, Comunal 276.1/210 (included in a delineation of Jaltepec's boundaries dated February 12, 1943).

where there are clouds" (*ytnu* or *itnu* = "slope"; *nu* or *ñu* = "place where something exists"; *vigo* or *huico* = "clouds"). I rather doubt that the frieze with clouds motif in the Belching Mountain sign refers to a boundary site per se, but it might well refer to a site, possibly a ceremonial site, in the western section of the municipality of Jaltepec, located on the same slope that today forms the boundary between Jaltepec and Tilantongo. Again, it would be helpful to have a document that surely identifies the name of the frieze with clouds—a document that shows the sign in conjunction with its Mixtec name written in European script.

In conclusion, it seems to me very likely that Codex Selden is from the Valley of Nochixtlán. First, the gloss on the cover of this codex includes the Mixtec name of Chachoapan, a town within the Nochixtlán Valley. Second, at the meeting of the first ruler of Belching Mountain with persons from 14 other towns, the three of these 14 place signs that can be surely identified represent names of towns in the Valley of Nochixtlán. Third, it is possible that the sign usually described as Belching Mountain—the sign of the town with which Codex Selden is primarily concerned—represents the Mixtec name of Magdalena Jaltepec in the Nochixtlán Valley.[8]

[8]Part of this topic was presented as a paper at the XLI International Congress of Americanists held in Mexico City September 2–7, 1974. A travel grant from the University of New Mexico enabled me to attend the Congress. Assistance, advice, and encouragement from Ross Parmenter, Emily Rabin, Nancy P. Troike, and Cecil R. Welte are gratefully acknowledged.

# TOPIC 75
## Postclassic Mixtec Kingdoms: Ethnohistoric and Archaeological Evidence

RONALD SPORES

## THE ETHNOHISTORIC MODEL

The most dynamic and pervasive of Mixtec sociopolitical institutions was the native kingdom, or *cacicazgo* (Spores 1967, 1974b). Mixtec *cacicazgos* were small, socially stratified states, each controlled by a privileged ruling aristocracy and consisting of a territory normally traversable by foot in a day, one or more agricultural settlements with adjacent farm plots and resource areas, and a resident population differentiated into a ruling lineage, a nobility, a class of commoners, and, in some cases, a group of tenant farmers subject to the direct control of the ruler. Rulers provided political leadership, were responsible for maintenance of the religious cult, saw to the general welfare, defense, and recreation of the citizenry, and represented the *cacicazgo* in external affairs. They, in return, were owed loyalty, personal service, and tribute by their subjects.

Matters of government, social control, and formalized ritual were channeled directly from the ruler through royal and noble representatives strategically located in populated centers of the kingdom, and through trained religious practitioners. Rulers, male and female, were recruited exclusively from ruling caste lineages and acquired political office by hereditary succession as the nearest direct descendant of previous rulers, by marriage, and by military conquest. Each kingdom, though independent, was a component of a system of political, social, and economic institutions existing throughout the Mixtec cultural–linguistic-geographical domain. The extent of political power, authority, and jurisdiction depended upon the personal abilities and ambitions of particular rulers, size and effectiveness of the political support group, the effectiveness of a relatively simplified, sub-bureaucratic political system, strategic marital alliances, and success in extension of domain through warfare and/or annexation. Conversely, political power could decline through ineffective leadership, lack of elite support, external conquest, succession of subject communities under locally powerful aristocratic leaders, or inability to arrange advantageous marriages, or through combinations of such factors contributing to a breakdown of political strategies or governmental institutions.

A Mixtec ruler was responsible for protection of his or her kingdom(s) and for adjudication of disputes among the nobility; the ruler served as final appellate authority in cases involving commoners that had been settled in the first instance by members of the nobility. The ruler also provided paraphernalia for the religious cult and furnished food, drink, and entertainment for the nobility on occasions when they were summoned or gathered at the royal household. Finally, the ruler represented the kingdom in negotiations and contracts with other political units or groups. Although it is quite clear in most cases that governmental activities were tempered by an inner council of advisors and close kinsmen and the nobility in general, the ruler was in control of the polity. The populations of the constituent communities of the kingdom(s) owed unquestioned allegiance and obedience as well as tribute and service to the ruler. The relationship, although obviously hierarchical, clearly had its reciprocal elements.

Once a ruler had succeeded to title, he or she was entitled to tribute and services from subject populations, to specified lands (normally the most productive of the kingdom) and their proceeds, and to the support of a nobility (and an inner council of four members, at least in some cases), who advised, administered the royal patrimony and domain, enforced royal orders, and oversaw tribute collection and performance of services. The ruler had the right to call up nobility and commoners for service in war; enjoyed special and exclusive dress, food, housing, and personal property; had monopolies on certain commodities prominent in the local or regional commercial network; supervised and controlled the religious cult and its priesthood; and had the respect, admiration, and obedience of the supporting nobility and commoners. All of the delineated functions and responsibilities fell to the ruler and remained with him or her until death, abdication, or removal from office, at which

FIGURE 8.11. The Mixteca, showing a sample of the Postclassic *cacicazgos* mentioned in the text.

time these passed to an heir through appropriate mechanisms of succession.

Centralized configurations of several states were in existence for at least 500 years prior to the Spanish Conquest. Some of the more important kingdoms in the Prehispanic period were centered at Acatlán in Puebla, and at Tequixtepec, Tonalá, Zacatepec, Tezoatlán, Silacayoapan, Tecomaxtlahuaca, Mixtepec, Tlaxiaco, Achiutla, Teposcolula, Tejupan, Tamazulapan, Coixtlahuaca, Yanhuitlán, Tilantongo, Mitlatongo, Teozacoalco, Chalcatongo, Putla, and Tututepec in Oaxaca (Figure 8.11). These and other Mixtec and non-Mixtec political entities of western Oaxaca were alternately combined, separated, and recombined during Postclassic times. Nahuas, Chochones, Cuicatecs, Triques, Amuzgos, Chatinos, and Zapotecs were incorporated into individual Mixtec *cacicazgos*, and Mixtec rulers were known to have held control over whole communities of foreigners in and around the Mixteca. Marriages among royal class Mixtecs and Oaxaca Valley Zapotecs are well documented. The individual *cacicazgos* and the larger constellations of *cacicazgos* were dynamic in their composition, showing growth, contraction, and a high level of adaptability to changing political and economic circumstances, including external conquest by the Mexican Tripartite Confederacy and later by Spain. It is, of course, conceivable that the adaptation of Mixtec *cacicazgos* to powerful external political powers extends back to the time of the Toltecs (see Flannery and Marcus, Topic 69), Teotihuacán and the apogee of Monte Albán, and that the composition of these polities at the time of the Conquest had been deeply influenced by these relationships.

## THE ARCHAEOLOGICAL EVIDENCE

### The Nochixtlán Valley

Five major kingdoms existed in the Nochixtlán Valley at the time of the Spanish Conquest. Capital settlements of these kingdoms were located adjacent to the modern and Colonial settlements of Yanhuitlán, Chachoapan, Nochixtlán, Etlatongo, and Jaltepec. The 175 localities occupied in the valley around A.D. 1520 were subject to one or another of these political centers.

*Yanhuitlán and Yucuita* The *cacicazgo* of Yanhuitlán was perhaps the largest and wealthiest in the Mixteca Alta, and the town of Yanhuitlán one of the two or three largest nucleated Indian settlements in sixteenth-century Oaxaca. Ayuxi, a large hillside and ridgetop site located approximately 2 km east–northeast of present Yanhuitlán, is a large and complex Late Postclassic site. Of the more than 70 Late Postclassic sites in the Yanhuitlán area, Ayuxi is the most likely candidate as the principal settlement or capital of the kingdom. Excavations (Spores 1974a) in the "palace" built during the early Colonial period for Don Gabriel de Guz-

mán, *cacique* of Yanhuitlán, suggest that it may overlie Prehispanic elite residential remains, but unexcavated complex structures in the 30-ha site of Ayuxi probably constitute the ancient royal residence and the core of the ancient capital before removal to the valley floor shortly after the Conquest.

Yanhuitlán controlled between 20 and 25 settlements in the Nochixtlán Valley. One was Yucuita. As suggested in earlier chapters, Yucuita is a massive site covering the Cerro de las Flores and adjacent lomas in the northern portion of the Nochixtlán Valley. As though to underline the shifting character of political organization and relations throughout the three millennia of settlement in the valley, the first great capital of the Classic period in the Mixteca was reduced to the level of a dependency of powerful Yanhuitlán in the Postclassic period. Excavations at Yanhuitlán, at Yucuita, and at a few of the dozens of Postclassic sites in the area will eventually clarify relations between a sixteenth-century capital and its dependencies.

*Chachoapan and Las Pilitas* Survey and excavations at Chachoapan Viejo (Spores 1974a; Lind 1979) revealed an area of mounds, stone alignments, plaster floors, and Natividad-phase ceramics and lithic industries covering nearly 1 km² of a high *loma* in the north Nochixtlán Valley. The principal structure excavated in 1970 was a carefully formed, multiroomed dwelling complex constructed of adobe, *ndeque* blocks, and faced stone, containing rich ceramic and lithic complexes. The structure, corresponding quite faithfully to cacique "palaces" described in the documents of the sixteenth century, was located at the "core" of the Late Postclassic (Natividad) and Early Colonial (Convento) capital settlement of Chachoapan. Remains of numerous one- and two-celled dwellings were recovered from the "common" residence areas lying concentrically around the "elite" central zone, in a fashion to be expected in a small *cacicazgo* settlement.

A smaller, internally homogeneous site (Las Pilitas) occupies an adjoining loma and gives every indication of having been a dependent barrio of the more complex capital settlement. Remains of closely spaced one- and two-celled houses are distributed along a low ridge measuring some 300 m by 1 km. Despite the discovery of a cache of several thousand sherds of Mixteca polychrome in 1937, the site configuration and artifact complexes are entirely consistent with the conclusion that Las Pilitas was a contiguous dependency, a barrio, of ancient Chachoapan.

*Nochixtlán: Pueblo Viejo and Loma de la Cruz Verde* Pueblo Viejo de Nochixtlán, the location of the ancient capital settlement of the Nochixtlán kingdom until the mid-sixteenth century, extends 1250 m north–south and 500–700 m east–west along a ridge located just northwest of the edge of the present *cabecera* of Nochixtlán. Mounds, patios, terraces, stone alignments, and exposed plaster floors appear in profusion along with abundant and highly diversified complexes of ceramics and lithic implements. There are two major concentrations of elevated structures along the spine of the ridge, with tightly concentrated single-room and multi-room structures in the immediately surrounding area. Occupational terraces descend to the valley, where they blend into agricultural terraces of the *lama–bordo* type.

In 1970, remains of a common house were cleared at Loma de la Cruz Verde, a homogeneous ridgetop site located approximately 1 km east of Pueblo Viejo. Many other such structures can be seen to cluster around the excavated area. The architectural complex, the undistinguished ceramic complex, and the general layout of the site indicate it to have been a common-status dependency of Nochixtlán. Again, there is clear conformity among the documentary and archaeological records as to settlement configurations that should be associated with an important kingdom like Nochixtlán.

## Teposcolula, Pueblo Viejo

The major Terminal Postclassic (Natividad) settlement at Teposcolula is situated on a ridgetop approximately 1.5 km east–northeast of and 250 m above present Teposcolula. The disposition of the site relative to Colonial and modern Teposcolula is entirely analogous to that observed at Nochixtlán and Chachoapan. The occupational zone covers only the upper one-quarter of the ridge, and extends some 1000 m east–west by 500 m north–south, and consists of numerous Natividad phase terraces, structural alignments, floors, pits, quadrangles, mounds, and artifacts. The variability of the architecture and the artifacts and the dimensions and layout of the site clearly suggest the existence of a relatively large and complex civic–ceremonial center. Other ridgetop sites adjacent to Teposcolula (i.e., Dos Arbolitos and La Fortaleza) date to the Late Classic period, with indications of very minor occupations during later times—suggesting that Pueblo Viejo was the most important late Postclassic site in the Teposcolula area (an area of 12–15 km²). Pueblo Viejo clearly had outlying dependencies, but the center may have consisted of only one large complex settlement. Despite the fact that the main settlement was moved down into the valley between A.D. 1540 and 1560, the existence of several Spanish Colonial structures indicates Posthispanic utilization of Pueblo Viejo.

## Tamazulapan Valley: Tamazulapan and Tejupan

Surveys by Bruce Byland reveal Postclassic settlement and demographic patterns in the Tamazulapan Valley that closely parallel those inferred for the Nochixtlán Valley. Two unusually large sites appear in the form of a concentrated 25–30-ha Late Postclassic site at Pueblo Viejo de Tamazulapan and a site of approximately 45 ha at Tejupan at the opposite (eastern) end of the valley. Pueblo Viejo de Tamazulapan is a complex settlement (quite analogous in general form and placement to Coixtlahuaca's Pueblo Viejo) of the exact type that would be inferred from historical documents

to have existed as the capital of a Mixtec kingdom. Nearby Yatachío, one of the largest of Classic sites in the Mixteca, is reduced to the status of a dependency of the Postclassic center located at Pueblo Viejo.

The Postclassic settlement of Tejupan is located on the higher portions of the loma occupied by Colonial and modern Tejupan. According to Byland (personal communication), the site is a complex cluster of elite and common houses, probable civic and ceremonial structures, alignments, platforms, patios, and terraces covering some 45 ha, making it the largest of approximately 200 Postclassic sites identified for the Tamazulapan Valley. Byland has also located several Postclassic settlements in the immediate vicinity of Tejupan that undoubtedly conform to the ancient barrios of Tejupan (Spores 1967:92–93). Ethnohistoric and archaeological data converge convincingly to indicate that Tejupan was the most important kingdom in the Tamazulapan Valley at the time of the Spanish Conquest and the clearest example of a tightly nucleated state–settlement yet identified for the Mixteca.

## Coixtlahuaca Viejo

Postclassic Coixtlahuaca, an open unfortified center, covers a ridge 1000 m long and 400 m wide located across a deep river gorge 1 km west of the Colonial and modern *cabecera*. Excavations by Ignacio Bernal (1949) revealed public buildings, private residences, numerous tombs and burials, and polychrome and Red-on-cream pottery in abundance. Public buildings are grouped around rectangular patios; Patio C is 34 by 16 m in extent and is flanked by mounds 20–30 m on a side. Patio B runs south from a platform 45 m long and supports two mounds. Private residences on the south slope of the ridge are composed of narrow rooms with pottery basins (*tlecuiles*) set in the floor, separated by cut-stone walls. Also on the slope was a series of curious "sepulchers," each consisting of a rectangular hole in whose north side a small vault had been excavated; in these vaults the deceased was buried, wrapped in his *petate* or sleeping mat, and accompanied by offerings. These presumably Mixtec burials contrasted with a cremation burial in the area of public buildings, which was accompanied by Aztec III ceramics. (It is considered possible that this burial is actually that of a person from the Valley of Mexico).

Because thin, gray Monte Albán V pottery of G3M type occurred intermixed with Mixtec polychromes at the site of Coixtlahuaca, for many years it was standard practice to refer to G3M pottery as Mixtec. More recent work, including the extensive surveys of Blanton, Spores, Brockington, and Hopkins, suggests that G3M pottery cannot so easily be assigned an ethnic identity. It does not occur with any frequency in the Nochixtlán–Yanhuitlán Valley, which is certainly Mixtec; it *does* seem to be coextensive with known Zapotec occupations of the Valley of Oaxaca, Miahuatlán, and the Isthmus of Tehuantepec. It also occurs as far up the

Tomellín Cañada (Topic 77) as Cuicatlán, and from there may have reached Coixtlahuaca, whose major commercial ties are with the Cañada.

## Tilantongo

Tilantongo was the seat of one of the most important kingdoms and was the residence of one of the most prestigious royal lineages in the Mixteca at the time of the Conquest. The Late Postclassic site is located on the low ridge occupied by the Colonial and modern *cabecera* of Tilantongo. Although the site is apparently relatively complex and contains abundant polychrome and other elite ceramics, it is quite small for a capital center, measuring no more than 300 m sq. The site appears pale by comparison to Postclassic sites in the Nochixtlán and Tamazulapan valleys, and reluctantly we must conclude that there is little in the archaeological evidence to reinforce, verify, or augment the historical documentation that indicates in unmistakable terms that Tilantongo was one of the most important kingdoms of the Mixteca.

## Other Mixteca Alta Sites

Other important Postclassic sites are known to exist in and around the Alta communities of Achiutla, Apoala, Tlaxiaco, Tayata, Cuquila, Sosola, Yolomécatl, Chalcatongo, and Teozacoalco (based on Contreras y Rodrigo 1972; García García and Palacios González 1976; and partial surveys by Spores). These and many other areas of the Mixteca Alta have not yet been systematically surveyed, and competent comment on several hundred Postclassic sites must await future study.

## Mixteca Baja: The North

Numerous Postclassic sites are known to exist in the northern Oaxaca–southern Puebla area, in and around such centers as Huajuapan, Suchixtepec, Tequixtepec, Chazumba, Chila, and Acatlán (Contreras y Rodrigo 1972; García García and Palacios González 1976; and partial survey by Spores). Because this important area has yet to be systematically surveyed for Postclassic sites, few conclusions regarding settlement and/or relationships among archaeological remains and historically known Postclassic *cacicazgos* can be made. Lomas, low ridges, and piedmont spurs adjoining broken valleys were favored settlement localities, suggesting patterns similar to those observed in the Nochixtlán and Tamazulapan valleys. The most intensively studied site in the general area is Tepexi el Viejo.

*Tepexi el Viejo* Tepexi el Viejo is a fortified Postclassic site on the northern end of a low hill near the Río Xamilpan, Puebla, not far from the border between the Mixteca and the Cholula region. The site is at 1700 m elevation in the tropical thorn scrub of the Mixteca Baja. Its excavator describes it as a "middle-sized" Mixtec center of some 2 km², with a fortified area of 22,400 m², and a tribute zone extending 50 km to the south (Gorenstein 1973).

Tepexi el Viejo is naturally fortified by precipitous canyons on three sides. In addition, its mounds and building complexes are enclosed by massive outer walls, which occur as a series of stepped terraces with differences in level of up to 6 m. The walls are of caliche blocks, perhaps from a quarry area 0.5 km away; outer walls are up to 1.5 m thick and 15 m high.

Tepexi was founded sometime around A.D. 1300, and grew to a population level estimated at 6000–12,500 persons. Ceramics included both polychromes (of Mixtec and/or Cholula types) and *fondo sellado*, or stamped-bottom, vessels like those of the Venta Salada phase in Tehuacán. Around A.D. 1438, there was a marriage between an Aztec noblewoman of Tlatelolco and a Mixtec nobleman of Tepexi. This marriage alliance, however, did not prevent the Aztec from attacking and conquering Tepexi in 1503. Scattered Aztec IV sherds suggest the site was not totally abandoned until the Spanish Conquest. During its final period, Tepexi was required to pay tribute to the Aztecs of Tepeaca (near the Tehuacán Valley) in maize, beans, sage, amaranth, lime, tobacco, deer hide, and cane for arrow shafts. Many of these products were probably grown on the ancient agricultural terraces of Mixtec *lama–bordo* type that Gorenstein (1973) found in the Xamilpan Valley. Tepexi el Viejo rests almost squarely astride the ancient frontier between Mixtec- and Nahuatl-speaking populations, which may somehow account for its rather unusual lofty and fortified position.

## Mixteca Baja: The South

The southern Mixteca Baja is a vast archaeological terra incognita extending from the area north of Silacayoapan to the mountains south of Juxtlahuaca, and from the Mixteca Alta to the Guerrero borderlands. Important Mixtec kingdoms are known to have existed at such places as Tezoatlán, Tonalá, Silacayoapan, Mixtepec, and Tecomaxtlahuaca–Juxtlahuaca. Large Postclassic sites are known to exist at Silacayoapan, Juxtlahuaca, and Tecomaxtlahuaca. Unfortunately, because the area has not yet been subjected to systematic survey or excavation, it is virtually impossible to comment on archaeological resources or to relate ancient sites to important Postclassic Baja kingdoms and communities. Clearly the southern Baja, like the north, is begging for immediate attention from archaeologists.

## Mixteca de la Costa

*Tututepec* The ancient kingdom of Tututepec was seated in and around the present center of Tututepec. Three major

Postclassic sites are reported for the area: Cerro de los Pájaros, La Soledad (Tututepec Viejo), and present Tututepec (DeCicco and Brockington 1956; Brockington 1974; Piña Chán 1960; García García and Palacios González 1976). The sites are relatively small and unelaborated; the superficial indicators are a few small mounds, a ceramic complex including a number of types associated with Mixtec society in other parts of Oaxaca, and several carved stones. Given the present state of knowledge, there is little suggestion of the known political and economic importance of the Tututepec kingdom in Late Postclassic times (Berlin 1947; Smith 1973a). At present, Cerro de los Pájaros, a terraced hilltop site containing abundant Mixteca polychrome, sculpture, and even metal work would be most favored as the ancient political capital of the Tututepec domain.

The apparent incongruities between abundant historical reference to a great expansionist state centered at Tututepec and the skimpy archaeological settlement data parallel the situation at Tilantongo; pictographic and conventional documentary evidence indicate an exalted political status but the archaeological data, such as they are, are quite unimpressive when compared to such localities as Yanhuitlán, Nochixtlán, Teposcolula, Tejupan, or Tamazulapan.

*Other Costa Sites* Other Postclassic, probably Mixtec, settlements are reported at Yugue, some 18–20 km southwest of Tututepec; Playa de Puerto Escondido; Bajos de Chila; Manialtepec; Puerto Angel; El Rincón No. 4, 3 km south of Tonameca; a dozen sites along the Río Tonameca; and two sites at El Zapotal, some 8 km east of the mouth of the Río Tonameca (Brockington and Long 1974; García García and Palacios González 1976). These and an untold number of other Costa sites contain materials that have been associated with Mixtec culture, but much additional survey and excavation must be carried out to determine ethnic identity, settlement patterns, intersite and interregional relations. Whether the dozens of Costa sites containing Mixtec artifacts were populated by Mixtec-speaking peoples, were settlements occupied by other ethnic groups (i.e., Chatino, Zapotec, Nahuatl) who were independent of the kingdom of Tututepec but received foods and other influences from Mixtec sources, or were communities conquered by Tututepec and were controlled through a simple bureaucracy, remains to be determined through skilled and persistent archaeological research in one of Oaxaca's most difficult and challenging regions.

## TOPIC 76
## Regional Points of View in the Mixtec Codices

MARY ELIZABETH SMITH

Over a quarter of a century ago, Alfonso Caso demonstrated that a group of Preconquest genealogical–historical manuscripts were from the Mixtec-speaking region of southern Mexico (Caso 1949). In his commentaries on several of these manuscripts, Caso (1950, 1960, 1964; Caso and Smith 1966) stressed correlations among the stories told in the various manuscripts and pointed out that many of the persons and events were recorded in more than one manuscript.

Prior to Caso's studies, other scholars had observed that the biographies of important individuals appeared in several manuscripts. In 1912 James Cooper Clark compiled some of the events in the life of the most frequently depicted Mixtec ruler, 8 Deer "Tiger Claw," and in 1935 Herbert J. Spinden presented the biography of the female ruler 6 Monkey "Serpent or Warband *Quechquemitl.*" Caso (1955) later summarized some of the data given in the various manuscripts concerning a ruler named 4 Wind "Fire Serpent."

The correlation and analysis of all the depictions in the manuscripts of a given individual or event are absolutely essential in obtaining a complete picture of a person's biography or the circumstances surrounding an important battle or diplomatic confrontation. Moreover, one manuscript will often provide important information—such as a birth or marriage date—that is omitted in other manuscripts.

As significant as the similarities among the various codices are, equally or more significant are the differences among the manuscripts in their presentation of a sequence of events or in their portrayal of the life of a ruler. In many cases, these differences reflect regional points of view. We assume that the painter of a manuscript was well aware of the story his patron wanted recorded, and that the events one ruler might wish to commemorate would differ considerably from events thought to be noteworthy by the ruler of a neighboring town or of a town in another region. Thus the emphases or omissions in the narrative are determined by what the rulers of a specific town or region within the Mixteca considered to be important or complimentary to their family and their predecessors.

An ideal manuscript in which to study a regional point of view is Codex Selden. This codex is concerned with the genealogy of only one town, and it traces this town's ruling line from its mythological origins through the mid-sixteenth century. Moreover, a probable provenience for this codex has been suggested: the town with which it is primarily concerned appears to be Magdalena Jaltepec in the Valley of Nochixtlán (Topic 74).

Some idea of the local character of Codex Selden may be gained from noting the high percentage of persons who appear in this codex but in no other manuscript. The total population of named persons in Selden—historical persons, priests, deities—is 204. Of these 204 different persons, only 50 appear in manuscripts other than Codex Selden, whereas 150 appear in Selden only. (At present, it is not possible to determine whether the remaining 4 appear only in Selden or are also in other manuscripts as well.) Thus three-fourths of the persons who are depicted in Codex Selden are of interest primarily to the rulers of Jaltepec and not to the other regions from which we have surviving codices.

By contrast, in the genealogical narrative presented on the Vienna reverse, a total of 151 different named persons appear, and 149 of these have counterparts in other codices, with only two being unique to the Vienna reverse. This genealogical manuscript seems to be derivative, and for the most part it confirms and complements the information given in other codices but provides little new information.

Codex Selden's regional point of view is also seen in its treatment of some of the persons who appear in manuscripts other than Selden. Among the most prominent Mixtec rulers, and one whose biography is narrated in great detail in other codices, is 8 Deer "Tiger Claw," ruler of the prestigious town of Tilantongo in the Mixteca Alta and also of Tututepec, the most powerful town in the coastal region of the Mixteca. Almost the entirety of Codex Colombino–Becker I is devoted to this ruler's life, as is one side of Codex Nuttall and over four pages of the encyclopedic Codex Bodley. However, if the only Mixtec codex that had survived were Codex Selden, 8 Deer would be considered a nonentity. He only appears once in Selden, as an "in-law"—that is, three of his daughters marry sons of the main ruling line shown in Selden.

A similar situation exists for 4 Wind "Fire Serpent," one of these sons who marries a daughter of 8 Deer. Because 4 Wind's younger brother is the son who inherits the town of Jaltepec, 4 Wind himself is given minimal treatment in Codex Selden: he is shown as being born and as marrying, but no other details of his life are provided. In Codex Bodley, however, his biography is given more space than that of any other individual, and the last few pages of Codex Colombino–Becker I also delineate his activities in detail.

To demonstrate further how Codex Selden differs from the other manuscripts in its point of view, I would like to discuss the biography of one ruler who appears in Selden and also in Codices Bodley, Nuttall, the Vienna reverse, and the 1580 Map of Teozacoalco. The person in question, ♂ 9 House "Tiger–Torch with Eye," appears five times in Selden, the largest number of appearances in this manuscript of a historical person not of the ruling line of Jaltepec.

In his first appearance on Selden 11-II (Figure 8.12), ♂ 9 House is shown with the figure of ♂ 9 Lizard "Flames–Face with Diagonal Black Lines." An umbilical cord is attached to the figure of ♂ 9 Lizard, who is depicted

as the first son and heir of ♂ 13 Wind "Warband Ballcourt" and ♀ 12 Rain "Feathers–Blood–Butterfly," rulers of Jaltepec. Because the figure of ♂ 9 House is placed directly following that of the first son, ♂ 9 Lizard, it might be assumed that ♂ 9 House is a second son of the rulers of Jaltepec and a younger brother of ♂ 9 Lizard. However, those familiar with the pictorial conventions used in Codex Selden would be aware that ♂ 9 House is not a biological brother of ♂ 9 Lizard because he lacks an umbilical cord. In this codex, when two or more male offspring of the same parents are shown together, each of them is shown with an umbilical cord.[1] Nonetheless, ♂ 9 House does function in the role of a brother to ♂ 9 Lizard during the early lives of both men, even though he is not actually ♂ 9 Lizard's brother. Indeed, in the next three lines of Selden (11-III through 12-I), ♂ 9 House seems to be the more active of the two because he appears three times and ♂ 9 Lizard appears only once.

On Selden 11-III, ♂ 9 House is shown making an offering at a cave, apparently as preparation for the battle to follow (Caso 1964:39, 86). Immediately following this offering, on the next line is a river with an entwined plumed serpent; seated on top of this river are a paired eagle and turtle/fire serpent and a paired coyote and tiger. This pairing also occurs in a dramatic sacrifice scene in Codex Nuttall (see following discussion), in which a descending fire-serpent plucks a heart from a coyote and an eagle hovers over a tiger. In Selden, too, the fire-serpent and eagle are shown later as victorious: on Selden 12-II (Figure 8.13), the turtle/fire-serpent and eagle offer hearts with blood to a sun deity who is appended to a sky band.

This offering to the sun deity follows a battle and sacrifice scene shown on Selden 12-I (Figure 8.13). On the left side of the line, the heir to Jaltepec, ♂ 9 Lizard, captures a prisoner who has no calendrical name but who has cornstalks in his hair that may function as a personal name or perhaps identify his town or region. At the right of this capture, ♂ 9 House is shown with another unnamed prisoner already tucked under his arm. He stands within a twin-peaked hill very similar to the twin-peaked hill that forms a platform for the sacrifice scene in Nuttall (Figure 8.15). In the last scene on the right of Selden 12-I (Figure 8.13), ♂ 9 House sacrifices an unnamed prisoner[2]; then, on the following line, the turtle/fire-serpent and eagle make

---

[1]This pictorial convention is seen in Selden 5-IV through 6-I, 8-IV, and 12-III.

[2]Caso (1964:39, 86) suggested that the date 13 Deer at the right of the sacrificed prisoner was his calendrical name, but it seems to me more likely that it is the day on which the sacrifice took place. The previous day-date given in Selden, the day 12 Death that appears on 11-IV just before the battle begins, is one day earlier than 13 Deer. Thus it is probable that the battle took place on the day 12 Death and the sacrifice was performed on the following day 13 Deer. Also, although the right side of Selden 12-I seems to be slightly damaged, the day-date 13 Deer does not appear to be attached to the prisoner by a connecting black line, and, as a general rule, calendrical names in Codex Selden are usually attached by a black line to the figures of the persons they name.

IV

III

II

I

FIGURE 8.12.  Codex Selden 11.

their offering to the sun deity in front of the place sign of Jaltepec.

In the discussion of this sequence in Codex Selden, several comparisons have been made between the events occurring in Selden and a sacrifice scene shown in Codex Nuttall as part of the biography of the famous ruler ♂ 8 Deer "Tiger Claw" (Figure 8.15). Even though some of the details shown in the two codices are different, the basic events are the same; the principal difference is the names of the participants. In Nuttall, ♂ 9 Flower "Arrow with Copal Ball" is shown performing a sacrifice on behalf of his brother ♂ 8 Deer; in Selden 12-I, ♂ 9 House, acting in the role of brother, performs a sacrifice on behalf of ♂ 9 Lizard of Jaltepec.

After this sacrifice scene, ♂ 9 Lizard of Jaltepec appears to carry on without the assistance of ♂ 9 House. In the remaining scenes on Selden 12, ♂ 9 Lizard is married and has three sons—two of whom die in battle or are sacrificed—and a daughter. On the first two lines of Selden 13 (Figure 8.14), ♂ 9 Lizard is shown as engaged in two battles, both without the aid of his former ally ♂ 9 House. The final appearance of ♂ 9 House in Codex Selden occurs on 13-III, where he is shown seated on the place sign of Teozacoalco, the first and only time he is associated with this town in Selden. He and his wife ♀ 3 Rabbit, who is seated on the place sign of Tilantongo, are depicted as the parents of ♀ 1 Serpent "Sun Helmet," who marries ♂ 2 Tiger "Smoking Earth Monster," the son of ♂ 9 Lizard of

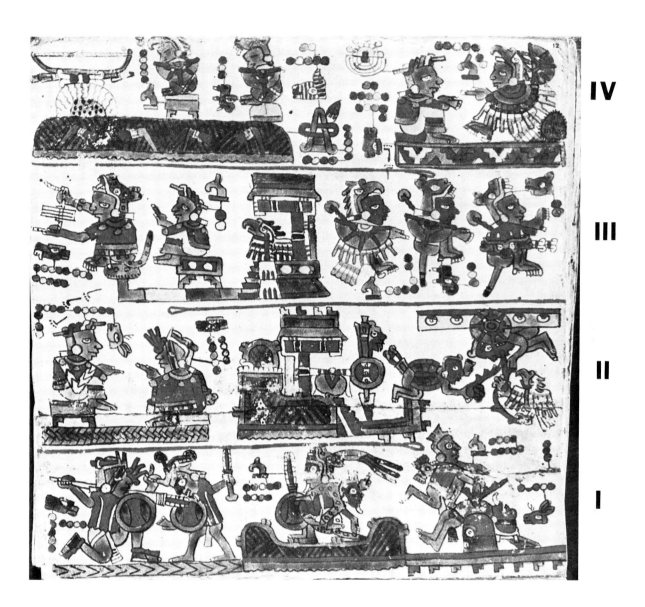

FIGURE 8.13.  Codex Selden 12.

Jaltepec. Thus the two former allies in battle seem to cement their relationship by the marriage of their offspring.

If our only source of information on the biography of ♂ 9 House "Tiger–Torch with Eye" were Codex Selden, all we would know about him is that he is a person of unspecified antecedents who seems to spend part of his early life in Jaltepec functioning in the role of brother to the heir to Jaltepec. Later he appears at Teozacoalco, married to a woman from Tilantongo, and their daughter marries the son of his former ally from Jaltepec. In other words, Codex Selden depicts only those events in ♂ 9 House's life that pertain directly to his relationship with Jaltepec, the town whose ruling line is the principal concern of this codex.

It is only from consulting the other Mixtec manuscripts in which ♂ 9 House appears that we learn something of his genealogy and gain some inkling as to why he might have spent the early part of his life in Jaltepec. According to Codices Bodley and Nuttall and the Map of Teozacoalco, ♂ 9 House is the son of ♂ 2 Dog "Strand of Flint Blades," ruler of Teozacoalco, and his wife ♀ 6 Reed "Feathered Serpent," who came from Tilantongo. (See accompanying genealogical chart, Figure 8.16). The text in Nuttall 32-I, however, informs us that ♂ 9 House is not the first offspring of this couple and that he has an older sister named ♀ 6 Water "Quetzal–Disk Jewel–Warbands with Flowers." At the time of this sister's first marriage to ♂ 4 Water "Bleeding Eagle" of Tilantongo, she is shown as the ruler of Teozacoalco (Bodley 15-IV), which she apparently inherited because she was the oldest offspring. On the death of her first husband and their son (Bodley 15-IV), ♀ 6 Water is shown as ruler of Tilantongo (Bodley 25-V), which she undoubtedly inherits not from her first husband (and her mother's brother), but from her mother ♀ 6 Reed, who was from Tilantongo and apparently the only ruler of her generation to produce heirs who survived.

Now ruler of Tilantongo, ♂ 9 House's sister ♀ 6 Water marries a second time, and the first offspring of this second marriage is ♀ 3 Rabbit "Xolotl [or Earth Man]–Cobweb," who inherits the town of Tilantongo from her mother and later marries her mother's brother ♂ 9 House. The birth of ♀ 3 Rabbit is shown in Bodley and the Vienna reverse as

taking place one year after the battle in Codex Selden in which ♂ 9 House is shown as an ally and "brother" of ♂ 9 Lizard of Jaltepec.

Thus we learn from manuscripts other than Selden that ♂ 9 House was the son of the rulers of Teozacoalco, but that the heir to this town was initially his older sister ♀ 6 Water. Once this sister inherits Tilantongo through her mother and after she produces an heir to succeed her as ruler of Tilantongo, she apparently relinquishes the ruler-ship of Teozacoalco to her younger brother ♂ 9 House. He then marries the daughter of his sister, and one of the daughters of his own marriage goes to Jaltepec to marry the son of ♂ 9 House's former companion-in-arms ♂ 9 Lizard.

FIGURE 8.14. Codex Selden 13.

FIGURE 8.15. Codex Nuttall 69.

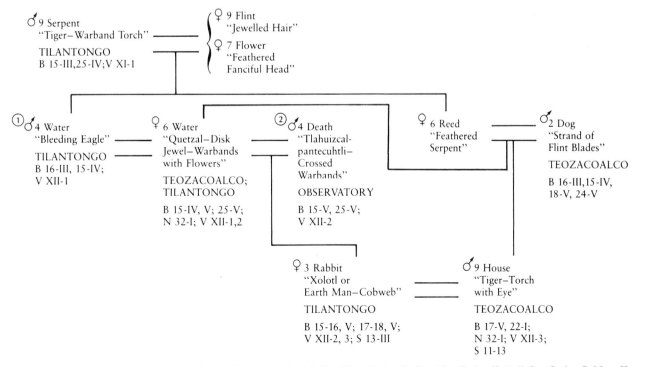

FIGURE 8.16. The genealogy of ♂ 9 House "Tiger–Torch with Eye." B = Codex Bodley; N = Codex Nuttall; S = Codex Selden; V = Codex Vienna.

If Codex Selden completely ignores virtually all the gene-alogical entanglements in which ♂ 9 House was involved, the manuscripts other than Selden are equally silent on ♂ 9 House's activities in Jaltepec. He is not shown at Jaltepec in any codex other than Selden, nor is the ruler of Jaltepec for whom ♂ 9 House functions as a brother—♂ 9 Lizard "Flames–Face with Black Diagonal Line"—ever depicted in any codex except Selden.

The presentation of ♂ 9 House in Codex Selden, as contrasted with the presentation of this ruler in manuscripts other than Selden, demonstrates very clearly Codex Selden's regional point of view. In this codex, ♂ 9 House appears prominently in the role of brother to the heir to Jaltepec, and in this role he performs activities that are extremely important to Jaltepec but are never mentioned in other codices. Moreover, because ♂ 9 House is not a biological brother of the heir to Jaltepec, it does not seem necessary to provide the names of his parents or his town of origin when he first appears in Selden. It is only when a son of the ruler of Jaltepec marries ♂ 9 House's daughter that the name of his town, as well as the name of his wife and her town, are given. Similarly, the only time the place sign of Jaltepec appears in ♂ 9 Houses's biography as it is depicted in codices other than Selden is when his daughter marries the future ruler of this town (Bodley 18-17, V).

For the most part, Codex Selden presents a very single-minded narrative of the rulers of one town, omitting information that is not important to these rulers and excluding events that would not show them in the most favorable light. Thus, until "one of their own" marries a ruler of Tilantongo or Teozacoalco, it is not necessary even to mention these towns, let alone relate in detail their genealogical embroilments.

Perhaps the best demonstration of Codex Selden's single-mindedness occurs in the closing pages of the manuscript. The latest date in this codex is A.D. 1556 (Caso 1964:14, 47, 52, 62, 94, 97), and at least the last two pages of the manuscript deal with persons who were alive at the time of the Spanish Conquest or were born in the early Colonial period. There is no indication whatsoever on these pages that the region in which these persons lived has been conquered by the Spaniards or that a major cultural upheaval is in progress.

# TOPIC 77
## The Tomellín Cañada and the Postclassic Cuicatec

JOSEPH W. HOPKINS III

The Cañada de Tomellín (Figure 8.17) is part of a deep trench that extends from the southern part of Puebla into the northern part of Oaxaca (see Topic 3). This trench is formed from the valleys of the Río Salado, flowing south from the Valley of Tehuacán, and the Río Grande, flowing north from the mountains on the northern periphery of the Valley of Oaxaca. The two rivers meet at Quiotepec and cut through the Sierra Madre Oriental to form a major tributary of the Río Papaloapan. The northern (or Río Salado) part of the trench was investigated as part of the Tehuacán Archaeological–Botanical Project, directed by R. S. MacNeish. The Cuicatecs occupied the southern (or Río Grande) part of the trench, called the Cañada de Tomellín. Quiotepec, at the junction of the Salado and the Río Grande (see Topic 35), was the northernmost Cuicatec town in the Cañada at the time of the Conquest.

The Cañada lies 600–800 m above sea level. To the east and west, mountains rise to 2000 m; the Cañada is thus in the rain shadow of the Sierra Madre Oriental. The highlands to the west of the Cañada are occupied by Mixtecs; to the south are Zapotecs. Chinantecs border the Cuicatecs to the southeast and the east. The highlands north of the Cuicatec area are occupied by Mazatecs, while the Valley of Tehuacán was inhabited by Nahuatl speakers at the time of the Conquest.

The Cañada is a major natural north–south route through the highlands of central Mexico. Today the railroad from Mexico City to Oaxaca goes through the Cañada, and a modern all-weather road has recently been completed. Earlier, the Colonial *Camino Real* passed down through the Cañada from Tehuacán to Oaxaca. The accounts of the Prehispanic expansion of the Aztec empire indicate that this route was important at that time also.

## ETHNOHISTORIC DATA

Although the Cuicatec Cañada is on a major historic and Prehispanic travel route and is in an area of considerable environmental diversity, anthropological work there was scanty until very recently. Frederick Starr (1900) passed through the region at the turn of the century. Robert Weitlaner, not surprisingly, was one of the few other ethnologists to visit the Cuicatecs (Weitlaner 1961, 1969). Only recently has a major ethnological and ethnohistorical study been made of the Cuicatecs. This is the work of Eva and Robert Hunt (E. Hunt 1972; R. Hunt and E. Hunt 1974, 1976).

From their ethnohistorical research, the Hunts picture the Conquest-period Cuicatec political unit as a *cabecera* with a few *sujeto* hamlets attached to it. The largest of the *cacicazgos*, Cuicatlán, was considerably under 5000 in population (including its *sujetos*), and the rest were well under 3000 (Hopkins 1974). The Cañada towns and the nearby highland towns were tied together in a system of exchange. The Cañada towns with their productive irrigation systems produced foodstuffs that the highland towns depended on in times of famine, and occasionally demanded. The highlands contributed products such as wood, charcoal, and woven cotton goods. In the sixteenth century, highland people rented lands in the Cañada, and worked for wages in Cañada fields (Hopkins 1974).

Each *cabecera* was occupied by members of a noble class and a larger commoner class. These were class-endogamous (E. Hunt 1972; Hopkins 1974). The *cacique* and his family were distinguished from the rest of the nobles. Since *caciques* could only marry into the families of other *caciques*, they were town-exogamous; some other nobles

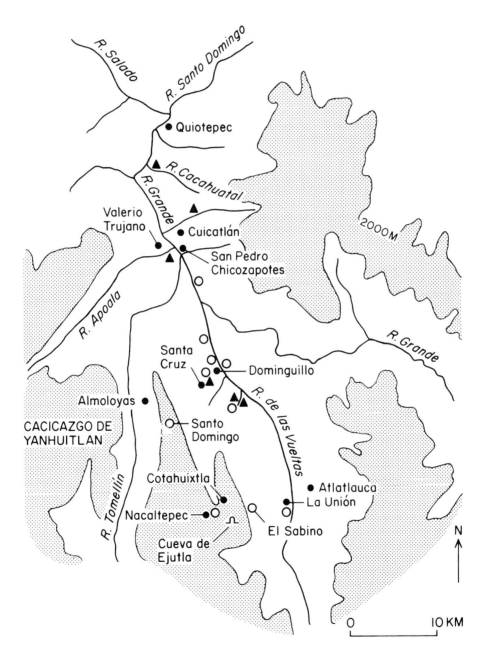

FIGURE 8.17. The Cañada de Tomellín, showing some of the Postclassic sites and irrigation localities mentioned in the text. Filled circles = modern towns; open circles = archaeological sites; filled triangles = canal remains. (Redrawn from Hopkins 1974.)

may also have married out of the town. This established weak ties among towns through members of the ruling elite. While these alliances tended to be with other Cuicatec towns, they were not limited to Cuicatecs; there are several cases of alliances with Mixtec and Chinantec towns. This loose network of marriage alliances in no sense tied the Cuicatec *cacicazgos* into a larger political unit. There is some evidence that Cuicatecs did not usually war with other Cuicatec towns (E. Hunt 1972); however, there is no evidence of a true Cuicatec "nation" or any other polity larger than the individual *cacicazgo*.

At the time of the Spanish Conquest, the Cuicatec towns were part of the Aztec Empire. The Mexican histories of the Aztec wars do not even take notice of the conquest of the Cañada towns. Certainly there is no way that the small Cuicatec *cacicazgos*, exposed as they were on a major north–south route, could have resisted the Aztec armies. Earlier, in fact, it appears that the Cuicatec towns were even unable to resist the aggression of their Mixtec neighbors. Burgoa (1674:387) reports that some of the Cuicatec Cañada tributaries of Almoloyas, a Mixtec town, once refused to pay their tribute in irrigated foodstuffs to Almoloyas. Almoloyas promptly enlisted help from Yanhuitlán and forced the Cañada towns to pay their tribute.

While the Cuicatecs seem to have been essential to a regional system of exchange, supplying foodstuffs that they could produce with their reliable irrigation systems, they were not able to muster the necessary numbers to parlay this economic role into any position of real power.

Were the Cuicatec *cacicazgos* at the peak of their development when the Spaniards arrived, or had they once been more important? Did their irrigation-based settlement allow them to assume a major role in the region earlier, until they were eventually outstripped by their neighbors? Or were the Cuicatec settlements, from their very inception, secondary parts of a larger system? With archaeological evidence we can examine these questions.

## ARCHAEOLOGICAL REMAINS

Very little archaeological work had been done before my research in the Cañada. Pareyón (1960) conducted a small excavation at Quiotepec. Unpublished surveys were carried out by Robert and Eva Hunt and Pedro Armillas. Since my research, the Oaxaca Regional Center of the INAH has tested an Early Formative site and begun work on Postclassic sites, and Charles Spencer and Elsa Redmond have carried out surveys and excavations relating to the Formative and Classic horizons in the Cañada (Topic 35).

From 1968 to 1970, I conducted surveys and excavations in the Cuicatec Cañada. My main interests were to understand the origin and nature of Cuicatec irrigation systems. A second goal of my fieldwork was to fill this gap in the Mesoamerican archaeological map. The field work consisted of three parts. The first part included making a careful survey of the land of the town of Cuicatlán and its surroundings, recording and making collections from all sites for dating. The second part was a 10-day reconnaissance of the rest of the Cañada and part of the neighboring highlands, to see if Cuicatlán was typical of the Postclassic Cañada towns. Finally, two small excavations were conducted in Cuicatlán, aimed at dating irrigation remnants and recovering remains from which the Prehispanic diet could be reconstructed.

From all this research, the general outline of the settlement and development of the Cuicatec Cañada can be reconstructed. Because Spencer and Redmond have concentrated on the Formative and Classic in Topic 35, I will concentrate on the general principles of Cañada settlement in Postclassic times.

The Cuicatec area breaks down into three basic zones:

1. A zone of lowland settlement along the alluvium of the Río Grande and the Río de las Vueltas at 600 to 800 m elevation. Almost without exception, irrigation is necessary in this zone because of the hot, dry, rain-shadow conditions. This seems to have been the first zone settled, and the earliest sites occur here at certain favorable riverine locations with higher-than-average soil humidity. This zone is not uniformly wide, however; in places it pinches down to nothing, while in others it expands to several kilometers wide. Perhaps the broadest expanse is the area between Cuicatlán and San Pedro Chicozapotes, where my survey recorded at least 25 sites with Postclassic material, presumably relatable to the Cuicatec. These sites varied from rock shelters or isolated residences to large towns with mounds, terraced plazas, and irrigation features.

2. A zone of rainfall agriculture along the mountain slopes east of the river at elevations from 1200 or 1400 m up to 2280 m. This zone, almost unknown archaeologically, has Postclassic settlements which were economically linked to the alluvium.

3. A no-man's-land between zones 1 and 2 at elevations of 800 to 1400 m. Neither irrigation nor dry farming is practiced in this zone today, though it is used for hunting and wild plant collecting trips. However, I found some small Postclassic sites and associated irrigation terraces in this zone.

By far the majority of the sites in the Cañada date to the Postclassic, and to the Late Postclassic at that. The ceramics of this phase are virtually a blend of Tehuacán and Oaxaca types. Particularly characteristic are (1) stamped-bottom (*fondo sellado*) vessels, probably *molcajetes*, that are indistinguishable from those of Venta Salada-phase Tehuacán, and (2) thin gray bowls with serpent-head tripod feet that are indistinguishable from G3M vessels of Monte Albán V (Hopkins 1973:Photos 1–3). Such pottery covers all hilltops and talus slopes above potentially irrigable land, and is so widespread as to suggest a Prehispanic population much greater than the current population.

Ancient Cuicatlán covers a long ridge above the floor of the Cañada as well as the talus slope south of this ridge and below the eastern wall of the Cañada. The ridge is called Iglesia Vieja, and the major building zone on the talus is called Ojo de Agua. Both overlook the Río Chiquito, which was used to irrigate the Cuicatlán alluvial plain. I was fortunate enough to be able to recover more than 1 km of the Prehispanic irrigation canal (see Topic 94). The ancient waterworks were higher than today's, and I have calculated that the ancient canal system at Cuicatlán may have irrigated up to 134 ha more than the present irrigation system (Hopkins 1974). Other major Prehispanic canals were found on the Río Cacahuatal between Cuicatlán and Quiotepec, and on the Río Apoala near Valerio Trujano.

On the Río de las Trancas, one of the small tributaries of the Río de las Vueltas (above Dominguillo), is the site of El Despoblado. Here a masonry canal attached to a vertical cliff leads water to a series of at least 28 terraces, associated with a hilltop Postclassic settlement.

Santa Cruz is another small site located above Dominguillo on land that belongs to Almoloyas. Here a few families are using canals that take water from a spring in a cave to irrigate a small area of fields. Beside the present canals are the mineralized remains of earlier canals, and a series of tanks used to store water through the dry season. The present users of the system live among the irrigated fields, but the Postclassic settlement is immediately above the irrigated fields and the spring.

Bernal (1966b) reports a Postclassic site, Santo Domingo, on the ridge dividing the Río Tomellín from the Río de las Vueltas. Santo Domingo is of considerable interest because of its architectural similarity to the ruins of Yagul and Mitla in the Valley of Oaxaca (see Topics 79, 80). It has a single pyramid surrounded by a number of apparently public buildings or palaces. Stone columns are composed of drum-shaped segments as at Yagul. All three sites share long, narrow rooms with multiple entrances divided by rectangular masonry columns. Because of the ethnohistoric connections between the Mixtecs of Almoloyas and the Valley Zapotec, Bernal and Gamio (1974) find the similarities of Santo Domingo, Yagul, and Mitla suggestive.

As described in Topics 11 and 35, the Cañada had modest occupation in the Early and Middle Formative, and its principal ties seem to have been with the valleys of Oaxaca and Tehuacán. Spencer and Redmond (Topic 35) and Marcus (Topic 29) have suggested a Zapotec takeover of the Cañada in the Late Formative and Early Classic. However, the main colonization of the Cañada, accompanied by a large population expansion, seems to have taken place during the Postclassic, and is presumably the work of the Cuicatec. It may be that this extensive type of development of the Cañada was not possible until a strong state organization or *cacicazgo* system of Mixtec–Cuicatec type was in existence in the area.

Late Postclassic settlements are everywhere associated with irrigation remains that are higher than the present systems and are therefore capable of watering greater areas

of land than the present irrigation systems. The settlements were invariably located high on hilltops or slopes, above any irrigation canals. This location could have been for defense; however, it seems that a primary concern was to not waste any potentially irrigable land.

It appears that the Cañada settlement process was part of an evolving feedback relationship between population growth and intensive agriculture which characterized the whole of the southern Mexican highlands. This pattern can be observed in the neighboring areas of the Valley of Oaxaca (Flannery et al. 1967; Kirkby 1973), the Mixteca Alta (Spores 1969, 1972), and the Valley of Tehuacán (Johnson [ed.] 1972; MacNeish et al. 1972), although the details in each valley are very different. With the rapid expansion of Mixtec *cacicazgos* at the start of the Postclassic, the irrigable alluvium of the Cañada once again became a strategic resource worthy of considerable labor investment, as it evidently had been to the Zapotec in Monte Albán II. This Postclassic investment was the work of the Cuicatec lords, but many of their Mixtec neighbors also reaped the benefits through tribute.

Once settled, the Cuicatec towns developed their irrigation systems to the greatest limit possible. The large Postclassic settlements that grew up on the hilltops and talus slopes of the Cañada were based on irrigation systems using the water of the small tributaries that ran down from the Sierra. Setting the absolute limits for each system were the amount of water in each small tributary and the amount of flat land on the Cañada floor over which the water could be deployed. In the case of Cuicatlán, in the widest part of the Cañada, the amount of land was probably greater than could be irrigated with the water resources of the dry season; thus parts of the system probably produced only one crop a year. In the case of El Despoblado, the problem of land on which to deploy irrigation water was solved by the construction of terraces that created flat land out of steep hillside. Both these suggest that the need for irrigated land—for subsistence, trade, and tribute in foodstuffs—was severe enough to justify construction both of canals (at great effort) that could only irrigate fields in the rainy season, and of fields out of hillsides. It would be interesting to know to what extent the tribute demands of Mixtec *cacicazgos* like Almoloyas and Coixtlahuaca were responsible for further Cuicatec intensification of irrigation. If the ethnohistoric documents are to be believed, areas like Almoloyas were either so overpopulated or had such poor land that they explored two alternatives: exacting tribute from the Cuicatecs, and sending surplus labor to the Valley of Oaxaca through royal marriage alliances.

Because the Postclassic Cañada towns were settled as part of a more widespread phenomenon of increasing population and reliance on intensive agriculture, their destiny was always tied into a larger regional system. Their existence depended, at least in part, on external demands for the food produced by intensive agriculture in the Cañada. Without the external demand for this food, there would have been less reason for the intensive agricultural systems necessary in the Cañada, and Postclassic settlement patterns might have been very different.

Archaeological remains indicate that, almost everywhere, Postclassic irrigation systems were more extensive than today's. However, the narrow Cañada and its limited tributary streams put a limit on the size of each settlement. Tied to the land by their investment in the irrigation systems, these settlements could not move. Thus the small, stationary Cañada settlements were invariably conquered by the Aztec armies who passed down the Cañada on their way south. They would have been just as unable to resist, much less dominate, highland states like Yanhuitlán, which Spores (1967) estimates to have had more than 12,000 people in 1548, after a decline in population; and their periodic subservience to Coixtlahuaca and Almoloyas has already been noted.

This same vulnerability made the Cuicatecs unlikely candidates for any "invasion" of the eastern Valley of Oaxaca, despite the architectural similarities among Santo Domingo, Yagul, and Mitla. Thus, although such similarities cannot be ignored, I doubt if they resulted from Cuicatec subjugation of Mitla; the Cuicatecs would have been at a distinct disadvantage in any conflict with Zapotec lords.

At this writing, further research on the Postclassic Cañada is being undertaken by Gilberto Hernández of the Oaxaca Regional Center (INAH). We await his results with interest, for the Cañada is an interesting area, its history inescapably tied to widespread processes in Postclassic Mesoamerica. The Cuicatec towns were settled and grew during this period, but they were probably always subsidiary parts of a complex whole, not prime movers. The Lord of Cuicatlán was never more than "an attendant lord, one that will do to swell a progress, start a scene or two" (Eliot 1917).

## TOPIC 78
## A Postclassic Burial Cave in the Southern Cañada

CHRISTOPHER L. MOSER

The Peña de Ejutla is a steep cliff overlooking the canyon of the Río de las Vueltas in the southern part of the Cuicatec Cañada (Figure 8.17). In this setting of rugged mountains, approximately 20 m up the sheer face of the cliff, is a large dry cavern, the Cueva de Ejutla, which can be reached conveniently only by rope ladder. When the cave was discovered by INAH inspector Rafael Vásquez it had already been extensively looted. During 1966 and 1967, at the urging of INAH representative Lorenzo Gamio, archaeologists from the University of Michigan made an effort to salvage as many as possible of the perishable artifacts left behind by the looters (Moser 1975, 1976).

Work in the cave was made difficult by the lack of light and poor ventilation in the main chamber, which is separated from the entrance by a long, tunnel-like passageway that must be traversed on hands and knees. Working by Coleman lantern light in the looters' backdirt, we were able to salvage such perishables as sandals, string, textiles, matting, basketry, bark paper, fire-drills, a cane arrow shaft with wooden foreshaft attached, brightly colored bird feathers, many plant remains, and the mummified foot of a child burial.

Among the more spectacular artifacts recovered were the left half of a wooden mask and part of a wooden earspool, both covered with turquoise mosaic (Moser 1975:Figure 5). The mask strongly resembles a group of mosaic-incrusted wooden masks collected by Marshall Saville (1922) for the Museum of the American Indian in New York. These 17 specimens are said to have come from a dry cave "in the mountains of the Mixtec region of the state of Puebla." The Cueva de Ejutla mask also resembles specimens excavated at Coixtlahuaca and Zaachila and recently restored by the INAH (*Boletín* 1967). The Coixtlahuaca and Zaachila masks are Late Postclassic, and the meager ceramic sample from Cueva de Ejutla is predominantly Monte Albán V gray ware. Also recovered from Cueva de Ejutla was a fragment of textile (Figure 8.18) with a somewhat stiff anthropomorphic central design, bordered by a series of *greca* motifs like those found on the palaces at Mitla and on Late Postclassic Mixtec Polychrome vessels (Moser 1975: Fig. 11).

The material left behind by the looters appears to have come from a series of crude stone masonry cells, probably tombs. These cells were circular to rectangular in plan, and each was large enough to have held one (or several) vertical burials or mummy bundles. The rectangular cells were built against the walls of the various cave chambers, with masons using the rock wall of the cave and/or the wall of an adjacent cell as the starting point for each new construction (Moser 1975:Figs. 2, 3). The circular cells are floor-to-ceiling constructions standing singly or in clusters in the central open space of the cave chambers (Moser 1975:Fig. 4). Before they were broken open by looters, there may have been as many as 45 or more of these cells—most of them in the main chamber, which was 10–12 meters in diameter. The rituals that accompanied the closing of each cell were hinted at by the countless discarded fragments of pine torches, colored feathers, and possible bloodletting equipment such as maguey spines, obsidian blades, strings of knotted cord, and many strips of stained and spotted bark paper (Moser 1975:Figure 10). Perhaps the most eco-

FIGURE 8.18. Fragment of Postclassic textile from Cueva de Ejutla, Oaxaca. (Drawing by Chris L. Moser.)

nomical explanation of the Cueva de Ejutla remains is that the cave was a burial site for nobles and their retainers from one of the Cuicatec (or Mixtec?) *cacicazgos* in the Cañada below, and that some burials were wrapped in textiles, given a turquoise mosaic funerary mask, and sealed up in stone masonry cells. This procedure would fit the ethnohistoric descriptions of Mixtec and Cuicatec funerary rites as well as portrayals in the Postclassic codices (Dahlgren de Jordán 1954:295; Spores 1967:24; Moser 1975).

## TOPIC 79
### Mixtec Impact on the Postclassic Valley of Oaxaca

JOHN PADDOCK

One of the most controversial topics in the history of Oaxaca archaeology is the nature of the Mixtec presence in the Late Postclassic Valley of Oaxaca; that is, during Monte Albán V. Some of the raw data on which the controversies have been based are summarized by the editors on pages 220–226, and more data are presented in Section 8b of this chapter. I have been asked by the editors to outline what I see as some reasonable alternative positions on the controversy. I do so in this topic in the context of two Monte Albán V sites where I have excavated—Yagul and Mitla, both in the Tlacolula arm of the valley.

## YAGUL

In order to understand the interpretations that have been made by me and others of Yagul and related finds, it is necessary to have in mind that they were offered in an atmosphere of intense hostility; sometimes they were given extra emphasis, or even pushed further than would have been the case otherwise, in defiant response to that hostility. Thus we first were forced to demonstrate that Yagul was, in fact, parallel to Mitla. A doctrine (whose source I do not know) maintained that Mitla was unique; thus, by definition, there could be no *greca* mosaics at Yagul. Another doctrine of equally mysterious roots proposed that there had been no Mixtec occupation, at least before the Spanish Conquest, in the Valley of Oaxaca.

One who had worked at Yagul, however, was confronted with some data hard to reconcile with that proposition. Some of these data, if taken one by one, could be dismissed as simple imports, booty, or local occurrences of a pan-Mesoamerican horizon style. Others resist such interpretations. It is many years since I last made such a list. There are some new items to add, and there are a few comments on it that are different now.

1. In Monte Albán V there are no recognizable representations of the deities that are found in Periods I through IV. There are no "urns" at all. Apparently filling their place are *penates* of stone (Bernal and Gamio 1974:Lám. 39), identical with those of the Mixteca Alta; there are also effigy vessels of a completely different kind, with examples known from Yagul, Cuilapan, and perhaps Huitzo. An incomplete one from Yagul Tomb 4 (Paddock 1955a:Fig. 14) and a complete one from Yagul Tomb 13 (Paddock 1955a: Figs. 21, 23) are quite different from Classic Zapotec urns, as is also the Cuilapan example of Saville (Bernal 1958b:Foto 44, upper right); the Huitzo examples, half a dozen magnificent perfect ones, are in the collections of the Frissell Museum in Mitla. Though attributed to Huitzo, some or all may have come from the Mixteca. But these examples leave a weird vacuum: they are few, and they represent Mixtec deities in any case; what happened to the gods of Monte Albán, represented in thousands of clay urns? Conquest-period documents say the Zapotecs of that time represented their deities in stone, wood, and other materials. Why do we not have one—even one—such image? I think perhaps we have a few, though they are not recognizable, at least not in the old terms. I have in mind here small stone figures, of which the Frissell Museum has a dozen or so on exhibit, and which I have called simply *ídolos de piedra*. The largest of them are less than 30 cm tall. They are of common stone, unpolished and unpolishable, sometimes ignimbrite. They virtually lack features interpretable as symbolic. They have often been thought to be fakes, but obviously they are not. When I first saw them I thought they might be idols from the early Colonial period, when details of iconography had been lost but ancient cults were still going on. Now, however, I think they may well be Prehispanic. Bernal's discovery of the head of one of them at Yagul (Bernal and Gamio 1974: Lám. 44) confirms my earlier conclusion that they are not fakes, and also my later idea that they are Prehispanic. But even if we include these figures, the point is that the abundance of clay effigies of the gods was replaced, in Period V, by a near-absence of such representations in any durable medium.

2. We do not know whom they represent, but in the Mixteca there are considerable numbers of greenstone, rarely jade, objects with faces indicated by the application of tubular drills to produce circles and part-circles. Other small greenstone objects, almost always perforated as if to be used in necklaces, may have simpler or more elaborate decoration, sometimes whole figures or even simple scenes. Considerable caches, and occasional single examples, have been found at Yagul (Paddock 1955a:Figs. 9, 10, 11). The

relation of these pieces to the jade plaques of late Monte Albán (Paddock 1966a:Figs. 159–164) and Tula (Caso 1965a:Figs. 20–30) remains unclear. Perhaps a revised definition of the IIIb–IV distinction at Monte Albán would place them in Period IV. But this whole question deserves a careful study. Meanwhile, we know what we see: another identity of Monte Albán V and the Mixteca.

3. Burials of persons in seated posture, with a *cajete* over the head like a skullcap, are not the rule anywhere. However, a number have been found in the Mixteca. In the Valley of Oaxaca, they are limited to Period V. I think they might all be burials of children, perhaps of girls. Note the way women at the Tlaxiaco market today wear *jícaras* on their heads.

4. Seated burials are the rule in the Mixteca, however, in Period V times at least. The Yagul tombs had at least one such, but had many more extended ones. Seated burials are present in the San José and Guadalupe phases, but for the later periods they are unknown in the valley, I believe, except in Period V. They are also unknown in the Valley of Mexico, except at Teotihuacán, where each corner of each body of the Pyramid of the Sun had such a burial, according to Batres (1906:22, 109, 111, 113).

5. Mixtec polychrome pottery of course was highly valued and surely was widely traded. It is, perhaps, worth noting that so thoroughly Mixtec a personage as Mixcoatl (Caso's identification) should turn up on a polychrome vessel at Yagul (Bernal and Gamio 1974:Lám. color 16). The Yagul polychrome in general differs somewhat from that of Coixtlahuaca and Chachoapan (Michael Lind, personal communication, 1975). Some fragments do seem to be like the Chachoapan variety, however. I think it might be possible to define a Valley of Oaxaca style, or perhaps several styles.

6. The G3M or Yagul Fine Gray pottery that is so dominant in Period V at Yagul is, according to Lind (personal communication, 1975) the same as what he has called Cacique Burnished in his report (Lind 1979) on excavations in immediately Pre- and Postconquest remains at Chachoapan and Yucuita during Spores's project. Its relation to his Miguelito Hard Fine Gray is a question I would like to see clarified. In any case, what he says of Cacique Burnished is a confirmation of what Bernal said of his Gris Pulido at Coixtlahuaca: "This type has not been common in the tombs, but is very abundant in some offerings and in the stratigraphy, appearing in all levels. It has been found in various places within the Mixteca Alta and in Monte Albán V" (Bernal 1949b:42). These opinions are of special weight because they were uttered before Bernal had ever seen or heard of Yagul—that is, before the Mixtec–Zapotec War (of which, happily, neither Mixtecs nor Zapotecs ever became aware) had begun. And, he adds,

we have sure resemblances to Monte Albán V, Mitla, and other Mixtec sites of the Valley of Oaxaca. Of course the exact relationships between Monte Albán V and the Mixteca present complexities that I will discuss on another occasion; for now it is enough to point out such resemblances as the cajetes of

compound silhouette, the polychrome, the polished gray tripods, and Tomb 7. The paintings of Mitla and the decoration of the palaces are strongly Mixtec [Bernal 1949b:72–73].

We all are aware of differences from one area to another in the polished gray ware. The *fondo sellado*, so common in Coixtlahuaca and the Cañada, is absent in the Nochixtlán and Oaxaca valleys; the proportions of various shapes differ from one area to another, as do details of color and finish. I have an impression that G3M pottery occurs in a wider variety of shapes and finishes in the Valley of Oaxaca than anywhere else, but that remains to be proven.

7. *Sahumador* lids of a highly peculiar shape and decoration have been found at Coixtlahuaca (Bernal 1949b:Lám. 9i-1), Chachoapan–Yucuita (Spores 1972:Figure 19e, f, g; Lind 1979), and the Yagul palace (Bernal and Gamio 1974:Lám. 27). These objects look like rather normal pot lids, except that they have three knobbed feet. Lind found that they fit perfectly over the bowls of the long-handled *sahumadores* of his area, and that they are thoroughly smoked on the inside.

8. Mixtec wall construction has not yet been the object of a proper study. This term refers to the use of large stones with the large face out, alternating with very small stones, small face out, to give a peculiar and highly distinctive effect. This type of construction has been found at a number of sites in the Mixteca Alta and Baja, and as far back as Ñuiñe times; in the Valley of Oaxaca it has occurred in Period V contexts at Monte Albán, Tlalixtac, Yagul, and Mitla. Both frequency and chronology indicate it as a Mixtec trait brought into the valley—and it is not portable. Further, because the walls in question were invariably covered with stucco, it was invisible once finished.

9. Bernal's discovery of architectural resemblances to the Mitla–Yagul style at Santo Domingo, as mentioned above, is another link, but not *just* another one. The absence of data on Mixteca architecture has often been leapt upon by critics of the "Mixtec interpretation" of Monte Albán V, and in extreme cases has even led to suggestions that there was no architecture worth mentioning in the Mixteca.

10. Caso's study linking the Zaachila Tomb 1 plaster reliefs with personages of the Yanhuitlán dynasty might be all wrong, but nobody seems to be challenging it.

11. There is a prominent absence—almost total—at Yagul of the red-on-cream ware that is so large a proportion of the late Mixteca Alta ceramic repertory. This absence always caused great puzzlement, and perhaps that will be sharpened by recent discoveries. The common, ill-made matte or unpolished red-on-cream of Coixtlahuaca, Tamazulapan, and Yanhuitlán is still uncommon in the Valley of Oaxaca[1], Drennan (Topic 84) traced the polished kind (my Huitzo Polished Cream) from the mountains north of the Etla Valley down into the Etla Valley itself,

---

[1]Spores (personal communication, 1980) has identified Yanhuitlán Red-on-cream sherds at San José Mogote.

and, as would be expected, it seems to become scarcer toward the south (Kowalewski 1974:4). I have cited earlier the occurrence of whole pieces in Zaachila Tomb 3 (Acosta 1972).

The list of reasons for not accepting some kind of Mixtec occupation in Yagul as an explanation of the above has not changed, I believe, since I last reviewed it (Paddock 1958a, b; 1966c:378). The lack of Mixtec speakers in the Tlacolula Valley, apparently since Colonial times, may be accounted for by the documented congregation of valley Mixtecs in Cuilapan and its subject towns, carried out at the orders of Cortés. Because it is found in the Mixe, Chinantec, and Cuicatec regions as a minimum, besides the Mixteca and the Valley of Oaxaca, the polished fine gray ware might well be dropped from the list of indicators of Mixtec occupation. The elimination won't help much; the list is formidable even without it. Our unanimous reluctance to appeal to migrations as explanations of culture change cannot be absolute, for we know migrations do take place sometimes. If some Mixtec ruler has carried out several successful conquests, the most recent of which brings his holdings right to the edge of the Valley of Oaxaca, will he stop there because the valley people speak a different language? I suspect he will covet the valley lands more than the mountains, and will attempt it. And if the time is ripe, he will be successful.

Nevertheless, there does exist some reason for reluctance to advocate Mixtec conquest in the valley as explanation, and that reason is not likely to go away. What do proper scientists do in such a situation? They make lists of the various possibilities, and then try to find ways to test them. Bernal had made such a list, though it is by no means always in print, and so have I (Bernal 1958a, 1958b, 1958c, 1964, 1966a, 1966b, 1974; Paddock 1955c, 1958a, 1958b, 1960, 1964, 1966c).

Unhappily, we do not always find a way to test all the propositions we would like to evaluate. And, even when the propositions are testable, the testing does not produce definitive answers—not in a world of human phenomena, not in a world where even the simplest phenomena, those of physics, are described in terms including uncertainty, relativity, and probability.

If we can accept the same limited success that other scientists have to content themselves with, we can proceed. If we are going to demand final, irrefutable, eternal proofs, we are not going anywhere. I assume the decision is to proceed.

The exploration—intensive, but limited to a very small area—of Lambityeco should teach us a general lesson in this form: just as we were almost entirely ignorant of early Monte Albán IV until Lambityeco was explored, other Valley of Oaxaca sites still to be examined may be holding the secrets of later stages of Period IV. We are not yet justified in assuming they do not exist, except as a trial formulation. Because we lack positive evidence for these later stages except that of Yuchacá–Cuilapan, which is not dated, we

are unable to say whether or not some form of Late Period IV existed in the Valley of Oaxaca after Monte Albán V had fully begun. (The appearance of single pottery vessels in Period V style during IIIb and early IV is not, in my opinion, sufficient evidence that V had fully begun.)

Thus we are faced with two major alternatives, and a large number of possible intermediate ones, or combinations of these two. The two polar choices are:

1. Vestiges of the Monte Albán culture remained in existence as the way of life of Zapotec populations (i.e., Monte Albán IV) throughout the span of Monte Albán V, and were extinguished only as a consequence of the Spanish Conquest. Monte Albán V was simply another province of Mixtec culture, brought into the valley by Mixtec invaders; it acquired its idiosyncrasies in the same way as did the other provinces of the Mixteca, through time and under the impact of distinctive exterior conditions that also affected the dialect of Mixteco spoken in the valley. Monte Albán V differs from the contemporary culture of Coixtlahuaca for the same reasons that Yanhuitlán and Tlaxiaco do, and in comparable degree.

2. Monte Albán V was not brought into the Valley of Oaxaca by an invasion, Mixtec or otherwise; rather, it evolved out of Monte Albán IV. Therefore, Monte Albán V is a culture carried, as it was created, by a Zapotec population. The resemblances it shows to the culture of the Mixteca Alta are a natural result of the fact that Mixtec style became a pan-Mesoamerican horizon style, and also of the fact that the Valley of Oaxaca has a long common border with the Mixteca Alta. Those objects made in the Mixteca that are found in the Valley of Oaxaca in Period V are the results of trade. Though intermarriages of ruling families may have occurred as early as A.D. 1280, no significant number of Mixtecs came into the valley until after 1500, and perhaps only after 1521.

Sound scientific procedure requires us to adopt each such possibility as a trial assumption and see what its consequences are, attempting to make the consequences into testable hypotheses and then testing them against existing or new data.

This has been amply done with respect to the first possibility. First Caso, then Bernal, and finally I have all put together (within the limits of data available at a given moment) comprehensive schemes based on the first assumption. Any such scheme at once produces many statements testable against data already in hand, so that even before we find ways to formulate testable hypotheses, and find resources with which to test them, the testing actually begins. The first alternative has been under constant examination for over 40 years. Because some of the important available data are in conflict—as I pointed out in reviewing the early chronicles—no formulation is going to fulfill the ideal condition of accommodating all available data.

From the beginning—say in Caso's first articles on Tomb 7 in 1932—the discussion has often been shrill, to say the least. Caso was attacked on ostensibly scientific, but in fact political, grounds; he was accused by some attackers of having stolen the best pieces from Tomb 7 at the same time that others were saying he had had the Tomb 7 offerings made to order to bring himself publicity.

A new wave of attacks on Position 1 was aroused by the Yagul discoveries and their interpretation in that framework. This time the accusations—usually directed at me because, I suppose, Caso and Bernal were insultingly considered capable of nonscientific reprisals—were approximately to the effect that Mixtec invasions of the Valley of Oaxaca were being promoted through false interpretations of history and archaeology as a means of denigrating the Zapotec people (the parallel with the Oscar Lewis scandal of 1965, in which Lewis was formally accused of "denigrating" the Mexican nation by publishing *The Children of Sánchez*, is irresistible).

No doubt we all are dismayed by these attacks, and would like to carry on our work in an atmosphere of lofty, objective, intellectual progress. But the questions considered here seem to be, for reasons that still baffle me after 20 years, only somewhat less hotly political than "Cuauhtemoc's" bones.

After 40 years of attacks on Position 1 as stated by Caso, and 20 years of the same on that position as elaborated by Bernal and by me, one would think there would exist an ample exposition of Position 2—an alternative scheme of late valley-culture history, accommodating all but the self-contradictory data and congruent with what we know of culture and of Mesoamerica in general. I have made a couple of tentative public attempts, and many unpublished ones. But the astonishing fact is that my rather abortive attempts have been the only ones; while there has been an unceasing chorus of attacks on Position 1, only a holder of Position 1 has taken Position 2 seriously enough to try to do something with it.

The Lambityeco discoveries, above all the dates, have seriously shaken one major foundation stone of Position 1—the long survival of Monte Albán IV. I have therefore given increased consideration to the alternatives. But I am not here going to embark on a major exposition of Position 2 and its consequences in the form of a comprehensive Mixtec-free scheme of late valley-culture history. I think it appropriate for those who reject Position 1 to do that.

Bernal has often expressed a belief that certain objects found in Period V contexts show traces of derivation from the culture of Period IV. Some of these, from tombs at Yagul and Monte Albán, seemed to me so nearly formless as to defy classification. This kind of pottery will not be found in the Monte Albán ceramics report, even though one batch of it was found at Monte Albán—an offering of dozens of miniature vessels, under the Mixtec-style stonework of the last repairs on Mound B on the North Platform.

Most of the examples we know from archaeological work are from Yagul. There are two colors, a cream and a red-brown, but both colors are often veiled by the ex-

tremely sketchy baking of the ware. As Bernal says (Bernal and Gamio 1974:68), referring to *cajetes* of this ware,

> We have found them both in the lower levels of Patio F and in Tombs 23 and 24, which suggests that this is a decadent Zapotec form of Monte Albán IV that was still in use later on, in fact until the end of occupation of the Palace. We have already mentioned the possibility that they may be objects made by relatives of the dead and not by professional potters.

Several shapes occur in this ware. It should be mentioned that, in my opinion, it cannot be a normal, functional pottery. It is so extremely ill-made and baked, and so thin, that great care is required to avoid breaking it in handling. Sherds of it are never found on the surface, not because it is rare, but because they have disintegrated. Apparently it was made especially for funerary, and possibly other, offerings (the tiny examples are found, for example, in the stone offering boxes). Long ago an ethnographic parallel was found and reported by Brockington (Paddock 1957:15n). At least some of its shapes may well be descendants of Monte Albán IV shapes—and in every such case, they are much more radically decadent than the Period IV predecessors, some of which were already decadent. Another point of great interest in this ware—for which Bernal has adopted our name of *amateur ware* along with his other terms for it—is that it is found side by side with the technically and esthetically excellent G3M in tombs. Bernal has not fully described its graininess: it is made with abundant, medium-coarse tempers, presumably because this formula assures minimum cracking on drying rapidly and in baking. Sometimes whole crystals of quartz, up to 3 mm in diameter, occur in it, as if the temper had been scooped up from the abundant anthills of Yagul where such crystals are common.

The shapes I am familiar with are *cajetes, sahumadores,* spiked vessels, claw vessels, vases or beakers, and miniatures of G3M forms including tripods (rare).

The *cajetes* are of three types. One, most commonly of red-brown paste, looks roughly subhemispherical on the inside, but has a small flattened base on the outside. This shape gives it the appearance of an incredibly bedraggled descendant of the G-35 bowl. But it is so poorly shaped that the rim, for instance, is utterly irregular; the rim is simply where the paste gave out. The exterior is vaguely classifiable as that of a conical *cajete.* Diameter is commonly around 15 cm.

The second *cajete* type is more commonly of the cream paste, and I have the impression it is slightly better shaped and thicker, though not always so. It is a subhemispherical shape with no flattening of the base. Examples in the Frissell Museum collections in Mitla range from 2 to 30 cm in diameter.

The third *cajete* type is always a miniature, with diameters of 3 to 6 cm. It is a subhemispherical bowl that has a strip of clay crossing its interior and dividing it into halves, and one of these halves is further divided by a second strip into quarters.

The *sahumadores* of this ware always seem to have a line

around the rim incised in their bowls, making a circle, and a cross made with two intersecting diameters. The handles are almost always solid, but very often have a perfunctory imitation of a lengthwise perforation. There may be imitations of perforations in the bowl as well, though these almost never go all the way through. Bowl diameters range from about 5 to over 15 cm. They are more often cream than red-brown.

Small and miniature spiked vessels (Bernal and Gamio 1974:Lám. 22c–g) are common, and were offered in large numbers in nonfunerary settings. They usually are from 2 to 4 cm in diameter. Almost equally common, and found in the same settings, are claw vessels, small and miniature (Bernal and Gamio:Lám. 22h–l; Paddock 1955a:Figure 13). These range in length from 4 to 10 cm. Vases and tumblers or beakers, about 3 to 8 cm tall, often have appliqué "worms," in simple squiggles, as decoration.

In the Frissell Museum collection I have seen tiny imitations in this ware of the polished gray tripod *cajete* and of the high, pear-shaped tripod gray *olla*. In addition, the thousands of tiny subhemispherical bowls (2–3 cm in diameter) may be imitations of the common G3M subhemispherical plate or bowl.

It appears (David Peterson, personal communication, 1975) that this same ware may have been used in Period V for boiling down brine into salt at the Yegüih salt deposits, but of course this was done in well-made vessels of enormous size.

Now if the "conical" *cajetes* of this crude ware are descendants of G-35, the subhemispherical ones of the common hemispherical flat-bottomed gray *cajete* of Period IV, and the claw vessels and the *sahumadores* also are descendants of the Period IV forms, we would have in absolutely Period V contexts some survivals of Period IV culture. And what a pathetic collection they make! The speculation that this group of traits is the product of an extremely low-ranking class or caste within the society is hardly consistent with the finding of these pitiable objects in otherwise rich offerings of tombs or as the only ceramic goods in important palaces having stone offering boxes. If these items were made by relatives of the deceased for a tomb, they are explained in a way, but their possible derivation from Period IV is not. And they are not usable. This is a typical point with which the scholars who wish to reject Position 1 may contend. If they succeed, with this and the others, I can be convinced.

No doubt the boldest attempt to grapple with this situation in scientific terms is that of Brockington (1973:1–5, 57–64, 80–86). Rather than adopting either Position 1 or Position 2 and then attempting to cope with the fairly ambitious enterprise of writing a cultural and ethnic history of late times in the Valley of Oaxaca congruent with that position, Brockington has prudently and usefully attacked another problem that is especially likely, if clarified, to help with the valley dilemma—the origins of late Mixtec culture. The Miahuatlán materials, scanty as they are, could hardly be more strategic.

1. They confirm the Lambityeco findings by coinciding almost point by point, making it clear that—quite possibly in opposition to a conservative IIIb enclave at and around Monte Albán—there is an early IV with many diagnostic traits.

2. They likewise show traces of a precocious V in the same period.

3. They show us a number of traits unique to Miahuatlán.

4. They suggest a potentially valuable distinction between the origin of Monte Albán V culture and the origin of Mixtec culture.

5. They confirm documentary indications of ties between Miahuatlán and the Coast Mixtec kingdom of Tututepec.

6. At the same time, they indicate that the Miahuatlán–Tututepec ties were late, and less intimate than expected; Miahuatlán seems to have been a Valley of Oaxaca center in the cultural sense to a degree rather surprising in view of its distance from Monte Albán and its nearness to the coast.

7. They show us, in Brockington's interpretation, a situation in which distinct IV and V traditions occur concurrently—a situation I believe is not to be seen at Yagul because of the brusque cutoff there of IV, and its replacement by V.

Brockington has thus neatly avoided committing himself to either Position 1 or Position 2, while contributing actively to the clarification of the problem. Some of his points favor one position, some another. Further work at Miahuatlán would surely be as promising as any approach we might take toward arriving at a satisfactory reformulation of late Valley of Oaxaca development.

Meanwhile, I think it is fair to ask anyone proposing the abandonment of Position 1 to present a constructive and reasonably complete alternative. We have had enough of simple nay-saying.

## MITLA

The quality of the Mitla architecture has long focused attention on the place, and the identity of its builders has been argued for at least 80 years, probably much longer. Saville asserted calmly that they were obviously Nahuas (1909:189). Of course many who discuss the matter consider it obvious that they were Zapotecs—just as, obviously, the British built Stonehenge, the Americans built Snaketown, the Tuaregs built Leptis Magna, and the Turks built Troy. This problem has led some of the more serious students of it to a certain formulation that requires a few words—no, it requires many, but will *get* only a few.

Spores speaks of "receding Mixtec influence" in 1521, and adds, "by that time the Zapotec, after allying themselves with the Mexicans, had reasserted control. . . . The Mixtec appear to have come in, built or taken over communities, occupied them for a period, and then moved out, leaving Zapotec culture relatively unaffected" (1965:965).

This is a very important idea, and apparently represents an attempt to grapple with the complications and contradictions I have tried to formulate above as Position 1 and Position 2—that is, a synthesis of the two.

Bernal had struggled with the problem in rather similar ways. Almost every paper he wrote from the beginning of the Yagul work until recently presented, if it dealt with late times in the Valley of Oaxaca, some new idea that he plainly hoped might lead to a synthesis resolving the contradictions of Position 1 and Position 2. At one time he proposed that in Mitla there were visible the beginnings of a Monte Albán VI—a fusion of IV and V resulting from a continued coexistence of Mixtecs and Zapotecs in the valley (Bernal 1966a:351). This may be the same phenomenon referred to by Spores.

In my first reports on Yagul (Paddock 1955c), I had—rather blindly and hopefully, and not impelled by any overwhelming accumulation of data—tried to list some possibilities, examine them in the light of what was known then, and assign relative probabilities to them. One result was the hypothesis that the cultural resurgence represented by the Mitla palaces had been caused by an analog of heterosis, an achievement beyond the capacity of either Mixtecs or Zapotecs alone, but resulting rather from their working together—whether as rivals or not—and produc-

ing something new. Whether such attempted syntheses go back further than that, I do not know; I don't think Caso tried that approach.

With respect to that approach, I want to make just one distinction. If we have, as one might interpret what Brockington found at Miahuatlán, an evolution of Monte Albán V ceramics out of those of IV, there will be intermediate forms—not hybrid forms that combine the traits of a more or less mature V with a mature IV, but a gradual reshaping of IV toward V. Brockington did not find such intermediate types.

If IV survives until V is fully formed, however, and then the two are combined by some process of fusion, we will get hybridization or acculturation—as occurred at Teotihuacán when purely Oaxaca-style vessels were succeeded by partly Oaxaca-style vessels having some Teotihuacán traits.

There is only one place from which I have seen pottery that seems to me to have this appearance: Guiengola. I have been searching for it for many years, and in the Frissell Museum collection I have set aside some possible examples. I wish I could accept all those Bernal has proposed, for example from Yagul and Monte Albán, as examples, but most of them seem to me to be shapeless pieces that he, as eager as I to find such specimens, has given the qualities he wishes they had.

# TOPIC 80
## An Editorial Opinion on the Mixtec Impact

KENT V. FLANNERY
JOYCE MARCUS

In our Introduction to the Postclassic (pages 217–226) we presented an outline of some of the controversies surrounding the Balkanization of Oaxaca, without explicitly taking sides. However, it would be deceptive to the reader to pretend that we are completely impartial. Having made a serious (and, we hope, successful) effort to keep our opinions out of the Introduction, we now want to make them explicit. We felt it would be inappropriate to do this until John Paddock had given his somewhat different perspective on the situation in Topic 79, providing us with needed balance as well as calling attention to some of the weaknesses in our position.

## THE ETHNOHISTORIC DATA

Our basic position on the ethnohistoric data is that, first, there can be no question about the presence of Mixtecs in the western Valley of Oaxaca; they were recorded by Spanish census-takers, and there were still Mixtec speakers at

Xoxocotlán when Marshall Saville (1899) excavated there. We propose that they originally entered the valley as the result of strategic marriage alliances between the Zapotec royalty of Zaachila and the Mixtec royalty of the Yanhuitlán–Almoloyas region. Whether these marriages were intended to establish peace following military conflict or to reinforce the power of certain Zapotec dynasties is not clear. However, they are independently documented in two different *relaciones* (Mata 1580; Salazar 1581) that share a significant number of details.

We suspect that most of the Mixtecs who came were *tay situndayu* who worked the lands given to the royal Mixtec marriage partner by his (or her) Zapotec in-laws. Our suspicion is reinforced by the fact that site C-V-132, which may well be ancient Sa'a Yucu, is without impressive palace architecture or public buildings (Topic 85). It is further reinforced by the Postclassic settlement pattern of the western Valley of Oaxaca, which most frequently consists of small farmsteads, hamlets, and isolated residences (Topic 83). This pattern is also seen in Drennan's "Mountain Survey" area located between the Valley of Oaxaca and the Yanhuitlán–Almoloyas area (Topic 84).

By the same token, we do not believe that these Mixtecs "invaded" the entire Valley of Oaxaca, or that Mitla and Yagul were built by "eastern Mixtecs." Whereas the *relaciones* of Cuilapan and Zaachila are very specific about Mixtec residents, the *relaciones* of Mitla, Tlacolula, Macuilxochitl, and Teotitlán del Valle mention only Zapotec residents (Canseco 1580; Asensio 1580a, 1580b). Moreover, we maintain that the *relación* of Mitla specifically attributes the religious structures to a Zapotec *bigaña,* the palaces to a Zapotec *coqui* (Topic 88; Canseco 1580). If we are to accept the *relaciones* as evidence for Mixtecs in the western valley, we must be consistent and accept them as evidence for Zapotecs in the eastern valley. However, we also accept Bernal's statement that the eastern valley was "Mixtec-influenced" (Bernal 1966a); because the Zapotec royalty had Mixtec in-laws, they would hardly be uninfluenced.

In this regard we are struck by one of the major points made in Topic 76 by M. E. Smith: all codices display a "regional point of view." Their authors were not producing objective, impartial history, but rather presenting only one side of each story. The same is probably true of most *relaciones*. Naturally the Mixtecs of Cuilapan told Salazar they had subdued the whole Valley of Oaxaca; naturally their descendants in the nearby Zaachila area, where Burgoa was vicar, told him they had expanded from Sa'a Yucu and forced the Zapotecs to flee to Tehuantepec. In the *relaciones* of "pure Zapotec" towns, one hears only about the exploits of Cocijoeza, and the way he outwitted both the Mixtecs and Aztecs.

Nowhere in the *relaciones* does it actually say that the Mixtecs "invaded" the Valley of Oaxaca. The *Relación de Cuylapa*, as we have seen, mentions the son of a "Mixtec woman" who escaped an assassination plot and "made war" against Zaachila. And Burgoa (1674) speaks of the Sa'a Yucu Mixtecs colonizing more and more of the Zaachila plain until they had encircled the Zapotec capital and forced the *coquitao* to leave. But this is not a wholesale conquest of Zapotecs by Mixtecs; it is a struggle between descendants of two royal houses already linked by marriage. Given the regional perspective of each *relación*, we feel the description of conflict at Cuilapan does not refer to a widespread state of war, but only to Cuilapan's conflict with Zaachila.

This situation leads us to what we feel is the most important general point we can make on Late Postclassic warfare among the Cloud People: it was *cacique* versus *cacique,* not nation versus nation. Nowhere is it imagined that "the Mixtec people" were at war with "the Zapotec people." Rather, the lord ♂ 5 Flower was at war with the lord ♂ 8 Serpent, and he allied himself with whatever other lords he could, regardless of their language. Thus the fact that Mitla had fought battles with Tlacolula (Canseco 1580:146), for example, does not convince us that Mitla was "Mixtec." Zapotec lords fought each other, Mixtec lords fought each other, and Zapotec and Mixtec lords fought the Aztec separately or together. In our opinion, the whole question of Zapotec–Mixtec relations sometimes has been obscured by being phrased in terms of clashing nations, such as the Allies versus the Axis in World War II.

## MONTE ALBÁN V CERAMICS

It is also our opinion that Postclassic studies have been confused by a general branding of Monte Albán V pottery as Mixtec. To call polychrome pottery or Yanhuitlán Red-on-cream pottery Mixtec is perhaps not so bad, but we feel that referring to the G3M gray wares in this way runs counter to all the archaeological evidence of the past 10 years. Brockington (1973) sees G3M growing out of the Classic Zapotec gray ware complex at Miahuatlán; we see the same thing at San Sebastián Abasolo (Topic 87). G3M jars were produced by the thousands in a cave outside Mitla (Topic 88); G3M pottery dominates the ruins of Guiengola (Topic 91), including the building that may be Cocijoeza's palace. Indeed, the major diversity of G3M occurs in the Valley of Oaxaca (Paddock, Topic 79), and it is more common in areas with Zapotec speakers than at Yanhuitlán in the Mixteca. In fact—to state the case most strongly—if G3M pottery is Mixtec, then the Zapotec did not exist at all during the Late Postclassic.

However, to call G3M Zapotec would also be an oversimplification: it reached Cuicatlán and Coixtlahuaca, and a reasonable facsimile occurred at Nochixtlán during the Natividad phase (Spores 1972), although it did not occur with the high frequency there that it did in the Valley of Oaxaca. Moreover, it is the main ceramic of C-V-132, the probable site of Mixtec Sa'a Yucu (Topic 85). We therefore propose to regard G3M gray ware simply as the dominant utilitarian ceramic made by the potters of the Valley of Oaxaca during Monte Albán V times, and we conclude that it was used by virtually everyone—Zapotec, Mixtec, or Aztec—who happened to be in the region at that time. In our opinion, its utility for determining the ethnicity of sites, residences, or burials is close to zero.

## MONTE ALBÁN V ARCHITECTURE

We believe that much the same can be said for the evidence from architecture, or architectural elements like the step-fret or *greca. Xicalcoliuhquis* or step-fret motifs occur on the pottery of Monte Albán II. There are architectural *grecas* on Monte Albán III buildings at Atzompa, and at sites as widely scattered as El Tajín and Chichén Itzá; they appear on Aztec seals, on textiles from Cueva de Ejutla (Topic 78), and in the Mixtec codices. Given their widespread distribution we feel it is unwarranted to designate them as Mixtec, and given their long history in the Valley of Oaxaca we do not find it surprising that they were used by the builders of Mitla, Yagul, Teotitlán del Valle, and the Zaachila tombs. In other words, we accept Acosta's framework for architectural evolution in Oaxaca, where the Mitla *grecas* represent the coming together of two concepts—the step-fret motif and the recessed *tablero*—already present in the Classic Zapotec architecture of Monte Albán.

To be sure, the architecture of Monte Albán V differs from that of Period III, just as the architecture of Period III differs from that of the Formative. But nowhere in the Mixteca—nor at Sa'a Yucu—do we see architectural prototypes that convince us that Monte Albán V architecture resulted from a Mixtec invasion. Presumably the Zapotec architects were aware of new trends and innovations over a wide area of Mesoamerica, and had they needed inspiration they were hardly restricted to the Mixteca—an area that has yet to produce a single Postclassic building as magnificent as the Hall of the Columns at Mitla. Even Santo Domingo, that mysterious site in the southern Cuicatec Cañada, is said to be less impressive than Yagul, which, in turn, is less impressive than Mitla (Bernal and Gamio 1974). Is it not just as likely that Mitla is the prototype for both Yagul and Santo Domingo, not to mention Tlalixtac, Teotitlán del Valle, and Matatlán?

And what of Mitla, and of Yagul, where the "civil buildings" are said to be more elegant than the "religious buildings" (Bernal 1966a:363), thereby reversing the situation in the Classic? In our opinion, Bernal has put his finger on an important trend here, but not necessarily one implying the arrival of a new ethnic group. The Postclassic state was, after all, a form of government integrated more by political power and military force than by state religion, and the escalated status of the Postclassic ruler demanded an elaborate residence. But is the difference really as great as some have suggested? None of the palaces at Mitla is really as large as the Period III palace on the east side of Monte Albán's Main Plaza. In fact, the largest single building at Mitla—the Hall of the Columns—is described in the *relaciones* as a religious structure (Topic 88; Canseco 1580), and Patio Four at Yagul, presumably an open area flanked by four temples, covers a larger space than the Palace of the Six Patios (Topic 87). Thus religion was hardly relegated to an insignificant position even in the "palace-oriented" cities of Monte Albán V.

In summary, we would not embrace either of the two "polar" positions given in Topic 79. We see a modest Mixtec presence in the Valley of Oaxaca as the result of strategic marriage alliances between Mixtec and Zapotec royal houses, and regard any "wars" as local conflicts of the kind typical of Balkanized regions. We are not very concerned by a Postclassic disappearance of Zapotec "deities" because we are not convinced that most Classic urns represent deities anyway (Topic 43); we are even less convinced that Period V *penates* are deities. Finally, we plead for a separation of two issues: Zapotec and Mixtec culture on the one hand, and Late Postclassic pottery on the other. Archaeological confusion increases in direct proportion to our inability to treat these as separate issues.

# SECTION 8b
# The Zapotec Response to Mixtec and Aztec Power

## TOPIC 81
## Monte Albán in Period V

RICHARD E. BLANTON

One of the great myths of Oaxaca archaeology is that during Period V Monte Albán lay abandoned, serving only as a necropolis for visitors from the valley floor who came to reuse the tombs and to bury offerings in the rubble of the abandoned public buildings. This illusion is caused by the fact that the Main Plaza was unoccupied. In fact, although considerably reduced in size relative to its maximum population in Period IIIb, Monte Albán was still an important community in Period V; it displays one of the largest concentrations of Period V pottery we have found in the course of our survey.

Figure 8.19 shows the distribution and density of Period V ceramics from our surface collections at Monte Albán. A striking feature of this period was the abandonment of the higher elevations, especially around the Main Plaza, in favor of the lower slopes of Monte Albán proper.

Surveys of the Central Valley by Kowalewski (Topics 83 and 85) also show substantial settlement around the base of Monte Albán. Period V occupation is scattered along the base of the hill in a giant C from the north slopes south along the west slopes, circling around the southern base. Since the exact relationship of these settlements to Monte Albán proper is not clear, my population estimates for the latter site do not include them.

The core of Period V settlement is located surrounding, and to the west of, the most highly accessible point in the city's ancient road system. I interpret this to mean that both a location closer to the valley floor and access to major roads were more important considerations for the population of Monte Albán in Period V than had been true earlier, which in turn suggests a more commercial orientation for the city during the Late Postclassic.

The distributions of some artifact scatters, interpreted as workshops, tend to support this interpretation. Six out of the seven mano and metate workshops we found have evidence of Period V occupation. Of 31 obsidian concentrations that may have been workshops, 18 had evidence of Period V occupation—a high proportion considering only a third of Monte Albán's terraces show any evidence for occupation during this time. Obsidian, in fact, is generally strongly associated with Period V ceramics at Monte Albán, producing a chi-square statistic of 58.2 with one degree of freedom, significant above the .00001 level.

During the Late Postclassic, Monte Albán was evidently still a very important place, probably a small commercial center and perhaps also a sacred place where people still deposited offerings and occasionally buried their dead, but it was no longer the center of decision making for a regional polity. The only important mound-group cluster in the core area of Period V settlement is the one referred to by Mexican archaeologists as El Pitahayo, where abundant ceramics of the period appear (Caso, Bernal, and Acosta 1967:17; Caso 1935:77).

A comparison of the dimensions of this mound-group

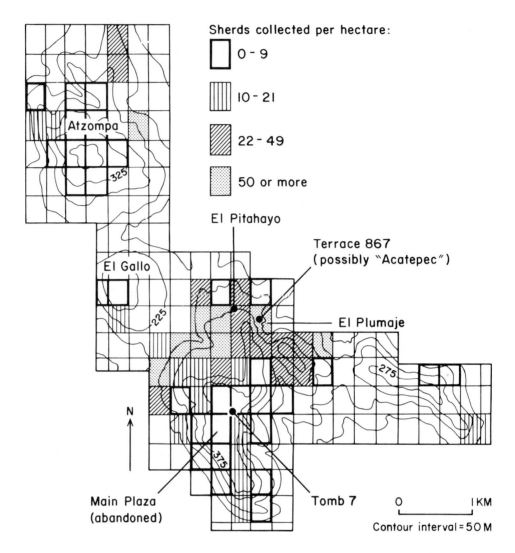

FIGURE 8.19. The extent of occupation at Monte Albán during Period V. (Redrawn, with modifications, from Blanton 1978.)

with those of the Main Plaza indicates the diminished role of the city. El Pitahayo covers an area of only 15,200 m², and has mounded platforms totaling only 9040 m³. The Main Plaza extended over an area of 160,500 m², and had

platform mounds totaling 723,646 m³. Also, although Monte Albán's Period IIIb population may have reached 30,000, by Period V it had been reduced to an estimated 4050 to 8100.

## TOPIC 82
## Monte Albán's Tomb 7

JOYCE MARCUS

As pointed out by Blanton (Topic 81), Late Postclassic Monte Albán was a nucleated settlement with a population estimated at 4050 to 8100 persons. On its southern flank lay a less densely nucleated settlement with an estimated

980–1960 persons, which may have been the Mixtec colony of Sa'a Yucu (Kowalewski, Topic 85). It is therefore no surprise that the area should contain numerous Monte Albán V tombs and burials. No one, however, was prepared for the extraordinary richness of Monte Albán's Tomb 7, which Alfonso Caso found in January of 1932. This tomb takes on additional significance in the light of Tombs 1 and 2 of Zaachila (Topic 87) and Tomb 1 at Huitzo (Topic 93), which appear to be contemporaneous.

Tomb 7 was one of several tombs discovered near System Y, several hundred meters to the northeast of the North Platform in an area called the Cementerio Norte (Caso 1969). Here a number of important rulers of the Classic period had been buried in royal tombs with commemorative buildings over them. Tomb 7 had originally been constructed as a standard Zapotec tomb of the Monte Albán IIIb period, with typical IIIb funerary urns and a carved door stone with Zapotec hieroglyphs, surmounted by a standard two-room temple with columns to either side of the doorway.

This Classic tomb had been discovered, partially emptied, and reused during Monte Albán V. At least 9 skeletons—all probably secondary "bundle" burials—were placed in the tomb, which has two chambers running east–west, united by a large vestibule. According to Rubín de la Borbolla (1969), the "principal" skeleton is that of a man approximately 55 years old with cranial deformation and filed teeth. Most of the other skeletons are also males between 16 to 20 years old and 45 to 55 years old, but there are also bones present from two women and an infant; however, Rubín de la Borbolla feels the latter may be intrusive bones included when the secondary remains were transferred to Tomb 7 from their earlier place of burial. After resealing the tomb, the Period V burial crew left an offering of 3 jade earspools, 36 jade beads, shell fragments, and a conch-shell trumpet in the earth above the crypt.

The secondary burials in Tomb 7 were accompanied by more than 500 items of exotic paraphernalia, not counting the thousands of individual beads which went into the various necklaces. There were pectorals of gold, silver, and gold and silver joined; some pectorals had the Mixtec A–O year-sign, whereas others show Nahuatl deities identified as Xochipilli and Xipe-Totec. There was a trophy skull covered with turquoise mosaic, similar to the masks from Zaachila (Topic 87) and Cueva de Ejutla (Topic 78), and there were lost-wax cast gold beads with carbon nuclei, similar to those found in Tomb 1 at Huitzo (Topic 93). Jade and gold fan handles, gold and silver cosmetic tweezers, gold and silver rings, gold and silver bells, earspools and "false fingernails" of gold, jade and gold lip plugs, and turquoise beads littered the floor of the tomb. Offerings included a gold diadem and "feather," bowls of silver and rock crystal and *tecali* (a kind of fine-grained travertine), and earspools of obsidian polished so thin that one could read newsprint through them. Necklaces of gold, silver, amber, jet, coral, pearl, and shell accompanied the skeletons. There were also more than a dozen bones carved in "codex" style, like those from the Zaachila tomb (Topic 87), some with bits of turquoise inlay serving as a blue background against which the figures could be seen more easily.

Caso understandably regarded Tomb 7 as "the greatest aboriginal treasure of the New World," and he considered its occupants to be Mixtec. The discovery of similar objects with "Mixtec" polychrome pottery at Zaachila only reinforced his interpretation (Caso 1969). Apparently, the fact that Xochipilli and Xipe-Totec were not Mixtec deities did not bother him, given the known political and military contact between the Mixtec and Nahua peoples dating back to Toltec times. We are left, however, with a number of unanswered questions. What was the relationship between the late Postclassic population of Monte Albán itself and the nearby colony of Sa'a Yucu? From which, if either, did the nine occupants of Tomb 7 come? What was their relationship to the occupants of Tomb 1 at Zaachila, whom Caso believed descended from the lords of Yanhuitlán? On a more general level, if a Mixtec lord from Yanhuitlán married a Zapotec princess from Zaachila, would his offspring be ethnically "Mixtec" or "Zapotec"? And would we be able to tell their ethnic affiliation just by looking at the objects in their tombs?

## THE CARVED BONES FROM TOMB 7

Certainly two of the interesting similarities between the Mixtec and Zapotec peoples were their sense of history and their interest in the genealogy of the nobility. The genealogical records of the Mixtec nobility were called *tonindeye*, "*historias de linajes.*" These records indicate that the origins of the royal ancestors of the Mixtec were linked to mythical places, dates, and events, sometimes represented in codices and sometimes on carved bones.

A great many carved bones were found in Tomb 7, although only 34 bore inscriptions or pictorial scenes. In terms of subject matter, there were basically three types of bones: (1) those including personages, names, places, and scenes similar to those found in the Mixtec codices; (2) those containing consecutive lists of years or of days in the 260-day calendar; and (3) those with alternating and repetitive iconographic elements, without actual writing. Caso (1969:179) has suggested that the majority of the bones were from jaguars, while others were from eagles. He also suggests that some of the carved bones found by Gallegos in Tomb 1 at Zaachila were carved by the same artist who carved the Tomb 7 bones. Although it is difficult to sustain this contention, the similarity of several artifacts and of the carving style does argue for relative contemporaneity between Tombs 1 and 2 at Zaachila and Tomb 7 at Monte Albán. (As for the artisan who might have carved these bones, Caso parenthetically mentions that during the 1936 season at Monte Albán he found a burial associated with a Mixtec polychrome olla that contained fragments of carved bone, four chisels or engravers of copper of different size and thickness, and a sharp-pointed polisher of shell—conceivably the burial of a bone carver.)

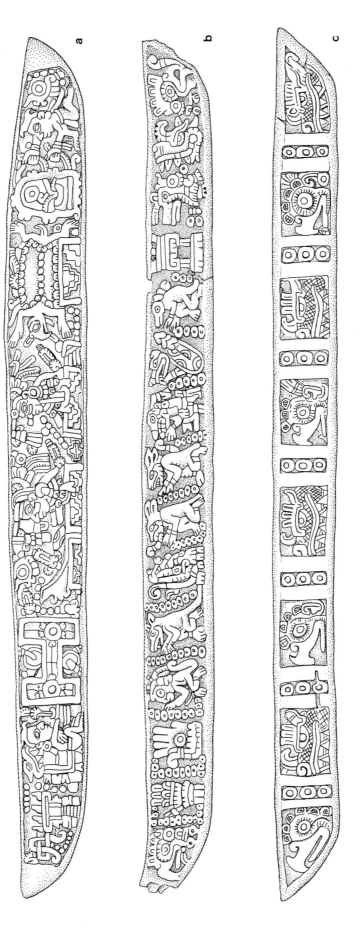

FIGURE 8.20. Examples of three categories of carved bones from Tomb 7 at Monte Albán: (a) Bone 203b; (b) Bone 172i; (c) Bone 203f. (Redrawn from Caso 1969.)

The carved bones of Tomb 7 constituted one of Caso's reasons for believing that the occupants of the tomb were ethnically Mixtec, the writing on the bones being quite different from that of the Zapotecs or Aztecs (Caso 1969:180). For example, the numerical coefficients accompanying the days in the 260-day calendar are written in dots even in the case of those numbers over 5. However, it is also true that during the Postclassic horizon the Aztecs (and perhaps other groups) employed dots alone for their system of numeration. Another of Caso's reasons for arguing that the occupants of the tomb were Mixtec was that there are bones, such as 203b (see following discussion), that bear many similarities to elements and places in the Mixtec codices, particularly the Codices Selden and Bodley.

Let us now look at an example of one bone from each type, beginning with Type 1. Bone 203b (Caso 1969:Fig. 170) was evidently intended to be read from right to left, beginning with the day 7 (?) Rain (Figure 8.20a). Next we see a man tugging on a hill sign with cord attached to it (the name of the hill is given within the hill sign). Following this, there are six localities that were apparently conquered; each place name has an arrow thrust into it, with the feathered nock of the arrow appearing above and to the right of the place name. The text ends on the left with the Mixtec year sign (interlocked A–O), the year 7 Reed, and the day 4 or 5 (?) House.

An example of a Type 2 carved bone listing days in the 260-day calendar in consecutive order is Bone 172i (Caso 1969:Fig. 213); an example listing years in consecutive order is Bone 37a (Caso 1969:Fig. 217a). In both cases, 13 days or 13 years are given in order. For example, on Bone 172i the text is intended to be read from right to left, giving us the first 13 days of the 260-day ritual calendar as follows (Figure 8.20b): 1 Crocodile, 2 Wind, 3 House, 4 Lizard, 5 Serpent, 6 Death, 7 Deer, 8 Rabbit, 9 Water, 10 Dog, 11 Monkey, 12 Grass, 13 Reed.

An example of Type 3, the carved bones showing only repetitive motifs, is Bone 203f (Caso 1969:Fig. 180). Here two animal heads are shown, the crocodile alternating with the vulture (Figure 8.20c).

We may suggest that Type 1 carved bones deal with genealogy and historical events related to the occupants of the tomb, and Types 2 and 3 may have been instruments for divination and its resultant decision making. If the skeletal remains of Tomb 7 can be interpreted as those of a lord and his retinue of retainers, it is likely that those retainers included a minor priest or diviner who was expected to continue his divination in the afterlife. It is also possible that the Type 1 bones represent records of marriage, conquest, and royal descent kept by a minor priest or scribe whose remains may also be among the retainers.

# TOPIC 83
## Monte Albán V Settlement Patterns in the Valley of Oaxaca

STEPHEN KOWALEWSKI

During Monte Albán V the Valley of Oaxaca reveals a series of apparent contrasts among subareas, with some parts of the valley showing nucleated centers and other parts mainly isolated residences and tiny hamlets. At the Santa Fe seminar it was suggested that these patterns might reflect the difference between nucleated Zapotec communities and areas where the land was worked by a Mixtec lord's *terrazgueros*, or *tay situndayu*. Some aspects of this contrast had already been noted by Bernal in his preliminary surveys—for example, the low numbers and small size of Monte Albán V sites in the Zimatlán region (Bernal 1966a:Map 1). Unfortunately, our intensive survey has not proceeded far enough to make meaningful comparisons among all parts of the valley.

## ETLA REGION

The amount of Period V occupation in the Etla region seems to have been considerably below the levels reached in the Late Classic (Figure 8.21). Between 4575 and 9150 people are estimated to have lived in 103 sites with a total occupied area of 348 ha (Varner 1974:126).

## CENTRAL VALLEY

In the Central Valley Survey region (Figure 8.22), populations were probably slightly larger in Monte Albán V than in IIIb, whereas the number of sites and the occupied area were much greater than in the Late Classic (an estimated 6407–14,658 persons living on 1156.2 ha divided among 339 sites). About one-third of the population in the two areas discussed so far lived at Monte Albán, but of the remaining rural population, 61% resided in the Central Valley region and only 39% in the Etla region.

Period V sites in the Etla and Central regions are almost always characterized by thin and spotty distributions of habitational debris, indicating a high degree of house dispersal within communities. Isolated residences and tiny

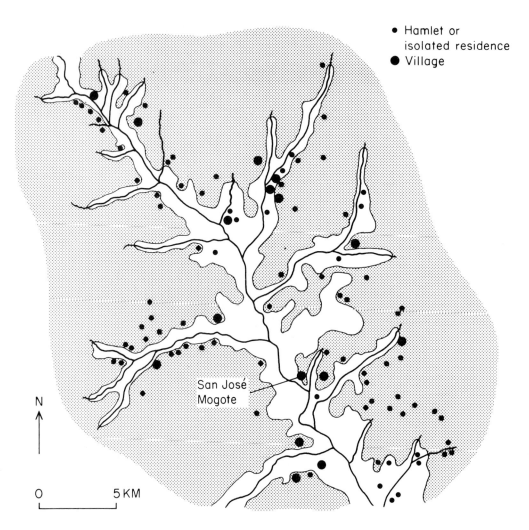

FIGURE 8.21.  The Etla region of the Valley of Oaxaca, showing settlements of the Monte Albán V period according to Varner. This is an area showing population decrease relative to the Classic period. (Redrawn, with modifications, from Varner 1974.)

hamlets were very common. In the Central region, for example, there were 232 settlements of a hectare or less (68% of the total number of sites in that area). Not only were Monte Albán V sites in this area not nucleated, but there was an almost total lack of mound construction. One exception to this pattern was a single, isolated ceremonial center located far away from any inhabited area, on a mountaintop north of Oaxaca City.

From the Late Postclassic we have the best evidence for local economic specialization in this region. In the rural areas, Monte Albán V ovens or maguey-roasting pits are fairly common, and at one site we were able to locate two obsidian workshops. The very common association between Period V pottery and green obsidian blade fragments suggests that even the humblest of isolated residences had easier access to obsidian than at any time since the Early Formative.

## THE TLACOLULA REGION

The situation is somewhat different in the Tlacolula arm of the valley during Monte Albán V. Mitla, Yagul, and Abasolo have all been mapped, and appear to have been nucleated centers with substantial public architecture (Topic 87). Teotitlán del Valle and Matatlán are less well known, but show traces of Mitla-style architecture. Macuilxochitl and Teitipac may be other examples, but more intensive survey is needed to confirm this.

## THE MIAHUATLAN VALLEY

Brockington (1973) reports 14–16 sites of this period from the Miahuatlán Valley, virtually all of them bordering the Río Miahuatlán and its upper tributary, the Río Ta-

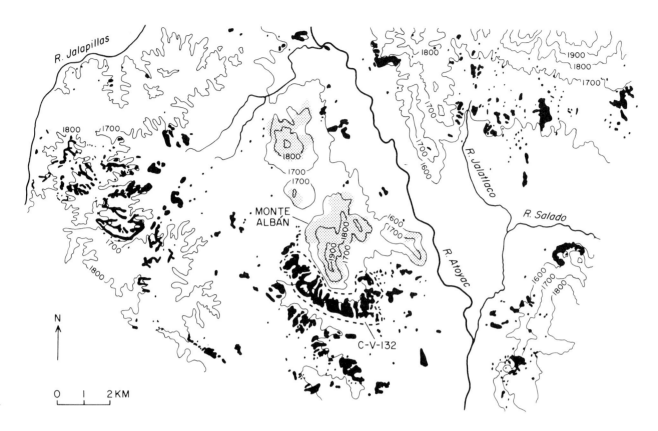

FIGURE 8.22. The Central region of the Valley of Oaxaca, showing settlements of the Monte Albán V period. This is an area showing population increase relative to the Classic period. The stippled area indicates the extent of occupation at Monte Albán itself according to Blanton 1978. Also indicated is site C-V-132, the possible location of Saʔa Yucu (see Topic 85).

mazulapan. Although site sizes are not always given, the pattern appears to resemble that of the Tlacolula area more than it does the Etla or Central regions of the Valley of Oaxaca; there are several nucleated sites with substantial elite or ceremonial–civic architecture (Figure 8.23).

For example, Brockington's Site 10 has a ceremonial and habitation zone 400 m long and 150 m wide, including 9 mounds and 2 patios. Surface sherds are between 70 and 98% Monte Albán V gray ware, with "absolutely no bichrome or polychrome sherds." Thick, red-painted stucco floors characterize some buildings. Site 1A, "the largest and most impressive site found" by Brockington, also has substantial Monte Albán V occupation and sits on a modified natural ridge at the south edge of Miahuatlán. This may be the original "Miahuapan" mentioned in the Codex Mendoza.

## SUMMARY

Because of the diversity of patterns in Late Postclassic Oaxaca, it would probably be premature to summarize the entire Valley of Oaxaca until our intensive surveys are com-

plete. The *relaciones* clearly indicate that we should expect nucleated Zapotec centers in some areas, Mixtec caciques with *tay situndayu* laborers in other areas, some fortified sites, and some places ruled by a royal pair—one of whom was Zapotec, one Mixtec.

In the Etla arm and the Central Valley, there seems to have been no single, dominant center of political administration able to control the entire region. The nature of the settlement distributions in the Etla and Central areas in fact suggest that production and exchange, rather than administration, were among the most outstanding activities carried on at these sites.

An alternative way of viewing the Central and Etla regions would be to suggest that the highly dispersed settlement pattern, the absence of a centralized regional state, and the emphasis on locally specialized production were functionally related (regardless of how the system came into being). The past history of the valley might indicate that the costs of administering the regional system tended to increase as populations were more dispersed. Significant amounts of the total population might then have been allowed to live in small communities distributed over the countryside—a pattern that does have its advantages,

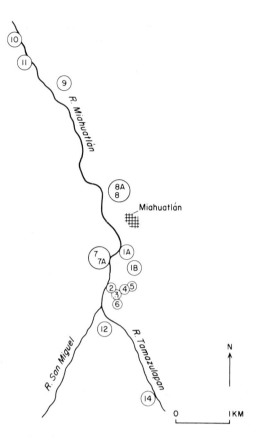

FIGURE 8.23. The Valley of Miahuatlán, showing settlements of the Monte Albán V period, according to Brockington 1973. (Redrawn with modifications.)

though not without incurring additional costs. In Periods I and IIIb, for example, rural expansion had been accompanied by absolute growth of the urban center. The implication for the Late Postclassic, then, would be that a still greater degree of rural expansion was accompanied by political decentralization. The burden of systems monitoring might then have been taken up by the ruling family and noble classes of small kingdoms, and by "hidden-hand" kinds of feedback loops involving military competition, marriage alliances, and marketing behavior (see Spores 1974b). Individual commoner households may have been controlled through the commercial exchange networks of the regional market, and by patron–client relationships with particular nobles or noble families.

The situation was clearly somewhat different in the Mitla–Yagul–Teotitlán region and in the case of Teozapotlan (Zaachila). While Zaachila would appear to have been a "small kingdom" relative to Monte Albán, the *relaciones* indicate there was hardly a Zapotec town in the valley that was not subservient to, and in a tributary relationship with, the lord of Teozapotlan; even Mitla and Tehuantepec were within his realm. In spite of this political clout, the Zapotec ruler Zaachila III apparently found it necessary to seek military aid from the Mixtec lord of Achiutla in order to defend Huitzo from the Aztecs (Topic 91). Unfortunately, there is almost no way that settlement pattern survey alone can clarify such a complex situation.

# TOPIC 84
# Late Postclassic Settlement in the Mountain Survey Zone between the Valleys of Oaxaca and Nochixtlán

ROBERT D. DRENNAN

During the Late Postclassic, equivalent in time to Monte Albán V, some 47 sites in the Mountain Survey area were certainly occupied, and 6 others possibly were. The relatively large number of sites for this period, however, is not directly comparable with the numbers for earlier periods because of a major change in the settlement pattern. The population was much more dispersed during Monte Albán V, with many people living in isolated residences scattered through the area. Such isolated residences cannot be compared with the more nucleated sites of earlier periods; however, most of the sites missed by our survey were probably Monte Albán V isolated residences as well. During this period, a change in ceramics was also evident. Considerable amounts of pottery like that of the Nochixtlán and Tehuacán valleys showed up together with Valley of Oaxaca

types, unlike earlier periods when the ceramics were almost exclusively like those of the Valley of Oaxaca.

These data fit reasonably well with Varner's survey of the Etla arm of the Valley of Oaxaca, and with the ethnohistoric data presented elsewhere in this volume. Varner (1974) reports a large number of isolated residences or tiny hamlets in the Etla region during Monte Albán V; many of these have Yanhuitlán style Red-on-cream ceramics and/or Paddock's Huitzo Polished Cream; one, at San Juan del Estado, had a stamped-bottom (*fondo sellado*) sherd of Tehuacán's Venta Salada style (found by Susan H. Lees, personal communication, 1969).

Although alternative interpretations should be kept in mind, these data from the Mountain Survey area would support a model of population movement toward the Valley of

Oaxaca from some region strongly in contact with both the *cacicazgo* of Yanhuitlán and the Cuicatec Cañada—a region like Almoloyas, which has already been suggested as a source of immigrants by various seminar participants. The Mountain Survey data would also suggest that the move- ment was one of farmers or *terrazgueros* (*tay situndayu*) who founded tiny settlements rather than nucleated towns, as has more or less been postulated in this volume for the adjacent Etla region during Monte Albán V.

# TOPIC 85
## The Archaeological Evidence for Sa'a Yucu

STEPHEN KOWALEWSKI

One of the places where archaeology and ethnohistory can combine to shed light on the Postclassic Valley of Oaxaca is in the *municipio* of Xoxocotlán. According to the *Relación de Cuylapa* (Salazar 1581), a group of Mixtecs from the region of Almoloyas entered the valley as the result of a royal marriage with the Zapotecs of Zaachila. These Mixtecs were given lands at the southern base of Monte Albán as a form of dowry, and they are said to have founded a settlement there called *Sa'a Yucu*, "At the Foot of the Mountain."

Archaeological site C-V-132, recovered by my intensive survey of the Central Valley of Oaxaca (Kowalewski 1976), may well be ancient Sa'a Yucu (Figure 8.19). The site extends over the heavily eroded and dissected slope between the southern base of Monte Albán and the alluvium of the Arrazola tributary stream, some 1850 m from Santa Cruz Xoxocotlán. The slope has the form of a 180° arc, measuring 600 to 900 m in width and 5 km long. C-V-132 covers 196 ha, of which roughly 75% has very sparse pottery, 24% has sparse pottery, and only 1% has a higher surface sherd density. Concentrations of pottery, obsidian, ground stone, burned adobe, and building stone were observed on areas of 18 by 18 m, 18 by 22 m, 30 by 30 m, and 35 by 40 m, probably indicating individual residences. I estimate the population at 980 to 1960 persons.

C-V-132 is not located in a very rich agricultural area. This fact would fit with the ethnohistoric account stating that when the opportunity presented itself the Mixtecs eagerly moved south to the vicinity of modern Cuilapan, where they founded a second settlement named Ynchaca (Salazar 1581). However, there were still some Mixtec speakers in Xoxocotlán when Marshall Saville excavated there in the late 1800s. Site C-V-132 may present a unique opportunity for comparing Mixtec settlement in the Valley of Oaxaca with contemporary Zapotec settlement in the same region.

# TOPIC 86
## San José Mogote and the *Tay Situndayu*

KENT V. FLANNERY
JOYCE MARCUS

As Kowalewski suggests (Topic 83), Monte Albán V occupation of the Central and Etla regions of the Valley of Oaxaca commonly takes the form of small hamlets and isolated residences. San José Mogote exhibits this type of settlement during Period V, and excavations there shed some light on the Late Postclassic occupation of the Etla region.

Mound 8 is a flat-topped, mesa-like eminence which includes the ruins of the Monte Albán II–IIIa palaces at the north end of the Main Plaza at San José Mogote. This artificial mesa was selected as the site for a small Monte Albán V hamlet or ranchería. Ash deposits, borrow pits filled with refuse, and storage jars buried flush with the old land surface have all survived; also discovered were the burials of more than a dozen adults, both primary and secondary interments. The primary burials occur in shallow pits or slab-lined graves, fully extended supine, and accompanied by fairly standardized lots of G3M gray bowls, jars, and pitchers. In some cases, a male and a female occur side by side.

Several hundred meters to the southwest, in a part of the site largely abandoned since the Middle Formative, is another group of Monte Albán V burials. These, however, include infant and child burials accompanied in some cases by Yanhuitlán Red-on-cream bowls or by Graphite-on-orange pottery similar to that of Spores's Natividad phase in the Nochixtlán region. It is suspected that this area was one of slightly higher-status residence; it is not known whether or not it was contemporaneous with the hamlet on Mound 8 or slightly more recent.

During Monte Albán V, the Protoclassic temples of Mound 1 at San José Mogote lay in ruins, presumably already covered by vegetation. Nevertheless, the Late Postclassic occupants of the site seemed to have recognized

Mound 1 as a place that had been sacred in ancient times; they climbed 15 m to the patio north of Structure 19 and buried a variety of offerings there, just below the surface of the earth now filling the patio. These offerings included two pottery Tlaloc effigies, several caches of miniature vessels, a number of greenstone beads and greenstone necklaces, isolated projectile points, and several lancet-like obsidian blades of the type used for ritual bloodletting at the time of the Conquest.

Elsewhere in this chapter we have suggested that Late Postclassic settlement patterns in the Central and Etla re-gions of the Valley of Oaxaca could be interpreted as resulting from Mixtec *tay situndayu*—commoners who worked the lands of the Mixtec lords who entered the valley as the result of marriage alliances, and who lived in scattered hamlets, farmsteads, or isolated residences near the best agricultural lands rather than in nucleated villages. The Yanhuitlán Red-on-cream pottery from San José Mogote could be used as additional support for this interpretation, as long as we keep in mind the perils of ascribing ethnicity on the basis of pottery styles.

# TOPIC 87
## Major Monte Albán V Sites: Zaachila, Xoxocotlán, Cuilapan, Yagul, and Abasolo

KENT V. FLANNERY

During Monte Albán V, important sites flourished in at least two different areas of the Valley of Oaxaca. In the broad plain south of Monte Albán, crucial sites included Zaachila (political capital of the sixteenth-century Zapotec), Xoxocotlán, and Cuilapan. In the Tlacolula arm of the valley, Mitla (religious capital of the sixteenth-century Zapotec), Yagul, Matatlán, Teotitlán, Macuilxochitl, Abasolo, and Teitipac were all important communities.

Not all these sites were nucleated centers (the actual area of Monte Albán V occupation at Zaachila was rather small), but many had impressive palaces, temples, and ballcourts. In the case of Zaachila, its importance as a place of royal residence outweighed its relatively small size. Mitla, however, was a town of major proportions in Period V (see Topic 88).

These sites have a number of features in common. All have long sequences stretching far back into Classic or Preclassic times. Their names are well known, and several are famous tourist attractions. In spite of this notoriety, most remain poorly known, their archaeological revelations shared only by a handful of Oaxacan specialists. I will attempt in this topic only to introduce the reader to a few of these extraordinary Late Postclassic sites.

## SITES IN THE ZAACHILA PLAIN

### Zaachila

The great mound of Zaachila is a *tell* in the Near Eastern sense, towering more than 20 m above the corn and carrizo of the sandy, flat alluvium south of the city of Oaxaca. The Zaachila plain is the widest part of the valley—9 km across—and the huge rock outcrop on which the site was founded must at times have seemed like an island in the high-water-table land to the west of the Atoyac. Even though some areas of the mound are natural bedrock outcrop, com-plete with small caves and rockshelters, the site is awesome. The massive Colonial church sits on Mound H, while the high acropolis of Mounds A–E alone covers 6 ha.

Like so many important places in the valley, Zaachila was occupied from Early Formative times on. A substantial Tierras Largas-phase site lies buried not far from the church, its sherds incorporated in the later adobes of the acropolis. There are traces of San José phase, Rosario phase, and some Monte Albán I occupation. Monte Albán II and the II–III Transition are well represented, and there are clear Monte Albán IIIa bowls with carved designs of G-23 type. During the decline of Monte Albán during periods IIIb and IV, Zaachila rose to be one of the most important places in the valley. A massive earthen platform, or series of platforms, was contoured to the hill by constructing terraces of adobe brick facing and *terre pisé* fill; then a coating of waterproof stucco was added to prevent erosion. Stone at Zaachila seems to have been used only sparingly, in places like tomb and building façades, and for sculptured tenons and carved stone monuments. A dominant theme in the stone monuments of IIIb–IV is the royal wedding scene Marcus already discussed in Topic 59, suggesting that some of Zaachila's political power was based on strategic marriage alliances. The sixteenth-century *relaciones* indicate that this pattern continued into Monte Albán V, with Zapotec rulers of Zaachila marrying Mixtec women, and Mixtec lords from Yanhuitlán and/or Almoloyas marrying royal Zapotec women from Zaachila.

In 1962, Roberto Gallegos excavated a building on Mound A of the Zaachila acropolis (Figure 8.24). Mound A is pure Monte Albán V, having been built over a terrace extending south from Mound B, which is stratigraphically earlier. There were at least two construction phases in Mound A, and a third phase which was merely repair. During the first phase, two important tombs were built, a stucco patio floor put over them, and a palace-like adobe structure with a stone foundation built. The east hall of the building is

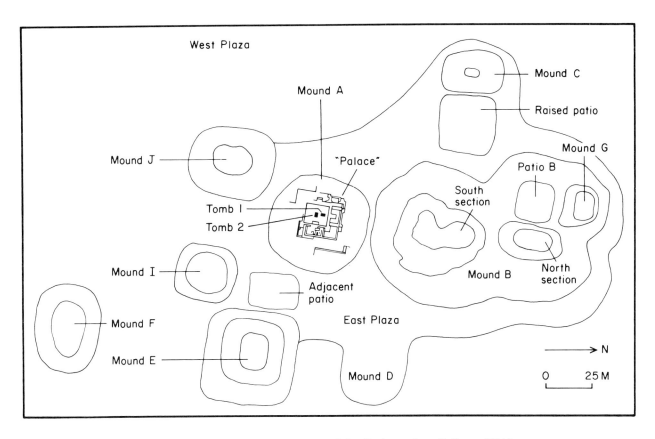

FIGURE 8.24. Mound complex at Zaachila. (Redrawn from Gallegos 1964.)

undistinguished; the north hall has an altar and the west hall a "sanctuary." These features, coupled with the fact that the tombs clearly preceded the building "as in the case of the Palenque tomb" (Gallegos 1964), suggest we are dealing with a Postclassic version of the Zapotec "commemorative palace" seen earlier at Monte Albán. This impression is strengthened by the tombs, which, like those at Mitla, begin in the patio, run under the rooms of the building, and have a complex series of stairways, vestibules, antechambers, chambers, and niches.

Tomb 1 runs north–south, opening at the south end. The vestibule has a *greca* frieze in Mitla style and two feline heads modeled in stucco. The antechamber originally had two stucco-modeled owls, one of which had fallen prior to excavation. In the main chamber were five more figures modeled in stucco, one of which, at the extreme north end, is a Late Postclassic version of the "flying turtle" seen on stone monuments of Monte Albán IIIb–IV at Zaachila (Figure 8.25), and thus almost a certain reference to the "cloud ancestors" of the tomb's occupants (see Marcus, Topic 59). Two of the remaining stucco figures are codex-style depictions of "Death"—one on the west wall of the main chamber, one on the east. Each of these "death figures" is accompanied by a named stucco figure bearing a pouch; the figure on the west is ♂ 5 Flower, the one on the east ♂ 9 Flower. Caso (1966) attempted to identify these stucco figures with

personages named and dressed similarly in the Codex Nuttall, expressing confidence that ♂ 5 Flower of Zaachila was the same ♂ 5 Flower mentioned on page 33 of Nuttall. If this was a named ancestor, at least one occupant of the Zaachila tomb would thus have been the descendant of a Yanhuitlán Mixtec royal lineage. Obviously, Caso was strongly influenced by the stories of royal marriage alliance in the *relaciones* of Zaachila and Cuilapan, and not all ethnohistorians are convinced by his reconstruction. Given the same evidence for marriage alliance, one could argue that even the "Zapotec" rulers of Zaachila in later times could have had

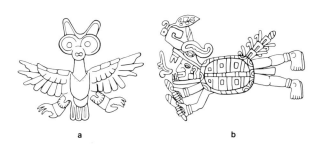

a                    b

FIGURE 8.25. Stucco-modeled figures on Tomb 1 at Zaachila. (Redrawn from Gallegos 1964).

FIGURE 8.26. Stucco-modeled figures on Tomb 1 at Zaachila. (Redrawn from Gallegos 1964.)

some royal Mixtecs in their genealogy, making ethnic identification next to impossible.

Tomb 1 contained a total of 11 skeletons. The two principal figures lay extended on their backs in the main chamber, accompanied by a secondary burial; in the antechamber were 6 extended and 2 semiflexed burials, possibly retainers. One of the principal burials wore obsidian earspools and a tiny gold ring with an eagle head and pendant bells; his companion had two gold plaques. They were accompanied by masterpieces of polychrome pottery, including one famous cup with a modelled blue hummingbird drinking from the rim (Paddock 1966a:Pl. 18–20). There were also Monte Albán V gray wares, turquoise mosaic masks, tiger claw vessels, and objects of bone and *tecali*. As has been customary for sites of this period, Gallegos refers to some offerings as Zapotec, to others as Mixtec.

Tomb 2 runs east–west, opening at the east end; it also has a *greca* frieze in the vestibule, but lacks the stucco modelling seen in Tomb 1. Inside the main chamber were at least 12 primary (but disturbed) burials, 1 secondary burial, and niches with 3 more crania and miscellaneous bones. In the antechamber were 5 more skeletons and an isolated skull, identified as belonging to adults, adolescents, and juveniles (at least one of which was a female). The offerings, almost all in the antechamber, included polychrome and Monte Albán V gray ware, jade fan handles, obsidian earspools, copal, shell ornaments, goldwork, and carved bones like those from Tomb 7 at Monte Albán. In addition, some of the skeletons in the main chamber had earspools, gold or shell rings, silver platelets, or bracelets.

Because of the ambiguities of ethnohistory and the high frequency of names like "5 Flower" in the Postclassic, we may never know exactly who was buried in Tombs 1 and 2 at Zaachila. Were "5 Flower" and "9 Flower" their names, or the names of their ancestors? Were male rulers buried in Tomb 1, wives and children in Tomb 2? Were they the last Zapotec rulers before Cocijoeza moved his capital to Tehuantepec, or were they incoming Mixtec royalty? Indeed, was that distinction even important after 200 years of royal intermarriage?

## Xoxocotlán and Cuilapan

In view of the ethnohistoric importance of the Xoxocotlán–Cuilapan region, it is a shame that so little is known of the Late Postclassic archaeology of either site. The ancient settlement of Sa'a Yucu, reportedly founded by Mixtecs from Almoloyas as the result of a marriage with the royal house at Zaachila, should lie at the southern foot of Monte Albán on lands belonging to modern Xoxocotlán. Kowalewski (Topic 85) reports a 196-ha settlement, C-V-132, at the southern foot of Monte Albán, but this likely candidate for Sa'a Yucu has yet to be excavated. Moreover, we do not know what relationship, if any, C-V-132 bears to the Period V settlement of Monte Albán itself, which Blanton estimates at 4050 to 8100 persons. Was the El Pitahayo mound-group, core of the late Postclassic occupation on the north slope of Monte Albán, a holdover from the Zapotec occupation of the latter site, or was it related to Mixtec Sa'a Yucu?

At Cuilapan de Guerrero, supposedly the site of the later Mixtec community of Ynchaca, Saville in 1902 found only superficial traces of Monte Albán V. Bernal (1958b) found "little to indicate clearly Mixtec occupation," but this is perhaps not surprising; the *Relación de Cuylapa* (Salazar 1581) states that the houses at Cuilapan were thinly scattered because of the barrancas and the unlevel terrain. Bernal did find a Monte Albán V tomb (Tomb 8), with two stone *penates* and some uninspiring vessels. He also found a ceramic assemblage in Mound II which contained a mixture of G-35 bowls from Monte Albán IV and finer G3M bowls from Monte Albán V. This assemblage, which was assigned by Bernal to the "end of Period IV," sounds like the material from Zone B at Abasolo which we have assigned to the Monte Albán IV–V transition (see discussion in this topic).

## SITES IN THE TLACOLULA REGION

### Yagul

The site of Yagul occupies a volcanic-tuff hill which rises out of the valley floor not far to the east of Lambityeco. As indicated in previous chapters, Yagul had been occupied sporadically from Monte Albán I times on, but its period of major occupation came during Monte Albán V. Since this surge of building activity took place at Yagul just about the time Lambityeco was abandoned, Paddock has suggested that the two events may have been related: perhaps the occupants of Lambityeco moved to Yagul in search of a more defensible location during the transition from Monte Albán IV to V. This view is supported by the fact that the rocky summit of the Yagul hill was fortified during Period V with the same kind of dry-laid stone masonry walls used at the Mitla Fortress.

This fortress is not the only similarity between Mitla and Yagul; the architecture and layout of the two sites are re-

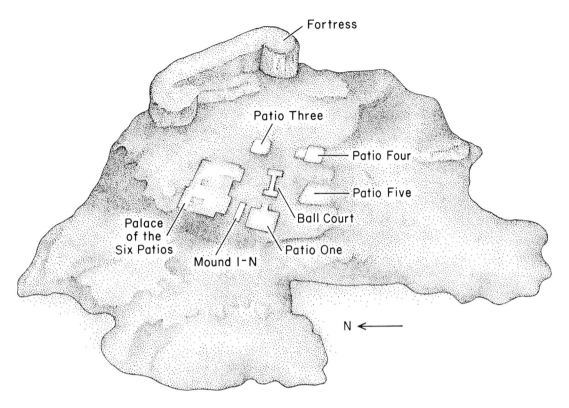

**FIGURE 8.27.** Three-dimensional view of the mesa of Yagul, showing the relationship of the Fortress, the Palace of the Six Patios, and related structures. (Drawing by Margaret Van Bolt, from an aerial photo by John Paddock.)

markably similar (Figure 8.27). Below the fortress is an elite residential complex called The Palace of the Six Patios which may be analogous to the Church Group at Mitla (see Topic 88). This complex of rooms, patios, and tombs is built on an artificial platform of some 5000 m² which levels a natural slope and covers some less impressive architecture of Monte Albán IV (Bernal and Gamio 1974; Bernal 1966a).

Downslope from the palace is a huge complex resembling the "Patio of the Tombs" at Mitla, and therefore possibly civic–administrative in function. It consists of a large patio ("Patio One") flanked on three sides by buildings and open to the south. The largest building on the north side is referred to by Bernal as the "Council Hall," and its back wall has remnants of a 40-m-long panel of stone mosaic *grecas*. Immediately to the east of Patio One is the Monte Albán V ballcourt already described by Wicke (1957), which has no counterpart at Mitla. On the next level downslope—just southeast of the ballcourt—is an apparent religious complex which superficially resembles the "Hall of the Columns" at Mitla. It consists of a large patio ("Patio Four") with a central adoratory and a series of four surrounding mounds, largely unexcavated, which probably supported temples. The tombs here and elsewhere on the site are described as displaying "a variant of the style found in the tombs at Monte Albán" (Bernal and Gamio 1974:356), but one out of every five tombs has a façade decorated with step-fret or *greca* motifs. In some cases, these *grecas* are true mosaics put

together from small stones; in other cases, they are "false mosaics" like the ones carved on single stones at Guiengola (Topic 93).

Bernal and Gamio's excavations into the Palace of the Six Patios has provided us with our best glimpse of an elite residence from the Monte Albán V period (Figure 8.28). Each of the patios (labeled A–F) consists of an open, unroofed court delimited by a bench 1.6 m wide and 30 cm high. On each of the four sides is a room whose entrance may be either single or divided into three spaces by pillars. The floors, the room walls, and the benches delimiting the patios are stuccoed, sometimes left white and sometimes painted red. Many rooms have *tlecuiles* or basins set in the floor, an architectural trait that goes back to the Terminal Formative.

Patio F was the largest of the six and perhaps the oldest, with several Monte Albán V building stages overlying a Monte Albán IV feature. In addition to the usual Monte Albán V gray ware, the building contained polychrome. Patio C, immediately to the north, had an offering box with an infant burial (perhaps a sacrifice) accompanied by an obsidian blade, necklaces, and pectorals of greenstone. Bernal and Gamio regard Patios C and F as the most "ceremonial" or "secret" of the whole palace complex, perhaps housing the persons whose residences were of most limited access.

Patios A and D, the westernmost, were smaller and contained a number of multioccupant tombs. Tomb 4 in Patio A had 16 skeletons "perhaps repeatedly moved as new skel-

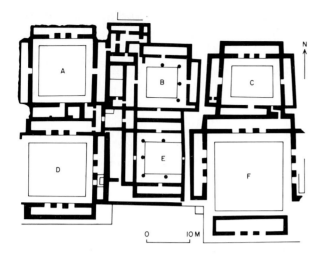

FIGURE 8.28. The Palace of the Six Patios at Yagul. (Redrawn from Bernal and Gamio 1974.)

etons were added" (Bernal and Gamio 1974:18). More than 25 vessels were present, mostly G3M bowls and jars, crude *sahumadores*, and a claw-shaped vessel; there were also jade beads, a shell *penate*, projectile points, and a grinding stone. Tombs 23 and 24 in Patio D also had multiple burials—both males and females—with one dog burial in each tomb. Similar tombs occur in other parts of the site (for example Tombs 25, 26, and 27 on Terrace C) and probably represent family or descent-line burial areas used over many years.

Patio E had a number of unusual features: several apparent pottery dumps, multiple ceramic offerings under the patio floor, and a blocked off room with burned human and animal bones, masses of charcoal, and pottery braziers. Bernal and Gamio interpret this area as "a type of enormous funerary pyre on which at least one person and some dogs and deer were burned" (or cooked?). In the overlying rubble of the building was a lone, rare, Aztec III black-on-red sherd.

Turning from the civic–ceremonial center of Yagul to the surrounding countryside, we find some striking resemblances to the rural sustaining area of Mitla. Hillsides flanking the Río Santo Domingo valley, to the north of Yagul, were extensively terraced, and in the hills and mountains around Díaz Ordaz are numerous caves with Monte Albán V occupation. Rural occupation of the plain between Yagul and Díaz Ordaz, while inadequately surveyed at this writing, seems not unlike the rural occupation of Mitla in Monte Albán V.

Before ending my summary of Yagul, I would like to add my two cents to the controversy surrounding its name. According to Bernal and Gamio, in the 1880s Bandelier was given the Zapotec name Gui-y-Baa, "Heaven," for the site.[1] In 1953 Bernal was given a variety of local names, from

which he arbitrarily selected "Yagul" or "Palo Viejo" as his favorite. This is derived from the Zapotec *yaga*, "tree," plus the suffix *gola* from *nagola*, "old"; in many parts of the Tlacolula valley this would be pronounced *Yag' gol'* = Yagul. As an alternative pronunciation, Bernal was given *yaguy*, which is suspiciously similar to Yegüih, the local name for the nearby extensive site of which Lambityeco is one small part. I see no reason to believe any of these names are ancient (or Mixtec or Cuicatec, as sometimes suggested), or anything but twentieth-century Zapotec peasant toponyms. My personal inclination is to opt for the simplest possible interpretation: that the Monte Albán IV population of Lambityeco moved to Yagul during Monte Albán V when military defense was a crucial consideration, and returned to the valley floor at Tlacolula shortly before the Spanish Conquest. No one doubts that the Monte Albán IV occupants of Lambityeco or the sixteenth-century occupants of Tlacolula were Zapotec. If there were any actual Mixtecs or Cuicatecs at Yagul in Monte Albán V—and I am not overwhelmed by the evidence—I suspect they were limited to royal marriage partners or occasional military allies.

### San Sebastián Abasolo

The site of Abasolo has already been mentioned in an earlier chapter because of its Formative remains; however, its Monte Albán V occupation is even more impressive. The site lies on a fertile, pot-irrigated alluvial plain in the central Tlacolula valley, near the point where the Río Salado temporarily disappears in a maze of distributaries and seasonal swamps.

Ignacio Bernal's survey in the 1950s recorded two areas of artificial mounds at Abasolo. One, site B-152, consisted of three mounds in the central part of the modern village. Steep enough to be temple mounds, these mounds were described in Bernal's notes as "partly destroyed, though superstructures, stucco, stones, and earth can be seen" (Bernal, unpublished survey notes).

A second cluster of structures, site B-153, lies near the Abasolo church on an almost imperceptible rise of higher ground which does not flood during the summer rains. Three mounds lie to the southwest and southeast of the church; still farther to the west is a large patio, open to the south, but flanked on its three other sides by low mounds which are littered with polychrome pottery, G3M gray ware, and fragments of red-painted stucco. My suspicion is that this is either a civic–administrative structure like Patio 1 at Yagul, or a massive "palace." The steeper mounds of B-152 may once have delimited a religious patio complex like Yagul's Patio Four. It would seem that Abasolo is another important Monte Albán V center, coeval with Mitla, Yagul, Matatlán, and Teotitlán, but constructed of adobe rather than of the less readily accessible volcanic tuff.

Our 1969 excavations in the large patio at site B-153 were aimed primarily at the underlying Formative deposits (Topic

---

[1]One wonders exactly where Bandelier was pointing when he was given this term.

16), but we recovered data on the Postclassic occupation as well. Most interesting was the succession of stratigraphic Zones B and A, which may well document two stages within Monte Albán V.

Stratigraphic Zone B varied in thickness between 40 cm (in Test A) and 1 m (in Test C). The sherds seem to reflect an early Monte Albán V assemblage that is without polychrome, and which includes G-35 bowls and other diagnostics of Monte Albán IV. The mixture of thin gray G3M types with thicker types reminiscent of Lambityeco is about what one would expect if Monte Albán V was an *in situ* development out of IV, as Brockington's Miahuatlán data suggest.

In Test C we found some of the architecture belonging to Zone B: a massive and very hard adobe wall preserved some 4–5 courses high, and associated with a plaster floor. In Test A, however, there were no traces of architecture in Zone B. This spot, only a dozen meters from Test C, appears to have been an open area away from any major buildings, but still rich in sherds. Two Monte Albán V wells, Features 1 and 5, had been dug down 1.5 m from this stratigraphic zone to a layer of fine sand that probably indicates where the water table was at that time. Each well had a shaft a meter in diameter and a funnel-like opening somewhat larger than that; the two features were spaced about 5 m apart. Given

the environmental setting of Abasolo, these may well have been facilities for pot irrigation.

Stratigraphic Zone A overlay both the adobe buildings and the middens and wells of Zone B; it varied in thickness between 20 cm (over the Test C buildings) and 120 cm (in Test A). Zone A is almost certainly a layer of collapsed debris from the buildings that surrounded the large patio on the north, east, and west, and apparently dates to a later stage of Monte Albán V. Along with the usual G3M gray ware, this zone had abundant sherds of polychrome and fragments of red-painted wall plaster or stucco.

Our evidence from Abasolo would support the notion that the thin gray pottery of Monte Albán V developed out of the thicker gray pottery of Period IV within the Valley of Oaxaca, rather than as a wholly "Mixtec" intrusion. It would also support the notion of an early Monte Albán V, lacking polychrome and Yanhuitlán Red-on-cream pottery. During this phase, which saw Lambityeco abandoned and Yagul enjoying its Postclassic "renaissance," Abasolo seems also to have been "rejuvenated" as an important administrative center for the Tlacolula valley. Still later in Monte Albán V, Abasolo went through a phase characterized by polychrome pottery and by adobe versions of the same ceremonial and elite-residential complexes seen in stone masonry at Yagul.

# TOPIC 88
## Urban Mitla and Its Rural Hinterland

KENT V. FLANNERY
JOYCE MARCUS

The ruins of Mitla are certainly among the best-known tourist attractions in the Valley of Oaxaca. Through a fortunate set of circumstances, Mitla is also one of the few Late Postclassic cities for which we have at least minimal information on the spatial relationships among the urban, suburban, and rural components of the population. These fortunate circumstances include the remarkable state of preservation of the Postclassic buildings; the functional descriptions of those buildings in the *Relación de Mitla;* the excavations of Batres, Saville, Caso and Rubín de la Borbolla, Bernal, and Paddock; the surveys of the surrounding area by Holmes, Williams and Heizer, and Lorenzo and Messmacher; and the cave excavations and pollen–stratigraphic research of our own University of Michigan group.

Before proceeding to our reconstruction of the city and its sustaining area, we should begin with a brief description of the setting of ancient Mitla, which lies at an elevation of 1688 m (5537 ft.) in a narrow river valley encircled by high mountains of Miocene volcanic tuff or ignimbrite.

The Río Grande de Mitla enters the Valley of Oaxaca through a barranca some 4.5 km east of the ruins. Near the

eastern outskirts of the town of Mitla it receives a tributary arroyo (usually dry) from nearby Hacienda Xaagá. For the next half-kilometer, the river is bordered on the north by rocky slopes and hills, and on the south by a 500-m-wide plain of silt alluvium. It then makes a loop to the south and, on the western outskirts of town, receives two more tributaries (usually dry) known as Gew Birush and Gew Rolatz. From here on its course is westward, toward Tlacolula.

The earliest settlement so far discovered at Mitla dates to the Early Formative period (ca. 1200 B.C.) and was located on the alluvial plain near the south bank of the river, a few hundred meters downstream from its confluence with the Xaagá arroyo. Mitla grew rapidly, and by late Monte Albán I times (200 B.C. [?]), a linear settlement nearly a kilometer long stretched westward beside the south bank of the river. By Monte Albán II times (ca. A.D. 1), this settlement had expanded to include house mounds on the north bank of the river as well. Deposits of Monte Albán II times are particularly well represented at a place called La Playa, not far from the western edge of the present town of Mitla.

The South Group, a series of pyramids around a rectangu-

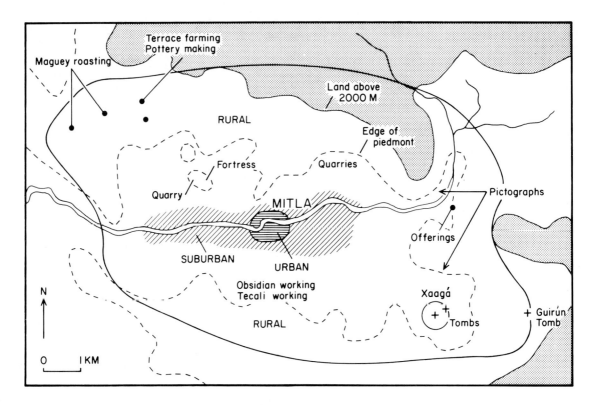

FIGURE 8.29. Schematic relationship of urban, suburban, and rural Mitla during the Postclassic. Caves are indicated by ●.

lar plaza, grew up as the center of this early settlement at Mitla. The South Group is the only known area of major construction on the left bank of the river, and it lies only 50 m west of Bala'h Bisyeh, where Early Formative deposits were first discovered (Figure 8.29). Features in the South Group include a Monte Albán IIIa tomb and constructions of Monte Albán IIIb–IV and V (Bernal 1966a). Mitla seems to have decreased in importance during the Classic period, for reasons as yet unknown; its renaissance came in the Postclassic, especially in Monte Albán V.

During the Late Postclassic, at least four important architectural complexes were built at Mitla, this time on the north side of the river. From northeast to southwest, these are called the Church Group, the Group of the Columns (including the two best-preserved buildings, the "Hall of Columns," and the "Patio of Tombs"), the Adobe Group, and the Arroyo Group. All these complexes seem to have been built on the bedrock of the slopes rising from the right bank of the river and are pure Monte Albán V (Paddock 1966a:213).

In Monte Albán V, Mitla once again stretched for several kilometers along the river. Its "urban" sector was perhaps as big as the present town, and beyond this was a zone of relatively level land with scattered house mounds. In 1967, Bion Griffin and John Cundiff (then of the University of Arizona) made a preliminary survey of this area and mapped all visible houses. Beyond they discovered still another zone, one of slopes covered with dry-laid stone agricultural ter-

races, ascending the nearby mountains to an elevation of at least 1800 m (5900 ft.). In all, this "sustaining area" covered at least 20 km², whereas the urban zone of Mitla may have been 1–2 km². We hope that further surveys by Kowalewski and Feinman can refine these figures, and perhaps break the area down into more rigorously defined sectors of differing settlement types.

## THE URBAN SECTOR

"There are in the town of Mitla," said Alonso de Canseco (1580) in the *Relación de Tlacolula y Mitla*, "two buildings of the greatest grandeur and fame that can be found in New Spain." Canseco was referring to the two remarkably preserved "palaces" of the Group of the Columns, which were probably the focal point of the ceremonial–civic center of urban Mitla. Each consists of a rectangular patio flanked on three sides by monumental buildings with intricate *greca* designs formed from individual stone mosaics. The small mosaic elements, as well as the giant lintels weighing up to 25 tons, are of sillar-type ignimbrite, a kind of volcanic tuff which is soft and easily worked. As Williams and Heizer have pointed out, "it is the geological setting of Mitla that has made possible the marvellous architectural forms and the beautiful mural mosaics with their intricate geometric designs for which the ruins are famous. Elaborate stone work of this kind would have been, for all practical purposes, impossible at the neighboring site of Monte Albán" (1965:41). Indeed, this contrast between the Yagul–Mitla ignimbrites and the geological formations elsewhere in the valley is rarely taken into consideration when attempts are made to account for the distinctive architecture of Mitla and Yagul.

According to Dupaix (quoted by del Paso y Troncoso 1905), the Mitla "palaces" were roofed with beams of *Taxodium* (ahuehuete or bald cypress) "as thick as a man," over which were laid flat stone slabs; then came a meter of lime, sand, and earth, all covered with a kind of Prehispanic concrete.

The most southern of the two buildings is the so-called Patio of the Tombs, which was evidently a civic–administrative structure. According to Canseco (1580), it was in the halls fronting this patio that problems of "government and republic" were dealt with, and the great lords of the region "came together to get drunk and enjoy themselves in their heathen way." Under the patio (and extending back under the halls) are the famous cruciform tombs which were for "burial of the great lords of this realm." It is not mentioned whether or not this building also served as a royal residence; there are other "palaces," such as the Church Group and the Arroyo Group, which could have served this purpose.

The most northern of the two buildings is the Hall of Columns, which was evidently a religious structure. "In this building they had their idols, and it was where they assembled for religious purposes, to make sacrifices to their idols, and to perform heathen rites" (Canseco 1580:152). There is an adoratory in the center of the patio, and the western and eastern halls have pairs of columns. The largest hall, on the north side of the patio, has six huge columns and is attached by means of a narrow, indirect passageway to an additional four-room structure with an interior courtyard. This additional structure, according to Canseco, was the residence of a Zapotec priest who was "like our pope": supreme head of the Precolumbian "church." The high priest's residence is described as windowless but elegant, clearly intended to have great privacy and extremely limited access (Figure 8.30).

It is, in fact, not hard to picture the evolution of this religious structure out of the less elaborate two-room temple of Monte Albán II–IIIb times. Both have an outer room, or antechamber, reached by a flight of stairs and entered by a wide doorway with large columns; this room would presumably have been accessible to secular nobility and perhaps even some commoners. Both also have an interior enclosure, reached by a narrow doorway, which would have been a windowless inner sanctum to which only priests had access. In both cases, antechamber and inner chamber are part of a "unitary" construction in Robertson's terms although the Hall of Columns is also part of a "unified" complex of three buildings sharing a common patio. And Marquina, in describing this very building at Mitla, writes that the famous *greca* mosaics occur in "*tableros* on the façades, similar to those of Monte Albán" (1951:Lám. 108).

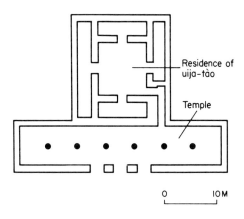

FIGURE 8.30. The Hall of Columns at Mitla. Columns are represented by ●. (Redrawn from Marcus 1978.)

## Religious Leadership

Although some authors have tried to attribute the palaces and temples of Mitla to the Mixtecs or Cuicatecs, such an ethnic ascription is contradicted by the ethnohistoric documents. For example, in discussing the high priest of Mitla, Canseco (1580) uses the Zapotec term *bigaña*, and there are suggestions that Mitla was a kind of Vatican City for the Zapotec nobility. Canseco was told by his sixteenth-century informants that Mitla was subject to the lord of Teozapotlan (Zaachila), but that their only tribute was to travel to Zaachila once in a while to sow some fields for him and to present him with turkeys and honey.

Father Burgoa (1674, Chapter 53) gives a somewhat different version of the high priest of Mitla. Pointing out that the *bigaña* were actually minor priests or students of the priesthood, Burgoa refers to the occupant of the Hall of Columns as a *uija-tào* or "great seer" (Marcus 1978:179). This is also a Zapotec, rather than a Mixtec or Cuicatec, term. Burgoa goes on to say that the *uija-tào* was treated by the Zapotec kings with "submissive veneration" and regarded as being closely connected with the supernatural; because he was the direct distributor of supernatural gifts and punishments, the kings turned to him for every need, and followed his advice with some diligence (Seler 1904:248). Burgoa (1674, Chapter 53) goes on to say:

I carefully examined these monuments some thirty years ago in the chambers above ground, which are constructed of the same size and in the same way as those below ground and, though single pieces were in ruins because some stones had become loosened, there was still much to admire. . . . There were four chambers above ground and four below. The latter were arranged according to their purpose in such a way that one front chamber served as a chapel and sanctuary for the idols, which were placed on a great stone which served as an altar. And for the more important feasts which they celebrated with sacrifices, or at the burial of a king or great lord, the high priest instructed the lesser priests or the subordinate temple officials who served him to prepare the chapel and his vestments and a large quantity of the incense used by them. And then he descended with a great retinue, while none of the common people saw him or dared to look in his face, convinced that if they did so they would fall dead to the earth as a punishment for their boldness.

We are told by Burgoa what garments the *uija-tào* put on, how he walked over to the altar bowing low before the idols, and how he prayed with grimaces, writhing, murmurings, and "inarticulate sounds." After he had come out of his "diabolical trance," he told his listeners "lies and fabrications which the spirit had imparted to him or which he had invented himself."

When human beings were sacrificed the ceremonies were multiplied, and the assistants of the high priest stretched the victim out upon a large stone, baring his breast, which they tore open with a great stone knife, while the body writhed in fearful convulsions and they laid the heart bare, ripping it out, and with it the soul, which the devil took, while they carried the heart to the high priest that he might offer it to the idols by holding it to their mouths, among other ceremonies; and the body was thrown into the burial place of their "blessed," as they called them.

. . . The second (underground) chamber was the burial place of these high priests, the third that of the kings of Theozapotlan, whom they brought thither richly dressed in their best attire. . . .

The last (underground) chamber had a second door at the rear, which led to a dark and grewsome [sic] room. This was closed with a stone slab, which occupied the whole entrance. Through this door they threw the bodies of the victims and of the great lords and chieftains who had fallen in battle. . . . Many who were oppressed by diseases and hardships begged this infamous priest to accept them as living sacrifices and allow them to enter through that portal and roam about in the dark interior of the mountain, to seek the great feasting places of their forefathers.

. . . One of the rooms above ground was the palace of the high priest, where he sat and slept, for the apartment offered room and opportunity for every thing. The throne was like a high cushion with a high back to lean against, all of tiger skin, stuffed entirely with delicate feathers or with fine grass which was used for this purpose. The other seats were smaller, even when the king came to visit them. The authority of this devilish priest was so great that there was no one who dared to cross the court, and to avoid this the other three chambers had doors in the rear, through which even the kings entered. For this purpose they had alleys and passageways on the outside above and below, by which people could enter and go out when they came to see the high priest.

These priests never married, nor did they hold intercourse with women. Only, at certain feasts, which they celebrated with great banqueting and much drunkenness, the kings brought to them the unmarried daughters of the chieftains, and if one of these became pregnant she was taken to a retired spot until her confinement, so that if a son should be born he could be brought up as the successor of the priest in his office, for this succession always fell to the son or nearest relative and was never elective.

The second chamber above ground was that of the priests and the assistants of the high priests. The third was that of the king when he came. The fourth was that of the other chieftains and captains, and though the space was small for so great a number and for so many different families, yet they accommodated themselves to each other out of respect for the place and avoided dissensions and factions. Furthermore, there was no other administration of justice in this place than that of the high priest, to whose unlimited power all bowed [Seler translation 1904:250–252].

In summary, Burgoa claimed that one of the underground chambers—in the front—had been a place for keeping idols,

the second had served as a burial place for the high priest, the third served as the tomb of kings and nobles, and the fourth chamber was thought to be connected with a "great cave," where they brought the sacrificial victims and the chiefs who had died in battle. The rooms above ground are said to have served as dwellings for (1) the high priest, (2) the subordinate members of the priesthood, (3) the king, and (4) the families of the nobles who came to Mitla as part of the king's retinue. Indeed, there may have been more than one relatively high-ranking priest at Mitla, for Burgoa (1674, Chapter 74) speaks of the Zapotec ruler Cocijopii summoning "several" high priests and lesser *bigaña* from Mitla to him when he was ruler at Tehuantepec.

### Secular Leadership

The secular ruler of Mitla was called "Coqui Gualaniça" by Canseco (*coqui* means "lord" and this phrase might be a corruption of *coquihualao,* "prince," plus a proper name, e.g., Niça). He was presumably the "*senor natural*" who convened the assemblies in the Patio of the Tombs, and whose word "was their only law." Once again, the name of the ruler is Zapotec, and his title suggests he would have been subordinate to the *coquitao* of Zaachila. The single most plausibly "Mixtec" feature of urban Mitla is a series of codex-style mural fragments in the palaces of the Church Group, which, not being portable (like the polychrome pottery of the same period), had to be painted *in situ*. Given the significant number of royal Mixtec spouses who married into Zapotec royal families during this period, however, the finding of such palace decoration need not represent Mixtec "conquest" or "domination." Indeed, all the murals could have been the work of a single court artist.

## THE SUBURBAN SECTOR

Beyond urban Mitla was a "suburban" sector stretching for at least a kilometer upstream and at least 2 km downstream. This settlement took the form of house mounds—some single, some in pairs, and sometimes three around a common patio. All have Monte Albán V pottery, dominated by G3M ollas and hemispherical bowls. It is possible that two other cruciform tombs, one at Hacienda Xaagá and one on Cerro Guirún, should be included in this sector. The tomb at Xaagá occurred below a "palace" like those at Mitla, and has similar *grecas;* however, Xaagá is separated from downtown Mitla by 5 km of open fields with no evidence of substantial architecture, and may simply have been a *sujeto* of Mitla.

## THE RURAL SECTOR

The rural sustaining area for Mitla extended for 5 km in every direction, and all indications are that agriculture was intensive. The slopes of the Dan Ro' mountain range to the north of Mitla, especially in the area of small drainages between Guilá Naquitz Cave and the Mitla Fortress, were extensively terraced up to an elevation of 1900 m. These terraces, all dating to Monte Albán V, show up on aerial photographs as a herringbone pattern of low stone walls climbing each drainage at right angles to the line of the arroyo. They differ from the *lama–bordo* systems of the Nochixtlán Valley (Topic 94) in that they seem only to have slowed runoff and retained soil humidity, rather than transporting soil from one region to another. According to Michael Kirkby (personal communication), these terraces predominate on the slopes which would most often have been in shadow, and where the evaporation rate would consequently have been lower.

Stratigraphic Zone A of Cueva Blanca was occupied at this time, and a series of five dry-laid stone masonry agricultural terraces were built on the talus slope below the cave, 4 km northwest of Mitla (Flannery [ed.] 1970:19). Additionally, the bank of an arroyo below the cave was terraced (amounting to a sixth terrace). During Monte Albán V, Cueva Blanca seems to have been part of a small farmstead (less than a hectare in size); the occupants, probably a single nuclear family, were engaged in farming and pottery production. Zone A was a layer of brown ash (with gray and black lenses) some 20 cm thick on the average, which covered the entire surface of the cave and yielded a radiocarbon date of A.D. 1430.

Inside the cave, Frank Hole and I found a series of medium-to-large storage pits, some of which still had preserved plant remains when excavated. Included in the debris of Zone A were maize, maguey, prickly pear, acorns, hackberries, susí nuts (*Jatropha*), and hawthorn fruits (*Crataegus*). The hawthorn or *tejocote* may have been a rural orchard crop, while some of the other plants were undoubtedly collected as wild products.

Two of the most important Monte Albán V discoveries, however, were Feature 6 (a maguey-roasting pit) and Feature 8 (a two-chambered pottery kiln; see Figure 8.31). Because the fire-cracked rock thrown out of Feature 6 formed a loose rubble layer in places under Zone A, it was initially distinguished as Zone B; further excavation showed it to be merely the first stage of Monte Albán V occupation. Feature 8 consisted of a pair of circular chambers a meter in diameter, connected by a stone-lined tunnel or flue 70 cm long. According to ceramicist William O. Payne (personal communication), this is the kind of indirect-firing kiln that could have maintained the even temperatures and reducing atmosphere necessary to fire the thin, well-made G3M gray ware of Monte Albán V; the fuel would have been placed in one chamber, the pottery in the other, with the heated air moving through the flue. Apparently, this particular kiln was used almost exclusively for thin gray G3M ollas with pattern-burnished designs of the type common at Mitla. Chris Moser's study of the ceramics from Zone A revealed more than 65,000 sherds of such ollas—so many that it seems likely that production far exceeded the demands of the Cueva Blanca farmstead, and may have served some of the

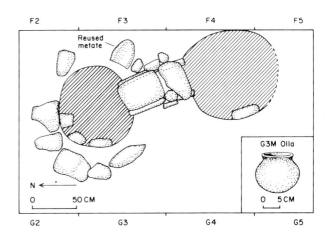

FIGURE 8.31. Feature 8, a Monte Albán V two-chambered pottery kiln from Cueva Blanca near Mitla. Lower right corner: reconstruction of a typical G3M olla of the type made at Cueva Blanca.

needs of urban Mitla (Moser, in preparation). This possibility is interesting because it suggests a continuation of the old Oaxaca pattern, in which craft specialists were not concentrated in urban centers.

Stratigraphic Zone Super-A of Guilá Naquitz Cave, 5 km northwest of Mitla, was also occupied during this period (Flannery et al. 1970:15). This zone was so named because it was not discovered until late in the excavation and occupied only a small area, near the southwest corner of the cave. It overlay Zone A, and associated ceramics placed it in the Monte Albán V period. Several features were prominent in Zone Super-A: a large maguey-roasting pit on the cave talus (Feature 7; see Figure 8.32), a storage pit containing an unused maguey heart (Feature 19), and two beds of grass and oak leaves (Features 6 and 16) which apparently had been used by two persons who occupied the cave while waiting for the maguey-roasting process to be completed (usually 24 to 72 hours). Because there is no associated farmstead, it appears that at this period Guilá Naquitz was used merely as a station for roasting one of the local maguey species (*Agave potatorum*), and that this activity was probably undertaken by a small group of people who came out from the town of Mitla, and later returned to Mitla with the baked maguey. Other caves in the same cliff also have maguey-roasting pits,

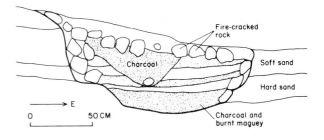

FIGURE 8.32. Feature 7, a Monte Albán V maguey-roasting pit from Guilá Naquitz Cave near Mitla.

most dating to the period A.D. 1250–1500. The fuel used in Feature 7 was all manzanita (*Arctostaphylos*), a slow-burning hardwood.

Artifacts from Zone Super-A included sherds of pattern-burnished thin gray ollas and G3M dishes with a dark-fired rim, which are identical to Monte Albán V pottery found at the site of Mitla itself. In addition, there were a number of bifaces and heavy denticulate scraper-planes, probably used in maguey shredding or processing. Many of these scraper-planes are similar to the ones that W. H. Holmes (1897) found at the ruins of Mitla and near the Mitla quarries. They superficially resemble Preceramic scraper-planes, but our stratigraphic evidence indicates they are in fact Postclassic, something already suggested by Williams and Heizer (1965).

Building-stone quarries were found in the Mitla rural sector by W. H. Holmes (1897), and revisited by Williams and Heizer (1965). The nearest of these quarries occurs only 2 km northeast of the ruins in a cliff of easily cut sillar-type ignimbrite; more distant quarries lie 10 km to the northeast and 300 m higher in elevation. Here one can still pick up the scraper-planes of highly indurated ignimbrite which Williams and Heizer (1965:Plate 7) believe were used to deflesh maguey fiber for manufacture of the ropes used to draw the giant quarry blocks to urban Mitla.

Chipped-stone quarries also are common in the Mitla sustaining area. The most famous of these is the one Holmes (1897) discovered on the slopes of the Mitla Fortress. According to Williams and Heizer (1965), this is a quarry of silicified volcanic tuff which has flint-like properties, and in many places is veined and replaced by chalcedony. Judging by the artifacts scattered around the quarry, it has been visited since at least 5000 B.C., and was certainly a major source during Monte Albán V.

An obsidian workshop has been reported by members of Paddock's project from the slopes near the Mitla airport 2 km south of the ruins. Paddock also reports that drill plugs of *tecali* (probably fine-grained travertine) are abundant in that area, suggesting other lapidary activities with imported stone types.

Pictographs in caves and rockshelters occur at Piedra Hueca near Hacienda Xaagá, and in the canyon of the Río Grande de Mitla some 5 km upstream from the ruins (Lorenzo and Messmacher 1963). The associated ceramics are all Monte Albán V, suggesting that the pictographs are Postclassic (if not more recent). Red is the usual color, and traced human hands are one of the common motifs.

Hilltop fortresses are another feature of the rural Mitla landscape. The *Relación de Tlacolula y Mitla* (Canseco 1580) says that Mitla and its associated villages had four fortresses or walled hilltops to which the people withdrew in times of war. One of these was surely the "Mitla Fortress," 2 km northwest of the ruins, which was described by Holmes (1897) and excavated by William G. Bittler during one of John Paddock's research projects in the 1960s. The fortress is a remnant of very hard, cliff-forming ignimbrite (including silicified and indurated tuffs), rising steeply above the cornfields north of the river. Natural wall-like outcrops of stone were connected by man-made walls of dry-laid stone mason-

ry, forming an impressive series of fortifications which are pure Monte Albán V.

Another of the fortresses mentioned in the *relaciones* may be Corral de Piedra, a still higher and more distant walled hilltop in the Dan Ro' range, 4–5 km north of Mitla. Still another may be the site of Yegoyachi, a fortified "bald mountain" in the rugged canyon between Hierve el Agua (Topic 94) and the Mixe region. In fact, we suspect that further survey will show many more Monte Albán V fortified hills than are mentioned in the ethnohistoric documents.

Dependent hamlets or *sujetos* are listed in the *Relación de Tlacolula y Mitla*, but most are difficult to identify with specific archaeological sites. Included among the hamlets which Canseco (1580:148) assigns to Mitla are "Santiago" (presumably Matatlán); "Quellabilla" (San Baltazar Guelavila); and "Santo Domingo," "San Miguel," "Santa Catalina," and "San Lorenzo" (all presumably Albarradas). Although many of these dependencies were in the mountains bordering Mixe territory, the *relación* specifically states that all *sujetos*, as well as the *cabecera* of Mitla, spoke Zapotec. Santiago Matatlán, the nearest *sujeto*, has Monte Albán V architecture in Mitla style; the most distant *sujetos*, "eight leagues from Mitla," have never been archaeologically surveyed.

## THE MITLA PATTERN: A SUMMARY

Settlement patterns at Mitla provide a significant contrast with the Monte Albán V occupation of the Etla region. While the latter is characterized by countless isolated residences and tiny hamlets, possibly reflecting the settlement of *terrazgueros*, Mitla seems to have had a nucleated urban center with elegant ceremonial and civic buildings, a substantial suburban residential area, a rural hinterland or "sustaining area" of 20 km², several hilltop forts, and a series of dependent hamlets up to 8 leagues distant. The rural sector of Mitla seems to have been terraced and intensively utilized in a way not seen in the Etla area. Thus, while settlement patterns in the Etla area would support a hypothesis of emigrant Mixtec royal marriage partners who assigned vast tracts of land to their *tay situndayu*, the Mitla area looks different. To us, at least, it looks like an attempt to maintain the ancient, nucleated Zapotec residential pattern by agricultural intensification. The assembly halls of the *coquihualao* at Mitla, with their *tableros* decorated in a way already seen at Atzompa; the elaborate tombs with niches, already seen at Classic Monte Albán; the windowless retreat of the *bigaña,* opening into a more accessible hall as did the two-room temples of Monte Albán IIIb—none of these features reminds us of the Mixteca.

As Blanton pointed out at the Santa Fe seminar, "The presence of strong Mixtec *caciques* at places like Cuilapan would put a lot of pressure on the remaining Zapotec lords to increase their own productivity and manpower if they wanted to remain autonomous." We suspect that the pattern of settlement we see at Mitla—and perhaps also at Yagul—is archaeological evidence for precisely that kind of increase.

# TOPIC 89
## The Reconstructed Chronology of the Later Zapotec Rulers, A.D. 1415–1563

JOYCE MARCUS

## INTRODUCTION

The only Zapotec rulers about whom we have any pseudohistorical knowledge are the last five, who ruled at Zaachila in the Valley of Oaxaca and later at Tehuantepec. And even this knowledge is presumably half fact, half legend; much of it was recorded by Fray Francisco de Burgoa, the vicar of Zaachila, one hundred years after the death of the last Zapotec *coqui*. In addition to Burgoa (1670, 1674), there are works by José Antonio Gay (1881), Bancroft (1882), and Martínez Gracida (1888a), the latter described by Paddock (Topic 90) as a "novelized history." Although I agree with Paddock that it would be foolish to rely on these sources as modern history is relied upon, some of the persons and events are given credence by the fact that they appear also in Aztec and Spanish documents. In this topic, I treat the story as an oral tradition that survived until Burgoa's time and was based on actual events whose precise details may have become fuzzy and romanticized through the passage of time. The chronology I give is a reconstruction, based on points of agreement among various authors; from A.D. 1520 onward, of course, it should prove to be more reliable.

## ZAACHILA I

The founder of the Zapotec royal dynasty at Zaachila (Teozapotlan) is said to have been Zaachila I, who must have ruled some time around the end of the fourteenth century and the beginning of the fifteenth. He reputedly was a "warrior king" who carried out military campaigns against the legendary Condoy, ruler of the Mixe, who lived in Totontepec (Gay 1881, I:175).

## ZAACHILA II

Zaachila I is said to have died in A.D. 1415; he was succeeded by his son Zaachila II. (Because we have no prece-

dents for Zapotec sons being given names identical to their fathers, it seems unlikely that this was his real name; more likely, it designates him as the second ruler in the dynasty. This observation would apply to Zaachila III also.) Zaachila II reportedly withdrew his forces from Totontepec and ended the hostilities with the Mixe. His reign was distinguished by intelligence and ingenuity rather than warfare, and is thought to have lasted for almost 40 years, from A.D. 1415 to 1454 (see Tables 8.2 and 8.3).

## ZAACHILA III

Zaachila III, "the Deceiver," is reported to have acceded to the throne after the death of his father in 1454. He ruled during the time of the Aztec king Ahuitzotl, and formed the military alliance with the Mixtec *cacique* of Achiutla to engage the Aztecs in battle at Huitzo in the northern Valley of Oaxaca (this battle is reported in Topic 91). He earned his nickname "the deceiver" because of the skillful way he managed to talk the Mixtecs into taking the full brunt of the Aztec attack, later allowing the army of Ahuitzotl to enter the valley by secret treaty (Gay 1881, I:177–179). Zaachila III died in 1487, and was succeeded by his son Cocijoeza, "Lightning-creator."

## COMMENTS ON ZAACHILA I–III

Before proceeding to the exploits of Cocijoeza, let us briefly consider the archaeological context of Zaachila I–III. These were the last Zapotec kings to die unbaptized by the Spaniards, and hence to have received a Precolumbian-style Zapotec burial. Might either of them be among the personages recovered by Gallegos (1964) in the spectacular tombs at Zaachila (discussed in Topic 87)? Caso (1966) has done his best to demonstrate that the occupants of those tombs were Mixtecs, descendants of the lords of Yanhuitlán, and his ethnic ascriptions are supported by the style of the stucco friezes, the carving of the bones, the goldwork, the use of five dots for the number 5, and so on. However, Tomb 1 has on its back wall a stucco version of the flying turtle that the Zapotec used as a metaphor for their royal ancestors, and it wears on its head the same curled-nose reptilian element and broad-bladed leaf seen on earlier Zapotec monuments in the Zaachila area (Figure 8.25; compare Caso 1966: Fig. 24 with Paddock 1966a: Fig. 285). This similarity suggests a strong continuity from Monte Albán IIIb–IV times, which it seems unlikely any Mixtec ruler would want to display.

Radiocarbon dates seem unlikely to resolve this problem.

### TABLE 8.2
Reconstructed Chronology of the Later Zapotec Rulers[a]

| King | Birthdate | Marriage | Accession | Death |
|------|-----------|----------|-----------|-------|
| Zaachila I | ? | ? | ? | 1415 |
| Zaachila II | ? | ? | 1415 | 1454 |
| Zaachila III | ? | ? | 1454 | 1487 |
| Cocijoeza | ? | 1496 | 1487 | 1529 |
| Cocijopii | 1502 | ? | 1518 | 1563 |

[a]Adapted from Taracena (1941). Years are A.D.

TABLE 8.3
Reconstructed Chronology of Events Involving the Later
Zapotec Rulers[a]

| Year (A.D.) | Event |
|---|---|
| 1415 | Death of Zaachila I; accession of Zaachila II |
| 1454 | Death of Zaachila II; accession of Zaachila III |
| 1469 | Initial conquest of Tehuantepec by Aztec ruler Axayacatl |
| 1486 | Battle of Huitzo (acc. to Gay) |
| 1487 | Death of Zaachila III; accession of Cocijoeza |
| 1494 | Sacking of Mitla and Zaachila by Aztec ruler Ahuitzotl |
| 1495 | Battle of Guiengola (acc. to Gay) |
| 1496 | Marriage of Coyolicatzin (daughter of Ahuitzotl) to Cocijoeza |
| 1498 | Bitoopaa, first son of Cocijoeza (by Zapotec wife?) born in Tehuantepec |
| 1500 | Natipaa, second son of Cocijoeza (by Zapotec wife?) born |
| 1502 | Cocijopii, third son of Cocijoeza (and offspring of Coyolicatzin), born |
| 1504 | Pinopiaa, first daughter of Cocijoeza, born |
| 1506 | Donají, last daughter of Cocijoeza, born |
| 1518 | Cocijopii named ruler of Tehuantepec; Pinopiaa dies in Isthmus |
| 1521 | Cocijoeza is baptized "Don Juan Cortés" by Spaniards; his daughter is baptized "Doña Juana Cortés" |
| 1522 | Princess Donají is sacrificed by the Mixtecs in revenge for her "treason"; this same year, Comiyuchi, last Mixtec ruler of Tututepec, dies, and Hernán Cortés bestows on Alvarado the señorío of Tututepec |
| 1527 | Cocijopii is baptized "Don Juan Cortés Cocijopii" by Spaniards |
| 1529 | Coyolicatzin dies in Zaachila; Natipaa dies in Tlacochahuaya while celebrating his wedding; Cocijoeza dies in Zaachila |
| 1561–1564 | Cocijopii is interrogated by Fray Juan de Córdova and Fray Juan de Mata concerning his "idolatrous practices" |
| 1563 | Cocijopii dies in Nejapa while returning to Tehuantepec |

[a]Adapted from Taracena (1941).

Caso presumably regarded the Zaachila tombs as those of Mixtec rulers who had driven the Zapotecs from Zaachila. If so, they would have to date to the time of Cocijoeza, for Zaachila III died in Zaachila unmolested by Mixtecs. This date would place the tombs roughly in the period A.D. 1490–1520, a period too short to be fixed by radiocarbon. If the tombs date to A.D. 1400–1490 or earlier, it would be very difficult to see them as Mixtec.

Although I am unable to resolve this question, I can see a compromise position. We have already suggested that royal marriage alliances between the Zapotecs and Mixtecs had begun to take place as early as 300 years before the 1579–1581 relaciones (see Introduction to Chapter 8). In one case (Mata 1580), a Mixtec prince from the cacicazgo of Yanhuitlán supposedly married a sister-in-law of the Zapotec ruler of Zaachila. If such marriages were taking place as early as A.D. 1280, any or all of the rulers called

Zaachila I–III could have had important Mixtec ancestors. Through their in-laws they would have had access to polychrome pottery, goldwork, carved bones, and any of the paraphernalia customarily thought of as "Mixtec." And their Zapotec ancestors, now Cloud People, might appear in their tombs as flying turtles. At such a point, it becomes futile to attempt to identify a specific royal skeleton as "Zapotec" or "Mixtec" in the ethnic sense.

Further complicating the archaeological context of these later rulers is that Zaachila itself was at that time little more than an area of royal residences. Blanton and Kowalewski's survey of the area shows no large Monte Albán V settlement; indeed, the Late Postclassic area of occupation is quite restricted when compared to the massive occupation of Monte Albán IIIb–IV. Whoever the occupants of Gallegos's tombs may have been, whatever their royal or ethnic identity, their residence was a palace atop a high artificial mound that had grown by accretion mainly in earlier periods. This royal residential area may have been the capital of a region, but it was evidently not the focus of a large urban center.

## COCIJOEZA, A.D. 1487–1529

Cocijoeza, son of Zaachila III, was perhaps the most famous of the later Zapotec rulers—a "brave hero and more astute than his father" (Gay 1881, I:184–185). It was he who, in league with the Mixtec cacique of Achiutla, successfully defended the Isthmus of Tehuantepec from the Aztec army under Ahuitzotl. The battle of Guiengola, focal point of this military success, is reported in Topic 91. This battle ended with a truce which prepared the way for the marriage of Cocijoeza with Coyolicatzin, daughter of Ahuitzotl, whose Zapotec name became Pelaxilla ("Cotton Flake"). This was an extremely important marriage, which linked the royal houses of the Zapotecs and the Mexica (see Figure 8.33). Through it, Cocijoeza became not only the son-in-law of Ahuitzotl but also the brother-in-law of Moctezuma II, who married another of Ahuitzotl's daughters. These events are better documented than those of previous Zapotec rulers because they are recorded by the Aztecs as well.

No event in Zapotec political history has been as romanticized as the wedding of Cocijoeza with Coyolicatzin. Although it seems likely that the marriage was one of political expediency, it has with the passage of time become a love story. According to Gay's version, Cocijoeza was unwilling to marry until he had seen the young lady, and so she arranged for him to see her bathing at Charcos de la Marquesa, a spring near a beautiful grove of trees near Tehuantepec. It was love at first sight.

As late as 1912, Paul Radin (1935) was able to record a lengthy story about the marriage of Cocijoeza from a Zapotec informant at Zaachila. Radin's version is truly romantic, having Cocijoeza travel conveniently by cloud wherever he wanted to go. Coyolicatzin was carried to Zaachila on a litter, and there was dancing for a week in preparation for the wedding. The dancers covered the ground around the

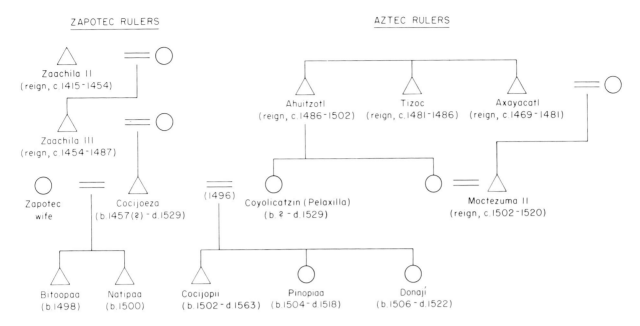

FIGURE 8.33. Kinship diagram showing the linking-up of the royal houses of the Zapotec and the Mexica.

palace with flowers, and prostrated themselves while the royal couple blessed them three times. In Bancroft's version (1876, V:445), Coyolicatzin was also carried to Zaachila on a litter borne on the shoulders of noblemen, where a succession of brilliant fetes were given in her honor, but the actual wedding took place in Tehuantepec.

Now living under her Zapotec name of Pelaxilla, Coyolicatzin is said to have loved Cocijoeza so much that she remained loyal to him when Ahuitzotl later plotted to assassinate him. Bancroft describes this turn of events as follows:

> It was, perhaps, not without hidden motives of future treachery that Ahuitzotl had insisted on a matrimonial alliance between the Aztecs and Zapotecs; at any rate, he is reported to have made an attempt some years later to assassinate Cociyoeza [sic] through the assistance of his wife. Ambassadors were sent to communicate with her on the matter, but Pelaxilla revealed the plot to her husband, who immediately sent back the embassy laden with gifts, and prepared his forts and his armies for war. The Aztecs, however, knowing that their plot was discovered, made no attack; they demanded permission to send troops through Zapotec territory for the conquest of Amaxtlan and Xuchitepec, south of the isthmus, which was granted; but Cociyoeza, suspecting treachery, took the precaution to furnish a large army to attend the Aztecs through his territory, both coming and going, under pretense of furnishing an escort [Bancroft 1876, V:447].

Cocijoeza had five legitimate children. His first two sons, Bitoopaa and Natipaa, were evidently the offspring of a Zapotec wife, and did not accede to the throne (Bitoopaa, his firstborn, died as an infant). His third son, Cocijopii, was the offspring of Pelaxilla and hence a grandson to Ahuitzotl; he was named ruler of Tehuantepec in A.D. 1518 at the age of 16. The fourth and fifth children were daughters (presum-

ably by Pelaxilla, although it is not always clear). These were Pinopiaa, a teenager of excellent qualities and rare virtues, who refused advantageous alliances and died a virgin in Tehuantepec, venerated by the Zapotecs after her death, and Donají, who was alive at the time of the Spanish Conquest. Donají is supposed to have married the Mixtec prince of Tilantongo, baptized Diego de Aguilar by the Spaniards; she was baptized Doña Juana Cortés. Refusing to betray her father to the Mixtecs, Donají was sacrificed "for treachery" and became a Zapotec heroine. She and her husband were buried in the convent at Cuilapan with the following inscription on the floor of the chapel: MAIOANA CORTES– DIEGO AGUILAR (Covarrubias 1946:202).

## COCIJOPII, A.D. 1502–1563

The birth of Cocijopii in A.D. 1502 was celebrated with public rejoicing. The Zapotec diviners declared that he would be happy in the first half of his life and would rule prosperously for some time, that he would be revered and feared by neighboring nations, but that in the end he would lose his throne and power, finishing up with unhappy events. Some say that because of these prognostications they named him Cocijopii ("Lightning-wind," which meant that he would begin to rule with the clamor and pomp of lightning, but would end like the vanishing wind—an accurate prediction, since he spent his latter years under Spanish "house arrest" in Tehuantepec).

When he was only 16 and already displayed rare talents, Cocijopii was named ruler of Tehuantepec by his father, Cocijoeza, who remained in Zaachila as *coquitao*. Cocijopii, who had inherited the prudence and bravery of Cocijoeza, began his reign by making alliances with the Chiapanecos. In 1527 he was baptized "Don Juan Cortés Cocijopii" by the Spaniards; however, during 1561–1563 he was found still to be practicing "idolatrous rites," and two Dominican priests were summoned to interrogate him. These were Fray Juan de Córdova, author of the great sixteenth-century Zapotec dictionary (Córdova 1578a) and Fray Juan de Mata, author of the *Relación de Teozapotlan* (Mata 1580). Both undoubtedly learned a great deal about Zapotec religion from Cocijopii, who eventually cleared himself of wrongdoing. The last of the great Zapotec rulers died in 1563 in Nejapa at the age of 61 while returning to Tehuantepec.

## TERRITORIAL ADMINISTRATION IN THE TEHUANTEPEC REGION

In the Precolumbian era, the administration of government and justice was based on a high regard for oral tradition and the spoken word. The territorial boundaries of Zapotec rulers' realms were generally landmarks such as named mountain peaks and rivers; these landmarks were referred to in settling disputes. Verbal honesty was highly valued and some forms of lying and deceit were punishable by sacrifice.

During 1535–1549, the Spaniards demanded that titles of land ownership be drawn up on paper to indicate which Indian communities owned which pieces of land. A great many *lienzos* or cartographic–genealogical documents were painted during this period by native artists. Very few of these survive for the Zapotec region or the holdings of Zapotec rulers, however. The few that have been published show this pattern of named mountain peaks, rivers, and other natural landmarks. I find the delimitation of Zapotec territory by named natural landmarks interesting, because it calls to mind the carved stones on Building J at Monte Albán, which list 40-odd places associated with "hill" or "mountain" glyphs. It reinforces my suspicion that Building J records the territorial boundaries of the Zapotec state in Monte Albán II by reference to a series of named landmarks.

In Topic 90, John Paddock discusses two of these documents, the *lienzos* of Huilotepec and Guevea. Both describe the territorial limits of communities in the Isthmus of Tehuantepec, within the area originally ruled by Cocijopii. I

will not duplicate here the comments made by Paddock. I will discuss only one of these documents—the *Lienzo de Guevea*—which has already been published by Eduard Seler (1908). It has two interesting aspects: a named series of natural landmarks which recalls the earlier series from Building J, and a genealogical list of Zapotec rulers ending with Cocijopii.

According to Seler, Santiago Guevea is a town situated "on the road running along the left bank of the Tehuantepec River through the mountains of the Mixes and beyond across Laoyago to Tehuantepec" (1908:123). There are two known copies, A and B. Noted on both copies, the original of the *lienzo* was produced in 1540 during the vice-regency of Don Antonio de Mendoza. Copy B records June 1, 1540 as the date while Copy A records the following:

Años del mapa original . . . . . . . . . . . . . . . . . . . . . . . . . . . . . 1540
Ydem de esta copia . . . . . . . . . . . . . . . . . . . . . . . . . . . . . 1820

Copy B provides the reader with an explanatory note in the middle of the page:

Para poder examinar en este Mapa con mas claridad la division ó linderos del Terreno de los Naturales del Pueblo de Santiago Guevea se busca el número 1 en el punto llamado en Castellano Cerro de Malacate, y alli mismo cierra la linia que circula al rededor de dho Terreno con el No. 18 parage nombrado Cerro de Chayote, con la ynteligencia de qe. cada punto ó parage contienen tres idiomas Mejicano, Zapoteco y traducido en Castellano.

In the middle of a ring of boundary landmarks appear the names *tani Guebiya* ("hill of Guevea") and *Serro de Guevea,* below a naturalistic hill with three "arrowheads." In front of the hill sign appear the words *rigula Guebiya* and *viejo de Guevea,* below a man sitting inside a structure. A road with footprints leading to Hill of Guebiya divides the town into two barrios—on Map A we read *yodo Santiago Guebiya* and *Yglesia de Santo Guevea,* and on the other side of the road are the words *yodo Santo Domingo* and *Yglesia de Santo Domingo.* Above each set of names is a church. Pickett (1959:69) gives *yu'du'* as Isthmus Zapotec for "church," which agrees well with this nineteenth-century copy.

The top half of the *lienzo* (Figure 8.34) provides us with 18 hieroglyphic landmarks, primarily "hills" and "rivers," which seem to delimit the territory surrounding the town of Guebiya—lands perhaps claimed by the Precolumbian ruler of Guevea. The 18 landmarks have bilingual inscriptions, as follows:

| Zapotec name | Spanish name | Translation of Zapotec name |
| --- | --- | --- |
| 1. Tani Guiebigoce | Serro [sic] de Malacate | Hill of the Stone Spindle Whorl |
| 2. Guietalaga | Piedra Ancha | Stone with a Leaf (= Broad?) |
| 3. Tani Guiexosa | Serro de Dos Puntas | Hill of Stone with Two Peaks |
| 4. Tani Guiegoxio | Cerro de Rayo | Hill of Stone of Lightning |
| 5. Nisa Guiegodaa | Agua del Río de Petapa | Water of the River of the Mat |
| 6. Tani Guiebituo | Serro de Santo | Hill of Stone with Great Spirit |
| 7. Tani Guieguiña | Serro de Caxa | Hill of Stone Box (Box Mountain) |
| 8. Tani Guiebiti | Serro de Penca | Hill of the Hide or Pelt (?) |
| 9. Tani Guegohue | Serro de Tinta | Hill of Dark Blue Color (?) |

| Zapotec name | Spanish name | Translation of Zapotec name |
|---|---|---|
| 10. Tani Guechohuy | Serro Quemado | Burnt Hill |
| 11. Nisa Guluga | Agua Xicopestle | Water of the Gourd Vessel (?) |
| 12. Guigo (?) Liasa | Río de Camalote | River of Camalote Grass |
| 13. Tani Guebeche | Serro de León | Hill of the "Puma" (literally, "fierce animal") |
| 14. Tani Guecheta | Piedras Opuestas | Hill of Stones Leaning Against One Another (?) |
| 15. Nisa Belole | Agua de Tempolcate | Water of the Tadpole (?) |
| 16. Guigo Xanaya | Río Debajo de la Tierra | River Beneath the Ground |
| 17. Guigo Iloxi | Río de Arena | River of Sand |
| 18. Tani Guiape | Serro o Piedra de Chayote | Hill or Stone of the Chayote (= Yape) |

One additional place, just north of Guevea and within the circle of boundary landmarks, is *tani quie cila*, "Serro de Columna." Martínez Gracida provides data that agree well with the placement of "Cerro de Columna" just to the north of Santiago Guevea: *"Al N. del pueblo queda el Cerro de Columna o Picacho á donde forman ramales los cerros más elevados que son: Xigana que queda al O. y Leellidoó o Sitio de Iglesia que está hácia al E."* (1883:139).

Another area of interest is the lower half of the *lienzo* (Glass 1964:Pl.2), which includes genealogical information about the Zapotec dynasty (Figure 8.35). Two columns of people are given, separated by a road (of footprints). The persons seated on the left side all have the same hairdo as the *viejo* or head man of the village of Guevea; they also wear very simple clothing, a piece of cloth tied together across one shoulder. Behind the first four head men are shields and lances. Their names are given as follows:

| Labels | Translation | Hieroglyph |
|---|---|---|
| 1. Logobicha | Face of the Sun | Sun disk plus snake |
| 2. Biciyatuo Rigula | Great Eagle, Old Man | Eagle's head |
| 3. Xûana Nece | Minor noble (Young Lord) | Snake's head |
| 4. Biciyatuo Rigula | Great Eagle, Old Man | Eagle's head |
| 5. Xûana Bechecha | Minor noble, "Puma" (Fierce Animal) | Puma and stone knife |
| 6. Pisialo | Eagle Eye | Deer's head (?) |
| 7. Xilacache Guiebisuño | Feathered Stone Rattle | Rattle and feathers |
| 8. Picezuño | Gourd Rattle | Rattle |

We can suspect that these eight men who wear no headdresses are officeholders of some kind, probably serving as representatives of towns paying tribute. In most cases, we are provided with a personal name for each (hieroglyphically attached to his cloak as well as given in Zapotec gloss) and his office or status. The two statuses indicated are (1) *xuana*, "minor noble" (*xoana* of Córdova 1578a) and (2) *rigula*, "old man or village elder" (from *gola*, "old"). The first four men, those associated with shields and lances, carry hieroglyphic names with snake's or eagle's heads, perhaps indicating some sort of warrior status.

Turning now to the lower right side of the *lienzo*, the later Zapotec rulers are shown. Starting from the bottom, we see a hill sign inside a six-stepped pyramid; the gloss immediately to the right is *Sachila*. There is a ruler seated upon a cushion-throne; he appears in a red robe, a red peaked cap, a black beard, and the gloss *Yobicoxi chalachi*. The second ruler given is glossed as *Rinicoxi chaleguesa*. These two men, then, are not actually named but simply referred to as "first son" and "second son."[1] We know from ethnohistoric

sources that the first two sons of Cocijoeza did not rule at Zaachila, either because they died early or because they were the offspring of less important (Zapotec) wives. The third ruler in sequence is glossed as *Cosiobi* (Cocijopii), who we know was the third son of Cocijoeza, the offspring of a royal marriage uniting Cocijoeza with the Aztec princess Coyolicatzin (Pelaxilla or Cotton Flake), daughter of Ahuitzotl. The fourth ruler shown is glossed as *Cosihuesa* (Cocijoeza), father of the three sons. In sum, these names may be roughly translated: Cosihuesa, "Lightning-creator"; Cosiobi, "Lightning-wind"; Rinicoxi chaleguesa, "Second-born son took . . . (?)"; Yobicoxi chalachi, "First-born son attracted suspicion." Proceeding upward, we encounter one more "ruler" of Zaachila, glossed as Penobiya (which may mean "12 Twisted"). His name is not mentioned in other ethnohistoric sources, and it is not at all clear when he might have "ruled" at Zaachila, unless he is an ancestor of Cocijoeza (see Paddock, Topic 90). Penobiya could be Cocijoeza's daughter Pinopiaa, who died in Tehuantepec.

Proceeding upward, the footprints and pathway lead to a ruler glossed as *Cosiobi* and associated with "the Hill of the Jaguar," glossed as *Tehuantepeque*. Ethnohistoric sources provide us with the data that Cocijopii was installed as ruler of Tehuantepec on January 10, 1518 by his father. The

---

[1]The Zapotec used the same name for "first finger" (*yobi*), "second finger" (*rini* or *tini*), "third finger" (*texi*), etc. for recording the birth order of their sons (Córdova 1578b). See also Paddock, Topic 90.

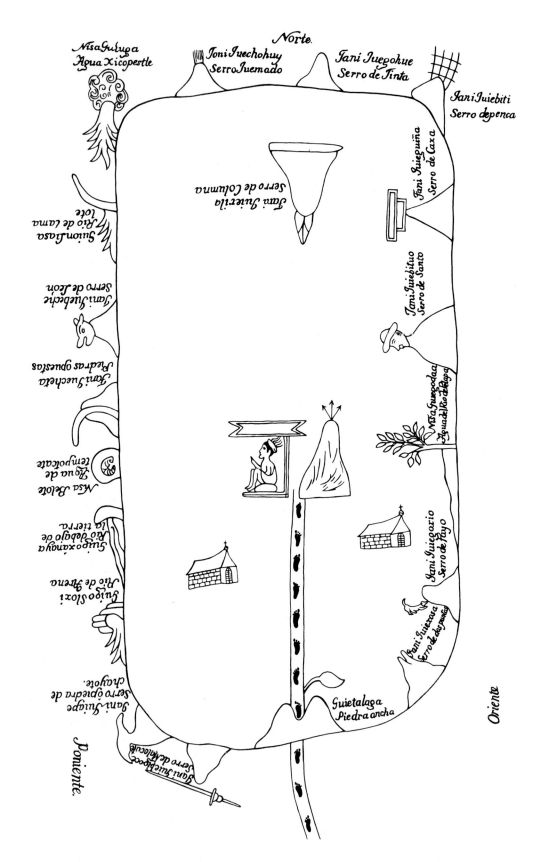

FIGURE 8.34. Upper half of Copy A of the Lienzo de Guevea, showing 18 named landmarks defining the territory claimed by Santiago Guevea.

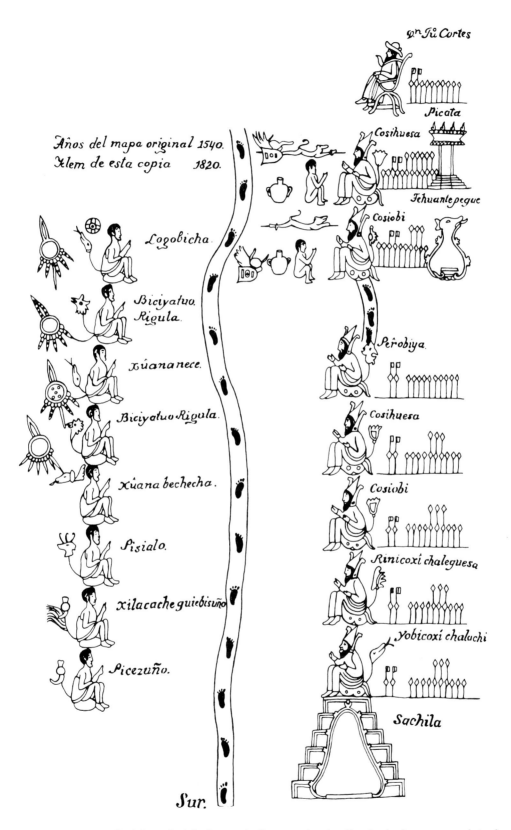

Dⁿ Jū Cortes

Picata

Cosihuesa

Años del mapa original 1540.
Ytem de esta copia      1820.

Tehuantepeque

Cosiobi

Logobicha.

Biciyatuo.
Rigula.

Xuananece.

Perobiya.

Biciyatuo Rigula.

Cosihuesa

Xuana bechecha.

Cosiobi

Pisialo.

Rinicoxi chaleguesa

Xilacache guiebisuño

Yobicoxi chaluchi

Picezuño.

Sachila

Sur.

FIGURE 8.35. Lower half of Copy A of the Lienzo de Guevea, showing Zapotec lords, *xuana*, and *rigula*.

Zaachila dynasty had two seats of power after 1518—Cocijoeza continued to rule at Zaachila, and Cocijopii ruled at Tehuantepec. Cocijoeza sits above Cocijopii in the *lienzo* as if legitimizing Cocijopii's right to rule at Tehuantepec. The Tehuantepec throne seems to have been very important for the receipt of tribute, as the rulers are shown receiving slaves (?), green feathers, an olla perhaps filled with a fermented beverage, and what appears to be meat. Finally, on the top of the dynastic list is shown an individual in European dress named Don Juan Cortés; Cocijopii received this name in December of 1521.

Despite the problems and omissions of the various ver-

sions of the Lienzo de Guevea (pointed out by Paddock in the following topic), the *lienzo* does provide some corroboration for otherwise ambiguous ethnohistoric sources. It seems to repeat the information that Cocijoeza's first two sons, Bitoopaa and Natipaa, did not accede to the throne, and that his third son Cocijopii ruled Tehuantepec. It shows that *xuana* or minor nobles and *rigula* or elders administered some towns, and that tribute was brought to the kings of the Zaachila dynasty. Finally, it shows that the territorial boundaries of the Zapotec realm were conceived of as a series of mountains or rivers with hieroglyphic names, a pattern of perhaps 2000 years' standing.

## TOPIC 90
## Comments on the *Lienzos* of Huilotepec and Guevea

JOHN PADDOCK

A number of documentary sources converge in implying that during Late Postclassic times the principal seat of Zapotec political power was transferred from Zaachila (Teozapotlan) in the Valley of Oaxaca to Tehuantepec in the Isthmus Zapotec region. What is surprising is how vague and ambiguous the details and chronology of this transfer of power become when the sources are examined critically.

It has been traditionally accepted that there was a dynasty of three rulers— Zaachila I, Zaachila II, and Zaachila III—who preceded the illustrious Zapotec ruler Cocijoeza. Cocijoeza, reportedly under Mixtec military pressure in the Valley of Oaxaca, placed his son Cocijopii in the rulership of Tehuantepec. Seler (1908:185), drawing on sources unknown to me and uncited by him, says that this took place in 1518. After the Spanish Conquest, Cocijopii was baptized Don Juan Cortés and continued to live in Tehuantepec. He was the last of the great Zapotec hereditary rulers.

The fragmentary data on the Zaachila "dynasty" within the Valley of Oaxaca may be augmented in two early colonial indigenous documents from the Isthmus—the *lienzos* of Huilotepec and Guevea—which give more specific information.

## DOCUMENTATION ON THE ZAACHILA RULERS

Turning first to the works of modern specialists who presumably have used whatever documentation is available—and who probably know it much more fully than I do—let's look at Taylor's history of Oaxaca land tenure during colonial times. As he notes, "The retention of substantial landholdings and high social status by the hereditary native chieftains is a distinguishing feature of colonial society in the Valley of Oaxaca" (Taylor 1972:35). Here, then, we should

find references to the ruling dynasty of Zaachila as the point of departure for colonial land tenure in Zaachila and throughout the Valley of Oaxaca. But Cocijoeza is not mentioned in the book, though caciques and *principales* of many valley towns turn up hundreds of times, and the role of the native nobility in Early Colonial land tenure is the object of special examination.

Spores has written on native institutions at the time of the Conquest. Though he discusses political organization (Spores 1965:965–967), he is cautious about the role of Teozapotlan–Zaachila: "It is certain that Teozapotlan had some kind of political control, but the precise nature of that control is not yet well known." Inferences about the Teozapotlan kings are equally cautious, and based on Burgoa and Gay.

Since the royal house of Teozapotlan was said to have been linked on two occasions by marriage with ruling houses of the Mixteca, Spores's book on the Mixtec kings is promising. But there is no reference to a Zapotec king by name, and only one brief mention of Teozapotlan. "Witnesses giving testimony in the Zapotec town of Miahuatlán in 1547 stated that there had been separate supreme lords [i.e., kings] in Mexico, in the Mixteca, and in Tehuantepec . . . the Zapotec king had moved from the capital of Teozapotlan (Zaachila) to Tehuantepec before the Spanish conquest" (Spores 1967:66–67). This statement makes it plain that we shall have to look not only at Zaachila, but also at Tehuantepec for traces of the Zapotec kings, and it hints that the center of power had been transferred to Tehuantepec.

Caso has studied the ruling family of Yanhuitlan and has given particular attention to its ties with the Teozapotlan rulers. Though his essay is accompanied by a long genealogy of the Mixtec rulers, there is not so much as a name for either of the Zaachila spouses (Caso 1966).

Judged quantitatively, the most considerable work on the Zapotec kings is by Martínez Gracida (1888a[1972]), but it is a novelized history in which the author has introduced fictional personages, events, and conversations. Since he goes to the trouble of citing sources when he has them, Martínez Gracida presumably would have written a history or biography if he had been able. Introducing the work, Ignacio Altamirano says that "the history of Mexico before the arrival of the Spanish is wrapped in legends, or rather, what we call History is a series of legends" (Martínez Gracida 1888a:1). But, even within the protection of the seminovel, Martínez Gracida really begins his work with Cocijoeza; of his antededents, he notes only that around A.D. 1390 Zaachila I founded Zaachila-yoo, and that in A.D. 1487 Cocijoeza inherited the throne from Zaachila III.

In order to impose this degree of restraint in his days, the doubts of Martínez Gracida must have been strong. The conspicuous absence of comment on these royal antecedents among later writers is, I suggest, caused by a lack of data.

The skepticism may be very old. The 1580 *Relación de Teozapotlan*, far from detailing the Prehispanic rulers in response to Questions 14 and 15: "*Cuyos eran en tiempo de su gentilidad, y el Señorío que sobre ellos tenian sus señores . . . Como se gobernauan . . .*" (del Paso y Troncoso 1905:IV, 4), though for other towns the response often included names of one or more rulers, maintains a discreet silence like that of a modern historian. It does affirm that the town seems to have been of special importance in the past, "for there was the capital of all this province from too many years back to be remembered, as is said by all the Indians of the Zapotecapan and also the Mixtecs of Cuilapan. . . . All of them agree on this, that Teozapotlan is the Zapotec court" (Mata 1580:190–191).

Insisting, as if he too were dubious, Fray Juan de Mata adds that "in ancient times it was a town of many people and many principales, a town such as a court would be, but today there are only a few inhabitants, and almost no principales" (Mata 1580:191). One mention of the Zapotec kings is in connection with the strong point to which other authors say Cocijoeza fled when Teozapotlan was attacked: "Near a place called Quiane in Zapoteco, and Suchitepec in Mexicano, the church of Santa Catarina, is a rock or headland . . . raised above the terrain like the crown of a hat. . . . It was in ancient times the fort of the kings of Teozapotlan" (Mata 1580:195). The remaining reference to the local royalty likewise fails to name any of the line; it refers to relations with the Aztecs: "And they say they did not give to these Mexicans any tribute, but simply out of friendship [they sent valuables to Moctezuma], and the king of Teozapotlan was the absolute ruler of his lands" (Mata 1580:194). But, as Barlow observes, "Tribute is tribute" (1949:121).

A much more imposing picture of Teozapotlan is gained from the *relaciones* of other places that record having paid tribute and given services to, in some cases almost being governed by, the Zapotec rulers there.

Even though he wrote 150 years after the Conquest, Burgoa remains the principal source for all later authors. We might dismiss him as simply having recorded tales, the legends Altamirano referred to, but Burgoa himself says he used ancient writings. These writings may have included codices, and the possibly much more common Early Colonial *lienzos*, as well as materials in ecclesiastical archives. Covarrubias gives an admirable brief summary of what Burgoa has to say about the Zapotec kings (1954:189–207). Perhaps with the aid of his friends Caso and Jiménez Moreno, Covarrubias seems to draw on sources other than Burgoa as well.

The notion that Teozapotlan was "founded" in very late times is neatly evaded: in "approximately A.D. 1390 a new dynasty was established at Zaachila Yoo. . . . About 1360, however, the Zapotecs had already occupied Tehuantepec" (Covarrubias 1954:189). Equally evaded is any other mention of the Teozapotlan royalty before Cocijoeza.

If we accept for the moment the existence of Zaachila I, II, and III, we can assume that Zaachila I was born just before the end of the thirteenth century. At that time, according to the *Relación de Cuilapan*, a Mixtec ruler had already come into the valley to marry "a daughter of Teozapotlan," surely implying that there was some dynasty ruling in Zaachila, even if not the same one from which Cocijoeza descended (Salazar 1581:23). The Teozapotlan *relación* disagrees on two points: it says that the marriage was between a Mixtec woman and a lord of Teozapotlan, and that at that time few other Mixtecs came into the valley (the Cuilapan version is that many came then). But the two *relaciones* agree perfectly on one important detail: the marriage took place more than 300 years before 1580, when they were written.

There is a confusing detail in the Chichicapa *relación*. Its elders said that Chichicapa in olden times had recognized as lord the ruler of Zaachila, whose name was Quieguela, "Lord of the Wine." (This name may mean "Rock or Hill of the Night," a toponym; but Quiaguela is Day 183 in the 260-day calendar.) Is he a predecessor of the three Zaachilas, or at least of Cocijoeza? Apparently not, for the *relación* adds that the Mixtecs were making war on this cacique when the Spaniards arrived (Espíndola 1580:116). Thus Quiaguela may be Cocijoeza's calendric name. Nevertheless, if we impute one fairly modest error to the witnesses or the scribe—and the contradictions among the *relaciones* suggest that such errors did occur—"Quieguela" just might have been something more interesting than the calendric name of Cocijoeza: a predecessor and perhaps ancestor.

A somewhat similar possibility lies in a citation for which I appeal to Gay (1881:I, 238–239). (Gay is citing Brasseur de Bourbourg, who is referring to the Codex Chimalpopoca.) Brasseur, says Gay, affirms that in 1351 a man named Ozomatli ("Monkey") ruled in Mitla. Brasseur adds that Zaachila I was a son of a Mitleño ruler named Huiyatóo or Huijatóo. However, Gay adds, this was a title given to the high priests at Mitla, and may not have been just the name of an individual ruler.[1] In any case, the Chimalpopoca may be committing here an error made famous by Durán and oth-

---

[1] The term *huija-tao* was, in fact, used for Zapotec high priests (see Marcus 1978).

ers, who tell firmly how a town named Mitla, near Oaxaca, was razed by the enraged Aztecs after some Aztec traders, on their way back to Mexico from Coatzacoalcos, were ambushed there. In fact, the place referred to seems to have been in the Huasteca.

Having apparently run out of gas as far as the valley is concerned, we may turn to the isthmus. Besides the chronicles that deal also with the valley, for the isthmus we have two early colonial indigenous documents that mention the Zaachila rulers: the *lienzos* of Huilotepec and of Guevea.

## THE *LIENZO DE HUILOTEPEC*

Huilotepec is a small town south of Tehuantepec, near the ocean and just west of the Lagunas Superior and Inferior. Its Early Colonial *lienzo* has been published, more or less, by Frederick Starr (1908), with maddeningly small photographs and a sketchy description. Barlow obtained Starr's plates, which reproduce two slightly different photographs, from the Bancroft Library and printed them again (1943). Seler had seen the *lienzo* in 1896, and had made a drawing of it from memory; he was not allowed to photograph it, but he has a few things to say about it in his publication on the *Lienzo de Guevea* (1908). Having only the plates at his disposal, Barlow could not enlarge the photographs, whose present location is seemingly unknown. With the partially legible photographs of the Huilotepec document at hand, one suspects that the strong resemblance Seler perceived between his memory of it and his copies of the Guevea *lienzo* is almost exclusively a matter of layout. The only content they have in common is representation of Cocijoeza, Cocijopii, and Tehuantepec.

Both are narrow, tall arrangements.[2] Huilotepec has the Pacific Ocean at the bottom. At the center bottom, the Tehuantepec River empties into it, after curving down from near the top left. Modern Huilotepec is on or near the left bank. At the appropriate spot there is a hill glyph with a building beside it and a bird perched on top. The gloss below the hill, in Zapoteco, is *tani que pito*. Because *tani* means "hill" and *que* probably refers to *quie*, "rock," the gloss for the bird must be *pito*. Barlow (a poet) called it "Hill of the Dove," but *pito* is actually closer to *peeti*, the word given by Córdova (1578a) for "pigeon." There are two pigeons native to the Tehuantepec area, the red-billed pigeon (*Columba flavirostris*) and the scaled pigeon (*Columba speciosa*), but neither is currently called a *huilota*. In Oaxaca, the term *huilota* is reserved for the mourning dove (*Zenaidura macroura*), which also occurs in the isthmus. However, this dove is referred to in Isthmus Zapoteco as *guugu huini,* and in Córdova's time would probably have been called *cògohuini* (Pickett 1959; Marcus and Flannery 1978:64). Thus, I feel that "Hill of the Pigeon" is the preferable reading.

Another gloss, to the north of the hill, may be mirror writing or a "print-through" from the reverse of the *lienzo*.

A small nearby body of water, probably the Laguna Superior, also has a bird on it, one that looks the same. Above it there is a small hill, with a gloss that may refer to the hill or the lagoon or both, but which is too nearly illegible for my inadequate Zapoteco; to the north of the hill is another gloss that includes one of my few words of Zapoteco, *niza,* "water."

The lower half of the *lienzo* is divided by horizontal lines into five strips, perhaps the lands of several persons or groups. It is curious that the east-west dividing lines cross the river or, perhaps better, that the river runs through these lands without affecting the divisions. Huilotepec is the second division up from the ocean, on the east side of the river. There are indications of settlements, people, buildings, hills, and vegetation, as well as glosses seemingly in Zapoteco, in the first (shore) and second (Huilotepec) divisions. A hill across the river from Huilotepec is named *tani que xopa.*

The three narrow strips of land above Huilotepec do not add up, all together, to as much as Huilotepec's strip. They seem to be divided besides, not by the river but by a north–south line to the east of it. In the resulting six areas, at least four have small named human figures that I assume are the owners; there are traces of drawing in the other two, but they are illegible and unnamed.

At the top, occupying just under half the *lienzo*, is a large rectangle, with the Tehuantepec River curving across the lower left (southwest) corner. A prominent feature here is the hill glyph, with a church below it and a (spotted) large feline on top. There is no doubt that this is Tehuantepec (*tecuani-tepetl,* "People Eater Hill").

Above the place glyph is, at last, our genealogy, a series of four seated figures enclosed in a vertical rectangle. All four are seated, like Mixtec rulers in the Prehispanic codices, on jaguar-skin cushions, though the topmost one seems to have his cushion placed on some kind of stool. And do we have a series of four rulers? I fear we may not.

Just as in verbal language, order of units often determines meaning ("A pays B" is not the same as "B pays A"). In the relatively abundant, relatively well-published, relatively well-studied Mixtec codices and *lienzos,* a succession of rulers at a given place is indicated by a succession of married pairs, often vertical and often with the latest ones in neat stratigraphy at the top. The four figures here at Tehuantepec have glosses, apparently their names, above their heads. Being competent in neither paleography nor Zapoteco, I am not about to utter a definitive reading.

We would hope that the topmost figure would be Cocijopii, and the three below would be his father, grandfather, and great-grandfather. But it isn't that way at all. The two upper figures wear a costume different from that of the two lower ones, and it appears to be a Spanish as distinguished from a Prehispanic one; they must be later. Nevertheless, the bottom figure seems to be Cocijopii, and no expert is required to read his name. The scribe does seem to have made an error; first he wrote Coyopee, and then he went back to

---

[2]Editors' note: The *Mapa de Huilotepec* is not reproduced here because available photographs exhibit such poor resolution that even our most talented artist despaired of copying it accurately. The reader is referred to Plate II of Barlow (1943).

add *ci* above the second and third letters, giving us Cociyopee. The second figure up from the bottom has a less legible name, but I think I see Cociyeh--ça. The final syllable may well be intended for *ça*, and I strongly suspect that we have here Cociyohoeça.

The third figure up from the bottom, the first in Spanish dress, has a gloss I cannot read. Barlow read it as Cortés; the *o* and the *t* seem to be almost unmistakable, and the C may be as he thought. However, Barlow knew that Cocijopii had become Don Juan Cortés by baptism, and he may have been seeing what he knew or thought ought to be there.

The topmost figure has a gloss that seems to me to name him José Irper- - - -s, or perhaps José Icpec- - - -s. The last six letters are easily interpretable as Cortés, though that reading is not the only possible one.

It appears, then, that the vertical line of four figures has Cocijoeza in second place from the bottom; below him, Cocijoeza has his son, Cocijopii, and above Cocijoeza the same son appears as Don Juan Cortés. Barlow thought the top figure was some descendant or successor, or both, of Cocijopii, which may well be the case. However, I think we ought to consider the possibility that he is rather a contemporary and subject of Cocijopii, perhaps a relative as well, who rules the subject village of Huilotepec.

Within the boundaries of the Huilotepec lands, but across the river from the place glyph, three small seated figures are arranged in front of the place glyph *Taniquexopa*. Their glosses are all but illegible for me, but I suspect they are Zapotec calendrical personal names. One other personage appears in this area, a figure below the hill glyph who seems to be seated on a road that runs from this area to the ocean (I can't make out which way the footprints point). These four are the only human figures within the Huilotepec area. There are no signs of hierarchy among them.

All the figures shown seated on the strips of land in the bottom half of the *lienzo* seem to be simply dressed. Only the 4 Tehuantepec personages who are set apart from all the rest of the *lienzo* by a frame are dressed in aristocratic fashion, and the contrast is plain when these 4 are compared with 11 people who sit facing them. All these have bare heads, whereas the rulers wear Prehispanic headdresses or Spanish-style hats. One of these persons seems to hold a child out toward Cocijoeza and, perhaps, Cocijopii, and also to have a feminine hairdo. All these persons are seated on cushions, which the people on the lands at the bottom of the *lienzo* lack, so they must be somebody; but their cushions are plain, so they must rank below the rulers on their jaguar-skin ones. Several of their glosses, which I assume are names, are legible even to me, for example *Piciopehe* and *Xito*.

## THE *LIENZO DE GUEVEA*

Santiago Guevea de Humboldt lies to the north of Tehuantepec, at the foot of the Sierra Mixe. Its Early Colonial *lienzo* is much easier to deal with than that of Huilotepec, having been more or less adequately reproduced

several times. There is also a study of it by Eduard Seler (1908).

Two copies of the *lienzo* are known. Both are shown, in photographic reproduction too small to permit reading the glosses, by Seler, who provides good-sized drawings of details. One of the copies, which is in the Museo Nacional de Antropología, is reproduced in black and white by Caso (1965c:943), and, especially with a reading glass, the glosses are legible. In most ways, however, the color copy-of-a-copy-of-a-copy in *Los Zapotecos* (Mendieta y Núñez [ed.] 1949:62) is better. Both because of the color and because of its size, it is thoroughly legible.

The copyist forgot five short glosses, and they are important: Don Pedro Santiago, the principal personage of the document, is named in front of his face as he sits in a profiled indigenous temple before a hill glyph. Below him is the gloss *Rigula Guebiya*, "Viejo de Guevea." Under the glyph of the place, the gloss is *Dani Guebiya*, "Serro de Guevea." Below this are two small churches, one on each side of the document. The left one is marked *Yodo Santiago Guebiya*, "Yglesia de Santo Guevea" (sic), and the right one is *Yodo Santo Domingo*, "Yglesia de Santo Domingo." With these omissions corrected, the Mendieta version is by a wide margin the best available one of the Museo Nacional copy.

The copy is dated 1820, though it is in fact a recopy made in the 1890s from the 1820 one. According to it, the original is dated 1540. Seler refers to this version—an oil painting on canvas, if I remember correctly from when it was exhibited in the old Museo Nacional—as Copy A.

Seler's Copy B is a photograph sent to him by a German who was working for the Mexican government. Seler believes it is a photograph of another copy, not of the original document, and that may be correct. He says the Museo Nacional version (Copy A) is much more primitive, but I think the style of Copy B—insofar as I can judge it in a small photograph—is much more like the indigenous style. Copy A is simplified in many ways; a number of interesting geographic features are left out, as is a long explanatory legend, and the road that leads from Zaachila to Guevea in Copy B comes from nowhere—the edge of the painting—in Copy A, and has been straightened out as well. The Nahuatl versions of the glosses are also eliminated in Copy A. In other words, Copy B is seemingly a much more complete, trustworthy version. Seler thinks it is a seventeenth- or eighteenth-century copy. Perhaps it is a predated original; but without knowing whether the original is still in Guevea, and what it looks like, we cannot be sure.

What interests us in the *Lienzo de Guevea* is the genealogy of the Zapotec rulers. Like many or most documents of its kind, it is highly parochial in viewpoint. The top half is a statement of local political geography, that is of boundaries (see Marcus, Topic 89). The lords of Teozapotlan are confined to the lower half. Tehuantepec is just one of 18 places on the boundaries of Guevea, and is given no special importance whatever in this part. (Guevea seems not to appear among the 31 subjects listed for Tehuantepec in its 1580 *relación*.)

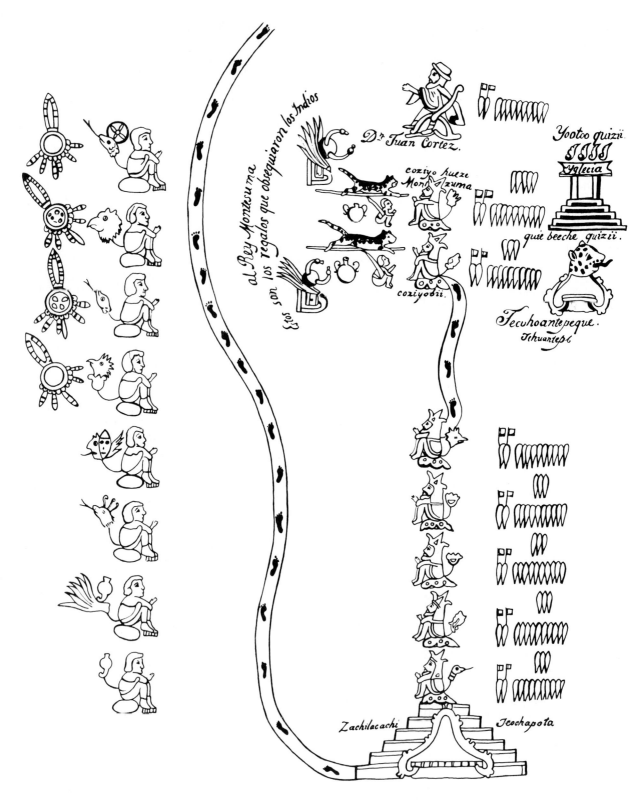

FIGURE 8.36. Lower half of Copy B of the Lienzo de Guevea, showing the later Zapotec rulers of Zaachila and Tehuantepec (compare with Figure 8.35).

One central difference between Seler's two copies is that in the earlier one (Copy B) the road comes right out of the Zaachila pyramid and goes to Guevea directly, not through Tehuantepec (Figure 8.36).

At the bottom right corner is a pyramid that encloses a hill glyph and is marked *Zachila*. Above this begins a column of five seated figures, followed by a short road that leads up to a sixth who is seated in front of the Tehuantepec glyph; above this figure is a seventh, seated in front of a Prehispanic temple, and the column ends with an eighth personage, seated in a chair and wearing Spanish-style clothing.

Thus the document makes a crucial point that Seler seems to have missed: there are two genealogies, a central one that traces the ruler of Guevea back to Zaachila (not to a person, but to the pyramid) without any intervening links, the road implying that he came from Zaachila; and a peripheral one that traces the rulers of Tehuantepec back to Zaachila through several intervening links.

All the eight personages of the Tehuantepec lineage are clearly named in Copy A (see Figure 8.35). The first, seated directly on top of the Zaachila pyramid, is *Yobicoxi chalochi*. Connected to him by a thin line (which would mean "this is his name" in a Mixtec codex) is a serpent head. Like all the others in this column except the last, he wears a fancy indigenous costume.

Second, directly above him, is *Rinicoxi chaleguesa*, whose glyphic name seems to be Alligator. This is not entirely clear in Copy A or in Seler's photograph of Copy B, but Seler's drawing of the detail in Copy B is (perhaps with a bit of bias in favor of the familiar calendar sign Cipactli?—one needs to see a good photograph) plainly the day-sign Alligator.

Third in line is *Cosiobi*, whose glyphic name is not very clear. Seler says Water, and his detail drawing shows a vessel with tiny hooked waves on top; the vessel is colored blue in Copy A, and Water seems reasonable.

Fourth from the bottom is *Cosihuesa*, and his glyphic name is the same: something like a vessel with drops of water at the rim.

The fifth figure is *Peñobiya* (Day 12 in the 260-day calendar), whose name glyph, I guessed at first, might be Stone Mask, but Seler's detail drawings are of the head of an animal that has a spiked crest. One might propose that an isthmus artist, familiar with iguanas, would thus render the day-sign Lizard.

From the fifth figure up to the sixth there is a space crossed by a road connecting them. The sixth figure is *Cosiobi* again, but this time he sits in front of the Tehuantepec place glyph. His glyphic name now is entirely different. From the reproductions I cannot make it out, but Seler's drawing from Copy A looks as if it may have been Eagle; his drawing from Copy B is an undecipherable blob. A naked man is seated in front of him (indicating a tribute of service?), and there is a pile of objects as well as a large feline bound to a pole.

The seventh figure up is *Cosihuesa* again. He is not seated in front of a Tehuantepec place glyph, but rather in front of an indigenous temple atop a small pyramid. It has *cuitlatl* (excrement: gold) symbols around the edge of its roof. In front of him are the same tribute symbols that Cocijopii has; that is, he enjoys his kingly income, and he is in indigenous costume.

The last figure of the series is *Cosijopii* again, but this time after baptism, now named Don Juan Cortés and now, perhaps significantly, with no tributes in front of him.

Cocijopii has appeared three times, and Cocijoeza twice. If there is any new genealogy here, it must be in the first, second, and fifth figures from the bottom. Seler offers a fascinating explanation of the first two. Burgoa says Cocijopii was the third son of Cocijoeza. Seler says that these first two personages, Yobicoxi and Rinicoxi, are the sons who were passed over. If his Zapoteco is reliable, their names mean "first son" and "second son," and the other words attached to them say that their father apparently did not trust them (see Topic 89).

As for Penobiya, though he is plainly shown in male costume in the *Lienzo de Guevea*, I think the name given to Cocijoeza's daughter by Burgoa, Pinobiaa, may be phonemically equal to, or cognate with, Penobiya. As Burgoa tells it, an Indian shepherd came by accident upon a hilltop where there was a clean-swept little plaza with fresh flowers on it, as well as a stone altar under which was a worked stone. He was holding this stone when a venerable-looking old man approached in great alarm and told him to put the stone back before lightning struck him. But he demanded to know what

> was this stone without figure or face. The evil idolater began with the fables they believe and told him this was the Virgin Queen, daughter of the Zapotec King of Zachiylla or Theozapotlan, named Cosijoeza, and when he conquered this area, sending his third son Cosijopii, he advised him to have special respect for his sister Pinopiaa, so that she might be with him in the kingdom he came to govern in Tehuantepeque and Soconusco, because she was a very devout lady in their way, very virtuous, devoted to their gods and not wishing to marry, and when they reached Jalapa she was taken with a mortal illness. . . . and when they were going to bury her body it disappeared with an immense thunder and was transformed into that stone [Burgoa 1674:II, 330].

Not being in a position to argue with Burgoa, I hereby give up on the genealogy of the Zapotec kings until significant new evidence is brought forward.[3]

---

[3] Soon after the seminar, a previously unknown print of Seler's photograph of Copy B (which presumably was destroyed in World War II) turned up in the U.S. My examination of this print confirms the opinions offered here about Copy B. In 1978 two old photographs of the original *Lienzo de Guevea* were discovered, confirming that Copy B is much more exact than Copy A. The Copy B print is in Peabody Museum, Harvard University; the photographs of the original are in the University of Texas Library, Austin.

## TOPIC 91
# Aztec Military Campaigns against the Zapotecs: The Documentary Evidence

JOYCE MARCUS

During the Late Postclassic, the Aztecs undertook several military campaigns in order to expand their territory and increase the number of towns paying tribute to them. Some of these towns were listed as defeated and tribute was exacted, presumably to be paid indefinitely. However, the frequency with which some towns were subdued or "reconquered" suggests that they were never effectively integrated into the Aztec "empire," and continued paying tribute only as a result of repeated military threats. Such was the case with much of Oaxaca.

In this paper I briefly consider the documentary evidence for some of the Aztec military campaigns against the Zapotec; in Topic 93, Flannery considers the archaeological evidence for two of the major battles. The Aztec versions of these campaigns are given in such documents as the Codex Chimalpopoca, the Anales de Tlatelolco, Torquemada, Ixtlilxochitl, and the Códice en Cruz. The Zapotec versions are given by writers such as Burgoa, Gay, and Martínez Gracida, but the ultimate source for most of these is Burgoa (1670, 1674) who was writing more than a century after the Spanish Conquest. It should be remembered, therefore, that we are dealing with legendary history rather than with accurate releases from the Associated Press.

## A.D. 1440–1486

Under the fourth Aztec ruler, Itzcoatl (ca. 1427–ca. 1440), Tenochtitlán emerged as a major power (Table 8.4). During the reign of his successor Moctezuma I (ca. 1440–ca. 1469), military campaigns were directed against central Puebla and Veracruz, with infiltrations into northern Oaxaca (Gibson 1971:379). Moctezuma I conquered Coix-

### TABLE 8.4
Chronology of the Aztec Rulers[a]

| Ruler | Reign in Years A.D. |
|---|---|
| Acamapichtli | ca. 1376–ca. 1396 |
| Huitzilihuitl | ca. 1396–ca. 1417 |
| Chimalpopoca | ca. 1417–ca. 1427 |
| Itzcoatl | ca. 1427–ca. 1440 |
| Moctezuma I (Ilhuicamina) | ca. 1440–ca. 1469 |
| Axayacatl | ca. 1469–ca. 1481 |
| Tizoc | ca. 1481–ca. 1486 |
| Ahuitzotl | ca. 1486–ca. 1502 |
| Moctezuma II (Xocoyotzin) | ca. 1502–ca. 1520 |
| Cuitlahuac | 1520 |
| Cuauhtemoc | 1520–24 |

[a]Reconstructed from Alvarado Tezozomoc (1949).

### TABLE 8.5
Oaxacan Localities Attacked or Subdued by the Aztec Ruler Ahuitzotl (ca. A.D. 1486–1502)

| Locality | Documentary source[a] |
|---|---|
| Cuicatlán (Ayotochcuitlatlan) | CC, AT, CM |
| Jaltepec de Candayoc (Xaltepec) | CC, AT, CM, TO, I |
| San Miguel Tiltepec (Tliltepec) | CC, I |
| Juchitán de Zaragoza (Xochtlan) | CC, AT, CM, TO, TE, I |
| Santo Domingo Tehuantepec (Tequantepec) | CC, AT, CM, TO, TE, I |
| Amatitlán (Amaxtlan) | CC, AT, CM, TO, TE, I |
| Zaachila (Tzapotlan; Teozapotlan) | CC, AT, CM, CTR, TO, CEC, I |
| San Pedro Tututepec (Tototepec) | CC, CM |
| San Jerónimo Sosola (Totollan; Tzottzollan) | CC, AT |
| San Francisco Ixhuatán (Izhuatlan) | CC, AT, CM, TE |
| Tlacotepec Plumas (Tlacotepec) | CC, AT, CM |
| San Bartolo Yautepec (Yauhtepec) | AT |
| San Pablo Mitla | CTR |
| Tlacolula de Matamoros | TO, TE |
| San Andrés Miahuatlán | TE |
| Huautla de Jiménez (Cuauhtlan) | CC, AT, CM, TO |

[a]CC = Codex Chimalpopoca, AT = Anales de Tlatelolco, CM = Colección de Mendoza, CTR = Codex Telleriano–Remensis, TO = Torquemada, TE = Tezozomoc, CEC = Códice en Cruz, I = Ixtlilxochitl; also, Kelly and Palerm (1952).

tlahuaca in the Mixteca, reportedly in the year 5 Rabbit (A.D. 1458) according to the Codex Chimalpopoca, the Anales de Tlatelolco, and the Códice en Cruz (Kelly and Palerm 1952:269–271). The infiltration of the Mixteca was crucial to the Aztec empire because it was related to their program of expansion toward the Pacific coast.

With the death of Moctezuma I, Axayacatl became ruler in A.D. 1469 and began raiding farther to the south. According to Torquemada, the purpose of these raids was "to obtain prisoners for sacrifice for Axayacatl's coronation" (1723:I, 172). Both Tehuantepec and Huatulco (on the Pacific coast of Oaxaca) are mentioned at this time, but there is no indication that they were incorporated into the Mexica "empire" at this time.

## THE CONQUESTS OF AHUITZOTL

In A.D. 1486 the ruler Tizoc died and was succeeded by Ahuitzotl. It is clear that although new military campaigns were frequently associated with any change of ruler,

Ahuitzotl was unusually aggressive in this respect. He reconquered many rebellious towns and pushed into distant areas, extending his "conquered" territory to the present borders of Guatemala. After a series of victories in Puebla and Oaxaca, the stage was set for a sweep through the Valley of Oaxaca to the Isthmus of Tehuantepec (see Table 8.5).

The Aztec versions of Ahuitzotl's conquests in the region of present-day Oaxaca are given in several sources. According to the Codex Chimalpopoca, he conquered Cuicatlán in A.D. 1493, Jaltepec in 1493 and 1500, Tiltepec in 1495, Juchitán in 1496, and Tehuantepec in 1497. The Anales de Tlatelolco give the conquests of Juchitán and Amatitlán as 1497 and of Tehuantepec as 1498 (Kelly and Palerm 1952:275–276). The Codex Telleriano–Remensis (Kingsborough 1830–1848:V, 153) gives 1495 as the conquest date for Zaachila, 1494 for Mitla. Torquemada provides conquest dates of 1500–1502 for Jaltepec; 1497–1500 for Tehuantepec and Amatitlán; 1500–1502 for Tlacolula; and 1486–1487 for the Zapotec area in general (Torquemada 1723:I, 192–193). From the Códice en Cruz we have a conquest date of 1496 for Zaachila (Dibble 1942:75, 146). Alva Ixtlilxochitl (1892:2, 271–289) gives us conquest dates of 1493–1500 for Jaltepec, 1495 for Tiltepec, 1486 and 1497 for Juchitán, 1496 and 1499 for Tehuantepec, 1486 and 1497 for Amatitlán, and 1492 for Zaachila. The interior regions on the way to coastal outposts remained incompletely controlled, and most of central and southern Oaxaca remained to be truly dominated. Some territories in coastal Guerrero and in the Isthmus of Tehuantepec, however, appear to have been enclaves of Aztec control (Gibson 1971:380).

Some of the more talked-about battles between the Aztecs and Zapotecs may have taken place during the reign of Ahuitzotl, at least according to some authors. Let us examine two of these.

## THE BATTLE OF HUITZO

Perhaps the most charming account of the battle of Huitzo is that of José Antonio Gay (1881). According to his version, the battle took place around A.D. 1486 during the reigns of the Aztec king Ahuitzotl and the Zapotec king Zaachila III; also involved was the Mixtec cacique of Achiutla, a descendant of the legendary Dzahuindanda (Gay 1881:Vol. 1:177–182). This account differs from other versions, in which Zaachila's ally was the cacique of Tilantongo. At any rate, Gay's account is a legendary history, which should be compared with the archaeological evidence given by Flannery in Topic 93.

For years, or so the story goes, the armies of the Aztec had marched through the Mixteca but then had to detour around the still-unconquered Valley of Oaxaca to reach Tehuantepec. They longed to be able to use the valley as the most direct route to the isthmus and beyond, to Soconusco and Guatemala. But Zaachila III and the cacique of Achiutla had

formed a military alliance to prevent this. As part of the agreement, Mixtec soldiers had entered the Valley of Oaxaca and set up garrisons "at Huitzo" (near the northern limits of the valley) and "at Cuilapan" (possibly at Sa'a Yucu rather than present-day Cuilapan; see Topic 85). The "Cuilapan" garrison, so near to his residence at the site of Zaachila, made the Zapotec ruler understandably nervous. In addition, the Mixtec are said to have had a strong garrison at Sosola, one of the localities within Drennan's Mountain Survey area (Topic 84). For his own part, Zaachila III is said to have fortified a high hill near Huitzo (probably Cerro de la Campana) with Zapotec soldiers, creating a redoubt called Güijazoo ("military watchtower") which could monitor not only the trail along the Atoyac River but also one of the major routes from the Cañada de Cuicatlán. It is thought that "Huitzo" is a corruption of this watchtower's Zapotec name.

Aztec ambassadors were sent to the unconquered territories of the Mixtecs and Zapotecs, requesting permission for Ahuitzotl's army to pass through. The Mixtecs refused, assuming the Zapotecs would do the same. But according to Gay, Zaachila III—who trusted the Mixtecs no further than he did the Aztecs—entered into discussions with the Mexica ambassadors which he kept secret even from the cacique of Achiutla. As was customary in those times, the Aztecs proclaimed themselves diplomatically insulted by the negative response from Oaxaca, and declared war.

Zaachila III knew that the Aztecs would attack either through the canyon of the Río San Antonio (which passed the Mixtec garrison of Sosola) or the Río de las Vueltas (in the Cuicatec Cañada). As he had hoped, the Aztec chose the first of these two routes and the Mixtec bore the full brunt of their attack; apparently, Zaachila expected the troops of Sosola and Achiutla to be so weakened by the Aztec campaign that they would no longer pose a threat to him. But the Mixtec forces held, and the Aztec army retreated back into the Cañada de Cuicatlán to regroup and try the second route, down the Río de las Vueltas toward the Zapotec army waiting at Güijazoo.

The Río de las Vueltas is so named because it runs a tortuous, serpentine route "crossing back on itself 163 times in 4 leagues" between perpendicular cliffs. Had Zaachila III decided to fight, according to Gay, "the Río de las Vueltas would have become Ahuitzotl's tomb." But the Aztec army reached Huitzo without a skirmish, apparently because of some secret treaty reached by the ambassadors of both peoples. The Aztec army named Huitzo Cuajilotitlan, "place of the cuajilote (Parmentiera) trees," and the nearby river Atoyac, "río caudaloso." They continued downriver 7 leagues to a place where the river entered a narrow passage lined with guaje (Leucaena) trees; from a high hill near the river they could see both the Etla valley, which they had left, and the Tlacolula valley, which they still had to cross on their way to Tehuantepec. Here the Aztecs are later supposed to have established a military garrison to protect their route, while clearing away trees to establish Huaxyacac, "at the nose of the guajes," the settlement which would later become Oaxaca City. (In Topic 92, Blanton discusses the difficulty of establishing the true location of the hilltop garrison). Finally, the Aztec army passed on its way to the isthmus past the fortified Zapotec strongholds of Nejapa and Quiegolani, which were apparently under orders from Zaachila III not to impede their progress. The battle of Huitzo, at least in Gay's version, had been a typical Zapotec diplomatic coup in which the Mixtec did all the fighting.

## THE BATTLE OF GUIENGOLA

The battle of Guiengola is one of the most heroic and romantic chapters in Zapotec legendary history, ending with a marriage alliance that linked the royal houses of Zaachila and Tenochtitlán. Once again, Gay (1881) has provided us with one of the most colorful accounts. His version, which places the battle around A.D. 1495, differs from that of other writers who have Cortés landing while the battle was in progress.

Is is said that the Zapotec king Cocijoeza, successor to his father Zaachila III, waited for a time when the armies of Ahuitzotl were in the Isthmus of Tehuantepec; he then sought a new alliance with the Mixtec cacique of Achiutla. His theory was that the Aztec army, divided as it now was, could not resist a joint Mixtec–Zapotec offensive. Like his father, he also hoped that the Mixtecs could be persuaded to do most of the fighting and take most of the losses, and that many of those from Sa'a Yucu would make the trip to Tehuantepec. The Mixtec did in fact send soldiers (Gay claims 24,000 Mixtec troops under 24 "brave captains"), but as was their custom they also left a contingent to guard the roads of their own *cacicazgos*, including the region of Cuilapan. Cocijoeza was left with no alternative but to lead his own Zapotec army to the isthmus, and after promising the Mixtec "land in the Tehuantepec area" for their aid in combat, he departed. Along the route, he designated Nejapa and Quiechapan as places where arms and provisions should be provided and where the wounded could later be treated.

As Flannery points out in Topic 93, we know from archaeological surveys that the mountaintop fortress of Guiengola, near Tehuantepec, had been used by the Zapotec as far back as the end of Monte Albán IV or the beginning of V. This high, rugged, hot, tropically forested mountain was chosen by Cocijoeza as his base of operations, whereas the Mixtec reportedly occupied the opposite bank of the river from Guiengola. Cocijoeza is said to have built extensive fortification walls, behind which were piles of river cobbles for throwing down on the enemy.[1] Aware of the scarcity of water on the mountain, he constructed huge water-storage tanks, even stocking some with fish. Maize, salted meat, and other provisions were stockpiled, and shipments of lances and armaments continued to arrive from Nejapa.

The Aztec soldiers were apprehensive. They were tired

from a journey of 120 leagues, they were used to the climate and altitude of the Valley of Mexico, and they regarded the muggy isthmus as unspeakably unhealthy. Caught between two hostile armies, they decided to starve the Zapotec out rather than attack. Ahuitzotl instructed his men to set up camp on the lower slopes of Guiengola to cut off the Zapotec supply lines, stalling for time until the Aztec troops who had marched on to Guatemala could return.

The Zapotec, who knew the region much more intimately, found secret routes through the Aztec lines, and along with their Mixtec allies waged a war of attrition on the enemy. One night, seeing that there were fewer Aztecs on guard than usual, the Zapotec crept down and fell upon them with no warning. The Aztec dead were carried up to the fortress and butchered like deer; the meat was cut into strips for salting or drying as future provisions. A captured Aztec officer was led to the top of the mountain, shown the skulls and bones of his devoured footsoldiers, and sent back to describe the grisly scene to Ahuitzotl.

Three times during a space of 7 months the Aztecs received reinforcements, but made no inroads into the Zapotec and Mixtec defenses. Finally Ahuitzotl, his troops depleted by death and illness and demoralized by the heat of Tehuantepec and the tenacity of their opponents, had had enough. Ambassadors were sent to arrange a truce and to feel out Cocijoeza on the possibility of a marriage alliance with one of Ahuitzotl's daughters, which it was felt could produce a lasting peace. The Zapotec ruler eventually married the Aztec princess Coyolicatzin, whose Zapotec name became *Pelaxilla*, "Cotton Flake," because of her extraordinary whiteness. As reported in Topic 90, Pelaxilla bore Cocijoeza a son, Cocijopii, whom he sent to Tehuantepec to rule that province.

So ended the battle of Guiengola, and the Mixtec allies patiently waited for the land they had been promised. In return for their aid, Cocijoeza granted them the Mixtequilla, one of the least fertile and desirable areas of the isthmus. It was a fitting move for the son of the ruler who had previously hoodwinked them at the battle of Huitzo.

## THE CONQUESTS OF MOCTEZUMA II

Moctezuma II, who succeeded Ahuitzotl in A.D. 1502, continued the process of southerly expansion. He concentrated his efforts in central and southern Oaxaca and pushed farther south to reconquer Soconusco (Colección de Mendoza in Kingsborough 1830–1848, 5:50). Following is a list of conquests in the Oaxaca area, attributed to Moctezuma II in various documents: the dates (A.D.) are given in parentheses. (The Oaxacan conquests are listed by locality in Table 8.6.)

1. *Codex Chimalpopoca:* Ixpantepec (1510), Tlaxiaco (1511), Quimixtlan (1512), Ocotlan (1514), Zenzontepec (1515)

---

[1]These walls and rock piles can still be seen by visitors to the mountain (see Topic 93).

TABLE 8.6
Oaxacan Localities Attacked or Subdued by the Aztec
Ruler Moctezuma II (ca. A.D. 1502–1520)

| Locality | Documentary source[a] |
|---|---|
| Ixtlán de Juárez (Itztitlan) | CC, AT, CM, TO |
| San Francisco Ixpantepec (Icpatepec) | CC, AT, CM, CTR, TO, TE, CEC, I |
| San Miguel Suchiltepec (Izquixochitepec) | CC, TO, I |
| Santa María Asunción Tlaxiaco (Tlachquiyauhcas) | CC, AT, CM, TO, TE, CEC, I |
| Ocotlán de Morelos (Macuilloctlan) | CC |
| Santa Cruz Zenzontepec (Çentzontepecas) | CC, AT, CM, TO |
| San Miguel Achiutla (Achiyotlan) | CC, AT, CM, TO |
| San Jerónimo Sosola (Çoçollan) | CC, AT, CM, CTR, TO, TE, I |
| Asunción Nochixtlán (Nochextlan) | CC, AT, CM |
| San Pedro Tututepec (Tototepec) | CC, AT, CTR, TO, TE, CEC, I |
| San Bartolo Yautepec (Quiyauhtepec) | CC |
| Santa Marta Chichihualtepec (Chichihualtatacallan) | CC, AT, CM |
| Ejutla de Crespo (Texotlan) | CC, AT |
| Santo Domingo Yanhuitlán (Yancuitlan) | CC, TE |
| San Miguel Tiltepec (Tliltepec) | CC, AT, CM |
| Santos Reyes Nopala (Nopallan) | CC, AT, CTR, TO, TE |
| Santiago Tejupan (Texopan) | CC |
| Tlaxiaco (Tlachquiyauhco) | CC |
| San Pedro Mixtepec (Quimichtepec) | CC, AT, CM, CTR |
| San Miguel Quetzaltepec (Quetzaltepec) | CC, AT?, CM, TO, TE, CEC |
| Ixtlahuaca (Cuezcomayxtlahuacan) | CC, AT, CM, TO |
| Santa María [or Santiago] Zacatepec (Çacatepec) | CC, CM, TO |
| San Raymundo Jalpan (Xallapam; Xalpan) | CC, AT, CM |
| Santa María Jaltianquis (Xaltianquizco) | CC, CM, CEC, I |
| Santiago Ixcuintepec (Itzcuintepec) | CC, AT, CM, TO |
| San Francisco Sola (Tzolla) | AT, CM, TO |
| Tlacotepec Plumas (Tlalotepec) | AT, I |
| San Luis Amatlán (Amoxtlan) | AT |
| Joluxtla (Tlacaxolotlan) | AT |
| San Pedro Huilotepec (Huilotepec) | CM, CEC? |
| San Juan Atepec (Atepec) | CM |
| San Pablo Villa de Mitla (Mictlan) | CM, TO, I |
| Santa Elena Comaltepec (Comaltepec) | CM |
| San Francisco Coatlán (Coatlayauhcan) | CM, TE |
| Zaachila (Teozapotlan, Teçapotitlan) | CM |
| Huautla de Jiménez (Quauhnelhuatlan) | TO |
| Santo Domingo Tehuantepec (Tecuantepec) | TO |
| Provincias Mixtecas | CC, AT, CM, CTR, TO, TE, I |
| San Juan Bautista Coixtlahuaca (Cohuaixtlahuacan) | TO, I |
| Amatitlán (Amatlan) | TO, I |
| Juchitán de Zaragoza (Izquixochtlan) | TO |
| Magdalena Jaltepec (Xaltepec) | TE |
| Tzapotecas | I |
| Oaxaca de Juárez (Huaxaca) | I |

[a]CC = Codex Chimalpopoca, AT = Anales de Tlatelolco, CM = Colección de Mendoza, CTR = Codex Telleriano–Remensis, TO = Torquemada, TE = Tezozomoc, CEC = Códice en Cruz, I = Ixtlilxochitl; also, Kelly and Palerm (1952).

2. *Anales de Tlatelolco:* Ixpantepec (1510), Achiutla (1504), Sosola (1505), Ixtlahuaca (1514)
3. *Codex Telleriano-Remensis:* Ixpantepec (1511), Sosola (1509), Tututepec (1513), Nopala (1512), Mixtepec (1512)
4. *Torquemada:* Ixpantepec (1510), Suchiltepec (1511), Tlaxiaco (1503, 1511), Zenzontepec (1516), Achiutla (1503), Sosola (1506), Tututepec (1506), Nopala (1512), Ixtlahuaca (1514)
5. *Códice en Cruz:* Ixpantepec (1510), Tlaxiaco (1503), Tututepec (1513)

## TRIBUTE FROM COYOLAPAN

Despite the best efforts of the Zapotec and their Mixtec allies, the Aztec ultimately succeeded in imposing a tributary status on the Valley of Oaxaca and much of the surrounding area. The Aztec called this the province of *Coyolapan* after its *cabecera* or administrative capital in the central valley. One Aztec tribute list, the Codex Mendoza, lists Camotlan, Etlan, Quauxilotitlan, Guaxacac, Macuilxochic, Tlalcuechahuaya, Teticpac, and Octlan as tribute-paying towns within the province of Coyolapan. Other documentary sources list the following additional towns as belonging to Coyolapan: Yoloxonecuilan, Atepec, Xaltianguisco, Tecuicuilco, Itztitlan, Çoquiapan, Iztepexi, Teotzacualco, Itzquintepec, Eztetlan (?), Quauxiloticpac, Huiztepec, Totomachapa, Xilotepec, Zenzontepec, Tlaliztacan, Teotitlán del Valle, Teozapotlan, Tlacolula, Mictlan, Chichicapan, Miahuatlán, Cuixtlán, and Coatlán (Barlow 1949:map).

The Mexica of the Triple Alliance received from the whole province of Coyolapan the following types of tribute (Barlow 1949:123):

1. *Cloth (semiannual payment)*
   400 bundles of richly worked mantles
   800 bundles of large mantles
2. *Food (annual payment)*
   4 wooden cribs (2 of maize, 1 of beans, and 1 of chía)
3. *Gold (annual payment)*
   20 gold disks—the size of an average plate, and as thick as a forefinger
4. *Cochineal (annual payment)*
   20 bags

Individual towns within the province also paid specific tributes, according to their available resources, in a wide variety of materials. For example, the towns of Çoquiapan, Atepec, Tecuicuilco, and Xaltianguisco gathered together their tribute—green feathers and green stones—by trading with other places (*Revista Mexicana de Estudios Históricos*, V. 2, Appendix, p. 123). Coatlán received military protection in return for paying the tribute of gold dust and woven mantles; to Moctezuma "*le tributaban oro en polbo y mantas, y el tenya quidado*" (Espíndola 1580:133). Guaxacac

(Barlow 1949:120) was mentioned as one of the garrison towns in the Codex Mendoza and said to have been governed by a "Hacatectli" and a "Hacochtectli." Iztepexi claimed that after the Mexica subjugated them, they paid double tribute, since the Mixtecs were already exploiting them (Ximénez Ortiz 1579:16). Macuilxochic (Macuil-xochitl) claimed to be subject to Teozapotlan (Zaachila), while Mictlan (Mitla), which was also subject to Teozapotlan, became subject to the Mexica as well.

Teotitlán del Valle was already subject to the Zapotec lords at Teozapotlan and later to the government in exile at Tehuantepec, after which it was reported to have become subject to the Mixtecs at Cuilapan (Asensio 1580b:105). Iztepexi had to pay the Mexica and Mixtecs in gold, green feathers, deer, maize, and turkeys; the gold and the feathers were obtained by going to the Isthmus of Tehuantepec and working for 6 months to a year cultivating lands (Ximénez Ortiz 1579:16).

## TOPIC 92
## The Aztec Garrison of "Acatepec"

RICHARD E. BLANTON

The *Relación de Teozapotlan* states that the Aztec ruler "Montecçuma" (presumably Moctezuma II) placed a garrison on a hill called Acatepec "near where the city of Antequera [Huaxyacac, or Oaxaca] is now" (Mata 1580:194). This garrison was said to have been placed there "in good will and without war" in order to protect the Aztec route to Tehuantepec and Guatemala.

This garrison has proved hard to discover archaeologically. Traditionally it had been thought that the Aztec soldiers were stationed on "Cerro del Fortín" above the present city of Oaxaca, but surveys by Kowalewski on that hill have revealed no occupation of any kind. Indeed, almost the only archaeological evidence for an Aztec presence in

Huaxyacac had been a small stone figure of Xipe, discovered in the course of digging the swimming pool of the Hotel Señorial (Paddock 1975:10).

During our survey of Monte Albán, we discovered approximately 10 Aztec III sherds in the vicinity of Terrace 867 on the spur known as El Plumaje (Figure 8.19). This spur overlooks the river from near the west bank (on the opposite side from Huaxyacac, but on the same side of the river as Teozapotlan [Zaachila] and Cuilapan). Although a concentration of 10 sherds is hardly convincing evidence for a garrison, it is so far the only significant concentration of Aztec sherds we have found anywhere in the valley.

## TOPIC 93
## Zapotec Warfare: Archaeological Evidence for the Battles of Huitzo and Guiengola

KENT V. FLANNERY

### INTRODUCTION

A picture of Zapotec warfare emerges from the sixteenth century *relaciones,* but the data are scattered through many documents from different parts of the valley, sierra, and coast. In virtually every case the scale of conflict is town versus town or *coqui* versus *coqui*, never nation versus nation. Huitzo fought against the Mixtec of Teocuicuilco, the Zapotec of Coatlán, Miahuatlán, Chichicapa, and Nexapa, and the Aztec under Moctezuma (Zárate 1581:199). Tlacolula warred with the Mixes and with Mitla (Canseco 1580:146). There were frequent alliances between towns, which cross-cut ethnic boundaries—such as Zapotec Zaachila with Mixtec Achiutla—but no campaign, not even the Aztec wars, seems to have unified the Postclassic Zapotec into one nation and one army.

The Zapotec conducted auguries before an important

combat, and are described as going into battle singing, carrying their principal "idol" (probably a deified royal ancestor), and playing the wooden drum (Ximénez Ortiz 1579:18). The officers, who were members of the nobility, wore quilted cotton armor and used cane shields, while the footsoldiers had only loincloths. The weapons were bow and arrow, lance, sling, and the macana or wooden broadsword edged with obsidian blades.

The first prisoner taken was sacrificed to the idol, while the rest were brought back to the victorious town (Ximénez Ortiz 1579:18). When a warrior captured a prisoner, "he tied the string of [the captive's] own bow around his genitals and thus led him back as a slave" (Espíndola 1580:128). Apart from the difficulty of escaping under such conditions, slaves rarely attempted to escape because if caught, "they would be cut into pieces" (Espíndola 1580:128). That is not to say that life was easy for docile slaves, since many of them were eaten following the battle. Some were kept for later sacrifice on particular religious holidays, or sold at markets for others to sacrifice. At Huitzo there was an annual festival at which one slave, taken in war, was selected to be sacrificed at a hilltop temple; the priests asked the "idols" to give them strength and courage in war, and later all those present ate the victim (Zárate 1581:198). The chest of the sacrificial victim was cut open "from nipple to nipple" with chipped stone knives (Espíndola 1580:127); the heart—that supreme locus of *pèe*—was removed; the idols were bathed with flowing blood (*tini*); and the bodies were quartered, cooked, and eaten (Ximénez Ortiz 1579:18).

The cosmological aspects of Zapotec warfare are unmistakable: the deified royal ancestor, whose influence on the supernatural was far beyond man's, had the power to give the warriors courage. And courage was a vital ingredient of this kind of warfare, where terror tactics and intimidation played as big a role as weaponry, and where soldiers entered battle knowing they had a good chance of being not merely defeated, but also eaten. But the royal *penigolazaa* would not respond unless their images had received two of the most precious commodities which could be sacrificed: the heart and *tini* of a human being.

For defense against this kind of warfare, the Zapotec towns frequently had fortifications. Usually the location was a high hill near the town, which was either naturally fortified by cliffs or artificially fortified with dry-laid stone masonry walls. Mitla is supposed to have had four of these (Canseco 1580:153), of which one has been archaeologically investigated (see Topic 88); Yagul has another. Huitzo had a similar mountaintop fortress from which its Zapotec name meaning "military lookout" was derived (see Topic 91). And Zaachila's defenders retired to a rocky hilltop "like the peak of a sombrero" near Quiane (Mata 1580:195).

Yet with all their weaponry and terror tactics, the Zapotec are most famous, not for their pitched battles, but for their strategy. It is clear that for the Zapotec, the whole battle plan of the Aztec campaigns was to get the Mixtecs to fight as many of their battles for them as possible, and ideally, to weaken both Aztecs and Mixtec. The nineteenth-century chronicler Gay (1881) is convinced that the Zapotec ruler Zaachila III, after convincing the *cacique* of Achiutla to help him defend Huitzo, made a secret treaty with the Aztec to throw the battle after the Mixtec had taken the brunt of the attack. And Zaachila III's successor Cocijoeza, after successfully defending Guiengola against the Aztec, "rewarded" his indispensable Mixtec allies with some of the most marginal land in the Isthmus of Tehuantepec. While all the facts are not yet in, future investigators may find this an interesting point of contrast between Mixtec and Zapotec warfare. While we should always take the romanticized stereotypes of the Colonial writers with a grain of salt, it is interesting that they invariably portray the Mixtec as "warlike, courageous mountain people" and the Zapotec as "devious, master diplomats, skilled at dissimulation." Perhaps, in this form of warfare, the word is mightier than the sword.

## THE BATTLE OF HUITZO: ARCHAEOLOGICAL EVIDENCE

In Topic 91, Marcus has outlined the ethnohistoric evidence for the battle of Huitzo. The Zapotec are said to have fortified a high hill near Huitzo (thought to be the archaeological site called Cerro de la Campana), while the Mixtec defended the Río Tomellín. Eventually Ahuitzotl's army marched down the Río de las Vueltas and entered the valley near Huitzo.

Cerro de la Campana is a low, volcanic-tuff mountain rising steeply from the left bank of the Atoyac River. It is covered with Precolumbian structures, but most of the surface sherds are earlier than Monte Albán V, and so far no excavations have been carried out there that would confirm the presence of Late Postclassic fortifications.

The casual visitor would certainly find no evidence that Huitzo had ever been the scene of a major battle. However, our 1967 excavations at a small, nearby mound in Huitzo's Barrio del Rosario (see Topic 15) produced some reasonable clues: 1 intrusive tomb and some 10 intrusive burials that could be construed as evidence for military activity during Monte Albán V.

Tomb 1 was a two-chambered stone masonry structure with a vaulted or corbelled roof (Moser 1969a, 1969b). The floor and lower walls were surfaced with red-painted stucco, the lintel was painted in codex style, and the tomb had a doorstone with a small offering box in front of it (Figure 8.37a). Several Postclassic-style carved stones had been reused in its construction, some of them set in place upside down or as broken fragments; the two largest were used as jambs for the antechamber (Figure 8.37b). As described by Moser (1969a:Fig. 9), the right jamb stone depicts a well-dressed lord with an atlatl in one hand and a shield and atlatl darts in the other (Figure 8.37c). Moser also calls attention to the resemblance between this jamb and a Mixtec stone monument from Tilantongo showing the lord ♂ 5 Death (Paddock 1966a:Fig. 248).

The principal skeleton in the chamber of the tomb was judged by Wilkinson and Heminger (n.d.) to be that of a man in his early twenties; he lay fully extended supine, accompanied by many offerings. Near his head was a group of backed and truncated obsidian blades which appeared to be from a *macana*, or obsidian-edged broadsword, like those used by both Zapotec and Mixtec military leaders. Small chips of turquoise indicated where his mosaic earplugs had disintegrated. Across his neck lay a series of beads from disintegrated necklaces: 35 beads of "lost-wax" cast gold over a carbon nucleus, 29 beads of jade, and 34 of amethyst. Three matched pairs of polychrome vessels and three vessels of G3M gray ware lay near his legs. At his feet were the partial remains of several other adults, both male and female, perhaps previous occupants of the tomb; more partial skeletons appeared in the fill outside the tomb. Analysis of bone strontium levels by Brown (1973) indicated that the principal skeleton and the two best-preserved partial skeletons in the tomb chamber had received significantly more meat in their diet than the fragmentary individuals outside. My interpretation of Tomb 1 is that the principal burial may be that of a young noble whose military role entitled him to a *macana*, and whose social rank entitled him to gold. The other tomb occupants were evidently also of high status, while the remains outside may be from lower-status sacrificed retainers.

Equally interesting were the 10 burials nearby because many seemed to be males between 17 and 35 years of age, accompanied by weaponry. Burial 4 was interred with a group of four quartz arrow-points (Harrell type); Burial 6 had an obsidian arrow-point and a T-shaped copper axe; and Burial 7 had four backed-and-truncated *macana* blades. Although not tall (Wilkinson and Heminger reconstruct Burial 6 as roughly 154 cm or 5' ½" in stature), these possible "footsoldiers" were very robust individuals, with Burials 8 and 9 described as particularly "rugged." Their bone strontium levels, on the average, showed them to have had less meat in the diet than the high-status individuals in Tomb 1.

The burials from Barrio del Rosario Huitzo, therefore,

FIGURE 8.37. Painted lintel and carved door-jamb stones from Tomb 1 at Huitzo. (Redrawn from Moser 1969a, 1969b, and from photographs.)

lend some support to the ethnohistoric accounts of military activity during Monte Albán V. Conceivably both noble "officers" and lower-status "footsoldiers" (in their late teens, twenties, and thirties) were killed by Ahuitzotl's troops and buried in the hills and mounds nearby. Assuming that this cause of death applies to the burials we found in 1967, however, the question arises: were these the Zapotec defenders of Huitzo or their Mixtec allies? On the basis of the associated polychrome, the lost-wax cast gold, the codex-style lintel and the various stone carvings, one could make a reasonable case for their being soldiers from the Mixteca. Most ethnohistoric accounts agree, however, that the Mixtec did their fighting at the entrances to the Cañada, while the Zapotec fortified Huitzo itself. Thus the ethnic identity of the Huitzo burials remains ambiguous.

## THE BATTLE OF GUIENGOLA: ARCHAEOLOGICAL EVIDENCE

In Topic 91, Marcus discussed the ethnohistoric evidence for the joint Zapotec–Mixtec defense of the Isthmus of Tehuantepec against the armies of Ahuitzotl. The battle of Guiengola remains the most famous in Zapotec history, culminating in the marriage of Cocijoeza and Coyolicatzin. Let us examine the archaeological evidence.

Fifteen km west of the town of Tehuantepec, the mountain of Guiengola rises 1000 m above the west bank of the Tehuantepec River. The mountain is solid limestone, with numerous caves, and is covered with dense, arid-tropical thorn forest. Its west side, connected to a nearby sierra, is almost sheer rock. The easiest approach is from the northeast, and these slopes were fortified by the Zapotec with several kilometers of dry-laid stone masonry walls; behind these walls one can still find piles of river cobbles intended to be thrown down on attackers.

Although the site of Guiengola has been known for more than a century (e.g., Bancroft 1875 and Seler 1904), not until David Peterson's work during 1970–1971 was the site extensively mapped and test-excavated (Peterson and Mac-Dougall 1974). The major buildings at Guiengola lie at 428 m elevation in a saddle-shaped hollow between stony peaks on the eastern flank of the mountain, about halfway to the summit. This "site center," as Peterson calls it, is clearly

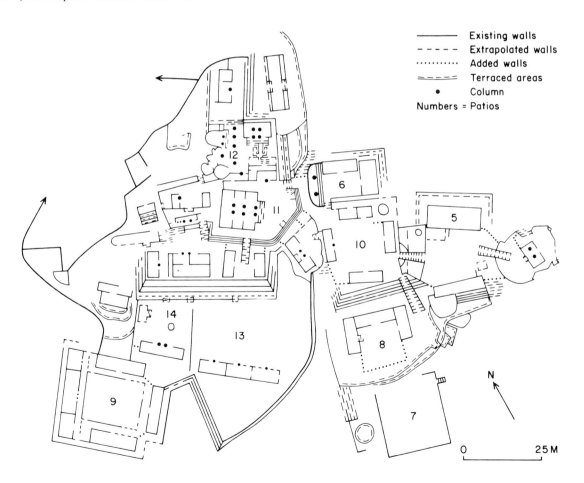

FIGURE 8.38. The site center area of Guiengola, near Tehuantepec, Oaxaca. (Redrawn, with modifications, from Peterson and MacDougall 1974.)

more than just a fort; it is a civic– ceremonial complex of 54,000 m² which includes 2 pyramids and more than 80 other structures, all protected by an extensive system of defensive walls. Peterson has divided the site center into three major components: an elite residential area on the east (with "palaces"), a northwest plaza, with pyramids and ballcourt, and a southeast building complex. In addition, outside the site center is a still larger area (as yet unmeasured), which includes nearby room and patio structures, small domestic habitations, buildings farther up on the mountain, caves with pictographs, and more defensive walls (Figure 8.38).

Clearly, Guiengola was not a mountain fortress hastily slapped together for the defense of Tehuantepec by Cocijoeza. At least 26 of the sherds discovered by Peterson are in Monte Albán IV style, suggesting that construction at the site began many centuries before Cocijoeza was born. Some 680 diagnostic sherds were of Monte Albán V gray wares, with polychrome rare but present. Paddock (1966a:223) notes that one pyramid–courtyard–adoratory complex at Guiengola looks "much like Systems M and IV of Monte Albán"; he also notes *greca* motifs carved on architectural stone at Guiengola in the false-mosaic style which "was used on Tomb 30 at Yagul . . . and for lintels and other elements where mosaic construction was impossible for technical reasons at both Mitla and Yagul" (Paddock 1966a:225). Because most construction at Guiengola was of limestone blocks quarried from the mountain itself—and resembling the stone block construction of the Yagul Fortress, the Mitla Fortress, and Tepexi el Viejo—the kind of mosaic work done at Mitla would have been virtually impossible there.

Let us now attempt, on the basis of admittedly fragmentary data, an interpretation for Guiengola. The Monte Albán style architecture and Period IV pottery reinforce the ethnohistoric evidence that the site was a Zapotec stronghold; indeed, the ethnohistoric evidence is so strong that it should lay to rest the idea that Monte Albán V gray ware and architectural *grecas* are Mixtec. But it seems unlikely that the Zapotecs would construct a 54,000-m² civic–ceremonial complex just to defend themselves against the Aztecs. It seems more reasonable to assume that Guiengola was originally built as a mountaintop Zapotec administrative center for the isthmus, complete with palaces, temples, ballcourts, pyramids, and courtyards with adoratories, in Postclassic imitation of Classic Monte Albán. It may even be that the fortification of the site center came later, when its 400-m elevation near the river made it a logical place for Cocijoeza's defense. Whether the original construction of the site was late in Monte Albán IV or early in V could only be determined by more extensive excavation. The significant points are that Guiengola is tied ethnohistorically to the royal Zapotec lineage of Zaachila, and its layout—an administrative center 400 m above the floodplain and defended by several kilometers of walls—finds its major precedent at Monte Albán.

## SUMMARY AND CONCLUSIONS

Archaeological evidence for ancient warfare is not always easy to come by. In 1966, several British newspapers reported that on the nine-hundredth anniversary of the Battle of Hastings a group of archaeologists had visited the battlefield and found little evidence to suggest that it had ever been the scene of a major conflict that forever changed the course of British history.

In Oaxaca, our best evidence comes from fortification walls at numerous sites, from piles of cobblestones stored as weapons, from *macana* blades and caches of arrow points buried with young male adults. However, without the ethnohistoric accounts it would be impossible to assess the significance of the battles fought at these localities. For their part, the archaeological data correct false impressions in the sixteenth-century documents. They show us, for example, that neither Guiengola nor Cerro de la Campana (Huitzo) was built from scratch as a Late Postclassic fort; both had been administrative centers used long before the battles which made them famous.

# Mixtec and Zapotec at the Time of the Spanish Conquest: Some Similarities and Differences

## Editors' Introduction

Our story is now almost told. We have traced the Cloud People from their Preceramic beginnings to the threshold of the Spanish Conquest; there remain only the tasks of describing some of the similarities and differences resulting from that long development and of attempting to account for them in terms of our evolutionary model.

There are perhaps a hundred ways in which the Mixtec and Zapotec could be compared and contrasted, but in this chapter we will consider only four. Those four topics have been chosen because they are all basic areas of anthropological inquiry, and because they cover a broad spectrum of human experience, from subsistence and technology to cosmology and psychology. They are farming systems, kinship and social organization, religion, and national character. In Chapter 10 we confront the more controversial problem of how the similarities and differences arose.

## TOPIC 94
### Precolumbian Farming in the Valleys of Oaxaca, Nochixtlán, Tehuacán, and Cuicatlán: A Comparative Study

KENT V. FLANNERY

Perhaps no aspect of Precolumbian culture is more appropriately viewed in a framework of adaptive radiation than farming. While such things as language, religion, architecture, and cosmology may display nonadaptive change or "drift," agriculture tends to show strong and obvious ties to the landscape, taking advantage of minor environmental dif-

ferences between valleys to produce major differences in farming systems. Such differences are all the more striking in the Otomanguean area, precisely because all these cultures had a common background and many millennia of interaction.

We have referred briefly to Precolumbian farming systems

throughout this book, but have deferred our detailed discussion until now for several reasons. For one, some systems are so long-lived that to discuss them at the Formative, Classic, and Postclassic levels would have involved needless repetition. For another, it seemed to us that the theme of this volume made it appropriate to consider the similarities and differences in Zapotec and Mixtec agriculture in the course of a single comparative–contrastive paper.

I have accordingly selected four areas within the Otomanguean region—the Valley of Oaxaca (Zapotec), the Valley of Nochixtlán–Yanhuitlán (Mixtec), the Cuicatlán Cañada (Cuicatec), and the Tehuacán Valley (Popoloca and/or Mazatec). Each of these areas is environmentally distinct and required its own special approach to dry farming, irrigation, and terracing. Although contacts were widespread, and all areas were probably aware of all the available techniques, each valley followed a slightly different pathway to agricultural success. I examine these different paths, and in keeping with the evolutionary perspective of the Santa Fe seminar, I discuss the various farming techniques in roughly the order in which it is thought they arose.

## THE VALLEY OF OAXACA

The Valley of Oaxaca has more than 700 km² of flat land, the largest expanse of any of the valleys I discuss. Its sources of water for agriculture include rainfall, springs, small streams and rivers, and the subsurface water table. It is best characterized as a region in which a tremendous variety of water-control techniques could be practiced, but where no single source of water was large enough to encourage, or benefit from, centralized control by a Prehispanic state. My discussion will lean heavily on studies by A. Kirkby (1973, 1974) and Lees (1973), supplemented by the archaeological record.

### Rainfall Farming

Rainfall farming is presumably the oldest type of farming practiced in the Valley of Oaxaca, perhaps going back to the Naquitz phase of the Preceramic era (prior to 6700 B.C.). It is also the most common type of farming; even today, water is applied to less than 20% of the cultivated land in the valley (A. Kirkby 1974:121). Finally, it is also the most risky type of farming. The Valley of Oaxaca receives 500–700 mm of mean annual rainfall, but even the annual mean "is barely adequate to support even one crop during the summer" (A. Kirkby 1973:35). Moreover, 3 years in 10 the rainfall is likely to dip below 500 mm, perhaps reaching levels that will not support a maize crop at all.

Because of these problems, the Zapotecs attempt to conserve water in the soil by careful weeding to reduce transpiration; they also try to minimize evaporation losses from the soil surface by concentrating surface storage and encouraging infiltration immediately around plants. Wherever this is still done by means of the Precolumbian digging stick (Zapotec *yagaquijxitanani*, Antillean *coa*), it is accomplished "by disturbing the surface as little as possible and confining cultivation to making shallow basins for each seed" (A. Kirkby 1973:35).

Despite these conservation methods, the Zapotec farmer who must rely totally on rainfall is unlucky indeed. Most try to have either a small area of land which can be irrigated or else a parcel of *tierra de humedad*. The latter is a type of valley-bottom land where the subsurface water table is so close to the surface (0.25–1.0 m) that the roots of the corn can abstract water continuously from the zone of high moisture content lying above the water table itself by capillary action (A. Kirkby 1973:41). *Tierra de humedad* is extremely restricted in its distribution throughout the valley, but it is prized for its ability to produce high yields continuously. In the frost-free areas that constitute most of the valley, it can produce two to three crops a year, one of maize and two of less demanding vegetables, with little or no fallowing; it does, however, require correspondingly more weeding.

Because every villager wants a share of this limited and highly productive land, individual holdings are frequently no more than 0.25–0.75 ha per family (A. Kirkby 1973:41). It is significant that many of the Valley of Oaxaca's most successful Formative villages, such as San José Mogote, Abasolo, Tierras Largas, Mitla, and San Lázaro Etla, are nestled up against *tierra de humedad*. It was the "infield" of an early agricultural system which included a larger "outfield" of less productive dry-farmed fields (see Wolf 1966:21).

Such areas of permanently humid bottomland could probably have supported a greater number of Early Formative hamlets than they did (Flannery 1976d:111). However, they would never have been extensive enough to support the populations of the Zapotec state centered at Monte Albán; for that, alternative moisture sources were needed. Interestingly enough, these alternative sources had probably been discovered well back in the Formative by hamlets such as Tomaltepec, Mitla, and Fábrica San José. In other words, not even the Early Formative farmers of the Valley of Oaxaca, for whom humid bottomland was widely available, chose to rely on it exclusively.

### The Origins of Irrigation

The position of the water table in the Valley of Oaxaca is not static but fluctuates throughout the year, following the rainfall pattern. When the water table falls below the effective reach of the plant roots, irrigation water drawn from shallow wells may be put on the plants; when the water table rises to the point where some fields become waterlogged, small canals are dug to lead the water off the land (A. Kirkby 1973:41).

In my opinion, the origins of irrigation might well have been found in these simple responses to the annual fluctuation of the water table in *tierra de humedad*. Once the technology of shallow wells was established, agriculture could be expanded to areas where the water table was 3 m (or more) below the surface. Once the technology of small gravity-flow canals was established, agriculture could be expanded to areas where surface water from springs or streams was more readily available than subsurface water. Both technologies were in evidence by the Early Formative, although we do not know when they were first applied to agriculture. Neither would have been practical while the Indians were still seminomadic, because they represent a considerable investment in the "improvement" of a specific locale. This being the case, these technologies may have more to do with the origins of the permanent village than they have been given credit for.

## Well Irrigation

Today, well irrigation is practiced on less than 10% of the cultivated land in the Valley of Oaxaca (A. Kirkby 1973:50). If we eliminate the modern well-irrigation systems which require pumps, plow furrows, or deep wells (greater than 4 m), the figure is reduced still further. I suspect that in Pre-Columbian times this technique was restricted to the zone where ground water lies within 3 m of the surface, and involved only the method called *riego a brazo* or "pot irrigation." The Zapotec phrase for this was *tiquilla niçaya*, translated by the sixteenth-century Spaniards as "to irrigate with

a *cántaro* as the Indians do" (Córdova 1578a). It consists of watering individual plants with a 10-liter jar drawn by hand from a shallow well dug right in the field.

Despite its restricted distribution, by today's standards, well irrigation remains a very important technique because it makes possible the growing of three crops a year on the same field; it could also have expanded the agricultural infield from the 0.25–1.0-m water table zone to the 3.0-m zone, an enormous increase. Formative sites in areas where the water table would have permitted well irrigation include Abasolo, Mitla, Zaachila, Santa Ana Zegache, Tierras Largas, San Lázaro Etla, and San José Mogote. Actual Formative wells have been found at Abasolo and Mitla (Figure 9.1; also see Topic 16). But as A. Kirkby points out, this "shows only that wells were used as a means of obtaining water, not necessarily that the water was used for irrigation" (1973:119). Whatever the case, the digging of wells at Abasolo had increased so much by Monte Albán V that in some excavations these features are found only 5–10 m apart. This seems like an excessive number of wells unless some were used for irrigation.

The intensity of production at Abasolo today is phenomenal; the same field produces a rainy season maize crop and two dry season vegetable crops. Crops such as chiles and bush beans are begun in seed beds (Spanish *almácigo;* sixteenth-century Zapoteco, *pillache;* twentieth-century Mitla Zapotec, *bilyáhts*) measuring 80 by 90 cm and spaced 10 cm apart. Such a seed bed will hold 1300–1500 chile plants for

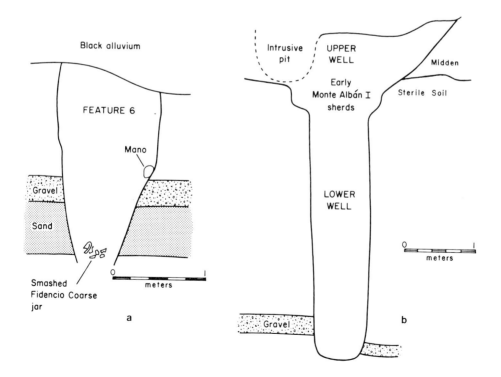

FIGURE 9.1. Formative wells from the Valley of Oaxaca: (a) cross-section of Feature 6, a San José-phase well from San Sebastián Abasolo; (b) cross-section of Monte Albán Ia well from Bala'h Bisyeh area of Mitla.

2–2.5 months; they will then be transplanted to cup-shaped depressions (Spanish, *cajete*) 15 cm in diameter and 2–3 cm deep, with a single *almácigo* supplying 160–180 m² of *cajetes*. The transplanted chiles are watered at the rate of 1 liter/plant every other day (3.5 days/week) for 1.0–1.5 months, after which two bean plants (from a different seed bed) are transplanted to each *cajete*, alongside the maturing chile. Since the beans grow faster, they are ready to harvest at the same time as the chiles; were the beans transplanted too soon, they would shade the chiles out. Beans require seven waterings a week, or twice as much work as the chiles, which may explain why they are rare in the archaeological debris from Abasolo. The productivity of such a field can perhaps be judged by one 1969 yield of 6400 bell-pepper-sized chiles from 100 m² (Flannery, unpublished data).

From a study conducted by A. Kirkby (1973:42) near Zimatlán, one can judge just how labor-intensive and water-intensive pot irrigation is. The farmer in question had a plot of chiles measuring 360 m², with wells excavated in it at 10-m intervals in every direction. Drawing a 10-liter jar from the nearest well he would water 4 earthen rectangles containing 2–8 plants; this was repeated until all 1800 rectangles had been watered. Working an average of 5.5 hr/day, he put an estimated 4500 liters of water/day on the 24-by-15-m plot. A. Kirkby estimates that this 0.6–1.4 cm/day of surface water was just enough to offset the 0.6–0.7 cm/day evaporation deficit typical of the valley floor during the dry season and "provide a little extra water for drainage of accumulating soluble salts from the root zone" (1973:42). By producing a microcosm in which the "rainy season" never ends, this constant watering also intensifies the labor needed in weeding. Fortunately, a number of weed genera such as *Amaranthus*, *Chenopodium*, and *Portulaca* are edible and add to the productivity of the system. Such edible herbs are probably reflected in the high numbers of "Cheno-Am" pollen grains from Formative village samples.

If pot irrigation is a labor-intensive farming technique, it is also one in which children can play an important role. More than half the watering of crops in Abasolo today is done by boys between 8 and 18 years old. Once pot irrigation had begun, therefore, there may have been increased selective advantage for families with large numbers of children. Even villages located in *tierra de humedad* could have used wells to increase the dry season productivity of their land, given adequate manpower. This selective advantage for larger households may be at the root of the Zapotec extended family, as well as the explosive population growth of the Formative period. At the same time, pot irrigation was not a technique that lent itself to "hydraulic despotism," since the water table beneath one man's field could hardly be controlled by his neighbors or improved by the Zapotec state.

## Canal Irrigation

Canal irrigation serves only 9% of the cultivated land in the Valley of Oaxaca today, but its regional distribution is interesting "because of the preeminence it gives to the Etla Valley in terms of concentration of water use and hence agricultural productivity" (A. Kirkby 1973:50). Twenty-five percent of the Etla region's cultivated land is canal irrigated, as compared with 7% in the Zaachila region and 3% in the Tlacolula region. Because the Etla region also had the largest population in the valley prior to the founding of Monte Albán, I suspect an early origin for canal irrigation.

I have suggested that canals may have begun as a response to waterlogging in the *tierra de humedad*. They might just as easily have their origin in the drainage ditches which prevented rain runoff from flooding houses in hillside villages. One such drainage ditch was found in a large open area uphill from San José phase House 1 at Tierras Largas; another was found next to Houses 16 and 17 at San José Mogote, in association with a large bedrock cistern (Flannery [ed.] 1976:30, Fig. 2.10). This simple technology moved agriculture out of the humid bottomlands into piedmont areas where small streams could be diverted to water downstream alluvium. Formative villages located in suitable areas for canal irrigation include Tomaltepec, Fábrica San José, Huitzo, Cuilapan, and Santa Ana Tlapacoyan.

During the course of Blanton's urban analysis of Monte Albán, James Neely (1972) discovered a Prehispanic irrigation system on the southeast flank of the site. Further work has dated the system, which consists of a dam and a 2-km canal, to Periods I and II of Monte Albán (Mason et al. 1977). The dam is situated in a large barranca below and to the east of the South Platform of the Main Plaza; the canal begins at the south end of the dam and follows the contour of the mountain flank along the side of the barranca, proceeding along the top of a gently convex piedmont spur toward the village of Xoxocotlán (Figure 9.2).

> Approximately 10 m high at its center and 80 m in overall length, the [dam] is V-shaped in plan view with the point of the V directed upstream. The ends of the dam abut a limestone outcrop on either side of the barranca, effectively blocking the channel and impounding water in a large reservoir. Construction material consisted primarily of unmodified boulder fill consolidated with a limestone cement. In addition, the uppermost portion of the construction, approximately one meter in height, was made of cut limestone blocks, fitted together very neatly. A thick limestone plaster was applied to the outer surface of the dam, probably to reduce water loss through seepage. . . . In a few places the canal is chiseled into bedrock but along most of its course it is only visible as a slight depression in the soil. Transverse test excavations indicated two distinct channels within the canal: a smaller one about 30 cm. wide by 12 cm. deep that had been excavated into the side-wall of a larger channel which was about 80 cm. by 25 cm. in size. . . . The two channel sizes may have been for the purpose of accommodating differing wet and dry season water volumes. . . . The irrigation system also included terraces, especially on the steeper upper portion of the piedmont ridge. These terraces would have made irrigation agriculture more efficient by retaining soil and water in the irrigated area [Mason et al. 1977:567; reproduced by permission of the Society for American Archaeology, *American Antiquity* 42(4):567–575, 1977].

Occupation around the canal consisted of a linear settlement that was founded in Monte Albán Ia, peaked in Period Ic, and declined during Period II. The cultivated area is estimated at about 50 ha, and the residential area as between 2.5

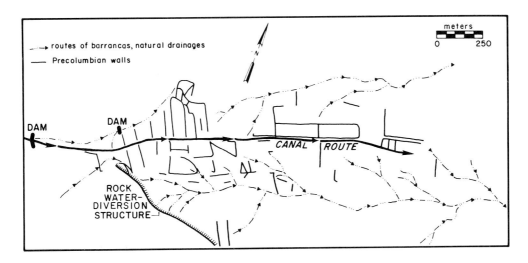

FIGURE 9.2. Monte Albán I–II dam and canal system near Xoxocotlán, below Monte Albán. (Redrawn from Mason et al. 1977.)

(Period Ia) and 10.2 ha (Period Ic). Such a cultivated area could probably not have supported more than 250 persons, so it is unlikely that the canal made much of a dent in the food requirements of Monte Albán (Mason et al. 1977:573). However, there could have been dozens of similar systems in the Central and Etla regions of the valley that have been obliterated by subsequent plowing.

An equally small, but extremely intricate, canal-and-terrace system can be seen at Hierve el Agua, near San Lorenzo Albarradas in the mountains east of Mitla (Figure 9.3) (Neely 1967; A. Kirkby 1973:Fig. 46; Flannery and Marcus 1976b:Fig. 2). Here half a square kilometer of artificially terraced hillside was served by a complex series of canals which descend from a permanent spring. The calcium carbonate and magnesium content of the water is so high that travertine deposition has literally turned the canals to stone, "fossilizing" the later stages of the system. Main canals descend from springs with a present flow of about 2 liters/sec during the summer months; distributary canals branch off them and run laterally across the terrace walls. At roughly regular intervals of 3.25 m there are circular basins (17 cm in diameter and 10 cm deep) called *pocitos*, cut in the lateral canals. Excavations by Neely (1967) into the terraces revealed a sequence extending from Monte Albán Ic (with radiocarbon dates of 420–310 B.C.) until Monte Albán V. Broken sections of travertine canals from various periods were included in the terrace fill.

A. Kirkby regards the *pocitos* as evidence for pot irrigation used in combination with canals, citing a modern system she observed in the Zaachila region where

the water was distributed through the field in an E-shaped canal system; and along each arm of the system, spaced 3 to 4 meters apart, were basins (cut into the earth canals) which were 50 cm. in diameter and 30 to 40 cm. deep. The rest of the field was laid out in circular hollows, each of which contained one tomato plant. When the canals were filled, water was taken from the nearest canal basin in a pot to each plant in the same way that

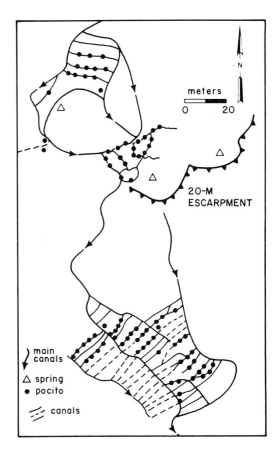

FIGURE 9.3. Canal and terrace system at Hierve el Agua near San Lorenzo Albarradas, Oaxaca. (Redrawn from A. Kirkby 1973: Figure 46.)

has been described for pot irrigation. . . . Such a sequence of water use might have been practiced at Hierve el Agua. The use of pot irrigation at all stages of plant growth would have had advantages in economy of applied water [A. Kirkby 1973:117–119].

In contrast to well irrigation, canal irrigation is a technique that has occasionally been singled out as a source of conflict and "hydraulic despotism" between upstream and downstream users. Lees (1973), however, found few examples of such conflict in the Valley of Oaxaca. For one thing, the traditional Oaxaca pattern is one of dozens of small streams (0.2–0.6 m³ water/sec), each of which has a small-scale irrigation system controlled by one village or by cooperation between two or three villages (A. Kirkby 1973:45–47). Most traditional dams are simple constructions of earth, stones, and brush, intended more to divert the water than to store it up. To date, no Prehispanic water control feature the size of the Tehuacán Valley's Purrón Dam (see discussion later in topic) has ever been found in the Valley of Oaxaca. The architects of Monte Albán surely did not lack the expertise to build such features; more likely, no single stream was considered worth the effort.

Although large dams were apparently lacking in the ancient Valley of Oaxaca, there is one area of the valley where Blanton's surveys have found evidence for water-control works on a larger scale than the Monte Albán (Xoxocotlán) canal. These works are in the southern half of the Zaachila–Zimatlán plain, far from any tributary streams, and apparently involved the main Atoyac River. Blanton describes the situation as follows:

> During our survey of the Zaachila–Zimatlán region, we noted some evidence for larger-scale water-control works south of Santa Inés Yatzeche [a town some 7 km downstream from Zimatlán]. It consisted of canals that would have directed water from the Atoyac to large flats of alluvium within meanders of the river. Today these canals are visible only as linear soil stains on the 1:5000 air photos. The placement of small sites near these canals suggests they were constructed and used during Monte Albán IIIa. This dating is reasonable, since Period IIIa was the time of highest population density of any Prehispanic period in the Zaachila–Zimatlán survey area [personal communication, 1975].

## Floodwater Farming

Floodwater farming is the most widespread water-control system in use in the Valley of Oaxaca today, but it varies from region to region. It forms the predominant method of water use in 52% of the Tlacolula region and 32% of the Zaachila region, but only 22% of the Etla region (A. Kirkby 1973:49). It is also the hardest technology to define, because "in their simplest forms floodwater techniques merge with those of dry farming. At the other end of the scale, floodwater distributary systems are similar to those of canal irrigation" (A. Kirkby 1973:36).

The basic principle behind floodwater farming is the artificial spreading of water from seasonally overflowing streams onto a wider area than it would normally reach.

This floodwater distribution may be accomplished by simple stone and brush diversion dams that take advantage of arroyos that carry water only once a year, or by canals dug to remove water from permanent streams when they reach their summer flood stage. The ephemeral nature of these features makes it almost impossible for archaeologists to document prehistoric floodwater farming. Most of the Formative villages I have listed as being in suitable localities for canal irrigation could just as easily have practiced floodwater farming. Even the Xoxocotlán canal described above might fall in this category; the low terraces that accompany it are not at all unlike the terraces used in areas like Macuil-xochitl to slow down the movement of floodwater, increase its penetration into the soil, and prevent erosion.

Perhaps the best clue comes from A. Kirkby's map showing the applicability of various farming techniques to the Valley of Oaxaca (A. Kirkby 1973:Fig. 18). According to this map, floodwater farming is the technique most likely to have supported a vast area of the Tlacolula plain, including the sites of Yagul and Caballito Blanco, Yegüih–Lambityeco, Dainzú, Macuilxochitl, and Teotitlán del Valle. It may also have played a role in the development of such southern valley centers as Santa Inés Yatzeche and Rancho Tejas. The dating of these sites suggests that floodwater farming was already in use by Monte Albán Ic and reached major proportions during Periods IIIb–IV and V.

## Hillside Terracing

During the Monte Albán V period (A.D. 1000–1500), small terrace walls of dry-laid stone masonry were constructed on hill and mountain slopes in certain parts of the Valley of Oaxaca. Mountains to the east of Díaz Ordaz and to the west, north, and east of Mitla were among the areas favored. The Period V occupation of Cueva Blanca (see Topic 5) included five terrace walls on the talus slope and a sixth in the arroyo below (Figure 9.4). Such terraces seem to be more common on slopes that are usually in the shade and have lower evaporation rates. They serve to conserve rain runoff from the cliffs and slopes above and, judging by our excavations in Terrace 3 at Cueva Blanca, do stay damp for a significant period following rains.

These terrace systems seem to have been used to intensify agriculture in the sustaining area around Postclassic centers like Mitla and Yagul. Some are so similar to Natividad-phase systems in the Mixteca Alta (see discussion later in topic) that it would be tempting to see them as a Postclassic introduction which accompanied the Mixtec "incursions" into the Valley of Oaxaca. However, we should bear in mind that terracing in the Valley of Oaxaca goes back at least to the Monte Albán I irrigation systems at Xoxocotlán and Hierve el Agua. An alternative explanation, which would fit both the Mixteca Alta and the Mitla–Yagul area, would be that hillside terracing was one of the ways that local *cabeceras* could increase the productivity of the limited land available to them in Balkanized Postclassic Oaxaca.

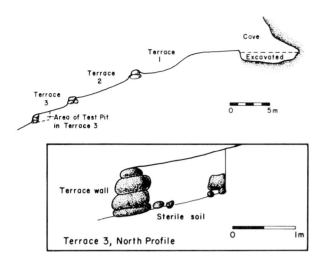

FIGURE 9.4. Cross-section of Postclassic hillside agricultural terraces at Cueva Blanca near Mitla, Oaxaca. The insert shows the cross-section of an excavation into Terrace 3.

### The Integration of Dry Farming and Irrigation

We have mentioned that most Zapotec villages have an "infield" of first-class land which is intensively farmed (by well irrigation, canal irrigation, or floodwater farming) and an "outfield" of marginal land which is dry farmed. Traditional Zapotec farmers integrate their use of prime and marginal land in intricate ways. A. Kirkby (1974) has shown that their strategy depends on certain predictions based on their perception of rainfall.

The Zapotecs believe they can detect cycles of greater rainfall at intervals of 3, 4, 5, or 7 years. This pattern is not borne out by local climatic records, and A. Kirkby feels it is partly a function of the way the Zapotecs perceive and remember rainy years; it also reflects a cosmology in which natural events are cyclic.

Perhaps the most important predictor used by the Zapotec today is the pattern of observed rainfall in the months immediately preceding the true rainy season, and in this they are supported by local meteorological records. According to A. Kirkby, if spring rainfall is greater than 80 mm, there is an 80% chance that growing-season precipitation will be above 600 mm; if spring rainfall is between 20 and 40 mm, there is a 50% chance that the crops will receive less than 420 mm. "By June reliability has increased so that if June rainfall is more than 150 millimeters . . . then rainfall throughout the growing season has an 85 percent chance of being above average" (A. Kirkby 1974:123).

When May–June rainfall indicates a wet year, the Zapotec response is not what a Western agronomist might expect, but it is consistent with their "satisficing" outlook. Predicting that yields will be higher than average, the Indian actually *reduces* his maize planting in the continuously culti-

vated main agricultural zone of the valley; in the much larger and only sporadically cultivated marginal zones, he will gamble on his prediction of a rainy year and increase his planting. In addition to reducing the differences in yield between wet and dry years, this strategy has a latent adaptive function detected by A. Kirkby: long-cultivated, underfallowed alluvium is allowed to rest during years when some yield can be expected from the long-fallowed, underused piedmont.

## THE VALLEY OF NOCHIXTLÁN

The Valley of Nochixtlán–Yanhuitlán has 250 km² of flat land, the second-largest expanse in the Oaxaca highlands. It also shows several significant differences from the Valley of Oaxaca. Because Nochixtlán (2200 m) is some 700 m higher than Oaxaca, frost is a more significant factor in the Mixteca Alta. And in spite of the abundant limestones in the Nochixtlán Valley, "it is somewhat surprising when comparison is made with the Tehuacán and Oaxaca Valleys that the Nochixtlán area lacks major springs issuing from the limestone, with or without travertine deposits" (M. Kirkby 1972:5). Perhaps it can best be characterized as an area where early farming depended on a compromise between the dangers of aridity and frost, and Postclassic farming depended on an unusual, highly productive, labor-intensive terracing system which took advantage of a unique feature in the Nochixtlán–Yanhuitlán environment.

### Rainfall Farming

It should be remembered that C. E. Smith (1976) has reconstructed the Nochixtlán Valley environment as pine–oak forest, so early rainfall farming there would initially have involved land clearance. Although it is possible that Formative agriculture included an infield–outfield pattern like that of the Valley of Oaxaca, Nochixtlán lacks the large areas of high subsurface water seen in the latter area. Consequently, there seems to have been less preoccupation with *tierra de humedad,* and no well-irrigation system evolved. Two early villages, Yucuita and Coyotepec, are on gently sloping, arable hills overlooking the valley floor, and the earliest deposits at Yucuita (ca. 1300 B.C.) actually occur on the opposite side of the hill from the river. Another early village, Etlatongo, lies at the confluence of two rivers in a tailor-made location for simple diversion irrigation, similar to the setting of Santa Ana Tlapacoyan in the Valley of Oaxaca.

But while the Valley of Oaxaca farmers searched for patches of high water table, Michael Kirkby's (1972) study suggests a different pattern for Nochixtlán. Annual precipitation there shows a marked increase with elevation, rising from 460 mm at 2200 m (Nochixtlán), through 690 mm at 2300 m (San Pedro Cántaros), to 1025 mm at 2560 m (Tiltepec) (M. Kirkby 1972:37). At the same time, risk of frost also increases with elevation, with winter crops in danger at 2100 m and even summer crops in danger at 2600 m. This gradient is complicated by the fact that, at lower elevations, valley-floor fields are in greater danger than hillslope fields because cold air settles to the valley floor—a phenomenon already noted for the Valley of Mexico by Sanders (1965).

The climatic limitations of rainfall farming are given by M. Kirkby (1972:Table 7) as follows: at 2200 m, the probabilities of total crop failure are 28% (from aridity); at 2300 m, only 6%; at 2400 m, about 15%; at 2600 m, back up to 21% (from frost). Thus the best elevation within the area for rainwater farming is at about 2300 m, where lower frost risk and 690 mm of rainfall overlap. Add to this fact the desirability of hillslope fields, and I believe we have a reasonable explanation for the settlement pattern at Yucuita and Coyotepec.

### Floodwater Farming and Canal Irrigation

The setting of Etlatongo suggests that simple diversion irrigation, probably with boulder and brush dams, was known in the Formative. Whether this system involved floodwater farming or canal irrigation has not yet been archaeologically determined. However, even as late as A.D. 500–700, the role of canal irrigation does not seem to have been crucial to this part of the Mixteca Alta. Spores (1969:563) speaks of an "apparently almost total dependence on rainfall and some diversion irrigation" prior to the rise of *lama–bordo* technology.

### The *Lama–Bordo* System

In the late 1940s, Cook (1949) pointed to a spectacular level of soil erosion in the Yanhuitlán area which he took to be evidence of agricultural practices reaching far back into Prehispanic times. Lorenzo (1958b) visited many of Cook's localities and tied the erosion geologically to the red soil of the "Yanhuitlán Beds," which he and Salas (1949) attribute to a series of landlocked Tertiary lakes. Now the studies of M. Kirkby (1972) and Spores (1969) have tied the erosion culturally to a unique system of agriculture.

> The Yanhuitlán Beds are typically highly calcareous, slightly compacted, shales and clays. The red to purple coloration and high $CaCO_3$ content indicate formation from limestone parent materials under conditions of rather low chemical solution, that is under arid or semi-arid conditions. Their fine grain size indicates deposition far from their source area, or, more probably, on a lake or playa floor. . . . These deposits are . . . highly erodible, so that they tend to be selectively removed, exposing more and more of the landscape on which they were originally deposited. The erodibility and high $CaCO_3$ content of the Yanhuitlán Beds form a recurring theme which . . . is perhaps the dominant influence on the physical environment of the Nochixtlán area, and gives the area its special character [M. Kirkby 1972:6].

During the era of pristine forests in the Nochixtlán–Yanhuitlán Valley, the erodible Yanhuitlán Beds were protected under a layer of calcrete (Hispanicized Mixtec *endeque,* Hispanicized Nahuatl caliche) which forms between the organic A horizon and the calcareous Tertiary clays. The areas of calcareous soils were selectively farmed because they were less acidic and more fertile than the volcanic soils elsewhere in the valley. Under the pressures of population growth, vast areas of forest were cleared from hills and slopes, hastening erosion. As gullies began to cut through the *endeque,* they exposed the even more highly erodible Yanhuitlán Beds. Soft red soil began to wash down the gullies into the narrow drainages, converting some of them from V-shaped to U-shaped valleys. It is believed that this process began prior to A.D. 1000, but probably did not become a major phenomenon until the Postclassic Natividad phase (A.D. 1000–1530).

At some point near the beginning of the Natividad phase, possibly under the demographic pressures of the buildup of Mixtec power, farmers realized that the red soil washing down into new parts of the valley was more alkaline, more fertile, and more moisture-retentive than the native soil of that area. Suddenly, also, unusable V-shaped gullies were becoming farmable U-shaped valleys. By "constructing stone and rubble dikes designed to trap water and eroding soils as they descended the natural drainage channels that extended from the mountain to the valley floor during the period of heavy summer runoff" (Spores 1969:563), they created a whole new system of agriculture: *lama–bordo* (see Figures 9.5 and 9.6.)

> These dikes, built of coursed stone and rubble, were 1 to 4 meters high and from 10 to 200 meters long. Modern farmers, who continue to construct these terrace systems, find that in 2 to 3 years sufficient soil (*lama*) can be accumulated in a new terrace (*terraza, trinchera,* or *bordo*) to form level and quite fertile farm plots, and they produce excellent yields of corn, grain, and vegetables. The plots, which range from a few hundred square feet to 10 hectares, can be worked for as long as the system is maintained, and many terraces have been worked since antiquity [Spores 1969:563; copyright 1969 by the American Association for the Advancement of Science].

It is also possible that intensification of farming during the Natividad phase led to deliberate attempts to increase erosion (and hence terrace formation) by stripping away of the *endeque.*

> Whether land pressure on hillside fields started erosion—and terracing was only a way to mitigate its effects—or erosion was deliberately started in order to provide material for terraces, is not known, but it appears that the combination of erosion and terracing proved to be a positive advantage for agriculture. The area of fairly level land was increased, and its quality improved both from the point of view of fertility and of moisture content. Because of this increase in available land, there is reason to suppose that a larger population *increase* from Las Flores to Natividad times could have been supported in the Nochixtlán Valley than elsewhere [M. Kirkby 1972:36].

Thus, the *lama–bordo* system must surely have contributed to the fact that Yanhuitlán was the richest and most powerful *cacicazgo* in the Mixteca Alta (Spores, Topic 75).

On the other side of the coin, the maintenance of the

system was undoubtedly improved by the cacique's constant demands and his power to enforce them. With the disruptions of the Spanish Conquest, much of the system fell into disuse and began to erode unchecked. M. Kirkby (1972:34) calculates that since the Spanish Conquest the rate of erosion in the Nochixtlán Valley (10 mm/year, for 500 years, for a drainage area of 0.4 km²) is among the highest recorded in the world. The *lama–bordo* system may be another classic example of a labor-intensive system which resulted from, and in turn supported, strongly centralized authority. It is also probably a classic example of the way a relatively small state can intensify the productivity of its immediate sustain-

ing area to the point where it has the manpower needed to exact tribute from weaker neighboring areas.

## Hillside Terracing

As early as the Las Flores phase (A.D. 300–1100), hillside terraces presumed to be agricultural are found adjacent to major centers. On aerial photographs these terraces, as well as those of the succeeding Natividad phase, frequently appear in concentric patterns, completely ringing an important center (see Spores 1967:Photo facing p. 62; Spores

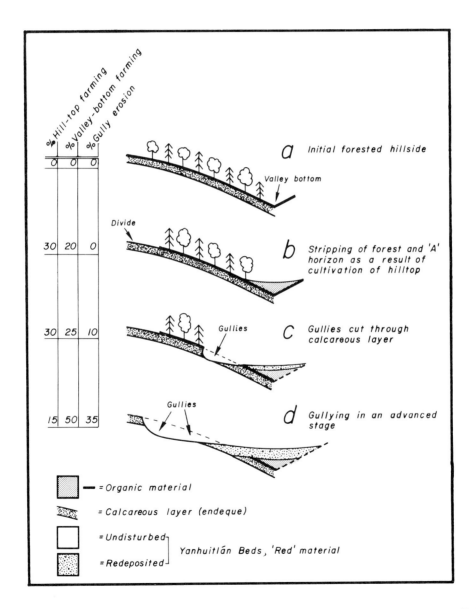

FIGURE 9.5. The sequence of stages in the development of a *lama–bordo* system for the Nochixtlán Valley. (Redrawn from M. Kirkby 1972.)

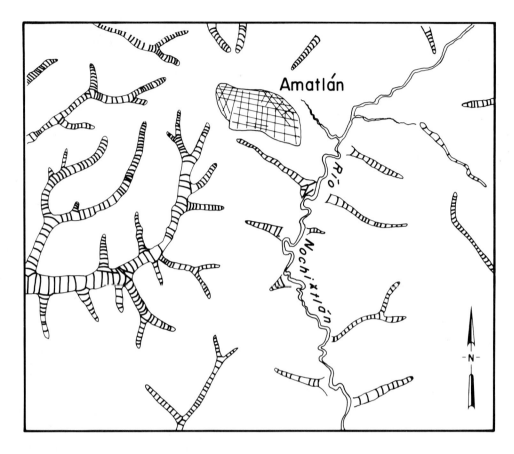

FIGURE 9.6. Pattern of ancient and modern *lama–bordo* terraces in gullies radiating out from the village of Amatlán in the Nochixtlán Valley. (Drawn from an aerial photograph published by Spores 1969: Figure 8.)

1969:Figs. 5, 6). From the location of these terraces, their main purpose must have been to increase soil humidity by slowing down and concentrating rain runoff.

### The Integration of Farming Techniques

According to Spores (1969:563), farming strategy in Natividad times was (1) to continue to work the valley lands, (2) to till limited areas on mountains and hilltops where the old dark soil overlying the caliche could be retained on more or less level plots, and (3) to expand and maintain the *lama–bordo* system with its more fertile reddish soil. Perhaps the greatest variety of techniques were employed in the immediate vicinity of the heavily occupied *cabeceras* of each *cacicazgo*, with the result that important Postclassic ruins often lie at the center of an intensely modified landscape.

## THE VALLEY OF TEHUACÁN

There are about 400 km² of relatively flat land in the area of the Tehuacán Valley surveyed by MacNeish (1964,

1972), making it roughly intermediate in size between the valleys of Oaxaca and Nochixtlán. Tehuacán has a lower annual rainfall than the latter two valleys, but has the advantage of considerable land at frost-free elevations below 1300 m. Its sources of water for agriculture included small piedmont arroyos, the Río Salado and its tributaries, and some vast but highly localized springs. The subsurface water level was too low for pot irrigation (although chain-wells of Persian *qanat* type were introduced by the Spaniards), and many springs and streams were too salty. Tehuacán is perhaps best described as a region where, in contrast to Oaxaca and Nochixtlán, large-scale canal and aqueduct systems running for dozens of kilometers and serving many different communities were appropriate. These systems often linked the monumental springs in the temperate northern valley (which today support five major soft-drink bottling companies) to the alluvial plains of the semitropical southern valley.

Because the water-control systems of the Tehuacán Valley have been extensively published by Woodbury and Neely (1972), there is no need for me to go into much detail. I briefly review their findings, concentrating on the systems which contrast with those described for Oaxaca and Nochixtlán.

## Rainfall Agriculture

Maize agriculture goes back to before 5000 B.C. in the Tehuacán Valley, and it is presumed that rainfall farming was the earliest kind. Much of the farming in Preceramic times may have taken the form of "barranca horticulture" or "barranca agriculture." MacNeish defines barranca horticulture as "the planting of individual hardy cultivars [especially cucurbits] in the barrancas near the cave sites," and barranca agriculture as "the planting of such grains as corn and amaranth in fields . . . in the arroyo bottoms, or on low terraces next to arroyos or barrancas where they would receive a supply of moisture from runoff during the rainy season" (1967b:306). Such farming would have taken advantage of the fact that some piedmont barrancas are among the most humid niches available in the otherwise arid Tehuacán Valley. Because Mesoamerican Indians frequently planted maize, cucurbits, and other cultivars in the same field, however, I suspect that in practice it may prove difficult to demonstrate a dichotomy between "horticulture" and "agriculture" in barrancas.

As MacNeish (1967b:306) pointed out, one of the first radical shifts in the agricultural pattern occurred at the start of the Ajalpan phase when "the proportion of improved corn derived from barranca or flood-plain agriculture rises to 35 percent of the bulk food stuffs" (recovered from caves and rock-shelters). Equally striking is the fact that during the Ajalpan phase (1500–900 B.C.), for the first time, most farmers in the Tehuacán Valley lived in hamlets of wattle-and-daub houses along the Río Salado rather than in piedmont barrancas. We do not know whether these Early Formative farmers depended on small patches of *tierra de humedad* along the Río Salado, or whether they diverted river water onto their fields with brush dams.

The arroyos of the Ríos Salado, Zapotitlán, and Calapilla can be considered a special "microenvironment" within the Tehuacán Valley, and perhaps even viewed as an extension of the barranca environment out onto the alluvial valley floor. Before the era of dam building and soft-drink bottling, the Río Salado must have carried much more water than it does now. Even today, in areas where it is deeply entrenched and carrying only 30 cm of water, its arroyo bed supports a river arroyo vegetation lusher than that of the surrounding plain. South of Ajalpan, where the river trickles between 5-m bluffs, there are dense thickets of quebracho (*Acacia unijuga*) and *chintoborrego* (*Vallesia glabra*) as well as reed beds, canebrakes, and vegetation-covered sloughs. In such areas, the roots of the corn can tap the subsurface water table of the floodplain below the bluffs. Like the *tierra de humedad* in the Valley of Oaxaca, however, this specialized riverine biotope constitutes a very small percentage of the total valley. Were it not for irrigation, population in the Tehuacán region could never have reached the level it did in the Late Formative and Classic periods.

## Small-Scale Dams

It is assumed that the earliest diversion dams in the Tehuacán Valley were simple brush-and-boulder constructs, but for obvious reasons none has survived to be studied. The oldest archaeologically documented dam dates to the early Santa María phase (Middle Formative, ca. 750–600 B.C.). It is found at site Tr435 in the Arroyo Lencho Diego and belongs to the series of structures known as the Purrón Dam complex (Woodbury and Neely 1972:82–99).

The normally dry Arroyo Lencho Diego descends from 2000- to 850-m elevation over the course of its 9-km canyon. The spot chosen for the dam is a point 1 km above the arroyo mouth, where the canyon narrows to 400 m in width between sheer cliffs 40–50 m high. The early Santa María dam (Figure 9.7, Part 2)

> was dome-shaped in cross-section, measured 6 m. wide and 2.8 m. high, and was primarily composed of earth and small stones laid over a foundation of large rocks. The eastern side [upstream] was faced with unmodified dry-laid stones of small to medium size. . . . Because of the small size of this dam as seen in profile, it quite likely did not extend completely across the 400-meter width of the canyon at this point. . . . It is quite probable . . . that the first dam was only about 175 m. in length, extending a little less than half the distance across the canyon narrows. . . . The small size of the dam would indicate a type of spillway utilized in small dams and the larger canal systems built by the local farmers today—that is, a narrow slot cut through the dam closed off with large logs, boulders, and mud. . . . Because the dam was small, the resulting catch basin was small, perhaps covering only an area of about 140 by 170 m. . . . Finely stratified layers of soil and small gravels were found behind (east of) this first dam. This silt and gravel, in fifteen to twenty horizontal layers of alluvial deposition, represents a period of some decades' use . . . before the basin silted nearly to the top of the dam, rendering it useless [Woodbury and Neely 1972:84–86].

To summarize: by 750 to 600 B.C., the villagers of the southern Tehuacán Valley had constructed a dam of some 2940 m³ of earth and stone, which backed up a 2.4-ha reservoir in the Arroyo Lencho Diego. Because the arroyo carries water only during a short period of the summer, the reservoir would probably seldom have been filled to the 37,000-m³ capacity estimated by Woodbury and Neely (1972:99). However, whatever water it backed up could have been used to irrigate the frost-free alluvial fan below the dam. Plant remains from Zone H of Purrón Cave, 900 m upstream from the dam, suggest that some of the Santa María-phase irrigation water was used to grow cotton, avocados, white zapotes (*Casimiroa edulis*), and black zapotes (*Diospyros digyna*).

As for the manpower requirements of the early Santa María-phase dam, Woodbury and Neely (1972:98) find it "conceivable that the first dam was built by cooperation within a single small village; ideally, ten men could have completed the construction in not much more than 100 days" of the dry season. Such an estimate would require that

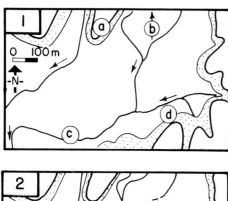

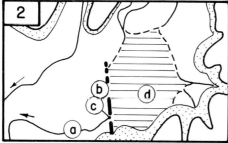

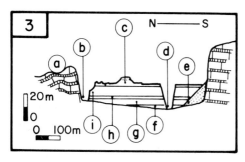

FIGURE 9.7. Stages in the development of the Purrón Dam, Tehuacán Valley. 1, Plan view of the Arroyo Lencho Diego prior to construction of the dam: (a) Cerro Lencho Diego; (b) direction of Purrón Cave; (c) Arroyo Lencho Diego; (d) talus slope. 2, Plan view of the Santa María-phase dam: (a) Arroyo Lencho Diego; (b) dam; (c) probable sluice gate; (d) impounded dam reservoir. 3, Cross-section of the Palo Blanco-phase dam: (a) Cerro Lencho Diego; (b), (d) eroded gullies; (c) superimposed Postclassic buildings; (e) talus slope; (i) final stage of Palo Blanco-phase dam; (f), (g), (h) earlier stages of dam. (Redrawn, with modifications, from a study by Jean Brunet [Byers 1967:86].)

each man move only 2.94 m³ dirt/day, a not unreasonable figure (see Erasmus 1965). In this case, it is clear that such dams were well within the capacity of Middle Formative societies, which presumably had some degree of hereditary community leadership but as yet no state organization.

## Large-Scale Dams

The dam described above was only the simple beginning of construction in the Arroyo Lencho Diego. There was a second period of construction during the middle Santa María phase (ca. 600 B.C.) that carried the dam to the full width of the canyon (400 m); then came a third period of construction in the late Santa María or early Palo Blanco phase (150 B.C.–A.D. 150) which "may represent repair . . . rather than a distinct building stage" (Woodbury and Neely 1972:90). A fourth period of construction during the early Palo Blanco phase (prior to A.D. 200) brought the Purrón dam to its maximum size: 18 m high, 100 m thick, and spanning the full 400 m of the canyon. This dam had an estimated 370,000 m³ of fill, of which the fourth construction stage alone contributed 192,000 m³ (Figure 9.7, Part 3). Much of the second and fourth stages consisted of fill well compacted into box-like "compartments" whose dry-laid stone masonry retaining walls give the dam a strong internal structure (Woodbury and Neely 1972:Figs. 6, 8, 10, 13). The fourth stage backed up a reservoir of some 400 by 700 m with an estimated capacity of 2.64 million m³—enough, by modern standards, to irrigate between 250 and 300 ha of the alluvial flats below the dam (Woodbury and Neely 1972:99). Woodbury and Neely estimate that a labor force of 4300 men would have been required to build the fourth stage of the dam during the 220 rain-free days of the dry season. "The magnitude of this construction thus suggests a sufficiently complex social organization to secure and control such a large body of laborers" (Woodbury and Neely 1972). Such a labor force would have to have been drawn from many different communities, if not the whole Tehuacán Valley (Woodbury and Neely 1972), suggesting a project directed by an early Palo Blanco-phase state. A detailed study of changing settlement patterns in the Arroyo Lencho Diego area, aimed at shedding light on this question, has been conducted by Charles S. Spencer (1979) since this topic was written.

## Large-Scale Canal Systems

The Postclassic canal systems of the Tehuacán Valley were vast and, because of "fossilization" by travertine deposition, they are extraordinarily well preserved. In some areas, solid travertine canals stand 3 m high, their successive depositional layers exposed by erosion of the surrounding soil. In other areas, modern cultivation has left only remnants of the Precolumbian canal networks. Woodbury and Neely found disconnected segments of what may have been "a huge single system, some 25 km in length" which began in the area of massive springs near the city of Tehuacán and ran southeast beyond Ajalpan to the village of San José Miahuatlán[1] (Woodbury and Neely 1972:130–131 and Fig. 51). The main canals appear to have been about 1.5–3.0 m wide, the smaller canals or distributaries about 0.3–1.0 m wide, and the whole system has a gradient of descent of about 1.5 to 1.8%. Beginning at an elevation of 1680 m near the giant San Lorenzo spring, the canals descend more than 500 m to

---

[1]Not to be confused with the town of Miahuatlán, south of the Valley of Oaxaca.

the frost-free southern valley, where some distributaries drain into the Río Salado, others into its tributary the Río Zapotitlán. As in the case of the Purrón dam, such a massive effort would have involved cooperation among many communities scattered over a 25-km stretch of the valley, suggesting administration at a supravillage or state level. The system also lends itself to theories of hydraulic "despotism," because downstream communities would have been dependent on upstream maintenance of the main canals by distant neighbors. Finally, a system of this size may have made possible the extensive cotton fields in the frost-free parts of the Tehuacán Valley during the sixteenth century (MacNeish 1967a:24).

### The Xiquila Aqueduct

Woodbury and Neely have described still another large-scale, multicommunity irrigation work. In this case the setting is the canyon of the Río Xiquila, a west-bank tributary of the Río Salado that joins the main river 50 km south of Tehuacán. At this point, the Tehuacán Valley has narrowed to a strip of alluvium only 500 m across, which cannot be served by the canal systems described above. During the late Palo Blanco phase and the subsequent Venta Salada phase (from roughly A.D. 400 to the Spanish Conquest), the Prehispanic occupants of the area built a stone-masonry aqueduct in the canyon to lead irrigation water east to the joint floodplain of the Xiquila and Salado (Woodbury and Neely 1972:102–113).

In the lower 2 km of its course, the Xiquila carries a flow of about 1100 liters/second. Approximately 4.7 km upstream from its confluence with the Salado, it was diverted into a canal estimated to have been 0.5–1.0 m wide and 50 cm deep and that followed the contours of the north side of the arroyo and descended at a grade of between 1.3 and 3.2% (except for a stretch where it circumvents an obstacle in the canyon wall at an 0.7% grade). In places there was a second canal, lower and shorter than the first (Figure 9.8). Both canals were supported by an aqueduct that has survived in places as a dry-laid masonry wall of some 10 courses of roughly dressed limestone blocks, reaching to a height of nearly 3 m.

Woodbury and Neely have provided us with figures that put the Xiquila aqueduct into perspective. The river has enough water to irrigate 3000–3500 ha of land, but a maximum of only 250 to 500 ha of farmland were available in the area. It is estimated that 10 men could have built the longer of the two canals over the course of 2.5 to 3.0 years (or 30 men over the course of 1 year). Such a canal would make possible the intensive, year-round farming of an area which was extremely marginal without irrigation; one need only compare the desertic, cactus-studded upper canyon with the irrigated alluvium to appreciate the difference (Woodbury and Neely 1972:Figs. 20, 26).

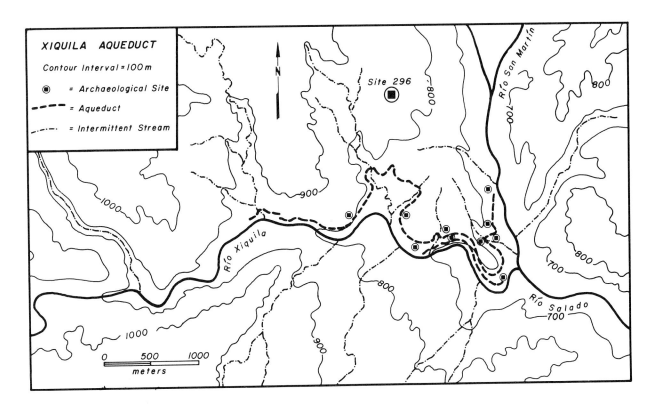

FIGURE 9.8. The Río Xiquila aqueduct, Tehuacán Valley. (Redrawn from Woodbury and Neely 1972.)

In its architectural details, the Xiquila aqueduct resembles the Río Chiquito canal discovered by Hopkins (1974) in the Cuicatec Cañada (see discussion in next section of this topic). The latter canal supported the *cacicazgo* of Cuicatlán and, appropriately, Woodbury and Neely compare the Xiquila canal to the efforts of the Cuicatec *cacicazgos* or smaller Mixtec kingdoms. They suggest that the longer canal may have been constructed by a local kingdom whose rulers resided at site Tr296, a large fortified Venta Salada-phase town on a mountaintop above the confluence of the Xiquila and Salado. Indeed, the similarities between the Xiquila and Cuicatlán canals and settlement systems are so great that it might almost have been more appropriate to discuss them both in the section on the Cañada, which follows.

**Hillside Terracing**

Terracing of hillsides for agriculture seems to have begun during the Palo Blanco phase in the Tehuacán Valley and reached its peak during Venta Salada times. This makes its history broadly parallel to the hillside terrace systems of the Nochixtlán–Yanhuitlán area. Much of the terracing at Tehuacán, however, seems to accompany small Postclassic sites which may be no more than farmsteads. Near Zapotitlán, west of the valley proper, there are linear terrace systems which from the air superficially resemble the *lama–bordo* system of Yanhuitlán (Woodbury and Neely 1972:Fig. 48). Closer inspection, however, reveals that these are mostly stone-bordered field systems rather than V-shaped barrancas converted to U-shaped *lama–bordo* terraces (Woodbury and Neely 1972:Fig. 50).

One could summarize the differences as follows. At Tehuacán, rulers intensified the productivity of their *cabeceras* by major works of canal irrigation, while farmsteads in the marginal "outfield" terraced their fields to reduce erosion and retain soil humidity. At Yanhuitlán, rulers intensified the productivity of their *cabeceras* by a radiating system of *lama–bordo* terraces, while farmers in the outfield diverted minor streams for small-scale irrigation. Both systems supported a state level of political organization.

## THE CUICATLÁN CAÑADA

There are about 100 km² of level or gently rolling land in the area of the Cuicatec Cañada surveyed by Hopkins (Topic 77). However, because of the low annual rainfall (under 400 mm at Cuicatlán) not all of this area is agriculturally useful. Most agriculture is confined to places where major tributaries of the Río Grande enter the Cañada, producing alluvial fans resulting in a wider, flatter valley floor that can be canal irrigated. The four major alluvial fans are those of Cuicatlán, Quiotepec, El Chilar, and Dominguillo, but there are numerous smaller fans. Because of the low elevation (500–700 m) the Cañada is totally frost-free, so irrigation makes it possible to grow two crops per year. We might best describe the area as one where agriculture is marginal-to-impossible without canal irrigation, and extraordinarily productive with it (Figure 9.9).

**Rainfall Farming**

Because of its role as the main Precolumbian corridor between Tehuacán and Oaxaca, it is assumed that the Cañada witnessed some early dry farming or barranca horticulture. However, this assumption will be difficult to prove

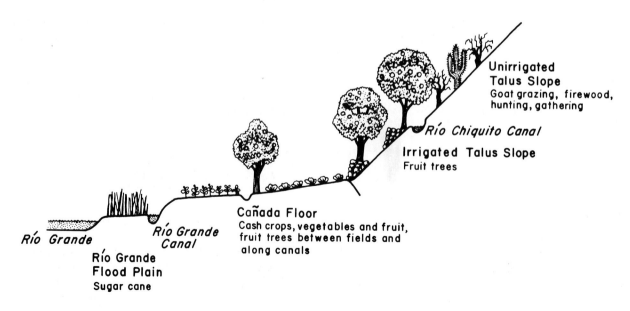

FIGURE 9.9. Environmental zonation and land use in the Cuicatlán Cañada. (Redrawn from Hopkins 1974.)

until more archaeology has been done there. The presence of an Early Formative site near San Pedro Chicozapotes (Topic 11) suggests that patches of *tierra de humedad* along the Río Grande de Cuicatlán may have been farmed as early as 1300 B.C. However, such patches are so rare that only tiny hamlets could have survived without irrigation.

### Simple Irrigation with Diversion Dams

The Formative occupants of the Cañada must have learned quite early that the best way to irrigate was to divert water from the higher tributaries of the Río Grande down onto the areas of low-lying alluvium produced by the main river. According to Hopkins, this is presently done by means of brush dams which are "constructed with teepee-like upright structures which support other brush and rocks to form the dam. These dams are reconstructed every year and gradually fill with sediment. Every year in the rainy season the dam is washed out. . . . When the water level falls a new diversion dam is constructed" (1974:203). Both the surveys by Hopkins (Topic 77) and by Spencer and Redmond (Topic 35) recovered Middle and Late Formative sites in settings where such irrigation could have been practiced, but concrete evidence (in the form of Prehispanic canals or floodwater farming terraces) is often lacking.

### Major Canal Irrigation

By Monte Albán Ic–II times, more sophisticated canal irrigation had been established in the Cuicatlán Cañada. Spencer and Redmond (Topic 35) report a large Precolumbian aqueduct that brought water down from a tributary barranca to the wide alluvium of the Río de las Vueltas, associated with the site of La Coyotera in the southern Cañada. This system seems to have been associated with a shift in settlement pattern between Periods Ia and Ic, not only at La Coyotera but elsewhere in the Cañada. The implication is that while Period Ia (and earlier) communities may have relied on a combination of *tierra de humedad* and simple diversion dams, settlements of Periods Ic and II were constructing more elaborate canal and aqueduct systems.

Obviously, this possibility raises the question of Monte Albán's role in the development of the Cañada. Was the Zapotec state responsible for this development, transferring to the Cañada many of the techniques already worked out in the Valley of Oaxaca? Or were the Zapotec attracted to the Cañada only after the local farmers had begun to increase its productivity through sophisticated canal irrigation? The evidence for a Monte Albán II subjugation of the Cañada (see Topics 29, 35) does not help us decide between these two alternatives; it merely indicates the military nature of the Zapotec frontier. The presence of the already-discussed Period Ia canal at Xoxocotlán near Monte Albán suggests that such techniques were employed at that site prior to the Period Ic–II aqueduct at La Coyotera, which could indicate a Zapotec role in the development of the Cañada—but we are still a long way from settling the issue.

Whatever the nature of Zapotec "influence" at earlier sites like Quiotepec and La Coyotera, canal irrigation in the Cañada seems to have reached its peak of development with the Postclassic Cuicatec. Hopkins (1974) discovered and partially excavated the main canal serving the Cuicatlán alluvial fan in Late Postclassic times (Figure 9.10). It drew water from the Río Chiquito, a north-bank tributary of the Río Grande, and carried it south past the Prehispanic site of Cuicatlán to an area of frost-free alluvium estimated at 134 ha (Hopkins 1974:241). Hopkins was able to trace the canal for more than a kilometer upstream to a place called Toma de los Gentiles, apparently the spot where it took off from the Río Chiquito.

> By leveling up from the highest fragment of the [Prehispanic] canal bed, I could establish roughly where the toma de agua [water takeoff] for this canal would have been. . . . One hundred and thirty meters below the estimated position of the toma de agua is a small fragment of mortar and stones. Below this another 25 to 30 meters downstream is a larger fragment, some 3 meters above the stream level and 22 meters long. This fragment had remnants of the channel bed of the canal preserved. . . . Another hundred meters downstream was another fragment, which also had the bed of the canal preserved. Leveling established that the canal bed dropped 1 meter 10 centimeters in the 100 meters. . . . This drop of 1.1 percent agrees closely with the 1.3 to 3.2 percent (with one section at 0.7 percent) reported by Woodbury and Neely for the Xiquila canal in the Tehuacán Valley. . . . The construction of the canal is also quite similar to that of the Xiquila aqueduct, except that the Cuicatlán aqueduct was constructed of rounded rocks that occur locally, while the Xiquila aqueduct was constructed of a local stone that fractured in rectangular shapes. . . . Following these fragments [of canal], I came to a point where the canyon of the Río Chiquito opened out to the main part of the Cañada. Here the canal crossed a small spur that stuck out from the cliff that forms the east side of the Cañada. . . . The canal seemed to cut a gap through the neck of this spur [Hopkins 1974:235–237].

It seems likely that similar Postclassic irrigation systems will be discovered as survey proceeds in the Cañada. There are numerous travertine springs in the region, some of which may have "fossilized" ancient canals. Hopkins (1974) reports such canals in the vicinity of Almoloyas, an important Mixtec *sujeto* of Yanhuitlán that warred occasionally with the nearby Cuicatec.

## ADAPTIVE RADIATION IN OTOMANGUEAN FARMING SYSTEMS: A RECONSTRUCTION

It is presumed that dry farming began sometime before 5000 B.C. throughout the Oaxaca–Puebla region. In its earliest stages it must have been a minor activity, perhaps confined to the "barranca horticulture" or "barranca agriculture" envisioned by MacNeish. Even at this stage, agriculture could have been spread all over the southern highlands of Mexico by judicious use of the most dependably

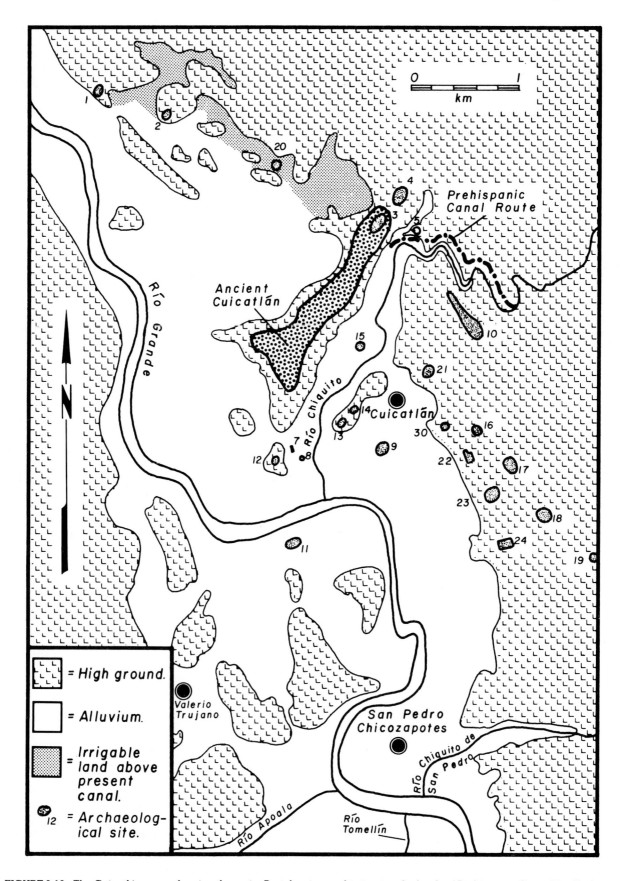

FIGURE 9.10. The Cuicatlán area, showing the major Postclassic canal irrigating the lands of Prehispanic Cuicatlán. (Redrawn from Hopkins 1974.)

humid habitats—piedmont barrancas, *tierra de humedad* along streams and rivers—however restricted in area they may have been.

The first real divergence of the four areas we have considered here came during the major expansion of agriculture in Formative times. The high water table of the Valley of Oaxaca—a product of the Atoyac River's inability to downcut the Ayoquesco gorge—made available substantial areas of humid bottomland which could be further enhanced by the simple technology of shallow well irrigation. The higher elevation of the Nochixtlán Valley was a mixed blessing, providing both greater rainfall and greater risk of frost; the strategy there was to find the 2300-m optimum zone. Neither approach was possible in the arid Cañada and the Tehuacán Valley, whose maximum development was to await more sophisticated irrigation technology.

Oaxaca was an area where dozens of small streams could be diverted with simple brush dams to provide canal or floodwater irrigation; a multiplicity of such small-scale systems arose during the Formative, none seemingly large enough to require the intervention of a centralized government. In the Tehuacán Valley, the Arroyo Lencho Diego was impounded between 750 and 600 B.C. with a dam that could have been built by a single community. By 400 B.C., a small dam and canal system had been built on the slopes of Monte Albán in the Valley of Oaxaca; still other canal-irrigation systems existed on the outskirts of the valley.

As late as 200 B.C., when the state had clearly formed in the Zapotec area (and perhaps in other parts of the Oaxaca–Puebla region as well), we still have no archaeological evidence for truly large-scale irrigation works. Indeed, they seem never to have been undertaken in the Prehispanic Valley of Oaxaca, where small-scale canals and floodwater farming systems remained the dominant strategy, and no single water source deserved valley-wide collaboration. The Tehuacán Valley was a different story: its massive resources could not be efficiently used until the state had arisen. By Palo Blanco times, the area's rulers had embarked on a series of ambitious projects such as the fourth stage of the Purrón dam, which required an estimated 4300 laborers.

It is interesting to note that the largest, most centralized, most militarily powerful state in the southern highlands—the Zapotec state centered at Monte Albán—seemingly concentrated on temples and defensive walls, leaving behind no impressive irrigation works. It extracted its tribute from thousands of small communities, each of which had its own small wells, canals, and floodwater terraces. In contrast, the somewhat smaller kingdoms of the Postclassic Mixtecs and Cuicatecs often left monumental records of their efforts to increase the productivity of their sustaining areas. The 5-km Xiquila aqueduct supported an isolated *cacicazgo* centered at Tr296. The Río Chiquito canal supported the ethnohistorically documented Cuicatec rulers. The Venta Salada phase rulers of Tehuacán apparently constructed a 25-km network of canals which turned arid tropical thorn forest into cotton plantations. And the *cacicazgo* of Postclassic Yanhuitlán turned useless V-shaped barrancas into fertile cornfields by encouraging the red clay of a long-vanished Tertiary lake to erode downslope into a series of carefully maintained stone masonry terraces. Each of these systems is beautifully adapted to the specific environmental features of one of our four regions, and would usually have been inappropriate for the other three.

If there is a lesson to be learned here, it is that very powerful states can be supported by rather simple farming techniques, and that very tiny states can produce some very impressive irrigation works. Consider the case of Zaachila, the most powerful Zapotec *cabecera* in the Late Postclassic Valley of Oaxaca. "There was no law except what [its] lord ordered"; it was supported by tribute from *estancias* "many leagues distant"; its ruins tower 20 m above the plain. A fertile plain, to be sure, but one on which the most spectacular irrigation feature anyone has ever found is a small, hand-dug well. Fortunately, the Postclassic rulers of towns like Zaachila had figured out what a state can do when its immediate environs aren't appropriate for a sophisticated irrigation system: find a neighbor who has one, get together an army, sacrifice the neighbor, and take over his land.

# TOPIC 95
## Sixteenth-Century Kinship and Social Organization

RONALD SPORES
KENT V. FLANNERY

We now address the question of the similarities and differences in kinship and social organization that might have characterized the Mixtec and Zapotec on the eve of the Conquest.

## SOCIAL STRATIFICATION

Both peoples show the same division into two broad social strata with internal subdivisions: the upper stratum was class-endogamous and largely community-exogamous, whereas the lower stratum was class-endogamous and largely community-endogamous. For the Mixtec, the upper stratum had at its apex a privileged kin group composed of the native cacique (*yaa tnuhu*), his siblings, his mate, his children, and perhaps an elderly parent; next came a more flexible contingent of supporting nobility (*tay toho*) of indeterminate, but relatively small, size. The lower stratum included the great mass of commoners (*tay yucu*) and below them a lesser number of tenant farmers, *tay situndayu*, servants, and slaves who cared for the lands and households of the ruler and high-ranking nobility. If we focus on marriage and courting patterns, ceremonial observances, income and acquisition of goods and property, freedom and servitude, and assessment of tribute and/or services, the class-endogamous strata could be divided into two (kings, lesser nobility) and three (free commoners, tenant farmer–servants, and slaves) groups, for a total of five social levels.

Zapotec society could be viewed in roughly the same way. At the time of the Conquest the royal family of Cocijoeza, along with other Zapotec lords (*coqui*) and minor nobility (*xoana*) who supported him, belonged to the upper stratum; commoners, servants and slaves made up the lower. Communities were ruled by a nobleman appointed by the king, and there were at least a few bureaucratic offices. One such office, held by a commoner appointed by the lord, was that of *golaba*, "the lord's solicitor." The *golaba*, usually an elder, seems to have been a kind of barrio head who collected tribute and corvée labor after the manner of the Aztec *tequitlato*.

Compared with the Aztec, however, neither the Mixtec nor the Zapotec had highly bureaucratic states. The sixteenth-century documents frequently state that "there was no law except what the lord ordered them to do," suggesting that his word did not pass through an elaborate hierarchy of officials, counselors, deputies, and the like. Nor was the lord elected by the elder nobility like some Aztec kings; he was born to his position, and was often prepared to fight near-relatives to defend it, or to kill near-relatives to obtain it. The Mixtec were more notorious in this regard than the Zapotec, and may have thought of themselves as more highly stratified; we have elsewhere mentioned the sixteenth-century belief that the Zapotec ruler's wife would grind her own corn, while the Mixtec ruler's wife would not. The Mixtec kingdom of Tututepec on the Pacific coast was perhaps our only example of a bureaucratized Oaxacan state, which may be because its founder, ♂ 8 Deer "Tiger Claw," drew on a Toltec model of statehood (see pp. 218–219).

## POLITICAL AND TERRITORIAL ORGANIZATION

A frequently mentioned difference among the Cloud People is the contrast between the numerous small, competing kingdoms or *cacicazgos* of the Mixteca and the larger Zapotec state. The Mixtec lords were not tied to one locality, moving from valley to valley and bringing in landless subjects to work their fields for them. The Zapotec may have been heading in this direction by the time of the Conquest, as evidenced by the shifting of the Zapotec capital from Zaachila to Tehuantepec. There remains, nonetheless, an impression of real differences in scale between the realm of Zaachila III and the average Mixtec *cacicazgo*. Considering the rise and fall of some Zapotec states, however, it may be that the Mixtec pattern of small competing kingdoms was a more resilient adaptation over long periods of time.

## ROYAL MARRIAGE

Although both the Zapotec and Mixtec used royal marriage as a means of consolidating power and arranging political and military alliances, the Mixtecs were almost unique in their frequency of marriage between closely related individuals. Dahlgren's analysis of the Prehispanic Mixtec codices lists eleven royal marriages between a male and his brother's daughter or a parallel cousin, fourteen marriages with a sister's daughter or a cross-cousin, one marriage to a half-sister, and four marriages to a full sister (Dahlgren 1954:149–151). There is no evidence to suggest marriages between comparably close relatives among the Zapotecs.

## KINSHIP TERMINOLOGY

We have already mentioned that both the Mixtec and Zapotec, like all Otomanguean groups, had a bilateral kinship system classified as "Hawaiian" in type. In Figure 9.11, Spores has attempted to reconstruct the kinship terms of the sixteenth-century Mixtecs (Reyes 1593); in Figure 9.12, Flannery has attempted to reconstruct those of the sixteenth-century Zapotecs (Córdova 1578a).[1] This task was fraught with uncertainties because the Spanish friars did not always indicate whether they had collected a descriptive term (e.g., "father") or a term of address (e.g., "Daddy"). However, we are encouraged by the strong similarities between our reconstructions and the modern Mixtec and Zapotec terms, despite four centuries of phonological change.

Our two sixteenth-century reconstructions share a significant number of features. Both Mixtec and Zapotec had three terms for siblings: "brother" (male speaking), "sister" (female speaking), and "my sibling of the opposite sex" (male or female speaking). This concept of "cross-sex sibling" (Mixtec *cuhua*, Zapotec *pizaana*) is widespread in other Otomanguean languages like Cuicatec and Chinantec, and may well be of great antiquity. Among the present day

---

[1] Since Flannery made this attempt, Whitecotton (1977:275–282) has published a similar sixteenth-century reconstruction, based in part on work by Harvey (1963). The similarities of all three schemes are more striking than the differences.

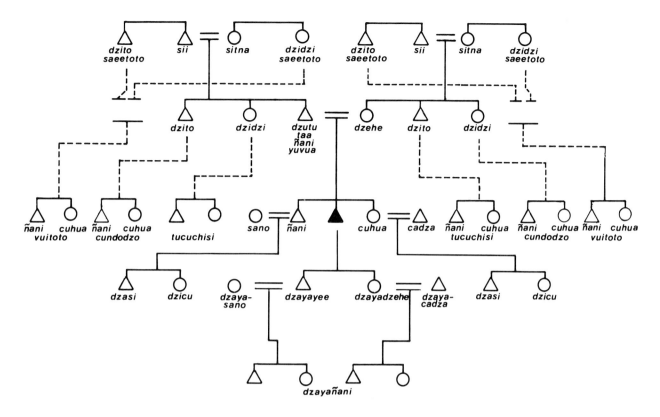

FIGURE 9.11. Reconstructed kinship terminology for the sixteenth-century Mixtecs, based on Fray Antonio de los Reyes (1593).

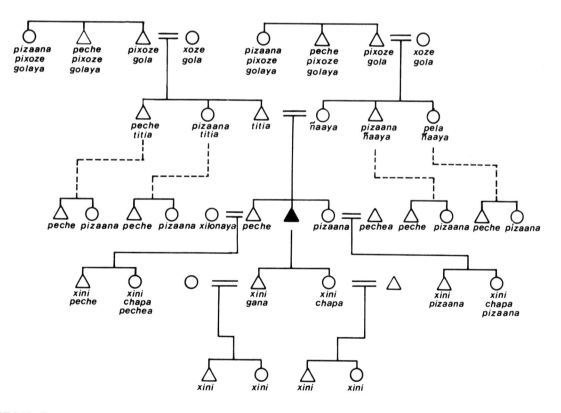

FIGURE 9.12. Reconstructed kinship terminology for the sixteenth-century Zapotecs, based on Fray Juan de Córdova (1578a).

Zapotec, *pizaana* has survived as *biza'na'* in the isthmus (Pickett 1959), *bisyana* in Mitla, and *zana?* among the Sierra Zapotec (Nader, quoted by Romney 1967).

Both Mixtec and Zapotec extended these three sibling terms to their cousins in the same generation, though the Mixtec might qualify this with an adjective. For example, a Mixtec male's first cousin, the son of his mother's brother, would be *ñanitucuchisi* (*ñani*, "brother" + *tucu*, "another" + *chisi*, "womb"). Both peoples addressed their grandparents as "old father" and "old mother" (Mixtec *taatnanu* = *taa*, "father" + *tna'nu*, "old"; Zapotec *pixozegola* = *pixoze*, "father" + *gola*, "old"). The latter expression has persisted in the isthmus as *bixhoze gola* (Pickett 1959) and in the Zapotec Sierra as *š oʷza? gul* (Nader, quoted by Romney 1967). Another similarity is the emphasis placed on birth order, both in the abstract and with regard to the person speaking. Among Mixtec brothers, first born, older, younger, and youngest could be distinguished by separate terms. Among the Zapotec there were terms for the birth order of sons from "first born" through at least "eighth born," and for daughters from "first born" through at least "sixth born."

There are a few differences between the two kinship systems that may be of evolutionary significance. The Zapotec referred to both son and daughter by the word *xini*, "child." When it was necessary to distinguish sex they used a modifier, for example, *xini gana*, "male child" or *xini chapa*, "female child"; these terms have persisted in the isthmus as *xiiñi' gaana* and *xiiñi' dxaapa'* respectively (Pickett 1959). The term *xini* was extended to all nieces and nephews in the same generation, a modifier being used only when it was necessary to specify a relationship (e.g., *xini pechea*, "my brother's child [male speaking]").

The Mixtecs also used one word, *dza'ya*, for their offspring, adding a modifier to specify whether the child was male (*dzayayee*) or female (*dzayadzehe*). In contrast to the Zapotec, however, they referred to their nephews and nieces by separate terms, *dzasi* and *dzicu* respectively. This dichotomy between one's own children and one's siblings' children—coupled with the previously mentioned modifiers used to distinguish between one's siblings and one's cousins—might be a reflection of the distinctive Mixtec sociopolitical system, in which direct descent seems to have been afforded much more importance than among the Zapotec. On the other hand, since Cuicatec and Trique share the same distinction between direct and collateral relatives in first ascending and first descending generations (Romney 1967:213), the dichotomy might go back even further than the origins of the Mixtec state.

As for the Zapotec system, with its extension of sibling terms to consanguineal–collateral relatives in all generations, Romney speculates that it may reflect a family organization characterized by loose bilateral extensions, producing a situation in which ego's parents are the only relatives that require differentiation. "During the age of socialization, all other relatives are roughly equivalent, e.g., those who are around the compound but do not have authority over ego" (Romney 1967:217). This could be a product of the period when the Zapotec began to live together in extended families, as in the 10–20 person "elaborate residences" Blanton reports at Monte Albán (Topic 39). Because it is shared by the Chinantec, however (Romney 1967:215), it could be a legacy of even more ancient times.

# TOPIC 96
## Mixtec Religion

RONALD SPORES

Mixtec formal religion centered on worshipful recognition of the forces and features of nature: life ("spirit of life" or "heart": *yni* or *ini*), death, and life hereafter. These universal forces, elements, events, and relationships were personified as spiritual things (*sasi ñuhu*) or deities (*ñuhu*). They were often represented as images (*naa ñuhu*), somewhat indiscriminately classed as *ídolos* by Spaniards (Avendaño 1579; Eras 1579; Pacho 1581; RMEH 1:174–178; RMEH 2:131–163; AGN Inquisición 37; Burgoa 1674, passim; Alvarado 1593, passim; AJT, leg. 34, exp. 1). They received such designations as *Cuaquisiqhi, Taadozo* (associated with warfare, the sun, and human sacrifice), and *Yocosituayuta* (associated with fertility and offerings of rich plumage and incense) at Juxtlahuaca–Tecomaxtlahuaca (RMEH 2:135–142); *Xiton* (associated with merchants), *Zaaguy* or *Zavui* (literally, "rain"), *Tizones* ("*corazón del pueblo*"), and *Toyna* [*Toyni?*] at Yanhuitlán (AGN, Inquisición 37); *Yaguinzi* ("aire," "wind" or "air") and *Yanacuu* ("lizard") at Tejupan (Avendaño 1579:55); and *Qhyosayo* ("deity") at Tilantongo (Eras 1579:73). There were numerous *Nubuy* ("deities") at Mitlantongo, but "the deity held in highest esteem was the sun [*el sol*]" (Eras 1579:78–79).

Most information on religion has to do with identification of activity areas; names and some of the attributes of spiritual forces and beings and their representative images; types of observances, passage rites, offerings, and sacrifices; treatment of the dead; accounts of some of the activities of the priests; and the social and ideological position of formal cult activities and practitioners (Herrera 1947:Dec. 3, lib. 3, caps. 12–13; AGN, Inquisición 37; Jiménez Moreno y Mateos Higuera 1940; Caso 1946; Spores 1965, 1967).

## SACRED PLACES

Temples, hermitages, and shrines were the primary loci of religious activity and were situated in civic centers, in subject communities, or in special ritually significant areas outside the population centers—in caves, along rivers, on rocky promontories, on mountaintops, or in abandoned settlements. Burgoa (1674, vol. 1:276) indicates that the temple (*huahi ñuhu*) containing the "idols" of the community of Achiutla was located on the west side of the *cabecera*, and that situated there was the "oracle" whom the natives consulted concerning their affairs, and to whom they directed their sacrifices. It is said that the *demonio* was held in such esteem that people came from distant provinces to ask favors and seek aid and direction in their activities from the son of a great "false" priest (*naha niñe*) of the pueblo. Even after the natives were baptized into Christianity, the caciques and *principales* continued to respect the traditional practitioner.

The Mixtecs are also said to have maintained an elaborate adoratory 4 leagues from Tilantongo in the middle of the spacious valley of Yanhuitlán. The shrine, located in a capacious cave under some hills, contained an idol that was attended by another priest acting as a patriarch "recognized by the other [priest of Achiutla]" (Burgoa 1674, vol. 1:277). Sacrifices were offered to this idol by those who were most remote, the incapacitated, and women who could not ascend the rugged mountains of Achiutla. Burgoa mentions the shrines of Achiutla and the Yanhuitlán Valley with reference to the important kingdom of Tilantongo, and states that the court of the lords and rulers of Tilantongo was advantageously situated halfway between the two important temple–sacrificial places.

Burgoa's account, the codices (e.g., Caso 1949, 1960), and other documents indicate that Tilantongo was a very important political center, but the two most important religious centers must have been in Achiutla and Yucuita (based on Burgoa, on testimony in AGN Inquisición 37, and on archaeological survey). Other localities frequently mentioned in the documents as important religious centers are Apoala and Sosola on the eastern edge of the Mixteca Alta.

Although there were important social and political ties between Tilantongo, Achiutla, and Yanhuitlán (which controlled the subject community of Yucuita), there is no indication that these religious centers came under the political control of Tilantongo. In fact, it appears that the three kingdoms were independent, albeit interrelated, polities. It is clear from Burgoa's account that these religious centers drew populations from all across the Mixteca (Burgoa 1674, vol. 1:278). The sacred caves, springs, peaks, groves, and unusual natural features associated with the supernatural realm had a great attraction for the Mixtecs and served as vital foci of social integration.

## PRACTITIONERS

As discussed in Topic 70, religious activities were directed by professional practitioners (*naha niñe; tay saque*) who were under the direct control and custody of the native rulers. Religious activities included fixed and movable feasts in and around ritual centers, prognostication, marriages, funerals and postfunerary observances, fertility rites in fields, and the training of boys and young men for priestly functions.

Boys, drawn from both social strata (e.g., Yanhuitlán) or only from the aristocracy (Tecomaxtlahuaca), normally entered training for priestly functions at around 7 years of age. Once an individual entered formal training, he was subject to a variety of requirements and restrictions: observance of rigorous ritual formulary, fasting, sexual abstinence, penance, isolation, and maintenance of cult centers and ritual paraphernalia.

After 4 years of training (Herrera 1947:Dec. 3, lib. 3, cap. 13), the practitioner went into the service of a particular native ruler, performing the rituals and recitations associated with priestly status, and continued these activities for an imprecisely stated period of time. Functions included dancing, singing, recitation, trance, receiving and presenting offerings (copal, dogs, doves, quail, feathers, precious stones, prepared foods, pulque, and clothing), performing marriages, baptizing (at 7 years), telling fortunes, reading omens, sacrificing animals and men, and performing autosacrifice. Fasting, penance, and sexual abstinence were also required.

## THE CALENDAR

Burgoa (1674, vol. 1:289) states that there were astronomers among the Mixtecs who possessed great knowledge of the stars, and thus were able to compute the years. Astronomers came from special "lineages" and were trained from boyhood. They learned the names of all of the days of the year and indicated each day with a separate sign. Their year consisted of 18 months of 20 days and another month of 5 days. Every 4 years the additional month contained 6 days in order to account for the 6 hours gained every year in the 365-day calendar. This 6-day month was known as the "useless month" (*mes menguado errático*).

The calendar-round period of 52 years was considered the ideal life span. The 52-year cycle was divided into four components of 13 years each, and each component was associated with one of the four directions. The fortunes of life and the seasons were in conformity with the 13-year periods and their corresponding directions. Years pertaining to the east were productive and healthy; those associated with the north were variable; those associated with the west were good for reproduction (*la generación*) and multiplication of mankind, but poor (*remisos*) for fruits of the land; years related to the south were associated with misfortune, particularly excessive heat and drought. Burgoa observed that since ancient times the natives had noticed that famine, pestilence, and war had been associated with the 13 years of the south. In their paintings, the time of the years of the south was depicted as a fire-breathing dragon (presumably, although it is not stated, similar pictographic devices were employed to depict the other 13-year components). When the 13 years of the south had passed, a new age began in the east. The new year "invariably began on March 13" because of the proximity of the equinox.

## COSMOGONY, ETHICS, AND SOCIAL ORDER

Information on the conceptual content of Mixtec religion is limited, but consultation of documents and linguistic study do reveal at least some aspects of Mixtec cosmology. The universe was mechanistically perceived, and associated with ancestors, nature, the present, and the future—a force field to be revered, honored, and influenced for the benefit of mankind. The afterlife, the sky, wind, water, the abode of the dead, clouds, lightning, thunder, fire, heat and cold, fertility, abundance, replenishment, renewal, birth, youth, age, and the continuity of life all figured prominently in Mixtec religion. Cosmogony, in the epistemic sense, was simple and embedded in history, legend, and the social charter of Mixtec peoples. It was believed that people emerged in antiquity from a world already in existence and functioning as a natural place. Little detail of what must have been complex philosophical conceptualizations has emerged from the documentation. Objects and acts of sacrifice, offering, burial, and curing are described repetitiously, but little of the conceptual background was taken down. Alas, there was no Sahagún for the Mixtecs.

Insofar as we can penetrate the Mixtec mind from available documentation, the universe existed in the past and continued to exist in the present; we can find no mention of the sequent creation, destruction, re-creation of the earth and its elements as conceptualized elsewhere in central Mexico. The Mixtec people were variably regarded to have sprung from the earth or to have originated elsewhere. But there seems (again, it is difficult to say what may have been left out of the documentation or native pictographic manuscripts) to have been little concern for elaboration upon the origins or nature of the universe, or of man. The earth exists, man exists, and further explanation was unnecessary. Accepting the world as it was, man was obliged to maintain the balance among men, nature, and the supernatural world through conscious acts of private and social ritual. The following are typical religious observances in the Mixteca.

The *relación* of Peñoles states that

> during the wet season a sizeable stream flows from the mouth of a cave. In ancient times the indigenous people were accustomed to making sacrifices in this cave, and the natives say that other people came to this cave to consult the *demonio* and to request that water be provided in times of need [RMEH 2:185–191].

Elsewhere, we read that

> in the time of their infidelity, the lord and the natives [of Guautla] had their deities and worshipped stone and wooden figures, and they sacrificed to these, removing blood from the ears and tongue, and they offered parrot feathers, quail, and other birds [*Relación de Guautla*].

In Xaltepetongo the natives worshipped stone and wooden idols covered with red mantles, practiced autosacrifice, held dances to the sound of flutes and other instruments, and held *borracheras* with pulque (Bernal 1962). At Teozacoalco, the natives worshipped the *demonio* and offered blood from the ears and tongues of humans, hearts of human sacrificial victims, and dogs, turkeys, and all manner of wild game. In Tamazola, adorations and rites were held in honor of the *demonio* and stone and wooden figures, "which they respected as their lords and gods," and

> they gave their priests copal to burn and turkeys and dogs in order that they be sacrificed to their idols . . . and they said that they kept their idols in the highest ramparts (*peñas*) in their hermitages and that they sacrificed adults and youths, slaying them alive and removing the heart and giving it to the priest for offering [Eras 1579:84].

Similar accounts are repeated for numerous other communities in the Mixteca as well as for Zapotec towns, the Spaniards' interpretations of the practices, observances, and concepts differing insubstantially from community to community and from one Oaxacan ethnic group to another (RMEH 1:174–178; RMEH 2:135–146, 159–163; Avendaño 1579; Eras 1579; Pacho 1581; AGN, Inquisición 37; Burgoa 1674, passim; Herrera 1947:Dec. 3, lib. 3, caps. 12–13; Jiménez Moreno and Mateos Higuera 1940; Dahlgren 1954; Spores 1965; Spores 1967:22–27). A statement from the 1580 *relación* of Zapotec Tecuicuilco could as easily come from any Mixtec community:

> All of the natives of these communities worshipped the *demonio* in the form of a statue made of wood and stones which they called deities. They had many of them designated by different names, some for health, and others for good weather, and others for the rains and for the women for childbirth and, finally, they had a deity to remedy all human needs; each pueblo, however, had a deity as its *patrón* which it revered above all the rest and thus there was in this pueblo of Tecuicuilco a deity that in their language they called *Coquebezelao*, which is to say chief of the demons (*Principal de los diablos*) [RMEH 2:125].

Atepec, Zoquiapa, and Xaltianguis, all subject to Tecuicuilco, are said to have had their own deities, despite the fact that they were politically bound to Tecuicuilco.

Ethics seem to have played a relatively insignificant role in Mixtec religion. The behavioral "models" of social interaction among supernatural beings such as described for the Aztecs (Sahagún: Florentine Codex) are missing in the accounts of Mixtec religion. Mixtec society was stratified, but there is no suggestion of a corresponding hierarchical principle in the supernatural universe. Deities and the forces of nature and the supernatural realm are individualistic and complementary, rather than hierarchically ordered: the deity (or force or element) of rain, of the community, of fertility, of the air, of the planets, of warfare, of merchants, of childbirth. The universe is organized into contrastive categories of existence, activities, and forces rather than being arranged incrementally or hierarchically as might be expected in a highly stratified society. Further, with the exception of the priests, whose behavior was quite circumscribed by rules of conduct and procedure, there is no indication of super-

naturally derived social controls or guides to human activity. Conduct was guided by social custom rather than by religious precept and thus it appears to have been until the arrival of Christianity in the Mixteca.

# TOPIC 97
## Zapotec Religion

JOYCE MARCUS

Spores (Topic 96) has described sixteenth-century Mixtec religion in terms of topics such as cosmogony, calendrics, religious practitioners, rituals, and sacred places. While I will organize my discussion of sixteenth-century Zapotec religion somewhat differently, I will touch on many of the same topics in order to provide a basis for comparison and contrast. I will, however, omit Zapotec calendrics because they are covered in Topic 23.

To begin with, we can characterize Zapotec religion as animatistic (Lowie 1924b:133–134), because it attributed life to many things we consider inanimate. This fact has sometimes been overlooked because of the unwarranted assumption that animatism could not be characteristic of a religion of "states" or "civilizations"; such "high cultures" are supposed to have a complex pantheon of gods or, occasionally, monotheism. While I would not describe the Zapotecs as monotheistic, they did recognize a supreme being who was without beginning or end, "who created everything but was not himself created," but he was so infinite and incorporeal that no images were ever made of him and no mortal came in direct contact with him (Flannery and Marcus 1976b). This supreme being had, in turn, created a series of powerful supernatural forces including lightning, sun, earthquake, fire, and clouds, which interacted with the Zapotecs but cannot be considered the equivalent of a Greco-Roman pantheon (Marcus 1978).

An important aspect of Zapotec religion was ancestor worship, especially the veneration of royal ancestors. This practice was widely misunderstood by the sixteenth-century Spaniards, who usually mistook the images of venerated, deceased rulers for the "idols" of "gods." Since the venerated rulers varied from town to town, the Spaniards wound up with dozens of "gods" (see following discussion), giving rise to the notion of an extensive anthropomorphized Zapotec pantheon. Such misconceptions pervade even the best accounts of Zapotec religion, including those of Fray Juan de Córdova (1578a, 1578b), Francisco de Burgoa (1670, 1674), Gonzalo de Balsalobre (1656), and the *Relaciones Geográficas* of 1579–1581 (del Paso y Troncoso 1905–1906).

## NATURAL AND SUPERNATURAL FORCES

In Topic 9, we discussed the fact that both Zapotecs and Mixtecs had the concept of a vital force that distinguished living from nonliving matter. For the Zapotecs it was *pèe,* "wind," "breath," or "spirit"; for the Mixtecs it was *yni* or *ini,* "spirit," "heart," or "heat." Similar concepts were known in other Mesoamerican cultures—for example, the Aztec *tona,* "vital energy," "heat" (González Torres 1977), and the Maya *ik,* "wind," "breath," or "life" (Marcus 1978).

To the Zapotecs, anything without *pèe* was inanimate and could be manipulated by technology, such as the variables of land and water discussed by Flannery in his synthesis of Oaxacan farming systems (Topic 94). Anything that moved had *pèe* and was therefore alive, to some degree sacred, and deserving of respect; it could not simply be manipulated, but had to be approached through ritual and reciprocity. Many "living" things had names that began with a *pe* or *pi* sound, reflecting their possession of the vital force. Examples include animals (*pichina,* deer; *picija,* eagle), men (*peni*), the 260-day ritual calendar (*pije, piye*), the moon (*peo*), light (*pianij*), and the effervescent foam on a cup of stirred hot chocolate (*pichijna*). Such phenomena as clouds (*zaa*), earthquakes (*xoo*), and lightning (*cocijo*) were also conceived of as living supernatural forces.

The difficulty in translating Zapotec cosmological terms becomes apparent when we consider the augmentative form of *pèe: pitào,* "great breath," "great spirit." For the sixteenth-century Spaniards, this term came to be translated as "god," and in their teachings and conversions they used the expression *Pitào Dios* to indicate the Christian deity (Córdova 1578a). *Pitào* had never referred to a specific deity, but rather to the great and sacred life force within lightning or a supernatural being; as Cruz pointed out (1946:45), it came to take on a meaning for the Spaniards that it had never had for the Zapotec, and this has colored our whole view of Zapotec religion. It seemed reasonable to the Spaniards because the Zapotec used it to refer to the stone statues (*pitào quie*) or wooden statues (*pitào yaga*) they kept in some temples, which the Spaniards took to be the "idols" of "gods." We will see in a later section, however, that many of these were the images of venerated royal ancestors; others were representations of great supernatural forces such as earthquakes and lightning, which were represented by combining aspects of different animals that would never have occurred together in nature (Marcus 1978).

A similar error was made by the Spaniards with the Mixtec term *ñuhu*, "divine," "sacred" (Alvarado 1593; Burgoa 1674; see Spores, Topic 96). According to Spores, Mixtec formal religion centered on the worshipful recognition of life forces, and such universal forces and elements were considered *ñuhu;* the term was used to convert "house" (*huahi*) to "temple" (*huahi ñuhu*), much as the Zapotec used *pèe* to change "house" (*yoho*) into "temple" (*yoho pèe*). The statues in Mixtec temples, *naa ñuhu*, were also viewed by the Spaniards as the idols of gods, leading to some sixteenth-century translations of *ñuhu* as "deity." Clearly, it was difficult for the Spaniards to realize that they were dealing with people whose world was filled with a greater variety of supernatural forces than theirs, but who had no word or concept of "god" in the European sense.

## Lightning

Lightning was perhaps the most powerful supernatural with which the Zapotecs dealt. The lightning bolt itself was *cocijo,* and thunder was *xoo cocijo,* "motion (earthquake) of lightning." When the Zapotec addressed the "great spirit" of which the lightning was a visible manifestation, however, they used the term *Pitào cocijo,* leading to the sixteenth-century Spanish notion of a Zapotec "god of rain." Lightning did have the power to cause rain (by splitting the clouds to release it) or withhold rain, but it is stretching the point to consider *cocijo* a "rain god" analogous to the Nahuatl *Tlaloc.* Lightning figured in the Zapotec ritual calendar, which we have seen (in Topic 23) was divided into four *cocijo,* and there are numerous other contexts in which four lightnings occupied the Zapotec cosmos. Offerings made to the various lightnings, either to express gratitude or to ask for some concession, included food and drink, one's own blood, or a sacrificed quail, turkey, dog, child, slave, or captive taken in war.

As recently as 35 years ago, Cruz (1946:33–35) was still able to collect Zapotec stories about lightning, such as the following:

FIGURE 9.13. Zapotec effigy vessel depicting Cocijo with four jars attached to him, possibly for clouds, rain, hail, and wind. Height of piece: 15 cm. (Drawn from a photo in Caso and Bernal 1952: Figure 54.)

On the summit of a mountain, long before the dawn of the world, lived Cocijoguí, the Old Lightning of Fire. He was the lord of all the "lightnings," large and small. At the foot of his dazzling throne he had in his custody four immense clay jars. In one, he kept the clouds shut up; in another, water (rain); in the third, hail; and in the fourth, wind. In turn, each one of these jars was watched over by a lesser lightning in the form of a *chintete* or small lizard. (There are Classic Zapotec vessels that may depict Cocijo with four jars attached to him; see Figure 9.13.)

In order to prove his power, Cocijoguí commanded the *chintete* Cocijozaa, the one in charge of the clouds, to uncover his jar and let them go free. A column of vapor was lifted to the skies and rapidly invaded the starry spaces. On earth, men stood marveling at the grandiose spectacle. The lesser lightning Cocijozaa meanwhile frolicked among the volutes of the great cloud mass, and his every movement was a lightning flash that at times vanished in the darkness of the night.

But men were thirsty, and raised their prayers to the Old Lightning of Fire in order to calm him. Cocijoguí ordered the second *chintete*, Cocijoniza, to open his jar. The waters came out of it and mounted on top of the clouds; they filled the terrestrial environment, and it began to rain. The rain lasted many days, until the men and the rest of these beings that were living with them began to be afraid. All the time this was happening, the lesser lightning Cocijoniza was enjoying himself making pirouettes in the skies, and each pirouette was a lightning flash that illuminated the world.

A chorus of voices was lifted up to the throne of Cocijoguí; the women asked him to order the other jar to be uncovered. The Old Lightning smiled maliciously, and at first did not want to satisfy the women's curiosity, but finally, proud of his power, he gave in. The third *chintete*, at the instruction of his master, let the hail escape from the other large earthen jar. Rough particles of ice, cold and stinging, fell on the terrified earth. The lesser lightnings illuminated the sky with their continuous flashes, and with their thunder they shook all space, while the storm of water and hail seemed to indicate the end of the world and the death of all its beings.

Men and women, beasts and birds, then terrified, took refuge in the steep rocks of the Cordillera, entreating the Old Lightning to calm the storm. But Cocijoguí did not listen to the public prayers of the world. Men and women, beasts and birds, then invoked Pitào, the Great Spirit.

Suddenly, toward the east the black curtain of clouds opened. A light illuminated the horizon, and the resplendent disk of the sun, Gobicha, appeared. Cocijoguí, who had indifferently contemplated the tempest and taken pleasure in his powers until then, felt a strange celestial fear in his heart. He recognized the importance of Gobicha and ordered the last *chintete* to open his jar and free the wind, in order to drive away the storm. Cocijopí obeyed, tearing into the heart of the clouds with a formidable wind, dazzling lightning, and gigantic thunder, calling upon his brothers to return submissive and obedient to their refuge on the summit of a high mountain.

And the Old Lightning of Fire, in order to render homage to the sun—compassionate, just, and good—stretched out on space a beautiful and multicolored bridge, whose bases were rooted in the heart of the earth. Thus the rainbow was born, a serpent adorned with feathers of the quetzal bird (Zapotec Pelaquetza, "quetzal serpent"), enemy of the storm, drinker of the rain, and since that day friend and protector of all beings.

While this story may include a great deal of acculturation (both from Nahua and Spanish sources), it tells us something about the celestial hierarchy. Under Old Lightning of Fire were the subordinate lightnings Cocijozaa (in charge of clouds), Cocijoniza (in charge of water), a *cocijo* in charge of hail, and Cocijopí (in charge of wind). When Cocijoguí would not respond to the entreaties of the people, they turned to the Great Spirit, or Pitào, who gave him life. We also learn about a beneficent being—the sun, Gobicha—and the rainbow Pelaquetza. We learn that Lightning resided on the summit of a mountain, and that the four lesser *cocijo* each had specific obligations. Given their power, it is not surprising that at least two sixteenth-century Zapotec rulers—Cocijoeza and Cocijopii—would have *cocijo* or lightning as part of their names.

The same reverence for lightning is clear in other ethnographic sources. E. C. Parsons (1936:211) reports a folk tale of two *compadres* who visited Lightning in his cave in the mountains; Lightning presented two corn maidens to them, and as a result of their choices the crops of the knowing *compadre* yielded only weeds. In another tale, obviously acculturated, Lightning is reported to have dropped grains of different colors of corn into the sacks of San Isidro, and thus created the different-colored ears of corn. The Cave of Lightning (Biliyär Gusi?), in the Dan Ro? mountains north of Mitla, was where offerings were made; when people ceased visiting the cave, drought and poor crops resulted. Before planting, a Mitla farmer would put down in the middle of his field a miniature tortilla for Lightning. In addition, according to Parsons,

> The stone in the strike-a-light, the hummingbird, and especially the lizard are associated with Lightning: the fire-making stone is called Lightning's stone; the hummingbird revives at first lightning; Lightning embodies himself as a lizard. When Lightning stays on earth as a lizard he re-ascends into the sky through fire; the lizard is placed in a little gourd of water which is thrown into a fire. If the gourd contains salt and if the fire is very hot, the lizard will be killed [1936:212; copyright 1936 by the University of Chicago Press].

## Clouds

Clouds (*zaa*) were important to the Zapotec, not only because of their relationship with lightning and rain, but also because they were regarded as the beings from which the Zapotec (Peni-Zaa, "cloud people") had descended, and to which their ancestors (*penigolazaa*, "old people of the clouds") would return after death. Providing one took care to honor his ancestors after death, the *penigolazaa* could intercede on one's behalf with lightning and the other supernaturals.

Even today a kind of veneration of the ancestors continues among the Zapotec. At Juchitán and other nearby isthmus localities there are important stories about the old people of the clouds (*binigulaza, binnigola, binizaa*). When figurines or other Precolumbian household objects are recovered, the contemporary Zapotecs say they have found objects that belonged to the ancestors, or say "we are the descendants of the *binizaa* who provided these" (Henestrosa 1936; Cruz 1936).

The *binigulaza* were men of great stature, and some say they were of gigantic size; they were magicians, doctors, and diviners and they knew how to read the caprices of the future in the starry skies. These ancestors were also the first to calm the ire of the beings causing calamities by offering penitence or sacrifices. The *binigulaza* knew mysterious beverages that they gave the dead (Cruz 1936).

## ROYAL ANCESTOR WORSHIP

Our discussion of the *penigolazaa* leads directly into the topic of royal ancestor worship, which was poorly understood by the Spaniards. The ancestors of royalty were even more important than those of common men, and they were often commemorated and sacrificed to as divine beings (Flannery and Marcus 1976b:381); frequently, temples or commemorative buildings were built above their tombs. We have suggested that the Spaniards often mistook the images of these ancestors as idols of gods; clues to this can be found in the names they collected for these deities, which frequently contain garbled versions of *coqui* ("male ruler"), *coquihualao* ("prince"), or *xonaxi* ("female ruler"). A second clue is that many have names taken from the 260-day ritual calendar, which we know from Córdova (1578b:16) and Burgoa (1674: Chapter 70, 316) were names given to human beings. A third clue is that the names of these personages vary tremendously from town to town and from period to period, which would not have been the case if they were Zapotec gods, members of a pantheon.

For example, the occupants of Taliztaca (now Tlalixtac de Cabrera, in the Tlacolula region) are said to have sacrificed children, adults, quail and quail feathers, parrot feathers, and little dogs to an idol named Coqui Huani (del Río 1580:179). At Macuilsuchil (now Macuilxochitl, only 13 km from Tlalixtac), villagers offered blood from their tongues and ears to an idol called Coquebila, presumably Coqui Bila (Asensio 1580a:101). At Tlacolula, only 10 km from Macuilxochitl, the villagers sacrificed dogs, turkeys, and people to an idol called Coqui Cehuiyo (Canseco 1580:145). In Mitla, only 13 km from Tlacolula, there was a male–female pair of idols called ♂ Coqui Bezelao[1] and ♀

Xonaxi Quecuya, to whom the occupants sacrificed children, adults, little dogs, turkeys, quail, and doves (Canseco 1580:149). Coatlán also had a male–female pair to whom dogs, turkeys, quail, and war captives were sacrificed (Espíndola 1580:134); their names are given (and roughly translated) by Espíndola as ♂ Benelaba, "7 Rabbit," and ♀ Xonaxi Belachina, "3 Deer."

It seems unlikely to me that all these personages were gods, or that so many towns in so small an area had such different gods. It seems particularly unlikely that personages with calendric names, especially male–female pairs with titles like Coqui and Xonaxi, were gods. It is more likely that what the Spaniards saw were the stone or wooden images of deceased rulers of those communities, who were honored as semidivine and sacrificed to in their roles as interceders with the supernatural.

Nowhere is this practice more clearly portrayed than in the *relación* from Ocelotepec (Espíndola 1580), a town in the mountainous region near Miahuatlán. Ocelotepec was another place where the nobility made sacrifices to a deity named Bezalao, drawing blood from their ears, noses, tongues, "and other members" with very fine (obsidian?) blades, and offering it "through the hands of the *bigaña*" (young priests), who "never left the temple." They are said to have had a god of war whom they painted as being very fierce, with bow and arrow in hand, but his name, Cozichacozee, sounds like a corruption of Cocijococii, which could be the name of a deceased ruler (cf. Cocijopii).

The ruler of Ocelotepec was Petela, renowned in legend as the member of a generation of men who had escaped a deluge like the one mentioned in Cruz's story of the Old Lightning of Fire. When he died after a rule of 10 to 12 years, the Zapotec "commemorated him as a god, for having come from that [line of] people, and they sacrificed to him as to a god" (Espíndola 1580:139). The Spanish vicar Bartolomé de Piza searched for and found Petela's remains "buried dry and embalmed, laid out in such a manner that all the bones were in place; he [de Piza] burned them publicly" to end such heathen practices.

Six months later, Ocelotepec was hit by a plague in which more than 1200 persons died. Immediately the Zapotec nobles "went back to making sacrifices to Petela over the ashes of the bones which de Piza had burned, for he [Petela] was an interceder with Bezalao, who they wanted to call off the plague." The nobles were jailed by the Spaniards for this offense (Espíndola 1580:140).

This *relación* makes it clear why we should be wary of the endless lists of Zapotec deities given to us by the sixteenth-century Spaniards. Bezalao may have been a legitimate su-

---

[1]This name appears in several *relaciones* as Bezalao (Ocelotepec), Beçaloo (Huitzo), or Bezelao (Mitla), usually translated as "the devil" or "Satan"; it appears in Córdova's dictionary as *Pezelào* or *Pezèelào*, "demonio" (Córdova 1578a:117). While such translations may represent sixteenth-century wishful thinking by concerned priests, this particular name is too widespread to be simply that of some venerated local ruler. If the etymology were clearer, it might be possible to explain this "lord of the afterlife" more clearly. The *pe* or *be* phoneme presumably refers to the life force; it is not clear whether *lào* in this context is an augmentative, or refers to sixteenth-century *lào*, "face." *Pezèelào* therefore remains untranslated.

pernatural, although even in this case I am not convinced we know exactly how he was envisioned. Petela, however, was clearly a deified royal ancestor, and the same is probably true of Cozichacozee, Xonaxi Belachina, Coqui Huani, and many of their contemporaries.

## THE "DEITY LISTS" OF CÓRDOVA AND BALSALOBRE

I have elsewhere maintained that the Zapotec did not have a vast, anthropomorphized, Greco-Roman style pantheon of gods (Marcus 1978). Nevertheless, there are in the literature several lists of Zapotec deities, the most notable of which are those of Fray Juan de Córdova (1578a) and Gonzalo de Balsalobre (1656). Both lists must be accounted for in any general model of Zapotec religion. Were these all gods, and if not, how many gods did the Zapotec have? I will attempt to deal with this question in light of the earlier sections of this topic.

Córdova (1578a) believed that the term *pitào* meant "god," and he accordingly listed some 24 gods, including Pitào Cocijo ("the god of rain"), Pitào Xoo ("the god of earthquakes"), Pitào Cozobi ("the god of harvests"), and Pitào Pijzi ("the god of divination"). I suspect that what we are dealing with here is the Zapotec way of addressing the life force within these phenomena, which were among the animate, supernatural forces of the Zapotec universe. For example, when a Zapotec wanted to express the idea of an abundant harvest, he used *cozobitào* ("harvest" + augmentative), but when making an offering or addressing the "breath" or "inner life" of the harvest, he uttered Pitào Cozobi; this is not the same concept as a deity who is in charge of harvests. Similarly, Pitào Cocijo was not a deity in charge of rain, but the "great spirit" or "inner life" within the lightning. Moreover, as we saw in the story collected by Cruz, there was not just one *cocijo* but several—in one case, a kind of "supreme lightning" under which there were four "lesser lightnings." Old Lightning of Fire was an important character in the story, but he was no more a god than was Old Man Coyote, who dominates so many North American Indian stories.

Significantly, none of the 24 Pitào listed by Córdova have names taken from the 260-day calendar, nor do they have titles like *coqui* or *xonaxi*. This situation is in striking contrast to the gods listed by several of the *relaciones*. I believe that Córdova actually understood Zapotec cosmology better than any writer of his time, and his list truly deals with important sacred or supernatural phenomena, although I would stop short of calling them gods.

Gonzalo de Balsalobre was the priest of Sola de Vega, a town some 80 km southwest of Oaxaca. During his 31-year stay (1634–1665) he recorded various "survivals of pagan beliefs" (Balsalobre 1656; Berlin 1957). Specifically, he elicited data from his informant Diego Luis about 13 deities that went with the 13 days of the *cocii*, a division of the 260-day calendar (see Topic 23). Two lists were obtained, one a 1635 declaration, the other a 1654 declaration. Heinrich Berlin (1957) suggests that the 1654 list of deities was more accurate, and he proposes the correct order of the 13 deities associated with each day as follows:

1. Liraaquitzino (God "13," god of all the 13 gods)
2. Licuicha Niyoa (God of Hunters)
3. Coqueelaa (God of Riches, Wealth)
4. Locucui (God of Maize, Food)
5. Leraa Huila (Devil, God of Hell)
6. Nohuichana (Goddess of River, Fish, Pregnancies, Births)
7. Lexee (God of Sorcerers, Thieves)
8. Nonachi (God of Illnesses)
9. Locio (God of Thunderbolts, or Lightning Flashes, that send the water for the cornfields)
10. Xonatzi Huilia (Woman of the Devil, to whom they sacrifice on behalf of the sick and dead)
11. Cosana (God of Ancestors, in deep water, to whom they light candles and burn copal before fishing)
12. Leraa Queche (God of Medicine)
13. Liraa Cuee (God of Medicine)

While this list is in the less-familiar Sola de Vega dialect of Zapotec, a number of points can be made. Two of the deities are feminine. None of the names appear to contain numbers between 1 and 13. *Locio* is the Sola pronunciation of *cocijo*,[1] "lightning." *Coqui* appears (in *Coqueelaa*), and *Xonatxi* is the Sola pronunciation of *Xonaxi*. None of Balsalobre's "deities" is prefaced by *Pitào*, and there is minimal overlap with the 24 deities of Córdova. Balsalobre's *Cosana* may be Córdova's Pitào Cozaana, "god of the animals," to whom sacrifices were made; Balsalobre's *Nohuichana* may be Córdova's *Pitào Huichana*,[2] "god or goddess of children." Balsalobre's *Licuicha* may correspond to Córdova's *Copijcha*, "sun" (see Berlin 1957:13). I suspect the list given by Balsalobre may represent the series of natural forces that influenced the 13 sacred numbers of the 260-day calendar, and helped to give each day its special character; whether they should really be called gods is open to debate.

## PRACTITIONERS

Among the sixteenth-century Zapotec the temple was known as *yohopèe* (literally "the house of *pèe*"). It was a two-room structure, frequently in an elevated location, and manned by full-time "priests." To the outer room came persons who wished to make an offering, but the actual sacrifice would be performed in the more sacred inner room by a

---

[1]It should be remembered that the *j* used by Córdova was a Latin *j*, so that *cocijo* would have been pronounced *co-si-yo*. The term is written *gosio* or *cosio* in several *relaciones*.

[2]Both *cozaana* and *huechaana* are given in Córdova (1578a) under the entry: "Linea colateral que sale de un linaje como decimos otra es mi linea"; *cozaana* also refers to a fertile woman who is "always giving birth."

TABLE 9.1.
Reconstruction of the Sixteenth-Century Zapotec Religious
Hierarchy[a]

| Rank | Zapotec title | Translation |
|---|---|---|
| First | *uija-tào, vuijatào* | "great seer" |
| Second | *copa pitào* | "priest" |
|  | *bigaña* | "young priest," "student priest" |
| Third | *ueza-eche, huetete* | "sacrificer" |
|  | *colanij* | "diviner" |

[a]After Burgoa (1670, 1674).

priest on an altar called *pecogo*, or *pe-quie* ("stone of *pèe*"). No layman ever entered the inner room, and the priests rarely left it (Espíndola 1580:139).

The Zapotec priesthood had a hierarchy composed of high priests (*uija-tào*), ordinary priests (*copa pitào*), lesser religious functionaries, and young men who were educated to enter the priesthood (*bigaña, pigaana, pixana;* see Table 9.1). Burgoa (1674) says that the *uija-tào* or "great seer" had as his chief function the consultation with the supernatural on important matters. This priest had the power to put himself into an ecstatic state, and believed and transmitted what he saw in his vision. The *uija-tào* was treated by the Zapotec lord with great respect and was regarded as closely connected with the supernatural; since he was the direct distributor of heavenly gifts and punishments, the lord turned to him for various needs, and is said to have followed his advice diligently (Seler 1904:248). Priests were recruited from among the children of the nobility, and there are some accounts suggesting that certain religious offices were inherited, or passed to sons or near relatives. While some priests were supposed to be chaste, Burgoa (1674) reports that at certain festivals when the high priest was forced to become intoxicated, virgins were brought to him; and if a son were then born, he ultimately succeeded to the position of high priest.

The ordinary priests were called *copa pitào* ("guardians of the great spirit"); still farther down the hierarchy were the *ueza-eche* ("sacrificers"), who constituted a specialized group. The *ueza-eche* apparently performed important sacrifices, particularly human sacrifices; after this activity, they brought the heart and blood to a higher priest, so that he could offer it to the supernatural.

Thus, the "great seer" served as a royal advisor as well as an intermediary between the ordinary priests, pupils, and commoners and the world of the supernatural. It does not appear that he performed the sacrifices himself, and in this regard the Zapotec are perhaps more similar to the Maya than to the Aztec. For the Maya, Landa (1941) lists two different positions called *(ah) nacom;* one refers to the position of "war chief" held for three years, but the other refers to a religious functionary with a lifelong obligation to perform human sacrifices, including cutting open the chest of the victim (see Marcus 1978).

Let us now turn to the students of the priesthood, called *bigaña* or *pixana.* They are the practitioners most frequently mentioned in the *relaciones,* perhaps because they had the most contact with laymen, or because the higher priests were the first to disappear after the Conquest. Their duties included the burning of incense, the offering of minor sacrifices (particularly small mammals and birds), and also the offering of their own blood drawn from the veins under the tongue and behind the ears (Burgoa 1674:Chapters 58, 64, 70).

For bloodletting, the priests employed a sharp bone or stingray spine, obsidian blade, stone knife, or a long fingernail grown especially for this purpose. The blood was caught on grass or bright feathers and then offered to sacred images. Burgoa says that human sacrifice was performed with "special solemnity and elaborate ceremonies." Córdova (1578a) adds that there were two or three occasions when human sacrifices were performed. Prisoners of war were sacrificed and the flesh (*pelapeni*) was cooked for eating. Humans were also sacrificed on the occasion of the harvest; finally, children (frequently) or adults (occasionally) were sacrificed to *cocijo.* This offering was seen as paying a debt to lightning for bringing rain, *ti quixe cocijo.*

The role of divination by the *colanij* (fortune-tellers or diviners) was also very important (Córdova 1578b:216). The *colanij* aided the individual with important decisions to be made—whom to marry, when to marry, the naming of one's children—and took the decision out of the hands of any individual. The actual decision maker was fate, whose will was determined by casting lots and by counting out beans by 2s, 3s, 4s, or 5s. The *colanij* may have been the Zapotec equivalent of the Maya *(a)hmen* (Marcus 1978:Table 1).

## RITUALS AND SACRED PLACES

The Zapotecs had sacred mountains, sacred caves, and certain cities that, like Mitla, were especially sacred. We have already mentioned the sacrifices of blood, captives, slaves, infants, mammals, birds, and feathers which were offered at the temples, and the "idols" which were curated by the *copa pitào* and *bigaña.* There were religious festivals at various times of the year, and sacred events keyed to the 260-day calendar. Some towns had a 40-day period during which they "ate only wild game" (Santamaría and Canseco 1580:34). Rituals were performed in connection with planting, harvesting, and warfare, and there were rites of penitence and deathbed confession.

Almost all *relaciones* describe ceremonies at which the Zapotec played music, danced, and engaged in drunkenness or the use of hallucinogenic plants. Pulque was a favored beverage, and tobacco was widely used. The main hallucinogens were the mushroom *Psilocybe* sp. (*peyaçoo*), the morning glory (*Rivea* sp.), and *Datura* sp. or jimson-weed (Marcus and Flannery 1978).

## ETHICS AND SOCIAL ORDER

Spores (Topic 96) has argued that among the Mixtec, "conduct was guided by social custom rather than by religious precept" and "there is no indication of supernaturally derived social controls." While the *Relación de Nexapa* (Santamaría and Canseco 1580) states that the Zapotec, from cradle to grave, were governed by "laws," with corporal punishment for lying, adultery, and fornication, there is also no suggestion that these sanctions were anything but civil. A *relación* from Huitzo (Zárate 1581) states that an adulterous wife was killed, then eaten by all present at her execution to publicize her punishment. It does not state, however, whether her death came at the hands of a *ueza-eche* or of her husband and his relatives; thus, as in the case of the Mixtec, we cannot yet state with any confidence that there were religious overtones to the punishment of human social misconduct.

## ZAPOTEC–MIXTEC COMPARISONS

The Zapotec and Mixtec religions show a number of interesting similarities. Both religions were based, as Spores has noted in Topic 96, on reverence for the forces and features of nature, life, death, the ancestors, and the hereafter. These forces were conceived of as spiritual phenomena, but it is debatable how many should be considered deities.

In Topic 9 we considered some of the important cosmological similarities of the Zapotec and Mixtec, including the concepts of *pèe* and *yni;* we noted the contrast between Zapotec *cocijo,* "lightning," and Mixtec *dzavui,* "rain," arguing that lightning might be the original Proto-Otomanguean supernatural, while rain's ascendence might show later Nahua influence.

While there may have been a hierarchy of lightnings for the Zapotec, in general I feel that Spores's observation about Mixtec religion—that there was no clear stratification of deities that approximated the stratification of human society—fits the Zapotec as well. The variety of deities recorded by the Spaniards for both Zapotec and Mixtec towns suggests a lack of standardization, which raises the question: what part of all this can be considered "state religion"? There are some clues in the role of both Mixtec and Zapotec high priests as advisors to the king, and in the year of religious training undergone by the ruler before his accession to the throne.

Parenthetically, I would add that there are two ways one can view the relationship of the ruler and the high priests. We can view the priest's political advisory role as making him a less-than-full-time religious functionary (Spores, Topic 70), or we can view him as a full-time religious functionary in a system where church and state were incompletely separated (my own view).

Zapotec and Mixtec rituals and sacred places were remarkably similar, whether from common ancestry, diffusion, or parallel evolution. The Zapotecs had their sacred cities (e.g., Mitla), the Mixtecs theirs (e.g., Achiutla, Yucuita); both had mountains, caves, and shrines which were also sacred, or where idols were kept. Ancestor worship may have been even more important for the Zapotecs than for the Mixtecs, although much more study needs to be done on this point. Both peoples used alcohol and hallucinogens in their rituals, both made extensive blood sacrifices, and in both systems the most important offerings could only be made by professional religious practitioners. Both had a sacred calendar in which units of 13 were not only important but also had supernatural associations, and both relied on divination to decide important issues.

Finally, neither Zapotec nor Mixtec religion fits the common anthropological notions of what a "state religion" should look like, such as a stratified series of gods whose social order resembles that of the men who worshipped them. That is no criticism of the Zapotec and Mixtec. Rather, it is a warning to broaden our notions about state religion.

## TOPIC 98
## Mixtec and Zapotec National Character: Some Early Views (A.D. 1580–1880)

JOHN PADDOCK

I have been presented with a virtually impossible task: to find significant differences in "national character" between the Mixtec and Zapotec at the time they were first contacted by Europeans. To make matters worse, my sources are Colonial Spanish administrators and early Mexican historians who were dedicated, but untrained, observers.

While in one sense I can say truthfully that I have no data comparing Zapotec and Mixtec personalities, that view overlooks characterizations that were often expressed by writers of the nineteenth century. A favorite device was to see the Zapotecs as typified by the Conquest-period ruler Cocijoeza, who

> prided himself on his triumph; he had achieved his desire: the Mixtecs had decimated the Aztecs [at Guiengola, and the Aztecs] had destroyed the Mixtecs. Cocijoeza was especially scornful of the Mixtecs because of their naïve simplicity, and, thinking they had been weakened to an extreme, he entered the fields and orchards of Cuilapan, taking whatever he wanted, claiming that the lands of the Valley were his [Gay 1881:I, 334].

It would be easy to cite page after page of similar materials; the Mixtecs are described as sincere, perhaps a little simple, though cautious and always warlike. The Zapotecs are described as astute, perfidious, capable of fighting when they have to but strongly preferring the ways of diplomacy. Well, perhaps. But these are only characterizations, and no analysis will be found to underlie them. They have been fabricated from a few scraps of data in Burgoa (1670, 1674) and the *relaciones,* with occasional references to the Aztec versions of some events as recounted by Durán (1867–1880) or Torquemada (1723). Carriedo (1846), Gay (1881), and Martínez Gracida (1883) are the principal authors. Both Carriedo and Gay professed their devotion to truth, and there is no reason to doubt their sincerity. But theirs was not a time of historiographic sophistication, nor did they have much in the way of data. Martínez Gracida openly confessed that, in writing of Cocijoeza and his family, he was novelizing (though of course he collected great quantities of raw data too, in other publications).

These materials cannot be dismissed with a phrase, however. Bernal, collecting local "historical" traditions in Oaxaca because so many historians have assured us of their value, found that, though the people who told him the stories sincerely believed they were ancient, in fact they came right out of the pages of the nineteenth-century Oaxacans mentioned here.

That is, these tales and "histories," consisting more of interpolations and extrapolations than of accounts based on records, have now been fed back into the streams of local oral tradition. They are affecting the self-images of modern Oaxacans—and not only in rural villages. These same unjustifiably detailed portraits and accounts are to be found daily in the newspapers of Oaxaca, in the classrooms of higher educational institutions, in the lore of the cultured. Probably they function as self-fulfilling hypotheses.

It would be grossly unjust to permit any hint of desire to mislead. Like Burgoa before them, Carriedo and Gay were men we can admire today for their morality, far more liberal and modern than was usual in their time. Their defects are plain, and innocent enough. A century ago, to be unwarlike was to be decadent; thus, even the "slyly scheming" Zapotecs (how many of them were like their rulers?) shed plenty of blood when the time came. An admiration for truth in history did not make our Oaxacans into twentieth-century historiographers, but it surely did make their work much better than it might have been and much better than that of many of their contemporaries. Nineteenth-century Oaxaca produced many admirable figures other than Juárez, and fortunately for us a number of them were historians. Since they often cite their sources, we can use them, at a minimum, as invaluable guides to the literature. Further, they were witnesses to much that is of interest, and one may have confidence in the accounts they give of what they saw.

One thing they saw was Indians—not Prehispanic ones, to be sure, but Indians much more conservative than any we know today.

The many races that populate the state, differing from each other in origin, language, habits, etc., form a heterogeneous and dis-

united body, brought together only by their beliefs. They do not have the national character, and only in a general sense may it be said that they are bellicose. The Indians are taciturn, hospitable, hard-working, sober, superstitious, docile in everything but religious matters, in which they are tenacious and stubborn; they are simple and good in their home life. Sometimes distrust and dissimulation may be seen in them. . . . In the army the Oaxaca Indian has always shown much serenity in the face of danger and heroic valor in facing it [Gay 1881:I, 28].

In the 1840s, Carriedo observed that in their holy images the Indians of the Department

seek out the one painted in the strongest colors, disfiguring the saints frightfully; in their churches there is no order or neatness. The Indian is timid, extremely distrustful, and superstitious; tireless in his work, simple and frugal; he goes to bed early, rises before dawn, and, lacking great passions, surrenders only to that of alcohol, which is his greatest pleasure . . . they are extremely strict in carrying out orders and tireless in pursuing wrongdoers; rigid in their own government, they capture the young man who has not married and deliver him to the draft; they never forget a grievance [Carriedo 1846:II, 125–126].

Ancient and modern are freely mixed in making group portraits.

The Zapotec nation was one of the most illustrious in prehispanic annals. Their kings were great and warlike, filling their histories with glorious deeds. . . . The Zapotecs may have been less rich and numerous than their [Mixtec] neighbors, but they made up for their lack of numbers and of gold with their exquisite and well calculated politics. By that means they took the Mixtec legions to throw out the Huaves of Tehuantepec, to sustain a terrible and admirable struggle against the Aztec monarch, in sum, they made the bodies of a multitude of allies serve them as a foundation on which to raise a throne of their house . . . with their shrewd politics the court of Zaachila made peace, made alliances, deceived, triumphed, and conquered. The Zapotec nation had a benign territory and its customs were less fierce than those of other nations, their laws were wiser, their rites less compulsive [Carriedo 1846:I, 115–116].

The Mixtec nation was brave and warlike; it conquered the Zapotecs many times . . . capturing even the court of Zaachila itself. It became known as great by these deeds and its name became feared. . . . The people [of Yanhuitlan] are clever, clean, reserved, and very courteous. . . . [At Tlaxiaco] the leaders in ancient times were brave and very skilled in military arts. . . . [Dzahuindanda of Achiutla], in order to start a campaign with a certain number of soldiers, used a woven *ixtle* bag he had . . . when he turned it upside down, out fell as many men as he needed, and with them in complete silence he set out to conquer whatever nation he wished [Carriedo 1846:I, 127–129].

That tenacious resistance to innovations is not open, for weakness is dominant in Indian character; nor is it all-embracing, being limited rather to certain points of general interest for their villages or which affect their social organization. The individual Indian is docile, lets himself be persuaded; it cannot be said that he is inaccessible to reason. A contrast in Indian character that has always caught the attention of observers is that, daring when together with others of his race, the Indian is soft and malleable as wax when he is alone . . . he lets himself be conquered and dominated personally . . . but struggles obstinately for the interests of his community. The private life of the Indian might be compared to a smooth current that flows without waves, not struggling with obstacles in its path or sweeping them out of the way, but rather flowing around them without commotion in order to continue its tranquil course. In Europe the peoples are agglomerations of individuals, each of whom has his own value and meaning, not lost by membership in society; in America, the Indian has no value, disappearing into the community, with which he forms a compact and united mass. Presumption, pride, and ambition, so common in the rest of the world, are unknown among the Indians. The Indian is not a degraded being, he is a man who does not think of himself but belongs wholly to his community [Gay 1881:I, 133–134].

Evidently Carriedo and Gay find it easier to speak of the Oaxaca Indians in general than of differences between the various groups, though both do some of that as well. No doubt the ethnic characterizations that still abound in our society were much more common in their day (Gay wrote around 1865–1875, Carriedo about 30 years earlier); in expressing what they do, that is, they surely were not carrying out fresh analyses from the beginning, but rather adopting—critically, we hope—a common wisdom of the time. In spite of our greater awareness of such factors, we too inevitably reflect the common wisdom of our day, and our profession, and our class.

Thus, while we may be tempted to reject entirely these ideas, it might be more productive to try making something of them. There is, perhaps, a grain of valid induction here. The contrasts between Mixtec and Zapotec leaders surely were much more complex than that of warrior versus diplomat. Cocijoeza did go to war when he had to, and among the many Mixtec leaders there must have been many different mixtures of Patton and Machiavelli. Cocijoeza was not the polar opposite of some "average Mixtec leader" reconstructed out of the many. Nevertheless, there surely were two different cultures and two different value systems involved here, and we have Spanish testimony of the sixteenth century to that effect (Salazar 1581).

In November of 1580, Fray Agustín de Salazar answered the questionnaire sent from Spain that resulted in the collection of the famous 1579–1581 *relaciones*. In Cuilapan, he said,

> The people of this town do not have their birth and origin here because they are newcomers and are known as such. Therefore the other Indians of the Zapotec region (where this town is located) are very different from these Indians in many ways. One is that these Indians are recently arrived Mixtecs. For another thing, they are more lordly in their ways, in their manners, in their dress, and in the way they treat their nobles. It appears that

a Zapotec women, even if she is noble, puts herself on a level with the plebeians by grinding [Salazar 1581:22–23].

Another *relación* of 1580, that of Chichicapa, confirms the differences: "the Mixtec Indians, who are another language and race of themselves" (Espíndola 1580:116). A native testimony to cultural difference appears in another of the same series, that of Coatlán, in which "the old natives say they did not have the custom of sacrifice until two of their nobles . . . went to the Mixteca . . . to see some nobles from there and offer their friendship, and there they had the custom of sacrifice showed them and taught them" (Espíndola 1580:134). (While this statement communicates a feeling of cultural difference, it would be well to have in mind that human sacrifice among Prehispanic Zapotecs is documented, especially perhaps in Bernal's find at San Luis Beltrán, a Monte Albán IV site, of some six or eight *cajetes* in a circle, each one containing a skull with mandible and the first two vertebrae.)

The literature of the past 50 years—that is, since the Monte Albán work began—is adorned with many statements to the effect, approximately, that the Prehispanic Zapotecs were architects, characterized by the grandness of their buildings, whereas the ancient Mixtecs were jewelers, whose distinctive taste and contribution are found in the preciosity of their small objects. These statements of course are based on comparing the architecture and planning of Period III Monte Albán with the Period V offerings of Tomb 7.

Comparing architecture with jewelry is not quite as mistaken as it would seem at first glance. Both are legitimate products of their cultures; to some extent they do express cultural aims or values, and to some extent their (sumptuary) purposes do overlap. If Mixtec architecture and Zapotec jewelry of goldworking times were added, of course, the comparison would be relatively easy. If then it turned out that architecture really were the chosen principal mode of expression of Zapotec culture, and small objects that of the Mixtec, comparison might proceed, though perhaps not very far. Such a comparison of two cultures is utterly legitimate, a device that, if cleaned up a bit as to method, might qualify as another version of Julian Steward's classification and comparison of cultures.

# Summary and Conclusions

TOPIC 99

A Synthesis of the Cultural Evolution of the Zapotec and Mixtec

JOYCE MARCUS

We do not feel that this seminar needs a lengthy summary and conclusion. Our introductions to the various chapters were designed to eliminate that need, and anyone who wants an extended summary need only skim through the volume reading those introductions.

I attempt in this topic to deal specifically with the *types* of cultural evolution we detected during the course of our survey of the archaeological sequence in Oaxaca. These were of three main kinds: (1) *general* evolution, or the ascent from one level of sociopolitical integration to another; (2) *divergent* evolution, through which the cultural differences between the ancestors of the present-day Mixtec and Zapotec grew more pronounced; and (3) *parallel* evolution—those cases in which the ancestors of the Mixtec and Zapotec seem to have evolved along similar trajectories for a period of time (without necessarily moving to a new level of integration). In the course of examining each case of divergent evolution, I usually suggest whether I feel the divergence is due to *adaptive radiation* or *nonadaptive drift*. For each major developmental period, I also suggest which aspects of Mixtec and Zapotec culture (as described at European contact) might be a legacy from that period. In a final section (Topic 100), Flannery will consider the possible role of such evolutionary studies for anthropology in general.

## THE PALEOINDIAN PERIOD

Data from this period are too scanty to allow any meaningful conclusions.

## THE ARCHAIC PERIOD

As might be expected at the present state of our knowledge, very few significant differences can be detected among the Archaic occupations in the various valleys comprising what is now the Otomanguean region. Data are particularly meager for the Early Archaic period, which preceded the separation of Proto-Zapotec-Chatino from Proto-Mixtec-Cuicatec (4100–3700 B.C. on the glottochronological scale). In Chapter 2 it was suggested that the Proto-Otomangueans may have constituted a "dialect tribe" of no more than 500 persons, ranging over a large area of mountains and valleys and camping in groups that seldom exceeded 25 persons. Even the introduction of small-scale agriculture between 8750 and 7840 B.C. (radiocarbon scale) does not appear to have changed the settlement pattern significantly for thousands of years. Here our analyses are hampered, however, by the small number of valleys (and sites) from which data are available.

Even in the Late Archaic, after Proto-Zapotec and Proto-Mixtec had presumably begun their separation, one can point to very few variations among valleys. There are differences in the popularity of various projectile point types between the valleys of Oaxaca and Tehuacán, but they are differences of proportion rather than presence–absence, and it is not clear how they might relate to ethnic or linguistic differences. For example, in her study of the !Kung San Bushmen, Weissner (1977) found significant variation in projectile-point styles among Bushman local bands all speaking the same language and engaged in the same reciprocal exchange network. We have suggested that one factor keeping all the early Otomangueans in linguistic contact was low population density, which made valley endogamy virtually impossible and linked vast areas into a single "effective breeding population." In other words, in this context, low population density could be seen as a factor delaying divergent evolution.

What were the cultural legacies of the Archaic period for the Mixtec and Zapotec? The most obvious legacy is technology. Many Archaic techniques of matting and basket weaving, sandal making, and net bag manufacture have persisted up to the present day. The fire-drills and atlatls of the Archaic differ insignificantly from those depicted in Postclassic codices. Many of the implements and facilities used today for processing food (metates, manos, mortars, pestles, maguey-roasting pits), or for trapping birds and small mammals, had their origins in the Archaic; so did the simplest techniques of dry farming.

The less obvious (but equally important) legacy is a whole series of intellectual and cosmological constructs, including schemes for classifying and describing the world. This was the period during which the Otomangueans defined their environment in detail, and we have already pointed out that many aspects of this definition are so thoroughly shared by the Zapotecs and Mixtecs as to suggest their presence in Proto-Otomanguean culture. These concepts begin with a rectangular universe with four great world quarters, each associated with one of four basic colors (red, white, black, and yellow)—a scheme so widespread among American Indians and the peoples of eastern Asia that it might have been part of the "cultural baggage" crossing the Bering Straits. The concepts proceed with a dichotomy of living–nonliving matter that hinges on a life force conceived of as "wind," "breath," or "heat"; a supreme creator who is incorporeal and timeless; and powerful supernaturals who take the form of lightning and produce rain. They continue with classificatory schemes which have a single word for "day" and "time," and a single word for "plant," "tree," and "wood," a category including plants classified either as "edible" and "useful" or "not eaten" and "useless." Certain prefixes are used to indicate that one is speaking of an animal, a category further divided into creatures "walking on four legs," "living in water," and "living in the air."

Finally, we have reconstructed the Archaic ancestors of the Zapotec and Mixtec as having an egalitarian, band-level society, probably (to judge by later developments) with a bilateral kinship terminology of Eskimo or simple Hawaiian type.

## THE FORMATIVE PERIOD

The Formative period in Oaxaca witnessed not only the first archaeologically observable general evolution within the Otomanguean area, but also the first observable divergent evolution. With the establishment of permanent villages, usually of only 10 families but in rare cases of up to 1000 persons, populations grew to the point where individual valleys had anywhere from 500 to several thousand inhabitants. The increasing opportunities for valley endogamy, coupled with a focusing of subsistence strategy on localized areas of farmland suitable for primitive races of maize, eventually helped to weaken the connections between valleys and lessen linguistic contact among Otomanguean speakers; an unusually high number of glottochronological separations are attributed to the early village period.

The most straightforward example of divergence during this period—and the one that can be most easily pictured as adaptive radiation—was the fitting of different agricultural strategies to the different environments of the Oaxaca–Puebla highlands. It is a process that was still going on 3000 years later, at the time of the Spanish Conquest. The Zapotec took advantage of the high water table and multiple small streams of the Valley of Oaxaca to establish irrigation with wells and small canals. The occupants of the Nochixtlán Valley found a crucial dry-farming zone that was just high enough for the necessary rainfall and just low enough to escape killing frosts. The occupants of the Tehuacán Valley learned how to dam small drainages to take advantage of brief floods in normally dry canyons. However, another whole group of intensive agricultural techniques were denied these valleys in the Formative period because they still lacked the manpower, perceived need, and/or centralized authority to carry them out.

There were repercussions from this adaptive radiation in other aspects of culture as well. For example, during the earlier Formative, the Valley of Oaxaca seems to have sprinted ahead of the Mixteca Alta in both population growth and general sociopolitical evolution. In part, this advance may have occurred because the Valley of Oaxaca is an area where so many simple techniques (wells, canals, and floodwater farming) can be applied to increase agricultural productivity dramatically. In part, it may be because the valley is a region where communication and interaction among villages occur relatively easily over an area of more than 700 km$^2$, thereby facilitating the development of multicommunity institutions. By 850 B.C., egalitarian society in the Valley of Oaxaca had given way to a society in which communities differed greatly in terms of size and public architecture, and households seemed to reflect a broad but continuous range of ascribed social statuses. Higher rank seems to have entitled its possessors to more elaborate burials, more elaborate residences, more venison, greater participation in the ritual life of the village, greater access to exotic raw materials and the artifacts thereof, and stronger exchange relationships with highly ranked people in other regions. Perhaps the most striking example of such differential advantage in interregional exchange was the apparent relationship between the Valley of Oaxaca (especially the community of San José Mogote) and the Olmec region of the Gulf Coast (especially the community of San Lorenzo). San José Mogote received most of its turtle-shell drums from the Gulf Coast; San Lorenzo received at least some of its magnetite mirrors from the Valley of Oaxaca. The two areas featured pottery with carved representations of the fire-serpent and were-jaguar, and although there are regional stylistic differences in the rendering, the shared cosmology and iconography are apparent. The virtual absence of such motifs in the Valleys of Nochixtlán and Tehuacán at this time stands in striking contrast to the situation in the Valley of Oaxaca, and emphasizes the divergence that had taken place. Clearly, certain large communities in the most highly populated areas of the Otomanguean region had virtually monopolized certain kinds of exchange relationships with the Gulf Coast.

Thus the Formative witnessed several key evolutionary processes: (1) loss of contact among previously related valleys, partly due to increasing valley endogamy; (2) "drift" resulting from this lack of contact, and perhaps reflected in stylistic and artifactual differences that were not necessarily adaptive; (3) truly adaptive divergence, particularly marked in agricultural and settlement systems, as the environmental potentials of each valley were explored; (4) emerging differences in general evolutionary level, as certain valleys achieved greater population density and sociopolitical complexity; and (5) further divergence caused by increased contact between these more sociopolitically complex valleys and important foreign areas, with the resultant introduction of changes which might be adaptive in some cases and drift-like in others.

Among the cultural legacies of the Formative, as pointed out in Chapter 3, one could include almost all the techniques of agriculture known in the Otomanguean area, and almost all the skills of village life—loom weaving, pottery making, adobe construction, and stone masonry. The use of a 260-day calendar, ceremonial bloodletting, human and animal sacrifice, formalized religious art, and a substantial body of ritual maintaining the involvement of ancestors in the ongoing life of the community could be cited as well. Both redistributive and reciprocal exchange systems were present, and many of the Precolumbian networks along which products moved from one valley to another had been permanently established.

## EARLY STATES IN THE ZAPOTEC AND MIXTEC REGIONS

Perhaps the major general evolutionary process of the Late Formative period was the rise of the Zapotec state in the Valley of Oaxaca. This process is outlined in Chapter 4 and summarized only briefly here. By 500 B.C. the population of the Valley of Oaxaca seems to have been organized into a series of apparently autonomous ascribed-status societies, each consisting of a relatively large village and a series of smaller hamlets. The largest (and best known) of these was the society centered on the 62-ha village of San José Mogote, whose acropolis of Rosario phase public buildings served an estimated 1300–1400 persons distributed through one large village and 18–20 outlying hamlets. The leaders of this society already exhibited a number of recognizable Zapotec patterns, including the use of a system of hieroglyphic writing to record important political events (such as the sacrifice of named individuals) on stone monuments. It would be interesting to know if the persons sacrificed were captives taken in combat, for this information would provide a reasonable background for the defensive works that appeared not long afterward.

Since none of the Rosario phase societies in the Valley of Oaxaca seems to have consisted of more than 1000 to 2000 persons, it is clear that the founding of Monte Albán had to represent the combined efforts of several such societies. Founded from the beginning as a major administrative center, Monte Albán had a population of 3600 to 7200 even in Period Ia. This population seems to have been divided into three different residential areas, perhaps representing at least three different polities that had participated in its founding. This division does not necessarily mean that all the participants were equal partners; in some confederacies, one partner may be more powerful, such as Tenochtitlán in its "Triple Alliance" with Texcoco and Tacuba.

Monte Albán represented a new administrative level in the Oaxaca site hierarchy, above secondary centers like San José Mogote and Dainzú, tertiary centers like Tomaltepec, and hamlets like Abasolo; it was the first administrative center of valley-wide significance. We have already suggested that a professional Zapotec ruling class evolved as the elite of Monte Albán allowed ties to their former valley-floor polities to wither, becoming instead "the lords of Monte Albán." Reverence for the ancestors continued, but the small hand-made figurines of the Formative vanished; now it was royal ancestors who were most important, represented by the more elaborate anthropomorphic urns of Classic-period Zapotec tombs. This pattern of ancestor worship survived into the Colonial period, and even today the *binigulaza* are important to the Zapotec.

The development of urban centers in the Mixteca Alta seems to have lagged a few centuries behind the Valley of Oaxaca, and such early centers were clearly influenced by their Zapotec counterparts. It is instructive to consider (1) the divergence between early Zapotec and Mixtec centers, (2) the common features they share, which suggest a form of parallel evolution, and (3) the contrasts between early Mixtec and Zapotec cities, on the one hand, and between Oaxacan cities and early cities in other regions such as Teotihuacán, on the other.

Early Zapotec centers, such as Period II Monte Albán and San José Mogote, had their major public buildings organized around a main plaza; early Mixtec centers, such as Monte Negro and Yucuñudahui, had a linear (or L-shaped) plan that lacks the main plaza. The Period Ia layout of Monte Albán suggests that this linear pattern may be earlier, and the divergence may have taken place in Period II. Early Zapotec temples were divided into an inner (more sacred) and outer (less sacred) room; early Mixtec temples were one-room structures. It is the two-room type that went on to be the more widespread in Mesoamerica, with examples from peoples as different as the Aztecs and the lowland Maya.

Equally striking, however, are the similarities. We have already pointed to the architectural similarities between San José Mogote and Monte Negro, and one could also point to similarities between the ballcourts at Monte Albán and Yucuñudahui. The hieroglyphic inscriptions at Huamelulpan follow Zapotec conventions, with a bar representing 5; this convention was to change with later Toltec influence on the Mixtecs.

Most important, all these early centers, whether Zapotec or Mixtec, share a number of characteristics that identify them as Oaxacan. Most are mountaintop cities in defensible locations, dominated by ritual and administrative structures; none shows the urban monopoly of craft specialists, market facilities, commercialization, large residential compounds, and grid or "quadrant" layout seen at Teotihuacán.

How are we to understand the sequential rise of mountaintop administrative centers, first in the Valley of Oaxaca, then at Huamelulpan and Yucuita, and then at Yucuñudahui? Was it strictly a form of parallel evolution, or was it also a chain reaction based on considerations of defense? Blanton has suggested that one incentive for maintaining a large, nucleated population at Monte Albán was to discourage economic or political expansion by Teotihuacán into the Valley of Oaxaca. If this is so, one incentive for maintaining a large, nucleated population at Yucuñudahui might have been to discourage economic or political expansion by the Zapotecs into the Nochixtlán Valley. Significantly, no Mixtec valley with a large mountaintop center seems to have suffered the kind of Zapotec takeover documented by Spencer and Redmond in the Cuicatlán Cañada.

Whatever the reasons behind this long series of Oaxacan mountaintop centers, one thing seems clear: none can be understood by considering only the events occurring within its valley. All these centers were in contact with each other, responding to military and economic changes in neighboring valleys and sharing an impressive series of architectural and organizational principles. Moreover (although we do not yet have the archaeological data to confirm this point), I seriously doubt that any small, sparsely populated valley in the Mixtec or Zapotec regions was able to retain its political autonomy during this period.

What was the legacy of the Classic period? A whole series of institutions that seem to conform well with what is known ethnohistorically about the Zapotec and Mixtec: a class-endogamous ruling stratum, including kings who lived in major palaces and nobles who lived in minor palaces; royal ancestor worship; temples staffed by professional priests, some of them possibly full-time specialists who actually resided in the temple; military conquest, with the possible conversion of captives into slaves for labor or sacrifice. To the Hawaiian kinship terms already characteristic of the Zapotecs and Mixtecs, there must now have been added a whole series of titles for social positions such as lord, great lord, royal heir, noble, slave, and many of the other categories encountered by the Spaniards.

## THE COLLAPSE OF THE EARLY CITIES AND THE RISE OF THE TOLTECS

The period between A.D. 700 and 1100 was also one in which organizational changes in each valley can only be understood in the context of the entire central and southern highlands of Mexico. The divergence between Mixtec and Zapotec cultures accelerated, but part of it was clearly due to the influence of third parties. The Mixtec and Zapotec also exhibited some continuing parallel evolution, but it too may reflect responses to political events of widespread significance.

The collapse of Teotihuacán around A.D. 600 might, in theory, have given the Zapotec state a chance to expand its sphere of economic, political, and military influence beyond places like Cuicatlán, Tututepec, and Miahuatlán. For reasons unknown, however, Monte Albán itself began to decline as well, shrinking from a peak of 30,000 persons in Period IIIb to only 4000 to 8000 persons by Period V. Its role as a major administrative center was probably over by A.D. 700, when public construction in the Main Plaza seems to have come to an end.

We have already mentioned the way the sequential rise of Monte Albán–Yucuita–Huamelulpan–Yucuñudahui resembles a chain reaction. A similar chain reaction seems to have followed the collapse of Teotihuacán. Monte Albán declined by A.D. 700, but the major centers of the Mixteca Alta hung on for another 200 years, finally fading between A.D. 900 and 1000. As the Mixteca Alta centers declined, the "Ñuiñe" centers of the Mixteca Baja rose, as if taking advantage of a power vacuum. To pursue the chain reaction analogy, however, these Ñuiñe centers themselves declined as Tula and the Toltec empire reached their apogee. Finally, as Bernal has already pointed out, the fall of Tula around A.D. 1160 allowed an expansion of Mixtec power that virtually rejuvenated the Mixteca Alta.

Mixtec culture, however, emerged from this rejuvenation greatly transformed, and even more divergent from that of the Zapotec. Major Mixtec dynasties claimed Toltec ancestry. The bar, which had stood for the number 5 since the days of Huamelulpan, was dropped in favor of five dots—a convention shared with the Postclassic Nahua. As argued by Caso, the Mixtec went over to the Toltec calendar, and years were henceforth named Reed, Flint, House, and Rabbit. It may also have been under Toltec influence that *Dzavui*, "rain," came to be stressed more than "lightning" in Mixtec religion. The mountaintop "multiplex" centers described for the Classic period by Spores gave way to valley-floor political centers, with the old mountaintops reduced to specialized religious–ritual precincts. The great Mixtec conqueror 8 Deer "Tiger Claw" went to Tula to have his nose ornament installed, then attempted to set up a bureaucratic state at Tututepec that may have been based on the Toltec model. What emerged were a series of small, intensely competitive petty states or *cacicazgos* that combined agricultural intensification specifically adapted to each valley of the Mixteca Alta (a continuing form of adaptive radiation) with a conscious effort to adopt institutions and organizational models from successful Nahua neighbors. The Monte Albán model had lost whatever appeal it might once have had for the Mixtec, and they had diverged still further from their old Otomanguean relatives.

In the Zapotec area, glottochronological data suggest the drifting apart of various regions, such as the sierra and the valley, after the integrative powers of Monte Albán had waned. Valley-floor centers such as Cuilapan, Zaachila, Noriega, Macuilxochitl, Lambityeco, Teotitlán, Mitla, and Matatlán began to grow, each more concerned with solidifying its own power base than with contributing to a Zapotec confederacy. The "special relationship" with Teotihuacán, which had been such a feature of Zapotec art and diplomacy during the Classic period, meant nothing anymore. Now the major political influence on the Zapotecs came from their Mixtec neighbors on the north and west, who were aggressive and land-hungry.

In this changed sociopolitical environment, one of the major concerns of the new Zapotec elite became the affirmation of their royal status and the arranging of the most politically and militarily advantageous royal marriage alliances. Their status was affirmed by means of genealogical registers, carved stone monuments recording the ruler's marriage and ancestry, displayed in some cases in the antechambers of royal tombs where they could be consulted by future generations. By the use of these registers, the Zapotecs accomplished some of the things their Mixtec neighbors accomplished with genealogical codices. Like the Mixtec manuscripts described by M. E. Smith, the Zapotec registers probably had a restricted or "regional" point of view, and some were laid out in boustrophedon style. Thus, there may be some convergent responses to the Balkanization of Oaxaca reflected here, although the Zapotec used stone as their medium and a bar for the number 5, whereas the Mixtec made use of deer hide and five dots.

One legacy of this period of Balkanization was the political unit known variously as a *cacicazgo*, or "city-state," consisting of one small urban center and a whole series of rural communities subject to one hereditary lord. While this type of polity was best known among the Mixtec, the sixteenth-century *relaciones* make it clear that much of the Zapotec area was organized the same way (see our discussion of Postclassic Mitla and its dependent hamlets). Many of the participants in the Santa Fe seminar felt this division of Oaxaca into a whole series of competitive, relatively autonomous small units, linked only by ephemeral alliances which fluctuated over time, may have been a more stable long-term adaptation for the region as a whole than the previous, highly nucleated polity centered at Monte Albán. In theory, the stability of the *cacicazgo* system lies in the fact that multiple small units should be more strongly buffered from perturbations in sister units (and hence more resilient to stress) than a more highly integrated system.

In the past, it has frequently been suggested that the *cacicazgo* system was an appropriate adaptation for the Mixteca Alta, with its multiplicity of tiny valleys that seem almost to defy unification. However, our data suggest that even the Valley of Oaxaca, with its 700 km² of broad, interconnecting, and previously unified plains, featured the same system of multiple small-scale units during Monte Albán IV and V. This fact (coupled with our realization that the Inca unified a region with an even greater multiplicity of tiny valleys) shows us that there is not a simplistic 1:1 relationship between the *cacicazgo* system and the topography of the Mixteca. It would perhaps be more accurate to say that the far-reaching political events of the Toltec and early Aztec periods elicited some convergent responses from the peoples of Oaxaca—the Mixtecs reacting primarily to their Nahua neighbors, the Zapotecs reacting to both the Nahua and Mixtecs.

## THE LATE POSTCLASSIC

Although the Classic period saw the buildup of the largest urban centers and the most centralized and regionally integrated states in Oaxaca, the Postclassic may in fact have seen the greatest escalation of social stratification. The Mixtecs evolved one of the most highly stratified systems in Mesoamerica, one in which differences were extreme even within the class-endogamous stratum of royalty and nobility. The Mixtec rulers were so highly ranked that there was literally a separate vocabulary for the various parts of the lord's body when contrasted with those of an ordinary man. The direct line of royal descent was so important that rulers sometimes married their full siblings, and first cousins were clearly distinguished from one's brother, sister, or "cross-sex sibling."

The Zapotecs also had a stratified society with Hawaiian kinship terms, but they did not distinguish between full siblings and first cousins, and placed less emphasis on direct descent. We know of no cases of full-sibling marriage within Zapotec royal houses, and there are in fact several cases where first-born sons were passed over because they were considered less talented or trustworthy than second sons. Despite their differences, however, both the Zapotec and Mixtec systems appear far less flexible than that of the Aztec, which placed even less emphasis on primogeniture and frequently allowed uncle-to-nephew succession. Moreover, both the Zapotec and Mixtec systems appear to have been much less bureaucratized than the Aztec system, with its dozens of administrative offices.

One of the probable factors selecting for the extreme stratification of the Mixtecs may have been the adaptive advantage enjoyed by a cacique with unlimited authority to control and direct manpower. Not only could such a cacique intensify agricultural production (as in the case of the incredible *lama–bordo* terrace systems of the Yanhuitlán *cacicazgo*), he could draft whole regional populations as footsoldiers, move whole farming communities from one valley to another, enforce the tribute of far-distant regions, and rule communities that did not even speak his language. Although the rulers of the Classic presumably drew much of their power from the populations of the regions where they had grown up, the Postclassic caciques seem to have transcended this: they traded communities, gave away lands, and relocated populations like participants in a giant Monopoly game.

What happened in the Late Postclassic went beyond convergence and parallel evolution. In a real sense, through the continual intermarriage of Zapotec and Mixtec rulers, the two cultures were becoming parts of a single political system whose internal geographic divisions were breaking down. In the Valley of Oaxaca, for example, we have reconstructed some Monte Albán V towns of the Tlacolula region as Zapotec communities. In the Etla region, however, many of the Period V hamlets and isolated residences may have been occupied by the *tay situndayu* or serf-farmers belonging to Mixtecs who had married into Zapotec royal families. Both the Zapotec and Mixtec had "religious capitals" or "pilgrimage centers" as well as politically important towns. At Mitla, a Zapotec "religious capital," we find both Zapotec-style two-room temples and Mixtec codex-style murals. Here we have come full circle: whereas the Protoclassic carvings of Huamelulpan in the Mixteca were Zapotec-influenced, the Postclassic murals of Mitla in the Valley of Oaxaca were now Mixtec-influenced.

In such a setting, it was inevitable that actual dislocations of ethnic groups would take place. Some may have resulted from parallel processes, as when the Mixtec drove to the Pacific coast at Tututepec (dislodging the Chatino) and the Zapotec drove to the Pacific coast at Tehuantepec (dislodging the Huave). Still others resulted from the growth of the huge multiethnic system already mentioned, as when Mixtec speakers were given land at Tehuantepec in return for their military aid to the Zapotec at Guiengola. Since this battle was followed by the marriage of a Zapotec ruler to an Aztec princess, there is no telling how complex the system might have become had the Spaniards not arrived when they did. In spite of their numerous political, marital, and military alliances, however, the Zapotec and Mixtec retained a great deal of ethnic diversity throughout the Postclassic, some of which is described in Chapter 9. For all their military prowess, the Mixtec caciques seemingly never caught on to the fact that their Zapotec allies were using them to fight all their major battles. And the Zapotec, perhaps drawing on a legacy that went back to their foreign relations with Teotihuacán, never ceased to favor skilled diplomacy over military confrontation.

## SUMMARY

This brief synthesis cannot do justice to 10,000 years of culture change in Oaxaca. The main point I have tried to make is that general evolution is only one of many evolutionary processes involved in the emergence of Zapotec and Mixtec culture as they were known at the Conquest. Even if we grant the rise of the Oaxaca peoples from band-level hunters and gatherers to state-level stratified societies, this rise is insufficient to explain the differences between Mixtec and Zapotec culture. Indeed, it is not even sufficient to explain all the similarities between them, for many of those are the result of common ancestry or close interaction, rather than the result of their having passed through similar general evolutionary stages. If we are genuinely interested in understanding individual Mesoamerican cultures, we cannot ignore drift, adaptive divergence, convergence, and parallel evolution while concentrating single-mindedly on advance through stages of sociopolitical organization.

A second point I hope we have made in this volume is that the familiar variables of agricultural intensification, population growth, warfare, and interregional trade are by themselves insufficient to explain the diversity of Mesoamerican cultures. We have found all these variables present in the history of the Mixtec and Zapotec, and we trust we have afforded them the recognition they are due. But what Mesoamerican culture was without them? Do they really explain the diversity of cultures—Mixtec, Zapotec, Aztec, Maya, Totonac, Huave, and Otomí—encountered by the Spaniards, or is there more to it than that?

Suppose I were a zoologist, and my task were to explain the class of birds. By diligent observation I might find that virtually all birds had feathers, laid eggs, had beaks, and featured air spaces in their major limb bones. That information alone would be insufficient either to explain how birds arose from reptiles or to account for the presence of hawks, penguins, parrots, and hummingbirds. Some would have us believe that explanations of human culture based solely on agricultural intensification, population growth, warfare, and trade are more "elegant" because they are more "simple." I would argue that such anthropologists, by diligent observation of the type seen in the biological analogy above, have merely identified four characteristics that virtually all complex societies share. They are certainly worth knowing, but they are insufficient either to explain how complex societies arose from simple ones, or to account for the observed diversity in complex societies.

# TOPIC 100
## Archaeology and Ethnology in the Context of Divergent Evolution

KENT V. FLANNERY

In Topic 99, Marcus has provided an overview of the evolution of Mixtec and Zapotec cultures from a common ancestral condition to their sixteenth-century states. It now remains to be seen whether there are wider implications to the use of an evolutionary model for examining cultural diversity.

If we were to ask 100 different anthropologists to define the goals of anthropology, we would certainly get many different answers. Nevertheless, one of the most common definitions would surely be "the explanation of sociocultural similarities and differences." It is a concern of anthropologists that has outlasted countless trends, fads, and "new directions."

Anthropologists are aware that sociocultural similarities and differences have histories, but their concern frequently extends no further than the acknowledgment of that fact. More often than not, they seek ad hoc explanations for the similarities and differences in the present-day adaptations of the peoples involved, when in fact the causes may lie far back in time. This tendency is particularly true for peoples whose past is preliterate. A colleague of mine, who has done outstanding ethnographic work with a group of North American Indians, once expressed to me his disappointment that his group "had no history." It was my impression, I said, that his area had a history extending back more than 10,000 years. "Oh, no," he replied, "just some archaeological sites."

The condescending view that archaeology is less than history—that it is, as one famous textbook of the late 1940s put it, "doomed always to be the lesser part of anthropology"— is at the root of a nagging inferiority complex that characterizes many anthropological archaeologists. Simply put, many archaeologists (and an even larger number of ethnologists) are programmed to play back the litanies: (1) "archaeologists can never recover the wealth of information on ancient cultures that ethnologists can recover from modern cultures" and (2) "archaeologists will always be dependent on ethnologists for their models of how cultures operate."

In order to gain some perspective on these litanies, let us consider the relationship between zoology and paleontology within the biological sciences.

One of the best-documented evolutionary stories in the fossil record is that of the horse, beginning with the tiny four-toed *Eohippus* in the Lower Eocene period, moving through the later forms *Mesohippus* and *Pliohippus*, and culminating with the genus *Equus* in the Pleistocene. Paleontologists are able to recognize all these forms as horses because of the detailed studies done on recent horses by zoologists. Based on anatomical principles discovered by those zoologists, paleontologists can reconstruct *Eohippus* as a forest-dwelling browser, whereas *Pliohippus* is considered more of a plains-dwelling grazer like the modern horse. Already in the Pleistocene record paleontologists recognize "caballine horses," "zebra-like horses," "ass-like horses," and "onager-like horses" on the basis of dentition and morphology. And zoologists, for their part, base part of their classification of recent equids on the fossil record, which shows them the ancestral relationships of these various forms. The two fields are thus complementary, one providing a wealth of data on modern species and the other documenting the history of evolutionary changes which led up to those species.

Zoologists do not make statements such as "paleontology is doomed always to be the lesser part of biology." They know that without it, they would have a devil of a time reconstructing the relationships of modern species. And though paleontologists do say "we can never recover the wealth of data on these fossils that zoologists can recover on the modern species," they say it matter-of-factly, without an inferiority complex. "Look," a paleontologist once told me, "zoologists know that the wild ass is buff with a brown stripe on the back, zebras are black-and-white striped, and caballine horses come in black, bay, chestnut, and sorrel. I can't tell you what the coat color of *Eohippus* was. But frankly, how important is it?"

Ethnologists know that tribal societies in various parts of the world may have Eskimo kinship terms, Crow kinship terms, Omaha kinship terms, or Hawaiian kinship terms. I can tell you with reasonable confidence that Tierras Largas-phase society in the Valley of Oaxaca was a tribal-level society, but I can't tell you what their kinship terms were. How important is it to know? About as important as knowing the coat color of *Eohippus*.

Of course, there have always been some ethnologists who understood the symbiotic relationship of archaeology and ethnology—Julian Steward, Eric Wolf, and Elman Service come immediately to mind. And Marvin Harris provided archaeology with a great shot of adrenalin at the 1965 meetings of the American Anthropological Association when he thundered from the podium:

> Archaeologists, shrive yourself of the notion that the units which you seek to reconstruct must match the units in social organization which contemporary ethnographers have attempted to tell you exist. . . . What we seek I presume in common, is the explanation of the differences and similarities in sociocultural phenomena. You are in a better position to provide such explanations because of your greater time span and because you can be relatively free from the mystifications which arise from the emic approach. You therefore ought not to permit your activities to be compressed into the narrow compass of attempting to link up with ethnographic data. Your operationally derived categories

and processes are superior to the unoperational definitions and categories of much of contemporary cultural anthropology [Harris 1968:360–361].

But such moments are rare. Far more common would be this situation: In 1974, a young ethnologist arrives in Oaxaca to do a comparative study of Zapotec and Mixtec communities. By 1979, after 5 years of fieldwork, he has a list of ways in which the Zapotec and Mixtec are similar and different. Their astonishingly similar classification of the cosmos he attributes to the fact that they have been in contact for centuries. The elaborate terraces of the Mixtec farmers he attributes to the lack of level land in their rugged mountain homeland; there is no way he can know that the Zapotecs had terraces even earlier, or that the Mixtec system resulted from the agricultural intensification of the Postclassic *cacicazgos*. The difference in cousin terms he attributes to modern inheritance preferences, without suspecting the differences in direct-line succession that once characterized the two political systems. The similarities in village craft production he attributes to the nature of Oaxaca's participation in the national economy of modern Mexico. The roots of the Zapotec extended family, the reasons for their two different terms for blood, their preoccupation with lightning, all escape him because their causes cannot be sought in the twentieth century. Zapotec ancestor worship he regards as somehow related to the Catholic saints, interlocked as it is today with *angelitos* and *difuntos* and the counting of rosary beads.

To put it another way, any ethnologist who attempted to "explain" the sociocultural similarities and differences between twentieth-century Zapotecs and Mixtecs without taking into account the past 6000 years of their history would have no more chance than a snowball in Hell. That does not mean we should abandon explanation as a goal. It simply means that in the search for certain explanations, ethnologists need archaeologists as badly as the archaeologists need them.

Perhaps the most important role the study of divergent evolution can play in the future is that of a bridge between these two disciplines, so they may one day display the symbiosis and mutual respect that zoology and paleontology have displayed for years. No one denies that there are aspects of culture which archaeology is poorly equipped to investigate, but as a discipline for the study of evolution it is second to none. No other branch of anthropology is so well equipped to deal with changes that took thousands of years. No other branch, over the last two decades, has taught us as much about the beginnings of food production or the origins of the state in such places as Mesopotamia, Mesoamerica, or the Andes. Marx and Engels? They identified some of the crucial theoretical questions, but they didn't know a Teotihuacán Thin Orange *florero* from an Uruk beveled-rim bowl.

If there is a message in all this, it is that archaeologists should shed their defensive behavior and their inferiority complex. We have accepted Willey and Phillips's revealed wisdom that "American archaeology is anthropology or it is nothing" (1958:2), but we have yet to accept the fact that there are some kinds of anthropology that archaeologists can do better than anyone else. Fellows: if evolution is what you are interested in, then anthropology includes archaeology or it is nothing.

# Appendix

## Radiocarbon Dates from the Oaxaca Region

ROBERT D. DRENNAN

The goal of this appendix is to make available in a single place all the radiocarbon evidence for the later periods of Oaxaca prehistory—that is, those phases with which ceramics are associated.[1] The only ceramic complex omitted is the Espiridión complex, for which no radiocarbon dates were available at the time the appendix was written.

The order of presentation of phases follows the sequence in the Valley of Oaxaca, with the phases in the Nochixtlán Valley and elsewhere in the Mixteca being tied to that sequence by ceramic cross-ties. Brief descriptions of the ceramic complexes used to define these phases are now available in this volume, in Caso, Bernal, and Acosta 1967, in Flannery 1968b, in Drennan 1976b, and in Spores 1972 and 1974a. It will be clear from Spores's contributions to this volume, as well as from the series of radiocarbon dates presented in Figures A.1 and A.2 that Spores's phases for the Nochixtlán Valley are not necessarily synchronized with the Valley of Oaxaca phases; often the phases in the Mixteca seem to start and end later than the Valley periods with which they show ceramic cross-ties.

All radiocarbon dates are presented according to the 5570-year half-life of $^{14}$C, subtracted from A.D. 1950 as recommended by the journal *Radiocarbon,* and with one standard deviation indicated.

When I began to collect the radiocarbon dates associated with the Pre-Hispanic ceramic sequences of Oaxaca, I had the impression that it would be a relatively brief task. After all, a consistent complaint of those dealing with Oaxaca chronologies (as of those working in other regions) had been the scarcity of good dates. Wistful reference is often made to

"securely dated" phases of other areas in an attempt to place Oaxaca phases correctly. The collection of nearly 100 dates which resulted from this effort, however, places the Oaxaca sequence among the best dated, or at least most dated, in Mesoamerica. Not only is this collection of dates surprisingly large, but the dates are rather well distributed through the length of the sequence—especially so considering the number of different and independent projects in the context of which the dates were obtained. It was thus a most pleasant surprise to see all the dates together in a single sequence.

Consideration of such a large group of dates from a series of diverse sites over a wide geographical area as if they belonged to a single set of phases, succeeding one another in orderly procession throughout Oaxaca, while perhaps heuristically justified, is an oversimplification. In an effort to make the geographical pattern, as well as the chronological pattern, of the dates clearer, the charts of dates (Figures A.1 and A.2) include a code for the site or region from which the carbon sample came. In addition, several instances are discussed in which the substantial deviation from the oversimplified view of synchronous phases is indicated.

Relationships between the Oaxaca ceramic sequence and those of other regions are not considered here, with one exception. The Tehuacán Valley sequence, from an area just on the Oaxaca state border, is also unusually well dated and, especially during certain phases, shows such strong ties to the Oaxaca sequence that an attempt has been made to link the two in order to clarify the dating. The Tehuacán ceramic sequence is described in MacNeish, Peterson, and Flannery (1970) and the radiocarbon sequence in Johnson and MacNeish (1972).

The procedure followed in making up the charts of dates which are the real heart of this section began with the subdivision of the dates according to the ceramic phase to which

---

[1] Editors' note: It was inevitable that new dates would appear while this appendix was in press. We have had to omit them because continual updating would have delayed the book.

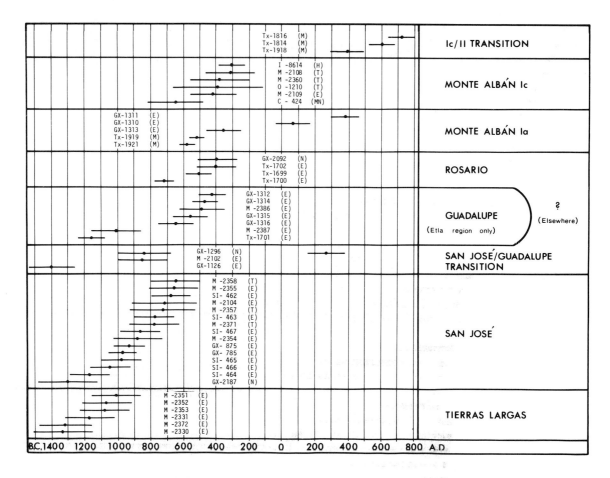

FIGURE A.1. Radiocarbon dates from Oaxaca, Part 1.

each date had been assigned. All dates were included in order to avoid the obvious (but all too common) circularity of supporting a chronology by reference to a set of radiocarbon dates from which all dates inconsistent with a preconceived idea of the chronology have been removed. Within each phase the dates were arranged in chronological order according to the mean of each. A few dates, which were identified by their excavators as from transitional contexts, were placed in special transitional categories. Figures A.1 and A.2 show the mean and one standard deviation for each date and include all dates of which I was aware at the time of writing the appendix. Table A.1 gives fuller information about each of the dates. Several investigators must be thanked for providing dates that are as yet unpublished, or special comments on dates published or unpublished, or both. They include Kent Flannery, John Paddock, Ronald Spores, and Marcus Winter. These individuals must not, of course, be held responsible for the conclusions which I base on their dates.

What follows, then, is a suggested set of dates for Oaxaca ceramic phases based on the consistency of the overall pattern of radiocarbon dates from Oaxaca and on connection to the radiocarbon dates from the Tehuacán Valley via the

ceramic sequence of that region. Unfortunately these dates are not the result of the application of a formally established procedure, but rather of a series of subjective judgments. By making clear what factors influenced those judgments, however, I hope to avoid the common kind of dubious reasoning in which dates are assigned to a ceramic phase because it is similar to one in another region, which in turn may have been dated on the basis of a chain of similar inferences, resulting in a dating that appears more solidly based than is really the case.

Many investigators will wish to modify these dates, being willing to make the assumptions and difficult judgments involved in considering similar ceramic types contemporaneous and in considering certain sherds trade items and the deposits in which they were found therefore contemporaneous with particular phases of other regions. In such an endeavor one must be careful not to ignore the solid evidence of a radiocarbon date pattern in favor of a chronological idea which, though strongly reinforced by long acceptance, may be less well supported. I suggest that the first step should be an independent consideration of the overall pattern of radiocarbon determinations for the region (together with other absolute dating measurements if available). From

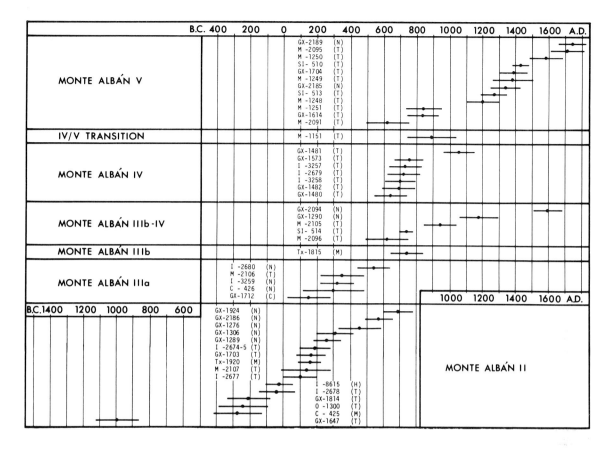

FIGURE A.2. Radiocarbon dates from Oaxaca, Part 2.

such an established base one can proceed to make whatever assumptions and judgments are considered justified and necessary to the aims of a particular study, whether that involves assuming certain kinds of contemporaneity and changing dates to match it, or the reverse process of assuming accuracy of dates and reaching conclusions about contemporaneity based on them. I offer the following, then, as a place to begin further study.

References to Caso, Bernal, and Acosta (1967), MacNeish, Peterson, and Flannery (1970), Flannery *et al.*, ([ed.] 1970), and Johnson and MacNeish (1972) are omitted from the following discussion because they would have become overly repetitive. Dates are given in radiocarbon years with no attempt to adjust them to calendar years.

Establishing a firm beginning for the Tierras Largas phase is impossible, because there are no dates for the recently discovered Espiridión ceramics that precede it. The earliest date for Tierras Largas phase materials is 1330 B.C. ± 180. These ceramics are similar to those of the Early Ajalpan phase in Tehuacán, the beginning of which has been placed at 1500 B.C. Thus it seems likely that the Tierras Largas phase began by 1350 or 1400 B.C., if not.earlier.

Considering only the Oaxaca radiocarbon dates, 1150 B.C. seems the most reasonable date for the end of the Tierras

Largas phase and the beginning of the San José phase. In terms of ceramic similarity, this boundary probably corresponds to the boundary between the Early and Late Ajalpan phases in Tehuacán, which was also set at 1150 B.C.

In Topic 14 Kowalewski, Fisch, and Flannery have discussed the problem of the Guadalupe phase, maintaining that "surveys and excavations now suggest that the complex of ceramic horizon markers used to define the Guadalupe phase may not extend far beyond the Etla arm of the Valley of Oaxaca." Hence, my conclusions about the dating of the Guadalupe phase should be seen as applying only to that region. The transition from San José to Guadalupe phase in the Etla region is marked by four radiocarbon readings, one of which is clearly much too early and one of which is clearly much too late. This leaves readings of 850 B.C. ± 150 and 840 B.C. ± 160 (the latter on the sample for which a reading of A.D. 265 ± 110 was also obtained). The dividing point most consistent with the radiocarbon measurements for the transition and for the two phases seems to be 800 B.C. The high frequency of Atoyac Yellow-white in late San José phase ceramics suggests that the boundary between San José and Guadalupe comes somewhat later than the boundary between Ajalpan and Santa María in Tehuacán, where similar types (Canoas White and Coatepec White) appear at the

TABLE A.1
Radiocarbon Dates for Oaxaca[a]

| Number[b] | Date | Phase | Site | Provenience | Reference |
|---|---|---|---|---|---|
| C-424 | 650 B.C. ± 170 | Monte Albán Ic | Monte Negro | Temple X | Libby 1955:130; Caso, Bernal, and Acosta 1967:267 |
| C-425 | 273 B.C. ± 145 | Monte Albán II | Monte Albán | Offering 3, Mound II | Libby 1955:130; Caso, Bernal, and Acosta 1967:267–268 |
| C-426 | A.D. 298 ± 185 | Las Flores | Yucuñudahui | Tomb 1 | Libby 1955:130; Paddock 1970a:120 |
| GX-785 | 975 B.C. ± 85 | San José | San José Mogote | Area A, Zone D1 | Flannery (ed.) 1970:43 |
| GX-875 | 930 B.C. ± 95 | San José | San José Mogote | Area A, Feature 2, Zone C3 | Flannery (ed.) 1970:43 |
| GX-1126 | 1400 B.C. ± 140 | San José–Guadalupe transition | Huitzo | Area A, Zone F3 | Flannery (ed.) 1970:33 |
| GX-1276 | A.D. 450 ± 130 | Ramos | Yucuita | N 203 D 0/0 2b, #17 | Spores 1972:172 |
| GX-1289 | A.D. 260 ± 85 | Ramos | Yucuita | N 217 D 0/0 5c, #32 | Spores 1972:172 |
| GX-1290 | A.D. 1175 ± 120 | Late Las Flores | Yucuita | N 217 B 0/0 2b, #7 | Spores 1972:172 |
| GX-1296 | 840 B.C. ± 160 A.D. 265 ± 110 | Early Cruz (cf. San José–Guadalupe) | Yucuita | N 203 B 0/0 3b F.5, #21 | Spores 1972:172 (two runs on the same sample) |
| GX-1306 | A.D. 310 ± 110 | Ramos | Yucuita | N 217 B 0/0 4b, #34 | Spores 1972:172 |
| GX-1310 | A.D. 65 ± 105 | Transition Rosario–Ia | Huitzo | Area B, Platform 1 | Flannery (ed.) 1970:35 |
| GX-1311 | A.D. 380 ± 85 | Transition Rosario–Ia | Huitzo | Area B, Platform 2 | Flannery (ed.) 1970:35 |
| GX-1312 | 425 B.C. ± 85 | Late Guadalupe | Huitzo | Area B, Feature 9, Zone C1 | Flannery (ed.) 1970:35 |
| GX-1313 | 355 B.C. ± 105 | Transition Rosario–Ia | Huitzo | Area B, Platform 3 | Flannery (ed.) 1970:35 |
| GX-1314 | 470 B.C. ± 80 | Guadalupe | Huitzo | Area A, House 3 | Flannery (ed.) 1970:33 |
| GX-1315 | 560 B.C. ± 110 | Guadalupe | Huitzo | Area A, House 5 | Flannery (ed.) 1970:33 |
| GX-1316 | 650 B.C. ± 110 | Guadalupe | Huitzo | Area A, Zone D | Flannery (ed.) 1970:33 |
| GX-1480 | A.D. 640 ± 100 | Monte Albán IV | Lambityeco | Mound 190, Floor 2 | Paddock 1970c:15 |
| GX-1481 | A.D. 1055 ± 95 | Monte Albán IV | Lambityeco | Building 195 sub | Paddock 1970c:15 |
| GX-1482 | A.D. 690 ± 100 | Monte Albán IV | Lambityeco | Tomb 6 | Paddock, Mogor, and Lind 1968:23; Paddock 1970c:15 |
| GX-1573 | A.D. 755 ± 90 | Monte Albán IV | Lambityeco | Building 195 sub | Paddock 1970c:15 |
| GX-1614 | A.D. 835 ± 95 | Monte Albán V | Pasa a Carrera | Mound 20-S | Paddock 1970c:15 |
| GX-1647 | 995 B.C. ± 130 | Monte Albán II | Brawbehl | Feature 69-20 | Paddock 1970c:14 |
| GX-1703 | A.D. 165 ± 90 | Monte Albán II | Brawbehl | Feature 69-21 | Paddock 1970c:14 |
| GX-1704 | A.D. 1385 ± 85 | Monte Albán V | Mitla Fortress | Building III | Paddock 1970c:15 |
| GX-1712 | A.D. 150 ± 130 | Cf. Monte Albán IIIa | Chila #1 | Stela #1, burial and offerings | Brockington, Jorrín, and Long 1974:62 |
| GX-1814 | 210 B.C. ± 130 | Monte Albán II | Brawbehl | Burial 69-10 | Paddock 1970c:14 |
| GX-1924 | A.D. 690 ± 90 | Late Ramos | Yucuita | N 203 K 2S/14E 2d, #86 | Spores 1972:172 |
| GX-2092 | 395 B.C. ± 120 | Late Cruz | Initiyu | N 233 A Test 2C, #3 | Spores 1972:172 |
| GX-2094 | A.D. 1595 ± 90 | Las Flores | Chachoapan: Iglesia Vieja | N 205 K 6S/0E 6A B, "C" | Spores 1972:172 |
| GX-2185 | A.D. 1340 ± 90 | Natividad | Yucuita | N 203 J 12S/6E 2A, F.10A #3 | Spores 1972:172 |
| GX-2186 | A.D. 570 ± 85 | Late Ramos | Yucuita | N 203 E 4N/6E F.15, #5 | Spores 1972:172 |
| GX-2187 | 1300 B.C. ± 180 | Early Cruz | Yucuita | N 203 K 2S/14E 3d, #135 | Spores 1972:172 |
| GX-2189 | A.D. 1745 ± 85 | Natividad | Chachoapan: Iglesia Vieja | N 205 K 6N/3E 2A, F.2A #1 | Spores 1972:172 |
| I-2674 I-2675 | A.D. 190 ± 95 | Monte Albán II | Caballito Blanco | Mound 1-S | Paddock 1970c:14 (average of two runs) |
| I-2677 | A.D. 100 ± 100 | Monte Albán II | Caballito Blanco | Mound 1-S | Paddock 1970c:14 |
| I-2678 | 40 B.C. ± 110 | Monte Albán II | Caballito Blanco | Mound 1-S | Radiocarbon 11:88; Paddock 1970c:14 |
| I-2679 | A.D. 720 ± 100 | Mounte Albán IV | Lambityeco | Mound 195 offering | Radiocarbon 11:88; Paddock 1970c:15 |

(continued)

TABLE A.1 *Continued*

| Number[b] | Date | Phase | Site | Provenience | Reference |
|---|---|---|---|---|---|
| I-2680 | A.D. 540 ± 100 | Las Flores | Yucuñudahui | Tomb 1 | Spores 1972:172 |
| I-3257 | A.D. 730 ± 100 | Monte Albán IV | Lambityeco | Mound 195 | *Radiocarbon* 11:88; Paddock 1970c:15 |
| I-3258 | A.D. 700 ± 95 | Monte Albán IV | Lambityeco | Mound 195 offering | *Radiocarbon* 11:88; Paddock, Mogor, and Lind 1968:23; Paddock 1970c:15 |
| I-3259 | A.D. 320 ± 100 | Las Flores | Yucuñudahui | Tomb 1 | *Radiocarbon* 11:88; Paddock 1970c:15 |
| I-8614 | 305 B.C. ± 80 | Huamelulpan I (cf. Monte Albán Ic) | Huamelulpan | Elemento 8, Capa VII | Gaxiola 1976 |
| I-8615 | 25 B.C. ± 80 | Huamelulpan II (cf. Monte Albán II) | Huamelulpan | Elemento 27, Capa II | Gaxiola 1976 |
| M-1151 | A.D. 890 ± 150 | Monte Albán IV–V transition | Yagul | Mound 5-W, above Tomb 10, below Tombs 11 and 13 | *Radiocarbon* 6:14–15 |
| M-1248 | A.D. 1200 ± 100 | Monte Albán V | Yagul | Cuarto 13, tlecuil norte | *Radiocarbon* 6:15; Bernal and Gamio 1974:92 |
| M-1249 | A.D. 1380 ± 100 | Monte Albán V | Yagul | Cuartos 16-17 | *Radiocarbon* 6:15; Bernal and Gamio 1974:93 |
| M-1250 | A.D. 1580 ± 100 | Monte Albán V | Yagul | Patio A, Cuarto Norte, tlecuil | *Radiocarbon* 6:15; Bernal and Gamio 1974:93–94 |
| M-1251 | A.D. 840 ± 110 | Monte Albán V | Mitla | South Group, Tomb 3 | *Radiocarbon* 6:15; (incorrectly given as A.D. 1110 in Paddock 1970c:15–1110 is the radiocarbon *age*) |
| M-2091 | A.D. 620 ± 130 | Monte Albán V | Cueva Blanca | Zone A | *Radiocarbon* 12:174; Flannery (ed.) 1970:20 |
| M-2095 | A.D. 1710 ± 100 | Monte Albán V | Guilá Naquitz | Feature 7 | *Radiocarbon* 12:175; Flannery (ed.) 1970:16 |
| M-2096 | A.D. 620 ± 130 | Monte Albán IIIb–IV | Guilá Naquitz | Zone A | *Radiocarbon* 12:175; Flannery (ed.) 1970:16 |
| M-2102 | 850 B.C. ± 150 | San José–Guadalupe transition | Huitzo | Area A, Zone F3 | *Radiocarbon* 14:186; Flannery (ed.) 1970:33 |
| M-2104 | 720 B.C. ± 200 | San José | San José Mogote | Area A, Zone D3 | *Radiocarbon* 14:185, Flannery (ed.) 1970:43 |
| M-2105 | A.D. 940 ± 100 | Monte Albán IIIb–IV | Hierve el Agua | Test 1, 75 cm | *Radiocarbon* 12:176; Flannery (ed.) 1970:87 |
| M-2106 | A.D. 350 ± 130 | Monte Albán IIIa | Hierve el Agua | Test 40, 113 cm | *Radiocarbon* 12:176; Flannery (ed.) 1970:87 |
| M-2107 | A.D. 140 ± 150 | Late Monte Albán II | Hierve el Agua | Test 40, 175 cm | *Radiocarbon* 12:176; Flannery (ed.) 1970:87 |
| M-2108 | 310 B.C. ± 150 | Monte Albán Ic | Hierve el Agua | Test 40, 190 cm | *Radiocarbon* 12:176; Flannery (ed.) 1970:87 |
| M-2109 | 420 B.C. ± 140 | Monte Albán Ic | Hierve el Agua | Test 41, 70 cm | *Radiocarbon* 12:176; Flannery (ed.) 1970:87 |
| M-2330 | 1330 B.C. ± 180 | Tierras Largas | San José Mogote | Area C, Feature 23 | *Radiocarbon* 14:185; Flannery (ed.) 1970:52 |
| M-2331 | 1170 B.C. ± 150 | Tierras Largas | San José Mogote | Area C, Zone G | *Radiocarbon* 14:185; Flannery (ed.) 1970:52 |
| M-2351 | 1010 B.C. ± 150 | Tierras Largas | Tierras Largas | Sq. 1995, Sample 1 | *Radiocarbon* 14:186; Flannery (ed.) 1970:66 |
| M-2352 | 1070 B.C. ± 150 | Tierras Largas | Tierras Largas | Sq. 1995, Sample 2 | *Radiocarbon* 14:186; Flannery (ed.) 1970:66 |
| M-2353 | 1080 B.C. ± 150 | Tierras Largas | Tierras Largas | Feature 116 | *Radiocarbon* 14:186; Flannery (ed.) 1970:66 |
| M-2354 | 890 B.C. ± 150 | San José | San José Mogote | Feature 24 | *Radiocarbon* 14:185; Flannery (ed.) 1970:52 |
| M-2355 | 660 B.C. ± 150 | San José | San José Mogote | Area C, Zone E | *Radiocarbon* 14:185; Flannery (ed.) 1970:52 |

*(continued)*

**TABLE A.1**  *Continued*

| Number[b] | Date | Phase | Site | Provenience | Reference |
|---|---|---|---|---|---|
| M-2357 | 730 B.C. ± 200 | Late San José | Abasolo | Test A, Sq. D13, Depth 220 cm, Zone D | *Radiocarbon* 14:186 |
| M-2358 | 650 B.C. ± 150 | San José | Abasolo | Test A, Feature 3 | *Radiocarbon* 14:186 |
| M-2360 | 380 B.C. ± 180 | Monte Albán Ic | Abasolo | Test B, Depth 120 cm | *Radiocarbon* 14:186 |
| M-2371 | 780 B.C. ± 150 | San José | Abasolo | Test A, Feature 3 | *Radiocarbon* 14:186 |
| M-2372 | 1320 B.C. ± 160 | Tierras Largas | San José Mogote | Area C, Platform 5, Zone F | *Radiocarbon* 14:185 |
| M-2386 | 490 B.C. ± 140 | Guadalupe | Huitzo | Area C, Zone D2 | *Radiocarbon* 14:187 |
| M-2387 | 1010 B.C. ± 150 | Guadalupe | Huitzo | Area A, House 7 | *Radiocarbon* 14:187 |
| O-1210 | 390 B.C. ± 275 | Monte Albán Ic | Yagul | Tomb 33 | Chadwick 1966:247; Paddock 1966a:120, 1970c:14 |
| O-1300 | 240 B.C. ± 150 | Monte Albán II | Caballito Blanco | Mound O | Paddock 1966a:120, 1970c:14 |
| SI-462 | 690 B.C. ± 120 | San José | San José Mogote | Area A, Zone C1 | *Radiocarbon* 11:172; Flannery (ed.) 1970:43 |
| SI-463 | 780 B.C. ± 120 | San José | San José Mogote | Area A, Zone C2 | *Radiocarbon* 11:172; Flannery (ed.) 1970:43 |
| SI-464 | 1170 B.C. ± 120 | San José | San José Mogote | Area A, Zone C3 | *Radiocarbon* 11:172; Flannery (ed.) 1970:43 |
| SI-465 | 980 B.C. ± 120 | San José | San José Mogote | Area A, Zone C4 | *Radiocarbon* 11:172; Flannery (ed.) 1970:43 |
| SI-466 | 1050 B.C. ± 120 | San José | San José Mogote | Area A, Zone D1 | *Radiocarbon* 11:172; Flannery (ed.) 1970:43 |
| SI-467 | 860 B.C. ± 120 | San José | San José Mogote | Area A, Zone D2 | *Radiocarbon* 11:173; Flannery (ed.) 1970:43 |
| SI-510 | A.D. 1430 ± 50 | Monte Albán V | Cueva Blanca | Zone A | *Radiocarbon* 12:196: Flannery (ed.) 1970:20 |
| SI-513 | A.D. 1270 ± 80 | Monte Albán V | Guilá Naquitz | Feature 7 | *Radiocarbon* 12:197; Flannery (ed.) 1970:16 |
| SI-514 | A.D. 740 ± 40 | Monte Albán IIIb–IV | Guilá Naquitz | Zone A | *Radiocarbon* 12:197; Flannery (ed.) 1970:16 |
| Tx-1699 | 510 B.C. ± 80 | Rosario | Fábrica San José | Feature 51 | *Radiocarbon* 17:92; Drennan 1976b |
| Tx-1700 | 720 B.C. ± 60 | Rosario | Fábrica San José | House 9(A) | *Radiocarbon* 17:92; Drennan 1976b |
| Tx-1701 | 1160 B.C. ± 80 | Late Guadalupe | Fábrica San José | Feature 61 | *Radiocarbon* 17:92; Drennan 1976b |
| Tx-1702 | 400 B.C. ± 120 | Rosario | Fábrica San José | Feature 58 | *Radiocarbon* 17:93; Drennan 1976b |
| Tx-1814 | A.D. 600 ± 80 | Monte Albán Ic–II transition | Monte Albán | Terrace 634-6, Feature 72-20 | Winter, personal communication |
| Tx-1815 | A.D. 740 ± 100 | Monte Albán IIIb | Monte Albán | Terrace 634-6, Feature 72-19 | Winter, personal communication |
| Tx-1816 | A.D. 720 ± 80 | Monte Albán Ic–II transition | Monte Albán | Terrace 634-6, Feature 72-20 | Winter, personal communication |
| Tx-1918 | A.D. 390 ± 100 | Monte Albán Ic–II transition | Monte Albán | Terrace 634-6, Feature 72-45 | Winter, personal communication |
| Tx-1919 | 520 B.C. ± 50 | Monte Albán Ia | Monte Albán | Terrace 634-6, Feature 73-69 | Winter, personal communication |
| Tx-1920 | A.D. 160 ± 70 | Monte Albán II | Monte Albán | Terrace 634–6, Feature 73–73 | Winter, personal communication |
| Tx-1921 | 580 B.C. ± 50 | Monte Albán Ia | Monte Albán | Terrace 634–6, Feature 73–77 | Winter, personal communication |

[a]This table makes no effort to include detailed comments concerning the contexts from which samples were taken. If more information is desired than the site and provenience information included here, the listed references should be consulted. The references include the official date list in which results have been reported for those dates which have been reported in this way. For the sake of simplicity and convenience, references to date lists in *Radiocarbon* are by volume and page number, rather than by author and date. Other sources are included in the reference section that follows. These other references do not comprise a comprehensive list of relevant sources, but indicate sources which provide information about the samples and their contexts to supplement that included in the date lists.

[b]Key to radiocarbon laboratories: C = Chicago; GX = Geochron; I = Isotopes, Inc.; M = Michigan; O = Humble Oil; SI = Smithsonian; Tx = Texas.

beginning of the Santa María phase. The end of the Ajalpan phase has been set at 850 B.C., although it is interesting to note that the Tehuacán radiocarbon dates alone, without reference to those of other regions, suggest a date of 800 B.C. for this division.

Elsewhere I have suggested the division of the Guadalupe phase into early and late segments of approximately equal duration (Drennan 1976b), but only one of the available radiocarbon dates can be securely assigned to either of the segments. The Early Santa María phase of Tehuacán has strong similarities to the Guadalupe phase, although the declining frequency of white-slipped ware and the increasing frequency of gray ware which mark the end of the Guadalupe phase begin to occur late in Early Santa María—suggesting that the end of the Guadalupe phase came before the end of the Early Santa María phase. This latter event has been placed at 500 B.C. Although 500 or 550 B.C. would be the date for the end of the Guadalupe phase in the Etla region that would be most consistent with our radiocarbon dates, the series of dates taken at face value would indicate that the entire Rosario and Monte Albán I phases fell within a period of 200 or 250 years. The amount of occupational debris and monumental construction datable to these phases in the Valley of Oaxaca, to say nothing of the magnitude of social change that took place, makes such a short period seem highly unlikely. This unlikelihood, together with the relation between the Guadalupe and Early Santa María phases suggested above, makes 600 B.C. seem a more reasonable ending date for Guadalupe; Flannery (personal communication) prefers an even earlier ending date.

Five hundred B.C. is the terminal date for the Rosario phase that fits best with the pattern of radiocarbon determinations. This date leaves only a century for that phase in the Etla region (which on further examination may seem an unacceptably short time); obviously, Rosario appears longer in those parts of the valley where Guadalupe material is rare. Rosario phase ceramics, however, also show extremely strong similarities to those of the early part of the Late Santa María phase in Tehuacán, which has been given a starting date of 500 B.C. Although these similarities do begin to appear toward the end of the Early Santa María phase, and although these ceramic traits may persist in Tehuacán after they were no longer used in the Valley of Oaxaca, it may become necessary to set a more recent date for the end of the Rosario phase.

The radiocarbon dates for Monte Albán Ia are few and very lacking in internal consistency. No known radiocarbon dates have been assigned by their excavators to Monte Albán Ib (if it, in fact, exists). Those for Monte Albán Ic, though internally consistent, are consistently too old to fit with preceding and following phases. The Monte Albán Ic dates would make a nice pattern directly following the Guadalupe or even the San José phase. They fail to overlap, however, as would be expected with the long series from Monte Albán II. Reference to the Tehuacán sequence is of little help here, since the Tehuacán ceramics which follow those so similar to Monte Albán Ia do not show such close

ties to Monte Albán Ic. It is undetermined if Monte Albán Ia-like traits persisted longer in Tehuacán or if they ended contemporaneously, followed by a course of development different from that of the Valley of Oaxaca. (Reference to the Tehuacán sequence is, in fact, less useful from this point onward because ceramic similarities are weaker, and because Oaxaca has approximately four times as many dates as Tehuacán for the period from Monte Albán Ic to the Conquest anyway.) On the basis of considerations of overall pattern, then, the terminal date for Monte Albán Ia is here set at 300 B.C., even though this date is not the most consistent with the radiocarbon determinations for Monte Albán Ia and Ic considered alone. The span from Rosario through Monte Albán Ic is probably the chronological segment most in need of further dates to eliminate ambiguities.

Three dates from Monte Albán Ic-II contexts fail to help set an ending date for Ic, as all are clearly too recent. Consideration of the sequence of dates for Ic and for II would indicate 250 or even 300 B.C. The implications of overall pattern discussed in the preceding paragraph, however, make 200 B.C. seem more reasonable, and perhaps further radiocarbon determinations will indicate an even more recent date.

The series of determinations for Monte Albán II indicates a somewhat longer phase than has usually been suggested. There are reasons, however, to suppose that this impression is at least partially inaccurate. For one thing, the large number of determinations for this phase may give, by its normal tendency to spread beyond the actual boundaries of the phase, an exaggerated impression of the duration, uncounteracted at the beginning at least because of the lack of substantial overlap between the Ic and II series.

Note that the latest five determinations, which make a large contribution to the spread, are actually Ramos-phase dates from the Nochixtlán Valley. This fact underscores our earlier statement that phases in the Valley of Oaxaca and the Nochixtlán Valley may share ceramic horizon markers without being closely synchronous. Spores has already argued that the Ramos phase, while sharing some traits with Monte Albán II, began later and ended later. This late adoption, however, seems curious in light of the relatively early Nochixtlán dates for ceramics related to Monte Albán IIIa. It may be that some of the Nochixtlán–Monte Albán II dates (particularly the last three) are out of line. All things considered, A.D. 200 seems a reasonable date for the end of Monte Albán II in the Valley of Oaxaca.

Monte Albán IIIa is the only period for which a majority of the radiocarbon determinations come from related material outside the Valley of Oaxaca, which, together with the rather small number of dates, makes assigning chronological boundaries to the phase more difficult than in some other cases. The date A.D. 450 has been selected for the end of the phase, although 50 years earlier or 50–100 years later would still be reasonably consistent with the pattern of radiocarbon determinations.

The single radiocarbon determination for Monte Albán IIIb is clearly an inadequate basis for establishing the length of the phase. The primarily nonceramic criteria according to which the division between IIIb and IV was originally defined have led some to combine the two into a single phase, resulting in the series of dates for Monte Albán IIIb–IV. Even this small set of dates is spread thinly over an excessively long period of time. The remarkably consistent series of Monte Albán IV dates from Lambityeco suggests that that phase began by A.D. 600 or shortly thereafter. In Topic 60, Paddock argues that the ceramic complex called Monte Albán IV began earlier in the Tlacolula arm of the valley than it did in the central region, in the immediate environs of Monte Albán. If that is the case, the radiocarbon determinations presently available are not adequate to fix the absolute end of IIIb. More determinations from various regions within the state, then, are needed for the Monte Albán IIIb–IV segment of the chronology in order to demonstrate conclusively the substantial geographical variation in the transition from one to the other seen by Paddock and, if the existence of such variation is substantiated, to specify the time periods and regions more precisely.

The final date to be determined is the boundary between Monte Albán IV and V. The date of a sample stratigraphically between a Monte Albán IV tomb and a pair of Monte Albán V tombs at Yagul was A.D. 890 ± 150. The most recent date for Monte Albán IV follows this, although the one standard deviation error ranges overlap. This late IV date, however, is separated from the rest of the dates for that phase by a substantial gap. Similarly, the earliest three dates for Monte Albán V are separated from the rest of the dates for that phase by a wide gap. These gaps might indicate that some or all of these four dates are out of line, or it might simply be the result of an inadequate number of determinations for the time period. Paddock (1970c:14) cites reasons to believe that the late IV date (GX-1481) is too recent.

It has in the past been suggested that Monte Albán IV and V overlapped within the Valley of Oaxaca, with IV persisting right up to the Conquest. None of the radiocarbon dates currently available indicates such a persistence of Monte Albán IV or conclusively rules out an overlap of the two

ceramic complexes. The overlap of radiocarbon dates, however, is no more extensive than that seen for other periods, or than that expected as the result of a normal tendency for the dates to be spread somewhat beyond the boundaries of a particular phase. There is thus not sufficient evidence from the radiocarbon determinations to postulate a major deviation from the simple assumption of successive phases that characterizes most regional chronologies. The date A.D. 950 has been selected as the beginning date for Period V most compatible with the overall pattern of radiocarbon dates available at the moment, although 50, 100, or even more years later than this would do no great violence to the pattern and might be indicated if more dates were run on Monte Albán IV and V materials.

In conclusion, two places in the chronological sequence showed indications of major deviations from the assumption of an orderly sequence of phases. There was tentative indication of a substantial lag between the adoption of the Monte Albán II ceramic complex at Monte Albán and the appearance of similar ceramics in the Ramos phase of the Nochixtlán Valley, and between the adoption of the Monte Albán IV ceramic complex at Lambityeco and its adoption in the central Valley of Oaxaca. Undoubtedly, as more radiocarbon determinations become available for different regions within the state, such temporal differences in the appearances of the various ceramic complexes can be better documented.

Two places in the chronological sequence stand out as having more ambiguities or contradictions than others. The Rosario–Monte Albán I section has a number of inconsistent dates, and those that are consistent seem too old to fit well with the preceding and following phases. The Monte Albán III–IV section has too few dates from too few regions to be defined precisely. It is hoped that this situation can be remedied in the future, and that continued accumulation of radiocarbon dates will continue to clarify the chronological sequence and connect it to revisions and refinements in the ceramic sequence.

# References

ACOSTA, JORGE R.
1956– "Interpretación de algunos de los datos obtenidos en Tula
1957 relativos a la época Tolteca," *Revista Mexicana de Estudios Antropológicos* 14(2):75–110.
1958– "Exploraciones arqueológicas en Monte Albán, XVIII
1959 temporada," *Revista Mexicana de Estudios Antropológicos* 15:7–50.
1965 "Preclassic and Classic Architecture of Oaxaca," in *Handbook of Middle American Indians*, vol. 3: *Archaeology of Southern Mesoamerica*, part 2, eds. Robert Wauchope and Gordon R. Willey (Austin: University of Texas Press), pp. 814–36.
1972 "Nuevos descubrimientos en Zaachila (1971)," *Boletín del Instituto Nacional de Antropología e Historia, Epoca II* 3:27–34.
n.d.*a* Exploraciones en Monte Negro, Oaxaca, manuscript, archives, Instituto Nacional de Antropología e Historia (México, D.F.).
n.d.*b* Informes de la XIII, XIV, XV, XVI, y XVII temporadas de exploraciones arqueológicas de Monte Albán de los años 1944 a 1949, manuscript, archives, Instituto Nacional de Antropología e Historia (México, D.F.).

ADAMS, ROBERT McC.
1966 *The Evolution of Urban Society* (Chicago: Aldine Publishing Co.).

ADAMS, ROBERT McC., AND HANS J. NISSEN
1972 *The Uruk Countryside* (Chicago: University of Chicago Press).

ADELHOFER, OTTO
1963 *Codex Vindobonensis Mexicanus 1* (Graz, Austria: Akademische Druck- u. Verlagsanstalt).

AGI (Archivo General de Indias, Sevilla) Escribanía de Cámara 162
1582– Los Indios del pueblo de Tecomatlan, Distrito de México
1584 con el Governador, alcaldes, y común de Yanhuitlan sobre que se declarase ser cabecera de por si, y no sujeto de Yanhuitlan.

AGN (Archivo General de la Nación, México) Tierras 985–86
1567/ Los naturales del pueblo de San Miguel Tecomatlan con
1820 tra los del de San Francisco Jaltepetongo y Martín José de Villagómez, cacique de Yanhuitlan, sobre propriedad de tierras.

AGN (Archivo General de la Nación, México) Tierras 2692, Exp. 16
1578 Tecomastlahuaca, Diligencias de información sobre el patrimonio que pide Don Francisco de Arellano, cacique del pueblo de Tecomastlahuaca.

AGN (Archivo General de la Nación, México) Civil 516

1580– Diligencias para declarar a cacique de Yanhuitlan a Don
1581 Gabriel de Guzmán.

AGN (Archivo General de la Nación, México) Tierras 44
1580– Autos que siguieron los indios de Tlaxiaco de la Mixteca
1583 Alta con los del pueblo de Atoyaquillo sobre estancias y tierras de Acatlixco.

AGN (Archivo General de la Nación, México) Tierras 400, Exp. 1
1567/ Títulos y probanzas de la descendencia de Teresa de la
1758 Cruz y Francisco de Guzmán, caciques de los pueblos de Yanhuitlan . . . contra los naturales del pueblo de Yanhuitlan sobre propriedad de tierras, etc.

AJT (Archivo del Juzgado, Teposcolula, Oaxaca, Mexico)

ALVA IXTLILXOCHITL, FERNANDO DE
1892 *Obras históricas*, ed. Alfredo Chavero, vol. 2: *Historia de la nación chichimeca*. México. (Reprinted 1952.)

ALVARADO, FRANCISCO DE
1593 *Vocabulario en lengua mixteca, hecho por los padres de la orden de predicadores, que residen en ella, y últimamente recopilado y acabado por el Padre . . . Vicario de Tamazulapa, de la misma orden.* [Facsimile ed., ed. Wigberto Jiménez Moreno. Instituto Nacional Indigenista and Instituto Nacional de Antropología e Historia (México), 1962]

ALVARADO TEZOZOMOC, FERNANDO
1949 Crónica mexicayotl, trans. Adrián León, Universidad Nacional Autónoma de México, *Publicación del Instituto Histórica, 1ª serie*, no. 10.

ASENSIO, GASPAR
1580*a* "Relación de Macuilsúchil y su partido," in *Papeles de Nueva España: segunda serie, Geografía y Estadística*, vol. 4, ed. Francisco del Paso y Troncoso (Madrid 1905), pp. 100–104.
1580*b* "El Pueblo Teutitlán," in *Papeles de Nueva España: segunda serie, Geografía y Estadística*, vol. 4, ed. Francisco del Paso y Troncoso (Madrid 1905), pp. 104–8.

AVELEYRA ARROYO DE ANDA, LUIS
1948 El hombre de Tamazulapan, *Memorias de la Academia Mexicana de la Historia*, vol. 7, no. 3 (México, D.F.).

AVENDAÑO, DIEGO DE
1579 "Relación de Texupa hecha el 20 de Octubre de 1579," in *Papeles de Nueva España: segunda serie, Geografía y Estadística*, vol. 4, ed. Francisco del Paso y Troncoso (Madrid 1905), pp. 53–57.

AVENI, ANTHONY F., AND ROBERT M. LINSLEY
1972 "Mound J, Monte Albán: possible astronomical orientation," *American Antiquity* 37:528–40.

BAILEY, JOYCE WADDELL
   1972   "Map of Texupa (Oaxaca, 1579): A Study of Form and Meaning," *Art Bulletin* 54:452–72.

BAIRD, ELLEN TAYLOR
   1973   "Tlaltecuhtli as a Personal Name in Mixtec Codices," unpublished paper prepared for a seminar in Mixtec codices, University of New Mexico.

BALSALOBRE, GONZALO DE
   1656   "Relación auténtica de las idolatrías, supersticiones, vanas observaciones de los indios del Obispado de Oaxaca," *Anales del Museo Nacional de Mexico, Primera Época* 6:225–60. [Reprinted 1892]

BANCROFT, HUBERT HOWE
   1874–76 The Native Races of the Pacific States of North America, 5 vols. (San Francisco and New York). [Reissued as his *Works,* vols. 1–5, 1882]
   1882–90 *Works,* 39 vols. (San Francisco).

BARLOW, ROBERT H.
   1943   "The Mapa de Huilotepec," *Tlalocan* 1(2):155–57.
   1945   "Dos relaciones del pueblo de Cuilapa, Estado de Oaxaca," *Tlalocan* 2(1):18–28 (Mexico). [English translation by Douglas S. Butterworth in *Boletín de Estudios Oaxaqueños* 23]
   1949   The Extent of the Empire of the Culhua Mexica, *Ibero-Americana,* no. 28 (Berkeley: University of California Press).

BARLOW, ROBERT H., AND BYRON MACAFEE
   1949   *Diccionario de elementos fonéticos en escritura jeroglífica (Códice Mendocino),* Publicaciones del Instituto de Historia, Primera Serie 9 (México: Universidad Nacional Autónoma de México).

BARTHEL, THOMAS S.
   1968   "El complejo 'emblema,'" *Estudios de Cultura Maya* 7:161–93.

BATRES, LEOPOLDO
   1902   *Exploraciones de Monte Albán* (México: Casa editorial Gante).
   1906   *Teotihuacán* (México: Memoria presentada al XV Congreso Internacional de Americanistas, Quebec).

BEADLE, GEORGE W.
   1972   "The Mystery of Maize," *Field Museum of Natural History Bulletin* 43(10):2–11.
   1977   "The Origin of *Zea mays*," in *Origins of Agriculture,* ed. Charles A. Reed (Chicago: Aldine Publishing Co.), pp. 615–35.

BEALS, RALPH L.
   1969   "Southern Mexican Highlands and Adjacent Coastal Regions: Introduction," in *Handbook of Middle American Indians,* vol. 7: *Ethnology,* eds. Robert Wauchope and Evon Z. Vogt (Austin: University of Texas Press), pp. 315–28.

BERLIN, HEINRICH
   1947   *Fragmentos Desconocidos del Códice de Yanhuitlán* (México: Antigua Librería Robredo).
   1951   "A Survey of the Sola Region in Oaxaca, Mexico," *Ethnos* 16:1–17.
   1957   "Las antiguas creencias en San Miguel Sola, Oaxaca, México," *Beiträge zur mittelamerikanischen Völkerkunde, Herausgegeben von Hamburgischen Museum für Völkerkunde und Vorgeschichte,* no. 4.
   1958   "El glifo 'emblema' en las inscripciones maya," *Journal de la Société des Américanistes* 52:91–99.

BERNAL, IGNACIO
   1946   "La cerámica preclásica de Monte Albán" (Master's thesis, Escuela Nacional de Antropología e Historia, México).
   1947   "Los calendarios de Durán," *Revista Mexicana de Estudios Antropológicos* 9:125–34.
   1949a   "La cerámica de Monte Albán IIIa" (Ph.D. diss., Universidad Nacional Autónoma de México, Mexico City).
   1949b   "Exploraciones en Coixtlahuaca, Oax.," *Revista Mexicana de Estudios Antropológicos* 10:5–76.
   1951   "Caso en Monte Albán," in *Homenaje a Doctor Alfonso Caso,* eds. Juan Comas et al. (México: Imprenta Nuevo Mundo, S.A.).
   1958a   "Archaeology of the Mixteca," *Boletín de Estudios Oaxaqueños* 7.
   1958b   "Exploraciones en Cuilapan de Guerrero, 1902–1954," *Informes* 7, Dirección de Monumentos Prehispánicos, Instituto Nacional de Antropología e Historia (México, D.F.).
   1958c   "Monte Albán and the Zapotecs," *Boletín de Estudios Oaxaqueños,* no. 1.
   1963   "Otra tumba cruciforme de Mitla," *Estudios de Cultura Nahuatl* 4:223–32.
   1964   "Arqueología mixteca del Valle de Oaxaca," in *Actas y Memorias del XXXV Congreso Internacional de Americanistas,* 1962, 1:453–60 (México).
   1965   "Archaeological Synthesis of Oaxaca," in *Handbook of Middle American Indians,* vol. 3: *Archaeology of Southern Mesoamerica,* part 2, eds. Robert Wauchope and Gordon R. Willey (Austin: University of Texas Press), pp. 788–813.
   1966a   "The Mixtecs in the Archaeology of the Valley of Oaxaca," in *Ancient Oaxaca: Discoveries in Mexican Archaeology and History,* ed. John Paddock (Stanford: Stanford University Press), pp. 345–66.
   1966b   "Ruinas de Santo Domingo, Oaxaca," *Boletín del Instituto Nacional de Antropología e Historia* 24:8–12.
   1968a   "The Olmec Presence in Oaxaca," *Mexico Quarterly Review* 3(1):5–22.
   1968b   "The Ball Players of Dainzú," *Archaeology* 21(4): 246–51.
   1968c   "Urna mixteca," *Boletín del Instituto Nacional de Antropología e Historia* 32:33 and color plate preceding.
   1973   "Stone Reliefs in the Dainzú Area," in *The Iconography of Middle American Sculpture* (New York: Metropolitan Museum of Art), pp. 13–23.
   1974   "Bajorrelieves en el Museo de Arte Zapoteco de Mitla, Oaxaca," *Corpus Antiquitatum Americanensium VII* (México: Instituto Nacional de Antropología e Historia).

BERNAL, IGNACIO, ED.
   1962   "Relación de Guautla," *Tlalocan* 4(1):3–16.

BERNAL, IGNACIO, AND LORENZO GAMIO
   1974   *Yagul, el palacio de los seis patios,* Instituto de Investigaciones Antropológicas, Serie Antropológica 16 (México, D.F.: Universidad Nacional Autónoma de México).

BERNAL, IGNACIO, JORGE GURRÍA, SANTIAGO GENOVÉS, AND LUIS AVELEYRA, EDS.
   1961   *Homenaje a Pablo Martínez del Río* (México: Instituto Nacional de Antropología e Historia).

BERNAL, IGNACIO, AND ANDY SEUFFERT
   1973   Esculturas Asociadas del Valle de Oaxaca, *Corpus Antiquitatum Americanensium VI* (México: Instituto Nacional de Antropología e Historia).

BERRY, BRIAN J. L.
   1961   "City Size Distributions and Economic Development," *Economic Development and Culture Change* 9:573–88.
   1967   *Geography of Market Centers and Retail Distribution* (Englewood Cliffs, N.J.: Prentice-Hall).

BINFORD, LEWIS R., AND W. J. CHASKO
   1976   "Nunamiut Demographic History: A Provocative Case," in *Demographic Anthropology,* ed. Ezra B.W. Zubrow (Albuquerque: University of New Mexico Press), pp. 63–143.

BIRDSELL, JOSEPH B.
   1968   "Some Predictions for the Pleistocene based on Equilibrium Systems Among Recent Hunter-gatherers," in *Man the Hunter,* eds. Richard B. Lee and Irven deVore (Chicago: Aldine Publishing Co.), pp. 229–40.

BITTLER, WILLIAM G.
1964, Reports on Excavations at the Mitla Fortress, manuscript
1968 on file, Instituto Nacional de Antropología e Historia.

BLANTON, RICHARD E.
1972 *Prehispanic Settlement Patterns of the Ixtapalapa Peninsula Region, Mexico,* Occasional Contributions to Anthropology 6, Department of Anthropology, Pennsylvania State University (University Park).
1976a "The Origins of Monte Albán," in *Cultural Change and Continuity: Essays in Honor of James Bennett Griffin,* ed. Charles E. Cleland (New York: Academic Press), pp. 223–32.
1976b "Anthropological Studies of Cities," *Annual Review of Anthropology* 5:249–64.
1976c "The Role of Symbiosis in Adaptation and Sociocultural Change in the Valley of Mexico," in *The Valley of Mexico: Studies in Pre-Hispanic Ecology and Society,* ed. Eric R. Wolf (Albuquerque: University of New Mexico Press), pp. 181–201.
1978 *Monte Albán: Settlement Patterns at the Ancient Zapotec Capital* (New York: Academic Press).
1980 "Cultural Ecology Reconsidered," *American Antiquity* 45(1):145–51.

BLANTON, RICHARD E., STEPHEN A. KOWALEWSKI, GARY FEINMAN, AND JILL APPEL
1982 Monte Albán's Hinterland, Part 1: Prehispanic Settlement Patterns of the Central and Southern Parts of the Valley of Oaxaca, Mexico. *Prehistory and Human Ecology of the Valley of Oaxaca,* vol. 7, eds. Kent V. Flannery and Richard E. Blanton, *Memoirs of the University of Michigan,* No. 15, Museum of Anthropology (Ann Arbor).

BOGUE, DONALD
1949 *The Structure of the Metropolitan Community* (Ann Arbor: Horace H. Rackham School of Graduate Studies, University of Michigan).

BOLETÍN
1975 *Boletín,* no. 2, Mayo 1975. [Centro Regional de Oaxaca, Instituto Nacional de Antropología e Historia, Oaxaca, Oaxaca, México]

BOOS, FRANK H.
1966 *The Ceramic Sculpture of Ancient Oaxaca* (New York: A.S. Barnes).

BORAH, WOODROW, AND SHERBURNE F. COOK
1960 "The Population of Central Mexico in 1548," *Ibero-Americana* 43 (Berkeley: University of California Press).

BORHEGYI, STEPHAN F. DE
1965 "Settlement Patterns of the Guatemalan Highlands," in *Handbook of Middle American Indians,* vol. 2: *Archaeology of Southern Mesoamerica,* eds. Robert Wauchope and Gordon R. Willey (Austin: University of Texas Press), pp. 59–75.

BOSERUP, ESTER
1965 *The Conditions of Agricultural Growth: The Economics of Agrarian Change under Population Pressure* (Chicago: Aldine Publishing Co.).

BROCKINGTON, DONALD L.
1957 "A Brief Report on an Archaeological Survey of the Oaxacan Coast," *Mesoamerican Notes* 5:98–104 (Mexico: Mexico City College).
1973 *Archaeological Investigations at Miahuatlán, Oaxaca,* Vanderbilt University Publications in Anthropology 7 (Nashville, Tenn.).

BROCKINGTON, DONALD L., MARÍA JORRÍN, AND J. ROBERT LONG
1974 *The Oaxaca Coast Project Reports: Part I,* Vanderbilt University Publications in Anthropology 8 (Nashville, Tenn.).

BROCKINGTON, DONALD L., AND J. ROBERT LONG
1974 *The Oaxaca Coast Project Reports: Part II,* Vanderbilt University Publications in Anthropology 9 (Nashville, Tenn.).

BROCKINGTON, DONALD L., AND JOSEPH B. MOUNTJOY, EDS.
n.d. Rise and Fall of the Mesoamerican Classic, symposium at the Thirty-Eighth Annual Meetings of the Society for American Archaeology, 1973, in press.

BROWN, ANTOINETTE B.
1973 "Bone Strontium as a Dietary Indicator in Human Skeletal Populations" (Ph.D. diss., Department of Anthropology, University of Michigan, Ann Arbor).

BRUMFIEL, ELIZABETH
1976 "Regional Growth in the Eastern Valley of Mexico: a Test of the 'Population Pressure' Hypothesis," in *The Early Mesoamerican Village,* ed. Kent V. Flannery (New York: Academic Press), pp. 234–48.

BULLARD, WILLIAM R., JR.
1960 "Maya Settlement Pattern in Northeastern Peten, Guatemala," *American Antiquity* 25:355–72.

BUNGE, WILLIAM W.
1966 *Theoretical Geography,* no. 1, 2nd ed. (Lund: Department of Geography, Royal University of Lund).

BURGOA, FRANCISCO DE
1670 *Palestra historial de virtudes y exemplares apostólicos . . .* Publicaciones del Archivo General de la Nación 24 (México: Talleres Gráficos de la Nación). [Reprinted 1934]
1674 *Geográfica descripción,* Publicaciones del Archivo General de la Nación 25–26 (México: Talleres Gráficos de la Nación). [Reprinted 1934]

BURLAND, COTTIE A.
1955 *The Selden Roll* (Berlin: Ibero-Americanischen Bibliothek zu Berlin).
1965 *Codex Egerton 2895* (Graz, Austria: Akademische Druck- u. Verlagsanstalt).

BYERS, DOUGLAS S., ED.
1967 *Environment and Subsistence, the Prehistory of the Tehuacán Valley,* vol. 1 (Austin: University of Texas Press).

CAJIGAS LANGNER, ALBERTO, ED.
1954 *Monografía de Tehuantepec* (México: author's edition).

CANSECO, ALONSO DE
1580 "Relación de Tlacolula y Mitla hecha en los días 12 y 23 de agosto respectivamente," *Papeles de Nueva España: Segunda serie, Geografía y Estadística,* vol. 4, ed. Francisco del Paso y Troncoso (Madrid 1905), pp. 144–54.

CANSECO, JUAN DE, AND FRAY BERNARDO DE SANTA MARÍA
1580 "Relación de Nexapa," in *Papeles de Nueva España: Segunda serie, Geografía y Estadística,* vol. 4, ed. Francisco del Paso y Troncoso (Madrid 1905), pp. 29–44.

CARMACK, ROBERT M.
1973 *Quichean Civilization: The Ethnohistoric, Ethnographic, and Archaeological Sources* (Berkeley and Los Angeles: University of California Press).

CARNEIRO, ROBERT L.
1970 "Theory of the Origin of the State," *Science* 169:733–38.

CARRASCO PIZANA, PEDRO
1950 *Los Otomíes: cultura e historia prehispánicas de los pueblos mesoamericanos de habla otomiana,* Publicación del Instituto de Historia, 1ª serie, no. 15, Universidad Nacional Autónoma de México.
1951 "Las culturas indígenas de Oaxaca, México," *América Indígena* 2:99–114.
1964 "Family Structure of Sixteenth-century Tepoztlán," in *Process and Pattern in Culture,* ed. Robert A. Manners (Chicago: Aldine Publishing Co.), pp. 185–210.
1970 "Las Clases Sociales en el México Antiguo," in *Verhandlungen des XXXVIII Internationalen Amerikanistenkongresses, Munchen,* vol. 2 (Munchen: Klaus Renner), pp. 371–76.

1971    "Social Organization in Ancient Mexico," in *Handbook of Middle American Indians*, vol. 10: *Archaeology of Northern Mesoamerica*, part 1, eds. Robert Wauchope, Gordon F. Ekholm, and Ignacio Bernal (Austin: University of Texas Press), pp. 349–75.

CARRIEDO, JUAN B.
1949    *Estudios históricos y estadísticos del estado oaxaqueño* (México: Biblioteca de Autores y de Asuntos Oaxaqueños, Prólogo de Jorge Fernando Iturribarría). [First ed. 1846]

CASO, ALFONSO
1928    *Las estelas zapotecas* (México: Secretaría de Educación Pública, Talleres Gráficos de la Nación).
1932a    "Monte Albán, Richest Archaeological Find in America," *National Geographic Magazine* 62(4):487–512.
1932b    "Reading the Riddle of Ancient Jewels," *Natural History* 32:464–80. [Translation of 1932c by George C. Vaillant, with a foreword by Vaillant]
1932c    "La tumba 7 de Monte Albán es mixteca," *Universidad de México* 4(20):117–50.
1935    *Las Exploraciones en Monte Albán, temporada 1934–35*, Instituto Panamericano de Geografía e Historia, Publicación 18 (México).
1938    *Exploraciones en Oaxaca, quinta y sexta temporadas, 1936–1937*, Instituto Panamericano de Geografía e Historia, Publicación 34 (México).
1942    "Resumen del informe de las exploraciones en Oaxaca durante la 7a y la 8a temporadas, 1937–1938 y 1938–1939," *Actas del XXVII Congreso Internacional de Americanistas*, 1939, 2:159–87 (México).
1946    "Los Dioses Zapotecas y Mixtecas," in *México Prehispánico, Antología de Esta Semana; This Week*, prólogo del Alfonso Caso, selección del Jorge A. Vivó (México: Impreso por Rafael Loera y Chávez para la Editorial Emma Hurtado), pp. 519–25.
1947    "Calendario y escritura de las antiguas culturas de Monte Albán," in *Obras completas de Miguel Othón de Mendizábal*, vol. 1 (México).
1949    "El Mapa de Teozacoalco," *Cuadernos Americanos* 8(5):145–81 (México).
1950    "Explicación del reverso del Codex Vindobonensis," *Memoria del Colegio Nacional* 5(5):9–46.
1951    "Base para la sincronología mixteca y cristiana," *Memoria del Colegio Nacional* 6(6):49–66.
1955    "La vida y aventuras de 4 Viento 'Serpiente de Fuego'," *Miscelánea de estudios dedicados al Dr. Fernando Ortíz* (La Habana), 1:291–98.
1956    "El calendario mixteco," *Historia mexicana* 5–20:481–97.
1960    *Interpretation of the Codex Bodley 2858*, trans. Ruth Morales and John Paddock (México: Sociedad Mexicana de Antropología).
1961    "Los lienzos mixtecos de Ihuitlán y Antonio de León," in *Homenaje a Pablo Martínez del Río*, eds. Ignacio Bernal, Jorge Gurría, Santiago Genovés, and Luis Aveleyra Arroyo de Anda (México: Instituto Nacional de Antropología e Historia), pp. 237–74.
1963    "Land Tenure Among the Ancient Mexicans," *American Anthropologist* 65:863–78.
1964    *Interpretación del Códice Selden 3135 (A.2)/Interpretation of the Codex Selden 3135 (A.2)* (México: Sociedad Mexicana de Antropología).
1965a    "Lapidary Work, Goldwork, and Copperwork from Oaxaca," in *Handbook of Middle American Indians*, vol. 3: *Archaeology of Southern Mesoamerica*, part 2, eds. Robert Wauchope and Gordon R. Willey (Austin: University of Texas Press), pp. 896–930.
1965b    "Sculpture and Mural Painting of Oaxaca," in *Handbook of Middle American Indians*, vol. 3: *Archaeology of Southern Mesoamerica*, part 2, eds. Robert Wauchope and Gordon R. Willey (Austin: University of Texas Press), pp. 849–70.
1965c    "Zapotec Writing and Calendar," in *Handbook of Middle American Indians*, vol. 3: *Archaeology of Southern Mesoamerica*, part 2, eds. Robert Wauchope and Gordon R. Willey (Austin: University of Texas Press), pp. 931–47.
1965d    "Mixtec Writing and Calendar," in *Handbook of Middle American Indians*, vol. 3: *Archaeology of Southern Mesoamerica*, part 2, eds. Robert Wauchope and Gordon R. Willey (Austin: University of Texas Press), pp. 948–61.
1966    "The Lords of Yanhuitlán," in *Ancient Oaxaca: Discoveries in Mexican Archaeology and History*, ed. John Paddock (Stanford: Stanford University Press), pp. 313–35.
1967    *Los calendarios prehispánicos* (México: Instituto de Investigaciones Históricas, Universidad Nacional Autónoma de México).
1969    *El Tesoro de Monte Albán*, Memorias del Instituto Nacional de Antropología e Historia 3 (México: Instituto Nacional de Antropología e Historia).

CASO, ALFONSO, AND IGNACIO BERNAL
1952    *Urnas de Oaxaca*, Memorias del Instituto de Antropología e Historia 2 (México: Instituto Nacional de Antropología e Historia).

CASO, ALFONSO, IGNACIO BERNAL, AND JORGE R. ACOSTA
1967    *La cerámica de Monte Albán*, Memorias del Instituto Nacional de Antropología e Historia 13 (México).

CASO, ALFONSO, AND LORENZO GAMIO
1961    "Informe de exploraciones en Huamelulpan," manuscript in Archivo del Instituto Nacional de Antropología e Historia, México.

CASO, ALFONSO, AND DANIEL F. RUBÍN DE LA BORBOLLA
1936    "Exploraciones en Mitla 1934–1935," *Instituto Panamericano de Geografía e Historia, Publicación 21*. México.

CASO, ALFONSO, AND MARY ELIZABETH SMITH
1966    *Interpretación del Códice Colombino/Interpretation of the Codex Colombino* [by Caso], *Las glosas del Códice Colombino/The Glosses of Codex Colombino* [by Smith] (México: Sociedad Mexicana de Antropología).

CHADWICK, ROBERT
1966    "The Tombs of Monte Albán I Style at Yagul," in *Ancient Oaxaca: Discoveries in Mexican Archaeology and History*, ed. John Paddock (Stanford: Stanford University Press), pp. 245–55.
1971    "Native Pre-Aztec History of Central Mexico," in *Handbook of Middle American Indians*, vol. 11: *Archaeology of Northern Mesoamerica*, part 2, eds. Robert Wauchope, Gordon F. Ekholm, and Ignacio Bernal (Austin: University of Texas Press), pp. 474–504.

CHISHOLM, MICHAEL
1962    *Rural Settlement and Land Use* (New York: John Wiley and Sons).

CHRISTALLER, WALTER
1966    *Central Places in Southern Germany* (Englewood Cliffs, N.J.: Prentice-Hall).

CLARK, JAMES COOPER
1912    *The Story of "Eight Deer" in Codex Colombino* (London: Taylor and Francis).
1938    *The Mexican Manuscript Known as the Collection of Mendoza and Preserved in the Bodleian Library* (London: Waterlow and Sons).

CLARK, P. J., AND FRANCIS C. EVANS
1954    "Distance to Nearest Neighbor as a Measure of Spatial Relationships in Populations," *Ecology* 35:445–53.

COBEAN, ROBERT
1974    "Archaeological Survey of the Tula Region," in *Studies of*

*Ancient Tollan: A Report of the University of Missouri Tula Archaeological Project*, ed. Richard A. Diehl, University of Missouri Monographs in Anthropology 1 (Columbia), pp. 6–10.

CODEX
Becker I and II: See Nowotny 1961a
Bodley: See Caso 1960
Colombino: See Caso and Smith 1966
Mendoza: See Clark 1938
Muro: See Smith 1973b
Nuttall: See Nuttall 1902
Sánchez Solís: See Burland 1965
Selden: See Caso 1964
Telleriano Remensis: See Hamy 1899
Teozacoalco (1580 Relación geográfica Map of): See Caso 1949
Vienna: See Adelhofer 1963
Xolotl: See Dibble 1951
Yanhuitlán: See Jiménez Moreno and Mateos Higuera 1940

COE, MICHAEL D.
1962  *Mexico* (New York: Praeger).
1965  "Archaeological Synthesis of Southern Veracruz and Tabasco," in *Handbook of Middle American Indians*, vol. 3: *Archaeology of Southern Mesoamerica*, part 2, eds. Robert Wauchope and Gordon R. Willey (Austin: University of Texas Press), pp. 679–715.
1968  "San Lorenzo and the Olmec Civilization," in *Dumbarton Oaks Conference on the Olmec*, ed. Elizabeth P. Benson (Washington, D.C.: Dumbarton Oaks Research Library and Collection and Trustees for Harvard University), pp. 41–78.
1977  "Archaeology Today: The New World," in *New Perspectives in Canadian Archaeology*, ed. A. G. McKay (The Royal Society of Canada), pp. 23–38.

COLBY, BENJAMIN N.
1967  "Psychological Orientations," in *Handbook of Middle American Indians*, vol. 6: *Social Anthropology*, eds. Robert Wauchope and Manning Nash (Austin: University of Texas Press), pp. 416–31.

COLECCIÓN DE MENDOZA
[In Kingsborough 5:39–126.]

CONTRERAS, EDUARDO, JR., AND LUIS RODRIGO
1972  *Informe del Recorrido Arqueológico por Oaxaca Rendido al Centro Regional de Oaxaca* (México: Instituto Nacional de Antropología e Historia).

COOK, SHERBURNE F.
1946  "Human Sacrifice and Warfare as Factors in the Demography of Precolonial Mexico," *Human Biology* 18:81–102.
1949  "Soil Erosion and Population in Central Mexico," *Ibero-Americana*, no. 34 (Berkeley: University of California Press).

COOK DE LEONARD, CARMEN, ED.
1959  *Esplendor del México Antiguo*, 2 vols. (México: Centro de Investigaciones Antropológicas de México).

CÓRDOVA, FRAY JUAN DE
1578a  *Vocabulario en Lengua Zapoteca* (México: Pedro Charte y Antonio Ricardo). [Reprinted 1942]
1578b  *Arte en Lengua Zapoteca* (México: Pedro Balli). [Reprinted 1886, Morelia.]
1942  *Vocabulario castellano-zapoteco* (México: Instituto Nacional de Antropología e Historia). [Facsimile of the original edition of 1578a]

COVARRUBIAS, MIGUEL
1946  *Mexico South: The Isthmus of Tehuantepec* (New York: Alfred Knopf).
1954  *Mexico South*, 2nd ed. (New York: Knopf).
1957  *Indian Art of Mexico and Central America* (New York: Knopf).

CRUZ, WILFRIDO C.
1936  Los Binigulaza, *Neza*, vol 2, no. 11 (México, D.F.:

Órgano Mensual de la Sociedad Nueva de Estudiantes Juchitecos).
1946  *Oaxaca Recóndita: Razas, Idiomas, Costumbres, Leyendas, y Tradiciones del Estado de Oaxaca, México* (México).

CURRAN, MARGARET E.
1978  "An Examination of the Relationship Between Population Density and Agricultural Productivity in the Prehispanic Valley of Oaxaca, Mexico," paper presented at the Forty-third Annual Meeting of the Society for American Archaeology, Tucson, Ariz.

CUTLER, HUGH C., AND THOMAS W. WHITAKER
1967  "Cucurbits from the Tehuacán Caves," in *Prehistory of the Tehuacán Valley*, vol. 1: *Environment and Subsistence*, ed. Douglas S. Byers (Austin: University of Texas Press), pp. 212–19.

DAHLGREN DE JORDÁN, BARBRO
1954  *La Mixteca: Su Cultura e Historia Prehispánicas* (México: Imprenta Universitaria).

DARK, PHILIP
1958  "Speculations on the Course of Mixtec History Prior to the Conquest," *Boletín de Estudios Oaxaqueños* 10 (Oaxaca).
1959  "Evidence for the Date of Painting and Provenience of Codex Selden and Codex Bodley," *Actas del XXXIII Congreso Internacional de Americanistas* 2:523–39 (San José de Costa Rica).

DE CICCO, GABRIEL, AND DONALD BROCKINGTON
1956  "Reconocimiento arqueológico en el Suroeste de Oaxaca," *Informe* 6 (México: Dirección de Monumentos Prehispánicos, Instituto Nacional de Antropología e Historia).

DE LA FUENTE, JULIO
1949a  "Documentos Para la Etnografía e Historia Zapotecas," *Anales del Instituto Nacional de Antropología e Historia*, 3:175–97.
1949b  *Yalalag: Una Villa Zapoteca Serrana*, Serie Científica 1 (México: Instituto Nacional de Antropología e Historia).
1960  "La Cultura Zapoteca," *Revista Mexicana de Estudios Antropológicos* 16:233–46.

DEL PASO Y TRONCOSO, FRANCISCO
1905–06  *Papeles de Nueva España: segunda serie, Geografía y Estadística*, 7 vols. (Madrid: Est. Tipográfico "Sucesores de Rivadeneyra").

DEL RÍO, JUAN
1580  "Relación de Taliztaca," in *Papeles de Nueva España: segunda serie, Geografía y Estadística*, vol. 4, ed. Francisco del Paso y Troncoso (Madrid 1905), pp. 177–82.

DÍAZ DEL CASTILLO, BERNAL
1962  *Historia de la Conquista de la Nueva España* (México: Editorial Porrúa).

DIBBLE, CHARLES E.
1942  *Códice en Cruz*, 1 vol. and atlas (México, D.F.: Talleres linotipográficos Numancia).
1951  *Códice Xolotl* (México: Universidad Nacional de México and the University of Utah).
1971  "Writing in Central Mexico," in *Handbook of Middle American Indians*, vol. 10: *Archaeology of Northern Mesoamerica*, part 1, eds. Robert Wauchope, Gordon F. Ekholm, and Ignacio Bernal (Austin: University of Texas Press), pp. 322–31.

DÍEZ DE MIRANDA, GUTIERRE
1579  "Relación de Xuchitepec," in *Papeles de Nueva España: segunda serie, Geografía y Estadística*, vol. 4, ed. Francisco del Paso y Troncoso (Madrid 1905), pp. 24–28.

DOXIADIS, CONSTANTINOS A.
1968  *Ekistics: An Introduction to the Science of Human Settlements* (New York: Oxford University Press).

DRENNAN, ROBERT D.
1976a  "Religion and Social Evolution in Formative Meso-

america," in *The Early Mesoamerican Village,* ed. Kent V. Flannery (New York: Academic Press), pp. 345–64.

1976*b* Fábrica San José and Middle Formative Society in the Valley of Oaxaca, *Prehistory and Human Ecology of the Valley of Oaxaca,* vol. 4, Memoirs of the University of Michigan Museum of Anthropology 8 (Ann Arbor).

1978 *Excavations at Quachilco: A Report on the 1977 Season of the Palo Blanco Project in the Tehuacán Valley,* Technical Reports of the University of Michigan, Museum of Anthropology 7 (Ann Arbor).

DUMOND, DONALD E.
1972 "Population Growth and Political Centralization," in *Population Growth: Anthropological Implications,* ed. Brian Spooner (Cambridge: M.I.T. Press), pp. 286–310.

DUNNELL, ROBERT C.
1980 "Evolutionary Theory and Archaeology," *Advances in Archaeological Method and Theory* 3:35–99.

DUPAIX, GUILLERMO
1969 *Expediciones acerca de los antiguos monumentos de la Nueva España, 1805–1808,* edición, introducción, y notas por José Alcina Franch, 2 vols. (Madrid: Ediciones José Porrúa Turanzas).

DURÁN, DIEGO
1867–80 *Historia de las Indias de Nueva España y Islas de Tierra Firme,* 2 vols. and atlas (México: J.M. Andrade y F. Escalante).

DURKHEIM, EMILE
1912 *The Elementary Forms of the Religious Life,* trans. Joseph Ward Swain (New York: Free Press) [1965].

EGGAN, FRED
1954 "Social Anthropology and the Method of Controlled Comparison," *American Anthropologist* 56(5):743–63.

ELIOT, THOMAS STEARNS
1917 "The Love Song of J. Alfred Prufrock," in *Prufrock and Other Observations* (London: The Egoist Ltd.).

ERAS, PEDRO DE LAS
1579 "Relación de Tilantongo y su Partido," in *Papeles de Nueva España: segunda serie, Geografía y Estadística,* vol. 4, ed. Francisco del Paso y Troncoso (Madrid 1905), pp. 69–87.

ERASMUS, CHARLES J.
1965 "Monument Building: Some Field Experiments," *Southwestern Journal of Anthropology* 21:277–301.

ESPÍNDOLA, NICOLÁS DE
1580 "Relación de Chichicapa y su Partido," in *Papeles de Nueva España: segunda serie, Geografía y Estadística,* vol. 4, ed. Francisco del Paso y Troncoso (Madrid 1905), pp. 115–43.

FALLERS, LLOYD A.
1965 *Bantu Bureaucracy* (Chicago: University of Chicago Press).

FEINMAN, GARY, AND STEPHEN A. KOWALEWSKI
1979 "Valley of Oaxaca Settlement Pattern Project Progress Report," report to the National Science Foundation (mimeographed).

FELDMAN, LAWRENCE
1974 "Tollan in Hidalgo: Native Accounts of the Central Mexican Tolteca," in *Studies of Ancient Tollan: A Report of the University of Missouri Tula Archaeological Project,* ed. Richard A. Diehl, University of Missouri Monographs in Anthropology 1 (Columbia, Missouri) pp. 130–49.

FERNÁNDEZ DE MIRANDA, MARÍA TERESA, MAURICIO SWADESH, AND ROBERTO J. WEITLANER
1960 "El Panorama Etno-Lingüístico de Oaxaca y el Istmo," *Revista Mexicana de Estudios Antropológicos* 16: 137–57.

FISCH, EVA
1978 "The Early Formative in the Valley of Oaxaca, Mexico: A Regional Analysis," paper presented at the Forty-third Annual Meeting of the Society for American Archaeology, Tucson, Ariz.

FISCHER, JOHN L.
1971 "Art Styles as Cultural Cognitive Maps," in *Art and Aesthetics in Primitive Societies,* ed. Carol F. Jopling (New York: Dutton), pp. 171–92.

FLANNERY, KENT V.
1966 "The Postglacial 'Readaptation' as Viewed from Mesoamerica," *American Antiquity* 31(6):800–805.

1967 "Vertebrate Fauna and Hunting Patterns," in *Prehistory of the Tehuacán Valley,* vol. 1: *Environment and Subsistence,* ed. Douglas S. Byers (Austin: University of Texas Press), pp. 132–77.

1968*a* "Archeological Systems Theory and Early Mesoamerica," in *Anthropological Archeology in the Americas,* ed. Betty J. Meggers (Washington, D.C.: Anthropological Society of Washington), pp. 67–87.

1968*b* "The Olmec and the Valley of Oaxaca: A Model for Inter-Regional Interaction in Formative Times," in *Dumbarton Oaks Conference on the Olmec,* ed. Elizabeth P. Benson (Washington, D.C.: Dumbarton Oaks), pp. 119–30.

1972*a* "Summary Comments: Evolutionary Trends in Social Exchange and Interaction," in *Social Exchange and Interaction,* ed. Edwin N. Wilmsen, Anthropological Papers of the University of Michigan Museum of Anthropology 46 (Ann Arbor), pp. 129–35.

1972*b* "The Origins of the Village as a Settlement Type in Mesoamerica and the Near East: A Comparative Study," in *Man, Settlement, and Urbanism,* eds. Peter J. Ucko, Ruth Tringham, and Geoffrey W. Dimbleby (London: Gerald Duckworth and Co.), pp. 23–53.

1972*c* "The Cultural Evolution of Civilizations," *Annual Review of Ecology and Systematics* 3:399–426.

1973 "The Origins of Agriculture," *Annual Review of Anthropology* 2:271–310.

1976*a* "The Early Formative Household Cluster on the Guatemalan Pacific Coast," in *The Early Mesoamerican Village,* ed. Kent V. Flannery (New York: Academic Press), pp. 31–34.

1976*b* "Contextual Analysis of Ritual Paraphernalia from Formative Oaxaca," in *The Early Mesoamerican Village,* ed. Kent V. Flannery (New York: Academic Press), pp. 333–45.

1976*c* "Evolution of Complex Settlement Systems," in *The Early Mesoamerican Village,* ed. Kent V. Flannery (New York: Academic Press), pp. 162–73.

1976*d* "Empirical Determination of Site Catchments in Oaxaca and Tehuacán," in *The Early Mesoamerican Village,* ed. Kent V. Flannery (New York: Academic Press), pp. 103–17.

FLANNERY, KENT V., ED.
1970 Preliminary Archaeological Investigations in the Valley of Oaxaca, Mexico, 1966 through 1969: Report to the Instituto Nacional de Antropología e Historia and the National Science Foundation, manuscript (Ann Arbor: University of Michigan, Museum of Anthropology).

1976 *The Early Mesoamerican Village* (New York: Academic Press).

n.d. "Guilá Naquitz Cave: A Study of Hunting, Gathering, and Incipient Agriculture in Preceramic Oaxaca, Mexico," in preparation.

FLANNERY, KENT V., AND JOYCE MARCUS
1976*a* "Evolution of the Public Building in Formative Oaxaca," in *Cultural Change and Continuity: Essays in Honor of James Bennett Griffin,* ed. Charles Cleland (New York: Academic Press), pp. 205–21.

1976*b* "Formative Oaxaca and the Zapotec Cosmos," *American Scientist* 64(4):374–83 (New Haven, Conn.: Sigma Xi, The Scientific Research Society of North America, Inc.).

FLANNERY, KENT V., ANNE V.T. KIRKBY, MICHAEL J. KIRKBY, AND AUBREY WILLIAMS, JR.
1967    "Farming Systems and Political Growth in Ancient Oaxaca," *Science* 158:445–54.

FLANNERY, KENT V., AND MARCUS C WINTER
1976    "Analyzing Household Activities," in *The Early Mesoamerican Village*, ed. Kent V. Flannery (New York: Academic Press), pp. 34–45.

FORD, RICHARD I.
1976    "Carbonized Plant Remains," in Fábrica San José and Middle Formative Society in the Valley of Oaxaca, by Robert D. Drennan, *Prehistory and Human Ecology of the Valley of Oaxaca*, vol. 4, Memoirs of the University of Michigan Museum of Anthropology 8 (Ann Arbor), pp. 261–68.

FOWLER, WILLIAM, AND JOHN PADDOCK
1973    "Nexos Teotihuacán-Monte Albán Vistos en la Cerámica," paper presented to the Mesa Redonda of the Sociedad Mexicana de Antropología, Xalapa, Veracruz, Mexico.

FRASER, DOUGLAS
1968    *Village Planning in the Primitive World* (New York: Braziller).

FRIED, MORTON H.
1960    "On the Evolution of Social Stratification and the State," in *Culture in History*, ed. Stanley Diamond (New York: Columbia University Press), pp. 713–31.
1967    *The Evolution of Political Society* (New York: Random House).

FURST, JILL LESLIE
1975    "Headdresses and Personal Names in Codex Zouche-Nuttall," paper presented at the Fortieth Annual Meeting of the Society for American Archaeology, Dallas, Tex.

GALINAT, WALTON C.
1970    "The Cupule and its Role in the Origin and Evolution of Maize," *Massachusetts Agricultural Experiment Station Bulletin* 585:1–18.
1971    "The Origin of Maize," *Annual Review of Genetics* 5:447–78.

GALINDO Y VILLA, JESÚS
1905    "Algo Sobre los Zapotecos y los Edificios de Mitla," Conferencia de Vulgarización dada por Jesús Galindo y Villa . . . Conferencias del Museo Nacional, Sección de arqueología, *Anales del Museo Nacional de Mexico 2a Epoca* 2:223, note 40 (Mexico: Umpr. del Museo Nacional).

GALLEGOS R., ROBERTO
1962    "Exploraciones en Zaachila, Oax.," *Boletín* 8:6–8 (México: Instituto Nacional de Antropología e Historia).
1963    "Zaachila: The First Season's Work," *Archaeology* 16(4):226–33 [trans. Dudley T. Easby, Jr.].
1964    "Exploraciones arqueológicas en Zaachila, Oaxaca, 1962" (M.A. thesis, Escuela Nacional de Antropología e Historia, México, D.F.).
1967    "Zaachila y la Tumba Siete de Monte Albán," lecture in a series entitled Culturas de Oaxaca, Museo Nacional de Antropología (México: Sección de Difusión Cultural).

GAMIO, LORENZO
1957    "Zona arqueológica de San Martín Huamelulpan," manuscript in Archivo del Instituto Nacional de Antropología e Historia (México).

GANN, THOMAS W. F.
1900    "Mounds in British Honduras," *Nineteenth Annual Report of the Bureau of American Ethnology, 1897–98*, part 2 (Washington: U.S. Government Printing Office), pp. 655–92.

GARCÍA GARCÍA, ROSA M., AND ELENA PALACIOS GONZÁLEZ
1976    *Atlas Arqueológico del Estado de Oaxaca*, Cuadernos de los Centros 23 (México: Instituto Nacional de Antropología e Historia).

GAXIOLA, MARGARITA
1976    "Excavaciones en San Martín Huamelulpan, Oaxaca, 1974" (tesis profesional, Escuela Nacional de Antropología, México, D.F.).

GAY, JOSÉ ANTONIO
1881    *Historia de Oaxaca*, 2 vols. (México).
1950    *Historia de Oaxaca*, 4 vols., prologue by Jorge Fernando Iturribarría (México: Biblioteca de Autores y de Asuntos Oaxaqueños). [First edition, 1881]

GELB, IGNACE J.
1963    *A Study of Writing*, rev. ed. (Chicago: University of Chicago Press).

GIBSON, CHARLES
1971    "Structure of the Aztec Empire," in *Handbook of Middle American Indians*, vol. 10: *Archaeology of Northern Mesoamerica*, part 1, eds. Robert Wauchope, Gordon F. Ekholm, and Ignacio Bernal (Austin: University of Texas Press), pp. 376–94.

GILLIN, JOHN
1952    "Ethos and Cultural Aspects of Personality," in *Heritage of Conquest*, ed. Sol Tax (New York: Cooper Square), pp. 193–222.

GLASS, JOHN B.
1964    *Catálogo de la Colección de Códices* (México: Museo Nacional de Antropología, Instituto Nacional de Antropología e Historia).
1975    "A Survey of Native Middle American Pictorial Manuscripts," in *Handbook of Middle American Indians*, vol. 14: *Guide to Ethnohistorical Sources*, ed. Howard F. Cline (Austin: University of Texas Press), pp. 3–80.

GONZÁLEZ TORRES, YÓLOTL
1977    "El Concepto del Tona en el México Antiguo," *Boletín* (México: Instituto de Antropología e Historia) vol. 19:13–16.

GOODENOUGH, WARD
1955    "A Problem in Malayo-Polynesian Social Organization," *American Anthropologist* 57:71–83.

GORENSTEIN, SHIRLEY
1973    "Tepexi el Viejo: A Postclassic Fortified Site in the Mixteca-Puebla Region of Mexico," *Transactions of the American Philosophical Society*, n.s., vol. 63, part 1 (Philadelphia).

GOULD, HAROLD A.
1969    "A Theory of Social Stratification and the Case of Indian Society," in *Anthropology and Archaeology: Essays in Commemoration of Verrier Elwin, 1902–1964*, eds. Mahesh C. Pradhan, R. D. Singh, P. K. Misra, and D. B. Sastry (London: Oxford University Press), pp. 142–53.

HAGGETT, PETER
1966    *Locational Analysis in Human Geography* (New York: St. Martin's Press).

HAMY, ERNEST THEODORE JULES, ED.
1899    *Codex Telleriano-Remensis, manuscrit Mexicain du Cabinet de Ch.-M. Le Tellier, Archveque de Reims à la Bibliothèque Nacionale* (MS mexicain, no. 385) (Paris).

HARNER, MICHAEL J.
1970    "Population Pressure and the Social Evolution of Agriculturalists," *Southwestern Journal of Anthropology* 26:67–86.

HARRIS, MARVIN
1968    "Comments" in *New Perspectives in Archeology*, ed. Sally R. Binford and Lewis R. Binford (Chicago: Aldine Press), pp. 359–61.

HARTUNG, HORST
1970    "Notes on the Oaxaca Tablero," *Bulletin of Oaxaca Studies* 27 (Oaxaca, Mexico).
1974    "Monte Albán—Concepto Espacial de Un Centro Cere-

monial Zapoteco," *Boletín* 19:9–27 (Caracas, Venezuela: Centro de Investigaciones Históricas y Estéticas, Universidad Central).

HARVEY, HERBERT R.
1963    "Términos de Parentesco en el Otomangue," *Departamento de Investigaciones Antropológicas Pub.* 13 (México: Instituto Nacional de Antropología e Historia).

HENESTROSA, ANDRES
1936    "Vini-Gundah-Zaa," *Neza* Año II, no. 10 (México, D.F.: Órgano Mensual de la Sociedad Nueva de Estudiantes Juchitecos).

HERRERA Y TORDESILLAS, ANTONIO DE
1601–15 *Historia General de los Hechos de los Castellanos en las Islas y Tierra Firme del Mar Océano* . . . , 4 vols.
1947    *Historia General de los Hechos de los Castellanos en las Islas y Tierra Firme del Mar Océano* 6 (Madrid: Academia de la Historia).

HOEBEL, E. ADAMSON
1949    *Anthropology: The Study of Man* (New York: McGraw-Hill).

HOLE, FRANK
n.d.    "The Chipped Stone Artifacts," in Guilá Naquitz Cave: A Study of Hunting, Gathering, and Incipient Agriculture in Preceramic Oaxaca, Mexico, ed. Kent V. Flannery, manuscript, University of Michigan, Museum of Anthropology (Ann Arbor).

HOLMES, WILLIAM H.
1897    Archaeological Studies Among the Ancient Cities of Mexico, Part II, Monuments of Chiapas, Oaxaca and the Valley of Mexico *Field Columbian Museum Anthropological Series*, vol. 1, no. 1. Chicago.

HOPKINS, JOSEPH W., III
1973    *Ceramics of La Cañada, Oaxaca, Mexico,* Vanderbilt University Publications in Anthropology 6 (Nashville, Tenn.).
1974    "Irrigation and the Cuicatec Ecosystem: A Study of Agriculture and Civilization in North Central Oaxaca, Mexico" (Ph.D. diss., University of Chicago, Department of Anthropology).

HUNT, EVA V.
1972    "Irrigation and the Socio-Political Organization of the Cuicatec Cacicazgos," in *The Prehistory of the Tehuacán Valley*, vol. 4: *Chronology and Irrigation*, ed. Frederick Johnson (Austin: University of Texas Press), pp. 162–248.

HUNT, ROBERT C., AND EVA HUNT
1974    "Irrigation, Conflict, and Politics: A Mexican Case," in *Irrigation's Impact on Society*, eds. Theodore Downing and McGuire Gibson (Tucson: University of Arizona Press), pp. 129–57.
1976    "Canal Irrigation and Local Social Organization," *Current Anthropology* 17:389–411.

HYMES, DELL
1960    "Lexicostatistics So Far," *Current Anthropology* 1:3–44.

JIMÉNEZ MORENO, WIGBERTO
1941    "Tula y los Toltecas Según las Fuentes Históricas," *Revista Mexicana de Estudios Antropológicos* 5:79–83.
1959    "Síntesis de la Historia Pretolteca de Mesoamérica," in *Esplendor del México Antiguo*, ed. Carmen Cook de Leonard (México: Centro de Investigaciones Antropológicas de México), vol. 2, pp. 1019–1108.
1966    "Mesoamerica before the Toltecs," in *Ancient Oaxaca: Discoveries in Mexican Archaeology and History*, ed. John Paddock (Stanford: Stanford University Press), pp. 1–82.

JIMÉNEZ MORENO, WIGBERTO, ED.
1962    *Vocabulario en Lengua Mixteca por Fray Francisco de Alvarado* (México: Instituto Nacional Indigenista and Instituto Nacional de Antropología e Historia).

JIMÉNEZ MORENO, WIGBERTO, AND SALVADOR MATEOS HIGUERA
1940    *Códice de Yanhuitlán* (México: Instituto Nacional de Antropología e Historia).

JOHNSON, FREDERICK, ED.
1972    The Prehistory of the Tehuacán Valley, vol. 4: *Chronology and Irrigation*, Robert S. Peabody Foundation (Austin: University of Texas Press).

JOHNSON, FREDERICK, AND RICHARD S. MAC NEISH
1972    "Chronometric Dating," in *The Prehistory of the Tehuacán Valley*, vol. 4: *Chronology and Irrigation*, ed. Frederick Johnson (Austin: University of Texas Press), pp. 3–55.

JOHNSON, GREGORY A.
1973    *Local Exchange and Early State Development in Southwestern Iran*, Anthropological Papers of the Museum of Anthropology, University of Michigan 51 (Ann Arbor).
1977    "Aspects of Regional Analysis in Archaeology," *Annual Review of Anthropology* 6:479–508.

JOPLING, CAROL F., ED.
1971    *Art and Aesthetics in Primitive Societies* (New York: Dutton).

JORALEMON, PETER DAVID
1971    *A Study of Olmec Iconography*, Studies in Pre-Columbian Art and Archaeology 7 (Washington, D.C.: Dumbarton Oaks).

JORRÍN, MARÍA
1974    "Stone Monuments," in *The Oaxaca Coast Project Reports: Part I*, eds. Donald L. Brockington, María Jorrín, and J. Robert Long, Vanderbilt University Publications in Anthropology 8 (Nashville, Tenn.), pp. 23–81.

KAPLAN, LAWRENCE
1967    "Archaeological *Phaseolus* from Tehuacán," in *Prehistory of the Tehuacán Valley*, vol. 1: *Environment and Subsistence*, ed. Douglas S. Byers (Austin: University of Texas Press), pp. 201–11.

KATZ, FRIEDRICH
1972    *The Ancient American Civilizations* (New York: Praeger).

KAUFMAN, TERRENCE
1976    "Archaeological and Linguistic Correlations in Mayaland and Associated Areas of Meso-America," *World Archaeology* 8(1):101–18.

KELLEY, DAVID H.
1962    "Glyphic Evidence for a Dynastic Sequence at Quiriguá, Guatemala," *American Antiquity* 27:323–35.

KELLY, ISABEL T., AND ÁNGEL PALERM
1952    *The Tajín Totonac, Part I: History, Subsistence, Shelter and Technology*, Smithsonian Institution, Institute of Social Anthropology, Publication 13 (Washington, D.C.: U.S. Government Printing Office).

KIDDER, ALFRED V., JESSE D. JENNINGS, AND EDWIN M. SHOOK
1946    *Excavations at Kaminaljuyú, Guatemala*, Carnegie Institution of Washington, Publication 561 (Washington, D.C.: Carnegie Institution of Washington).

KINGSBOROUGH, EDWARD KING, LORD
1830–48 *Antiquities of Mexico*, 9 vols. (London: A. Aglio).
1831    *Antiquities of Mexico: Comprising Facsimiles of Ancient Mexican Paintings and Hieroglyphs*, vol. I (London).

KIRKBY, ANNE V. T.
1973    "The Use of Land and Water Resources in the Past and Present Valley of Oaxaca, Mexico," in *Prehistory and Human Ecology of the Valley of Oaxaca*, vol. 1, ed. Kent V. Flannery, Memoirs of the University of Michigan Museum of Anthropology 5 (Ann Arbor).

1974 "Individual and Community Responses to Rainfall Variability in Oaxaca, Mexico," in *Natural Hazards: Local, Regional, and Global,* ed. Gilbert F. White (New York: Oxford University Press), pp. 119–128.

KIRKBY, MICHAEL J.
1972 *The Physical Environment of the Nochixtlán Valley, Oaxaca,* Vanderbilt University Publications in Anthropology 2 (Nashville, Tenn.).

KIRKBY, MICHAEL J., AND ANNE V. T. WHYTE
n.d. "The Physical Environment of Guilá Naquitz Cave," in Guilá Naquitz Cave, ed. Kent V. Flannery, in preparation.

KOTTAK, CONRAD P.
1972 "A Cultural Adaptive Approach to Malagasy Political Organization," in *Social Exchange and Interaction,* ed. Edwin N. Wilmsen, Anthropological Papers of the University of Michigan Museum of Anthropology 46 (Ann Arbor), pp. 107–28.

KOWALEWSKI, STEPHEN A.
1974 "Ancient Settlement Patterns in the Central Valley of Oaxaca, Mexico," paper presented to the Seventy-third Annual Meeting of the American Anthropological Association, Mexico City.
1976 "Prehispanic Settlement Patterns of the Central Part of the Valley of Oaxaca, Mexico" (Ph.D. diss., University of Arizona, Department of Anthropology).
1980 "Population-resource Balances in Period I of Oaxaca, Mexico," *American Antiquity* 45(1):151–65.

KOWALEWSKI, STEPHEN A., RICHARD E. BLANTON, AND DUDLEY M. VARNER
1975 "Early Classic Economic Formations in the Valley of Oaxaca, Mexico," paper presented to the Seventy-fourth Annual Meeting of the American Anthropological Association, San Francisco, Ca.

KOWALEWSKI, STEPHEN A., AND MARCIA TRUELL
1970 "'Tlaloc' in the Valley of Oaxaca," *Boletín de Estudios Oaxaqueños* 31.

KRAPF-ASKARI, EVA
1969 *Yoruba Towns and Cities* (London: Oxford University Press).

KUBLER, GEORGE
1961 "Chichén-Itzá y Tula," *Estudios de Cultura Maya,* 1:47–80 (México, D.F.: Universidad Nacional Autónoma de México).
1962 *The Art and Architecture of Ancient America* (Harmondsworth: Penguin Books).
1964 "Polygenesis and Diffusion: Courtyards in Mesoamerican Architecture," *Actas y Memorias del XXV Congreso Internacional de Americanistas,* 1962, 1:345–57 (Mexico City).

KUTTRUFF, CARL, AND WILLIAM O. AUTRY, JR.
1978 "Test Excavations at Terrace 1227," in *Monte Albán: Settlement Patterns at the Ancient Zapotec Capital,* ed. Richard E. Blanton (New York: Academic Press), pp. 403–15.

LACK, DAVID
1947 *Darwin's Finches* (London: Cambridge University Press).

LANDA, FRAY DIEGO DE
1941 *Relación de las Cosas de Yucatán,* trans. and ed. Alfred M. Tozzer, Papers of the Peabody Museum of American Archaeology and Ethnology, Harvard University, 18 (Cambridge, Mass.).

LATHRAP, DONALD W.
1976 "Radiation: The Application to Cultural Development of a Model from Biological Evolution," in *The Measures of Man,* eds. Eugene Giles and Jonathan S. Friedlaender (Cambridge, Mass.: Peabody Museum Press), pp. 494–532.

LEACH, EDMUND R.
1965 *Political Systems of Highland Burma* (Boston: Beacon Press).

LEES, SUSAN
1973 "Sociopolitical Aspects of Canal Irrigation in the Valley of Oaxaca, Mexico," in *Prehistory and Human Ecology of the Valley of Oaxaca,* vol. 2, ed. Kent V. Flannery, Memoirs of the University of Michigan Museum of Anthropology 6 (Ann Arbor).

LEHMANN, WALTER, AND OTTOKAR SMITAL
1929 *Codex Vindobonensis Mexic, 1* (Vienna: Verlag für Nord u. Sudamerika Kunstanstalt M. Jaffé).

LEIGH, HOWARD
1966 "The Evolution of Zapotec Glyph C," in *Ancient Oaxaca: Discoveries in Mexican Archaeology and History,* ed. John Paddock (Stanford: Stanford University Press), pp. 256–69.

LENSKI, GERHARD E.
1966 *Power and Privilege* (New York: McGraw-Hill).

LEÓN, NICOLÁS
1901 *Lyobaa ó Mictlan: Guía Histórico-Descriptiva* (México: Tip. y Lit. "La Europea").

LEVEY, WILL T.
1966 "Early Teotihuacán: An Achieving Society," *Mesoamerican Notes* 7–8:25–68.

LEVINS, RICHARD
1968 *Evolution in Changing Environments: Some Theoretical Explorations* (Princeton, N.J.: Princeton University Press).

LEWIS, OSCAR
1951 *Life in a Mexican Village: Tepoztlán Restudied* (Urbana: University of Illinois Press).

LIBBY, WILLARD F.
1955 *Radiocarbon Dating,* 2nd ed. (Chicago: University of Chicago Press).

LINARES, OLGA F.
1977 "Adaptive Strategies in Western Panama," *World Archaeology* 8(3):304–19.

LIND, MICHAEL
1979 *Postclassic and Early Colonial Mixtec Houses in the Nochixtlán Valley, Oaxaca,* Vanderbilt University Publications in Anthropology 23 (Nashville, Tenn.).

LINNÉ, SIGVALD
1934 *Archaeological Researches at Teotihuacán. Mexico,* The Ethnographic Museum of Sweden, new series, Publication no. 1 (Stockholm).
1942 *Mexican Highland Cultures: Archaeological Researches at Teotihuacán, Calpulalpan, and Chalchicomula in 1934–35,* Ethnographic Museum of Sweden, new series, Publication no. 7 (Stockholm).

LLOYD, PETER C.
1965 "The Political Structure of African Kingdoms: An Exploratory Model," in *Political Systems and the Distribution of Power,* ed. M. Banton (London: Tavistock), pp. 63–112.

LONG, RICHARD C.E.
1926 "The Zouche Codex," *Journal of the Royal Anthropological Institute of Great Britain and Ireland* 56:239–58.

LONGACRE, ROBERT
1967 "Systemic Comparison and Reconstruction," in *Handbook of Middle American Indians,* vol. 5: *Linguistics,* ed. Norman A. McQuown (Austin: University of Texas Press), pp. 117–59.

LONGACRE, ROBERT E., AND RENÉ MILLON
1961 "Proto-Mixtecan and Proto-Amuzgan-Mixtecan Vocabularies: A Preliminary Cultural Analysis," *Anthropological Linguistics* 3(4):1–44.

380    References

LORENZO, JOSÉ LUIS
  1958a   "Un Sitio Precerámico en Yanhuitlán, Oaxaca," *Instituto Nacional de Antropología e Historia, Dirección Prehistoria, Pub.* 6 (México).
  1958b   "Aspectos Físicos del Valle de Oaxaca," *Revista Mexicana de Estudios Antropológicos* 7:49–63.
LORENZO, JOSÉ LUIS, AND MIGUEL MESSMACHER
  1963   "Hallazgo de Horizontes Culturales Precerámicos en el Valle de Oaxaca," *Homenaje a Pedro Bosch-Gimpera,* ed. Santiago Genovés (México, D.F.: Instituto Nacional de Antropología e Historia and Universidad Nacional Autónoma de México), pp. 289–301.
LOWE, GARETH W.
  1959   *Archaeological Exploration of the Upper Grijalva River, Chiapas, Mexico,* Papers of the New World Archaeological Foundation 2 (Provo, Utah: Brigham Young University).
LOWIE, ROBERT H.
  1915   *Dances and Societies of the Plains Shoshone,* Anthropological Papers of the American Museum of Natural History, vol. 11, part 10 (New York).
  1924a   "Notes on Shoshonean Ethnography," *Anthropological Papers of the American Museum of Natural History,* vol. 20, part 3 (New York).
  1924b   *Primitive Religion* (New York: Boni and Liveright).
MAC NEISH, RICHARD S.
  1962   *Second Annual Report of the Tehuacán Archaeological-Botanical Project,* R.S. Peabody Foundation for Archaeology (Andover, Mass.: Phillips Academy).
  1964   "Ancient Mesoamerican Civilization," *Science* 143(3606):531–37.
  1967a   "An Interdisciplinary Approach to an Archaeological Problem," in *The Prehistory of the Tehuacán Valley,* vol. 1: *Environment and Subsistence,* ed. Douglas S. Byers (Austin: University of Texas Press), pp. 14–24.
  1967b   "A Summary of the Subsistence," in *The Prehistory of the Tehuacán Valley,* vol. 1: *Environment and Subsistence,* ed. Douglas S. Byers (Austin: University of Texas Press), pp. 290–309.
  1972   "The Evolution of Community Patterns in the Tehuacán Valley of Mexico and Speculations about the Cultural Processes," in *Man, Settlement, and Urbanism,* ed. Peter J. Ucko, Ruth Tringham, and Geoffrey W. Dimbleby (London: Gerald Duckworth and Co.), pp. 67–93.
MAC NEISH, RICHARD S., MELVIN L. FOWLER, ANGEL GARCÍA COOK, FREDERICK A. PETERSON, ANTOINETTE NELKEN-TERNER, AND JAMES A. NEELY
  1972   *The Prehistory of the Tehuacán Valley,* vol. 5: *Excavations and Reconnaissance* (Austin: University of Texas Press).
MAC NEISH, RICHARD S., AND ANGEL GARCÍA COOK
  1972   "Excavations in the San Marcos Locality in the Travertine Slopes," in *Prehistory of the Tehuacán Valley* vol. 5: *Excavations and Reconnaissance,* by Richard S. MacNeish, Melvin L. Fowler, Angel García Cook, Frederick A. Peterson, Antoinette Nelken-Terner, and James A. Neely. (Austin: University of Texas Press), pp. 137–60.
MAC NEISH, RICHARD S., ANTOINETTE NELKEN-TERNER, AND IRMGARD W. JOHNSON
  1967   *The Prehistory of the Tehuacán Valley,* vol. 2: *Nonceramic Artifacts* (Austin: University of Texas Press).
MAC NEISH, RICHARD S., FREDERICK A. PETERSON, AND KENT V. FLANNERY
  1970   *The Prehistory of the Tehuacán Valley,* vol. 3: *Ceramics* (Austin: University of Texas Press).
MANGELSDORF, PAUL C.
  1974   *Corn: Its Origin, Evolution, and Improvement* (Cambridge, Mass.: Harvard University Press).

MANGELSDORF, PAUL C., RICHARD S. MAC NEISH, AND WALTON C. GALINAT
  1967   "Prehistoric Wild and Cultivated Maize," in *The Prehistory of the Tehuacán Valley,* vol. 1: *Environment and Subsistence,* ed. Douglas S. Byers (Austin: University of Texas Press), pp. 178–200.
MARCUS, JOYCE
  1970   An Analysis of the Color-Direction Symbolism Among the Maya, manuscript, Harvard University, Peabody Museum (Cambridge, Mass.).
  1973   "Territorial Organization of the Lowland Classic Maya," *Science* 180:911–16.
  1974   "The Iconography of Power among the Classic Maya," *World Archaeology* 6(1):83–94.
  1976a   *Emblem and State in the Classic Maya Lowlands: An Epigraphic Approach to Territorial Organization* (Washington, D.C.: Dumbarton Oaks Research Library and Collection and Trustees for Harvard University).
  1976b   "The Size of the Early Mesoamerican Village," in *The Early Mesoamerican Village,* ed. Kent V. Flannery (New York: Academic Press), pp. 79–90.
  1976c   "The Origins of Mesoamerican Writing," *Annual Review of Anthropology* 5:35–67.
  1976d   "The Iconography of Militarism at Monte Albán and Neighboring Sites in the Valley of Oaxaca," in *The Origins of Religious Art and Iconography in Preclassic Mesoamerica,* ed. Henry B. Nicholson (Los Angeles: University of California at Los Angeles, Latin American Center), pp. 123–39.
  1978   "Archaeology and Religion: A Comparison of the Zapotec and Maya," *World Archaeology* 10(2):172–91.
  1980   "Zapotec Writing," *Scientific American* 242:50–64.
MARCUS, JOYCE, AND KENT V. FLANNERY
  1978   "Ethnoscience of the Sixteenth-Century Valley Zapotec," in *The Nature and Status of Ethnobotany,* ed. Richard I. Ford, Anthropological Papers of the University of Michigan Museum of Anthropology 67 (Ann Arbor), pp. 51–79.
MARQUINA, IGNACIO
  1951   *Arquitectura Prehispánica, Memorias* 1 (México, D.F.: Instituto Nacional de Antropología e Historia).
MARTÍNEZ GRACIDA, MANUEL
  1883   Colección de cuadros sinópticos, Anexo no. 50 a la memoria administrativa. (Oaxaca).
  1888a   *El rey Cocijoeza y su familia* (México: Oficina Tipográfico de la Secretaría de Fomento). [reprinted 1972]
  1888b   "Catálogo etimológico de los nombres de los pueblos, haciendas y ranchos del Estado de Oaxaca," *Boletín de la Sociedad Mexicana de Geografía y Estadística,* 4a. época 1(5–6):285–438 (México).
  1905   Civilización Mixteca, Historia antigua de la Mixteca (Manuscrito en Colección Martínez Gracida de la Casa de Cultura, Oaxaca, México).
  1972   *El rey Cocijoeza y su familia* (Oaxaca: Sociedad Cultural Pro-Zaachila, second edition, mimeographed. First edition: 1888).
MASON, ROGER D., DENNIS E. LEWARCH, MICHAEL J. O'BRIEN, AND JAMES A. NEELY
  1977   "An Archaeological Survey on the Xoxocotlán Piedmont, Oaxaca, Mexico," *American Antiquity* 42(4):567–75.
MATA, FRAY JUAN DE
  1580   "Relación de Teozapotlan," in *Papeles de Nueva España: segunda serie, Geografía y Estadística,* vol. 4, ed. Francisco del Paso y Troncoso (Madrid 1905), pp. 190–95.
Mc CLELLAND, DAVID C.
  1967   *The Achieving Society* (New York: Free Press). [First edition, Van Nostrand, 1961]
Mc QUOWN, NORMAN A., AND JULIAN PITT-RIVERS, EDS.

1970    *Ensayos de Antropología en la Zona Central de Chiapas* (México, D.F.: Instituto Nacional Indigenista).

MENDIETA Y NÚÑEZ, LUCIO, (ED.)
1949    *Los zapotecos: monografía histórica, etnográfica y económica* (México: Imprenta Universitaria).

MESSER, ELLEN
1978    Zapotec Plant Knowledge: Classification, Uses, and Communication about Plants in Mitla, Oaxaca, Mexico, *Prehistory and Human Ecology of the Valley of Oaxaca,* vol. 5, part 2, eds. Kent V. Flannery and Richard E. Blanton, Memoirs of the University of Michigan Museum of Anthropology 10 (Ann Arbor).

METCALFE, GRACE
1946    "Indice de la Palestra Historial y la Geográfica Descripción de Burgoa," *Boletín del Archivo General de la Nación* 17:4 (México: Archivo General de la Nación).

MILES, SUZANNE W.
1965    "Sculpture of the Guatemala-Chiapas Highlands and Pacific Slopes, and Associated Hieroglyphs," in *Handbook of Middle American Indians,* vol. 2: *Archaeology of Southern Mesoamerica,* part 1, eds. Robert Wauchope and Gordon R. Willey (Austin: University of Texas Press), pp. 237–87.

MILLER, ARTHUR G.
1973    *The Mural Painting of Teotihuacán* (Washington, D.C.: Dumbarton Oaks Research Library and Collection and Trustees for Harvard University).

MILLON, CLARA
1973    "Painting, Writing, and Polity at Teotihuacán, Mexico," *American Antiquity* 38(3):294–314.

MILLON, RENÉ
1967a    "Teotihuacán," *Scientific American* 216(6):38–48.
1967b    "Urna de Monte Albán IIIA encontrada en Teotihuacán," *Boletín del Instituto Nacional de Antropología e Historia* 29:42–44.
1973    *Urbanization at Teotihuacán, Mexico, vol. 1, The Teotihuacán Map, part 1: Text* (Austin: University of Texas Press).
1976    "Social Relations in Ancient Teotihuacán," in *The Valley of Mexico: Studies in Pre-Hispanic Ecology and Society,* ed. Eric R. Wolf (Albuquerque: School of American Research, University of New Mexico Press), pp. 205–48.

MOLINA, ALONSO DE
1944    *Vocabulario en lengua castellana y mexicana* (Madrid: Ediciones Cultura Hispánica). [First edition 1571]

MORISON, SAMUEL ELIOT
1965    *The Oxford History of the American People* (New York: Oxford University Press).

MORLEY, FRANCES R., AND SYLVANUS G. MORLEY
1938    *The Age and Provenance of the Leyden Plate,* Carnegie Institution of Washington, Contributions to American Anthropology and History, Pub. 509, Contrib. 24 (Washington, D.C.).

MORLEY, SYLVANUS G. (REVISED BY GEORGE W. BRAINERD)
1956    *The Ancient Maya,* 3rd edition (Stanford: Stanford University Press).

MOSER, CHRISTOPHER L.
1969a    "Tomb 1 at Barrio del Rosario, Huitzo, Oaxaca," *Katunob* 7(1):17–21.
1969b    "La Tumba 1 del Barrio del Rosario, Huitzo, Oaxaca," *Boletín* 36:41–47 (México, D.F.: Instituto Nacional de Antropología e Historia).
1972    "Ñuiñe Hieroglyphics of the Mixteca Baja," in *Religión en Mesoamérica, Twelfth Mesa Redonda* (México, D.F.: Sociedad Mexicana de Antropología), pp. 269–73.
1975    "Cueva de Ejutla: una cueva funeraria postclasica?" *Boletín del Instituto Nacional de Antropología e Historia*

14(July–Sept.): 25–36.
1976    "Cueva de Ejutla: A Postclassic Burial Cave?" *Katunob* 9(1):22–28. [English translation of Moser 1975 without illustrations]
1977a    *Ñuiñe Writing and Iconography of the Mixteca Baja,* Vanderbilt University Publications in Anthropology 19 (Nashville, Tenn.).
1977b    "The Head-Effigies of the Mixteca Baja," *Katunob* 10(2):1–18.
n.d.    "Descriptive Analysis of the Ceramic Headlets of the Mixteca Baja, unpublished manuscript (1969).

MURDOCK, GEORGE PETER
1949    *Social Structure* (New York: The Macmillan Co.).

NADEL, SIEGFRIED FREDERICK
1942    *A Black Byzantium: The Kingdom of Nupe in Nigeria* (London: Oxford University Press).

NADER, LAURA
1969    "The Zapotec of Oaxaca," in *Handbook of Middle American Indians,* vol. 7: *Ethnology,* part 1, eds. Robert Wauchope and Evon Z. Vogt (Austin: University of Texas Press), pp. 329–59.

NAVARRETE, CARLOS
1966    *The Chiapanec History and Culture,* New World Archaeological Foundation, Paper 21 (Provo, Ut.: Brigham Young University).

NEELY, JAMES A.
1967    "Organización hidráulica y sistemas de irrigación prehistóricos en el Valle de Oaxaca," *Boletín del Instituto Nacional de Antropología e Historia* 27:15–17 (México, D.F.).
1972    "Prehistoric Domestic Water Supplies and Irrigation Systems at Monte Albán, Oaxaca, Mexico," paper presented at the Thirty-seventh Annual Meeting of the Society for American Archaeology, Miami, Fla.

NETTING, ROBERT M.
1972    "Sacred Power and Centralization: Aspects of Political Adaptation in Africa," in *Population Growth: Anthropological Implications,* ed. Brian Spooner (Cambridge, Mass.: M.I.T. Press), pp. 219–44.

NICHOLSON, HENRY B.
1959    "The Chapultepec Cliff Sculpture of Motecuhzoma Xocoyotzin," *El México Antiguo* 9:379–444.
1960    "The Mixteca-Puebla Concept in Mesoamerican Archaeology: A Re-examination," in *Men and Cultures: Selected Papers from the Fifth International Congress of Anthropological and Ethnological Sciences,* ed. Anthony F. C. Wallace (Philadelphia: University of Pennsylvania Press), pp. 612–17.
1967    "Review of Interpretación del Codice Selden 3135 (A.2) by Alfonso Caso," *American Antiquity* 32:257–58.
1971    "Religion in pre-Hispanic Central Mexico," in *Handbook of Middle American Indians,* vol. 10: *Archaeology of Northern Mesoamerica,* part 1, eds. Robert Wauchope, Gordon F. Ekholm, and Ignacio Bernal (Austin: University of Texas Press), pp. 395–446.

NIEDERBERGER, CHRISTINE B.
1969    "Paleoecología humana y playas lacustres postpleistocénicas en Tlapacoya," *Boletín del Instituto Nacional de Antropología e Historia* 37:19–24 (México, D.F.).

NOWOTNY, KARL A.
1948    "Erläuterungen zum Codex Vindobonensis (Vorderseite)," *Archiv für Völkerkunde* 3:156–200.
1961a    *Codices Becker I/II* (Graz, Austria: Akademische Druck- u. Verlagsanstalt).
1961b    *Tlacuilolli: Die mexikanischen Bilderhandschriften: Stil und Inhalt* (Berlin: Verlag Gebr. Mann).
1970    *Beiträge zur Geschichte des Weltbildes: Farben und Weltrichtungen* (Vienna: Ferdinand Berger & Söhne).

NUTTALL, ZELIA
1902 *Codex Nuttall: Facsimile of an Ancient Mexican Codex Belonging to Lord Zouche of Harynworth, England* (Cambridge, Mass.: Peabody Museum, Harvard University).

OKADA, FERDINAND E.
1954 "A Comparative Study of Marginal Societies" (Ph.D. diss., Columbia University).

OLSSON, INGRID U., ED.
1970 *Radiocarbon Variations and Absolute Chronology, Proceedings of the Twelfth Nobel Symposium, Uppsala, Sweden, Aug. 11–15, 1969* (Stockholm: Almquist and Wiksell; New York: Wiley Interscience Division, John Wiley and Sons).

PACHO, RODRIGO
1581 "Relación de Nochiztlán," in *Papeles de Nueva España: segunda serie, Geografía y Estadística,* vol. 4, ed. Francisco del Paso y Troncoso (Madrid 1905), pp. 206–12.

PADDOCK, JOHN
1953 "Excavations in the Mixteca Alta," *Mesoamerican Notes* 3:1–50.
1955a "The First Three Seasons at Yagul," *Mesoamerican Notes* 4:25–47.
1955b "Place Names," *Mesoamerican Notes* 4:68–69.
1955c "Some Observations," *Mesoamerican Notes* 4:80–90.
1957 "The 1956 Season at Yagul," *Mesoamerican Notes* 5:13–35.
1958a "Clarifications and Suggestions," *Boletín de Estudios Oaxaqueños* 8:9–18.
1958b "Comments on Some Problems of Oaxaca Archeology," *Boletín de Estudios Oaxaqueños* 4.
1959 "Tomorrow in Ancient Mesoamerica," *Texas Quarterly* 2(1):78–98.
1960 "Exploración en Yagul, Oaxaca," *Revista Mexicana de Estudios Antropológicos* 16:91–96.
1961 "A Neglected Viewpoint on Humanity and Science in Archaeology," in *Homenaje a Pablo Martínez del Río,* eds. Ignacio Bernal, Jorge Gurría, Santiago Genovés, and Luis Aveleyra Arroyo de Anda (Mexico: Instituto Nacional de Antropología e Historia), pp. 323–35.
1964 "La etnohistoria mixteca y Monte Albán V," in *Actas y Memorias del XXXV Congreso Internacional de Americanistas,* 1962, 1:461–78 (Mexico).
1965 "Current Research: Western Mesoamerica," *American Antiquity* 31(1):133–36.
1966a "Oaxaca in Ancient Mesoamerica," in *Ancient Oaxaca: Discoveries in Mexican Archaeology and History,* ed. John Paddock (Stanford: Stanford University Press), pp. 83–242.
1966b "La idea del imperio aplicada a Mesoamérica," *Revista Mexicana de Estudios Antropológicos* 20:83–94.
1966c "Mixtec Ethnohistory and Monte Albán V," in *Ancient Oaxaca: Discoveries in Mexican Archaeology and History,* ed. John Paddock (Stanford: Stanford University Press), pp. 367–85.
1966d "Monte Albán: ¿Sede de imperio?" *Revista Mexicana de Estudios Antropológicos* 20:117–46.
1966e *Ancient Oaxaca: Discoveries in Mexican Archaeology* (ED.) *and History* (Stanford: Stanford University Press).
1966f "The Mixteca in Early Urban Times," in *Ancient Oaxaca: Discoveries in Mexican Archaeology and History,* ed. John Paddock (Stanford: Stanford University Press), pp. 174–99.
1967 "Current Research: Western Mesoamerica," *American Antiquity* 32(3):422–27.
1968a "Current Research: Western Mesoamerica," *American Antiquity* 33(1):122–28.
1968b "Una tumba en Ñuyoo, Huajuapan de León, Oaxaca,"

*Boletín del Instituto Nacional de Antropología e Historia,* Epoca 1, 33: 51–54 (México, D.F.).
1970a "A Beginning in the Ñuiñe: Salvage Excavations at Ñuyoo, Huajuapan," *Boletín de Estudios Oaxaqueños* 26.
1970b "More Ñuiñe Materials," *Boletín de Estudios Oaxaqueños* 28.
1970c "Radiocarbon Dates of Monte Albán I–V," *Boletín de Estudios Oaxaqueños* 33:14–15 (Mitla, Oaxaca: Museo Frissell de Arte Zapoteca).
1972a "Distribución de rasgos teotihuacanos en Mesoamérica," *Teotihuacán: XI Mesa Redonda* (México: Sociedad Mexicana de Antropología), pp. 223–39.
1972b "Religión antigua oaxaqueña: ensayo y lección," *Religión en Mesoamérica* (México: Sociedad Mexicana de Antropología), pp. 247–68.
1973 "Pristine Urbanism in Mesoamerica," paper presented at the Thirty-eighth Annual Meetings of the Society for American Archaeology, San Francisco, Cal.
1975 "Comments on Ancient Huaxyacac," *Boletín* (Oaxaca, México: Centro Regional de Oaxaca, Instituto Nacional de Antropología e Historia).
1978 "The Middle Classic Period in Oaxaca," in *Middle Class Mesoamerica: A.D. 400–700,* ed. Esther Pasztory (New York: Columbia University Press), pp. 45–62.

PADDOCK, JOHN, JOSEPH R. MOGOR, AND MICHAEL D. LIND
1968 "Lambityeco Tomb 2: A Preliminary Report," *Boletín de Estudios Oaxaqueños* 25 (Mitla, Oaxaca: Museo Frissell de Arte Zapoteca).

PANOFSKY, ERWIN
1964 "Iconography and Iconology," in *Art and Philosophy: Readings in Aesthetics,* ed. W. E. Kennick (New York: St. Martin's Press), pp. 391–402.

PAREYÓN MORENO, EDUARDO
1960 "Exploraciones arqueológicas en Ciudad Vieja de Quiotepec, Oaxaca," *Revista Mexicana de Estudios Antropológicos* 16:97–104.

PARMENTER, ROSS
1961 "20th century adventures of a 16th century sheet: the literature on the Mixtec lienzo in the Royal Ontario Museum," *Boletín de Estudios Oaxaqueños* 20 (Mitla, Oaxaca: Museo Frissell de Arte Zapoteca).

PARSONS, ELSIE CLEWS
1936 *Mitla: Town of the Souls and other Zapotec-speaking Pueblos of Oaxaca, Mexico* (Chicago: University of Chicago Press).

PARSONS, JEFFREY R.
1968 "Teotihuacán, Mexico, and its Impact on Regional Demography," *Science* 162(3856):872–77.
1971a Prehistoric Settlement Patterns in the Texcoco Region, Mexico. Memoirs of the University of Michigan Museum of Anthropology 3 (Ann Arbor).
1971b "Pre-Hispanic Settlement Patterns in the Chalco Region, Mexico, 1969 Season," report presented to the Instituto Nacional de Antropología e Historia, Mexico City.
1974 "The Development of a Prehistoric Complex Society: A Regional Perspective from the Valley of Mexico," *Journal of Field Archaeology* 1:81–108.

PARSONS, LEE A.
1969 *Bilbao, Guatemala: An Archaeological Study of the Pacific Coast Cotzumalhuapa Region,* vol. 2, Publications in Anthropology 12 (Milwaukee: Milwaukee Public Museum).

PASO Y TRONCOSO., SEE DEL PASO Y TRONCOSO

PASZTORY, ESTHER, ED.
1978 *Middle Classic Mesoamerica: A.D. 400–700* (New York: Columbia University Press).

PAYNE, WILLIAM O.
1970 "A Potter's Analysis of the Pottery from Lambityeco Tomb 2," *Boletín de Estudios Oaxaqueños* 29 (Mitla, Oaxaca: Museo Frissell de Arte Zapoteca).

PEÑAFIEL, ANTONIO
1885 *Nombres geográficos de México . . .* (Mexico: Secretaría de Fomento).

PÉREZ DE ZAMORA, PEDRO
1580 "Relación de Teticpac," in *Papeles de Nueva España: segunda serie, Geografía y Estadística,* vol. 4, ed. Francisco del Paso y Troncoso (Madrid 1905), pp. 109–14.

PÉREZ GARCÍA, ROSENDO
1956 *La Sierra Juárez,* 2 vols. (México: Comisión del Papaloapan).

PETERSON, DAVID ANDREW
1976 "Ancient Commerce" (unpublished Ph.D. diss., State University of New York at Binghamton).

PETERSON, DAVID ANDREW, AND THOMAS B. MAC DOUGALL
1974 *Guiengola: A Fortified Site in the Isthmus of Tehuantepec,* Vanderbilt University Publications in Anthropology 10 (Nashville, Tenn.).

PICKETT, VELMA B.
1959 *Castellano-Zapoteco y Zapoteco-Castellano, dialecto del Zapoteco del Istmo,* Serie de Vocabularios Indígenas Mariano Silva y Aceves 3 (México, D.F.: Secretaría de Educación Pública).

PIKE, KENNETH L.
1945 "Tone puns in Mixteco," *International Journal of American Linguistics* 11:129–39.

PIÑA CHAN, ROMÁN
1960 "Algunos sitios arqueológicos de Oaxaca y Guerrero," *Revista Mexicana de Estudios Antropológicos* 16:65–76.

PIRES-FERREIRA, JANE WHEELER
1975 "Formative Mesoamerican Exchange Networks with Special Reference to the Valley of Oaxaca," *Prehistory and Human Ecology of the Valley of Oaxaca,* ed. Kent V. Flannery, vol. 3, Memoirs of the University of Michigan Museum of Anthropology 7 (Ann Arbor).
1976 "Shell and Iron-ore Mirror Exchange in Formative Mesoamerica, with Comments on other Commodities," in *The Early Mesoamerican Village,* ed. Kent V. Flannery (New York: Academic Press), pp. 311–26.

PLOG, STEPHEN
1976 "The Measurement of Prehistoric Interaction between Communities," in *The Early Mesoamerican Village,* ed. Kent V. Flannery (New York: Academic Press), pp. 255–72.

PROSKOURIAKOFF, TATIANA
1960 "Historical Implications of a Pattern of Dates at Piedras Negras, Guatemala," *American Antiquity* 25:454–75.
1963 "Historical Data in the Inscriptions of Yaxchilán, part I," *Estudios de Cultura Maya* 3:149–66.
1964 "Historical Data in the Inscriptions of Yaxchilán, part II," *Estudios de Cultura Maya* 4:177–201.

PYNE, NANETTE M.
1976 "The Fire-Serpent and Were-Jaguar in Formative Oaxaca: a Contingency Table Analysis," in *The Early Mesoamerican Village,* ed. Kent V. Flannery (New York: Academic Press), pp. 272–80.

QUIRARTE, JACINTO
1973 *El estilo artístico de Izapa* (México: Instituto de Investigaciones Estéticas, Universidad Nacional Autónoma de México).

RABIN, EMILY
1970 "The Lambityeco Friezes: Notes on Their Content, With an Appendix on C$_{14}$ Dates," *Boletín de Estudios Oaxaqueños* 33.

1974 "Some Problems of Chronology in the Mixtec Historical Manuscripts," paper presented at the XLI International Congress of Americanists, Mexico, D.F.
1975 "Calendrical Names in the Mixtec Historical Manuscripts: A Preliminary Study," paper presented at the Fortieth Annual Meeting of the Society for American Archaeology, Dallas, Tex.
1976 "Some Problems of Chronology in the Mixtec Historical Manuscripts, Part II" (to be published in *Tlacuilolli* II).

RADIOCARBON
(New Haven: American Journal of Science)

RADIN, PAUL
1935 "An Historical Legend of the Zapotecs," *Ibero-Americana* 9 (Berkeley: University of California Press).

RALPH, ELIZABETH K., H. N. MICHAEL, AND M. C. HAN
1973 "Radiocarbon Dates and Reality," *MASCA Newsletter* 9(1):1–20 (Philadelphia: University Museum, University of Pennsylvania).

RAMSEY, JAMES R.
1975 "An Analysis of Mixtec Minor Art, with a Catalogue" (unpublished PhD. diss., Tulane University).

RAPPAPORT, ROY A.
1968 *Pigs for the Ancestors: Ritual in the Ecology of a New Guinea People* (New Haven: Yale University Press).
1971a "Ritual, Sanctity, and Cybernetics," *American Anthropologist* 73:59–76.
1971b "The Sacred in Human Evolution," *Annual Review of Ecology and Systematics* 2:23–44.

REED, VERNER Z.
1896 "The Ute Bear Dance," *American Anthropologist* (old series) 9:237–44.

RENDÓN, JUAN JOSÉ
1975 "Estudio de los factores sociales en la diversificación del zapoteco," *Anales de Antropología* 12:283–318.

REYES, ANTONIO DE LOS
1593 *Arte en lengua mixteca . . .* (México). [Reprinted in Vanderbilt University Publications in Anthropology 14 (Nashville, Tenn.), 1976]
1890 "Arte en lengua mixteca," *Actes de la Société Philologique,* vol. 18 (Paris 1888).

RICKARDS, CONSTANTINE GEORGE
1910 *The Ruins of Mexico* (London).

RMEH (REVISTA MEXICANA DE ESTUDIOS HISTÓRICOS)
1927–28 (Publication suspended 1929; resumed as *Revista Mexicana de Estudios Antropológicos* in 1939), vols. 1–2.

ROBERTSON, DONALD
1959a *Mexican Manuscript Painting of the Early Colonial Period: The Metropolitan Schools* (New Haven: Yale University Press).
1959b "The Relaciones Geográficas of Mexico," *Actas del 33rd Congreso Internacional de Americanistas* 2:540–47 (San José de Costa Rica).
1966 "The Mixtec Religious Manuscripts," in *Ancient Oaxaca: Discoveries in Mexican Archaeology and History,* ed. John Paddock (Stanford: Stanford University Press), pp. 298–312.

ROJAS GONZALEZ, FRANCISCO
1949 "Los zapotecos en la época prehispánica," in *Los zapotecos: monografía histórica, etnográfica, y económica,* ed. Lucio Mendieta y Núñez (México: Imprenta Universitaria), pp. 35–102.

ROMNEY, A. KIMBALL
1957 "The Genetic Model and Uto-Aztecan Time Perspective," *Davidson Journal of Anthropology* 3(2):35–41.
1967 "Kinship and Family," in *Handbook of Middle American Indians,* vol. 6: *Social Anthropology,* eds. Robert Wauchope and Manning Nash (Austin: University of Texas Press), pp. 207–37.

ROYS, LAWRENCE
1934   *The Engineering Knowledge of the Maya,* Carnegie Institution of Washington, pub. 436, contrib. 6 (Washington, D.C.).

RUBÍN DE LA BORBOLLA, DANIEL F.
1969   "La osamenta humana encontrada en la Tumba 7," in *El tesoro de Monte Albán,* Memorias del Instituto Nacional de Antropología e Historia 3:275–324 (México, D.F.).

SAALMAN, HOWARD
1968   *Medieval Cities* (New York: George Braziller).

SÁENZ, CÉSAR A.
1961   "Tres estelas en Xochicalco," *Revista Mexicana de Estudios Antropológicos* 17:39–66.

SAHLINS, MARSHALL D.
1958   *Social Stratification in Polynesia,* American Ethnological Society, monograph 29 (Seattle: University of Washington Press).
1972   *Stone Age Economics* (Chicago: Aldine-Atherton).

SAHLINS, MARSHALL D., AND ELMAN R. SERVICE, EDS.
1960   *Evolution and Culture* (Ann Arbor: University of Michigan Press).

SALAS, G. P.
1949   "Bosquejo geológico de la cuenca sedimentaria de Oaxaca," *Boletín Asociación Mexicana de Geología y Petroleo* 1(2):79–156.

SALAZAR, AGUSTÍN DE
1581   "Descripción del pueblo de Cuylapa," in *Dos relaciones antiguas del pueblo de Cuilapa, estado de Oaxaca,* ed. Robert H. Barlow, *Tlalocan* 2(1):18–28 [1945].

SANDERS, WILLIAM T.
1956   "The Central Mexican Symbiotic Region," in *Prehistoric Settlement Patterns in the New World,* ed. Gordon R. Willey, Viking Fund Publications in Anthropology, vol. 23 (New York: Wenner-Gren Foundation for Anthropological Research), pp. 115–27.
1965   The Cultural Ecology of the Teotihuacán Valley: a Preliminary Report of the Results of the Teotihuacán Valley Project, manuscript, Department of Sociology and Anthropology, Pennsylvania State University (University Park).
1966   "Review of *Desarrollo Cultural de los Mayas,* eds. Evon Z. Vogt and Alberto Ruz L.," *American Anthropologist* 68:1068–71.
1971   "Settlement Patterns in Central Mexico," in *Handbook of Middle American Indians,* vol. 10: *Archaeology of Northern Mesoamerica,* part 1, eds. Robert Wauchope, Gordon F. Ekholm, and Ignacio Bernal (Austin: University of Texas Press), pp. 3–44.
1972   "Population, Agricultural History and Societal Evolution in Mesoamerica," in *Population Growth: Anthropological Implications,* ed. Brian Spooner (Cambridge, Mass.: M.I.T. Press), pp. 101–53.
1974   "Chiefdom to State: Political Evolution at Kaminaljuyú, Guatemala," in *Reconstructing Complex Societies: An Archaeological Colloquium,* ed. Charlotte B. Moore, Supplement to the Bulletin of the American Schools of Oriental Research 20:97–116.

SANDERS, WILLIAM T., AND BARBARA J. PRICE
1968   *Mesoamerica: The Evolution of a Civilization* (New York: Random House).

SANDERS, WILLIAM T., AND ROBERT SANTLEY
1978   "Review of *Monte Albán: Settlement Patterns at the Ancient Zapotec Capital* by Richard Blanton," *Science* 202(4365):303–4.

SANDERS, WILLIAM T., MICHAEL WEST, CHARLES FLETCHER, AND JOSEPH MARINO
1975   *The Formative Period Occupation of the Valley,* The Teotihuacán Valley Project Final Report, vol. 2, Occasional Papers in Anthropology 10, Department of Sociology and Anthropology, Pennsylvania State University (University Park).

SANTAMARÍA, BERNARDO DE, AND JUAN DE CANSECO
1580   "Relación de Nexapa," in *Papeles de Nueva España: segunda serie, Geografía e Estadística,* vol. 4, ed. Francisco del Paso y Troncoso (Madrid 1905), pp. 29–44.

SANTLEY, ROBERT S.
1980   "Disembedded Capitals Reconsidered," *American Antiquity* 45(1):132–45.

SAPIR, EDWARD
1916   *Time Perspective in Aboriginal American Culture: A Study in Method,* Anthropological Series 13, Memoir 90, (Canada: Department of Mines).

SAVILLE, MARSHALL HOWARD
1899   "Exploration of Zapotecan Tombs in Southern Mexico," *American Anthropologist* (n.s.) 1:350–62.
1904   "Funeral Urns from Oaxaca," *The American Museum Journal* 4:49–60.
1909   *The Cruciform Structures of Mitla and Vicinity* (New York: author's edition, reprint from Putnam Anniversary Volume).
1922   *Turquoise Mosaic Art in Ancient Mexico,* Contribution VI, Museum of the American Indian (New York: Heye Foundation).

SCHMIDT, JOHANNES
1872   *Die Verwandschaftsverhältnisse der Indo-Germanischen Sprachen* (Weimar: H. Böhlau).

SCHOENWETTER, JAMES
1974   "Pollen Records of Guilá Naquitz Cave," *American Antiquity* 39(2):292–303.

SCHOENWETTER, JAMES, AND LANDON D. SMITH
n.d.   "Pollen Analysis of the Oaxacan Preceramic," in *Guilá Naquitz Cave: A Study of Hunting, Gathering, and Incipient Agriculture in Preceramic Oaxaca, Mexico,* ed. Kent V. Flannery, in preparation.

SCHUCHARDT, HUGO ERNST M.
1900   *Über die Klassifikation der Romanischen Mundarten* (Graz, Austria: Gedruckt von der K.K. Universitätbuchdr. "Styria").

SCOTT, JOHN F.
1971   "Post-Olmec Art in Preclassic Oaxaca, Mexico" (Ph.D. diss., Columbia University).

SÉJOURNÉ, LAURETTE
1960   "El simbolismo de los rituales funerarios en Monte Albán," *Revista Mexicana de Estudios Antropológicos* 16:77–90.
1966a  *El lenguaje de las formas en Teotihuacán* (México: Gabriel Mancera 65).
1966b  *Arqueología de Teotihuacán: La Cerámica* (México: Fondo de Cultura Económica).
1966c  *Arquitectura y pintura en Teotihuacán,* Siglo Veintiuno editores, S.A.

SELER, EDUARD
1902–  *Gesammelte Abhandlungen zur Amerikanischen Sprach-
1923   und Alterthums-kunde,* 5 vols. (Berlin: A. Asher & Co. and Behrend & Co.).
1904   "The Wall Paintings of Mitla, a Mexican Picture Writing in Fresco," in *Mexican and Central American Antiquities, Calendar Systems, and History:* 24 papers by Seler, Förstemann, Schellhas, Sapper, Dieseldorff, translated from the German under supervision of Charles P. Bowditch, Bureau of American Ethnology, Bulletin 28:247–324 (Washington, D.C.: U.S. Government Printing Office).
1908   "Das Dorfbuch von Santiago Guevea," in *Gesammelte Abhandlungen,* vol. 3 (Graz, Austria), pp. 157–93. [reprinted, 1960]

SERVICE, ELMAN R.
1962   *Primitive Social Organization: An Evolutionary Perspective* (New York: Random House).

1975    *Origins of the State and Civilization* (New York: Norton).

SHAPLIN, PHILIPPA D.
1975    "An Introduction to the Stylistic Study of Oaxaca Urns" (unpublished Master's thesis, Wellesley College).

SHARP, ROSEMARY
1970    "Early Architectural Grecas in the Valley of Oaxaca," *Boletín de Estudios Oaxaqueños* 32.

SJOBERG, GIDEON
1960    *The Preindustrial City: Past and Present* (First Free Press paperback edition 1965).

SKINNER, ELLIOTT P.
1964    *The Mossi of the Upper Volta* (Stanford: Stanford University Press).

SMITH, CAROL A.
1975    "Examining Stratification Systems Through Peasant Marketing Arrangements: An Application of Some Models from Economic Geography," *Man* 10:95–122.

SMITH, C. EARLE, JR.
1967    "Plant Remains," in *The Prehistory of the Tehuacán Valley*, vol. 1: *Environment and Subsistence*, ed. Douglas S. Byers (Austin: University of Texas Press), pp. 220–55.
1976    *Modern Vegetation and Ancient Plant Remains of the Nochixtlán Valley, Oaxaca*, Vanderbilt University Publications in Anthropology 16 (Nashville, Tenn.).
1978    "The Vegetational History of the Oaxaca Valley," in *Prehistory and Human Ecology of the Valley of Oaxaca*, vol. 5, part 1, eds. Kent V. Flannery and Richard E. Blanton, Memoirs of the University of Michigan Museum of Anthropology 10 (Ann Arbor).
n.d.    "Early Adaptations to Environmental Differences in Mexico," manuscript, Department of Anthropology, University of Alabama (University).

SMITH, MARY ELIZABETH
1963    "The Codex Colombino, A Document of the South Coast of Oaxaca," *Tlalocan* 4(3):276–88.
1973a   *Picture Writing from Ancient Southern Mexico: Mixtec Place Signs and Maps* (Norman: University of Oklahoma Press).
1973b   "The Relationship between Mixtec Manuscript Painting and the Mixtec Language: A Study of Some Personal Names in Codices Muro and Sánchez Solís," in *Mesoamerican Writing Systems: A Conference at Dumbarton Oaks, October 30th and 31st, 1971*, ed. Elizabeth P. Benson (Washington: Dumbarton Oaks, Trustees for Harvard University), pp. 47–98.
1974    "Codex Selden: A Manuscript from the Valley of Nochixtlán?" paper presented at the Forty-first International Congress of Americanists, México, D.F.

SMITH, MICHAEL G.
1960    *Government in Zazzau* (London: Oxford University Press).

SPENCE, MICHAEL W.
1976    "Human Skeletal Material from the Oaxaca Barrio in Teotihuacán, Mexico," in *Archaeological Frontiers: Papers on New World High Cultures in Honor of J. Charles Kelley*, ed. Robert B. Pickering, Southern Illinois University, University Museum Studies 4, pp. 129–48.

SPENCER, CHARLES S.
1979    "Irrigation, Administration, and Society in Formative Tehuacán," in *Prehistoric Social, Political, and Economic Development in the Area of the Tehuacán Valley*, ed. Robert D. Drennan, Technical Reports of the University of Michigan Museum of Anthropology 11 (Ann Arbor), pp. 13–109.

SPINDEN, HERBERT J.
1924    "The Reduction of Mayan Dates," *Papers of the Peabody Museum of American Archaeology and Ethnology, Har-*

*vard University*, vol. 6, no. 4 (Cambridge, Massachusetts: Peabody Museum).
1935    "Indian Manuscripts of Southern Mexico," *Annual Report of the Smithsonian Institution, 1933* (Washington, D.C.: The Smithsonian Institution), pp. 429–51.

SPOONER, BRIAN, ED.
1972    *Population Growth: Anthropological Implications* (Cambridge, Mass.: M.I.T. Press).

SPORES, RONALD
1965    "The Zapotec and Mixtec at Spanish Contact," in *Handbook of Middle American Indians*, vol. 3: *Archaeology of Southern Mesoamerica*, part 2, eds. Robert Wauchope and Gordon R. Willey (Austin: University of Texas Press), pp. 962–87.
1967    *The Mixtec Kings and Their People* (Norman: University of Oklahoma Press).
1969    "Settlement, Farming Technology, and Environment in the Nochixtlán Valley," *Science* 166:557–69.
1972    *An Archaeological Settlement Survey of the Nochixtlán Valley, Oaxaca*, Vanderbilt University Publications in Anthropology 1 (Nashville, Tenn.).
1974a   *Stratigraphic Excavations in the Nochixtlán Valley, Oaxaca*, Vanderbilt University Publications in Anthropology 11 (Nashville, Tenn.).
1974b   "Marital Alliances in the Political Integration of Mixtec Kingdoms," *American Anthropologist* 76:297–311.

SPORES, RONALD, AND MIGUEL SALDAÑA
1973    *Documentos Para la Etnohistoria del Estado de Oaxaca: Indice del Ramo de Mercedes del Archivo General de la Nación, Mexico*, Vanderbilt University Publications in Anthropology 5 (Nashville, Tenn.).
1975    *Documentos Para la Etnohistoria del Estado de Oaxaca: Indice del Ramo de Indios del Archivo General de la Nación, México*, Vanderbilt University Publications in Anthropology 13 (Nashville, Tenn.).

STARR, FREDERICK
1900    "Notes upon the Ethnography of Southern Mexico," 2 parts: *Proceedings of the Davenport Academy of Natural Science*, vols. 8, 9.
1908    *In Indian Mexico: A Narrative of Travel and Labor* (Chicago: Forbes and Co.).

STEWARD, JULIAN
1938    *Basin-Plateau Aboriginal Sociopolitical Groups*, *Bureau of American Ethnology Bulletin* of the Smithsonian Institution 120 (Washington, D.C.).
1955    *Theory of Culture Change* (Urbana: University of Illinois Press).

STIRLING, MATTHEW W.
1943    *Stone Monuments of Southern Mexico*, *Bureau of American Ethnology Bulletin* 138 (Washington, D.C.: U.S. Government Printing Office).
1965    "Monumental Sculpture of Southern Veracruz and Tabasco," in *Handbook of Middle American Indians*, vol. 3: *Archaeology of Southern Mesoamerica*, part 2, eds. Robert Wauchope and Gordon R. Willey (Austin: University of Texas Press), pp. 716–38.

SUÁREZ, MELCHIOR
1962    "Relación de Guautla," *Tlalocan* 4(1):3–16 (ed. Ignacio Bernal).

SUESS, H. E.
1970    "Bristlecone Pine Calibration of the Radiocarbon Time-Scale 5200 B.C. to the Present," in *Radiocarbon Variations and Absolute Chronology, Proceedings of the Twelfth Nobel Symposium, Uppsala, Sweden, August 11–15, 1969* (Stockholm: Almquist and Wiksell [New York: Wiley Interscience Division, John Wiley and Sons]), pp. 303–11.

SWADESH, MORRIS
1949    "El Idioma de los Zapotecos," in *Los Zapotecos: Mono-*

*grafía histórica, Etnográfica, y Económica,* ed. Lucio Mendieta y Núñez (México: Imprenta Universitaria), pp. 415–48.

1951 "Lexicostatistic Dating of Prehistoric Contacts," *Proceedings of the American Philosophical Society,* vol. 96.

1967 "Lexicostatistic Classification," in *Handbook of Middle American Indians,* vol. 5: *Linguistics,* ed. Norman A. McQuown (Austin: University of Texas Press), pp. 79–115.

TARACENA, ÁNGEL
1941 *Efemérides Oaxaqueñas.* Oaxaca, Mexico.

TAX, SOL, ED.
1968 *Heritage of Conquest* (New York: Cooper Square). [Facsimile of first edition, 1952]

TAYLOR, WILLIAM B.
1972 *Landlord and Peasant in Colonial Oaxaca* (Stanford: Stanford University Press).

TELLERIANO-REMENSIS
[In *Kingsborough* 5:129–58.]

THOMPSON, J. ERIC S.
1948 "An Archaeological Reconnaissance in the Cotzumalhuapa Region, Escuintla, Guatemala," *Contributions to American Anthropology and History* 44, Carnegie Institution of Washington Publication 574 (Washington, D.C.).

1950 *Maya Hieroglyphic Writing: Introduction,* Carnegie Institution of Washington, Publication 589 (Washington, D.C.).

1962 *A Catalogue of Maya Hieroglyphs* (Norman: University of Oklahoma Press).

1966 "Merchant Gods of Middle America," in *Summa Antropológica en Homenaje a Roberto J. Weitlaner,* ed. Antonio Pompa y Pompa (México: Instituto Nacional de Antropología e Historia), pp. 159–85.

TORQUEMADA, JUAN DE
1723 *Los Veinte i un Libros Rituales i Monarchía Indiana,* 2nd edition, 3 vols. (Madrid). [first edition 1615, Sevilla]

TORRES DE LAGUNAS, JUAN
1954 "Relación de Tecuantepeque," in *Monografía de Tehuantepec,* ed. Alberto Cajigas Langner (Mexico: author's edition), pp. 47–57.

TROIKE, NANCY P.
1974 "The Codex Colombino-Becker" (Ph.D. diss., University of London).

1975 "The Meanings of Postures and Gestures in Mixtec Codices," paper presented at the Fortieth Annual Meeting of the Society for American Archaeology, Dallas, Tex.

1978 "Fundamental Changes in the Interpretations of the Mixtec Codices," *American Antiquity* 43(4):553–68.

VARNER, DUDLEY M.
1974 "Prehispanic Settlement Patterns in the Valley of Oaxaca, Mexico: The Etla Arm" (Ph.D. diss., University of Arizona, Department of Anthropology, Tucson).

VERA, JUAN DE
1581 "Relación de Acatlán y su Partido," in *Papeles de Nueva España: segunda serie, Geografía y Estadística,* vol. 4, ed. Francisco del Paso y Troncoso (Madrid 1905), pp. 55–80.

VOGT, EVON Z.
1963 "Courses of Regional Scope," in *The Teaching of Anthropology,* eds. David G. Mandelbaum, Gabriel W. Lasker, and Ethel M. Albert, American Anthropological Association, Memoir 94, vol. 1, pp. 183–90.

1964 "The Genetic Model and Maya Cultural Development," in *Desarrollo Cultural de Los Mayas,* eds. Evon Z. Vogt and Alberto Ruz Lhuillier (México, D.F.: Universidad Nacional Autónoma de México), pp. 9–48.

VOGT, EVON Z., AND ALBERTO RUZ LHUILLIER, EDS.
1964 *Desarrollo Cultural de Los Mayas* (México: Universidad Nacional Autónoma de México).

VON WINNING, HASSO
1947 "Representations of Temple Buildings as Decorative Patterns on Teotihuacán Pottery and Figurines." *Carnegie Institution of Washington, Notes on Middle American Anthropology and Ethnology* 3(83):170–77 (Washington, D.C.).

WARNER, ROSE ELLA, AND C. EARLE SMITH, JR.
1968 "Boll Weevil Found in Pre-Columbian Cotton from Mexico," *Science* 162:911–12.

WAUCHOPE, ROBERT, AND NORMAN A. Mc QUOWN, EDS.
1967 *Linguistics. Handbook of Middle American Indians,* vol. 5 (Austin: University of Texas Press).

WAUCHOPE, ROBERT, AND MANNING NASH, EDS.
1967 *Social Anthropology, Handbook of Middle American Indians,* vol. 6 (Austin: University of Texas Press).

WAUCHOPE, ROBERT AND GORDON R. WILLEY, EDS.
1965 *Archaeology of Southern Mesoamerica,* part 2, *Handbook of Middle American Indians,* vol. 3 (Austin: University of Texas Press).

WEAVER, MURIEL PORTER
1972 *The Aztecs, Maya, and Their Predecessors: Archaeology of Mesoamerica* (New York: Seminar Press).

WEBSTER, DAVID
1975 "Warfare and the Origin of the State: A Reconsideration," *American Antiquity* 40:464–70.

WEISS, BRIAN
1975 "The New Archaeology," *Psychology Today* 8(12): 50–58.

WEISSNER, PAULINE
1977 "Hxaro: a Regional System of Reciprocity among the !Kung San for Reducing Risk" (Ph.D. diss., Department of Anthropology, University of Michigan).

WEITLANER, ROBERT J.
1941 "Los Pueblos no Nahuas de la Historia Tolteca y el Grupo Lingüístico Macro-Oto-Mangue," *Revista Mexicana de Estudios Antropológicos* 5(2–3):249–69.

1961 *Datos Diagnósticos Para la Etnohistoria del Norte de Oaxaca,* Instituto Nacional de Antropología e Historia, Dirección de Investigaciones Antropológicas, Publicación 6.

1969 "The Cuicatec," in *Handbook of Middle American Indians,* vol. 7: *Ethnology,* part 1, eds. Robert Wauchope and Evon Z. Vogt (Austin: University of Texas Press), pp. 434–47.

WEITLANER, ROBERT J., AND GABRIEL de CICCO
1962 "La Jerarquía de los Dioses Zapotecos del Sur," *Proceedings of the 34th International Congress of Americanists,* pp. 695–710.

WEITZ, MORRIS
1964 "The Form-Content Distinction," in *Art in Philosophy: Readings in Aesthetics,* ed. W. E. Kennick (New York: St. Martin's Press) pp. 339–50.

WHALEN, MICHAEL E.
1976a "Zoning Within an Early Formative Community in the Valley of Oaxaca," in *The Early Mesoamerican Village,* ed. Kent V. Flannery (New York: Academic Press), pp. 75–79.

1976b "Excavations at Santo Domingo Tomaltepec: Evolution of a Formative Community in the Valley of Oaxaca, Mexico" (Ph.D. diss., Department of Anthropology, University of Michigan).

1981 "Excavations at Santo Domingo Tomaltepec: Evolution of a Formative Community in the Valley of Oaxaca, Mexico," in *Prehistory and Human Ecology of the Valley of Oaxaca,* vol. 6, Memoirs of the University of Michigan Museum of Anthropology 12 (Ann Arbor).

WHALLON, ROBERT
1973 "Spatial Analysis of Occupation Floors I: Application of Dimensional Analysis of Variance," *American Antiquity* 38(3):266–78.

WHITAKER, THOMAS
n.d.    "Cucurbits from Guilá Naquitz Cave," in Guilá Naquitz Cave: A Study of Hunting, Gathering and Incipient Agriculture in Preceramic Oaxaca, Mexico, ed. Kent V. Flannery (in preparation).

WHITECOTTON, JOSEPH
1977    *The Zapotecs: Princes, Priests, and Peasants* (Norman: University of Oklahoma Press).

WICKE, CHARLES R.
1957    "The Ball Court at Yagul, Oaxaca: A Comparative Study," *Mesoamerican Notes* 5:37–78.
1966    "Tomb 38 at Yagul and the Zaachila Tombs," in *Ancient Oaxaca: Discoveries in Mexican Archaeology and History,* ed. John Paddock (Stanford: Stanford University Press), pp. 245–55.
1971    *Olmec: An Early Art Style of Precolumbian Mexico* (Tucson: University of Arizona Press).

WILKES, H. GARRISON
1972    "Maize and its Wild Relatives," *Science* 177:1071–77.

WILKINSON, RICHARD G., AND BARBARA L. HEMINGER
n.d.    "Human Skeletal Remains from Barrio del Rosario Huitzo, Oaxaca," unpublished manuscript to appear in a future Memoir of the University of Michigan Museum of Anthropology (Ann Arbor).

WILKINSON, RICHARD G., AND RICHARD J. NORELLI
1981    "A Biocultural Analysis of Social Organization at Monte Albán," *American Antiquity* 46(4):743–58.

WILLEY, GORDON R., AND PHILIP PHILLIPS
1958    *Method and Theory in American Archaeology* (Chicago: University of Chicago Press).

WILLIAMS, HOWEL, AND ROBERT F. HEIZER
1965    "Geological Notes on the Ruins of Mitla and Other Oaxacan Sites, Mexico," *Contributions of the University of California Archaeological Research Facility* 1:40–54.

WINTER, MARCUS C.
1972    "Tierras Largas: A Formative Community in the Valley of Oaxaca, Mexico" (Ph.D. diss., University of Arizona, Department of Anthropology).
1974    "Residential Patterns at Monte Albán, Oaxaca, Mexico," *Science* 186:981–87.
1975    "Reportes Breves de Excavaciones, La Cañada," *Boletín* (Oaxaca: Centro Regional de Oaxaca, INAH), no. 2.
1976a   "The Archaeological Household Cluster in the Valley of Oaxaca," in *The Early Mesoamerican Village,* ed. Kent V. Flannery (New York: Academic Press), pp. 25–31.
1976b   "Differential Patterns of Community Growth in Oaxaca," in *The Early Mesoamerican Village,* ed. Kent V. Flannery (New York: Academic Press), pp. 227–34.
1976c   "Excavating a Shallow Community by Random Sampling Quadrats," in *The Early Mesoamerican Village,* ed. Kent V. Flannery (New York: Academic Press), pp. 62–67.
1978    "Dos Fechas de Carbón 14 de la Época I de Monte Albán, Oaxaca," *Estudios de Antropología e Historia,* no. 7 (Oaxaca: Centro Regional de Oaxaca, Instituto Nacional de Antropología e Historia).

WINTER, MARCUS C., DARIA DERAGA, AND RODOLFO FERNÁNDEZ
1976    "Cerro de la Codorniz: Una Zona Arqueológica Ñuiñe en Santiago Chilixtlahuaca, Huajuapan, Oaxaca," *Boletín I.N.A.H.,* Época II, 17:29–40 (México, D.F.: Instituto Nacional de Antropología e Historia).

WINTER, MARCUS C., AND WILLIAM O. PAYNE
1976    "Hornos Para Cerámica Hallados en Monte Albán," *Boletín* 16:37–40 (México, D.F.: Instituto Nacional de Antropología e Historia).

WINTER, MARCUS C., AND JANE WHEELER PIRES-FERREIRA
1976    "Distribution of Obsidian Among Households in Two Oaxacan Villages," in *The Early Mesoamerican Village,* ed. Kent V. Flannery (New York: Academic Press), pp. 306–11.

WOBST, H. MARTIN
1974    "Boundary Conditions for Paleolithic Social Systems: A Simulation Approach," *American Antiquity* 39(2) (part 1):147–78.

WOLF, ERIC R.
1959    *Sons of the Shaking Earth* (Chicago: University of Chicago Press).
1966    *Peasants* (Englewood Cliffs, N.J.: Prentice-Hall).

WOLF, ERIC R., ED.
1976    *The Valley of Mexico: Studies in Pre-Hispanic Ecology and Society* (Albuquerque: University of New Mexico Press).

WOODBURY, RICHARD B., AND JAMES A. NEELY
1972    "Water Control Systems of the Tehuacán Valley," in *The Prehistory of the Tehuacán Valley,* vol. 4: *Chronology and Irrigation,* ed. Frederick Johnson (Austin: University of Texas Press), pp. 81–153.

WRIGHT, HENRY T.
1977    "Recent Research on the Origins of the State," *Annual Review of Anthropology* 6:379–97.

WRIGHT, HENRY T., AND GREGORY A. JOHNSON
1975    "Population, Exchange, and Early State Formation in Southwestern Iran," *American Anthropologist* 77:267–89.

WRIGHT, HENRY T., AND SUSAN KUS
1979    "An Archaeological Reconnaissance of Ancient Imerina," in *Madagascar in History: Essays from the 1970's,* ed. Raymond K. Kent (Albany, Cal.: Foundation for Malagasy Studies), pp. 1–31.

WRIGHT, SEWALL
1939    "Statistical Genetics in Relation to Evolution," *Actualités Scientifiques et Industrielles* 802:37–60 (Paris: Hermann).

XIMÉNEZ ORTÍZ, JUAN
1579    "Relación de Iztepexi," in *Papeles de Nueva España: segunda serie, Geografía y Estadística,* vol. 4, ed. Francisco del Paso y Troncoso (Madrid 1905), pp. 9–23.

YENGOYAN, ARAM A.
1972    "Ritual and Exchange in Aboriginal Australia: An Adaptive Interpretation of Male Initiation Rites," in *Social Exchange and Interaction,* ed. Edwin N. Wilmsen, Anthropological Papers, of the University of Michigan Museum of Anthropology 46 (Ann Arbor), pp. 5–9.

YOFFEE, NORMAN
1979    "The Decline and Rise of Mesopotamian Civilization: An Ethnoarchaeological Perspective on the Evolution of Social Complexity," *American Antiquity* 44(1):5–35.

ZÁRATE, BARTOLOMÉ DE
1581    "Relación de Guaxilotitlán," in *Papeles de Nueva España: segunda serie, Geografía y Estadística,* vol. 4, ed. Francisco del Paso y Troncoso (Madrid 1905), pp. 196–205.

ZEITLIN, JUDITH F.
1978    "Changing Patterns of Resource Exploitation, Settlement Distribution, and Demography on the Southern Isthmus of Tehuantepec, Mexico," in *Prehistoric Coastal Adaptations,* eds. Barbara L. Stark and Barbara Voorhies (New York: Academic Press), pp. 151–78.

ZEITLIN, ROBERT N.
1978    "Long-Distance Exchange and the Growth of a Regional Center on the Southern Isthmus of Tehuantepec, Mexico," in *Prehistoric Coastal Adaptations,* eds. Barbara L. Stark and Barbara Voorhies (New York: Academic Press), pp. 183–210.

ZIPF, GEORGE K.
1949    *Human Behavior and the Principle of Least Effort* (Cambridge, Mass.: Harvard University Press).

# Index